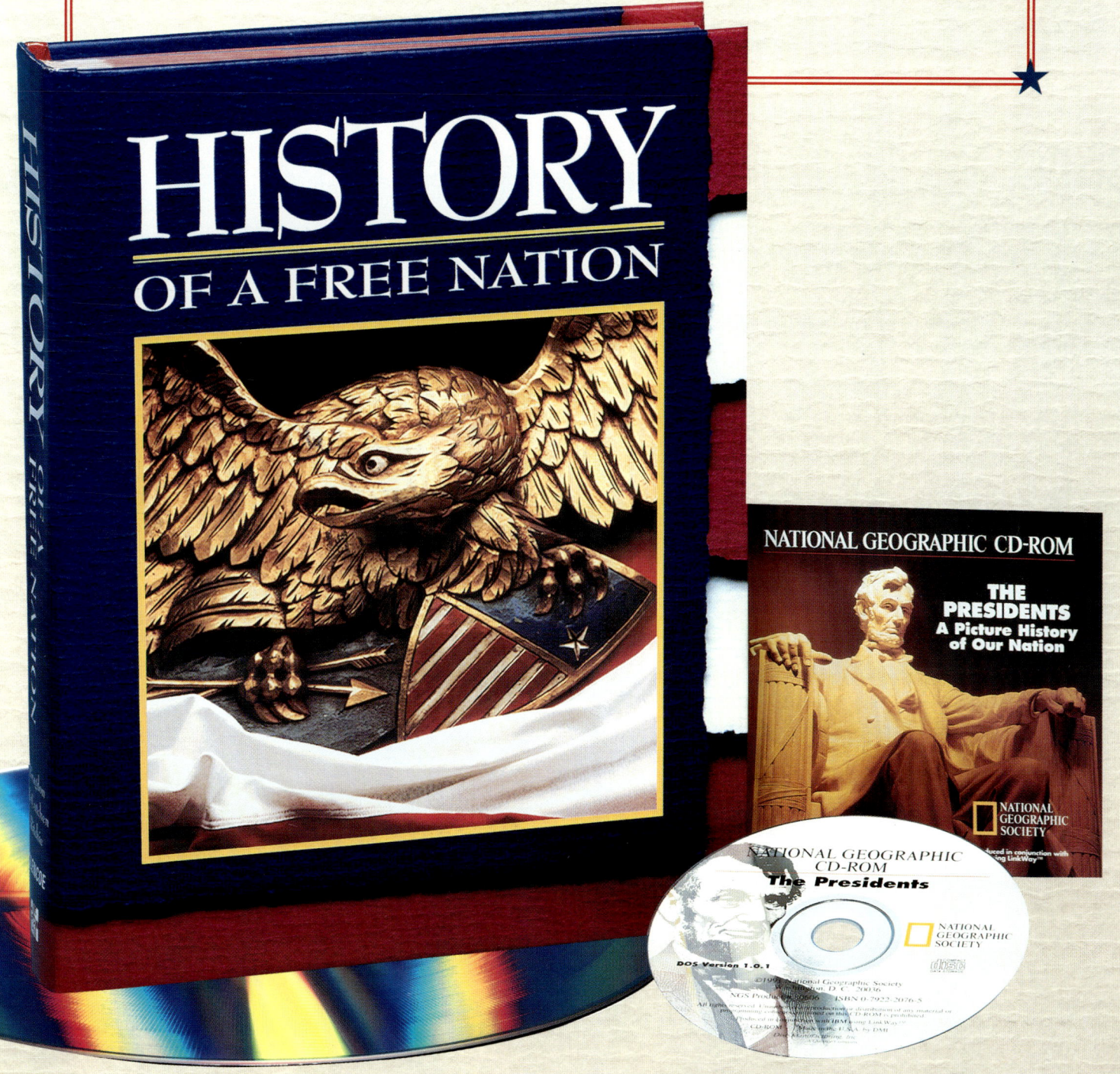

★ **Historical Integrity**

★ **Appealing Presentation**

★ **Dynamic Resources**

The Thorough Historical Presentation You Need
History of a Free Nation is a dramatic re-telling of our nation's history, from its earliest beginnings to the present. A compelling narration integrates primary sources for a truly first-person account of historical events. Your students don't just *read* history—they *experience* it.

A Dramatic Format Your Students Will Enjoy
The inviting, full-color visual program includes new maps, charts, and illustrations that entice your students to explore the many facets of United States history.

Connections Add Richness to Historical Details
Integrated humanities and cross-curricular topics demonstrate that history isn't just a dusty collection of facts. It's a living story told in the nation's art, music, and literature.

Resources Create Limitless Possibilities
From transparencies to CD-ROMs, videodiscs, and videotapes, *History of a Free Nation* brings you endless instructional choices. Now you can teach the way you want to and still meet the needs of all your students.

Complete Program

The American story. Nobody tells it better than this.

A Student-Friendly Text Relates the American Story—Beautifully

History of a Free Nation delivers the full, rich panorama of American history, and its superb visual presentation makes your students eager to read and to learn.

SECTION 3

War on the Home Front

Setting the Scene

Section Focus

In order to raise and equip vast armies, increase the size of the navy elevenfold, and keep munitions and food flowing to the Allies, massive reorganization of American business, industry, and agriculture was needed. Victory in World War I was due, in large part, to the great efforts and sacrifices made on the home front.

Objectives

After studying this section, you should be able to

★ explain how the war was financed.
★ describe how public opinion was shaped by the government.
★ discuss the goals of Wilson's Fourteen Points.

Key Term

victory garden

▲ WORLD WAR I POSTER, 1918

The United States found itself ill-equipped for battle when it entered World War I. The most immediate domestic concern that Congress faced was to keep the United States and Allied armies supplied by gearing United States industry to the war machine. In addition, the federal government needed to raise money to pay for the war and to mobilize the American people to support the war effort.

■ Mobilizing the Economy

To accomplish these goals, Wilson and Congress applied the Progressive Era's ideals of efficiency, control, and conformity in society to the war effort at home. "It is not an army that we must shape and train for war," said the President, "it is a nation."

Organizing Industries

The government's solution to the problem of supplying the troops was to place most industries under the control of federal agencies. The most important of these—the War Industries Board—handled purchasing for both the Allies and the United States. Under the leadership of Bernard Baruch, a Wall Street stockbroker, the War Industries Board attempted "to operate the whole United States as a single factory dominated by one management." Enlisting the most able businesspeople in America to direct the war effort, the government received the cooperation of business to convert factories to war production. Federal officials determined how raw materials would be allocated and what prices should be fixed.

The Fuel Administration was in charge of boosting coal and oil production, while encouraging people to conserve. The agency introduced such conservation methods as daylight savings time and shortened workweeks for nonwar-related factories. The Railroad Administration took charge of the railroads and ran them as a single system. The War Labor Board worked to prevent labor disputes.

Labor unions generally supported the war effort, hoping that cooperation would result in goodwill from the government and big business. Union leaders saw in the war opportunities for higher pay, better working conditions, and the right to organize and bargain collectively. Membership in unions doubled, and unions won concessions, such as the eight-hour day that industries had long opposed.

Involvement of Women

Wartime also meant increased opportunities for American women. Millions of jobs given up by men who volunteered or were drafted were filled by women. For the first time, women were welcomed in many occupations. Female workers became an essential part of the nation's war effort in war industries and defense plants.

Despite the progress toward social and economic equality the war offered them, many women wondered how the United States could be fighting to save democracy and still deny them the vote at home. Activists for woman suffrage continued to work during the war.

Involvement of African Americans

African Americans might well have asked similar questions because Southern states continued to deny them the right to vote. Also, African American soldiers fighting in Europe encountered far less discrimination from Europeans than they had experienced in their own country.

Nevertheless, the war offered new opportunities for African Americans at home. Job opportunities and high wages during the

 Visualizing History ▲ **AT HOME** During the war more and more women became a vital part of the labor force. In addition, women volunteered for noncombat duty on the war front or for a military Home Guard in the United States. *What happened to the suffrage movement during the war?*

- The clean, open layout with numerous heads to outline the story aids students' understanding.

- Increased coverage of recent American history focuses your students' attention on events that have affected their own lives.

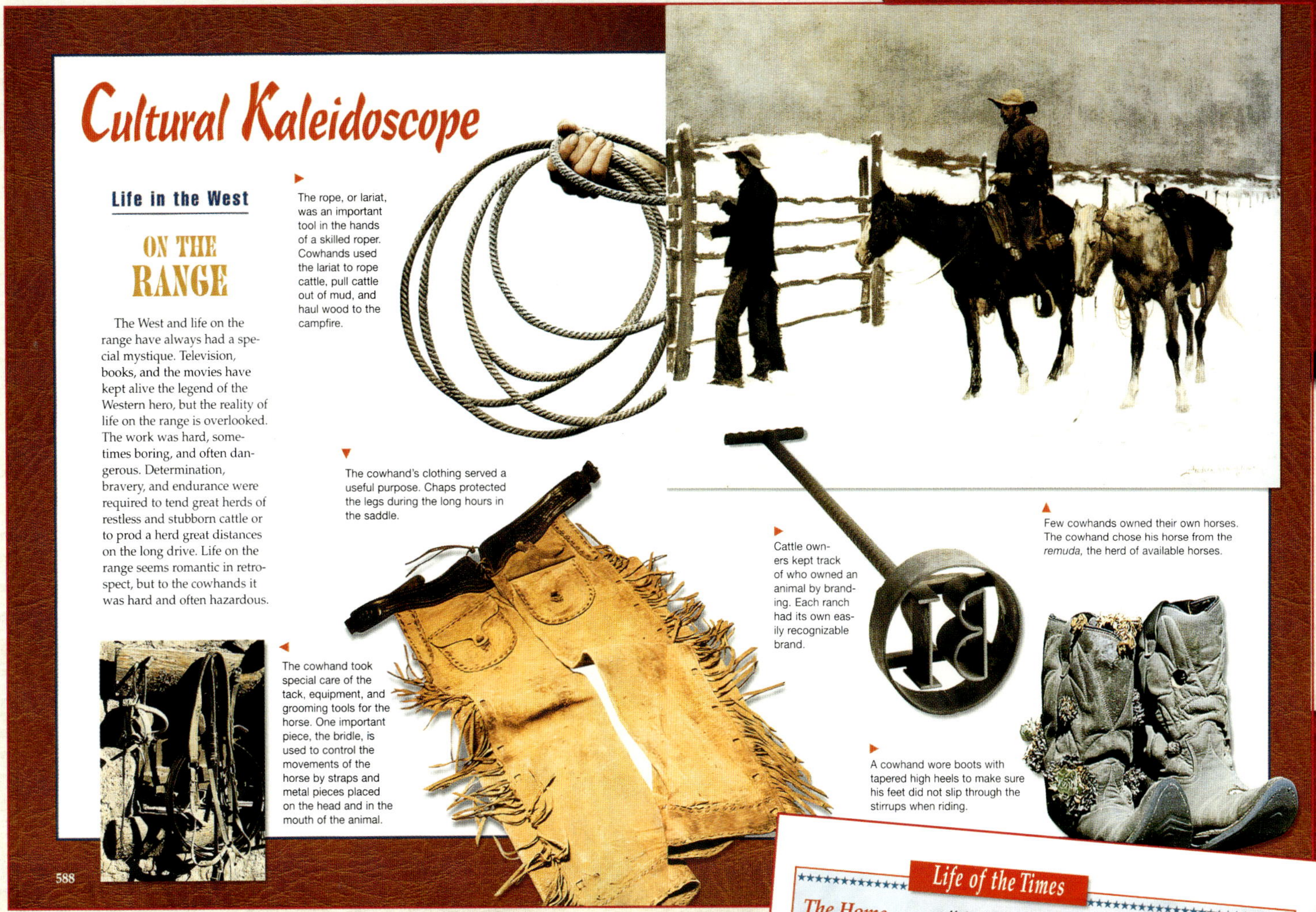

Student Edition

Cultural Kaleidoscope

Life in the West

ON THE RANGE

The West and life on the range have always had a special mystique. Television, books, and the movies have kept alive the legend of the Western hero, but the reality of life on the range is overlooked. The work was hard, sometimes boring, and often dangerous. Determination, bravery, and endurance were required to tend great herds of restless and stubborn cattle or to prod a herd great distances on the long drive. Life on the range seems romantic in retrospect, but to the cowhands it was hard and often hazardous.

▶ The rope, or lariat, was an important tool in the hands of a skilled roper. Cowhands used the lariat to rope cattle, pull cattle out of mud, and haul wood to the campfire.

▶ The cowhand's clothing served a useful purpose. Chaps protected the legs during the long hours in the saddle.

▶ Cattle owners kept track of who owned an animal by branding. Each ranch had its own easily recognizable brand.

▶ Few cowhands owned their own horses. The cowhand chose his horse from the *remuda*, the herd of available horses.

▶ The cowhand took special care of the tack, equipment, and grooming tools for the horse. One important piece, the bridle, is used to control the movements of the horse by straps and metal pieces placed on the head and in the mouth of the animal.

▶ A cowhand wore boots with tapered high heels to make sure his feet did not slip through the stirrups when riding.

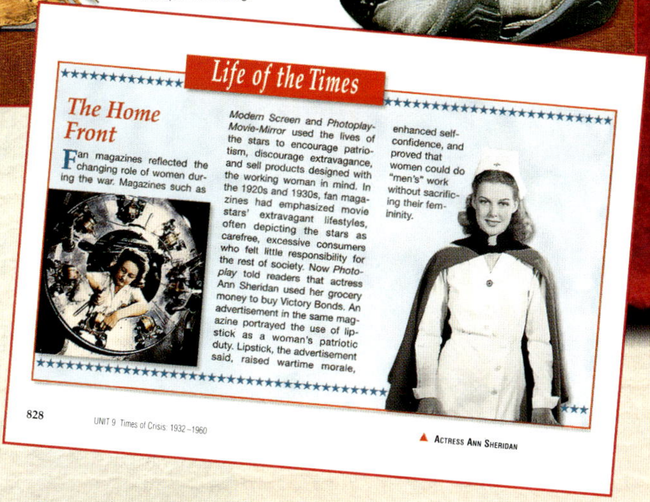

Life of the Times

The Home Front

Fan magazines reflected the changing role of women during the war. Magazines such as *Modern Screen* and *Photoplay-Movie-Mirror* used the lives of the stars to encourage patriotism, discourage extravagance, and sell products designed with the working woman in mind. In the 1920s and 1930s, fan magazines had emphasized movie stars' extravagant lifestyles, often depicting the stars as carefree, excessive consumers who felt little responsibility for the rest of society. Now *Photoplay* told readers that actress Ann Sheridan used her grocery money to buy Victory Bonds. An advertisement in the same magazine portrayed the use of lipstick as a woman's patriotic duty. Lipstick, the advertisement said, raised wartime morale, enhanced self-confidence, and proved that women could do "men's" work without sacrificing their femininity.

▲ Actress Ann Sheridan

- **Cultural Kaleidoscope** and **Life of the Times** make history relevant to your students by showing them how the art, music, language, customs, and activities of other eras in American history tell the story of our nation's past.

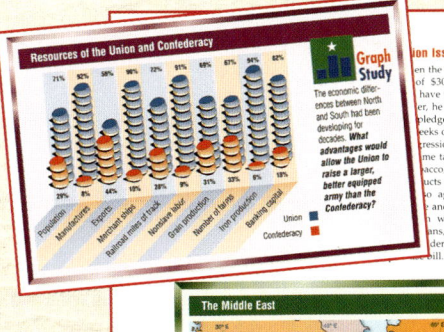

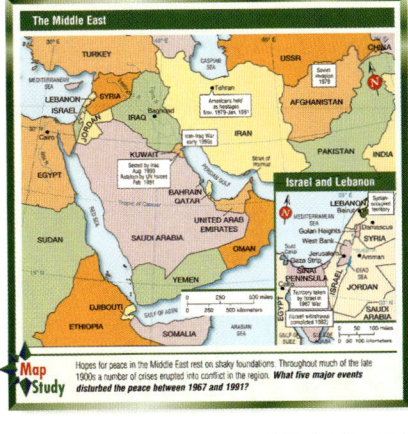

- Dynamic, colorful time lines, graphs, charts, maps, illustrations, and photographs with corresponding questions, complement the narrative and offer additional opportunities for learning.

Student Edition

Cross-Curricular Connections Tie History to Other Disciplines

American Literary Heritage

▲ RIDE FOR LIBERTY, BY EASTMAN JOHNSON, 1862

Follow the Drinking Gourd

When the sun comes back and the first quail calls,
Follow the drinking gourd,
For the old man is a-waiting for to carry you to freedom
If you follow the drinking gourd.

Follow the drinking gourd,
Follow the drinking gourd,
For the old man is a-waiting for to carry you to freedom
If you follow the drinking gourd.

The river bank will make a very good road,
The dead trees show you the way,
Left foot, peg foot traveling on
Follow the drinking gourd.

The river ends between two hills
Follow the drinking gourd,
There's another river on the other side,
Follow the drinking gourd.

Where the little river meets the great big river,
Follow the drinking gourd,
For the old man is a-waiting for to carry you to freedom
If you follow the drinking gourd.

Go Down, Moses

When Israel was in Egypt land,
Let my people go!
Oppressed so hard they could not stand,
Let my people go!

CHORUS
Go down, Moses,
Way down in Egypt land
Tell ole Pharaoh,
Let my people go!

Thus say the Lord, bold Moses said,
Let my people go!
If not I'll smite your first-born dead,
Let my people go!

No more shall they in bondage toil,
Let my people go!
Let them come out with Egypt's spoil,
Let my people go!

Swing Low, Sweet Chariot

Swing low, sweet chariot,
Coming for to carry me home,
Swing low, sweet chariot,
Coming to carry me home.

I looked over Jordan and what did I see
Coming for to carry me home,
A band of angels coming after me,
Coming to carry me home.

If you get there before I do,
Coming for to carry me home,
Tell all my friends I'm coming too,
Coming to carry me home.

Swing low, sweet chariot,
Coming for to carry me home,
Swing low, sweet chariot,
Coming to carry me home.

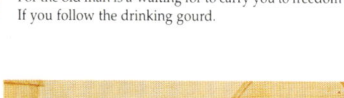
▲ MOTHER AND CHILD

The struggles that tore the nation apart at mid-century were reflected in much of the period's writing. Spirituals—songs of salvation—provided the African Americans who wrote and chanted them not only with a measure of solace in bleak times but with a means for communicating secretly among themselves under their masters' watchful eye.

▲ MUSIC ON THE PLANTATION

Interpreting Literature
1. What is the message from one enslaved person to another in "Follow the Drinking Gourd"?
2. Which spiritual equates the plight of the African Americans with that of another group? Which group?

Making Evaluations
3. Describe the mood of the spirituals.

- **American Literary Heritage** helps your students see how the literary works of an era reflect the life and the times of the period.

- **Connections** to economics, geography, science, and other disciplines place events in a wider context and demonstrate the interplay of history and the other disciplines.

The Barcoded Teacher's Wraparound Edition Gives You Flexibility and Instant Access to Technology

Barcoded Teacher's Wraparound Edition

Barcodes provide a fast, easy link to an impressive assortment of videodisc programs, and CD-ROM programs are referenced throughout the textbook. In seconds, you can integrate the latest technology into your classroom presentations. (See pages 10-11 for more discussion of these exciting resources.)

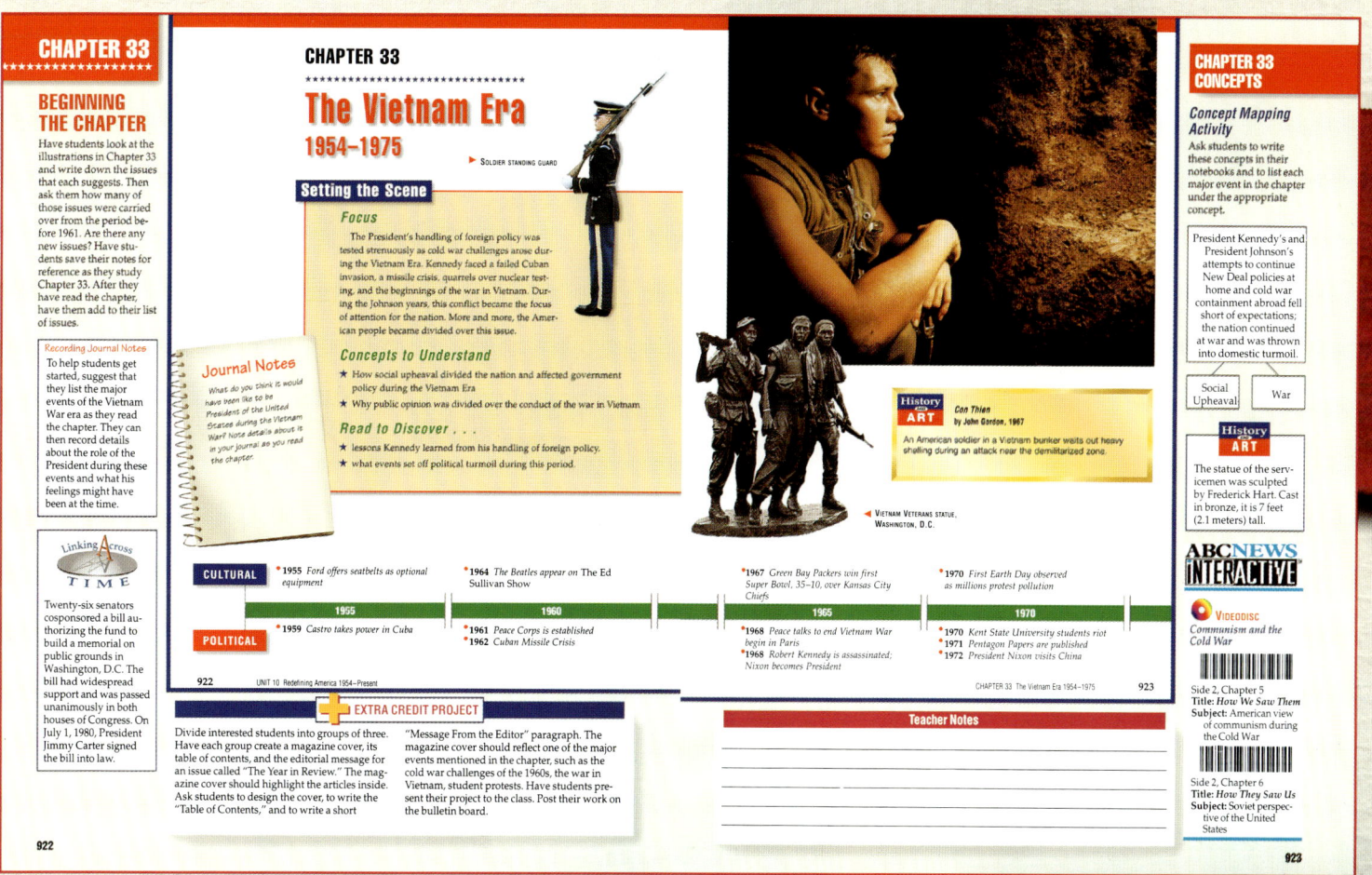

A wide range of teaching strategies lets you select the approaches that fit your teaching style and classroom needs. Strategies include:

- Linking Past and Present
- Cooperative Learning Activities
- Fact or Fiction
- Performance Assessment
- Food of the Times
- Multicultural Perspectives—And More!

The Resources You Need to Teach Your Way

High-Interest Extension Activities

- **Concept Mapping Activities** provide visual organizers that reinforce important chapter concepts and themes.
- **Cooperative Learning Activities** offer easy-to-use activities that add the dimension of collaborative learning without added preparation time.
- **The Spirit of American Art and Music** includes activities and profiles of American artists, musicians, and architects who made significant contributions to American history.
- **Political Cartoons in American History** enrich lessons and motivate students by providing activities that add a visual perspective on key issues.
- **Geography in History Activities** give students graphic opportunities to understand the impact of geography on the historical development of the United States.
- **Supreme Court Cases** contain background information, case summaries, and debate/discussion questions about some of the country's most significant court cases.

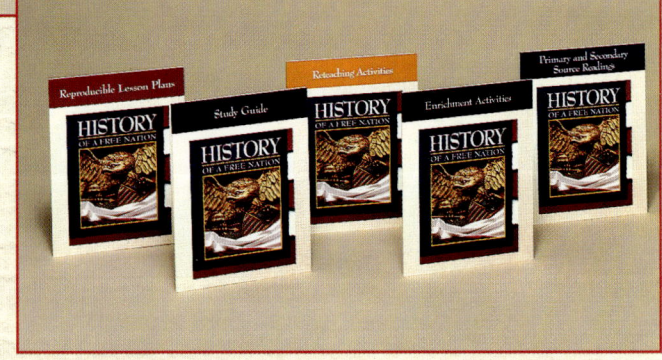

Chapter Resources

Now you can plan, teach, reteach, and enrich all your lessons more effectively.
- **Reproducible Lesson Plans**
- **Study Guide**
- **Reteaching Activities**
- **Enrichment Activities**
- **Primary and Secondary Source Readings**

Links to the Humanities

- **American Music: Cultural Traditions** is an audio program (available on cassettes or CD) that explores the nation's heritage through the music of the times—from the Colonial period to the present. It includes a Teacher's Guide and student activity sheets.

- **United States History and Art Transparencies** offer a multifaceted look at our nation's history through its art and include teaching strategies, learning objectives, teacher-guided activities, and student worksheets.

- **American History Fine Art Prints** includes display-quality, laminated posters that present the cultural heritage of America. Complete with a Teacher's Guide and Student Worksheets.

Assessment Resources

- **Performance Assessment Strategies and Activities** provide alternative assessment activities for each chapter. Scoring rubrics and suggestions for implementation are included.

- **Section Quizzes** are quick, effective measures of daily progress.

- **Chapter and Unit Tests: Forms A and B** are ready-made resources for assessing content mastery.

- **Testmaker Software (Apple, IBM, and Macintosh)** contains more than 3,000 questions and gives you the flexibility to edit them or to add your own.

And More . . .

Spanish Resources Binder provides the extra support Spanish-speaking students need to succeed. The Binder includes:
- Chapter Summaries and Glossary
- Reteaching Activities
- Section Quizzes
- Unit Digest Transparencies

United States History and Glencoe Social Studies Enrichment Series offers seven booklets that make it easy for you to enrich and enhance your classroom lessons.
- **Map and Graph Skill Activities**
- **Reinforcing Social Studies Skills**
- **American Literary Heritage**
- **American Portraits**
- **Writer's Guidebook**
- **Outline Map Resource Book**
- **New SAT Test Practice**

Technology Brings the Past to Life

Videodisc Programs

*National Geographic Society
Award-Winning Videodisc Programs*
- **GTV: A Geographic Perspective on American History** gives an exciting exploration of American history, from pre-Columbian days to the present.
- **GTV: The American People: Fabric of a Nation** allows you to present an inclusive story of American history, highlighting the contributions of all Americans.

- **Set on Freedom: The American Civil Rights Movement™ Videodisc** lets your students meet the movement's greatest leaders, hear the major speeches, and witness pivotal events of the Civil Rights era.

ABCNEWS InterACTIVE™
Award-Winning Videodisc Programs

- **Lessons of War** offers explanations of the causes of war, how wars are fought, and what measures can be taken to resolve them.
- **Communism and the Cold War** helps your students understand the historical context of the U.S.-Soviet rivalry and portrays the events that led to the collapse of communism and the end of the Cold War.
- **Martin Luther King, Jr.** is a tribute to the life and work of one of America's greatest civil rights advocates. The program provides a chronology of his participation in the Civil Rights Movement and explores the impact of the movement on today's society.
- **Powers of the U.S. Government Videodisc Series (3 videodiscs)** details the powers of the Supreme Court, the Congress, and the Presidency. Chief Justice William Rehnquist, former Speaker of the House Tom Foley, and former President Jimmy Carter lead the discussions of their respective branches of government.

Media/Technology

CD-ROM / Software Programs

NATIONAL GEOGRAPHIC SOCIETY

- **The Presidents: A Picture History of Our Nation CD-ROM Program** offers a spellbinding look at the presidency in an easy-to-use interactive format.
- **NGS PictureShow: Native American CD-ROM Programs**
  Part One introduces the major Native American tribes that inhabited the eastern woodlands and the Great Plains.
  Part Two introduces the Native Americans of the Southwest, Northwest Coast, and Arctic.
- **ZipZapMap USA Software** is a fast-paced game that quickly increases your students' grasp of U.S. geography.

- **Facts on File CD-ROM Programs**
  Landmark Documents in American History
  The American Indian
- **Student Self-Test: A Software Review** lets students review the key concepts of every chapter at their own pace. Incorrect responses activate a built-in tutorial function.
- **Vocabulary PuzzleMaker Software** allows you to create various types of word puzzles that help students learn vocabulary terms from each chapter.

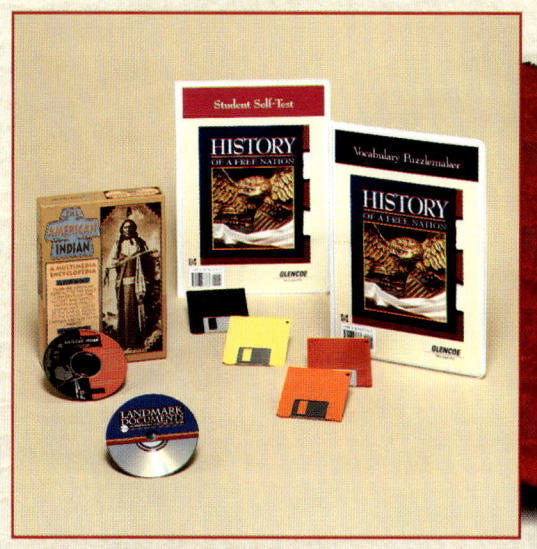

Transparencies, Audiocassettes, and Compact Discs

- **Teaching Transparencies with Strategies and Activities** allow you to introduce, reteach, and reinforce chapter and unit concepts. This handy binder includes:
  Map Transparencies
  Skills Transparencies
  U.S. History Diagraph Transparencies
  Unit Digest Transparencies

- **Section Focus Transparencies with Strategies and Activities** give you easy-to-use motivational activities to begin every lesson in the textbook.

- **Chapter Digest Audiocassettes (English and Spanish)** reinforce major concepts. Perfect for auditory learners and for students who need to review or catch up because of missed classes. Includes reproducible student activities and tests.

- **American Music: Cultural Traditions** (Audiocassettes and compact disc version) provide a musical look at the major time periods of American history.

Your Students Won't Just *Read* History–They'll *Experience* It.

Student Edition	0-02-823776-5
Teacher's Wraparound Edition	0-02-823777-3
Teacher's Classroom Resources	0-02-823780-3
Teaching Transparencies Package*	0-02-823816-8
Section Focus Transparency Package*	0-02-823817-6
U.S. History and Art Transparencies	0-02-662292-0
Focus on American History Fine Art Prints	0-02-823800-1
American Music: Cultural Traditions	
(CD Version Package)	0-02-823803-6
(Cassette Version)	0-02-823805-2
Chapter Digests Audiocassette Package	0-02-823813-3
Spanish Chapter Digests Audiocassette Package	0-02-823815-X
Spanish Resource Binder	0-02-823789-7
Vocabulary PuzzleMaker IBM Version	0-02-823809-5
Vocabulary PuzzleMaker MAC Version	0-02-823810-9
Student Self-Test: A Software Review MAC Version	0-02-823807-9
Student Self-Test: A Software Review IBM Version	0-02-823808-7
Apple Testmaker	0-02-823797-8
IBM Testmaker	0-02-823799-4
Macintosh Testmaker	0-02-823801-X
The National Geographic Society Programs	
GTV: A Geographic Perspective on American History Videodisc	
• Level I	0-02-823631-9
• Level III for Macintosh	0-02-823632-7
• Level III for DOS	0-02-823633-5
GTV: The American People: Fabric of a Nation Videodisc	
• Level I	0-02-823639-4
• Level III for Macintosh	0-02-823640-8
The Presidents: A Picture of Our Nation	
CD-ROM Program, DOS Version	0-02-823657-2
NGS PictureShow: Native Americans	
CD-ROM Program, Part I	0-02-823679-3
NGS PictureShow: Native Americans	
CD-ROM Program, Part II	0-02-823692-0
ZipZapMap USA Software	
• Windows Version	0-02-823646-7
• DOS Version	0-02-823647-5
• Macintosh Version	0-02-823648-3
ABCNews InterActive™ Videodiscs	
Lessons of War	
• Level I	0-02-822926-6
• Level III Macintosh	0-02-822930-4
Communism and the Cold War	
• Level I	0-02-822925-8
• Level III Macintosh	0-02-822929-0
Martin Luther King, Jr.	
• Level I	0-02-822932-0
• Level III Macintosh	0-02-822933-9
Powers of the U.S. Government Videodisc Series	0-02-823690-4
Set on Freedom: The American Civil Rights Movement™ Videodisc Program	
• Level I Videodisc Program	0-02-823432-4
• Level III MS-DOS Videodisc Program	0-02-823433-2
The American Indian CD-ROM	0-02-823462-6
Landmark Documents in American History CD-ROM	0-02-822773-5

*Also included in Teacher's Classroom Resources

FOR MORE INFORMATION CONTACT YOUR NEAREST GLENCOE REGIONAL OFFICE OR CALL 1-800-334-7344

1. Northeast Region
Glencoe/McGraw-Hill
15 Trafalgar Square #201
Nashua, NH 03063-1968
Phone: 603-880-4701
Phone: 800-424-3451
Fax: 603-595-0204
(CT, MA, ME, NH, NY, RI, VT)

2. Mid-Atlantic Region
Glencoe/McGraw-Hill
P.O. Box 458
Hightstown, NJ 08520-0458
Phone: 609-426-5560
Phone: 800-553-7515
Fax: 609-426-7063
(DC, DE, MD, NJ, PA)

3. Atlantic-Southeast Region
Glencoe/McGraw-Hill
Brookside Park
One Harbison Way
Suite 101
Columbia, SC 29212
Phone: 803-732-2365
Phone: 800-731-2365
Fax: 803-732-4582
(KY, NC, SC, VA, WV)

4. Southeast Region
Glencoe/McGraw-Hill
6510 Jimmy Carter Boulevard
Norcross, GA 30071
Phone: 404-446-7493
Phone: 800-982-3992
Fax: 404-446-2356
(AL, FL, GA, TN)

5. Mid-America Region
Glencoe/McGraw-Hill
936 Eastwind Drive
Westerville, OH 43081
Phone: 614-890-1111
Phone: 800-848-1567
Fax: 614-899-4905
(IN, MI, OH)

6. Great Lakes Region
Glencoe/McGraw-Hill
846 East Algonquin Road
Schaumburg, IL 60173
Phone: 708-397-8448
Phone: 800-762-4876
Fax: 708-397-9472
(IL, MN, WI)

7. Mid-Continent Region
Glencoe/McGraw-Hill
846 East Algonquin Road
Schaumburg, IL 60173
Phone: 708-397-8448
Phone: 800-762-4876
Fax: 708-397-9472
(IA, KS, MO, ND, NE, SD)

8. Southwest Region
Glencoe/McGraw-Hill
320 Westway Place,
Suite 550
Arlington, TX 76018
Phone: 817-784-2113
Phone: 800-828-5096
Fax: 817-784-2116
(AR, LA, MS, NM, OK)

9. Texas Region
Glencoe/McGraw-Hill
320 Westway Place,
Suite 550
Arlington, TX 76018
Phone: 817-784-2100
Phone: 800-828-5096
Fax: 817-784-2116
(TX)

10. Western Region
Glencoe/McGraw-Hill
709 E. Riverpark Lane,
Suite 150
Boise, ID 83706
Phone: 208-368-0300
Phone: 800-452-6126
Fax: 208-368-0303
(AK, AZ, CO, ID, MT, NV, OR, UT, WA, WY)

11. California Region
Glencoe/McGraw-Hill
15319 Chatsworth Street
P. O. Box 9609
Mission Hills, CA 91346
Phone: 818-898-1391
Phone: 800-423-9534
Fax: 818-365-5489
(CA, HI)

Glencoe Catholic School Region
Glencoe/McGraw-Hill
25 Crescent Street, 1st Floor
Stamford, CT 06906
Phone: 203-964-9109
Phone: 800-551-8766
Fax: 203-967-3108

Canada
McGraw-Hill Ryerson Ltd.
300 Water Street
Whitby, Ontario
Canada L1N 9B6
Phone: 905-430-5000
Phone: 800-565-5758
Fax: 905-430-5020

International
McGraw-Hill, Inc.
International Group
Princeton-Hightstown Road
Hightstown, NJ 08520
Phone: 609-426-5934
Fax: 609-426-7917

DoDDS and Pacific Territories
McGraw-Hill School Publishing Company
1221 Avenue of the Americas
13th Floor
New York, NY 10020
Phone: 212-512-6128
Fax: 212-512-6050

 Printed on recycled paper.

VIDEODISC EDITION

Teacher's Wraparound Edition

HISTORY
OF A FREE NATION

Henry W. Bragdon

Samuel P. McCutchen

Donald A. Ritchie

GLENCOE
McGraw-Hill

New York, New York   Columbus, Ohio   Mission Hills, California   Peoria, Illinois

Authors

Henry W. Bragdon was for many years a much-admired teacher at the Phillips Exeter Academy in Exeter, New Hampshire, winding up his career there as Cowles Professor in the Humanities Emeritus. In addition to his work on this textbook, he is the author of a biography of President Woodrow Wilson, *Woodrow Wilson: The Academic Years*, which was nominated for a National Book Award. Bragdon also served as president of the New England History Teachers' Association, chief examiner in Social Studies for the College Entrance Examination Board, and lecturer at Harvard College.

Samuel P. McCutchen spent a long career as a teacher of high school social studies and as a teacher of social studies teachers. He was professor of education at New York University. On the high school level, he taught at Fayette (Mississippi) High School and was chairperson of the social studies department of the John Burroughs School, St. Louis, Missouri. McCutchen also served as president of the National Council for the Social Studies.

Donald A. Ritchie is Associate Historian of the United States Senate Historical Office. Dr. Ritchie received his doctorate in American history from the University of Maryland, after service in the U.S. Marine Corps. He has taught American history at various levels, from high school to the university. He edits the Historical Series of the Senate Foreign Relations Committee and is the author of several books, including *Press Gallery: Congress and the Washington Correspondents*, which received the Organization of American Historians' Richard W. Leopold Prize. Dr. Ritchie has served as president of the Oral History Association and as a council member of the American Historical Association.

Send all inquiries to:

Glencoe/McGraw-Hill
936 Eastwind Drive
Westerville, Ohio 43081

ISBN 0-02-823776-5 (Student Edition)
ISBN 0-02-823777-3 (Teacher's Wraparound Edition)

Copyright © 1996 by Glencoe/McGraw-Hill.

All rights reserved.
Except as permitted under the United States Copyright Act, no part of this publication may be reproduced or distributed in any form or by any means, or stored in a database or retrieval system, without prior written permission of the publisher.

Printed in the United States of America

1 2 3 4 5 6 7 8 9 RRD-W/LH-P 00 99 98 97 96 95

Academic Consultants

Delbert A. Jurden, M.A.
Instructor of History
Johnson County Community College
Overland Park, Kansas

Keith Ian Polaloff, Ph.D.
Assistant Vice President for Academic
Affairs and Dean of Graduate Studies
California State University, Long Beach
Long Beach, California

Sarah Witham Bednarz
Visiting Assistant Professor
Department of Geography
Texas A&M University
College Station, Texas

Yolanda Elaine Childers
Reviewer/Consultant
Austin Community College
Austin, Texas

John Waukeshon, M.A.
Member
American Indian Resource and
Education Coalition
Austin, Texas

K. Austin Kerr, Ph.D.
Professor of History
The Ohio State University
Columbus, Ohio

Teacher Reviewers

Mary C. Burkett
Social Studies Teacher
Jackson City Schools
Jackson, Mississippi

Rose Marie Floyd
Social Studies Teacher
Jefferson Davis High School
Montgomery, Alabama

George W. Henry, Jr.
Teacher, Chair History Department
St. Mark's School
Salt Lake City, Utah

Marjorie B. Hollowell
Chair, Social Studies Department
John A. Holmes High School
Edenton, North Carolina

Michael L. Manson, Ed.D.
Teacher of Social Studies (retired)
Townsend Harris High School
New York City, New York

Simmie G. Plummer
History Teacher
Valley High School
Albuquerque, New Mexico

Irene Ramnarine
Secondary Social Studies
Resource Teacher
Brevard County School District
Melbourne, Florida

James M. Wolfe
History Teacher
Suitland University High School
Forestville, Maryland

Teacher's Wraparound Edition Contents

CONTENTS STUDENT EDITION	T6
SCOPE AND SEQUENCE	T18
PROFESSIONAL NOTES	T24
Cooperative Learning	T24
Block Scheduling	T25
Multicultural Perspective	T28
Critical Thinking	T28
Different Learning Styles	T29
At-Risk Students	T29
Performance Assessment	T30
Technology in the Classroom	T32

Teacher's Classroom Resources   T33

Study Guide T33
Concept Mapping Activities T34
Reteaching Activities T35
Enrichment Activities T36
Cooperative Learning Activities T37
Interpreting Political Cartoons T38
Primary and Secondary Source Readings T39
Supreme Court Case Studies T40
Geography in History Activities T41
Spirit of American Art and Music T42
American Music: Cultural Traditions T43
Focus on American Fine Art Prints T44
Spanish Resources T45
Section Quizzes and Performance Assessment T46
Tests and Testmaker Software T47
Student Self-Test: A Software Review T48
Unit Digest Transparencies T49
Section Focus Transparencies T50
Skills and Map Transparencies T51
U.S. History and Art Transparencies T52
U.S. History Diagraph Transparencies T53
English and Spanish Audiocassettes T54
Vocabulary PuzzleMaker T55
Student Self-Test: A Software Review T56
Videodiscs and CD-ROMs T57
Testmaker Software T58
Reproducible Lesson Plans 1

Student Edition Table of Contents

UNIT ONE
A New World
Prehistory to 1776

CHAPTER 1

The World in Transition, Prehistory to 1500s — 6
1. The First Americans — 8
2. The New Europe — 15
3. Medieval Asia and Africa — 20
4. Europeans Seek the East — 26

CHAPTER 2

The Age of Exploration, 1000–1682 — 34
1. Voyages of Columbus — 36
2. Spain in America — 42
3. New Ventures — 47

CHAPTER 3

Colonial America, 1578–1776 — 54
1. The Southern Colonies — 56
2. New England — 63
3. The Middle Colonies — 69
4. People of the Colonies — 73

UNIT TWO
Creating a Nation
1650–1789

CHAPTER 4

The Road to Revolution, 1650–1775 — 90
1. Struggle for Empire — 92
2. Control and Protest — 98
3. The Breach Widens — 104

CHAPTER 5

War for Independence, 1775–1783 — 114
1. Foundations of Freedom — 116
2. Fighting for Independence — 126
3. The War Deepens — 130
4. The War Ends — 136

CHAPTER 6

A More Perfect Union, 1775–1789 — 142
1. Government in Transition — 144
2. The Confederation — 149
3. Toward a New Constitution — 155
   THE CONSTITUTION TODAY — 168
   THE CONSTITUTION OF THE UNITED STATES — 172

UNIT THREE
Launching the Republic
1789–1824

CHAPTER 7

The Federalist Era, 1789–1800 — 202
1. Organizing the Government — 204
2. Solving National Problems — 208
3. Foreign Affairs Under Washington — 216
4. President John Adams — 222

Chapter 8

Age of Jefferson, 1800–1815 — 228
1. The Changing Political Scene — 230
2. Looking Westward — 237
3. Foreign Affairs — 244
4. The War of 1812 — 248

Chapter 9

Nationalism and Change, 1816–1824 — 256
1. The Era of Good Feelings — 258
2. Tying the Nation Together — 263
3. Monroe and Foreign Affairs — 271

UNIT FOUR
Toward a Democracy 1820–1854

Chapter 10

Sectionalism, 1820–1842 — 286
1. Growth in the North — 288
2. Growth in the South and West — 294
3. Rivalry and Compromise — 300

Chapter 11

Age of Jackson, 1828–1842 — 308
1. Growth of Democracy — 310
2. Jacksonian Democracy — 315
3. Political Controversies — 319
4. The Bank and the Whigs — 323

Chapter 12

The Spirit of Reform, 1820–1854 — 332
1. Advances in Education — 334
2. Struggle for Rights — 339
3. Social and Cultural Change — 346

UNIT FIVE
Division and Reunion 1825–1877

Chapter 13

Manifest Destiny, 1825–1854 — 364
1. The Thirst for New Lands — 366
2. War With Mexico — 374
3. Global Interests — 380

Chapter 14

Compromise and Conflict, 1848–1861 — 386
1. A Union in Danger — 388
2. Dispute Over Slavery — 396
3. Drifting Toward War — 402

Chapter 15

The Civil War, 1861–1865 — 410
1. The Outbreak of War — 412
2. The War on the Battlefield — 417
3. Behind the Lines — 424
4. Ending the War — 431

Chapter 16

Reconstruction, 1865–1877 — 438
1. After Slavery — 440
2. Reconstructing the South — 445
3. Restoring Southern Power — 453

Student Edition Table of Contents

UNIT SIX
New Horizons
1860–1900

CHAPTER 17
Into the West, 1860–1890 — 468
1. People of the Plains — 470
2. Ranching and Mining — 477
3. Farming Moves West — 484

CHAPTER 18
The Rise of Industry, 1860–1900 — 492
1. Industrialization Takes Hold — 494
2. Growth of Big Business — 502
3. Captains of Industry — 506

CHAPTER 19
An Urban Society, 1860–1900 — 516
1. The Workers' Plight — 518
2. The Rise of New Unions — 524
3. Patterns of Immigration — 528
4. City Life and Problems — 533

CHAPTER 20
The Gilded Age, 1865–1900 — 542
1. A Tarnished Image — 544
2. Calls for Good Government — 551
3. Cultural Life — 557

CHAPTER 21
Politics and Protest, 1865–1900 — 566
1. Agrarian Unrest — 568
2. Rise and Fall of Populism — 573
3. Other Forces for Reform — 580

UNIT SEVEN
Entering a New Century
1867–1920

CHAPTER 22
Imperialism, 1867–1908 — 596
1. America Looks Abroad — 598
2. The Spanish-American War — 603
3. Becoming a World Power — 608
4. A New Arena — 615

CHAPTER 23
The Progressive Era, 1893–1920 — 622
1. Sources of Progressivism — 624
2. Progressive Reforms — 632
3. Limits of Progressivism — 640

CHAPTER 24
White House Reformers, 1900–1914 — 648
1. The Square Deal — 650
2. The Taft Presidency — 656
3. The Election of 1912 — 660
4. Wilson's Progressivism — 665

UNIT EIGHT
Crusade and Disillusion
1914–1932

CHAPTER 25
World War I Era, 1914–1920 — 682
1. Prelude to War — 684
2. America Enters the War — 690
3. War on the Home Front — 696
4. After the War — 701

Chapter 26
The Decade of Normalcy, 1920–1928   710
1 The Harding Years   712
2 The Coolidge Era   719
3 The "Roaring Twenties"   728

Chapter 27
The Depression Begins, 1928–1932   738
1 The Stock Market Crashes   740
2 Hoover's Policies   747
3 The Depression Worsens   754

UNIT NINE
Times of Crisis 1932–1960

Chapter 28
The New Deal, 1932–1939   772
1 Roosevelt Takes Charge   774
2 Reform, Relief, and Recovery   779
3 The Second New Deal   787
4 The Impact of the New Deal   795

Chapter 29
World War II, 1933–1945   804
1 World Affairs, 1933–1939   806
2 Moving Closer to War   811
3 The United States at War   817
4 War on the Home Front   827

Chapter 30
The Cold War, 1945–1952   836
1 The Start of the Cold War   838
2 The Cold War in Asia   845
3 Cold War America   850

Chapter 31
Search for Stability, 1952–1960   860
1 The Eisenhower Years   862
2 The Straight Road   867
3 An Affluent Society   871
4 Foreign Policy   878

UNIT TEN
Redefining America 1954–Present

Chapter 32
The Civil Rights Era, 1954–1975   896
1 A New Beginning   898
2 Successes and Setbacks   904
3 New Directions   910
4 The Impact of Civil Rights   915

Chapter 33
The Vietnam Era, 1954–1975   922
1 Cold War Challenges   924
2 War in Vietnam   930
3 Protest and Reaction   936
4 Secrecy and Summitry   941

Chapter 34
Camelot to Watergate, 1960–1975   948
1 Kennedy's New Frontiers   950
2 The Great Society   956
3 An Imperial Presidency   962
4 The Watergate Scandal   967

Chapter 35
Search for Solutions, 1976–1992   974
1 Crisis of Confidence   976
2 A Conservative Shift   982
3 A New Presidency   990

Chapter 36
Toward a New Century, 1992–Present   1000
1 Reinventing Government   1002
2 America in a Changing World   1008
3 Challenges and Opportunities   1015

T9

Features

★★★★★★★★★★ AMERICAN PORTRAITS

Hiawatha 10	Joseph Pulitzer 606
Junípero Serra 44	Ida Tarbell 627
Margaret Brent 60	W.E.B. Du Bois 670
Crispus Attucks 106	George M. Cohan 699
Haym Salomon 128	Will Rogers 721
Thomas Jefferson 156	Dorothea Lange 757
Benjamin Banneker 224	Eleanor Roosevelt 777
Dolley Madison 249	Charles Drew 831
Henry Clay 259	Douglas MacArthur 846
Elizabeth Ann Seton 292	Betty Friedan 869
Sequoya 317	Malcolm X 912
Amelia Bloomer 344	Maya Lin 944
Narciso López 381	Cesar Chavez 958
Harriet Tubman 397	Jesse Jackson 992
Clara Barton 428	Ruth Bader Ginsberg. 1005
Frederick Douglass 442	
Charles M. Russell 480	
Gutavus Swift 503	
Jane Addams 534	
Susan B. Anthony 553	
Willa Cather 571	

Life of the Times

Golden Age of Mali	23
French Fur Traders	49
Bride Ships	58
Colonial Dance	94
Yankee Peddler	133
Home Remedies	152
Fontier Weddings	211
Telling Time	234
Seminole Survival	273
Moving West	297
Getting Out the Vote	312
The Language of Etiquette	340
Mountain Men	370
Forty-Niners	390
Mess Call	427
Southern Pride	447
Native American Schools	473
Working-Class Tenements	497
Italian Cuisine	530
Personal Hygiene	559
Boardinghouses	583
Imperial Fruits	611
Boy Scouts	637
The Elderly in Greenwich Village	658
Doughboys	694
Radio	731
Depression Needy	756
Sit-down Strikes	782
The Home Front	828
Veterans Return	853
Child Rearing by Spock	875
School Desegregation	900
Letters from Vietnam	938
Shopping Malls	964
Physical Fitness	987
Volunteers	1012

Features

Social Studies Skills

Interpreting Primary Sources
Women in the Colonies 68
The Stamp Act Crisis 103
Female Equality 236
The Light 314
Migration 379
Political Corruption 550
Anti-Imperialist Politics 614
The Harlem Renaissance and Visual Arts 735
Who Is an American? 833
Collage Art in the 1960s 961

Map and Graph Skills
Drawing Conclusions From Maps 275
Classifying Information 401
Reading a Line Graph 513
Supporting Generalizations 664
Interpreting a Political Map 689
Hypothesizing 844
Interpreting Military Maps 935
Reading a Bar Graph 989
Reading a Bar Graph 1014

Study and Writing Skills
Using Literature as a Historical Source 25
Asking Effective Questions 46
Taking Notes 148
Using Reference Works in Research 305
Analyzing Illustrations 430
Summarizing 523
Recognizing Ideologies 585
Writing a Persuasive Argument 753
Predicting Consequences 794

Critical Thinking Skills
Identifying Alternatives 135
Distinguishing Between Fact and
   Value Judgement 215
Making Comparisons 338
Making Predictions 452
Reconizing Fallacies in a Line of Reasoning 645
Discovering Symbolism in History 866
Identifying Cause and Effect 909

Cultural Kaleidoscope

Native American Life: Sports and Games	82
Colonial Life: In the Kitchen	164
The Early Republic: Transportation	278
Clothing: High Fashion	356
Education: The One-Room Schoolhouse	460
Life in the West: On the Range	588
Transportation: Moving Into the Fast Lanes	674
The 1920s: Fashions in the 1920s	764
A Changing Society: Innovations	888
The World of Music: Rocking Into the Future	1026

Features

CONNECTIONS

HISTORY AND ECONOMICS
Stock Exchanges 62
Banks and the Money Supply 329
Growth of Southern Manufacturing 457
The Stock Market 746

HISTORY AND ENVIRONMENT
Urban Pollution and Public Health 539
The Conservation Movement 655
The Dust Bowl 786
Environmental Issues
  of the Twenty-First Century 1021

HISTORY AND GEOGRAPHY
"'Twas a Small World," Columbus Thought 41
Native American and European Land Values 97
Exploring the Louisiana Purchase 253
The Battle of Vicksburg 423
The Great American Desert 489
Standard Time Zones 501
Changing the Map of Europe 707
African American Migration 857

HISTORY AND MUSIC
Songs of Slavery 299
Folk Songs of Protest 579
Origins of Rock and Roll 877

HISTORY AND RELIGION
The Revolutionary Pulpit 121
American Missionaries 373
Reform Judaism 639
African American Churches and
  the Civil Rights Movement 903

CONNECTIONS

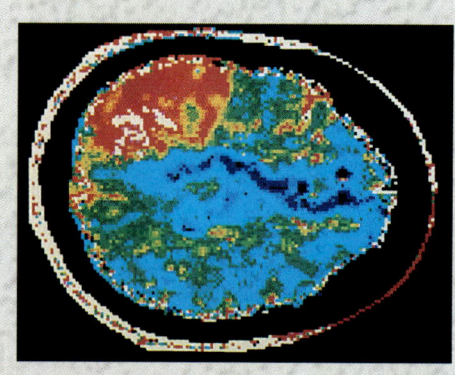

HISTORY AND SCIENCE
Prehistory and Archaeology 14
Astronomy and the Constitution 161
Planning Washington, D.C. 221
The Scientists of New Harmony 345
The Atomic Bomb 826
Space Race 955
As the Brain Grows Older 997

HISTORY AND TECHNOLOGY
Canal Locks 270
Industrial Innovation 395
Improvements in Printing 563
Coaling Stations and Colonies 602
Household Technology 719
Changing Nature of Warfare 929

American Literary Heritage

from *The Constitution of the Five Nations* 30
Navajo Song of the Rain Chant 31
from *The American Crisis, Number 1*
by Thomas Paine 110
from *The Prairie* by James Fenimore Cooper 242
from *Walden* by Henry David Thoreau 352
African American Spirituals 406
from *Roughing It* by Mark Twain 482
from *Sister Carrie* by Theodore Dreiser 630
"Recuerdo" by Edna St. Vincent Millay 726
"Dream Boogie" by Langston Hughes 727
from *The Grapes of Wrath* by John Steinbeck 800
from *Hunger of Memory* by Richard Rodgriuez .. 1022

Features

MAPS

Native American Cultures	12
Prehistoric Migration Route	12
Trade Routes, 1400s	22
African Trading Kingdoms	33
Voyages of Exploration	39
European Exploration of the New World	50
Settlement of the Colonies, 1587–1760	57
Economy of the Colonies	59
National Origins of the American Colonists, 1760	74
New England Land Grants, 1609–1732	81
Land Claims in North America	95
The French and Indian War, 1754–1763	96
The Proclamation of 1763	99
Lexington and Concord	113
The Revolutionary War in the North, 1775–1777	131
The Revolutionary War in the South, 1778–1781	137
Western Land Claims of the Original States	146
North America, 1783	150
Northwest Territory and the Land Ordinance of 1785	153
Native American Campaigns	212
The Westward Movement, 1790–1820	213
The Election of 1800	231
Exploring the Louisiana Purchase, 1804–1807	238
The War of 1812	251
The Barbary States	255
Roads, Canals, and Waterways, 1840	265
The Acquisition of Florida	275
Latin America, 1825	277
The Missouri Compromise, 1820	302
The United States in 1824	303
Removal of Native Americans, 1820–1840	316
Trails West	368
Texas War for Independence, 1835–1836	371
The Mexican War, 1846–1848	376
Territorial Expansion of the United States	378
Slave Population and the Underground Railroad	398
Kansas-Nebraska Act, 1854	399
Compromise of 1850	401
The Election of 1860	404
The Union and the Confederacy	405
The War in the East, 1861–1863	419
The War in the West, 1862–1863	421
The Final Campaigns, 1864–1865	437
Reconstruction in the South	449
Election of 1876	459
Precipitation in the Late 1800s	476
The Opening of the West, 1865–1900	478
The Disappearing Frontier	487
Railroad Lines, 1860 and 1890	498
Time Zones of the United States	501
The Election of 1896	587
The Spanish-American War	605
United States Overseas Possessions, 1900	610
The Panama Canal	621
The Progressive Movement and State Government	633
The Election of 1912	664
Regions of the Federal Reserve System	669
Europe in 1914	689
The World at War: World War I	693
The Western Front	693
The Eastern Front	693
Europe After World War I	702
Woman Suffrage Before 1920	705
The Tennessee Valley Authority	781
World War II in Europe and Africa	819
World War II in the Pacific	822
Europe After World War II	841
The Occupation of Berlin	844
The Korean War: June 25–November 25, 1950	848
The Korean War: November 26, 1950–July 27, 1953	848
The Election of 1948	854
The Cold War in the 1950s	883
The Election of 1960	952
Registration of African American Voters in the South, 1960 and 1966	908
The Vietnam War	933

The Election of 1968 973	North America 1036
The Tet Offensive, 1968 935	Latin America 1037
Khe Sanh, Vietnam: January 21–April 7, 1968 947	Eurasia 1038
The Middle East 995	The Middle East 1040
Israel and Lebanon 995	Africa 1042
The Election of 1992 1004	Southeast Asia 1043
The World 1032	United States Climate Regions 1044
United States 1034	

CHARTS, GRAPHS, and TABLES

The American Colonies, 1607–1776 66	Immigration, 1921–1930 716
American Casualties in the Revolution 141	Auto Sales, 1920–1929 722
Ratification of the Constitution 163	Immigration, 1921–1930 737
Division of Powers 168	Stock Prices, 1920–1932 743
The American System of Checks and Balances . . . 169	GNP, Stock Values, and Unemployment 745
How a Bill Becomes a Law 170	Farm Prices, 1910–1935 763
Kinds of Historical Reasoning 227	Labor Union Membership, 1900–1940 785
The Marshall Court and the National Interest 261	The Federal Budget and Deficit, 1932–1940 803
Election of 1824 307	Women in the Labor Force, 1900–1950 835
Growth of the Labor Force 307	Marshall Plan, 1948–1952 859
Population by Region, 1800 and 1840 331	European Recovery, 1948–1952 859
U.S. Student Enrollment, 1840–1860 336	Suburbanization, 1901–1980 873
Population in Urban and Rural Territory 355	Income Distribution by Families 887
Immigration, 1820–1860 392	Race and Hispanic Origin for the United States, 1990 . 921
Resources of the Union and Confederacy 415	The United States in Vietnam, 1950–1975 943
Agricultural Production in the South, 1850–1900 . . 455	Gasoline Consumption and Prices 978
The Election of 1876 459	United States Exports and Imports, 1971–1993 989
Native American Population 472	Federal Budget, 1945–1994 999
Corn and Wheat Production and Prices, 1870–1900 . . 491	Total Assets, Selected Multinationals 1014
Production of Raw Steel, 1860–1900 513	Foreign Assets, Selected Multinationals 1014
Production of Crude Oil, 1860–1900 513	Foreign Sales as a Percentage of Total Sales, Selected Multinationals 1014
Production of Bituminous Coal, 1860–1900 515	The Labor Force, 1983–1993 1025
Immigration to the United States, 1861–1920 529	Population of the United States 1045
The Popular Vote for President, 1860–1900 548	Population Distribution by Age 1045
Farm Prices, 1860–1900 569	Major Religions in the United States 1045
U.S. Territorial Expansion to 1917 612	Political Parties in Power 1046
Weekly Wages in the Woolen Industry 625	Graduation Rates 1046
Imports and Tariff Duties, 1880–1920 673	Life Expectancy 1046
American Mobilization, 1917–1918 709	The United States 1047
Employee Earnings, 1920–1929 714	

SCOPE AND SEQUENCE

	Chapter 1	Chapter 2	Chapter 3	Chapter 4	Chapter 5
Themes and Concepts					
American Democracy			Sec. 2	Sec. 1-3	Sec. 1-4
Humanities and Religion	ALH, Sec. 1-3	Sec. 1-3	Sec. 1-4, UD	ALH, Sec. 1, 3	Sec. 1
Cultural Diversity	Sec. 1-4	Sec. 1-3	Sec. 1-4, UD	Sec. 1, CK	
Geography and Environment	Sec. 1-4	Sec. 1-3	Sec. 1-4, UD	Sec. 1, 2, 3	Sec. 3, 4
Conflict and Cooperation	Sec. 1-4	Sec. 2, 3	Sec. 1-3	Sec. 1-3	Sec. 1-4
Influence of Technology	Sec. 1-4	Sec. 1			
The Individual and Family Life	Sec. 1-4	Sec. 2, 3	Sec. 1-4, UD	Sec. 1, 3	Sec. 2-4
U.S. Role in World Affairs	GP			GP	
Civil Rights and Liberties		Sec. 2	Sec. 1, 2, 4	Sec. 1-3	Sec. 1-4
Economic Development	Sec. 1-4	Sec. 1-3	Sec. 1-4	Sec. 1-3	Sec. 2-4
Social Studies Skills					
Study and Writing	Sec. 1, CR	Sec. 2, CR	CR	Sec. 2, CR	CR
Map and Graph	Sec. 1, 4	Sec. 1, 3, CR	Sec. 1, CR	Sec. 1, 2, CR	Sec. 3, 4
Interpreting Primary Sources			Sec. 2, 4	Sec. 1-3	Sec. 1
Making Connections	Sec. 1-4	Sec. 1-3	Sec. 1-4	Sec. 1-3	Sec. 1-4
Critical Thinking Skills					
Knowledge	Sec. 1-4, CR	Sec. 1-3, CR	Sec. 1-4, CR	Sec. 1-3, CR	Sec. 1-4, CR
Comprehension	Sec. 1-4, CR	Sec. 1-3, CR	Sec. 1-4, CR	Sec. 1-3, CR	Sec. 1-4, CR
Application	Sec. 3	Sec. 2	Sec. 2, 3, 4	Sec. 3, CR	Sec. 2
Analysis	Sec. 1-4, CR	Sec. 1-3, CR	Sec. 1-4	Sec. 1-3, CR	Sec. 1-4
Synthesis			CR, UD	Sec. 2	
Evaluation	Sec. 1, 2, 4	Sec. 1	Sec. 1, 4	Sec. 1-3	

Key to Abbreviations

Chapter 6	Chapter 7	Chapter 8	Chapter 9	Chapter 10	Chapter 11	Chapter 12
Sec. 1-3, UD	Sec. 1-4	Sec. 1-4	Sec. 1-3, UD	Sec. 1-3	Sec. 1-4	Sec. 1-3, UD
Sec. 1	ALH	Sec. 4		ALH, Sec. 1-3	Sec. 1, 2	Sec. 1-3, UD
Sec. 2, 3	Sec. 2, 4	Sec. 2, CK	Sec. 3	Sec. 2, 3	Sec. 3	Sec. 2, 3
Sec. 2	Sec. 1-3	Sec. 2-4	Sec. 2, 3, UD	Sec. 1-3	Sec. 2	Sec. 3
Sec. 1-3, UD	Sec. 1-4	Sec. 1-4	Sec. 1-3, UD	Sec. 1-3	Sec. 1-4	Sec. 1-3, UD
Sec. 3		Sec. 4	Sec. 2	Sec. 1, 2		Sec. 3
Sec. 2	Sec. 2	Sec. 1, 4	Sec. 2	Sec. 1, 2	Sec. 1	Sec. 1-3
Sec. 2	GP, Sec. 2, 4	Sec. 2, 4	Sec. 3, UD	GP		
Sec. 1-3, UD	Sec. 2, 4	Sec. 1, 2		Sec. 1-3	Sec. 1, 2	Sec. 1, 2
Sec. 1-3, UD	Sec. 2	Sec. 1-3	Sec. 1, 2	Sec. 1-3	Sec. 1, 3, 4	Sec. 2, 3, UD
Sec. 3, CR	Sec. 1, 4, CR	CR	CR	Sec. 3, CR	Sec. 3, CR	Sec. 1, CR
Sec. 1, 2	Sec. 2	Sec. 1, 2, 4	Sec. 2, 3	Sec. 3	Sec. 3	
Sec. 1, 3, CR	Sec. 3, 4	Sec. 1	Sec. 1	Sec. 3	Sec. 3	
Sec. 1-3	Sec. 1-4	Sec. 1-4	Sec. 1-3	Sec. 1-3	Sec. 1-4	Sec. 1-3
Sec. 1-3, CR	Sec. 1-4, CR	Sec. 1-4, CR	Sec. 1-3, CR	Sec. 1-3, CR	Sec. 1-4, CR	Sec. 1-3, CR
Sec. 1-3, CR	Sec. 1-4, CR	Sec. 1-4, CR	Sec. 1-3, CR	Sec. 1-3, CR	Sec. 1-4, CR	Sec. 1-3, CR
Sec. 1	Sec. 2, 3, CR	Sec. 1, 2, CR	Sec. 3, CR	Sec. 2, 3		
Sec. 1-3	Sec. 1-3, CR	Sec. 1-4, CR	Sec. 1-3	Sec. 1-3, CR	Sec. 1-4, CR	Sec. 1-3
Sec. 3, CR, UD	Sec. 1, CR		Sec. 3, UD			UD
	Sec. 1, 4	Sec. 4	CR	CR	Sec. 2, 4, CR	Sec. 2, 3

CR–Chapter Review • **UD**–Unit Digest • **ALH**–American Literary Heritage • **CK**–Cultural Kaleidoscope • **GP**–Global Perspectives

SCOPE AND SEQUENCE

	Chapter 13	Chapter 14	Chapter 15	Chapter 16	Chapter 17
Themes and Concepts					
American Democracy	Sec. 2	Sec. 1, 3	Sec. 1, 3, 4	Sec. 2, 3	
Humanities and Religion	**ALH**, Sec. 1		Sec. 4	Sec. 1, 3	**ALH**, Sec. 1, 3
Cultural Diversity	Sec. 1, 3	Sec. 1, 3, **CK**	Sec. 1-4	Sec. 1-3, **UD**	Sec. 1-3
Geography and Environment	Sec. 1, 2	Sec. 1-3	Sec. 1, 2, 4	**UD**	Sec. 1-3
Conflict and Cooperation	Sec. 1-3	Sec. 1-3	Sec. 1-4	Sec. 1-3, **UD**	Sec. 1-3
Influence of Technology	Sec. 3	Sec. 1	Sec. 2		Sec. 1-3
The Individual and Family Life	Sec. 1-3	Sec. 1, 2	Sec. 3	Sec. 1, 2	Sec. 1-3
U.S. Role in World Affairs	**GP**, Sec. 1-3	Sec. 1	Sec. 1	**UD**	**GP**
Civil Rights and Liberties	Sec. 1-3	Sec. 1-3	Sec. 1-4	Sec. 1-3, **UD**	Sec. 1
Economic Development	Sec. 1-3	Sec. 1, 2	Sec. 1, 3	Sec. 1-3	Sec. 1
Social Studies Skills					
Study and Writing	**CR**	Sec. 1, 3, **CR**	**CR**	**CR**	**CR**
Map and Graph	Sec. 1, 2	Sec. 1-3	Sec. 1, 2	Sec. 2, 3	Sec. 1-3
Interpreting Primary Sources	Sec. 2		Sec. 4	Sec. 2	
Making Connections	Sec. 1-3	Sec. 1-3	Sec. 1-4	Sec. 1-3	Sec. 1-3
Critical Thinking Skills					
Knowledge	Sec. 1-3, **CR**	Sec. 1-3, **CR**	Sec. 1-4, **CR**	Sec. 1-3, **CR**	Sec. 1-3, **CR**
Comprehension	Sec. 1-3, **CR**	Sec. 1-3, **CR**	Sec. 1-4, **CR**	Sec. 1-3, **CR**	Sec. 1-3, **CR**
Application	Sec. 3	**CR**		Sec. 2	Sec. 2
Analysis	Sec. 1, 2, **CR**	Sec. 1-3, **CR**	Sec. 1-4, **CR**	Sec. 1-3	Sec. 1, 3, **CR**
Synthesis			Sec. 1	**UD**	Sec. 1
Evaluation	Sec. 2, **CR**	Sec. 1, **CR**	Sec. 3, 4, **CR**	Sec. 1, **CR**	**CR**

Key to Abbreviations

Chapter 18	Chapter 19	Chapter 20	Chapter 21	Chapter 22	Chapter 23	Chapter 24
		Sec. 1-3	Sec. 1-3	Sec. 1-4	Sec. 1-3	Sec. 1-4, UD
	Sec. 3, 4	Sec. 3	Sec. 2, 3	ALH, Sec. 3	Sec. 1, 3	
Sec. 1, 3	Sec. 3, 4	Sec. 1-3	Sec. 1-3, UD	Sec. 2, 3, CK	Sec. 3	Sec. 4
Sec. 1	Sec. 1, 3, 4		Sec. 1, 2, UD	Sec. 2-4		Sec. 1, 3
Sec. 1-3	Sec. 1-4	Sec. 1, 2	Sec. 1-3, UD	Sec. 1-4	Sec. 1-3	
Sec. 1-3	Sec. 1, 4	Sec. 3	Sec. 1, 2, UD	Sec. 1, 4	Sec. 2	Sec. 1
Sec. 1-3	Sec. 1, 3, 4	Sec. 2, 3	Sec. 1, 3	Sec. 2	Sec. 1-3	Sec. 1-3, UD
Sec. 3	Sec. 3	Sec. 2	Sec. 3	GP, Sec. 1-4	Sec. 3	Sec. 3, 4, UD
Sec. 3	Sec. 1-4	Sec. 1	Sec. 3	Sec. 2	Sec. 1-3	Sec. 1, 3, 4
Sec. 1-3	Sec. 1, 2	Sec. 2	Sec. 1-3	Sec. 1-4	Sec. 1-3	Sec. 1-4, UD
CR	Sec. 1, CR	CR	CR	CR	CR	Sec. 3, CR
Sec. 1, 3	Sec. 3, 4		Sec. 1	Sec. 2-4	Sec. 1	Sec. 3, 4
Sec. 2	Sec. 2, 3	Sec. 1-3	Sec. 1, 2	Sec. 4		Sec. 2
Sec. 1-3	Sec. 1-4	Sec. 1-3	Sec. 1-3	Sec. 1-4	Sec. 1-3	Sec. 1-4
Sec. 1-3, CR	Sec. 1-4, CR	Sec. 1-3, CR	Sec. 1-3, CR	Sec. 1-4, CR	Sec. 1-3, CR	Sec. 1-4, CR
Sec. 1-3, CR	Sec. 1-4, CR	Sec. 1-3, CR	Sec. 1-3, CR	Sec. 1-4, CR	Sec. 1-3, CR	Sec. 1-4, CR
Sec. 1, 2	Sec. 1, 2, CR	Sec. 3	Sec. 1		CR	Sec. 3, CR
Sec. 1, 3, CR	Sec. 1-4, CR	Sec. 1-3, CR	Sec. 1-3	Sec. 1-4, CR	Sec. 1-3, CR	Sec. 1, 2
	Sec. 4		Sec. 2, CR, UD			UD
Sec. 2, 3, CR	CR	Sec. 2	Sec. 3	Sec. 2, 4, CR		Sec. 2, 4, CR

CR–Chapter Review • **UD**–Unit Digest • **ALH**–American Literary Heritage • **CK**–Cultural Kaleidoscope • **GP**–Global Perspectives

SCOPE AND SEQUENCE

	Chapter 25	Chapter 26	Chapter 27	Chapter 28	Chapter 29
Themes and Concepts					
American Democracy	Sec. 3, 4	Sec. 1, 2	Sec. 2, 3	Sec. 1-4	Sec. 1, 4
Humanities and Religion	ALH	Sec. 1, 3	Sec. 2	ALH, Sec. 4	
Cultural Diversity		Sec. 1	Sec. 1	Sec. 4	Sec. 4
Geography and Environment	Sec. 1, 2, 4	Sec. 1		Sec. 2	Sec. 2, 3
Conflict and Cooperation	Sec. 1-4	Sec. 1-3	Sec. 2, 3, UD	Sec. 1-4	Sec. 1-4
Influence of Technology	Sec. 1-4	Sec. 1-3	Sec. 1, 2, UD		Sec. 3, 4
The Individual and Family Life	Sec. 4	Sec. 1-3	Sec. 1-3, UD	Sec. 1-4	Sec. 4
U.S. Role in World Affairs	GP, Sec. 1-4	Sec. 1, 2	Sec. 2, UD	GP	Sec. 1-4
Civil Rights and Liberties	Sec. 2, 3	Sec. 1, 3	Sec. 3	Sec. 2-4	Sec. 4
Economic Development	Sec. 2	Sec. 1, 2	Sec. 1-3	Sec. 1-4	Sec. 4
Social Studies Skills					
Study and Writing	CR	Sec. 1, CR	Sec. 2, CR	CR	CR
Map and Graph	Sec. 1, 2, 4, CR	Sec. 1, 2	Sec. 1, 2	Sec. 2	Sec. 3, 4
Interpreting Primary Sources	Sec. 1-3	Sec. 1-3	Sec. 1	Sec. 1-3, CR	Sec. 4
Making Connections	Sec. 1-4	Sec. 1-3	Sec. 1-3	Sec. 1-4	Sec. 1-4
Critical Thinking Skills					
Knowledge	Sec. 1-4, CR	Sec. 1-3, CR	Sec. 1-3, CR	Sec. 1-4, CR	Sec. 1-4, CR
Comprehension	Sec. 1-4, CR	Sec. 1-3, CR	Sec. 1-3, CR	Sec. 1-4, CR	Sec. 1-4, CR
Application	Sec. 1, 3, CR	Sec. 2, 3	Sec. 2, 3		Sec. 4
Analysis	Sec. 3, 4, CR	Sec. 1-3, CR	Sec. 1-3	Sec. 1-4, CR	Sec. 1-4, CR
Synthesis	Sec. 2	CR	Sec. 1, CR, UD		Sec. 4
Evaluation	Sec. 1, 2, CR	Sec. 1, 3, CR		Sec. 2, CR	Sec. 1, 3, CR

Key to Abbreviations

Chapter 30	Chapter 31	Chapter 32	Chapter 33	Chapter 34	Chapter 35	Chapter 36
Sec. 1, 3	Sec. 1-4, UD	Sec. 1-4	Sec. 3, 4	Sec. 1, 2, 4	Sec. 2	Sec. 1, 3
Sec. 1	Sec. 3	ALH, Sec. 1	Sec. 3	Sec. 1		Sec. 2, ALH
Sec. 1, 3	Sec. 3	Sec. 1-4	Sec. 1-3	CK	Sec. 2	Sec. 2, 3, ALH, UD
Sec. 1-3	Sec. 1, 4		Sec. 1, 2, 4	Sec. 2	Sec. 1-3	Sec. 2, 3
Sec. 1-3	Sec. 1-4, UD	Sec. 1-4	Sec. 1-4	Sec. 1-4	Sec. 1-3	Sec. 1-4, UD
Sec. 1	Sec. 3, 4		Sec. 2	Sec. 1	Sec. 2	
Sec. 1, 3	Sec. 2, 3	Sec. 1, 2, 4	Sec. 3			Sec. 3
Sec. 3	Sec. 1, 4, UD	GP	Sec. 1-4	Sec. 1, 3, 4	Sec. 1-3	Sec. 2, UD
Sec. 1-3	Sec. 2, 3, UD	Sec. 1-4	Sec. 3		Sec. 3	Sec. 1, 3, UD
Sec. 1, 3	Sec. 2	Sec. 4	Sec. 1	Sec. 1-4	Sec. 1-3	Sec. 1-3
CR	CR	CR	CR	CR	CR	CR
Sec. 1-3	Sec. 3, 4	CR	Sec. 2, 4, CR	CR	Sec. 2, 3, CR	Sec. 1, 2, CR
		CR	CR	Sec. 2, 4	CR	CR
Sec. 1-3	Sec. 1-4	Sec. 1	Sec. 1	Sec. 1	Sec. 3	Sec. 3
Sec. 1-3, CR	Sec. 1-4, CR	Sec. 1-4	Sec. 1-4, CR	Sec. 1-4, CR	Sec. 1-3, CR	Sec. 1-3, CR
Sec. 1-3, CR	Sec. 1-4, CR	Sec. 1-4	Sec. 1-4, CR	Sec. 1-4, CR	Sec. 1-3, CR	Sec. 1-3, CR
Sec. 2, 3, CR	Sec. 1, 4, CR	Sec. 1, 4	Sec. 1, CR	Sec. 1, 2	Sec. 3	Sec. 1, 3, CR
Sec. 1-3, CR	Sec. 1-4	Sec. 1, 4	Sec. 1, 2, 4, CR	Sec. 1-4, CR	Sec. 2, 3, CR	Sec. 2, 3
Sec. 1	UD		Sec. 3			CR, UD
Sec. 1	Sec. 1, 2, 4, CR	Sec. 2, CR	Sec. 2, 4, CR	Sec. 2, 3, CR	Sec. 1, 2, CR	Sec. 2, 3

CR–Chapter Review • **UD**–Unit Digest • **ALH**–American Literary Heritage • **CK**–Cultural Kaleidoscope • **GP**–Global Perspectives

Professional Notes

Cooperative Learning

Although cooperative learning is a useful teaching strategy in many subjects, it occupies a special place in the social studies curriculum because of its success in imparting the abilities needed to work effectively in a group. Such social studies skills are beneficial for all citizens living in a democracy.

Research suggests that mixed ability grouping in learning activities leads to higher student achievement, especially for lower ability level students. More able students benefit as well, however, from the reinforcement of learning that occurs as they assist their peers or justify their opinions.

■ Defining Cooperative Learning

Cooperative learning requires students to work together to pursue a common goal. Each member of the group has a specific task to accomplish in achieving the group's goal. Because part of each student's evaluation is determined by the overall quality of the group's work, there are incentives for students to help one another accomplish tasks assigned to the group as a whole. In such approaches, cooperation replaces the competitiveness of more traditional classroom activities, and students learn effective interpersonal communication skills.

Cooperative learning requires careful structuring and monitoring by the teacher if it is to be something more than a group activity. Characteristics of cooperative learning include the following:

- Students work face-to-face in heterogeneous groups.
- The activity promotes a sense of positive interdependence.
- Each member of a group has individual accountability.
- The group has a common product or goal.

■ Role of the Teacher

Although successful Cooperative Learning groups may appear to work independently, this is no doubt due to the astute coaching of a good teacher. Groups may need the teacher's assistance at key moments during a project, such as in agreeing on goals, establishing a structure of accountability, or evaluating their success. In particular, the teacher needs to assure that no one student in a group does most of the work.

In their efforts to achieve group goals or objectives, students practice such social skills as listening critically, consensus building, conflict resolution, and offering and accepting constructive feedback.

■ Cooperative Learning in the *History of a Free Nation* Program

Throughout the *History of a Free Nation* program, students are asked to work together to address significant questions and resolve pertinent issues raised in their study. Activities require students to work together to analyze, synthesize, and apply lesson content. These cooperative learning activities challenge groups to solve problems, to make decisions, and to explain or justify conclusions. Many activities involve students in hands-on research and in presenting learning to others.

Depending on the nature of the activity, the strategies suggest that students approach tasks in pairs, small groups, or larger groups. Generally, the ideal group size will be four to six students. The teacher should structure each group to obtain a mix of high, average, and low achievers. In addition, gender and ethnic balance should be sought.

The **Student Edition** includes cooperative learning activities in each of the **Chapter Reviews**. They provide a variety of opportunities for students to work together on activities related to the chapter content.

The **Teacher's Wraparound Edition** contains both individual and cooperative learning activities. The cooperative learning suggestions, found in the bottom channel throughout the lessons, offer a variety of interesting, activity-based teaching ideas.

The **Teacher's Classroom Resources** includes a **Cooperative Learning Acivities** booklet containing blackline master cooperative learnng activities for each chapter. These activities reinforce learning and build mangement and interpersonal skills by requiring students to work together to acquire, organize, and present information.

Block Scheduling

Block scheduling differs from traditional scheduling in that fewer class sessions are scheduled for larger blocks of time over fewer days. For example, in block scheduling, a course might meet for 90 minutes a day for 90 days, or half a school year. Does this type of scheduling have any advantage over more traditional scheduling methods? Those schools that have tried it believe that it does.

■ Advantages for School Systems

For the schools themselves, the greatest advantage of block scheduling is that there is a better use of resources. No additional teachers or classrooms may be needed, and more efficient use is made of those resources presently in schools. These advantages are accompanied by an increase in the quality of teacher instruction and students' time on task.

■ Advantages for Teachers

The advantages for teachers who are in schools that use block scheduling are many. Teacher-student relationships are improved. In traditional scheduling, teachers may teach five or six (or more) classes a day with as many different preparations. They are expected to know and teach 150 or more students in a day's time. With block scheduling, teachers have responsibility for a smaller number of students at a time, so students and teachers get to know each other better. With more time, teachers are able to provide additional time and resources for meeting the individual needs of students.

Teachers can also be more focused on what they are teaching. In fact, block scheduling seems to result in changes in teaching approaches, classrooms that are more student-centered, improved teacher morale, and increased teacher effectiveness. Teachers feel free to venture away from discussion and lecture to use more productive models of teaching.

If school days are of the same length as those that are more traditionally scheduled, teachers find the block approach more time-efficient. Block scheduling cuts in half the time needed for introducing and closing classes. Block scheduling also eliminates half of the time needed for class changes. If two six-minute class changes are eliminated each day, an hour of teaching time is gained in just one week. Fewer class changes also result in fewer discipline problems.

■ Advantages for Students

The benefits of block scheduling are not limited to teachers. Student success rate is found to be greater than is found with traditional scheduling because students seem to learn more and retain it better. Problem-solving skills are better developed, grades are improved, and the failure rate is lower.

Some of the advantages for teachers also are advantages for students. Improved student-teacher relationships and a more manageable work load help students. Students feel better about what they are learning, outside interference is reduced, and students are better able to concentrate. Generally, students feel better organized and are more aware of their progress in the class.

Parents report that there are many home-related benefits to block scheduling. There are fewer hassles about school, and students have a more positive attitude in general and take more responsibility for their homework. All of this results in a more relaxed family environment.

■ Modified Block Scheduling

Some schools use a modified form of block scheduling that combines two core classes. Under this system students might study social studies for 90 minutes each day during the first semester, science during the second semester. Another modification has students take English and social studies blocks in one semester and science and mathematics blocks the second. Such scheduling encourages the teachers to institute team teaching or similar interdisciplinary approaches.

90-Minute Block Schedule Planning Guide

The following is a suggested planning guide for using *History of a Free Nation* in 90-minute periods for a total of 90 days. It can easily be adjusted for alternative lengths or for varied course emphasis.

Unit/Chapter/Section	Days
Unit 1 *A New World: Prehistory to 1776*	**8**
CHAPTER 1 The World in Transition	3
Section 1: The First Americans	1
Section 2: The New Europe	½
Section 3: Medieval Asia and Africa	½
Section 4: Europeans Seek the East	½
Chapter Review and Test	½
CHAPTER 2 The Age of Exploration	2
Section 1: Voyages of Columbus	½
Section 2: Spain in America	½
Section 3: New Ventures	½
Chapter Review and Test	½
CHAPTER 3 Colonial America	3
Section 1: The Southern Colonies	½
Section 2: New England	½
Section 3: The Middle Colonies	½
Section 4: People of the Colonies	1
Chapter Review and Test	½
Unit 2 *Creating a Nation: 1650–1789*	**9**
CHAPTER 4 The Road to Revolution	2½
Section 1: Struggle for Empire	½
Section 2: Control and Protest	½
Section 3: The Breach Widens	1
Chapter Review and Test	½
CHAPTER 5 War for Independence	4
Section 1: Foundations of Freedom	1
Section 2: Fighting for Independence	1
Section 3: The War Deepens	1
Section 4: The War Ends	½
Chapter Review and Test	½
CHAPTER 6 A More Perfect Union	2½
Section 1: Government in Transition	½
Section 2: The Confederation	½
Section 3: Toward a New Constitution	1
Chapter Review and Test	½
Unit 3 *Launching the Republic: 1789–1824*	**8½**
CHAPTER 7 The Federalist Era	3
Section 1: Organizing the Government	½
Section 2: Solving National Problems	1
Section 3: Foreign Affairs Under Washington	½
Section 4: President John Adams	½
Chapter Review and Test	½
CHAPTER 8 Age of Jefferson	3
Section 1: The Changing Political Scene	½
Section 2: Looking Westward	1
Section 3: Foreign Affairs	½
Section 4: The War of 1812	½
Chapter Review and Test	½

Unit/Chapter/Section	Days
CHAPTER 9 Nationalism and Change	2½
Section 1: The Era of Good Feeling	½
Section 2: Tying the Nation Together	1
Section 3: Monroe and Foreign Affairs	½
Chapter Review and Test	½
Unit 4 *Toward a Democracy: 1820–1854*	**7**
CHAPTER 10 Sectionalism and Growth	2
Section 1: Growth in the North	½
Section 2: Growth in the South and West	½
Section 3: Rivalry and Compromise	½
Chapter Review and Test	½
CHAPTER 11 Age of Jackson	3
Section 1: Growth of Democracy	1
Section 2: Jacksonian Democracy	½
Section 3: Political Controversies	½
Section 4: The Bank and the Whigs	½
Chapter Review and Test	½
CHAPTER 12 The Spirit of Reform	2
Section 1: Advances in Education	½
Section 2: Struggle for Rights	½
Section 3: Social and Cultural Change	½
Chapter Review and Test	½
Unit 5 *Division and Reunion: 1825–1877*	**10**
CHAPTER 13 Manifest Destiny	2
Section 1: The Thirst for New Lands	½
Section 2: War With Mexico	½
Section 3: Global Interests	½
Chapter Review and Test	½
CHAPTER 14 Compromise and Conflict	2
Section 1: A Union in Danger	½
Section 2: Dispute Over Slavery	½
Section 3: Drifting Toward War	½
Chapter Review and Test	½
CHAPTER 15 The Civil War	4
Section 1: The Outbreak of War	1
Section 2: The War on the Battlefield	1
Section 3: Behind the Lines	½
Section 4: Ending the War	1
Chapter Review and Test	½
CHAPTER 16 Reconstruction	2
Section 1: After Slavery	½
Section 2: Reconstructing the South	½
Section 3: Restoring Southern Power	½
Chapter Review and Test	½
Unit 6 *New Horizons: 1860–1900*	**10**
CHAPTER 17 Into the West	2
Section 1: People of the Plains	½
Section 2: Ranching and Mining	½
Section 3: Farming Moves West	½
Chapter Review and Test	½

Unit/Chapter/Section	Days
CHAPTER 18 The Rise of Industry	**2**
Section 1: Industrialization Takes Hold	½
Section 2: Growth of Big Business	½
Section 3: Captains of Industry	½
Chapter Review and Test	½
CHAPTER 19 An Urban Society	**2**
Section 1: The Workers' Plight	½
Section 2: The Rise of New Unions	½
Section 3: City Life and Problems	½
Chapter Review and Test	½
CHAPTER 20 The Gilded Age	**2**
Section 1: A Tarnished Image	½
Section 2: Calls for Good Government	½
Section 3: Cultural Life	½
Chapter Review and Test	½
CHAPTER 21 Politics and Protest	**2**
Section 1: Agrarian Unrest	½
Section 2: Rise and Fall of Populism	½
Section 3: Other Forces for Reform	½
Chapter Review and Test	½
Unit 7 *Entering a New Century: 1867–1920*	**6 ½**
CHAPTER 22 Imperialism	**2 ½**
Section 1: America Looks Abroad	½
Section 2: The Spanish-American War	½
Section 3: Becoming a World Power	½
Section 4: A New Arena	½
Chapter Review and Test	½
CHAPTER 23 The Progressive Era	**2**
Section 1: Sources of Progressivism	½
Section 2: Progressive Reforms	½
Section 3: Limits of Progressivism	½
Chapter Review and Test	½
CHAPTER 24 White House Reformers	**2**
Section 1: The Square Deal	½
Section 2: The Taft Presidency	½
Section 3: The Election of 1912	½
Chapter Review and Test	½
Unit 8 *Crusade and Disillusion: 1914–1932*	**7**
CHAPTER 25 World War I Era	**3**
Section 1: Prelude to War	½
Section 2: America Enters the War	1
Section 3: War on the Home Front	½
Section 4: After the War	½
Chapter Review and Test	½
CHAPTER 26 The Decade of Normalcy	**2**
Section 1: The Harding Years	½
Section 2: The Coolidge Era	½
Section 3: The "Roaring Twenties"	½
Chapter Review and Test	½
CHAPTER 27 The Depression Begins	**2**
Section 1: The Stock Market Crashes	½
Section 2: Hoover's Policies	½
Section 3: The Depression Worsens	½
Chapter Review and Test	½

Unit/Chapter/Section	Days
Unit 9 *Times of Crisis: 1932–1960*	**10**
CHAPTER 28 The New Deal	**2 ½**
Section 1: Roosevelt Takes Charge	½
Section 2: Reform, Relief, and Recovery	½
Section 3: The Second New Deal	½
Section 4: The Impact of the New Deal	½
Chapter Review and Test	½
CHAPTER 29 World War II	**3**
Section 1: World Affairs, 1933-1939	½
Section 2: Moving Closer to War	½
Section 3: The United States at War	1
Section 4: War on the Home Front	½
Chapter Review and Test	½
CHAPTER 30 The Cold War	**2**
Section 1: The Start of the Cold War	½
Section 2: The Cold War in Asia	½
Section 3: Cold War America	½
Chapter Review and Test	½
CHAPTER 31 Search for Stability	**2 ½**
Section 1: The Eisenhower Years	½
Section 2: The Straight Road	½
Section 3: An Affluent Society	½
Section 4: Foreign Policy	½
Chapter Review and Test	½
Unit 10 *Redefining America: 1954 to Present*	**13**
CHAPTER 32 The Civil Rights Era	**3 ½**
Section 1: A New Beginning	1
Section 2: Successes and Setbacks	1
Section 3: New Directions	½
Section 4: The Impact of Civil Rights	½
Chapter Review and Test	½
CHAPTER 33 The Vietnam Era	**3**
Section 1: Cold War Challenges	½
Section 2: War in Vietnam	1
Section 3: Protest and Reaction	½
Section 4: Secrecy and Summitry	½
Chapter Review and Test	½
CHAPTER 34 Camelot to Watergate	**2 ½**
Section 1: Kennedy's New Frontier	½
Section 2: The Great Society	½
Section 3: An Imperial Presidency	½
Section 4: The Watergate Scandal	½
Chapter Review and Test	½
CHAPTER 35 Search for Solutions	**2**
Section 1: Crisis of Confidence	½
Section 2: A Conservative Shift	½
Section 3: A New Presidency	½
Chapter Review and Test	½
CHAPTER 36 Toward a New Century	**2**
Section 1: Reinventing Government	½
Section 2: America in a Changing World	½
Section 3: Challenges and Opportunities	½
Chapter Review and Test	½

Professional Notes

Multicultural Perspective

The study of history furnishes a wealth of material than can help students learn to appreciate the multicultural diversity of the United States. By reading *History of a Free Nation*, students receive a broad view of the people and events that have contributed to the foundation of this country and the smooth operation of our system of democracy.

As immigration continues to make the United States a multicultural society, it is increasingly important for students to see peoples different from themselves as interesting neighbors who have different ideas, customs, and languages, but who also share many of the same values. By studying all aspects of our multicultural society, students gain a keen understanding of the roles that all Americans have played and continue to play in our government.

The following five points have been identified as some of the major goals of multicultural education:

- Promoting the strength and value of cultural diversity.
- Promoting human rights and respect for those who are different from oneself.
- Promoting alternative life choices for people.
- Promoting social justice and equal opportunity for all people.
- Promoting equity in the distribution of power among groups.

—from *Making Choices for Multicultural Education: Five Approaches to Race, Class, and Gender* by Sleeter, Grant. Columbus: Merrill Publishing, 1988.

Critical Thinking

To learn about history in a way that prepares students to become thoughtful participants in our society, students must learn to think critically. They need to be able to evaluate and to question the meaning of what they see, read, and hear. The teacher plays a crucial role in this development by creating a classroom climate that actively encourages critical thinking. To help teach critical thinking, teachers may wish to refer to Benjamin Bloom's Taxonomy of Cognitive Behavior. Bloom's Taxonomy organizes cognitive learning into six hierarchical classes:

- Knowledge involves recalling, identifying, and defining.
- Comprehension includes describing, explaining, summarizing and interpreting.
- Application entails applying, solving, and predicting.
- Analysis involves organizing, comparing, differentiating, relating, and inferring.
- Synthesis includes combining, producing, proposing, and hypothesizing.
- Evaluation entails appraising, judging, and deciding.

■ THE CLASSROOM CLIMATE

The teacher can promote critical thinking in the classroom by asking questions that encourage students to analyze, synthesize, apply, and evaluate the information they hear and read daily. Sources for critical thinking activities or discussions range from the textbooks to newspaper and magazine stories and television news reports. Questions dealing with what happened, when it happened, or who was involved check the student's comprehension of facts. Questions that ask them to compare or explain events require that they dig deeper.

■ CRITICAL THINKING IN THE HISTORY OF A FREE NATION PROGRAM

Critical thinking is taught, reviewed, and reinforced throughout the *History of a Free Nation* program. The **Student Edition** teaches the skills used in critical thinking, such as distinguishing between fact and opinion, determining cause and effect, and recognizing bias. Each of the skill pages provides opportunities for students to both learn and practice the skill being taught. Additional practice is provided in each **Section Review**, **Chapter Review**, and **Unit Review** to continually reinforce the critical thinking process.

The **Teacher's Wraparound Edition** includes additional critical thinking activities. These are found in the bottom channel throughout the lessons.

Different Learning Styles

Your classroom undoubtedly contains students from a variety of backgrounds and with a variety of learning styles. In order to reach all of your students and make their learning experiences the most rewarding for their individual needs, *History of a Free Nation* provides a wealth of instructional approaches and strategies.

■ VISUAL LEARNERS

Visual learners benefit the most when they can carefully look at the material to be studied. In general, visual learners retain more information if they are able to visualize what they are learning. These types of learners benefit from laserdisc presentations as well as from CD-ROMs. Visual learners also benefit from reading the text and studying the accompanying visuals.

■ AUDITORY LEARNERS

Auditory learners retain the most information when they hear what they are to learn. Oral instructions from the teacher are ideal ways to introduce these learners to new concepts. Technology also plays an essential role in helping these learners master the course content. For example, audiocassette transcripts of chapters or lessons provide these students with invaluable learning aids. These students also benefit from laserdisc presentations because the soundtracks help them comprehend the information with a higher retention rate. These learners also benefit from CD-ROMs, which provide them with instant auditory directions and feedback.

■ KINESTHETIC LEARNERS

Kinesthetic learners retain information more easily when they can actually perform basic tasks using the information. For these students, individual or group projects in which they construct models, charts, or graphs are ideal.

At-Risk Students

Most educators today agree that the nation's schools are facing an epidemic of students who are at risk of failure. If their special needs are not met, these students usually drop out of school. Without a high school education, these young people face a life of low wages and menial jobs. Occupying the lowest ranks of our society, these young people seldom have the opportunity to enjoy the advantages that most Americans take for granted. These young people also make up a disproportionate number of prison inmates, with little hope for escape from the cycle of poverty.

■ IDENTIFYING AT-RISK STUDENTS

It is difficult to define exactly what constitutes an at-risk student because being at risk is not linked to a single cause. Rather it is often linked to several environmental causes such as limited English proficiency, poverty, low self-esteem, homelessness, substance abuse, or pregnancy. Whatever the causes, at-risk students share a common characteristic. They have extreme difficulty with learning and are almost always low achievers.

■ TEACHING METHODS

Current educational research has shown that certain teaching methods can make a difference with at-risk students and help keep them from dropping out. One method is to maximize time-on-task. By doing so, teachers can help students overcome the outside stimuli that distract them from academic work.

Another method is to establish high expectations and a school climate that supports learning. Expecting students to succeed will help them believe that they are capable of succeeding. Many schools actively involve parents in this process so that the expectations for success are not left inside the classroom after school is out. By including the parents in decision making, many teachers have found that the entire school community benefits.

Because at-risk students have often failed in school, it is important to give them as much positive feedback as possible. Many teachers try to give this feedback at the end of each successfully completed assignment and regularly include awards ceremonies for those students who are meeting expectations.

Professional Notes

Performance Assessment

■ DEFINING PERFORMANCE ASSESSMENT

In response to the growing demand for accountability in the classroom, many educators are advocating new approaches to assessment. One such approach is performance assessment, which measures student achievement in a more constructive and interactive manner than traditional tests do. In general, performance assessment includes performance-based activities and tests, and portfolios.

Performance tests ask students to effectively and creatively apply the knowledge they have gained. These tests require the application of problem-solving skills rather than mere recall. Instead of using a multiple-choice test to assess knowledge of a specific government concept, for example, a performance-based test asks students to actually utilize the concept. In designing performance-based tests, educators devise tasks that have more than one correct answer and that require more than one answer to complete. A key element in scoring such tests is to analyze the process the students use to clarify and solve the problem. Scoring involves rating students' performance on multiple factors, resulting in a descriptive profile of performance.

The portfolio approach is often used with performance-based assessment. Portfolios contain samples of students' work collected over a period of time—an entire grading period or even a semester. Students often help choose which items will be included in their portfolios. Portfolios allow for assessing a broad range of skills. Students can see how much progress they are making by comparing the work that they have completed throughout the course.

■ PERFORMANCE ASSESSMENT ACTIVITIES

Performance assessment is a way of teaching and learning that involves both process and product. It is not just a testing strategy.

Performance assessment activities provide "hands-on" approaches to learning concepts. Through the activities students are able to actually experience these concepts rather than just reading, writing, and listening about them. Each performance assessment is designed to allow the teacher to give a guided practice of the concepts being taught. At the end of each activity, the student is assigned a performance task that checks understanding of the lesson's concepts.

Performance assessment tasks get students involved in constructing various types of products for diverse audiences. Students also are involved in developing the process that leads to the finished product.

Performance assessment measures what you can do with what you know, not how much you know. Performance assessment tasks are based on what is most essential in the curriculum and what is interesting to a student.

■ MORE LIKE PLAYING BASEBALL THAN JUST PLAYING CATCH

Many concepts, skills, and attitudes are important if an athlete is to develop into an accomplished baseball player. A coach teaches and drills players and promotes appropriate attitudes. However, if the training stopped there, the players would never learn the game. They must *play* baseball. Similarly, teachers can present the information and skills of a discipline and quiz the students on the details, but students also must "play the game." Students need the opportunity to put the concepts, skills, and attitudes together. Performance assessment allows students to demonstrate how effectively they can put the pieces together in ways similar to how information is used in the larger world.

■ LOOKING AT AUTHENTIC USE OF INFORMATION

A common model of assessment is to teach the chapter, then stop and test the students.

Performance assessment changes this pattern. Performance assessment is an approach to learning that changes what the teacher and students do in class. The textbook becomes a resource for learning; it becomes a means to an end rather than the end in itself.

When students leave school they will need to use books and other sources to find information on specific subjects. Perhaps they will need to make an oral presentation to a specific audience, design a display, produce a video, or research a consumer question and write a persuasive letter.

These kinds of tasks all use information in an authentic way. With performance assessment, students are engaged in tasks in which they are crafting products. The teacher is the coach who is guiding the students' work, providing models of excellent work, and giving feedback all along the way. Performance assessment tasks get students highly involved in constructing all types of products, and this active involvement results in meaningful learning.

The word *authentic* used with performance assessment means that the performance uses information, concepts, and skills in ways that people use them in the larger world. School should be a valid preparation for what is required in the larger world.

■ PERFORMANCE ASSESSMENT REQUIRES THINKING SKILLS

Thinking skills provide the "verbs" that direct the action in performance assessment tasks. These include getting information, processing it, and using it to make a product. Thinking skills include those activities related to understanding the audience and crafting a product that fulfills a certain purpose with that audience. The assessment of the students' work should not only look at the final product, but should also assess the processes that lead to it.

■ PERFORMANCE ASSESSMENT MAKES USE OF DIFFERENT LEARNING STYLES AND PREFERENCES

Some learners prefer to understand the connections between ideas and excel in the skills of critical analysis. These students are good at predicting, comparing and contrasting, and analyzing. Other learners enjoy organizing information and excel in remembering the details. A third group of learners engages in creative problem solving and uses productive, divergent thinking skills. A fourth group is best at tasks that require interpersonal skills. This group is good at interviewing and working in teams. They focus on attitudes, motivations, feelings, and opinions and are more self-aware than most. Some students prefer to write while others like oral presentations; still others enjoy drawing or constructing.

All learning styles are important and students should not use only the style in which they excel, but should also work on tasks that require other styles so that they can expand their competency. The student who prefers to write detailed, factual information pamphlets for peers should also be given the opportunity to become better at making persuasive posters for adult groups. Some performance tasks will dictate what the product is to be like. Other performance tasks will involve all students with the same information, but will allow them to choose the format, purpose, and audience for their product.

■ PERFORMANCE ASSESSMENT INVOLVES COOPERATIVE LEARNING

Cooperative learning simulates how teamwork is used in a business environment. Effectively managed cooperative learning not only develops essential lifelong interpersonal skills, it also gets the students to spend more time actively thinking. Performance assessment often uses a combination of individual and group cooperative learning. Group work may be used as the initial step to get students actively engaged and to allow for a diversity of ideas to emerge. Sometimes, the whole project is done through group work and, in this case, individuals should have specific tasks for which they are accountable. For example, if the group's task is to write a booklet for elementary school children on the topic of European governments, each person in the group should have a chapter to create. The whole group can work together to plan the sequence of chapters, the cover, an author's page, and other elements while each individual is responsible for a specific chapter. The individual's assessment is for the chapter. There is no group grade for the entire book. If the entire book is well done, then the group's reward is that the book will be sent to an elementary school. Individuals are accountable for their work and the group has a goal for overall quality.

■ PERFORMANCE ASSESSMENT IN THE HISTORY OF A FREE NATION PROGRAM

The *History of a Free Nation* program provides a variety of performance assessment suggestions and options. The **Teacher's Wraparound Edition** provides **Portfolio Project** suggestions at the beginning of each unit. **Performance Assessment Activities** are included on each Chapter Planning Guide. Additional performance assessment activities and rubrics are provided in the **Performance Assessment Strategies and Activities** booklet found in the **Teacher's Classroom Resources**.

Professional Notes

Technology in the Classroom

Advances in technology are continually being made, and these advances dramatically affect all aspects of the social studies. Social studies instruction should include an awareness of advances in technology. Wherever possible, discuss technology with your students as an ongoing part of the social studies courses.

■ Using Software with Limited Hardware

As with many other types of instructional tools, the more equipment available, the more flexibility your program can have. The ideal situation is to have one computer for each member of the class. You also might have access several times a week to a school computer lab. If either of these situations exists, you have unlimited opportunities for providing a wide range of computer activities. It is possible, however, to provide some computer activities with limited computer hardware.

- **One Computer for Twenty-five Students.** With one computer, three to five students can be accommodated in an average class period by rotating students at the computer. Rather than have each student complete a specific exercise, form teams of two or possibly three students and assign each a portion of the software for the chapter. All students can then gain some computer experience without taking an excessive amount of classroom time. The one-computer classroom is also ideal for demonstration using an electronic display device hooked up to a computer and an overhead projector. Remember that computerized student demonstrations of social studies concepts are excellent learning situations that develop not only content knowledge, but also software and communication skills as well.

- **Three to Five Computers for Twenty-five Students.** Three to five students can be accommodated at each computer in an average class period. All students should be able to complete review and reinforcement activities and become familiar with computers.

- **Seven to Ten Computers for Twenty-five Students.** Review and reinforcement programs can all be completed on an individual basis. With proper scheduling, students should have sufficient time to complete several computer activities without intruding on instructional time.

■ Multimedia

As a social studies teacher, you know that your students have varying learning styles. Some students are print-dominant learners; others are non-print-dominant learners. To help you accommodate these varying learning styles and to integrate listening, hands-on application, and more frequent stimulation and interactivity into the classroom, Glencoe offers a variety of multimedia programs, including software, laserdiscs, CD-ROMs, and audiocassettes.

■ Laserdiscs

If your school has a basic system consisting of a videodisc player and a television receiver, Glencoe laserdiscs provide an effective tool for classroom presentations. Students can see the connection between concepts and the real world. Students are also given opportunities to apply what they have learned.

■ CD-ROMs

CD-ROM programs provide large databases of information, as well as sound and motion. A display panel allows for large-screen display.

■ Computer Training for Teachers

You must have a general knowledge of computer operation, but you do not have to have a knowledge of internal hardware elements or programming languages. Resources exist in every school or district for help in using any troubleshooting equipment. These resources include other computer teachers, lab assistants, and technology supervisors. Concentrate on becoming familiar with the operation of your software programs. Remember that software hotlines are one of your best resources when using any type of software. Glencoe's software HOTLINE is 1-800-437-3715.

Teacher's Classroom Resources

Study Guide

Reading Comprehension

Study Guide is a complete set of focused study materials that systematically review key terms, ideas, and events in every section of the textbook.

Name _____ Date _____ Class _____

CHAPTER 12
Study Guide

THE SPIRIT OF REFORM

SECTION ONE Learning Key Terms
1. Write the term that fits each description.
   a. State senator who signed a bill in 1837 creating a state board of education in Massachusetts and served as secretary of that board for 12 years _____
   b. Author of *American Spelling Book* and dictionaries who favored using language to promote national spirit _____
   c. Cleric and college president who introduced reading anthologies filled with moral instructions and patriotic sayings _____
2. Write the meaning of each of the following term:
   lyceum: _____

Understanding Important Ideas and Events
3. Write two sentences describing important ideas and events from Section One.
_____
_____

SECTION TWO Learning Key Terms
1. Write the term that fits each description.
   a. Saw mental illness as a disease rather than a crime, advocated establishment of asylums _____
   b. Gathering of women reformers who drew up resolutions supporting women's rights _____
   c. Black antislavery reformer who also supported women's rights _____
   d. Editor of *The Liberator* who attacked the Constitution for its support of slavery _____
   e. Former slave called "Black Moses" because she guided more than 300 slaves to freedom via Underground Railroad _____
2. Write the meaning of each of the following terms:
   abolitionists: _____
   Underground Railroad: _____

Understanding Important Ideas and Events
3. Write two sentences describing important ideas and events from Section Two.
_____
_____

History of a Free Nation

Study Guide 23

Name _____

SECTION THREE Learning Key Terms
1. Write the term that fits each description.
   a. A group of eastern romantic landscape painters _____
   b. New England architect who developed distinctiv_ architecture and helped complete design of Capi_
   c. Distinctly American philosophical movement e_ between human beings and nature _____
   d. Immense renewal and growth of Protestantism
2. Write the meaning of each of the following term_
   socialism: _____

Understanding Important Ideas and Events
3. Write two sentences describing important ideas

IDENTIFYING ACCOMPLISHMENTS
Fill in the chart below by adding the names _ ers and other contributors to educational a_

Reformer	
Horace Mann	opened _
	wrote s_
William McGuffey	helped _
Mary Lyon	esta_
Elizabeth Blackwell	or_
William Lloyd Garrison	_
Mother Ann Lee	founder of American Peace Society

24 Study Guide

T33

Teacher's Classroom Resources

Reading Comprehension

Concept Mapping Activities

Concept Mapping Activities provide graphic organizers that help students structure conceptually the knowledge they have gained from the textbook.

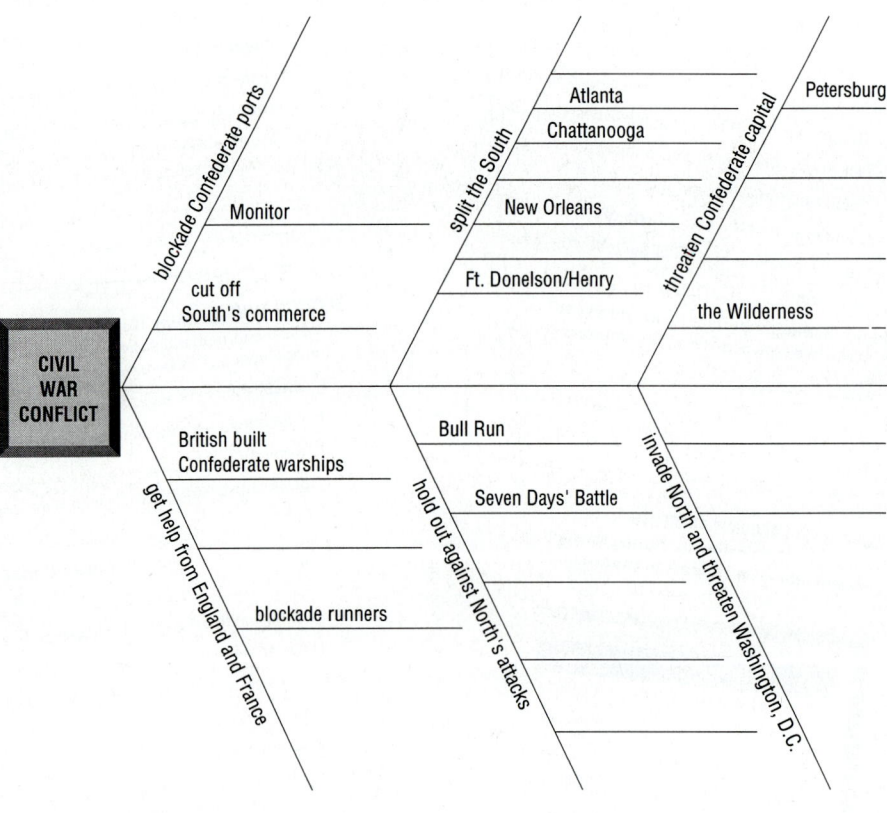

Name _____ Date _____ Class _____

CHAPTER 15
Concept Mapping Activity 1   THE CIVIL WAR

Concept: Conflict

In any conflict, each side has a strategy for winning the dispute. During the Civil War, both North and South developed and attempted to use several military strategies with different degrees of success. The fishbone map below illustrates the strategies each side hoped would carry it to victory in the conflict. Complete the map and read the generalization about the conflict that has been written from the map.

Concept Generalization: The strategies each side chose to fight the Civil War reflected their strengths or weaknesses when they began the conflict.

History of a Free Nation — Concept Mapping Activity 29

Name _____ Date _____ Class _____

CHAPTER 8 SECTION 3
Reteaching Activity

FOREIGN AFFAIRS

Key Concept

In the early 1800s, Americans struggled to establish an independent national identity. France and Great Britain, the two strongest military powers in the world, were opponents in an epic struggle for empire in Europe and around the world. Each took turns pressuring the United States to cooperate to destroy the other. Americans took steps to remain neutral in the conflict, but with every European act and American reaction, the United States drew closer to war.

Directions: Complete the chart below by describing the results of the foreign policy steps taken by the French, British, or Americans from 1806 to 1811.

Year	Act	Results for Americans
1807	Congress passed Embargo Act, forbidding American ships to sail for all foreign ports.	1.
1807	British orders in Council forbade neutral ships to trade in Europe unless they stopped first in Britain.	2.
1809	U. S. Congress repealed the Embargo Act and passed the Non-Intercourse Act.	3.
1810	Congress passed Macon's Bill No. 2.	4.
1811	U.S. cut off trade with Great Britain in compliance with the provisions of Macon's Bill No. 2.	5.

28 History of a Free Nation

Teacher's Classroom Resources

Extension and Enrichment

Enrichment Activities

Extension and enrichment activities provide a wide variety of materials to motivate and challenge students while building skills and expanding understanding.

Enrichment Activities for every chapter expand historical concepts, motivate students, and help build thinking skills.

Name _____ Date _____ Class _____

CHAPTER 24
Enrichment Activity

WHITE HOUSE REFORMERS

Connection

In the early 1900s Americans were preoccupied with the economic problem of continuing their remarkable development while finding ways to insure that they created an atmosphere of fair competition in the business place. Economic competition took place between companies and between men, women, and children in the workplace.

DIRECTIONS: The following statistics describe the labor force in the United States from 1890 to 1920. To get a more graphic idea of these statistics, convert them into a bar graph in the space below. Then answer the questions.

Year	Total Labor Force	Total Males (%)	Boys/Young Men Ages 14–19 (%)	Total Females (%)	Girls/Young Women Ages 14–19 (%)
1920	40,282,000	32,053,000 (79.6)	2,947,000 (7.3)	8,229,000 (20.4)	1,540,000 (4.1)
1900	27,640,000	22,641,000 (81.9)	2,834,000 (10.3)	4,999,000 (18.1)	1,230,000 (4.5)
1890	21,833,000	18,129,000 (83.0)	1,997,000 (9.1)	3,704,000 (17.0)	984,000 (4.5)

Historical Statistics of the United States, United States Government, 1975.

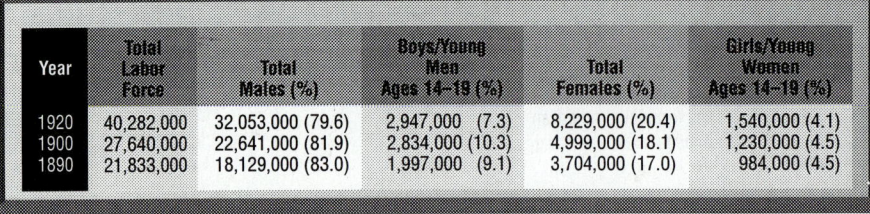

History of a Free Nation

Enrichment Activity 47

Cooperative Learning Activities

Extension and Enrichment

Name _____ Date _____ Class _____

ACTIVITY 1
Cooperative Learning

EFFECTS OF TRADE

Group Project

Prior to the exploration of the New World, the civilizations within Europe, Asia and Africa were undergoing significant changes. Governments and people who had basically kept to themselves started to trade, explore, and conquer new lands. Work with members of your group to design a flowchart that demonstrates what life was like, what were the motivations for opening up trade, what changes trading had on the culture and lives of your people, and the effects those changes had on the New World.

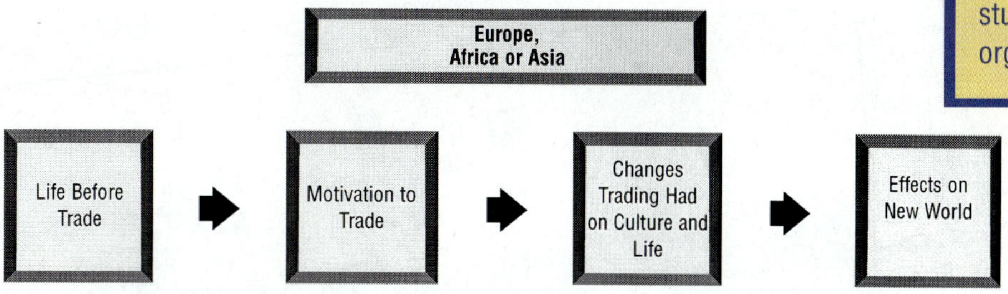

> **Cooperative Learning Activities** for each chapter reinforce learning and build management and interpersonal skills by requiring students to work together to acquire, organize, and present information.

Europe, Africa or Asia

Life Before Trade → Motivation to Trade → Changes Trading Had on Culture and Life → Effects on New World

Cooperative Group Process

1. **Defining Tasks** Form three groups. Group 1 will represent Europe, Group 2 will represent Asia, and Group 3 will represent Africa.
2. **Decision-Making** Each group member selects a section of the flowchart to research. A group-appointed manager makes sure all four boxes have members assigned and that members know their assignments.
3. **Individual Work** Research the topic you volunteered for and take notes.
4. **Group Sharing/Decision-Making** Group members reassemble and share their research. Decide which information needs to be included on the chart. If further research is thought to be necessary, have the group manager assign members to return to the text for additional research. Then select a writer, editor, and proofreader to put members' notes into the form of a rough draft of a flowchart similar to the one above. All group members read the draft and decide if additional changes are needed before a final copy is made.
5. **Analysis** Select a presenter to share your group's efforts with the class. After each group has presented its chart, discuss the similarities and differences among the contents and outcomes of each group's chart. What conclusions can be drawn about how trade influenced the discovery of the New World?

Group Process Questions

Did the group agree on the assignment of tasks?

Did members respect each other's point of view?

Did each member share information?

What would you change to make group work more enjoyable?

History of a Free Nation

Teacher's Classroom Resources

Extension and Enrichment

Interpreting Political Cartoons Activities

Interpreting Political Cartoons Activities enrich and motivate by providing visual activities that challenge students with provocative perspectives on key issues.

Name _____ Date _____ Class _____

ACTIVITY 15
Interpreting Political Cartoons

Urban Corruption

Perhaps the most dishonest of all politicians in the "Gilded Age" was William M. Tweed, called "Boss" Tweed. Tweed held various offices in New York City and New York state between 1851 and 1871. The most famous example of his dishonesty was the building of the "Tweed Courthouse" in New York City. During construction, Tweed ordered all contractors to add 100 percent to their bills and give the amount that was overcharged to the Tammany Ring. Under this system, New York City ended up paying $170,730 for 40 tables and chairs. When word began to reach the public, Thomas Nast drew the cartoon on the opposite page for The New York Times.

Study the cartoon, then answer the questions that follow.

"WHO STOLE THE PEOPLES MONEY?" — DO TELL. N.Y.TIMES.
'TWAS HIM.

Courtesy of the New York Historical Society, New York

Analyzing the Cartoon

1. What does the caption "Who Stole the Pe... point of view of the cartoonist?

2. Which of the men is Boss Tweed? How ... ing him look ridiculous?

3. From the looks of the men in Tweed ... to be part of the ring? How does th...

4. What do you think is Nast's opi... the time of Boss Tweed?

★★★ CRITICAL THINKING ★★★

5. Understanding Cause and E... time periods to have greater ...

6. Predicting Consequences ... ous consequences of wide...

Primary and Secondary Source Readings

Extension and Enrichment

Name_____ Date_____ Class_____

CHAPTER 29
Primary Source Reading

WORLD WAR II

A Marine at Nagasaki After the Atomic Blast

In this interview, former marine Victor Tolley recalls being sent to Nagasaki just a few weeks after the city was destroyed by an atomic explosion. Nagasaki was the second—and final—Japanese city to be leveled by an atomic blast. Tolley describes the sobering sights he saw while walking up Nagasaki's main street.

As you read, think about:
1. Why did the marines cheer when they heard that Hiroshima and Nagasaki had been attacked with atomic bombs?
2. Why were the marines sent to Nagasaki?

★★★

I'll never forget August 6, 1945. I'm standing in a chow line on Saipan at approximately eleven-thirty in the morning. On the armed-services radio I heard: "The President of the United States just announced that a terrible new weapon has been used on the city of Hiroshima, Japan. It'll be a hundred years before anybody will be able to enter that city. The new weapon is called the atomic bomb."

We cheered and we hollered and we grabbed each other and we jumped up and down. Maybe this. . . war's gonna end and we won't have to invade Japan. We all felt that way. On August 9, they dropped another bomb on the city of Nagasaki. The armed-services radio came out with the same report. It will be a hundred years before you could enter the city.

A few weeks later, we found ourselves aboard a troop transport. We laid out in the harbor for about three days. A young lieutenant said, "We're gonna occupy Nagasaki." I asked him a dumb question: "How can we occupy Nagasaki when they told us it would be a hundred years before anybody could go into that city?" He said, "Marine, you don't have anything to worry about. The scientists have gone in there. It's very safe."

On September 23, 1945, the ships pulled into the harbor of Nagasaki. The first sight I remember is the Mitsubishi factory. It looked like somebody had taken an erector set and stepped on it with both feet.

The next morning, I said to five of my buddies, "Let's get off this ship and go ashore. Let's see what's in Nagasaki and what the bomb did.". . . It was just like walking into a tomb. There was total silence. You could smell this death all around ya. There was a terrible odor. You could feel the eyes peering at you from the buildings that were left standing. We were less than a mile from ground zero, where they dropped the bomb.

For the next three months, we lived in Nagasaki. We helped tear down the buildings. We helped clean up the rubble. . . . We were instructed not to touch or go near any Japanese that we saw.

Source: From *The Good War: An Oral History of World War Two* by Studs Terkel. Copyright © 1984 by Studs Terkel. Reprinted by permission of Pantheon Books, a Division of Random House, Inc.

Answer the following questions on a separate sheet of paper.

Analyzing the Reading
1. Why was Tolley surprised to be sent to Nagasaki?
2. What was Tolley's "first sight" of Nagasaki?

★★★ **CRITICAL THINKING** ★★★
3. **Drawing Conclusions** Why do you think the marines seemingly accepted the idea of entering Nagasaki even after the radio report stated it would not be possible?

Primary and Secondary Source Readings for each chapter provide insights into government by policymakers and expert observers, and ask students to analyze and apply this information.

Teacher's Classroom Resources

Extension and Enrichment

Supreme Court Case Studies

Supreme Court Case Studies activities reinforce themes and concepts by presenting Supreme Court cases that consider fundamental constitutional questions.

Name Class Date

SUPREME COURT CASE 44

WASHINGTON V. DAVIS (1976)

Background of the Case

In 1970, African American police officers in the District of Columbia filed suit against the police commissioner and other city officials. They claimed that the police department's hiring and promotion policies were racially discriminatory. At issue was Test 21, an examination intended to test verbal ability, vocabulary, reading, and comprehension. The African American officers claimed that Test 21 was discriminatory because a higher percentage of African Americans failed the test than did whites.

A federal district court disagreed. The case went to the Court of Appeals, which ruled in the officers' favor. That decision was based solely on the fact that four times as many African Americans failed the test as did whites. The Court of Appeals held that the test was discriminatory without requiring that any additional discriminatory intent be shown or proved. City officials appealed this ruling to the United States Supreme Court.

Constitutional Issue

Several points were in question. Did the due process clause of the Fifth and Fourteenth Amendments, and the equal protection clause of the Fourteenth Amendment, prohibit racially disproportionate results? Was it necessary to prove an attempt to purposefully discriminate?

The Court's Decision

The Court ruled 7 to 2 that Test 21 did not violate the due process or equal protection clauses. Justice Byron R. White wrote for the Court.

The Court held that "the central purpose of the equal protection clause of the Fourteenth Amendment is the prevention of official conduct discriminating on the basis of race. . . . But our cases have not embraced the proposition that a law or other official act, without regard to whether it reflects a racially discriminatory purpose, is unconstitutional <u>solely</u> because it has a racially disproportionate impact."

Other Court decisions had held that the establishment of purpose was vital to determine discrimination. Even so, White stated, "a statute, otherwise neutral on its face, must not be applied so as invidiously to discriminate on the basis of race." The same was true for actions. The Court agreed it was even possible to infer discrimination "from the totality of the relevant facts, including the fact, if it is true, that the law bears more heavily on one race than another."

On the issue of Test 21, however, the Court found that African Americans no more than whites could blame failing the test on a denial of equal protection. The Court maintained that "it is untenable that the Constitution prevents the government from seeking modestly to up-grade the communicative abilities of its employees rather than to be satisfied with some lower level of competence." The Court ruled that Test 21 was "neutral on its face." Moreover, its disproportionate impact did not "warrant the conclusion that it is a purposeful device to discriminate against Negroes and hence an infringement of the constitutional rights of respondents as well as other black applicants."

Concurring, Justice Stevens wrote, "There are two reasons why I am convinced that the challenge to Test 21 is insufficient. First, the test serves the neutral and legitimate purpose of requiring all applicants to meet a uniform minimum standard of literacy. Reading ability is manifestly relevant to the police function, there is no evidence that the required passing grade was set at an arbitrarily high level, and there is sufficient disparity among high schools and high school graduates to justify the use of a separate uniform test.

Geography in History Activities

Extension and Enrichment

Name _____ Date _____ Class _____

CHAPTER 1
Geography in History

★★★★★★★★★★★★★★★★★★★★★★★★★★★★★★★

THE WORLD IN TRANSITION

The First American Highways

A fundamental theme of geography is the movement of people, things, and ideas across the earth's surface. Nowhere is this movement more apparent than on the world's roads. Some of the world's first roads were created by the Native Americans. And many of these ancient routes are still being used today! Read about these roads in the passage below. Then answer the questions that follow.

★★★

Geography in History Activities provide a link between geography—the study of the earth and how people use its natural resources—and history.

This story begins in a countryside still recovering from lengthy glaciation and as yet untouched by human ingenuity. It is a countryside populated by many species, who by now depend on movement over the ground for their very survival. But nature has not made that movement easy: the terrain is difficult, the obstacles enormous, and the ground cover impenetrable. The species have two survival options: either to continue to adapt to the world as they find it, or to modify that world and make their own way within it...

The first pathways to cross the countryside were created by animals pushing aside vegetation and pounding the earth with their feet...a Kentucky settler noted in his journal in 1756, "We came to a large road which the buffaloes have beaten spacious enough for a wagon to go abreast." A major American commentator subsequently observed that "the buffalo because of this sagacious selection of the most sure and direct courses, has influenced the routes of trade and travel of the white race as much, possibly, as he influenced the course of red men in earlier days. [The buffalo blazed] the course of many of our roads"...

Although animals could push and trample, they could not actively construct. People, on the other hand, could construct ways but needed both incentive and organizational support. The manufactured path was thus a consequence of increased social and economic pressures exerted by a growing civilization.

Indeed, the first human pathways led to campsites, food, and water. In time the travel needs became more than local, and extended pathways used fords [stream crossing], mountain passes, routes through swamps, and bypassed dangerous areas. The subsequent growth [of com]munities created the first major need for [orga]nized travel, the catalysts being the requ[irements] for trade and the collection of superimposed taxation...

When Europeans arrived in North America they found the land traversed by a myriad of narrow footpaths up to 600mm [24 inches] wide and intended for single-file human use. The most famous of these was possibly the Iroquois/Mohawk Trail, which was a 600km (372 mile) beaten path between Buffalo and Albany in New York State and which is now New York Route 5. American government documents [as late as] 1808 were still referring to roads that did not follow Indian trails as artificial roads...

...many of the early pathways rose quickly out of waterlogged valleys to follow high contours and ridges, which were firmer, less densely vegetated, and safer. These ridgeways were also protected from the destructive effect of running water, the major destroyer of roadmaking efforts...

Ridgeways were...common in North America prior to European settlement—one of the most famous was the Natchez Trace [a route between Natchez, Mississippi and Memphis, Tennessee]...

The influence of [Indian] pathways canalso be seen in the urban New World. For example, the street system of Newark, New Jersey, is based on pre-existing Indian trails, and Detroit's main street follows the Indian Saginaw Trail...

from Ways of the World, A History of the World's Roads and of the Vehicles That Used Them by M.G. Lay (New Brunswick; Rutgers University Press, 1992)

History of a Free Nation   Geography in History   13

Teacher's Classroom Resources

Extension and Enrichment

Spirit of American Art and Music

Spirit of American Art and Music blackline masters provide biographical material on American artists, musicians, and architects who made significant contributions throughout American history.

Name _____ Date _____ Class _____

**UNIT 3
American Art and Music**

THOMAS JEFFERSON (1743–1826)

Architect for a New Nation

When you hear the name Thomas Jefferson, do you think of this prominent American as our country's third President or as our nation's first Secretary of State? Or perhaps you think of Thomas Jefferson as the author of The Declaration of Independence. The truth is Thomas Jefferson was all of these things and more. In fact, Jefferson himself might have wished to be remembered in an entirely different way—as an accomplished and free-thinking architect of his time.

If you've heard of Monticello, Thomas Jefferson's home in Virginia, then you might already know that Jefferson designed this and several other important buildings. In fact, architecture was one of Jefferson's most passionate avocations. It represented all the things he valued most in life—culture, intelligence, education, and logic.

After leaving college to practice law, Jefferson embarked on a new project—to design a house for himself. The site he chose was a mountaintop near Charlottesville, Virginia. He called his new home, built between 1769 and 1782, Monticello. This first exercise in architecture was based on eighteenth-century English design, with large, boxlike rooms. Later, as Jefferson's knowledge of architectural design broadened, he was to become disenchanted with this English style, and Monticello would be rebuilt.

In 1785, Jefferson was appointed Minister of France and took up residence in Paris. While there, a new style of architecture, called neoclassical, captured his imagination. The neoclassic style was based on ancient Greek and Roman designs that incorporated Ionic and Doric columns, porches, pediments, and towering interior spaces, similar to the Greek and Roman temples these structures resembled.

So powerful and graceful was this style of architecture to Jefferson that when the Virginia legislature asked him to find a new design for its state capitol in Richmond, he produced the design himself—using the neoclassic style. Jefferson's plans incorporated much of the Greek and Roman forms that he had learned to appreciate in the neoclassic buildings of Paris. With the design for the Virginia capitol building approved, Jefferson introduced the neoclassic style of architecture into American culture. It would remain a powerful force in American architecture for decades to come.

Jefferson's most inclusive project was in the design of a new university for his home state—the University of Virginia in Charlottesville. As chief architect, and the creative force in developing the new university's curriculum, Jefferson had the opportunity to use all his knowledge in architecture and education to create a powerful institution. Jefferson faced the enormous task with gusto. His ideas—to incorporate the new nation's democratic ideals with a university that would foster learning at the highest level—spurred his creative imagination. The result was a series of buildings not rooted in traditional English design but rather in a neoclassical one.

For Thomas Jefferson, architecture was more than just piles of brick, stone, wood, and glass. Architecture was the means by which he could exhibit all that he had learned and express his cultivated tastes that extended far beyond the original thirteen colonies. Architecture represented Jefferson's quest for building a new democratic society in which only the highest ideals were tolerated and which only a master architect could ultimately have helped to shape.

1. **Evaluating Information** In what ways is Jefferson's architectural talent, especially in the design of the University of Virginia, similar to his talent as a statesman in a new nation?

2. **Synthesizing Information** How were Jefferson's architectural designs instrumental in reviving a classical Greek and Roman style of architecture here in the United States?

6 Spirit of American Art and Music

History of a Free Nation

American Music: Cultural Traditions

Extension and Enrichment

American Music: Cultural Traditions brings students into contact with American music from the pre-colonial period through today's rap music.

Teacher's Classroom Resources

Extension and Enrichment

Focus on American Fine Art Prints

Focus on American Fine Art Prints includes 20 colorful, laminated fine-art posters that decorate your classroom and show students how the cultural heritage of the United States is reflected through the arts.

Spanish Resources

Extension and Enrichment

Spanish Resources include Spanish translations of *Reteaching Activities*, *Chapter Summaries and Glossary*, *Section Quizzes*, and *Unit Digest Transparencies*. Spanish Chapter Digests Audiocassettes with Activities and Tests are also available.

T45

Teacher's Classroom Resources

Evaluation

Section Quizzes and Performance Assessment

Evaluation material helps you measure the progress of your students through a large selection of testing and assessment resources.

Section Quizzes provide a quick and effective way to check understanding and monitor daily progress.

Performance Assessment Strategies and Activities provide alternative assessment strategies for greater flexibility in evaluation. The booklet also contains classroom assessment lists and scoring rubrics.

Name _____

CHAPTER 1 SECTION 1
Section Quiz

THE WORLD IN TRANSITION

SCORE

Key Facts
From the list below choose the term that best matches each of the following descriptions.
Write the letter of each term chosen in the blank provided.

A. Cahokia
B. Olmecs
C. Maya
D. Aztecs
E. Anasazi
F. Iroquois

_____ 1. alliance of Native Americans who lived in Northeastern United States, often in long houses

_____ 2. built large multistory apartment-like buildings of adobe

_____ 3. had a written language with books written on bark paper

_____ 4. city of moundbuilders near present-day St. Louis

_____ 5. first Mesoamerican people to build with large masses of stone

Key Concepts
Write the letter of the phrase that best completes each statement in the blank provided.

_____ 6. Tenochtitlán was
  a. a Mayan god.
  b. the Aztec city near present-day Mexico City.
  c. the founder of the Anasazi civilization.
  d. a famous temple mound in the Ohio River Valley.

_____ 7. The confederation of Creeks, Cherokees, and other tribes in the Southeastern United States was called the
  a. Five Civilized Tribes.
  b. Iroquois.
  c. Hopewell culture.
  d. Pueblo.

_____ 8. The achievements of the Mayan culture include
  a. mathematical concepts, including the number zero.
  b. building a large city of 100,000 people in central Mexico.
  c. building the pueblos.
  d. opening an extensive trade with parts of Asia.

_____ 9. The purpose of the Iroquois League according to its constitution was to
  a. defeat neighboring people.
  b. engage in trade.
  c. unite against Europeans.
  d. establish peace.

_____ 10. Mesoamerica is best defined as
  a. the Southwestern United States.
  b. Central and South America.
  c. Peru and Ecuador
  d. Central Mexico and Central America.

History of a Free Nation

Section Quiz 1

Name _____ Date _____

CHAPTER 1
Performance Assessment Activity

What in the World Was Happening?

Information
By the year 1000 B.C., groups in the Americas had settl[ed] and Ecuador and had begun to develop cultures. At th[e] of the Islamic empire led to the Crusades and a renew[al] Europeans in the East. In the 1400s, the Mesoamerica[n] a population of 100,000 people, much larger than any time. During the Middle Ages, between A.D. 500 and of discovery altered the political and social structur[e] African communities. Trade led to the breakup of th[e] emergence of a middle class that supported explor[ation] Mali to Italy became important centers of culture a[nd]

Exhibit
You are going to create a map of historic civilizat[ions] important empires or kingdoms that existed in [the] Americas. Choose a time from before A.D. 1500. your map that will identify the political, econom[ic] forces that were in effect in each civilization at Include your map in a class exhibit showing th[e] cal order. Write a report further explaining the and give reasons why you chose the date tha[t]

Target Audience
The target audience are students in your cla[ss]

Purpose
The purpose of this activity is to provide a ic location and the range of influence of fo[reign] tinents during a specific time period. By civilizations, you will gain a better under[standing] cultural, and religious systems changed

Procedure
1. Review your information about wo[rld] on the line below choose a year or your map of historic civilizations. for interesting contrasts and corre[spondences] parts of the world.

T46

Evaluation

Tests and Testmaker Software

Name _____ Date _____ Class _____

CHAPTER 3
Test A

COLONIAL AMERICA

SCORE

Identifying People, Places, and Terms
Match each item in the right column with its best description in the left column. Write the letter of each item in the blank provided. (3 points each)

_____ 1. first permanent English settlement in North America
_____ 2. first representative assembly in America
_____ 3. person who had authority over the government of a colony
_____ 4. people who protested against the Church of England
_____ 5. document signed by the Pilgrims in 1620 in which they agreed to live under the laws of the community
_____ 6. Dutch governor of New Netherland in 1664
_____ 7. people who believed that every person could know God's will through his or her own "inner light"
_____ 8. German religious sect who denounced slavery
_____ 9. widespread religious revival in the 1740s
_____ 10. early colonial college founded to train young men for the ministry
_____ 11. philosophic movement in the eighteenth century marked by an interest in science
_____ 12. most direct form of democracy in the colonies
_____ 13. sent settlers to Roanoke Island and named Virginia
_____ 14. began successful religious colony in Pennsylvania
_____ 15. trading company bought by the Puritans

a. Great Awakenings
b. House of Burgess
c. Jamestown
d. Mennonites
e. Harvard
f. John Locke
g. Peter Stuyvesant
h. congregation
i. Quakers
j. town meeting
k. dissenters
l. naval stores
m. the Enlighten...
n. proprietor
o. Mayflowe...
p. William ...

Understanding Concepts
Choose the item that best completes the statement. Write the lett... the blank provided. (5 points each)

_____ 16. The settlers in Virginia learned to raise tobacco becau...
    a. it was the only crop that would grow there.
    b. it was a profitable cash crop.
    c. fe...
    d. the...

_____ 17. Puritans decided to migrate to New England for
    a. religious freedom.
    b. better soil for farming.
    c. preci...
    d. trade...

_____ 18. Proprietors in the Middle Colonies permitted their colo... blies because
    a. they were free there.
    b. they found work in the industries.
    c. they prefe...
    d. slave lab... plantations.

8 Chapter Test   History of a Free Nation

Tests in two forms for each chapter and unit evaluate student understanding of key facts, history themes, and thnking skills through objective and essay questions.

Testmaker Software (IBM, Apple, or Macintosh) offers a bank of more than 3,000 questions, and provides the flexibility to edit existing questions and add new ones.

Teacher's Classroom Resources

Evaluation

Student Self-Test: A Software Review

Student Self-Test: A Software Review (IBM and Macintosh) allows students to test their understanding of basic concepts at the unit, chapter, and section levels. A tutorial explains why incorrect answers to the questions are wrong.

Unit Digest Transparencies

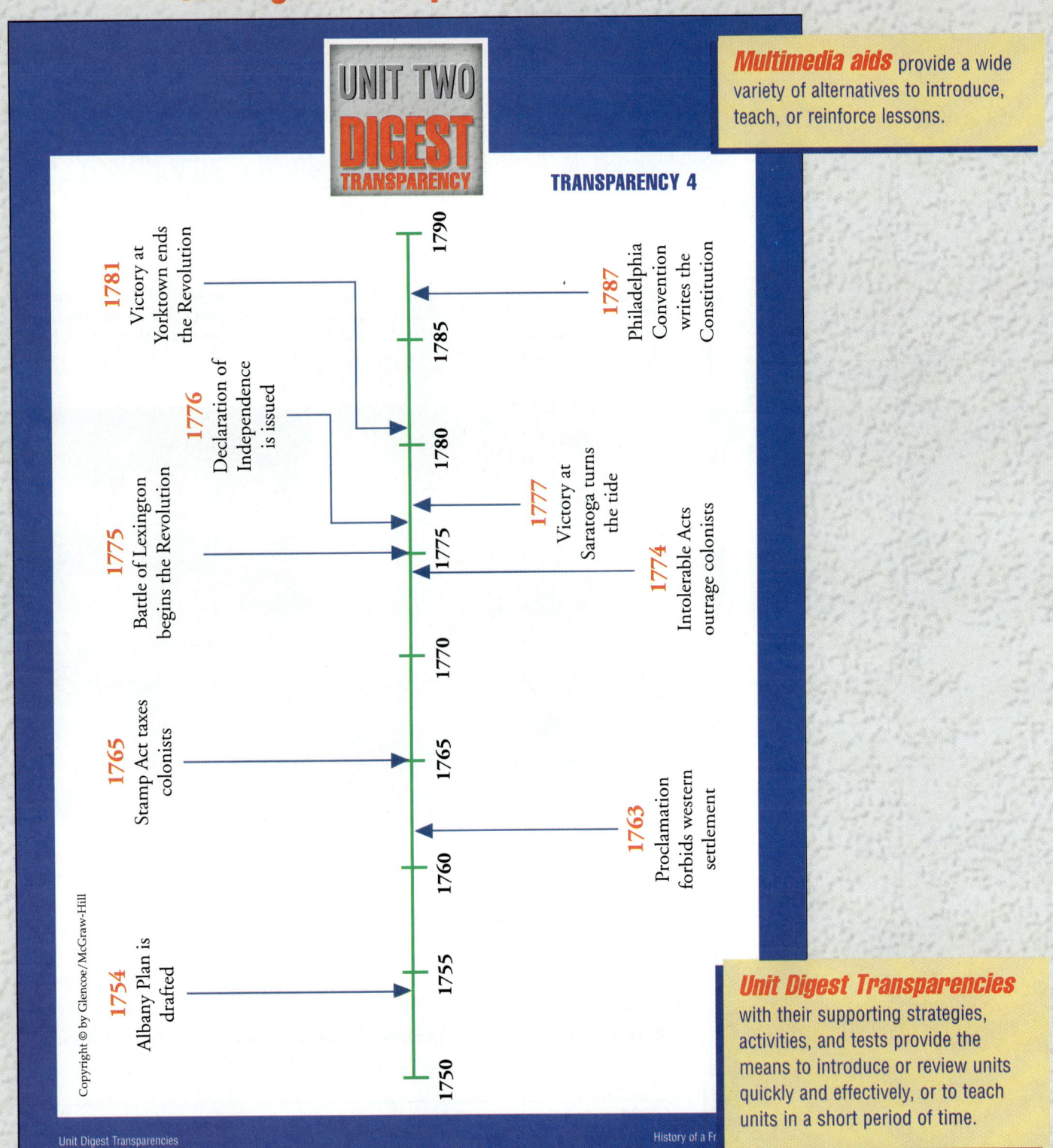

Multimedia

Multimedia aids provide a wide variety of alternatives to introduce, teach, or reinforce lessons.

Unit Digest Transparencies with their supporting strategies, activities, and tests provide the means to introduce or review units quickly and effectively, or to teach units in a short period of time.

Teacher's Classroom Resources

Multimedia

Section Focus Transparencies

Section Focus Transparencies offer a variety of formats that may be used as Bell-ringer Motivational Activities.

Focus Activities
TRANSPARENCY 35

Documenting Native American Culture

Before the widespread use of photography, artists served as visual historians, creating for posterity colorful records of their time. In 1832, artist George Catlin completed a bold 2,000-mile journey along the Missouri River. His purpose was to paint the Native Americans living in the region.

Left: *Horse Chief, Grand Pawnee Head Chief.* 1834. National Museum of American Art, Washington DC/Art Resource, New York. Gift of Mrs. Joseph Harrison, Jr. Accession number 1985.1.99 **Right:** *George Catlin.* 1849. National Portrait Gallery, Smithsonian Institution, Washington DC/Art Resource, New York. Gift of Miss May C. Kinney, Ernest C. Kinney and Bradford Wickes, 1945. Accession number NPG. 70.14

Questions

1. How do you think Americans living in the East would have reacted upon first seeing the portrait of Horse Chief? Why?
2. Which elements in the portrait of the artist himself (at right) provide evidence of the subject's occupation and purpose?

Chapter 10, Section 3, Transparency 35

Multimedia

Skills and Map Transparencies

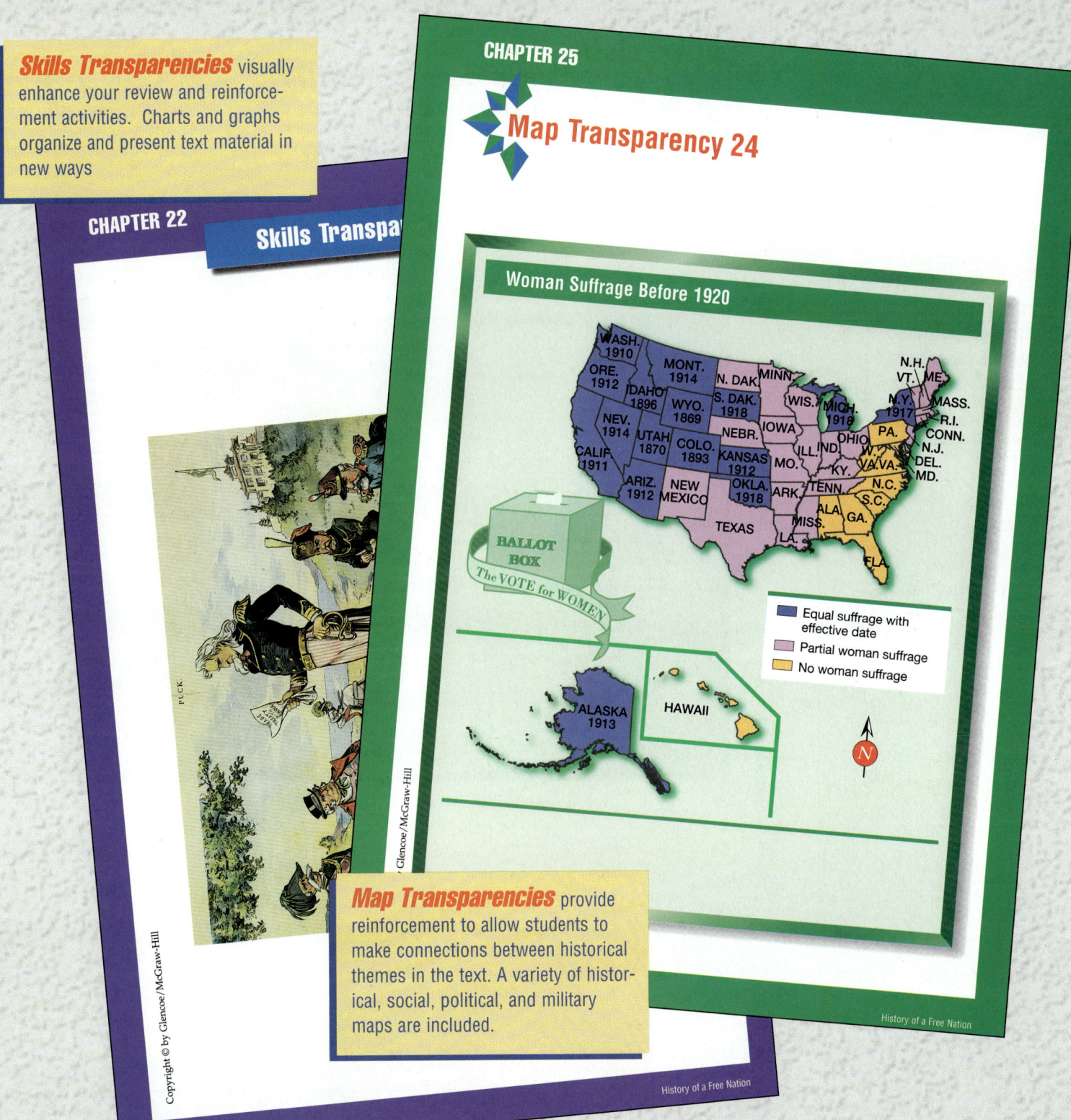

Skills Transparencies visually enhance your review and reinforcement activities. Charts and graphs organize and present text material in new ways

Map Transparencies provide reinforcement to allow students to make connections between historical themes in the text. A variety of historical, social, political, and military maps are included.

T51

Teacher's Classroom Resources

Multimedia

U.S. History and Art Transparencies

The Declaration of Independence (1786-97)
John Trumbull

Transparency 4

U.S. History and Art Transparencies are designed to enrich and extend the *History of a Free Nation* textbook by giving students an understanding of how art acts as a tool when learning about history.

© Yale University Art Gallery

Multimedia

U.S. History Diagraph Transparencies

U.S. History Diagraph Transparencies provide detailed information about specific innovations and themes in history.

Teacher's Classroom Resources

Multimedia

English and Spanish Audiocassettes

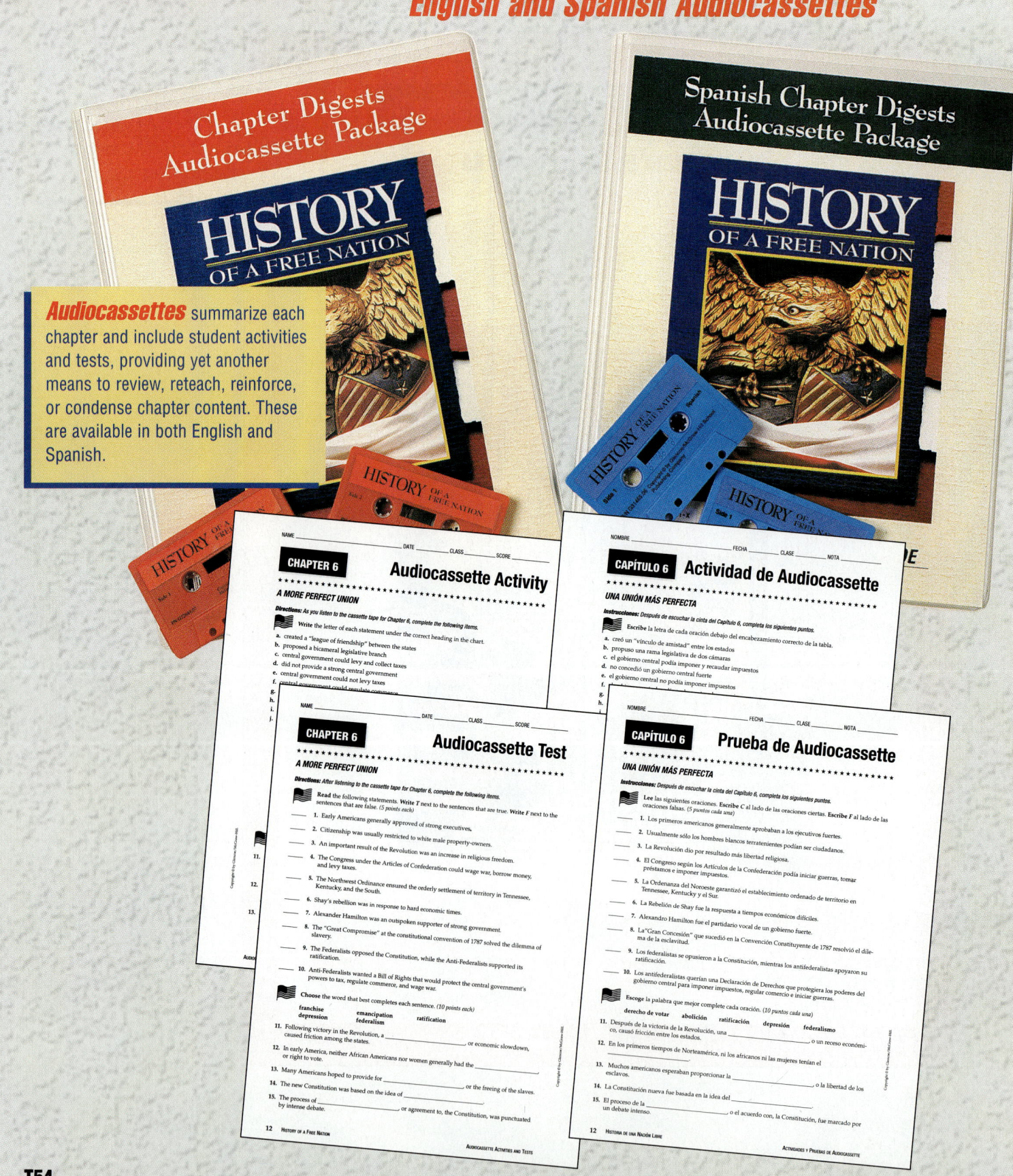

Audiocassettes summarize each chapter and include student activities and tests, providing yet another means to review, reteach, reinforce, or condense chapter content. These are available in both English and Spanish.

Multimedia

Vocabulary PuzzleMaker Software

Vocabulary PuzzleMaker reinforces chapter vocabulary terms by allowing you to generate your own crossword puzzles and word searches, so students can have fun while they learn the language of history.

Teacher's Classroom Resources

Multimedia

Student Self-Test: A Software Review

Student Self-Test: A Software Review (IBM and Macintosh) allows students to test their understanding of basic concepts at the unit, chapter, and section levels. A tutorial explains why incorrect answers to the questions are wrong.

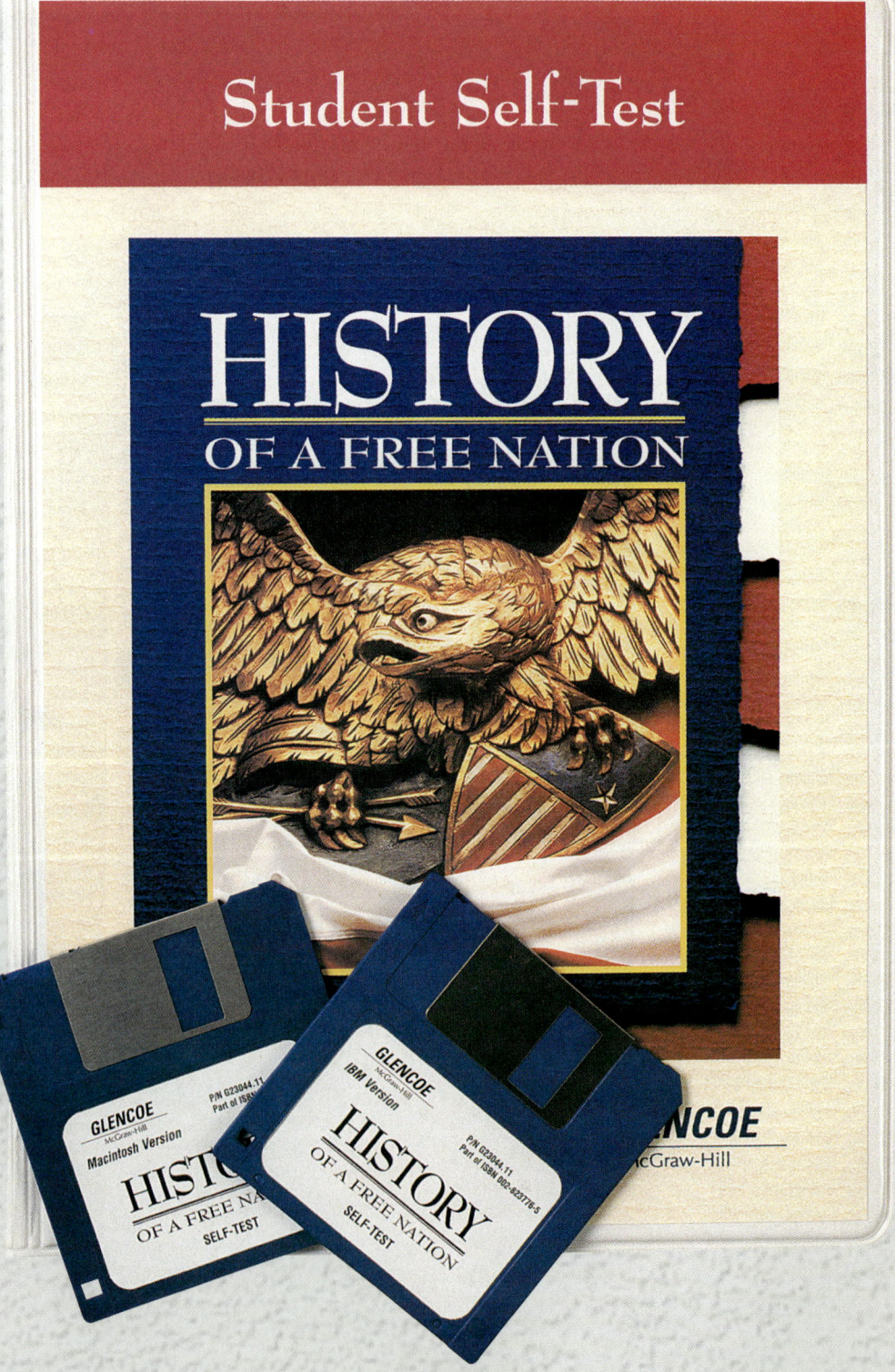

Videodiscs and CD-ROMs

Multimedia

Interactive Videodiscs from Glencoe, National Geographic Society, and ABCNews InterActive™ contain electronic field trips as well as segments designed to help students make connections with historical concepts and themes.

The National Geographic Society CD-ROM program *The Presidents: A Picture History of Our Nation* and the Facts on File CD-ROM *Landmark Documents in American History* will enrich your students' study of United States history.

Teacher's Classroom Resources

Multimedia

Testmaker Software

Testmaker Software (IBM, Apple, or Macintosh) offers a bank of more than 3,000 questions, and provides the flexbility to edit existing questions and add new ones.

Reproducible Lesson Plans

Other Teacher Support

CHAPTER 8
Lesson Plan

SECTION 1 (pp. 254-257)

Teacher's Name _____ Date _____ Grade _____

Class(es) _____ Date _____ M Tu W Th

Focus

_____ Bell Ringer, *TWE*, p. 254
_____ Objectives, *SE*, p. 254
        1. Compare the views of the Federalist and Republican parties on the economy, democracy, and the role of government.
        2. Explain Thomas Jefferson's views on government.
_____ Motivating Activity, *TWE*, p. 254

Teach

■ **Guided Practice**

_____ Chapter Opening, *TWE*, pp. 252-252
_____ Interpreting Primary Sources, *TWE*, p. 258
_____ Activities, *TWE*, pp. 254-255
_____ Special Needs Strategy, *TWE*, p. 255
_____ Cooperative Learning Activity, *TWE*, p. 256
_____ Critical Thinking Activity, *TWE*, p. 257
_____ *TCR* Chapter 8 Map Transparencies
_____ *TCR* American Literary Heritage Unit 3
_____ *TCR* Chapter 8 Skills Transparencies
_____ *TCR* Chapter 8 Concept Mapping Activity

■ **Independent Practice**

_____ Activities, *TWE*, p. 256
_____ History Writer's Handbook, *SE*, p.1127
_____ *TCR* Study Guide
_____ Interpreting Primary Sources, *TWE*, p. 258
_____ *TCR* Writer's Guidebook Lessons 2-5

★★ HOMEWORK ASSIGNMENTS ★★

_____
_____
_____
_____
_____
_____
_____
_____
_____
_____
_____
_____
_____
_____

Assess

_____ Check Understanding, *TWE*, p. 256
_____ Evaluate, *TWE*, p. 256
_____ *TCR* Section Quiz
_____ Testmaker
_____ Reteach, *TWE*, p. 256
_____ *TCR* Reteaching Activity 8-1
_____ Enrich, *TWE*, p. 257
_____ Close, *TWE*, p. 257

History of a Free Nation   Activity   2

Reproducible Lesson Plans let you spend less time planning and more time teaching.

INTRODUCING UNIT 1

BEGINNING THE UNIT

Provide this cause and effect chart to students with the effects omitted. Assign students to complete the chart as they read the chapters in the unit.

Event
- Christopher Columbus's first voyage

Causes
- The growth of trade with Asia
- The rise of strong monarchs
- The growth of cities
- The Renaissance

Effects
- Competition for power among European nations
- Native Americans forced from their lands or enslaved
- European colonies in the Americas
- Africans enslaved

History AND ART

Drawings found on rocks and in caves reveal much about the earliest Americans. Similar drawings have been found in other parts of the world. Encourage students to find out about rock and cave paintings in Europe and Asia.

OUT OF TIME? If time does not permit teaching the entire unit, use the Unit Digest on pages 84–85.

UNIT ONE
A NEW WORLD
PREHISTORY TO 1776

CHAPTER 1
The World in Transition
Prehistory–1500s

CHAPTER 2
The Age of Exploration
1000–1682

CHAPTER 3
Colonial America
1578–1776

▼ ARROWHEAD, HAND-CHIPPED STONE

History AND ART
Prehistoric Drawing
Baja California, Mexico

Native Americans came to the Western Hemisphere thousands of years ago. Artists have provided a glimpse of their way of life through cave and rock paintings.

Exploring Unit Themes

Geography and the Environment The Native American peoples created varied and distinct cultures as they adapted to the geography and environment where they settled. European settlers, too, had to adapt to the environments they found in the Western Hemisphere.

The Individual and Family Life While a social hierarchy existed in Colonial America, it was far less rigid than in Europe. Success in the colonies required individual effort, so people with drive and ambition could rise to the top of American society. There was one exception—enslaved persons were held in bondage for life.

Setting the Scene

The Americas were inhabited by a rich variety of cultures. Almost 500 years ago, however, other peoples—Europeans, filled with dreams of adventure and wealth, and enslaved Africans—set foot in what to them was a New World.

Themes
- Geography and the Environment
- The Individual and Family Life
- Humanities and Religion
- Cultural Diversity

Key Events
- First Americans cross the Bering Strait
- Hopewells build mounds in the Ohio River valley
- Height of Maya culture
- Norse seafarers land at Newfoundland
- Voyages of Columbus
- Spanish conquer Aztec and Incan empires
- Spanish bring enslaved Africans to America
- Founding of New France
- Founding of English colonies

Major Issues
- The environment influences the development of Native American cultures and European colonies in the Americas.
- The search for wealth and a direct route to Asia prompts European exploration and settlement.
- Interaction among Native Americans, European colonists, and African Americans leads to the creation of a new American society.

▼ JAPANESE MILITARY EQUIPMENT

 SIR WALTER RALEIGH

◀ ASTROLABE, ITALY 1500s

Portfolio Project
Prepare a short report on a Native American culture in the United States today. Describe its peoples' occupations, living standards, and social life as well as traditional crafts, legends, and beliefs.

INTRODUCING UNIT 1

UNIT 1 Independent Study Project
Point out that American culture is a rich tapestry woven with threads from all over the world. Have students work together to construct a wall chart. As they read Unit 1, have students enter on the chart aspects of American culture that derive from these various groups.

Unit Digest Transparencies:
Show Transparency 1.

Portfolio Project
After students have completed the first draft of their report, ask each to edit a classmate's work. Try not to pair students who have chosen the same culture.

History and the Humanities

- History & Art Transparency 1
- Focus on American Art Prints 1 and 2
- American Music: Cultural Traditions
- Spirit of American Art and Music 1, 2, and 3

Exploring Unit Themes

Humanities and Religion Scientific inquiry generated by the Renaissance led to an age of exploration and discovery. Many Europeans settled in the Americas because they wanted the freedom to worship as they pleased.

Cultural Diversity The Europeans' interactions with many different groups of Native Americans and their adaptation to the new environment led to a new and unique American culture.

Examining the Themes Point out that this unit describes the peopling of the Americas. Have students identify the various groups that settled in the Western Hemisphere.

LESSON PLAN
Global Perspectives

FOCUS
Motivating Activity
Point out that the exchange of beliefs and knowledge among civilizations is called *cultural diffusion*. The peanut might serve as an illustration of this process. The Spanish first encountered the peanut in Hispaniola in the early 1500s. They later introduced the crop to their possessions in the Philippines and the Malay Archipelago. By the end of the century, it had spread to the Asian mainland. Today, the peanut is an important aspect of the cuisine of China, Thailand, and many other Southeast Asian countries. Ask students to suggest recent examples of cultural diffusion involving food. (Most students will suggest that recent immigrants to the United States have introduced their cuisine to Americans.)

TEACH
Guided Practice
Exploring the Time Line
Ask students to study the time line and note the European nations that explored or colonized the Americas. Then mention that the Russians, too, were interested in the Americas. During the 1700s, a Russian fleet regularly visited Monterey Bay in California to hunt the bay's sea otters. In 1812 they built a trading post and fort at Fort Ross. They sold it to John Sutter in 1841. **L1**

Global Perspectives

The World

	Prehistory		500 B.C.
Asia and Oceania		▼ 660 B.C. Jimmu becomes first emperor of Japan	
Europe	c. 4000 B.C. Civilizations develop in Asia and Africa		509 B.C. Romans set up a republic
Africa	c. 1,750,000 B.C. First groups of people appear in Africa		200s B.C. Axum emerges as a trading power
South America			
North and Central America	c. 35,000–20,000 B.C. First migrants from Asia cross the Bering Strait	1500 B.C. Olmec civilization begins	

The United States

	Prehistory		500 B.C.
Pacific and Northwest		c. 1500 B.C. People learn metalworking techniques	
Southeast			
Midwest		◄ 200 B.C.–A.D. 400 Hopewell culture reaches its zenith	
Southwest			
Atlantic Northeast			

UNIT 1 A New World: Prehistory to 1776

Cultural Diversity

Native Americans have left an indelible mark on American English. Over 125 Algonquin words are in common use today. They include chipmunk, skunk, moose, opossum, raccoon, caribou, hominy, pecan, squash, succotash, and terrapin. Those words became a part of the language as a result of direct contacts between the English and Native Americans.

Other words have entered the language through indirect contacts. From the Spanish, English-speaking colonists learned such Native American words as coyote, mesquite, avocado, tomato, and barbecue.

Linking Across Time

Native Americans have left an indelible mark on American life. Perhaps the most obvious sign of our country's Native American heritage is the hundreds of place names that dot the map. Some of these names offer a vivid physical description of the place. Chattanooga, for example, means "rock rising to a point," while Nantucket means "the faraway place." Other names indicate what went on at the place. Milwaukee was the "gathering place by the river" and Kalamazoo was the "boiling pot."

Timeline: 1400 A.D. – 1700 A.D.

- **1368** Ming Dynasty begins rule of China 
- **1400s** Explorers set out, and Age of Exploration begins
- **1400s** Inca and Aztec empires flourish 
- **1492** Columbus lands in the Americas
- **1578** Sir Francis Drake explores the California coast 
- **1607** First permanent English settlement is formed at Jamestown
- **1050–1200** Great Pueblo period
- **1684** LaSalle establishes Fort St. Louis
- **1620** Pilgrims found Plymouth

UNIT 1 A New World: Prehistory to 1776   5

Cooperative Learning

Divide the class into five groups and assign one of the following continents to each: North America, South America, Africa, Asia, Europe. Ask groups to research what was happening in their assigned area at the time Columbus made his voyage of discovery. They should then write a brief narrative on their area for an imaginary radio broadcast titled "At This Time." Have groups select representatives to make their broadcasts. **L3**

LESSON PLAN
Global Perspectives

Independent Practice

World Events and the U.S. Direct students' attention to the time line entry on the founding of Plymouth. Then mention that 10 years before this event, there was a thriving Spanish colony in the Southwest, centered on what today is Santa Fe, New Mexico. Have students research and write a report on Spanish settlement in the Southwest prior to the establishment of English colonies in North America. **L2**

ASSESS

Studying the Time Line

1. What was happening in China at about the time the burial-mound culture in America was beginning to wane? (Ming Dynasty began its rule.)

2. What event began the age of exploration? (opening of Prince Henry of Portugal's school for navigators)

3. What event shown on the time line do you think was the most important for the development of the United States? Why? (Answers will vary but may include the first permanent English settlements at Jamestown and Plymouth.)

5

PLANNING GUIDE Chapter 1 The World in Transition

Daily Lesson Objectives	Teacher Classroom Resources	Multimedia
SECTION 1 **The First Americans** 1 Day pp. 8–13 1. Explain the origins and paths of settlement of the first immigrants to the Americas. 2. Compare the cultures in Mexico and South America to those in North America.	Chapter 1 Study Guide Reproducible Lesson Plan Reteaching Activity 1-1 Section Quiz Chapter 1 Cooperative Learning Activity Chapter 1 Concept Mapping Activity Chapter 1 Primary & Secondary Source Readings Reinforcing Social Studies Skills 3, 35, 51, 56, 59, 61 American Portraits 1, 2 Writer's Guidebook, Lesson 6 Building Skills in Geography	Student Self-Test Software Section Focus Transparency 1 Chapter 1 Skills Transparency Unit 1 Digest Transparency Chapter 1 Map Transparency U.S. History & Art Transparency 1 American Music: Cultural Traditions The American People: Fabric of a Nation PictureShow: Native Americans
SECTION 2 **The New Europe** 1 Day pp. 15–19 1. Describe how European society changed from medieval times. 2. Explain the significance of the Renaissance and the Reformation.	Reproducible Lesson Plan Reteaching Activity 1-2 Section Quiz Reinforcing Social Studies Skills 32, 56 Building Skills in Geography	Student Self-Test Software Testmaker Section Focus Transparency 2
SECTION 3 **Medieval Asia and Africa** 1 Day pp. 20–24 1. Explain the impact of Islam. 2. Describe the extent and importance of the Mongol Empire. 3. Identify some of the trading kingdoms of Africa.	Reproducible Lesson Plan Reteaching Activity 1-3 Section Quiz Reinforcing Social Studies Skills 23, 32, 40, 69, 70 SAT Practice Tests 5-14 Writer's Guidebook, Lesson 6	Student Self-Test Software Testmaker Section Focus Transparency 3
SECTION 4 **Europeans Seek the East** 1 Day pp. 26–29 1. Explain the changes in commerce and in technology that enabled Europeans to sponsor long ocean voyages. 2. State the importance of the Portuguese discovery of a sea route to Asia.	Reproducible Lesson Plan Reteaching Activity 1-4 Section Quiz Chapter 1 Enrichment Activity Reinforcing Social Studies Skills 2, 32 Building Skills in Geography Spanish Summaries & Glossary	Student Self-Test Software Testmaker Vocabulary Puzzlemaker Section Focus Transparency 4 Audiocassette, Chapter 1 The American People: Fabric of a Nation
CHAPTER REVIEW AND EVALUATION 1 Day	Chapter 1 Test Chapter 1 Performance Assessment Activity	Student Self-Test Software Testmaker

 **OUT OF TIME?** If time does not permit teaching the entire chapter, use the Chapter 1 Summary on pages 84–85 and the Chapter 1 audiocassette (English and Spanish) to point out the main ideas of the chapter.

PLANNING GUIDE

Cultural Diversity Activity

Cooperative Learning Point out that Native Americans are often erroneously treated as though they were a single ethnic group. Scholars believe that before European colonization, Native Americans spoke from 300 to 550 different languages. These languages reflected their cultural as well as linguistic diversity. Divide students into small groups. Have each choose a medium (newspapers and magazines, advertisements, television, films, or children's books) and explore the ways it has contributed to the view that Native Americans are all alike. How does this perception lead to stereotyping? Have each group also look for ways some filmmakers, writers, artists, etc. are challenging that perception. Discuss why it is important to do so.

Performance Assessment Activity

Cultural Highlights Ask students to research the way of life of a group that made its home in North America in the 1500s and prepare a poster highlighting their findings. The posters should express a main idea supported by appropriate detail. For example, one poster might focus on the importance of the woodland environment to the Iroquois; another might feature the artistic achievements of the Pueblo people of the Southwest. Encourage students to share their posters with the class. This activity may be done individually or in small groups.

POSSIBLE RUBRIC FEATURES: Content information, organization, written and pictorial communication skills, creativity

Chapter Resources

Literature from the Period

Brandon, William, ed., *The Magic World: American Indian Songs and Poems.* William Morrow, 1971.

Callaway, Sydney M., et al. *Grandfather Stories of the Navajos.* Navajo Curriculum Press, 1979.

Gibbs, H.A.R., ed. *Travels of ibn Battuta.* Cambridge University Press, 1962.

Machiavelli, Niccolo. *The Prince.* Quentin Skinner and Russell Price, eds. Cambridge University Press, 1988.

Readings for the Student

Brandon, William. *Indians.* American Heritage, 1985.

Robinson, David, and Douglas Smith. *Sources of the African Past.* Holmes & Meier, 1979.

Swanson, Earl H., et al. *The Ancient Americas.* Peter Bedrick Books, 1990.

Readings for the Teacher

Billings, Malcolm. *The Cross and the Crescent: A History of the Crusades.* Sterling Publishing, 1988.

Cardini, Franco. *Europe 1492: Portrait of a Continent Five Hundred Years Ago.* Facts on File, 1989.

Harris, Joseph E. *Africans and Their History,* rev. ed., Mentor, 1987.

Holmes, George, ed. *The Oxford Illustrated History of Medieval Europe.* Oxford University Press, 1988.

Multimedia Resources

Asia, 1600–1800. Landmark Films. (VHS, 26 minutes)

Mexico Before Cortez. Social Studies School Service. (VHS, 14 minutes)

Peru: Inca Heritage. Social Studies School Service. (VHS, 18 minutes)

Rise of Nations in Europe. Coronet Instructional Films. (VHS, 13 minutes)

Key to Ability Levels

Teaching strategies have been coded for varying learning styles and abilities.

- **L1** Basic activities for all students
- **L2** Average activities for average to above-average students
- **L3** Challenging activities for above-average students
- **LEP** Limited English Proficiency activities

Glencoe Links to the Humanities

Link to Art
- U.S. History and Art Transparency 1

Link to Literature
- Macmillan Literature: American Literature Audiotapes Side 1
- Macmillan Literature: American Literature Text—Early Indians

Link to Music
- American Music: Cultural Traditions

CHAPTER 1

BEGINNING THE CHAPTER

Display a large world relief map on the wall. Point to the Americas, Europe, Africa, and Asia and mention that until the late 1400s these regions largely developed in isolation. Ask students to suggest what physical features may have helped to create this isolation. (oceans, mountain ranges, vast deserts, and so on) Tell students that Chapter 1 details the ways of life that developed in the various world regions.

Point out that until 1492, the peoples of the Americas were isolated from the rest of the world but not from one another. They developed hundreds of regional trade networks. Along those routes groups exchanged not only goods but also ideas and technology. Many of the innovations in technology developed by the Native Americans still shape the way people live today.

Recording Journal Notes

Tell students that a journal is a place where they can not only record their notes but also reflect on the ideas expressed in the chapter.

CHAPTER 1

The World in Transition
Prehistory–1500s

Setting the Scene

▶ INCAN KNIFE, 1100s

Focus

The first immigrants came to North America long before written history. They arrived by walking across a broad grassy "land bridge" where the Bering Strait now separates Siberia and Alaska. These Native Americans developed unique cultures in North and South America. Then a series of events in Europe, Asia, and Africa opened the way to European voyages of discovery and exploration across the Atlantic. From these ventures, the United States was born.

Concepts to Understand

★ Why diverse cultures among Native Americans came into being
★ How economic change developed from trade with East Asia

Read to Discover . . .

★ who were the major native North American groups.
★ what circumstances in Europe, Asia, and Africa led to voyages of exploration.

Journal Notes

How do the accomplishments and ideas of a culture reflect values? Note important details about various cultures in your journal as you read the chapter.

CULTURAL	• c. 1150 B.C. Olmec civilization begins in Mexico	• 200 B.C. Hopewell culture begins to build burial mounds	• 900 Mayan civilization begins to decline
	1000 B.C.	500 B.C.	A.D. 500
POLITICAL	• 1000 B.C. People inhabit present-day Peru and Ecuador	• 507 B.C. Athenians establish democracy	• 618 Tang Dynasty is founded in China

6   UNIT 1 A New World: Prehistory to 1776

✚ EXTRA CREDIT PROJECT

The world in the 1400s looked very different from the way it looks today. The eastern part of North America was covered by thick forests. Marshland stretched along much of Europe's Mediterranean coast and covered vast areas of northern Germany and Russia. Ask interested students to research the environment of each continent in the 1400s. Have students present their findings to the class in the form of a map. Encourage them to research when those environments began to change and the consequences of those changes. Ask them to discuss those findings as they explain their maps to their classmates.

History AND ART

Pawnee Village
unknown artist

The Pawnee were one of many Native American peoples who lived in the present-day midwestern United States.

▲ SOUTHWESTERN POTTERY

- 1085 Anasazi build pueblos, oldest standing buildings in North America
- 1210 Genghis Khan controls a vast empire
- 1300 Cahokia is largest North American community
- 1433 Ming rulers in China stop outside trade
- 1500 Aztec and Incan empires are at their height
- 1500 European expeditions reach Venezuela and Brazil

1000 — 1250 — 1500

CHAPTER 1 The World in Transition   7

CHAPTER 1 CONCEPTS

Concept Mapping Activity

Reproduce the following generalization and concepts map on the chalkboard. Ask students to hypothesize what topics may be covered in Chapter 1.

Continents separated by great oceans developed cultures in relative isolation until European contacts opened the gates to exploration and discovery.

- Diverse Cultures
- Economic Changes

History AND ART

This drawing by an unknown artist suggests the complex social structure found in many Native American cultures.

 VIDEODISC

- *GTV: A Geographic Perspective on American History*

Side 1, Chapter 2
Title: *Linking Life and Land*
Subject: The first Americans and the effects of geography on their lives

See GTV Guide page 33 for complete lesson plan.

Teacher Notes

LESSON PLAN
SECTION 1, 8–14

FOCUS

Bellringer
Display Focus Activity Transparency 1 on the overhead projector and assign the accompanying Focus Activity Sheet.

Objectives
Point out the objectives on this page to students in previewing the section content.

Motivating Activity
Ask for volunteers to tell what they know about Native Americans—their dress, homes, religious customs, and so on. Because of the impact of movies and television, students probably will give descriptions of the Plains peoples—feathered headdresses, tepees, hunting buffalo, worshipping the Great Spirit, and so on. Refer students to the map on page 12 and stress that the Plains Indian culture was only one of many.

- *GTV: The American People: Fabric of a Nation*

Side 1, Chapter 2
Title: *Kaleidoscope*
Subject: A look at the diversity of Native Americans

See GTV Guide page 42 for complete lesson plan.

SECTION 1

The First Americans

Setting the Scene

Section Focus
The first people to come to the Americas are called Native Americans. Over time they formed many rich and diverse cultures. Some cultures became elaborate empires, while others remained simple in organization.

Objectives
After studying this section, you should be able to
★ explain the origins and paths of settlement of the first immigrants to the Americas.
★ compare the cultures in Mexico and South America to those in North America.

Key Terms
maize, pueblos, confederation

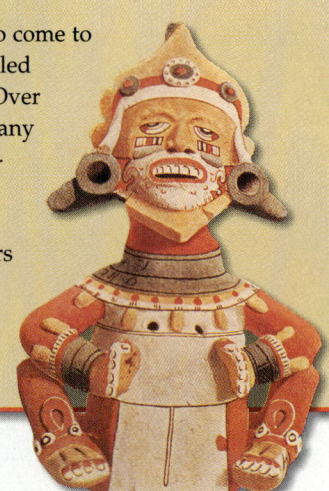

◀ PAINTED CLAY IMAGE

Twenty thousand years ago, much of the water in today's oceans was frozen. Huge ice sheets covered much of present-day Canada and the northern United States. Scientists today believe that people from Asia walked across a "land bridge" that once connected Alaska and Asia. They did not come all at once but in waves often hundreds or thousands of years apart. Most were groups of several families, following great herds of game animals. As groups reached North America, they moved south along the coasts and mountain valleys. Migrations continued until about 12,000 years ago when rising seawater destroyed the land bridge.

The first Americans gathered wild plants and hunted large animals—mammoths, giant sloths, and beavers. Their spear points have been found with the bones of many animals now extinct in America: mastodons, tapirs, and giant bison. In addition to these and other large animals, people hunted deer, antelope, and elks.

Groups of the earliest Americans moved south slowly until they reached the tip of South America. Over time these people adapted to their "New World" environments and became the peoples known today as Native Americans.

For many thousands of years, humans lived in bands of hunter-gatherers, adapting to the land or moving on. Some groups felt so close to their land that they came to believe that they had always been there.

■ Empires in America

Over time some hunters took up different ways of living. In South America groups moved onto the dry seacoast of Peru and Ecuador. By harvesting the rich oceans and farming the river valleys, they developed

8   UNIT 1   A New World: Prehistory to 1776

Classroom Resources for SECTION 1

Teacher's Classroom Resources
- Chapter 1 Study Guide
- Reproducible Lesson Plan
- Reteaching Activity 1-1
- Chapter 1 Cooperative Learning Activity
- Chapter 1 Primary & Secondary Source Readings
- Section Quiz

Multimedia
- Section Focus Transparency 1
- Chapter 1 Skills Transparency
- Chapter 1 Map Transparency
- Testmaker
- Student Self-Test Software
- The American People: Fabric of a Nation
- PictureShow: Native Americans, Part 1 & 2

a more complicated culture. By about 1000 B.C., they and the mountain peoples above them began to draw on the abundance of both the jungles and sea. From the jungles they got dyes and medicine. Skillful farming of the mountainsides provided potatoes, peanuts, squash, and beans. Fine engineers designed and built great cities—some of which were larger than those of Europe at the time—with canals, pyramids, temples, and markets. Their way of life became more complex, with bureaucrats and taxes, and city-states and empires that rose and fell. Because these people had no written language, however, precise knowledge of this history is uncertain.

The Inca

The last of the great empires in the Andes was the Inca. The Inca were a mountain culture who, about 100 years before Columbus, controlled a 3,000-mile stretch of South America from its northern coast to the middle of Chile. The empire was linked through its 10,000-mile-long road system. Woven suspension bridges crossed canyons and rivers. Terraced hillside farms with complicated irrigation systems produced abundant food. The Incan government provided for orphans, the aged, and the sick.

To the north, in the area called Mesoamerica—parts of the modern nations of Mexico, Guatemala, and Honduras—similar developments occurred. About the time the fishing people of Peru began to settle down, the gathering people in the central valley of Mexico were cultivating a large-seeded grass, **maize**, the forerunner of corn.

The Olmec

Along the Gulf of Mexico coast, a group called the Olmec developed a much more complex society with large villages, temple complexes, and pyramids. The Olmec were the first Mesoamerican people to use large masses of stone, sculpting it into large monuments. Their civilization strongly influenced their neighbors.

 ▲ **EARLY PEOPLES** People had spread throughout the Western Hemisphere and had developed cultures in keeping with the different terrains and climates in which they had settled. *How did the first people come to the Americas?*

CHAPTER 1 The World in Transition

CHAPTER 1 SECTION 1

Independent Practice

Linking Past and Present
Ask students to research examples of the legacy of the Native Americans. **L1**

Teaching American Portraits

Point out that each of the five nations ran its own internal affairs, but foreign affairs—especially the declaration of war—were decided by the League. Then ask students why Hiawatha referred to the Iroquois Confederacy as the "Great Peace." (It ended war among the Five Nations.)

Did You Know?

Leaders of the League of Five Nations would often end their speeches with "Horoquoue!"—an exclamation meaning "I have spoken with great emotion!"

 **CD-ROM**

PictureShow: Native Americans, Part 1

Subject: Introduces the major Native American cultures in the eastern woodlands and Great Plains

PictureShow: Native Americans, Part 2

Subject: Introduces the Native Americans of the Southwest, Northwest Coast, and Arctic

AMERICAN PORTRAITS

Hiawatha
c. 1570

The character in the poem "The Song of Hiawatha" is not based on the life of the actual Native American leader. The real Hiawatha, a Mohawk, enjoyed a reputation as a magician and a prophet.

Dedicated to ending violence and warfare, Hiawatha devoted his final years to creating a union from among hostile Native American nations. About 1570, he brought together the Mohawk, Onondaga, Oneida, Cayuga, and Seneca into the League of the Five Nations, also known as the Iroquois Confederacy. One remarkable aspect of the league was its ruling council in which each nation had a single vote. This early form of "government based on the consent of the governed" influenced the course of early American democracy. The United States began as a confederacy of states much like the Iroquois Confederacy.

The Maya

Farther south the Maya were building ever larger pyramids and villages. Their trade networks spread along the coasts. Corn, cocoa, cotton, tomatoes, beans, and squash were traded both north and south. Mayan seeds and cloth were traded for the pottery and precious stones of the South Americans. Both peoples became skilled at metalwork and pottery. No doubt ideas also moved back and forth from group to group.

As people increased their food supply, societies became more and more complex. Small groups grew into city-states and small countries. Market and trade centers sprang up. The Maya developed a vast group of city-states that competed with one another in battle and in building grand public works. Then about A.D. 1000, the Maya changed and scattered over their area. The Maya and their trade routes continued but on a smaller scale.

Throughout this era the Maya were fascinated with mathematics. They invented the concept of zero. They developed complicated calendars linked to the study of the stars. Their temple-pyramids reflect an understanding of the earth's relation to the sun.

The Aztec

Many other equally advanced groups rose in Mesoamerica. The last group were the Aztec. In about 1325 they settled on islands in the middle of Lake Texcoco and built their city, Tenochtitlán, the site of modern Mexico City. Tenochtitlán was connected to the mainland by causeways. By the late 1400s, it had gold-adorned temples, floating gardens, and an enormous market. Its population of 100,000 was far larger than that of any city in Europe at the time.

■ Cultures North of Mexico

The people living north of Mexico traded with the natives of Mexico. By 400 B.C., maize had been introduced into what would become the southwestern United States and the fertile Mississippi Valley. From these two areas, knowledge of maize cultivation spread.

North of Mexico, the population was only one-tenth that of Mexico and the Incan empire. The way of life was also much different. Most people lived in small villages and bands.

UNIT 1 A New World: Prehistory to 1776

Cooperative Learning

Divide the class into groups of four or five. Assign each group one of the Native American cultures discussed in this section. Have group members brainstorm to come up with as much information as they can about their assigned culture. Then ask group members to work together to identify the most important points in the information they have gathered. Next, have each group write a sentence that summarizes these important points. Groups should select a representative to read their sentences to the rest of the class. **L2**

Southwestern Communities

About the time of the fall of the classic Maya and the rise of cultures in Mexico, people in the present-day southwestern United States began to form larger groups with more complex village structures. Several groups began to build large, close-knit villages in the area where present-day Utah, Colorado, Arizona, and New Mexico come together. These people, called Anasazi, built large, multistory apartment-like buildings of adobe and cut stone with connecting causeways and elaborate ceremonial rooms. Early Spanish explorers called these houses **pueblos**, the Spanish word for "villages."

To the south in Arizona, the Hohokam were building large villages with elaborate irrigation canals, ball-playing courts, and temple mounds. Their trade goods and decorations show close contact with northern Mexico. Other groups in the area also built large villages and developed trade.

Then, in A.D. 1300, all this changed. Perhaps a severe drought and climate change took place. The Hohokam vanished; other groups scattered and moved closer to established water. The Anasazi moved to the springs on the Hopi mesas and the Rio Grande. Other groups moved to similar places. Their descendants remain as the Pueblo people of New Mexico and Arizona.

The Moundbuilders

Another area that showed a great growth in population was the Mississippi Valley. Around A.D. 900, people along the Mississippi River flourished as farmers and traders. They built great temple mounds of earth similar to those in Mexico. Settlements along the river grew into large towns. Cahokia (near present-day St. Louis) had a population of perhaps 10,000 people, with hundreds of temple mounds.

An earlier group of moundbuilders, the Hopewell culture, grew up in the Ohio River valley about 200 B.C. and lasted about 700 years. The Hopewell people farmed their rich land and traded across the Midwest for copper and shells. They built huge mounds of earth as both ceremonial centers and burial sites. Some of the Hopewells' elaborate and enormous mounds—as high as 30 feet—are in the shapes of snakes, turtles, and other animals. Inside the burial mounds, archaeologists have found pearl beads, woven cloth, copper ornaments, and striking objects of stone and mica.

On the Great Plains, the last of the hunter-gatherers still hunted the enormous herds of buffalo, which were all that remained of the mighty herds their ancestors had followed from Asia. With the arrival of the Spanish and their horses, these people would also undergo a tremendous change. With horses to ride, the buffalo hunters would become a powerful force on the plains.

In other parts of the country, other groups also flourished: the rich fishing cultures of the Pacific Northwest, the seed gatherers of California, and the farmers of the Southeast.

Visualizing History ▼ **EARLY DWELLINGS** Housing styles of Native Americans were as varied as their cultures. The Cliff Palace, Mesa Verde, is one of the grandest of all cliff dwellings. It was the hub of a Colorado chiefdom nearly 1,000 years ago. **What are pueblos?**

CHAPTER 1 SECTION 1

Linking Across Time

Like their forebears, Native Americans today believe that their ancestors' graves are sacred. Yet, for years archaeologists and others have dug up thousands of Native American remains. In 1989 the Smithsonian Institution in Washington, D.C., met the demands of Native American activists and agreed to return properly identified skeletons from their Native American collection to groups who could prove at least a "cultural affiliation" with the remains.

Food of the Times

According to the United Nations, the four staples of diets around the world are wheat, rice, maize, and potatoes. Two of the four—maize and potatoes—were developed by Native Americans.

Visualizing History

Point out that today Mesa Verde is a 52,000-acre national park. It contains hundreds of cliff dwellings, mesa-top pit houses, and pueblos.
Answer to Caption: Pueblos are multistory buildings of adobe and stone.

Sidelights: Inca Engineers

The Incas were highly sophisticated engineers. They linked their empire with over 10,000 miles of roads. They also slung rope suspension bridges across the deep ravines that cut through their mountainous land. One bridge built in 1350 was in daily use for over 500 years. In addition, without cement, the Incas constructed intricate stone buildings that remain standing to this day.

CHAPTER 1
SECTION 1

**Using Maps**

Answers: Navajo, Hopi, Zuni, Pima, Papago, Pueblo, Comanche

Skills Practice

Have students determine which part of the Americas was settled last. Why did it take Native Americans so long to settle this area? (The southernmost part of South America. It was the farthest point from the "land bridge" that connected the Americas to Asia.)

Did You Know?

The Acoma pueblo, established in about 1300, is believed to be the oldest continuously occupied settlement in the present-day United States. The Spaniards first discovered the settlement in 1540, but it would take them a century to conquer it. Today the pueblo, a national historic landmark, is still home to a few families.

Native American Cultures

Long before Europeans arrived, people had migrated from the continent of Asia and spread throughout the Americas. **What groups settled in southwest North America?**

12   UNIT 1 A New World: Prehistory to 1776

Sidelights: Iroquois Women

Contrary to popular belief, women wielded considerable power in many Native American societies north of Mexico. Among the Iroquois, for example, women owned the houses, fields, and crops, and descent was traced through the female line. While Iroquois women did not hold any leadership positions, it was their task to choose the leaders. Further, they decided whether or not a leader was effective. If, after a number of warnings, his performance did not improve, the women could demand that he be removed.

The Iroquois

The Iroquois, an alliance of farming people, dominated the Northeast in the 1500s and 1600s. They were made up of Mohawk, Seneca, Oneida, Onondaga, and Cayuga nations. Large groups of several families shared a "long house" of poles and bark. A large village might have 50 or more long houses and 300 to 400 people. Their league was a representative **confederation**, or government made up of independent units, probably formed about 1580. It was founded by two of the culture's heroes, Dekanawida and Hiawatha. The female leaders of each clan chose their chief, who would attend league councils. The confederation worked to maintain peace between the various tribes.

The Five Civilized Tribes

In the southeastern United States, the Creek, Cherokee, Choctaw, Seminole, and Chickasaw formed another confederation, which they called the Five Civilized Tribes. This group later devised a written language and a dictionary. They practiced a loose-knit form of democracy.

Just as the people of Europe and Asia were aware of each other, so groups within the Americas knew about each other and shared similar ideas. For example, despite their diversity, the Native American people felt a close relationship to the land and their environment. They felt that all things, themselves included, were part of a universal spirit.

A Clash of Values

In the 1400s Native Americans and Europeans were unaware of each other. Native Americans continued to develop their ways of life isolated from other peoples of the world. Similarly, the people of other continents were unaware of America. Then a chain of events began, moving the peoples of Europe, Asia, and Africa toward interdependence. European nations initiated the ventures that led to the colonization of America. By the late 1400s the world stood on the brink of enormous changes.

The Native American way of life was one that the Europeans who arrived seeking wealth were unable to understand. The Europeans' values seemed strange to the Native Americans as well. For example, during the conquest of Peru, an Incan citizen asked a European, "What do you do with gold? Do you eat it?" Reportedly, during the conquest of Mexico, Cortés told the ambassador to the Aztec ruler Moctezuma, "We have an illness only gold will cure."

These two different viewpoints and the conviction that there was only one valid outlook would lead to misunderstandings for centuries to come.

▲ TOTEM BY TLINGIT-TSMISYAN CARVER

Section 1 ★ Review

Checking for Understanding

1. **Identify** Olmec, Hopewell, Iroquois League, Mesoamerica.
2. **Define** maize, pueblos, confederation.
3. **Summarize** the process by which the Americas were first settled.
4. **Discuss** three elements of Aztec and Incan cultures.

Critical Thinking

5. **Evaluating Causes** Why would towns and complex societies tend to grow up among farmers, rather than among hunter-gatherers?

CHAPTER 1 The World in Transition

CHAPTER 1
SECTION 1

ASSESS

Check Understanding

Assign the Section 1 Review as homework or an in-class activity.

Evaluate

Assign the Section 1 Quiz in the TCR or use the History of a Free Nation Testmaker to create a customized quiz.

Reteach

Have students complete Reteaching Activity 1-1.

Enrich

Have students conduct research for a report on the Native American cultures of their area.

CLOSE

Have students repeat the motivating activity on page 8 of these teacher's notes. Ask them to compare their responses to those they gave before they read this section.

• *GTV: The American People: Fabric of a Nation*

Side 1, Chapter 3
Title: *Change of Scene*
Subject: Why Europeans sought a new home

See GTV Guide page 44 for complete lesson plan.

Answers to SECTION 1 REVIEW

1. Olmec, 10; Iroquois League, 13; Mesoamerica, 9
2. All vocabulary words are defined in the Glossary.
3. Asians cross a "land bridge" between Siberia and Alaska, spread through Americas.
4. empires of conquered people, accumulate precious metals and wealth, beautiful temples and cities, religious. Aztec sacrifice humans.
5. Farmers are in one place long enough to build towns and plan for future.

CHAPTER 1 CONNECTIONS

Teaching Making Connections

Native American groups are seeking to have relics and remains of ancestors removed from museums and returned for burial. In 1989 the Smithsonian Institution agreed to return all remains that were identifiable as belonging to a certain Native American group. That same year, Congress passed the Repatriation Act in an effort to protect Native American grave sites and return remains.

Did You Know?

The word *archaeology* comes from two Latin words that mean "study of antiquity." Today the word refers to the systematic recovery and scientific study of past cultures.

CONNECTIONS  CONNECTIONS

Prehistory and Archaeology

Collectors of Native American relics buy and sell arrowheads, spear points, and bits of pottery and jewelry for prices ranging from 50 cents for common arrowheads to hundreds of thousands of dollars for rare ancient specimens. Native Americans and archaeologists object to this practice. They claim that "pothunters" destroy America's historic legacy and that an isolated artifact can add little to the understanding of prehistoric cultures.

Some native people also object to the work of archaeologists, claiming that sacred sites are destroyed. Archaeologists defend their work. They say their digs aid historical understanding. As they excavate they observe and note details about the placement of each object. Their observations, combined with scientific techniques of dating and classification, can tell much about a particular culture. Archaeologists

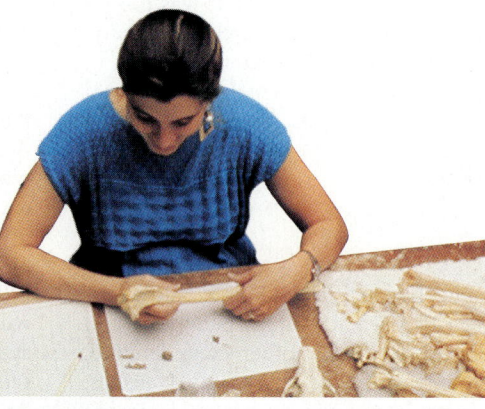

ARCHAEOLOGISTS AT WORK

can show how people got their food, whether they built permanent homes, what they used to make tools, and whether they traded with others. Theories can then be developed about a culture's ideas and beliefs. This helps to preserve the prehistoric culture, even though the artifacts have been removed from their original sites.

Making the Science Connection

1. What can archaeologists learn about a particular culture from excavating a prehistoric site?
2. Why do archaeologists object to "pothunters"?

Linking Past and Present

3. What are some artifacts of our own culture?

Answers to CONNECTIONS

1. They can determine how people got their food, whether they built permanent homes, what they used to make tools, and whether they traded with others. Theories can then be developed about a culture's ideas and beliefs.
2. They destroy Americans' historic legacy, and an isolated artifact can add little to the understanding of prehistoric cultures.

3. Possible answers: computers, VCRs, and automobiles, televisions, bicycles, clothing, frozen or canned food, fast food containers, CDs, lawnmowers, and so forth.

SECTION 2

The New Europe

Setting the Scene

Section Focus

During the Middle Ages, the western part of the old Roman Empire recovered from decline and developed a new civilization rooted in Christianity. Powerful monarchs emerged in several countries, and contacts with the Middle East and East Asia stimulated trade, learning, and national rivalries.

Objectives

After studying this section, you should be able to

★ describe how European society changed from medieval times.

★ explain the significance of the Renaissance and the Reformation.

Key Terms

feudalism, manor, serf, charter, parliament, Renaissance, classical, humanism, dynasty

◀ CROSS OF LOTHAR, C. 1000

The collapse of the Roman Empire was nearly complete by A.D. 550. With the collapse of the western Roman empire's government, western Europe entered the Middle Ages. During this period, from about A.D. 500 to 1500, **feudalism**—a system in which powerful lords gave land to nobles in return for pledges of loyalty—replaced centralized government. The Roman Catholic Church, the western branch of Christianity, became a powerful force in Europe.

■ The Middle Ages

During the Middle Ages—A.D. 500 to 1500—most of European society was organized by the manorial system. The majority of the people of Europe were peasants who worked on farmlands that belonged to a **manor**, or large estate, held by a noble.

Peasants lived in a village on the manor. Most were **serfs**, who were "bound to the soil"; that is, they were considered part of the property. A manor also included woods; common fields and pastures; a church; and shops for weavers, blacksmiths, and others who made the manor nearly self-sufficient.

In this period, the Church was the center of life in western Europe. Catholic clergy not only performed religious ceremonies but also helped govern the small feudal manors and the larger emerging kingdoms.

In 1095 Pope Urban II, head of the Roman Catholic Church, called for a "holy war" against the Seljuk (sehl•JOOK) Turks, a Muslim people who held the Christian shrines in Palestine. The Church began a series of wars called Crusades to recapture the Holy Land, including Jerusalem. Over the next 200 years, Crusaders went to war in the Holy Land. By 1291, however, the Muslims had driven out the Crusaders.

CHAPTER 1 The World in Transition

CHAPTER 1 SECTION 2

TEACH
Guided Practice

Writing Have students write an essay that compares the Italian Renaissance with the Northern Renaissance. Ask students to focus on three areas in the essay: major writers and their works, major artists and their works, and important inventions and developments. Have students discuss which Renaissance—Italian or Northern—made the greatest contribution to European culture. **L3**

 Although the Crusaders did not intend to change life in Europe, their experiences had long-lasting effects. Perhaps the most important was that they brought home an assortment of luxury goods. Discuss with students how that one change led to many others.
Answer to Caption: encouraged the growth of trade

Did You Know?
The English government assemblies took their name from the French word *parler,* which means "to talk." Over time, *parler* changed to *parliament.*

 **THE CRUSADES** Beginning in the 1000s, western European forces carried out a series of religious wars to win Palestine from Muslim rule. *What effect did the Crusades have on trade?*

▲ **ILLUMINATED MANUSCRIPT,** illustrated and handwritten document

Although the Crusades were a failure, their effects upon western Europe were enormous. They helped bring western Europe out of isolation and into contact with other parts of the world. Trade for Eastern luxury goods started a series of events that completely changed Europe's economic, political, and social life.

When cities began to serve as trade centers, new job opportunities developed. The manorial system began to break down as competition enabled some serfs to demand higher wages and benefits to stay on the manor. Eventually, many could afford to buy their own land. Others began to pay rent for land with money rather than labor or produce. Farming for profit increased agricultural production, and better living conditions enabled the population to grow.

Because of their access to trade routes, towns along the Mediterranean Sea—in Italy, southern France, and Spain—grew first. As early as 1200, Venice and Genoa were strong city-states with busy shipyards. Cities in northern Europe also emerged as centers for trade, shipping, and profitable craft industries such as weaving. Those with access to the sea would eventually rival the growth of Italian cities.

■ The Late Middle Ages

The rise of commerce brought prosperity to much of western and central Europe. The use of money and the need for credit turned some merchants into bankers. They lent money to finance new business and provided credit for shipments of goods. Well-to-do bankers, merchants, and master craftsworkers made up a new part of the social system—the middle class—which stood between the nobility at the top of the social system and the peasants at the bottom.

The Decline of Feudalism

The middle class supported the king—who represented stable government—against the feudal nobility, who disrupted trade by conducting local wars. As towns

16   UNIT 1 A New World: Prehistory to 1776

Special Needs

Study Strategies The objectives given in the "Setting the Scene" feature provide a valuable tool for focusing reading on main ideas. Point out that the tasks required by the objectives are usually signaled in the first word. Some emphasize information collection ("List," "Identify"), while others call for description ("Describe," "Explain"), and still others ask students to compare and contrast. Ask students to look through each chapter objective and note the first word. Discuss the kinds of responses required.

grew in population and wealth, some townspeople were able to buy a **charter** from the local lord and win the right to control their own affairs. In England, townspeople and knights gained a voice in government, sending representatives to meetings of a **parliament**, or assembly.

The Renaissance

The power of the towns helped weaken the feudal system and strengthen national governments. Townspeople used their financial power to win rights and favors from ambitious monarchs. In return they supplied funds for ships or soldiers. Powerful bankers dealt on almost equal terms with European rulers who needed to borrow money. Prosperity, optimism, and an emphasis on human potential set the mood for far-reaching social and cultural changes in the 1400s and 1500s. This period is known as the **Renaissance**, a French word for the "rebirth" of interest in the culture and learning of ancient Greece and Rome. The meaning of the Renaissance, however, went far beyond this definition. Even today, people marvel at the accomplishments of Renaissance artists and scholars.

The Renaissance began about 1350 in the city-states of northern Italy. Wealthy families bought books and paintings, hired architects to design buildings, and supported painters and sculptors. These wealthy patrons were especially interested in **classical** culture—the arts, literature, and knowledge of ancient Greece and Rome. This interest in the classics came to be called **humanism**.

While the Middle Ages had emphasized the human inner or spiritual nature and the need for self-discipline, the Renaissance awakened human creativity and demanded an outward expression of talent. Renaissance writers, artists, and thinkers were brimming with new ideas. Writers tried new styles, writing in everyday language instead of scholarly Latin. Painters developed new techniques and tried to portray people realistically. Humanism took on a broader meaning, including an appreciation for all aspects of human life.

The Renaissance in Italy reached its height in the late 1400s. Three of the most famous of the many Italian artists working at that time were Raphael, Michelangelo, and Leonardo da Vinci. Around 1500, Renaissance ideas spread northward into France, the Holy Roman Empire, the Netherlands, and England.

The new craft of printing with movable type, invented about 1440 by a German, Johannes Gutenberg, helped spread ideas. Because more people could afford books, they were exposed to new thoughts.

▼ **REAPING AND SHEARING IN JULY** Miniature from Très Riches Heures, by Jean duc de Berry, c. 1413 During feudal times, power was based on the ownership of land. The land was divided into manors, or farming communities. **Does the artist view feudalism in a favorable light?**

CHAPTER 1 The World in Transition 17

CHAPTER 1
SECTION 2

Independent Practice

Religion The play *Luther*, by John Osborne, portrays the life of Martin Luther. Have students read the scene in which Johann Eck confronts Luther at the Diet of Worms. Ask them to write in their own words a monologue that Luther might have given in defense of his beliefs. Some students might like to present their monologues to the class. **L3**

Visualizing History

The painting, which was created in about 1413, shows the work done on a manor in the summer. Point out that a manor was a self-sufficient community with its own mill, blacksmith shop, and church. Its people could produce almost everything they needed. They raised pigs, chickens, and cattle for meat and grew grain, fruits, and vegetables. They also raised sheep for wool and spun the wool into cloth.
Answer to Caption: The artist's portrayal of an orderly and prosperous community seems to suggest a positive view of feudalism.

Making Connections: History and Art

The most distinctive artistic technique of the Renaissance was perspective. Its use in painting makes objects and scenes look three-dimensional. To achieve that look, artists use converging visual rays to give the illusion of a unified and infinite three-dimensional space on a two-dimensional canvas. The idea originated in Florence in about 1420. It was the result of a collaboration between architects, painters, and sculptors. In the years that followed, artists in many parts of Europe tried the technique and refined its basic principles. From the 1400s until today, perspective has remained a distinguishing characteristic of Western art. It does exist in the art of other civilizations.

CHAPTER 1
SECTION 2

Visualizing History During the Crusades merchants in northern Italy built ships to transport people and goods across the Mediterranean. As trading grew, so did the wealth of those merchants.
Answer to Caption: Wealthy merchants and bankers financed painting and sculpture and developed an interest in the classics.

Fact or Fiction?
During the Renaissance a person's clothing was a mark of his or her wealth.

FICTION: Clothing was the mark of a person's class. During the Renaissance, laws were passed that prohibited commoners from wearing certain clothing. In England they could not wear a ruff. In Florence women of the lower classes could not have buttons of certain shapes and materials.

Visualizing History ▲ NEW MARKETS By the 1400s trade had created markets in Europe where Eastern goods sold for great profit. *How did this trade bring a Renaissance to northern Italy?*

End of Religious Unity

For most Europeans in the Middle Ages, the Roman Catholic Church was the center of life and the most stable and unifying influence. But by the late 1400s, Europe was in the early stages of a religious upheaval.

What would later be known as the Protestant Reformation began simply with demands for reforms in the Roman Catholic Church. Among the leading early reformers were John Wycliffe in England and John Huss in Bohemia, part of the Holy Roman Empire. These early reformers criticized the Church's wealth and the luxurious lifestyles of some clergy. They also printed Bibles in the language of the common people rather than the official Latin. The Church feared widespread rebellion against its leadership. Soon arguments broke out between Church supporters and reformers.

In the early 1500s, Martin Luther, a Catholic and a professor in a German university, challenged several Church practices. Luther believed that salvation was achieved by faith, not by good works. In 1521, when he was called before Emperor Charles V to answer charges brought against him by Church authorities, Luther declared:

> *Unless I be convinced by Scripture and reason, I neither can nor dare retract anything, for my conscience is a captive to God's word, and it is neither safe nor right to go against conscience.*

This stand marked Luther's separation from the Catholic Church. The first Protestant faith, Lutheranism, was born. Soon other Protestant sects developed and grew in Scandinavia, parts of modern Germany, the Netherlands, and England. In other parts of Europe, particularly Spain and the Holy Roman Empire, Catholic rulers became the Church's defenders.

■ Emerging Nations

During most of the Middle Ages, Europe was splintered into many small states. Ruled by princes and other lords, these small states were part of the feudal system. This system rested on ties of protection and obligation between landowning nobles and those who lived on their lands.

During the late Middle Ages, strong monarchs began to replace feudalism in western Europe. Rulers brought unity to their countries and gained authority over the powerful nobles.

In England it took 30 years of bloody civil war from 1455 to 1485 to unify the kingdom. Hundreds of English nobles died in the fighting. The winning Lancastrian leader, Henry Tudor, came to the throne in 1485 as King Henry VII. He married Elizabeth of York, the daughter of one of his defeated rivals, unifying the kingdom. Henry VII's ruling house, or **dynasty**, produced several outstanding rulers.

UNIT 1 A New World: Prehistory to 1776

Making Connections: History and Political Science

One of the most influential works produced during the Renaissance was Niccolo Machiavelli's *The Prince* (1517). Considered a primer on political science, *The Prince* is a discussion of power—how to get it and how to keep it. Machiavelli suggested that princes should use any means necessary—lies, cunning, and even violence—to gain and hold on to power. Today a scheming, deceitful, and unscrupulous politician is often called *Machiavellian*.

The monarchs of France, too, gradually consolidated their power and territory. As the French fought the English in the Hundred Years' War from 1337 to 1453, French rulers won the confidence of the people. France's victory in the war, aided by the heroism of Joan of Arc, increased the people's feeling of patriotism and unity.

A different motivation brought political unity to Spain. In about A.D. 711, Muslims, or Moors, from North Africa conquered most of the Iberian peninsula—Spain and Portugal—and established a sophisticated culture. Christian rulers, led by the kingdom of Castile, tried continuously to drive the Moors out of Spain. By the mid-1400s, the Muslims held only the territory around Granada on the southeast coast.

In 1469 Christian unity in Spain was aided by the marriage of the heirs to the largest kingdoms: Isabella of Castile and Leon, and Ferdinand of Aragon. "The Catholic monarchs" believed that Christianity would unify the country. In 1492 they ordered all Jews to leave Spain. In the same year, their armies took Granada from the Moors.

Once part of Spain, Portugal won its independence in the twelfth century. By the late 1300s the country was unified under King John I. In the late 1400s, the Holy Roman Empire, which included parts of the modern nations of Germany, Austria, and Italy as well as Poland and Russia, would lack the unified direction to participate in exploration and discovery with the western European kingdoms: Spain, Portugal, France, and England. All four had seaports on the Atlantic Ocean—soon to become a great avenue of trade and exploration.

Europeans, once isolated and bound by a rigid feudal system, were developing a spirit of curiosity and adventure. Unified monarchies and national rivalry led to competition for trade with Asia. The search for an all-water route to East Asia encouraged explorers to cross unknown oceans and seek new lands.

▲ ARMED KNIGHT, 1300s

Section 2 ★ Review

Checking for Understanding

1. **Identify** Martin Luther, Henry Tudor, Moors, Isabella of Castile and Leon, Ferdinand of Aragon.
2. **Define** feudalism, manor, serf, charter, parliament, Renaissance, classical, humanism, dynasty.
3. **Discuss** the political changes in Europe in the late 1400s.
4. **Explain** the broad meaning of the term *Renaissance* as it applies to the art, science, and culture of the period.

Critical Thinking

5. **Analyzing Cause and Effect** Why did the growth of towns and a middle class of bankers and merchants lessen the influence of feudal lords?

CHAPTER 1 The World in Transition 19

CHAPTER 1 SECTION 2

ASSESS

Check Understanding
Assign Section 2 as homework or an in-class activity.

Evaluate
Assign the TCR or use the History of a Free Nation Testmaker to create a customized quiz.

Reteach
Ask students to reread the section. Test their retention of information by holding an oral quiz. Add an element of competition to the quiz by organizing the students into two teams.
Have students complete Reteaching Activity 1-2.

Enrich
Leonardo da Vinci drew designs for machines and contraptions—the helicopter and the parachute, for example—that did not become a reality for hundreds of years. Have students write a research paper on some of Leonardo's far-sighted ideas.

CLOSE

Ask students to trace the events that signaled the end of the Middle Ages and the development of the "New Europe."

Answers to SECTION 2 REVIEW

1. Martin Luther, 18; Henry Tudor, 19; Moors, 19; Isabella of Castile and Leon, 19; Ferdinand of Aragon, 19
2. All vocabulary words are defined in the Glossary.
3. Leadership passed from feudal lords to the monarchs of European nations.
4. Rebirth of interest in classics, achievements in arts, science, and scholarship.
5. This class, not attached to or economically dependent on land or under power of landowner.

LESSON PLAN
SECTION 3, 20–25

FOCUS

Bellringer
Prior to taking roll at the beginning of the class period, display Focus Activity Transparency 3 on the overhead projector and assign the accompanying Focus Activity Sheet.

Objectives
Point out the objectives on this page to students in previewing the section content.

Motivating Activity
Ask students to read the quotation by Marco Polo in this section (page 23). Then have them write in their own words the kind of ruler Kublai Khan was and the extent of the empire over which he ruled. Select a number of students to read their responses to the class. Then discuss why Marco Polo's book had such an impact on the European imagination. Point out that this section describes some of the great Asian and African kingdoms that existed at the dawn of the Age of Exploration.

SECTION 3

Medieval Asia and Africa

Setting the Scene

Section Focus
Europeans' desire for trade provided a compelling reason for contact with the East. Trade between Asia and Africa, however, had transpired for centuries. The rise of Islam was a major influence on contacts between Europe, Asia, and Africa.

Objectives
After studying this section, you should be able to
★ explain the impact of Islam.
★ describe the extent and importance of the Mongol Empire.
★ identify some of the trading kingdoms of Africa.

Key Terms
samurai, shogun

◀ MIDDLE EASTERN METAL HELMET

Since ancient times, trade had linked the different peoples and cultures of the "Old World"—Europe, Asia, and Africa. Both the Greeks and Romans had established profitable routes of trade with Asia and Africa. Seeking slaves and luxuries such as silks, spices, and precious stones, traders also carried ideas and information over great distances.

With the fall of the Roman Empire, Europe's participation in foreign trade had declined. Roads and bridges fell into disrepair, and robbers preyed on travelers because there was no government to keep order. While most people in Europe lived in the country, isolated into small villages, trade between Asia and Africa continued. African merchants, for example, traded iron, skins, and ebony for goods from the Red Sea region. They also conducted trade throughout the Indian Ocean area.

■ Spread of Muslim Ideals

The most important influence in medieval Asia and Africa—with consequences for Europe as well—was the rise of the religion of Islam in the 600s. Inspired by the teachings of the prophet Muhammad, the prophet's followers spread Islam quickly from the Arabian Peninsula through the Middle East to Asia and North Africa into Spain and the Mediterranean region. About 682 an Arab general, Achbar Ben Nafi Al-Fahri, and his warriors had reached the Atlantic in North Africa. Achbar expressed his zeal for Islam:

❝ Did not these waters present an insuperable barrier, I would carry the faith and the law of the faithful to countries reaching from the rising of the sun to the setting thereof! ❞

Classroom Resources for SECTION 3

Teacher's Classroom Resources
- Reproducible Lesson Plan
- Reteaching Activity 1-3
- Section Quiz

Multimedia
- Section Focus Transparency 3
- Testmaker
- Student Self-Test Software

 ▲ **INNOVATIONS** Islamic doctors' discoveries helped develop European medicine in the 1100s. **Where did Arabic numbers originate?**

The original Islamic empire led by Arabs was soon divided. Rival groups of Muslims—the name for followers of Islam—organized and took control over different areas in Asia, Africa, and parts of Europe. In some places—for example, Spain—they met fierce resistance and eventually lost power.

By the late 1400s, the rapidly growing empire of the Ottoman Turks was the leading Muslim power. From their base in Asia Minor—modern Turkey—the Ottomans had taken over Greece and much of the Balkan Peninsula.

Contact Between Muslims and Christians

As Islam spread, Muslims and Christians came into direct conflict. Knights from Christian Europe fought to recapture lands that the Muslims occupied in Spain and Sicily. In 1095, at the urging of the Pope, the knights' main goal became control of Palestine and its Christian shrines.

In the long run, the Crusades into the Holy Land, which was sacred to both Christians and Muslims, influenced trade and learning. From Middle Eastern and Islamic cultures, the returning knights and soldiers brought back new foods and products—spices, sugar, silk, cotton, dyes, perfumes, and fruits such as peaches and melons. Increased trade enriched the Italian city-states.

Contact also brought new ideas. Arab scholars had made advances in medicine, astronomy, mathematics, and other sciences. From the Arabs, Europeans learned algebra and the system of Arabic numerals, which the Arabs had learned in India. In Spain the Muslims introduced the Arabian horse as well as oranges and lemons.

Expansion into India

One of the early areas of Muslim expansion was India. Beginning in A.D. 712, groups of Muslims from Persia (Iran) and Afghanistan occupied parts of northern India. The beliefs of the Muslim people clashed with the ancient Hindu traditions of India. While some Indians converted to Islam, conflict led to divisions within the country.

In the late 1400s, a weak Muslim kingdom was in power in northern India. The rest of the country was divided among many small states and kingdoms controlled by princes and rajas, most of whom were Hindu. Early in the 1500s, another group of

CHAPTER 1
SECTION 3

Independent Practice

Word Origin To illustrate the impact of the Arab world on Europe, give the following list of words—all derived from Arabic—to students: apricot, cotton, damask, lemon, muslin, and orange.

Have students look up each of the words in an etymological dictionary and note its origins and meanings. Then ask students to suggest how these words came into the English language. (They were the names of unfamiliar products brought to Europe by traders.) **L1**

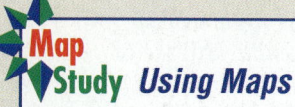

Study *Using Maps*
Answer: by traveling overland

Skills Practice
Ask students to trace the route merchants might take on a journey from Calicut to Genoa. (From Calicut across the Arabian Sea to the Persian Gulf, or Red Sea; then overland to the Mediterranean coast, then across the Mediterranean to Genoa.)

Map Study
Italian cities controlled trade through the Mediterranean, forcing northern Europe to take more difficult land routes. **How else could northern Europeans reach China?**

Muslims established the powerful Mogul Empire, which would unite and rule India for several hundred years.

■ Empires of the East

In the early 1200s, the ancient empire of China was conquered by the invading "Golden Horde" of Mongols from central Asia. Under the strong leadership of Genghis Khan, the Mongol army of fierce, swift riders also swept westward across central Asia, through Russia, terrorizing the Slavic people of Poland, Hungary, and Austria. For nearly 200 years, the Mongols ruled an enormous empire, including China, central Asia, Russia, and the Middle East.

▶ ASTROLABE

China

Although the Chinese considered the Mongols "barbarians," China prospered under their rule. Overland travel was safe while the Mongols controlled the huge central Eurasian plain. East-west trade was revived, along with cultural exchanges among China, Europe, and Muslim Asia. European traders, travelers, and missionaries were welcome in China. They returned not only with silks and spices but also with important inventions such as the compass, printing, and gunpowder.

European traders also brought back exciting descriptions of the wonders they had seen in Asia. Marco Polo was a young merchant from Venice who traveled to the court of Kublai Khan in 1275. His description of

22   UNIT 1 A New World: Prehistory to 1776

Critical Thinking

Making Generalizations Point out that trade among countries is a major focus of this section. Then ask students to write a generalization concerning the relationship between trade and a country's rise to power. Suggest that they use information on one of the countries, empires, or kingdoms discussed in this section to support their generalization. **L3**

the luxury of the "Great Khan's" palace stirred the imaginations of his readers in Europe:

> *Inside, the walls and halls and chambers are all covered with gold and silver and decorated with pictures of dragons and birds and horsemen and various breeds of beasts and scenes of battle.... The hall is so vast that a meal might be served there for more than 6,000 men.*

In the late 1400s, when the spirit of the Renaissance was transforming Europe, the mood in China was to preserve tradition. Following the death of the Great Khan in 1294, the Chinese overthrew their Mongol rulers. The rulers of the new Ming Dynasty wanted to restore their traditional Chinese heritage. New ideas were discouraged, and students studied only the ancient, classic books. At first the Ming rulers encouraged trade, sending expeditions around the Indian Ocean and to the coast of east Africa. Then in 1433 the Ming rulers cut China's contacts with the outside world. China would remain relatively isolated for centuries.

Japan

Like medieval Europe, Japan had a feudal society, based on the bonds between landowning nobles and the knights who served them. **Samurai**, the warriors of feudal Japan, lived by a strict code of honor. Since the 1100s, the country had been led by **shoguns**, military dictators who had far more power than the emperor.

Japan's island location had helped protect it from conquest during Mongol rule in China. When Kublai Khan's navy tried to invade Japan in 1281, a typhoon destroyed the fleet. Fighting off the Mongols, however, weakened the shoguns' government. In the late 1400s, local lords, backed by their private armies of samurai, were almost constantly at war. Nonetheless, towns and trade prospered in medieval Japan.

Life of the Times

Golden Age of Mali

A firsthand account of life in Mali was given by the Arab geographer ibn-Battutu. Traveling through Mali in the fourteenth century, he marveled at the law, order, and racial tolerance of the African kingdom.

"The Negroes possess some admirable qualities. They are seldom unjust and have a greater abhorrence of injustice than any other people. Their Sultan shows no mercy to any one guilty of the least act of it. There is complete security in their country. Neither traveler nor inhabitant in it has anything to fear from robbers or men of violence. They do not confiscate the property of any white man who dies in their country, even if it be uncounted wealth. On the contrary, they give it into the charge of some trustworthy person among the whites, until the rightful heir takes possession of it."

▶ **CARVED RITUAL STOOL**

▲ **ANTELOPE FIGURINE**

CHAPTER 1 SECTION 3

Did You Know?

The empire of Mali grew rich from the trade in salt and gold, even though people there had neither commodity. Mali was located on a major trade route between north and central Africa. As a result, the empire was able to tax merchants who made their way from one part of the continent to another. In return, the leaders of Mali protected the network of caravan routes that crisscrossed the region.

Teaching Life of the Times

Mention that ibn-Battutu visited other African kingdoms including Ethiopia and Kilwa. His travels also took him across the Russian steppes, over the Hindu Kush to India, and finally to China. In his 30 years of travel, ibn-Battutu covered close to 75,000 miles. Ask students to speculate what impact news of ibn-Battutu's travels had on people in Europe.

Sidelights: The Salt Trade In West Africa

One of the most important commodities that changed hands in the trading centers of West Africa was common salt. The grasslands of the Western Sudan had no natural supplies of salt, and people from there were willing to part with sacks of gold—which they had in plentiful supply—pound for pound for blocks of the mineral. Salt was needed to preserve meat, which quickly spoiled in the hot climate. More importantly, it was a necessity of life. People lose some of their body salts when they sweat. A diet containing common salt helps replace those lost body salts.

CHAPTER 1
SECTION 3

ASSESS
Check Understanding
Assign Section 3 Review as homework or an in-class activity.

Evaluate
Assign Section 3 Quiz in the TRC or use the History of a Free Nation Testmaker to create a customized text.

Reteach
Have students complete Reteaching Activity 1-3.

Enrich
Point out that Europeans knew little of the kingdoms of West Africa until the pilgrimage of the great Malian ruler, Mansa Musa, in the 1320s. Have students write a report on Mansa Musa's hajj to Makkah and the impact it had on North Africa. Ricky Rosenthal's *The Splendor That Was Africa* (1967) is a useful source of information for this report.

CLOSE
Have students construct a time line of the events and developments covered in the first three sections of this chapter. Suggest that they divide it into four sections: The Americas, Europe, Africa, and Asia.

▲ BENIN IVORY MASK, SIXTEENTH CENTURY

■ African Trading Kingdoms

From ancient times, trade linked areas of the continent of Africa with other cultures. While Egypt and parts of North Africa traded with others around the Mediterranean, North African merchants also followed caravan trails south across the Sahara to exchange precious salt for gold and slaves.

Early African Civilizations

The earliest African civilizations developed east of the Sahara. Egypt dominated the region for more than 2,000 years. Kushites from the southern Nile then became an independent kingdom. During the time of the Roman Empire, another powerful state, Axum, expanded to challenge the Kushite rule. Axum made Christianity the official religion of the kingdom in A.D. 330. When Islam spread across northern Africa in the 600s, Axum lost much of its coastal territory. Its rulers set up the Christian kingdom of Ethiopia. While Ethiopian rulers attempted to spread Christianity throughout Africa, civil war and Muslim expansion weakened the nation.

Islamic Expansion

Between A.D. 500 and 1500, three wealthy trading kingdoms—Ghana, Mali, and Songhai—developed one after the other in the western Sudan, the grasslands south of the Sahara. The Muslim conquest of North Africa greatly increased trade, and Muslim culture spread to the area.

In the 1300s the trading city of Timbuktu in Mali became a center of Islamic culture, with a university and a great mosque. In 1468 the Songhai people rebelled and captured Timbuktu. Askia Mohammed, a general and devout Muslim, ruled Songhai between 1493 and 1528.

East Africa, on the other hand, looked eastward, trading with Arabia, Persia, India, and China. Wealthy city-states such as Kilwa were centers for gold, ivory, cinnamon, palm oil, and slaves. Swahili, an African-based language mixed with Arabic words, was widely used in trade.

Civil wars brought internal disorder to Bantu nations in central and southern Africa. The resulting loss of power left little defense against Europeans who arrived in the 1500s.

Section 3 ★ Review

Checking for Understanding
1. **Identify** Muslims, Ottomans, Crusades, Marco Polo, Axum, Swahili.
2. **Define** samurai, shogun.
3. **Analyze** the way in which the spread of Islam affected Europe, Asia, and Africa.
4. **Discuss** the importance of the Mongol Empire.

Critical Thinking
5. **Predicting Outcomes** How might interest in exploration have increased as a result of the Crusades?

---

24   UNIT 1 A New World: Prehistory to 1776

Answers to SECTION 3 REVIEW

1. Muslims, 21; Ottomans, 21; Crusades, 21; Marco Polo, 22; Axum, 24; Swahili, 24
2. All vocabulary words are defined in the Glossary.
3. Established empires in Africa and Asia. Conquests of Holy Land prompted Crusades, brought Eastern goods and ideas back to Europe, fueled interest in exploration.
4. Covered China, central Asia, Russia, Middle East. Revived world trade.
5. Crusaders bring back goods, ideas, stories of sights, more people want goods and knowledge and to visit.

Social Studies Skills

Study and Writing Skills

Using Literature as a Historical Source

Literature is imaginative or creative writing in all its forms. It can be poetry or prose, fiction or nonfiction. Some of what we now consider literature actually began in oral form—the legends, histories, and stories told and retold before written language developed.

Each culture's literature is unique. Through its literature, a culture reveals the values it holds important, as well as its beliefs and customs. Each unit of this textbook presents a piece of literature selected to help you better understand the people and period you are studying.

The reading that follows is a creation legend from the Ibibio people of Nigeria. As you read this selection, observe how the characters' actions reveal the beliefs of the ancient Ibibio.

▲ Ibibio carved wood mask

Years ago the sun, the moon, and the water lived on the earth together. The sun often visited the house where water lived and they would sit talking for hours. But the water never came to visit the sun.

One day the sun asked, "Why don't you and your family ever visit my house? My wife and I would be pleased to welcome you."

The water answered, "I'm sorry I have not visited you, but your house is small. I was afraid that if I and my people came to see you, we would drive you and your wife away."

"We are going to build a larger home," replied the sun. "Then will you come to visit us?"

The sun seemed so sad that the water promised to visit when the new house was complete.

The sun and his wife, the moon, set to work, and with the help of their friends, built a magnificent home.

"Come and visit us now," urged the sun.

The water was still doubtful, but the sun begged so hard that the water decided to enter. Through the door into the house he flowed, bringing with him hundreds of fish, some water rats, and even a few water snakes.

When the water was knee-deep, he asked the sun, "Do you still want us to come in?"

"Yes," cried the foolish sun.

The water continued to stream in, and the sun and the moon climbed onto the roof to stay dry.

"Do you still want my people and me to come into your home?" asked the water once more.

The sun did not want to go back on his word, so he replied, "Yes, let them all come in."

Soon the water reached the very top of the roof. The sun and moon were forced into the sky, where they have lived ever since.

Practicing the Skill

1. What is the theme of the literature selection?
2. Do the events help you understand the historical setting, circumstance, or specific culture? Explain.
3. What have you learned from this work about a particular period or culture?
4. For further practice in using literature as a historical source, read the excerpts on pages 30 and 31 of this book, and answer the suggested questions for each selection.

LESSON PLAN
Mastering Social Studies Skills

Teaching Study and Writing Skills

Be sure students understand that a legend is an explanation of a phenomenon of nature. Ask students what the story of creation is as described in this legend. (Water forced the sun and moon into the sky.) What parts of the legend were related to the environment of the Ibibio? (water, sun, moon)

Encourage students to find creation stories from other cultures. What do they have in common with this story? How and why do the stories differ?

Discuss the questions students can ask as they read literature selections, using the legend as an example.

Did You Know?

African masks, bronze sculptures, and textiles have inspired artists in many parts of the world. Pablo Picasso was one of many famous artists who used elements of African art in their work.

Answers to SOCIAL STUDIES SKILLS

1. The theme is how the sun and moon got to the sky.
2. Yes, the legend provides information about Ibibio values and beliefs, such as the importance of friendship and personal promises.
3. Legends helped the Ibibio people explain occurrences in nature.
4. See pages 30–31 for answers.

LESSON PLAN
SECTION 4, 26–29

FOCUS

Bellringer
Prior to taking roll at the beginning of the class period, display Focus Activity Transparency 4 on the overhead projector and assign the accompanying Focus Activity Sheet.

Objectives
Point out the objectives on this page to students in previewing the section content.

Motivating Activity
Tell students that many fifteenth-century Europeans believed that somewhere in Asia or Africa lay a paradise. Surrounded by walls of crystal, gold, and precious stones, this "lost" land was the source of all the world's great rivers. Then say: Imagine you are a fifteenth-century European. Write a paragraph describing this paradise.

• GTV: *The American People: Fabric of a Nation*

Side 1, Chapter 3
Title: *Change of Scene*
Subject: Why Europeans sought a new home

See GTV Guide page 44 for complete lesson plan.

SECTION 4

Europeans Seek the East

Setting the Scene

Section Focus
By the last decades of the fifteenth century, technological and economic changes in Europe made long sea voyages possible. The prime goal of these ventures was a sea route from Europe to Asia. Encouraged by their rulers, Portuguese sea captains were the first to find this route.

Objectives
After studying this section, you should be able to
★ explain the changes in commerce and in technology that enabled Europeans to sponsor long ocean voyages.
★ state the importance of the Portuguese discovery of a sea route to Asia.

Key Terms
joint-stock company, stock, capital, compass, astrolabe, quadrant, carrack, caravel, scurvy

◀ BINOCULARS AND COMPASS

The Renaissance spirit of curiosity and adventure that swept over Europe helped launch the bold voyages of the Age of Exploration. Many other motivations sent travelers across unknown oceans: Europeans wanted luxury goods from Asia, as well as the spices—pepper, nutmeg, cinnamon, cloves—that preserved foods and made them taste better. European merchants hoped to break the monopoly that Arab traders and Venetian merchants had on the overland routes to Asia. European monarchs hoped to enrich and strengthen their countries—and themselves. The Roman Catholic Church sent missionaries to bring Christianity to millions of new souls.

While six countries on the Atlantic coast—Portugal, Spain, France, the Netherlands, Sweden, and England—would eventually undertake voyages of discovery, the pioneer in these ventures was Portugal.

■ A Revolution in Commerce
Italian city-states had proven that great profit awaited those willing to take risks to trade with the distant East. They had a monopoly on trade through the Mediterranean, but northern European merchants and bankers would soon sponsor voyages.

Financing Exploration
The great expense of ocean voyages made new ways of raising finances necessary. In England, France, and the Netherlands, the **joint-stock company** became a useful form for raising money. The company sold shares, called **stock,** to investors, thus providing money or **capital** for its venture. Each shareowner then received a portion of the venture's profits—or losses.

UNIT 1 A New World: Prehistory to 1776

Classroom Resources for SECTION 4

Teacher's Classroom Resources
- Reproducible Lesson Plan
- Reteaching Activity 1-4
- Chapter 1 Enrichment Activity
- Chapter 1 Performance Assessment Activity
- Spanish Summaries and Glossary
- Section Quiz

Multimedia
- Section Focus Transparency 4
- Vocabulary Puzzlemaker
- Testmaker
- Student Self-Test Software
- The American People: Fabric of a Nation

HISTORY AND ART

▲ *THE MONEYCHANGER AND HIS WIFE* by Quentin Metys, 1514 Increased trade demanded changes in the organization and operation of commercial activities. **What do you think is happening in this painting?**

▲ FLORINS, ITALIAN COINS

The joint-stock company let small investors, who could not afford to outfit an entire ship, take part in overseas commercial ventures by buying shares of stock. It also enabled wealthy people to spread their risks by investing in several joint-stock companies at the same time. A joint-stock company might have hundreds of shareholders, thus creating enough wealth to support long expeditions or found colonies.

New Technology

No matter how well financed, long voyages could not have succeeded without better technology. With sailors ready to strike out in new directions, advances in shipbuilding and navigation were important. For thousands of years, Mediterranean ship captains had tried to sail within sight of land, guided mainly by written descriptions of coasts and harbors.

By the fifteenth century, captains were using precise maps for both the Mediterranean and the Atlantic coasts of Europe and North Africa. In addition, Arab sailors taught Europeans how to use several improved navigational instruments. The **compass**, which was invented in China, reliably showed the direction of magnetic north—even at night or in cloudy weather. The **astrolabe** and the **quadrant** measured the positions of the sun and stars, allowing the navigator to determine distance north and south from a given point.

Ships built to new designs were faster and more seaworthy. The **carrack**, for example, had several masts and a rudder. Smaller but easier to handle was the Portuguese **caravel**, a double-rigged ship with both square and triangular sails. On Christopher Columbus's first voyage, the flagship *Santa Maria* was a carrack; the *Niña* and the *Pinta* were caravels.

■ Pioneering Portuguese

Portugal was the first European country to search for a sea route to Asia. This small nation had a long Atlantic coast with good ports and a rich seafaring tradition.

CHAPTER 1 The World in Transition 27

CHAPTER 1
SECTION 4

Independent Practice

Geography Have students skim the section to discover geographic terms in the text. Provide examples such as ocean, coast, harbor, equator, island, currents, sea, and cape. To make certain they understand the geographic definitions of the terms they find, ask students to use each term in a sentence. **LEP, L1**

Visualizing History Prince Henry was the younger brother of King John I of Portugal. He set up a center for astronomical and geographical studies at Sagres on the southwestern tip of Portugal.
Answer to Caption: Portugal was the first to send explorers in search of a sea route to Asia.

Did You Know?

As early as the eighth century, Arab and Moorish traders drove enslaved people across the Sahara for delivery to Mediterranean ports.

Did You Know?

Portugal was the first European nation to build an overseas colony organized around slave labor. The colony was Madeira, an island off the coast of Africa.

Prince Henry's Expeditions

The groundwork for Portugal's accomplishments was laid in the early 1400s by Prince Henry, an individual who neither sailed to other lands nor explored any new areas. Yet his efforts kindled the fires of exploration.

Through exploration, Henry wanted to bring Portugal more trade and power and to spread Christianity. In his mind, the key to reaching these goals lay in the open seas. Henry's first step was to bring together mapmakers, astronomers, and shipbuilders from throughout the Mediterranean world to study and plan voyages of exploration. These experts pooled their talents to uncover knowledge about the seas and to extend the art of navigation.

Drawing on this collected expertise, Prince Henry sent expeditions beyond the safety of the Mediterranean. One of Henry's plans was to have his ships sail around Africa and find a path to India and the Spice Islands. Such a route might lead to Prester John, the legendary Christian monarch said to rule a rich, powerful kingdom. The new route also might reveal the source of the gold dust and other precious goods the Moors brought to Mediterranean ports. Portuguese ships traveled southward along the African coast. As expeditions returned, Henry's mapmakers corrected and improved their sailing charts.

Bit by bit, expedition after expedition, the Portuguese inched their way down the coast of Africa. For people at that time, these were fearsome voyages. Europeans were convinced that great dangers awaited in the open ocean: a Sea of Darkness, sea monsters, oceans that boiled at the equator. A big obstacle was exploring new areas where geographical knowledge stopped and myth took over. Said one Portuguese sailor about reaching these limits:

> Beyond this there is no race of men or place of inhabitants. Nor is the land less sandy than the deserts of Libya, where there is no water, no tree, no green herb. And the sea is so shallow that a whole league from land is only a fathom deep, while the currents are so terrible that no ship, having once passed the Cape, will ever be able to return.

There were, in fact, some dangerous currents and treacherously shallow waters along the African coast. By the time Prince Henry—known as "the Navigator"—died in 1460, his ships had reached just beyond Cape Verde, the westernmost tip of Africa.

The Slave Trade

By this time, the Portuguese had well-established trade patterns with African merchants for gold, ivory, pepper, palm oil, and slaves. Soon they added profitable trading posts on the West African coast and built sugar plantations.

Slavery and the slave trade were not new in the region. Using war captives as slaves had long been a practice in North Africa and

▼ **HENRY THE NAVIGATOR** Shown in this detail of the painting, *Panel of the Infanta*, is Prince Henry. **What role did Portugal play in navigation?**

UNIT 1 A New World: Prehistory to 1776

Critical Thinking

Classifying Information Have students identify and list all the motives that prompted the Europeans to make voyages of exploration and discovery. Then ask students to think of classifications into which they might organize their lists. Provide the following examples: Geographic motives—location on the sea, better maps, more sophisticated navigational instruments; Economic motives—desire for financial gain, demand for luxury goods from Asia. **L2**

in other parts of the world as well. The first African slaves were taken to Portugal as servants in 1441. Probably 1,000 Africans were taken to Portugal over the next 5 years. But by the 1490s, the growth and profits of the African sugar plantations had increased the demand for local slave labor. To meet the new demand, slave traders turned to kidnapping and "slave raids" in the African interior.

Rounding the Tip of Africa

In 1487 and 1488 a Portuguese expedition led by Bartholomeu Dias was caught in a storm that blew the ships off course near the southern tip of Africa. As the skies cleared, Dias realized from the position of the sun that they had rounded the tip of Africa without knowing it. The Portuguese ruler, King John II, named the area the "Cape of Good Hope" because it seemed to promise the existence of a new sea route to India.

Crossing the Indian Ocean

Ten years later another Portuguese expedition set sail, headed by Vasco da Gama. After almost a year's travel, they rounded the Cape of Good Hope and sailed up the eastern coast of Africa past the rich Muslim city-states of Kilwa and Malindi. With an Arab pilot, the expedition crossed the Indian Ocean to Calicut on the coast of India.

The voyage home took another year and was much more difficult. Many sailors died of **scurvy**, a sickness caused by a lack of vitamin C. Da Gama finally returned home to Portugal in September 1499. It is said that the profits on his cargo of cinnamon, cloves, nutmeg, ginger, and pepper covered the cost of his expedition 60 times over.

▶ CARAVEL

Growing Rivalry

The trade rivalry among Italian city-states had been intense. Now Portugal's sea venture could cost the Italian cities their monopoly on trade. When news of da Gama's voyage reached Venice, the effect was dramatic. A writer reported:

> ... if this voyage should continue, the King of Portugal could call himself the King of Money, because all would convene to that country to obtain spices, and the money would accumulate greatly in Portugal.... this news was held by the learned to be the worst news which the Venetian Republic could have had....

Da Gama's ships had traveled 24,000 miles. The sea route that he opened challenged the other European nations to make their own explorations. In the following four centuries, western Europe's quest for wealth and empire would affect the lives of people on every continent.

Section 4 ★ Review

Checking for Understanding

1. **Identify** Prince Henry "the Navigator," Bartholomeu Dias, Vasco da Gama.
2. **Define** joint-stock company, stock, capital, compass, astrolabe, quadrant, carrack, caravel, scurvy.
3. **Enumerate** the reasons the Europeans undertook voyages of discovery.
4. **Describe** the effects on other nations of the Portuguese discovery of a sea route around Africa to Asia.

Critical Thinking

5. **Making Deductions** Why would wealthy investors want to buy a small share in several overseas voyages rather than a large share in one?

INTEGRATING Language Arts

American Literary Heritage

Historical Setting
The Iroquois originally comprised five warring nations—the Seneca, Oneida, Mohawk, Cayuga, Onondaga, and, later, the Tuscarara. When infighting became particularly vicious, Dekanawidah emerged to promote peace and unity. In contrast, the Navajo believed humans should live harmoniously with nature and generally were peaceful. The Navajo raised crops and sheep in the present-day southwestern United States.

Background
Native Americans "passed down" their literature in the oral tradition.

The literary device of repetition is used in the "Rain Chant" with the refrain "Comes the rain/Comes the rain with me." This repetition stresses the oneness of nature (rain) and humans (me).

About the Oral Tradition
The excerpt from *The Constitution of the Five Nations,* unlike the Navajo "Song of the Rain Chant," is unique in that it possesses an originator. Dekanawidah is a legendary figure. A prophet who preached peace, he managed at some time between 1575 and 1600 to convince the nations to unite.

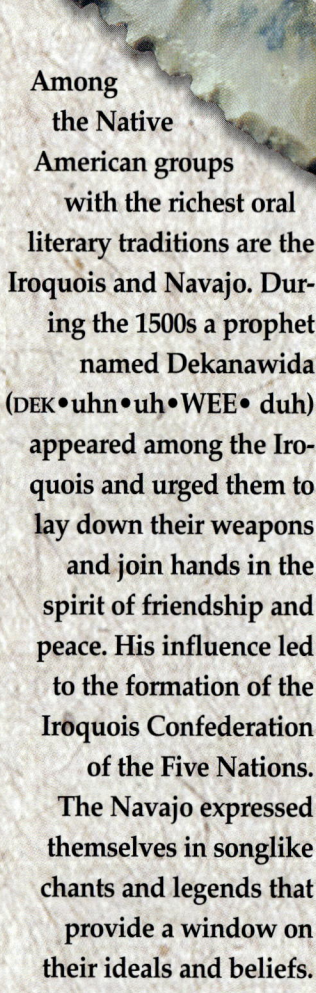

Among the Native American groups with the richest oral literary traditions are the Iroquois and Navajo. During the 1500s a prophet named Dekanawida (DEK•uhn•uh•WEE• duh) appeared among the Iroquois and urged them to lay down their weapons and join hands in the spirit of friendship and peace. His influence led to the formation of the Iroquois Confederation of the Five Nations. The Navajo expressed themselves in songlike chants and legends that provide a window on their ideals and beliefs.

The Constitution of the Five Nations (excerpts)

I am Dekanawida and with the Five Nations confederate lords I plant the Tree of the Great Peace. I name the tree the Tree of the Great Long Leaves. Under the shade of this Tree of the Great Peace we spread the soft white feathery down of the globe thistle as seats for you . . . and your cousin lords.

We place . . . at the top of the Tree of the Long Leaves an eagle who is able to see afar. If he sees in the distance any evil approaching or any danger threatening he will at once warn the people of the confederacy. . . .

All lords of the Five Nations Confederacy must be honest in all things. . . . It shall be a serious wrong for anyone to lead a lord into trivial affairs, for the people must ever hold their lords high in estimation out of respect to their honorable positions. . . .

We now do crown you with the sacred emblem of the deer's antlers, the emblem of your lordship. You shall now become a mentor of the people of the Five Nations. The thickness of your skin shall be seven spans—which is to say that you shall be proof against anger, offensive actions and criticism. Your heart shall be filled with peace and good will and your mind filled with a yearning for the welfare of the people of the confederacy. With endless patience you shall carry out your duty and your firmness shall be tempered with tenderness for your people. Neither anger nor fury shall find lodgement in your mind and all your words and actions shall be marked with calm deliberation. . . .

▲ IROQUOIS NOTCHED STAFF

UNIT 1 A New World: Prehistory to 1776

Cultural Diversity
Point out that every culture has an oral tradition, which consists of stories, songs, and poems that have been passed from one generation to the next. Each generation adds new details and deletes those that no longer seem meaningful. As a result versions may vary greatly not only over time but also from place to place. Encourage students to collect folklore from various sources to make comparisons.

Navajo Song of the Rain Chant

Far as man can see,
Comes the rain,
Comes the rain with me.

From the Rain-Mount,
Rain-Mount far away,
Comes the rain,
Comes the rain with me.

O'er the corn,
O'er the corn, the tall corn,
Comes the rain,
Comes the rain with me.

'Mid the lightnings,
'Mid the lightning zigzag,
'Mid the lightning flashing
Comes the rain,
Comes the rain with me.

'Mid the swallows,
'Mid the swallows blue
Chirping glad together,
Comes the rain,
Comes the rain with me.

Through the pollen,
Through the pollen blest,
All in pollen hidden,
Comes the rain,
Comes the rain with me.

Far as man can see,
Comes the rain,
Comes the rain with me.

▲ NAVAJO RUG

Interpreting Literature

1. In the Iroquois Constitution, what is the function of the eagle that sits atop the Tree of the Long Leaves?

2. How does the Rain Chant reflect Navajo beliefs about nature?

Analyzing Culture

3. In what ways are the qualities desired for Iroquois leaders similar to or different from those desired for today's leaders in the United States government?

Other Works of Native American Folklore

Because of the nature of the oral tradition, which was shared through word-of-mouth, it is difficult to identify other pieces of literature directly linked to this period. However, recent Native American authors, such as Rosebud Yellow Robe, have retold and preserved in writing some myths and legends that have been handed down. Related works include *North American Indian Mythology* by Cottie Burland and *The Red Swan: Myths and Tales of the American Indians* edited by John Bierhorst.

INTEGRATING Language Arts

Developing Student Understanding

Explain that family histories often are shared in the oral tradition. Ask volunteers to share family stories. Then ask how the stories provide insight into certain periods of time.

Interpreting Literature

1. The eagle is a watchguard and warns the confederacy of approaching evil or danger.
2. Rain is a central part of nature and the cycle of growth. It comes from afar but is part of everything and covers everything.
3. Both are to be honest in all things and live in accordance with the laws. Both should strive to be leaders of peace and goodwill, whose concern is the welfare of the people.

 VIDEODISC

- *GTV: A Geographic Perspective on American History*

Side 1, Chapter 2
Title: *Linking Life and Land*
Subject: The first Americans and the effects of geography on their lives

See GTV Guide page 33 for complete lesson plan.

REVIEW CHAPTER 1

Reviewing Facts

1. Leadership passes from feudal lords to national monarchs, manorial system breaks down, serfs become free farmers or paying tenants, middle class of merchants grows in towns.
2. rebirth of interest in classics; achievements in arts, science, and scholarship; new styles evolve.
3. China, Ottoman Empire, Japan, Ghana, Mali. Source of gold, spices, silks, slaves, ivory, etc. Impetus for voyages of exploration.
4. Protestant Reformation and split in Christian Church, Crusades and the cultural effects.
5. Mesoamerican: cultures centered on religion, had written language, number system, calendar, temples, some large cities and great wealth, mined precious metals and gems, agricultural; North American: no written language, mix of hunter-gatherer and agricultural, some similar architecture, no large cities or great wealth.
6. obtain luxury goods and spices, break Venetian and Arab monopoly of trade routes, enrich and strengthen nations
7. Towns grow, merchants gain power, wealth, independence from feudal landholders, support monarchs, accumulate wealth, joint ventures to finance expeditions for goods to trade or as loans.
8. Better maps and sea charts, discover route around Africa and sail by it to India.

Understanding Concepts

1. Both Medieval Europe and Medieval Japan were feudal societies. Trade eroded feudalism in Europe. West Africans and Aztecs built cities as trading centers. The Aztec empire grew in peace until the Europeans arrived, while the northern part of West Africa experienced a Muslim conquest.
2. European scholars were open to new ideas and reaching for knowledge for its own sake. Ming Dynasty limited study to the classics to discourage new ideas.
3. accumulate wealth through trade, have money to lend when credit needed
4. Joint-stock venture. Made it possible for more people to profit from trade with a smaller investment.

CHAPTER 1 ★ REVIEW

Using Vocabulary

Classify each of the terms listed below into one of the following categories: Political Structures and Systems, Economic Activity and Systems, Inventions and Technology, Religion and Culture

astrolabe
capital
caravel
carrack
charter
classical
compass
confederation
dynasty
feudal system
humanism
joint-stock company
manor
parliament
pueblos
quadrant
Renaissance
samurai
serfs
shoguns

Reviewing Facts

1. **Discuss** the major changes in the political and social structure of Europe in the late 1400s.
2. **Describe** the characteristics of the Renaissance.
3. **Identify** advanced cultures of Africa and Asia and the importance of their trade with Europe.
4. **Report** on the effects of religious conflicts during the Middle Ages.
5. **Compare** the cultures of Mesoamerican and North American native peoples.
6. **List** the motives of the nations interested in voyages of discovery.
7. **Summarize** the development of the middle class and its role in the voyages of exploration.
8. **Enumerate** the achievements of the Portuguese voyages of discovery.

Understanding Concepts

Diverse Cultures

1. Compare the differences and similarities between each of the following sets of cultures: medieval European and medieval Japanese culture; the West African trading kingdoms and the Aztec empire.

2. Both European Renaissance scholars and Ming Dynasty rulers restored interest in ancient classic works of their cultures. How did their motives differ?

Economic Change

3. How did the middle class gain economic power comparable to that of feudal landowners?
4. What new form of investment made more voyages of exploration possible? In what ways did these new forms affect economic opportunity in general?

Critical Thinking

1. **Classifying Causes** What factors facilitated the change from feudalism to nationalism? Label each cause political, economic, or religious.
2. **Analyzing Motivation** What forces and events motivated voyages of exploration?
3. **Understanding Global Events** How did the spread of Islam contribute to the growth of nationalism? To the Renaissance? To the interest in exploration?
4. **Analyzing Artifacts** Examine the picture of the Renaissance shield on this page and answer the questions that follow.
   a. How many men and how many women are portrayed on the shield?
   b. What seems to be the attitude of the people in the picture?
   c. What conclusions can you draw about the artist's feelings toward the Renaissance? Explain your answer.

▶ RENAISSANCE SHIELD

Writing About History

Narration

Imagine you are captain of one of Vasco da Gama's ships. Write a few days' entries in the ship's log book, relating the day's events and challenges

32   UNIT 1 The New World: Prehistory to 1776

CHAPTER 1 ★ REVIEW

and detailing the crew's reactions. You may need to conduct research at your school or local library for authentic details, but imaginary details are also acceptable.

Cooperative Learning

Working in a group of four, make a set of four parallel time lines covering the years 600 to 1500. Indicate major events and developments in China, among the Native Americans in present-day Mexico, among the Europeans in present-day Italy, and among major Arab Muslim groups. Each member should research the history of one culture and show the major events on that culture's time line.

Social Studies Skills

Reading a Travel Route Map

A map can convey travel route information more accurately and efficiently than verbal description alone. To maximize the information gained from a travel route map, follow these steps:

- Read the map legend. The legend is the mapmaker's means of drawing attention to key data.
- Study the map scale to gain perspective on the distance traveled.
- Look at the physical features portrayed on the map. Can you make inferences about the difficulty of the travel?
- Evaluate the travel routes. Do some cities on the map serve as hubs where several travel routes intersect?

Practicing the Skill

Use the map of the African trading kingdoms to answer the following questions.

1. What map scale is used?
2. What physical features are shown on the map?
3. What city is the easternmost trade partner? The westernmost trade partner?
4. What two cities show the largest number of intersecting trade routes?
5. Other than the information on trade routes, what key historic information is supplied by the map?

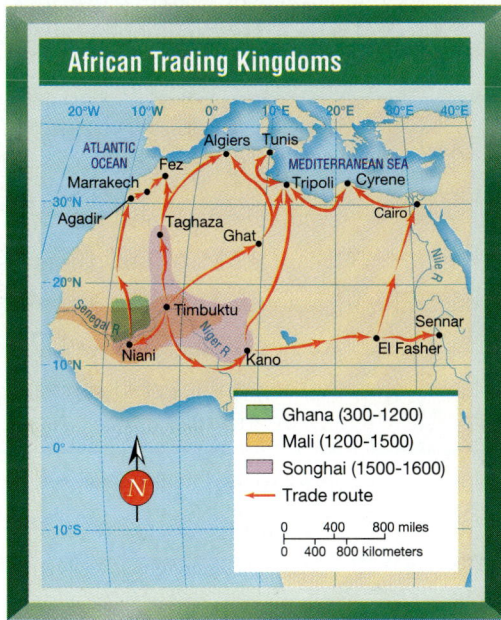

Using Your Journal
Compare the accomplishments and values of two different cultures. Write a paragraph explaining similarities and differences.

REVIEW CHAPTER 1

? Chapter Bonus Test Question

Most of what is known about the earliest Americans comes from archaeological analysis of various artifacts. Imagine that you are an archaeologist in the 2990s and you are studying the 1990s. What artifacts would tell you the most about life in the United States in the 1990s? (Answers will vary but should include objects that do not decompose over time—anything made of plastic, metal, or bone.)

Using Your Journal

The ideas students present in their paragraphs will vary but should include specific similarities and differences. You might call on volunteers to read their paragraphs to the class and then have students contrast their varying views of the cultures they studied.

CHAPTER 1 The World in Transition

Critical Thinking

1. Need to unite against common enemy—political; break of serfs from land—economic; rise of middle class economic and political; independence of towns—political; Islamic threat in Spain—religious.
2. Desire for goods and rise of nationalism.
3. Pose threat that unites Spain. Islamic traders bring goods from the East, but control routes.
4. a. one man and another figure
   b. solemn or grave
   c. Answers will vary, but might include the artist's views of the Renaissance.

Practicing the Skill

1. 1 inch = 800 miles
2. rivers, Atlantic Ocean, Mediterranean Sea
3. Sennar; Agadir
4. Timbuktu; Tripoli
5. location, size, and names of each trading kingdom; location and name of major cities

PLANNING GUIDE Chapter 2   The Age of Exploration

Daily Lesson Objectives	Teacher Classroom Resources	Multimedia
SECTION 1 **Voyages of Columbus** 1 Day pp. 36–40 1. Compare the purposes and results of the four voyages of Columbus. 2. Discuss the purpose and results of Magellan's expedition.	Chapter 2 Study Guide Reproducible Lesson Plan Reteaching Activity 2-1 Section Quiz Chapter 2 Cooperative Learning Activity Chapter 2 Concept Mapping Activity Reinforcing Social Studies Skills 28, 51, 69–72 American Portraits 3 Writer's Guidebook, Lesson 2-6 SAT Practice Tests 10-13 Building Skills in Geography	Student Self-Test Software Testmaker Section Focus Transparency 5 Chapter 2 Skills Transparency Chapter 2 Map Transparencies The American People: Fabric of a Nation
SECTION 2 **Spain in America** 1 Day pp. 42–45 1. Describe the Spanish exploration and conquest of the South and Central American mainlands. 2. Discuss life in the Spanish colonies.	Reproducible Lesson Plan Reteaching Activity 2-2 Section Quiz Reinforcing Social Studies Skills 70–72 Chapter 2 Primary and Secondary Source Readings American Portraits 4 Writer's Guidebook, Lesson 2-5	Student Self-Test Software Testmaker Section Focus Transparency 6 Chapter 2 Map Transparencies U.S. History & Art Transparency 2 The American People: Fabric of a Nation
SECTION 3 **English, French, and Dutch Ventures** 1 Day pp. 47–51 1. Describe early English exploration of North America. 2. Discuss French and Dutch colonization in North America.	Reproducible Lesson Plan Reteaching Activity 2-3 Section Quiz Chapter 2 Enrichment Activity Reinforcing Social Studies Skills 2, 32 Building Skills in Geography Spanish Summaries & Glossary	Student Self-Test Software Testmaker Section Focus Transparency 7 Chapter 2 Map Transparencies Vocabulary Puzzlemaker Audiocassette, Chapter 2 A Geographic Perspective on American History
CHAPTER REVIEW AND EVALUATION 1 Day	Chapter 2 Test Chapter 2 Performance Assessment Activity	Student Self-Test Software Testmaker

OUT OF TIME? If time does not permit teaching the entire chapter, use the Chapter 2 Summary on pages 84–85 and the Chapter 2 audiocassette (English and Spanish) to point out the main ideas of the chapter.

PLANNING GUIDE

Cultural Diversity Activity

Cooperative Learning European settlers of North America left their mark on their new homeland in the place names of cities and towns. Plymouth, Raleigh, and New London are named for English towns or leaders. Brooklyn and Harlem were named by the Dutch, whereas towns like Berlin, New Hampshire and New Sweden, Pennsylvania reflect the influence of German or Swedish colonists.

Divide students into groups and give each group a road map of the eastern United States. Have groups compete to see how many place names of European origin they can find in one of the eastern seaboard states. An alternative activity is to have one group find English place names, while others look for French, Spanish, or Dutch names. One group might serve as a resource team, using books such as *American Place-Names* by George Stewart to verify origins of names chosen.

Performance Assessment Activity

Comparing Explorations Divide the class into small groups and have each select a country that participated in the Age of Exploration. Ask each to prepare a booklet that emphasizes its successes and achievements. Possibilities include England, France, the Netherlands, Portugal, Spain, and Sweden. Point out that groups may have different ideas about success and achievement. Students should be encouraged to research the goals as well as the outcomes of each exploration.

POSSIBLE RUBRIC FEATURES: Content information, main idea, creativity, clarity, visual and written communication, organization

Chapter Resources

Literature from the Period

Columbus, Christopher. *The Log of Christopher Columbus.* Translated by Robert H. Fuson. International Marine Publishing, 1987.

Nabakov, Peter, ed. *Native American Testimony: An Anthology of Indian and White Relations: First Encounter to Dispossession.* Crowell, 1978.

Readings for the Student

Boorstin, Daniel J. *The Discoverers.* Vintage, 1985.

Brandon, William. *Indians.* American Heritage, 1985.

Leon, George deLucenay. *Explorers of the Americas Before Columbus.* Franklin Watts, 1989.

Readings for the Teacher

Cardini, Franco. *Europe 1492: Portrait of a Continent Five Hundred Years Ago.* Facts On File, 1989.

Lang, James. *Conquest and Commerce: Spain and England in the Americas.* Academic Press, 1975.

Multimedia Resources

Discoverers. National Film Board of America. (VHS, 43 minutes)

Decisions, Decisions: Colonization. Tom Snyder Productions. (Apple or IBM PC diskette)

Who Really Discovered America? Interact. (Simulation)

Key to Ability Levels

Teaching strategies have been coded for varying learning styles and abilities.

- **L1** Basic activities for all students
- **L2** Average activities for average to above-average students
- **L3** Challenging activities for above-average students
- **LEP** Limited English Proficiency activities

Glencoe Links to the Humanities

Link to Art
- U.S. History & Art Transparency 3

Link to Literature
- Macmillan Literature: American Literature Text— Christopher Columbus, John Smith, William Bradford

Link to Music
- American Music: Cultural Traditions

CHAPTER 2

BEGINNING THE CHAPTER

Provide students with the following information:

Average rate at which ships left Spain for the Americas—in 1506, one every 17 days; in 1512, one every 11 days; in 1533, one every 6 days; and in 1542, one every 4 days.

Ask students to speculate what these figures indicate about Spain's relationship with the Americas in the 50 years after Columbus's first transatlantic voyage. Tell them that in Chapter 2 they will learn that not only Spain, but also other European nations established strong ties with the Western Hemisphere.

Linking Across TIME

Point out that during the Age of Exploration, explorers did not always sail for their original homelands. In this century, people born in one country have worked for another. For example, physicist Enrico Fermi, from Italy, directed the first controlled nuclear chain reaction for the United States.

Recording Journal Notes

To help students review their journal notes, discuss the aims and outcomes of the various expeditions.

CHAPTER 2

The Age of Exploration
1000–1682

▶ EXPLORER'S LOG BOOK

Setting the Scene

Focus

The first Europeans to visit North America were Norse seafarers who reached Newfoundland about 1000. Interest in exploration and settlement of the Americas, however, did not truly begin until the first voyage of Christopher Columbus in 1492. Thereafter, until the early 1600s, various nations—Spain, Portugal, France, England, and the Netherlands—sent explorers to the Americas.

Concepts to Understand

★ How European nations sought wealth through voyages of discovery and exploration to the New World

★ How European values and beliefs differed from those of the Native American population

Read to Discover . . .

★ why European nations wanted to explore the Americas.

★ how the Spanish and French treated Native Americans.

Journal Notes

Did European explorers usually find what they were looking for? Note the aims of various expeditions and their degree of success in your journal as you read the chapter.

CULTURAL
- 1050 European traders bring technology from East Asia
- 1400 Incan and Aztec empires flourish
- 1470s Marco Polo travels to China

| 1000 | 1400 | 1450 |

POLITICAL
- 1000 Norse seafarers establish settlements in Iceland, Greenland, and Newfoundland
- 1400s Age of Exploration begins
- 1492 First voyage of Christopher Columbus begins

34 UNIT 1 A New World: Prehistory to 1776

➕ EXTRA CREDIT PROJECT

It took great daring for explorers to brave the dangers of the unknown. Ask interested students to research the payments and other rewards that Christopher Columbus, John Cabot, Henry Hudson (for his Dutch voyage), and Jacques Cartier received for their efforts. Have students present their findings to the class in the form of a chart. Ask them to discuss their research as they explain the chart to their classmates.

Cabot's Departure, 1497
by Ernest Board, 1906

English merchants persuaded their king to send John Cabot, an Italian navigator, to Asia by a northwest route. This painting, completed more than 400 years after the event, communicates a feeling of solemn pageantry.

◀ VIKING HELMET

- **1540** Ignatius of Loyola founds the Society of Jesus, or Jesuits
- **1539** Hernando de Soto explores North America

1500

- **1556** *Ordinary of the Mass* is first book printed in the Americas
- **1570** Iroquois form League of Five Nations

1550

- **1593** John White publishes detailed drawings of Native Americans
- **1608** Samuel de Champlain founds Quebec

1600

CHAPTER 2 The Age of Exploration 1000–1682

CHAPTER 2 CONCEPTS

Concept Mapping Activity

Reproduce the following concept map on the chalkboard, and have students copy it in their notebooks. As they read Chapter 2, have students enter major events, ideas, people, and places in the most appropriate concept column.

European nations sought economic gains through exploration, conquest, and settlement.
- Exploration
- Values and Beliefs

History AND ART

An artist's depiction of a historical event can influence a viewer's ideas about the past. The pageantry of this painting contains no hint that Cabot's first voyage for England in 1496 ended in failure.

 VIDEODISC

- *GTV: The American People: Fabric of a Nation*

Side 1, Chapter 3
Title: *Change of Scene*
Subject: Why Europeans sought a new home

See GTV Guide page 44 for complete lesson plan.

Teacher Notes

LESSON PLAN
SECTION 1, 36–41

FOCUS

Bellringer
Display Focus Activity Transparency 5 on the overhead projector, and assign the accompanying Focus Activity Sheet.

Objectives
Point out the objectives on this page to students in previewing the section content.

Motivating Activity
Ask students to imagine they have just signed on as crew for Christopher Columbus's "enterprise of the Indies." Then announce: Many people believe that if you sail westward, eventually you'll fall off the edge of the earth!

Point out that this was a widely accepted view in Columbus's day. Then ask: Given this belief, why would someone want to make such a voyage?

Use Chapter 2 Skills Transparency.

- *GTV: The American People: Fabric of a Nation*

Side 1, Chapter 4
Title: *Wealth Enough*
Subject: Europeans in the Americas

See GTV Guide page 46 for complete lesson plan.

SECTION 1

Voyages of Columbus

Setting the Scene

Section Focus
In their eagerness to find easier routes for trade in Asia, some Europeans had a new idea: instead of sailing south and east around Africa, they could sail west. The idea led to discoveries that brought drastic change to those who lived on the continents that lay between Europe and Asia.

Objectives
After studying this section, you should be able to
★ compare the purposes and results of the four voyages of Columbus.
★ discuss the purpose and results of Magellan's expedition.

Key Terms
saga, line of demarcation, isthmus, strait

◀ CUBICAL SUNDIAL

The first Europeans to arrive in the Americas were Norse seafarers from Scandinavia. Between A.D. 800 and 1100, the Norse established settlements in Iceland, Greenland, and present-day Newfoundland, which they called Vinland. The Norse settlements in Vinland were unsuccessful because of conflicts with Native Americans and lack of support from home. The Vinland settlements soon disappeared—forgotten except in Norse **sagas**, or long, heroic stories.

Not until the voyage of Christopher Columbus in 1492 did European exploration of the Americas begin in earnest. After Europeans learned that Columbus had sailed to continents not yet known to them, Spain, Portugal, France, the Netherlands, and England sent expeditions to the New World. They pursued a passage to Asia through or around the giant landmass. In time these nations all established colonies in the Americas.

■ Columbus's First Venture

Christopher Columbus was born in Genoa, Italy, in 1451. His early interest in navigation led him to Lisbon, Portugal, in 1477. There, Portuguese explorations of the Atlantic coast of Africa brought him new knowledge of geography and cartography.

Preparing for the Expedition
Columbus studied the atlas of the ancient Greek geographer, Ptolemy, who had greatly underestimated the size of the earth. In 1477, Columbus was one of the first to read the newly printed "Travels" of Marco Polo. On the basis of this information, Columbus shrank Ptolemy's calculations. He figured the distance between Japan and the Canary Islands, off the northeastern coast of Africa,

---

Classroom Resources for SECTION 1

Teacher's Classroom Resources
- Chapter 2 Study Guide
- Reproducible Lesson Plan
- Reteaching Activity 2-1
- Chapter 2 Cooperative Learning Activity
- Section Quiz

Multimedia
- Section Focus Transparency 5
- Chapter 2 Skills Transparency
- Chapter 2 Map Transparency
- Testmaker
- Student Self-Test Software
- The American People: Fabric of a Nation

at only 2,400 miles. His calculations resulted in an obsession to undertake a voyage to Asia by sailing west.

For years Columbus sought financial backing. Having no success with the kings of Portugal, France, and England, he spent six years trying to persuade Ferdinand and Isabella of Spain that his scheme would bring them wealth, empire, and converts to Catholicism. Finally, Isabella and Ferdinand provided Columbus with three ships, the *Niña*, the *Pinta*, and the *Santa Maria*.

Voyage Into the Unknown

Columbus left Spain in August 1492 with about 90 sailors. He sailed south to the Canary Islands, where he repaired his ships and took on fresh supplies. Columbus then charted his course westward, noting ". . . nothing to the north, nothing to the south."

By early October the fleet had already gone farther than Columbus had thought would be necessary to reach Japan. The sailors were frightened and wanted to turn back. On October 9 the crew "heard birds passing all night long" and believed they were close to land. On October 11 Columbus wrote in his log:

> *The crew of the Pinta spotted some . . . reeds and some other plants; they also saw what looked like a small board or plank. A stick was recovered that looks man-made, perhaps carved with an iron tool. . . . but even these few [things] made the crew breathe easier; in fact the men have even become cheerful.*

In the early morning of October 12, 1492, the lookout aboard the *Pinta* saw white cliffs glistening in the moonlight. At dawn, Columbus went ashore onto a small island in the Bahamas (San Salvador) and claimed it for Spain. Believing he had reached the East Indies off the coast of Asia, he called the native people Indians.

▶ CHRISTOPHER COLUMBUS

▲ VOYAGES OF COLUMBUS An Italian sailor and mapmaker, Christopher Columbus believed that Asia could be reached by sailing directly west from Europe. **Why do you think Columbus did not realize that he had reached a new world?**

Marvels of a New World

In April 1493, Columbus returned triumphantly to the Spanish court. The king and queen gave him the titles "Admiral of the Ocean Sea" and "Viceroy and Governor of the Indies." All were fascinated by both the copper-skinned people Columbus brought back and his reports of lands where every bird, tree, and flower was new to Europeans. Isabella and Ferdinand were most interested in the reports of gold and in trade.

Columbus made three more voyages across the Atlantic. Despite his achievements, Columbus died in 1506 a broken, frustrated dreamer, unaware that he had reached new continents in the Western Hemisphere.

CHAPTER 2
SECTION 1

Independent Practice

Drama Some students might like to write and perform a brief play on Columbus's audience at the court of Ferdinand and Isabella after his triumphant return from the Americas. Music of the period might add atmosphere to their performance. The record *Music from the Court of Ferdinand and Isabella* by David Munrow and the Early Music Consort of London (Angel S-36926) is a possible source. **L3**

Visualizing History

The Italian merchant and explorer Amerigo Vespucci sailed from Portugal in a 1501–2 expedition that traveled south along the coast of Brazil and Argentina.

Did You Know?

A recent study that analyzed Columbus's route across the Atlantic and compared his geographic descriptions with present-day geography suggested that he made landfall at Grand Turk in the Turks and Caicos Islands, a present-day British colony.

■ Spain and Portugal Divide the World

Accounts of Columbus's travels soon set off a flurry of exploration, particularly by Spain and Portugal. Seafaring explorers considered the lands reached by Columbus to be a barrier between Europe and Asia, and they sought to find a way around them. They clearly were uncertain how to deal with this world.

Treaty of Tordesillas

Columbus's exploration put Spain and Portugal in direct competition for trade and empire-building. In 1493, because of potential conflict, Pope Alexander VI convinced the two Catholic nations to divide any new overseas trading interests between them. A **line of demarcation**, a north-south line drawn on a map through the Atlantic Ocean by the pope, gave Spain all the non-Christian lands to the west of the line and Portugal all those to the east. In 1494 Spain and Portugal resolved their differences "for the sake of peace and concord" in the Treaty of Tordesillas (TAWR•duh•SEE•yuhs). The treaty established the demarcation line at about 48° west longitude and extended it around the earth to secure Portuguese claims in Asia.

In 1500 a fleet of Portuguese ships under the command of Pedro Álvares Cabral (PAY•droh AHL•vuh•REHZ kuh•BRAHL) set out for India by going east around the coast of Africa. Swinging west to get favorable winds, Cabral's expedition was blown off course and unintentionally reached present-day Brazil. Because a part of Brazil's coastline lay to the east of the line set by the treaty, Portugal claimed it.

America Is Named

In 1499 another Portuguese expedition, with an Italian-born navigator and merchant, Amerigo Vespucci (vay•SPOO•chee), sailed along the coast of South America. Vespucci concluded that this land was a vast new continent. In 1504 Vespucci's sensational account was published, and he erroneously received credit for reaching the mainland of this land before Columbus. German mapmakers named the New World "America," and the name stuck.

A Vast New Ocean Revealed

On expeditions into what is now Panama, Vasco Núñez de Balboa (VAHS•koh NOO•nyayth day bal•BOH•uh) learned from the native people of "great waters" to the west. Balboa led an expedition to find this body of water, guided by the Indians who knew trails through the difficult countryside.

They did indeed reach a huge body of water, which Balboa claimed for Spain. Having climbed a peak alone to see the water first, Balboa in 1513 became the first European to see the eastern coast of the Pacific Ocean. It now appeared that the lands Columbus had reached were separated from Asia by this seemingly endless ocean.

▲ AMERIGO VESPUCCI

Cooperative Learning

Organize students into groups of five; have each group select a representative. Have these representatives read the material on Magellan's voyage of circumnavigation on page 40. Then have them work together to construct maps that show the route of this voyage. Ask the representatives to return to their groups. Next, have them use the maps to teach what they have learned to their groups. Test group members' retention of the information by having them write a paragraph describing the voyage. **L2**

CHAPTER 2 SECTION 1

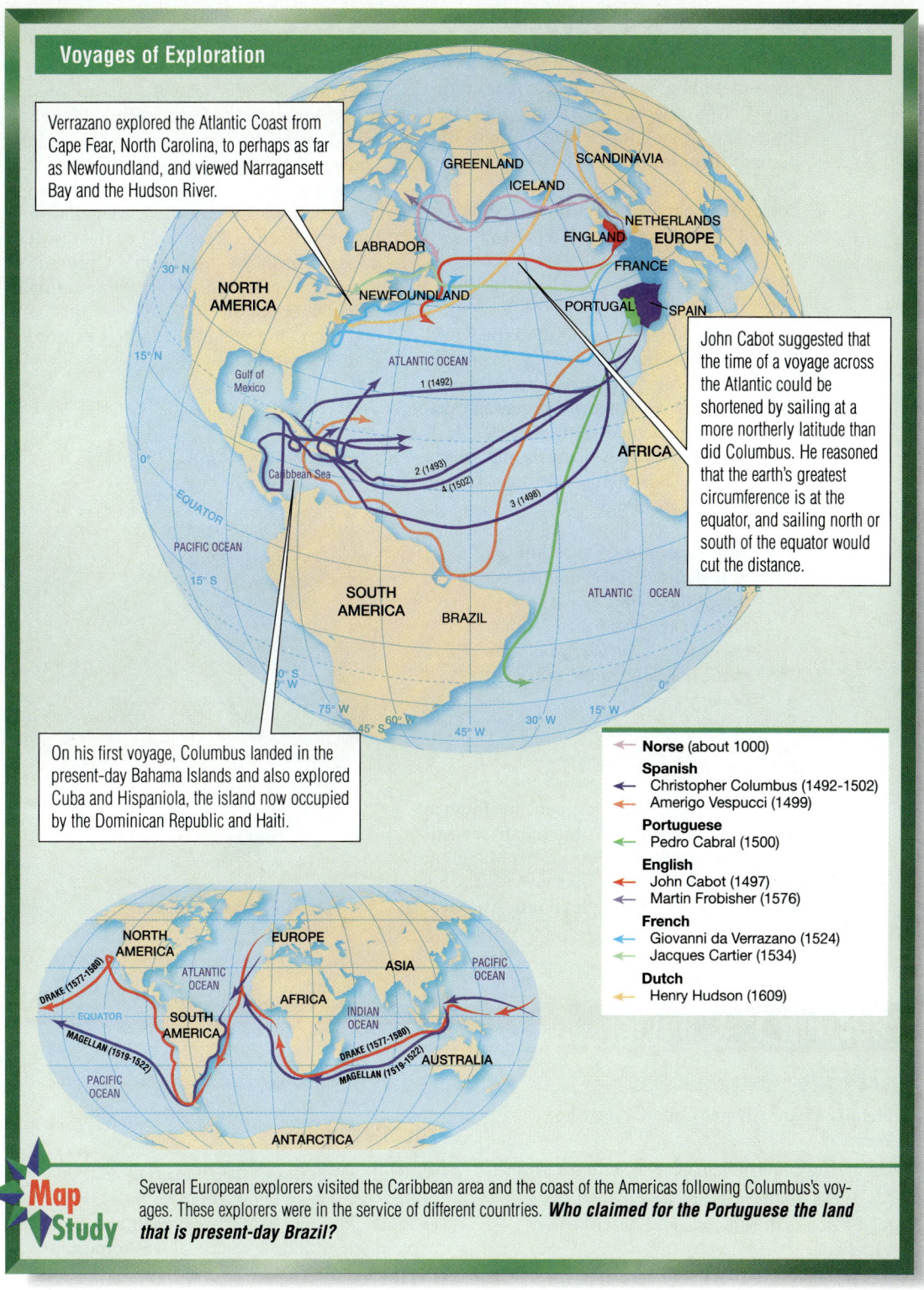

Voyages of Exploration

Verrazano explored the Atlantic Coast from Cape Fear, North Carolina, to perhaps as far as Newfoundland, and viewed Narragansett Bay and the Hudson River.

John Cabot suggested that the time of a voyage across the Atlantic could be shortened by sailing at a more northerly latitude than did Columbus. He reasoned that the earth's greatest circumference is at the equator, and sailing north or south of the equator would cut the distance.

On his first voyage, Columbus landed in the present-day Bahama Islands and also explored Cuba and Hispaniola, the island now occupied by the Dominican Republic and Haiti.

← Norse (about 1000)
Spanish
← Christopher Columbus (1492-1502)
← Amerigo Vespucci (1499)
Portuguese
← Pedro Cabral (1500)
English
← John Cabot (1497)
← Martin Frobisher (1576)
French
← Giovanni da Verrazano (1524)
← Jacques Cartier (1534)
Dutch
← Henry Hudson (1609)

Map Study Several European explorers visited the Caribbean area and the coast of the Americas following Columbus's voyages. These explorers were in the service of different countries. **Who claimed for the Portuguese the land that is present-day Brazil?**

Map Study Using Maps

Answer:
Pedro Cabral

Skills Practice
On the voyages of which explorers did England and Spain base their claims to the Americas? (England—Cabot, Spain—Columbus)

FACT or FICTION?
Magellan's expedition was a financial success.

FACT: On arriving in the Spice Islands, the survivors took on a cargo of cloves worth more than the whole cost of the voyage.

CHAPTER 2 The Age of Exploration 1000–1682   **39**

Critical Thinking

Making Connections Point out that Columbus's voyages to the Americas had a major impact on the Americas and on Europe. Then ask students to complete the following sentences:

The greatest impact of Columbus's voyages on the Americas was . . . .

The greatest impact of Columbus's voyages on Europe was . . . .

Have students write brief paragraphs supporting their sentence completions. **L1, L2**

39

CHAPTER 2 SECTION 1

ASSESS

Check Understanding
Assign Section 1 Review as homework or an in-class activity.

Evaluate
▼ ■ Assign the Section 1 Quiz in the TCR, or use the History of a Free Nation Testmaker to create a customized quiz.

Reteach
▼ Have students complete Reteaching Activity 2-1.

Enrich
Some students might undertake research on the early life of Christopher Columbus or Ferdinand Magellan. Suggest that students write a brief report on Magellan's early life.

CLOSE
Ask students to speculate on which was of greater geographical significance: Columbus's reaching the Americas or Magellan's circumnavigation of the world.

■ Magellan's Voyage

Balboa's expedition did, however, revive hope of sailing west to reach Asia. Since only a strip of land, or **isthmus**, separated the oceans at Panama, it was thought that perhaps there was a **strait**, or narrow waterway, connecting the two bodies of water. Portuguese navigator Ferdinand Magellan believed he could find such a passage.

Magellan's Plan

Magellan hoped to sail around the world to the Spice Islands, a center for the valuable spice trade located in what is now Indonesia. Out of favor in the Portuguese court, Magellan approached King Charles I of Spain with his plan. A Spanish missionary to America, Bartolemé de Las Casas, described this meeting:

> ❝ Magellan brought with him a well-painted globe, and thereon traced the course he proposed to take . . . he intended to follow the coast . . . until he found the strait [passage to the other ocean]. ❞

Difficult Passage

The Spanish king agreed to finance Magellan, and in 1519 Magellan set sail with 5 ships. By October 1520, Magellan had reached the strait that now bears his name at the southern tip of South America. The strait, with its fierce winds and strong tides, was so difficult to navigate that it took over a month for the expedition to pass through. Because the ocean on the other side seemed so calm, Magellan called it the Pacific, meaning "peaceful." During the voyage across the Pacific that followed, the sailors suffered extreme hardships, and many died. Magellan met his own death in April 1521 as the result of a local war in the Philippines. Only one of his ships, carrying 18 survivors, finally reached Spain in 1522. These survivors and their ship were the first to circumnavigate the world.

▲ FERDINAND MAGELLAN

Section 1 ★ Review

Checking for Understanding

1. **Identify** Pedro Álvares Cabral, Amerigo Vespucci.
2. **Define** saga, line of demarcation, isthmus, strait.
3. **Name** the first Europeans to establish settlements in North America, and describe their experience.
4. **Evaluate** Columbus's achievements.

Critical Thinking

5. **Analyzing Solutions** The Panama Canal was built at great cost. On the map on page 39, examine the route Magellan opened and explain why building the canal was important.

---

40   UNIT 1 A New World: Prehistory to 1776

Answers to SECTION 1 REVIEW

1. Pedro Álveres Cabral—38; Amerigo Vespucci—38
2. All vocabulary terms are defined in the Glossary.
3. Norse seafarers settled Iceland, Greenland, and parts of North America. Settlements died out.
4. Reached islands and coasts of the Americas, but failed to recognize new continents. Found new sources of wealth and encouraged further ocean voyages west in hopes of finding Asia.
5. From Europe, or the North American coast, trip around America extremely long. Canal cut distance considerably; rough sailing around Cape.

CONNECTIONS  CONNECTIONS

▲ MAP OF THE WORLD, C. 1502

"'Twas a Small World," Columbus Thought

Around the sixth century B.C., the Greek philosopher Thales proposed the idea that the earth was a disc floating in water. Shortly after, Pythagoras advanced a different idea, that the earth was a sphere. Several centuries later Aristotle tested this idea by observing the circular shadow of the earth on the moon during eclipses.

The size of the earth was more difficult to determine than its shape. Greek geographer Eratosthenes, however, almost correctly calculated the circumference of the earth at about 25,000 miles by measuring the angles of the sun's rays at separated points. This figure was known by Columbus, but he chose to use the calculations made by a number of later scholars who underestimated the size of the earth by nearly one-half. Mapmakers compounded the errors by showing Europe, Asia, and Africa much larger than they actually are and by showing the Atlantic Ocean as a narrow gulf.

Columbus made four voyages in all. He explored the coasts of Venezuela and Central America. He returned from his last voyage in 1504. He died two years later, still convinced he had found an accurate route to Asia. After all, he had found it just where he had calculated it to be.

Magellan's voyage was a great achievement. By circumnavigating, or sailing completely around the world, Magellan proved that the earth is indeed round. The voyage opened the Pacific Ocean to European ships. It also proved that Columbus had not landed in Asia but in the Americas.

Making the Geography Connection

1. What contributions did early Greeks make to geography?
2. Why did Columbus think he had reached Asia?

Linking Past and Present

3. Compare the level of technology Columbus used with that used by modern astronauts.

CHAPTER 2 CONNECTIONS

Teaching Making Connections

Point out that from the 900s to 1100s, Arab scholars, using direct observation rather than mathematical calculations, made major contributions to people's understanding of geography. Ask students to suggest why direct observation is so important in establishing the validity of scientific theories.

In 1522 circumnavigating the globe was an amazing achievement, though the voyage had taken almost three years. Today the excitement lies in setting— and breaking— speed records. One such record holder is American Dodge Morgan.

Did You Know?

The *Catalan Atlas*, drawn in 1375, summarized Europe's geographic knowledge of the world in the century before Columbus. It shows Europe, parts of Africa, the Middle East, India, China, and some of the rich islands that Columbus later tried to reach by sailing west.

Answers to CONNECTIONS

1. Made observations and calculations about shape and size of the earth.
2. His calculations of distance based on works of scholars who underestimated earth's size by one-half.
3. DME (distance-measuring equipment) for aerial navigation, radio telescopes, X-ray telescopes used on space satellites, gamma-ray telescopes.

LESSON PLAN
SECTION 2, 42–46

FOCUS

Bellringer
Before taking roll at the beginning of the class period, display Focus Activity Transparency 6 on the overhead projector, and assign the accompanying Focus Activity Sheet.

Objectives
Point out the objectives on this page to students in previewing the section content.

Motivating Activity
Ask students to suggest what reasons they think influenced the conquistadors to come to the Americas. (Most students will say conquistadors came simply to get rich.) Mention that while greed for gold was a major motivation for the young Spaniards who flocked to the Americas in the 1500s, other forces were also at work. Point out that in this section, students will learn that many conquistadors were driven by the desire to serve the Roman Catholic Church and the king of Spain.

Food of the Times
European explorers encountered many new foods in the Americas. These included maize (corn); sweet potatoes; white potatoes; snap, kidney, and lima beans; peanuts; pumpkins; pineapples; chocolate; avocados; tomatoes; and turkeys.

SECTION 2

Spain in America

Setting the Scene

Section Focus

Europeans had not found a new trade route to Asia, but they soon began to look upon the Americas as a source of wealth. Explorers heard stories of fabulously rich cities in the interior. Among the most vigorous in searching for treasure in the Americas were Spanish explorers. Their activities, along with those of the Christian missionaries, changed the world of the native peoples of the Americas.

Objectives

After studying this section, you should be able to
★ describe the Spanish exploration and conquest of the South and Central American mainlands.
★ discuss life in the Spanish colonies.

Key Terms

conquistador, *peninsulares*, creole, mestizo, mulatto, *encomienda*, viceroy, presidio

◀ COMPASS, 1500s

In the 25 years after Columbus's first voyage, Spaniards carved out small outposts through the West Indies—on Cuba, Jamaica, Puerto Rico, and Hispaniola. Generally they were not interested in creating permanent settlements in the Americas. Instead, they flocked to the islands in search of land and precious metals. The peoples of these islands suffered greatly, however, because of Spanish ambition.

■ The Conquistadors

The many **conquistadors** (kohn•KEES•tuh•dohrs)—Spanish conquerors who made their way to the Caribbean islands in the early 1500s—were eager to find great wealth, especially gold and silver. They did not hesitate to use harsh means to obtain this end. The natives of the Caribbean, many of whom were enslaved and put to work washing for gold or raising crops, were virtually exterminated in less than 20 years. Most succumbed to such European diseases as smallpox and measles, from which they had no immunity. By 1520 the Spanish were importing Africans as slaves to replace the Native American populations.

The Spaniards did not confine themselves to the Caribbean islands for very long. Fantastic stories from the mainland soon sent bold Spanish adventurers into the interior of Mexico, Central America, and South America.

42   UNIT 1   A New World: Prehistory to 1776

Classroom Resources for SECTION 2

Teacher's Classroom Resources
- Reproducible Lesson Plan
- Reteaching Activity 2-2
- Chapter 2 Primary and Secondary Source Readings
- Section Quiz

Multimedia
- Section Focus Transparency 6
- Chapter 2 Map Transparency
- Chapter 2 History and Art Transparency
- Testmaker
- Student Self-Test Software
- The American People: Fabric of a Nation

Cortés and Moctezuma

Among the most successful of these conquistadors was Hernán Cortés (kawr•TEHZ). In 1519 Cortés led an expedition from Cuba to the eastern shore of Mexico. Although Cortés's army numbered only 600, the Spaniards had luck—and sophisticated weapons—on their side. The Spanish also had horses, which the Indians had never seen, that they used in cavalry charges.

Cortés gained invaluable help from Malinche, an enslaved native who quickly learned Spanish. She may have told Cortés of Quetzalcoatl (keht•SAHL•KWAHT•uhl), the legendary god who had promised to return as a fair-skinned man.

When Cortés landed on the Mexican coast, reports of "floating mountains bearing fair-skinned gods" were sent to Moctezuma, the Aztec emperor. Moctezuma believed that Cortés might indeed be Quetzalcoatl, and he sent the Spaniards dazzling gifts.

As Cortés marched inland toward the Aztec capital of Tenochtitlán (tay•NAWCH•teet•LAHN), subjects of the Aztec allied with him, hoping to free themselves from Aztec rule. At first Moctezuma reluctantly welcomed the Spaniards and lodged them in Tenochtitlán. Cortés wrote:

> *The city itself is as big as Seville or Córdoba.... [it] has many squares where ... markets are held continuously.... There are ... many temples.... Amongst these temples there is one ... whose great size and magnificence no human tongue could describe.*

To insure their safety, the Spaniards took Moctezuma captive. They also looted the city of gold and silver. Eight months later, when Moctezuma was killed by a stone thrown by one of his subjects, the Aztec rose up against the Spanish. Many Spaniards were killed during a retreat.

In 1521 Cortés returned to the Aztec capital, having amassed huge numbers of allies among the native peoples. He cut off supplies to Tenochtitlán and, after a long siege, destroyed this city whose magnificence had so impressed him. Mexico City was built on its ruins, and the area's rich silver mines soon produced vast wealth.

Destruction of the Incan Empire

The conquest of Mexico encouraged other conquistadors to seek their furtune in the Americas. One such conquistador was Francisco Pizarro, an illiterate soldier who had been stirred by rumors of fabulously rich cities on the Pacific coast of South America.

In 1531 Pizarro set sail from Panama with an army of only 180 soldiers. His destination was the Incan empire in present-day Peru. After an exhausting journey, the Spaniards reached the city of Cajamarca (KAH•huh•MAHR•kuh). The Incan empire had been badly weakened by a civil war from which the new emperor Atahualpa (AH•tah•WAHL•pah) had emerged victorious. The Spaniards greeted him with swords and guns, taking him captive. In an effort to save his life, Atahualpa gave the Spaniards a room filled with gold objects and other treasures. Despite the ransom, the Spanish later executed Atahualpa. Within a short time many Spanish settlers had immigrated to Peru, where they mined silver and gold.

▲ **FALL OF THE AZTEC EMPIRE** Cortés, with only a small army, marched on the Aztec capital of Tenochtitlán in 1519 and eventually destroyed this magnificent city. **What new city was built on its site?**

CHAPTER 2 SECTION 2

TEACH
Guided Practice

Debate Have students debate the following statement:

The *encomienda* system was little more than slavery by another name.

(The basic pro argument might be that the system led to the large-scale exploitation of the Native American population. The basic con argument might be that, in theory, the system was established to protect the Native Americans.) **L3**

Visualizing History This illustration shows the Spanish conquistadors trading with Native Americans. **Answer to Caption:** Mexico City

NATIONAL GEOGRAPHIC SOCIETY

VIDEODISC

• *GTV: The American People: Fabric of a Nation*

Side 1, Chapter 5
Title: *When Worlds Collide*
Subject: European and Native American encounters

See GTV Guide page 48 for complete lesson plan.

Critical Thinking

Analyzing a Point of View On the chalkboard, write the following quotation from *In the American Grain* by William Carlos Williams:

"Cortés was neither malicious, stupid nor blind, but a conqueror like other conquerors.... He was one among the rest."

Ask students to write a brief paper that answers the following questions: What point of view is being expressed? What evidence might be used in support of this view? What evidence might challenge it? Do you agree or disagree with the author? **L3**

American Portraits

Junípero Serra
1713–1784

Most Spanish conquests in the New World were marked by a terrible slaughter of the local people. In contrast, a gentle priest established Spanish control in California by setting up a string of missions to care for and convert the Native Americans.

Born on an island off the Spanish coast, Junípero Serra became a Franciscan priest and professor of philosophy. Because he wanted to work as a missionary among Native Americans, in 1749 he left Spain to travel to Mexico.

At the age of 55, he was sent to take control of Upper California. He established a mission at San Diego, and later founded several missions stretching up the California coast to San Francisco. Taking as his motto "Always go forward and never turn back," Junípero Serra traveled by foot from mission to mission, making sure that Native Americans were not abused.

Elusive Fountain of Youth

Other Spanish conquistadors explored areas to the north. Juan Ponce de León, the governor of Puerto Rico, was one of the first to head to northern lands. De León had heard native tales of a wondrous fountain whose water would restore youth. In 1513 he set sail in search of this magical fountain. When the Spaniards reached land near what is now the city of St. Augustine, they named the area Florida for the blooming wild flowers and fragrant plants. De León never found the mythical "Fountain of Youth," but he claimed the land for Spain.

After 1542 the Spanish worked to consolidate their empire in the Americas. Because the northern lands appeared so inhospitable, the Spanish considered these borderlands unsuitable for colonization.

■ Colonial Life

The people of Spain's American colonies formed a structured society, where position was determined predominately by birth. At the top were *peninsulares*—high government and church officials who had been born in Spain. Below the *peninsulares* were **creoles**—those born in the Spanish colonies of Spanish parents. **Mestizos** (meh•STEE•zohs), those born of Native American and Spanish parents, made up the next level of colonial society. At the lowest levels of society were Native Americans, African slaves, and **mulattoes**—people of Spanish and African or Native American and African ancestry.

Land and Agriculture

Through the *encomienda* system, the Spanish monarch rewarded conquistadors and others with vast tracts of land and the right to demand both taxes and labor from the Native Americans who lived there. The *encomenderos* were supposed to protect the Native Americans, teach them Catholicism, and pay them for their labor. In reality, the Spanish colonists often treated the natives cruelly, overworking them and using their forced labor to gain vast personal wealth.

The mingling of Spanish and Native American cultures produced a new kind of society in the Spanish colonies. Spanish became the language of the colonies, though many Native Americans continued to speak their original languages. The Spanish introduced European crops, such as wheat, alfalfa, oranges, and figs, as well as horses, cattle, and firearms.

Likewise, products from the Americas made significant changes in Europe when the Spaniards returned with plants such as potatoes, tomatoes, and corn. For example, the potato decreased Europeans' reliance on flour—to the extent that towns and cities whose economies centered around mills declined.

Colonial Administration and Religious Missions

Spain's system for governing its huge colonial empire included the appointment of **viceroys**—Spanish nobles appointed by the monarch to look after the interests of the crown. The Spanish monarch also set up a special court in Mexico City known as the *audiencia*. The purpose of the court was to oversee the viceroys and control the behavior of the conquistadors. It also was supposed to provide a forum for justice to the native peoples.

The Spaniards established missions in their colonies to help convince Native Americans to become loyal Spanish subjects and Catholics. Some priests sought to protect the natives from the conquistadors. Father Bartolomé de Las Casas insisted that, like all humans, Native Americans were children of God and therefore should be protected by the Church and the king.

Beginning in 1769 Father Junípero Serra began a chain of missions in California, the northern part of Spain's empire. A road called The Royal Highway, or *El Camino Real* (EHL kah•MEE•noh ray•AHL), linked

▲ **SPAIN IN THE AMERICAS** By the middle of the 1500s, Spain had established the base of a colonial empire in the Americas. Spain's empire was first settled by soldiers, adventurers, and missionaries. **What was the encomienda system?**

these missions. **Presidios,** or forts, were generally built nearby to protect the missions. Native peoples were brought to the missions to be fed, clothed, taught European methods of agriculture, and to attend religious instruction and services.

Section 2 ★ Review

Checking for Understanding

1. **Identify** Hernán Cortés, Francisco Pizarro, Junípero Serra, *El Camino Real*.
2. **Define** conquistador, *peninsulares*, creole, mestizo, mulatto, *encomienda*, viceroy, presidio.
3. **Discuss** the effects of Spanish colonization on the peoples of the West Indies.
4. **Summarize** the Spanish exploration and conquest of the American mainland.

Critical Thinking

5. **Verifying Predictions** Spanish explorers introduced horses to Native Americans. Predict how the lives of the Plains peoples in North America might have been significantly altered by having horses.

CHAPTER 2 The Age of Exploration 1000–1682

LESSON PLAN
Mastering Social Studies Skills

Teaching Study and Writing Skills

Discuss the article, pointing out the key questions students should ask before beginning to research any topic. (Students should ask who, what, and where questions.) Ask: Did your group ask these kinds of questions? How can asking effective questions help you focus your research? How can asking good questions lead you to the right resources? (They specify the scope of the research.) You may wish to select one of the topics listed at the end of the article and complete Practicing the Skill as a group activity.

Did You Know?

The conquistadors in one generation acquired more new territory than the ancient Romans did in 500 years. Although Genghis Khan swept over a larger area, he and his followers were unable to administer the lands they conquered. The Spaniards established a colonial system that lasted more than 300 years.

Social Studies Skills

Study and Writing Skills

Asking Effective Questions

Effective questions are questions that serve a specific purpose and provide desired information. Asking effective questions involves a three-step process. If you ask questions without having a carefully planned strategy for doing so, much time can be wasted and confusion may result. Effective questions help you "get to the point" and allow you to better understand any given topic.

The three steps involved in developing effective questions are:

a. Determine what information you need to know.
b. Decide what materials or people you should consult.
c. Consider what questions you should ask.

For a report on the conquistadors, for example, important questions include: Who were the conquistadors? What were they doing in Spain before they came to America? How were they funded? What were their specific goals?

Having determined what it is you need to understand, the sources of information, and the topics that could be covered, you are prepared to ask questions as you read and absorb materials during your study of American history. By following these guidelines, the questions you ask will be effective ones.

▲ PONCE DE LEÓN

▲ CONQUISTADORS IN AMERICA

Practicing the Skill

For further practice in asking effective questions, apply the three steps to preparing a research report on one of the following:
a. Spanish conquistadors
b. the exploration of Amerigo Vespucci
c. Spanish missions in the Americas
d. life in Tenochtitlán
e. Ponce de León

SECTION 3

New Ventures

Setting the Scene

Section Focus

Like the Spanish, the English, French, and Dutch sought a water route through the New World. In this search they explored the northern regions of the continent. Unlike the Spanish, though, they did not quickly establish colonies. For the first century or so, these nations' activities in the New World were neither as far-reaching nor as forceful as those of Spain.

Objectives

After studying this section, you should be able to

★ describe early English exploration of North America.

★ discuss French and Dutch colonization in North America.

Key Terms

northwest passage, Spanish Armada, mercantilism

◀ FRENCH HELMET

Although the English participated in early voyages of exploration, they failed to establish permanent colonies in America until the early 1600s. Poor finances, religious conflict, the colonization of Ireland, and the threat of war with Spain overshadowed English interest in the Americas.

In 1497 King Henry VII of England authorized John Cabot "to sayle to all partes, countreys, and seas, of the East, of the West, and of the North" and to discover new lands unknown to Christians. English merchants hoped that Cabot would discover a route to Asia. Cabot explored the shores of present-day Nova Scotia, Newfoundland, and Labrador. Like Columbus, Cabot believed he had found Asia. But when a second expedition found only the barren coasts of Labrador and Greenland, English interest in westward exploration and settlement waned.

■ Rivalry Between England and Spain

By the 1570s, however, Queen Elizabeth I had become increasingly anxious about Spain's growing global power. Wishing to challenge Spain's influence in the Americas—but fearing to do so openly—she secretly financed voyages by Martin Frobisher, whose purpose was to search for a **northwest passage** through North America to Asia. Frobisher explored the Atlantic coast of what is now Canada, but he too failed to find a route to the East.

On the High Seas

Elizabeth also gave her unofficial approval to piracy against Spanish ships and settlements. Daring English sea captains, such as Francis Drake, cruised the

CHAPTER 2 The Age of Exploration 1000–1682

LESSON PLAN
SECTION 3, 47–51

FOCUS

Bellringer
Display Focus Activity Transparency 7 on the overhead projector, and assign the accompanying Focus Activity Sheet.

Objectives
Point out the objectives on this page to students in previewing the section content.

Motivating Activity
Ask students who they think might have said the following:
"I would like to see the clause of Adam's will that excludes me from a share of the world."
(Students probably will suggest the statement was made by an explorer or a monarch who had been prevented from laying claim to the Americas.) Point out that this was the response of King Francis I of France when told that the Treaty of Tordesillas divided the "unknown" world between Spain and Portugal.

 VIDEODISC

• *GTV: A Geographic Perspective on American History*

Side 1, Chapter 4
Title: *Land of Opportunity*
Subject: Europeans gain a foothold in the Americas

See GTV Guide page 34 for complete lesson plan.

Classroom Resources for SECTION 3

Teacher's Classroom Resources
- Reproducible Lesson Plan
- Reteaching Activity 2-3
- Chapter 2 Enrichment Activity
- Chapter 2 Performance Assessment Activity
- Spanish Summaries and Glossary
- Section Quiz

Multimedia
- Section Focus Transparency 7
- Chapter 2 Map Transparency
- Vocabulary Puzzlemaker
- Testmaker
- A Geographic Perspective on American History

CHAPTER 2 SECTION 3

TEACH
Guided Practice

Geography Remind students that the French undertook explorations of the Great Lakes and Mississippi Valley in the early 1600s. The legacy of that period in American history can be seen in the many French place names in those regions. Ask students to use atlases to locate and list about 10 such place names. (Lists might include: Marquette, Detroit, Bois Blanc Island, La Salle, Charlevoix, Joliet, St. Louis, Champaign, and Sault Ste. Marie.) **L1, L2**

Did You Know?

In Louisiana, two ethnic groups, both famous for their cuisine, boast French ancestry. The Cajuns descended from French settlers driven from Acadia in 1755. Creoles are a mix of early French and Spanish settlers.

Visualizing History Point out that those relatively few French settlers who came to farm settled along the St. Lawrence River.
Answer to Caption: St. Lawrence River valley

shores of Spanish America, capturing treasure ships, looting towns, and inflicting heavy damage to the Spanish. Because Spain was still the strongest power in Europe, however, the English did not attempt colonization in America or take any open action against the Spanish.

Defeat of the Spanish Armada

The eventual challenge to open conflict came from Spain rather than England. In 1588, seeking revenge for English attacks on Spanish ships and colonies, King Phillip II of Spain dispatched a huge fleet of ships, known as the **Spanish Armada**, to sail against the English fleet. The "invincible armada" included 130 ships and 27,000 troops.

Although the English fleet was greatly outnumbered, their ships were faster and far easier to handle than the slow, heavy Spanish galleons. The English ships attacked the Spanish vessels one by one. Before a Spanish galleon could get close enough for its soldiers to board an English warship, it was pounded by artillery. The result was devastating to the Spanish fleet. The badly damaged armada was forced up the English Channel and into the North Sea. A fierce storm off the coast of Scotland further crippled the Spanish fleet. Only 60 to 70 ships returned to Spain. In a single battle, Spain had lost most of its naval forces. The way was now cleared for English colonization in the Americas.

Mercantilism

The age of exploration and colonization brought sweeping changes to European society and culture. Beginning in the 1600s, many European nations, including England, followed a theory of national economic policy called **mercantilism.** This theory held that a state's power depended on its wealth. Accordingly, the aim of every nation was to become as wealthy as possible.

Colonies played an important role in the mercantilist system. They were the sources of raw materials and provided markets for manufactured goods from the parent country. The goal of the colonies was to make the parent country self-sufficient. Mercantilism

▲ QUEEN ELIZABETH I

helped England amass enormous national wealth that it used to build a colonial empire. Some other nations, however, found it more difficult to establish colonies.

■ French Presence in America

In 1524 the French king, Francis I, had sent Italian sea captain Giovanni da Verrazano to search for a northwest passage. Verrazano sailed the Atlantic coast from Newfoundland south to North Carolina. In 1534 Jacques Cartier made the first of three voyages to northern North America, searching for the elusive passage. Although he explored the St. Lawrence River as far as what is now Montreal, he also failed to find the passage. While French fishers sometimes visited North American waters, it was not until the early 1600s that the French made a serious attempt to establish a colony. In 1608 Samuel de Champlain founded Quebec on the banks of the St. Lawrence River. Few French settlers, however, were attracted to this northern outpost. In 1609 Champlain joined the Algonquian and Huron peoples in a raid against the Iroquois confederacy. Champlain described the hostilities:

Cultural Diversity

During the 1500s the French tried to found colonies south of Canada. In 1562 French Huguenots set up a colony in present-day South Carolina, but it failed because of internal disagreements. In 1564 the French established Fort Caroline in Florida. The Spanish who viewed the Protestant French fort as a threat, attacked and drove out the French. Then Spain founded St. Augustine, Florida, in 1565.

Life of the Times

French Fur Traders

In the early 1700s, the most stylish Europeans wore hats and other garments fashioned from felt

◀ FUR TRADER

cloth. Beaver furs from North America produced the highest quality and most durable felt. Pelts supplied by French fur traders were therefore highly prized. To keep the supply of furs constant, French traders maintained a close relationship with Native Americans who trapped the beaver.

The French government, hoping to keep the lucrative fur trade from the English, encouraged traders and settlers to live with the Algonquin. Many traders and missionaries moved into Algonquin villages.

As a result, the Algonquin changed the French colonists in America. Frenchmen married Algonquin women and raised their children as Algonquin. Other French settlers adopted Algonquin ways. In 1749 a Swedish traveler observed:

▲ FRENCH MAP OF NORTH AMERICA, 1550

"The French in Canada in many respects follow the customs of the Indians, with whom they have constant relations. They use the tobacco pipes, shoes, gaiters [leg coverings], and girdles [loincloths] of the Indians. They follow the Indian way of waging war exactly and have adopted many other Indian fashions."

> "When I saw them getting ready to shoot their arrows at us, I leveled my arquebuse [gun] . . . and aimed straight at one of the three chiefs. The shot brought down two and wounded another. . . . The Iroquois were greatly astonished and frightened to see two of their men killed so quickly . . . they abandoned the field and fled into the depth of the forest."

As a result of this battle, the formidable Iroquois warriors became sworn enemies of the French.

Exploration of the Mississippi

The French were generally confined to present-day Canada until the late 1600s. In 1673 Louis Joliet, an American-born fur trader, and the Jesuit priest Jacques Marquette embarked on a search for a river known to native Americans as the "big river"—the Mississippi. They canoed from St. Ignace on the northern tip of Lake Michigan to the Mississippi along inland waterways and followed it as far as the Arkansas River. In 1682 Robert de La Salle followed the Mississippi to its delta and claimed the vast lands drained by it for France. He named the region Louisiana.

Fur Trappers and Priests

The colonies established by France in North America formed a long string of outposts, extending from the Gulf of Mexico to Canada. French interests were directed largely toward the development of the fur trade. Beaver skins sent to France and made into hats were a particularly profitable item.

CHAPTER 2 SECTION 3

Making Comparisons The approaches of the Spanish and the French to colonization in America were very different. Ask students to write an essay that compares these approaches. Suggest that they cover in their essays such topics as purpose of colonization, time period of colonization, impact on the environment, and relations with the native populations. **L3**

Independent Practice

Chronology Have students use information from all three sections of Chapter 2 to construct a time line titled "Exploration in the Americas, 1492–1682." Suggest that students retain their time lines for review purposes. **L1, LEP**

Teaching Life of the Times

People born of French and Native American parents were called *métis* (may TEE). Ask students what similar word was used to describe people with Spanish and Native American heritage. (*Mestizos*) Point out that *méti* and *mestizo* both derive from the Latin word *miscere*, which means "to mix."

Cooperative Learning

Ask students to think of an answer to the following question: Why were France and the Netherlands relatively unsuccessful in developing colonies in the Americas?

Have students form pairs to discuss their answers. Then have each pair develop a composite response to the question. Select pairs to share their answers with the rest of the class. **L1, L2**

CHAPTER 2
SECTION 3

Using Maps

Answer:
Arkansas River valley

Skills Practice
Who explored the Mississippi River as far south as the Arkansas River? (Marquette and Joliet)

Did You Know?

The first 10,000 French settlers in Canada included 4,500 indentured servants; 3,500 retired soldiers; 1,000 prisoners, mostly smugglers; and 1,000 women.

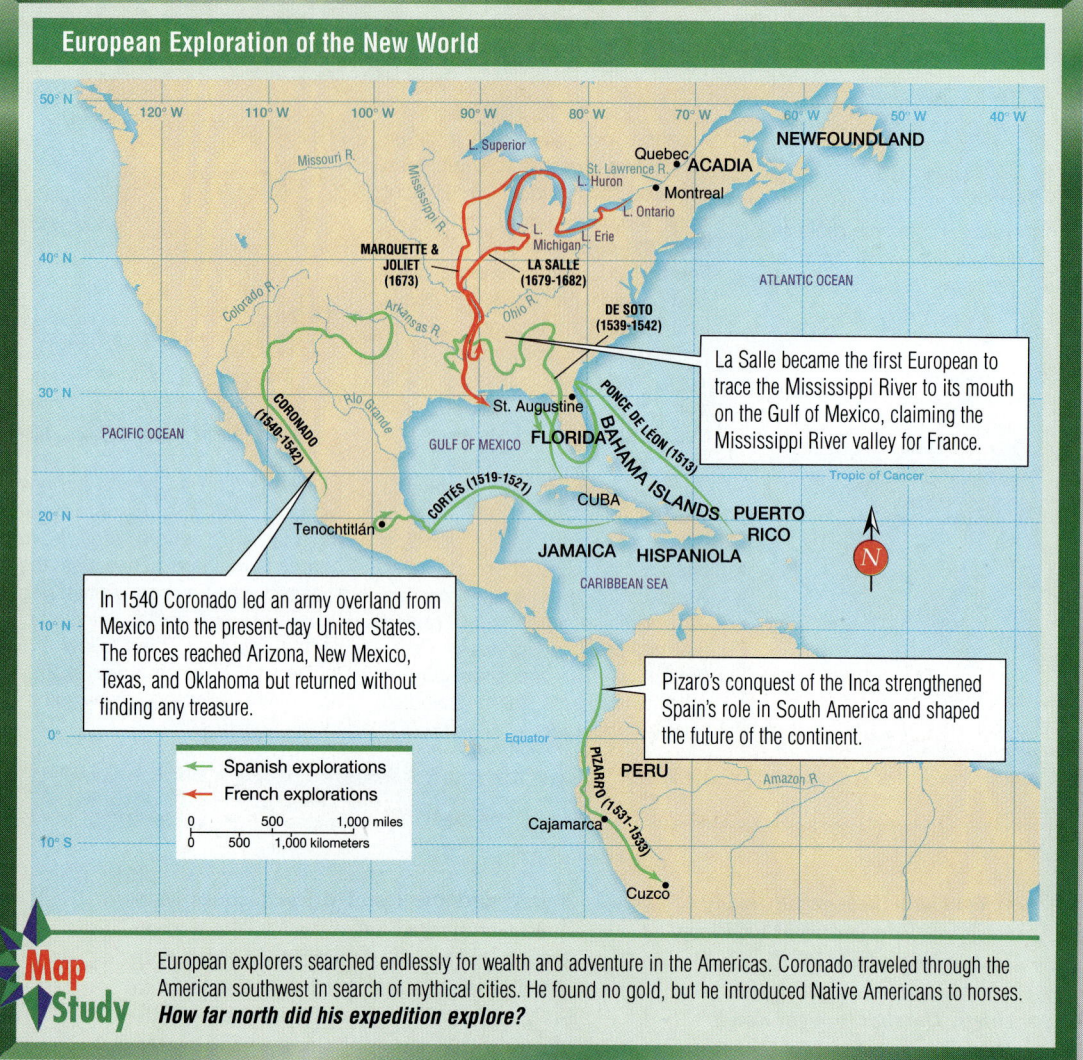

European Exploration of the New World

La Salle became the first European to trace the Mississippi River to its mouth on the Gulf of Mexico, claiming the Mississippi River valley for France.

In 1540 Coronado led an army overland from Mexico into the present-day United States. The forces reached Arizona, New Mexico, Texas, and Oklahoma but returned without finding any treasure.

Pizaro's conquest of the Inca strengthened Spain's role in South America and shaped the future of the continent.

Map Study European explorers searched endlessly for wealth and adventure in the Americas. Coronado traveled through the American southwest in search of mythical cities. He found no gold, but he introduced Native Americans to horses. *How far north did his expedition explore?*

Except with the Iroquois, the French generally had better relations with Native Americans than did the Spanish. French trappers and traders known as *coureurs de bois*—"runners of the woods"—did not threaten to take over Native American lands. They lived among the Native Americans, learned their ways, spoke their languages, and often married among them.

French missionaries, who were known to Native American peoples as "black robes," journeyed into the North American wilderness to convert Native Americans to Catholicism. Not accompanied by armies as the Spanish missionaries were, the French Jesuits often suffered torture and death. In spite of their troubles, most of the Jesuits did not despair. One French priest wrote in the mid-1600s:

> *Do not imagine that the . . . loss of many Christians can bring to nought the mystery of the cross of Jesus Christ. . . . We shall die; we shall be captured, burned, butchered: be it so. Those who die in their beds do not always die the best death.*

UNIT 1 A New World: Prehistory to 1776

Sidelights: French North America

The French population in North America grew very slowly. By 1670, some 60 years after Champlain's founding of Quebec, there were a little more than 8,000 French in New France. As a comparison, at that time the population of Boston was around 5,000. Over the next 100 years, the French population grew some tenfold—but through natural increase rather than immigration. At this time, most French Americans were *habitants,* poor farm workers employed on the lands owned by the nobility.

Disinterest in the Colonies

The French government had difficulty recruiting colonists for its North American settlements for several reasons. First of all, these colonies were not as valuable as French possessions in the West Indies—the islands of Guadeloupe, Martinique, and Saint Dominique, which all produced rich sugar crops. Second, most French rulers were more interested in extending their rule over European territory than in settling North America. In addition, the French missed an opportunity to gain an energetic group of settlers when they forbade French Protestants, known as Huguenots, to settle in America. Persecuted in France, many Huguenots would have gladly emigrated to America.

■ The Dutch in America

The Netherlands, which had won its independence from Spain in the late 1500s, was also interested in expansion. This small country had few natural resources and limited farmland. The key to survival, then, was to increase trade and commerce.

The period of the 1600s was the golden age of the Netherlands. Dutch ships were efficient, carrying more cargo and smaller crews than other ships, and the Dutch enjoyed a high standard of living.

Like the French, the Dutch were late in setting up colonies in North America. They were, however, making great strides in other parts of the world. The first Dutch expedition to the Far East returned in 1599. Three years later Dutch companies expanded trade with Asia. In 1619 Dutch traders set up headquarters in present-day Indonesia. Soon, the Dutch controlled island trade in sugar, spices, coffee, and tea.

They controlled the East Indies; set up the only trading post in Japan; maintained many West African slave ports; established a colony in Cape Town, South Africa; and had holdings in the Caribbean islands.

New Amsterdam

Dutch ventures on the North American continent were not nearly so impressive. In 1609 the Dutch East India Company funded an expedition by an English navigator, Henry Hudson. He reached New York Harbor and sailed up the river, which today bears his name, as far as present-day Albany, New York. The Dutch soon set up trading posts on Manhattan Island, which they named New Amsterdam, and along the Hudson River. A profitable fur trade was established with the Native Americans.

To attract settlers, the Dutch West Indies Company promised to give huge tracts of land along the Hudson and Delaware rivers to proprietors if at least 50 people could be hired and kept on the land. Few settlers, however, were interested. Although the Dutch colony was small, it contained a remarkable ethnic mix. One visitor reported that he had heard "eighteen different languages" being spoken in New Amsterdam in the mid-1600s. Because of poor leadership and weak government, though, the Dutch colony easily fell to the growing colonial influence of England in 1664.

Section 3 ★ Review

Checking for Understanding

1. **Identify** John Cabot, Jacques Cartier, Samuel de Champlain, Robert de La Salle, Henry Hudson.
2. **Define** northwest passage, Spanish Armada, mercantilism.
3. **Summarize** English voyages of exploration in North America.
4. **Contrast** patterns of French settlement with colonization patterns of other European nations.

Critical Thinking

5. **Citing Evidence** What evidence can you find of the importance of the Catholic faith to the French?

REVIEW CHAPTER 2

Using Vocabulary
1. b 5. h
2. g 6. a
3. d 7. f
4. c 8. e

Reviewing Facts
1. Norse seafarers
2. Columbus reached, but failed to recognize, new continent. He brought back gold and encouraged further ocean voyages west in hopes of finding Asia. Vespucci recognized South America as a new continent, renewing the search for a water route to Asia.
3. Stratification with Spanish at top, blend of Spanish and Native American cultures, ruled by appointed governors, courts established, land and Native American labor granted to conquistadors; establishment of missions.
4. Established Quebec and small outposts, initiated the fur trade. Changed environment little, coexisted with most Native American groups.

Understanding Concepts
1. Searches for Northwest Passage, search for Fountain of Youth by de León, gold by Coronado.
2. The Americas in search for Asian route, fur trade—by French in search of Northwest Passage, Brazil in search for Asia.
3. French and Spanish missionaries explored and established missions to convert Native Americans.
4. Would not let Huguenots, who would have migrated, settle in America.

52

CHAPTER 2 ★ REVIEW

Using Vocabulary

Match each word or phrase with the correct definition below.

a. saga   e. strait
b. creole   f. *peninsulares*
c. *encomienda* g. mestizo
d. armada   h. northwest passage

1. people born in the Spanish colonies of Spanish parents
2. people with Native American and Spanish parents
3. a fleet of ships
4. system of awarding conquistadors land and the right to collect taxes and labor
5. fabled water route through North America to the Pacific
6. long narratives
7. in the Spanish colonies, high officials born in Spain
8. a narrow body of water between two landmasses

Reviewing Facts

1. **Identify** the first Europeans to attempt to settle North America.
2. **Summarize** Spanish exploration, exploitation, and colonization in America.
3. **Describe** the class system in the Spanish colonies.
4. **Discuss** French exploration and settlement patterns in North America.

Understanding Concepts

Discovery and Exploration
1. What explorations were undertaken in search of something that was never found?
2. What discoveries were made when searching for something else?

52   UNIT 1 A New World: Prehistory to 1776

Values and Beliefs
3. What role did religion play in the colonization of the Americas?
4. How did the religious values of the French rulers interfere with their efforts to attract French colonists to North America?

Critical Thinking

1. **Analyzing Motivation** Compare the motives of the early European explorers with those who explore areas such as outer space and the ocean floor today.
2. **Comparing Effects** Compare the effects of French and Spanish settlers on Native American peoples.
3. **Analyzing Art** Spanish priest Bartolomé de Las Casas devoted most of his life to speaking out for Native American peoples and condemning the brutality of Spanish troops in the Americas.
   a. Do you think this is a realistic portrait of Las Casas?
   b. Do you think the artist has captured the dignity of his subject? Explain.

▲ BARTOLOMÉ DE LAS CASAS

Critical Thinking
1. Early Europeans sought wealth and domination. Today explorers search for knowledge for its own sake.
2. The Spanish enslaved Native Americans, claimed large tracts of land for mining and agriculture, and established missions. The French established the fur trade with Native Americans and brought priests to convert them. They did not change the environment by starting large farms or mining operations.
3. Little gold found in North America to attract fortune seekers.

CHAPTER 2 ★ REVIEW

Writing About History

Argumentation
Imagine you are a friend of Columbus. He is frustrated by his failure to persuade the monarchs of Europe to fund a voyage to find a water route around the world to Asia and has asked you to write a persuasive letter to King Ferdinand and Queen Isabella of Spain. Begin by describing the hardships of the land route to Asia, then present your solution.

Cooperative Learning
Work in a group of five to map the routes of Columbus, Magellan, Cabral, Cabot, and La Salle. Each member should research one explorer, then trace the route of that explorer on a single map large enough to display in the classroom or elsewhere in the school. Each member of the group should write a short paragraph on the explorer, describing his motivations, exploits, and significance.

Social Studies Skills

Using a Gazetteer
What if you wanted to find Cuba on a map, but you had no idea where it was located? To find out, you could look up *Cuba* in a gazetteer, a dictionary of geographical names.

A gazetteer lists geographical place-names in alphabetical order. Gazetteers differ somewhat, but most entries include a description, relative location, and exact location with map coordinates—latitude and longitude. The coordinates for Cuba are 22°N/79°W. To find this exact location on a map, simply find the correct latitudinal and longitudinal lines and follow them until they intersect.

Practicing the Skill
Study the gazetteer entries in the next column, then answer the questions that follow:
1. Which of the locations are found in the United States? Which are outside the United States?
2. What is the exact location of the Columbia River?
3. If Cuzco, the Incan capital in Peru, had been listed in the gazetteer, where would it have been placed?
4. Choose four geographic locations from the maps on pages 39 and 50, and write gazetteer entries for each of them, including latitude and longitude coordinates where possible.
5. Choose two cities that are in your home state and write complete gazetteer entries for them.

Columbia River river flowing through southwest Canada and northwestern United States into the Pacific Ocean (46°15′N/124°W)

Concord village northeast of Boston, Massachusetts; site of first battle of the American Revolution in 1775 (42°N/71°W)

Connecticut state in the northeastern United States (41°45′N/73°15′W)

Cuba country in the West Indies, North America (22°N/79°W)

Using Your Journal

Based on your notes, write a paragraph about the nature of exploration. What do you think are some of the basic concerns and hazards of exploring the unknown?

CHAPTER 2 The Age of Exploration 1000–1682

---

a. Las Casas meant that Native Americans were people and should be treated with dignity and fairness.
b. Most Spaniards of the 1400s viewed Native Americans as inferior to Europeans and as people suited for slavery.
c. A pious man determined by his faith to seek justice for Native Americans by writing protests.

Practicing the Skill
1. Concord, Columbia River, and Connecticut are inside the United States; Cuba and the Czech Republic outside the United States.
2. 46° 15′ N/124° W
3. Cuba and the Czech Republic

REVIEW CHAPTER 2

4. Answers may vary.
Samples:
Map on page 39:
Netherlands—Country in NW Europe, bounded by the North Sea, Belgium, and Germany; 53°N/4°E
Newfoundland—Island in the Atlantic Ocean off the coast of Canada, site of Norse settlement around 1000; 45°N/56°W
Map on page 50:
Quebec—City on the N side of the St. Lawrence River in Canada, founded in 1608; 46°N/71°W
St. Augustine—City on the N Florida coast, founded by the Spanish in 1565; 30°N/81°51′W

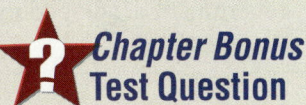

Chapter Bonus Test Question
Suppose you are the leader of a Native American people in the late 1400s or early 1500s. How would you react to your first encounter with European explorers? Be sure to give reasons for your actions.
(Answers will vary. Some may counsel retreat to the hinterland; others may suggest using force against the outsiders; still others may attempt to reach agreements with the Europeans.)

Using Your Journal
The paragraphs should reflect not only the hazards all sailors face but also those associated with exploring unmapped regions.

PLANNING GUIDE Chapter 3 Colonial America

Daily Lesson Objectives	Teacher Classroom Resources	Multimedia
SECTION 1 **The Southern Colonies** 1 Day pp. 56–61 1. Explain the effect of the environment on Virginia's settlement and lifestyle. 2. Describe the economic conditions that influenced the development of the Southern Colonies.	Chapter 3 Study Guide Reproducible Lesson Plan Reteaching Activity 3-1 Section Quiz Chapter 3 Cooperative Learning Activity Chapter 3 Concept Mapping Activity Chapter 3 Primary & Secondary Source Readings	Student Self-Test Software Testmaker Section Focus Transparency 8 Chapter 3 Skills Transparency Unit 3 Digest Transparency Chapter 3 Map Transparency A Geographic Perspective on American History
SECTION 2 **New England** 1 Day pp. 63–67 1. Explain the relationship of church and state in the New England colonies. 2. List three reasons why self-government developed in New England.	Reproducible Lesson Plan Reteaching Activity 3-2 Section Quiz American Portraits 5 Reinforcing Social Studies Skills 32, 37 American Literary Heritage, Unit 1	Student Self-Test Software Testmaker Section Focus Transparency 9 The American People: Fabric of a Nation
SECTION 3 **The Middle Colonies** 1 Day pp. 69–72 1. Describe the role of proprietors in the development of the Middle Colonies. 2. Give reasons for Pennsylvania's rapid growth.	Reproducible Lesson Plan Reteaching Activity 3-3 Section Quiz Writer's Guidebook, Lesson 6	Student Self-Test Software Testmaker Section Focus Transparency 10 U.S. History & Art Transparency 3 The American People: Fabric of a Nation
SECTION 4 **People of the Colonies** 1 Day pp. 73–79 1. Describe social class and the role of women, indentured servants, and African Americans. 2. Discuss the relationship between English colonists and African Americans. 3. Explain why religious toleration and freedom developed during the colonial period.	Reproducible Lesson Plan Reteaching Activity 3-4 Section Quiz Chapter 3 Enrichment Activity Reinforcing Social Studies Skills 3, 27, 38, 40 American Portraits 6 Spanish Summaries & Glossary	Student Self-Test Software Testmaker Section Focus Transparency 11 Unit Digest Transparency Vocabulary Puzzlemaker Audiocassette, Chapter 3 The American People: Fabric of a Nation A Geographic Perspective on American History
CHAPTER REVIEW AND EVALUATION 1 Day	Chapter 3 Test Chapter 3 Performance Assessment Activity	Student Self-Test Software Testmaker

OUT OF TIME? If time does not permit teaching the entire chapter, use the Chapter 3 Summary on pages 84–85 and the Chapter 3 audiocassette (English and Spanish) to point out the main ideas of the chapter.

PLANNING GUIDE

Cultural Diversity Activity

Critical Thinking By 1775 American colonists could be divided into three groups. A third were of English origin. Another third were of various European nationalities and religions—Scotch Presbyterians, Irish Catholics, French Huguenots, Spanish Jews, German Lutherans. The rest were African Americans, slave and free. Have students research what members within each group had in common. For example, British settlers shared a common language, legal system, customs. Many other Europeans were dissenting or minority religious groups who had experienced persecution or minority status. African Americans came against their will and shared the memory of forced removal and of slavery. Have students speculate on the adjustments each group had to make to life in the colonies. What customs, skills, or traditions would help members make that adjustment? What customs or traditions might complicate or hamper that adjustment?

Performance Assessment Activity

Broadsides and Brochures Point out to students that promoters of the British colonies produced broadsides and brochures designed to entice people into becoming settlers. Organize students into groups of four or five to develop a broadside or brochure. Each group should select a specific colony and prepare an appropriate brochure illustrating the benefits that will accrue to those who settle there. Have each group present its broadside or brochure to the class.

POSSIBLE RUBRIC FEATURES: Content information, creativity, organization, written and pictorial communication skills, collaborative skills

Chapter Resources

Literature from the Period

Franklin, Benjamin. *Poor Richard's Almanac.* Houghton Mifflin, 1986.

Hammon, Jupiter. *America's First Negro Poet: The Complete Works of Jupiter Hammon of Long Island.* Stanley Austin Ransom, Jr., Kennikat Press, 1970.

Miller, Perry, and Thomas H. Johnson, eds. *The Puritans: A Source Book of Their Writings.* Harper & Row, 1963.

Readings for the Student

Boorstin, Daniel J. *The Americans: The Colonial Experience.* Random House, 1964.

Brandon, William. *Indians.* American Heritage, 1985.

Nash, Gary B. *Red, White, and Black: The Peoples of Early America*, 2nd ed. Prentice-Hall, 1982.

Ziner, Feenie. *Stories About the Pilgrims: Squanto.* Linnet Books, 1988.

Readings for the Teacher

Brandon, William. *The Last Americans: The Indian in American Culture.* McGraw-Hill, 1974.

Hawke, David Freeman. *Everyday Life in Early America.* Perennial Library, 1988.

Multimedia Resources

Colonial America. Mastervision. (VHS, 60 minutes)

Colonial Merchant. Educational Activities. (2 Apple diskettes)

Colonization: Exploring the New World. Tom Snyder Productions. (Apple or IBM PC diskette)

Key to Ability Levels

Teaching strategies have been coded for varying learning styles and abilities.

L1 Basic activities for all students

L2 Average activities for average to above-average students

L3 Challenging activities for above-average students

LEP Limited English Proficiency activities

Glencoe Links to the Humanities

Links to Art
- U.S. History & Art Transparency 3
- Focus on American History: Fine Art Prints, Unit 1

Link to Literature
- Macmillan Literature: American Literature Audiotapes Side 1
- Macmillan Literature: Novel Guides—*The Scarlet Letter* and *The Crucible*
- Macmillan Literature: American Literature Text—Anne Bradstreet, Edward Taylor, William Byrd

Link to Music
- American Music: Cultural Traditions

CHAPTER 3

BEGINNING THE CHAPTER

Ask students to imagine that they are about to make a long, hazardous journey to a new land of which they know nothing. Then ask: Why would you decide to make such a journey? What do you expect to find? Tell students that as they read this chapter they will discover how the first colonists answered these questions.

Recording Journal Notes

Tell students that their journal is a useful place to record their responses to the chapter events. Point out that history often has involved both conflict and consensus—general agreement about opinions and beliefs. Ask students to record ways in which people in the colonies came into conflict with one another and ways in which they reached a consensus.

Point out that the movement of people from Europe and Africa to North America in the 1600s and 1700s helped shape the character of colonial society. Today people coming from countries in Latin America and Asia are helping to shape American society.

CHAPTER 3

Colonial America
1578–1776

▶ Doctor's saddlebag

Setting the Scene

Focus

The British entered the race for colonial empire in the Americas in the early 1600s. Although their early efforts were not as dramatic as those of the Spanish, the British colonies became the most populous American settlements within a century of colonization. The British used their colonies as a source of raw materials and a market for manufactured goods. In time, a distinctly new American society emerged. This in turn led to tensions and strained relations between the colonies and Great Britain.

Concepts to Understand

★ How migration from Europe shaped the character of colonial society
★ What political, social, and religious values and beliefs the colonists brought to America

Read to Discover . . .

★ what contributed to the growth and success of the Middle Colonies, New England, and the Southern Colonies.
★ in what ways Americans differed from the British by 1750.

Journal Notes

In what ways did religious groups exert their influence? Note details about it in your journal as you read the chapter.

CULTURAL
- 1598 Spanish establish missions in present-day New Mexico
- 1647 Massachusetts establishes elementary schools
- 1654 First Jewish colonists arrive in New Amsterdam from Brazil

1570 — 1610 — 1650

POLITICAL
- 1607 English found Jamestown
- 1630 Massachusetts Bay becomes a haven for Puritan dissenters
- 1660 Navigation Acts passed

➕ EXTRA CREDIT PROJECT

Ask interested students to select one of the following groups and research the main economic, political, social, or religious factors that influenced or affected its settlements in the colonies: English, Scots, Irish, Scotch-Irish, Welsh, French, Germans, Dutch, Swedes, Finns, Spanish, Jews, Africans. Have students present their findings to the class in the form of a chart listing the original homeland, the reasons for coming, and the destination. Ask them to discuss those findings as they explain their charts to their classmates.

▼ COLONIAL GRINDSTONE

History AND ART

Hooker and Company Journeying through the Wilderness from Plymouth to Hartford in 1636
by Frederic Edwin Church, 1846

Many of Church's paintings show nature in repose. Like other artists aligned with the Hudson River School, Church focused on scenes of nature untouched by settlement.

- **1690** New England Primer, *first elementary textbook, published*
- **1701** French establish Fort Detroit
- **1733** *Georgia, last British colony in North America, founded*
- **1741** *Height of "Great Awakening" religious revival*
- **1772** *Americans set up committees of correspondence*
- **1774** *Mozart writes Mass in F Major*

| 1690 | 1730 | 1770 |

CHAPTER 3 Colonial America 1578–1776   55

Teacher Notes

CHAPTER 3 CONCEPTS

Concept Mapping Activity

Reproduce the following concept map on the chalkboard. Ask students to underscore the key words in the generalization. Then have students hypothesize about what topics may be covered in this chapter.

> A new culture took root in North America. The values and beliefs of this new culture developed as peoples from several parts of the world migrated to the continent.

| Migration | Values and Beliefs |

History AND ART

Settlers who wanted more freedom and richer farmland followed Thomas Hooker, a Puritan minister, to the fertile valley of the Connecticut River.

 VIDEODISC

- *GTV: A Geographic Perspective on American History*

Side 1, Chapter 6
Title: *Hoping for the Best in America*
Subject: Trials and triumphs of English settlers

See GTV Guide page 35 for complete lesson plan.

55

LESSON PLAN
SECTION 1, 56–62

FOCUS

Bellringer
Display Focus Activity Transparency 8 on the overhead projector and assign the accompanying Focus Activity Sheet.

Objectives
Point out the objectives on this page in previewing the section content.

Motivating Activity
Write on the chalkboard: "He that will not work shall not eat."

Have students write a sentence answering each of the following questions: What is your initial reaction to such a statement? What challenges do you think people were facing when this statement was issued? Tell students that the statement was a directive issued in 1608 to the people of Jamestown by Captain John Smith.

Use Skills Transparency 3.

NATIONAL GEOGRAPHIC SOCIETY

VIDEODISC
- *GTV: A Geographic Perspective on American History*

Side 1, Chapter 9
Title: *Settling Down, Moving On*
Subject: Regional differences emerge in the Colonies

See GTV Guide page 36 for complete lesson plan.

SECTION 1

The Southern Colonies

Setting the Scene

Section Focus

In the 1500s England's response to Spanish enterprise in America was nothing more creative than piracy of Spanish sea trade. By 1600, however, England had a naval power in the Atlantic, adequate finances for colonization, and a surplus population willing to take risks for religious, political, or economic reasons.

Objectives

After studying this section, you should be able to
★ explain the effect of the environment on Virginia's settlement and lifestyle.
★ describe the economic conditions that influenced the development of the Southern Colonies.

Key Terms

indentured servant, proprietor, subsistence farming, naval stores

▲ WOOD PLANE, 1600S

As early as 1578, Sir Humphrey Gilbert and Sir Walter Raleigh, his half brother, tried to plant a permanent English colony in North America. But on Gilbert's voyage back to England, his ships were lost at sea. In 1587 Raleigh sent 91 men, 17 women, and 9 children to settle on Roanoke Island near the coast of what is now North Carolina. He named the land "Virginia" in honor of the "Virgin Queen," Elizabeth I. This effort to build a colony failed because Spanish control of the Atlantic delayed Raleigh's efforts to resupply the settlement until after England defeated the Spanish Armada in 1588.

When English ships returned to Roanoke, they found none of the settlers. The only clue was a word carved on a tree—CROATOAN, the name of a Native American group and of a nearby island. The fate of the "Lost Colony" remains a mystery.

■ Jamestown, 1607

In 1606 King James I created the Virginia Company from two separate groups of merchants who had petitioned for permission to found colonies. Two divisions, the Virginia Company of London and the Virginia Company of Plymouth, were granted exclusive settlement rights in North America. The London group's charter permitted the planting of a colony in Virginia, where, it was believed, precious metals abounded.

The Struggle to Survive

In 1607 the London Company sent out 3 ships carrying 144 settlers. After being driven back by Native Americans on the first attempted landing in Virginia, they sought a more secure place for a settlement on a peninsula 60 miles up the James River. There they founded Jamestown.

Classroom Resources for SECTION 1

Teacher's Classroom Resources
- Chapter 3 Study Guide
- Reproducible Lesson Plan
- Reteaching Activity 3-1
- Chapter 3 Cooperative Learning Activity
- Chapter 3 Primary and Secondary Source Readings
- Section Quiz

Multimedia
- Section Focus Transparency 8
- Chapter 3 Skills Transparency
- Chapter 3 Map Transparency
- Testmaker
- Student Self-Test Software
- A Geographic Perspective on American History

The long ocean voyage, an outbreak of disease in the swampy and unhealthy settlement site, attacks, and starvation worked against the colonists. Captain John Smith led the colony through some of its most trying times. Mixing friendship, force, bluff, and bargaining, he saved the starving colony by trading beads, knives, pots, and fish hooks for corn, vegetables, turkeys, and venison from Native Americans.

Some of Jamestown's difficulties resulted from the London Company's poor management. Houses and buildings were the immediate need for the colonists, but the company had sent only four carpenters. Jamestown was a business venture for the London Company, expected to make a profit for its shareholders. For this reason the company supplied jewelers and goldsmiths and "gentlemen" who wanted to look for gold—not carpenters to build houses or farmers to raise crops for survival.

The tragic result was that most of the 500 colonists who came in the first few years died. George Percy, one of the survivors, wrote of the sufferings at Jamestown:

> Our men were destroyed with cruell diseases as Swellings, Flixes, Burning Fevers, and by warres, and some departed suddenly, but for the most part they died of mere famine. There were never Englishmen left in a forreigne Countrey in such miserie....

Effective leadership might have spared Jamestown these hardships. As it was, John Smith, injured in a gunpowder explosion, had returned to England in 1609, and not until 1611 did the company supply a new governor.

The End of the London Company

Mismanagement eventually cost the London Company its charter. By 1616 the investment made by company shareholders had brought no real profits. The company's reform program of 1618 expanded land sales, extended English law and rights to colonists, and allowed settlers to elect a representative assembly. Soon after, new recruits, including various craftspeople, arrived in Virginia. Even an additional 4,000 settlers did not end Virginia's troubles, however. Poor treatment of nearby Native Americans resulted in an attack that cost 350 lives. A royal investigation found that the badly governed settlers were dying faster

Settlement of the Colonies, 1587–1760

Legend: Settled by 1660 / Settled by 1700 / Settled by 1760 / Regional boundary

Map Study England's American colonies were founded along the Atlantic coast from present-day Maine to Georgia. **How did rivers and natural harbors influence settlement?**

CHAPTER 3 Colonial America 1578–1776 57

CHAPTER 3 SECTION 1

Fact or Fiction?

Virginia colonial law made slavery a permanent condition.

FACT: In 1662, the Virginia legislature passed a law declaring that an African American woman's newborn child would have the same status as the mother. Thus, the children of an enslaved woman would be enslaved too.

Did You Know?

Physicians (with university degrees), surgeons, and apothecaries (makers of medicine) came to Virginia on London Company ships.

Teaching Life of the Times

The "bride ship" was a joint stock venture, financed by a number of London Company officials. They made a 47-percent profit on their investment. Ask students to discuss why families would be important to the survival of a new colony.

Life of the Times

Bride Ships

The first colonists of the London Company in 1607 to inhabit Jamestown were men. Women did not arrive until several years later. The population remained heavily male for nearly two decades. A ratio of 15 men to 1 woman was the norm.

The London Company decided that "The Plantacion can never flourish till families be planted and the respect of wives and Children fix the people on the Soyle." In 1619 the members of the first legislative assembly agreed: "In a newe plantation it is not knowen whether man or women be more necessary." To solve the problem of the shortage of women, the London Company sent the first "bride ship" to America. Its passengers included nearly 100 "young, handsome, and honestly educated maids" suitable for marriage.

Cost of transport for these maidens was paid by the London Company. The average payment for a bride by a Virginia colonist was 120 pounds of tobacco, or about $20.

After a few instances in which a woman became engaged to two men at the same time, the London Company stopped sending bride ships. Instead, a type of travel brochure was written boasting of the advantages of living in the Americas.

▶ BRIDE SHIP ARRIVING AT JAMESTOWN

than they could be replaced. King James I dissolved the company and took control of the colony in 1624.

■ Growth of Virginia

From the native peoples, the settlers learned to grow corn, beans, squash, and tobacco. Despite the fact that King James I loathed tobacco, its use soon spread in England. As a result, tobacco became a profitable cash crop for Virginia. The native Virginia tobacco was of poor quality compared with that from the Spanish Caribbean islands, but in 1612 John Rolfe secured and planted some West Indies tobacco seeds. After this change, Virginia's tobacco exports grew rapidly. In 1640 almost 1.5 million pounds of tobacco entered the port of London.

Meeting the Demand for Labor

Tobacco, a labor-intensive crop, produced a great demand for colonists and farmers. Thousands of settlers streamed into Virginia, lured by the promise of free, abundant farmland. This source of labor was not enough, however.

To provide a work force, homeless children from the streets of London were sent to serve as apprentices to tradespeople in the colony. Convicts, farmers who had lost their lands, and the poor also came to share this opportunity.

A source of workers for wealthy settlers and tobacco farmers were the **indentured servants.** Indentured servants worked from four to seven years to pay off their passage across the Atlantic. After the period of indenture was completed, they were free to start their own farms.

Sidelights: Reluctant Immigrants

Not all those who set foot in the Americas came of their own free will. Among the unwilling immigrants were large numbers of British convicts. Beginning in the early 1600s, a steady flow of criminals—mostly those found guilty of capital crimes—were brought to the colonies to work on the farms and plantations. Thousands of felons were transported to North America, serving sentences of 7 or 14 years at hard labor. This practice came to an end in 1775 with the outbreak of the Revolutionary War.

The Introduction of Slave Labor

In 1619 a Dutch warship brought 20 enslaved Africans to Jamestown. Virginians, desiring an additional source of labor for their tobacco fields, purchased them. At first Africans were treated somewhat like indentured servants, many earning their freedom by several years of work. Slavery was first recognized in Virginia law in 1661. The following year, Virginia law declared that the status of a newborn child depended on the status of the mother. Slavery became a permanent, inherited condition. From 1600 to 1850, Europeans brought 15 million enslaved West Africans to the Americas.

■ Governing Virginia

In the 1660s an oversupply of tobacco pushed down its price. Only the very largest plantations were able to remain profitable. Many former indentured servants, now free, had to rent farmland or move west to

Economy of the Colonies

The American colonies carried on trade among themselves and with distant ports across the Atlantic. **Make a list of the items that the colonies imported and those they exported.**

CHAPTER 3 SECTION 1

Independent Practice

Science One of the Roanoke colonists, John White, painted pictures of the wildlife and native population of North America. Have students research and write a brief report on the impact that these paintings had on 16th-century science. **L2**

Map Study Using Maps
Answer:
imported: manufactured goods, enslaved people, molasses, coins; exported: tobacco, fur, fish, rum, rice, flour, meat, iron bars, lumber, indigo, naval stores

Skills Practice
Ask students to identify the major export crop of the West Indies. (sugar)

Linking Across TIME

Modern science has shown that James I's opinion of tobacco was correct. Medical research has found direct links between smoking tobacco and lung cancer and other respiratory diseases. What present-day protections exist against the development and sale of products that might be harmful to one's health? (Federal agencies like the Food and Drug Administration conduct extensive tests to ensure safety of new drugs.)

Critical Thinking

Identifying Cause and Effect Copy the following onto the chalkboard: 1. Jamestown's settlers searched for gold rather than building houses and raising crops. 2. The tobacco boom in Virginia created a great demand for labor. 3. The London Company permitted Virginia settlers to elect representatives to a legislative assembly.

Ask students to write an effect for each of these causes. (1. Many original settlers died, or settlement almost failed. 2. Thousands of men and women came to Virginia. 3. People of Virginia had a greater say in government.) **L1, L2**

CHAPTER 3 SECTION 1

Teaching American Portraits

Although members of the colonial assembly backed the governor's decision to deny Margaret Brent the vote, they recognized her ability. At the time of the rebellion, the colonial assembly issued a statement saying "it was better for the colony's safety at that time in her hands than in any man's else in the whole province." Ask students why they think the Maryland governor and colonial assembly denied Margaret Brent the vote. (The governor was following 17th-century standards: women were considered to be unfit to play a role in government.)

Did You Know?

By the end of the 1600s, enslaved people from Africa made up 11 percent of Maryland's population, 28 percent of Virginia's population, and 43 percent of the population of South Carolina.

Fact or Fiction?

Nathaniel Bacon and his followers briefly controlled most of Virginia.

FACT: Before his sudden death, wealthy planter Nathaniel Bacon burned the estates of his rivals and controlled most of Virginia.

AMERICAN PORTRAITS

Margaret Brent
1601–1671

Born a Roman Catholic at a time when England was denying Catholics many civil rights, Margaret Brent moved to Maryland in 1638. She quickly became one of the largest landowners, and, according to colonial records, was the first woman to own land in her own name.

Brave and forceful, Brent helped put down a rebellion from neighboring Virginia, and she took charge of paying Maryland's troops. Refusing to be confined to the restricted life of most colonial women, she later served as attorney for Lord Baltimore, Maryland's proprietor.

Brent came into conflict with the colonial government when she appeared before the assembly and demanded the right to vote. After the governor denied her claim, she moved to a large plantation in Virginia. There, the woman some call "America's first feminist" lived the rest of her life.

the interior, where they were exposed to attack. These depressed economic conditions produced bands of homeless people who wandered through the colony. In June 1676, Nathaniel Bacon brought together many people who were angry with the government of Virginia. In September Bacon's force burned Jamestown; Bacon died of dysentery, however, in October. Leaderless, the rebellion lost its momentum.

Changes in Labor

Wealthy planters began to rely less upon indentured servants and more upon enslaved people. Unlike indentured servants, enslaved persons could be denied their freedom permanently and could be punished without appeal to the courts. Because they were black, identification was easy and escape difficult. African slavery expanded rapidly in Virginia after 1670.

The Growth of Self-Government

In the beginning Virginia had been ruled by a council and an appointed governor. In 1619, however, the London Company gave the settlers a voice in the government by permitting the first representative assembly in America, the House of Burgesses. These burgesses and a council appointed by the governor together made the laws. When King James I took control from the London Company, making Virginia a royal colony, he appointed the governor but allowed the House of Burgesses to continue.

Over the years the House of Burgesses gained more power. It assumed control over taxes that paid the governor's and other officials' salaries—the "power of the purse."

■ Other Southern Colonies

Proprietors colonized Maryland, the Carolinas, and Georgia. Like Virginia, these colonies built their economies on crops suited to the land.

Maryland

In 1632 King Charles I gave his friend George Calvert, Lord Baltimore, a grant of 10 million acres north of Virginia. Calvert became **proprietor** of the Maryland colony, meaning that he had authority over its government. By 1634 his son, Cecil Calvert, sent

60 UNIT 1 A New World: Prehistory to 1776

Sidelights: Sports in the Colonies in the 1600s

The most popular spectator sports in the colonies during the 1600s were bull baiting, cockfighting, and horse racing. Bull baiting and cockfighting were open to all social classes, from the humblest farmhand to the wealthiest plantation owner. But horse racing was strictly for the gentry. One Chesapeake tailor, for example, was fined 100 pounds of tobacco for taking part in a race that was designated "for gentlemen only."

the first 200 settlers there. The Calverts intended Maryland to be a refuge for Catholics. Soon, however, more Protestants than Catholics were arriving. To protect Catholics from persecution, Cecil offered religious freedom to all Christian settlers. Later the legislative assembly of Maryland affirmed this freedom by the Toleration Act of 1649, the first of its kind in America.

Like Virginia, Maryland grew tobacco. Because of extensive farming, its towns were few and small. Baltimore, the chief city, had only 7,000 inhabitants by 1765.

The Carolinas

Profits from tobacco in Virginia and Maryland lured others to areas farther south along the Atlantic coast. In 1663 eight nobles received a grant to settle Carolina. From the start, northern Carolina was an area for **subsistence farming** where farmers grew only enough to live on. As northern Carolina grew, its principal exports became **naval stores**—tar, pitch, and turpentine—products of its pine forests that are used in shipbuilding.

Southern Carolina offered a better harbor than in the north and attracted more settlers. The first English colonists came from the West Indies island of Barbados to found the only major city in the South, Charles Town—present-day Charleston—in 1669. Some of these settlers had used slave labor on their sugar plantations in the Caribbean. With the thorough knowledge of rice-growing that the enslaved Africans brought, these settlers built plantations. Eliza Lucas, a settler from the West Indies, introduced the growing of indigo, a plant that produced a blue dye. By 1746 indigo had become an important cash crop.

Anthony Cooper, one of the proprietors, persuaded John Locke, an English political philosopher, to write a framework of government for South Carolina. The result was The Fundamental Constitutions of Carolina, providing for a legislature of wealthy nobles chosen by landholders. The proprietors surrendered control in 1729, and the king made both Carolinas royal colonies.

Georgia

Georgia, named after King George II, was the last of the 13 English colonies. Its proprietor, James Oglethorpe, a wealthy philanthropist and soldier, wanted Georgia to be both a refuge for debtors and a military outpost against the Spaniards in Florida. The first settlement, founded in 1733, was Savannah.

At first, Oglethorpe governed with strict controls, forbidding slavery and rum and controlling land sales. These restrictions limited Georgia's growth. In the 1740s the trustees who controlled Georgia lifted the restrictions against slavery and rum. They also let the colonists elect an assembly, but Georgia failed to prosper until after control was returned to the king in 1752.

Section 1 ★ Review

Checking for Understanding

1. **Define** indentured servant, proprietor, subsistence farming, naval stores.
2. **Compare** the organizations that established and governed the Southern Colonies with those that governed European nations.
3. **Explain** the factors that created hardships and initially limited the success of the Virginia colonies.
4. **Relate** the economic activity and conditions that prevailed in early Virginia to the development of the class system and slavery.

Critical Thinking

5. **Evaluating Social Changes** Planters prospered by growing tobacco. Today we know tobacco is an unhealthy substance. If tobacco were discovered today, do you think our government would permit its sale? Explain.

CHAPTER 3
SECTION 1

ASSESS

Check Understanding
Assign Section 1 Review as homework or an in-class activity.

Evaluate
Assign the Section 1 Quiz in the TCR or use the History of a Free Nation Testmaker to create a customized quiz.

Reteach
Have students complete Reteaching Activity 3-1.

Enrich
Read this quotation from a seventeenth-century colonist:
   "Tobacco is the current coin of Maryland and will sooner purchase commodities from the merchant than money."
   Then ask students to write a report on the role that tobacco played in the economy of the Southern colonies.

CLOSE
Ask students to discuss the role that Smith's leadership played in Jamestown's survival.

Answers to SECTION 1 REVIEW

1. All vocabulary terms are defined in the Glossary.
2. Private individuals or companies ran the colonies as business ventures. Nations and states were run by monarchs or other governmental bodies.
3. distance from England—hard to supply; hostility of Native Americans; swampy, unhealthy site; lack of skills among colonists and disinclination to work
4. Crops appropriate for the region were labor intensive and suited to large-scale production.
5. Answers may vary, with some saying no, because most addictive and cancer-causing substances are restricted or banned today. Others may believe tobacco to be more benign than most prohibited substances.

CHAPTER 3 CONNECTIONS

Teaching Making Connections

An investor in the first English joint-stock company noted that individual backing brought "cold comfort to adventures." Ask: What do you think he meant? (Individual investors could not provide comfort, in the form of funds, for colonial ventures.)

Did You Know?

By the 1630s, Dutch joint-stock companies dominated overseas trade in Western Europe. According to one estimate, Dutch traders owned four out of every five merchant ships in Europe.

CONNECTIONS  CONNECTIONS

Stock Exchanges

The age of exploration brought sweeping changes to European society and to culture. Overseas trade and colonial ventures stimulated the European economy and helped it develop and grow. Business practices and banking practices soon became more sophisticated in order to facilitate profit from the flourishing world trade.

Launching an overseas trading venture was a major financial undertaking. Merchants in the sixteenth century reduced the risks of ocean trade by forming trading companies. Governments of western European states controlled the trade of their merchants and provided company charters that included the rights of stock ownership. Shares of stock allow the buyer a certain part of the future profits and assets of the company selling the stock. The person buying stock, therefore, becomes part owner of a company.

The early trading companies eventually led to the establishment of joint-stock companies such as the Dutch United East India Company, formed in the early 1600s. In order to sell large blocks of shares to investors, this company created a stock exchange in Amsterdam. The money raised became a permanent fund the company could draw money from when it initiated trading ventures.

In 1650 the English adopted the Dutch method of creating a permanent fund to finance trading enterprises. Before 1773, however, when English investors wanted to buy or sell shares of stock, they had to locate a broker to carry out their transactions. Then the London brokers founded the first English stock exchange. The first stock exchanges in the United States were organized in Philadelphia in 1791 and in New York City a year later.

Not all the trading companies made money. England's Virginia Company was a costly failure, as were other European companies. By 1700, however, joint-stock companies had proved that free enterprise could raise the capital necessary for costly ventures, regardless of the risk.

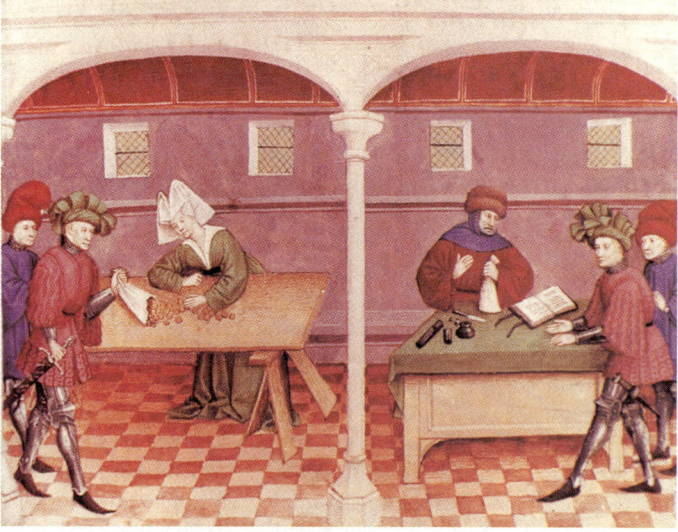

▲ COUNTING HOUSE

Making the Economics Connection

1. Why did merchants form joint-stock companies?
2. What advantage did the Dutch United East India Company have over English companies in 1690?

Linking Past And Present

3. What is a stock exchange? Do you consider buying stock today a form of investment or savings? Explain.

Answers to CONNECTIONS

1. to raise money for trading ventures
2. Sold shares on stock exchange and had permanent fund for future ventures.
3. place in which shares of stock in companies are sold

SECTION 2

New England

Setting the Scene

Section Focus

The Virginia Company of Plymouth sent Captain John Smith to explore the region north of Virginia, which he named "New England." When New England was settled, it was by accident rather than design by people seeking a religious haven, not investors seeking a fortune.

Objectives

After studying this section, you should be able to

★ explain the relationship of church and state in the New England colonies.

★ list three reasons why self-government developed in New England.

Key Terms

dissenter, congregation, commonwealth, constitution

▲ WILLIAM BRADFORD'S BIBLE

The Church of England—the Anglican Church—broke away from the Catholic Church in 1534. Some Anglicans, called Puritans, believed that the Church of England had not done enough to "purify" itself of all symbols of Catholic worship. Most Puritans wanted to reform the Church of England. One group, called Separatists, believed that it was better to separate themselves entirely and to form their own church. Because the Anglican Church was the official state church, Separatists, like all other religious **dissenters,** or protesters, faced persecution, jail, and even death.

In 1607 a group of Separatists, soon to be known as Pilgrims, left England to escape persecution. They settled in Holland (known today as the Netherlands), where, despite the freedom to worship as they pleased, they were dissatisfied. Their children grew up speaking a different language and learning new customs. Where might they maintain their language, customs, and form of worship? America beckoned.

■ On to Plymouth

In 1619 the Pilgrims secured a grant of land in Virginia from the London Company. After much preparation, in September 1620, 73 men and boys and 29 women and girls set sail on the *Mayflower* from Plymouth, England. Violent storms blew the ship off course. In November the ship landed far to the north of Virginia on the Massachusetts coast. Because they had no charter for an area outside the control of the London Company, the Pilgrims drew up the Mayflower Compact. It was a simple document that expressed their feelings that a government derives its just powers from the people who are governed.

CHAPTER 3 Colonial America 1578–1776   63

Classroom Resources for SECTION 2

Teacher's Classroom Resources
- Reproducible Lesson Plan
- Reteaching Activity 3-2
- Section Quiz

Multimedia
- Section Focus Transparency 9
- Testmaker
- Student Self-Test Software
- The American People: Fabric of a Nation

LESSON PLAN
SECTION 2, 63–67

FOCUS

Bellringer

Prior to taking roll at the beginning of the class period, display Focus Activity 9 on the overhead projector and assign the accompanying Focus Activity Sheet.

Objectives

Point out the objectives on this page to students in previewing the section content.

Motivating Activity

Ask students to imagine that they are religious dissenters in England in the early 1600s. Read to them the following statement made by James I:

"I will make [the dissenters] conform themselves or I will harry [force] them out of the land."

Have students discuss the options open to them by asking: What will you do? Why? As they read this section, ask students to note how the Pilgrims and the Puritans answered these questions.

 **VIDEODISC**

- *GTV: The American People: Fabric of a Nation*

Side 1, Chapter 6
Title: *A New England?*
Subject: English ways dominate colonial life

See GTV Guide page 50 for complete lesson plan.

63

CHAPTER 3 SECTION 2

TEACH

Guided Practice

Geography Have students write a brief essay comparing the settlements at Jamestown and Plymouth from a geographical perspective. Suggest that their essays cover points such as location, landforms, natural vegetation, and climate. **L2**

Fact or Fiction?

In the description of the first Thanksgiving celebrated by the Pilgrims, William Bradford mentioned turkeys.

FACT: Besides wild turkey, he listed as food cod, bass, "other fish," waterfowl, venison, meal, and Indian corn.

Visualizing History Unlike the leaders and owners of other colonies, the Pilgrims never obtained a charter of government from the English.
Answer to Caption: an agreement to obey laws made by leaders they chose

Did You Know?

Most of the passengers aboard the *Mayflower* were not Pilgrims. Only 35 of the 101 passengers were members of the Separatist group that had settled in the Netherlands.

The First Year's Hardships

In the bleak, cold, snowy New England winter, the Pilgrims, like the Virginia colonists, had their "starving time." By spring almost half of them had died. Even the few survivors might have starved if it had not been for Squanto of the Pawtuxet people, who taught them about their new environment. William Bradford, one of the colonists, wrote that Squanto "directed them how to set their corn, where to take fish, and to procure other commodities" and that he was also their pilot "to bring them to unknown places for their profit, and never left them until he died."

The First Thanksgiving

The Pilgrims' deep sense of religious purpose and determination to endure hardships sustained the colony. In 1621 the survivors elected Bradford governor, a post that he would hold for more than 30 years. In the spring they planted crops. A good harvest in the autumn and the arrival of more provisions on the ship *Fortune* inspired a day of thanksgiving to God.

More Settlers Arrive

Additional settlers from England built a cluster of small villages near Plymouth, but the colony never became very large. It elected its own officials and ran its own affairs until 1691, when it became part of the larger Massachusetts Bay Colony.

■ Puritan Massachusetts

In 1625 when Charles I became king of England, he decided to rule without Parliament and to suppress Puritanism. When Puritan ministers were deprived of their pulpits, the dissenters turned their thoughts

 ▲ **SIGNING THE MAYFLOWER COMPACT** Pilgrims on board the *Mayflower* signed a compact, or agreement, to obey the officers elected and the laws passed. All those who signed received the right to share in the government. *What was the intent of the Compact?*

UNIT 1 A New World: Prehistory to 1776

Sidelights: The Puritan Ethic

The qualities that helped the settlers of the Massachusetts Bay Colony to succeed—discipline, industry, learning, and stubbornness—are usually referred to as the "Puritan ethic." Some historians have suggested that this ethic has become deeply embedded in the American character, emerging in varying forms at different historical periods. The "rugged individualism" of those who settled the West and the self-sacrifice of Americans during World War II, these historians argue, are but two aspects of the Puritan ethic.

 ▲ PILGRIMS GOING TO CHURCH by George H. Boughton, 1867 Religion was important in Pilgrim life. *What evidence shown in this picture suggests that the settlers did not yet feel safe?*

to America. Several prominent Puritans bought a trading company, changed its name to the Massachusetts Bay Company, and secured a charter directly from the king. Twelve members signed an agreement at Cambridge in 1629.

This marked the beginning of the great Puritan migrations to New England to build a Christian society they believed would be a lighthouse for all the world. The first governor of Massachusetts, John Winthrop, made their intentions clear:

> We shall be as a city upon a hill. The eyes of all people are upon us.

In 1630, 17 ships with about 1,000 Puritan settlers sailed for Massachusetts. During the next 10 years, 20,000 settlers followed. Boston, the leading town, and surrounding settlements such as Dorchester, Roxbury, Watertown, and Charlestown, flourished.

Congregationalists

When they left England, the Puritans thought of themselves as members of the Anglican Church. As they settled Massachusetts, they organized their churches under ministers elected by each **congregation,** or a body of church members. The ministers set about reforming religious ceremonies, while the congregation became the final authority on church decisions. Compared to the Anglican clergy, the New England minister had limited authority. He was to teach, preach, pray, and administer; but the congregation held power over membership and church discipline. In the colonies, the Puritans became known as Congregationalists.

From Trading Company to Commonwealth

The Massachusetts Bay charter, unlike those of other colonies, did not specify the location of the company's headquarters or where its shareholders' meetings would be held. Taking advantage of this loophole, the shareholders voted to move the company from England to Massachusetts. Governor John Winthrop carried the charter across the Atlantic Ocean, where shareholders would have more freedom from the king's control. Winthrop transformed the Massachusetts Bay Company from a trading company into a **commonwealth**, a self-governing political unit, the first of its kind in America.

In the beginning, the few shareholders of the Massachusetts Bay Company, called "freemen," held all the power in the colony. Under Governor Winthrop, these shareholders made up the General Court, or the lawmaking body. Soon, however, more

CHAPTER 3 SECTION 2

Did You Know?

Even though he was a vociferous supporter of Native Americans, Roger Williams still looked on them as inferior and flawed. For example, he felt that deviousness and treachery were natural qualities of all Native Americans.

Using Charts

From 1701 to 1710, the Southern Colonies were responsible for about 67 percent of the combined value of the total overseas trade (imports and exports) between the colonies and Britain; the New England Colonies for about 22 percent; and the Middle Colonies for only about 11 percent.
Answer:
seven

Food of the Times

Few colonists treated sugar casually. One observer notes that families kept their sugar loaves under lock and key. Popular and less costly substitutes were molasses, maple sugar, and honey.

The American Colonies, 1607–1776

Colony and date of settlement	Founders	Type of government
NEW ENGLAND		
Plymouth Colony 1620	Pilgrims	Charter, 1620–1686; Part of Massachusetts, 1691–1776
New Hampshire 1623	Puritans, Proprietors	Proprietary, 1629–1679; Royal, 1679–1776
Massachusetts Colony 1630	Puritans	Charter, 1629–1686; Royal, 1691–1776
Rhode Island 1636	Roger Williams	Charter, 1644–1776
Connecticut 1636	Thomas Hooker	Charter, 1662–1776
MIDDLE COLONIES		
New York (New Netherland) 1626	Dutch West India Company	Dutch charter, 1626–1664; Proprietary, 1664–1685; Royal, 1685–1776
New Jersey (as part of New Netherland) 1626	Dutch West India Company	Dutch charter, 1626–1664; Proprietary, 1664–1702; Royal, 1702–1776
Delaware (New Sweden) 1638	Swedish West India Company	Swedish charter, 1638–1655; Dutch charter, 1655–1664; Proprietary, 1664–1776
Pennsylvania 1682	William Penn	Proprietary, 1681–1776
SOUTHERN COLONIES		
Virginia 1607	London Company	Charter, 1606–1624; Royal, 1624–1776
Maryland 1634	George Calvert (Lord Baltimore)	Proprietary, 1632–1691; Royal, 1691–1715; Proprietary, 1715–1776
North Carolina 1650	Proprietors	Proprietary, 1663–1729; Royal, 1729–1776
South Carolina 1670	Proprietors	Proprietary, 1663–1729; Royal, 1729–1776
Georgia 1733	James Oglethorpe	Proprietary, 1732–1752; Royal, 1752–1776

Chart Study Most of the 13 colonies (Plymouth became part of Massachusetts) were founded under charters issued to investing companies. By 1752, however, 8 colonies had come under the direct control of the monarch. *How many colonies that were once controlled by proprietors became royal colonies?*

than 100 colonists demanded to be admitted to the company as freemen. Under pressure, Governor Winthrop consented to the demands of the freemen.

A law passed in 1631 gave all Puritan men who were church members admission to the General Court as freemen. When the population grew too large to operate the government in this way, the Massachusetts Bay Company made a change. The company allowed the freemen in each town to elect two representatives to the General Court. What began as a directors' meeting of a trading company ended up as a colonial legislature with power to make law.

■ Dissent and Division

The Puritans who came to Massachusetts to worship as they pleased had no intention of granting this freedom to others. They drove out Baptists, Quakers, and others who disagreed with them. Others simply left to find more fertile land. Those who left founded other colonies in New England.

Rhode Island

Roger Williams arrived in the Massachusetts Bay Colony in 1631. According to William Bradford, Williams was "a man

---

Critical Thinking

Recognizing Bias Point out that the word *puritan* originally meant "pure of heart." Over time, however, it came to mean someone who is narrow-minded and excessively attached to certain beliefs. Read the following quotation by the essayist H.L. Mencken:

"Puritanism is the haunting fear that someone, somewhere, may be happy."

Then ask: Judging from your knowledge of the Puritans, is this a fair comment? Why might people feel this way about Puritanism? **L2, L3**

godly and zealous but very unsettled in judgment." When Williams became pastor of a church in Salem, he began to raise embarrassing issues. He preached that the church and government should remain separate because involvement in political affairs would corrupt the church. He also asserted that the colonists had no right to settle on the land unless the land was purchased from the Native American people. Finally, he challenged the right of Puritan rulers to compel people to take part in religious services. Because Williams's views threatened basic Puritan ideas, Winthrop and the General Court banished him from the colony.

Facing deportation to England, Williams fled south and spent the winter with friendly Narragansetts. In 1636 he started the colony of Rhode Island on land purchased from the Native Americans. The new colony, chartered in 1644, welcomed Jews as well as all Christians and guaranteed their religious freedom. In Rhode Island church and state were completely separate, a principle that was to become an important part of America's political heritage.

▲ ANNE HUTCHINSON

New Settlements

Not long after Williams departed, Massachusetts faced a similar challenge. Anne Hutchinson began to openly challenge Puritan ministers and their interpretations of the Bible. When her teachings attracted a growing band of disciples, authorities brought her to trial. Ordered to leave the colony, she went to Rhode Island to begin a new settlement later called Portsmouth.

In 1637 the Reverend John Wheelwright, one of the few ministers Anne Hutchinson admired, was also expelled from Massachusetts for criticizing Puritan teaching. He and his followers settled in New Hampshire. Following the example of the Mayflower Compact, they created and signed the Exeter Compact and set up a civil government. In 1679 New Hampshire obtained a charter from King Charles II. Other pioneer settlers pushed farther north into Maine, which remained part of Massachusetts until 1820.

In 1636 settlers who wanted richer farmland and more freedom followed Thomas Hooker, a Puritan minister, to the fertile valley of the Connecticut River. Hartford and a series of other "river towns" sprang up along the river. Later, these communities annexed New Haven and other towns to form the colony of Connecticut. In 1639 the colony adopted the Fundamental Orders of Connecticut, the first written **constitution**, or plan of government, in America. It provided for a representative government similar to the one in Massachusetts, except that voting for representatives and government was not limited to church members.

Section 2 ★ Review

Checking for Understanding

1. **Identify** Mayflower Compact, Squanto, Roger Williams, Anne Hutchinson, Exeter Compact.
2. **Define** dissenter, congregation, commonwealth, constitution.
3. **Explain** the objectives of the Puritans and Pilgrims in settling the Massachusetts Bay Colony.
4. **Discuss** the relationship of church and state in New England.

Critical Thinking

5. **Analyzing Motives** Most New England colonies were settled by people escaping religious persecution. Which of these groups sought true religious freedom? How did they differ from the others?

CHAPTER 3 Colonial America 1578–1776

LESSON PLAN
Mastering Social Studies Skills

Teaching Interpreting Primary Sources

Have students choose a document they have filled out—for example, a tax form or a school or job application—and list the kinds of information one could learn about the student by reading it. (Answers could include personal data, interests, job and educational background, and so on.) Discuss students' responses. Ask: What information do such documents provide about our culture? Do they provide a definitive story or do they tell just part of the story? Point out that historians use documents to gain information about individuals and about society as a whole.

Did You Know?

Husbands in colonial society controlled the property of their wives. If a woman worked for money—for example, as a tavern keeper, printer, upholsterer, or silversmith—she was probably single or a widow carrying on her husband's business.

Social Studies Skills

Interpreting Primary Sources

▲ PURITANS SUBJECTING WRONGDOERS TO PUBLIC RIDICULE

Women in the Colonies

Historians have used documents, such as the following from the records of the Suffolk County Court in Massachusetts, to uncover information about colonial women. Read the excerpts below and answer the questions.

Order abt Hitt (8 July, 1674)
In Answer to the request of Anne Hitt widdow . . . that Shee might have Liberty to dispose of & put to Sale some part of [her husband's] Estate for the paiment of debts & Legacies & maintenance of herselfe & Children: The Court Orders & Empowres the saide Anne Hitt (with the consent & advice) of those that are Sureties for her true Administracion upon the saide Estate) to dispose of & put to Sale the house & ground at Charlestown valued in the Inventory at £:170. Shee rendring an Account of Sd Sale unto the Court of this County.

Walsebee's discharge (28 April, 1674)
The wife of David Walsebee of Brantery being presented for her Idleness and sottish carriage [drunken behavior]. *upon hearing of the case The Court judge there is noe ground for the presentment & soe discharge her.*

Examining the Primary Source

1. List examples in the colonial documents of alphabetical, spelling, and capitalization changes that have appeared in the English language since these documents were written.
2. What freedom was originally denied Anne Hitt that resulted in the court order?

Critical Thinking

3. **Drawing Conclusions** What does the charge against the wife of David Walsebee indicate about the manners expected of women?

Answers to SOCIAL STUDIES SKILLS

1. Answers may vary but should include: A *u* was employed, where today we might use a *v* (*respectiuely*); conversely, a *v* was sometimes used where we would use a *u* (*vnder*); the word *license* is no longer capitalized; the final *e* has been dropped in *shee, childe,* and *herselfe.*
2. She did not own the property jointly with her husband. The court had to grant her the right to own and dispose of property.
3. The charge indicates that women could be arrested for looking idle or not carrying themselves properly. Also that people were brought to court for what we regard as moral rather than legal matters.

SECTION 3

The Middle Colonies

Setting the Scene

Section Focus

From 1640 to 1660 a bitter struggle for power between the king and Parliament postponed further colonization in America. Parliament overthrew King Charles I in 1649 and established a commonwealth under Puritan Oliver Cromwell. When the monarchy was restored in 1660, the new king, Charles II, revived English interest in starting new colonies. He rewarded some of his supporters by granting them proprietorships. These became the Middle Colonies.

Objectives

After studying this section, you should be able to
★ describe the role of proprietors in the development of the Middle Colonies.
★ give reasons for Pennsylvania's rapid growth.

Key Term

patroon

▶ PINE TREE SHILLING, 1652

England's neglect of the American colonies between 1640 and 1660 enabled traditions of self-government to develop firmly in America. Colonial legislatures in New England and the South made their own laws, and local courts enforced them. Colonists frequently defied or ignored orders from England and even from their own colonial governors. The Middle Colonies also developed a degree of independence from England.

■ New York

In 1664 King Charles II granted his brother James, the Duke of York, the land west and south of New England, from the Connecticut River to the Delaware River. He did this even though the territory had already been settled by the Dutch. For years the English had viewed the Dutch colony as a threat because of its trade, its expanding settlements, and its location as a wedge between New England to the north and Virginia to the south. Consequently, in 1664 the Duke of York sent a fleet of four English warships to capture the settlement of New Amsterdam. Peter Stuyvesant (STY•vuh•sant), the Dutch governor of New Netherland, tried to defend the colony. But he lacked the support of his own colonists and was forced to surrender New Netherland without a struggle. The Duke of York did not hesitate to change the colony's name to New York.

Colonial Government

Governors appointed by the Duke of York ruled New York until 1683, when the Duke agreed to demands for an elected representative assembly. Two years later, however, the Duke of York became King James II,

CHAPTER 3 Colonial America 1578–1776   **69**

Classroom Resources for SECTION 3

Teacher's Classroom Resources
- Reproducible Lesson Plan
- Reteaching Activity 3-3
- Section Quiz

Multimedia
- Section Focus Transparency 10
- Chapter 3 History and Art Transparency
- Testmaker
- Student Self-Test Software

LESSON PLAN
SECTION 3, 69–72

FOCUS

Bellringer
Prior to taking roll at the beginning of the class period, display Focus Activity 10 on the overhead projector and assign the accompanying Focus Activity Sheet.

Objectives
Point out the objectives on this page to students in previewing the section content.

Motivating Activity
William Penn said that Pennsylvania would be "a commonwealth founded on the principle of brotherly love."
Ask students to infer what impact Penn's statement had on the growth of Pennsylvania.

TEACH

Guided Practice
Cultural Diversity The Dutch influence in American history can be seen in some of the place names in New Jersey and New York—Kinderhook and Hoboken, for example. Have students use atlases to locate and list 10 Dutch place names. **L1**

Independent Practice
Government Have students compare and contrast the three types of colonies: corporate, proprietary, royal. **L1**

69

CHAPTER 3
SECTION 3

Visualizing History  The influence of early Dutch architecture is still evident in some American buildings, both old and new, in the use of Dutch stepped gables and Flemish curvilinear gables.

Answer to Caption: The Dutch set up trading companies to explore and claim land and to establish settlements.

 **VIDEODISC**

- *GTV: The American People: Fabric of a Nation*

Side 1, Chapter 7
Title: *A Mixed Bag*
Subject: Diversity in the Colonies

See GTV Guide page 52 for complete lesson plan.

 ▲ **CLAIMS FOR THE NETHERLANDS** While the Spaniards searched for gold and the French searched for furs, Dutch leaders wanted new lands for trade centers. *How did the Dutch acquire claims?*

making New York a royal colony. He dissolved the assembly and returned full power to the governor.

When the English overthrew James II in the Glorious Revolution of 1688, Jacob Leisler, a German trader, led a rebellion in New York. He established a government with an elected assembly that lasted until 1690, when a new British royal governor arrived. The new governor captured Leisler and put him on trial. Leisler was convicted and the governor had him hanged. The governor, however, permitted the colony to continue to elect an assembly.

Limited Growth

Several factors delayed New York's rapid growth. Few settlers came because large landowners, called **patroons,** still held much of the land along the Hudson River. The French in Canada prevented expansion to the north, and the Iroquois Confederacy blocked expansion westward. New York City's magnificent harbor made it a natural trade center, but for many years the small population of the colony did not supply enough goods for export.

A Diverse Population

New York's varied population included Dutch, Swedes, Native Americans, Africans, Jews, some English and French settlers, and people of many other nationalities. But Dutch customs remained strong, and the Dutch Calvinist churches endured. The city, as it appeared in 1679, was described by a Dutch traveler, Jasper Dankers:

> [The fort] has only one gate, and that is on the land side, opening upon a broad plain or street, called the Broadway or Beaverway. Over this gate are the arms of the Duke of York.... We went on up the hill, along open roads and a little woods, through the first village, called Breukelen [Brooklyn]....

■ New Jersey

Shortly after the Duke of York received his grant of land in 1664, he started giving out parts of it to his friends. He gave New

70 UNIT 1 A New World: Prehistory to 1776

Cultural Diversity

A trading company owned by Dutch and Swedish investors founded the colony of New Sweden in 1638 in a region inhabited by the Delaware, a Native American people. There settlers built Fort Christiana (present-day Wilmington, Delaware). Three years later, Swedish investors bought control of the company. Increasing conflict between the Swedish settlement and nearby Dutch forts led to the end of Swedish rule in 1655. The British, in turn, took control from the Dutch a few years later.

Jersey to John Lord Berkeley and Sir George Carteret. Finding it sparsely inhabited, these proprietors offered religious freedom and large land grants.

In 1674 Berkeley sold his proprietary rights in western New Jersey to members of a religious group called the Society of Friends, or Quakers, who were seeking escape from persecution. In 1682 Carteret's heirs sold eastern New Jersey to another Quaker group. The English government created the royal colony of New Jersey by combining the two parts, placing it under the authority of New York's governor in 1702.

Penn's Colonies

William Penn started the most successful colony in America. The son of a British admiral, Penn won the favor of both King Charles II and King James II. To his father's dismay, however, Penn had joined the Quakers when he was a student at Oxford. Quakers were considered religious radicals in England because they believed that paid clergy were unnecessary and that every person could know God's will through his or her own "inner light." They were detested in England and persecuted as anarchists in America.

Pennsylvania

Neither his father's anger nor jail could make Penn give up his views, and King Charles II remained his friend. Penn wanted to start a colony in America that would serve as a refuge for persecuted Quakers. After his father's death, Penn took advantage of a debt that Charles II owed Admiral Penn, asking the king for land in America. In 1681 Charles II made Penn the proprietor of a vast area west of the Delaware named "Penn's Woods," or Pennsylvania.

Arriving in Pennsylvania in 1682, Penn worked out a plan for a "city of brotherly love," Philadelphia. His agents advertised

▲ **WILLIAM PENN**

▲ **WILLIAM PENN'S TREATY WITH THE INDIANS** by Edward Hicks, 1830–1840 Although the overall English policy toward Native Americans was harsh, some settlers did treat the Native Americans favorably. **What details in the painting give you clues about the Native Americans' relationship with William Penn?**

CHAPTER 3 SECTION 3

History AND ART

Hicks created about 100 versions of this painting, thus showing his Quaker belief that Pennsylvania was a place in which the biblical prophecy of justice and peace on earth would be fulfilled. **Answer to Caption:** Pennsylvania leaders and Native Americans sign a peace treaty.

Did You Know?

In present-day Delaware, place names still reflect the cultural diversity of its early inhabitants: Delaware (Native American), Christiana (Swedish), Vandyke (Dutch), and Dover (English).

FACT or FICTION?

Descendants of the Dutch people who settled in eastern Pennsylvania in the 1700s are known as the Pennsylvania Dutch.

FICTION: The Pennsylvania Dutch are descendants of German, not Dutch, settlers. The confusion arose because the German word for "German" is *Deutsch*.

Cooperative Learning

Organize students into groups of five, and assign a number from one through five to the members of each group. Have the groups work on preparing answers for the Section Review questions on page 72. After the work is completed, call out a number and have all students with that number stand. Select one of these students to answer one of the questions. If the answer is incomplete, call on another student with that number to complete it. Continue calling out numbers until all questions have been answered satisfactorily. **L2, L3**

CHAPTER 3
SECTION 3

Visualizing History William Penn had originally planned that each house in the new city of Philadelphia would be built in the center of a plot of land, surrounded by gardens, fruit trees, and greenery.
Answer to Caption: to attract settlers

ASSESS
Check Understanding
Assign Section 3 Review as homework or an in-class activity.

Evaluate
Assign the Section 3 Quiz in the TCR or use the History of a Free Nation Testmaker to create a customized quiz.

Reteach
Have students complete Reteaching Activity 3-3.

Enrich
Ask students to complete the following sentence:
   William Penn's vision of America was different because....

CLOSE
Have students compare the reasons that the Middle Colonies were founded with the reasons that the Southern and New England Colonies were founded.

 ▲ **PHILADELPHIA** William Penn founded Philadelphia on the west banks of the Delaware River not far from the Atlantic coast. The city grew quickly and by the middle of the 1700s was the largest city in the American colonies. *What was the first major task in a new settlement?*

for settlers from Europe. Their promises of religious freedom and tolerance attracted many other groups besides the Quakers, especially Germans.

Because Penn believed in equality, he drew up a "Frame of Government" that provided for an elected council and an assembly. Pennsylvania gave the right to vote to a large number of colonists. Penn also insisted that Native Americans be paid for their land.

These measures meant rapid growth for the colony. By the time Penn left for England in 1684, there were 7,000 colonists. When he returned in 1699, Philadelphia rivaled Boston and New York City as both a commercial and cultural center. Thousands of prosperous farms dotted the countryside.

A boundary dispute with Maryland to the south led to the hiring of two surveyors, Mason and Dixon, to draw borders between the two colonies. This border became known as the Mason-Dixon Line.

Delaware

In 1682 William Penn bought the three counties south of Pennsylvania along the Atlantic Coast from the Duke of York. These "lower counties," known as Delaware, had first been settled by the Dutch, then the Swedes, before the English captured them in 1664. Although Delaware was not part of Penn's grant from the king, he allowed the lower counties to elect their own assembly.

Section 3 ★ Review

Checking for Understanding
1. **Identify** Quakers, Duke of York, William Penn, Mason and Dixon.
2. **Define** patroon.
3. **Discuss** the role of proprietors in the political and economic development of the Middle Colonies. Compare how they pursued their personal goals.
4. **Explain** the conditions, in England and in the Middle Colonies, that supported the development of self-government in the Middle Colonies.

Critical Thinking
5. **Supporting an Opinion** Argue for or against this statement: In the Middle Colonies, democracy developed more because of its economic advantages than because of ideology.

UNIT 1 A New World: Prehistory to 1776

Answers to SECTION 3 REVIEW
1. Duke of York, 69; Quakers, 71; William Penn, 71; Mason and Dixon, 72
2. All vocabulary words are defined in the Glossary.
3. Colonies founded by proprietors with grants from king, pursued various personal goals.
4. England preoccupied by internal struggle for power, leave colonies alone, democracy and self-government attract settlers and increase profits, Penn's values and beliefs.
5. Answers may vary. Supporters may say democracy was expedient to attract settlers and boost profits. Others may credit idealists such as Penn.

SECTION 4

People of the Colonies

Setting the Scene

Focus

By the mid-1700s, colonial society differed from Britain in many ways. A diversity of peoples and new economic opportunities helped to produce a society uniquely American. The history of social development in America is a story of progress for many. It is blemished by the enslavement of Africans and the eviction of Native Americans from their lands.

Objectives

After studying this section, you should be able to
★ describe social class and the role of women, indentured servants, and African Americans.
★ discuss the relationship between English colonists and Native Americans.
★ explain why religious toleration and freedom developed during the colonial period.

Key Term

gentry

◀ CHILDREN'S DOLLS

By European standards the society of Elizabethan England was remarkably mobile. An apprentice might become rich and marry his daughter to a noble. In turn, a noble's younger son, who inherited no property, might become an apprentice or hire himself out as a soldier. Like England, the colonies' social structure had many classes, but from the start it was more democratic.

■ Colonial Social Classes

In each of the 13 colonies there was an upper class. In New England, merchants, shipowners, and the clergy composed this class. In the South and along the Hudson River in New York, great landowners imitated the country **gentry**, or upper class, of England. Early colonial laws permitted only upper-class men to wear silver buttons and upper-class women and girls to wear silk dresses. Social rank was indicated on marriage certificates and even on tombstones.

Near the bottom of society were indentured servants, bound by contract to work in the colonies in return for their passage to America. When the contract expired, the servant was free to work for wages. Because labor was scarce, wages in the colonies were 2 or 3 times those in England. Indentured servants could move up in society. For example, in the 1660s, 13 of 28 members of the Virginia House of Burgesses had come to the colony as indentured servants.

Life in the Colonies

For most people, life in colonial America was better than it had been in Europe. Still, many died within the first year because of hardships encountered during the ocean voyage. Frontier settlements faced conflict

CHAPTER 3 Colonial America 1578–1776   73

Classroom Resources for SECTION 4

Teacher's Classroom Resources
- Reproducible Lesson Plan
- Reteaching Activity 3-4
- Chapter 3 Enrichment Activity
- Chapter 3 Performance Assessment Activity
- Spanish Summaries and Glossary
- Section Quiz

Multimedia
- Section Focus Transparency 11
- Chapter 3 Unit Digest Transparency
- Vocabulary Puzzlemaker
- Student Self-Test Software
- The American People: Fabric of a Nation
- A Geographic Perspective on American History

LESSON PLAN
SECTION 4, 73–79

FOCUS

Bellringer
Prior to taking roll at the beginning of the class period, display Focus Activity 11 on the overhead projector and assign the accompanying Focus Activity Sheet.

Objectives
Point out the objectives on this page to students in previewing the section content.

Motivating Activity
Have students carefully read the following quotation from Benjamin Franklin's *Poor Richard's Almanac* (1775): "The day is short, the work great, the workmen lazy, the wages high, the master urgeth. Up then, and be doing." Then ask: What word would you use to characterize the life described in the quotation? Tough? Challenging? Boring? Rewarding? Give reasons for your choice.

 VIDEODISC
- *GTV: A Geographic Perspective on American History*

Side 1, Chapter 12
Title: *The Rise of Cities*
Subject: Urban life in the colonies

See GTV Guide page 37 for complete lesson plan.

73

CHAPTER 3 SECTION 4

TEACH

Guided Practice
Sociology
Ask students to write a sentence that makes a generalization about each of the following subjects: colonial social classes, women in the colonies, slavery in the colonies, and Native Americans and colonists. **L2**

Map Study Using Maps
Answer:
the English

Skills Practice
Ask students which immigrant group was predominant along the eastern side of the Appalachian Mountains in the Southern Colonies. (Scotch-Irish)

Independent Practice
Literature Have students use Benjamin Franklin's *Poor Richard's Almanac* to locate and list five or ten sayings that are well-known American proverbs. Offer the following examples: "God helps them that help themselves" and "Necessity never made a good bargain." Use the students' lists as the starting point for a class discussion on the following: Benjamin Franklin was a man of the "most useful and ingenious" learning. **L2**

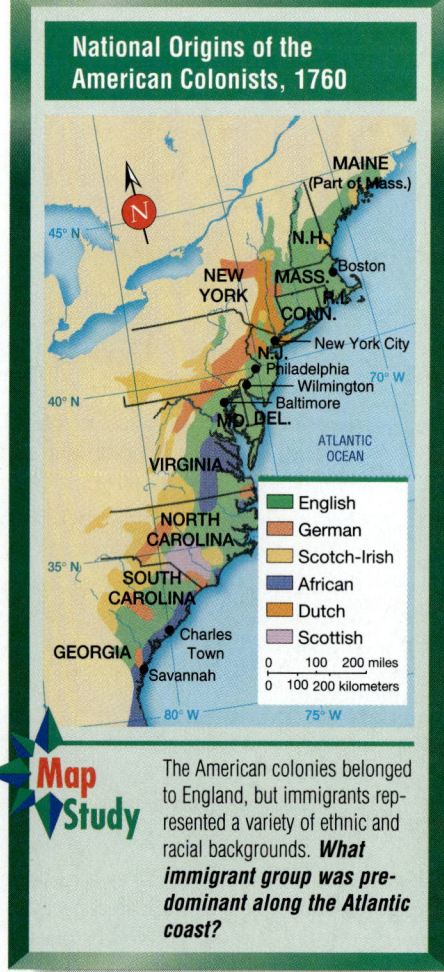

National Origins of the American Colonists, 1760

Legend: English, German, Scotch-Irish, African, Dutch, Scottish

Map Study The American colonies belonged to England, but immigrants represented a variety of ethnic and racial backgrounds. **What immigrant group was predominant along the Atlantic coast?**

---

per woman in New England—and the long period of colonial history—1607 to 1776—meant that most of these were born in the colonies. From about the time of the founding of Pennsylvania in 1681, people of different nationalities and religions—Scots, Irish Catholics, French Huguenots, Spanish Jews, and German Protestants—arrived in increasing numbers. Together with the Dutch in New York, these accounted for nearly one-third of the colonists.

Beginning in Virginia in 1619, the first enslaved Africans were brought by the Dutch from the West Indies. Africans, both enslaved and free, made up about 20 percent of the total population. The proportion of African Americans was highest in the Southern Colonies because slave labor proved profitable on rice and tobacco plantations. In South Carolina three out of four people were enslaved Africans.

■ Women in the Colonies

English colonial population grew rapidly because proportionately there were more women than in the Spanish and French colonies. The only respectable option for women at that time was thought to be marriage. As in all European societies of the time, women were denied higher education. Women generally married in their early twenties and had five or six children. Their principal task was rearing children, although most women died during the child-bearing years.

The second occupation for most women was farming. A farm could not carry on without the skills of women in making cloth, garments, candles, soap, and breadstuffs. A visitor to the North Carolina-Virginia border region in 1710 gave this description of a frontierswoman:

> ❝ ... [S]he is a very civil woman and shows nothing of ruggedness or Immodesty in her carriage, yett she will carry a gunn in the woods and kill deer, turkeys, etc., shoot down wild cattle, catch and tye hoggs. ... ❞

---

with Native Americans, starvation due to crop failures, disastrous fires, and epidemics of smallpox, dysentery, malaria, diphtheria, and yellow fever.

By the 1700s conditions had improved, although epidemics continued to make life uncertain. There was widespread prosperity—a product of cheap land, a ready market for colonial exports, and hard work. Idleness was generally regarded as a sin like drunkenness or gluttony.

The Colonies' Varied Population

By 1775 people of English origin accounted for just under half the population. The high birthrate—an average of seven births

---

Cooperative Learning

Organize students into three or four groups. Have the groups work on developing a "theme" sentence that describes life in Colonial America. Suggest that they do this in three stages: brainstorming ideas, first draft, and final theme sentence. After all groups complete a stage, select a student to report on each group's progress. When all three stages have been completed, have all students work together to develop a class theme sentence. **L2, L3**

In the South plantation wives helped direct the work force. When seafaring New England husbands left their wives, sometimes for years at a time, women were successful as merchants or storekeepers. Widespread home manufacturing allowed women to learn trades. Some women were printers, publishers, druggists, and doctors.

Slavery in the Colonies

At first it was not clear that enslaved Africans were to be treated differently from white indentured servants. Gradually legal distinctions were adopted. Indentured servants retained the rights of English people and the protection of the law. Africans were protected by no law or tradition. The South gave marriages between enslaved persons no legality, and children could be sold away from their mothers. Enslaved persons could own no property and had little legal protection against irresponsible or cruel owners.

Slavery and the Southern Plantation System

Slave labor was adopted for the southern plantations, where the work was done in fields and easily overseen. The profits of large plantations made slavery seem necessary to the South's prosperity. Southern colonial laws declared Africans to be enslaved for life. It was illegal to teach Africans to read for fear that learning would spoil them for physical labor.

There were, in the South, slaveholders who disapproved of slavery but hesitated to act on their feelings because free blacks faced serious discrimination. In addition, whites feared them as possible leaders of slave insurrections. Most southern colonies passed laws that made it difficult to give enslaved people their freedom.

Slavery in the North

In the North, slavery was less profitable and enslaved people less numerous. New England not only allowed, but required, people who were enslaved to marry; they could acquire property and testify in court. An owner might punish a slave, but an owner who killed a slave could be charged with murder. A growing number of people argued that slavery was a moral wrong.

In Pennsylvania, Quakers and Mennonites, a German religious sect, denounced slavery. The number of free African Americans increased. In Jaffrey, New Hampshire, Amos Fortune bought other African Americans out of slavery and left money for the town school. But the northern colonies did not permit equality to free African Americans. Custom usually kept them in menial positions, and the laws denied them the right to vote or hold office.

Native Americans

The first meetings between English settlers and Native Americans gave little evidence of the eventual destruction of the Native Americans' ways of life. A few colonial leaders, notably Roger Williams and William Penn, tried to treat them fairly, and

▲ **THE SLAVE TRADE** Trade that furnished Africans to American markets was a horrible example of inhumanity. It has been estimated that about 30 percent of the enslaved Africans died crossing the Atlantic. **How were Africans treated in the northern colonies?**

CHAPTER 3
SECTION 4

Visualizing History Most colonial women worked in the home as housewives and also worked on the family farm. **Answer to Caption:** housewives, farmers, and servants; a very few were merchants, printers, or artisans.

 **VIDEODISC**

- *GTV: The American People: Fabric of a Nation*

Side 1, Chapter 5
Title: *When Worlds Collide*
Subject: European and Native American encounters

See GTV Guide page 48 for complete lesson plan.

---

some Protestant ministers regarded the native people principally as souls to be brought to knowledge of Christ.

Who Owns the Land?

The expansion of colonial farms became the principal cause of numerous conflicts. The colonists reasoned that since Native Americans did not have settled dwellings, but were on the move like "the foxes and wild beasts . . . so it is lawful now to take a land which none useth; and make use of it."

Some of the conflicts resulted from misunderstandings each culture had of the other's values. Europeans viewed land ownership as essential to progress.

Individual native peoples did not own land, but jointly shared territory with all the members of the group. In general, Native Americans adapted their lifestyles to suit the physical surroundings. Native Americans viewed the land as a resource to be used and left unchanged. Native Americans who sold or by treaty gave up lands did so without any authority, since no chief could dispose of land.

Visualizing History ▼ **COLONIAL POLITICS** A twentieth-century artist provided this view of a political discussion in colonial America. **What options did colonial women have for careers?**

Colonists justified wars against Native Americans in many ways. Some Puritan ministers even claimed that Native Americans were children of the devil, so they could be killed in good conscience.

Weapons of Conquest

Individually, a colonist may not have been a match for a brave who had learned the art of war in struggles over territory, but because of sheer numbers and weapons the whites were destined to win. They also had grim allies in diseases such as smallpox. European diseases sometimes wiped out whole Native American communities that had not developed immunities. Of the estimated 120,000 Native Americans who had lived in the area occupied by the 13 colonies, perhaps only 20,000 survived. Most native nations, too small to resist, simply disappeared as social units. The Iroquois Confederacy was the only group that had the ability to protect its members from destruction.

■ The Colonial Mind

Although many came to America to worship as they pleased, they were not ready to grant others the same privilege. In New England and the Southern Colonies, a single official church was "established"—that is, supported by taxes. Massachusetts Puritans believed that religious toleration was a weakness inspired by the devil. Anyone who advocated it would suffer the consequences. While they expelled many like Roger Williams, they hanged Quakers on Boston Common. Virginia, on the other hand, expelled ministers from Massachusetts.

The Great Awakening

In the 1740s the colonies experienced a religious revival called the Great Awakening. Some Puritan ministers in Massachusetts, concerned over declining religious fervor in their communities, began to preach sermons that warned of the impending dangers of hell. They were influenced by Jonathan Edwards, one of America's greatest

UNIT 1 A New World: Prehistory to 1776

Critical Thinking

Applying Principles Have students consider the ideas of Jean-Jacques Rousseau, a French philosopher, who blamed European society's evils on "the first man who, having enclosed a piece of ground, bethought himself of saying 'This is mine'. . . ." To this he added, "You are undone if you once forget that the fruits of the earth belong to us all, and the earth itself to nobody." Ask students to write a brief paragraph describing how Rousseau might have helped the colonists understand Native Americans. **L3**

colonial Christian theologians. As ministers took sides favoring or opposing the revivalists, new churches sprang up. The diversity of churches helped to make religious toleration even more essential. Other products of the revival were new colleges such as Princeton, Brown, Rutgers, and Dartmouth.

By the late 1700s, open religious persecution in the colonies was largely a thing of the past, although not all religious groups were equal before the law. Visitors from other countries were especially struck by the freedom granted Jews, who still suffered severe persecution in most European countries.

Education in the Colonies

The Puritans believed that citizens should learn enough English to read the Bible and understand the laws. The Massachusetts General School Act of 1647 stated two principles of education that remain today: local communities have a duty to set up schools, and this duty is enforced by law.

In the Middle Colonies, schooling was not as universal as in New England, but it was widespread. In the Southern Colonies, formal education was generally limited to children of large landowners and professionals. Even where schools were desired, the widely separated plantations and farms of the South made them impractical.

By modern standards schools in the colonies were primitive. There were few books, and instruction was given only two or three months a year. Most girls received little formal education. Two-thirds of the women whose names appear on Massachusetts legal documents in the early 1700s could not write their signatures. Despite these shortcomings, no other region of equal size in the world had such a high proportion of the population that could read and write.

▲ **THE MASON CHILDREN: DAVID, JOANNA, AND ABIGAIL** unknown artist, c. 1670 Usually a person's place in colonial society was obvious from his or her appearance and dress. **What can you conclude about the children's family from this painting?**

Religion was the principal force behind most institutions of higher learning in the colonies. The earliest colleges—Harvard, William and Mary, and Yale—were founded to train young men for the ministry.

The Influence of the Enlightenment

By the middle of the eighteenth century, the college curriculum began to change, as interest in science and a demand for practical subjects arose. When King's College—later Columbia—opened in New York City in 1754, it announced that studies would include not only the traditional Latin, Greek, and Hebrew, but also:

> Surveying and Navigation, Geography, History, Husbandry, Commerce, Government, the Knowledge of All Nature in the Heavens above us and in the Air, Water, and Earth Around us. . . .

CHAPTER 3 SECTION 4

Did You Know?

American values and beliefs such as "liberty," "democracy," "freedom of speech," and "freedom of worship" were already being established as part of colonial values in the mid-1700s.

History AND ART

Many families commissioned family portraits—sometimes done by untrained painters—to preserve accurate likenesses of family members for future generations, as well as to decorate their homes.
Answer to Caption: displays family's prosperity

Fact or Fiction?

The leading textbook for young schoolchildren in the colonies combined lessons in religion and grammar.

FACT: The book, entitled *The New England Primer*, first appeared in 1688. The 1748 edition contained "Now I Lay Me Down to Sleep," then a newly published prayer.

Special Needs

Inefficient Readers Scanning a passage before reading can help students develop a time frame for the events or ideas that are presented. Have students scan "The Colonial Mind" passages for time markers. Note that many paragraphs contain these markers. Examples are: "By the 1770s . . ." (paragraph 3); "By the late 1700s . . ." (paragraph 4); ". . . in the early 1700s" (paragraph 7), and "By the middle of the eighteenth century . . ." (paragraph 9).

CHAPTER 3
SECTION 4

FREEDOM OF THE PRESS In 1735 John Peter Zenger faced charges of libel for printing a critical report about the royal governor of New York. Andrew Hamilton defended Zenger in court by asking the jury to base its decision on whether the charges were true, not whether they were offensive. The jury found Zenger not guilty. Freedom of the press was included in the Bill of Rights, ratified in 1791. In 1931 the Supreme Court expanded this right by declaring "prior restraint" laws against malicious or slanderous articles unconstitutional.

 Like many undemocratic governments, that of the New York colony censored publications of which it disapproved. The Zenger case helped establish the right to publish criticisms of government.
Answer to Caption: found not guilty

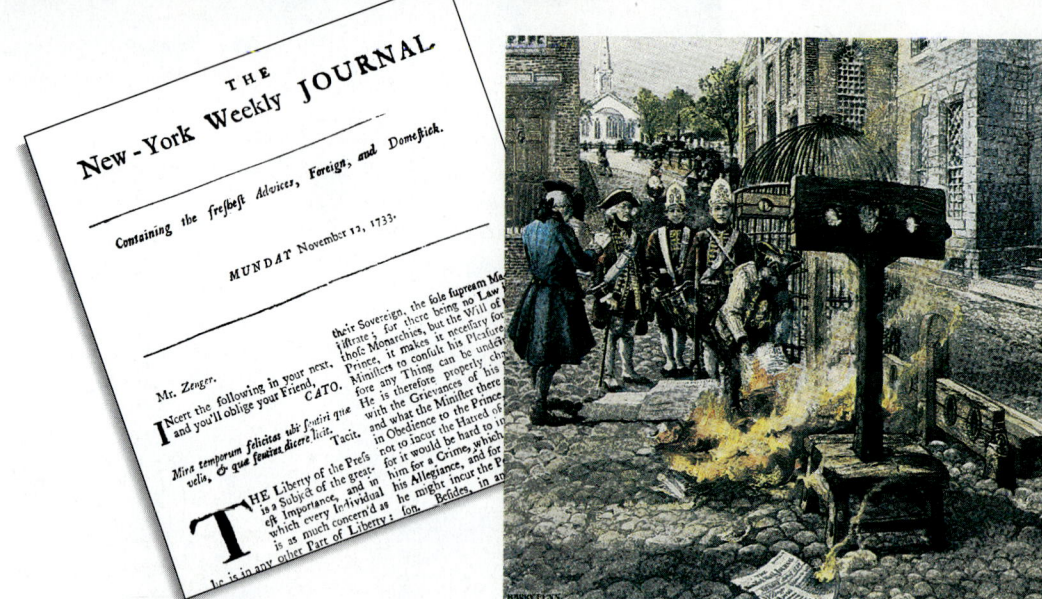

 ▲ **FREEDOM OF THE PRESS** John Peter Zenger, publisher of the *New York Weekly Journal*, was arrested and imprisoned for criticizing the governor of New York, and copies of the newspaper were burned in Wall Street. Andrew Hamilton, Zenger's lawyer, argued that the publisher had the right to speak and write the truth and to oppose arbitrary power. **What was the result of the trial?**

This interest in science originated in Europe, where it was known as the Enlightenment. English philosopher John Locke produced works that were widely read in America. In *An Essay Concerning Human Understanding*, Locke maintained that people could best gain knowledge of the universe by observing and by experimenting. This knowledge would guide them in developing a reasonable society. In the second of two *Treatises on Government*, Locke taught that people were born with certain natural rights to life, liberty, and property; that people formed governments to protect these rights; and that a government interfering with these might rightfully be overthrown. Many readily accepted the idea that government was the agent of the people, not their ruler.

The Press in America

In addition to schools and colleges, newspapers, almanacs, and books helped raise the level of public information. Because paper and type were expensive and the reading public in America small, most books came from Britain. But by 1750 there were 25 or 30 American newspapers, mostly 4 pages long, printed weekly. Printed on tough rag paper, these newspapers were passed from hand to hand at the local inn until often half the men in a village had read a single copy. European travelers in the colonies were amazed to find that political discussions in public inns were joined intelligently by everybody from the college educated to stable help.

The Zenger Case

Colonial editors occasionally criticized British laws or officials. In 1735 John Peter Zenger of the *New York Weekly Journal* accused the royal governor of corruption. As a result, copies of the paper were publicly burned by the sheriff, and Zenger was brought to trial on a charge of libel. His lawyer, Andrew Hamilton, argued that the editor was not guilty since the charges were true and since free speech was a basic right

---

Cooperative Learning

Organize students into groups of 10. Take 10 blank index cards, write a key term from the section on 5 cards and a definition of each term on the other cards. Make copies of the cards for all groups. Distribute a card to each member of each group. Have students pair off within their group with the group member who has a matching term or definition card. **L1, L2**

of English people. As a result, Zenger was acquitted. At the time the case attracted little attention, but today it is regarded as a landmark in the development of free press in America.

New Directions

By 1776 America was well on its way to establishing economic independence. Thirty percent of the ships in the British merchant marine were American, and most of these sailed from New England ports.

The Economy

New Englanders carried on a share of the African slave trade. They were the first to hunt whales in the Antarctic; in 1774, 360 whaling ships sailed from the island of Nantucket alone. While New England was a formidable competitor in trade, no colony offered much competition to the British in manufacturing. The American colonists usually obtained manufactured goods from Britain.

To pay for fine European goods such as clothing, books, wine, and cutlery, the colonies had to trade staples that Europeans needed or to pay in gold or silver. Trade with the West Indies netted Spanish dollars, the common colonial currency. Later the new nation, the United States, would adopt the dollar instead of the British pound as its monetary unit. Gradually the colonies developed a culture distinctly different from that of Europe.

Stirrings of Independence

The degree of power exercised by British officials varied from colony to colony, but it was limited everywhere. In all colonies the voters elected their own legislature, and in charter colonies, their governor as well. In proprietary colonies the governor was appointed by the proprietor or by his heirs; in royal or crown colonies the governor was chosen by the king. The governor of a proprietary or crown colony had wide powers, such as a veto over the legislature and control of land grants.

Government at the town and county levels was run entirely by the colonists themselves. In New England, the important local unit was the township. Decisions were made at the town meeting, which most heads of families had a right to attend. The town meeting was the most direct form of democracy in the colonies. In the Southern and Middle colonies, local government was usually less democratic but, nevertheless, entirely independent of British control.

None of the colonies was so democratic as to allow full political rights to all men or to any women. Active citizenship and the right to vote and hold office were limited to adult white males owning property, who usually had to be members of the established church. In spite of these limitations, a higher proportion of people were involved in government in the British colonies than anywhere in the European world. This wide participation gave Americans training that was valuable when the colonies later became independent.

Section 4 ★ Review

Checking for Understanding

1. **Identify** the Iroquois Confederacy, the Great Awakening, John Locke.
2. **Define** gentry.
3. **Describe** the position of indentured servants, women, and African Americans in the colonies.
4. **Give** reasons for the development of religious freedom and toleration in the British colonies.

Critical Thinking

5. **Evaluating Causes** Most colonists were common people, rather than titled aristocracy. What became the new basis for class structure, and how did it lead to class mobility?

CHAPTER 3 Colonial America 1578–1776

REVIEW CHAPTER 3

Answers

Reviewing Facts
1. Religious groups settled seeking religious freedom, established many institutions.
2. Distance from England and English neglect, representative government demanded by colonists and to attract settlers, Enlightenment philosophers such as Locke, local self-rule, free press and available newspapers, some colonies settled by idealists.
3. Motivated settlement by companies and determined lifestyle and values, for example, slavery.
4. Royal—governor appointed by king, wide powers; proprietary—control by proprietors who appoint governor; charter—legislature and governor elected
5. Crops suited to it were labor intensive, making slavery profitable.

Understanding Concepts
1. Religious freedom, profit, land, escape undesirable condition or status at home
2. Enlightenment philosophy, religious convictions such as Friends, growing acceptance of established self-government traditions

Critical Thinking
1. Answers may vary. Possible concentration of development in small but high-density sections of territory, or widely scattered settlements without fences that do not restrict access or interfere with game.
2. a) Answers will vary, but students should note that the hammer and clothing of the man indicates that he is a shoemaker and the spinning wheel indicates that the woman is a clothes maker.
b) Answers will vary, but students might note that the paintings indicate that: workers toiled in solitude rather than in groups, people worked at home, the demeanor of the workers shows work to be a serious pursuit.

CHAPTER 3 ★ REVIEW

Using Vocabulary

Use all the terms below in one of four sentences or paragraphs, each about one of the following: the class hierarchy in the colonies, the religious groups who colonized New England, government in the colonies, major exports.

congregation
commonwealth
constitution
dissenters
gentry
indentured servants
naval stores
patroons
proprietor
subsistence farming

Reviewing Facts
1. **Describe** the role of religion in settling the American colonies.
2. **Summarize** the growth of self-government in the colonies.
3. **Explain** the role economics played in the settlement of the colonies.
4. **Detail** the government in three types of colonies.
5. **Analyze** why slavery became more prevalent in the South than in New England.

Understanding Concepts

Migration
1. The colonists who left England to settle in America endured formidable hardships. List three reasons why different groups of colonists migrated to America in the face of these risks and hardships. How do their motives compare to the reasons people migrate today?

Values and Beliefs
2. What values and beliefs were instrumental in establishing democratic institutions in the American colonies?

Critical Thinking
1. **Proposing Solutions** Imagine you are appointed to resolve disputes between Native Americans and colonists who want farmland. Propose a fair plan for expansion. Remember that Native Americans did not own land.
2. **Analyzing Fine Art** Analyze the two paintings on this page and answer the questions that follow.
   a. What details in the paintings give you clues about the people's occupations?
   b. What can you tell about town life by looking at these paintings?

80   UNIT 1 A New World: Prehistory to 1776

CHAPTER 3 ★ REVIEW

Writing About History

Description

Imagine you are an author who traveled in the first supply ship to reach Jamestown the year after it was settled. Write a description, to be published in Britain, of the condition of the colony when you arrived.

Cooperative Learning

Working in a group with four members, study slavery around the world and throughout history. Assign each member one or more cultures or geographic areas to study. Report your findings and conduct a discussion comparing and contrasting slavery in other cultures with slavery of African Americans in the colonies.

Social Studies Skills

Reading a Thematic Map

No doubt you have seen and studied maps in textbooks, magazines, atlases, even on television weather or news reports. Although there is almost no limit to the kinds of information that maps can show, most maps, depending on the type of information they present, fit into one of two broad categories. Maps that show general information such as countries, cities, rivers, and other features are called general reference maps. A second category of maps is thematic maps. These maps depict or emphasize more specific information than general reference maps. Often the information is on a single topic. The map below is a thematic map because it depicts information about a particular topic—land holdings in New England during the 1600s and early 1700s.

Practicing the Skill

Use the map and what you have read in the chapter to answer the following questions.
1. Based on the title, what can you learn from the map?
2. In what year was the Rhode Island Grant bestowed?
3. What grants of land were made in 1629?
4. **Drawing Conclusions** The map shows that there were many grants of land made during the 1600s and early 1700s. What do you think the British Crown was trying to accomplish by making these land grants?

Using Your Journal
Compare the details you have noted about the influence of different religious groups with the way religious groups today try to exert political influence. Write a paragraph explaining the similarities and differences.

REVIEW CHAPTER 3

4. Answers may vary, but might include: accelerate settlement; establish British control over land that might be settled by French; to provide natural resources, goods, and trading posts for the British; as gifts or favors to certain individuals or groups

❓ Chapter Bonus Test Question

Suppose it is 1730 and you are planning to settle in one of Britain's North American colonies. Briefly describe your social, economic, and political status. Which colony interests you most? For what reasons? (Answers may vary but should include a discussion of how the character of a particular colony matches a potential settler's political, social, and religious beliefs.)

Using Your Journal

The ideas students present in their paragraphs may vary but should include specific similarities and differences. You might call on volunteers to read their paragraphs to the class. Then have students contrast their varying views on the political influence exerted by the various religious groups they studied.

CHAPTER 3 Colonial America 1578–1776

Practicing the Skill
1. grants of land in New England given to individuals and groups by the British government
2. 1663
3. the Mason Grant and the Massachusetts Bay "Sea to Sea" Grant

Cultural Kaleidoscope

Making Connections
History and Archaeology

Discoveries by archaeologists have revealed much about the Mayan culture, a Native American way of life that flourished on Yucatan peninsulas of Mexico before the coming of Europeans. A curious feature of Mayan culture was the ball court, a level space with a carved stone ring mounted high up on one wall. Apparently, opposing players used their hips to try and knock a ball through the ring. Competitions in the Mayan ball courts probably had some ceremonial significance.

More About
Lacrosse

Although this game was invented by Native Americans, its name is French. (*La crosse* means "the stick.") Among the Native Americans, as many as a thousand warriors might take part in a game, which could range over several miles of territory.

Cultural Kaleidoscope

Native American Life
Sports and Games

From the earliest recorded history, people have taken part in play and games. Athletic competition has served as a way for individuals to interact with others and to display skills and physical ability as well as provide an expression for the love of competition. The first people of the Americas invented and enjoyed games of competition that tested skill and bravery.

▼ The game of Arrows was a popular competition. One by one, each contestant would shoot arrows into the air trying to put the largest number in the air before the first struck the ground. There were other competitions in marksmanship with bow and arrow.

◄ California peoples' game tray with acorn dice, eighteenth century

Cooperative Learning

Divide the class into four or five groups. Ask each group to select a common American sport, such as baseball, basketball, or football. Each group should then explain the goal and the rules of its game to the others; the audience should pretend to be Native Americans who have never heard of the game before (and should feel free to ask questions about it). **L1**

Cultural Kaleidoscope

Portfolio Project

Ask students to collect newspaper pictures and/or stories about their favorite leisure activity (other than a sport). What would its counterpart have been in pre-Columbian times? For example, watching television or going to the movies could be compared to storytelling around a campfire. What are the advantages and disadvantages of the modern activity as compared to the older one?

▲ Lacrosse is an authentic Native American sport and the oldest game in North America. Some Canadian groups called the game bagataway, and the Seneca knew it as otada-jish-qua-age. The Mandan game of Tchungkee (above) was another of the many forms of lacrosse.

▲ Lacrosse is a popular sport in many schools today.

▶ Jim Thorpe won both the pentathlon and decathlon medals at the 1912 Olympics. Thorpe of the Sac and Fox was a superb athlete who was an All-American football player, an outfielder for the New York Giants, and an important figure in the emergence of professional football. Sportswriters selected Thorpe the best football player of the first half of the twentieth century.

◀ CEREMONIAL BOW

The Historian's Craft

None of the Native Americans who lived in the present-day United States had a written language. So historians rely on other evidence to learn about their past. One source is *myths and legends*. For instance, Iroquois stories about a famous hero, Hiawatha, commemorate a real-life statesman who helped found the Iroquois League. Another source of information is *language*. Because of similarities between the Navajo tongue and languages spoken in Canada, it seems clear that the Navajo moved into the Southwest from the far north a long time ago.

UNIT 1 DIGEST

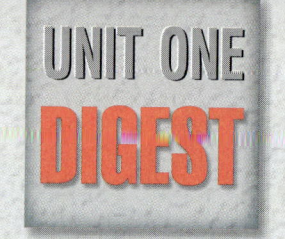

UNIT ONE DIGEST

Unit 1 Digest can be used to teach unit coverage when time is limited, to review unit content, or to link content of one unit to another.

 Unit Digest Transparencies

Use Transparency 1.

Chapter 1

Organize the students into small groups, and give to each a copy of the reproducible Unit 1 Test. Ask each group to complete the Understanding Concepts section and to be prepared to support their answers with specific information. Then review the answers and supporting evidence with the entire class.

Chapter 2

Read the following statement made by Bartolomé de Las Casas:

"The Indians were totally deprived of their freedom and were put in the harshest, fiercest, most horrible servitude and captivity. . . ." Ask students to discuss what both the conquistadors' actions and Las Casas' protests reveal about European values and beliefs.

Chapter 3

Provide students with copies of the outline map of the Thirteen Colonies from the Glencoe Social Studies Resource Book. Ask students to label the 13 colonies and to insert a dot and label for the 4 largest towns in 1750: Boston, Philadelphia, New York, and Charlestown. Discuss what role location played in the growth of these colonial towns.

Chapter 1
The World in Transition

The first Americans traveled across a land bridge that once connected Siberia and Alaska and spread throughout North and South America. The Olmec, Maya, Aztec, and Incan civilizations developed highly organized and sophisticated societies. The monuments of the Anasazi and the Hopewell people attest to their level of cultural sophistication.

Across the Atlantic Ocean, a new Europe was emerging as strong monarchs unified their territories. A wealthy middle class developed from the increase in commerce and growth of cities. A rebirth of interest in the classical heritage of Greece and Rome brought a profound cultural awakening known as the Renaissance. Religious leaders called for the reform of the Roman Catholic Church, which led to the Reformation.

In Asia and Africa, Muslim empires expanded their territories. Ancient trade routes continued to flourish. Ming China, however, turned inward, halting trade to shield its people from outside influences.

Many factors caused Europeans to turn outward. Improved technology gave navigators the compass; the astrolabe; and faster, more seaworthy ships. Bankers, merchants, and joint-stock companies provided the money to finance expeditions. In search of spices and luxury goods, explorers braved the uncharted seas to find an all-water route from Europe to Asia. Portuguese sailors rounded the tip of Africa to reach India.

Chapter 2
The Age of Exploration

Not until the voyages of Christopher Columbus in the 1490s were Europeans aware that the Americas existed. Spain and Portugal were competing for

▼ RECONSTRUCTION OF JAMESTOWN SETTLEMENT

◀ SIR WALTER RALEIGH

84 UNIT 1 A New World: Prehistory to 1776

Cooperative Learning

The Royal Hunt of the Sun by Peter Shaffer is a play about Pizarro's conquest of the Inca Empire. Have students read selections from the play, especially the exchanges between Pizarro and Atahualpa. Then ask students to work in pairs to write a similar dialogue that might have taken place between Cortés and Moctezuma or between Ponce de León and the Native Americans he encountered in his search for the Fountain of Youth. Ask pairs to volunteer to perform their dialogues for the rest of the class. **L1 L2**

▲ HUSKING BEE, 1700s

exclusive rights for trade. The pope drew a line of demarcation between Portuguese and Spanish interests that extended around the earth. Meanwhile, Portugal prospered because it controlled the eastern route to the Indies. In 1519 Spain sent Ferdinand Magellan to find a westerly route to Asia. His expedition was the first to circumnavigate the world.

Commerce led to empire building. The Spaniards wanted to acquire wealth and to spread Christianity in the Americas. In 1521 Hernán Cortés conquered the Aztecs and shipped huge amounts of Aztec gold to Spain. His success encouraged other conquistadors such as Francisco Pizarro, who conquered the Incan empire, to seek their fortunes in the Americas. In the process, the Spaniards claimed vast territories that eventually formed a great colonial empire.

France, England, and the Netherlands searched for a northwest passage to Asia during the 1500s and 1600s. As a result, the French established permanent colonies along the St. Lawrence River and developed a lucrative fur trade. By 1682 French explorers had claimed the Mississippi River basin. The Dutch settled in the rich Hudson River valley.

Chapter 3

Colonial America

In 1607 the English founded Jamestown in Virginia—their first permanent settlement in the Americas. Despite many hardships the colonists survived, and their success lured new settlers to Virginia. In time, the colonists formed a representative government body, the House of Burgesses. The first enslaved Africans were brought to Jamestown in 1619.

The Pilgrim and Puritan settlers in New England wanted freedom from religious persecution. Upon arrival in North America in 1620, the Pilgrims signed the Mayflower Compact and established the Plymouth colony in present-day Massachusetts. However, religious differences soon forced some of them to move on and found settlements in Rhode Island and Connecticut.

Other colonies were created when the king granted huge tracts of land to proprietors. These proprietorships included the Southern Colonies of Maryland, the Carolinas, and Georgia, and the Middle Colonies of New York, New Jersey, Pennsylvania, and Delaware.

New England, Middle, and Southern colonies developed differently. Diverse economies were built on crops or enterprises suited to regional climates. England largely left the colonies to govern themselves. Religious diversity eventually made religious toleration necessary. With a thriving export and trade economy, many people moved up in class.

Women could not vote, but they were full partners in running farms and sometimes businesses. Enslaved persons became property with no legal protection in the South. Native Americans suffered from battles with colonists over land and from epidemics of European diseases. At first, churches provided most schools and colleges, but later public education began to emerge, especially in New England.

Understanding Unit Themes

1. **Geography and the Environment** How did the location of Asian centers of trade relative to Europe lead to colonies in the Americas?
2. **The Individual and Family Life** Compare the lives and obligations of medieval serfs and colonial indentured servants.
3. **Humanities and Religion** What roles did religion play in motivating voyages of exploration and in colonizing America?
4. **Cultural Diversity** What role did cultural diversity play in the colonization of North and South America?

UNIT 1 A New World: Prehistory to 1776   85

UNIT 1 DIGEST

Understanding Unit Themes

1. Asian centers of trade were separated from Europe by hundreds or thousands of miles of rugged territory, making ocean routes desirable.
2. Serfs were bound to the land for life. Indentured servants worked off their debt after several years.
3. Crusades whetted appetites for Eastern goods and ideas; Church wanted to spread Christianity; dissenters wanted religious freedom.
4. Answers may vary. Native Americans and Europeans clashed over cultural differences such as those relating to religion, wealth, exploitation of peoples and resources, and slavery.

Student Self-Test Software allows students to test their understanding of historical concepts in this unit.

Have students listen to the Chapter Digests on the audiocassettes.

 VIDEODISC

- GTV: *The American People: Fabric of a Nation*

Side 1, Chapter 7
Title: *A Mixed Bag*
Subject: Diversity in the Colonies

See GTV Guide page 52 for complete lesson plan.

The Historian's Craft

Synthesizing Information Point out that historians have synthesized information to explain why, by the mid-1700s, the English were the group with the strongest foothold in North America. Ask students to write a paragraph explaining why the English were so much more successful than other Europeans in colonizing North America. Suggest that they explore subjects such as motivation, goals, and methods of colonization in their paragraphs. Have volunteers read their paragraphs to the class.

85

INTRODUCING UNIT 2

BEGINNING THE UNIT

Present this cause-and-effect chart to students with the effects omitted. Assign them to complete the chart as they read the chapters in the unit.

Event
- The American Revolution

Causes
- Britain gains North America.
- Colonies become resentful of Britain.
- Tensions increase.
- Open conflict begins.

Effects
- Colonies unite.
- Central government is formed.
- Britain is defeated.
- An independent nation emerges.
- Internal problems bring disputes.
- New Constitution is written.
- Federal union is created.

History AND ART

A few days before the battle at Yorktown, Washington made his only wartime visit to Mount Vernon. From there he marched south to win the final battle of the Revolution.

00:00 OUT OF TIME? If time does not permit teaching the entire unit, use the Unit Digest on pages 166–167.

UNIT TWO
CREATING A NATION
1650–1789

CHAPTER 4
The Road to Revolution
1650–1775

CHAPTER 5
War for Independence
1775–1783

CHAPTER 6
A More Perfect Union
1775–1789

▲ SWORDS AND SABERS

▲ COLONIAL HORNBOOK, SEVENTEENTH CENTURY

History AND ART
George Washington Before Yorktown, 1781
by Rembrandt Peale, 1824

Rembrandt Peale was one of 17 children, many of whom became artists. Peale was only 17 when he painted his first portrait of Washington in 1795.

Exploring Unit Themes

American Democracy Colonists claimed that Britain's despotic acts denied them their rights to representative self-government. After the war they formed a system of federal government containing checks and balances that would preclude future despotism.

Civil Rights and Liberties In the Declaration of Independence, American leaders stated that all people possess the inalienable rights of life, liberty, and the pursuit of happiness. To protect these rights, they attached the Bill of Rights to the Constitution.

Economic Development Britain's mercantile economy was based on the colonies as a source of raw materials and a dumping ground for British manufactured goods. After indepen-

Setting the Scene

Harsh measures passed by Parliament in an effort to control the American colonies were met with outrage and hostile countermeasures. Gradually united, the colonists rebelled against their parent country. Their independence secured, Americans created for themselves a remarkable new form of democratic government.

Themes
- American Democracy
- Civil Rights and Liberties
- Economic Development
- Conflict and Cooperation

Key Events
- French and Indian War
- Fall of Quebec
- Treaty of Paris, 1763
- Stamp Act
- Boston Tea Party
- Battles of Lexington and Concord
- Declaration of Independence
- Battle of Saratoga
- British defeat at Yorktown
- Treaty of Paris, 1783
- Ratification of the Constitution

▲ **AMERICAN BATTLE FLAG**

Major Issues
- British defeat of the French in North America prompts Parliament to attempt tightening commercial and political control of the 13 English colonies.
- Patriot determinism, military skill, and French aid enable the colonies to win independence from Britain.
- Key compromises lead to the formation of a strong and democratic central government.

◄ MOLLY PITCHER

Portfolio Project
Compare the events of the American Revolution to the circumstances of a political or social upheaval that has taken place elsewhere in the world. Outline the major developments in both and identify some of the causes and effects.

INTRODUCING UNIT 2

UNIT 2 Independent Study Project
Divide the class into three groups, and ask each to construct a large-scale time line on one of the following: the events leading up to the outbreak of war between Britain and the American colonies; the major events of the Revolutionary War; the major events of the postwar years up to the ratification of the Constitution.

Unit Digest Transparencies
Strategies and Activities
Use Transparency 2, "George Washington Before the Battle of Trenton" by John Trumbull.

Portfolio Project
After students have completed their outlines, initiate a discussion of the similarities and differences between the American Revolution and other world upheavals.

History and the Humanities
 History and Art Transparency 2

Focus on American Art Prints 3, 4

 American Music: Cultural Traditions

Spirit of American Art and Music 4, 5, 6

---

dence, Britain severed economic ties with the United States and refused to sign any trade agreements.
Cooperation and Conflict Britain's imposition of more stringent colonial policies in the 1760s caused dissent among American colonists. Dissent turned to open rebellion and a war for independence. During this rebellion the colonies slowly began to work together, creating a new American nation.
Examining Unit Themes Point out that this unit tells how colonial conflicts with British policies led to American independence. Have students trace the developments that led to the founding of the United States.

87

LESSON PLAN
Global Perspectives

FOCUS
Motivating Activity

Point out that the French Revolution occurred 13 years after the American Revolution began. Then provide students with these facts: The French government gave aid to the Americans by heavily taxing the French people. A respected French noble, the marquis de Lafayette, played a leading role in the American Revolution. The philosophy of the Declaration of Independence influenced French reformers. Ask students to speculate on how each fact relates to the French Revolution. (Heavy taxes caused discontent and demands for changes in government. Lafayette was prepared to take a similar leading role in France. The Declaration of Independence provided French reformers with justification for revolution in France.)

TEACH
Guided Practice
Exploring the Time Line

Direct students to the United States part of the time line, and have them identify European nations that were gaining footholds in North America between 1650 and 1800. Ask how this might affect a newly independent United States. (Answers may include: prevent U.S. expansion; encourage European colonies to encroach on U.S. territory, which no longer had British protection; cause conflict with parent nations in Europe.)

Global Perspectives

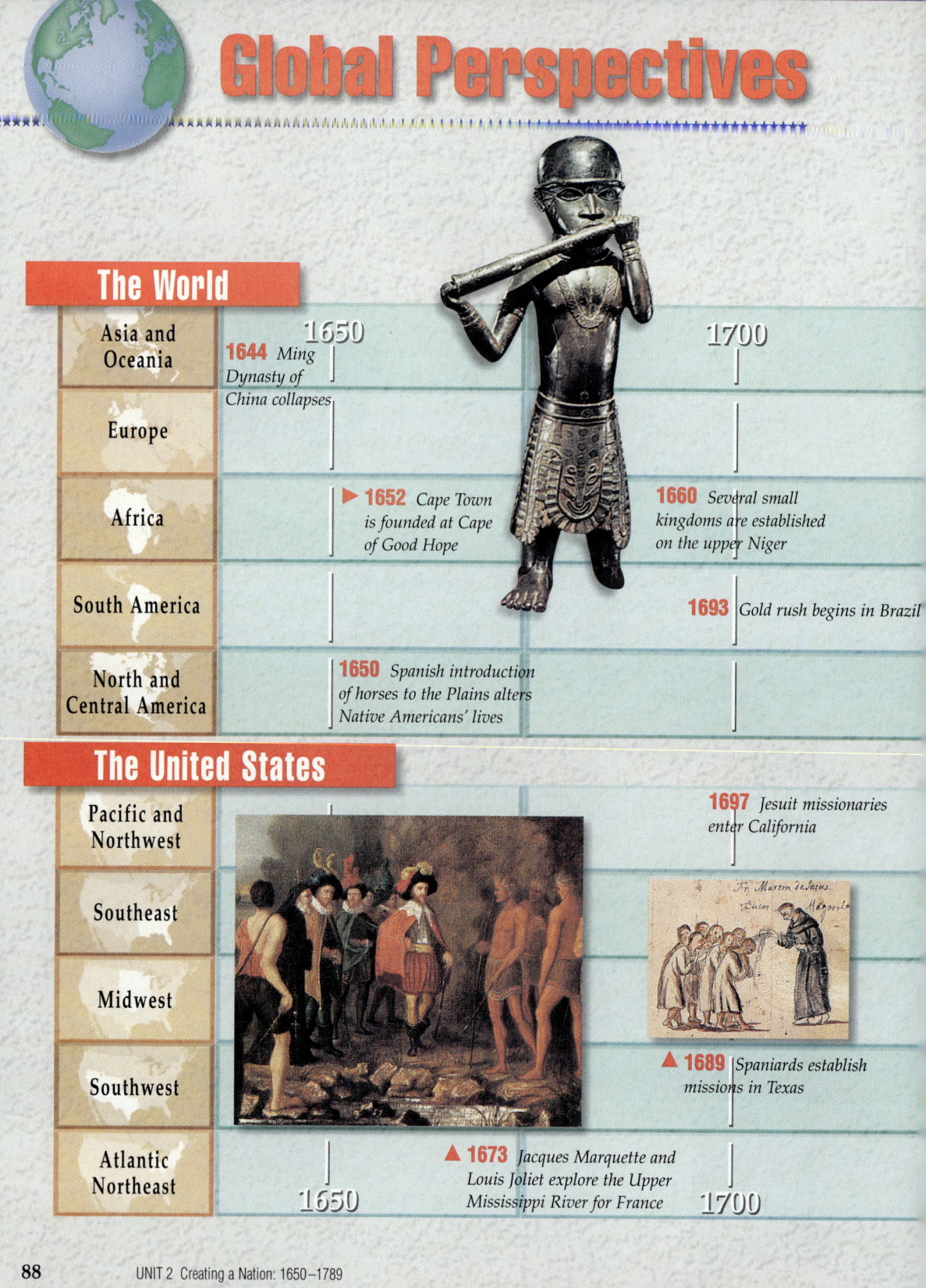

The World

	1650		1700
Asia and Oceania	**1644** Ming Dynasty of China collapses		
Europe			
Africa	▶ **1652** Cape Town is founded at Cape of Good Hope	**1660** Several small kingdoms are established on the upper Niger	
South America		**1693** Gold rush begins in Brazil	
North and Central America	**1650** Spanish introduction of horses to the Plains alters Native Americans' lives		

The United States

Pacific and Northwest		**1697** Jesuit missionaries enter California	
Southeast			
Midwest			
Southwest		▲ **1689** Spaniards establish missions in Texas	
Atlantic Northeast	1650	▲ **1673** Jacques Marquette and Louis Joliet explore the Upper Mississippi River for France	1700

UNIT 2 Creating a Nation: 1650–1789

Cultural Diversity

Songs of the revolutionary period were generally derived from old English, Scottish, or Irish tunes. John Dickenson's "Liberty Song" is believed to be the first patriotic song published in British North America (1768). Its lyrics are American, but its tune is from an English song, "Hearts of Oak." The tune for "Yankee Doodle Dandy" might be English, Irish, or Dutch. One of the nation's popular patriotic songs, "My Country 'Tis of Thee," takes its tune from Britain's national anthem, "God Save the King."

Linking Across Time

The English, the first Europeans to settle the eastern seaboard, gave our country its language. The adoption of Native American words and the contributions of successive waves of immigrants have created a truly *American* form of English. However, people in isolated areas of Chesapeake Bay, Maryland, and the Outer Banks in North Carolina still speak in a similar fashion to the first English settlers. For example, they pronounce *s* and the soft *c* as *z*, and the long *i* as *oi*. So cider, a popular drink in the region, is pronounced *zoider*.

1750 — **1770** Captain James Cook discovers Australia — 1800

1727 Robert Walpole becomes Britain's first prime minister

▼ **1769** James Watt perfects the steam engine

1789 Revolution breaks out in France

1789 Alexander Mackenzie reaches Arctic Ocean

1778 Captain James Cook discovers Hawaiian Islands

1718 French found city of New Orleans

▲ **1754** French and Indian War begins

▲ **1776** Declaration of Independence signed

1750 — 1800

UNIT 2 Creating a Nation: 1650–1789   89

LESSON PLAN
Global Perspectives

Independent Practice

Linking World Events Tell students that another revolution in the 1700s marked a period of many inventions and technological advances. Known as the Industrial Revolution, it began in Britain and then spread to Europe and the American colonies. Ask students to research a particular invention of the Industrial Revolution—for instance, Watt's perfection of the steam engine. Have them present their research in the form of a report. You might have volunteers read their reports and discuss them with the class.

ASSESS

Studying the Time Line

1. What was happening in Africa around the time that Marquette and Joliet were exploring the Mississippi? (Several small kingdoms were established on the Niger.)
2. When James Cook was exploring the Hawaiian Islands, what was going on in the colonies? (the American Revolution)
3. How did the development of the steam engine affect the location of factories? (Location became more flexible because factories did not have to depend on fast-flowing rivers for power.)

Cooperative Learning

Inform students that some political scientists recognize four stages of revolution: a crisis, a challenge to authority, an armed insurrection, and a political settlement. Organize students into groups of four. Ask group members to select one of the stages above and research details of that stage in the American Revolution. Then have group members work together to construct a flow chart showing the details of the four stages of the American Revolution. Suggest that groups display their flow charts on the bulletin board. **L1**

PLANNING GUIDE Chapter 4 The Road to Revolution

Daily Lesson Objectives	Teacher Classroom Resources	Multimedia
SECTION 1 **Struggle for Empire** 1 Day pp. 92–96 1. Explain the economic motives that shaped British colonial policy. 2. Explain the causes and results of the French and Indian War.	Chapter 4 Study Guide Reproducible Lesson Plan Reteaching Activity 4-1 Section Quiz Chapter 4 Cooperative Learning Activity Chapter 4 Concept Mapping Activity Reinforcing Social Studies Skills 28, 32, 52 Writer's Guidebook, Lesson 6 Building Skills in Geography	Student Self-Test Software Testmaker Section Focus Transparency 9 Chapter 4 Skills Transparency Unit 2 Digest Transparency
SECTION 2 **Control and Protest** 1 Day pp. 98–102 1. List and explain British attempts to tighten control over the colonies. 2. Identify the ways in which the colonies resisted British control.	Reproducible Lesson Plan Reteaching Activity 4-2 Reinforcing Social Studies Skills 32, 52 Section Quiz	Student Self-Test Software Testmaker Section Focus Transparency 10 Chapter 4 Map Transparency Powers of the Congress A Geographic Perspective on American History
SECTION 3 **The Breach Widens** 1 Day pp. 104–109 1. List the Intolerable Acts, and describe how the colonists responded to them. 2. Describe the events that led to war between Great Britain and the American colonies.	Reproducible Lesson Plan Reteaching Activity 4-3 Section Quiz Chapter 4 Primary and Secondary Source Readings Chapter 4 Enrichment Activity American Portraits 7 Reinforcing Social Studies Skills 2, 32 Spanish Summaries & Glossary	Student Self-Test Software Testmaker Vocabulary Puzzlemaker Section Focus Transparency 11 Audiocassette, Chapter 4 A Geographic Perspective on American History
CHAPTER REVIEW AND EVALUATION 1 Day	Chapter 4 Test Chapter 4 Performance Assessment Activity	Student Self-Test Software Testmaker

00:00 OUT OF TIME? If time does not permit teaching the entire chapter, use the Chapter 4 Summary on pages 166–167 and the Chapter 4 audiocassette (English and Spanish) to point out the main ideas of the chapter.

PLANNING GUIDE

Cultural Diversity Activity

Research The first person to propose a union of all the colonies was Iroquois chief Canassatego. He suggested the colonists form a union like the Iroquois League, made up of the Onondaga, Mohawk, Seneca, Oneida, and Cayuga nations. Ben Franklin first presented a plan of government modeled on the Iroquois League at a conference in 1754. He called it the Albany Plan of Union. Although the colonial and British governments rejected his proposals, some aspects of the Albany Plan survived in the later Articles of Confederation.

Have students research the origin of the Iroquois League, how its delegates were chosen, the League's powers, and its similarities to the Albany Plan. An excellent resource for this and other Native American contributions to American life is *Indian Givers* by Jack Weatherford.

Performance Assessment Activity

Propaganda Colonists used cartoons, broadsides, and pamphlets to criticize British policies and urge other Americans to resist them. Organize students into small groups to select a British policy they would like to protest and develop an appropriate cartoon, broadside, or pamphlet to express their views. Have each group present its work to the class. Encourage students to use research illustrations and primary sources appropriate to the topic.

POSSIBLE RUBRIC FEATURES: Content information, visual and written communication skills, main idea, creativity, clarity

Chapter Resources

Literature from the Period

Burke, Edmund. "Speech on Moving His Resolutions for Conciliation with the Colonies." 1775.

Franklin, Benjamin. *The Autobiography.* 1771.

Readings for the Student

Collier, James L. *My Brother Sam is Dead.* School Book Services, 1977.

Langguth, A. J. *Patriots: The Men Who Started the American Revolution.* Simon and Schuster, 1988.

Readings for the Teacher

Christie, Ian R. *Crisis of Empire: Great Britain and the American Colonies, 1754–1783.* Norton, 1966.

Greene, Jack P. *The Reinterpretation of the American Revolution, 1763–1789.* Greenwood Press, 1979.

Lipman, Jean, Elizabeth V. Warren, and Robert Bishop. *Young America: A Folk-Art History.* Museum of American Folk-Art, 1987.

Multimedia Resources

Colonial Merchant. Educational Activities. (2 Apple diskettes)

The French and Indian Wars. Multi-Media Productions. (2 sound filmstrips)

The Inventory. Maryland Center for Public Broadcasting. (VHS, 28 minutes.)

My Brother Sam Is Dead. Random House. (VHS, 26 minutes)

To Keep Our Liberty. National Park Service. (VHS, 23 minutes)

Key to Ability Levels

Teaching strategies have been coded for varying learning styles and abilities.

- **L1** Basic activities for all students
- **L2** Average activities for average to above-average students
- **L3** Challenging activities for above-average students
- **LEP** Limited English Proficiency activities

Glencoe Links to the Humanities

Link to Art
- U.S. History & Art Transparency 2

Link to Literature
- Macmillan Literature: American Literature Audiotapes Side 1
- Macmillan Literature: Novel Guide—*The Light in the Forest*
- Macmillan Literature: American Literature Text—Jonathan Edwards

Link to Music
- 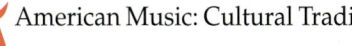American Music: Cultural Traditions

CHAPTER 4

BEGINNING THE CHAPTER

Read students a statement written by John Adams many years after the American Revolution: "The Revolution was effected before the war commenced. It was in the hearts and minds of the people . . . ." As students read Chapter 4, ask them to decide whether they agree with John Adams's assessment of the American colonists.

Recording Journal Notes

To help students get started, have them list the products various colonial merchants exported. Ask them to choose one to write about.

Point out that the Americans' discontent with and subsequent rebellion over British imperial policy set a precedent for the eventual overthrow of European colonial powers around the world. In the 200 years following the American Revolution, European empires in South America, Africa, and Asia fell, and scores of independent nations emerged.

CHAPTER 4

The Road to Revolution
1650–1775

▶ BEDFORD FLAG

Setting the Scene

Focus

Through hard work, the colonists created a prosperous economy based on agriculture and trade, and they learned to govern themselves. In settling this new land, colonists also developed a sense that they were taking part in the birth of a new society, different from Europe, where men and women were able to better themselves. Once their need for British protection ended, the road to independence was not far behind.

Journal Notes

Put yourself in the role of a colonial merchant with a product to export. As you read the chapter, keep notes on your position on the issues.

Concepts to Understand

★ How Parliament sought to tighten political control over the colonies
★ Why colonists resorted to political protest against British policies

Read to Discover . . .

★ the causes and results of the French and Indian War.
★ the events that led the colonists to armed resistance to British control over the colonies.

CULTURAL
- 1763 Benjamin Franklin perfects the harmonica
- 1767 *Letters from a Farmer in Pennsylvania* published by John Dickinson

1760 — 1765

POLITICAL
- 1763 French and Indian War ends
- 1765 Stamp Act passed
- 1767 Townshend Acts passed

90   UNIT 2 Creating a Nation: 1650–1789

✚ EXTRA CREDIT PROJECT

Civil Disobedience Interested students might research the history of civil disobedience as a way of bringing about changes in government policies. Or suggest they find examples of civil disobedience in American society today. Ask them to focus on such questions as: Is civil disobedience ever justified? Is it justified in this case? If it is, what form should it take? How far may a group go to protest against what it believes to be injustices? Have students write essays describing their findings and share them with the class.

▲ COLONIAL NEWSPAPER ATTACKING STAMP ACT

History AND ART

Patrick Henry Before the Virginia House of Burgesses
by Peter F. Rothermel, 1851

Best known for his historical works, Rothermel also turned out paintings based on religious and literary themes. This work illustrates Rothermel's technique of combining sharp details with shadowy forms in a single painting.

- 1774 Shakers settle in Watervliet, New York
- 1770 Boston Massacre takes place
- 1773 Colonists dump tea into Boston Harbor

1770

- 1775 Quakers establish first antislavery society in the United States
- 1775 Revolutionary War begins

1775

CHAPTER 4 The Road to Revolution 1650–1775 91

CHAPTER 4 CONCEPTS

Concept Mapping Activity

Display the following diagram on the chalkboard. Ask students to copy the diagram into their notebooks. As they read Chapter 4, have them list in their notebooks the major topics, main ideas, and supporting details related to the two concepts shown in the diagram.

> The idea of political separation grows from the misunderstandings between two divergent cultures
>
> Political Control   Political Protest

History AND ART

Peter F. Rothermel's earliest works were portraits, but in the 1840s he began to focus on historical subjects.

 VIDEODISC

- **GTV: The American People: Fabric of a Nation**

Side 1, Chapter 9
Title: *The Winds of Warfare!*
Subject: Cultural diversity in the Colonies

See GTV Guide page 56 for complete lesson plan.

Teacher Notes

91

LESSON PLAN
SECTION 1, 92–97

FOCUS

Bellringer
Before taking roll at the beginning of the class period, display Focus Activity Transparency 12 on the overhead projector, and assign the accompanying Focus Activity Sheet.

Objectives
Point out the objectives on this page to students in previewing the section content.

Motivating Activity
Ask students to list possible reasons for conflict in North America between Britain and France. (territorial, economic, political rivalry) Ask them to speculate on how such a conflict might affect the colonists. Tell them that this section focuses on those questions. After they have read the section, ask them to compare their ideas with what actually happened.

Use Skills Transparency 4.

SECTION 1

Struggle for Empire

Setting the Scene

Section Focus
The colonies needed to trade with other countries. When Parliament passed a series of laws restricting their right to trade freely, the colonists found ways to evade the restrictions. In 1689 England and France began a struggle for the control of North America.

Objectives
After studying this section, you should be able to
★ explain the economic motives that shaped British colonial policy.
★ explain the causes and results of the French and Indian War.

Key Terms
enumerated commodity, duty, salutary neglect, militia

▲ Cartoon promoting colonial unity

While allowing the colonies to run local affairs with little interference, Great Britain attempted to control their foreign trade. From the British point of view, the colonies existed to supply raw materials and to provide markets for British goods.

■ New Policies

Beginning in 1651, Parliament passed a series of laws known as Trade and Navigation Acts. The Navigation Act of 1651 stated that all goods shipped between England and the colonies had to be carried in ships built either in England or in the colonies. Then in 1660 Parliament listed, or enumerated, specific colonial products that could be shipped only to Britain. These **enumerated commodities** included tobacco, cotton, indigo, and sugar.

Another measure required American ships returning from Europe to make a "broken voyage," stopping at an English port to pay a **duty,** or tax, on the goods they had purchased. As a result, the colonies received less for some of their exports and paid more for some of their imports than if they had been permitted to trade freely.

Colonial Response

A number of other laws were designed to help special groups. For example, the Molasses Act of 1733 helped the owners of sugar plantations in the British West Indies by putting a heavy tax on the importation of sugar and molasses. Development of colonial industry was slowed by the Woolen Act of 1699, which forbade the colonies to export woolen goods; the Hat Act of 1732, which made it illegal for hatmakers to sell their goods outside the colonies; and the

UNIT 2 Creating a Nation: 1650–1789

Classroom Resources for SECTION 1

Teacher's Classroom Resources
- Chapter 4 Study Guide
- Chapter 4 Cooperative Learning Activity
- Reproducible Lesson Plan
- Reteaching Activity 4-1
- Chapter 4 Cooperative Learning Activity
- Section Quiz

Multimedia
- Section Focus Transparency 12
- Unit 2 Digest Transparency
- Chapter 4 Skills Transparency
- Testmaker
- Student Self-Test Software

Iron Act of 1750, which restricted the manufacture of iron.

Often, these restrictions were the result of pressure on Parliament by British manufacturers who wanted to kill colonial competition. Benjamin Franklin's reaction was typical of the Americans' views:

> A colonist cannot make a button, a horse shoe, nor a hobnail but some sooty ironmonger or respectable buttonmaker of Britain shall bawl . . . that his honor's worship is . . . injured, cheated and robbed by the rascally Americans.

Salutary Neglect

During the early colonial years, Parliament opted for a policy of **salutary neglect,** or non-interference, which allowed the colonists to do what they wished. One reason for the policy was distance—it was simply too difficult to control a situation 3,000 miles away. Another reason was that few revenue officers bothered to go to America; instead they appointed deputies, who were often lax in their duties. Soon colonists began to evade British laws, and smuggling became an accepted practice.

The French and Indian War

The Anglo-French contest for North America had two phases. The wars fought between 1689 and 1713 were known in the colonies as King William's War (1689–1697) and Queen Anne's War (1702–1713). At the close of this first phase, Great Britain gained Nova Scotia, Newfoundland, and Hudson's Bay Territory. The second phase, from 1742 to 1763, included the wars known in the colonies as King George's War (1742–1748) and the French and Indian War (1754–1763). In Europe they were called the War of the Austrian Succession and the Seven Years' War.

▲ **FRANKLIN IN LONDON** Benjamin Franklin journeyed to London to present the colonists' views on taxation to the Lords of the Privy Council. *Why was it difficult for the British government to enforce laws strictly in the colonies?*

Life of the Times

Colonial Dance

The long work week of most colonists was often filled with physically draining labor. The few moments spent on leisure activities generally centered around quiet activities such as reading or card games. Spectator sports for men—horse racing and turkey shoots—were also popular. Dancing, too, was a popular pastime.

From rural farms to urban mansions, dance in colonial America was a common recreation. While some clergy members condemned dancing as evil, others recommended it as healthy exercise. "Dancing masters"—teachers—opened schools in communities and were often employed by wealthy families to demonstrate the latest steps.

Taverns were often the site of impromptu dances. Couples performed line dances such as the reel to the accompaniment of a fiddler. The reel soon gave way to a more daring dance called the cotillion, a dance imported from the courts of France. In this forerunner of modern square dancing, four couples formed a group and moved to the directions of a "caller."

▲ DANCING THE MINUET

The Albany Plan

In 1754 delegates from seven northern colonies met with representatives of the Iroquois nations in Albany, New York. The stated purpose was to persuade the Iroquois to ally with the British against the French. But many delegates hoped to create a union of the colonies. Benjamin Franklin presented the Albany Plan of Union, a proposal that the colonies form a council with the power to levy taxes, raise troops, and regulate trade.

Although Franklin's plan was adopted by the delegates, it was rejected by both the colonial and British governments who feared loss of power. The lack of cooperation seriously handicapped the war effort. Americans seldom consented to fight outside their own colonies, and colonies ignored taxes imposed by Britain for their own defense. Nor would they tax themselves.

War Begins

The final struggle between England and France for control of North America began in the Ohio Valley. The French drove out English fur traders and in 1754 built Fort Duquesne (doo•KAYN) at the point where the Monongahela (muh•NAHN•guh•HEE•luh) and Allegheny rivers meet to form the Ohio River. The fort, located in territory claimed by both Virginia and Pennsylvania, was a threat to the safety of these colonies.

Facing this threat, the colonists sent a force of Virginia **militia**—a group of civilians trained as soldiers to fight in emergencies—to attack the fort. Under the command of an inexperienced 22-year-old major from Virginia named George Washington, the militia advanced on the fort and ambushed a French scouting party. The French later captured Washington's entire force but released them. War had begun even though there had been no formal declaration.

UNIT 2 Creating a Nation: 1650–1789

CHAPTER 4 SECTION 1

Independent Practice

Recognizing Cause and Effect Ask students to make cause-event-effect charts for the following events: William Pitt becomes Britain's minister of war in 1758 (Cause—early British defeats by the French; Effect—tide of war turns in favor of British). Braddock's defeat (Cause—British try to take Fort Duquesne; Effect—many Native Americans shift support to the French, weakening the British war effort). **L2**

Teaching Life of the Times

As well as dancing, the churches frowned upon drama and some forms of musical entertainment. Have students discuss why the churches did not speak out against such cruel pastimes as cockfighting.

Did You Know?

The present-day city of Pittsburgh, Pennsylvania, stands on the site of the old Fort Duquesne. When the British finally took the fort, they renamed it Fort Pitt.

Cooperative Learning

Divide students into groups of three. One student is to be an interviewer; the second, a colonial farmer or manufacturer; the third, a British counterpart. The interviewer in turn asks each of the other two to respond to the various trade and navigation acts imposed by the British to control the American colonies. At the close of the activity, the interviewer should select one act and report to the class the two responses to it. **L2, L3**

In the summer of 1755, British General Edward Braddock led 1,450 British and colonial soldiers in another attack on Fort Duquesne. Once more, the British forces were driven back.

Native American Support Shifts

Braddock's defeat caused many Native Americans to switch their support from the British to the French. The French were winning the war, and French fur traders, who mixed peacefully with the Native Americans, seemed less a threat to their way of life than did the land-hungry English settlers.

William Pitt

Disasters continued after Great Britain and France formally declared war in 1756. British generals were no match for French commander Louis Montcalm. British expeditions that tried to control the St. Lawrence River failed.

The tide shifted, however, when William Pitt became Britain's minister of war in 1758. By giving aid to France's enemies in Europe, Pitt forced France to split its forces. Pitt also sent talented, young officers to lead the campaigns in North America. By the end of 1758, Louisburg and Fort Duquesne were in British hands; and in June 1759, a British army of 9,000 was encamped on the St. Lawrence River a few miles below Quebec.

British commander James Wolfe had tried in vain to find a weak spot in the French defenses at Quebec. Finally, Wolfe proposed to have his troops land at night and scale a wooded cliff located under the guns of the fortress. Wolfe had observed Canadian women washing clothes in the river and hanging them to dry on the cliffs above. He realized that there had to be a pathway up the cliffs to the fortress! Wolfe suspected that the French would not have a strong guard at a point considered safe from attack.

Quebec Falls

Wolfe's soldiers climbed the cliffs and overpowered the few guards. Before daybreak 4,500 soldiers were prepared for battle on the fields at the top of the cliffs known as the Plains of Abraham. Commander Montcalm quickly gathered his forces to meet them. In the battle that followed, the French were forced to surrender.

■ Treaty of Paris, 1763

Great Britain won its war with France—in America, Europe, and Asia. Under the terms of the Treaty of Paris of 1763, Great Britain obtained all of Canada it did not already control and all the land east of the Mississippi River. From Spain, France's ally, Great Britain gained Florida. To repay Spain for its losses and to avoid losing it to Great Britain, France transferred the Louisiana Territory to Spain. North America was now

Map Study In 1754 Great Britain, France, Spain, and Russia all claimed land in North America. **Which two countries controlled the most land on the continent?**

CHAPTER 4
SECTION 1

The colonists' desire for unlimited trade with other nations helped spark revolution. This desire did not end with separation from Britain. From the start, however, Americans were divided over how much protection their industries should have from foreign competition. Although the U.S. government today has a number of agreements with other nations that promote free trade, the issue is still being debated.

Map Study Using Maps
Answer: France and Spain

Skills Practice
Have students use information from the text and the map on page 95 to create a new map showing European land claims in North America after the French and Indian War.

CHAPTER 4 The Road to Revolution 1650–1775 **95**

Cultural Diversity

A Varied Society Visitors to the American colonies were usually surprised by the diversity they observed. One could encounter English, Irish, Scottish, Dutch, and German inhabitants, all speaking their own language. Roman Catholics, Anglicans, Methodists, Presbyterians, Quakers, and Jews freely practiced their religion.

CHAPTER 4 SECTION 1

ASSESS

Check Understanding
Assign Section 1 review as homework or an in-class activity.

Evaluate
Assign the Section 1 quiz in the TCR or use the History of a Free Nation Testmaker to create a customized quiz.

Reteach
Have students complete Reteaching Activity 4-1.

Enrich
Ask students to reread the material on General Wolfe's battle plan at Quebec. Have them write a brief report on the role that geography played in Wolfe's strategy.

CLOSE
Refer students to the list of reasons for conflict between Britain and France that they drew up at the beginning of this section. Ask them to review their speculations on how the conflict might affect the colonists.

Map Study Using Maps
Answer: from Cape Breton Island through the Gulf of St. Lawrence and up the St. Lawrence River

Skills Practice
Ask student in which direction Murray traveled. (southwest)

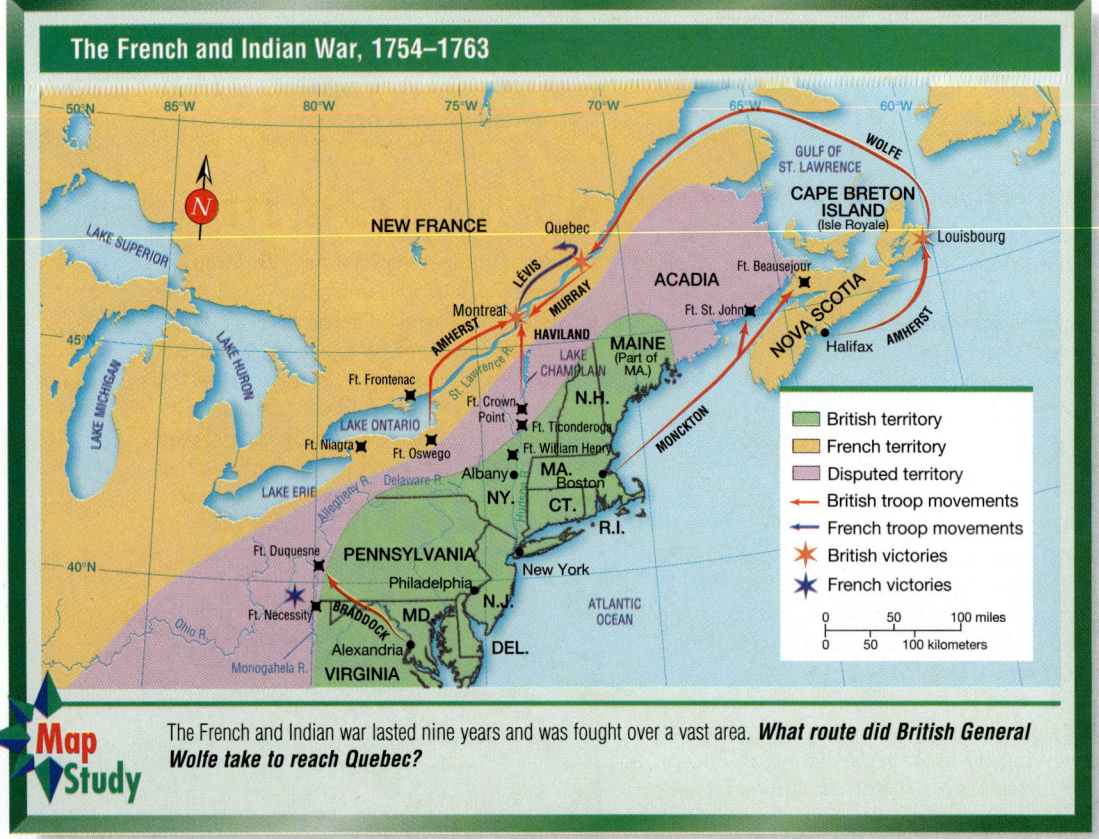

The French and Indian War, 1754–1763

The French and Indian war lasted nine years and was fought over a vast area. **What route did British General Wolfe take to reach Quebec?**

divided between Great Britain and Spain with the Mississippi River forming the boundary.

For the French, defeat was bitter. France was left with no land on the continent of North America. After 150 years of colonization, the enterprise and heroism of French pioneers, missionaries, and soldiers were halted. There was only one small crumb of comfort—the 13 colonies might revolt. A French leader likened them to a "ripe fruit," ready to drop off the branch.

Section 1 ★ Review

Checking for Understanding
1. **Identify** Albany Plan of Union, George Washington, Treaty of Paris.
2. **Define** enumerated commodity, duty, salutary neglect, militia.
3. **State** two ways in which the interests of the British and the colonists differed.
4. **Explain** why control of the Ohio Valley was important.

Critical Thinking
5. **Recognizing Stereotypes** In a war, the two sides are usually categorized as good and bad or the right side and the wrong side. In the French and Indian War, the British and the American colonists who fought for them are usually portrayed as the right side, while the French and their Native American allies are portrayed as the wrong side. Discuss how this results in stereotyping.

Answers to SECTION 1 REVIEW
1. Albany Plan of Union, 94; George Washington, 94; Treaty of Paris, 95
2. All vocabulary words are defined in the Glossary.
3. Colonists wanted unrestricted trade with other nations; Britain wanted to control trade for its own benefit. Britain wanted to expand its empire by gaining French territory; colonists were reluctant to fight Britain's wars.
4. The area had an extensive river system and was a rich source of furs.
5. Responses may include that categorizing one group of people as good and another as bad leads people to believe that everyone in that group is either good or bad.

CONNECTIONS — History and Geography — CONNECTIONS

Native American and European Land Values

Struggles between white settlers and Native Americans continued intermittently from the time Europeans first came to the Americas until the end of the 1800s. A major underlying cause of these struggles was conflict over land. Native Americans were quick to understand European desire for their own territory, but colonists seemed unable—or unwilling—to understand how deeply the Native Americans valued the land. Chief Pontiac, of the Ottawa people, speaking to Englishman Alexander Henry, explained: *"These lakes, these woods, and mountains were left us by our ancestors. They are our inheritances, and we will part with them to no one. . . . you ought to know that He, the Great Spirit and Master of Life, has provided food for us in these spacious lakes and on the woody mountains. . . ."*

Englishman George Thomas, when negotiating the price paid to the Iroquois for lands in New York, stated a very different view: *"It is very true, that the lands are of late become more valuable, but what raises their value? Is it not entirely owing to the industry and labor used by the white people, in their cultivation and improvement? Had not they come amongst you, these lands would have been of no use to you . . . and the value of land is no more than it is worth in money."*

The steady expansion of colonial settlements transformed the Native American way of life. Few among the colonists were willing to treat the Native Americans as equals or acknowledge their rights to the land. In 1635 the Pequot people of southern New England rose up against the colonists and were defeated. A combined force of settlers from Plymouth, Massachusetts, and Connecticut followed and attacked the Pequots who fled.

▲ NATIVE AMERICAN VILLAGE

Increasingly feeling the pressure of colonial expansion, five Native American peoples formed an alliance in 1675. Under the alliance's leader Metacomet, called King Philip by the Puritans, the Native Americans were also defeated. Native Americans continued to raid frontier villages, however, and their bitterness against the English grew.

Making the Geography Connection

1. What was the value of the land to Native Americans?
2. How did the colonists' idea of land value differ from the Native Americans' view?

Linking Past and Present

3. How does Thomas's view compare with the current practice of valuing land?

CHAPTER 4 CONNECTIONS

Teaching Making Connections

Ask students to suggest how the Americas might have been settled differently if Europeans had shared the Native Americans' philosophy of land ownership.

FACT or FICTION?

William Penn, the Quaker founder of Pennsylvania, was one of the few early colonists who refused to buy land from Native Americans.

FACT: Penn negotiated treaties with Native Americans for the use of their lands, writing that "great Promises pass between us of Kindness and good Neighborhood . . . ."

Did You Know?

Not until the late twentieth century were Native Americans able to regain rights to some of the lands taken from them. Although the government has made payments to some groups to settle their land claims, most Native Americans want their land, not money.

Answers to CONNECTIONS

1. provided their living and was part of their heritage
2. Colonists viewed land as valuable only in its ability to make money for people.
3. Answers will vary, but most students will probably respond that Thomas's view is in line with the modern view of the value of land.

LESSON PLAN
SECTION 2, 98–102

FOCUS

Bellringer

Before taking roll at the beginning of the class period, display Focus Activity Transparency 13 on the overhead projector, and assign the accompanying Focus Activity Sheet.

Objectives

Point out the objectives on this page to students in previewing the section content.

Motivating Activity

Write these slogans on the chalkboard: "Taxation without representation is tyranny!" "Give me liberty or give me death!" "Don't tread on me!" Discuss the meanings of these slogans with students. Tell them slogans like these were prompted by British policies after the French and Indian War. Point out that as students read this section they will find out which British actions prompted these and other slogans.

- *GTV: A Geographic Perspective on American History*

Side 1, Chapter 15
Title: *Laying Down the Law*
Subject: The rise of revolutionary feelings

See GTV Guide page 38 for complete lesson plan.

SECTION 2

Control and Protest

Setting the Scene

Section Focus

Although the colonists did not realize it at the time, the French and Indian War changed their relationship with Britain forever. Freed from danger of French attack, Americans no longer needed British protection.

Objectives

After studying this section, you should be able to

★ list and explain British attempts to tighten control over the colonies.

★ identify the ways in which the colonies resisted British control.

Key Terms

land speculator, writ of assistance, specie, direct tax, boycott, nonimportation agreement, redcoat

▲ **WARNING TO THE BRITISH**

After the French and Indian War, Britain turned its attention to America. Victory had brought Britain vast new territories—and new problems. The British government first had to cope with the huge debt left by the war. Then it needed to decide what to do with the recently acquired western territory beyond the Appalachian and Allegheny mountains.

Proclamation of 1763

In 1763 Pontiac's Rebellion broke out in the West. Pontiac, chief of the Ottawa people, had foreseen that Britain's defeat of France meant a hard fate for his people. The French had traded with the Native Americans and lived among them. By contrast, the ever-advancing settlers of the British colonies threatened to wipe them out. Pontiac welded several Native American peoples into a fighting force and formed a confederacy in the Ohio Valley. Pontiac's forces captured a chain of British forts northwest of the Ohio River but failed to drive the settlers back across the Appalachian Mountains.

During Pontiac's Rebellion, the British government issued the Proclamation of 1763, which ended all settlement west of the Appalachian Mountains. The government also maintained thousands of troops along the frontier—as much to protect the Native Americans from the settlers as the settlers from the native peoples.

Although Americans at first accepted the Proclamation of 1763, they soon resented it. Colonists protested that the Proclamation deprived them of land they had a right to settle and interfered with charter rights of colonies whose grants extended "from sea to sea." Perhaps the biggest outcry came

98   UNIT 2 Creating a Nation: 1650–1789

Classroom Resources for SECTION 2

Teacher's Classroom Resources
- Reproducible Lesson Plan
- Reteaching Activity 4-2
- Section Quiz

Multimedia
 Section Focus Transparency 13
- Testmaker
- Student Self-Test Software
- A Geographic Perspective on American History

from **land speculators**—people who purchased land to resell it for profit. They claimed American interests were being sacrificed to fill the pockets of the British fur traders who wished to leave the Native Americans undisturbed.

■ Stricter Enforcement

The selection of George Grenville as Britain's minister of finance in 1763 signaled a change in policy. Grenville was an energetic administrator who believed that laws should be strictly enforced. He was said to be the first minister in a generation who read dispatches from American revenue collectors and was aware of the extent of smuggling in the colonies. In addition, Grenville noted that the revenue service in the 13 colonies was costing the British government 4 times as much as it collected.

Grenville required customs officers to go to their posts in America rather than stay in England and hire deputies as before. These officers were armed with **writs of assistance**—general search warrants allowing them to seek smuggled goods without swearing out a particular warrant for every building they entered. Grenville also mandated that colonists accused of smuggling be tried in admiralty courts, where the accused was denied the right of trial by jury and the judges pocketed a percentage of the fines they imposed.

■ New Taxes

Between 1764 and 1767, Parliament levied new taxes that shifted part of the burden of the war debt to the colonies. With the acquisition of Canada and other territories after the war, the size of the British Empire had more than doubled, and the problems of governing it grew more complicated and expensive. The war left the British government with a national debt more than twice what it was in 1754, and the people of Britain objected strongly to paying any more in taxes. They felt it was only fair that the colonists pay a part of the cost of defending and administering the empire.

The Sugar Act

Grenville also persuaded Parliament to levy duties on colonial imports, the most important of these being the Sugar Act of

The Proclamation of 1763

Map Study The Proclamation of 1763 forbade colonists from settling west of an imaginary line along the crest of the Appalachian Mountains. **Why did the British government want to halt westward movement?**

CHAPTER 4
SECTION 2

TEACH
Guided Practice
Civics Ask students to consider how the British government and the colonists viewed the concept of representation. Then have them make a concept map that shows the difference between these two views. Ask a volunteer to present and explain the concept map to the class. **L3**

Map Study Using Maps
Answer: to avoid conflict with Native Americans who lived west of the Appalachians

Skills Practice
As a result of the Proclamation of 1763, what river was closed to British colonists? (Mississippi)

Food of the Times
Most American colonists avoided drinking water because it was often tainted. The chief drink was cider, consumed at every meal, including breakfast. There were many special beverages as well. A concoction called syllabub, made of sweetened cider, nutmeg, milk, and cream, was a traditional Christmas drink.

Special Needs

Inefficient Readers This section is especially adaptable to role-playing, which can greatly aid students whose reading skills are weak. Organize students into two groups. Have one group imagine they are members of the British government and the other group imagine they are American colonial leaders. Have each group present its case on imposing taxes on the colonies, making certain the group provides arguments supporting its point of view. Discuss with students the possible outcomes if their views on taxation are adopted.

1764. Although this law cut the rates of the Molasses Act of 1733, the British government had always winked at evasions of the Molasses Act of 1733. The troubling thing about the Sugar Act was that the British intended to enforce it. Colonial merchants realized that strict enforcement would wipe out the profits of the trade with the Spanish and French West Indies that brought much-needed **specie**—gold and silver coins—into the colonies. In that same year, Parliament forbade colonial governments to issue paper money. Caught in a two-way squeeze of lower profits and scarcity of hard currency, many merchants faced bankruptcy.

▲ **PONTIAC IN COUNCIL** Pontiac's forces, which included members from many different Native American nations, captured most of the British outposts west of Fort Niagara. *How did the British change their settlement policy?*

The Stamp Act

In 1765 Parliament passed another revenue law called the Stamp Act. This law differed from previous tax measures because it was a **direct tax**—a tax paid directly to the government rather than being included in the price of goods. It required that stamps be placed on many kinds of articles and documents, including wills, playing cards, newspapers, dice, almanacs, and licenses. Duties ranged from 1 cent on newspapers to $10 for college diplomas, and payment had to be made in specie.

Protest

While Grenville's previous tax laws had affected those engaged in foreign trade, namely New England merchants and shippers, the Stamp Act affected colonists everywhere. It especially offended the most powerful and articulate groups in the colonies: lawyers, newspaper editors, and ministers. On the day the Stamp Act was to go into effect, men and women wore mourning clothes and church bells tolled all the way from Portsmouth, New Hampshire, to Savannah, Georgia.

Colonists backed their protests with a **boycott**—a refusal to buy British goods. Men and women made solemn promises to wear homespun clothing instead of British woolens. Colonial merchants signed **nonimportation agreements,** promising not to buy British goods until Parliament repealed the unpopular law. Soon imports from Britain dropped, and British merchants, saying that they were faced with "utter ruin," besieged Parliament with petitions against the Stamp Act. Under such pressure, Parliament backed down and repealed the law in 1766.

The Townshend Acts

The next year Parliament tried to raise revenue through the Townshend (TOWN•zehnd) Acts, which placed import duties on tea, paper, glass, and paint. The British could not effectively collect these taxes either, and all the Townshend duties were

UNIT 2 Creating a Nation: 1650–1789

repealed in 1770, except the tax on tea, which was retained to assert the principle of Parliament's authority.

Threats to Colonial Self-Government

Grenville's new customs collectors and admiralty judges were followed by 10,000 British soldiers. These troops were sent, it was said, to protect the Americans. But to protect them from whom? The French had been defeated, and the Native Americans were at peace. Colonists noted that the British soldiers, called **redcoats** because of the color of their uniforms, were not stationed in frontier posts, but in towns such as Boston and New York where there was no more danger from Native Americans than in London. But the presence of the redcoats served other purposes—to strengthen the hand of colonial governors and to frighten colonial legislatures into line.

It was also clear that the British wanted to free royal officials from colonial control. For this reason, the British government shifted customs cases to the admiralty courts and ruled that royal judges and governors were to be paid out of customs revenues that British revenue officers collected. Now colonial legislatures could no longer check the power of royal governors by holding up their salaries.

Disobedience to British Laws

The efforts of the British government to tighten control met such swift and determined resistance that it surprised even the Americans themselves. The resistance took a variety of forms, including disobedience to British laws, protests, increased cooperation among the 13 colonies, boycotts, and violence.

The Americans, long accustomed to evading British revenue laws, did not hesitate to disobey new ones. In spite of a much stronger British customs service, smuggling went on much as usual. The long coast of America prevented revenue officers from inspecting all incoming ships, especially when the local inhabitants were constantly trying to thwart them.

In 1765 Parliament passed the Quartering Act directing the colonies to provide barracks and supplies for the thousands of British troops ordered to America. The New York and Massachusetts legislatures regarded the act as concealed taxation and flatly refused to provide funds. Most of the other colonies found other ways to disobey the law.

After 1765 many colonists crossed the Appalachian Mountains and began to establish settlements in the western lands. Led by Daniel Boone and others, settlers spilled into western New York, Kentucky, and Tennessee, staking their land claims on Native American land. Although this westward movement met the colonists' need for expansion, it violated the Proclamation of 1763.

▲ **COLONIAL RESPONSE** Patrick Henry attacked the Stamp Act in a speech given before the Virginia legislature. *What did the colonists mean by "no taxation without representation"?*

Visualizing History
A French observer noted that in spite of Patrick Henry's rousing oratory, the fiery speaker did express his loyalty to Britain and to the king. The "resolves" that Henry persuaded the Virginia legislature to pass against the Stamp Act were printed by newspapers throughout the colonies.
Answer to Caption: The colonists did not believe they should be taxed, because they did not elect representatives to the British Parliament.

Did You Know?
The word *boycott* comes from the name of an infamous English landlord in Ireland named Captain James Boycott. People responded to his acts of cruelty by refusing to have anything to do with him.

Fact or Fiction?
When the British learned of American resistance to the Stamp Act, they united against the Americans.

FICTION: Word of American resistance touched off a heated debate in Britain over the wisdom of the act. The debate began in the press and among ordinary people and reached Parliament itself in December 1765.

Making Connections: History and Politics

The Stamp Act was not the first restrictive British law, but it was the first to arouse unanimous colonial opposition. During the furor over the act, a tradition of peaceful protest by Americans was established. The groups most directly affected by the Stamp Act were ministers, lawyers, and newspaper editors. These powerful people with access to methods of mass communication helped lay the groundwork for the widespread protests that would lead to the Revolutionary War. In so doing they helped lay the basis for the nation's freedoms of speech and press.

CHAPTER 4 SECTION 2

ASSESS

Check Understanding
Assign Section 2 Review as homework or an in-class assignment.

Evaluate
 Assign the TCR or use the History of a Free Nation Testmaker to create a customized quiz.

Reteach
 Have students complete Reteaching Activity 4-2.

Enrich
Ask students to make up their own slogans in response to various British actions. Students may wish to display their slogans on a bulletin board.

CLOSE
Have students trace the developments that brought the colonists to challenge British authority.

ABCNEWS INTERACTIVE

The following material is available from Glencoe and may be used to introduce or enrich Chapter 4:

VIDEODISC
Powers of the Congress

Side 1
Chapter 8: Comparing Governments 7754–8851

The Question of Representation

One of the first public colonial protests took place in Virginia in May 1765 when the House of Burgesses met to consider the Stamp Act. Patrick Henry introduced the Virginia Resolutions protesting Parliament's action. Henry claimed that, since Americans elected no members to the British Parliament, they could not be taxed by that body. The House of Burgesses had "the only exclusive right and power to lay taxes" upon Virginians. This bold stand by the largest of the colonies encouraged the other colonies to follow suit, and the principle of "no taxation without representation" was accepted as a basic right.

Virtual Representation

To most people in Britain the argument against "taxation without representation" was faulty. The colonies were represented under the principle of "virtual" representation. It did not matter that Americans did not elect members to the House of Commons, the only branch of the government that could tax. Many other citizens were not directly represented either. It did not matter where these citizens lived or even if they had the right to vote because the House of Commons was pledged to represent every person in Britain and the empire. Americans had little regard for the idea of virtual representation, largely because, since the time of the earliest settlements, the people had always had direct representation—electing colonial assembly members to represent their interests.

The Stamp Act Congress

Resistance to the Stamp Act brought about the first real cooperation among the 13 colonies. A committee of the Massachusetts legislature sent letters to leaders of the other colonial legislatures urging them to send delegates to a convention to decide on a common policy toward the British government. As a result, the Stamp Act Congress met in New York in October 1765. Nine colonial legislatures were represented, and the colonies that did not participate sent messages of support.

The delegates drew up resolutions and organized a boycott of British-made goods. In 1768 the Massachusetts legislature issued a Circular Letter calling on all the other colonial legislatures to join in protest against the measure.

John Dickinson helped promote colonial unity in his *Letters from a Farmer in Pennsylvania* published in 1767 and 1768. Dickinson argued that the people of the American colonies, "separated from the rest of the world, and firmly held together by the same rights, interests, and dangers," creating "one political body of which each colony is a member."

▶ JOHN DICKINSON

Section 2 ★ Review

Checking for Understanding
1. **Identify** Pontiac, Proclamation of 1763, Stamp Act, Townshend Acts, Stamp Act Congress.
2. **Define** land speculator, writ of assistance, specie, direct tax, boycott, nonimportation agreement, redcoat.
3. **Explain** why Great Britain ended salutary neglect of the colonies after 1763.
4. **State** the primary reason American colonists opposed direct taxes.

Critical Thinking
5. **Understanding Cause and Effect** Compose a series of American newspaper headlines that describe British actions (causes) and American reactions (effects) between 1763 and 1770.

102   UNIT 2 Creating a Nation: 1650–1789

Answers to SECTION 2 REVIEW

1. Pontiac; 98; Proclamation of 1763, 98; Stamp Act, 100; Townshend Acts, 100; Stamp Act Congress, 102
2. All vocabulary words are defined in the Glossary.
3. Stricter enforcement was necessary to raise revenue to pay Britain's war debt and to regulate Britain's new territories.
4. Taxes were levied by a distant government body in which colonists had no voice.
5. Responses might include: "British Close Western Frontier"; "Americans Angered Over Restrictions"; "British Pass Despicable Stamp Act"; "Americans Boycott British Goods."

Social Studies Skills

Interpreting Primary Sources

The Stamp Act Crisis

During the decade between the passage of the Stamp Act in 1765 and the outbreak of the Revolution, colonial resistance to Parliament took several forms. Colonial legislatures issued many resolutions and petitions to the Crown criticizing their perceived loss of some rights and "taxation without representation." Early colonial successes, though—notably the repeal of the Stamp Act—came from boycotts and other acts of defiance by ordinary citizens.

Open protest against unjust rulers and laws had long been an accepted part of English political life. In the colonies, efforts to bring about political change through protest were aided by weak British control. Although colonial officials had the authority to suppress "disturbances of the peace," they frequently did not have the means to do so. In rural areas, police power consisted only of a county sheriff and, sometimes, a deputy. In towns, the sheriff might have had a night watch, but this was seldom effective. In New York, for example, the night watch was described as a "parcel of idle, drinking, vigilant snorers who never quelled any nocturnal tumult in their lives."

The hated Stamp Act placed a tax on every type of legal document, newspapers, almanacs—even playing cards and dice. A stamp on the paper testified that the tax had been paid. Money raised from the sale of stamps was to be used to help pay for British soldiers stationed in the colonies. The measure created a great protest because it was Parliament's first attempt to tax the colonists directly. Previously, each colony had been assessed a portion of the revenue needed, and the assemblies raised the money by whatever means they chose.

Colonists reacted swiftly. Radical groups formed, riots broke out, and delegates from most of the colonies declared at a Stamp Act Congress that Parliament had no legal right to tax the colonists.

▲ BURNING STAMPS TO PROTEST THE STAMP ACT

The illustration on this page depicts the unrest that convinced stamp agents throughout the colonies to resign their posts. Images such as this also served to justify violent action.

Examining the Primary Source

1. Describe the mood of the crowd. What details in the picture help you determine this?
2. Would publicity of such a protest reinforce or strengthen colonial resistance? Explain.

Critical Thinking

3. **Demonstrating Reasoned Judgment** What circumstances today might justify using intimidation tactics to protest unjust laws? Explain.

103

LESSON PLAN
Mastering Social Studies Skills

Teaching Interpreting Primary Sources

Remind students that symbols are often used in political cartoons. Discuss the purpose of a political cartoon. (present a definite viewpoint about an event, persuade people to see the subject of the cartoon from a certain viewpoint) Ask: Why can cartoons be a powerful way to communicate? (They get a message across in a simple and humorous way—often with few words.)

Have students describe the cartoon shown. What is the artist's view of the Stamp Act? How do you know? (Negative; the crowd stones a stamp agent. A coffin is shown, possibly symbolizing the desire to rid the colony of the law.) Whose point of view is shown in the cartoon? What might a cartoon portraying the opposite point of view look like? (Answers will vary but would indicate the British point of view.)

Did You Know?

Only four colonies failed to send representatives to the Stamp Act Congress. No one came from New Hampshire. Many in Virginia, North Carolina, and Georgia supported the protests, but their governors refused to call their legislative assemblies into session so that members could choose representatives.

Answers to SOCIAL STUDIES SKILLS

1. The hats raised high in the air indicate that the crowd is in a lively, jovial mood.
2. reinforced by showing people in a mood of excitement and readiness to resist
3. Answers will vary. Some students may say that circumstances never justify using tactics of fear and intimidation because innocent people could be hurt. Others may suggest that using such tactics are justified if political leaders are using the same methods to enforce their authority.

103

LESSON PLAN
SECTION 3, 104–111

FOCUS

Bellringer
Before taking roll at the beginning of the class period, display Focus Activity Transparency 14 on the overhead projector, and assign the accompanying Focus Activity Sheet.

Objectives
Point out the objectives on this page to students in previewing the section content.

Motivating Activity
Have students define in their own words the concept of "resistance." Ask them to list examples of resistance from their knowledge of history. Discuss students' examples, and encourage them to predict what will happen next as the colonists continue to resist British policies. As students read the section, have them trace the way resistance escalates into a shooting war.

- *GTV: A Geographic Perspective on American History*

Side 1, Chapter 15
Title: *Laying Down the Law*
Subject: The rise of revolutionary feelings

See GTV Guide page 38 for complete lesson plan.

SECTION 3

The Breach Widens

Setting the Scene

Section Focus
The period between 1770 and 1773 marked a slowdown in the struggle between the colonies and Great Britain. This respite ended when Parliament granted a monopoly on the sale of tea in the colonies to the East India Company. After that every British action triggered an American response—the Boston Tea Party, the Intolerable Acts, and the First Continental Congress. Even as late as the winter of 1775, many colonists hoped for a reconciliation with Britain.

Objectives
After studying this section, you should be able to
★ list the Intolerable Acts and describe how the colonists responded to them.
★ describe the events that led to war between Great Britain and the American colonies.

Key Terms
effigy, monopoly

▶ PAUL REVERE'S RIDE

Resistance to taxation caused a new spirit of cooperation and a rising spirit of patriotism. In a speech to the Stamp Act Congress, Christopher Gadsden of South Carolina declared, "There ought to be no New England Man, no New Yorker, known on the continent, but all of us Americans."

■ Boycotts and Violence

Although most colonial leaders who opposed efforts of the British Parliament to tax Americans were from the wealthy planter and merchant classes, they were supported and aided by many others. Among those who fueled the resistance were shopkeepers, clerks, and laborers. These colonists were the driving force behind two vital resistance groups—the Sons and Daughters of Liberty.

Sons of Liberty

The Sons of Liberty carried out organized resistance by keeping watch on shopkeepers suspected of selling British goods. They publicly denounced or threatened those they caught. When the Sons of Liberty learned that Andrew Oliver was going to be appointed Distributor of Stamps for Boston, they hung his **effigy**, or likeness, on the Liberty Tree and stoned it. Then they looted his house and coerced him to refuse the job.

American and British opposition to the Stamp Act forced Parliament to repeal it. In an effort to save face, Parliament passed the Declaratory Act, which affirmed its rights as the supreme legislator of the British empire.

Parliament was following the principle of this law when it passed the Townshend Acts in 1767, but the colonists argued that any

UNIT 2 Creating a Nation: 1650–1789

Classroom Resources for SECTION 3

Teacher's Classroom Resources
- Reproducible Lesson Plan
- Reteaching Activity 4-3
- Chapter 4 Primary and Secondary Source Readings
- Chapter 4 Enrichment Activity
- Chapter 4 Performance Assessment Activity
- Section Quiz

Multimedia
- Section Focus Transparency 14
- Vocabulary Puzzlemaker
- Testmaker
- Student Self-Test Software
- A Geographic Perspective on American History

▲ Mercy Otis Warren

▲ **Revolutionary Actions** Some Americans used force against British sympathizers. Mercy Otis Warren of the Daughters of Liberty was a witty and skillful propagandist for the American cause. *In what other way did the Sons and Daughters of Liberty help the resistance?*

law designed to raise revenue from them without their consent was a violation of their liberties.

Daughters of Liberty

Colonial women organized the Daughters of Liberty to boycott British goods. The Daughters of Liberty gave up imported clothes, made tea out of local herbs, and produced homespun cloth. One of the most influential of the Daughters was Mercy Otis Warren, who published pamphlets supporting the resistance—although she had to use a man's name to be published.

The Boston Massacre

In the same year that Parliament repealed the Townshend duties, the first clash between Americans and British troops took place. On the night of March 5, 1770, a crowd of 50 or 60 men and boys gathered to taunt British soldiers outside the Boston Customs House. When the crowd threw sticks and snowballs at the redcoats, the soldiers panicked and opened fire, killing five men. News of the event, which became known as the "Boston Massacre," spread throughout the colonies. It soon became a symbol of British force and tyranny.

An Uneasy Calm

From 1770 to 1773 a lull quieted the controversy between Great Britain and the 13 colonies. Having won relief from some taxes, the Americans allowed the British to collect others. Imports of British goods rose—from $8 million in 1768 to $21 million in 1771.

The calm was interrupted periodically by acts of violence. In 1771 a British customs schooner that had taken a smugglers' ship into custody was attacked at night. When another British revenue boat, the *Gaspée*, ran aground off Rhode Island, "persons unknown" attacked and burned it.

Meanwhile, leaders of the American resistance were busy forming a variety of organizations to translate popular discontent into action. The most effective of these

CHAPTER 4 The Road to Revolution 1650–1775   **105**

Sidelights: Mercy Otis Warren

Mercy Otis Warren was an important Revolutionary figure. The sister of one resistance leader and wife of another, she was an accomplished writer of scholarly history and witty satirical plays. She created devastating portraits of the British in works such as *The Defeat* (1773) and *The Group* (1775). She also carried on widespread correspondence with noted people of the time, including John Adams. A champion of political freedom, she opposed ratification of the Constitution because she believed it gave too much power to the federal government.

CHAPTER 4 SECTION 3

Teaching American Portraits
What role did Crispus Attucks play in the Boston Massacre? Some members of the mob said he was an innocent bystander. However, an eyewitness claimed to have seen Attucks disarm and knock down a redcoat. Others charged that he actually organized and led the mob. Discuss why there is so much confusion about what happened on March 5, 1770.

Independent Practice
Military History Have students write a paragraph to explain why each of the following battles was important for the Americans: Lexington and Concord, Bunker Hill, Crown Point, and Ticonderoga. (At Lexington and Concord, they learned about British fighting style; at Bunker Hill the untrained colonial militia stood up to professional British troops; Crown Point and Ticonderoga were strategically placed on a water route and had large stores of military supplies.) **L1, LEP**

---

were the committees of correspondence. Keeping in contact with each other, these committees helped keep the resistance movement going.

■ The Boston Tea Party

The period of calm between the colonies and Britain came to an end with the Boston Tea Party. This dramatic event started a chain reaction that led to war and broke the ties between Great Britain and the colonies.

Monopoly
By 1773 the British East India Company was experiencing severe financial problems. Facing bankruptcy, the company appealed to Parliament for assistance. Parliament quickly voted to grant it a **monopoly**, or sole control of the trade, for tea in America.

Announcement of the plan produced an outcry in America. Colonists objected to the tea monopoly because they suspected its real purpose was to bribe them into acknowledging Parliament's right to tax the colonies.

Opposition
Opposition groups mobilized to prevent the sale of the East India tea. Ships arriving in the Atlantic ports were unable to sell a pound of tea. At New York and Philadelphia the tea ships were forced to turn back.

In Boston, however, Governor Hutchinson ordered that no ship could leave the harbor without unloading its tea. Colonists led by Sam Adams were just as determined that no tea would come ashore. For days, crowds milled in the street and attended rallies discussing what action to take. Then on December 16, about 8,000 people attended a meeting where they learned that Hutchinson would not back down. On a signal from Sam Adams, a group of colonists, disguised as Mohawks, rushed to the wharf. Before a cheering crowd, they boarded the tea ships and heaved 342 chests of tea into the harbor.

■ The Intolerable Acts

Benjamin Franklin called the Boston Tea Party "an act of violent injustice." Some Boston merchants were willing to start a collection to pay for the damage.

Crispus Attucks
1723(?)–1770

AMERICAN PORTRAITS

Little is known about the life of Crispus Attucks before the evening of March 5, 1770. Attucks may well have been a runaway slave in Boston, where he probably worked on the docks; but for one brief moment that night, Attucks stood at the forefront of American resistance to British rule.

After Attucks finished his dinner in an inn, he joined a nearby crowd that had formed on King Street. Young boys were taunting a group of British soldiers, hurling snowballs and sticks. Tensions grew between the soldiers and the unruly mob. A soldier's musket suddenly fired, and Attucks fell to the ground and died instantly.

Four others were also killed, and several were wounded in what has become known as the Boston Massacre. Attucks became a martyr to the patriot cause—an African American who gave his life in the name of liberty.

106 UNIT 2 Creating a Nation: 1650–1789

Making Connections: History and Art

Today Crispus Attucks's presence at the Boston Massacre is well known and unquestioned. Paul Revere's engraving of the time clearly shows that one of the dead colonists in the square is black. Copies of the engraving were widely shown throughout the colonies to enlist support for the cause. However, in the southern colonies, the engravings pictured all the dead men lying in the Boston snow as white.

▲ JOHN ADAMS

 ▲ THE BOSTON MASSACRE Bitter feelings erupted in bloodshed on March 5, 1770 in Boston, when British soldiers fired into a crowd, killing five. **What happened when news of the Boston Massacre spread?**

Visualizing History Some eyewitnesses told a different story about the Boston Massacre than the one depicted here. According to them, frightened British soldiers fired in self-defense after being threatened by a mob wielding clubs and hurling insults. The victims of the massacre are buried in the same graveyard in Boston along with Paul Revere, John Adams, and other Revolutionary heroes.
Answer to Caption: fear and distrust of the British spread

The Coercive Acts

To the British government, however, the Boston Tea Party was an act of lawlessness that deserved swift and severe punishment. In March 1774, Parliament passed a series of laws known as the Coercive Acts. One of the acts closed the port of Boston until payment was made for the tea. Another act stipulated that British officials accused of a crime were to be tried in English rather than American courts. Still another provided that British troops could be quartered in any town in Massachusetts—even in private homes. Finally, the Massachusetts charter was amended to greatly reduce the colony's right of self-government. Colonists considered the provisions of the Coercive Acts so harsh that they called them the "Intolerable Acts."

The Quebec Act

Passed at the same time, and considered by the colonists as one of the Intolerable Acts, was the Quebec Act, which extended the Canadian province of Quebec south to the Ohio River. It also allowed French Canadians use of their own legal system, which did not provide for trial by jury, and which recognized the legality of the Roman Catholic Church. Americans saw the Quebec Act as the first step toward doing away with jury trials and Protestantism in the 13 colonies. They also believed the boundary changes were made to keep American settlers out of western lands forever.

The Intolerable Acts revealed that the British government intended to show the colonists who had authority.

■ The First Continental Congress

When Parliament passed the Coercive Acts, British leaders expected that the other colonies would agree that Massachusetts deserved punishment. William Pitt had warned, however, that the acts would give the colonies a new reason to unite.

Did You Know?

The word *green* refers to a large open area in the center of a village. It derives from the Old English word *growan*, which means "to grow" or "to become green." New England towns were organized around a central area of uncleared land owned in common by all.

Critical Thinking

Analyzing Cause and Effect Have students consider the Intolerable, or Coercive, Acts as they would a single stone thrown into a silent pool; it causes countless ripples to form. Have the class discuss and list as many effects of the four acts as they can. They might wish to divide the effects into these general categories: effects on individuals and families, effects on the colonial legal system, effects on the colonial political system, effects on colonial resistance, and so forth. **L2**

▲ KING GEORGE III

 ▲ DEATH OF GENERAL WARREN AT THE BATTLE OF BUNKER HILL by JOHN TRUMBULL, 1786 The bright red uniforms, the stormy sky, and the heroic scene reflect the patriotic temper of the times. **Why was the battle symbolic for the colonists?**

Declaration of Rights and Grievances

Pitt proved to be right. The acts convinced many Americans that the leaders of Britain were conspiring to take away their liberties. In response, the 56 delegates to the First Continental Congress met in Philadelphia in September 1774.

The Congress petitioned the king for relief from the Intolerable Acts and vowed to stop trade with Britain until the acts were repealed. A Declaration of Rights and Grievances denounced every revenue-raising or power-limiting step taken by Britain since 1763 as a violation of colonial charters and the rights of colonists as British citizens.

"The Association"

Congress tried to enforce its boycott by setting up "in every county, city, and town" an organization known as "The Association." The Association exerted a surprising degree of control over Americans, telling them what they should eat, drink, and wear, as well as how they should behave in public. The Association did its work effectively; imports of British goods into New York, for example, dropped from more than $2 million in 1774 to $6,000 in 1775.

■ The Final Break

Meanwhile, every colony was organizing. In New England, "minutemen" assembled to drill on village greens, while town officials collected ammunition, uniforms, and food. In the Southern Colonies, planters undertook to recruit and equip companies of soldiers at their own expense. It appeared that the dispute between Great Britain and the colonies would be settled only by force.

Lexington and Concord

Fighting between the Americans and the British broke out near Boston, which had been occupied in 1774 by a British army under General Thomas Gage. Early on April 19, 1775, 700 British soldiers were secretly sent to destroy the military supplies colonists had collected at Concord, 21 miles from Boston. Learning of the soldiers' destination, the Boston Sons of Liberty sent Paul Revere and William Dawes to alert the minutemen in the towns and villages along the way. When the British reached the town of Lexington, about 70 armed minutemen awaited them. The colonists were ordered to drop their weapons and disperse. Then someone fired a shot. A spontaneous skirmish ensued,

108 UNIT 2 Creating a Nation: 1650–1789

and the colonists fled. Eight colonists were killed, and ten were wounded; only one British soldier was wounded. The British pushed on to Concord and burned what little gunpowder the colonists had not used for themselves.

By the time the British began their march toward Boston, the countryside was swarming with minutemen, who fired at the redcoats from behind trees, buildings, and stone walls. Only a brigade sent out from Boston saved the British troops from complete annihilation. About 250 British and 100 Americans were killed or wounded at Concord.

The Colonists Mobilize

News of Lexington and Concord, carried by riders on horseback, electrified the colonies. The Massachusetts Committee of Public Safety called for an army of 30,000 men "to defend our wives and children from the butchering hands of an inhuman soldiery." Groups of militia from all over New England marched toward Boston. General Gage found himself besieged.

Battle of Bunker Hill

On June 17, 1775, the British discovered that American troops occupied Breed's Hill, a peninsula overlooking the city of Boston from the north. The American army could easily have been trapped from behind, but the British commander decided to make a frontal attack uphill. Because the range of a musket was scarcely more than 50 yards, the Americans were ordered to hold their fire until they could see the "whites of their enemies' eyes."

The Americans turned back two British attacks but finally ran out of ammunition. The Battle of Bunker Hill, as it came to be called, was a moral victory for the Americans because their untrained militia had stood up to professional troops. The British, whose casualties in the battle were more than 40 percent, made no further attempt to attack.

Second Continental Congress

On May 10, 1775, a Second Continental Congress met in Philadelphia. The Congress assumed the powers of a central government and took steps to conduct the war that had, in fact, begun at Lexington. The Congress voted to ask the colonies for supplies and troops.

For commander in chief, Congress chose George Washington. It valued his experience and ability, but the fact that he was a Virginian was also important because it would keep the Southern and Middle colonies from thinking of the conflict as New England's war. Although it would be more than a year until independence was declared, the American Revolution had begun.

Section 3 ★ Review

Checking for Understanding

1. **Identify** Declaratory Act, Boston Massacre, Boston Tea Party, Intolerable (Coercive) Acts, Lexington and Concord, Breed's Hill, Second Continental Congress.
2. **Define** effigy, monopoly.
3. **Compare** the British reason for giving the East India Company a monopoly on tea with the colonists' reasons for opposing it.
4. **Explain** the purpose and significance of the two Continental Congresses.

Critical Thinking

5. **Supporting an Opinion** Some historians place the cause of the Revolution on the series of tax laws passed after 1763. Others believe that the cause was a growing national consciousness of Americans. Point out the strengths of each theory.

CHAPTER 4 The Road to Revolution 1650–1775

CHAPTER 4
SECTION 3

ASSESS

Check Understanding
Assign Section 3 Review as homework or as an in-class assignment.

Evaluate
Assign the TCR, or use the History of a Free Nation Testmaker to create a customized quiz.

Reteach
Have students prepare an events-chain map of the events leading to the Boston Tea Party, starting with Parliament's granting of a monopoly to the British East India Company to 1773.
Have students complete Reteaching Activity 4-3.

Enrich
Ask students to imagine they are press officers for the Continental Congress. Have them write a press release announcing the beginning of the war with Britain.
Have students complete Chapter 4 Enrichment Activity in the TCR.

CLOSE
Refer students to the list of major topics, main ideas, and supporting details they were asked to note in the Chapter 4 Concepts activity on page 91. Ask them to use their lists to develop maps for both concepts.

Answers to SECTION 3 REVIEW

1. Declaratory Act, 104; Boston Massacre, 105; Boston Tea Party, 106; Intolerable (Coercive) Acts, 106; Lexington and Concord, 108; Breed's Hill, 109; Second Continental Congress, 109
2. All vocabulary words are defined in the Glossary.
3. British wanted to save company from bankruptcy while colonists saw it as a precedent for other monopolies.
4. Purpose was to protest British policies; significance was cooperation of all colonies.
5. Answers may include tax laws created resentment and tried to subjugate colonies to British authority; growing national consciousness gave sense of being different from Britain and sharing common traits and ideals.

INTEGRATING Language Arts

American Literary Heritage

Historical Setting
By 1776, although increasingly disenchanted with Britain, American suffered split loyalties, torn between fidelity to the Crown and desire for independence. *Common Sense* served as a catalyst for Americans to more decisively identify their stance. It paved the way for a final break with Britain—and for the Declaration of Independence.

Background
Common Sense illustrates the power of persuasive, emotional words. Arguing with strength and passion, Paine swayed public opinion.

About Paine's Work
Invite volunteers to name historical and political figures who are considered to be persuasive speakers. (Samples: Winston Churchill, John F. Kennedy, Dr. Martin Luther King, Jr., Jesse Jackson) Explain that effective users of language, whether spoken or written, can stir the thoughts and emotions of others, moving them to action.

▲ **THOMAS PAINE** *Common Sense* was important in swaying the colonists toward the idea of separation from Great Britain.

The call to arms during the Revolution was heard not only on fields of battle but off, echoed by the leading writers of the day. Some of the most inspiring words that rang out against British tyranny were those of Thomas Paine. As you read this excerpt, notice the language Paine uses to rally support for the American cause.

The American Crisis, Number 1 (excerpt)

These are the times that try men's souls. The summer soldier and the sunshine patriot will in this crisis, shrink from the service of his country; but he that stands it now deserves the love and thanks of man and woman. Tyranny, like hell, is not easily conquered; yet we have this consolation with us, that the harder the conflict, the more glorious the triumph. What we obtain too cheap, we esteem too lightly; 'tis dearness only that gives everything its value. Heaven knows how to put a proper price upon its goods; and it would be strange indeed, if so celestial an article as FREEDOM should not be highly rated. Britain, with an army to enforce her tyranny, has declared that she has a right (not only to tax) but "to bind us in all cases whatsoever," and if being bound in that manner, is not slavery, then is there not such a thing as slavery upon earth. Even the expression is impious, for so unlimited a power can belong only to God. . . .

I have as little superstition in me as any man living, but my secret opinion has ever been, and still is, that God Almighty will not give up a people to military destruction, or leave them unsupportedly to perish, who have so earnestly and so repeatedly sought to avoid the calamities of war, by every decent method which wisdom could invent. Neither have I so much of the infidel in me, as to suppose that he has relinquished the government of the world, and given us up to the care of devils; and as I do not, I cannot see on what grounds the king of Britain can look up to heaven for help against us: a common murderer, a highwayman, or a housebreaker, has as good a pretense as he. . . .

Not a place upon earth might be so happy as America. Her situation is remote from all the wrangling world, and she has nothing to do but to trade with them. A man can distinguish himself between temper and principle, and I am as confident, as I am that God governs the world, that America will never be happy

Cultural Diversity

Thomas Paine was dedicated to freedom, equality, and dignity for all. Much of Paine's writing illustrates that he was a truly modern thinker whose ideas have reached out to people everywhere who love freedom. The *American Crisis*, whose first sentence has become a famous quotation, has withstood the test of time. Current American political thought, as well as that of other democratic nations, echoes Paine's beliefs.

▲ WASHINGTON CROSSING THE DELAWARE by Emanuel Gottlieb Leutze, 1851

till she gets clear of foreign domination. Wars, without ceasing, will break out till that period arrives, and the continent must in the end be conqueror; for though the flame of liberty may sometimes cease to shine, the coal can never expire. . . .

. . . Let it be told to the future world that in the depth of winter, when nothing but hope and virtue could survive, that the city and the country, alarmed at one common danger, came forth to meet and to repulse it. Say not that thousands are gone, turn out your tens of thousands; throw not the burden of the day upon Providence, but *"show your faith by your works,"* that God may bless you. . . .

▶ TITLE PAGE OF COMMON SENSE

Interpreting Literature

1. What does Paine mean by the phrase "the summer soldier and the sunshine patriot"?
2. What does Paine believe must be accomplished before America can be happy?

Identifying Viewpoints

3. Point to several sentences that give evidence of Paine's views about the British cause and the American cause.

INTEGRATING Language Arts

Developing Student Understanding

Explain that Paine's essay rallied the colonists and united them in the goal of independence. Read aloud the passage on page 111, ". . . Let it be told . . . that God may bless you. . . ." Ask: How might these words have influenced and inspired others? (encouraged unity among all states and all Americans, emphasized a common goal and cause)

Other Works by the Author

Thomas Paine (1737–1808) is perhaps the most effective political essayist the colonies produced. After arriving in the colonies in 1774, he edited *Pennsylvania Magazine*. His ardent patriotic work *Common Sense* rallied the colonists against the British. Later, as a supporter of the French Revolution, his *Rights of Man* garnered support for that great upheaval as well.

Answers to INTERPRETING LITERATURE

1. He refers to "patriots" who support their nation only in peacetime, when little personal sacrifice is necessary.
2. "Foreign domination" must end before the nation can be content.
3. Answers may include: Paine found the British to be tyrants. "Britain, with an army to enforce her tyranny . . ." Britain holds people in slavery: ". . . if being bound in that manner, is not slavery, then there is not such a thing as slavery upon Earth." He believed in the justness of the Revolution, claiming God would bless the Patriot effort. "Not a place upon Earth might be so happy as America. Her situation is remote from all the wrangling world . . .".

CHAPTER 4 ★ REVIEW

Using Vocabulary

Using the words below, write an editorial for the *Boston Gazette* that might have appeared the day after the battle at Lexington.

salutary neglect	direct tax
duty	boycott
writ of assistance	redcoat

Reviewing Facts

1. **Describe** the British strategy and execution of the battle fought against the French at Quebec.
2. **State** how the series of laws passed by Parliament after 1763 differed from those passed before 1763.
3. **Explain** how the Proclamation of 1763 affected the colonists and tell why they were angry over it.
4. **Identify** the incidents that became turning points in the relationship between the colonies and Britain.
5. **List** the acts of Parliament between 1763 and 1774 that colonists considered direct taxes.
6. **List** the organizations that came into being in the colonies to protest British tax laws and describe the ways in which the colonists defied those laws.

Understanding Concepts

Political Control

1. When the colonists refused to pay the taxes imposed by Parliament, the crown took measures to force obedience. List these measures and tell what effect they had on British-American relations.

Political Protest

2. Describe three forms of political protest used by the colonists.
3. Protest documents helped unite Americans against the British crown. Cite two of these documents, along with the names of their authors and a summary of their contents.

Critical Thinking

1. **Identifying Alternatives** Historians argue whether any war is inevitable. How could war between Britain and the American colonies have been avoided?
2. **Interpreting Illustrations** Examine closely the picture of the painting *A View of the Town of Concord, 1775*, attributed to Ralph Earl. In the background, the British are destroying barrels of gunpowder and throwing them into the river. What was the objective of the British march on Concord, and did it meet its objective?

Writing About History

Definition

Write a letter from Benjamin Franklin to Parliament following passage of the Coercive Acts. In the letter, attempt to explain the reasons for the Boston Tea Party and the colonial position on taxation.

REVIEW CHAPTER 4

Answers

Reviewing Facts

1. British scaled a cliff and assembled on the Plains of Abraham. British infantry drove the French back into Quebec and forced their surrender.
2. Laws passed after 1763 imposed taxes and duties on colonial trade and commerce, whereas laws before 1763 regulated trade and commerce.
3. Prevented colonists from moving into lands west of the Appalachians. Deprived them of land they had a right to settle and interfered with land grants given in colonial charters.
4. Answers will vary but may include: Stamp Act, quartering of soldiers, Stamp Act Congress, Boston Tea Party, Coercive or Intolerable Acts, First Continental Congress, Lexington and Concord.
5. Stamp Act, Townshend Acts
6. Stamp Act Congress—organized a boycott of British goods; Sons of Liberty—monitored shops selling British goods; Daughters of Liberty—boycotted British goods

Understanding Concepts

1. Sugar Act—placed import duty on sugar; Stamp Act—placed duties on documents, wills, newspapers, and so on; Townshend Acts—placed import duties on tea, paper, glass, paint
2. Answers will vary but should include boycotts, disobedience, violence, colonial delegate conventions.
3. Virginia Resolutions—Patrick Henry—no taxation without representation; Letters from a Farmer in Pennsylvania—John Dickinson—colonies formed one political body, of which each colony was a member.

Critical Thinking

1. Answers will vary but may include: Britain could have permitted colonies a say in recommending how to share government burden and expenses, allowed duties to have been collected by colonial officers and used for colonial purposes, prohibited direct taxes, and made no show of force by sending British troops.
2. British objective was to destroy military supplies the colonists had collected. The supplies were destroyed, but the skirmish aroused the countryside.

CHAPTER 4 ★ REVIEW

Cooperative Learning

Your group will write a play in three acts about the incidents leading to the American Revolution. Your play should have British and American characters. Each act should have one scene that takes place in Britain and one that follows it in America. Use these time periods in writing the acts: Act I, 1763–1767; Act II, 1767–1773; Act III, 1773–1776.

Social Studies Skills

Reading Military Maps

Military maps, besides giving you a visual representation of an event, can provide helpful information that sometimes the text does not include. For example, a map might show what kind of terrain is involved. You could tell if the soldiers had to march over hills or through rivers. A military map could also show which ports had to be protected, how much area the soldiers covered, and what their advances and retreats were.

Practicing the Skill

To help you read military maps, follow these guidelines.

- Look at the title to determine the subject.
- Find the legend. It will include symbols to help you find routes and battle sites.
- Study the mileage chart to get an idea of how much land they covered. For example, in this map, you can see that it is about 21 miles from Boston to Concord. Remember that Paul Revere and the other riders were covering this distance on horseback.
- If the map is *topographical,* or shows land features, consider what the soldiers had to deal with in marching and fighting battles.

Study the map and then answer the questions that follow.

1. Who took over for Paul Revere when he was captured?

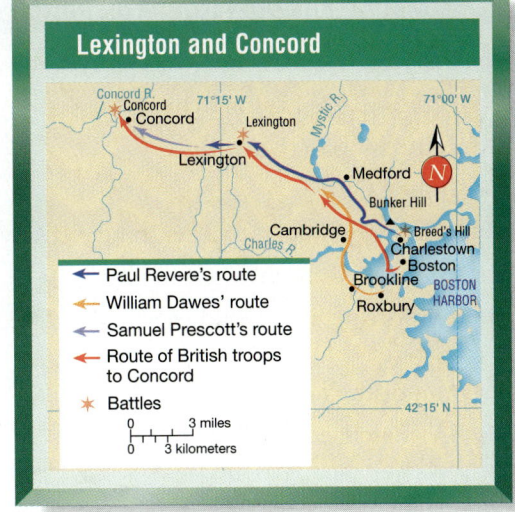

2. Why did Paul Revere and William Dawes take different routes?
3. **Making Inferences** Considering what you've read about trade between England and the colonies, why would it be important for the colonists to control Boston and its harbor?

Using Your Journal

Review your notes on the issues and answer the following questions. Do you pay the British taxes? Why or why not? When boycotts are organized, do you participate? When war is declared, do you support the revolution?

CHAPTER 4 The Road to Revolution 1650–1775

REVIEW CHAPTER 4

 Chapter Bonus Test Question

This question may be used for extra credit on the chapter test. Choose the letter of the correct response.

The actions of the British government and British soldiers encouraged colonists to
a. fight in the French and Indian War.
b. strictly obey British trade laws.
c. unite in opposition to Britain.
d. give up their rights as British subjects.
(Answer: b)

Using Your Journal
Answers will vary, but opinions should be supported with facts and reasoned arguments.

Practicing the Skill
1. Samuel Prescott
2. Sample answer: to cover the most distance possible; if one was captured, the other might be able to get through
3. to control the ships coming into and out of the harbor

PLANNING GUIDE Chapter 5 War for Independence

Daily Lesson Objectives	Teacher Classroom Resources	Multimedia
SECTION 1 **Foundations of Freedom** 1 Day pp. 116–120 1. List the arguments for American independence. 2. Explain the purposes and principles of the Declaration of Independence.	Chapter 5 Study Guide Reproducible Lesson Plan Reteaching Activity 5-1 Section Quiz Chapter 5 Cooperative Learning Activity Chapter 5 Concept Mapping Activity Reinforcing Social Studies Skills 25, 27, 32, 37, 59, 62 American Portraits 8 SAT Practice Tests 10-13	Student Self-Test Software Testmaker Section Focus Transparency 12 U.S. History & Art Transparency 4 Chapter 5 Skills Transparency A Geographic Perspective on American History Landmark Documents in American History
SECTION 2 **Fighting for Independence** 1 Day pp. 126–129 1. List two reasons why the American victories at Trenton and Princeton were important. 2. Compare the difficulties faced by the Americans and the British in the Revolutionary War.	Reproducible Lesson Plan Reteaching Activity 5-2 Section Quiz Reinforcing Social Studies Skills 56, 65 Writer's Guidebook, Lessons 3-5 American Literary Heritage Unit 1	Student Self-Test Software Testmaker Section Focus Transparency 13 A Geographic Perspective on American History
SECTION 3 **The War Deepens** 1 Day pp. 130–134 1. List two reasons why France supported the American Revolution. 2. Describe the roles of women, African Americans, and Native Americans in the war.	Reproducible Lesson Plan Reteaching Activity 5-3 Section Quiz Chapter 5 Primary and Secondary Source Readings Reinforcing Social Studies Skills 2, 32 American Portrait 10 Writer's Guidebook, Lesson 3-5 American Heritage Literary Heritage Unit 1	Student Self-Test Software Testmaker Section Focus Transparency 14 Chapter 5 Map Transparencies U.S. History & Art Transparency 5 A Geographic Perspective on American History
SECTION 4 **The War Ends** 1 Day pp. 136–139 1. Identify the problems that the British and Americans faced in continuing the war effort. 2. Explain the military strategy that defeated Lord Cornwallis.	Reproducible Lesson Plan Reteaching Activity 5-4 Section Quiz Chapter 5 Enrichment Activity Chapter 5 Primary and Secondary Source Readings Reinforcing Social Studies Skills 23, 40, 53, 59 American Portraits 9 Spanish Summaries & Glossary	Student Self-Test Software Testmaker Section Focus Transparency 15 Unit 2 Digest Transparency Vocabulary Puzzlemaker Audiocassette, Chapter 5 A Geographic Perspective on American History
CHAPTER REVIEW AND EVALUATION 1 Day	Chapter 5 Test Chapter 5 Performance Assessment Activity	Student Self-Test Software Testmaker

 **OUT OF TIME?** If time does not permit teaching the entire chapter, use the Chapter 5 Summary on pages 166–167 and the Chapter 5 audiocassette (English and Spanish) to point out the main ideas of the chapter.

PLANNING GUIDE

Cultural Diversity Activity

Critical Thinking Phillis Wheatley is the best known of the early African American poets. Kidnapped by African slave traders at the age of 8, she arrived in Boston speaking only Senegalese. She was educated by the Wheatley family in Boston. Five years later she wrote her first poem, and in 1773 her first book was published, the second volume of poetry published by a woman in British North America. Her poems can be found in *The Poems of Phillis Wheatley* edited by Julian D. Mason.

Have students read "On Being Brought from Africa to America" and contrast it with works by modern African American authors on the forced removal of Africans from their homelands and their subsequent enslavement in the Americas.

Performance Assessment Activity

Spreading the News Divide the class into groups. Assign each group one of the political events shown on the time life on pages 114–115. Ask each group to prepare a TV news broadcast about the event. Have each group choose reporters to describe the event and news analysts to discuss its meaning. Invite each group to present its broadcast to the class.

POSSIBLE RUBRIC FEATURES: Content, main idea, creativity, clarity, visual and written communication skills, organization, use of maps and illustrations

Chapter Resources

Literature from the Period

Jefferson, Thomas. "The Declaration of Independence." 1776

Paine, Thomas. *Common Sense.* 1776

Wheatley, Phillis. "To His Excellency, General Washington." 1775

Readings for the Student

Applebaum, Diane Karter. *The Glorious Fourth.* Facts On File, 1989.

Bober, Natalie S. *Thomas Jefferson: Man on a Mountain.* Atheneum, 1988.

DePauw, Linda Grant. *Founding Mothers: Women in the Revolutionary Era.* Houghton Mifflin, 1975.

Randel, William Pierce. *The American Revolution: Mirror of the People.* Rutledge Books, 1973.

Readings for the Teacher

Gross, Robert. *The Minutemen and Their World.* Hill and Wang, 1976.

Wood, W. J. *Battles of the Revolutionary War, 1775–1781.* Algonquin, 1990.

Multimedia Resources

Independence: Birth of a Free Nation. Finley-Holiday Film Corporation. (VHS, 28 minutes)

Paul Revere: The Messenger of Liberty. (VHS, 24 minutes)

The Revolution. Westport Media (5 filmstrips, teacher's guide)

Revolution '76. Britannica Software. (Apple IIGS or IBM diskette)

Revolutionary Wars: Choosing Sides. Tom Snyder Productions. (Apple diskette)

Key to Ability Levels

Teaching strategies have been coded for varying learning styles and abilities.

- **L1** Basic activities for all students
- **L2** Average activities for average to above-average students
- **L3** Challenging activities for above-average students
- **LEP** Limited English Proficiency activities

Glencoe Links to the Humanities

Link to Literature

- Macmillan Literature: Novel Guides—*Johnny Tremain*
- Macmillan Literature: American Literature Text—Benjamin Franklin, Patrick Henry, Thomas Paine, Thomas Jefferson

Link to Music

- American Music: Cultural Traditions

CHAPTER 5

BEGINNING THE CHAPTER

Discuss the advantages and disadvantages of the British and Americans in the war. (British—large well-trained army, strong navy, but far from home; Americans—used to frontier fighting, knew the land, fighting for liberty but not trained as soldiers, often short of food and supplies)

The American Revolution created a new political order in which government is by the consent of the governed and rights are protected by written constitutions. Despite conflicts, this compact between government and the American people still endures.

- GTV: A Geographic Perspective on American History

Side 1, Chapter 17
Title: *The American Revolution*
Subject: The impact of geography and aid from France on the American Revolution

See GTV Guide page 39 for complete lesson plan.

CHAPTER 5

War for Independence
1775–1783

◀ EAGLE AND CROSSED FLAGS

Setting the Scene

Focus

Even after the first skirmishes, the colonists still hoped to reconcile with the British crown. Events during the winter of 1775–1776, however, moved them toward separation. The writings of Thomas Paine, the king's inflexible attitude, and Britain's use of German mercenaries all led the Second Continental Congress to issue a Declaration of Independence on July 4, 1776. Under George Washington's leadership, the new United States fought its war for independence over six long years.

Concepts to Understand

★ Why revolution against Great Britain seemed the only option left for the colonies

★ How colonists believed their civil rights and liberties could be secured and protected

Read to Discover . . .

★ what factors caused the American Revolution.

★ why the Americans were able to win the war.

Journal Notes

What contributions did women, African Americans, and Native Americans make to the American Revolution? Note details in your journal as you read the chapter.

CULTURAL
- 1776 Thomas Paine writes *Common Sense*
- 1778 William Brown publishes first American book about medicines

1775 — **1778**

POLITICAL
- 1776 Declaration of Independence is signed
- 1777 Continental Army victorious at Saratoga
- 1778 George Rogers Clark's forces capture Kaskaskia

✚ EXTRA CREDIT PROJECT

Influence of the Revolution The American Revolution has influenced people around the world in their struggles for freedom. Interested students might research other revolutions, comparing causes, the course of the revolutions, and their outcomes. Have them note similarities and differences and evaluate the results of these revolutions in terms of the changes they brought. Ask them to share their findings with the class.

History AND ART

Molly Pitcher at the Battle of Monmouth
by Dennis Malone Carter, 1854

Several women took an active part in the fighting. At the Battle of Monmouth, New Jersey, in 1778, Molly Pitcher takes her husband's place firing a cannon.

◀ REVOLUTIONARY WAR DRUM

- **1783** Noah Webster publishes first spelling book

1781

- **1781** Cornwallis surrenders at Yorktown
- **1783** Treaty of Paris signed

- **1784** American Methodist Church formed in Baltimore, Maryland

1784

- **1784** Congress drafts land ordinance

CHAPTER 5 War for Independence 1775–1783

CHAPTER 5 CONCEPTS

Concept Mapping Activity

Reproduce the following generalization and concepts map on the chalkboard and have students copy it in their notebooks. Have students look for examples of each concept as they work through the chapter.

> A revolution based on the principles of freedom and rights leads to independence.

| Revolution | Civil Rights and Liberties |

Recording Journal Notes
Students might categorize contributions under Military and Home Front.

History AND ART

The battle at Monmouth, depicted here, was waged on July 4, 1778, and was the longest battle of the war.

Teacher Notes

LESSON PLAN
SECTION 1, 116–120

FOCUS

Bellringer
Prior to taking roll at the beginning of the class period, display Focus Activity Transparency 15 on the overhead projector and assign the accompanying Focus Activity Sheet.

Objectives
Point out the objectives on this page to students in previewing the section content.

Motivating Activity
Direct students to Jefferson's statement about equality from the Declaration of Independence on page 119. Ask them to write in their own words what this sentence means to them.

• GTV: A Geographic Perspective on American History

Side 1, Chapter 15
Title: *Laying Down the Law*
Subject: The rise of revolutionary feelings

See GTV Guide page 38 for complete lesson plan.

SECTION 1

Foundations of Freedom

Setting the Scene

Section Focus
Delegates to the Second Continental Congress faced a difficult decision—whether to separate from or to seek reconciliation with Great Britain. The delegates would weigh carefully any official action announcing independence, since they would be committing treason against the British crown.

Objectives
After studying this section, you should be able to
★ list the arguments for American independence.
★ explain the purposes and principles of the Declaration of Independence.

Key Terms
treason, mercenary, Patriot, Loyalist, artillery, grievance, preamble, social contract, right of self-determination

▲ **BETSY ROSS FLAG**

After the bloodshed in Massachusetts, colonial leaders such as Patrick Henry of Virginia appealed for separation from Great Britain. Most colonists, however, were not ready for independence, and neither was the Second Continental Congress that convened in Philadelphia in May 1775.

■ Moving Toward Independence

Most of the members of the Continental Congress wanted the colonies to remain part of the British Empire but rule themselves through their own legislatures. In a petition that tried to appease the king, the delegates blamed all their troubles on his ministers.

Charge of Treason

King George III refused to read the conciliatory petition from the Continental Congress and denounced the "diverse wicked and desperate persons" leading the rebels. He called on loyal subjects to charge the American leaders with **treason,** or attempting to overthrow the government, and to punish them according to British law.

The king then took direct action. In October 1775, a British naval force burned the defenseless port of Falmouth, Maine. In December, George III declared the American colonies entirely outside his protection and placed all their ports under blockade by the British fleet. Unable to raise sufficient troops in Great Britain because the war was unpopular, the king hired **mercenaries,** or paid soldiers, from the rulers of small German states. They were generally known as "Hessians," because a large number were supplied by the

UNIT 2 Creating a Nation: 1650–1789

Classroom Resources for SECTION 1

Teacher's Classroom Resources
- Chapter 5 Study Guide
- Reproducible Lesson Plan
- Reteaching Activity 5-1
- Chapter 5 Cooperative Learning Activity
- Chapter 5 Primary and Secondary Source Readings
- Section Quiz

Multimedia
- Section Focus Transparency 15
- Chapter 5 Skills Transparency
- Chapter 5 Map Transparency
- U.S. History and Art Transparency 5
- Student Self-Test Software
- A Geographic Perspective on American History
- Landmark Documents in American History

Prince of Hesse. By 1776 it was becoming obvious that compromise between the colonies and Britain was impossible. Yet the American Congress held back, unwilling to declare the final separation.

Thomas Paine and *Common Sense*

At this critical moment, *Common Sense* was published. It was written in January 1776 by Thomas Paine, who had recently arrived in America from England. Paine attacked the strongest bond tying America to Britain—loyalty to the king. He assaulted monarchy in general and George III in particular, discrediting hereditary kingship as superstition.

Paine pointed to the advantages Americans might gain if they were free of British commercial restrictions and of Britain's quarrels with its European neighbors. He appealed to the Americans' belief that they were a chosen people, pioneers of liberty.

Common Sense divided Americans into either **Patriots**, those who favored separation, or **Loyalists**, those who supported the British government. The early successes of American Patriots supported Paine's arguments. In Virginia they expelled the royal governor and the soldiers defending him; in North Carolina the militia repulsed an attempted landing of redcoats; in South Carolina a British attack on Charleston was driven back.

The greatest American success occurred in the New England region. When George Washington arrived to take charge of the Continental Army near Boston, he had almost no **artillery**, or large guns to use against British forces. During the winter rebels seized more than 50 cannons from Fort Ticonderoga. Weighing 2 to 6 tons apiece, they were lashed to sledges and dragged by oxen 200 miles over snowy trails and frozen rivers to Dorchester Heights overlooking Boston. During the night of March 4, 1776, about 2,000 militiamen positioned groups of these cannons. In the morning this threat greeted General William Howe. He was left with no choice but to abandon the city.

 ▲ **Symbols of Freedom** "Raising the Liberty Pole" symbolizes the idea of freedom that was growing in the American colonies. *On what European philosophy were the ideas expressed in the Declaration of Independence based?*

CHAPTER 5 SECTION 1

TEACH

Guided Practice
Recognizing Cause and Effect Provide copies of the cause and effect chart below to students, omitting the cause and effects. Then ask students to complete the chart. **L1, LEP**

Event
- Continental Congress writes petition to King George III

Cause
- Colonies desire to remain part of the British Empire

Effects
- King George III accuses colonists of treason
- Orders Falmouth burned
- Blockades colonies
- Hires Hessian mercenaries

Visualizing History To express their feelings over the Declaration of Independence, Americans throughout the colonies erected liberty poles.
Answer to Caption: Enlightenment philosophy

Critical Thinking

Comparing and Contrasting In the twentieth century, the world has witnessed such violent protests against totalitarian governments as World War II. It has also seen the successful use of nonviolent action in the drive for independence in India and in the American civil rights movement. The American colonists used both violent and nonviolent protest in the period preceding the Revolutionary War. List two examples of each type of protest and their outcomes. In your opinion, which form of protest was more successful? Do you think that form generally achieves better results? Explain your answer. **L3**

CHAPTER 5 SECTION 1

Independent Practice

Journalism Have students create newspaper headlines and related opening paragraphs about one or more of the following: George III's response to the congressional petition, the publication of *Common Sense*, Washington's victory in Boston, the signing of the Declaration of Independence. Students might create a bulletin board display of their headlines. **L1**

Visualizing History In New York City, mobs pulled down a statue of George III and sent parts of it to a munitions factory in Connecticut. There the pieces were made into bullets.
Answer to Caption: The English had deposed James II in 1688.

Did You Know?

Against Thomas Jefferson's wishes, Congress deleted a scathing attack on the slave trade from the Declaration. This deletion was engineered by a coalition of Southern slaveholders and Northern merchants whose ships transported slaves.

 ▲ **COLONIAL REACTION** Colonists pull down the statue of King George III in New York on July 9, 1776. **On what grounds could the colonists argue that English subjects had the right to overthrow a king?**

Arguments for Independence

Colonists made strong arguments for independence from their need for military supplies and for reopening foreign trade. The Americans lacked guns, gunpowder, ammunition, uniforms, tents, and medical supplies. The cutoff of trade with the British Empire caused acute distress among American shippers and merchants, who had to find new markets. However, commercial treaties with other nations could be written only by an independent nation—not by rebellious colonies.

Members of the Continental Congress hoped for aid from France. Since 1763 the French had desired revenge on Great Britain for the terrible defeat they suffered in the Seven Years' War. As early as November 1775, a French agent had secretly conferred with members of the Congress. Within a few months the French government had started to smuggle arms to the Americans. France, nevertheless, refused to enter into a formal alliance or sign a commercial treaty until the Americans declared independence.

The Colonies Declare Independence

Beginning with North Carolina in April 1776, the colonies advised their delegates in Congress to vote for independence. On June 7, Richard Henry Lee of Virginia introduced a brief "Resolution of Independence." The delegates debated for nearly a month while the moderates in Congress made a last stand for reconciliation. On July 2, 1776, the Continental Congress adopted Lee's resolution "that these united colonies are, and of right ought to be free and independent states." The official Declaration of Independence was agreed upon by Congress on July 4. Its purpose was to justify the revolution, to state that the colonies were independent, and to express the new nation's principles.

UNIT 2 Creating a Nation: 1650–1789

Sidelights: The Fourth of July

While July 4 is celebrated as Independence Day, the process of declaring independence took close to six months. A formal resolution to separate from Britain was adopted by the Continental Congress on July 2, 1776. Two days later the Congress adopted the Declaration of Independence. The Declaration was proclaimed on July 8, and most of the delegates signed the document on August 2. However, it was January 19, 1777, before the Declaration and a complete list of its signatories were published.

The Declaration of Independence

The Declaration of Independence was principally the work of Thomas Jefferson, a young Virginian who had been an inconspicuous member of Congress. A poor public speaker and shy by nature, Jefferson was known as an able writer. When Congress appointed a committee to draw up a public statement justifying independence, he was asked to write the first draft of the Declaration.

Writing the Declaration

Since time was limited, Jefferson drew upon several sources—a declaration of **grievances**, or complaints, he had written earlier; the new Virginia Bill of Rights; Lee's resolution; and writings by European political philosophers. Jefferson was influenced by the ideas of "natural rights" and government by social contract written by the English philosopher John Locke. Jefferson gave the idea of natural rights its most eloquent expression in the Declaration.

Jefferson submitted his draft to Benjamin Franklin, who made a few changes before sending it to Congress. There, additional changes were made before its acceptance.

Preamble

The Declaration has four main parts: the **preamble**, or introduction, which states why the Continental Congress chose to explain their separation from Britain formally and publicly; a declaration of rights, which describes the general theories of government upon which the American Revolution was founded; a long list of grievances against George III; and finally, the formal resolution of independence. The declaration of rights sets forth a philosophy of human rights that has influenced generations.

Declaration of Rights

After a statement in the preamble that the Americans were publishing the Declaration out of "a decent respect to the opinions of mankind," Jefferson wrote this famous sentence, the basis for all that follows:

> We hold these truths to be self-evident, that all men are created equal, that they are endowed by their Creator with certain unalienable Rights, that among these are Life, Liberty, and the pursuit of Happiness.

Jefferson did not mean that everyone has the same abilities or the same circumstances. True equality of condition for men and women was not a subject for consideration by even the most enlightened leaders. The self-evident truths to which Jefferson referred were that rights are God-given or "natural," not subject to the whim of a monarch or even an elected government.

The next lines of the Declaration set forth the idea of government by social contract:

> That to secure these rights, Governments are instituted among Men, deriving their just powers from the consent of the governed, That whenever any Form of Government becomes destructive of these ends, it is the Right of the People to alter or to abolish it. . . .

Like Locke, Jefferson suggested that the purpose of government is to secure natural rights. Locke had argued that in a "state of nature" people were all free, equal, and independent. They gave up their complete freedom in order to join a community for their own safety and comfort. Jefferson agreed that the origin of government was a **social contract** in which people granted power to the rulers in exchange for protection of their rights. Jefferson insisted that the only rightful aim of government is to protect the individual, and that government is the agent of the people.

If a just government rests on popular consent, the document continues, the people may refuse their consent to an unjust government, may "alter or abolish it," and may set up another government. This passage,

CHAPTER 5 War for Independence 1775–1783   119

CHAPTER 5
SECTION 1

Interpreting Primary Sources

Have students read the quotations from the Declaration on this page. Ask them to note the lines "That whenever any form of Government becomes destructive of these ends, it is the Right of the People to alter or to abolish it, and to institute new Government . . ." The British government would consider this an act of treason. Americans considered it justified. Conduct a class discussion on situations in which students think the alteration or abolition of a government is justified. **L3**

TECHNOLOGY

The following material is available from Glencoe and may be used to study the Declaration of Independence.

 CD-ROM
Facts On File, Inc. Landmark Documents in American History
Declaration of Independence

Cooperative Learning

Divide the class into groups of five or six students. Have each group discuss the points presented in the Declaration and consider how adopting the Declaration will affect the colonies. Have each group summarize its conclusions and present them to the class. **L2**

CHAPTER 5 SECTION 1

ASSESS

Check Understanding
Assign Section 1 Review as homework or an in-class assignment.

Evaluate
Assign the Section 1 Quiz in the TCR or use the History of a Free Nation Testmaker to create a customized quiz.

Reteach
Have students summarize the Declaration of Independence by making a concept map of the four sections of the document.
Have students complete Reteaching Activity 5-1.

Enrich
Have students take turns reading sections of the Declaration of Independence aloud, as if they were presenting it to a large town meeting in 1776. Encourage them to use their voices to stress the formal language and communicate the serious tone of the document.

CLOSE
Ask students to discuss the meaning of the phrase "point of no return." Then have them discuss the following question: Had the signers of the Declaration of Independence reached such a point? Why or why not?

---

then, justified revolution. In the twentieth century it has sometimes been called the **right of self-determination**, meaning the right of people to be free from foreign rule.

Next the Declaration charges that the British government had attempted to put Americans under the king's power. An early version of the document blamed Parliament, but this was altered to read "the present King of Great Britain." This change increased the document's effectiveness because revolt against a tyrannical monarch was more powerful than was a revolt against Parliament.

List of Grievances

The largest section of the Declaration is a list of grievances against George III. Jefferson heaped wrong upon wrong. Note his use of repetition: "He has refused. . . . He has forbidden. . . . He has utterly neglected. . . . He has obstructed. . . . He has plundered. . . ." These charges were not entirely fair. George III did not begin the quarrel with the colonies, nor did he play an important role in shaping policy toward America until 1774. From that point on, however, the king resisted conciliation.

Formal Declaration of Independence

The Declaration of Independence closes by maintaining that the American colonies did everything possible to preserve peace but were spurned by Great Britain. In their mind, there was no other choice for them but to declare the colonies "Free and Independent States." To defend this action, the Americans pledged their lives, their fortunes, and their honor.

■ Influence of the Declaration

The Declaration of Independence became one of the world's most important political documents. In it Americans made a commitment, as Lincoln later stated in the Gettysburg Address, "to the proposition that all men are created equal." The Declaration has been a lever for change—toward equal rights, equal opportunities, and equal voice in government. At different times in our history, it has operated toward ending slavery, giving women the right to vote, enlarging job opportunities, and extending opportunities for education. With his genius for simple and eloquent prose, Jefferson managed to plant the ideals of equality and self-government in the American tradition.

The Declaration demanded independence from Britain on the basis of the natural, inborn rights of all persons. Thus, the Declaration acquired worldwide significance. When the Spanish-American colonies revolted in the early nineteenth century, several drew up declarations based on the United States' model. In the twentieth century, Jawaharlal Nehru, the first prime minister of India, called the Declaration of Independence a "landmark in human freedom."

Section 1 ★ Review

Checking for Understanding

1. **Identify** Hessians, Thomas Paine, General William Howe, Richard Henry Lee.
2. **Define** treason, mercenary, Patriot, Loyalist, artillery, grievance, preamble, social contract, right of self-determination.
3. **Name** three reasons for separating from Great Britain as described in *Common Sense*.
4. **Cite** the four main sections of the Declaration of Independence and tell what each contains.

Critical Thinking

5. **Making Value Judgments** Explain why unalienable rights were so important that the colonists were willing to fight a war to preserve them.

---

120   UNIT 2 Creating a Nation: 1650–1789

Answers to SECTION 1 REVIEW

1. Hessians, 116, 117; Thomas Paine, 117; General William Howe, 117; Richard Henry Lee, 118; Thomas Jefferson, 119; John Locke, 119
2. All vocabulary words are defined in the Glossary.
3. Hereditary kingship was a superstitious lie. George III was a ruffian.
4. Preamble—states reasons for separation; Declaration of rights—describes theories of government justifying separation; Grievances—lists complaints against the king; Resolution of independence—declares separation
5. Answers will vary but should include that such rights were essentially human and thus not subject to bestowal or withdrawal on a government's whim.

History and Religion Connections

The Revolutionary Pulpit

The origins of the American Revolution can be traced to changes and developments from the early 1700s. Ideas of self-government were transplanted to the American colonies, and these ideas took root and thrived. The colonial economy, though still sustaining itself through its economic ties with England, was flourishing. Colonial cities were bustling with activity and developing into powerful centers of commerce and trade.

Changes could also be seen in colonial culture. Public schools and institutions of higher learning were on the increase. Colonists set up libraries, and creative thinkers made enduring contributions to knowledge.

Among the most influential thinkers were religious leaders. Their efforts led to a rekindling of religious faith, known as the Great Awakening, which reached its peak around 1740. In New England the fiery sermons of Jonathan Edwards spread the ideas of religious revival. Preacher George Whitefield took the message of revivalism to countless communities.

"If the Americans shall be taught to believe Resistance to be lawful . . . it will not be long before . . . [they] publicly appear in Arms," remarked an English citizen in 1774. His fears were well-founded. The Revolutionary War effort drew powerful support from Congregational, Presbyterian, and other Christian churches, whose clergy had no official ties with England. Boston minister Samuel West interpreted the New Testament discussion on submitting to civil authority as applying only to those leaders who "punish the wicked and encourage the good." Those who do not, he continued, "forfeit their authority to govern the people."

In contrast, the Episcopal Church in America had strong ties with the Church of England. Episcopal clergy, who were ordained in England, saw opposition to British rule as a danger to all authority. Their support of the Crown drew widespread acceptance among the colonial aristocracy, particularly in the Southern colonies.

◀ GEORGE WHITEFIELD PREACHING

Making the Religion Connection

1. How did the strength of their ties with England affect the support or opposition of American clergy to the Revolution?
2. In what ways did Jonathan Edwards and George Whitefield influence Americans?

Linking Past and Present

3. Describe a current political issue on which American clergy are divided.

CHAPTER 5 MAKING CONNECTIONS

Teaching Making Connections

Point out that religious freedom played a major role in the settlement of Britain's North American colonies. The Puritans who settled in Massachusetts were dissenters from the Church of England. The Quakers who founded Pennsylvania also fled persecution in England. In addition, Roman Catholics found the freedom to worship in the colony of Maryland.

Did You Know?

George Whitefield broke away from the Church of England and embraced the doctrine of Methodism, the religious view that people were responsible for their own salvation. Touring the colonies, Whitefield gave rousing sermons that appealed to ordinary people, who wanted to be free from a rigid church authority.

Answers to CONNECTIONS

1. Clergy with strong ties to Britain opposed the Revolution. Clergy with weak or no ties tended to support the Revolution.
2. Their efforts led to a rekindling of religious faith.
3. Answers will vary but may include such issues as prayer in schools, gay and lesbian rights, abortion, and the ordination of women.

LESSON PLAN
The Declaration of Independence

FOCUS
Motivating Activity

Ask students if they would risk their lives for an idea and, if so, for what idea. Remind them that the American Revolution involved great risks for the people who fought it. Ask what ideas were being fought for in the American Revolution. (self-government, freedom, representation, equality) Direct students to read the first paragraph of the Declaration of Independence on page 122. Ask them to describe the tone of this document. They should note that the Declaration is not addressed to King George III or to the English Parliament specifically, but to the entire world. Led by thinkers such as Thomas Jefferson and Thomas Paine, Americans came to view their revolution as more than a political squabble between governments. The American Revolution was a fight over ideas and beliefs.

TEACH
Guided Practice

Writing Choose a student to read aloud the first paragraph under "Declaration of Natural Rights" on page 122. Discuss some of the more difficult terms such as *self-evident* and *unalienable*. Assign students to write a paraphrase of the paragraph. **LEP, L1**

The Declaration of Independence

Delegates at the Second Continental Congress faced an enormous task. The war against Great Britain had begun, but to many colonists the purpose for fighting was unclear. As sentiment increased for a complete break with Britain, Congress decided to act. A committee was appointed to prepare a document that declared the 13 colonies free and independent from Britain. More important, the committee needed to explain why separation was the only fitting solution to long-standing disputes with Parliament and the British Crown. Thomas Jefferson was assigned to prepare a working draft of this document, which was then revised. It was officially adopted on July 4, 1776. More than any other action of the Congress, the Declaration of Independence served to make the American colonists one people.

★★

The printed text of the document shows the spelling and punctuation of the parchment original. To aid in comprehension, selected words and their definitions appear in the side margin, along with other explanatory notes.

impel *force*

endowed *provided*

People create governments to ensure that their natural rights are protected.

If a government does not serve its purpose, the people have a right to abolish it. Then the people have the right and duty to create a new government that will safeguard their security.

Despotism *unlimited power*

In Congress, July 4, 1776. The unanimous Declaration of the thirteen united States of America,

Preamble
When in the Course of human events, it becomes necessary for one people to dissolve the political bands which have connected them with another, and to assume among the powers of the earth, the separate and equal station to which the Laws of Nature and Nature's God entitle them, a decent respect to the opinions of mankind requires that they should declare the causes which impel them to the separation.—

Declaration of Natural Rights
We hold these truths to be self-evident, that all men are created equal, that they are endowed by their Creator with certain unalienable Rights, that among these are Life, Liberty, and the pursuit of Happiness.—

That to secure these rights, Governments are instituted among Men, deriving their just powers from the consent of the governed,—

That whenever any Form of Government becomes destructive of these ends, it is the Right of the People to alter or to abolish it, and to institute new Government, laying its foundation on such principles and organizing its powers in such form, as to them shall seem most likely to effect their Safety and Happiness. Prudence, indeed, will dictate that Governments long established should not be changed for light and transient causes; and accordingly all experience hath shewn, that mankind are more disposed to suffer, while evils are sufferable, than to right themselves by abolishing the forms to which they are accustomed. But when a long train of abuses and usurpations, pursuing invariably the same Object evinces a design to reduce them under absolute Despotism, it is their right, it is their duty, to throw off such Government, and to provide new Guards for their future security.—

The Declaration of Independence

Sidelights: The Real Title of the Declaration of Independence

Strictly speaking, the title of this famous document is not the "Declaration of Independence" but rather "The Unanimous Declaration of the Thirteen United States of America." The original document does not bear that title, and it was not the act by which independence was declared. That had been done on July 2 when the Continental Congress adopted Lee's resolution.

▲ DECLARATION OF INDEPENDENCE IN CONGRESS by John Trumbull, 1824

List of Grievances

Such has been the patient sufferance of these Colonies; and such is now the necessity which constrains them to alter their former Systems of Government. The history of the present King of Great Britain is a history of repeated injuries and usurpations, all having in direct object the establishment of an absolute Tyranny over these States. To prove this, let Facts be submitted to a candid world.—

He has refused his Assent to Laws, the most wholesome and necessary for the public good.—

He has forbidden his Governors to pass Laws of immediate and pressing importance, unless suspended in their operation till his Assent should be obtained; and when so suspended, he has utterly neglected to attend to them.—

He has refused to pass other Laws for the accommodation of large districts of people, unless those people would relinquish the right of Representation in the Legislature, a right inestimable to them and formidable to tyrants only.—

He has called together legislative bodies at places unusual, uncomfortable, and distant from the depository of their public Records, for the sole purpose of fatiguing them into compliance with his measures.—

He has dissolved Representative Houses repeatedly, for opposing with manly firmness his invasions on the rights of the people.—

He has refused for a long time, after such dissolutions, to cause others to be elected; whereby the Legislative powers, incapable of Annihilation, have returned to the People at large for their exercise; the State remaining in the meantime exposed to all the dangers of invasion from without, and convulsions within.—

He has endeavoured to prevent the population of these States; for

usurpations *unjust uses of power*

Each paragraph lists alleged injustices of George III.

relinquish *give up*
inestimable *priceless*

Annihilation *destruction*

convulsions *violent disturbances*

The Declaration of Independence 123

The Declaration of Independence

Identifying Central Issues
Refer students to the painting on this page. Mention that the painting includes many of the delegates who also signed the Constitution. Discuss differences and similarities between this group and current members of the United States Congress. The discussion can include observations about numbers, gender, ethnicity, age, style of dress, and so forth. Conclude by pointing out that the calmness of the setting obscures the desperateness of this step. In the eyes of the British government, each of these representatives was guilty of treason. For some time after, the names of the signers were kept secret, presumably to protect them from British reprisal. **L2**

Language Select a volunteer to read the preamble aloud. Lead a discussion on its meaning. (The preamble makes it clear that the document was designed to sway the "opinions of mankind.") **L1**

Analyzing Information
Point out that the statements in the Declaration of Natural Rights voice some of the most important ideas of governments. Ask students to identify the important statements. (Answers will vary but should include: All people are created equal; all people have certain basic rights; the purpose of government is to secure these basic rights for the people; the power and sovereignty that governments have come from the people.)

Cultural Diversity

Once it was adopted, the Declaration of Independence exerted a strong influence upon others. With its democratic principle that "all men are created equal," it stimulated humanitarian movements in the United States and inspired leaders of the French Revolution and Latin American independence movements. For the short term, it led to increased foreign aid for the rebels' cause and paved the way for French intervention on their side. It also steeled Americans to carry on their struggle until they reached the goal stated in the Declaration. Encourage students to find out more about the effects the Declaration of Independence had on peoples around the world.

123

The Declaration of Independence

Determining Cause and Effect Ask students to think about the impact of the Declaration on the colonists. Have them list as many different effects as they can resulting from news that the Congress had issued the Declaration. (Answers will vary, but might include the following: The time for indecision was over. It forced Americans to decide whether they supported independence or the king. It rallied support and boosted morale. It also raised the conflict above the level of discontent over economic issues.) **L2**

Independent Practice

Research Organize students into groups of three. Have students find out in what ways the French Revolution was different from the American Revolution and report their findings to the class. **L3**

TECHNOLOGY

The following material is available from Glencoe and may be used to study the Declaration of Independence.

 CD-ROM
Facts On File, Inc. Landmark Documents in American History Declaration of Independence

---

Naturalization of Foreigners *process by which foreign-born persons become citizens*

tenure *term*

Refers to the British troops sent to the colonies after the French and Indian War.

Refers to the 1766 Declaratory Act.

quartering *lodging*

Refers to the 1774 Quebec Act.

render *make*

abdicated *given up*

perfidy *violation of trust*

insurrections *rebellions*

Petitioned for Redress *asked formally for a correction of wrongs*

---

that purpose obstructing the Laws for Naturalization of Foreigners; refusing to pass others to encourage their migrations hither, and raising the conditions of new Appropriations of Lands.—

He has obstructed the Administration of Justice, by refusing his Assent to Laws for establishing Judiciary powers.—

He has made Judges dependent on his Will alone, for the tenure of their offices, and the amount and payment of their salaries.—

He has erected a multitude of New Offices, and sent hither swarms of Officers to harass our people, and eat out their substance.—

He has kept among us, in times of peace, Standing Armies without the Consent of our legislatures.—

He has affected to render the Military independent of and superior to the Civil power.—

He has combined with others to subject us to a jurisdiction foreign to our constitution, and unacknowledged by our laws; giving his Assent to their Acts of pretended Legislation:—

For quartering large bodies of troops among us:—

For protecting them, by a mock Trial, from punishment for any Murders which they should commit on the Inhabitants of these States:—

For cutting off our Trade with all parts of the world:—

For imposing Taxes on us without our Consent:—

For depriving us in many cases, of the benefits of Trial by Jury:—

For transporting us beyond Seas to be tried for pretended offences:—

For abolishing the free System of English Laws in a neighbouring Province, establishing therein an Arbitrary government, and enlarging its Boundaries so as to render it at once an example and fit instrument for introducing the same absolute rule into these Colonies:—

For taking away our Charters, abolishing our most valuable Laws, and altering fundamentally the Forms of our Governments:—

For suspending our own Legislatures, and declaring themselves invested with power to legislate for us in all cases whatsoever.—

He has abdicated Government here, by declaring us out of his Protection and waging War against us.—

He has plundered our seas, ravaged our Coasts, burnt our towns, and destroyed the Lives of our people.—

He is at this time transporting large Armies of foreign Mercenaries to compleat the works of death, desolation and tyranny, already begun with circumstances of Cruelty & perfidy scarcely paralleled in the most barbarous ages, and totally unworthy the Head of a civilized nation.—

He has constrained our fellow Citizens taken Captive on the high Seas to bear Arms against their Country, to become the executioners of their friends and Brethren, or to fall themselves by their Hands.—

He has excited domestic insurrections amongst us, and has endeavoured to bring on the inhabitants of our frontiers, the merciless Indian Savages, whose known rule of warfare, is an undistinguished destruction of all ages, sexes and conditions.

In every stage of these Oppressions We have Petitioned for Redress in the most humble terms: Our repeated Petitions have been answered only by repeated injury. A Prince, whose character is thus marked by every act which may define a Tyrant, is unfit to be the ruler of a free people.

Critical Thinking

Making Comparisons Have students read the Seneca Falls Declaration of 1848 on page 341 of the text. Compare and contrast the words and ideas expressed in this document with those in the Declaration of Independence. Then have students discuss why the writers of the Seneca Falls Declaration modeled their work on that of the Declaration of Independence. **L2, L3**

Nor have We been wanting in attentions to our British brethren. We have warned them from time to time of attempts by their legislature to extend an unwarrantable jurisdiction over us. We have reminded them of the circumstances of our emigration and settlement here. We have appealed to their native justice and magnanimity, and we have conjured them by the ties of our common kindred to disavow these usurpations, which would inevitably interrupt our connections and correspondence. They too have been deaf to the voice of justice and of consanguinity. We must, therefore, acquiesce in the necessity, which denounces our Separation, and hold them, as we hold the rest of mankind, Enemies in War, in Peace Friends.—

unwarrantable jurisdiction *unjustified authority*

consanguinity *originating from the same ancestor*

Resolution of Independence by the United States

We, therefore, the Representatives of the united States of America, in General Congress, Assembled, appealing to the Supreme Judge of the world for the rectitude of our intentions, do, in the Name, and by Authority of the good People of these Colonies, solemnly publish and declare, That these United Colonies are, and of Right ought to be Free and Independent States; that they are Absolved from all Allegiance to the British Crown, and that all political connection between them and the State of Great Britain, is and ought to be totally dissolved; and that as Free and Independent States, they have full Power to levy War, conclude Peace, contract Alliances, establish Commerce, and to do all other Acts and Things which Independent States may of right do.—

And for the support of this Declaration, with a firm reliance on the protection of divine Providence, we mutually pledge to each other our Lives, our Fortunes and our sacred Honour.

rectitude *rightness*

The signers, as representatives of the American people, declared the colonies independent from Great Britain. Most members signed the document on August 2, 1776.

John Hancock
 President from
 Massachusetts

Georgia
Button Gwinnett
Lyman Hall
George Walton

North Carolina
William Hooper
Joseph Hewes
John Penn

South Carolina
Edward Rutledge
Thomas Heyward, Jr.
Thomas Lynch, Jr.
Arthur Middleton

Maryland
Samuel Chase
William Paca
Thomas Stone
Charles Carroll
 of Carrollton

Virginia
George Wythe
Richard Henry Lee
Thomas Jefferson
Benjamin Harrison
Thomas Nelson Jr.
Francis Lightfoot Lee
Carter Braxton

Pennsylvania
Robert Morris
Benjamin Rush
Benjamin Franklin
John Morton
George Clymer
James Smith
George Taylor
James Wilson
George Ross

Delaware
Caesar Rodney
George Read
Thomas McKean

New York
William Floyd
Philip Livingston
Francis Lewis
Lewis Morris

New Jersey
Richard Stockton
John Witherspoon
Francis Hopkinson
John Hart
Abraham Clark

New Hampshire
Josiah Bartlett
William Whipple
Matthew Thornton

Massachusetts
Samuel Adams
John Adams
Robert Treat Paine
Elbridge Gerry

Rhode Island
Stephen Hopkins
William Ellery

Connecticut
Samuel Huntington
William Williams
Oliver Wolcott
Roger Sherman

The Declaration of Independence

Did You Know?

Roger Sherman was the only person who signed all of the four most important documents of the Revolution: the Articles of Association, the Declaration of Independence, the Articles of Confederation, and the Constitution.

Research Organize students into groups of four. Point out that the Declaration has been a force for change in the United States. People have used its words and its ideas to promote such measures as the abolition of slavery and equal rights for women. Have each group do research to find three examples in which an individual or a group used the words and ideas expressed in the Declaration to promote change or reform. **L2**

Determining Relevance Ask students to write a paragraph stating which idea Jefferson expressed in the Declaration is the single most important one. (Answers will vary but may be modeled as follows: Jefferson's words express the basic ideas of American democracy—that the government draws its powers from the people, and it exists to preserve their rights.) **L3**

Critical Thinking

Identifying Central Issues On June 7, 1776, Richard Henry Lee submitted a resolution to the Continental Congress stating that "these United Colonies are, and of right ought to be, free and independent states." Ask: Why did the members of the Continental Congress believe it was necessary to also issue a longer declaration? (More was required than a simple statement of withdrawal from the British Empire. It also required a statement of causes and principles.) **L2**

LESSON PLAN
SECTION 2, 126–129

FOCUS

Bellringer
Prior to taking roll at the beginning of the class period, display Focus Activity Transparency 16 on the overhead projector and assign the accompanying Focus Activity Sheet.

Objectives
Point out the objectives on this page to students in previewing the section content.

Motivating Activity
Tell students that Thomas Paine referred to those colonists who would shrink from serving their country as "summer soldiers" and "sunshine patriots." Ask students to define these terms in their own words. Suggest that students look for examples of people who fit these descriptions as they read this section.

- GTV: A Geographic Perspective on American History

Side 1, Chapter 17
Title: *The American Revolution*
Subject: The impact of geography and aid from France on the American Revolution

See GTV Guide page 39 for complete lesson plan.

SECTION 2

Fighting for Independence

Setting the Scene

Section Focus
Having announced their separation from Britain, the Americans faced a draining military struggle to maintain independence. The British would not willingly surrender so large a part of their colonial empire to a band of rebels. During the early stages of the war, it was all Washington could do to prevent the capture of his entire army.

Objectives
After studying this section, you should be able to
★ list two reasons why the American victories at Trenton and Princeton were important.
★ compare the difficulties faced by the Americans and the British in the Revolutionary War.

Key Term
Continental

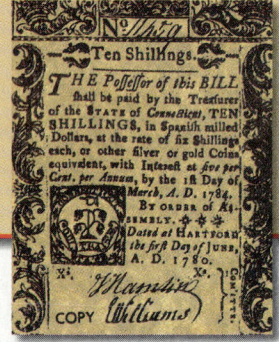

◀ CONTINENTAL MONEY

Early in 1776 Parliament authorized an army of 55,000, including 30,000 German mercenaries. In August 1776, perhaps the largest single military force ever sent from Europe to America appeared off the coast of New York City—more than 400 transports bearing 32,000 troops, guarded by 30 warships, under the command of Sir William Howe.

With his brother, Admiral Richard Howe, he addressed a conciliatory letter to "George Washington, Esq.," offering to pardon the rebels if they laid down their arms, restored the local governments that existed before 1775, and accepted royal governors and councils. Washington adamantly refused to consider proposals that offered nothing but pardons.

After Washington's refusal, the British war machine moved into action. Easily defeating an ill-trained militia of 20,000 under Washington's command, the British took New York City and held it until the war ended seven years later.

■ British Army Invades America

The British forces followed Washington's army up the Hudson River and, when he crossed to New Jersey, pursued him southward to the Delaware River. Through desertions, deaths, and captures, the American army was now reduced to 5,000, and the Continental Congress was forced to flee from Philadelphia to Baltimore.

Trenton
When all seemed lost, Washington planned a bold move. On the evening of December 25, the first issue of *The Crisis* by

---

Classroom Resources for SECTION 2

Teacher's Classroom Resources
- Reproducible Lesson Plan
- Reteaching Activity 5-2
- Section Quiz

Multimedia
- Section Focus Transparency 16
- Testmaker
- Student Self-Test Software
- A Geographic Perspective on American History

Thomas Paine was read to the troops ("These are the times that try men's souls...."). Hoping to win at least one battle before his troops' terms were up, Washington ferried his soldiers back across the Delaware River in a freezing winter wind.

Nine miles away lay Trenton, held by 1,300 Hessians under the command of Colonel Johann Gottlieb Rall, who regarded the Americans as "country clowns." Rall had taken few precautions against attack. Washington guessed correctly that these German troops would celebrate Christmas by getting thoroughly drunk and took a chance on surprising them the morning after. He attacked at dawn on December 26, killing or capturing more than 1,000 Hessians in only 45 minutes.

Rall, gravely wounded, was carried back to his headquarters. As doctors cut away his clothes to treat his wounds, they found an unopened note from a Loyalist who had tried to warn him the night before that Washington was coming. Had the colonel read this note, he might have ambushed Washington and changed the course of history.

Princeton

When General Howe heard of the defeat at Trenton, he sent General Charles Cornwallis from New York with 8,000 soldiers to capture Washington's force. Washington, whose troops now numbered only 1,500, pretended to be trapped, then slipped away and surprised a British force at Princeton on January 3, 1777. He then moved his army into the highlands of New Jersey out of Cornwallis's reach.

These victories saved the American cause. Philadelphia celebrated when the captured Hessians were paraded through the streets. Because of his earlier failures, Washington had been in danger of being removed from command. Now Congress gave him more power, and new enlistees joined his army as it moved to winter quarters at Morristown, New Jersey.

Visualizing History

▲ **VICTORY AT TRENTON** With morale sinking among his troops, Washington launched a surprise attack on Christmas night. Crossing the Delaware River into New Jersey, his army captured the British garrison at Trenton and then defeated a second British force at Princeton on January 3, 1777. **Why were the victories at Trenton and Princeton important to the American cause?**

Sidelights: The American Navy

At the beginning of the Revolutionary War, the colonists had no navy, so they began to commission private ships to attack British vessels. Owners of these ships could keep half the cargo of any captured enemy vessels. This arrangement greatly aided the American cause by cutting deeply into British supply routes. One ingenious Yankee captain, Jonathan Haraden, instructed his crew to cover the ship's gun ports with canvas to make the vessel look like a vulnerable merchant ship. However, when an unsuspecting British ship neared, it was met with gunfire from the disguised gun ports.

CHAPTER 5
SECTION 2

Independent Practice
Writing Letters Have students imagine they are Continental soldiers writing home to their families. How would they describe the strengths and weaknesses of the army's commander, George Washington? **L1**

Evaluating
Direct students to list British and American failures and successes in the first phase of the war. Invite volunteers to present their lists to the class. Ask: Do the failures outweigh the successes or do the successes outweigh the failures? Have students explain their conclusions with evidence from the text. **L2**

Teaching American Portraits
At his death, the American government owed Haym Salomon about $650,000. Not all financiers of the Revolution were as unfortunate as Salomon, however. Robert Morris, for example, profited greatly from the war and died a wealthy man.

Ask students what criminal penalties, if any, there should be for making high profits from the misery of a war.

AMERICAN PORTRAITS

Haym Salomon
1740(?)–1785

Forced to flee from his native Poland after championing the cause of Polish freedom, Haym Salomon went first to England and then to America. Arriving in New York in 1772, he soon joined the Patriot struggle.

A Jewish businessman of remarkable ability, Salomon acquired wealth, all of which he risked during the American Revolution. Twice arrested as a spy, Salomon was condemned to death for plotting to burn British ships at anchor outside New York City. He escaped by bribing his jailer and fled to Philadelphia. There he opened a prosperous private banking business and donated thousands of dollars for military supplies and government salaries. He also worked with Robert Morris to secure loans for the war effort. As a result of his devotion to America—and business problems after the war—Salomon died penniless.

■ Financial Problems

Victory was sweet, but harder tests of Patriot endurance lay ahead. Raising a volunteer army for short-term duty was difficult enough; keeping troops in service was nearly impossible. Although some 300,000 persons eventually took up arms as Patriots, Washington could never count on more than 20,000 under his command at any point. Most soldiers served during the winter months, then returned home for the spring planting, and many refused to fight outside their own home areas. Throughout the war Washington begged for more troops, but Congress was powerless to do anything more than pass these requests along to the states.

Paying for the war was equally difficult. Lacking the power to tax, Congress issued **Continentals**, or paper money to be used as currency instead of British coins. These Continentals, which had nothing to support their value, soon became nearly worthless, forcing many American merchants and farmers to sell goods to the British. Fortunately, Robert Morris, a Pennsylvania merchant and banker, personally pledged large amounts of money for the war effort.

A member of the Continental Congress, Morris was elected superintendent of finance in 1781, a position that earned him the title "financier of the American Revolution." Largely through his efforts, sufficient funds were raised to move Washington's army from New York to the final campaign at Yorktown.

■ American Advantages

The Americans faced financial problems and a larger, better-equipped army. However, the American army also held several advantages.

Washington Commands Respect

Washington's leadership was undoubtedly America's greatest asset, even though he lost more battles than he won. He may have been mistaken in training his army on strictly European lines. He sometimes annoyed his troops by his stiff manner and a tendency to talk as though all were lost. Yet no one on the American side did more to win the war.

While British commanders often returned to England for the winter, Washington remained at his post. He saw his home at Mount Vernon only once during the war, and then only for a few hours. He alone

UNIT 2 Creating a Nation: 1650–1789

Cooperative Learning

Divide the class into groups of five, each group to represent a subcommittee of Parliament. The members are concerned about the war in America and wish to present a case for ending it to the entire Parliament. What are the members' reasons for wanting to end the war? Have each group member contribute to a discussion of this question. At the end of a set time period, have a group reporter present his or her group's arguments to the class as if it were a session of Parliament. (This activity may be an appropriate method of authentic assessment and may be placed in students' portfolios). **L2**

commanded sufficient respect to keep the frail Continental Army from dissolving. As one former soldier later told his grandchildren, "He was a fine man, General Washington—he was everything a man should be."

The British People and the War

Great Britain's military strength should have been sufficient to defeat the rebels. The British government had hard cash to pay its troops and to buy food from Loyalist farmers. The disciplined army, well-trained officers, and a strong navy kept supplies flowing. But the British faced several major hurdles. First, the war was unpopular in Britain. General Gage, who was relieved of his command in 1775, observed:

> They [colonists] give out that they expect peace on their own terms through the inability of Britain to contend with them; and it is no wonder that such reports gain credit with the people, when letters from England and English newspapers give so much encouragement to rebellion.

Britain's Military Strength Divided

In addition, Britain's sprawling colonial empire, threatened by other European powers, demanded that troops be stationed around the globe. While American soldiers defended their homes, the British, thousands of miles from home, fought for a cause that many did not understand or even support. Finally, in order to win, the British had to gain control of a vast American territory. This task was especially difficult because the Americans' hit-and-run tactics frustrated British generals, and Washington established an effective spy system that brought information from behind British lines at critical times.

Despite these problems, British generals believed they could defeat the poorly equipped Americans. Lieutenant General John Burgoyne devised a plan to divide and conquer the rebels. Neither he nor the Americans could foresee that this effort would backfire, resulting in America's obtaining the key ingredient for its success—French aid.

▲ GENERAL GEORGE WASHINGTON AMONG HIS TROOPS

Section 2 ★ Review

Checking for Understanding

1. **Identify** Trenton, Princeton, General Cornwallis, Robert Morris, General Thomas Gage.
2. **Define** Continental.
3. **List** the American and British advantages at the beginning of the war. Which side do you think had the better chance of winning?

Critical Thinking

4. **Analyzing Ideas** It has been said that George Washington was America's greatest asset in winning the Revolution. Analyze this thesis using the battles at Trenton and Princeton, the winter at Valley Forge, and Washington's personal commitment to duty to support your argument.

CHAPTER 5 War for Independence 1775–1783   129

LESSON PLAN
SECTION 3, 130–135

FOCUS

Bellringer
Prior to taking roll at the beginning of the class period, display Focus Activity Transparency 17 on the overhead projector and assign the accompanying Focus Activity Sheet.

Motivating Activity
Write the following on the chalkboard:

The enemy of my enemy is my friend.

Have students explain how this might apply to political alliances. (When looking for support against an opponent, look for other enemies of that opponent.)

Assign students the Chapter 5 Reading entitled "Changing the Hearts and Minds of the People" in Primary and Secondary Source Readings.

Use Chapter 5 Map Transparency.

- *GTV: A Geographic Perspective on American History*

Side 1, Chapter 17
Title: *The American Revolution*
Subject: The impact of geography and aid from France on the American Revolution.

See GTV Guide page 39 for complete lesson plan.

SECTION 3

The War Deepens

Setting the Scene

Section Focus
The American Revolution divided opinion both in America and in Europe. Although European rulers hoped that Britain would be humbled and the balance of power restored, they were concerned that their open support for a revolution might encourage rebellion in their own colonies or even at home.

Objectives
After studying this section, you should be able to
★ list two reasons why France supported the American Revolution.
★ describe the roles of women, African Americans, and Native Americans in the war.

Key Term
envoy

◀ BENJAMIN FRANKLIN

The first efforts to secure French assistance came as early as 1776 when Silas Deane was sent to Paris. Deane was successful in securing secret aid, but after the Declaration of Independence, the United States desired open support. Benjamin Franklin became the principal American **envoy** [EHN•voy], or delegated representative, to France. Perhaps no foreign diplomat in history was as popular as Franklin in Paris. However, France would not provide funds for the American struggle unless there was some hope of success.

■ British Strategy

Although an American attempt to conquer Canada in 1776 had failed, it forced the British to divert to Canada troops that might have been better used in New York and New Jersey. In 1777 General John Burgoyne planned a great three-pronged attack that would divide the colonies along the line of Lake Champlain and the Hudson Valley. According to the plan, while General Howe moved up the Hudson River from New York City, Burgoyne's army would move south from Montreal. A force under British officer Barry St. Leger would invade by way of Lake Ontario and the Mohawk River. The three armies would meet near Albany.

Because the British war office failed to keep in touch with him, Howe's army never participated in the plan. Hoping to catch Washington, Howe led an expedition from New York to Philadelphia, the capital. He captured Philadelphia in September, overcoming Washington at the Battle of Brandywine and inflicting a further defeat on the Americans at Germantown, Pennsylvania, in October. This time Congress fled to York, Pennsylvania.

UNIT 2 Creating a Nation: 1650–1789

Classroom Resources for SECTION 3

Teacher's Classroom Resources
- Reproducible Lesson Plan
- Reteaching Activity 5-3
- Chapter 5 Primary and Secondary Source Reading
- Section Quiz

Multimedia
- Section Focus Transparency 17
- U.S. History and Art
- Chapter 5 Map Transparency
- Testmaker
- Student Self-Test Software
- A Geographic Perspective on American History

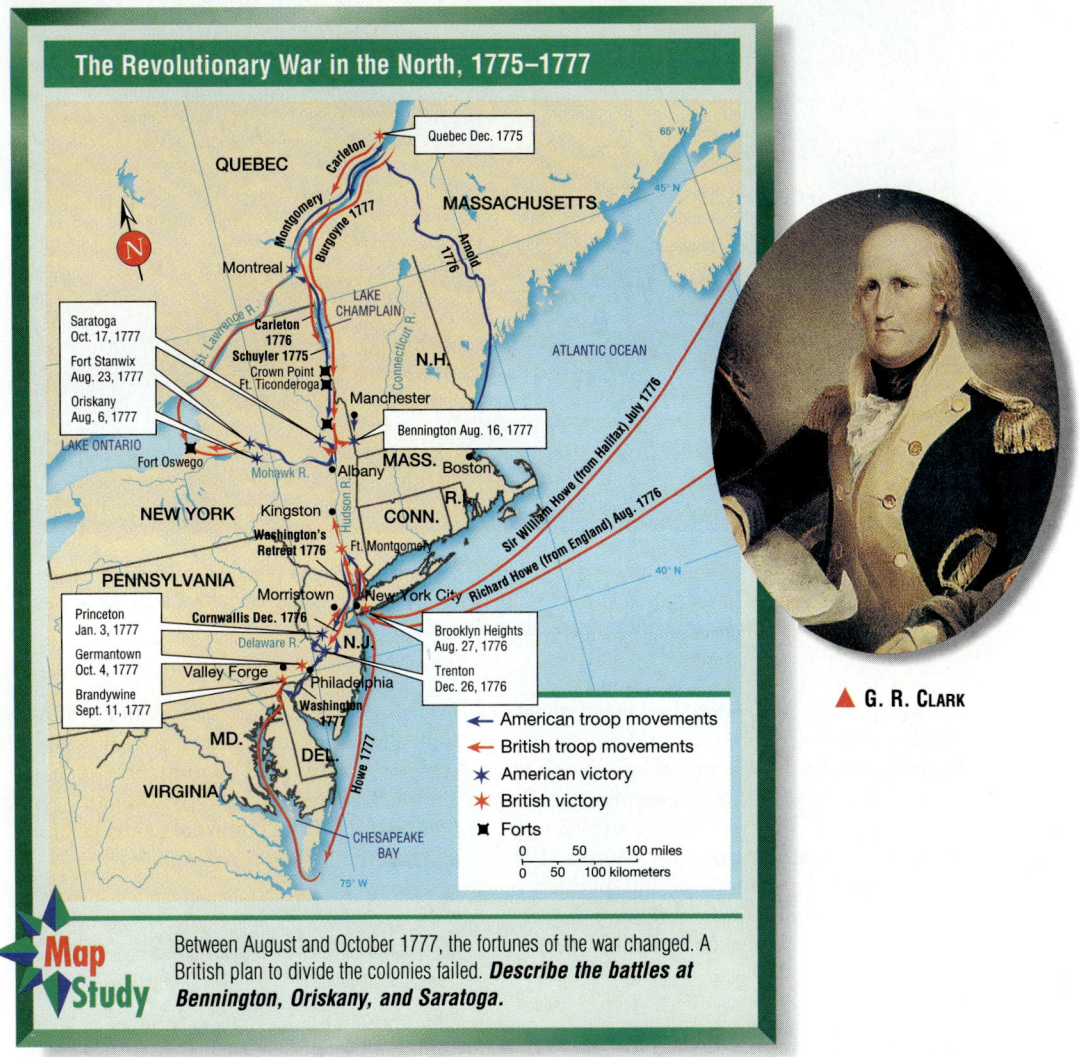

The Revolutionary War in the North, 1775–1777

▲ G. R. CLARK

Map Study Between August and October 1777, the fortunes of the war changed. A British plan to divide the colonies failed. *Describe the battles at Bennington, Oriskany, and Saratoga.*

Meanwhile, Burgoyne's force of 8,000 troops, unaware that Howe's army would not meet them, started south toward Albany. They easily recaptured Fort Ticonderoga in midsummer.

After such an effortless victory, however, Burgoyne faced one obstacle after another. A force of 1,000 Americans felled trees across the only road to Albany, so that Burgoyne's army could move no more than 1 mile a day.

To further delay Burgoyne's plan, St. Leger's advance from Lake Ontario was slowed by his own troops' bloody ambush of Americans at Oriskany, New York. The stage was set for a dramatic American victory.

Saratoga

In spite of his difficulties near Philadelphia, Washington sent some of his best troops to General Horatio Gates, commanding officer for the northern campaigns. Meanwhile, with their homes threatened by the British advance and Burgoyne's Native American allies, New York and New England militia began to gather at Bemis Heights. Eventually, Burgoyne was surrounded by a force nearly twice as large as his own. He was unable to get food, to retreat to Ticonderoga, or to advance on Albany. His force surrendered at Saratoga in October 1777.

▶ **BATTLE OF SARATOGA** Short of supplies, Burgoyne's forces withdrew to Saratoga where Gates's forces surrounded them. On October 17, 1777, Burgoyne surrendered. *What was the significance of the American victory at Saratoga?*

The victory at Saratoga proved crucial. British ministers offered to grant the Americans generous rights of self-government within the British Empire. Fearing that the offer might be accepted, France signed two treaties with the Continental Congress. The first recognized American independence and granted commercial privileges; the second offered an alliance on favorable terms.

Valley Forge

Before French aid reached America, Washington's army had to endure the unusually harsh winter of 1777 and 1778 encamped at Valley Forge, Pennsylvania. Many of the soldiers lacked food, shoes, and coats. Huddled together in small huts, they wrapped themselves in blankets. By spring nearly one-fourth of the original 10,000 soldiers had died. Others had deserted.

The Prussian Baron Friedrich W.A. von Steuben and the French Marquis de Lafayette joined Washington at Valley Forge, bringing discipline and encouragement. By spring, the tattered army began to regain morale as new provisions arrived from France. Several European nations joined with France to lend financial and military support. Individual volunteers such as Count Casimir Pulaski of Poland, von Steuben, and Lafayette were evidence of the support the Revolution generated.

Difficult Choices

When the Declaration of Independence called the United States "one people," it expressed a hope rather than a fact. Only about one-third of the American people actively supported the war. Another third were indifferent to the Patriot cause. The rest supported the British.

Americans Choose Sides

The American Revolution was a civil war as well as a war against Great Britain. Loyalists, sometimes called Tories, refused to abandon allegiance to the king, and many joined the British army. The struggle between the Patriots and the Loyalists was as bitter as the struggle between the rebels and the British. Patriots thought of the Loyalists as traitors to the American cause.

African Americans

From the beginning of the war, at Lexington, Concord, and Bunker Hill, African American soldiers fought for the American cause. Slaveholders were afraid to give guns to African Americans, however, whether enslaved or free.

In November 1775, orders went out to discharge all African American soldiers in the Continental Army and not to permit others to enlist. Soon after, the royal governor of Virginia promised to free any enslaved person who joined the British army. Many slaves were reportedly crossing into the British lines. As a result, the Continental Congress reversed its policy and allowed free African Americans to reenlist.

Jehu Grant, a slave in Rhode Island, joined the American army fearing that his Loyalist master planned to send him to work on a British ship. Jehu Grant served for 10 months and later achieved freedom. Other slaves who were recruited into the army either won freedom from the start or at the end of their military service.

Native Americans

Some groups of Native Americans remained neutral, but many joined the British. They knew the Americans opposed the Proclamation of 1763, which reserved the land west of the Appalachian Mountains for Native Americans. British agents encouraged the Native Americans to attack settlements on the frontier. They provided weapons and ammunition to Cherokee to raid the Virginia, Georgia, and Carolina frontiers. These actions diverted many state militia from fighting against British troops. The British stirred up similar trouble throughout the Northwest.

In New York four nations of the Iroquois Confederation supported the British. General Washington sent troops against the Iroquois and broke their confederation. Many

Life of the Times

Yankee Peddler

Farm families during the Revolution had difficulty producing all the materials required for food, shelter, and clothing. Peddlers—traveling hawkers of dry goods—canvased the countryside with pack horses and wagons laden with merchandise. Such Yankee vendors dated from early colonial times and were a prominent fixture in rural America for generations.

Wherever crowds assembled, a peddler selling wares was usually present. In between times the peddler traveled house to house and was a welcome visitor. His inventory varied, of course, but goods ranged from such notions as pins, combs, buttons, and ribbon to necessities such as clocks, tinware, drugs, shoes, spices, cloth, even books. The peddler brought news and gossip, gave advice, and sometimes even treated the sick. Due to customary shortages of currency and coin, barter for goods was the usual practice. Some successful peddlers eventually established themselves in a general store. For others the appeal of the road was simply too great to resist.

▲ YANKEE PEDDLER DISPLAYING GOODS

CHAPTER 5 War for Independence 1775–1783

Sidelights: Patriot Colonial Women

Colonial women asserted themselves as Patriots as best they could within the restrictive social and political framework of the time. In 1780, for example, women in Philadelphia, New Jersey, Maryland, and Virginia went from door to door collecting money for the troops. When General Washington denied their request that the money go straight to the soldiers, they refused to hand over the funds. Instead, they bought material, sewed shirts, and sent these directly to the troops.

CHAPTER 5 SECTION 3

Teaching Life of the Times

In general, Yankee peddlers had a bad name. According to one colonial observer, they were "proverbial for their dishonesty." However, such a notable American as Stephen Girard, the financier who provided funds for the United States during the 1812 War, began as a peddler. Also many of today's great department stores were founded by former peddlers.

Ask students to speculate as to why the peddler was such a welcome visitor in rural areas and frontier towns.

Food of the Times

A broth called Philadelphia Pepper Pot has been called the soup of the Revolution. It was invented for Washington's troops to give them a hot and filling food at Valley Forge. Made of peppercorns, tripe, and scraps, it saved many soldiers from starving.

 **WOMEN AND RIGHTS** Abigail Adams was a crusader for women's rights, demonstrating the careful thought of educated women of this period. *To what group did the new state bill of rights reserve the full privileges of citizenship?*

Native Americans—including almost all of the Mohawk—moved permanently to Canada.

Women

Many women actively served the American cause. Women often served as secret agents supplying information about British positions and plans. They raised money to equip troops. They ran farms and businesses while their husbands were away at war. John Adams's family would have gone bankrupt had not Abigail Adams capably managed their family farm in Braintree, Massachusetts.

During the war it was common for women to accompany the troops—both American and British—serving as cooks, medics, laundresses, and guides. Sarah Osburn went with her husband's regiment from West Point to Yorktown, washing, mending, and cooking for the soldiers.

A few women fought in the ranks, the most famous being Mary Ludwig Hays, better known as Molly Pitcher. Carrying water to the gunners during the battle of Monmouth, New Jersey, in 1778, she saw her husband fall and took his place at the cannon. For her services she later received a pension of $50 a year. Deborah Sampson disguised herself as a man and enlisted in a Massachusetts regiment. She fought in many battles and was seriously wounded. Sampson was honorably discharged from the army and returned home to marry and raise a family.

Women who supported the Revolution expected to gain from its ideals of democracy and equality. However, the American Revolution did very little to change the political rights of women. Although new state bills of rights declared that all people are equal, they reserved full privileges of citizenship for white males.

▶ **DEBORAH SAMPSON**

Section 3 ★ Review

Checking for Understanding

1. **Identify** Silas Deane, John Burgoyne, Saratoga, Horatio Gates, Baron Friedrich W.A. von Steuben, Count Casimir Pulaski, Marquis de Lafayette, Tories, Molly Pitcher, Abigail Adams.
2. **Define** envoy.
3. **Cite** both military and diplomatic reasons why the victory at Saratoga was crucial to the American cause.
4. **Explain** the decisions facing African Americans and Native Americans during the Revolutionary War.

Critical Thinking

5. **Analyzing Beliefs** The Revolution has been described as a civil war as well as a rebellion against Great Britain. Analyze this theory based on the conflict between Loyalists and Patriots. Consider each group's political beliefs.

134   UNIT 2 Creating a Nation: 1650–1789

Social Studies Skills

Study and Writing Skills

Identifying Alternatives

In order to make an informed decision, you must identify the alternatives or the possible options in each situation. Almost any decision you make has alternatives, even if the choices are unpleasant.

Use the following steps to identify and evaluate alternatives:

- **State** the problem or decision to be made.
- **List** all the possible options you can think of.
- **Gather** information to evaluate the alternatives. Map out both positive and negative consequences of each alternative.

Revolutionary leader and public official Samuel Adams early on took a firm position for independence. In 1765 he was elected to the Massachusetts House of Representatives, where he was linked with the colonists arousing public feeling against British measures. As one of the main spokespersons for this position, Adams agitated against the Stamp Act, the Townshend duties, and other measures imposed by Parliament.

Adams wrote many articles alerting Americans of Parliament's actions and helped organize the committees of correspondence in New England.

In 1772 Adams wrote *A List of Infringements and Violations of Rights*, detailing what he considered to be the wrongs committed by Great Britain against the colonists. Adams wrote to convince other colonists of his position:

> "We cannot help thinking, that an enumeration [list] of some of the most open infringements of our rights [by Great Britain], will by every candid person be judged sufficient to justify whatever measures have been already taken, or may be thought proper to be taken, in order to obtain a redress of the grievances under which we labour. . . ."

▲ Samuel Adams

Practicing the Skill

1. What is the topic Adams is discussing?
2. What position does Adams advocate?
3. Identify at least two alternative viewpoints to Adams's position.
4. Following Adams's advice might lead to war with Great Britain. What are some possible consequences of the alternative positions you listed in question 3 above?
5. In August 1776, King George III sent 32,000 troops to the colonies, along with a letter offering pardon for any rebels who laid down their arms. How else could King George III have responded to the Declaration of Independence? In other words, identify Great Britain's alternatives.

LESSON PLAN
Mastering Social Studies Skills

Teaching Study and Writing Skills

Ask students to read the text explaining the steps involved in identifying and evaluating alternatives. Using their lists, have them write all the possible alternatives they can think of involving their decisions. Ask: Based on the steps you have read, did you make the best informed decision?

Did You Know?

Although he fought long and hard for independence, Samuel Adams refused to attend the convention held in 1787 to form a new Constitution. Adams feared a strong central government and was suspicious of many of the delegates' intentions.

Answers to SOCIAL STUDIES SKILLS

1. wrongs Adams believed Britain committed
2. whatever Patriots did was justified
3. Responses will vary but examples may be that Britain did not commit any wrongs; Patriots could decide to compromise; Britain could compromise.
4. Responses will vary depending on alternatives given. Answers should be reasonable and probable.
5. Britain could have sent the offer of pardon without troops or the troops without the pardon.

LESSON PLAN
SECTION 4, 136–139

FOCUS

Bellringer

 Display Focus Activity Transparency 18 on the overhead projector and assign the accompanying Focus Activity Sheet.

Objectives

Point out the objectives on this page in previewing the section content.

Motivating Activity

Write the following headlines on the chalkboard: "Troops Mutiny, Demand Pay"; "Hero of Saratoga Turns Traitor." Have students imagine seeing these headlines in colonial newspapers during the war. Ask them if they would expect a country faced with such problems to win the war.

 Assign students the Chapter 5 Reading on Valley Forge in Primary and Secondary Source Readings.

NATIONAL GEOGRAPHIC SOCIETY

 **VIDEODISC**

- *GTV: A Geographic Perspective on American History*

Side 1, Chapter 17
Title: *The American Revolution*
Subject: The impact of geography and aid from France on the American Revolution

See GTV Guide page 39 for complete lesson plan.

SECTION 4

The War Ends

Setting the Scene

Section Focus

Britain hoped to prevent the rebels from securing arms from France and other nations. Yet the rebels held on by avoiding direct confrontation and capture. The rebellion had broken out in the north, but the conclusion would be played out in the south at Yorktown, Virginia.

Objectives

After studying this section, you should be able to

★ identify the problems that the British and Americans faced in continuing the war effort.

★ explain the military strategy that defeated Lord Cornwallis.

Key Term

traitor

◀ COLONIAL SOLDIER

In 1778 the British evacuated Philadelphia and marched across New Jersey toward New York. At Monmouth, Washington attacked General Henry Clinton's baggage train. A mistaken order and perhaps treachery prevented an American victory, but Clinton was not able to take advantage of American blunders. While New York City remained in British hands, Washington kept an eye on the enemy from his camp in nearby White Plains.

■ The Final Years

Unable to capture Washington's army or to put down the rebellion in the north, the British turned their main military efforts to the south. For three years, beginning in 1778, the redcoats marched through Georgia, the Carolinas, and Virginia, never suffering major defeat.

Spain Enters the War

The British were not as successful in the southwest. General Bernardo de Galvez, the governor of Spanish Louisiana, helped Americans ship supplies up the Mississippi River. When Spain officially entered the war in 1779, Galvez's troops defeated the British at Baton Rouge, Natchez, and Pensacola. These battles forced the British to divert troops from their campaigns along the Atlantic coast.

Poor Morale and a Traitor

The American cause suffered a year of gloom in 1780. When 6,000 French troops landed at Newport, Rhode Island, a British fleet promptly blockaded them. The Continental Army had not been paid for a month and was on the verge of mutiny. Civilians suffered from high prices as a result of the

UNIT 2 Creating a Nation: 1650–1789

Classroom Resources for SECTION 4

Teacher's Classroom Resources
- Reproducible Lesson Plan
- Reteaching Activity 5-4
- Section Quiz
- Chapter 5 Primary and Secondary Source Reading
- Spanish Summaries and Glossary
- Chapter 5 Enrichment Activity

Multimedia
- Section Focus Transparency 3
- Testmaker
- Student Self-Test Software
- Vocabulary Puzzlemaker
- A Geographic Perspective on American History

flood of paper money that had been printed. American morale received its most severe blow when a major general turned **traitor**—one who commits treason.

Benedict Arnold, a brilliant military leader, had won several battles for the American cause. In 1780 he attempted to turn over to the British the American fort at West Point. Arnold tried to deliver a secret message to the head of British secret service, but three American militiamen intercepted his notes. Washington was given the evidence in Arnold's own writing.

The British were having their troubles, too. Ireland had rebelled, and pro-American riots erupted in London. The British armies could not keep their conquests in the south because they could not win the loyalty of the inhabitants. The British were also harassed by guerrilla fighters under the leadership of Francis Marion, "the Swamp Fox." Sometimes commanding as few as 30 men, Marion repeatedly surprised and defeated small British forces.

Beginning of the End

Believing that Georgia and South Carolina were secure, Lord Cornwallis, the British commander of forces in the south, moved

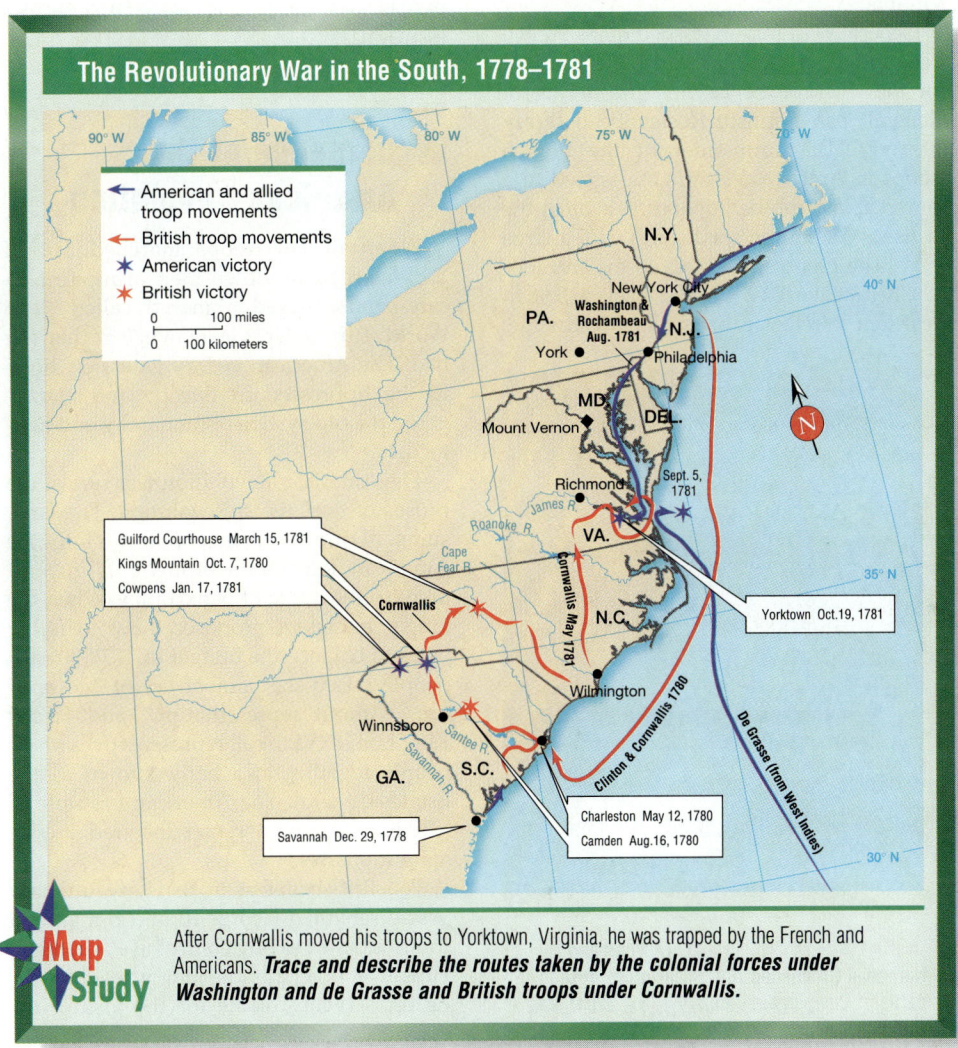

The Revolutionary War in the South, 1778–1781

Map Study After Cornwallis moved his troops to Yorktown, Virginia, he was trapped by the French and Americans. *Trace and describe the routes taken by the colonial forces under Washington and de Grasse and British troops under Cornwallis.*

CHAPTER 5 War for Independence 1775–1783 137

CHAPTER 5 SECTION 4

TEACH

Guided Practice

Political Science Have students make a wall chart showing the difficulties encountered by the British and the Americans as they fought the war. Each problem should be labeled political, economic, military, or a combination of factors.

Have students discuss which problem was most detrimental to morale for each side. **L1, LEP**

Did You Know?

At 13 years of age, Andrew Jackson was arrested as a rebel in South Carolina. When the future President refused to clean a British officer's boots, he was slashed with a sword and marched off to prison. He later regained his freedom and fought the British in the War of 1812 and became the seventh President.

Map Study Using Maps

Answer: Washington: south overland from New York; De Grasse: north by sea from West Indies; Cornwallis: north from Carolinas then east to Yorktown.

Skills Practice:

What role did the location of Yorktown play in Cornwallis's surrender? (British troops' land retreat was cut off by French and American troops; French fleet prevented escape by sea.)

Cooperative Learning

Organize students into small groups and pose the following question: How could the colonies, deep into the war, raise more money to pay Continental Army troops and avoid a mutiny? Have one student in each group contribute a suggestion by writing it down and then passing the paper to the left. When all students in each group have contributed a suggestion, have the groups discuss their choices and vote on the best one. Ask a representative from each group to announce the group's decision to the class. **L2**

137

CHAPTER 5 SECTION 4

Independent Practice

Law Suggest students write a transcript of an imaginary courtroom exchange between Benedict Arnold and a colonial prosecutor. Ask them to focus their transcripts on the arguments that Arnold uses in his defense. **L2**

Visualizing History Cowpens was named for an open area where cattle were rounded up. The Patriots scored a victory when they outflanked the British, whose commander fled. He was chased by Colonel William Washington, a cousin of the general.
Answer to Caption: turned back British forces in the South

Fact or Fiction?
At the Yorktown surrender, the British band played the tune "The World Turned Upside Down."

FICTION: The incident has never been verified. An eyewitness did report, however, that when a British officer offered his sword to French general Rochambeau instead of Washington, Lafayette was so angry at the insult that he asked the American band to play "Yankee Doodle" in derision of the British.

---

into North Carolina. At Kings Mountain on October 7, 1780, rebels ambushed an army of 1,100 Loyalists. After this victory Daniel Morgan and General Nathaniel Greene defeated part of a British force under Cornwallis at Cowpens in January, but were forced to retreat at Guilford Courthouse in March 1781.

The most serious setbacks for the British in 1780 and 1781 were naval defeats at the hands of the French, causing them to lose command of the Atlantic. This made possible the capture of the principal British force in the south under Lord Cornwallis, who had moved out of North Carolina to what he believed to be the safety of Yorktown, Virginia.

General Washington learned that a French fleet under Admiral de Grasse was heading for the Chesapeake Bay. At the urging of General Jean Baptiste Rochambeau (ROH•SHAM•BOH), commander of the French troops in America, Washington agreed to a remarkable combined operation against the British. Washington sped south with a large force. The French fleet blocked the entrance to Chesapeake Bay, beating back a British fleet sent to relieve Cornwallis. Meanwhile,

▲ **BATTLE OF COWPENS** Daniel Morgan and Nathaniel Greene led American forces at the battle of Cowpens in January 1781. *What was the result of this battle?*

a French army sailed from Rhode Island to Virginia. Additional forces under Anthony Wayne and Lafayette converged on Yorktown. Besieged on land and hemmed in by sea, Cornwallis was forced to surrender on October 19, 1781.

The Treaty of Paris, 1783

The Treaty of Paris in 1783 acknowledged American independence and granted the new nation land from the Atlantic Ocean to the Mississippi River. Although several provisions of the treaty led to later disputes, it was a great diplomatic victory. The United States gained an area four times the size of France and nearly ten times that of the British Isles.

■ Influence of the American Revolution

When British troops marched out of Yorktown to lay down their arms, American bands played a march called "The World Turn'd Upside Down." Perhaps it had. The American victory gave new hope to the oppressed in Europe and endangered the old system of monarchy and aristocracy.

The American Revolution was one of the causes of the French Revolution. The large sums of money France poured into the American Revolution brought its government to the verge of bankruptcy. When the king's ministers proposed new loans or taxes to balance the budget in 1778, French people raised the familiar cry of "no taxation without representation" and forced King Louis XVI to call representatives of the people together in a body known as the Estates-General. The American example of rebellion against a tyrant inspired French revolutionaries.

The British defeat in the Revolutionary War discredited George III and put an end to his attempt to buy control of Parliament. However, in a letter the king wrote in 1782, he refused any blame for the loss of the colonies:

Critical Thinking

Summarizing Events Ask students to summarize the chain of events leading to the American victory at Yorktown, beginning with the move by Cornwallis and the British into North Carolina. Suggest that students present their summaries in flow-chart form. **L2**

▼ THE MARQUIS DE LAFAYETTE

History AND ART

▲ **SURRENDER OF LORD CORNWALLIS AT YORKTOWN** by John Trumbull, 1824 Surrounded by American and French forces, General Charles Cornwallis was forced to surrender. Although other skirmishes followed, the victory at Yorktown assured America's independence. **Why did Britain offer generous peace terms?**

> " I cannot conclude without mentioning how sensibly I feel the dismemberment of America from this empire, and that I should be miserable indeed if I did not feel that no blame can be laid at my door.... "

After the defeat at Yorktown, Parliament voted Lord North, George III's prime minister, out of office and took steps to ensure that no king could ever again corrupt and control its members as George III had done. Thus, the American Revolution helped to make the British monarch a figurehead. It also persuaded the British to allow their remaining colonies more self-government. Ralph Waldo Emerson did not exaggerate when he wrote in the "Concord Hymn" that the shot fired by the minutemen on April 19, 1775, was "heard 'round the world."

Section 4 ★ Review

Checking for Understanding

1. **Identify** Benedict Arnold, Francis Marion, Yorktown, General Clinton, Lord Cornwallis, Treaty of Paris.
2. **Define** traitor.
3. **List** three problems that the Americans and the British each faced toward the end of the war.
4. **Detail** the French-American operation that brought about the end of the war.

Critical Thinking

5. **Analyzing Results** A military band played "The World Turn'd Upside Down" when British troops marched out of Yorktown to surrender. Analyze and explain how the world had been turned upside down by the United States's victory in the Revolution and how the course of British and American history was changed.

CHAPTER 5 War for Independence 1775–1783

REVIEW CHAPTER 5

Answers

Reviewing Facts

1. Both plans involved the multidirectional movement of forces, but the 1777 plan involved only land forces, whereas the 1780 plan involved land and naval forces.
2. Guerrilla tactics consisted of unexpected hit-and-run attacks on small British forces, which resulted in repeated surprise and defeat.
3. Answers will vary but may include: Americans: Washington—command and strategy; Marion—guerrilla tactics; de Grasse—naval blockade. British: Burgoyne—lost at Saratoga; Howe—his huge army won no major victories; Cornwallis—surrendered at Yorktown
4. Women raised money, ran farms and businesses, served in army support positions, served as secret agents, and fought as soldiers.
5. Answers will vary but may include that African American participation gave added meaning to the principle of liberty, for which the war was being fought.
6. money, an alliance agreement, and military forces
7. Britain acknowledged American independence and ceded territory west to the Mississippi River. Diplomatic victory for America; U.S. gained valuable territory.

CHAPTER 5 ★ REVIEW

Using Vocabulary

Each of the following terms pertains to the Declaration of Independence. Use these terms to explain the four parts of the Declaration.

grievance
social contract
preamble
right of self-determination

Reviewing Facts

1. **Compare** the plan the British devised to win the war in 1777 with that of the Americans and French in 1780, noting similarities and differences in the two plans.
2. **Describe** the guerrilla tactics used by General Francis Marion and the effect of these methods on the British army.
3. **List** three important military leaders on each side of the conflict, and tell how each influenced the war's outcome.
4. **Explain** the many significant contributions and achievements made by women to the war effort.
5. **Tell** how the participation of African American soldiers in the war enhanced the American cause.

Understanding Concepts

Revolution

1. The American Revolution has been described as the most conservative revolution in history. After looking up the definition of *conservative*, prove or refute the above statement based on what Americans wanted to "conserve," as stated in the Declaration of Independence, and how successful they were in their endeavor.

Civil Rights and Liberties

2. Jefferson turned to natural rights and the contract theory of government when he was writing the Declaration of Independence. Explain why he used these particular concepts.

Critical Thinking

1. **Linking Past and Present** Detail the relationship you see between the theory of government as outlined in the Declaration of Independence and political changes that have occurred in Eastern Europe in recent years.
2. **Understanding Cause and Effect** Analyze the effects of a long and indecisive war on citizen morale and war support. Describe the factors that produce positive effects and negative effects.
3. **Analyzing Artifacts** Study the artifact below and answer the questions that follow.
    a. What is the artifact?
    b. What is its purpose?
    c. How might a modern recruitment poster differ in appearance from this poster?

Writing About History

Narration

Imagine that you are George Washington, Commander in Chief of the Continental Army. Keep a diary of your thoughts and experiences during the awful winter at Valley Forge, 1777–1778. Include items from your expense ledger and accounts of how the

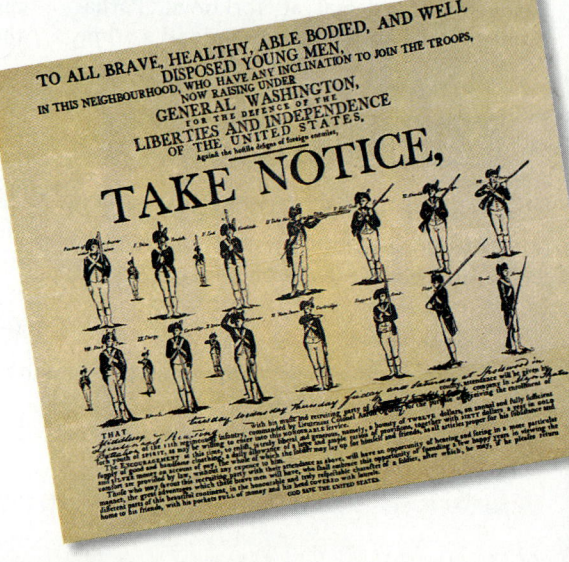

140 UNIT 2 Creating a Nation: 1650–1789

Understanding Concepts

1. It would inspire other colonies to seek independence and provide basic arguments for individual rights.
2. Answers will vary but may include that the American Revolution was conservative in that it sought to keep basic English rights long enjoyed by colonists, as stated in the list of grievances, or was not conservative in that it sought to overthrow English government authority over the colonies, as stated in the Declaration of Rights.
3. Magna Carta: monarch was subject to the law; English Bill of Rights: trial by jury and representation by Parliament; Mayflower Compact: agreement to live under laws of the community; Declaration of Independence: adopted position of the Glorious Revolution of 1688.

CHAPTER 5 ★ REVIEW

men reacted to the cold, the scarcity of food and clothing, the lack of pay, and the failure of Congress to provide even basic necessities for fighting the war.

Cooperative Learning

You and a partner will take sides in the Revolutionary cause. Decide which one will assume the Loyalist position and which the Patriot position. Adopt an appropriate name for the characters you portray and choose a role that includes personal information such as your occupation, your family, and your community. Write a series of letters to your partner in which you convey your feelings before, during, and after the war. Include your reactions to such events as the Stamp Act, the Boston Massacre, the Boston Tea Party, the Declaration of Independence, the various campaigns and battles of the war, and the Treaty of Paris.

Date your letters so that they follow each event that you discuss. Remember that your personal circumstances and your age will change over the course of the 20 years in which these events took place. In reacting to the events, explain how each relates to the position you took as a Patriot or a Loyalist. Write a final letter that concludes by telling what happened to you and your family at the end of the war. When you finish, present several letters to the class as if it were a script of a play.

Social Studies Skills

Interpreting a Table

Study the table on this page. On a separate sheet of paper, answer the questions that follow.
1. What is the title of the table?
2. How is the table organized?
3. Read the following statements. Write a *T* on your paper if the statement is true based on the information in the table. Write an *F* if the statement is false based on the information. Write an *X* if the validity of the statement cannot be determined from the information.
   a. More than 10,000 Americans died in service.
   b. Fewer than 20,000 Americans were captured.
   c. Deaths due to naval engagements outnumber deaths from militia engagements.
   d. More American troops than British troops were killed during the Revolution.

American Casualties in the Revolution

	Militia	Naval	Total
Killed in action	5,992	832	6,824
Died as prisoners	—	—	8,500
Total American deaths in service 15,324			
Wounded	7,988	457	8,445
Captured	15,427	2,725	18,152
Missing	1,426	—	1,426
Deserted	99	1	100

Source: Howard H. Peckham. *The Toll of Independence.* Chicago: University of Chicago Press, 1974.

Using Your Journal
Review your notes on contributions made by women, African Americans, and Native Americans. What did these groups hope to gain by joining the fight for equality? Write a paragraph explaining the outcomes.

CHAPTER 5 War for Independence: 1775–1783

Critical Thinking

1. Answers will vary but may include that since the authority of communist governments in Eastern Europe did not rest on consent of their citizens, the people rose against them and set up new governments more respectful of citizens' rights.
2. Long, indecisive wars weaken morale and popular support. Answers will vary but may include: battle victories, and patriotic fervor.
3. a. poster b. to recruit soldiers c. Answers will vary but may include appeal to opportunities in the military, advancement to better positions.

Practicing a Skill

1. American Casualties in the Revolution
2. by militia and naval casualties
3. a. T
   b. T
   c. F
   d. X

REVIEW CHAPTER 5

4. Answers will vary but may include that Jefferson made use of these terms because John Locke employed them to justify overthrow of monarchy.

Chapter Bonus Test Question

This question may be used for extra credit on the chapter test. Choose the letter of the correct response.

Which of the following explains the basic principle upon which the Declaration of Independence is based?
a. the right of appeal to a monarch
b. the right of people to be governed by their own consent
c. the right to peaceful protest
d. the right to be a rich nation
(Answer: b)

Using Your Journal

Ideas may include equality or at least a higher status in society; recognition of their rights as human beings; economic benefits; for Native Americans, protection of their land rights. Have students share their paragraphs and discuss their conclusions.

PLANNING GUIDE Chapter 6   A More Perfect Union

Daily Lesson Objectives	Teacher Classroom Resources	Multimedia
SECTION 1 **Government in Transition** **1 Day** pp. 144–147 1. Describe the governments that resulted from state constitutions. 2. List the strengths and weaknesses of the Articles of Confederation.	Chapter 6 Study Guide Reproducible Lesson Plan Reteaching Activity 6-1 Reinforcing Social Studies Skills 25, 27, 32, 35, 59, 62 Writer's Guidebook Lessons 2-6 Section Quiz Chapter 6 Cooperative Learning Activity Chapter 6 Concept Mapping Activity	Student Self-Test Software Testmaker Section Focus Transparency 15 Chapter 6 Skills Transparency Powers of the Congress
SECTION 2 **The Confederation** **1 Day** pp. 149–154 1. Discuss the problems between the United States and other nations. 2. Explain the process of settling the West. 3. Identify the domestic problems of the new nation.	Reproducible Lesson Plan Reteaching Activity 6-2 Section Quiz Reinforcing Social Studies Skills 46, 55 Outline Map 9 Building Skills in Geography	Student Self-Test Software Testmaker Section Focus Transparency 16 U.S. History & Art Transparencies 5, 10
SECTION 3 **Toward a New Constitution** **1 Day** pp. 155–160 1. Explain the arguments for and against the new constitution. 2. Explain how the Constitution corrected the weaknesses of the Confederation government.	Reproducible Lesson Plan Reteaching Activity 6-3 Section Quiz Chapter 6 Enrichment Activity Chapter 6 Primary & Secondary Source Readings Reinforcing Social Studies Skills 32, 34, 40, 67 American Portraits 11, 12 Outline Map 10 The Living Constitution Spanish Summaries & Glossary	Student Self-Test Software Testmaker Section Focus Transparency 17 Unit 3 Digest Transparency Vocabulary Puzzlemaker Audiocassette, Chapter 6 Focus on Government Powers of the Congress Landmark Documents in American History
Constitution Handbook **2 Days** pp. 168–197	The Living Constitution	
CHAPTER REVIEW AND EVALUATION **1 Day**	Chapter 6 Test Chapter 6 Performance Assessment Activity	Student Self-Test Software Testmaker

00:00 **OUT OF TIME?** If time does not permit teaching the entire chapter, use the Chapter 6 Summary on pages 166–167 and the Chapter 6 audiocassette (English and Spanish) to point out the main ideas of the chapter.

PLANNING GUIDE

Cultural Diversity Activity

Critical Thinking Refer students to pages 187–189. Have students review the freedoms granted Americans by the Bill of Rights. Point out that throughout the history of the United States, immigrants have been drawn to the nation by the constitutional rights granted to American citizens by the first ten amendments to the Constitution. Note that in many parts of the world today such rights are routinely denied by the government.

Divide the class into groups and assign each a region of the world (Europe, the former Soviet republics, the Middle East, Africa, East Asia, South Asia, Central America, South America). Encourage groups to research the status of political freedoms in one country in the region and report their findings to the class. As a class, compare and contrast political rights in each of the countries selected with those guaranteed by the Bill of Rights.

Performance Assessment Activity

The Structure of Government Ask students to work in pairs or small groups to make charts of the structure of the government established under the Articles of Confederation, the structure defined in the Constitution, and the United States government today. Ask each group to prepare a brief report analyzing the three structures, explaining the changes over time, and describing the reasons for these changes.

POSSIBLE RUBRIC FEATURES: Content, organization, clarity, critical thinking skills, research skills, charting and graphing skills, collaborative skills

Chapter Resources

Literature from the Period

Henry, Patrick. "Speech in the Virginia Ratifying Convention."

Jefferson, Thomas. *Notes on the State of Virginia.* 1787.

Madison, James. "Federalist, No. 51." 1788.

Readings for the Student

Hauptly, Denis, J. *A Convention of Delegates: The Creation of the Constitution.* Macmillan, 1987.

Kennedy, Caroline, and Ellen Alderman. *In Our Defense: The Bill Of Rights in Action.* Morrow, 1991

Rossiter, Clinton. *1787: The Grand Convention.* Norton, 1987.

Readings for the Teacher

Gaustad, Edwin S. *Faith of Our Fathers: Religion and the New Nation.* Harper, 1987.

Norton, Mary Beth. *Liberty's Daughters: The Revolutionary Experiences of American Women, 1750–1800.* Scott, Foresman, 1980.

Multimedia Resources

The Constitution as a Living Document. Close-Up Foundation. (VHS, 57 minutes)

Creating the U.S. Constitution. Educational Activities. (Apple diskette, backup, guide)

To Form a More Perfect Union. National Geographic. (film, teacher's guide)

Meet George Washington. NBC Project 20 Series. (VHS, 54 minutes)

U.S. Constitution Tutor. Micro Learn/Word Associates. (Apple or IBM diskette)

Key to Ability Levels

Teaching strategies have been coded for varying learning styles and abilities.

- **L1** Basic activities for all students
- **L2** Average activities for average to above-average students
- **L3** Challenging activities for above-average students
- **LEP** Limited English Proficiency activities

Glencoe Links to the Humanities

Links to Art
- US History & Art Transparencies 5, 10

Writer's Choice (Grade 11) Fine Art Transparency 2

Link to Literature
- Macmillan Literature: American Literature Text—Phyllis Wheatley, William Bartram, Jean De Crevecoeur

Link to Music

- American Music: Cultural Traditions

CHAPTER 6

BEGINNING THE CHAPTER

Have students use their own words to define the term *authority*. Ask if all expressions of authority are harmful. In a discussion of their responses, help students see that some authority is necessary and beneficial. Point out that the colonists' negative feelings about authority caused problems immediately after the Revolution. Ask students to identify these problems as they read Chapter 6.

Recording Journal Notes
Suggest that students list their findings under regions of the new nation: New England, Middle Atlantic states, Southern states, the Western Frontier.

During the Revolution, colonists were divided over the relationship between the central government and the new state governments. Some wanted a strong federal government; others wanted power to reside with the states. Today these divisions are still visible in the debate over reducing the power of the federal government and giving states more control.

CHAPTER 6

A More Perfect Union
1775–1789

▼ FARMERS PLOWING

Setting the Scene

Focus
Americans successfully met the challenge of establishing state governments and a national government under the Articles of Confederation. It soon became apparent, however, that weaknesses of this new national government might break it apart. During this period of experiment and uncertainty, farsighted American political leaders laid the foundations of a free and democratic government embodied in a new constitution.

Concepts to Understand
★ How political control was allocated within the government under the Articles of Confederation
★ Why a strong central authority was needed to keep the republic intact

Read to Discover . . .
★ why people considered the government under the Articles of Confederation weak.
★ what important compromises made the Constitution possible.

Journal Notes
As you read, note in your journal ways in which Americans continued to be divided following the Revolution.

CULTURAL
- 1775 Smallpox epidemic strikes colonies
- 1780 The first Universalist Church in the nation built in Gloucester, Massachusetts

1775 — 1779

POLITICAL
- 1776 New Hampshire adopts the first written state constitution
- 1781 Articles of Confederation ratified

142 UNIT 2 Creating a Nation: 1650–1789

✚ EXTRA CREDIT PROJECT

During the Revolution, the newly proclaimed states created their own constitutions. As more states were added to the growing nation, they too drew up constitutions. Suggest that interested students look up their state's constitution and outline its provisions. What rights does the state have? What are its responsibilities? Conduct a class discussion based on the students' findings.

History AND ART

The Signing of the Constitution
by Helen Clark Chandler, 1940

The delegates sign the final draft of the Constitution in Independence Hall. Despite mixed feelings regarding some aspects of the Constitution, most of those present were hopeful about the future.

◄ Coin, 1787

- **1784** *Empress of China* sails from New York to Canton, China
- **1787** *The Contrast* is first successful stage comedy in New York City
- **1789** University of North Carolina founded

1783 — **1787**

- **1785** Land Ordinance passed
- **1787** Constitutional Convention held in Philadelphia
- **1788** Constitution is ratified

CHAPTER 6 A More Perfect Union 1775–1789

CHAPTER 6 CONCEPTS

Concept Mapping Activity

On the chalkboard, reproduce the following generalization and concepts map, and have students copy it in their notebooks.

> Consensus on cherished political values leads to the formation of a new government
>
> Political Control — Central Authority

History AND ART

Chandler's painting suggests the artist's admiration for Washington. He is shown standing above the other delegates at the signing of the Constitution.

ABC NEWS INTERACTIVE™

VIDEODISC
Powers of the Congress

Side 1, Chapter 4
Title: *Articles of Confederation*
Subject: Preamble to Articles of Confederation

Side 1, Chapter 5
Title: *Preamble to the Constitution*
Subject: Students reading the Preamble to the Constitution

Teacher Notes

LESSON PLAN
SECTION 1, 144–148

FOCUS

Bellringer
Prior to taking roll at the beginning of the class period, display Focus Activity Transparency 19 on the overhead projector and assign the accompanying Focus Activity Sheet.

Objectives
Point out the objectives on this page to students in previewing the section content.

Motivating Activity
Josiah Tucker, an English clergyman, claimed that once the British government was gone, "the Americans will have no center of union among them, and no common interests to pursue." Ask students if they think Tucker was accurate in his description of Americans in the 1780s. Have them give reasons for their answers. Point out that Section 1 deals with the Americans' struggle to hold together the fragile union of separate states that had been formed during the Revolutionary War.

Use Skills Transparency 6.

Did You Know?
The Massachusetts state constitution made church attendance compulsory.

SECTION 1

Government in Transition

Setting the Scene

Section Focus
As the Revolution progressed, some Americans recognized the need for unity, as well as the need to maintain law. While soldiers fought for freedom, their leaders struggled to create a government to replace British authority. The result was a unique blend of British political heritage and the American experience.

Objectives
After studying this section, you should be able to
★ describe the governments that resulted from state constitutions.
★ list the strengths and weaknesses of the Articles of Confederation.

Key Terms
bicameral, veto, emancipation, disestablished, ratify, public land, unicameral

◀ SLAVE SHACKLES, 1700S

As the fighting spread from Massachusetts in 1775, royal governors throughout the colonies watched their authority collapse. At first a few tried to organize Loyalist resistance, but eventually all royal governors abandoned their offices and fled. In May 1776, Congress urged the colonies to replace their colonial charters with new constitutions.

■ New State Governments
Most state constitutions established state governments similar to the colonial governments they replaced. All states except Pennsylvania and Georgia created **bicameral**, or two-house, legislatures. Members of each house represented geographic districts and, in nearly all the states, were directly elected by the voters.

Major changes were made in the executive branch, however. Many Americans had come to distrust strong executive power. So most state governors were elected to one-year terms by their legislatures and had no power to **veto,** or reject, bills passed.

Citizenship Restrictions
For the most part, citizenship was restricted to white male property owners. Neither women nor African Americans could vote in most states.

Although the Revolution did not win full equality for all Americans, it did move American society in that direction. Because it was difficult to claim that "all men are created equal" in a society where some people were enslaved, many Americans began to question the institution of slavery. Some states passed laws to prohibit the

UNIT 2 Creating a Nation: 1650–1789

Classroom Resources for SECTION 1

Teacher's Classroom Resources
- Chapter 6 Study Guide
- Reproducible Lesson Plan
- Reteaching Activity 6-1
- Chapter 6 Cooperative Learning Activity
- Chapter 6 Primary and Secondary Source Readings
- Section Quiz

Multimedia
- Section Focus Transparency 19
- Chapter 6 Skills Transparency
- U.S. History and Art Transparency 6
- Student Self-Test Software
- Testmaker
- Powers of the Congress

importation of more slaves, and by 1804 every state north of Maryland had provided for the **emancipation**, or freeing, of African American slaves.

Religious Freedom

As the Southern colonies gained independence, the Church of England was **disestablished**—that is, no longer supported by taxation. In Virginia a bill for religious freedom written by Jefferson proclaimed that:

> ❝ ... [N]o man shall be compelled to frequent or support any religious worship, place or ministry ... nor shall otherwise suffer on account of his religious opinions or belief, but that all men shall be free to profess, and by argument to maintain, their opinion in matters of religion. ❞

In New England, however, the descendants of the Puritans continued tax support of the Congregational Church and allowed only Protestants to vote. In addition, Roman Catholics could not hold office in five states, and Jews were barred from office in nine.

Although states discriminated against their residents on the basis of race, sex, religion, and economic standing, most state constitutions included bills of rights spelling out the "unalienable rights" that government must recognize and protect. State bills of rights guaranteed trial by jury and freedom of the press.

The Articles of Confederation

While the individual states were drafting their constitutions, Congress developed a plan to unite the states and establish its own legal authority. In 1777 Congress completed the document, called the Articles of Confederation, and proposed that it go into effect only after every state had approved it.

Claims on the West

Not until 1781, however, did all the states **ratify**, or agree to, the Articles of Confederation. The main reason for delay was that several states claimed large tracts of western land. Based mainly on colonial charters that had granted land "from sea to sea,"

▲ RELIGION, CHURCHES, AND THE COLONIES Churches played a central role in the lives of most early Americans. Virginia's Old Bruton Church is shown in this nineteenth century painting by New York artist A. Wordsworth Thompson. *What was the established church in Virginia before independence?*

CHAPTER 6 A More Perfect Union 1775–1789   145

CHAPTER 6 SECTION 1

Independent Practice

Have students read the Chapter 6 readings in Primary and Secondary Source Readings in the TCR.

American distrust of a strong executive branch exists to this day. Many states limit the number of terms a governor may serve. In 1951 the Constitution was amended to limit Presidents to two terms in office.

Did You Know?

Each of the states had its own army, and nine states had a navy.

Map Study Using Maps

Answer: Virginia

Map Skills Practice

Have students compare this map with a map of the United States today by listing the present-day states carved out of the western land.

Western Land Claims of the Original States

Map Study: States without western land claims feared that states with western lands would expand to become so rich and powerful that they would dominate any central government. Therefore, states without western lands refused to agree to a central government until the other states surrendered their land claims. **Which state had the largest land claims in the West?**

these claims often overlapped, causing confusion and conflict. In addition, the six states without western land claims argued that the West should become **public land**, or land belonging to the national government. Maryland refused to ratify the Articles until this demand was met. Virginia, which had huge claims—the present-day states of Kentucky, West Virginia, Ohio, Indiana, Illinois, Michigan, and Wisconsin—also refused to cooperate. Finally, in 1781, with Lord Cornwallis and the British army moving toward Virginia, the state agreed to give up its land claims. Maryland ratified the Articles, and at last the rebelling states were united.

UNIT 2 Creating a Nation: 1650–1789

Critical Thinking

Analyzing Ideas Have students reread the Section Focus. Direct them to work in pairs to analyze how the newly created government was "a unique blend of British political heritage and the American experience." (British Political Heritage: state constitutions established state governments similar to the colonial governments they replaced. American Experience: Major changes in the executive branch due to the distrust of strong executive powers because of the unhappy experience with royal governors and George III; new state governors elected to one-year terms only and had no veto power.) **L3**

Fear of Centralized Power

Most members of the Continental Congress were quite wary of a strong central government. They took Benjamin Franklin's Albany Plan of Union as their guide and created what John Dickinson, the main author of the Articles, called a "firm league of friendship" among the states. Governing authority was placed in a **unicameral**, or one-house, Congress in which each state had one vote. Congress could wage war and make treaties. It could raise an army and navy, borrow money, establish a postal system, and manage Native American affairs.

National Government Ineffective

Despite these features, the national government under the Articles proved too weak to operate effectively. There was no executive branch to carry out laws, and no federal courts to interpret them. Executive power was divided among several congressional committees. Two important functions were denied to Congress—the power to tax and the power to regulate commerce.

Unable to collect taxes, Congress had to depend on the generosity of the states for its income. Between 1781 and 1789, however, the states gave Congress only about one-sixth of the funds it requested. Without

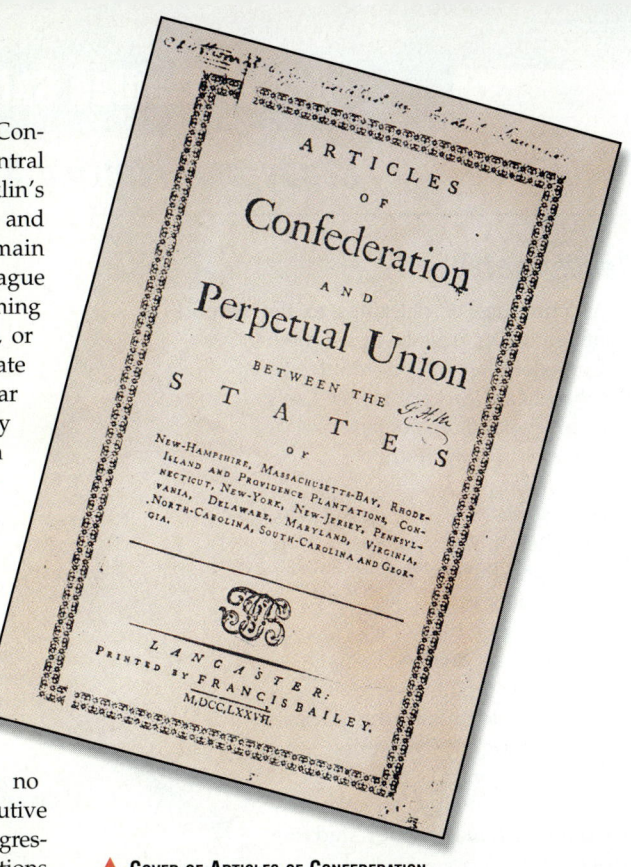

▲ COVER OF ARTICLES OF CONFEDERATION

money or real power over the states, the Confederation Congress commanded so little respect that its members often did not bother to attend sessions. In 1783 it was difficult even to convene enough members to ratify the treaty ending the Revolutionary War.

Section 1 ★ Review

Checking for Understanding

1. **Identify** Articles of Confederation, Confederation Congress.
2. **Define** bicameral, veto, emancipation, disestablished, ratify, public land, unicameral.
3. **Explain** why the newly formed states made major changes in their executive branches.
4. **Describe** the positive and negative features of the Articles of Confederation.

Critical Thinking

5. **Expressing Viewpoints** Imagine that you live in the new United States after the Revolution. Based on your own sex, race, and religion, tell to what extent the Revolution has brought about equality for you.

CHAPTER 6 A More Perfect Union 1775–1789

LESSON PLAN
Mastering Social Studies Skills

Teaching Study and Writing Skills

With the class, generate a list of reasons why it is helpful to be able to take good notes. (to remember details or main ideas at a later date; to avoid returning to a source)

Discuss the guidelines for taking notes, asking students to summarize the points. (Identify subject; be selective in what you write; paraphrase; be legible.) Have a student read the notes on page 148 aloud. Ask if students would add or delete information.

You may wish to work through all or part of "The Ratification Struggle" with students, depending on the time available or the abilities of your students. Stress that note-taking is personal and that, as long as the notes are clear to the writer, any form of shorthand is acceptable.

Did You Know?

James Madison was the major notetaker at the Constitutional Convention in 1787. His *Journal of the Constitutional Convention* relates the conflicts and struggles among the delegates creating a new government.

Social Studies Skills
Study and Writing Skills

Taking Notes

A committee of delegates to the Second Continental Congress designed the Articles of Confederation. The committee members had heard Richard Henry Lee's original proposal of a confederation. No doubt, while they were listening to Lee, delegates dashed down notes about the plan and their opinions about it.

Experts agree that one of the best ways to remember something is to write it down. Taking notes—writing down information in an orderly and brief form—not only helps you remember, but it also makes your studying easier.

▲ Lap desk invented by Thomas Jefferson

There are several styles of note taking, but all clarify and put information in a logical order. When taking notes, it will help to keep in mind these guidelines:

- **Identify** the subject and write it at the top of the page. In your text, for example, look at the chapter title, section title, or subsection headings.

- **Select** specific information for your notes. For example, anything your teacher writes on the chalkboard or shows you from a transparency should be included. If your teacher emphasizes a point or spends a considerable amount of time on a given topic, this is also a clue to its importance.

- **Paraphrase** the information. That is, put the information in your own words rather than trying to take it down word for word. That will make you think about what the author or speaker meant.

In order to save time, you might want to develop different strategies. One way is to create a personal "shorthand." For example, eliminate vowels from words: "develop" becomes "dvlp," "government" changes to "gov." Use symbols, arrows, or rough drawings: "+" for "and." Practice your shorthand in all of your classes.

- **Write** legible and neat notes so that you will be able to understand them when you read them again.

Practicing the Skill

Review the guidelines for taking notes. Then read Section 2, entitled "The Confederation." After you have carefully analyzed the section, follow the guidelines and create shorthand notes for the subsection entitled "Settling the West," which begins on page 151.

148

Answer to SOCIAL STUDIES SKILLS

After students have read the section, ask volunteers to share their notes with the class to point out the varying personal styles for taking notes.

SECTION 2

The Confederation

Setting the Scene

Section Focus

The United States, under the Articles of Confederation, was an unstable nation. America expanded westward, but it continued to have problems with other nations. There was constant bickering among the states, and many groups in society were discontented.

◀ FARMER HARROWING FIELDS

Objectives

After studying this section, you should be able to

★ discuss the problems between the United States and other nations.

★ explain the process of settling the West.

★ identify the domestic problems of the new nation.

Key Terms

right of deposit, tribute, seceding, depression, currency

One of the blessings of independence predicted by Thomas Paine in *Common Sense* was that America would at last be free of European rivalries. Even before the Treaty of Paris was ratified, the Confederation Congress resolved that "the true interest of these states requires that they should be as little as possible entangled in the politics and controversies of European nations." Yet total isolation from Europe was impossible.

The prosperity of the United States depended, as before the Revolution, on trade with European nations and their colonies. Satisfactory trading arrangements required that the United States make commercial treaties with those nations. There also were problems with the Spanish in Florida and New Orleans to the south, and with the British in the north. These problems, too, could be settled only through diplomatic efforts.

■ Foreign Relations

Predictably, the United States did not enjoy good relations with Great Britain. The British agreed to receive John Adams as minister from the United States, even though he had been a prominent rebel during the war. They refused, however, to send a minister to the United States, explaining that they did not know whether to send 1 or 13—a representative for each individual state.

Treaty Violations

Neither country carried out the terms of the Treaty of Paris. The United States had agreed that British creditors could recover prewar debts by suing in American courts, and that Congress would ask the states to cease persecution of Loyalists. But when British merchants sued in state courts, unfriendly judges and juries usually sided

CHAPTER 6 A More Perfect Union 1775–1789

CHAPTER 6 SECTION 2

TEACH
Guided Practice

Foreign Relations Write the following on the chalkboard:

Great Britain, Spain, France, North Africa.

Ask students to write a brief paragraph that describes the problems the United States had with each nation after the Revolution. Then have students identify the foreign-relations problem that they believe presented the greatest threat to the new nation. Ask them to write another paragraph explaining their choices.

Using Maps

Answer: over the border between Georgia and Spanish Florida

Skills Practice

Have students note the lands owned by Spain and Britain on the North American continent. Ask how each might respond to a weak United States government. (might encourage those nations to expand at the expense of the new nation)

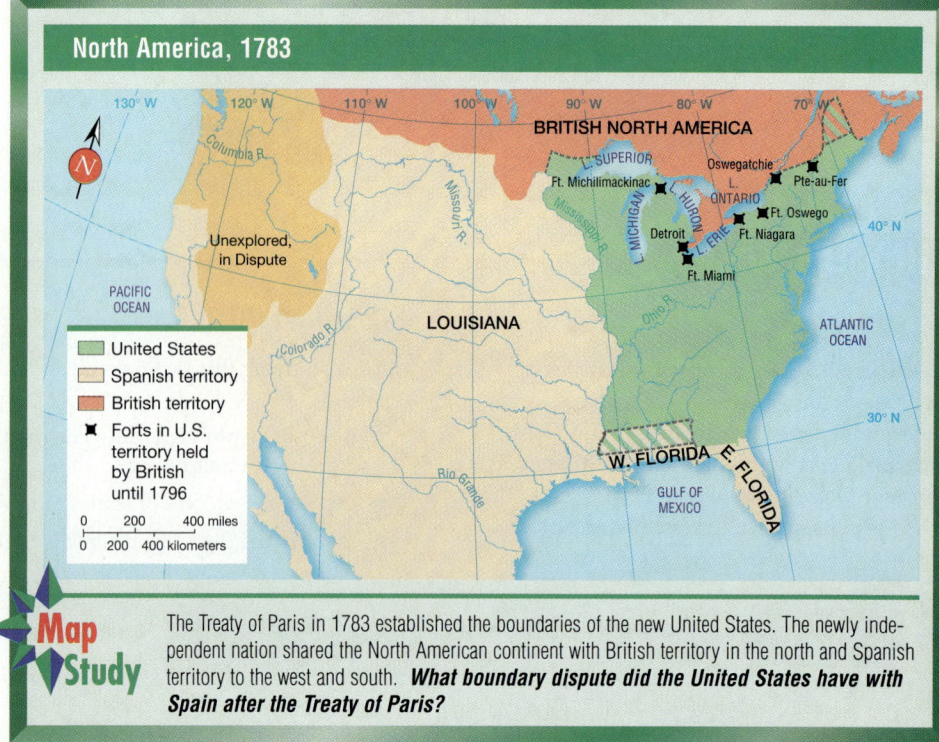

The Treaty of Paris in 1783 established the boundaries of the new United States. The newly independent nation shared the North American continent with British territory in the north and Spanish territory to the west and south. **What boundary dispute did the United States have with Spain after the Treaty of Paris?**

with American debtors. The states also ignored Congress and continued to treat Loyalists harshly. The British government used these treaty violations as an excuse to remain in northern forts they had agreed to abandon. These posts were the centers of a million-dollar annual fur trade that Great Britain was determined to keep.

American Trade Suffers

Tobacco and naval stores no longer enjoyed a preferred position in British markets. American ships were banned from the British West Indies, and they were allowed to enter English ports only with the products of their home states. When the United States tried to negotiate, Britain showed little desire to grant economic privileges.

Trouble With Spain

The Spanish were unhappy about the vast western lands the United States acquired in the Treaty of Paris, fearing that future expansion would threaten the Spanish empire in America. Spain insisted that the southern boundary of the United States was not the border described in the Treaty of Paris, but a line nearly 100 miles to the north. To protect its claims, Spain formed alliances with the Cherokee, Creek, and Chickasaw nations and incited them against American settlers in the disputed territory.

By controlling the mouth of the Mississippi River, Spain also was able to threaten western trade. Bulky goods from the West—lumber, grain, and deerskins—could not be easily carried over the mountains to the East, but had to float down the Ohio and Mississippi rivers on rafts and flatboats. Westerners wanted the **right of deposit** at New Orleans—that is, permission to put goods ashore for transfer to ocean-going ships without paying duties. When Spain refused this request, westerners asked Congress for a treaty with Spain that would grant free navigation along the Mississippi River. Although a treaty was proposed, it did not address western interests.

UNIT 2 Creating a Nation: 1650–1789

Critical Thinking

The Articles of Confederation marked a first step toward a central government for the new United States. The Articles had strengths and weaknesses. Have students list the strengths and weaknesses of the Articles and then answer the following questions: Why were the Articles acceptable to many Americans when they were first adopted? How adequate were the Articles for the needs of a new nation? (accepted because they gave states a great deal of freedom; answers will vary but many will suggest not adequate because the central government was weak and could not resolve conflicts among the states) **L3**

Strained Relations with France

During the Revolutionary War, French loans helped the Americans. Now rising debt interest on loans created serious problems in France. Hoping to stave off bankruptcy, the government introduced reforms and universal land taxes. The French were also disappointed that few commercial opportunities resulted from American independence.

The Barbary Pirates

The most humiliating foreign relations problem for the nation was its treatment by the Barbary Pirates. Four North African states—Morocco, Tunis, Tripoli, and Algiers—made a practice of capturing the ships and crews of nations who refused to pay them an annual **tribute**, a payment to sail in their waters. No longer protected by the British fleet and treasury, American ships were subject to attack.

■ Settling the West

Until the end of the 1800s, "the West" was not a specific geographic region of the United States. Instead, it was a term for the next area of settlement, as pioneers invaded the territory of Native Americans and moved them off the land. During the Confederation period, the West lay just beyond the Appalachian Mountains. Between 1780 and 1790 the western population grew from 2,000 to 100,000.

Congress was powerless to meet these westerners' needs. It could not dislodge the British from their forts in the North or persuade Spain to grant the right of deposit in the South. Without money, Congress could neither purchase Native American land nor provide troops to protect settlers.

Westerners had other grievances with the national government as well. Many resented that eastern speculators held large tracts of western land.

▲ *Daniel Boone Escorting Settlers Through the Cumberland Gap* by George Caleb Bingham, 1851–2 In many of his works, George Caleb Bingham depicts life along the Missouri and Mississippi rivers. **Who was living on the land settled by these pioneers?**

CHAPTER 6
SECTION 2

Teaching Life of the Times
Point out that some of the plant and herbal remedies used by Native Americans were later adopted by Europeans. The Inca, for example, found that boiling a certain kind of tree bark in water alleviated the symptoms of malaria. But it was not until 1820 that the active ingredient—quinine—was finally isolated. Ask: What does the feature identify as the major cause of disease? (germs and poor sanitation)

Independent Practice
Geography Distribute blank U.S. maps to the class. Ask students to locate and label the "West." Then have them label potential "trouble spots" on the western borders where the United States might come into conflict with foreign powers. **L1, LEP**

THEORY OF EMPIRE
The Land Ordinance of 1785 established a system of land survey and settlement that we still use today. The Northwest Ordinance of 1787 created a procedure by which territories could become self-governing and achieve equal status with the founding states. Thirty-seven states have entered the Union through this procedure.

152

Talk of Secession
In 1784, after making a journey to the West, George Washington reported that the region was hanging to the Confederation by a thread. In present-day Tennessee, settlers created a government called the State of Franklin. Unable to obtain statehood from Congress, some Tennessee leaders considered **seceding**, or withdrawing, from the Union. Settlers in the Kentucky territory also talked of secession. The Confederation Congress responded with two laws that established a precedent for the future growth of the nation.

The Land Ordinance of 1785
Determined not to repeat the problems in Kentucky and Tennessee—and also to raise money—Congress passed the Land Ordinance of 1785. This law provided a more orderly method for settling public land north of the Ohio River. The land would be surveyed and divided into townships six miles square. Every township was to contain 36 sections of one square mile, 640 acres, each. The land would sell for $1 per acre. To attract land speculators, the law required that buyers take at least one whole section. Speculators could divide their sections into smaller rectangular tracts and sell them to settlers at a profit.

The Northwest Ordinance of 1787
To provide for a strong government, Congress passed the Northwest Ordinance of 1787. The region bounded by the Ohio River, the Great Lakes, and the Mississippi River was to be divided into not fewer than three territories nor more than five. Whenever 5,000 adult male citizens settled in a territory, they could set up a territorial government modeled on a British royal colony. The settlers would elect a territorial legislature. The national government

Life of the Times

Home Remedies

In an age before germs and proper sanitation were understood, home remedies for illness became an everyday, and perhaps necessary, part of pioneer life. While some folk remedies, such as herbal teas, might have had positive effects, other cures could make the patient worse. Consider these examples.

For venomous snakebite, a part of the reptile that inflicted the wound was placed on top of the incision. This, it was thought, would draw out the poison.

Mumps were treated by rubbing the ill person's spine with garlic. One cure for measles was to make a warm broth of water and sheep dung. The patient sipped the broth until recovery.

Indigestion was a common problem. A mixture of cayenne pepper and alcohol applied to the stomach supposedly spelled relief.

Worms in children could be treated by boiling sage in milk, turning it to whey with vinegar or alum, then having the child drink it. If the worms did not harden in the stomach, the child would live.

Some of the best cures were learned from the Native Americans, who used native plants in pastes and teas.

152 UNIT 2 Creating a Nation: 1650–1789

Critical Thinking

Supporting Generalizations Present this generalization to students: Despite the long struggle to break free of Britain, most Americans after the Revolutionary War continued to think of themselves either as individuals or as inhabitants of states, not as members of a nation. Ask students to list at least four facts that support this generalization, as well as any facts they have read or can think of that may offer a counterargument. **L3**

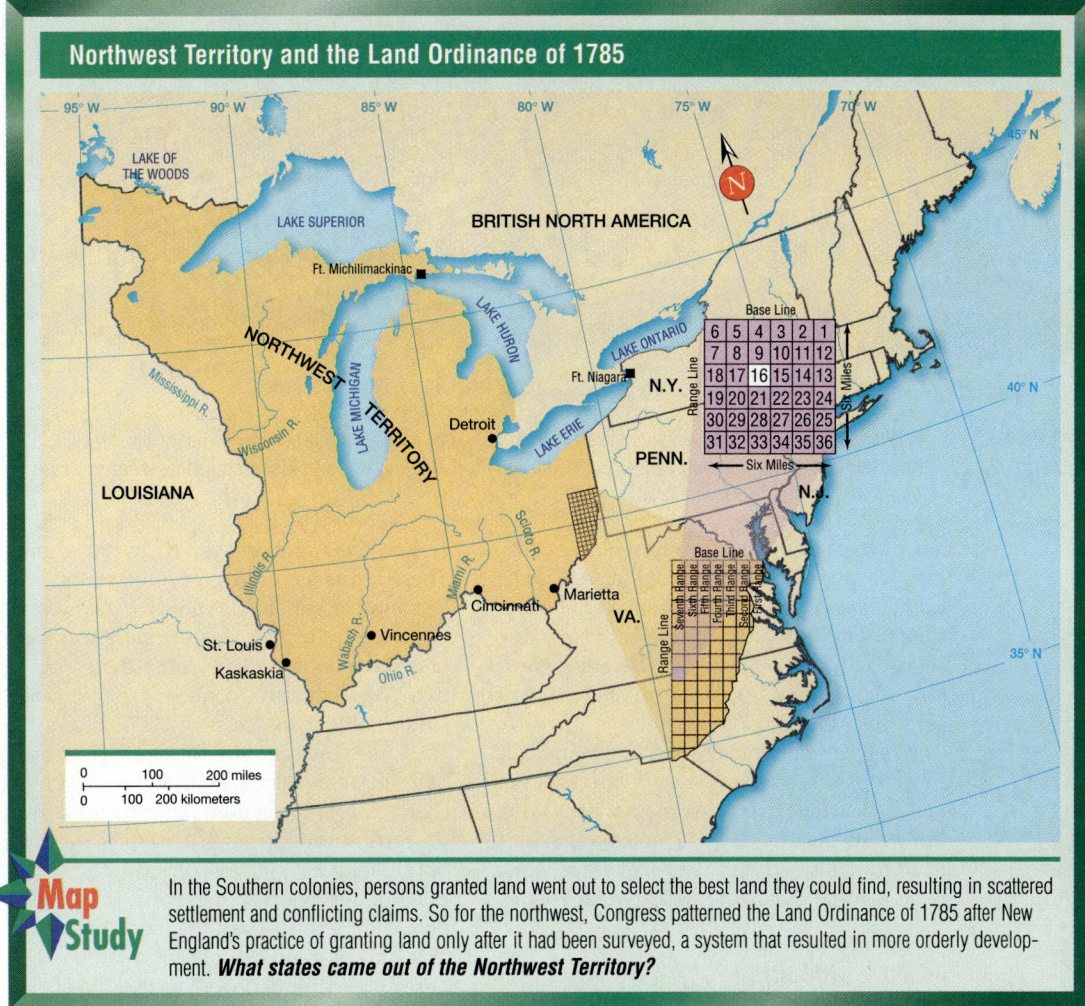

Northwest Territory and the Land Ordinance of 1785

Map Study In the Southern colonies, persons granted land went out to select the best land they could find, resulting in scattered settlement and conflicting claims. So for the northwest, Congress patterned the Land Ordinance of 1785 after New England's practice of granting land only after it had been surveyed, a system that resulted in more orderly development. **What states came out of the Northwest Territory?**

Map Study Using Maps
Answer: Illinois, Michigan, Indiana, Ohio, Wisconsin

Skills Practice
Give students a blank map of the Northwest Territory. Have them draw in the boundaries of the states that were carved out of the territory.

Did You Know?

The neat squared-off pattern of farms that is seen in much of the Midwest dates to the system of land survey adopted in the Ordinance of 1785.

Fact or Fiction?

Europeans did not think that the government established under the Articles of Confederation would be successful.

FACT: Europeans were gloomy about the success of the new nation. In 1784, France's Comte de Vergennes said: "The American Confederation has a great tendency toward dissolution [dissolving]." Not surprisingly, King George III expressed the opinion that the United States "certainly for many years cannot have any stable government."

---

appointed and paid judges and a territorial governor.

The Northwest Ordinance provided a democratic model for national expansion. When the population of a territory reached 60,000, its people could organize a new state and apply for admission to the Union as the equal of the other states.

The Northwest Ordinance also extended into the territories personal rights guaranteed in the constitutions of the original 13 states, such as freedom of religion, speech, and assembly. Perhaps more important, it prohibited slavery north of the Ohio River, an act that had a lasting effect on the political geography of the United States.

State Disputes

While the Confederation Congress was providing for stability in the West, the eastern states engaged in disputes with one another. These difficulties resulted from suspicion and rivalry, from the postwar **depression**—or economic slowdown—and from the weak central government.

Boundary and Tax Disputes

Conflicts erupted as states engaged in boundary disputes. Parts of present-day Vermont were claimed by other states. A serious conflict between Connecticut and Pennsylvania almost resulted in war.

CHAPTER 6 A More Perfect Union 1775–1789   153

Sidelights: Secession During the Revolutionary Era

Most people associate secession with the Civil War, but threats of secession abounded both during and after the Revolution. While the fighting raged, Ethan Allen schemed to make Vermont a province of Canada, although he may have been trying to force Congress to recognize Vermont as a separate state, rather than a territory of New York. At the same time, James Wilkinson, a Revolutionary officer working secretly for Spain, tried to annex Kentucky to Spain. Although these schemes came to nothing, they illustrate the deep divisions that existed in the Revolutionary era.

▲ RHODE ISLAND CURRENCY

 ▲ SHAYS'S REBELLION Some states printed so much paper money that it became virtually worthless. Jacobb Shattucks and Daniel Shays led the farmers' rebellion in western Massachusetts. *What grievances did these rebelling farmers have?*

Congress was powerless to regulate commerce, so each state passed laws taxing goods from its neighbors. New York taxed firewood from Connecticut and cabbage from New Jersey. New Jersey retaliated by charging New York for a harbor lighthouse on the New Jersey side of the Hudson River.

When the Continentals issued during the Revolution lost their value, there was no national **currency**, or paper money. Each state printed its own money. The notes' value differed from state to state, and they often were not accepted outside the states issuing them.

Shays's Rebellion

In Massachusetts the economic situation became explosive. Unable to pay their debts, farmers in western Massachusetts were jailed or had their property seized by the courts. These farmers felt the new government was just another variety of tyranny. In September 1786, led by former Continental Army captain Daniel Shays, they closed the courts in two Massachusetts counties and stopped land confiscations. In early 1787, Shays led 1,000 men against the Springfield arsenal. Only through donations from wealthy merchants was Massachusetts able to raise a militia force strong enough to meet Shays at Springfield.

Although his rag-tag band was easily defeated by the militia, the rebellion caused great alarm, and people who believed in orderly government were fearful. It seemed that the prophecies of those who said the United States could not form an effective system of government were coming true.

Section 2 ★ Review

Checking For Understanding

1. **Identify** John Adams, Cherokee, New Orleans, Barbary Pirates.
2. **Define** right of deposit, tribute, secede, depression, currency.
3. **Describe** the difficulty between the United States and Spain over right of deposit at New Orleans.
4. **Specify** the reasons for Shays's Rebellion and show how it led to the Constitutional Convention.

Critical Thinking

5. **Contrasting Ideas** This period saw the beginnings of a "sectional" awareness within the new United States. Contrast the economic interests in various areas of the country at this time.

154   UNIT 2 Creating a Nation: 1650–1789

SECTION 3

Toward a New Constitution

Setting the Scene

Section Focus

Some Americans became convinced that the Articles of Confederation were an inadequate framework for government. At a convention to address this problem, a new constitution was drawn up. Acceptance of the new government by the public, however, was not assured.

Objectives

After studying this section, you should be able to
★ explain the arguments for and against the new constitution.
★ explain how the Constitution corrected the weaknesses of the Confederation government.

Key Terms

federalism, amendment

◀ CELEBRATING THE CONSTITUTION

After the war, George Washington had retired to Mount Vernon, his Virginia estate on the Potomac River. But concern about the nation's problems moved him to action once again. In 1785 he invited representatives of Virginia and Maryland to Mount Vernon to discuss their differences. The meeting's success inspired Maryland and Virginia to invite all states to meet at Annapolis, Maryland, to discuss common problems.

When the Annapolis Convention met in September 1786, delegates from only five states were present, so they could do little. Included in this group, however, was Alexander Hamilton of New York, an outspoken supporter of a strong national government. Hamilton persuaded the delegates to propose another convention. Its purpose would be to regulate commerce and to propose measures making the national government more effective. Congress responded by calling a meeting of the states in Philadelphia, "for the sole and express purpose of revising the Articles of Confederation."

■ The Philadelphia Convention

The date set for the Philadelphia Convention was May 14, 1787, but it was May 24 before enough delegates arrived to do business. Eventually 12 of the 13 states were represented. Only Rhode Island was not represented.

Assembling the Delegates

The 55 delegates at the convention included many of the most able political leaders in the United States. Most were lawyers or judges; 21 had college degrees, a high

CHAPTER 6 A More Perfect Union 1775–1789 **155**

LESSON PLAN
SECTION 3, 155–161

FOCUS

Prior to taking roll call at the beginning of the class period, display Focus Activity 21 on the overhead projector and assign the accompanying Focus Activity Sheet.

Objectives

Point out the objectives on this page to students in previewing the section content.

Motivating Activity

Write the word *compromise* on the chalkboard and ask students to define it in their own words. Encourage students to look up the word in a dictionary and a thesaurus. Ask them to think of a time when they compromised. What did they give up? What did they gain? How did the agreement they finally reached differ from their initial idea?

Powers of the Congress

Side 1, Chapter 3
Title: *Constitutional Government*
Subject: Overview of constitutional government

Side 1, Chapter 5
Title: *Preamble to the Constitution*
Subject: Students reading the Preamble to the Constitution

Classroom Resources for SECTION 3

Teacher's Classroom Resources
- Reproducible Lesson Plan
- Reteaching Activity 6-3
- Chapter 6 Primary and Secondary Source Readings
- Section Quiz
- Chapter 6 Spanish Summaries and Glossary
- Chapter 6 Enrichment Activity
- Chapter 6 Performance Assessment Activity

Multimedia
- Section Focus Transparency 21
- Student Self-Test Software
- Unit 2 Digest Transparency
- Vocabulary Puzzlemaker
- Focus on Government
- Powers of the Congress
- Landmark Documents in American History

155

CHAPTER 6 SECTION 3

TEACH

Guided Practice

Political Science Have students create a Constitution chart, using the horizontal headings of Representation, Slavery, and Trade, and the vertical headings of Conflicts, Compromise. (Representation: Conflicts—large vs. small states; Compromise—Great Compromise. Slavery: Conflicts—North wanted to count slaves for taxation but not representation—South wanted opposite and no limits on slave trade; Compromise—five enslaved persons to equal three free persons for representation and taxation; no limit to slave trade for 20 years. Trade: Conflict—North wanted navigation laws to protect American shipping, while South feared high price of such laws, export tax; Compromise—navigation laws subject to South veto; no export taxes) **L2**

Teaching American Portraits

Add that Jefferson's love of learning is also reflected in his founding of the University of Virginia. He believed that this action was far more important for the future of the United States than anything he did as President.

Ask students what they think John Adams meant by Jefferson's "peculiar felicity of style." In their opinion, was it a compliment or was it a criticism?

AMERICAN PORTRAITS

Thomas Jefferson
1743–1826

The young Virginia lawyer first came to public attention in 1774 as a political thinker and writer when he penned a pamphlet in defense of colonial rights. Jefferson acquired his lifelong love of books on science, philosophy, and literature from his childhood teachers and as a student at William and Mary College.

Jefferson's effectiveness as a writer went far beyond his literary style. His writings reflected careful reading and study. Jefferson loved ideas—as well as book collecting. His enormous library later became the basis of the Library of Congress. As minister to France from 1785 to 1789, he shipped nearly 200 volumes to his good friend James Madison. These books—mostly works on political theory—had a profound impact on Madison's thinking about a new government for the United States.

---

number in a time when few people had any formal education. Nearly all the delegates had practical experience in government. Most had helped write their state constitutions. More than half had sat in the Continental Congress and so had seen for themselves the unhappy consequences of a weak central government.

Franklin, the oldest delegate at 81, was in poor health and did not attend regularly. Washington was elected to preside over the proceedings, so, like Franklin, his participation in the discussions was limited. But they were the best-known Americans of their time and their presence gave the convention great prestige.

The Virginia Plan

James Madison, a 36-year-old Virginian, was the first delegate to arrive at the convention, and he was the most prepared. He came to Philadelphia with a draft of a completely new framework of government. Virginia governor Edmund Randolph immediately presented Madison's proposal, known as the Virginia Plan. This document became the basis for discussion in the convention; it is the foundation for the Constitution of the United States.

■ Conflicting Plans

Almost all delegates at the convention agreed that the Articles were hopelessly weak, but there were two serious conflicts that proved difficult to resolve. Differences developed between large states and small states over representation in Congress and between northern and southern states over economic issues and the institution of slavery.

Representation

The dispute between large and small states nearly broke up the convention. The large states demanded that each state be represented by population in the bicameral Congress Madison had proposed. By what possible right, they asked, should Delaware's 59,000 inhabitants have equality with Virginia's 692,000? The small states insisted that they would never give up the equal power they enjoyed under the Articles of Confederation to be swallowed up by the large states. William Paterson of New Jersey presented an alternative proposal, known as the New Jersey Plan, which would have merely strengthened the Articles of Confederation.

Special Needs

Language Delayed The beautifully written Preamble to the Constitution offers students an example of how the English language can be used concisely. Committing the Preamble to memory provides a useful language model for students whose spoken-language development is slow. To aid in this memory task, structure the activity by asking students to copy the words *who*, *why*, and *what* in their notebooks. Have students write the various phrases of the Preamble under the words to which they are most closely related.

Disagreement also arose over the structure of the new government. Large-state delegates generally favored Madison's plan for a national government with separate executive, legislative, and judicial branches and with the states subordinate to the national government. Most small-state delegates supported the New Jersey Plan, which continued the Confederation and left the states supreme.

For two weeks, bitter debate raged over these differences. There seemed no middle ground between the large and the small states. Washington wrote a friend that he had lost all hope for the convention and regretted having anything to do with it. Franklin proposed that each session be opened with prayer, to ask divine guidance in finding an acceptable compromise.

The deadlock was broken when the delegates took a day off to celebrate the Fourth of July. During the recess, a committee worked out what became known as the "Great Compromise." According to this agreement, state representation in the lower house of Congress would be based on population; in the upper house each state would have an equal vote. The delegates' ability to resolve this dispute increased their confidence in compromise as the key to a successful convention. For this reason, the Constitution that emerged from Philadelphia has been called a "bundle of compromises." Compromise can be found in nearly every section of the document.

Economic Interests

A dispute arose between the commercial interests of the North and the plantation interests of the South. Southerners wanted to count slaves to determine representation to Congress but not for direct taxation. The North wanted to count slaves for taxation but not for representation. A "three-fifths compromise" established that five slaves would be equal to three free persons for both representation and taxation.

South Carolina and Georgia, afraid that a strong national government might act against slavery, insisted that the Constitution forbid interference with the slave trade. The delegates agreed that for 20 years the national government would not prevent the importation of slaves nor charge an import duty of more than ten dollars a head.

Compromises Yield a New Government

These compromises allowed the delegates to complete their two essential tasks: to give the national government more power and to provide a framework for a workable government. The delegates granted to the central government the powers it had needed most under the Articles of Confederation. The new government could levy and collect taxes, provided such taxes were "uniform throughout the United States." It could regulate commerce with foreign nations and between the states. Thus it could write and enforce commercial treaties that would increase foreign trade, and it could keep trade among the states free of barriers. It could also coin money and regulate its value, so there could be a national standard of money instead of state currencies with differing values.

▲ **JAMES MADISON** As one of the delegates from Virginia, James Madison participated in the lengthy, often heated debates that created a foundation of government for the United States. *What other contributions did Madison make to the Constitution?*

157

CHAPTER 6 SECTION 3

Identifying Main Ideas

Write the following on the chalkboard: Anti-Federalists; Bill of Rights; Alexander Hamilton, James Madison, and John Jay. Ask students to write questions that should accompany these answers for a "Jeopardy"-type game. (What was the name of the group opposing ratification? What was added to the Constitution to protect people's liberties? Who wrote the Federalist Papers?) Invite students to read their questions to the class. **L1**

Visualizing History

George Washington was so greatly admired and respected that his very presence at the convention encouraged compromise. Ask students to suggest why opposing factions might be willing to listen to Washington. **Answer to Caption:** He gave dignity to the proceedings.

Did You Know?

Roger Sherman, a lawyer from Connecticut, was the only person to participate in the writing of all three: the Declaration of Independence, the Articles of Confederation, and the Constitution.

The Executive Branch

Although the greatest disputes at the convention were over the structure and powers of the legislative branch, the delegates also disagreed about the executive branch. Everyone at the convention agreed on the need for an executive branch to operate the government, but some delegates favored a group executive, so that no one individual could become too powerful. The executive committees of the Confederation Congress had not worked out well, and Hamilton's proposal for a single executive chosen by Congress for life was too reminiscent of monarchy. In the final weeks of the convention, two more compromises were achieved. A single executive would serve a four-year term. This person would be chosen not directly by the people but indirectly by special electors named by the legislature of each state.

The Judicial Branch

As the long hot summer drew to a close, the exhausted delegates merely roughed out the framework of the judicial branch. In so doing, they created only a Supreme Court and empowered the new government to create "such inferior Courts as the Congress may from time to time ordain and establish."

Their work concluded, the delegates reviewed their efforts. No one was completely happy with the final plan, but most agreed it was a vast improvement on the Articles. Madison recorded the reaction of Benjamin Franklin:

> Doctor Franklin, looking toward the President's chair, at the back of which a rising sun happened to be painted... "I have," said he, "often and often in the course of the Session... looked at that [sun] behind the President without being able to tell whether it was rising or setting; but now, at length I have the happiness to know it is a rising and not a setting Sun."

■ The Ratification Struggle

On September 17, 1787, after four months of work, the delegates to the Constitutional Convention gathered one last time to sign their work. Of the 55 who had come to Philadelphia that spring, 42 were still on hand, and all but 3 agreed to sign the

▲ **INDEPENDENCE HALL** George Washington sat at this platform desk in Philadelphia's Independence Hall to preside over the Constitutional Convention. *Why was Washington's presence so important?*

UNIT 2 Creating a Nation: 1650–1789

Cooperative Learning

Have students imagine that they represent groups not included at the Constitutional Convention in Philadelphia (women, Native Americans, African Americans, men who did not own property). How might they react to the decisions made at the convention? Have students pair up and discuss their responses. Then ask students to share their findings with the class. **L2, L3**

 ▲ **SUPPORT FOR RATIFICATION** A 1788 cartoon celebrates Virginia and New York's becoming the tenth and eleventh states to ratify the Constitution. **When approval of only nine states was needed, why was the approval of Virginia and New York so important?**

document. Then the delegates adjourned to a nearby tavern for a farewell dinner before beginning their journeys home to campaign for ratification.

The Framers of the Constitution anticipated that ratification would be difficult. Rhode Island, which had boycotted the convention, certainly would not approve. So it seemed foolish to insist on the unanimous approval required to amend the Articles. Instead, the Constitution provided that "the ratification of nine States shall be sufficient for the establishment of this Constitution."

The Constitution Opposed

To get even nine states to ratify the Constitution was no small task. Some states objected to surrendering their power and independence to the national government. Mercy Otis Warren, an influential political writer, observed:

> *Not one legislature in the United States had any idea when they sent delegates to the convention at Philadelphia that it would destroy their state governments and offer them a consolidated system instead.*

Nor were supporters of states' rights pleased that the new Constitution bypassed state governments in the ratification process. Ratification was to be decided by special conventions to be called in each state, a process implementing the idea expressed in the Declaration of Independence that governments "derive their just powers from the consent of the governed."

Even among the "governed," however, opposition was strong. Debtors and paper-money advocates were opposed to any plan forcing full payment of debts and restoring sound currency. There was certainly suspicion of a powerful central government. Why revolt from Great Britain, people asked, simply to fall under a new kind of tyranny? Popular leaders such as John Hancock, Samuel Adams, and Patrick Henry opposed it.

Support Organized

Those who favored the new plan of government called themselves "Federalists." They took this name to emphasize that the Constitution was based on the principle of **federalism**, a system in which power is divided between a central government and regional governments, and to remind Americans that the states would retain many of their powers. Of course, those who opposed the Constitution were "Federalists" too, because the league of states created by the Articles also was based on federalism. The real issue was whether the national government or the state governments would be supreme. By taking the name "Federalists,"

CHAPTER 6 A More Perfect Union 1775–1789   **159**

CHAPTER 6 SECTION 3

ASSESS

Check Understanding

Assign Section 3 Review as homework or an in-class activity.

Evaluate

Assign the Section 3 Quiz in the TCR or use the History of a Free Nation Testmaker to create a customized Quiz.

Reteach

Have students complete Reteaching Activity 6-3.

Enrich

Have students work in groups to discuss how the Constitution might have been different if John and Sam Adams, Thomas Paine, and Patrick Henry had been present to help write it.

CLOSE

Write the chapter concepts—political control, central authority—on the chalkboard. Ask students to give examples of how each concept is exemplified in the chapter content.

---

however, the supporters of the Constitution caused their opponents to be tagged with the negative label "Anti-Federalists."

Although the two sides were almost equally divided, several factors worked against the Anti-Federalists. Their campaign was a negative one. They attacked almost everything about the Constitution and complained that it failed to protect basic liberties such as freedom of speech and religion. But the Anti-Federalists had nothing to offer in its place.

The Federalists, on the other hand, presented a definite program to meet the difficulties facing the nation. They promised that if the Constitution were ratified, **amendments**, or additions and changes, would be made to provide a Bill of Rights to protect the people.

The Federalists

The Federalists also made better use of communications. They were supported by most of the nation's newspapers. They presented their case more convincingly in sermons, pamphlets, and debates in state conventions.

The Federalists' campaign for ratification produced one of the finest pieces of political writing in the history of the world, *The Federalist*—a collection of 85 essays written by Hamilton, Madison, and John Jay. Originally published as newspaper articles in the *New York Journal*, the essays explained in detail the importance of the Constitution to the success of the nation.

The Constitution Is Ratified

The Federalists succeeded in getting the Constitution ratified not merely because they were good speakers and writers, but because they were politically shrewd. In the states where strong opposition existed, the Federalists were able to outmaneuver their opponents.

In Pennsylvania, the Federalists called the election for the state's ratifying convention before the Anti-Federalists had an opportunity to organize. In Massachusetts, the Federalists used influential Anti-Federalist leader John Hancock to gain support for the Constitution. They suggested that if the Constitution were ratified, Hancock could be the first President of the United States.

In New York, two-thirds of the State Convention were Anti-Federalists. But the persuasiveness of John Jay and the news that 10 states had already ratified the Constitution convinced enough Anti-Federalists to change sides so that New York became the "eleventh pillar" of the new federal roof.

The vote in several key states was extremely close: in the Massachusetts ratifying convention, 187 voted in favor of the Constitution, 168 voted in opposition to it; in Virginia the vote was 89 to 79; and in New York 30 to 27. By July 1788, however, all the states except Rhode Island and North Carolina had ratified, and preparations were made to launch the new government without them.

Section 3 ★ Review

Checking for Understanding

1. **Identify** Philadelphia Convention, Virginia Plan, New Jersey Plan, Federalists, Anti-Federalists.
2. **Define** federalism, amendment.
3. **Describe** the key compromises that were made in the Constitution concerning representation, slavery, and the executive branch.
4. **Distinguish** between the positions of the Federalists and the Anti-Federalists.

Critical Thinking

5. **Making Inferences** Why would it have been considered significant when people such as John Hancock, Samuel Adams, and Patrick Henry opposed the new Constitution?

160 UNIT 2 Creating a Nation: 1650–1789

Answers to SECTION 3 REVIEW

1. Philadelphia Convention, 155; Virginia Plan, 156; New Jersey Plan, 161; Federalists, 160; Anti-Federalists, 160
2. All vocabulary words are defined in the Glossary.
3. States would be represented in lower house of Congress based on their population; in the upper house, each state would have an equal vote; five enslaved persons would be equal to three free persons for purposes of taxation and representation.
4. Federalists: favored constitutional government, had program to meet nation's problems; Anti-Federalists: attacked constitutional plan, offered no positive proposals.
5. Answers will vary; since all three associated with Revolution, their opposition could be interpreted as saying the Constitution betrayed the ideals of the Revolution.

History and Science CONNECTIONS

Astronomy and the Constitution

Like most delegates to the Constitutional Convention, James Madison was greatly influenced by the ideas of the European Enlightenment. Madison recognized the Enlightenment idea of the need for careful investigation of accepted principles and authorities, whether in politics, religion, or science. Madison also endorsed the theory that the universe was an orderly machine that worked according to natural laws. Like other Enlightenment thinkers, Madison also believed that there were "natural laws" that governed human behavior. These natural laws operated much like the laws that governed the physical universe.

Madison was much impressed by an intricate working model of the solar system, an orrery (AWR•uh•ree), built in 1767 by Philadelphia astronomer David Rittenhouse. Rittenhouse was one of the prominent leaders in American science. He built the first observatory in the colonies and constructed a telescope that may have been the first made in the colonies. After the American Revolution, Rittenhouse served as treasurer of Pennsylvania and director of the United States Mint. Rittenhouse used the orrery to illustrate the theories of Isaac Newton. Newton believed that the solar system was held in place by a balance between centrifugal force and the power of gravity. Centrifugal force is the force that tends to move an object outward from a center of rotation.

Just as the solar system was stabilized by equal but opposing forces, Madison reasoned, so might a stable government result from a balance of political powers. Thus Madison found in the theories of Isaac Newton support for federalism—a strong national government balanced by the power of the states.

▼ RITTENHOUSE'S ORRERY

Making the Science Connection

1. What was Rittenhouse's orrery supposed to demonstrate?
2. How did Newtonian theory influence Madison?

Linking Past and Present

3. What other examples of balances in power are there in national government today?

CHAPTER 6 CONNECTIONS

Teaching Making Connections

Point out that the first orrery was constructed in 1700 by the English inventor and mechanic George Graham. He named the machine for his patron, Charles Boyle, the Earl of Orrery.

Did You Know?

David Rittenhouse, who created the orrery pictured on this page, marked out several state boundaries. He also determined part of the famous Mason-Dixon line. Rittenhouse Square in the city of Philadelphia is named for him.

Answers to Connections

1. The orrery was to demonstrate that the solar system was held in place by centrifugal force and gravity.
2. Newton's theory that the solar system's stability resulted from a balance between opposing forces suggested to Madison that a stable government could be achieved in the same way.
3. Answers may vary but could include the system of checks and balances among federal government branches.

REVIEW CHAPTER 6

Answers

Reviewing Facts
1. Answers will vary but should include those relating to the weak central government, relations with foreign countries, trade, western territories, relations between the states, and the economy.
2. England saw no reason to give America trade privileges since it was no longer a colony. Spain opposed American western expansion as a threat to its holdings in America.
3. It provided the only outlet for bulky goods sent down the Ohio and Mississippi rivers for transferral to oceangoing trade ships.
4. Land Ordinance of 1785: provided a means for settling and selling western lands. Northwest Ordinance of 1787: provided procedures for setting up a territorial government and applying for admission to the Union.
5. Their backgrounds in law, politics, learning, and government provided experience for drawing up a new framework of government.
6. representation between large and small states, structure of the national government and its relation to the states, way in which enslaved persons were to be counted, slave trade, regulating commerce, executive branch
7. Written by prominent people, they appeared as newspaper articles and explained why the Constitution was important to the success of the nation.

CHAPTER 6 ★ REVIEW

Using Vocabulary

Each of the following terms has a meaning that relates to government. Find the definition of each word and then write a sentence in which you give an example of its meaning.

bicameral
federalism
ratify
franchise
veto
amendments

Reviewing Facts

1. **Describe** the problems faced by the United States under the Articles of Confederation.
2. **List** reasons why England and Spain refused to negotiate trade treaties with the United States after the Revolution.
3. **Explain** why right of deposit at New Orleans was essential to western farmers.
4. **State** the main purposes for passage of the Land Ordinance of 1785 and the Northwest Ordinance of 1787.
5. **Explain** why the delegates' backgrounds at the Constitutional Convention were helpful.
6. **Identify** the disagreements that divided the delegates at the Constitutional Convention.
7. **Detail** why *The Federalist* helped win public support for the new Constitution.

Understanding Concepts

Political Control
1. How were the political values of the newly independent states reflected in the form of government created under the Articles?
2. Show how the changes made by the Framers of the Constitution preserved those same values.

Authority
3. The states gave their legislatures a great deal of power after the war. Explain the view of authority that prompted them to do so.

162 UNIT 2 Creating a Nation: 1650–1789

4. Propose possible reasons why a distrust of strong central authority after the Revolutionary War gradually gave way to its acceptance at the Constitutional Convention.

Critical Thinking

1. **Analyzing Ideas** Explain why phrases such as "government by supplication" and "a shadow without substance" so well described the Confederation government.
2. **Formulating Alternatives** If Tennessee settlers had seceded from the Union and Shays's Rebellion had succeeded, what immediate effects do you think they would have had on Americans?
3. **Analyzing Illustrations** Study the illustration on this page and answer the questions that follow.
   a. What two groups are shown in the painting?
   b. What are each of the two groups doing?
   c. Does the artist give the work a central focus?
   d. What clues in the painting suggest a particular period of time or era? Explain.

▲ TRANSPORTING TOBACCO

Understanding Concepts

1. Answers will vary but may include: value of representation was reflected in the Confederation Congress in which each state was equally represented; value of weak executive power was reflected in establishing only a legislative branch in which the states shared governing authority.
2. Answers will vary but may include: Framers preserved representation by setting up a lower house in which representation was based on population and an upper house in which representation was equally apportioned; the framers preserved weak executive power by requiring Senate approval for appointments and allowing Congress to override presidential veto.

CHAPTER 6 ★ REVIEW

Writing About History

Cause and Effect

Imagine that you are an observer at the Constitutional Convention listening to the delegates argue about how to set up a legislative branch. Record their various proposals and the effect each proposal would have.

Cooperative Learning

In order for people to operate effectively in a free society, individuals must give up some personal freedoms and agree to live by rules that operate in the best interests of all citizens. Imagine that you are part of a group that is being sent to the moon in order to establish a colony there. Together, write a constitution by which you agree to be governed while you are living on the moon. Decide which portions of the United States Constitution will work for your new situation and the changes that will need to be made to serve the best interests of your group.

Social Studies Skills

Organizing in a Table

A table presents information in a visually appealing, easy-to-use format. Tables organize data into a series of columns and rows, so they are especially useful tools when comparing information. The table's title supplies the subject under study. Headings over the columns tell the category of information listed in each column. Read each row in the table from left to right.

Practicing the Skill

Use this table and your knowledge from the chapter to answer the questions.

1. What information is found in this table?
2. How is color used to organize the table?
3. What determines the order in which the states are listed in the table? Explain one other criterion that could have been used to order the states.
4. How much time passed between the first state's ratification and the last?
5. Which state had the closest vote?
6. How was Rhode Island's voting pattern consistent with its position on the Constitutional Convention?

Ratification of the Constitution

State	Date	Vote
Delaware	Dec. 7, 1787	30-0
Pennsylvania	Dec. 12, 1787	46-23
New Jersey	Dec. 18, 1787	38-0
Georgia	Jan. 2, 1788	26-0
Connecticut	Jan. 9, 1788	128-40
Massachusetts	Feb. 6, 1788	187-168
Maryland	Apr. 28, 1788	63-11
South Carolina	May 23, 1788	149-73
New Hampshire	June 21, 1788	57-47
Virginia	June 25, 1788	89-79
New York	July 26, 1788	30-27
North Carolina	Nov. 21, 1789	194-77
Rhode Island	May 29, 1790	34-32

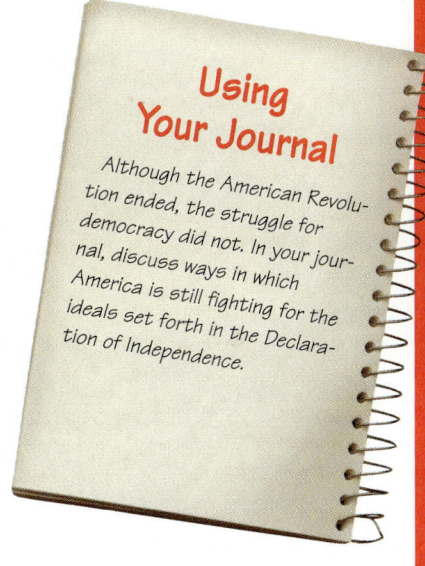

Using Your Journal

Although the American Revolution ended, the struggle for democracy did not. In your journal, discuss ways in which America is still fighting for the ideals set forth in the Declaration of Independence.

CHAPTER 6 A More Perfect Union 1775–1789

REVIEW CHAPTER 6

3. a. Slaveholders and slaves
   b. The slaveholders are overseeing the work of enslaved workers
   c. Yes, enslaved workers
   d. The clothing suggests late 1700s and early 1800s

Practicing the Skill

1. When states ratified the Constitution.
2. Each column is a different color.
3. By date of ratification. Alphabetical order.
4. Two and a half years.

Chapter Bonus Test Question

This question may be used for extra credit on the chapter test.
During the Constitutional Convention, Benjamin Franklin observed a sun painted on the President's chair and wondered whether it was a rising or setting sun. As the convention ended, he was convinced it was a rising sun. Ask students to write a sentence explaining why. (Constitution established a government that would help the nation prosper.)

Using Your Journal

Have students organize the discussion around issues currently in debate. Ask them to identify one that can be traced back to the Revolutionary era.

---

3. Answers will vary but may include that this view was prompted by belief that government authority was derived from consent of the governed.
4. Answers will vary but may include that memory of British tyranny was receding; the new union of states required strong overriding authority to meet its needs; weakened central authority had created crises and lack of confidence.

Critical Thinking

1. Answers will vary but may include that the Confederation government was constantly at the mercy of the states for money and had more the appearance than the actuality of authority.
2. Answers will vary but may include that Americans could have lost confidence in the central government, other states could have seceded, other people could have resorted to armed rebellion.

Cultural Kaleidoscope

Making Connections
History and Economics

Work in colonial times—when each family unit was largely self-sufficient—was very different from what it is today. Children were responsible for many chores, such as taking care of younger children and tending animals. Women handled many jobs later thought of as men's work. Some also worked alongside their husbands in the fields.

More About . . .
Eating

In colonial times most family members ate out of a single, common wooden bowl that was placed in the middle of the table. Forks were rare. Most people used a knife to spear their food. They also ate with their hands. That is why colonial households were well supplied with napkins.

Cultural Kaleidoscope

Colonial Life

In The Kitchen

When Europeans first settled in America, they found no great treasures of gold or rare spices. From Native American peoples, however, they did gain something more vital for survival—plentiful foods and methods of cultivation. For early colonists, Indian corn, or maize, was the main food staple. Gradually, the colonists came to appreciate other native foods.

▶ Children performed chores to help prepare the day's meals. In many colonial households, children had no place at the table. They stood to eat and were not allowed to speak.

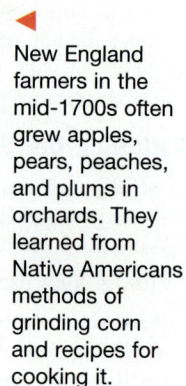

◀ New England farmers in the mid-1700s often grew apples, pears, peaches, and plums in orchards. They learned from Native Americans methods of grinding corn and recipes for cooking it.

Cooperative Learning

Divide the class into several small groups. Ask each to research a basic colonial food, such as hominy, game birds, rabbit, dried fruits, pumpkins, and cider. The groups should report to the class on how each food was obtained and prepared. As a class project, the groups may want to join efforts to prepare a typical colonial meal.

▶ During the summer, maize was eaten green, but colonists usually allowed it to ripen and then ground it into cornmeal. Sometimes it was hulled and eaten whole as hominy.

▲ Cooking in the early 1700s was done over an open fire, and utensils for cooking necessarily had long handles. Metal was usually reserved for cooking tools. Utensils that today are made of metal, ceramic, or plastic, were made of wood.

▶ Table, cutting board, and bowl

Cultural Kaleidoscope

Portfolio Project

Ask students to collect pictures of their favorite foods. For each one, the student should determine whether it would have been available to settlers in the English colonies of North America.

The Historian's Craft

Although the colonial diet was limited in many ways, it was of better quality than that of the European diet. Historians believe that this is the main reason colonists lived longer. While life expectancy for a European in the late 1600s was about 40 years, that of an American colonist was closer to 60. Because there was no census at this time, historians use tax records, church records, and registrations for the militia to arrive at their population estimates.

UNIT 2 DIGEST

Unit 2 Digest can be used to teach unit coverage when time is limited, to review unit content, or to link content of one unit to another.

 Unit Digest Transparencies

Use Transparency 4.

■ Chapter 4

Tell students that some historians speculate that if Governor Thomas Hutchinson of Massachusetts had allowed the British tea ship to return to England, rather than insisting that its cargo be unloaded, American history might have taken a different course. Pose the following questions to students: Was the Boston Tea Party a pivotal event on the road to revolution? If the incident had not occurred, could the Revolution have been averted? Discuss these questions with students, asking them to present evidence to support their speculations.

■ Chapter 5

Remind students that many of the paintings depicting the Revolutionary War are representative of the theme of Chapter 5: the colonies striving for and achieving independence. Have students research paintings other than those in the chapter, and ask them to write a paragraph on how these paintings reflect the theme.

■ Chapter 6

Provide students with copies of a diagram or chart of the United States

Chapter 4
The Road to Revolution

The road from colonies to nation began with Parliament's attempt to control the colonies' foreign trade. Most of these laws, however, were not enforced. Parliament's concern was part of a larger issue, the struggle between Britain and France over control of North America. In the French and Indian War, Britain emerged victorious and, with the Treaty of Paris in 1763, France was eliminated as a contender for power in North America.

Britain's victory brought it a host of new problems, among them a huge war debt and a question of how to administer their newly acquired territory. Parliament levied new taxes that shifted part of the financial burden onto the colonies and passed the Proclamation of 1763, which forbade all settlement west of the Appalachians. The colonists protested, and as tensions grew, so did the means of protest. In their challenge to British authority, the colonies discovered a sense of unity and patriotism.

King George III refused to compromise, arguing that the colonies must "submit or triumph." The colonists responded by calling the First Continental Congress and organizing volunteer armies. Soon fighting broke out between Massachusetts "minutemen" and British troops at Concord. Although it would be another year before the colonies formally declared their independence, the American Revolution had begun.

Chapter 5
War for Independence

Most colonists wanted to remain part of the British empire as long as they could govern themselves through their own legislatures. The British government, though, was inflexible and wanted to punish the rebels.

In January 1776, Thomas Paine published the persuasive and widely read pamphlet *Common Sense*. In it, Paine argued for separation from Britain and appealed to the Americans' belief that they were a select people.

Beginning in April 1776, the colonies advised their delegates in Congress to vote for independence. The Declaration of Independence formally notified the world on July 4 that the colonies were indeed independent.

Announcing their independence was not as challenging as maintaining it. Britain, unwilling to surrender its large territory in North America, dispatched a large military force to America. George Washington's early victories at Trenton and Princeton helped save the American cause. Nevertheless, the Americans faced a long struggle with a volunteer army and insufficient funds to pay for the war. The struggle was eased when France allied itself with the American cause following a major victory over British forces at Saratoga.

166 UNIT 2 Creating a Nation: 1650–1789

Cooperative Learning

Remind students that during the American Revolution various patriotic groups penned American slogans, poems, and songs in support of the cause. Divide the class into groups of five. Ask groups to compose a slogan, poem, or song on one of the following: the boycott of British goods, the Boston Tea Party, the battles at Lexington and Concord, the Declaration of Independence, the winter at Valley Forge, or the British surrender at Yorktown. Encourage students to find or create illustrations for their compositions. Have each group select a representative to read its work to the class.

Many women courageously served the American war effort, in some cases fighting in the ranks. African Americans and Native Americans also served in the Revolutionary War. In 1780, British General Cornwallis surrendered at Yorktown, Virginia, marking the last significant battle of the war. The colonies were, at last, independent.

Chapter 6
A More Perfect Union

With independence, the colonies needed new state constitutions to replace colonial charters. Most adopted a bicameral, or two-house, legislature and restricted the executive branch. The right to vote, however, was restricted to white males who were property owners. Some of the states also began to question the institution of slavery.

Meanwhile, Congress developed a plan to unite them. Known as the Articles of Confederation, this document placed governing authority in Congress, in which each state had one vote.

Under the Articles, the national government was weak. Domestically, it was unable to collect taxes, enforce the laws, or interpret them. It also faced difficulties dealing with settling the West, although Congress passed two important documents—the Land Ordinance of 1785 and the Northwest Ordinance of 1787. In addition, the government had difficulty mediating disputes between the states over boundaries, commerce, and currency. Internationally, the new nation experienced difficulties with Britain, Spain, France, and the Barbary States.

Because of these problems, it became apparent that a new framework for government was needed. Before political anarchy and financial irresponsibility destroyed the ideals for which Americans had fought, a bold group of leaders met and drafted a new plan of government over the summer of 1787. States put aside jealousies and compromised on the crucial issues of representation and slavery and created a powerful two-house Congress, a strong chief executive, and a national judicial system. Most delegates believed that the new Constitution was a vast improvement over the Articles.

Some states were cautious about surrendering their power. Finally, though, supporters of the Constitution, the Federalists, emerged victorious. The new government was set to be launched in 1789.

Understanding Unit Themes

1. **American Democracy** How did the new state constitutions strive for democratic ideals?
2. **Civil Rights and Liberties** What civil rights were denied colonists by British laws and actions before the Revolutionary War?
3. **Economic Development** How did Great Britain's view of the American colonies before the Revolution and its view of the new United States after the war affect trade relations between the two nations?
4. **Conflict and Cooperation** How did the conflicting interests of the British and Americans lead to the Revolutionary War?

UNIT 2 DIGEST

federal government, and ask them to study its structure. After students have studied the diagram, ask them to construct a similar one showing how the government was organized under the Articles of Confederation. Ask students to write a report comparing the two different organizations. Their reports should explain why government under the Articles was weak and inefficient, and why government under the Constitution was successful.

Understanding Unit Themes

1. Answers will vary but may include that state constitutions established bicameral legislatures and restricted executive powers to ensure majority rule.
2. trial by jury, taxation by elected representatives, rights of privacy, right to make a living without interference
3. Before the Revolution Britain regulated trade with the colonies. After the war, Britain viewed the colonies as no longer part of its political or economic sphere, closed markets to American trade, and refused to enter into a trade treaty.
4. Britain wanted to legislate for the colonies that wanted to make their own laws. British wanted to regulate American trade, but colonists wanted freedom to pursue their own economic interests. Britain wanted military control over colonies, which colonists opposed.

The Historian's Craft

Analyzing Viewpoints Point out that not all American leaders were convinced of the need for a written constitution. Then read this view of written constitutions by Thomas Jefferson: "We might as well require a man to wear still the coat which fitted him when a boy, as civilized society to remain ever under the regime of their barbarous ancestors." Ask students to discuss whether Jefferson's view could be applied to the United States Constitution.

LESSON PLAN
THE CONSTITUTION TODAY

FOCUS
Motivating Activity

Have students recall some of the aspects of self-government with which the American colonists had experimented. (Possible responses: In the 1600s Mayflower Compact and organizations such as Virginia House of Burgesses had given colonists their first experience in self-government. Later, Stamp Act Congress of 1765, Committees of Correspondence [1722–1776], and Continental Congresses [1774–1775] were necessitated by colonists' growing dissatisfaction with English domination. Finally, Articles of Confederation and the U.S. Constitution took root, almost 170 years after the first colonial experiment in self-government.)

Tell students that in this Constitutional Handbook they will see how those early experiments shaped the American system of government.

Using Charts
Answer: the people

Skills Practice
Ask students what the powers granted to the federal government have in common. (regulate relations between the United States and other nations and relations among the states)

The Constitution Today

The entire system of federal government in the United States rests on a single document: the Constitution. It has served as the "supreme law of the land" for more than 200 years, making it the oldest written constitution in the world. Institutions that we take for granted—the Congress, the President, the Supreme Court—were created by the Constitution. Major governmental decisions that are made every day depend upon constitutional authority.

The authors of the Constitution created a strong central government. Article I, Section 8, which has been called the "heart of the Constitution," gave the new Congress various powers not possessed by the Confederation Congress, including the authority to levy taxes and regulate interstate commerce. The power to levy taxes enabled Congress to finance the federal government.

Through its authority over interstate commerce, Congress has enacted laws ranging from prohibitions against racial discrimination to regulations on consumer credit.

The "elastic clause" that appears in Article I, Section 8, says that Congress shall make all laws "necessary and proper" for putting into effect its enumerated powers. Determining what laws are necessary and proper has provided for ongoing debate and controversy over the years, beginning with the debate over the National Bank in 1790.

The Constitution reinforced the idea that the states were to remain sovereign in some matters. Through their authority in common law and criminal law, the state governments were left in control of local affairs. Their separate identities were protected, and their authority in matters not specifically given to the national government was limited only by the rights of the people within each state. The Tenth Amendment assured this basic protection of each state's sovereignty.

Another assurance of state and popular sovereignty is provided by the amending process. Because the Constitution and the states both derive their authority from the people, provisions for changing the Constitution depend upon the will of the people. This careful arrangement has resulted in only 27 amendments. The first 10 were added almost immediately—in 1791—as a Bill of Rights to protect against national government encroachments on individual freedom.

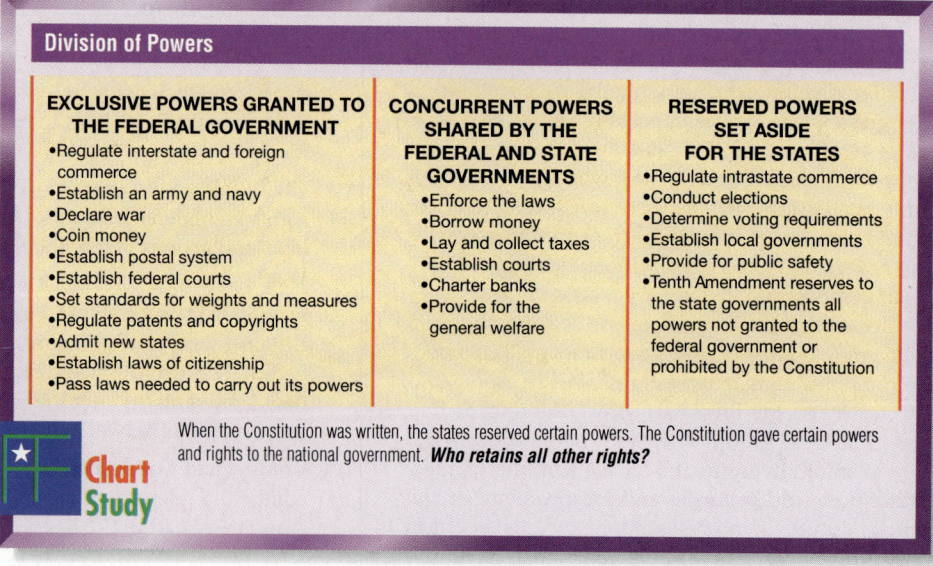

Division of Powers

EXCLUSIVE POWERS GRANTED TO THE FEDERAL GOVERNMENT	CONCURRENT POWERS SHARED BY THE FEDERAL AND STATE GOVERNMENTS	RESERVED POWERS SET ASIDE FOR THE STATES
•Regulate interstate and foreign commerce •Establish an army and navy •Declare war •Coin money •Establish postal system •Establish federal courts •Set standards for weights and measures •Regulate patents and copyrights •Admit new states •Establish laws of citizenship •Pass laws needed to carry out its powers	•Enforce the laws •Borrow money •Lay and collect taxes •Establish courts •Charter banks •Provide for the general welfare	•Regulate intrastate commerce •Conduct elections •Determine voting requirements •Establish local governments •Provide for public safety •Tenth Amendment reserves to the state governments all powers not granted to the federal government or prohibited by the Constitution

Chart Study When the Constitution was written, the states reserved certain powers. The Constitution gave certain powers and rights to the national government. **Who retains all other rights?**

Cooperative Learning

Applying Ideas Have students work together to develop a set of five rules for use in the classroom. Offer the following as an example of the type of rule they should develop: During class discussion, students should not talk unless they raise their hands and are recognized by the teacher. Point out that the rules should be acceptable to a two-thirds majority of the class. Also, students should set up some system of adjusting the rules if they prove unworkable. After they have completed the task, ask them to discuss the most difficult problems they faced in establishing the rules. **L1, LEP**

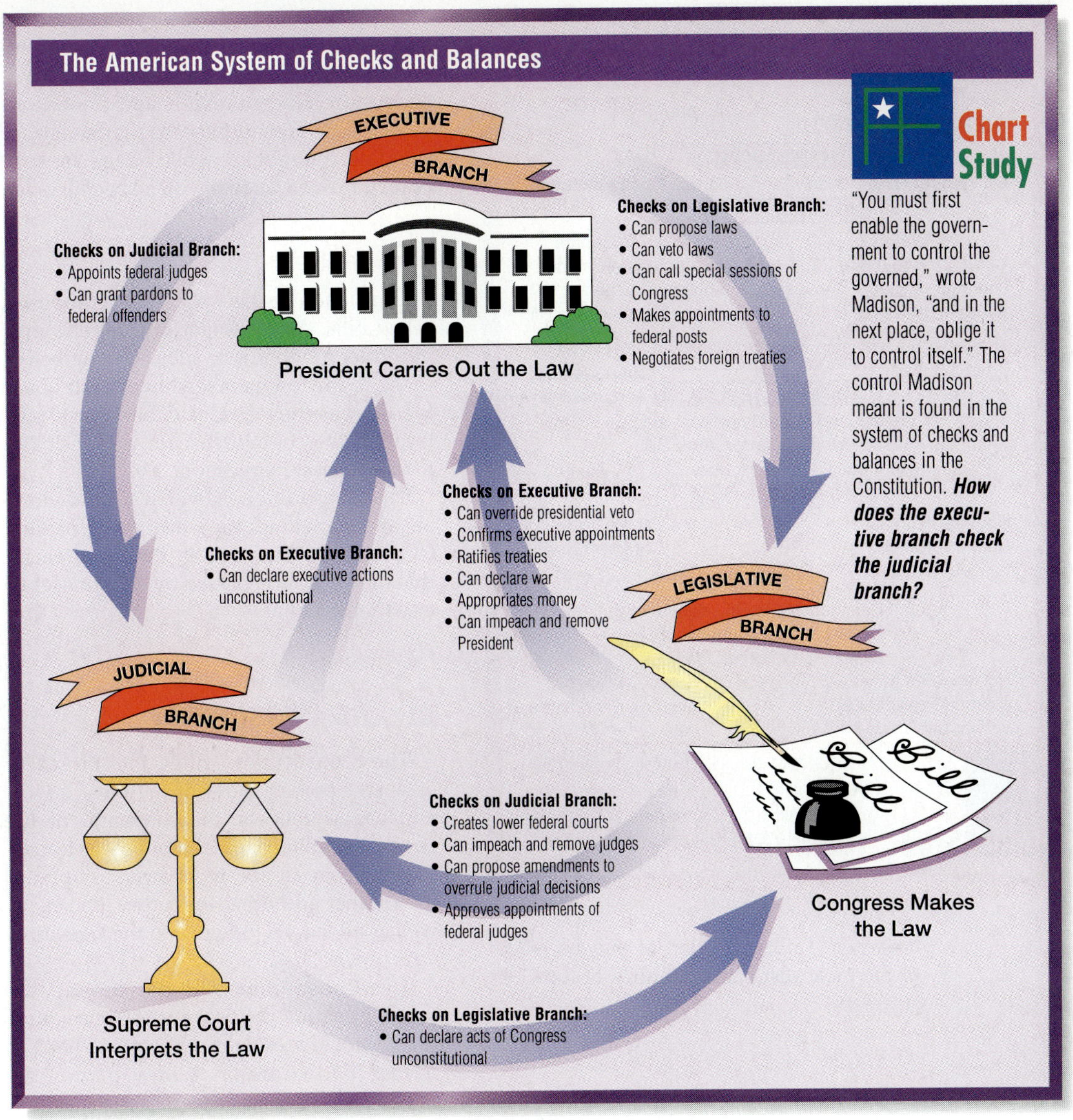

The American System of Checks and Balances

EXECUTIVE BRANCH — President Carries Out the Law

Checks on Judicial Branch:
- Appoints federal judges
- Can grant pardons to federal offenders

Checks on Legislative Branch:
- Can propose laws
- Can veto laws
- Can call special sessions of Congress
- Makes appointments to federal posts
- Negotiates foreign treaties

LEGISLATIVE BRANCH — Congress Makes the Law

Checks on Executive Branch:
- Can override presidential veto
- Confirms executive appointments
- Ratifies treaties
- Can declare war
- Appropriates money
- Can impeach and remove President

Checks on Judicial Branch:
- Creates lower federal courts
- Can impeach and remove judges
- Can propose amendments to overrule judicial decisions
- Approves appointments of federal judges

JUDICIAL BRANCH — Supreme Court Interprets the Law

Checks on Executive Branch:
- Can declare executive actions unconstitutional

Checks on Legislative Branch:
- Can declare acts of Congress unconstitutional

Chart Study

"You must first enable the government to control the governed," wrote Madison, "and in the next place, oblige it to control itself." The control Madison meant is found in the system of checks and balances in the Constitution. **How does the executive branch check the judicial branch?**

Congress

The Constitution provided different legislative powers for the Senate and House. The Senate approves treaties and presidential appointments and tries all **impeachment** cases of government officials formally accused of wrongdoing in office; the House originates all revenue bills, and has the power to impeach members of the executive and judicial branches. Legislation must pass both Houses before it can be sent to the President to be signed into law.

Most of the enumerated powers of Congress leave little room for interpretation. When the constitutional authority of Congress seems to conflict with the authority of the President, it is often because of a deliberate effort by the Constitutional Convention to limit the power of government. The framers of the Constitution chose to divide government powers among three separate

The Constitution Today 169

THE CONSTITUTION TODAY

TEACH
Guided Practice
Analyzing Information
Point out how each house of Congress has powers denied the other. Then ask students to find newspaper or magazine articles that reflect the differences between these two branches of the legislature. Have them discuss which powers have been at the center of recent debates. **L1, LEP**

Using Charts
Answer: appoints federal judges, grants pardons to federal offenders

Skills Practice
Ask students to explain how the legislative branch checks the judicial branch (by creating lower federal courts, impeaching and removing judges, proposing amendments to overrule judicial decisions; approving appointment of judges)

TECHNOLOGY

The following is available from Glencoe and may be used to introduce The Constitutional Handbook

 CD ROM

Facts on File, Inc. Landmark Documents in American History
The Constitution

Critical Thinking

Debate Have the class debate the merits of setting term limits for members of Congress. Supporters may wish to stress such advantages as limiting the powers of incumbency and seniority, whereas opponents may emphasize the advantages of experience. **L2**

THE CONSTITUTION TODAY

Independent Practice

Journalism Have students imagine they are journalists following the progress of a bill through Congress. They may focus on a bill currently in Congress or one that Congress considered in the past. Remind them that they are to write news stories, not editorials, and thus be as objective as possible. **L3**

Using Charts

Answer: The federal government might shut down.

Skills Practice

Ask: Can a bill become law if the President does not sign it into law? (yes, unless he vetoes it. It can still become law if both the House and the Senate vote to override the President's veto.)

Did You Know?

When George Washington became the nation's first President, no one knew what to call him. John Adams, the first Vice President, suggested "His Highness, The President of the United States and Protector of the Rights of the Same." The House of Representatives finally settled on "the President of the United States."

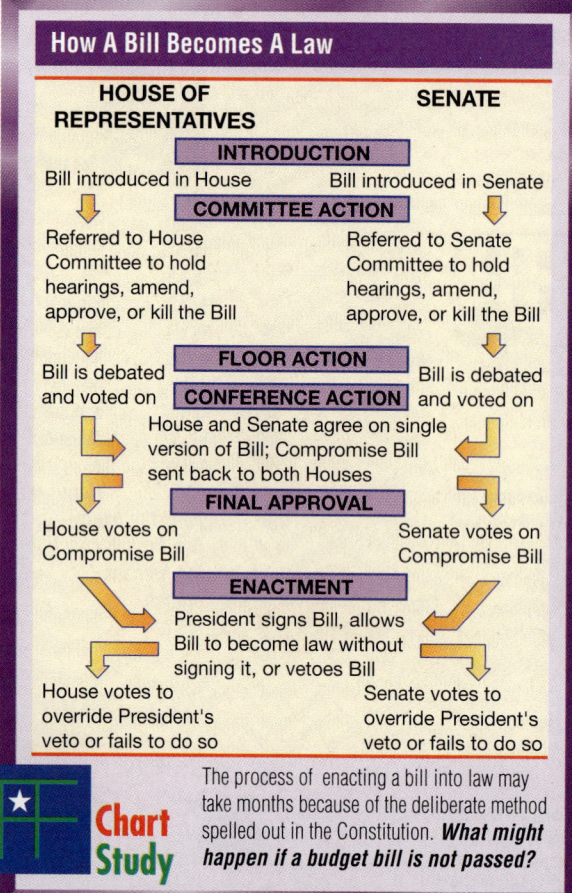

Chart Study The process of enacting a bill into law may take months because of the deliberate method spelled out in the Constitution. **What might happen if a budget bill is not passed?**

branches. This separation of powers is one of the most distinctive features of the Constitution.

Duties

The federal government is separated into legislative, executive, and judicial branches. These branches, described in the first three articles of the Constitution, are each given separate authority. Under this **separation of powers**, each branch exercises a check on the powers of the other two.

The Constitution describes the duties of the three branches, but it does not detail how those duties are to be carried out. To handle the heavy volume of legislation efficiently, both houses of Congress, from the very beginning, divided into committees.

These smaller units do most of the work of both houses. Each committee deals with particular problems, such as labor, banking, agriculture, foreign affairs, and armed services. Some committees are permanent, or standing committees, while others are temporary, formed to deal with a specific issue.

Legislation

Legislation begins with written proposals called bills. Any member of Congress may introduce a bill on any subject. Long before going to the full membership of each house for a vote, however, the bill must pass through the committee with responsibility for the subject in question.

The Constitution provided for a deliberate and sometimes slow method of passing legislation. One factor is the requirement that the legislation passed by both houses be exactly the same.

■ The Presidency

The Constitution gives the President extensive powers. Four of the most important are as follows: the command of the country's military forces; the power to conduct foreign affairs; the power to appoint the cabinet and other executive officers, as well as all federal judges; and the legislative veto power.

The Constitution did not foresee the development of political parties, one source of additional presidential power. As head of one of the two major political parties, the President can exert pressure for legislation and can give or withhold support for a senator's or representative's reelection.

Presidential power increases during crises involving actual or perceived danger from abroad. It is affected by the tendency of Congress to yield much of its power to the President for the duration of the crisis.

The President, who has access to a vast military and foreign service network, can control information that Congress receives. In addition, Congress, working as a whole or through committees, is inherently less capable of exercising decisive action quickly.

Cooperative Learning

Organize students in groups of five. Have groups select one of the following Presidents: George Washington, Andrew Jackson, Abraham Lincoln, Franklin D. Roosevelt, Harry Truman, John F. Kennedy, Lyndon Johnson, or Ronald Reagan. Have each group compose a letter to its selected President explaining how his actions in office have contributed to the way the executive office operates today. Have groups choose representatives to read the letters to the class. **L2, L3**

In domestic policy the Constitution clearly gives "the power of the purse" to Congress. Over time, the President has come to dominate many processes of allocating the government's money. The creation of the Bureau of the Budget in 1921 (now the Office of Management and Budget), whose director was appointed by the President, heralded the transfer of major budgetary power out of the hands of Congress.

The Courts

The judiciary is only briefly described in the Constitution. Article III provides that there shall be "one Supreme Court" and such lower courts as Congress may establish.

The Court System

The first Congress passed the Judiciary Act of 1789. This law set up the federal court system, the basics of which are still in place today. The federal judiciary may be envisioned as a three-tiered pyramid, with many district courts at the bottom, a smaller number of circuit courts in the middle, and one Supreme Court at the top.

Cases from a district court may be appealed, or taken for review, to the circuit court for the area in which the district court is located. Cases may be appealed to the Supreme Court, which currently consists of nine members: eight associate justices and one Chief Justice. Because the cases that reach them are so complex, the justices must decline to rule upon all but a small fraction of the cases they are asked to hear.

The main purpose of the federal judiciary is to provide a forum for disputes involving federal laws. The most important power of the federal courts, that of **judicial review**, is not stated in the Constitution. This is the power of the Court to decide whether a given law, federal or state, conflicts with the Constitution. If so, the law can be declared unconstitutional and ceases to have effect. This acts as a form of veto power over laws. If the Supreme Court rules a law unconstitutional, the Congress or the states may initiate an amendment to the Constitution.

The Court cannot rule on just any law, but only on those that come before it. In this sense its role is passive; it cannot take the initiative to correct problems that the justices see or hear about, but must wait for others to file lawsuits. The Court also must rely on the President to enforce its rulings.

Unlike Congress and the President, federal judges do not have to face reelection. The Constitution provides that they shall hold office "during good behavior"—which generally means for life or until they choose to resign—and that their salaries may not be reduced. The Framers wanted to protect federal judges from political pressures so they could rule fairly and wisely, without fear of popular hostility. A federal judge can be removed through the difficult process of impeachment by Congress.

A Living Document

When the Constitution reached its bicentennial year in 1989, it inspired interest in the significance of the document. Two broadly different views emerged. Some people saw the limitations and problems that the federal government faced and suggested a new constitutional convention to restructure the government to meet today's difficult challenges. Others emphasized the remarkable enduring quality of the Constitution and its basic principles that remain important today.

It is likely that if changes are to be made in basic principles of government, they will come by amendment or interpretation. Amendment, however, has historically been approached with caution. The founders wanted the Constitution to be safe from the passions of the public and political schemes.

The Constitution's adaptability to new circumstances has made it a lasting framework of government. It has permitted, perhaps even encouraged, debate over the proper role of each branch of government, or of government itself. Through the first two centuries of federal government, the Constitution has served to moderate change in government. It has also ably guarded those freedoms that we the people have entrusted it to preserve.

THE CONSTITUTION TODAY

Independent Practice
Conducting an Opinion Poll
Point out that the Supreme Court has ruled that televising court proceedings does not necessarily deny defendants their right to a fair trial. Have the students conduct an opinion poll to determine whether class members favor or oppose television in the courtroom, and why. Post and discuss the results.
L1, LEP

Fact or Fiction?
The President must sign a constitutional amendment before it becomes law.

FICTION: An amendment becomes part of the Constitution on the date when the last state required to ratify it does so.

Did You Know?
The Constitution does not specify any requirements for a Supreme Court justice—not even a law degree. So far, however, all the justices have been lawyers, and the majority have served as judges.

Sidelights: English Common Law

The U.S. judicial system is based in large part on English common law. The latter began to develop in the 1100s, when the rulers of England tried to set up one system of justice for the entire country. The system relied not so much on laws as on decisions of judges. For example, any judge trying a case involving treason would look for precedents—judges' decisions in earlier, similar cases.

GLENCOE TECHNOLOGY

VIDEODISC
Focus on Government

Side 1, Chapter 1
Title: *Electronic Field Trip to Independence Hall*
Subject: Understand the role of Independence Hall in American history

ABC NEWS INTERACTIVE

VIDEODISC
Powers of the Congress

Side 1, Chapter 3
Title: *Constitutional Government*
Subject: Overview of constitutional government

ABC NEWS INTERACTIVE

VIDEODISC
Powers of the Congress

Side 1, Chapter 5
Title: *Preamble to the Constitution*
Subject: Identify six goals of our government

The Constitution of the United States

The Constitution of the United States is truly a remarkable document. It was one of the first written constitutions in modern history. The Framers wanted to devise a plan for a strong central government that would unify the country, as well as preserve the ideals of the Declaration of Independence. The document they wrote created a representative legislature, the office of president, a system of courts, and a process for adding amendments. For over 200 years, the flexibility and strength of the Constitution has guided the nation's political leaders. The document has become a symbol of pride and a force for national unity. For easier study of the Constitution, those passages that have been set aside or changed by the adoption of amendments are printed in blue. Also included are explanatory notes that will help clarify the meaning of each article and section.

▲ THE CAPITOL, WASHINGTON, D.C.

Preamble

We, the people of the United States, in Order to form a more perfect Union, establish Justice, insure domestic Tranquility, provide for the common defence, promote the general Welfare, and secure the Blessings of Liberty to ourselves and our Posterity, do ordain and establish this Constitution for the United States of America.

The Preamble introduces the Constitution and sets forth the general purposes for which the government was established. The preamble also declares that the power of the government comes from the people.

The printed text of the document shows the spelling and punctuation of the parchment original.

Article I

Section 1
All legislative Powers herein granted shall be vested in a Congress of the United States, which shall consist of a Senate and House of Representatives.

Section 2
1. The House of Representatives shall be composed of Members chosen every second Year by the People of the several States, and the Electors in each State shall have the Qualifications requisite for Electors of the most numerous Branch of the State Legislature.

2. No Person shall be a Representative who shall not have attained to the Age of twenty-five Years, and been seven Years a Citizen of the United States, and who shall not, when elected, be an Inhabitant of that State in which he shall be chosen.

3. Representatives and direct Taxes shall be apportioned among the several states which may be included within this Union, according to the respective Numbers, which shall be determined by adding to the whole Number of free Persons, including those bound to Service for a Term of Years, and excluding Indians not taxed, three-fifths of all other Persons. The actual Enumeration shall be made within three Years after the first Meeting of the Congress of the United States, and within every subsequent Term of ten Years, in such Manner as they shall by Law direct. The Number of Representatives shall not exceed one for every thirty Thousand, but each state shall have at Least one Representative; and until such enumeration shall be made, the State of New Hampshire shall be entitled to chuse three; Massachusetts eight, Rhode Island and Providence Plantations one, Connecticut five, New York six, New Jersey four, Pennsylvania eight, Delaware one, Maryland six, Virginia ten, North Carolina five, South Carolina five, and Georgia three.

4. When vacancies happen in the Representation from any State, the Executive Authority thereof shall issue Writs of Election to fill such Vacancies.

5. The House of Representatives shall chuse their Speaker and other Officers; and shall have the sole Power of Impeachment.

Article I. The Legislative Branch

Section 1. Congress
The power to make laws is given to a Congress made up of two chambers to represent different interests: the Senate to represent the states; the House to be more responsive to the people's will.

Section 2. House of Representatives

1. Election and Term of Office
"Electors" means voters. Every two years the voters choose new Congress members to serve in the House of Representatives. The Constitution states that each state may specify who can vote. But the 15th, 19th, 24th, and 26th Amendments have established guidelines that all states must follow regarding the right to vote.

2. Qualifications
Representatives must be 25 years old, citizens of the United States for 7 years, and residents of the state they represent.

3. Division of Representatives Among the States
The number of representatives from each state is based on the size of the state's population. Each state is divided into congressional districts, with each district required to be equal in population. Each state is entitled to at least one representative. The number of representatives in the House was set at 435 in 1929. Since then, there has been a reapportionment of seats based on population shifts rather than on addition of seats.

Only three-fifths of a state's slave population was to be counted in determining the number of representatives elected by the state. Native Americans were not counted at all.

The "enumeration" referred to is the census, the population count taken every 10 years since 1790.

4. Vacancies
Vacancies in the House are filled through special elections called by the state's governor.

5. Officers
The speaker is the leader of the majority party in the House and is responsible for choosing the heads of various House committees. "Impeachment" means indictment, or bringing charges against an official.

The Constitution of the United States 173

LESSON PLAN
Article I
The Legislative Branch

FOCUS
Motivating Activity
Ask students to read the introduction to the Constitution known as the Preamble. Then ask them to read again the Declaration of Independence on pages 122–123.

Have students discuss the similarities and connections between the Declaration and the Preamble to the Constitution. (Tell students that the Constitution was written with the Declaration of Independence in mind. The connection comes out most strongly in the Preamble. Like the Declaration, the Preamble is concerned with liberty, and places responsibility for government in the hands of "We the People.")

Explain that the Framers of the Constitution were concerned that states as well as individuals should receive fair representation in making the nation's laws. Article I shows how these concerns were finally resolved.

Did You Know?
Before Congress limited the size of the House of Representatives, it grew from 65 to 435 members. In the beginning, a state elected a representative for every 30,000 persons living there. If that rule were still in effect, the House today would have over 8,000 members!

Cooperative Learning
Divide the class into four groups. Assign each one a section of Article I—2, 3, 4, or 9—that has been modified by amendment. Have each group explain how, why, and when the change was made. **L2**

Article I
The Legislative Branch

TEACH

Guided Practice

Analyzing Information
Write on the chalkboard this statement attributed to George Washington: "We pour legislation into the senatorial saucer to cool it." (Washington apparently said this when he was defending the creation of the Senate to Thomas Jefferson.) Ask students to explain what the statement means. (Answers should include the fact that the Senate was seen as a more deliberative body.) How does the Constitution provide for this difference? (Senators are older: they serve for six years instead of two.) **L1, LEP**

FACT or FICTION?
The oldest senator from each state is known as the senior senator.

FICTION: Because every state has two senators, the one who has served longer is known as the senior senator. The other, appropriately enough, is called the junior senator.

Section 3. The Senate
1. Number of Members, Terms of Office, and Voting Procedure
Originally, senators were chosen by the state legislators of their own states. The 17th Amendment changed this, so that senators are now elected directly by the people. There are 100 senators, 2 from each state.

2. Staggered Elections; Vacancies
One-third of the Senate is elected every two years. The terms of the first Senate's membership was staggered: one group served two years, one four, and one six. All senators now serve a six-year term.
The 17th Amendment changed the method of filling vacancies in the Senate.

3. Qualifications
Qualifications for the Senate are more restrictive than those for the House. Senators must be at least 30 years old and they must have been citizens of the United States for at least 9 years. The Framers of the Constitution made the Senate a more elite body in order to produce a further check on the powers of the House of Representatives.

4. President of the Senate
The Vice President's only duty listed in the Constitution is to preside over the Senate. The only real power the Vice President has is to cast the deciding vote when there is a tie. However, modern Presidents have given their Vice Presidents new responsibilities.

5. Other Officers
The Senate selects its other officers, including a presiding officer (president pro tempore) who serves when the Vice President is absent or has become President of the United States.

6. Trial of Impeachments
When trying a case of impeachment brought by the House, the Senate convenes as a court. The Chief Justice of the Supreme Court acts as the presiding judge, and the Senate acts as the jury. A two-thirds vote of the members present is necessary to convict officials under impeachment charges.

7. Penalty for Conviction
If the Senate convicts an official, it may only remove the official from office and prevent that person from holding another federal position. However, the convicted official may still be tried for the same offense in a regular court of law.

Section 4. Elections and Meetings
1. Holding Elections
In 1842 Congress required members of the House to be elected from districts in states having more than one Representative rather than at large. In 1845 it set the first Tuesday after the first Monday in November as the day for selecting presidential electors.

2. Meetings
The 20th Amendment, ratified in 1933, has changed the date of the opening of the regular session of Congress to January 3.

Section 3
1. The Senate of the United States shall be composed of two Senators from each State, chosen by the Legislature thereof; for six Years; and each Senator shall have one Vote.
2. Immediately after they shall be assembled in Consequence of the first Election, they shall be divided as equally as may be into three Classes. The Seats of the Senators of the first Class shall be vacated at the Expiration of the second Year, of the second Class at the Expiration of the fourth Year, and of the third Class at the Expiration of the sixth Year, so that one-third may be chosen every second Year; and if Vacancies happen by Resignations, or otherwise, during the Recess of the Legislature of any State, the Executive thereof may make temporary Appointments until the next Meeting of the Legislature, which shall then fill such Vacancies.
3. No person shall be a Senator who shall not have attained the Age of thirty Years, and been nine Years a Citizen of the United States, and who shall not, when elected, be an Inhabitant of that State in which he shall be chosen.
4. The Vice President of the United States shall be President of the Senate, but shall have no vote, unless they be equally divided.
5. The Senate shall chuse their Officers, and also a President pro tempore, in the absence of the Vice-President or when he shall exercise the Office of the President of the United States.
6. The Senate shall have the sole Power to try all impeachments. When sitting for that purpose they shall be on Oath or Affirmation. When the President of the United States is tried, the Chief Justice shall preside: And no person shall be convicted without the Concurrence of two-thirds of the Members present.
7. Judgment in Cases of Impeachment shall not extend further than to removal from Office, and disqualification to hold and enjoy any Office of Honor, Trust or Profit under the United States: but the Party convicted shall nevertheless be liable and subject to Indictment, Trial, Judgment and Punishment, according to Law.

Section 4
1. The Times, Places, and Manner of holding Elections for Senators and Representatives, shall be prescribed in each state by the Legislature thereof; but the Congress may at any time by Law make or alter such Regulations, except as to the Places of Chusing Senators.
2. The Congress shall assemble at least once in every Year, and such Meeting shall be on the first Monday in December, unless they shall by Law appoint a different Day.

Critical Thinking

Analyzing Information Have students ascertain the number of members currently representing your state in the House of Representatives and also the number in 1990 and 1985. This information is readily available in many almanacs or on request from the secretary of state's office in your state. Point out that representation in the House is based on each state's population. Ask students to compare the numbers and indicate changes in representation. Then ask students to discuss how a change in the number of House seats might affect a state. **L1**

 ▲ **THE WILL OF THE PEOPLE** The idea of representative democracy works well when the legislature is responsive to the citizens. *Which chamber was not originally elected by the people?*

Section 5

1. Each House shall be the Judge of the Elections, Returns and Qualifications of its own Members, and a Majority of each shall constitute a Quorum to do Business; but a smaller Number may adjourn from day to day, and may be authorized to compel the Attendance of absent Members, in such Manner, and under such Penalties as each House may provide.

2. Each House may determine the Rules of its Proceedings, punish its Members for disorderly Behaviour, and, with the Concurrence of two-thirds, expel a Member.

3. Each House shall keep a Journal of its Proceedings, and from time to time publish the same, excepting such Parts as may in their Judgment require Secrecy; and the Yeas and Nays of the Members of either House on any question shall, at the desire of one-fifth of those Present, be entered on the Journal.

4. Neither House during the Session of Congress, shall, without the Consent of the other, adjourn for more than three days, nor to any other Place than that in which the two Houses shall be sitting.

Section 6

1. The Senators and Representatives shall receive a Compensation for their Services, to be ascertained by Law, and paid out of the Treasury of the United States. They shall in all Cases, except Treason, Felony and Breach of the Peace be privileged from Arrest during their attendance at the Session of their respective Houses, and in

Section 5. Organization and Rules of Procedure

1. Organization
Until 1969 Congress acted as the sole judge of qualifications of its own members. In that year, the Supreme Court ruled that Congress could not legally exclude victorious candidates who met all the requirements listed in Article I, Section 2.

A "quorum" is the minimum number of members that must be present for the House or Senate to conduct sessions. For a regular House session, a quorum consists of the majority of the House, or 218 of the 435 members.

2. Rules
Each house sets its own rules, can punish its members for disorderly behavior, and can expel a member by a two-thirds vote.

3. Journals
In addition to the journals, a complete official record of everything said on the floor, as well as the roll call votes on all bills or issues, is available in the *Congressional Record*, published daily by the Government Printing Office.

4. Adjournment
Neither house may adjourn for more than three days or move to another location without the approval of the other house.

Section 6. Privileges and Restrictions
1. Pay and Privileges
To strengthen the federal government, the Founders set congressional salaries to be paid by the United States Treasury rather than by members' respective states. Originally, members were paid $6 per day. Salaries for Senators and Representatives are $129,500.

The Constitution of the United States

Article I
The Legislative Branch

Independent Practice
Creating a Chart Have students create a chart that categorizes the legislative powers of Congress. Instruct them to list the items under these categories: Monetary, Commerce, Regulatory, Judicial, War, Implied. **L1**

Visualizing History Point out that the Senate was originally intended to resemble the British House of Lords in its separation from popular control. **Answer to Caption:** the Senate

Did You Know?
When the first Congress was called to assemble in New York City, early in March 1789, there were not enough representatives or senators to form a quorum. Only after a month did enough members show up so that Congress could officially convene.

Powers of the Congress

Side 1, Chapter 38
Title: *Powers of the House and Senate*
Subject: Understand the powers of each House

Critical Thinking
Demonstrating Reasoned Judgment Have students state the qualifications for serving in Congress as set forth in the Constitution. Then ask if they can think of any other qualifications that should be applied to members of Congress. For example, should lawmakers have certain legal or technical training? Why or why not? **L1, LEP**

Article I
The Legislative Branch

Making Comparisons In addition to the enumerated powers, Congress has certain implied powers that are not stated in the Constitution. Instead, they are based on the "necessary and proper" clause. This clause is also known as the "elastic clause." In it, Congress is granted the power to make any laws "necessary and proper" in carrying out its duties. Throughout American history, Supreme Court decisions have expanded the authority of Congress to act under this clause. Have students discuss the advantages and disadvantages of doing so. (Possible answers: Because it is impossible to list all enumerated powers, the elastic clause provides the flexibility to address changing and unforeseen political and social conditions; the addition of powers might weaken the balance of powers between the branches.) **L2**

GLENCOE TECHNOLOGY

VIDEODISC

Focus on Government

Side 2, Chapter 22
Title: *Electronic Field Trip to the Capitol*
Subject: Tour the Capitol

The "immunity" privilege means members cannot be sued or be prosecuted for anything they say in Congress. They cannot be arrested while Congress is in session, except for treason, major crimes, or breaking the peace.

2. Restrictions
"Emoluments" means salaries. The purpose of this clause is to prevent members of Congress from passing laws that would benefit them personally. It also prevents the President from promising them jobs in other branches of the federal government.

Section 7. Passing Laws
1. Revenue Bills
"Revenue" is income raised by the government. The chief source of government revenue is taxes. All tax laws must originate in the House of Representatives. This insures that the branch of Congress which is elected by the people every two years has the major role in determining taxes. This clause does not prevent the Senate from amending tax bills.

2. How Bills Become Laws
A bill may become a law only by passing both houses of Congress and by being signed by the President. If the President disapproves, or vetoes, the bill, it is returned to the house where it originated, along with a written statement of the President's objections. If two-thirds of each house approves the bill after the President has vetoed it, it becomes law. In voting to override a President's veto, the votes of all members of Congress must be recorded in the journals or official records. If the President does not sign or veto a bill within 10 days (excluding Sundays), it becomes law. However, if Congress has adjourned during this 10-day period, the bill does not become law. This is known as a "pocket veto."

---

going to and returning from the same; and for any Speech or Debate in either House, they shall not be questioned in any other place.

2. No Senator or Representative shall, during the Time for which he was elected, be appointed to any civil Office under the Authority of the United States, which shall have been created, or the Emoluments whereof shall have been encreased, during such time; and no Person holding any Office under the United States, shall be a Member of either House during his continuance in Office.

Section 7
1. All Bills for raising Revenue shall originate in the House of Representatives; but the Senate may propose or concur with Amendments as on other bills.

2. Every Bill which shall have passed the House of Representatives and the Senate, shall, before it become a Law, be presented to the President of the United States; If he approve he shall sign it, but if not he shall return it, with his Objections, to that House in which it shall have originated, who shall enter the Objections at large on their Journal, and proceed to reconsider it. If after such Reconsideration two-thirds of that House shall agree to pass the bill, it shall be sent, together with the objections, to the other House, by which it shall likewise be reconsidered, and if approved by two-thirds of that House, it shall become a Law. But in all such Cases the Votes of both Houses shall be determined by Yeas and Nays, and the Names of the Persons voting for and against the Bill shall be entered on the Journal of each House respectively. If any Bill shall not be returned by the President within ten Days (Sundays excepted) after it shall have been presented to him, the Same shall be a Law, in like Manner as if he had signed it, unless the Congress by their Adjournment prevent its Return, in which Case it shall not be a Law.

▲ Preamble of the Constitution

176   The Constitution of the United States

Sidelights: The Capitol

The Capitol so familiar today—with the huge rotunda dome—was not completed until the 1860s. Today, each house of Congress meets in its own wing of the Capitol. Although many of the furnishings and works of art are the same as in the 1800s, signs of modern technology are everywhere. Roll call votes are counted electronically. In addition, members of both houses have access to computers and other information services. There are even underground tunnels with electric subways connecting many of the office buildings on Capitol Hill.

 **THE WORK OF CONGRESS** Although some of the work of the legislature is done on the floor of Congress, most of it is done outside the chambers by committees. Each member of Congress has a staff of legislative assistants and other aides who research issues, draft bills, and organize the member's office. **How does a resolution differ from a bill?**

3. Every Order, Resolution, or Vote to which the Concurrence of the Senate and House of Representatives may be necessary (except on a question of Adjournment) shall be presented to the President of the United States; and before the Same shall take Effect, shall be approved by him, or, being disapproved by him, shall be repassed by two-thirds of the Senate and House of Representatives, according to the Rules and Limitations prescribed in the case of a Bill.

Section 8
The Congress shall have the Power
1. To lay and collect Taxes, Duties, Imposts and Excises, to pay the Debts and provide for the common Defence and general Welfare of the United States; but all Duties, Imposts and Excises shall be uniform throughout the United States;
2. To borrow money on the credit of the United States;
3. To regulate Commerce with foreign Nations, and among the several States, and with the Indian Tribes;
4. To establish an uniform Rule of Naturalization, and uniform Laws on the subject of Bankruptcies throughout the United States.
5. To coin Money, regulate the Value thereof, and of foreign Coin, and fix the Standard of Weights and Measures;
6. To provide for the Punishment of counterfeiting the Securities and current Coin of the United States;

3. Presidential Approval or Veto
The Framers included this paragraph to prevent Congress from passing joint resolutions instead of bills to avoid the possibility of a presidential veto. A bill is a draft of a proposed law, whereas a resolution is the legislature's formal expression of opinion or intent on a matter.

Section 8. Powers Granted to Congress
1. Revenue
This clause gives Congress the power to raise and spend revenue. Taxes must be levied at the same rate throughout the nation.
2. Borrowing
The federal government borrows money by issuing bonds.
3. Commerce
The exact meaning of "commerce" has caused controversy. The trend has been to expand its meaning and, consequently, the extent of Congress's powers.
4. Naturalization and Bankruptcy
"Naturalization" refers to the procedure by which a citizen of a foreign nation becomes a citizen of the United States.
5. Currency
Control over money is an exclusive federal power; the states are forbidden to issue currency.
6. Counterfeiting
"Counterfeiting" means illegally imitating or forging.

The Constitution of the United States

Article I The Legislative Branch

Analyzing Information
Point out that because of the heavy volume of legislation, both houses of Congress have committees that do much of the work. Each committee deals with a particular issue, such as banking, foreign affairs, or natural resources. Ask students to bring in newspaper or magazine articles that deal with current congressional committees. In each case, ask them to indicate (1) whether the committee is standing or temporary, and (2) who is the committee chairman. **L2**

Did You Know?
Expertise can win committee members standing among their colleagues and enhance their committee roles. For example, Sam Nunn, the Democratic senator from Georgia, built a reputation for being very well prepared for Defense Committee meetings—so much so that Republican members often sought his advice.

Visualizing History Bills are discussed on the House and Senate floors only after they come out of committee hearings. Before debate begins, many important decisions have already been made.
Answer to Caption: A resolution expresses congressional opinion or intent; a bill is a draft of a proposed law.

Cooperative Learning
Organize the class into groups of five to consider one of the expressed powers of Congress—taxing and spending, regulating commerce, foreign policy and national defense, providing for nation's growth, and other powers. Have each group discuss why its power was delegated to Congress rather than to the executive branch. Have a reporter from each group summarize its conclusions for the class. **L2, L3**

Article I
The Legislative Branch

Analyzing Information
Explain that the powers of Congress are great, but they are not unlimited. Congress has only those powers that are expressly granted to it by the Constitution. Some, such as the power to tax, are legislative powers. Others are described as non-legislative powers. Ask students to study Article I, Section 8, to identify some of Congress's non-legislative powers. (Answers include conducting investigations; amending the Constitution; admitting new states; governing federal lands; choosing executive officials; impeaching officials; and giving advice and consent.) **L1**

Did You Know?

On many occasions when the United States has intervened militarily, Congress did not actually declare war. Among the so-called "undeclared wars" were the twentieth-century conflicts in Korea and Vietnam. Both wars were fought on the President's authority to support regimes against external aggression.

7. Post Office
In 1970 the United States Postal Service replaced the Post Office Department.

8. Copyrights and Patents
Under this provision, Congress has passed copyright and patent laws.

9. Courts
This provision allows Congress to establish a federal court system.

10. Piracy
Congress has the power to protect American ships on the high seas.

11. Declare War
While the Constitution gives Congress the right to declare war, the United States has sent troops into combat without a congressional declaration.

12. Army
This provision reveals the Framers' fears of a standing army.

13. Navy
This clause allows Congress to establish a navy.

14. Rules for Armed Forces
Congress may pass regulations that deal with military discipline.

15. Militia
The "militia" is now called the National Guard. It is organized by the states.

16. National Guard
Even though the National Guard is organized by the states, Congress has the authority to pass rules for governing its behavior.

17. Nation's Capital
This clause grants Congress the right to make laws for Washington, D.C.

18. Elastic Clause
This is the so-called "elastic clause" of the Constitution and one of its most important provisions. The "necessary and proper" laws must be related to one of the 17 enumerated powers.

Section 9. Powers Denied to the Federal Government.

1. Slave Trade
This paragraph contains the compromise the Framers reached regarding regulation of the slave trade in exchange for Congress's exclusive control over interstate commerce.

2. Habeas Corpus
Habeas corpus is a Latin term meaning "you may have the body." A writ of habeas corpus issued by a judge requires a law official to bring a prisoner to court and show cause for holding the prisoner. The writ may be suspended only during wartime.

3. Bills of Attainder
A "bill of attainder" is a bill that punishes a person without a jury trial. An "ex post facto" law is one that makes an act a crime after the act has been committed.

7. To establish Post Offices and post Roads;
8. To promote the Progress of Science and useful Arts, by securing for limited Times to Authors and Inventors the exclusive Right to their respective Writings and Discoveries;
9. To constitute Tribunals inferior to the Supreme Court;
10. To define and punish Piracies and Felonies committed on the high Seas, and Offenses against the Law of Nations.
11. To declare War, grant Letters of Marque and Reprisal, and make Rules concerning Captures on Land and Water;
12. To raise and support Armies, but no Appropriation of Money to that Use shall be for a longer Term than two Years;
13. To provide and maintain a Navy;
14. To make Rules for the Government and Regulation of the land and naval forces;
15. To provide for calling forth the Militia to execute the Laws of the Union, suppress Insurrections, and repel Invasions;
16. To provide for organizing, arming, and disciplining, the Militia, and for governing such Part of them as may be employed in the Service of the United States, reserving to the States respectively, the Appointment of the Officers, and the Authority of training the Militia according to the discipline prescribed by Congress;
17. To exercise exclusive Legislation in all Cases whatsoever, over such District (not exceeding ten Miles square) as may, by Cession of particular States, and the acceptance of Congress, become the Seat of Government of the United States, and to exercise like Authority over all Places purchased by the Consent of the Legislature of the State in which the Same shall be, for the Erection of Forts, Magazines, Arsenals, dock-Yards, and other needful Buildings;—And
18. To make all Laws which shall be necessary and proper for carrying into Execution the foregoing Powers, and all other Powers vested by this Constitution in the Government of the United States, or in any Department or Officer thereof.

Section 9

1. The Migration or Importation of such Persons as any of the States now existing shall think proper to admit, shall not be prohibited by the Congress prior to the Year one thousand eight hundred and eight, but a tax or duty may be imposed on such importation, not exceeding ten dollars for each Person.
2. The privilege of the Writ of Habeas Corpus shall not be suspended, unless when in Cases of Rebellion or Invasion the public Safety may require it.
3. No Bill of Attainder or ex post facto Law shall be passed.

Sidelights: Slavery

Although the first paragraph of Article I, Section 9 deals with the slave trade, note that the language of the Constitution does not use the term *slave*, but instead refers to "such persons." In fact, the word *slave* does not occur anywhere in the document. Elsewhere, enslaved people are referred to as "other persons" (Art. I, Sect. 2) and "person[s] held to service" (Art. IV, Sect. 2).

▲ **INAUGURATION OF THE PRESIDENT** The inauguration is held on January 20 following a presidential election. Generally held on the steps of the Capitol, the ceremony centers on swearing into office the new President. **What does Article II, Section 5 describe?**

4. No capitation, or other direct, Tax shall be laid unless in Proportion to the Census or Enumeration herein before directed to be taken.

5. No Tax or Duty shall be laid on Articles exported from any State.

6. No Preference shall be given by any Regulation of Commerce or Revenue to the Ports of one State over those of another: nor shall Vessels bound to, or from, one State, be obliged to enter, clear, or pay Duties in another.

7. No Money shall be drawn from the Treasury, but in Consequence of Appropriations made by Law; and a regular Statement and Account of the Receipts and Expenditures of all public Money shall be published from time to time.

8. No Title of Nobility shall be granted by the United States:—And no Person holding any Office of Profit or Trust under them, shall, without the Consent of the Congress, accept of any present, Emolument, Office, or Title, of any kind whatever, from any King, Prince, or foreign State.

Section 10
1. No State shall enter into any Treaty, Alliance, or Confederation; grant Letters of Marque and Reprisal; coin Money; emit Bills of Credit; make any Thing but gold and silver Coin a Tender in Payment of Debts; pass any Bill of Attainder; ex post facto Law, or Law impairing the Obligation of Contracts, or grant any Title of Nobility.

4. Direct Taxes
The 16th Amendment allowed Congress to pass an income tax.

5. Tax on Exports
Congress may not tax goods that move from one state to another.

6. Uniformity of Treatment
This prohibition prevents Congress from favoring one state or region over another in the regulation of trade.

7. Appropriation Law
This clause protects against the misuse of funds. All of the President's expenditures must be made with the permission of Congress.

8. Titles of Nobility
This clause prevents the development of a nobility in the United States.

Section 10. Powers Denied to the States
1. Limitations on Power
The states are prohibited from conducting foreign affairs, carrying on a war, or controlling interstate and foreign commerce. States are also not allowed to pass laws that the federal government is prohibited from passing, such as enacting ex post facto laws or bills of attainder. These restrictions on the states were designed, in part, to prevent an overlapping in functions and authority with the federal government that could create conflict and chaos.

Article I
The Legislative Branch

Evaluating Issues Article I, Section 10 prohibits the states from signing a treaty with another country. Ask students to explain why the Framers did not want states to have this right. (to make sure the nation acted as a unit; under the Articles of Confederation some states acted on their own, resulting in problems) **L2**

Visualizing History Presidents are now inaugurated on January 20, but George Washington took the oath of office on April 30, 1789, following John Adams's inauguration as Vice President nine days earlier. Congress passed the first law outlining a procedure for administering oaths of office in June of that year.
Answer to Caption: the qualifications for President

Sidelights: The Income Tax

Originally the Constitution did not allow Congress to levy direct taxes that were not divided equally among the states according to population. Thus, Congress could not raise money through income taxes because the income taxes would not be equally divided among the states. As the United States expanded and the amount of money required by government grew, this taxing limit became a serious problem. Congress found that it needed more sources of revenue. The Sixteenth Amendment, ratified in 1913, provided that income taxes could be collected without regard to a state's population.

LESSON PLAN
Article II
The Executive Branch

FOCUS
Motivating Activity
Point out that one of the difficult questions facing the Framers was that of a chief executive. Clearly, a single leader with broad but limited powers was needed to carry on the daily business of government. Ask students: Why did the Framers set up an office of President with limited powers? (Answers will vary but might include: Most delegates decided against having a king or any leader with uncontrolled powers; the people wanted an elected official who would work for the interests of a majority of the citizens.)

Visualizing History Although Article II, Section 3 requires that the President report to Congress on the State of the Union, it does not require a speech. The President's annual State of the Union Address has, however, become a tradition.
Answer to Caption: Article II, Sections 2 and 3

Side 1, Chapter 3
Title: *Constitution and the President*
Subject: Understand the basic duties of the President

2. Export and Import Taxes
This clause prevents states from levying duties on exports and imports. If states were permitted to tax imports and exports they could use their taxing power in a way that weakens or destroys Congress's power to control interstate and foreign commerce.

3. Duties, Armed Forces, War
This clause prohibits states from maintaining an army or navy and from going to war, except in cases where a state is directly attacked. It also forbids states from collecting fees from foreign vessels or from making treaties with other nations. All of these powers are reserved for the federal government.

Article II. The Executive Branch
Section 1. President and Vice President
1. Term of Office
The President is given power to enforce the laws passed by Congress. Both the President and the Vice President serve four-year terms. The 22nd Amendment limits the number of terms the President may serve to two.

2. Election
The Philadelphia Convention had trouble deciding how the President was to be chosen. The system finally agreed upon was indirect election by "electors" chosen for that purpose. The President and Vice President are not directly elected. Instead, the President and Vice President are elected by presidential electors from each state who form the electoral college. Each state has the number of presidential electors equal to the total number of its senators and representatives. State legislatures determine how the electors are chosen. Originally, the state legislatures chose the electors, but today they are nominated by political parties and elected by the voters. No senator, representative, or any other federal officeholder can serve as an elector.

2. No State shall, without the Consent of the Congress, lay any Imposts or Duties on Imports or Exports, except what may be absolutely necessary for executing its inspection Laws: and the net Produce of all Duties and Imposts, laid by any State on Imports and Exports, shall be for the Use of the Treasury of the United States; and all such Laws shall be subject to the Revision and Controul of the Congress.

3. No State shall, without the Consent of Congress, lay any duty on Tonnage, keep Troops, or Ships of War in time of Peace, enter into any Agreement or Compact with another State, or with a foreign Power, or engage in War, unless actually invaded, or in such imminent Danger as will not admit of delay.

Article II
Section 1
1. The executive Power shall be vested in a President of the United States of America. He shall hold his Office during the Term of four years, and together with the Vice-President chosen for the same Term, be elected, as follows:

2. Each State shall appoint, in such Manner as the Legislature thereof may direct, a Number of Electors, equal to the whole Number of Senators and Representatives to which the State may be entitled in the Congress: but no Senator or Representative, or Person holding an Office of Trust or Profit under the United States, shall be appointed an Elector.

▲ **STATE OF THE UNION** Presidents use the annual State of the Union Address to outline yearly goals. *In which sections of the Constitution are the President's powers and duties defined?*

180   The Constitution of the United States

Sidelights: Presidential Term of Office

The Constitution originally did not limit the number of terms the chief executive could serve. George Washington served two terms and established a tradition that all Presidents followed until Franklin D. Roosevelt. Many people opposed Roosevelt's four terms in office.

This opposition eventually led to ratification of the Twenty-second Amendment in 1951, limiting the President to two terms. Since Roosevelt, however, only Eisenhower and Reagan have served two full terms.

3. The Electors shall meet in their respective States, and vote by Ballot for two Persons, of whom one at least shall not be an Inhabitant of the same State with themselves. And they shall make a List of all the Persons voted for and of the Number of Votes for each; which List they shall sign and certify, and transmit sealed to the Seat of the Government of the United States, directed to the President of the Senate. The President of the Senate shall, in the Presence of the Senate and House of Representatives, open all the Certificates, and the Votes shall then be counted. The Person having the greatest Number of Votes shall be the President, if such Number be a Majority of the whole Number of Electors appointed; and if there be more than one who have such Majority, and have an equal Number of Votes, then the House of Representatives shall immediately chuse by Ballot one of them for President; and if no Person have a Majority, then from the five highest on the List the said House shall in like Manner chuse the President. But in chusing the President, the Votes shall be taken by States, the Representation from each State having one Vote; a quorum for this Purpose shall consist of a Member or Members from two-thirds of the States, and a Majority of all the States shall be necessary to a Choice. In every Case, after the Choice of the President, the Person having the greatest Number of Votes of the Electors shall be the Vice-President. But if there should remain two or more who have equal votes, the Senate shall chuse from them by Ballot the Vice President.

4. The Congress may determine the Time of chusing the Electors, and the Day on which they shall give their Votes; which Day shall be the same throughout the United States.

5. No person except a natural born Citizen, or a Citizen of the United States, at the time of the Adoption of this Constitution, shall be eligible to the Office of President; neither shall any Person be eligible to that Office who shall not have attained to the Age of thirty-five Years, and been fourteen Years a Resident within the United States.

6. In Case of the Removal of the President from Office, or of his Death, Resignation, or Inability to discharge the Powers and Duties of the said Office, the same shall devolve on the Vice-President, and the Congress may by Law provide for the Case of Removal, Death, Resignation or Inability, both of the President and Vice-President, declaring what Officer shall then act as President, and such Officer shall act accordingly, until the disability be removed, or a President shall be elected.

7. The President shall, at stated Times, receive for his Services a Compensation, which shall neither be encreased nor diminished during the Period for which he shall have been elected, and he shall not receive within that Period any other Emolument from the United States, or any of them.

8. Before he enter on the execution of his office, he shall take the following Oath or Affirmation "I do solemnly swear (or affirm) that I will faithfully execute the Office of President of the United States, and will to the best of my Ability, preserve, protect and defend the Constitution of the United States.

3. Former Method of Election
This clause describes the original method of electing the President and Vice President. According to this method, each elector voted for two candidates. The candidate with the most votes (as long as it was a majority) became President. The candidate with the second highest number of votes became Vice President. In the election of 1800, the two top candidates received the same number of votes, making it necessary for the House of Representatives to decide the election. To prevent such a situation from recurring, the 12th Amendment was added in 1804.

4. Date of Elections
Congress selects the date when the presidential electors are chosen and when they vote for President and Vice President. All electors must vote on the same day. The first Tuesday after the first Monday in November has been set as the date for presidential elections. Electors cast their votes on the Monday after the second Wednesday in December.

5. Qualifications
The President must be a citizen of the United States by birth, at least 35 years old, and a resident of the United States for 14 years. See Amendment 22.

6. Vacancies
If the President dies, resigns, is removed from office by impeachment, or is unable to carry out the duties of the office, the Vice President becomes President. (Amendment 25 deals with presidential disability.) If both the President and Vice President are unable to serve, Congress has the power to declare by law who acts as President. Congress set the line of succession in the Presidential Succession Act of 1947.

7. Salary
Originally, the President's salary was $25,000 per year. The President's current salary of $200,000 plus a $50,000 taxable expense account per year was enacted in 1969. The President also receives numerous fringe benefits including a $120,000 nontaxable allowance for travel and entertainment, and living accommodations in two residences—the White House and Camp David. However, the President cannot receive any other income from the United States Government or state governments while in office.

8. Oath of Office
The oath of office is generally administered by the chief justice, but can be administered by any official authorized to administer oaths. All Presidents-elect except Washington have been sworn into office by the chief justice. Only Vice Presidents John Tyler, Calvin Coolidge, and Lyndon Johnson in succeeding to the office have been sworn in by someone else.

The Constitution of the United States **181**

Article II
The Executive Branch

TEACH
Guided Practice
Classifying Point out that Article II of the Constitution outlines the powers of the President. Their nature and extent have been shaped by the historical development of the office. Explain that these powers can be grouped under five headings—executive, legislative, diplomatic, military, and judicial. Although these powers are limited by the checks and balances of the other branches of government, the President can use them in a variety of formal and informal ways. Assign students to read Article II and find and classify the powers of the President under the appropriate headings. **L1**

Fact or Fiction?
Under the veto power, the President must veto the entire bill.

FACT: The President does not have a line-item veto as most state governors do.

Did You Know?
Some Presidents have used the veto sparingly, whereas others used it often. Franklin Roosevelt, for example, vetoed 635 pieces of legislation, only 9 of which were overridden. On the other hand, Richard Nixon vetoed 42 bills (5 overrides) and John F. Kennedy, 21 (no overrides).

Critical Thinking

Determining Cause and Effect Write the following statement on the chalkboard:

"The increase in presidential power during this century has been largely related to crises, whether domestic or foreign."

Then ask: Do you think this is the true cause of the increase in presidential power? Why or why not? If not, what in your opinion did cause this increase? **L3**

Article II
The Executive Branch

Independent Practice

Making Judgments Ask: Why did the Framers of the Constitution make the President commander in chief of the armed forces and of any state militia called to serve the United States? (They wanted to ensure civilian control of the military.) **L2**

Visualizing History
In wartime Presidents have stretched their power as commander in chief. Discuss why this happens. (Wars are a state of emergency. Presidents have tended to act quickly without always consulting Congress.)
Answer to Caption: All treaties have to be approved by two-thirds of the senators present.

Did You Know?
Two former Presidents were elected to Congress after leaving the presidency. John Quincy Adams served in the U.S. House of Representatives from 1830 until 1848. Andrew Johnson was elected to the Senate in 1874 and served briefly before his death.

▲ **THE PRESIDENT'S POWER** As commander in chief of the United States armed forces, the President is the people's check on the power of the military. *What limits are placed on the President's power to make treaties?*

Section 2. Powers of the President
1. Military, Cabinet, Pardons
Mention of "the principal officer in each of the executive departments" is the only suggestion of the President's Cabinet to be found in the Constitution. The Cabinet is a purely advisory body, and its power depends on the President. Each Cabinet member is appointed by the President and must be confirmed by the Senate. This clause also makes the President, a civilian, the head of the armed services. This established the principle of civilian control of the military.

2. Treaties and Appointments
The President is the chief architect of American foreign policy. He or she is responsible for the conduct of foreign relations, or dealings with other countries. All treaties, however, require approval of two-thirds of the senators present. Most federal positions today are filled under the rules and regulations of the civil service system. Most presidential appointees serve at the pleasure of the President. Removal of an official by the President is not subject to congressional approval. But the power can be restricted by conditions set in creating the office.

3. Vacancies in Offices
The President can temporarily appoint officials to fill vacancies when the Senate is not in session.

Section 2
1. The President shall be Commander in Chief of the Army and Navy of the United States, and of the Militia of the several States, when called into the actual Service of the United States; he may require the Opinion, in writing, of the principal Officer in each of the executive Departments, upon any subject relating to the Duties of their respective Offices, and he shall have Power to Grant Reprieves and Pardons for Offences against the United States, except in Cases of Impeachment.

2. He shall have Power, by and with the Advice and Consent of the Senate, to make Treaties, provided two-thirds of the Senators present concur; and he shall nominate, and by and with the Advice and Consent of the Senate, shall appoint Ambassadors, other public Ministers and Consuls, Judges of the supreme Court, and all other Officers of the United States, whose Appointments are not herein otherwise provided for, and which shall be established by Law. But the Congress may by Law vest the Appointment of such inferior Officers, as they think proper, in the President alone, in the Courts of Law, or in the Heads of Departments.

3. The President shall have Power to fill up all Vacancies that may happen during the Recess of the Senate, by granting Commissions which shall expire at the End of their next Session.

Cultural Diversity

Until the 1930s no President had selected a woman or a member of a minority to serve in the cabinet. Franklin D. Roosevelt appointed the first woman to serve in the cabinet. In 1933 he chose Frances T. Perkins to serve as secretary of labor. In 1966 Robert C. Weaver became the first African American appointed to the cabinet. Lyndon B. Johnson named him to head the newly created Department of Housing and Urban Development.

Section 3

He shall from time to time give to Congress Information of the State of the Union, and recommend to their Consideration such Measures as he shall judge necessary and expedient; he may, on extraordinary occasions, convene both Houses, or either of them, and in Case of Disagreement between them, with respect to the Time of Adjournment, he may adjourn them to such Time as he shall think proper; he shall receive Ambassadors and other public Ministers; he shall take Care that the Laws be faithfully executed, and shall Commission all the Officers of the United States.

Section 4

The President, Vice-President and all civil Officers of the United States, shall be removed from Office on Impeachment for, and Conviction of, Treason, Bribery, or other high Crimes and Misdemeanors.

Article III

Section 1

The Judicial Power of the United States, shall be vested in one supreme Court, and in such inferior Courts as the Congress may from time to time ordain and establish. The judges, both of the supreme and inferior Courts, shall hold their Offices during good Behaviour, and shall, at stated Times, receive for their Services, a Compensation, which shall not be diminished during their Continuance in Office.

Section 3. Duties of the President

Under this provision the President delivers annual State-of-the-Union messages. On occasion, Presidents have called Congress into special session to consider particular problems.

The President's duty to receive foreign diplomats also includes the power to ask a foreign country to withdraw its diplomatic officials from this country. This is called "breaking diplomatic relations" and often carries with it the implied threat of more drastic action, even war. The President likewise has the power of deciding whether or not to recognize foreign governments.

Section 4. Impeachment

This section states the reasons for which the President and Vice President may be impeached and removed from office. (See annotations of Article I, Section 2, Clauses 6 and 7.)

Article III. The Judicial Branch

Section 1. Federal Courts

The term *judicial* refers to courts. The Constitution set up only the Supreme Court but provided for the establishment of other federal courts. There are presently nine justices on the Supreme Court. Congress has created a system of federal district courts and courts of appeals, which review certain district court cases. Judges of these courts serve during "good behavior," which means that they usually serve for life or until they choose to retire.

 ▲ **THE SUPREME COURT** Supreme Court proceedings are held in this room. The Constitution established the jurisdiction of the federal courts by defining the kinds of cases these courts may hear. **What is statute law?**

The Constitution of the United States **183**

LESSON PLAN
Article III
The Judicial Branch

FOCUS

Motivating Activity

Ask students to consider the meaning of the phrase "respect for the law." Questions to address during the discussion might include: What is law? How can the law affect individuals and society? What is meant by the phrase "respect for the law"?

Stress that the law is the foundation of representative democracy in the United States.

 VIDEODISC
Powers of the Supreme Court

Side 1, Chapter 3
Title: *Constitution and the Court*
Subject: Understand the separation of powers and checks and balances

 The judiciary is only briefly described in the Constitution. The Judiciary Act of 1789 set up the federal court system. That system has been amended by later acts of Congress and by tradition.
Answer to Caption: laws passed by Congress

Critical Thinking

Analyzing Ideas Show the film *Twelve Angry Men*. Before the jury takes its second vote on the case, stop the film. Divide the class into small groups. Have students in each group decide which juror they believe will be next to change his vote. Next, have students answer the question, If all jurors switched their votes, which juror would be the last to change his vote to not guilty? Have each group present its ideas. Complete the showing of the film. Conclude by leading a discussion in which students analyze the real outcome of the film. **L2**

Article III
The Judicial Branch

TEACH

Guided Practice

Demonstrating Reasoned Judgment Point out that federal judges are appointed for life and can only be removed by their death, resignation, or impeachment. Have students discuss why the Framers decided to do this. (Answers will vary but might include: the Framers wanted to free judges to make their best determinations without worrying that they might be punished for making unpopular decisions.) **L2**

Independent Practice

Simulation Hold a mock trial in which students assume the roles of prosecuting and defense attorneys, members of the jury, witnesses, and a judge. The issue at stake could be an issue of local concern, an issue identified by earlier activities, or an issue resulting in a landmark Supreme Court decision.

Visualizing History Point out that until the late 1900s, all justices of the Supreme Court were white males. Discuss why the court has been slow to change. (Justices are replaced only when they die or retire.)
Answer to Caption: specified as "good behavior," meaning service for life or until retirement

▲ **JUSTICES OF THE SUPREME COURT** Because we have judicial review, the Supreme Court is the official interpreter of the Constitution and has the final say in deciding what the Constitution means. ***What is the term of office for a Supreme Court Justice?***

Section 2. Jurisdiction

1. General Jurisdiction
Use of the words *in law and equity* reflects the fact that American courts took over two kinds of traditional law from Great Britain. The basic law was the "common law," which was based on over five centuries of judicial decisions. "Equity" was a special branch of British law developed to handle cases where common law did not apply.

Federal courts deal mostly with "statute law," or laws passed by Congress, treaties, and cases involving the Constitution itself. "Admiralty and maritime jurisdiction" covers all sorts of cases involving ships and shipping on the high seas and on rivers, canals, and lakes.

2. The Supreme Court
When a court has "original jurisdiction" over certain kinds of cases, it means that the court has the authority to be the first court to hear a case. A court with "appellate jurisdiction" hears cases that have been appealed from lower courts. Most Supreme Court cases are heard on appeal from lower courts.

3. Jury Trials
Except in cases of impeachment, anyone accused of a crime has the right to a trial by jury. The trial must be held in the state where the crime was committed. Jury trial guarantees were strengthened in the 6th, 7th, 8th, and 9th Amendments.

The Constitution of the United States

Section 2

1. The judicial Power shall extend to all Cases, in Law and Equity, arising under this Constitution, the Laws of the United States, and treaties made, or which shall be made, under their Authority; to all Cases affecting ambassadors, other public ministers and consuls; to all cases of admiralty and maritime Jurisdiction; to Controversies to which the United States shall be a party; to Controversies between two or more states; between a State and Citizens of another State; between Citizens of different States; between Citizens of the same State claiming Lands under Grants of different States, and between a State, or the Citizens thereof, and foreign States, Citizens or Subjects.

2. In all Cases affecting Ambassadors, other public Ministers and Consuls, and those in which a State shall be Party, the supreme Court shall have original Jurisdiction. In all the other Cases before mentioned, the supreme Court shall have appellate Jurisdiction, both as to Law and Fact, with such Exceptions, and under such Regulations as the Congress shall make.

3. The trial of all Crimes, except in Cases of Impeachment, shall be by Jury; and such Trial shall be held in the State where the said Crimes shall have been committed; but when not committed within any State, the Trial shall be at such Place or Places as the Congress may by Law have directed.

Critical Thinking

Predicting Outcomes Have students discuss the pros and cons of federal judges being elected instead of appointed. Have them include a discussion of the concept of "the tyranny of the majority" in their preparation. Then have them make a list of possible outcomes they foresee if the federal judiciary were to be subject to the electoral process. **L3**

Section 3
1. Treason against the United States, shall consist only in levying War against them, or in adhering to their Enemies, giving them Aid and Comfort. No Person shall be convicted of Treason unless on the Testimony of two Witnesses to the same overt Act, or on Confession in open Court.
2. The Congress shall have power to declare the Punishment of Treason, but no Attainder of Treason shall work Corruption of Blood, or Forfeiture except during the Life of the Person attainted.

Article IV
Section 1
Full Faith and Credit shall be given in each State to the public Acts, Records, and judicial Proceedings of every other State. And the Congress may by general Laws prescribe the Manner in which such Acts, Records, and Proceedings shall be proved, and the Effect thereof.

Section 2
1. The Citizens of each State shall be entitled to all Privileges and Immunities of Citizens in the several States.
2. A Person charged in any State with Treason, Felony, or other Crime, who shall flee from Justice, and be found in another State, shall on demand of the executive Authority of the State from which he fled, be delivered up, to be removed to the State having Jurisdiction of the crime.
3. No Person held to Service or Labour in one State, under the Laws thereof, escaping into another, shall, in Consequence of any Law or Regulation therein, be discharged from such Service or Labour, but shall be delivered up on Claim of the Party to whom such Service or Labour may be due.

Section 3
1. New States may be admitted by the Congress into this Union; but no new State shall be formed or erected within the Jurisdiction of any other State; nor any State be formed by the Junction of two or more States, or parts of States, without the Consent of the Legislatures of the States concerned as well as of the Congress.
2. The Congress shall have Power to dispose of and make all needful Rules and Regulations respecting the Territory or other Property belonging to the United States; and nothing in this Constitution shall be so construed as to Prejudice any Claims of the United States, or of any particular State.

Section 4
The United States shall guarantee to every State in this Union a Republican Form of Government, and shall protect each of them against Invasion; and on Application of the Legislature, or of the Executive (when the Legislature cannot be convened) against domestic Violence.

Section 3. Treason
1. Definition
Knowing that the charge of treason often had been used by monarchs to get rid of people who opposed them, the Framers of the Constitution defined treason carefully, requiring that at least two witnesses be present to testify in court that a treasonable act was committed.

2. Punishment
Congress is given the power to determine the punishment for treason. The children of a person convicted of treason may not be punished nor may the convicted person's property be taken away from the children. Convictions for treason have been relatively rare in the nation's history.

Article IV. Relations Among the States
Section 1. Official Acts
This provision insures that each state recognize the laws, court decisions, and records of all other states. For example, a marriage license or corporation charter issued by one state must be accepted in other states.

Section 2. Mutual Duties of States
1. Privileges
The "privileges and immunities," or rights of citizens, guarantee each state's citizens equal treatment in all states.

2. Extradition
"Extradition" means that a person convicted of a crime or a person accused of a crime must be returned to the state where the crime was committed. Thus, a person cannot flee to another state hoping to escape the law.

3. Fugitive-Slave Clause
Formerly this clause meant that slaves could not become free persons by escaping to free states.

Section 3. New States and Territories
1. New States
Congress has the power to admit new states. It also determines the basic guidelines for applying for statehood. One state, Maine, was created within the original boundaries of another state (Massachusetts) with the consent of Congress and the state.

2. Territories
Congress has power over federal land. But neither in this clause nor anywhere else in the Constitution is the federal government explicitly empowered to acquire new territory.

Section 4. Federal Protection for States
This section allows the federal government to send troops into a state to guarantee law and order. The President may send in troops even without the consent of the state government involved.

The Constitution of the United States

LESSON PLAN
ARTICLES IV–VII

FOCUS
Motivating Activity
Point out that one political scientist has called the supremacy clause—Article VI, Section 2—"the most important single provision of the Constitution." Ask students to think about why this might be so as they read Articles IV–VI and reflect on Articles I–III. (This clause, by making it clear that the national Constitution and laws are supreme over state constitutions and laws, prevented what could have been devastating conflicts between Congress and the states.)

TEACH
Guided Practice
Expressing Viewpoints
Review the amendment process.

Have students discuss whether the amendment process should be simpler and why the Framers established this particular system. (Answers will vary but might include: The Articles of Confederation had been too difficult to amend. Yet the Framers worried that if they made the Constitution too easy to amend, it would not be respected.) **L2**

Sidelights: Articles IV–VII

The Articles of Confederation had concentrated power in the hands of the states. The Constitution reversed this by concentrating power at the federal level. If the new system was to be accepted, the states needed to know that their rights and the rights of their citizens would be protected. Article IV provides these guarantees. In Article V, the Framers provided a way to change the Constitution. Article VI established the Constitution as the supreme law over individuals and states. Finally, Article VII provides a system for ratifying the Constitution.

ARTICLES IV–VII

Independent Practice

Writing Ask students to research and write a brief report on the life of one of the signers of the Constitution. Tell students that when writing their reports, they should focus on such factors as background, education, family life, etc., that might reveal the signer's motivations in taking part. **L2**

Did You Know?

Of the 55 delegates who attended the convention, only 38 signed the document. The 39th signature—that of John Dickinson—was written by George Read at Dickinson's request. Elbridge Gerry of Massachusetts and Edmund Randolph and George Mason of Virginia refused to sign. Thirteen delegates left the convention before it ended. Rhode Island sent no delegates to the convention.

Article V. The Amending Process

There are now 27 Amendments to the Constitution. The Framers of the Constitution deliberately made it difficult to amend or change the Constitution. Two methods of proposing and ratifying amendments are provided for. A two-thirds majority is needed in Congress to propose an amendment, and at least three-fourths of the states (38 states) must accept the amendment before it can become law. No amendment has yet been proposed by a national convention called by the states, though in the 1980s a convention to propose an amendment requiring a balanced budget had been approved by 32 states.

Article VI. National Supremacy

1. Public Debts and Treaties
This section promised that all debts the colonies had incurred during the Revolution and under the Articles of Confederation would be honored by the new United States government.

2. The Supreme Law
The "supremacy clause" recognized the Constitution and federal laws as supreme when in conflict with those of the states. It was largely based on this clause that Chief Justice John Marshall wrote his historic decision in *McCulloch* v. *Maryland*. The 14th Amendment reinforced the supremacy of federal law over state laws.

3. Oaths of Office
This clause also declares that no religious test shall be required as a qualification for holding public office. This principle is also asserted in the First Amendment, which forbids Congress to set up an established church or to interfere with the religious freedom of Americans.

Article VII. Ratification of the Constitution

Unlike the Articles of Confederation, which required approval of all thirteen states for adoption, the Constitution required approval of only nine of thirteen states. Thirty-nine of the 55 delegates at the Constitutional Convention signed the Constitution. The Constitution went into effect in June 1788.

Article V

The Congress, whenever two-thirds of both Houses shall deem it necessary, shall propose Amendments to this Constitution, or, on the Application of the Legislatures of two-thirds of the several States, shall call a Convention for proposing Amendments, which, in either Case, shall be valid to all Intents and Purposes, as part of this Constitution, when ratified by the Legislatures of three-fourths of the several States, or by Conventions in three-fourths thereof, as the one or the other Mode of Ratification may be proposed by the Congress; Provided that no Amendment which may be made prior to the Year One thousand eight hundred and eight shall in any Manner affect the first and fourth clauses in the Ninth Section of the first Article; and that no State, without its Consent, shall be deprived of its equal Suffrage in the Senate.

Article VI

1. All Debts contracted and Engagements entered into, before the Adoption of this Constitution, shall be as valid against the United States under this Constitution as under the Confederation.

2. This Constitution, and the Laws of the United States which shall be made in Pursuance thereof; and all Treaties made, or which shall be made, under the Authority of the United States, shall be the supreme Law of the Land; and the Judges in every State shall be bound thereby, any Thing in the Constitution or Laws of any State to the Contrary notwithstanding.

3. The Senators and Representatives before mentioned, and the Members of the several State Legislatures, and all executive and judicial Officers, both of the United States and of the several States, shall be bound by Oath or Affirmation, to support this Constitution; but no religious Test shall ever be required as a Qualification to any Office or public Trust under the United States.

Article VII

The Ratification of the Conventions of nine States shall be sufficient for the Establishment of this Constitution between the States so ratifying the same.

Done in Convention, by the Unanimous Consent of the States present, the Seventeenth Day of September, in the Year of our Lord one thousand seven hundred and Eighty-seven, and of the Independence of the United States of America the Twelfth. In Witness whereof We have hereunto subscribed our Names.

Sidelights: Ratification

The first five states to ratify the Constitution—Delaware, Pennsylvania, New Jersey, Georgia, and Connecticut—did so quickly and by large majorities. Eleven states had ratified the Constitution by the time George Washington was inaugurated on April 30, 1789.

Signers

George Washington, **President and Deputy from Virginia**

New Hampshire
John Langdon
Nicholas Gilman

Massachusetts
Nathaniel Gorham
Rufus King

Connecticut
William Samuel Johnson
Roger Sherman

New York
Alexander Hamilton

New Jersey
William Livingston
David Brearley
William Paterson
Jonathan Dayton

Pennsylvania
Benjamin Franklin
Thomas Mifflin
Robert Morris
George Clymer
Thomas FitzSimons
Jared Ingersoll
James Wilson
Gouverneur Morris

Delaware
George Read
Gunning Bedford, Jr.
John Dickinson
Richard Bassett
Jacob Broom

Maryland
James McHenry
Daniel of St. Thomas Jenifer
Daniel Carroll

Virginia
John Blair
James Madison, Jr.

North Carolina
William Blount
Richard Dobbs Spaight
Hugh Williamson

South Carolina
John Rutledge
Charles Cotesworth Pinckney
Charles Pinckney
Pierce Butler

Georgia
William Few
Abraham Baldwin

Attest: William Jackson, **Secretary**

Amendment I

Congress shall make no law respecting an establishment of religion, or prohibiting the free exercise thereof; or abridging the freedom of speech, or of the press; or the right of the people peaceably to assemble, and to petition the Government for a redress of grievances.

Amendment II

A well-regulated Militia, being necessary to the security of a free State, the right of the people to keep and bear Arms, shall not be infringed.

Amendment III

No soldier shall, in time of peace be quartered in any house, without the consent of the Owner, nor in time of war, but in a manner to be prescribed by law.

Amendment IV

The right of the people to be secure in their persons, houses, papers, and effects, against unreasonable searches and seizures, shall not be violated, and no Warrants shall issue, but upon probable cause, supported by Oath or affirmation, and particularly describing the place to be searched, and the persons or things to be seized.

Amendment 1.
Freedom of Religion, Speech, Press, and Assembly (1791)

The 1st Amendment protects the civil liberties of individuals in the United States. The 1st Amendment freedoms are not absolute, however. They are limited by the rights of other individuals.

Amendment 2.
Right to Bear Arms (1791)

The purpose of this amendment is to guarantee states the right to keep a militia.

Amendment 3.
Quartering Troops (1791)

This amendment is based on the principle that people have a right to privacy in their own homes. It also reflects the colonists' grievances against the British government before the Revolution. Britain had angered Americans by quartering (housing) troops in private homes.

Amendment 4.
Searches and Seizures (1791)

Like the 3rd Amendment, the 4th amendment reflects the colonists' desire to protect their privacy. Britain had used writs of assistance (general search warrants) to seek out smuggled goods. Americans wanted to make sure that such searches and seizures would be conducted only when a judge felt that there was "reasonable cause" to conduct them. The Supreme Court has ruled that evidence seized illegally without a search warrant may not be used in court.

THE AMENDMENTS

Motivating Activity
Analyzing Information

Write the word *Change* on the chalkboard. Have students discuss why the Framers included a process to change the Constitution. (They realized the needs of the people would change. This, in turn, would make changes in the Constitution necessary.)

Point out that the United States Constitution is the oldest written national constitution still in operation. One of the reasons for its survival is its flexibility. The Constitution is easy enough to amend to meet the real needs of the people. Yet it is difficult enough to amend that changes cannot be made without care and thought. As a result, the Constitution has provided for a government that is stable and responsive to the needs of the people as those needs change.

Linking Past and Present

Making the process for amending the Constitution easier continues to be a subject of some debate. Many Americans feel a simple majority vote should be all that is required. Others feel the process should remain complicated to prevent trivial matters becoming the subject of amendments. Some people in this latter group suggest the concerns of many amendments might have been dealt with more properly through legislation.

Sidelights: The Bill of Rights

Critics felt the Constitution did not go far enough in protecting individual rights and liberties. To meet their objections, supporters of the Constitution promised to introduce a series of amendments listing these rights. On September 25, 1789, James Madison kept this promise by proposing 12 amendments to the Constitution. The 10 amendments that were adopted are known as the Bill of Rights. One of the two amendments that did not become part of the Constitution in 1789 eventually became the Twenty-seventh Amendment.

THE AMENDMENTS

TEACH
Guided Practice
Analyzing Ideas
Ask students to give areas of concern they would like to see addressed by a Constitutional amendment. Write suggestions on the chalkboard and have the class discuss each in terms of the following questions: Why is an amendment needed? Might it be better to allow Congress to pass laws or the courts to establish precedents on this issue? What would be the best way to lobby for such an amendment?

Visualizing History Ask which amendment addresses bail and fines. (the Eighth Amendment)
Answer to Caption: Amendment 6

Did You Know?
One important requirement for a fair trial is that the judge must be impartial and disinterested. The Supreme Court has also held that a trial is unfair if it is dominated by a mob or if publicity has poisoned the jurors' minds.

Amendment 5.
Rights of Accused Persons (1791)
To bring a "presentment" or "indictment" means to formally charge a person with committing a crime. It is the function of a grand jury to see whether there is enough evidence to bring the accused person to trial. A person may not be tried more than once for the same crime (double jeopardy).

Members of the armed services are subject to military law. They may be tried in a court martial. In times of war or a natural disaster, civilians may also be put under martial law.

The 5th Amendment also guarantees that persons may not be forced in any criminal case to be a witness against themselves. That is, accused persons may refuse to answer questions on the ground that the answers might tend to incriminate them.

Amendment 6.
Right to Speedy, Fair Trial (1791)
The requirement of a "speedy" trial insures that an accused person will not be held in jail for a lengthy period as a means of punishing the accused without a trial. A "fair" trial means that the trial must be open to the public and that a jury must hear witnesses and evidence on both sides before deciding the guilt or innocence of a person charged with a crime. This amendment also provides that legal counsel must be provided to a defendant. In 1963, the Supreme Court ruled, in *Gideon v. Wainwright*, that if a defendant cannot afford a lawyer, the government must provide one to defend the accused person.

Amendment V
No person shall be held to answer for a capital, or otherwise infamous crime, unless on a presentment or indictment of a Grand Jury, except in cases arising in the land or naval forces, or in the Militia, when in actual service in time of War or public danger; nor shall any person be subject for the same offence to be twice put in jeopardy of life or limb; nor shall be compelled in any criminal case to be a witness against himself, nor be deprived of life, liberty, or property, without due process of law; nor shall private property be taken for public use, without just compensation.

Amendment VI
In all criminal prosecutions, the accused shall enjoy the right to a speedy and public trail, by an impartial jury of the State and district wherein the crime shall have been committed, which district shall have been previously ascertained by law, and to be informed of the nature and cause of the accusation; to be confronted with the witnesses against him; to have compulsory process for obtaining witnesses in his favor, and to have the Assistance of Counsel for his defence.

Visualizing History ▶ **RIGHTS OF THE ACCUSED** Several amendments protect the rights of the accused. While awaiting trial, a defendant may be released by posting bail, a procedure regulated by the Eighth Amendment. *Which amendment guarantees the right to a speedy and fair trial?*

The Constitution of the United States

Critical Thinking
Analyzing Points of View Point out that there is disagreement about the amending process. Some people feel that it should be made easier, whereas others think that the process should remain complicated. Have students discuss the merits of each position, using specific amendments and/or proposed amendments to support their point of view. **L3**

Amendment VII

In suits at common law, where the value in controversy shall exceed twenty dollars, the right of trial by jury shall be preserved, and no fact tried by a jury, shall be otherwise reexamined in any Courts of the United States, than according to the rules of common law.

Amendment VIII

Excessive bail shall not be required, nor excessive fines imposed, nor cruel and unusual punishments inflicted.

Amendment IX

The enumeration in the Constitution, of certain rights, shall not be construed to deny or disparage others retained by the people.

Amendment X

The powers not delegated to the United States by the Constitution, nor prohibited by it to the States, are reserved to the States respectively, or to the people.

Amendment XI

The Judicial power of the United States shall not be construed to extend to any suit in law or equity, commenced or prosecuted against one of the United States by Citizens of another State, or by Citizens or Subjects of any Foreign State.

Amendment XII

The Electors shall meet in their respective States and vote by ballot for President and Vice-President, one of whom, at least, shall not be an inhabitant of the same State with themselves; they shall name in their ballots the person voted for as President, and in distinct ballots the person voted for as Vice-President, and they shall make distinct lists of all persons voted for as President, and of all persons voted for as Vice-President, and of the number of votes for each, which lists they shall sign and certify, and transmit sealed to the seat of the government of the United States, directed to the President of the Senate;—The President of the Senate shall, in the presence of the Senate and House of Representatives, open all the certificates and the votes shall then be counted;—The person having the greatest number of votes for President, shall be the President, if such number be a majority of the whole number of Electors appointed; and if no person have such majority, then from the persons having the highest numbers not exceeding three on the list of those voted for as President, the House of Representatives shall choose immediately, by ballot, the President. But

Amendment 7.
Civil Suits (1791)

"Common law" means the law established by previous court decisions. In civil cases where one person sues another for more than $20, a jury trial is provided for. But customarily, federal courts do not hear civil cases unless they involve a good deal more money.

Amendment 8.
Bail and Punishment (1791)

"Bail" is money that an accused person provides to the court as a guarantee that he or she will be present for a trial. This amendment insures that neither bail nor punishment for a crime shall be unreasonably severe.

Amendment 9.
Powers Reserved to the People (1791)

This amendment provides that the people's rights are not limited to those mentioned in the Constitution.

Amendment 10.
Powers Reserved to the States (1791)

This amendment protects the states and the people from an all-powerful federal government. It provides that the states or the people retain all powers except those denied them or those specifically granted to the federal government. This "reserved powers" provision is a check on the "necessary and proper" power of the federal government provided in the "elastic clause" in Article I, Section 8, Clause 18.

Amendment 11.
Suits Against States (1795)

This amendment provides that a lawsuit brought by a citizen of the United States or a foreign nation against a state must be tried in a state court, not in a federal court. This amendment was passed after the Supreme Court ruled that a federal court could try a lawsuit brought by citizens of South Carolina against a citizen of Georgia. This case, *Chisholm* v. *Georgia*, decided in 1793, was protected by many Americans, who insisted states would lose authority if they could be sued in federal courts.

Amendment 12.
Election of President and Vice President (1804)

This amendment changes the procedure for electing the President and Vice President as outlined in Article II, Section 1, Paragraph 3.

To prevent the recurrence of the election of 1800 whereby a candidate running for Vice President (Aaron Burr) could tie a candidate running for President (Thomas Jefferson) and thus force the election into the House of Representatives, the Twelfth Amendment specifies that the electors are to cast separate ballots for each office. The votes for each office are counted and listed separately. The results are signed, sealed, and sent to the president of the senate. At a joint session of Congress, the votes are

The Constitution of the United States   **189**

THE AMENDMENTS

Independent Practice

Interpreting Primary Sources Have students discuss the meaning of Amendment 9. (Not all the rights of the people have necessarily been listed in the Constitution.) Ask why the Framers believed it was necessary to include this amendment. (could not list all rights; made it clear that those listed were not the people's only rights)

FACT or FICTION?

Freedom of speech, as guaranteed by the First Amendment, has limits.

FACT: Among other things, the amendment does not protect slander (a spoken lie meant to damage another person's reputation) or libel (slander that is published).

Did You Know?

The Framers regarded torture and such means of execution as beheading and drawing and quartering as "cruel and unusual punishments." More recently, opponents of the death penalty have argued that capital punishment as such is cruel and unusual; the Supreme Court has not upheld this view.

Sidelights: Due Process of Law

References to due process of law are found in the Fifth and Fourteenth Amendments. As a result of Supreme Court rulings, two kinds of due process have developed: procedural and substantive. Procedural due process requires that government use fair procedures in enforcing the law. Substantive due process requires that the laws under which government acts be fair.

THE AMENDMENTS

Identifying Alternatives
Point out that the electoral college has been criticized as obsolete, and various reforms have been suggested for changing it or doing away with it completely. Ask students to discuss whether some other method of election should replace the electoral college—for example, direct election of the President. **L3**

Did You Know?
In slightly more than 200 years, about 10,000 amendments have been introduced in Congress, but only 27 have been adopted. One proposal concerned limiting the scope of the federal treaty power. Senator John Bricker of Ohio proposed that "Congress shall have the power to regulate all Executive and other agreements with any foreign power...." Opponents of the proposal asserted that such a law would seriously damage the President's ability to negotiate effectively. In February 1954, the Senate voted 60-31, one vote short of the required two-thirds majority, for a slightly different version of the Bricker amendment.

---

counted. The candidate who receives the most votes, providing it is a majority, is elected President. Other changes include: (1) a reduction from five to the three highest candidates receiving votes among whom the House is to choose if no candidate receives a majority of the electoral votes, and (2) provision for the Senate to choose the Vice President from the two highest candidates if neither has received a majority of the electoral votes.

The Twelfth Amendment does place one restriction on electors. It prohibits electors from voting for two candidates (President and Vice President) from their home state.

Amendment 13.
Abolition of Slavery (1865)
This amendment was the final act in ending slavery in the United States. It also prohibits the binding of a person to perform a personal service due to debt. In addition to imprisonment for crime, the Supreme Court has held that the draft is not a violation of the amendment.

This amendment is the first adopted to be divided into sections. It is also the first to contain specifically a provision granting Congress power to enforce it by appropriate legislation.

Amendment 14.
Rights of Citizens (1868)
The clauses of this amendment were intended 1) to penalize southern states that refused to grant African Americans the vote, 2) to keep former Confederate leaders from serving in government, 3) to forbid payment of the Confederacy's debt by the federal government, and 4) to insure payment of the war debts owed the federal government.

Section 1. Citizenship Defined By granting citizenship to all persons born in the United States, this amendment granted citizenship to former slaves. The amendment also guaranteed "due process of law." By the 1950s, Supreme Court rulings used the due process clause to protect civil liberties. The last part of Section 1 establishes the doctrine that all citizens are entitled to equal protection of the laws. In 1954 the Supreme Court ruled, in *Brown v. Board of Education* of Topeka, that segregation in public schools was unconstitutional because it denied equal protection.

Section 2. Representation in Congress This section reduced the number of members a state had in the House of Representatives if it denied its citizens the right to vote. This section

190   The Constitution of the United States

---

in choosing the President, the votes shall be taken by states, the representation from each state having one vote; a quorum for this purpose shall consist of a member or members from two-thirds of the states, and a majority of all the states shall be necessary to a choice. And if the House of Representatives shall not choose a President whenever the right of choice shall devolve upon them, *before the fourth day of March next following,* then the Vice-President shall act as President, as in the case of the death or other constitutional disability of the President.—The person having the greatest number of votes as Vice-President, shall be the Vice-President, if such number be a majority of the whole number of Electors appointed, and if no person have a majority, then from the two highest numbers on the list, the Senate shall choose the Vice-President; a quorum for the purpose shall consist of two-thirds of the whole number of Senators, and a majority of the whole number shall be necessary to a choice. But no person constitutionally ineligible to the office of President shall be eligible to that of Vice-President of the United States.

Amendment XIII

Section 1
Neither slavery nor involuntary servitude, except as a punishment for crime whereof the party shall have been duly convicted, shall exist within the United States, or any place subject to their jurisdiction.

Section 2
Congress shall have power to enforce this article by appropriate legislation.

Amendment XIV

Section 1
All persons born or naturalized in the United States, and subject to the jurisdiction thereof, are citizens of the United States and of the State wherein they reside. No State shall make or enforce any law which shall abridge the privileges or immunities of citizens of the United States; nor shall any State deprive any person of life, liberty, or property, without due process of law, nor deny to any person within its jurisdiction the equal protection of the laws.

Section 2
Representatives shall be apportioned among the several States according to their respective numbers, counting the whole number of persons in each State, excluding Indians not taxed. But when the right to vote at any election for the choice of electors for President and Vice-President of the United States, Representatives in Congress, the Executive and Judicial officers of a

---

Cultural Diversity

Amendments 13, 14, and 15 represented attempts to use the Constitution to end slavery, extend citizenship to former enslaved persons, and guarantee African Americans the right to vote. Although the intent of these amendments was to prohibit racial discrimination, they failed to do so. For instance, literacy tests, poll taxes, and property taxes kept many African Americans from voting. In just 10 years (1896 to 1906), the number of African Americans registered to vote in Louisiana fell from 130,334 to 1,342.

▲ **POLITICAL PARTIES** The Constitution did not provide for the existence of political parties, which today play a major role in the election of the President and Vice President. *What restrictions does the Twelfth Amendment place on electors?*

State, or the members of the Legislature thereof, is denied to any of the male inhabitants of such State, being twenty-one years of age, and citizens of the United States, or in any way abridged, except for participation in rebellion, or other crime, the basis of representation therein shall be reduced in the proportion which the number of such male citizens shall bear to the whole number of male citizens twenty-one years of age in such State.

Section 3

No person shall be a Senator or Representative in Congress, or elector of President and Vice-President, or hold any office, civil or military, under the United States, or under any State, who, having previously taken an oath, as a member of Congress, or as an officer of the United States, or as a member of any State legislature, or as an executive or judicial officer of any State, to support the Constitution of the United States, shall have engaged in insurrection or rebellion against the same, or given aid or comfort to the enemies thereof. But Congress may by a vote of two-thirds of each House, remove such disability.

was not implemented, however. Later civil rights laws and the 24th Amendment guaranteed the vote to African Americans.

Section 3. Penalty for Engaging in Insurrection The leaders of the Confederacy were barred from state or federal offices unless Congress agreed to revoke this ban. By the end of Reconstruction all but a few Confederate leaders were allowed to return to public life.

The Constitution of the United States

THE AMENDMENTS

Creating a Time Line Have students make a time line that includes each of the amendments, the year of ratification, and significant concurrent political, economic, and social events. After completing the activity, have students display and compare their time lines. **L2**

Visualizing History Not until the 1830s did political parties organize conventions to name their candidates for President and Vice President.
Answer to Caption: They must cast separate ballots for President and Vice President, one of whom must not come from their state.

Did You Know?

The Fourteenth Amendment's guarantee of equal protection of the laws is the Constitution's first mention of equality.

Sidelights: The Poll Tax

Explain that a poll tax is a special tax paid as a qualification for voting. After the Civil War, poll taxes were levied in many southern states. Although taxes kept many low-income white males from voting, the major purpose of the poll tax was to keep African Americans from voting. Not until the 1960s did Congress take firm action to enforce the guarantee of the Fifteenth Amendment and end this kind of voter discrimination.

THE AMENDMENTS

Expressing Viewpoints
Delegates to the Constitutional Convention were divided into two groups: those who wanted a strong central government and those who wanted more power invested in the states. Some leaders, like Patrick Henry, feared the Constitution was a trap to give power to the educated and aristocratic elements of society. He argued for a bill of rights to guarantee individual liberties and freedom. Tell students that this difference of opinion is still voiced in political elections and debates today. Ask students to suggest reasons why some citizens prefer power to be concentrated at the local level. (Federal government is insensitive to local issues and practices.) Challenge students to think of occasions when a strong central government is preferable to local control. Point out that during the civil rights movement of the 1950s and 1960s, activists turned towards the federal government to enforce the rulings of the Supreme Court. **L2**

Did You Know?
Thomas Jefferson said, "The Constitution belongs to the living, not the dead."

Section 4. Public Debt The public debt incurred by the federal government during the Civil War was valid and could not be questioned by the South. However, the debts of the Confederacy were declared to be illegal. And former slave owners could not collect compensation for the loss of their slaves.

Section 5. Enforcement Congress was empowered to pass civil rights bills to guarantee the provisions of the amendment.

Amendment 15.
The Right to Vote (1870)
Section 1. Suffrage for African Americans The 15th Amendment replaced Section 2 of the 14th Amendment in guaranteeing African Americans the right to vote, that is, the right of African Americans to vote was not to be left to the states. Yet, despite this prohibition, African Americans were denied the right to vote by many states by such means as poll taxes, literacy tests, and white primaries.

Section 2. Enforcement Congress was given the power to enforce this amendment. During the 1950s and 1960s, it passed successively stronger laws to end racial discrimination in voting rights.

Amendment 16.
Income Tax (1913)
The origins of this amendment went back to 1895, when the Supreme Court declared a federal income tax unconstitutional. To overcome this Supreme Court decision, this amendment authorized an income tax that was levied on a direct basis.

Amendment 17.
Direct Election of Senators (1913)
Section 1. Method of Election The right to elect senators was given directly to the people of each state. It replaced Article I, Section 2, Clause 1, which empowered state legislatures to elect senators. This amendment was designed not only to make the choice of senators more democratic but also to cut down on corruption and to improve state government.

Section 2. Vacancies A state must order an election to fill a senate vacancy. A state may empower its governor to appoint a person to fill a Senate seat if a vacancy occurs until an election can be held.

Section 4
The validity of the public debt of the United States incurred for payment of pensions and bounties for service, authorized by law, including debts in suppressing insurrections or rebellion, shall not be questioned. But neither the United States nor any State shall assume or pay any debt or obligation incurred in aid of insurrection or rebellion against the United States, or any claim for the loss or emancipation of any slave; but all such debts, obligations and claims shall be held illegal and void.

Section 5
The Congress shall have power to enforce, by appropriate legislation, the provisions of this article.

Amendment XV

Section 1
The right of citizens of the United States to vote shall not be denied or abridged by the United States or by any State on account of race, color, or previous condition of servitude.

Section 2
The Congress shall have power to enforce this article by appropriate legislation.

Amendment XVI

The Congress shall have power to lay and collect taxes on incomes, from whatever source derived, without apportionment among several States, and without regard to any census or enumeration.

Amendment XVII

Section 1
The Senate of the United States shall be composed of two Senators from each State, elected by the people thereof, for six years; and each Senator shall have one vote. The electors in each state shall have the qualifications requisite for electors of the most numerous branch of the state legislatures.

Section 2
When vacancies happen in the representation of any State in the Senate, the executive authority of such State shall issue writs of election to fill such vacancies: *Provided*, that the legislature of any State may empower the executive thereof to make temporary appointments until the people fill the vacancies by election as the legislature may direct.

The Constitution of the United States

Critical Thinking

Analyzing Information Make sure that students understand the issue regarding "lame ducks." (Lame ducks are Presidents and members of Congress waiting to leave office after failing reelection or retiring. Because lame ducks generally represented the policies of the defeated party, they were in a position to affect legislation even though they no longer spoke for the majority of voters.) Then ask students how the Twentieth Amendment addressed this problem. (It shortened the waiting time between Election Day and the beginning of a new term.) **L1**

Section 3
This amendment shall not be so construed as to affect the election or term of any Senator chosen before it becomes valid as part of the Constitution.

Amendment XVIII

Section 1
After one year from ratification of this article the manufacture, sale, or transportation of intoxicating liquors within, the importation thereof into, or the exportation thereof from the United States and all territory subject to the jurisdiction thereof for beverage purposes is hereby prohibited.

Section 2
The Congress and the several states shall have concurrent power to enforce this article by appropriate legislation.

Section 3
This article shall be inoperative unless it shall have been ratified as an amendment to the Constitution by the legislatures of the several States, as provided in the Constitution, within seven years from the date of the submission hereof to the states of the Congress.

Amendment XIX

Section 1
The right of citizens of the United States to vote shall not be denied or abridged by the United States or by any state on account of sex.

Section 2
Congress shall have power to enforce this article by appropriate legislation.

Amendment XX

Section 1
The terms of the President and Vice President shall end at noon on the 20th day of January, and the terms of the Senators and Representatives at noon on the 3rd day of January, of the years in which such terms would have ended if this article had not been ratified; and the terms of their successors shall then begin.

Section 3. Time in Effect This amendment was not to affect any senate election or temporary appointment until it was in effect.

Amendment 18.
Prohibition of Alcoholic Beverages (1919)
This amendment prohibited the production, sale, or transportation of alcoholic beverages in the United States. Prohibition proved to be difficult to enforce, especially in states with large urban populations. This amendment was later repealed by the 21st Amendment.

Amendment 19.
Women's Suffrage (1920)
This amendment, extending the vote to all qualified women in federal and state elections, was a landmark victory for the women's suffrage movement, which had worked to achieve this goal for many years. The women's movement had earlier gained full voting rights for women in four western states in the late nineteenth century.

Amendment 20.
"Lame-Duck" Amendment (1933)
Section 1. New Dates of Terms This amendment had two major purposes: 1) to shorten the time between the President's and Vice President's election and inauguration, and 2) to end "lame-duck" sessions of Congress.

When the Constitution first went into effect, transportation and communication were slow and uncertain. It often took many months after the election in November for the President and Vice President to travel to Washington, D.C., and prepare for their inauguration on March 4. This amendment ended this long wait for a new administration by fixing January 20 as inauguration day.

THE AMENDMENTS

Demonstrating Reasoned Judgment Tell students that at times our constitutional provisions protecting personal liberties have been sorely tested. One such test occurred during World War II. After the bombing of Pearl Harbor, more than 100,000 Japanese Americans, many of whom were citizens of the United States, were put into "detention camps." The United States government justified its action by claiming they were a security risk, even though there was no evidence of disloyalty. The Supreme Court upheld the action. Ask students if times of crisis, such as wartime, justify the suspension of personal liberties. Tell students that in the 1980s courts in the United States began to award sums of money to the families who had been affected by the detention program. **L2**

Did You Know?
Early in our history, women in one state—New Jersey—had the vote. The state's first constitution granted the suffrage to "any person" who met certain property qualifications. Many women took advantage of this provision to vote. However, the state legislature took away this right from women in 1807.

Critical Thinking

Making Comparisons Have students list advantages and disadvantages to the two-term limit for Presidents. Ask volunteers to present their list to the class and provide reasons for their choices. Finally, have students determine by vote whether or not they support presidential term limits. **L3**

THE AMENDMENTS

Civil Disobedience

Tell students that before the passage of the Twenty-fourth Amendment, state and local governments could require people to pay a poll tax before being allowed to vote. This tax was often used to discriminate against voters with little money. Among those who opposed the poll tax was one of the nation's best writers and essayists, Henry David Thoreau.

In his "Essay on Civil Disobedience," Thoreau stressed that government can be a positive force in bettering society, but that the machinery of government at times appears unjust. When this happened, Thoreau believed a person had a right and a duty to take action. For Thoreau this meant not paying the poll tax and then using every public means to speak or write against it. The ideas expressed in "Civil Disobedience" became significant in the defense of minority rights in the twentieth century. Discuss with students the right to "disobey" government. Challenge them to determine when this tactic is appropriate. **L3**

Did You Know?

Although Prohibition caused many problems, it did succeed in reducing alcohol consumption, thus decreasing the number of alcohol-related deaths and accidents.

Section 2. Meeting Time of Congress
"Lame-duck" sessions occurred every two years, after the November congressional election. That is, the Congress that held its session in December of an election year was not the newly elected Congress but the old Congress that had been elected two years earlier. This Congress continued to serve for several more months, usually until March of the next year. Often many of its members had failed to be re-elected and were called "lame-ducks." The 20th Amendment abolished this lame-duck session, and provided that the new Congress hold its first session soon after the November election, on January 3.

Section 3. Succession of President and Vice President This amendment provides that if the President-elect dies before taking office, the Vice President-elect becomes President. In the cases described, Congress will decide on a temporary President.

Section 4. Filling Presidential Vacancy
If a presidential candidate dies while an election is being decided in the House, Congress may pass legislation to deal with the situation. Congress has similar power if this occurs when the Senate is deciding a vice-presidential election.

Section 5. Beginning the New Dates Sections 1 and 2 affected the Congress elected in 1934 and President Roosevelt, elected in 1936.

Section 6. Time Limit on Ratification
The period for ratification by the states was limited to seven years.

Amendment 21.
Repeal of Prohibition Amendment (1933)

This amendment nullified the 18th Amendment. It is the only amendment ever passed to overturn an earlier amendment. It remained unlawful to transport alcoholic beverages into states that forbade their use. It is the only amendment ratified by special state conventions instead of state legislatures.

Section 2
The Congress shall assemble at least once in every year, and such meeting shall begin at noon on the 3rd day of January, unless they shall by law appoint a different day.

Section 3
If, at the time fixed for the beginning of the term of the President, the President elect shall have died, the Vice President elect shall become President. If a President shall not have been chosen before the time fixed for the beginning of his term, or if the President elect shall have failed to qualify, then the Vice President elect shall act as President until a President shall have qualified; and the Congress may by law provide for the case wherein neither a President elect nor a Vice President elect shall have qualified, declaring who shall then act as President, or the manner in which one who is to act shall be selected, and such person shall act accordingly until a President or Vice President shall have qualified.

Section 4
The Congress may by law provide for the case of the death of any of the persons from whom the House of Representatives may choose a President whenever the right of choice shall have devolved upon them, and for the case of the death of any of the persons from whom the Senate may choose a Vice President whenever the right of choice shall have devolved upon them.

Section 5
Sections 1 and 2 shall take effect on the 15th day of October following the ratification of this article.

Section 6
This article shall be inoperative unless it shall have been ratified as an amendment to the Constitution by the legislatures of three-fourths of the several States within seven years from the date of its submission.

Amendment XXI

Section 1
The eighteenth article of amendment to the Constitution of the United States is hereby repealed.

Section 2
The transportation or importation into any State, Territory, or possession of the United States for delivery or use therein of intoxicating liquors, in violation of the laws thereof, is hereby prohibited.

Section 3
This article shall be inoperative unless it shall have been ratified as an amendment to the Constitution by conventions in the several States, as provided in the Constitution, within seven years from the date of the submission hereof to the States by the Congress.

The Constitution of the United States

Critical Thinking

Analyzing Ideas Have students debate the following topic:

"The principles of the Constitution have less and less impact on a government in which special-interest groups and their lobbies influence and control much of the legislation."

Have opposing sides present their arguments to the class. **L3**

Amendment XXII

Section 1

No person shall be elected to the office of the President more than twice, and no person who had held the office of President, or acted as President, for more than two years of a term to which some other person was elected President shall be elected to the office of the President more than once.

But this Article shall not apply to any person holding the office of President when this Article was proposed by the Congress, and shall not prevent any person who may be holding the office of President, or acting as President, during the term within which this Article becomes operative from holding the office of President or acting as President during the remainder of such term.

Section 2

This article shall be inoperative unless it shall have been ratified as an amendment to the Constitution by the legislatures of three-fourths of the several States within seven years from the date of its submission to the States by the Congress.

Amendment XXIII

Section 1

The District constituting the seat of Government of the United States shall appoint in such manner as the Congress may direct:

A number of electors of President and Vice President equal to the whole number of Senators and Representatives in Congress to which the District would be entitled if it were a State, but in no event more than the least populous State; they shall be in addition to those appointed by the States, but they shall be considered, for the purposes of the election of President and Vice President, to be electors appointed by a State; and they shall meet in the District and perform such duties as provided by the twelfth article of amendment.

Section 2

The Congress shall have power to enforce this article by appropriate legislation.

Amendment 22.
Limit on Presidential Terms (1951)

This amendment wrote into the Constitution a custom started by Washington, Jefferson, and Madison, whereby Presidents limited themselves to two terms in office. Although both Ulysses S. Grant and Theodore Roosevelt sought third terms, the two-term precedent was not broken until Franklin D. Roosevelt was elected to a third term in 1940 and then a fourth term in 1944. The passage of the 22nd amendment insures that no President is to be considered indispensable. It also provides that anyone who succeeds to the presidency and serves for more than two years of the term may not be elected more than one more time.

Amendment 23.
Presidential Electors for the District of Columbia (1961)

This amendment granted people living in the District of Columbia the right to vote in presidential elections. The District casts three electoral votes. The people of Washington, D.C., still are without representation in Congress.

THE AMENDMENTS

Classifying Information

Write the headings that follow on the chalkboard:
- State-state and state-nation relations
- Executive branch
- Basic freedoms
- Extension of rights
- Congress and legislative procedures
- Military protection and rights
- Rights of the accused

Ask students to discuss what kinds of changes the amendments have produced. Have students review the amendments and categorize them according to the headings.

(Answers may vary slightly. The Twenty-third Amendment, for example, might be seen as either an extension of rights or a legislative procedure. Possible answers include: State-state (9, 10, 11); Executive branch (12, 20, 22, 25); Basic freedoms (1); Extension of rights (13, 14, 15, 19, 26); Procedures (16, 17, 23, 24); Military (2, 3); Rights: (5-8, 14)) **L3**

Did You Know?

During the 1960s the Supreme Court was dominated by Democratic appointees and made very broad interpretations in civil rights cases. In the 1990s a conservative-dominated Court made much narrower interpretations of civil rights issues.

Sidelights: The Twenty-fifth Amendment

When President Kennedy was assassinated in 1963, the need for a constitutional amendment dealing with presidential disability was obvious. Kennedy's successor, Lyndon B. Johnson, had once suffered a heart attack, and the two men in the line of succession after Johnson were both more than 70 years old. Congress passed the Twenty-fifth Amendment, which was submitted to the states in July 1965 and was ratified early in 1967.

THE AMENDMENTS

State Constitutions Each of the states has a state constitution. Have students discuss why it is necessary that states have a constitution although there is a national Constitution. (The national Constitution is the supreme law of the land. On the state level, unless it is in conflict with national law, the state constitution is the supreme law of the state. State constitutions provide the basic framework for the state government itself. State constitutions also establish systems of local government and a variety of state boards, agencies, and institutions as well as a revenue system for operation of the state government.) **L3**

Did You Know?

The Twenty-seventh Amendment was proposed by James Madison and approved by Congress in 1798. It then went to the states for approval. It did not gain the approval of three-fourths of the states until May 7, 1992, when the Michigan Legislature approved it.

Amendment 24.
Abolition of the Poll Tax (1964)
A "poll tax" was a fee that persons were required to pay in order to vote in a number of Southern states. This amendment ended poll taxes as a requirement to vote in any presidential or congressional election. In 1966 the Supreme Court voided poll taxes in state elections as well.

Amendment 25.
Presidential Disability and Succession (1967)
Section 1. Replacing the President The Vice President becomes President if the President dies, resigns, or is removed from office.
Section 2. Replacing the Vice President The President is to appoint a new Vice President in case of a vacancy in that office, with the approval of the Congress.

The 25th Amendment is unusually precise and explicit because it was intended to solve a serious constitutional problem. Sixteen times in American history, before passage of this amendment, the office of Vice President was vacant, but fortunately in none of these cases did the President die or resign.

This amendment was used in 1973, when Vice President Spiro Agnew resigned from office after being charged with accepting bribes. President Nixon then appointed Gerald R. Ford as Vice President in accordance with the provisions of the 25th Amendment. A year later, President Richard Nixon resigned during the Watergate scandal, and Ford became President. President Ford then had to fill the Vice Presidency, which he had left vacant upon assuming the Presidency. He named Nelson A. Rockefeller as Vice President. Thus both the presidency and vice-presidency were held by men who had not been elected to their offices.

Section 3 Replacing the President With Consent If the President informs Congress, in writing, that he or she cannot carry out the duties of the office of President, the Vice President becomes Acting President.

196 The Constitution of the United States

Amendment XXIV

Section 1
The right of citizens of the United States to vote in any primary or other election for President or Vice President, for electors for President or Vice President, or for Senator or Representative in Congress, shall not be denied or abridged by the United States or any State by reason of failure to pay any poll tax or other tax.

Section 2
The Congress shall have power to enforce this article by appropriate legislation.

Amendment XXV

Section 1
In case of the removal of the President from office or his death or resignation, the Vice President shall become President.

Section 2
Whenever there is a vacancy in the office of the Vice President, the President shall nominate a Vice President who shall take the office upon confirmation by a majority vote of both houses of Congress.

Section 3
Whenever the President transmits to the President pro tempore of the Senate and the Speaker of the House of Representatives his written declaration that he is unable to discharge the powers and duties of his office, and until he transmits to them a written declaration to the contrary, such powers and duties shall be discharged by the Vice President as Acting President.

Section 4
Whenever the Vice President and a majority of either the principal officers of the executive departments or of such other body as Congress may by law provide, transmit to the President pro tempore of the Senate and the Speaker of the House of Representatives their written declaration that the President is unable to discharge the powers and duties of his office, the Vice President shall immediately assume the power and duties of the office of Acting President.

Thereafter, when the President transmits to the President pro tempore of the Senate and the Speaker of the House of Representatives his written declaration that no inability exists, he shall resume the powers and duties of his office unless the Vice President and a majority of either the principal officers of the executive departments or of such other body as Congress may by law provide, transmit within four days to the President pro tempore of the Senate and the Speaker of the House of Represe

---

Critical Thinking

Research Point out that compared to other written constitutions from around the world, the United States Constitution might be characterized as succinct. The average federal constitution has about 26,500 words, whereas the United States Constitution—with all its amendments—has less than 7,500 words. Have students research and write a brief report comparing the United States Constitution with the constitutions of other nations. Suggest that they focus on such points as length, time in effective use, and political values espoused. Resource: *Written Constitutions: A Computerized Comparative Study* by Hene van Maarseveen and Ger van der Tang.

tives their written declaration that the President is unable to discharge the powers and duties of his office. Thereupon Congress shall decide the issue, assembling within forty-eight hours for that purpose if not in session. If the Congress within twenty-one days after receipt of the latter written declaration, or, if Congress is not in session, within twenty-one days after Congress is required to assemble, determines by two-thirds vote of both houses that the President is unable to discharge the powers and duties of his office, the Vice President shall continue to discharge the same as Acting President; otherwise, the President shall resume the power and duties of his office.

Amendment XXVI

Section 1
The right of citizens of the United States, who are eighteen years of age or older, to vote shall not be denied or abridged by the United States or by any State on account of age.

Section 2
The Congress shall have power to enforce this article by appropriate legislation.

Amendment XXVII
No law, varying the compensation for the services of Senators and Representatives, shall take effect, until an election of Representatives shall have intervened.

Section 4 Replacing the President Without Consent If the President is unable to carry out the duties of the office but is unable or unwilling to so notify Congress, the Cabinet and the Vice President are to inform Congress of this fact. The Vice President then becomes Acting President. The procedure by which the President may regain the office if he or she recovers is also spelled out in this amendment.

Amendment 26.
Eighteen-Year-Old Vote (1971)
This amendment made 18-year-olds eligible to vote in all federal, state, and local elections. Until then, the minimum age had been 21 in most states.

Amendment 27.
Restraint on Congressional Salaries (1992)
Any increase in the salaries of members of Congress will take effect in the subsequent session of Congress.

▲ **VOTING RIGHTS** The Twenty-sixth Amendment, ratified in 1971, extended the right and the responsibility of voting. *In what way did the amendment change voting eligibility?*

THE AMENDMENTS

Did You Know?
The United States had had a disabled President several times in its history. In the 1880s James Garfield lingered 80 days in a coma before succumbing to an assassin's bullet. In this century Woodrow Wilson suffered a stroke that incapacitated him for the last several months of his presidency.

Visualizing History Point out to students that the amendment was passed during the Vietnam War. Many Americans argued that those old enough to fight were old enough to vote.
Answer to Caption: It lowered the minimum voting age from 21 to 18.

The Constitution of the United States

INTRODUCING UNIT 3

BEGINNING THE UNIT

Provide this cause and effect chart to students with the effects omitted. Assign students to complete the chart as they read the chapters in the unit.

Event
- War of 1812

Causes
- Conflict with British-supported Native Americans in the Northwest Territory
- Demands for conquest of Canada
- British impressment of American sailors
- British violation of U.S. neutral rights during Britain's conflict with France

Effects
- Growth of U.S. nationalism
- American control of Spanish West Florida
- More active military policy against Native American groups
- The Era of Good Feelings

Portfolio Project
After students have completed their report, ask each to design and create a poster that summarizes the pertinent information about the state he or she selected.

OUT OF TIME?
If time does not permit teaching the entire unit, use the Unit Digest on pages 280–281.

UNIT THREE
LAUNCHING THE REPUBLIC
1789–1824

CHAPTER 7 The Federalist Era 1789–1800

CHAPTER 8 Age of Jefferson 1800–1815

CHAPTER 9 Nationalism and Change 1816–1824

▲ CHEROKEE BEADED SHOULDER BAG

History AND ART

Liberty in the Form of the Goddess of Youth based on an engraving by Edward Savage, 1796

The hope and sense of adventure that most Americans felt at the launching of their new nation are expressed in this illustration.

Exploring Unit Themes

American Democracy The plan of government set forth in the Constitution had to be turned into a working entity. Decisions taken by the country's first leaders established precedents and procedures for how the government would function. The early years of the republic saw the development of the two-party system.

Geography and the Environment Acquisitions of new territory helped the United States grow rapidly in the early 1800s. Settlers soon began to stream west into the new territories, forever changing the American environment.

Conflict and Cooperation In the early 1800s, an intense feeling of nationalism largely submerged the differences that existed among Americans. However, the seeds of disagree-

Setting the Scene

The American people faced an uncertain future, but the new government put finances in order, witnessed the birth of political parties, improved its transportation system, and more than doubled its territory. By 1824 the United States had been transformed into a strong, independent nation.

Themes
- American Democracy
- Geography and Environment
- Conflict and Cooperation
- United States Role in World Affairs

Key Events
- Washington's Inauguration
- Bill of Rights ratified
- Whiskey Rebellion
- Treaty of Greenville
- "Revolution of 1800"
- *Marbury* v. *Madison*
- Louisiana Purchase
- Lewis and Clark Expedition
- War of 1812
- Battle of New Orleans
- Acquisition of Florida
- The Monroe Doctrine

▲ PRO-WASHINGTON POLITICAL BUTTONS

▲ POCKET WATCH, EARLY 1800S

Major Issues
- The plan for a strong central government, as set forth in the Constitution, becomes a reality.
- Disagreements within Congress and Washington's cabinet result in the formation of political parties.
- Backed by the Supreme Court, the power and authority of the national government grow at the expense of the states.

Portfolio Project
Prepare a report on 1 of the 10 states admitted to the Union between 1791 and 1821. Describe its admission to statehood and details of the first legislature, governor, and state capital.

◄ FLAG FLOWN AT FORT MCHENRY

INTRODUCING
UNIT 3

UNIT 3 Independent Study Project
Organize the class into two groups. Assign the topic "Domestic Policy Issues" to one group and the topic "Foreign Policy Issues" to the other. Tell students to prepare a written report detailing which issues in their topic area were settled in the first 48 years of our nation's history.

Unit Digest Transparencies:
Strategies and Activities
Use Transparency 3, *Liberty in the Form of the Goddess of Youth*, based on an engraving by Edward Savage.

History AND ART
Edward Savage (1761–1816) was an American painter and engraver known for his portraits of prominent Americans such as George and Martha Washington and Thomas Jefferson.

History and the Humanities

 History and Art Transparencies 4, 5, 6

Focus on American Art Prints 7, 8, 9

♪ American Music: Cultural Traditions

Spirit of American Art and Music 7, 8, 9

---

ments that would have a great impact on life in America had already been sown.

U.S. Role in World Affairs Despite Americans' efforts to heed George Washington's warning, they found themselves increasingly drawn into the bitter conflict between Britain and France. Later, however, through the Monroe Doctrine the United States and Britain cooperated to prevent further encroachment of other European powers into the Western Hemisphere.

Examining the Themes Have students identify how growing nationalism affected Americans domestically and internationally.

LESSON PLAN
Global Perspectives

FOCUS
Motivating Activity

Write the following statement on the chalkboard:
"Keep out of my backyard!"

After students have studied this feature, ask them which American foreign-policy development the above statement might describe. (The Monroe Doctrine) Then ask: Is this an accurate description of the Monroe Doctrine? Why or why not? (Some students might respond: Yes, because it warned Europeans not to get involved in the Western Hemisphere. Others might say: No, Latin America is not the United States' backyard.) Point out that stopping the development of communism in "our backyard" was used as a justification for overt and covert intervention by the United States in Central America in the 1980s.

TEACH
Guided Practice
Exploring the Time Line

Direct students' attention to the time line entry on the slave revolt led by Toussaint L'Ouverture. Then ask them to speculate on the impact news of L'Ouverture's victory had on life in the southern United States. (Enslaved peoples might have been encouraged to revolt. Slaveholders might have clamped down harder on slaves to prevent revolt.)

Global Perspectives

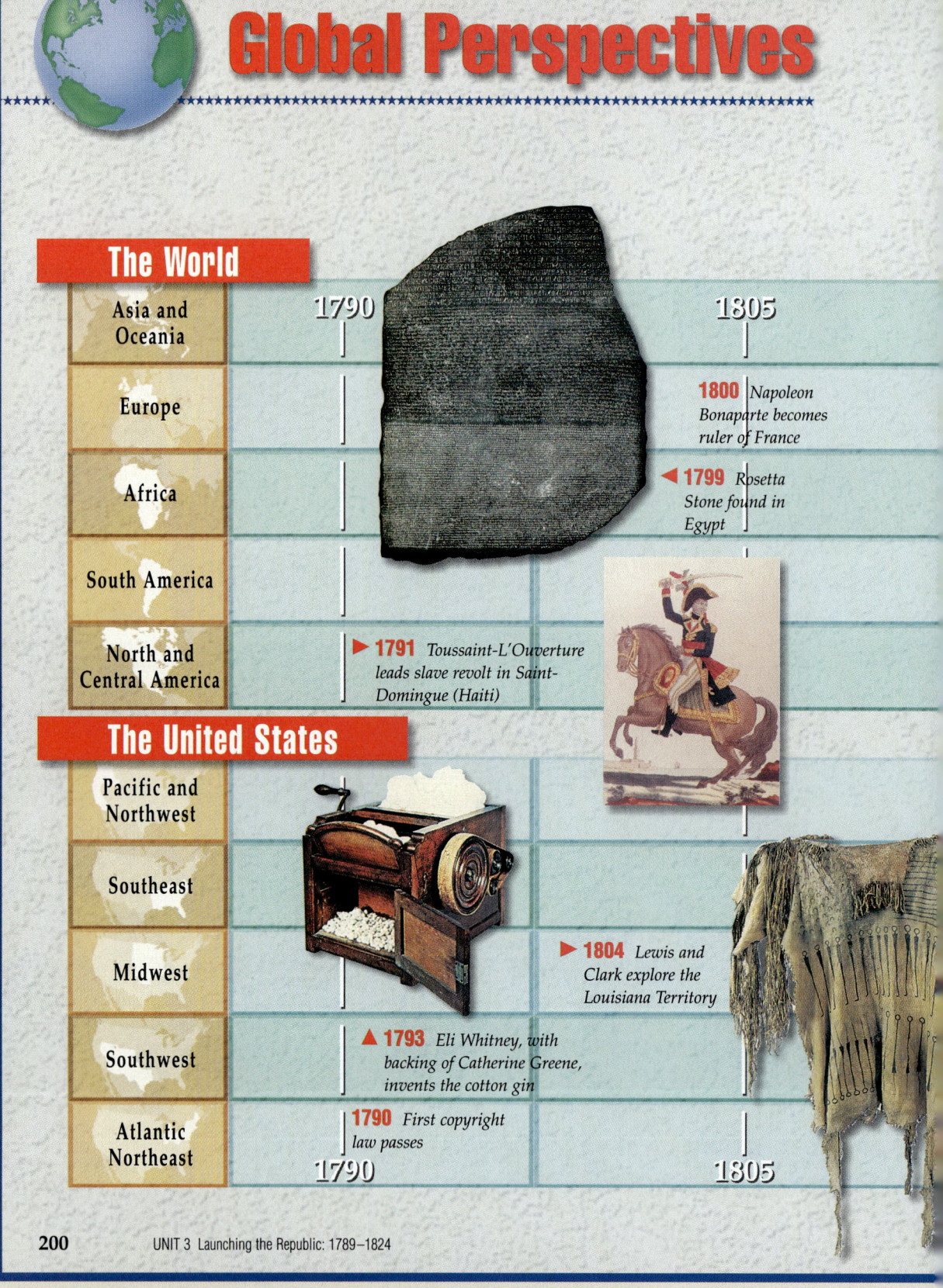

The World

| | 1790 | | 1805 |

- Asia and Oceania
- Europe — **1800** Napoleon Bonaparte becomes ruler of France
- Africa — ◄ **1799** Rosetta Stone found in Egypt
- South America
- North and Central America — ► **1791** Toussaint-L'Ouverture leads slave revolt in Saint-Domingue (Haiti)

The United States

- Pacific and Northwest
- Southeast
- Midwest — ► **1804** Lewis and Clark explore the Louisiana Territory
- Southwest — ▲ **1793** Eli Whitney, with backing of Catherine Greene, invents the cotton gin
- Atlantic Northeast — **1790** First copyright law passes

| 1790 | | 1805 |

200 UNIT 3 Launching the Republic: 1789–1824

Cultural Diversity

In 1820, people of English descent were the main ethnic group in Delaware, although it was originally settled by the Lenni Lappe, the Minqua, and other Native American groups. The Dutch, Swedes, and Finns were the first European settlers, followed by the English and Welsh. By the early 1700s, the Scotch-Irish, the English, and Africans were the major groups in the colony. By 1775, Germans were living in northwestern Delaware, and some French people had arrived from the West Indies and France.

Linking Across Time

Henry Wadsworth Longfellow's poem "Evangeline" tells of the British expulsion of French settlers from Acadia—present-day Nova Scotia and Prince Edward Island—in 1755. Most of these settlers migrated to Louisiana, where they became known as Cajuns—a slurring of the word *Acadians*. Today, Cajuns continue to exhibit their French heritage through their Creole language (a French dialect), their special cuisine, and their *joie de vivre* (zestful enjoyment of life).

1820 — **1835**

1819 Thomas Raffles obtains Singapore for Britain

▼ **1815** Napoleon defeated at Waterloo

▶ **1824** Simón Bolívar frees Peru and Bolivia from Spanish rule

1823 Monroe Doctrine proclaimed

1820 First Christian missionaries reach Hawaii

1819 Florida is purchased from Spain

1813 Oliver H. Perry defeats the British in Battle of Lake Erie in War of 1812

▶ **1821** Stephen Austin settles Americans in Texas

1807 Robert Fulton's steamboat *Clermont* speeds river travel

1821 Public schools open in Massachusetts

UNIT 3 Launching the Republic: 1789–1824

LESSON PLAN
Global Perspectives

Independent Practice

Linking World Events Ask students to research and write a report on the impact that world events had on the expansion of the United States during the period covered by this feature. To help students get started, direct their attention to entries for 1804 and 1819 on the United States section of the time line. **L2**

ASSESS
Studying the Time Line

1. Which person made the greatest contribution to the liberation of Central and South America? (Simón Bolívar)

2. How did the United States signal its support for the independence movements in Latin America? (issued the Monroe Doctrine)

3. Based on information in this feature, which decade could be called the "Decade of Independence"? (1820s)

Cooperative Learning

Organize students in groups of five. Ask groups to select one of the following topics: George Washington's policy of avoiding "foreign entanglements," Thomas Jefferson's belief that the United States' economic future lay in agriculture, and James Monroe's warning to European powers to stay out of the Western Hemisphere. Then have groups write a letter to Washington, Jefferson, or Monroe telling them how their noted actions or ideas have affected United States history. **L1, L2**

PLANNING GUIDE — Chapter 7 The Federalist Era

Daily Lesson Objectives	Teacher Classroom Resources	Multimedia
SECTION 1 **Organizing the Government** 1 Day pp. 204–207 1. List the precedents set by Washington as first President. 2. Describe the first Congress under the Constitution.	Chapter 7 Study Guide Reproducible Lesson Plan Reteaching Activity 7-1 Section Quiz Chapter 7 Cooperative Learning Activity Chapter 7 Concept Mapping Activity The Living Constitution Reinforcing Social Studies Skills 31, 36, 48 Writer's Guidebook, Lesson 6	Student Self-Test Software Testmaker Section Focus Transparency 18 Chapter 7 Skills Transparency U.S. History and Art Transparency 8 Unit 3 Digest Transparency The Presidents: A Picture History of Our Nation
SECTION 2 **Solving National Problems** 1 Day pp. 208–214 1. Discuss Hamilton's financial program for the United States and the opposition to it. 2. Describe the problems settlers faced during western expansion.	Reproducible Lesson Plan Reteaching Activity 7-2 Section Quiz Chapter 7 Primary and Secondary Source Readings Reinforcing Social Studies Skills 31, 35, 53 Building Skills in Geography	Student Self-Test Software Testmaker Section Focus Transparency 19 Chapter 7 Map Transparency U.S. History Digraph 1 The American People: Fabric of a Nation A Geographic Perspective on American History
SECTION 3 **Foreign Affairs Under Washington** 1 Day pp. 216–220 1. Describe the effects of the French Revolution on the United States. 2. Explain the importance of the Jay and Pickney treaties.	Reproducible Lesson Plan Reteaching Activity 7-3 Section Quiz Chapter 7 Primary and Secondary Source Readings Reinforcing Social Studies Skills 31, 35, 53	Student Self-Test Software Testmaker Section Focus Transparency 20 U.S. History and Art Transparency 9
SECTION 4 **President John Adams** 1 Day pp. 222–225 1. Explain why political parties arose. 2. Describe the problems John Adams encountered as President.	Reproducible Lesson Plan Reteaching Activity 7-4 Section Quiz Chapter 7 Primary and Secondary Source Readings Chapter 7 Enrichment Activity Reinforcing Social Studies Skills 40, 46 Map and Graph Skill Activity Spanish Summaries & Glossary	Student Self-Test Software Testmaker Vocabulary Puzzlemaker Section Focus Transparency 21 Audiocassette, Chapter 7
CHAPTER REVIEW AND EVALUATION 1 Day	Chapter 7 Test Chapter 7 Performance Assessment Activity	Student Self-Test Software Testmaker

00:00 OUT OF TIME? If time does not permit teaching the entire chapter, use the Chapter 7 Summary on pages 280–281 and the Chapter 7 audiocassette (English and Spanish) to point out the main ideas of the chapter.

PLANNING GUIDE

Cultural Diversity Activity

Linking Past and Present Ask a volunteer to define the term *alien*. (a person who is not a citizen of the country in which he or she lives) Then have students describe the circumstances that led to the passage of the Alien Act. Note reasons why suspicions of French citizens increased during this period.

Compare the feelings of Americans in 1789 toward French immigrants with those of Americans toward immigrants today. How do wars and other crises affect the attitudes of Americans toward immigrants? What protections should immigrants have against deportation? Does the government have the right to deport noncitizens in times of war or other crises? Why or why not? Interested students might research the response of Americans to refugees from Nazi Germany in the 1930s and 1940s, immigrants from Japan in the same period, as well as responses to refugees from Vietnam, Haiti, and Cuba in more recent times. Encourage them to account for differences in the way the Americans responded to each group of newcomers.

Performance Assessment Activity

Debate Organize students into teams of four or five to prepare for a debate on the issues that divided Alexander Hamilton and the Federalists from Thomas Jefferson, James Madison, and the Anti-Federalists. Then organize a series of debates so that each Federalist team can debate at least one Anti-Federalist team.

POSSIBLE RUBRIC FEATURES: Content, presentation of information with a historical context, communication skills, collaborative skills, clarity

Chapter Resources

Literature from the Period

Hamilton, Alexander. "First Report on Public Credit." 1790.

Jefferson, Thomas, and James Madison. "The Kentucky Resolutions." 1789.

Washington, George. "Farewell Address." 1796.

Readings for the Student

Farber, Doris and Harold. *The Birth of a Nation.* Scribner's, 1989.

Flexner, James T. *Washington: The Indispensable Man.* Mentor, 1979.

Musselman, Lloyd. *The Federalist Period, 1790–1800.* Glencoe, 1980.

Readings for the Teacher

Miller, John C. *The Federalist Era 1789–1801.* Harper, 1960.

Rakove, Jack N. *The Beginning of National Politics: An Interpretive History of the Continental Congress.* Johns Hopkins, 1982.

Multimedia Resources

George Washington and the Whiskey Rebellion. LCA. (film, 27 minutes)

Launching the New Government, 1789–1800. Coronet. (color film, 13 minutes)

U.S. Constitution Tutor. Micro Learn/Word Associates. (Apple or IBM diskette)

Key to Ability Levels

Teaching strategies have been coded for varying learning styles and abilities.

- **L1** Basic activities for all students
- **L2** Average activities for average to above-average students
- **L3** Challenging activities for above-average students
- **LEP** Limited English Proficiency activities

Glencoe Links to the Humanities

Links to Art
- Focus on American Fine Art Prints 5, 6
- U.S. History & Art Transparencies 5, 8, 10

Link to Literature
- Macmillan Literature: American Literature Text—Washington Irving

Link to Music
- American Music: Cultural Traditions

CHAPTER 7

BEGINNING THE CHAPTER

Divide the class into interest groups representing farmers, trappers, trades people, and merchants, new immigrants, and so on. Ask students to imagine that they are inhabitants of the United States at the time the nation came into being. Have each group discuss and report its expectations of the new government. Discuss why the government might have difficulties fulfilling them.

Recording Journal Notes
Before students read Chapter 7, ask them to list in their journals characteristics and beliefs elected officials ought to have. When students have completed reading the chapter, encourage them to see how closely early leaders matched the lists students prepared.

Linking Across Time

Point out that George Washington served two terms as President. That tradition of presidential term limits held for almost a century and a half. The crises of the Great Depression and World War II convinced voters to elect Franklin D. Roosevelt to a third and then a fourth term.

CHAPTER 7

The Federalist Era
1789–1800

Setting the Scene

Focus
With the ratification of the Constitution and national elections, a new government was in place by the spring of 1789. One of the most urgent problems it faced was the poor financial condition of the country. Largely through the efforts of Alexander Hamilton and Federalist leaders, sound policies were implemented. Controversy developed over Hamilton's program, however, resulting in the formation of political parties.

▲ HOOKED RUG, 1790S

Journal Notes
What were the personal characteristics and beliefs of the country's early leaders? Note details about them in your journal as you read the chapter.

Concepts to Understand
★ How George Washington's strong leadership brought stability to the new government
★ How political values shaped the formation of political parties

Read to Discover . . .
★ some of the major issues that Washington faced as President.
★ how foreign affairs contributed to the growth of American political parties.

CULTURAL
- 1789 Church of England becomes the Protestant Episcopal Church
- 1790 Samuel Slater builds first cotton mill
- 1791 Washington, D.C., is surveyed

1785 — **1789**

POLITICAL
- 1787 Northwest Ordinance passes
- 1789 George Washington is inaugurated
- 1791 Bank of the United States is chartered

UNIT 3 Launching the Republic: 1789–1824

✚ EXTRA CREDIT PROJECT

Within six months of Washington's taking office, Congress had passed the first ten amendments to the Constitution, known collectively as the Bill of Rights. Then three-fourths of the states had to ratify those amendments. That process took more than two years. Ask interested students to work as a group to research the arguments used for and against approving the Bill of Rights. Have students present their findings to the class, listing the main points of each amendment and the arguments for and against it.

CHAPTER 7 CONCEPTS

Concept Mapping Activity

Draw the concept map below on the chalkboard for students to copy. Have students underline the key words in the generalization and predict what topics will be covered in the chapter.

Government affects political and economic values as it establishes the power of the new nation.

- Political Values
- Leadership

History AND ART

Savage painted George and Martha Washington and their two grandchildren after Martha's daughter died in the 1770s. The map represents their vast landholdings, and the African American symbolizes the enslaved people who worked their estates.

VIDEODISC

- *GTV: A Geographic Perspective on American History*

Side 2, Chapter 1
Title: *A Fresh Start*
Subject: The Constitution

See GTV Guide page 40 for complete lesson plan.

History AND ART

The Washington Family
by Edward Savage, c. 1798

When Washington took the oath of office on April 30, 1789, the machinery of government did not exist. There were no federal laws, no federal courts, and no federal law-enforcement officials.

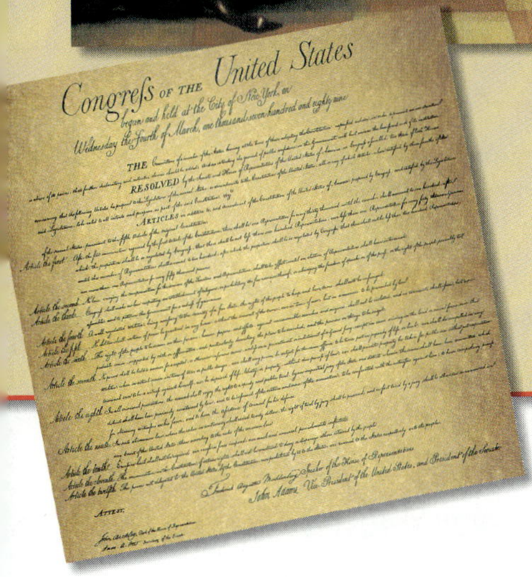

◀ BILL OF RIGHTS

- **1794** Connecticut inventor Eli Whitney patents cotton gin

1793	1797

- **1794** Whiskey Rebellion breaks out
- **1795** Northwest Territory opens for settlement
- **1799** American Review and Literary Journal *published; first quarterly literary review*
- **1797** John Adams is inaugurated
- **1798** Undeclared naval war with France rages

CHAPTER 7 The Federalist Era 1789–1800

Teacher Notes

LESSON PLAN
SECTION 1, 204–207

FOCUS

Bellringer
Prior to taking roll at the beginning of the class period, display Focus Activity Transparency 22 on the overhead projector and assign the accompanying Focus Activity Sheet.

Objectives
Point out the objectives on this page to students in previewing the section content.

Motivating Activity
Organize students into two groups. Have one group compile lists naming the areas of knowledge a President needs. (Examples: politics, foreign policy, economics) Have the other group list the qualities an effective leader should possess. (Examples: intelligence, trustworthiness, sensitivity to people's needs) Discuss why the first President of any new government would need outstanding skills.

Use Skills Transparency 7.

The following material is available from Glencoe and may be used to enrich Chapter 7.

CD-ROM
- *The Presidents: A Picture History of Our Nation*

SECTION 1

Organizing the Government

Setting the Scene

Section Focus
With the ratification of the Constitution in 1788, a new framework of government was in place. The obvious choice as leader of the new government was the hero of the Revolution, George Washington. Although he was reluctant to take the job, his reputation and stature were critical to the nation's success.

Objectives
After studying this section, you should be able to
★ list the precedents set by Washington as first President.
★ describe the first Congress under the Constitution.

Key Terms
cabinet, quorum

◀ BIBLE USED FOR WASHINGTON'S OATH OF OFFICE

eorge Washington accepted the presidency reluctantly. On the day he left for his inauguration, he wrote in his diary:

❝ *About ten o'clock I bade adieu to Mt. Vernon, to private life, and to domestic felicity, and with a mind oppressed with more anxious and painful sensations than I care to express, set out for New York.* ❞

At almost every town and village on the way from Virginia to the nation's temporary capital, Washington was met by welcoming speeches, cheering crowds, and troops of cavalry. When he reached New York on April 23, 1789, he was rowed across the Hudson River on a barge built especially for the occasion. Most of New York's 33,000 residents lined the wharves and cheered as the barge neared shore. Seven days later, Washington took the oath of office and gave the first Inaugural Address.

After the inauguration ceremony concluded, the festivities began with the ringing of church bells and the firing of cannons. Throughout the land there was public rejoicing for the man many believed to be the United States's greatest national asset.

■ Washington as President

Washington's background was as plantation manager and soldier. Because he lacked experience in government and had only limited knowledge of political theory and history, he felt he was unprepared to be the chief executive. Although Washington doubted his own qualifications, many

204   UNIT 3 Launching the Republic: 1789–1824

Classroom Resources for SECTION 1

Teacher's Classroom Resources
- Chapter 7 Study Guide
- Reproducible Lesson Plan
- Reteaching Activity 7-1
- Chapter 7 Cooperative Learning Activity
- Section Quiz

Multimedia
- Section Focus Transparency 22
- Chapter 7 Skills Transparency
- Chapter 7 U.S. History & Art Transparency
- Unit 3 Digest Transparency
- Testmaker
- Student Self-Test Software
- The Presidents: A Picture History of Our Nation

Americans regarded him with admiration bordering on awe. As early in his career as his first military victories at Trenton and Princeton, a Philadelphia newspaper wrote of Washington: "If there are any spots in his character they are like the spots on the sun, only discernible through a telescope." Such hero worship had its value to the new government. As a visible symbol of unity and power, Washington provided a focus for loyalty to the nation.

Washington's Qualifications

Washington was far more than a national symbol or figurehead. He knew the United States as well as any person alive, having traveled in every state except Georgia and having met or exchanged letters with most of the nation's prominent leaders. From the time he took charge of the Continental Army in 1775, he worked, as he said, to "discourage all local attachments" and to substitute "the greater name of American."

Organizing the New Government

Even with Washington in office and Congress in session, the Constitution was still little more than a paper plan. It would be months before the government could be functioning effectively. Laws had to be passed to establish executive departments such as the Treasury and the Post Office. A federal court system was needed to fill the gap left by the Framers of the Constitution.

Once federal offices were established, hundreds of people had to be found who were willing to give up their current jobs to serve as judges, tax collectors, and postmasters. Here, Washington's wide range of acquaintances and his reputation were invaluable in helping him find competent government officials.

Washington himself proved to be a first-rate administrator. On important matters, he sought the advice of his department heads, establishing what became known as the **cabinet**, a group of advisers to the President that continues to serve the same function today.

▲ PRESIDENTIAL SEAL

Visualizing History ▲ THE FIRST CABINET Washington's original cabinet included Henry Knox, Thomas Jefferson, Edmund Randolph, and Alexander Hamilton. Washington held no regular meetings with these officers but did rely on their expert opinions. Hamilton became the most influential because the Treasury post gave him a strong position in proposing legislation. Washington claimed to have no particular political expertise. **What other qualifications did he bring to the presidency?**

CHAPTER 7 The Federalist Era 1789–1800

CHAPTER 7
SECTION 1

Independent Practice

Vocabulary Write the following on the chalkboard or distribute as a handout.

Match each term with its correct definition.
  a. inauguration
  b. quorum
  c. figurehead
  d. ratify

(a) 1. the installing of an official in office with a ceremony
(d) 2. to approve formally
(c) 3. person who is head of a business or government in name only
(b) 4. number of members required to be present in order to conduct business

Discuss definitions with students. **LEP, L1**

Did You Know?

Congress voted George Washington a yearly salary of $25,000. At the time the average skilled artisan earned about $300 a year. Unskilled laborers earned about $160 a year.

Fact or Fiction?

John Jay, who served as the first chief justice of the United States, resigned that position.

FACT: Jay resigned in 1795 to become the governor of New York State.

Setting Precedents

Creating a cabinet was only one of several precedents set by Washington in areas where the Constitution was silent or unclear. He determined that the Senate's approval power over presidential appointments did not extend to their removal from office. He took control of foreign affairs, limiting the Senate's role of advice and consent to ratifying or rejecting treaties only after they were made.

Although he headed the executive branch, Washington assumed leadership in legislative affairs as well. In written messages to Congress and indirectly through reports prepared by Secretary of the Treasury Alexander Hamilton, Washington urged passage of laws he believed were in the public interest. With such encouragement Congress almost invariably followed his lead. Later Presidents would follow suit and become what some have called "chief legislator."

■ The First Congress

When the Confederation came to an end in 1788, it left behind 70 unpaid clerks, a military of 672 soldiers, and millions of dollars in debts. Before it disbanded, the Confederation Congress had arranged for the new government to be elected in November 1788 and start work on March 4, 1789. When March arrived, however, fewer than one-third of the senators and one-fourth of the representatives had reached New York. "The people will forget the new government before it is born," lamented a senator from Massachusetts. Not until April did each house of Congress have a **quorum**, or a majority of its members present in order to conduct business.

The Senate

The Senate was a small body consisting of two members from each state elected by their state legislature. The Framers of the Constitution had expected the Senate to serve as an advisory body to the President. With this in mind, Washington came to the Senate in August 1789 with a treaty with the Creek people and asked for the senators' advice as well as their consent to the treaty. Because some senators felt uncomfortable discussing the treaty in the presence of the President, they instead referred it to a committee for study. Washington then left the Senate, departing, wrote Senator William Maclay, "with a discontented air." Although he returned later to watch the Senate debate, amend, and ratify the treaty, it was the last time that any President formally sought the advice of the Senate.

The Senate was a quiet and formal body. Its members dressed in powdered wigs, lace, and velvet. For its first five years, the Senate conducted its business in private. Not until 1794 was a gallery built for the public and the press.

The House of Representatives

The House of Representatives was more informal. Elected by the people, the House welcomed the public and the press from the beginning. Debate was loud, and members often wore their hats inside the chamber. The House took the lead in legislative matters, especially in dealing with the nation's troubled finances and in providing a Bill of Rights.

Executive Departments

After debates that lasted through the summer of 1789, Congress established three executive departments: a Department of State to take charge of foreign affairs, a Department of the Treasury to handle the nation's finances, and a Department of War to manage the military. Congress also created the position of Attorney General to handle the government's legal matters. None of these offices was specifically called for in the Constitution.

Creation of the Judiciary

Congress then turned its attention to the judicial branch and passed the Judiciary Act of 1789, setting up the Supreme Court and

---

Cooperative Learning

Organize students into groups of four. Ask each group to discuss George Washington's reasons for taking on the enormous task of setting up a new government. Have each group choose a person to record the main points of the discussion and present them to the class. Ask each group to also choose a timekeeper who will be responsible for keeping the discussion within the allowed time frame. Call on students in random order to present the main points to the class. **L1, L2**

 ▲ THE INSPECTION OF THE FIRST U.S. COINS by John W. Dunsmore, 1914 The half disme [dime] was the first coin struck by the United States government in July 1792. **What cabinet department was created to handle the government's legal matters?**

lower federal courts as called for by the Constitution. President Washington quickly named the first Supreme Court justices, deliberately choosing three from Northern and three from Southern states.

The Bill of Rights

Although a majority in both the Senate and the House had supported ratification of the Constitution, the Anti-Federalist minority insisted that Congress quickly provide the Bill of Rights promised during the ratification campaign. In his Inaugural Address, Washington also urged that careful attention be given to such demands. Finally in September 1789, after much debate, Congress proposed 12 amendments. Of these, 10 were ratified by the states and added to the Constitution in 1791.

▶ MEMORIAL TANKARD

Section 1 ★ Review

Checking for Understanding

1. **Identify** Department of State, Judiciary Act of 1789.
2. **Define** cabinet, quorum.
3. **List** the characteristics that made George Washington the ideal choice to become the first President of the United States.
4. **Describe** the precedents set by Washington that are still practiced by Presidents today.

Critical Thinking

5. **Evaluating Performance** Given his lack of experience in government and politics, explain why Washington was able to head a new framework of government.

CHAPTER 7 The Federalist Era 1789–1800   207

LESSON PLAN
SECTION 2, 208–215

FOCUS

Bellringer

Prior to taking roll at the beginning of the class period, display Focus Activity Transparency 23 on the overhead projector and assign the accompanying Focus Activity Sheet.

Objectives

Point out the objectives on this page to students in previewing the section content.

Motivating Activity

Read aloud the following quotation by Alexander Hamilton, Secretary to the Treasury:

"The support of government—the support of troops for the common defense—the payment of the public debt, are the true final causes for raising money."

Then have the students complete one of the following incomplete statements:
1. I agree with Alexander Hamilton's assessment because . . . .
2. I disagree with Hamilton's assessment because . . . .

Ask students to look for arguments and evidence that support or refute their views as they read Section 2.

Did You Know?

According to the U.S. Constitution, only Congress can impose tariffs. The Tariff of 1789 placed import taxes on commodities such as hemp, molasses, steel, and nails.

SECTION 2

Solving National Problems

Setting the Scene

Section Focus

The United States needed money to pay its war debts and to finance national growth. Raising these funds was the huge but vital task of Secretary of the Treasury Alexander Hamilton. His plans would bring financial stability to the new government. The plans also rekindled debate over the amount of power exercised by the national government.

Objectives

After studying this section, you should be able to
★ discuss Hamilton's financial program for the United States and the opposition to it.
★ describe the problems settlers faced during western expansion.

Key Terms

tariff, protective tariff, revenue tariff, bond, excise tax, enumerated power, implied power, suffrage

◄ UNITED STATES GOLD QUARTER EAGLE, 1796

*I*f the United States were to survive, the new government had to be able to pay its way. All members in both houses of Congress agreed that as soon as possible the federal government should begin to collect **tariffs,** or taxes on imports.

A tariff law was not passed, though, until July 1789 because some sections of the nation wanted a **protective tariff**—a high tax on imports to protect their products from foreign competition—while they opposed protection for goods produced in other sections. For example, the South wanted a high tariff on imported hemp, which was used in making rope, to protect its own hemp crop. New England opposed this because it would cost more to rig ships. New England, in turn, wanted a high tariff to protect its rum distilleries, while the South preferred to import rum directly from Jamaica.

The tariff of 1789 represented a compromise between the South and New England. Representatives to Congress from both sections of the country dropped their demands for protection and agreed to a **revenue tariff**, a low tax on imports designed to provide income for the government rather than protection for private business. Although there were a few exceptions, tariffs on imports averaged between 5 percent and 8 percent.

■ Hamilton's Program

Most of the money raised by the tariff was needed to pay off the $54 million national debt. The United States owed $12 million to France and the Netherlands for loans made during and after the Revolutionary War. The Continental Congress also had borrowed more than $40 million from

208   UNIT 3 Launching the Republic: 1789–1824

Classroom Resources for SECTION 2

Teacher's Classroom Resources
- Reproducible Lesson Plan
- Reteaching Activity 7-2
- Chapter 7 Primary and Secondary Source Readings
- Section Quiz

Multimedia
- Section Focus Transparency 23
- Chapter 7 Map Transparency
- Testmaker
- Student Self-Test Software
- The American People: Fabric of a Nation
- A Geographic Perspective on American History

individual Americans by selling them **bonds,** or certificates that promised repayment with interest. In addition, the government felt responsible for paying soldiers and army suppliers as the Continental Congress had promised. Finally, the individual states owed money totaling $25 million.

A Strong Federal Hand

In the debate over federal finances, the dominant figure was 33-year-old Alexander Hamilton. An aide to General Washington during the American Revolution, Hamilton had now been chosen by Washington to be secretary of the treasury. A poor man who married into a wealthy family, Hamilton believed in a strong government that favored prosperous merchants and large landowners. He had grown to distrust small farmers and laborers and expressed this view in writing:

> *All communities divide themselves into the few and the many. The first are the rich and well-born, the other the mass of the people. . . . The people are turbulent and changing; they seldom judge or determine right.*

When Congress asked Hamilton to prepare a financial plan, his proposals reflected his attitudes about wealth, power, and government. In a two-part *Report on the Public Credit* and a *Report on Manufactures*, he convinced Congress to pass a series of laws in 1790 and 1791. His recommendations, however, produced conflict and controversy.

Hamilton believed it was vital to the nation that the government have enough income to operate, pay the interest on the national debt, and gradually reduce the debt itself. So, in addition to the tariff, Hamilton proposed an **excise tax** on American whiskey. An excise tax is a tax paid by the manufacturer of a product and passed on to those who buy the product. In 1791 Congress approved Hamilton's proposal by enacting an excise tax on whiskey.

Paying Debts in Full

In dealing with the national debt, Hamilton proposed that foreign creditors be paid at once. As long as the United States owed money to other nations, he argued, it could not be truly independent. Congress responded by repaying France and the Netherlands by 1796.

Hamilton believed that the domestic debt also should be paid in full, even though the value of the bonds issued by the Continental Congress had fallen in value to as little as 20 cents on the dollar. Hamilton argued that in paying these bonds in full, the United States would tell its citizens and the world that its promises were good. After much debate, Congress passed the Funding Bill in 1790.

Hamilton also proposed that the federal government pay the states' debts. The states had fought for the entire nation, he argued, so the cost of their help during the Revolution should be assumed by the national government. Hamilton believed that federal

Visualizing History ▲ **ALEXANDER HAMILTON** Educated at King's College, Alexander Hamilton served Washington during the Revolutionary War and married into a rich and powerful New York family. Hamilton later served as Washington's secretary of the treasury. **What did he propose to make the nation wealthier?**

CHAPTER 7 The Federalist Era 1789–1800

CHAPTER 7 SECTION 2

Independent Practice

Vocabulary Write the following terms on the chalkboard. Ask students to work with partners to locate the definitions of the words in the dictionary.
a. tariff (import tax on goods)
b. principal (of a debt) (the sum borrowed on which interest is paid)
c. interest (a charge for borrowed money)
d. capital (sum) (accumulated money)

Then challenge students to study the word origin of *tariff*. (from the Arabic *tariff*, meaning "notification" or "information") Ask students to discuss how the origin reflects the present-day usage. (The origin reflects the fact that people are notified or informed of a schedule of taxes.) **L1, LEP**

Did You Know?

Private investors purchased 80 percent of the stock of the first Bank of the United States and named 20 of its 25 directors.

Visualizing History Philadelphia was the capital of the United States from 1790 to 1800 and the nation's financial center until about 1836.
Answer to Caption: He said it was unconstitutional because it was not among the enumerated or implied powers of Congress.

 ▲ **THE FIRST BANK** The Bank of the United States was built on Third Street in Philadelphia. *On what grounds did Madison oppose the Bank?*

payment of state debts would give the states a strong commitment to the success of the central government. Congress agreed and in 1790 passed the Assumption Act.

The National Bank

A key element of Hamilton's proposals was that the federal government establish a national bank modeled on the Bank of England. The bank would be a place for the federal government to deposit its tax receipts, as well as a place where tax revenues and private deposits could be used for large loans to government and to businesses.

Most important, the proposed bank would issue paper money backed by gold and silver in the bank's vaults. The public could have confidence in this currency because it could be exchanged for coins on demand.

Hamilton believed that the federal government should encourage development of American industries. He contended that industrial growth would make the country wealthier, because manufacturing often yielded higher profits than agriculture. Industrial growth would also encourage the immigration of skilled laborers. He proposed protective tariffs and government aid to new or expanding businesses. Although Congress did not act on this part of Hamilton's program, later events would prove that his vision was a clear one.

On the whole, Hamilton's program had immediate success in restoring the credit of the United States. By 1792, for example, bonds that had sold at a discount just four years earlier were selling for 120 percent to 125 percent of face value.

There was another, more personal, motive behind Hamilton's proposals. Because he believed in government by the wealthy and distrusted common people, his plans were intended to enlist the "rich and well-born" to support the federal government. He hoped to make such people personally interested in its survival. Although most of his proposals were enacted by Congress, the debate over many of them became bitter and divisive.

Cooperative Learning

To review the problems in the West, group students into teams of four, and appoint a team leader for each group. Assign the three other team members in each group one of the following topics: the Native Americans and their defeat at the Battle of Fallen Timbers, the Whiskey Rebellion, and the settlement of the West in the late 1700s. Allow team members 15 minutes to study and summarize the key concepts of their topics and teach them to the members of their teams. Have team leaders make outlines of the key concepts that each group member teaches. **L1, L2**

CHAPTER 7
SECTION 2

■ Opposition to Hamilton's Program

Despite its merits, Alexander Hamilton's program encountered a great deal of opposition. Much of the opposition was led by Thomas Jefferson, Washington's secretary of state. These tensions between Hamilton and Jefferson involved a personal struggle for power in Washington's cabinet. In addition, their conflict also reflected larger differences in the vision each man had for the nation's future.

The self-made Hamilton called democracy "poison" and characterized the general public as selfish, unreasonable, and violent. He believed that a powerful central government was necessary to keep law and order. Also, he wanted to reduce the power of the states.

Thomas Jefferson

Jefferson, born to wealth and social position, believed that if people were given the opportunity, they would be decent and reasonable. A defender of liberty, Jefferson believed in a minimum of government and favored power at the local level. Because Jefferson could not block Hamilton in the executive branch, the conflict was played out in Congress, where Jefferson's ally, James Madison, represented Virginia.

James Madison

Led by Madison, Hamilton's critics attacked the Funding Bill as unfair to the original purchasers of the bonds issued by the Continental Congress—"the warworn soldiers" and their "widows and orphans," one anti-Hamilton newspaper called them.

Linking Across Time

In every period, one or two architectural styles seem to be favored over others. In the early years of the Republic, architects borrowed features from ancient times. Greek and Roman columns, semicircular domes, and round domes were especially popular. Jefferson's Monticello was built in this neoclassical style.

Life of the Times

Frontier Weddings

Weddings were major social events on the frontier. Often a justice of the peace would hear the couple's vows. This union was followed with festivities orchestrated by neighbors and friends that lasted for days.

The party began at the bride's home when her father placed a jug of whiskey on his doorstep. Male guests positioned themselves one mile from the house, then raced to seize the jug. The winner carried the jug to the groom, who took the first drink. Next, the groom and his party traveled to the bride's home for a daylong party. Around 9 o'clock in the evening, the female guests carried the bride to a bed in her parents' cabin. Later the male guests brought the groom to the bed. Guests would continue their party outside the cabin, often looking in on the newlyweds.

The next morning the couple led a procession of the guests to the cabin of the groom's parents. Another daylong party, or "infare," followed. On the third day the new couple moved into their own cabin. In the evening a "shivaree," or housewarming, took place. Guests surrounded the cabin armed with noise-making devices. On a designated signal, the woods erupted in a din of noise. The newlyweds opened their home for yet another party that generally ended near dawn. This party marked the end of the wedding celebration.

▼ WEDDING PARTY IN KENTUCKY

CHAPTER 7 The Federalist Era 1789–1800   211

Teaching Life of the Times

Eating and dancing were favorite pastimes at weddings and at other types of neighborly get-togethers. The food was usually very simple, and may have consisted of bread and butter, fried pork or other meat, coffee, and sauces made of wild fruits. The dances were held almost anywhere, such as schoolrooms, cabins, or just a clearing near a cabin. People wore their Sunday best, and men, women, and children came to enjoy themselves. Discuss how weddings and other get-togethers served the frontier people as a means of recreation and a way to exchange news and information.

Critical Thinking

Analyzing Viewpoints Divide the class into two groups and have them conduct an informal debate. Ask one group to attack Hamilton's economic plan for assuming the national debt, and have the other group defend the plan. As students prepare, have them take the following questions into consideration:

1. What group(s) and section(s) would be helped by the plan? hurt by the plan?
2. What other viable solutions could have been used? **L2**

CHAPTER 7 SECTION 2

Map Study Using Maps

Answer: near Fort Miami and the Maumee River

Skills Practice

Ask students in which general direction Wayne and St. Clair traveled in their campaigns against the Native Americans (north)

Food of the Times

European settlers brought the custom of making ice cream to the United States in the late 1700s. (The dish was invented in Paris.) Ice cream did not become popular with Americans until Thomas Jefferson, George Washington, and James Madison served it to their guests.

- GTV: *The American People: Fabric of a Nation*

Side 2, Chapter 2
Title: *Between Worlds*
Subject: For Native Americans, a shrinking realm

See GTV Guide page 60 for complete lesson plan.

As time had passed, the original holders of these bonds, facing hard times and fearing that they would never be paid, had sold their bonds to speculators at a discount. Madison was outraged that New England merchants who had paid as little as $10 for a $100 bond now would receive full value. In addition, because federal funds would pay these speculators, tax money from the South would end up in the pockets of New Englanders.

Settling the Dispute

Madison's objection to the Assumption Bill was based on similar sectional concerns. Most of the Southern states had already paid their debts in full and did not want their taxes used to pay the debts of the Northern states. This major dispute was settled only when Hamilton, Madison, and Jefferson struck a deal. Southerners in Congress would vote for Hamilton's Assumption Bill. In return, the nation's capital would move from New York to Philadelphia for a period of 10 years and then to a new federal city on the Potomac River between Maryland and Virginia.

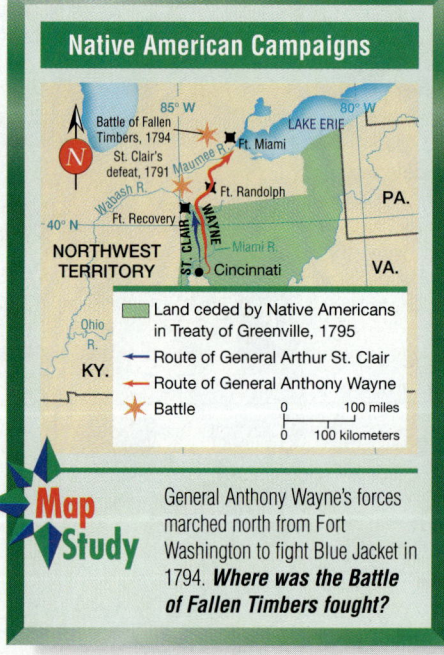

Map Study

General Anthony Wayne's forces marched north from Fort Washington to fight Blue Jacket in 1794. **Where was the Battle of Fallen Timbers fought?**

A Question of Power

When Congress debated the bill to establish a national bank, Madison attacked it on constitutional grounds. Congress had no power to establish a bank, he argued, because it was not among the **enumerated powers**, or powers mentioned specifically, in the Constitution. Nor was it an **implied power**, a power that, while not directly stated in the Constitution, is suggested and does allow Congress to exercise its stated powers. If the federal government established a national bank, he feared there would be no limits to federal power.

Despite Madison's arguments, Congress passed the Bank Bill by an almost two-to-one majority. Washington hesitated to act, however, realizing that whether he signed this controversial bill or vetoed it, he would be setting an important precedent. Instead, he asked Attorney General Edmund Randolph and Secretary of State Jefferson, both fellow Virginians, for written opinions on the constitutionality of a national bank. Each opposed it using the same argument as Madison—that it was an overextension of federal power.

Washington passed Jefferson's and Randolph's opinions on to Hamilton. Working day and night, Hamilton composed a reply that convinced President Washington he should sign the Bank Bill. In a classic statement of implied powers, Hamilton argued that because the bank's functions were among the powers given Congress, the Constitution gave Congress the right to choose any legal means to carry out those functions. In 1791 the Bank of the United States was established.

■ Problems in the West

In addition to its financial problems, the new government faced continuing concerns about the western territories. The most immediate cause for alarm was relations with Native American nations. Armed to defend their lands, encouraged by the British and Spanish, and unimpressed by the federal government, Native Americans battled settlers over frontier land. Thousands of people were killed. Washington hoped to improve relations, but the bloodshed had to stop.

212 UNIT 3 Launching the Republic: 1789–1824

Cultural Diversity

Settlers to North America brought a variety of customs with them. By studying the origin of the names they gave those customs, students can discover the cultural origins of each. *Shivaree,* the noisy serenade to newly married couples, is derived from a French word with the same meaning—*charivari.* The first part of the word is derived from a Latin word meaning "headache." The last part of the word comes from *Infare,* which means a reception for newly-wed couples. It is based on the Old English word meaning "to go in."

South of the Ohio River, treaties were signed with the Cherokee in 1791 and the Chickamauga in 1794—and the Creek asked the federal government for protection from the settlers. Once relations in the southern regions had been stabilized, the bluegrass meadows of Kentucky and the rich bottomlands along the rivers of Tennessee began to draw more settlers. Population increases enabled Kentucky to gain admission to the Union in 1792 and Tennessee to do so in 1796.

St. Clair Defeated

After a military expedition into the Northwest Territory was badly beaten by Miami Chief Little Turtle, Washington ordered the governor of the territory, General Arthur St. Clair, to the area with the largest force the West had ever seen—2,300 regular troops plus several companies of militia. As St. Clair moved north from Cincinnati, desertion and disease reduced his army to 1,400. Underestimating his enemy and rejecting the pleas of his weakened troops, St. Clair continued into Native American territory. In November 1791, near the present-day Ohio-Indiana border, he was attacked. Only 500 of his command survived one of the worst defeats in American military history.

Blue Jacket Defeated

The Native Americans demanded that all settlers north of the Ohio River leave the territory. Washington turned to General

CHAPTER 7
SECTION 2

Map Study *Using Maps*
Answer: Ohio River
Skills Practice
Ask students to identify the geographic feature along which main settlements are located. (oceans, rivers)

NATIONAL GEOGRAPHIC SOCIETY

Videodisc
- *GTV: A Geographic Perspective on American History*

Side 2, Chapter 3
Title: *Map Rap*
Subject: The growth of the United States, 1776–1867

See GTV Guide page 41 for complete lesson plan.

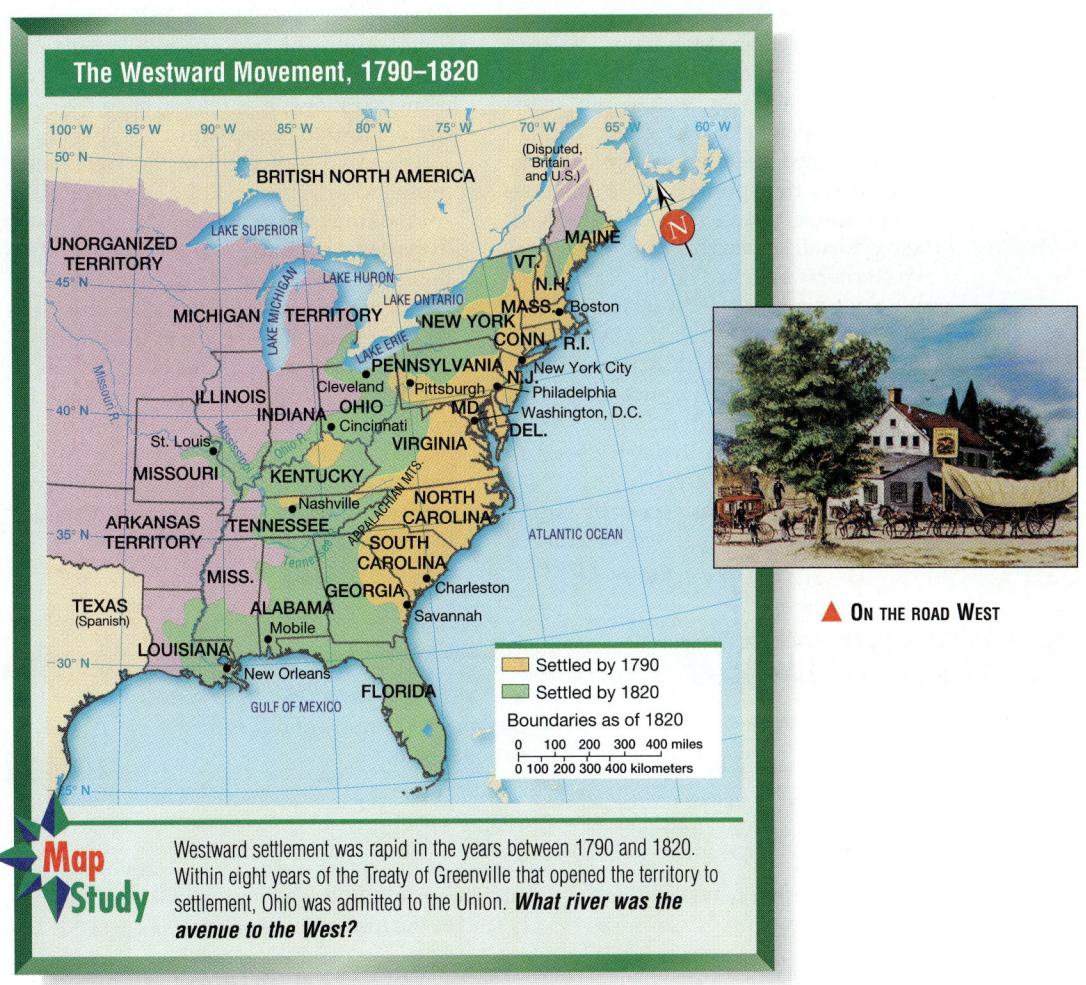

The Westward Movement, 1790–1820

▲ On the Road West

Settled by 1790
Settled by 1820
Boundaries as of 1820

Map Study Westward settlement was rapid in the years between 1790 and 1820. Within eight years of the Treaty of Greenville that opened the territory to settlement, Ohio was admitted to the Union. **What river was the avenue to the West?**

CHAPTER 7 The Federalist Era 1789–1800   213

Sidelights: Political

Controversy in the Eighteenth Century A rift between Hamilton and Jefferson developed when Jefferson, fearing Hamilton's influence with Washington, declared unconstitutional Hamilton's plan to create a central bank. Another rift occurred when Jefferson recommended Tench Coxe, an associate, for a high position in the treasury. Jefferson also sought to persuade George Washington to appoint Thomas Paine as postmaster general. This would have transferred the Post Office from Hamilton's influence to Jefferson's.

CHAPTER 7 SECTION 2

FACT or FICTION?
George Washington is the only U.S. President who led troops into a combat zone while he held the office of President.

FACT: during the 1794 Whiskey Rebellion

ASSESS

Check Understanding
Assign the Section 2 Review as homework or an in-class activity.

Evaluate
Assign the Section 2 Quiz in the TCR or use the History of a Free Nation Testmaker to create a customized quiz.

Reteach
Have students complete Reteaching Activity 7-2.

Enrich
Have students write newspaper headlines and brief editorials that reflect the conflicts created by Hamilton's central bank plan.

CLOSE
Summarize this section by holding an informal debate on whether the United States should have helped France fight the British.

Anthony Wayne, who had distinguished himself in the Revolutionary War. In August 1794, his force defeated 800 Native Americans under Shawnee Chief Blue Jacket at the Battle of Fallen Timbers. Wayne pursued his foes all the way to Fort Miami, near present-day Toledo, Ohio, a British fur post that had been supplying weapons to the Native Americans. In 1795 the Native Americans agreed to surrender most of the present-day state of Ohio. As a result, settlers flocked to the new land, and in 1803 Ohio was admitted to the Union.

The Whiskey Rebellion

While settlers and Native Americans fought, another uprising was occurring in the West. In the days before canals and railroads, Westerners did not sell their grain east of the Appalachian Mountains because wagon transportation was costly. Since a wagonload of whiskey was worth much more than a wagonload of grain, Western farmers distilled their grain into whiskey before they transported it to market. Whiskey also served as currency in the West, where gold and silver coins were scarce.

Westerners believed that Hamilton's excise tax on whiskey, first levied in 1791, was aimed directly at them. There may have been some truth to this claim. Hamilton viewed the excise tax not only as a source of revenue for the national government but also as a way to get the West to recognize federal authority.

Antitax sentiment was especially strong in western Pennsylvania, where citizens refused to pay the tax, attacked revenue officers, and burned the barns of neighbors who told authorities where stills were located. Known as the Whiskey Rebellion, this revolt was as much a challenge to law and order as Shays's Rebellion had been eight years before. The outcome of the Whiskey Rebellion under the new government, however, was very different. The Massachusetts militia had suppressed Shays without help from the nearly bankrupt Confederation government.

When the governor of Pennsylvania hesitated to take action against the Whiskey Rebellion, the federal government stepped in and crushed it. President Washington, with Hamilton at his side, personally led 12,000 militia into western Pennsylvania. Some rebellion leaders were seized and taken to Philadelphia for trial. Two were found guilty of treason, but Washington pardoned both of them. The new government had shown its strength, he felt. Now it could afford to be merciful.

The rapid settlement of the West had a profound effect on politics. Reflecting the spirit of the frontier, the new Western states extended **suffrage**, or voting rights. Because land was so plentiful in the West, the constitutions of Kentucky and Tennessee required no property qualifications for voting. All white males over 21 years of age had the franchise. The argument for extending suffrage was that any man who helped clear the land and fight Native Americans had a right to a say in the government. Like Jefferson, Westerners tended to believe in common people.

Section 2 ★ Review

Checking for Understanding
1. **Identify** Fallen Timbers, Whiskey Rebellion.
2. **Define** tariff, protective tariff, revenue tariff, bond, excise tax, enumerated power, implied power, suffrage.
3. **Describe** why protective tariffs created sectional disagreements.
4. **Explain** the purpose and function of the national bank.

Critical Thinking
5. **Predicting Outcomes** Predict why Hamilton's and Jefferson's differing views might eventually lead to the formation of political parties.

---

214 UNIT 3 Launching the Republic: 1789–1824

Answers to SECTION 2 REVIEW
1. Fallen Timbers, 214; Whiskey Rebellion, 214
2. All vocabulary words are defined in the Glossary.
3. Each section wanted a tariff to protect its products from outside competition, but each opposed protection for goods produced in other sections.
4. A depository for federal tax receipts and private deposits to be used for loans to government and businesses; would issue paper currency backed by the bank's gold and silver.
5. Answers will vary but may include: As more people come to accept Hamilton's view of strong government or Jefferson's view of limited government, they may band together to politically agitate for their view and to offer candidates for office who support their view.

Social Studies Skills

Critical Thinking Skills

Distinguishing Between Fact and Value Judgment

A fact is a statement that can be proved by evidence. This evidence can be empirical (something you can actually see or feel) or a reliable written account as in a book or document. In contrast, a value judgment is a statement that includes a person's opinions based on one's values or feelings.

At one time or another, everyone is faced with the need to make a decision based on facts and value judgments. The following guidelines will help you in distinguishing between these two kinds of statements:

a. When reading or listening to any statement, keep in mind the definitions of fact and value judgment. Could the statement be supported with evidence?

b. Which statements are you being asked to accept as fact without evidence?

Read the following statements and note how the guidelines have been applied.

1. Hamilton said in 1790 that a central bank of the United States would be "an institution of primary importance to the prosperous administration of the finances." Could this statement have been supported with evidence?

   (*No. This is a value judgment. The statement reflected Hamilton's belief that a central bank would be of primary importance, yet there was no evidence or proof to support it.*)

2. Hamilton stated that the bank and its branches would provide places where the government could deposit money obtained through taxes.

   (*This is a fact. If created, the bank would provide such places.*)

3. Madison, however, argued that the federal government had no right to establish a central bank because it was not among the enumerated powers of Congress found in the Constitution.

   (*This is a fact. Such authority was not among the powers of Congress. Evidence, therefore, supported it.*)

4. Madison stated that if the federal government were allowed to set up a central bank, there would be no limits to the power of the federal government. What evidence did Madison have to support this statement?

   (*None. He was personally against too much governmental control over the states and was, therefore, suspicious of federal power.*)

▲ CONGRESS HALL, PHILADELPHIA

Practicing the Skill

For practice in this skill, find two examples of both factual statements and value judgments or opinions of the authors in Section 1 of this chapter.

215

LESSON PLAN
Mastering Social Studies Skills

Teaching Critical Thinking Skills

Have students work in pairs to answer the following: What makes a statement a fact? What makes a statement a value judgment? What is an example of each?

Discuss student responses. Can facts be true or untrue? (Not by definition: a fact is a statement that can be proved by evidence.) Can a value judgment be true or untrue? Are some value judgments fact? (Yes, even though a value judgment is one person's feeling, it may be shown true by evidence.)

Ask students to give examples of value judgments they have made in their conversations with others. (Examples: the cafeteria food is awful; he doesn't know how to pick out clothes; our football team is the best in the country.)

Did You Know?

Alexander Hamilton believed in the strict enforcement of laws. He wrote, "It is essential to the idea of a law, that it be attended with a sanction; or, in other words, a penalty or punishment for disobedience."

Answers to SOCIAL STUDIES SKILLS

Answers taken from Section 1 will vary but may include: *Factual Statements:* "Washington's background was as plantation manager and soldier." (Page 204) "Although he headed the executive branch, Washington assumed leadership in legislative affairs as well." (Page 206) *Value Judgments:* "He knew the United States as well as any person alive." (Page 205) "The people will forget the new government before it is born." (Page 206)

LESSON PLAN
SECTION 3, 216–220

FOCUS

Bellringer
Prior to taking roll at the beginning of the class period, display Focus Activity Transparency 24 on the overhead projector and assign the accompanying Focus Activity Sheet.

Objectives
Point out the objectives on this page to students in previewing the section content.

Motivating Activity
Write the following on the chalkboard:
  Causes of French-British Rivalry—desire to be the strongest world power, to colonize the largest area, to find new markets for goods, and to rule the seas
  Then ask: Where will the French-British rivalries impact the United States? Why? (on land because both countries claim land on the American continent, on the seas because the United States sails the seas, in the trading of goods because both countries are trading partners)

Did You Know?
American public opinion toward France became sharply divided in early 1793 after French revolutionaries voted for and carried out the execution of King Louis XVI.

SECTION 3

Foreign Affairs Under Washington

Setting the Scene

Section Focus
Although an ocean away from Europe, the United States could not hope to exist in isolation, and the nation had to forge a response to overseas pressures. Treaties improved relations, but the end of Washington's presidency found the United States facing renewed problems with other nations.

Objectives
After studying this section, you should be able to
★ describe the effects of the French Revolution on the United States.
★ explain the importance of the Jay and Pinckney treaties.

Key Term
privateer

◀ GLASSWARE HONORING PRESIDENT WASHINGTON

Shortly after Washington was inaugurated in 1789, the French Revolution began. Americans sympathized with the French revolutionaries because they were demanding the same rights that Americans had won a few years earlier. The French "Declaration of the Rights of Man and the Citizen" proclaimed that all "men are born and remain free and equal in rights," and declared the rights of "liberty, property, security and resistance to oppression." The French revolutionaries readily acknowledged their debt to the United States in the expression and defense of these rights.

In this country, popular enthusiasm for France became almost a madness. Americans sang French revolutionary songs such as the "Marseillaise," erected "liberty poles" and wore "liberty caps," and even took to calling each other Citizen and Citizeness instead of Mr. and Mrs. In New York, King Street was renamed Liberty Street, and in Boston, Royal Exchange Alley became Equality Lane.

Cheers for France were often joined with damnation of Britain. Not only was the memory of the American Revolution still strong, but there was resentment because of the British refusal to give up the fur posts and to stop arming the Native Americans of the Northwest.

■ America's European Problems

When France and Great Britain went to war in 1793, the French expected American aid. According to treaties signed in 1778 between France and the American revolutionaries, France would have been justified in asking for American military assistance.

216 UNIT 3 Launching the Republic: 1789–1824

Classroom Resources for SECTION 3

Teacher's Classroom Resources
- Reproducible Lesson Plan
- Reteaching Activity 7-3
- Section Quiz

Multimedia
- Section Focus Transparency 24
- Chapter 7 U.S. History and Art Transparency
- Testmaker
- Student Self-Test Software

They did not go that far, but they hoped to recruit American volunteers for the French army and navy and to use American ports as bases to attack British merchant ships.

France's expectations placed the United States in a difficult position. Three-fourths of America's trade was with Britain, and tariff duties on British products provided the bulk of federal revenues. Because the British fleet controlled the seas, war would have ended foreign trade and meant bankruptcy for the new government.

Proclamation of Neutrality

When the war began, Washington called a cabinet meeting to discuss whether he should issue a declaration of neutrality. All cabinet members supported neutrality, even though Jefferson did so reluctantly. Jefferson, who had served as American minister to France and greatly respected the French people, believed that a formal declaration of neutrality would help Britain, and so he cautioned Washington against it. Hamilton, who despised the democracy of the French Revolution, argued that Britain was more to be feared than France, and he urged Washington to announce America's neutrality. Again, Hamilton's arguments prevailed, and in April 1793, Washington issued a Proclamation of Neutrality. The President declared that the United States would be "friendly and impartial." He warned that Americans who helped either side would be denied the protection of the government and would be subject to punishment.

A Visit from the French Minister

The arrival of a new French minister, Citizen Edmond Genet (zhuh•NAY), put Washington's neutrality proclamation to the test. Genet traveled to the capital at Philadelphia. Along the way he was invited to so many pro-French celebrations that his journey became a triumphant procession. He arranged to place American crews on French **privateers**, or armed private ships, and offered George Rogers Clark a commission in the French army. Arriving confidently in Philadelphia, Genet demanded that the United States advance him money to pay his new recruits.

▲ STORMING THE BASTILLE The French Revolution of 1789, in which the French people overthrew their king to establish a republic, found most Americans sympathetic to a cause that seemed much like their own. As the French Revolution became more radical, however, American opinion divided sharply. **What action did the United States government take when war began between France and Britain?**

CHAPTER 7 SECTION 3

Fact or Fiction?

Despite the American victory in the Revolutionary War, Britain occupied parts of the United States for 13 years after the peace treaty was signed.

FACT: Britain occupied American land, including forts around Lake Champlain and at Oswegatchie, Oswego, and Niagara in New York State and Detroit and Michilimackinac (present-day Mackinac) in Michigan until 1796, 13 years after the peace treaty was signed.

Visualizing History

In the 1790s, Philadelphia was the most important U.S. port and the largest U.S. city. Philadelphia had an informally organized stock market, the main office of the First Bank of the United States, the first general hospital, and an important medical school.

Answer to Caption: After issuing orders forbidding neutral ships to trade with France, Britain seized hundreds of American vessels and confiscated their cargoes.

Did You Know?

The best-selling American books of 1794 and 1795 were Benjamin Franklin's *Autobiography* and Thomas Paine's *Age of Reason*.

▲ **The Arch Street Ferry** by William Birch This engraving shows a busy trade center in Philadelphia. **How did Britain threaten American trade?**

The French minister's efforts to involve the United States in war were soon thwarted. Washington received him with icy politeness. Hamilton used all his influence against Genet. Even Jefferson flatly refused Genet's demands and came to dislike him intensely. Finally, an outraged Washington demanded that France recall the diplomat. Genet, however, begged to remain in the United States, because changes in France's government caused him to fear for his life. Washington granted the request, and Genet remained in America.

British Provocation

Great Britain also tested American foreign policy. When the British realized that the new federal government was more powerful than its predecessor, they at last consented to send a minister to the United States. Once war began in Europe, however, they issued a series of orders forbidding neutral ships to trade with the French West Indies, to carry French West Indian produce, or to carry any weapons or food to France. These restrictions fell most heavily on the United States, which had the largest neutral merchant marine. British warships seized hundreds of American vessels and confiscated their cargoes, a clear violation of the rights of a neutral nation under international law.

In the spring of 1794, these provocations, coupled with news of British support for Native Americans in the Northwest Territory, pushed Congress to the brink of war. Hamilton urged Washington to make one last effort to come to a peaceful solution to the disputes by sending John Jay, Chief Justice of the Supreme Court, as a special envoy to Great Britain.

■ Treaties with Britain and Spain

The British were willing to sign a treaty. A war with the United States would only make it harder to carry on the war with France, and the United States was Britain's

UNIT 3 Launching the Republic: 1789–1824

Sidelights: The French Revolution

After the American Revolution, the French sought major changes in their own nation. In many ways French society of the late 1700s was feudal. By law, people belonged to one of three classes, or estates. A person's social status, political rights, and economic privileges were determined by which estate he or she belonged to. Many people in all of the estates were dissatisfied with their positions because of unequal privileges. This and the heavy burden of taxation placed on the poor were major causes of the French Revolution.

best market. Jay got rather poor treaty terms, however, partly because Alexander Hamilton committed a serious mistake: he let the British know Jay's instructions.

Treaty with Britain

The Jay Treaty was completed late in 1794. The British promised once again to evacuate their forts in American territory if the United States let them keep the fur trade with the Native Americans. American ships were allowed into ports in the British Isles on the same terms as British ships in American ports. The treaty permitted the United States a very limited trade with the British West Indies but none with Canadian ports. On the whole, it seemed that the British gave fewer concessions than they received. There was no promise that the violation of American neutral rights at sea would cease. Nor was there any assurance that British agents would stop giving weapons to Native Americans.

When the news of the Jay Treaty became known, there was a tremendous outcry against it. Jay's effigy was hanged in city squares. Hamilton, speaking in support of the treaty in New York City, was stoned by a mob. Despite the public's outrage, the Senate narrowly ratified the treaty by a two-thirds vote, 20 to 10. Dissatisfied with the treaty and dismayed by public reaction, Washington reluctantly signed it. Resistance continued in the House, where opponents of the treaty refused to vote funds necessary to put it into effect. Because a growing fear that the alternative to an unsatisfactory treaty was war with Britain, a 50-to-49 vote to release the funds resulted.

Treaty with Spain

When the treaty's terms became public, Spain's government suspected that a secret agreement had been made providing British support for an American attack on Spanish New Orleans and Florida. Thomas Pinckney was sent to Spain to try to settle long-standing differences between the two nations. In 1795 the Pinckney Treaty granted the United States all the concessions it had been seeking since the end of the Revolutionary War—free navigation of the Mississippi River, the right of deposit at New Orleans, and acknowledgment of the United States's southern boundary at the 31st parallel and western boundary at the Mississippi.

Washington Steps Down

Washington had wanted to retire after his first term as President, saying he would rather dig ditches than continue. He agreed to serve a second term only after leaders, including both Jefferson and Hamilton, urged him to do so. In 1792, as in 1789, he received no opposition in the electoral college. Washington, however, enjoyed his second term even less than his first.

Jefferson Resigns from the Cabinet

Forced to choose in the bitter conflict between Jefferson and Hamilton, Washington continued to favor Hamilton. When Jefferson resigned from the cabinet in 1793, Washington was harshly attacked by Jefferson's supporters. By the end of his second term, Washington had become more and more sensitive to criticism. He confessed that he wished to

◀ CHIEF JUSTICE JOHN JAY

CHAPTER 7
SECTION 3

Independent Practice

Constructing a Flowchart Have students construct vertical flowcharts to show the causes, events, and effects of the Jay and Pinckney treaties. **L2**

FACT or FICTION?

John Jay favored the continuation of slavery in the United States.

FICTION: Jay opposed slavery. As governor of New York State, he signed into law a 1799 law gradually ending it in that state.

Did You Know?

Alexander Hamilton wrote most of George Washington's famous "Farewell Address." The President never delivered it but had it printed in a newspaper.

Did You Know?

Before the American Revolution, George Washington bought expensive London-made clothing. As President, Washington would attend receptions wearing yellow gloves, a black velvet suit with gold buckles, and a cocked hat with ostrich plumes.

Critical Thinking

Analyzing Viewpoints In his "Farewell Address," George Washington wrote: " 'Tis our true policy to steer clear of permanent alliances, with any portion of the foreign world. . . . There can be no greater error than to expect or calculate upon real favors from nation to nation." Ask students to write a paragraph analyzing why Washington thought the United States should avoid permanent foreign alliances and why he thought the nation would be able to avoid such alliances. **L2**

escape these attacks made "in such exaggerated and indecent terms as could scarce be applied to a Nero, a notorious defaulter, or even a common pickpocket."

Farewell Address

The last major act of Washington's presidency was his Farewell Address, which was published in the *American Daily Advertiser* on September 17, 1796. This address was Washington's explanation for not seeking a third term as President. Even more important, he gave the young republic his best advice on the conduct of politics and foreign affairs.

Upon returning to his beloved Mount Vernon, Washington had every reason to feel proud of his administration's achievements. Most of the difficulties of the Confederation had been overcome, and the credit of the United States was as solid as any European nation's.

The suppression of the Whiskey Rebellion had demonstrated the power of the new government. The major demands of the West had been fulfilled. In the difficult situation presented by war between France and Britain, Washington had steered a course that kept the United States prosperous and at peace.

▲ **GEORGE WASHINGTON'S FAREWELL** Washington, feeling that the government had been safely launched, refused nomination for a third term. The poster (above) and the painting (right) celebrate Washington's success in office. *What advice did he give Americans in his Farewell Address?*

Section 3 ★ Review

Checking for Understanding

1. **Identify** Declaration of the Rights of Man and the Citizen, Proclamation of Neutrality, Citizen Edmond Genet, Jay Treaty, Pinckney Treaty, Farewell Address.
2. **Define** privateer.
3. **Describe** the activities of Citizen Genet that caused President Washington to demand his recall.
4. **Show** how Great Britain's actions against the United States nearly resulted in war.

Critical Thinking

5. **Supporting Positions** Washington warned of political divisions at home and entanglements abroad. Cite three events in American history that prove his warnings were not heeded.

History AND Science CONNECTIONS

Planning Washington, D.C.

By using inspiration, imagination, and his skill in geometry, engineer Pierre Charles L'Enfant created the design for a national capital unlike any other. When L'Enfant, who fought in the Revolution, heard that Congress was planning a new national capital, he quickly offered his services. President Washington hired L'Enfant, and the President himself negotiated purchase from the farmers who owned the land where the capital was to rise.

Although L'Enfant's design was soon modified, his basic plan allowed a spacious, modern city to develop. He envisioned a rationally laid-out metropolis that would embody the new nation's republican ideals, with wide boulevards connecting the branches of government, national monuments, parks, and entry gates.

L'Enfant began by choosing the spots for the Capitol and President's house. The Congress building became the central point in a square grid of streets occupying the terrain between the Potomac and Anacostia rivers. The grid was

▲ WASHINGTON AND L'ENFANT AT CAPITOL SITE, 1791

slashed by avenues that radiated from the capitol hill like spokes on a wheel. These avenues provided a direct route to different parts of the city. At strategic spots, L'Enfant's unique blend of topography and geometric symmetry called for circular intersections to join three or more avenues.

◀ THE CAPITOL, 1824

Making the Science Connection

1. What geometric forms did L'Enfant use in planning the design of Washington, D.C.?
2. What are the advantages of locating a capital in a planned city? What might be some disadvantages?

Linking Past and Present

3. What kinds of geometric shapes are used in the design of modern government buildings?

CHAPTER 7 CONNECTIONS

Teaching Making Connections

Because of disagreements with government planners and massive cost overruns, L'Enfant was dismissed in 1792 and his plans for the national capital were shelved. Some 100 years later, his original designs were readopted as guidelines for all future developments in the city. Ask students why L'Enfant's plan for the capital proved to be a success. (The capital is accessible and has provided a logical arrangement for key structures.)

Did You Know?

French-born American engineer Pierre Charles L'Enfant completed the plan for the capital city of Washington in 1791, but Congress paid him only $3,800 of the $95,500 he thought was due to him. L'Enfant died in poverty.

Answers to CONNECTIONS

1. squares, circles, angles, triangles, rectangles.
2. the ability to site important buildings and monuments for best effect and to create an overall sense of order and dignity.
3. Answers will vary but may include rectangles and circles.

LESSON PLAN
SECTION 4, 222–225

FOCUS

Bellringer
Prior to taking roll at the beginning of the class period, display Focus Activity Transparency 25 on the overhead projector and assign the accompanying Focus Activity Sheet.

Objectives
Point out the objectives on this page to students in previewing the section content.

Motivating Activity
Ask students to discuss how they would feel if they had no choice in their everyday lives—they could only buy one style of clothes, for example. Explain that in a democratic society, people are theoretically able to make choices that affect their lives.

Then write "Republican Party" and "Democratic Party" on the chalkboard. Ask students why people like to have a choice in voting for either party. (represent different points of view and different platforms)

Did You Know?
In 1796, for the first time in the United States an election was held in which the winning candidate for President represented one party and the Vice President another.

SECTION 4

President John Adams

Setting the Scene

Section Focus
It was inevitable that a nation of people holding different political philosophies would establish political parties. Foreign affairs provided further reasons for partisan politics. Led by a new President, the government would soon have to deal with problems on foreign soil as well as suspected treason at home.

Objectives
After studying this section, you should be able to
★ explain why political parties arose in the United States.
★ describe the problems John Adams encountered as President.

Key Terms
nonpartisan, nullification

◀ FROM A CARTOON ABOUT THE XYZ AFFAIR

The origins of America's two-party political system are found in the conflicts within Washington's cabinet and in congressional debates over Hamilton's financial program. Shortly after Washington took office, it became clear that Hamilton had the President's ear on almost every government matter. To counter Hamilton's strong influence, Madison and Jefferson began to gather support for their views both inside the government and outside.

■ Formation of Parties

Washington's first administration was **nonpartisan**—that is, there were no permanent divisions based on politics or causes. Differences arose over specific issues, which were hotly debated, but harmony returned after a cause triumphed or lost. Jefferson's resignation from Washington's cabinet, however, signaled a formal split in the ranks of the nation's political leadership.

The Republicans
After resigning, Jefferson openly allied with Madison, who was already opposing the Washington administration in Congress, to form what they called the "Republican" interest. They chose this name to suggest that they were defending freedom and self-government from the antidemocratic influence of Hamilton.

The Federalists
Hamilton's supporters took the name "Federalists," the label used by supporters of the Constitution during the ratification

---

Classroom Resources for SECTION 4

Teacher's Classroom Resources
- Reproducible Lesson Plan
- Reteaching Activity 7-4
- Chapter 7 Primary and Secondary Source Readings
- Spanish Summaries and Glossary
- Chapter 7 Enrichment Activity
- Chapter 7 Performance Assessment Activity
- Section Quiz

Multimedia
- Section Focus Transparency 25
- Vocabulary Puzzlemaker
- Testmaker
- Student Self-Test Software

campaign. This maneuver was intended to imply that the Republicans were anti-Federalists and that they did not support the Constitution.

The Federalists included people who stood to profit from Hamilton's financial program—creditors, merchants, and bondholders. Federalists gained support from wage earners in the shipping industry and from residents of states that benefited when the federal government assumed state debts. Reflecting Hamilton's distrust of the people, the Federalists hoped to put the direction of government into the hands of the "rich, well-born, and able." The Republicans' strength was among Southern planters, subsistence farmers of the backcountry, and "mechanics" such as carpenters, shoemakers, and masons. Republican leaders advocated limiting the power of the central government.

Election of 1796

As the presidential election of 1796 drew near, both sides planned strategy. Under Madison's leadership, the Republicans tried to gain public support by opposing the unpopular Jay Treaty. Washington gave the Federalists an election advantage by delaying his retirement announcement. The Republicans were unwilling to offer any candidate to oppose a national hero.

When Washington withdrew two months before the election, the Federalists selected Vice President John Adams to run. The Republicans countered with a candidate of equal national reputation and sectional strength—Thomas Jefferson. In selecting its candidate for Vice President, each party tried to achieve geographic balance between its candidates. The Federalists chose Thomas Pinckney of South Carolina, who was currently popular because of his successful treaty negotiations with Spain. The Republicans balanced Jefferson, the Virginian, with Aaron Burr of New York.

Because the Framers of the Constitution had not anticipated political parties, the nation's first partisan presidential election was a confusing contest. The Constitution provided that the candidate with the highest number of votes in the electoral college would become President and the runner-up, Vice President. Therefore, some New England Federalist electors left Pinckney off their ballots in order to make sure that Adams would get the highest vote. The result was that Adams, a Federalist, was elected President with 71 electoral votes, while Jefferson, a Republican, became Vice President with 68.

■ Adams in Office

John Adams had spent most of his life in public service. An early leader of the revolutionary movement in Massachusetts, he was a prominent member of the First and Second Continental Congresses. During the war, he served as envoy to France and Holland and was a representative at the Treaty of Paris. He later became the nation's first minister to Great Britain. Under Washington, he served two terms as Vice President. In each office, he served with distinction.

Visualizing History

▲ **ADAMS IN OFFICE** John Adams's influence in the Constitutional Convention helped to produce the strong office of the President. *As President, Adams faced opposition from what political party?*

CHAPTER 7 The Federalist Era 1789–1800

Cooperative Learning

Organize students into groups of four or five. Give each group the topic "John Adams as President." Using one piece of paper per group, have each person take a turn writing a statement about Adams's presidency. Have each group critique and change statements that do not relate to the topic. Then have each group share its statements with the class. Discuss any missing information. **LEP, L1**

American Portraits

Benjamin Banneker
1731–1806

Born into a free family in Maryland, Benjamin Banneker was largely self-educated. When his father died, Banneker sold the family farm and devoted the rest of his life to mathematics and natural science.

Banneker's skill in mathematics prompted Thomas Jefferson to secure him a job surveying the land for the new national capital at Washington, D.C. Legend has it that when the French architect Pierre L'Enfant quit the project and took his detailed maps with him, Banneker reproduced L'Enfant's plans from memory.

Later, Banneker wrote and published a most successful almanac. His picture on the cover proclaimed it as the work of an African American. Banneker's efforts and his achievements brought attention to racial injustice in a land not yet willing to grant him rights of citizenship.

Tension with France

When Adams took office, he inherited the dispute with France. French disappointment over Washington's Neutrality Proclamation turned to hostility after the Jay Treaty. During the election of 1796, the French minister to the United States actively campaigned against Adams. When Charles C. Pinckney was sent as minister to France in 1796, he was ordered out of the country. Meanwhile, the French navy started to prey on American shipping.

Adams was anxious to make peace. Immediately after taking office, he sent envoys to Paris to negotiate a treaty. When the Americans arrived, they were approached by three representatives of Charles Maurice de Talleyrand, the French minister of foreign affairs. The agents demanded that a bribe be paid to Talleyrand.

An Undeclared War

Unwilling to pay the bribe, the Americans broke off negotiations. Because their reports labeled Talleyrand's agents as X, Y, and Z, this situation came to be known as the XYZ Affair, and it produced an outburst of popular anger against France. Adams was cheered in Congress when he declared that he would never send another minister without France assuring its respect to "the representative of a great, free, powerful, and independent nation." The slogan of the day became: "Millions for defense, but not one cent for tribute." Congress created a Department of the Navy in May 1798, and soon warships and privateers were waging an undeclared naval war with France.

War fever suited Federalist party leaders. The national emergency strengthened the federal government, made the Federalists popular, and discredited the pro-French Republicans. If war continued, Federalists expected to win reelection in 1800, but President Adams refused to let election politicking dominate American foreign policy. When Talleyrand changed his mind and decided to receive American diplomats, Adams opposed others in his party and sent an American minister to France. Federalist senators were furious, but they could not long oppose an effort to make peace. By the end of Adams's presidency, peace with France had been restored.

Adams's action in making peace against the wishes of most of his party was a courageous act. Proud of his nonpartisan action, Adams wrote that on his gravestone he wanted written "Here lies John Adams who took upon himself the responsibility of the peace with France in the year 1800."

Cultural Diversity

The Naturalization Act of 1798 changed the period of legal residency required for becoming a citizen from 5 years to 14 years. That law was repealed in 1802. Persons who wish to become naturalized citizens today must maintain legal residency for five years before making application. Foreign spouses of U.S. citizens can apply after three years. Applicants must be at least 18 years old; be able to speak, read, and write English; be of good moral character; and demonstrate a knowledge of U.S. history. They also must pay a small fee and take an oath of allegiance to the United States.

Partisan Legislation

Many Federalists were convinced that prominent Republicans were actively in league with France. So in 1798, in the midst of war fever, the Federalist majority in Congress pushed through three laws designed to hurt the Republican party—a Naturalization Act, an Alien Act, and a Sedition Act.

Many French and Irish refugees had recently come to America. Because they were anti-British, most supported the Republican party. The Naturalization Act tried to weaken this Republican strength by extending the residency requirement for citizenship from 5 to 14 years. The Alien Act required all immigrants to register with the federal government and allowed the President to deport without trial any alien whom he considered "dangerous." The Sedition Act attempted to muzzle the Republican press by making it a crime to speak or publish anything false or malicious against the federal government or any of its officers.

Instead of weakening the Republican party, these laws gave Republicans the issues that broadened their support. Republicans were horrified by these attacks on freedom of speech and press. In 1798 and 1799, the Republican legislatures of both Kentucky and Virginia passed resolutions denouncing the Sedition Act as unconstitutional. The Kentucky Resolutions presented the theory of **nullification**. According to this theory, the Constitution was an agreement among the states to establish a central government. If an act of the government exceeded the powers granted by the Constitution, a state had the right to refuse to obey.

The nullification theory was denounced by other state legislatures as threatening to the Union. If a state could nullify any federal law it considered unconstitutional, the power of the federal government would cease.

 ▲ **HOT-TEMPERED REPRESENTATIVES** In *Congressional Pugilists*, 1798, Roger Griswold, wielding a cane, fights with Matthew Lyon, the most notable victim of the Sedition Act of 1798. **What was the aim of the Sedition Act?**

Section 4 ★ Review

Checking for Understanding

1. **Identify** XYZ Affair, Naturalization Act, Alien and Sedition acts, Kentucky and Virginia resolutions.
2. **Define** nonpartisan, nullification.
3. **List** the main differences between the Republicans and the Federalists.
4. **Describe** the effects of the XYZ Affair.

Critical Thinking

5. **Evaluating Ideas** List what you consider to be the strengths and weaknesses of having political parties. Use your list to write an opinion statement of 3 to 4 sentences explaining why you favor or oppose having political parties.

CHAPTER 7 The Federalist Era 1789–1800

REVIEW CHAPTER 7

Answers
Reviewing Facts

1. established a cabinet as part of the executive branch, paid off foreign debt, assumed state debts, established a national bank, made treaties with and took military actions against Native Americans, suppressed the Whiskey Rebellion
2. opposition to Hamilton's program; Hamilton's and Jefferson's opposing views on democracy, people, and the role of government; split between pro-French and pro-British feelings; Jefferson's resignation from the cabinet; political criticism against Washington
3. National debt was addressed by repaying France and the Netherlands and by the Funding Bill; state debts were addressed by the Assumption Act; lack of a national currency was addressed by establishing a national bank.
4. War with Britain led France to expect American aid and resulted in the Proclamation of Neutrality. British trade restrictions, seizure of American ships, and Native American involvement led to American war sentiment and resulted in the Jay Treaty. French dismissal of an American minister, attacks on American ships, and the XYZ Affair led to American war sentiment and resulted in sending a minister to France.
5. Washington signed treaties and sent military forces to quell Native Americans; signed treaties with Britain and Spain, both of which had armed and encouraged Native Americans, reducing their influence in the West and with the Native Americans.

Understanding Concepts

1. Answers will vary but may include that he was a good leader and selected good officials.
2. Answers will vary but may include that the Federalists provided decisive leadership, whereas the Confederation government had little power or respect.
3. Answers will vary but may include that he was motivated by a desire to make the new government work.
4. Answers will vary but may include limited government as compared to strong government, democracy as compared to authority.

Critical Thinking

1. Answers will vary, but may include that generals are already considered leaders, are

---

CHAPTER 7 ★ REVIEW

Understanding Vocabulary

For each term below, write a sentence explaining why it had either a unifying effect or a divisive effect on the new government.

cabinet
protective tariff
revenue tariff
excise tax
enumerated powers
implied powers
nonpartisan
nullification

Reviewing Facts

1. **List** the actions taken during Washington's presidency that reflected the Federalist principle of strong central government authority.
2. **Outline** the causes that gradually led to the development of political parties.
3. **Identify** the economic problems facing the nation in 1789, and tell how Hamilton's financial program addressed those problems.
4. **State** the causes, their effects, and the final outcomes of the problems that the United States faced with France and Britain between 1789 and 1800.
5. **Show** how the actions of George Washington and improved foreign relations opened up the West for settlement.

Understanding Concepts

Leadership

1. **Characterize** the leadership style that George Washington exercised as President.
2. **Describe** the kind of leadership the Federalists provided in relation to the kind provided in the Confederation government.

Political Values

3. **Describe** the political values that motivated President Washington.
4. **Explain** the ideals of the Republicans under Thomas Jefferson, and compare them with Federalist principles.

226   UNIT 3 Launching the Republic: 1789–1824

Critical Thinking

1. **Drawing Conclusions** Washington was the first of several generals who later became President. Why do people think that a good general will make a good President?
2. **Analyzing Illustrations** Study the illustration below and answer these questions.
   a. What do you think the two individuals are doing?
   b. What tools are they using?
   c. What feeling about their work do the individuals' physical stances and expressions convey?

Writing About History

Classification and Division

Read an encyclopedia article about the life of George Washington. Then, divide the many facts about Washington's life into several different periods or categories. Write a report on George Washington's life and be prepared to explain why you have classified Washington's life into the categories you have chosen.

▲ AMERICAN SURVEYORS, NINETEENTH CENTURY

CHAPTER 7 ★ REVIEW

Cooperative Learning

You and four class members will portray a banker and the following persons asking for a loan: 1) a New England manufacturer wanting to build a furniture factory, 2) a Western farmer wanting to buy 100 acres of land, 3) a Southern plantation owner wanting to acquire more land and enslaved persons, 4) a land speculator wanting to buy a million acres of land in the West. Each team member should portray a different person. After interviews are finished, decide together whether and why each of the loans should be granted or denied.

Social Studies Skills

Recognizing Historical Reasoning When historians write about history, they often use certain words to connect the facts to other words that help the reader understand their meaning. These clue words point out the deductions they have made.

The chart that follows lists four kinds of historical reasoning. By learning to recognize these four methods, you can better determine for yourself whether or not a historian has supported his or her argument adequately.

Kinds of Historical Reasoning

KIND	CLUE WORDS
Cause and Effect	led to, brought on, resulted in

Example: *The ratification of the Constitution in 1788 resulted in a new framework for government.*

Analogies	like, as, similar to, different from

Example: *Westerners tended, like Jefferson, to believe in common people.*

Generalizations	some, most, all, few

Example: *Most people were opposed to the Jay Treaty.*

Proof	for example, this statement shows

Example: *Washington made it clear that he wanted to retire after his first term. For example, he pointed out that he would rather dig ditches than continue.*

Practicing the Skill

After studying the chapter and the kinds of historical reasoning shown in the chart, answer the following questions concerning the story told about the Federalist Era by this text's authors.

1. What statements in Section 1 give *proof* to Washington's leadership skills?
2. How is *cause and effect* used in Section 2 to explain how settlement north of the Ohio River caused conflict with Native Americans?
3. Read the following statement Thomas Jefferson made in regard to his differences with Hamilton.

   "Every difference of opinion is not a difference in principle. We have called by different names brethren of the same principle. We are all Republicans, we are all Federalists."

   What kind of reasoning do you think Jefferson was using to make his point? Explain your answer.

Using Your Journal
Compare the details you have noted about the character and beliefs of early leaders with those of two political leaders of today.

REVIEW CHAPTER 7

? Chapter Bonus Test Question

In 1798 Congress passed the Sedition Act. Present Federalist arguments in favor of the law and Republican arguments against it. (Answers will vary, but Federalists might say criticisms undermined authority and Republicans might say the law violated the First Amendment.)

Using Your Journal

The ideas students present in their comparisons will vary depending upon the political leaders they selected.

CHAPTER 7 The Federalist Era 1789–1800   227

---

used to exercising authority, and frequently command great respect.
2. Answers will vary. Accept all reasonable arguments.
Analyzing Illustrations
3. a. Surveying new land
   b. Answers may vary, but should include surveyor's tools.
   c. Answers may vary, but they seem to take their work seriously.

Practicing the Skill
1. Military victories, character, knew the country
2. Native Americans battled settlers, Washington sent troops.
3. Generalization; uses clue words *every* and *all*

PLANNING GUIDE — Chapter 8   Jefferson and the Republicans

Daily Lesson Objectives	Teacher Classroom Resources	Multimedia
SECTION 1 **The Changing Political Scene** **1 Day** pp. 230–235 1. Explain Thomas Jefferson's views on government. 2. Compare similarities and differences between Jefferson's administration and those of Washington and Adams. 3. Discuss the significance of judicial review.	Chapter 8 Study Guide Reproducible Lesson Plan Reteaching Activity 8-1 Section Quiz Chapter 8 Cooperative Learning Activity Chapter 8 Concept Mapping Activity Reinforcing Social Studies Skills 35, 44 The Living Constitution American Literary Heritage Unit 3	Student Self-Test Software Testmaker Section Focus Transparency 22 Chapter 8 Map Transparency Chapter 8 Skills Transparency The Presidents: A Picture History of Our Nation
SECTION 2 **Looking Westward** **1 Day** pp. 237–241 1. Explain the significance of the Louisiana Purchase. 2. Identify the reasons why unrest between Native Americans and the American government was increasing.	Reproducible Lesson Plan Reteaching Activity 8-2 Section Quiz American Portrait 15 Chapter 8 Primary and Secondary Source Readings American Heritage Literary Heritage Unit 3	Student Self-Test Software Testmaker Section Focus Transparency 23 A Geographic Perspective on American History
SECTION 3 **Foreign Affairs** **1 Day** pp. 244–247 1. Identify the problems that the United States faced in its attempt to remain neutral in the conflict between Great Britain and France. 2. Identify three ways the United States tried to maintain its freedom of the seas. 3. Explain the reasons for the increasing demand for war.	Reproducible Lesson Plan Reteaching Activity 8-3 Section Quiz Reinforcing Social Studies Skills 31, 52	Student Self-Test Software Testmaker Section Focus Transparency 24
SECTION 4 **War of 1812** **1 Day** pp. 248–252 1. Describe the major campaigns of the War of 1812. 2. Summarize the results of the War of 1812 and the Treaty of Ghent.	Reproducible Lesson Plan Reteaching Activity 8-4 Section Quiz American Portrait 16 Chapter 8 Enrichment Activity Chapter 8 Primary and Secondary Source Readings SAT Practice Test Spanish Summaries & Glossary	Student Self-Test Software Testmaker Section Focus Transparency 25 Vocabulary Puzzlemaker Audiocassette, Chapter 8
CHAPTER REVIEW AND EVALUATION **1 Day**	Chapter 8 Test Chapter 8 Performance Assessment Activity	Student Self-Test Software Testmaker

 **OUT OF TIME?** If time does not permit teaching the entire chapter, use the Chapter 8 Summary on pages 280–281 and the Chapter 8 audiocassette (English and Spanish) to point out the main ideas of the chapter.

PLANNING GUIDE

Cultural Diversity Activity

Cooperative Learning While William Henry Harrison is described on page 241 as "the most talented American at depriving the Indians from their ancestral lands," Harrison described Tecumseh, the Shawnee leader, as "one of those uncommon geniuses which spring up occasionally to produce revolutions and overturn the established order of things...."

Divide students into groups. Have each group research the life of Tecumseh and his brother Tenskwatawa (known as the Prophet) and their efforts to create a confederation of Native American nations. Then have groups write a series of questions for a TV-style interview show with Tecumseh. The focus should be U.S. policies toward Native Americans and relations with U.S. settlers. Ask each group to select a spokesperson to take part in the show. Have one of those students role play Tecumseh, while the others act as reporters. Encourage broader participation by allowing time for the "audience" to ask questions.

Performance Assessment Activity

Political Analysis Ask students to work with a partner to identify similarities and differences between Washington's administration and Jefferson's. Encourage partners to develop a list of areas they might feature in their analysis: foreign policies, domestic policies, quality of political appointments, leadership and style. Encourage students to find an appropriate way of sharing their findings with the class. Possibilities include charts and diagrams as well as oral and written reports.

POSSIBLE RUBRIC FEATURES: Content, creativity, clarity, visual and written communication skills, organization, use of diagrams, cooperative skills

Chapter Resources

Literature from the Period

Jefferson, Thomas. "The Inaugural Address." March 4, 1801.

Madison, Dolley. "Letters." 1814.

Readings for the Student

Folsom, Franklin. "Jobless Jack-Tars (1808)." *Labor's Heritage*, Vol. 2, No. 4, October 1990.

McCall, Edith. *Biography of a River: The Mississippi.* Walker and Company, 1990.

Readings for the Teacher

Adams, Henry. *History of the United States of America During the Administrations of Thomas Jefferson and James Madison.* Library of America, 1986.

DeConde, Alexander. *The Affairs of Louisiana.* Louisiana State University Press, 1976.

Hickey, Donald R. *The War of 1812: A Forgotten Conflict.* University of Illinois Press, 1990.

Rokove, Jack N. *James Madison and the Creation of the American Republic.* Scott Foresman/Little Brown, 1990.

Multimedia Resources

America Moves West. Orange Cherry. (2 Apple diskettes, backups, guide)

The Defense of Fort McHenry. National Park Service (VHS, 17 minutes)

On the Campaign Trail: Decisions, Decisions. Tom Snyder (Apple or IBM diskette, backup, guide, booklets)

The Supreme Court in American Life, A History. Multi-Media Productions. (VHS, 45 minutes)

Key to Ability Levels

Teaching strategies have been coded for varying learning styles and abilities.

- **L1** Basic activities for all students
- **L2** Average activities for average to above-average students
- **L3** Challenging activities for above-average students
- **LEP** Limited English Proficiency activities

Glencoe Links to the Humanities

Link to Art
- U.S. History & Art Transparency 5

Link to Literature
- Macmillan Literature: American Literature Text—James Fenimore Cooper

Link to Music
- American Music: Cultural Traditions

CHAPTER 8

BEGINNING THE CHAPTER

Point out that without a single shot being fired and without one colonial power being offended, the land area of the United States more than doubled in size in the early 1800s. Ask: How have most countries increased their land area? (through war and conquest)

Tell students that in this chapter they will read how geographic expansion, economic change, and conflict unified Americans.

Jeffersonians gained strength by using propaganda. They developed slogans about "monocrats" and tried to appeal to the sense of nostalgia in people by talking about the simplicity of the past. They promised a glorious future. Point out the many types of propaganda, such as TV ads, that presidential candidates use today.

Recording Journal Notes
Tell students that a journal is a useful place to compare and contrast differences in opinions about historical figures.

CHAPTER 8

Age of Jefferson
1800–1815

▶ THE SECOND U.S. FLAG, 1795–1818

Setting the Scene

Focus

Between 1800 and 1815, the United States experienced rapid expansion as well as the challenge of war. The Louisiana Territory doubled the size of the nation, creating remarkable new opportunities, and Americans looked to the future confidently. However, when war between France and Great Britain was renewed, the United States found its peace and neutrality threatened. By 1812 the United States and Great Britain had once more plunged into war.

Concepts to Understand

★ How geographic expansion changed the social and economic character of the United States

★ How expansion, economic change, and conflict unified Americans and helped them form a national identity

Read to Discover . . .

★ the opportunities that resulted from the Louisiana Purchase.

★ the factors that caused the War of 1812.

Journal Notes
How did the Republican views held by Jefferson differ from the Federalist views held by Washington and Adams? Note the differences as you read the chapter.

CULTURAL
- 1801 "Second Great Awakening" religious revival in the West begins
- 1807 Inventor Robert Fulton perfects the steamboat *Clermont*

1800 | 1805

POLITICAL
- 1801 Jefferson is elected President
- 1803 Louisiana Purchase completed
- 1807 The *Chesapeake* is attacked
- 1809 Embargo Act is repealed

UNIT 3 Launching the Republic: 1789–1824

✚ EXTRA CREDIT PROJECT

Thomas Jefferson wanted to be remembered for three things and requested that his tombstone list them thus: "Here was buried Thomas Jefferson, author of the Declaration of Independence, of the statute of Virginia for religious freedom, and father of the University of Virginia." Ask interested students to select one of these three achievements, and to research Jefferson's role in it and its importance to the present-day United States. Ask students to give a brief presentation of their findings to the class.

☆UNDER ☆MY☆ ☆WINGS☆ ☆EVERY ☆THING ☆PROSPERS☆

◀ HUNTING SHIRT

History AND ART

A View of New Orleans
by John L. Boqueta de Woiseri, 1803

This aquatint of New Orleans was painted in celebration of the purchase of the Louisiana Territory from France in 1803. The American eagle holds what some called a prophetic banner.

- 1810 *Boston Philharmonic Society formed*
- 1813 *Francis Scott Key writes "The Star-Spangled Banner"*
- 1815 *North American Review is published*

1810 ———————————— **1815**

- 1812 *War with Great Britain begins*
- 1815 *Treaty of Ghent ratified*

CHAPTER 8 Age of Jefferson 1800–1815

Teacher Notes

CHAPTER 8 CONCEPTS

Concept Mapping Activity

Copy the diagram below on the chalkboard and tell students that it represents the organizing concepts for the chapter. Ask students to write the concepts in their notebooks and list the major events under the appropriate concept as they read the chapter.

Seeds of democracy develop along with geographic expansion.
- National Identity
- Geographic Expansion

History AND ART

Boqueta de Woiseri was known for his watercolors and aquatints of American cities. This aquatint celebrates the purchase of the Louisiana Territory from France in 1803. The city of New Orleans, first laid out by a French company in 1718, had been destroyed by fires in 1788 and 1794 and then rebuilt.

NATIONAL GEOGRAPHIC SOCIETY

The following material is available from Glencoe and may be used to enrich Chapter 8.

 CD-ROM
- *The Presidents: A Picture History of Our Nation*

229

LESSON PLAN
SECTION 1, 230–236

FOCUS

Bellringer

Prior to taking roll at the beginning of the class period, display Focus Activity Transparency 26 on the overhead projector and assign the accompanying Focus Activity Sheet.

Objectives

Point out the objectives on this page to students in previewing the section content.

Motivating Activity

Discuss the campaign methods of the 1800s compared with those of today. Ask for volunteers to offer ways in which political candidates today and in the 1800s could make their views known. (Today and in the 1800s: campaign brochures; speeches; newspapers. Today only: advertisements on radio and TV; campaign offices; door-to-door campaign workers; mailings) Tell students that in the 1800s it took weeks for people to find out the election results.

Use Skills Transparency 8.

Did You Know?

Unlike Presidents Washington and Adams, who had traveled on official duties with servants and a fancy carriage drawn by six horses, President Jefferson, often unaccompanied, rode around the city on horseback.

230

SECTION 1

The Changing Political Scene

Setting the Scene

Section Focus

The election of 1800 marked a turning point for the United States. For the first time, the Federalist party was not in power. The growing democratic spirit of the nation found its expression in the Republican party. Jefferson's primary task was to unite the nation and prove that he would represent all Americans. Partly for this reason, Jefferson left intact many Federalist programs.

Objectives

After studying this section, you should be able to

★ explain Thomas Jefferson's views on government.

★ compare similarities and differences between Jefferson's administration and those of Washington and Adams.

★ discuss the significance of judicial review.

Key Terms

laissez-faire, judicial review, writ of mandamus

◀ THOMAS JEFFERSON

As Vice President under John Adams, Thomas Jefferson became the active leader of the Republican party. He was in an ideal situation for the task—at the center of the government—and yet his job as Vice President carried with it very few official duties.

■ The Election of 1800

As the presidential election of 1800 approached, the Federalists selected John Adams and Charles Pinckney as their candidates; the Republicans, Jefferson and Aaron Burr. During the campaign, Jefferson and his followers concentrated their fire on the Sedition Act and heavier taxes brought on by the undeclared war with France. The Federalists countered by predicting that Jefferson would cancel the public debt and abolish the navy. Republicans pictured Adams as a tyrant who wanted to be king. Federalists portrayed Jefferson as a drunkard, an atheist, and a French agent. A leading Federalist newspaper, *The Hartford Courant*, voiced the opinion that

> *Mr. Jefferson has long felt a spirit of deadly hostility against the Federal Constitution. . . . If he should be elected President, the Constitution will inevitably fall. . . . The result will be dreadful to the people of the United States.*

Jefferson Defeats Adams

Realizing that lack of support in all the states north of Pennsylvania had cost them the election in 1796, the Republicans worked

230   UNIT 3 Launching the Republic: 1789–1824

Classroom Resources for SECTION 1

Teacher's Classroom Resources
- Chapter 8 Study Guide
- Reproducible Lesson Plan
- Reteaching Activity 8-1
- Chapter 8 Cooperative Learning Activity
- Section Quiz

Multimedia
- Section Focus Transparency 26
- Chapter 8 Skills Transparency
- Chapter 8 Map Transparency
- Testmaker
- Student Self-Test Software
- The Presidents: A Picture History of Our Nation

hard in 1800 to gain the backing of laborers and immigrants in northeastern cities. The vote was so close that the voters in New York state would determine which candidate would win. Aaron Burr's organization was so effective in getting out the vote in New York City that the Republicans carried every district in the city. That victory gave them the state and, with it, the national election.

The election results posed a new question: the Republicans had won, but *which* Republican candidate became President? There was no doubt that the party had intended Jefferson as President and Burr as Vice President. But unlike today's election practices, candidates in 1800 were not designated as the candidate for President or the candidate for Vice President. Because every Republican elector had two votes and voted separately for both Jefferson and Burr, each candidate received 73 electoral votes. Where there is no majority, the Constitution stipulates that the House of Representatives selects the President. Some Federalists schemed to deny Jefferson the presidency and elect Burr—and came close to doing so. The House was so evenly divided that it took 6 days and 36 ballots. The deadlock was broken after a group of Federalists led by Hamilton supported Jefferson because they considered him better suited for the job and abler than Burr.

Transfer of Political Control

Although the Federalists were unhappy at losing the presidency, they accepted their loss and surrendered control of the federal government. This marked the first time in modern history that the political control of a country had been transferred through a democratic election. Despite animosity between Federalists and Republicans, the party system was beginning to work for the nation. The political parties that Washington had feared and warned against had developed national organizations that selected competent candidates for public office, maintained communications between federal officials and their constituents, and dealt effectively with factional and sectional differences.

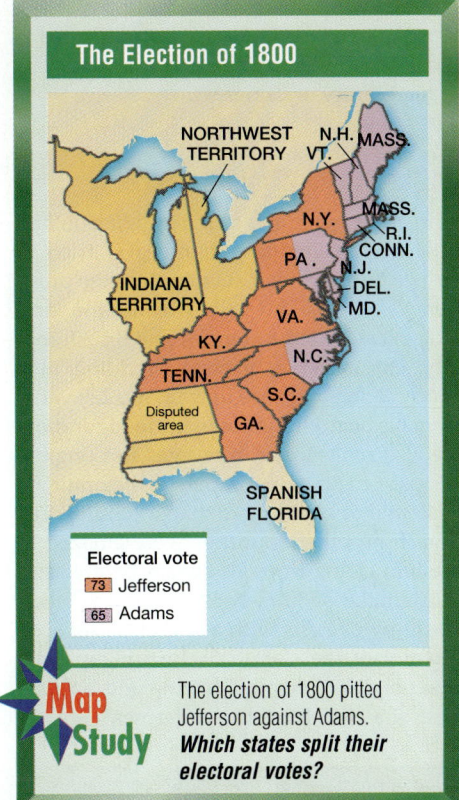

The Election of 1800

Electoral vote
- 73 Jefferson
- 65 Adams

Map Study The election of 1800 pitted Jefferson against Adams. **Which states split their electoral votes?**

Jefferson the Individual

If the Washington, D.C., of 1801—with its muddy streets and half-finished buildings—was an odd sort of national capital, the first President inaugurated there was in many ways an odd sort of man to be the founder of a political party and head of state. Thomas Jefferson hated crowds, avoided making speeches, and was too thin-skinned to enjoy rough-and-tumble politics.

Jefferson's Accomplishments

Jefferson's interest in agriculture led him to import hundreds of foreign plants into this country and to send hundreds of American plants abroad. One of the finest architects of his day, Jefferson designed his own home, Monticello, and was the chief architect of the Virginia Capitol and a complex of buildings for the University of Virginia. His many inventions included an improved

CHAPTER 8 Age of Jefferson 1800–1815

CHAPTER 8 SECTION 1

TEACH
Guided Practice

Language Write the term *mudslinging* on the chalkboard and explain that it means "using unflattering and insulting language in describing a political candidate or his or her beliefs." Ask students to write an example of mudslinging during the Jefferson-Adams campaign and also an example from a modern-day campaign. **L1, LEP**

Map Study Using Maps
Answers:
Pennsylvania, North Carolina, Maryland
Skills Practice
Which candidate won the election in Tennessee? (Jefferson)

Did You Know?

By 1800, slavery had been completely outlawed in the Northwest Territory, Massachusetts (which included present-day Maine), Vermont, New Hampshire, and Rhode Island. Gradual emancipation was underway in New York, Pennsylvania, New Jersey, and Connecticut.

Use Chapter 8 Map Transparency.

Critical Thinking

Making Comparisons Ask students to make two lists, one with the heading Federalists' Views of Government and the other with the heading Republicans' Views of Government. Ask students to compare the two views. (Sample entries: Federalists' Views: democracy in its natural operation to be the worst kind of government, general population incapable of making honest deductions. Republicans' Views: trusted common people, praised the farmers.) **L2**

CHAPTER 8 SECTION 1

Visualizing History As a young man, Jefferson used illustrated books to teach himself about architecture. His interest in ancient Greece and Rome also influenced the architectural designs he created.
Answer to Caption: to show that the Republicans did not propose to destroy the federal government and that all Americans needed to work together

Independent Practice

Political Science Organize the class into two groups. Ask one group to prepare campaign materials for Thomas Jefferson, and the other group to prepare campaign materials for John Adams. Groups should create posters, cartoons, written speeches, and editorials that reflect their candidate's beliefs. **L3**

The following material is available from Glencoe and may be used to enrich Chapter 8.

 CD-ROM
- *The Presidents: A Picture History of Our Nation*

---

plow, a swivel chair, and a folding carriage top. A lover of literature, he collected a library that eventually became the nucleus of the Library of Congress.

Jefferson in Washington, D.C.

In appearance and manner, Jefferson had little of Washington's dignity. He tried to reduce the ceremony surrounding the presidency because he felt Washington and Adams had acted too much like British royalty. For example, instead of riding in a coach, Jefferson chose to walk the 200 yards from his boardinghouse to his inauguration. He also sent written messages to Congress instead of appearing in person, beginning a custom that lasted more than a century. Visitors from other countries were amazed to see him riding through the dusty streets of Washington on horseback, dressed in faded corduroy overalls with a bag of clover seed in front of the saddle. A British diplomat described Jefferson as having the appearance of a "tall, large-boned farmer."

Jefferson and Government

Jefferson brought both a political and a philosophical change to the presidency. He believed the people were the source of a government's power, an idea he expressed in his Inaugural Address. Pleading for national harmony after the bitter election, Jefferson said:

> *Let us restore to social intercourse that harmony and affection without which liberty and even life itself are but dreary things. . . . We are all Republicans, we are all Federalists.*

By this he meant that despite their distrust of democracy, Federalists recognized the principle that problems are finally settled by the will of the people, and that despite their distrust of centralized power, the Republicans did not propose to destroy the federal government.

▲ **Visualizing History** **JEFFERSON'S ACCOMPLISHMENTS** In addition to being an inventor and a scientist, Thomas Jefferson helped design the University of Virginia. Jefferson brought a new outlook to the presidency as well. **Why did the new President focus on the theme of unity in his Inaugural Address?**

Cooperative Learning

Place students into groups of four and give each student a number from one to four. Have groups compare and contrast Hamilton's and Jefferson's beliefs about government. At various points in students' discussions, call upon number 1 students and ask them to report on their group's progress. Continue this procedure at varying intervals until all students have responded. **L1, L2**

 ▲ **THE NATION'S CAPITAL** Washington, D.C., at the time of Jefferson's presidency, did not resemble the capital city familiar to citizens today. *How did Jefferson attempt to quiet the fears of his opponents?*

Laissez-faire

Jefferson described what he thought were the principles of "wise and frugal government." In contrast to Hamilton's idea that the government should actively promote banking, commerce, and industry, Jefferson advocated a "hands-off" policy called **laissez-faire,** meaning generally, "let people do as they choose." A government should not control the way people do business or farm but should keep its role to restraining people from injuring each other and allowing them to be "free to regulate their own pursuits."

Quieting Fears

Jefferson's views on democracy and individual freedom quieted the fears of the Federalists. He called for "the preservation of the General Government in its whole constitutional vigor," which surely did not suggest his earlier theory of nullification. He also spoke of "the honest payment of our debts." This came as a great relief to owners of federal bonds who feared that Jefferson would prevent repayment to the bondholders.

■ Jefferson the Leader

Jefferson liked to speak of his election in 1800 as a "revolution." Perhaps in the sense that leaders who distrusted democracy were replaced by those who believed in it, it was a mild revolution.

Congressional Leadership

Before he became President, Jefferson had argued that the executive branch held too much power. In his Inaugural Address, he hinted that he would allow Congress to guide policy. As President, Jefferson made gestures toward giving Congress more control over day-to-day affairs of government. However, he had to provide strong leadership or watch his party divide into factions.

For this reason Jefferson used his position as party leader to influence legislation. By working with Republican leaders in Congress and by giving his supporters key positions, Jefferson became just as much chief legislator as Washington had been.

The Judiciary

The congressional elections of 1800 gave the Republicans solid majorities in both the House and Senate, enabling them to repeal Federalist legislation they disliked. The only change they attempted to make, however, was to cut the power of the federal judiciary and remove some federal judges.

Republicans feared the judiciary for three reasons. One was that federal judges, holding their positions "during good behavior," or for life, were beyond the people's control. Another was that federal courts had declared several state laws unconstitutional, thereby strengthening the power of the federal government while reducing that of the

---

CHAPTER 8 SECTION 1

Visualizing History Jefferson carried out his plans for a "wise and frugal government" by reducing the national debt and by cutting the size and cost of the army and navy.
Answer to Caption: left the major features of Hamilton's financial program untouched

Did You Know?

In 1802, Thomas Jefferson said, "I contemplate with solemn reverence that act of the American people [the First Amendment] which declared that their legislature should 'make no law respecting an establishment of religion or prohibiting the free exercise thereof,' thus building a wall of separation between church and state."

Critical Thinking

Verifying Information Provide the statements below and ask students which sources would be most useful for verifying the content:
(a) Federalist newspaper; (b) *Statistical Abstracts of the United States*; (c) biography, autobiography, or diary; (d) painting of the time.
1. Every Republican elector had voted for both Jefferson and Burr. (b)
2. In appearance and manner, Jefferson did not have Washington's dignity. (c, d)
3. Jefferson was portrayed as a drunkard and an atheist, and his election, his opponents contended, would undermine the Constitution. (a)
L1, L2

CHAPTER 8
SECTION 1

Teaching Life of the Times

Ask students to compare the pace of life in the early 1800s with the pace of life today. Ask students to speculate why most people today have little leisure time, even though they have many time-saving devices.

Did You Know?

The Marquis de Chastellux, who met Jefferson near the end of the Revolutionary War, was amazed at finding him in backcountry Virginia: "an American, who without ever having quitted [left] his own country, is at once a musician, skilled in drawing, a geometrician, an astronomer, a natural philosopher, legislator, and statesman."

---

states. Finally, Federalists had "packed" the judiciary. The number of federal judges was increased by the Judiciary Act of 1801, and Adams had filled many positions with members of his party. These judges were known as "midnight judges" because Adams supposedly signed appointments until midnight of his last day in office.

One of the first acts of Congress after Jefferson took office was to repeal the Judiciary Act. After doing away with the "midnight judges" by abolishing their offices, the Republicans tried to remove other Federalist judges by impeachment.

In 1804 a Federalist district judge from New Hampshire, John Pickering, was impeached by the House and convicted by the Senate for actions that indicated he was unfit to serve. The House then impeached Associate Justice Samuel Chase of the Supreme Court for biased conduct. He had attacked democracy in general and Jefferson in particular while addressing a Baltimore jury. The Senate, however, refused to convict Chase because it was not convinced that he had been proved guilty of "treason, bribery, or other high crimes and misdemeanors." (See Article II, Section 4 of the Constitution.)

The failure to remove Chase reduced the use of impeachment in the future to serious wrongdoing. Only once more, in the case of President Andrew Johnson in 1868, was it used as a political weapon.

■ Judicial Review

Shortly before leaving office, President Adams appointed John Marshall Chief Justice of the United States. Marshall was a Federalist and detested his cousin, Thomas Jefferson. In *Marbury* v. *Madison* (1803), Marshall greatly strengthened the power of the federal judiciary. In his decision he claimed that the federal courts had the power of **judicial review** over acts of Congress—that is, the power to decide whether laws passed by Congress were constitutional.

Marbury v. Madison

When James Madison took over as Jefferson's secretary of state, he found on his desk the commissions of several justices of the peace for the new District of Columbia. President Adams had signed the commissions,

---

Life of the Times

Telling Time

Whether rich or poor, urban or rural, Americans measured their activity primarily in days, months, and seasons—not in hours or minutes.

Most families in the early 1800s could afford neither clocks nor watches. Although accurate clocks existed, the few timepieces within a community often told different times. People used the position of the sun during the various seasons to estimate time during the day and to determine when they slept and rose from bed. Church bells tolled to announce worship services and town meetings, not the hour of the day.

The routine of daily life moved at a different pace without standardized time. Nature, for example, arranged a farmer's schedule. Farm families planted, cultivated, and harvested their crops according to the cycle of the seasons. Weather patterns influenced when families could set out for town or market—by wagon, over dirt roads—or when visitors were likely to arrive. A storm could easily upset plans by turning the roads to mud.

▼ Box clock, c. 1815

234   UNIT 3 Launching the Republic: 1789–1824

Sidelights: John Marshall and Thomas Jefferson

Thomas Jefferson and John Marshall held two different views of government. Marshall believed that the Constitution established a government of law, not of people. In his view, no one ought to be above the law; therefore, it was the duty of the Court "to say what the law is." It was the duty of the American people and their elected officials, including the President, to obey the law. To Jefferson and his followers, such ideas were undemocratic. They believed that elections registered the wishes of the people, and elected officials had a duty to carry out those wishes. The Supreme Court, an appointed institution, had no right to interfere with the will of the people.

but they had not been delivered. Jefferson instructed Madison to withhold the commissions. One of the appointees, William Marbury, petitioned the Supreme Court for a **writ of mandamus**—a court order requiring specific action—instructing Madison to give him his commission.

The Supreme Court was faced with a difficult decision. If it ruled that Marbury was entitled to be a judge and issued a writ, Jefferson and Madison could simply ignore it, diminishing the power and prestige of the Court. If the Court did not issue a writ, the Republicans would win by default. Marshall came up with a brilliant solution.

Acknowledging that Marbury had a legal right to his commission, Marshall argued that the Supreme Court could not issue the writ because the Constitution specifically listed the cases in which the Court had *original* jurisdiction. The writ of mandamus was not among them. In attempting to extend the Court's original jurisdiction to issue writs, the Judiciary Act of 1789 violated the Constitution, so the law was void.

Marshall said that the Constitution was the supreme law of the land. It could not be changed at the whim of the legislative branch. In this way Marshall had sidestepped his political dilemma. He gave the Republicans the result they sought by not issuing the writ. He even limited the original jurisdiction of the Court. Far more important, he laid down the cornerstone of the Court's power, judicial review—the authority to interpret the Constitution—which gives the judicial branch a "check of the legislative branch" in the system of checks and balances.

▲ JOHN MARSHALL

A New Term

Aside from this setback, Jefferson viewed his first term as a success. War had broken out in Europe, but its first effect in the United States was to increase foreign trade. Taxes had been reduced, and the income of the federal government from tariffs was sufficient to pay everyday expenses and reduce the national debt. Nearly everything that had happened during President Jefferson's first term added to the popularity of the Republican party, and Jefferson's reelection was assured. Running against Charles Pinckney of South Carolina, Jefferson received 162 of 176 electoral votes. The prospects for continuing what he had started looked good, but Jefferson's second term was to be far less successful than his first.

Section 1 ★ Review

Checking for Understanding

1. **Identify** Charles Pinckney, Aaron Burr, John Marshall, *Marbury* v. *Madison*.
2. **Define** laissez-faire, judicial review, writ of mandamus.
3. **State** the main points of Jefferson's political philosophy.
4. **Name** three important accomplishments of Jefferson during his first term in office.

Critical Thinking

5. **Analyzing Issues** How did Marshall go beyond the issues of his case to establish the power of the Supreme Court for all time?

CHAPTER 8 Age of Jefferson 1800–1815

Social Studies Skills

Interpreting Primary Sources

Female Equality

In the early 1800s, some American women began to challenge the accepted notion of female inferiority to men. They began to demand a greater role in public life. They also worked for better opportunities in education and in the workplace for women. An organized movement for woman's rights—with a substantial number of supporters—did not begin until the Seneca Falls Convention in 1848, however.

The following letter shows a young woman trying to make sense of the contradictory doctrines of female subordination and sexual equality. Eliza Southgate wrote to a male cousin in 1801:

▲ MOTHER AND DAUGHTER, 1790s

But every human being who has contemplated human nature on a large scale will certainly justify me when I declare that the inequality of privilege between the sexes is very sensibly felt by us females, and in no instance is it greater than in the liberty of choosing a partner in marriage; true, we have the liberty of refusing those we don't like, but not of selecting those we do. This is undoubtedly as it should be. . . .

I never was of opinion that the pursuits of the sexes ought to be the same; on the contrary, I believe it would be destructive to happiness, there would a degree of rivalry exist[;] each should have a separate sphere of action—in such a case there could be no clashing unless one or the other should leap their respective bounds. Yet to cultivate the qualities with which we are endowed can never be called infringing the prerogatives of man. . . .

The cultivation of the power we possess, I have ever thought a privilege (or I may say duty) that belonged to the human species, and not man's exclusive prerogative. Far from destroying the harmony that ought to subsist, it would fix it on a foundation that would not totter at every jar. Women would be under the same degree of subordination that they now are; enlighten and expand their minds, and they would perceive the necessity of such a regulation to preserve the order and happiness of society. . . .

Examining the Primary Source

1. What does Southgate suggest is a prime example of the inequality of privilege between the sexes?
2. What disadvantage does Southgate see to men and women following the same pursuits?

Critical Thinking

3. Do you agree or disagree with Southgate's assertion that competition between men and women creates unhappiness in male-female relationships? Explain your answer.

SECTION 2

Looking Westward

Setting the Scene

Section Focus

The Louisiana Purchase was a notable achievement of the Jefferson administration. Committed to interpreting the Constitution in its strictest sense, Jefferson doubted that he possessed the power to make the purchase. On the other hand, the opportunity to gain the land west of the Mississippi River might never come again.

Objectives

After studying this section, you should be able to
★ explain the significance of the Louisiana Purchase.
★ identify the reasons why unrest between Native Americans and the American government was increasing.

Key Term

expedition

◀ THE LOUISIANA PURCHASE TREATY

The news that Spain had ceded Louisiana, including New Orleans, to France in 1800 was of great concern to the United States. The French were now ruled by Napoleon Bonaparte, whose conquests kept Europe in turmoil for many years. Napoleon increased France's power in Europe and planned to create a new French empire in North America.

The Louisiana Purchase

Jefferson was alarmed at the prospect of New Orleans being in French hands. The city was a major trade center for the United States, especially as a market for Western goods. Jefferson feared that the French might close New Orleans to American trade, thus blocking the development of the American West. He authorized Robert Livingston, United States minister stationed in Paris, to offer France $10 million for New Orleans and West Florida and sent James Monroe as a special envoy to Paris to negotiate the purchase.

Trouble in Sainte Domingue

It is unlikely that American dollars would have moved Napoleon if his plans for a French empire had not suffered a great defeat in the most valuable of France's American colonies, Sainte Domingue (Haiti). During the 1700s, its exports of sugar, indigo, coffee, and cotton were almost equal in value to the combined exports of the 13 colonies. In 1791 its enslaved people rebelled. Under the leadership of Pierre Toussaint-L'Ouverture (TOO•SAN LOO•vuhr•TYUR), "the black Napoleon," Haitian blacks attempted to make their island an independent state.

CHAPTER 8 Age of Jefferson 1800–1815   **237**

Classroom Resources for SECTION 2

Teacher's Classroom Resources
- Reproducible Lesson Plan
- Reteaching Activity 8-2
- Chapter 8 Primary and Secondary Source Readings
- Section Quiz

Multimedia
- Section Focus Transparency 27
- Testmaker
- Student Self-Test Software
- A Geographic Perspective on American History

LESSON PLAN
SECTION 2, 237–243

FOCUS

Bellringer

Prior to taking roll at the beginning of the class period, display Focus Activity Transparency 27 on the overhead projector and assign the accompanying Focus Activity Sheet.

Objectives

Point out the objectives on this page to students in previewing the section content.

Motivating Activity

Write "Britain," "France," and "Spain" on the chalkboard. Ask students to speculate how stable the United States was after the American Revolution in the eyes of these countries. (Unstable because each of these countries thought that the U.S. government, under the Articles of Confederation, was weak. However, these countries might have respected the U.S. military power.)

 VIDEODISC
• *GTV: A Geographic Perspective on American History*

Side 2, Chapter 4
Title: *Lewis and Clark*
Subject: The Lewis and Clark Expedition

See GTV Guide page 42 for complete lesson plan.

237

CHAPTER 8 SECTION 2

TEACH
Guided Practice

Political Science Have students write a paragraph in response to the following:

According to Hamilton, Aaron Burr said to him in 1800: "General, you are now at the head of the Army.... Our Constitution is a miserable paper machine. You have it in your powers to demolish it, and give us a proper one, and you owe it to your friends and the country to do it." **L2**

Study Using Maps

Answer: Fort Clatsop on the Pacific

Skills Practice

Ask students which area was disputed by the United States and Spain. (area west of Orleans Territory in what is now Texas)

• *GTV: A Geographic Perspective on American History*

Side 2, Chapter 6
Title: *The Advancing Frontier: The Near West*
Subject: Settlement between the Appalachians and the Mississippi

See GTV Guide page 43 for complete lesson plan.

238

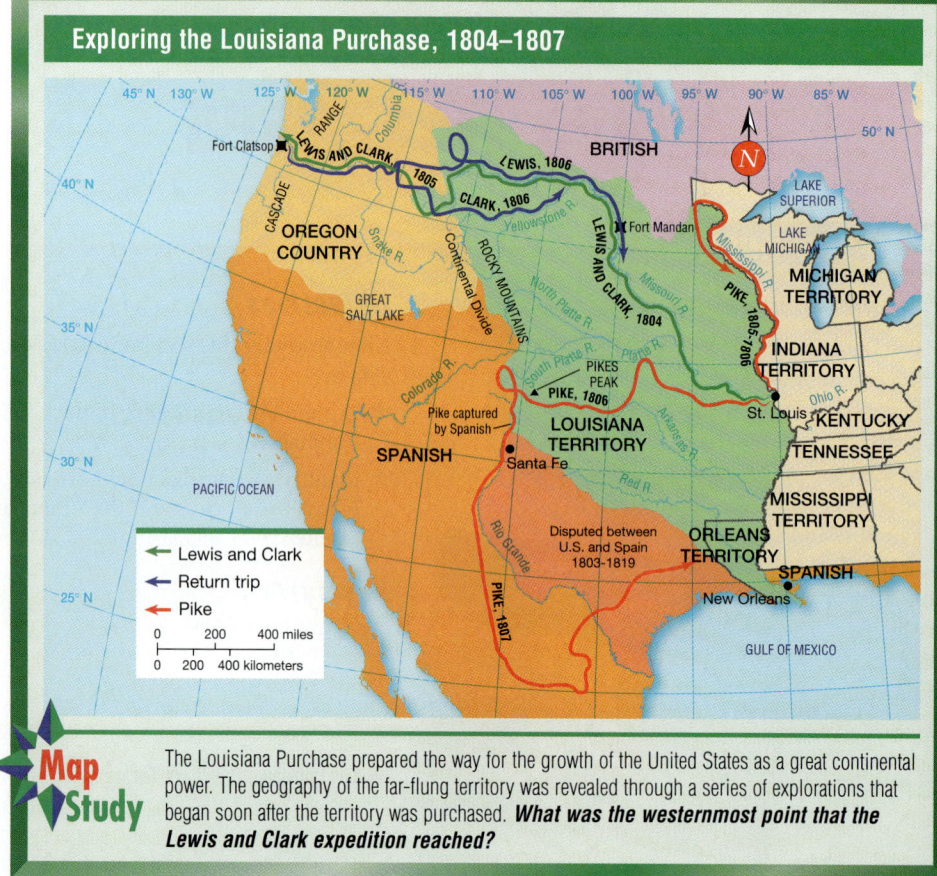

Exploring the Louisiana Purchase, 1804–1807

Map Study: The Louisiana Purchase prepared the way for the growth of the United States as a great continental power. The geography of the far-flung territory was revealed through a series of explorations that began soon after the territory was purchased. **What was the westernmost point that the Lewis and Clark expedition reached?**

In 1801 Napoleon sent soldiers to put down the Haitian revolt. Toussaint-L'Ouverture organized such effective resistance that the French expedition failed, although he himself was captured. When the French lost almost all their troops to battle and yellow fever, Napoleon was forced to abandon his American ambitions.

French Offer to Sell Louisiana Territory

Meanwhile, Livingston had been urging the French to sell New Orleans. In April 1803, Talleyrand, the French foreign minister, asked Livingston how much the United States would pay for the entire Louisiana Territory. Livingston, who had been joined by James Monroe, took only a few days to negotiate an agreement by which the United States was to pay about $15 million for the territory—about 4 cents an acre.

Jefferson was torn between a desire to extend the nation's boundaries and concern over whether the government could legally acquire foreign territory. Finally, Jefferson decided to ask the Senate to ratify the treaty and the Senate gave its consent, despite opposition from New England Federalists. Although this action did not follow Jefferson's belief in strict construction of the Constitution, he justified the acquisition on the grounds that it was part of the President's implied powers to protect the nation. The Louisiana Purchase doubled the size of the United States and opened the way for westward expansion by removing the threat of French interference.

UNIT 3 Launching the Republic: 1789–1824

Critical Thinking

Finding Supporting Evidence Provide this statement:

Jefferson justified the acquisition of the Louisiana Territory on the grounds that it was part of the President's implied powers to protect the nation.

Ask students whether they think Jefferson's justification was valid. Have them write several sentences supporting their answers. (Most will answer "Yes." It provided unhindered access to Mississippi River and port of New Orleans; eliminated France as a potential threat to the United States; eliminated the need to become an ally of Britain to gain protection against France.) **L1, LEP**

Lewis and Clark

Very little was known about the area west of the Mississippi, and it excited Jefferson's curiosity. He sent an **expedition,** a journey with a specific purpose, led by two officers in the United States Army—Meriwether Lewis and William Clark—up the Missouri River to explore the new territory. The expedition was the first scientific project to receive federal funds, and Jefferson himself drew up their instructions. He told Lewis and Clark to find the sources of the Missouri River, to try to find a usable route across the Rocky Mountains to the Pacific Ocean, and to observe the customs of the Native Americans they met. They were also instructed to note carefully the features of the land, the weather, and the plants and animals they saw.

The expedition left St. Louis in May 1804. It returned over two years later with its mission accomplished, having surmounted hardships that ranged from "ticks and musquiters" to near starvation and floods.

Among the members of the expedition was York, an enslaved person. York's skills in hunting and fishing made him a valuable member of the expedition. He was particularly successful in making friends with the Native Americans they met along the way. Sacajawea (SA•kuh•juh•WEE•uh), a Shoshone woman, and her French-Canadian husband later joined the party as interpreters and guides. Her role was important because Lewis and Clark wanted to build peaceful relations with the Native Americans living in the newly acquired territory.

The Lewis and Clark expedition added immensely to the knowledge of the huge area that had been purchased. It also helped the United States lay claim to the northern region between the Rocky Mountains and the Pacific Ocean known as Oregon. Within a few years, fur traders based in St. Louis were traveling to and settling in the Rockies, and by 1812 there were about 70,000 people living in the southern section of the Louisiana Territory.

▼ **COMMEMORATIVE STAMP**

▲ **EXPLORING THE NEW LANDS** After the Louisiana Territory became part of the United States, Jefferson authorized an army expedition to the territory. Sacajawea accompanied Lewis and Clark on the trip westward, acting as guide and interpreter. **Why was the expedition important?**

CHAPTER 8 Age of Jefferson 1800–1815

CHAPTER 8
SECTION 2

Rivalry between Britain and France for domination of North America and Europe helped the young United States. France, following the loss of its North American empire in the French and Indian War, was anxious to aid the 13 colonies in their struggle against Britain. Later, after France took Louisiana from Spain, the young United States acquired this vast inland domain. In 1803, following the defeat of French troops in Haiti, Napoleon sold Louisiana, partially to prevent the British from seizing it.

Did You Know?

In 1806 President Thomas Jefferson urged Congress to pass a law prohibiting the importation of enslaved people. The next year, Congress passed a law making the slave trade illegal as of January 1, 1808. Nevertheless, smuggling of slaves continued.

▶ AARON BURR

■ Burr's Conspiracies

The Louisiana Purchase troubled diehard Federalists in the Northeast. They feared that westward expansion would weaken New England's power in national affairs and would subordinate its commercial interests to the agricultural interests of the South and West.

Burr and Hamilton

A group of Federalists drafted a plan to take New England out of the Union and form a northern confederacy. The plotters realized that, if the confederacy were to last, it had to include New York as well as New England. They found an ally in Aaron Burr, who was willing to desert the Republican party and run for governor of New York on the Federalist ticket in 1804.

The plan went awry, however, when Burr was soundly defeated. Alexander Hamilton, who had worked to prevent Burr's election to the presidency in 1800, campaigned against him.

When Hamilton continued after the election to criticize his integrity, Burr challenged Hamilton to a duel. Hamilton accepted the challenge.

On a July morning in 1804, Hamilton, Burr, their assistants, and a physician rowed across the Hudson River to a rock shelf at the foot of the Palisades. At the signal Burr fired a bullet into Hamilton's body. Hamilton died the next day.

Western Conspiracy

When a New York coroner's jury indicted Burr for murder, he escaped from New York but not from his troubles. He headed west and took part in arranging a conspiracy. Sometimes Burr talked of secession of the western territories, sometimes of the conquest of Mexico—with himself as emperor. Whatever Burr's final goal, he collected arms, bought flatboats on the Ohio River, and floated down toward New Orleans with between 80 and 100 followers. His movements became so widely known, however, that the federal government had time to prepare for anything he might do. When President Jefferson ordered his arrest, Burr fled to Spanish Florida.

Burr was captured in 1807 and taken to Richmond, Virginia, to stand trial for treason. At the trial, Chief Justice Marshall, following the Constitution's provisions regarding the rights of a person accused of treason, insisted that the prosecution produce two witnesses to an "overt act" on Burr's part. Because there were no trustworthy witnesses against him, Burr was acquitted and went into exile.

■ Conflict with Native Americans

During both Jefferson's and James Madison's administrations, settlers, hunters, and land speculators pressured the Native Americans hard. Jefferson, himself, favored moving Native Americans who lived east of the Mississippi River to unoccupied lands in the Louisiana Territory. He insisted that the Chickasaw and Cherokee nations give up their lands in Alabama and Georgia and move to present-day Arkansas.

North of the Ohio River, the Treaty of Greenville had not satisfied the pioneers' desire for land. By persuasion, force, and

UNIT 3 Launching the Republic: 1789–1824

Cultural Diversity

French people from eastern Canada moved to the bayou region of Spanish-controlled Louisiana after the British took over Canada in 1763. Their descendants are called Cajuns (originally Acadians). By 1800, most of the population of Louisiana (by then French controlled) lived on the lower banks of the Mississippi. The majority were Creoles (descendants of Spanish and French settlers) and African Americans, both enslaved and free. The area north of the Orleans Territory was populated by the Osage, Pawnee, Apache, and Dakota.

fraud, Native Americans were forced to give up more and more land. In spite of treaty promises that were to last "as long as the sun shall climb the heavens or the waters shall run in the streams," white settlers persisted in moving into Native American land. William Henry Harrison, governor of the Indiana Territory, has been described as "the most talented American at depriving the Native Americans of their ancestral lands." In the 15 treaties he negotiated, Native Americans gave up nearly all of present-day Indiana and Illinois.

During these difficult times, a remarkable leader named Tecumseh (tuh•KUHM•suh) became chief of the Shawnee. He wanted to unite all the peoples of the Mississippi Valley into a great federation to protect themselves against the white intruders. Tecumseh went to Harrison and urged that the United States give up some recently "purchased" territory on the grounds that the chiefs who signed the treaty had no authority to do so. Harrison replied that only the President of the United States could answer such a request. Tecumseh answered:

 ▲ **TECUMSEH** Shawnee chief Tecumseh was a bold and imaginative leader along the frontiers of the northwest. *What did Tecumseh hope to achieve by establishing a confederation?*

❝ *Well, as the great chief is to decide the matter, I hope the Great Spirit will put sense enough into his head to induce him to give up this land. It is true, he is so far off he will not be injured by the war; he may sit still in his town and drink his wine, while you and I will have to fight it out.* ❞

The prediction came true. In 1811 Harrison launched a war against Tecumseh's followers, knowing that the great leader had journeyed south to persuade Native American communities to join the confederation. Harrison became a national hero after leading American troops in battle at Tippecanoe near present-day West Lafayette, Indiana. Tecumseh's death in 1813 destroyed the dream of a Native American confederation. Afterward, several Native American nations made peace with Harrison.

Section 2 ★ Review

Checking for Understanding
1. **Identify** Louisiana Purchase, Lewis and Clark, York, Sacajawea, Tecumseh.
2. **Define** expedition.
3. **State** why New Orleans was a city important to the nation.
4. **Specify** Jefferson's reasons for making the Louisiana Purchase.

Critical Thinking
5. **Predicting Outcomes** Aaron Burr was tried for treason but was acquitted. How did his acquittal affect future treason charges?

CHAPTER 8 Age of Jefferson 1800–1815   **241**

CHAPTER 8
SECTION 2

ASSESS
Check Understanding
Assign Section 2 Review as homework or an in-class activity.

Evaluate
Assign the Section 2 Quiz in the TCR or use the History of a Free Nation Testmaker to create a customized quiz.

Reteach
Have students complete Reteaching Activity 8-2.

Enrich
Have students read a book about Tecumseh and report on his efforts to build a Native American confederation.

CLOSE
Some historians consider Jefferson's purchase of the Louisiana Territory to be his greatest accomplishment. Ask students if they agree with this assessment.

Visualizing History The Native American hope of a vast confederation organized to protect their lands from American settlers was crushed when Tecumseh was killed in 1813. He died while serving as a brigadier general, leading Native Americans who supported the British during the War of 1812. **Answer to Caption:** protection of Native Americans from white settlers

---

Answers to SECTION 2 REVIEW
1. Louisiana Purchase, 237; Lewis and Clark, 239; York, 239; Sacajawea, 239; Tecumseh, 241
2. All vocabulary words are defined in the Glossary.
3. was a major trade center
4. wanted to extend the boundaries of the U.S. westward and rid the U.S. of foreign interference.
5. Answers will vary but may include: a strict interpretation of the Constitution regarding treason has resulted in few treason trials.

American Literary Heritage

INTEGRATING Language Arts

Historical Setting

During James Monroe's presidency, the Era of Good Feelings flourished. The Monroe Doctrine, a reflection of nationalism, both reinforced and promoted national pride. By the time John Quincy Adams became President, the "good feelings" had begun to fade. Nationalism, too, was waning; however, its effects were long-lasting, as evidenced by the literary works of the era.

Background

In the nineteenth century, American literature became more "American." Writers, reflecting a sense of national pride, began to break with their Eurocentric backgrounds and establish a decidedly American tone. They began to emphasize American history, settings, and themes in their works. Romantic writers of the era included Washington Irving, James Fenimore Cooper, and Edgar Allan Poe.

About the Author

Born in 1789 in New Jersey, James Fenimore Cooper was reared in upstate New York. He served for a short time in the navy and returned to New York, where he became a gentleman farmer. Although he wrote many works, Cooper is best known for his novels about Natty Bumppo's frontier life, *The Leather-Stocking Tales,* set in the huge expanse of the New York State frontier, now immortalized in his works.

▲ **JAMES FENIMORE COOPER**

Romanticism, a movement that emphasized imagination and inner feelings, won adherents among many writers of the era. One of the most celebrated was James Fenimore Cooper. Cooper left a legacy of five novels whose central character, Natty Bumppo, is a trapper forced increasingly westward by the encroachment of civilization on his beloved frontier. In the following excerpt, Natty Bumppo, surrounded by the Pawnee who have become his family, is near death.

The Prairie (excerpts)

When he had placed his guests in front of the dying man, Hard-Heart . . . [a young Pawnee chief and Natty Bumppo's adopted son] leaned a little forward and demanded: "Does my father hear the words of his son?"

. . . "Let the wise chief have no cares for his journey," continued Hard-Heart with an earnest solicitude that led him to forget, for the moment, that others were waiting to address his adopted parent; "a hundred . . . [Pawnee] shall clear his path from briars."

"Pawnee, I die as I have lived, a Christian man," resumed the trapper with a force of voice that had the same startling effect upon his hearers as is produced by the trumpet when its blast rises suddenly and freely on the air after its obstructed sounds have been heard struggling in the distance: "as I came into life so will I leave it. Horses and arms are not needed to stand in the presence of the Great Spirit of my people. He knows my color, and according to my gifts will he judge my deeds. . . ."

Middleton [an army officer whose life Natty Bumppo has saved] took one of the meager hands of the trapper, and, struggling to command his voice, he succeeded in announcing his presence. . . .

[Bumppo said,] "Will you do a favor to an old and dying man?"

"Name it," said Middleton; "it shall be done."

"It is a far journey to send such trifles," resumed the old man, who spoke at short intervals, as strength and breath permitted; "a far and weary journey is the same; but kindnesses and friendships are things not to be forgotten. There is a settlement among the Otsego hills—"

"I know the place," interrupted

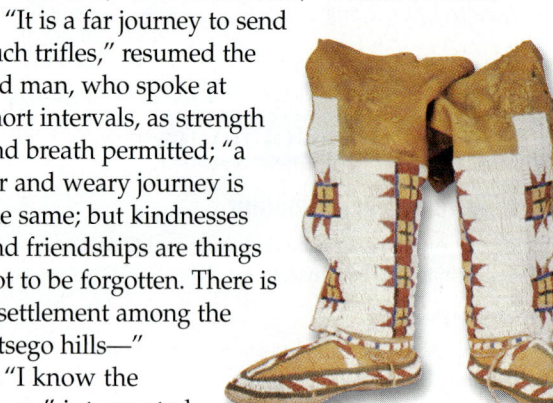

▲ **BEADED BUCKSKIN LEGGING MOCCASINS**

242 UNIT 3 Launching the Republic: 1789–1824

Cultural Diversity

Washington Irving gained worldwide recognition as an author. Many of his works, such as the stories "The Legend of Sleepy Hollow" and "Rip Van Winkle," took place in the Hudson Valley, which was settled by the Dutch. Edgar Allan Poe, regarded as the father of the modern detective story, wrote "The Murders in the Rue Morgue" and "The Purloined Letter." Poe is best known for his macabre horror stories, including "The Tell-Tale Heart," "The Black Cat," and "The Fall of the House of Usher." He also penned classic works of poetry, including "The Raven" and "Annabel Lee." Translations helped make Poe's writings extremely popular in France.

Middleton, observing that he spoke with increasing difficulty; "proceed to tell me what you would have done."

"Take this rifle and pouch and horn, and send them to the person whose name is graven on the plates of the stock—a trader cut the letters with his knife—for it is long that I have intended to send him such a token of my love."

"It shall be so. Is there more that you could wish?"

"Little else have I to bestow. My traps I give to my Indian son; for honestly and kindly has he kept his faith. Let him stand before me.". . .

"Pawnee," continued the old man, always changing his language to suit the person he addressed, and not infrequently according to the ideas he expressed, "it is a custom of my people for the father to leave his blessing with the son before he shuts his eyes forever. This blessing I give to you; take it, for the prayers of a Christian man will never make the path of a just warrior to the blessed prairies either longer or more tangled. May the God of a white man look on your deeds with friendly eyes, and may you never commit an act that shall cause him to darken his face. I know not whether we shall ever meet again. There are many traditions concerning the place of Good Spirits. It is not for one like me, old and experienced though I am, to set up my opinions against a nation's. You believe in the blessed prairies, and I have faith in the sayings of my fathers. If both are true, our parting will be final; but if it should prove that the same meaning is hid under different words, we shall yet stand together. . . ."

▲ Fur traders

Interpreting Literature

1. What requests does Natty Bumppo make of his friend Middleton?
2. Describe the trapper's feelings about Pawnee customs and traditions.
3. What support can you find for the view that Natty Bumppo is a product of the prairie?

Determining Relevance

4. What symbolism can be witnessed in Natty Bumppo's death?

CHAPTER 8 Age of Jefferson 1800–1815

LESSON PLAN
SECTION 3, 244–247

FOCUS

Bellringer
Prior to taking roll at the beginning of the class period, display Focus Activity Transparency 28 on the overhead projector and assign the accompanying Focus Activity Sheet.

Objectives
Point out the objectives on this page to students in previewing the section content.

Motivating Activity
Present this scenario to students:
You are the captain of an American ship. Your ship, loaded with goods, is in the Strait of Gibraltar. Pirates in the narrow strait will prey on your ship unless you pay a ransom. What are your options? (to pay or not to pay) What will you do? Why?
Tell students that in this section they will read about ways in which the United States tried to maintain its freedom of the seas.

Did You Know?
At the time of the XYZ Affair, when Americans were chanting "Millions for defense, but not one cent for tribute," a United States warship was on its way to Algiers, carrying 26 barrels of silver dollars to pay the Barbary pirates for their "protection."

SECTION 3

Foreign Affairs

Setting the Scene

Section Focus
Thomas Jefferson had entered the presidency committed to Washington's policy of neutrality. Yet, the United States and Europe were dependent upon each other. When Britain and France each tried to manipulate trade with the United States as a weapon against the other, the United States sought ways to fight back.

Objectives
After studying this section, you should be able to
★ identify the problems that the United States faced in its attempt to remain neutral in the conflict between Great Britain and France.
★ identify three ways the United States tried to maintain its freedom of the seas.
★ explain the reasons for the increasing demand for war.

Key Terms
piracy, impressment

◀ AMERICAN SAILORS

*J*efferson hoped that "nature and a wide ocean" would keep the United States entirely isolated from European rivalries. "Peace," he wrote to an English friend, "is our passion."

■ Barbary Coast Piracy

The first threat to peace came not from one of the great powers of Europe, but from Tripoli (part of present-day Libya), a small country on the north coast of Africa. **Piracy**, or preying on ships at sea, was a principal business of Tripoli and the other Barbary Coast states of Morocco, Algiers, and Tunis. The ships of countries that did not pay tribute to the Barbary States were likely to be captured and their sailors enslaved. Between 1789 and 1801, the United States paid over $2 million in tribute.

Despite his desire for peace, Jefferson was determined that the United States would not be robbed by the Barbary pirates. Consequently, he carried on a four-year war with Tripoli. The American navy eventually had 14 ships stationed in the Mediterranean Sea.

In 1805 the ruler of Tripoli made peace after receiving a ransom of $60,000 for captured American sailors. For a time, this discouraged the other Barbary Coast states from asking for additional tribute. Still, in 1807 after President Jefferson withdrew the American navy, attacks started again. The piracy ended in 1815 when an American fleet of ships under Stephen Decatur, joined by warships of European nations, put an end to the practice.

UNIT 3 Launching the Republic: 1789–1824

Classroom Resources for SECTION 3

Teacher's Classroom Resources
- Reproducible Lesson Plan
- Reteaching Activity 8-3
- Section Quiz

Multimedia
- Section Focus Transparency 28
- Testmaker
- Student Self-Test Software

Britain and France

Most of Jefferson's second term, coinciding with war in Europe, was spent trying to maintain American neutrality. In 1803 Great Britain and France had once again gone to war.

Neutrality

The United States was an important source of supply to both sides. Each side tried to limit what it saw as aid to the enemy and, in doing so, violated American freedom of the seas. Napoleon issued the Berlin and Milan decrees, which forbade any country under French control to import British goods or to allow British ships to enter its harbors. Neutral ships bringing British goods, stopping at British ports, or even submitting to search by British naval vessels were to be seized.

Great Britain answered the Napoleonic decrees with the Orders in Council. British traders feared that the United States would take over the trade with Europe forbidden to the British by Napoleon and replace Britain as the greatest trading nation in the world. Therefore, the Orders in Council of 1807 forbade neutral ships to trade with Europe unless they stopped in Britain first.

Impressment

Even more distressing than the attempt to cut off the United States trade was the British practice of taking sailors from American ships. For centuries Britain had secured sailors by a legalized form of kidnapping known as **impressment**. Sailors were impressed in port and taken off merchant ships at sea. British sailors frequently deserted and signed on with American vessels, where the conditions and pay were better. Sometimes a British warship calling in an American port found it difficult to sail away because so many of the crew had deserted. To combat this problem, Britain claimed the right to stop American ships, search for former British subjects, and force them back into service.

 ▲ **IMPRESSMENT** Americans resented the British method of recruiting for their navy by impressment. *How did public opinion change after the British ship* Leopard *attacked the American frigate* Chesapeake*?*

CHAPTER 8 Age of Jefferson 1800–1815

CHAPTER 8
SECTION 3

The plight of the sailors thrown into unemployment by the embargo prompted a 13-year-old Massachusetts boy to write a poem in 1808.

The writer, William Cullen Bryant, went on to become one of America's leading poets and newspaper editors. He was editor of the *New York Evening Post* from 1829 until his death in 1878.

Visualizing History In 1807, the British ship *Leopard* attacked the American frigate *Chesapeake*, killing three people and seizing four seamen.
Answer to Caption: caused loss of jobs by sailors, dockworkers; financial losses by shipowners and growers of wheat, cotton, tobacco

ASSESS
Check Understanding
Assign Section 3 Review as homework or an in-class activity.

Evaluate
Assign the Section 3 Quiz in the TCR or use the History of a Free Nation Testmaker to create a customized quiz.

Reteach
Have students complete Reteaching Activity 8-3.

 ▲ **THE APPROACH OF WAR** The United States was not well prepared for war. The British Royal Navy, with frigates like the 38-gun *Shannon*, vastly outnumbered the United States Navy. **How did the Embargo Act affect the United States?**

In June 1807, a United States warship, the *Chesapeake*, was leaving the United States for the Mediterranean Sea when it was stopped by a British naval vessel, the *Leopard*. The commander of the *Leopard* demanded that he be allowed to search the *Chesapeake* for British deserters. When he was refused, the British ship fired 3 broadsides at the *Chesapeake*, killing 3 and wounding 18. After the *Chesapeake* surrendered, the British boarded the ship and carried off 4 sailors.

The attack on the *Chesapeake* aroused great anger, and American newspapers clamored for war. Jefferson, however, delayed calling Congress into session until tempers had had time to cool. Although the President did not intend to let these actions by the British go unanswered, he sought a course of action other than war.

The Embargo Act

Jefferson reasoned that both Britain and France were so dependent upon American goods that if the United States cut off trade with them, they would stop violating the nation's neutral rights. With the President's urging, Congress passed the Embargo Act in December 1807, forbidding United States ships to sail for any foreign ports.

The Embargo Act caused some suffering in Britain, hurt France very little, but was almost disastrous for the United States. Wheat, cotton, and tobacco piled up on wharves. Thousands of sailors were put out of work. Ships rotted at the docks. Exports fell from $198 million in 1807 to $22 million in 1808. Imports fell from $138 million to $55 million.

The law was bitterly resisted. Merchant ships made secret runs to European ports. Smuggling between the northeastern states and Canada flourished. To stop violations of the embargo, Jefferson stationed militia along the Canadian border and permitted officials to search for smuggled goods without proper warrants. Ironically, President Jefferson was accused of using his great power at the expense of the Bill of Rights, which he himself had championed years before as a check against tyranny.

UNIT 3 Launching the Republic: 1789–1824

Critical Thinking

Expressing an Opinion Ask students to reread the first paragraph under the head "Drifting Into War" on page 247. Ask students to identify ways in which they think Jefferson violated his principles of individual freedom and limited federal power. Do they think that Presidents should violate their principles for the good of the country as a whole? Why or why not? Why do they think Jefferson chose to be remembered as the author of the Declaration of Independence rather than as the President of the United States? **L1**

Drifting Into War

After two terms, Jefferson was glad to retire to Monticello. He used his influence to secure the nomination of his close friend and secretary of state, James Madison. In the election of 1808, Madison easily defeated the Federalist candidate, Charles Pinckney.

Economic Warfare

Before Jefferson left office in March 1809, Congress repealed the Embargo Act and replaced it with the Non-Intercourse Act, which banned trade with ports under British or French control but allowed trade with the rest of the world. Although less harmful to American trade than the Embargo Act, the Non-Intercourse Act was no more successful in forcing France and Britain to respect the rights of the United States.

In May 1810, Congress tried another tactic by passing Macon's Bill No. 2, which stated that, if either France or Britain agreed to respect neutral rights, the United States would cut off trade with the other nation. In August Napoleon responded with offers to remove his decrees. Not even waiting for the actual repeal of the French decrees, Madison cut off trade with Great Britain, effective March 2, 1811. Napoleon revealed how insincere his offer had been when the French navy continued to seize American ships.

The War Hawks

Although neither Britain nor the United States really wanted war, their actions steered them in that direction. In May 1811, an American ship attacked a British warship. Americans saw it as revenge for the British attack on the *Chesapeake*.

Some young members of Congress, most of them Republicans from the West and the South, called for war. Hunger for land heightened this war fever. Westerners were eager to take Canada, while Southerners wanted Spanish Florida.

Alone, the war hawks did not have enough votes in Congress to pass a declaration of war. More Americans became angry over seizure of American sailors and ships, and pressure to fight increased. Finally, Congress decided that the United States must accept the risks of war rather than be pushed around.

▶ Dock at Portland, Maine

Section 3 ★ Review

Checking for Understanding

1. **Identify** Tripoli, Stephen Decatur, Berlin and Milan decrees, *Chesapeake*, *Leopard*, Embargo Act, Non-Intercourse Act, Macon's Bill No. 2.
2. **Define** piracy, impressment.
3. **Describe** the conflicts with the Barbary pirates that inhibited American trade in North Africa.
4. **Explain** how the Berlin and Milan decrees and the Orders in Council interfered with American neutrality.

Critical Thinking

5. **Analyzing Events** There were a number of opposing influences leading to the War of 1812. Explain the sectional interests to be served by war with England.

LESSON PLAN
SECTION 4, 248–253

FOCUS

Bellringer
Prior to taking roll at the beginning of the class period, display Focus Activity Transparency 29 on the overhead projector and assign the accompanying Focus Activity Sheet.

Objectives
Point out the objectives on this page to students in previewing the section content.

Motivating Activity
Have students read the section introduction and list Madison's grievances against Britain. (impressment, blockades, inciting Native American uprisings, rejecting diplomatic efforts)

Ask students to vote for or against war with Britain. Count and record the number of doves and the number of hawks in the class. Explain that people who are in favor of peace are often called doves, which are symbols of peace. Those in favor of war are called hawks, which are predatory, aggressive birds. Then ask: Why did you vote for or against the war?

Did You Know?
In April 1813, American troops attacked, looted, and occupied York (present-day Toronto), the British capital of Canada. York at that time had a population of 700.

SECTION 4

The War of 1812

Setting the Scene

Section Focus

President Madison listed a number of grievances against Great Britain in his war message, including impressment, blockades, inciting Native American uprisings, and rejecting diplomatic efforts. Yet the war was not a popular one, especially in New England. The fighting ended in 1814 with the Treaty of Ghent, but it did not settle the issues that had caused the war.

Objectives

After studying this section, you should be able to
★ describe the major campaigns of the War of 1812.
★ summarize the results of the War of 1812 and the Treaty of Ghent.

Key Term
frigate

▶ AMERICAN MILITIA COAT, 1812

The British government repealed the Orders in Council on June 23, 1812. British harvests had been poor, and the British desperately needed grain from the United States. British manufacturers had bombarded Parliament with pleas that they faced utter ruin unless trade with the United States was reestablished. The repeal came too late, however. The United States had declared war four days earlier. Declaring war against Great Britain did not suggest an alliance with France. A proposal to include France in the declaration was defeated in the Senate by a vote of 18 to 14.

■ The War in Canada

General Andrew Jackson expressed a popular opinion when he predicted that the conquest of Canada by the United States would be a "mere military promenade." There were several reasons why an attack northward was feasible. Canada was sparsely populated, and French Canadians were lukewarm toward their British rulers. The narrow strip of settlement along the St. Lawrence River and north of Lake Ontario was close to the United States and open to attack. Montreal, the strategic center of Canada, was only 30 miles from New York state.

Lack of Preparation

The conquest of Canada stalled, however, because the military forces of the United States were unprepared. The regular army, numbering about 6,000 soldiers, was scattered throughout the frontier posts. The top commanders, veterans of the Revolution, were too old for warfare. There was no single commanding general and no overall strategy.

UNIT 3 Launching the Republic: 1789–1824

Classroom Resources for SECTION 4

Teacher's Classroom Resources
- Reproducible Lesson Plan
- Reteaching Activity 8-4
- Chapter 8 Primary and Secondary Source Readings
- Chapter 8 Enrichment Activity
- Chapter 8 Performance Assessment Activity
- Spanish Summaries & Glossary
- Section Quiz

Multimedia
- Section Focus Transparency 29
- Vocabulary Puzzlemaker
- Testmaker
- Student Self-Test Software

To compensate for the small size of the army, Madison called on the states to furnish militia. Some New England governors refused to supply any troops because they were opposed to "Mr. Madison's War." Members of New York's militia refused to cross the Niagara River into Canada because they had enlisted only to defend their state from invasion.

Failures and Successes

The lack of preparation was evident when small but ably led Canadian forces took Detroit and two forts on Lake Michigan. An American attack across the Niagara River was turned back.

In 1813 matters improved at the western end of the war zone. Commodore Oliver Hazard Perry, having constructed a small fleet, won a brilliant victory over a British squadron and established American control of Lake Erie. Perry's victory made possible an invasion of Canada by way of Detroit. Kentucky volunteers under William Henry Harrison advanced into Canada and defeated a British army at the Battle of the Thames, about 60 miles northeast of Detroit. In the East, however, attempted invasions of Canada from Sackett Harbor and Lake Champlain failed.

During 1812 and 1813, the British, preoccupied with the war against France, had put little effort into the war against the United States. But when Napoleon was defeated and forced into exile in 1814, the British were free to strike hard at the United States. In late summer an army of more than 14,000 British veterans advanced southward from Montreal to invade New York. Blocking its way was an American army stationed at Plattsburg on Lake Champlain. Although outnumbered nearly 3 to 1, American forces drove back the attacks, and the British retreated to Montreal. The northern border of the United States was safe.

■ The British Offensive

In 1814 the British sent two other expeditions into the United States—one to attack Washington, D.C., and Baltimore, the other to take New Orleans.

Washington, D.C., and Baltimore

In August British transports landed an army of about 4,000 soldiers at Chesapeake Bay. It marched into the capital and very nearly captured the President. To retaliate

AMERICAN PORTRAITS

Dolley Madison
1768–1849

Born in North Carolina, Dolley Payne grew up in Virginia until, at age 15, she moved with her parents to Philadelphia. There she married John Todd, Jr. Dolley Todd gave birth to two children, but in the yellow-fever epidemic in 1793, she lost one of her children and her husband.

The following year Dolley Todd married James Madison. When James became secretary of state, Dolley served as unofficial first lady, entertaining White House guests of widower Thomas Jefferson. As official first lady from 1809 to 1817, Dolley was known for her elaborate parties—including the first inaugural ball. She also displayed remarkable bravery during the War of 1812. Packing up Gilbert Stuart's famous painting of George Washington and White House belongings, she conveyed them safely out of town before the British burned the White House in 1814.

CHAPTER 8 Age of Jefferson 1800–1815   **249**

Special Needs

Specialized Learners Ask students who learn best by reading to research one of the maritime battles of the War of 1812, such as the engagement between HMS *Shannon* and USS *Chesapeake* off Boston. Have students who prefer visual or hands-on learning experiences draw a detailed picture of a battleship of the period. Have students who undertook research projects read them to the class, and ask students who made drawings to display them on the bulletin board.

CHAPTER 8 SECTION 4

Independent Practice

Vocabulary Tell students that Francis Scott Key wrote the "Star-Spangled Banner" while near Fort Henry in Baltimore. Ask students to study the words of the song. Have them look up in a dictionary the meaning of these words from the song: hailed, perilous, ramparts, and gallantly. Have students use the words in sentences. **L1, LEP**

Visualizing History Of the 2,260 American battle deaths during the War of 1812, there were 265 people killed while serving in the navy.
Answer to Caption: The British navy had long been regarded as invincible.

Did You Know?

During the War of 1812, a meatpacker named Samuel Adams shipped beef to the U.S. Army with "U.S." stamped on the shipments. The initials stood for "United States," but those who opposed the war said the initials stood for "Uncle Sam." Curiously, today, "Uncle Sam" is a symbol of national pride.

---

against the burning of public buildings in York (now Toronto) in 1813, the British burned the public buildings of Washington, destroying the Capitol and the White House.

From Washington the British proceeded to Baltimore but were turned back by the forces guarding the city. During the bombardment of Fort McHenry in Baltimore harbor, Francis Scott Key wrote "The Star-Spangled Banner."

New Orleans

Unable to crack the defenses at Baltimore, the British army joined forces with the expedition attempting to capture New Orleans. The British, now almost 10,000 strong, reached the mouth of the Mississippi River in December 1814. Awaiting them were 4,500 Americans under the command of Andrew Jackson of Tennessee. His army consisted of regular soldiers and militia, with a few pirates recruited for their ability to handle artillery. Jackson also called upon the free African Americans of New Orleans to volunteer for service, promising them the same wages as the white soldiers. Two all-African American battalions contributed to the American victory at New Orleans.

When the final British attack came on January 8, 1815, American forces were sheltered behind a barricade of cotton bales. The British, advancing in the open, were no match for Jackson's well-protected soldiers. More than 2,000 soldiers were killed or wounded before the British surrendered. However, the Battle of New Orleans, the greatest American victory of the war, was a useless slaughter. News traveled slowly in those days, and it was learned only after the battle that a peace treaty had been signed in Europe two weeks earlier.

▲ **WAR ON THE SEAS** On August 19, 1812, the United States frigate *Constitution* decisively defeated the British warship *Guerriere*. **Why was it surprising that American ships were victorious in many early battles?**

UNIT 3 Launching the Republic: 1789–1824

Cooperative Learning

Have students form groups of three to review events of the War of 1812. Assign each member one of the following topics: the reasons for going to war with Britain, the main land battles, and the main sea battles. Set a time limit for students to study, summarize, and teach the key facts of their topics to the other members of the group. **L1, L2**

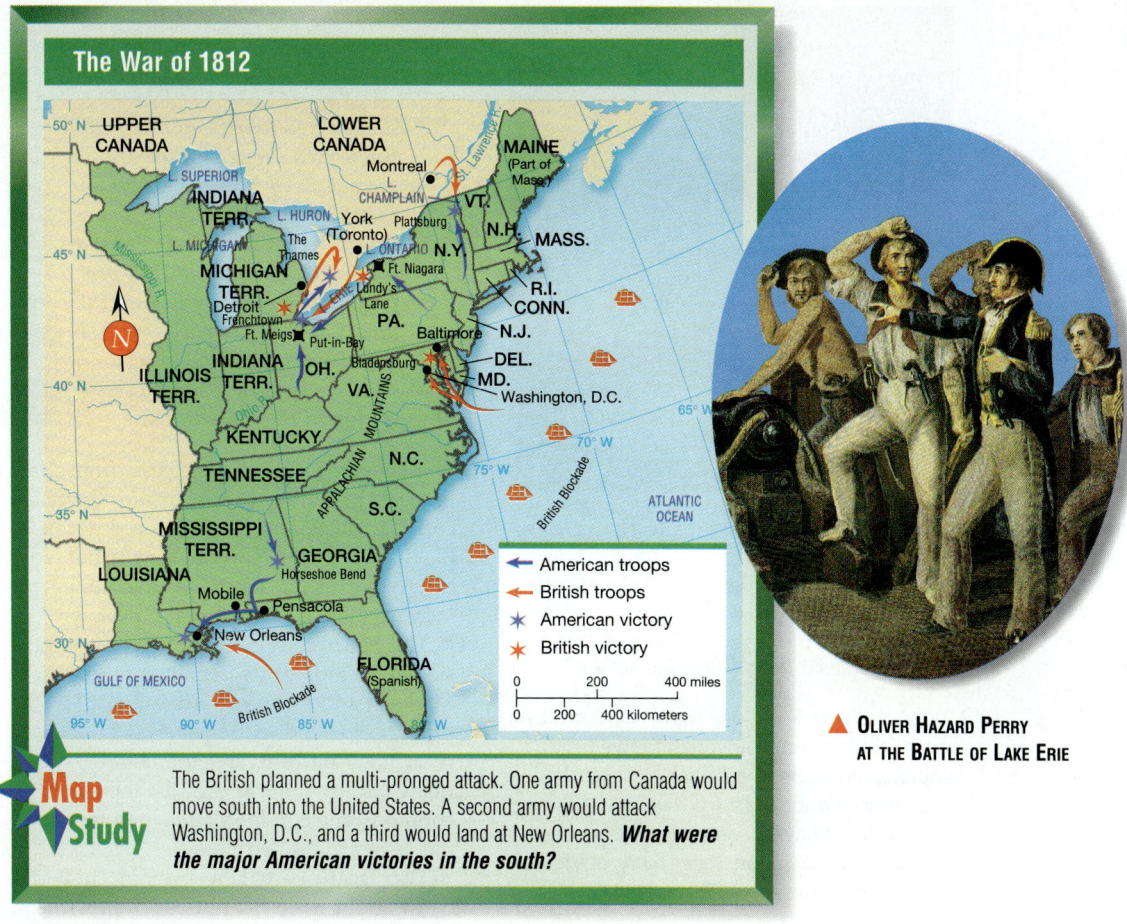

Map Study

The British planned a multi-pronged attack. One army from Canada would move south into the United States. A second army would attack Washington, D.C., and a third would land at New Orleans. **What were the major American victories in the south?**

▲ OLIVER HAZARD PERRY AT THE BATTLE OF LAKE ERIE

■ The War at Sea

At the beginning of the war, the small navy of the United States appeared to be no match for the British fleet. Only four small ships plus a few small gunboats for coastal defense had been built during the administrations of Jefferson and Madison. During John Adams's term in office, however, half a dozen excellent **frigates**—medium-sized warships—had been built. These frigates had more firepower than any European ships of the same size and were speedy enough to escape from larger warships.

When war broke out, the frigates put to sea and within a few months had won a series of victories in battles with British vessels. The victories had little effect on Britain, however, since its navy outnumbered that of the United States at least 20 to 1. Still, Britain had ruled the sea so long that even a few defeats by the United States came as a shock to British leaders. After yet another loss, a British newspaper lamented:

> ❝ Can this be true? Will the English people read this unmoved? Any man who foretold such disasters this day last year would have been treated as a madman or a traitor. . . [U.S. frigates] leave their ports when they choose and return when it suits their convenience. ❞

In addition to the frigates, the United States sent more than 500 privateers to sea. They captured more than 1,300 British vessels, some within sight of Britain.

Sidelights: Military History

When British troops took over Washington D.C., in 1814, British admiral Sir George Cockburn ordered them to burn the Capitol, the White House, and the Navy Arsenal. Destruction to the city was not total, because a violent rainstorm struck the same night, and the accompanying winds destroyed houses, killed 30 British soldiers, and dismantled cannons. An accidental gunpowder explosion and a false rumor that American troops were mustering to retake Washington so demoralized the British that the redcoats left the city, never to return.

CHAPTER 8 SECTION 4

Map Study **Using Maps**

Answers: Horseshoe Bend and New Orleans

Skills Practice

Ask students to identify the sites of British victories in the War of 1812. (Frenchtown, Lundy's Lane, Washington, D.C.)

Did You Know?

After Oliver Hazard Perry's victory at the Battle of Lake Erie in 1813, he sent the following famous message to General William Harrison: "We have met the enemy, and they are ours."

ASSESS

Check Understanding

Assign Section 4 Review as homework or an in-class activity.

Evaluate

Assign the Section 4 Quiz in the TCR or use the History of a Free Nation Testmaker to create a customized quiz.

Reteach

Have students complete Reteaching Activity 8-4.

▲ **JACKSON AT NEW ORLEANS** American forces under Andrew Jackson resoundingly defeated the British troops at the Battle of New Orleans, fought on January 8, 1815. **What effect did the battle have on the treaty that ended the war?**

As the war went on, however, American victories at sea grew fewer and fewer. With its superior numbers, the British fleet blockaded the entire Atlantic coast from Boston to Savannah. United States trade with other countries ceased, and the United States navy, bottled up in port, could not repeat its early successes.

The War's End

As the war dragged on, opposition grew, especially in New England, where people balked at buying United States bonds issued to cover the cost of the war. Public meetings were held to protest the conflict. Above all, they foresaw that the war would be damaging, even ruinous to their economies:

> About three-fourths of our townsmen depend on the sea for the means of subsistence for themselves and their families. By the recent declaration of war more than one-half of that proportion is liable to fall into the hands of the enemy.... We feel therefore most strongly incumbent.... to seek a speedy termination of the present war.

In December 1814, delegates from New England met in secret at Hartford, Connecticut. The Hartford Convention did not insist that New England leave the Union, but it did demand seven constitutional amendments to increase the region's political power.

The Hartford Convention sent commissioners to present its demands to President Madison and Congress. Their arrival in the capital coincided with the news of the victory at New Orleans and the signing of the treaty ending the war. Amidst the great celebrations, the commissioners had no choice but to return to their homes.

The Treaty of Ghent did not contain a word about neutral rights or impressment. Not a square mile of territory changed hands. The warring nations simply agreed to stop fighting, to restore the old boundaries, and to put other problems off for future settlement. Signed on Christmas Eve, 1814, the treaty was unanimously ratified by the Senate in February 1815.

Section 4 ★ Review

Checking for Understanding

1. **Identify** Andrew Jackson, Mr. Madison's War, Oliver Perry, Francis Scott Key, Battle of New Orleans, Hartford Convention, Treaty of Ghent.
2. **Define** frigate.
3. **Explain** why American troops failed to capture Canada.
4. **State** why the battle of New Orleans was a useless slaughter.

Critical Thinking

5. **Comparing Actions** The United States entered the war in Vietnam and left it without winning or losing. Compare the War of 1812 and the Vietnam War.

CONNECTIONS  CONNECTIONS

Exploring the Louisiana Purchase

Even before the Louisiana Purchase was considered, President Thomas Jefferson was interested in exploring the lands west of the United States. Meriwether Lewis, Jefferson's private secretary, shared that dream. After the Louisiana Territory became part of the United States, Jefferson made plans to send an exploration party to the territory. He selected Lewis to lead the expedition.

William Clark, the brother of Revolutionary War hero George Rogers Clark, was chosen to be second in command. William Clark had resigned from the army but reenlisted in order to go on the expedition.

than 7,600 miles to the Pacific. They returned with maps and information that helped make possible the great western migration during the mid-1800s.

William Clark constructed 60 maps—some eight feet in length—depicting the expedition's route. Although the expedition carried various surveying and measuring instruments, Clark seems to have relied primarily on the compass and his own estimates of distances in making his maps. It is likely that Clark took a series of back sightings to render his maps. For example, after reaching an easily identifiable landmark such as a bend in a stream, Clark would turn and take a compass reading back to his previous point of sighting. Clark could then plot each shift in the route on the map.

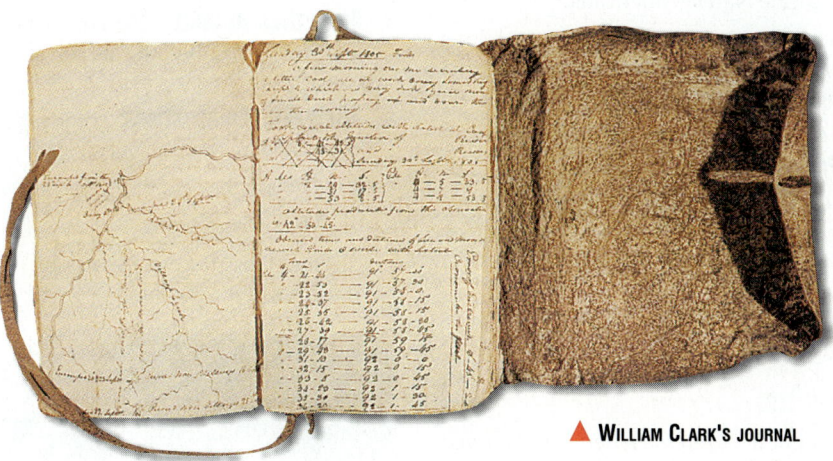

▲ WILLIAM CLARK'S JOURNAL

What lay in the vast Louisiana Territory? How far was it to the Pacific Ocean? Certainly, the members of the Lewis and Clark expedition had little idea of what distances and difficulties they would face on their trek. Starting from St. Louis, the expedition traveled northward up the Missouri River into present-day North Dakota. Eventually, it crossed the Rocky Mountains and sailed on the Columbia River to the Pacific Ocean. The members had traveled more

Making the Geography Connection

1. What do you think was the major obstacle facing Lewis and Clark?
2. Would you classify Clark's method of mapmaking as scientific? Explain.

Linking Past and Present

3. How might an unknown region of the earth be mapped today?

CHAPTER 8 CONNECTIONS

Teaching Making Connections

Although the maps of Lewis and Clark were primitive by today's standards, considering their tools and methods of mapping they are remarkably accurate. The map of the Mississippi River system shows the tributaries quite accurately in relation to one another, and the configuration of the river system is immediately recognizable.

Did You Know?

On January 18, 1803, months before France offered to sell the entire Louisiana territory, Jefferson secretly asked Congress for money for an expedition to be led by Lewis and Clark. Its purpose was to explore the Missouri River region and lands "even to the western ocean [the Pacific]."

Answers to Connections

1. Answers will vary; traveling into unknown region, great distances, crossing Rocky Mountains, rivers.
2. Clark's mapping activities were not scientific, because he relied mainly upon his own estimates.
3. Answers will vary but might include remote sensing using satellite imagery.

REVIEW CHAPTER 8

Answers
Reviewing Facts

1. Hamilton's views: government should support industry and trade; government should support wealthy manufacturing interests; population based in cities; strong central government, weak state legislatures; Jefferson's views: government should promote farming and small businesses; common people should have greater government role; strong state, weak central government.
2. Marshall, a staunch Federalist and Chief Justice for life, carried out the Federalist principles and established judicial review.
3. Jefferson favored removing Native Americans from lands east of the Mississippi to unoccupied lands west of the Mississippi.
4. New England Federalists believed that the Louisiana Purchase was unconstitutional; western expansion would weaken New England's economic and political position, would subordinate New England's commercial interests to those of agrarian South. Federalists took position that the sale was illegal because there was nothing in the Constitution authorizing it.
5. Andrew Jackson defeated Creeks and Cherokees in Florida; he defeated a superior British force in New Orleans in 1815.
6. Both Jefferson and Madison wanted to move the Native Americans west of the Mississippi River. They forced the signing of the treaties ceding valuable Native American lands to the government.

Understanding Concepts

1. Jefferson wanted to assure New England Federalists that he needed their support and that his measures would not harm them.
2. Europe acknowledged the United States' right to exist as an independent nation.
3. Many Americans believed that God had allowed them to come through the War of 1812 with honor.
4. Harrison negotiated 15 treaties forcing Native Americans to give up lands in Indiana and Illinois. He also fought those who resisted.

Critical Thinking

1. Answers will vary but may include that Jefferson would represent all people.

CHAPTER 8 ★ REVIEW

Using Vocabulary

Use the vocabulary words to create a newspaper article on the main events of the War of 1812.

laissez-faire
judicial review
impressment
writ of mandamus
piracy
frigate

Reviewing Facts

1. **Compare** the views of Thomas Jefferson and Alexander Hamilton on the role of government and society.
2. **Explain** why *Marbury* v. *Madison* was a great victory for Federalists and the judiciary.
3. **Indicate** how Jefferson planned to use some of the territory gained within the Louisiana Purchase to relocate Native Americans.
4. **Explain** how the Louisiana Purchase caused the champions of implied powers to become strict constructionists.
5. **Describe** the military accomplishments of Andrew Jackson between 1813 and 1815.
6. **State** where the Republicans wanted Native Americans to move and the measures Jefferson and Madison took to force that move.

Understanding Concepts

National Identity

1. In his Inaugural Address, Jefferson reminded Americans, "We are all Republicans, we are all Federalists." Explain how that statement was meant to create a national identity.
2. Show how the Treaty of Ghent enhanced the nation's identity even though the United States gained none of its goals in fighting the war.

Geographic Expansion

3. When Jefferson doubled the size of the United States through the Louisiana Purchase, many people believed it was God's will that the United States should extend from sea to sea. Explain why Americans held this belief.

4. American expansion also occurred through the cession of Native American lands. How did William Henry Harrison handle the conflict with the Native Americans?

Critical Thinking

1. **Making Judgments** Imagine that you are walking along a Washington street and see President Jefferson dressed in faded corduroy overalls. How would you feel about Jefferson running the country today? On what criteria have you based your judgment?
2. **Comparing Policy** Describe ways Jefferson was like Washington.
3. **Cause and Effect** What effects did the Louisiana Purchase have on the United States politically and economically?
4. **Analyzing Results** Explain why neither side won or lost under the terms of the Treaty of Ghent.
5. **Analyzing Illustrations** Study the illustration below and answer the questions.
    a. Who are the central figures in the picture?
    b. What is happening?
    c. Does the artist express a point of view in this illustration? Explain.

▲ IMPRESSMENT OF AMERICAN SAILORS

254 UNIT 3 Launching the Republic: 1789–1824

CHAPTER 8 ★ REVIEW

Writing About History

Narration

Although they were political enemies in office, Thomas Jefferson, a Republican, and John Adams, a Federalist, later became friends. They kept up a correspondence until they died. Select a partner and write a series of letters that Adams and Jefferson might have written to each other on the state of the nation after 1808—about the War of 1812, Native American affairs, and the settlement of the West.

Cooperative Learning

Organize a group within your classroom to simulate a discussion among Bill Clinton, John Adams, and Thomas Jefferson. Possible discussion topics might include the budget deficit, the situation in the Middle East, civil rights, and any other foreign or domestic issues you think relevant. Present the group discussion to your class.

Social Studies Skills

Describing Exact and Relative Location

Geographers use lines of latitude and longitude to locate places on Earth's surface. The degrees at which the latitude and longitude lines meet are the exact location of that place. For example, to describe the exact location of a city, geographers would first find on the map the line of latitude nearest to the city. Then they would follow this line until it intersects the nearest line of longitude. The latitude and longitude coordinates together provide the city's exact location. On the map of the Barbary States, the exact location of Tripoli is 32° N, 13° E.

Besides exact location, places also have relative location. Relative location is indicated by using the cardinal directions—north, south, east, and west—as well as the intermediate directions—northeast, southeast, northwest, and southwest—to describe the location of one place in relation to another. For example, Tripoli is located west of the city of Derna and southeast of Algiers. The use of latitude and longitude can also be helpful in determining the relative location of one place to another.

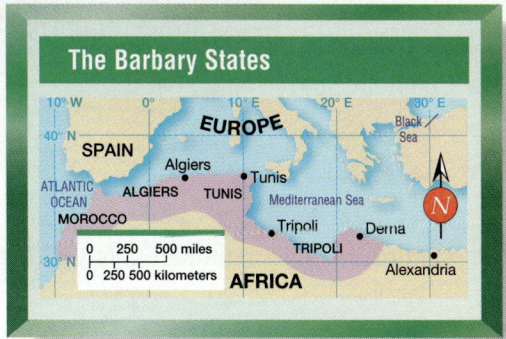

Practicing the Skill

Study the map and then answer the questions.
1. What body of water borders the Barbary States to the north?
2. What is the exact location of Tunis?
3. In which direction would a traveler go from Tunis to reach Tripoli?
4. In between approximately which lines of longitude do the Barbary States fall?
5. Use a map of the world to describe the relative location of Tripoli to these cities: Moscow, Russia; Johannesburg, South Africa; and Bombay, India.

Using Your Journal

Use your notes of differences between Republican and Federalist views to summarize the major differences between Republicans and Federalists.

REVIEW CHAPTER 8

Practicing the Skill
1. Mediterranean Sea
2. 37° N and 10° E
3. southeast
4. 10° W and 25° E
5. southwest of Moscow; north of Johannesburg and slightly west of it and northwest of Bombay

Chapter Bonus Test Question

At the end of Thomas Jefferson's second term of office, which European countries controlled land that bordered on the United States? (Spain in Florida and the Southwest; Britain in Canada and claims to Oregon Country.)

Using Your Journal

The ideas that students present in their summaries should include specific differences and similarities.

---

2. Jefferson, like Washington, became the chief legislator. He worked with the Republican leaders in Congress and gave his supporters key positions in government.
3. The Louisiana Purchase doubled the size of the United States and opened the way for settlers to move westward. Politically and economically, the Louisiana Purchase stretched the interpretation of the Constitution; made New England Federalists fearful that their power would weaken and their economy would suffer.
4. The terms of the Treaty of Ghent did not address neutral rights or impressment and did not change any land boundaries.
5. a. Two British soldiers and an American sailor
   b. The British soldiers are taking the sailor prisoner.
   c. Answers will vary, but include the illustration shows the imperialist nature of Britain.

PLANNING GUIDE   Chapter 9   Nationalism and Change

Daily Lesson Objectives	Teacher Classroom Resources	Multimedia
SECTION 1 **The Era of Good Feelings** **1 Day** pp. 258–262 1. Identify events after the War of 1812 that showed a spirit of nationalism. 2. Explain how the Supreme Court increased the national government's power.	Chapter 9 Study Guide Reproducible Lesson Plan Section Quiz Reteaching Activity 9-1 LEP Reinforcing Social Studies Skills 27, 30, 32, 36, 38, 62 LEP Chapter 9 Primary and Secondary Source Readings American Portraits, 17 The Living Constitution Chapter 9 Cooperative Learning Activity Chapter 9 Concept Mapping Activity	Student Self-Test Software Chapter 9 Testmaker Section Focus Transparency 26 Chapter 9 Skills Transparency
SECTION 2 **Tying the Nation Together** **1 Day** pp. 263–269 1. Explain the advantages and disadvantages of each type of transportation improvement. 2. Discuss the ways that internal improvements changed the nation.	Reproducible Lesson Plan Reteaching Activity 9-2 LEP Section Quiz Reinforcing Social Studies Skills 9, 27, 50, 61, 64 LEP Map and Graph Skill Activity 16 American Portraits, 18	Student Self-Test Software Chapter 9 Testmaker Section Focus Transparency 27 Chapter 9 Map Transparency U.S. History & Art Transparency 6
SECTION 3 **Monroe and Foreign Affairs** **1 Day** pp. 271–274 1. Describe America's problems with Britain and Spain and how they were settled. 2. Explain the foreign policy principles established by the Monroe Doctrine.	Reproducible Lesson Plan Reteaching Activity 9-3 LEP Section Quiz Chapter 9 Enrichment Activity Chapter 9 Primary & Secondary Source Readings Reinforcing Social Studies Skills 23, 32, 40 LEP Map and Graph Skill Activity 23 LEP American Literary Heritage, Unit 3 Outline Maps 5, 6 Spanish Summaries & Glossary	Student Self-Test Software Chapter 9 Testmaker Section Focus Transparency 28 Unit 3 Digest Transparencies Vocabulary Puzzlemaker Audiocassette, Chapter 9 A Geographic Perspective on American History
CHAPTER REVIEW AND EVALUATION **1 Day**	Chapter 9 Test Chapter 9 Performance Assessment Activity	Student Self-Test Software Chapter 9 Testmaker

00:00   OUT OF TIME? If time does not permit teaching the entire chapter, use the Chapter 9 Summary on pages 280–281 and the Chapter 9 audiocassette (English and Spanish) to point out the main ideas of the chapter.

PLANNING GUIDE

Cultural Diversity Activity

Research In 1810, a Philadelphian boasted, "In no country in the world is the practice of music more universally extended." By the early 1800s, Americans had already developed a rich musical tradition. It was an integral part of life throughout the nation, and it reflected the nation's cultural diversity. Encourage students to divide into groups and research some of that music and trace its ethnic origins. One group might focus on ballads and love songs. Another might explore the music played at both elegant balls and country barn dances. Others might gather examples of work songs. Other possibilities include patriotic songs, military marches, and church music. Set aside a day for students to share their findings with the class.

Performance Assessment Activity

Cultural Highlights Divide the class into four groups. Assign a different bestseller to research from the early 1800s. (Possibilities include: Washington Irving's *Sketch Book*; James Fenimore Cooper's *The Spy*, *The Pilot*, and *The Pioneer*.) Ask each group to create a poster or write a book review that would encourage Americans to buy the book.

POSSIBLE RUBRIC FEATURES: Content, organization, clarity, critical thinking skills, creativity, cooperative skills, written and visual communication skills

Chapter Resources

Literature from the Period

Clinton, DeWitt. "Annual Message of the Governor." 1825.

Irving, Washington. "The Legend of Sleepy Hollow." 1819–1820.

Readings for the Student

"Robert Fulton Through Nineteenth Century Eyes." *American History Illustrated.* Vol. 21, No. 8, December 1986.

Shank, William. *Towpaths to Tugboats: A History of American Canal Engineering.* American Canal and Transportation Center, 1982.

Readings for the Teacher

Brown, Richard D. *Modernization: The Transformation of American Life: 1600–1865.* Hill and Wang, 1976.

Dangerfield, George. *The Awakening of American Nationalism: 1815–1828.* Harper, 1980.

Multimedia Resources

American Foreign Policy. Focus Media. (Apple diskette.)

The Monroe Doctrine Applied: US Policy Toward Latin America. VMA. (VHS, 16 minutes)

South America: A Unit of Study. United Learning. (6 color filmstrips)

Supreme Court Decision. Queue. (Apple or IBM diskettes, guide)

Key to Ability Levels

Teaching strategies have been coded for varying learning styles and abilities.

L1   Basic activities for all students

L2   Average activities for average to above-average students

L3   Challenging activities for above-average students

LEP   Limited English Proficiency activities

Glencoe Links to the Humanities

Link to Art
- U.S. History & Art Transparency 6

Link to Literature
- Macmillan Literature: American Literature Text— William Cullen Bryant

Link to Music
- American Music: Cultural Traditions

CHAPTER 9

BEGINNING THE CHAPTER

Direct students' attention to the time line on pages 256–257. Ask them to identify the political event that had economic connections. (Second Bank of the United States chartered) Have students speculate why the chartering of the Second Bank of the United States might have become necessary. (to print national currency, to provide money to run the federal government) Tell students to check the accuracy of their speculations as they study this chapter.

Recording Journal Notes

Tell students that one way to make efficient use of a journal is to record notes in the form of charts. Suggest that they create a chart with three columns: Nationalistic Legislation, Court Decisions, and Internal Improvements.

Linking Across TIME

Most of the symbols through which we express our American identity—heroes, songs, legends, flags, monuments—developed in the early 1800s. Some of our holidays, such as the Fourth of July, and the ways we celebrate them with parades, speeches, and picnics, became established during that time.

CHAPTER 9

Nationalism and Change
1816–1824

▶ Quilt, sunburst pattern

Setting the Scene

Focus

During the peacetime that followed the War of 1812, a powerful spirit of nationalism swept through American life. Nationalism was reflected in many ways. It included the push for internal improvements, better economic ties among sections of the country, and a strengthening of the central government. Many Federalist ideals were implemented in spite of the disappearance of the Federalist party. This new sense of American pride also resulted in a more forceful foreign policy.

Concepts to Understand

★ How a feeling of national community emerged during the presidency of James Monroe

★ How foreign policy helped shape the United States as an emerging world power

Read to Discover . . .

★ the forces that helped unite the United States after the War of 1812.

★ what circumstances prompted the Monroe Doctrine.

Journal Notes

What impact did the nationalistic legislation, court decisions, and internal improvements of this era have on state governments? Note examples in your journal as you read the chapter.

CULTURAL	• 1816 African Methodist Episcopal Church organized	• 1819 University of Virginia founded	• 1820 United States missionaries travel to Hawaii
	1816	**1818**	**1820**
POLITICAL	• 1816 Second Bank of the United States chartered	• 1818 National Road reaches Wheeling	• 1821 Moses Austin receives land grant in Texas

256   UNIT 3 Launching the Republic: 1789–1824

✚ EXTRA CREDIT PROJECT

The federal government has often intervened in the national economy. Ask interested students to work as a committee to research the provisions of the charter of the Second Bank of the United States, including the percentage of its stock owned by the federal government and the number of its 25 directors named by the government. The committee should present its findings to the class, noting how the bank aided private businesses and the nation's prosperity.

256

CHAPTER 9 CONCEPTS

Concept Mapping Activity

Draw this concept map on the chalkboard, and ask students to hypothesize what era of history and what concepts they will be studying. Have them copy the concept map in their notebooks and list pertinent events found in the chapter.

```
A spirit of nationalism
supports western
expansion and an end
to interference from
European countries.
         /        \
National      World
Community     Power
```

History AND ART

John Lewis Krimmel (1786–1821) was born in Germany and immigrated to Philadelphia in 1810. This picture depicts a Fourth of July celebration in Philadelphia shortly after the War of 1812.

NATIONAL GEOGRAPHIC SOCIETY

The following materials are available from Glencoe and may be used to enrich Chapter 9:

VIDEODISC

- *GTV: A Geographic Perspective on American History*

Any side, Frame 52673
Subject: Map showing acquisition of Florida

History AND ART

Fourth of July Celebration in Center Square, Philadelphia
by John Lewis Krimmel, 1819

Celebrations on the Fourth of July show that the Fourth had become a national tradition less than 50 years after the nation gained its independence.

◀ NATIONAL ROAD MILE MARKER

- **1823** "Twas the Night Before Christmas" published
- **1823** Monroe Doctrine proclaimed
- **1824** Robert Owen founds New Harmony, Indiana
- **1824** Gibbons v. Ogden
- **1828** American Peace Society forms
- **1826** Pan-American Conference held

CHAPTER 9 Nationalism and Change 1816–1824

Teacher Notes

LESSON PLAN
SECTION 1, 258–262

FOCUS

Bellringer
Before taking roll at the beginning of the class period, display Focus Activity Transparency 30 on the overhead projector, and assign the accompanying Focus Activity Sheet.

Objectives
Point out the objectives on this page to students in previewing the section content.

Motivating Activity
Have students list their school's symbols. (examples: school colors; school uniforms for sports or other activities; school emblem and motto) Ask why these symbols are important to students. (They make students feel special, provide a feeling of belonging, and help create pride in attending a school.) Then ask and discuss: What are some examples of national symbols that create in Americans feelings of belonging? (examples: national flag, national anthem) Point out that this section deals with the spirit of nationalism as a powerful force in the development of the United States.

Use Skills Transparency 9.

SECTION 1

The Era of Good Feelings

Setting the Scene

Section Focus
After the War of 1812, United States economic growth continued to be limited by geography. Because long-range commercial activity was difficult, most Americans traded close to home. As industry grew in Northern cities, manufacturers wanted to expand their markets and enjoy conditions that encouraged growth. Rural Americans also desired prosperity. New government legislation was directed toward meeting these goals.

Objectives
After studying this section, you should be able to
★ list events that showed a spirit of nationalism.
★ explain how the Supreme Court increased the national government's power.

Key Terms
nationalism, internal improvement

▶ CANDLE MOLD

Nationalism is a feeling of intense loyalty and devotion to one's country. It is a spirit that unifies into one nation diverse groups who share a geographic area. Nationalism can be demonstrated by people's actions; illustrated by such symbols as a flag; and expressed in a nation's art, literature, and music.

■ Nationalistic Legislation

In the United States, the spirit of nationalism declined after the Revolution but was revived by the War of 1812. The conduct of the war revealed the dangers of disunion, and the war's outcome increased national pride and self-confidence. Albert Gallatin, one of the United States commissioners at the peace conference in Ghent, recognized the revival of nationalism in a letter written shortly after the war's end:

66 *The war had renewed & reinstated the National feelings & character, which the Revolution had given, & which were daily lessened. The people . . . are more American: they feel & act more as a Nation, and I hope that the permanency of the Union is thereby better secured.* 99

In 1816 James Monroe, a Virginia Republican, was elected President over New York Federalist Rufus King. On a national goodwill tour, the new President promoted a spirit of unity everywhere he went. His warm reception by cheering crowds in Boston caused a local Federalist newspaper to proclaim that an "Era of Good Feelings" had begun. By 1820 the Federalists, discredited by their antiwar position during the War of 1812, had vanished from national politics, and President Monroe was reelected without opposition.

UNIT 3 Launching the Republic: 1789–1824

Classroom Resources for SECTION 1

Teacher's Classroom Resources
- Chapter 9 Study Guide
- Reproducible Lesson Plan
- Reteaching Activity 9-1
- Chapter 9 Primary and Secondary Source Readings
- Chapter 9 Cooperative Learning Activity
- Section Quiz

Multimedia
- Section Focus Transparency 30
- Chapter 9 Skills Transparency
- Testmaker
- Student Self-Test Software

Postwar nationalism was revealed in legislation as well as in politics. The War of 1812 had clearly demonstrated that Jefferson's ideal of a central government with strictly limited functions could not meet the needs of a nation in crisis. After the war, a Republican Congress passed a series of laws that sounded as though they had been written by Federalists.

The "American System"

Henry Clay of Kentucky and John C. Calhoun of South Carolina proposed an ambitious program that Clay called the "American System," based on protection and **internal improvements**—roads, canals, and other transportation needs. They advocated a protective tariff for manufacturers, an improved market for farmers, and better transportation for agricultural and industrial goods. Transportation improvements would be financed with money raised by the tariff. Both leaders wanted to reinstate the national bank to create a national currency and encourage economic growth. They hoped that this nationalistic program would bring prosperity to all sections of the country and, to the nation, economic independence from the rest of the world.

Establishment of a National Currency

Republicans traditionally had opposed the idea of a national bank. They blocked the recharter of the first Bank of the United States in 1811 and substituted nothing in its place. The results were disastrous because the notes of the Bank of the United States already had become the national currency. Without a currency and lacking sufficient gold and silver for coins, the country had only the notes of state-chartered banks, which had little or no value beyond the localities where they were issued. Without a national bank, the federal government also had a difficult time borrowing money during the War of 1812.

Because of the nation's financial problems, the Republicans changed their minds and supported creation of a new national bank. In 1816 Congress passed a bill to establish a second Bank of the United States. Like its predecessor, the second Bank of the United States could issue notes to be used as national currency and could act in a number of ways to control state banks.

Trade Protection

During the War of 1812, Americans had difficulty obtaining British products and thus encouraged the growth of American

Henry Clay
1777–1852

AMERICAN PORTRAITS

Virginia-born and raised, Henry Clay moved to Kentucky, a state that kept him in Congress—and in the forefront of national politics—for nearly 50 years.

A fierce political rivalry soon developed between Clay and another Westerner, Andrew Jackson of Tennessee. The two first clashed in 1819 when Clay blasted Jackson's Florida invasion. The election of 1824 made them bitter enemies. Ignoring instructions from Kentucky to back Jackson for President, Clay supported John Quincy Adams, who appointed Clay secretary of state. Jackson's revenge came when he defeated Clay in the presidential election of 1832. Clay sought the presidency three more times before retiring. In 1849, however, he returned to Congress and put together a compromise between North and South that helped delay the Civil War.

CHAPTER 9 Nationalism and Change 1816–1824

Sidelights: Entertainment in the Early Nineteenth Century

People took every opportunity they could to relieve the monotony of isolation on the frontier. Because there was always work to be done, farmers combined working and socializing. Farmers came together to help construct cabins and farm buildings for one another, to put up roofs, or to help with a particularly difficult chore. Women met to beat flax, make quilts, or cook for other workers. Singing, dancing, and swapping tales were among the favorite activities on the frontier.

CHAPTER 9
SECTION 1

Visualizing History

After gaining independence from Britain, the United States developed national tariff policies. In general, tariffs mounted until 1828 and then declined through 1857.
Answer to Caption: to protect them from foreign competition and provide money to finance internal improvements

Did You Know?

People in the early 1800s could be imprisoned if they were unable to pay their debts. An 1817 New York law prevented people who owed less than $25 from being put into debtor's prison. Kentucky, in 1821, was the first state to abolish imprisonment for debt.

Fact or Fiction?

The University of Virginia was the first university in the United States that did not require students to attend chapel.

FACT: In 1819 Thomas Jefferson established the university with this policy.

---

industry. But once the war was over, Britain dumped goods in the United States at such low prices that they threatened to put American companies out of business. Protecting American industry meant that consumers would pay more for imported products, but to business leaders and nationalists alike this price seemed a fair exchange for economic independence.

Congress responded with the Tariff of 1816. Unlike earlier revenue tariffs, which had provided income for the federal government, this tariff was designed to protect American manufacturers by placing high taxes on imports.

■ Supreme Court Nationalism

Nationalism also was demonstrated in a series of Supreme Court decisions by Chief Justice John Marshall. Marshall was appointed in 1801 as one of the last acts of President John Adams, a Federalist. By 1815 the majority of the justices had been appointed by Republican Presidents, but Marshall still dominated the Court. He was a brilliant debater and possessed such strong convictions, friendliness, and persuasiveness that, according to one historian, he "molded his fellow judges like putty." During his 34 years as Chief Justice, Marshall was in the minority on only one case dealing with a constitutional issue. Between 1819 and 1824, Marshall ruled in three important Court cases that established the dominance of the nation over the states and that shaped the future of American government.

"Necessary and Proper" Powers

McCulloch v. *Maryland* (1819) involved an attempt by Maryland to tax the Baltimore branch of the newly created second Bank of the United States. The case answered basic questions about the federal government's power and its relationship with the states.

The national bank was constitutional, Marshall said, even though the Constitution did not specifically give Congress the power to create one. He repeated Alexander Hamilton's 25-year-old argument that the federal government was not limited to the powers listed in the Constitution. Marshall observed that the Constitution specifically permitted Congress to issue money, borrow money, and

▲ **THE TARIFF QUESTION** The unity of the North was related to the development of an economy based primarily on manufacturing. **Why did manufacturing interests favor a protective tariff?**

UNIT 3 Launching the Republic: 1789–1824

Cooperative Learning

Have students discuss in groups of four the precedent-setting cases of the Marshall Court that are covered in detail in this section and in the chart on page 261. Assign numbers and the following tasks to individual students in each group: (1) to present the opposing sides of the case, (2) to analyze the issue, (3) to state the outcome, and (4) to speculate on the effect the outcome would have on future cases. Tell students that you will call on them by number and that they are to carry out their assigned task for the class. **L1, L2**

The Marshall Court and the National Interest

Case and Year	Issue and Decision
Marbury v. Madison (1803)	Declared an act of Congress unconstitutional. Court given power of judicial review and power to declare congressional and state legislation unconstitutional.
Fletcher v. Peck (Yazoo land fraud case, 1810)	Declared sanctity of contracts. Gave Supreme Court right to overturn state laws that ran counter to specific provisions of Constitution.
Martin v. Hunter's Lessee (1816)	Gave Supreme Court right to reverse decisions of state courts.
Trustees of Dartmouth College v. Woodward (1819)	Reaffirmed sanctity of contracts. Protected banks and corporations with state charters from meddling by state legislators.
Sturges v. Crowninshield (1819)	Tested constitutionality of state bankruptcy laws. Court determined that in absence of federal regulation, states were free to legislate.
McCulloch v. Maryland (1819)	Challenged constitutionality of Bank of the United States. Court said "implied powers" enabled Congress to enact any legislation within letter and spirit of Constitution.
Cohens v. Virginia (1821)	Tested constitutionality of Judiciary Act of 1789. Court said states gave up some sovereignty in ratifying Constitution so state courts must accept federal jurisdiction.
Gibbons v. Ogden (1824)	Invalidated a state monopoly. Court gave Congress right to regulate interstate commerce, a decision of great importance for national development.

Source: *The Guide to American Law*, vol. 7 (1984).

Chart Study Chief Justice John Marshall dominated the Supreme Court until his death in 1835. The Marshall Court handed down a series of decisions that increased federal power over state governments. **What was significant about the Martin decision?**

collect taxes. He noted that the national bank would assist in exercising these enumerated powers. Therefore, he concluded, the federal government could choose any method that was "necessary and proper" to exercise the powers the Constitution had given it.

Marshall noted that the people, acting collectively, had created the federal government. Thus it was a truly "national" government, not created by the states or subordinate to them. Therefore, he reasoned, no state had the power to tax the national bank, a legal creation of the federal government.

Contracts and Property Rights

The second important decision of the Marshall Court during this period was *Dartmouth College* v. *Woodward* (1819). This case was one of several in which the Court handed down decisions protecting contracts and property rights from state power. Dartmouth College was a private school chartered in 1769 by King George III. In 1815 the New Hampshire state legislature passed a law to change the charter, allowing Dartmouth to become a state college. But Dartmouth officials did not want to give up their private school, and they refused to turn over college records and funds to the state. When New Hampshire courts upheld the legislature, Dartmouth appealed to the Supreme Court. In writing the Court's decision, Marshall noted that "the state legislatures were forbidden 'to pass any law impairing the obligation of contracts,' that is, of contracts respecting property." A college charter is a contract, he said, and a state has no right to interfere with it. Thus, the state's attempt to seize this private college was unconstitutional.

CHAPTER 9 Nationalism and Change 1816–1824

▲ **COMMERCE** As transportation grew, questions over state and federal rights grew. The case of *Gibbons* v. *Ogden* concerned an attempt by New York to grant a monopoly over steamboat traffic on the Hudson River. **How did the Court rule in this case?**

Interstate Commerce

Gibbons v. *Ogden* (1824) involved a company that operated steamboats in New York. The company had been given a monopoly over steamboat traffic in New York waters. The company took it upon itself to extend its monopoly to include traffic across the Hudson River between New York and New Jersey.

Marshall declared this monopoly was unconstitutional. In his decision, Marshall stated that in allowing the extension, the state legislature had overstepped its power, according to the Constitution, which gave the federal government control over interstate commerce.

In writing the Court's decision, Marshall defined interstate commerce in a way that went far beyond the mere exchange of trade goods between states. By ruling, in effect, that anything crossing state boundaries comes under federal control, Marshall provided the federal government with the constitutional basis for many of the broad and sweeping powers it exercises today.

In these cases and others, Marshall's nationalism strengthened the power of the federal government at the expense of the states. Although he was attacked for his decisions by defenders of states' rights, Marshall's views made the Constitution flexible enough to meet the nation's changing needs.

Section 1 ★ Review

Checking for Understanding

1. **Identify** Era of Good Feelings, American System, Tariff of 1816, John Marshall, *McCulloch* v. *Maryland*, *Gibbons* v. *Ogden*.
2. **Define** nationalism, internal improvement.
3. **Compare** the powers of the second Bank of the United States with the powers of the first Bank.
4. **List** two ways in which the Republicans adopted a Federalist point of view of government after 1812.

Critical Thinking

5. **Determining Relevance** Explain how John Marshall's ruling in *McCulloch* v. *Maryland* was an example of "the end justifies the means."

SECTION 2

Tying the Nation Together

Setting the Scene

Section Focus

The United States had a need for better transportation. The number of states had nearly doubled by 1820, and many new states were west of the Appalachians. Yet there was no easy way to move products long distances. As a transportation network began to crisscross the country, it stimulated movement of people and products and helped build a stronger nation.

Objectives

After studying this section, you should be able to

★ explain the advantages and disadvantages of each type of transportation improvement.

★ discuss the ways that internal improvements changed the nation.

Key Terms

turnpike, toll, lock

◀ FIRST UNITED STATES GENERAL ISSUE POSTAGE STAMPS

The War of 1812 made the need for a better transportation system clear. It had been extremely difficult to move armies, cannons, and supplies from one place to another. Indeed, American plans to invade and annex Canada during the war had failed, in part because America lacked good roads. Now, in peacetime, the only way to move products long distances overland was in wagons on roads that weather made impassable much of the year. With the steamboat in its infancy, travel on the Mississippi River was still one-way. Goods could be floated downriver on flatboats or keelboats, but very little could be powered upstream. Some Americans, especially in the West, felt it was the federal government's responsibility to improve transportation. One such Westerner was Henry Clay.

Not all of Clay's fellow Republicans were ready to support federal financing of internal improvements. In 1816 Representative John C. Calhoun of South Carolina proposed a "Bonus Bill" to build roads and canals with the $1.5 million fee paid by the Bank of the United States for its charter. The bill passed, but President Madison vetoed it, arguing that to spend money improving transportation was an unconstitutional extension of federal power.

■ Transportation by Road

A vital east-west road was already underway when Madison vetoed the Bonus Bill. In 1806 Congress funded the National Road from the sale of Western lands, and construction started from the Potomac River at Cumberland, Maryland, in 1811. By 1818 the road reached Wheeling, Virginia (in present-day West Virginia), spanning the Ohio River on the longest suspension bridge in the

CHAPTER 9 Nationalism and Change 1816–1824   **263**

LESSON PLAN
SECTION 2, 263–270

FOCUS

Bellringer

Before taking roll at the beginning of the class period, display Focus Activity Transparency 31 on the overhead projector, and assign the accompanying Focus Activity Sheet.

Objectives

Point out the objectives on this page to students in previewing the section content.

Motivating Activity

Discuss with students the relationship between the location of the original 13 states and ease or difficulty of transportation among these states, Europe, and the areas west of the Appalachian Mountains.

Tell students that in this section they will study how the building of roads, canals, and railroads contributed to the development of the nation.

 VIDEODISC

• *GTV: A Geographic Perspective on American History*

Side 2, Chapter 9
Title: *Getting Up to Speed*
Subject: Transportation and the growing nation, 1825–1850

See GTV Guide page 44 for complete lesson plan.

Classroom Resources for SECTION 2

Teacher's Classroom Resources
- Reproducible Lesson Plan
- Reteaching Activity 9-2
- Section Quiz

Multimedia
- Section Focus Transparency 31
- Chapter 9 Map Transparency
- Testmaker
- Student Self-Test Software
- A Geographic Perspective on American History

263

CHAPTER 9 SECTION 2

TEACH
Guided Practice
Evaluating Technology

Ask each student to select either the period before the War of 1812 or the period from 1812 to 1840 and write a brief evaluation of the means of transportation in terms of safety, ease, and speed of moving people and products. (Before 1812: horse and wagon—difficult and slow; flatboat or keelboat—faster, cheaper than land transportation but could only float downstream. 1812–40: National Road, turnpikes, and state roads—most not surfaced, muddy in spring, inadequate bridges; steamboats—high-risk, but much faster and more efficient; canals—superior to roads, enabled horses to pull canal boats with 50-ton loads; railroads—best means of transportation, initially dangerous) **L1, L2**

- *GTV: A Geographic Perspective on American History*

Any side, Frame 52561
Subject: Picture of settlers moving west in 1840

world—an engineering marvel. The bridge was 1,010 feet long and hung from towers rising 153 feet above the river.

The National Road went west to Vandalia, Illinois, cutting a path 80 feet wide through the wilderness. The center 30 feet were "paved" with crushed stone, and the road crossed streams and rivers on stone bridges. Great Conestoga wagons drawn by oxen or teams of 4, 6, or 8 horses moved westward along this route.

State Road-Building Projects

In general, states or private businesses undertook improvements in transportation. State-chartered private companies constructed hundreds of miles of **turnpikes**, roads that were barricaded at intervals by poles that stopped travelers until they paid a **toll**, or fee. However, turnpikes were profitable only on main routes, such as between Albany and Lake Erie, or in populated areas where traffic was heavy. In the West, highways usually were constructed by the states themselves, at times with the aid of federal funds.

The Ordeal of Overland Travel

Although by 1840 the country was crisscrossed with roads, they did not provide satisfactory transportation. Except in the East, few were surfaced or spanned by adequate bridges. When the routes passed through woods, foot-high stumps remained in the roadbed. Spring rains turned roads to mud and mired wagons up to their axles. In swampy places, "corduroy"—logs laid sideways across the roadbed—hurt horses' legs and jolted wagons to pieces.

David Stevenson described a journey by stagecoach along a typical route of the time in his book *Sketch of the Civil Engineering of North America*, published in 1838:

> "Sometimes our way lay for miles through extensive marshes, which we crossed by corduroy-roads.... At others the coach stuck fast in mud, from which it could be extricated only by the combined efforts of the coachman and passengers; and at one place we traveled ... through a forest flooded with water, which stood to a height of several feet.... The distance of the route from Pittsburgh to Erie is 128 miles, which was accomplished in forty-six hours ... although the conveyance by which I traveled carried the mail, and stopped only for breakfast, dinner, and tea, but there was considerable delay by the coach being once upset and several times 'mired.'"

Such difficult travel was necessary for families moving west with their belongings and for farmers herding cattle and hogs to market. But bulky goods, such as farm crops or manufactured products, could not be quickly or profitably moved long distances by land. The price of products was out of reach for many people because merchants passed shipping costs on to consumers. Far more important to commerce, therefore, were America's inland waterways.

▼ **CONESTOGA WAGON**

264   UNIT 3 Launching the Republic: 1789–1824

Special Needs

Reading Disability Reading comprehension is often greatly aided by presentation of background information or "schema." The schema is developed from the reader's current knowledge and then extended with new information from text, lecture, pictures, and media. Have students with reading comprehension problems read only the Section Focus. Then discuss our present transportation systems. Continue by having students think about the types of transportation available in the early 1800s. Then have them read Section 2, "Tying the Nation Together."

Map Study

By 1840, the United States east of the Mississippi River was crisscrossed by a network of roads and canals. **By what route could farm goods from Lexington, Kentucky, reach New York City?**

Transportation by Water

Rivers had long been the primary means of moving commercial goods, but travel was one-way—flatboats and rafts floated only downstream. Trips against the current were slow and difficult. Although steamboats were built before 1800, they initially did not attract much attention. In 1807, however, Robert Fulton's steamboat, the *Clermont*, made its first voyages on the Hudson River, chugging the 150 miles from New York City to upstream Albany in an amazing 32 hours. By demonstrating the practicality of two-way river travel, Fulton launched the steamboat era.

The Growth of Steamboat Travel

In 1811 the first steamboat in Western waters steamed down the Ohio and Mississippi rivers from Pittsburgh to New Orleans and then returned upriver as far as Louisville. Steamboats proved their ability to carry passengers and goods quickly and efficiently,

---

Map Study Using Maps

Answer:
North on Maysville Turnpike to Ohio River; either east or west on river to the Ohio and Erie Canal or the Miami and Erie Canal; north on either canal to Lake Erie at Cleveland or Toledo; east on lake to Erie Canal at Buffalo; east on canal to Hudson River; south on river to New York City.

Skills Practice
Ask students which canal connects Troy and Buffalo. (Erie Canal) Which is the westernmost canal? (the Illinois and Michigan)

Use Chapter 9 Project Map Transparency.

Did You Know?

The Conestoga wagon took its name from the Conestoga Valley in Pennsylvania, where it was first made in 1750. The Conestoga Valley, in turn, derived its name from the Conestoga people, a Native American group whose population was reduced by epidemics from about 5,000 in 1600 to 20 people in 1763. Those last few were massacred by white settlers.

Cooperative Learning

Divide students into groups of five. Assign each group one of these topics to discuss: railroads, canals, and roads and turnpikes. Give each student a set of colored chips and each group a container to place the chips into and a one-minute timer. Explain that when a student wishes to participate in the discussion, he or she must give up a chip and place it in the container. Tell students that they must spend all their chips in 15 minutes and that one minute is the longest a person can talk. **L1, L2**

CHAPTER 9
SECTION 2

Another great federal road project was completed much later for similar reasons as the National Road. In the 1950s truckers asked Congress for modern, high-speed highways. In addition, increased car use on such highways would benefit the construction industry, the oil industry, large auto producers, and the thousands of other businesses that supplied the auto industry with glass, rubber, steel, and car parts.

To finance the interstate highway system with federal funds, Congress decided that interstates were necessary for defense.

Visualizing History George Catlin (1796–1872) painted this Mississippi riverboat scene. He is famous for his hundreds of paintings of Native American peoples. Catlin wished to record their traditional ways of life before they were gone forever.
Answer to Caption: By connecting the Hudson River to the Great Lakes, the canal made the city the commercial center for the area north and west of the Ohio River.

and by 1850 nearly 800 of them regularly traveled the Mississippi and its tributaries. Flat-bottomed steamboats were developed to navigate rivers less than three feet deep.

The benefits of steamboat travel were great, but risks were high. The average life of a river steamboat was three to six years—not surprising considering the dangers presented by snags, ice, bursting boilers, collisions, fires, and sandbars. About one-third of the steamboats built before 1850 were lost in accidents. In 1839 Michael Chevalier, a French traveler in America, noted that his Mississippi steamboat trip posed more dangers than his Atlantic crossing:

> There have been many accidents by fire in the steamers, and many persons have perished in this way.... The Brandywine was burnt near Memphis, in 1832, and every soul on board, to the number of 110, was lost.

> The Americans show a singular indifference in regard to fire... they smoke without the least concern in the midst of half-open cotton bales... they ship gunpowder with no more precaution than if it were so much maize or salt pork.... it matters little, if they move at a rapid rate, and are navigated at little expense.

The Erie Canal

For moving heavy goods, the thousands of miles of canals built during the first part of the nineteenth century were far more efficient than even the best roads. On a good road, it took 4 horses to haul a 1.5-ton load; 2 horses or mules could pull a canal boat with a load of 50 tons. Before 1815 a number of short canals had been built, most of them

 ▲ **ON THE RIVER** by George Catlin Steamboats and canal boats speeded the movement of people and the transportation of goods. **How did New York City benefit from the Erie Canal?**

UNIT 3 Launching the Republic: 1789–1824

Critical Thinking

Recognizing Values Distribute copies of the following information:

The writers of the Constitution left control of public schools to the states. States did not have to support education financially, however, so each community provided its own school. While many village schools had hired masters, there were no trained teachers until 1823, when the first school for teachers was opened in Concord, Vermont.

Ask students to use the paragraph to explain the value people placed on education. **L1, L2**

bypassing rapids and falls in rivers or linking natural waterways. The canal-building craze did not really begin, however, until completion of the Erie Canal in 1825.

Begun by New York state in 1817, the Erie Canal was 40 feet wide, 4 feet deep, and 363 miles long—running from Albany on the Hudson River to Buffalo on Lake Erie. The canal lowered the cost of moving a ton of goods from almost 20 cents per mile to less than 2 cents and reduced travel time from 20 days to 6. It quickly made New York City the greatest port in America and brought instant prosperity to rural areas upstate.

The success of the Erie Canal encouraged other states to invest in canals. Pennsylvania built a canal system across the Appalachian Mountains, linking Pittsburgh with the East and allowing Philadelphia to challenge New York as the nation's major port. Ohio went deeply into debt to build 500 miles of canals connecting the Ohio River and Lake Erie. Indiana's canal-building program nearly bankrupted the state.

Canal Construction

In an era before dynamite, concrete, and steel, building canals took astonishing physical effort by countless workers. By 1840 more than 3,000 miles of canals had been dug by workers using shovels and scoops pulled by horses and oxen. **Locks**—enclosures with gates at each end to raise or lower the water level—were constructed as canals crossed hills and valleys. The stone for these locks had to be cut and set completely by hand.

Construction workers labored on the canals from dawn to dusk for wages that averaged less than $1 a day. Many farmers earned extra income by working on nearby canal projects. But farmers were not available during the growing season, and frequently the population was too small to supply enough workers. So construction depended on thousands of Irish immigrants who moved from project to project as canal building spread. Canals also created opportunities for new businesses to supply food, shelter, and other necessities to workers—and later to travelers on the canals. In rural areas, towns sprang up along canals, especially at locks, which were typical stopping points for boats. Soon, however, an even quicker means of transportation was developing.

▲ POLICE ALARM RATTLE, EARLY 1800S

■ Transportation by Rail

Railroads proved the most practical of all internal improvements. They were faster than roads and were passable in almost all weather. They did not freeze in winter or dry up in summer like canals and rivers; nor were they limited by topography.

Early trains were nearly as unsafe as steamboats. Engineers operated locomotives at top speed down hills and around curves, giving passengers the nineteenth-century equivalent of a roller-coaster ride. Sparks from belching smokestacks ignited wooden railroad cars, haystacks, and buildings along the track. To save money, only a single set of tracks was laid to carry trains in both directions, so collisions were frequent. Experienced travelers rode in the middle cars.

Despite their dangers, railroads excited Americans. In his book *Walden*, Henry David Thoreau captured this spirit:

> "When I hear the iron horse make the hills echo with his snort like thunder, shaking the earth with his feet and breathing fire and smoke from his nostrils . . . it seems as if the earth had got a race now worthy to inhabit it."

Nevertheless, railroads were slow to take hold, mainly because of opposition from state governments, which had heavy investments in roads and canals. New York, for example, attempted to protect the Erie Canal by prohibiting trains from carrying freight. By 1840 the number of miles

CHAPTER 9 Nationalism and Change 1816–1824   **267**

CHAPTER 9
SECTION 2

Independent Practice

Expressing Ideas Ask students to draw cartoons depicting the opening of the West. Their drawings might show what traveling on early roads, steamboats, or railroads was like. Remind students to base their drawings on fact. Have them display their cartoons on the bulletin board. **L2**

Food of the Times

In the early 1800s, diets were limited by techniques for preserving food. Most families stored potatoes and other root crops underground. They dried, smoked, and salted meat. Only in the fall did many families enjoy fresh meat. For most of the year, they pulled salted meat out of a barrel, cut a slab of smoked bacon, or ate dried fish.

Sidelights: Medical Beliefs in the Early 1800s

Medical professionals of the 1800s were unaware that diseases were caused by microorganisms, and they scoffed at the notion that diseases were contagious. In fact, they viewed those who held such views as shockingly superstitious. Thus, infectious diseases were rampant. Scarlet fever, typhoid fever, and whooping cough were prevalent. Such diseases became the primary cause of death for people living on the frontier.

CHAPTER 9 SECTION 2

Visualizing History In 1820 about 72 percent of all workers in the United States worked on farms. For the most part, field work was a man's responsibility; women were responsible for child care, candlemaking, spinning, weaving, and sewing.
Answer to Caption: By the 1840s railroads had lowered the cost of transporting farm produce from and manufactured goods to previously isolated areas.

Did You Know?
There was no home mail delivery in the early 1800s as there is today. Letters were held until they were picked up. The person receiving the letter commonly paid for its transportation.

 ▲ **EXPANSION** Settlements grew in rural areas, partly because of improved means of transportation. **Why was railway travel practical?**

of track laid equaled the number of miles of canals that had been dug. But not until the second half of the century would railroads dominate the nation's transportation system.

■ Transportation and Daily Life

Roads, canals, steamboats, and railroads had created a truly national economy in the United States by the mid-1800s. People could now buy goods produced in distant places. Rural Americans could have glass windows in their homes and hang curtains sewn from cloth manufactured in the mills of New England. Citizens of Illinois could enjoy the same foods, fashions, and household furnishings as residents of Vermont.

The Accessibility of Information

Transportation changed America in other ways as well. Information joined the flow of products as mail became deliverable throughout the nation. In 1825 Congress established home delivery of letters and in 1847 created the first national postage stamps. With the mail came newspapers, which brought national issues to the attention of the most remote rural communities. Improved transportation also brought circuit-riding preachers more frequently. No longer did isolated areas wait months for formal religious services, marriage ceremonies, or baptisms.

An American Culture

As technology and the accessibility of information changed the way people worked and lived, American artists and writers were beginning to explore American topics and developing styles that reflected American scenes. Beginning in the 1820s, a group of realistic landscape painters, called the Hudson River School, focused on scenes of the Hudson River valley and the Adirondack and Catskill mountains.

Other artists worked in other forms. Among the most popular were printmakers Nathaniel Currier and James Merritt Ives, whose works celebrated holidays, sporting events, and American rural life.

American writers were turning away from European influences and writing about contemporary America. Writers such as James Fenimore Cooper and Washington Irving reveal the spirit of the expanding American frontier and of the possibilities for improvement and change. Cooper produced one of the first truly American heroes, Natty Bumppo, in his *Leatherstocking Tales.* Bumppo was a frontier scout who was constantly in conflict; he was drawn to life in the wilderness as well as life among American settlers. Irving's romantic tales explored the legends of New York. His stories "The Legend of Sleepy Hollow" and "Rip Van Winkle" are adaptations of folktales with American characters and locales.

268   UNIT 3 Launching the Republic: 1789–1824

Sidelights: Settlement of the West

The transportation revolution helped to open the West. Since Congress followed an open land policy, farmers bought land cheaply in the 1800s—between $1.25 and $2.00 an acre. Squatters, settlers intruding on public land, cleared and cultivated the land. Congressional legislation provided penalties, but they were never enforced, since the nation benefited from squatters' work. In 1841 Congress passed the Pre-Emption Act, allowing squatters to lay claim to their cultivated lands. They could buy it at $1.25 an acre or sell their preemption rights to the highest bidder.

 ▲ CONNECTING ONE PLACE TO ANOTHER Although it provided a bumpy trip for travelers, the safety coach averaged the trek from Washington, D.C., to Baltimore in about 5 hours. *How did improved transportation affect relations between the West and the Northeast?*

Women in the Labor Force

For women, the effects of the transportation revolution were mixed. The constant need to make household necessities once required the help of the whole family. The availability of manufactured goods, however, changed the division of labor. Household work required less time and became the sole responsibility of women. It also became less valued than labor that produced income, and many women moved into paid employment outside the home.

An important result of the transportation system was that it forged a link between the Northeast and the old Northwest Territory. The natural geographic connection of the West was with the South by way of the Mississippi River. But the best market for Western farm products was the populous industrial Northeast. Food prices fell in the Northeast, while farm production more than doubled. By 1840 more Western farm products were being shipped on the Erie Canal than down the Mississippi River. Building roads, canals, and railroads created a strong economic tie between the West and the Northeast that later would have important consequences for the nation.

Section 2 ★ Review

Checking for Understanding

1. **Identify** Bonus Bill, National Road, Robert Fulton, Erie Canal.
2. **Define** turnpike, toll, lock.
3. **Describe** the environmental problems that were involved in building early roads and canals.
4. **Explain** the effect the transportation revolution had on women.

Critical Thinking

5. **Linking Past and Present** Roads, canals, and railroads were early transportation links between East and West. What major links tie different sections of the country together today?

CHAPTER 9
CONNECTIONS

Teaching Making Connections

In building the Erie Canal, enormous volumes of earth and rock had to be moved largely by mule and human muscle power, with the aid of dynamite. As the project progressed, new, huge, horse-drawn scrapers loosened and moved the earth, and horse-powered winches uprooted tree stumps. Ask: What recently developed equipment is being used in construction today? (Possible answers: computers to make soil analyses or generate designs; lasers to detect depth to dig)

Did You Know?

A skilled carpenter, mason, or mule-team driver on the Erie Canal could earn between $1.00 and $1.50 a day.

• *GTV: A Geographic Perspective on American History*

Any side, Frame 52829
Subject: Canal lock at Johnstown, Pennsylvania

CONNECTIONS  CONNECTIONS

▲ VIEW OF LOCKPORT, NEW YORK

Canal Locks

Get up there mule, here comes a lock
We'll make Rome 'fore 6 o'clock
And back we'll go to our home dock
Right back home to Buffalo.

The "lock" in the verse of this early nineteenth-century song was one of 83 along the Erie Canal. Locks are chambers, with gates at each end, that raise and lower ships to compensate for elevation changes along a waterway.

A ship traveling downstream enters a lock and remains there while a gate is closed behind it, creating a watertight chamber. Water is slowly released through the downstream gate to lower the water level in the lock. The downstream gate is then opened, and the ship continues on its way at a lower elevation. To raise a ship, water is added to the lock through the upstream gate.

In places where elevation changes are great, such as at a waterfall, locks are combined in a sort of water staircase. Ships pass from one lock to another, each lock like a step on the staircase.

Among the earliest canals in the United States were the Great Lakes canals begun in the 1700s. The first locks between Lakes Huron and Superior were constructed in 1798.

Locks remain important even today on the Ohio and Mississippi rivers. Many locks from times past can be found still standing in towns, forests, and fields—remnants of the nineteenth century.

Making the Technology Connection

1. What do canal locks do?
2. What materials and technologies common today were not available for building or operating nineteenth-century locks?

Linking Past and Present

3. What canals are important in world commerce today?

270

Answers to CONNECTIONS

1. compensate for changes in elevation by raising or lowering water level
2. Metal alloys, reinforced concrete, electronic control systems not available
3. Panama Canal, Suez Canal, St. Lawrence Seaway

SECTION 3

Monroe and Foreign Affairs

Setting the Scene

Section Focus
Nationalism also affected the young nation's foreign affairs. Americans approved as Spain's colonies in Latin America gained independence. At the same time, the United States worked to establish peace along its borders and to expand them where possible. Out of these events came a policy that for the next 150 years guided America's attitude toward affairs in the Western Hemisphere.

Objectives
After studying this section, you should be able to
★ describe America's problems with Britain and Spain and how they were settled.
★ explain the foreign policy principles established by the Monroe Doctrine.

Key Term
ultimatum

◀ JAMES MONROE

United States foreign affairs after the War of 1812 were dominated by John Quincy Adams, Monroe's secretary of state until he became President himself in 1825. Few Americans could match his qualifications. He had spent 18 years abroad in diplomatic service as the United States minister to the Netherlands, Portugal, Russia, and Great Britain. Furthermore, as the son of a former Federalist President and a native New Englander, his appointment to the cabinet was in the spirit of national unity sought by President Monroe.

■ Disputes and Diplomacy

Although peace with Great Britain had been achieved in 1815, bitter feelings remained. The Treaty of Ghent was widely regarded as a mere truce because it had not resolved the differences between the two nations. "That man must be blind to the indications of the future," declared Henry Clay in 1816, "who cannot see that we are destined to have war after war with Great Britain." Disputes over fishing rights at the mouth of the St. Lawrence River led to violence between Canadians and New Englanders. Britain and the United States competed for naval supremacy on the Great Lakes. From Maine to Oregon the boundary between the United States and Canada was unsettled, and in several places it was disputed.

Tensions with Britain Ease

There were strong reasons for improving relations with Great Britain. Chief among these was trade. Britain remained a buyer of American raw materials and America a market for British manufactured goods. Realizing that neither country had anything

CHAPTER 9 Nationalism and Change 1816–1824   271

LESSON PLAN
SECTION 3, 271–275

FOCUS

Bellringer
Before taking roll at the beginning of the class period, display Focus Activity Transparency 32 on the overhead projector, and assign the accompanying Focus Activity Sheet.

Objectives
Point out the objectives on this page to students in previewing the section content.

Motivating Activity
Display a map of North America. Show students the areas controlled by the United States, Britain, and Spain after the War of 1812. Then write "Predictions" on the board. Ask students to predict what conflicts in foreign affairs might have arisen after the War of 1812 and why. (Possible answer: Border disputes might have become an issue.) Discuss answers, and then have students note those most likely to be correct. Have students refer to these predictions as they read Section 3.

The following material is available from Glencoe and may be used to introduce or enrich Chapter 9.

  CD-ROM
• *The Presidents: A Picture History of Our Nation*

Classroom Resources for SECTION 3

Teacher's Classroom Resources
- Reproducible Lesson Plan
- Reteaching Activity 9-3
- Chapter 9 Primary and Secondary Source Readings
- Chapter 9 Enrichment Activity
- Chapter 9 Performance Assessment Activity
- Spanish Summaries and Glossary
- Section Quiz

Multimedia
- Section Focus Transparency 32
- Unit 3 Digest Transparency
- Vocabulary Puzzlemaker
- Student Self-Test Software
- A Geographic Perspective on American History
- The Presidents: A Picture History of Our Nation

271

CHAPTER 9 SECTION 3

TEACH
Guided Practice

Political Science Write the word *doctrine* on the chalkboard. Invite volunteers to define it. (possible answer: position statement) Then have students write a paper discussing why the Monroe Doctrine is not an agreement but a declaration or policy statement. **L3**

Did You Know?

In the mid-1820s, people in northern towns began to replace kitchen fireplaces with cookstoves, which burned about one-third as much firewood as old-fashioned fireplaces. Some historians consider this one of the most radical changes in heating and cooking technology in hundreds of years.

The following materials are available from Glencoe and may be used to enrich Chapter 9.

 **VIDEODISC**

- *GTV: A Geographic Perspective on American History*

Any side, Frame 52673
Subject: Map showing acquisition of Florida

---

to gain by continued hostilities, Britain made attempts to smooth out relations. Between 1815 and 1817, Great Britain and the United States worked out several of their disputes peacefully.

The Rush-Bagot Agreement

As minister to England, John Quincy Adams used Great Britain's desire for better relations with the United States to negotiate the Rush-Bagot Agreement of 1817, the first mutual naval disarmament in history. The United States and Britain agreed to remove all warships from the Great Lakes except for a few small vessels to control smuggling. This precedent later encouraged the United States and Canada to demilitarize their entire 3,000-mile border, creating what continues to be the longest unfortified international boundary in the world.

The Rush-Bagot Agreement also set the stage for the Convention of 1818, which specified where American ships could fish in Canadian waters and set the northern boundary of the Louisiana Purchase along the forty-ninth parallel from the Lake of the Woods in Minnesota to the Rocky Mountains. Beyond the Rockies, the treaty provided "joint occupation" of the disputed Oregon territory for 10 years. Each country would be free to carry on fur trade and settle the region without interference from the other.

Florida Border Dispute

Spanish Florida remained a source of friction. Spain insisted that Florida's western boundary was the Mississippi River, while the United States claimed that it was the Perdido River 200 miles farther east. During the War of 1812, the United States resolved the controversy by simply seizing the disputed territory.

Because Spain was an ally of Great Britain in the War of 1812, Florida became a base of British and Native American operations against the United States. After the war, it remained a refuge for Seminoles and Creeks, who continued to battle Georgia settlers. In 1818 Andrew Jackson, commanding the Tennessee militia, pursued a Seminole force into Florida, where he seized Spanish settlements at Pensacola and St. Marks.

The Adams-Onís Treaty

The Spanish government demanded that the United States pay for the "outrage." But Adams defended Jackson and argued that true blame lay in Spain's failure to keep order in Florida. He convinced Monroe to issue Spain an **ultimatum,** a demand that would have serious consequences if ignored, likely a resort to force: either govern Florida effectively or surrender it to the United States.

Occupied with problems throughout its Latin American empire, Spain ceded Florida to the United States in the Adams-Onís Treaty of 1819. In return the United States agreed to reimburse American citizens who had claims against Spain. The treaty also set the western boundary of the Louisiana Purchase: it ran from the Gulf of Mexico northwest to the Oregon Territory and then west to the Pacific. The United States gave up a weak claim to Texas, while Spain gave up a much stronger claim to Oregon.

■ The Monroe Doctrine

The most significant accomplishment of Secretary of State Adams was the Monroe Doctrine of 1823. This famous statement of foreign policy had a complex background that involved events in Latin America, in Europe, and on the Pacific coast of North America.

Between 1814 and 1824, Spain's Latin American colonies declared independence. Armies led by Simón Bolívar (see•MOHN buh•LEE•VAHR) and José de San Martín (hoh• SAY day SAHN mahr•TEEN) exceeded even the Patriots' heroics in the American Revolution and captured the attention of the American people.

Threat from Europe

After defeating Napoleon at Waterloo in 1815, the victorious monarchies of Europe—Russia, Austria, Prussia, and Britain—formed

272 UNIT 3 Launching the Republic: 1789–1824

Cultural Diversity

Some of the Native Americans of the Creek people moved south from Georgia beginning about 1750. They were joined by runaway enslaved Native Americans and African Americans. By 1775 the group began calling itself by the Creek word *Seminole*, meaning "separatist" or "runaway." The United States wanted to recapture escaped enslaved people, prevent the fleeing of more, and eventually obtain Seminole lands.

Life of the Times

Seminole Survival

In order to avoid defeat by Andrew Jackson in 1818 and 1819, many Seminoles of the Southeast fled deep into the swamps of the Florida Everglades. Isolated from the world, the Seminoles had to adapt to a new environment.

Seminole houses called *chickees* were made from the palmetto trees that flourished in the swamp. The floor of the house was raised off the ground on poles to keep it dry. Open walls and thatched roofs kept the dwelling cool.

The Seminoles' birchbark canoes were replaced by sleek dugouts. These were made by throwing embers from a fire along the center of prepared logs and then scraping out the charred wood. The walls of the dugouts were thin, sometimes no more than one inch thick. Using streams as trails, the pilots stood on platforms at the rear of the dugouts. From this vantage point, they used long poles to push the vessels through the swamps. The hunters who rode in the dugout could spear fish, which provided the Seminoles with a rich supply of food. Seminoles continue to live in the Everglades today.

▶ SEMINOLE LEADER TUKO-SEE-MATHLA

▲ PRESENT-DAY SEMINOLES

---

the Quadruple Alliance to suppress the democratic ideas of the French Revolution. Klemens von Metternich (MEHT•uhr•nihk), prime minister of Austria, branded democracy "the disease which must be cured, the volcano which must be extinguished, the gangrene which must be burned out with the hot iron." The Quadruple Alliance, with France or a new member replacing Britain, helped defeat revolutions in Italy and Spain.

The success of the Quadruple Alliance caused some European leaders to talk of taking similar action in the Americas. Although there was little chance that they could carry out such action, rumors of it caused concern in the United States and Great Britain. Both the British and the Americans were enjoying a profitable trade with Latin American nations. If the Quadruple Alliance returned the region to Spain, restrictions would reappear and this trade would be lost. The British government looked for a way to discourage moves to restore Spanish rule in Latin America.

British Initiative

In August 1823, the British foreign minister suggested to the United States minister in London that the two nations issue a joint statement about the independence of Latin America. The statement would say that the United States and Britain opposed intervention in Latin America by any power and that neither nation would acquire any part of Latin America for itself—a surprising proposal from an old enemy. The American minister informed President Monroe.

The British proposal was an attractive and timely one. The Monroe administration was wrestling with a number of foreign-policy concerns. Russia already claimed Alaska and was making aggressive moves on the

CHAPTER 9 Nationalism and Change 1816–1824

Critical Thinking

Primary Sources Write on the chalkboard the following quotation from Jackson's 1830 message to Congress on Native American removal:

"The waves of population and civilization are rolling to the westward, and we now propose to acquire the countries occupied by the red men . . . and to send them to a land where their existence may be prolonged and perhaps made perpetual."

Ask students to write a paragraph explaining Jackson's attitude toward the Native Americans. **L2**

CHAPTER 9 SECTION 3

Independent Practice

📁 Have students read the editorial on Protective Tariffs in Primary and Secondary Source Readings. **L1, L2**

 Secretary of State John Quincy Adams played a significant role in developing the wording of the declaration, and he influenced the doctrine's overall shape. **Answer to Caption:** The United States opposed any further European colonization in the Western Hemisphere.

ASSESS

Check Understanding

Assign Section 3 Review as homework or an in-class activity.

Evaluate

📁 💿 Assign the Section 3 Quiz in the TCR, or use the History of a Free Nation Testmaker to create a customized quiz.

Reteach

📁 Have students complete Reteaching Activity 9-3.

Enrich

📁 Have students complete Chapter 9 Enrichment Activity.

CLOSE

Have students discuss why they think historians do not consider James Monroe an outstanding President.

274

▲ **THE MONROE DOCTRINE** President Monroe consulted his cabinet before issuing the Monroe Doctrine. *What warning did the Doctrine contain?*

Pacific coast. In 1821 the Russian czar announced that his empire extended south into Oregon, a claim that conflicted with American and British claims there.

Should the United States allow Russia to expand its holdings in the Western Hemisphere? How should the United States meet the threat of intervention in Latin America—accept the British offer of cooperation or act alone? President Monroe discussed these questions with his cabinet and consulted Jefferson and Madison, who favored a joint statement with Great Britain. But Secretary of State Adams argued that it would look as though the United States were following "in the wake of the British man-of-war." He urged that the United States act on its own. The nationalism of John Quincy Adams prevailed.

Statement of American Resolve

For what would become a landmark of American foreign policy, the Monroe Doctrine was presented in an undramatic way. It appeared in two widely separated passages in President Monroe's annual message to Congress on December 2, 1823. The Monroe Doctrine provided both a warning and a reassurance to European countries regarding their conduct in the Western Hemisphere (see Appendix).

If the nations of the Quadruple Alliance ever seriously contemplated intervention in the Americas, it was the British navy, not Monroe's warning, that made them back down. In 1824 the Russians, already in possession of more land than they could effectively govern, agreed to withdraw from Oregon.

The significance of the Monroe Doctrine is in later events. Its bold warnings gained meaning only when the United States became a major sea power—a development that took nearly a century. Nor did the Monroe Doctrine restrict the nationalism, expansion, and intervention of the United States itself over the next 150 years.

Section 3 ★ Review

Checking for Understanding

1. **Identify** John Quincy Adams, Rush-Bagot Agreement, Adams-Onís Treaty, Simón Bolívar, José de San Martín, Quadruple Alliance, Monroe Doctrine.
2. **Define** ultimatum.
3. **List** the disputes that the United States had with Britain and Spain.
4. **Describe** the chain of events that formed the background to the Monroe Doctrine.

Critical Thinking

5. **Applying Principles** Argue how United States government involvement in Central American affairs could be interpreted as violating the principles of the Monroe Doctrine.

UNIT 3 Launching the Republic: 1789–1824

Answers to SECTION 3 REVIEW

1. John Quincy Adams, 271; Rush-Bagot Agreement, 272; Adams-Onís Treaty, 272; Simón Bolívar, 272; José San Martín, 272; Quadruple Alliance, 272–73; Monroe Doctrine, 274
2. All vocabulary terms are defined in the Glossary.
3. Britain: fishing rights on St. Lawrence, naval rivalry on Great Lakes; Spain: Florida's western boundary and Native American attacks against the Georgia settlers
4. Latin America's quest for independence won American sympathy. Quadruple Alliance was antidemocratic, suppressed revolutions.
5. Answers will vary but may include that the U.S. sometimes treats these countries too much as dependents; U.S. influence is often viewed as too pervasive in the region.

Social Studies Skills

Map and Graph Skills

Drawing Conclusions from Maps

Your best friend comes back from a hiking trip to Colorado. Taking out a map, she describes a dangerous situation she survived near the top of Pikes Peak. After talking about all the factors that could have created the situation and looking closely at the map, you conclude that she must have lost the trail at about 10,000 feet.

Drawing conclusions is a process of making decisions through analysis of available information. To draw a conclusion, you make a series of inferences, or deductions based on facts or circumstances. Inferences act as clues that help in making decisions or judgments. In this situation you reached a conclusion based on your knowledge of Pikes Peak and experience reading a map.

The following guidelines will help you draw conclusions from maps:
a. **Analyze** the map for bodies of water. How might they be used in the future? Are they strategic for trade or defense?
b. **Study** the landscape. Is it mountainous or flat? Is the land suitable for farming?
c. **Study** the boundaries. Do physical boundaries match natural boundaries? Are there any border disputes?
d. **Examine** other map data. Examine routes, resources, labels, etc.

Examine the historical map of Florida on this page. Following the guidelines, you can draw a conclusion as to why Florida was acquired by the United States in 1819:
a. Bodies of water—all locations along these waterways would provide ports for trade and strategic locations for defense.

The Acquisition of Florida

b. Landscape—Florida is a peninsula, and most land lies near coasts; land would be too wet for farming.
c. The borders are clearly defined, except for the New Orleans area. Spain, England, France, and the United States all had interests in this area.
d. Data primarily deal with border disputes—land in three different areas between the Mississippi River and the eastern coast of Florida was annexed or ceded.

You conclude that the need to expand to its natural borders, obtain good ports, and gain a strategic position for defense made the acquisition of Florida appealing for the United States.

Practicing the Skill

Apply these same guidelines to the map of roads, canals, and rivers in 1840 in this chapter, and draw conclusions as to why the states of New York, Ohio, and Indiana had the most mileage of canals.

LESSON PLAN
Mastering Social Studies Skills

Teaching Map and Graph Skills

Ask students to assemble in small groups and list 10 reasons why their community is located where it is. (Answers should include location near rivers, railroads, highways, canals, natural resources, farm supply centers.) Have students discuss the reasons for their answers. Remind them that they can draw similar conclusions by looking at and analyzing the information on maps.

Assign students the Chapter 9 Reading describing a French economist's views on doing business in the United States in 1839 in Primary and Secondary Source Readings.

Did You Know?

The term "Era of Good Feelings," now applied to the period of one-party rule on the national level during President Monroe's two terms, was first used by the Boston *Columbian Centinel* in 1817.

Answers to SOCIAL STUDIES SKILLS

Conclusion: The northern states had more canal construction than did the southern states.
Conclusion is based on:
a. The North did not have as many navigable rivers as the South. The North had to build a system of canals in order to engage in efficient commerce. This would have cost the northern states a good deal of money.
b. Flat land characteristics allowed easy canal construction in places.
c. There is no evidence of border disputes.
d. Great Lakes and rivers linked up canals for effective long water routes.

REVIEW CHAPTER 9

Answers

Reviewing Facts
1. It created a national currency to encourage and finance economic growth in all sections.
2. Favored establishing a national bank, federally financed internal improvements, and strong central government; reversed earlier positions.
3. Established dominance of the national government by ruling in favor of implied powers and against states interfering with federal agencies and private contracts, and by broadly defining interstate commerce.
4. He claimed that spending money on improving transportation was an unconstitutional extension of federal power.
5. westward movement, movement of goods, passenger travel, immigrant labor
6. Roads: Advantages—connected towns and cities, brought goods to people. Disadvantages—bad roads often caused equipment breakdowns. River steamboats: Advantages—carried passengers and goods quickly and efficiently. Disadvantages—high-risk dangers of snags, ice, bursting boilers, collisions, fires, and sandbars. Canals: Advantages—moved heavy goods. Disadvantages—needed many people to build. Rail: Advantages—faster, more efficient. Disadvantages—dangerous, risky, breakdowns, expensive.

CHAPTER 9 ★ REVIEW

Using Vocabulary

Write a paragraph describing the awakening of American nationalism from 1812 to 1823 using the following terms:

internal improvement
protective tariff
turnpike
Era of Good Feelings
American System
Monroe Doctrine

Reviewing Facts

1. **Describe** how establishing the second Bank of the United States contributed to the spirit of nationalism.
2. **Compare** the Republicans' attitudes on internal improvements, banking, and federal power with their previous positions on these issues.
3. **Explain** how the federal judiciary strengthened nationalism in key decisions between 1819 and 1824.
4. **Cite** Madison's reason for vetoing the Bonus Bill.
5. **Summarize** the changes that resulted from internal improvements in transportation.
6. **List** transportation improvements of the era and the advantages and disadvantages of each.

Understanding Concepts

National Community
1. How did the United States begin to change from local communities to a more national community in the Era of Good Feelings?

World Power
2. What perception of United States power resulted from the Monroe Doctrine?

Critical Thinking

1. **Understanding Cause and Effect** How did the transportation revolution bring about a communications revolution in the West?
2. **Interpreting Illustrations** Study the illustration of the city of New York during the early-to-mid-1800s on this page and answer the questions that follow.
   a. Do you think this artist's portrayal of New York would make a good illustration for a travel poster designed to attract tourists to the city? Why or why not?
   b. Do you think the illustration is an accurate portrayal of the city? Explain.

Writing About History

Comparison
Compare the advantages of each of the following means of transportation during the early 1800s: roads, rivers, canals, railroads.

Cooperative Learning

Imagine that you work for a local newspaper in Cincinnati, Ohio, in 1823. Like most newspapers

276 UNIT 3 Launching the Republic: 1789–1824

Understanding Concepts

1. Answers will vary but may include a sense of national pride over the outcome of the War of 1812.
2. Answers will vary but may include that Britain gained respect for the United States as a power after the War of 1812. Spain's agreeing to sell Florida and settle boundary disputes with the U.S. was hastened by American military action taken in Florida.

CHAPTER 9 ★ REVIEW

even today, your news staff holds daily meetings to discuss which news items to print in the upcoming edition. Discuss with other members of your staff what international, national, and local topics should be included in tomorrow's newspaper. Also determine on what you will base your decision to include certain articles.

Social Studies Skills

Interpreting Historical Maps

Historical maps might resemble modern maps in style and content, but they show a geography of the past. Because they show the past, they can confuse or disorient you unless you study them carefully. The following guidelines will help you interpret a historical map:

- Read the map title and any information contained in legends, keys, or captions. It is essential to know precisely what time period the map portrays.
- Pay close attention to the use of color, pattern, line, or text since this will help you distinguish various pieces of information.
- Compare the historical map to a modern map of the same region and look for differences. Place names may have changed, borders may have shifted, and roads and towns disappeared. The physical landscape may be different. Often these changes are important in explaining historical developments.

Practicing the Skill

Study the map of Latin America on this page and answer the questions.
1. Why was the year 1825 selected as the time to show the political situation occurring in Latin America?
2. Independence movements in Latin America had been taking place for approximately how many years?
3. Describe some of the changes you see when comparing this map to a modern map of Latin America. What do the changes suggest about independence movements in Latin America after 1825?

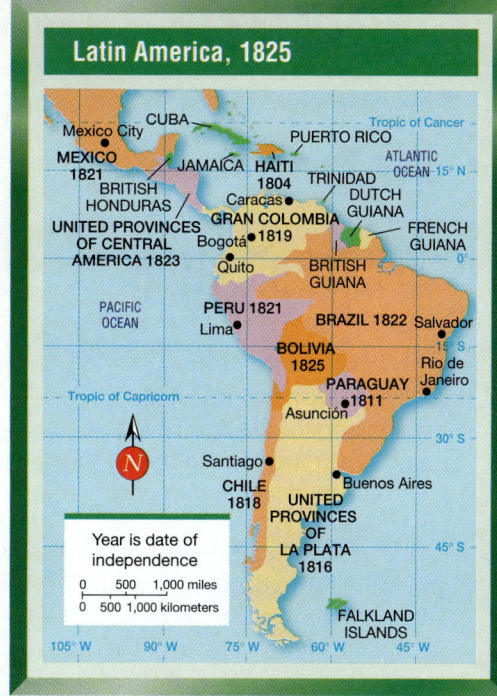

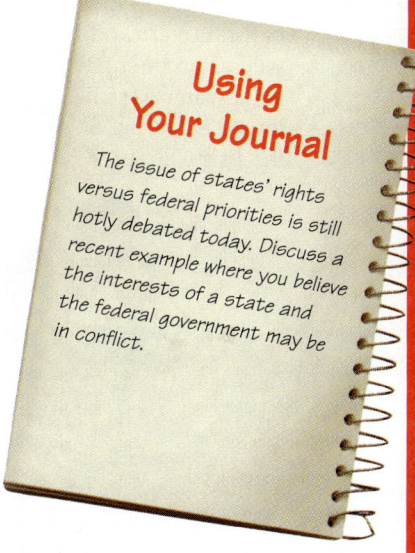

Using Your Journal

The issue of states' rights versus federal priorities is still hotly debated today. Discuss a recent example where you believe the interests of a state and the federal government may be in conflict.

REVIEW ★ CHAPTER 9

Practicing the Skill
1. Most Latin American countries had achieved independence by 1825.
2. 20 years
3. Gran Columbia has split into Colombia, Ecuador, and Venezuela. Uruguay is located at the southern end of Brazil. Chile took over some of Bolivia's area. The movements continued to take place.

Chapter Bonus Test Question

This question may be used for extra credit on the chapter test. Choose the letter of the correct response.

The U.S. military leader who gained fame by invading foreign-controlled territory was
a. Thomas Jefferson
b. Andrew Jackson
c. James Madison
d. John Quincy Adams
(Answer: b)

Using Your Journal
Clearly expressed ideas in students' journals can be used in formulating a presentation to a group.

CHAPTER 9 Nationalism and Change 1816–1824   277

Critical Thinking
1. Answers will vary but may include that newspapers, magazines, pamphlets, books, letters, and personal conversations traveled faster and were less expensive as a result of improved roads and canals.
2. Answers will vary. It would make a good poster since it conveys the bustle and excitement of a cosmopolitan center.
   b. Answers will vary. The illustration seems accurate since it shows lower Manhattan and the New Jersey side of the Hudson built up.

Cultural Kaleidoscope

The Early Republic

Transportation

The Louisiana Purchase and victory in the War of 1812 sent a clear message to the world: Americans were going to control their own destinies. An ever-growing freedom of mobility infused Americans in the period from 1789 to 1824. People moved westward in a variety of ways. Many traveled on foot and horseback, their possessions piled in handcarts or wagons. Still others traveled via America's waterways on the nation's natural rivers and lakes as well as on the network of artificial waterways that followed construction of the Erie Canal.

▲ Trade began to increase rapidly with the development of bigger and quicker merchant ships. Clipper ships made the voyage from New York City to San Francisco around the tip of South America in 3 to 4 months—about twice as fast as the overland journey.

◀ The canoe, which was developed from the seagoing vessels of the Carib people and played an important part in the exploration of North America, was still an important means of travel.

Making Connections
History and Immigration

Many "American" innovations actually owe their beginnings to the Pennsylvania Dutch, as newcomers from Germany were then known. For example, they developed the flatboat common on American rivers. They also perfected the Conestoga wagon, with its canvas top and wide-rimmed wheels. We are also indebted to the Pennsylvania Dutch for the Kentucky rifle, the box stove, and such dishes as coleslaw and sauerkraut.

More About...
Transportation

Accommodations for travelers in the early 1800s were crude and uncomfortable. In most inns, everyone ate at one big table. The bedrooms usually had several beds, and guests often had to share their bedrooms with one or more complete strangers. About the only way to avoid bedbugs was to sleep on the floor.

Cooperative Learning

Divide the class into four or five groups. Assign each one an early method of transportation discussed in the text. Ask the group to research the item—where and when it originated, where and how long it was used—and have each group report its findings to the class.

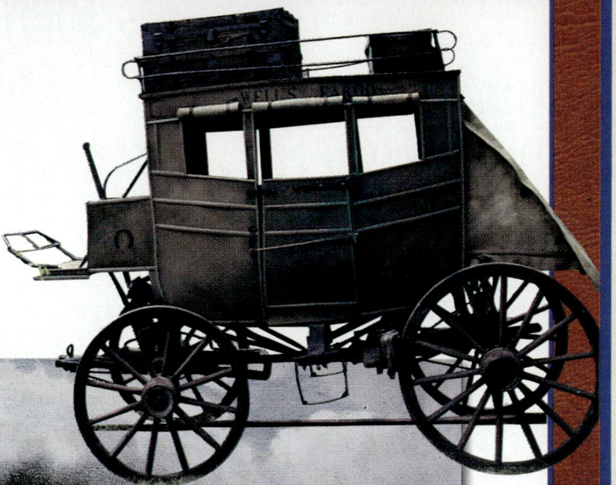

From its opening in 1818, the National Road was heavily traveled by stagecoaches, Conestoga wagons, and other vehicles, besides droves of cattle, sheep, and hogs. Pennsylvania Dutch wagon drivers preferred handling a team from the left, which provided better visibility when the vehicle kept to the right. This may have been the start of the custom of vehicles driving on the right side of the road in later years.

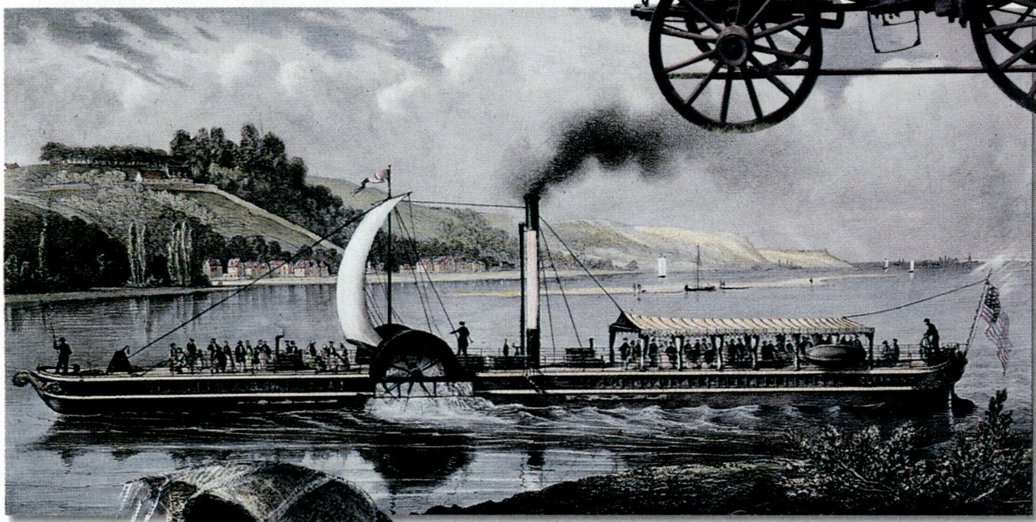

While stagecoaches might make 6 miles per hour, steamboats reached upwards of 12 miles per hour—and the engines were just as fresh and energetic as ever after hundreds of miles.

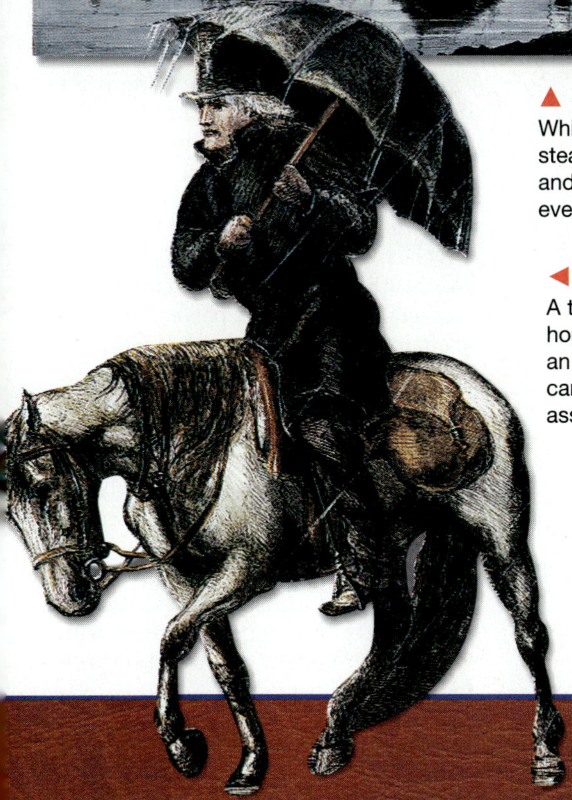

A typical toll fee for a rider on horseback traveling 10 miles on an early turnpike was $6\frac{1}{2}$ cents. A carriage with 2 horses was assessed 25 cents.

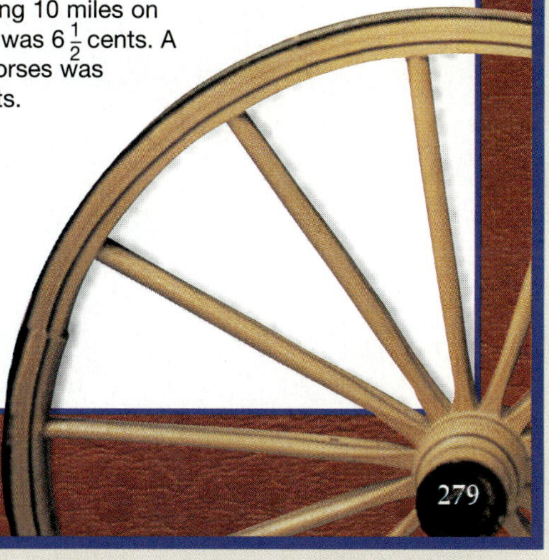

Cultural Kaleidoscope

Portfolio Project
Ask students to list distances from their community to several other towns or cities. How long does a trip between home and each of these other locations take today? How long would it have taken in the early days of the American republic?

- *GTV: A Geographic Perspective on American History*

Side 2, Chapter 9
Title: *Getting Up to Speed*
Subject: Transportation and the growing nation, 1825–1850

See GTV Guide page 44 for complete lesson plan.

The Historian's Craft

What was it like to travel on early American roads? Good sources of information for the historian are accounts by travelers themselves. One man, Charles Fenno Hoffman, wrote about the National Road in 1833: "It appears to have been originally constructed of large round stones, thrown without much arrangement on the surface of the soil, after the road was first levelled…. The ruts are so broad and deep by heavy travel, that an army of pigmies might march into the bosom of the country under the cover they would afford."

UNIT 3 DIGEST

Unit 3 Digest can be used to teach unit coverage when time is limited, to review unit content, or to link content of one unit to another.

 Unit Digest Transparencies

Use Transparency 3.

■ Chapter 7

Write the following on the chalkboard:

George Washington's greatest achievement as President was that he was the first—he set the standards and precedents for those who followed. His greatest failure was that he did not anticipate the development of political parties.

Have students write a paragraph explaining why they agree or disagree with this statement. Ask those who disagree to suggest what they think were Washington's greatest achievement and failure.

■ Chapter 8

Have students construct a chart with two columns—Successes and Failures. Then have them enter the major foreign-policy events of the presidencies of Thomas Jefferson and James Madison in what they believe is the appropriate column. Then have them discuss whether or not the overall foreign policy of these years was successful. Remind them to offer reasons supporting their views.

UNIT THREE DIGEST

Chapter 7

The Federalist Era

The people elected George Washington, the hero of the Revolution, to lead the new nation. Washington set several precedents as the first President, such as creating a cabinet, directing foreign affairs, and serving as "chief legislator."

Washington also tackled the nation's war debts. He delegated much of the nation's financial policy to Alexander Hamilton, his secretary of the treasury. On the whole, Hamilton's program restored the credit of the United States, although it met with bitter opposition from people who believed the federal government should not wield such power.

The defeat of the Miami Confederation and the Treaty of Greenville pushed Native Americans out of Ohio and opened the way for settlement in the Northwest. Washington also snuffed out the Whiskey Rebellion.

At the outbreak of the Anglo-French War, Washington issued the Proclamation of Neutrality, which stated that the nation would be "friendly and impartial" toward both warring parties. However, it was still necessary to negotiate the Jay Treaty in order to escape a war with England and the Pinckney Treaty to resolve a border dispute with Spain.

John Adams, who succeeded Washington as the nation's leader, faced a difficult term in office. Adams's tenure was marked by the XYZ Affair, an undeclared war with France, and anti-Republican legislation that ultimately hurt Adams's Federalist party.

Chapter 8

Age of Jefferson

Republican Thomas Jefferson brought a political and philosophical change to the presidency in 1800. The thrust of his beliefs was that the people were the source of a government's power. Once in office, however, Jefferson found that he had to provide strong leadership to prevent his party from dividing into factions.

During Jefferson's first term, much of the earlier Federalist legislation remained in effect. In addition, foreign trade was increased, taxes and the national debt were reduced, and the principle of judicial review was established. Jefferson's accomplishments led to an easy victory for a second term.

A major event during Jefferson's presidency was the Louisiana Purchase. The new territory doubled the size of the United States by extending its boundaries west of the Mississippi. Not all people supported the purchase of Louisiana, however. In particular, Federalists in the Northeast feared that it would ultimately weaken New England's power in national affairs.

During Jefferson's presidency, he tried to remain neutral in foreign affairs despite the threat of foreign attacks on American ships. In response to British policies, Congress passed the Embargo Act, which sanctioned an economic boycott that was later repealed.

Under James Madison, Jefferson's successor, the United States became embroiled in an unpopular war with Britain, which finally ended in 1814 with the Treaty of Ghent.

280 UNIT 3 Launching the Republic: 1789–1824

Cooperative Learning

Organize students in groups of five. Ask groups to select one of the following topics: George Washington's policy of avoiding "foreign entanglements," Thomas Jefferson's belief that America's economic future lay in agriculture, and James Monroe's warning to European powers to stay out of the Western Hemisphere. Then have groups write a letter to Washington, Jefferson, or Monroe telling him how his noted actions or ideas have affected United States history. **L1, L2**

Chapter 9

Nationalism and Change

The period following the War of 1812 was marked by a spirit of nationalism. Internal improvements were encouraged, a new national bank stimulated the economy, and tariffs protected American manufacturers from foreign goods. Nationalism was also demonstrated in a series of Supreme Court decisions that strengthened the power of the federal government at the expense of the states. The early 1800s were also marked by a transportation revolution on America's inland waterways while highway and railroad development were in their infancy. Fulton's steamboat turned rivers into two-way routes. This, along with the building of thousands of miles of canals, dramatically lowered the time and cost required to ship goods from place to place.

Transportation improvements helped unite Americans and increased the spread of information and the changes to the geographic landscape of the country.

The United States was also looking after its foreign affairs. Relations improved with Britain following the Rush-Bagot Agreement and with Spain following the Adams-Onís Treaty. The Monroe Doctrine proclaimed that the Western Hemisphere was closed to further European colonization. Although insignificant when it was issued, it has had lasting importance in American foreign policy.

Understanding Unit Themes

1. **American Democracy**   What beliefs held by Jefferson furthered the spirit of democracy?
2. **Geography and Environment**   As settlers poured into the country's expanded Western lands, what effects did they have on the American environment?
3. **Conflict and Cooperation**   Why did some issues threaten to disrupt the spirit of American nationalism and unity?
4. **United States Role in World Affairs**   Explain George Washington's rationale for recommending noninvolvement in Europe.

UNIT 3 DIGEST

■ Chapter 9

Write the following on the chalkboard: Roads, Canals, Other Innovations in Transportation. Have students write in their notebooks the major developments in these three areas and the ways in which these developments changed everyday life. Then ask students to discuss which of these developments had the most far-reaching impact.

Understanding Unit Themes

1. Answers will vary but may include Jefferson's belief in people's ability to govern themselves, his belief that people were the source of the government's power, and his belief in separation of church and state.
2. They cleared forests and hills to make way for roads, canals, bridges, farms, and towns. Pristine areas became developed.
3. Issues such as slavery, tariffs, the role of the federal government, political parties, and foreign policy tended to divide along sectional lines.
4. United States was not strong enough to become involved in foreign wars, American interests were unique to itself.

Student Self-Test Software allows students to test their understanding of historical concepts at the unit, chapter, or section levels.

Have students listen to the Chapter Digests on the audiocassettes.

The Historian's Craft

Making Judgments   Point out that many historians feel that the actions taken in the first few months of an administration set the style and standards for the future. Ask students to judge what actions taken by the first five Presidents set the style and standard for future Presidents. Have them organize the actions they chose into order of importance. Select students to share their lists with the rest of the class.

INTRODUCING UNIT 4

BEGINNING THE UNIT

Provide this cause and effect chart to students, omitting the effects. Assign students to complete the chart as they read the chapters in the unit.

Event
- Election of Andrew Jackson

Causes
- Northeast becomes industrial.
- South develops agriculture.
- Western frontier expands.

Effects
- Presidential power increases.
- Political democracy advances.
- Sectional differences arise.
- Economic issues cause conflict.
- Reform movements bring change.

Portfolio Project
To help students get started, suggest they organize their sources into categories such as primary sources and secondary sources.

 OUT OF TIME? If time does not permit teaching the entire unit, use the Unit Digest on pages 358–359.

UNIT FOUR
TOWARD A DEMOCRACY
1820–1854

CHAPTER 10 Sectionalism and Growth 1820–1842

CHAPTER 11 Age of Jackson 1828–1842

CHAPTER 12 The Spirit of Reform 1820–1854

◀ JACKSON CAMPAIGN BOX

History AND ART

The County Election
by George Caleb Bingham, 1852

While many artists of the mid-1800s made the frontier appear romantic and picturesque, George Caleb Bingham painted it realistically. As a result, his pictures show the frontier as a way of life.

Exploring Unit Themes

American Democracy During this period many more Americans gained the right to vote. At the same time, such reforms as national nominating conventions and the direct election of presidential electors increased voter participation in the political process. Women, African Americans, and Native Americans, however, benefited little from these changes.

Economic Development The Industrial Revolution brought changes throughout the United States. In the Northeast the textile industry switched from home production to factory production. Textile workers, once independent craftspeople, now worked long hours on the production line. In the South, cotton became the leading cash crop as the textile mills increased demand.

Setting the Scene

The years between 1820 and 1854 were a time of national optimism and the growth of democracy. At the same time, the nation's economy grew. Confident of their future, Americans experimented with social reform movements aimed at bettering society.

Themes
- American Democracy
- Economic Development
- Humanities and Religion
- Conflict and Cooperation

Key Events
- Missouri Compromise
- Founding of New Harmony
- Tariff of Abominations
- Maysville Road veto
- *The Liberator* published
- Native American Removal
- Nullification Crisis
- Bank Recharter Bill veto
- American Anti-Slavery Society
- Panic of 1837
- Seneca Falls Convention

Major Issues
- Distinct sections—North, South, and West—cooperate and compete for economic development.
- Jacksonian democracy results in increased power of the President and popular participation in political life.
- Religious motivation and democratic ideals spark the abolitionist movement and other efforts for social reform.

▲ **CEDAR AND DEERSKIN DRUM**

▲ **CORN HUSK DOLL**

◀ **IDENTIFICATION TAGS**

Portfolio Project
Use the library to locate sources about one of the important individuals, events, or developments discussed in this unit. Organize information about these sources to create an efficient reference guide for someone interested in writing an in-depth study of the subject.

INTRODUCING UNIT 4

UNIT 4 Independent Study Project
Organize the class into three groups and assign one of the three sections of the United States—North, South, West—to each. Have each group develop a report on the major social, economic, and political changes that took place in its section during the period covered in Unit 4.

Unit Digest Transparencies
Use Unit Digest Transparencies for Unit 4.

History and the Humanities
 History and Art Transparency 9

 Focus on American Fine Art Prints 7, 8

 Spirit of American Art & Music 10, 11, 12

 American Music: Cultural Traditions

History AND ART
Elections in early America were usually colorful events. Discuss with students how Bingham's painting reflects the makeup of voters during this era. (All white males; no women, African Americans, or Native Americans are depicted.)

Humanities and Religion In the mid-1800s the focus of religion changed from preparing for the hereafter to bettering life on earth. This necessarily involved people in the social reform movement. They attempted to increase economic and educational opportunities and improve the moral tone of society in general.

Conflict and Cooperation Three distinct sections—the increasingly industrialized North, the agricultural South, and the frontier West—developed during this period. Each section had its own interests and, as a result, often differed on important national issues.

283

LESSON PLAN
Global Perspectives

FOCUS
Motivating Activity

Point out to students that the years between 1828 and 1840 were a period of transition and conflict around the world. In the Western Hemisphere, revolutions against colonial rule took place throughout Latin America. In Europe, revolution overturned monarchies and established republics. Tell students that the era has been referred to as the Age of Revolution. Ask what recent examples they can suggest of similar change and conflict in the world. (Responses may include the fall of communism in the former Soviet Union and the nations of Eastern Europe; the establishment of majority rule in South Africa; and ethnic conflicts in the former nation of Yugoslavia.)

TEACH
Guided Practice
Exploring the Time Line
On the chalkboard draw a chart with two vertical columns, one headed The World and the other The United States, and two horizontal columns headed Conflict and Cooperation respectively. Direct students to study the time line and then enter appropriate events from the time line onto the chart. (Examples: World, Conflict—Opium War; Cooperation—Pan-Americanism; U.S., Conflict—Trail of Tears; Cooperation—Missouri Compromise)

Global Perspectives

The World

	1820		1830
Asia and Oceania			
Europe			◄ **1830** July Revolution in France
Africa			**1835** Boer farmers start the "Great Trek"
South America		**1821** Peru becomes independent of Spain	**1830** Venezuela and Ecuador become nations
North and Central America			**1826** Pan-Americanism gets underway at Panama Congress

The United States

	1820		1830
Pacific and Northwest		**1821** California becomes a Mexican province	
Southeast			
Midwest		**1820** Missouri Compromise creates a balance between slave and free states	
Southwest			▲ **1827** Mission era ends with expulsion of all Franciscans from present-day New Mexico and Arizona
Atlantic Northeast			**1826** Educational lyceum movement begins in Massachusetts

284 UNIT 4 Toward a Democracy: 1820–1854

Cultural Diversity

Point out to students the influence of different cultures on the architecture of the United States. In New Orleans, Louisiana, both the Spanish and French styles of building are reflected in the open courtyards and graceful balconies of the old quarter of the city. In the Southwest, adobe buildings are a combination of Spanish styles and Native American materials. Americans in cold, snowy regions still build homes made of logs, a heritage of the cabins introduced by the Swedes who settled in the Northeast.

Linking Across Time

African Americans have made major contributions to our country's music. Gospel, an exuberant and joyous celebration of faith through music, grew out of the religious services held by enslaved African Americans. Blues, which grew out of work songs and chants, had a strong impact on the pioneers of rock 'n roll. Jazz, which some people consider the only new art form to be developed in the twentieth century, was influenced by both gospel and the blues.

▶ **1839** Britain and China battle in First Opium War

▼ **1837** Victoria becomes Queen of Great Britain

1847 Liberia becomes an independent republic

1845 Peruvian President Ramón Castilla becomes one of the first mestizos to hold high public office

1840 Act of Union unites Upper and Lower Canada

▶ **1838** Cherokee endure the "Trail of Tears"

1845 Texas annexed

1839 Charles Goodyear makes first vulcanized rubber

UNIT 4 Toward a Democracy: 1820–1854   285

LESSON PLAN
Global Perspectives

Independent Practice
Linking World Events
A French observer of events in the United States in the early nineteenth century was Alexis de Tocqueville. His book, *Democracy in America,* had a tremendous influence on the leaders of revolutions that swept through Europe in the mid-1800s. Ask students to research European revolutions of the period and create a time line of these revolutions.

ASSESS
Studying the Time Line

1. What two efforts at unity took place between 1820 and 1850?
2. What religious development took place in the United States in 1830?
3. What event on the time line do you think had the greatest impact on life in the United States? Why?

Answers to Questions

1. Pan-Americanism and Act of Union in Canada
2. Founding of Church of Latter-Day Saints
3. Answers will vary but should take into account the Missouri Compromise, which postponed rather than resolved the issue of slavery.

Cooperative Learning

Organize students into small groups and tell them their task is to design a T-shirt that might have been sold in conjunction with one of the events mentioned in the time line. Have half the groups select world events and the other half United States events. Suggest that their designs include illustrations and some form of slogan. Display the finished designs on the bulletin board. **L2**

PLANNING GUIDE — Chapter 10   Sectionalism and Growth

Daily Lesson Objectives	Teacher Classroom Resources	Multimedia
SECTION 1 **Growth in the North** **1 Day** pp. 288–293 1. Discuss the impact of the Industrial Revolution on American life. 2. Examine the conditions that prompted the formation of trade societies. 3. Explain why early attempts at unionization in the United States failed.	Chapter 10 Study Guide Reproducible Lesson Plan Reteaching Activity 10-1 Section Quiz Chapter 10 Cooperative Learning Activity Chapter 10 Concept Mapping Activity Reinforcing Social Studies Skills 25, 32, 36, 41 American Portrait 19 Outline Map 2 Writer's Guidebook, Lessons 2–6 American Literary Heritage Unit 4	Student Self-Test Software Testmaker Section Focus Transparency 29 Chapter 10 Skills Transparency U.S. History and Art Transparency 8 Unit 4 Digest Transparency A Geographic Perspective on American History
SECTION 2 **Growth in the South and West** **1 Day** pp. 294–298 1. Explain how industrialization contributed to wider acceptance of slavery in southern states. 2. Describe the importance of cotton to the South. 3. Identify reasons for the rapid growth experienced by the Northwest.	Reproducible Lesson Plan Reteaching Activity 10-2 Section Quiz Chapter 10 Primary and Secondary Source Readings Reinforcing Social Studies Skills 25, 40 American Portraits 14, 20 American Literary Heritage Unit 4 SAT Practice Tests 9–14 Building Skills in Geography	Student Self-Test Software Testmaker Section Focus Transparency 30 U.S. History and Art Transparency 9 U.S. History Digraph 2 A Geographic Perspective on American History
SECTION 3 **Sectional Rivalry and Compromise** **1 Day** pp. 300–305 1. Identify four areas of sectional conflict. 2. Explain how the Missouri Compromise temporarily maintained a balance between slave states and free states. 3. Explain how John Quincy Adams won the 1824 presidential election.	Reproducible Lesson Plan Reteaching Activity 10-3 Section Quiz Chapter 10 Primary and Secondary Source Readings Chapter 10 Enrichment Activity Reinforcing Social Studies Skills 40, 46 American Literary Heritage Unit 4 Spanish Summaries & Glossary	Student Self-Test Software Testmaker Section Focus Transparency 31 Chapter 10 Map Transparency Vocabulary Puzzlemaker Audiocassette, Chapter 10 The Presidents: A Picture History of Our Nation
CHAPTER REVIEW AND EVALUATION **1 Day**	Chapter 10 Test Chapter 10 Performance Assessment Activity	Student Self-Test Software Testmaker

OUT OF TIME? If time does not permit teaching the entire chapter, use the Chapter 10 Summary on pages 358–359 and the Chapter 10 audiocassette (English and Spanish) to point out the main ideas of the chapter.

PLANNING GUIDE

Cultural Diversity Activity

Cooperative Learning Beginning in the late 1820s, German immigrants contributed significantly to the growth of many midwestern towns. In such cities as Cincinnati, Ohio; Milwaukee, Wisconsin; Louisville, Kentucky; and St. Louis, Missouri; German immigrants started libraries, concert halls, schools, and newspapers. Skilled artisans found jobs in such farm-related industries as milling, brewing, meatpacking, and tanning.

Have students identify the various ethnic groups that settled in their community or a nearby larger city. Divide the class into teams, and have each choose one ethnic group to research. Teams should look for examples of the way its group enriched life in the community and contributed to its economic, social, and political vitality. Have each team report its findings in the form of a poster or collage.

Performance Assessment Activity

Reporting Changes As the United States grew and expanded, so did its transportation network. Ask students to work alone or in small groups to research and report on one form of transportation (railroads, stagecoach service, canals, rivers). Encourage them to use maps, graphs, and other illustrations in their reports. As students present their findings, discuss the importance of transportation and how it linked the regions of the nation together.

POSSIBLE RUBRIC FEATURES: Content, written and visual communication skills, organization, interdependence of geography and economics

Chapter Resources

Literature from the Period

Slavery. Social Studies School Service. (14 Documentary Photoaids)

Readings for the Student

Marsh, Carole. *Out of the Mouths of Slaves.* Gallopade, 1989.

Whitman, Sylvia. "Black Folk Artists of the South." *Cobblestone*, Vol. 9, No. 2, February 1988.

Readings for the Teacher

Eaton, Clement. *Henry Clay and the Art of American Politics.* Scott, Foresman, 1962.

Tyler, Alice Felt. *Freedom's Ferment: Phases of American Social History From the Revolution to the Outbreak of the Civil War.* Harper, 1962.

Multimedia Resources

Industrializing America: A Game of American Industrial Development. Perfection Form. (Apple diskette, backup, guide)

Mill Girls, Intellectuals and the Southern Myth. Random House. (color, sound filmstrip)

The New American Worker. Random House. (color, sound filmstrip)

Slavery: America's Peculiar Institution. Zenger Productions. (VHS, 30 minutes)

Views of Vanishing Frontier. Metropolitan Museum of Art. (VHS, 27 minutes)

Key to Ability Levels

Teaching strategies have been coded for varying learning styles and abilities.

- **L1** Basic activities for all students
- **L2** Average activities for average to above-average students
- **L3** Challenging activities for above-average students
- **LEP** Limited English Proficiency activities

Glencoe Links to the Humanities

Link to Art
- U.S. History and Art Transparency 9

Link to Literature
- Macmillan Literature: American Literature Text—Edgar Allan Poe

Link to Music
- American Music: Cultural Traditions

CHAPTER 10

BEGINNING THE CHAPTER

Read to students these statements by a French observer of life in the United States in the early 1800s: "No people in the world has made such progress in trade and manufacturing...." "[The farmer] brings land into tillage in order to sell it again...." "...inhabitants of the North arrive ...and settle in the parts where the cotton plant and the sugar cane grow." Ask students to which sections of the nation these statements apply. (North, West, South) Tell students that as they read the chapter they will discover how accurate an observer Alexis de Tocqueville was.

Recording Journal Notes
As students note details about regional responses, they might also record reasons a region responded in a particular way.

Linking Across Time

In the early 1800s, the industrial age in the United States was just beginning. In the late 1900s, it is argued that the United States is entering a post-industrial era. Ask: What might be the reasons for this shift? (foreign competition, automation)

CHAPTER 10

Sectionalism
1820–1842

▼ **COLLECTION OF WRITINGS BY WOMEN WORKERS**

Setting the Scene

Focus

At the same time that national spirit and pride were evident throughout the country, a strong sectional rivalry was also developing. Each region—the North, South, and West—wanted to further its own economic and political interests. Issues such as land policy, the tariff, and internal improvements were favored or opposed by different regions. The question of extending slavery, however, became the issue that proved the most difficult to resolve.

Journal Notes
How did different regions respond to the idea of protective tariffs? Note details about how they responded in your journal as you read the chapter.

Concepts to Understand
★ Why early labor movements challenged the free enterprise system
★ How economic and cultural change brought about by the Industrial Revolution led to the creation of the factory system

Read to Discover...
★ how the Industrial Revolution affected the textile industry.
★ how each section viewed the major issues faced by the nation.

CULTURAL
- 1790 Samuel Slater builds first cotton mill at Pawtucket, Rhode Island
- 1800 Library of Congress founded
- 1816 African Colonization Society formed

1790 | 1805

POLITICAL
- 1791 Bill of Rights ratified
- 1800 Nation's capital moved from Philadelphia to Washington, D.C.
- 1819 Slavery prohibited in Missouri

286   UNIT 4 Toward a Democracy: 1820–1854

✚ **EXTRA CREDIT PROJECT**

Population Growth During the early nineteenth century, the population of the United States grew rapidly. Ask interested students to research population growth in the North, South, and West for the period from 1790 to 1820. Have them present their findings to the class in the form of a graph comparing growth in the three sections. Conduct a class discussion on the relationship between the Industrial Revolution and population growth.

CHAPTER 10 CONCEPTS

Concept Mapping Activity

Reproduce the following generalization and map concepts on the chalkboard. Have students define "sectionalism" (loyalty to state or section). Ask why an uneven rate of industrial growth in different sections of the country might increase sectionalism. (sections would become less alike, with different resources and economic needs)

As the nation grew, differences in economic activities and needs increased sectionalism.

- Free Enterprise
- Economic and Cultural Change

History AND ART

Where Cotton Is King
by Konstantin Rodko, 1908

This work depicts a style of art called "folk art," a term almost interchangeable with "primitive art" or "naive art." One art scholar defines folk art as "the expression of the common people, made by them and intended for their use and enjoyment."

History AND ART

Ask students what Rodko's painting suggests about agricultural growth in the South. (It was basically a one-crop economy based on cotton.)

◀ FACTORY WORKER

- 1825 Erie Canal completed
- 1839 Edgar Allan Poe publishes first book

1820 | **1835**

- 1820 Missouri Compromise reached
- 1824 House decides presidential election
- 1837 Financial panic sweeps nation

CHAPTER 10 Sectionalism 1820–1842   287

NATIONAL GEOGRAPHIC SOCIETY

 VIDEODISC

- **GTV: A Geographic Perspective on American History**

Any side, frame 52928
Subject: The steam engine replaced the power of horses with the power of steam

Teacher Notes

_____
_____
_____
_____
_____

287

LESSON PLAN
SECTION 1, 288–293

FOCUS

Bellringer
Prior to taking roll at the beginning of the class period, display Focus Activity Transparency 33 on the overhead projector and assign the accompanying Focus Activity Sheet.

Objectives
Point out the objectives on this page to students in previewing section content.

Motivating Activity
Have students list the ways their lives today would be different if the only major sources of power in the world were horses, oxen and other draft animals, and falling water. Ask volunteers to read their lists aloud. Then point out that their lists describe life in the United States in the preindustrial age and that this section looks at the ways the North was transformed from an agricultural to an industrial region.

Use Skills Transparency 10.

SECTION 1

Growth in the North

Setting the Scene

Section Focus
The late eighteenth and early nineteenth centuries brought developments that would forever change life in all regions of the United States. With newly developed machines, goods could be produced more quickly and efficiently than ever before. With the growth of industry, however, came new problems.

Objectives
After studying this section, you should be able to
★ discuss the impact of the Industrial Revolution on American life.
★ examine the formation of trade societies.
★ explain why early attempts at unionization in the United States failed.

Key Terms
textile, emigration, closed shop, mechanics' lien law

◀ SAMUEL SLATER

In the thousands of years between the building of the first pyramids in 2650 B.C. and the construction of log cabins in the eighteenth century, there was not much change with regard to building tools or sources of power. Then came the Industrial Revolution—a revolution that would change ways of life more in the next 200 years than they had changed in the previous 4,500 years.

■ The Industrial Revolution

The Industrial Revolution consisted of several basic developments: in industry there were shifts from simple tools to complex machines; from natural sources of power, such as draft animals and falling water, to artificial sources, such as the steam engine and the electric motor; and from regional to nationwide distribution of products. Jobs became more specialized, so that many workers concentrated on particular, narrow tasks rather than on creating an entire product. In addition, new inventions made transportation and communication faster and more efficient.

From Britain to America

The Industrial Revolution began in Great Britain. Between 1730 and 1800, new mechanical methods of spinning and weaving cotton cloth transformed Britain's clothing industry. These machines operated so efficiently that cotton cloth, formerly a luxury, became the cheapest **textile,** or woven fabric, in the world.

Initially, manufacturing was a British monopoly; many of the machines that characterized the Industrial Revolution were developed by British inventors. Furthermore, British laws forbade the export of this

---

Classroom Resources for SECTION 1

Teacher's Classroom Resources
- Chapter 10 Study Guide
- Reproducible Lesson Plan
- Reteaching Activity 10-1
- Chapter 10 Cooperative Learning Activity
- Section Quiz

Multimedia
- Section Focus Transparency 33
- Unit 4 Digest Transparency
- Chapter 10 Skills Transparency
- Testmaker
- Student Self-Test Software

machinery, as well as the **emigration**—the leaving of one's country permanently for another country—of skilled workers. Many Americans believed it was time to start producing their own goods. As Thomas Jefferson wrote in 1816:

> ... to be independent for the comforts of life we must fabricate them ourselves.... [S]hall we make our own comforts or go without them at the will of a foreign nation?

The new technology finally reached America in 1789 with the arrival of Samuel Slater. While a young man in Britain, Slater apprenticed in a textile factory, where he memorized every detail of the finest textile machinery. Soon after arriving on American soil, he formed a partnership with two other men in Providence, Rhode Island, and began to duplicate British textile machinery from memory. In 1790 America's first textile mill, built on the banks of the Seekonk River, opened its doors for business. The Industrial Revolution had come to America.

New England and the Middle Atlantic States

The embargo against England in 1812 had given the cotton-textile industry a chance to develop in the United States. This industry, which soon became more prosperous than the North's lucrative trade, was centered in New England for a number of reasons. The region boasted many swift-flowing streams, an abundant source of waterpower. New England's shippers were seeking additional enterprises in which to invest their profits. Also, after the 1820s, European immigration to the region provided a large labor force. By 1840, 800 cotton mills and 500 woolen mills in New England employed nearly 50,000 workers. Shipping continued to thrive, and many small factories were turning out such products as shoes, clocks, carriages, and paper.

Manufacturing also took hold in the Middle Atlantic states—Pennsylvania, New Jersey, and New York. Although there were textile mills in this region, too, the area was better known for its coal and iron ore resources. Improved roads and expansion of the nation's railway systems opened

 ▲ **SLATER'S MILL** Technology from the Industrial Revolution was used by Samuel Slater in a mill he built at Pawtucket, Rhode Island, in 1790. *How was Slater's textile mill powered?*

CHAPTER 10 SECTION 1

Linking Across Time

As was the case in the early decades of the nineteenth century, the United States continues to import more textiles than it manufactures. Great Britain, however, has been replaced as the major supplier. Imported textiles today come primarily from the Pacific Rim countries, which include Singapore, Malaysia, the Philippines, Indonesia, Taiwan, and South Korea. This region, like New England in the early nineteenth century, has an abundance of cheap labor.

Visualizing History

Point out that many New England towns sprang up around factories such as this one. **Answer to Caption:** cotton, textiles, shoes, clocks, carriages, paper

Did You Know?

In a period of only 12 years, from 1834 to 1846, several significant advances were made in technology: Cyrus McCormick patented the mechanical reaper; John Deere introduced the steel plow; Charles Goodyear developed a way to vulcanize rubber.

 **Visualizing History** ▲ **RISE OF AMERICAN FACTORIES** As the Industrial Revolution spread, factories sprang up in many cities and towns in New England. *What types of products did these new factories produce?*

Western markets, and increased the demand for machinery. It was discovered that coal could be used in the manufacture of iron, which was used to make machines. The coalfields of Pennsylvania turned the area into a great center for the iron industry and for the manufacture of machinery. Pittsburgh, located near plentiful deposits of coal and iron ore, became a center for these industries.

■ Early Effects

The Industrial Revolution transformed the Northeast from a region where families lived and worked together at farming, crafts, and home-based businesses to one in which people lived mostly in cities and earned their livings by working for others in industry. Factories that required a large labor force and nearby sources of power sprang up in existing cities, such as New York and Philadelphia. Such new cities as Lowell and Lawrence in Massachusetts were built along the falls and rapids of New England's rivers. As the cities grew, so did the demand for better transportation to carry raw materials to the factories and finished products to markets. Improved transportation brought food into the cities to feed the thousands of factory workers.

Industrialization created two new classes of people—the industrial capitalists who built and owned the factories and the industrial laborers who worked in them. These new owners and workers performed distinctly different functions. The differences even extended to their dress, and these differences became symbols that are still understood today: in political cartoons, a top hat and frock coat designate a capitalist; a cap and overalls, a factory worker.

Much of the profit from the Northeast's manufacturing and shipping went back into business, but a great deal of money was also invested all over the country. Banks loaned money to speculators in the West, to companies building Mississippi River steamboats, and to Alabama cotton producers. Thus, even though the regions of the nation developed in different ways, the whole country began to be tied together by a web of credit.

UNIT 4 Toward a Democracy: 1820–1854

Sidelights: Working in Factories

Between 1820 and 1850, manufacturing was the fastest growing sector of the American economy. But growth was very uneven. In the North the textile industry by 1850 had 564 cotton mills with 62,000 workers. By contrast the South had 166 mills with 10,000 workers. In the 1820s about half the cotton textile workers in New England were children under age 16. As competition grew, factory owners used the following methods to boost productivity: increased the speed of machines and the number of machines each worker had to run, and paid premiums to overseers whose departments produced the most cloth.

The Labor Movement

As machines replaced hand tools, jobs for skilled craftsworkers became scarcer, and many such workers were reduced to performing unskilled labor. Before industrialization, there had been enjoyment in skilled work and pride in good handicraft. Now, though, tending machines proved monotonous, and workers could take little pride in the completed product.

The First Labor Unions

In an effort to improve working conditions, workers organized into labor unions. In the United States, the first labor unions were formed by skilled craftspeople, such as carpenters, shoemakers, and printers. By 1830 most of the major crafts had "trade societies" in all the major Northeastern cities. The trade societies worked to improve the lives of their members by demanding higher wages, shorter hours, and the **closed shop**—a place of employment open only to union members.

In some cities, different crafts joined together to form citywide federations. In 1835 the Philadelphia trade societies called a citywide strike to force employers to grant members a 10-hour workday. In addition, city trade societies from several cities formed a National Trades Union, which claimed 300,000 members.

Unskilled factory workers were less successful in forming unions. Strikes could be easily broken by employers who simply hired recent immigrants to fill vacant factory positions. Incentive to organize was low, too, among textile workers, many of whom were young women from poor farms. To these hardworking young women, $3 a week was good pay and a 12- or 13-hour workday not unusual. Some factory owners even provided these women with educational opportunities, comfortable quarters, and chaperones.

 ▲ **MORNING BELL** by Winslow Homer, 1866 After the Civil War, Winslow Homer often painted scenes of everyday life. Homer's painting *Morning Bell* depicts young women carrying their lunches going off to work in a New England textile mill. **About how many hours per day did laborers such as these young women work?**

CHAPTER 10 SECTION 1

Independent Practice

Writing Have students give reasons why each of the following contributed to industrial growth: embargo, streams, shippers, immigrants. (allowed new American industries to develop by reducing competition from Britain; source of water power; capital for investment; labor supply) Then have students write a letter to a British cloth manufacturer explaining why New England would be a good choice for an American mill. Invite volunteers to read their letters to the class. **L2**

History AND ART

Winslow Homer's painting offers an idyllic view of early New England factory life. Suggest that students consider how a factory worker of the period might view his or her working conditions. **Answer to Caption:** 12 to 13 hours

Critical Thinking

Drawing Conclusions Farm girls saw mill work as a chance to be independent and to save for a wedding; most expected to return to farms after marriage. How might the belief that work was short term affect attitudes toward working conditions? toward joining labor unions? (willing to accept conditions, no interest in working for change) Early unions favored public schools and public lands for settlers in the West. How did unions expect northern workers to benefit from each? (Schools: less competition from children for jobs; land: settlers moving West reduce labor supply in North, wages rise) **L2**

CHAPTER 10 SECTION 1

Teaching American Portraits

What event in Mother Seton's life helped bring about her conversion to Catholicism? (her husband's death) In what ways was the elementary school founded by Mother Seton in 1809 unique? (It was a free school which provided secular education as well as religious instruction for students.)

Did You Know?

"Strike" was first used in the context of the labor movement in 1768 when British sailors showed their dissatisfaction with working conditions by refusing to work and by "striking" or taking down their ship's sails.

American Portraits

Elizabeth Ann Seton
1774-1821

Elizabeth Ann Seton was 31 years old when she converted from the Episcopal Church to Roman Catholicism. Newly widowed with five young children, she drew strength from her new faith and determined to see that her children would receive a Catholic education.

Seton opened a free Catholic elementary school—the first such school in the United States—in Baltimore, Maryland, in 1809. She not only provided the children of newly arrived immigrants with schooling, but she also fed them lunch! Seton later founded the American Sisters of Charity, one of the earliest American religious societies.

Elizabeth Ann Seton guided the Sisters into aiding the sick, founding orphanages, and bringing new converts to the Roman Catholic faith. In 1975, "Mother Seton" became the first native-born American to be declared a Roman Catholic saint.

Female Workers Unionize

As competition for jobs in the textile mills increased, however, conditions worsened, and some of the female workers decided to organize. This led to the first women's strike, which occurred in 1824 among the weavers of Pawtucket, Rhode Island. In 1833 a union for female factory workers appeared in Lynn, Massachusetts, followed shortly by a "Factory Girls' Association" open to all female workers.

Often these early labor unions were ineffective. As Harriet Hanson Robinson wrote of an 1836 textile strike in Lowell, where she had worked as a child:

> *It is hardly necessary to say that so far as results were concerned this strike did no good... . [T]hough the authorities did not accede to their demands, the majority returned to their work, and the corporation went on cutting down the wages.*

Nonetheless, such unions represented the first attempts at large-scale organization of women workers in the United States.

■ Demands of Labor

The unions stood behind many demands for reform. No groups were more interested in the founding of public schools than the trade societies, whose members wanted to eliminate competition from children in the labor market. Unions also led the movement to abolish imprisonment for being unable to pay one's debts. In the 1830s, an estimated 75,000 people were thrown into jail for unpaid debts each year, often for trifling amounts. Another labor demand was for **mechanics' lien** (LEEN) **laws,** which would require that the wages owed to workers be the first payments a bankrupt employer would have to make.

Labor and Politics

In order to obtain their goals, laborers began to enter politics. In 1829 the Workingmen's party put up candidates for local offices in New York City and won a surprising 6,000 out of 20,000 votes. This party and others like it did not last long, for they were torn apart by infighting between radicals and moderates and between representatives of different unions. Professional politicians

UNIT 4 Toward a Democracy: 1820–1854

Cooperative Learning

Divide the class into four groups. Assign each group one of the demands of the labor movement: 10-hour workday, public schools, mechanics' lien laws, abolition of imprisonment for debt. Have each group make a list of arguments in support of the change it favors and create a comic strip or political cartoon explaining why this change is needed or highlighting injustices of existing conditions. Display students' work and conduct a class discussion so that students can obtain feedback regarding the effectiveness of their cartoons in influencing opinion. **L1, L2**

lured many workers into the major parties by including some of labor's demands in their platforms. The Democrats were especially successful in encouraging workers to support Andrew Jackson. In 1840 Martin Van Buren revealed his debt to the labor vote by establishing a 10-hour workday for federal government workers.

Legal Opposition

The early trade societies faced severe legal difficulties. In 1806 a Pennsylvania court ruled against a strike by Philadelphia's shoemakers' union—the Federal Society of Journeymen Cordwainers—stating that workers organizing to force employers to raise wages constituted criminal conspiracy, punishable by fines or imprisonment. This ruling became a precedent followed in other states.

In 1835 employers prosecuted another group of shoemakers, this time in Geneva, New York. In finding the workers guilty of conspiracy because their trade society demanded that they be paid at least $1 to make a pair of shoes, the court said:

> *Competition is the life of trade. If the defendants cannot make coarse boots for less than one dollar per pair, let them refuse to do so: but let them not directly or indirectly undertake to say that others shall not do the same work for less price.*

Limited Gains

The legal right of trade societies to carry on collective action against employers was finally recognized in 1842 in the case of *Commonwealth* v. *Hunt*. The Massachusetts Supreme Court held that an attempt by a trade society to improve the lot of its members through organized pressure, such as a strike or a boycott, might be legal if the methods employed were peaceful. This rather cautious tolerance of trade societies had force only in Massachusetts, however, and employers were still able to use the courts to break many strikes.

In any event, the decision came too late to help most of the early unions. The Panic of 1837 had already caused the collapse of many trade unions. Unemployment was so widespread that in order to avoid starvation, workers accepted whatever wages were offered. It would be nearly a generation before labor again tried to organize on a large scale.

The labor movement did secure some permanent gains, however. Labor was a major force in promoting public schools and in making it easier for settlers to acquire public lands. Several states passed laws limiting the workday to 10 hours. In 1840 President Van Buren declared a 10-hour day for work done for the federal government. Some states also limited child labor. Many states passed mechanics' lien laws, and imprisonment for debt was almost universally abandoned.

Section 1 ★ Review

Checking for Understanding

1. **Identify** Samuel Slater, National Trades Union, Factory Girls' Association, *Commonwealth* v. *Hunt*.
2. **Define** textile, emigration, closed shop, mechanics' lien law.
3. **Describe** the effects of the Industrial Revolution on the economy and lifestyles of the Northeast.
4. **Explain** the conditions that led workers to form trade societies.

Critical Thinking

5. **Analyzing Viewpoints** United States law prohibits "industrial espionage," or theft of technology between firms, and the export of certain technologies to foreign countries. Give your opinion of such laws and of Slater's conduct.

CHAPTER 10 Sectionalism 1820–1842   293

Answers to SECTION 1 REVIEW

1. Samuel Slater, 289; National Trades Union, 291; Factory Girl's Association, 292; *Commonwealth* v. *Hunt*, 293
2. All vocabulary words are defined in the Glossary.
3. Economic—rapid growth to textile and iron industries, increased manufacturing, and improved transportation. Life styles—Many moved to city to labor in factories, where they worked long hours.
4. competition for jobs, lack of security, low pay, long hours, poor working conditions, lack of public education, debtor's prison
5. Answers will vary. Supporters may disapprove of Slater's conduct.

CHAPTER 10
SECTION 1

ASSESS
Check Understanding
Assign Section 1 Review as homework or an in-class activity.

Evaluate
Assign the Section 1 Quiz in the TCR or use the History of a Free Nation Testmaker to create a customized quiz.

Reteach
Have students complete Reteaching Activity 10-1.

Enrich
Write on the chalkboard the following statement from a Northern newspaper in 1847 concerning demands of workers for a 10-hour workday:
"To be idle several of the most useful hours of the morning and evening will surely lead to intemperance and ruin."
Have students write a response that might be given by a member of the "Factory Girl's Association."

CLOSE
Have students complete the following sentence:
For the North the Industrial Revolution was revolutionary because it . . . .

LESSON PLAN
SECTION 2, 294–299

FOCUS

Bellringer
Prior to taking roll at the beginning of the class period, display Focus Activity Transparency 34 on the overhead projector and assign the accompanying Focus Activity Sheet.

Objectives
Point out the objectives on this page in previewing section content.

Motivating Activity
Draw three large overlapping circles on the chalkboard. Label the circles North, West, South. Have students fill in the circle for the North with phrases describing the changes in economic activities and population taking place there. Ask students to preview Section 2 and suggest phrases describing life in the South and West. Place key phrases in the appropriate circle or overlapping areas.

- GTV: A Geographic Perspective on American History

Any side, frame 52789
Subject: Slaves use a cotton gin to separate seeds and fiber. Whitney's invention did the job 50 times faster than it could be done by hand.

SECTION 2

Growth in the South and West

Setting the Scene

Section Focus
During this time of industry, ingenuity, and migration, Americans quickly adapted to the changing times. They altered production methods to take advantage of new technology and redefined the westward-moving frontier. In doing so they influenced American life and society for years to come.

Objectives
After studying this section, you should be able to
★ explain how industrialization contributed to wider acceptance of slavery in Southern states.
★ describe the importance of cotton to the South.
★ identify reasons for the rapid growth experienced by the Northwest.

Key Term
cotton gin

◀ COTTON GIN

The effects of the Industrial Revolution were felt in the South even earlier than they were felt in the Northeast. As British cotton mills produced cheaper goods for a worldwide market, they demanded more and more raw cotton. Much of this cotton came from the Southern states. To produce more cotton, Southern planters needed a technological advancement.

■ Plantation Slavery

Before the Industrial Revolution, some Southern planters profited greatly from their use of enslaved people—especially owners of large rice fields and tobacco plantations. Most other planters, however, made little profit from slave labor. Keeping enslaved persons fed and clothed was costly. To prevent them from attempting to run away from the cruel and harsh working conditions, slaveholders had to supervise their workforce continually.

With Eli Whitney's invention of the cotton gin in 1793, however, slave labor was made profitable throughout the South. The **cotton gin,** a machine that cleaned the seeds from the cotton fibers, made it possible to process cotton much more quickly, cheaply, and efficiently than by hand. Now, rather than cleaning 1 pound of cotton per day, a worker could clean 50. If the cotton gin were operated with waterpower, this total was increased to 1,000 pounds a day.

Cotton production proved to be ideally suited to the use of enslaved labor. The planting, hoeing, picking, and ginning all required manual labor, and enslaved persons provided a fairly cheap source. Furthermore, most of the field work was done in groups and could thus be easily supervised. Because the growing and harvesting

UNIT 4 Toward a Democracy: 1820–1854

Classroom Resources for SECTION 2

Teacher's Classroom Resources
- Reproducible Lesson Plan
- Reteaching Activity 10-2
- Chapter 10 Primary & Secondary Source Readings
- Section Quiz

Multimedia
- Section Focus Transparency 34
- U.S. History and Art Transparency
- Testmaker
- Student Self-Test Software
- A Geographic Perspective on American History

of cotton continued throughout much of the year in the Deep South, there were no long periods of idleness. Thus, slave labor suddenly became profitable for cotton growers. Between the invention of the cotton gin and the beginning of the Civil War, the number of enslaved persons in the United States more than quintupled, even though enslaved Africans could not be legally imported after 1808, when the slave trade was ended.

Cotton Is King

"Cotton is king" was a common Southern phrase that accurately reflected the importance of cotton to the South's economy. Because the South had few factories, cotton continued to be sent out of the region for manufacture. Cotton was the greatest export, especially to Britain, the center of world textile production.

Class Structure

The profound influence of cotton on the South was reflected in the class structure of Southern society. At the top were a few wealthy planters, who enslaved 50 to 200 or more people and cultivated the best land. Below these rich owners was a larger class of less wealthy planters who owned medium-sized farms and usually had fewer than 20 enslaved persons. Then there were the owners of small farms, who made up a large majority of Southern farmers and owned either a few enslaved

 ELI WHITNEY

 ▲ THE PLANTATION SYSTEM The invention of the cotton gin by Eli Whitney helped make cotton the most important Southern agricultural product. Bountiful cotton harvests, particularly in the newer growing regions of Alabama and Mississippi, were the basis of the South's increasing prosperity. The cultivation of cotton, however, required intensive hand labor. **What tasks in cotton production did enslaved people perform?**

CHAPTER 10 Sectionalism 1820–1842   295

Cooperative Learning

Divide students into pairs. Have each pair write a letter to Eli Whitney describing to the inventor the impact of his cotton gin on life in the South and on other parts of the United States. Letters might include opinions on who might be grateful or ungrateful to Whitney for his ingenuity and how the pair thinks the history of the period might have been different if the cotton gin had not been invented. If time allows, pairs can exchange letters and write responses from Whitney to the letter writers, expressing his feelings about the effects of his invention on life in the South. **L2**

CHAPTER 10
SECTION 2

TEACH
Guided Practice
Analyzing Cause and Effect
Provide the cause and effect chart below, omitting the effects. Ask students to complete the chart. **L1, LEP**

Events
- Cotton processing becomes faster, cheaper, easier.
- Slave labor becomes profitable for cotton-growers.
- Cotton production moves South and West.

Causes
- invention of cotton gin
- British mills demand more cotton.
- Repeated plantings reduce the fertility of the soil.

Effects
- Farmers plant more cotton.
- Support for slavery in South increases.
- Mississippi, Alabama, and Arkansas grow rapidly and apply for statehood.

 Visualizing History Eli Whitney never made much money from his cotton gin. It was so easy to build that few planters bothered to buy one. **Answer to Caption:** planted, hoed, picked cotton in the fields, operated cotton gin

CHAPTER 10
SECTION 2

Fact or Fiction?
The slave trade in the United States ended on January 1, 1808, when it became illegal to import enslaved Africans.

FICTION: As many as 250,000 enslaved Africans entered the United States from abroad between 1808 and 1860. They were smuggled in by northern shipowners.

Visualizing History
Point out that Native Americans blazed the Wilderness Trail and other routes across the mountains. Later arrivals turned these trails into roads. Discuss the difficulties of an overland trail to the West.
Answer to Caption: yoked oxen

▲ **THE WILDERNESS TRAIL** The journey across the mountains into the Ohio Valley on roads such as the Wilderness Trail was difficult and often took several weeks. *What draft animals were used to pull carts and wagons?*

persons or none at all. Many cotton farmers also raised crops and meat for their own needs and some cash crops, as a way to combat low cotton prices.

Near the bottom of the social scale was a class of impoverished white people, about 1 percent of the white population. They were usually illiterate and did not have regular employment, obtaining food by hunting, raising a few hogs or cows, and farming the exhausted soils for which cotton growers had no use. Seen as lowest on this cotton-created scale were the African Americans. All but a few were enslaved, and nearly all performed heavy labor or menial tasks.

Cotton Production Moves West

To keep up with the demand for raw cotton, cotton plantations sprang up to the west, in the fertile "black belt" (so called for its rich, black soil) of Mississippi and Alabama, and in the rich bottomlands along the Mississippi River and its tributaries. This westward movement of the cotton crop contributed to the population growth that led to statehood for Mississippi in 1817, for Alabama in 1819, and for Arkansas in 1836.

The rapid movement of cotton production was not just the result of increasing demand. It also came from the movement of plantation owners, who depleted the soil by planting one cotton crop after another in the same location. When the fertility of the soil was exhausted, the planters had to find new land. It was cheaper to migrate than to restore the soil's fertility.

Slavery and the Founding of Liberia

Many Southerners, including Thomas Jefferson, George Washington, and Patrick Henry, publicly condemned slavery. In 1787 many Southerners even supported passage of the Northwest Ordinance, which prohibited slavery north of the Ohio River. This same group advocated the abolition of the slave trade at the earliest date allowed by the Constitution.

Few Southern planters were as enthusiastic about freeing their enslaved workers. Many Southerners feared that if too many African Americans were freed in the South, it would create social and cultural problems. In addition, most did not believe that freed African Americans should have equality with whites. As a result, in 1817 slaveholders in Virginia, Maryland, and Kentucky formed the American Colonization Society, whose purpose was to send freed slaves to Africa, from which continent their ancestors had been forcibly transported.

Members of the society encouraged free African Americans to emigrate. In 1819 Congress appropriated $100,000 to support the project, and in 1822 the society founded the republic of Liberia—"land of freedom"—on the west coast of Africa as a haven for American ex-slaves. However, the society lacked the necessary funds to relocate more than a few thousand people. More important, most African Americans felt that America, not Africa, was their home. One group wrote:

Cultural Diversity

Music of the Times One of the most popular composers of the times was Stephen Foster, famous for his songs idealizing the South. Foster used African American melodies to create lively songs. He wrote mostly for the popular minstrel shows, which incorporated the songs, dances, and instruments of African Americans. In the cities, opera was beginning to be popular. European musicians, mostly German immigrants, delighted audiences with band concerts. Other European performers, such as the singer Jenny Lind, the "Swedish nightingale," toured the country and drew huge crowds.

> *This is our home, and this is our country. Beneath its sod lies the bones of our fathers: for it, some of them fought, bled, and died. Here we were born, and here we will die.*

Settlement of the Northwest

Because of the hostilities between settlers and Native Americans, settlement of the Northwest had been tentative until the end of the War of 1812. That war resulted in the breakup of Tecumseh's league and put an end to British support of the northern nations. After the defeat of the Sauk (SAWK) leader, Chief Black Hawk, in 1832, the Native Americans were driven west of the Mississippi.

Perhaps the greatest lure of the Northwest was vast, rich, unsettled land. Available land was cheap. Many settlers "squatted" on whatever unoccupied acres they could find. The settlers poured in. From the South came independent farmers and impoverished whites anxious to acquire land and to move to the new frontier. From the Northeast came farmers lured by tales of the fertility of the land. Eventually, Europe supplied a third stream of immigrants, often arriving in New York or Philadelphia and traveling west by the Erie Canal or the Ohio River to the nation's frontier.

Growth of Towns

Farmers alone did not develop the West. They needed sawmills for lumber and flour mills for grain, barges and wagons to carry produce to market, merchants to buy it, and storekeepers to provide the goods they could not make themselves. These suppliers gathered in towns where cargo was transferred, such as Cincinnati (where three tributaries flow into the Ohio River) and Louisville (at the falls of the Ohio River).

Life of the Times

Moving West

Rich soil and cheap land drew farmers to the Northwest like a magnet. Between 1800 and 1840, thousands of settlers poured into the region. They came from all sections of the United States—cotton planters from the South, cattle and sheep farmers from New England, grain farmers from Virginia. All were looking for new economic opportunities.

Conestoga wagons, developed by Pennsylvania's German Americans during the colonial era, carried all the family's possessions on their journey west. These sturdy wagons, pulled by yoked oxen, had canvas tops.

Once the pioneers arrived, their survival depended upon the long-handled axe and rifle. With the axe the farmer not only cleared trees from the land but fashioned the wood from those trees into cabins and crude furniture.

A good rifle was essential for people moving West. It was used for defense from enemies—human and otherwise—and for providing game for food. Until the 1840s, the weapon most settlers chose was the "Kentucky Rifle." With its long barrel, small bore, and accurate sights, a skilled pioneer could split a sapling at 200 yards.

CHAPTER 10 Sectionalism 1820–1842

Critical Thinking

Interpreting Ideas Review with the class the concepts of specialization and interdependence. Then write this statement on the chalkboard:

"By the Jacksonian era economic specialization made the sections of the United States at once more different and more dependent on one another."

Have students identify the seeming contradiction in this statement (sections more different and more dependent) and write a paragraph explaining it, noting sectional economic differences and how they contributed to interdependence. (growth of northern textile mills provided market for southern cotton) **L3**

CHAPTER 10
SECTION 2

ASSESS
Check Understanding
Assign Section 2 Review as homework or an in-class activity.

Evaluate
Assign the Section 2 Quiz in the TCR or use the History of a Free Nation Testmaker to create a customized quiz.

Reteach
Have students complete Reteaching Activity 10-2.

Enrich
Have students complete the Chapter 10 Enrichment Activity in the TCR.

CLOSE
Direct students to complete the diagram introduced in this section's Motivating Activity on page 294. Ask why the West is the "middle" section in the diagram. Have students give reasons for their opinions. (because it had both farmers like the South and manufacturers like the North; settlers came from the North and the South, bringing own attitudes on such issues as slavery)

Visualizing History Point out that most early cities developed along lakes, rivers, and other transportation routes.
Answer to Caption: steamboats

Visualizing History ▲ GROWTH OF CITIES Cincinnati, the "Queen City of the West," had become a major transportation and manufacturing center by the 1840s. *What was the major form of commercial travel on the Ohio River during this period?*

Thus, manufacturing began to develop in these cities. At one time Cincinnati's showpiece was a combined flour and textile mill run by steam. This stone and brick mill reached an amazing nine stories high. The West's largest manufacturing center, however, was Pittsburgh. Located at the site where the Allegheny and Monongahela rivers flow into the Ohio River, Pittsburgh had access to the area's mineral resources. Here were glass factories, which in 1815 produced glassware worth $235,000. The entire region derived benefits from Pittsburgh's ironworks.

In Western towns, people could often make more money in manufacturing than they could on the farms. Such skilled workers as masons and wheelwrights were so scarce that they commanded high wages. Manufacturers could charge high prices because of the increasing demand for their articles and because of the cost of transporting products across or around the Appalachians. Western towns offered such prospects of wealth that selling lots in future cities of the West became a standard way for speculators to make money.

Section 2 ★ Review

Checking for Understanding
1. **Identify** Eli Whitney, Northwest Ordinance, American Colonization Society, Liberia.
2. **Define** cotton gin.
3. **Explain** the importance of cotton to the South and its effect on the region's way of life.
4. **Summarize** the reasons for the rapid growth of the Northwest and Western cities.

Critical Thinking
5. **Examining Causes** In what way did industry and the plantation system encourage settlement in the Northwest?

298 UNIT 4 Toward a Democracy: 1820–1854

Answers to SECTION 2 REVIEW
1. Eli Whitney, 294; Northwest Ordinance, 296; American Colonization Society, 296; Liberia, 296
2. All vocabulary words are defined in the Glossary.
3. Cotton became the section's most important crop and export, entrenching the plantation system and the resulting class structure.
4. abundant fertile but cheap land, improved transportation, dissatisfaction with the plantation and slavery system in the South, the need for goods and services and high prices
5. The plantation and slavery system made it difficult for small farmers and landless workers to compete in the agricultural market and find

CONNECTIONS  CONNECTIONS

▲ Cotton pickers by Ethel Magafan

Songs of Slavery

Enslaved African Americans used music to help endure long, tedious hours of forced labor and to relax when they were released from chores. Although slaveholders forbade enslaved Africans from playing horns or drums, for fear that these could be used to send messages about planned rebellions, they were permitted to sing.

One kind of African American music that developed in the early 1800s was the spiritual. Sung in a lively style with strong rhythms and rich harmonies, the spirituals usually express themes of redemption from sin and from slavery and of a better life waiting in the future. Well-known spirituals include "Jacob's Ladder" and "Many a Thousand Gone."

The repertoire of songs African Americans sang was much more extensive than the slaveholders knew. It was not uncommon for African Americans to slip out of their quarters at night for secret meetings. In these secret gatherings, they poked fun at the slaveholders by telling folktales and singing songs such as "They Give Us the Husk."

They Give Us the Husk
We raise the wheat,
They give us the corn;
We bake the bread,
They give us the crust;
We sift the meal,
They give us the husk;
We peel the meat,
They give us the skin;
And that's the way
They take us in.

Making the Music Connection
1. Identify the "we" and "they" in this song.
2. What response might enslaved persons make to the idea that the slaveholders cared for them? Why do you think this is the case?

Linking Past and Present
3. How might workers today protest unfair treatment?

CHAPTER 10 CONNECTIONS

Teaching Making Connections
One of the few ways African Americans who were enslaved could express their creativity and feelings was through music. Their songs were also a form of protest.

Food of the Times
What today we call "soul food" comes from the kinds of food that African Americans created from the meager rations they received or could grow on plantations.

Did You Know?
African Americans also passed on folktales that reminded them of their homeland. Many tales described their ancestors or enslaved people who had outwitted their owners. Tales about animals often featured weaker creatures who got the best of stronger animals. One such series of tales is that of the clever Brer Rabbit who always outsmarted the fox.

Answers to CONNECTIONS
1. we: African slaves; they: white masters
2. Slaves would disagree. They get the leftovers masters do not want.
3. by striking, picketing, going to a grievance committee, suing, working for legislative change, organizing boycotts

LESSON PLAN
SECTION 3, 300–305

FOCUS

Bellringer

Prior to taking roll at the beginning of the class period, display Focus Activity Transparency 35 on the overhead projector and assign the accompanying Focus Activity Sheet.

Objectives

Point out the objectives on this page to students in previewing section content.

Motivating Activity

Ask each student to list three types of decisions on which they find it easy to compromise (where to go for lunch, what movie to see, what tape to buy) and three issues they might find it hard to compromise on (freedom of speech, abortion, pollution, drug use). Have students review their lists and suggest reasons why it might be easier to reach compromises on some issues than on others. (Conflicts that involve moral issues are often harder to resolve than purely economic or political ones.)

Tell students that in this section they will look at four major issues that led to sectional differences and learn how the nation's leaders tried to use compromise.

Assign students the Chapter 10 Reading entitled "Fire Bell in the Night" in Primary and Secondary Source Readings.

SECTION 3

Rivalry and Compromise

Setting the Scene

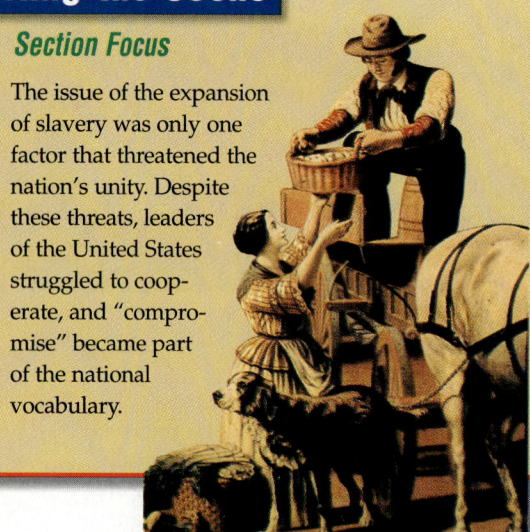

Section Focus

The issue of the expansion of slavery was only one factor that threatened the nation's unity. Despite these threats, leaders of the United States struggled to cooperate, and "compromise" became part of the national vocabulary.

Objectives

After studying this section, you should be able to

★ identify four areas of sectional conflict.

★ explain how the Missouri Compromise temporarily maintained a balance between slave states and free states.

★ explain how John Quincy Adams won the 1824 presidential election.

Key Term

favorite son

▶ PREPARING FOR MARKET

Given the physical differences between the regions of the United States—the harsh and unforgiving land of certain areas of the Northeast; the warm, fertile Southern region; and the forests and mountains of the West—it is not surprising that Americans in these regions had different concerns and reacted differently to important issues. How to apportion public lands, how to protect American products, how to improve life in the United States, and what to do about slavery were questions whose resolutions would affect each region differently.

■ Points of Conflict

Political leaders were the ones who assumed the task of finding compromises to smooth over the sectional differences that threatened the Union. One of the issues they tackled was public land policy. Should land be offered to settlers at a low price or a high one? Should land be opened for settlement rapidly or slowly? Should squatters, who had occupied lands before they were opened for sale, have any rights to the lands they farmed?

Each region of the nation had different answers to these questions. Western frontier farmers naturally favored cheap land, rapid settlement, and "squatters' rights." Eastern manufacturers, on the other hand, opposed such policies for fear the West would draw off their labor supply. Eastern farmers believed that cheap Western lands would result in unfair competition.

Southerners were divided on this issue. Plantation owners wanted lands opened for sale but opposed "squatters' rights" because the squatters might claim the best lands.

UNIT 4 Toward a Democracy: 1820–1854

Classroom Resources for SECTION 3

Teacher's Classroom Resources
- Reproducible Lesson Plan
- Reteaching Activity 10-3
- Chapter 10 Primary & Secondary Source Reading
- Chapter 10 Enrichment Activity
- Chapter 10 Performance Assessment Activity
- Spanish Summaries and Glossaries
- Section Quiz

Multimedia
- Section Focus Transparency 35
- Chapter 10 Map Transparency
- Vocabulary Puzzlemaker
- Testmaker
- Student Self-Test Software
- The Presidents: A Picture History of Our Nation

Protective Tariffs

Another caustic issue was protective tariffs. Should there be high tariffs to protect United States industries? Should tariffs be kept low to allow foreign goods to come into the country cheaply? Northeastern manufacturers and laborers naturally favored protective tariffs to ensure that their factories could compete successfully with foreign manufacturers. As Southerners came to realize that their region would not become a manufacturing center, they became opposed to the system of protection. High tariffs caused them to pay more for imported manufactured goods.

Surprisingly, the Northwest, a farming region, was the section most completely in favor of protection. This was because they thought that the growth of industrial cities would increase the market for farm products. In addition, Westerners believed that protection might encourage manufacturing west of the Appalachians; revenue from the tariffs could then be used for building needed roads and canals.

Money was at the core of arguments over internal improvements. Should the federal government spend money to build roads and canals or at least help states and private companies to build them? The West was overwhelmingly in favor of using federal money for such purposes because it needed roads and canals to get its goods to market. The South, with a fine river system for transportation, was opposed. The Northeast generally favored internal improvements, partly because tariffs would be required to pay for them.

The Issue of Slavery

Among all the issues, the extension of slavery into territories seemed to raise the most feverish emotion. Should the territories be closed to slavery following the precedent set in the Northwest Ordinance? Because cotton production demanded the movement of plantations onto new lands and the plantation system depended on slave labor, Southerners insisted that they be allowed to take their enslaved workers with them anywhere but into the free states.

In the Northern and Western states, which were not economically dependent on the slave system, there was an increasing conviction that slavery was a moral wrong. While conceding that Southern states had a right to maintain slavery where it already existed, Northerners protested it should not be allowed to be extended to the territories. To Southerners, this meant that no new slave states could be formed, and the political power of the South would decrease.

▼ **IRON LADLES**

▲ **THE TARIFF QUESTION** Generally, Northeastern manufacturers and laborers favored protective tariffs while Southerners did not. **Why did the people of the Northwest support tariffs?**

CHAPTER 10 Sectionalism 1820–1842

Cooperative Learning

Have students work as partners or in small groups and choose one of the following roles: Northern factory owner, Northern union organizer and factory worker, Northern farmer, Southern planter, Southern slave, Western farmer, Western merchant, Western Native American. Ask pairs to decide how the person they have chosen would feel about one of the sectional conflicts facing the nation and write a two-minute television editorial expressing the person's point of view. Have groups with opposing points of view present their opinions in a TV interview or panel discussion format. **L2**

CHAPTER 10 SECTION 3

Map Study Using Maps
Answer: border between Missouri and Arkansas Territory; extended west to Spanish territory

Skills Practice
How does the map help explain why the Missouri Compromise is seen as a postponement of the slavery issue? (A vast region south of the parallel had potential for American expansion and settlement. Its future would test the compromise.)

Did You Know?
John Quincy Adams was the first President to wear long pants at his inauguration ceremony. All previous Presidents had worn knee-length breeches with white stockings and black shoes topped with silver buckles.

The following material is available from Glencoe and may be used to enrich Chapter 10:

 **CD-ROM**
• *The Presidents: A Picture History of Our Nation*

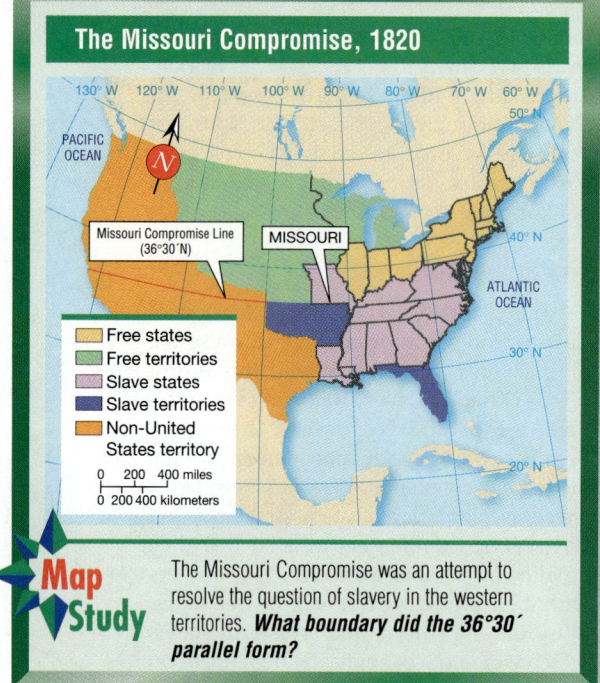

The Missouri Compromise, 1820

- Free states
- Free territories
- Slave states
- Slave territories
- Non-United States territory

Map Study The Missouri Compromise was an attempt to resolve the question of slavery in the western territories. **What boundary did the 36°30´ parallel form?**

The Missouri Compromise

The question of the expansion of slavery became politically controversial in 1819 when Missouri applied for admission to the Union as a slave state. As soon as the bill reached the floor of Congress, Representative James Tallmadge of New York proposed an amendment that would gradually abolish slavery in Missouri and forbid future importation of slaves into the state. His amendment stated, in part:

> ... That the further introduction of slavery or involuntary servitude be prohibited ... and that all children of slaves, born within the said state ... shall be free....

Reaching a Compromise

The Tallmadge Amendment would gradually end slavery in an area where it already existed. A new twist to the debate was introduced when Maine petitioned to be separated from Massachusetts and admitted to the Union as a free state. At this time slave and nonslave states were evenly represented in the Senate, although the North's population gave it a majority in the House of Representatives. If Missouri alone were admitted, the slave states would enjoy an important advantage in the Senate. However, if Maine were admitted as a free state at the same time, the balance would remain unchanged.

As a compromise, Missouri and Maine were admitted together. In the unsettled portions of the Louisiana Purchase, slavery would be forbidden north of the parallel 36° 30´, a line running west from the southern boundary of Missouri.

The Spread of Slavery

This solution gave Southerners their immediate goal—the admission of Missouri as a slave state. The area closed to the future expansion of slavery was still far greater than the area potentially open to slaveholders. The South allowed the North this advantage partly because of a widely held belief that the prairie region west of the Mississippi River was unfit for human settlement. When Southerners realized that this region was not "a great American desert," they began to demand changes in the provisions of the Missouri Compromise.

The Election of 1824

The four candidates who ran for President in 1824 were **favorite sons**—candidates supported by the political leaders from their own state and region. Two of the candidates, Henry Clay of Kentucky and Andrew Jackson of Tennessee, were from the West. John Quincy Adams of Massachusetts received his strongest support from New England, while William Crawford of Georgia represented the South. John C. Calhoun of South Carolina withdrew from the race early and ran for the vice presidency, which he easily won.

Only one-fourth of the electorate bothered to vote. When the results were tallied,

UNIT 4 Toward a Democracy: 1820–1854

Critical Thinking

Predicting Have students name sections of the United States today and describe distinctive features of each. What are some issues on which these regions might disagree? (Possible answers: sharing water resources, illegal immigration, pollution, waste disposal, nuclear energy) Could any of these issues lead to the kind of sectionalism students read about in Section 3? Why or why not? (Probably not, because such factors as the mobility of the Americans, modern communications, and transportation have lessened sectional differences and made regions' concerns more alike.) **L2**

Jackson had received a plurality of the popular vote, but he did not have a majority in the electoral college. Here he led with 99 votes, followed by Adams with 84. Crawford and Clay were far in the rear with 41 and 37, respectively.

The House Votes

In such situations, the Twelfth Amendment to the Constitution provides that the President is to be chosen by the House of Representatives, each state having one vote. The state delegations are to select the President from the three candidates with the highest number of electoral votes.

Clay was eliminated because he had placed fourth. Crawford was President Monroe's favorite, but illness took him out of the running. The choice was between Jackson and Adams. As speaker of the house, Clay was in a position to swing the election either way. Not wanting to aid the fortunes of a rival Westerner, he threw his support to Adams. Adams easily won on the first ballot,

▲ JOHN CALHOUN

which was taken February 9, 1825. Clay was even able to convince his own Kentucky delegation—under clear instructions from the state legislature to support Jackson—to

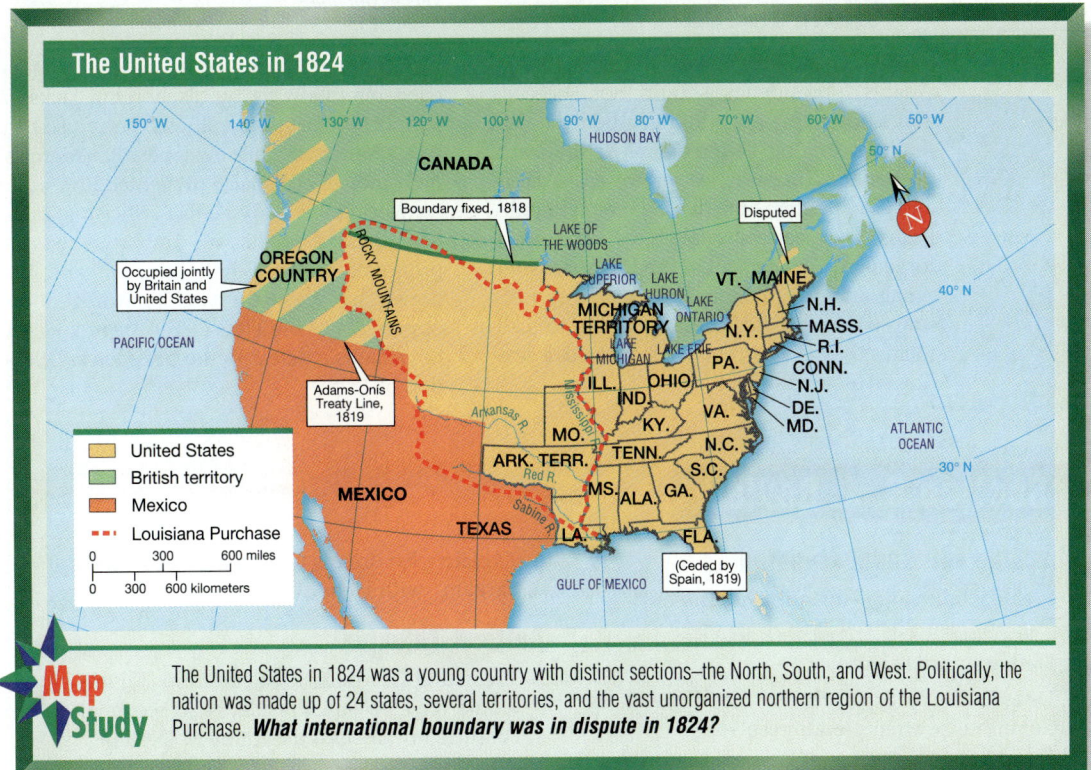

Map Study The United States in 1824 was a young country with distinct sections—the North, South, and West. Politically, the nation was made up of 24 states, several territories, and the vast unorganized northern region of the Louisiana Purchase. **What international boundary was in dispute in 1824?**

CHAPTER 10 Sectionalism 1820–1842   **303**

Sidelights: History and Politics

For his part in helping John Quincy Adams win the 1824 election, Clay earned the nickname "President Maker." His support for the Missouri Compromise of 1820 led to his nickname "The Great Pacificator," and his efforts to avert civil war in 1850 gave him his most famous title, the "Great Compromiser." Clay's name is famous for another reason as well. The first nationally newsworthy message sent by telegraph concerned Henry Clay. In May 1844, the wires tapped out the message that Clay had won the nomination for President.

switch their vote. The tally was 13 states for Adams against only 7 for Jackson and 4 for Crawford.

Charges of a "Corrupt Bargain"

The new President named Clay his secretary of state, a position then considered to be an important stepping-stone to the presidency. An anonymous letter to the newspapers charged that Clay was given the job as the result of a "corrupt bargain." The story claimed that Adams had promised to make Clay secretary of state in return for his leverage over key votes in the House of Representatives. Adams, a devoutly religious man, protested his innocence, as did Clay. Their denials, however, failed to remove suspicion. For the next three years, critics of the Adams administration repeated the cry of the "bargain and corruption" that had betrayed the will of the people.

Adams in the White House

Jackson supporters were determined that Adams's presidency should not succeed, and throughout his administration the differences among Jeffersonian Republicans deepened. Those who supported Adams and Clay became known as National Republicans. They generally favored a strong role for federal government in funding roads and canals and other national projects. In opposition were the Jacksonians, soon to call themselves Democrats, who favored a less powerful government.

 ▲ JOHN QUINCY ADAMS By the time of his election in 1824, John Quincy Adams was already an established figure in American political life. *Why was Adams's presidency not a successful one?*

Although Adams could have strengthened his following by discharging Jackson supporters from federal jobs, he refused to play politics on his own behalf. Adams's own code of ethics also prevented him from answering his opponents' criticisms publicly. Because of this, his ambitious federal programs received little support, and his power as President was neutralized by opponents in the House. The stage was set for Adams's defeat in the presidential election of 1828.

Section 3 ★ Review

Checking for Understanding
1. **Identify** Tallmadge Amendment, Missouri Compromise, Henry Clay.
2. **Define** favorite son.
3. **Describe** the sectional conflict the Missouri Compromise attempted to resolve.
4. **Explain** why Adams was accused of a "corrupt bargain" with Henry Clay.

Critical Thinking
5. **Predicting Outcomes** Do you think Adams would have become President had sectional conflicts not divided the country? Explain.

Social Studies Skills

Study and Writing Skills

Using Reference Works in Research

Standard reference works are general encyclopedias, biographical dictionaries, periodical guides, books of quotations, atlases, and almanacs. These are found in the reference section of the library.

General encyclopedias are sets of books that contain relatively short articles on many subjects. Because encyclopedia reading levels and the amount of detail in content coverage vary, check several to see which is the most appropriate for you.

Biographical dictionaries offer condensed biographies of famous individuals. They are useful when you need more information than an encyclopedia provides, but less than a full biography or autobiography.

Periodical guides help you find articles in magazines and newspapers. Articles are indexed by subject or by the author's last name. Under a subject heading the entry will contain the title of the article; author name(s); and the title of the publication, date, and page number(s). Periodical guides are especially helpful when you need to have current information.

Books of quotations contain statements by individuals. Quotations may be arranged by the author's last name or by subject. Make it a habit to use quotations to support your main ideas and "add color" to your writing.

Atlases contain maps and charts, and *almanacs* contain statistics. Each also includes additional data that may give supporting evidence for your report. If the report is to contain illustrations, atlases and almanacs may provide ideas or suggestions.

A term paper has been assigned, and you decide to research the presidency of John Quincy Adams. For a report on John Quincy Adams, follow these steps:

- **Check** several encyclopedias to see which one has the appropriate reading level and best coverage of Adams.
- **Locate** and read about Adams in a biographical dictionary. Does the material add to what was in the encyclopedia?
- **Look up** "Adams, John Q." in a periodical guide under "Subjects." With the assistance of a librarian, obtain the periodicals listed.
- **Locate** books of quotations, and scan the index for quotes by Adams. Read them and decide if any could be used in your report.
- **Check** atlases and almanacs on United States history or United States Presidents for illustrations or maps pertaining to Adams's administration.

Practicing the Skill

For further practice, make a list of the titles of all the reference works in your school library that you could use to complete a report on Samuel Slater and the early American textile industry.

LESSON PLAN
Mastering Social Studies Skills

Teaching Study and Writing Skills

Review the kinds of information each listed source contains, providing the actual sources if possible. What other sources do students use? (newspaper guides, special purpose encyclopedias, special purpose dictionaries) Suppose you needed to find information on a topic about which you had no clues. How would you start? (general purpose dictionary, general encyclopedia, data base or card catalog, library personnel) Once you understand what you are going to research, what do you do then? (Go to the special purpose sources to find details)

Did You Know?

At the age of 7, John Quincy Adams was taken by his mother, Abigail Adams, to observe the Battle of Bunker Hill from a nearby promontory. By 11 years old, he was frequently riding to Boston to gather the latest news. He went to school in both France and the Netherlands, where his father served on diplomatic missions. At the age of 14, young Adams was the secretary to the United States minister to Russia.

Answers to SOCIAL STUDIES SKILLS

Answers will vary depending on school or public library resources but should include the kinds of resources listed in the feature.

CHAPTER 10 ★ REVIEW

Using Vocabulary

Use each vocabulary word in a sentence about the Industrial Revolution or its effect on sectional conflict.

closed shop
cotton gin
emigration
favorite sons
mechanics' lien law
textile

Reviewing Facts

1. **Compare** the effects of the Industrial Revolution on different sections.
2. **Describe** the conditions that organized workers tried to change and what limited their success.
3. **List** four issues on which the sections had major differences.
4. **Identify** factors that led to the rapid development of the Northwest.
5. **Explain** why "Cotton [was] King" in the South.
6. **Name** the plan that temporarily resolved sectional conflict over slavery.
7. **State** why the Tallmadge Amendment angered Southerners.
8. **Summarize** the events that brought John Q. Adams to the presidency.

Understanding Concepts

Free Enterprise
1. What were some of the abuses of the free enterprise system that factory workers experienced? In what way did the government and citizens address these abuses?

Economic and Cultural Change
2. What factors caused a shift from small-scale production by independent workers to large-scale production in factories owned by a few capitalists?

Critical Thinking

1. **Making Comparisons** Compare the capitalist factory system and the plantation system with the class structures they created and related human rights issues.
2. **Analyzing Art** Study the illustration on this page and answer the questions that follow.
   a. What kind of work are the individuals doing?
   b. Do you think this is a realistic portrayal? Explain.

▼ WORKING AT HOME

UNIT 4 Toward a Democracy: 1820–1854

CHAPTER 10 ★ REVIEW

Writing About History

Description

Imagine it is 1800. You have moved to the city to work in a factory or textile mill. Write a letter to your family on the farm, describing something they have not seen, such as a spinning frame, a factory, a tenement, or the city.

Cooperative Learning

Working in a group of three, research the current status of NAFTA and GATT. Examine the arguments that put these policies into effect and point out any criticisms. Choose a spokesperson to share your findings with other groups.

Social Studies Skills

Analyzing Tabular Data

Analyzing involves breaking information into smaller pieces so that it can be examined more easily. Information presented in tables, or tabular data, can often help you analyze information because tables summarize a large amount of information in a small space. Tabular data is presented in rows and columns to make it easy to read.

Practicing the Skill

Use the tables on this page and your understanding of Chapter 10 content to answer the two questions that follow.

Election of 1824

Candidate	Electoral Vote	Popular Vote	House Vote
Jackson	99	153,544	7
Adams	84	108,740	13
Crawford	41	46,618	4
Clay	37	47,136	—

1. How did Adams succeed in winning the presidency in 1824?
2. How could Clay have received more popular votes but fewer electoral votes than Crawford?
3. Why did the industrial labor force grow more rapidly between 1800 and 1830 than did slave labor?
4. How many laborers worked on farms by 1810? How many laborers performed industrial work by 1820?

Growth of the Labor Force (In Thousands)

Year	Free	Slave	Farm	Industrial
1800	1,370	530	1,400	1
1810	1,590	740	1,950	15
1820	2,185	950	2,470	17
1830	3,020	1,180	2,965	75

Using Your Journal

Controversy still exists over tariffs and other legislation to protect American industry from foreign competition. In a paragraph, discuss how such measures affect American consumers and workers.

REVIEW ★ CHAPTER 10

Chapter Bonus Test Question

This question may be used for extra credit on the chapter test. What did Americans gain and lose because of the rapid growth of the nation in the early nineteenth century? (Gains: prosperity, linking of sections, growth of towns and cities, national pride, creation of jobs, opportunities for land in the West. Losses: sectional antagonism in spite of nationalistic feelings; growth of slavery; conflict over trade and slavery that weakened national bonds.)

Using Your Journal

Although student responses may vary, they should reflect an understanding that consumers will pay higher prices for manufactured goods.

Practicing the Skill

1. The election was thrown into the House of Representatives, where Clay threw his support to Adams.
2. Remind students of what they know about the electoral college. The number of electors is determined by a state's representation in Congress.
3. immigration
4. 1,950,000; 17,000

PLANNING GUIDE — Chapter 11 Age of Jackson

Daily Lesson Objectives	Teacher Classroom Resources	Multimedia
SECTION 1 **Growth of Democracy** 1 Day pp. 310–313 1. Describe campaign methods used by both political parties in the election of 1828. 2. Summarize the life and political career of Andrew Jackson.	Chapter 11 Study Guide Reproducible Lesson Plan Reteaching Activity 11-1 Section Quiz Chapter 11 Cooperative Learning Activity Chapter 11 Concept Mapping Activity Map and Graph Skill Activity 15 Chapter 11 Primary and Secondary Source Readings	Student Self-Test Software Testmaker Section Focus Transparency 32 Chapter 11 Skills Transparency The Presidents: A Picture History of Our Nation
SECTION 2 **Jacksonian Democracy** 1 Day pp. 311–318 1. List three democratic changes that developed during this period. 2. Describe attitudes toward Native Americans and African Americans during this period.	Reproducible Lesson Plan Reteaching Activity 11-2 Section Quiz American Portrait 21 Chapter 11 Primary and Secondary Source Readings	Student Self-Test Software Testmaker Section Focus Transparency 33 Chapter 11 Map Transparency U.S. History and Art Transparency 9
SECTION 3 **Political Controversies** 1 Day pp. 319–322 1. Identify the problems that the United States faced in its attempt to remain neutral in the conflict between Great Britain and France. 2. Identify three ways the United States tried to maintain its freedom of the seas. 3. Explain the reasons for the increasing demand for war.	Reproducible Lesson Plan Reteaching Activity 11-3 Section Quiz American Portrait 22 Reinforcing Social Studies Skills 32 SAT Practice Tests 9–14 Writer's Guidebook Lessons 2–6	Student Self-Test Software Testmaker Section Focus Transparency 34
SECTION 4 **The Bank and the Whigs** 1 Day pp. 323–328 1. Explain the role of the Bank of the United States in the election of 1832. 2. List three causes of the Panic of 1837.	Reproducible Lesson Plan Reteaching Activity 11-4 Section Quiz American Portrait 16 Reinforcing Social Studies Skills 24, 25, 67 Chapter 11 Enrichment Activity Chapter 11 Primary and Secondary Source Readings American Literary Heritage Unit 4 Spanish Summaries & Glossary	Student Self-Test Software Testmaker Section Focus Transparency 35 Vocabulary Puzzlemaker Audiocassette, Chapter 11 Economics in Action The Presidents: A Picture History of Our Nation
CHAPTER REVIEW AND EVALUATION 1 Day	Chapter 11 Test Chapter 11 Performance Assessment Activity	Student Self-Test Software Testmaker

OUT OF TIME? If time does not permit teaching the entire chapter, use the Chapter 11 Summary on pages 358–359 and the Chapter 11 audiocassette (English and Spanish) to point out the main ideas of the chapter.

PLANNING GUIDE

Cultural Diversity Activity

Critical Thinking Help students define the word *racism*. (the belief that a particular race is inherently superior to others) Then provide students with this statement by Lewis Cass, the secretary of war in the Jackson administration. Lewis wrote an 1830 article that appeared in the *North American Review*. In that article he reminded readers of "the progress of civilization . . . the triumph of industry and art, by which [Native American lands] have been reclaimed and over which freedom, religion, and science are extending their sway." Native Americans were, he went on to say, a "barbarous people depending for existence upon the scanty supplies furnished by the chase, [who] cannot live in contact with a civilized community."

Ask: What are Cass's arguments for pushing Native Americans further west? Why might his statements be considered racist? How might a Native American respond to Cass's charge that Native Americans were "barbarous" and whites "civilized"?

Performance Assessment Activity

The Jacksonian Era Have students write an essay that answers the following question: Was the Jacksonian period the Era of the Common Man? Suggest students research the topic by reviewing primary sources (newspapers, cartoons, voting records, paintings, autobiographies, journals, and so on) as well as secondary sources (reference works, historical interpretations, biographies). Be sure students provide evidence in support of their conclusions. Urge them to use charts, graphs, and other illustration to document their findings. Encourage students who reached different conclusions to debate their ideas before the class.

POSSIBLE RUBRIC FEATURES: Content, creativity, clarity, use of supporting evidence, written and oral communication skills, organization

Chapter Resources

Literature from the Period
De Tocqueville, Alexis. *Democracy in America, I.* 1835.

Jackson, Andrew. "Farewell Address." March 4, 1837.

Readings for the Student
Hilton, Suzanne. *The World of Young Andrew Jackson.* Walker and Company, 1988.

Remini, Robert. *The Revolutionary Age of Andrew Jackson.* Harper, 1976.

Readings for the Teacher
Fressen, Edward. *Jacksonian America: Society, Personality and Politics.* Dorsey Press, 1979.

Schlesinger, Arthur, Jr. *The Age of Jackson.* Little, Brown, 1988.

Multimedia Resources
America Moves West. Orange Cherry. (two Apple diskettes, backups, guide)

Andrew Jackson: The People's President. Westport Media. (VHS, 15 minutes)

Key to Ability Levels

Teaching strategies have been coded for varying learning styles and abilities.

- **L1** Basic activities for all students
- **L2** Average activities for average to above-average students
- **L3** Challenging activities for above-average students
- **LEP** Limited English Proficiency activities

Glencoe Links to the Humanities

Link to Art
- U.S. History and Art Transparencies 7, 9

Links to Literature
- Macmillan Literature: American Literature Text—Ralph Waldo Emerson
- Macmillan Literature: American Literature Audiotapes Side 1

Link to Music
- American Music: Cultural Traditions

CHAPTER 11

BEGINNING THE CHAPTER

Explain to students that in the 1824 presidential election, only 25 percent of eligible voters actually voted. In 1840, more than 80 percent went to the polls. As students read Chapter 11, have them look for reasons that voters were more involved in national politics in 1840 than they were in 1824.

During the Age of Jackson, voters came to believe that elected officials should reflect the wishes of the people they represented. Ask students how they think voters today view elected officials. What do students think is the role of an elected official, to represent the views of voters or the officials' own views?

Recording Journal Notes

Students might organize their information into a chart with the name of each political party listed at the top of each column. As students read about the various campaigns, they can fill in the chart.

CHAPTER 11

Age of Jackson
1828–1842

▶ CHEROKEE LEADER BLACK COAT

Setting the Scene

Focus

Andrew Jackson's victory in the election of 1828 marked the beginning of a new era. His election symbolized the growth of popular democracy, and Jackson himself became a symbol for the age. Although a Westerner, he fought sectionalism by insisting upon the supremacy of federal laws over the states. He also fought economic injustice and social inequality. Jackson's political movement resulted in the formation of the Democratic party and also an opposition party, the Whigs.

Concepts to Understand

★ How political change in state voting laws advanced democracy

★ How economic policy shaped controversies over the tariff and the national banking system

Read to Discover . . .

★ in what ways Andrew Jackson was a symbol of his times.

★ how Jackson's nationalism was shown during the nullification crisis and his war on the national bank.

Journal Notes

What kind of campaigns did political parties wage against presidential candidates of the opposing party? Jot down the information in your journal.

CULTURAL
- 1828 *Cherokee Phoenix,* first newspaper in a Native American language, published
- 1830 Church of Jesus Christ of Latter-day Saints (Mormons) organized in New York

| 1825 | 1830 |

POLITICAL
- 1825 Democratic Republican and National Republican parties emerge
- 1828 Andrew Jackson elected
- 1830 Webster debates Hayne
- 1832 South Carolina adopts Nullification Ordinance

UNIT 4 Toward a Democracy: 1820–1854

✚ EXTRA CREDIT PROJECT

Comparing Presidents Point out to students that Andrew Jackson was the first President from a western state. Suggest that interested students research the lives of the six preceding Presidents as well as that of Andrew Jackson. Have them compare Jackson with the other Presidents. Ask students to present their findings in a report and to draw conclusions about Jackson's election and the expansion of democracy in the early nineteenth century.

History AND ART

Stump Speaking
by George Caleb Bingham, 1854–1855

Bingham's series of election paintings expresses faith in the democratic process. For nearly five years, the artist devoted his talent to illustrating the human aspect of the political process.

◀ PORCELAIN DOLL

- **1837** Nathaniel Hawthorne publishes *Twice-Told Tales*
- **1842** American Agriculturalist first published

1835	1840

- **1836** Bank of the United States charter expires
- **1837** Worldwide economic depression strikes
- **1840** Whigs nominate Harrison

CHAPTER 11 Age of Jackson 1828–1842   309

CHAPTER 11 CONCEPTS

Concept Mapping Activity

Write the chapter concepts on the chalkboard. Have students copy the concepts in their notebooks and briefly define them. Then place the generalization below on the board. Ask students what change in political life is suggested by the generalization. (emergence of democracy)

> Despite sectional differences, democracy emerged as the leading force in American political life
> - Political Change
> - Economic Policy

History AND ART

Point out that George Caleb Bingham drew most of his subjects from everyday life. Discuss how this painting reflects the spirit of the times as Americans entered the Age of Jackson.

The following material is available from Glencoe and may be used to introduce or enrich Chapter 11.

 CD-ROM

- *The Presidents: A Picture History of Our Nation*

Teacher Notes

LESSON PLAN
SECTION 1, 310–314

FOCUS

Bellringer

 Prior to taking roll at the beginning of the class period, display Focus Activity Transparency 36 on the overhead projector and assign the accompanying Focus Activity Sheet.

Objectives

Point out the objectives on this page to students in previewing the section content.

Motivating Activity

Ask students to imagine they are all 18 years old. Have all students eligible to vote in the next election stand. (all but non-citizens) Have those eligible to vote in the 1824 election stand. (white males only) Inform students who are standing that half of them must sit down. Only white males who owned property could vote in 1824. Tell students that in Chapter 11 they will read about the beginnings of the movement toward universal suffrage.

 Use Skills Transparency 11.

The following material is available from Glencoe and may be used to introduce or enrich Chapter 11.

CD-ROM

• *The Presidents: A Picture History of Our Nation*

SECTION 1

Growth of Democracy

Setting the Scene

Section Focus

Although sectional rivalries overshadowed the national spirit and proved divisive during John Quincy Adams's presidency, a powerful force was rising that would influence American politics more than sectionalism or nationalism. The spirit of democracy soon would significantly influence voters, election rules, and government decisions. The presidency of Andrew Jackson would give this spirit momentum and would itself be carried along by democracy's swelling tide.

Objectives

After studying this section, you should be able to

★ describe campaign methods used by both political parties in the election of 1828.

★ summarize the life and political career of Andrew Jackson.

Key Term

mudslinging

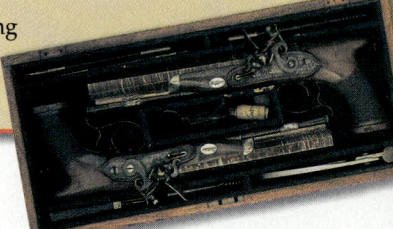

▶ ANDREW JACKSON'S DUELING PISTOLS

Well before the presidential election of 1828, it was clear that President John Quincy Adams and challenger Andrew Jackson would be the only candidates. Without much help from the President, Adams's supporters had built a loosely organized following, primarily in the Northeast. They tended to represent established property interests and favored nationalist legislation. Jackson's supporters, on the other hand, included farmers of the South and West, skilled workers, and owners of small businesses. Like the Republican party of Jefferson's time, Jacksonians favored limiting federal power. The Adams supporters called themselves National Republicans in order to emphasize the President's commitment to a national program. Jacksonians took the name Democratic Republicans, or simply Democrats, to stress their ties to the common people.

■ The Election of 1828

The United States in the 1820s was undergoing rapid change. Conflicting sectional interests and a shifting population made political forecasts difficult. In this environment both political parties decided not to risk the presidential election of 1828 by taking a strong position on any issue. Instead, they focused on comparisons of the candidates' personal traits.

A Mudslinging Campaign

The electioneering soon turned to **mudslinging**, making malicious, often untrue, charges against an opponent. The National Republicans portrayed Jackson as a barbarian who "misspelled every fourth word," a Julius Caesar who would destroy American liberties, and a "butcher" who had murdered a number of people. The Democrats

310   UNIT 4 Toward a Democracy: 1820–1854

Classroom Resources for SECTION 1

Teacher's Classroom Resources
- Chapter 11 Study Guide
- Reproducible Lesson Plan
- Reteaching Activity 11-1
- Chapter 11 Cooperative Learning Activity
- Chapter 11 Primary and Secondary Source Readings
- Section Quiz

Multimedia
- Section Focus Transparency 36
- Chapter 11 Skills Transparency
- Testmaker
- Student Self-Test Software
- The Presidents: A Picture History of Our Nation

revived the "bargain and corruption" smear from the 1824 election. They went on to charge that Adams had allowed the federal civil service to become scandalously dishonest and had wasted the people's money on "gaming tables"—actually a billiard table and a chess set bought with Adams's own money for the White House. Adams's backers went so far as to accuse Jackson of adultery based on a technicality concerning his wife's divorce from a former husband years earlier. Rachel Jackson suffered terribly from this attack and died shortly after the election—a tragedy for which Jackson never forgave the slanderers.

While both parties were equally adept at misrepresentation, the Democrats found an advantage in their candidate's humble beginnings. Democratic newspapers began to call Andrew Jackson "the candidate of the people."

"The Candidate of the People" Wins

The election of 1828 was a decisive victory for Jackson—178 electoral votes to 83. Adams was strong only in New England. Jackson swept nearly every Southern and Western state and carried Pennsylvania and New York.

Although the campaign was a national disgrace, the election was one of the most significant in American history. For the first time, a candidate from the region west of the Appalachians was elected President. The rapid growth of the Western states was swinging the political center of gravity away from the Eastern seaboard. The results also showed the developing political split between the nation's sections.

New Voters

Three times as many people voted for President in 1828 as had in 1824. This was partly because many states had lowered or eliminated property ownership as a voting qualification and also because twice as many eligible voters participated. Many reasons have been given for the elimination of property ownership as a qualification for voting in the early 1800s, including the ideals of the Declaration of Independence and the social equality of frontier life. In addition, as cities and towns grew, the percentage of working people who did not own property increased. These people paid taxes and had an interest in the political affairs of their communities. By the 1820s Pennsylvania, Massachusetts, and New York recognized this interest and substituted the payment of taxes for property ownership as a basis for voting rights. By 1852 the last state, Virginia, had given the franchise to all adult white males.

Andrew Jackson's victory in 1828 was partly the result of his party's appeal to the new voters. Jackson's supporters believed that he represented the "common man." All former Presidents had enjoyed the advantages of inherited wealth or education or both. Jackson, orphaned at 14, had made his way entirely on his own. He became the symbol of the growing power of democracy.

Visualizing History ▲ **KING ANDREW** His supporters viewed Jackson as a strong President who represented the common people. Critics denounced him as a would-be tyrant. They called him "King Andrew the First," and he is shown in this cartoon trampling on the Constitution and ruling by veto. **What was significant about the election of 1828?**

CHAPTER 11 SECTION 1

Independent Practice

Politics Point out that mudslinging mixes fact and fiction. Have students find the facts on which each of the following fictions is based.
1. Adams wasted the people's money on gaming tables for the White House. (He bought a billiard table and chess set with his own money.)
2. Jackson was uneducated. (He spelled poorly but enjoyed reading and practiced law.)
3. Jackson was a violent man and a murderer. (He once killed a man in a duel.) **L3**

Teaching Life of the Times

Tell students that entertaining voters was not new to American politics in the 1820s. However, in the Jacksonian era it was more widely and more effectively used. Efficient party "machines" also were created in Jackson's time to support candidates and get out the vote. Ask students to consider whether these changes advanced or hindered democracy.

Life of the Times

Getting Out the Vote

The election of Andrew Jackson in 1828 signaled a new era in politics. Property-holding qualifications for voting had been gradually abolished by the states, which extended the franchise to most adult white males. With this increase in voters, political party organizations and candidates soon learned to make appeals tailored for mass audiences.

Candidates and political parties participated in every kind of community gathering. Political rallies featuring parades, flags, speeches, and free-flowing liquor became hallmarks of electioneering.

The potential for vote fraud was everywhere. The polls might be open for several days, which made it easier for enterprising voters to cast more than one ballot. None of the states used a secret ballot. Rather, parties printed their own ballots, or "tickets" with the names of candidates. Voters going to the polls might be harassed by high-pressure ballot hawkers from rival parties into accepting their ticket.

State nominating conventions also encouraged participation in elections. Convention proceedings were reported in the local press, which aroused citizens to work for their party's choices.

▶ ANDREW JACKSON ON HORSEBACK

Andrew Jackson was such a controversial figure that it is difficult to find the truth between the slander of his enemies and the praise of his admirers. According to James Parton, his first important biographer, the evidence could be interpreted to show Jackson as either a patriot or a traitor:

> He was one of the greatest of generals and wholly ignorant of the art of war. A writer, brilliant, elegant, eloquent, without being able to compose a correct sentence or spell words of four syllables. . . . A democratic autocrat. An urbane savage. An atrocious saint.

■ A Symbol of His Times

Born in a log cabin on the North Carolina frontier, Jackson rose to the highest office—visible evidence of the American success story. In his time Jackson became almost a mythical figure. George Bancroft, a New Englander and an ardent Democrat, wrote:

> Behold, then, the unlettered man of the West, the nursling of the wilds, the farmer of the Hermitage, little versed in books, unconnected by science with the tradition of the past, raised by the will of the people to the highest pinnacle of honor, to the central post of republican freedom, to the station where all the nations of the earth would watch his actions—where his words would vibrate through the civilized world, and his spirit be the moving-star to guide the nations.

Jackson's Early Career

Jackson was elected Tennessee's first representative to Congress before the age of 30. In the War of 1812, he had been one of the few generals who could get ill-trained militia to stand up to the British redcoats. His most obvious trait was his force of will, a characteristic that became evident when someone tried to defy him.

Critical Thinking

Evaluating Election Campaigns Some observers have called the election campaign of 1828 "a national disgrace." Why was the campaigning disgraceful? (smear tactics, comparison of candidates' personal traits rather than their views on issues) Why did both parties stress personalities rather than issues? (Politicians feared that taking strong positions on issues would expose what they actually believed, thereby risking the loss of votes.) Point out that today such tactics are called "negative campaigning." Have students research examples from newspapers or television. Ask them to compare their examples to those given in the textbook. Ask: Why do you think such tactics are still used today? **L3**

Jackson's early life was notable for violent personal quarrels. He took part in five duels, once killing a man. From that encounter, a bullet that lodged next to his heart remained with him for the rest of his life, surgeons believing it too dangerous to risk removing. As Jackson grew older, his temper and actions became milder.

The Inauguration

As the time for Jackson's inauguration approached, his supporters poured into Washington, D.C. Men slept five or six in a room; when no more beds were available, they spent the night on sofas, billiard tables, and floors. John Quincy Adams left the city rather than attend the ceremony that Jackson's detractors thought could mean the end of the republic. A typical reaction was that of Daniel Webster, senator from Massachusetts:

> *Nobody knows what he will do when he does come. . . . My fear is stronger than my hope.*

Jackson followed Jefferson's precedent of walking to the inaugural ceremony. His hands shook as he read a rather cautious and colorless Inaugural Address. What happened later, however, seemed to justify those who had gloomily predicted that Jackson's election would mean the reign of "King Mob." From the Capitol, he rode on horseback to the White House surrounded by a cheering crowd. There, a reception had been prepared only for invited guests and officials. There were no means, however, to prevent the crowd from pushing in. Chairs and china were broken; several people fainted. The crowd pressing around Jackson was so great that he had to be helped to escape through a back window.

"A Gentleman and a Soldier"

By the time Jackson reached the White House, he had become a person of dignity and courtesy. A visiting Englishwoman at his inauguration said he looked like "a gentleman and a soldier."

Jackson surely did not have the training or education that Thomas Jefferson or John Quincy Adams had. In addition, his political opinions were sometimes vague and continually changing. Yet when questions came to him for decision, he showed quick and firm judgment.

Like Washington, he often sought advice from several sources, and as President, he had a group of personal friends, called by his enemies the "kitchen cabinet," who advised him on all major decisions. "The character of his mind," wrote his friend Senator Thomas H. Benton of Missouri, "was that of judgment, with a rapid and almost intuitive perception, followed by instant and decisive action."

Entering office at age 62, Jackson was tortured by several physical agonies. He suffered from headaches, digestive disorders, coughing spells, and old wounds. His wife Rachel's death before the inauguration in 1829 added bereavement and loneliness. Still, his inner toughness enabled him to perform the duties of the office with a firm and steady hand.

Section 1 ★ Review

Checking for Understanding

1. **Identify** National Republicans, Democratic Republicans.
2. **Define** mudslinging.
3. **Describe** the central focus of the 1828 election.
4. **Explain** why the campaigning parties chose not to take positions on the issues.

Critical Thinking

5. **Analyzing Results** How might changes during the Industrial Revolution have become factors in the extension of voting privileges?

CHAPTER 11 Age of Jackson 1828–1842   **313**

LESSON PLAN
Mastering Social Studies Skills

Teaching Interpreting Primary Sources

Remind students that a work of art expresses the artist's point of view. Discuss how a portrait painter indicates a point of view. (colors create moods; postures show attitudes; choice of subject matter, and so on)

Have students study *The Light* by George Catlin. What differences are there in the backgrounds and clothing of the figures? Ask: What do these differences symbolize? (the difficulty that two cultures have in coming together)

Did You Know?

George Catlin gave up a law career in 1823 to become a portrait painter. By 1837 he had completed 500 portraits and sketches of Native Americans.

Social Studies Skills
Interpreting Primary Sources

▲ PIGEON'S EGG HEAD GOING TO AND RETURNING FROM WASHINGTON BY GEORGE CATLIN, 1832

The Light

A self-taught artist, George Catlin (1796–1872) devoted his life to documenting the history and culture of Native Americans through the art of painting. Catlin moved westward from Pennsylvania in 1830 and became the first painter to shape the national image of the proud Plains peoples. During the mid-1830s, Catlin spent several summers among various Native American peoples. He saw and recorded with his brush the earthen lodge villages of the Pawnee, the scalp dance of the Sioux, and the practices of Blackfoot medicine men. He was so accurate and detailed in his paintings that descendants of those he immortalized easily recognized their ancestors.

By 1840 Catlin had made almost 500 portraits and sketches. He established Catlin's Indian Gallery, a traveling exhibition of paintings, costumes, and artifacts that toured major cities in Great Britain and France as well as the United States. During the 1850s Catlin traveled to South America and to the Pacific coast of North America and recorded the appearances, surroundings, and ways of life of the Native Americans of these regions. Many of the paintings Catlin produced can be viewed in the Smithsonian Institution in Washington, D.C., and in the American Museum of Natural History in New York.

The two-pose painting shown here is of Wi-jun-jon, or Pigeon's Egg Head—also known as The Light—the son of an Assiniboin chief, whom Catlin painted in 1832. The Assiniboin lived on the northern Plains and were distant relatives of the Dakota Sioux. Wi-jun-jon was part of a delegation of Plains peoples who, in 1831, traveled to Washington, D.C., where they met with President Jackson.

Catlin shows Wi-jun-jon resplendent in Native American dress upon his arrival in Washington and ridiculous in a colonel's uniform (a gift from the President) on his way back to his people. The Assiniboin barely recognized Wi-jun-jon when he arrived and dismissed his stories of the life he had seen in Washington as preposterous lies. Once respected by his people, The Light lost his credibility while in the white man's land.

Examining the Primary Source

1. Compare the clothing, accessories, and posture in each pose.
2. Identify and explain the significance of the scenery that The Light faces in each pose.

Critical Thinking

3. **Identifying Central Issues** What point does the artist make by showing back-to-back poses?

Answers to SOCIAL STUDIES SKILLS

1. Both poses show The Light in clothing that symbolizes a way of life. On the left, he stands erect, one knee bent to step forward, conveying dignity and ease. On the right, he leans back—off balance—on an umbrella, trying to work the fan in his right hand. The pose at right depicts The Light as ill-at-ease and displaced.
2. On the left, The Light faces a river and, in the distance, the Capitol. On the right, he faces a line of tepees. The scenery indicates his destinations—to Washington, D.C., and then to his home.
3. The artist suggests that the two worlds indicated by The Light's clothing are incompatible. The Light must choose one.

SECTION 2

Jacksonian Democracy

Setting the Scene

Section Focus

While Jackson's name is used to describe this period of American history, American democracy in these years had much broader sources than the character of the President. Jacksonian democracy is also defined by the political optimism of his time. It was a period of celebration for the rights of the "common man."

Objectives

After studying this section, you should be able to

★ list three democratic changes that developed during this period.

★ describe attitudes toward Native Americans and African Americans during this period.

Key Terms

spoils system, pocket veto

▶ BLACK HAWK, SAC AND FOX LEADER

During the administration of Andrew Jackson, the United States was a nation of change, a nation on the move—socially and economically as well as politically. American society was viewed as a society of opportunity. Americans felt that, given a chance, they could make a better life for themselves. This was the era of the common people, and Andrew Jackson appealed to the American people because he stood for values that many regarded with favor.

■ The People's Government

Before Jackson's time, voters expected public officials to use their own best judgment. Now they came to believe that officials should act according to the demands of the people. To make government respond more directly to popular will, state and local governments began to fill some positions such as judges, constables, and public surveyors by election rather than appointment. The terms of office were also shortened so that popular opinion had a more direct effect on the actions of elected officials.

The Spoils System

As new voters made demands on government, they learned the power of political organization. National issues became as much topics of conversation as local issues had always been. As national parties built stronger state and local ties, they began to rely upon a growing number of professional or career politicians. These changes helped to initiate the **spoils system,** the practice of appointing people to government positions on the basis of party

CHAPTER 11 Age of Jackson 1828–1842   **315**

CHAPTER 11 SECTION 2

TEACH
Guided Practice
Making Generalizations
Have students list two supporting statements for each generalization below.
1. Jacksonian democracy had nothing to offer Native Americans. (initiated Indian Removal, refused to enforce Supreme Court decision upholding rights of Georgia Cherokee)
2. Jackson asserted his power over Congress. (use of pocket veto, greater use of veto than all previous Presidents)
L1, LEP

Map Study *Using Maps*
Answers: Sauk Fox, Ojibway, Potawatomi, Miami, Shawnee, Cherokee, Creek, Seminole, Chickasaw, Choctaw

Map Skills
Have students locate and identify on the map the area to which Native Americans were forced to move.

Fact or Fiction?
Andrew Jackson was the first man of ordinary means to become President.

FICTION: By the 1820s, Jackson was a wealthy planter who held many enslaved persons.

---

loyalty and party service. This was not an entirely new development, but Jackson was the first to oust large numbers of government employees in order to appoint his followers to office. He argued that there should be rotation in office—a point he emphasized in his first State of the Union message:

> *The duties of all public officers are ... so plain and simple that men of intelligence may readily qualify themselves for their performance; and I cannot but believe that more is lost by the long continuance of men in office than is generally to be gained by their experience.*

Some believed that the spoils system set a poor precedent. A contemporary observer not unfriendly to Jackson noted that "office-seeking and office-getting was becoming a regular business, where impudence [boldness] triumphed over worth." Jackson amplified presidential power by using the veto more than all previous Presidents. He was also one of the first Presidents to use the **pocket veto**, killing a bill by taking no action on it and waiting for Congress to adjourn.

Removal of Native Americans, 1820–1840

- Lands ceded by Native Americans
- Native American reservations
- Cherokee Trail of Tears
- Migration route

Map Study The federal government relocated Native Americans living in the United States to reservations in Indian Territory. *Identify the peoples that were removed according to the map.*

316 UNIT 4 Toward a Democracy: 1820–1854

Cultural Diversity

Jacksonian democracy did not benefit all Americans. Even when the courts sided with Native Americans, President Andrew Jackson refused to enforce the rulings. African Americans also lost ground. Southern states severely limited their mobility, rights, and opportunities.

Free African Americans in the South could not vote, bear arms, buy liquor, speak in public, form organizations, or testify against whites in court. African Americans in the North were only marginally better off.

AMERICAN PORTRAITS

Sequoya 1760(?)–1843

Although he was the son of a white trader, Sequoya was raised among his mother's Cherokee people. He never learned English, but he was fascinated by the "talking leaves" of books.

Sequoya was convinced that reading and writing gave whites power. After being disabled by an accident, he dedicated himself to creating written symbols for the Cherokee language. At first, Sequoya tried to create simple pictures to represent Cherokee words, but later he developed 86 symbols to represent all syllables in Cherokee speech. He then had his six-year-old daughter demonstrate his system of reading and writing to Cherokee leaders.

Following their approval of his system, thousands of the Cherokee learned how to read and write. Sequoya even published a Cherokee newspaper and translated parts of the Bible into Cherokee.

Some Gains for Women

Jacksonian democracy did not offer women suffrage, but women did make some gains. Emma Willard, Catharine Beecher, and Mary Lyon established female academies promoting education among women. During the 1830s some states passed the first women's property acts, guaranteeing women the right to control property.

■ Minorities

Whereas women made some strides under Jackson's presidency, Native Americans and African Americans did not. Jacksonian democracy had nothing to offer these two oppressed minorities.

Removal

Most Americans believed that the area between the Missouri River and the Rocky Mountains, "the Great American Desert," would provide a permanent Native American reservation. Jackson and, later, President Van Buren spoke of protecting the Native Americans from fraud and of how humane the government's removal policy was, but the policy as carried out was cruel.

The Cherokee

In Georgia the Cherokee had developed a lifestyle that included schools, mills, and turnpikes. In the 1820s, under pressure from the state to give up their lands, they wrote a constitution, hired lawyers, and sued in the Supreme Court. Chief Justice John Marshall upheld the rights of the Cherokee against Georgia. However, Jackson refused to carry out the decision that ordered Georgia to return Cherokee lands. "Marshall has made his opinion," he reportedly said, "now let him enforce it."

When the Cherokee resisted the government's "generous" offer of lands farther west, Jackson sent in the army. Forced to move from their homes to what is now Arkansas and Oklahoma, an estimated 4,000 died of starvation, disease, or exposure on the march that the Cherokee called the "Trail of Tears."

Mistreatment Continues

Another tragedy took place in Illinois. The Sac and Fox people were forced to move to Iowa, where the Sioux and the settlers harassed them. In 1832 Black Hawk, the leader of the Sac and Fox, moved them back into Illinois to recover their lands. When

CHAPTER 11 Age of Jackson 1828–1842

CHAPTER 11 SECTION 2

Independent Practice

Comparing Have students research recent government policies toward Native Americans. Ask students to write two or three paragraphs comparing these policies with those of the Jacksonian period. How do they differ? Are there any similarities? **L1, L2**

Teaching American Portraits

Before 1821, Native American groups did not have written languages. Traditions, ideas, and history were transmitted orally or in pictures from one generation to the next. Sequoya believed that a written language would help the Cherokee preserve their culture and their independence. Discuss with students how Sequoya's system would help the Cherokee and why it is an important contribution to American history.

Linking Across TIME

The state of Oklahoma entered the Union in 1907. It was created from the Indian and the Oklahoma territories. The state seal displays a large circle in whose center is a five-pointed star. Within the points of the star are five symbols, one for each seal of the "Five Civilized Tribes."

Critical Thinking

Making Predictions Review the quotation from Andrew Jackson on page 316, in which he states his views on the process of rotation in office. Point out that during the early 1800s government had a much smaller role in American life, providing few of the services it offers today. Have students describe some of the differences between the roles of civil servants during Jackson's presidency and the roles of civil servants today. **L2**

 ▲ **THE TRAIL OF TEARS** Native Americans who were forced from their land traveled west in the 1830s. **Why did the Cherokee call the forced march from their land the "Trail of Tears"?**

farmers in Illinois panicked, the state militia massacred Black Hawk's entire group.

By 1840 the government had moved the few Native Americans still living east of the Mississippi to reservations, except for the Seminoles of Florida. After years of fighting, Osceola, their chief, was captured and later died in prison. Some Seminoles settled deep in the Everglades.

Although most citizens supported Jackson's Native American removals, a few leaders, like Henry Clay, said that Jackson's attitude stained the nation's honor. Religious denominations, especially Methodists and Quakers, also denounced the harsh treatment of Native Americans, but these voices were a small minority.

"The Great Silence"

In the 1830s the cotton culture in the South had firmly established the institution of slavery, and criticism of the system became increasingly unwise. Those who spoke out against slavery risked physical harm. In the North, African Americans were free, but they were generally second-class citizens.

The debates of the 1820s leading to the Missouri Compromise had shown the slavery issue to be so explosive that a policy called "the great silence" began, and discussion of slavery as a national issue faded. Antislavery literature was often barred from the mails. From 1836 to 1844, antislavery petitions to Congress were ignored.

Section 2 ★ Review

Checking for Understanding

1. **Identify** John Marshall, the Trail of Tears, Black Hawk, Osceola.
2. **Define** spoils system, pocket veto.
3. **Summarize** the political changes that took place in the United States during the Jacksonian period.
4. **Compare** the fates of African Americans and Native Americans during this era.

Critical Thinking

5. **Evaluating Leadership** In what way did the Jackson administration violate the constitutional system of checks and balances?

318 UNIT 4 Toward a Democracy: 1820–1854

SECTION 3

Political Controversies

Setting the Scene

Section Focus

Although Andrew Jackson was the people's President, Americans in 1828 had diverse interests. Westerners believed that Jackson would favor internal improvements and curb the power of the Bank of the United States while inflating the currency. Southern Democrats began to oppose high tariffs and national spending on internal improvements. The Northeastern wing of the party was split on the tariff issue but strongly opposed inflationary money policies. It was a setting ripe for conflict that would test Jackson's leadership.

Objectives

After studying this section, you should be able to
★ identify the various sectional interests of the nation in this period.
★ explain how the tariff and nullification issue developed into a crisis.

Key Terms

nullification, compact

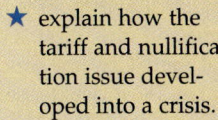

▶ ANTI-JACKSON IMAGE

Both supporters and opponents were interested in President Jackson's position on such matters as internal improvements, the question of tariffs, and banking. In his first term of office, Jackson made bold decisions on these issues—sometimes delighting, sometimes dismaying, members of his own Democratic party.

Jackson surprised the West with his answer to the issue of federally financed roads. Congress had passed a bill promising to pay for half the cost of extending the Cumberland Road inside the state of Kentucky. This legislation, known as the Maysville Road Bill, was vetoed by Jackson. He said that the Constitution did not grant the federal government power to spend money on local transportation—the road was to be entirely inside one state. In his veto message he explained that grants of federal money

> ... [h]ave always been professedly under the control of the general principle that the works which might be thus aided should be 'of a general, not local; national, not state,' character. A disregard of that distinction would of necessity lead to the subversion of the federal system.

While Westerners were dismayed at Jackson's decision, the veto pleased Southerners, who opposed federal support of internal improvements. The veto demonstrated that although Jackson was a strong nationalist,

CHAPTER 11 Age of Jackson 1828–1842

CHAPTER 11
SECTION 3

TEACH
Guided Practice

Law Have students use the index to locate the Kentucky and Virginia Resolutions, read the information, and write a paragraph explaining why these resolutions were written (to oppose the Sedition Act), and what they had in common with the tariff controversy of 1832 (used the theory of nullification to oppose actions by the federal government, raised question of whether the federal government or states were sovereign). **L2**

Visualizing History
Point out that Daniel Webster was considered to be the finest orator of the time. He could hold listeners spellbound for hours. **Answer to Caption:** The federal government was created by a compact of the states. If Congress passes a law that infringes on the rights of states, the states can declare the law null and void.

Did You Know?
Daniel Webster's final words in his famous debate with Haynes were "Liberty and Union, now and forever, one and inseparable."

---

he also believed in a strict interpretation of the Constitution. The fact that the proposed extension was to be inside the home state of Henry Clay, Jackson's chief political adversary, probably influenced his strict interpretation of the Constitution.

■ Sectional Issues

The Northeast and the West were divided over federal land policy. Senator Samuel A. Foot of Connecticut represented Eastern manufacturers who were worried about losing their labor supply. In 1830 he proposed a limit on Western land sales to discourage people from moving west. Senator Thomas Hart Benton of Missouri angrily attacked Foot for promoting the interests of the Northeast at the expense of the West. Senator Robert Y. Hayne of South Carolina supported Benton. In several days of debate, senators from both the South and the Northeast attempted to win the support of Western politicians. With Vice President Calhoun of South Carolina presiding, Hayne and Daniel Webster of Massachusetts eventually engaged in a full-scale discussion of many of the issues.

Webster and Calhoun

Webster's political career followed a course exactly opposite Calhoun's. Calhoun had been a War Hawk during the War of 1812. Webster had opposed the war, even to the extent of considering **nullification**, or making null and void federal laws calling for raising troops. When Calhoun supported nationalist legislation after the war, Webster supported the Northeast. By 1830, however, the two had reversed positions. To preserve his political future in South Carolina, Calhoun changed his views. South Carolina was suffering from low cotton prices and a depressed economy. Calhoun could no longer support high tariffs because the people of his home state believed that high tariffs were a cause of their local economic

▲ **STATES' RIGHTS OR UNION** During the Webster-Hayne debate in the Senate, Daniel Webster argued that the Union was a national government of all people in all states, and if it passed laws that infringed on the rights of the states, the Supreme Court would declare the laws unconstitutional. **What was Robert Hayne's major argument?**

UNIT 4 Toward a Democracy: 1820–1854

Special Needs

Learning Disability For students with learning disabilities, review the concepts of main ideas and details by having them locate the main ideas in the section "The Nullification Crisis." Explain that main ideas usually are located in the first sentences of each paragraph. Have students write each main idea on an index card. Then ask them to write the following words or dates on separate cards: 1832, Ordinance of Nullification, secession, Proclamation to the People of South Carolina, resignations, Force Bill, Henry Clay, Tariff of 1833. Have students arrange the words under main ideas and check for accuracy.

problems. Opposing the tariff, Calhoun became a states' rights advocate, while Webster's support for a protective tariff made him favor a strong federal government.

In a "Second Reply to Hayne," Webster pointed out that nullification could only mean the end of the Union. Webster said the Union was not a creature of the states: it was the people's government, forged for their own welfare and meant to endure.

The greatness of Webster's speech lay in his use of American patriotism to support the idea of a Constitution flexible enough to meet the needs of a growing country. His audience was not so much the Senate as the people at large.

Thousands of copies of the speech were published. Schoolchildren memorized the closing paragraph with the famous final words: "Liberty and Union, now and forever, one and inseparable!"

The antitariff forces rallied around Calhoun's ideas published anonymously in a work called *The South Carolina Exposition*. Calhoun denounced the Tariff of 1828, claiming that it made the South a servant of Northern industrialists. In brief, Calhoun's argument was that the federal government was created by a **compact**, or contract among the states. Each state gave up only such powers as were expressly granted in the Constitution. If the federal government passed laws that infringed on the remaining state powers, each individual state, not the Supreme Court, had the right to decide whether or not that federal law was constitutional. A state could declare the law null and void within its own borders. Behind this doctrine of nullification lurked the threat to secede from the Union.

The Tariff of 1828

The protective tariff of 1816 was not costly enough to satisfy American manufacturers. In response to their demands, duties on imported manufactures and on some raw materials were raised twice more—in 1824 and 1828. These laws aroused increasing resentment in the South, especially in South Carolina where the cotton economy was depressed. Increased cotton production on rich lands farther west had reduced cotton

▲ **PEGGY EATON** President Jackson viewed the refusal of cabinet members and spouses to meet socially with Peggy Eaton as a plot to discredit him politically. **What caused Jackson's final break with John Calhoun?**

prices. Instead of blaming local causes, South Carolinians attributed their ills to the tariff.

When news of the Tariff of 1828, often called the "Tariff of Abominations," reached Charleston, people were indignant. Flags were hung at half-mast; college students threatened to buy no Northern goods; and there was talk of leaving the Union. South Carolina, however, held back from acting against the tariff because John C. Calhoun, the state's leading politician, was Andrew Jackson's running mate for Vice President. Calhoun's influence in a new administration might bring about tariff reduction.

The Nullification Crisis

Which side would Jackson take in the argument over nullification? Southerners hoped that the President, a slaveholder and planter himself, would support their interests. The nullifiers tried to get Jackson to show his hand at a dinner celebrating Jefferson's birthday on April 13, 1830. Controlling

CHAPTER 11
SECTION 3

ASSESS
Check Understanding
Assign Section 3 Review as homework or an in-class activity.

Evaluate
Assign the Section 3 Quiz in the TCR or use the History of a Free Nation Testmaker to create a customized quiz.

Reteach
Have students complete Reteaching Activity 11-3.

Enrich
Ask students to write a paragraph describing how they think American history might have been different if Jackson had allowed South Carolina to nullify the Tariff of 1832.

CLOSE
Have students explain how Jackson chose the nation's interest over the states' interest in the nullification crisis.

There is controversy today, as there was in Jackson's time, over the value of protective tariffs. Many business leaders and political figures argue that free trade will create jobs by opening markets abroad for American goods. Others believe that free trade will flood the market.

---

the committee in charge of the banquet, they printed on the menu 24 toasts, many of them expressing sentiments against the tariff and for nullification. When Jackson's turn came to make a toast, the Old Warrior asked everyone to rise, looked straight at Calhoun, and echoed Webster when he stated, "Our Federal Union: it must be preserved." Calhoun, pale and trembling, responded, "Our Union, next to our liberty, the most dear."

Jackson and Calhoun

The break between Jackson and Calhoun was personal as well as political. Major John Eaton, Jackson's secretary of war, had married a young woman who was not socially accepted by Mrs. Calhoun and the other cabinet members' wives. Of the cabinet members, only Martin Van Buren was pleasant to Peggy Eaton. Jackson, remembering his own wife's suffering from slander, stopped meeting with most of his cabinet advisers. Jackson's final break with Calhoun came when he discovered that, years earlier, Calhoun had wanted to have "Old Hickory" censured for mistreatment of the Seminoles in Florida. From this point on, Van Buren became Jackson's choice to succeed him in office.

The Tariff of 1832

In 1832 Congress passed a new tariff law. The rates, while lower than those of 1828, were still high. South Carolina called a special convention that passed an Ordinance of Nullification declaring that the tariff was "null, void, and no law." The ordinance threatened secession, and the state began to arm and drill a volunteer military force.

In response, Jackson issued a "Proclamation to the People of South Carolina" pointing out that nullification meant disunion and disunion meant treason. Privately, he warned Senator Hayne that if there was bloodshed he would hang the first nullificationist he could get his hands on from the first tree he could find. Hayne resigned from the Senate to become governor of South Carolina, and Calhoun resigned the vice presidency to lead the fight in the Senate.

Compromise Tariff

Compromise settled the crisis. Jackson asked Congress to pass a Force Bill to give him the powers necessary to suppress disunion in South Carolina. While Congress debated the measure, Henry Clay introduced a compromise tariff bill. It provided for gradual scaling down of duties. The Tariff of 1833, supported by both Webster and Calhoun, and the Force Bill were passed the same day. Thus Congress removed South Carolina's grievance about the tariff and at the same time denied its right to nullify a law.

Jackson agreed to the compromise, yet he felt it was probably a mistake to give in at all. "The nullifiers in the South intend to blow up a storm on the slave question next," he wrote a friend. "This ought to be met." The next step, predicted Jackson, would be an attempt to form a Southern confederacy bounded on the north by the Potomac River.

Section 3 ★ Review

Checking for Understanding
1. **Identify** Daniel Webster, John C. Calhoun, Ordinance of Nullification.
2. **Define** nullification, compact.
3. **Describe** the differing sectional interests during Jackson's presidency.
4. **Summarize** the crisis over the tariff and nullification and its resolution.

Critical Thinking
5. **Inferring Values** At a celebration, President Andrew Jackson and Vice President John Calhoun exchanged toasts to the Union. Although they used similar words, they planted themselves firmly on opposing sides of a sensitive issue. In your own words, restate the implied messages these two leaders were giving to one another.

Answers to SECTION 3 REVIEW

1. Daniel Webster, 320; John C. Calhoun, 320–321; Ordinance of Nullification, 322
2. All vocabulary words are defined in the Glossary.
3. Southern and northwestern farmers favored cheap land, eastern factory owners and eastern farmers did not; South opposed tariffs, Northeast and Northwest favored; West favored federal funds for transportation, South opposed; extension of slavery opposed except in South
4. High tariff antagonized South Carolina so passed Ordinance of Nullification; Jackson threatened force; Clay proposed compromise; South Carolina withdrew the ordinance.
5. Jackson asserted preservation of Union; Calhoun implied states' rights came first.

SECTION 4

The Bank and the Whigs

Setting the Scene

Section Focus

The fight over the second Bank of the United States divided the nation. This issue caused panic and depression. Opposition to Jackson resulted in the formation of the Whig party. After electing two Presidents, the Whig party split over slavery in the 1850s.

Objectives

After studying this section, you should be able to
★ explain the role that the Bank of the United States played in political debate and in the election of 1832.
★ list three factors that helped cause the Panic of 1837.

Key Term

platform

▲ Gold quarter eagles, c. 1834

At the time the question of nullification was dividing the nation, Jackson was also engaged in a dramatic struggle with the Bank of the United States. Chartered in 1816, the "B.U.S.," as it was nicknamed, was a useful institution. Like the original Bank of the United States, it performed much of the financial business of the country and controlled the supply of currency.

■ Popular Distrust of Banks

Despite its importance, the Bank had many enemies. Opposition came from smaller banks chartered by state legislatures, because the B.U.S. was a powerful competitor and because it prevented state banks from lending too freely. Another group, mostly farmers, were against all banks. They believed the only honest currency was "hard money"—silver and gold. Farmers respected real wealth—corn, hogs, grain, cotton, tobacco—and resented paying tribute to those who controlled paper wealth, such as mortgages and banknotes.

The Bank also suffered because of a rising feeling against monopolies. Although 80 percent of the Bank of the United States was owned by private individuals, it enjoyed a monopoly of all government business. State legislatures granted somewhat similar privileges to state banks and also made monopoly grants to companies running toll bridges, steamship lines, and turnpikes. Feeling against this sort of privilege was strong in the Northeast among small businesses and workers, who believed that monopolistic charters created an unfair advantage. Such people said monopolistic charters made certain people wealthy and kept others from acquiring property.

CHAPTER 11 SECTION 4

TEACH
Guided Practice
Political Science Have groups of students plan and conduct an imaginary interview with Henry Clay right after the election of 1832. Students should choose someone to act as Clay and make a list of questions and answers that they would ask him, such as: What did you hope to gain from introducing a recharter bill for the Bank? (embarrass Jackson; force him to veto bill) How did you misjudge public opinion about the Bank? (thought most people favored Bank) How did your plan backfire? (Jackson's veto won him the election.) **L2, L3**

Visualizing History
Have students compare the way the cartoonist portrays Jackson with the way he depicts Biddle and the Bank. (Jackson is shown as a determined fighter waving his veto stick at a monster with many heads symbolizing the Bank's many branches.)
Answer to Caption: The Bank's strict lending policy made it difficult for farmers to obtain credit; laborers did not like paper money because it resulted in higher prices.

■ Jackson versus the Bank

Jackson, like most Westerners, was a hard-money man who distrusted all banks and all paper money. While the President believed that high finance was dangerous, he also remembered that the Bank had opposed his candidacy in 1828 and had refused jobs and loans to his supporters.

■ A Campaign Issue

For the first three years of his presidency, Jackson took no action against the Bank. The President's inaction may have encouraged Bank president Nicholas Biddle's supporters to use the difference of opinion on the Bank issue to challenge Jackson in the election of 1832.

The National Republicans fired the first shot in the Bank war when they made the Bank the main issue of the election. Henry Clay, the likely presidential challenger, introduced a bill to give the Bank a new charter even though the old one would not run out until 1836. Clay hoped to embarrass Jackson by forcing him either to sign a bill he disliked or to veto it. He did not believe Jackson could defend a veto in the presidential campaign.

Jackson Vetoes the Bill

When Congress passed the Recharter Bill, Jackson remarked, "The Bank, Mr. Van Buren, is trying to kill me; but I will kill it." His veto message to Congress showed little

GENERAL JACKSON SLAYING THE MANY HEADED MONSTER.

 ▲ **JACKSON VS. THE BANK** One of Jackson's biggest political battles was fought over the Bank of the United States. The Bank issue provided a rich source for cartoonists. **Why did many Americans distrust the Bank?**

324 UNIT 4 Toward a Democracy: 1820–1854

Cooperative Learning
Divide the class into ten groups and assign to each one of the headings in Section 4. Ask each group to identify the main ideas under each heading, define unfamiliar or difficult terms, and make up questions for the class about its section. Then invite each group to teach its section to the class and to check the class's understanding by having students answer the group's questions. **L1**

knowledge of banking but great understanding of why many people disliked the B.U.S. Jackson wrote that the Bank favored the few against the many; it made "the rich richer and the potent more powerful." He called it un-American because more than one-fourth of its stock had been purchased by foreigners. Finally, he said it was an overextension of federal power because the Constitution nowhere explicitly granted the government the right to establish a central bank.

Election of 1832

The Bank issue did determine the presidential election, but not in the way Henry Clay had anticipated. The National Republicans accused Jackson of "appealing to the worst passions of the uninformed part of the people and endeavoring to stir up the poor against the rich." They produced arguments to show the value of the Bank to the nation's finances, but the Bank issue backfired. When the returns were counted, they showed that Jackson had won an overwhelming victory. He received 687,000 popular votes to Clay's 530,000 and carried the electoral college 219 to 49.

Jackson Destroys the Bank

Jackson took his reelection as a directive from the people to destroy the power of the Bank at once, even though its charter ran until 1836. Although the law required funds of the federal government to be deposited in the Bank, Jackson resolved to remove them. This required an order from the secretary of the treasury. Two secretaries resigned rather than sign the order. Finally, a third secretary agreed, and the government gradually began to withdraw deposits from the vaults of the B.U.S. New funds from taxation and land sales were placed in strong state banks that National Republicans scornfully called "pet banks."

The removal of the deposits caused a great outcry among Jackson's opponents. Nicholas Biddle claimed that removal of the deposits forced him to call in the B.U.S.'s loans and stop lending. Biddle's policy created such a scarcity of credit that hundreds

▲ **NICHOLAS BIDDLE**

of businesspeople were driven into bankruptcy and scores of banks failed. Factories closed down and workers were laid off. Since Jackson had vetoed the Bank Bill, businesspeople sent petitions urging him to save the country from depression. The President replied, "Go to Nicholas Biddle!" Eventually, Democrats shifted the blame to Biddle, arguing that if one man at the head of a private institution could drive the country into depression, then Jackson was right in saying the Bank had too much power.

Finally Biddle surrendered. The B.U.S. reversed its policies and began to extend easy credit to state banks. With money once again plentiful, the administration threw millions of acres of public land on the market. The resulting land boom sparked a time of reckless investment. Congress stimulated the boom by issuing $30 million in surplus funds to the states, triggering a host of internal improvement schemes in turnpikes, canals, and railroads.

A Change in Policy

The free spending, speculation, and resulting inflation worried Jackson's hard-money supporters. Jackson decided to halt

CHAPTER 11
SECTION 4

Linking Across TIME

In the early years of Jackson's presidency, a group of friends acted as close advisers to the President. They are often referred to as Jackson's "Kitchen Cabinet." The name probably comes from the idea of people gathering informally in a kitchen to talk. The practice continued, with succeeding Presidents surrounding themselves with friends who offered advice and suggestions, not always to the benefit of the President.

The following material is available from Glencoe and may be used to enrich Chapter 11.

 CD-ROM
- *The Presidents: A Picture History of Our Nation*

Critical Thinking

Evaluating Evidence To find out how popular or unpopular Andrew Jackson was, suggest that students research the public opinion of the time. They will find evidence in contemporary political cartoons, voting records, newspaper articles, journal or diary entries, letters, and so on. When students have completed their research, have them present their findings to the class and draw conclusions about Jackson's popularity from the evidence. **L3**

CHAPTER 11
SECTION 4

Independent Practice

Analyzing Cause and Effect
Have students work in groups to list causes for the panic and depression of 1837. Have students discuss which of the causes they listed might cause a depression today.
L2

Van Buren is reported to have said that the two happiest days of his life were those when he took the office of President and when he left it. Discuss with students why Van Buren should feel this way. (He was blamed for doing nothing about the depression and was vilified personally.)
Answer to Caption: the Panic of 1837

Did You Know?

Andrew Jackson's home in Tennessee is called the Hermitage and was modeled after George Washington's home at Mount Vernon.

NATIONAL GEOGRAPHIC SOCIETY

The following material is available from Glencoe and may be used to enrich Chapter 11.

 CD-ROM
- *The Presidents: A Picture History of Our Nation*

---

the trend by issuing the Specie Circular, ordering that all payments for public lands be made in silver or gold. This drastic reversal of policy virtually stopped land sales, eliminated easy credit, and set the stage for a severe panic and depression in 1837.

The Election of 1836

As the election of 1836 approached, Jackson used his control of the Democratic party to pick his successor. His choice was Martin Van Buren, the Vice President, a New York politician whose reputation for craftiness had earned him the nickname "the Fox of Kinderhook."

The Whigs were so divided they could not agree on any single candidate. Instead, they nominated three favorite sons, or leading politicians from different states, hoping to divide the electoral college vote. The Whig candidates were William Henry Harrison of Ohio, Daniel Webster of Massachusetts, and Hugh Lawson White of Tennessee. If the three candidates could prevent Van Buren from getting a majority, the election would be thrown into the House of Representatives, which was controlled by the Whigs. Jackson's continuing popularity and the nation's perceived prosperity were enough to give the Democrats the election. Van Buren won 170 electoral votes against a combined total of 124 votes for all his opponents, although his edge in the popular vote was small.

The Panic of 1837

Van Buren had hardly taken office when the country was hit by the Panic of 1837 and one of the most severe depressions in American history. Jackson's Specie Circular had sent the economy into a tailspin, but like most depressions that of 1837 had several causes. One factor was a withdrawal of British investments. British gold and silver deposits in American banks had supported American economic growth in the 1830s. In 1837 Great Britain suffered from hard times, and British investors became more cautious.

A Deepening Depression

As British and American investors in state banks withdrew deposits, banks failed. There was no Bank of the United States to restore confidence in the banking system. People hoarded their gold and silver, merchandise went unsold, crops found no markets, and businesses closed. Thousands of farmers lost their farms through mortgage foreclosures. Unemployment soared among Eastern factory workers, and work on canals and railroads nearly ceased. As the depression deepened, workers fought over the meager relief that city governments provided.

Today, faced with such a crisis, the people would demand action by the federal government, and the federal government would respond with legislation. In the 1830s, however, a depression was regarded as an act of nature like a drought or a hurricane. Instead of recognizing that both state

▲ **MARTIN VAN BUREN** Jackson used his influence to have Vice President Martin Van Buren nominated for President in 1836. *What economic woes struck the nation soon after Van Buren took office?*

326 UNIT 4 Toward a Democracy: 1820–1854

Sidelights: Van Buren's Nicknames

Martin Van Buren had several nicknames, one of which was "Little Van," because he was five feet, six inches tall. Other nicknames were based on his character and personality. Because he was a master at political wheeling and dealing, he earned the titles "Red Fox" and "Little Magician." One of his magician's tricks was to outmaneuver John C. Calhoun for the vice presidency, thus leaving himself in line as Jackson's successor.

▲ GENERAL WILLIAM HENRY HARRISON

▲ THE LOG CABIN CAMPAIGN The 1840 election campaign was full of slogans, banners, rallies, and parades. **What was the Whigs' campaign plan?**

Van Buren's Term of Office

In his Inaugural Address, Van Buren emphasized the laissez-faire policy when he said that "all communities are apt to look to government for too much." His one great legislative effort was to try to get the federal government entirely out of banking. He shared Jackson's disapproval of a great central bank like the B.U.S. but recognized that depositing federal funds in pet banks had also failed.

Van Buren proposed an Independent Treasury System, under which the federal government would collect its taxes in specie to be stored in vaults throughout the country. Federal expenditures would be paid in specie, making federal credit literally as good as gold. This would discourage inflated bank notes because state banks would have to keep a sufficient reserve to allow their depositors and those holding their notes to do business with the government. The Independent Treasury Act successfully passed in 1840.

and federal governments had helped to cause the depression, laissez-faire philosophers said it was not the function of the government to do much about the problem.

The "Log Cabin" Campaign of 1840

The Whigs eagerly looked forward to the election of 1840, even though they were so divided on major issues that they did not even try to write a **platform,** or statement of beliefs. Their campaign plan was simple: nominate a military hero and attack Van Buren. For their presidential candidate they passed over known leaders of the party and chose General William Henry Harrison, whose principal attraction was that he had fought Native Americans at the Battle of Tippecanoe in 1811.

Democrats jeered that all Harrison was fit for was to sit in front of a log cabin, drink hard cider, and draw a pension. The Whigs adopted the very methods the Jacksonians had used against Adams in 1828. Harrison—born to wealth and social position—was pictured as a simple frontiersman, while Van Buren—born in humble circumstances—was portrayed as a champagne-drinking aristocrat with cologne-scented whiskers. John Tyler, a former Democrat who had left the party in protest over Jackson's policy against nullification, was selected as Harrison's running mate. The Whigs' campaign slogan became "Tippecanoe and Tyler too." The result of this campaign was a decisive victory for Harrison—234 electoral votes to 60—although the popular vote was quite close.

The election of 1840 was the first to illustrate a recurring principle of American politics: during a depression, the party in power is likely to be punished at the polls. Twelve years before, when Jackson had defeated Adams, a little more than 50 percent of the eligible voters had gone to the polls. In 1840 nearly 80 percent of those eligible voted—in some states almost 90 percent. The high turnout revealed that the party organizations had penetrated every county, village, and city precinct. Parties had set up machinery for informing the electorate and had ensured that voters came to the polling places.

■ Tyler and Whigs Split

The elderly Harrison was expected to be a figurehead while Clay and Webster ran the party. Clay, now in the Senate, had worked out a legislative program designed to appeal to as many different interests as possible. However, only a month after Harrison's inauguration the President died of pneumonia.

John Tyler of Virginia became the first Vice President to become President by the death of the incumbent. Having been placed on the Whig ticket simply to attract Southern support, Tyler was opposed to most of the Clay and Webster programs. They were nationalists; the new President was a believer in states' rights. Nevertheless, he did sign the first of several bills in Clay's program. The Tariff of 1842 pleased Eastern manufacturers by raising the rates to about what they had been ten years earlier. The Pre-emption Act of 1841 satisfied the Western demand that "squatters" on public lands have first right to buy the lands they had settled. Tyler, however, vetoed a bill establishing another national bank and vetoed a second bill that was drawn up to meet his objections. In disgust at the President's actions, all the Whigs except Daniel Webster resigned from the cabinet, and Clay resigned from the Senate. Divided, without a program or leadership, the Whigs lost heavily in the congressional elections of 1842, and John Tyler became a President without a party.

▲ THE LOG CABIN SONG BOOK

Section 4 ★ Review

Checking for Understanding

1. **Identify** Specie Circular, Whigs, Martin Van Buren, John Tyler.
2. **Define** platform.
3. **Describe** the role the Bank of the United States played in the election of 1832.
4. **List** factors that led to the panic and depression of 1837.

Critical Thinking

5. **Evaluating Political Systems** Several Vice Presidents, starting with John Tyler, have succeeded to the presidency during another's term. In effect, they have been chosen by the presidential candidate, not by the voters. Suggest another method by which the Vice President might be chosen.

CONNECTIONS  CONNECTIONS

Banks and the Money Supply

In the 1800s a bank served three functions in the community: it provided a secure place to deposit gold and silver coins; it loaned its deposits to individuals and local businesses; and it issued paper notes to borrowers—the value on each banknote representing a like amount of coins in its vault. These notes then circulated in the economy as money.

In theory, a bank's loans could not exceed its deposits. However, the interest on loans was profit, and by issuing more notes banks could loan many times the specie in their vaults. If enough people who held a bank's notes wanted hard cash, however, all its assets would be paid out and its depositors' funds would be lost.

The second Bank of the United States sought to regulate the nation's economy by controlling banknotes. By purchasing huge amounts of notes and redeeming them at the issuing banks, the B.U.S. could exhaust the assets of unsound banks and force them to close. Even this crude central banking system ended when the B.U.S. lost its charter. Not until the Federal Reserve System was created in 1913 was banking brought under effective control.

This system, which is still in effect today, was created by the Federal Reserve Act of 1913. The act divided the United States into 12 banking districts, each with a Federal Reserve bank. All national banks—those chartered by the federal government—are required to become members. Banks chartered by the states may also join if they choose to do so. Each member bank has to deposit a certain amount of money in the district Federal Reserve bank. This reserve requirement helps protect people's deposits.

Federal Reserve banks do not do business with individuals but are bankers' banks. They serve as clearinghouses for checks, make loans to member banks, and provide a more flexible currency. The Federal Reserve Board is appointed by the President. The board has the power to set interest rates on loans that the district

▲ BANKNOTE ISSUED IN 1840

banks make to member banks. This power gives the Board control over the credit supply. If the Board lowers rates, that makes loans easier to obtain. This increases the money supply and stimulates the economy. If the Federal Reserve Board raises rates, that tightens the supply and slows economic growth.

Making the Economics Connection
1. How did banks get the paper money they printed into the nation's money supply?

Linking Past and Present
2. What clues on today's paper money show that the government is involved in banking?

CHAPTER 11 CONNECTIONS

Teaching Making Connections
Remind students that the First Bank of the United States was founded by Alexander Hamilton and was a source of conflict between him and Jefferson. Although the B.U.S. handled only one-third of the nation's total deposits, it was a symbol of wealth and power and as such was hated by Jackson and his supporters. Display some United States currency and discuss how government is involved in banking.

Did You Know?
Many bankers themselves opposed the Bank of the United States. Eastern bankers wanted the money and power of the B.U.S. to flow into New York City. They often called the Bank the "Monster of Chestnut Street" because of its location in Philadelphia. Western and Southern bankers resented its restrictions over the expansion of state banks and what they regarded as eastern control.

Answers to CONNECTIONS
1. When borrowers took out loans, they received paper money from the bank.
2. "United States of America" and "Federal Reserve Note" printed on every bill; portraits of Presidents and signature of secretary of the treasury is on the bills.

REVIEW CHAPTER 11

Answers

Reviewing Facts

1. In both campaigns, candidates avoided issues and focused on personalities; made misleading allegations
2. Vote extended; politicians sought support of ordinary people
3. right to vote not extended to Native Americans, who were removed from their lands; African Americans, who were enslaved or regarded as second class citizens; women, who were judged as inferior to men and incapable of participating in political life
4. spoils system, ignoring court decision to relocate the Cherokee, use of pocket veto, threat of force over nullification
5. unconstitutional, too powerful, favored the rich
6. Jackson withdrew Bank funds; shutdown credit, business failure, unemployment; return to easy credit; administration put land up for sale and gave $30 million to states; many improvement projects; overspeculation and inflation; Specie Circular dried up credit, stopped land sales; British withdrew deposits; banks failed; consumers panicked, hoarded, and stopped buying; business failures and unemployment
7. organized in opposition to Jackson, chose Harrison as figurehead, represented him as common man, nominated Tyler for Vice President to appease South, stuck with states' rights, President when Harrison died, could not agree with Tyler

CHAPTER 11 ★ REVIEW

Using Vocabulary

Use the following terms to write a short essay about presidential leadership style.

platform pocket veto
spoils system

Reviewing Facts

1. **Compare** the campaigns of 1828 and 1840.
2. **Identify** the important democratic changes that developed during the Jackson era.
3. **Identify** the groups that did not benefit from democracy under Jackson and explain why.
4. **List** examples of Jackson's authoritative style and extension of presidential power.
5. **State** the reasons Jackson and others objected to the second Bank of the United States.
6. **Describe** the Panic of 1837 and its causes.
7. **Summarize** the rise and fall of the Whigs.

▲ SEMINOLE LEADER OSCEOLA

Understanding Concepts

Political Change

1. What political and democratic changes helped bring about Andrew Jackson's election victory in 1828?
2. In what ways was the presidential election of 1840 significant?

Economic Policy

3. How did the tariff and nullification issue develop into a crisis?
4. What changes, both in the United States as well as in other countries, contributed to the Panic of 1837?

Critical Thinking

1. **Linking Past and Present** Political parties often choose vice-presidential candidates for the reasons the Whigs selected Tyler: to attract voters with views different from those of the presidential candidate. Review news accounts of the 1992 presidential election. Do you think the Republicans should have chosen Robert Dole as George Bush's running mate instead of Dan Quayle? Explain your answer.
2. **Analyzing Executive Performance** How did Andrew Jackson's conduct as President reflect the growing spirit of democracy? Cite specific examples.
3. **Evaluating Policy** Argue for or against the spoils system.
4. **Comparing Institutions** Compare the Bank of the United States with the Independent Treasury System created to replace it. What were the advantages of each?
5. **Analyzing Art** When the Seminoles were told to give up their land and move west, Osceola refused. He led a series of guerrilla raids against federal troops. Osceola was captured after being invited to peace talks and died in prison. What qualities and attributes does the artist portray in this painting of Osceola?

---

or among themselves, lost leadership and power

Understanding Concepts

1. extension of vote to landless workers, influence of common man, development and emerging influence of West
2. It was the first to illustrate a principle of American politics: during a depression, the party in power is likely to be punished at the polls.
3. People were indignant over the tariff of 1828. Flags were hung at half-mast. College students threatened to buy no northern goods. Although the tariff law of 1832 lowered rates, South Carolina voted for an Ordinance of Nullification, threatening secession from the Union. A compromise settled the issue. Tariff rates were gradually scaled down to the 1816 level.
4. economic downturn in Great Britain, federal policy change (withdrew funds from B.U.S.), changes in money policy, alternate tight and liberal credit, increase in land for sale

CHAPTER 11 ★ REVIEW

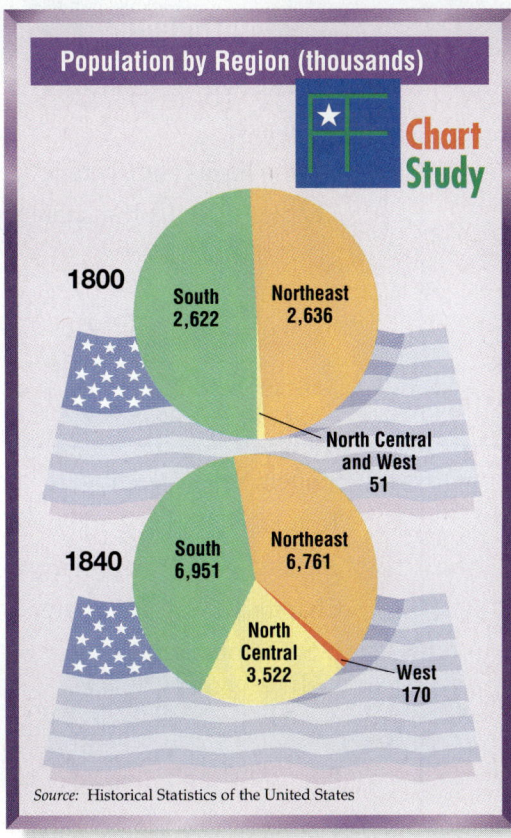

Population by Region (thousands)

Chart Study

1800
- South 2,622
- Northeast 2,636
- North Central and West 51

1840
- South 6,951
- Northeast 6,761
- North Central 3,522
- West 170

Source: Historical Statistics of the United States

Social Studies Skills

Reading a Circle Graph

One way to present numerical information is to use a circle graph. Circle graphs make it easy both to compare parts of a whole and to compare changes in the relationships of the parts. For example, the two circle graphs on this page compare population by region in the United States for 1800 and 1840.

Practicing the Skill

Use the circle graphs and information from the chapter to answer the following questions.

1. In the circle graph for 1800, which region has the largest population?
2. Which region decreased the most in percentage of the total population between 1800 and 1840?
3. In terms of numbers of people, how did the population of the Northeast change between 1800 and 1840?
4. The text notes that in the 1820s "conflicting sectional interests and a shifting population made political forecasts difficult." According to the circle graphs, how was the population shifting? What effect might a shift in the population have on sectional interests?

Writing About History

Cause and Effect

Imagine you are a financial reporter. Write an article explaining to your readers the chain of causes and effects that led to the Panic of 1837. Prepare before you begin writing by organizing your ideas.

Cooperative Learning

Working in pairs, research the history of the government's and settlers' dealings with Black Hawk's nation. Imagine it is 1832 and Black Hawk has returned with his followers to reclaim Iowa lands that farmers now hold. You and your partner have been appointed by Jackson to recommend a solution. Agree on a fair plan and present it to your class.

Using Your Journal

Briefly describe whether political campaign tactics today differ from those used in the presidential campaigns of 1832 and 1840. If so, discuss in what ways they differ.

CHAPTER 11 Age of Jackson 1828–1842

REVIEW ★ CHAPTER 11

Practicing the Skill

1. Northeast
2. Northeast
3. grew by more than 4 million
4. South and North Central showed the greatest growth. Answers will vary but should reflect an understanding of the sectional interests of Westerners.

❓ Chapter Bonus Test Question

This question may be used for extra credit on the chapter test. How did the political life of the nation become more democratic during the Jacksonian period? (suffrage extended, political reforms made, frontier expanded, more economic opportunities)

Using Your Journal

Most students may mention negative campaigning. Students should support their conclusions with examples.

Critical Thinking

1. Responses will vary. Students favoring Dole may cite political experience and ability to work with Congress. Opponents may cite party unity.
2. Some students may regard his opposition to the bank as motivated by democratic principles, though most would regard his methods of fighting it more dictatorial than democratic.
3. The spoils system could make the President too powerful and reduce personnel selection to a political prize system.
4. Both held federal funds, stabilized currency, conducted federal financial business.
5. Responses will vary but may include pride, dignity, courage, and determination to fight for his cause.

PLANNING GUIDE Chapter 12   The Spirit of Reform

Daily Lesson Objectives	Teacher Classroom Resources	Multimedia
SECTION 1 **Advances in Education** 1 Day pp. 334–337 1. Identify improvements in education made in the 1800s. 2. Discuss the obstacles to establishing public schools.	Chapter 12 Study Guide Reproducible Lesson Plan Section Quiz Reteaching Activity 12-1 Reinforcing Social Studies Skills 27, 32, 36, 50, 53 LEP American Literary Heritage Unit 4 Chapter 12 Cooperative Learning Activity Chapter 12 Concept Mapping Activity	Student Self-Test Software Testmaker Section Focus Transparency 36 Chapter 12 Skills Transparency
SECTION 2 **Struggle for Rights** 1 Day pp. 339–344 1. List reform movements of the 1800s and discuss their achievements. 2. Explain the ways in which women were treated as second-class citizens. 3. Discuss the efforts to end slavery.	Reproducible Lesson Plan Reteaching Activity 12-2 Section Quiz Reinforcing Social Studies Skills 32, 51, 69 American Portraits 23, 24 Chapter 12 Primary and Secondary Source Readings SAT Practice Tests 11–13 Building Skills in Geography	Student Self-Test Software Testmaker Section Focus Transparency 37 Chapter 12 Map Transparency U.S. History and Art Transparency 6 Powers of the Supreme Court
SECTION 3 **Social and Cultural Change** 1 Day pp. 346–351 1. Identify the prominent artists, writers, and scientists of the 1800s. 2. Explain the goals of nineteenth-century religious movements. 3. Discuss the temperance movement.	Reproducible Lesson Plan Reteaching Activity 12-3 Section Quiz Chapter 12 Enrichment Activity Chapter 12 Primary and Secondary Source Readings Reinforcing Social Studies Skills 49 Writer's Guidebook Lesson 6 Spanish Summaries & Glossary	Student Self-Test Software Testmaker Section Focus Transparency 38 Unit 4 Digest Transparencies Vocabulary Puzzlemaker Audiocassette, Chapter 12 U.S. History and Art Transparencies 6, 12
CHAPTER REVIEW AND EVALUATION 1 Day	Chapter 12 Test Chapter 12 Performance Assessment Activity	Student Self-Test Software Testmaker

00:00 **OUT OF TIME?** If time does not permit teaching the entire chapter, use the Chapter 12 Summary on pages 358–359 and the Chapter 12 audiocassette (English and Spanish) to point out the main ideas of the chapter.

PLANNING GUIDE

Cultural Diversity Activity

Cooperative Learning Divide students into groups. Have each group read a primary source account of slave life or escape on the Underground Railroad. Ask each group to write a short skit or create a poster that might be used by antislavery groups to publicize the evils of slavery. Two useful sources are Charles Blockson's *The Underground Railroad* and *The Classic Slave Narratives* edited by Henry Louis Gates. It contains the stories of Frederick Douglass and Harriet Jacobs (alias Linda Brent).

Performance Assessment Activity

Mass Culture Students may be divided into small groups or pairs to research the "mass" culture of the period: magazines, romantic novels, songs, theater, entertainments such as circuses. Ask groups to present their research in the form of a picture essay. Invite each group to share its work with the class.

POSSIBLE RUBRIC FEATURES: Content, organization, creativity, written and visual communication skills

Chapter Resources

Literature from the Period

Emerson, Ralph Waldo. *Self-Reliance.* 1841.

Thoreau, Henry David. "Civil Disobedience." 1849.
_____. *Walden.* 1854.

Readings for the Student

Abel, Ernest L. "The Most Hated Man in America." *American History Illustrated,* Vol. 22, No. 8, December 1987.

Blockson, Charles L., *The Underground Railroad: First Person Narratives of Escapes to Freedom in the North.* Prentice Hall, 1987.

Germer, Lucie. "Dorothea Dix: Quiet Crusader." *Cobblestone,* Vol. 10, No. 6, June 1989.

Jacobs, William Jay. *Mother, Aunt Susan, and Me: The First Fight for Women's Rights.* Coward, 1979.

"The Transcendentalists and Their Message." *Cobblestone,* Vol. 8, No. 6, 1987.

Readings for the Teacher

Cremin, Lawrence A. *American Education: The National Experience, 1783–1876.* Harper, 1980.

Gausted, Edwin S., ed. *Rise of Adventism: Religion and Society in Mid-Nineteenth Century America.* Harper, 1974.

Rose, Anne C. *Transcendentalism as a Social Movement, 1830–1850.* Yale University Press, 1986.

Multimedia Resources

American Art and Architecture. Alarion. (VHS, three videos)

The American Image. Zenger Films. (VHS, 54 minutes)

The American Woman: A Social Chronicle. Social Studies School Service. (six color filmstrips)

Black Fugitive. National Film Board of Canada. (color filmstrip, cassette)

Frederick Douglass. Zenger Films. (VHS, 50 minutes)

A Woman's Place. Time. (VHS, 25 minutes)

Women in History. Tom Snyder. (Apple or IBM diskette)

Key to Ability Levels

Teaching strategies have been coded for varying learning styles and abilities.

- **L1** Basic activities for all students
- **L2** Average activities for average to above-average students
- **L3** Challenging activities for above-average students
- **LEP** Limited English Proficiency activities

Glencoe Links to the Humanities

Link to Art
- U.S. History and Art Transparencies 6, 12

Link to Literature
- Macmillan Literature: American Literature Text—Henry David Thoreau, Nathaniel Hawthorne, Herman Melville

Link to Music

American Music: Cultural Traditions

CHAPTER 12

BEGINNING THE CHAPTER

Write on the chalkboard the following statement by New England philosopher Ralph Waldo Emerson: "What is man born for but to be a Reformer, a Re-maker of what man has made, a renouncer . . . ."

Discuss the quotation, asking students to describe Emerson's idea of a reformer. How is it like their own views of a reformer? How does it differ? Tell students that in Chapter 12, they will learn how reformers attempted to remake American society politically and socially.

The National American Lyceum, a mutual improvement society, was formed in 1831. Lyceums provided a platform for reformers and for statespersons and writers such as Daniel Webster and Ralph Waldo Emerson.

Recording Journal Notes
Suggest students organize their notes under headings such as Education, Slavery, Women's Rights, Religion, Peace Movement, Social Experiments.

00:00 OUT OF TIME? If time does not permit teaching the entire unit, use the Unit Digest on pages 462–463.

CHAPTER 12

The Spirit of Reform
1820–1854

Setting the Scene

Focus
American reformers during the first half of the nineteenth century worked selflessly to create a more perfect society. Many reformers were religiously motivated, while others traced their reform spirit to ideas in the Declaration of Independence. In either case, the noble goal of achieving a just American society would serve as a model for the rest of the world.

▲ NATHANIEL HAWTHORNE

Concepts to Understand
★ Why social reform movements were so widespread during this period
★ How new values and beliefs influenced educators, artists, and writers

Read to Discover . . .
★ the factors that motivated a wide variety of reform movements.
★ how the spirit of reform affected the status of prisoners, women, and African Americans.

Journal Notes
As you read the chapter, make notes about the types of reform that occurred during the first half of the nineteenth century.

CULTURAL
- 1825 Robert Owen organizes utopian community at New Harmony, Indiana
- 1833 National temperance movement founded

1820 — **1830**

POLITICAL
- 1825 John Quincy Adams inaugurated as sixth U.S. President
- 1830 Maysville Road Bill is vetoed
- 1832 Black Hawk War fought
- 1837 Panic strikes the economy

UNIT 4 Toward a Democracy: 1820–1854

✚ EXTRA CREDIT PROJECT

Ask interested students to choose an issue that concerns them today (environment, health care, education, civil rights, big government, taxes, homelessness, poverty) and research reform efforts related to that issue. Have them address the goals of reformers, their techniques, and their successes and/or failures. When the chapter is completed, students might compare current reform efforts with those of reformers in the 1800s.

CHAPTER 12 CONCEPTS

Concept Mapping Activity
Reproduce the concept map below on the chalkboard. Review the generalization and ask students how democracy widened during the Age of Jackson.

> Widening democracy provided a setting in which educational progress and other social reform movements flourished.

- Social Reform
- Values and Beliefs

History AND ART
Melchers's work is an example of "genre" art, paintings that tell a story. Genre painters chose ordinary people and activities as their subjects.

History AND ART
The Sermon
by Julius Gari Melchers, 1886

Melchers often portrayed villagers in scenes of everyday life. Many of his works stressed religion and worship.

◀ JOHN J. AUDUBON PAINTING

- 1846 Smithsonian Institution founded
- 1846 United States and Mexico go to war
- 1852 Harriet Beecher Stowe's Uncle Tom's Cabin published
- 1850 Compromise of 1850 reached

1840 — **1850**

CHAPTER 12 The Spirit of Reform 1820–1854

Teacher Notes

LESSON PLAN
SECTION 1, 334–338

FOCUS

Bellringer
🔸 Prior to taking roll at the beginning of the class period, display Focus Activity Transparency 40 on the overhead projector and assign the accompanying Focus Activity Sheet.

Objectives
Point out the objectives on this page to students in previewing section content.

Motivating Activity
Read aloud the following response made by a Cincinnati, Ohio, milk deliverer when he was asked why Americans spent so much time reading newspapers.

"How should freemen spend their time, but looking after their government and watching that them fellers as we gives offices to, doos their duty and gives themselves no airs?"

Paraphrase the milk deliverer's explanation and discuss the links between education and democracy suggested by it.

🔸 Use Skills Transparency 12.

SECTION 1

Advances in Education

Setting the Scene

Section Focus
Americans began examining their society on the basis of ideas in the Declaration of Independence. During the early 1800s, many Americans in search of a better, more democratic world formed organizations to persuade others to their way of thinking. Perhaps never before or since the Jacksonian period have Americans shown such optimistic faith in improving the quality of life.

Objectives
After studying this section, you should be able to
★ identify improvements and reforms that were made at various levels of education during the 1800s.
★ discuss the obstacles to establishing public schools.

Key Term
lyceum

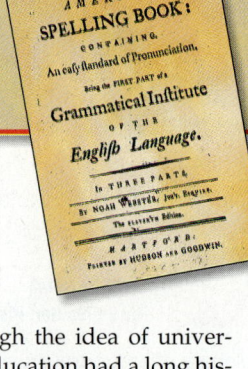
◀ WEBSTER'S SPELLING BOOK

Although the idea of universal education had a long history, dating back as far as the Massachusetts General School Act of 1647, public school systems had not developed adequately. As late as 1834, 250,000 of the 400,000 children in Pennsylvania did not attend school. In the 1830s and 1840s, however, there was a tremendous increase in the number of tax-supported schools.

■ Need for Education

As more people gained the right to vote, the need for education grew. Nonwhites, women, and white men without property had all been denied the vote in the early days of the Republic. In the 1820s and 1830s, however, most states amended their laws, extending the vote to white men who did not own land. In addition, it became necessary to educate the increasing number of immigrants who came to the United States in the mid-1800s. Thus, the increase in the number of eligible voters became a compelling reason for free public education. Democracy demanded an informed, educated electorate, a goal not easy to achieve.

Horace Mann, president of the Massachusetts Senate, pressed for public education and signed a bill in 1837 creating a state board of education in Massachusetts. He served as secretary of the state board of education for 12 years. During that time he doubled teachers' salaries, opened 50 new high schools, grouped students by grades, and established schools for teacher training called "normal schools." Massachusetts quickly became the model for all other Northern states.

UNIT 4 Toward a Democracy: 1820–1854

Classroom Resources for SECTION 1

Teacher's Classroom Resources
- Chapter 12 Study Guide
- Reproducible Lesson Plan
- Reteaching Activity 12-1
- Chapter 12 Cooperative Learning Activity
- Section Quiz

Multimedia
- Section Focus Transparency 40
- Skills Transparency 12
- Testmaker
- Student Self-Test Software

Resistance to Public Education

The establishment of public schools was not achieved without a fight. Communities that declared themselves in favor of public schools were often unwilling to tax their citizens to raise the necessary money. Lutherans, Roman Catholics, and other religious groups ran private schools of their own. Many of these people wondered why they should pay taxes to support public schools. Many people without children were also opposed.

Educating African Americans presented even more difficult problems. It was illegal in the South, and in the Northern states, people wavered on the need to provide education for African Americans. Although there were 15,000 African Americans in New York City in 1828, there were only 2 schools for them; in Philadelphia, there were only 3 schools for 20,000 students.

Efforts to educate African Americans sometimes met with violence. Prudence Crandall's white students withdrew when she admitted one African American girl to her Connecticut school in 1831. When her school filled with African American girls from all over the Northeast, the school was vandalized. Food had to be brought in secretly to the students. Connecticut then made it illegal to educate "a person of color" from out of state, which led to Crandall's arrest and conviction. The verdict, however, was reversed. When Crandall reopened the school, it was again attacked, and she was forced to give up her efforts there.

Others, especially in the West, saw no reason why children should learn more than the "three Rs." As an Indiana newspaper put it:

> ... Give them a little spelling, a little ciphering, and a little handwriting, with a liberal sprinkling of the rod, and they'll have more than their fathers had before them. Did Tippecanoe Harrison graduate from a seminary? Did Old Hickory Jackson know any Latin or Greek?...

▲ THE COUNTRY SCHOOL by Winslow Homer By the mid-1800s, public elementary schools were being established in many states, and public high schools were also growing in number. Horace Mann was one of the leaders in educational reform. **Why did some groups resist Mann's ideas about public education?**

CHAPTER 12 SECTION 1

Independent Practice

Language Arts Tell students that Noah Webster's good friend Ben Franklin desired some rather drastic reforms in spelling. He wanted to add new letters to the alphabet and drop all silent letters. Franklin's proposal would change *give* to *giv*, *will* to *wil*, and *wrong* to *rong*. Have students try rewriting a textbook paragraph using Franklin's spelling rules. **L1**

Using Charts

Answer: from 1850 to 1860

Skills Practice
Based on the graph, what is the correlation between total population and student enrollment during this period? (As the population increased, so did the number and percentage of students.)

Did You Know?

Harriet Beecher Stowe, the author of *Uncle Tom's Cabin*, was tutored by her older but less famous sister, Catherine Beecher, who attended a private school. She went on to study mathematics, Latin, and science on her own.

U.S. Student Enrollment, 1840–1860

	1840	1850	1860
Total population (in millions)	17.1	23.2	31.4
Total students: primary, secondary, and higher education (in millions)	2.0	3.6	5.5
Students as percent of total population	11.7	15.5	17.5
Total white population, ages 5–19 (in millions)	5.3	7.2	9.5
Students as percent of total white population, ages 5–19	37.7	50.0	57.8

Source: Lawrence A. Cremin, *American Education: The National Experience, 1783–1876* (1980).

Chart Study The number of students enrolled in school more than doubled between 1840 and 1860. *In which 10-year period covered in the table did enrollments increase the fastest?*

Special Needs Education

There was even less public support for education for children with special needs. Reformers who worked for this cause went to great lengths to give these children an equal opportunity for a better life. Reverend Thomas Gallaudet traveled to Europe to learn how to help people with impaired hearing. In 1817 he opened a school in Hartford, Connecticut, that became a model in education for the hearing impaired.

Samuel Gridley Howe, head of the New England Asylum for the Blind, taught the unsighted to read by pasting string on cards to make raised letters. His prize student was Laura Bridgman, a girl who entered the school at age eight and learned to read, write, and sew. She became the first sight- and hearing-impaired person to be successfully educated.

▲ LAURA BRIDGMAN

Teachers and Education

Often teachers were untrained young men or women. Since teachers were paid salaries of only $155 a year for men and as little as one-third of that for women, schools could not attract skilled professionals. Classroom instruction was characterized by memorization and harsh discipline.

Fortunately, the spirit of reform was strong enough to influence lawmakers. By 1850 most free states provided tuition-free elementary education. Free high schools had replaced many private academies.

Critical Thinking

Analyzing Ideas Have students bring to class news articles on modern educational reform issues. As a class, list some current criticisms of public education (not preparing students for global economy, multicultural curriculum, mainstreaming for the challenged, inadequate education of minorities, too much or not enough bilingual education). Compare reform issues of today with those of Horace Mann's time. Ask: How do the demands of reformers today show ways in which American society has changed since the early 1800s? (greater heterogeneity, more ethnic and international concerns) **L3**

An American Language

Despite a popular mistrust of "book learning," Noah Webster's *American Spelling Book* became a bestseller after it was first published in 1783. By 1837 sales had reached 15 million copies.

Webster was dedicated to "a uniformity and purity of language." He was eager not simply to preserve the language for its own sake; he saw it as a way to promote national spirit. His spelling book contained a preface encouraging Americans to respect their own literature. Webster also wrote the famous dictionaries that bore his name.

William McGuffey, a cleric and college president, had similar ideas. In 1836 he introduced the first of six McGuffey's Readers. Filled with moral instructions and patriotic sayings, these literature anthologies influenced schoolchildren for generations.

Higher Education

Interest in training teachers helped the cause of higher education for women. One argument for training women as teachers was that it was more economical because women teachers could be paid less than men. Although many men feared that higher education for women would disrupt home life, feminist leaders such as Emma Willard, Catharine Beecher, and Mary Lyon argued that chemistry could be used in cooking and math in household finance.

Oberlin College in Ohio, the first coeducational school, saw its first female student graduate in 1841. Oberlin and Bowdoin College in Maine were the first institutions to allow African Americans to attend as students. Because African American men and women were generally barred from educational opportunities, there were fewer than 15 African American college students in the United States before 1840. Aside from one African American college, Lincoln University, which opened in Pennsylvania in 1854, there was little progress in education for African Americans until the years after the Civil War.

Other Adult Education

While opportunities for formal higher education were limited for most people, there was a move toward adult education for the common person. Libraries began to take hold as free public institutions. The first was established in Peterboro, New Hampshire, in 1833.

Even more popular was the **lyceum** (ly•SEE•uhm) movement begun in 1826. A lyceum was a voluntary organization designed to promote "the improvement of its members in useful knowledge." Supporting their organization with small membership fees, the group used the money they collected to purchase books, scientific equipment, and specimens for study.

▶ Page from *McGuffey's Reader*

Section 1 ★ Review

Checking for Understanding

1. **Identify** Noah Webster, William McGuffey, Horace Mann.
2. **Define** lyceum.
3. **Summarize** the progress in public education, including the problems facing those who wanted to educate African American children.
4. **List** the groups that objected to public education and the reasons for their objections.

Critical Thinking

5. **Analyzing Causes** In what ways did the *McGuffey's Reader* and Webster's dictionaries and spelling book play a part in keeping American English uniform?

CHAPTER 12 The Spirit of Reform 1820–1854

LESSON PLAN
Mastering Social Studies Skills

Teaching Critical Thinking Skills

Point out that the ability to consider similarities and differences is important in studying history. Emphasize, however, that a comparison is not a conclusion or a judgment.

Call on volunteers to locate in Section 1 the information needed to answer each of the questions. Emphasize the need to focus on one area of commonality so that students' comparisons will be fair. Ask: Why do you think choosing one area to compare is more effective than comparing along general lines? (One is able to compare specifics, not generalities.) You might suggest that students create a chart to organize the information needed to answer the last question.

Did You Know?

In 1833, seven African American women and eleven white women formed the Female Anti-Slavery Society of Philadelphia. Enraged by the sight of white and African American women working together, a mob tried to burn down their meeting hall in Philadelphia in 1838. The white women responded by declaring that it was their duty to identify "with these oppressed Americans by . . . receiving them as we do our white fellow citizens."

Social Studies Skills

Critical Thinking Skills

Making Comparisons

Imagine that your younger brother cannot decide between joining the debate team or playing intramural baseball. He has limited free time, so he asks you to help him compare the two. You tell him that you cannot because that is "like comparing apples and oranges." Your friend hears the conversation and comes in to tell you that you indeed can compare the debate team to baseball.

▶ EARLY AMERICAN SCHOOL

To compare means to examine in order to identify similarities and differences. You can compare any two things. To get an accurate comparison, however, you must note at least one similarity and one difference.

Making comparisons does not involve analysis or evaluation. There are no judgments being made, and no conclusions being drawn.

In the example you just read, there are obvious differences between debating and baseball. Yet, you can identify at least two similarities. Both are group activities, and both are competitive in the nature in which points are scored. This means that a comparison is possible.

No matter what you are comparing, there are questions that can be asked that help in making effective comparisons. They are:
- What is it that I want to compare?
- What do they have in common that I can compare?
- On which common area do I want to concentrate?
- What similarities are there in this common area? What differences are there in this common area?

Note that these questions can be applied in a variety of ways. For practice, apply these questions in making a comparison between public and private schools in the 1800s.

In addition, this method can be applied to other movements or institutions in your study of history.

Practicing the Skill

For further practice in making comparisons, read Section 2 entitled "Struggle for Rights" and apply the above questions in making a comparison between the woman's rights movement and the antislavery movement.

338

Answers to SOCIAL STUDIES SKILLS

a. The women's rights movement is being compared to the antislavery movement.
b. What they have in common: both were made up of volunteers; both demanded equal rights.
c. Concentration can be on the common area of both demanding equal rights.
d. Similarities of this common area: both groups urged that all humans be judged on their abilities. Differences: women's rights had a secular origin; the antislavery movement grew at least in part from religious beliefs. Women's rights' movement leadership came almost entirely from within; antislavery was generally led by whites, or at least leadership was shared.

SECTION 2

Struggle for Rights

Setting the Scene

Section Focus

Numerous reforms were advocated during the Jacksonian period. There were organizations to do away with flogging in the navy, drinking alcohol, and eating meat. The great reform movements of the 1830s and 1840s could boast of solid achievement, especially in state legislation dealing with such problems as prisons, the mentally ill, child labor, liquor, and public schools.

Objectives

After studying this section, you should be able to

★ list reform movements of the 1800s and discuss their achievements.

★ explain the ways in which women were treated as second-class citizens.

★ discuss the efforts made to end slavery.

Key Terms

abolitionist, Underground Railroad

◀ SOJOURNER TRUTH

Calling for action on such issues as care for the mentally ill, woman's rights, and abolition of slavery, reformers appealed to their state legislatures and the federal government with little success. The persistent message of the reformers eventually awakened the United States to many of the needs of more than one-half of the population.

■ Prison Reform

As Emerson had suggested, there was a wealth of opportunity for reform; one had only to turn a critical eye to the world and make a choice.

Prisons began to experiment with ways to reform criminals. Unfortunately, the results were more severe punishments. For example, in Pennsylvania criminals were put in solitary confinement day and night to allow convicts to meditate on their crimes and, thus, reform. At Auburn, New York, treatment was less severe. There group labor in absolute silence was allowed. Instead of public hangings—commonplace before the 1830s—reformers sought more humane private executions.

Obviously, much reform remained to be done. When Dorothea Dix began visiting prisons in 1841, she found that mentally ill persons were still treated as criminals. In her report to the Massachusetts legislature, she wrote:

> *I proceed, gentlemen, briefly to call your attention to the present state of insane persons confined within this commonwealth, in cages, closets, cellars, stalls, pens! Chained, naked, beaten with rods, and lashed into obedience....*

CHAPTER 12 The Spirit of Reform 1820–1854

Classroom Resources for SECTION 2

Teacher's Classroom Resources
- Reproducible Lesson Plan
- Reteaching Activity 12-2
- Chapter 12 Primary and Secondary Source Readings
- Section Quiz

Multimedia
- Section Focus Transparency 41
- Testmaker
- Student Self-Test Software
- Powers of the Supreme Court

LESSON PLAN
SECTION 2, 339–345

FOCUS

Bellringer

Prior to taking roll at the beginning of the class period, display Focus Activity 41 on the overhead projector and assign the accompanying Focus Activity Sheet.

Objectives

Point out the objectives on this page to students in previewing section content.

Motivating Activity

Write the following sentences on the chalkboard and ask students to write an ending for each: A woman's place is . . . . A woman's work is . . . . Invite volunteers to read their answers aloud. Have students complete these sentences as they think most Americans would have done in the early 1800s. Discuss reasons for differences in responses for the 1990s and the early 1800s. Have students suggest possible explanations for changes in attitudes toward women between the 1830s and the 1990s. Point out that this section tells about the many ways reformers sought to change the treatment of women, enslaved persons, and the mentally ill.

Assign students the Chapter 12 reading by Sarah Grimké in Primary and Secondary Source Readings.

CHAPTER 12 SECTION 2

TEACH

Guided Practice

Biography Ask students to choose the name in each pair below that best completes the sentence. Then have students describe the reform efforts of the other person in each pair.
1. (*Dorothea Dix*, Sarah Grimké) worked for better treatment of the mentally ill.
2. The most famous African American abolitionist and publisher of *The North Star* was (William Lloyd Garrison, *Frederick Douglass*).
3. Along with Elizabeth Cady Stanton, (James G. Birney, *Lucretia Mott*) helped organize the Seneca Falls women's rights convention. **L1, LEP**

Teaching Life of the Times

It was not considered polite to speak of one's *stomach*. Instead people referred to it as the "chest." Thus, "a pain in the chest" was a stomach ache. In all-male gatherings, however, language was more outspoken and less polite.

Did You Know?

Despite the horrors detailed by Dorothea Dix, conditions in American prisons and asylums were considered better than those in Europe.

Life of the Times

The Language of Etiquette

In the early 1800s a strict code of behavior governed relationships between unmarried men and women. Public displays of affection of any sort were prohibited. Modesty required that words referring to body parts were never spoken in mixed company.

In 1839 the English novelist Frederick Marryat toured the United States. His journals provide a glimpse of the obsession with modesty that pervaded American social etiquette. While visiting Niagara Falls, a female companion of Mr. Marryat's fell and grazed her leg. The novelist asked if she had "hurt her leg." Much to his astonishment, she was deeply offended by his question. She later explained that the word "leg" was not used in mixed company. Rather, the novelist should have asked if she had "hurt her limb."

If Mr. Marryat was not fully convinced of the lengths to which Americans would take this social modesty, a trip to a girls school a few months later probably persuaded him. In the parlor of the school stood a grand piano with four "limbs." Much to his surprise, each piano leg had been covered with a frilly trouser!

▼ YOUNG COUPLE, MID-1800S

Dix's findings led Massachusetts to pass a law establishing asylums where mental illness could be treated as a disease rather than as a crime. Dix traveled throughout the United States visiting more than 800 jails and almshouses, or homes for the poor. Largely as a result of her influence, 20 more states founded insane asylums.

Later she traveled to other countries, helping to promote better treatment of the mentally ill in European nations. Through her influence and friendship with a Japanese diplomat, the first insane asylums in Japan were built.

■ Woman's Rights Movement

Even though the Declaration of Independence promised equality for all, the promise rang hollow for women. Women had actually lost ground in their political equality since colonial times.

Status of Women

While certain women had the right to vote under colonial charters, that privilege was revoked after the colonies declared their independence. Despite the fact that by 1850 nearly all white males could vote, women were still denied an active part in politics.

Women were perceived as "second-class citizens" in other ways, too. According to the English common law that formed the basis of American law, "husband and wife are one and that one is the husband." Similarly, a woman had no legal right to manage the affairs of her own children, and only in the state of Ohio was a woman given the right to make a will.

As factories opened in the Northeast, many new jobs for women were created. As in teaching, women received considerably less pay than men did, and when they took it home, the money became their husbands'. Women also felt social pressures directed against those who took these jobs.

340   UNIT 4 Toward a Democracy: 1820–1854

Cooperative Learning

Direct students to work in small groups to research current ideas about prison reform or reform of care for the mentally ill. Then ask students to imagine that they have been asked to form a commission to review these ideas and make recommendations. Have the groups draw up position papers on current problems and suggest what they would do to resolve these problems. **L2, L3**

▲ LUCRETIA MOTT

Almost all institutions of higher education and most professional careers were closed to women. It took Elizabeth Blackwell years to be allowed to take medical courses. When she finally completed her training to become the country's first female physician, sexist prejudice nearly kept her from practicing.

Even in the reform movements themselves, women were often forced to defer to men. It was considered improper, for example, for a woman to address a mixed audience. When nine women went as United States delegates to the World Antislavery Convention, they were greeted with cries of "Turn out the women!" from American clerics. The women, Lucretia Mott and Elizabeth Cady Stanton among them, refused to leave and, as a compromise, were seated behind a curtain and allowed only to listen.

Seneca Falls Convention

Frustrated by the limits on their actions, female reformers began a campaign for their own rights. In 1848 Mott and Stanton organized the Seneca Falls Convention. This gathering of female reformers drew up a "Declaration of Sentiments and Resolutions" that echoed the words of the Declaration of Independence:

> We hold these truths to be self-evident: that all men and women are created equal; that they are endowed by their Creator with certain inalienable rights; that among these are life, liberty, and the pursuit of happiness....

Stanton shocked many of the women when she proposed a resolution that they devote themselves to gaining the right to vote. Frederick Douglass, an African American antislavery reformer, seconded the resolution and gave a speech in support. The resolution narrowly passed.

Most politicians were either indifferent or hostile to the issue of woman's rights. During this time women gained neither the right to vote nor admission to professions; most colleges continued to exclude them. They did, however, gain relief from some of their worst legal handicaps. For example, many states passed laws permitting women to retain and manage their own property.

▲ **ELIZABETH BLACKWELL** Elizabeth Blackwell was a noted physician, educator, and writer. **What examples of prejudice did Blackwell face?**

CHAPTER 12 The Spirit of Reform 1820–1854

Antislavery Crusade

A glaring violation of democratic principles in the United States was African American slavery. How could the nation claim to be "the land of the free" when human beings were bought and sold like common property? The question had become increasingly acute by 1840. By then most Latin American countries had abolished slavery, and Great Britain had banned the practice. It is not surprising, then, that the upsurge of democratic feeling in the Jacksonian period made antislavery the dominant reform effort.

Abolitionists

The organized movement to abolish slavery began among religious groups. As early as 1776, the Quakers—in both the South and the North—agreed not to enslave people. In Virginia in 1789 the Baptists recommended "every legal measure to extirpate this horrid evil from the land." The abolition movement at first made many converts in the South. Benjamin Lundy, a native of New Jersey, spent most of his active career organizing antislavery societies in Southern communities. James G. Birney, an Alabama lawyer and cotton planter, freed his slaves and attempted to get others to do the same.

The voices of **abolitionists,** or those persons in favor of doing away with slavery, grew stronger. On January 1, 1831, the first edition of *The Liberator,* a Boston antislavery newspaper, was published. Editor William Lloyd Garrison wrote in a strong, unrelenting tone:

▶ FREDERICK DOUGLASS

▲ **MOVING TOWARD FREEDOM** Before the Civil War, thousands of enslaved people fled hundreds of miles and endangered their lives to reach the first station on the Underground Railroad. Frederick Douglass (inset) published *The North Star* and spoke on behalf of the emancipation of women as well as of enslaved people. **Who were the abolitionists?**

> "I will be as harsh as truth, and as uncompromising as justice. On this subject, I do not wish to think, or speak, or write, with moderation.... I am in earnest. I will not equivocate. I will not excuse. I will not retreat a single inch. AND I WILL BE HEARD."

Garrison denounced both Northerners who refused to be shocked by slavery and Southerners who held enslaved people. He demanded immediate freedom for enslaved African Americans without compensation for the slaveholders. Garrison and his followers made no attempt to win their way by political action. They were willing to divide the Union to rid the free states of the shame of being tied to the slave states.

A group who proposed to abolish slavery by the use of the ballot box founded the Liberty party. It nominated James G. Birney for the presidency in 1840 and 1844, but Birney received only a few thousand votes.

The Underground Railroad

Another leader who favored political action was Frederick Douglass, self-educated and formerly enslaved, who edited an abolitionist newspaper, *The North Star*. The title was meant to remind people of the **Underground Railroad.** This secret abolitionist organization, which had hiding places, or stations, throughout the Northern states and even into Canada, brought enslaved people out of the South and thus ensured their freedom. Moving at night, the agents of the Underground Railroad had only Polaris, the fixed star in the northern skies, to guide them. They not only took care of African Americans after they had come North, but they risked their lives to go into the slave states and lead enslaved others to freedom.

One of the most successful agents was Harriet Tubman, the "Black Moses," who herself had been born into slavery. After escaping, she returned to the South many times, liberating more than 300 enslaved people. Tubman avoided arrest, despite a reward of $40,000 offered for her capture.

▲ **THE ANTISLAVERY MOVEMENT** Sarah and Angelina Grimké played a major role in the antislavery crusade of the 1800s. *How did some Southerners combat the spread of abolitionist literature?*

Southern Reaction to Abolition

The first edition of *The Liberator* coincided with a slave insurrection in Virginia in 1831. That revolt was led by Nat Turner, an African American preacher and enslaved person who believed himself divinely inspired to lead his people from bondage. Turner's rebellion was quelled, but only after about 60 white persons had been killed. The revolt spread panic throughout the South. The belief that Turner had been inspired by abolitionist propaganda effectively ended the antislavery movement in the South. From that time on, Southerners who favored abolition usually remained silent or moved north.

Among Southern abolitionists who fled to the North were sisters Sarah and Angelina Grimké (GRIHM•kee). As daughters of a slaveholder in South Carolina, they had learned through firsthand experience to abhor slavery. They moved to Philadelphia, became Quakers, and were among the first women to speak out for both abolition and woman's rights.

One of the few Southerners who did not leave was Cassius Marcellus Clay, a distant relative of Henry Clay, who edited abolitionist newspapers in Kentucky. As a Southerner who held unpopular beliefs, Clay carried

CHAPTER 12 SECTION 2

Linking Across Time

In the 1920s, after they received the vote, many women reflected their new freedom by casting off their tight corsets and long skirts and adopting short skirts, silk stockings, and bobbed hair. As women pressed for equal rights in the 1960s, they too adopted freer styles of clothing.

Visualizing History
Point out that it took great courage for southerners to oppose slavery and speak out against it.
Answer to Caption: demanded abolitionist literature be suppressed; attempted to persuade Congress to bar it from the mail

Fact or Fiction?
The Underground Railroad saved up to 100,000 slaves.

FICTION: Historians believe that abolitionists greatly overestimated the successes of the Underground Railroad. They have concluded that only a few thousand slaves used this route to freedom.

Sidelights: Slave Rebellion

At least three large-scale slave revolts took place in the period before the Civil War. In 1800 Gabriel Prosser organized a slave army and tried to take Richmond, Virginia. In 1822 Denmark Vesey attempted to seize Charleston, South Carolina. In 1831 Nat Turner led a rebellion that killed about 60 whites. Many small-scale uprisings and individual acts of resistance went unreported.

CHAPTER 12 SECTION 2

ASSESS

Check Understanding
Assign Section 2 Review as homework or an in-class activity.

Evaluate
Assign the Section 2 Quiz in the TCR or use the History of a Free Nation Testmaker to create a customized quiz.

Reteach
Have students complete Reteaching Activity 12-2.

Enrich
Ask students to make a list of the grievances they would include in a modern-day version of the "Declaration of Sentiments and Resolutions" and rewrite this document to reflect conditions today.

CLOSE
Have students give some modern examples of human rights violations. (torture or murder of prisoners, imprisonment for opposition to the government)

Teaching American Portraits
In 1851 when Amelia put on her "bloomers," women were wearing tightly laced corsets, petticoats, and long dresses that had to be held up when walking on muddy streets. Discuss with students what statement about equal rights Bloomer was making with her clothing? (women have the same right as men to freedom of movement)

AMERICAN PORTRAITS

Amelia Bloomer
1818–1894

A single episode in Amelia Bloomer's life so catapulted her to fame that today few remember she was a leading reformer. Publisher of *The Lily*, her own newspaper, Bloomer called for just marriage laws, temperance, and woman's suffrage.

It was, however, the clothing she first wore in 1851 that made Amelia Bloomer a household name. Seeking a more practical style than the hoopskirt, she donned a short skirt over loose pants gathered at the ankles. She did not invent the fashion, but her insistence on wearing it—despite ridicule—led to the outfit's becoming known as "bloomers." Large crowds came to hear her lecture. The novelty of seeing a woman wearing pants accounted for much of her popularity. She finally concluded that her bloomers distracted attention from her reform efforts, and she returned to more traditional garb.

two pistols and a bowie knife. He even fortified his office with two cannons and a keg of gunpowder set to go off. When he was absent one day, however, a mob seized his presses and sent them across the Ohio River to Cincinnati.

Southern hostility to abolition grew stronger. The South demanded the suppression of abolitionist material as a condition for remaining in the Union. Southern postal workers refused to deliver abolitionist newspapers. In 1835 a bill to bar abolitionist literature from the mails passed the United States Senate but eventually was abandoned. In 1836, under Southern pressure, the House of Representatives passed a "gag rule" providing that all abolitionist petitions should be shelved without debate.

Despite the excitement it aroused, the antislavery movement affected politics very little at first. The Missouri Compromise had supposedly averted civil war by fixing the boundary between slave and free territory. No prominent politician, however, proposed endangering the Union by attacking slavery where it was protected by law.

▲ **WOMAN IN BLOOMERS**

Section 2 ★ Review

Checking for Understanding
1. **Identify** Dorothea Dix, Seneca Falls Declaration, Frederick Douglass, William Lloyd Garrison, Harriet Tubman.
2. **Define** abolitionist, Underground Railroad.
3. **Discuss** the reform movements of the 1800s and their achievements.
4. **Describe** the contributions of three key individuals to the antislavery movement.

Critical Thinking
5. **Making Decisions** Imagine that you are a Northern male teacher who has strong feelings against slavery. Would you join the abolitionists? Why or why not?

344   UNIT 4 Toward a Democracy: 1820–1854

Answers to SECTION 2 REVIEW
1. Dorothea Dix, 339; Seneca Falls Declaration, 341; Frederick Douglass, 343; William Lloyd Garrison, 342; Harriet Tubman, 343
2. All vocabulary words are defined in the Glossary.
3. established public schools; education for the visually and hearing impaired; reformed asylums.
4. Garrison—antislavery newspaper; Douglass—editor, antislavery paper; Tubman—liberated many slaves; Grimké—spoke against slavery; Clay—editor, abolitionist newspapers.
5. Answers will vary. Those who would join—strongly oppose slavery; nonjoiners—fear loss of jobs or taking stand against sensitive issue.

CONNECTIONS  CONNECTIONS

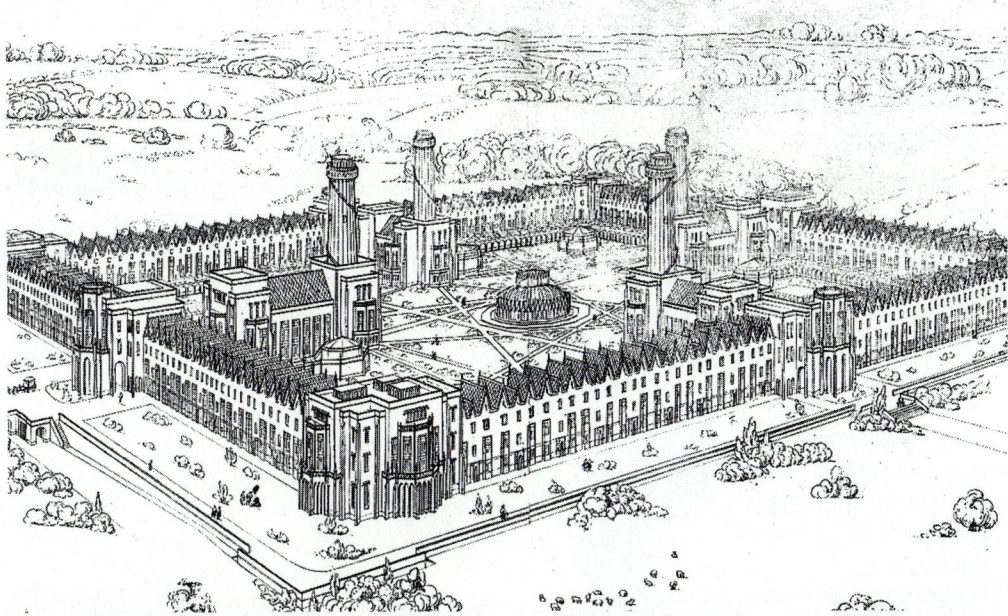

▲ COMMUNITY OF NEW HARMONY, INDIANA

The Scientists of New Harmony

The short-lived economic community that Robert Owen founded at New Harmony, Indiana, in 1825 was an exciting place. Although isolated, it boasted an excellent library, school, musical societies, art collections, even a public lecture series. This environment attracted some of the finest scientific minds of the day. Primarily naturalists, these scientists collected and classified specimens, and wrote on biological and geological subjects.

A key supporter of Owen's community was geologist William Maclure. In 1817 Maclure had produced a detailed United States geological map, the first of its scope. A member of New Harmony until its failure in 1827, he had hoped to put into practice new European teaching methods. Another New Harmony geologist, Gerard Troost, a native of Holland, acquired an impressive mineral collection.

Entomologist Thomas Say settled at New Harmony permanently and published a descriptive work on insects, the third volume of *American Entomology*. Say later edited books on shells and birds.

Making the Science Connection

1. Why were scientists like Maclure, Troost, and Say attracted to life at New Harmony?
2. What scientific interests did the New Harmony naturalists pursue?

Linking Past and Present

3. What is the interest of naturalists today?

CHAPTER 12
MAKING CONNECTIONS

Teaching Making Connections

At Robert Owen's New Harmony community all property was held in common. Owen wanted to create a self-sufficient agricultural and industrial community that would provide an alternative way of life to the growing industrial society and its exploitation and abuse of workers. Its participants would work not for the enrichment of others but for the good of all. New Harmony eventually failed partly because many of its members were less interested in working than in benefiting from Owen's fortune.

Did You Know?

Although New Harmony did not succeed as a utopian community, it did establish several "firsts" in the United States. The community created the first kindergarten; founded the first trade school, free library, and community-supported free school.

Answers to CONNECTIONS

1. The community had a school, library, lectures, art collections.
2. collected and classified mineral and biological specimens; published papers
3. Some interpret phenomena; some are employed by natural resources agencies or museums; others are advocates for ecological awareness.

LESSON PLAN
SECTION 3, 346–353

FOCUS

Bellringer
Prior to taking roll at the beginning of the class period, display Focus Activity Transparency 42 on the overhead projector and assign the accompanying Focus Activity Sheet.

Objectives
Point out the objectives on this page to students in previewing section content.

Motivating Activity
Have students consider why Americans in the early 1800s might feel culturally inferior to Europeans. (The new nation still drew on European ideas and cultural traditions in music, painting, literature, and the sciences.) Then point out that by the middle of the nineteenth century, this sense of inferiority had greatly diminished. Tell students that in Section 3 they will learn how Americans created a distinct national culture.

SECTION 3

Social and Cultural Change

Setting the Scene

Section Focus
The Pilgrims had come to the New World with a vision of a different life. The years that followed were filled with the work of carving out an existence in a new land. Americans wanted to prove that their country was truly independent of Europe. They wanted to create a distinct civilization rivaling that of the Old World. They were concerned not only with rights but with the quality and flavor of life in the United States.

◀ RIP VAN WINKLE

Objectives
After studying this section, you should be able to
★ identify the prominent artists, writers, and scientists of the 1800s and their important contributions.
★ explain the goals of nineteenth-century religious movements.
★ discuss the temperance movement.

Key Term
socialism

---

*A*mericans themselves had a sense of inferiority. People could not write poetry without "a legendary past nor a poetic present," remarked one young scholar. "Large mountains, extensive prairies, tall cataracts, long rivers [and] millions of dirty acres" did not seem suitable subjects for literature. James Fenimore Cooper set the scene of his first novel, *Precaution* (1820), in England and tried to attract readers by promoting himself as "a prominent Englishman." In 1820 the Reverend Sydney Smith, writing in a British magazine, sneered at the low cultural level of Americans and their lack of artistic and scientific achievement.

The second quarter of the nineteenth century saw many advances by American scientists and an outpouring of books by American writers that are still read on both sides of the Atlantic.

■ Writers and the American Scene

Editors such as Garrison, Clay, and Douglass used their talents to directly influence social reform. American writers had different motivations—to reform America's attitude toward itself.

Washington Irving invented a literary past out of the history of the Hudson River valley, once an area of Dutch settlement. With this material he created characters such as Rip Van Winkle. As a result of reading James Fenimore Cooper's novels, generations of children—not only here but in France and Great Britain—gloried in the drama of Native Americans and pioneers on the New York frontier. In his novels and short stories, Nathaniel Hawthorne mined the Puritan history of his native New England. In *Moby*

UNIT 4 Toward a Democracy: 1820–1854

Classroom Resources for SECTION 3

Teacher's Classroom Resources
- Reproducible Lesson Plan
- Reteaching Activity 12-3
- Chapter 12 Enrichment Activity
- Chapter 12 Performance Assessment Activity
- Spanish Summaries and Glossary
- Section Quiz

Multimedia
- Section Focus Transparency 42
- U.S. History & Art Transparencies 6, 12
- Unit 4 Digest Transparency
- Vocabulary Puzzlemaker
- Testmaker
- Student Self-Test Software
- Powers of the Supreme Court

Dick, Herman Melville used his experience as a sailor to write a fascinating account of whaling that was also an allegorical drama of the human struggle itself.

American poets, too, began to use American subjects. Henry Wadsworth Longfellow immortalized the Native American hero Hiawatha. John Greenleaf Whittier in "Snow-Bound" described winter on a New England farm. William Cullen Bryant in "To a Waterfowl" drew a haunting picture of sunset over a lonely marsh. Edgar Allan Poe wrote of the terrors that lurk in the world of imagination and dreams.

Many American writers took an active part in reform movements. Whittier and Longfellow joined the crusade against slavery, as did poet James Russell Lowell and poet and novelist Lydia Maria Child. Henry David Thoreau himself spent a night in jail rather than pay taxes to support the Mexican War.

Scientific Advances

Men and women in the United States also won fame in the field of science. As a child Maria Mitchell taught herself astronomy while checking navigational instruments

▲ **AMERICAN LITERATURE** James Fenimore Cooper's series of books about the frontier, the *Leatherstocking Tales,* included *The Last of the Mohicans* (1826) and *The Deerslayer* (1841). **How did Cooper's new series differ from his first novel, Precaution?**

for whaling captains. She discovered a new comet, several groups of distant stars, and wrote important studies of Jupiter and Saturn. Mitchell was the first woman elected to several learned societies. Joseph Henry, the inventor of the electromagnetic motor, headed the Smithsonian Institution, established in 1846. Research there laid the basis for the accurate prediction of weather.

Matthew Maury, an officer of the United States Navy, developed tables predicting winds and ocean tides at different seasons and gave directions for the shortest travel time. These tables helped reduce the average sailing time from New York to San Francisco by 47 days. His findings aided worldwide navigation so greatly that 13 foreign nations honored him. Known as the founder of the science of oceanography, Maury also made a systematic study of the ocean bottom and selected the route for the first transatlantic cable.

▲ **MARIA MITCHELL** Maria Mitchell taught herself astronomy and made a name for herself by discovering a comet in 1847. **What advances did the physicians Long and Morton make to the field of medicine?**

Cooperative Learning

Creating Categories Divide students into small groups and give each group 10 notecards. Ask each group to write 10 questions that can be answered with the name of a writer, scientist, artist, religious leader, or social reform movement discussed in this section. Direct the groups to arrange their questions into categories such as literature, art and architecture, science, and religion. Collect the questions and have groups take turns picking categories and providing the questions that go with each answer. **L1**

CHAPTER 12 SECTION 3

Independent Practice

Literature Have students read a poem by Henry Wadsworth Longfellow, Ralph Waldo Emerson, or John Greenleaf Whittier and write a paragraph explaining in what sense the poem is about an American subject and how it might help "reform America's attitude toward itself" as the text suggests on page 346. Possible choices for poems include Longfellow's "Evangeline," "Song of Hiawatha," "Courtship of Miles Standish," "Paul Revere's Ride," and Emerson's "The Concord Hymn," and Whittier's "Barbara Freitchie." **L2**

History AND ART

One group of landscape artists was known as the Hudson River School because members often painted that river. Albert Bierstadt and other artists inspired by that school focused on the grandeur of the Rocky Mountains and other western landscapes.
Answer to Caption: to refute the charge that the United States had produced no people of genius

Did You Know?

Charles Bulfinch finished the Capitol when the first architect, Benjamin Latrobe, resigned in 1817. Bulfinch was the first American to receive this appointment.

▲ **AMONG THE SIERRA NEVADA MOUNTAINS** by Albert Bierstadt, 1868 Albert Bierstadt's most popular works deal with the frontier, reflecting both Americans' pride in their country's natural beauty and their love of nature. **Why did painters, including Samuel F. B. Morse, seek to excel in their art?**

An important advance in medicine is credited to two physicians from the United States. Working independently, Dr. Crawford W. Long of Georgia in 1842 and Dr. W. T. G. Morton of Boston in 1846 were the first physicians to use ether as an anesthetic during surgery.

■ The Arts

American painters and sculptors were eager to produce works as great as those of Europe. The artists of the time set a standard that served to inspire later artists.

Artists

Samuel F. B. Morse, the inventor of the telegraph, began his career as a painter who wanted to "rival the genius of a Raphael, a Michelangelo, a Titian," in order to refute the charge that the United States "has produced no men of genius." American art, however, did not develop quickly. American artists had little opportunity for the skilled training available abroad, and European styles were still the standard by which art was judged.

American artists did best when, like the writers, they turned their attention to the American scene. George Caleb Bingham painted the life he had seen on the Missouri frontier as a boy. A group of landscape painters in the East was known as the Hudson River School. Their romantic paintings of the Catskill Mountains and Hudson River are highly prized.

Architects

Early nineteenth-century American architects continued to use classical models developed in the Renaissance. In New England, Charles Bulfinch, influenced by English models, developed a distinctive "Federal" style of architecture that can be seen in the Massachusetts State House, the largest building in America at the time it was designed. Bulfinch later worked for 14 years in Washington, D.C., and helped to complete the design of the Capitol. His influence can be seen in architecture in the Northeast.

Cultural Diversity

The works of writers such as Cooper, Hawthorne, and Longfellow glorified the American past, idealizing the wilderness and the frontier. At the same time, the poet Walt Whitman captured the hopefulness and idealism of the early years of the nineteenth century. Sometimes called the "poet of democracy," Whitman passionately believed in democracy. His poetry expresses the virtues of ordinary people and everyday life. Whitman was also unique in that he wrote of the vitality of the nation's growing cities, largely ignored by his contemporaries.

The type of architecture that most appealed to the American taste, however, was the style known as "Greek Revival." Based on classical Greek and Roman forms, it was used both in domestic architecture and in public and private buildings, the most famous of which is Virginia's State Capitol.

Social Experiments

From Europe came a new idea—**socialism.** Socialists believed that the means of production should be owned by society, not by private individuals. They believed that business competition and individual ownership of property caused poverty and inequality. Socialists proposed to substitute cooperation for competition and common ownership for individual ownership. Early followers of the idea wanted to start small, voluntary communities where their ideas could be put into practice.

Most of these experiments took place in the United States where land was easy to acquire. A famous English socialist, Robert Owen, started a cooperative venture at New Harmony, Indiana. Charles Fourier, a Frenchman, proposed to organize society into "phalanxes" of just 1,620 people living in villages called "phalansteries." His converts included Horace Greeley, editor of the *New York Tribune,* the most widely read newspaper in the United States.

The goal of the Brook Farm community in Massachusetts, founded by George Ripley, was to free its members for intellectual activity by running a self-sufficient farm. Members became disillusioned, however, because of the time, energy, and hard work required by farm labor. Nathaniel Hawthorne was persuaded to live at Brook Farm for a time. He, too, found it difficult to write—his primary aim—because of the hard work. He wrote to his fiancée:

> *It is my opinion ... that a man's soul may be buried under a dungheap, or in a furrow of the field, just as well as under a pile of money....*

The Brook Farm community ultimately collapsed after a large fire left the group greatly in debt.

Religious Movements

A great ferment in religious thought occurred in the first half of the nineteenth century. During this period a number of new religious denominations and religious bodies arose, including some that practiced communal living. Among these were the Church of Jesus Christ of Latter-day Saints and the Shakers.

Religious Communal Groups

Religious groups, having an additional basis for unity, were successful in community living. One rapidly growing religious body was the Church of Jesus Christ of Latter-day Saints, or the Mormon Church. This church was founded in 1830 by a New Englander, Joseph Smith, who believed he had been called to restore the Christian church to its original form. Smith wrote the *Book of Mormon* from golden plates that he said an angel had led him to discover. Mormonism enjoyed rapid growth and established a distinctive pattern of communal living at Kirtland, Ohio. Persecution drove the Mormons west to Utah.

The Shakers were founded by Mother Ann Lee in 1772 as an offshoot of the Quakers. Supporting themselves by small industries in orderly communities that were isolated from the rest of the world, the Shakers reached their peak in the mid-1800s with some 6,000 members. They did not marry or have children; the society survived by making converts. Few Shakers are left, but their handiwork—especially Shaker furniture, with its clean lines—is highly valued by collectors today.

The Oneida Community in central New York state was another group that aspired to found a successful utopian society. Practicing a form of Christian socialism, members supported themselves by manufacturing steel game traps and silver plate. The group prospered for some 30 years but then broke up.

CHAPTER 12 The Spirit of Reform 1820–1854   349

CHAPTER 12
SECTION 3

Linking Across TIME

The temperance movement continued under the guidance of the National Women's Christian Temperance Union (WCTU), formed in 1874. The WCTU worked for state laws that required public schools to teach about the harmful effects of alcohol and drugs.

Special Needs

Language Disability In taking notes, many students with language difficulties have trouble finding the relationships among words which set up a sequence of ideas. Explain that good notes require careful attention to these relationships. Read the seventh paragraph under "Religious Movements" aloud, stopping after each sentence to ask if there are key ideas or transition words presented. Point out the use of "no longer" and "instead." Demonstrate a way of writing the information in this paragraph in note form. For example: "DeTocqueville on Religion—religion emphasized present environment, not hereafter."

CHAPTER 12
SECTION 3

Visualizing History Point out that "camp meetings" such as this one were known as "revivals" because they revived people's religious zeal.
Answer to Caption: built thousands of new churches; founded scores of colleges

Food of the Times

Sylvester Graham was an eighteenth-century vegetarian who traveled the country preaching dietary reform. Spurning meat, processed flour, and alcohol, Graham insisted that a healthy diet consisted of vegetables, fresh fruit, and whole-wheat bread. (The graham cracker is named for him.)

ASSESS

Check Understanding
Assign Section 3 Review as homework or an in-class activity.

Evaluate
Assign the Section 3 Quiz in the TCR or use the History of a Free Nation Testmaker to create a customized quiz.

 ▲ **REVIVAL MEETINGS** The first half of the nineteenth century saw a great variety of religious movements in the United States. Throughout the country, the immense growth of Protestant denominations was marked by great revival meetings. *In what other ways did the Protestant faith spread?*

Other Religious Activity

The creed for the Unitarian Church was formulated in New England in 1819 by Reverend William Ellery Channing. Breaking away from the Congregational Church, Unitarians rejected the doctrine of the Trinity, preferring the concept of the oneness of Deity. The Unitarians also believed that human beings were by nature good, not evil.

Unitarians were attracted to Transcendentalism, an American movement that emphasized the relationship between human beings and nature as well as the importance of the individual conscience. Writers such as Margaret Fuller, Ralph Waldo Emerson, and Henry David Thoreau were among the leading Transcendentalist thinkers. Through her life and writings, Fuller advocated rights for women. In his poems and essays, Emerson urged people to trust themselves, to listen to the inner voice of conscience, and to break the bonds of prejudice. In *Walden* (1854) Thoreau extolled a life of thoughtful solitude.

Protestantism experienced a renewal, a "Second Great Awakening." Throughout the country, beginning in New England and spreading westward, growth of Protestant denominations was marked by great revival meetings, the building of thousands of new churches, and the founding of scores of colleges and universities.

In cities a similar stirring of religious activity arose in the Catholic churches. In Boston and New York, for example, the Roman Catholic Church provided not only places of worship for Catholic European immigrants, but also schools, orphanages, and charitable organizations.

350   UNIT 4 Toward a Democracy: 1820–1854

Sidelights: Popular Sayings

The phrase "on the wagon," referring to a recovering alcoholic, originated during the temperance movement. To publicize their cause, reformers pulled a water wagon through the streets and urged people to climb on. Over time "going on the wagon" came to mean accepting the temperance cause and staying sober.

The Temperance Movement

While some religious groups attempted to revise their philosophies or create alternative societies, others put their energies into changing what they felt undermined the quality of life. This was how many groups, especially Baptists and Methodists, viewed liquor. The temperance movement, which began in the United States and spread to England, attempted to ban the use of alcohol.

Most of the movement's leaders were clergy interested in doing away with social evils, poverty, and crime that were often brought on by heavy drinking. Like many other reform groups, temperance groups founded a national organization, the United States Temperance Union, in 1833. Heavy drinkers were persuaded to "take the pledge" to give up alcohol. Temperance propaganda even included a "Cold Water Army" of children with uniforms and marching songs.

In addition to trying to persuade people not to drink, temperance societies demanded laws to put an end to the sale of liquor. They were able to convince many politicians of the justice of their cause. Abraham Lincoln, for example, favored prohibition by state action, arguing that just as the American Revolution freed people from the tyranny of Britain, so would prohibition free people from the tyranny of alcohol. In 1851 Maine passed the first state prohibition law, an example followed by about a dozen states. Other states passed "local option" laws, which allowed towns and villages to prohibit the sale of liquor.

The achievements of the 1830s and 1840s had beneficial and long-lasting results. The years of reform helped establish the spirit of free thinking in the American character.

 ▲ **THE TRANSCENDENTALISTS** Margaret Fuller was a leader in the Transcendentalist movement. *What ideas did Transcendentalists express?*

Section 3 ★ Review

Checking for Understanding

1. **Identify** Hudson River School, Maria Mitchell, Charles Bulfinch, Greek Revival, Brook Farm community, Transcendentalism, Second Great Awakening.
2. **Define** socialism.
3. **List** the prominent American artists and writers of the 1800s.
4. **Describe** the temperance movement in the 1800s.

Critical Thinking

5. **Analyzing Reform** The reform movements of the 1800s were initiated to extend rights and freedom of choice. What movement was an exception? What laws exist today that have similar goals to those of this movement?

CHAPTER 12 The Spirit of Reform 1820–1854

INTEGRATING Language Arts

American Literary Heritage

Historical Setting
Henry David Thoreau lived in a time of political, social, and intellectual ferment. Transcendentalism was but one movement of that time.

Background
Thoreau was one of the most influential philosophers and writers in American history. At Walden, Thoreau lived out his philosophy of freedom of the individual. He observed nature, walked, read, and expanded his Transcendental ideas. The journal he kept became his most famous book, *Walden*, published in 1854.

About the Journal
Thoreau believed that a person could only realize his full potential by contemplating himself and his place in the universe. Thoreau's two years at Walden were the ultimate rejection of the material world around him. Have students read this excerpt from *Walden* and summarize in their own words Thoreau's criticisms of society, his call for personal freedom, and his view of how individuals must live in society.

▲ HENRY DAVID THOREAU

Part journal, part social commentary, and part sermon, this work summarizes and enlarges upon Thoreau's experiences at Walden Pond, near Concord, Massachusetts, where he built a cabin and lived in solitude for two years.

As you read this passage, look for Thoreau's criticisms of American society, his call for personal freedom, and what he says we must do to live in society.

Walden (excerpt)

I went to the woods because I wished to live deliberately, to front only the essential facts of life, and see if I could not learn what it had to teach, and not, when I came to die, discover that I had not lived. I did not wish to live what was not life, living is so dear; nor did I wish to practice resignation, unless it was quite necessary. I wanted to live deep and suck out all the marrow of life, to live so sturdily and Spartan-like as to put to rout all that was not life, to cut a broad swath and shave close, to drive life into a corner, and reduce it to its lowest terms, and, if it proved to be mean, why then to get the whole and genuine meanness of it, and publish its meanness to the world; or if it were sublime, to know it by experience, and be able to give a true account of it in my next excursion. For most men, it appears to me, are in a strange uncertainty about it, whether it is of the devil or of God, and have *somewhat hastily* concluded that it is the chief end of man here to "glorify God and enjoy him forever."

Still we live meanly, like ants. . . . Our life is frittered away by detail. An honest man has hardly need to count more than his ten fingers, or in extreme cases he may add his ten toes, and lump the rest. Simplicity, simplicity, simplicity! I say, let your affairs be as two or three, and not a hundred or a thousand; instead of a million count half a dozen, and keep your accounts on your thumb-nail. In the midst of this chopping sea of civilized life, such are the clouds and storms and quicksands and thousand-and-one items to be allowed for, that a man has to live, if he would not founder and go to the bottom and not make his port at all, by dead reckoning, and he must be a great calculator indeed who succeeds. Simplify, simplify. Instead of three meals a day, if it be necessary eat but one; instead of a hundred dishes, five; and reduce other things in proportion. Our life is like a German Confederacy, made up of petty states, with its boundary forever fluctuating, so that even a German cannot tell you how it is bounded at any moment. The nation

Cultural Diversity

Many of the ideas expressed by Thoreau had a far-reaching impact. In India during the mid-twentieth century, the leader Mahatma Ghandi used Thoreau's ideas of civil disobedience through nonviolence to win eventual freedom for his nation. The nonviolent protests of Martin Luther King, Jr., in the civil rights movement of the 1960s were also based, in part, on ideas expressed by Thoreau.

▲ WALDEN POND

itself, with all its so-called internal improvements, which, by the way, are all grown establishment, cluttered with furniture and tripped up by its own traps, ruined by luxury and heedless expense, by want of calculation and a worthy aim, as the million house-holds in the land; and the only cure for it, as for them, is in a rigid economy, a stern and more than Spartan simplicity of life and elevation of purpose. It lives too fast. Men think that it is essential that the *Nation* have commerce, and export ice, and talk through a telegraph, and ride thirty miles an hour, without a doubt, whether *they* do or not; but whether we should live like baboons or like men, is a little uncertain. . . .

Interpreting Literature
1. What motivated Thoreau to go and live alone in the wilderness?
2. What is Thoreau's assessment of life at mid-century? To what does he compare life?

Seeing Relationships
3. What trends and tendencies of the period go hand in hand with the ideals Thoreau expresses?

INTEGRATING Language Arts

Developing Student Understanding
Ask students why they think Thoreau wanted to isolate himself for two years from all human society. (He wanted to be at one with nature, to find peace and simplicity.) Explain that this selection from *Walden* expresses Thoreau's ideas of humans, nature, and a person's place in the natural world.

Other Works of Thoreau
As well as a philosopher, Thoreau was also a dedicated naturalist. His first book, *A Week on the Concord and Merrimack Rivers,* and later works, *Excursions* and *Cape Cod,* grew out of his Walden journal and express his observations and ideas about nature. As a social critic, Thoreau wrote the essay "Civil Disobedience," a protest against the Mexican War and a powerful condemnation of slavery.

Answers to INTERPRETING LITERATURE
1. He wanted to see only the fundamental things of life and shut out all that was not necessary to life.
2. Most people are uncertain of their lives; they live like ants and waste their lives in details.
3. Answers will vary but may include the rapid growth of the nation—society moving too fast, people wanting material things.

REVIEW CHAPTER 12

Answers

Reviewing Facts
1. The number of public schools increased; women trained as teachers; few colleges admitted women and African Americans. Standard readers, spellers, and dictionaries became part of the American education system.
2. They established abolitionist newspapers, brought the horrors of slavery to public attention, perhaps helped limit the spread of slavery.
3. The movement resolved to press for enfranchisement, property rights, and entrance to professions. It gained property rights and limited access to education and professions.
4. Mormons, Shakers, Oneida Community, Unitarians, Transcendentalists were some of the major religious groups. Also, reform movements saw expansion of services in established religions, social reform, and the establishment of alternative societies.

Understanding Concepts
1. Abolition; slavery was too profitable.
2. Answers will vary. Some may say when laws are immoral or inhumane, such as legal genocide, they should be broken. Others may say people should work through legal channels for reform.

Critical Thinking
1. In the United States, enlightenment and spirit of reform was outweighed by the economic interests of the cotton industry.

CHAPTER 12 ★ REVIEW

Using Vocabulary

Context clues help a reader determine the meaning of an unfamiliar word. A clue might take the form of a definition, an explanation, a synonym or antonym, or further details that make the meaning clear. Write a sentence for each of the terms below. Include context clues so that the meaning of the words are clear to a reader unfamiliar with them.

lyceum
abolitionist
socialism
Underground Railroad

Reviewing Facts

1. **Summarize** advances in American education in the early 1800s.
2. **Describe** how Garrison, Douglass, and Clay influenced the abolitionist movement.
3. **Specify** the goals and achievements of the woman's rights movement during this period.
4. **Identify** the major religious groups and movements that emerged during the 1800s.

Understanding Concepts

Reform
1. Which of the nineteenth-century reform movements were hampered by opposition from groups concerned about their own economic interests? Explain.

Values and Beliefs
2. The Underground Railroad was run by decent people who broke the law. Under the law these people were technically stealing property. What values did they consider to be above the law? Do you think breaking the law is ever justified under certain circumstances? Explain.

Critical Thinking

1. **Making Global Comparisons** Slavery was abolished in Great Britain, France, and Latin America before it was abolished in the United States. What economic and political differences probably account for this?
2. **Comparing Fine Art** Compare this painting by James Hamilton, entitled *Scene on the Hudson*, with the painting *Among the Sierra Nevada Mountains* on page 348. Do the artists differ in the way they painted their scenes? How does the environment in Hamilton's painting differ from that in Bierstadt's work?

▲ SCENE ON THE HUDSON BY JAMES HAMILTON

Writing About History

Examples
Imagine you are the editor of a prominent newspaper in 1830. Write an editorial pointing out injustices that exist even as democratic changes are sweeping the country. Give examples of failure to provide freedom and equal opportunity for all people in the United States.

Cooperative Learning

Working in pairs, research the life of one American writer or poet of the 1800s, and review one of the writer's works. Have one partner write a biography and a description of the writer's contribution to American culture. Have the other partner write a review of the writer's work. Bind them into one booklet with the writer's name as a title. Display the booklets for other students to read.

Slavery was not as attractive economically in other countries. Slavery became a political issue dividing North and South.
2. Answers will vary but may include that the style of both is a romantic landscape reflecting the natural beauty of the American landscape but that Hamilton's does not show such grandeur as Bierstadt's. Hamilton's is more tamed and "civilized."

Practicing the Skill
1. 1790–1860
2. percentage of population
3. rural
4. percentage of urban population
5. Answers will vary but students are likely to suggest a growing interest in reforms that affect city life.

CHAPTER 12 ★ REVIEW

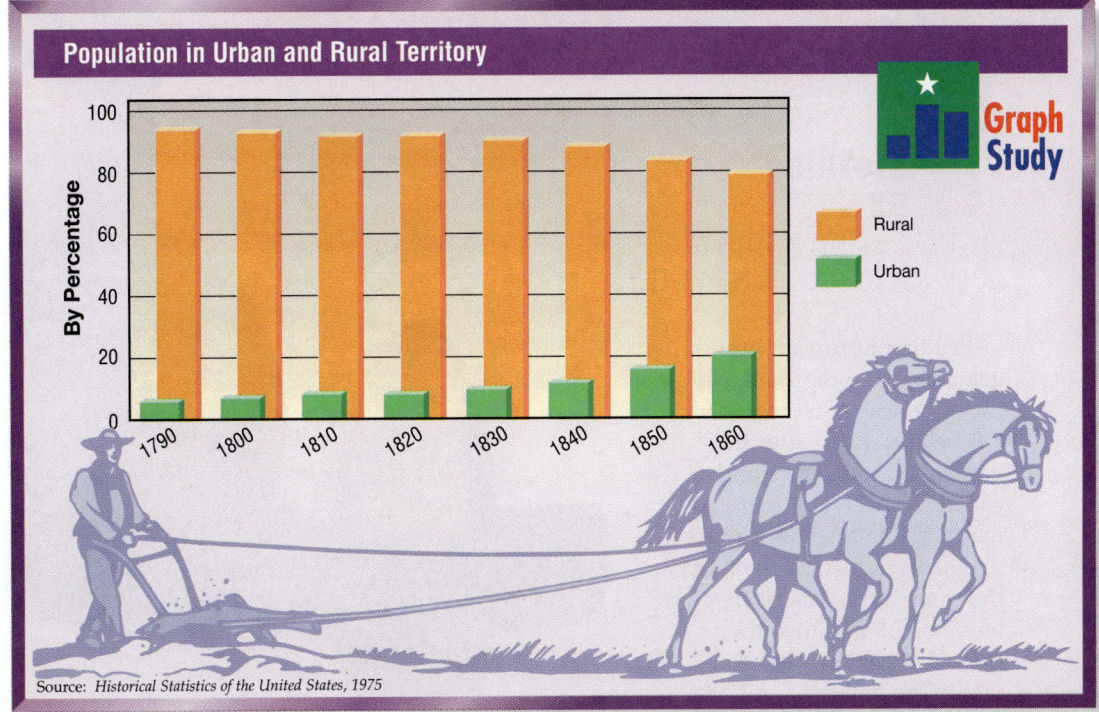

Social Studies Skills

Reading a Bar Graph

A bar graph is used to show relationships. A bar graph can be used to show how something changes over time. For example, the bar graph on this page shows how urban and rural populations changed during a certain time period.

Practicing the Skill

Use the bar graph and your understanding of Chapter 12 content to answer the following questions.
1. What time period is covered in the graph?
2. What do the vertical bars of the graph represent?
3. Throughout the time period covered, is the majority of the population urban or rural?
4. How is the population changing during the time period covered?
5. How might the trend shown in the bar graph affect the reforms discussed in the chapter?

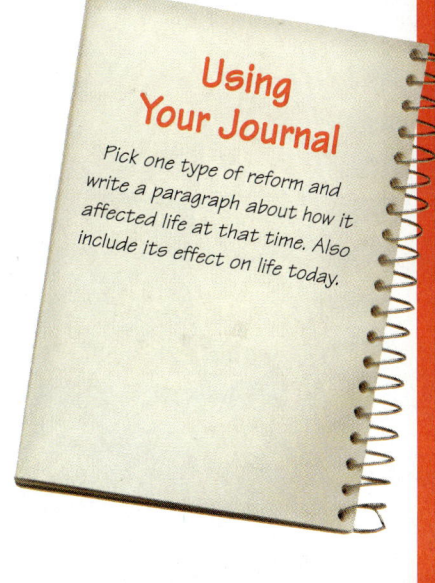

Using Your Journal
Pick one type of reform and write a paragraph about how it affected life at that time. Also include its effect on life today.

REVIEW CHAPTER 12

Chapter Bonus Test Question

This question may be used for extra credit on the chapter test. What basic values are reflected in the reform movements of this period? (belief in expanding democracy, optimism that society could be improved, ideas of equality)

Using Your Journal

Paragraphs should not only express an opinion but also include evidence to support ways that reforms have affected life then and now. You might have students read their paragraphs and share their conclusions with the class.

CHAPTER 12 The Spirit of Reform 1820–1854

Cultural Kaleidoscope

Making Connections
History and Art Portraits provide information about the fashions favored by Americans of the past, especially in the years before photography. Even though they may not be outstanding as art, such works detail not only clothing but also hairstyles, footwear, and interior decoration. Two words of caution, however: Most portraits portray only the middle and upper classes, who could afford to commission art. Also the subjects of a portrait were usually shown in their "Sunday best," not the clothes they wore every day.

More About...
Clothing
In the pre–Civil War years, boots and shoes were still made by shoemakers. Except in rare cases, right and left shoes of a given pair were identical. Although this did not make for comfort, the wearer could alternate the shoes from day to day, thus minimizing wear and tear on the heels.

Cultural Kaleidoscope

Clothing

High Fashion

The first European immigrants tried to reproduce in the Americas what they had left behind. Even after they gained independence and called themselves Americans, many still followed Europe's lead in matters of fashion. At the same time, Americans were forced to adjust their lifestyles to a new environment. The development of a unique American style in clothing and fashions was beginning.

▲ Nineteenth-century slippers and perfume

Hatboxes came in a variety of shapes and sizes. The well-dressed woman often wore an oversized hat or bonnet.
▼

Cooperative Learning
Divide the class into small groups, one for each of the items of clothing shown in this essay. Have each group compare its item with a comparable one from colonial times. How does it differ? Is the change for the better or not?

Cultural Kaleidoscope

Portfolio Project

In today's world, unlike that of the pre–Civil War years, children's clothing differs from that of adults. Have students collect pictures showing typical clothing for young children, teenagers, young adults, and older adults. What is the message conveyed by each style?

▲ A variety of styles is shown in *The Sailor's Wedding*. During the 1830s and 1840s, more and more women wore full-skirted gowns with petticoats. One interesting fashion note is that for nearly 200 years moustaches and beards were almost never worn. Only in the 1850s did American men in large numbers begin to let their facial hair grow.

▲ Jewelry box

► Into the early 1800s, children, at least those in families wealthy enough to have portraits painted, wore the same kind of clothing their parents wore.

► Beginning in the 1820s, most well-dressed men wore top hats and ankle-length trousers rather than knee breeches.

The Historian's Craft

A topic of special interest to modern historians is the effect of mechanization on the life of a nation. One invention of the mid-1800s that had a broad impact was the sewing machine. It made life easier for the average homemaker. It stimulated factory production of clothes and shoes. With a sewing machine, a man's shirt could be made in about an hour, compared to 14 hours by hand. Because the machine was a costly purchase, it also led to two marketing innovations: installment buying and the trade-in.

UNIT 4 DIGEST

Unit 4 Digest can be used to teach unit coverage when time is limited, to review unit content, or to link content of one unit to another.

Unit Digest Transparencies: Strategies and Activities

Use Transparency 4.

■ Chapter 10

Remind students that in spite of the growth of a national economy, sectional conflicts produced antagonisms that were not easily overcome. Have students list factors that bound the nation together and factors that tended to pull the nation apart. Ask which factors were strongest and why.

■ Chapter 11

Read the following assessment of Andrew Jackson by historian John Spencer Basset. "Jackson accepted democracy with relentless logic. Some others believed that wise leaders could best determine the policies of government, but he more than anyone else of his day threw the task of judging upon the common man...." Ask students to write a paragraph explaining whether they agree or disagree with this analysis of Andrew Jackson.

■ Chapter 12

The idea of reforming American society to make life better for people had strong roots in the religious and political heritage of the nation. Ask students to write a paragraph tracing the reform

UNIT FOUR DIGEST

Chapter 10

Sectionalism

The Industrial Revolution brought changes to all sections of the United States. In the Northeast, the textile industry expanded rapidly. Other manufacturing and shipping industries also grew in importance. As a result, goods became cheaper and more widely available. Craft workers organized trade societies, and unskilled workers formed labor unions to improve their lives.

In the South the cotton gin and Britain's increased demand for cotton boosted the economy. Cotton became the major export not only of the South but of the nation. As a result, many Southerners' disapproval of slavery faded away.

In the Northwest, pioneers streamed over the Appalachian Mountains to settle the region. Soon towns became cities, and in these cities manufacturing sprang up. By 1820 more than one-fourth of the people in the United States lived west of the Appalachian Plateau.

Each section of the country had its own wants and needs. Often people in different sections quarreled over whether the national government should support a particular issue. These quarrels threatened American unity.

Henry Clay's "American System" was designed to benefit the economies of all sections, but this compromise brought unity for only a while. In the presidential election of 1824, four National Republicans, representing different sections, sought the office. In a close election, the House of Representatives decided on John Quincy Adams, much to the disgust of Andrew Jackson, who had received the most popular votes.

Chapter 11

Age of Jackson

By the election of 1828, sectional interests had strengthened, and the population was shifting from the Northeast to the South and the Northwest.

The new President, Andrew Jackson, was a man of the people, and his supporters became known as Democrats. During his administration, the power of

the presidency increased, the American definition of democracy broadened, and the people began to expect more from their political system.

However, the new democracy did not extend to Native Americans and African Americans. The government forced Native Americans to move from their lands. African Americans remained enslaved in the South; they were second-class citizens in the North.

Meanwhile, tariffs, banking, and internal improvements still triggered sectional disputes. During debates on the issues of nullification and high tariffs, many feared that the Southern states might secede. Jackson's stand against the second Bank of the United States helped him win the 1832 election but, in the end, led to the Panic of 1837.

In the election of 1840, the Whig party captured the presidency for its candidate, William Henry Harrison, by trying to overcome sectionalism. However, Harrison died after only a month in office, and Vice President John Tyler became President. Unfortunately, Tyler disagreed with the Whigs on many issues, especially states' rights.

Cooperative Learning

Construct a large wall chart with six vertical columns labeled Education, Social Issues, Women's Rights, African American Rights, Arts, and Literature. Divide the class into six groups and assign one vertical column to each group. Have groups use this text and other resources to enter on the chart all the developments in their assigned area between 1820 and 1850. Display the chart on the bulletin board and have groups enter further developments as they study later historical periods. **L2**

Chapter 12
The Spirit of Reform

Between 1820 and 1854, many Americans focused on social needs rather than political issues. Reformers wanted to better their world.

Thanks in part to Horace Mann, many states were providing free elementary education by 1850. State universities began to spring up, and some of the first schools for the academic education of women were founded. Programs for adult education and free public libraries became widespread.

Other reformers championed the causes of prisoners and the disabled. Many states opened insane asylums to care for the mentally ill, who formerly lived in jails.

Women began to organize for their rights. They failed to gain universal suffrage or general acceptance into professions, but for the first time many states allowed women to retain and to manage their property.

The dominant reform effort of the time was the abolitionist movement. Meanwhile, the Underground Railroad quietly smuggled enslaved African Americans out of the South.

American culture reflected the social changes going on. Poets, artists, and novelists described the American scene. Part of the scene was a religious renewal, a "Second Great Awakening." Among the new religious organizations were several utopian communities, such as the Shakers.

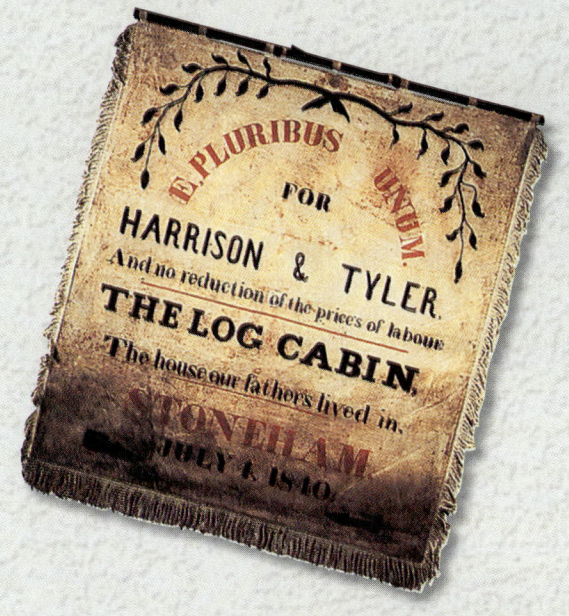

Understanding Unit Themes

1. **American Democracy** What important democratic changes began to develop during the period of the Industrial Revolution?
2. **Economic Development** How did the Industrial Revolution lead to changes in the American economy, its lifestyle, and its values?
3. **Humanities and Religion** How did changes in religious philosophy relate to the growing leadership of religious groups in social reform?
4. **Conflict and Cooperation** How did sectional interests over economic issues develop into conflicts and division within the United States?

UNIT 4 Toward a Democracy: 1820–1854

UNIT 4 DIGEST

movements of this period to political and religious beliefs.

Understanding Unit Themes

1. Extension of voting rights, political influence of the common man, labor movement, education reforms.
2. Economically, Americans experienced cheaper and more abundant goods; the factory system replaced skilled craftsworkers. Lifestyles changed, creating two new classes of people—the capitalists and the workers. Many workers were landless. Changes in values led to a focus on the rights of the common person.
3. The focus of religious philosophy changed from preparing for the hereafter to improving the lives of the people. This zeal was often tied to the spirit of reform.
4. When tariff laws and laws restricting slavery were passed by the federal government, the states asserted their right to oppose federal legislation that was not in their interest, describing the Union as a contract of the states. Nationalists contended the Union was an entity of the people.

● Student Self-Test Software allows students to test their understanding of historical concepts at the unit, chapter, or section levels.

● Have students listen to the chapter digests on the audiocassettes.

The Historian's Craft

Remind students that comparing events, issues, movements, or people is a way of analyzing information to find similarities. Direct students to review material in Chapter 3 on religious movements in colonial times with religious movements described in this chapter. Ask students to consider the following questions in making their comparisons: Who were the leaders of these movements? What were their aims? How successful were they? What impact did these religious movements have on life in the United States?

INTRODUCING UNIT 5

BEGINNING THE UNIT

Provide this cause-and-effect chart to students with the effects omitted. Assign students to complete the chart as they read the chapters in the unit.

Event
- Civil War

Causes
- Growth and spread of institution of slavery
- Growth in antislavery sentiment
- Dependence on cotton in the South
- Growth of belief in political philosophy of states' rights
- Differing rates of industrialization in the North and South

Effects
- Abolition of slavery
- Preservation of the United States
- Primacy of the national government
- Deaths of about 620,000 Americans
- Extension of civil rights to African Americans
- Rapid industrialization due to war effort

History AND ART

Henry Ossawa Tanner (1859–1937) studied at the Philadelphia Academy of Fine Arts. He painted this picture in 1893 in Paris, using sketches he had made earlier. Its theme is teaching and learning.

UNIT FIVE
DIVISION AND REUNION
1825–1877

CHAPTER 13
Manifest Destiny
1825–1854

CHAPTER 14
Compromise and Conflict 1848–1861

CHAPTER 15
The Civil War
1861–1865

CHAPTER 16
Reconstruction
1865–1877

▲ Brass candlestick, 1850s

History AND ART
The Banjo Lesson
by Henry Tanner, 1893

American artist Henry Ossawa Tanner produced a number of realistic studies of American life. After he moved to Europe in the early 1900s, he found another source of inspiration—the Bible.

Exploring Unit Themes

Civil Rights and Liberties During Reconstruction, the Freedmen's Bureau was established to assist African Americans in their transition from slavery to freedom. Congress also passed three constitutional amendments to protect African American rights. However, terror tactics essentially returned African Americans to a position of servility.

Conflict and Cooperation For almost 40 years, political compromises provided a temporary solution to the issue of slavery. In the 1860s compromises failed, and the country plunged into a bloody civil war. A period of postwar Reconstruction in the South was brought to a close by the Compromise of 1877.

Cultural Diversity The annexation of Texas and

Setting the Scene

The slavery issue dominated American life during the first half of the nineteenth century. Compromise had worked in the past, but a growing antislavery movement would not let the moral shame of slavery die.

Themes
- Civil Rights and Liberties
- Conflict and Cooperation
- Cultural Diversity
- U.S. Role in World Affairs

Key Events
- Monroe Doctrine
- Treaty of Guadalupe Hidalgo
- Compromise of 1850
- Confederate States formed
- Battles of Gettysburg and Vicksburg
- Surrender of General Lee
- Assassination of Lincoln
- Radical Reconstruction
- Compromise of 1877

▲ UNION SOLDIER

▲ HONORARY BANNER, 1860

Major Issues
- A belief in Manifest Destiny results in war with Mexico.
- The breakdown of the political party system with the death of the Whigs produces an inability to compromise over slavery.
- During the Civil War, the nation's welfare versus individual rights leads to a suspension of civil liberties.
- Although harsh, reconstruction of the Southern states gradually leads to a renewed Union.

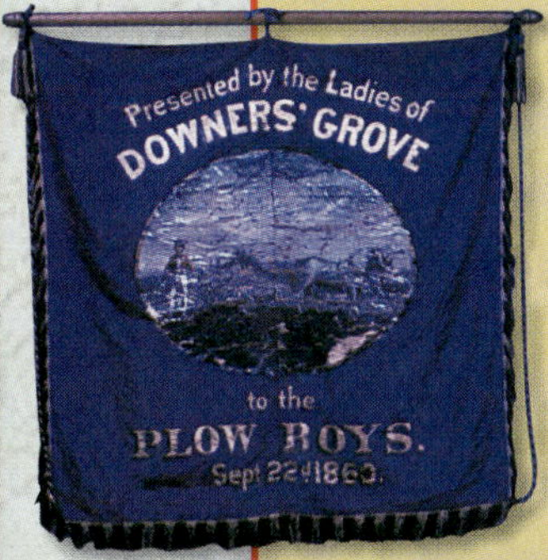

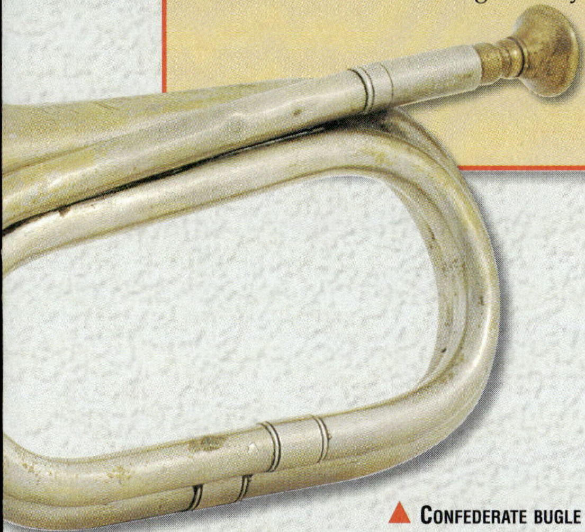

Portfolio Project
Research one of the Latin American countries formed from the United Provinces of Central America. Create a time line of important events in the history of that country, from its inception to current time.

▲ CONFEDERATE BUGLE

the Mexican Cession added a new thread to the cloth of American cultural life. These land acquisitions brought many people of Spanish heritage into the Union.
U.S. Role in World Affairs Territorial expansion brought the United States into conflict with other nations. A disagreement with Britain over the Oregon Territory was settled diplomatically.

The United States' annexation of Texas, however, led to a war with Mexico.
Examining the Themes Ask students to select one of the themes and jot down notes dealing with it as they read this unit. Upon completion of the unit, students should write one paragraph summarizing the theme.

INTRODUCING
UNIT 5

Independent Study Project
Divide the class into two groups. Ask each group to build a history portfolio. The subject of one portfolio should be major figures of the period covered in Unit 5. The subject of the other portfolio should be important locations discussed in the unit—the Alamo, Oregon Territory, Buena Vista, Gettysburg, Appomattox Court House, and so on. Remind groups to provide captions for all illustrations in their portfolios. Display the portfolios.

Unit Digest Transparencies
Use Transparency 5.

Portfolio Project
After students have completed the first draft of their time line, ask them to edit one another's work. Encourage partners to find similarities and differences in the countries they chose.

History and the Humanities

U.S. History and Art Transparencies 7, 8, and 9

Focus on American Fine Art Prints 9, 10

Spirit of American Art and Music 13, 14, 15, 16

American Music: Cultural Traditions

LESSON PLAN
Global Perspectives

FOCUS
Motivating Activity

Ask students why the years between the late 1840s and the early 1850s have been called "the springtime of peoples." Ask students to discuss what might be meant by this phrase. (In many parts of the world, nationalist revolutions sought to end political absolutism, and, like spring flowers, these revolutions soon faded and died.)

TEACH
Guided Practice
World Events and the U.S.

Refer students to the entry for 1869 on the world section of the time line. Point out that French engineer Ferdinand de Lesseps designed and built the Suez Canal. In 1881, de Lesseps tried to build a canal across the Isthmus of Panama. However, poor planning and lack of finance caused him to abandon the attempt some years later.

Global Perspectives

The World

	1825	1845	
Asia and Oceania			**1853** Commodore Matthew Perry arrives in Japan
Europe		◀ **1848** Nationalist revolutions occur throughout Europe	
Africa			
South America			**1850** Slave trade, but not slavery, ends in Brazil
North and Central America			

The United States

	1825	1845	
Pacific and Northwest	**1830** Fur traders open the Oregon Trail	**1848** Gold discovered in California	
Southeast	**1831** Cyrus McCormick invents the reaper		
Midwest			
Southwest	◀ **1836** Texas Revolution, Battle of the Alamo fought	**1848** United States acquires Mexican Cession	
Atlantic Northeast	**1825** Erie Canal completed	**1852** Uncle Tom's Cabin published	

362   UNIT 5 Division and Reunion: 1825–1877

Cultural Diversity

The first massive wave of nineteenth-century European immigration occurred between 1845 and 1860 as the U.S. economy improved after a deep economic depression. More than 2.6 million immigrants arrived, most of them Roman Catholics. The Irish made up the largest ethnic group. Many were fleeing the disastrous Irish potato famine of the late 1840s. The Germans, the second-largest group, were fleeing for economic and political reasons, particularly the repression that followed the failed revolutions of 1848.

African Americans have made major contributions to our country's cultural life, especially in the area of music. Gospel, an exuberant and joyous celebration of faith through music, grew out of the religious services held by enslaved people. Blues, which grew out of their work songs and chants, had an indelible impact on the pioneers of rock 'n roll. Jazz, which some people consider the only new art form to be developed in the twentieth century, was influenced by both gospel and the blues.

1865 **1885**

▶ **1869** Suez Canal opens

▲ **1861** Benito Juárez becomes President of Mexico

1867 Dominion of Canada is formed

1867 Alaska purchased from Russia

1877 Nez Percé War fought

1872 Yellowstone National Park created

1875 Black Hills opens to gold seekers

▲ **1861** Civil War begins

1865 **1885**

UNIT 5 Division and Reunion: 1825–1877   363

Cooperative Learning

Divide the class into groups of five. Ask the groups to put together two time capsules for the period 1825 to 1875, one for the world and one for the United States. Suggest that capsules include events, people, and ideas. Have group members write their capsule ideas—pictures, words, slogans, and artifacts (a maple leaf flag to indicate the founding of the Dominion of Canada, for example)—on a sheet of paper. Have groups compare the contents of their time capsules. **L1, L2**

LESSON PLAN
Global Perspectives

Independent Practice
World Events and the U.S.
At the Battle of Balaclava, in October 1854, 600 members of a British cavalry unit—even though they knew the order was folly—charged the Russian line and were cut to pieces. This most famous action of the Crimean War was commemorated in the poem "The Charge of the Light Brigade" by Alfred, Lord Tennyson. After they have read Chapter 15, ask students to compare this charge to Pickett's charge at the Battle of Gettysburg.

ASSESS
Studying the Time Line

1. What event revolutionized American transportation?
2. What war may have contributed to Russia's willingness to sell Alaska to the United States? Why?
3. Which world event and which United States event had the greatest impact on U.S. history? Explain your answers.

Answers to Questions

1. completion of Erie Canal
2. the Crimean War
3. Answers will vary. Sample answers: World—Commodore Perry's arrival in Japan, established United States influence in Asia; United States—discovery of gold in California, brought expansion of slavery to political forefront.

363

PLANNING GUIDE — Chapter 13 Manifest Destiny

Daily Lesson Objectives	Teacher Classroom Resources	Multimedia
SECTION 1 **The Thirst for New Lands** 1 Day pp. 366–372 1. Give reasons Americans wanted to expand their territory to the Pacific. 2. Describe negotiations with Britain over disputed lands. 3. Describe the overland migrations to Oregon and Utah. 4. Explain why Texans wanted independence from Mexico and how Texas became part of the United States.	Chapter 13 Study Guide Reproducible Lesson Plan Reteaching Activity 13-1 Section Quiz Chapter 13 Cooperative Learning Activity Chapter 13 Concept Mapping Activity Chapter 13 Primary and Secondary Source Readings Reinforcing Social Studies Skills 25, 28, 31, 49, 53, 59 American Portrait 26	Student Self-Test Software Testmaker Section Focus Transparency 39 Chapter 13 Skills Transparency Chapter 13 Map Transparencies Unit 5 Digest Transparencies The American People: Fabric of a Nation
SECTION 2 **War with Mexico** 1 Day pp. 374–378 1. Contrast the United States' short-term and long-range goals in the war with Mexico. 2. List the terms of the treaty of Guadalupe Hidalgo.	Reproducible Lesson Plan Reteaching Activity 13-2 Section Quiz Reinforcing Social Studies Skills 31, 32 Building Skills in Geography	Student Self-Test Software Testmaker Section Focus Transparency 40
SECTION 3 **Global Interests** 1 Day pp. 380–383 1. Explain the events that brought about the Clayton-Bulwer Treaty. 2. Compare the motivations for American interest in Cuba, Central America, China, and Japan in the mid-1800s.	Reproducible Lesson Plan Reteaching Activity 13-3 Section Quiz Chapter 13 Enrichment Activity Reinforcing Social Studies Skills 25, 32, 55 Outline Map 4 Spanish Summaries & Glossary	Student Self-Test Software Testmaker Section Focus Transparency 41 Vocabulary Puzzlemaker Audiocassette, Chapter 10 The Presidents: A Picture History of Our Nation
CHAPTER REVIEW AND EVALUATION 1 Day	Chapter 13 Test Chapter 13 Performance Assessment Activity	Student Self-Test Software Testmaker

OUT OF TIME? If time does not permit teaching the entire chapter, use the Chapter 13 Summary on pages 462–463 and the Chapter 13 audiocassette (English and Spanish) to point out the main ideas of the chapter.

PLANNING GUIDE

Cultural Diversity Activity

Journalism Have students reread John O'Sullivan's quotation on manifest destiny on page 367. Then point out that many Americans also felt they had a "civilizing mission" that justified land seizures. This group argued that Mexicans and Native Americans would benefit from the superior talents, democratic institutions, and culture of those who were taking control of the land.

Taking the perspective of a Native American group or Mexican settlers in Texas, have students write editors responding to the assertion that "rights of discovery, exploration, settlement" were "cobweb issues." Editorials might stress that the "superiority" of one culture over another is in the "eye of the beholder." Or they might focus on the treaties that guaranteed land rights to Native Americans and Mexicans.

Performance Assessment Activity

Boosting Immigration Ask students to research the reasons for the enormous influx of German and Irish immigrants to the United States in the 1830s and 1840s. Then have students work in small groups to prepare a brochure promoting immigration aimed at the Irish or the Germans. Ask groups to exchange brochures and evaluate the effectiveness of the one they reviewed.

POSSIBLE RUBRIC FEATURES: Content information, written and visual communication skills, organization, creativity, cooperative skills

Chapter Resources

Literature from the Period

Corwin, Thomas. "Speech in the U.S. Senate." February 11, 1847.

Polk, James. "Message to Congress." May 11, 1846.

Readings for the Student

Morrison, Dorothy Nafus. *Under a Strong Wind: The Adventures of Jessie Benton Fremont.* Atheneum, 1983.

Slate, Dorothy. "Levi's Gold: The Original Blue Jeans." *Cobblestone,* Vol. 10, No. 5, May 1989.

West, Elliott. "The Youngest Pioneers." *American Heritage,* Vol. 37, No. 1, December 1985.

Readings for the Teacher

Arrington, Leonard J., and Davis Bitton. *The Mormon Experience: A History of the Latter-day Saints.* Knopf, 1979.

Johnson, Charles A. *The Frontier Camp Meeting: Religion's Harvest Time.* Southern Methodist University Press, 1985.

Multimedia Resources

American Moves West. Orange Cherry. (2 Apple diskettes, backups, guide)

Ghosts of Cape Horn. ABC Wide World of Learning. (VHS, documentary film)

The Missions: Mission Life, Missions of the Southwest. Arthur Barr Productions (VHS, 30 minutes)

The New American Worker. Random House. (color, sound filmstrip)

The Revival of Manifest Destiny. Multi-Media Productions. (color filmstrip, cassette, guide)

Key to Ability Levels

Teaching strategies have been coded for varying learning styles and abilities.

L1	Basic activities for all students
L2	Average activities for average to above-average students
L3	Challenging activities for above-average students
LEP	Limited English Proficiency activities

Glencoe Links to the Humanities

Links to Art
- U.S. History & Art Transparencies 7, 8, 9
- Focus on American Fine Art Prints 9, 10

Links to Literature
- Macmillan Literature: Understanding Literature Audiotapes Side 6
- Macmillan Literature: Appreciating Literature Audiotapes Sides 3, 6
- Macmillan Literature: American Literature Audiotapes Side 2
- Macmillan Literature: American Literature Text—Oliver Wendell Holmes, Henry Wadsworth Longfellow, James Russell Lowell

Link to Music
- American Music: Cultural Traditions

CHAPTER 13

BEGINNING THE CHAPTER

Have students refer to the map on page 377 and locate the 98th meridian that divided the United States from the "Great American Desert." Tell them that the territorial expansion of the United States in the mid-1800s would concern these areas. Ask students to predict what problems with other nations and peoples the nation might encounter in trying to expand. (threats from Great Britain over Canada, rebellions by Native Americans on the Great Plains, war with Mexico)

History AND Art

Artist Francis William Edmonds (1806–1863) was also a banker and director of the New York and Erie Railroad. He specialized in scenes of middle-class life in urban America in the mid-nineteenth century.

In 1820, enslaved African Americans made up about 16 percent of the population; by 1840, they made up about 14.5 percent of the population.

CHAPTER 13

Manifest Destiny
1825–1854

▼ Miniature books of the 1830s

Setting the Scene

Focus

The drive to expand the boundaries of the United States across North America became a single-minded goal for many Americans in the 1830s and 1840s. Through war with Mexico and diplomatic negotiations with Great Britain, the United States acquired Texas, Oregon, California, Utah, and the remainder of the Southwest. By 1850 thousands of settlers had crossed the Great Plains for new homes.

Concepts to Understand

★ Why geographic expansion to the Pacific became a national mission
★ How westward migration shaped the political development of Oregon and California

Read to Discover . . .

★ what made Americans determined to expand the size of the country.
★ the causes and results of the Mexican War.

Journal Notes

Why did people want to expand the territory of the United States? Record the various reasons as you read the chapter.

CULTURAL
- 1839 Charles Goodyear develops vulcanized rubber
- 1844 First telegraph message sent

1835 — 1840

POLITICAL
- 1836 Battle of the Alamo fought
- 1836 Texas wins independence
- 1842 Webster-Ashburton Treaty ratified

✚ EXTRA CREDIT PROJECT

The Mexican War was one of the most controversial wars in U.S. history. Ask interested students to research the way one of the following Americans viewed the war and the way other Americans responded to that point of view: John C. Frémont, Henry Thoreau, Abraham Lincoln, Charles Sumner, James K. Polk. Have students present their findings to the class in the form of a panel discussion. Each should be prepared to defend the viewpoint of the person she or he researched.

History AND ART

The Speculator
by Francis W. Edmonds, 1852

A native of New York and a banker as well as an artist, Francis Edmonds specialized in scenes of everyday life, illustrating themes that are distinctly American.

▲ FLAG OF THE REPUBLIC OF TEXAS

- 1847 Brigham Young leads Mormons to the Great Salt Lake valley
- 1846 United States and Britain set Oregon boundary
- 1846 Mexican War begins

1845

- 1853 Stephen Foster pens "My Old Kentucky Home"
- 1853 United States makes Gadsden Purchase

1850

CHAPTER 13 Manifest Destiny 1825–1854

CHAPTER 13 CONCEPTS

Concept Mapping Activity

Write the chapter concepts on the chalkboard. Ask students to write these concepts in their notebook and to list each major event in the chapter under the appropriate concept.

```
      Western expansion
     leads to conflict with
         other nations
         /          \
   Expansion     Migration
```

Recording Journal Notes
After listing reasons some Americans wanted to expand the territory of the United States, ask students to record their response to each reason and provide reasons or evidence in support of that opinion.

NATIONAL GEOGRAPHIC SOCIETY

 **VIDEODISC**

- *GTV: A Geographic Perspective on American History*

Side 2, Chapter 11
Title: *Going to Extremes: the Far West*
Subject: Settlement in the Far West, 1820–1850

See GTV Guide page 45 for complete lesson plan.

Teacher Notes

LESSON PLAN
SECTION 1, 366–373

FOCUS

Bellringer

Before taking roll at the beginning of the class period, display Focus Activity Transparency 43 on the overhead projector, and assign the accompanying Focus Activity Sheet.

Objectives

Point out the objectives on this page to students in previewing the section content.

Motivating Activity

Present the following diary account to students:

"Killing buffaloes, hunting wild horses, sleeping every night on the ground for a whole month, and depending from day to day for the means of existence upon the deer, wild turkey, and bears . . . are matters of thrilling interest to citizens who read of them in their green slippers seated before a shining grate, the neatly printed page illuminated by a bronze astral lamp."

Philip Hone, April 14, 1835

Before students read the section, ask them to write their own impressions of frontier life and compare them with their impressions after reading the section.

Use Skills Transparency 13.

SECTION 1

The Thirst for New Lands

Setting the Scene

Section Focus

The idea that the United States was bound to extend its borders from the Atlantic Ocean to the Pacific Ocean became known as "Manifest Destiny." Americans had begun moving to Texas in the 1820s. By the 1830s and 1840s, they were making their way to Oregon, California, and Utah. What began as a trickle of immigrants swelled to a flood; these American settlements, in turn, gave weight to arguments in favor of expansion and annexation.

Objectives

After studying this section, you should be able to
★ give reasons Americans wanted to expand their territory to the Pacific.
★ describe negotiations with Britain over disputed lands.
★ describe the overland migrations to Oregon and Utah.
★ explain why Texans wanted independence from Mexico and how Texas became part of the United States.

Key Terms

dark horse, joint resolution

◀ THE PRAIRIE HUNTER

Several factors combined to produce the expansionist movement known as Manifest Destiny. Chief among these was the seemingly habitual ambition, nurtured by the restlessness of the American pioneer spirit, to move on to new land.

■ Westward to the Pacific

Expanding the United States to the Pacific involved risks, for it meant taking land claimed or settled by other peoples. The United States, with limited military power, had to weigh carefully the possibility of hostilities with Native Americans on the plains, with Mexico in Texas, and with Britain.

Rivals for the Land

The first area where the advance of American settlement caused serious friction with Britain was in the Northeast. Because of confusing language in the Treaty of Paris after the Revolution, the northern and eastern boundaries of Maine had been uncertain. As long as the region was unoccupied, this was not a serious matter.

In 1838, however, the British decided to construct an overland road to connect St. John on the Bay of Fundy with Montreal and Quebec. In February 1839, settlers from Maine, pushing into the fertile Aroostook (uh•ROOS•tuhk) Valley, clashed with British workers who were felling trees for the road project. The struggle, fought mostly

UNIT 5 Division and Reunion: 1825–1877

Classroom Resources for SECTION 1

Teacher's Classroom Resources
- Chapter 13 Study Guide
- Reproducible Lesson Plan
- Reteaching Activity 13-1
- Chapter 13 Cooperative Learning Activity
- Chapter 13 Primary and Secondary Source Readings
- Section Quiz

Multimedia
- Section Focus Transparency 43
- Chapter 13 Skills Transparency
- Chapter 13 Map Transparency
- Unit 5 Digest Transparency
- Testmaker
- Student Self-Test Software

with fists, is known as the Aroostook War. It nearly led to something more serious when Maine and New Brunswick called out their militias, and Congress authorized President Van Buren to call for 50,000 soldiers in case of war.

The Webster-Ashburton Treaty

In spite of friction and ill feeling, there were practical reasons for pursuing peace. The most important reason was that the United States and Great Britain each profited from the other's trade.

The negotiators—Daniel Webster, the American secretary of state, and Lord Ashburton, the husband of an American heiress—decided that it was impossible to fix the correct boundary of Maine. Instead, the 1842 treaty divided the disputed territory as fairly as they could. Great Britain got what it wanted most: enough land to make possible a direct land route from the St. Lawrence River to New Brunswick. The United States received what it wanted—the Aroostook Valley—along with other concessions on the northern boundaries of New Hampshire, Vermont, and New York.

Settlers Move West

The Oregon Territory extended from the Pacific Ocean to the Rocky Mountains, bordering Russian Alaska to the north and California to the south. Oregon was originally claimed by four countries—the United

▲ **SPIRIT OF THE FRONTIER** by John Gast, 1872 Driven by a sense of Manifest Destiny, Americans moved west. By 1848 the United States stretched unchallenged from sea to sea. **Over what area did the United States-British confrontation take place in the late 1830s?**

CHAPTER 13 Manifest Destiny 1825–1854   **367**

CHAPTER 13
SECTION 1

Independent Practice

Mathematics Ask students to make a chart of the results of the 1844 election. Write the following information on the board:

Polk won 1,339,368 popular votes and 170 electoral votes. Clay won 1,300,687 popular votes and 105 electoral votes.

Ask students to calculate the percentage of electoral and popular votes for each candidate. Then have them use the chart and the information in the text on each candidate's platform and slogan to present a postmortem of the presidential campaign as if they were a news anchor on national television. **L2**

Map Study Using Maps

Answer: Arkansas River, Rocky Mountains, Colorado River, desert

Map Skills

Ask students to determine in what city the Oregon Trail began. (Independence, Missouri)

Map Study

By the late 1840s, large amounts of new territory came under American control. Soon after, thousands of Americans moved to settle this land. **What were the geographic hazards on the trail from Independence to Los Angeles?**

States, Great Britain, Spain, and Russia. By 1824, however, only the Americans and the British were left to compete for control of Oregon.

To Oregon

Until shortly before 1840 the joint occupation of Oregon was almost entirely a British affair. In the mid-1830s, however, American churches sent missionaries to Christianize the Native Americans. When the missionaries began to farm, they sent back glowing reports of the fertility of the soil.

In 1838 a party of American pioneers arrived by ship in the valley of the Willamette River; most newcomers, however, came by covered wagon over the Oregon Trail. By 1842 there were perhaps 500 Americans in Oregon, and in the next year a single party of immigrants numbered 900.

By 1843 so many Americans had arrived in Oregon that they set up a government of their own. Like the Pilgrims and the Mayflower Compact, they drew up their own constitution. Its preamble, similar to the United States Constitution Preamble, read:

> We the people of Oregon Territory, for the purpose of mutual protection and to secure peace and prosperity among ourselves, agree to adopt the following laws and regulations until such time as the United States of America extend their jurisdiction over us.

368 UNIT 5 Division and Reunion: 1825–1877

Cooperative Learning

To review the different conflicts that arose during the westward movement, divide the class into discussion panels made up of four students each. Assign one student in each group to represent each of the following: the United States, the Native American peoples of the Plains, Mexico, and Great Britain. Have each student present the reasons why he or she opposes the westward expansion of the United States. Ask the student representing the United States to defend the movement westward. Each group should hold a panel discussion to summarize their arguments and then answer questions from the class. **L1, L2**

The last phrase shows that the settlers were determined that the United States and not Britain should rule Oregon. By 1845, 5,000 Americans were living south of the Columbia River and demanding that their government take possession of the Oregon Territory.

To Utah

Another group of settlers moved west, not to expand United States territory but to escape from it. The Mormon Church and its founder Joseph Smith were forced to move several times to escape persecution. Many people resented the new religion because of its communal organization and Smith's teachings that a man could have more than one wife. The Mormons moved first to Ohio, then to Missouri, and then to Illinois. At Nauvoo, Illinois, they built a thriving community of 20,000 people. In 1844, however, Joseph Smith was jailed for ordering the destruction of a printing press that belonged to people who disagreed with him. An angry mob then killed Smith and his brother. Brigham Young, the new leader, believing that no safe refuge could be found in the United States, sought an isolated haven in territory that belonged to Mexico.

The move took place in 1847. The Mormons soon established flourishing settlements near the Great Salt Lake in Utah. They developed an advanced system for controlling the water supply in the semiarid regions of the Far West. Around Salt Lake City, irrigation transformed the desert into a garden spot.

■ Texas Independence

Texas—a vast, ill-defined area extending southwest from Louisiana to the Rio Grande and west to the foothills of the Rocky Mountains—belonged to Mexico. The original Spanish settlements in Texas were limited to a few hundred people and a dozen missions.

Visualizing History

▲ **MORMONS MOVE WEST** The Mormons ventured west across the Missouri River to the valley of the Great Salt Lake. Some poorer Mormons traveled to Utah in handcarts. *Who led the Mormons to Utah?*

CHAPTER 13 Manifest Destiny 1825–1854

Critical Thinking

Expressing Point of View Ask students to write a sentence expressing the point of view on the United States expansion westward of each of the following: a young American settler migrating to Oregon, a frontiersman living in the Rocky Mountains, a Native American living on the Great Plains, a Mexican citizen farming in Texas, and a British shipowner operating off the Oregon coast. Have volunteers read their sentences aloud to the class. **L1, L2**

CHAPTER 13
SECTION 1

Visualizing History The religious beliefs of the Mormons ran counter to the democratic pluralism of American society. This difference of opinion led to many difficulties with their neighbors.
Answer to Caption: Brigham Young

Did You Know?

Haitian artist John James Audubon (1785–1851), is best known for his numerous paintings of North American birds in their natural habitat. His book *Birds of America* contains 435 hand-colored engravings. He also traveled westward to the Rocky Mountains in the 1830s and 1840s to sketch the mammals and scenery of the West.

NATIONAL GEOGRAPHIC SOCIETY

VIDEODISC

• *GTV: The American People: Fabric of a Nation*

Side 2, Chapter 6
Title: *No Place Like Home*
Subject: The turbulent history of Texas

See GTV Guide page 68 for complete lesson plan.

CHAPTER 13 SECTION 1

Food of the Times

In the summer, most people lived on barreled salt pork and beef because fresh meat spoiled in the heat. By the 1840s rich people used boxes filled with cut ice to keep their fresh meat, butter, and milk from spoiling.

Fact or Fiction?

Most Americans who migrated to the West did so to escape economic hardship.

FICTION: Fairly prosperous Americans found it easier to afford to move West. The trip cost from $700 to $1,500. Land cost from $1.25 to $10 an acre. Clearing the land and tools cost $100 to $400. Building a log cabin cost as much as $50.

Teaching Life of the Times

When the fur trade declined, many mountain men moved to British Columbia or went back to St. Louis. There they hired themselves out as guides along the Oregon Trail. Ask students to investigate the decline in fur trade today due to the protests of animal rights groups. Ask students if they agree or disagree with these protesters. Why or why not?

Life of the Times

Mountain Men

In the early nineteenth century, fashionable Europeans wore felt hats made of beaver fur. At one time milliners obtained their furs from Russia, but hunters exhausted the supply of beaver there. The next source was the woodlands of eastern North America until the beaver was hunted out there too. Then beaver were discovered in the Rocky Mountains.

Fur companies hired freelance trappers who over time became known as mountain men. As year-round wilderness residents, they learned to live independently. They also knew everything about capturing beavers.

A mountain man called the bait he used to lure the beaver "medicine." Actually it was a musky liquid that came from the glands of other beavers. The mountain man spread the liquid on a branch suspended above the trap.

Since beavers are water animals, a mountain man set his trap under water to mask smell. An animal caught in the underwater trap drowned quickly, and so the trapper did not have to worry about struggling with his catch and possibly getting hurt or damaging the pelt of the animal.

American Settlement of Texas

When Mexico broke away from Spain in 1821, its government sought migrants to come and develop Texas. In 1822 Stephen Austin, an American settler, took over a grant of land that the Spanish government had given his father. Mexican officials agreed that Austin could bring American settlers into Texas, provided that they became Roman Catholics and obeyed Mexican law.

Austin's settlement proved so successful that by 1830 Texas had attracted almost 30,000 Americans. In that year Mexico passed a law restricting further immigration because it was concerned about developments in Texas. Americans, knowing that Mexico's law against slavery was not strictly enforced in Texas, had brought thousands of enslaved people. In addition, they had failed to become Catholics, and the flood of settlers now outnumbered local Mexicans 10 to 1.

The Lone Star Republic

In 1833 Mexico elected General Antonio Santa Anna as president. When the new president abolished local rights, rebellion broke out in Texas. Late in 1835 Santa Anna marched his army north to subdue the rebels. In February 1836, with more than 2,000 troops, Santa Anna besieged 188 Texans in the Alamo, a mission station in San Antonio. After two weeks of resistance, the defenders of the Alamo were defeated.

The Mexican army pursued Sam Houston, the military leader of the Texans, and his troops toward the United States border. Then at San Jacinto (SAN juh•SIHN•tuh) Creek, Houston's forces turned and attacked. Crying "Remember the Alamo!" they surprised and defeated the Mexican troops and captured Santa Anna. Under pressure, Santa Anna signed a treaty accepting the independence of Texas. As soon as he was free, however, Santa Anna refused to be bound by the terms.

Sidelights: Mapping the West

By the 1840s a team of government explorers had conducted scientific explorations of the West. One of these, Colonel John C. Frémont of the United States Corps of Topographical Engineers, described the Salt Lake Valley in such glowing terms—"still and solitary grandeur"—that Brigham Young moved his Mormons from Illinois to the deserts of Utah. During the Mexican War, United States Army explorers accompanied American cavalry. Their journeys resulted in the first detailed maps of the Southwest and a great regional survey of the geology, flora, fauna, and Native American peoples of the region.

CHAPTER 13
SECTION 1

Texas Statehood

In 1836 Texas declared itself the Lone Star Republic and immediately voted to seek admission to the United States. Although there was strong Southern support to extend the area of cotton-growing by annexing Texas, Northern abolitionists charged that the whole history of Texas was a slaveholders' plot to enlarge their power.

Statehood Denied

Although Presidents Jackson and Van Buren refused to recommend annexation, the issue arose again in 1843. President John Tyler feared that Texas would ally itself with Great Britain. The British were interested in Texas as a new source of cotton—and as a market for their manufactured goods. Moreover, British antislavery societies hoped that the new country might be persuaded to free its enslaved workers.

The threat of Texas as a competing source of cotton and a possible haven for runaways alarmed Southerners. Secretary of State John C. Calhoun presented an annexation treaty to the Senate, but a 35–16 vote did not meet the two-thirds majority needed. The rejection of annexation sprang from Northern opposition to adding more slave territory to the Union and from fears that admission of Texas would bring on a war with Mexico.

Election of 1844

As the presidential election of 1844 approached, the issue of territorial expansion took center stage. Former President Van Buren, a Democrat, and Henry Clay, a Whig, were expected to be the rival candidates. Then the unexpected happened: Van Buren failed to receive the Democratic nomination.

▲ GENERAL SAM HOUSTON

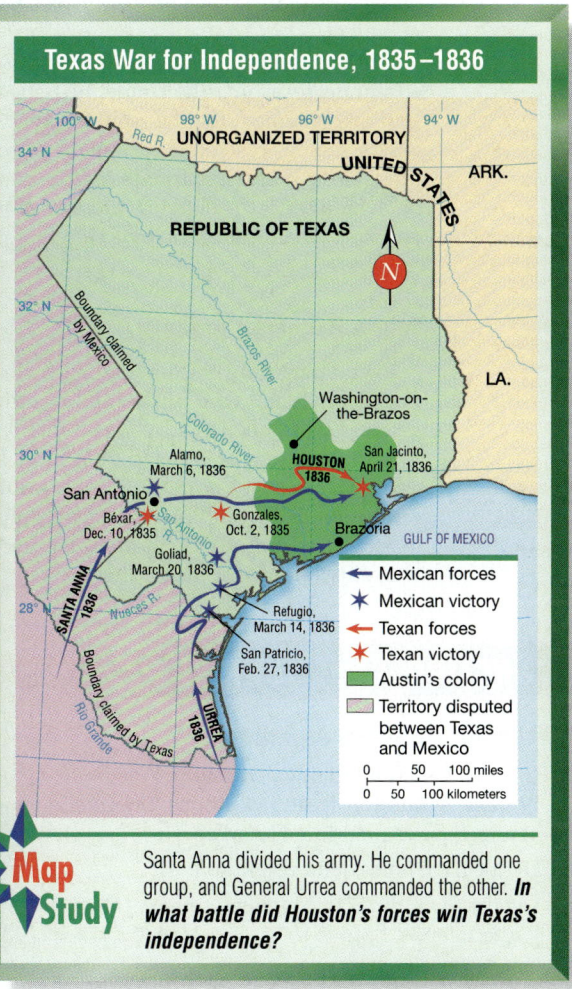

Texas War for Independence, 1835–1836

Santa Anna divided his army. He commanded one group, and General Urrea commanded the other. *In what battle did Houston's forces win Texas's independence?*

Did You Know?

Ex-President Van Buren was expected to be the Democratic candidate in the 1844 presidential election. Texas's annexation, with its threat of disunion over slavery, alarmed him so much that he wrote a letter to the press opposing it. Van Buren then failed to receive the Democratic nomination.

Map Study Using Maps
Answer: San Jacinto
Skills Practice
Ask: Which river is farther south, the Nueces or the Rio Grande? (Rio Grande)

Did You Know?

During the 1844 presidential campaign, the Democrats dramatized their demand for all of Oregon with the campaign slogan "Fifty-four forty or fight!" The parallel 54° 40' was the boundary between Canada and Alaska.

CHAPTER 13 Manifest Destiny 1825–1854

Sidelights: George Catlin

In 1829 artist and author George Catlin began a series of visits to various Native American peoples, mostly on the Great Plains. He sketched, painted scenes, and wrote detailed accounts of Native American life. Catlin was a lawyer and had never studied art. However, by the mid-1800s he was exhibiting paintings and sketches along with Native American costumes, weapons, and ritual objects, to audiences across the United States and in Europe. Show students Transparency 7, *The Buffalo Chase, Mouth of the Yellowstone* by Catlin in United States History and Art.

CHAPTER 13
SECTION 1

ASSESS

Check Understanding
Assign Section 1 Review as homework or an in-class activity.

Evaluate
Assign the Section 1 Quiz in the TCR, or use the History of a Free Nation Testmaker to create a customized quiz.

Reteach
Have students complete Reteaching Activity 13-1.

Enrich
Ask students to pretend they are tour guides describing American culture at this time to visitors from other nations. Have them develop a presentation to give to the visitors. Have volunteers share their presentations with the class.

CLOSE
Summarize the section by asking students in what way the westward expansion was the story of the continuous rebirth of American society. Ask: What forms of political organization did the newcomers take to the West? (democracy, elections) How did they "Americanize" the West? (They brought their culture and ideas.)

A coalition of Westerners who wanted Oregon and Southerners who wanted Texas nominated the first **dark horse,** or unexpected candidate, in the history of the presidency—James K. Polk of Tennessee.

The Democrats dodged the slavery issue by linking the demands for Texas and Oregon. They placed their main emphasis on taking all of Oregon, where slavery would certainly never be established. This was dramatized by the campaign slogan "Fifty-four forty or fight!" (The parallel 54°40′ was the southern boundary of Alaska.)

Manifest Destiny became the principal issue of the campaign. To counter this unexpected challenge, the Whigs had only Henry Clay's great personal popularity and the slogan, "Who is James K. Polk?" which called attention to the obscurity of Clay's opponent.

Although Clay had earlier opposed admitting Texas into the Union, he issued a cautious statement that he would be glad to see the region annexed if the American people so desired and if war with Mexico could be avoided. Clay's hedging did not work, and Polk won the election by a slim margin.

Texas Becomes a State

Even though the election had been close, President Tyler, who was still in office, asserted that Polk's victory was a mandate for the admission of Texas to the Union. He asked Congress to admit Texas by a **joint resolution** that would require only a simple majority, instead of a treaty that required a vote of two-thirds of the Senate.

On Tyler's initiative in February 1845, both houses of Congress, by very narrow majorities, passed the joint resolution. In December 1845, the Lone Star Republic became the twenty-eighth state. The boundary between Mexico and Texas remained undetermined, and the Mexican government threatened war.

■ Division of Oregon

The risk of war with Mexico put pressure on the United States to settle the Oregon question. It was one thing to shout, "Fifty-four forty or fight!" in an election campaign. It was quite another to take on Great Britain, the greatest sea power in the world, and prepare to fight Mexico.

Great Britain also had reasons to settle the Oregon question peacefully. By 1846 the number of American settlers in Oregon had risen to 10,000 and United States expansionists were calling for "thirty thousand rifles" in Oregon to protect American interests. Rather than losing all of the territory, the British government was willing to relinquish the southern half.

The Hudson's Bay Company had trapped the beavers from the region there and had moved its principal base from the Columbia River to Vancouver Island. In 1846 Polk submitted to the Senate a British proposal to divide Oregon along the 49th parallel. In spite of the objections of Westerners, who accused the President of backing down on his demand for all of Oregon, the Senate approved the treaty, which was signed on June 15, 1846.

Section 1 ★ Review

Checking for Understanding
1. **Identify** Manifest Destiny, Aroostook War, Webster-Ashburton Treaty, Mormons, Brigham Young, Santa Anna, Sam Houston.
2. **Define** dark horse, joint resolution.
3. **List** the three rivals to American settlers for Western lands.
4. **Cite** two reasons why James K. Polk won the 1844 election.

Critical Thinking
5. **Identifying Assumptions** What assumptions did the idea of Manifest Destiny make about the rights of Native Americans and others to this land?

Answers to SECTION 1 REVIEW
1. Manifest Destiny, 366; Aroostook War, 367; Webster-Ashburton Treaty, 367; *Columbia,* 369; Mormons, 369; Brigham Young, 369; Sam Houston, 372
2. All vocabulary words are defined in the Glossary.
3. Native Americans, Mexico, Britain
4. Democrats' interest in annexing Texas and taking all of Oregon
5. Answers will vary. Many Americans assumed they had the right to take land from Native Americans and Mexico. They also assumed their government and political system were superior.

History and Religion CONNECTIONS

American Missionaries

The Spanish were the first Europeans to establish missions in the Americas. In sparsely populated regions of New Spain, the Spanish missionaries set up small communities that usually included a village, farmland, a fort, and a church.

In the 1800s, Americans called for missionaries to move beyond the frontier. Lyman Beecher, Congregationalist pastor and seminary president, in his *Plea for the West* (1832), argued that the future of the nation depended on Christianizing the West. Protestant and Catholic missionaries heeded Beecher's call. Organizations were founded to send missionaries and Bibles to remote Western settlements. Along with the strong challenge to repent and accept Christian beliefs, missionaries taught people to read and write.

A few Protestant missionaries also began to work among Native Americans in the West—a calling that Franciscans and Jesuits had felt since the early days of exploration. A pioneer Methodist missionary effort began in the Oregon Territory when Marcus and Narcissa Whitman helped establish a string of mission stations along the Columbia River in the 1830s.

The reports from the missionaries and poor economic conditions in the East drew more and more farmers west. Attracted by land, high prices, favorable markets, and rivers for transportation, Americans in large numbers became infected with "Oregon fever." In the 1840s and 1850s, thousands of settlers moved to Oregon to start a new life. Most people settled in the Willamette Valley.

Missionaries often tried to secure special protection for Native Americans, but they found it difficult to serve the needs of both the Native Americans and the advancing settlers. Missionaries also at times imposed their own values and traditions, which often led to few converts and deep resentment among Native Americans.

▲ MISSION IN THE SOUTHWEST, 1820s

Making the Religion Connection

1. Why did Lyman Beecher call for missionary work in the West?
2. Why might missionaries have found it difficult to serve the needs of Native Americans and settlers?

Linking Past and Present

3. How does missionary activity today differ from that of the 1800s? Describe what you think the primary responsibilities of missionaries are.

CHAPTER 13 CONNECTIONS

Teaching Making Connections

The lives of Native Americans who lived in missions were regimented by ringing bells and strict overseers. Discipline was often administered by flogging. Native Americans at San Diego attempted a large-scale rebellion. Some historians believe their failure was the reason Native Americans in that region never again attempted a major assault on their conquerors.

Did You Know?

In the Oregon territory, which was called Oregon Country, Great Britain's ambition had been to make the Columbia River the boundary between Canada and the United States. This would have given Britain control of the fur trade. The United States had offered to divide the land along the 49th parallel. Hence, the area under dispute lay between the 49th parallel and the Columbia River. The number of American settlers and the fact that beaver hats went out of style finally settled the American claim.

Answers to CONNECTIONS

1. Lyman argued that the future of the United States depended on Christianizing the West.
2. Needs of the two groups were very different.
3. Answers will vary. Students may mention that modern communication aids contemporary missionaries.

LESSON PLAN
SECTION 2, 374–379

FOCUS

Bellringer

Before taking roll at the beginning of the class period, display Focus Activity Transparency 44 on the overhead projector, and assign the accompanying Focus Activity Sheet.

Objectives

Point out the objectives on this page to students in previewing the section content.

Motivating Activity

Present the following description to students:

Imagine that it is 1849. You have just trekked through a Navajo canyon searching for a wagon route. As you search the canyon, you are the first person to come across a lost cliff dwelling of the ancient Anasazi people.

Ask: What do you think the early settlers who traveled through the Southwest felt? (a tremendous pride in the new lands they were settling) Tell students that the war with Mexico in 1846 also led a great number of United States Army explorers into the Southwest. As they read this section, ask students to keep in mind that the Southwest boundary of the United States would be drawn on the basis of the nation's territorial claims.

SECTION 2

War With Mexico

Setting the Scene

Section Focus

James K. Polk had been chosen as a presidential candidate because of his clear commitment to territorial expansion. He was determined to fulfill the pledges he made to his party during the campaign. In undertaking a war with Mexico, however, he would face stiff resistance from Northerners and Whigs in Congress.

Objectives

After studying this section, you should be able to

★ contrast the United States's short-term and long-range goals in the war with Mexico.

★ list the terms of the treaty of Guadalupe Hidalgo.

Key Term

consul

◀ Oil lamp, 1840s

James K. Polk was a man who knew what he wanted. On his first day in office, he told a member of his cabinet that he had four great purposes: settle the Oregon question, lower the tariff, reestablish the independent treasury system abolished by the Whigs in 1842, and annex California. By his third year in office, Polk's strong will and hard work had accomplished his first three goals. Annexing California was more difficult.

■ Polk Attempts to Purchase California

New Englanders had traded with California for cattle hides and tallow for 50 years and had described the region as "the richest, the most beautiful, the healthiest country in the world." In the 1840s, it seemed that control of the region might soon change hands. The native population had staged four rebellions against the Mexican government, which was too distant and too disorganized to govern the region effectively. American officials feared that Great Britain, or even France, might annex California to acquire the great harbor of San Francisco.

In his annual message to Congress in December 1845, Polk cautioned Great Britain and France by repeating the "no colonization" principle of the Monroe Doctrine. He also urged the United States **consul**, or official representative, in Monterey, California, to "arouse in the bosoms of the Californians that love of liberty so natural to the American continent"—in other words, to stir up a revolution. Late in 1845 he sent John Slidell as envoy to Mexico to discuss the Texas question and to offer up to $25 million for California. So great was

UNIT 5 Division and Reunion: 1825–1877

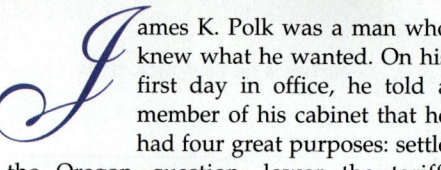

Classroom Resources for SECTION 2

Teacher's Classroom Resources
- Reproducible Lesson Plan
- Reteaching Activity 13-2
- Section Quiz

Multimedia
- Section Focus Transparency 44
- Chapter 13 Map Transparency
- Testmaker
- Student Self-Test Software

Mexican anger at the loss of Texas that any Mexican official who dared to talk with the American diplomat could have lost his position and possibly his life. Slidell's visit, however, inspired a successful revolt against the Mexican government by those who opposed any negotiations with the United States. The new leaders were determined to go to war to win back Texas, and President Mariano Paredes refused to see Slidell. Because he could not present his case, Slidell returned to Washington, D.C. The Mexican government broke off diplomatic relations when the United States annexed Texas, making further negotiations impossible.

The failure of Slidell's mission did not end attempts by the United States to annex California. Mexico's leaders, already angry with the United States, might easily be provoked into war.

Outbreak of War

The spark that ignited the war between Mexico and the United States resulted from a dispute over the southern boundary of Texas. Mexico claimed it was the Nueces (nu•AY•suhs) River, while the United States said it was the Rio Grande 130 miles to the south. On hearing of the failure of Slidell's mission to Mexico City, Polk ordered General Zachary Taylor to move his troops south to the Rio Grande. Taylor's troops were, in effect, sent looking for trouble, waiting for an incident justifying retaliation.

War Begins

Late in April 1846, Mexican soldiers crossed the Rio Grande and attacked a small detachment of United States cavalry, which was in Mexican territory according to the Mexican point of view. When news of this attack on Taylor's force reached Washington, D.C., the President hastily revised a war message that he had been preparing in response to Slidell's rejection in Mexico City. Pointing out that his effort to negotiate peaceably with Mexico had failed, Polk argued that war had been begun "by the act of Mexico herself." On May 13, 1846, Congress declared war by overwhelming majorities in both houses.

Many Americans refused to support a war of aggression against a weaker neighbor. It was, wrote the New England author James Russell Lowell, simply a Southern scheme to steal "bigger pens to cram in slaves." Whig members of Congress, including Abraham Lincoln, then a representative from Illinois, challenged Polk's statement that American blood had been spilled on American soil. Lincoln invited Polk to point out the spot where this had occurred.

Even American soldiers had their doubts about the legitimacy of the war. In 1846 Colonel Ethan Allen Hitchcock wrote:

❝ *I have said from the first that the United States are the aggressors.... We have not one particle of right to be here. It looks as if the government sent a small force on purpose to bring on a war, so as to have a pretext for taking California and as much of this country as it chooses, for, whatever becomes of this army, there is no doubt of a war between the United States and Mexico.... My heart is not in this business... but, as a military man, I am bound to execute orders.* ❞

◀ JAMES KNOX POLK

CHAPTER 13 Manifest Destiny 1825–1854

CHAPTER 13
SECTION 2

TEACH
Guided Practice
History Divide students into groups of four to discuss the Treaty of Guadalupe Hidalgo. Ask each group to negotiate the terms of the treaty. Two students should represent the United States' interests and two Mexico's interests. Point out that American troops controlled a large portion of Mexico, and that Mexico was concerned about citizens' rights, land titles, and religion for Mexicans in the Southwest. Have students present their ideas. **L2**

Did You Know?
Santa Anna, who had fought the United States during the Mexican War, sold Mexican lands (called the Gadsden Purchase) to the United States in 1853 in order to raise money for his army.

Cooperative Learning
To review the issues of conflict between Mexico and the United States, divide the class into groups of four. Have two students in each group research the Mexican view that the United States was provoking a war by encroaching on Mexican territory in California and Texas. Have the other two students research points made by Polk's administration that it had tried to negotiate with the Mexican government. Following the sharing of information from both sides, have each group come to a consensus on which side provoked the Mexican War and why. **L1, LEP**

CHAPTER 13
SECTION 2

In 1845 American military forces in territory that Mexico regarded as its own provoked an attack. That attack permitted President Polk to demand and obtain from Congress a declaration of war. A similar event occurred 119 years later when U.S. ships provoked a North Vietnamese attack, which led President Lyndon Johnson to demand and obtain quickly from Congress a resolution permitting U.S. fighting without the constitutionally required declaration of war. To prevent this from ever happening again, Congress passed the War Powers Act in 1973.

 **Using Maps**

Answer: Feb. 1847

Skills Practice

Ask: What is the southernmost city in which fighting occurred? (Mexico City)

Did You Know?

President Polk was the first president to inform Congress that war existed before Congress formally declared war.

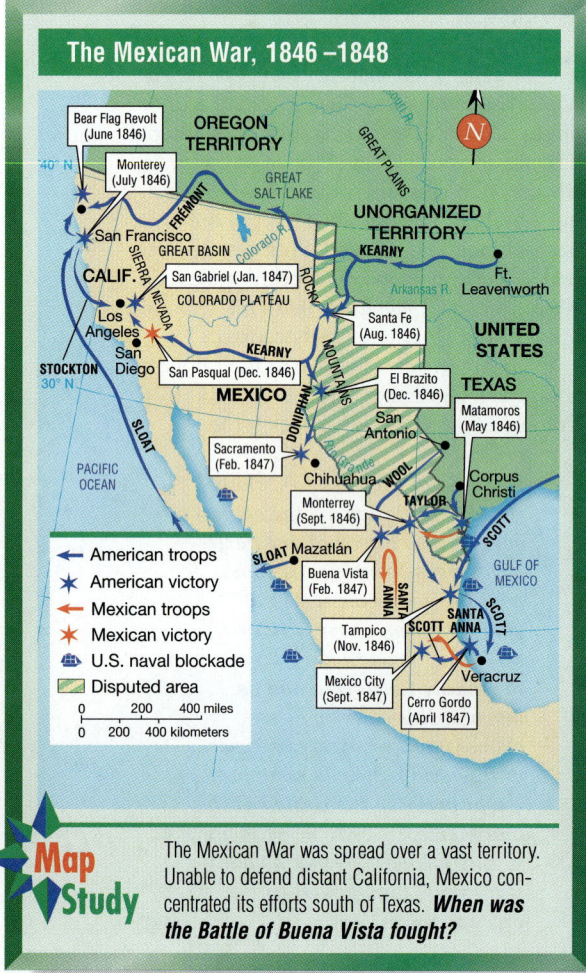

Map Study

The Mexican War was spread over a vast territory. Unable to defend distant California, Mexico concentrated its efforts south of Texas. **When was the Battle of Buena Vista fought?**

Although attacking Polk for starting the war, the Whigs in Congress supported it by voting for supplies and troops. This action was not as illogical as it may seem, because it is not certain that war could have been prevented. Several months before Polk's message to Congress, the Mexican government had declared itself in favor of "a necessary and glorious war." Aware of the dismal failure of American efforts to invade Canada in the War of 1812, the Mexicans expected victory.

Polk's War Strategy

President Polk planned the military campaigns of the Mexican War as a three-part strategy. First, General Taylor and his troops invaded northern Mexico. In May they pushed the Mexican army across the Rio Grande and by September had taken the city of Monterrey. Taylor and his men then penetrated nearly 300 miles into Mexico and won the Battle of Buena Vista in February 1847.

As the second part of the war strategy, General Stephen Kearny headed west from Missouri with a small force of young recruits in July 1846. In August they took Santa Fe with hardly a shot fired in its defense. Kearny and his troops marched on to California, where they helped the Pacific Squadron defeat the Mexicans in Los Angeles in January 1847. A local revolt in northern California, with the assistance of a handful of American troops and a small fleet, had already shaken off Mexican authority. Thus California came under United States control, and fighting in the West ended.

When Mexico still refused to make peace, Polk launched the third part of his war strategy, sending General Winfield Scott to conquer Mexico City. With a force of 10,000, Scott sailed south and landed at Veracruz. In September 1847, after six months of difficult fighting, he occupied the capital.

Working to the Americans' advantage was the disorganization of the Mexican government. One group after another seized power in Mexico, so that sometimes it was difficult to know who headed the government; once three different men claimed to be president. Alfonso Toro, a Mexican historian, wrote of his country's hapless condition:

> Although Mexico had an enormous war budget, she really lacked an army; for hardly worthy of the name was the assemblage of drafted men, badly armed, and ... without confidence in their leaders. The soldiers, who were almost never paid but were maltreated and exploited by their chiefs, deserted whenever they could and even rebelled with arms in their hands when they were ordered to march....

Critical Thinking

Making Predictions Divide students into pairs. Ask each pair to predict what would have happened in American history if James K. Polk had not been elected president in 1844. Would the war with Mexico have occurred? Why or why not? What effect would this have had on the United States acquisition of California and New Mexico? How about the establishment of our political boundaries? Ask students to write their predictions in a short statement. Discuss student answers. **L2, L3**

376

Treaty of Guadalupe Hidalgo

After the capture of Mexico City, some months passed before a Mexican government could be organized to sign a peace treaty. Meanwhile, advocates of Manifest Destiny, including two members of Polk's cabinet, urged that the United States annex all of Mexico.

Trist in Mexico

President Polk, anticipating Scott's victory in Mexico City, sent Nicholas P. Trist, a clerk in the state department, to Mexico with instructions to offer the same terms that Slidell had offered earlier. After a long delay, Polk's patience with Trist gave out, and the President ordered him back to Washington, D.C. Trist, knowing that he was on the verge of a successful treaty, ignored the orders and stayed on to complete the negotiations.

In February 1848, before the movement for total annexation had proceeded very far, a peace treaty was signed at Guadalupe Hidalgo, outside Mexico City. While President Polk denounced the "exceptional conduct" of Nicholas Trist, he saw no alternative to submitting this treaty to the Senate. After a round of expansionist arguments by those who favored annexing all of Mexico, the Senate finally voted 38 to 14 in favor of the treaty.

Terms of the Treaty

The United States gained full title to Texas (with the Rio Grande as a boundary). The United States also gained California and all of what was then called New Mexico. In a later purchase, the nation gained the

 ▲ **ENTERING MEXICO CITY** After six months of difficult fighting, General Winfield Scott forced his way into Mexico City. Scott's troops included young military officers Ulysses S. Grant and Robert E. Lee. *Why did some of the troops oppose the war?*

CHAPTER 13 Manifest Destiny 1825–1854 377

Sidelights: The Boy Heroes of Mexico

By August 1847 the Mexican War had almost ended. In September 1847, as General Winfield Scott marched into Mexico City, six young Mexicans called *Los Niños Héroes* (The Boy Heroes) tried to fight off the conquerors and leapt to their deaths. Under the Guadalupe Hidalgo Treaty, Mexicans living in the United States were given one year to consider returning to Mexico. Only 2,000 Mexican Americans chose to return. Those who remained were guaranteed rights under the U.S. Constitution, but the article protecting land titles and property rights was omitted from the treaty.

CHAPTER 13
SECTION 2

Map Study Using Maps

Answer: Kansas

Skills Practice

Ask: What land was the last to be added to the contiguous part of the United States? (the Gadsden Purchase)

ASSESS

Check Understanding

Assign Section 2 as homework or an in-class activity.

Evaluate

Assign the Section 2 Quiz in the TCR, or use the History of a Free Nation Testmaker to create a customized quiz.

Reteach

Ask students to write a paragraph answering the following question: Why were antislavery Whigs opposed to Polk's actions?

Have students complete Reteaching Activity 13-2.

Enrich

Have students research minorities who fought in the Mexican War. Students should use outside reference materials. Have volunteers present their reports.

CLOSE

Discuss the extent to which diplomatic negotiations should take place before people risk their lives in a war.

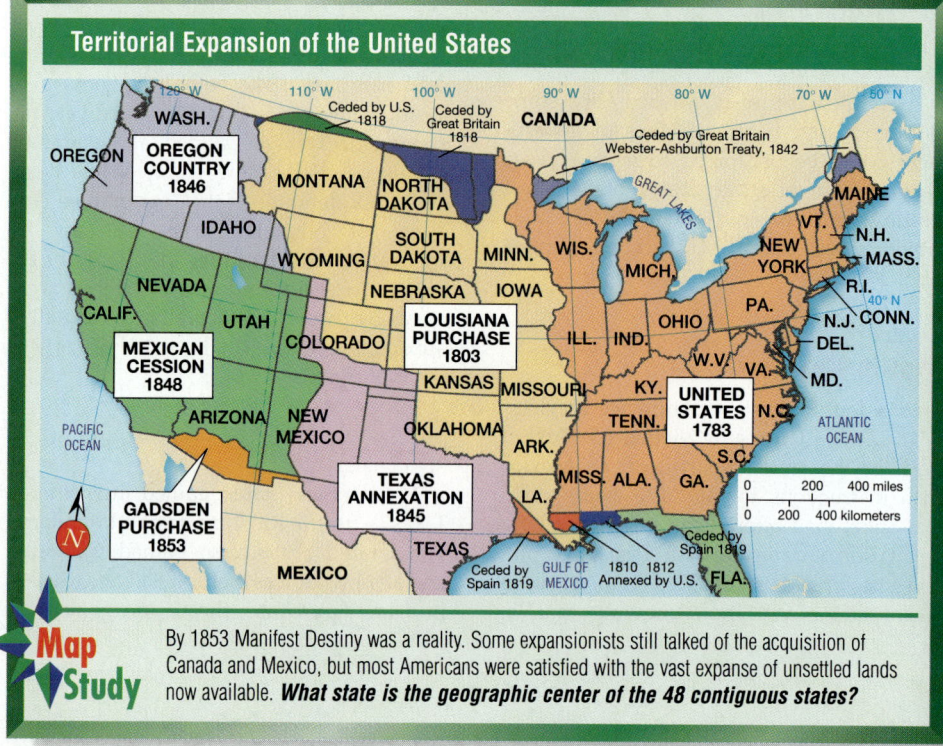

Map Study By 1853 Manifest Destiny was a reality. Some expansionists still talked of the acquisition of Canada and Mexico, but most Americans were satisfied with the vast expanse of unsettled lands now available. *What state is the geographic center of the 48 contiguous states?*

southern portion of the New Mexico territory as part of the Gadsden Purchase in 1853. The United States paid $15 million outright for New Mexico and California and agreed to pay debts of the Mexican government amounting to $3,250,000. Mexico lost only 1 percent of its population but half of its territory.

In 1853 the United States completed expansion across the continent with the Gadsden Purchase for $10 million. As a result, the nation stretched from the Atlantic Ocean to the Pacific Ocean. This land provided a route where the Rocky Mountains were low enough to build a railroad across the southern part of the country to California. Once the United States gained control of large areas of the West, Americans began moving into these regions in greater and greater numbers.

Section 2 ★ Review

Checking for Understanding

1. **Identify** John Slidell, Zachary Taylor, Winfield Scott, Treaty of Guadalupe Hidalgo.
2. **Define** consul.
3. **List** two reasons for the war between Mexico and the United States.
4. **Summarize** the provisions of the Treaty of Guadalupe Hidalgo.

Critical Thinking

5. **Evaluating an Action** Imagine you are a newspaper editor in the mid-1840s. Write your opinion on whether the United States's actions to wage war against Mexico were justified. Include your conclusion on what part Manifest Destiny played in the United States's decision to take these actions.

378   UNIT 5 Division and Reunion: 1825–1877

Answers to SECTION 2 REVIEW

1. John Slidell, 374; Zachary Taylor, 375; Winfield Scott, 376; Treaty of Guadalupe Hidalgo, 377
2. All vocabulary words are defined in the Glossary.
3. Polk's desire to annex California, dispute over southern boundary of Texas
4. California and New Mexico became part of the United States in return for $15 million; southern border of Texas was set at the Rio Grande.
5. Answers will vary. *Yes:* The United States was justified because Mexico was seeking revenge for Texas and was the first to attack. *No:* Polk deliberately provoked the war in order to acquire California.

Social Studies Skills

Interpreting Primary Sources

Migration

Shortly after California became United States territory, the gold rush began. Among the thousands of people who made the long and dangerous trek west was Alvin Coffey, an enslaved man. His holder took away all the money that Coffey made in the mines and later sold him to another man. Coffey eventually earned freedom for himself and his family. His account of the trip to California suggests some of the dangers and hardships faced by many of the forty-niners.

from *Reminiscences* by Alvin Coffey:

I started from St. Louis, Missouri, on the 2nd of April in 1849. There was quite a crowd of neighbors who drove through the mud and rain to St. Joe to see us off. About the first of May we organized the train . . . We crossed the Missouri River at Savanna Landing. . . . At six in the morning, there were three more went to relieve those on guard. One of the three that came in had cholera so bad that he was in lots of misery. Dr. Bassett, the captain of the train, did all he could for him, but he died at 10 o'clock and we buried him. . . . We got news every day that people were dying by the hundreds in St. Joe and St. Louis. It was alarming. When we hitched up and got ready to move, [the] Dr. said, "Boys, we will have to drive day and night." . . . We drove night and day and got out of reach of the cholera. . . . We got across the plains to Fort Lar[a]mie, the 16th of June and the ignorant driver broke down a good many oxen on the trains. There were a good many ahead of us, who had doubled up their trains and left tons upon tons of bacon and other provisions. . . . We crossed the South Pass on the Fourth of July. The ice next morning was as thick as a dinner-plate. On the morning of the 15th, we went to dry-digging mining. We dug and dug to the first of November, at night it commenced raining, and rained and snowed pretty much all the winter. We had a tent but it barely kept us all dry. There were from eight to twelve in one camp. We cut down pine trees for stakes to make a cabin. It was a whole week before we had a cabin to keep us dry.

The wagon train went through Honey Lake to Deer Creek in Sacramento Valley and then to Redding Springs on October 13, 1849.

▲ GOLD MINING IN CALIFORNIA, 1850s

Examining the Primary Source

1. What danger did travelers face in St. Louis and St. Joseph?
2. What does the description of ice on the Fourth of July reveal about South Pass?

Critical Thinking

3. **Drawing Conclusions** Do you think that people in 1850 were more willing to take risks than they are today? Explain.

LESSON PLAN
Mastering Social Studies Skills

Teaching Interpreting Primary Sources

Ask students to summarize each paragraph of Coffey's text. Have them ask themselves: What is happening? Who and what are described? Help students draw conclusions about what the trip was like. Why does Coffey's text seem accurate? (He was an eyewitness.)

Did You Know?

More than 78,000 American troops fought in the Mexican War; 1,733 American soldiers died in battle.

Answers to SOCIAL STUDIES SKILLS

1. The primary danger they faced was from a cholera epidemic.
2. It was a high elevation that remained cold all year.
3. Those who say that people were more willing should refer to the danger of death from disease, exposure, and so on. Those who disagree should give examples of risks people take today.

LESSON PLAN
SECTION 3, 380–383

FOCUS

Bellringer
Before taking roll at the beginning of the class period, display Focus Activity Transparency 45 on the overhead projector, and assign the accompanying Focus Activity Sheet.

Objectives
Point out the objectives on this page to students in previewing the section content.

Motivating Activity
Ask students to tell how the actions of Presidents Tyler and Polk influenced U.S. expansion. Discuss students' responses, and tell them that the next President, Franklin Pierce, would continue this expansionary trend.

Did You Know?
The term *filibusters* comes from the Spanish *filibustero*—used to describe sixteenth-century buccaneers who robbed Spanish colonies.

SECTION 3

Global Interests

Setting the Scene

Section Focus
Victory in the Mexican War and the acquisition of Oregon gave the United States vast new territories but also raised new issues. How would the United States connect its Pacific settlements with the East? Would expansion continue southward? Would Manifest Destiny continue to move American interests beyond North America?

Objectives
After studying this section, you should be able to
★ explain the events that brought about the Clayton-Bulwer Treaty.
★ compare the motivations for American interest in Cuba, Central America, China, and Japan in the mid-1800s.

Key Term
extraterritoriality

▲ **CHINESE FAN**

The acquisition of territory from Mexico and the division of Oregon completed United States expansion across the continent. The spirit of Manifest Destiny subsided in the North but not in the South.

■ The Caribbean and Central America

Whether dictated by law or by geography, the portion of the United States open to slavery was far smaller than the area closed to slavery. Many Southerners thought the only way to maintain the sectional balance was to expand southward. In 1848 a writer for *De Bow's Review*, a New Orleans financial journal, declared, "We have New Mexico and California. We *will* have old Mexico and Cuba!"

Cuba

Lying so close to Florida, Cuba offered tempting benefits—rich sugar plantations worked by thousands of enslaved people and a strategic location at the mouth of the Caribbean. So strong was the desire for Cuba among Southerners and some Northern investors that in 1848 the United States offered to buy Cuba from Spain for $100 million. The Spanish foreign minister refused, saying that he would rather see the island sink than sell it.

When negotiations failed, determined expansionists supported armed adventurers called "filibusters," who set off to gain territory that might later be annexed to the United States. One of the best-known filibusters was Narciso López. With the aid of prominent Southerners, López attempted three armed landings in Cuba with small bands of Americans. His goal was to start a revolt

380 UNIT 5 Division and Reunion: 1825–1877

Classroom Resources for SECTION 3

Teacher's Classroom Resources
- Reproducible Lesson Plan
- Reteaching Activity 13-3
- Chapter 13 Enrichment Activity
- Spanish Summaries and Glossary
- Section Quiz

Multimedia
- Section Focus Transparency 45
- Vocabulary Puzzlemaker
- Testmaker
- Student Self-Test Software

against Spanish rule, but he was captured swiftly and executed on his third try in 1851.

Interest in expansion to the south did not die with López, however. Prominent Northern Democrats such as President Franklin Pierce sought southern expansion. He raised America's offering price for Cuba to $130 million. When Spain still refused, Secretary of State William Marcy instructed United States ministers to Spain, Britain, and France to meet and decide how to obtain Cuba. The three diplomats drew up a statement known as the Ostend Manifesto, which declared that if Spain would not sell the island, the United States should take it by force. In part it said:

> After we shall have offered Spain a price for Cuba far beyond its present value, and this shall have been refused, it will then be time to consider the question, does Cuba, in the possession of Spain, seriously endanger our internal peace...? Should this question be answered in the affirmative, then, by every law, human and divine, we shall be justified in wresting it from Spain....

Published in 1854, this infamous document caused such protest that the secretary of state repudiated it, and the effort to buy Cuba was abandoned. Future attempts to expand slave territory were doomed because of Northern opposition.

Desire for a Canal Across Central America

American ambitions turned from expansion to development of the newly acquired territories. Hundreds made the long journey overland across the plains and the Rocky Mountains, but the longest route, by sea around Cape Horn, South America, was the safest. In January 1848, gold was discovered in California at Sutter's mill near Sacramento. Stories of instant riches led to a gold rush from the eastern United States and Europe. Many fortune seekers who took the ocean route saved time by crossing the narrow isthmus at Panama to board one of the few ships that would carry them to California. The gold rush aroused interest in the construction of a canal across Central America to connect the Atlantic and Pacific oceans. In 1846 the United States signed a treaty with

AMERICAN PORTRAITS

Narcisco López 1798?–1851

Narcisco López, a Venezuelan, fought for Spain against Simón Bolívar's South American independence forces, rising to the rank of general in the Spanish Army. Later he took up residence in Cuba, married, and became devoted to the interests of the Cuban people.

In 1848 he planned a revolt against Spanish rule, hoping for help from American supporters and for annexation of the island to the United States. When the revolt failed, he fled to America. López visited New Orleans where, in 1850, he asked for volunteers to join an expedition to win the island from Spain. His force of 600 landed in Cuba but found few Cubans willing to risk revolution. On a later expedition López was captured by the Spanish and executed.

In 1902 an independent Cuba raised its flag—one originally designed by López in red, white, and blue.

CHAPTER 13 Manifest Destiny 1825–1854

 **PERRY IN JAPAN** This work of art painted on three separate panels shows Commodore Perry, accompanied by his color-bearer, delivering gifts to the emperor of Japan. *What favor did Perry seek?*

New Granada (later Colombia) by which it gained the right to preserve "free transit" across the Isthmus of Panama.

The British were also interested in controlling canal routes and in extending their influence along the entire Atlantic coast of Central America. Rival ambitions caused such tension that in 1850 Great Britain sent a special agent, Sir Henry Bulwer, to Washington, D.C., to confer with Secretary of State John M. Clayton. In the resulting Clayton-Bulwer Treaty, the United States and Britain agreed to jointly support the building of a canal through either Nicaragua or Panama. The cost and risks of such a venture delayed action by either country until after 1900.

The Opening of China and Japan

The acquisition of California gave the United States valuable ports from which to launch its Pacific trade. For centuries the prospect of trade with China had stirred people's imaginations because China produced valuable commodities and its potential 300 million customers were the largest untapped market in the world. United States trade with China had grown since the late eighteenth century, but until the 1840s this trade was limited to the port of Canton. As the oldest civilization in the world, the Chinese did not think they had much to gain from the outside world.

Trade with China

A weakened Chinese government could not long resist foreign trade, however. Through most of the early 1800s, British merchants found a way to break China's trade barriers and make enormous profits. In exchange for Chinese tea, silk, and porcelain, the merchants smuggled into China a drug called opium, which they acquired from Turkey and India. In 1839 Chinese forces tried to halt the smuggling. When the British resisted, war broke out. From 1839 to 1842, the British fought the First Opium War with China. When Great Britain won, it acquired the port of Hong Kong and various privileges for its merchants and missionaries.

Among these was the right of **extraterritoriality,** or the right of a foreigner accused of a crime to be tried under his or her own law rather than under Chinese law by Chinese courts. Later the British, aided by other European nations, forced China to grant special privileges to Christian missionaries, to set aside 16 "treaty ports" run by Westerners, and to allow European gunboats to patrol Chinese rivers.

The United States also secured privileges in China. In 1844 President Tyler sent Caleb Cushing, a diplomat, to China with four warships. Cushing persuaded the Chinese to grant generous trade arrangements. Because the United States was not interested in annexing parts of China, the Chinese were friendlier to Americans than to others. By 1850 American clipper ships carried most of the Chinese tea exported to Europe. American missionaries followed the traders; 88 of the 150 Protestant missionaries in China in 1851 were American.

Japan as a Port of Call

American ships sailing to China needed ports to take on fuel and supplies. Japan's location made it ideal for such ports of call. European traders had first come to the island country in the 1500s. Like the Chinese, the Japanese were uninterested in European goods, and they cut off almost all trade with Europe in the early 1600s. At the time, a military leader called a shogun ruled Japan. Although Japan also had an emperor, he held no real power.

Japan, however, had shut itself off from contact with most of the outside world for hundreds of years. The Japanese distrusted foreigners so intensely that sailors from shipwrecked whaling vessels had no guarantee of protection if they washed up on Japanese shores.

Japan did not trade again with the outside world until 1853 when a small United States fleet under Commodore Matthew C. Perry sailed into Tokyo harbor. Perry stayed only 10 days but left a message for the Mikado, or emperor, of Japan from President Millard Fillmore, who wrote:

> *These are the only objects for which I have sent Commodore Perry, with a powerful squadron, to pay a visit to your imperial majesty's renowned city of Yedo: Friendship, commerce, a supply of coal and provisions, and protection for our shipwrecked people. . . .*

Perry returned the next year with more warships, all guns prepared for action. Perry also brought elaborate presents for the ruler of Japan, including a miniature telegraph and steam railroad. By this mixture of courtesy and threat, the Japanese were persuaded to open relations with the rest of the world.

Within five years after Perry's arrival, the shogun signed treaties with several nations, including Britain, Russia, Holland, and France as well as with the United States. Soon, Japanese leaders were convinced that they should adopt the industrial technology of Western nations, and Japan moved quickly to catch up with the West. Within one century Japanese influence rivaled American influence in the Pacific.

Section 3 ★ Review

Checking for Understanding

1. **Identify** Narcisco López, Franklin Pierce, Ostend Manifesto, Clayton-Bulwer Treaty, Matthew Perry.
2. **Define** extraterritoriality.
3. **Explain** how the Ostend Manifesto raised controversy.
4. **List** two reasons the United States government expressed an interest in China and Japan in the mid-1800s.

Critical Thinking

5. **Evaluating Foreign Policy** Evaluate Commodore Perry's strategy in Japan. What was the underlying message of Perry's visit?

CHAPTER 13 Manifest Destiny 1825–1854

CHAPTER 13 SECTION 3

ASSESS

Check Understanding
Assign Section 3 as homework or an in-class activity.

Evaluate
Assign the Section 4 Quiz in the TCR, or use the History of a Free Nation Testmaker to create a customized quiz.

Reteach
Ask each student to write 10 interesting questions on this section's content. Use the questions to play Historical Pursuit.

Have students complete Reteaching Activity 13-3.

Enrich
Have students complete Chapter 13 Enrichment Activity in the Teacher's Classroom Resources.

CLOSE

Summarize the section by asking students how the doctrine of Manifest Destiny led to conflicts with other nations.

Answers to SECTION 3 REVIEW

1. Narcisco López, 380; Franklin Pierce, 381; Ostend Manifesto, 381; Clayton-Bulwer Treaty, 382; Matthew Perry, 383
2. All vocabulary terms are defined in the Glossary.
3. Instead of allowing expansionists to acquire Cuba, it set off public opinion against the expansionist attempt.
4. China was an important market for trade and possessed valuable commodities. Japan was an important location for fuel and supplies for shipping.
5. Perry used the threat of violence to force the opening of Japanese ports. The strategy, though perhaps morally questionable, was effective.

REVIEW CHAPTER 13

Answers

Using Vocabulary
Answers will vary but should reflect an understanding of both terms.

Reviewing Facts
1. Agrarian: the wish to farm western lands. Commercial: use West Coast ports for trade with China.
2. The war was precipitated by border clashes along the southern Texas border, but was the result of Polk's wish to annex California.
3. Battle of the Alamo, capture of Santa Anna by Houston
4. Armed invasions failed; Spain would not sell; the Ostend Manifesto turned public opinion against the acquisition.
5. British victory in First Opium War weakened Chinese government; implied threat of force by Matthew Perry.

Understanding Concepts
1. Answers will vary. One could argue that, geographically, the Pacific Ocean is the "natural" western boundary of the United States. This thinking was part of the Manifest Destiny movement.
2. Answers will vary. The migration westward is part of Americans' fondness for the frontier spirit. The trip to Oregon required courage, nerve, and skill—traits many associate with American spirit.

CHAPTER 13 ★ REVIEW

Using Vocabulary

Imagine that you are an American diplomat in the 1840s. You have been assigned to negotiate trade agreements with the leaders of China and Japan. Explain the challenges and duties of your job, using the terms *consul* and *extraterritoriality*.

Reviewing Facts

1. **Specify** both agrarian and commercial reasons that promoted Manifest Destiny.
2. **Explain** the reasons for the war between the United States and Mexico.
3. **Name** two important events in the Texas independence movement.
4. **Summarize** why the United States was not able to acquire Cuba.
5. **Cite** two reasons why the nations of China and Japan were forced to initiate trade with Western countries.

Understanding Concepts

Expansion
1. Geography often plays a role in defining the borders of a nation. Explain the role of geography in supporting the belief that it was "natural" for the United States to expand to the Pacific Ocean.

Migration
2. The westward migration of pioneers in Conestoga wagons is a cherished part of American folklore. What factors made this migration such an adventure? Why do you think Americans continue to be fascinated by stories about these travels?

Critical Thinking

1. **Assessing Causes** Was war with Mexico inevitable? Explain the causes that made negotiations between the United States and Mexico nearly impossible, including the Mexican viewpoint.
2. **Analyzing Fine Art** Study the painting on this page entitled *October, 1867* by John Whetton Ehninger and answer the questions that follow.
   a. What does the painting tell you about these individuals and their time?
   b. What is your emotional reaction to the painting?

Writing About History
Definition

Write four separate definitions of the concept of Manifest Destiny as each of these four people might have defined it: James K. Polk, Santa Anna, a Native American of the plains, and a mountain man.

Cooperative Learning

Was President Polk a shrewd and visionary leader who expanded the power and borders of the United States, or was he a bully who took what he wanted

▲ *OCTOBER, 1867* BY JOHN WHETTON EHNINGER

UNIT 5 Division and Reunion: 1825–1877

Critical Thinking
1. Answers will vary. Tensions over California and Texas made conflict almost inevitable. Mexicans were aware that the United States failed to take over Canada in 1812.
2. a. Answers will vary, but may include they were self-sufficient and met the challenge of the land. b. Answers will vary, but may include respect for their hard work and cooperative spirit.

CHAPTER 13 ★ REVIEW

without regard for other people's rights? You and a partner will evaluate Polk's presidency to answer this question. One of you will be a Polk supporter and the other an opponent. First, work together to compile a list of Polk's achievements. Then work separately and write an evaluation of each action according to your role of supporter or opponent. When you have finished writing, exchange and discuss each other's evaluations. Then present your findings to the class.

Social Studies Skills

Preparing Notecards for a Research Report

An important step to writing a research paper is preparing notecards from your research before writing your first draft. The following guidelines will help you prepare notecards with the critical information you will need to write your report well. Included is an example of what might appear on your notecard if your topic is "Pioneer Life."

Practicing the Skill

- On the first card, write the name of the author of the resource, the title, location, publisher, copyright date, and page number, according to the bibliographic style approved by your teacher. Later, you will use this same card when preparing your bibliography.

- Start the next card with the author's last name (and first name, if more than one author has the same last name). Include the title, too, if you are using more than one resource from this author. Also include the page number.

- Underneath the author's name and page number, take notes of one main idea only. Start by writing a sentence that summarizes the main idea—a generalization. Then list supporting statements.

- After you have taken notes from all your resources using a separate card for each main idea, sort through your cards, placing them in the order you will use to address the main ideas as you write. Now you are ready to write a rough draft of your report.

For further practice, research and prepare notecards for a report on the history of one of the Western states.

Weaver, page 439
Main Idea: The pioneers could not buy soap, so they had to make their own.
Supporting Statements:
1. The pioneers saved wood ashes in a barrel and fats and grease from cooking and butchering.
2. In the spring the pioneers poured water over the ashes in the barrel and allowed it to trickle out through a hole near the bottom.
3. This brown liquid called lye was collected and boiled in a kettle with fats and grease until it thickened to form a soft, jellylike, yellow soap.

Weaver, Robert B. "Pioneer Life." *World Book Encyclopedia*. Vol. 14. Chicago: Field Enterprises, 1991, pages 428–442.

Using Your Journal
Group and summarize the reasons for expansion in a paragraph explaining Manifest Destiny.

CHAPTER 13 Manifest Destiny 1825–1854 — 385

REVIEW CHAPTER 13

Using Your Journal
The reasons for expansionism that students present may vary; the following may be among them: room for growing population; land for increased agriculture; protection against the possibility of powerful neighbors; extension of slavery to new areas; source of raw materials.

Practicing the Skill
Answers will vary. Remind students to take complete notes on bibliographical information so that they will not have to go back a second time to sources in order to obtain missing information such as copyright dates.

 **Chapter Bonus Test Question**
This question may be used for extra credit on the chapter test. Which of the following Americans contributed the most to fulfilling the nation's dreams of "Manifest Destiny"? Give at least one reason for your answer. (Answers will vary but should be supported with at least one fact.)
Winfield Scott
Zachary Taylor
John C. Frémont

385

PLANNING GUIDE — Chapter 14 Compromise and Conflict

Daily Lesson Objectives	Teacher Classroom Resources	Multimedia
SECTION 1 **A Union in Danger** 1 Day pp. 388–394 1. Evaluate the impact of the issue of slavery on the 1848 presidential election. 2. Explain why California's application for admission to the United incited heated debates on the question of slavery and how the Compromise of 1850 temporarily reunited the nation. 3. Explain how inventions and increased immigration affected the economic growth of the United States.	Chapter 14 Study Guide Reproducible Lesson Plan Reteaching Activity 14-1 Section Quiz Chapter 14 Cooperative Learning Activity Chapter 14 Concept Mapping Activity Reinforcing Social Studies Skills 32, 35, 53 Map and Graph Skill Activity 18 Chapter 14 Primary and Secondary Source Readings Writer's Guidebook Lesson 8–14	Student Self-Test Software Testmaker Section Focus Transparency 42 Chapter 14 Skills Transparency Chapter 14 Map Transparencies U.S. History Diagraph 2 The American People: Fabric of a Nation
SECTION 2 **Dispute Over Slavery** 1 Day pp. 396–400 1. Discuss how the majority of southerners viewed and defended the institution of slavery. 2. Explain the significance of the Kansas-Nebraska Act. 3. Examine the reactions of both the North and the South to the Supreme Court's *Dred Scott* decision.	Reproducible Lesson Plan Reteaching Activity 14-2 Section Quiz Reinforcing Social Studies Skills 25, 27, 32, 40 American Portrait 28 American Literary Heritage, Unit 5 Writer's Guidebook Lesson 6	Student Self-Test Software Testmaker Section Focus Transparency 43 Chapter 14 Map Transparencies The American People: Fabric of a Nation
SECTION 3 **Drifting Toward War** 1 Day pp. 402–405 1. Evaluate the importance of the Lincoln-Douglas debates. 2. Identify the purpose of John Brown's raid at Harpers Ferry and reactions to it. 3. List the political events that led to the secession of seven southern states.	Reproducible Lesson Plan Reteaching Activity 14-3 Section Quiz Chapter 14 Enrichment Activity Chapter 14 Primary and Secondary Source Readings American Portrait 27 American Literary Heritage Unit 5 Writer's Guidebook Lesson 6 SAT Practice Tests Spanish Summaries & Glossary	Student Self-Test Software Testmaker Section Focus Transparency 44 Chapter 14 Map Transparencies Vocabulary Puzzlemaker Audiocassette, Chapter 14 The Presidents: A Picture History of Our Nation
CHAPTER REVIEW AND EVALUATION 1 Day	Chapter 14 Test Chapter 14 Performance Assessment Activity	Student Self-Test Software Testmaker

OUT OF TIME? If time does not permit teaching the entire chapter, use the Chapter 14 Summary on pages 462–463 and the Chapter 14 audiocassette (English and Spanish) to point out the main ideas of the chapter.

PLANNING GUIDE

Cultural Diversity Activity

Interpreting Graphs The rise of the "Know Nothings" in 1849 is an early example of the anti-immigrant attitude known as *nativism*. Nativists were people who wanted to preserve the United States for white, native-born Protestants. Know Nothings were anti-Catholic and anti-foreign. Nativist sentiment often arises in periods of economic depression. It may reflect concern that immigrant workers will take jobs from native-born workers or work at lower pay. It also reflects fear or intolerance of languages and customs different from one's own.

Have students look at the graph on page 392 (Immigration 1820–1860) and suggest reasons for the rise of nativism in the 1840s. Against which ethnic groups might it have been directed? How are nativism and racism similar? Does nativist sentiment exist today? If so, against which groups is it directed?

Performance Assessment Activity

Political Highlights Assign students to one of three groups representing section divisions in the United States and its territories between 1848 and 1860: the North, the South, and the West. Ask each group to develop ten cleverly worded and easy-to-remember slogans that encapsulate its section's political beliefs and goals on separate sheets of paper. Draw the slogans randomly from a box and ask the class to identify the region it represents.

POSSIBLE RUBRIC FEATURES: Content information, summary skills, creativity, clarity, written communication skills, cooperative learning skills.

Chapter Resources

Literature from the Period

Douglass, Frederick. *Narrative of the Life of Frederick Douglass: An American Slave.* 1845.

Pennington, James, W.C. "Escape: A Slave Narrative." 1850.

Stowe, Harriet Beecher. *Uncle Tom's Cabin.* 1852.

Truth, Sojourner. "Ain't I a Woman?" 1851.

Readings for the Student

Carlson, Judy. *Harriet Tubman: Call to Freedom.* Fawcett, 1989.

Levine, I.E. *The Many Faces of Slavery.* Messner, 1975.

Oates, Stephen B. "God's Angry Man." *American History Illustrated,* Vol. 20, No. 9, January 1986.

Readings for the Teacher

Genovese, Eugene D. *Roll, Jordan, Roll: The World the Slaves Made.* Vintage Books, 1974.

Smith, H. Shelton. *In His Image, But . . .: Racism in Southern Religion, 1780–1910.* Duke University Press, 1972.

Stampp, Kenneth M. *America in 1857: A Nation on the Brink.* Oxford University Press, 1990.

Multimedia Resources

Half Slave, Half Free. Sony (VHS, 113 minutes)

The Time Tunnel: American History Series I. Focus Media. (Apple or IBM diskette, backup, guide)

Key to Ability Levels

Teaching strategies have been coded for varying learning styles and abilities.

- **L1** Basic activities for all students
- **L2** Average activities for average to above-average students
- **L3** Challenging activities for above-average students
- **LEP** Limited English Proficiency activities

Glencoe Links to the Humanities

Links to Literature

- Macmillan Literature: Understanding Literature Audiotapes Sides 3, 4
- Macmillan Literature: Appreciating Literature Audiotapes Side 3
- Macmillan Literature: American Literature Audiotapes Sides 2, 3
- Macmillan Literature: American Literature Video—*The Adventures of Huckleberry Finn*
- Macmillan Literature: Novel Guide—*Island of the Blue Dolphins*
- Macmillan Literature: American Literature Text—John Greenleaf Whittier

Link to Music

♪ American Music: Cultural Traditions

CHAPTER 14

BEGINNING THE CHAPTER

Give students the following information. The total population of the United States increased during the 1850s by 8 million, growing from 23 to 31 million. With railroads solving the transportation problems in the Midwest, its population grew rapidly, and people began moving from the Midwest to the West. Ask students to speculate on what effect this westward expansion would have on the possible extension of slavery to the territories.

Recording Journal Notes
Tell students to read the chapter and record events that contributed to the Union's division. Upon completing the chapter, ask them to rank in importance the events leading to war.

In 1850 the United States was not a nation as we know it today. Tensions between the states divided the nation into three separate regions. Fierce differences of opinion, geographic diversity, economic inequalities, and slavery contributed to this sectionalism.

CHAPTER 14

Compromise and Conflict
1848–1861

Setting the Scene

▶ LINCOLN CAMPAIGN TORCH

Focus
Even though the nation as a whole was prosperous, deep political and social divisions could no longer be ignored. By the late 1840s, Southerners were defending slavery as a "positive good," while antislavery feelings in the North and West intensified. Political compromise worked in 1850, but by 1860 compromise was no longer possible. The election of Lincoln convinced Southerners that slavery would not be protected within the Union. Secession, they felt, was the only option left.

Concepts to Understand
★ How economic diversity led to differing views on slavery
★ How political conflict over slavery and the nature of the Union led to secession

Read to Discover . . .
★ the major differences between the North and the South.
★ the events that led seven Southern states to secede from the Union.

Journal Notes
What contributed to division of the Union? As you read the chapter, record the events, decisions, acts, and other activities that answer the question.

CULTURAL
- 1846 Elias Howe patents sewing machine
- 1851 Herman Melville publishes *Moby Dick*

1845 — **1850**

POLITICAL
- 1848 First presidential election to be held on the same day in all states
- 1850 Compromise of 1850 passed

UNIT 5 Division and Reunion: 1825–1877

✚ EXTRA CREDIT PROJECT

The lives of John C. Calhoun and John Brown were over before the Civil War began. Yet both helped shape forces that eventually led to war. Ask interested students to research the life of either man, investigating in particular activities that made that individual a hero or a villain to some Americans. Have students present their findings to the class in the form of a wanted or hero poster. Ask them to discuss their research as they explain the posters to the class.

View of Harpers Ferry
by Ferdinand Richardt, 1858

Danish artist Ferdinand Richardt captured a serene view of Harpers Ferry, Virginia—the location of the armory targeted for assault by abolitionist John Brown in 1859.

◀ DIARIST MARY CHESNUT OF SOUTH CAROLINA

- **1857** National Teacher's Association organized
- **1854** Kansas-Nebraska Act passed
- **1857** Supreme Court rules Missouri Compromise unconstitutional

1855

- **1860** Repeating rifle introduced
- **1860** South Carolina secedes from the Union

1860

CHAPTER 14 Compromise and Conflict 1848–1861

CHAPTER 14 CONCEPTS

Concept Mapping Activity

Write the chapter concepts on the chalkboard. Ask students to write these concepts in their notebooks and to list each major event in the chapter under the appropriate concept.

> Growing Sectional tensions lead to differences that cannot be resolved by compromise.

- Economic Diversity
- Political Conflict

History AND ART

In 1859 Harpers Ferry was a town of about 2,000 people. Located on Virginia's northern border with Maryland, the town was bounded on the south by the Shenandoah River and on the north by the Potomac.

 VIDEODISC

- *GTV: A Geographic Perspective on American History*

Side 2, Chapter 13
Title: *One Nation, Still?*
Subject: Regional differences deepen

See GTV Guide page 46 for complete lesson plan.

Teacher Notes

LESSON PLAN
SECTION 1, 388–395

FOCUS

Bellringer
Before taking roll at the beginning of the class period, display Focus Activity Transparency 46 on the overhead projector, and assign the accompanying Focus Activity Sheet.

Objectives
Point out the objectives on this page to students in previewing the section content.

Motivating Activity
Present the following: Town Meeting to Be Held!

All citizens are invited to attend a meeting this Sunday to discuss our urgent need for a state constitution to support California's admission as a free state.

Ask: What reasons would you have for voting for or against slavery?

Use Skills Transparency 14.

VIDEODISC
- *GTV: A Geographic Perspective on American History*

Side 2, Chapter 15
Title: *The Gathering Storm*
Subject: Conflict and compromise before the Civil War

See GTV Guide page 47 for complete lesson plan.

SECTION 1

A Union in Danger

Setting the Scene

Section Focus
The acquisition of New Mexico and California brought into the open the slavery issue. It became clear that some decision had to be made regarding the legality of slavery in these new areas. During this period there was remarkable national prosperity. Every major economic interest—cotton planting, wheat farming, manufacturing, and transportation—was booming. The huge gold strike in California paid for imports; the flood of gold expanded United States currency. Also, increasing numbers of immigrants began arriving.

Objectives
After studying this section, you should be able to
★ evaluate the impact of the issue of slavery on the 1848 presidential election.
★ explain why California's application for admission to the Union incited heated debates on the question of slavery and how the Compromise of 1850 temporarily reunited the nation.
★ explain how inventions and increased immigration affected the economic growth of the United States.

Key Term
popular sovereignty

◀ KEG USED ON THE ERIE CANAL

Even before the war with Mexico had ended, growing antislavery sentiment in the North led the House of Representatives, with its Northern majority, to pass the Wilmot Proviso. This bill provided that all territory acquired from Mexico should be closed to slavery.

The Wilmot Proviso was defeated in the Senate, where the North and South were equally represented. Many Southern senators argued that Congress had no constitutional power to forbid slavery in the territories. If the representatives did outlaw slavery there, they would be denying slaveholders their rights as citizens.

■ The Election of 1848
There seemed to be no way of reconciling these opposing views on the issue of slavery in the new territories. When the Polk administration ended in 1849, no steps had been taken to provide for civil government in New Mexico and California.

Democrats and Whigs
In the presidential election of 1848, both Northerners and Southerners took precautions to play down discussion of slavery. The Democrats, although controlled by their

UNIT 5 Division and Reunion: 1825–1877

Classroom Resources for SECTION 1

Teacher's Classroom Resources
- Chapter 14 Study Guide
- Reproducible Lesson Plan
- Reteaching Activity 14-1
- Chapter 14 Cooperative Learning Activity
- Chapter 14 Primary and Secondary Source Readings
- Section Quiz

Multimedia
- Section Focus Transparency 46
- Chapter 14 Skills Transparency
- Chapter 14 Map Transparency
- Testmaker
- Student Self-Test Software
- The American People: Fabric of a Nation
- A Geographic Perspective on American History

Southern wing, nominated a Northern senator, Lewis Cass of Michigan. Cass supported a compromise solution known as **popular sovereignty,** whereby voters within the territories would decide whether slavery would be permitted inside their borders. The Whigs, whose principal stronghold was in the North, nominated Zachary Taylor from Louisiana, a slaveholder himself. The Whig platform avoided the issue of slavery by focusing on Taylor's military accomplishments in the Mexican War.

The Free-Soil Party

Efforts to keep slavery out of the campaign failed, however. A third party emerged when a group of antislavery Northern Democrats and "conscience Whigs" united with the former Liberty party to form the Free-Soil party. This party, whose motto was "Free soil, free speech, free labor, and free men," nominated former President Martin Van Buren. Although the Free-Soil party gained no electoral votes, it received more popular votes than the Democrats had in New York, Vermont, and Massachusetts. In New York the Free-Soilers received enough Democratic votes to deprive Cass of that state's 36 electoral votes, which gave the election to Taylor with 163 electoral votes—exactly 36 more than Cass had.

■ The California Question

The issue of slavery in the new territories intensified after gold was discovered in California in 1848. By the end of 1849, an estimated 95,000 "forty-niners" from all over the world had settled in northern California.

Application for Statehood

With this tremendous growth in population came an urgent need for government. Crime and violence had become common in mining camps and towns, and military authorities could not control it. At the suggestion of President Taylor, a convention met in Monterey, California, in the fall of 1849 and adopted a constitution that, in part, provided a structure for the new government and outlined state boundaries. It also prohibited slavery. The newly created government immediately applied for admission to the Union as a free state in which slavery was forbidden. California's application for statehood touched off a long and bitter debate. Admission of California would tip the balance of power in the Senate in favor of the free states, already in the majority in the House. If California were admitted as a free state, Southern leaders warned, their states would leave the Union.

Compromise of 1850

To deal with this alarming situation, Henry Clay, who had been in retirement since his defeat in the presidential election of 1844, successfully ran for reelection as senator. The Whig senator from Kentucky, a master of negotiation, proceeded to arrange his last great intersectional compromise.

▲ **TOWARD COMPROMISE** The intense debate in the Senate sparked by the California question led to yet another important political compromise. *Who arranged this last great intersectional agreement?*

CHAPTER 14 Compromise and Conflict 1848–1861

CHAPTER 14 SECTION 1

Independent Practice

Social History Have students write an essay describing pre–Civil War conditions for incoming immigrants who came through Boston or New York. The essay could be written as a diary entry of a British, Irish, or German immigrant. **L3**

Teaching Life of the Times

Many of the gold miners came from Asia. Chinese miners called California the "Golden Mountain."

Did You Know?

The debates over Clay's proposals were so important that the dying Senator Calhoun insisted on attending so he could protect Southern rights. He was so weak that a friend read his speech for him. Daniel Webster urged compromise in an emotional speech in which he spoke "not as a Massachusetts man, nor as a northern man, but as an American."

Life of the Times

Forty-Niners

Skeletons of horses and oxen marked the toll of death from exhaustion or starvation. The hardships, according to John Lloyd Stephens who described his own struggle, ". . . are beyond conception. Care and suspense, pained anxiety, fear of losing animals and leaving one to foot it and pack his 'duds' on his back, begging provisions, fear of being left in the mountains to starve and freeze to death . . . are things of which I may write and you may read, but they are nothing to the reality."

President Polk referred to the rich gold discovery in California in his annual message to Congress in December 1848. The secret was out. Within a year the gold fever attracted some 95,000 people to California. The three principal routes were across the Isthmus of Panama, around Cape Horn, or overland. Half of the forty-niners crossed the plains and mountains. Along the California Trail inexperienced travelers died by the hundreds. Those who survived the trail found life in California nearly as demanding.

▶ **TRAVELING WEST**

Clay's compromise was a series of measures intended to satisfy Northern and Southern demands. The principal provisions favoring the North were that California be admitted as a free state and that the slave trade—but not slavery—be forbidden in the District of Columbia. The South, in turn, would gain a stronger Fugitive Slave Law, designed to suppress the Underground Railroad. In addition, the Mexico Cession, gained at the end of the Mexican War, would be divided into two territories, Utah and New Mexico, with the question of slavery to be decided by popular sovereignty when the territories were organized with territorial legislatures.

At first, Clay's proposals failed to receive sufficient support to pass. President Taylor opposed Clay and offered proposals of his own. However, Taylor died suddenly in the summer of 1850. His successor, Vice President Millard Fillmore, favored the compromise. The young Illinois senator Stephen A. Douglas, a Democrat, skillfully put through the compromise as five separate bills, which Fillmore duly signed. The Compromise of 1850 averted immediate disaster but, unhappily, turned out to be just a temporary truce.

■ Inventions and Industry

During the 20 years from 1840 to 1860, rapid growth became the dominant characteristic of the nation's economy. Among the reasons for this growth were new inventions, sufficient capital with which to build new factories, a class of businesspeople willing to start new enterprises, an increase in agricultural productivity, a growing labor supply, and a transportation system that connected farms to factories.

In 1850 two-thirds of the nation's people were engaged in agriculture. Industry was growing, though, partly because of a flood

---

Cooperative Learning

To discuss the doctrine of popular sovereignty, divide students into groups of three or four. Have each group explain why Northern Democrats left their party in 1848 and joined the Free-Soil party. Students should note events leading up to the split in the party. Have each group conclude by preparing a statement explaining how popular sovereignty affected the election. Have them share their statements with the class. Then discuss their conclusions. For accountability, number the members of each group, and call upon students at random. **L1, L2**

of new inventions. By 1861 the telegraph had made possible rapid communication throughout the continent and across the Atlantic. The rotary press allowed newspapers to publish far larger editions than ever before. Some inventions, however, had their greatest impact on Northern industries. For example, the sewing machine, invented by Elias Howe in 1846, revolutionized shirt-making by reducing the time it took to make one shirt from more than 14 hours to little more than an hour; when the technique was adapted for shoemaking, it made possible the mass production of shoes. Charles Goodyear's invention of vulcanized rubber in 1839 was widely used in industry and in the manufacture of waterproof garments.

Textile factories, powered by more efficient steam engines, increased in size as several operations were combined under a single roof. The techniques invented by Eli Whitney and Simeon North for making interchangeable parts and breaking down manufacturing into simple operations now found applications in the mass production of clocks, watches, farm machinery, and sewing machines.

■ Developments in Agriculture

Inventions, innovations, and government policies allowed agricultural productivity to keep pace with the nation's fast-growing industries.

The Middle West, with its fertile plains, attracted farmers from the rocky and hilly lands of the Northeast as well as immigrants from Europe. Public lands could be purchased for as little as 25 cents an acre, and the Pre-emption Act of 1841 allowed squatters the opportunity to buy their land before someone else did.

The first great need was for plows that could cut through tree roots in recently cleared forest land and turn the tough sod of the prairies. In 1825 Jethro Wood began the

 ▲ **COMMUNICATIONS AND TRANSPORTATION** Westward expansion during the years 1820 through 1860 created an urgent need for better connections between locations. A canal boom was ushered in with the completion of the Erie Canal. *What innovations helped improve communications?*

CHAPTER 14
SECTION 1

Most of the immigrants who arrived in the United States before 1860 came from western and northern Europe, particularly Germany and Ireland. By the 1890s, however, most of the millions of immigrants were from eastern and southern Europe, notably Russia and Italy. By the 1990s most immigrants were from Latin America and Asia. Regardless of the country of origin, reasons for coming to the United States remained much the same, political freedom and economic opportunity.

Did You Know?

The first Pony Express between Sacramento, California, and St. Joseph, Missouri, began April 1860 and ended 18 months later when the first transcontinental telegraph line was completed.

Visualizing History It cost New York State $7 million to build the 363-mile-long Erie Canal.
Answer to Caption: steamboats, telegraph, canals, railroads

Sidelights: Labor Unions

Between 1840 and 1860, various groups tried unsuccessfully to organize labor unions. Government workers started a movement for an eight-hour working day. New England shoe workers held a successful strike for higher wages, but the first to formally organize was the National Union of Iron Molders, formed in 1859. In 1863 the locomotive engineers formed the first of the four big railroad unions, the Locomotive Engineers Union. During the Civil War, low wages paid by employing women, children, and immigrants caused labor union activity to increase.

CHAPTER 14 SECTION 1

- GTV: *The American People: Fabric of a Nation*

Side 2, Chapter 3
Title: *At Home in America*
Subject: The immigrant experiences of the Irish

See GTV Guide page 62 for complete lesson plan.

Using Graphs
Answer: 1851 and 1854

Skills Practice
For which group did immigration peak between 1820 and 1860? (the Irish)

Did You Know?
A 21-year-old German immigrant arrived in San Francisco in 1850 to sell dry goods to gold-rush miners. He saw the need for durable trousers. At first Levi Strauss made trousers out of tent canvas. Then he tried brown denim. Later he used blue denim with copper rivets to strengthen the pockets. The trousers became one of the nation's most famous products—known as dungarees, levis, or blue jeans.

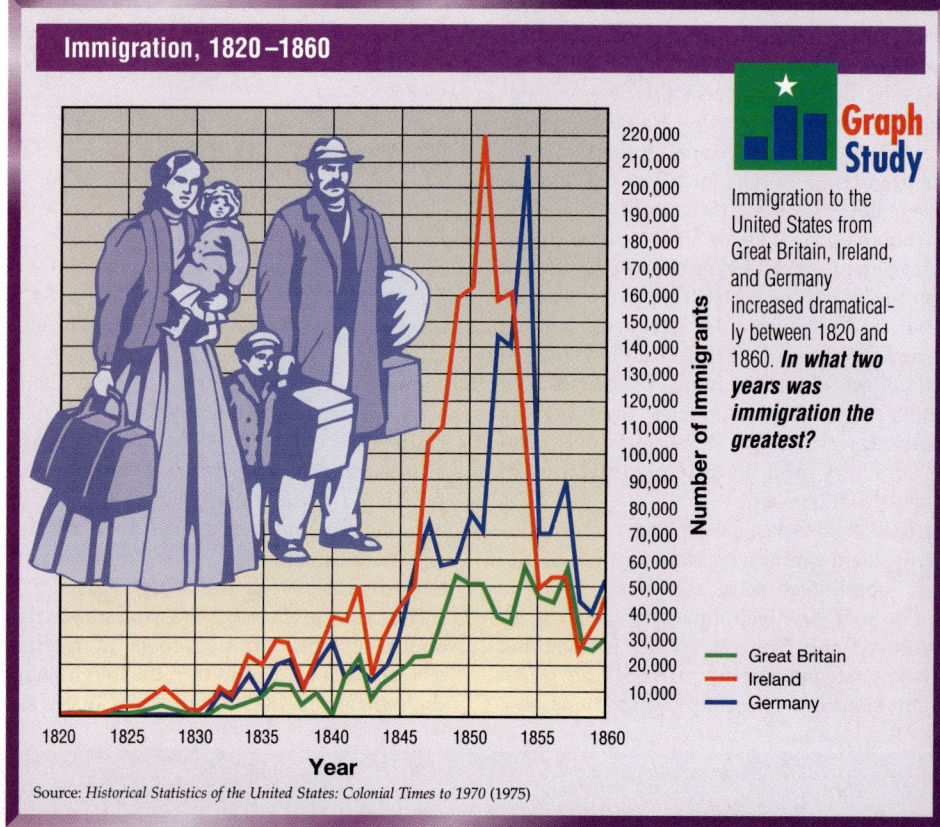

Graph Study
Immigration to the United States from Great Britain, Ireland, and Germany increased dramatically between 1820 and 1860. *In what two years was immigration the greatest?*

manufacture of an iron plow with replaceable parts. John Deere of Moline, Illinois, soon developed a much-improved version made of steel instead of iron; by 1850 the Deere factories were turning out as many as 10,000 plows per year. The new plows enabled farmers to plant more land than they could harvest. To solve this problem, Cyrus McCormick, a Virginia blacksmith, took out a patent in 1834 on a mechanical "reaper," or grain harvester. By 1860 more than 100,000 of McCormick's reapers were in use. These inventions were accompanied by still others: a mechanical drill to plant grain, the threshing machine, and the horse-drawn hay rake.

Although the West benefited more from these inventions than did the South, which still depended on slave labor, the Southern economy also improved. Increased demand for raw cotton by an efficient British textile industry brought prosperity to the Deep South. In the 1850s, cotton production broke all previous records. By 1860 seven-eighths of the world's supply of cotton came from the United States, and raw cotton comprised three-fifths of the nation's exports.

■ Increased Immigration Fuels Factories

A necessity for sustained industrial growth is a sizable labor supply. Until about 1800, immigrants came to the United States at a rate of about 8,000 per year.

Coming to America
During the second quarter of the nineteenth century, however, a great migration from Europe to America began. Between 1840 and 1860, an average of more than

UNIT 5 Division and Reunion: 1825–1877

Cooperative Learning
Divide students into groups of three to research pre–Civil War topics of interest. Groups may choose to study architecture, literature, music, art, industry, religion, fashion, immigration, politics, or communications. Appoint a group leader to report the progress of the group. Have each group present their research to the class. Before their presentation the group should prepare a handout for the class listing five key points. **L2**

200,000 immigrants reached American shores every year. The reasons for this were both political and economic. Thousands of immigrants made the often perilous voyage to escape poverty.

Many English craftworkers, made jobless by the Industrial Revolution, sailed to America. The Scandinavians and the Dutch, whose native soil could not support rapidly growing populations, also came. So did the Irish, after a failure of their potato crop resulted in economic hardship and the starvation of thousands. Others, like the Germans, came to avoid political persecution. By 1860 one out of every eight Americans was foreign-born.

Hardships and Resentment

The move to America was difficult and dangerous. Immigrants, packed into overcrowded ships, often faced terrible conditions. Many times they suffered from malnutrition and disease, which resulted in the death of an estimated 10 percent of the passengers. Unfortunately, the problems of the immigrants continued even after they had found jobs and places to live—immigrants were forced to confront the bigotry of some established Americans who resented their different languages, religions, and customs.

Such resentment, along with the fear that immigrants would bring new and radical political ideas into the United States, led to the formation of secret societies. One of these was a nationwide secret political society called The Order of the Star-Spangled Banner, founded in 1849. Nicknamed "Know-Nothings" because members replied "I know nothing" when asked about their organization, they tried to keep recent immigrants from political office. They also demanded that immigration be restricted and that the naturalization period be extended to 21 years.

In spite of such hardships and prejudice, immigrants continued to flock to the United States. Although some migrated West to its rich farmlands, many immigrants remained in the North, often in such port cities as New York and Boston, where their ships had docked. One reason for this was that they had little money to continue their journeys. Also, the South already had a source of cheap labor—enslaved African Americans. The result was that immigrants supplied the North's growing industries with a steady stream of low-paid workers.

■ Transportation Ties North and West

With rapidly expanding markets came great advances in transportation. In the 1850s the United States built the largest merchant marine fleet in the world, inland navigation reached its peak, and railroad track mileage was increased.

▲ "Know-Nothing" song sheet cover

CHAPTER 14 SECTION 1

In the early 1800s, inland waterways carried most freight and passengers. By the 1850s the nation had built 4,500 miles (7,240 km) of canals. The growth of the railroads caused a sudden decline in the use of inland waterways. Today inland waterways are a major mode of freight transportation along with railroads, pipelines, trucks, and airways.

Did You Know?

During the 1850s New Orleans and New York City tied for first place in *exports* among major U.S. ports. However, 70 percent of all imports entered the United States through New York City.

Fact or Fiction?

Nathaniel Hawthorne's *The Scarlet Letter* and *The House of the Seven Gables* and Herman Melville's *Moby-Dick* were best-selling books in the early 1850s.

FICTION: Although published in the early 1850s, they did not gain popularity until years later, when they were republished as cheap reprints.

Critical Thinking

Summarize Tell students that many historians link the growth of slavery in the South to Eli Whitney's invention of the cotton gin. Have students work in small groups to analyze the economic factors that would have made this possible. Have them discuss how the cotton gin stimulated the South's economy and indirectly contributed to the institution of slavery. Ask groups to summarize their ideas in short statements and present them to the class. Discuss students' answers. **L1**

CHAPTER 14 SECTION 1

ASSESS

Check Understanding
Assign Section 1 Review as homework or an in-class activity.

Evaluate
Assign the Section 1 Quiz in the TCR, or use the History of a Free Nation Testmaker to create a customized quiz.

Reteach
On the chalkboard write the six factors that spurred economic growth. (Inventions, Available Capital, Entrepreneurs, Increased Agricultural Production, Transportation Advances, Growing Labor Supply) Discuss how each contributed to growth.

Have students complete Reteaching Activity 14-1.

Enrich
Ask students to research secret societies such as The Order of the Star-Spangled Banner, mentioned on page 393.

CLOSE
In 1850 Daniel Webster told the U.S. Senate: "I can now sleep of nights. We have gone through the most important crisis that has occurred since the founding of the government, and whatever party may prevail, hereafter the Union stands firm." Ask: Do you think Webster's prediction was realistic for the time?

Clipper Ships

In 1849 Great Britain repealed the Navigation Laws that had given special protection to British ships trading within its empire. The United States, however, continued to allow only its own ships to carry cargo between American ports. These advantages helped United States ships increase their total tonnage from 943,000 tons in 1846 to 2,226,000 tons in 1857.

The greatest triumph at sea for the United States was the clipper ship, which made its mark between 1845 and 1860. Characterized by very sharp bows, an immense spread of sail, and masts 200 feet high, clippers soon became the fastest oceangoing sailing vessels ever built. The clipper *Lightning* once logged over 500 miles in a 24-hour period.

Inland Waterways

During this decade inland navigation also reached its peak. The Erie Canal carried so much traffic that it had to be widened and deepened. The Great Lakes gained such importance as a water route that 6,000 ships sailed from Chicago in a single year. This was also the great period of steamboats on the Mississippi River. Mark Twain's *Life on the Mississippi* and *Huckleberry Finn* bear witness to the importance of the great river as a route for trade and commerce.

The days of great river traffic were numbered, however. As inventor Oliver Evans predicted in 1813:

> " *The time will come when people will travel in stages moved by steam engines, from one city to another, almost as fast as birds fly, fifteen or twenty miles an hour.* "

Railroads

Railroads were able to reach places that riverboats could not. By 1860 railroads tied the agricultural areas of the Northwest to the cities and ports of the Northeast. The first successful use of the steam locomotive in the United States occurred on the Charleston and Hamburg railroad line in South Carolina in 1831. Other lines began operation almost simultaneously.

Early railroads, however, were extremely expensive to build and maintain. Whereas state governments had funded the building of canals, private enterprise provided the money for the railroads. The new railroads cost what were then colossal sums. The Erie Railroad cost about $23 million to build, half as much as the United States paid for New Mexico and California.

By 1850 an era of great expansion began. By this time 9,000 miles of track had been laid; 10 years later the number of miles had increased to over 30,000, and railroads connecting the Atlantic seaboard to the Mississippi River crisscrossed the East. What continued to set the South apart from the North, however, was its "peculiar institution," slavery.

Section 1 ★ Review

Checking for Understanding
1. **Identify** Wilmot Proviso, Lewis Cass, Zachary Taylor, Free-Soil party, Stephen A. Douglas, Compromise of 1850, Elias Howe, John Deere, Cyrus McCormick, "Know-Nothings," clipper ship.
2. **Define** popular sovereignty.
3. **List** four provisions of the Compromise of 1850.
4. **Identify** two differences between the economic systems of the North and the South.

Critical Thinking
5. **Evaluating Policies** Explain why acceptance of the idea of popular sovereignty would have been unacceptable to abolitionists.

Answers to SECTION 1 REVIEW

1. Proviso, 388; Cass, 389; Taylor, 389; Free-Soil party, 389; Douglas, 390; Compromise of 1850, 390; Howe, 391; Deere, 392; McCormick, 392; "Know-Nothings," 393; clipper ship, 394
2. All vocabulary terms are defined in the Glossary.
3. admitted California as free state, forbade slave trade (but not slavery) in District of Columbia, stricter Fugitive Slave Law, Mexico Cession divided into two territories
4. North was industrial, used immigrant labor. South was agricultural, used slave labor.
5. Answers may vary. Abolitionists demanded immediate emancipation of all enslaved people. Popular sovereignty might force abolitionists to become more militant.

CONNECTIONS — History AND TECHNOLOGY — CONNECTIONS

Industrial Innovation

"What is the North," asked a Southerner in the 1850s, "but a conglomeration of greasy mechanics, filthy operatives, small-fisted farmers, and moonstruck theorists?" Southerners may have looked scornfully at manufacturing in the North, but Europeans were fascinated by "Yankee Notions" like machine-made clocks and buckets, canned food, and handguns with revolving chambers. These products were the result of Yankee ingenuity and the machine-tool industry, which mass-produced interchangeable parts.

▲ CRYSTAL PALACE, INDUSTRIAL EXHIBITION IN LONDON, 1851

The British called this industry "the American system of manufacturing," but "the Northeastern American system" would have been more accurate. More than half of America's 140,000 factories were concentrated between New York and Massachusetts, and they were the country's largest and most productive. The South had 20,000 factories, but they were small and concentrated on processing local products like cotton or tobacco rather than manufacturing.

In 1820 most manufacturing was done in homes or small shops. After 1820, however, the factory system began to take over. In factories the total process of manufacturing took place at one location. The need for a single location was due to the new sources of power—water and steam. The first factories used waterpower and were built in rural areas along rivers and streams.

Improved transportation and communication increased the importance of Northern cities as centers of trade. As city merchants grew wealthier, they sought investments that would further increase their business. Much of their capital, or investment money, went into new manufacturing industries.

Connecticut inventor Eli Whitney started the use of interchangeable parts. These were identical machine parts that could be quickly put together to make a complete product. Because all the parts were alike, they could be manufactured with less skilled labor, and they made machine repair easier.

Making the Technology Connection
1. How might the level of industrialization affect the ability of the North and the South to wage war?

Linking Past and Present
2. Hypothesize why the South in the 1990s is not among the top few manufacturing centers.

CHAPTER 14 CONNECTIONS

Teaching Making Connections
The difference in development between the North and South created fierce differences of opinion and economic inequalities.

Did You Know?
Between 1850 and 1860, the number of nonfarm workers increased by an astounding 55 percent. By 1860 about 4 out of every 10 workers no longer worked on farms.

Fact or Fiction?
In the 1840s and 1850s, the average American factory worker worked about eight hours a day, six days a week

FICTION: In 1840 the average daily hours of work for factory workers was 11.4 hours, six days a week. In the late 1840s and early 1850s, laws in the North and in California attempted to limit work hours to 10 hours a day.

Answers to CONNECTIONS
1. Northern armies would be better supplied and equipped owing to manufacturing capability.
2. Until the mid-1900s, the Southern economy was based on agriculture. Today large Southern cities are often service and information centers.

LESSON PLAN
SECTION 2, 396–402

FOCUS

Bellringer
Before taking roll at the beginning of the class period, display Focus Activity Transparency 47 on the overhead projector, and assign the accompanying Focus Activity Sheet.

Objectives
Point out the objectives on this page to students in previewing the section content.

Motivating Activity
Present the following to students.

Official Notice: Join the Missouri River Company—move to Kansas! We're leaving in Spring and need 10 more families. Come live where the prairies stretch before you like a sea of grass, soil is good, and land is ready for the taking.

Ask: Do you think Kansas was accurately described? (No, the advertisement does not mention the hardships of the travel nor the hot summers and icy cold winters.)

Did You Know?
Slavery was supported by many of the established institutions of society. For example, North Carolina's Supreme Court ruled as early as 1829 that the purpose of slavery "is the profit of the Master" and the purpose of the enslaved person was "to toil that another may reap the fruits."

SECTION 2

Dispute Over Slavery

Setting the Scene

Section Focus
The 1850s found the South feeling increasingly isolated—isolated from the industrial boom of the North and from the new technologies that were redefining agriculture in the West, and isolated by its support of the slave system. Was the Union doomed to be torn apart by the vast political and economic differences that separated the North and South?

Objectives
After studying this section, you should be able to

★ discuss how the majority of Southerners viewed and defended the institution of slavery.

★ explain the significance of the Kansas-Nebraska Act.

★ examine the reactions of both the North and the South to the Supreme Court's *Dred Scott* decision.

Key Term
obiter dictum

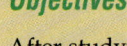
◀ COTTON CARDING PADDLES

Southern legislatures made it increasingly difficult for slaveholders to emancipate their enslaved men and women. Some states decreed that free African Americans must either go somewhere else or be sold back into slavery. All African Americans, enslaved or free, had to carry identification passes when away from their homes. At night, patrols equipped with dogs and guns watched for runaways.

■ The South and Slavery
Although slavery was common in the South, the majority of people were not slaveholders. In addition, the bondage of African Americans assumed many different forms.

Forms of Slavery
Between house servants and their masters and mistresses, there was often a sense of trust and affection. Some enslaved people, especially in the cities, were hired out to other employers and thus were afforded some freedom of movement. The workforce of the successful Tredegar Iron Works in Richmond, Virginia, was African American.

Most African Americans, however, worked on plantations and lived lives marked by hard labor, cruel discipline, and isolation. Marriages between enslaved persons were not legally recognized. Families could be broken up by sale. It was against the law to teach enslaved persons to read, although some white Southerners broke that law.

UNIT 5 Division and Reunion: 1825–1877

Classroom Resources for SECTION 2

Teacher's Classroom Resources
- Reproducible Lesson Plan
- Reteaching Activity 14-2
- Section Quiz

Multimedia
- Section Focus Transparency 47
- Chapter 14 Map Transparency
- Testmaker
- Student Self-Test Software
- The American People: Fabric of a Nation

In Defense of Slavery

To support the system, many Southerners developed an elaborate defense of slavery. Southerners argued that slavery was necessary to provide an adequate labor supply and was "a positive good" because all the enslaved person's material needs were provided. Finally, defenders of slavery tried to use arguments from science and the Bible to show that slavery was acceptable.

The Rift Widens

For a few years it looked as though the Compromise of 1850 might provide a permanent solution to the slavery controversy. In the North, however, opposition to the stringent Fugitive Slave Law included in the Compromise of 1850 increased. Under this law, the word of a slaveholder, or even one who claimed to be, was taken as conclusive proof of identity of the runaway. A suspected runaway (who might in fact be a free person) had no right to testify on his or her own behalf. Any citizen might be required to join in pursuit of a runaway.

To fight this injustice, most free state legislatures passed personal liberty laws that nullified the Fugitive Slave Law by forbidding state officials to assist in the capture of runaways. Antislavery feeling in the North was also stimulated by Harriet Beecher Stowe's *Uncle Tom's Cabin,* a novel portraying slavery at its worst. The book sold 300,000 copies in 1852, its first year of publication.

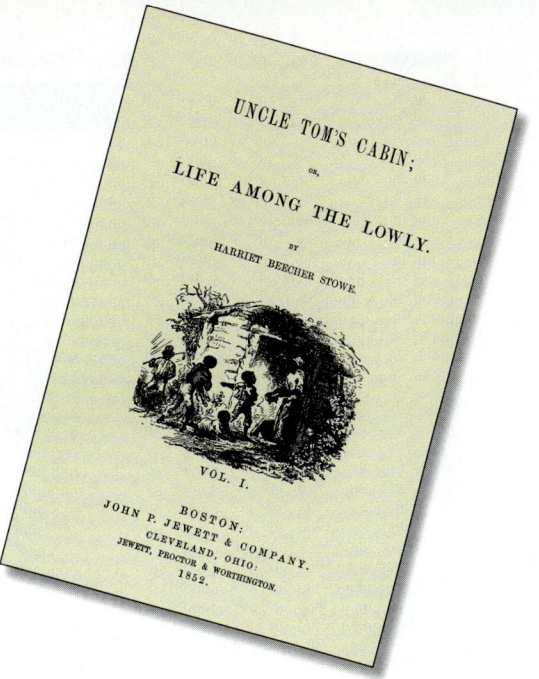

▲ Harriet Beecher Stowe's *Uncle Tom's Cabin*

AMERICAN PORTRAITS

Harriet Tubman
1820–1913

Born to enslaved parents in Maryland, Harriet Tubman worked as a plantation field hand until she was nearly 30 years old. Then she made her break for freedom, escaping to the North with the help of the Underground Railroad.

Knowing full well the risks of being captured, Tubman nonetheless made 19 trips back into the South during the 1850s to help other enslaved people escape. Altogether she assisted more than 300 African Americans—including her aged parents—to escape bondage. While not the founder of the Underground Railroad, she certainly became its most famous and successful conductor. Known as the "Moses" of her people, Tubman maintained iron discipline among the escapees, and—despite huge rewards offered in the South for her capture and arrest—she always managed to elude her enemies.

CHAPTER 14
SECTION 2

TEACH

Guided Practice
Political Science Have students discuss the reasons the North and South disagreed on the Kansas-Nebraska Act. List the reasons on the chalkboard under headings North, South. Tell students that much of the reasoning was the result of nationalism versus states' rights. Conclude by emphasizing the differences between Northerners and Southerners. **L2**

Teaching American Portraits
Slaveholders offered $40,000 for Harriet Tubman's capture. After the Civil War began, she worked as a nurse and as a Union spy.

Did You Know?
According to the 1850 Fugitive Slave Law, anyone convicted of helping an enslaved person escape could be fined $1,000 and sentenced to jail. Bystanders could be deputized and forced to help search for anyone who had escaped from slavery. If they refused to help, they too could be fined $1,000—at a time when yearly wages averaged about $300 to $400.

Cooperative Learning

To review the *Dred Scott* decision, organize students into groups of four. Have each student present one aspect of the event to the rest of the group. Among possible choices are President Buchanan's reasons for not deciding on the issue, the reasons for the Supreme Court's decision, and Northern and Southern reactions. To conclude, have the group draw up a hypothesis stating what might have happened had Northerners not challenged the Court's decision. **L1, L2**

CHAPTER 14
SECTION 2

Independent Practice

History Using the headings of the subsections as a guide, have students list the major events described in Section 2. **L1, LEP**

Map Study Using Maps

Answer: into Northern states and from there into Canada

Skills Practice

Ask: How did people trying to escape from slavery get from Charleston, South Carolina, to Canada? (sailed along the coast, then went overland)

Did You Know?

In the early 1850s, Indiana, Iowa, and Illinois bordered slave states. All three had laws that banned African Americans, whether free or enslaved, from entering their states.

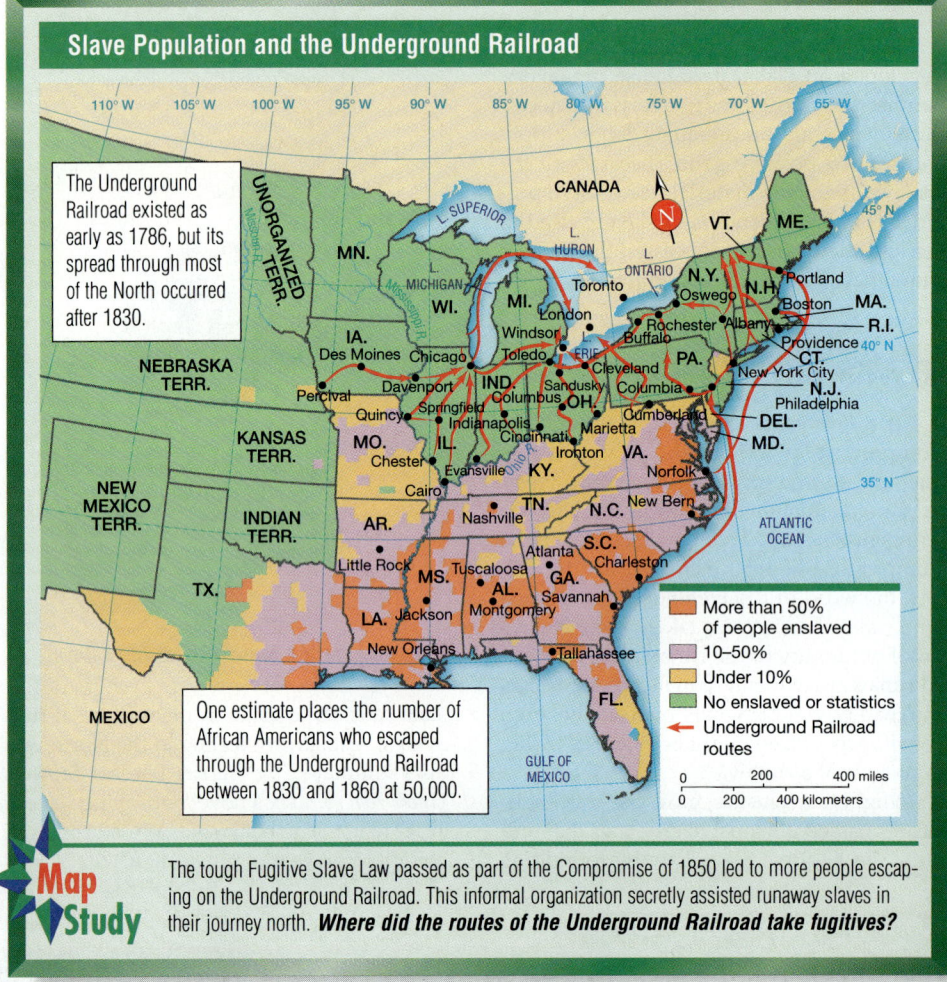

Map Study The tough Fugitive Slave Law passed as part of the Compromise of 1850 led to more people escaping on the Underground Railroad. This informal organization secretly assisted runaway slaves in their journey north. **Where did the routes of the Underground Railroad take fugitives?**

Bloodshed on Free Soil

In 1854 the political truce over slavery ended with the passage of the Kansas-Nebraska Act. Senator Stephen A. Douglas of Illinois proposed the Kansas-Nebraska Act to encourage the rapid settlement of the trans-Missouri region and the building of a transcontinental railroad with terminals at St. Louis and Chicago. However, the act reopened intersectional controversy. It provided that the region be divided into two new territories, Nebraska and Kansas. The question of whether or not slavery would exist in the new territories was to be decided by popular sovereignty. This part of the act negated the Missouri Compromise, because both territories lay above latitude 36° 30′. A clause specifically repealing the Missouri ban on slavery north of that line was added.

The Kansas-Nebraska Act was criticized. The repeal of the Missouri Compromise was denounced in the North. The South continued to demand that the North recognize the rights of slaveholders in the territories of the United States.

Bleeding Kansas

Settlers started at once to move into the Kansas Territory. Because the slavery issue was to be decided by popular vote, a race developed to see whether the majority of settlers would come from slave or free states.

398 UNIT 5 Division and Reunion: 1825–1877

Critical Thinking

Analyzing Consequences Ask students to answer the following question: Passage of the Kansas-Nebraska Act of 1854 had what important consequence for the history of American political parties? Have students write their answers in three paragraphs. Discuss student answers. (The Republican party was formed. Because antislavery Northerners were shocked by the passage of the act, many broke away from the Whig party and formed the Republican party to keep slavery out of all of the territories.) **L3**

A bloody struggle between the proslavery and antislavery factions assumed the proportions of a civil war. The violence in "bleeding Kansas" reached its peak on the eve of the presidential election of 1856.

Election of 1856

In the two years since the passage of the Kansas-Nebraska Act, the Whig party had broken up over the slavery issue. To fill the void, two new parties—the Americans and the Republicans—appeared. The American party, composed of Know-Nothings and some ex-Whigs, tried to divert people's minds from the slavery issue by whipping up feeling against immigrants. Its candidate in 1856 was former President Fillmore. The basic principle of the Republicans (who took their name from the party of Thomas Jefferson) based its platform on "free soil," or keeping slavery out of the territories. Strongly organized in every free state, the Republican party nominated General John C. Frémont.

Meanwhile, the Democrats dodged the slavery issue. To balance Southerners' dominance of the party, they nominated a Northerner, James Buchanan of Pennsylvania. With only a minority of the popular vote, Buchanan won the election with 174 electoral votes against 114 for Frémont and 8 for

CHAPTER 14 SECTION 2

FACT or FICTION?

During the 1850s, enslaved laborers in the United States worked only on farms and plantations.

FICTION: One out of four worked as house servants, factory and construction workers, miners, lumberers, or artisans.

Map Study — Using Maps

Answer: The agricultural frontier of the nation moved farther and farther west. Kansas is directly west of Missouri, a slave state.

Skills Practice

Ask students to compare the map on page 401 with the map on this page. Ask: What new territories were organized between 1850 and 1854? (Washington, Nebraska, and Kansas territories)

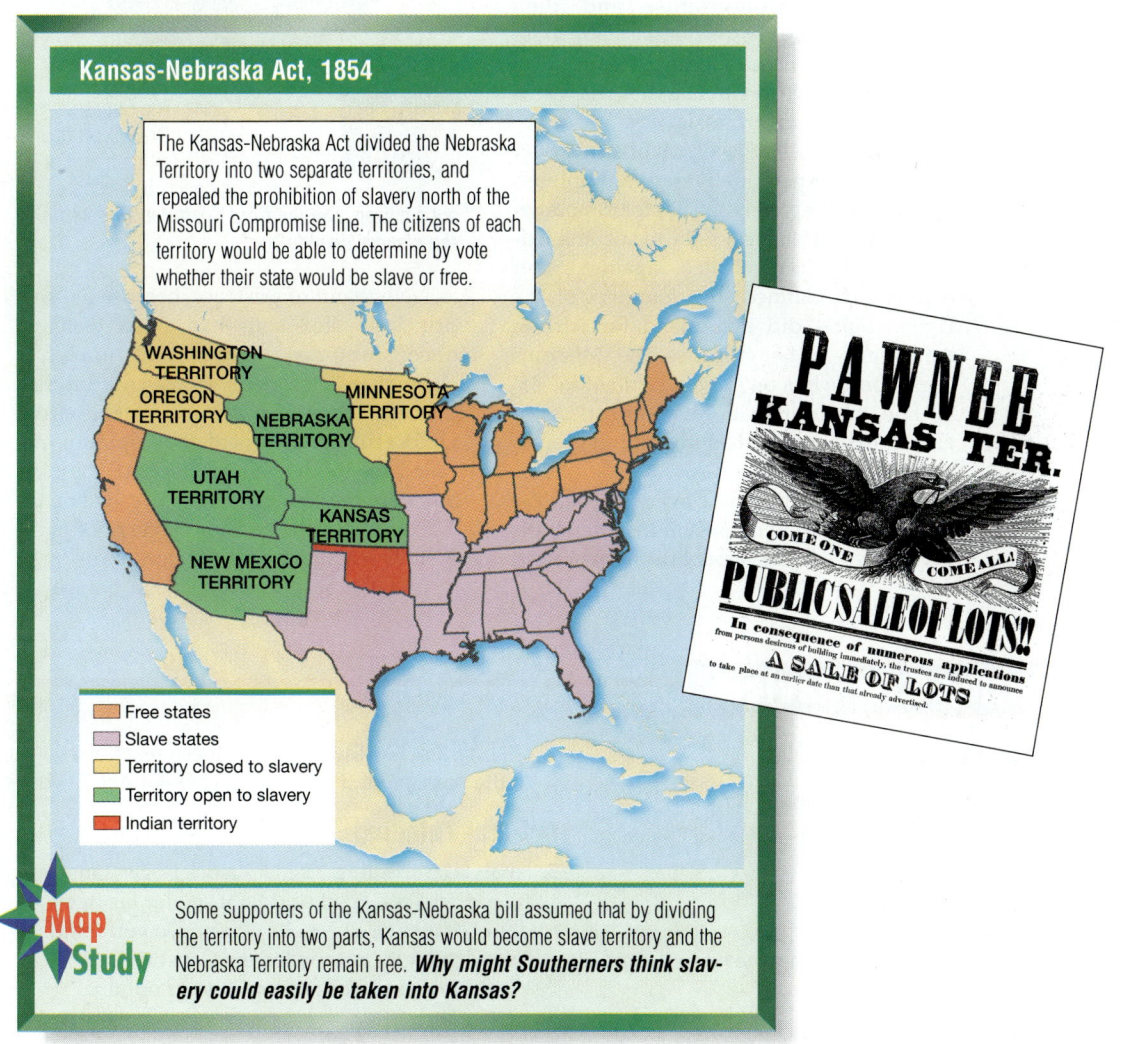

Kansas-Nebraska Act, 1854

The Kansas-Nebraska Act divided the Nebraska Territory into two separate territories, and repealed the prohibition of slavery north of the Missouri Compromise line. The citizens of each territory would be able to determine by vote whether their state would be slave or free.

- Free states
- Slave states
- Territory closed to slavery
- Territory open to slavery
- Indian territory

Map Study Some supporters of the Kansas-Nebraska bill assumed that by dividing the territory into two parts, Kansas would become slave territory and the Nebraska Territory remain free. **Why might Southerners think slavery could easily be taken into Kansas?**

CHAPTER 14 Compromise and Conflict 1848–1861

Sidelights: The Debates in Virginia

Nat Turner's rebellion in the 1830s touched off critical debates in the Virginia House of Delegates on how to forestall further rebellions. Moderates from western Virginia proposed abolishing slavery and sending enslaved people to colonize other lands. Their failure to persuade the Virginia House led to a turning point in Southern attitudes toward slavery. Up to this time, Southern leaders had argued only that slavery be tolerated. After the rebellion they began to argue that slavery was a "positive good."

Fillmore. The Democrats swept the South and gained enough votes to win, while the Republican Frémont won two-thirds of the electoral votes of the free states.

The Dred Scott Decision

In his Inaugural Address in March 1857, President Buchanan suggested that the controversy over slavery in the territories be left to the Supreme Court, which had recently heard a case on this question and was expected to render a decision soon.

Dred Scott was an enslaved man taken by a former master from the state of Missouri into territory closed to slavery by the Missouri Compromise and then brought back to Missouri again. For more than 10 years, Scott sued for freedom on the grounds that residence in a free territory released him from slavery.

On March 6, 1857, Chief Justice Roger Taney (TAW•nee) delivered an opinion upholding completely the Southern point of view that Scott had no right to sue in a federal court. Taney ruled against Scott because, he claimed, the founders of the United States did not intend for African Americans to be citizens. The Missouri Compromise ban on slavery north of the 36° 30' line, the Court said, was unconstitutional because Congress had no right to prohibit slavery in the territories.

Instead of settling the slavery dispute, the *Dred Scott* decision made it more bitter. If the decision stood, the Republican party might

▲ **DRED SCOTT** The Supreme Court ruled that Dred Scott had no right to sue for his freedom in the federal courts because he was not a citizen. *Did the Dred Scott decision settle the slavery dispute?*

as well go out of existence, because its basic principle—free soil—had been declared unconstitutional. Republicans therefore claimed that the decision was not binding but was an *obiter dictum* (OH•buh•tuhr DIHK•tuhm), an incidental opinion not called for by the circumstances of the case. Southerners, on the other hand, called on the North to obey the decision as the price of the South's remaining in the Union.

Section 2 ★ Review

Checking for Understanding

1. **Identify** Harriet Beecher Stowe, James Buchanan, Dred Scott, *Uncle Tom's Cabin*, Republican party.

2. **Define** *obiter dictum*.

3. **State** three reasons Southerners used to defend slavery.

4. **Distinguish** Northern and Southern reactions to the passage of the Kansas-Nebraska Act.

Critical Thinking

5. **Analyzing a Ruling** Chief Justice Roger Taney ruled that Dred Scott could not sue for his freedom because he was not a citizen. Do you think Taney correctly interpreted the Constitution? Write two sentences to support your opinion.

UNIT 5 Division and Reunion: 1825–1877

Social Studies Skills

Map and Graph Skills

Classifying Information

Look at a map of the United States. As you read the names of the states, various thoughts float through your mind. Perhaps you picture the places you would someday like to visit, or maybe you remember locations that have been in the news lately. As you scan the map, you organize the information in your mind by sorting the data into a pattern. In other words, you classify the map's information.

Classifying is a process of separating and arranging information into related groups or categories. Before you begin the process, you need to set up a classification system. You do this by defining the categories. When you evaluate a map in terms of the places you would like to visit, you classify the information into two categories: places you like to see and places you would not care to see. Frequently, a map legend defines the map's classification system and categories.

One of the many sources of information about history is maps. This map of the Compromise of 1850, for example, will be helpful in understanding the results of the compromise.

After examining the data on the map, follow these guidelines to help classify its information. Then complete the practice.

- **Determine** what information you need to classify.
- **Decide** on the major categories by looking closely at how the information can be broken down into parts.
- **Write** the data that fits in each category or, if you are making a chart, place the appropriate information in columns under each category.
- **Determine** what conclusions you can make after studying the information in each category.

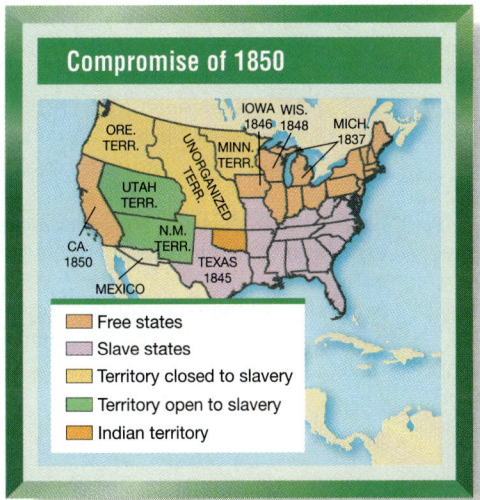

Practicing the Skill

1. How many categories does the legend define for this map?
2. How does the map convey each distinct classification?
3. Keep the same classifications as shown on the legend. Make a chart, placing the appropriate information in columns under each category.
4. Based on the map and your prior knowledge of the subject, what conclusions could you draw about the Compromise of 1850?
5. Define another classification system and legend for the Compromise of 1850 map. Does your system provide more or less information than that shown on the existing map?
6. Study the map on page 399 that shows the results of the Kansas-Nebraska Act. Make a chart, using the map legend's classification system. Compare the chart and map with those of the Compromise of 1850. What conclusions can you draw?

LESSON PLAN
Mastering Social Studies Skills

Teaching Map and Graph Skills

Ask students to list the kinds of maps they are familiar with. Once the lists are complete, have them categorize the maps into groups. Let the students develop their own categories. Examples might include travel maps: highway, campground. Ask: How are the maps in your groups similar? How are they different?

Use Chapter 14 Map Transparency. Assign the accompanying activity from Map Transparencies: Strategies and Activities.

Did You Know?

The anti–Roman Catholic, anti-immigrant Know-Nothing party reached its peak in 1855. That year 43 members of Congress belonged to the party. They were against allowing foreign-born or Roman Catholic citizens to vote. This party also wanted to take away from these Americans the right to hold political office.

Answers to SOCIAL STUDIES SKILLS

1. five categories: free states, slave states, territory closed to slavery, territory open to slavery, Indian Territory
2. by color
3. free states: Calif., Conn., Del., Ill., Ind., Iowa, Maine, Mass., Mich., N.H., N.J., N.Y., Ohio, Pa., R.I., Vt., Wisc.; free territories: Minn., Oreg., Unorganized Territory; slave states: Ala., Ark., Fla., Ga., Ky., La., Md., Miss., Mo., N.C., S.C., Tenn., Tex., Va.; territories open to slavery: N.M., Utah; Indian Territory
4. Answers will vary, but may include: Free States and territories were in the northern half of the country.
5. Answers will vary depending on the classification system used.
6. Indian Territory extended into Oklahoma panhandle; former Unorganized Territory, previously closed to slavery, now called Nebraska Territory and Kansas Territory with the possibility of slavery at the time of eventual statehood.

LESSON PLAN
SECTION 3, 402–407

FOCUS

Bellringer
Before taking roll at the beginning of the class period, display Focus Activity Transparency 48 on the overhead projector, and assign the accompanying Focus Activity Sheet.

Objectives
Point out the objectives on this page to students in previewing the section content.

Motivating Activity
Present the following advertisement to students:

Wanted: Dedicated individual to work for abolitionist organization. Long hours (14–16 hours a day) and low pay ($35 weekly). Must enjoy public speaking and be dedicated to abolishing slavery.

Ask: Would you apply for this job? Why or why not? (Dedicated students might apply for this well-meaning position.)

Fact or Fiction?
Stephen A. Douglas of Illinois made the following statement in 1858: "'A house divided against itself cannot stand. I believe this government cannot endure permanently half slave and half free.'"

FICTION: Abraham Lincoln of Illinois made the statement in 1858 at the Republican State Convention.

SECTION 3

Drifting Toward War

Setting the Scene

Section Focus
Both the North and the South watched with dread as events surrounding the election of 1860 led toward the dissolution of the Union. For Southerners, the election of Abraham Lincoln as President signaled that slavery could not be extended.

Objectives
After studying this section, you should be able to
★ evaluate the importance of the Lincoln-Douglas debates.
★ identify the purpose of John Brown's raid at Harpers Ferry and reactions to it.
★ list the political events that led to the secession of seven Southern states.

Key Term
secession

◀ CANNED FOODS AND MEDICINE, MID-1800S

The question of slavery in the territories left the nation in a state of almost hopeless confusion. The *Dred Scott* decision, supported in the South, was flatly opposed by the Republicans, dominant in the North.

■ Lincoln and Douglas

What effect did the *Dred Scott* decision have on the principle of popular sovereignty? Did the decision forbid the people of a territory to decide whether or not they wanted slavery?

Stephen A. Douglas and Abraham Lincoln were rival candidates in the election for senator from Illinois in 1858. Douglas—a short, thickset man nicknamed "The Little Giant" for his size and political influence—served in the Senate for 12 years and had a national reputation for his commitment to popular sovereignty. The most prominent Democrat in Congress, he hoped to be elected President in 1860.

Abraham Lincoln was a man whose tall, angular frame inspired ridicule. Lincoln had served only a single undistinguished term in the House of Representatives. He defended the Compromise of 1850—even to the point of enforcing the Fugitive Slave Law. Although Lincoln was not an abolitionist, he believed that if slavery were confined to its existing area, Southerners themselves might eventually abolish it. As a former Whig who had only recently joined the Republican party, Lincoln enjoyed a local reputation as a clever lawyer and keen debater.

Debates

During the campaign Lincoln and Douglas traveled to seven Illinois towns to debate critical issues. Douglas attempted to

402   UNIT 5 Division and Reunion: 1825–1877

Classroom Resources for SECTION 3

Teacher's Classroom Resources
- Reproducible Lesson Plan
- Reteaching Activity 14-3
- Chapter 14 Enrichment Activity
- Chapter 14 Performance Assessment Activity
- Spanish Summaries and Glossary
- Section Quiz

Multimedia
- Section Focus Transparency 48
- Chapter 14 Map Transparency
- Vocabulary Puzzlemaker
- Testmaker
- Student Self-Test Software
- The Presidents: A Picture History of Our Nation

show that Republicans in general—and Lincoln in particular—were abolitionists in disguise, bent on destroying the Union. During their debate at Freeport, Illinois, Lincoln put Douglas in a difficult position by asking the question, "Can the people of a territory in any lawful way . . . exclude slavery from their limits prior to the formation of a State Constitution?" Douglas was trapped. If he answered "Yes," he would appear to support popular sovereignty, thereby opposing the *Dred Scott* decision. A "yes" answer would improve his chances for reelection as senator, but cost him Southern support for the 1860 presidency. A "no" answer would make it seem as if he had abandoned popular sovereignty, on which he had based his political career. This answer would be welcomed by the South but could cost him the senatorial election.

Freeport Doctrine

To solve this dilemma, Douglas formulated the so-called Freeport Doctrine. Douglas said he accepted the *Dred Scott* decision that forbade Congress to bar slavery from the territories. However, he pointed out, a territorial legislature might effectively discourage slavery if it failed to pass laws to keep enslaved persons under control. Said Douglas, "Slavery cannot exist a day, or an hour, anywhere, unless it is supported by local police regulations." By admitting that a territorial legislature could practically nullify the *Dred Scott* decision, Douglas won a narrow victory in the election but lost Southern support for the presidency in 1860. Lincoln lost the election but gained a national reputation.

John Brown's Raid

John Brown, a fiery abolitionist, regarded himself as a heaven-sent agent whose mission was to liberate enslaved people and punish slaveholders. Brown had participated in the armed struggle against proslavery forces in Kansas. On October 16, 1859, with 21 followers, he seized the federal arsenal at Harpers Ferry, Virginia, intending to free and arm the enslaved men and women of the surrounding countryside. The siege ended with the capture of Brown by Colonel Robert E. Lee and the death of 10 of his men. At his Virginia trial for treason and murder, Brown expressed no remorse.

Found guilty, John Brown was hanged on December 2. Many Northerners regarded Brown as a martyr to the cause of freedom. The New England poet Ralph Waldo Emerson said that Brown had "made the gallows glorious like the cross." Southerners regarded Brown's punishment as just. They feared nothing so much as a slave revolt.

The Election of 1860

As the election of 1860 approached, Democrats split over the issue of slavery in the territories. A Northern wing of the party nominated Douglas for the presidency and backed popular sovereignty; a Southern wing nominated John C. Breckinridge of Kentucky and supported the *Dred Scott* decision. The Constitutional Union party, a third group composed mostly of former Southern Whigs, nominated

▲ CAMPAIGN BANNER

CHAPTER 14
SECTION 3

Independent Practice

Political Science Ask students to research information to write a three-page report comparing the stated political principles of the 1854–1876 Republican party and those of the Republican party of today. **L2, L3**

ASSESS

Check Understanding

Assign Section 3 Review as homework or an in-class activity.

Evaluate

Assign Section 3 Review in the TCR, or use the History of a Free Nation Testmaker to create a customized test.

Map Study Using Maps

Answer: Missouri (also received three of New Jersey's seven electoral votes).

Skills Practice

Ask: What percentage of the popular vote did Lincoln receive? (almost 40 percent)

Did You Know?

Abraham Lincoln was famous for his good sense of humor. When someone asked him if he had consulted his cabinet about a particular decision, Lincoln replied, "I never consult my cabinet, they all disagree too much."

John Bell of Tennessee and attempted to avoid the slavery issue.

With such division among their opponents, the door to the presidency stood open for the Republicans. Their platform, designed to attract votes from many quarters, was that slavery should be left undisturbed where it existed, but that it should be excluded from the territories. They denounced John Brown's raid and also called for a protective tariff, free homesteads for settlers, and federal funds for internal improvements, including a railroad to the Pacific. In an attempt to attract recent immigrants, they were harshly critical of Know-Nothing attempts to make naturalization more difficult.

The Republicans nominated Abraham Lincoln as their candidate. Lincoln, the only one of the candidates to make no speeches, stayed quietly at his home in Springfield, Illinois.

The election was a clear victory for the Republicans. Lincoln gained a majority in the electoral college, winning more votes than all three of his opponents combined. Not even listed on the ballot in some Southern states, he carried every free state except New Jersey, where the vote was split between Lincoln and Douglas. Breckinridge carried the Deep South, and Bell and Douglas divided the border states.

■ The South Secedes

The Republican victory caused great alarm in the Deep South. Many Southerners felt that they had no other recourse but to leave the Union. Leadership there passed to the secessionists, some of whom had long been threatening to leave the Union. They looked on Lincoln as "a daring and reckless leader of the abolitionists." They predicted his election meant abolition and rebellion by those who were enslaved. Mississippi Senator Albert Gallatin Brown told a Southern audience:

> *The North is accumulating power, and it means to use that power [for emancipation].... When that is done, no pen can describe, no tongue can depict, no pencil can paint the horrors that will overspread this country.... Disunion is a fearful thing, but emancipation is worse.*

The Confederacy

During the four-month interval between Lincoln's election in November 1860 and his inauguration in March 1861, the seven states of the Deep South (South Carolina, Mississippi, Florida, Alabama, Georgia, Louisiana, and Texas) voted for **secession**—withdrawal from the Union.

These states based their right to secede on the theory of states' rights: the Constitution, they argued, was a contract among sovereign states. The free states had broken that contract by refusing to enforce the Fugitive Slave Law and by denying the Southern states their equal rights in the territories. Together the seven states drafted a

---

The Election of 1860

Popular vote: 4,689,568 — Electoral vote: 303

Candidate	Popular vote	Electoral vote
Lincoln	1,865,593	180
Breckinridge	848,536	72
Bell	592,906	39
Douglas	1,382,713	12

Map Study The presidential election of 1860 split along sectional lines. Lincoln did not win in any states south of Pennsylvania and the Ohio River. **How many states did Douglas carry?**

Critical Thinking

Analyzing Effects Divide students into pairs to analyze the effects of the growth of slavery. Tell them that in 1790 there were 698,000 slaves in the entire United States. By 1860 there were 3,954,000 slaves in the South. Ask each pair to list reasons why political compromise over the slavery question would have been easier right after the American Revolution than during the 1850s. Discuss student answers. (Slavery had spread throughout the South by the 1850s, and the economy of the South depended on slavery. A better political climate for compromise existed after the Revolution.) **L1, L2**

constitution for their new alliance—the Confederate States of America—and called on the other slave states to join them.

Uneasy Truce

Government leaders made last-minute attempts at compromise. The most promising was a proposal by Senator John J. Crittenden of Kentucky. The keystone of the Crittenden Compromise was reestablishment of the 36° 30' line, dividing the territories into slave and nonslave regions. Lincoln refused to agree to this proposal.

When Lincoln reached Washington, D.C., in late February 1861, eight slave states remained in the Union. Although the North generally agreed with Buchanan's view that states did not have the right to leave the Union, no one wished to fight to force them back in. General Winfield Scott expressed widespread public sentiment when he said, "Wayward sisters, depart in peace."

Lincoln's Position

Lincoln disagreed. In his first Inaugural Address, he said that "no state upon its own mere motion can lawfully get out of the Union." He argued that secession was a blow to the basic democratic principle that the will of the majority should prevail. Yet, like Buchanan before him, Lincoln suggested no active measures to force the Confederate states back into the Union. He proposed only to hold military posts not yet taken by the Confederates, to enforce federal laws where federal agents were not "obnoxious" to the local population, and to deliver the mail "unless repelled." Although Lincoln still refused to make any concession regarding slavery in the territories, his address did not explicitly object to a constitutional amendment forbidding federal interference with slavery in the Southern states. Finally, he pleaded that the North and South be "not enemies, but friends" and said that "there need be no bloodshed or violence." Sadly, these hopes were soon dashed.

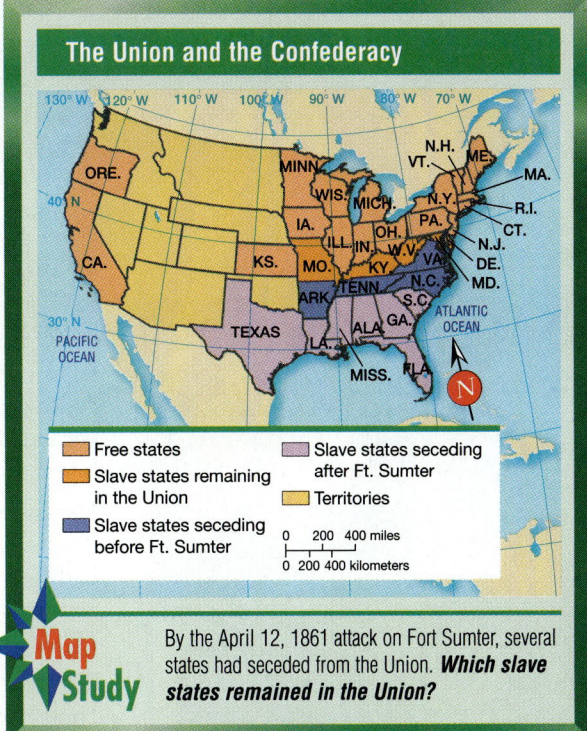

The Union and the Confederacy

Map Study
By the April 12, 1861 attack on Fort Sumter, several states had seceded from the Union. **Which slave states remained in the Union?**

- Free states
- Slave states remaining in the Union
- Slave states seceding before Ft. Sumter
- Slave states seceding after Ft. Sumter
- Territories

Section 3 ★ Review

Checking for Understanding

1. **Identify** Abraham Lincoln, John Brown, Crittenden Compromise, Confederate States of America.
2. **Define** secession.
3. **Identify** the opposing viewpoints demonstrated during the Lincoln-Douglas debates.
4. **List** three issues the Republicans used to their advantage in the election of 1860.

Critical Thinking

5. **Analyzing Choices** Compile a list of events, other than the election of Lincoln, that might have led the seven Southern states to secede from the Union.

CHAPTER 14 Compromise and Conflict 1848–1861

INTEGRATING Language Arts

American Literary Heritage

Historical Setting

By 1860 there were about four million enslaved African Americans in the United States. When the Civil War commenced, enslaved people made up more than one-third of the South's population.

Background

Struggling to achieve a sense of unity and to promote support within deplorable living conditions, enslaved African Americans turned to music. They had embraced Christianity, cherishing the teachings of the Bible. Spirituals provided a way for slaves to create unity and to protest the actions of their oppressors. The songs were often sung as work songs. Passed down through the oral tradition, spirituals helped to form an African American culture.

About the Oral Tradition

As with much of the literature derived from the oral tradition, the spirituals have no known authors or originators. Folk songs primarily were produced in cultures in which formal education was limited. Perhaps the spirituals were the results of collaborations among various authors. No one can be certain. However, subsequent generations were responsible for preserving in writing some of these songs.

▲ MOTHER AND CHILD

The struggles that tore the nation apart at mid-century were reflected in much of the period's writing. Spirituals—songs of salvation—provided the African Americans who wrote and chanted them not only with a measure of solace in bleak times but with a means for communicating secretly among themselves under their masters' watchful eye.

Follow the Drinking Gourd

When the sun comes back and the first quail calls,
Follow the drinking gourd,
For the old man is a-waiting for to carry you to freedom
If you follow the drinking gourd.

Follow the drinking gourd,
Follow the drinking gourd,
For the old man is a-waiting for to carry you to freedom
If you follow the drinking gourd.

The river bank will make a very good road,
The dead trees show you the way,
Left foot, peg foot traveling on
Follow the drinking gourd,

The river ends between two hills
Follow the drinking gourd,
There's another river on the other side,
Follow the drinking gourd,

Where the little river meets the great big river,
Follow the drinking gourd,
For the old man is a-waiting for to carry you to freedom
If you follow the drinking gourd.

▲ MUSIC ON THE PLANTATION

UNIT 5 Division and Reunion: 1825–1877

Cultural Diversity

Historians of music have tried to trace the history of African American spirituals. Much of the imagery is drawn from the Hebrew Scriptures and the New Testament. African traditions are evident in the vocal style, polyrhythmic accompaniment, choral singing, and the call-and-response pattern. Many historians also believe there is a relationship between African American spirituals and hymns popular among rural white Southerners in the late eighteenth-century, especially those sung at religious revival camp meetings.

Go Down, Moses

When Israel was in Egypt land,
Let my people go!
Oppressed so hard they could not stand,
Let my people go!

CHORUS
Go down, Moses,
Way down in Egypt land
Tell ole Pharaoh,
Let my people go!

Thus say the Lord, bold Moses said,
Let my people go!
If not I'll smite your first-born dead,
Let my people go!

No more shall they in bondage toil,
Let my people go!
Let them come out with Egypt's spoil,
Let my people go!

▲ *Ride For Liberty*, by Eastman Johnson, 1862

Swing Low, Sweet Chariot

Swing low, sweet chariot,
Coming for to carry me home,
Swing low, sweet chariot,
Coming to carry me home.

I looked over Jordan and what did I see
Coming for to carry me home,
A band of angels coming after me,
Coming to carry me home.

If you get there before I do,
Coming for to carry me home,
Tell all my friends I'm coming too,
Coming to carry me home.

Swing low, sweet chariot,
Coming for to carry me home,
Swing low, sweet chariot,
Coming to carry me home.

Interpreting Literature

1. What is the message from one enslaved person to another in "Follow the Drinking Gourd"?
2. Which spiritual equates the plight of the African Americans with that of another group? Which group?

Making Evaluations

3. Describe the mood of the spirituals.

INTEGRATING
Language Arts

Developing Student Understanding

Explain that the selections show how enslaved African Americans struggled to achieve a sense of unity and culture during a grim era.

Other Works of African American Folklore

Spirituals were a combination of gospel songs that slaves heard their Christian masters singing and traditional African music. Most spirituals appear in four-part harmony. A collection of spirituals is *The Books of American Negro Spirituals* by James Weldon Johnson and J. Rosamond Johnson. African American author Virginia Hamilton, a Newberry medalist, has published a collection of African American folklore, *The People Could Fly: American Black Folktales.*

Answers to INTERPRETING LITERATURE

1. The directions are possible instructions on escape routes
2. "Go Down, Moses"; the Hebrews of ancient Egypt
3. Answers may vary. Appropriate responses should be words like *plaintive, angry, hopeful, resigned,* and *religious.*

REVIEW CHAPTER 14

Answers

Reviewing Facts

1. Although Democrats and Whigs tried to downplay the slavery issue, the Free-Soil party brought it into the open. The votes received by Free-Soilers gave the election to Taylor.
2. To please the South: stricter Fugitive Slave Law, popular sovereignty for Utah and New Mexico. To please the North: California admitted as a free state, ending of the slave trade in District of Columbia.
3. sewing machine, telegraph, improved steam locomotive, interchangeable parts, steel plow, mechanical reaper
4. employment, letters from relatives, escape poverty and political persecution
5. By negating clauses of the Missouri Compromise, Northerners were enraged and conflict broke out as proslavery and antislavery settlers raced into Kansas.
6. Scott was not a citizen and could not bring suit in court. As property, slaves could be taken into the territories, thus the Missouri Compromise was unconstitutional.
7. Douglas argued for popular sovereignty to decide whether slavery could be extended into the territories. Lincoln wanted to confine slavery to the areas where it already existed.
8. Answers may vary. It is likely that Brown's raid made a Southern compromise with the North less possible.

408

CHAPTER 14 ★ REVIEW

Using Vocabulary

Each of the following terms can be considered a "cause" and an "effect." Define the terms below by writing two sentences for each. Write one sentence that explains the term as a cause and another sentence using the term as an effect. Here is an example: "*Secession* by Southern states was one cause of the Civil War." "One effect of the election of Abraham Lincoln was the Southern states' *secession*."

popular sovereignty   platform

Reviewing Facts

1. **Explain** how the slavery issue affected the presidential election of 1848.
2. **Classify** the provisions of the Compromise of 1850 into those that appealed to Southern states and those that appealed to Northern states.
3. **List** five inventions that hastened economic development between 1830 and 1860.
4. **State** three reasons why large numbers of immigrants came to the United States between 1830 and 1860.
5. **Explain** why the Kansas-Nebraska Act resulted in renewed fighting between slavery and antislavery forces.
6. **Summarize** the *Dred Scott* decision.
7. **Relate** the issue of popular sovereignty to the Lincoln-Douglas debates.
8. **Correlate** Brown's raid at Harpers Ferry to Southern attitudes about the North.

Understanding Concepts

Economic Diversity

1. Explain how economic diversity might have affected Northern and Southern views on slavery. Include in your answer differences between the Northern and Southern economies.
2. What role did improved transportation play in the expanding United States economy?

408   UNIT 5 Division and Reunion: 1825–1877

Political Conflict

3. How did the Southern states explain their right to secede from the Union?
4. Evaluate the impact of John Brown's attack at Harpers Ferry on Southern attitudes toward compromise with abolitionists.

Critical Thinking

1. **Linking Past and Present** The issues of slavery and popular sovereignty divided Americans in the 1850s. What are some issues today that divide Americans? What distinguishes a divisive issue from one that can be resolved through compromise?
2. **Analyzing Fine Art** Study the painting of John Brown and answer the questions that follow.
    a. Do you think the painting is realistic or idealized? Explain.
    b. Can you tell from the painting how the artist feels about John Brown? Explain.

▲ JOHN BROWN

Understanding Concepts

1. Answers may vary. The South's economy was primarily agricultural. It depended on cotton production and slave labor. The North's economy was more diversified. The manufacturing of the North relied on inexpensive labor.
2. Answers may vary. Improved link between different facets of the economy such as raw materials, production, and distribution.
3. Answers may vary. Southern states had long espoused the company theory of government, states' rights, and nullification, all of which challenged the idea of a strong federal union.
4. Answers may vary. Brown's attack probably further strengthened the South's already defensive attitude toward slavery, isolating it even further from any possible compromise with antislavery advocates.

CHAPTER 14 ★ REVIEW

Writing About History

Classification

Compile a list of changes that took place in the years between 1840 and 1860. Divide these changes into three categories: political, technological, and social. Next, create a subcategory that enumerates all the items that created conflict and tension between the North and South. Use these classifications to write an essay entitled "Factors That Divided North and South."

Cooperative Learning

You will work with two others in a group to conduct a mock trial to determine whether or not John Brown should be found guilty. Each member in your group will assume one of the following roles: defending attorney, prosecuting attorney, and judge. The defense and prosecution attorneys must prepare their cases to present before the judge. The judge must prepare at least two questions to ask each attorney. Present your trial to the class and poll them to determine John Brown's innocence or guilt.

Social Studies Skills

Making Inferences

You make an inference when you use facts to draw a conclusion that is not stated directly. Good inferences are based on sound reasoning and careful analysis of information.

Practicing the Skill

The following steps will help you make inferences from information presented in this passage about Southern slaveholders.

- Read the information carefully.

Slaveholders, called planters, were actually a very small percentage of the southern population. To be considered a planter, a person had to hold at least 20 slaves. Only about 4 percent of slaveholders had this many slaves. An extremely small percentage of slaveholders had more than 100 slaves. Jefferson Davis, who became the future President of the Confederacy, held as many as 3,000 slaves. The majority of slaveholders, however, were farmers who kept about 5 slaves.

About three-fourths of the Southerners had no slaves at all. These Southerners owned small farms on which they grew their own food and perhaps a cash crop such as tobacco or cotton. About 10 percent of this non-slave-holding southern population were poor whites. They supported themselves by hunting and fishing.

- Summarize the information:

The majority of the people in the South did not hold slaves. Those who did had very few. Only a few planters had large numbers of slaves.

- Decide what inferences or conclusions can be made based on what was read or heard but was not stated directly. Read the following inference based on the summary.

Slavery directly benefited economically only a few Southerners.

Use the three steps and what you have learned in this chapter to determine which of the following inferences seems reasonable.

1. Before the Civil War, the prosperity of the South depended on slave labor.
2. The absence of slavery in the North meant that Northerners were not prejudiced.
3. The Southern economy grew because of advances in farming equipment such as Deere's steel plow and McCormick's grain harvester.

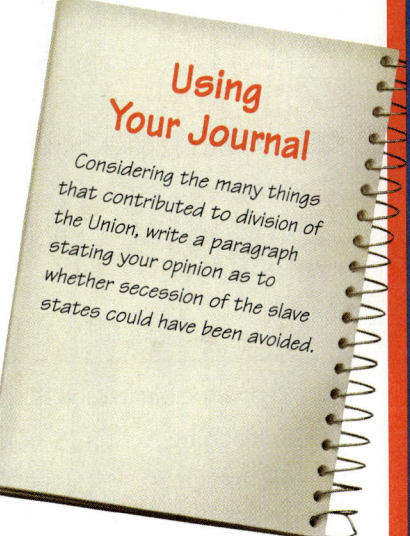

Using Your Journal

Considering the many things that contributed to division of the Union, write a paragraph stating your opinion as to whether secession of the slave states could have been avoided.

REVIEW ★ CHAPTER 14

Practicing the Skill

The first answer is reasonable.

? Chapter Bonus Test Question

This question may be used for extra credit on the chapter test.

By 1860 the number of African Americans enslaved in the United States was about

a. 1 million
b. 4 million
c. 8 million
d. 16 million

(Answer: b)

Using Your Journal

Opinions will vary but should include specific details supporting students' viewpoint. Invite volunteers to read their paragraphs to the class, and have the class discuss major points.

Critical Thinking

1. Answers may vary. Extremely divisive issues are usually emotional and are perceived by people as either morally right or wrong. Slavery could not be tolerated in any form by abolitionists who perceived it as a moral evil. In the present-day United States, issues such as reproductive rights, school prayer, and the death penalty are extremely divisive issues with moral aspects.

2. a. realistic but explanations may vary
   b. Answers will vary but should be supported with details from the painting.

PLANNING GUIDE — Chapter 15 The Civil War

Daily Lesson Objectives	Teacher Classroom Resources	Multimedia
SECTION 1 **The Outbreak of War** 1 Day pp. 412–416 1. Explain the strategies of the North and South. 2. Discuss the role of wartime diplomacy.	Chapter 15 Study Guide Reproducible Lesson Plan Section Quiz Reteaching Activity 15-1 Reinforcing Social Studies Skills 25, 29, 40 Outline Map 9 Chapter 15 Cooperative Learning Activity Chapter 15 Concept Mapping Activity Writer's Guidebook Lessons 3–5	Student Self-Test Software Testmaker Section Focus Transparency 45 Chapter 15 Skills Transparency U.S. History Diagraph 2 Focus on Government The Presidents: A Picture History of Our Nation A Geographic Perspective on American History
SECTION 2 **The War on the Battlefield** 1 Day pp. 417–422 1. Identify the major battles of the war. 2. Explain the significance of the battles of Antietam, Gettysburg, and Vicksburg.	Reproducible Lesson Plan Reteaching Activity 15-2 Section Quiz Reinforcing Social Studies Skills 1, 8, 25 American Portrait 30 Writer's Guidebook Lesson 2 Building Skills in Geography	Student Self-Test Software Testmaker Section Focus Transparency 46 Chapter 15 Map Transparency U.S. History & Art Transparency 11 A Geographic Perspective on American History
SECTION 3 **Behind the Lines** 1 Day pp. 424–429 1. Discuss behind-the-lines activity in the North and South. 2. Explain the wartime roles played by women, African Americans, and Native Americans.	Reproducible Lesson Plan Reteaching Activity 15-3 Section Quiz Reinforcing Social Studies Skills 32, 35 American Portrait 29 Chapter 15 Primary and Secondary Source Readings Writer's Guidebook Lesson 6	Student Self-Test Software Testmaker Section Focus Transparency 47 Landmark Documents in American History
SECTION 4 **Ending the War** 1 Day pp. 431–435 1. Explain the changes in Union military strategy after Grant took command. 2. Discuss the issues in the election of 1864.	Reproducible Lesson Plan Reteaching Activity 15-4 Section Quiz Chapter 15 Enrichment Activity Chapter 15 Primary and Secondary Source Readings Reinforcing Social Studies Skills 27, 62 Spanish Summaries & Glossary	Student Self-Test Software Testmaker Section Focus Transparency 48 Vocabulary Puzzlemaker Audiocassette, Chapter 15
CHAPTER REVIEW AND EVALUATION 1 Day	Chapter 15 Test Chapter 15 Performance Assessment Activity	Student Self-Test Software Testmaker

00:00 OUT OF TIME? If time does not permit teaching the entire chapter, use the Chapter 15 Summary on pages 462–463 and the Chapter 15 audiocassette (English and Spanish) to point out the main ideas of the chapter.

PLANNING GUIDE

Cultural Diversity Activity

Interpreting Media According to John Hope Franklin's *From Slavery to Freedom*, more than 186,000 African Americans served in the Union Army during the Civil War. Many came from Confederate or border slave states. About 53,000 were from free states. Most regiments were all-black units led by white officers. African American soldiers received lower pay than white soldiers of the same rank. However, in 1864, after many protests, the War Department granted equal pay to African American soldiers. Have students view the film *Glory*, available on videocassette, which chronicles the experiences of the all-black Fifty-fourth Massachusetts Infantry. As students watch, have them note ways in which the wartime experiences of African American soldiers differed from that of their white counterparts. What forms of discrimination did African American soldiers face? What motivated them to fight for the Union? Discuss also the ways a movie of a historical event differs from a written account.

Performance Assessment Activity

Popular Culture Organize students into groups of four or five to research the popular culture of 1861–1865. Among the possible choices are art (Winslow Homer), patriotic prints (Currier and Ives), battle or religious hymns ("Dixie" and the "Cumberland Cap"), or patriotic literature (Edward Everett Hale and John Greenleaf Whittier). Have the groups present their individual reports to the class. Encourage them to use illustrations, recordings, and primary sources.

POSSIBLE RUBRIC FEATURES: Content information, collaborative skills, written and oral communication skills, creativity, interdependence of history and culture

Chapter Resources

Literature from the Period

Alcott, Louisa May. *Hospital Sketches*. 1863.

Lincoln, Abraham. "Emancipation Proclamation." 1863.

_____. "Gettysburg Address." 1863.

Lee, Robert E. "Letter to His Son." 1863.

Readings for the Student

Catton, Bruce. *The Civil War*. American Heritage, 1971.

Holzer, Harold. "A Few Appropriate Remarks." *American History Illustrated*, Vol. 23, No. 7, November 1988.

Readings for the Teacher

Catton, Bruce. *A Stillness at Appomattox*. Washington Square, 1970.

Foote, Shelby. *The Civil War*. Random House, 1958.

Ward, Geoffrey C., with Ric and Ken Burns. *The Civil War: An Illustrated History*. Knopf, 1990.

Multimedia Resources

Abraham Lincoln. Atlas Video. (VHS, 35 minutes)

The Civil War. Time-Life Video. (VHS, 9 episodes)

The Civil War. Westport Media. (5 filmstrips)

Living American History Series. U.S. History II: 1840–1875. Priven Learning Systems (2 Apple diskettes, guide)

Key to Ability Levels

Teaching strategies have been coded for varying learning styles and abilities.

- **L1** Basic activities for all students
- **L2** Average activities for average to above-average students
- **L3** Challenging activities for above-average students
- **LEP** Limited English Proficiency activities

Glencoe Links to the Humanities

Links to Art
- U.S. History & Art Transparencies 11

Links to Literature
- Macmillan Literature: Understanding Literature Audiotapes Side 3
- Macmillan Literature: American Literature Video—*The Red Badge of Courage*
- Macmillan Literature: Novel Guide—*The Red Badge of Courage*
- Macmillan Literature: American Literature Text—Frederick Douglass, Mary Chesnut, Robert E. Lee, Abraham Lincoln

Link to Music
- American Music: Cultural Traditions

CHAPTER 15

BEGINNING THE CHAPTER

Give students the following information. At the beginning of the Civil War, 21 million people lived in the North, and 9 million lived in the South. Of those living in the South, 4 million were enslaved. Ask students to speculate about how these factors would affect the odds of the South winning the war.

Recording Journal Notes
To help students get started, suggest that they list their findings under separate categories such as Union soldier, Confederate soldier, civilian, nurse, child.

- **GTV: A Geographic Perspective on American History**

Side 2, Chapter 16
Title: *The Civil War*
Subject: Summary of the Civil War and how geography played a role in the outcome

See GTV Guide page 48 for complete lesson plan.

CHAPTER 15

The Civil War
1861–1865

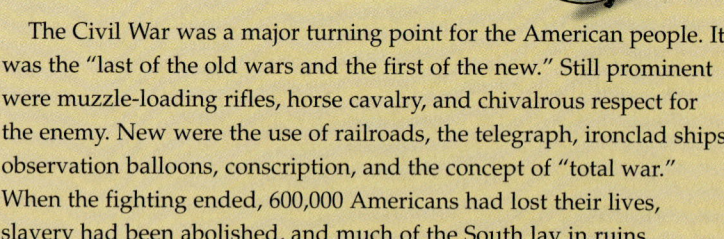

Setting the Scene

▶ CONFEDERATE CANNON

Focus
The Civil War was a major turning point for the American people. It was the "last of the old wars and the first of the new." Still prominent were muzzle-loading rifles, horse cavalry, and chivalrous respect for the enemy. New were the use of railroads, the telegraph, ironclad ships, observation balloons, conscription, and the concept of "total war." When the fighting ended, 600,000 Americans had lost their lives, slavery had been abolished, and much of the South lay in ruins.

Concepts to Understand
★ Why it became necessary to curtail civil rights and freedoms during the Civil War
★ How military conflict led to total war between the North and South

Read to Discover . . .
★ the advantages of the Union and the Confederacy in the war.
★ how Lincoln's choice of Grant as commander of the Union armies helped the Union war effort.

Journal Notes
What was life like during the Civil War? Note details about it as you read the chapter.

CULTURAL	• The Pony Express links Missouri with California	• First transcontinental telegraph message is sent	• Julia Ward Howe's "Battle Hymn of the Republic" is published
	1860	**1861**	**1862**
POLITICAL	• Buchanan sends relief supplies to Ft. Sumter	• Eleven states secede and form the Confederate States of America	• Emancipation Proclamation issued

410 UNIT 5 Division and Reunion 1825–1877

✚ EXTRA CREDIT PROJECT

Presidential Powers President Lincoln was the first U.S. President to expand presidential war powers. Without consulting Congress, Lincoln spent millions of dollars enlarging the army and navy. Ask interested students to conduct research to find examples of U.S. Presidents sending armed forces into conflict without a declaration of war from the Congress and discover what law Congress passed in 1973 to remedy this problem. Have students present their findings to the rest of the class.

History AND ART
Battle of Fredericksburg
by C. Rochling

During the battle, a Pennsylvania regiment helped save the left Union flank from disaster. Colonel Charles Collis rides holding the colors among his troops.

▲ UNION OFFICER'S HAT

- First national currency goes into circulation
- Quakers found Swarthmore College in Pennsylvania
- Mark Twain publishes "The Celebrated Jumping Frog of Calaveras County"

1863 — **1864** — **1865**

- Union victories at Gettysburg and Vicksburg
- Lincoln reelected
- Lincoln assassinated
- Lee surrenders to Grant
- Andrew Johnson becomes President

CHAPTER 15 The Civil War   411

Teacher Notes

CHAPTER 15 CONCEPTS

Concept Mapping Activity
Write the chapter concepts on the chalkboard. Ask students to write these concepts in their notebooks and to list each major event in the chapter under the appropriate concept.

Civil War challenges the survival of the nation.
- Civil Rights and Liberties
- Military Conflict

History AND ART
Because color photography had not yet been invented, many of our full-color images of the Civil War are derived from artists' conceptions. Artist C. Rochling depicts Union soldiers, some of whom wore bright, decorative Zouave uniforms similar to those worn by French infantry units in North Africa.

The Civil War was a turning point in American history. Its legacy includes changes in government and in society. It ended the issue of federal authority versus states' rights and abolished slavery.

LESSON PLAN
SECTION 1, 412–416

FOCUS

Bellringer

 Prior to taking roll at the beginning of the class period, display Focus Activity Transparency 49 on the overhead projector and assign the accompanying Focus Activity Sheet.

Objectives

Point out the objectives on this page to students in previewing the section content.

Motivating Activity

Present the following announcement to students:

Wanted—Soldiers to fight for the Union!

Sharpshooters needed for the 9th Regiment of Boston. Volunteer! Sign up today.

Discuss with students whether they would enlist and why or why not.

 Use Skills Transparency 15.

GLENCOE TECHNOLOGY

The following material is available from Glencoe and may be used to introduce or enrich Chapter 15:

VIDEODISC

Focus on Government

Chapter 5
The Federal System
Disc 1, Video 5

SECTION 1

The Outbreak of War

Setting the Scene

Section Focus

The new President of the United States and his counterpart in the Confederacy each faced a formidable task. With the attack on Fort Sumter, war became the solution to the longstanding differences between the North and South. The war aims of both sides were simple. The goal of the South was to defend its independence. The goal of the North was to restore the Union by force. Each leader was determined to do what was necessary to win a quick victory. Neither could predict the terrible cost of the long war that was to come.

Objectives

After studying this section, you should be able to

★ explain the strategies of the North and South.

★ discuss the role of wartime diplomacy.

Key Terms

martial law, blockade

▶ UNION RECRUITMENT POSTER, 1861

As the Southern states seceded, they seized United States arsenals, mints, fortresses, and other public property within their borders. Fort Sumter, on a rocky island in the harbor of Charleston, South Carolina, was one of only two Southern forts still under federal control. By April 1861, the fort was running short of provisions because a supply ship sent by President Buchanan in January had been turned back by artillery fire from shore. Lincoln decided to resupply Fort Sumter, and he told South Carolina authorities of his decision.

Lincoln's decision placed Jefferson Davis, president of the Confederacy, in a difficult position. How long could the Confederates tolerate the fort of a "foreign" nation in the harbor of their major Atlantic port? If Davis allowed the fort to be resupplied, he would appear to be giving in to Lincoln. If he ordered that Fort Sumter or the relief ships be fired upon, he risked war. Davis chose to take the fort before the ships arrived.

On April 12, 1861, shore batteries of the South Carolina militia opened fire on Fort Sumter. From inside the fort, Captain Abner Doubleday described the attack:

66 *Showers of balls ... and shells ... poured into the fort in one incessant stream, causing great flakes of masonry to fall in all directions. When the immense mortar shells, after sailing high in the air, came down in a vertical direction, and buried themselves in the parade ground, their explosion shook the fort like an earthquake.* 99

After 34 hours of bombardment, but no loss of life, Fort Sumter surrendered.

UNIT 5 Division and Reunion 1825–1877

Classroom Resources for SECTION 1

Teacher's Classroom Resources
- Chapter 15 Study Guide
- Chapter 15 Cooperative Learning Activity
- Reproducible Lesson Plan
- Reteaching Activity 15-1
- Section Quiz

Multimedia
- Section Focus Activity Transparency 49
- Chapter 15 Skills Transparency
- Student Self-Test Software
- Testmaker
- Focus on Government
- The Presidents: A Picture History of Our Nation

Preparing to Fight

News of the attack on Fort Sumter stirred nationalism in the North. When Lincoln requested 75,000 volunteers for 90 days to suppress the rebellion, more responded than could be equipped or trained. "I never knew what popular excitement could be," wrote a Bostonian to a friend in England. "The whole population, men, women, and children, seem to be in the streets with Union flags. . . . Nobody holds back." A similar wave of nationalism swept the South, as Jefferson Davis called for 100,000 volunteers. A visitor to the South found "revolutionary fervor in full sway. . . . Young men are dying to fight."

More Southern States Secede

Lincoln knew that conflicting forces existed in the eight slaveholding states that had not yet seceded. Nationalism worked for the Union, while the strongest argument for secession was slavery. He considered Delaware to be safe for the Union. But to remind the others that the war was to preserve the nation, and not to end slavery, the President declared:

> The central idea pervading this struggle is the necessity of proving that popular government is not an absurdity. We must settle this question now, whether, in a free government, the minority have the right to break up the government whenever they choose.

Faced with the prospect of fighting their neighbors, however, four more states—Virginia, Arkansas, North Carolina, and Tennessee—abandoned the Union. Virginia's secession put Washington, D.C., in danger. To its west was Virginia. To the east was Maryland, where many people owned

▲ SUNSET AT FORT SUMTER by Conrad Wise Chapman, 1864 Chapman produced some of the most brilliant paintings associated with the Civil War. This work displays the artist's use of strong light and shade contrasts. Chapman, an enlisted soldier, was 22 years old when he painted this scene. **When did the bombardment begin?**

CHAPTER 15
SECTION 1

Independent Practice
Presenting Ideas
Ask students to write an announcement of the attack on Fort Sumter as if it were being reported on national television. Ask students to speculate on the effects modern communication would have on a civil war in the United States today. **L2**

 Point out that Confederates burned the *Virginia* (formerly known as the *Merrimac*) later that year to keep the ironclad from falling into Union hands.
Answer to Caption: It deprived the South of income derived by selling cotton to Great Britain and prevented the South from importing British manufactures needed to maintain the war effort.

The following material is available from Glencoe and may be used to introduce or enrich Chapter 15:

CD-ROM
- *The Presidents: A Picture History of Our Nation*

▲ **THE IRONCLADS** In the first battle of ironclad ships, the Union's Monitor defeated the South's Merrimac off Virginia in March 1862. The Union's blockade was saved, but the era of wooden warships was over. **Why was the blockade important?**

slaves and supported the Confederacy. If Maryland seceded, the Union capital would be in enemy territory. Lincoln determined to hold Maryland at all costs.

Riots in Baltimore

Only a week after Fort Sumter, as Union troops passed through Baltimore on their way to Washington, D.C., they were attacked by a mob aroused by pro-Confederate newspapers. The President responded by placing Baltimore under **martial law**, a form of military rule that includes suspending Bill of Rights guarantees. Persons who advocated secession or otherwise openly supported the Confederacy were arrested and held without trials. Although tensions in Maryland remained high throughout the war, Lincoln's action kept this strategically important state in the Union.

"I hope to have God on my side," Lincoln said, "but I must have Kentucky." The President's native state and Missouri were important because they controlled the Mississippi and Ohio rivers. Although Kentucky had a pro-Union government, Lincoln eventually put the state under martial law to stabilize it. In Missouri, where slaveholders controlled the state, he supported rebellion against the pro-Confederate elected state government.

■ Strategies and Advantages

The Civil War was fought across the continent from southern Pennsylvania in the Northeast to New Mexico in the Southwest. Almost 3 million soldiers wore the uniforms of the Union or the Confederacy. Countless other men and women supported these troops—on the farms, in the factories, on the battlefields, and behind the lines.

The South's Leaders

The South had the better army, especially during the early years of the war. Because of a strong military tradition in the South, many Confederate officers had attended the United States Military Academy at West Point in New York. Most of the top officers in the United States Army resigned their commissions to fight for the Confederacy, among them Robert E. Lee. After his native Virginia seceded, Lee decided that he could not "raise my hand against my relatives, my children, my

UNIT 5 Division and Reunion 1825–1877

Cooperative Learning

Organize the class into groups of four or five students. Have each group hold a roundtable discussion on the strengths and weaknesses of the North and of the South and how their strategies compensated for or took advantage of these strengths and weaknesses. Students should summarize their conclusions. A recorder for the group should write the summaries and present them to the class. **L1, L2**

home." He rejected Lincoln's offer to lead the Union armies and took command of Confederate forces in Virginia.

The Union's Three-Pronged Strategy

The Union's military strategy was simple: **blockade,** or close off, Confederate ports and ruin its economy; invade the South and split it into thirds at the Mississippi River and through Tennessee and Georgia; and capture the Confederate capital at Richmond, Virginia. Southern strategy was even simpler. Southerners would be fighting for their independence on familiar terrain. To win, the South did not have to do anything except hold out against enemy attacks.

The South, formerly a region within a nation, became a "nation in arms." Men from 17 to 50 were drafted into the army and farmers were told what to plant. Women bore a large part of the burden of supplying clothing and medical supplies for the troops. Southerners felt they were fighting to preserve the cotton economy and the plantation culture. Because Europe was the major market for their cotton, they counted on European nations to provide war materials and other supplies.

Differences in Resources

The South would need Europe's help because the North was superior in nearly every type of resource. The Union had more than 80 percent of the manufacturing plants and most of America's merchant ships, railroad track, banks, minerals, grain crops, and meat. The Confederacy had less than one-half as many people as the North, and more than one-third of these were enslaved persons. The Confederacy was open to attack all along its border with the Union and along its extensive coastline. In short, the South was ill-equipped to wage war, even in its own defense.

The Confederacy also suffered from the very political theories that had created it. The Confederate constitution limited the authority of the central government and emphasized states' rights, a framework of government that was contrary to what was needed in wartime. As the war progressed, some state governments resisted the Confederacy's efforts to raise troops. Not until 1863 was the central government able to levy taxes to finance the war. It was forced to borrow and to issue worthless paper money to pay its bills. State governments also printed paper money and added to the economic chaos, which encouraged hoarding and damaged morale.

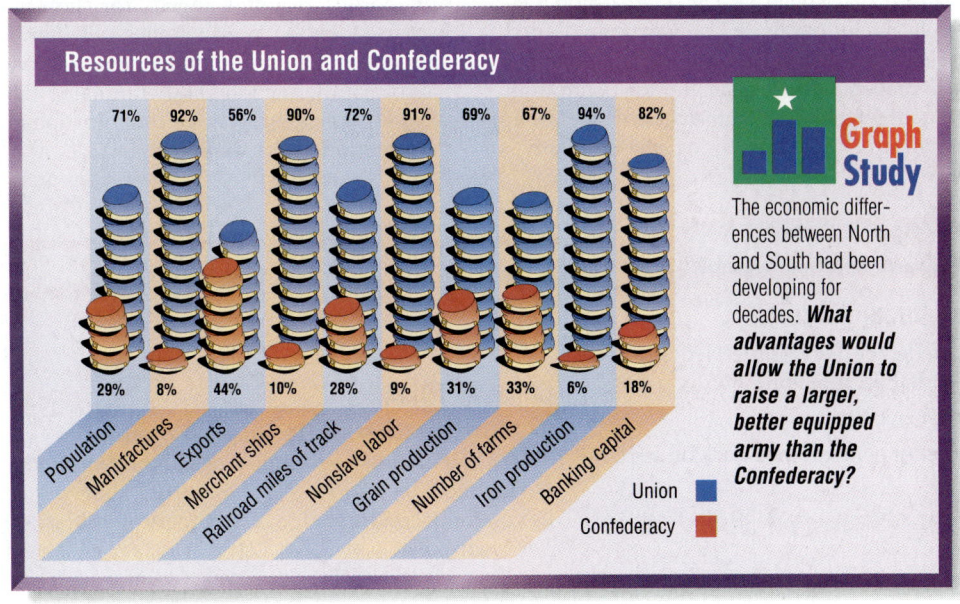

Resources of the Union and Confederacy

 **Graph Study**

The economic differences between North and South had been developing for decades. **What advantages would allow the Union to raise a larger, better equipped army than the Confederacy?**

CHAPTER 15 SECTION 1

 Using Graphs

Answers:
Answers will vary, but should include population, manufactures, and banking capital.

Skills Practice
Have students use the information presented in the bar graphs on page 415 to create circle graphs.

Linking Across TIME

Cotton remains a vital part of the Southern economy. Because it is processed when grown, cotton has a higher return than other field crops. It is still among the largest cash crops in Alabama, Mississippi, Arkansas, and Louisiana.

Did You Know?

More than a few Northern regiments were more like private clubs than military units. Recruits were admitted only after they were voted in.

Critical Thinking

Analyzing Decisions When war appeared inevitable, President Lincoln asked Robert E. Lee to command the Union troops. Lee decided to defend his homeland of Virginia rather than lead the Union forces. To analyze Lee's decision, have students discuss the pros and cons of fighting for the Union. Pros: Lee was neither pro-secession nor pro-slavery, would have more resources, West Point education. Cons: attachment to the Southern culture and to his home in Virginia, would have to fight his friends and neighbors. **L1, L2**

CHAPTER 15
SECTION 1

Did You Know?
The Civil War was the first war to be documented by photographs. Mathew Brady and other photographers carried their bulky cameras to camps and battlefields, leaving us a record of the war.

ASSESS
Check Understanding
Assign Section 1 Review as homework or an in-class activity.

Evaluate
Assign the Section 1 Quiz in the TCR or use the History of a Free Nation Testmaker to create a customized quiz.

Reteach
Have students complete Reteaching Activity 15-1.

Enrich
Have students research events in France and Great Britain during the U.S. Civil War.

CLOSE
Ask students if they agree or disagree with the following statement and why: The Civil War began as a struggle to keep the Union together; however, it ended as a struggle over the meaning of freedom.

▲ **BLOCKADE RUNNERS**

Wartime Diplomacy

The principal task of Union diplomacy during the Civil War was to prevent European nations from supporting the Confederacy. Europe's ruling classes continued to be concerned about maintaining their power and status at home, and they were not upset by the disintegration of the world's largest democracy. The British and French governments, in particular, were openly sympathetic to the Confederacy.

The South and Great Britain

The South expected Britain's aid because British textile mills used Southern cotton. Lincoln reminded the British that they needed Union wheat as much as Confederate cotton. To prevent Great Britain and the South from developing closer commercial ties, the President struck his first blow against the South.

The Blockade Begins

Six days after Fort Sumter fell, Lincoln announced a blockade of Southern ports. At the time, the action seemed foolish and impossible to enforce. To patrol a Confederate coastline 3,500 miles long, the United States Navy had just 42 wooden ships and fewer than 9,000 sailors, so at first the blockade was selective. But as the Union navy grew to 626 ships and about 59,000 sailors, the blockade reduced Confederate imports and exports to what could be carried in by "blockade runners"—small, fast vessels designed to sneak through openings in the sandbars that lined much of the Southern coast. Blockade runners could not begin to replace regular commerce, however, and Southern trade eventually shrank to a fraction of what it had been before the war, depriving Confederate armies of vital supplies.

Unable to break the blockade militarily, Southern leaders hoped to accomplish it diplomatically. If Britain recognized Confederate independence, its powerful navy could keep Southern cotton flowing to British textile mills. Southern diplomats arranged for British shipyards to build and outfit Confederate warships to prey on Northern shipping. These vessels, however, could not break the Union blockade, nor could Britain's need for cotton. Increased cotton production by Britain's colonies in Egypt and India replaced the loss of Southern cotton and eliminated the Confederacy's best hope for European intervention in the Civil War.

Section 1 ★ Review

Checking for Understanding

1. **Identify** Confederacy, Fort Sumter, Jefferson Davis, Robert E. Lee, three-pronged strategy.
2. **Define** martial law, blockade.
3. **List** three consequences of the attack on Fort Sumter.
4. **Summarize** the advantages of the North and South.
5. **Describe** the effects of the Union blockade and the Southern response to it.

Critical Thinking

6. **Analyzing Causes** The attack on Fort Sumter aroused intense patriotic feelings in the North. Comment on two aspects of this attack that you think contributed to Northerners' outburst of patriotism.

---

416   UNIT 5   Division and Reunion 1825–1877

Answers to SECTION 1 REVIEW

1. Confederacy, 412; Fort Sumter, 412; Jefferson Davis, 412; Robert E. Lee, 414; three-pronged strategy, 415
2. All vocabulary words are defined in the Glossary.
3. Stirred patriotic feelings in the North and South, four more Southern states seceded, Lincoln asked for volunteers.
4. North: more manufacturing ability, resources, and food. South: experienced soldiers and officers, defensive military posture.
5. Greatly reduced Southern trade and vital military supplies; encouraged "blockade runners"
6. Answers will vary but may include that Northerners rallied around their soldiers.

SECTION 2

The War on the Battlefield

Setting the Scene

Section Focus

The fighting began with two armies of immigrants, farm boys, schoolteachers, and store clerks. At first there was a curious, almost eager anticipation of battle. Yet when blood began to spill and young men on both sides fell wounded and dying, both the North and South began to confront the grim reality of a long and bitter war.

Objectives

After studying this section, you should be able to
★ identify the major battles of the war.
★ explain the significance of the battles of Antietam, Gettysburg, and Vicksburg.

Key Term

proclamation

▲ UNION SOLDIER'S GLOVE AND REVOLVER

There were two major areas of land warfare. The eastern theater, east of the Appalachians, centered on the region surrounding the two capitals, Washington, D.C., and Richmond, Virginia. Because the two cities were less than 100 miles apart, many battles occurred in this area.

The western theater centered around the Mississippi River and its tributaries. In many ways, the West was critical to victory. If Union armies gained control of the Mississippi River, the Confederacy would lose its western food supplies.

■ The War in Virginia

On July 21, 1861, with Lincoln's 90-day volunteers nearing the end of their enlistments, the Union army invaded Virginia to capture Richmond. About 30 miles from Washington, D.C., 30,000 Northern troops met a smaller Confederate force near a stream called Bull Run. Expecting victory and a quick end to the war, members of Congress and Washington civilians came along to picnic and watch the battle. What they saw was a confusing clash of two untrained armies. Union troops fought well at first, but the Confederates proved better organized. Using the railroad and telegraph, Confederate officers were able to quickly supply reinforcements. The Union army's retreat was reported for the London Times by a correspondent on the scene:

> 66 I perceived several wagons coming from the direction of the battlefield; . . . a thick cloud of dust rose behind them, and running by the side of the wagons were a number of men in uniform. . . . Every moment the crowd increased, drivers and men cried out with the most vehement gestures, 'Turn back! Turn back! We are whipped!' 99

CHAPTER 15 The Civil War 417

LESSON PLAN
SECTION 2, 417–423

FOCUS

Bellringer
Prior to taking roll at the beginning of the class period, display Focus Activity 50 on the overhead projector and assign the accompanying Focus Activity Sheet.

Objectives
Point out the objectives on this page to students in previewing the section content.

Motivating Activity
Show the following video segment about the Civil War. Discuss the different emotions that a partisan piece of music such as "The Battle Hymn of the Republic" can evoke.

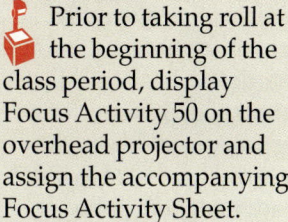

 VIDEODISC
- *GTV: A Geographic Perspective on American History*

Side 2, Chapter 16
Title: *The Civil War*
Subject: Summary of the Civil War and how geography played a role in the outcome

See GTV Guide page 48 for complete lesson plan.

Classroom Resources for SECTION 2

Teacher's Classroom Resources
- Reproducible Lesson Plan
- Reteaching Activity 15-2
- Section Quiz

Multimedia
- Section Focus Activity Transparency 50
- U.S. History and Art Transparency 11
- Chapter 15 Map Transparency
- Testmaker
- Student Self-Test Software
- A Geographic Perspective on American History

417

CHAPTER 15 SECTION 2

TEACH
Guided Practice
Sociology Hold a discussion with students on the characteristics of a military leader. List student responses on the chalkboard. Then ask: How did leadership affect the North's and the South's campaigns? (North: Lincoln's difficulty in finding a superior general prolonged the war; Grant's determination in the West brought costly and harsh Union victories. South: Well-trained generals sustained the war at the beginning.) **L2**

Visualizing History
"Stonewall" Jackson earned his nickname during the first Bull Run when Confederate troops held off a strong Union assault. Confederate general Barnard E. Bee rallied his troops by shouting, "There is Jackson standing like a stone wall. Let us determine to die here, and we will conquer." After Bull Run, Jackson was known as "Stonewall," and his brigade as the "Stonewall Brigade."
Answer to Caption: McDowell, McClellan, Pope, Burnside, and Hooker

---

Together, panic-stricken soldiers and civilians fled back to Washington. Indeed, Yankee predictions of a quick war could have come true. "Give me 10,000 fresh troops, and I will be in Washington tomorrow," Confederate General Thomas "Stonewall" Jackson said after Bull Run. Jefferson Davis, however, insisted on a defensive war, and the Union was saved.

After the disaster at Bull Run, Lincoln replaced General Irvin McDowell with General George McClellan, who trained and reorganized the Union army. But in 1862 the Confederates turned back McClellan at the Seven Days' Battle, General John Pope at the Second Battle of Bull Run, and General Ambrose Burnside at Fredericksburg. In May 1863, at Chancellorsville, Virginia, Lee smashed General Joe Hooker, who lost 17,000 men to an army half the size of his. "My God, my God," Lincoln cried when he learned of Hooker's terrible defeat, "What will the country say!"

■ Antietam and Gettysburg

Confederate military success in the eastern theater did not extend onto Northern soil. Lee's victory over bungling Union generals at the Second Battle of Bull Run in August 1862 encouraged him to invade the Union. His plan was to surprise Washington, D.C., from the north and destroy Northern morale. In September 1862, his 45,000 troops slipped into Maryland and disappeared into the mountains, where he split his army and sent "Stonewall" Jackson to seize the federal arsenal at Harpers Ferry. McClellan, who was to protect Washington by keeping between Lee and the capital, frantically chased after his enemy.

Antietam

At this point, incredible good luck befell McClellan. On a Maryland road, a Union

 ▲ **ROBERT E. LEE** While Lincoln searched desperately for a general who could win in the east, the Confederates remained under the able command of General Robert E. Lee (on the white horse). But Lee's brilliant strategist, General Thomas "Stonewall" Jackson, was mortally wounded at Chancellorsville, and Lee mourned the loss of "my right arm." **Which Union generals did Lee defeat in Virginia?**

Sidelights: Military History

Estimates of the effectiveness of the Union blockade show that in general the blockade was a failure until the end of the war. Historians estimate that between 1861 and 1865 only one in every six blockade runners was captured. As a result, half the Southern cotton crop made it through the Union blockade after 1862. By comparison, records show that the British blockade of the United States during the War of 1812 was far more effective in stopping trade.

patrol found 3 cigars wrapped in a copy of Lee's plans. McClellan realized that the Confederate forces were divided and that he could destroy Lee's army. On September 17, 1862, McClellan attacked Lee at Antietam (An•TEE•tuhm) Creek near Sharpsburg, Maryland. In the bloodiest single day of the war, McClellan forced Lee to retreat back into Virginia. The Confederates suffered more than 11,000 casualties. McClellan lost even more, and his army was too damaged to pursue Lee and finish him.

When news of Antietam was telegraphed to Lincoln, he called his cabinet together and told them:

> ... several weeks ago, I read to you an Order I had prepared.... I think the time has come now. I wish it were a better time.... The action of the army against the Rebels has not been quite what I should have best liked. But they have been driven out of Maryland.

The Emancipation Proclamation

The order was in the form of a **proclamation,** or official public announcement, and known as the Emancipation Proclamation. Lincoln's order, issued on September 22, 1862, to free the slaves of the Confederacy made this conflict a war against slavery.

Encouraged by almost destroying Hooker's army of 130,000 at Chancellorsville, Lee crossed the Potomac again in June 1863, and moved into southern Pennsylvania. He was shadowed, however, by a Union army under General George G. Meade. An accidental clash between small units at Gettysburg developed into a bloody battle that marked the turning point of the war.

Gettysburg

As both armies gathered to do battle, Union troops took up positions on the crest of a low ridge. It became the Confederates' task to dislodge them from this high ground. Desperate Confederate attacks—concluding on July 3 in a gallant but suicidal charge across an open field by General George Pickett's 15,000 troops—were all repulsed. After 3 days of fighting, Union casualties were more than 23,000. More than 28,000 Confederates were killed or wounded, about 7,000 of them in Pickett's charge. "Do not let the enemy escape," Lincoln wired the victorious Meade.

On July 4, Lee retreated into Virginia. Once again, the Union army failed to pursue him. "Our army held the war in the hollow of its hand," cried a frustrated Lincoln. "We had only to stretch forth our hands and they were ours. And nothing I could say or do could make the army move."

The Gettysburg Address

Although both sides suffered heavy casualties at Gettysburg, it was a devastating loss of life from which the sparsely populated South could not recover. On November 19, 1863, President Lincoln visited Gettysburg to dedicate the battlefield cemetery and to honor the soldiers buried there. In

The War in the East, 1861–1863

Map Study The Union's military strategy in the eastern theater of the war is shown on the map. **What battle took place in Pennsylvania?**

CHAPTER 15
SECTION 2

Fact or Fiction?
The U.S. government commissioned "Taps" as a patriotic hymn to honor its fighting men during the Civil War.

FICTION: General David Butterfield, a Union officer, didn't like the sound of the traditional "lights out" bugle call, so he whistled a new tune for his bugler to play.

Did You Know?
More soldiers died from sickness during the Civil War than from bullets. Improper food and sanitation caused diarrhea, dysentery, measles, smallpox, typhoid, gangrene, and chicken pox, killing more than 400,000 of the 618,000 who died.

Fact or Fiction?
The writer of the realistic novel of the Civil War, *The Red Badge of Courage*, did not fight in the Civil War.

FACT: Crane had no war experience and based his book on tales told by veterans and on the photographs by Mathew Brady.

---

this Gettysburg address, the President promised that "these dead shall not have died in vain" (see Appendix).

■ War in the West

In 1861 the war in the west was a struggle for control of the border states. In Missouri the pro-Union state government that Lincoln supported waged its own civil war against Confederate sympathizers. Thousands were killed in fighting in Missouri before the first shots were fired at Bull Run in the east.

The western counties of Virginia, where pro-Union sentiment ran strong, were detached from the state after it seceded, and in 1863 they were admitted to the Union as the new state of West Virginia. Despite Kentucky's strong pro-Confederate leanings, the Union army held the state throughout the war. Thus, Union strategy in the border states deprived the South of a strong line of defense along the Ohio River.

In the following year, the Confederacy was squeezed from both north and south, as opposing forces battled for control of the Mississippi River. The Union advance began when General Ulysses S. Grant attacked two Confederate forts on the Kentucky-Tennessee border. First taking Fort Henry, on the Tennessee River, Grant surrounded Fort Donelson, on the Cumberland River, in February 1862. When the Confederate commander at Fort Donelson tried to negotiate, Grant's reply created his reputation as a tough, no-nonsense soldier: "No terms except unconditional and immediate surrender can be accepted."

The fall of Fort Donelson, with about 13,000 Confederate prisoners, opened the way for a Union advance south toward a railroad center at Corinth, Mississippi. From there Grant planned to move west along the railroad to capture Memphis, Tennessee, on the Mississippi River.

The Slaughter at Shiloh

The Union advance was slowed in April 1862 by the bloody, two-day battle of Shiloh on the Tennessee-Mississippi border. Grant's army was surprised near Corinth by the Confederates under General Albert Sidney Johnston. Union forces escaped disaster when reinforcements arrived and Johnston was killed.

Grant lost 13,000 of his 63,000 troops, and Confederate casualties numbered 11,000 of 40,000. Impressed by the determination of his enemy, Grant later wrote that after Shiloh, "I gave up all idea of saving the Union except by complete conquest."

The Union Takes New Orleans

Meanwhile, Flag Officer David Farragut was ordered to capture New Orleans. To reach the city, his warships had to move upriver from the Gulf of Mexico past 2 Confederate forts. After failing to destroy the forts, Farragut decided to pass under cover of darkness. As the maneuver began, the moon rose and the forts opened fire, hitting the first ship 42 times. After a 90-minute battle, 20 of the 24 Union ships made it past the forts, and New Orleans surrendered without firing a shot.

By the end of 1862, Union armies occupied all of western Tennessee and were probing south into Mississippi. Other armies were advancing north from New Orleans. Only the strongly fortified city of Vicksburg, Mississippi, blocked Union control of the river and success of the Union's western strategy.

■ Vicksburg and Chattanooga

As 1863 began, Union victory on the Mississippi River depended on taking the city of Vicksburg, and in late 1862 and early 1863, Grant made five attempts to capture the city. Finally, in May 1863, he began one of his most daring campaigns. After marching his army down the west bank of the Mississippi, below Vicksburg, he started inland. The Confederate commander at Vicksburg, thinking Grant was trying to trick him into the field, stayed behind his fortifications.

Critical Thinking

Identifying Cause and Effect Tell students that Southerners, when asked why they were fighting the war, often replied that they were defending themselves against the Yankees. Union soldiers arrested civilians, forced citizens to take loyalty oaths, stole and destroyed property, burned plantations, and set slaves free. What caused these actions? (mob mentality, unauthorized orders, breaches of discipline) What guarantees of security exist in modern international law to prevent such actions from happening? (United Nations charter for international warfare) **L2, L3**

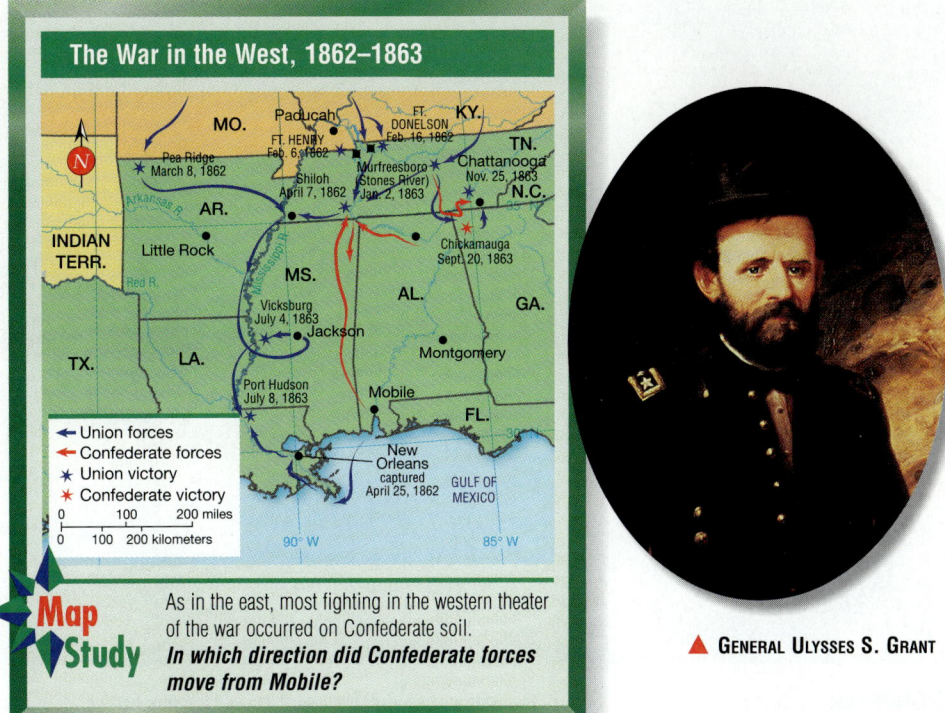

The War in the West, 1862–1863

Map Study: As in the east, most fighting in the western theater of the war occurred on Confederate soil. **In which direction did Confederate forces move from Mobile?**

▲ GENERAL ULYSSES S. GRANT

Map Study Using Maps
Answer: North

Skills Practice
Ask: What southernmost city on the Mississippi River controls the movement of ships from the Gulf of Mexico northward up the river? (New Orleans)

Did You Know?
More than a few officers were either appointed by state governments, regardless of their military experience, or were elected by their troops.

Vicksburg Under Siege

Moving quickly, Union forces reached Jackson, the capital of Mississippi, almost without opposition. Then Grant turned and fought his way back west to the outskirts of Vicksburg. In 17 days his troops marched 180 miles and won 5 battles against larger forces. Then he laid siege to Vicksburg. It was a terrifying time for the population. Starving residents ate horses, mules, and dogs. As Union artillery bombarded the city, a woman wrote in her diary:

> We are utterly cut off from the world, surrounded by a circle of fire.... The fiery shower of shells goes on day and night.... A shell came tearing through the roof, burst upstairs, tore up that room; ... the pieces coming through both floors down into the cellar....

On July 4, 1863, the same day that Lee began his retreat from Gettysburg, the starving city of Vicksburg surrendered. Five days later Port Hudson, the last Confederate port on the Mississippi River, also fell. Texas and Arkansas, the South's leading food producers, were now cut off from the rest of the Confederacy.

Battle for Chattanooga

Union forces now attempted to cut the Confederacy again—through eastern Tennessee and Georgia. The key was Chattanooga, a rail center on the Tennessee-Georgia border. In September 1863, a Union army under General William Rosecrans was badly defeated by Confederate General Braxton Bragg at the Battle of Chickamauga, in northwest Georgia. A Union officer described his army's retreat:

> The march was a melancholy one. All along the road for miles, wounded men were lying. They had crawled or hobbled slowly away from the fury of the battle, become exhausted, and lain down by the roadside to die.

Sidelights: Weapons of War

Weapons of war have become more efficient, distant, and impersonal since the time of the American Revolution. During the Revolution, colonists carried smooth-bore muskets. During the Civil War, soldiers used the rifled musket, railroad mines, land mines, and telescopic sites for the first time. The U.S. government issued a total of 240 military patents. Weapons such as mines made war more impersonal. Modern weapons such as guided missiles have continued this trend.

CHAPTER 15
SECTION 2

Visualizing History After being driven from Lookout Mountain, Confederate forces were routed from their position on Missionary Ridge. **Answer to Caption:** The North's victory enabled it to divide the eastern portion of the Confederacy by marching through Georgia.

ASSESS

Check Understanding
Assign Section 2 Review as homework or an in-class activity.

Evaluate
Assign the Section 2 Quiz in the History of a Free Nation Testmaker to create a customized quiz.

Reteach
Have students complete Reteaching Activity 15-2.

Enrich
Assign students American Portrait 30 on Thomas "Stonewall" Jackson. After students read the selection, have them write one paragraph in their journals, explaining why they think Jackson was a superior military leader.

CLOSE
Summarize the section and discuss why historians have called the Civil War the "end of American innocence."

 **Visualizing History** ▲ **OVERLOOKING CHATTANOOGA** The Battle of Chattanooga was one of the few battles in which Confederate forces outnumbered Union troops, 70,000 to 56,000. At first, Confederate troops forced their foes to retreat to the city. *What was the significance of the Battle of Chattanooga?*

Rosecrans retreated to Chattanooga, where the Confederates laid siege to his army and cut off its supplies. The Union forces were saved when Grant arrived with fresh supplies and reinforcements in late October and drove Confederate forces from the heights around the city. By the end of November, the Union forces had driven Bragg into Georgia and Tennessee was in Union hands. By the end of 1863, only four states—Georgia, South Carolina, North Carolina, and Virginia—remained to be subdued. In early 1864, Lincoln gave General William T. Sherman command in the west and summoned Grant to accomplish what none of his other generals could do—crush Robert E. Lee.

Section 2 ★ Review

Checking for Understanding
1. **Identify** Bull Run, George McClellan, Antietam, Emancipation Proclamation, Gettysburg, Ulysses S. Grant, Vicksburg.
2. **List** early Confederate victories and when they occurred.
3. **Explain** Lincoln's timing in issuing the Emancipation Proclamation.
4. **State** why the Battle of Gettysburg was so significant.

Critical Thinking
5. **Making Inferences** Bull Run changed people's perception of the war. From this reaction, what can you infer about the way people on both sides viewed the war before Bull Run?

422 UNIT 5 Division and Reunion 1825–1877

Answers to SECTION 2 REVIEW
1. Bull Run, 417; George McClellan, 418; Antietam, 419; Emancipation Proclamation, 419; Gettysburg, 419; Ulysses S. Grant, 420; Vicksburg, 420
2. Bull Run—1861; Seven Days—1862; Second Bull Run—1862; Fredericksburg—1862; Chancellorsville—1863
3. Issued within a week of the Union's first major victory at Antietam, thus bolstering morale and broadening the war's aims
4. Forced Southern retreat from the North
5. Answers will vary but may include that people believed the war would be efficiently conducted, not very bloody, and over quickly.

CONNECTIONS  CONNECTIONS

The Battle of Vicksburg

Control of the Mississippi River was critical to success for both the Union and Confederacy. As long as the South held Vicksburg, it controlled the 150 miles of river between that city and Baton Rouge. Vital supplies from western states flowed into the Confederacy across this stretch.

Unable to track Grant's army, Vicksburg's defenders were taken by surprise when he attacked from the south and east. Pinned against the river and swamp, the Confederates surrendered after a six-week siege.

▲ PRESENT-DAY VICKSBURG

◀ FIRST AT VICKSBURG by H. Charles McBarron The first battalion of the 13th U.S. Infantry fighting its way to the top of the Confederate lines at Vicksburg, Mississippi, May 19, 1863.

Before Grant could seize Vicksburg, however, he had to deal with a greater enemy—the wicked geography of the delta. Heavily fortified, Vicksburg was perched on a high bluff on the east side of a sharp bend in the Mississippi. North of Vicksburg lay the Yazoo Delta, a vast area of flat, swampy land half under water.

Grant descended the river from Memphis, where he sought unsuccessfully to approach the city through the delta. Grant then boldly crossed the Mississippi to the west bank, slipped south, and recrossed below Vicksburg. Contrary to established military strategy, and against the unanimous advice of his staff, Grant cut his supply lines, allowing only what food they could carry or get along the way.

Making the Geography Connection

1. What hazards might Grant have encountered in the delta?
2. Why was control of the Mississippi River important for the Union?
3. What tactic did Grant use to lay siege to Vicksburg?

Linking Past and Present

4. What places do you know of today where geography would pose problems for American troops?

CHAPTER 15 CONNECTIONS

Teaching Making Connections

For six months Grant's troops around Vicksburg dug ditches in waist-deep mud, slept in soaked fields, and endured plagues of malaria, measles, mumps, and smallpox.

Did You Know?

One result of the successes of African American units in the Vicksburg campaign was increased support for the policy of emancipation in the North.

Answers to Connections

1. Swampy land and water made troop movement difficult.
2. Cut western Confederate states, and important sources of food, from rest of Confederacy.
3. Cut his own supply lines, allowing only what food his troops could carry or get along the way.
4. Answers will vary, but students may mention geography-influenced climate such as heat in the Middle East, heat and humidity in Southeast Asia.

LESSON PLAN
SECTION 3, 424–429

FOCUS

Bellringer
Prior to taking roll at the beginning of the class period, display Focus Activity Transparency 51 on the overhead projector and assign the accompanying Focus Activity Sheet.

Objectives
Point out the objectives on this page to students in previewing the section content.

Motivating Activity
Present the following advertisement to students:

Wanted: Volunteers to help out at a refreshment saloon for the city of Philadelphia to welcome battle-bound units. Volunteers will dispense free meals and clothing to soldiers. Staff should expect to serve at least 100,000 soldiers over a period of three to four days. Join us for the Union Cause! Sign up at 312 No. Elm Street.

Ask: What benefit did the above action have on soldiers? (boosted morale and provided needed meals and clothing) Tell students that during the Civil War, groups of women in the North served as volunteers at events such as this. As students read, tell them to be aware of women's achievements.

SECTION 3

Behind the Lines

Setting the Scene

Section Focus
Financial, agricultural, and industrial resources played a major role in determining which side would win the war. But people were the most important resource. The war provided opportunities for African Americans and women to make additional contributions to their nation's vital interests.

Objectives
After studying this section, you should be able to
★ discuss behind-the-lines activity in the North and South.
★ explain the wartime roles played by women, African Americans, and Native Americans.

Key Terms
habeas corpus, conscription, bounty, greenback

◀ POWDER HORN

The Civil War was the largest war ever fought on the North American continent. Of the 1.5 million Southern white males of fighting age, about 900,000 served in the Confederate armies. Of 4 million such males in the North, about half fought in the war. In addition, more than 200,000 African Americans fought and served in the Union military, and thousands more performed manual labor for Confederate armies.

More Americans were killed in this war than in any other conflict in the history of the United States. Even in the early battles, the losses were shockingly high. As the war dragged on, the Union suffered terrible casualties but grew stronger. Confederate losses, however, gradually weakened the South's will to fight.

■ Wartime Government Power

Opposition to the war existed from the very beginning in both North and South. To carry on the war, President Lincoln and President Davis each exerted so much power that both were accused of acting like dictators. The Confederate government seized mules, wagons, food, and slaves for its armies. The Union government took over and operated private telegraph lines and railroads near war zones. Both Presidents suppressed opposition to the war by abusing the civil rights of citizens. Davis declared martial law in parts of the Confederacy, and he suspended the right of habeas corpus, which requires that persons who are arrested be brought to court to show why they should be held.

UNIT 5 Division and Reunion 1825–1877

Classroom Resources for SECTION 3

Teacher's Classroom Resources
- Reproducible Lesson Plan
- Reteaching Activity 15-3
- Section Quiz
- Chapter 15 Primary and Secondary Source Readings

Multimedia
- Section Focus Activity Transparency 51
- Chapter 15 Map Transparency
- Student Self-Test Software
- Testmaker
- Landmark Documents in American History

Discontent Grows

The North was a hotbed of discontent about the war. Abolitionists were irate over Lincoln's accommodating attitude toward slavery and about his refusal to make the end of slavery a goal of the war. They were joined by members of Lincoln's own party in Congress, a faction called the Radical Republicans, who opposed Lincoln's view that the war was only to preserve the Union.

The Copperheads

At the other extreme were the "Copperheads," mainly Democrats, who called for ending the war at any price, even if that meant welcoming the South and slavery back into the Union, or letting the slave states leave in peace. Some Copperheads encouraged Northerners to resist the war and others openly supported the South.

The Issue of Rights

Many of the measures Lincoln used to quiet opposition to the war violated constitutional guarantees of free speech, press, and assembly. He prevented a state legislature from meeting. He denied some opposition newspapers use of the mails and used the army to shut others down. And he ordered hundreds of suspected Confederate sympathizers jailed without the right of habeas corpus.

President Lincoln agonized over his decisions to deny American citizens their civil rights. He believed, though, that the survival of the nation during an emergency overrode the Constitution. In May 1863, Clement Vallandigham, a former Ohio congressman, made a speech in which he blamed the President for prolonging the war. He was arrested and sentenced to prison for the remainder of the war by a military court in Cincinnati. Vallandigham appealed to the Supreme Court for his release. But in 1864, in *Ex parte Vallandigham*, the Court refused to challenge the President and ruled that its authority did not extend to military courts.

■ Effects of the Emancipation Proclamation

When the Civil War began, there was not universal support in the North for a war to free enslaved persons. In many areas of the North there was open hostility to African Americans and laws that limited their rights. Slavery still existed in Washington, D.C., and in five states that remained in the Union.

Lincoln's Position

Lincoln, himself, was not an abolitionist. He regarded slavery as a moral wrong and a disaster for both blacks and whites, but he recognized the constitutional guarantees for slavery. He assured the South that he had "no purpose, directly or indirectly, to interfere with the institution of slavery where it now exists" but that he only opposed its extension into the territories. Again and again Lincoln declared that his goal was "to save the Union . . . not either to save or destroy slavery." If he acted any other way, he feared that the border states might join the Confederacy.

 President Abraham Lincoln

CHAPTER 15 The Civil War 425

Sidelights: Baseball

Baseball is said to have originated in a seventeenth-century English game called rounder played by the American colonists. In 1839, Abner Doubleday of Cooperstown, New York, perfected the game and called it base ball (two words). Baseball spread during the Civil War largely because Union soldiers played it for recreation between battles. Confederate prisoners and other troops watched the game and learned it. Before long, people around the country were playing baseball.

CHAPTER 15
SECTION 3

Independent Practice

Interpreting Primary Sources Refer students to the photograph of African American soldiers on page 427 and read the quotation that follows by Abraham Lincoln below on the importance of black Americans to the war effort.

"Keep it and you can save the Union. Throw it away, and the Union goes with it."

Ask: Why might Lincoln have placed such importance on African American soldiers? (good soldiers, increased size of Union army, deprived South of workers) Have students write a paragraph contrasting Lincoln's views on using black troops with the prejudiced view of those who opposed him. **L2**

Did You Know?

The two songs that many people identify with the Civil War, "Dixie" and "The Battle Hymn of the Republic," ironically were each borrowed from the other side. Dan Emmett, the son of an Ohio abolitionist, wrote "Dixie" as a Northern minstrel tune. Julia Ward Howe wrote the words to "The Battle Hymn" to the melody of a Southern camp-meeting hymn.

Pressure Mounts

As time passed, however, Lincoln came under increasing pressure to turn the war into a crusade against slavery. The abolitionists and the Radical Republicans demanded that Southern slaveholders be punished for the war by loss of their property. As the number of battlefield casualties grew, Northerners increasingly began to feel that such bloodshed was justified only if it destroyed an institution that violated human principles of freedom and dignity. In addition, Great Britain talked of mediating a settlement of the war. Lincoln realized that public opinion in Europe—and in Britain especially—was strongly opposed to slavery, and that no European government would defend the South in a war to abolish slavery.

The Proclamation Renews Spirit

After Lee's defeat at Antietam in 1862, Lincoln announced that he would free enslaved people in the Confederate states on January 1, 1863. But the Emancipation Proclamation did not immediately free anyone, because it applied only to the areas held by the enemy. The Proclamation, however, turned the war into a moral crusade and aroused a renewed spirit in the North. The number of African American volunteers for the army increased dramatically. As news of the Proclamation spread through the Confederacy, whenever Northern armies occupied Southern territory, thousands of African Americans poured into Union lines. The Emancipation Proclamation is "the greatest event of our nation's history, if not the greatest event of the century," said abolitionist editor Frederick Douglass.

Slavery in areas where the Emancipation Proclamation did not apply remained a problem, however. There were 800,000 enslaved persons in the border states and many more in areas of the South that the Union armies already had conquered. For these areas Lincoln recommended a policy of compensated emancipation—setting the enslaved free, but paying their owners for them. Congress, however, adopted this idea only for the District of Columbia, where there were just 3,000 enslaved people. Elsewhere, slavery was abolished by the Thirteenth Amendment to the Constitution, ratified in 1865.

■ Raising the Armies

At first, both North and South relied on volunteers and Lincoln's original 90-day volunteers were replaced by 3-year enlistments. But mounting casualties reduced enthusiasm for the war, and enlistments decreased.

Desertions

As the South's economy collapsed, and the scarcity of clothing and medicine was matched by shortages of food and shelter, Confederate desertions increased. "I am so tired for I never get any rest night or day, and I don't think I will last much longer," wrote a Georgia woman in despair. When Confederate soldiers received such letters, many saw no disgrace in going home to aid their suffering families.

The Draft

Both North and South were forced to resort to **conscription,** or the drafting of men for military service. In April 1862, the South, with less than one-half the population of the North, began drafting men aged 18 to 35. Later, as the need to maintain its armies increased, the Confederate congress raised the upper age limit to 50. In March 1863, the United States Congress created a military draft in the North.

The draft laws were incomplete and discriminatory. A draftee could avoid service by hiring a substitute, and a Union draftee could buy his way out by paying the government $300. Such provisions aroused criticism that it was "a rich man's war and a poor man's fight."

In the South, some state governors helped their citizens evade the draft. In the North, opposition to conscription led to riots in New York City in July 1863. A resident reported that for four days:

UNIT 5 Division and Reunion 1825–1877

Critical Thinking

Finding Supporting Evidence Write the following phrase on the board:

... all men are created equal ...

Tell students that President Lincoln used this phrase. Ask them to write three paragraphs explaining the meaning of the phrase for a democratic government and in what ways this philosophy affects their lives. **L2**

Life of the Times

Mess Call

One of the more unpleasant features of life in the Civil War armies was the food. Neither the Confederacy nor the Union enlisted men as cooks and no training was available to those who received this assignment.

When in quarters, a company would receive a government issue of flour, pork, beans, potatoes, coffee, and the like. Initially, six or eight recruits would form a mess team and take turns cooking. If any of them actually knew anything about preparing meals, the group was fortunate. Later, the commanding officer assigned men to the cook tent, as often as not, to get them out of the ranks.

On the march, rations typically consisted of dried salt pork, hardtack (a saltless hard biscuit made from flour), and coffee. Southern soldiers usually went without coffee, and cornmeal was substituted for hardtack. Veteran soldiers found fresh hardtack palatable enough.

With age, however, it might become infested with weevils. Some thought it better to eat it in the dark. Soldiers from both armies frequently supplemented meager rations by stealing crops and livestock from nearby farms.

▼ HARDTACK

▲ SOLDIER'S CANTEEN

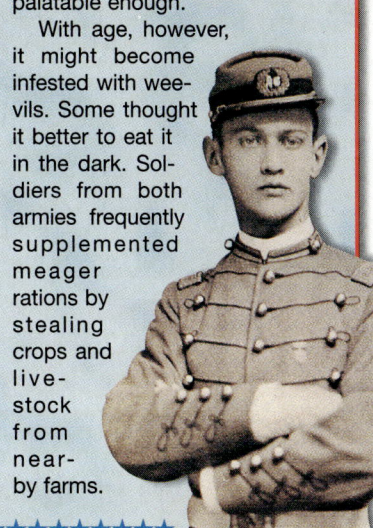
▲ UNION SOLDIER PHOTOGRAPHED BY MATHEW BRADY

African Americans Fight for the Union

President Lincoln at first resisted appeals to enlist African Americans in the Union armies because he feared that such a policy would be resented in the border states. After the Emancipation Proclamation, the policy was changed. Nearly 200,000 African Americans enlisted for military service and an additional 150,000 served in the quartermaster and engineering corps. Black soldiers were commanded by white officers, were paid less, and were segregated from white troops, who often resented them. Many African American regiments distinguished themselves in combat, however, and 23 soldiers won the Congressional Medal of Honor during the war.

Until the very end of the war, the South refused to accept African Americans for military service. Confederate armies often used enslaved persons to dig fortifications, cook, drive wagons, and perform other labor, but there was widespread opposition to arming them for combat.

> " ... there were dreadful scenes enacted in the city. The police were successfully opposed; many were killed, many houses were gutted and burned: the ... asylum was burned and all the furniture was carried off by women .... "

To those who enlisted, the North paid a **bounty**, or lump sum of money, of as much as $1,500 for a single 3-year enlistment. This led to the practice of "bounty jumping," whereby a man would enlist, collect his bounty and then desert, only to reenlist somewhere else.

CHAPTER 15 SECTION 3

Did You Know?

The Draft Riot of 1863 began in New York City with the drawing of names for those who had to serve in the Union army. Wealthy residential areas were looted by mobs, made up mainly of recent immigrants from Ireland.

Teaching Life of the Times

Soldiers called the pickled beef they received "salt horse" because it was stringy and salty. They told stories about how the square biscuits called hardtack saved soldiers' lives by stopping bullets.

Critical Thinking

Analyzing Change Before the 1860s the majority of women working outside their homes or farms were employed as household servants and public school teachers. During the war, however, women performed many of the tasks previously done by men. After the war many women returned to their traditional roles. Why were the changes in women's status so short-lived? (men and women alike were comfortable with the status quo, many believed they benefited from the status quo, cultural roles are difficult to change) **L1**

**CHAPTER 15
SECTION 3**

Teaching American Portraits

Tell students that Clara Barton was called the "Angel of the Battlefield" because she led search parties to look for the wounded. Once a bullet went through her sleeve and killed the patient she was attending. Discuss the contributions of women during the war.

Did You Know?

Elizabeth Blackwell and Clara Barton helped improve conditions in military hospitals. Blackwell, the first female medical graduate in the United States, had received an M.D. from the Geneva (New York) Medical College in 1849.

Did You Know?

The Confederate and Union armies both encountered difficulties in obtaining supplies for their troops. Confederate army officers improperly seized civilians' food, horses, animal feed, and other property. In 1863, the Confederate government passed a law trying to end these abuses. The efforts of the Union government to supply its armies were hindered by overcharging and corruption. Union army contractors sometimes supplied shoddy clothing, rotten meat, and defective shoes.

AMERICAN PORTRAITS

Clara Barton
1821–1912

Clara Barton grew up loving sports and intended to make teaching her career. After 18 years in education, however, she went to work for the U.S Patent Office. She was in the nation's capital when the guns of the Civil War started blazing.

Though lacking medical training, Clara Barton left her desk job to care for sick and wounded Union soldiers. Traveling to the sites of some of the worst carnage of the war, she even ventured deep into the Confederacy to assist federal forces laying siege to Charleston. She regularly risked her life by passing through the front lines to deliver supplies and nurse the wounded.

After the war—before she founded the American Red Cross in 1877—Clara Barton worked to identify thousands of soldiers who had perished at the Andersonville prison camp in Georgia.

Native Americans and the War

The Civil War also dramatically affected Native Americans. The South acted quickly to gain support, sending commissioners to the Indian Territory to sign peace treaties. The Cherokee even fought on the Confederate side.

In 1864 the Union sent troops to restore its authority over the Native Americans. Federal victories over forces in Arkansas and in the Indian Territory showed the Native Americans the weakness of their Confederate allies.

The North then renegotiated treaties with their nations and took land away from those who had fought for the Confederacy.

■ Women Behind the Lines

The demands the war placed on civilian populations created new roles for women. Southern women were required to run plantations. On smaller farms, women plowed the fields and handled other chores. Southern households became miniature factories, with spinning wheels and looms turning out clothing for the Confederacy.

Changing Roles

The war forced many Southerners to abandon their romantic view of women as "belles" to be protected from rough work. Many women worked as government clerks and factory workers—including dangerous work in munitions factories, making weapons and ammunition for the troops. Some women accompanied the armies in the field, cooking, sewing, and washing.

On Farms and in Factories

Although most Northern women did not suffer from invading armies, they also were deeply affected by the war. In the North, the mechanical reaper and the sulky plow—where the operator rode on top of the plow itself rather than pushed it from behind—allowed women to take the place of husbands and sons. Industry's need for labor opened other opportunities in Northern factories. Many women needed such work to support their families.

On the Battlefield

Nurses were exposed to the worst horrors of the war. Dorothea Dix became

UNIT 5 Division and Reunion 1825–1877

Cooperative Learning

Writing Have students work in groups of four to research and write a two-page report on the Sand Creek massacre of Cheyenne and Arapaho in 1864. Ask students to include possible reasons why the relationship between Native Americans and the federal government deteriorated during the Civil War. Each group should present its findings to the class. Compare and contrast the findings of the different groups, and discuss how researchers often reach different conclusions. **L3**

superintendent of female nurses in the Union army and in this position fought corruption and prejudice against her sex. Even more effective in widening the role of women in hospitals was Clara Barton, who founded the American Red Cross.

Women also played a large part in America's first great private relief organization—the United States Sanitary Commission. This organization collected millions of dollars for projects to improve the living conditions of Union soldiers. It is little wonder that after the Civil War there was a renewed demand for woman suffrage.

Supplying the Armies

In a long war fought on a vast scale, victors are decided as much behind the lines as on the battlefield. The Confederacy was defeated largely because of its inability to produce industrial goods. Through war contracts, the Confederate government helped to stimulate industry in the South. It encouraged factories to supply its troops with arms and ammunition, but it lacked the industrial capacity to provide other necessities.

Graft and Corruption

The efforts of the Union government to supply its armies were hindered by overcharging and corruption. Army contractors sometimes supplied shoddy clothing, rotten meat, and defective shoes. The productivity of Northern factories was so great, though, that in spite of the graft, Union armies were better equipped than their enemy.

Financing the War

The Confederacy also was less able to finance the war than was the North. The South had intended to obtain money by selling cotton to Europe, but the Union blockade prevented this. To raise money, the Confederacy enacted an income tax and demanded 10 percent of all crops produced. The most important way that the Confederacy and its state governments raised money was simply by printing more of it. The Confederate government was able to operate only by forcing its citizens to accept its worthless currency in exchange for supplies.

The North was far more successful in financing the war. About one-fourth of the $4 billion needed came from taxation, and the rest from borrowing and issuing paper money.

During the war the federal government issued more than $2.5 billion worth of bonds. Like the Confederacy, the Union government also inflated its currency, but not to the point where it became worthless. The federal government issued $400 million worth of **greenbacks,** paper money that was not backed by gold or silver, but whose value rose and fell with the success of Union armies in the field.

Section 3 ★ Review

Checking for Understanding

1. **Identify** Clara Barton, Radical Republicans, Copperheads, Ex parte Vallandigham, Dorothea Dix.
2. **Define** habeas corpus, conscription, bounty, greenback.
3. **State** what factors caused Lincoln to change his war goals to include freeing the enslaved persons.
4. **List** the contributions made by African Americans to the war effort on both sides.
5. **Explain** how women supported the war effort behind the lines.

Critical Thinking

6. **Assessing Cause and Effect** The war provided women opportunities that were not open to them before. What effect do you think this had on their views about their status in society?

CHAPTER 15 The Civil War 429

Answers to SECTION 3 REVIEW

1. Clara Barton, 428; Radical Republicans, 425; Copperheads, 425; *Ex parte Vallandigham*, 425.
2. All vocabulary terms are defined in the Glossary.
3. Pressure from abolitionists and Radical Republicans, need to justify battlefield casualties, threat of British intervention on behalf of the South.
4. 200,000 African Americans enlisted for Union military service; 150,000 served in Union support services; enslaved African Americans were forced to support the Confederate armies in various ways, including manual labor.
5. Women ran plantations and farms.
6. Answers will vary, but may include that these experiences spurred women to seek equality.

CHAPTER 15
SECTION 3

ASSESS
Check Understanding
Assign Section 3 Review as homework or an in-class activity.

Evaluate
Assign the Section 3 Quiz in the TCR or use the History of a Free Nation Testmaker to create a customized quiz.

Reteach
Ask students to list three sectors of the economy that welcomed women during the Civil War and to explain the jobs women held. Discuss students' answers. (industry: factory workers; nursing: replaced men in caring for sick and wounded; agriculture: ran plantations and plowed fields)
Have students complete Reteaching Activity 15-3.

Enrich
Have students write a biographical sketch describing the wartime contributions made by an important minority figure.

CLOSE
Summarize the section. Then discuss with students the effect of having Confederate money that did not have adequate backing of the people of the South during the Civil War.

LESSON PLAN
Mastering Social Studies Skills

Teaching Study and Writing Skills

Ask: Why is it more difficult to analyze pictures than is at first apparent? Point out that sometimes the photographer's or artist's motivation in making the picture may not be obvious. A supposedly objective historical painting might, in fact, convey a political message. A supposedly candid photo may be computer-enhanced (or carefully composed, as were some Civil War photos in which the photographers re-arranged bodies to influence viewers.)

Did You Know?

Both the Union and the Confederacy raised taxes and borrowed to help pay war expenses. They also printed lots of paper money. Dollar U.S. "greenbacks" decreased in value to 39 cents by 1864. Some Confederate treasury notes were worth only 1.6 cents by early 1865.

Social Studies Skills

Study and Writing Skills

▲ **COMPANY E, 4TH U.S. INFANTRY** at Fort Lincoln, District of Columbia, 1865

Analyzing Illustrations

The photographs and illustrations that appear throughout this book contain special information. They aid in your understanding of each chapter. The pictures identify the focus of the material, and they make the book more interesting.

Look carefully at each picture to analyze its content. The steps you can take to analyze the picture are simple.

1. **Look** at the picture to get a general sense of what the subject is about. The picture could give useful evidence about aspects of daily life.
2. **Read** the caption that goes with each picture or group of pictures.
3. **Decide** if the picture is a drawing, a painting, or a photograph. (There will be no photographs before the middle of the 1800s when photography was developed.)
4. **Decide,** if possible, whether a drawing or a painting was done by someone who lived at the time or someone who lived at a later time.
5. **Decide** whether a drawing is a posed portrait or an unposed photograph.
6. **Consider** the main theme and the general message of the picture.
7. **Identify** the main focus of the picture.
8. **Consider** how the figures in the picture support the main theme.
9. **Consider** how the use of color or lack of color supports the theme of the picture.
10. **Decide** why you think the picture is used at its location in the book.

Practicing the Skill

Using such a list can make understanding pictures easier. As an example, use the list to analyze the picture on this page. As you study the picture, consider the following questions.

1. All of the figures in the picture are African American soldiers. What does this tell you about the makeup of the Union army?
2. Study the expressions of the soldiers. What information does this give you?

As you look at the other pictures in this book, develop your own list of questions.

Answers to SOCIAL STUDIES SKILLS

1. Answers will vary, but students should note that the forces are segregated.
2. Answers will vary. Most students will note that the expressions are serious or grave and typical of soldiers.

SECTION 4

Ending the War

Setting the Scene

Section Focus

In March 1864, it became Ulysses S. Grant's turn to face the brilliant Confederate general, Robert E. Lee. Lincoln brought Grant east and gave him command of all Union forces. At last the President found a commander who could win the war. The President, however, would not live to see the war's end.

Objectives

After studying this section, you should be able to
★ explain the changes in Union military strategy after Grant took command.
★ discuss the issues in the election of 1864.

Key Term

forage

◀ Confederate hat

General Grant determined that to win the war he would utilize the Union's biggest advantages over the South—its overwhelming superiority in population and in production capacity. To end the South's ability to fight, he would not only defeat Confederate armies, but would destroy them. To end the South's will to fight, he would engage in "total war"—war against civilians and resources as well as against armies.

■ Grant in the East

Moving south into Virginia, in May and June 1864, Grant's force of 120,000 engaged the Confederate army of 60,000 almost continuously. At the Battle of the Wilderness, Lee stopped Grant in a forest where the fighting was so heavy that the woods caught fire, trapping the wounded in the flames and burning them to death. But instead of retreating after a defeat, as previous Union commanders had done, Grant kept advancing. He attacked Lee at Spotsylvania in a bloody battle that one soldier called "the most terrible twenty-four hours of our service in the war." In early June, Grant attacked Lee again, at Cold Harbor, where he ordered suicidal charges against fortified Confederate positions.

In less than a month, Union forces had suffered casualties greater in number than Lee's entire army. A Union officer protested that "our men have, in many instances, been foolishly and wantonly sacrificed." Grant knew that he could replace his losses while his enemy could not, and he promised "to fight it out along this line if it takes all summer."

In mid-June Lee retreated to Petersburg, south of Richmond, where Grant surrounded the Confederates and their capital and laid siege to the city. In July Lee attempted to break the siege by instructing General Jubal Early to move through Virginia's Shenandoah River valley to threaten Washington, D.C. Grant dispatched the Union cavalry under General Philip Sheridan to

CHAPTER 15 The Civil War 431

CHAPTER 15 SECTION 4

Teach

Guided Practice

Critical Thinking Have students reread "Sherman's March." Discuss Sherman's methods and whether they were extreme. Have students write three paragraphs explaining why civilian guarantees broke down during the Civil War. **L3**

Did You Know?

When Sherman entered Savannah he wired President Lincoln: "I beg to present you, as a Christmas gift, the city of Savannah, with 150 heavy guns, plenty of ammunition, and 25,000 bales of cotton."

Visualizing History The city of Richmond is actively dedicated to preserving its rich history. Civil War monuments may be seen in many areas, such as the Richmond National Battlefield Park, which contains sites of seven sieges against the Confederate capital. Meadow Farm, an 1850s living history museum, presents authentic reenactments of major Civil War battles. The Museum of the Confederacy boasts the world's largest collection of Civil War artifacts.

Answer to Caption: to destroy its productive capacity and to bring the horrors of war to the civilian population

---

drive the Confederates from the area and told him "nothing should be left to invite the enemy to return." He ordered Sheridan to make the valley "a barren waste." By March 1865, Sheridan had carried out his orders so well, he reported to Grant, that a crow flying across the valley would have to carry its food. Meanwhile, Grant continued his siege of Richmond.

■ Sherman's March

In May 1864, as Grant invaded Virginia, he ordered General William T. Sherman and his 100,000 troops posted in Chattanooga, Tennessee, to engage and destroy the Confederate army in the west. The Confederates were forced to retreat toward Atlanta, Georgia, which Sherman captured in September and occupied until November, when he ordered the city evacuated and destroyed. City officials begged that Atlanta be spared, but Sherman replied:

> *You might as well appeal against the thunderstorm as against these terrible hardships of war. They are inevitable, and the only way the people of Atlanta can hope once more to live in peace and quiet at home, is to stop the war....*

As the Northern army abandoned the city, a Union officer described its destruction:

> *The heaven is one expanse of lurid fire; the air is filled with flying, burning cinders; buildings covering two hundred acres are in ruins or in flames; every instant there is the sharp detonation or the smothered booming sound of exploding shells and powder....*

To divide the South a second time, Sherman adopted Grant's tactics before Vicksburg—strike into enemy territory and **forage,** or

◀ **HISTORIC DISTRICT, RICHMOND TODAY**

▲ **DESTRUCTION IN THE SOUTH** By April 1865 many major cities of the Confederacy, including Atlanta and the capital city of Richmond (above), had felt the full force of war. **Why did Sherman burn Atlanta?**

432 UNIT 5 Division and Reunion 1825–1877

Sidelights: Sherman's Legacy

When Sherman marched through Georgia, the weather was warm and dry, allowing his army and cannons to move easily across the countryside. The Confederates hoped in vain for rain to mire the roads and slow the advance. Because of the destruction Sherman caused, his name lives on in the South. During the 1988 Democratic National Convention in Atlanta, a barbecue was held for Ohio delegates. One Atlanta resident is said to have commented, "I never thought I would see the day that I would be lighting a fire in Atlanta for a bunch of people from Sherman's home state."

live off the land. His army marched southeast and for a month carved a path of destruction 60 miles wide through one of the richest agricultural regions of the South. Sherman reached the Atlantic coast at Savannah, Georgia, and reported to Grant that he had destroyed $100 million of property in Georgia—$20 million in military damage and "the remainder is simply waste and destruction."

As he entered Savannah on December 20, 1864, Sherman learned that five days before, outside Nashville, Tennessee, General George Thomas had destroyed the Confederates' western army. The war in the west was over. In February 1865, Sherman left Savannah and marched north through the Carolinas, destroying everything in his path and planning to link up with Grant at Richmond.

 ▲ **Sherman** Union General William T. Sherman brought the horror of war to the civilian population of Georgia and the Carolinas. *How did Sherman affect the outcome of the election of 1864?*

■ The Election of 1864

Throughout the war, federal, state, and city elections continued to be held in the North, but the war divided both major parties into War Democrats and Peace Democrats, Radical Republicans and Conservative Republicans. In the presidential election of 1864, the Republican party temporarily changed its name to the Union party to attract Democrats who supported the war.

Lincoln Runs for Reelection

The Unionists renominated Lincoln for President and chose a War Democrat for Vice President, Andrew Johnson, military governor of Tennessee. The Democrats nominated George McClellan, the popular general whom Lincoln had twice removed from command. But the Democrats drew up a peace platform that branded the war a failure and called for the immediate restoration of the Union.

Lincoln's chances for victory largely depended on the fortunes of the Union armies in the field. In mid-1864 the war was going badly, and Lincoln was certain that he would be defeated. But Sherman's capture of Atlanta in September, coupled with McClellan's refusal to support his party's platform, gave Lincoln the victory. The voters had decided that "it was not best to swap horses while crossing the river," Lincoln said.

"With Malice Toward None"

In his second Inaugural Address in March 1865, Lincoln reviewed the causes of the war and hoped for a peace without bitterness. Both sides "read the same Bible and pray to the same God," he noted, so "let us judge not that we be not judged." It may be, Lincoln said, that the war was divine vengeance on both North and South for two centuries of wrong to African American people.

Lincoln concluded his short address by extending charity to the defeated South. He directed his generals to offer the Confederate armies the most liberal terms of surrender and asked Northerners:

> *With malice toward none, with charity for all . . . let us strive on to finish the work we are in, to bind up the nation's wounds, . . . to do all which may achieve and cherish a just and lasting peace among ourselves and with all nations.*

CHAPTER 15
SECTION 4

Visualizing History Lee wore his best uniform at Appomattox. Grant's was disheveled and spattered with mud. Nevertheless, the two men, so different in many ways, possessed mutual respect for one another. **Answer to Caption:** Lincoln wanted lenient treatment for the defeated South, and Grant's surrender terms were in that spirit.

Fact or Fiction?

Life in prison camps was dangerous because of the conditions and disease.

FACT: After the war, federal government figures showed more than 26,000 fatalities among the 220,000 Confederate prisoners held in the North and more than 22,000 among the 126,000 Union captives in the South.

ASSESS

Check Understanding
Assign Section 4 Review as homework or an in-class activity.

Evaluate
Assign the Section 4 Quiz in the TCR or use the History of a Free Nation Testmaker to create a customized quiz.

In the four years since the untried prairie lawyer delivered his first Inaugural Address, his stock had risen. In spite of violent attacks in Congress and in the press, Lincoln inspired affection and trust, as shown by the nicknames "Uncle Abe" and "Father Abraham." Many people had begun to appreciate the ability and strength of character hidden behind Lincoln's homely exterior. One of these was the novelist Nathaniel Hawthorne, who wrote about the President:

> *There is no describing the lengthy awkwardness nor the uncouthness of his movement; and yet it seemed as if I had been in the habit of seeing him daily, and had shaken hands with him a thousand times in some village street.... If put to guess his calling and livelihood, I should have taken him for a country schoolmaster as soon as anything else ... [Yet, I like his appearance] ... and, for my small share in the matter, would as [soon] have Uncle Abe for a ruler as any man whom it would have been practicable to put in his place.*

The Final Days

While Lincoln was delivering his second Inaugural Address in March 1865, Grant was pressing in on Richmond and Sherman was marching through the Carolinas. Aware that the situation was hopeless, General Lee advised President Davis that he could no longer defend Richmond. The Confederate government fled south, and Lee's army finally evacuated the city. By April 4, 1865, President Lincoln was able to walk through the streets of the former Confederate capital.

▲ **Visualizing History** LEE (RIGHT) SURRENDERS TO GRANT AT APPOMATTOX COURT HOUSE Grant ordered Union troops not to celebrate. "The war is over," he said, "the rebels are our countrymen again." **How did Grant's surrender terms compare with Lincoln's attitude toward the South?**

434 UNIT 5 Division and Reunion 1825–1877

Critical Thinking

Making Comparisons Compare life in the agricultural South with life in the industrial North during the Civil War. Compare clothes, houses, food, types and availability of jobs. (South: living conditions deteriorated, lack of clothing and material, lack of workers to plant and harvest crops, cotton crop shifted to food crops, little industry; North: living conditions improved, food and clothes available, industry prospered, jobs increased) **L2**

Lee Surrenders

Just days later, Grant's forces cut off Lee's troops as they attempted to unite with other Confederate armies. Grant urged Lee to surrender in order to prevent "further effusion of blood." On April 9, 1865, the two men met at Appomattox Court House in central Virginia. Grant offered Lee generous terms: Southern soldiers could go home if they pledged not to fight again. The officers would keep their pistols and the men their horses.

When Lee's army came to lay down their arms, Union troops saluted each division as it appeared. As the Confederate forces marched before them, the Union troops watched silently, with "not a cheer, nor a word, nor whisper of vainglory," one Union officer described it, "but an awed stillness rather, a breath-holding, as if it were the passing of the dead."

Defying orders from President Davis, by June, all other Confederate generals also surrendered. The long, bitter struggle that split the nation finally came to an end.

Lincoln is Assassinated

President Lincoln did not live to see the end of the war, however. On April 14, 1865, just five days after Lee's surrender, Lincoln was assassinated by John Wilkes Booth, a fanatical Confederate sympathizer. Booth's deed was a tragedy for both North and South, for it removed the one person best equipped to "bind up the nation's wounds."

A Richmond newspaper called Lincoln's death "the heaviest blow which has ever fallen upon the people of the South." A young Southern woman confided to her diary, "The most terrible part of the war is now to come."

▶ JOHN WILKES BOOTH (BELOW) AND WANTED POSTER

Visualizing History ▲ President Lincoln was shot and killed while attending a play at Ford's Theater. An eyewitness later recalled that the theater was filled with "the shouts, groans, curses, smashing of seats, screams, and cries of terror." The items shown below the wanted poster and Booth's photo are the contents of Lincoln's pockets the day he died. **Why did many Southerners as well as Northerners mourn the loss of the President?**

Section 4 ★ Review

Checking for Understanding
1. **Identify** William T. Sherman, Andrew Johnson, Appomattox, John Wilkes Booth.
2. **Define** forage.
3. **Explain** the strategy that Grant adopted to defeat the Confederacy.
4. **Examine** how the tactics used by Union generals Philip Sheridan and William Sherman broadened the scope of the war beyond purely military engagements.

Critical Thinking
5. **Analyzing a Quotation** To explain his reelection, Lincoln stated, "it was not best to swap horses while crossing the river." Explain the meaning of Lincoln's quotation and how it applied to him.

REVIEW CHAPTER 15

Answers

Reviewing Facts

1. Southern: superior military leadership, familiarity with the terrain. Northern: superior industrial production, more people.
2. Blockade the South, invade and divide the South, capture Richmond
3. Utilizing railroads and the telegraph enabled a quick supply of reinforcements, resulting in a Confederate victory. The invasion of the North was repulsed and the enormous loss of men severely crippled the South.
4. For the first time, the war was now being fought over human rights—putting an end to human slavery.
5. conscription, bounty payments
6. Sherman's capture of Atlanta bolstered Union morale. The Democratic candidate refused to support his party's platform condemning the war and calling for immediate restoration of the Union.

CHAPTER 15 ★ REVIEW

Using Vocabulary

For the first time, photography was used extensively to record history during the American Civil War. Regard each of the terms below as captions for a pictorial history of the Civil War. After each term, describe a photograph that would explain the concept or identify the term.

- martial law
- greenbacks
- bounty
- conscription
- habeas corpus

Reviewing Facts

1. **List** two Southern military advantages and two Northern military advantages.
2. **State** the Union army's three principal goals.
3. **Explain** how technology played a role in determining the victor at Bull Run. Describe the results of Antietam and Gettysburg for the Southern army.
4. **Summarize** the effects the Emancipation Proclamation had on the war.
5. **State** two methods the North used to raise troops.
6. **State** two reasons Lincoln was reelected.

Understanding Concepts

Rights and Freedom

1. How did Lincoln violate constitutional rights during the war and for what reasons?
2. Why would African Americans be eager to fight for the Union army? Why was Lincoln initially reluctant to use African American soldiers?

Conflict

3. Why did Union victory come only after its generals decided to fight a ruthless war?
4. How did attitudes about the kind and extent of the war change after Bull Run?

Critical Thinking

1. **Evaluating Causes** List five factors that affected the military ability of both the Northern and Southern armies. Rank the items according to their importance in determining the outcome of the Civil War.
2. **Evaluating an Action** Grant's campaign against Vicksburg was a calculated risk. List the pros and cons of Grant's strategy. If he had failed, what likely consequences would he have faced?
3. **Analyzing Artifacts** Supporters for Lincoln expressed their support during the 1860 presidential election campaign with posters such as this one. Why did the creators of the poster choose those particular symbols to represent Lincoln? What other symbols can you suggest?

Writing About History

Argumentation

The Civil War resulted in enormous loss of life. Do you believe this loss was justified? Write an essay stating whether you believe the war was worth the cost. Write your argument from the perspective of a disabled Union or Confederate soldier or a Union or Confederate wife whose husband died fighting in the war.

Understanding Concepts

1. He violated rights of free speech, press, assembly, and habeas corpus. Answers will vary but may include that war necessitates decisions for reasons of security and survival, although many believe such actions should never be allowed to override the Constitution.
2. African Americans were eager to contribute to the military effort that would win their people's freedom. Lincoln did not want to anger the border states or to start slave uprisings in the South.
3. Union generals realized that their manpower and resources outnumbered those of the Confederacy. Such ruthless measures as throwing countless Union soldiers into battles and laying areas of the South to waste would have the effect of wearing down the Confederacy.

CHAPTER 15 ★ REVIEW

Cooperative Learning

Each member in your group takes one of these roles: Union soldier, Confederate soldier, and British journalist. The journalist would like to get both viewpoints on the war. Each group member must prepare one question to be asked by the journalist. If you are the Union soldier, write a question for the journalist to ask the Confederate soldier and vice versa. If you are the journalist, write one question that you will ask each soldier. Conduct the interview in front of your classmates.

Social Studies Skills

Drawing Conclusions Drawing conclusions—that is, making judgments or decisions after deliberation—can help you in your studies. After reviewing what you know, ask yourself such questions as:

- Do I have all the information I need to make a valid conclusion?
- Have I weighed all the information fairly?
- How and why might new information cause me to change or modify my conclusion?

The map on this page shows the final campaigns of the Civil War. Like the early battles, the final struggles between the Union and the Confederacy took place in the eastern theater. From this information, you could conclude that it might have been unwise for the Confederacy to move their capital to Richmond, which appears to be a poor strategic location.

Practicing the Skill

Study the map, and then draw further conclusions by answering the questions that follow.

1. What conclusions can you make about what life must have been like for people living in Virginia during the final months of the war?
2. What conclusions can you make about whether or not the Confederates were fighting offensive or defensive battles?
3. **Analyzing Choices** What conclusions do you think led General Lee to finally surrender?

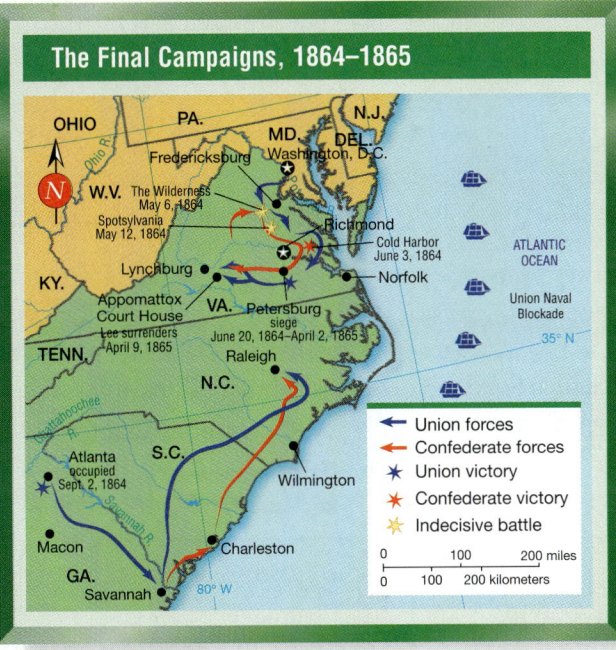

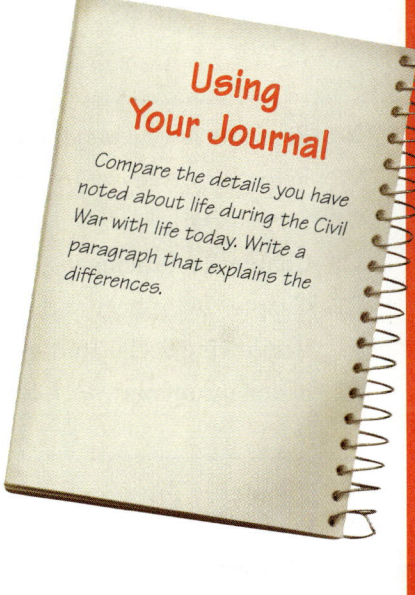

Using Your Journal
Compare the details you have noted about life during the Civil War with life today. Write a paragraph that explains the differences.

CHAPTER 15 The Civil War 437

REVIEW CHAPTER 15

Practicing the Skill

1. Life must have been very difficult because they were constantly surrounded by the fighting.
2. The Union forces kept pushing southward; in effect they were chasing the Confederate forces, putting the Confederates on the defensive.
3. Sample Answer: Richmond had fallen and his forces were surrounded.

? Chapter Bonus Test Question

This question may be used for extra credit on the chapter test. Choose the letter of the correct response.

The Emancipation Proclamation laid the basis for
a. allowing the former slaves to serve in the Union army.
b. freeing the slaves as the Union army took control over areas formerly under Confederate control.
c. calling for troops to put down the rebellion.
d. ordering supplies and forces to Fort Sumter in South Carolina.

(Answer: b)

Using Your Journal

The ideas that students present in their paragraphs will vary but should include references to specific details. You might call on volunteers to read their paragraphs to the class and have the class discuss major points.

---

4. Americans on both sides realized that the war would be long and bloody.

Critical Thinking

1. Answers will vary but may include: Wealth—1. Industrial production—2. Military leadership—3. Size of population—4. Support of population—5. Agricultural production
2. Answers will vary but may include—Pros: was daring and could not be anticipated. Cons: dangerous and put lives of his troops in jeopardy. If Grant failed, the entire western campaign might have been turned back, the Mississippi would not have come under Union control, the war would have been prolonged.
3. Answers will vary but may include the idea that symbols of national unity and strength would help win the election.

437

PLANNING GUIDE — Chapter 16   Reconstruction

Daily Lesson Objectives	Teacher Classroom Resources	Multimedia
SECTION 1 **After Slavery** 1 Day pp. 440–444 1. Explain the changes in Southern society that occurred after the Civil War. 2. Discuss the changes that freedom brought to African American families.	Chapter 16 Study Guide Reproducible Lesson Plan Reteaching Activity 16-1 Section Quiz Chapter 16 Primary and Secondary Source Readings Reinforcing Social Studies Skills 26, 31, 32, 67 American Portraits 31, 32 Chapter 16 Cooperative Learning Activity Chapter 16 Concept Mapping Activity Writer's Guidebook Lesson 6	Student Self-Test Software Testmaker Section Focus Transparency 49 Chapter 16 Skills Transparency A Geographic Perspective on American History
SECTION 2 **Reconstructing the South** 1 Day pp. 445–451 1. Compare the Lincoln-Johnson plans for Reconstruction with the plans of the Radical Republicans. 2. Explain how the black codes and the return of former Confederates to power affected Reconstruction.	Reproducible Lesson Plan Reteaching Activity 16-2 Section Quiz Reinforcing Social Studies Skills 26, 28, 31, 53, 55, 59 LEP American Portraits 31, 32 The Living Constitution	Student Self-Test Software Testmaker Section Focus Transparency 50 Chapter 16 Map Transparency The American People: Fabric of a Nation The Presidents: A Picture History of Our Nation
SECTION 3 **Restoring Southern Power** 1 Day pp. 453–456 1. Describe Southern resistance to Reconstruction. 2. Discuss political and economic change in the South after Reconstruction.	Reproducible Lesson Plan Reteaching Activity 16-3 Section Quiz Chapter 16 Enrichment Activity Chapter 16 Primary and Secondary Source Readings Reinforcing Social Studies Skills 27, 30, 31, 50 Spanish Summaries & Glossary	Student Self-Test Software Testmaker Section Focus Transparency 51 Unit 5 Digest Transparencies Vocabulary Puzzlemaker Audiocassette, Chapter 16 The Presidents: A Picture History of Our Nation
CHAPTER REVIEW AND EVALUATION 1 Day	Chapter 16 Test Chapter 16 Performance Assessment Activity	Student Self-Test Software Testmaker

OUT OF TIME? If time does not permit teaching the entire chapter, use the Chapter 16 Summary on pages 462–463 and the Chapter 16 audiocassette (English and Spanish) to point out the main ideas of the chapter.

PLANNING GUIDE

Cultural Diversity Activity

Analyzing an Opinion Write historian Edgar Toppin's assessment of Reconstruction on the chalkboard:

"The greatest shame of Reconstruction was the failure to provide for the freedmen, after centuries of unpaid toil, with land and assistance to make a sound start economically. This failure left a legacy of future troubles."

Have students speculate about what Toppin means by the reference to "future troubles." Then discuss what students consider the greatest successes and failures of Reconstruction. Then have students consider how the legacy of Reconstruction might have been different if formerly enslaved Americans had been provided with land and start-up money.

Performance Assessment Activity

Education Organize students into groups of four or five and assign each a different state in existence in 1870. Tell students that by 1870 about 43 percent of children between the ages of 5 and 17 were enrolled in an elementary or secondary school. Ask each group to research the status and quality of elementary education in their assigned state from 1865 to 1876. Ask each group to prepare a poster highlighting its findings. As a class, use the information on the posters to assess the education in the United States in the years after the Civil War.

POSSIBLE RUBRIC FEATURES: Content, research skills, organization, creativity, written and visual communication skills, collaborative skills

Chapter Resources

Literature from the Period

Douglass, Frederick. "What the Black Man Wants." 1865.

Stevens, Thaddeus. "Speech in the U.S. House of Representatives." January 3, 1867.

Readings for the Student

Cook, Fred. *The Ku Klux Klan: America's Recurring Nightmare.* Messner, 1989.

Morris, Roy, Jr. "Master Fraud of the Century." *American History Illustrated,* Vol. 23, No. 7, November 1988.

Woodward, C. Vann. *The Strange Career of Jim Crow.* Oxford. 1974.

Readings for the Teacher

Foner, Eric. *Reconstruction: America's Unfinished Revolution.* Harper, 1988.

Sernett, Milton C., ed. *Afro-American Religious History: A Documentary Witness.* Duke University Press, 1985.

Stampp, Kenneth M. *The Era of Reconstruction, 1865–1877.* Random House, 1967.

Multimedia Resources

Frederick Douglass: An American Life. Your World Video. (VHS, 30 minutes)

Living American History Series. U.S. History II: 1840–1875. Priven Learning Systems (2 Apple diskettes, guide)

Rebuilding the American Nation, 1865–1890. Guidance Associates. (2 filmstrips)

Reconstruction. Dallas Community College. (VHS, 30 minutes)

Key to Ability Levels

Teaching strategies have been coded for varying learning styles and abilities.

- **L1** Basic activities for all students
- **L2** Average activities for average to above-average students
- **L3** Challenging activities for above-average students
- **LEP** Limited English Proficiency activities

Glencoe Links to the Humanities

Links to Literature

- Macmillan Literature: Novel Guide—*When Legends Die*
- Macmillan Literature: American Literature Text—Walt Whitman, Emily Dickinson

Link to Music

 American Music: Cultural Traditions

CHAPTER 16

BEGINNING THE CHAPTER

After the Civil War, the great question facing the nation was how to readmit the Confederate states to the Union. Lincoln's policy was generous, making reentry as easy as possible. But Radical Republicans demanded a policy that would punish the South so that it would never again take up arms in rebellion. Ask students to predict which political issues might arise during Reconstruction.

Linking Across Time

One outcome of the Civil War was the rise of independent African American churches. By 1870, four—the Colored Primitive Baptist Church, the Colored Methodist Episcopal Church, the African Methodist Episcopal Church, and the Zion Church—had been formed.

Recording Journal Notes

Encourage students to use their journals to make comparisons between present-day life and the events presented in the chapter. As they record the events that inhibited racial equality during Reconstruction, ask them to draw parallels and contrasts with events from the mid-1960s to the present.

CHAPTER 16

Reconstruction
1865–1877

▶ ELECTION CAMPAIGN RIBBON, 1868

Setting the Scene

Focus

Confederate war veterans who returned home after the war found their land devastated. African Americans quickly discovered that freedom did not mean equality. The first order of business for the federal government, however, was to readmit the Southern states to the Union. This proved difficult because white Southerners were bitter and Radical Republicans in Congress worked to keep their party in power.

Concepts to Understand

★ Why adaptation to new social conditions was necessary for newly freed men and women and white planters
★ How Radical Republicans sought to exercise power and authority over the Reconstruction process

Read to Discover . . .

★ why Reconstruction policies differed.
★ what the Compromise of 1877 established.

Journal Notes

As you read the chapter, note how racial equality was inhibited during Reconstruction. Write your findings in your journal.

CULTURAL
- 1866 Fisk School, later Fisk University, founded in Nashville, Tennessee
- 1871 P. T. Barnum opens circus in Brooklyn, New York

1865 ———————————————— 1869

POLITICAL
- 1868 President Johnson impeached by House; Senate fails to convict him
- 1869 Federal government completes Great Western Survey

438 UNIT 5 Division and Reunion: 1825–1877

✚ EXTRA CREDIT PROJECT

The Fourteenth Amendment (1868) protected citizens from being deprived of their rights as citizens. The Fifteenth Amendment (1870) protected voting rights. Both were ratified during Reconstruction. Ask interested students to research specific protections in each amendment. Have students prepare and present charts comparing these with the provisions of the Civil Rights Act of 1964 and the Voting Rights Act of 1965.

History AND ART

Dog Swap by R.N. Brooke

Artist R.N. Brooke skillfully captured the details of daily life during Reconstruction.

◀ TOY WHEELED HORSE, LATE 1800s

- **1876** Alexander Graham Bell transmits message on telephone
- **1879** The Church of Christ, Scientist, chartered

1873 — **1877**

- **1873** New York Stock Exchange closes for 10 days after economic panic begins
- **1877** Compromise of 1877 completed
- **1881** Kansas passes a prohibition law

CHAPTER 16 Reconstruction 1865–1877

CHAPTER 16 CONCEPTS

Concept Mapping Activity

Write the chapter concepts on the chalkboard. Ask students to write these concepts in their notebooks and to list each major event in the chapter under the appropriate concept.

Northerners and Southerners move to rebuild the nation.
→ Adaptation
→ Power and Authority

History AND ART

Richard Norris Brooke (1847–1920) was born in Virginia, studied at the Pennsylvania Academy of Fine Arts, and served as a U.S. consul in France in the mid-1870s. He was noted for his nostalgic paintings of African Americans.

NATIONAL GEOGRAPHIC SOCIETY

- **GTV:** *The American People: Fabric of a Nation*

Side 2, Chapter 8
Title: *The Dream, Deferred*
Subject: Equal rights during Reconstruction—and now

See GTV Guide page 72 for complete lesson plan.

Teacher Notes

LESSON PLAN
SECTION 1, 440–444

FOCUS

Bellringer
Before taking roll at the beginning of the class period, display Focus Activity Transparency 53 on the overhead projector, and assign the accompanying Focus Activity Sheet.

Objectives
Point out the objectives on this page to students in previewing the section content.

Motivating Activity
Present the following letter to students:

> July 15, 1867
> You, my friends,
> A generous enemy will forgive us for taking a minute to remember what will fade from our memories . . . a lingering look on our Southern homes as they existed before the red hand of war made them desolate.
> Mary Lenox, Columbus, GA

Ask: What do you think this Southern writer was feeling at this moment? (deep sadness for the loss of life as it had been) Tell students that during Reconstruction many Southern writers romanticized life in the pre–Civil War South. As they read have them note the changes that would take place in Southern society.

Use Skills Transparency 16.

SECTION 1

After Slavery

Setting the Scene

Section Focus

The Civil War saved the Union but shook the nation to its roots. The fall of the Confederacy toppled the planter aristocracy that had ruled the South. Also gone was slavery, the labor system that was the basis of Southern society. The end of slavery, however, did not solve the problems that the newly freed African Americans were to face.

Objectives

After studying this section, you should be able to
★ explain the changes in Southern society that occurred after the Civil War.
★ discuss the changes that freedom brought to African American families.

Key Terms

tenant farmer, sharecropper

◀ BADGE WORN BY FREED AFRICAN AMERICANS

When Confederate veterans—tired, ragged, and hungry—went home at the end of the Civil War, they returned to a ravaged land. Large areas of land had been systematically laid to waste by the armies of Sherman and Sheridan. One Mississippi woman remembered her father's homecoming after the war:

> 66 He had come home to a house stripped of every article of furniture. The plantation was stripped of the means of cultivating any but a small portion of it. A few mules and one cow made up the stock. . . . He owned nothing that could be turned into money without great sacrifice but five bales of cotton. 99

The wreckage stretched from South Carolina's Atlantic coast in the east to Tennessee in the west and from Virginia's Shenandoah Valley in the north through Georgia in the south. It was not only the land that was in ruin, however. Economically, politically, and socially, the South was in total disarray. Confederate money was worthless, and Southern banks were ruined. Government at every level had all but disappeared. There were no courts, no judges, no sheriffs, and no police—no law or authority except when groups of people took matters into their own hands. The war also left the South's transportation system in complete disorder. Roads were impassable, bridges had been destroyed or had washed away, and railroad tracks had been rendered unusable. For planters, the greatest economic blow was the loss of their enslaved workers, an investment worth more than $2 billion. When the workers were freed, the plantation system collapsed.

Classroom Resources for SECTION 1

Teacher's Classroom Resources
- Chapter 16 Study Guide
- Reproducible Lesson Plan
- Chapter 16 Primary and Secondary Source Readings
- Reteaching Activity 16-1
- Chapter 16 Cooperative Learning Activity
- Section Quiz

Multimedia
- Section Focus Transparency 53
- Chapter 16 Skills Transparency
- Testmaker
- Student Self-Test Software
- A Geographic Perspective on American History

New Ways of Life

The devastation of war affected all levels of Southern society. For landowners it meant that their old way of life had been swept away.

The Plight of the Landowners

After his regiment surrendered at Appomattox, the planter Harry Hammond said he had "a pipe, some tobacco, and literally nothing else." Although Hammond owned a large plantation, he could find no one who could afford to buy his land when he put it up for sale. Hammond was saved from total ruin when most of the 300 African Americans on the plantation agreed to stay and work the land. In return for their labor, Hammond provided his formerly enslaved workers with housing, firewood, weekly food allotments, every other Saturday off, and $15 a year in cash after the crops were harvested. Hammond also agreed to provide the loan of a mule and a plow so that the workers could grow their own crops.

Not every planter was so fortunate. Southerners who had invested heavily in Confederate currency and bonds were wiped out financially when Confederate funds became worthless after the war. Many lost their land because of taxes or other debts they could not pay. Some sold their acres to anyone who could pay the outrageously low prices for which Southern farms and plantations were advertised in Northern newspapers. On other plantations and on small farms throughout the South, war widows struggled to hold on to their property and keep it producing.

The Plight of Workers

Poor African Americans and whites realized that social and economic status in the South was tied to the land, but few had money to buy land, even at such low prices. So some became **tenant farmers**, farming land that they rented. But even this was beyond the means of many poor Southerners, and more often they became **sharecroppers**, persons who worked the owner's land—sometimes using the owner's tools, animals, and seed—and received a share of the crops in return.

Although these arrangements seemed a solution that would provide a living for both workers and landowners, the system contained serious defects. For example, debt-ridden landowners wanted to get the highest possible return, so they pressured tenants to grow only cotton or tobacco, cash crops that paid the most. To prevent depletion of the soil, however, tenants should have planted a variety of crops, including food crops.

Tenants, black and white alike, usually had to buy seed, fertilizer, work animals, and food on credit, at interest rates as high as 40 percent. Thus, no matter how hard they worked, many tenants fell deeply into debt and remained trapped on the land until they paid those debts—no freer to leave than enslaved workers had been. As late as 1907,

 ▲ **THE WAY THEY LIVE** by Thomas Pollock Anshutz, 1879 Painter and teacher Thomas Anshutz concentrated on everyday scenes in the lives of rural and city workers. **How did tenant farmers make a living?**

CHAPTER 16 SECTION 1

Independent Practice

Analyzing Statistical Data
Ask students to use *Statistical Abstracts of the United States* to find information on the percentages of blacks enrolled in schools from 1860 to 1990. Ask them to use this information to create a bar graph using 10-year increments. **L2**

Teaching American Portraits

Frederick Douglass was born enslaved in 1817. He escaped to freedom and became an important abolitionist, writing and giving public lectures against slavery. In the three decades after the Civil War, Douglass was a leading supporter of the women's rights movement, fought against racial segregation laws and practices, and held important government posts such as U.S. minister and consul general to Haiti.

Founded in 1867 by the Freedmen's Bureau, Howard University now consists of 18 schools and 12 research institutes. Not only do the university's libraries hold the finest collection of materials on African American life in the United States, but the institution also has one of the very few laser chemistry laboratories in the eastern part of the country.

AMERICAN PORTRAITS

Frederick Douglass
1817–1895

Born enslaved, Frederick Douglass escaped (after one failed attempt) in 1838 and quickly emerged as a leading abolitionist. During the Civil War, he prodded President Lincoln to free African Americans, and he helped organize them to fight for freedom.

After Lincoln was assassinated, Douglass opposed the Reconstruction program of President Johnson. Instead he backed the Radical Republican plan. He used his oratorical ability to insist on full equality for African Americans in all parts of the nation, and he was a vigorous backer of the Fourteenth Amendment. He was particularly outspoken in support of the Fifteenth Amendment, guaranteeing African American men the right to vote. To Douglass, being able to vote meant that African Americans would not only be full citizens but would also have a weapon to protect their rights.

---

a federal investigator estimated that one-third of the farms in the Cotton Belt depended on the labor of tenants tied to the land by their debts. Years later a former enslaved person recalled the frustration that many African Americans felt about the system:

> *Lincoln got praise for freeing us, but did he do it? He gave us freedom without giving us any chance to live to ourselves and we still had to depend on the southern white man for work, food, clothing, and he held us through our necessity and want in a state of servitude but little better than slavery.*

From Slavery to Freedom

Even before the end of the war, some slaveholders noticed a change in the attitude of African Americans as they sensed freedom close at hand. Other planters were stunned, however, when enslaved workers they thought were content left without a word to try to reach the Union lines.

Freedom strengthened African American family ties. Families that had been separated were now reunited. Newspapers carried advertisements from African Americans seeking information about missing relatives:

> *$200 reward. During the year 1849, Thomas Sample carried away from this city, as his slaves, our daughter Polly, and son, Geo. Washington, to the State of Mississippi, and subsequently to Texas.... We will give $100 each for them, to any person who assist them, or either of them, to get to Nashville, or get word to us of their whereabouts, if they are alive.*

Freed men and women, many of whom had only first names, now went about choosing family names. Some chose the name of an ancestor or the name of a hero, like Lincoln. Some adopted their former slaveholder's family name, but many African Americans rejected such an idea. "That's my old rebel master's title," said one young man, "and I don't see any use in being called for him."

Newly freed workers who remained on the plantations as paid laborers usually refused to live in their old quarters. They

UNIT 5 Division and Reunion: 1825–1877

Cooperative Learning

To review the changes in Southern society that occurred after the Civil War, organize students into three groups. Assign each group to represent a segment of Southern society: planters, African American sharecroppers, or poor white farmers and tenant farmers. Have each group review the material about their assigned topic in Section 1. Then have them develop a short play, a dialogue, a radio show, a graphic, or another creative presentation to illustrate social changes in the South. Each group should be prepared to answer questions after their presentation. **L1, L2**

objected to the common areas for cooking and washing and sought the privacy of separate cabins. For others, freedom meant leaving the plantation and their former masters and starting a new life. Some settled on the Great Plains and farmed land of their own. Others headed for large cities, hoping to find jobs there.

The Freedmen's Bureau

At the close of the war, Congress had created within the War Department a Bureau of Refugees, Freedmen, and Abandoned Lands, which became popularly known as the Freedmen's Bureau. Led by General O. Howard, the Bureau at first gave food and clothing to all families in the war-ravaged South. Its primary mission, however, was to help African Americans adjust to their new freedom. In addition, the Bureau provided medical help and founded 45 hospitals in 14 states.

Education

Sponsored by the Freedmen's Bureau and the American Missionary Association, hundreds of Northern school teachers went South after the war. Many were young women who had been active in the antislavery and women's rights movements, who now dedicated themselves to educating the newly freed African Americans. The teachers frequently found their students just as dedicated to getting an education. One African American teacher from Philadelphia who taught school in Georgia noted that many of her students worked in the fields in the morning and came to class "after their hard toil in the hot sun, as bright and as anxious to learn as ever." At the end of the day, these same classrooms were filled with adults, equally hungry for the education that had been denied to them. The Freedmen's Bureau also worked to establish colleges to train African American teachers, contributing to the founding of Howard University, Hampton Institute, Fisk University, and other colleges for African Americans.

Jobs

In addition, the Freedmen's Bureau tried to find jobs for formerly enslaved workers. It encouraged them to sign labor contracts

CHAPTER 16 SECTION 1

Linking Across TIME

The Freedmen's Bureau was the first United States federal agency to provide aid mainly to a particular group of people. Today the government assists many groups of people. Ask students to identify some of these groups. (elderly, handicapped, homeless)

Visualizing History The U.S. Bureau of Refugees, Freedmen, and Abandoned Lands (known as the Freedmen's Bureau) gave more than 21 million rations to impoverished Southerners—white and black. **Answer to Caption:** providing food, clothing, shelter, and medical help

Did You Know?

During Reconstruction thousands of people were able to attend college because of the Morrill Act of 1862. The national government gave each state 30,000 acres of federal land for each member of Congress from that state. States sold the land and used the profits to set up agricultural and other colleges.

 ▲ **FREEDMEN'S BUREAU SCHOOL** The Freedmen's Bureau set up hundreds of schools in the South for African American children and adults. *In what other ways did the Bureau help African Americans adjust to a new life?*

Critical Thinking

Assessing Outcomes Imagine that you are a Confederate soldier returning home in 1865. Before the war you were a blacksmith employed on a plantation outside Richmond, Virginia. Describe your home before and after the war, and explain how you are going to support yourself, your wife, and your two children. What will you use for money? (Answers will vary but should include descriptions of a desolate area and should mention problems such as the lack of employment opportunities, schools, and transportation.) **L1**

CHAPTER 16
SECTION 1

ASSESS
Check Understanding
Assign Section 1 Review as homework or an in-class activity.

Evaluate
Assign the Section 1 Quiz in the TCR, or use the History of a Free Nation Testmaker to create a customized quiz.

Reteach
Have students complete Reteaching Activity 16-1.

Enrich
Have students create a bulletin-board display based on this period. Possible topics: a black farming family, an impoverished Southern planter family, or a poor white tenant family.

CLOSE
Have students discuss the following statement: The status of black Americans was the focal problem of Reconstruction.

History AND ART
Homer sought his subjects in the everyday world. Common elements in his work are precise observation and deep sympathy with the subject.
Answer to Caption: Students should note that both paintings focus on sharecropping or tenant-farming life.

---

with planters to provide work in return for wages or a share of the crops. Because most formerly enslaved men and women could neither read nor write, Bureau agents tried to prevent them from being cheated in these contracts, but the Bureau never had enough agents to do this job fully.

Land

The dream of most freed men and women was to own land. During the war Union troops had seized large amounts of land from Southern planters, and Congress decided to distribute some of this land to formerly enslaved workers. On the Sea Islands of South Carolina, the Freedmen's Bureau was permitted to sell or lease confiscated land in parcels of up to 40 acres. Many newly freed African American families hoped that 40 acres and a mule would help them start their lives anew. However, when President Andrew Johnson decided to pardon Confederates, he restored their property rights. If their land had been distributed to African Americans, it was returned to its former owners.

General Howard went to the Sea Islands to tell African American farmers that their land was being returned to pardoned Confederates. He urged them to sign labor contracts to work on the land they briefly had owned. Most of the farmers refused to sign contracts, and a large number refused to give up their land. They were evicted against their will—some at bayonet point—by Union troops.

 ▲ **UPLAND COTTON** by Winslow Homer, 1879 Winslow Homer was one of the leaders in naturalism, painting realistic scenes of everyday life. Compare Homer's work with *The Way They Live* on page 441. *In what way are the paintings similar?*

Section 1 ★ Review

Checking for Understanding
1. **Identify** Freedmen's Bureau.
2. **Define** tenant farmer, sharecropper.
3. **List** three drawbacks to tenant farming.
4. **Describe** three changes in family life for African Americans after the war.

Critical Thinking
5. **Assessing Outcomes** Imagine that you are a newly freed worker living in the South. Write a short account of how freedom affects your life. Include ideas about the Freedmen's Bureau, segregation, former masters, and your chances to own land.

444 UNIT 5 Division and Reunion: 1825–1877

Answers to SECTION 1 REVIEW
1. Freedmen's Bureau—443–444
2. All vocabulary words are defined in the Glossary.
3. Tenants could not own land; landowners forced tenants to plant crops that exhausted the soil; tenants became totally dependent on landowners.
4. Family ties were renewed; family names were chosen; many left plantations and moved to cities.
5. Answers will vary. Accept all reasonable assessments.

SECTION 2

Reconstructing the South

Setting the Scene

Section Focus

Northern leaders varied in their opinions of the best way to deal with the defeated South. President Lincoln contended that the task was to restore the nation quickly and without bitterness. Others, however, felt that the South should be punished.

Objectives

After studying this section, you should be able to
★ compare the Lincoln and Johnson plans for Reconstruction with the plans of the Radical Republicans.
★ explain how the black codes and the return of former Confederates to power affected Reconstruction.

Key Terms

amnesty, mandate, disenfranchise, impeach

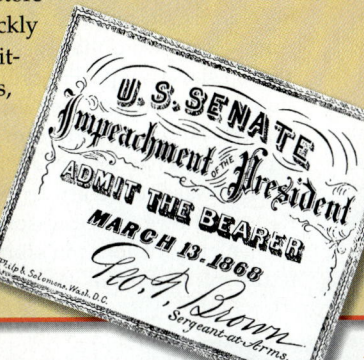

◀ TICKET TO IMPEACHMENT TRIAL

Reconstruction did involve much more than merely rebuilding and repairing the war damage inflicted on the South. It also meant restructuring Southern society by granting rights to formerly enslaved persons and restoring the nation by readmitting Southern states to the Union.

Presidential Reconstruction

Between 1865 and 1877, Congress and the President struggled with, and frequently clashed over, Reconstruction policies and programs.

Some believed that the South should be punished. President Lincoln argued that the task before the country was to restore the Union.

Lincoln's Plan

Before the war ended, Lincoln began to plan for the peace that would follow the war. Because his primary goal was to restore the Union as quickly as possible, the President favored a generous policy. Except for a few high-ranking Confederate officials, he offered **amnesty**, or pardon, to all Southerners who pledged an oath of loyalty to the United States. Lincoln proposed that when 10 percent of a state's voters in the 1860 presidential election had taken this oath, Congress would readmit the state to the Union.

Lincoln's plan did not address the plight of the newly freed African Americans. Although Lincoln strongly supported the Thirteenth Amendment, for a long time he personally had favored colonization of free African Americans in Africa and the Caribbean. He was willing, though, to let the

CHAPTER 16 Reconstruction 1865–1877   **445**

LESSON PLAN
SECTION 2, 445–452

FOCUS
Bellringer
Display Focus Activity Transparency 54 on the overhead projector, and assign the accompanying Focus Activity Sheet.

Objectives
Point out the objectives on this page in previewing the section content.

Motivating Activity
Present the following information to students:
In 1867 and 1868, voters elected delegates to state constitutional conventions in the South. The constitutions they wrote provided for state governments that allowed homesteading so poor people could obtain land and offered help to small farmers deep in debt.
Ask: What might have been your attitude toward the new state government if you had been a plantation owner before the war?

NATIONAL GEOGRAPHIC SOCIETY

VIDEODISC
• *GTV: The American People: Fabric of a Nation*

Side 2, Chapter 8
Title: *The Dream, Deferred*
Subject: Equal rights during Reconstruction —and now

See GTV Guide page 72 for complete lesson plan.

Classroom Resources for SECTION 2

Teacher's Classroom Resources
- Reproducible Lesson Plan
- Reteaching Activity 16-2
- Section Quiz

Multimedia
- Section Focus Transparency 54
- Chapter 16 Map Transparency
- Testmaker
- Student Self-Test Software
- The American People: Fabric of a Nation
- The Presidents: A Picture History of Our Nation

445

South handle the matter. The President urged, however, that African Americans who could read and write and those who had served in the Union army be allowed to vote.

The Radical Republicans' Plan

Resistance to Lincoln's plan surfaced at once from his Radical Republican opponents in Congress. The Radicals' alternative to Lincoln's plan came in the Wade-Davis Bill of 1864. This legislation proposed putting the South under military rule and required a majority of a state's electorate to take the loyalty oath as a condition for the state's readmission. Lincoln killed this bill with a pocket veto—he let the session of Congress expire without signing the legislation. However, when the states of Arkansas, Tennessee, and Louisiana met the conditions of Lincoln's plan, Congress refused to readmit them to the Union. The President then realized that a peace based on "malice toward none and charity for all" was not possible, and he began to negotiate with Radical congressional leaders. At this critical point, Lincoln was assassinated.

Johnson's Program

Andrew Johnson, who succeeded to the presidency, attempted to carry out Lincoln's Reconstruction policies. He was hampered in this effort because, as an unelected President, he had little popular following. In addition, as a former Democrat, he could not command the support of the Republican majority in Congress, and as a Tennesseean and former slaveholder, he offended the Radicals. If these handicaps were not enough, he was viewed by his critics as being self-righteous, hot-tempered, stubborn, and crude.

In the summer of 1865, with Congress in recess, Johnson began to implement his Reconstruction program. His conditions for readmission were that each Southern state abolish slavery, repeal its ordinance of secession, and repudiate its war debts. When Congress returned in December, every state except Texas had followed Johnson's formula and asked to return to the Union. The Radicals, however, expressed alarm because the leniency of Johnson's plan allowed the return of traditional leadership in each of

▼ CARPETBAG

▲ CONGRESSIONAL ACTION Controlled by the Radical Republicans, the Joint Committee on Reconstruction maintained the authority of Congress over Reconstruction. *What was the goal of the Civil Rights Bill of 1866?*

Cooperative Learning

Organize the class into groups of six students each. Have students work in pairs, with each pair representing one of the following points of view: Johnson's moderate Reconstruction policy, the Republicans' radical Reconstruction policy, and a Southern Democrat's reactionary Reconstruction policy. Students should prepare a short defense of their policy. To stimulate discussion, ask: Should the South be left alone to manage its own affairs? Have the groups make their presentations to the class in the form of a television panel discussion. **L2**

CHAPTER 16
SECTION 2

Life of the Times

Southern Pride

Soon after General Lee's surrender, the occupying Union army issued certain ordinances that were aimed at erasing all loyalty to the Confederacy. Many of these laws added insult to the injury of the defeated South. Ingenious Southerners, however, often found ways to circumvent these rules and keep their pride intact.

A "Button Order," for example, prohibited the wearing of Confederate military buttons. Because buttons of any type were scarce, Southerners resorted to using thorns from thornbushes as fastenings. Because replacement buttons were difficult to find, a clause permitted the "covering of formerly used buttons with cloth." Ingenious women draped Confederate buttons with black cloth. Thus, in obeying the Button Order, Southerners found a way that they could publicly display mourning for the Confederacy.

Another ordinance stated that the courts of Virginia could not issue any marriage license unless both parties took the oath of allegiance to the United States. More than one former Confederate prospective groom bristled at such an idea. Under much pressure, the Union general who issued the ordinance delayed its effective date for three days. During this interval, many hastily planned weddings took place.

▶ **Confederate military hat**

▼ **Military buttons**

Did You Know?

Andrew Johnson's policy for Reconstruction was announced in two proclamations issued on May 29, 1865. The first included amnesty and pardon for all who pledged a loyalty oath. The second stated that Southern owners of taxable property valued at more than $20,000 had to apply individually for presidential pardons.

Teaching Life of the Times

Many such ordinances were passed because Radical Republican leaders, such as Massachusetts Senator Charles Sumner, believed that the Confederate states had committed political suicide and were subject to whatever form of control the Union wished to impose. Thaddeus Stevens noted that the Confederacy were "conquered provinces" and that Congress was not limited by the Constitution in dealing with the defeated states.

Fact or Fiction?
President Andrew Johnson called powerful Radical Republican leaders traitors.

FACT: Johnson claimed they were "opposed to the restoration of the Union of these States."

---

these states, and Southern voters elected former Confederate officials to power. As a result, Congress refused to seat members from the Southern states.

White Men and Black Codes

The Radicals were also concerned about the status of African Americans in the South. Like Lincoln, President Johnson believed that this was a state matter and that federal jurisdiction stopped with the abolition of slavery. Consequently, the new Southern state governments endorsed the principle stated by the governor of Mississippi, "Ours is and ever shall be a government of white men."

The new Southern state legislatures passed a series of laws known as "black codes" that severely limited the rights of African Americans and made it plain that African Americans were still to have a subordinate status in the South. State governments made few provisions for African Americans' schools.

In no Southern state were African Americans permitted to vote, testify against whites, handle weapons, or serve on juries. In some states, all African Americans were required by law to have steady work. Those who did not were arrested as vagrants and their labor sold to the highest bidder. Some states permitted African Americans to work only as farmers and servants and denied them many of the rights enjoyed by whites.

The North Responds

Northerners were outraged by the black codes, and even Johnson's supporters were alarmed by the actions of the Southern states. Their fears proved well founded. Events in the South increasingly led moderate Northerners to support the Radicals in Congress against the President.

CHAPTER 16 Reconstruction 1865–1877 447

Cultural Diversity

Motion pictures have created powerful popular images of the antebellum South and Reconstruction. In 1915 the silent film *Birth of a Nation* retold the story of the Civil War and the Ku Klux Klan from a reactionary white Southern viewpoint. The film, considered a technological breakthrough, was boycotted by those protesting against its racism. *Gone With the Wind*, a four-hour dramatization of Margaret Mitchell's book, opened to popular acclaim in Atlanta, Georgia, in 1939. The four-hour film told the story of how two Southern women survived in a war-ravaged South. Historians have criticized its presentation of stereotypes of African Americans and carpetbaggers.

CHAPTER 16 SECTION 2

Independent Practice

Mathematics Present students with the following information on the 1868 election. *Candidate:* Ulysses S. Grant; Republican; 214 electoral votes; 3,013,421 popular votes. *Candidate:* Horatio Seymour; Democrat; 80 electoral votes; 2,706,829 popular votes.

Ask students to calculate the percentage of popular votes Grant and Seymour received. (Grant: 52.7%; Seymour: 47.3%—divide 5,717,250, total popular votes into the popular vote received by each candidate) Then ask students to draw a circle graph to illustrate the results. **L2**

Food of the Times

Americans in the 1860s and 1870s ate potatoes with almost every meal. Southerners preferred sweet potatoes; Northerners ate white potatoes, also known as Irish potatoes. Until the mid-1860s Americans ate their potatoes boiled, roasted, baked, or fried. Then cooks began preparing potatoes in a new way: french-fried.

In 1865, House and Senate leaders created a Joint Committee on Reconstruction to set congressional policy for restoring the Union. The Joint Committee proposed bills providing economic aid for African Americans and protection of their civil rights. Congress passed these bills, but President Johnson vetoed each one. Finally, in April 1866, Congress passed the Civil Rights Bill, which granted citizenship to African Americans and gave the federal government the power to intervene to protect the rights of freed men and women. When Johnson also vetoed this bill, Congress overrode his veto.

The Fourteenth Amendment

Fearing that the Civil Rights Act might be overturned in court, however, Congress passed the Fourteenth Amendment to the Constitution in June 1866. The amendment defined citizenship to include African Americans and required that no state deny any person "the equal protection of the laws." In addition, the amendment barred many Confederate political leaders from holding public office and prohibited any state from paying Confederate war debts.

President Johnson attacked the Fourteenth Amendment and campaigned against its ratification. As the 1866 congressional elections neared, it was clear that they would reveal whether the President or Congress would control the direction of Reconstruction.

The November election provided an overwhelming victory for the Radicals, who gained control of both the House and Senate. They now had the strength to override any presidential veto and could claim that they had been given a **mandate,** or command, from the public to enact their own Reconstruction program.

■ Radical Reconstruction

Now firmly in control, the Radical Republicans began implementing their policies for Reconstruction.

One goal was to sweep away the new state governments in the South and to replace them with military rule. Other goals were to ensure that former Confederate leaders would have no role in governing the South and that the freed African Americans' right to vote was protected.

Reconstruction Plans

Radical plans were inspired by self-interest as well as by concern for the freed African Americans and a desire to punish the South. The Radicals expected that African Americans would express their gratitude for freedom by voting Republican. Radical plans also were supported by Northern business leaders, who feared that a Congress controlled by Democrats might lower tariffs or destroy the newly established national banking system.

Many Radicals genuinely cared about the plight of the freed men and women, of course. They had been abolitionists and had pushed Lincoln into making emancipation a goal of the war. They believed in a right to equality and that government must rest on the consent of the governed. Senator Henry Wilson of Massachusetts summarized their position by saying:

> [Congress] must see to it that the man made free by the Constitution is a freeman indeed; that he can go where he pleases, work when and for whom he pleases . . . go into the schools and educate himself and his children; that the rights and guarantees of the common law are his, and that he walks the earth proud and erect in the conscious dignity of a free man.

Reconstruction Legislation

In March 1867, Congress passed a Reconstruction Act that abolished the South's new state governments and put them under military rule. Except for Tennessee, the former Confederacy was divided into five military districts, each under command of a Union general. To be restored to the Union, each of the states was required to hold a

448 UNIT 5 Division and Reunion: 1825–1877

Critical Thinking

Making Inferences Lincoln believed that the Southern states had never legally seceded. Lincoln also believed that he could set the terms for restoring the rights of Southerners. Ask: On what did Lincoln base these beliefs? (Answers will vary. In responding to the first point, students should mention that the Constitution had no provision for secession. In responding to the second point, students should remember that the Constitution gives the President the power to pardon individuals. Since individuals had rebelled, Lincoln could pardon them and restore their rights.) **L2, L3**

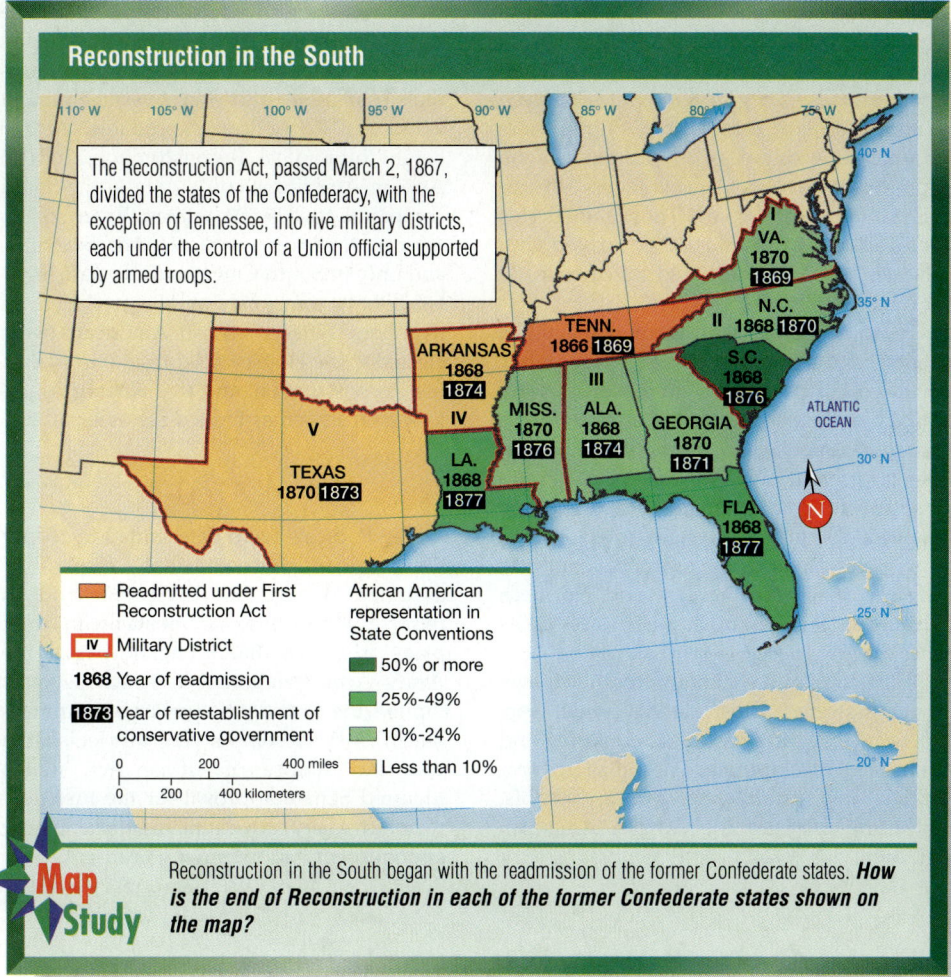

Reconstruction in the South

Reconstruction in the South began with the readmission of the former Confederate states. **How is the end of Reconstruction in each of the former Confederate states shown on the map?**

CHAPTER 16 SECTION 2

Map Study Using Maps

Answer: The year is indicated under the state's name.

Skills Practice

Ask: What state was the first to be readmitted to the Union? (Tennessee)

Did You Know?

Carpetbaggers were named for the luggage that they brought with them from the North. The word was connected to greedy, unprincipled people even before Reconstruction. In Britain crooked bankers often stashed their loot in carpetbags. So, over time, *carpetbagger* came to mean any kind of embezzler.

Scalawag comes from a term used by western ranchers to describe skinny, useless cattle. The word's origin is unknown, but one suggestion is that it comes from the Latin *scurra vagas*, which means "wandering buffoon."

---

constitutional convention with delegates elected by all adult males and to frame a state constitution that gave African Americans the right to vote. If the voters ratified the constitution, a state government could be elected. Finally, if Congress approved the constitution, if the state legislature ratified the Fourteenth Amendment, and if the amendment became a part of the Constitution, then the state would be readmitted to the Union. By 1868 Louisiana, Alabama, Arkansas, Florida, North Carolina, and South Carolina had met these requirements and regained statehood.

In 1869 Congress protected African American suffrage by passing the Fifteenth Amendment to the Constitution, providing that the right to vote "shall not be denied . . . on account of race, color, or previous condition of servitude." Congress required that states not yet complying with the Reconstruction Act—Virginia, Georgia, Mississippi, and Texas—ratify the Fifteenth Amendment as a further condition for readmission to the Union.

Carpetbag Government

By 1870 each of the 10 states under military rule had been readmitted to the Union. However, Radical Reconstruction had **disenfranchised**—or taken the right to vote from—many former Confederates. In addi-

CHAPTER 16 Reconstruction 1865–1877   **449**

Critical Thinking

Making Decisions If you had been a member of the House of Representatives in 1868, would you have voted for or against impeaching President Johnson? Explain the reasons for your choice. (Students' answers should show an understanding of the issues involved such as the political climate of the time and the Tenure of Office Act.) Tell students that after leaving the presidency, Johnson ran for election to the Senate three times. The third time he succeeded; and when he entered the Senate chamber, he received a standing ovation. **L1, L2**

CHAPTER 16 SECTION 2

Visualizing History Among the accomplishments of the Reconstruction state governments were the setting up of public schools and the rebuilding of infrastructure.
Answer to Caption: encourage rebuilding; establish public schools

Linking Across Time

President Richard M. Nixon is the only other President who was charged with grounds for impeachment. The House Judiciary Committee voted three articles of impeachment, but before the full House could vote on them, Nixon, unlike Andrew Johnson, resigned from office in 1974.

---

tion, many other Southern white men boycotted elections. As a result, government in the Southern states was left to two small groups. One was a group of white Southern Union sympathizers whom Southerners nicknamed "scalawags." Northerners who came South—called "carpetbaggers"—comprised the other group. They gained this derogatory name because they arrived with all their belongings in cheap suitcases made of carpet fabric.

Some carpetbaggers were respectable, honest, and sincerely devoted to the public interest. However, enough of them were greedy and self-seeking so as to give the phrase "carpetbag governments" a reputation for graft, fraud, and waste. One carpetbag governor admitted to accepting more than $40,000 in bribes. Railroad franchises, public lands, and government contracts went to white Northerners and Northern businesses. As a result, Southern state debts rose sharply.

Carpetbag rule was not without achievement, however. Most public funds were spent honestly to encourage rebuilding and industrial development. Carpetbag governments also established public schools, including facilities for African American children.

Many Southern whites despised carpetbag governments. African American voters, however, saw the carpetbag governments as their best hope, and they overwhelmingly voted for Republican candidates. At the height of Radical Reconstruction, 700,000 African Americans could vote in the South compared to 625,000 whites. Even so, no African Americans were elected governors, and only in South Carolina did a state legislature have a majority of African American members. Fifteen African Americans were elected to the House of Representatives during Reconstruction, and two African American men served as United States senators.

The Radicals in Power

The Radicals were determined to reduce the presidential power that Lincoln had assumed during the Civil War and to remove Johnson as an obstacle to their plans. In March 1867, Congress passed the Army Appropriation Act, which severely limited the President's power as commander in chief. Accompanying this legislation was the Tenure of Office Act, which required Senate approval for the President to remove any government official whose appointment had required its consent.

Visualizing History ▲ **MEMBERS OF CONGRESS** The first African American members of Congress are shown in this Currier and Ives print. The first African American senator, Hiram R. Revels, is at the far left. *What were the major achievements of Southern governments during this period?*

450 UNIT 5 Division and Reunion: 1825–1877

Sidelights: Women's Occupations

While the Civil War gave women a chance to show their skills, few opportunities opened up for them in the postwar years. For example, in 1870 only 5 of the United States' 40,736 lawyers, 67 of 43,874 ministers, and 525 of 62,383 doctors were women. Further, none of these women professionals received salaries approaching those of their male counterparts. In 1870 most of the 1.9 million American women who worked outside the home were farm workers or household servants.

Challenging the Tenure Law

The Radicals knew that President Johnson wanted to remove Edwin Stanton, Lincoln's secretary of war, who remained in Johnson's cabinet but who openly sided with the Radicals. Characteristically, Johnson ignored these warnings. He continued trying to block Radical Reconstruction. Johnson also removed commanders in the Southern military districts who supported the Radicals and, while Congress was in recess, he fired Stanton.

To replace Stanton, Johnson appointed General Grant, but when the Senate reconvened it rejected Grant's nomination, and Grant resigned in favor of Stanton. Outraged, Johnson fired Stanton again—on February 21, 1868—this time replacing him with General Lorenzo Thomas. In answer, Stanton barricaded himself inside his office and refused to leave.

Johnson Impeached

The Radicals came to Stanton's support. Three days later, the House of Representatives voted to **impeach**, or charge, Johnson with "high crimes and misdemeanors" in office. As provided in the Constitution, the President was tried by the Senate. A two-thirds majority vote was needed for a conviction.

For more than two months amid intense public excitement, the Senate debated the President's fate. Radical members of the House, led by Thaddeus Stevens, presented the case against Johnson. Johnson's lawyers argued that Lincoln, not Johnson, had appointed Stanton to the Cabinet and, therefore, that the Tenure of Office Act did not apply.

On May 16, 1868, the Senate voted 35 to 19 to find Johnson guilty, just 1 vote short of conviction. Seven Republican senators were not able to find honest evidence that Johnson was guilty. Under tremendous political pressure, they refused to give in to partisan politics. Although Johnson remained in office for the last few months of his term, he was powerless to challenge the Radicals' policies.

The 1868 Election

The Radical Republicans sought a candidate in the 1868 presidential election who could sweep the country and keep them in power. They chose General Grant. The Democrats nominated Horatio Seymour, former governor of New York, and their platform condemned Radical Republican actions.

Although Grant won easily, by a vote of 214 to 80 in the electoral college, a small shift in the popular vote in key states would have given Seymour the election. Grant won because he was supported by the carpetbag governments of the South and because three Southern states had not yet been readmitted.

Section 2 ★ Review

Checking for Understanding

1. **Identify** Radical Republicans, Andrew Johnson, Fourteenth Amendment, Fifteenth Amendment, Tenure of Office Act.
2. **Define** amnesty, mandate, disenfranchise, impeach.
3. **List** two objections the Radicals had to Lincoln's Reconstruction plans.
4. **Explain** the purpose of the black codes.

Critical Thinking

5. **Determining Cause and Effect** The 1866 congressional elections served as a contest between President Andrew Johnson and the Radical Republicans for control of Reconstruction. What happened in the 1866 election? How do congressional elections during a President's term of office act as a barometer of presidential policies and popularity? Give specific examples.

CHAPTER 16 Reconstruction 1865–1877   **451**

CHAPTER 16
SECTION 2

ASSESS

Check Understanding
Assign Section 2 Review as homework or an in-class activity.

Evaluate
Assign the Section 2 Quiz in the TCR, or use the History of a Free Nation Testmaker to create a customized quiz.

Reteach
Have students complete Reteaching Activity 16-2.

Enrich
Have students illustrate the Fifteenth Amendment by drawing a political cartoon.

CLOSE

What problems did Lincoln foresee in reconstructing the Union? Ask: Had Lincoln lived, what might have been the outcome of Reconstruction?

NATIONAL GEOGRAPHIC SOCIETY

The following material is available from Glencoe and may be used to enrich Chapter 16:

CD-ROM
- *The Presidents: A Picture History of Our Nation*

Answers to SECTION 2 REVIEW

1. Radical Republicans, 446; Andrew Johnson, 446; Fourteenth Amendment, 448; Fifteenth Amendment, 449; Tenure of Office Act, 450
2. All vocabulary words are defined in the Glossary.
3. Southerners could not be trusted; state governments should not be based on the Ten Percent Plan.
4. The purpose was to subordinate blacks by reducing and restricting their rights.
5. Presidential elections are held every four years. Congressional elections are held every two years. In midterm congressional elections, voters can show approval or objection to the President by voting for or against members of the President's political party.

LESSON PLAN
Mastering Social Studies Skills

Teaching Critical Thinking Skills

Remind students that making predictions is different from guessing and that often very accurate predictions can be made if one takes into account both past and present conditions and information.

Go through the exercise using the Fourteenth Amendment. Ask: Where does the information come from? How does the information help you make an accurate prediction? Was your prediction correct?

Did You Know?

Under the Reconstruction Act, each former Confederate state had to set up a government that guaranteed African American men the right to vote. If the state did not do so, it could not be fully restored to the Union. By 1868 most Southern states had complied. Not until the Fifteenth Amendment was ratified in 1870 did African American men gain suffrage in many Northern states.

Social Studies Skills

Critical Thinking Skills

Making Predictions

A *prediction* is a foretelling of something before it happens. When you predict something, you are stating what you believe will happen in the future. Good predictions are based on present conditions as well as what has happened in the past.

Asking the questions that follow can help you predict the possible results of any historical event:
a. What related conditions existed prior to the event being studied?
b. What caused these conditions?
c. What was the event supposed to accomplish?
d. Based on the answers to these questions, what is your prediction about what will happen as a result of the event?

Note how the questions have been applied in predicting the results of the passage of the Fourteenth Amendment:
a. What conditions existed prior to the passing of the Fourteenth Amendment?
 • African Americans were considered by many to be inferior to whites.
 • African Americans were denied rights guaranteed to whites.
 • Many people spoke out against the institution of slavery.
b. What caused these conditions?
 • the belief of many people that African Americans were inferior
 • the belief by many that African Americans should be considered equal
c. What was the amendment supposed to accomplish?
 • All persons born and naturalized in the United States would have all the rights due them under the Constitution.

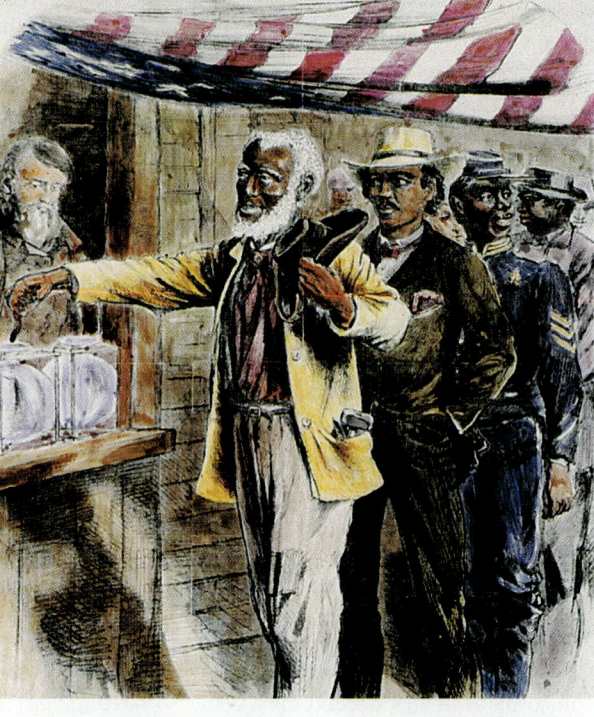

▲ FREED AFRICAN AMERICANS CAST THEIR FIRST BALLOTS

d. Predict what will happen as a result of the passage of the Fourteenth Amendment.
 • Passage will cause conflict, unrest, and confusion.
 • Equality for African Americans will have to come gradually.

Practicing the Skill

For practice in making predictions, apply these questions and make a prediction about the success of Lincoln's plan for Reconstruction had he lived to carry out his program.

452

Answers to SOCIAL STUDIES SKILLS

a. What were the related conditions? a) a defeated South; b) free African Americans; c) continued discrimination against African Americans
b. What caused these conditions? a) the North's victory in the Civil War; b) the continuing belief by many that African Americans were inferior
c. What was Lincoln's plan supposed to accomplish? integration of African Americans and the South into the United States
d. What prediction could be intelligently made? The South, in reentering the Union, and the integration of African Americans into free society will encounter many difficulties.

SECTION 3

Restoring Southern Power

Setting the Scene

Section Focus

Reconstruction allowed the South to begin rebuilding its economy but proved to be of only temporary help to African American Southerners. As political and civil rights were restored to former Confederates, they were increasingly denied to African Americans.

Objectives

After studying this section, you should be able to

★ describe Southern resistance to Reconstruction.

★ discuss political and economic change in the South after Reconstruction.

Key Term

segregation

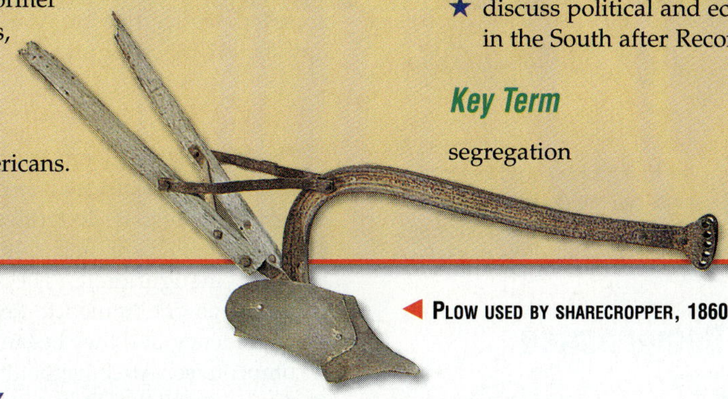

◀ **PLOW USED BY SHARECROPPER, 1860S**

Unable to strike openly at the federal government, opponents of Reconstruction organized secret resistance societies. The largest of these groups was the Ku Klux Klan. Started in Tennessee in 1866, the Klan spread throughout the former Confederacy. Hooded, white-robed Klan members rode in bands at night and threatened carpetbaggers, teachers in African American schools, and African Americans themselves. Using beatings, murder, and other violence to back up their threats, Klansmen broke up Republican meetings, tried to drive Freedmen's Bureau officials out of their communities, and tried to keep freed African Americans from voting.

Although by 1872 it had been greatly suppressed by federal troops, the Klan and similar organizations contributed to the establishment of Southern governments opposed to the Radicals. Democrats, often called "Redeemers," gained control of one Southern state after another, until by 1876 only South Carolina, Florida, and Louisiana did not have governments controlled by white Democrats, many of whom were former Confederates.

One reason for these Democratic successes in the South was that Northerners were becoming weary of Radical Reconstruction. In 1872 a group called the Liberal Republicans, including several prominent Republican leaders, opposed the Radicals and refused to support Grant for reelection because they considered him unfit for the presidency. The Liberal Republicans joined with the Democrats to nominate newspaper publisher Horace Greeley for President. Although Grant won reelection, the Radicals' power was weakened, and Grant's administration loosened its controls over the South. As fewer troops were sent to protect African American voters during Southern elections, white political power was restored.

Classroom Resources for SECTION 3

Teacher's Classroom Resources

- Reproducible Lesson Plan
- Reteaching Activity 16-3
- Chapter 16 Primary and Secondary Source Readings
- Chapter 16 Enrichment Activity
- Spanish Summaries and Glossary
- Section Quiz

Multimedia

- Section Focus Transparency 55
- Unit 5 Digest Transparency
- Chapter 16 Vocabulary Puzzlemaker
- Student Self-Test Software
- The Presidents: A Picture History of Our Nation
- The American People: Fabric of a Nation

LESSON PLAN
SECTION 3, 453–456

FOCUS

Bellringer

Before taking roll at the beginning of the class period, display Focus Activity Transparency 55 on the overhead projector, and assign the accompanying Focus Activity Sheet.

Objectives

Point out the objectives on this page to students in previewing the section content.

Motivating Activity

Present the following:

In every part of the South during Reconstruction, schools, both day and night, were filled to overflowing with people of all ages . . . .

Booker T. Washington
Up From Slavery

Ask: What do you think was the most important gain made by black Americans during Reconstruction? (Answers will vary and may include education, citizenship, right to vote.)

NATIONAL GEOGRAPHIC SOCIETY

VIDEODISC

- *GTV: The American People: Fabric of a Nation*

Side 3, Chapter 7
Title: *Enter the Klan*
Subject: Prejudice and intolerance in America

See GTV Guide page 86 for complete lesson plan.

▲ **THE KU KLUX KLAN** Members of the Ku Klux Klan used threats, beatings, and murder to keep African Americans and Republicans from voting. **Who were the Redeemers?**

The Compromise of 1877

The presidential election of 1876 brought the end of Radical Reconstruction. In the campaign the Republicans "waved the bloody shirt," or attempted to stir up bitter memories of the war. Democrats countered by attacking the excesses of Radical Reconstruction and the corruption they claimed was rampant in the Grant administration.

On Election Day, Democratic candidate Samuel J. Tilden, governor of New York, polled 250,000 more popular votes than the Republican Rutherford B. Hayes, Ohio's governor. Tilden was a vote short of a majority in the electoral college, but 20 electoral votes were disputed. One of these electoral votes was from Oregon, and it was challenged on a technicality. The other 19 involved disputed results from the 3 Southern states still under carpetbag rule—Florida, South Carolina, and Louisiana—where charges of massive voting fraud flew.

Electoral Commission

Republicans complained that Democrats had prevented African Americans from voting, and Democrats accused Republicans of using federal troops to raise its vote totals. These 3 states each filed 2 sets of election returns, 1 for Tilden and another for Hayes.

Because the Constitution did not provide for settling such a dispute, Congress appointed a commission of 5 members each from the House, the Senate, and the Supreme Court to settle the matter. Tilden needed only 1 of the disputed electoral votes to become President, but Hayes needed all of them. Voting strictly along party lines, the commission awarded all 20 disputed electoral votes to Hayes. Congress accepted the verdict on March 2, 1877, 2 days before the inauguration.

Reaching an Agreement

The Democrats were outraged at the commission's decisions, and they were determined not to be defrauded. There were threats of civil war and talk of blocking Hayes's inauguration. The Republicans were just as determined to keep control of the presidency, and they began to talk about a compromise. After negotiations between party leaders, the Democrats agreed to accept the election results and the Republicans agreed to several demands. Democrats were assured that a Southerner would become postmaster general, an important position because of the many federal jobs it controlled. Republicans also promised federal funds for internal improvements in the South. Most important, Republicans agreed to withdraw the remaining federal troops from the South. Without soldiers to protect them, the three remaining carpetbag governments collapsed and Reconstruction officially came to an end.

After Reconstruction

In many ways, the South after Reconstruction was similar to the South before the Civil War. As white Southern Democrats returned to power, African Americans lost many of their civil rights.

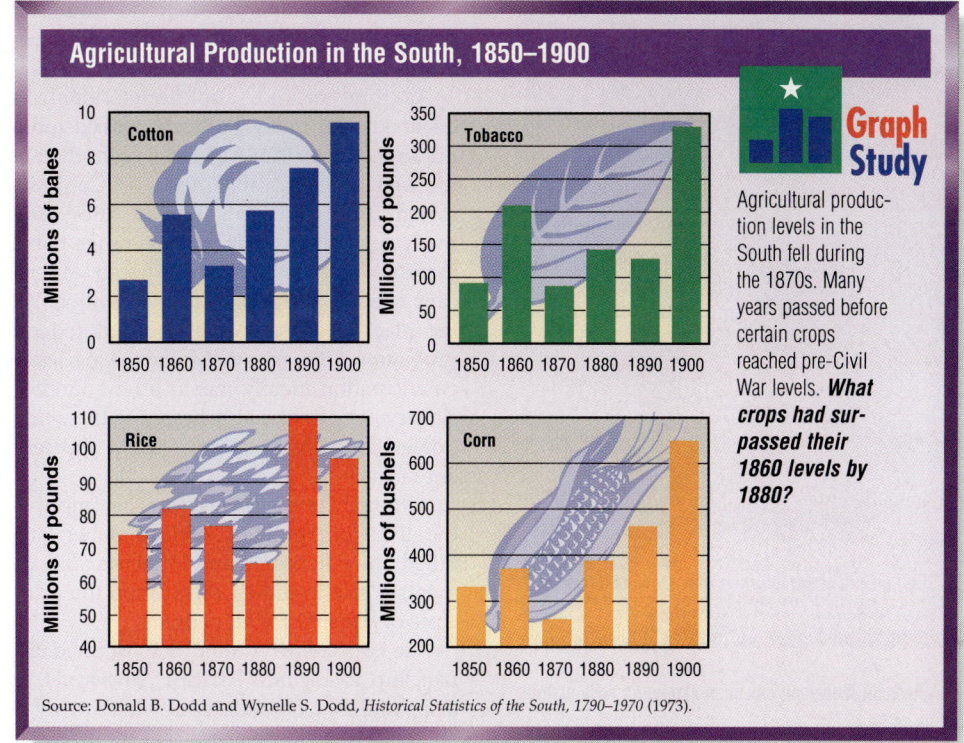

Graph Study

Agricultural production levels in the South fell during the 1870s. Many years passed before certain crops reached pre-Civil War levels. **What crops had surpassed their 1860 levels by 1880?**

Source: Donald B. Dodd and Wynelle S. Dodd, *Historical Statistics of the South, 1790–1970* (1973).

Segregation

For years, in the North as well as the South, **segregation,** or the practice of separating people on the basis of race, had been an accepted way of life. Even before the Civil War, custom in the North had separated African American and white travelers on railroads, coaches, and steamboats and in hotels. Such segregation also existed in Northern schools, churches, hospitals, and cemeteries. After Reconstruction, however, the South began to pass "Jim Crow" laws, which legally segregated blacks from whites in daily life.

Where possible, African Americans protested segregation. These protests helped to integrate the streetcar lines of Washington, D.C.; Richmond, Virginia; and Charleston, South Carolina. In 1875 Congress passed a Civil Rights Act requiring that all people have equal access to public places and transportation facilities. In 1883, however, the Supreme Court ruled that the act was unconstitutional, and by the 1890s Jim Crow laws were common throughout the South.

The "New South"

Despite the South's return to white supremacy, by the late 1870s there was increasing talk of a "New South." An alliance between powerful white Southerners and Northern financiers brought about the economic rebuilding of the South. Northern capital helped to build railroads, and by 1890 the South had twice the railroad mileage that it had had in 1860.

Better transportation encouraged the industrialization of the South. A growing iron and steel industry developed around Birmingham, Alabama, and in North Carolina tobacco processing became big business. Cotton mills appeared in countless small towns throughout the South. Nevertheless, far from populous Northern markets and paying high freight rates, Southern industries faced serious problems. To compete, Southern factory owners generally paid lower wages than did factories in the North.

With these developments in transportation and industry and with the spread of

CHAPTER 16 Reconstruction 1865–1877 455

CHAPTER 16
SECTION 3

Independent Practice

Identifying Point of View
Have students write a brief essay about citizenship from the point of view of one of these: a Northern black factory worker, a Northern white factory worker, a Southern white small farm owner, or a Southern black sharecropper. Ask students to utilize the redefinition of citizenship after the Civil War. **L2, L3**

Using Graphs

Answers: cotton and corn

Skills Practice
Ask: When did rice surpass its 1860 level? (1890)

Did You Know?

At some point between 1870 and 1880 for the first time in American history more workers were working in nonfarm jobs than on farms.

The following material is available from Glencoe and may be used to enrich Chapter 16:

CD-Rom
- *The Presidents: A Picture History of Our Nation*

Critical Thinking

The issues of Reconstruction are as old as the American Republic. The enforcement of the rights of citizens and the problems of economic and racial justice were the central themes in this period. Have these issues been solved in our contemporary society? (no) What Reconstruction issues still exist? (inequalities of economic and racial justice) **L1, LEP**

▲ AFRICAN AMERICAN CHILDREN ATTENDING FREE SCHOOL

sharecropping in agriculture, the South's economy gradually revived. By 1900 Southern industrial production was four times what it had been in 1860.

Few Gains for African Americans

In many ways, Reconstruction aided the South. However, it also caused much bitterness in that region, helping to create the "Solid South"—a voting bloc dominated by the Democrats that did not break up for a century. Reconstruction also provided only limited and temporary help to Southern African Americans, whose rights it professed to defend.

As time passed, abolitionist idealism declined, and many Radicals proved more interested in African American votes than in the welfare of African Americans. Congress closed the Freedmen's Bureau after only five years, and it made no long-range plans to provide what the freed African Americans needed most—land and education. As the black codes revealed, without federal protection, for many African Americans emancipation merely meant a new kind of slavery—continued attachment to the white power structure as sharecroppers and tenant farmers.

Although immediate efforts to improve the lives of Southern African Americans failed, the Fourteenth and Fifteenth amendments wrote into the Constitution the principle of equality for all people.

The Fourteenth Amendment defined citizenship to include African Americans. It also said that no state could take away a citizen's life, liberty, or property without due process of law, and that every citizen was entitled to equal protection of the laws. The Fifteenth Amendment stated that the right to vote "shall not be denied . . . on account of race, color, or previous condition of servitude."

For many years these amendments remained almost a dead letter, but in the 1900s they provided the legal basis and, in part, the inspiration for movements to obtain for African Americans their full rights as citizens.

Section 3 ★ Review

Checking for Understanding
1. **Identify** Ku Klux Klan, Compromise of 1877, "Solid South."
2. **Define** segregation.
3. **Describe** the strategies and tactics used by the Ku Klux Klan. Discuss the reaction of African Americans to that organization.
4. **Explain** two important concessions that were made in the Compromise of 1877.

Critical Thinking
5. **Distinguishing Fact from Opinion** Describe the images of the South created by motion pictures and novels. What facts from the era refute these images?

History and Economics Connections

▲ Foundry, Birmingham, Alabama, 1887

▶ Sewing machine, mid-1800s

Growth of Southern Manufacturing

Many factors pushed the postwar South toward industrialization. Most important, however, was the surplus labor supply. Widows, orphans, and displaced formerly enslaved workers needed work, and agriculture could not employ them all. This meant there was a large pool of cheap labor. In addition, Northerners and Europeans invested capital in fledgling Southern industries, as did a number of Southerners themselves.

Two industries that made spectacular advances in the postwar South were textiles and tobacco processing. Cotton mills sprang up in the major cotton-growing areas of the South. By 1900 there were 400 mills in operation. The postwar demand for a new product—cigarettes—and the invention of the cigarette-rolling machine in 1880 were the catalysts that fueled the development of the tobacco-processing industry.

Other industries based on agriculture or minerals also developed, such as steel manufacturing and making cottonseed oil. Still, despite gains in industrialization, the South remained primarily rural and agricultural until the industrial advances of the mid-twentieth century.

Making the Economics Connection

1. What factors led to the development of industry in the postwar South?
2. What Southern cities of the 1900s are noted as industrial centers?

Linking Past and Present

3. Why was the region's economy primarily agricultural until the mid-1900s?

CHAPTER 16 CONNECTIONS

Teaching Making Connections

In the late 1870s Southern male workers who worked in the coal mines, iron and steel foundries, and cotton mills earned from $1.25 to $1.50 a day. Women and children earned much less but had to work for the family to survive.

Did You Know?

Most foreign investment in the United States in the 1860s and 1870s came from Britain. British investors put a lot of their money into the new American railroads.

Fact or Fiction?

By the 1870s half of all females who worked outside their homes or farms were household servants.

FACT: In towns and cities the percentage was even greater.

Answers to CONNECTIONS

1. A large pool of cheap labor existed. Also, Northerners and Europeans, as well as Southerners, invested capital in fledgling Southern industry.
2. Answers will vary but may include Atlanta, Georgia, and Baltimore, Maryland.
3. Not until the mid-1900s was the South able to take advantage of industrial advances.

REVIEW CHAPTER 16

Answers

Reviewing Facts
1. Laborers could not afford to purchase farms. Landowners could not afford to pay wages.
2. supplied food, clothing, and medicine; provided education; found employment
3. Both sides disagreed over: which branch of government should carry out Reconstruction, amnesty for former Confederates, requirements for readmitting Southern states, the political status of African Americans.
4. successes: passage of the Fourteenth and Fifteenth amendments; failures: no real protection of African American civil rights, no education, no opportunity to own land, no meaningful employment

Understanding Concepts
1. Southern landowners had no money. This tenant-farming system gave them a source of workers who did not have to be paid directly.
2. Grew as a result of their perception of Southern arrogance and their lack of respect for Johnson. Diminished when they failed to convict Johnson of impeachment charges, which led to an erosion of support.

Critical Thinking
1. Federal government tried to improve the status of African Americans by providing relief, education, and employment services. Southern state governments, especially before 1868 and after the late 1870s, tried to maintain the former status quo of keeping African Americans in a subordinate status by passing black codes and segregation laws.
2. **a.** white female former slaveholder and African American woman who was previously enslaved;
b. They confront each other uneasily; the white woman is well-dressed and the black woman poorly clothed.
c. that the Civil War has changed the relative status between Southern whites and blacks.

CHAPTER 16 ★ REVIEW

Using Vocabulary

Create a classification system that demonstrates how these words below are related. First, write *Reconstruction* as your main heading. Under the main heading create several smaller categories. Challenge yourself to see how many different classifications you can devise.

tenant farmer · sharecropper
segregation · black code
amnesty · carpetbagger
mandate · concession
impeach

Reviewing Facts

1. **Cite** two reasons why tenant farming and sharecropping were used in the South.
2. **List** three services provided by the Freedmen's Bureau.
3. **Specify** two differences between the Reconstruction plans of Presidents Lincoln and Johnson and those of the Radical Republicans.
4. **List** the long-term successes and failures of Reconstruction for Southern African Americans.

Understanding Concepts

Adaptation
1. Explain how tenant farming and sharecropping were a means for Southern landowners to adjust to new conditions after the Civil War.

Power and Authority
2. What are the significant reasons that explain how the power of the Radical Republicans first grew and later diminished?

Critical Thinking

1. **Identifying Central Issues** The 1860s were a time of radical change. Summarize the string of events that caused so much political and social turbulence during the 1860s.

2. **Analyzing Fine Art** Study the painting on this page, entitled *A Visit from the Old Mistress* by Winslow Homer, and answer the questions that follow.
   a. Identify the two main figures.
   b. How does the artist contrast these figures?
   c. What idea do you think the artist is expressing?

Writing About History

Comparison
Imagine that you are a newly freed African American living in the South during Reconstruction. You have learned to read and write at a Freedmen's Bureau school. You write a letter to a long-lost relative living in the North describing the changes in your life. In your letter compare your life before the Civil War to life during Reconstruction. Include information about your work, your way of life, and your relations with whites.

Cooperative Learning

You belong to a group analyzing Reconstruction policies. Each member of your group will assume one of these roles: a Southern landowner, a Northern carpetbagger, and an African American sharecropper. Your goal is to write two Reconstruction

458 UNIT 5 Division and Reunion: 1825–1877

CHAPTER 16 ★ REVIEW

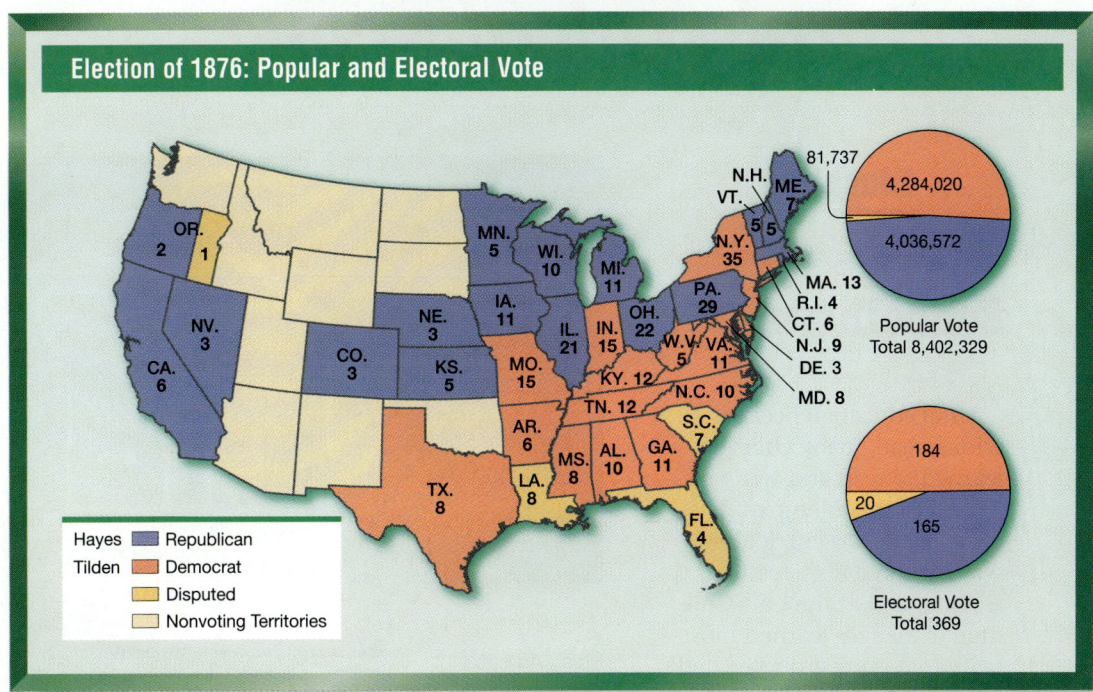

Election of 1876: Popular and Electoral Vote

laws that are acceptable to all. Write one law on voting rights for African Americans and a second law on the treatment of former Confederate soldiers.

4. On the basis of the popular vote, who should have won the election?

Social Studies Skills

Interpreting an Election Map

Election maps let you see at a glance how different states voted. They also show trends in voting. For example, the election map on this page shows that people in the Far West voted primarily for Tilden.

Practicing the Skills

Use the election map and the information in the chapter to answer the following questions.

1. What do the numbers on the map indicate?
2. Is there a geographical trend in the way the states voted? If so, what is it?
3. Why is it helpful to include the two circle graphs along with the map?

Using Your Journal

Despite great strides, African Americans are still under-represented in government and in higher-paying jobs. Note in your journal what present-day factors inhibit equality and how those factors compare with the factors you noted for the Reconstruction era.

CHAPTER 16 Reconstruction 1865–1877   459

Cultural Kaleidoscope

Making Connections
History and Economics

Merchants and manufacturers were among those who advocated more and better public schools. They would sooner or later be employing many of the school graduates. They wanted the schools to teach young Americans not only the three Rs but also the virtues of discipline, honesty, and perseverance that would make them better workers.

More About...
Hornbooks

Hornbooks were developed in the Middle Ages because paper and books were expensive. The standard hornbook was a wooden paddle-shaped board on which was pasted a sheet of paper; the board was then covered with a thin sheet of animal horn to protect it. Typically, the paper was printed with the letters of the alphabet, a benediction, and the Lord's Prayer.

Cultural Kaleidoscope

Education

The One-Room Schoolhouse

Until education became widespread, many children learned to read and write in one-room schoolhouses. The backbone of the curriculum was the three R's—reading, writing, and arithmetic. Children of all ages learned mostly by rote—one group recited while the rest studied their lessons. Students today might view the one-room schoolhouse as primitive. Chalkboards and maps were rare, and students, lacking even paper and pen, used a slate and a slate pencil. Despite its drawbacks, the one-room schoolhouse provided many with their only opportunity for an education.

▲ Many American leaders saw in public schools a means of promoting national spirit.

▶ Many students received their learning from church schools, proprietary institutions, private tutors, or members of their own families.

◀ The hornbook for learning the alphabet was still in use during the 1800s in many schoolhouses.

Cooperative Learning

Divide the class into five groups. Assign each a notable figure in American education: Horace Mann, Henry Barnard, Emma Willard, Prudence Crandall, Catharine Beecher (or others of your own choosing). Ask each group to research its educator and then report its findings to the class.

Cultural Kaleidoscope

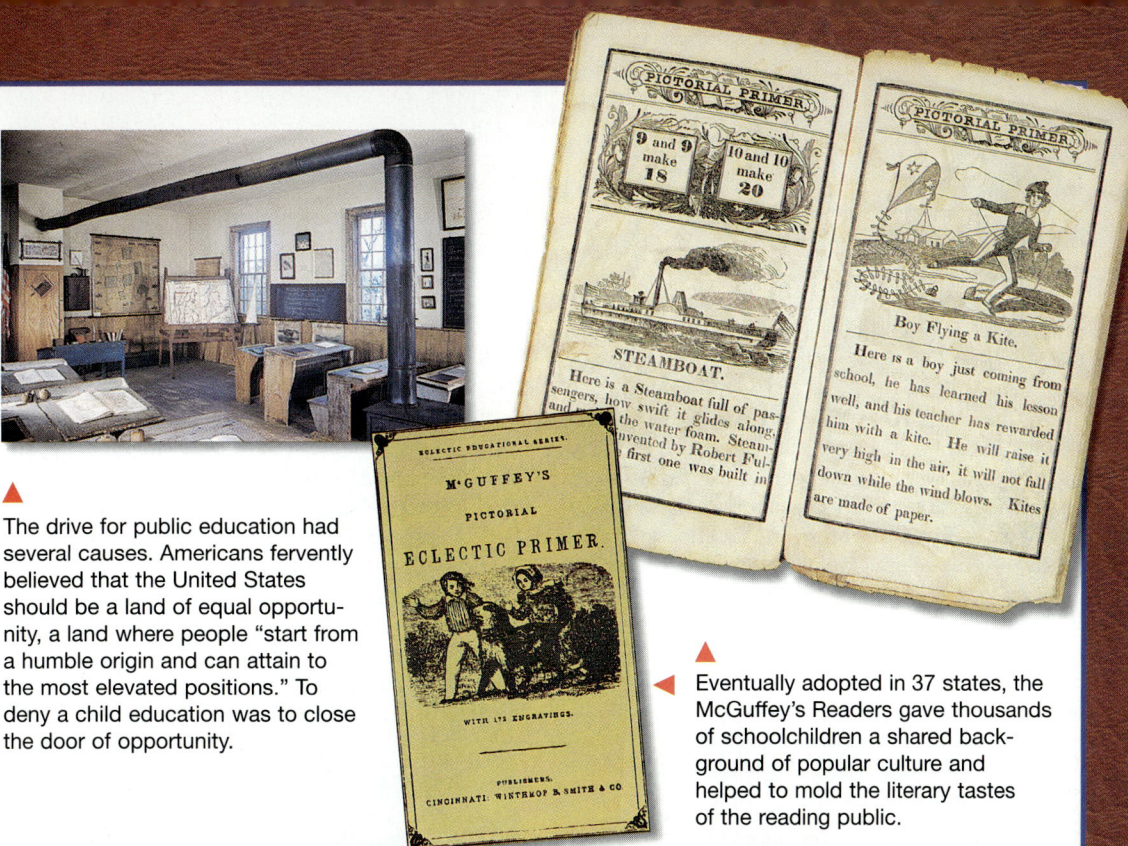

▲ The drive for public education had several causes. Americans fervently believed that the United States should be a land of equal opportunity, a land where people "start from a humble origin and can attain to the most elevated positions." To deny a child education was to close the door of opportunity.

◄ Eventually adopted in 37 states, the McGuffey's Readers gave thousands of schoolchildren a shared background of popular culture and helped to mold the literary tastes of the reading public.

▲ More and more schools provided desks in the 1800s. Earlier, students sat on backless wooden benches. The teacher's desk was often on a raised platform.

◄ "And as for teachers—can't any young lawyer or preacher teach the boys and girls all they need to know?" With widespread acceptance of such views, it is not surprising that in the early nineteenth century most secondary education was supplied not by public, but by private schools.

Portfolio Project

Have students pretend that they are living around 1850 and attending a one-room schoolhouse in the country. Ask them to write a letter to a friend or relative in a distant city, describing how they get to school, what it's like inside, what they are studying, and how they like school.

The Historian's Craft

Many complex issues are associated with education in the United States today, among them student performance, the curriculum, school financing, teacher training, discipline, bilingualism, and segregation. Almost all of these concerns have their roots in the past, and educational historians use many kinds of evidence to analyze that history. In studying teacher training, for example, they may explore the development of normal schools, school-district records, and the experiences of individual teachers.

UNIT 5 DIGEST

The Unit 5 Digest can be used to teach unit coverage when time is limited, to review unit content, or to link content of one unit to another

Unit Digest Transparencies
Use Transparency 10.

■ Chapter 13
Ask students to mark on copies of the outline map of the United States from the Map and Graph Skills Activities in the TCR the areas the United States acquired between 1825 and 1877 and when and how these areas were acquired.

■ Chapter 14
Point out that historian Daniel Boorstin has referred to the growing sectional strife in the mid-1800s as "the failure of the politicians." Ask students to write a paragraph in support of one of these statements:
  Politicians failed to explore every avenue of compromise.
  Compromise exhausted, conflict was inevitable.

■ Chapter 15
Read the following statement by Shelby Foote: "The Civil War defined us as what we are and it opened us to being what we became.... It was the crossroads of our being...."
  Then ask students to discuss whether the Civil War made us what we are as Americans.

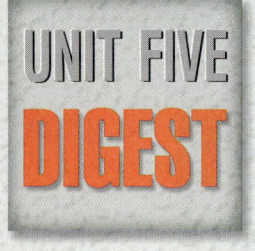

Chapter 13
Manifest Destiny
Several factors influenced the American drive to the Pacific, including the desire to move onto new land, the belief that the plains were unsuitable for farming, commercial interests, and patriotism.

In Texas, disputes between American settlers and the Mexican government led to several conflicts. In 1836 Texas became independent, and in 1846 the United States and Mexico clashed over the southern boundary of Texas. The Mexican War ended with the Treaty of Guadalupe Hidalgo, which granted the United States full title to Texas, California, and what was then New Mexico territory.

Americans also sought to acquire Cuba but abandoned their efforts after several unsuccessful attempts. Americans did, however, succeed in laying the groundwork for a canal across the Isthmus of Panama. In East Asia, Americans opened up China and Japan for trade.

Chapter 14
Compromise and Conflict
Once the United States acquired New Mexico and California, the question arose concerning slavery in the new territories. The issue became more acute after the discovery of gold in California led to California's application for statehood as a free state. The solution, the Compromise of 1850, temporarily staved off further problems.

By 1850 the United States was booming economically, but many of the new developments benefited only the North. The South's feelings of isolation were intensified by its reliance on slavery, which created further tension. The rush among settlers from both slave and free states to populate the Kansas Territory culminated in bloodshed. The nation was further torn apart by the Dred Scott decision.

In the election of 1860, slavery was the key issue, with the Republican candidate, Lincoln, who was viewed as an abolitionist, victorious. In response, most of the Southern states seceded from the Union.

Chapter 15
The Civil War
The fall of Fort Sumter kindled patriotism in both North and South and started their preparation for war. The North drew upon advantages in manufacturing, population, transportation, and wealth, whereas the South relied on superior generals.

UNIT 5 Division and Reunion: 1825–1877

Cooperative Learning
Point out that the Civil War is often characterized as "the first modern war." Organize students into three groups, and assign each group one of the following topics: military technology, military tactics, the home front. Ask the groups to use resources in the school and public libraries to find information about their topics that would support or refute the above characterization. Have the groups present their findings to the rest of the class. **L1**

At first, Southern armies outmaneuvered Union forces in the east, awakening the nation to the reality that it would be a long and costly war. Southern invasions of the North were unsuccessful, however. In the western theater, Union armies gained control of border states. Grant's victory at Vicksburg segmented the South, while Sherman's march subdivided it again.

As the war dragged on, both sides were forced to conscript soldiers. Lincoln reversed an earlier decision and allowed African Americans to enlist. The character of the war also changed when Lincoln issued the Emancipation Proclamation, thereby making the end to slavery a reason for the conflict. Shortly after Lincoln was reelected, Lee surrendered. But chances for a peaceful reconciliation were weakened by Lincoln's assassination just five days later.

Chapter 16
Reconstruction

The Civil War had left the South in disarray, with the land, government, and transportation system in ruin. African Americans and whites set out to rebuild the South. Economically and politically, however, African Americans were thwarted by segregation and black codes.

The Radical Republicans' version of Reconstruction, advocating voting rights for African Americans and harsh treatment of former Confederates, was set in motion when the Radical Republicans gained control of Congress. Reconstruction governments were often handicapped by corruption. Eventually, white Southerners regained control of Southern government. Although Reconstruction was only partially effective for African Americans, a degree of cooperation was achieved between the North and the South.

Understanding Unit Themes

1. **United States Role in World Affairs** How did the spirit of Manifest Destiny affect the role of the United States in world affairs?
2. **Cultural Diversity** How were cultural differences between Northerners and Southerners a factor that caused the Civil War?
3. **Conflict and Compromise** Was a compromise on the slavery issue ever a feasible tactic? Why or why not?
4. **Civil Rights and Liberties** Compare the legal and social status of African Americans before and after the Civil War.

UNIT 5 DIGEST

Chapter 16

Ask students to write a paragraph explaining why they support or oppose this statement:

The North won the war, but the South won the peace.

Understanding Unit Themes

1. Answers will vary, but may include that Manifest Destiny naturally led to an increase in American involvement in world affairs.
2. Economies differed—North was more industrial, South more agricultural; more immigration to the North; North was more urban, South more rural. The North was more diverse ethnically and more pluralistic and open to changes in ways of living, working, and learning. South wanted to preserve its way of life against most changes.
3. Answers will vary. Compromises such as the one made in 1850 did not directly address the problem of slavery, but merely delayed solving it.
4. Answers will vary. Emancipation created little change for many African Americans. The inability or lack of desire on the part of the federal government to enforce the provisions of the Thirteenth, Fourteenth, and Fifteenth amendments negated their effect.

Student Self-Test Software allows students to test their understanding of historical concepts at the unit, chapter, or section levels.

Have students listen to the Chapter Digests on the audiocassettes.

The Historian's Craft

Good historians need to be very careful when analyzing historical documents. Almost everyone has certain opinions, ideas, or beliefs about particular topics or subjects. For this reason, written material is not always objective and may show the bias, a set idea or opinion about something or someone. Bias may be in favor of or against an idea or person. Ask students to read a magazine article and then answer these questions: When and why was the article written? Are certain phrases used in order to have emotional impact? Does the writer show the group as good and the other group as evil? Have the class discuss their findings.

INTRODUCING UNIT 6

BEGINNING THE UNIT

Provide this cause and effect chart to students with the effects omitted. Assign students to complete the chart as they read the chapters in the unit.

Event
- United States becomes industrialized.

Causes
- Abundant natural resources and labor
- Standardization and consolidation of railroads
- New forms of business organization

Effects
- Rapid settlement of the Great Plains
- Removal of buffalo and Native Americans from the plains
- American Federation of Labor formed.
- Populist party formed.

History AND ART

The first gold rush was in California in 1849. When the gold boom there ended in 1852, miners moved eastward to the Rocky Mountains. The first big gold strike there came in 1859 near Pikes Peak in what is now Colorado.

00:00 OUT OF TIME? If time does not permit teaching the entire unit, use the Unit Digest on pages 590–591.

UNIT SIX
NEW HORIZONS
1860–1900

CHAPTER 17	CHAPTER 18	CHAPTER 19	CHAPTER 20	CHAPTER 21
Into the West 1860–1900	The Rise of Industry 1860–1900	An Urban Society 1860–1900	The Gilded Age 1865–1900	Politics and Protest 1865–1900

History AND ART
Miners in the Sierra
by Charles Nahl and Frederick August Wenderoth, 1851–1852

An abundance and variety of natural resources were utilized for industrial production.

▲ Horatio Alger cover

464

Exploring Unit Themes

Geography and the Environment As the West opened up, vast stores of natural resources became available. Newcomers set up farms in the central plains area, extracted minerals from the mountains, and grazed sheep and cattle on the western plains. However, lack of trees and water and climate variations created problems for western settlers.

Conflict and Cooperation As settlers moved westward, they laid claim to Native American hunting grounds and decimated the buffalo. The Native Americans fought to stay on their lands, but most ended up on government reservations. As the railroads spread across the country, so did their economic power. As a result, farmers united and called for needed reform.

Setting the Scene

This was an age of optimism, coupled with a belief in the certainty of human progress. As pioneers continued to spread across the continent and immigrants flocked to industrial centers, Americans adapted to the rapidly changing environment in which they found themselves.

Themes
- Geography and Environment
- Conflict and Cooperation
- Influence of Technology
- Cultural Diversity

Key Events
- First transcontinental railroad
- Interstate Commerce Act
- Civil Service reform
- American Federation of Labor formed
- Sherman Antitrust Act
- Battle at Wounded Knee
- Populist party formed
- Pullman strike

 ▲ Sioux shield

▲ Early phonograph

Major Issues
- Transcontinental railroads allow the rapid settlement of the Great Plains.
- A wealth of natural resources and abundant labor makes the United States a major industrial power.
- The swift growth of industry creates a demand for new labor unions.
- The alliance between government and big business leads to widespread political corruption.
- Agrarian unrest promotes new political movements that seek to regulate commerce.

 ▼ Riding plow, c. 1880s

Portfolio Project
Design a political cartoon that shows the contrasting sides of one of the divisive issues of this era; for example, Native American and settler; labor and big business, or political machine and reformer.

INTRODUCING UNIT 6

UNIT 6 Independent Study Project
Divide the class into four research and study groups. Assign each group one of the following topics: cattle ranchers, miners, farmers, or Native Americans in the late 1800s. Ask the groups to present a research report on their topic to the class after the unit has been completed.

Unit Digest Transparencies
Use Transparency 6.

Portfolio Project
After students have completed their political cartoons, ask them to share their cartoons with the class. Have the class identify the issue referred to by each cartoon and discuss differing points of view.

History and the Humanities

U.S. History and Art Transparencies 9, 12, 13, 14, 15, 18

Focus on American Fine Art Prints 11, 12

American Music: Cultural Traditions

Spirit of American Art and Music 17, 18, 19, 20, 21

Influence of Technology Improved farming and manufacturing processes and transportation systems made available to the public items that once were considered luxuries. Other developments, such as electricity and the telephone, helped to spur industrial growth.

Cultural Diversity Until the late 1800s, the vast majority of immigrants came from northern Europe. After this time, "new immigrants"—people from southern and eastern Europe and China—came in large numbers.

Examining the Themes Tell students that during the period covered by this unit, the United States experienced a great surge in economic growth. Have students trace the development of economic growth in the United States and speculate about its benefits and disadvantages.

LESSON PLAN
Global Perspectives

FOCUS
Motivating Activity

Refer students to the entry on the opening of Ellis Island in the United States section of the time line. Then point out that a refurbished Ellis Island was opened as a museum in 1990. This opening, an observer said, was a powerful reminder to "Americans of where they came from and for what their nation stood."

Have students discuss what this statement means. Close the discussion by telling students that during the time period covered by Unit 6, millions of people from all over the world immigrated to the United States.

TEACH
Guided Practice

Exploring the Time Line
The Native Americans' struggle to hold back the advance of settlement from the United States was not unique. The Maoris of New Zealand, for example, were engaged in a similar struggle with British settlers. Like their American counterparts, the Maoris felt that their only course of action was to fight. And like Native Americans, by the 1890s the Maoris had been forced from their ancestral lands on to bleak and desolate reservations.

L1

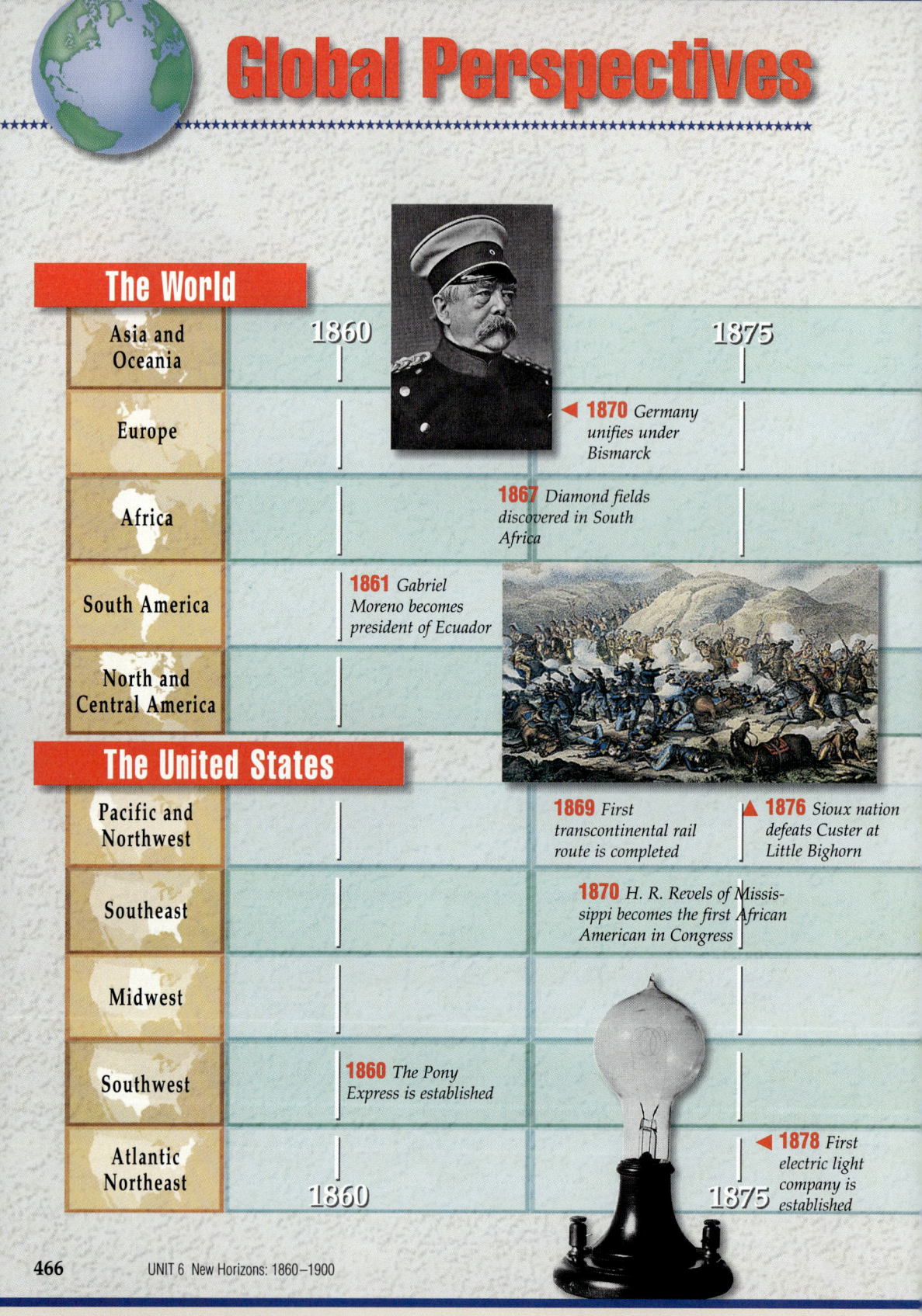

Global Perspectives

The World

	1860		1875
Asia and Oceania			
Europe		**1870** Germany unifies under Bismarck	
Africa		**1867** Diamond fields discovered in South Africa	
South America	**1861** Gabriel Moreno becomes president of Ecuador		
North and Central America			

The United States

Pacific and Northwest		**1869** First transcontinental rail route is completed	▲ **1876** Sioux nation defeats Custer at Little Bighorn
Southeast		**1870** H. R. Revels of Mississippi becomes the first African American in Congress	
Midwest			
Southwest	**1860** The Pony Express is established		
Atlantic Northeast			◀ **1878** First electric light company is established
	1860		1875

466   UNIT 6 New Horizons: 1860–1900

Cultural Diversity

From 1882 on, immigration from China was severely limited. Later Congress also sharply curtailed immigration from Japan and other parts of East Asia. Those restrictions were not removed until the 1940s. The few East Asians who were able to enter the nation between 1910 and 1940 passed through an immigration center at Angel Island in San Francisco Bay. There inspectors studied their papers and questioned the immigrants for inconsistencies in their stories in hope of finding grounds for denying them entry. The questioning could drag on for weeks, and in some cases even months and years. During this time, the immigrants were prisoners on the island. Today Angel Island is a California state park.

Linking Across Time

There has been a Jewish presence in North America for hundreds of years. Jews tended to gravitate to areas where they met little prejudice—Rhode Island, Pennsylvania, and South Carolina, for example. By the mid-1700s the largest concentration of Jews was found in South Carolina's major city, Charleston. The Jewish population in the United States remained relatively small until the late 1800s, when there was an influx of Jews from central and eastern Europe. Today, the United States has the largest Jewish population in the world.

1882 Germany, Austria, and Italy form the Triple Alliance

1890

1894 Sino-Japanese War begins

1900 Boxer rebellion begins

1905

1899 Boer War starts

1895 Cubans revolt against Spanish rule

1884 First steel-skeleton construction is begun, making it possible to build skyscrapers

1892 Ellis Island becomes a receiving station for immigrants

1890   **1905**

UNIT 6 New Horizons: 1860–1900   467

LESSON PLAN
Global Perspectives

Independent Practice
World Events and the U.S.
Point out that the struggle for unification in Italy left the country politically unstable. This instability led to the emigration of some 5 million Italians to the Americas. Ask students to research the impact of nationalism in other European countries on immigration to the United States. **L2**

ASSESS
Studying the Time Line
Study the time line on pages 466 and 467 and answer the questions that follow.
1. What political-first occurred in the United States at about the same time Bismarck unified Germany? (The first African American was elected to Congress.)
2. What major transportation development occurred in 1869? (The first transcontinental railroad route was completed.)

Cooperative Learning

Point out that in 1885, some 16 years after the completion of the United States transcontinental rail route, a rail route across Canada was opened. Divide the class into two groups. Have one group construct a large-scale map of the United States route and the other construct a large-scale map of the Canadian route. Suggest that the groups include illustrations, captions, and a detailed key on their maps. Display the maps and then lead the class in a discussion on the similarities and differences between the two routes. **L2**

467

PLANNING GUIDE — Chapter 17   Forces Shaping the West

Daily Lesson Objectives	Teacher Classroom Resources	Multimedia
SECTION 1 **People of the Plains** 1 Day pp. 470–475 1. Describe the Plains peoples' way of life. 2. Give three reasons the Plains peoples' way of life came to an end.	Chapter 17 Study Guide Reproducible Lesson Plan Reteaching Activity 17-1 Section Quiz Chapter 17 Cooperative Learning Activity Chapter 17 Concept Mapping Activity Reinforcing Social Studies Skills 9, 38, 40, 44 American Portrait 33 Writer's Guidebook Lessons 8-14	Student Self-Test Software Testmaker Section Focus Transparency 52 Chapter 17 Skills Transparency Chapter 17 Map Transparencies Unit 6 Digest Transparencies The American People: Fabric of a Nation A Geographic Perspective on American History
SECTION 2 **Ranching and Mining** 1 Day pp. 477–481 1. Explain the role of the environment in the rise and fall of the long drive. 2. Identify the realities behind the myths of the Old West.	Reproducible Lesson Plan Reteaching Activity 17-2 Section Quiz Reinforcing Social Studies Skills 27, 32, 40 Outline Maps 9, 14 American Portrait 33 Writer's Guidebook Lesson 1 SAT Practice Tests 4-9	Student Self-Test Software Testmaker Section Focus Transparency 53 Chapter 17 Map Transparencies U.S. History and Art Transparencies 7, 9, 13 The American People: Fabric of a Nation
SECTION 3 **Farming Moves West** 1 Day pp. 484–488 1. List three factors that made farming the Plains possible. 2. Summarize the problems faced by Plains farmers.	Reproducible Lesson Plan Reteaching Activity 17-3 Section Quiz Chapter 17 Enrichment Activity Chapter 17 Primary and Secondary Source Readings Reinforcing Social Studies Skills 31, 32, 50, 67 American Portrait 34 American Literary Heritage Unit 6 Building Skills in Geography Spanish Summaries & Glossary	Student Self-Test Software Testmaker Section Focus Transparency 54 Vocabulary Puzzlemaker Chapter 17 Map Transparencies Audiocassette, Chapter 17
CHAPTER REVIEW AND EVALUATION 1 Day	Chapter 17 Test Chapter 17 Performance Assessment Activity	Student Self-Test Software Testmaker

00:00   OUT OF TIME? If time does not permit teaching the entire chapter, use the Chapter 17 Summary on pages 590–591 and the Chapter 17 audiocassette (English and Spanish) to point out the main ideas of the chapter.

PLANNING GUIDE

Cultural Diversity Activity

Interpreting Media Point out that in real life many cowboys were Mexican or African American, especially in Texas, which was a slaveholding state before the Civil War. After the war, many freed slaves found work as professional cowhands. Most Texas trail outfits included African American cowboys, and some were entirely African American. Mexican cowhands, descendants of the *vaqueros*, the first cowboys, were common in south Texas.

Have students watch an older movie or Western series on TV. Such films are often shown as reruns on cable television stations or can be rented from video stores. As students view the film, ask them to look critically at the portrayal of Native Americans and cowboys. Then have students suggest ways the movie could be changed to give a truer picture of the West.

Performance Assessment Activity

Picturing the West Have students work in small groups to create a poster that shows life in the West in the late 1800s. Encourage each group to depict the West from a particular point of view. For example, one group might show how the West looked to Native Americans; another might describe it from a farmer's point of view; and still another might focus on the way in which miners viewed the region. After each group has completed its poster, discuss similarities and differences in points of view.

POSSIBLE RUBRIC FEATURES: Content information, main idea, creativity, clarity, visual and written communication skills, collaborative skills

Chapter Resources

Literature from the Period

Chief Joseph. *Chief Joseph's Own Story.* Montana Council for Indian Education, 1983.

_____. "I Will Fight No More Forever." 1877.

Harte, Bret. "The Outcasts of Poker Flat." 1869.

Readings for the Student

Freedman, Russell. *Buffalo Hunt.* Holiday House, 1988.

Hoig, Stan. "The Great Oklahoma Land Rush of 1889." *American History Illustrated*, Vol. 24, No. 1, March 1989.

"Joseph, A Chief of the Nez Perce." *Cobblestone*, Vol. 2, No. 9, September 1990.

Readings for the Teacher

Dale, Edward E. *Frontier Ways: Sketches of Life in the Old West.* University of Texas, 1989.

Moyniham, Ruth B., et. al., eds. *So Much to Be Done: Women Settlers on the Mining and Ranching Frontier.* University of Nebraska Press, 1990.

Schlissel, Lillian, et al. *Far From Home: Families of the Westward Journey.* Schocken, 1989.

Vine, Robert V. *Community on the American Frontier: Separate But Not Alone.* University of Oklahoma Press, 1980.

Multimedia Resources

Famous Women of the West. Multi-Media Productions. (filmstrip, cassette, guide)

Nez Perce: Portrait of a People. National Park Service. (VHS, 23 minutes)

Vaquero: The Forgotten Cowboy. PBS (VHS, 60 minutes)

Key to Ability Levels

Teaching strategies have been coded for varying learning styles and abilities.

L1 Basic activities for all students

L2 Average activities for average to above-average students

L3 Challenging activities for above-average students

LEP Limited English Proficiency activities

Glencoe Links to the Humanities

Links to Art
- U.S. History and Art Transparencies 9, 12, 13, 18
- Focus on American Fine Art Prints 11, 12

Links to Literature
- Macmillan Literature: Appreciating Literature Audiotapes Side 1
- Macmillan Literature: American Literature Audiotapes Side 3
- Macmillan Literature: American Literature Video—*The Adventures of Huckleberry Finn*
- Macmillan Literature: Novel Guide—*The Adventures of Tom Sawyer, Old Yeller, Shane*
- Macmillan Literature: American Literature Text—Mark Twain, Bret Harte

Link to Music
- American Music: Cultural Traditions

CHAPTER 17

BEGINNING THE CHAPTER

Have students use the map of the United States on page 487 to identify the area that was mostly unsettled in 1870. (most of the area west of the Mississippi River to the Pacific Ocean) Then have them speculate why settling this area might have proved difficult. (difficult to get to by wagon, might have less desirable farmland, more remote, Native Americans might be unfriendly) Point out that the problems of settling the West will be explored in this chapter.

Linking Across Time

A number of plains states' names are of Native American origin. Among them are *Dakota*, meaning "allies"; *Kansas*, meaning "south wind people"; and *Nebraska*, meaning "flat water."

Recording Journal Notes

To help students get started, suggest that they categorize their findings under two headings: Geographic Features and Environmental Features.

CHAPTER 17

Into the West
1860–1900

Setting the Scene

Focus
The settlement of the Far West frontier was filled with hardships and tragedy as well as adventure. For Native Americans, the slaughter of the buffalo and gradual expansion of white settlement meant the end of their way of life. For miners, ranchers, and farmers, life on the Great Plains meant long hours of work, a harsh climate, and isolation.

▲ **LANTERN, LATE 1800S**

Concepts to Understand
★ Why national expansion developed in the Great Plains region
★ How conflict between the Plains peoples and settlers led to the destruction of Native American society

Read to Discover . . .
★ the role of the railroads in the settlement of the Great Plains.
★ how life on the Great Plains measured up to settlers' expectations.

Journal Notes
What geographic and environmental features created hardships for those who settled and farmed the West? Make notes in your journal as you read the chapter.

CULTURAL
- 1866 First major "long drive" moves Texas longhorns to Missouri
- 1872 Yellowstone National Park is created in Wyoming Territory

1860 | **1870**

POLITICAL
- 1862 Homestead Act passes
- 1869 First transcontinental railroad is constructed

468 UNIT 6 New Horizons: 1860–1900

✚ EXTRA CREDIT PROJECT

The building of the transcontinental railroad was a mammoth undertaking. Ask interested students to research aspects of the task. Some might focus on the physical obstacles work crews had to overcome. Others might find out about the Chinese, the Irish, and others who laid the tracks across the nation. Still other students might focus on the entrepreneurs who owned the Central Pacific and the Union Pacific railroads, the race across the West between the two companies, or the role the federal government played in the building of the railroad. Have students share their written reports by organizing them into a book.

▲ SIOUX WAR CLUB

The Last of the Buffalo
by Albert Bierstadt, 1889

Bierstadt sat on the banks of the Republican River in north central Kansas and worked out his idea for *The Last of the Buffalo*.

- **1883** "Buffalo Bill" Cody opens his first wild west show
- **1884** United States government prohibits Native American Sun Dance
- **1895** The Red Badge of Courage published
- **1890** Census Department declares the frontier closed

1880 — **1890**

CHAPTER 17 Into the West 1860–1900

CHAPTER 17 CONCEPTS

Concept Mapping Activity

Reproduce the following generalization and concepts map on the chalkboard, and have students copy it in their notebooks. Ask students what words in the concept generalization express or mean the same thing as *expansion* and *conflict*.

> People from the United States moved west because of unlimited opportunity but had to fight for survival in a harsh environment.

Expansion — Conflict

History AND ART

Albert Bierstadt joined a buffalo hunt as an observer and painted this dramatic confrontation between hunter and buffalo.

- *GTV: A Geographic Perspective on American History*

Side 3, Chapter 3
Title: *A World of Change*
Subject: Settlement on the Great Plains

See GTV Guide page 50 for complete lesson plan.

Teacher Notes

LESSON PLAN
SECTION 1, 470–476

FOCUS

Bellringer
Before taking roll at the beginning of the class period, display Focus Activity 56 on the overhead projector, and assign the accompanying Focus Activity Sheet.

Objectives
Point out the objectives on this page to students in previewing the section content.

Motivating Activity
Have students study the illustration of the buffalo hunt on page 471. Then ask them to consider the following questions: Who participated in the hunt? (Difficult to say, but probably men.) How was the hunt conducted? (The hunters wore wolves' skins as disguises, creeping up on grazing buffalo herds.) Did this hunt take place before or after the coming of the Europeans? Why? (Probably before, since the hunters are not using horses.) Write students' responses on the chalkboard, and discuss them with the class. Tell students that in this section they will learn that the buffalo was the major focus of the Plains peoples' way of life.

Use Skills Transparency 17.

SECTION 1

People of the Plains

Setting the Scene

Section Focus
The steady push of settlement across North America skipped over a thousand miles of treeless expanse before resuming again at the Pacific Coast. For a few years the United States government reserved most of the vast interior of the country to Native Americans because it believed these "Great Plains" to be too dry for farming. When settlers began to infringe on these territories, they met determined resistance from the Plains peoples.

Objectives
After studying this section, you should be able to
★ describe the Plains peoples' way of life.
★ give three reasons the Plains peoples' way of life came to an end.

Key Term
nomadic

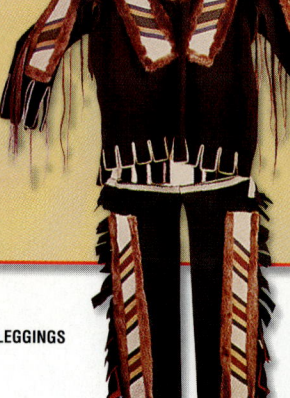

▶ PLAINS WOOLEN JACKET AND LEGGINGS

The United States government had assigned Major Stephen H. Long the exploration of the region beyond the Mississippi River in 1820. In his report, Long used the term "Great American Desert" to describe the territory—a term that soon appeared on all the maps of the West. Believing the land to be completely desolate, many who ventured to California and Oregon completely avoided it, choosing to travel by clipper ship around Cape Horn at the tip of South America.

■ A Nomadic Life
The territory that early European explorers believed to be a desert was home to countless species of wildlife. Hundreds of millions of jackrabbits and prairie dogs, millions of wolves and coyotes, and an estimated 12 to 15 million American bison—usually called buffalo—roamed the Great Plains.

The region was also home to many different Native American nations. Some, like the Omaha and the Osage nations, lived in communities as farmers and hunters. Most of the Native Americans, however, including the Sioux [SOO], the Comanche [kuh•MAN•chee], and the Blackfeet, were **nomadic** peoples. They roamed vast distances, following their main source of food: the great herds of buffalo that lived on the plains.

For generations the nomadic peoples of the plains had only dogs to haul their possessions as they traveled from one hunting area to another. In the 1600s, horses, either

UNIT 6 New Horizons 1860–1900

Classroom Resources for SECTION 1

Teacher's Classroom Resources
- Chapter 17 Study Guide
- Reproducible Lesson Plan
- Reteaching Activity 17-1
- Chapter 17 Cooperative Learning Activity
- Section Quiz

Multimedia
- Section Focus Transparency 56
- Chapter 17 Skills Transparency
- Chapter 17 Map Transparency 1
- Student Self-Test Software
- A Geographic Perspective on American History
- The American People: Fabric of a Nation

traded or stolen from Spanish settlers in the Southwest, changed the Plains peoples' way of life. By the mid-1750s, almost every Plains people rode on horseback. Horses became a vital part of their social, economic, and political life. The Comanche were perhaps the best riders, but the Sioux, Cheyenne [shy•AN], Pawnee, Blackfoot, and Crow nations were nearly as skilled. In the deserts of the region that are the present-day states of Arizona and New Mexico, the Apache [uh•PA•chee] and Navajo [NAH•vuh•hoh] captured horses to sell to northern peoples.

The horse made the Plains people much more effective hunters than they had been on foot. It became easier to follow the buffalo, which provided the main source of food, skins for clothing and shelter, and bones for tools. The buffalo hunt not only yielded life's necessities, it also provided sport, ritual, worship, and training for war. Fighting from horseback, Native American warriors were better able to resist the encroachments of settlers and railroads.

Railroads Open the West

A Dakota newspaper editor wrote, "Without the railroad it would have required a century to accomplish what has been done in five years." What was "accomplished" was the killing of nearly all the buffalo and other prairie life, obstruction of the Plains peoples' way of life, and removal of any surviving peoples to reservations.

First Transcontinental Railroad

Railroad building in the West began at a furious pace during the Civil War. The most dramatic achievement was the completion of the first transcontinental line in 1869. Discussion of this project started when gold was discovered in California in 1848.

During the 1850s at least 10 routes were surveyed, and the Gadsden Purchase was acquired from Mexico principally because the Gila River valley provided the easiest route across the western plateau. Congress wanted to finance this gigantic project, but

▼ APACHE LEADER

▲ **PLAINS LIFE** Native Americans faced many hardships on the plains. *How did the extinction of the buffalo affect the Plains peoples' way of life?*

CHAPTER 17 Into the West 1860–1900

Sidelights: The Horse

Spanish settlers first introduced the horse to the Native Americans. The Spanish used horses at their missions, and it was there that the Native Americans learned why the animal was useful. Not having a name for the horse they called it "mystery dog" or "mystery elk." In 1680 a revolt among Native Americans in the Southwest so terrified the Spanish that they fled the territory, releasing their horses into the wild. In the wilderness the horse quickly multiplied and, within a short time, became an important part of Native American life on the Great Plains.

CHAPTER 17 SECTION 1

TEACH
Guided Practice

History Divide students into groups of three. Have each group list the ways in which the horse changed the Native Americans' way of life. (improved transportation; made hunting buffalo easier) Discuss the lists, and then have each student write one paragraph explaining how the cultures of the Plains peoples were related to the buffalo and the horse. **L1, LEP**

Visualizing History Buffalo hunting methods included donning buffalo skins and luring the animals over a cliff, or in winter driving the buffalo into deep snow, where they were much easier to approach and kill. **Answer to Caption:** eliminated their main source of food and other necessities of life

In the nineteenth century, the United States negotiated hundreds of treaties with various Native American nations. These treaties were usually enforced very selectively, if at all.

In the last half of the twentieth century, many Native American groups have gone to court seeking to redress grievances caused by unequal enforcement of treaties.

CHAPTER 17
SECTION 1

Independent Practice

Religion Have students research and write short papers on the religious beliefs of the Plains peoples. **L2**

Using Graphs

Answer: 1880–1890

Skills Practice

Have students determine by how much the Native American population declined between 1850 and 1900. (about 160,000)

VIDEODISC

• *GTV: A Geographic Perspective on American History*

Side 3, Chapter 3
Title: *A World of Change*
Subject: Settlement on the Great Plains

See GTV Guide page 50 for complete lesson plan.

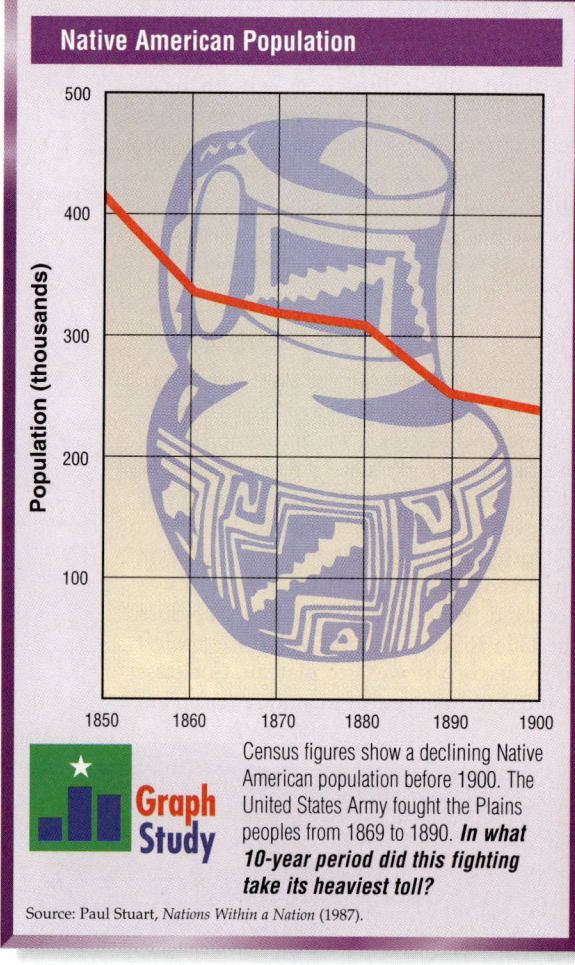

Native American Population

Census figures show a declining Native American population before 1900. The United States Army fought the Plains peoples from 1869 to 1890. *In what 10-year period did this fighting take its heaviest toll?*

Source: Paul Stuart, *Nations Within a Nation* (1987).

Construction proceeded rapidly as the 2 lines raced to get more government money and land. At the height of the competition, the Union Pacific builders employed 10,000 workers. Irish immigrant crews working for the Union Pacific and Chinese immigrants working for the Central Pacific sometimes laid as much as 10 miles of track a day—a remarkable feat because the digging and grading were done by hand. The Central Pacific had a difficult time in the Sierra Nevada ranges with snow that sometimes collected in drifts 60 feet deep. Its heavy equipment was carried from the East 19,000 miles around Cape Horn to California by a fleet of 30 ships.

On May 10, 1869, the "wedding of the rails" took place at Promontory Point, Utah. The whole country celebrated as a transcontinental telegraph reported the blow of a silver sledgehammer driving a golden spike to complete the railroad. A magnetic ball dropped from a pole on the top of the Capitol in Washington, D.C.; in Chicago a seven-mile procession paraded through the streets; in small towns citizens rang church bells.

Other Railroads

The first transcontinental line was soon followed by others—the Northern Pacific; the Atchison, Topeka, and Santa Fe; the Southern Pacific; and the Great Northern. Like other big businesses, the railroads needed people of ability, imagination, and drive. The greatest of the Western builders was James J. Hill, a small, short-tempered, red-bearded man of enthusiasm and energy. Beginning in 1879, Hill built the Great Northern, connecting the state of Minnesota and the Washington Territory, without government help. By encouraging settlement as soon as the rails were laid, Hill ensured that his line would have customers. He offered free transportation from Eastern ports, credit, farm machinery, and even free advice on how to improve crops. Hill's careful construction of the Great Northern kept maintenance costs down and enabled him to charge lower rates. As a result, his railroad became the leading carrier in the Northwest.

sectional rivalry caused delays. The South preferred that the eastern terminal be located at New Orleans; the North argued for St. Louis or Chicago. In 1862, with Southern representation temporarily withdrawn from Congress, the government passed an act to encourage the building of a Pacific Railroad.

The Union Pacific Company was to build west from Omaha, while the Central Pacific Company was to run lines east from Sacramento. The federal government loaned money to both companies at the rate of $16,000, $32,000, or $48,000 per mile, according to the terrain. Each company also received land grants along the right-of-way averaging 640 acres per mile.

Cooperative Learning

Organize the class into small groups. For each group provide a map showing the location of the various Native American nations. Have students compare that map with the one on page 478 that shows railroad lines. Then ask them to decide what conflicts could have been predicted before the railroads were built. Ask each student to write a creative proposal of how to avoid conflict. Have the group provide constructive suggestions on how to improve the content of the proposal. Finally ask the groups to present their proposals to the class. **L3**

Believing passionately in the life of the farmers on the plains, Hill wanted to promote maximum settlement. He expressed the idea that

> *Population without the Prairie is a mob, and the Prairie without Population is a desert.*

Killing of Buffalo

The railroads played a major role in the extermination of the buffalo. Though buffalo had formerly ranged eastward as far as Pennsylvania and the Carolinas, their natural habitat was the Great Plains, where they migrated north and south with the seasons. The Union Pacific Railroad effectively cut the huge herds in half. At first buffalo hunting supplied meat for railroad workers, but later it became "sport" for city vacationers to shoot the animals from train windows. In 1871 it was discovered that buffalo leather could be sold at a profit. Professional hunters killed millions for their hides. Train loads of bones were shipped east to make fertilizer or charcoal. By 1886 only a few hundred buffalo were left, deep in the Canadian woods.

■ Plains Wars

To protect their lands and to stop the waste of the buffalo, Plains people had to fight. For two and one-half centuries they had maintained their way of life against Spanish, English, French, and American invaders. The last battles against overwhelming forces proved futile. The military effort to remove Native Americans from the plains was relentless, with the United States spending an estimated million dollars for each adult male Native American killed.

Taking of Native American Land

The first concentrated fighting broke out in Colorado just after the Civil War started in the East. Government officials tried to

---

Life of the Times

Native American Schools

In the 1870s and 1880s, the federal government passed legislation and instituted policies designed to assimilate Native Americans into white society.

Most of the 106 day and boarding schools operated by the federal government in 1881 were on or adjacent to reservation land. However, white educators believed that Native American children would learn more and be assimilated more quickly if they attended non-reservation boarding schools.

Many Native American parents showed reluctance when whites came to recruit their children for boarding school. For example, parents were particularly reluctant to send their daughters away from home. They understood that it would change the children's values. One mother of an especially bright 10-year-old girl refused to let her daughter go off to an industrial training school without her. Education and civilization, the mother explained, would make the child regard her mother as a savage. In the end, this mother was allowed to accompany her child to school.

▲ PINE RIDGE, SOUTH DAKOTA, SCHOOL

CHAPTER 17 Into the West 1860–1900

Critical Thinking

Synthesizing Information In 1879 Chief Joseph of the Nez Percés, in an appeal to President Rutherford B. Hayes, said:

"Let me be a free man—free to travel, free to stop, free to work, free to trade where I choose, free to choose my own teachers, free to follow the religion of my father, free to think and talk and act for myself—and I will obey every law or submit to the penalty."

Ask: Which of these requests are guaranteed in the Bill of Rights? (all) How were these rights denied to Native Americans? (had to live on reservations) **L2**

CHAPTER 17
SECTION 1

Teaching Life of the Times

Native American students were forbidden to speak their own languages in school. This practice greatly contributed to the destruction of Native American cultures and loss of identity. Ask students how they might feel if they were forbidden to speak their own language in school.

Approximately 755,000 Native Americans live on reservations in the United States today. Most of the land is located in remote, barren desert areas. Most Native Americans live in extreme poverty, without running water or electricity.

 VIDEODISC

- *GTV: The American People: Fabric of a Nation*

Side 2, Chapter 2
Title: *Between Worlds*
Subject: For Native Americans, a shrinking realm

See GTV Guide page 60 for complete lesson plan.

CHAPTER 17
SECTION 1

History AND ART

Tell students that in 1829, Speckled Snake, a Creek, said on hearing that President Jackson planned to move all Native Americans west of the Mississippi: "Brother, I have listened to a great many talks from our great father. But they always began and ended in this—'Get a little further; you are too near me.'"

Answer to Caption: Plains people knew little about farming and were demoralized by reservation life.

Fact or Fiction?

Sitting Bull commanded the Sioux at the Battle of Little Big Horn.

FICTION–Sitting Bull stayed behind the battle lines during the skirmish. Two Oglala Sioux war chiefs, Crazy Horse and Gall, won the battle.

▲ **BLANKET SIGNAL** by Frederic Remington Artist Frederic Remington captured dramatic and compelling images of the vanishing Western frontier. **Why did the Dawes Act fail?**

force the Arapaho and Cheyenne from an area that had been granted to them "forever" 10 years earlier. Warfare continued for 3 years until Black Kettle, the Cheyenne chief, was trapped at Sand Creek in eastern Colorado by Colonel John Chivington. The militia ignored Black Kettle's repeated attempts to surrender and killed men, women, and children.

In 1862 the Santee Sioux of Minnesota attacked a group of settlers who had moved into their hunting lands. After the militia defeated them, the Sioux were forced to move to reservations in the Dakota Territory. A short time later, the Oglala [oh•GLA•lah] Sioux became enraged at the territorial government's plans to build a road through their sacred lands. Led by Red Cloud, they successfully resisted for several years. In the end, however, the Sioux lost their land to miners searching for gold in the Black Hills.

Efforts Toward Peace

After the bloody war with the Sioux, humanitarians in the East called for a change of government policies. The United States divided responsibility for the Native Americans between the Department of the Interior and the War Department. The Department of the Interior first was to placate Native Americans with gifts and to establish reservations; the War Department was to make war on those who resisted.

In 1867 the federal government sent a peace commission to meet with representatives of several nations, including the Comanche, Kiowa [KY•uh•WAW], Cheyenne, and Arapaho. This effort to end the constant warfare produced agreements that stipulated that the Native Americans were to live on two major reservations on the Great Plains, one in Oklahoma and one in the Dakota Territory. Not all nations were involved, however, so conflicts between Native Americans and the army continued.

Hostilities Resume

With the discovery of gold in the Dakota Territory in 1874, miners flooded into Sioux and Cheyenne lands. Two years later the Sioux, led by Chiefs Sitting Bull and Crazy Horse, attacked the miners and settlers. The conflict came to a climax in June 1876 at the Little Bighorn River, where a large group of Cheyenne and Sioux were camped. General George Custer attacked, but the Native Americans killed Custer and all of his troops at the Battle of the Little Bighorn. The Sioux victory meant only a brief reprieve. In 1881 they surrendered for a final time to the United States Army.

▶ **NATIVE AMERICAN CRADLE**

Sidelights: The Ghost Dance

Early in 1889 a Paiute leader named Wovoka began to preach that a messiah was coming who would drive the whites out of North America and return the Native Americans to their former glory. To hasten the messiah's arrival, Wovoka said, the Native Americans must perform a ritual called the Ghost Dance. Native Americans all over the West quickly began to follow Wovoka's advice. American military authorities, believing the Ghost Dance was more a declaration of war than a ritual, dispatched troops to put a stop to it. At Wounded Knee in December 1890, the troops did just that.

The final clash occurred at Wounded Knee, South Dakota, in December of 1890, where more than 190 unarmed Native Americans were killed. With this tragic encounter, the wars came to an end.

Although Plains nations fought hundreds of battles from 1860 to 1890, their cause was doomed because they were dependent on the buffalo for food, clothing, fuel, and shelter. When the herds were wiped out, resistance became impossible. In spite of some victories and heroic deeds, such as the 1,500-mile march of the Nez Percé (NEHZ PUHRS) under Chief Joseph in 1877 to avoid capture, the result was inevitable. Chief Joseph's speech at his surrender summarized the hopelessness of the cause:

> Our chiefs are killed. . . . The little children are freezing to death. My people . . . have no blankets, no food. . . . Hear me, my chiefs; I am tired; my heart is sick and sad. From where the sun now stands, I will fight no more forever.

The Dawes Act

In 1887, three years before Wounded Knee, Congress passed the Dawes Act, which broke up Native American nations, even on the reservations. The Dawes Act gave each family 160 acres to cultivate. After a probation period of 25 years, Native Americans would be granted ownership of the land and United States citizenship.

The Dawes Act was the result of humanitarian opposition to the United States Army's extermination policy. In 1881 Helen Hunt Jackson had written *A Century of Dishonor*, a book that criticized the government policy toward Native Americans. Unfortunately, the new legislation did more harm than good. Plains peoples were nomads whose way of life was based on the buffalo hunt. They did not understand legal technicalities of land ownership, knew little about farming, and were demoralized by reservation life. Between 1887 and 1943, Native Americans lost to real estate speculators and dishonest government agents an estimated 86 million acres of the 138 million acres that had been set aside for them.

▲ GHOST DANCE SHIRT

Section 1 ★ Review

Checking for Understanding

1. **Identify** Sioux, Promontory Point, James J. Hill, Sitting Bull, Little Bighorn, Wounded Knee.
2. **Define** nomadic.
3. **Explain** how the expansion of the railroads benefited some people at the expense of others.
4. **Enumerate** the events that eventually brought an end to the Plains peoples' way of life.

Critical Thinking

5. **Formulating Hypotheses** Why did the United States government fight wars against Plains peoples in spite of the human costs?

CHAPTER 17 Into the West 1860–1900   475

LESSON PLAN
Mastering Social Studies Skills

Teaching Map and Graph Skills

Relate weather maps to the map shown. How are the two maps alike? (Both show how different kinds of data are related.) Why are the title and key crucial to using the map accurately? (These parts tell what data are provided, how the data are separated, and the time the data represent.)

Discuss the conclusions students could make with this map. What can you say about climates of the United States? (There are huge areas of similar climates and pockets of certain other kinds of climates.) What similarities do some regions have? (Sample: Both desert and steppe regions are dry.) Of what historical significance would this map be? (Based on the date, one could speculate about economic prosperity, agricultural potential, and possible population centers.)

🔖 Use Chapter 17 Map Transparency. Assign the accompanying activity from Map Transparencies: Strategies and Activities.

Did You Know?
The Mojave is the largest desert within the United States. Covering 15,000 square miles (24,135 square kilometers) in southern California, it receives only 5 inches of rain per year.

Social Studies Skills
Map and Graph Skills

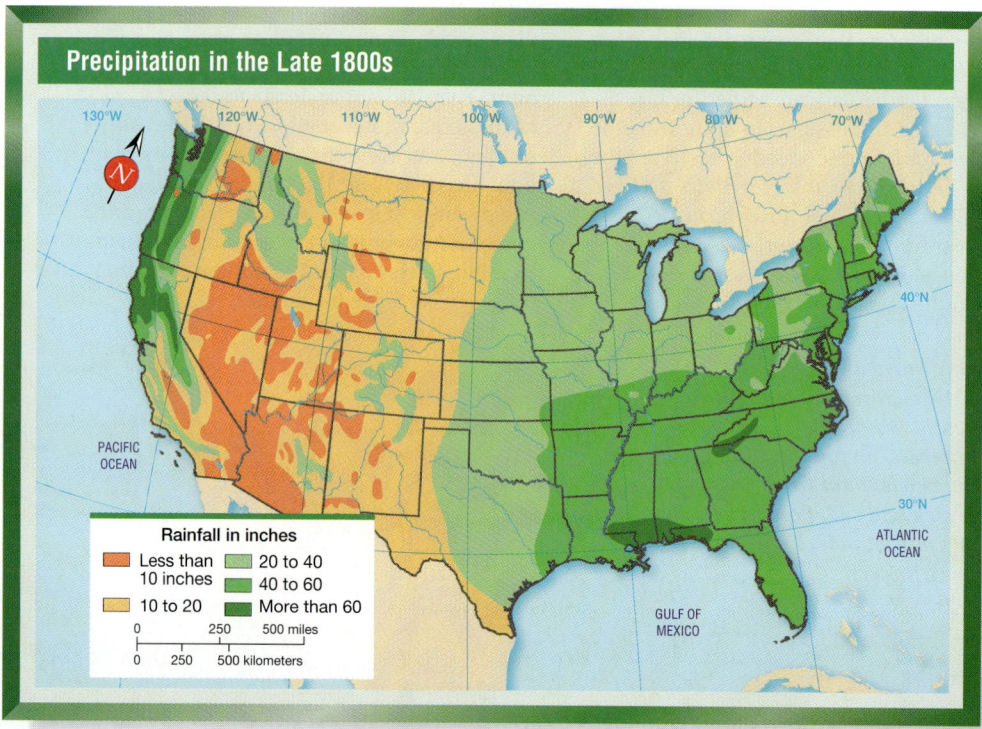

Analyzing Map Data

One way to tell the state of agriculture in a region is to study the amount of rainfall it receives. Studying data on rainfall helps you judge whether a region's agricultural potential is good, fair, or poor. The plains farmers had no way of doing this because accurate records of rainfall did not then exist.

Analysis is the process of separating data into its various parts and seeing how they relate to one another. Once you have analyzed data, you can then make better judgments based on it. For example, instruments exist today that collect data about rainfall. This data can be separated and organized so that it provides a comparison of different amounts and different geographic areas. This gives a basis by which to judge the agricultural potential of different areas.

Practicing the Skill
Analyze the data on the climate map of the United States by answering the following questions:
1. What data is shown on the map?
2. How is the data separated?
3. How is the data related?
4. What judgments can you make?

For further practice in analyzing map data, answer the same questions while studying the map on page 478.

Answers to SOCIAL STUDIES SKILLS
1. the amount of rainfall in inches that fell over all of the United States during the 1800s
2. into five areas with each representing a certain range of measured rainfall
3. Some areas show very little rainfall; others increasingly more; others show extensive amounts. The areas relate to one another on a scale from driest to wettest.
4. Answers will vary, but students are likely to suggest that agricultural potential was best in areas with plenty of rain.

SECTION 2

Ranching and Mining

Setting the Scene

Section Focus

The "Old West" that inspired romantic tales for over a century is based on the realities of cattle ranching and mining. Removal of buffalo and Native Americans from the plains and the opening of Eastern markets by the railroad introduced the great days of the cattle ranchers. Discoveries of more gold and silver in mountains of the West lured thousands of fortune seekers to the mining towns.

Objectives

After studying this section, you should be able to

★ explain the role of the environment in the rise and fall of the long drive.

★ identify the realities behind the myths of the Old West.

Key Terms

maverick, long drive, vigilance committee, vaudeville, "Western"

◀ NAT LOVE

The open-range cattle industry started in Spanish Texas. The Spanish brought the techniques of herding on horseback, roping, and the roundup to the Americas. From the Spanish, too, came the distinctive dress and equipment of the cowhand. The cattle in Texas were mainly Spanish in origin, although some were brought by American and French settlers to Texas when it was part of Mexico. The Great Plains, with its vast open grasslands, was well suited for raising cattle. Faced with such an opportunity, ranchers rapidly moved into the last frontier.

■ The Cattle Kingdom

After the Texas Revolution in 1836, **mavericks,** or unbranded cattle, multiplied on the open range. An estimated 330,000 head of cattle in 1850 grew to between 3 and 4 million head by 1860. There were so many that they could be bought for as little as $3 or $4 a head in Texas.

Cattle Drives

After the Civil War, opportunity developed for great profit in the cattle industry as growing cities of the North provided huge

CHAPTER 17 Into the West 1860–1900   477

Classroom Resources for SECTION 2

Teacher's Classroom Resources
- Reproducible Lesson Plan
- Reteaching Activity 17-2
- Section Quiz

Multimedia
- Section Focus Transparency 57
- Chapter 17 Map Skills Transparency 2
- U.S. History and Art Transparency
- Testmaker
- Student Self-Test Software
- The American People: Fabric of a Nation

LESSON PLAN
SECTION 2, 477–483

FOCUS

Bellringer
Before taking roll at the beginning of the class period, display Focus Activity Transparency 57 on the overhead projector, and assign the accompanying Focus Activity Sheet.

Objectives
Point out the objectives on this page to students in previewing the section content.

Motivating Activity
Write the following quotation on the chalkboard:
"There's gold from the grass roots down, but there's more gold from the grass roots up."
Students should quickly gather what "gold from the grass roots down" means. Have them speculate what "gold from the grass roots up" might refer to. (cattle) Then ask: Why might there be "more gold from the grass roots up"? (Gold must be mined, may be hard to find, may be in limited supply. Huge herds of cattle could be grazed across the extensive plains.)

Did You Know?
Many African Americans worked as cowhands. Some were brought to the West as slaves to herd cattle. Others headed west after emancipation in search of a better life. Unlike African Americans in other occupations, they experienced little discrimination.

477

CHAPTER 17 SECTION 2

TEACH
Guided Practice

Economics Have students formulate generalizations on the impact of supply and demand on the boom and bust in the Texas cattle industry. (Example: Because of a large supply of cattle and a huge demand for meat, profits in the cattle industry increased. Profits decreased when there was supply of meat greater than demand for it.) Discuss students' generalizations. **L2**

Map Study Using Maps

Answer: on the northern plains in what today is Montana and Wyoming

Skills Practice

Ask students to determine which state held the most extensive mining area. (California)

Did You Know?

Nearly one out of three cowhands were either Mexican or African American. Nat Love, an ex-slave from Tennessee, began a 20-year career as a cowhand working a trail herd at age 15. Later he became a rodeo celebrity.

Assign the Chapter 17 Primary and Secondary Source Readings on the "Hard Life of American Farmers."

markets for meat. There were, however, no direct railroad lines from Texas to the North. The result was the **long drive.** As the spring of 1866 turned the grasslands green, cowhands drove herds of steers to railroad shipping centers in Missouri and Kansas. The routes of the long drives became known as trails—such as the Chisholm Trail from near San Antonio to Abilene, a station on the Kansas Pacific Railroad.

A single herd might number 2,500 and be attended by 8 to 10 cowhands, a trail boss, and wranglers to care for the horses. The life of a cowhand on the trail demanded discipline, endurance, and courage, but it paid well to those who survived. More than 30,000 cowhands may have ridden the trails to deliver cattle from Texas to the North. Several thousand of these were African Americans, free to earn their first wages after the Civil War.

Life in the cattle towns was exciting, but many cowhands told exaggerated tales of daring that multiplied as dime novels—books of stories that sold for a dime—spread the myths of the "Wild West" in Eastern towns and cities. A typical tale was *The Life and Adventures of Nat Love: Better Known in the Cattle Country as "Deadwood Dick"—By Himself.* Love was an authentic African American cowboy whose story became part of the romance of the West.

For the investor, the profits obtained from a successful cattle drive were enormous.

The Opening of the West, 1865–1900

Map Study Although 35 years of settlement had changed the face of the West, by 1900 much of this territory remained unsettled. The 27 percent of the nation's population that lived there remained concentrated in larger towns such as San Francisco, Los Angeles, and Denver. The population was growing rapidly, however. Between the end of the Civil War and the turn of the twentieth century, nearly every state in the West had been touched by railroad building, precious metals mining, and battles. *In what area were most of these battles concentrated?*

UNIT 6 New Horizons: 1860–1900

Special Needs

Language Disability Help students with poor language development by structuring a response to the question about the myths and realities of the "Old West" presented in the section objectives. Tell students to use the skimming skills they learned earlier to find a single sentence that signals the shift from myth to reality. Refer them to the sentence "The romance of the Wild West conceals some of the truth," which begins the last paragraph on page 481. Discuss the sentence's role in marking the transition.

As the buffalo were cleared from the plains, the Cattle Kingdom expanded northward until, by 1885, it covered an area half as large as Europe, extending from Texas to Montana. From the East, even from Great Britain and France, people with cash to invest and a taste for adventure put their money in cattle.

Decline of the Cattle Industry

Although offering vast profits, the industry was beset by difficulties. Steers could go blind from drought, drown in flash floods, die in stampedes, or get infected by the dreaded Texas fever. They might be stolen by rustlers or shot by angry homesteaders trying to protect their crops. The open-range cattle industry collapsed even more rapidly than it had risen. Too many animals were put on the ranges, and overgrazing resulted. Overproduction drove prices down. Sheepherders and homesteaders competed with the cattle ranchers for land.

Nature helped to end the long drives. The cold winter of 1885 and 1886 was followed by a summer so dry that the grass withered and streams disappeared. In the winter of 1886–1887, terrible blizzards covered the ground with snow so deep that the cattle could not paw down to grass. Next came an unprecedented cold spell, with temperatures ranging as low as –60°F. "When spring finally came," wrote historian Ray Allen Billington,

> ... cattlemen saw a sight they spent the rest of their lives trying to forget. Carcass piled upon carcass in every ravine, gaunt skeletons staggering about on frozen feet, trees stripped bare of their bark....

The cattle industry survived this terrible blow, but the day of the open range was over. From then on herds were raised on fenced-in ranches, English Herefords replaced longhorns, and the cowhand became a ranch hand.

The Mining Frontier

The discovery of gold in California was just the beginning of prospecting in the West. Inspired fortune seekers moved to California.

Mining and Mining Towns

From California the fortune seekers spread east into the Great Basin and Rocky Mountain regions. A gold strike in Colorado in 1858 set off a stampede to the region the next year.

> The first breath of spring started the hordes westward. Steamboats crowded to the rails poured throngs of immigrants ashore at every Missouri River town.... All through April, May, and June they left the jumping-off places in a regular parade of Conestoga wagons, hand carts, men on horseback, men on foot—each with "Pikes Peak or Bust" crudely pinned on their packs and wagon canvas.... By the end of June more than 100,000 "fifty-niners" were in the Pikes Peak country.

The Colorado strike was followed by many other finds: gold in the Black Hills of South Dakota, copper in Montana, and silver in many places. The Comstock Lode at Virginia City, Nevada, yielded about $300 million worth of silver ore between 1859 and 1877. These discoveries attracted swarms of fortune seekers, and new mining towns appeared overnight.

The discovery of precious metals brought thousands of miners into a single area, giving rise first to makeshift camps and later to towns and cities. People from a variety of backgrounds mingled in these places. A study of one Western camp revealed that the population consisted of 37 from China, 35 from Great Britain, 29 from Mexico, 24 from other nations, and 81 from other parts of the United States. In addition, other newcomers, including a substantial number of women, set up businesses to serve the miners.

CHAPTER 17
SECTION 2

Independent Practice

Ecology Divide the class into three groups—cattle ranchers, miners, and homesteaders. Have each group list on the chalkboard the ways in which they contributed to the destruction of natural resources. Have the class discuss the long-term effects of the actions of these three groups. **L3**

Did You Know?

The Comstock Lode was discovered by Henry T.P. Comstock but not in the way he claimed. Comstock rode past two prospectors hard at work. Noticing that they had found some gold, he informed them that they were working on his ground. His partners eventually discovered that the land taken by Comstock was rich in gold.

 VIDEODISC

- *GTV: The American People: Fabric of a Nation*

Side 2, Chapter 5
Title: *Close-up U.S.A.*
Subject: The Gold Rush, microcosm of the West

See GTV Guide page 66 for complete lesson plan.

Cooperative Learning

Have students work in pairs to create maps of cattle trails. Ask them to research in a historical atlas the names and locations of the main cattle trails from Texas to the various railroads and the names of the major railroad towns to which the cattle were driven. Have students indicate and label on an outline map of the United States the cattle trails, the important railroad towns, and the railroads. Tell them to make a map key for their map. Have the pairs exchange maps and correct or add to them. **L2**

CHAPTER 17
SECTION 2

Teaching American Portraits

Charles Russell's wife, Nancy Cooper, contributed greatly to his success. As his sales agent, she worked tirelessly to bring his paintings to the notice of the American public. Ask students to discuss why they think Russell's work became so popular.

Food of the Times

The last great gold rush occurred in 1896 in the Klondike region of Canada's Yukon Territory. Because of its remoteness, there were often shortages of food for the miners. Salt sold for its weight in gold. Although no one starved, there were numerous cases of scurvy among the miners, whose diets rarely varied from flapjacks and beans.

Did You Know?

Some cattle ranches in the West were enormous, covering more land than Massachusetts and Vermont combined.

Despite differences in background, all of the miners shared one goal: an unbending desire to mine that lucky strike that would bring them wealth. After the minerals in one area were exhausted, miners would leave town, and a once-lively center of trade and commerce would become a deserted ghost town almost overnight. While the wealth lasted, however, mining communities could be spirited—as well as dangerous—places. One observer described one such mining town in this way:

> This human hive, numbering at least 10,000 people, was the product of 90 days. Into it were crowded all the elements of a rough and active civilization.... [F]illed with gambling tables and gamblers, and the miner who was bold enough to enter one of them with his day's earnings in his pocket seldom left until thoroughly fleeced.... Not a day or night passed which did not yield its full fruition of fights, quarrels, wounds or murders.... Street fights were frequent ... and everyone was on his guard against a random shot.

Human life was cheap in these communities of tents and crude dwellings, with their rows of saloons and gambling houses. There was a vital need for law enforcement agencies to settle disputes over mining claims and to punish or prevent crime. Self-appointed volunteers called **vigilance committees** sometimes provided law and order. Other times mass meetings drew up their own rules and elected their own officials. Soon the different communities of a region such as Colorado or Nevada would band together and demand territorial status or statehood. Usually the actual grant of statehood came after the arrival of homesteaders and miners, because cattle raisers were too nomadic to provide stable government.

The "Wild West"

The "Wild West" captured the imagination of Americans immediately. Dime novels and popular ballads spread the adventures of Wild Bill Hickok, Billy the Kid, and Jesse James. A Wild West Show became part of Barnum and Bailey's circus; and Annie Oakley, the sharpshooter, appeared on **vaudeville,** or live variety show, stages everywhere. The Wild West period lasted little more than 30 years, yet

AMERICAN PORTRAITS

Charles M. Russell
1864–1926

Born in St. Louis, Charles Russell much preferred to watch the fur traders and men who worked along the Mississippi River than to attend school.

In 1880, at the age of 16, Russell set out for Montana to work as a cowhand and to observe Native American life. He began to paint life as he saw it, creating realistic scenes of the untamed West. Among Russell's favorite subjects were cowhands riding bucking broncos, Native Americans hunting buffalo, and outlaws holding up stagecoaches.

Little realizing the value of his paintings, he often gave them away. By the early 1890s, however, Russell was able to stop cowpunching and devote himself solely to art. By 1920 Russell's portrayals of "cowboys and Indians" commanded high prices, and he was recognized as one of the finest artists of the American West.

Critical Thinking

Analyzing Quotations Write on the chalkboard the following quotation, taken from *Land Grab* by John Upton Terrell:

"The Cattle Barons were despots and tyrants who held their domains not by legal right but by force of arms and criminal violence. The enormous region of the so-called Cattle Kingdom did not produce many cows."

Ask students to study the quotation and identify the words that are "loaded," that is, that indicate that the author is trying to sway the reader to accept his opinion. (despots, tyrants, criminal violence, so-called Cattle Kingdom) **L3**

▲ **MINING TOWNS** The discovery of gold in Colorado and silver in Nevada started a rush to the West. Thousands flocked into "boom towns" like Creede, Colorado, to strike it rich. *How many "fifty-niners" went to Pikes Peak country?*

its fascination has continued in storybooks and comics, Western songs and costumes, and **"Westerns"**—movies produced by Hollywood and shown at movie theaters or on television.

The romance of the Wild West conceals some of the truth. The conquest of the plains and the Rockies by the invading cattle ranchers, miners, and homesteaders destroyed natural resources, wildlife, and human beings. Charles Marion Russell, a frontier artist, gave this sobering message in a speech to "forward-looking citizens" in Helena, Montana:

> I have been called a pioneer. . . . a pioneer is a man who comes to a virgin country, traps off all the fur, kills off all the wild meat, cuts down all the trees, grazes off all the grass, plows the roots up, and strings ten million miles of wire. A pioneer destroys things and calls it civilization. I wish to God this country was just like it was when I first saw it and that none of you folks were here at all.

Section 2 ★ Review

Checking for Understanding

1. **Identify** Chisholm Trail, Nat Love, Cattle Kingdom, Comstock Lode, Annie Oakley.
2. **Define** maverick, long drive, vigilance committee, vaudeville, "Western."
3. **Summarize** the rise and fall of the open-range cattle industry.
4. **Examine** the realities of life that inspired the romanticized myths of the "Old West."

Critical Thinking

5. **Predicting Outcomes** Had the open-range system continued, what conflicts could have developed as the farmers settled the plains?

CHAPTER 17 Into the West 1860–1900   **481**

INTEGRATING Language Arts

Historical Setting

In the second half of the nineteenth century, an unfortunate series of events led to widespread cynicism in the United States. The Civil War had torn the nation apart. Meant to heal the nation, Reconstruction further divided it. To the nation's horror, President Lincoln was assassinated in 1865. Later U.S. Grant's presidency was characterized by corruption and scandal. The Golden Age proved to be an era of rampant political corruption. The American perspective was altered drastically in light of these events.

Background

Realism was a reaction against romanticism and transcendentalism. Realism dispensed with the idealized notions of the transcendentalists and scrutinized the individual under the harsh light of reality. The "warts and all" method of writing sought to reveal the truth in what the writer observed.

About the Author

Mark Twain was the pen name of Samuel Clemens (1835–1910). He worked as a journeyman printer and piloted a riverboat before embarking on a prolific career as a writer, lecturer, and journalist. Clemens is credited with changing the tone of American literature, writing in a relaxed, humorous, colloquial fashion that struck a responsive chord in his readers and in subsequent authors who emulated him.

American Literary Heritage

The Civil War shattered the illusions of many Americans, including writers. They had little use for the idealism of antebellum books. This postwar generation of writers depicted events and characters in the hard, cold light of reality. One master of the new realism was Mark Twain. In the following selection, Twain applies a light touch to his account of a journey to Carson City with two miners. As you read, determine what Twain is implying about human nature.

Roughing It (excerpts)

The snow lay so deep on the ground that there was no sign of a road perceptible, and the snowfall was so thick that we could not see more than a hundred yards ahead, else we could have guided our course by the mountain ranges. The case looked dubious, but Ollendorff said his instinct was as sensitive as any compass, and that he could "strike a beeline" for Carson City and never diverge from it. . . . For half an hour we poked along warily enough, but at the end of that time we came upon a fresh trail, and Ollendorff shouted proudly:

"I knew I was as dead certain as a compass, boys! Here we are, right in somebody's tracks that will hunt the way for us without any trouble. Let's hurry up and join company with the party."

So we put the horses into as much of a trot as the deep snow would allow, and before long it was evident that we were gaining on our predecessors, for the tracks grew more distinct. We hurried along and at the end of an hour the tracks looked still newer and fresher—but what surprised us was, that the *number* of travelers in advance of us seemed to steadily increase. We wondered how so large a party came to be traveling at such a time and in such a solitude. . . . Presently [Ballou] stopped his horse and said:

"Boys, these are our own tracks, and we've actually been circussing round and round in a circle for more than two hours, out here in the blind desert! By George this is perfectly hydraulic!". . .

All agreed that a campfire was what would come nearest to saving us, now, and so we set about building it. We could find no matches. . . . This was distressing, but it paled before a greater horror—the horses were gone! I had been appointed to hold the bridles, but in my absorbing anxiety . . . I had unconsciously dropped them and the released animals had walked off in the storm. . . .

▲ COLORADO GHOST TOWN

UNIT 6 New Horizons: 1860–1900

Cultural Diversity

Lured by Native American legends of gold in the Black Hills, prospectors flocked to the Dakotas. However, the 6,000-square-mile (9,654-square-kilometer) region belonged to the Teton Sioux according to a treaty that recognized the area as their sacred place. The United States government offered the Sioux $6 million for the land. When negotiations failed, the government stopped protecting the Sioux's treaty rights, and prospectors overran the region.

We were miserable enough, before; we felt still more forlorn, now.... At this critical moment Mr. Ballou fished four matches from the rubbish of an overlooked pocket.... when Mr. Ballou prepared to light the first match, there was an amount of interest centered upon him that pages of writing could not describe. The match burned hopefully a moment, and then went out. It could not have carried more regret with it if it had been a human life. The next match simply flashed and died. The wind puffed the third one out just as it was on the imminent verge of success. We gathered together closer than ever, and developed a solicitude that was rapt and painful, as Mr. Ballou scratched our last hope on his leg. It lit, burned blue and sickly, and then budded into a robust flame. Shading it with his hands, the old gentleman bent gradually down and every heart went with him.... The flame touched the sticks at last, took gradual hold upon them—hesitated—took a stronger hold—hesitated again—held its breath five heart-breaking seconds, then gave a sort of human gasp and went out.

Nobody said a word for several minutes. It was a solemn sort of silence; even the wind put on a stealthy, sinister quiet, and made no more noise than the falling flakes of snow....

Then [next morning] came a white upheaval at my side, and a voice said, with bitterness: "Will some gentleman be so good as to kick me behind?" It was Ballou—at least it was a tousled snow image in a sitting posture, with Ballou's voice.

I rose up, and there in the gray dawn, not fifteen steps from us, were the frame buildings of a stage station and under a shed stood our still saddled and bridled horses!

▶ PANNING FOR GOLD IN THE DAKOTA TERRITORY

Interpreting Literature
1. Were the men in *Roughing It* experienced Western travelers? Explain.
2. Why does the narrator find the group's situation humiliating?

Analyzing Material
3. How does Twain's tone in this selection contribute to its humor?

CHAPTER 17 Into the West 1860–1900

INTEGRATING Language Arts

Developing Student Understanding
Explain that the United States "grew up" during the nineteenth century. It lost its innocence, and this was reflected in its literature.

Explain that the realists sought honestly to expose human existence, presenting an unsanitized, often ugly view of life.

Read aloud the passage on page 482, "All agreed that... in the storm...." Ask: What happened to the bumbling group of men? (The men could not start a fire, and the horses escaped when someone dropped the bridles.)

Explain that Twain leaves the unhappy band in the snow, without a fire, and expecting to die. Ask: Instead of death, what did the men experience? (They realized that they were in front of a stage station and that their horses were there.) Ask: Why didn't the men realize this? (As Twain states in the opening passage, the men "could not see more than a hundred yards ahead.")

Other Works of the Author
Mark Twain is perhaps best known for his celebrations of boyhood recollections along the Mississippi River, *Tom Sawyer* (1876) and *Huckleberry Finn* (1885). In 1889 he wrote *A Connecticut Yankee in King Arthur's Court*, a social satire.

Answers to INTERPRETING LITERATURE
1. No; they did not know how to track in the snow, keep their horses nearby, or light a fire in the storm.
2. They were afraid they would freeze to death; yet they were only steps from a town.
3. Twain's light tone adds to the humor.

LESSON PLAN
SECTION 3, 484–489

FOCUS

Bellringer
Before taking roll at the beginning of the class period, display Focus Activity 58 on the overhead projector, and assign the accompanying Focus Activity Sheet.

Objectives
Point out the objectives on this page to students in previewing the section content.

Motivating Activity
Display wall maps showing the landforms, climate, and natural vegetation of the United States. Ask for volunteers to describe the physical characteristics of the Great Plains. (Landforms: large, flat plain; Climate: little rainfall, hot in summer, cold in winter; Vegetation: few trees, mostly short grasses)

Then ask students to speculate why people from the East may have thought the plains were unsuitable for settlement. (People from the East would be used to woodland areas with wetter, warmer climate; dryness of plains and lack of trees for building materials would make it appear unsuitable.)

SECTION 3

Farming Moves West

Setting the Scene

Section Focus

For years the Great Plains resisted settlement. The main reason for farmers' unwillingness to venture into the plains was the totally new environment. Three forces worked to overcome the farmers' hesitation: new agricultural technology, westward expansion of the railroads, and European immigration.

Objectives

After studying this section, you should be able to

★ list three factors that made farming the plains possible.

★ summarize the problems faced by plains farmers.

Key Terms

meridian, commodity

◀ McCORMICK HARVESTING MACHINE

In 1862 Congress passed the Homestead Act, enabling a head of a family to acquire a 160-acre farm for $10. To ensure that the land went to actual settlers, the act required that the owner must reside on or cultivate the land for 5 years. The act was passed as a result of nearly half a century of agitation by Western farmers and Eastern laborers.

■ Farming the Great Plains

The Homestead Act did not work out as planned. Through fraud, speculators rather than actual settlers gained possession of much land. The law required that a would-be homesteader put up a home and cultivate the land. Speculators paid relatives or employees to lay down a few logs as a "foundation" and scatter a few grains of corn. After five years they collected title to a large tract. A more important reason for the ineffectiveness of the Homestead Act was that much of the most desirable land near the railroad lines was usually controlled by the railroad companies themselves.

Technology

Before the plains could be settled, farmers had to be convinced that they could overcome the disadvantages of the dry environment. In the East a farmer could get water from a stream or by digging a well 10 to 20 feet deep. In the plains few streams ran year-round, and underground water was 30 to 300 feet down. The American farmer had always depended on trees for fuel, buildings, and fences. On the plains, trees were found only in the bottomlands near rivers.

484   UNIT 6 New Horizons: 1860–1900

Classroom Resources for SECTION 3

Teacher's Classroom Resources
- Reproducible Lesson Plan
- Chapter 17 Primary and Secondary Source Readings
- Reteaching Activity 17-3
- Spanish Summaries and Glossary
- Chapter 17 Enrichment Activity

Multimedia
- Section Focus Transparency 58
- Vocabulary Puzzlemaker
- Chapter 17 Map Transparency
- Section Quiz
- Student Self-Test Software
- Testmaker

484

Some of the difficulties of farming the plains were overcome by technology from the Industrial Revolution. Cheap iron and steel made possible the iron-encased, drilled well and the cast-iron windmill. Joseph Glidden sold his first barbed wire in 1874, making up for the lack of wooden fence rails.

Improved agricultural machinery cut the cost of raising crops. The reaper, in general use by 1865, was followed by the mechanical binder, which tied the grain into sheaves as fast as it was cut. By the 1880s 2 people and a team of horses could harvest and bind 20 acres of wheat a day. The steam-driven threshing machine also came into general use. In addition to solving technical problems, the Industrial Revolution created a vast new urban population and expanded the market for food, both in America and Europe.

Railroads

The ineffectiveness of the Homestead Act provided Westerners with a grievance but did not interfere with settlement. Although railroads sometimes discouraged the acquisition of free land, they actively promoted the sale of their own. They did not charge high prices because they wanted settlers to get the land into production. In fact, the most important factor in promoting settlement was the railroad.

Land-grant railroads had "Bureaus of Immigration" to persuade farmers to settle along their lines. They maintained offices in the principal European cities and agents in Eastern seaports to meet immigrants as they left the boat. Steamship companies and Western states advertised the region as so healthy that it cured all known diseases. The industrious person could expect to become wealthy; an $8,000 investment, it was claimed, might soon result in a steady income of $11,000 per year—an enormous sum considering that a 160-acre farm was homesteaded for $10. The West was pictured as a place where unmarried women would easily find husbands. "When a daughter of the East is once beyond the Missouri," said one railroad advertisement, "she rarely recrosses it except on a bridal tour."

To offset the myth of the "Great American Desert," a new myth was created. Some "experts" said that rainfall on the Great Plains would increase with the planting of

 ▲ **Sod Houses** Lack of trees on the Great Plains forced homesteaders to build homes from materials other than wood. One of the most common was sod cut from the grassy turf. *What were the environmental realities that farmers on the plains faced?*

CHAPTER 17 Into the West 1860–1900 **485**

Sidelights: Sod Houses

The idea for the sod house probably came from English turf houses and earth-covered Native American lodges. To build a sod house, pioneers chose an area of prairie where grassroots were firmly enmeshed and intertwined. Using a special plow, they cut the turf into blocks. They laid these giant grass blocks like bricks and filled the cracks with loose dirt. Space was left for windows and a door. These accessories were bought from stores or ordered through mail-order catalogs. A sod house took about a week to build and usually lasted for 10 years.

CHAPTER 17
SECTION 3

Independent Practice

Economics Have students create advertisements that would entice European farmers to emigrate to the Great Plains region, sell Great Plains' farm products, or sell railroad transportation to or from the Great Plains region. Tell them that in their brochures they can include charts, graphs, or any other graphic devices to pitch the region, product, or service. Have students present their advertisements to the class. **L2**

Visualizing History In the late 1880s, the open range for cattle ranchers was near its end. Large herds of cattle, fenced in by barbed wire, could no longer roam freely across the plains. Then in the winter of 1886–1887, blizzards blanketed the region. Only about 10 percent of the cattle on the open range survived.
Answer to Caption: agricultural machinery, like the plow and reaper; windmills for water; fencing

---

trees or with simple cultivation; a Nebraska promoter summed it up in the catchy epigram, "Rain follows the plow."

As the plains were opened, the production of wheat—centering in Minnesota, the Dakotas, Kansas, and Nebraska—quadrupled. Wisconsin, too far from the market to send fresh dairy products, used its surplus milk for cheese production. Near every great city, truck gardens provided supplies of fresh vegetables.

■ Sod House Reality

The life of a Great Plains farmer seldom approached the railroad agents' glowing prophecies. The realities of the weather and economic conditions combined to make life on the plains hard.

Weather

The climate that was supposed to cure all known diseases turned out to be severe. In the summer the temperature might go over 100°F for days at a time. In winter there were periods of extreme cold, and terrible blizzards drove the snow through every chink in doors and windows. Families could be stranded in sod houses for many days.

Prairie fires were a constant danger in the spring and fall. Sometimes grasshoppers appeared in huge numbers and destroyed the crops.

Worst of all disasters was drought. The normal rainfall of the Plains region was markedly less than that of the wooded East, dropping from about 30 to 40 inches along the 98th **meridian,** or line of longitude, to as little as 10 inches just east of the Rockies.

The greatest push westward into the Great Plains took place in the early 1880s, during a cycle of wet years that offered false promises of abundant crops. In the late 1880s, drought returned to drive thousands back east in despair.

In spite of all the difficulties, most settlers managed to adjust to their physical environment. Water from deep wells enabled them to plant gardens and trees around their homes. Railroads brought lumber and brick for houses to replace sod huts and coal to replace cornstalks or hay as fuel.

▲ **BARBED WIRE** The introduction of barbed wire, perfected in 1874, was a blessing for farmers. Previously farmers had made do with earth embankments and hedges to keep cattle out of their crops. **What equipment and materials were needed to farm on the plains?**

486 UNIT 6 New Horizons: 1860–1900

Critical Thinking

Constructing a Plan Have students work in groups to plan the building of a 1860s prairie town. Tell them to consider the following in preparing their plan: what buildings to build and where to locate them, what building materials to use, what energy sources to use, the kinds of landscaping to use, and so on. Ask students to draw pictorial maps of their town and label the buildings. Then have them write a short report explaining the planning choices they made. **L2**

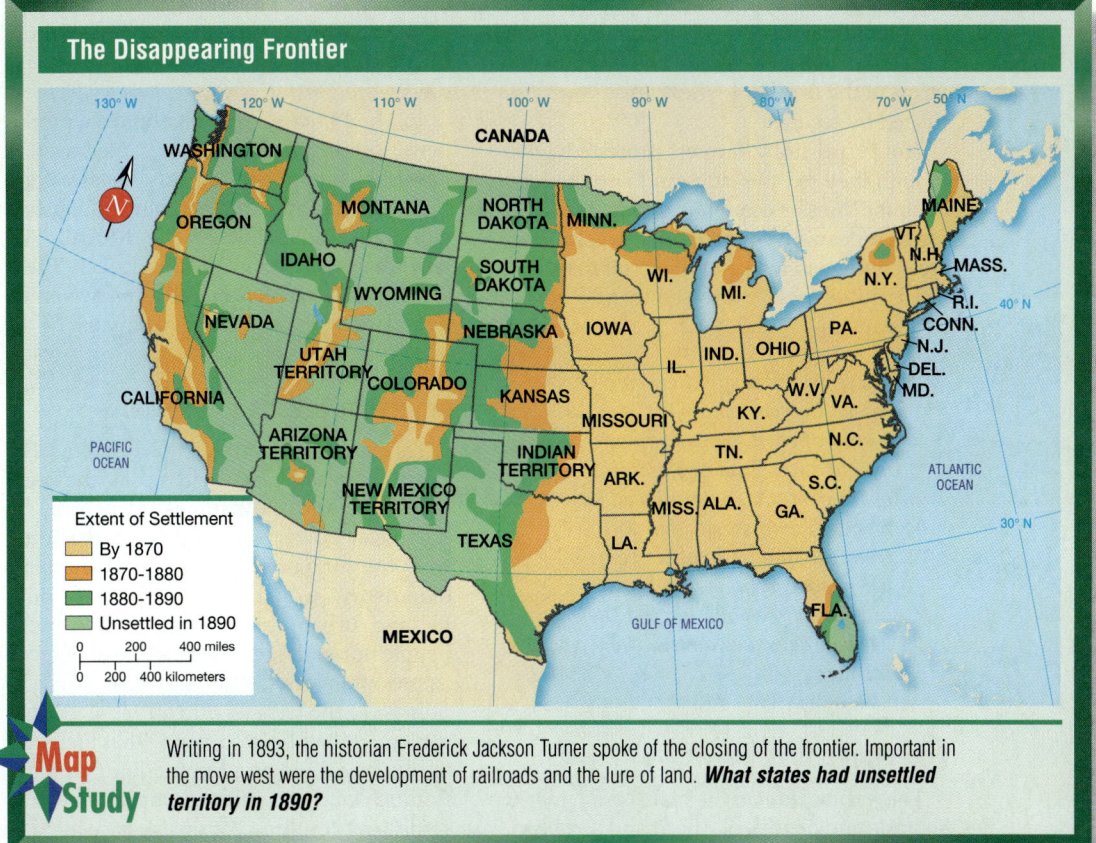

The Disappearing Frontier

Extent of Settlement
- By 1870
- 1870–1880
- 1880–1890
- Unsettled in 1890

Map Study Writing in 1893, the historian Frederick Jackson Turner spoke of the closing of the frontier. Important in the move west were the development of railroads and the lure of land. **What states had unsettled territory in 1890?**

CHAPTER 17 SECTION 3

FACT or FICTION?
The wheat that made the Great Plains the world's breadbasket was not the same kind of wheat grown in the eastern United States.

FACT–This hardier strain, which needed less water and could withstand great extremes of temperature, was brought to the Great Plains by immigrants from northern Europe and Russia.

Map Study Using Maps
Answers: Maine, Florida, Minnesota, Nebraska, Texas, Nevada, California, Oregon, Kansas, Colorado, North Dakota, South Dakota, Montana, Washington, Idaho, and Wyoming

Skills Practice
Ask students why they think the Census Bureau declared the frontier closed after 1890. (Settlement was so extensive that a true frontier line was unrecognizable.)

Economics

Plains farmers faced a second problem at least as frustrating as the weather. They were in the grip of economic forces beyond their control. Formerly, out of necessity as subsistence farmers, they had produced almost everything they needed. The independent farmer was admired in literature and melodramas, especially when contrasted with unhappy factory hands, the idle rich, or "city slickers." With the opening of great urban markets, however, farmers tended to specialize. Some farmers grew a single cash crop, such as wheat or corn; others might specialize in dairy production or cattle raising. Their incomes went up, but so did their expenses. Large-scale farming required a great deal of agricultural machinery. The need to buy clothing and food made farmers less independent.

A farmer's prosperity, perhaps even the ownership of the farm, might depend on the unpredictable price of grain in an international market. Farmers also became dependent on the railroad, which carried their crops to market, on the commission merchant who marketed it, and on the owners of grain elevators who stored it. Farmers who raised hogs or beef cattle were in a similar situation; they had little bargaining power and were forced to take whatever the meat packers paid.

Farming on the plains demanded large investments of money to drill wells, put up windmills, enclose fields in barbed wire, and buy machinery. Because few farmers could pay with cash, they had to borrow by mortgaging their land. Then, to pay interest on the mortgages, they were forced to concentrate more than ever on raising cash

CHAPTER 17 Into the West 1860–1900 487

Did You Know?
In 1890 about 250,000 women were running their own ranches and farms in the West. Besides gaining property rights, these women were the first to win the right to vote. The first seven states to grant women suffrage were in the West.

Sidelights: The "Sooner" State

On April 22, 1889, over 60,000 settlers waited impatiently on the borders of the Oklahoma Territory. At noon a bugle call sent thousands in wagons, on horses, on bicycles, and on foot racing across the prairie to stake out their homestead on the most desirable land. A few people, however, had sneaked in before the bugle call. Other settlers disparagingly called them "sooners." To this day Oklahoma is known as the "Sooner State."

487

CHAPTER 17
SECTION 3

ASSESS
Check Understanding
Assign Section 3 Review as homework or an in-class activity.

Evaluate
Assign the Section 3 Quiz in the TCR, or use the History of a Free Nation Testmaker to create a customized quiz.

Reteach
Have students complete Reteaching Activity 17-3.

Enrich
Ask students to read first-person accounts of frontier life, such as *Little House on the Prairie* by Laura Ingalls Wilder or *My Ántonia* by Willa Cather, *Pioneer Women: Voices From the Kansas Frontier* by Joanna L. Stratton, or novels by O.E. Rolvaag. Have them write a book report for presentation to the class.

Have students complete Chapter 17 Enrichment Activity in the Teacher's Classroom Resources.

CLOSE
Have students name some factors that contributed to making the Great Plains "the breadbasket of the world."

---

crops. If prices dropped or a lean year came, they could not meet their payments and lost their land. By 1900 about one-third of the farms in the corn and wheat areas were cultivated by tenants.

Not surprisingly, farmers protested. Even though they fed the cities and supplied the **commodities**, or economic goods, that paid for European investments, the wealth they created seemed to be siphoned off to others. Their attitude was expressed by a Nebraska newspaper:

> There are three great crops raised in Nebraska. One is a crop of corn, one a crop of freight rates, and one a crop of interest. One is produced by farmers, who sweat and toil, from the land. The other two are produced by men who sit in their offices and behind their bank counters and farm the farmers.

The Plains Women
For women, life on the plains often meant solitude and drudgery. "Born and scrubbed, suffered and died," is the epitaph given a woman in one of Hamlin Garland's poems. Yet the settlement of the West owed much to the endless toil of frontier women.

Women have written some of the best accounts of plains life, such as *Cimarron* by Edna Ferber and *My Ántonia* by Willa Cather. While not minimizing the sufferings of pioneering, these novels reveal how much easier life became after the sod house days were past.

In *My Ántonia* Cather mentioned a prominent building in Black Hawk, Nebraska, a new brick high school. As soon as farm communities had the funds, they established churches and schools. The Morrill Act helped states to establish universities. These were open to women as well as men; women had gained a new position of equality.

Declining Status of Farmers
Farmers, however, were losing status. For years they had been held up as the most admirable and the happiest of people. By the 1880s power and prestige had shifted from the rural areas to the cities. "Captains of industry" won the admiration of the public, and urban America regarded country people not as the backbone of the nation but as unsophisticated and backward.

In 1890 the Census Bureau reported that settlement had been so rapid "that there can hardly be said to be a frontier line." In reality, much land was still unoccupied, and new settlement continued at a brisk pace into the twentieth century, but the news that the frontier was closing encouraged prophets of doom, who saw the end of an era. They believed that the existence of unoccupied land at the frontier had provided a "safety-valve of social discontent," the idea that Americans could always make a fresh start.

Section 3 ★ Review

Checking for Understanding
1. **Identify** the Homestead Act, the Morrill Act, Willa Cather, Hamlin Garland.
2. **Define** meridian, commodity.
3. **Describe** the changes that made the West profitable for farmers.
4. **List** the problems the environment created for farmers on the plains.

Critical Thinking
5. **Analyzing Transfer of Risk** In the 1800s farmers began to sell "futures," or to contract months in advance to sell a crop to a grain merchant for a certain price. What are the advantages and disadvantages to the farmer of selling crops this way? What are the problems to the grain merchant?

Answers to SECTION 3 REVIEW
1. Homestead Act, 484; Morrill Act, 488; Willa Cather, 488; Hamlin Garland, 488
2. All vocabulary words are defined in the Glossary
3. Homestead Act, new farm machinery, growing urban population, railroads
4. little standing water and rainfall, few trees, hot summers, cold winters, blizzards, fires, grasshoppers, drought
5. Farmer—assured of profit while planning and planting but may miss out on higher prevailing market price; Grain merchant—able to plan and control wholesale costs but may pay more than the market price

History and Geography Connections

The Great American Desert

To Americans accustomed to well-watered, timbered lands east of the Mississippi River, the Great Plains seemed a vast and forbidding desert. The 100th meridian marked the line west of which annual rainfall was less than 20 inches. Farther west the annual rainfall was even less. Aquifers—strata of water-bearing rock—lay much farther below the surface than they did in the East, making hand-dug wells impractical.

The general aridity of the Great Plains region had caused explorers to label the area a desert. Major Stephen Long, leading an army expedition to explore the Great Plains in 1820, stated that ". . . it is almost wholly unfit for cultivation. . . . The scarcity of wood and water, almost uniformly prevalent, will prove an insuperable obstacle in the way of settling the country." Long prepared a map, labeled the region the Great American Desert, and influenced Americans' perception of the plains for decades. Almost every map published between 1820 and 1860 used Long's label. Americans' misconception about the plains delayed settlement until new technology—drilling machines and the windmill—tapped deep aquifers. Until the water runs out, technology has conquered geography.

▲ HOMESTEADERS, COBURG, NEBRASKA, 1887

▲ NEBRASKA WHEAT FIELD

Making the Geography Connection

1. The absence of which resources led people to think of the Great Plains as a desert?
2. How could settlers adapt to the environment?

Linking Past and Present

3. How might the "mining" of aquifers affect people on the Great Plains today?

CHAPTER 17 CONNECTIONS

Teaching Making Connections

The label *Great American Desert* was being widely used in newspapers and geography texts by the mid-1830s. So firm was the belief in the existence of a desert that some people imported camels for use in the West.

Did You Know?

Since water was scarce, some farmers used the "dry farming" method. Steel-tipped plows cut through the dry, hard-baked surface to reach the moist soil underneath. The moisture would rise through the plowed soil to the plants' roots. Farmers then packed down the topsoil to keep the moisture from rising to the surface and evaporating.

Fact or Fiction?

The Great Plains region has been labeled both "America's Breadbasket" and the "Dust Bowl."

FACT: After farmers covered the plains with wheat fields, the region became known as "America's Breadbasket." In the 1930s the plains suffered a drought, and winds blew away the dry soil. The plains were once again renamed, this time as the "Dust Bowl."

Answers to CONNECTIONS

1. trees and water
2. They dug wells and used windmills to get water; sod was used to build houses, for example.
3. As underground water supplies are diminished, both urban and rural people have to conserve water. Farmers must grow crops that need less water and must use more efficient irrigation methods.

REVIEW CHAPTER 17

Answers

Reviewing Facts

1. They ranged over vast areas following and hunting the buffalo.
2. encroachment of settlers, building of railroads, slaughter of buffalo, conflicts with settlers and military, search for precious metals on Native American lands, placing Native Americans on reservations
3. abundant inexpensive land, precious metals, availability of cattle and open range, opportunities for profitable investments, railroads' convenience and inducements
4. Open-range cattle industry consisted of cowhands driving cattle over unclaimed land to railroad centers. It was replaced by a system that raised cattle on fenced-in ranches.
5. technology that made possible deep well digging and windmills, barbed wire fences, machinery that made farming more efficient, railroads that carried people, materials, and supplies
6. long journeys, severe climate, harsh environment, drought, conflicts with Native Americans, primitive living conditions, solitude, drudgery, hard work

Understanding Concepts

1. Answers will vary but may include demand for land and food, discovery of precious metals, new technology to farm the plains, and completion of transcontinental railroads.
2. Answers will vary but may include that railroads made moving, building, farming, and provisioning easier; provided transportation, land, means of doing business, and other inducements.
3. Native Americans depended on the buffalo and access to expansive territory; settlers owned and fenced off land, contributed to slaughter of the buffalo. Environmental groups, people who want to keep rural areas unspoiled, those who enjoy public access to wilderness areas.
4. Cattle industry needed large areas of open land accessible to cattle. Settlers wanted to fence in farms and homes to convey ownership as well as to protect crops from roaming cattle.

CHAPTER 17 ★ REVIEW

Using Vocabulary

Explain why each of these terms is used in a chapter about opening the West.

nomadic
long drive
"Western"
commodity
maverick
vigilance committees
meridian
vaudeville

Reviewing Facts

1. **Describe** the lives of the nomadic Plains peoples.
2. **Give** reasons why the Plains peoples' way of life came to an end.
3. **List** the factors that drew settlers to the West.
4. **Contrast** the open-range cattle industry with the system that replaced it.
5. **Specify** the changes that made farming attractive on the Great Plains.
6. **Discuss** the hardships faced in settling the Old West.

Understanding Concepts

Expansion

1. During the 1700s and early 1800s, most expansion took place east of the Mississippi. What changes and developments accelerated expansion west of the Mississippi?
2. What part did railroads play in the westward expansion?

Conflict

3. Explain the conflicts between Native Americans and settlers. What groups today might oppose unrestrained development and fencing of wilderness areas?
4. Conflict on the plains was not confined to wars with Native Americans. Open-range cattle ranchers often came into conflict with sheepherders and homesteaders. How might the interests of an open-range cattle industry conflict with those of other settlers?

490 UNIT 6 New Horizons: 1860–1900

Critical Thinking

1. **Recognizing Effects** How did the railroads benefit from encouraging farmers and immigrants to settle near their rail lines?
2. **Analyzing Art** Study the rendering on this page by a Cheyenne artist. It depicts a Ghost Dance, which was performed as a ritual that was believed would bring back the buffalo and restore the Native American way of life. In December 1890, United States soldiers tried to break up a large band of Ghost Dancers gathered at Wounded Knee Creek on the Pine Ridge Reservation in South Dakota. In the resulting massacre, many Native Americans were killed.
   a. Which part of the picture seems to be the most important? How does the artist draw your attention to it?
   b. What is unusual about the artist's portrayal of the Native Americans?

▲ CHEYENNE PICTOGRAPH HIDE, LATE 1800S

Writing About History

Narration

Write a day's entry in the diary of a 17-year-old traveling west by rail in 1870. Include details about the geographic features, the hardships, and the traveler's reactions.

CHAPTER 17 ★ REVIEW

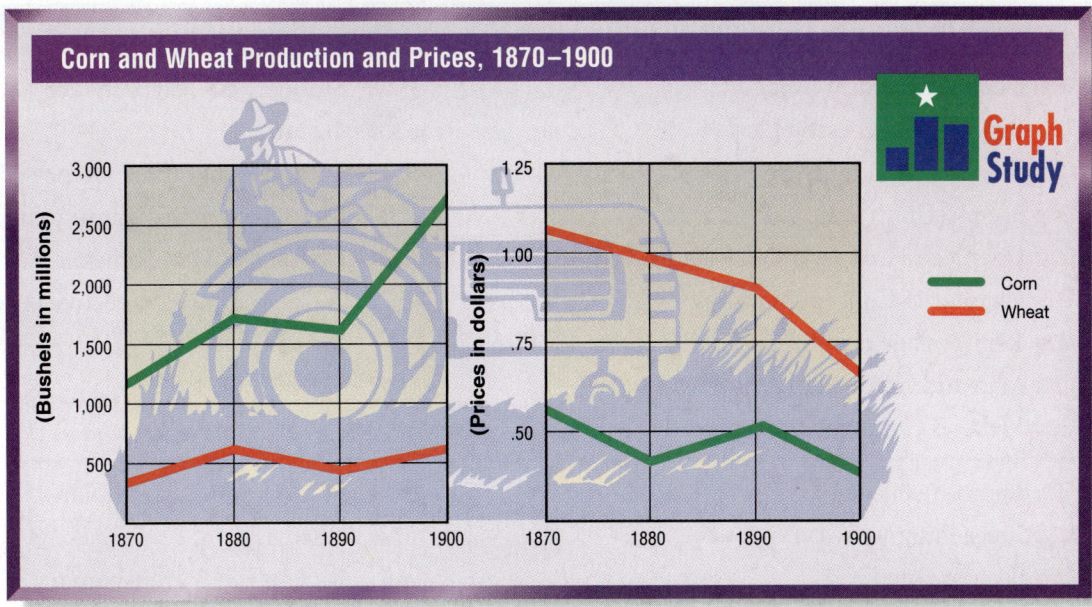

Corn and Wheat Production and Prices, 1870–1900

Cooperative Learning

Your group will research either the details of life during the days of the open-range cattle industry or the same details as depicted in "Westerns." Divide the research assignments so that each group member is responsible for a different aspect of real life or life in a "Western."

Social Studies Skills

Reading a Line Graph

Like a bar graph, a line graph is used to show a relationship between two variables. Study the graph on this page, then answer the questions.

Practicing the Skill

1. What is the time period in the graphs?
2. What is the independent variable in both graphs?
3. What are the dependent variables in the graphs?
4. What does each graph show?
5. What is the overall trend in the production of corn and wheat?
6. According to the chapter, what factors contributed to this trend?
7. What appears to be the trend in prices of corn and wheat between 1870 and 1900?

Using Your Journal
Compare and contrast the hardships for the settlers in the West with those faced by the colonists in the 1600s.

REVIEW CHAPTER 17

Chapter Bonus Test Question

Choose one of the events below, and explain how it contributed to changes in the West in the late 1800s.
• First transcontinental railroad (brought people and supplies to the West; led to development of towns and destruction of Native American way of life)
• Homestead Act (encouraged settlement on the plains)
• Dawes Act (broke up Native American nations)

Using Your Journal

Both experienced long journeys, harsh environment, conflicts with Native Americans, solitude, and hard work.

Critical Thinking

1. Answers will vary but may include that the railroads profited by charging people to ride West; by selling land that had been granted the railroads free of charge; by charging farmers to ship their crops; and, as more farmers developed the land, business increased for the railroads.

2. a) Answers will vary. Students may note that the artist focuses on the individuals in the center. b) Answers will vary. Students may note that the elements are arranged assymetrically or in an unbalanced manner; that little perspective is provided; that no background or geographical features are provided.

Practicing the Skill

1. 1870–1990
2. time span
3. Bushels in millions; prices in dollars
4. Production and prices
5. It rose.
6. improved machinery
7. down slightly

PLANNING GUIDE Chapter 18   The Rise of Industrial America

Daily Lesson Objectives	Teacher Classroom Resources	Multimedia
SECTION 1 **Industrialism Takes Hold** 1 Day pp. 494–500 1. Identify and explain the factors that encouraged industrial growth. 2. Discuss the railroad's role in the growth of industry.	Chapter 18 Study Guide Reproducible Lesson Plan Reteaching Activity 18-1 Section Quiz Chapter 18 Cooperative Learning Activity Chapter 18 Concept Mapping Activity Reinforcing Social Studies Skills 26, 36, 40, 46, 69-72 Map and Graph Skill Activities 35, 36 Writer's Guidebook Lessons 9-14	Student Self-Test Software Testmaker Section Focus Transparency 55 Chapter 18 Skills Transparency Chapter 18 Map Transparencies A Geographic Perspective on American History
SECTION 2 **Growth of Big Business** 1 Day pp. 502–505 1. Discuss the methods big business used to become successful. 2. Explain why incorporation encouraged business growth.	Reproducible Lesson Plan Reteaching Activity 18-2 Section Quiz Reinforcing Social Studies Skills 55, 62, 67-72 Outline Map 4 Chapter 18 Primary and Secondary Source Readings American Portraits 35, 36 American Literary Heritage Unit 6 Writer's Guidebook Lessons 9-14	Student Self-Test Software Testmaker Section Focus Transparency 56 Powers of the Congress
SECTION 3 **Captains of Industry** 1 Day pp. 506–512 1. Compare the methods used by Carnegie and Rockefeller to achieve success. 2. Explain Social Darwinism and the Gospel of Wealth.	Reproducible Lesson Plan Reteaching Activity 18-3 Section Quiz Chapter 18 Enrichment Activity Chapter 18 Primary and Secondary Source Readings Reinforcing Social Studies Skills 27, 32, 52, 62 Map and Graph Skills Activities 26, 31, 52, 62 Writer's Guidebook Lessons 9-14 Spanish Summaries & Glossary	Student Self-Test Software Testmaker Section Focus Transparency 57 Vocabulary Puzzlemaker Audiocassette, Chapter 18
CHAPTER REVIEW AND EVALUATION 1 Day	Chapter 18 Test Chapter 18 Performance Assessment Activity	Student Self-Test Software Testmaker

OUT OF TIME? If time does not permit teaching the entire chapter, use the Chapter 18 Summary on pages 590–591 and the Chapter 18 audiocassette (English and Spanish) to point out the main ideas of the chapter.

PLANNING GUIDE

Cultural Diversity Activity

Research Over 10,000 Chinese workers helped build the first transcontinental railroad. In this often dangerous work more than 1,200 were killed by avalanches and other accidents. Others went on to become the main builders of the Southern Pacific and Northwest Pacific railroads. Chinese workers were also instrumental in turning California's San Joaquin and Sacramento River valleys from swampland into farmland. Despite these and other contributions, Chinese had few rights in the United States. They could not become citizens. And after 1882, Congress excluded further immigration from China.

Have students find out what led Congress to pass the Chinese Exclusion Act. Students might also research the effects of the act on Chinese already living in the United States. Encourage them to share their findings orally with the class.

Performance Assessment Activity

Economics Working in small groups, have students imagine that they are entrepreneurs who want to start a medium-sized business in the late 1800s. Ask them to decide what type of business they wish to establish, how they might finance the day-to-day operation without investing personal capital (sell shares to investors), and how they would run the company. Who would manage the company? Have groups also plan for a vertical combination to take place within a few years. Ask a spokesperson from each group to present its plan to the class. Discuss the viability of each venture.

POSSIBLE RUBRIC FEATURES: Content information, organization, creativity, clarity, oral communication skills, collaborative skills

Chapter Resources

Literature from the Period
Carnegie, Andrew. "Steel Manufacture in the United States in the Nineteenth Century." 1902.

Readings for the Student
Brown, Dee. *Hear That Lonesome Whistle Blow*. Holt, 1977.

"Entrepreneurs of the Past." *Cobblestone*, Vol. 10, No. 5, May 1989.

Jennings, Walter Wilson. *20 Giants of American Business*. Exposition Press, 1953.

Walker, Robert H. *Everyday Life in the Age of Enterprise: 1865–1900*. Putnam, 1967.

Wilson, Everett B. *America's Vanishing Folkways*. Barnes, 1965.

Readings for the Teacher
Higgs, Robert. *Competition and Coercion: Blacks in the American Economy, 1865–1914*. University of Chicago, 1980.

Livesay, Harold C. *Andrew Carnegie and the Rise of Big Business*. Little, Brown, 1975.

Takaki, Ronald. *Strangers From a Different Shore*. Little, Brown, 1989.

Multimedia Resources
Cartels and Cutthroats. Micro Center. (Apple diskette)

The Entrepreneurs: An American Adventure. Martin Sandler. (6 VHS, 5 hours)

Urbanization: The Growth of Cities. Tom Snyder. (Apple or IBM diskette)

Key to Ability Levels

Teaching strategies have been coded for varying learning styles and abilities.

- **L1** Basic activities for all students
- **L2** Average activities for average to above-average students
- **L3** Challenging activities for above-average students
- **LEP** Limited English Proficiency activities

Glencoe Links to the Humanities

Link to Art
- U.S. History & Art Transparencies 14, 15

Links to Literature
- Macmillan Literature: Appreciating Literature Audiotapes Side 3
- Macmillan Literature: American Literature Audiotapes Side 3
- Macmillan Literature: American Literature Text—Kate Chopin, Hamlin Garland, Jack London, Stephen Crane, Sidney Lanier

Link to Music
- American Music: Cultural Traditions

CHAPTER 18

BEGINNING THE CHAPTER

Have students read "Setting the Scene" and identify the factors that were responsible for the remarkable economic growth in the late 1800s. (cheap labor, abundant raw materials, new technology, new forms of business organization) Ask students to speculate how these factors together might create economic growth. Tell them that they will find out the accuracy of their answers as they read Chapter 18.

Recording Journal Notes
As students record information about Carnegie and Rockefeller, encourage them to write thoughts about their contributions.

Linking Across TIME

Until the early 1800s, most businesses in the United States were operated as sole proprietorships and partnerships. A few merchants began to experiment with business organization. One of the most successful was the corporation. It allowed businesses to accumulate large amounts of capital by selling stock. By the late 1800s, corporations were dominating the American economy. Today, they account for more than three-fourths of all business profits.

492

CHAPTER 18

The Rise of Industry
1860–1900

Setting the Scene

Focus

The United States developed into a great industrial power in the latter decades of the nineteenth century. By the year 1900, United States industrial production was the strongest in the world. This remarkable growth was the result of many different factors—cheap labor, abundant raw materials, new technology—but also of new forms of business organization.

▲ SPINDLETOP OIL FIELD, BEAUMONT, TEXAS

Journal Notes
When you read about Rockefeller and Carnegie, look for instances when they gave away some of their wealth. Note these instances in your journal.

Concepts to Understand

★ Why business leaders believed that individual initiative benefited all of society

★ How lack of restrictions helped large companies but hurt small ones

Read to Discover . . .

★ what factors caused American industry to grow so rapidly.

★ how Andrew Carnegie and John D. Rockefeller were able to become industrial giants.

CULTURAL
- 1869 Mark Twain publishes *Innocents Abroad*
- 1879 Thomas Edison invents the first practical electric light

POLITICAL
- 1865 Civil War ends
- 1873 Panic of 1873 strikes

UNIT 6 New Horizons: 1860–1900

✚ EXTRA CREDIT PROJECT

Have interested students research a modern-day invention of their choice (computer, laser, optic fiber). Ask them to prepare a talk with accompanying visuals in which they present information about the invention and the inventor. Their talks should also include information on how the invention has changed people's lives.

History AND ART
Factory Chimneys
by Maximillian Luce, 1896

Mass production—production of large quantities of goods at low cost—was the heart of the new industrial system.

◀ INVENTOR THOMAS ALVA EDISON

- **1882** Standard Oil Trust formed
- **1884** Congress establishes the Federal Bureau of Labor
- **1893** First successful gasoline-powered car operated
- **1893** Colorado grants women the right to vote

1880 | **1890**

CHAPTER 18 The Rise of Industry 1860–1900

CHAPTER 18 CONCEPTS

Concept Mapping Activity
Write the concept generalization and the concepts below on the chalkboard. Tell students that as they read, they should list laws and policies about new U.S. industries under the concept "Government Restriction."

> New industries emerge as a result of new opportunities, ambitious individuals, vast natural resources, and technological change.

> Government Restriction

> Individual Initiative

History AND ART
From 1860 to 1890, the value of manufactured goods rose from less than $2 billion to over $9 billion. *Factory Chimneys* by Maximillian Luce captures this brisk growth of industry.

 VIDEODISC

- *GTV: A Geographic Perspective on American History*

Side 3, Chapter 8
Title: *The March of Industry*
Subject: Growth of American industry

See GTV Guide page 52 for complete lesson plan.

Teacher Notes

LESSON PLAN
SECTION 1, 494–501

FOCUS

Bellringer
Before taking roll at the beginning of the class period, display Focus Activity 59 on the overhead projector, and assign the accompanying Focus Activity Sheet.

Objectives
Point out the objectives on this page to students in previewing the section content.

Motivating Activity
Ask students to imagine that they will be choosing outstanding modern inventions—machines, processes, materials, medicinal drugs, and so on—to exhibit at a technical fair in the year 2000. Discuss what inventions might be included in such a fair.

Use Skills Transparency 18.

VIDEODISC
- *GTV: A Geographic Perspective on American History*

Side 3, Chapter 8
Title: *The March of Industry*
Subject: Growth of American industry

See GTV Guide page 52 for complete lesson plan.

SECTION 1

Industrialization Takes Hold

Setting the Scene

Section Focus
The tremendous industrial growth that occurred in the United States after the Civil War resulted from foundations that had been laid over the previous half-century. Agriculture flourished in the South and Midwest, and manufacturing increased in the Northeast. A transportation network spread people, products, and information across the nation. Yet greater growth was ahead.

Objectives
After studying this section, you should be able to
★ identify and explain the factors that encouraged industrial growth.
★ discuss the railroad's role in the growth of industry.

Key Terms
entrepreneur, economies of scale

◀ CASH REGISTER, 1878

Unlike the South, the North emerged virtually undamaged by the Civil War, its railroads and factories intact. Furthermore, the war and Reconstruction eliminated Southern planters as rivals to Northern industrialists for political power, allowing industrial growth to proceed at an even greater pace. Although interrupted by depressions from 1873 to 1878, 1882 to 1884, and 1893 to 1896, America's industrial production doubled every 12 to 14 years. By the 1880s the United States had overtaken Great Britain as the world's industrial leader.

■ Resources

The change from a primarily agricultural society to an industrial one was possible because the United States had the means necessary for a changing and growing economy. Among these were an abundance and variety of natural resources and large numbers of workers to turn raw materials into goods.

A Wealth of Natural Resources

Before the war, natural resources such as coal, iron ore, and petroleum had scarcely been touched. By the 1860s, however, methods for extracting and utilizing these resources were well developed.

As a result, the amount of coal mined in the United States more than doubled in every decade between 1840 and 1890. By the 1870s, vast deposits throughout the Appalachians from Pennsylvania to Alabama were being mined. Completion of the Soo Canal between Lake Superior and Lake Huron in 1855 allowed ships to move iron ore mined in Michigan and Wisconsin to iron and steel mills on the lower Great Lakes.

Classroom Resources for SECTION 1

Teacher's Classroom Resources
- Chapter 18 Study Guide
- Reproducible Lesson Plan
- Reteaching Activity 18-1
- Chapter 18 Cooperative Learning Activity
- Section Quiz

Multimedia
- Section Focus Transparency 59
- Chapter 18 Skills Transparency
- Chapter 18 Map Transparency
- Testmaker
- Student Self-Test Software
- A Geographic Perspective on American History

The American oil industry got its start in 1859 in western Pennsylvania when the first successful well was drilled. By 1900 oil fields extended as far west as Texas. Production had risen from 2,000 barrels per year in 1859 to 64 million barrels per year in 1900.

A Growing Labor Force

The human resources available to American industry were as important as the mineral resources. European capitalists sometimes had difficulty recruiting labor for new industries. Children of working-class families often were raised to follow traditional occupations, and in the European countryside peasants frequently were reluctant to leave their home villages. In the United States, however, labor was more mobile. Workers came to new jobs in cities the way pioneers moved to new lands.

Between 1860 and 1890, America's population more than doubled, rising from 31 million to nearly 75 million. The flood of immigration that had begun in the 1840s continued, contributing to this growth. Pulled by opportunities in America—and pushed out by the lack of them at home—14 million immigrants arrived between 1860 and 1900, more than twice the number of the previous 40 years. Many of these immigrants were adult males eager to find employment. These newcomers enlarged the labor pools that accumulated wherever jobs were available, and that helped keep industrial wages low.

■ Public Policies and Private Investment

American industry developed within a free enterprise system. Americans embraced a philosophy of laissez-faire, which comes from the French phrase meaning "let alone." As a result, American industries developed with few government restraints. In fact, some government policies actually encouraged industrialization. **Entrepreneurs,** or business organizers, sought and received special favors from Congress. Liberal immigration laws ensured a steady supply of cheap labor. High protective tariffs encouraged American industries and raised manufacturers' profits by keeping out foreign goods. The federal government sold public lands containing vast mineral resources for a small proportion of their true value and assumed about one-third of the cost of building Western railroads. It gave railroads grants of money totaling more than $700 million and gave them public lands throughout the West equaling the size of Texas.

While European entrepreneurs often retired when they acquired enough money to buy their way into the upper class, Americans regarded moneymaking itself as a worthwhile goal. "Such opportunities for making money," wrote Thomas Mellon, a Pittsburgh judge who later became a banker, "never existed before in all my former experience."

The money to be made in American manufacturing and transportation attracted private investors. The savings of New Englanders—accumulated from the West Indies and China trade, from clippers and whalers, from textile mills and shoe manufactures—helped build hundreds of factories and thousands of miles of railroad track. An equally important source of private capital was Europe, especially Great Britain. By 1900 British investors owned

◀ **OFFICE SECRETARY IN THE LATE 1800s**

CHAPTER 18 The Rise of Industry 1860–1900   495

CHAPTER 18
SECTION 1

TEACH
Guided Practice

Economics Draw a hierarchical flowchart. In the top box, write "Industrial Development in the United States." Draw six boxes in a horizontal line below the top box, and attach them to the top box with arrows. Ask students to fill in the six boxes with the main factors that encouraged industrial growth. (transportation, resources, science and technology, government, private investments, markets) Discuss their flowcharts. Challenge them to suggest ways of showing graphically the interdependence of each of the factors. (Sample answer: overlapping circles) **L1, L2**

Did You Know?

To supplement their income, many families rented rooms and provided meals to boarders. In 1890, 44,000 families reported that they shared housing with one or more boarders. By 1900 the figure had almost doubled.

Special Needs

Writing Disability Many students with writing disabilities have difficulty organizing answers to questions that require written responses. Although they have usually studied "topic" or "lead" sentences, they often do not know how to form one independently. Read just the headings in this section aloud. Then, as a group have students write a topic sentence related to the increase in industrialization after the Civil War. For the Section Focus, for example, students may write "There were several factors that affected the growth of industry after the Civil War." **LEP, L1**

CHAPTER 18 SECTION 1

Independent Practice

Constructing a Graph
Have students work with a partner to create bar graphs showing the increase in the number of northern European immigrants between 1861 and 1900. Tell them to use the following information in their graphs:

   1861–1870—2,065,000
   1871–1880—2,272,000
   1881–1890—4,737,000
   1891–1900—3,559,000

Discuss students' graphs. Ask: If the total number of immigrants between 1861 and 1900 was about 14 million, about how many million came from countries other than those in northern Europe? (approximately 1.5 million) **L2**

Visualizing History Between 1860 and 1900, about 676,000 inventions were registered at the U.S. Patent Office. Ask students to list the inventions that have changed office work in the 1990s. (computers, fax machines, copiers, etc.)
Answer to Caption: The man because few women were given positions of responsibility during this era.

$2.5 billion in American railroad securities—more than twice the national debt of the United States.

Science and Technology

A flood of important inventions helped increase America's productive capacity and improved the network of transportation and communications that was vital to the nation's industrial growth. As American universities extended their activities beyond teaching, they became important centers of scientific research.

The Typewriter and the Telephone

The American public knew little of the university professors who extended the boundaries of science. People were greatly impressed, however, with inventors such as C. Latham Sholes, a Wisconsin printer whose idea for a typewriter in 1868 revolutionized business communications.

Equally inventive was Alexander Graham Bell, an immigrant from Scotland. Bell's profession was teaching deaf children to speak. He applied his speech training to developing the principles upon which the telephone is based. In 1876 he sent the first telephone communication to his laboratory assistant in the next room: "Mr. Watson, come here; I want you."

A year later he demonstrated the commercial value of his invention by sitting in Boston and talking with Watson in New York City—and the Bell Telephone Company was founded. By 1886 more than 250,000 phones were in use, mostly in businesses. This rapid growth created jobs for thousands of women as switchboard operators. By 1900 telephone rates had been lowered, and telephones increasingly began to appear in American homes.

▲ **CANDLESTICK TELEPHONE, 1890s**

Visualizing History ▲ **THE INFLUENCE OF THE TELEPHONE** The telephone made business communications quick and personal. The job of the telephone operator was the first American occupation considered to be strictly "women's work." *Which person in this photograph is probably the manager? Why do you think this is so?*

496   UNIT 6 New Horizons: 1860–1900

Cooperative Learning

Organize students into groups of four. Each group will be entrepreneurs in the industrial climate of the late 1800s. Have each group decide what product or service it wants to provide. Assign each student in each group one of the following research topics: what human and mineral resources they need to use in their business, which of the newest scientific methods and inventions they plan to use, how they want to ship their product or sell their service, and what public policies and private investment practices they plan to follow. Have the group as a whole review and revise each other's work. **L2**

Life of the Times

Working-class Tenements

Working-class incomes varied greatly during the late nineteenth century. For example, in 1889 a carpenter earned $686 annually; a laborer, $384; and a young woman in a silk mill, only $130. Most working-class people lived crowded together in tenements designed to house as many families as possible.

Living conditions in tenements were primitive. Beds often consisted of boxes filled with straw. Few buildings had indoor plumbing, and in those that did, several families shared a bathroom. Living areas were cramped.

Rags, bones, and other garbage piled up outside, freezing in winter and reeking in summer. Disease festered because of the pervasive dirt and vermin.

Working-class men and women developed a community life as vibrant as their physical surroundings were bleak. Frequently this life was based on ethnic ties. Irish Americans gathered in taverns and parish churches. Jewish Americans organized Hebrew schools and Yiddish-speaking literary groups. Most immigrant groups and African Americans developed social clubs, storefront churches, and mutual-aid societies.

▲ WORKING-CLASS FAMILY

◀ THE EVICTION

Edison's Contributions

Perhaps even more famous than Bell was Thomas Alva Edison, who has been erroneously credited with inventing the electric light and moving pictures. Edison actually made few original discoveries. Instead, he was a great innovator who put the inventions of others to practical use. For example, Edison's redesign of Sholes's typewriter permitted people to type faster than they could write. His improvement of Bell's telephone allowed voices to be transmitted longer distances. His work on improving the telegraph led to one of his few actual inventions, the phonograph.

The incandescent electric light had been demonstrated in Britain in 1840. But it was Edison who, in 1879, developed cheap methods of supplying power and wire, as well as filaments that lasted more than just a few minutes. The incandescent bulb lighted America's cities and made industrial production possible 24 hours a day.

The Canning Industry

During the Civil War, soldiers in the Union army had received some rations in cans, an innovation that demonstrated the value of canned food. After the war the canning industry improved its methods, and by 1900 machines had been designed to make, fill, and seal cans. A large variety of canned foods began to appear on the shelves of the nation's stores.

Textiles, Clothing, and Shoes

America's textile industry had long depended on machines to turn fibers into cloth. In 1893 the invention of the Northrup automatic loom led to the manufacture of cloth at an even faster rate. Bobbins, which had previously been changed by hand while the loom was stopped, were now changed automatically without stopping the loom.

Great changes also occurred in the clothing industry. Standard sizes, developed

CHAPTER 18
SECTION 1

Teaching Life of the Times

In the 1890s more than 1,000,000 people were living in fewer than 40,000 tenements in lower Manhattan. The slums were a result of increased immigration, corrupt city governments, and employers who exploited workers. Ask students to speculate why they think the working class developed a vibrant community life.

Did You Know?

Some of the inventions in the 1800s were just plain peculiar. One of these looked like a cow, but was a hunting decoy. Two hunters would climb into it and could roam the fields looking for ducks or other game birds. To shoot, the hunters had to unhinge the head of the cow and aim.

Sidelights: Computers

The U.S. population for the 1890 census was tabulated on machines invented by Herman Hollerith. These tabulating machines eventually brought about the "Computer Age." Hollerith was visiting a friend's home where he met her father, head of the Vital Statistics Department for the 1880 census. The father suggested that a machine using notched cards could take over the chore of counting census figures by hand. Hollerith devised a machine to electrically "read" or sort these cards. Since the machines were twice as fast as the hand method, Hollerith was given a contract.

CHAPTER 18
SECTION 1

Did You Know?

In the late 1800s, railroads became the nation's largest industry, surpassing all others as a buyer of iron, steel, and coal, and the nation's largest employer. By 1910 there were 1.7 million railroad workers. They expanded the size of the market for products, facilitated the acquisition of raw materials, and transported the labor pool to places where jobs existed.

Map Study Using Maps

Answer: They expanded the size of the market for products, facilitated the acquisition of raw materials, and transported the labor pool to places where jobs existed.

Skills Practice

Ask students to trace the Union Pacific Railroad route westward from Omaha to Promontory Point. Have them list the states the route crosses. (Nebraska, Wyoming, Utah)

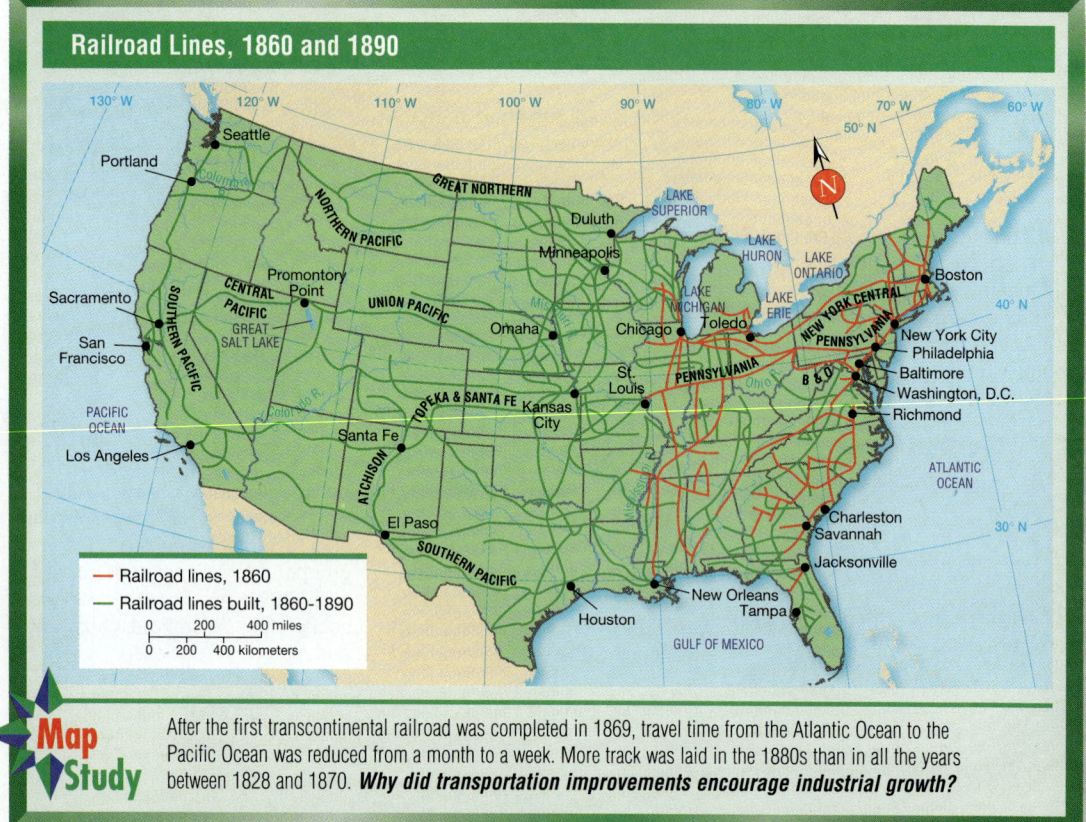

Railroad Lines, 1860 and 1890

Map Study After the first transcontinental railroad was completed in 1869, travel time from the Atlantic Ocean to the Pacific Ocean was reduced from a month to a week. More track was laid in the 1880s than in all the years between 1828 and 1870. **Why did transportation improvements encourage industrial growth?**

from measurements taken of Union soldiers during the Civil War, were used in the manufacture of ready-made clothes. The use of power-driven sewing machines and cloth cutters moved the clothing business from small tailor shops to large factories.

Similar changes took place in shoe making. New processes and inventions made **economies of scale** possible. In other words, large factories could mass-produce shoes more cheaply and efficiently than smaller companies. These factories could also pass these savings on to their customers in the form of lower prices. By the turn of the century, local cobblers had nearly disappeared.

Steel, Oil, and Trains

Industrial growth was tied to advances in specific industries. The Bessemer process revolutionized American steelmaking in the 1870s. As steel was increasingly used for products such as machines, rails, and building beams, industry in general began to expand. The boom in the oil industry, along with the development of oil-lubricated machine tools—metal lathes, punches, and drill presses used to make other machines—brought tremendous growth in industrial capability.

New technology also stimulated the growth of the railroad industry. The Bessemer process was a factor in the expansion of railroad operations. This process allowed the railroad companies to replace iron rails with steel, which held up better and was able to carry heavier loads.

Another innovation was the Westinghouse air brake. The brake allowed the cars and locomotives to stop simultaneously—another factor making longer trains and heavier loads possible. Kerosene lamps, and later electric lights, provided better headlights for nighttime travel.

498 UNIT 6 New Horizons: 1860–1900

Cultural Diversity

Many of the inventions and ideas that helped industry to expand in the United States in the late 1800s were the work of immigrants. For example, Ottmar Mergenthaler, a German immigrant, invented the linotype machine in 1884. The machine made it possible to cast a "line of type" for a printing press in a few seconds. It sharply reduced the cost of printing books, magazines, and newspapers. Jan Matzeliger, an immigrant of African descent from Dutch Guiana, invented a machine that attached the uppers of a shoe to the soles as efficiently as workers could by hand. Patented in 1883, his revolutionary machine cut the cost of a pair of shoes in half.

■ Railroad Building

Perhaps no other single factor was more responsible for the growth of American industry than the expansion of the nation's railroads. At the end of the Civil War, there were 35,000 miles of railroad track in the United States, all of various gauges, or widths between the two rails.

Standardization and Consolidation

By the mid-1870s the amount of track had doubled, and by 1890 it had more than doubled again. In 1900 passenger and freight trains steamed along almost 200,000 miles of rails. By then track also was laid according to a standard gauge—4 feet, 8½ inches wide—so that freight could move from line to line without having to be unloaded from one car and reloaded onto another. This standardized railroad network bound all sections of the country into one market and one nation. Trains could carry bulky products long distances quickly and cheaply, making it possible for businesses to sell their goods across the continent. In 1860 railroads carried less than half as much freight as inland waterways. By 1890 railroads carried five times as much.

Railroads were not only the biggest shippers of industrial products; they were also American industry's best customers. In the mid-1880s, for example, rails were the single most important product of American steel companies. In addition, construction and operation of railroads required huge amounts of coal to power locomotives, lumber for ties and cars, iron for bridges, and petroleum products to lubricate moving parts.

Consolidating of smaller lines in the Midwest, East, and South was as important to development as the building of railroads spanning the West. Railroad building in the East was intended to promote specific cities or to serve local needs. As a result, hundreds of unconnected small lines, with tracks of varying gauges, were in use. The South had more than 400 railroads averaging less than 40 miles each. The challenge facing Eastern capitalists was to create a single rail system from this maze of small companies.

 ▲ **ACROSS THE CONTINENT** by Currier and Ives, 1868 Currier and Ives produced America's most popular and successful prints of the 1800s. **Why did rail transport surpass water transport in the late 1800s?**

CHAPTER 18 SECTION 1

Rising fuel costs and ecological concerns have revived interest in trains, especially for mass transit. Commuter rail lines can carry 70 times as many people as highways, yet cost one-tenth as much to build and use only 1 percent of the fuel.

History AND ART

Railroads brought eastern tourists to places that were once remote and inaccessible, places like the Grand Tetons in Wyoming. The Chicago, Burlington, and Quincy railroads, for example, conducted escorted tour groups. **Answer to Caption:** faster, cheaper, and more efficient

---

Sidelights: Trunks and Carpetbags

Since most traveling in the late 1800s was done by railroad or ship, various sizes of trunks were used to transport personal belongings. One could pack an entire wardrobe in the Saratoga trunk. The more affluent had trunks made of deer hide and pigskin, while the less fortunate used wooden trunks with hinges and locks. For hand luggage people carried cases made of cardboard or carpetbags made from a piece of old carpet. For hats and collars, people carried a bandbox, which was a container made of wood or cardboard.

CHAPTER 18
SECTION 1

ASSESS
Check Understanding
Assign Section 1 Review as homework or an in-class activity.

Evaluate
Assign the Section 1 Quiz in the TCR, or use the History of a Free Nation Testmaker to create a customized quiz.

Reteach
Write these terms on the chalkboard: *expansion, consolidation, standardization.* Have students use these terms to write a paragraph about the development of the railroad.
Have students complete Reteaching Activity 18-1.

Enrich
Have students research one of the following subjects: the development of the steam locomotive in the United States, custom Pullman cars, or the architecture of railroad terminals.

CLOSE
Refer to the quotation in this section by Francis Adams, Jr., on corruption in the railroad industry. Have students give their opinions on whether a *laissez-faire* attitude toward business regulation breeds corruption and why.

Railroad consolidation proceeded rapidly from the end of the Civil War to the turn of the century. By 1890 the Pennsylvania Railroad was a consolidation of 73 smaller companies with more than 5,000 miles of track. The Southern Pacific Railway had pieced together companies with 8,500 miles of lines. Eventually most rail traffic was controlled by 7 giant systems with terminals in major cities and scores of branches reaching into the countryside.

Getting a "Share of the Business"

In gaining and using such power, many railroad builders became tough, ruthless, and unethical competitors who amassed fortunes in the course of their activities. Railroad consolidator Jay Gould sold small lines that he owned to large railroads that he controlled at prices far above the small railroads' actual worth. When railroad builder Collis Huntington remarked, "It takes money to fix things," he meant bribing government officials, not repairing equipment! In describing his industry, railroad executive Charles Francis Adams, Jr., observed:

> *Honesty and good faith are scarcely regarded. Certainly they are not tolerated at all if they interfere with a man's getting his "share of the business." Gradually this demoralizing spirit of low cunning has pervaded the entire system. Its moral tone is deplorably low....*

Cornelius Vanderbilt

One of the most successful railroad consolidators was Cornelius Vanderbilt, who built the New York Central system. By the mid-1850s, he had built the largest steamboat fleet in America. Yet Vanderbilt saw that the future of transportation was in railroads. So at age 73 he merged 3 short New York railroads he had purchased to form the New York Central, which ran from New York City to Buffalo. Within 4 years Vanderbilt extended his control over lines all the way to Chicago. In addition to bringing many lines under one management, Vanderbilt made great improvements in service. He was one of the first to use the Westinghouse air brake and the very first to lay a four-track main line—two tracks for freight and two for passenger traffic.

Vanderbilt, like other railroad tycoons, was a combination of shrewd speculator, ruthless competitor, and visionary. Yet Vanderbilt and other railroad entrepreneurs provided great benefits, too. Standard-gauge track was universally accepted, and standard time zones were established to simplify scheduling. The big systems were able to improve equipment, to shift cars from one section of the country to another according to seasonal needs, and to speed long-distance transportation. They made railroad operation so much more efficient that the average rate per mile for a ton of freight dropped from 2 cents in 1860 to less than 1 cent in 1900. The railroad executives also showed entrepreneurs how to operate large companies across great distances.

Section 1 ★ Review

Checking for Understanding
1. **Identify** Alexander Graham Bell, Thomas Alva Edison, Cornelius Vanderbilt.
2. **Define** entrepreneur, economies of scale.
3. **List** reasons for the growth of industry.
4. **Describe** how specific technology accelerated the growth of industry.

Critical Thinking
5. **Applying Ideas** One writer noted that, "This standardized railroad network bound all sections of the country into one market and one nation." Explain what the writer meant by this statement and why this was so. Then name some standardizing influences that exist in the United States today.

UNIT 6 New Horizons: 1860–1900

Answers to SECTION 1 REVIEW

1. Alexander Graham Bell, 496; Thomas Alva Edison, 497; Cornelius Vanderbilt, 500
2. All vocabulary words are defined in the Glossary.
3. abundant resources, available labor, immigration, favorable government policies, protective tariffs, private and foreign investment, advances in technology, communications, and transportation.
4. Typewriter and telephone improved communications, electric lighting allowed industrial production at night; power-driven machines created large clothing and shoe factories; Bessemer steel process spurred growth of railroads.
5. Answers may vary but should include the idea that standardization promotes efficiency and quicker turnaround.

CONNECTIONS  CONNECTIONS

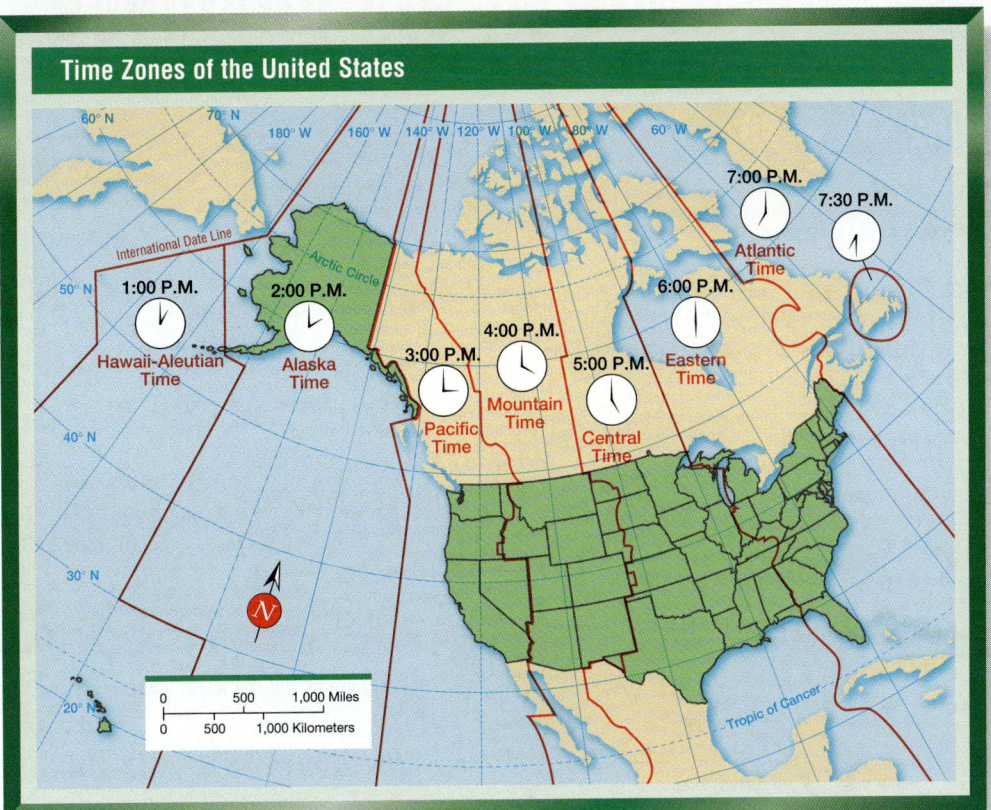

Standard Time Zones

Throughout most of the nineteenth century, few Americans could agree on the time of day because every community determined its own time by the position of the sun. When it was noon in New York City, for example, it was 11:55 A.M. in Philadelphia and 11:47 A.M. in Washington, D.C. Railways, however, required a single standard of time for scheduling and routing. In 1883 American and Canadian railroads established standardized time zones.

In 1884 delegates from 27 nations met in Washington, D.C., and divided the earth into 24 time zones. The base time zone was established with the Prime Meridian (0° longitude) as its midpoint. This zone extended about 7½ degrees on either side of the Prime Meridian. Since the Prime Meridian ran through Greenwich in Britain, the time in the base zone became known as Greenwich time.

Making the Geography Connection
1. Why did standardized time zones become necessary in the 1800s?

Linking Past and Present
2. If time zones were being set up today, do you think the base zone would be in Britain? Why or why not?

CHAPTER 18 CONNECTIONS

Teaching Making Connections
Have students refer to the time zone map on page 501 and locate the time zone in which they live. Ask them to locate the International Date Line, and ask them if they traveled east across the Date Line, what the present day would be.

Did You Know?
Opponents of standard time called local time "God's time" because it was based on the laws of nature—the sun's position in the sky—rather than on human criteria. They referred to standard time as "railroad time," and blocked attempts to create time zones. Not until 1918 was Congress able to pass a law that standardized time zones.

Answers to CONNECTIONS
1. Railroads and the need for standardized time for scheduling and routing, especially in countries covering a large area, led to the establishment of standardized time zones.
2. In answering, students should be aware that Britain is no longer the major world power it was in 1884. Also, other countries would likely object to making Britain the center of the world. On the other hand, the location of the International Date Line, in the sparsely settled mid-Pacific, could not be conveniently moved.

LESSON PLAN
SECTION 2, 502–505

FOCUS

Bellringer
Before taking roll at the beginning of the class period, display Focus Activity Transparency 60 on the overhead projector, and assign the accompanying Focus Activity Sheet.

Objectives
Point out the objectives on this page to students in previewing the section content.

Motivating Activity
Tell students that in this section they will read about how consolidation in business encouraged economic growth.

Ask students to define *consolidation*. Discuss their definitions. (the process of uniting or merging something)

VIDEODISC
Powers of the Congress

The following material is available from Glencoe and may be used to introduce or enrich Chapter 18:

Side 2
Chapter 10: Capitalism

SECTION 2

Growth of Big Business

Setting the Scene

Section Focus
As railroads gave industrialists access to raw materials and markets, great opportunities developed for business expansion. The result was "Big Business." By 1900 gigantic companies owned scores of plants, sold products nationwide, and had hundreds of millions of dollars in capital and credit behind them.

Objectives
After studying this section, you should be able to

★ discuss the methods big business used to become successful.

★ explain why incorporation encouraged business growth.

Key Terms
corporation, holding company, trust, horizontal integration, vertical integration

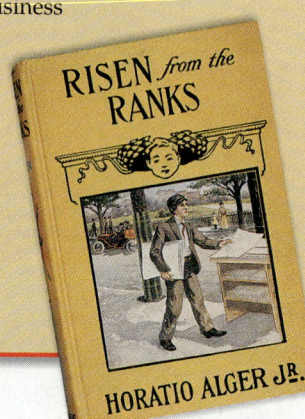

◀ COVER OF HORATIO ALGER NOVEL

The railroads were America's first "Big Business." Founding a major railroad consumed larger sums of money than any previous American enterprise. The investment required was so great that no one individual could make it. Instead, a large railroad line was organized as a **corporation**—a company formed by a group of investors who each receive a share of ownership in proportion to the amount they invested. Investors also enjoyed the protection of limited liability: they risked only the amount of their investment, even if the corporation went bankrupt and could not pay its bills.

The expansion of the railroads, along with other improvements in transportation and communication, created the mass market. No longer were manufacturers limited to local or regional sales. The mass market made mass production practical.

■ Benefits of Big Business
Corporate structure allowed entrepreneurs in many industries to raise the money they needed to launch or expand companies as opportunities arose. Big business enjoyed many advantages.

Efficiency in Production and Labor
Large companies could manufacture enough products to meet the demands of a national market. They produced better products at lower cost than their smaller competitors through the economies of scale that resulted from using the newest processes and combining operations formerly performed by separate companies. High salaries were offered in order to get expert managers. At the same time, they increased efficiency by establishing separate departments for specialized functions such as purchasing, production, research, distribution, and sales.

UNIT 6 New Horizons: 1860–1900

Classroom Resources for SECTION 2

Teacher's Classroom Resources
- Reproducible Lesson Plan
- Chapter 18 Primary and Secondary Source Readings
- Reteaching Activity 18-2
- Section Quiz

Multimedia
- Section Focus Transparency 60
- Testmaker
- Student Self-Test Software
- Powers of the Congress

In conducting their operations, big companies organized work to gain maximum production from their employees. A steel company engineer, Frederick W. Taylor, developed a system to study and time workers and to make changes so their jobs could be performed more efficiently. Such studies even included counting the steps a worker took in moving from one place to another on the job and determining what size shovels were best for shoveling coal, rice, and iron ore!

The Big Business of Meatpacking

The advantages of big business were shown dramatically by the development of large meatpacking companies. In the past, fresh meat had been slaughtered locally, and every town had at least one slaughterhouse. When the refrigerated railroad car made it possible to ship fresh meat over long distances, huge companies such as Swift and Armour appeared, selling their products throughout the country. The big packers were so highly organized and efficient that they could sell meat at a loss and make their profit from the rest of the carcass. Chicago humorist Finley Peter Dunne, writing under the name of the fictional Irish saloon keeper "Mr. Dooley," hardly exaggerated about Armour when he noted:

> *A cow goes lowin' softly into Armour's an' comes out glue, gelatin, fertylizer, celooloid, joolry, sofy cushions, hair restorer, washin' sody, soap, lithrachoor an' bed springs so quick that while aft she's still cow, for'ard she may be anything fr'm buttons to pannyma hats.*

Big Business Tactics

Because of their efficiency, organization, and size, large businesses were frequently in a position to take advantage of their competitors and sometimes of the public. Big companies could demand volume discounts from shippers. They could sell their products in an area at a loss until local competitors were forced to shut down or sell out. If a large company succeeded in getting a monopoly in its industry, it could raise consumer prices and pay less to suppliers of raw materials.

Big business in the late nineteenth century resulted from the vision of people who

Gustavus Swift
1839–1903

AMERICAN PORTRAITS

At the age of 16, Gustavus Swift borrowed $25, bought a cow, slaughtered it, and sold the beef at a $10 profit. From that point on, Swift devoted his life to making money from meat.

Swift first opened several butcher shops. With a talent for buying only the best cattle, he next moved to Chicago—capital of the cattle market—and went into business shipping livestock by rail to Eastern cities. He soon realized, however, that he could make more money butchering the cattle in Chicago and shipping the meat.

At first, to prevent spoilage, Swift could ship only during winter months. But then he hired an engineer who developed a refrigerated railroad car that made it possible to ship year-round. As hungry workers swelled the size of Eastern cities, Swift & Co. made great profits by shipping huge quantities of meat to feed them.

CHAPTER 18 The Rise of Industry 1860–1900   503

Critical Thinking

Analyzing Quotations Write the following quotation from the Rev. Russell H. Conwell's sermon "Acres of Diamonds" on the chalkboard:

"It is cruel to slander the rich because they have been successful . . . . They are not scoundrels because they have gotten money. They have gone into great enterprises that have enriched the nation and the nation has enriched them."

Have students write a paragraph giving their opinions on whether or not Rev. Conwell's defense is justified in regard to entrepreneurs in the late nineteenth century. Tell students to back up their opinions with facts. **L2, L3**

CHAPTER 18
SECTION 2

TEACH

Guided Practice
Linking Past and Present
Ask students to list some of the nineteenth-century business practices entrepreneurs engaged in that would today be punishable by fines or imprisonment. (forcing competitors out of business through unfair business practices, evading the law, bribing officials, destroying labor unions, devastating the environment) Discuss students' lists, and have them speculate why people allowed entrepreneurs to get away with such abuses. **L1, LEP**

Teaching American Portraits
Gustavus Swift was preoccupied with increasing profits. In order to detect wasted motion, waste in materials, and identify potential trouble spots, Swift often observed the workers on the packinghouse floor. Through systematic organization of work he increased productivity. Ask students how they feel when someone watches them work.

Food of the Times
By 1900 H.J. Heinz's company was the nation's largest food processor. The company manufactured more than two hundred food products, including such items as baked beans and tomato ketchup. Those inexpensive canned goods added variety to the diet of city families.

503

CHAPTER 18
SECTION 2

Independent Practice

Contrasting Ideas Have students form opinions on whether big business should or should not be allowed to function without restraints on size, competition, hiring policies, ways of obtaining investment capital, and so on. Ask them to present their opinions to the class. **L2**

Visualizing History

Have students compare the advertisement on page 504 with modern advertisements. Ask: How does the older advertisement differ from ads today? (Answers will vary, but may include that the older ad differs by being more melodramatic, less artistically sophisticated, makes no use of humor.)
Answers to Caption: because of their efficiency and "buying power"

Did You Know?

Magazines of the late 1800s carried some unique advertisements, often for patent medicines. Like magazines today there was a multitude of advertisements for weight loss. One ad for Allan's Anti-Fat—which included the familiar before-and-after pictures—assured consumers that the contents of the remedy were purely vegetable.

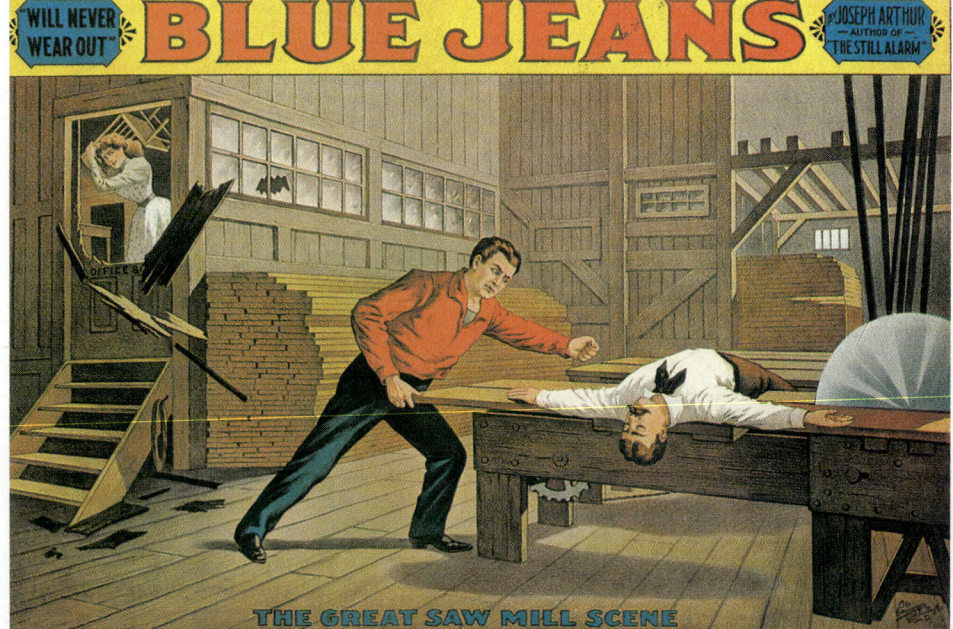

Visualizing History ▲ **MARKETING GOODS** Mass production of consumer goods, such as blue jeans, combined with transportation improvements inspired entrepreneurs to print merchandise catalogs and open mail-order stores. *Why were big businesses able to sell for less than local companies?*

recognized great opportunities for wealth and were willing to take risks to get it. The companies they organized—American Tobacco, General Electric, and United Fruit, among them—came to dominate their industries and sold products not just nationwide but to the entire world.

In attaining success, however, many entrepreneurs showed few scruples in driving competitors out of business. Their tactics included evading the law, bribing officials, destroying labor unions, and devastating the environment. Some entrepreneurs commonly sold products at below their cost until local businesses were forced to close down or sell out.

The American public, therefore, had mixed feelings about big business and its leaders. Americans worried about the corrupting influence of wealth and power. Yet others admitted that they benefited from big business's efficiency, its lower prices, and the jobs it created. Historian Vernon L. Parrington said of the entrepreneurs:

> These new Americans were primitive souls, ruthless, predatory, capable, single-minded men; rogues and rascals often, but never feeble, never hindered by petty scruples, never given to puling [whimpering] or whining. . . . Analyze the most talked-of men of the age and one is likely to find a splendid audacity coupled with immense wastefulness. A note of tough-mindedness marks them. . . . They fought their way encased in rhinoceros hides.

Success in business became a best-selling theme in popular fiction. Horatio Alger became wealthy himself when he wrote novels like *Mark the Match Boy*, *Tattered Tom*, and more than 100 others—all "rags-to-riches" stories of young men who became successful in business because of hard work and lucky breaks.

Cooperative Learning

Organize students into groups of four. Assign each group member a well-known old-time company for study, such as Singer Sewing Machine Company, American Tobacco, General Electric, or United Fruit. Have individuals obtain information and take notes on how these companies came to dominate the other companies in their field. Ask each student to present his or her notes to the group and decide if information needs to be added or deleted. **L2**

■ The Role of Corporations

American law allowed the formation of business corporations, and conditions in the United States encouraged their existence. As a business form, the corporation offered a number of advantages over a partnership or a sole proprietorship. The corporation had a permanence that lasted beyond the lives of its owners or stockholders. That meant company managers could confidently plan far into the future.

Kinds of Companies

By selling stocks and bonds, a corporation could raise the capital, or investment money, for its operations. Small amounts of capital from many individual investors could be pooled into the huge sums needed to start or expand a large company. In that way no one investor would have to take a big financial risk. To reduce risk even more, investors could spread it out by purchasing stock in several corporations. One specialized form of corporation, the **holding company,** became very popular. Holding companies manufactured no products and had no customers. They existed only to own stock in other corporations. Through holding companies, wealthy capitalists could own controlling interests in many businesses.

Other companies were organized into trusts. **A trust** was formed when several companies gave control of their operations to a single board of trustees. The shareholders of each individual company continued to own it and keep its profits, but management of all companies in the trust was in the same hands. Through holding companies and trusts, entrepreneurs formed the huge business combinations that dominated the late nineteenth century. Some combinations were able to restrict or prevent competition among their members.

Ways to Combine Companies

Business consolidation—combining companies into one unit—took various forms. Sometimes companies were consolidated by **horizontal integration,** in which several firms engaged in the same kind of business were joined together. If a horizontal combination became large enough, it could achieve a monopoly of that industry.

Companies also were consolidated by **vertical integration,** which joined businesses engaged in different but related activities. A vertical combination, for example, might include under the same ownership individual companies that provided raw materials, transported those raw materials to factories, manufactured a product from those raw materials, and distributed and sold the finished product.

A horizontal combination, once established, was able to expand vertically because of the control its size gave it over both suppliers and distributors. Similarly, a vertical combination could become so efficient that it expanded horizontally by buying its competitors, forcing them into trusts, or driving them out of business.

Section 2 ★ Review

Checking for Understanding

1. **Identify** Frederick W. Taylor, Horatio Alger.
2. **Define** corporation, holding company, trust, horizontal integration, vertical integration.
3. **Describe** the practices that made big business successful, but at the same time open to criticism from many Americans.
4. **List** the various ways businesses can be organized.

Critical Thinking

5. **Evaluating Change** How might the shift to the prevalence of big business work to the advantage or disadvantage of a consumer? A worker? An owner of a small business?

CHAPTER 18 The Rise of Industry 1860–1900 505

Answers to SECTION 2 REVIEW

1. Frederick W. Taylor, 503; Horatio Alger, 504
2. All vocabulary words are defined in the Glossary.
3. Successful: produced greater volume, better products, at lower cost; used newest processes; combined operations; hired expert managers; departmentalized; created jobs. Objectionable: demanded discounts and forced smaller competitors out of business.
4. corporations, holding companies, trusts, horizontal or vertical combinations
5. Answers will vary: consumer—lower prices, monopolistic price gouging; worker—more jobs, impersonal working conditions, and regulations; owner—personalized service, less variety, higher prices

---

CHAPTER 18 SECTION 2

ASSESS
Check Understanding
Assign Section 2 Review as homework or an in-class activity.

Evaluate
Assign the Section 2 Quiz in the TCR, or use the History of a Free Nation Testmaker to create a customized quiz.

Reteach
Pair students; have one partner list methods big business used in the 1800s to become successful, and the other list reasons incorporation encouraged business growth.
Have students complete Reteaching Activity 18-2.

Enrich
Have students read stories by Horatio Alger and then write their own rags-to-riches story using an Alger story as a model. Ask them to create an imaginative plot but to make the setting and the references historically accurate.

CLOSE
John D. Rockefeller claimed that consolidation protected businesses from "wasteful conditions." He insisted that "individualism has gone, never to return." Ask students if they agree. Have them give facts and arguments in support of their point of view.

505

LESSON PLAN
SECTION 3, 506–513

FOCUS

Bellringer
Before taking roll at the beginning of the class period, display Focus Activity Transparency 61 on the overhead projector, and assign the accompanying Focus Activity Sheet.

Objectives
Point out the objectives on this page to students in previewing the section content.

Motivating Activity
Have students list ways in which oil is used today. (gasoline for cars, ships, airplanes; oil for heating homes; to generate electricity; to manufacture chemicals to produce cloth and paint) Have students explain why a rise in oil prices today might have a serious impact on America's economy.

SECTION 3

Captains of Industry

Setting the Scene

Section Focus

The oil and steel industries were each dominated by a man as ruthless as he was efficient. Rising from poverty to attain great wealth and power, John D. Rockefeller and Andrew Carnegie represented to many the American Dream.

Objectives

After studying this section, you should be able to

★ compare the methods used by Carnegie and Rockefeller to achieve success.

★ explain social Darwinism.

Key Terms

rebate, social Darwinism, philanthropy

◀ COVER OF *McCLURE'S MAGAZINE*

Although giant combinations arose to control the beef, flour, whiskey, tobacco, lead, and sugar industries, as well as many others, by 1900 the American economy ran on oil, and its backbone was steel. No industrialists exemplified the principles of doing "big business" in late-nineteenth-century America more than the entrepreneurs who dominated these two basic industries—John D. Rockefeller in oil and Andrew Carnegie in steel.

■ Rockefeller and the Standard Oil Trust

The most successful example of horizontal consolidation was the Standard Oil Trust, which gained a near monopoly of oil refineries and pipelines. The guiding genius behind Standard Oil was John D. Rockefeller, who during his 98 years, from 1839 to 1937, amassed what was at the time the world's largest fortune—almost $1 billion.

The Early Years

Rockefeller went to work at age 16 as a bookkeeper in a wholesale commission and produce company in Cleveland, Ohio. Dominated by the idea that he was "bound to be rich," he saved $800 in 3 years on a salary of $15 per week. At 19 he left his job and opened his own commission house. In only 4 years he increased his capital to about $100,000. Then in 1862, at age 23, he put all his money into a new and growing industry—petroleum refining.

Until the 1850s, petroleum, then called "rock oil," had been used only as a patent medicine. In 1855 scientists discovered that petroleum, when refined into kerosene, gave

UNIT 6 New Horizons: 1860–1900

Classroom Resources for SECTION 2

Teacher's Classroom Resources
- Reproducible Lesson Plan
- Reteaching Activity 18-3
- Chapter 18 Primary and Secondary Source Readings
- Chapter 18 Enrichment Activity
- Chapter 18 Performance Assessment Activity
- Spanish Summaries and Glossary
- Section Quiz

Multimedia
- Section Focus Transparency 61
- Vocabulary Puzzlemaker
- Testmaker
- Student Self-Test Software

better light than whale oil in lamps and made a much better lubricant than animal fat.

The first oil well, drilled in 1859, set off a stampede to western Pennsylvania much like the California gold rush of 1849. Land values jumped from a few dollars an acre to hundreds of dollars a square foot, new towns appeared overnight, and the demand for kerosene spread worldwide. In spite of the Civil War, the petroleum industry grew so fast that by 1865 oil products had risen to fourth place among American exports.

Drilling for oil was always a big gamble, and Rockefeller realized oil refining was a safer investment. The entire oil business was highly disorganized, however. Fortunes were made and lost overnight as the price of oil fluctuated wildly. Rockefeller believed such unstable conditions resulted from competition among thousands of small producers and hundreds of small refiners.

Standard Oil Becomes a Giant

By 1870 Rockefeller's firm, the Standard Oil Company of Ohio, was the largest of 26 refineries in Cleveland, processing 2 or 3 percent of the crude oil produced in the United States. Over the next 9 years, Rockefeller gained control of more than 90 percent of the nation's refining business and brought order to a chaotic industry. But to achieve stability and efficiency in the oil business, Rockefeller used methods so shrewdly brutal that when they were revealed he became one of the most hated men in America.

One of Standard Oil's major weapons was the **rebate,** or discount, on freight charges. In 1872 the company offered to give certain railroads all its shipping business if those railroads secretly agreed to charge Standard Oil 25 to 50 percent less than they charged its competitors. In return for its business, these railroads also promised to tell Rockefeller the destinations of all his competitors' shipments. This information gave him valuable insights into his rivals' business dealings. These secret arrangements gave Standard Oil such an advantage over other Cleveland refineries that within 3 months all but 5 were forced to sell out to Rockefeller. Once it controlled oil refining in Cleveland, Standard Oil moved rapidly toward a nationwide monopoly by allying with the strongest companies throughout the industry. In 1880 a committee of the New York legislature reported on the extent of Standard Oil's domination of the oil business:

> *It owns and controls the pipe lines of the producing regions that connect with the railroads. It controls both ends of these roads. It ships 95 percent of all oil.... It dictates terms and rates to the railroads. It has bought out and frozen out refiners all over the country. By means of the superior facilities for transportation which it thus possessed, it could overbid [its competitors for crude oil] in the producing regions and undersell [its competitors] in the markets of the world.*

Visualizing History ▲ **JOHN D. ROCKEFELLER** Although he was ruthless in business dealings, John D. Rockefeller always carried dimes in his pockets to give to small children he encountered on the street. **What changes did Rockefeller bring to the oil industry?**

Sidelights: The Oil Industry

Much like Standard Oil, the Organization of Petroleum Exporting Countries (OPEC) tries to maintain stability in the oil industry to ensure profits. Since 1970 OPEC has controlled approximately one-third to one-half of the world's oil supply. In 1994 member nations included Algeria, Gabon, Indonesia, Iran, Iraq, Kuwait, Libya, Nigeria, Qatar, Saudi Arabia, United Arab Emirates, and Venezuela.

CHAPTER 18 SECTION 3

Guided Practice

Economics Write the following on the chalkboard:
Date	Price per Barrel
1858	$30
1861	$1.35
1864	$14
1870	$2.70

Ask students to study the swings in oil prices and hypothesize why such wide swings were unsettling to the oil producers, oil refiners, oil towns, and oil users. (Making a reasonable profit was not predictable, creating planning problems for producers and refiners. Towns were in boom or bust cycles. Users could not predict outlay for oil.)

Have students explain how John D. Rockefeller brought the wild oil price fluctuation to an end. (First he took over competitors' oil refineries, and then he took over control of the oil fields.) **L2**

Did You Know?

Not all of the nineteenth-century business tycoons were comfortable with their wealth. J.P. Morgan, for example, spent almost 20 years giving money away.

Visualizing History During his 98 years, from 1839 to 1932, John D. Rockefeller amassed what was at the time the world's largest fortune—almost $1 billion.

Answer to Caption: stability, efficiency, consolidation

CHAPTER 18 SECTION 3

Independent Practice

Making a Map Provide an outline map of the world found in the Teacher's Classroom Resources, and ask students to label the areas where oil fields are located. Have them also investigate what percentage of oil the United States buys from other countries and what percentage is produced domestically. **LEP, L1**

Did You Know?

When he retired in 1897, John D. Rockefeller, Sr., dedicated the remainder of his life to philanthropic work. He gave over $35 million to the University of Chicago and also established the General Education Board. Through this board, established for the promotion of education throughout the United States, Rockefeller gave over $60 million for medical research, $78 million to colleges and universities, $18 million for African American education, and $18 million for other educational purposes. Before his death in 1937, Rockefeller had given away over $520 million.

 **Visualizing History** Point out that important muckrakers of the period included Charles E. Russell who wrote on the beef trust and Ray Stannard Baker on railroads.
Answer to Caption: Standard Oil.

▲ **IDA TARBELL** Ida Tarbell was one of several American writers who played a major part in exposing social problems. **What company did Tarbell target in her series of articles for** *McClure's Magazine?*

By a secret agreement that became known as the Standard Oil Trust, Rockefeller moved in 1882 to consolidate his control of the oil industry further by combining 40 companies under a single management. Once in control of most of the refining and transportation of oil in the United States, Standard Oil expanded vertically. It gained control of oil fields to have an independent supply source, and it marketed natural gas. At the other end of the production process, Standard Oil moved into the distribution of petroleum products, both in the United States and overseas. Eventually Standard Oil controlled a fleet of oceangoing tankers and door-to-door delivery wagons in Europe. It even manufactured and sold cooking stoves to increase the demand for kerosene!

Following Standard Oil's Lead

Standard Oil's spectacular success led others to establish horizontal combinations of companies in industries as varied as whiskey, bituminous coal, and rope. The purpose of these combinations was mainly to prevent overproduction and to keep prices up. Yet it was difficult to control an entire industry and to keep new firms out of the market. Such efforts to obtain monopolies were greatly resented by small business people and consumers. Vertical combinations, on the other hand, were not monopolistic. The savings that resulted from the economies they brought to production were passed on to consumers in lower prices. Vertical combination thus became a common form of business organization.

Business Tactics Exposed

Although Rockefeller's rivals in the oil industry were painfully aware of his ruthless methods, it was an investigative journalist who exposed them to the public. This courageous woman was Ida Tarbell.

In 1903, in a series of brilliant articles in *McClure's Magazine,* Tarbell revealed Rockefeller's secret deals and his high-pressure tactics. She explained how companies controlled by Standard Oil continued to do business under their former names. She documented how, to conceal his control of these companies, Rockefeller appointed "dummy directors," who were sometimes employees such as errand-runners or secretaries.

Rockefeller, a devout churchgoer and Sunday school teacher, did not think that his actions were wrong. He pointed out that what he had done to destroy his competitors had not been illegal when he first did it. Rebates, for example, were granted by railroads to big shippers in many other industries. When buying out his competitors, Rockefeller offered to pay them in either cash or Standard Oil stock, advising them to take the stock. Those who took his advice became rich.

Much of Rockefeller's advantage over competitors came from his passion for efficiency and his hatred of waste. Standard Oil continuously improved its product. The company had few labor troubles because it paid its workers well. It tried to protect their jobs in times of depression and was one of the first companies to pay old-age pensions.

UNIT 6 New Horizons: 1860–1900

Critical Thinking

Analyzing Quotations Write the following quotation from *Early Days of Oil* by P.H. Giddens on the chalkboard:
"Wells are sinking in every direction and strangers are flocking in from all parts of the country . . . every son of Pennsylvania should rejoice in the good Providence that has enriched the state . . . with rivers of oil."
Have students read the quotation and write a paragraph comparing the excitement created by the discovery of oil in Pennsylvania with the excitement of the gold strike in California. **L3**

Andrew Carnegie, Master of Steel

The most remarkable example of the creation of a vertical combination was the giant steel corporation built by Andrew Carnegie.

Coming to Pittsburgh from Scotland at the age of 13, Carnegie went to work in a cotton factory where he earned $1.20 for working a 72-hour week. He saw an opportunity to grow with the railroad, however, and in 1853 he went to work as a clerk and telegraph operator for the Pennsylvania Railroad. His ability, energy, and ambition were so great that at age 23 he became superintendent of the railroad's western division.

Looking to the Future

While working for the railroad, Carnegie wisely invested his earnings in iron companies. As the railroads grew, Carnegie foresaw his opportunity for personal success in the increasing demand for rails, bridges, and locomotives. By age 30, when he left the railroad to manage an iron bridge company, his investments were producing an annual income of nearly $50,000.

After seven years making iron bridges, Carnegie again looked at the future and saw it was in steel. In 1873 he formed a group of investors to build the largest and most modern steel mill in the world near Pittsburgh. Carnegie was the first person in the United States to use two new ways of making steel—the Bessemer process and the open-hearth process. These processes enabled him to produce steel so cheaply that it could now be used for rails and construction girders, as well as for cutlery and precision machines.

Another Giant Is Born

Almost overnight Carnegie changed the character of the industry. Previously iron and steel had been manufactured at hundreds of small furnaces all over the country. But Bessemer converters and open-hearth furnaces required heavy investments of capital and huge amounts of coke and ore to keep them going. Small companies were soon forced out of business by big ones.

In less than 20 years, Carnegie was the greatest steelmaker in the world. One reason for his phenomenal success was that he took the guesswork out of making steel by getting the best technical and scientific experts he could find. Carnegie liked to boast that he "was smart enough to surround himself with men far cleverer than himself." For example, his managers were able to determine almost to the penny what it cost to produce a ton of steel. With this knowledge, Carnegie could set prices below his competitors and still make a profit. His chemists found uses for by-products previously considered to be industrial waste, and they discovered how to use low-grade ores.

 ▲ *The Steel Mill* by Maximillian Luce, 1895
Although the growth of the oil industry after the Civil War was phenomenal, the steel industry achieved even greater growth. **What benefits did the success of these industries bring to the nation?**

Cases in the 1990s involving unethical business practices such as those of Michael Milken, Ivan Boesky, and Dennis Levine—Wall Street millionaires—have stirred business schools to offer business ethics courses in their MBA programs. The Harvard Business School received a $30 million gift from alumnus John S. R. Shad, head of the bankrupt investment firm Drexel Burnham Lambert, that he targeted for a business ethics curriculum.

History AND ART

Between 1866 and 1876, the production of American steel jumped from 20,000 to 600,000 tons; by 1897 it had skyrocketed to more than 7 million tons.
Answer to Caption: Their efficiency in production brought more goods and lower prices to consumers.

Did You Know?

In 1802 Pittsburgh was described by a French traveler as a town of 40 to 50 acres with 400 homes. In 1890 a team of British ironworkers noted that Pittsburgh had 21 blast furnaces, 40 iron foundries, 15,000 coke ovens, and 33 rolling mills.

Cooperative Learning

Divide the class into small groups, and provide each group with a large piece of paper. Have group members work together to research how such by-products of oil as kerosene, paint, or paraffin are processed. Ask students to show the process on a poster, using explanatory labels. **L1**

CHAPTER 18
SECTION 3

Visualizing History Captains of industry like Rockefeller and Carnegie believed that competition in industry was wasteful. They argued that consolidated companies were more efficient than many, small, competing companies in the same industry.
Answer to Caption: His railroad job made him realize the importance of these products.

Fact or Fiction?
Andrew Carnegie, like other wealthy people, had the deep conviction that if individuals worked hard in the United States, saved their earnings, and invested prudently, they would become wealthy in no time at all.

FICTION: Immigrant workers had little opportunity to amass wealth because they had neither political nor social connections. They were given no lands, other than homesteads, and received no grants from the government as the railroad builders had. Actually, some of the later immigrants were denied entry into schools and jobs and also into better neighborhoods.

In his constant effort to be more efficient, Carnegie combined all of the processes required for making steel into one great vertical combination. In addition to blast furnaces and steel mills, the Carnegie Steel Company controlled rich iron ore deposits near Lake Superior, fleets of ships to carry the ore over the Great Lakes, a railroad to carry the ore from the Lake Erie region to Pittsburgh, coal mines in Pennsylvania to fire the blast furnaces, and factories for producing finished steel products such as wire.

Crushing Labor and Gobbling the Competition

Seeking out the ablest people in the industry, Carnegie bought their loyalty by making them partners. Equally alert for ability inside his companies, he rapidly promoted exceptional employees. Common laborers in his mills fared less well, however, as he drove wages down and hours up. In 1892, with his partner, Henry C. Frick, he crushed the steelworkers' union, so that the 12-hour day remained standard for many years.

During the three major depressions of the late 1800s, while other steel companies closed down, Carnegie expanded. He rebuilt his factories to be even more efficient and acquired his weakened competitors.

■ Social Darwinism and the Industrialists

Andrew Carnegie was making $25 million a year at a time when there was no income tax. His workers, on the other hand, earned $8 or $9 a week. He made steel so cheaply and competed so mercilessly that remaining steel companies faced bankruptcy. Carnegie and most other great industrialists found justification for these actions and their consequences in a philosophy known as **social Darwinism**, which applied the biological theories of naturalist Charles Darwin to human society.

Darwin believed that in nature a competition exists in which only the fittest—the strongest, most clever, most efficient— plants and animals survive. The weak individuals die out, and each species thereby remains strong and healthy. Philosophers such as Yale professor William Graham Sumner argued that this competition also operated in human society, and that industrialists like Rockefeller and Carnegie had succeeded because of their rare talents. "The millionaires are a product of natural selection," Sumner wrote. "They get high wages and live in luxury, but the bargain is a good one for society." Not surprisingly, Andrew Carnegie and John D. Rockefeller both believed wholeheartedly in the philosophy of social Darwinism. Carnegie called it a method better than elections for selecting leaders. "By a process of pitiless testing we discover who are the strong and who are the weak," he wrote. "To the strong we give power in the form of the autocratic control of industry and of wealth." Rockefeller told his Sunday school class that his business practices merely demonstrated "the survival of the fittest . . . a law of nature and a law of God."

Visualizing History ▲ **ANDREW CARNEGIE** If any entrepreneur symbolized the rags-to-riches legend, it was Andrew Carnegie. The son of poor immigrants, Carnegie built a company that by 1900 was making one-fourth of the nation's steel and serving a world market. *What caused Carnegie to believe the future was in iron and steel?*

UNIT 6 New Horizons: 1860–1900

Critical Thinking

Analyzing Quotations Write on the chalkboard the following quotation attributed to Andrew Carnegie:

"Those who are most successful in the acquisition of property and who acquire it to such an enormous extent are the very men who are able to control it, to invest it, and to handle it in the way most useful to society."

Ask students to study the quotation and explain why the sentiment expressed in it was acceptable in the late 1800s but not today. **L2**

CHAPTER 18
SECTION 3

 ▲ **THE HATCH FAMILY** by Jonathan Eastman Johnson, 1871 The artist portrays a family in fine clothing enjoying a comfortable afternoon at home. Note that parents, children, and grandchildren live in the household—a typical arrangement for the times among the rich as well as the poor. **What is philanthropy?**

But for Carnegie the achievement of great power and wealth was not enough. He looked beyond success to question whether those who profited from society owed anything to it in return.

Writing in the *North American Review* in 1889, Carnegie maintained that a wealthy person should:

> ... [c]onsider all surplus revenues which come to him simply as trust funds, which he is called upon to administer . . . in a manner which, in his judgment, is best calculated to produce the most beneficial results for the community . . . becoming the mere agent and trustee for his poorer brethren, bringing to their service his superior wisdom, experience, and ability to administer, doing for them better than they would or could do for themselves.

Carnegie practiced what he preached. In 1901 he sold his steel properties to the newly formed United States Steel Corporation for $250 million and withdrew from business to devote the rest of his life to **philanthropy,** or actions benefiting society. By the time he died in 1919, he had donated $350 million—mostly to building public libraries, improving education, and promoting research. Rockefeller also returned much of his fortune to society in gifts that totaled more than $500 million.

Sherman Antitrust Act

In 1881 *The Atlantic Monthly* published an article entitled "The Story of a Great Monopoly," by Henry Demarest Lloyd, telling how the Standard Oil Company had monopolized the oil-refining business. The article caused such a sensation that the magazine had to print three times as many copies as usual. Throughout the next decade, as it was revealed that many industries were in

Visualizing History The homes of the wealthy contained much bric-a-brac, knickknacks, and trinkets of every type. Most of these objects had little or no function and merely graced the table or shelves because people felt that space should be filled up. Many of the items were very ornate and indisputably inane. For example, lamps were held up by figures of winged nymphs or cupids, teapots of superb china did not pour, and clocks often came in the belly of a figure. **Answer to Caption:** actions benefiting society

Did You Know?

Elizabeth "Cassie" Bigley was born poor. To support the lifestyle she had chosen she convinced a variety of people, including bankers and lawyers, that she was Andrew Carnegie's illegitimate daughter. Using credit against money she supposedly had, she spent about a million dollars. Once a banker sued Carnegie for the money she used, the sham was discovered, and Cassie was arrested and sent to prison.

Cultural Diversity

The immigrants who crossed the ocean to come to the United States in the 1800s left their homeland for a variety of reasons. Many Germans came to avoid compulsory military service; many Jews to escape pogroms in Russia; crop failures brought Italians; and many people came to find religious freedom or just out of a sense of adventure. Most immigrants came in steerage, where conditions were crowded and filthy. The trip took up to 10 days and was unpleasant at best and dangerous in bad weather. On disembarking from the ship, emigrants had to cope with a new language, new customs, and a new land.

CHAPTER 18 SECTION 3

ASSESS

Check Understanding
Assign Section 3 Review as homework or an in-class activity.

Evaluate
📁 💻 Assign the Section 3 Quiz in the TCR, or use the History of a Free Nation Testmaker to create a customized quiz.

Reteach
📁 Have students complete Reteaching Activity 18-3.

Enrich
📁 Have students complete Chapter 18 Enrichment Activity in the Teacher's Classroom Resources.

CLOSE
Ask students to name some present-day abuses in business. Have them compare the abuses with those of the 1800s. Discuss the need for ethics in business.

---

danger of being monopolized, demands for federal regulation came from many groups—small businesses, farmers, consumers, laborers, and even some big businesses.

Even officials of the great corporations began to have concerns about growing public cries for reform. Henry O. Havemeyer, head of the American Sugar Refining Company, which controlled a trust producing more than 90 percent of the nation's sugar, urged that manufacturers of products in general use should submit to some federal regulation.

In the election of 1888, both the Democratic and the Republican political parties promised action. Then in 1890, with only one dissenting vote, Congress passed the Sherman Antitrust Act. The Sherman Act wrote into federal law a traditional principle of English common law. This is the idea that private monopolies and artificial restrictions on trade were wrong. In the words of the act:

> *Every contract, combination, in the form of trust or otherwise, or conspiracy, in restraint of trade or commerce among the several states or with foreign nations, is hereby declared to be illegal.*

The Sherman Act had little effect on preventing business consolidation. It was not strictly enforced and was so loosely worded that its meaning was doubtful. Did the law mean, for example, that all mergers were unlawful, that all business transactions must be open and public, that any contract that permitted one company to take business from another was illegal?

Under the Constitution, the answers to such questions are left to the federal courts, which in the 1890s were probably more favorable to business interests than at any other time in American history. In *United States v. E. C. Knight Company*, the Supreme Court in 1895 agreed that the American Sugar Refining Company was a trust and that it enjoyed a near monopoly in the manufacture of sugar. But the Court ruled that the company's activities did not violate the Sherman Act because manufacturing was not interstate commerce.

The Supreme Court's decision in the *Knight* case was followed by one of the greatest periods of business consolidation in American history. In 1890 there had been 24 trusts worth a total of $436 million. In 1900 there were 183 huge combinations with a total worth of more than $3 billion. At the same time, big business simply turned away from trusts and toward holding companies in creating combinations.

In spite of its early failures, the Sherman Act was an important law. It signaled to large corporations to be more aware of how their activities looked to the public. As a result, corporate image and public relations became important business concerns. Later regulation of big business and industry would depend on additional legislation, on the interpretations of future courts, and on attitudes in the executive branch about enforcement.

Section 3 ★ Review

Checking for Understanding
1. **Identify** John D. Rockefeller, Standard Oil, Ida Tarbell, Andrew Carnegie, Sherman Antitrust Act.
2. **Define** rebate, social Darwinism, philanthropy.
3. **Compare** the methods used by Rockefeller and Carnegie to build their industrial empires.
4. **Explain** why the Sherman Antitrust Act failed to control big business.

Critical Thinking
5. **Judging Actions** Would the United States have been better off with or without industrial giants such as John D. Rockefeller and Andrew Carnegie? Explain.

512 UNIT 6 New Horizons: 1860–1900

Answers to SECTION 3 REVIEW

1. John D. Rockefeller, 506; Standard Oil, 506; Ida Tarbell, 508; Andrew Carnegie, 509; Sherman Antitrust Act, 512
2. All vocabulary words are defined in the Glossary
3. Beginning with nothing, both built enormous industrial monopolies.
4. not strictly enforced; too vague; interpreted by federal courts favorable to business
5. Answers will vary but may include: Positive effects—making goods available, lowering prices, providing jobs, improving the economy. Negative effects—greed, materialism, unethical practices.

Social Studies Skills

Map and Graph Skills

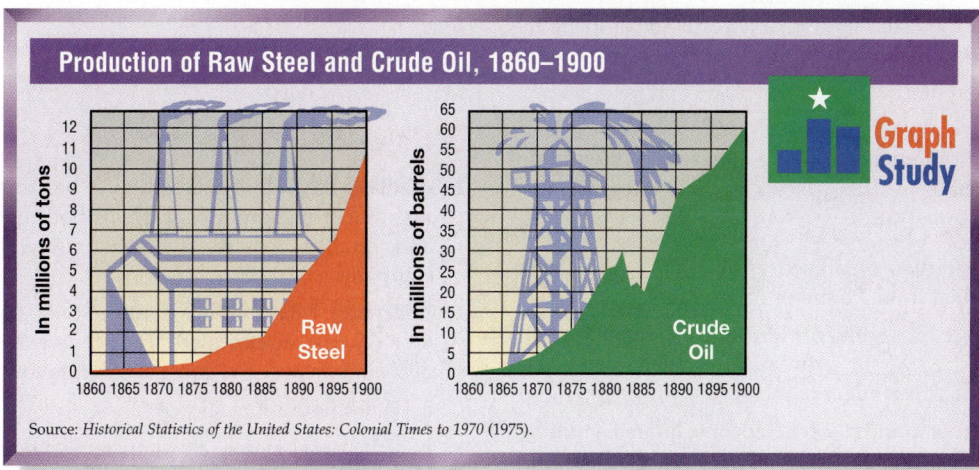

Production of Raw Steel and Crude Oil, 1860–1900

Source: *Historical Statistics of the United States: Colonial Times to 1970* (1975).

Reading a Line Graph

When historical information involves numbers and statistics, it often is presented on a graph. Graphic data can be presented in the form of circle graphs, bar graphs, or line graphs.

A line graph charts information about two variables. Line graphs typically show how one variable, depicted on the vertical axis, changes over time. Time, the second variable—whether minutes, hours, days, or years—is recorded on the horizontal axis. To maximize the information you obtain from a line graph, follow this procedure:

- **Read** the title to get a general idea of what the graph shows.
- **Examine** the labels. Labels define the two variables and explain what the lines and/or points on the graph represent. Labels also specify the units of measurement.
- **Analyze** the graph. Look for increases, decreases, and sudden shifts. Analyze the *amount* and the *rate* of change.
- **Draw** conclusions or generalizations from the statistics presented on the graph. What trends or patterns appear?

Practicing the Skill

1. Apply the steps on reading a line graph to analyze the two graphs on this page.
    a. What time period is under study in the graph?
    b. How many units are represented by each point on the vertical axis of each of the graphs? How much time is represented by each point on the horizontal axis of each graph?
    c. Approximately how much did steel and oil production increase between 1885 and 1890? During what 5-year period did the largest dip in oil production occur?
    d. What generalization can be made about steel and oil production between 1860 and 1875?
2. Explain why the statistics are shown on two different graphs.

LESSON PLAN
Mastering Social Studies Skills

Teaching Map and Graph Skills

Ask students what the two graphs show. Tell them that although the growth of the oil industry after the Civil War was phenomenal, the growth of the steel industry, which started later, was nearly 30 times greater. Discuss the benefits the success of these industries brought to the nation.

Did You Know?

In 1898, although Carnegie Steel's output had risen threefold over the previous few years, the number of workers needed to produce the steel had decreased by 400. The use of electricity to drive automatic machinery was largely responsible for the decline in the workforce.

Answers to Social Studies Skills

1. **a.** 1860–1900;
b. millions of tons; millions of barrels; five years; five years;
c. about 3 million tons; about 20 million barrels; 1880–1885;
d. There was relatively little growth in steel production between 1860 and 1875. There was steady growth in oil production from 1860 to 1875.
2. It would be difficult to read the data if both were on the same graph.

REVIEW CHAPTER 18

Using Vocabulary
1. corporations
2. entrepreneurs
3. horizontal intergration; vertical intergration

Reviewing Facts
1. abundant resources; available labor; immigration; favorable government policies; protective tariffs; private and foreign investment; advances in technology, communications, and transportation
2. unifier, distributor, carrier, customer, consolidator
3. production volume, efficient organization and use of labor, best equipment, combined operations, expert management
4. built large businesses in areas critical to industry and the economy; forced competitors out; manipulated prices; disregarded the law
5. Prohibited combining or conspiring to restrict trade. Little impact at first because it was not enforced, was vague, and was ruled on in courts that were pro-business.

Understanding Concepts
1. Vanderbilt: consolidated local railroad lines into a statewide and later an interstate line. Rockefeller: offered to give all his business to a railroad in exchange for a rebate and information on his competitors. Carnegie: utilized the newest steelmaking processes.
2. Answers will vary but may include that as a result of Vanderbilt's initiative, his consolidated railroad line acted as a trade link among business owners in a statewide and regional area and pro-

vided an example of the benefits of consolidation to other segments of country's economy.
3. would support them because policies would not interfere with economic competition, thus allowing the most able to rise to the top, which benefits society

CHAPTER 18 ★ REVIEW

Using Vocabulary

Use the listed vocabulary words to complete the sentences that follow. You will use all but one of the words. Write an original sentence using the remaining word.

entrepreneur   horizontal integration
rebate   vertical integration
corporation

1. Businesses organized as _____ can raise capital from a number of investors.
2. When governments practice laissez-faire policies, _____ can run businesses with very little government regulation.
3. Carnegie and Rockefeller consolidated a number of businesses using both _____ and _____.

Reviewing Facts

1. **Enumerate** the factors that boosted industrial growth in the United States.
2. **State** the roles played by the railroad in the growth of American industry.
3. **Identify** the strategies that big business used to become successful.
4. **Summarize** the common elements in the strategies of Rockefeller, Carnegie, and Vanderbilt.
5. **Describe** the provisions of the Sherman Antitrust Act and its effects.

Understanding Concepts

Individual Initiative
1. Cite examples of individuals and how they used their initiative to shape industrial growth.
2. In what ways did Vanderbilt's individual initiative benefit others?

Government Restriction
3. Would a social Darwinist support or oppose laissez-faire government policies? Explain why.

4. Entrepreneurs who developed big businesses benefited. Those who were driven out by monopolies and ruthless practices could have benefited from protective legislation.

4. Lack of government restriction benefited some businesses and hurt others. Which types of businesses benefited, and which might have been more successful with some protection?

Critical Thinking

1. **Judging Effects** Discuss how a big company manufacturing products high in both quantity and quality benefits the consumer and the company.
2. **Analyzing Political Cartoons** Study the cartoon on this page entitled "The Monster Monopoly," and answer the questions that follow.
   a. What figures are shown?
   b. Who or what does the monster symbolize?
   c. What does the cartoon suggest about big business?

▲ THE MONSTER MONOPOLY, 1884

Critical Thinking

1. Answers will vary but might include: Products made in large supply kept prices low. Well-made products satisfied consumers. Low prices and customer

CHAPTER 18 ★ REVIEW

Writing About History

Cause and Effect

Imagine you are a nineteenth-century writer who hopes to publish a collection of true rags-to-riches stories. Write a brief biography of a nineteenth-century captain of industry who began with little and built an industrial empire. Choose an entrepreneur from this chapter, or conduct research about another from the same period.

Focus on what you believe to be the causes of your subject's success. Write about the traits and experiences that influenced this person's growth. What decisions were the key to success? What risks did the entrepreneur take, and what were the results of those risks? Were there mistakes and failures along the road to success?

Cooperative Learning

Work with a partner to research the history of the Bell telephone system from the parent company's formation to its breakup into smaller companies. Then discuss between yourselves what the company's contributions to the nation were and why the system was broken up by the government. Present your findings to the class, with one partner explaining Bell's contributions and the other explaining why it was broken up. Compare your findings with those presented by other class pairs.

Social Studies Skills

Making Comparisons

To *compare* means to examine data in order to identify similarities and/or differences. You can compare things that are very different or that are very much alike. To make a comparison accurate, however, you must note at least one similarity and one difference.

Practicing the Skill

The graph on this page shows the production of bituminous coal from 1860 to 1900. Compare this graph with the graphs of raw steel and crude oil production found on page 513.

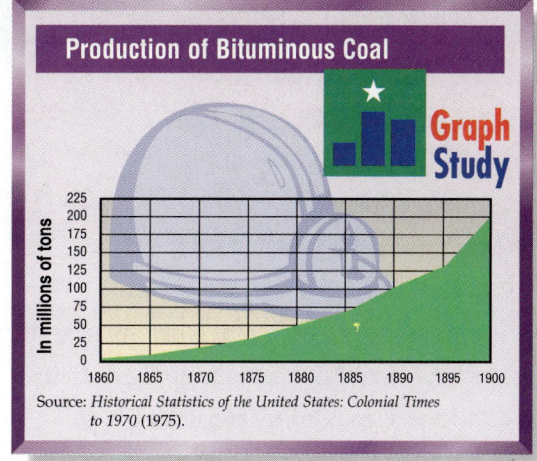

1. What three subjects can you compare by using these graphs?
2. Why is it easier to compare the production of coal and raw steel than that of coal and oil?
3. For the production of raw steel, what trend does the graph show? How does this trend compare with the production trends in the other two graphs?

Using Your Journal

Read over your notes about Rockefeller and Carnegie. Do you think that people who make enormous amounts of money have an obligation to donate some of it to society? Can you think of any modern-day "Rockefellers" and "Carnegies"? Organize your thoughts into a paragraph in your journal.

REVIEW CHAPTER 18

❓ Chapter Bonus Test Question

John D. Rockefeller told his Sunday school classes that his business practices demonstrated "survival of the fittest." What example might he give to support that point of view? (Answers will vary, but students are likely to refer to the way he forced out competitors to create a monopoly.) How might Ida Tarbell have responded to Rockefeller's boast? (Answers will vary, but she would probably have suggested that his successes were due less to social Darwinism than to secret deals with high-pressure tactics.)

Using Your Journal

The ideas students present in their paragraphs will vary but may include reference to present-day movie and television personalities, athletes, musicians, and well-known businesspeople.

---

satisfaction had the effects of winning consumer loyalty to a company's products.
2. a. a tentacled monster and various other implements and edifices
b. Answers will vary, but students should note that it symbolizes Standard Oil or any other large trust.
c. Answers will vary, but students should note that the cartoonist seems to feel big business controls smaller businesses.

Practicing the Skill

1. coal, oil, steel production
2. Steel and coal are shown in millions of tons produced. Oil is shown in a different measure: millions of barrels.
3. a sharp drop from the early 1860s to the early 1870s, then a steep rise in production; neither of the other two graphs shows such a sharp drop during the period

PLANNING GUIDE — Chapter 19 Labor, Immigrants, and Urban Life

Daily Lesson Objectives	Teacher Classroom Resources	Multimedia
SECTION 1 **The Workers' Plight** 1 Day pp. 518–522 1. Describe the conditions under which people worked during the late 1800s. 2. Explain the obstacles faced by labor unions during this period.	Chapter 19 Study Guide Reproducible Lesson Plan Section Quiz Reteaching Activity 19-1 Reinforcing Social Studies Skills 31, 32, 53, 67 Outline Map 4 Chapter 19 Cooperative Learning Activity Chapter 19 Concept Mapping Activity American Literary Heritage Unit 6 SAT Practice Tests 11-13	Student Self-Test Software Testmaker Section Focus Transparency 58 Chapter 19 Skills Transparency
SECTION 2 **The Rise of New Unions** 1 Day pp. 524–527 1. Identify two of the strongest labor unions of the late 1800s. 2. Evaluate the gains labor unions achieved during this period.	Reproducible Lesson Plan Reteaching Activity 19-2 Section Quiz Reinforcing Social Studies Skills 26, 55, 59, 67, 69-72 American Portrait 37 Chapter 19 Primary and Secondary Source Readings SAT Practice Tests 5-9	Student Self-Test Software Testmaker Section Focus Transparency 59
SECTION 3 **Changing Patterns of Immigration** 1 Day pp. 528–532 1. Identify the reasons that immigrants came to the United States. 2. Distinguish between the "old" and the "new" immigration.	Reproducible Lesson Plan Reteaching Activity 19-3 Section Quiz Reinforcing Social Studies Skills 32, 38, 40, 49, 53 American Portrait 38 Chapter 19 Primary and Secondary Source Readings American Literary Heritage Unit 6	Student Self-Test Software Testmaker Section Focus Transparency 60 Chapter 19 Map Transparency The American People: Fabric of a Nation A Geographic Perspective on American History
SECTION 4 **City Life and Problems** 1 Day pp. 533–538 1. Identify the factors that led to the growth of cities during the late 1800s. 2. List the problems resulting from an increase in the urban population.	Reproducible Lesson Plan Reteaching Activity 19-4 Section Quiz Chapter 19 Enrichment Activity Reinforcing Social Studies Skills 26, 27, 32, 61 American Portrait 38 Writer's Guidebook Lessons 9-14 Spanish Summaries & Glossary	Student Self-Test Software Testmaker Section Focus Transparency 61 Chapter 19 Map Transparency Vocabulary Puzzlemaker Audiocassette, Chapter 19 The American People: Fabric of a Nation A Geographic Perspective on American History
CHAPTER REVIEW AND EVALUATION 1 Day	Chapter 19 Test Chapter 19 Performance Assessment Activity	Student Self-Test Software Testmaker

OUT OF TIME? If time does not permit teaching the entire chapter, use the Chapter 19 Summary on pages 590–591 and the Chapter 19 audiocassette (English and Spanish) to point out the main ideas of the chapter.

PLANNING GUIDE

Cultural Diversity Activity

Critical Thinking Write the terms *Old Immigrants* and *New Immigrants* on the chalkboard. Have students list differences between the two groups, focusing on countries of origin, reasons for emigrating, social and economic status. Point out that despite the rhetoric of the period, the "new immigrants" were as skilled and as well-educated as most Americans of their day. Ask students to consider why many people focused on the ways the newcomers differed from other Americans rather than on similarities.

Define the term *assimilate* (absorb into the system or make similar). Why did many Americans fear that the newcomers would never assimilate? Was assimilation a reasonable goal then? Is it a reasonable goal for immigration today? Why or why not?

Performance Assessment Activity

Recognizing Differing Points of View Organize students into small groups. One member of each group should represent one of the following: worker, union leader, employer, government official, and a journalist. Give students time to research how their character would respond to the right of workers to strike. Be sure they gather evidence to support that position. Then ask each group to debate the topic. Encourage students to seek allies within their group. Have a spokesperson from each group summarize the outcome of its discussion. Which position prevailed? For what reasons?

POSSIBLE RUBRIC FEATURES: Content information, research skills, organization, collaborative skills, oral communication skills, creativity

Chapter Resources

Literature from the Period

Bellamy, Francis. "Pledge of Allegiance." 1892.

Wheeler, Thomas C., ed. *The Immigrant Experience: The Anguish of Becoming American.* Penguin, 1972.

Readings for the Student

Oxford, Edward. "Hope, Tears, and Remembrance." *American History Illustrated,* Vol. 25, No. 4, September/October 1990.

Robbins, Peggy. "Alas Memphis." *American History Illustrated,* Vol. 26, No. 9, January 1982.

"The Working American." *American Heritage,* Vol. 31, No. 4, June/July 1980.

Readings for the Teacher

Higham, John. *Strangers in the Land: Patterns of American Nativism, 1860–1925.* Atheneum, 1963.

Numbers, R. L., and D.W. Amundsen, eds. *Caring and Curing: Historical Essays on Health, Medicine, and the Faith Traditions.* Macmillan, 1986.

Wetheimer, Barbara Meyer. *We Were There: The Story of Working Women in America.* Pantheon, 1977.

Multimedia Resources

The Immigrant Experience: The Long, Long Journey. LCA. (VHS, 30 minutes)

Immigration: Maintaining the Open Door. Tom Snyder. (Apple or IBM diskette)

The Inheritance. Harold Mayer Productions. (VHS, 45 minutes)

The Rise of the American Labor Movement: Toil and Struggle. Educational Enrichment. (2 color filmstrips)

Urbanization: The Growth of American Cities. Tom Snyder. (Apple or IBM diskette)

Key to Ability Levels

Teaching strategies have been coded for varying learning styles and abilities.

L1   Basic activities for all students

L2   Average activities for average to above-average students

L3   Challenging activities for above-average students

LEP   Limited English Proficiency activities

Glencoe Links to the Humanities

Link to Art
- U.S. History and Art Transparency 15

Link to Literature
- Macmillan Literature: American Literature Text—Edwin Robinson, Paul Dunbar

Link to Music
- American Music: Cultural Traditions

CHAPTER 19

BEGINNING THE CHAPTER

Tell students that before 1890 most immigrants to the United States were from northern and western Europe. Between 1890 and 1914, the majority came from Italy, Russia, Poland, Austria-Hungary, Greece, Romania, and Turkey. Have students locate these places on a map of the world. Ask students to speculate why the dramatic shift in emigration occurred.

Linking Across Time

By the late 1800s, the way people worked had changed drastically because of industrialization. Today, major changes are again shaping the ways people work. These changes are brought about by new communications networks: computers, telephones, and satellite links.

Recording Journal Notes

To get students started, have them categorize the obstacles under such heads as Working Conditions, Family Life, City Life, Social Life.

CHAPTER 19

An Urban Society
1860–1900

▶ UNION SYMBOL

Setting the Scene

Focus

One factor supporting industrialization in the late nineteenth century was the abundant labor supply. For workers, poor pay and working conditions led to a renewed interest in labor unions. Efforts by unions such as the Knights of Labor to improve conditions, however, were only modestly successful. The union movement was also influenced by the influx of millions of immigrants. These new arrivals crowded into America's cities and brought with them the cultural heritage of their old world.

Concepts to Understand

★ How unity among workers led to the growth of unions
★ How conflict between workers and employees resulted in unrest

Read to Discover . . .

★ the difficulties experienced by labor unions in the late 1800s.
★ the major factors behind the migration to American cities.

Journal Notes

What were some of the major obstacles facing immigrants coming to the United States in the late 1800s? Note examples as you read the chapter.

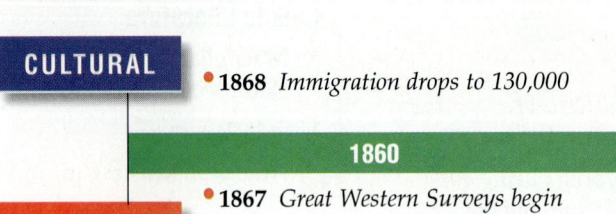

CULTURAL
- 1868 *Immigration drops to 130,000*
- 1876 *Central Park opens in New York City*

| 1860 | 1870 |

POLITICAL
- 1867 *Great Western Surveys begin*
- 1872 *Victoria Claflin Woodhull, first woman presidential candidate, is nominated*

516   UNIT 6 New Horizons: 1860–1900

✚ EXTRA CREDIT PROJECT

Ask interested students to find out more about Terence Powderly, Samuel Gompers, or some other union leader of the period. What prompted that individual to form a union? What were his or her goals? What values guided the methods used to achieve those goals? What contribution did that individual make to American life? Invite students who prepared reports to share their information with the class by participating in a panel discussion entitled "Early Labor Leaders—Successes and Failures."

CHAPTER 19 CONCEPTS

Concept Mapping Activity

Write the concept generalization and the concepts below on the chalkboard. Ask them to think of factors other than migration and immigration that contributed to urban growth.

> Urban growth and change took place in the United States because of migration of people from rural areas to cities and because of immigration.

- Social Change
- Urban Growth

◄ FAMILY AT ELLIS ISLAND, EARLY 1900S

History AND ART

Hester Street
by George Luks, 1905

Hester Street in New York City—part of a Jewish immigrant neighborhood—was filled with vitality and color.

History AND ART

Hester Street in New York City—part of a Jewish immigrant neighborhood—was filled with vitality and color as shown by artist George Luks.

• GTV: *The American People: Fabric of a Nation*

Side 3, Chapter 2
Title: *Going to Town!*
Subject: Migration to cities

See GTV Guide page 76 for complete lesson plan.

- **1883** Brooklyn Bridge in New York City is completed
- **1886** Haymarket Square riot takes place in Chicago
- **1893** Columbian Exposition opens in Chicago
- **1892** Steelworkers' strike put down at the Homestead mill
- **1894** Pullman strike ends

CHAPTER 19 An Urban Society 1860–1900

Teacher Notes

LESSON PLAN
SECTION 1, 518–523

FOCUS

Bellringer
Before taking roll at the beginning of the class period, display Focus Activity 62 on the overhead projector, and assign the accompanying Focus Activity Sheet.

Objectives
Point out the objectives on this page to students in previewing the section content.

Motivating Activity
Present the following:
"Last year [1892], I made only 4.5% profit and this year it will be less than 4%. I am entitled to make more money than that. My workers will have to take a pay cut."
— George Pullman

Ask students whether they think Pullman was justified in asking his workers to take a cut in pay and, if so, why? Discuss why present-day companies ask employees to take pay cuts. Examine the hardships that pay cuts create for workers.

Use Skills Transparency 19.

SECTION 1

The Workers' Plight

Setting the Scene

Section Focus
The new industrial age brought many problems for workers, who toiled long hours for low wages. In an attempt to improve working conditions, workers began to organize. In spite of rapid growth after the Civil War, unions encountered many difficulties.

Objectives
After studying this section, you should be able to
★ describe the conditions under which people worked during the late 1800s.
★ explain the obstacles faced by labor unions during this period.

Key Terms
real wages, company town, scrip, business cycle, blacklist, lockout, scab, collective bargaining

▲ COAL MINER'S HELMET

With the growth of industry, the number of factory workers rose from about 900,000 in 1860 to more than 3.2 million in 1890. Industrialization affected various aspects of workers' lives—where they worked and lived, the size of the workforce, and the nature of work itself. Many workers were forced to make the transition from skilled to semiskilled or unskilled labor. The experience and skill of such artisans as carpenters, silversmiths, and furniture makers no longer gave them any advantage over the unskilled. It took little training to tend a machine.

■ Problems
With machines taking the place of human skills, work became monotonous. Workers concentrated on highly specific, repetitive tasks and could take little pride in the fruits of their labor. As factories increased the efficiency of production, more and more people worked for fewer and fewer employers. The workers began to feel like "cogs in a wheel." Machines were designed to work at a given pace, and the workers were forced to try and keep up.

Unfair Conditions of Employment
Low wages and long hours posed additional burdens for industrial workers. Workdays of 10 to 14 hours were common. Although **real wages**—wages adjusted for inflation—rose more than 10 percent between 1870 and 1900, the average income remained inadequate. Most industrial workers earned between $400 and $500 a year during the 1890s; $600 was the minimum annual income needed to maintain a decent standard of living.

UNIT 6 New Horizons: 1860–1900

Classroom Resources for SECTION 1

Teacher's Classroom Resources
- Chapter 19 Study Guide
- Reproducible Lesson Plan
- Reteaching Activity 19-1
- Chapter 19 Cooperative Learning Activity
- Section Quiz

Multimedia
- Section Focus Transparency 62
- Chapter 19 Skills Transparency
- Testmaker
- Student Self-Test Software

▲ ELEMENTARY SCHOOL, EARLY 1900s

 ▲ CHILD LABOR Children were often employed in small, makeshift factories in which workers were hired on a piecework basis. **How were state labor laws evaded?**

In some industries workers were required to live in **company towns,** built and run by the companies. The best known was the town of Pullman, Illinois, where every citizen worked for the Pullman Palace Car Company. The usual practice was for companies to deduct money from the workers' pay for rent and advances to the company store as well as medical and fuel fees. Some companies paid their workers in **scrip,** or company money, that could be redeemed only at the company store. This store usually charged higher prices than did stores in other towns, and many workers remained in constant debt.

Health and Safety Hazards

Factory work was unhealthful as well as dangerous. Miners breathed coal dust all day. Factory workers breathed sawdust, stone dust, cotton dust, or toxic fumes. Heavy machines, grouped together on shop and mill floors for the sake of efficiency, caused an appallingly high injury rate among workers. An 1884 government report described working conditions for women in a small factory in Boston:

> " The work is dangerous ... [they] are liable to get their fingers jammed under the bench, or caught in the die when it comes down to press the parts of the buttons together. A man (although not a surgeon) is provided to dress wounds three times for each individual without charge; afterwards, the person injured must pay all expenses. There are 35 machines in use, and accidents are of very frequent occurrence. "

Child Labor

Children, some as young as six, were regularly employed as factory workers. Throughout the 1800s there were some efforts to restrict child labor, but state laws were usually worded in such a way that they could be easily evaded both by employers and by parents who needed the income. In 1885 in New Jersey, there were 340,000 children of school age. About 90,000

CHAPTER 19 An Urban Society 1860–1900

Sidelights: Home Alone

At the turn of the century, many parents working 12 hours or longer a day often had to leave young children home all alone or in the care of older children. Some parents unable to care for their children abandoned them. Reporter Jacob Riis, an immigrant from Denmark, described how one little boy had been found with this note: "Take care of Johnny, for God's sake. I cannot." According to Riis, by 1889 the Children's Aid Society had taken in about 300,000 children who had been outcast, homeless, or orphaned.

of them did not attend school; most worked full-time jobs. Industrial work was neither less difficult nor less dangerous for children than it was for adults. As a Pennsylvania newspaper, the *Luzerne Union,* reported in January 1876:

> During the past week, nearly one boy a day has been killed, and the public has become so familiar with these calamities that no attention is given them after the first announcement through a newspaper or friend.

Job Insecurity

Always looming was the threat of pay cuts or layoffs. Workers were vulnerable to the **business cycle**—a recurring sequence of change in business activity. Beginning with a period of prosperity, business activity declines until a low point, or depression, is reached. A period of recovery follows when business conditions become more active. A period of prosperity is again reached. The cycle is then repeated.

In the late 1800s, business went through many such cycles. During slack periods employers kept their costs down by reducing wages or laying off workers. Millions of people lost their jobs or had their wages slashed during the depressions of 1873, 1882, and 1893. Workers looked to labor unions for protection.

The Revival of Labor Unions

The growth of labor unions during the early 1800s had been halting and sporadic, but conditions during the Civil War spurred the revival of unionism. With hundreds of thousands of workers not available while serving in the army, unions were in a strong position to demand better pay. During the war the number of local unions rose dramatically. To strengthen local unions, labor also began to organize on a national scale.

Problems With Organizing

Labor unions faced serious difficulties in organizing because of the mobility and diversity of the American labor force. Workers who did not "stay hitched," but moved from job to job were difficult to organize.

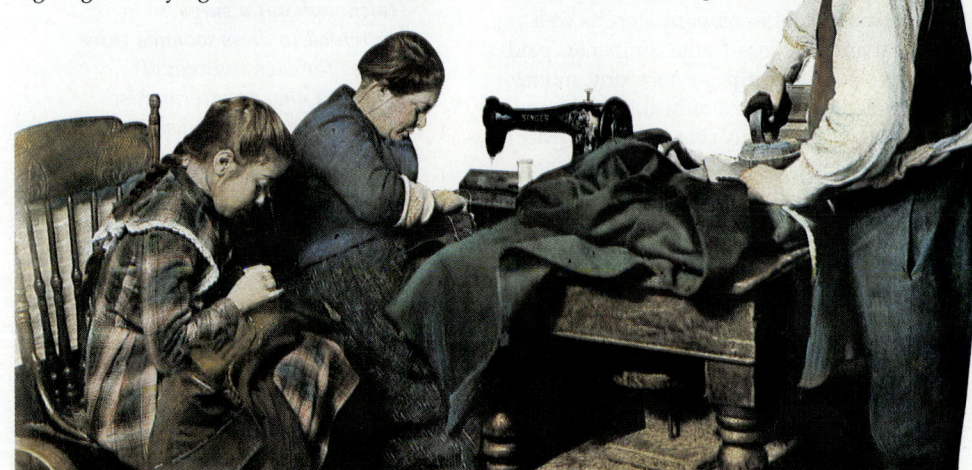

▲ ORGANIZING THE WORKERS Union leaders hoped to improve conditions for workers, such as these immigrants working at home. *What were the difficulties that unions encountered in organizing immigrants?*

 **RAILWAY STRIKE** The railway strike of 1877 resulted in one of the most violent upheavals in the history of American labor. **How did the strike start?**

CHAPTER 19
SECTION 1

Visualizing History During the Railway Strike, one newspaper reported, "It is wrong to call this a strike, it is a labor revolution." **Answer to Caption:** Several railroad companies cut workers' wages.

Did You Know?

Almost one hundred years after the railroad strike of 1877, another group of transportation workers, air traffic controllers, went on strike demanding higher wages and fewer working hours.

Did You Know?

Railroads and locomotives have achieved a special place in American literature, song, and folklore. Emily Dickinson and Walt Whitman could not resist writing about the mighty locomotive. Folk songs like "I Been Working on the Railroad" paid tribute to the building of the road. "Chattanooga Choo-Choo" and "The Atchison, Topeka, and the Santa Fe" were popular tunes that celebrated the railroads themselves. Jelly Roll Morton, the man who supposedly invented jazz, traces the first blues he heard in his mind to the sound of southern railway trains.

The constant influx of large numbers of immigrants—averaging more than one-third of a million a year between 1870 and 1900—also presented a problem. Differences in language, religion, and customs among the immigrants made it hard to unite them into an effective union.

Another problem was that different labor leaders had different goals. Some leaders envisioned uniting all workers into one large union in order to promote widespread reforms. Others believed that unions should be organized by particular crafts or industries and work only for short-term benefits.

Unions also faced strong opposition from employers. Workers were often required to take oaths swearing they would not join a union. If found to have been involved in union activity, a worker would be fired and often could not get another job because of **blacklists,** or records kept by employers of "troublemakers." Once blacklisted a laborer could get a job only by changing residence, trade, or even name. Another way employers retaliated against union organizing in a workplace was the **lockout**—whereby the factory was shut down—or by firing union members and hiring **scabs,** or replacement workers. In any lockout or strike, the odds favored employers. Few unions had enough money to support their members through the long period of unemployment caused by a strike.

Problems With Public Image

Labor unions also had to fight public opinion. Many Americans viewed fixing wages and hours by **collective bargaining**—negation between an employer and a labor union—as violating the right of an individual to deal personally with the employer. Only infrequently did public opinion condemn employers when labor disputes resulted in violence. This happened during the Homestead lockout in 1892 when the Carnegie Steel Company hired a private army of 300 Pinkerton detectives armed with repeating rifles. Generally, however, labor unions were held responsible when disorder occurred.

Another problem for unions was that law enforcement agencies usually sided with the employers. Employers suffered no penalties for lockouts and blacklists. Union strikes and boycotts, on the other hand, were judged to

CHAPTER 19 An Urban Society 1860–1900 **521**

Critical Thinking

Identifying Problems Present the following description by Sadie Frowne from *Plain Folk: The Life Stories of Undistinguished Americans*, and ask students to suggest changes that they think are needed in the condition of the sweatshop.

"The [sewing] machines [are loud and] go like mad all day, because the faster you work the more money you get. Sometimes in my haste I get my finger caught and the needle goes right through it.... I bind the finger up... and go on working. We all have accidents like that.... Sometimes a finger has to come off."
L3

CHAPTER 19
SECTION 1

ASSESS
Check Understanding
Assign Section 1 Review as homework or an in-class activity.

Evaluate
Assign the Section 1 Quiz in the TCR, or use the History of a Free Nation Testmaker to create a customized quiz.

Reteach
Have students complete Reteaching Activity 19-1.

Enrich
Have students complete the Chaper 19 Enrichment Activity in the TCR.

CLOSE
Hold a discussion with students on child labor laws today.

---

be "conspiracies in restraint of trade" for which labor leaders might be jailed or fined. Contracts between employers and unions were not usually enforceable by law. When violence occurred, or was even threatened, the police—and sometimes armed troops—were sent to the aid of employers.

■ Railroad Strike of 1877

Despite these obstacles labor unions survived—sometimes just barely. Membership in the union fluctuated according to business conditions. Following the depression of 1873, 5,000 businesses closed, causing widespread unemployment and homelessness.

Union membership dropped from more than 300,000 to 50,000. Three million workers were unemployed. At this time there were no unemployment or relief benefits available from either the state or federal government. Tramps and hobos roamed the countryside; workers' rallies to demand relief were stopped or suppressed by mounted police.

Labor Responds to Wage Cuts

The hard times of the 1870s reached a climax in the railroad strike of 1877, which shook the nation as no labor conflict in its history had done before. It began when four Eastern railroads cut workers' wages. To protest the cuts, the workers went on strike. As other railroads cut wages, the strike spread to Chicago and beyond.

In city after city, strikers seized and sometimes destroyed railroad property. In Pittsburgh alone the Pennsylvania Railroad lost 2,000 cars, 25 locomotives, 2 roundhouses, and a railroad station. At the height of the strike, more than one-half of the freight on the nation's 76,000 miles of track had stopped running. Troops and workers clashed in the streets of Martinsburg, West Virginia, as well as Pittsburgh and Baltimore. Although the clashes were usually spontaneous, newspapers viewed them collectively as

> " . . . an insurrection, a revolution, an attempt of Communists and vagabonds to coerce society and endeavor to undermine American institutions. "

Management Gains a Costly Victory

In several cities order was restored only after President Rutherford B. Hayes had sent in federal troops. Hayes himself, however, was troubled. He felt railroad officials had brought on the crisis by their own ruthless actions. The President confided in his diary, "Shall the railroads govern the country or shall the people govern the railroads?"

When the railroad strike was over, more than 100 persons were dead, 1,000 had been jailed, and 100,000 workers had gone on strike. In addition there was such fear of violent revolution that state militia were reorganized. National Guard armories were built in many large cities as fortresses, where troops could hold out against strikers if necessary. Union leaders learned from the strike that they were not united or strong enough to defeat the powerful combination of business and government.

Section 1 ★ Review

Checking for Understanding
1. **Identify** 1877 railroad strike.
2. **Define** real wages, company town, scrip, business cycle, blacklist, lockout, scab, collective bargaining.
3. **Discuss** the hardships facing industrial workers during the late 1800s.
4. **Give** examples of problems unions faced once they were organized.

Critical Thinking
5. **Weighing Options**   Imagine that you are an industrial worker in 1870. List the advantages and disadvantages of joining a union.

---

522   UNIT 6 New Horizons: 1860–1900

Answers to SECTION 1 REVIEW

1. 1877 railroad strike, 522
2. All vocabulary words are defined in the Glossary.
3. monotony, low wages, long hours, unhealthful conditions, unemployment
4. lockouts, hiring of strikebreakers, negative siding of law enforcement agencies with employers
5. Answers will vary. Advantages: union will fight for better wages, hours, and conditions; will help during hard times. Disadvantages: poor public opinion about unions, risk employer sanctions such as blacklisting and lockouts.

Social Studies Skills

Study and Writing Skills

Summarizing

Imagine that you have received an expensive camera for your birthday. The instructions are complicated with at least 12 pages describing how to adjust the camera for certain shots. The more you read, the more confused you become. Finally, you discover a *summary* of the main steps, and your confusion disappears.

Summarizing is the process of recapping main ideas by bringing together the major points and excluding the minor ones. Knowing how to summarize is a useful skill for students who have to answer essay questions, take notes, and write research papers.

Read the following material carefully. Then answer the questions that follow.

▲ MOVING ASSEMBLY LINE, HIGHLAND PARK, MICHIGAN

During the late 1800s, the United States, like other modernized nations, was experiencing societal changes brought on by the shift from an agriculture-based economy to one based on industrial production. American life up to this time had been based on a rugged self-determinism, a belief that one should take care of one's self and family. This was largely done through owning and farming land.

To encourage settlement in the frontier, Congress passed laws that provided land to settlers who would cultivate it and pay a fee. Farmers moved west in greater and greater numbers. More land was occupied and improved in the closing years of the 1800s than had been occupied and improved during the first 250 years of American history.

The growth of industry lured many people to the cities and into jobs that required a new set of values. In new industrial centers, such as Pittsburgh and Chicago, there was work available for thousands. People in the industrial labor force faced profound changes in their lives. Often a man did not so much work for his family as he did for his boss. Further, working conditions and pay were often a source of discontent.

Long hours were another burden to workers. During the late 1800s, 65- and 70-hour workweeks were common. Labor unions began to organize, and although their intent was to lend support to exploited employees, it often made workers feel they were helpless to take care of themselves.

Practicing the Skill

1. Locate and list in order of appearance the main ideas expressed in the material.
2. Summarize the text by rewriting the main ideas in your own words.
3. For further practice in this skill, read the material under the subhead "Urbanization" in Section 4 of this chapter. Then, following the guidelines suggested in the example, list the main ideas of the material and write a short summary of the material presented.

LESSON PLAN
Mastering Social Studies Skills

Teaching Study and Writing Skills

Discuss the guidelines for summarizing articles. Ask: What should you do first? (List the main points of the article.) How do you determine what the main points of an article are? (Determine what the article is mostly about.) What parts of an article can you use as clues? (Students should mention these: titles, subheads, highlighted terms, topic sentences.)

You may wish to do the Practice activity as a class. Write the main points on the chalkboard and prepare a summary together. Point out the need for combining ideas in a summary.

Did You Know?

Many bosses forbade singing, drinking, joking, smoking, or conversation on the job. They also denied immigrant workers time to celebrate their national holidays and holy days or to keep the Sunday Sabbath.

Answers to SOCIAL STUDIES SKILLS

1. Main ideas: Between 1860–1900, urban areas grew twice as fast as the total population. Urbanization was related to industrialization. Cities grew through a self-generating process: banks and warehouses were built, and this attracted more industry, which made the cities grow.
2. Summary: Between 1860–1900, American cities grew quite quickly. They grew through a self-generating process by which certain facilities were built that would attract more industry, such as banks, insurance companies, and warehouses. This in turn seemed inviting to other industries, so they would build in a given city. These industries caused more related facilities to be built, and so on.
3. Answers will vary but will include urbanization, problems of city life, and beautifying the city.

LESSON PLAN
SECTION 2, 524–527

FOCUS

Bellringer
Before taking roll at the beginning of the class period, display Focus Activity 63 on the overhead projector, and assign the accompanying Focus Activity Sheet.

Objectives
Point out the objectives on this page to students in previewing the section content.

Motivating Activity
Write the following job description on the chalkboard:

Wanted: Woman to make linings for caps. Hours 8 A.M. to 6 P.M. Pay is 3½ cents to 10 cents a dozen.... Earn an average of $5 a week. Must provide your own machine, which costs $45.

Ask students what they would find objectionable about this job if they had to take it. (low pay, number of working hours per day, having to buy one's own machine) Discuss why women took these jobs in the late 1800s. (It was difficult to make a living, especially for immigrant women who did not speak English well.) Point out that this description was for a job that Rose Schneiderman had around the turn of the century. When her bosses kept reducing women's pay, she left the sweatshop to organize women workers.

SECTION 2

The Rise of New Unions

Setting the Scene

Section Focus
Individually, workers were powerless to change hazardous working conditions, low pay, and long hours. When little was done to improve their lot, workers in growing numbers came to accept the idea of forming new, better-organized unions.

Objectives
After studying this section, you should be able to
★ identify two of the strongest labor unions of the late 1800s.
★ evaluate the gains labor unions achieved during this period.

Key Terms
arbitration, industrial union, injunction

▲ JUDGE'S GAVEL

As industrialization was an urban phenomenon, so too were unions. Those states with the highest percentage of workers in industry had the greatest urban populations. It was in these industrial areas of the North and the Midwest that a score of new labor organizations were established in the late 1860s.

■ The Knights of Labor and the AFL Unions

By far the most influential labor organization was the Noble Order of the Knights of Labor. Founded in 1869 the Knights of Labor attempted to bring all laboring people—skilled and unskilled, black and white, men and women, white-collar and blue-collar—into one big union.

The Desire for Widespread Reform
Terence V. Powderly, an immigrant and a former railway switchtender, led the Knights of Labor after 1879. An eloquent speaker and a tireless organizer, Powderly believed a single, powerful union was the best means of gaining concessions from employers for better working conditions.

Powderly persuaded the Knights to support equal pay for women, temperance, abolition of child labor and, above all, establishment of cooperatively owned industrial plants. A man of peace, he opposed strikes and wished to submit labor disputes to **arbitration**—a process whereby an impartial third party helps workers and management reach an agreement.

Membership in the Knights grew rapidly in the early 1880s—especially after the striking Knights won the dispute against Jay Gould's Wabash Railway. Membership in

---

Classroom Resources for SECTION 2

Teacher's Classroom Resources
- Reproducible Lesson Plan
- Reteaching Activity 19-2
- Chapter 19 Primary and Secondary Source Readings
- Section Quiz

Multimedia
- Section Focus Transparency 63
- Testmaker
- Student Self-Test Software

the Knights soared from 100,000 in 1885 to 700,000 in less than a year. Some newspapers feared that Powderly would become stronger than the President.

The Knights of Labor, however, were soon swamped with troubles. The union had wasted its funds in unsuccessful attempts to set up cooperative businesses. Moreover, the effort to unite different kinds of labor into one big union had failed. Workers in different crafts and industries often had little in common with one another and little interest in working for the same goals.

Haymarket Square Riot

The decline of the Knights was hastened by the Haymarket Square riot in Chicago on May 4, 1886. This event followed a peaceful meeting of some 3,000 workers who gathered together to protest the shooting of striking McCormick Harvester Company workers by the police. As the meeting was breaking up, someone threw a bomb into a group of police officers. Seven persons were killed and more than 60 were injured. Although the identity of the bomb-thrower was never established, 8 anarchist leaders were arrested and found guilty of taking part in the crime. Four were later executed for murder. Although the Knights of Labor could in no way be held responsible for the Haymarket affair, it became identified with radicals and violence. From then on the Knights of Labor declined rapidly.

Foundation of the AFL

In 1886, the year the Knights began to decline, the American Federation of Labor (AFL) was organized. In its principles as well as its structure, the AFL differed greatly from the Knights. While the Knights had accepted a large number of unskilled workers, the AFL accepted only skilled workers. This policy indicated the reluctance of the

▲ **TROUBLE AT THE HAYMARKET** On the night of May 4, 1886, a crowd gathered in Chicago's Haymarket Square to protest police violence. As the meeting was breaking up, a bomb was thrown into a group of police and the police fired into the crowd. **What effect did the Haymarket affair have on the labor movement?**

CHAPTER 19
SECTION 2

Independent Practice

Writing Have students write one paragraph evaluating Pullman Company's treatment of the workers and its attitude toward them. Have them write a second paragraph suggesting what Pullman could have done to avoid cutting off the income of two-thirds of its workers. **L3**

ASSESS

Check Understanding

Assign Section 2 Review as homework or an in-class activity.

Evaluate

Assign the Section 2 Quiz in the TCR, or use the History of a Free Nation Testmaker to create a customized quiz.

Reteach

Divide students into four groups. Have the students in each group work together to write five main idea questions about one of the following: the Knights of Labor, the AFL, the American Railway Union, or the Pullman Company. Collect the questions, and put them in a container. Have students take turns answering the questions.

Have students complete Reteaching Activity 19-2.

AFL to accept women, African Americans, and immigrants—the majority of whom were unskilled—into their union. Also, the AFL organized workers into separate unions, each covering a particular craft.

Each union managed its own affairs with only occasional help from the national organization. The AFL's fees were relatively high, in order to restrict membership, build up strike funds, and provide benefits to members and their families in cases of sickness, unemployment, or death.

The AFL might never have enjoyed the success it did were it not for Samuel Gompers, its president for 37 years. Born in London, Gompers adapted some ideas of British trade unions, the best established in the world. Gompers, who prided himself on being practical, was interested only in day-to-day gains of AFL members—higher wages, shorter hours, and benefits for disabled workers.

So effective was the organization and leadership of the AFL that when hard times hit again in 1893, its member unions not only survived but thrived. Between 1890 and 1900, when other labor organizations lost members, AFL membership rose from 190,000 to 500,000.

■ The Pullman Strike

To address the needs of unskilled and semiskilled labor—and yet avoid the "one big union" approach—a new type of labor organization developed. This was the **industrial union,** in which all classes of workers in a single industry are joined together. Among those who saw the advantages of an industrial union was Eugene V. Debs, an officer of the Brotherhood of Locomotive Firemen, one of several railway unions. He felt that the separation of railway workers into different unions weakened their power. Conductors and engineers, the "aristocracy of labor," looked down on less skilled and lower paid workers, and the unskilled had no organization at all. Debs, therefore, started a new organization in 1893—the American Railway Union. This union included all types of railroad workers—from conductors, firemen, and engineers to telegraph operators and station clerks. By 1894 the American Railway Union was powerful enough to force James J. Hill, the owner of the Great Northern Railway, to restore wage cuts.

Protest Leads to Walkout

Hardly had the Great Northern strike ended than the Pullman strike began in Pullman, Illinois, the company town built by George M. Pullman for his workers. Losing profit because of a reduced demand for its railroad cars, the Pullman Palace Car Company laid off two-thirds of its employees and cut the wages of the rest. It did not, however, reduce either the dividends it paid to stockholders or the rents charged to workers in the town. When a delegation of workers met with Pullman to protest the pay cuts, they were fired. At noon the following day, 10,000 Pullman workers walked off the job.

The American Railway Union took up the Pullman workers' cause. Debs's first move was to propose that the dispute be referred to arbitration. Pullman, however, replied, "There is nothing to arbitrate." Realizing that negotiating with Pullman was futile, the union called for members to refuse to work on any train that included a Pullman car. Railway workers answered

▲ PULLMAN AD

526 UNIT 6 New Horizons: 1860–1900

Cooperative Learning

Organize students into groups of four. Have each group write a skit and role-play the pre-strike negotiations of a company representative, two union workers, and a union representative. The dialogue should reflect the attitudes of the characters and should include the vocabulary in the section. Each group member should write the dialogue for his or her character. Have several groups present their skits. **L2**

 ▲ **THE PULLMAN STRIKE** An economic depression gripped the nation in the 1890s. Layoffs and pay cuts made workers desperate. In the company town of Pullman, Illinois, a strike began that led to a tie-up of the nation's railroad system. **How was the strike broken?**

the union's call. Within 5 days 100,000 railroad workers had walked off the job. Railway traffic west of Chicago was almost paralyzed. Debs warned his followers not to interfere with the mail and appealed to them to be "orderly and law-abiding." A few mail trains were delayed, but there were few disturbances.

Federal Intervention Turns the Tide

Quickly, President Grover Cleveland stepped in. Over protests by the mayor of Chicago and the governor of Illinois, President Cleveland sent federal troops to guard mail trains. Immediately, rioting broke out as angry mobs, sympathetic to the strikers, taunted the soldiers. Members of the American Railway Union kept out of trouble but nevertheless received the blame. Even before the troops had arrived, the federal government obtained an **injunction,** or court order, forbidding the union to continue the strike. Debs refused to obey the injunction and was imprisoned.

Without Debs's leadership, the Pullman strike collapsed and with it the American Railway Union. From that point on, employers used the injunction as a means of breaking up strikes.

Although labor unions lost more disputes than they won, and most workers remained unorganized (only 4 percent of American workers belonged to unions in 1900), workers made some gains in the late 1800s. Federal and state legislation reflected the growing political influence of labor. Wages began to increase slowly, and the workday was shortened. Moreover, nearly every state passed laws regulating working conditions and requiring minimum standards of health and safety.

Section 2 ★ Review

Checking for Understanding

1. **Identify** Knights of Labor, American Federation of Labor, Terence V. Powderly, Samuel Gompers, Eugene Debs.
2. **Define** arbitration, industrial union, injunction.
3. **Summarize** the difficulties faced by the Knights of Labor and the American Railway Union.
4. **Examine** the achievements of labor unions during the late 1800s.

Critical Thinking

5. **Supporting an Opinion** Do you agree with Debs that an industrial union was more powerful than separate unions of craft workers? Why or why not?

LESSON PLAN
SECTION 3, 528–532

FOCUS

Bellringer

Display Focus Activity 64 on the overhead projector, and assign the accompanying Focus Activity Sheet.

Objectives
Point out the objectives on this page in previewing the section content.

Motivating Activity
Use the following videos to introduce immigration in the late 1800s. Or, point out the photograph on page 528 and ask students to discuss what it would be like to move to a country where you cannot speak the language.

NATIONAL GEOGRAPHIC SOCIETY

 VIDEODISC

- *GTV: A Geographic Perspective on American History*

Side 3, Chapter 5
Title: *Making a Mark*
Subject: The impact of immigration, 1870–1910

See GTV Guide page 51 for complete lesson plan.

- *GTV: The American People: Fabric of a Nation*

Side 3, Chapter 1
Title: *The Golden Door*
Subject: The flood of immigration between 1880 and 1920

See GTV Guide page 74 for complete lesson plan.

528

SECTION 3

Patterns of Immigration

Setting the Scene

Section Focus

Between 1860 and 1900 almost 14 million people came to America. Another 14.5 million came between 1900 and 1915. Even more significant than the increase in numbers was the changing character of immigration during these years. The vast majority no longer came from northern and western Europe but from southern and eastern Europe.

Objectives

After studying this section, you should be able to

★ identify the reasons that immigrants came to the United States.

★ distinguish between the "old" and the "new" immigration.

Key Term

pogrom, anarchism

◀ IMMIGRANT MOTHER AND DAUGHTERS, C. 1900

The thirteen colonies had been settled mainly by English settlers. Other settlers from Holland, Sweden, France, Scotland, Ireland, and Germany came later. After 1815, however, increasing numbers of immigrants started to arrive from Ireland. During these early years, a total of only about 400,000 immigrants had come to America. Beginning in the 1850s and continuing after the Civil War, immigration rose sharply.

■ The "Old Immigration"

During the period of "Old Immigration," which started in the 1830s and reached a high point in the 1840s, there was a great wave of immigration to America's shores. Between 1840 and 1850, an additional 1.5 million newcomers journeyed to the United States. Nearly one-half were from Ireland, which was suffering from a potato famine. Between 1846 and 1860, about 1.5 million Irish immigrated to America, settling in New York and Boston, which functioned as ports of entry into the United States.

In the 1840s large numbers of Germans also began to come to America. Some left their homeland because of crop failures. Others came to escape political persecution after the failure of the Revolution of 1848. Still others were German Jews seeking religious freedom. Large numbers of German immigrants settled on farms and in cities in the Midwest—areas that were rapidly growing and had job opportunities. The Germans gave a distinctive flavor to such cities as Cincinnati, Milwaukee, and St. Louis. Then, in the 1850s, after the Gold Rush, Chinese immigrants began to come to the Pacific Coast. Many were hired to help build the railroads. About 100,000 Chinese had settled in the West by the mid-1870s.

528   UNIT 6 New Horizons: 1860–1900

Classroom Resources for SECTION 3

Teacher's Classroom Resources
- Reproducible Lesson Plan
- Reteaching Activity 19-3
- Chapter 19 Primary and Secondary Source Readings
- Section Quiz

Multimedia
- Section Focus Transparency 64
- Chapter 19 Map Transparency
- Testmaker
- Student Self-Test Software
- The American People: Fabric of a Nation
- A Geographic Perspective on American History

During the colonial period, most immigrants were readily accepted. Workers were badly needed in all the colonies.

European agents of railroad companies and steamship lines described America as a land where riches could be had almost for the asking. Perhaps the most persuasive arguments for others to come to this country were the "America letters" written by recent immigrants to their family and friends. "If you wish to be happy and independent, then come here," wrote a German farmer from his new home in Missouri. In the 1840s and 1850s, however, some native-born Americans began to resent the newcomers, especially the Irish immigrants. Some Americans resented them because they dressed and sounded "different" and because they were Catholics.

The "New Immigration"

Until the 1880s most newcomers had come from the nations of western Europe. After 1885, however, large numbers came from nations of southern and eastern Europe. The new immigrants were from Italy, Russia, and Poland as well as from the nations of the Austro-Hungarian Empire.

Italians were one of the largest groups of new immigrants. Many came from Sicily and the southern part of Italy. People in this region faced economic misfortune. Unemployment and overpopulation made existence perilous. As a result, millions of Italian Catholics chose to go to America.

Eastern European Jews were another sizeable group of new immigrants. Although scattered throughout many countries, the

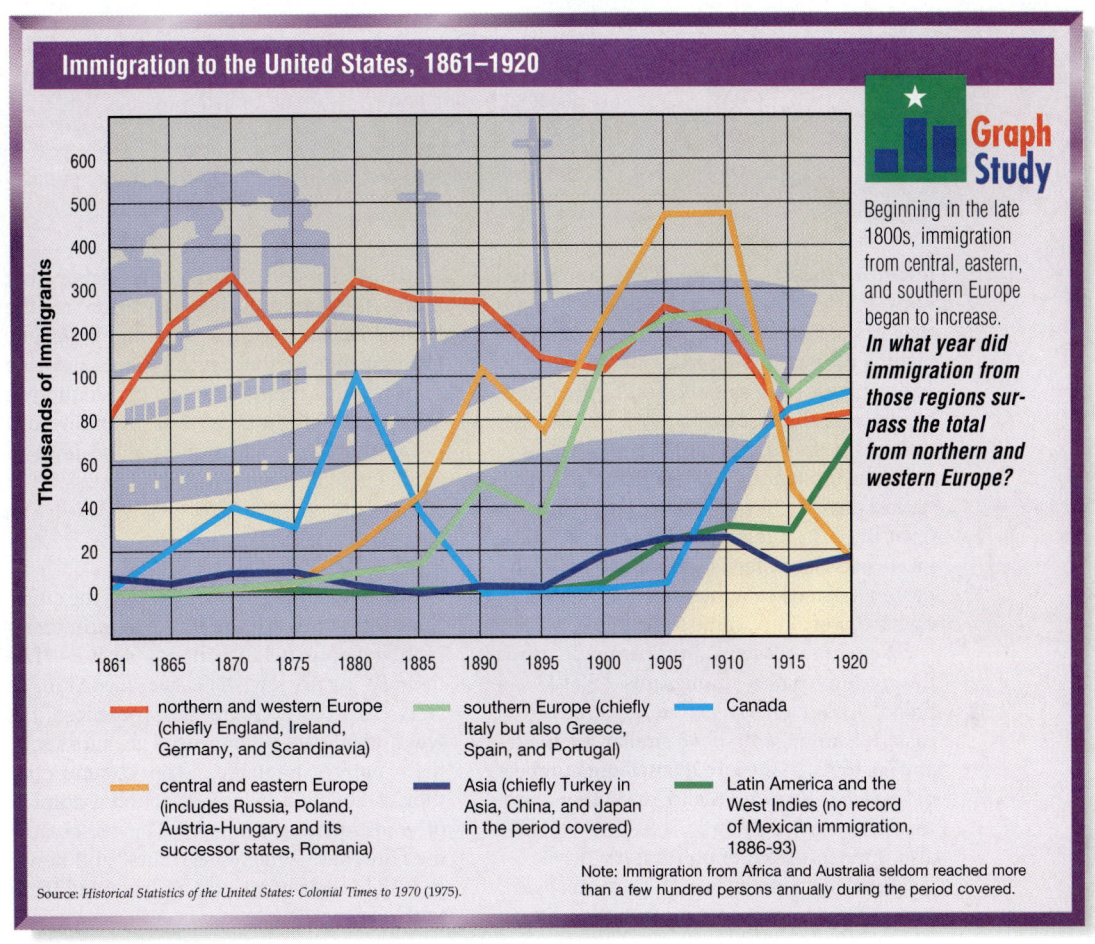

Immigration to the United States, 1861–1920

 Graph Study

Beginning in the late 1800s, immigration from central, eastern, and southern Europe began to increase. **In what year did immigration from those regions surpass the total from northern and western Europe?**

- northern and western Europe (chiefly England, Ireland, Germany, and Scandinavia)
- central and eastern Europe (includes Russia, Poland, Austria-Hungary and its successor states, Romania)
- southern Europe (chiefly Italy but also Greece, Spain, and Portugal)
- Asia (chiefly Turkey in Asia, China, and Japan in the period covered)
- Canada
- Latin America and the West Indies (no record of Mexican immigration, 1886-93)

Note: Immigration from Africa and Australia seldom reached more than a few hundred persons annually during the period covered.

Source: *Historical Statistics of the United States: Colonial Times to 1970* (1975).

CHAPTER 19 An Urban Society 1860–1900

CHAPTER 19 SECTION 3

Independent Practice
Conducting an Interview
Have students interview a relative, friend, or acquaintance who immigrated to the United States. Have them find out where the person came from, why the person emigrated, what adjustment problems the person experienced, and what humorous misunderstandings may have occurred because of difficulties with English. **L1**

Did You Know?
Since immigrants from northern Europe had more access to education, Lodge concluded that a literacy test would "bear most heavily upon the Italians, Russians, Poles, Hungarians, Greeks, and Asiatics."

Teaching Life of the Times
According to popular belief, pasta was introduced into Italy by Marco Polo, who brought it back from China. Fifty years before Marco Polo even left for China, however, both the Indians and the Arabs were already eating noodles. Since the Arabs were important traders in Venice during the Middle Ages, it is possible that pasta came to Italy via the Arab lands rather than China.

Discuss food as an important aspect of a national culture.

Life of the Times

Italian Cuisine

Between 1890 and 1910 about 2.7 million southern Italians immigrated to the United States. Coming from farms in Italy, they settled primarily in the cities on America's East Coast. By 1920 New York City had become home to more Italians than there were living in Venice, Genoa, and Florence combined. Italian Americans adjusted to many changes in their adopted country, and they adapted their cooking to substitute some more readily available ingredients.

Italian dishes became a lasting contribution to American culture. Pasta was enjoyed by everyone, sometimes several times a week. Macaroni, manicotti, spaghetti, and lasagna were first introduced to Americans by the little shops nestled among the blocks of tenements.

Italian bakery ovens produced the first pizzas, which had been a strictly Neapolitan item back in Italy. Opening in 1905, "G Lombardi" on Spring Street in New York's Little Italy became the first known pizzeria in the United States. Deep-dish, Chicago-style pizza, cooked in a black skillet, did not come along until 1943, when it was created by Ike Sewell and Ric Riccardo at Pizzeria Uno in Chicago. After World War II, the pizza industry boomed in the United States.

Jews of eastern Europe were confronted with many common problems wherever they lived. For one thing they were often the victims of religious discrimination. In many regions Jews were not allowed to own land, work in certain trades, or move out of areas that had been set aside for them.

These limitations on Jews created widespread poverty. In addition eastern European Jews lived in danger of **pogroms,** or organized massacres. Jewish immigrants seeking personal safety, religious freedom, and economic opportunity, came to America.

Slavs from eastern Europe made up a third group of new immigrants. "Slavs" is a broad label given to a people, generally from eastern Europe, who have similar languages and customs. In the late 1800s, large numbers of Slavs left Russia, Poland, and other countries to escape economic woes. Many Slavs also came in search of political freedom.

These newcomers were, for the most part, poor. They hoped to find a better life in America. In part it was their labor that made the rapid industrialization of the United States possible. For many people, immigrating to the United States was the only way for them to escape persecution in their homeland. One Jewish immigrant noted that "the only hope for the Jews in Russia is to become Jews out of Russia."

Ethnic Neighborhoods

The new immigrants flocked to the cities. There they lived together in ethnically homogeneous neighborhoods such as "Little Italy" or the Jewish "Lower East Side" in New York City. There they practiced the ways of life they were used to and spoke their native languages. The communities they established revolved around a number of traditional institutions. They re-created the churches, synagogues, clubs, and newspapers of their homeland and adapted them to their new environment.

Cooperative Learning
Organize students into groups of four to research immigrants in their area. Have each group choose a member who will represent them at meetings. The group representatives should plan together what nationality groups they want to study, what information they want to gather, and how information is to be presented. Students could tape and write first-person accounts of the immigrants' experiences, research what important immigrants are associated with their area, and provide cultural data on the immigrants. **L2**

Public Resentment

This huge influx of immigrants created special social problems. Because immigrants lived in their own neighborhoods, practiced their own customs, and spoke their own languages, many Americans wondered if they could ever be assimilated into American life. Some people, especially workers, blamed them for low wages. Others resented that many immigrants were Catholics or Jews.

The railroad strike of 1877 and the Haymarket Square riot of 1886 resulted in many people's fear of immigrants who, it was thought, believed in socialism or even **anarchism**, a belief in no direct government authority over society. A few politicians, notably Senator Henry Cabot Lodge of Massachusetts, were strongly reactionary in their response to the issue of immigration. They wanted immigration from southern and eastern Europe to be stopped completely. In 1896 Lodge argued for a bill that would exclude all prospective immigrants who could not read or write 25 words of the United States Constitution in some language. Lodge concluded that such a test would

> ... bear most heavily upon the Italians, Russians, Poles, Hungarians, Greeks, and Asiatics ... races most affected by the test are those who[m] emigration has ... swelled rapidly ... and who are most alien to the great body of the United States.

In the late 1800s, hostility grew toward many of the new racial and ethnic groups coming into the new country. The differences in customs, dress, and language of the new arrivals created a basic distrust of the foreign born by many native-born Americans. Some historians believe that this reaction was a response to the rapid changes occurring in America because of industrialization. For those native-born Americans who were uncertain and disturbed by social change, immigrants became easy targets of hostility.

Organized Opposition

Some Americans formed groups to counter what they considered the immigrant threat. One of these groups, the American Protective Association, was founded in

 ▲ **THE NEW IMMIGRANTS** During the late 1800s, new immigrants poured into the United States, braving the long and difficult journey to start a new life. *Why did many people view these newcomers as a threat?*

CHAPTER 19 An Urban Society 1860–1900

Cultural Diversity

In the late 1800s, people from other countries in the Americas could enter and leave the United States without passports whenever they wished. All they had to do was report their name, place of birth, and destination to an immigration officer. In fact, entry was even easier. Mexicans and Canadians could simply walk across the border, and many did so every day.

CHAPTER 19 SECTION 3

VIDEODISC

• *GTV: The American People: Fabric of a Nation*

Side 3, Chapter 4
Title: *Generation Gap*
Subject: The immigration experience—for kids

See GTV Guide page 80 for complete lesson plan.

Today, the flow of immigrants to America is higher than in any decade since 1900–1910. Six hundred thousand immigrants arrive yearly. Like those of the late 1800s and early 1900s, today's immigrants also come to escape oppression or to make a better life for themselves and their children.

Visualizing History Discuss the kinds of jobs open to newly arrived immigrants unable to speak English. **Answer to Caption:** They feared the new immigrants would take away their jobs. They also were suspicious of the immigrants' culture and customs.

CHAPTER 19
SECTION 3

ASSESS
Check Understanding
Assign Section 3 Review as homework or an in-class activity.

Evaluate
📁 💿 Assign the Section 3 Quiz in the TCR, or use the History of a Free Nation Testmaker to create a customized quiz.

Reteach
📁 Have students complete Reteaching Activity 19-3.

Enrich
Have students research and write a report on Ellis Island that gives such information as how long the island was used, which immigrants passed through the port, and what procedures were followed. Resource: *Ellis Island: Echoes from a Nation's Past,* edited by Susan Jones.

CLOSE
Discuss why new immigrants often experience discrimination in the United States. Have students discuss why some people resent foreigners.

1887 to protest the large number of Catholic immigrants. In some parts of the country, local laws were passed that prohibited immigrants from holding certain kinds of jobs and denied them other rights. Jewish immigrants, for example, were denied admission to some universities. In addition the immigrants faced actual physical attacks.

The anti-immigration movement was not limited to groups such as the American Protective Association. Some well-known scholars of the time were susceptible to these feelings as well. Historian and future President Woodrow Wilson and frontier historian Frederick Jackson Turner lamented the lessening flow of immigration from northern Europe and the rise in numbers of "inferior stocks" coming to America. One writer considered the new immigration a plot by European governments to "unload the sweepings of their jails and asylums."

Anti-Chinese Sentiment

Public resentment was not limited to newcomers from Europe, however. The Chinese, too, suffered discrimination on the Pacific Coast. The discovery of gold in 1849 and the subsequent demand for cheap labor first brought the Chinese to California. Many found work in the gold fields or on the construction of the Central Pacific Railroad. By 1852 there were some 25,000 Chinese men, women, and children living on the Pacific Coast and thereafter they came at the rate of 4,000 a year. By the end of the 1870s, there were almost 75,000 Chinese in California alone. Their willingness to work for low wages prompted a violent anti-Chinese movement among the white workers of California. Such feelings intensified during hard economic times. During the depression that followed the Panic of 1873, unemployed workers in California attacked the Chinese. Some Americans began to demand that Chinese immigrants be excluded from the United States.

In 1879 Congress forbade the importing of foreign workers under contract—a law aimed primarily at the Chinese. Then, in 1882, Congress, responding to pressure from the western states, suspended nearly all immigration from China for 10 years.

▼ CHINESE AMERICAN CHILDREN

Section 3 ★ Review

Checking for Understanding
1. **Identify** Henry Cabot Lodge.
2. **Define** pogrom, anarchism.
3. **Explain** why people migrated from Europe to the United States.
4. **Differentiate** the "Old Immigration" from the "New Immigration."

Critical Thinking
5. **Understanding Bias** Throughout history people suffering hardship have found "scapegoats" on whom to blame their troubles. Explain why immigrants were chosen as scapegoats by native-born residents during the 1800s.

532 UNIT 6 New Horizons: 1860–1900

Answers to SECTION 3 REVIEW

1. Henry Cabot Lodge, 531
2. All vocabulary words are defined in the Glossary.
3. Reasons for immigration include crop failures in homeland, escape from religious and political persecution, search for a better life.
4. "Old Immigration" came from northern and western Europe and lasted up until 1885. "New Immigration" began after 1885 and came from southern and eastern Europe.
5. Immigrants were different, relatively powerless, and easily identifiable.

SECTION 4

City Life and Problems

Setting the Scene

Section Focus

With the rise of industrialism, the landscape of the nation changed. Railroads crisscrossed the continent. Where farms once stood, factories spewed forth black smoke. Thousands of Americans left the nation's farms hoping to make their fortunes in the city. Millions of immigrants came to better their lives and share in the benefits of the new industrial age.

Objectives

After studying this section, you should be able to

★ identify the factors that led to the growth of cities during the late 1800s.

★ list the problems resulting from an increase in the urban population.

Key Term

merchandising

◀ BOOK ON URBAN LIFE BY JACOB RIIS

All over the nation—but especially in the Northeast—cities were growing rapidly. This urban growth was a result of industrialization. In 1840, 1 out of every 12 Americans lived in a city with a population of more than 8,000. By 1900, however, 1 out of every 3 Americans lived in a large city.

Why were so many people attracted to the cities? One reason was that rising new industries held out the promise of jobs and opportunity. Where else could immigrants—or other Americans, for that matter—fulfill the "rags to riches" dream of making a fortune overnight? The cities of the 1890s held the promise of excitement and activity, in contrast to the isolation of rural farm life. There was running water, modern plumbing, museums, libraries, theaters, shops, convenient transportation, and countless things to see and do.

■ Urbanization

Between 1860 and 1900 American urban areas grew twice as fast as the total population. Chicago, which in the 1830s had been a frontier town with a few hundred residents, became a vast metropolis of almost 2 million people. New York became the second-largest city in the world. During the same span of years, Philadelphia grew from less than 600,000 people to about 1.3 million. Both Boston's and Baltimore's populations increased from about 200,000 to more than one-half million.

Industrial cities were essentially the product of mines, factories, steamships, and railroads. New cities appeared, or old ones mushroomed, near coal and iron deposits (Birmingham, Alabama, and Pittsburgh), sources of water power (Lowell and Lawrence, Massachusetts), shipping centers

CHAPTER 19 An Urban Society 1860–1900   **533**

LESSON PLAN
SECTION 4, 533–539

FOCUS

Bellringer
Before taking roll at the beginning of the class period, display Focus Activity 65 on the overhead projector, and assign the accompanying Focus Activity Sheet.

Objectives
Point out the objectives on this page to students in previewing the section content.

Motivating Activity
Tell students that between 1850 and 1901 New York City's growth was 460 percent and Chicago's 5,500 percent. Ask them to speculate what problems such rapid growth might have created. (example answer: overcrowding and unhealthy living conditions, overcrowded schools, an inadequate sewer system, inadequate fire protection)

 VIDEODISC

• *GTV: The American People: Fabric of a Nation*

Side 3, Chapter 3
Title: Home Sweet Home?
Subject: The urban immigration experience

See GTV Guide page 78 for complete lesson plan.

Classroom Resources for SECTION 4

Teacher's Classroom Resources
- Reproducible Lesson Plan
- Reteaching Activity 19-4
- Chapter 19 Enrichment Activity
- Chapter 19 Performance Assessment Activity
- Spanish Summaries and Glossary
- Section Quiz

Multimedia
- Section Focus Transparency 65
- Chapter 19 Map Transparency
- Vocabulary Puzzlemaker
- Testmaker
- Student Self-Test Software
- The American People: Fabric of a Nation
- A Geographic Perspective on American History

533

CHAPTER 19 SECTION 4

TEACH

Guided Practice
Constructing an Outline Provide the following outline:

City Life and Problems
I. Factors that led to the growth of cities
II. Problems caused by rapid urbanization
III. Needs of urban dwellers

Divide the class into groups of three. Have each group list subtopics and details for the main topics listed. **L2**

Teaching American Portraits
Jane Addams's (1860–1935) goal in establishing the Hull-House was to "share the lives of the poor" and to humanize the city. She believed strongly in the importance of education and had the Hull-House staff teach classes in everything from beginning English to cooking to the history of art.

 **VIDEODISC**

- *GTV: A Geographic Perspective on American History*

Side 3, Chapter 10
Title: *A New Life*
Subject: Migration from rural to urban areas, 1890–1920

See GTV Guide page 53 for complete lesson plan.

Jane Addams
1860–1935

AMERICAN PORTRAITS

By the time the guns of World War I began blazing in 1914, Jane Addams was already famous as the founder of Hull House—the settlement house that served Chicago's immigrants and urban poor. By then peace had become her passion.

In 1915 Addams urged European leaders to find a way to end the mounting carnage. When the United States entered the war, she was labeled unpatriotic for holding true to her pacifist ideals. After the war ended in 1918, Addams worked to ensure no repetition of the "war to end all wars."

Addams was elected president of the Women's International League for Peace and Freedom in 1915 and held that office until 1929. Her devotion to world peace was recognized in 1931 when she was named corecipient, with educator Nicholas Murray Butler, of the Nobel Peace Prize.

(Baltimore and New York City), and at railroad centers (Omaha and Chicago). Industrial cities, especially in the Northeast, had the greatest growth, but cities in all regions experienced rapid growth. Between 1860 and 1900, Nashville grew from 16,000 to more than 80,000, Minneapolis from 2,500 to more than 200,000, and Los Angeles from 4,000 to more than 100,000.

Once established, cities seemed to generate their own growth. To serve industry such facilities as banks, insurance companies, docks, and warehouses developed. These, in turn, attracted more industry and workers. Immigrants could often find employment only in urban industrialized areas. Yet an even greater number of new workers came from rural areas of the United States.

■ Problems of City Life

The modern industrial city confronted many people with an unfamiliar and often unattractive environment. The new cities were built with less concern for the comforts of the inhabitants than for the profits of builders and real-estate speculators. People poured into the cities faster than housing could be built to accommodate them. Many had no choice but to live in tenements, poorly constructed and cramped five- or six-story buildings, which housed many families. Many of the rooms and tenements had no windows and were often dark, narrow, and airless.

As more and more people were crowded together and the buildings began to deteriorate, city slums developed. Lacking proper sanitation, tenements became foul-smelling and vermin-infested. Typhoid and other diseases often spread rapidly.

Lack of Social Services

Besides inadequate housing, there was a shortage of police and firefighters. City water was impure and sewers were often clogged. Garbage collection was sporadic. In addition there were no attempts at city planning. Little was done to provide for open spaces, parks, and playgrounds or to take advantage of rivers and other natural features. The few open spaces were often used as garbage dumps or left vacant with a scanty growth of grass and weeds competing with cinders and tin cans.

Rivers and harbors were polluted by sewage and factory wastes, and the air was

---

Special Needs

Writing Disability Some students with writing disabilities feel most comfortable when they are permitted to tape lectures and discussions. This helps bypass the writing problem but creates another problem—time needed to review the lecture and sift through information. This process can be made more efficient if students are cued by the teacher as to when to turn on the recorder for new information. As you discuss the problems resulting from urban population increases, use a prearranged cuing system to help students record appropriate parts of the discussion. **L1, LEP**

fouled by smoke from thousands of chimneys. The new environment cut off people from sun, air, and natural beauty.

New Concerns Arise

The growth of cities created a demand for new sources of water because wells and brooks provided too scanty a supply and were often polluted. New York City, the first of the major cities to meet this problem head-on, built the Croton Aqueduct 25 miles outside the city limits.

Cities also had to come up with more efficient means of intercity transportation. This was accomplished by the horse car and later by the elevated railway, the trolley car, and the subway. The demand for space in preferred localities such as Wall Street in New York or the Loop in Chicago resulted in the creation of huge skyscrapers, which, in turn, added a vertical dimension to transportation—in the form of the elevator.

Rise in Crime

An unexpected problem of urban life, however, was the increase in crime. There had always been occasional violence and theft, but never on a scale demanding an organized police force. There had been nothing resembling modern police until the formation of the Metropolitan Police of London, known as "bobbies," around 1830.

Because the problems experienced by growing urban centers were new, old solutions could not be relied upon. It seemed as if the answers were as varied as the problems. Some people looked back to an earlier morality and sought to enforce the Puritan Sabbath as a means of regenerating the city. As a result restaurants and amusement places were closed. There were even efforts to forbid the running of trains and streetcars.

Public Awareness Spurs Legislation

One who faced the realities of life in factories, shops, and slums was Jacob A. Riis (REES), a Danish-American police reporter for New York newspapers. In the course of his work, Riis had seen again and again the connection between slums and human degradation. In 1890 he focused public attention on the problem in a best-selling book, *How the Other Half Lives*. By appealing to public conscience, Riis secured legislation that reduced the worst slum conditions, along with other measures that improved

Visualizing History ▲ **URBAN PROBLEMS** Poverty and overcrowding brought on many social problems in large cities throughout the United States. *What problems did residents of tenements in the nation's larger cities face?*

CHAPTER 19 An Urban Society 1860–1900

Sidelights: Tenements

According to Jacob Riis, 1,500,000 people were living in 43,000 tenements in New York City in the 1890s. Tenements were large residences in once-respectable neighborhoods that had been abandoned by their owners and were subdivided for use by several families rather than one. Dividing often led to the shutting off of some levels from other levels, making the use of water and plumbing unavailable to some tenants and dividing rooms into windowless areas. When landlords ran out of residences to subdivide, they built flimsy housing with an eye to heavy use and low maintenance.

CHAPTER 19 SECTION 4

Visualizing History Electric street railways were introduced in 1888. New York City installed its first elevated train in 1870. Have students identify these and other innovations in the illustration. Discuss how these innovations affected people's lives.
Answer to Caption: Cities are drab and ugly, with no concern for recreation.

Fact or Fiction?
One of the greatest problems of cities in the late 1800s was fire.

FACT: Buildings were usually constructed of wood and were erected with little space between them. These factors were a major reason why Pittsburgh, San Francisco, Boston, and Chicago all had devastating fires.

Did You Know?
Frederick L. Olmsted also laid out the estate grounds for George W. Vanderbilt in Asheville, North Carolina. Known as Biltmore Estates, it consists of over 11,000 acres and to this day is one of America's horticultural showplaces.

Visualizing History ▲ **A Nation of Cities** As the United States became a nation of cities, public services expanded to serve the needs of the people. Paved roads, electric street lights, and streetcars improved transportation. **What did critics say about the appearance of cities?**

the lives of city dwellers, such as playgrounds for schools. Among his close friends was a rising young Republican politician, Theodore Roosevelt, whom he "educated" by taking him into tenements, sweatshops, and jails.

Settlement Houses Assist Communities

The year before *How the Other Half Lives* was published, Jane Addams founded, in a Chicago slum, the most famous settlement house in the United States, Hull House. About this neighborhood, Addams wrote:

> [T]he streets were inexpressibly dirty . . . the street lighting bad. . . . Many houses have no water save the faucet in the back yard; there are no fire escapes. . . .

Addams, a deeply religious woman, was inspired by a passionate desire to put her faith to work. Modeling her endeavor on Toynbee Hall, a settlement house in England, Jane Addams was determined to improve the life of the "other half." Hull House soon had activities as varied as an art gallery and a gymnasium as well as hot lunches for factory workers and classes in English. Above all Addams was interested in helping children, believing that "a fence at the top of a precipice is better than an ambulance at the bottom." Addams surrounded herself with young people who were glad to enlist in a war against human suffering.

Similar convictions were the motivating forces behind the founding of other settlement houses, including the Henry Street Settlement in New York City, the Santa Maria Institute in Cincinnati, and the South End House in Boston. In addition to providing immediate services to neighborhood people, settlement houses were schools where hundreds of men and women learned social responsibility.

Many of these people later helped to promote reform legislation, either as political lobbyists or officeholders. "Graduates" of Hull House, for example, were instrumental in securing the first playgrounds in Chicago,

UNIT 6 New Horizons: 1860–1900

Critical Thinking

Interpreting Primary Sources Have students obtain a copy of Jacob A. Riis's book *How the Other Half Lives* and investigate the legislation that Riis secured in order to improve slum conditions. Have them research how he went about securing this legislation. Ask students to present their findings as if they were asking Congress to pass a law to protect urban dwellers. **L3**

better garbage collection, and the first Illinois factory inspection law. Frances Perkins, trained in a New York settlement house, embarked on a political career that led to her appointment as secretary of labor, the first woman to serve on a presidential cabinet.

Beautifying the City

Among the indictments against sprawling industrial cities were their ugliness and their lack of provision for rest and recreation. Architects and landscape designers were among those who sought remedies.

Public Buildings and Open Spaces

In 1876 New York City opened Central Park, designed by Frederick L. Olmsted and Calvert Vaux, as "a great breathing space for the toiling masses." Olmstead was the first person to use the term *landscape architect* as the name of this kind of work. Olmsted also designed Prospect Park in Brooklyn. Many other cities followed New York's example. In 1892 and 1893 Chicago hosted a World's Fair on fairgrounds designed by Olmsted, with buildings in the classical style surrounded by lagoons and landscaped grassy areas.

The Chicago World's Fair revealed that American architecture was dynamic and original. The best architects now thoroughly understood European styles and adapted them for modern use. The firm of McKim, Mead, and White used the Italian Renaissance style in their design for the Boston Public Library. Henry Richardson adapted Romanesque style in his design for churches, libraries, warehouses, and even department stores.

New Functional Architecture

The Transportation Building at the Chicago Fair, designed by Louis Sullivan, however, was based on a new concept: form follows function. Sullivan believed an architect should create designs that reveal a building's purpose and method of construction. He was one of the first architects to design skyscrapers. His influence, both directly and later through the work of his pupil Frank Lloyd Wright, reached worldwide.

The finest example of a structure in which form expressed function was the Brooklyn Bridge. Completed in 1883, 16 years after it was begun, it was the largest suspension bridge in the world at that time. Hung from great steel cables with a span half again as long as that of any previous bridge, it was designed and constructed by two German Americans, John Roebling and his son Washington Roebling. During the project, John was killed on the job. His son continued directing the work until he himself was injured. The work was then taken over by John's wife who, with her son's direction, completed the project.

Public Libraries

For those who wished to continue their education, American cities provided opportunities that had never existed before. In 1876 the American Library Association was founded to encourage "the best reading for the largest number at the least expense." By 1900 the public libraries, which receive support from taxes, revenues, and private donations, came to be recognized as "no less important than the schoolhouse in the system of popular education."

Downtown Shopping Districts

New means of **merchandising,** or the buying and selling of goods, were created to meet the growing needs of urban populations. One striking example was the department store. Stores such as A. T. Stewart and John Wanamaker were retail centers where nearly all kinds of goods were sold in one location. These stores had an enormous appeal to people of all classes. As a

▶ Flatiron Building, New York City

William Le Baron Jenney designed the first metal-framed skyscraper—a 10-story building erected in Chicago in 1884–1885. By 1931, the Empire State Building dwarfed all other buildings in the world at 102 stories. Today the world's tallest building is the Sears Tower in Chicago. It is 1454 feet high and has 110 stories.

Did You Know?

During construction of the Brooklyn Bridge, John Roebling was killed on the job. His son continued directing the work until he was injured. The work was then taken over by John's wife, who completed the project with her son's direction.

Sidelights: City Planning

When Chicago burned to the ground in 1871, it was both a curse and a blessing. The curse was that most of the city was destroyed; the blessing was that it could be rebuilt with wide straight streets and modern buildings that would serve people better in the next century. Daniel Burnham, one of the architects who gave Chicago the skyscraper, emphasized modern parks, residential areas, and an efficient transportation system in his "Plan of Chicago," which he presented in 1904. Much of his plan was implemented, making Chicago one of the greenest cities today.

CHAPTER 19 SECTION 4

ASSESS

Check Understanding
Assign Section 4 Review as homework or an in-class activity.

Evaluate
Assign the Section 4 Quiz in the TCR, or use the History of a Free Nation Testmaker to create a customized quiz.

Reteach
Have students work in groups to describe the problems of living in a large city from the viewpoint of one of the following: a recent immigrant, a police officer, Louis Sullivan, Jane Addams, or Jacob Riis.

Have students complete Reteaching Activity 19-4.

Enrich
Have students research the "dumbbell tenements" in the library. Have them find out how and why they were built and why they were so terrible to live in. Have volunteers share their findings with the class.

CLOSE
Have students give reasons why the sentiments expressed in the quotation by Jacqueline Shaw Lowell that ends this chapter are still valid today.

---

result the downtown areas of cities became centers where people came to shop. Merchants who wanted this new business were active in making sure that the areas were kept clean and attractive. New streets, sidewalks, and buildings were constructed.

Despite some setbacks, citizens made progress solving some of the problems facing the major cities. The availability of electricity enabled shops and factories to remain open after dark and thus stimulated urban nightlife as well.

Efforts by Municipal Governments

Throughout the late 1800s, city governments turned their efforts toward providing the services needed for their citizens. Steps were taken by city leaders to reduce crime, to improve recreational opportunities and living conditions, and to solve some of the public health problems that accompanied the rapid growth of the cities. Methods of identifying criminals, such as the use of photographs, were improved. Electric streetlights added a large measure of safety on city streets.

Many parks were built, usually toward the edges of already congested cities. Public utilities provided electricity, clean water, and sewage services for many urban areas. By 1898 approximately 350 communities had built publicly owned electric light companies, and by 1900 more than 3,500 public waterworks had been constructed nationwide.

The need for better communication spurred the use of a new innovation, the telephone. Within a few years after the telephone was invented in 1876, telephone exchanges were established in more than 80 cities. Within 20 years nearly 800,000 telephones were in use throughout the United States, twice as many as were in use in Europe. The impact of the telephone upon American life was enormous, linking many of the urban and rural areas of the nation almost instantly.

Despite these changes for the better, many social reformers felt that this was only a start. They contended that it was essential to find solutions for problems before the problems ever occurred. More and more reformers urged government to deal with the causes of social and economic problems. Jacqueline Shaw Lowell, the founder of the New York Charity Organization Society, expressed this attitude about the city's problems when she noted:

> [There are] five hundred thousand wage earners in this city, 200,000 of them women, and 75,000 of those working under dreadful conditions. . . . If the working people had all they ought to have, we should not have the paupers and the criminals. . . . It is better to save them before they go under than to spend your life . . . taking care of them afterwards.

Section 4 ★ Review

Checking for Understanding

1. **Identify** Jacob A. Riis, Jane Addams, Louis Sullivan.
2. **Define** merchandising.
3. **List** the factors that led to the growth of cities during the late 1800s and summarize the problems that developed as the population grew.
4. **Describe** the efforts made to improve life and conditions in the cities.

Critical Thinking

5. **Understanding Analogies** How does Jane Addams's theory that "a fence at the top of a precipice is better than an ambulance at the bottom" explain her focus on children?

538 UNIT 6 New Horizons: 1860–1900

Answers to SECTION 4 REVIEW

1. Jacob A. Riis, 535; Jane Addams, 534; Louis Sullivan, 537
2. All vocabulary words are defined in the Glossary.
3. new industries, jobs and opportunities, amenities of city life, excitement and activities, immigration, migration from rural areas
4. aqueducts, better transportation, police departments, legislation, playgrounds, settlement houses, parks, architectural buildings, libraries, department stores
5. Answers will vary. She wants to help children develop so they stay out of trouble rather than help them out of trouble as adults.

CONNECTIONS  CONNECTIONS

Urban Pollution and Public Health

Citizens who complain about air pollution, poor water quality, and inadequate garbage disposal in modern cities might feel at home if transported to the New York City of 1866. A report on the sanitary conditions of the city in that year identified the following problems. (1) filthy streets; (2) neglected garbage and domestic refuse; (3) obstructed and faulty sewers and drains; (4) neglected privies and stables; (5) cattle pens and large stables in the more populous districts; (6) neglected and filthy markets; (7) slaughterhouses and hide and fat depots in close proximity to populous streets; (8) droves of cattle and swine in crowded streets; (9) swill-milk stables; . . . (10) bone boiling, fat melting . . . within the city limits; (11) . . . offensive exhalations . . . in gas manufacture; . . . (12) . . . dumping grounds and manure yards in vicinity of populous streets; (13) . . . management of refuse and junk materials; . . . (14) overcrowding of . . . public conveyances; . . . (15) neglect of dead animals in the streets and gutters of the city.

Such urban problems were not new. Examples can be found even in ancient times. Many cities, having become centers for trade, government, and religion, were large and crowded. Some historians place Rome's population at more than 1 million by the start of the first century A.D. Within 100 years overcrowding resulted in many of Rome's citizens living in apartment houses. Some apartments were 5 or 6 stories high and sheltered about 200 people each. Many of the cities' residential structures were flimsy and poorly constructed, and living conditions paralleled those in the impoverished sections of nineteenth-century New York.

The living conditions of the urban poor left a great deal to be desired. Life in the crowded tenements was hazardous at best. Fires were an ever-present threat. In the late 1800s, the amount of damage from urban fires was on the rise.

▲ CITY STOREFRONT, C. 1910

Much of Chicago's downtown area burned in 1871, and two years later Boston experienced a devastating fire.

Another threat was illness. One reason for this was poor diet. Another was unsanitary conditions. Most tenement houses had neither indoor plumbing nor good ventilation.

Making the Environment Connection

1. Categorize the pollution problems under air, soil, and water.
2. Why do you think the speed of urban growth contributes to environmental problems?

Linking Past and Present

3. Which of these problems are unlikely to occur in modern cities?

CHAPTER 19 CONNECTIONS

Teaching Making Connections

Point out that modern-day cities have additional pollution problems that were nonexistent in the late 1800s—noise pollution and visual pollution. Ask students to give examples of each. (noise: airplanes, rock bands, jackhammers; visual: graffiti, neon signs, roadside billboards)

 VIDEODISC

- *GTV: A Geographic Perspective on American History*

Side 3, Chapter 12
Title: *The Price of Progress*
Subject: Investigate the price of progress in the Industrial Age

See GTV Guide page 54 for complete lesson plan.

 VIDEODISC

- *GTV: A Geographic Perspective on American History*

Side 3, Chapter 15
Title: *A Progress Report*
Subject: Early environmental reforms, 1870–1920

See GTV Guide page 55 for complete lesson plan.

Answers to CONNECTIONS

1. Air pollution would include such things as odors from bone boiling and fat melting and offensive exhalations in gas manufacture. Soil pollution might include filthy streets, garbage, stables and cattle pens, animals in the streets, dumping of manure and other refuse, and dead animals. Water pollution could derive from runoff or discharges from any of the items listed.

2. Overcrowding of the cities overtaxes the inadequate disposal systems for removing waste. City services can't expand rapidly enough to keep pace.

3. Fewer problems from animals in the streets would be found.

REVIEW CHAPTER 19

Answers

Reviewing Facts
1. monotony, low wages, long hours, unhealthful conditions, unemployment
2. mobility and diversity of workers, differing goals, public opinion, opposition from employers and law enforcement agencies, lockouts
3. wage increases, shorter hours, health and safety standards, and restriction of immigration
4. famine, opportunity, crop failures, political persecution, religious freedom
5. new industries, jobs and opportunities, amenities of city life, excitement and activities, immigration, migration from rural areas
6. tenements, crowding, slums, crime, disease, poor sanitation, pollution
7. aqueducts, improved transportation, police, playgrounds, legislation, settlement houses, parks, buildings, libraries, department stores

Understanding Concepts
1. By enlisting members from each and every facet of society, big business would be confronted by a union representing all the people.
2. Employers, law enforcement, the public. Unions were blamed for unrest and disorder; were associated with anarchists and political extremists.

CHAPTER 19 ★ REVIEW

Using Vocabulary

Use the following terms in sentences or short paragraphs. Relate them by using two or more of the terms in each sentence or paragraph.

real wages	company town
business cycle	blacklist
lockout	collective bargaining
arbitration	industrial union
injunction	tenement

Reviewing Facts

1. **Discuss** the hardships and problems that plagued industrial workers in the late 1800s and early 1900s.
2. **Report** on the problems facing labor unions in the late 1800s.
3. **Summarize** the achievements of labor unions during the late 1800s.
4. **List** the reasons why people immigrated to the United States.
5. **Cite** reasons for the growth of cities during the late 1800s.
6. **Identify** the problems created by growth in urban populations.
7. **Describe** efforts to improve nineteenth-century city life.

Understanding Concepts

Unity
1. How did Terence Powderly envision the Knights of Labor as being capable of confronting big business? How did his methods and goals differ from other union leaders'?

Conflict
2. With what groups did labor unions have conflict once they were organized? What were some of the reasons for the conflict? Explain how the conflict was resolved.

Critical Thinking

1. **Understanding Stereotypes** What stereotypes of labor unions were created because of the actions of a few union members or nonunion strikers? How did they work against the efforts of organized labor?
2. **Analyzing Photographs** Study the photograph on this page of an alley playground taken in the early 1900s and answer the questions that follow.
   a. What are the individuals in the photograph doing?
   b. What evidence do you see that conveys economic conditions?
   c. What title would you give this photograph?

Writing About History

Description
Imagine you are a reporter assigned to cover the railroad strike of 1877. Write an article describing the scene of the strike as you arrive. Include enough sensory details so that your readers can share your experience and sense the mood and emotions of the strikers and onlookers.

▲ Tenement Alley Playground, c. 1910

540 UNIT 6 New Horizons: 1860–1900

Critical Thinking
1. Union members were stereotyped as anarchists and radical socialists who preached violent overthrow of the existing order. Became associated with instances of violence during strikes.

2. a. Playing and watching a ballgame; b. Answers may vary, but might include: drab surroundings, wash hanging on lines, children playing ball in alley; c. Answers may center on life in the city.

Practicing the Skill
1. U.S. was heavily populated in North (OH, PA, NY)
2. illustrates the growth of U.S. from east to west
3. Maryland. GA: 2,216,000; MA: 2,805,000
4. Geologists. Agriculturalists, health organizations.

CHAPTER 19 ★ REVIEW

Cooperative Learning

Work with a partner to research a major strike that occurred in the United States within the last five years. Find information on the workers' grievances. In addition find information on the company's position in the strike. Use this information to take turns as a union representative and a company representative questioning one another during an arbitration meeting.

Social Studies Skills

Reading a Cartogram

At first glance you may not have recognized the image on this page as a map of the United States; in fact, you may not have thought it was a map at all. Nevertheless, it is a striking indication of the vast differences in population among the various regions of the United States in 1900.

A cartogram is a type of map that purposely distorts physical space in order to highlight one aspect of physical, cultural, or human geography. Most maps, by contrast, try to minimize or disguise any sort of distortion.

Cartograms can show just about anything: population, income, highways, nuclear power, natural disasters, or food consumption. What is critical is that the size of individual areas reflects importance solely in relation to the information that the map-maker wishes to emphasize. These maps have very specific uses.

Cartograms of today's population in the United States, based perhaps on age or gender, would be useful to someone in politics or marketing who needs to identify demographic trends.

Practicing the Skill

Use the cartogram on this page and your knowledge from the chapter to answer the questions below.

1. What fact about the United States population in 1900 is most evident from a quick glance at the cartogram?
2. In what ways might the information on the cartogram enhance your understanding of the text?
3. Which state was larger in 1900—Georgia or Maryland? How many people lived in each of these states?
4. Who might find a cartogram of natural disasters useful? Of food consumption? Explain your reasoning for each example you provide.

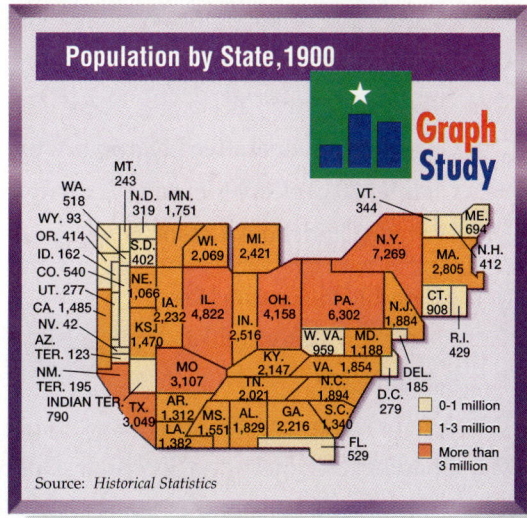

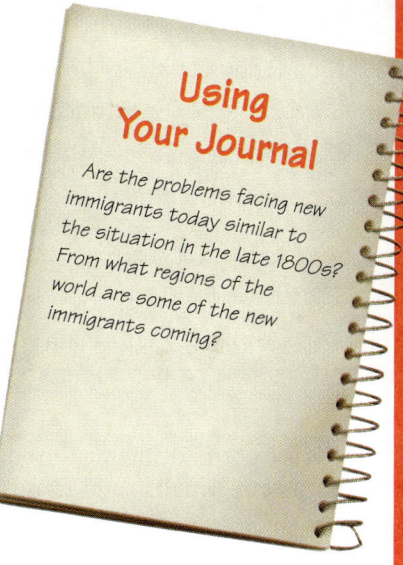

Using Your Journal

Are the problems facing new immigrants today similar to the situation in the late 1800s? From what regions of the world are some of the new immigrants coming?

CHAPTER 19 An Urban Society: 1860–1900   **541**

REVIEW CHAPTER 19

Chapter Bonus Test Question

In each of the following pairs, the two terms are related in some way. Write a sentence for each pair that explains how the terms are related. (Sample answers: Employers used a *lockout* to retaliate against a *labor union*. A bill was proposed that would require all *immigrants* to pass a *literacy test*.

1. labor union, lockout
2. literacy test, immigrants

Using Your Journal

The ideas students present will vary, but they may mention that many of today's immigrants are Southeast Asians, Central Americans, and Russian Jews. Many of the problems are the same, including adjustment to new customs and language, and job and housing discrimination.

PLANNING GUIDE   Chapter 20   The Gilded Age

Daily Lesson Objectives	Teacher Classroom Resources	Multimedia
SECTION 1 **A Tarnished Image** 1 Day pp. 544–549 1. Identify the major causes of increased political corruption. 2. Give examples of corruption at local, state, and national levels.	Chapter 20 Study Guide Reproducible Lesson Plan Section Quiz Reteaching Activity 20-1 Chapter 20 Primary and Secondary Source Readings Reinforcing Social Studies Skills 53, 62, 65 American Portrait 40 Chapter 20 Cooperative Learning Activity Chapter 20 Concept Mapping Activity Writer's Guidebook Lesson 6	Student Self-Test Software Testmaker Section Focus Transparency 62 Chapter 20 Skills Transparency U.S. History and Art Transparency 15
SECTION 2 **Calls for Good Government** 1 Day pp. 551–556 1. Identify the reforms made during the 1870s and 1880s. 2. Describe the tariff controversy.	Reproducible Lesson Plan Reteaching Activity 20-2 Section Quiz American Portrait 40 Chapter 20 Primary and Secondary Source Readings Reinforcing Social Studies Skills 22, 32, 49, 63	Student Self-Test Software Testmaker Section Focus Transparency 63
SECTION 3 **Cultural Life** 1 Day pp. 557–562 1. Discuss developments in literature, art, and higher education. 2. Describe how various leisure activities expanded.	Reproducible Lesson Plan Reteaching Activity 20-3 Section Quiz Chapter 20 Enrichment Activity Reinforcing Social Studies Skills 24, 25, 26, 27 Spanish Summaries & Glossary	Student Self-Test Software Testmaker Section Focus Transparency 64 U.S. History and Art Transparencies 11, 16, 17, 19 Vocabulary Puzzlemaker Audiocassette, Chapter 20
CHAPTER REVIEW AND EVALUATION 1 Day	Chapter 20 Test Chapter 20 Performance Assessment Activity	Student Self-Test Software Testmaker

OUT OF TIME? If time does not permit teaching the entire chapter, use the Chapter 20 Summary on pages 590–591 and the Chapter 20 audiocassette (English and Spanish) to point out the main ideas of the chapter.

PLANNING GUIDE

Cultural Diversity Activity

Critical Thinking Examine reasons many urban immigrants found political machines appealing. Point out that during the frigid winter of 1870, Boss Tweed dumped $50,000 worth of coal on street corners in the poorest parts of New York. Members of political machines paid condolence calls when someone died in a family, sent gifts for newborns, and celebrated First Holy Communions and bar mitzvahs. What were the needs of the immigrants who flooded into large cities in the late 1800s? What difficulties did they face in adjusting to American life? Why might the personal attention of political leaders have special appeal to these newcomers? Despite their awareness of political corruption, why did many immigrants support machine candidates?

Performance Assessment Activity

Everyday Life Have the class work together to create a newspaper or TV newscast that describes an imaginary day in the late 1800s. Divide the class into groups and assign a student from each group to form an editorial board. The board should decide what news, special features, and advertisements to include. Ask the board to assign tasks to each group and then review the work submitted by the various groups. The board might duplicate the newspaper for distribution or videotape the newscast for broadcast.

POSSIBLE RUBRIC FEATURES: Content, organization, written and visual communication skills, creativity, collaborative skills

Chapter Resources

Literature from the Period
Anthony, Susan B. *History of Woman's Suffrage.* 1902.
Twain, Mark. *Life on the Mississippi.* 1975.

Readings for the Student
Tower, Samuel A. *Cartoons and Lampoons: The Art of Political Satire.* Messner, 1982.

Readings for the Teacher
Callow, Alexander B,. Jr. *The Tweed Ring.* Oxford, 1966.
Dobson, John M. *Politics in the Gilded Age.* Praeger, 1972.

Multimedia Resources
The Abuse of Political Power. Guidance Associates.
Living American History Series. U.S. History III, 1876–1914. Priven Learning Systems. (2 Apple diskettes)
Women in American Life, 1880–1920. National Women's History Project. (VHS, 15 minutes.)

Key to Ability Levels

Teaching strategies have been coded for varying learning styles and abilities.

- **L1** Basic activities for all students
- **L2** Average activities for average to above-average students
- **L3** Challenging activities for above-average students
- **LEP** Limited English Proficiency activities

Glencoe Links to the Humanities

Link to Art
- U.S. History and Art Transparency 14, 15, 16, 17

Link to Literature
- Macmillan Literature: Understanding Literature Audiotapes Side 1

Link to Music
- American Music: Cultural Traditions

CHAPTER 20

BEGINNING THE CHAPTER

Tell students that in this chapter they will learn about the Tweed Ring, a group of corrupt New York politicians. Have students discuss the problems that arise when people in government use their positions for personal gain.

Recording Journal Notes

After students have noted abuses such as kickbacks, graft, bribes, and influence peddling, ask them to categorize their findings. One way of doing so is by level of government. Which type took place at the local level? state level? national level?

Perhaps the last great political machine was the Cook County Democratic party, run by Chicago Mayor Richard J. Daley. Coming to power in 1955, Daley adopted many of the tactics of the nineteenth-century political bosses. He rewarded loyal party workers with government jobs. In return, the party workers brought in huge voting majorities for Daley's candidates on Election Day. Daley remained in control of the machine until his death in 1976.

CHAPTER 20

The Gilded Age
1865–1900

▶ TIFFANY LAMP

Setting the Scene

Focus

American political life reached a low point between 1865 and 1900. Corruption in the form of graft and bribery became almost routine in local, state, and national governments. Both political parties came under the influence of lobbyists and other special interests. Neither party was ready for change, although the assassination of President Garfield prompted civil service reform.

Concepts to Understand

★ How the spoils system and lobbyists fostered corruption in government
★ How public protest by a free press worked to end political corruption

Read to Discover . . .

★ the major forms of political corruption.
★ new forms of leisure pastimes and amusements that attracted the interest of Americans before 1900.

Journal Notes

As you read the chapter, note the types of corruption and questionable ethics in government during the Gilded Age.

CULTURAL
- 1873 One of the first schools of nursing opens at Bellevue Hospital in New York
- 1876 National Baseball League formed
- 1883 Joseph Pulitzer buys the New York World

POLITICAL
- 1872 Crédit Mobilier scheme uncovered
- 1883 Pendleton Act passes
- 1884 Cleveland elected President

✚ EXTRA CREDIT PROJECT

Ask interested students to read one of the works of literature mentioned in this chapter—*The Adventures of Tom Sawyer* and *The Adventures of Huckleberry Finn*, by Mark Twain; *The Rise of Silas Lapham*, by William Dean Howells, or *The Red Badge of Courage*, by Stephen Crane—or some other novel of the period. Have students write a brief essay in which they explain how the book they read enhances their understanding of the period.

CHAPTER 20 CONCEPTS

Concept Mapping Activity

Write the concept map below on the chalkboard. Have students copy the map into their notebooks. Then ask them to study the time line on pages 542–543 and hypothesize what types of political corruption and protest they might study in this chapter.

```
        Political corruption
        and scandal lead to
           needed reforms.
           /            \
    Political         Corruption
    Protest
```

History AND ART

Visitors to the World's Fair could ride several types of railroads, ascend 1,500 feet in a tethered hot air balloon, or pay fifty cents for two revolutions on the Ferris wheel.

History AND ART

World's Columbian Exposition, Chicago
by F.C. Jones, 1893

The artist paints a view of the grounds and buildings at the Chicago World's Fair. The fairgrounds included a one-mile-long entertainment strip.

◀ CROQUET DRESS, LATE 1800s

- 1890 Reporter Nelly Bly circles globe by train and steamship in 72 days
- 1890 McKinley Tariff passes
- 1895 William Randolph Hearst purchases the New York Morning Journal
- 1896 McKinley elected President

1885 — 1895

CHAPTER 20 The Gilded Age 1865–1900   543

GLENCOE TECHNOLOGY

VIDEODISC

Focus on Government

Videodisc 1, Chapter 20
The Media and Politics

Teacher Notes

_____ _____
_____ _____
_____ _____
_____ _____
_____ _____

543

LESSON PLAN
SECTION 1, 544–550

FOCUS

Bellringer
Before taking roll at the beginning of the class period, display Focus Activity Transparency 65 on the overhead projector, and assign the accompanying Focus Activity Sheet.

Objectives
Point out the objectives on this page to students in previewing the section content.

Motivating Activity
Ask students to name some present-day political wrongdoings of corrupt officials in their city or state. Write students' responses on the chalkboard. (sample answers: taking kickbacks from companies in return for awarding government contracts, accepting money for overlooking city code violations, fixing parking tickets) Then have students discuss the following question: Can government reform completely eradicate political corruption? Why or why not?

Use Skills Transparency 20.

SECTION 1

A Tarnished Image

Setting the Scene

Section Focus
In the late 1800s, there were scandals at all levels of government. In the eyes of many critics, politics reached a low point. Although that low point was not maintained, it dealt a lasting blow to the image of politicians.

Objectives
After studying this section, you should be able to
★ identify the major causes of increased political corruption.
★ give examples of corruption at local, state, and national levels.

Key Terms
graft, political machine, kickback, ward, lobbyist, township

▶ THE BRAINS, BY THOMAS NAST, 1871

The Gilded Age was a phrase coined by two authors of the period—Mark Twain and Charles Dudley Warner—in a novel about the corruption of the Grant administration. In the years following the Civil War, the quality of American government left much to be desired. Politicians were irresponsible, loyalties were shallow, and money was tainted.

In this post-Civil War period, the most ambitious and talented people were no longer attracted to politics but to business. Indeed, politics itself became something of a business. The goal of political entrepreneurs was to achieve power and position through political office. Often politicians were able to line their pockets with money. Corruption seemed to flourish at every level of government. At first the corruption was not apparent. Material progress had produced a society that appeared to be bright and attractive. Society and government were not what they appeared to be on the surface, however.

■ Political Machines

Some of the most outrageous examples of **graft**, or thievery in office, were those at the grass-roots level of city government. A factor that contributed to corrupt city government was the rapid growth of cities.

Growth of Cities

In 1840 there were only 131 cities in the United States; by 1880 there were 939. In addition cities often doubled, tripled, or even quadrupled in size within a decade. Services for these large populations had to be expanded at a rate never experienced before. Providing increased police and fire

UNIT 6 New Horizons: 1860–1900

Classroom Resources for SECTION 1

Teacher's Classroom Resources
- Chapter 20 Study Guide
- Reproducible Lesson Plan
- Reteaching Activity 20-1
- Chapter 20 Cooperative Learning Activity
- Chapter 20 Primary and Secondary Source Readings
- Section Quiz

Multimedia
- Section Focus Transparency 65
- Chapter 20 Skills Transparency
- U.S. History and Art Transparency 15
- Testmaker
- Student Self-Test Software

protection, water supplies, and sewage disposal was a daunting task for what often were untrained and ill-paid city officials. At the same time, businesses were eager to get lucrative contracts for paving streets and building new schools. An alliance between business and politics that fostered corruption resulted.

Maintaining Control

The usual democratic restraints on abuses of power did not work well in the cities of this era. Large portions of the population of cities were immigrants who had little or no experience with urban living or with democratic government. Many were accustomed to corruption in government. Both poor immigrants and native-born residents had little time to worry about abstract notions of government. They worked from dawn to dusk just to keep food on the table. Those more well-off, who might have gone into politics, were busy making money in business and real estate. As a result, almost every major city was dominated by a **political machine**—a party-linked political organization that maintained power by controlling votes, controlling the courts, and controlling the police as well.

The strength of a political machine came from the bottom up, not from the top down. Local politicians took care of the needs of their voters. They often provided groceries to families who were needy, organized free celebrations on important national holidays, attended ethnic religious and social events, and even helped get people out of jail. In this way politicians earned the loyalty of their neighborhood citizens. When election time came around, the votes were always there, keeping the helpful politicians in power.

The "Tweed Ring"

The most notorious city machine was the "Tweed Ring" in New York City. In 1868 "Boss" William M. Tweed gained control of New York's Democratic machine, known locally by the name of its central meeting place—Tammany Hall. For the next 3 years, he and his underlings managed to steal millions of dollars of city funds. The usual way this was done involved a process known as the "kickback." A **kickback** was an arrangement whereby contractors would pad, or increase, the amount of their bills for city work and pay or "kick back" a percentage of that amount to politicians in the ring. In one

 ▲ **THE TRUSTS** Powerful trusts dominate the United States Senate in this 1889 cartoon by Joseph Keppler. The people's entrance to the Senate chambers (upper left) is shown bolted shut. **How did the trusts influence senators?**

CHAPTER 20 SECTION 1

Independent Practice

Political Science Have students work in small groups to develop a campaign for an honest big-city mayor, a reform-minded senator, or a presidential candidate in the 1880 election. Ask students to decide what reforms their candidates need to address, what campaign promises they should make, and how they should convey their campaign messages. Invite each group to present its campaign to the class. **L3**

Visualizing History

Thomas Nast, a Republican, used his savage cartoons to expose the corrupt "Boss" Tweed. Interestingly enough, after Tweed fled to Spain to avoid arrest, he was identified and apprehended through one of Nast's cartoons. **Answer to Caption:** Although personally honest, Grant seemed unable to distinguish between honest and dishonest government officials.

Did You Know?

Thomas Nast was responsible for creating the symbols of the Democratic and Republican parties. The donkey came to symbolize Democrats and the elephant Republicans.

---

example a county courthouse that should have cost taxpayers $250,000 actually cost $11 million. One plastering contractor was paid almost $3 million for 9 months' work.

In 1871 *The New York Times* published evidence of Tweed's rampant greed. At the same time, Thomas Nast, a brilliant political cartoonist, ridiculed Tweed in his cartoons for *Harper's Weekly*. Nast's cartoons found their mark and were devastating. Tweed was driven to complain: "I don't care a straw for your newspaper articles: my people don't know how to read, but they can't help seeing them . . . pictures." Tweed and his cronies were convicted of criminal conduct and driven from office.

In spite of Tweed's removal, Tammany Hall continued to be an active influence in New York politics. This was true because local machine leaders drew their power from the local neighborhoods that they served 24 hours a day. A good deal of the graft, however, was used to help needy residents of the neighborhood **wards,** small administrative divisions of a city.

Occasionally city graft became so flagrant that voters were driven to "throw the rascals out" and put in a reform administration. Such movements often failed. Reform candidates focused on economy and honest administration but failed to understand the reasons why the political machines commandeered so much loyalty and met with such success.

■ Widespread Corruption

Corruption was not limited to local governments. It also occurred at the state and federal levels. In addition to the corruption, government in the late 1800s was affected by a marked lack of leadership. Neither Congress nor the President provided the direction the nation needed.

▲ **NAST AND TWEED** Thomas Nast (left) entertained Americans with biting political cartoons in the late 1800s. The most well-known political machine was run by "Boss" William M. Tweed (right). *Why did corruption in the federal government spread during the Grant administration?*

546 UNIT 6 New Horizons: 1860–1900

Cooperative Learning

Organize students into groups of three. Assign one member in each group to obtain copies of three different cartoons by Thomas Nast that ridicule William M. Tweed or another corrupt politician. Have the group determine what and who is shown in each cartoon, what the message of each cartoon is, and how the caption helps convey the message. Then have the groups, using Nast's cartoons as models, create political cartoons criticizing a current political situation. **L2, L3**

In State Government

Politics at the state level was nearly as corrupt as in the cities. In many states big business stood to gain or lose large amounts of money as a result of legislative votes on various matters, such as tax rates and internal improvements. Thus, companies spent large sums to influence votes.

In pre-Civil War times, businesspeople influenced politicians by writing letters and inviting them to expensive dinners. After the war the demands on government increased to the point that the amount of money spent by state governments was huge, and the stakes for those seeking state contracts were high. Businesses now began to employ **lobbyists**—people paid to represent a company or a special interest group. Sometimes they tried to influence votes by offering money in the form of campaign contributions. If it was unclear who would win a race, contributions were given to both parties. Such payments were regarded by legislators and lobbyists alike as "insurance" against unfavorable legislation.

At other times money was offered in the form of outright bribes. When Jay Gould controlled the Erie Railroad, he was reported to have spent $500,000 in bribes during a single session of the New York state legislature. Of the relations between the Standard Oil Company and the government of Pennsylvania, one observer wrote, "The Standard has done everything with the Pennsylvania legislature except to refine it."

In Federal Government

In general there was more corruption in state and local politics than in national politics. By far the worst misconduct in the federal government occurred when Grant was President.

Grant had been a great general, but he was a poor President. Although he was personally honest, he seemed unable to distinguish decent people from the dishonest. Dazzled by wealth, he fell under the sway of the financial speculators James J. Fisk and Jay Gould, who reaped millions of dollars from their relationship with the President. Members of Grant's family, personal staff, and cabinet peddled influence and jobs in return for cash. At one time Grant's brother managed to hold four jobs by farming out the duties to other men.

▲ **MR. DOOLEY** Humorist Finley Peter Dunne is dwarfed by his creation, Mr. Dooley. Like Nast, Dunne was a shrewd observer of political events at the turn of the century. **Which political party were new immigrants likely to join?**

Crédit Mobilier

In 1872 the scandals spread to Congress as well. A New York newspaper revealed that officers of the Union Pacific Railroad had formed their own construction company called the Crédit Mobilier. The contracts this company received enabled the railroad officers to reap enormous personal profits. To forestall investigation, the company distributed shares of stock "where it would do the most good." Grant's Vice President and several prominent members of Congress turned out to have accepted these thinly disguised bribes.

When the graft in his administration was uncovered, Grant declared that he would "let no guilty man escape." However, he protected many accused of wrongdoing from both investigation and punishment.

CHAPTER 20 The Gilded Age 1865–1900

CHAPTER 20 SECTION 1

Visualizing History Mr. Dooley, the talkative Irish barkeeper, first appeared in a Chicago newspaper in the 1890s. Dooley spoke for the common man and woman. He provided a humorous perspective on events of the day.
Answer to Caption: the Democratic party, because Democrats actively sought the immigrant vote

By the time of the Gilded Age, the pool of citizens eligible to vote had expanded considerably. In the early days of the Republic, only white male property owners over age 21 could vote. By the 1850s, property—and in some states religious—restrictions had disappeared, and most white adult males could vote. In 1870 the Fifteenth Amendment gave African American males the franchise. With the addition of women voters in 1920 and 18-year-old voters in 1971, the voter pool reached its contemporary constituency: all American citizens 18 years and older.

Critical Thinking

Analyzing a Quotation Have students write in their own words the meaning of the following verse written by James Russell Lowell:
*Show your State Legislatures; show your Rings;
And challenge Europe to produce such things
As high officials sitting half in sight
To share the plunder and to fix things right;
If that don't fetch her, why you only need
To show your latest style in martyrs,—Tweed!*
L2

CHAPTER 20
SECTION 1

Did You Know?

Grant's real name was Hiram Ulysses Grant. He was named for his maternal grandfather and a hero of Greek mythology. The prospect of entering West Point with the initials H.U.G. embarrassed him, so he began reversing the two names. When he learned that he was erroneously enrolled at West Point under the name Ulysses Simpson Grant, he went along with the change. He thereafter was known as Ulysses S. Grant.

Using Graphs

Answer: The elections of 1864, 1868, 1872, 1896, and 1900.

Skills Practice

In which presidential elections did the Democrats win the popular vote? (1876, 1892)

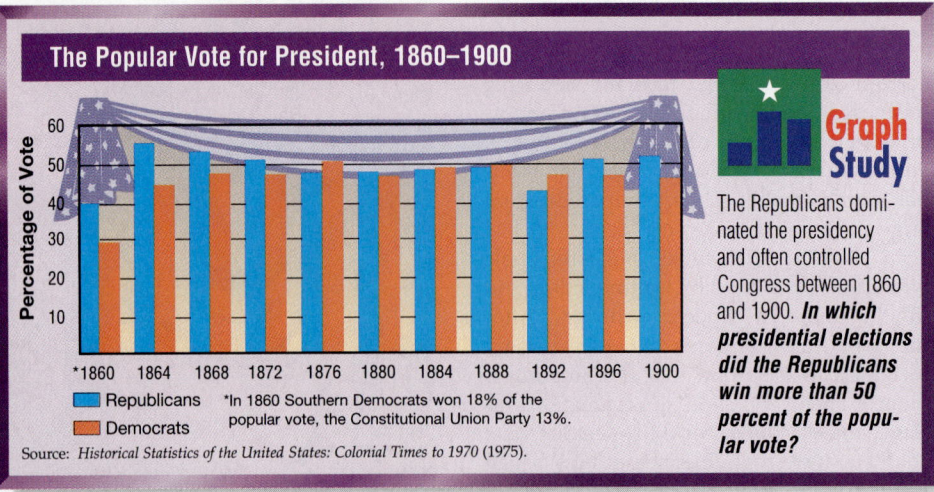

The Popular Vote for President, 1860–1900

*In 1860 Southern Democrats won 18% of the popular vote, the Constitutional Union Party 13%.

Source: *Historical Statistics of the United States: Colonial Times to 1970* (1975).

Graph Study

The Republicans dominated the presidency and often controlled Congress between 1860 and 1900. **In which presidential elections did the Republicans win more than 50 percent of the popular vote?**

Postwar Political Parties

Even political analysts often found it difficult to explain the positions Democrats and Republicans took on major issues such as the tariff and railroad regulation. English writer James Bryce wrote:

> *Neither party has, as a party, anything to say on these issues, neither party has any clean-cut principles. . . . All has been lost except office or the hope of it.*

Issues Split Parties

One reason that parties seemed so similar was that they both reflected sectional differences so accurately. At every level, from wards to **townships,** or smaller divisions of a county broken up into local government districts, political parties were popular, and democratic participation was high. They did not avoid any of the issues; rather they were split internally on most of them. In the Northeast, for example, with its strong banking system, both parties favored the gold standard. In the Midwest both parties favored increasing the amount of money in circulation. Republicans in the developing Midwest were protariff, while Southern Democrats were antitariff. Both parties in the Northeast were divided on the tariff issue.

The humorist "Mr. Dooley," created by Finley Peter Dunne, described a hypothetical candidate for President as someone who was pulled in different directions by varied interests and needed to be all things to all people.

> *Wanted: a good, active Dimmycrat, sthrong iv lung an' limb; must be . . . a sympathizer with th' crushed an' down throdden people but not be anny means hostile to vested inthrests; must advocate sthrikes, gover'mint be injunction, free silver, sound money, greenbacks, a single tax, a tariff f'r rivinoo . . . at home in Wall sthreet an' th' stock yards, in th' parlors iv th' r-rich an' th' kitchens iv th' poor.*

Although fairly evenly matched in strength, the two parties were hardly identical. Though both parties received support from people in every walk of life, each had a distinctive base of support.

Republicans

The Republicans were supported by Western farmers and merchants, who benefited from Republicans' internal improvements and liberal land policies, and Eastern

548   UNIT 6 New Horizons: 1860–1900

Sidelights: Literature

The corruption of the post–Civil War years inspired a number of novels. In *Democracy* (1880), Henry Adams—whose grandfather and great-grandfather were Presidents—ridiculed the "practical" politics of the day. Through the words of a leading character, Adams vividly showed his contempt: "I declare to you, that . . . I have found no society which has had elements of corruption like the United States. The children in the street are corrupt. . . . The cities are all corrupt, and also the towns and the counties and the States' legislatures and the judges."

businesspeople, who benefited from high tariffs and national banks. The Republicans tended to be old-immigrant Protestants—Presbyterians, Methodists, Congregationalists, or Baptists. The Republicans' problem was to keep together its Eastern and Western wings, which differed on such issues as greenbacks, free silver, tariffs, and banking.

The Republicans' "patron saint" was Abraham Lincoln, whose birthday they honored with banquets and oratory. As the party that had led during the Civil War, they had great prestige in the North and the West. "The party that saved the nation must rule it," they proclaimed.

While critics attacked the Republicans for keeping alive war hatreds by "waving the bloody shirt," appeals to the memory of the Civil War were much more than that. Republican strength came from genuine devotion to the idea of the United States as a nation rather than as a federation of states. Many Republicans continued to be inspired by the party's early idealism. They felt that government existed to advance the public good.

Democrats

Democrats, too, looked back to the Civil War. From the end of radical Reconstruction until well into the twentieth century, Southern states formed the "Solid South," never wavering in its allegiance to the Democrats.

The Democrats could not have remained a national party with only Southern support, however. The party depended on an alliance between white Southerners and Northern city machines. Democrats tended to get the support of recent immigrants, many of whom were Catholics or liturgical Protestants, such as Lutherans or Episcopalians. Their religious and cultural background was quite different from that of evangelical Protestants, such as Methodists and Baptists, who formed the core of the Republican party. The Democrats had allies among Western farmers, especially when crop prices were low, and among certain groups of businesspeople and owners of import companies who favored a lower tariff.

The Democratic party had two "patron saints"—Thomas Jefferson and Andrew Jackson. Like these leaders the Democrats claimed to represent the interests of ordinary Americans. The Democrats took issue with the Republican view of the United States as a nation. "This is no nation," said one Democrat. "We are free and independent states." In contrast to the Republicans' view that the federal government should take an active role in helping the needy and shaping national growth, the Democrats wanted to keep the federal government on a skimpy allowance and a short leash. "That government governs best which governs least" remained their motto.

During the entire period from 1865 to 1900, Democrats held the presidency for only two terms. Although they usually lost the White House, the Democrats were seldom far out of the running. Democratic candidates often got almost as many popular votes as their victorious opponents, and it was rare that the Republicans did not have to deal with Democrats in control of at least one house of Congress.

Section 1 ★ Review

Checking for Understanding

1. **Identify** William M. Tweed, Thomas Nast, Finley Peter Dunne.
2. **Define** graft, political machine, kickback, ward, lobbyist, township.
3. **Cite** examples of corruption that occurred in government.
4. **State** how Republicans and Democrats viewed the role of the federal government.

Critical Thinking

5. **Interpreting Satire** In his description of the ideal campaign candidate on page 548, what was Mr. Dooley expressing about politicians?

LESSON PLAN
Mastering Social Studies Skills

Teaching Interpreting Primary Sources

Discuss the cartoon described, having students point out the meanings of symbols and words in the cartoon. Ask: Why is a political cartoon a good primary source? (It reflects issues and feelings of a certain time and point of view.) How can you determine whether a cartoon portrays a valid point of view? (Details should reflect the period, such as clothing and political issues. You should be able to find facts to back up the point of view shown.)

Students might work together to create political cartoons based on current issues. Have them compare their cartoons for validity and accuracy.

Did You Know?

Before it was exposed in 1871, the Tweed Ring is believed to have stolen as much as $200 million from the city treasury.

Social Studies Skills

Interpreting Primary Sources

Political Corruption

None of William "Boss" Tweed's critics leveled more scathing attacks at his notorious Tammany Hall machine than did Thomas Nast, a cartoonist for *Harper's Weekly*. *Harper's* magazine pioneered the use of illustrations and cartoons to comment on significant political issues of the day. Under Nast's pen, Tweed and his cronies were depicted as vultures, jailed criminals, and smiling deceivers.

Tweed was well aware of the political damage that Nast's cartoons could do to him and the Tammany Hall political machine. He ordered his men to stop Nast from drawing his cartoons. Tweed cared little what the papers wrote about him because most of his constituents could not read. However, they could see and understand the message of the cartoons.

In this cartoon, "Who Stole the People's Money?" the answer is "'Twas Him." Tweed appears as the heavyset man in the left foreground of the cartoon.

On Tweed's right a man holds a hat labeled "chairs," a reference to the $179,000 New York City paid for 40 chairs and 3 tables. Other contractors and cheats—their names on their coats—complete the circle.

Articles and cartoons published in *Harper's Weekly* and *The New York Times* led to the downfall of the Tweed Ring. Citizens worked to remove Tweed and his accomplices from political office. Several members of the ring left the country, and Tweed himself was arrested in 1871. His first trial resulted in a hung jury, but a second trial brought a conviction. He died in jail in 1878.

▼ WHO STOLE THE PEOPLE'S MONEY? 'TWAS HIM

Thomas Nast was born in Germany but was brought to the United States as a child and spent most of his life there. Nast worked as a news illustrator for a number of national magazines, gaining a national reputation for his cartoons during the Civil War. Nast is also credited with creating the elephant and donkey symbols of the Republican and Democratic parties.

Examining the Primary Source

1. What label identifies the group in the circle?
2. What does clothing show in this cartoon?
3. How does the cartoon visually answer the question posed in its title, "Who Stole the People's Money?"

Critical Thinking

4. **Analyzing Information** What statement does Nast make in his cartoon about the extent of political corruption in New York City?

Answers to SOCIAL STUDIES SKILLS

1. The circle is identified as the Tammany Ring at the bottom of the cartoon.
2. The white coats of the men at the top of the circle reveal their occupations ("carpenter"), and the dress clothes of the men facing forward reveal their superior economic status.
3. Each man is pointing a finger or thumb at someone else.
4. Nast asserts—by the variety of businesses represented and the high proportion of unidentifiable Tweed Ring associates—that the corruption in New York City is pervasive. The circle indicates that the organization protects the members by allowing them to "pass the buck."

SECTION 2

Calls for Good Government

Setting the Scene

Section Focus
During the 1870s and the 1880s, social reformers like Henry George tried to raise the alarm that official corruption threatened democracy in the United States. If reformers wanted rebellion, they were disappointed, but through their efforts, a slow and steady movement away from the abuses of the Grant administration began. The first hopeful sign was the election of Rutherford B. Hayes in 1876.

Objectives
After studying this section, you should be able to
★ identify the reforms made during the 1870s and the 1880s.
★ describe the tariff controversy.

Key Terms
patronage, rider, free-trader, protectionist

◀ DEMOCRATIC BANNER, 1888

Before the administration of Rutherford B. Hayes, one of the common practices had been **patronage**—the assumed right of elected officials to control political appointments to unelected positions. Patronage employees made the federal government the epitome of apathy and astonishingly idle.

■ Civil Service Reforms

With the election of Hayes, the tone of national politics began to change. Hayes made some steps toward rescuing the presidency from congressional domination.

Hayes Begins Reforms
After his inauguration in 1877, Hayes named Carl Schurz, owner of a German-language newspaper in St. Louis, Missouri, and United States Senator from Missouri, to take charge of the Department of the Interior, which had previously been the scene of some of the worst examples of patronage. This practice was soon curbed. Hayes also forbade the practice of "shaking down" federal workers—forcing them to make political campaign contributions.

Hayes also defied congressional leaders by blocking important appointments favored by individual members of Congress. In addition he refused to sign otherwise acceptable legislation if Congress had attached **riders**—irrelevant amendments—of which he disapproved. He vetoed several appropriations bills with riders attached and finally won a clear-cut victory. Through his actions Hayes not only cut down on corruption but began to restore the balance of power between Congress and the President.

CHAPTER 20 The Gilded Age 1865–1900

Classroom Resources for SECTION 2

Teacher's Classroom Resources
- Reproducible Lesson Plan
- Cooperative Learning Activity
- Reteaching Activity 20-1
- Chapter 20 Primary and Secondary Source Readings
- Section Quiz

Multimedia
- Section Focus Transparency 66
- Testmaker
- Student Self-Test Software

Election of 1880

Hayes's reforms brought him enemies among the Stalwarts, a group of Republican machine politicians who strongly opposed civil service reform. After Hayes declined to run for a second term, the party became divided between the Stalwarts, who wanted to nominate Grant for a third term, and the "Halfbreeds," who opposed Grant. After a prolonged deadlock at the national convention, the Republicans nominated dark horse James A. Garfield, a former Union general.

To blunt the old charge of disloyalty in wartime, the Democrats nominated General Winfield S. Hancock, a Union hero of the Battle of Gettysburg. The intellectual level of the ensuing campaign may be judged by the following excerpt from the speech of a Republican orator:

> I belong to a party that believes in good crops; that is glad when a fellow finds a gold mine; that rejoices when there are forty bushels of wheat to the acre.... [T]he Democratic party is a party of famine; it is a good friend of an early frost; it believes in the Colorado beetle and in the weevil.

Despite such inflammatory rhetoric, Garfield narrowly won the election.

The Pendleton Act

Under Hayes and Garfield, government was cleaner than it had been during the Grant administration, but the spoils system remained a constant source of inefficiency and graft. Disputes over patronage poisoned the relationship between the President and Congress. There was little momentum for reform.

In July 1881, however, as President Garfield entered the Washington, D.C., railroad station, he was shot by a disappointed office seeker. The unbalanced man cried, "I am a Stalwart and Arthur is President now." Garfield clung to life for two months, but in September Vice President Chester A. Arthur, a New York Stalwart, succeeded to the presidency.

Garfield's assassination excited public opinion against the spoils system. In 1883 Congress passed the Pendleton Act, which has been called (with some exaggeration) "the Magna Carta of civil service reform." This law allowed the President to decree which federal jobs would be filled according to rules laid down by a bipartisan Civil Service Commission. Candidates competed for

▲ **ASSASSINATION OF THE PRESIDENT** President Garfield was shot only four months after his inauguration by a frustrated patronage seeker, Charles J. Guiteau. In this engraving, Guiteau flees while James G. Blaine, secretary of state, supports Garfield. **After Garfield's death, who became President?**

AMERICAN PORTRAITS

Susan B. Anthony
1820–1906

From her Quaker upbringing, Susan B. Anthony learned that men and women were equal before God. She spent most of her 86 years trying to convince others of that equality.

After teaching school for several years, Anthony returned home to help run the family farm. While living in her father's house, she began to focus on the great reform movements of the day. Anthony first joined a temperance group and experienced gender discrimination firsthand when she was refused permission to speak at a temperance rally. Realizing that as long as women were propertyless and voteless they would also remain powerless, Anthony began devoting her considerable energies to securing equal rights for women. Throughout the four decades from the end of the Civil War to her death, she was the nation's foremost crusader for a woman's right to vote.

---

these jobs through examinations. Appointments could be made only from the list of those who took the exams. A civil service official could not be removed for political reasons.

Although President Arthur was a veteran of machine politics, he supported the Pendleton Act, placing 14,000 jobs (about one-tenth of the total) under the control of the civil service. The federal government had finally begun a shift away from the spoils system.

■ Cleveland in Office

The reform movement begun by Hayes and continued by Garfield and Arthur did not stop. Thus, the major theme of the presidential election of 1884 was honesty in politics.

Election of 1884

The Republican nominee, Representative James G. Blaine, was a man of great ability and personal charm. However, his reputation was clouded by charges that he had taken money for helping a railroad. As a result some independent reformers in the Republican party, called "Mugwumps," did not support him. The Democrats won Mugwump support by nominating Grover Cleveland, who earned a reputation for integrity as mayor of Buffalo and governor of New York.

The campaign of 1884 was a negative one, focusing less on issues and more on character assassination. Blaine was portrayed as a "tattooed man" with railroad stocks and bonds indelibly engraved on his skin. Cleveland was attacked on the grounds that he had hired a substitute to fight for him in the Civil War and that he had fathered an illegitimate child. Republicans chanted:

> Ma! Ma! Where's my pa?
> Gone to the White House,
> Ha! Ha! Ha!

To which the Democrats countered:

> Blaine, Blaine, James G. Blaine,
> The continental liar from the
> State of Maine.

Cleveland won the election by a narrow margin, becoming the first Democratic President elected since 1856. Balloting in New York was close. Had 600 voters switched to Blaine, he would have won the state—and the presidency. The Republicans retained control of the Senate, but the Democrats gained a majority in the House of Representatives.

CHAPTER 20 The Gilded Age 1865–1900   553

Critical Thinking

Detecting Points of View Read the following excerpt from Grover Cleveland's second inaugural address:

"The lessons of paternalism ought to be unlearned and the better lesson taught that while the people should patriotically and cheerfully support the government, its functions do not include support of the people."

Ask: Do you think Cleveland would be a supporter of "big government"? Why or why not? (No, he did not believe that the government should provide support for the people.)
L2

CHAPTER 20
SECTION 2

Fact or Fiction?
A woman's name appeared on the presidential ballot in 1884.

FACT: Belva Lockwood was nominated for President in 1884 and 1888 by the Equal Rights party. She campaigned for women's rights and civil service reform. She was the first woman to appear on a presidential ballot, and received about 4,000 votes in the election of 1884.

Visualizing History
James G. Blaine, secretary of state during Benjamin Harrison's presidency, hoped to promote cooperation among Western Hemisphere nations under American leadership. Toward this end, he helped to create the Pan American Union, an organization that worked to improve relations among the nations of the Americas.
Answer to Caption: focused less on issues than on character assassination

▲ **Grover Cleveland**

Visualizing History ▲ **Blaine** This cartoon portrays James G. Blaine as a protector of tariffs. The person in the kilt is industrialist Andrew Carnegie. *In what ways was the campaign of 1884 a negative campaign?*

Reforms Continue

Unskillful in political maneuvering, Cleveland often met defeat in his dealings with Congress. Nevertheless, his devotion to the public good did much to restore the prestige of the presidency. Cleveland's first problem was to deal with the Democratic officeseekers who swarmed to Washington seeking the fruits of his victory. If he were to make appointments on merit alone, he would split his party wide open. If he were to give in to the spoils system, he would lose the support of the Mugwumps and other reformers who had played a decisive part in electing him. As a compromise Cleveland appointed many "deserving Democrats" to office. He also made every effort to see that the new appointees were qualified.

Cleveland entered office with a weak understanding of most national issues but worked intensely at the job. Few Presidents have put in more study to determine what course of action to follow. His Republican predecessors, for example, had signed hundreds of private bills giving pensions to veterans unable to qualify under regular laws. Examining such bills with care, Cleveland found many of them fraudulent. One veteran, for example, asked for a pension for an injury suffered while *intending* to enlist. Cleveland disapproved of so many pension bills that his vetoes totaled more than those of all previous Presidents.

Cleveland worked to improve government efficiency and integrity. He supported the Presidential Succession Act, which established a line of succession to the presidency in the event of the death of the Vice President. He also won repeal of the Tenure of Office Act, which strengthened presidential independence. Interested in preserving public lands, Cleveland reclaimed land from private companies that had not lived up to the terms of their land grants.

■ Tariffs and the Election of 1888

The public question that Cleveland studied most seriously was the tariff. During the Civil War, duties had been raised from an average of 19 percent in 1861 to more than 40 percent in 1865.

554 UNIT 6 New Horizons: 1860–1900

Critical Thinking

Identifying Points of View Point out that many companies in the United States today are moving their manufacturing to foreign countries where labor is cheaper. The manufactured goods are then imported to the United States. Discuss the economic impact of a tariff on such imported goods. Then have students write a paragraph, from the perspective of a manufacturer, worker, or consumer, on whether tariffs should be levied on imported goods. **L2**

Different Views on Tariffs

High tariff rates, which benefited manufacturers, were constantly attacked by farmers, consumers, shippers, and importers. These **free-traders** argued that a protective tariff was unfair government interference with the normal laws of supply and demand. Tariffs, they said, were subsidies paid to manufacturers out of the pockets of consumers.

Protectionists, on the other hand, defended the tariff as a means of nurturing fledgling industries in the United States. They argued that tariffs kept wages high by shielding them from competition with cheap foreign labor. Previous bills to lower the tariff had been defeated.

Shortly after Cleveland took office, Carl Schurz asked him about his views on the tariff issue. "You know I really don't know anything about it," replied the President. "In my political career as sherriff of Buffalo County, mayor of Buffalo, and governor of New York, it has, of course, not been an issue." Cleveland investigated the problem thoroughly. His studies convinced him that the existing tariff was responsible for the treasury's large surplus. Cleveland argued that the surplus was a sign of overtaxation. He proposed a reduction of the tariff—not because he was a free-trader, but because he was in favor of limited government. Excess money in the treasury, he said, was not good for the economy; it was a temptation to Congress, which was apt to spend it wastefully. The President's dramatic effort to lower the tariff was blocked by House Republicans.

Harrison Elected President

The tariff became the major issue in the presidential election of 1888. Openly avowing protection for the first time, the Republicans collected a record-breaking campaign fund. "Put all the manufacturers of Pennsylvania under the fire," said a Republican campaign manager, "and fry that fat out of them." The Republicans revived Henry Clay's name for the protective tariff, calling their economic program the "American system." Renominating Cleveland, the Democrats campaigned against unnecessary taxation. As in 1880 and 1884, the result was extremely close.

Although he got fewer popular votes than Cleveland, the Republican candidate, Benjamin Harrison, won a majority in the electoral college.

The new President was a quiet, reserved man, whom one observer called a "human iceberg." Harrison was too reserved to make a good Gilded Age politician. Still, he had an able legal mind and a distinguished career as an attorney in Indiana. He had been elected to the Senate in 1881.

Harrison had fought under Sherman at Atlanta and was not shy about "waving the bloody shirt" for votes. An ardent protectionist, he was conservative in fiscal policy and liberal when it came to veterans' pensions.

Treasury Surplus and the Tariffs

Once in office the Republicans promptly disposed of the treasury surplus by spending it, and it was the last time in history that the government held a surplus. Within two years the "Billion-Dollar Congress" had

Visualizing History ▲ **PRESIDENT HARRISON** Unlike Cleveland before him, President Benjamin Harrison favored attempts to freely spend the mounting treasury surplus. *How long did it take the "Billion-Dollar Congress" to convert the surplus into a deficit?*

CHAPTER 20
SECTION 2

Visualizing History Benjamin Harrison's grandfather was William Henry Harrison, elected President in 1840.
Answer to Caption: less than two years

Did You Know?

Cleveland was originally named Steven Grover Cleveland. By the age of 19, he began signing his name S. Grover Cleveland. A few years later, he dropped the initial.

Sidelights: Etiquette

Rules on how people should behave in public were laid down in books on etiquette. Among the most popular of these books was *Manners and Social Etiquette* (1884), by Mrs. John Sherwood. A sample of the advice she provided: To the question of whether young ladies should allow gentlemen to pay for their theater tickets, Mrs. Sherwood replied, "No." For "in permitting a gentleman to expend money for her pleasures, a lady assumes an obligation to him which time and chance may render oppressive."

CHAPTER 20 SECTION 2

ASSESS

Check Understanding
Assign Section 2 Review as homework or an in-class activity.

Evaluate
Assign the Section 2 Quiz in the TCR or use the History of a Free Nation Testmaker to create a customized quiz.

Reteach
Ask students to write five questions on the main ideas in this section. Have students exchange their questions with a partner and answer the questions. Ask the partners to check each other's answers.

Have students complete Reteaching Activity 20-2.

Enrich
Have students draw political cartoons of their own expressing their views of the corruption in the federal government during the late 1800s.

CLOSE
Ask students to name some local issues that played a role in the most recent congressional election and helped one of the candidates to gain or lose votes.

---

created a deficit, mostly through handouts to special-interest groups. The number of Civil War pensioners increased by more than half—many of them the same ones whom Cleveland had turned down.

Moving on to the election-winning tariff issue, the Republicans passed the McKinley Tariff of 1890, which was the highest in the country's history. It dried up revenue by levying rates so high that some foreign products were kept entirely out of the country.

Nearly every foreign product that competed with American-made products was heavily taxed, including such items as food, clothing, furniture, and tools. Western silver states supported the tariff in exchange for the passage of the Sherman Silver Purchase Act, which authorized the federal government to buy up 4.5 million ounces of silver a month.

Millions of dollars were spent on the improvement of harbors and waterways, coastal defenses, federal buildings, and naval expansion. Congress also passed the Sherman Antitrust Act and provided for admission to the Union of North and South Dakota, Montana, Washington, Idaho, and Wyoming.

Several Issues Hurt Republicans

The Republicans' position on protective tariffs, which had helped them win the presidency in 1888, hurt them two years later. Because there was little competition in the market, prices generally were falling; thus, depts were harder to repay.

Republicans also were hurt nationally by local Republicans in such states as Wisconsin and Massachusetts, who supported compulsory public school attendance where instruction was in English. Many Catholic and Lutheran immigrant families residing in these states wanted public funding for their parochial schools, in which students were taught in their first language. Republicans also pushed Prohibition at the grassroots level.

Democrats used these issues, together with that of a backfiring tariff, to attack the Republicans. The congressional elections of 1890 resulted in a Democratic landslide.

By 1892 the Republicans' position was even worse. Disspiritedly, they renominated Harrison, and the Democrats nominated Grover Cleveland again. Popular discontent with the Republicans was so high that for the first time since before the Civil War Democrats won not only the White House but both houses of Congress.

This time, however, Cleveland won by more than 350,000 popular votes and an electoral majority of 277 to 145. Cleveland became the only President in American history to serve two nonconsecutive terms.

Of larger importance than Cleveland's margin of victory was the support given to a third-party candidate, James B. Weaver. Weaver, who had been the candidate for the Greenback party in 1880, ran in 1892 under the banner of the new People's party, better known as the Populist party. By this time, a large part of the American electorate was already responding to the Populist philosophy.

Section 2 ★ Review

Checking for Understanding
1. **Identify** Rutherford B. Hayes, James Garfield, Chester Arthur, Grover Cleveland.
2. **Define** patronage, rider, free-trader, protectionist.
3. **Describe** political reforms made during the 1870s and the 1880s.
4. **Explain** the controversy over raising or lowering the tariff.

Critical Thinking
5. **Evaluating Reforms** How could the civil service system limit the patronage system and cut down on corruption?

556   UNIT 6 New Horizons: 1860–1900

Answers to SECTION 2 REVIEW

1. Rutherford B. Hayes, 551; James Garfield, 552; Chester Arthur, 552; Grover Cleveland, 553
2. All vocabulary words are defined in the Glossary.
3. curbed patronage and "shaking down" of federal workers, restored balance between Congress and the presidency, reformed civil service
4. Pro: protectionists said tariffs nurtured new industry and kept wages high. Con: free-traders said tariffs interfered with laws of supply and demand.
5. It prevented the removal of government staff for political reasons; the exam allowed jobs to be awarded on merit rather than as political payoffs.

SECTION 3

Cultural Life

Setting the Scene

Section Focus

The Civil War was also a turning point in cultural life. The period after the war was a time of rapid change. Some satirized the values of post-Civil War society, as in Twain and Warner's description of a poorly maintained Washington Monument. Others celebrated the country's emergence as an industrial giant.

◀ THE BATH BY MARY CASSATT

Objectives

After studying this section, you should be able to
★ discuss developments in literature, art, and higher education.
★ describe how various leisure activities expanded.

Key Terms

antebellum, realism, expatriate, yellow journalism

The United States was quickly becoming an urban, industrialized society. It needed citizens who could understand complex political and economic questions, and it needed literate workers and managers who could staff its offices, shops, and factories.

■ Education

In the late nineteenth century, the nation reformed its educational system. Public education and higher education benefited from the reforms.

Public Education

By 1900 many states had or were working toward compulsory school attendance. In cities, graded schools replaced one-room school houses. The school year, which had traditionally been squeezed in between fall harvest and spring planting, was lengthened. Many cities also introduced free secondary education, and the number of public high schools increased from a few hundred in 1860 to more than 2,500 in 1890. Yet there remained much room for improvement. In 1900 the average child received only 5 years of schooling.

Private Colleges and Universities

The most far-reaching development in education during the late 1800s was the expansion of higher education. At mid-century most colleges and universities in the United States had poor equipment, scanty libraries, and ill-trained, overworked faculties. Fixed curricula that emphasized ancient Greek and Roman thought included little training in modern languages, history, or science. There were no first-rate graduate

CHAPTER 20 The Gilded Age 1865–1900   **557**

Classroom Resources for SECTION 3

Teacher's Classroom Resources
- Reproducible Lesson Plan
- Reteaching Activity 20-3
- Chapter 20 Enrichment Activity
- Chapter 20 Performance Assessment Activity
- Spanish Summaries and Glossary
- Section Quiz

Multimedia
- Section Focus Transparency 67
- U.S. History and Art Transparency 11, 16, 17, 19
- Vocabulary Puzzlemaker
- Testmaker
- Student Self-Test Software

LESSON PLAN
SECTION 3, 557–563

FOCUS

Bellringer

Before taking roll at the beginning of the class period, display Focus Activity Transparency 67 on the overhead projector, and assign the accompanying Focus Activity Sheet.

Objectives

Point out the objectives on this page to students in previewing the section content.

Motivating Activity

Write the headings Education, Literature, Art, and Architecture on the chalkboard. Ask students to hypothesize how each of these aspects of culture might have changed during the last century. Write students' responses on the chalkboard. Tell them to check their hypotheses as they read this section.

In 1876 Congress voted funds to complete the Washington Monument. Designed by Robert Mills, a neoclassical architect, the monument was begun in 1848 and completed in 1884. The length of time it took to construct led Mark Twain to suggest that it should carry the title "The Great-Great-Grandfather of His Country."

CHAPTER 20
SECTION 3

TEACH

Guided Practice

Linking Past and Present
Have students work in small groups to discuss why changes were necessary in education in the late nineteenth century. Have them identify the educational problems that had to be overcome. (poorly trained, overworked staff, outdated curriculum, poor equipment) Ask students to compare these problems with the problems inherent in today's educational system. Have students propose some possible solutions to today's educational problems.

History AND ART

Ungraded schools were common in rural areas. Children from 3 to 18 were often taught in the same classroom. **Answer to Caption:** romanticism and classicism

Did You Know?

In the years after the Civil War, educational opportunities expanded for women. By 1890, 13 percent of all college graduates were women. By 1900, that figure increased to nearly 20 percent.

---

schools in law, medicine, or the liberal arts. No American scientific school compared well with the best in Europe.

By 1900 these weaknesses had been vigorously attacked. Responding to the need for more practical education, colleges in the United States reformed their fields of study. Courses in the social and natural sciences were made available, and the elective system, first introduced at Harvard, made it possible for students to choose an individual course of study.

Young scholars from the United States who were trained in the world's best universities—in Germany—brought back higher standards of scholarship and scientific research. Existing private universities were greatly expanded, and new ones were founded—most with the aid of wealthy businesspeople who supported the trend toward making education more useful. More than two dozen new schools were devoted specifically to technical training. The Massachusetts Institute of Technology and others like it supplied industry with highly trained engineers, metallurgists, and chemists. Also during this period the first graduate schools of business, such as the Wharton School of Finance, were established.

State Universities

Along with the growth of privately endowed universities and technical schools came an expansion of state universities. Such institutions owed a great deal to the Morrill Act of 1862, which gave public lands to each state as a grant to finance the endowment of colleges. While the main goal of these schools was to extend knowledge of "agriculture and mechanic arts," they were funded to teach science and classical studies as well. The University of California, Texas A&M, and most of the large state universities of the Midwest began as land-grant colleges.

Universities in the Midwest also played an important role in opening higher education to women for the first time. In the pre-Civil War era, women had been admitted to Oberlin and Antioch colleges in Ohio. After the war, coeducation became common west of the Appalachians. In the more conservative East, women founded private colleges of their own, such as Mount Holyoke, Vassar, Smith, Radcliffe, and Bryn Mawr. These colleges shared the same educational goals as all-male institutions.

The adult public also cried out for more learning. Beginning in 1874 as a summer program to train Sunday school teachers,

 **SNAP THE WHIP** by Winslow Homer, 1872 Winslow Homer's painting captures the joy of a school recess. Homer is known for his vivid use of color and attention to detail. *What European artistic styles did he reject?*

Special Needs

Language Disability It is important for students with language processing weaknesses to hear a variety of language styles accompanied by interpretations so that meanings are clear. This section introduces a number of authors—William Dean Howells, Stephen Crane, and Mark Twain—who wrote in very different styles. Read aloud selections from these authors. (See selection from *Roughing It* by Mark Twain on page 482.) Then ask students to suggest what might make these authors' language difficult to understand. Rewrite selections in contemporary language to assist students' comprehension.

Life of the Times

Personal Hygiene

For polite society in the late nineteenth century, a virtual wall of silence surrounded the bathroom and related subjects. Such modesty would have been unthinkable in colonial America, or even on the farm, where privacy was rare. The invention of indoor plumbing—and with it the flush toilet—exemplified a revolution in personal hygiene and habits that transpired during the Gilded Age.

The word *toilet* reflected this change. Americans borrowed it from the French word *toilette*, which referred to grooming, as a euphemism for the British water closet, or simply, W.C.

Only when privy facilities were moved indoors did it become possible to treat this most human of topics with delicacy. The first bathroom in a household was installed in the New York residence of George Vanderbilt in 1855. Other wealthy families soon followed suit, although early plumbing systems were far from sanitary.

With the mass production of enamel-coated fixtures around the turn of the century, indoor plumbing in private homes became more commonplace. After cities acquired water and sewage systems, piping was run first to the kitchen. Next connected were washbasins and, finally, the bathtub and toilet. The bathroom thus became a room of genuine privacy.

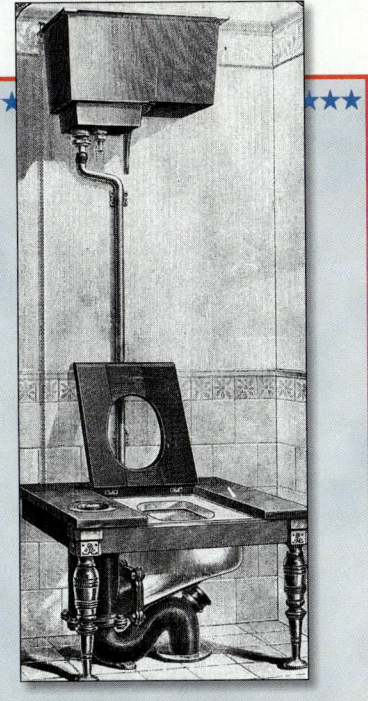

▲ Bathroom, c. 1880

---

the Chautauqua (shuh•TAW•kwuh) Institute in western New York sparked a movement that provided the masses with instruction in such subjects as literature, economics, science, and government through summer school instruction and correspondence school.

■ Literature

United States writers responded to the post-Civil War era in different ways. One popular school of postwar writers looked backward, striving to capture the romance of vanishing rural traditions. A center of such "local-color" writing was the South. Civil War and Reconstruction had swept away an entire way of life, leaving poverty and destruction in its wake. In the 1870s and the 1880s, Southern local colorists wrote nostalgically about **antebellum**—or pre-Civil War—manners, customs, and institutions.

Local colorists also wrote of vanishing ways of life in the small towns and fishing villages of New England, on the farms of the Midwest, on the ranches of the plains, and in the mining camps and boomtowns of the Wild West.

One of America's greatest writers was a local colorist named Samuel Clemens who wrote under the name Mark Twain. Twain wrote vivid and hilarious stories about his travels in the West. His most enduring works—*The Adventures of Tom Sawyer* and *The Adventures of Huckleberry Finn*—are tales of his boyhood home on the Mississippi River. Twain's books were not only acclaimed by critics but loved by the public. He combined shrewd observation and irreverent wit.

Twain's writing bridged the gap between popular and highbrow literature, between ordinary local-color writing and **realism**, a European-influenced movement that strove for accurate representation.

CHAPTER 20
SECTION 3

History AND ART

James McNeill Whistler was equally skilled in several media, including oil, watercolor, and etching. He traveled extensively and, after the 1860s, did most of his work in England. **Answer to Caption:** real people in everyday, normal activities

Fact or Fiction?

Only the very wealthy could afford to decorate their homes with works of art.

FICTION: Currier and Ives, the New York lithographers, produced inexpensive paintings that practically every household could afford. Their catalog, which in the 1870s included 2,800 items, boasted that their "pictures are the cheapest ornaments in the world."

Realist writers wanted to get away from the emotional preoccupations of the romantic movement and the pretty, sentimental themes of popular literature. Realist writers took a close look at real people's lives and problems. William Dean Howells declared that novels should "speak the dialect, the language, that most Americans know." In *The Rise of Silas Lapham,* Howells depicted a crude but likeable bumpkin—the new American millionaire. In *The Red Badge of Courage,* Stephen Crane depicted a Union soldier's fear and cowardice under fire. Other realists exposed the seamy underside of urban life. Critics of realism argued that realistic fiction was not uplifting, that its subject matter was often ordinary or even ugly, and that its characters' misdeeds were not always suitably punished.

 ▲ **THE LITTLE WHITE GIRL** by James Abbott McNeill Whistler, **1864** James Whistler adapted the concepts of Japanese color prints to his own style. **What subjects did realist artists seek to portray?**

■ Art and Architecture

Realism was also an important force in American painting during the Gilded Age. Rejecting the classicism and romanticism of the first half of the century, realist painters portrayed ordinary people in everyday activities. Winslow Homer moved from painting Civil War scenes to subjects such as a schoolyard full of boys playing a rowdy game, a hunter and his dogs, or sailors at sea. Of another great realist painter, Walt Whitman said:

> *I never knew of but one artist, and that's Tom Eakins, who could resist the temptation to see what they thought ought to be rather than what is.*

Some of America's greatest painters, however, became **expatriates**—people who choose to live outside their native country. John Singer Sargent, a portraitist of Europe's upper classes, lived in England. James Abbott McNeill Whistler and Mary Cassatt also lived in Europe. Cassatt was influenced by a style of painting called impressionism. Impressionists tried to capture the play of light, color, and pattern as they made immediate impressions on the senses.

The architecture of the Gilded Age was heavy and ornate. It is often called "Victorian," after Queen Victoria of Great Britain who reigned from 1837 to 1901. On the outside, Victorian houses had turrets, towers, porches, and gables. The development of better woodworking machines made it possible to add elaborate "gingerbread" decorations to roofs and porches of houses. The interior decor was similarly ornamented. Rooms were crowded with dark, thickly carved furniture, plush carpeting, heavy curtains, and countless knickknacks on ornate shelves.

Some dismissed the Victorian style as vulgar—a symbol of greed that characterized the Gilded Age. Others have celebrated the gaudiness as a symbol of the period's vitality and exuberance.

Cultural Diversity

Joseph Pulitzer emigrated from Hungary to the United States after being rejected for military service. He served in the Union army, and after the war became a reporter for Carl Schurz's German-language daily. In 1878 Pulitzer bought the *St. Louis Dispatch.* Later he acquired the *St. Louis Post,* the *New York World,* the *Evening World,* and other newspapers. Pulitzer is credited with fashioning the modern American newspaper. He founded mass circulation journalism, and revolutionized the newspaper to fit the needs of urban society.

CHAPTER 20
SECTION 3

■ The Yellow Press and the Dime Novel

The Industrial Revolution brought some Americans unaccustomed leisure time. As machines took over the work of more and more hands, the time required to produce a shirt, a bucket, a pin, or a table was reduced to a fraction of what it had been. Hours of work, although still long by the standards of the twentieth century, were gradually reduced. As leisure time increased, new forms of entertainment developed.

Penny Newspapers

Journalism took new forms. In the late 1800s, improvements in papermaking and printing made it possible to produce newspapers more cheaply than before. At the same time, newspapers could make their profits entirely from advertisers. Copies were sold below cost to attract the greatest number of readers. These penny newspapers strove to amuse readers as much as to inform them. Their intended audience was not the educated middle and upper classes but clerks, laborers, and homemakers.

The pioneer among the penny newspapers was the *New York World*, purchased by Joseph Pulitzer in 1883. In 15 years its circulation rose from 15,000 to more than 1 million. Pulitzer, dedicating his paper "to the cause of the people rather than the purse-proud potentates," attacked unfair employers and grafting politicians with vigor. The real source of Pulitzer's success, however, was not politics but sensationalism. He was one of the first to use "scare headlines" like "Baptized in Blood" and "Death Rides the Rails." He also introduced the colorized Sunday supplement and the serialized comic strip. From the yellow ink he used in his comics came the term **"yellow journalism,"** which critics applied to the subject matter and style of the *World* and all its imitators. If he could not find news, Pulitzer made it. Once he sent a young reporter, Nelly Bly, to travel around the globe in less time than it took the hero of Jules Verne's popular novel, *Around the World in Eighty Days*.

▲ The "Yellow Kid" comic strip, 1896

Dime Novels

Another form of reading matter produced for a mass market was the dime novel, which was designed especially to interest boys. These were adventure stories where heroes such as Mustang Sam and Deadwood Dick fought cattle rustlers and outlaws. Dime novels also portrayed the worlds of business and crime. Moralists suspected that these early paperbacks would corrupt the young. Defenders pointed out, however, that because dime novels were not the work of realists, no bad deed ever went unpunished; no good boy went without his just reward.

■ Sports and Entertainment

As work became less strenuous, many looked for leisure activities that involved physical exercise. Golf, croquet, and lawn tennis from Great Britain were popular sports with the middle and upper classes. College students brought in other British sports, including rowing, track, and rugby (from which American football was derived).

Did You Know?

Although organized baseball was played as early as the 1850s, the game really took off after the Civil War. Returning veterans helped to form teams, and by 1866 there were 202 teams in 17 states.

Football became an important spectator sport during the Gilded Age, with college competitions being the biggest draw. The first collegiate game took place in 1869, between Rutgers and Princeton. Seven years later, representatives from eastern colleges gathered to develop a set of rules. The standard design of today's game was established at this meeting. Throughout the 1800s the three big eastern colleges—Harvard, Yale, and Princeton—dominated the sport. Thanksgiving Day games involving these teams drew huge, festive crowds.

Food of the Times

In 1893, at the Chicago World's Fair, Americans were introduced to such processed foods as Cream of Wheat cereal, Aunt Jemima pancake mix, Juicy Fruit gum, and Nabisco's Shredded Wheat.

Sidelights: Circuses

In the late 1800s, circuses were among the most popular forms of entertainment. People seemed to be especially attracted to the oddities—the 120-year-old woman, the bearded lady, the two-headed monster, and so on—that were presented as sideshows. Most of these oddities were frauds, but occasionally they were real. For example, circus owner P. T. Barnum reportedly paid $250,000 for a real white elephant from Siam. Not to be outdone, competitor Adam Forepaugh created his own by painting an Indian elephant with whitewash.

CHAPTER 20 SECTION 3

ASSESS

Check Understanding
Assign Section 3 Review as homework or an in-class activity.

Evaluate
📁 💻 Assign the Section 3 Quiz in the TCR or use the History of a Free Nation Testmaker to create a customized quiz.

Reteach
📁 Have students complete Reteaching Activity 20-3.

Enrich
📁 Have students complete the Chapter 20 Enrichment Activity in the TCR.

CLOSE

Tell students that between 1870 and 1900 the workday for most people had decreased from 12 to 10 hours and that yearly per capita income rose from $779 to $1,164. Ask students to discuss the impact of these changes on people's lives.

Fact or Fiction?
Vassar College had women's baseball teams in the 1860s.

FACT: Many people were shocked that a college would allow such rough behavior by its students. By 1876 the sport was abandoned, a victim of public outcry.

Baseball, however, was a truly American invention—its earliest form was played before the Civil War. College and club teams sprang up all over the country in the late 1800s. The first professional team was the Cincinnati Red Stockings in 1869; in 1876 the National League was organized. Professional baseball found a ready audience and loyal fans in crowded urban areas where working-class people had little money for entertainment.

The enthusiasm for baseball had started during the Civil War, and it appeared that everyone was playing ball. A writer for a Nevada Territory newspaper noted:

> ❝ The rage for ball playing is very apparent. Old fellows whose hair and teeth are going and gone and young ones who have just got their first breeches and boots on are knocking and tossing and catching ball on the plaza and the streets from daybreak to dark. ❞

Towns that had no baseball called for teams. In an article in the Walla Walla *Statesman*, one writer explained why a team was needed.

> ❝ There is scarce a one-horse town . . . that has not one or more ball clubs. The practice of these clubs affords healthful exercise—something required by young men too closely confined to workshops and stores. In view of this advantage, cannot we have a baseball club at Walla Walla? In these dull times an organization of the kind would serve to drive away the blues. ❞

After the modern safety bicycle was substituted for the dangerous "high wheeler," bicycling became a craze. There were hundreds of bicycle clubs; special trains carried cyclists into the country on Sundays, and special bicycle paths were built in parks and suburbs. A transcontinental bicycle route was wanted.

Cities became centers of cultural life. In a day when the motion picture had not yet been invented, theater and vaudeville shows enjoyed great popularity. Large cities boasted opera companies and symphony orchestras, theaters, and museums of fine art.

In 1891 Peter Tchaikovsky, the Russian composer, came to America and conducted one of his own works at the new Carnegie Music Hall in New York City. He wrote home that everything went wonderfully, and that he was received with even greater enthusiasm than he had been in his native land.

▶ CAP ANSON OF THE CHICAGO WHITE SOX

Section 3 ★ Review

Checking for Understanding

1. **Identify** Mark Twain, Stephen Crane, James Abbott McNeill Whistler, Joseph Pulitzer, Thomas Eakins.
2. **Define** antebellum, realism, expatriate, yellow journalism.
3. **Characterize** the local-color and realist styles of literature.
4. **Give** examples of how Americans entertained themselves.

Critical Thinking

5. **Supporting Opinions** Argue for or against compulsory education in a democratic society. Support your opinion with facts or arguments that show how your position supports democratic goals.

Answers to SECTION 3 REVIEW

1. Mark Twain, 559; Stephen Crane, 560; James Abbott McNeill Whistler, 560; Joseph Pulitzer, 561; Thomas Eakins, 560
2. All vocabulary words are defined in the Glossary.
3. Local-color: nostalgic, romantic, sentimental, idealized; Realist: accurate, realistic, ordinary, gritty.
4. Penny newspapers, dime novels, magazines, sporting activities, museums, music, theaters
5. Answers will vary. Supporters may say that it provides all children with an education. Opponents may say democracy means choice.

CONNECTIONS — History and Technology — CONNECTIONS

Improvements in Printing

During the late 1800s, improvements in printing led to the inexpensive mass production of newspapers, magazines, and books. In 1863 American inventor William A. Bullock produced the first web-fed press. This press printed on huge rolls of paper rather than single sheets. Printer Richard March Hoe perfected the continuous-roll press in 1871. This device made it possible to produce up to 12,000 full newspapers an hour.

In 1886 linotype typesetting machines cut the time required to set type to a fraction of that required to set it by hand. The linotype operator sat at a keyboard. When the operator touched a letter on the keyboard, a lead mold was placed in line with other letters. Each complete line of type was molded onto a single slug, and the slugs were made into printing plates. The linotype allowed text to be assembled much faster into columns and pages.

Improved printing technology led to rapid growth of the publishing industry. It also led to increased competition among newspaper publishers to get out the "latest edition."

Improvements in printing also aided the magazine industry. For nearly 20 years after the Civil War, the magazine industry was limited by technology. For the most part, magazines were monthlies or weeklies that reached a small readership. The leaders in the field included the *Atlantic Monthly* and *Harper's Magazine*.

Improvements in the printing process, however, led to a new form of magazine in the 1880s. Such popular magazines as the *Ladies' Home Journal* and the *Saturday Evening Post* reached larger audiences.

Another development leading directly from improvements in printing concerned the Sunday edition. Throughout the country major city newspapers created Sunday papers of 50 or more pages. Comic strips, which began as Sunday features, were moved into separate colored supplements. By 1900 the formula of the American newspaper—daily and Sunday—was in place. In addition the new techniques helped magazines such as *McClure's* and the *Saturday Evening Post* achieve mass circulation.

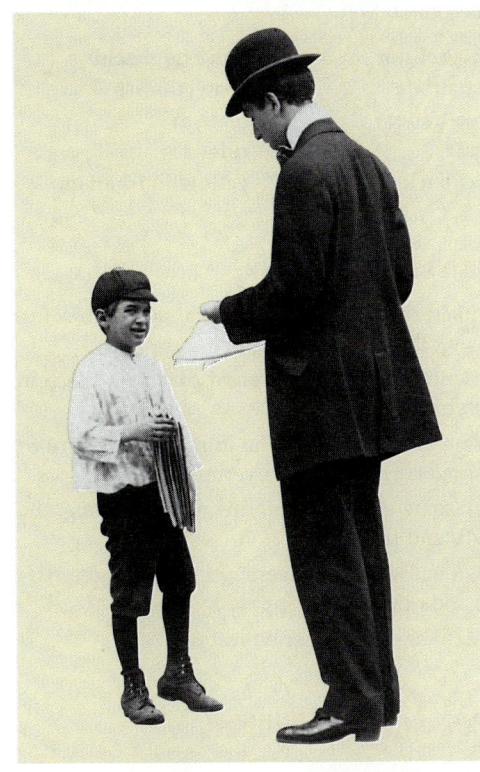

▲ Newsboy in the early 1900s

Making the Technology Connection
1. What is a linotype machine?
2. How did improved methods of printing and typesetting affect the publishing industry?

Linking Past and Present
3. How is most publishing done today?

CHAPTER 20 CONNECTIONS

Teaching Making Connections
Improvements in printing led to an explosion in published materials. For example, the number of daily newspapers in the United States grew from 1,000 in 1880 to about 2,200 by 1900. And the number of bookstores and libraries grew rapidly. Ask students what impact such developments would have on the spread of knowledge. (They would aid the spread of knowledge.)

Did You Know?
To boost readership, newspapers added a comics section. They quickly attracted a loyal following.

Did You Know?
In 1869 the first professional team, the Cincinnati Red Stockings, went on a barnstorming tour of the country, paying its players between $800 and $1,400 for the season. In a few years, the professional game had taken off and baseball was well on its way to being "the great national pastime."

Answers to CONNECTIONS
1. machine that sets type from a keyboard using hot lead slugs
2. they led to growth in the publishing industry and an increase in competition among publishers, especially newspaper publishers
3. Today, almost all commercial publishing is done by computer.

CHAPTER 20 ★ REVIEW

Using Vocabulary

Each term below has one of the following connotations: *political*, *economic*, or *cultural*. Classify each term under its respective connotation. Write a sentence that explains the connection between the term and its connotation.

antebellum	political machine
expatriate	protectionist
free-trader	realism
graft	rider
kickback	yellow journalism

Reviewing Facts

1. **Explain** the increase in political corruption following the Civil War.
2. **Describe** types of corruption that took place in government.
3. **Name** the Presidents who introduced reform or resisted corruption in government.
4. **List** some political reforms made during the 1870s and the 1880s.
5. **Point out** why some were in favor of higher tariffs and others were opposed.
6. **List** changes in higher education.

Understanding Concepts

Corruption
1. How might patronage and the spoils system have allowed for more corruption in government?

Public Protest
2. What events described in this chapter suggest that a free press can inspire public protest of corruption in government?

Critical Thinking

1. **Linking Past and Present** What businesses today depend on people having leisure time? Would all these businesses exist if work hours had not been shortened? Explain.

2. **Analyzing Illustrations** Study the advertisement on this page and answer the questions that follow.
   a. What is the product that is featured in the advertisement?
   b. This advertisement appeared in 1885. In what ways would a modern advertisement differ from this example? In what ways would the ads be similar?

Writing About History

Definition
Imagine that you are an art critic attending the first showing of a group of American realist painters. Write a definition of realism that would be appropriate to include in an art review. To help your readers understand realism, use examples and comments about how this style contrasts with other schools of painting.

REVIEW CHAPTER 20

Answers

Reviewing Facts
1. Growth of cities, alliance between business and politics, immigrants unfamiliar with democracy, few restraints on abuses of power.
2. kickbacks, overly expensive contracts, party machine control, bribes, conflict of interest, influence peddling
3. Hayes, Garfield, Arthur, and Cleveland.
4. reform of civil service, balancing of power between the presidency and Congress, improving government efficiency and integrity
5. Some favored tariffs as a means of protecting growing industries and keeping wages high. Others were opposed because government was seen as interfering in the laws of supply and demand and because tariffs amounted to subsidies paid to manufacturers.
6. made compulsory, state-supported colleges, expanded college curricula, higher education opened to women

Understanding Concepts
1. Answers will vary. Jobs were offered or sold as rewards for political support. Elected officials could surround themselves with corrupt jobholders who would conspire on graft and kickbacks.
2. Published evidence of Tweed's greed, Nast's cartoons about Tweed, revelation of Crédit Mobilier's bribes to members of Congress. Answers will vary. Watergate was a particularly dramatic example.

Critical Thinking
1. Amusement parks, cinemas, organized sports, television, restaurants, night clubs. Some that appeal mainly to the working class might be absent or limited if work hours had not been shortened.
2. Silk Hats. Ads would include price and information about quality. Appealing graphics and typefaces are used.

CHAPTER 20 ★ REVIEW

Cooperative Learning

Work with a partner to act out an interview between a newspaper reporter and a local political boss or a machine politician. Decide which role each of you will assume. The reporter should review information on corrupt government practices as were presented in the chapter. The politician should review information on party machines. The reporter should prepare a list of questions to ask the politician. The politician should prepare a list of answers to questions that he or she feels may be asked. After the interview, both of you should list what were the most pertinent points brought out in the interview. Compare your findings with those of other groups.

Social Studies Skills

Reading and Interpreting Political Cartoons

A political cartoon is meant to entertain as well as make a point about a current issue. Such cartoons often use caricatures, symbols, and/or analogies. Understanding a political cartoon involves understanding these caricatures, symbols, and analogies and determining the point of the cartoon.

Practicing the Skill

Use the following questions to help you interpret this political cartoon.
1. From the title, the words on the ladder, and the ladder's placement, what do the ladder and tree represent?
2. What are the keys to fortune?
3. What activities do not lead to success?
4. What are the rewards of climbing the ladder of fortune?
5. What people climb the ladder of fortune?
6. Why do you think the tree and the people in the foreground are in bright colors, whereas the people in the background are in black and white or dull colors?
7. Summarize in a sentence or two the point being made by this cartoon.

Using Your Journal

From your Journal notes and knowledge of recent problems with some government officials, write a paragraph comparing the corruption and questionable ethics during the Gilded Age with today's problems.

CHAPTER 20 The Gilded Age 1865–1900 565

REVIEW CHAPTER 1

❓ Chapter Bonus Test Question

Americans in the 1800s passed laws to solve each of the following problems. Identify the law associated with them. Which was most successful?
(a) spoils system (Pendleton Act of 1883)
(b) foreign products competing with American products (McKinley Tariff)
(c) trusts too powerful (Sherman Antitrust Act)
(d) no line of succession to the presidency (Presidential Succession Act)
(Answers to the last question will vary, but students should recognize that none of the four completely ended the problem it was passed to resolve.)

Using Your Journal

Students' paragraphs may include questions about campaign contributions, gifts to officeholders, lobbyists' activities, speaking fees for legislators, and other perceived conflicts of interest.

Practicing the Skill
1. Hard work and good morals would bring rewards.
2. perseverance, courage, punctuality, economy, integrity, prudence, temperance, industry
3. lottery (chance), betting, gambling, striking
4. influence, contentment, a good conscience, the favor of God, riches, reputation, self-respect, success, good will to men
5. businesspeople, hard workers, professional people, educated people, entrepreneurs
6. The bright colors indicate success, the dull colors signify failure.
7. The point of this cartoon is that success comes from hard work and good morals, whereas idle schemes lead to poverty and ruin.

565

PLANNING GUIDE   Chapter 21   Politics and Protest

Daily Lesson Objectives	Teacher Classroom Resources	Multimedia
SECTION 1 **Agrarian Unrest** 1 Day pp. 568–572 1. Identify the problems farmers faced during the late 1800s. 2. Discuss the rise and fall of the Grange. 3. Analyze the impact of the Interstate Commerce Act.	Chapter 21 Study Guide Reproducible Lesson Plan Reteaching Activity 21-1 Section Quiz American Portrait 42 Chapter 21 Primary and Secondary Source Readings Reinforcing Social Studies Skills 6, 25, 27, 31, 37 Chapter 21 Cooperative Learning Activity Chapter 21 Concept Mapping Activity American Literary Heritage Unit 6 Writer's Guidebook Lessons 6 SAT Practice Tests 11-13	Student Self-Test Software Testmaker Section Focus Transparency 65 Chapter 20 Skills Transparency Chapter 21 Map Transparency
SECTION 2 **Rise and Fall of Populism** 1 Day pp. 573–578 1. Explain the motivations of the groups that supported greenbacks and free silver. 2. Describe the campaign and results of the election of 1896. 3. Discuss the Populist movement.	Reproducible Lesson Plan Reteaching Activity 20-2 Section Quiz American Portrait 44 Chapter 21 Primary and Secondary Source Readings Reinforcing Social Studies Skills 32, 45, 46, 49, 53, 67	Student Self-Test Software Testmaker Section Focus Transparency 66 GTV: A Geographic Perspective on American History The Presidents: A Picture History of Our Nation
SECTION 3 **Other Forces for Reform** 1 Day pp. 580–504 1. Trace women's involvement in the temperance and suffrage movements. 2. Discuss the political ideas of Karl Marx and Henry George.	Reproducible Lesson Plan Reteaching Activity 21-3 Section Quiz Chapter 21 Enrichment Activity American Portrait 41 Reinforcing Social Studies Skills 28, 31, 32, 37, 63 Spanish Summaries & Glossary	Student Self-Test Software Testmaker Section Focus Transparency 67 Unit 6 Digest Transparencies Vocabulary Puzzlemaker Audiocassette, Chapter 20 Powers of the Supreme Court
CHAPTER REVIEW AND EVALUATION 1 Day	Chapter 21 Test Chapter 21 Performance Assessment Activity	Student Self-Test Software Testmaker

00:00   OUT OF TIME? If time does not permit teaching the entire chapter, use the Chapter 21 Summary on pages 590–591 and the Chapter 21 audiocassette (English and Spanish) to point out the main ideas of the chapter.

PLANNING GUIDE

Cultural Diversity Activity

Interpreting Primary Sources After students have read about the radical solutions to the problems created by industrialism, write the following statement on the chalkboard: "The settlement of America shifted the emphasis from nobility to ability." Have students explain how this quotation applied to the European immigrant experience in the United States. Note that greater economic opportunity and changes for upward social mobility reduced the appeal of radical movements to immigrants. Then ask how it applied to the experience of Chinese Americans, African Americans, and Native Americans. Have students also consider whether more recent immigrants from Southeast Asia, Mexico, Central and South America, and the Caribbean share earlier immigrants' views of the United States as the "land of ability." Why or why not?

Performance Assessment Activity

Taking a Stand Have pairs of students create posters advocating or opposing one of the following: Granger laws, the Omaha platform, unlimited coinage of silver, temperance, or the women's suffrage movement. Suggest that partners begin by reviewing the issue they chose and then decide on their point of view. They might afterward list topics that relate to that issue and determine how best to illustrate them. Have the class evaluate the posters in terms of how well each succeeds in presenting the point of view.

POSSIBLE RUBRIC FEATURES: Content, organization, research, visual communication skills, creativity, collaborative skills

Chapter Resources

Literature from the Period
Addams, Jane. *Twenty Years at Hull House.* 1910.

Cather, Willa. *My Antonia.* 1918

Readings for the Student
Meltzer, Milton. *Bread and Roses: The Struggle of American Labor, 1865-1915.* Facts on File. 1990.

Walker, Robert Harris. *Everyday Life in the Age of Enterprise 1865-1900.* Putnam, 1967.

Readings for the Teacher
Grob, Gerald N. *Workers and Uptopia.* Quadrangle, 1961.

Wilson, Charles Morrow. *The Commoner: William Jennings Bryan.* Doubleday, 1970.

Multimedia Resources
Labor Movement: Beginnings and Growth in America. Coronet. (13 1/2 minutes.)

Living American History Series. U.S. History III, 1876-1914. Priven Learning Systems. (2 Apple diskettes)

Progressives, Populists, and Reform in America. Guidance Associates. (VHS, 32 minutes)

Key to Ability Levels

Teaching strategies have been coded for varying learning styles and abilities.

- **L1** Basic activities for all students
- **L2** Average activities for average to above-average students
- **L3** Challenging activities for above-average students
- **LEP** Limited English Proficiency activities

Glencoe Links to the Humanities

Link to Art
- U.S. History and Art Transparencies 16, 17

Link to Literature
- Macmillan Literature: Appreciating Literature Audiotapes Side 4

Link to Music
- American Music: Cultural Traditions

CHAPTER 21

BEGINNING THE CHAPTER

Give students the following information. The center of population in 1790 was about 23 miles east of Baltimore, Maryland. In 1850 it was 23 miles southeast of Parkersburg, West Virginia. By 1900 it had moved to 6 miles southeast of Columbus, Indiana. Ask students to speculate on the cause of this dramatic shift in population.

Recording Journal Notes

Students are likely to mention in their journals that many Democrats agreed with the principles of the Populist party, thereby raising fears that the third party would divide the Democratic vote. When the Populist party supported the Democratic party's narrow focus on free silver in 1896, the Democrats split, and the Republicans won the election.

CHAPTER 21
Politics and Protest
1865–1900

▶ **POLITICAL CAMPAIGN BUTTONS**

Setting the Scene

Focus

In the late nineteenth century, most Americans continued to live on the farm. By the 1880s, however, agriculture was in crisis. Farmers blamed their difficulties on abuses by the railroads, greedy bankers, and eastern industrialists. Farmers began to band together to fight these problems, which in turn led to the creation of a new political party, the Populists. Populism shared some goals with a larger movement aimed at redistributing the wealth and political power in the United States.

Concepts to Understand

★ Why economic inequity developed between farmers and urban workers
★ Why many reformers believed that social change would result in a more just and equitable society

Read to Discover . . .

★ some of the problems that American farmers faced in the 1880s.
★ what were the major goals of the Populist party.

Journal Notes

As you read the chapter, note in your journal the answers to these questions: Why was the Democratic party divided in 1896? What effect did this division have on the presidential election?

CULTURAL
- 1874 National Woman's Christian Temperance Union formed in Cleveland
- 1881 Clara Barton founds the American Red Cross

1865 — **1875**

POLITICAL
- 1871 Civil Service Reform Act passed
- 1877 Munn v. Illinois
- 1878 Bland-Allison Act passes

566   UNIT 6   New Horizons: 1860–1900

➕ EXTRA CREDIT PROJECT

Divide interested students into two groups: defenders of Granger laws and defenders of private businesses. Have the two groups hold a mock court session. The defenders of the Granger laws can represent the viewpoint of the farmers, and the defenders of private businesses can represent the railroads.

I Feed You All
Lithograph, American Oleograph Company, 1875

During the mid- and late 1800s, the lithograph, made by printing from designs on stone or other surfaces, was a popular art form.

▲ Railroad conductor's badge

- **1891** Hamlin Garland publishes Main-Travelled Roads
- **1896** Henry Ford builds his first automobile

| 1885 | 1895 |

- **1892** Populist national convention held in Omaha
- **1896** William J. Bryan delivers "Cross of Gold" speech

CHAPTER 21 Politics and Protest 1865–1900

CHAPTER 21 CONCEPTS

Concept Mapping Activity
Write the concept generalization and the concepts below on the chalkboard. Ask students to copy the generalization and the concepts into their notebooks. Have them enter ideas about economic integrity and social change they read about under the appropriate concept.

> People united to have their economic and political needs met.
> → Economic Integrity
> → Social Change

History AND ART
For the first time in American history, the 1870 census counted farmers as a minority in the workforce. They constituted about 47 percent of all employed workers. Their shrinking numbers and the expanding food supply were testimony to their efficiency.

GLENCOE TECHNOLOGY

VIDEODISC

Economics in Action

Videodisc 1, Side 2, Chapter 14
Competition and Monopolies

Teacher Notes

LESSON PLAN
SECTION 1, 568–572

FOCUS

Bellringer
Before taking roll at the beginning of the class period, display Focus Activity 68 on the overhead projector, and assign the accompanying Focus Activity Sheet.

Objectives
Point out the objectives on this page to students in previewing the section content.

Motivating Activity
Present the following job description to students:

Wanted: Person to own and manage small business. Applicant must be willing to do physical labor for long hours (12–14), especially during spring and summer. Wages based on current market price of product minus cost of shipment to customers. Payment for services made at point of sale of product.

Ask students: Would you apply for the job described above? Why or why not? (probably not, because of the long hours, the hard work, and the uncertain salary)

Tell students that the job describes the work of a farmer in the late 1800s. Discuss why some people might choose such a life. Tell students that they will learn about the problems of farmers in the late 1800s in this section.

Use Skills Transparency 21.

SECTION 1

Agrarian Unrest

Setting the Scene

Section Focus

In the late 1800s, most people in the United States still lived in rural areas, but the balance was rapidly shifting. The country's attention was on the future—on booming industry and bustling cities. While much of America prospered, farmers were struggling. As conditions grew worse, they organized to protest their exclusion from the table of plenty.

Objectives

After studying this section, you should be able to
★ identify the problems farmers faced during the late 1800s.
★ discuss the rise and fall of the Grange.
★ analyze the impact of the Interstate Commerce Act.

Key Terms

pooling, cooperative

◀ MOWER ADVERTISEMENT, C. 1868

There appeared, as if from nowhere, a plague of grasshoppers that destroyed not only the wheat but the morale of farmers on the Great Plains. The Norwegian American writer, Ole Rolvaag, described the coming of the grasshoppers in his novel *Giants in the Earth*:

> They actually hurt me as they flew against my face and hands. The wagon ... was literally filled with them. The road was seething. ... I saw Father standing almost in despair. So thick were the grasshoppers in the cornfield of which both of us had been so proud, that not a spot of green was left to be seen. And within two hours ... not a leaf was left. ...

The grasshoppers ate anything green, choked wells to the brim, broke the branches off fruit trees by their weight, and even devoured harnesses and tool handles. They came in clouds that darkened the sky and covered the ground.

■ The Plight of the Farmers

Even clouds of grasshoppers were only one of the hazards of life on the plains. There was always the threat of prairie fires, dust storms, and, worst of all, drought, which combined with hot winds and temperatures over 100°F to bake crops in the ground and to cake farmers' faces with the salt of their sweat.

Farm prices began to decline in the 1880s; the price of wheat fell from 91 cents a bushel in 1883 to 69 cents in 1886. This decline was

568 UNIT 6 New Horizons: 1860–1900

Classroom Resources for SECTION 1

Teacher's Classroom Resources
- Chapter 21 Study Guide
- Reproducible Lesson Plan
- Chapter 21 Cooperative Learning Activity
- Reteaching Activity 21-1
- Chapter 21 Primary and Secondary Source Readings
- Section Quiz

Multimedia
- Section Focus Transparency 68
- Chapter 21 Skills Transparency
- Chapter 21 Map Transparency
- Testmaker
- Student Self-Test Software

largely the result of overproduction of crops. New inventions, such as steam-powered harvesting and threshing machines, had improved crop yields, and more efficient techniques greatly increased farm production. As prices declined farmers had to borrow more and more money. Costs of the new farm machinery that assisted with large harvests were high. Often farmers could afford such equipment only on a mortgage. High, too, were the costs of shipping crops to market. The more farm prices fell, the harder it became for farmers to pay back their loans.

Even farmers who were not investing in mechanized equipment frequently had to borrow money. They had to live for a full year on the payments they received for their crops in the fall. If the money did not last, they were forced to borrow. This meant they were at the mercy of interest rates. It also meant that farmers were pretty much forced to sell their crops as soon as they came in. At that time, of course, because of the large supply, prices were always low. This is why farmer organizations, most notably the Southern Alliance, began to look for other ways to finance and market crops. Many farmers also began to call for railroad regulations for a variety of reasons.

Railroad Abuses

Railroads opened vast stretches of the West to settlement, making it possible for farmers to get their crops to markets and to get manufactured goods from the East. Huge sums of money were required to finance the building of a railway system. The promise of quick profits made the railroad an attractive investment for shrewd business leaders. Millions of dollars were raised through the sale of stock to private investors, both American and European.

Because a railroad promised growth and prosperity for those along its path, state and local governments offered loans and land grants in order to obtain railroad connections. Not all the dealings were legal, however.

Unethical Business Practices

Some railroad companies spent millions of dollars in bribes to state legislators and other public officials in exchange for special favors, such as land grants, cash subsidies, pro-railroad laws, and tax exemptions. But they often evaded laws designed to make them provide services in return for the benefits they were granted.

Graph Study
Farm prices peaked during the Civil War. **What crop declined the most by 1900?**

▼ FIGHTING GRASSHOPPERS IN KANSAS, 1875

CHAPTER 21 Politics and Protest 1865–1900

CHAPTER 21 SECTION 1

TEACH
Guided Practice
Science Ask what types of natural factors have an effect on the success of a crop. (weather, pests, diseases, rainfall, fire) Write "Supply" and "Demand" on the chalkboard. Have students make up a generalization of how natural factors influence the supply of a farm product. (When growing conditions are favorable, supply of a crop increases.) Ask: What happens to a crop's price if supply exceeds demand? (Prices fall.) **L1, LEP**

Using Graphs
Answer: wheat
Skills Practice: Why did farm prices peak during the Civil War? (Supplies were low; demand was great.)

Assign students the Chapter 21 reading on "The Farmer's Right" in Primary and Secondary Source Readings.

Today's high-tech farm equipment has increased farm efficiency over 1960 levels almost as dramatically as the steam-powered equipment of the 1900s advanced farm productivity over its 1860 level.

Sidelights: The General Store

The general store was probably the most frequented place in a rural town. It was usually located on Main Street and was stocked with everything from hand tools to quinine to calico for a dress. Farmers came to the store from long distances to load up on supplies and to sell their farm products. Often farm women brought eggs and vegetables that they grew in their gardens. However, a trip to the general store met more than economic needs. It provided a chance to get away from ever-present chores, to see one's friends, to catch up on the local gossip, and to receive mail.

CHAPTER 21 SECTION 1

Independent Practice

Writing Have students write two- or three-paragraph editorials, condemning or promoting either railroad practices during the late 1800s or the Interstate Commerce Act. Tell students to assume that the editorial would appear in a newspaper distributed by the Grange. Have several volunteers read their editorials. **L2**

Did You Know?

In 1872 Aaron Montgomery Ward started a mail-order business, sending out a 1-page list of items for sale. By 1874 people were ordering goods from his 72-page catalog. Before long Sears, Roebuck and Company also recognized the vast rural market and began a mail-order business that promised "satisfaction or your money back."

Food of the Times

Americans in the late 1800s consumed huge quantities of baked goods made from wheat or corn. Northerners ate more wheat bread than westerners or southerners. Biscuits were a more popular way of preparing wheat in the West and South.

▲ SEARS AND ROEBUCK CATALOG, EARLY 1900s

Another abuse was called "stock watering," the practice of increasing the number of shares of a company without adding to the company's assets. For example, when Jay Gould and James J. Fisk gained control of the Erie Railroad in 1868, they issued $71 million of stock on property worth $20 million. They made money by selling this "watered stock" to the public who did not know of the stock's actual lower value. Such action cheated all the stockholders. It also hurt the public because the railroads had to keep their rates high to pay dividends.

Unfair Pricing

In a day when trucks and highways were not yet dreamed of, railroads often enjoyed a natural monopoly; that is, in certain places there was no competition for services. Railroads took advantage of this situation by charging more for short hauls where they had a monopoly than for long hauls where they faced competition from other railroad lines. Thus, it cost shippers more to send goods from Poughkeepsie, New York, to New York City than to send goods from Chicago to New York City.

Sometimes competing railroad lines divided up traffic serving the same route, a practice known as **pooling.** Railroads pooled to make sure each line had enough traffic to pay costs and debts.

■ The Grange

Feelings against railroad abuses ran high all over the country but were especially strong in the West where there was almost no competition from other forms of transportation. This was because railroads had been favored by huge government subsidies in the form of land. Business owners and workers in the cities as well as farmers resented the railroads.

It was a nationwide farm organization, however, that began a movement against the unfair practices of the railroads. This organization tried to end railroad abuses with laws passed by state legislatures.

From Social Support to Political Action

The Patrons of Husbandry, commonly called the Grange, was an early national farm organization. It was founded in 1867 by Oliver Hudson Kelley. At first the main purpose of the Grange was to relieve the isolation and loneliness in the lives of farm families by providing social activities. Also, recognizing the importance of women on the farm, the Grange was the first fraternal organization to admit women on an equal basis.

The panic of 1873, however, turned the Grange into a reform lobby. As crop prices fell and credit became scarce, farmers began to talk about how to solve their common problems. Local Grange organizations pooled farmers' resources to set up mills, factories, banks, insurance companies, grain elevators, and **cooperatives,** or nonprofit stores owned by farmers. The local Granges involved themselves in local and national politics and pressed for state laws to help farmers.

UNIT 6 New Horizons: 1860–1900

Cooperative Learning

Divide students into groups of four or five. Give each group the topic the Grange. Using one piece of paper per group, have each student write a statement about the history of the Grange during the late 1800s. Have them pass the paper around several times until they have written down all they know about the Grange. Then have students review the statements and add any information that is missing. Have each group share one statement with the class. **L1, L2**

By 1874 the Grange had 1.5 million members in states throughout the Midwest, the South, and the West. Its solidarity met with such success that several states passed "Granger laws" that fixed maximum freight and passenger rates, forbade railroads to discriminate between places or shippers, and attempted to regulate monopolies of such farmer necessities as grain elevators and warehouses.

Granger Laws Versus Business Interests

Private businesses protested loudly against the Granger laws. Their main argument was that government should not interfere with private enterprise. Railroad lawyers argued that Granger laws were unconstitutional because the Fourteenth Amendment forbade a state to "deprive any person of life, liberty, or property, without due process of law." They viewed a railroad corporation as a legal "person" that should not be deprived of its property by being forced to lower its rates.

Defenders of the Granger laws said railroads that had accepted generous aid from government should not claim to be devotees of laissez-faire capitalism. Further, they argued that laissez-faire rules did not apply to natural monopolies because there was no competition to keep prices down. The Grangers maintained that government must regulate railroads and other such monopolies in order to protect the public.

Supreme Court Decisions

In 1877 the Supreme Court decided in favor of the Granger laws in the case of *Munn* v. *Illinois*. The Court stated that common carriers, such as railroads, and public utilities, such as grain elevators, "stand in the very gateway of commerce" and "take toll of all who pass." Therefore these carriers must "submit to being controlled by the public for the common good."

In spite of such Court decisions, the Granger laws were unsuccessful. The railroads fought the laws by cutting services or threatening to lay no more track until the acts were repealed. Moreover, in the late 1870s, membership in the Grange declined and so did its political activity. The main cause of the Grange's collapse was its venture into business activities. The Grange set up plow and reaper factories, grain elevators, packing plants, and banks. Bitterly opposed by private companies and often not well run, these

AMERICAN PORTRAITS

Willa Cather
1873–1947

Life on the prairie was a memorable experience for a young girl in the 1880s and the 1890s. The beauty of the land and the hardy determination of the pioneers lasted long in the memory of Willa Cather.

Born in Virginia in 1873, Willa moved with her family to a farm near Red Cloud, Nebraska, at the age of nine. The next eight years would provide the reflections for several novels, written years later.

Cather tried her hand at writing while teaching school in Pittsburgh in 1901 and then became an editor for *McClure's Magazine*. However, her real success did not begin until she started writing about life on the plains. Many of her famous novels, such as *O Pioneers!* (1913), tell of the tough, yet sensitive, nature of the immigrants who matched their determination against the demanding and lonely life on a plains farm.

CHAPTER 21 Politics and Protest 1865–1900   571

CHAPTER 21 SECTION 1

Teaching American Portraits

When Willa Cather moved with her family to Nebraska, she lived among immigrants and came to admire and respect them. In her novels she draws on her experiences of living among newcomers to the United States. Ask: In Willa Cather's lifetime, what inventions changed life on the farm most, in your opinion?

Did You Know?

Between 1889 and 1893, banks and mortgage companies foreclosed on more than 11,000 farms in Kansas alone. In the late 1970s and early 1980s, thousands of U.S. farmers also lost their land. They, too, had overborrowed. When the price of land dropped and interest rates increased, they defaulted on their loans, and the banks foreclosed.

Critical Thinking

Detecting Bias Write on the chalkboard the following quotation, left incomplete, taken from a Nebraska newspaper.

"There are three great crops raised in Nebraska. One is a crop of corn, one a crop of freight rates, and one a crop of interest. One is produced by farmers, who sweat and toil on the land. The other two are produced by . . . ."

Ask students to study the incomplete quotation and suggest how it might be concluded. (possible answer: railroads and bankers) Ask if the author of the quotation displays a bias. (Yes. The author favors the farmer.) **L3**

CHAPTER 21
SECTION 1

ASSESS

Check Understanding
Assign Section 1 Review as homework or an in-class activity.

Evaluate
📁 💻 Assign the Section 1 Quiz in the TCR, or use the History of a Free Nation Testmaker to create a customized quiz.

Reteach
📁 Have students complete Reteaching Activity 21-1.

Enrich
Have students research the impact of the Interstate Commerce Act on American business today and write a short report on it. Ask volunteers to present their papers to the class.

CLOSE
Ask students to explain how the farmers in the late nineteenth century were benefactors as well as victims of the Industrial Revolution.

Remind students that not only farmers but also railroads and other businesses had to adjust to an industrial economy.

Granger businesses usually failed. Their collapse discredited the Grange, and by 1880 its membership was less than one-fourth of what it had been in 1874. This effort of the Grangers to undercut the marketers had one favorable long-term result, however: the development of mail-order department stores, selling directly to the consumer. Montgomery Ward & Co., of Chicago, was founded in 1872 especially "to meet the wants of the Patrons of Husbandry."

The remaining Granger laws were dealt a mortal blow in 1886. In the Wabash Railway decision, the Supreme Court held that the states could control railroad traffic only within each state's own borders. They did not have the power to regulate railroad traffic that crossed state borders. Because most railroad traffic crossed state boundaries, the Court's decision effectively wiped out states' regulation of railroad rates.

The fall of the Grangers did not stop other organizations from taking its place. In the late 1800s, farmers' alliances, first formed locally, called for reform. One especially important local group was started in Texas in the mid-1870s. This group, guided by Dr. C. W. Macune, soon joined with similar groups in Arkansas and Louisiana to form a national alliance. It was called the National Farmers' Alliance and Industrial Union and was referred to as the Southern Alliance.

■ Interstate Commerce Act

The Supreme Court's ruling in the Wabash decision made it clear that regulation would have to come at the national level. In 1887 Congress passed the first federal law to regulate interstate commerce. The Interstate Commerce Act declared that the rates that railroads charged must be "reasonable and just"; it forbade pooling, rebates, and higher rates for short rather than long hauls.

The railroad companies were required to publish rates, give advance notice of all rate changes, and make annual financial reports available to the federal government. Violations of these provisions were punishable by fines of up to $5,000 for each offense. Enforcement of the law was placed under the Interstate Commerce Commission (ICC), a five-member panel appointed by the President.

As far as its immediate purpose was concerned, the Interstate Commerce Act was a failure. The ICC, lacking power to set rates, could only make recommendations or bring suits in the federal courts. Of 16 such cases that reached the Supreme Court, the Court held for the railroads in 15.

In 1892 Richard Olney, a corporate lawyer who later served as attorney general and secretary of state, wrote to a railroad official urging him not to advocate repeal of the Interstate Commerce Act. "It satisfies popular clamor for government supervision of the railroads," observed Olney, "at the same time that such supervision is almost entirely nominal."

In retrospect, though, the Interstate Commerce Act was a very important law. It established the precedent that the federal government might control large-scale private enterprise if the public good seemed to require it. It also provided a model for the regulatory commissions of today.

Section 1 ★ Review

Checking for Understanding
1. **Identify** the Grange, Interstate Commerce Act.
2. **Define** pooling, cooperative.
3. **Explain** why farmers failed to share in the economy's prosperity.
4. **Describe** the purposes of the Grange.

Critical Thinking
5. **Applying Principles** Some farmers believed their prosperity depended on producing more crops. State in your own words the law of supply and demand. Then explain how the law worked against farmers.

---

572   UNIT 6 New Horizons: 1860–1900

Answers to SECTION 1 REVIEW

1. The Grange, 570; Interstate Commerce Act, 572
2. All vocabulary words are defined in the Glossary.
3. overproduction, low prices, indebtedness due to loans, high costs, natural disasters
4. communal social outlet, educational, means of discussing solutions to farmers' problems, setting up cooperatives, lobby for political pressure
5. Farmers produced more crops to meet increased demand, but received lower prices when the supply of crops exceeded the demand.

SECTION 2

Rise and Fall of Populism

Setting the Scene

Section Focus

After the collapse of the Granger movement, farmers in the South and West began to form new organizations. In the 1890s these farmers' alliances grew into a new national political party. American farmers prepared to do battle to maintain their political power against the growing influence of industry.

Objectives

After studying this section, you should be able to
★ explain the motivations of the groups that supported greenbacks and free silver.
★ describe the campaign and results of the election of 1896.
★ discuss the Populist movement.

Key Terms

inflation, deflation, gold standard, third party

◀ GRANGE FARMER

"In God we trusted, in Kansas we busted," and "Going home to Mother"—so read signs on the wagons of "busted" farm families returning east during the hard times of the 1880s. Discontent grew to new heights in rural areas. Farm prices continued to fall, money was in short supply, and more and more people were losing their land to creditors.

Many blamed their problems not only on the drought but on human forces as well: greedy bankers, industrialists, and railroad companies that were accused of controlling government policies and bleeding rural areas dry. Like the Grangers, these men and women turned to politics to solve the problems caused by rapid economic change. The farmers' alliances, which spawned the Populist Party, succeeded beyond the dreams of the Grangers.

■ Greenbacks and Free Silver

If there was anything that farmers in the late nineteenth century demanded more strongly than the regulation of natural monopolies or the reduction of the marketers' profits, it was "cheap money." The value of money, like that of any other commodity, changes according to the supply. If the number of dollars in circulation increases while there is no increase in the amount of goods and services for sale, the dollar buys *less,* and prices go up. This situation is called **inflation.** On the other hand, if the number of dollars in circulation decreases while there is no decrease in the amount of goods and services for sale, the dollar buys *more,* and prices go down. This situation is

CHAPTER 21 Politics and Protest 1865–1900 **573**

LESSON PLAN
SECTION 2, 573–579

FOCUS

Bellringer
Before taking roll at the beginning of the class period, display Focus Activity 69 on the overhead projector, and assign the accompanying Focus Activity Sheet.

Objectives
Point out the objectives on this page to students in previewing the section content.

Motivating Activity
Write the following quotation by Mary Ellen Lease, a Kansas lawyer, on the chalkboard, and ask students to name the individuals for whom Lease spoke. (farmers)

"We want money, land, and transportation. We want the abolition of National Banks, and we want the power to make loans direct from the government. We want the accursed foreclosure system wiped out."

Ask students: What groups are being attacked in the quotations (railroads, banks, businesses)

Tell students that this section tells about farmers' attempts to solve their economic problems through political means.

Did You Know?

Due to frost and drought, crops failed every year but two from 1886 to 1895.

Classroom Resources for SECTION 2

Teacher's Classroom Resources
- Reproducible Lesson Plan
- Reteaching Activity 21-2
- Chapter 17 Primary and Secondary Source Readings
- Section Quiz

Multimedia
- Section Focus Transparency 69
- Testmaker
- Student Self-Test Software
- GTV: A Geographic Perspective on American History
- The Presidents: A Picture History of Our Nation

573

CHAPTER 21 SECTION 2

TEACH
Guided Practice
Summarizing Content
Have students write a short summary explaining why McKinley won the election, and why Bryan lost it. Then hold a discussion on the following topic: If the election were held today, which candidate would win? Have students support their responses with examples.
L3

History AND ART

Between 1870 and 1900, more acres of land—431 million—came under new cultivation than in all the nation's history. By 1900 American farmers were producing up to 150 percent more staple crops—cotton, wheat, and corn—than they had in 1870.
Answer to Caption: to help farmers

📁 Assign students the Chapter 21 reading in Primary and Secondary Source Readings.

Did You Know?
For many years American coins were made of gold and silver. Since 1965 the silver was removed from the dime and quarter and reduced to 40 percent in the half dollar. Today only commemorative coins are made of gold.

---

called **deflation.** In the three decades after the Civil War, the production of agricultural staples, such as wheat and cotton, nearly quadrupled while the supply of money increased very little. Thus, the prices received by farmers dropped by nearly two-thirds.

The Gold Standard

In 1865, with the value of currency inflated by the wartime issuance of United States notes, or greenbacks, there was $10.60 in circulation for every person in the country. By 1895 per capita circulation had sunk to $4.50. This was partly the result of a movement toward adoption of the **gold standard** in many nations. A country that adopted the gold standard made all its currency convertible into gold. Formerly, most countries had been on a bimetallic standard of both gold and silver.

The difficulty with the gold standard in the late nineteenth century was that world production of gold did not increase as fast as world production of goods. This restricted the currency supply and drove prices down. Deflation was hard on farmers, who borrowed money more heavily than ever before. This resulted in thousands of farm owners losing their land.

As soon as greenbacks began to be called in during the late 1860s and prices began to drop, farmers started to demand inflation. They protested that bankers and bondholders had lent "50-cent dollars" during the war; they now wanted to be repaid in 100-cent dollars. In the midterm election of 1878, a Greenback party polled more than 1 million votes, electing 15 members to Congress.

The Demand for Free Silver

The Greenback movement declined after the mid-1870s as inflationists turned to free silver. Ever since the gold rush of 1849 had lowered the price of gold, silver miners had sold their silver commercially rather than selling it to the Treasury. In 1873 Congress, unaware of the potential of new silver mines, decided to stop coining silver money and adopted the gold standard. Six years later, after building up a gold reserve, the federal government resumed specie, or coin, payments. These events caused a howl of protest from Western silver miners because new mines, especially the famous Comstock Lode, produced a flood of silver that would no longer be coined. Denouncing what they called "the Crime of '73," silver miners demanded a policy of free silver, meaning that the government should coin all silver brought to the mint. They were joined by farmers of the West and the South who expected that free silver would mean a cheaper dollar and higher prices.

The strength of the silver movement was shown by the Bland-Allison Act of 1878, which was passed over President Hayes's veto. This law required that the treasury

 ▲ *A Prayer for Rain* by A. B. Frost, 1894 On the Great Plains, farming had its agonies. Bumper crops brought low prices, and drought brought no crops. **What was the goal of the Populist party?**

574 UNIT 6 New Horizons: 1860–1900

Special Needs

Oral Expression Disability Students with oral expression problems often do not ask questions in class. Tell all the students in the class you want them to write down two or three questions based on the information presented in each portion of Section 2. Their questions should relate to something they *do not* understand, such as a word's meaning or the way to answer a question from the Objectives section. Any question related to the material is acceptable. Collect the questions, read them aloud, and discuss ways of finding the answers.

buy from $2 million to $4 million worth of silver a month and issue currency against it. Although adding to the money supply, the Bland-Allison Act did not halt deflation.

The Populist Movement

The election of 1892 was notable because for the first time since 1860, a **third party,** a minor political party, won electoral votes. The new organization, the People's, or Populist party, was principally an expression of farmers' grievances.

Government Policies

Ever since the Civil War, federal policies had favored industry over agriculture and the city over the country. In spite of the clamor for a cheaper dollar, the United States remained on the gold standard—to the advantage of creditors—and farm prices went steadily down—to the advantage of urban consumers. The protective tariff raised the price of the goods farmers bought, to the advantage of manufacturers, but American agricultural staples were sold overseas in an unprotected market. Legislation that favored agrarian, or farming, interests proved ineffective. State and federal regulation of railroads had been frustrated by adverse judicial decisions. When drought hit the Great Plains region in the late 1880s, the farmers were in a rebellious mood. In the West in general, economic distress was widespread; after the depression of 1893, feelings became so bitter that many citizens feared a revolution.

Forming a Party

The Populist party originated from two great farmers' organizations, which were formed after the decline of the Grange—the Southern Alliance, which covered the cotton and tobacco belt, and the Northern Alliance, especially strong in the Plains region. Although the two alliances failed to merge, they made similar demands—free silver, more paper money, cheaper credit, government ownership of railroads, and the restoration of railroad bounty lands to the federal government. After several congressional election successes and conferences in Cincinnati in 1891 and St. Louis in February 1892, a new political party was formed. The People's party held a national convention in Omaha in July 1892. Although mostly from farm organizations, delegates also represented the Knights of Labor and the followers of social reformers Henry George and Edward Bellamy.

Following the custom of the time, the convention nominated for President a Civil War veteran, James B. Weaver. There was nothing customary, however, about the Populist party's platform.

▲ Mary Ellen Lease

The Omaha Platform

The preamble of the Omaha platform expressed indignation at the existing political and economic conditions. It condemned the political corruption, the newspapers dominated by business interests, the mortgage burden, and the condition of labor. The influence of social reformers was seen in the statements that "the land is concentrating in the hands of the capitalists" and that governmental injustice breeds "two great classes—tramps and millionaires." Turning to money and banking, the Populists characterized worldwide adoption of the gold standard as "a vast conspiracy against mankind . . . organized on two continents."

The following was perhaps the most zealously radical statement in the preamble of the Omaha platform:

> ❝ We believe that the powers of government—in other words, of the people—should be expanded . . . as rapidly and as far as the good sense of an intelligent people and the teachings of experience shall justify. ❞

The Omaha platform revealed that it was the agriculturalists—not organized labor—who dominated the Populist party.

CHAPTER 21
SECTION 2

Visualizing History Read to students part of Bryan's spellbinding speech at the 1896 Democratic convention: "You come to tell us that the great cities are in favor of the gold standard. We reply that the great cities rest upon our broad and fertile plains. Burn down your cities and leave our farms, and your cities will spring up again as if by magic; but destroy our farms and grass will grow in the streets of every city in the country." Discuss why these words stirred emotions in support of free silver.
Answer to Caption: farmers, some laborers, and most debtors

Did You Know?
In 1892 Populist governors were elected in Kansas and North Dakota, and the Populist party swept the state of Colorado.

GLENCOE TECHNOLOGY
The following materials are available from Glencoe and may be used to enrich Chapter 21:

VIDEODISC
Economics in Action

Money and Banking Videodisc 2, Side 1, Chapter 20

The demands of organized labor were given a subordinate position. Excluded from the platform proper, labor's demands were placed among a miscellaneous list of resolutions that were given the title "Expression of Sentiments."

The Omaha platform seems less radical now than it did at that time. The Populists proposed not to overthrow the capitalist system but simply to change the rules. They aimed to achieve their ends not through revolution but through the orderly process of free elections. The Populist platform reveals an important function of third parties in the United States—to bring to public attention measures that the major parties later adopt as their own.

Election of 1892

The Populists' enthusiasm as they entered the campaign of 1892 had a religious tone. They adapted revival meeting hymns as party songs. Huge rallies were addressed not only by men but also by "women with skins tanned to parchment by the hot winds, with bony hands of toil, and clad in faded calico." The balloting revealed the distinct character of various regions in the People's party. All of its 22 electoral votes came from states lying west of the Mississippi River. In the South sympathy with Populist aims was widespread, but there was fear that the new party might divide the Democratic vote and

▲ **BRYAN AND SILVER** The British humor magazine *Puck* shows candidate William Jennings Bryan as a puppet being controlled by the silver-mine owners. **Besides the mine owners, who supported free silver?**

576 UNIT 6 New Horizons: 1860–1900

Sidelights: The Panic of 1893

President Cleveland had barely begun his second term when a series of bank failures and industrial collapses signaled the Panic of 1893. The gold reserve in the U.S. Treasury was depleted due to an excess import of goods, liquidation of U.S. securities in London, and the useless purchase of silver, required by the Sherman Silver Purchase Act. Cleveland called on Congress to repeal the act in order to uphold the gold standard. Farmers felt betrayed by this action, and when Cleveland later borrowed money from J. P. Morgan, they believed that he had sold out to Wall Street.

let the Republican party back into power. Southern Democrats with Populist principles—"Popocrats"—nonetheless helped elect their own party's candidate, Grover Cleveland.

Cleveland's Second Term

Cleveland's second term proved difficult. Inheriting a treasury deficit from the Harrison administration, he had scarcely taken office when the panic of 1893 burst upon the country. Although Cleveland could not have prevented this disaster, he was blamed for it. Furthermore, he managed to antagonize almost every element in his party. For example, he angered "machine" politicians by putting 120,000 civil service jobs on the merit system. Cleveland also infuriated workers by using troops in the 1894 Pullman strike.

Cleveland Loses Democratic Support

Above all, Cleveland antagonized farmers by defending the gold standard. Fearful that the Sherman Silver Purchase Act would flood the United States Treasury with so much silver that it could not be redeemed in gold, he called a special session of Congress in 1893 and forced repeal of the law. Because most Western and Southern Democrats opposed him, he was able to do this only with Republican support. Even after federal buying of silver ceased, the gold standard was endangered because it was difficult for the government to keep an adequate gold reserve in the treasury. To obtain the precious metal, the Treasury Department sold United States bonds.

In one transaction J. Pierpont Morgan, the most powerful banker on Wall Street, obtained federal bonds so far below their market value that he and the bankers associated with him made $1.5 million. Western fury at the Morgan bond transaction was unbounded. The gold standard was bad enough, but to pay bankers to preserve it seemed to them almost treasonable.

▲ PRESIDENT GROVER CLEVELAND

The President's hope of lowering the prohibitive duties of the McKinley Tariff faded when a few Democratic senators joined the Republicans in tacking 633 amendments on a new tariff bill, thereby keeping rates almost at former levels. Cleveland let the resulting Wilson-Gorman Tariff of 1894 become a law without his signature, but he denounced the action of the rebellious senators as "a piece of party perfidy and dishonor."

Republicans Nominate McKinley

Meanwhile the Republicans had become, more than ever, identified with business interests. A dominant figure in the party was Mark Hanna, an Ohio businessman-politician. Big, bluff, and low-browed, Hanna became, perhaps unjustly, a symbol of the alliance between corporate wealth and politics. Anti-Republican cartoons habitually portrayed him in a suit covered with dollar signs. In 1896 Hanna used his great organizing talents to secure the Republican nomination for his friend William McKinley on a platform pledging high tariffs and maintenance of the gold standard.

CHAPTER 21 SECTION 2

Linking Across TIME

The Populist party had an impact on politics and government far beyond its showing in national elections. Minor parties have served as vehicles for reform by taking clear-cut stands on controversial issues and proposing bold and original solutions. Among the Populist proposals that were adopted and are still in place today are the federal income tax (Sixteenth Amendment, 1913), direct election of U.S. senators (Seventeenth Amendment, 1913), the secret ballot (late 1890s), and primary elections (Wisconsin, 1903).

Did You Know?

After William Jennings Bryan delivered his speech at the Democratic convention in 1896, people were crying and rejoicing for an hour.

Sidelights: Thieves and the Campaign

During William Jennings Bryan's presidential campaign, he was faithfully followed by a band of pickpockets. To make the point that silver was as widely accepted as gold, he would first ask people who carried gold to lift their hands and then those who carried silver to do the same. The thieves worked the packed crowd, relieving both groups of their money.

CHAPTER 21
SECTION 2

ASSESS
Check Understanding

Assign Section 2 Review as homework or an in-class activity.

Evaluate

Assign the Section 2 Quiz in the TCR, or use the History of a Free Nation Testmaker to create a customized quiz.

Reteach

Have students describe each of the following in a summary statement: support for greenbacks and free silver, Populist party, Omaha platform, James B. Weaver, and William Jennings Bryan.

Have students complete Reteaching Activity 21-2.

Enrich

Have students research Mary Lease's life and present one of her speeches to the class.

CLOSE

Call attention to the quotation by William Jennings Bryan on page 578. Ask students to explain in their own words the meaning of the quotation.

Democrats Nominate Bryan

The Democratic national convention opened with such a bitter fight between Gold Democrats and Silver Democrats that it was almost impossible to keep a semblance of order. Then, with dramatic suddenness, the party found a leader in a rather obscure presidential candidate, William Jennings Bryan of Nebraska. Bryan combined a romantic devotion to free silver with a personality, voice, and presence that made him literally a spellbinder:

> *Burn down your cities and leave our farms, and your cities will spring up again as if by magic; but destroy our farms, and the grass will grow in the streets of every city in the country.*

Speaking at the convention, Bryan used images that seemed to identify the gold standard with evil itself:

> *You shall not press down upon the brow of labor this crown of thorns—you shall not crucify mankind upon a cross of gold!*

This speech contained hardly a single fact-based argument for a bimetallic standard. It was so charged with emotion that it made free silver a crusade—with Bryan as its standard bearer. Although only 36 years old, he received the Democratic nomination. Most Populists also agreed to support Bryan.

The Campaign for the Presidency

Breaking with tradition, which held that political campaigning was beneath the dignity of one who aspired to the presidency, Bryan traveled the country in search of support. In spite of all his efforts, though, Bryan's cause was doomed. Most large Democratic newspapers abandoned him; the Gold Democrats deserted the Democratic party and ran a separate candidate. Collecting an immense campaign fund, Hanna hired speakers and issued pamphlets aimed at countering the free silver arguments. McKinley was helped by the fact that prices of grain and cotton rose.

The most serious weakness in Bryan's campaign was that free silver was a poor issue on which to base an entire campaign. No one knew what the result of free coinage of silver would be; it would not have ended fluctuation in the value of money, and it might have caused a business panic.

McKinley Wins

The Republicans won the election of 1896 by a decisive margin, carrying all the thickly populated states of the Northeast and Midwest. It was a victory for industry over agriculture, city over country, North and East over West and South.

After their defeat in the election of 1896, the Populists ceased to be a force in politics. Though many at the time felt that all their efforts had failed, those who lived long enough saw most of the planks of their party's platform signed into law.

Section 2 ★ Review

Checking for Understanding

1. **Identify** Populist party, Mark Hanna, William McKinley, William Jennings Bryan.
2. **Define** inflation, deflation, gold standard, third party.
3. **Analyze** the causes of more rapid price declines on farm crops than on many other goods and services.
4. **List** two of the important objectives for the Populist party.

Critical Thinking

5. **Recognizing Common Goals** The alliance between laborers and farmers was hampered by each group's different interests. What did the two groups have in common that encouraged such an alliance?

---

578   UNIT 6 New Horizons: 1860–1900

Answers to SECTION 2 REVIEW

1. Populist party, 575; Mark Hanna, 577; William McKinley, 577; William Jennings Bryan, 578
2. All vocabulary words are defined in the Glossary.
3. While farmers greatly increased the amount of crops they grew, money supply increased very little, creating deflation, which lowered prices for farm products.
4. opposed the gold standard; favored government ownership of railroads
5. both poor, felt victimized by big business and government support of it

CONNECTIONS  CONNECTIONS

Folk Songs of Protest

Songs of protest are threaded throughout American History. In 1777 Americans marched to battle at Saratoga singing "Yankee Doodle." During the 1960s protesters marched for civil rights singing "We Shall Overcome." In the 1890s, too, Populists sang a protest song against bankers called "The Kansas Fool."

THE KANSAS FOOL

We have the land to raise the wheat
And everything that's good to eat;
And when we had no bonds or debt,
We were a jolly, happy set.
With abundant crops raised everywhere,
'Tis a mystery, I do declare,
Why farmers all should fume and fret,
And why we are so deep in debt.

The bankers followed us out west,
And did in mortgages invest;
They looked ahead and shrewdly planned,
and soon they'll have our Kansas land.

CHORUS

Oh Kansas fools! Poor Kansas Fools!
The banker makes of you a tool;
I look across the fertile plain,
Big crops—made so by gentle rain;
But twelve-cent corn gives me alarm,
And makes me want to sell my farm.

Other works expressed a tone that was partly serious and partly humorous.

STARVING TO DEATH ON MY GOVERNMENT CLAIM

My name is Tom Hight,
An old bach'lor I am;
You'll find me out west
   in the county of fame,
You'll find me out west
   on an elegant plain,
Starving to death
   on my government claim.

Hurrah for Green County!
   the land of the free;
The land of the bedbug,
   grasshopper, and flea;
I'll sing of its praises,
   I'll tell of its fame,
While starving to death
   on my government claim.

Making the Music Connection

1. What complaints do farmers make in the first song?
2. How do these protest songs reflect the fears and concerns of farmers that organized interests were acting against them?

Linking Past and Present

3. Describe the complaints found in a current protest song.

CHAPTER 21 CONNECTIONS

Teaching Making Connections

Songs of protest are also associated with the union movement. The Industrial Workers of the World used music to get its message across to attract mine, farm, and textile workers to its ranks. Joe Hill, one of the union's members honored through song, was unjustly executed as a murderer.

Did You Know?

The word *populist* comes from a Latin word meaning "people." Thus a populist is a member of a party claiming to represent the common people.

Answers to CONNECTIONS

1. Most of the protest is aimed at banking practices, including high interest rates that leave farmers with no money.
2. The second stanza of the first song makes it clear that farmers believed the banks were systematically trying to destroy them. Bankers "followed" them west, "looked ahead and shrewdly planned" to take their land.
3. Answers will vary. Folk music of the 1960s and 1970s, such as Bob Dylan's "Blowing in the Wind," was filled with protest against war and the materialism of society. "We Shall Overcome" is considered an anthem for the civil rights movement. Popular music of the 1980s and 1990s often reflects concerns for the environment and hunger.

LESSON PLAN
SECTION 3, 580–585

FOCUS

Bellringer
Display Focus Activity 70 on the overhead projector and assign the accompanying Focus Activity Sheet.

Objectives
Point out the objectives on this page in previewing the section content.

Motivating Activity
Provide the following verse by George Francis Train:
"Kansas will win the
  World's applause
As the sole champion of
  the woman's cause
So light the bonfires, have
  the flags unfurled
To the banner state of all
  the world."
Ask students what feelings and beliefs the writer expresses about women's rights. (hope and belief that woman's suffrage will pass)

VIDEODISC
Powers of the Supreme Court

Side 1, Chapter 25
Title: *Amendment 18, Prohibition of Liquor*
Subject: Problems during prohibition

Side 1, Chapter 26
Title: *Amendment 19, Woman Suffrage*
Subject: Brief history of women's suffrage

SECTION 3

Other Forces for Reform

Setting the Scene

Section Focus

Though the Gilded Age is often thought of as a period of greed, corruption, and self-centered individualism, it was also a period of reform. Like the Populists, whose strength lay mainly in the West, reformers in other areas were trying to call attention to problems.

Objectives

After studying this section, you should be able to
★ trace women's involvement in the temperance and suffrage movements.
★ discuss the political ideas of Karl Marx and Henry George.

Key Term

conspicuous consumption

◀ CARRIE NATION, FIGHTER FOR PROHIBITION

Reforms of the Civil War and Reconstruction periods encouraged people in the United States to look to government as the agent of social change. In the years of its unquestioned dominance, the Republican party had freed slaves, imposed a new way of life on the South, and opened the West to settlement. After the war, reformers who were dissatisfied with various aspects of life in the Gilded Age also looked to the government for action.

■ Temperance and Woman's Rights

The period after the Civil War was not just a time of industrial progress, urban growth, and agrarian and labor discontent. Like the Jacksonian period, it also produced reforms designed to cure the ills of the new industrial society of the United States.

The Temperance Movement

Several reform movements that had begun earlier continued to reach toward their goals. Supporters of Prohibition, for example, formed a national political party in 1869; in 1872 they ran a presidential candidate. The temperance movement had never been more active.

Most effective were two national organizations that waged a ceaseless campaign against the evils of liquor and the saloon: the Anti-Saloon League and the Woman's Christian Temperance Union (WCTU). The WCTU revealed that women were learning the techniques of large-scale organization. Frances Willard, the head of the WCTU, made her group an effective force for causes other than temperance, such as prison reform and protective labor laws. Because women were far more likely than men to favor temperance, temperance advocates usually favored woman suffrage.

UNIT 6 New Horizons: 1860–1900

Classroom Resources for SECTION 3

Teacher's Classroom Resources
- Reproducible Lesson Plan
- Reteaching Activity 21-3
- Chapter 21 Enrichment Activity
- Spanish Summaries and Glossary
- Section Quiz

Multimedia
- Section Focus Transparency 70
- Vocabulary Puzzlemaker
- Unit 7 Digest Transparency
- Testmaker
- Student Self-Test Software
- Powers of the Supreme Court

Woman Suffrage

Woman suffrage had its beginnings in the antebellum period; its first leaders were female abolitionists like Elizabeth Cady Stanton, who decided to put the antislavery cause ahead of their own. After the war woman suffrage was championed with renewed vigor.

In 1878 Susan B. Anthony of the National Woman Suffrage Association (NWSA) persuaded a sympathetic senator to propose the first woman suffrage amendment to the Constitution. It was voted down many times in the next 40 years. These defeats reflected the opinion of the majority of the people at the time, both male and female.

At the state level, suffragists had better success. By 1900 about half the states allowed women to vote on school issues, where their special knowledge of children was presumed to be a benefit. On the frontier, where women shared the hardships and dangers equally with men, support for woman suffrage was more widespread. By 1900, four states—Colorado, Wyoming, Utah, and Idaho—had granted women the right to vote.

▼ ELIZABETH CADY STANTON

Women and Unions

Women workers especially suffered exploitation during the new industrial age. By 1900 almost 5 million women were employed in the United States. It was not uncommon for women to work in "sweat shops" for 10 to 14 hours a day, often for less than $4 a week. Most unions, however, refused to accept women as members. One exception, the International Ladies' Garment Workers Union, had women leaders as well as women members. In 1903 a group of women formed the National Women's Trade Union League to campaign for better working conditions.

■ Socialism

Wherever industrialism appeared, there were people driven toward extreme solutions for the problems it created. Something seemed wrong with a system that produced

▲ **WOMEN AND THE VOTE** The West led the way in granting woman suffrage. These women voted in Cheyenne, Wyoming, in 1888. *What other reform movement was reaching toward its goals before 1900?*

Cultural Diversity

In the late 1800s, discrimination in the workplace was the rule rather than the exception. Women were always paid less than men, even when they did the same work. The best jobs went to native-born white males. African American men were virtually unable to get any factory jobs. Many African American women could find jobs only as domestic workers.

CHAPTER 21
SECTION 3

Independent Practice

Analyzing Ideas Have students work in pairs to analyze the ideas of Henry George and Thorstein Veblen. Ask pairs to list the basic premises of each writer's proposal and explain the responses to each one. Have pairs develop their own ideas for remaking the society of the late 1800s. Have each pair present their ideas and develop a class plan for remaking society. **L3**

Visualizing History By 1900 female wage earners made up one-fifth of the nation's workforce. Two million of these women were domestics—maids, cooks, nurses, and laundresses. Have students research the numbers of women in the workforce today and the types of jobs they hold. What is the percentage of women in various occupations? Students can present their findings in the form of graphs.
Answer to Caption: about 5 million

Did You Know?

In the 1870s people thought it was too strenuous for a woman to type all day and also too intellectually difficult. Male secretaries, though, were well paid. In the early 1900s, once women were hired as secretaries, typing became a menial, poorly paid job.

---

both the idle rich, who lived in mansions, and the unemployed poor, who lived in slums. Some were impelled toward socialism.

Experiments in Socialism

Socialists in the early 1800s did not attempt to change the economic system by gaining control of the government. Instead they tried to effect change by experimenting with cooperative communities. Robert Owen brought his idea of cooperative control of industry from England to New Harmony, Indiana, in 1825. Such socialist communities reached their peak in America in the 1840s.

Karl Marx and Socialism

Socialists of the late nineteenth century were dedicated to changing the entire social and political system, partly because of the influence of Karl Marx. Marx had been a student at the University of Berlin during the emergence of a new philosophical and literary movement that questioned established values. Searching for meaning in history, Marx finally wrote his economic philosophy in *The Communist Manifesto* in 1847 and in *Das Kapital*, the first volume of which was published in 1867. Marx predicted that capitalism was doomed. Fewer and fewer capitalists, he said, would control all wealth, while the mass of the people would be pushed into the ranks of the proletariat (people without property). Eventually the proletarians would rise and overthrow their masters. History, said Marx, had seen continual class struggles, but the conflict between industrial workers and capitalists would be the last. When the workers eventually took control of society, Marx believed they would establish a classless society.

Marxist socialism appealed to many workers in the industrial countries of Europe. In the United States, however, it gained only a small following.

The American Socialist Party

Eugene V. Debs became a lifelong convert to socialism because of unjust treatment after his imprisonment in an Illinois jail during the Pullman strike. Declaring that in a democracy workers could gain control of the government and use it to change the free enterprise system, he organized the American Socialist party.

■ Dissenting Voices

Socialism was not the only remedy proposed at the time. Other solutions to fix society's ills included a single tax on land and a classless society.

 ▲ **AT THE OFFICE** In the early 1900s, professional careers were largely reserved for men, while secretarial jobs were thought to be women's work. *How many women were employed by 1900?*

582   UNIT 6 New Horizons: 1860–1900

Cooperative Learning

Have students work in groups. Assign one student from each group to be part of a planning committee and plan a women's suffrage "convention." The planning committee assigns various tasks to each group, such as giving speeches, making posters, providing advice, writing plays or skits, role-playing how to deal with politicians. Have students in each group decide how they want to divide the work. The groups should discuss and solve any problems they have with the planning committee. Have each group present its project to the class. **L2**

Life of the Times

Boardinghouses

Beginning in the 1830s, farm girls moved to Lowell, Massachusetts, to work in the textile mills there. The mill owners set up boardinghouses with strict curfews and comfortable if sparse accommodations for the women.

The practice of boarding offended the sensibilities of some middle-class reformers. They complained that boarding weakened the family unit and helped spread disease. But many immigrants had a different point of view. They knew that all boardinghouses differed. In some tenements as many as 10 immigrants slept in a room.

But other boardinghouses were like the establishment of one immigrant woman who thought she would own her own home in America. Having difficulty just making ends meet shortly after she arrived in the United States, she cooked for four boarders. Initially she resented having to share her home, prepare meals, and attend to the needs of people she did not even know. However, the woman's attitude changed. She began to enjoy providing a home for new immigrants who otherwise would have no place to stay.

▼ Ridge Street, New York City

CHAPTER 21 SECTION 3

Teaching Life of the Times

The Kohler family in Kohler, Wisconsin, was one of the factory owners who provided boardinghouses for unmarried immigrant men. For immigrant families the Kohlers built small houses in an area that became a company town. The houses were built so well that the Kohler family turned them into an upscale resort in the 1970s.

Did You Know?

Boardinghouses were known by different names in various cities—"furnished-room houses" in Philadelphia, "rooming houses" in Chicago, and "lodging houses" in San Francisco.

Henry George and the Single Tax

Another writer with a proposal for remaking society was Henry George, whose major work *Progress and Poverty* was published in 1879. George attacked the central problem posed by the socialists: Why should the advance of the industrial revolution, with more and more machinery for producing wealth, apparently result in more poverty? George said the problem was that ownership of land—the source of all wealth—was being concentrated in the hands of speculators. These speculators did not put the land to use. They merely waited for it to increase in value, meanwhile charging high rents that drove down wages and business profits. George criticized the growing gap between rich and poor:

> We need not look far from the palace to find the hovel. When people can charter special steamboats to take them to watering places . . . build marble stables for their horses and give dinner parties which cost . . . a thousand dollars a head, we may know that there are poor girls on the street . . . [facing] starvation.

George did not propose socialism as a remedy. Instead he urged what he called the "single tax" on land values. The rate of the single tax would be based not on existing value but on *potential* value if the land were used efficiently. Thus there would be no profit in keeping land out of use and waiting for it to increase in worth; owners would either have to develop it themselves or sell it to someone else who would do so. George argued that this would cause prosperity by promoting maximum productivity and by plowing the profits of the land monopoly back into society. Although George's ideas had great appeal, the single-tax idea was too radical a change to be accepted completely. However, it did influence methods of taxation both in this country and abroad.

Sidelights: Architecture

The "conspicuous consumption" of the upper class described by Veblen (page 584) was most evident in housing. The dream houses of the upper class were transformed into reality by architect Richard M. Hunt, who had studied at L'Ecole des Beaux-Arts in Paris. He designed both the chateau at Vanderbilt's Biltmore Estates in North Carolina and The Breakers in Newport, Rhode Island. It is said Hunt never had to worry about the cost of his labor or voluminous and expensive construction materials—in other words, he was given a "blank check."

CHAPTER 21
SECTION 3

ASSESS
Check Understanding
Assign Section 3 Review as homework or an in-class activity.

Evaluate
▼ ● Assign the Section 3 Quiz in the TCR, or use the History of a Free Nation Testmaker to create a customized quiz.

Reteach
▼ Have students complete Reteaching Activity 21-3.

Enrich
Have students research the changes that were made by various progressive reformers of the early 1900s in the areas of work, living conditions, and government. Have them present their findings in an oral report to the class.

▼ Have students complete Chapter 21 Enrichment Activity in the Teacher's Classroom Resources.

CLOSE
Discuss with students how taxation is a means of redistributing wealth. Ask them whether they think taxes should be raised considerably for the wealthy in order to redistribute wealth.

Thorstein Veblen and "Conspicuous Consumption"

Another widely read book, *The Theory of the Leisure Class,* was published in 1899 by Thorstein Veblen. The son of Norwegian immigrants, Veblen had been influenced by Populism in his early days in Wisconsin. Attending Yale and Johns Hopkins University, he became interested in the social sciences, especially economics. His appreciation for science led him to write with the cool detachment of an observer, not a fiery revolutionary.

Influenced by Darwin's theory of evolution, Veblen believed in the process of natural selection. He contended that the "leisure class," which was made up of those people who had great wealth, was *not* an example of the most fit. In fact Veblen argued that the leisure class hindered progress and evolution. Veblen believed that, like the dinosaur, the leisure class would eventually disappear.

Veblen used the phrase **conspicuous consumption** to describe the life of the upper class. Veblen described conspicuous consumption as the use of vast resources just for show. The phrase had deep meaning because the contrast between wealth and poverty was not hidden in the United States. The mansions that lined the streets of cities like New York and Chicago were within a few blocks of immigrant ghettos. However, Veblen's vision of a community of equals governed by an elite group of social planners was judged impractical by most Americans of his time.

Limited Support for Radical Changes

Probably the reason why radical formulas for altering society did not gain wide support was that many Americans did not want change. Even those at the bottom rung of the economic ladder often felt they had bettered their position from an earlier time.

A New England farm boy might find drawing wages of a dollar a day for a 60-hour week in a factory preferable to working from dawn to dark trying to make a living from a rocky farm. An immigrant might be living with her family in a single room and working in a windowless sweatshop, but for the first time in her life she was wearing shoes.

Even the poorest workers believed that in time they would also be able to "get ahead" and become property owners. They fervently believed in the "rags-to-riches" story and felt, like the heroes of the Horatio Alger series, that they could by work, perseverance, and luck rise to a higher station in life. If property rights were destroyed, what would happen to the American dream?

Working Through the Political Process

Also, the United States was so large and had so many different interests that no one idea attained universal appeal. Its citizens, wanting to improve their economic situation, worked through the political party process. These parties tried to appeal to as many groups as possible.

Section 3 ★ Review

Checking for Understanding
1. **Identify** Susan B. Anthony, Eugene V. Debs.
2. **Define** conspicuous consumption.
3. **Describe** the movements to gain voting rights for women.
4. **Compare** the solutions proposed by Karl Marx, Henry George, and Thorstein Veblen.

Critical Thinking
5. **Arguing an Opinion** Women fought for the right to vote but had had success in only four states by 1900. Why did many states refuse them the right to vote? What arguments would you propose to justify women's right to vote in the late 1800s?

---

584 UNIT 6 New Horizons: 1860–1900

Answers to SECTION 3 REVIEW

1. Susan B. Anthony, 581; Eugene V. Debs, 582
2. All vocabulary words are defined in the Glossary.
3. formation of National Woman's Suffrage Association, proposal of first woman's suffrage amendment, granting women the right to vote in four western states by 1900
4. Marx predicted overthrow of capitalism by industrial workers and establishment of a classless society. Veblen believed in a society of equals governed by an elite group of experts. George proposed taxing privately owned land's potential value to encourage productivity and discourage speculators.
5. Answers will vary: Women had already involved themselves in important social issues, vote had been extended to black males, who had formerly been disenfranchised.

Social Studies Skills

Study and Writing Skills

Recognizing Ideologies

Identifying the motives or belief system behind a particular political position may help you form an opinion. One effective way to identify motives and beliefs is to analyze the benefits and costs associated with the issue. Ask questions, such as:

- Which people benefit if the issue passes? How do they benefit?
- Which people benefit if the issue fails? How do they benefit?
- Which people pay or suffer if the issue passes? How do they pay or suffer?
- Which people pay or suffer if the issue fails? How do they pay or suffer?

Throughout United States history, numerous minor political parties have initiated social or political reform. The goals of the minor party often centered on a single issue, and as popular support grew for that issue and public opinion changed, the "cause" was adopted by either the Democratic or Republican party. The minor party thus faded out as its goals were achieved.

The Populist party had an impact far beyond its showing in national elections. Several Populist proposals are in use today. The federal income tax, adopted as part of the Sixteenth Amendment in 1913, accounts for one-half of the monies collected at all levels of government. The Seventeenth Amendment, placed into law the direct election of United States senators. The secret ballot, first used in the late 1890s, became standard practice in all elections. Primary elections are used to settle virtually all contests for majority-party nominations for state and congressional offices and for many local offices. Hundreds of cities and many states permit citizens to use the initiative and referendum, used in South Dakota in the late 1890s, to introduce legislation and vote on proposed laws.

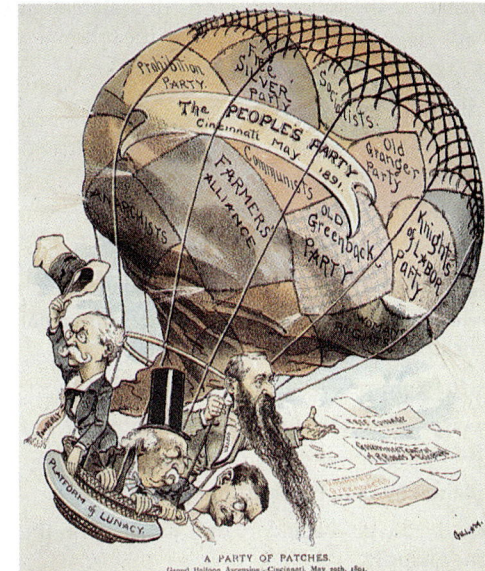

▲ 1891 POLITICAL CARTOON, PARTY OF PATCHES

Practicing the Skill

Use the guidelines on recognizing ideologies mentioned in this skill and information from the chapter to analyze the proposals.

1. What benefits are associated with the use of a secret ballot? Who might oppose its use? Why?
2. In what way is the proposal for a secret ballot consistent with Populist goals?
3. Who benefits from the initiative and referendum proposal? Explain how these systems work.
4. Does the proposal for a federal income tax seem like a Populist idea? Explain.

REVIEW CHAPTER 21

Answers

Reviewing Facts
1. overproduction, low prices, debt, high costs, and natural disasters
2. fixed maximum railway rates, forbade railroad discrimination between places or shippers, regulated other farm-related monopolies (grain elevators, etc.)
3. forbade pooling, rebates, and higher rates for short hauls; required published rates with advance notice of change, financial reports to government
4. lowered prices for crops, made it harder to repay loans
5. Money must be backed by gold. Money supply could not increase faster than the gold supply.
6. elimination of national banks and the gold standard, more government powers, regulation of railroads
7. Marx advocated overthrowing capitalism and establishing a classless society. George advocated taxing land's potential value, which would reduce speculation by the rich.

CHAPTER 21 ★ REVIEW

Using Vocabulary

Use each of the following terms in a statement that might have been made by each of the following people:

- Railroad owner: pooling
- Farmer: cooperatives
- Banker: inflation

Reviewing Facts

1. **Summarize** the factors that created financial hardships for farmers in the late 1800s.
2. **List** three purposes of the Granger laws.
3. **Specify** what the Interstate Commerce Act required of the railroads.
4. **Explain** why deflation hurt the farmers.
5. **Describe** the gold standard and its effect on the money supply.
6. **State** the reforms the Populists demanded in their platform.
7. **Compare** Karl Marx's solution to poverty with Henry George's.

Understanding Concepts

Economic Inequity
1. In the farmers' view, what groups enriched themselves at the farmers' expense?

Social Change
2. Which groups of people might be expected to support extreme solutions for social problems? What groups would likely oppose such solutions? Why did most Americans vote for more moderate candidates in the late 1900s?
3. What did the Populist party, the Grange, and the followers of Marx, George, and Veblen have in common?

Critical Thinking

1. **Understanding Cause and Effect** Explain how new agricultural technology helped the farmers. How did it financially hurt some farmers?
2. **Linking Past and Present** Today banks and lending institutions offer variable-rate loans with an interest rate that varies as prices rise and fall. What problem is this intended to solve?
3. **Proposing Strategy** Assume you are William Jennings Bryan's campaign manager in the 1896 election. Draw up a plan of recommendations to improve Bryan's chances of success.
4. **Contrasting Ideas** How did the Marxist theory of reform contrast with the methods used or envisioned by the other reform proposals discussed in this chapter?
5. **Comparing Fine Art** Study the two paintings on this page by artist John Singer Sargent. Then answer the questions.
    a. What is the mood in each of these works?
    b. What adjectives would you use to describe these paintings?
    c. Compare the use of color and light in these paintings.
    d. Which painting do you prefer? Explain.

586 UNIT 6 New Horizons: 1860–1900

Understanding Concepts
1. railroad owners, manufacturers, banks
2. the unemployed and poorly paid workers; the well-to-do; answers will vary
3. All championed the poor and exploited and targeted the practices of big business and capitalists, and of government that favored the rich.

Critical Thinking
1. More production with less labor, and sometimes more profit. Expensive, caused debt, overproduction, and price drop.
2. People borrow and pay back in either inflated or deflated dollars. Variable interest rates help compensate for varying rates of inflation or deflation.
3. Answers will vary. Perhaps a more balanced focus on money policy; persuade farmers to accept workers' demands and emphasize them in the campaign to win the labor vote.

CHAPTER 21 ★ REVIEW

Writing About History

Comparison

Assume you are a European tourist attending a rally at which the Populists describe their platform. Write a letter to a Marxist friend in Europe, comparing and contrasting the Populist approach to reform with the Marxist formula. You may wish to research additional details about Marx's theory.

Cooperative Learning

You will be part of a discussion between four people meeting in a Great Plains town in the year 1886. Divide the following roles among yourselves: a farmer, a banker, a railroad owner, and a politician. The purpose of this meeting is to discuss the problems of the farmer. Review Section 1 to gain background information on your role. The farmer will begin the meeting by stating his or her main concerns. The other members should discuss ways to answer the farmer's problems, although each individual should be prepared to argue why he or she cannot agree to a recommended change. End the meeting by having all members agree on two recommendations for helping the farmer.

Social Studies Skills

Reviewing Map Basics

Maps can be used to show many different kinds of information. For example, political maps show countries, states, and cities. Transportation maps show means of transportation such as train or plane routes; physical maps show geographical features such as mountains and lakes. In addition, there are military maps, weather maps, and building maps—and this is just a partial list.

Practicing the Skill

Look at the map on this page and answer the following questions.
1. What kind of map is shown?
2. What does the legend tell you?
3. How would you interpret voting in the states of California and Kentucky?

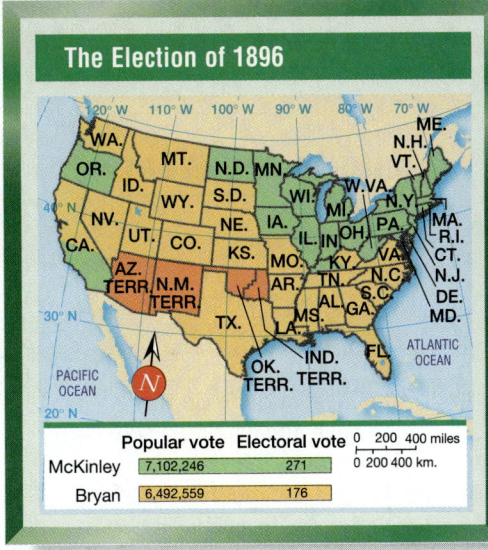

4. Could this map also be a political map? Why or why not?
5. How is this map different from the map on page 459? List at least four differences.

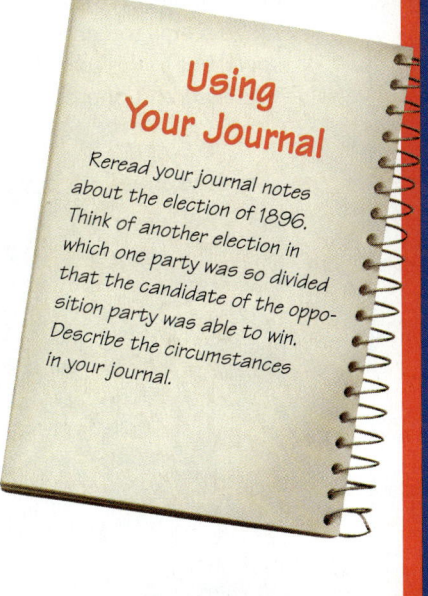

Using Your Journal

Reread your journal notes about the election of 1896. Think of another election in which one party was so divided that the candidate of the opposition party was able to win. Describe the circumstances in your journal.

REVIEW CHAPTER 21

Chapter Bonus Test Question

Based on what you have read in the chapter, decide whether each of the following is true or false. If it is true, explain why. If it is false, correct it to make it true.
1. Third parties have never been a force in U.S. politics. (False; many third-party proposals bring to the public's attention measures that the major parties later adopt as their own.)
2. Populism never gained much support outside farming areas. (True; Populism was primarily a farmers' movement.)

Using Your Journal

Answers will vary. Students may cite several examples. Among the elections are: John Quincy Adams's victory in 1824 when Andrew Jackson, William Crawford, and Henry Clay split the Democratic vote; Martin Van Buren's victory in 1836 over Whigs William Henry Harrison, Hugh White, and Daniel Webster; Abraham Lincoln's victory in 1860 over Democrats John Breckinridge and Stephen Douglas; Ulysses S. Grant's 1868 victory over Horatio Seymour.

---

4. Most others wanted to work within the system to reform it, not overthrow it.
5. a. Answers will vary, but students should note that the paintings depict a serene mood.
b. Answers will vary but include *calm, relaxed, friendly.*
c. Answers will vary, but students should point out that the artist's use of the elements of color and light emphasize the central focus of the paintings.
d. Answers will vary, but students should provide reasons for their responses.

Practicing the Skill

1. election map
2. popular vote and electoral vote for candidates McKinley and Bryan
3. divided between McKinley and Bryan
4. Yes, because it shows state and territorial boundaries.
5. Answers will vary, but students should provide details.

Cultural Kaleidoscope

Making Connections

History and Popular Culture Although the era of the open range lasted only about 20 years, the cowboy has remained an extremely popular American symbol. One milestone in popularizing the cowhand was Buffalo Bill's Wild West Show, first staged in 1883. Another landmark was *The Virginian* (1902), a best-selling novel by Owen Wister. Its strong, silent cowpuncher hero set the pattern for hundreds to follow. Movie and television "westerns" got their start with one of the very first feature-length films, *The Squaw Man* (1914).

More About... Cowboys

Mexicans were the first cowboys; thus much of the vocabulary of the range is Spanish in origin. For example:
bronco (Spanish for "rough")
chaps (Spanish, *chaparejos*)
cinch (Spanish, *cincha*)
corral (Spanish for "enclosure")
lariat (Spanish, *la reata*)
lasso (Spanish, *lazo*)
mustang (Spanish, *mesteño*)
pinto (Spanish for "painted")

Cultural Kaleidoscope

Life in the West

ON THE RANGE

The West and life on the range have always had a special mystique. Television, books, and the movies have kept alive the legend of the Western hero, but the reality of life on the range is overlooked. The work was hard, sometimes boring, and often dangerous. Determination, bravery, and endurance were required to tend great herds of restless and stubborn cattle or to prod a herd great distances on the long drive. Life on the range seems romantic in retrospect, but to the cowhands it was hard and often hazardous.

▶ The rope, or lariat, was an important tool in the hands of a skilled roper. Cowhands used the lariat to rope cattle, pull cattle out of mud, and haul wood to the campfire.

▼ The cowhand's clothing served a useful purpose. Chaps protected the legs during the long hours in the saddle.

◀ The cowhand took special care of the tack, equipment, and grooming tools for the horse. One important piece, the bridle, is used to control the movements of the horse by straps and metal pieces placed on the head and in the mouth of the animal.

Cooperative Learning

Divide the class into small groups. Ask each to research a famous Western figure, such as Andy Adams, Buffalo Bill, Deadwood Dick, Wyatt Earp, Annie Oakley, or Will Rogers (or others of your choosing). Have each group report its findings to the class.

Cultural Kaleidoscope

Portfolio Project
Ask students to note representations of cowboys in current advertising and popular culture. With each example, they should try to judge how true to life the image seems.

▶ Cattle owners kept track of who owned an animal by branding. Each ranch had its own easily recognizable brand.

▲ Few cowhands owned their own horses. The cowhand chose his horse from the *remuda*, the herd of available horses.

▶ A cowhand wore boots with tapered high heels to make sure his feet did not slip through the stirrups when riding.

The Historian's Craft

For decades, cowboys were portrayed almost exclusively as white westerners. Historians have explored this stereotype and learned that at least a third of the ranch hands during the height of the cattle kingdom were African Americans or Mexicans. Many were southerners, who moved west after the defeat of the Confederacy during the Civil War. A useful study of this subject is Joseph B. Frantz and Julian E. Choate, *The American Cowboy: The Myth and the Reality* (1968).

UNIT 6 DIGEST

Exploring Unit Themes

The Unit Digest may be used to teach unit coverage when time is limited, to review unit content, or to relate the content of one unit to that of another.

Unit Digest Transparencies
Use the Unit 6 Digest Transparency.

■ Chapter 17
Have students create a time line showing the major events in the struggle of the Plains peoples against the encroachment of white settlers.

■ Chapter 18
Divide the chalkboard into two columns, heading one Captains of Industry and the other Robber Barons. Lead the class in a discussion of the usefulness of these two "labels."

■ Chapter 19
Point out that the Knights of Labor welcomed women members. Further, leaders argued that "homemakers" were workers eligible for membership. Ask students to research the role of women in the labor movement of the late 1800s.

■ Chapter 20
Read aloud Henry Adams's view of American politics in the last 30 years of the 1800s:
   "The period was poor in purpose and barren in results."
   Have students use information from the text to write an essay supporting or opposing Adams's statement.

UNIT SIX DIGEST

Chapter 17

Forces Shaping the West

In the early 1860s, many Native American nations lived on the Great Plains with the vast buffalo herds. Then, beginning in 1869, transcontinental railway lines opened the West. The Homestead Act made land easy to obtain, and the railroads actively promoted settlement. Pioneer farmers poured onto the plains by the thousands. The discovery of gold and other minerals and the promise of wealth from cattle also lured many people.

Native Americans fought this intrusion, but their cause was doomed. White hunters slaughtered the buffalo almost to extinction, and farmers, miners, and ranchers took much of their land. In 1890 at Wounded Knee, their resistance came to an end.

Chapter 18

The Rise of Industrial America

The United States had all the necessary ingredients for industry to grow—abundant natural and human resources, investment money, free enterprise economic system, and new inventions and technology.

By 1900 huge companies dominated the economy. Their efficiency resulted in cheaper production, higher quality, and lower prices that drove smaller competitors out of business. Corporations, monopolies, and trusts became the norm. Industrial leaders used social Darwinism to justify their actions. The Sherman Antitrust Act, passed in 1890, did little to control business practices.

Chapter 19

Labor, Immigrants, and Urban Life

With industrialization the work force grew and the workers' lives changed. Machines took over many traditional tasks of the worker. Hours were long, wages were low, and work places were hazardous. Unable to improve their lot individually, workers turned to labor unions.

Opposed by the big corporations, management and, to a certain extent, the government, labor unions resorted to strikes. However, even major strikes like the 1894 Pullman strike failed to win significant gains.

An important influence on labor were the large numbers of immigrants who provided unskilled labor for urban industries. They were primarily southern and eastern European and Chinese immigrants who flocked to the cities, where they created their own ethnic communities. Their unfamiliar languages and customs aroused anti-immigration sentiment.

Along with the influx of immigrants, rural Americans came to the rapidly growing cities. In this urban environment that was faced with daunting human and technical problems, a new way of life evolved.

UNIT 6 New Horizons: 1860–1900

Cooperative Learning

Divide the class into three groups and assign each group one of the following: A major personality, an important event, or an important technological development of the time period covered in Unit 6. Ask groups to design a museum exhibit illustrating their selected personality, event, or technological development. Suggest that groups use models, sketches, maps, quotations, eyewitness accounts, and so on in their exhibits. Have the groups display their finished exhibits in class. **L2**

Chapter 20

The Gilded Age

With industrialization and urbanization came political corruption. Scandals arose at every level of government. Political machines dominated almost all major cities.

Government in general lacked leadership, and reform efforts met with limited success. Civil service reform finally came in 1883 with passage of the Pendleton Act.

The society and culture changed as well. Education expanded and improved. Local-color writers like Mark Twain described their locals with realsim and detail. Sporting events became a favorite leisure-time activity, as did vaudeville, penny newspapers, and dime novels.

Chapter 21

Politics and Protest

The prosperity of the Gilded Age did not extend to farmers, who were burdened with high costs, low incomes, and heavy debts. They organized into groups such as Granges and farmers' alliances. Ultimately these groups turned to politics.

The farmers joined with labor and other reform groups to form a new national political party—the Populist party. The Omaha platform of the Populist party in 1892 clearly reflected the interests of the farmer. The Populist party had some successes, but the movement died soon after William Jennings Bryan lost the 1896 presidential election.

Farmers were not the only ones seeking reform. The temperance movement had never been more active, and woman suffrage became a popularly debated issue across the country. At the same time, writers such as Karl Marx proposed socialism as an economic remedy while Henry George favored a "single tax" on land values. However, Americans on the whole were not interested in instituting radical change.

Understanding Unit Themes

1. **Geography and Environment** Compare the American landscape and the environment in 1860 and 1900.

2. **Conflict and Cooperation** How did the settlement of the West affect Native Americans? The nation as a whole? How might cooperation have resolved many conflicts?

3. **Influence of Technology** In what ways did technology influence American life and society between 1860 and 1900?

4. **Cultural Diversity** What ethnic groups played a role in the settlement of the West and in industrialization?

UNIT 6 DIGEST

Chapter 21

Remind students of the words spoken by William Jennings Bryan at the 1896 Democratic Convention (page 577), especially the second sentence: "We reply that the great cities rest upon our broad and fertile plains."

Use Bryan's statement as a starting point for a class discussion of the importance of agriculture in the United States in the late 1800s.

Analyzing Unit Themes Answers

1. In 1860 the United States was primarily rural, and the Great Plains was considered the "Great American Desert." In 1900, the United States was an urban nation crisscrossed by railroad tracks and the Great Plains was mostly farmland.

2. Destroyed their way of life. Opened up opportunity and led to economic expansion. Could have preserved buffalo and Native American hunting lands.

3. Technology enabled railroads to open the West and farmers to cultivate the Great Plains, cities to grow, American production to increase, and transportation and communication to improve.

4. Western settlement: Native Americans, settlers from eastern states, and U.S. soldiers. Industrialization: Chinese and Irish immigrant railroad workers, immigrants from northern and western Europe followed by those from southern and eastern Europe.

The Historian's Craft

In *The Shame of the Cities*, an indictment of corruption in local government, Lincoln Steffens blamed "all the citizens of all the cities in the United States" for the problem. Have students analyze Steffens's accusation by answering these questions: How could citizens be held accountable for the wrongdoing of their political leaders? If a city is free of corruption, why should its citizens be held accountable for the actions of leaders in another city? Do you agree or disagree with Steffens? Why?

INTRODUCING UNIT 7

BEGINNING THE UNIT

Present this cause-and-effect chart to students with the effects omitted. Assign students to complete the chart as they read the chapters in the unit.

Event
- Spanish-American War

Causes
- Economic growth of United States
- Expansion of overseas markets
- Shift away from isolationist policy

Effects
- American dominance in the Caribbean
- Expansionist policies in the Pacific and Far East
- Building of Panama Canal
- Emergence as a world power
- Growth of anti-imperialism

Portfolio Project

After students rewrite the amendment they chose, ask them to consider whether it accomplished its objective. Explain that when they have completed the unit, they will be better able to answer that question.

 OUT OF TIME? If time does not permit teaching the entire unit, use the Unit Digest on pages 676–677.

UNIT 7
ENTERING A NEW CENTURY
1867–1920

CHAPTER 22
Imperialism
1867–1908

CHAPTER 23
The Progressive Era
1893–1920

CHAPTER 24
White House Reformers
1900–1914

▲ BANJO, LATE 1800s

History AND ART
Cliff Dwellers by George Wesley Bellows, 1913
Bellows's works often show elements of humor and adventure. His favorite themes, which include landscapes and athletic events, mark him as a uniquely American painter.

Exploring Unit Themes

American Democracy Progressive reforms such as the direct election of senators, the direct primary, municipal government reform, and the initiative, referendum, and recall all gave voters a greater say in the political process. A number of states granted women full suffrage. Jim Crow laws in the South, however, all but denied African Americans the right to vote.

Economic Development The early years of the twentieth century saw greater government involvement in the economy. The power of the trusts was restricted. Laws were passed to improve working conditions and to protect consumers from fraud and poor-quality goods.

The Individual and Family Life Progressive reforms prohibited child labor, mandated work-

INTRODUCING UNIT 7

Setting the Scene

In an age of optimism, United States foreign policy shifted away from isolationism, and the nation became a major power in international affairs. Americans also took a look at their political institutions and concluded that change was necessary. Progressive-minded reformers sought a more democratic government while working to end a host of social ills.

Themes
- American Democracy
- Economic Development
- The Individual and Family Life
- U.S. Role in World Affairs

▲ TRAVEL TRUNK

Key Events
- Purchase of Alaska and annexation of Hawaii
- Spanish-American War
- Building of the Panama Canal
- States institute direct primary, initiative, and referendum
- Formation of the National Association for the Advancement of Colored People
- Income taxes enacted
- "Bull Moose" party formed
- Federal Reserve System created
- Federal Trade Commission established

◀ EARLY AIRPLANE

Major Issues
- Commercial interests and war with Spain lead to the acquisition of a colonial empire.
- Muckraking literature inspires a new generation of reformers who seek to correct social inequities.
- Reform-minded Presidents extend democracy and protect Americans from big business.

◀ CHILD'S TOY, EARLY 1900S

Portfolio Project
Read the amendments that passed during the time between 1867 and 1920. Choose one and rewrite it in your own words, making clear what the amendment is expected to accomplish.

Unit 7 Independent Study Project
Have students work together to develop a newspaper covering the historical developments discussed in Unit 7. Suggest that they divide their newspaper into sections: local politics, national politics, international affairs, editorial and op-ed, sports, entertainment.

Unit Digest Transparencies
Use Unit 7 Digest Transparencies

History and the Humanities

History and Art Transparency 18

Focus on American Art Prints 13, 14

American Music: Cultural Traditions

Spirit of American Art and Music 22, 23, 24

History AND ART

Cliff Dwellers
George Wesley Bellows was born in Columbus, Ohio, and attended Ohio State University, where he developed his skills in music and athletics as well as in art. He left college in 1904 to study art in New York, where he quickly won national recognition.

---

er's compensation insurance, and ensured the quality of consumer goods. These reforms, and the provision of health clinics and recreation parks, improved the quality of life for most Americans. Progressive reforms, however, were of little benefit to African Americans and Native Americans.

U.S. Role in World Affairs After the Spanish-American War, the United States began to take on the responsibilities of a world power. Many Americans nonetheless expressed reservations about the country's new role.

Examining the Themes Tell students that this unit traces the emergence of the United States as an industrial giant and a major world power.

LESSON PLAN
Global Perspectives

FOCUS
Motivating Activity

Tell students that one historian has said of the United States in the late nineteenth and early twentieth centuries that "an exhilarating new spirit of Manifest Destiny swept the nation."

Discuss with students the idea of Manifest Destiny. Ask them to suggest reasons the United States might be caught up in such a spirit during this period. (becoming a great industrial power; new markets needed for products; western frontier closing, new areas for expansion sought)

TEACH
Guided Practice

Exploring the Time Line
Refer students to the world section of the time line. Ask them to identify worldwide conflicts. (Sino-Japanese War, Russo-Japanese War, Spanish-American War) Ask students to consider how these events might affect the United States. (U.S. could become involved in affairs in the Pacific and in Latin America.) Tell students that as they read this unit, they will learn how these and other worldwide events interacted with events in the United States.

UNIT 7 Entering a New Century: 1867–1920

Cultural Diversity

Tell students that the overseas expansion of the United States, which they will read about in this unit, brought the nation into contact with many different groups of people, from the Caribbean and Latin America to East Asia. Many of these people would accept and adapt to ways of life brought by Americans. Americans would also change. They, too, would accept and adapt to the ways of life of the people they encountered.

Linking Across Time

A trip to the grocery store gives an indication of the Italian influence on American life. Foods like pizza, spaghetti, macaroni, minestrone, parmesan cheese, broccoli, and zucchini are all part of the American diet. However, they were all introduced by the Italian immigrants who came to the United States around the turn of the century. Make a list of all the kinds of Italian foods found in the local supermarket.

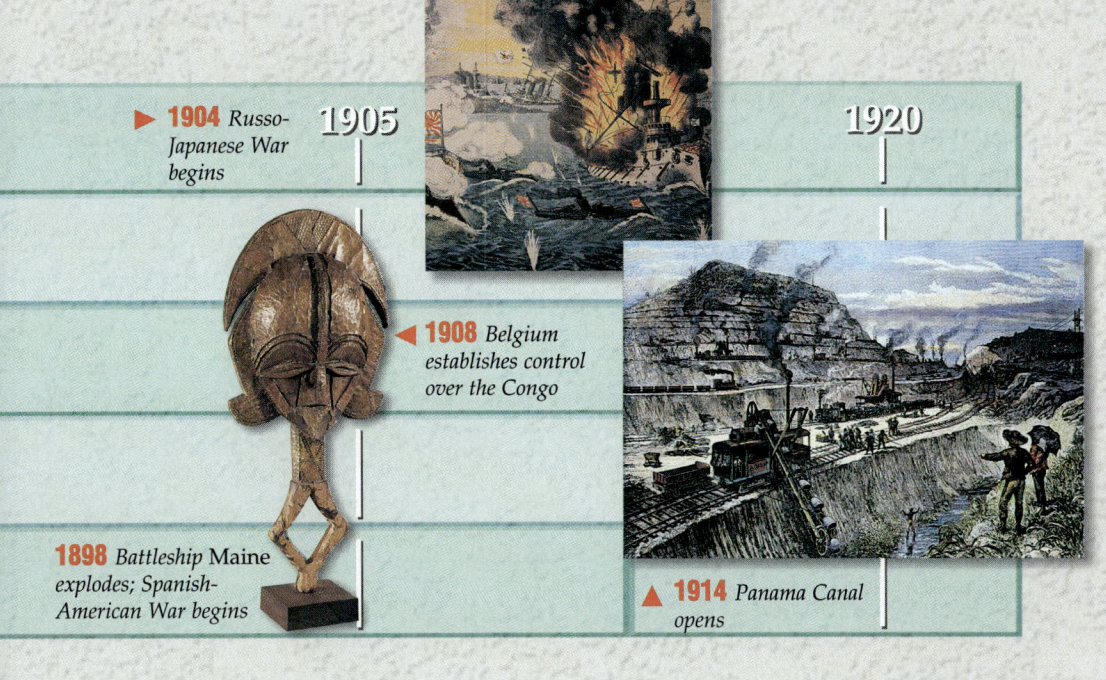

▶ **1904** Russo-Japanese War begins

◀ **1908** Belgium establishes control over the Congo

1898 Battleship *Maine* explodes; Spanish-American War begins

▲ **1914** Panama Canal opens

1898 Gold discovered at Nome

▼ **1903** Wright brothers' first flight

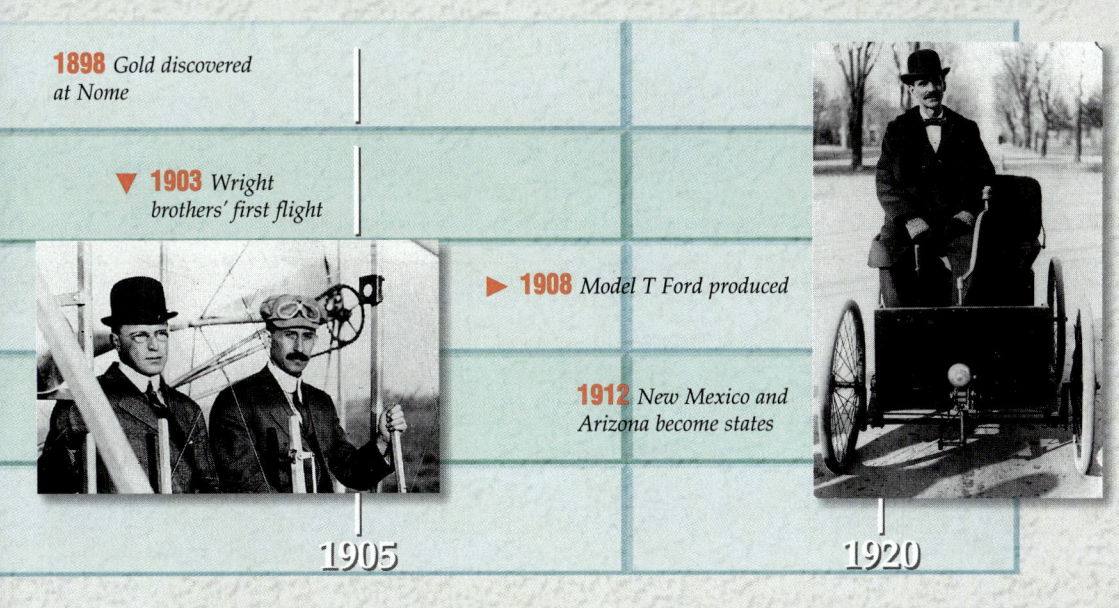

▶ **1908** Model T Ford produced

1912 New Mexico and Arizona become states

UNIT 7 Entering a New Century: 1867–1920   **595**

LESSON PLAN
Global Perspectives

Independent Practice
World Events and the U.S.
Remind students that United States involvement in Latin American affairs was a long-standing tradition. Ask them to review the history of United States–Latin American relations from the late nineteenth century to World War I. A useful source of information is *Latin America and the United States* by Graham H. Stuart and James L. Tigner. Have students outline their findings or present them in the form of a chart for class discussion.

ASSESS
Studying the Time Line
1. Which world event drew the United States into a war? (explosion on the *Maine*)
2. Which region of the country was the location of the two new states admitted to the Union in the early 1900s? (Southwest)
3. Based on information in this feature, which nation would be the major Asian power? Why? (Japan; within 10 years it had defeated its main rival—China—in Asia and had dealt a crushing blow to a major Western power—Russia)

Cooperative Learning

Point out to students that before the construction of the Panama Canal, a plan to build a canal across Nicaragua had been considered. Ask them to work in groups to develop a blueprint for this Nicaraguan canal. Tasks should be shared—one group of students might do research, another group might draw diagrams, and another might write captions for the diagrams. The blueprint should include a map of the canal, the dimensions of the canal, the problems that construction workers would face, and so on. **L3**

595

PLANNING GUIDE — Chapter 22 Imperialism

Daily Lesson Objectives	Teacher Classroom Resources	Multimedia
SECTION 1 **America Looks Abroad** 1 Day pp. 598–601 1. Discuss the emergence of the United States from isolationism. 2. Cite two examples of arbitration averting war.	Chapter 22 Study Guide Reproducible Lesson Plan Reteaching Activity 22-1 Section Quiz Chapter 22 Cooperative Learning Activity Chapter 22 Concept Mapping Activity SAT Practice Tests	Student Self-Test Software Testmaker Section Focus Transparency 68 Chapter 22 Skills Transparency Chapter 22 Map Transparencies Unit 7 Digest Transparencies GTV: A Geographic Perspective on American History
SECTION 2 **The Spanish-American War** 1 Day pp. 603–607 1. List the events that led to the Spanish-American War. 2. Explain the reason for the involvement of the Philippines in the war.	Reproducible Lesson Plan Reteaching Activity 22-2 Section Quiz Chapter 22 Primary and Secondary Source Readings Map and Graph Skill Activity 17 Writer's Guidebook Lesson 6	Student Self-Test Software Testmaker Section Focus Transparency 69 GTV: A Geographic Perspective on American History
SECTION 3 **The United States Becomes a World Power** 1 Day pp. 608–613 1. Explain why the Philippine Islands were difficult to govern. 2. Discuss the constitutional difficulties involved in colonization.	Reproducible Lesson Plan Reteaching Activity 22-3 Section Quiz American Portrait 43 Reinforcing Social Studies Skills 22, 28, 67	Student Self-Test Software Testmaker Section Focus Transparency 70 Chapter 22 Map Transparencies
SECTION 4 **Theodore Roosevelt and Foreign Affairs** 1 Day pp. 615–619 1. Give examples of Roosevelt's "Big Stick" diplomacy. 2. Discuss the goals and results of the "Open Door" policy in China. 3. Discuss America's concerns over the Russo-Japanese War.	Reproducible Lesson Plan Reteaching Activity 22-4 Section Quiz Chapter 22 Enrichment Activity American Portrait 44 Chapter 22 Primary and Secondary Source Readings Building Skills in Geography Outline Map 4, 39, 44 Spanish Summaries & Glossary	Student Self-Test Software Testmaker Vocabulary Puzzlemaker Section Focus Transparency 71 Chapter 22 Map Transparencies Audiocassette, Chapter 22 The Presidents: A Picture History of Our Nation
CHAPTER REVIEW AND EVALUATION 1 Day	Chapter 22 Test Chapter 22 Performance Assessment Activity	Student Self-Test Software Testmaker

OUT OF TIME? If time does not permit teaching the entire chapter, use the Chapter 22 Summary on pages 676-677 and the Chapter 22 audiocassette (English and Spanish) to point out the main ideas of the chapter.

PLANNING GUIDE

Cultural Diversity Activity

Interpreting Primary Sources The resentment of Japanese immigrants that led to the Gentleman's Agreement of 1908 was fueled by newspaper claims that Japan was using immigrants to prepare a secret attack on the United States. Write on the chalkboard the following quotation, typical of the times, from San Francisco Mayor James Phelan:

"The Chinese and Japanese are not bona fide citizens. They are not the stuff of which American citizens can be made. . . .[Since] they will not assimilate with us and their social life is so different from ours, let them keep at a respectful distance."

Discuss how the mayor defines a "bona fide citizen." What evidence of racism can students find in his remarks? Ask how they would define a "bona fide citizen."

Chapter Resources

Literature from the Period

Crane, Stephen. "The Open Boat." 1897.

Roosevelt, Theodore. *Autobiography*. 1913.

Readings for the Student

Boorstin, Daniel J. *The Landmark History of the American People, Volume 2*. Random House, 1987.

O'Toole, G.J.A. *The Spanish War: An American Epic, 1898*. Norton, 1986.

Readings for the Teacher

Hutchison, William R. *Errand to the World: American Protestant Thought & Foreign Missions*. University of Chicago Press, 1987.

Milton, Joyce. *The Yellow Kids: Foreign Correspondents in the Heyday of Yellow Journalism*. Harper & Row, 1989.

Multimedia Resources

American Foreign Policy. Focus Media. (Apple diskette, backup, guide)

Becoming a Modern Nation. Video Knowledge. (VHS, 28 minutes)

Foreign Policy: The Burdens of World Power. Tom Snyder. (Apple or IBM diskette)

The Philippine-American War. Multi-Media Productions. (Filmstrip, cassette, guide)

The Spanish-American War. Multi-Media Productions. (sound filmstrip)

The Spanish-American War: The Dynamics of Change. Multi-Media Productions. (VHS, 30 minutes)

Performance Assessment Activity

Connecting Past and Present Ask students to draw up a list of territories acquired by the United States in the years between 1865 and 1901. Ask them to locate each on an outline map of the world and then answer the following questions: What is the territory's status today? How does its status today differ from its status in the years between 1854 and 1901? Ask students to choose one territory and research its history since 1900 for a more detailed report on how its status has changed over the years.

POSSIBLE RUBRIC FEATURES: Content information, main idea, organization skills, map skills, written communication skills

Key to Ability Levels

Teaching strategies have been coded for varying learning styles and abilities.

- **L1** Basic activities for all students
- **L2** Average activities for average to above-average students
- **L3** Challenging activities for above-average students
- **LEP** Limited English Proficiency activities

Glencoe Links to the Humanities

Links to Art
- U.S. History and Art Transparency 18
- Focus on American Fine Art Prints 13, 14

Links to Literature
- Macmillan Literature: Appreciating Literature Audiotapes Side 4
- Macmillan Literature: Understanding Literature Video— *Call of the Wild*
- Macmillan Literature: American Literature Text—Ezra Pound, T. S. Eliot, William Carlos Williams, Hilda Doolittle

Link to Music
- American Music: Cultural Traditions

CHAPTER 22

BEGINNING THE CHAPTER

Read to students this statement made by Senator Henry Cabot Lodge in 1895:

"The great nations are rapidly absorbing for their future expansion and their present defense, all the waste places of the earth. It is a movement which makes for civilization and the advancement of the race. As one of the great nations of the world the United States must not fall out of line of march."

What is Lodge proposing that the United States do? (expand its territory in order to build an empire) Ask students how they think such a statement would be received today. (Present U.S. foreign policy does not include colonization or empire building.) Tell students that at the time Lodge's argument was widely accepted. Chapter 22 describes how and why the United States began to build an overseas empire.

Recording Journal Notes
Suggest students divide the countries into two categories: Western Hemisphere and Eastern Hemisphere.

CHAPTER 22

Imperialism
1867–1908

▼ RED LEATHER BOOTS AND BUTTON HOOK

Setting the Scene

Focus
Foreign policy before the late nineteenth century had been dominated by two ideas. The first was President Washington's isolationist warning against entering into "entangling alliances." The second was President Monroe's warning to Europe against interference in the Americas. War with Spain, however, resulted in a more aggressive foreign policy and the acquisition of overseas colonies. Suddenly, the United States had become a major world power.

Concepts to Understand
★ How increased United States economic and political power led to the acquisition of an overseas empire
★ How confrontation with Spain resulted in war over Cuba

Read to Discover . . .
★ why Americans moved away from a policy of isolationism.
★ the problems and responsibilities that victory in the Spanish-American War brought the United States.

Journal Notes
Why did the United States become involved in the affairs of other countries? Record each country and the reasons for each as you read this chapter.

CULTURAL
- 1880 "General" William Booth organizes the Salvation Army
- 1891 University of Chicago founded
- 1893 World's Columbian Exposition is held in Chicago

1875 | 1885

POLITICAL
- 1882 Chinese Exclusion Act is passed
- 1893 Queen Liliuokalani of Hawaii is overthrown

596 UNIT 7 Entering a New Century: 1867–1920

✚ EXTRA CREDIT PROJECT

Although United States foreign policy is no longer imperialist, the United States still intervenes in conflicts around the world. Suggest interested students research an example of recent American intervention. Ask them to report their findings, including reasons for the intervention and its outcome. You might conduct a class debate on whether students think the intervention was justified.

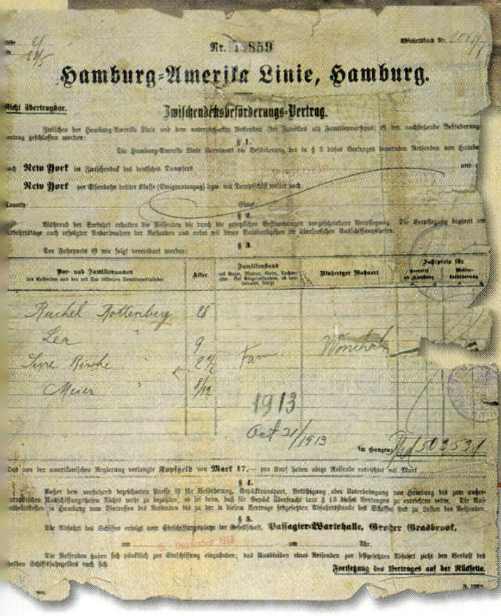

The Return of the Conquerors
by Edward Moran, 1898

Edward Moran painted this work to commemorate the American victory over Spain in the Spanish-American War. In the foreground is Admiral Dewey's flagship *Olympia*.

◀ EUROPEAN STEAMSHIP TICKET

- **1903** The Great Train Robbery motion picture produced; first to have a fully developed plot
- **1910** Women make up 21 percent of the workforce

1895 — **1905**

- **1898** Spanish-American War begins
- **1899** Hay initiates Open Door policy
- **1900** Boxer Rebellion in China
- **1904** Roosevelt Corollary announced
- **1905** Roosevelt arbitrates Russo-Japanese War

CHAPTER 22 Imperialism 1867–1908

CHAPTER 22 CONCEPTS

Concept Mapping Activity
Reproduce the following generalization-and-concepts map on the chalkboard, and have students copy it in their notebooks. Ask them to hypothesize about what topics may be covered in Chapter 22 based on this information.

> As a world power, the United States becomes increasingly involved in foreign affairs and establishes an empire.
>
> - Economic and Political Power
> - Confrontation

History AND ART
Edward Moran commemorated Admiral Dewey's victory over Spain in the Philippines with his dramatic *Return of the Conquerors*, painted in 1898.

The following material is available from Glencoe and may be used to introduce or enrich Chapter 22:

 VIDEODISC
- *GTV: A Geographic Perspective on American History*

53461

Teacher Notes

LESSON PLAN
SECTION 1, 598–602

FOCUS

Bellringer
Before taking roll at the beginning of the class period, display Focus Activity Transparency 72 on the overhead projector, and assign the accompanying Focus Activity Sheet.

Objectives
Point out the objectives on this page to students in previewing section content.

Motivating Activity
Ask students to name the President who stated that the independent nations of the Americas were "henceforth not to be considered as subjects for further colonization by any European powers." (Monroe, in what became known as the Monroe Doctrine) Tell students as they read Section 1 to look for ways in which the Monroe Doctrine was challenged during the late 1800s.

Use Skills Transparency 22.

The following material is available from Glencoe:

VIDEODISC
- *GTV: A Geographic Perspective on American History*

53461

SECTION 1

America Looks Abroad

Setting the Scene

Section Focus

Beginning in the 1500s, European nations built vast colonial empires. By the mid-1800s, many of these colonies had become independent. The Industrial Revolution caused new empire building. Germany, France, Belgium, Portugal, and Japan joined the race for colonies. The United States had grown entirely by expansion. Would the race for empire tempt a once-colonial people to seek colonies?

Objectives

After studying this section, you should be able to
★ discuss the emergence of the United States from isolationism.
★ cite two examples of arbitration averting war.

Key Terms

imperialism, isolationism, reciprocity, arbitration

 QUEEN LILIUOKALANI OF HAWAII

European colonialism was motivated by trade and adventure, power and profit, idealism and national patriotism. These nations also believed they had a "civilizing mission" toward nonwhite populations. The Industrial Revolution generated a need for markets for manufactured goods and new sources of raw materials. **Imperialism**—the policy of establishing colonies and building empires—answered these needs.

Isolationism, or separation from the political affairs of other countries, was a policy established by George Washington. In his farewell address, he warned against entangling alliances. Later the Monroe Doctrine emphasized the United States's desire to keep the Americas separate from Europe. Another factor affecting American foreign policy was the Declaration of Independence—the idea that people had the right to govern themselves.

■ Securing an American Continent

European control of parts of North America by France and Russia ended in the 1860s. The United States challenged a French expansion effort in 1861 and bought Russian territory in 1867.

End of French Expansion

Mexico's reform government under Benito Juárez (HWAHR•uhs) stopped payment of its foreign debts. French, Spanish, and British troops entered the country to force payment. The debts were collected and Spain and Britain left, but the French remained. Ignoring the Monroe Doctrine and taking advantage of the American Civil War, the French emperor Napoleon III overthrew the Republic of Mexico. In 1864

598 UNIT 7 Entering a New Century: 1867–1920

Classroom Resources for SECTION 1

Teacher's Classroom Resources
- Chapter 22 Study Guide
- Reproducible Lesson Plan
- Reteaching Activity 22-1
- Chapter 22 Cooperative Learning Activity
- Section Quiz

Multimedia
- Section Focus Transparency 72
- Skills Transparency 22
- Unit 7 Digest Transparency
- Testmaker
- Student Self-Test Software
- GTV: A Geographic Perspective on American History

Napoleon III installed Austrian prince Maximilian as Mexico's emperor.

The United States protested and, after the Civil War, sent nearly 50,000 troops to the border at the Rio Grande. Napoleon's forces withdrew. The Mexicans promptly defeated Maximilian's army and executed Maximilian. The United States proved its willingness to back the Monroe Doctrine with force.

Acquisition of Alaska

Secretary of State William H. Seward believed in Manifest Destiny. He envisioned a United States empire and wanted to annex Canada, Hawaii, and several Caribbean islands.

Seward's only major achievement along this line was the purchase of Alaska in 1867. The undeveloped territory of Alaska, twice the size of Texas, was held by Russia, but the czar saw little value in the territory.

In 1867, when the Russian minister to the United States informed Seward that the czar wanted to sell Alaska, the secretary of state jumped at the chance. In a few hours, Seward arranged a treaty in which the United States would buy Alaska for $7.2 million—less than two cents an acre. After four months of selling the idea to Congress, the transaction was completed.

■ Economic Empire Building

At one time the United States had little need to look beyond its own borders for growth. Raw materials were abundant, and the home market was immense. By the 1890s, the country had developed into a great industrial nation, able to compete with European producers.

Reciprocity

James G. Blaine, secretary of state under Presidents Garfield and Harrison, wanted to open up new markets not by taking on

Visualizing History ▲ **MINING GOLD IN THE YUKON** Many settlers and prospectors came to Alaska after gold was discovered in the region in the late 1800s. *Why did many Americans criticize the Alaska purchase?*

CHAPTER 22 SECTION 1

Independent Practice

Geography Provide students with an outline map of Alaska. Have them complete the map by showing the state's natural resources and industries. Make sure they include a legend on their maps. When the maps are completed, ask students if they agree that "Seward's icebox" was worth purchasing. Discuss why or why not. **L2**

Hawaii's strategic position made the islands highly attractive to the United States. The U.S. government eventually turned its coaling stop at Pearl Harbor into a naval base that proved invaluable in World War II. Attacked by the Japanese on December 7, 1941, the base sustained crippling casualties. The base not only was rebuilt but also became the center of the victorious Pacific campaign.

Visualizing History **Alaska** Miners found vast reserves of copper in the Copper River area. Other newcomers developed Alaska's fishing industry by building canneries.

Answer to Caption: to protect trade and growing number of Americans living in Hawaii

▲ ANCHORAGE, ALASKA

 **Visualizing History** ▲ **ALASKA** The wealth of resources found in this scenic state proved Alaska's worth, even though its purchase was originally called Seward's Folly. *Why did some Americans call for the annexation of Hawaii?*

colonies, but by increasing American trade through **reciprocity**—the mutual lowering of tariff barriers. He tried, without much success, to include reciprocity provisions in the McKinley Tariff of 1890. He was able to chair a Pan-American Congress in Washington, D.C., in 1889. The goal of the group, which later became the Pan-American Union, was to promote economic cooperation and trade among the Americas. Success was limited, however, because the United States intervened, often forcibly, in Latin American affairs.

Should Hawaii Be Annexed?

American missionaries and traders first ventured to Hawaii in the early 1800s. American sugar growers followed. By the 1890s Hawaii was closely connected to the United States through commerce and the many Americans living there.

While many nationalities lived in Hawaii, native Hawaiian rulers were controlled by the American business community until the Hawaiian Queen Liliuokalani (lih•LEE•uh•woh•kuh•LAH•nee) came into power in 1891. She was determined to return control to her own people. In response, some American business leaders, with the help of marines from the cruiser *Boston*, took over the government.

The American minister to Hawaii wrote the Department of State that Hawaii was ready to annex. President Cleveland disagreed. He decided that the use of American troops to overthrow the Hawaiian government was a violation of "national honesty." Despite criticism, Cleveland withdrew American soldiers from Hawaii. He also tried, but failed, to oust the revolutionary provisional government and put Liliuokalani back on her throne.

■ Challenging Great Britain

After the Civil War, the United States appeared ready to take a position among the powers of the world. Twice the United States forced Britain to submit to **arbitration**, or the settlement of a dispute by an impartial group.

Civil War Damages

In 1868 Charles Sumner, head of the Senate Foreign Relations Committee, claimed that Great Britain owed the United States more than $2 billion in damages for allowing Confederate ships to use British ports during the Civil War. If the British would not pay, Senator Sumner declared, the United States should take British-controlled Canada.

In 1871 Secretary of State Hamilton Fish arranged for arbitration. Britain did not want to risk war in Canada and feared that a hostile United States might supply Britain's

UNIT 7 Entering a New Century: 1867–1920

Sidelights: United States Economic Expansion

The late 1800s witnessed a tremendous surge in American agricultural and industrial production. Between 1870 and 1892, for example, the United States increased its gross national product (GNP) from approximately $7.4 billion per year to $14.3 billion per year. The rapid growth in production led, in turn, to increased foreign trade since American markets could not absorb the large quantities of agricultural and manufactured goods that were produced. Between 1870 and 1892, the value of American exports rose from $451 million to $1.1 billion.

enemies with warships. The United States backed down on its demand for "indirect" damages. In the Treaty of Washington, the United States was awarded $15.5 million, which Britain paid.

Venezuela Border Dispute

President Cleveland requested that the British put a long-standing Venezuela–British Guiana boundary dispute to arbitration. In July 1895 Secretary of State Richard Olney wrote the British government that their refusal to arbitrate violated the Monroe Doctrine. He warned:

> *The United States is practically sovereign on this continent and its fiat is law upon the subjects to which it confines its interposition.*

Britain answered that the Monroe Doctrine had no standing in international law and did not apply to the situation.

Aware of the possibility of war, Cleveland asked Congress for authorization to appoint a commission to determine the boundary without consulting Britain. Americans responded with excitement, but Britain thought it "monstrous and insulting." For a few days, war seemed a strong possibility.

Fortunately, the British government backed down. Early in January 1896, Britain's attention was diverted from Venezuela by a dispute with Germany involving South Africa. Seeking to improve relations with the United States, Britain agreed to arbitration. The boundary settlement turned out in Britain's favor and a new era of Anglo-American understanding emerged.

Strengthening the Navy

The Venezuelan crisis called attention to the fact that the United States had only three modern battleships. The crisis also popularized the writings of an American naval officer, Captain Alfred T. Mahan. Mahan believed that as America developed its industrial strength, the nation should look outward. Great nations of the past had built up foreign markets, expanded their merchant fleets, constructed navies to protect their commerce, and planted colonies in distant territories. Mahan argued that a modern nation needed sea power in order to become great.

At first Mahan had more influence abroad. Kaiser (Emperor) Wilhelm II of Germany studied his books and instructed German naval officers to read them. In Great Britain Mahan was showered with honors. Mahan influenced rising American leaders such as Senator Henry Cabot Lodge and Theodore Roosevelt and helped to shape United States naval policy.

Congress established a Naval Advisory Board in 1881 that pressed for larger naval appropriations. In 1883 Congress authorized construction of 1 more cruiser and 3 battleships. By adding 3 heavier and more powerful ships in 1890 and by voting for 13 new ships in 1895, Congress made it clear that it intended to have a navy capable of matching any enemy on the high seas.

Section 1 ★ Review

Checking for Understanding

1. **Identify** Maximilian, William Seward, Queen Liliuokalani, Charles Sumner.
2. **Define** imperialism, isolationism, reciprocity, arbitration.
3. **Show** how the French challenged the Monroe Doctrine in 1861.
4. **Describe** two instances of confrontation with Great Britain that were settled by arbitration.

Critical Thinking

5. **Understanding Cause and Effect** How did the writings of Captain Alfred T. Mahan lead to expanding the American navy?

CHAPTER 22
SECTION 1

ASSESS

Check Understanding

Assign Section 1 Review as homework or an in-class activity.

Evaluate

Assign the Section 1 Quiz in the TCR, or use the History of a Free Nation Testmaker to create a customized quiz.

Reteach

Have students complete Reteaching Activity 22-1.

Enrich

Ask students to research the role of the U.S. secretary of state. Have them identify the current secretary, and outline his duties, including the role he plays in foreign and economic policy and his decision-making authority.

CLOSE

Have students identify the foreign affairs discussed in Section 1 that were settled based on a policy of isolationism and the foreign affairs that were settled based on a policy of imperialism.

CHAPTER 22 Imperialism 1867–1908

Answers to SECTION 1 REVIEW

1. Maximilian, 599; William Seward, 599; Queen Liliuokalani, 600; Charles Sumner, 600
2. All vocabulary words are defined in the Glossary.
3. French troops invaded Mexico with Spain and Britain to collect debts. Spain and Britain left. France occupied Mexico City and installed Maximilian emperor.
4. (a.) In 1868 U.S. government claimed $2 million damages for British aid to Confederacy. If Britain refused to pay, U.S. threatened to take control of Canada. Britain negotiated and paid $1.5 million. (b.) President Cleveland asked Britain to put boundary dispute between Venezuela and British Guiana to arbitration. Britain first refused, then backed down.
5. showed that a nation needed a strong navy to be great

CHAPTER 22 CONNECTIONS

Teaching Making Connections

Point out to students that the United States today maintains naval and air bases throughout the world. Discuss with students the advantages and disadvantages of operating bases in distant lands. Ask them if they think it is necessary for the United States to maintain bases in far-flung places. Why or why not?

Did You Know?

Until the last decade of the nineteenth century, the United States had no battleships. In 1890 Congress authorized the construction of the first three: the *Oregon*, the *Indiana*, and the *Massachusetts*. Each was more than 10,000 tons and bristled with guns.

Fact or Fiction?

Proposals to admit Hawaii as a state began as early as the 1850s.

FACT: In 1854 the U.S. government negotiated a treaty of annexation with the kingdom of Hawaii. It was rejected by the Senate, however, because it contained a provision for immediate statehood. Hawaii did not enter the Union until more than 150 years later when in 1959 it became the fiftieth state.

CONNECTIONS  CONNECTIONS

Coaling Stations and Colonies

By the end of the 1800s, Americans began to think in terms of a different and broader Manifest Destiny. The original concept was changed to include overseas as well as westward expansion. The idea that it was the fate of the United States to extend its boundaries beyond the seas has been called the new Manifest Destiny.

The change in attitude toward foreign affairs was due to certain ideas and developments that occurred in the late 1800s. One such development was imperialism. Nations began to establish empires around the globe to build important new sources of raw materials and provide new avenues for investment.

More justification for imperialism was provided by Captain Alfred Thayer Mahan. Mahan believed that for a country to become a major sea power, its ships needed remote sources of supplies that could not be carried for an entire voyage. While commercial shipping required these supply stations, an armed navy needed them even more. The supplies, according to Mahan, were "first, fuel; second, ammunition; last of all, food."

Fuel became essential to shipping as nations switched from sail to steam power at the turn of the century. No ship could steam away from its home port for any great distance without refueling. A fleet that wanted to trade or fight very far beyond its home waters needed coaling stations in distant lands.

Mahan did not favor unchecked expansionism. Too many supply and fueling bases in foreign lands, he warned, could drain the resources

▲ **U.S.S. *Iowa*, c. 1900**

of the parent country and could become "a source of weakness, multiplying exposed points, and entailing division of force."

The United States had made some strides earlier in the century. One of these was the development of ironclad ships during the Civil War. However, after the war, the United States allowed its navy to deteriorate.

Mahan's ideas provided a real impetus for change. Influenced by Mahan's concepts, Congress passed the Naval Act of 1890, which appropriated additional money for battleships. By 1900 the United States had the naval power it needed to back up an expanded role in foreign affairs.

Making the Technology Connection

1. What supplies did coaling stations provide?
2. How did new technology influence American foreign policy?

Linking Past and Present

3. In what areas of the world does the United States have refueling stations today?

Answers to CONNECTIONS

1. Coaling stations provided fuel, ammunition, and food.
2. The switch to steam-powered ships made it important for the U.S. to have bases for refueling in different lands.
3. Students should be aware that one factor in U.S. policies toward the Philippines, Australia, and New Zealand is the need for secure bases in the Pacific.

SECTION 2

The Spanish-American War

Setting the Scene

Section Focus

Struggling for freedom under Spanish rule for years, Cubans had gained only greater repression. When a new revolution took place in 1895, Americans were moved by two impulses to intervene. Many urged American support for the repressed Cuban people, while others saw the revolt as an opportunity to expand the American empire.

Objectives

After studying this section, you should be able to
★ list the events that led to the United States's involvement in the Spanish-American War.
★ explain the reason for the involvement of the Philippines in the war.

Key Term

neutrality

◀ TIN TRAY WITH LIKENESS OF THEODORE ROOSEVELT

Americans were outraged when they found that the Spanish Governor-General Valeriano Weyler had ordered Cuban men, women, and children into "reconcentration camps." Weyler, unable to tell civilians from rebels, had set up the camps where 200,000 Cubans, an estimated one-eighth of the population, died of illness and starvation. Some leaders of the Cuban independence movement were naturalized American citizens who had returned to work in Cuba. When captured by Spanish authorities, they demanded protection by the United States.

Not all sentiment supported the Cubans, however. American business interests had invested more than $30 million in Cuba—mostly in sugar plantations—and wanted the revolt to end. Some plantation owners, doubting the capacity of the Cubans for self-government, favored the restoration of Spanish rule. The force of public opinion, however, caused many in the business community to change their minds.

■ Drawn Into War

Although President Cleveland preserved strict **neutrality,** or the refusal to take sides, in the Cuban struggle, he warned that if "the useless sacrifice of human life" went on, the United States might have to abandon the policy of "patient waiting." President McKinley, who came into office in the middle of the conflict, was also committed to neutrality. He even offered to buy Cuba, but was rejected. A peaceful solution seemed possible when Spain recalled General Weyler and offered Cuba a measure of local self-government. Assistant Secretary of the Navy Theodore Roosevelt was impatient

CHAPTER 22 Imperialism 1867–1908 **603**

Classroom Resources for SECTION 2

Teacher's Classroom Resources
- Reproducible Lesson Plan
- Reteaching Activity 22-2
- Chapter 22 Primary and Secondary Source Readings
- Section Quiz

Multimedia
- Section Focus Transparency 73
- Student Self-Test Software
- Testmaker
- GTV: A Geographic Perspective on American History

LESSON PLAN
SECTION 2, 603–607

FOCUS

Bellringer
Before taking roll at the beginning of the class period, display Focus Activity Transparency 73 on the overhead projector, and assign the accompanying Focus Activity Sheet.

Objectives
Point out the objectives on this page to students in previewing section content.

Motivating Activity
Ask students to name some slogans that are used today to promote various causes. ("Just say no." "Only you can prevent forest fires.") Discuss the pros and cons of using a rallying cry to get one's ideas across. Tell students that in Section 2 they will learn how a famous slogan helped propel the United States into war.

Assign students the Chapter 22 Reading on Enthusiasms for War and Expansion in Primary and Secondary Source Readings.

 **VIDEODISC**

- **GTV: A Geographic Perspective on American History**

Any side, Frame 53459
Subject: Picture of *Maine* exploding at Havana, Cuba

603

CHAPTER 22 SECTION 2

TEACH

Guided Practice
Evaluating
Have students list developments leading up to the Spanish-American War. (Cuban revolution, sensational media reporting, de Lôme letter, explosion on the *Maine*) Then ask them to evaluate these developments and tell which they think were the most important to the United States's declaration of war with Spain. Have them explain their reasons. **L2**

Visualizing History
Coverage of the *Maine* explosion raised American anger against Spain. President McKinley was trying to resolve American differences with Spain through diplomacy when the explosion occurred. It ended all hope of a negotiated settlement. **Answer to Caption:** No one knows. Each side blamed the other.

Did You Know?
William Randolph Hearst sent artist Frederic Remington to Cuba to cover events after the explosion on the *Maine*. When the expected conflict between the United States and Spain did not immediately materialize, the artist asked if he should return home. Hearst cabled back, "You furnish the pictures, I'll furnish the war."

 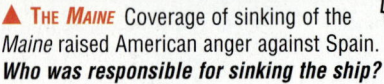 ▲ **THE MAINE** Coverage of sinking of the *Maine* raised American anger against Spain. **Who was responsible for sinking the ship?**

with McKinley's negotiation with Spain and described the President as having "no more backbone than a chocolate eclair." William Randolph Hearst's *New York Journal* and Joseph Pulitzer's *New York World* fanned public anger with exaggerated and sometimes fabricated stories of Spanish atrocities in Cuba. This "yellow journalism" helped sell papers and encouraged war:

> How long are the Spaniards to drench Cuba with the blood and tears of her people? . . . How long shall old men and women and children be murdered by the score, the innocent victims of Spanish rage against the patriot armies they cannot conquer?
> . . . How long shall the United States sit idle and indifferent?

"Remember the *Maine!*"

Public sentiment in favor of war was growing when, on February 9, 1898, the *Journal* printed a private letter written by Enrique Dupuy de Lôme, the Spanish ambassador to the United States, in which he called McKinley "weak and a bidder for the admiration of the crowd. . . . " This comment was a national insult. The ambassador resigned, but the damage to United States–Spanish relations was done.

Six days later the United States battleship *Maine*, anchored off the Cuban capital, Havana, exploded, killing 260 crew members. United States naval experts declared that the explosion came from outside the ship. Spanish experts replied that there were no mines.

The "yellow press" in 1898 expressed no indecision. Papers promptly blamed Spain and even printed diagrams showing just how the deed was done. "Remember the *Maine!*" became the battle cry throughout the United States.

Preparing for War

Congress responded to a torrent of public indignation against Spain by allocating $50 million for war preparations. McKinley, meanwhile, demanded that Spain give Cuba independence. Although at the last moment Spain claimed it was trying to comply, McKinley nevertheless delivered a warlike message to Congress. Congress demanded that Spain evacuate the island. When no reply to this ultimatum was received, Congress declared war on April 25.

While expansionists were excited about the prospects of gaining Cuba, humanitarian forces in Congress attached the Teller Amendment to the declaration of war. In it Congress pledged "to leave the government and control of the Island to the people" as soon as peace was established there.

604 UNIT 7 Entering a New Century: 1867–1920

Special Needs

Summarizing Problems Summarizing requires students to choose key ideas or events and state them in a concise way. Important events and reactions to these events are related in the subsection "Remember the *Maine*." Ask students to pick one of these key events and draw it. (Most students will choose the explosion on the battleship *Maine*.) Then have them write a sentence that explains one event that preceded the event they drew and one event that came after it. Label the sequence 1, 2, and 3. Explain that they have summarized a section of text.

"A Splendid Little War"

While the army prepared to invade Cuba, the conflict, called by Secretary of State John Hay a "splendid little war," began in the Pacific. Although the McKinley administration had no thought of expanding the territories of the United States, some officials believed that this was a prime opportunity to do so. One such person was Theodore Roosevelt.

The Philippine Connection

When John D. Long, secretary of the navy, was out of his Washington office, Roosevelt took charge. On February 25, 1898, he ordered on his own authority a Pacific squadron stationed in Hong Kong to sail for the Philippine Islands, a Spanish colony for 300 years, if war broke out. Commodore George Dewey, commander of the United States fleet, would try to prevent a Spanish fleet in Manila Bay from going to sea. As soon as war was declared, Dewey's fleet set sail; it penetrated Manila Bay on May 1 and rapidly destroyed the weaker Spanish fleet. The quick victory surprised the President, and an army of occupation was hastily organized to sail from San Francisco to the Philippines.

A native Filipino, Emilio Aguinaldo (AH•gee•NAHL•doh), had led an uprising against Spanish rule of the Philippines in 1896. Aguinaldo was exiled in Hong Kong, where Dewey met him and provided supplies so he could lead a revolt against the Spanish forces that remained in the islands. By the time the American army arrived in the

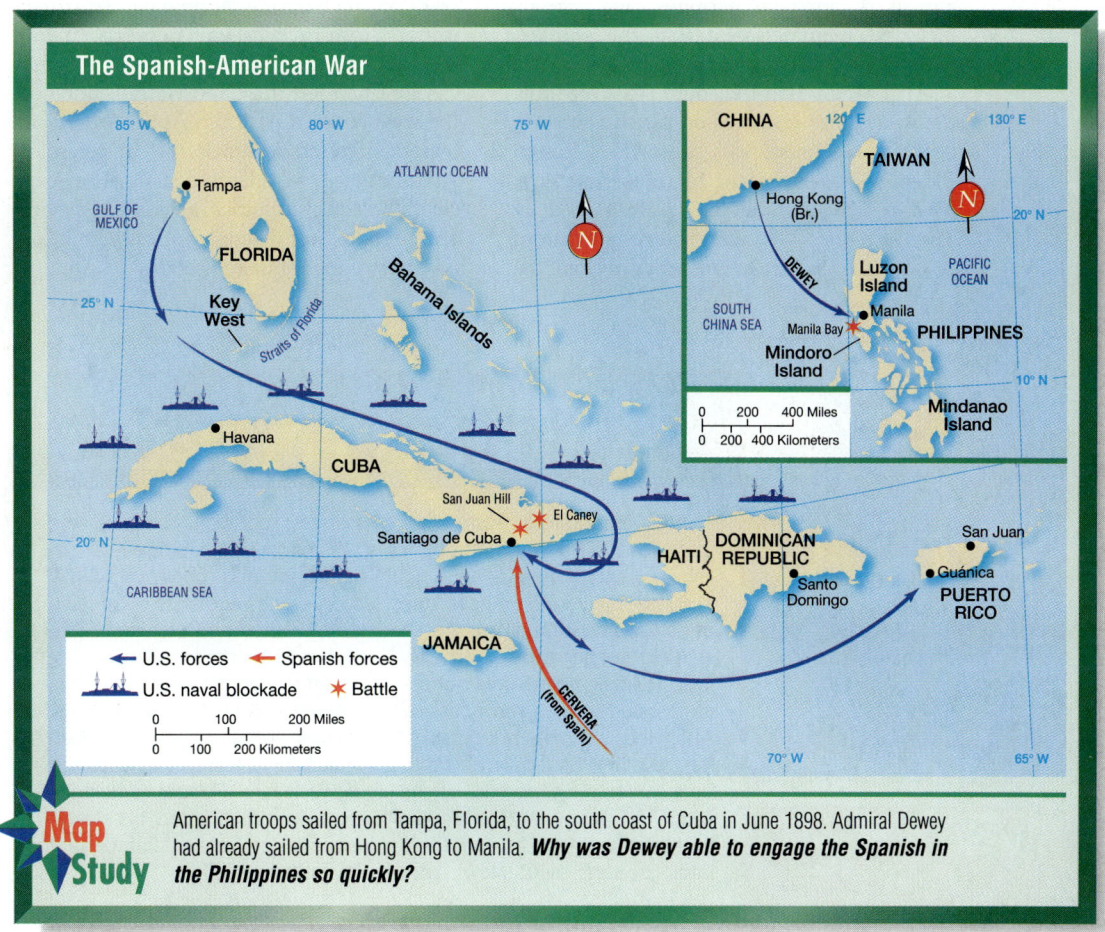

The Spanish-American War

American troops sailed from Tampa, Florida, to the south coast of Cuba in June 1898. Admiral Dewey had already sailed from Hong Kong to Manila. **Why was Dewey able to engage the Spanish in the Philippines so quickly?**

CHAPTER 22 SECTION 2

Teaching American Portraits

Joseph Pulitzer established the Graduate School of Journalism at Columbia University with a million dollar gift and left another million dollars to the school at his death. He endowed a special fund for the Pulitzer Prizes—16 awards given each year for outstanding accomplishments in journalism, literature, music, and art. Ask students why a newspaper publisher would be interested in giving these awards. (to encourage writers and artists)

Linking Across Time

The Tenth Cavalry was one of four African American units to serve in Cuba. Although African Americans have fought in every war, and although their courage in Cuba was highly praised, African American soldiers were not considered equals. It was not until 1954 that the army finally abolished segregated units. Until 1941 fewer than 1 percent of African Americans were promoted to officer rank. In 1940 Benjamin O. Davis broke a military race barrier to become the first African American brigadier general.

Philippines, Aguinaldo's forces controlled all the territory except the city of Manila. When the Spanish surrendered and turned the Philippines over to the United States Army, it left unanswered the question of who would rule the islands after the war.

Fighting in Cuba

When war was first declared, McKinley had called for 200,000 volunteers to supplement the regular army, which numbered only 28,000. The War Department was inefficient. Nevertheless, 17,000 troops were declared ready to sail from Tampa, Florida, to Cuba by the middle of June. To fight a war in the tropics, they were issued heavy woolen uniforms left over from the western wars against the Plains peoples. Their ammunition was out-of-date; there were almost no medical supplies; and rations included inedible meat that the soldiers nicknamed "embalmed beef."

After landing on the south coast of Cuba, the Americans advanced on the city of Santiago. One regiment was called the "Rough Riders"—an assortment of college athletes, cowboys, miners, and law officers—led by Theodore Roosevelt, who had resigned from the Navy Department in order to join the fight. On foot because their horses were still in Florida, they charged up San Juan Hill. By securing the heights overlooking Santiago, they helped capture the city.

The Rough Riders were not alone in this attack. Among the other regiments was the all-black 10th Cavalry Regiment. Many African Americans had responded to the call for soldiers both because they identified with the Cubans' struggle for freedom and because they hoped it would improve their own lot. At least four of these African American soldiers were awarded the Congressional Medal of Honor.

Naval Encounters

At the outbreak of hostilities, an American squadron of new battleships under Admiral William T. Sampson was given the task of intercepting a Spanish squadron under Admiral Pascual Cervera (pahs•KWAHL suhr•VEHR•uh). Knowing that Cervera had left the Cape Verde Islands off the west coast of Africa in April, Americans feared he would attack the undefended Atlantic coast of the United States. They canceled hotel reservations at seaside resorts and prepared for defense, but Cervera headed directly for Santiago harbor.

Joseph Pulitzer 1847–1911

AMERICAN PORTRAITS

After emigrating from Hungary, Joseph Pulitzer made publishing history—and a personal fortune—by creating a new form of newspaper journalism.

As a soldier during the Civil War, Pulitzer noted how Americans loved to read newspapers. After the war, he bought and merged two St. Louis newspapers. Circulation soared as he filled his paper with scandals and attacks on big business. He later bought two New York papers, bringing to them the same successful recipe—sensationalism and controversy. He won a mass audience by running comic strips and covering fashions and sports.

After retiring, he saw his papers engage in "yellow journalism" to compete with William Randolph Hearst's flag-waving newspapers. Pulitzer took back control and returned his newspapers to their flamboyant investigative style.

UNIT 7 Entering a New Century: 1867–1920

Sidelights: Economics and War with Cuba

By the mid-1890s, tension between Spain and Cuba increased in part because of the Wilson-Gorman Tariff, which the U.S. Congress passed in 1894. This tariff imposed heavy duties on Cuba's major export and economic base—sugar. Before the new tariff, the United States had been the chief market for Cuban sugar. Because these new duties raised the price of Cuban sugar to prohibitive levels, the sale of Cuban sugar in the United States fell sharply. Decreased sugar sales brought a severe depression to Cuba, which led to discontent and revolts.

MANILA BAY United States naval ships in the Pacific, under Commodore George Dewey, sailed into Manila Bay on May 1, 1898. **When did Spain and the United States agree to an armistice?**

Sampson's superior force found the Spanish fleet at Santiago and blockaded the harbor. Once the American army took the heights overlooking Santiago, Cervera could surrender or try to break the blockade. On July 3, with little hope of victory, Cervera ordered his ships out of Santiago harbor. In the ensuing battle, all Spanish vessels were sunk. Only one American was killed and one was wounded. Effective Spanish resistance in Cuba ceased with the surrender of Santiago two weeks later. American troops went on to occupy another Spanish possession, the island of Puerto Rico. On August 12 Spain and the United States agreed to an armistice.

The "splendid little war" cost 5,000 American lives, mostly due to disease and food poisoning. The flag of the United States, an emerging world power, flew over distant islands. Had American isolationism ended?

Section 2 ★ Review

Checking for Understanding

1. **Identify** William Randolph Hearst, Joseph Pulitzer, Dupuy de Lôme, the *Maine,* Theodore Roosevelt, Rough Riders.
2. **Define** neutrality.
3. **List** the key events leading to war with Spain over Cuba.
4. **State** the importance of the naval battle between Admiral William T. Sampson and Admiral Pascual Cervera.

Critical Thinking

5. **Making Judgments** How did the United States justify going to war with Spain given a previous policy of noninvolvement?

LESSON PLAN
SECTION 3, 608–614

FOCUS

Bellringer
🔶 Before taking roll at the beginning of the class period, display Focus Activity Transparency 74 on the overhead projector, and assign the accompanying Focus Activity Sheet.

Objectives
Point out the objectives on this page to the students in previewing section content.

Motivating Activity
Direct students to the two statements on pages 609 and 610, one by President William McKinley and the other by Andrew Carnegie. Ask them to interpret each statement. (McKinley believed Filipino people were basically inferior to whites; Carnegie was deploring how such an attitude led to violence and the death of Filipinos.) Tell students that Section 3 traces the conflict between the United States's colonial policies and its commitment to democratic government.

🔶 Use Chapter 22 Map Transparency. Assign the accompanying activity from Map Transparencies: Strategies and Activities.

SECTION 3

Becoming a World Power

Setting the Scene

Section Focus
After the Spanish-American War the United States was confronted by a host of questions and responsibilities. Congress debated what to do about the Philippine Islands. Commercial and industrial interests argued for annexation, but how could colonialism be reconciled with the principles of the Declaration of Independence?

Objectives
After studying this section, you should be able to
★ explain why the Philippine Islands were difficult to govern.
★ discuss the constitutional difficulties involved in colonization.

Key Term
protectorate

◀ ARMY RECRUITMENT POSTER

The Spanish-American War and the prospect of expanding in the Pacific brought a change of policy toward the Hawaiian Islands. Cleveland had resisted a move to annex them in 1893, and in 1897 the Senate had turned down an annexation treaty presented by McKinley. Hawaii, the halfway point between California and the Philippines, would be valuable as a naval base, however. In July 1898, before the war ended, the Hawaiian Islands were annexed by a joint resolution of Congress.

■ The Philippines
The armistice left Americans in control of the Spanish-owned Philippine Islands. The debate over whether to acquire and annex the Philippines was a stormy one.

Arguments For and Against Annexing the Philippines
Before entering the Spanish-American War, most Americans had no idea of annexing territory, particularly a territory 6,000 miles from the Pacific coast. McKinley confessed that before Dewey's victory he could not have come within 2,000 miles of placing the Philippine Islands on a map. Once he said, "If old Dewey had just sailed away when he smashed that Spanish fleet, what a lot of strong feelings he would have saved us."

Strong feelings developed against acquiring the islands. Several leading Democrats, including former President Grover Cleveland, were opposed. Many influential private citizens agreed with them. Prominent Republicans such as Speaker of the House Thomas B. Reed and several senators fought annexation as a violation of American tradition.

UNIT 7 Entering a New Century: 1867–1920

Classroom Resources for SECTION 3

Teacher's Classroom Resources
- Reproducible Lesson Plan
- Reteaching Activity 22-3
- Section Quiz

Multimedia
- Section Focus Transparency 74
- Chapter 22 Map Transparency
- Testmaker
- Student Self-Test Software

Senator Henry Cabot Lodge spoke for those who wanted a larger American role in world affairs. Business interests thought of new markets and fields of investment. Public opinion was excited by the prospect of acquiring an empire. Patriotism merged with belief in social Darwinism, or the belief in the "survival of the fittest." If the United States was the most fit to govern the Philippines, why should it haul down the Stars and Stripes and allow Japan or Germany or some other power to step in and take them?

For others, like Reverend Josiah Strong, there was a sense of mission based on racial and religious bias. Strong, in his book *Our Country*, blended social Darwinism with his interest in spreading Christianity. He felt the nationality groups were in a competition from which Anglo-Saxons were destined to emerge victorious.

Settlement with Spain

McKinley, a deeply religious man, wrestled with the problem, then reported that through prayer he had decided to:

> ... [E]ducate the Filipinos, and uplift and civilize and Christianize them, and by God's grace, do the very best we could by them, as our fellow men for whom Christ died.

Actually, Catholic missions had been started in the Philippines in the 1500s. McKinley instructed his peace commissioners to ask for all of the Philippine Islands. When Spain resisted, the United States offered to pay $20 million for them. In the treaty, signed December 10, 1898, Spain gave up control over Cuba and surrendered Puerto Rico, the Pacific island of Guam, and the Philippine Islands. Anti-imperialist feeling in the Senate was so strong that the treaty was ratified by only a two-vote margin. A Senate resolution promising eventual independence to the Filipino people was defeated only by the tie-breaking vote of the Vice President.

The United States encountered problems in trying to govern the Philippines. The

 ▲ **THE BIG STICK** To many people around the world, the United States in the late 1800s and early 1900s used its power to spread its influence. *Why did the United States encounter difficult problems in trying to govern the Philippines?*

CHAPTER 22 SECTION 3

Independent Practice

History Have students use reference books to determine the current status of Puerto Rico, the Philippine Islands, and Cuba. They should organize information into charts that contain the following: Government, Major Industries, Chief Crops, Major Trade Partners.

When charts are completed, have students discuss the current relationship each nation or area has with the United States. Ask how the relationships differ from those at the turn of the century. **L2, L3**

Map Study Using Maps

Answer: the Philippines

Skills Practice
Have students study the map and create a then-and-now chart showing the political status of United States possessions in 1900 and the current political status of these areas.

Did You Know?

According to the Treaty of Paris, signed in December 1898, the United States gave $20,000,000 for the Philippines. The treaty was only ratified by a two-vote margin because of anti-imperialist feelings in the Senate.

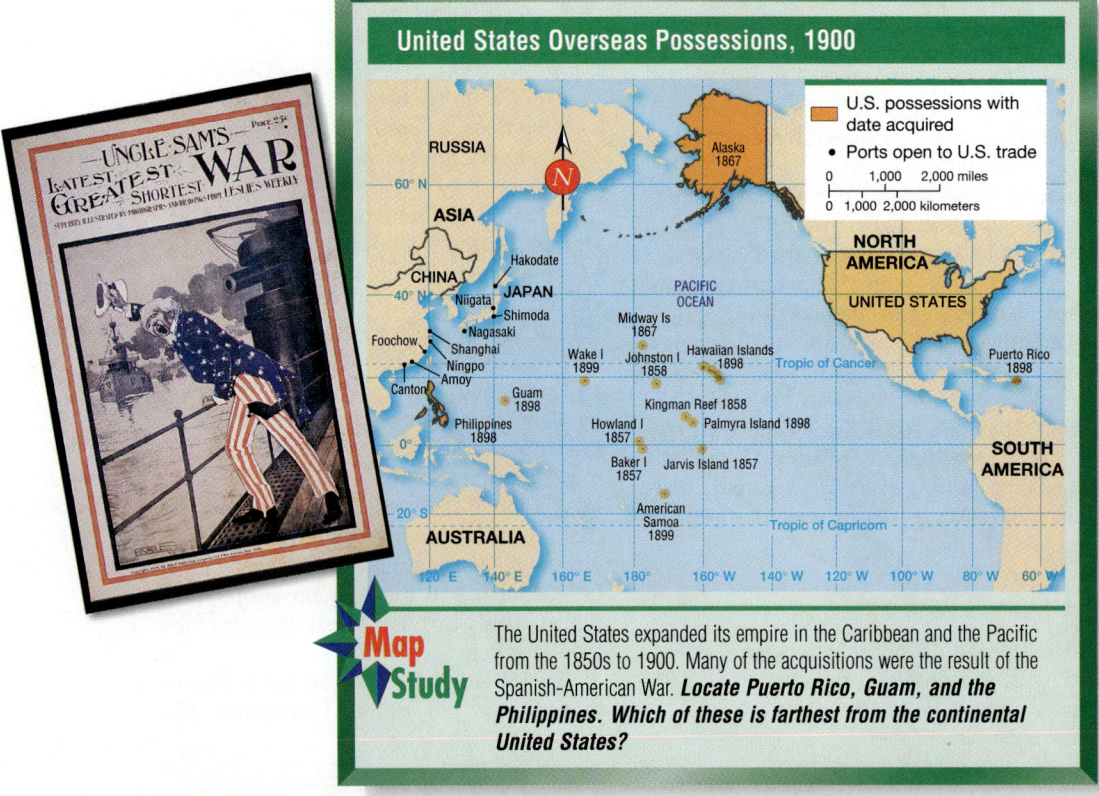

Map Study

The United States expanded its empire in the Caribbean and the Pacific from the 1850s to 1900. Many of the acquisitions were the result of the Spanish-American War. **Locate Puerto Rico, Guam, and the Philippines. Which of these is farthest from the continental United States?**

7,100 islands had 7.5 million people, who were divided into 43 ethnic groups speaking 87 different languages and dialects. The Filipinos ranged from people living in the forests to highly literate city dwellers.

Filipino Resistance

Filipino patriots had helped the American forces capture the islands. Once it became clear that the United States intended to annex the Philippines, however, a new uprising broke out—this time against the Americans. Feeling that they had been cheated out of their independence, Filipino soldiers took to the hills. A revolutionary government was set up under Emilio Aguinaldo. The congress adopted its own republican constitution. Aguinaldo and the other Filipino leaders knew that if the republic were to succeed, they must gain the loyalty of the people and set up diplomatic relations with other countries.

Fighting between Filipino and United States forces broke out in February 1899. Within two months, the Filipinos had been driven from their capital city, and the government fled. Aguinaldo continued to carry on guerrilla operations that produced some success. Aguinaldo's capture in March 1901, however, for all practical purposes ended the Filipinos' military efforts. More than 60,000 troops—four times the number sent to Cuba—and three years of fighting were required to suppress the Filipino patriots and put down the revolt.

At the conclusion of the fighting, Andrew Carnegie commented to a friend in the government:

> You seem to have finished your work of civilizing the Filipinos; it is thought about 8,000 of them have been completely civilized and sent to heaven. I hope you like it.

610 UNIT 7 Entering a New Century: 1867–1920

Cultural Diversity

The overseas expansion of the United States brought with it great cultural diversity. Today many people from former American colonies live and work in the United States. Suggest that students investigate the cultural diversity of their community, the various peoples who live there and their customs and traditions, their food, music, and so on. Ask students to report their research by describing the contributions of the various groups to the community. **L3**

Many Americans were distressed to find their country at war with an independence movement. Mark Twain suggested that Old Glory should have its white stripes painted black and its stars replaced with skull and crossbones.

Even before the Filipino uprising was put down, President McKinley declared that American policy toward the islands would be for the good of the Filipinos. The President stated,

> The Philippines are ours, not to exploit but to develop, to civilize, to educate, to train in the science of self-government.

President McKinley sent two commissions to investigate the conditions in the Philippines and set up a civil government.

There were several changes during the first years of United States rule in the Philippines. The English language replaced Spanish as the language of general usage. The number of American business enterprises grew quickly, largely because Americans were permitted to sell their goods tariff-free in the Philippines. Street names were Americanized.

Resentment against American rule in the Philippines was moderately relieved in 1901 when President Theodore Roosevelt appointed William Howard Taft as the first civilian governor. Genuinely devoted to the interests of the island people, Taft started a program to prepare the Filipinos for self-government, and public schools were established. The United States bought out large foreign landowners and passed laws to keep property in the hands of the Filipinos.

Taft did not believe that the Philippines would be ready for independence for many years, though. In 1907 an elective legislature was set up, and in 1916 the United States promised that the Philippines would have independence eventually. That independence was finally granted in 1946.

Life of the Times

Imperial Fruits

Tropical fruits, such as lemons and oranges, first came to North America in the 1500s by way of the Spanish explorers and missionaries in Florida. More exotic tropical fruits were unavailable to the average person until the late nineteenth century.

Tropical fruits such as bananas, coconuts, and pineapples appeared on the breakfast tables of ordinary Americans for the first time when steamships reduced travel time from the tropics. Foods such as bananas, which easily rotted, could be transported expeditiously by steamship from the Caribbean islands to the United States. The imperialistic impulse that brought the United States distant colonies also inspired business entrepreneurs to build plantations. In 1899 Lorenzo Dow Baker and Minor Keith founded the United Fruit Company; their goal was to own and operate banana plantations in Central America. Baker and Keith realized enormous profits and indirectly helped coin the term "banana republics" for Costa Rica, Guatemala, and Nicaragua—where American corporations often influenced United States policy.

CHAPTER 22
SECTION 3

Teaching Life of the Times

Generally only the fruit of the banana plant is used and transported to other countries, but some banana trees produce useful fiber that can be used to make baskets. What other crops that are "imperial fruits" does the United States import? (sugar, coffee)

Did You Know?

Secretary of State Elihu Root answered the question "Does the Constitution follow the flag?" by saying "Je-es, as near as I can make out the Constitution follows the flag—but doesn't quite catch up with it."

FACT or FICTION?

Only reformers opposed imperialism.

FICTION: Opponents of imperialism included not only Jane Addams and Samuel Gompers but also ex-Presidents Benjamin Harrison and Grover Cleveland, industrialist Andrew Carnegie, writers Mark Twain and William James, and many others.

Cooperative Learning

Conducting a Panel Discussion Invite volunteers to form three groups, one assuming the role of traders or businesspeople, another the role of missionaries, and a third the role of people whose country has just been colonized by the United States. Ask a volunteer to act as the panel arbitrator. Have each group prepare arguments for its viewpoint on colonization and select a spokesperson to present that view. When all views have been presented, ask the class to decide who gave the most convincing argument for or against colonization. **L2, L3**

CHAPTER 22
SECTION 3

Using Graphs

Answer: 31 years, 1867–1898

Skills Practice

Using the graph, have students work in groups to create a large wall map of the United States and the areas covered in the graph.

Linking Across TIME

Despite the violence and bloodshed that accompanied the United States acquisition of the Philippines, both the United States and the Philippines gradually began to work toward Philippine independence. In 1916 Filipinos began electing both houses of their legislature and were promised eventual independence. In 1946 independence day finally arrived.

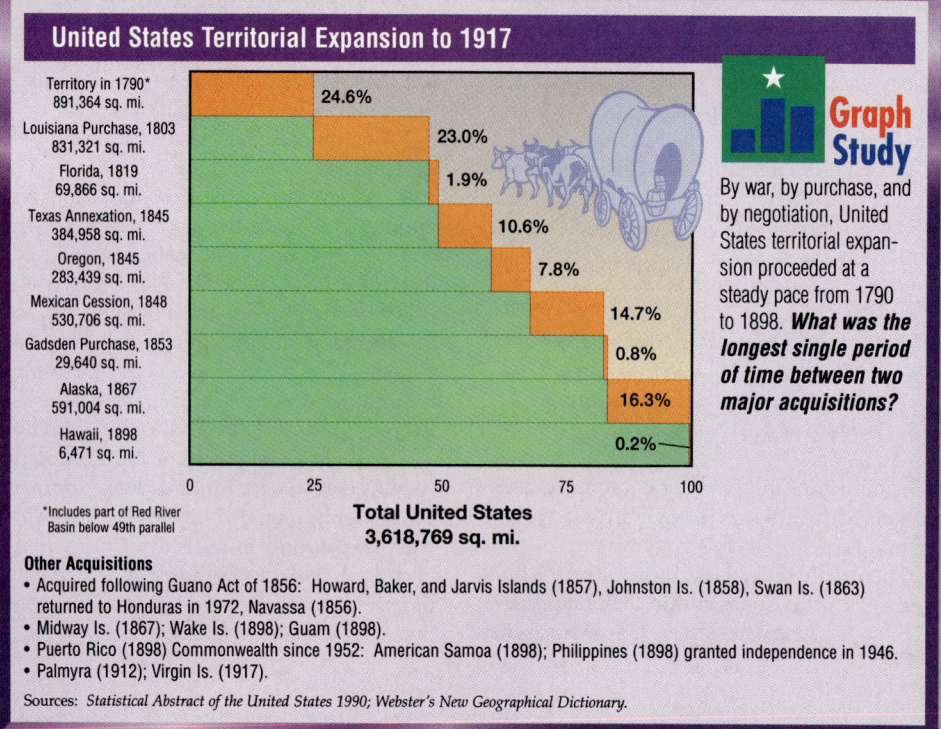

United States Territorial Expansion to 1917

Acquisition	Area	Percent
Territory in 1790*	891,364 sq. mi.	24.6%
Louisiana Purchase, 1803	831,321 sq. mi.	23.0%
Florida, 1819	69,866 sq. mi.	1.9%
Texas Annexation, 1845	384,958 sq. mi.	10.6%
Oregon, 1845	283,439 sq. mi.	7.8%
Mexican Cession, 1848	530,706 sq. mi.	14.7%
Gadsden Purchase, 1853	29,640 sq. mi.	0.8%
Alaska, 1867	591,004 sq. mi.	16.3%
Hawaii, 1898	6,471 sq. mi.	0.2%

Total United States 3,618,769 sq. mi.

*Includes part of Red River Basin below 49th parallel

Other Acquisitions
- Acquired following Guano Act of 1856: Howard, Baker, and Jarvis Islands (1857), Johnston Is. (1858), Swan Is. (1863) returned to Honduras in 1972, Navassa (1856).
- Midway Is. (1867); Wake Is. (1898); Guam (1898).
- Puerto Rico (1898) Commonwealth since 1952: American Samoa (1898); Philippines (1898) granted independence in 1946.
- Palmyra (1912); Virgin Is. (1917).

Sources: *Statistical Abstract of the United States 1990; Webster's New Geographical Dictionary.*

Graph Study

By war, by purchase, and by negotiation, United States territorial expansion proceeded at a steady pace from 1790 to 1898. **What was the longest single period of time between two major acquisitions?**

■ Problems of an Overseas Empire

The new possessions posed constitutional problems summarized in the question, "Does the Constitution follow the flag?" Congress, according to the Constitution, may not set tariff duties on goods carried from one part of the United States to another. Did this mean that no duties would be laid on goods from American colonies? The Constitution guarantees to all American citizens certain civil rights. Did constitutional guarantees of civil rights extend to the people of the new colonies who knew nothing of American justice?

The Supreme Court decided that the Constitution did not cover overseas possessions. Puerto Rico, the Court ruled, was a dependency; therefore Congress could set tariffs on its products. Other decisions determined that inhabitants of dependencies enjoyed full civil rights only if granted them by congressional legislation.

Cuba

According to the Teller Amendment, the United States pledged to withdraw from Cuba when order was restored. After three years of civil war, however, the island was in terrible condition. The United States Army remained in Cuba to set up a republican government, oversee Cuban finances, and establish public health and sanitation programs.

In 1901, to protect its interests in Cuba, the United States Congress added the Platt Amendment to an army bill. This amendment, which governed the relations between Cuba and the United States for 33 years, provided that: (1) Cuba should not make any treaty with another nation that weakened its independence; (2) Cuba should allow the United States the right to buy or lease naval stations; (3) Cuba's public debt should not exceed its capacity to pay; and (4) the United States should have the right to intervene to protect Cuban independence and keep order. These conditions,

UNIT 7 Entering a New Century: 1867–1920

Sidelights: Government for Puerto Rico

The Foraker Act, which settled the status of Puerto Rico, gave that island a governor appointed by the United States, an upper house also appointed by the United States, and a lower house elected by the people. Those who opposed the colonization of Puerto Rico pointed out that this arrangement was very similar to that of British rule over the American colonies.

written into Cuba's constitution and into a treaty with the United States, made Cuba an American **protectorate**—a nation or region controlled by a stronger state. The attitude that Cuba was part of "the white man's burden" was reflected in an editorial by William Allen White in Kansas's *Emporia Gazette:*

> *Only Anglo-Saxons can govern themselves. The Cubans will need despotic government for many years to restrain anarchy until Cuba is filled with Yankees.*

For almost four years, Cuba was under military rule directed by General Leonard Wood. The greatest achievement of Wood's administration was the suppression of yellow fever. An American medical team under Dr. Walter Reed proved the theory of a Cuban physician, Carlos J. Finlay: that yellow fever is transmitted by the stegomyia mosquito. American doctors and volunteers allowed themselves to be bitten by mosquitoes, and some of them died as martyrs to medical progress. Major William C. Gorgas, an Army doctor, carried on a campaign to eliminate mosquitoes from Havana. By 1901, for the first time in centuries, there was no yellow fever in the Cuban capital.

Puerto Rico

The United States had made no prior commitment to withdraw from Puerto Rico as it had done in Cuba. That island's cultural ties

 ▲ **AN OVERSEAS EMPIRE** As in most wars, the civilians suffered many hardships. Thousands of Filipinos perished from sickness, starvation, and other indirect effects of war. The Philippines gained independence in 1946. **When was Puerto Rico granted territorial status?**

with Spain and Latin America through the Roman Catholic Church, the Spanish language, and other traditions had existed for nearly 300 years. Yet, the United States chose to keep the island as its territory.

After a brief period of military rule, Congress gradually allowed Puerto Rico a degree of self-government. The Puerto Rican people demanded either independence or complete self-rule under the American flag. In 1917 they were granted territorial status and made citizens of the United States.

Section 3 ★ Review

Checking for Understanding

1. **Identify** William Gorgas, Walter Reed, "white man's burden," Platt Amendment.
2. **Define** protectorate.
3. **Explain** ways in which the President and Congress resolved the annexation difficulties in the Philippines.
4. **Describe** how problems with Cuba and Puerto Rico were resolved.

Critical Thinking

5. **Making Decisions** Analyze the reasoning of the Supreme Court on constitutional guarantees for overseas possessions. Do you agree with their conclusions? Explain.

CHAPTER 22 Imperialism 1867–1908

LESSON PLAN
Mastering Social Studies Skills

Teaching Interpreting Primary Sources

Review the basic ideas behind imperialism and anti-imperialism. Point out that as on many political issues, Americans were divided on this one. Ask students to present arguments for and against imperialism. Write their responses on the chalkboard.

After students have read Bryan's speech, discuss how he presented his point of view. Have students who opposed the imperialism argument list ways they could change the minds of those who supported imperialism.

Did You Know?

William Jennings Bryan was nominated three times for President: in 1896, 1900, and 1908. In part his anti-imperialist stand helped defeat him. He did go on, however, to become secretary of state under President Woodrow Wilson. In that post he continued to oppose U.S. expansionist policies.

Social Studies Skills

Interpreting Primary Sources

Anti-Imperialist Politics

As the Democratic presidential candidate in 1900, William Jennings Bryan became a leader of the anti-imperialist cause. The following passage illustrates the cause's major arguments.

From William Jennings Bryan's speech to the Democratic National Convention, 1900—

The principal arguments . . . advanced by those who enter upon a defense of imperialism are:

First—That we must improve the present opportunity to become a world power and enter into international politics.

Second—That our commercial interests in the Philippine Islands and in the Orient make it necessary for us to hold the islands permanently.

Third—That the spread of the Christian religion will be facilitated by a colonial policy.

Fourth—That there is no honorable retreat from the position which the nation has taken. . . .

It is sufficient answer to the first argument to say that for more than a century this nation has been a world power. . . .

It is not necessary to own people in order to trade with them We do not own Japan or China, but we trade with their people. . . .

The religious argument varies . . . from a passive belief that Providence delivered the Filipinos into our hands, for their good and our glory, to the exultation of the minister who said that we ought to "thrash the natives (Filipinos) until they understand who we are," and that "every bullet sent, every cannon shot and every flag waved means righteousness."

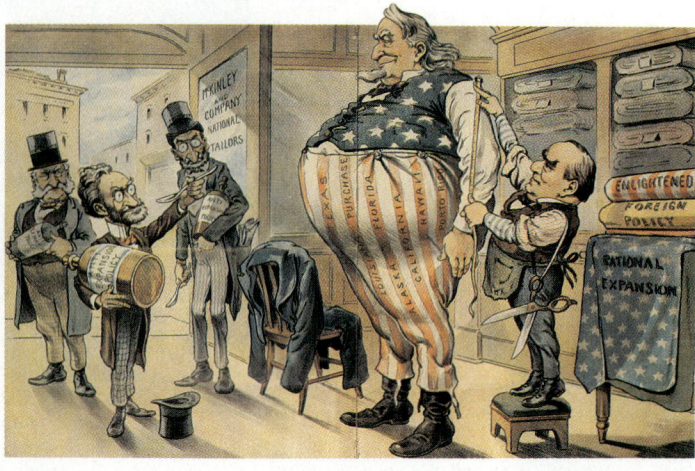

▲ McKINLEY TAILORS AN EXPANDING UNCLE SAM

. . . If true Christianity consists in carrying out in our daily lives the teachings of Christ, who will say that we are commanded to civilize with dynamite and proselyte with the sword?

Examining the Primary Source

1. Identify the sentences that introduce Bryan's answers to the four arguments he cites.
2. What evidence does Bryan give to refute the argument that commercial interests necessitate control of the Philippines?

Critical Thinking

3. **Making Comparisons** Analyze Bryan's description of the imperialists' attitude toward the Filipinos. Then compare that attitude with the attitude of those who embraced the idea of Manifest Destiny toward Native Americans.

614

Answers to SOCIAL STUDIES SKILLS

1. Argument 1: "It is sufficient answer . . . ."; argument 2: "It is not necessary to own . . . ."; argument 3: "The religious argument varies . . . ."; argument 4: ". . . who will say that we are commanded . . . ?"

2. The United States has successfully pursued commercial interests without exerting political control elsewhere, for example, in Japan and China.

3. Sample: Those who supported imperialism had much in common with those who supported Manifest Destiny: both regarded people of European ancestry as culturally superior.

SECTION 4

A New Arena

Setting the Scene

Section Focus

Americans expected President Roosevelt to adopt an aggressive foreign policy. Roosevelt was resolved that the United States should be a great power. In the Western Hemisphere, he enlarged the scope of the Monroe Doctrine and secured United States domination of the Caribbean. In the Pacific and East Asia, he attempted to keep a balance of power and restrain first Russian, then Japanese, ambitions.

Objectives

After studying this section, you should be able to

★ give examples of Roosevelt's "Big Stick" diplomacy.

★ discuss the goals and results of the "Open Door" policy in China.

★ discuss America's concerns over the Russo-Japanese War.

Key Terms

anarchist, corollary, partitioned, sphere of influence, indemnity

◀ THEODORE ROOSEVELT, BRONZE RELIEF

In the Western Hemisphere, the acquisition of Puerto Rico and the establishment of a protectorate over Cuba gave the United States a new interest in this region. American expansion into the Pacific brought closer contact with East Asian nations, particularly China. Several European countries, along with Japan, were fiercely competing for trading rights in China. The United States entered a new and complex arena of international politics.

■ The Election of 1900

In 1900 William Jennings Bryan, again the Democratic candidate, attempted to make imperialism the paramount issue of the presidential campaign. The Republicans again nominated McKinley for President. Theodore Roosevelt, who had become governor of New York, received the nomination for Vice President. As much as possible, the Republicans avoided discussion of imperialism because they were divided. The result was an even greater Republican victory than that in 1896.

Six months after his second inauguration, McKinley spoke of the United States's new position in the world. Previously a strong supporter of isolationism, he announced a change of heart, saying:

❝ *Isolation is no longer possible or desirable. God and man have linked the nations together. No nation can longer be indifferent to any other....* ❞

CHAPTER 22 Imperialism 1867–1908   615

CHAPTER 22
SECTION 4

TEACH
Guided Practice

Geography On a world map, have students trace the water route from San Francisco to New York around Cape Horn and use the map's scale to calculate the approximate distance. (13,000 miles) Next, have students trace the route by ship from San Francisco to New York City via the Panama Canal and calculate that distance. (5,200 miles) Ask students to write a paragraph explaining how the Panama Canal improved United States trade and business. **L1, LEP**

Did You Know?

Theodore Roosevelt was the youngest President in the White House, succeeding McKinley at the age of 42. He was not, however, the youngest *elected* President. John F. Kennedy was 46 years old when he was inaugurated.

Food of the Times

In the early 1800s, the United States was not noted for its cuisine or its fine restaurants. In the latter part of the century, however, a Swiss family named Delmonico brought French cooking to the nation. The family opened a chain of restaurants in New York City. Their success inspired restaurant owners in other cities.

He explained that America's diversity of products and its efficiency in producing them had so increased that there was an urgent need for more markets. He proposed reciprocity treaties with foreign nations, providing for mutual lowering of tariffs.

McKinley did not live to put his new policy into effect. The day after delivering his speech he was shot by an **anarchist,** one who opposes all forms of government. Just short of 43 years old, Roosevelt became the youngest President.

■ The Big Stick

Theodore Roosevelt had a genius for the dramatic gesture. He told young men, "Don't flinch, don't foul, hit the line hard." Roosevelt's actions were sometimes impulsive, sometimes unwise, but he firmly believed that power imposed responsibility. One of Roosevelt's mottoes in foreign policy was a West African saying, "Speak softly and carry a big stick."

The Panama Canal

The "Big Stick" was most in evidence in the Caribbean. Roosevelt and others believed that in addition to saving time for commercial shipping, a canal would answer the strategic need to shuttle warships between the Atlantic and the Pacific oceans.

This was clearly demonstrated during the Spanish-American War. The battleship *Oregon*, ordered from Puget Sound to Cuba, was forced to steam 14,000 miles around Cape Horn—3 times as far as if there had been a canal.

In the 1800s a French company had made a vain and costly effort to cut through Panama. Early in the 1890s, an American company started to dig a canal through Nicaragua but soon abandoned the attempt. In 1901 Britain, which also had an interest in the canal, agreed that the United States could build, control, and fortify a canal, provided that ships of all nations were charged equal toll.

Immediately, Secretary of State John Hay offered Colombia, which controlled Panama, $10 million and a yearly rent of $250,000 for the right to construct a canal through Panama and control a narrow strip of land on either side. However, feeling that the price was too low and fearful of losing control of Panama, the Colombian senate unanimously refused to ratify the agreement.

Roosevelt was furious. He let it be known privately that he would not mind if Panama revolted. On November 3, 1903, a revolution broke out, and an independent Republic of Panama was proclaimed. On November 6 the United States recognized Panama's independence. Less than two weeks later the United States and Panama signed a treaty for the canal.

Roosevelt defended his Big Stick diplomacy in Panama on the ground that he advanced "the needs of collective civilization" by speeding up the building of an inter-ocean canal. His action was widely condemned in the United States as unjustifiable aggression. In Latin America it aroused dislike and distrust of the United States.

The engineering difficulties involved in cutting through the Isthmus of Panama were enormous and were compounded by the tremendous health problems encountered in the tropics. In 1885 an English writer wrote of Panama:

> *In all the world there is not perhaps now concentrated in any so much foul disease. . . . The Isthmus is a damp, tropical jungle, intensely hot, swarming with mosquitoes . . . the home, even as Nature made it, of yellow fever, typhus, and dysentery.*

George W. Goethals, a colonel in the Corps of Engineers, directed the engineering feat that completed the canal in 1914. Dr. William C. Gorgas, who had cleaned up Havana, reduced the health threats in Panama.

Venezuela

Roosevelt, like Cleveland, defended Venezuela from possible European aggression, strengthening the Monroe Doctrine. By 1902 Venezuela owed money to citizens of several European countries. Cipriano Castro,

UNIT 7 Entering a New Century: 1867–1920

Cooperative Learning

Creating Cartoons Tell students that Theodore Roosevelt's personality and style made him a favorite with cartoonists. Divide students into groups, and have each portray Roosevelt in a cartoon in which he is involved in an event or an issue. (Students might want to do some research on political cartoons.) Have groups exchange cartoons and explain their meanings. Display the cartoons on a bulletin board. **L2, L3**

the Venezuelan dictator-president, refused either to pay the debts or submit them to arbitration. Roosevelt said the Monroe Doctrine did not protect Latin American nations against punishment for misbehavior.

After consultation with the American State Department, Great Britain and Germany, Venezuela's two principal creditors, blockaded Venezuelan ports to force payment. The blockade was very unpopular in the United States because it was perceived as a violation of the Monroe Doctrine. Feeling was intensified when Venezuelan gunboats were sunk and Venezuelan ports bombarded. Public anger moved Roosevelt to press for an end of the blockade and the submission of the dispute to arbitration. Although both parties agreed to arbitration, Great Britain was quicker to respond than Germany was. This added to Roosevelt's distrust of the rising German empire.

Roosevelt Corollary

In 1903 Argentine foreign minister Luis Drago urged that forcibly collecting debts from bankrupt countries be made a violation of international law. If the United States opposed Drago and allowed foreign nations to block the coasts and bombard the cities of defaulting Latin American nations, the door was left open to further aggression. If, however, the United States outlawed forcible collection of debts, it might be pushed into defending financial dishonesty. The President's reply to the Drago Doctrine became known as the Roosevelt **Corollary,** or addition, to the Monroe Doctrine. Whenever an American republic was guilty of "chronic wrongdoing," said Roosevelt, the United States might have to intervene itself.

Dominican Republic

The Roosevelt Corollary was first applied in the Dominican Republic. In 1905 the United States assumed the responsibility of collecting Dominican customs. The United States Marine Corps collected the duties and divided them to support the Dominican government and to pay that nation's debts to European countries.

Roosevelt's successor, President William Howard Taft, continued Roosevelt's policies but with a shift of emphasis. Taft's secretary of state, Philander C. Knox, promoted American business interests abroad with the slogan, "Every diplomat a salesman." In Latin America this "dollar diplomacy" resulted in increased sales of United States goods—including warships—and in efforts to increase American investments there.

Although Taft described his brand of diplomacy as "substituting dollars for bullets," sometimes he used both. In 1912 he sent marines to Nicaragua to install a more friendly government and to force acceptance of a loan from New York bankers. Such policies increased the unpopularity of the United States in Latin America.

■ The Balance of Power in East Asia

Roosevelt realized that the position of the United States in East Asia was weak. He called the Philippines the "Achilles' heel" of

 ▲ **THE PANAMA CANAL** Work on the Panama Canal began in 1904 and lasted 10 years. *What difficulties were encountered?*

CHAPTER 22 Imperialism 1867–1908   **617**

Sidelights: Technology

The job of constructing the Panama Canal involved three major engineering projects. First the workers had to excavate the Gaillard Cut, which was 300 feet (91 meters) wide across the isthmus. Next they had to build a dam across the Charges River to create an artificial lake. Finally they had to construct the canal's locks.

The hardest job was digging the Gaillard Cut because the hills through which the cut runs consist of soft volcanic material. When workers dug a hole, more rock and earth would slide into the space or push up from below.

CHAPTER 22
SECTION 4

Soon after the Panama Canal was completed, many Panamanians began to insist that the United States did not have the right to control the Canal Zone. The United States disagreed, claiming that the treaty of 1903 gave it that right. Over the years the United States set up bases not only in the zone but throughout Panama. Progress toward settling the issue was finally made in 1977, when the United States and Panama signed a treaty. The treaty states that all nations have the right to use the canal but that United States warships have the right to sail through the canal first.

Visualizing History Hay's "Open Door" policy opened the way for a larger American role in Asia. **Answer to Caption:** Both nations wanted control of resource-rich Manchuria.

Did You Know?
John Hay studied law in an office next to Abraham Lincoln. He was Lincoln's assistant private secretary when Lincoln was President.

Visualizing History ▲ **SPHERES OF INFLUENCE** Cities in China grew into centers of trade. Major international powers divided China into spheres of influence. *What clash of interest led to the Russo-Japanese War?*

American defense; they were easily vulnerable to attack by Japan. China and Russia also posed problems.

China and the Open Door

At the close of the nineteenth century, it looked as though China, like Africa, would be **partitioned**, or divided among stronger powers. In 1898 and 1899, Russia, Germany, France, and Great Britain forced China to lease its ports, some of them for 99 years. Each "leasehold" was expected to become the center of a **sphere of influence**—an area where a European nation controlled economic development.

The United States and Great Britain, in order to ensure open avenues of trade with China, decided to oppose the parceling out of Chinese territory. Early in 1898 the British government proposed a joint declaration with the United States in favor of the "Open Door"—with the goal of preserving equal trading opportunities in China for all foreign nations. At that time the United States was cool to the idea, but its annexation of the Philippines changed the American attitude.

John Hay, secretary of state, thought that the days of American isolationism must end. Having defended the acquisition of an overseas empire, he agreed with Great Britain on the policy of an Open Door in China. In September 1899, Hay sent notes to countries with leaseholds in China asking that they keep the ports open to vessels of all nations on equal terms.

Boxer Rebellion

While foreign countries debated control of China, Chinese secret societies were organizing to oust foreign control. One of these was called "the Boxers" by Westerners because of the physical exercises they practiced.

When a falsified story was printed in America suggesting that Westerners were negotiating the dismantling of a Chinese monument, the Boxer Rebellion broke out. With secret aid from the Chinese government, the Boxers intended to wipe out

UNIT 7 Entering a New Century: 1867–1920

Critical Thinking

Comparing Remind students that from the time the Monroe Doctrine was adopted to the present time, the United States has always had an interest in the Caribbean and Latin America.

Have students research policies of recent Presidents and compare them with those of Theodore Roosevelt. **L3**

"foreign devils" and their Christian converts. They killed more than 200 foreigners, mostly missionaries and their families. For 7 weeks the Boxers laid siege to foreign embassies in Beijing.

During this crisis Hay worked to prevent full-scale retaliation and war against China and to persuade the leaseholding powers not to use the Boxer Rebellion as an excuse to partition the country. In July 1900, he sent a second set of Open Door notes. This time he declared that the policy of the United States was to seek ways to "preserve Chinese territorial and administrative entity."

The United States lacked sufficient military power to enforce Hay's Open Door notes of 1899 and 1900. Equal trading opportunities in China and the preservation of China's territorial integrity lay in maintaining a "balance of power" among the nations with ambitions in East Asia.

Russo-Japanese War

China's two closest neighbors, Japan and Russia, were especially threatening. In 1893 Japan established a protectorate over the independent kingdom of Korea and obtained Formosa and other islands off China's northeast coast. Japan had designs on the resource-rich Chinese province of Manchuria, in which Russia was already established. The Russians hoped to move into Korea. This clash of interests led to the Russo-Japanese War in 1904.

Japan won victories over Russia on both land and sea. By the summer of 1905, both countries were ready to make peace. The Japanese secretly asked Roosevelt if he would serve as go-between. After consulting the czar, Roosevelt formally offered to help make peace. Both nations accepted the President's proposals and sent diplomats to a peace conference in Portsmouth, New Hampshire, in August 1905.

Treaty of Portsmouth

The President induced Japan to give up claims for a money **indemnity,** or payment for damages, and Russia to give up the southern half of the island of Sakhalin (SA•kuh•LEEN). Japan also took over Russian interests in southern Manchuria.

The war altered the balance of power in East Asia. Now it was no longer Russian expansion that was most to be feared, but Japanese. Roosevelt himself believed that there was potential danger of war.

Roosevelt arranged a compromise in 1907 and 1908, known as the Gentlemen's Agreement. In a complicated series of maneuvers, he soothed Japanese anger and showed the Japanese that he was not afraid of them. To check Japanese expansion toward the Philippines, Roosevelt recognized Japan as dominant in Korea and Manchuria.

The resolution of the Russo-Japanese War was an example of Roosevelt's efforts to use arbitration rather than war to settle controversies. Although he upgraded America's military power, he believed that the United States had an obligation as a leader of an interdependent world to act responsibly.

Section 4 ★ Review

Checking for Understanding

1. **Identify** Big Stick diplomacy, John Hay, Drago Doctrine, Roosevelt Corollary, Open Door, Boxer Rebellion, Russo-Japanese War, Gentlemen's Agreement.
2. **Define** anarchist, corollary, indemnity.
3. **State** instances where Theodore Roosevelt used Big Stick diplomacy.
4. **Indicate** how President Theodore Roosevelt acted as peacemaker in the Russo-Japanese War.

Critical Thinking

5. **Understanding Cause and Effect** Explain how Roosevelt's Big Stick diplomacy led to ill feeling against the United States throughout Latin America.

CHAPTER 22 Imperialism 1867–1908

Answers to SECTION 4 REVIEW

1. Big Stick diplomacy, 616; John Hay, 618; Drago Doctrine, 617; Roosevelt Corollary, 617; Open Door, 618; Boxer Rebellion, 618–619; Russo-Japanese War, 619; Gentlemen's Agreement, 619
2. All vocabulary words are defined in the Glossary.
3. in Colombia, Nicaragua, Venezuela
4. Organized the peace conference in Portsmouth, NH. Japan ceded money claims; Russia ceded Sakhalin and allowed Japan to take over its Manchurian interests in Japan.
5. Such diplomacy created resentment and anger by the U.S. attempting to dominate the economic and political policies of Latin America.

CHAPTER 22
SECTION 4

ASSESS
Check Understanding
Assign Section 4 Review as homework or an in-class activity.

Evaluate
Assign the Section 4 Quiz in the TCR, or use the History of a Free Nation Testmaker to create a customized quiz.

Reteach
Have students write several examples of Roosevelt's Big Stick diplomacy. Then discuss how this diplomacy style affected the United States both economically and politically. (Economically: made U.S. wealthy because acquired additional markets and sources of raw material. Politically: showed U.S. had power to back up its claims)
Have students complete Reteaching Activity 22-5.

Enrich
Theodore Roosevelt said that he considered the presidency a "bully pulpit." Ask students what they think this expression means and if and how Roosevelt's actions reflected this phrase.

CLOSE
Have students read the last paragraph in this section. Ask: Do you agree with its assessment of Roosevelt? Why or why not?

REVIEW CHAPTER 22

Answers

Reviewing Facts

1. Industrialization increased the number of products for sale and the need for new markets. Other countries were practicing imperialist policies—expanding their empires and gaining trade advantages over the United States. Opportunity existed to acquire territory to increase sources of raw materials. Kept other countries from encroaching on the Western Hemisphere.
2. British had a powerful navy. The threat of war over the Venezuelan situation of 1895 revealed a weakness of the United States Navy. With only three battleships to go up against, Congress approved money for 13 new ships.
3. McKinley wanted to preserve neutrality. The press wanted to go to war to show the strength of the country. McKinley believed that Spain would not grant Cuban independence, and he wanted to intervene to protect Cuban people.
4. the atrocities against Cuban independence leaders, the many accusations of yellow press, and protection of American business investments and expansion of overseas markets
5. Hawaii was dominated by American interests; many of its people spoke English; had ties with United States. Americans wanted Hawaiian products; Hawaii wanted American manufactures. Puerto Rico, on the other hand, had closer ties to Spain. Philippines were too diverse, too far away, and the least developed country.
6. The United States believed its trading interests would be advanced if each nation had equal rights to trade in China.
7. The United States believed that in addition to saving time for commercial shipping, the Panama Canal would answer the strategic need to shuttle warships between the Atlantic and the Pacific oceans. Moreover, the United States could establish control over the Canal Zone.

Understanding Concepts

1. Economically the use of Big Stick diplomacy made the United States wealthy through acquisition of additional markets and sources of raw materials. Politically it gave the United States status

---

CHAPTER 22 ★ REVIEW

Using Vocabulary

Assume that you are a reporter for an antiadministration newspaper covering the Latin American situation in 1903. Write a feature article describing Theodore Roosevelt's policies using the following vocabulary terms.

imperialism
isolationism
reciprocity
protectorate
sphere of influence
corollary

Reviewing Facts

1. **State** three reasons why the United States abandoned isolationist policies after the Civil War.
2. **Explain** how confrontation with Great Britain in 1895–1896 led to strengthening the American navy.
3. **Describe** the position of the President and press regarding war with Spain over Cuba. Why did McKinley change his mind?
4. **List** three reasons America went to war over Cuba. Which was most important?
5. **Discuss** why Hawaii had fewer difficulties accepting its position as a United States possession than did Puerto Rico or the Philippines.
6. **Show** why Americans favored an Open Door policy in China.
7. **Indicate** why the United States needed to build the Panama Canal.

Understanding Concepts

Economic and Political Power

1. How did the use of the Big Stick in Latin America increase American wealth and political power?
2. How did a show of force with Great Britain and Germany enhance the American position in Latin America?
3. Why was the United States unable to avoid military confrontation in Cuba?

Critical Thinking

1. **Recognizing Stereotypes** How did adherence to social Darwinism cause the United States to stereotype people who lived in countries under their possession? In what ways did stereotyped thinking influence political and economic policies toward these territories?
2. **Analyzing Fine Art** The painting on this page by Frederic Remington depicts the bravado of the Rough Riders. Analyze the painting and answer the questions that follow.
   a. What is happening in the painting?
   b. What details do you see in this scene?
   c. Do you think Remington has captured the reality of battle? Why or why not?

▲ CHARGE OF SAN JUAN HILL BY FREDERIC REMINGTON

Writing About History

Argumentation

Write a headline and article for a Hearst newspaper urging war with Spain over Cuba. Remember, the article is designed to stir up public opinion in favor of conflict. Take into account national honor; persecuted people wanting freedom; business interests in Cuba; the superior economy and government of the United States; and the strategic position of Cuba.

UNIT 7 Entering a New Century: 1867–1920

CHAPTER 22 ★ REVIEW

Cooperative Learning

Organize into three groups representing diplomats charged with negotiating the conclusion to the Russo-Japanese War. Consider:
- What points are on the table for negotiation?
- What does each team hope to gain?
- What is each willing to concede in order to reach its objectives?
- What is the conclusion of the negotiations?
- What is the special role of the United States in the proceedings?

Social Studies Skills

Reading a Special-Purpose Map

There are many kinds of maps, such as physical, political, and land-use maps. However, some maps do not fit any of these categories. They are called special-purpose maps. They are drawn to show a specific feature, area, or situation. For example, this map shows the Panama Canal.

Because special-purpose maps are unique, each must be analyzed on its own. Each map will have a unique legend, scale, grid, and style. Depending on what a map shows, it may have elements you have not encountered before.

Practicing the Skill

Use the map and what you have read in the chapter to answer the following questions.
1. In what country is the Panama Canal located?
2. What is the land on both sides of the canal called?
3. What are the approximate geographical coordinates of the canal?
4. How many sets of locks are part of the canal?
5. About 22 miles of the canal is situated on what lake?
6. To go from the Atlantic Ocean to the Pacific Ocean, what general direction would a ship travel?
7. About how long is the Panama Canal according to the map?

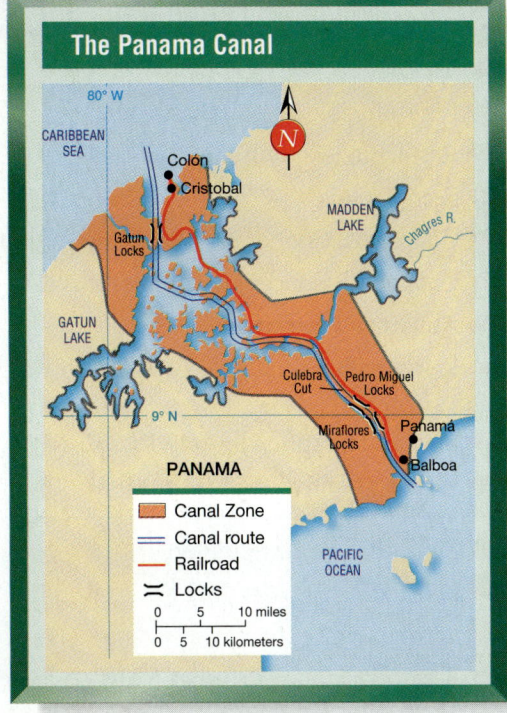

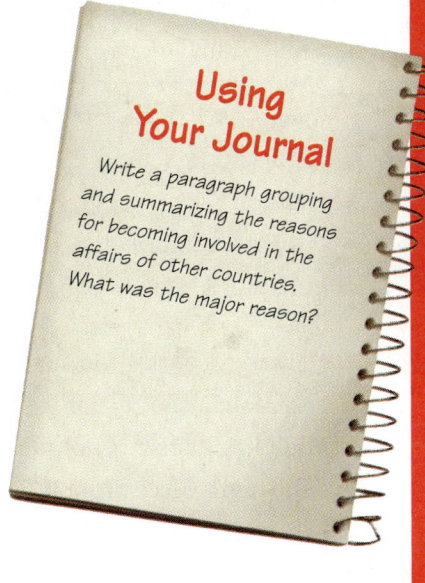

Using Your Journal

Write a paragraph grouping and summarizing the reasons for becoming involved in the affairs of other countries. What was the major reason?

CHAPTER 22 Imperialism 1867–1908   **621**

REVIEW ★ CHAPTER 22

Critical Thinking

1. The idea of superior people ruling led to a belief that people in these countries were backward, less advanced, and less competent than Americans. McKinley believed in civilizing, educating, and training them to be self-governing.
2. a. Rough Riders seize the hill under heavy fire.
  b. Answers will vary, but students might note such details as troops are in open area; few trees or places for cover; soldiers are in relatively close proximity; most soldiers are on foot; there are casualties; soldiers are determined to take objective.
  c. Answers will vary, but students should provide reasons to support their answer.

Practicing the Skill

1. Panama **2.** the Canal Zone **3.** 9°N latitude, 80°W longitude **4.** 3 **5.** Gatun Lake **6.** southeast **7.** approximately 50 miles, or 80 km

? Chapter Bonus Test Question

This question may be used for extra credit on the chapter test.
Describe the relationship between U.S. expansionism and the economic expansion of the nation. (Expanding industry and business needed more trade and more markets.)

Using Your Journal
Student paragraphs should refer to specific reasons. Answers may vary but will probably say for economic or strategic reasons.

among nations, showing that the United States had clout to back up its claims. Also it made the United States a dominant force in Latin America.
2. The United States used its superior wealth and political organization as justification for establishing protectorates over less powerful and advanced nations. The United States believed it was destined to rule by virtue of superior intelligence and achievement.
3. The presence of the United States in Latin American affairs showed its willingness to fight to maintain its superior position there. Others preferred negotiation when confronted with ultimatum.

621

PLANNING GUIDE   Chapter 23 The Progressive Era

Daily Lesson Objectives	Teacher Classroom Resources	Multimedia
SECTION 1 **Sources of Progressivism** **1 Day** pp. 624–629 1. Discuss the role of the muckrakers in promoting social change. 2. Explain how methods used in business and education influenced social reform.	Chapter 23 Study Guide Reproducible Lesson Plan Reteaching Activity 23-1 Section Quiz Chapter 23 Cooperative Learning Activity Chapter 23 Concept Mapping Activity American Portrait 48 Reinforcing Social Studies Skills, 28, 32, 53, 67, 69–72 Map and Graph Skill Activity 28 Writer's Guidebook Lessons 9–14	Student Self-Test Software Testmaker Section Focus Transparency 72 Chapter 23 Skills Transparency Chapter 23 Map Transparencies
SECTION 2 **Progressive Reforms** **1 Day** pp. 632–638 1. Explain how reforms strengthened democracy. 2. Describe the advances made in protecting adult and child workers.	Reproducible Lesson Plan Reteaching Activity 23-2 Section Quiz Reinforcing Social Studies Skills 49, 53, 61, 67, 69–72 Chapter 23 Primary and Secondary Source Readings The Living Constitution American Literary Heritage Unit 6	Student Self-Test Software Testmaker Section Focus Transparency 73
SECTION 3 **Limits of Progressivism** **1 Day** pp. 640–644 1. Describe progressive attitudes about immigrants and racial minorities. 2. Explain why African American leadership changed.	Reproducible Lesson Plan Reteaching Activity 23-3 Section Quiz Chapter 23 Enrichment Activity Chapter 23 Primary and Secondary Source Readings American Portrait 46 Reinforcing Social Studies Skills 32, 37, 55, 63 Building Skills in Geography The Living Constitution Writer's Guidebook Lessons 9–14 Spanish Summaries & Glossary	Student Self-Test Software Testmaker Section Focus Transparency 74 Vocabulary Puzzlemaker Audiocassette, Chapter 23 The American People: Fabric of a Nation
CHAPTER REVIEW AND EVALUATION **1 Day**	Chapter 23 Test Chapter 23 Performance Assessment Activity	Student Self-Test Software Testmaker

OUT OF TIME? If time does not permit teaching the entire chapter, use the Chapter 23 Summary on pages 676-677 and the Chapter 23 audiocassette (English and Spanish) to point out the main ideas of the chapter.

PLANNING GUIDE

Cultural Diversity Activity

Analyzing Ideas Write the following assessment of the progressives from student text page 645 on the chalkboard: "Although they excluded large groups from their efforts, the progressives expanded democracy, reformed education, and improved the quality of life for millions of men, women, and children."

Have students research the views of African American progressives like W.E.B. Du Bois and Ida Baker Wells Barnett. Ask: Would they have agreed with this assessment of progressivism? Why or why not? Do you agree? Give reasons in support of your point of view.

Performance Assessment Activity

A Picture Essay The Progressive Era was a time of tremendous innovation in painting, as exemplified by the Ashcan School. Divide the class into small groups and assign each one of these artists: Robert Henri, John Sloan, George Luks, William Glackens, Everett Shinn, Ernest Lawson, Arthur Davies, and Maurice Prendergast—the "Eight" of the Ashcan School. Ask each group to create a picture essay of its artist's works with descriptions of his paintings and an analysis of what the artist reveals about American life through his work. Students might also explain how the Ashcan School influenced other American artists.

POSSIBLE RUBRIC FEATURES: Research skills, content information, organization, written and visual communication skills, creativity, collaborative skills

Chapter Resources

Literature from the Period
Sinclair, Upton. *The Jungle.* 1906.

Tarbell, Ida. *History of the Standard Oil Company.* 1904.

Readings for the Student
Marshall, Megan. "Three Sisters Who Showed the Way." *American Heritage,* Vol. 38, No. 6, September/October 1987.

Mitelman, Bonnie. "Rose Schneiderman and the Triangle Fire." *American History Illustrated.* Vol. 16, No. 4, July 1981.

Readings for the Teacher
Abell, Aaron I. ed. *American Catholic Thought on Social Questions.* Bobbs-Merrill, 1968.

Filler, Louis. *The Muckrackers.* Rev. ed. Pennsylvania State University, 1980.

Hopkins, C. Howard. *The Rise of the Social Gospel in American Protestantism, 1865–1895.* Yale University Press, 1967.

Multimedia Resources
The Cross of Gold—William Jennings Bryan and the Politics of Progressivism. Multi-Media Productions (sound filmstrip)

Progressives, Populists, and Reform in America. Guidance Associates (VHS, 32 minutes)

Key to Ability Levels

Teaching strategies have been coded for varying learning styles and abilities.

- **L1** Basic activities for all students
- **L2** Average activities for average to above-average students
- **L3** Challenging activities for above-average students
- **LEP** Limited English Proficiency activities

Glencoe Links to the Humanities

Link to Art
- U.S. History and Art Transparency 19

Link to Literature
- Macmillan Literature: American Literature Text— Gertrude Stein, Carl Sandburg, Edna St. Vincent Millay

Link to Music
- American Music: Cultural Traditions

CHAPTER 23

BEGINNING THE CHAPTER

Read to students the following lines written by poet Sarah Cleghorn in the early twentieth century:

> The golf links lie so near the mill
> That almost every day
> The laboring children can look out
> And see the men at play.

Ask students what this tells them about economic and social conditions in the United States at the time. (The stanza depicts the marked contrast between the leisure-class rich and the children of the poor, who, despite some progress, still worked in factories.)

Tell students Chapter 23 describes conditions in industrial cities and explains how a movement arose to fight these conditions and reform society.

Recording Journal Notes
Suggest that students organize their notes under the names of leaders active in the woman's suffrage movement.

CHAPTER 23

The Progressive Era
1893–1920

Setting the Scene

Focus
In the late 1800s, the Grangers and Populists had sought to resist corrupt government and unfair business practices. By 1900 their stalled efforts were given fresh life by a new group of reformers—the progressives. These optimistic, largely urban, middle-class reformers were confident in their ability to improve government and the quality of life. Their reforms were based not only on traditional democratic values but also on the new philosophy of pragmatism and study of the social sciences.

▲ WOOD AND LEATHER ROCKING HORSE

Journal Notes
Note in your journal, as you read the chapter, how women continued to push for the right to vote.

Concepts to Understand
★ How values and beliefs shaped the program of the Progressive Era
★ Why reform efforts were successful in correcting the worst abuses of big business and government

Read to Discover . . .
★ the types of reform that progressive leaders advocated.
★ the limitations of progressivism.

CULTURAL
- 1890 Census shows population of the United States at 63 million
- 1897 The first subway system is completed in Boston

1890 — **1900**

POLITICAL
- 1890 Sherman Silver Purchase Act passes
- 1902 Oregon adopts the initiative and referendum

UNIT 7 Entering a New Century: 1867–1920

✚ EXTRA CREDIT PROJECT

Reform movements have emerged throughout American history in response to economic, political, and social problems. Interested students might research and report on current reform efforts. Ask them to identify the issue or problem and analyze the movement—its leaders, objectives, and outcomes. Students might conclude their reports by deciding if reform is needed and why. Have them share their work with the class.

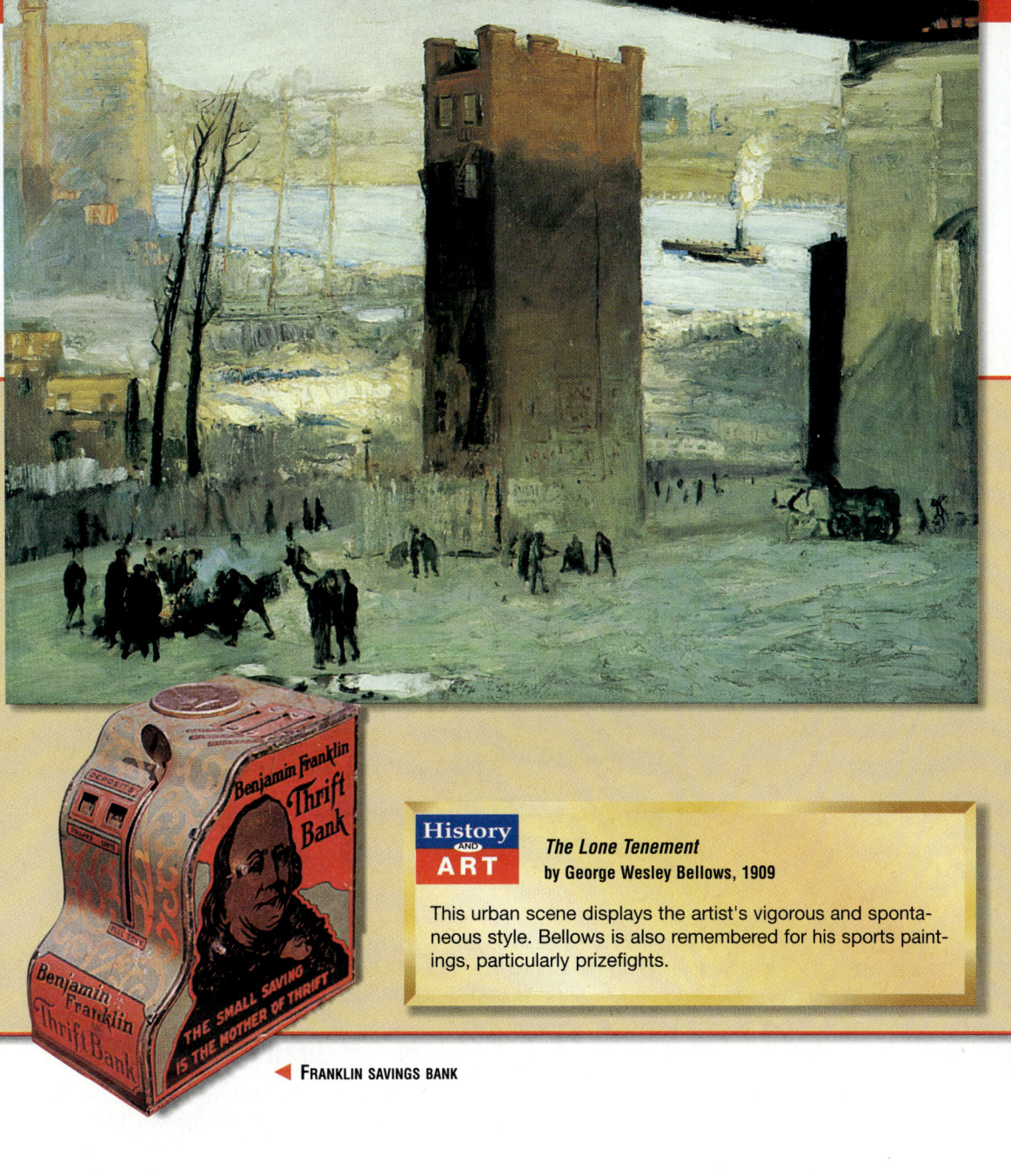

The Lone Tenement
by George Wesley Bellows, 1909

This urban scene displays the artist's vigorous and spontaneous style. Bellows is also remembered for his sports paintings, particularly prizefights.

◀ FRANKLIN SAVINGS BANK

- **1909** National Association for the Advancement of Colored People (NAACP) is formed
- **1917** United States declares war on Germany
- **1920** Sinclair Lewis's Main Street is bestseller
- **1920** Ratification of woman suffrage

| 1910 | 1920 |

CHAPTER 23 The Progressive Era 1893–1920   **623**

CHAPTER 23 CONCEPTS

Reproduce the following generalization and concepts map on the chalkboard, and have students copy it in their notebooks. Ask them to hypothesize about what topics may be covered in Chapter 23 based on this information.

A new group of reformers emerges to battle the injustices that had come about as a result of industrialization and urbanization

- Values and Beliefs
- Reform

History AND ART

The Lone Tenement, by George Bellows, depicts life in the city in 1911. Bellows was influenced by the so-called Ashcan school, an art movement in the early 1900s that advocated realistic portrayals of urban life.

Teacher Notes

LESSON PLAN
SECTION 1, 624–631

FOCUS

Bellringer

Before taking roll at the beginning of the class period, display Focus Activity Transparency 76 on the overhead projector, and assign the accompanying Focus Activity Sheet.

Objectives

Point out the objectives on this page to students in previewing the section content.

Motivating Activity

Read this statement by Jacob Riis, an American journalist: "The poor we shall have always with us, but the slum we need not have." Point out that Jacob Riis was one of the strongest advocates of social reform. He spent part of his career as a police reporter in New York City and often followed detectives into tenement districts, observing firsthand the horrors of slum conditions. Riis photographed and wrote about what he saw.

Discuss with students whether they think it is possible to do away with all slums, and if so, what proposals they would offer to abolish slums.

Use Skills Transparency 23.

SECTION 1

Sources of Progressivism

Setting the Scene

Section Focus

The 1900s saw many challenges and opportunities for change. As city populations exploded with immigrants and rural Americans attracted by jobs, squalid slums and worker discontent also grew. In the face of threats of radical change, a variety of moderate reformers worked to protect, preserve, and improve American society.

Objectives

After studying this section, you should be able to

★ discuss the role of the muckrakers in identifying social ills and promoting social change.

★ explain how methods and strategies used in business and education influenced social reform.

Key Terms

social gospel, pragmatism

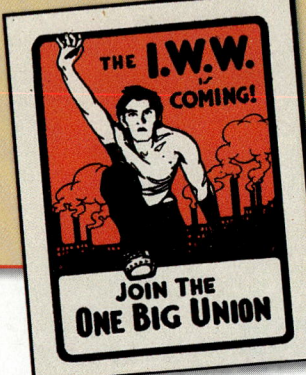
◀ LABOR UNION POSTER

Despite widespread social, political, and economic change in the late 1800s, the Gilded Age produced no broad effort to improve society. Populism was a large movement, but it was farm based and did not attract urban workers to its goals. The labor movement was also large, but it involved itself primarily with issues related to workers' jobs, wages, and working conditions.

Alternating periods of prosperity and depression accompanied industrialization in the late nineteenth century. Economic contractions shook the United States in the mid-1870s and well into the mid-1880s. The depression that followed the Panic of 1893, however, was the worst the nation had yet seen. As the split between rich and poor became too wide to ignore, Americans of all classes began to ask hard questions about the nation's political and economic systems, and they saw much that alarmed them.

■ Inequality in America

Not until the 1890s did Americans begin to show widespread concern about the direction in which their society was moving. Increasing poverty was one area of concern.

The Gap Between the Rich and Poor

Millions of American laborers worked long hours for low wages in the late 1800s. Wages of industrial workers averaged $10 to $12 for a 60- to 80-hour week. One of every 5 women worked, frequently for as little as

624   UNIT 7 Entering a New Century: 1867–1920

Classroom Resources for SECTION 1

Teacher's Classroom Resources
- Chapter 23 Study Guide
- Reproducible Lesson Plan
- Reteaching Activity 23-1
- Chapter 23 Cooperative Learning Activity
- Section Quiz

Multimedia
- Section Focus Transparency 76
- Chapter 23 Skill Transparency
- Testmaker
- Student Self-Test Software

$6 to $8 a week, and children received even less. If workers were injured in industrial accidents, were laid off when business slowed, or became unemployed for any reason at all, their income completely stopped. At the other end of the scale were the immensely rich, the people who owned huge yachts, palatial estates, private railroad cars, and summer retreats covering thousands of acres. In 1900, when Andrew Carnegie earned $25 million from his steel company, the average worker made $500.

While 20 percent of the nation's families lived in comfort, 80 percent barely subsisted. A 1904 study estimated that 10 million Americans—12 percent of the nation's population—were "underfed, underclothed, and poorly housed." Relief for the poor was of little help because it was local, unsystematic, and largely dependent on private charity for funds.

It was not just the disparity of wealth that was alarming but also the distribution of political power. Not only did wealthy industrialists seem beyond the reach of government, they even appeared to dominate it. With such vast wealth and power at the top of society and such grinding poverty at the bottom, many Americans feared revolution.

Socialist Solutions

Some Americans turned to socialism as the answer. Edward Bellamy's 1887 novel *Looking Backward 2000–1887* made socialism seem an attractive alternative to the existing industrial society. His book tells the story of a nineteenth-century person in the United States who awakens from a prolonged hypnotic trance to find himself alive in a socialist paradise in the year 2000. All business has been merged into one big trust run by the people themselves; there is work and leisure for all without a trace of poverty or crime. Bellamy's vision of a socialist utopia made such an impact that his book sold 1 million copies, and numerous Nationalist Clubs were founded to advance his ideas.

Bellamy had no real program for action, however, and his followers eventually drifted toward other reform movements. Bellamy's influence, though, was reinforced by other socialist writers. Socialist ideas were widely circulated by popular authors such as Jack London and Upton Sinclair.

Popular labor leader Eugene V. Debs also lost faith in capitalism after being jailed during the Pullman strike of 1894. Declaring that in a democracy workers could gain control of the government and use it to change the free enterprise system, he organized the American Socialist party.

Opposed to Debs and other moderates were radical socialists such as Daniel De Leon, who preached that democratic reform was useless. "We Socialists are not reformers; we are Revolutionists," he

Weekly Wages in the Woolen Industry

Occupation and Location	Men 1890	Men 1900	Women 1890	Women 1900
New England	Median weekly rates in dollars			
Bobbin hands, doffers, and filling and roving carriers..............	4.50	5.00	3.00	4.00
Dresser tenders and beamers...............	12.00	8.00	6.00	6.50
General hands, helpers, and laborers..............	6.50	7.00	5.00	5.50
Loom fixers................	12.50	13.50	—	—
Overseers and foreman..	19.50	19.50	—	—
Spinners....................	7.50	9.50	5.50	6.00
Weavers....................	7.50	9.00	6.50	7.50
All Occupations..........	7.50	8.00	6.50	6.50
Middle States				
All Occupations..........	7.50	9.00	5.00	5.00
Southern States				
All Occupations..........	6.50	6.50	3.50	3.50
Central States				
All Occupations..........	8.50	8.00	4.00	4.00
Pacific States				
All Occupations..........	9.50	9.50	5.00	5.00
All Sections				
All Occupations for workers under 16......	3.00	3.50	3.00	3.50

Source: Twelfth Census of the United States, 1900 *Special Reports: Employees and Wages (1903).*

Chart Study

Note the differences in pay rates for skilled and unskilled labor for men and women, the regional variations in pay, and the lower wages for children. **Why are no rates shown for female supervisors?**

Cultural Diversity

An English Social Thinker Edward Bellamy's English counterpart H. G. Wells envisioned the effects of socialism differently. In his 1895 book *The Time Machine,* Wells's hero, a scientist, propels himself into a future world of languid, indifferent people for whom work has been abolished altogether. In the subterranean depths, however, lurk the subhumans who operate the society's machinery. They emerge from the darkness to feed upon the unresisting elite. Wells's pessimistic vision of the "beasts" created by the extremes of socialism was in sharp contrast to Bellamy's paradise.

CHAPTER 23 SECTION 1

Independent Practice

Ask students to list the goals of the progressives. Then have students find examples of problems or developments in American society that prompted these objectives. Suggest they focus on such questions as What problems did workers face? Farmers? What was life like for the urban poor? How was wealth distributed? How did progressives respond to corruption in government? Invite students to present the problems they found and explain how each led to a goal or goals of the Progressive Movement. **L2**

Visualizing History

Point out that the Salvation Army was based on ideals of Christian charity. Today it provides counseling and aid to people in need throughout the world.
Answer to Caption: religious services, counseling, aid to the needy

Did You Know?

The Salvation Army was founded in London in 1865 and was established in the United States in 1880. It has about 25,000 officers, each an ordained minister, in over 85 countries. The Salvation Army provides religious services, counseling, and aid to prisoners and their families.

▲ **THE SOCIAL GOSPEL** The Salvation Army, after being established in England by General William Booth, was organized in the United States in 1880. It helped provide food, lodging, and hope for the urban needy. **What else did the Salvation Army provide?**

declared. "We care nothing for forms. We want a change of the inside of the mechanism of society. . . ." De Leon argued that even labor unions were traitors to the working class because they compromised with the industrialists. He proposed to organize all workers into new industrial unions that would eventually take over American business.

The Wobblies

Debs and De Leon briefly cooperated in 1905 in founding such a labor union, the Industrial Workers of the World, or "Wobblies." Debs soon withdrew, however, and the IWW rejected De Leon in favor of more radical leaders who preached murder and sabotage. The preamble of the IWW's constitution declared, "The working class and the employing class have nothing in common. There can be no peace so long as hunger and want are found among millions of working people. . . ."

Wherever the IWW existed, there were confrontations, strikes, sabotage, and often violence. The IWW remained strong, however, until after World War I, when Americans rejected radical politics.

More Moderate Voices

Most socialists were more moderate than the Wobblies, however, and the socialist movement gained strength throughout the early 1900s. At its height in 1912, Debs polled nearly 1 million votes as the Socialist party candidate for President. Although this was less than 10 percent of the total votes cast, the socialist movement had an importance greater than its numbers indicated. Other more moderate reformers called "progressives" owed much of their success to a growing public feeling that the only way to save the capitalist system was to improve it.

■ Progressive Leadership

The Progressive Era occupied the first 15 years of the twentieth century. Although the reforms of this period are sometimes called

Cooperative Learning

Have students work in groups to find photographs that were used by muckrakers to illustrate the problems resulting from the rapid growth of cities. Direct each group to choose one muckraker mentioned in the section, research the person, and look for photographs that showed the problems the muckraker addressed. Have the groups present their findings to the class. Discuss how the pictures would influence those who saw them. A source for a description of the muckrakers' investigations is *Years of Conscience: The Muckrakers*, edited by Harvey Swados. **L2, L3**

the Progressive movement, that label can be misleading. Unlike the Populists, the progressives were not a political party.

Who the Progressives Were

Although a Progressive party was formed in 1912, progressives also were found in both major parties. Nor were progressives united by a geographic section or by an occupation. Instead, they were a broad and largely unorganized group of reformers who often worked independently, each seeking solutions to a specific problem. Some were local reformers, while others worked for change at state or national levels. The reforms progressives advocated sometimes even conflicted.

Also unlike the Populists, the progressives were generally not the victims of existing conditions. They were mostly urban middle-class professionals who worked as journalists, social workers, educators, and clergy. Although they themselves were not suffering, they sympathized with those who were.

The Social Gospel

Progressives among Catholic priests, Jewish rabbis, and Protestant ministers began to preach a new **social gospel:** that religious organizations should work to improve society as well as to meet the spiritual needs of their congregations. Leaders such as Washington Gladden, Josiah Strong, and Walter Rauschenbush were concerned about social problems. Rauschenbush explained his view:

> *Our business is to make over an antiquated and immoral economic system.... Our inherited Christian faith dealt with individuals; our present task deals with society.*

In 1908 the National Council of the Churches of Christ was founded to support social reform. In every large city the Salvation Army—a religious group devoted to helping the needy—provided food, lodging, and hope for the despairing and poor. Like the settlement houses of the late 1800s, urban churches began to consider the whole person by providing recreational facilities, adult-education classes, nurseries, and counseling.

Women Reformers

Women also became a driving force for progressive reform. That women figured so largely in the Progressive movement was an indication that their status was improving.

AMERICAN PORTRAITS

Ida Tarbell 1857–1944

After teaching school briefly, Ida Tarbell made her career as a writer and editor. She wrote hundreds of articles and many books, but her reputation as a "muckraker" rests on one book, *The History of the Standard Oil Company*, initially published as articles in *McClure's Magazine*.

Her interest in Standard Oil was deeply personal. Her father claimed that the company had forced him out of the oil tank business and had caused his partner to commit suicide. *McClure's* asked her to write about Standard Oil because of her knowledge of the oil business and because of her flair for writing.

For two years she researched Standard Oil's practices. Her revelations created such a popular furor that Standard Oil was investigated and eventually broken up by the Supreme Court for violating federal antitrust laws.

CHAPTER 23 The Progressive Era 1893–1920

Sidelights: Jane Addams's Objectives

As a result of Jane Addams's Hull House, the first juvenile court in the United States, the first public playground in Chicago, pensions for mothers, the beginning of industrial medicine, and the union label came about. In 1935 Addams summed up her goals, "To marshal the moral forces capable of breaking what must be broken and building what must be rebuilt; to reconstruct our social relationships through regeneration of the heart; to repair a world shattered by war and sodden self-seeking; to establish moral control over a mass of mechanical achievements."

CHAPTER 23
SECTION 1

Teaching American Portraits

As an editor at *McClure's*, Ida Tarbell exercised great influence over its writers. Lincoln Steffens described her as a tactful, affectionate mediator of their squabbles. Allan Nevins, a biographer of Rockefeller, called her book on Standard Oil "the most spectacular success of the muckraking period...." Ask students what current writers they can think of whose work has revealed information that led to investigative proceedings.

Did You Know?

During the early 1900s, only Colorado, Idaho, Utah, and Wyoming gave women full suffrage in state elections. In 1905 membership in the National American Woman Suffrage Association (NAWSA) was 17,000. This number increased to over 2 million by 1917. Carrie Chapman Catt and most suffragettes used persuasion and political pressure to win backing for a constitutional amendment allowing women to vote. Alice Paul, who formed the National Woman's Party (NWP) in 1915, however, led marches, disrupted meetings, and picketed the White House to call attention to the suffrage crusade.

CHAPTER 23
SECTION 1

Since the early 1900s, the Supreme Court has strengthened and expanded the rights of working women. A 1986 ruling declared that sexual harassment in the workplace violates the 1964 Civil Rights Act. This ruling also makes companies liable for such behavior by any employee and allows women the right to seek trial by jury and punitive damages for harassment.

By 1900 women's colleges in the North and East had been turning out well-trained graduates for two generations. These women were aware of and interested in the various issues of the day. National women's clubs devoted to the study of such issues were common. By 1910 these clubs had nearly 1 million members.

Furthermore, the rights of women were expanding. By 1900 every state recognized the right of women to make a will. Most states recognized the right of women to dispose of their own wages, and some states had given them the right to equal guardianship of children. More importantly, five Western states had adopted woman suffrage.

The settlement-house movement, which women continued to lead, expanded into broader areas of reform such as slum clearance and legislation to limit working hours and outlaw child labor. Florence Kelley left Jane Addams and Hull House in Chicago and founded the National Consumers League, where she organized boycotts of goods produced by children or by workers in unsafe or unhealthful conditions. Another former Hull House social worker, Julia Lathrop, became the first head of the federal Children's Bureau, created in the Department of Labor in 1912 and now part of Health and Human Services. Other female progressives included Carrie Chapman Catt, widely known for her work in the woman's suffrage movement. Elizabeth Platt Decker headed the General Federation of Women's Clubs, which attracted nearly 1 million women in the early 1900s to promote the arts, education, and community health.

Striving for Big-Business Efficiency

Ironically, progressive reformers owed a great debt to the big businesses that so many of them detested. Unlike Populists, who believed that common people could solve society's problems, progressives put their faith in experts. Although critical of the methods and power of business leaders, progressives admired their ability to run large companies smoothly and efficiently. Progressives were confident that just like the trained managers, scientists, and efficiency experts who solved business problems, expert reformers could analyze and solve problems that kept society from running smoothly.

Educators and Investigators

In the mid-1800s, most American colleges were small, church-supported institutions less concerned with knowledge than with shaping the character of their students. Graduates who wanted to pursue further studies often went to Germany, where universities awarded an advanced degree, the Ph.D. These students brought back to America a learning style that emphasized questioning and research instead of memorizing facts. They pioneered changes in American colleges.

The Influence of Pragmatism

Coupled with educational reform was a new way of thinking known as **pragmatism**, an approach to problem solving that was popularized by Harvard philosopher William James. Pragmatists questioned the absolute truth of science. They believed that scientific laws stated only what was *probably* true and that ideas must be tested to see if they worked.

By the late 1800s many American colleges offered courses in social work, economics, political science, and sociology and granted advanced degrees. Professors such as social scientist Richard Ely at the University of Wisconsin taught students to solve problems pragmatically. At Johns Hopkins University, historian Henry Adams taught students how to do research and told them, "By the instrumentality of scholars great improvement of society is to be made." American colleges thus provided a core of reformers to study society and change it.

Pragmatist John Dewey, who taught at the University of Chicago, argued that the value of government actions should be measured by the good they do. Harvard Law School professor Oliver Wendell Holmes, Jr., was a pragmatist. In his book *The Common*

Critical Thinking

Evaluating Tell students that muckrakers were criticized by many for what was often seen as exaggerated writings. Theodore Roosevelt, although a progressive himself, once called them "liars for hire." Ask students to research primary sources to find some articles by muckraking writers and select a passage or passages to read. Ask students how, if they had lived at the time, they would have reacted to such revelations about social conditions. Do they agree or disagree with Roosevelt's assessment of muckrakers? **L2, L3**

Law, he wrote that law should not be an absolute set of principles but a tool to meet the needs of society. When Holmes was appointed to the Supreme Court in 1902, his ideas began to influence its decisions.

The Muckrakers

Other, more popular, writers played a major role in investigating and exposing a variety of social problems. President Theodore Roosevelt compared these writers to a character in John Bunyan's book, *Pilgrim's Progress,* who constantly looked downward and raked filth, and he labeled them "muckrakers."

Most muckrakers were journalists who wrote for popular magazines like *McClure's Magazine, Cosmopolitan,* and *Collier's.* Although similar to the "yellow journalism" of the period, these articles were not written to boost sales but to expose conditions the writers had found deeply disturbing. For example, in 1902 Lincoln Steffens wrote a series of articles for *McClure's Magazine* that described shocking graft and corruption in city governments across the nation. He was followed in the same magazine by Ida Tarbell's exposé of the corrupt business practices of the Standard Oil Company. In 1906 David Phillips shocked the nation with a series in *Cosmopolitan* about links between big business and 75 United States senators.

Other muckrakers revealed the results of their investigations in books. In 1906 John Spargo's *Bitter Cry of the Children* wrote about abuses of child labor, and two years later, Ray Stannard Baker's *Following the Color Line* revealed the long pattern of discrimination against African Americans in both the North and the South. Still other muckrakers were novelists who used fiction to criticize existing social conditions. In *The Octopus,* Frank Norris told how railroads dominated wheat farmers in a rich Western valley. Despite their revelations of society's ills, most muckrakers were not activists. They merely identified problems and argued for reform but counted on others to accomplish it.

 ▲ **THE MUCKRAKERS** The investigative reporting of journalists such as Ida Tarbell, Ray Stannard Baker, and Lincoln Steffens (above) made them frequent contributors. **Why did President Roosevelt call such reporters "muckrakers"?**

Section 1 ★ Review

Checking for Understanding

1. **Identify** *Looking Backward,* Wobblies, Ida Tarbell, John Dewey, Oliver Wendell Holmes, muckrakers.
2. **Define** social gospel, pragmatism.
3. **Describe** the inequities in society in the late 1800s.
4. **List** five social problems exposed by the muckrakers.

Critical Thinking

5. **Understanding Cause and Effect** What relationship do the ideas of philosophy professor William James have to progressive reform?

INTEGRATING Language Arts

American Literary Heritage

Historical Setting

At the end of the Civil War, the population of the United States was nearly 40 million. By 1910 it had doubled. This growth, coupled with increased industrialization, led to massive urbanization. By 1900 close to 40 percent of all Americans lived in cities. With the surge in population came the criticism that cities had grown too rapidly and become bleak and soulless.

Background

New literary movements are usually a reaction to their predecessors. Naturalism, however, did not abandon realism but rather took it a step further. Naturalist writers explored basic human drives but saw people as tossed about by fate and their environment, powerless to control their lives.

About the Author

Born in 1871 Theodore Dreiser worked as a journalist in his native Midwest and eventually settled in New York City. His first novel, *Sister Carrie*, published in 1900, drew on the city life he observed around him. The novel was considered objectionable because of its subject matter, and to Dreiser's dissatisfaction, received limited exposure. In 1911 Dreiser published *Jennie Gerhardt*. Again he experienced censorship when others viewed this work as perverse and immoral. Dreiser, who died in 1945, is credited with being a major American naturalist writer.

▲ THEODORE DREISER

A major literary development in the late nineteenth century was naturalism, which developed out of realist fiction. Naturalist writers carried the vivid detail of realism a step further by depicting environmental factors. In his first novel, *Sister Carrie*, published in 1900, Theodore Dreiser describes the compelling attraction as well as the cold indifference of life in growing cities.

Sister Carrie (excerpts)

To Carrie, the sound of the little bells upon the horse-cars, as they tinkled in and out of hearing, was as pleasing as it was novel. She gazed into the lighted street when Minnie brought her into the front room, and wondered at the sounds, the movement, the murmur of the vast city which stretched for miles and miles in every direction.

Mrs. Hanson, after the first greetings were over, gave Carrie the baby and proceeded to get supper. Her husband asked a few questions and sat down to read the evening paper. He was a silent man, American born, of a Swede father, and now employed as a cleaner of refrigerator cars at the stock-yards. To him the presence or absence of his wife's sister was a matter of indifference. Her personal appearance did not affect him one way or the other. His one observation to the point was concerning the chances of work in Chicago.

"It's a big place," he said. "You can get in somewhere in a few days. Everybody does."

It had been tacitly understood beforehand that she was to get work and pay her board. He was of a clean, saving disposition, and had already paid a number of monthly installments on two lots far out on the West Side. His ambition was some day to build a house on them....

"You'll want to see the city first, won't you?" said Minnie, when they were eating. "Well, we'll go out Sunday and see Lincoln Park."

Carrie noticed that Hanson had said nothing to this. He seemed to be thinking of something else.

"Well," she said, "I think I'll look around tomorrow. I've got Friday and Saturday, and it won't be any trouble. Which way is the business part?"

Minnie began to explain, but her husband took this part of the conversation to himself.

"It's that way," he said, pointing east. "That's east." Then he went off into the longest speech he had yet indulged in, concerning the lay of Chicago. "You'd better look in those big manufacturing houses along

UNIT 7 Entering a New Century: 1867–1920

Cultural Diversity

The naturalist school was represented not only in novels but also in poetry. The preeminent poet of the period was Edward Arlington Robinson. Although his style was traditional, his work reflects a spirit of courage in the face of tragedy. Robinson was concerned with human relationships and how and why people acted the way they did. He was awarded the Pulitzer Prize in 1922, 1925, and 1928.

Franklin Street and just the other side of the river," he concluded. "Lots of girls work there. You could get home easy, too. It isn't very far." . . .

In 1889 Chicago had the peculiar qualifications of growth which made such adventuresome pilgrimages even on the part of young girls plausible. . . . It was a city of over 500,000, with the ambition, the daring, the activity of a metropolis of a million. Its streets and houses were already scattered over an area of seventy-five square miles. Its population was not so much thriving upon established commerce as upon the industries which prepared for the arrival of others. The sound of the hammer engaged upon the erection of new structures was everywhere heard. . . .

The entire metropolitan center possessed a high and mighty air calculated to overawe and abash the common applicant, and to make the gulf between poverty and success seem both wide and deep.

Into this important commercial region the timid Carrie went. She walked east along Van Buren Street through a region of lessening importance, until it deteriorated into a mass of shanties and coalyards, and finally verged upon the river. She walked bravely forward, led by an honest desire to find employment and delayed at every step by the interest of the unfolding scene, and a sense of helplessness amid so much evidence of power and force which she did not understand. . . .

Through the open windows she could see the figures of men and women in working aprons, moving busily about. The great streets were wall-lined mysteries to her. . . .

▶ WORKER IN SHOE FACTORY, 1895

Interpreting Literature

1. Why do you think Carrie came to live with her sister?
2. What kind of attitude about life in the city at this time does Mr. Hanson exemplify?
3. Do large cities today hold the attraction that they held for Carrie and other ambitious men and women at the turn of the century? Why or why not?

INTEGRATING Language Arts

Other Works of Naturalist Writers

Naturalist writers included Upton Sinclair, whose 1906 novel, *The Jungle,* presented a stomach-churning and unforgettable portrait of the meatpacking industry. Frank Norris's 1901 novel, *The Octopus,* exposed a corrupt railroad industry that cheated small businesses while favoring large businesses. Stephen Crane in *The Red Badge of Courage* (1895) explored fear as a basic motive for human behavior, and in *Maggie, A Girl of the Streets* (1893) describes the violence and degradation of city slums. Jack London offered the most extreme examples of the idea of the survival of the fittest in novels like *The Call of the Wild* (1903) and *The Sea Wolf* (1904).

Developing Student Understanding

Ask students to name some positive and negative characteristics of city life, as compared with rural life. (Positive: more employment and cultural opportunities, greater exposure to multicultural living, more diverse educational opportunities; Negative: overcrowding, greater ethnic and racial tensions, a more hectic pace of life)

Explain that many naturalist writers of the early 1900s explored the lives of people in the cities, examining not only what made cities exciting but also the forces that overwhelmed people and often led to tragedy.

Answers to INTERPRETING LITERATURE

1. She believes that she will find new opportunities and a new life in the city.
2. His life revolves around work and money.
3. Answers will vary. Students might argue that cities have employment, educational, and social opportunities not available in small towns or rural areas. Others might defend the values of small town life, such as a healthy environment, a relaxed pace, more concerned people.

SECTION 2

Progressive Reforms

Setting the Scene

Section Focus

Progressive reforms affected government, consumer's rights, and education. People began to speak out against children working in mines, mills, and factories and to back temperance and woman suffrage. Although early accomplishments were mainly local changes, later reforms occurred at state and national levels.

Objectives

After studying this section, you should be able to
★ explain how reforms strengthened democracy.
★ describe the advances made by social reformers and government in protecting adult and child workers.

Key Terms

direct primary, initiative, referendum, recall

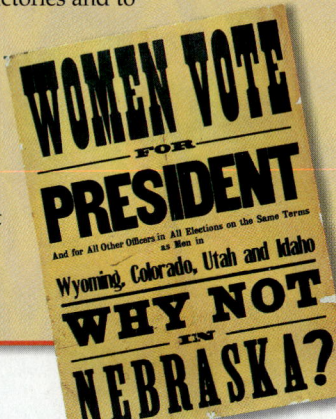

◀ WOMAN SUFFRAGE POSTER

It is fitting that the earliest evidence of progressive activism dealt with cities. Being primarily city residents, progressives were viewed as representative of the increasing importance of the nation's urban centers. What is perceived as the initial progressive reform came even before the muckrakers began to write. This reform was inspired not by a book or a magazine article but by a natural disaster.

■ Reforms in Government

In 1900 a hurricane roared in from the Gulf of Mexico and devastated the coastal city of Galveston, Texas. When the political machine that controlled city government proved incapable of responding to the disaster, local reformers and business leaders convinced the state legislature to allow them to take control. In April 1901, the mayor and city council were replaced by five commissioners chosen in a nonpartisan election. Four of the commissioners were local business leaders who applied their management experience to running the city, and it quickly recovered. Reformers in other cities were impressed. Galveston's experience demonstrated the benefits of running a city like a business.

Changes in City Government

From the commission plan developed another progressive reform—the city-manager plan. In this reform an elected city council hired a professional manager to run city government, much as the directors of a business would hire a superintendent to run a factory.

UNIT 7 Entering a New Century: 1867–1920

Early city managers often were engineers, because much of the business of running a modern city—such as sewage disposal, water supply, and paving streets—was technical. By 1915 more than 400 cities had adopted commission or city-manager plans.

Even in cities where progressives could not reshape government, reform mayors fought powerful combinations of political bosses, unethical business leaders, and corrupt city officials. Reform mayors such as Tom Johnson in Cleveland, Samuel "Golden Rule" Jones in Toledo, and Hazen Pingree in Detroit gained national attention. All three left successful businesses to battle corruption in city government and to force streetcar lines, electric companies, and other utilities to behave in the public interest.

Voting Reforms

At the state level, political reform was first achieved in Wisconsin. Robert La Follette, after twice failing to become Republican

The Progressive Movement and State Government

Women won the right to vote in Wyoming (1869), Utah (1870) and, by the end of the 1800s, in Colorado and Idaho. By 1914 women could vote in several other Western states, including Montana, Kansas, Washington, and Arizona. Montana elected the first woman to the House of Representatives in 1916.

South Dakota (1898), Utah (1900), and Oregon (1902) adopted the initiative and referendum. By 1918 more than 20 states had adopted these reforms in one form or another.

Mississippi (1902), Wisconsin (1903), and Oregon (1905) adopted the direct primary. By 1915 two-thirds of the states had adopted direct primary laws.

- Reformers control state offices
- Reformers influence state government
- Reformers not effective
- 1890 Date reformers came to power

Map Study Although they achieved notable success at the state level, in most industrial states progressive reformers were unable to completely break the power of the bosses and their political machines. **Why was Wisconsin called the "laboratory of democracy"?**

CHAPTER 23 The Progressive Era 1893–1920   633

CHAPTER 23 SECTION 2

Independent Practice

Government Have students research their community's form of government. Explain that many meetings of town or city governments are open to the public. Suggest that students attend such a meeting to watch their government in operation. Have them note the kinds of problems that are raised and the suggestions for solving them. **L2**

Visualizing History

Some suffragists went on hunger strikes when they were jailed for demonstrating. The force-feeding they endured brought widespread publicity and helped dramatize the suffrage movement. **Answer to Caption:** the West

Food of the Times

Urban families no longer depended on local farmers to supply their fresh milk, butter, or meat. It was cheaper and more convenient to get milk from a dealer, who often diluted it with water. Butter and cheese were sometimes processed in plants that blended bleach with animal parts to produce the products. A saying of the time noted that butter was axle grease, and cheese was made of lard and soap. These health hazards led to the Pure Food and Drug Act.

▲ **Visualizing History** **THE RIGHT TO VOTE** Women parade for the right to vote in New York. Suffragists (left) are forced to eat during a hunger strike. *Which region of the nation was first to grant woman suffrage?*

candidate for governor, finally was elected in 1900. He used his office to attack the tradition of party nominating conventions. Because party bosses controlled the selection of convention delegates, they also controlled the selection of election candidates. From his own experience, La Follette knew that reformers had little chance of being chosen to run for office. In 1903 he pressured the state legislature to require that each party hold a **direct primary,** a preliminary election in which voters choose candidates for the general election. This reform took the nomination of party candidates from the bosses and their political machines and gave it to the people.

To reduce the control that big business and the party bosses had over state legislators, La Follette introduced three other reforms. The **initiative** allowed a group of citizens to introduce legislation and required the legislature to vote on it. The **referendum** allowed proposed legislation to be submitted to the voters for approval, and the **recall** allowed voters to remove an elected official from office by holding a special election. Although none of these ideas originated in Wisconsin, La Follette's great success in enacting them there gave the state a reputation as "the laboratory of democracy," and progressives in other states copied Wisconsin's reforms.

The most significant political reform that the progressives accomplished at the national level was the direct election of senators. Because they were chosen by their state legislatures, senators were shielded from direct public pressure. Progressive reformers felt that if its members were elected, the Senate would be more responsive to the public will and less influenced by powerful business interests. The call for this reform became so great that in 1913 the Seventeenth Amendment to the Constitution provided for direct election of senators.

Slow Progress for Women

It was difficult to argue that the people should have a greater voice in government affairs without including women, especially

634 UNIT 7 Entering a New Century: 1867–1920

Sidelight: Reformers in the Cities

Three notable progressives were responsible for urban reform. When he became mayor of Detroit in 1898, Hazen Pingree improved the quality of life with new parks and schools and work for the unemployed. Samuel Jones, mayor of Toledo, established municipal ownership of public utilities and cleaned up corruption in the police at the turn of the century. In 1901 in Cleveland, Tom Johnson placed higher taxes on railroad and utility properties, lowered streetcar fares, and built recreational facilities.

because they were increasingly holding jobs in factories, business offices, and schools, as well as taking prominent roles in reform movements. In addition, some progressives believed that if women gained the right to vote, their influence would help push through other reforms. By 1914, 11 Western states had granted women full suffrage. In the East, women promoted their cause by holding parades and circulating petitions. Many women believed, however, that a constitutional amendment would be needed to gain the vote nationwide.

Consumer Protection

A basic principle that American business inherited from Great Britain was *caveat emptor*, Latin for "let the buyer beware." This meant that people who purchased worthless life insurance, bread made with sawdust, or colored water labeled as medicine had only themselves to blame for not being more careful. Progressives argued that consumers had no way of knowing when meat was prepared under unsanitary conditions, children's cough syrup was dosed with opium, or other products were similarly misrepresented.

Regulating the Insurance Industry

In 1905 Charles Evans Hughes, a lawyer who worked for the New York legislature, investigated the insurance industry. He uncovered bribery of elected officials and huge salaries insurance executives paid to themselves and to family members they hired. Consequently, New York—and later other states—passed laws to regulate insurance companies and to protect the interests of policyholders.

Making Buildings Safer

At the local level, protection for consumers often came in the form of city zoning laws. The laws regulated how land and buildings could be used. Building codes prohibited some of the worst features of tenements by setting minimum requirements for light and air, fire escapes, room size, and sanitation.

Ensuring the Safety of Food and Medicine

Passage of pure food and drug laws demonstrated the effectiveness of the muckrakers in influencing consumer protection. Articles in *Collier's* about harmful medicines in 1906 convinced the chief chemist of the Department of Agriculture to perform experiments on himself and then to call for regulation. Even more sensational was the publication in 1906 of Upton Sinclair's best-selling book, *The Jungle,* a fact-based novel that portrayed horribly unsanitary conditions in slaughterhouses:

> *There would be meat that had tumbled out on the floor, in the dirt and sawdust, where workers had tramped and spit uncounted billions of [tuberculosis] germs. There would be meat stored in great piles in rooms; and the water from leaky roofs would drip over it, and thousands of rats would race about on it.*

An outraged President Theodore Roosevelt demanded reform, and Congress responded with legislation. The Pure Food and Drug Act established a government agency, the Food and Drug Administration, to protect consumers from unsafe medicines and foods. The Meat Inspection Act was passed on the same day in 1906. These laws regulated the content and inspection of food, prohibited the use of addictive drugs in nonprescription medicines, and required accurate labels on food and drug products. State governments followed with similar legislation to regulate food and drugs that did not cross state lines.

Protecting Workers

"I aimed at the public's heart," Upton Sinclair complained, "and by accident I hit it in the stomach." Sinclair did not intend *The Jungle* to focus public attention on impure food. Instead he wanted to expose

CHAPTER 23
SECTION 2

Linking Across TIME

A legacy of the progressives' concern with protecting people from harmful substances can be seen in the work of the Food and Drug Administration (FDA) and the Environmental Protection Agency (EPA). The EPA, which regulates toxic substances, registers some 22,000 pesticides and requires some 75 toxicity tests for each pesticide. Companies are often required to wait several years for a substance to be approved and licensed for sale and use.

Sidelights: Mother Jones and Child Labor

Mary Harris Jones ("Mother Jones") was a well-known labor leader in the late 1800s and early 1900s. She devoted much of her life to speaking and organizing efforts to help improve the conditions of workers, especially children. At the age of 73, Jones organized and led the March of the Mill Children from Pennsylvania to New York. Three children dressed as Revolutionary soldiers led the group and carried signs that read, "We Want to Go to School" and "Prosperity, Where Is Our Share?" The marchers were seeking the President's support for a law prohibiting child labor.

CHAPTER 23
SECTION 2

Visualizing History Young "breaker boys" in the coal mines ranged in age from 10 to 15. These youngsters picked the pieces of slag out of the coal. Many had little schooling beyond the eighth grade.
Answer to Caption: through the efforts of the National Child Labor Committee, muckrakers like John Spargo, and the federal Children's Bureau, which investigated and published information about the abuses of child labor

Did You Know?

The 1908 *Muller* v. *Oregon* Supreme Court decision stated that "for a long time on her feet at work, repeating this from day to day, tends to injurious effects upon the body, and as healthy mothers are essential to vigorous offspring, the physical well-being of woman becomes an object of public interest and care in order to preserve the strength and vigor of the race." Have students express their opinions about the validity of this quote. Ask if such an assessment would cause controversy today. Why or why not?

▲ **CHILD LABOR** One concern for reformers was protecting children, such as these workers in a Pennsylvania coal mine. Because canaries are very sensitive to poisonous gases, they were used to detect such gases in coal mines. *How was child labor reform achieved?*

the terrible working conditions in slaughterhouses. One of the grim realities of industrialization was the frequency of industrial accidents.

Workers' Compensation

Workers who suffered industrial accidents had little protection. Employers argued that industrial accidents were not caused by unsafe conditions but by carelessness, and they often fired employees who were seriously disabled. Progressives joined labor union leaders to pressure state legislatures for workers' compensation laws. These laws established insurance funds into which employers made payments. Workers who were injured by industrial accidents were paid from the fund. In 1902 Maryland was first to pass such legislation, and by 1911 10 of the states had workers' compensation laws on the books. Workers' compensation laws not only helped injured workers, they improved working conditions for all workers because employers with low accident rates paid lower insurance premiums. Related progressive legislation established state agencies to inspect factories, limited workers' hours, and attempted to end crowded, unsanitary work environments.

Protecting Women: *Muller v. Oregon*

Many progressives were especially interested in improving working conditions for women. By 1900 about 20 percent of all workers were women, and progressive reformers believed women workers needed special protection. In 1903 Oregon passed a law limiting female factory workers to a 10-hour day. Employers challenged the law as violating a woman's civil right to work as long as she chose, and in 1908 the case was appealed to the Supreme Court.

636 UNIT 7 Entering a New Century: 1867–1920

Critical Thinking

Evaluating Effectiveness Have students research some social-service organizations that are active in their community. Suggest they focus on such questions as how these organizations help the people of the community. Which organization is the most important, and why do you think so? What kind of organization do you think your community needs that it does not have? Have students write a report answering these questions. When students present their reports, conduct a class discussion on how students think social-service organizations in their community might be improved. **L3**

To defend the law in *Muller* v. *Oregon*, progressive attorney Louis D. Brandeis presented research that convinced the Court that long working hours damaged women's health, and the Oregon law was upheld. After the *Muller* decision, several other states quickly passed similar laws.

Muller v. *Oregon* was a revolutionary legal decision. For the first time, the Court looked beyond legal principles and precedents and applied pragmatism to the law. The Court began to weigh what was best for society when it decided cases. In so doing, it took the first step toward becoming an instrument of social reform.

Protecting Children

Probably the most emotional progressive labor reform was the campaign against child labor. Although children had always worked on family farms, urban children found factory work dangerously monotonous and conditions often unhealthy or unsafe. Reformers established a National Child Labor Committee in 1904 to campaign for the abolition of child labor.

Muckraker John Spargo's 1906 book, *The Bitter Cry of the Children*, presented detailed evidence of the conditions of child labor in America. He told of anthracite coal mines, where thousands of "breaker boys" were hired at age 9 or 10 to pick slag out of coal and were paid 60 cents for a 10-hour day. He described how the work permanently bent their backs and often crippled their hands. He revealed that in textile mills more than one-eighth of the employees were less than 16 years old and that some children entered cotton factories at age 7 or 8. Public opinion was so stirred by such information that by 1914 all but one state set a minimum age for employment and many established other limits on child labor as well. At the federal level, the newly established Children's Bureau had few powers, but it investigated and published information that helped the campaign to improve the well-being of child workers.

Life of the Times

Boy Scouts

While many progressive reformers focused on social issues, others concentrated on keeping the nation's youth under control.

Organizations such as the Boy Scouts of America (BSA) arose to provide supervised activities that stressed old-fashioned values and sheltered adolescents from the lures of the city. Scouts hiked in the school year, camped in the summer, and attended weekly meetings packed with instruction, drills, and games. Scouting channeled adolescent energy into the wholesome pursuit of specialized merit badges acquired by passing tests on woodcraft, reconnaissance, and citizenship skills.

The Boy Scouts of America was designed, in part, to reinforce what were perceived at the time to be traditional American male values. BSA executives and scoutmasters strongly opposed girl scouting and were reluctant to involve the Boy Scouts in service projects on which Boy and Girl Scouts worked as equals.

CHAPTER 23 The Progressive Era 1893–1920   637

CHAPTER 23 SECTION 2

Teaching Life of the Times

The Boy Scouts was organized in Great Britain in 1907 by Robert Baden-Powell in order to give boys training in citizenship. The organization was brought to the United States by American businessman William D. Boyce in 1910 after a British Boy Scout helped Boyce find his way in a London fog. Baden-Powell helped work out a similar program for girls called the Girl Guides. Girl Guiding was established in the United States in 1912 by Juliette Gordon Low. The name of the group was later changed to Girl Scouting. Ask students who among them belonged to the Boy or Girl Scouts and what positive values they learned from the experience.

Did You Know?

Governor Robert La Follette founded *La Follette's Weekly Magazine* in 1909. By 1912 it was considered the country's leading progressive journal. The magazine supported most of the reform programs of the day. During the next two decades, both the Republicans and the Democrats put into effect many of the programs first presented in La Follette's magazine.

Cooperative Learning

Comparing Reforms Remind students that the Woman's Christian Temperance Union (WCTU) still exists today. Divide the class into four groups, and assign each group one of the following organizations: WCTU, Alcoholics Anonymous, Mothers Against Drunk Driving (MADD), and Students Against Drunk Driving (SADD). Ask students to research the groups and report on the backgrounds of the groups, their major goals, how they work to achieve these goals, and their effectiveness. Have students compare these current groups with earlier attempts at temperance reform and identify their similarities and differences. **L2**

CHAPTER 23 SECTION 2

ASSESS

Check Understanding
Assign Section 2 Review as homework or an in-class activity.

Evaluate
Assign the Section 2 Quiz in the TCR, or use the History of a Free Nation Testmaker to create a customized quiz.

Reteach
Ask students to identify and explain the ways in which progressives attempted to make government more democratic and efficient.

Have students complete Reteaching Activity 23-2.

Enrich
Tell students that in the latter part of the twentieth century the direct primary has been severely criticized for a variety of reasons. One is that because primaries are stretched out over a period of time, only wealthy candidates can afford to go the distance. Also, voters lose interest after a while. Ask students to write letters to their representatives in Congress suggesting ways that direct primaries might be reformed to address the charges of the critics.

CLOSE
Ask the students to discuss the elements of direct democracy that have survived from the Progressive Era.

■ Varieties of Reform

In addition to reforming labor practices, many progressives insisted that business be regulated in ways to protect the public interest. Because of their great influence and power, large corporations commonly gained tax breaks from state legislatures.

Robert La Follette, the governor of Wisconsin, determined that railroads paid less than half the property taxes of other businesses. He obtained reform laws to tax railroads on a more equal basis. La Follette also established a commission to regulate the railroads in the state. Other states followed Wisconsin's lead.

On the federal level, Congress began to tax corporate profits in 1909. Although the Supreme Court in 1895 had declared an income tax unconstitutional, in 1913 the Sixteenth Amendment empowered the federal government to levy such a tax.

Public Utilities

The Progressive Era also was a time when reformers called for regulation of public utilities such as streetcar lines, waterworks, and electric-light companies. Many states set up public service commissions with the power to control the rates charged by public utilities. Some city reformers, doubtful that regulation could force utility companies to act in the public interest, called for city governments to buy them out and run the utilities directly. By 1915, for example, all but 1 of the 36 largest cities owned or operated their own waterworks.

Health, Recreation, and Education

Progressive reform was also felt in other areas. It resulted in playgrounds and dental clinics for children. Private charities multiplied and broadened their social usefulness. The Rockefeller Foundation, for example, led a campaign to eradicate hookworm, which was causing serious health problems in rural areas of the South. Juvenile courts and reform schools were set up to care for young lawbreakers. Progressives began to show concern about America's natural resources. State and federal governments passed conservation laws and set aside public recreation areas.

The reform impulse also resulted in great progress in education. Many states passed laws requiring children to attend school, and the number of high schools more than doubled between 1900 and 1920. The school year was lengthened and the curriculum enriched by courses in music, art, home economics, and industrial arts.

The Fight Against Alcohol Use

Long at the forefront of the temperance movement was the Woman's Christian Temperance Union (WCTU), founded in 1874. By 1890, it already had 150,000 members.

Like so many progressive reforms, temperance was first accomplished at the local level. By 1914 nearly half the people of the United States lived in areas where the sale of alcohol was illegal, and 12 states had passed statewide Prohibition laws. In 1919 Prohibition became nationwide when the Eighteenth Amendment was added to the Constitution.

Section 2 ★ Review

Checking for Understanding
1. **Identify** Galveston, Seventeenth Amendment, Charles Evans Hughes, Upton Sinclair, *Muller* v. *Oregon*, John Spargo, WCTU.
2. **Define** direct primary, initiative, referendum, recall.
3. **Describe** the commission plan as a form of city government.
4. **Discuss** three reforms that came out of the Progressive movement that promoted stronger and more direct involvement by citizens in government.

Critical Thinking
5. **Understanding Cause and Effect** Explain why progressive reforms strengthened the cause of woman's suffrage.

Answers to SECTION 2 REVIEW
1. Galveston, 632; Seventeenth Amendment, 634; Charles Evans Hughes, 635; Upton Sinclair, 635–636; *Muller* v. *Oregon*, 637; John Spargo, 638; WCTU, 638
2. All vocabulary words are defined in the Glossary.
3. City government is divided into departments; mayor and city council are replaced by elected commissioners.
4. direct primary, initiative, referendum, recall, and the direct elections of senators
5. Many reformers were women, and it was difficult to reform society and extend democracy without confronting the irony that about half of society was denied the vote on the basis of its gender.

History and Religion Connections

Reform Judaism

By 1880 about 250,000 Jews lived in America; most were of German ancestry. Many practiced Reform Judaism, a form of Judaism that arose in the 1800s in answer to the changing conditions of emancipated Jews in Germany.

Isaac Mayer Wise organized Reform Judaism in the United States in the mid-1800s. Wise initiated reforms in worship that became important elements of this form of Judaism. These reforms included family pews, baring of the head, and abolishing non-Biblical festival days. In comparison to Orthodox Judaism, Reform Judaism maintains only those traditional ceremonies considered meaningful to the modern Jew.

Influenced by liberal Protestantism and the social gospel of reformers, many Jews began to adapt their religious customs and rituals to the American way of life. For example, they adopted a congregation structure similar to that of American Christians. Like their liberal Christian counterparts, Reform Jews supported such progressive social reforms as child labor laws and collective bargaining. Attorney and later Supreme Court justice Louis D. Brandeis, for example, was an ardent champion of progressive causes.

After 1880 Jewish immigrants flooded into America, many escaping persecution in Russia. Reform Jews helped these newcomers make their way in the United States. The help was given partly because of their belief in social reform and partly because they feared that these poor, old-fashioned, Yiddish-speaking Jews would create an anti-Jewish reaction among American Christians. The Russian Jews were Orthodox—observing traditional Jewish beliefs and rituals. In turn, Orthodox Jews reintroduced the Reform Jews to a number of customs and rituals that had been discarded by their parents.

▲ A POSTER CELEBRATING JEWISH CONTRIBUTIONS TO AMERICA

Making the Religion Connection

1. In what ways were Reform Jews influenced by the American way of life?
2. For what reasons did Reform Jews help Russian Jewish immigrants?

Linking Past and Present

3. How have American Jews helped Russian Jewish immigrants in recent times?

Chapter 23 Connections

Teaching Making Connections

Reform Judaism developed many organizations aimed at helping all Jews, including educational groups and self-help societies. The Young Men's and Women's Hebrew Associations attended to the moral needs of young people. The first Jewish summer camp was started to take Jewish children away from the city slums. Many of the activities sponsored by Reform Jews were less religious and emphasized, instead, a common cultural heritage.

Did You Know?

Newspapers written in the Yiddish language helped Jewish immigrants adapt to a new way of life. In such newspapers as the *Jewish Daily Forward*, newcomers could read about issues that deeply affected their lives. The papers also served as a forum for discussion of everyday life. The *Forward*'s Letters to the Editor section, called "Bintel Briefs," gave immigrants the chance to express their views on everything from work to marriage to religion, children, and education.

Answers to CONNECTIONS

1. influenced by liberal Protestantism and the social gospel of reformers
2. partly because of their belief in social reform and partly because they feared these poor, Yiddish-speaking Jews would create an anti-Jewish reaction among American Christians
3. American Jews pressured the United States government to help Jews leave the Soviet Union. Soviet Jews had been persecuted for a number of years. American Jewish congregations helped the Soviet Jews who came to the United States adjust to the American way of life. They also gave the immigrants economic help.

LESSON PLAN
SECTION 3, 640–645

FOCUS

Bellringer
Before taking roll at the beginning of the class period, display Focus Activity Transparency 78 on the overhead projector, and assign the accompanying Focus Activity Sheet.

Objectives
Point out the objectives on this page to students in previewing the section content.

Motivating Activity
Read to students the following statement by Booker T. Washington:
"In all things that are purely social we [the two races] can be as separate as the fingers, yet one as the hand in all things essential to mutual progress."
Point out to students that Washington was the most influential black leader at the turn of the century. He thought African Americans could not gain equality with whites all at once. Ask students to interpret Washington's statement. Tell students that in this section they will learn how progressives viewed African Americans as well as new immigrants and how these views affected minority groups.

Assign students the Chapter 23 Reading on Booker T. Washington's Advice to Black Americans in Primary and Secondary Source Readings.

SECTION 3

Limits of Progressivism

Setting the Scene

Section Focus
While progressivism resulted in many lasting changes, reform had its limits. Much progressive reform was based on traditional American attitudes about race, sex, and nationalism. As a result, not all Americans shared equally in the benefits of reform.

Objectives
After studying this section, you should be able to
★ describe progressive attitudes about immigrants and racial minorities.
★ explain why African American leadership changed.

Key Term
literacy test

◀ WOODEN ICE SKATES, EARLY 1900S

The achievements of progressive reform at the national level were less far-reaching than its successes at local and state levels. It was more difficult to create nationwide demands for reform than to organize effective campaigns on a smaller scale. The federal government also was more difficult to prod into action. The Senate, chosen by boss-dominated state legislatures until 1913, was a highly conservative body. In the House of Representatives, powerful figures such as committee heads and the speaker usually resisted change.

The Supreme Court became somewhat less conservative than it had been in the 1890s, as progressives Oliver Wendell Holmes (1902), Charles Evans Hughes (1910), and Louis D. Brandeis (1916) were appointed to the Court. Yet the majority of justices seldom were willing to extend federal power into new areas.

Partly because of the attitude of the courts, many of the evils described by the muckrakers were considered outside the constitutional sphere of the federal government's powers, making national reform nearly impossible.

The benefits of progressivism were spread unevenly in other ways, too. Many middle-class progressives feared labor unions almost as much as they did trusts. So although progressives worked with labor leaders to improve working conditions, few objected when businesses organized effectively to prevent unions in their plants—often with cooperation from local courts and police. Therefore, wage gains during the Progressive Era went only to skilled workers. The earning power of unskilled workers actually dropped because prices increased more rapidly than their rates of pay.

UNIT 7 Entering a New Century: 1867–1920

Classroom Resources for SECTION 3

Teacher's Classroom Resources
- Reproducible Lesson Plan
- Reteaching Activity 23-3
- Chapter 23 Enrichment Activity
- Chapter 23 Primary and Secondary Source Reading
- Spanish Summaries and Glossary
- Section Quiz

Multimedia
- Section Focus Transparency 78
- Vocabulary Puzzlemaker
- Student Self-Test Software
- Testmaker
- The American People: Fabric of a Nation

Reformers and Immigrants

Among the many factors that held down the wages of unskilled workers was the continuing flood of immigrants to the United States, averaging one million a year during the Progressive Era—largely from southern and eastern Europe. This "New Immigration" caused widespread alarm, as immigrant men and women competed for unskilled jobs in American mines, mills, and factories.

In addition, the newcomers seemed to have more difficulty fitting in to established American culture than the "old immigrants" from northern and western Europe. Pressure from labor-union leaders and such organizations as the Immigration Restriction League persuaded Congress in 1897, 1913, and 1915 to enact laws requiring all immigrants to pass **literacy tests,** tests to show they could read English. All three laws were vetoed, but such a law passed over President Woodrow Wilson's veto in 1917.

Reform and Immigrant Cultures

Many progressives feared the socialist ideas that immigrants brought from Europe. As middle-class reformers, progressives wanted to change capitalism, not abolish it. Many also worried about preserving existing values and culture. Therefore, many progressive reforms were aimed at weakening the political strength of immigrant numbers and instilled in newcomers what reformers thought were proper American values.

In calling for reform of city government, one writer complained about:

> [t]he mass of ignorant voters, who now help the vicious bosses to govern our cities.... A colony of Italians, Scandinavians, Germans, or Irish, preserving their national language and their national ideas, and living as foreigners among us is very difficult to reach, but their votes count just as much as the votes of the most highly educated men among us.

▲ **Adult Classes** Many businesses organized English classes for their employees. The classes were held in the plant so that workers could attend at the end of their shift. *Why would employers consider learning English important?*

CHAPTER 23 The Progressive Era 1893–1920 641

Cooperative Learning

Divide the class into groups, and assign each group one of the following roles: a newly arrived immigrant, a progressive reformer, a political boss, a labor-union leader. Direct students to formulate the views of each of these people concerning immigration and reform. Ask each group to present its viewpoint to the class and answer questions. You might suggest that students write a summary of each of the viewpoints presented and discuss the merits of each. **L2, L3**

CHAPTER 23
SECTION 3

Independent Practice

Debate Ask students to summarize the arguments of Booker T. Washington and those of W.E.B. Du Bois. After they have completed their summaries, ask them to write a few paragraphs explaining with whose views they most agree and why. You might suggest they conclude by comparing the arguments of Washington and Du Bois with those of African American leaders today. **L2**

Visualizing History Although progressives largely ignored the problems of African Americans, some were actively involved in the founding of the National Association for the Advancement of Colored People (NAACP). In fact, with the exception of Du Bois, all of the founders were white. However, the group's leaders and members were mainly African Americans.
Answer to Caption: the NAACP

▲ **STRIVING FOR JUSTICE** Booker T. Washington (right) and W.E.B. Du Bois were among the most important African American leaders of the period. Both men had the same goals, but they took different approaches to those goals. *What organization did Du Bois help form?*

When progressives reformed government by defeating political bosses and machines, they also destroyed the system that provided immigrant groups with a political voice, political jobs, and political power.

Education and Resistance

As reformers obtained child labor laws and school attendance laws, they forced immigrant children out of factories and into classrooms. Many states made the study of American history a required course in public schools during the Progressive Era. Educator John Dewey advised that it was essential to teach students to be good citizens.

With the great increase in immigration in the late 1800s, other functions were thrust upon the schools. Besides teaching intellectual skills and citizenship, the schools taught patriotism and gave Americans a sense of unity. In this way, schools assisted in the work of assimilating newcomers into American culture by teaching the English language and stressing American values.

In the late 1800s American education was rapidly becoming free, public, and almost universal. In fact, by 1900 most states had compulsory education laws. These laws required that children attend school for a certain part of each year.

As a result, enrollment increased. In 1870 less than 60 percent of all children ages 5 to 17 were enrolled in elementary and secondary schools. By 1900 the figure was over 72 percent. The number of public high schools increased from about 150 in 1870 to nearly 6,000 by 1900. The greatest growth occurred in the Northeast and the Midwest.

The benefits of public school education, however, were not shared by everyone. Most pupils were middle- and upper-class children who chose to go to a public school rather than to be privately educated. Many immigrant children did not complete their schooling. Many poor immigrants needed their children to work to add to the family income. Forced to work at an early age, they sometimes did not even finish elementary school.

■ Progressives and Race

The most conspicuous limit to progressivism was its attitude about race. Like most white Americans at that time, most progressives believed that nonwhite races were inferior. Therefore, reformers did not object to the

642   UNIT 7 Entering a New Century: 1867–1920

Cultural Diversity

Immigrants to the United States formed groups to help them adjust to their new country and to overcome the prejudices of native-born Americans. These groups usually were connected to churches, synagogues, and schools and were often social and athletic clubs. The immigrants formed their own ethnic societies, such as German-American clubs, Slovak-American clubs, the Polish National Alliance, the Italian-American Society, and the National Council of Jewish Women. Newspapers in the immigrants' native languages served as a link among the newcomers. Many of these newspapers still exist in large American cities.

segregation of Japanese Americans in San Francisco schools in 1906, nor did they oppose sharp cuts in Japanese immigration that began in 1907.

Ignoring the Problems of African Americans

In addition, progressives accepted widespread discrimination against African Americans. Although many progressives sympathized with their plight, most reformers agreed with Theodore Roosevelt, who stated that Africans "as a race and in the mass are altogether inferior to whites."

Few progressives objected to the Jim Crow laws that Southern states had passed after Reconstruction to restore segregation. In 1896, when the Supreme Court ruled in *Plessy* v. *Ferguson* that segregation was constitutional as long as separate facilities were equal, no progressive campaign was launched for reform. While Southern whites were lynching African Americans and barring them from voting or holding public office, progressives were crusading for primary elections, direct election of senators, and other reforms to spread democracy. Like most whites, progressives generally accepted the South's Jim Crow system, partly because of indifference and partly because African Americans in the North also were restricted to low-paying jobs, segregation, and inferior social status.

The Struggle for Equality Continues

These circumstances help explain a shift in African American leadership during the Progressive Era. At the turn of the century the most influential African American leader was Booker T. Washington. Formerly enslaved, Washington founded Alabama's Tuskegee Institute in 1881 to train African Americans in 30 trades. Washington argued that equality would be achieved not through campaigns for reform but when African Americans gained the education and skills to become valuable members of their communities. In 1895 he spelled out this view:

> "... [T]he agitation of questions of social equality is the extremist folly.... [P]rogress in the enjoyment of all privileges that will come to use must be the result of severe and constant struggle rather than of artificial forcing. No race that has anything to contribute to the market of the world is long in any degree ostracized."

Yet as the great changes in society that accompanied progressive reform largely bypassed African Americans, a new leadership arose that rejected Washington's approach to achieving equality. The most prominent new African American leader was W.E.B. Du Bois, a Harvard-educated history professor at Atlanta University. Du Bois argued that suffrage was the way to end white supremacy, stop the lynching of

▲ **EDUCATION** Progressives believed in compulsory public education to keep children out of factories and to provide them with proper values. **Why did many states require high school students to study American history?**

CHAPTER 23 The Progressive Era 1893–1920

The NAACP was not the first African American national civil rights organization. In 1890 newspaper editor Thomas Fortune formed the Afro-American League of the United States. Located in Chicago it worked to promote civil rights. More radical in its approach was the Niagara Movement, whose members demanded an immediate end to racial discrimination, equal justice and housing, and full voting rights. Its views were attacked by moderates like Booker T. Washington, and it failed to attract much support, but it helped to lay the foundation for the emergence of the NAACP.

CHAPTER 23 SECTION 3

ASSESS

Check Understanding
Assign Section 3 Review as homework or an in-class activity.

Evaluate
Assign the Section 3 Quiz in the TCR, or use the History of a Free Nation Testmaker to create a customized quiz.

Reteach
Have students complete Reteaching Activity 23-3.

Enrich
Suggest students research a current social problem in cities, such as deteriorating housing, homelessness, or substance abuse, and suggest ways in which reform movements could attack the problem and how government could aid in solving it.

CLOSE
Discuss the measures that could have been taken by progressives to provide assistance to both immigrants and African Americans.

Visualizing History Point out that Progressives feared the immigrants' values and culture would overshadow the "American" way of life.
Answer to Caption: expanded democracy and reformed education

Visualizing History ▶ **IN THE CITIES** The rapid growth of cities led to a push for building codes and zoning laws. Other areas of progressive reform included child labor and foods. *In what other areas did progressives help change American society?*

African Americans, and gain better schools. In 1905 Du Bois and 28 other leaders convened at Niagara Falls to demand full political rights and responsibilities for African Americans as well as an end to racial discrimination.

This call eventually resulted in the founding of the National Association for the Advancement of Colored People (NAACP) in 1909. "The power of the ballot we need in sheer self-defense," Du Bois said, "else what shall save us from a second slavery?" Du Bois became the editor of the NAACP's magazine, *The Crisis*. In fiery editorials he called for African Americans to fight openly against injustice and discrimination.

The End of the Progressive Era

Despite the failure of most progressives to be concerned about such questions, progressive reform helped change American society in many ways. Although they excluded large groups from their efforts, the progressives expanded democracy, reformed education, and improved the quality of life for millions of men, women, and children. Except for the two amendments to the Constitution in 1919 and 1920, progressivism in America ended as the United States entered World War I. Americans turned from reforming their own society to a crusade to "make the world safe for democracy."

Section 3 ★ Review

Checking for Understanding
1. **Identify** Booker T. Washington, W.E.B. Du Bois, *Plessy* v. *Ferguson*.
2. **Define** literacy test.
3. **Describe** how some progressive reforms worked to limit the political power of immigrants.
4. **Discuss** the status of African Americans during the Progressive Era.

Critical Thinking
5. **Making Comparisons** Compare the methods of Booker T. Washington and W.E.B. Du Bois for increasing African Americans' participation in society.

UNIT 7 Entering a New Century: 1867–1920

Answers to SECTION 3 REVIEW
1. Booker T. Washington, 643; W.E.B. Du Bois, 643; *Plessy* v. *Ferguson*, 643
2. All vocabulary words are defined in the Glossary.
3. City government reform and the direct primary weakened political bosses, whose power base often was in the immigrant community.
4. Discrimination and segregation continued. Progressives considered African Americans to be inferior to whites, and with few exceptions, their problems were ignored. African Americans formed their own reform organizations, such as the NAACP.
5. Washington believed that African Americans were not prepared to achieve equality immediately. He wanted them to learn skills, acquire property, and develop habits of thrift and industry. DuBois wanted equal rights immediately.

Social Studies Skills

Critical Thinking Skills

▲ A GROUP OF IMMIGRANT WOMEN AT WORK

Recognizing Fallacies in a Line of Reasoning

A fallacy in a line of reasoning is an error in thinking something out. The fallacy may be an unsupported argument or a mistaken conclusion.

To determine whether there is a fallacy in a line of reasoning, ask the following questions:
- Is there any connection between the facts and the conclusion? If not, the statement contains a fallacy. If there is a connection, go on to the next question.
- Is there only a loose connection between the facts and the conclusion? If there is, go on to the next question.
- Are there enough facts given to reach the conclusion, or is additional information needed? If more facts are needed, the statement contains a fallacy.

The following example contains a statement of fact and a conclusion. Read the statement and note how the three steps have been applied:

In the early 1900s, the managers of women workers were almost always men. This was because women lacked the ability to direct others. (There is a loose connection between the fact that men were managers and the conclusion that women did not have the ability. But more facts are needed to support that inability was the reason. What roles did lack of educational opportunities for women and biases of male bosses play? The conclusion that women did not have management ability is not supported. The reasoning contains a fallacy.)

Practicing the Skill

For further practice in this skill, read the following sentences, and determine if a fallacy exists. If so, explain why a fallacy is present.

1. The Constitution did not contain provisions against child labor, so the government was powerless to do anything about it.
2. The muckrakers published many books and articles, so the entire public became more aware of social injustices.
3. It was difficult to operate a democratic government and not allow women to vote, so many Western states granted women full suffrage by 1914.

LESSON PLAN
Mastering Social Studies Skills

Teaching Recognizing Fallacies in a Line of Reasoning

Have students read the examples and apply the questions. Ask: What possible conclusion might be drawn from the fact that the managers of women in 1900 were almost always men? (Women were not considered competent enough to manage others.) What information would be needed to prove this? (Sample: facts comparing management ability of men and women) What is the more probable conclusion? (fewer opportunities due to discrimination against women)

Did You Know?

The term *sweatshop* comes from what was called the *sweating system*, a system of subcontracting. A garment manufacturer, for instance, gave materials to a middleman, who then subcontracted the work to tailors and seamstresses who worked at home or in small shops.

Answers to SOCIAL STUDIES SKILLS

1. The statement contains a fallacy. There is a definite connection between the fact and the conclusion, yet it is a mistaken conclusion because the Constitution is a flexible document and provides for measures that are "necessary and proper." More information is needed to support the conclusion.
2. The conclusion is false. There would seem to be a definite connection between the fact and the conclusion; however, the fact that books and magazines are published does not necessarily mean that the entire public will be better informed. The word *entire* is the key word.
3. No fallacy. There is a definite connection between the fact and the conclusion, and no other information is needed to support the claim.

REVIEW CHAPTER 23

Answers

Reviewing Facts

1. The muckrakers exposed unsafe working conditions, corruption in politics, and other social problems through books and magazine articles. Public pressure following such reports resulted in many of the problems being addressed through regulations or laws.
2. Twenty percent of society lived in comfort, 25 percent lived in dire poverty, and 55 percent just survived. Exploitation of the powerless—workers, women, children, and immigrants—was widespread.
3. Improvements included commission plan and city manager form of government and public ownership or regulation of public utilities.
4. It was more difficult to convince people nationwide of the need for a reform; a conservative Supreme Court and Senate moved slowly on reform, and until the Seventeenth Amendment (1913) senators were not directly elected; the Constitution limited any national reform legislation to areas falling under Congress's interstate commerce power.
5. Reformers admired big business's methods and expert management and applied them to solving social problems.
6. Reforms included minimum employment age and other laws to reform child labor, workers' compensation for workers injured in industrial accidents, regulation of working conditions and hours for women, and an attack on overcrowded, unsanitary sweatshops.
7. Although most socialist goals were not realized, socialists made progressive reforms seem mild—and thus more acceptable—in comparison.
8. Most progressives believed in reforming capitalism rather than abolishing it.

Understanding Concepts

1. It reduced the power of political bosses and gave voters more power by providing a direct voice in legislation and in nomination and election of officeholders.
2. Workers' compensation laws eased the poverty of injured workers and their families and resulted in safer workplaces; child labor reform increased school enrollment as interest in children's welfare was manifested by a

CHAPTER 23 ★ REVIEW

Using Vocabulary

Imagine that you are a muckraker who is investigating the need for urban reform. Use the following words to write an article summarizing the corruption and stating your recommendations.

social gospel   referendum
recall   pragmatism
direct primary   initiative

Reviewing Facts

1. **Discuss** the role of the muckrakers in promoting social change.
2. **Describe** the inequalities that existed between the upper and lower classes of society.
3. **List** the improvements in city government achieved through progressive reform efforts.
4. **Explain** why reform was more successful at state and local levels than at the national level.
5. **State** the connection between progressive reform and big business management methods.
6. **Identify** reforms that improved the lives of industrial workers.
7. **Indicate** the importance of the socialist movement in early twentieth-century reform.
8. **Discuss** why progressives were not considered to be radical reformers.

Understanding Concepts

Reform

1. To what extent did reform in government extend democracy in the Progressive Era?
2. What changes did labor reforms bring to other areas of society in the early 1900s?

Values and Beliefs

3. Describe the values of the people who preached the social gospel and pioneered social programs.
4. How did progressives' beliefs about immigrant cultures influence their reform activities?

Critical Thinking

1. **Understanding Cause and Effect** To what extent were progressive reformers inspired by the Populists? Consider the membership, goals, and approach to problem solving of each reform group.
2. **Analyzing Artifacts** Study the picture on this page from *Harper's Weekly* and answer the questions that follow.
   a. What is the purpose of this picture?
   b. What is the central focus of the picture?
   c. Do you think this picture is effective? Explain your answer.

Writing About History

Classification

Classification is the writing method that organizes information about a complex whole into smaller, more useful categories.

646 UNIT 7 Entering a New Century: 1867–1920

CHAPTER 23 ★ REVIEW

Use classification to organize all the progressive reforms discussed in this chapter and to write an essay on how progressive reform changed society. Your teacher will give you specific instructions on the essay's length and the assignment's due date.

Cooperative Learning

Working in a group of three, organize a debate among candidates for governor during the early 1900s. Select one student to be a socialist follower of Eugene Debs, another to be a socialist follower of Daniel De Leon, and the third student to be a progressive reform candidate. Candidates should prepare statements expressing their views regarding reform, what they will do once elected, and why voters should support them. After completing their statements, students should exchange them with the other group members so that each candidate can prepare a rebuttal statement to the other candidates' positions.

Social Studies Skills

Understanding History Through Political Cartoons

In a single picture, a political cartoon from the past can provide special insight into the issues that concerned the public. When you look at a political cartoon, study all the details—the setting, the faces, the clothing, the potential action—and they will help you understand history when it was current news.

Practicing the Skill

Analyze the political cartoon on this page, then answer the questions that follow.
1. What is the setting for the cartoon?
2. How does it tell you who the "good guys" and the "bad guys" are?
3. On each of the giants is printed a different name: J.J. Hill, Morgan, Gould, Oxnard, and Rockefeller. Do you know who these "giants" are? Would your answer be different if you were in high school in 1904? Explain.
4. What does the cartoon tell you about what was happening at the time?

Using Your Journal

As your notes show, women were successful in getting the right to vote in several Western states. Why, then, do you think some felt that a constitutional amendment granting women the right to vote was needed? Write your answer in your journal.

REVIEW CHAPTER 23

b. the man in the foreground
c. Answers may vary, but students should support their opinions.

Practicing the Skill

1. Some students may say a city; others may recognize the setting as Wall Street.
2. The giants are the bad guys, and Roosevelt is the good guy, the little "giant-killer."
3. Most students will recognize Rockefeller. They were obviously prominent businessmen, and they would likely have been featured in the news.
4. There were giant, powerful trusts that Roosevelt was trying to cut down to size.

❓ Chapter Bonus Test Question

This question may be used for extra credit on the chapter test. What was the significance of the Progressive Movement? (The innovations and reforms progressives championed paved the way for later reforms.)

Using Your Journal

Students should recognize that a constitutional amendment has the power of the federal government behind it to enforce it and provides equal voting rights for women throughout the nation.

---

juvenile justice system and in the formation of organizations for young people.
3. Many reformers sympathized with the sufferings of others. Some reformers wanted to change the values and behavior of the less fortunate.
4. Their reforms were designed to make immigrants' values and behavior more "American."

Critical Thinking

1. Although progressives supported some Populist reforms, progressivism was city-based and national in appeal, and Populism was regional and rural; Populists were victims of the need for reform, progressives were not; Populists believed that the people could solve social problems; progressives believed in expert problem solvers.
2. a. to show changes bought about by the automobile

PLANNING GUIDE Chapter 24 White House Reformers

Daily Lesson Objectives	Teacher Classroom Resources	Multimedia
SECTION 1 **Roosevelt's Progressive Domestic Policies** 1 Day pp. 650–654 1. Explain why Theodore Roosevelt became known as a "trust buster." 2. Identify the series of events that led to the settlement of the 1902 coal strike.	Chapter 24 Study Guide Reproducible Lesson Plan Section Quiz Reteaching Activity 24-1 Chapter 24 Primary and Secondary Source Readings Chapter 24 Cooperative Learning Activity	Student Self-Test Software Testmaker Section Focus Transparency 75 Chapter 24 Skills Transparency
SECTION 2 **The Taft Presidency** 1 Day pp. 656–659 1. Explain the impact of the Payne-Aldrich Tariff. 2. Describe the reactions of Roosevelt and the public to Taft's leadership.	Reproducible Lesson Plan Reteaching Activity 24-2 Section Quiz	Student Self-Test Software Testmaker Section Focus Transparency 76 The Presidents: A Picture History of Our Nation
SECTION 3 **The Election of 1912** 1 Day pp. 660–663 1. Relate the events that led to the formation of the Progressive party. 2. Explain how a split in the Republican party helped lead to Woodrow Wilson's election in 1912.	Reproducible Lesson Plan Reteaching Activity 24-3 Section Quiz American Portrait 45 Chapter 24 Primary and Secondary Source Readings Reinforcing Social Studies Skills 25, 28, 32, 55, 69–72	Student Self-Test Software Testmaker Section Focus Transparency 77 Chapter 24 Map Transparency Powers of the President The Presidents: A Picture History of Our Nation
SECTION 4 **Wilson's Progressivism** 1 Day pp. 665–671 1. Explain why Wilson had congressional support for his programs. 2. List the accomplishments of Wilson's domestic program.	Reproducible Lesson Plan Reteaching Activity 24-4 Section Quiz Chapter 24 Enrichment Activity Reinforcing Social Studies Skills 69–72 Writer's Guidebook Spanish Summaries & Glossary	Student Self-Test Software Testmaker Section Focus Transparency 78 Chapter 24 Map Transparency Unit 7 Digest Transparencies Vocabulary Puzzlemaker Audiocassette, Chapter 24 Economics in Action
CHAPTER REVIEW AND EVALUATION 1 Day	Chapter 24 Test Chapter 24 Performance Assessment Activity	Student Self-Test Software Testmaker

00:00 OUT OF TIME? If time does not permit teaching the entire chapter, use the Chapter 24 Summary on pages 676-677 and the Chapter 24 audiocassette (English and Spanish) to point out the main ideas of the chapter.

PLANNING GUIDE

Cultural Diversity Activity

Critical Thinking Between 1880 and 1924, over 27 million immigrants entered the United States. The numbers alarmed nativists and awakened anti-immigrant feeling. In 1917 nativists succeeded in getting Congress to pass a bill requiring that all immigrants over the age of 16 pass a test demonstrating their literacy in any one language. The bill became law over President Wilson's veto. He argued that illiteracy shows a lack of opportunity, not a lack of ability. Ask students to research the nation's immigration laws from 1790 to 1917. Ask them to consider the causes and the effects of each law. Then ask students to consider what restrictions, if any, they would place on immigration today. Ask the class to justify restrictions and brainstorm possible consequences.

Performance Assessment Activity

Linking Past and Present Ask students to choose one of the following reforms addressed by progressive presidents: regulation of business, protection of workers, social issues, the environment. Then have them create a report that shows how that issue was addressed in the early 1900s and the way it is viewed today. Each report should account for similarities and differences in the way the problem is defined and in proposed solutions to it. This activity may be done individually or in small groups.

POSSIBLE RUBRIC FEATURES: Content information, research skills, organization, collaborative skills, written and visual communication skills, presentation

Chapter Resources

Literature from the Period

Dreiser, Theodore. *The Financier.* 1912.

Du Bois, W.E.B. "Of the Meaning of Progress." 1903.

Readings for the Student

Dillion, Richard H. "The Most Unique and Majestic of Nature's Marvels." *American History Illustrated,* Vol. 25, No. 4, September/October 1990.

"Environmentalism." *Cobblestone,* Vol. 10, No. 8, August 1988.

Morris, Edmund. *The Rise of Theodore Roosevelt.* Ballantine Books, 1980.

Readings for the Teacher

Harbaugh, William H. *The Life and Times of Teddy Roosevelt.* Oxford University Press, 1975.

Link, Arthur S. *Woodrow Wilson: Revolution, War and Peace.* Harlan Davidson, 1979.

Multimedia Resources

The Federal Reserve System. Federal Reserve Board. (VHS, 30 minutes)

Focus 1900–1909. ABC Wide World of Learning. (color, 58 minutes)

Theodore Roosevelt—Cowboy in the White House. Centron (29 minutes)

Theodore Roosevelt: A Portrait of Power. Prentice-Hall Media. (color, sound filmstrip)

The Time Tunnel: American History Series 2. Focus Media. (Apple diskette, backup)

The U.S. Economic System. United Learning. (VHS, 75 minutes)

Key to Ability Levels

Teaching strategies have been coded for varying learning styles and abilities.

L1 Basic activities for all students

L2 Average activities for average to above-average students

L3 Challenging activities for above-average students

LEP Limited English Proficiency activities

Glencoe Links to the Humanities

Link to Literature

- Macmillan Literature: American Literature Text—Edgar Lee Masters, Jean Toomer, Countee Cullen

Link to Music

American Music: Cultural Traditions

CHAPTER 24

BEGINNING THE CHAPTER

Ask students what kinds of legislation progressives wanted the government to pass. (Answers may vary, but students should note antitrust legislation, legislation to regulate the railroads and the banking industry, labor legislation.) Then ask them which reform they believe was the most necessary and why.

Linking Across Time

Although the reforms instituted and carried out by the progressive Presidents addressed specific issues of their time, the major areas that concerned them—controlling big business, protecting workers, and correcting social ills—remain concerns today. Among contemporary problems are the organization of global communications (regulating big business), issues relating to discrimination in the workplace (worker protection), and the disposal of hazardous waste (correcting a social ill).

Recording Journal Notes

To help students get started, ask them to list the three progressive Presidents—Roosevelt, Taft, and Wilson—leaving space for specific information on each one.

CHAPTER 24

White House Reformers
1900–1914

▶ **EARLY TELETYPEWRITER**

Setting the Scene

Focus

From 1900 to 1917, progressive reforms at the national level were aided by three strong-minded Presidents: Theodore Roosevelt, William Howard Taft, and Woodrow Wilson. These Presidents had different political philosophies, styles, and temperaments. Yet each worked to control big business, gain protection for workers, and protect the American people from social ills.

Concepts to Understand

★ How interests and positions of the progressives were translated into federal legislation
★ How business practices worked to limit economic competition

Read to Discover . . .

★ in what ways Roosevelt was successful or disappointing as a progressive leader.
★ what progressive reforms were achieved by Wilson as President.

Journal Notes

Note instances in your reading where Presidents appealed directly to the nation in order to gain support for new or controversial programs.

CULTURAL
- 1902 First Rose Bowl game played
- 1903 Orville Wright flies first heavier-than-air airplane
- 1906 San Francisco earthquake causes extensive damage
- 1907 Electric washing machine invented

1900 — **1904**

POLITICAL
- 1901 Theodore Roosevelt becomes President
- 1906 Pure Food and Drug Act passed

648 UNIT 7 Entering a New Century: 1867–1920

✚ EXTRA CREDIT PROJECT

Theodore Roosevelt had a varied career before he became President. Among other things, he served as a New York State representative, a rancher, a New York City police commissioner, an officer in the Spanish-American War, and governor of New York. Ask interested students to research what Roosevelt accomplished in each of these careers, with particular emphasis on the way each related to his progressivism. Have students present their findings to the class in the form of brief oral reports.

History AND ART
The Grand Canyon of the Yellowstone
by Thomas Moran, 1872

On a government expedition to the West, Moran made sketches for a series of paintings. His work prompted Congress to designate Yellowstone a national park.

◀ BASEBALL CAP, EARLY 1900s

- **1908** First Model T Ford automobile produced
- **1908** William Howard Taft elected President

1908

- **1913** Congress designates Mother's Day as the second Sunday in May
- **1912** Woodrow Wilson elected President
- **1912** Progressive party is formed
- **1913** Federal Reserve System created

1912

Teacher Notes

CHAPTER 24 CONCEPTS

Concept Mapping Activity

Draw the following concept map on the chalkboard, and have students copy it into their notebooks. Ask them to underline the key words in the generalization. Emphasize that the details of these topics will help them understand more about the influence of special-interest groups.

```
    Reformers make some
    progress in solving
     economic and social
          problems
          /        \
   Interests/     Economic
   Positions     Competi-
                    tion
```

History AND ART

Thomas Moran said of this painting, "I cast all my claims to being an artist into this one picture of the Great Canyon and am willing to abide by the judgment of it."

- *GTV: A Geographic Perspective on American History*

Side 3, Chapter 15
Title: *A Progress Report*
Subject: Early environmental reforms, 1870–1920

See GTV Guide page 55 for complete lesson plan.

LESSON PLAN
SECTION 1, 650–655

FOCUS

Bellringer
Before taking roll at the beginning of the class period, display Focus Transparency 78 on the overhead projector, and assign the accompanying Focus Activity Sheet.

Objectives
Point out the objectives on this page to students in previewing the section content.

Motivating Activity
Remind students that they have studied 25 Presidents so far in this text. Ask them to identify those they feel were effective. Have them suggest what special qualities made these Presidents good leaders.

Then ask volunteers to read aloud the lists they made for the Bellringer activity. Discuss whether these qualities would make Roosevelt an effective leader. Mention that President Roosevelt, the twenty-sixth President, has been described as "the most perfectly equipped and the most effective politician" of the first 26 Presidents. Tell students that as they read this section, they will learn about the qualities that contributed to Roosevelt's success.

Use Skills Transparency 24.

Assign students the Chapter 24 Reading in Primary and Secondary Source Readings.

SECTION 1

The Square Deal

Setting the Scene

Section Focus

When Theodore Roosevelt succeeded William McKinley as President, leaders of industry feared that he would use the power of his office to break up existing trusts. With Roosevelt's first speeches, their worst fears were realized. The President made it clear that he intended to carry out his "Square Deal," based on the idea that every individual is "entitled to no more and to receive no less."

Objectives

After studying this section, you should be able to
★ explain why Theodore Roosevelt became known as a "trustbuster."
★ identify the series of events that led to settlement of the 1902 coal strike.
★ examine Roosevelt's efforts for conservation of wilderness areas.
★ discuss Roosevelt's legacy to the United States.

Key Term

conservation

◀ INDUSTRIAL FLATIRON

When Theodore Roosevelt received the Republican vice-presidential nomination in 1900, the powerful Republican leader Mark Hanna warned that there would be only one life between "that cowboy" and the White House. When the election resulted in a Republican victory, Hanna turned to McKinley and said, "Now it is up to you to live." However, after McKinley's assassination in 1901, Theodore Roosevelt—the "cowboy," the reformer, the progressive—did indeed become President of the United States.

■ The Trustbuster

Roosevelt described his approach to social problems as the "Square Deal," a belief that all people should have an equal opportunity to succeed through strong personal ethics, a sense of fairness, and adherence to the spirit of the law. Roosevelt also promised America that he would continue McKinley's policies unbroken. Not having become President by election, Roosevelt felt he did not have the authority to push a general program of reform through Congress. During this time, however, industries were merging at an all-time high rate. This rash of mergers prompted Roosevelt to urge Congress to pass legislation regulating big business.

Popular Support for Regulation

When Congress did not respond, Roosevelt turned to the American people to garner support for his program. The response was overwhelming. Government leaders responded with a series of moves designed

650   UNIT 7 Entering a New Century: 1867–1920

Classroom Resources for SECTION 1

Teacher's Classroom Resources
- Chapter 24 Study Guide
- Reproducible Lesson Plan
- Reteaching Activity 24-1
- Chapter 24 Cooperative Learning Activity
- Chapter 24 Primary and Secondary Source Readings
- Section Quiz

Multimedia
- Section Focus Transparency 78
- Chapter 24 Skills Transparency
- Testmaker
- Student Self-Test Software

to limit the trusts. First, the attorney general took the Northern Securities Company to court. In 1904 the Supreme Court overturned previous court decisions and ruled that Northern Securities, which had tried to attain a monopoly of northwestern railroads, had violated the Sherman Act.

Legislation to Assist Antitrust Suits

Roosevelt was not opposed to all trusts. He believed the government should leave honest corporations alone. Only the trusts that damaged the public or worked outside the law should be regulated or broken up. In his own words, "We draw the line against misconduct, not against wealth."

Roosevelt also understood that trust-busting suits could not prevent monopolies. Well-considered cases brought to court at the appropriate time, however, could force even the most powerful trust to obey the law. Roosevelt's reputation as a trustbuster grew.

Eventually, Congress followed Roosevelt's lead and, in 1903, passed the Expedition Act, which gave federal antitrust suits precedence on the dockets of circuit courts. An act of Congress also established the Department of Commerce and Labor, empowered to investigate interstate commerce. In addition, the Department of Justice started more trust-busting suits against corporations than they had at any time during the three previous administrations.

■ The Coal Strike of 1902

One of the most prolonged strikes in United States history started in May 1902, when nearly 150,000 workers walked out of the anthracite mines of eastern Pennsylvania. Terrible conditions precipitated this strike: low wages, frequent layoffs, and the requirement to live in cheaply built company towns. The strikers drew widespread public support.

▲ **On Strike** The major weapon for men and women workers against management was the strike. Coal miners at Shenandoah, Pennsylvania, demonstrate to win better pay and working conditions during the 1902 coal strike. *How was the strike settled?*

CHAPTER 24 White House Reformers 1900–1914 651

CHAPTER 24 SECTION 1

TEACH

Guided Practice
Recognizing Cause and Effect Provide students with copies of the following cause-and-effect chart, omitting the causes and effects. Have them complete the chart. **L1**

Events
- Roosevelt asked Congress to pass legislation regulating big business.
- Roosevelt made speeches to the American people asking for support of his reform program.

Causes
- Industrial mergers reached an all-time high.
- U.S. Steel Corporation tried to attain a monopoly of northwestern railroads.

Effects
- Congress passed the Expedition Act.
- Congress established the Department of Commerce and Labor.

Visualizing History In 1869 about half of the nation's industrial power came from water; by 1900 steam engines supplied 80 percent of the nation's industrial power. Coal kept those steam engines running.
Answer to Caption: Roosevelt's representative, Root, met with Morgan, who forced the mine operators to back down.

Special Needs

Reading Disability One problem many students with reading comprehension or attention problems have is working through a section of material in a timely fashion. They tend to lose their sense of purpose in the reading or become distracted by movement or noise. One way to help them stay focused on their objectives is to set both a goal and a time limit. Start students in Section 1 with a search for the names of the representative of the United Mine Workers and the spokesperson for the mine employers. Give one minute as the time goal.

CHAPTER 24
SECTION 1

Did You Know?

Theodore Roosevelt had a high opinion of himself. When he published his memoirs of the Spanish-American War, the publisher ordered an extra supply of the letter "I."

Food of the Times

As early as 1883, the federal government was investigating the use of additives to prevent spoilage of canned and processed foods. Government agents tested the preservatives used in milk, meat, butter, and cocoa as well as in canned vegetables and fruits. Their findings and Upton Sinclair's novel *The Jungle* led to the Pure Food and Drug Act of 1906.

▲ FACTORY WORKERS ON STRIKE

Management and Labor in a Deadlock

John Mitchell, who represented the United Mine Workers, asked mine operators to consider allowing an independent party to determine whether miners' wages were adequate. But George F. Baer, principal spokesperson for the mine employers, refused Mitchell's suggestion, saying that "anthracite mining is a business and not a religious, sentimental, or academic proposition." Baer further alienated a public already sympathetic to the workers when he refused to listen to the miners' complaints, to submit to arbitration, or to recognize the United Mine Workers as the true representative of the mine workers. This attitude and the strong conviction behind the miners' position caused the strike to drag on, with no prospect of settlement. Appeals for action poured in to the President.

Presidential Action Helps Resolve the Strike

Roosevelt had no power to force an agreement, yet he resolved to use whatever influence he had to end the strike. Early in October, Roosevelt invited representatives of the operators to meet union representative Mitchell at the White House. Nothing was accomplished in a stormy session, but public opinion soured even more toward the employers.

Faced with this deadlock, Roosevelt considered a legally questionable seizure of the mines by federal troops, but after a conference between Elihu Root, the President's representative, and J. Pierpont Morgan, whose banking firm indirectly controlled most of the anthracite mines, Morgan was able to put enough pressure on the operators to force them to back down. Morgan's action was apparently prompted by concern that United States businesses would suffer if the strike continued. Roosevelt's action in using the prestige of his office and his personal influence to settle the strike was recognized in this country and abroad as an important precedent. The London *Times* commented:

> *The President has done a very big and entirely new thing. We are witnessing not merely the end of the coal strike, but the definite entry of a powerful government on a novel sphere of operation.*

■ Efforts at Conservation

Even before Theodore Roosevelt became President, the nation was adopting a policy of **conservation**, the planned management of natural resources to prevent destruction or neglect. In 1872 an act of Congress created Yellowstone National Park, and the 1890s saw the establishment of four more national parks. In 1891 Congress enacted the Forest Reserve Act, empowering Presidents to set aside land for national forests and withdraw forest lands from the public domain. In this way, land could be set aside for preservation rather than left available for private claim or purchase.

Action Based on Personal Commitment

Roosevelt's efforts to preserve the nation's natural resources stemmed from a deep love for America's wilderness. His beliefs made conservation popular. He stimulated public

---

Cooperative Learning

Organize students into groups of four. Have each group focus on the topic "Conservation became a household word during Roosevelt's presidency." Give each student a set of colored chips. When a student wishes to speak, he or she must place a chip in the center of the table. Give the groups 10 or 15 minutes to discuss what measures are being taken toward conservation in their communities and across the country today. All students must spend their chips in the time given for discussion. Ask one student in each group to summarize his or her group's discussion. **L2, L3**

interest in the subject by writing, by taking publicized holiday trips to the West, and by constantly pushing for better conservation laws. Roosevelt also used the power and prestige of the presidential office to promote the cause.

Laws to Preserve Our Natural Legacy

The Newlands Act of 1902, supported by Roosevelt, provided federal aid to irrigation projects in arid states. He also enforced laws against the illegal occupation of public lands. Using the Forest Reserve Act, Roosevelt more than tripled the amount of land previously set aside for national forests.

Roosevelt also enlisted states' aid in the conservation effort. In May 1908 he called a national conference on conservation that resulted in the creation of more than 40 state conservation commissions and a National Conservation Commission, which began an inventory of the nation's natural resources.

Wisconsin senator Robert La Follette, though often critical of Roosevelt, predicted that future historians would conclude that Roosevelt's greatest achievement was not the Square Deal, but the preservation of the nation's natural resources for the benefit of all.

■ Further Regulation

As the presidential election of 1904 approached, the "Old Guard" of the Republican party was unhappy at the prospect of four more years of the Rough Rider in the White House. The New York *Sun* accused Roosevelt of "bringing wealth to its knees" and "putting labor unions above the law." It seemed possible that Mark Hanna might try to block Roosevelt's nomination, but Hanna died in February 1904. Roosevelt had popular opinion behind him and was, as even his enemies admitted, the ablest politician of the day. He received the unanimous nomination from the Republican national convention.

After being elected to a full term in 1904, Roosevelt felt confident enough to respond to the growing public clamor for stricter regulation of the railroads. The Interstate Commerce Commission had only limited success in controlling the unfair practices and political influence of these powerful businesses. Newspaper editor William Allen White spoke for many when he wrote.

> *The railroads cannot name senators, pack state conventions, run legislatures, and boss politics generally . . . and then successfully maintain that they are private carriers doing a private business.*

Visualizing History ▲ CONSERVATION Theodore Roosevelt was an avid supporter of the conservation movement. Roosevelt worked to protect wildlife and scenic areas. *What was the purpose of the Newlands Act?*

CHAPTER 24 SECTION 1

Did You Know?

On one occasion when President Theodore Roosevelt was hunting, he supposedly refused to shoot a bear cub that crossed his line of fire. Following the incident, *Washington Post* cartoonist Clifford K. Berryman drew a cartoon of Roosevelt turning away from the helpless cub. Seeing the cartoon, candy-store owner Morris Michtom began to make toy bear cubs in 1903, naming them "Teddy Bears." The teddy bears soon gained wide popularity, making Michtom a rich man.

Visualizing History Naturalists like John Muir led the campaign to create Yosemite National Park in California. Roosevelt supported that effort. **Answer to Caption:** He provided federal aid for irrigation projects.

Sidelights: *The Jungle*

Perhaps no book can match Upton Sinclair's *The Jungle* in terms of public popularity *and* impact on government policy. Sinclair continued his muckraking ways, publishing a number of controversial novels. He also ran for Congress and the governorship of California on the Socialist ticket.

CHAPTER 24 SECTION 1

ASSESS

Check Understanding

Assign Section 1 Review as homework or an in-class activity.

Evaluate

Assign the Section 1 quiz in the TCR, or use the History of a Free Nation Testmaker to create a customized quiz.

Reteach

Have students write a paragraph summarizing Roosevelt's "Square Deal" achievements.

Have students complete Reteaching Activity 24-1.

Enrich

Have students research and write a report about the other reform legislation passed during Theodore Roosevelt's presidency.

CLOSE

Ask students if they think Roosevelt would have been reelected based on his accomplishments. Have them give reasons for their answers.

Some leaders proposed that the railroads be owned and operated by the government. Thinking such a step would lead to far-reaching disaster, Roosevelt urged tighter regulation as an alternative. As a result of popular support, clever politics, and willingness to compromise, Roosevelt was able to push the Hepburn Bill through the Senate 18 months after he urged Congress to act.

The Hepburn Act of 1906 strengthened the Interstate Commerce Act of 1887 in several ways. It abolished the "free pass" that railroads granted to politicians and other influential people such as newspaper editors. It widened the jurisdiction of the Interstate Commerce Commission to include express companies, pipelines, ferries, and sleeping-car companies. Railroad corporations were restrained from operating other businesses.

Most important of all, the Interstate Commerce Commission was granted power to fix rates, although its decisions could be appealed to the courts. Complaints to the commission soon multiplied 40 times, and a great many rates were lowered.

Roosevelt also urged legislation to address abuses in the food and meatpacking industries. The Meat Inspection Act of 1906 gave government the right to inspect meats sold in interstate commerce and the right to enforce cleaner conditions in meatpacking plants.

■ Assessing Roosevelt's Progressive Policies

In spite of Roosevelt's many accomplishments, Congress offered much resistance to his ideas. His legislative achievement was so unimpressive that some critics accused Roosevelt of producing "more noise than accomplishment."

Roosevelt and Politics

Roosevelt failed to effect a revision of the tariff, regarding the issue as "political dynamite." He did use the issue to his advantage, however, occasionally threatening to bring it up unless congressional leaders supported other legislative measures. Roosevelt also never seriously supported long-overdue efforts to make the banking system more stable and the currency system more flexible.

One reason for the failure to produce much reform legislation was Roosevelt's feeling that politics was "the art of the possible." His philosophy of reform was one of gradualism: he was willing to accept half a loaf if he could not get the whole. Furthermore, the Republican leaders in Congress, carryovers from the McKinley-Hanna period, were unsympathetic to progressive legislation.

Roosevelt and History

Although Roosevelt accomplished less than he seemed to promise, he restored the people's faith in the power of the federal government to serve their interests. Through his Square Deal philosophy, he promoted the idea that the cure for the evils of unrestrained individualism was not socialism but moderate reform. Above all he created a demand for reform. According to one historian, "Roosevelt was the best publicity man progressivism ever had."

Section 1 ★ Review

Checking for Understanding

1. **Identify** J. Pierpont Morgan, Expedition Act, Forest Reserve Act, Hepburn Act, Square Deal.
2. **Define** conservation.
3. **Explain** why Roosevelt preferred regulation to trust-busting.
4. **State** how Roosevelt influenced the solution of the 1902 coal strike.

Critical Thinking

5. **Understanding Cause and Effect** Analyze how Roosevelt's conservation policies grew out of his love for the American wilderness.

---

654 UNIT 7 Entering a New Century: 1867–1920

Answers to SECTION 1 REVIEW

1. J. Pierpont Morgan, 652; Expedition Act, 651; Forest Reserve Act, 653; Hepburn Act, 654; Square Deal, 650
2. All vocabulary words are defined in the Glossary.
3. Roosevelt believed that trust busting did not stop the rise of monopolies. It broke them up after the fact. Regulation forced business leaders to obey laws.
4. Roosevelt brought together the mine operators, the miners, and J.P. Morgan, who indirectly controlled the mines. Morgan forced the operators to compromise and settle the strike.
5. Roosevelt was a lover of the wilderness. He wrote about conservation, took holiday trips to the West, and constantly pushed for better conservation laws. He used the power and prestige of his office to promote the cause.

CONNECTIONS — History AND Environment — CONNECTIONS

The Conservation Movement

By the beginning of the twentieth century it was becoming clear that the natural resources Americans had long taken for granted were—in fact—in danger of being used up. Theodore Roosevelt, a champion of conservation, made an effective case for the wise and scientific use of natural resources by people of all ages.

To the Society of American Foresters in 1903, Roosevelt said, "First and foremost, you can never afford to forget for one moment what is the object of forest policy.... Your attention should be directed not to the preservation of the forests as an end in itself, but as the means for preserving and increasing the prosperity of the nation."

Roosevelt's 1907 Arbor Day message to schoolchildren said in part, "Within your lifetime the nation's need for trees will become serious.... You will want what nature once so bountifully supplied and man so thoughtlessly destroyed; and because of that want you will reproach us, not for what we have used, but for what we have wasted...."

Roosevelt abhorred the way the country's national resources were being exploited. For example, irreplaceable resources such as natural gas were wasted, and fires and floods, caused by poor management of land and water services, were common. Roosevelt wanted not only to protect wildlife and scenic areas, but also to ensure efficient use of soil, minerals, and forests.

The National Reclamation Act, also known as the Newlands Act of 1902, was the first major conservation law passed under Roosevelt. It provided for replacing natural services and set aside funds from public land sales for irrigation projects in the West.

During Roosevelt's terms, the size of the national forests were increased from about 40 million acres to more than 190 million acres. Roosevelt also worked to preserve other valuable lands as well. At his direction, the Department of the Interior set aside 80 million acres of coal lands.

▼ ARAPAHO NATIONAL FOREST, COLORADO

Making the Environment Connection

1. What did Roosevelt suggest was the object of forest policy?
2. How did Roosevelt's conservation program relate to the Square Deal?

Linking Past and Present

3. Why has forest conservation received renewed emphasis in recent years?

CHAPTER 24 CONNECTIONS

Teaching Making Connections

Point out that Roosevelt was both a conservationist and an avid hunter. On one East African safari, he and his son shot 17 lions, 12 elephants, 11 buffalo, and 20 rhinoceroses—including 9 rare white rhinoceroses. Ask students if they think one can be both a conservationist and a hunter.

Did You Know?

In 1908 Roosevelt called a National Conservation Congress. It was attended by 44 governors and hundreds of experts. It led to annual governors' meeting and the creation of state conservation commissions.

 VIDEODISC

- *GTV: A Geographic Perspective on American History*

Side 3, Chapter 15
Title: *A Progress Report*
Subject: Early environmental reforms, 1870–1920

See GTV Guide page 55 for complete lesson plan.

Answers to CONNECTIONS

1. To preserve and increase the prosperity of the nation.
2. Government regulation and protection of forests and other natural resources were necessary to conserve them for the benefit of all people and prevent their exploitation by a select few.
3. Concern over global warming brought on by increased carbon dioxide in the atmosphere, which is removed by trees, has led to efforts to slow forest clearing and to the planting of new trees.

LESSON PLAN
SECTION 2, 656–659

FOCUS

Bellringer
Before taking roll at the beginning of the class period, display Focus Activity Transparency 79 on the overhead projector, and assign the accompanying Focus Activity Sheet.

Objectives
Point out the objectives on this page to students in previewing the section content.

Motivating Activity
Review with students the meaning of the words *lobbyists* (well-organized pressure groups) and *insurgents* (people who act contrary to the policies and decisions of their political party). Ask students to name lobby groups today and what these groups do.

The following material is available from Glencoe and may be used to enrich Chapter 24:

CD-Rom
- *The Presidents: A Picture History of Our Nation*

SECTION 2

The Taft Presidency

Setting the Scene

Section Focus
In 1908 Theodore Roosevelt declined to run for reelection, accepting the custom that limited Presidents to two terms. Although his successor, William Howard Taft, was a supporter of Roosevelt's progressive policies, Taft's presidency led not only to a split between Taft and Roosevelt but also to a division of the Republican party itself.

Objectives
After studying this section, you should be able to
★ explain the impact of the Payne-Aldrich Tariff.
★ examine the public reaction to the Ballinger-Pinchot controversy.
★ describe the reactions of Roosevelt and the public to Taft's leadership.

Key Term
income tax

◀ ROOSEVELT AND TAFT IN CONFLICT

Although a distinguished public servant, having served as a judge, as governor of the Philippines, and as Roosevelt's secretary of war, Taft was a reluctant President. His true ambition lay in the judicial, not the executive, branch of government. Remarking on the snow, sleet, and rain that pelted the people coming to his Inaugural Address, Taft said, "Even the elements do protest."

■ Taft in Difficulty

Taft began his term as President by addressing the tariff issue, largely ignored during Roosevelt's eight-year term. Since passage of the Dingley Tariff of 1897, prices had advanced more rapidly than wages, and many blamed the resulting high cost of living on unduly high tariff rates. Some, including Taft, also believed that high rates encouraged monopoly.

Subversion of Tariff Reform
Congress met in March 1909, and within less than a month the House of Representatives passed a measure, introduced by Sereno Payne of New York, that provided for substantial reductions in the tariff without abandoning the principle of protection. Under the leadership of conservative Senator Nelson W. Aldrich of Rhode Island, however, more than 800 amendments were tacked onto the House bill. Many of these amendments were designed to conceal higher rates, such as changing a duty on certain small articles from so much "per hundredweight" to so much "per hundred."

656   UNIT 7 Entering a New Century: 1867–1920

Classroom Resources for SECTION 2

Teacher's Classroom Resources
- Reproducible Lesson Plan
- Reteaching Activity 24-2
- Section Quiz

Multimedia
- Focus Activity Transparency 79
- Testmaker
- Student Self-Test Software
- The Presidents: A Picture History of Our Nation

When Aldrich attempted to railroad the amended bill through the Senate, he was met with resistance in his own party. Several Republican senators, nicknamed "the Insurgents," used their privilege of unlimited debate to reveal the way Aldrich and his allies were carrying out the demands of high-tariff lobbyists instead of the people. Too late, Taft attempted to persuade the Old Guard leaders to reduce the rates, but they made only slight concessions before the bill received Senate approval.

By the time the bill reached Taft's desk, the Payne-Aldrich Tariff contained high duties on iron ore, coal, and hides and increases on other materials. The bill, however, allowed for a corporation tax, established a tariff commission to make a scientific study of rates, and provided for some flexibility in rates at the discretion of the President. For these reasons, and because he feared a split between the Old Guard and the Insurgents in his own party, Taft signed the bill despite its weaknesses.

The public saw Taft's action as a betrayal of his campaign promise. On a speaking tour in the Midwest, Taft argued that the bill fulfilled the Republican platform, adding:

> *If the country . . . wishes the manufacturers all over the country to go out of business, and to have cheaper prices at the expense of the sacrifice of many of our manufacturing interests, then it ought to . . . put the Democratic party in power. . . .*

Despite his efforts, there continued to be widespread dissatisfaction with the tariff and with Taft for supporting it.

Controversy Over an Administrative Dispute

Another blow was dealt to Taft's popularity when a conflict developed between Taft's secretary of the interior, Richard A. Ballinger, and the chief forester, Gifford Pinchot. Ballinger reopened for private purchase certain lands in Montana, Wyoming, and Alaska that had been withdrawn while Roosevelt was President. Pinchot, a well-known conservationist, protested these actions and publicly accused Ballinger of fraud. Taft, convinced of Ballinger's innocence—later confirmed by a congressional investigating committee—dismissed Pinchot for insubordination. But the public viewed Taft's action as a move against the conservation effort begun by Roosevelt, and Taft's popularity plummeted. Even though Ballinger was exonerated of the charges, he eventually resigned his post.

Unpopular Alignment with the Old Guard

Immediately following the Ballinger-Pinchot controversy came an outbreak of Insurgent Republicanism in the House of Representatives, which took the form of an attack on the Old Guard Speaker of the House, Joseph G. "Uncle Joe" Cannon. The speaker had come to enjoy a power over legislation greater in some ways than that of the President. He appointed all committees, he decided what bills should be referred to which committees, and by almost absolute control over debate he could push some measures through without discussion and see that others never reached the floor.

▲ **ROOSEVELT AND TAFT** In this cartoon, a smiling Roosevelt celebrates with Taft, his chosen successor. Soon, however, Roosevelt and Taft found themselves at odds. **Why did Taft dismiss Gifford Pinchot?**

CHAPTER 24 White House Reformers 1900–1914 657

CHAPTER 24 SECTION 2

TEACH

Independent Practice

Journalism Have students imagine they work as newspaper reporters. Their assignment is to cover the speech that Theodore Roosevelt is giving at Osawatomie, Kansas, during the congressional election of 1910. In their articles students should include the subject, content, delivery of the speech, and audience response. **L3**

Fact or Fiction?

Taft and Roosevelt, his predecessor, had been at odds from the beginning of Taft's term as President.

FICTION: Roosevelt had selected Taft as his successor, using his powerful influence to have Taft nominated at the Republican National Convention of 1908. Roosevelt did not break with Taft until 1911, in the wake of the Ballinger-Pinchot controversy.

Teaching Life of the Times

Point out that the first national comprehensive senior-citizen pension plan was set up by the Social Security Act of 1935. Then have students discuss the benefits senior citizens enjoy today as compared with the few benefits they had in the early 1900s.

Life of the Times

The Elderly in Greenwich Village

Although Progressive leaders used the power of government to improve society, not all Americans benefited from reform efforts. Growing old for many Americans in the early 1900s meant a life of poverty, or near poverty, and dependence for many Americans.

The aged poor showed imagination in making ends meet. For example, a survey of elderly residents of New York's Greenwich Village in 1914 showed 74-year-old Mrs. S. working as a janitor in exchange for free rooms and 75-year-old Miss F. subletting one of her three rooms to cover $10 of her $16 monthly rent. Seventy-year-old Mrs. N. took in sewing and washing.

Even when entirely dependent on charity, many aged people managed to create opportunities for recreation. Miss M., financially supported by her church, lived "in proud isolation, scorning her neighbors," and repeated poetry that she had learned as a child in Canada. "I used to go to lectures at [the public] school," she said, "but the only lectures they have now are economical, and I have enough of that at home, and I don't like it!"

The conservative Cannon used the powers of this office to hold up progressive legislation. He also cooperated with Aldrich during the tariff debacle in 1909. Furthermore, Cannon had long been an opponent of conservation. With the motto "Not one cent for scenery," he had stalled the creation of national parks and forests.

Finally, in March 1910, a coalition of Democrats and Republican Insurgents forced a change in the rules of the House that stripped the speaker of much of his power. This attack on Cannon hurt Taft, who in order to keep party harmony aligned himself with the speaker. Thus, by signing the Payne-Aldrich Tariff, by supporting Ballinger against Pinchot, and by backing Cannon, Taft gave the impression that he had "sold the Square Deal down the river." An Insurgent senator described Taft as "a large good-natured body entirely surrounded by people who know exactly what they want." Popular indignation was so great that the congressional elections of 1910 resulted in a sweeping Democratic victory, with Democrats taking the majority in the House and Democrats and Republican Insurgents wresting control of the Senate from the Old Guard.

■ Roosevelt Proclaims "New Nationalism"

During his retirement Roosevelt tried hard to maintain faith in the man he had chosen as his successor, but he found public opinion toward Taft had worsened. In spite of Roosevelt's intention to remain out of politics, Taft's disappointing performance as President soon drew Roosevelt back into the political arena.

Roosevelt aligned himself with the Insurgents in the Republican party, who had started to call themselves "Progressive Republicans," or simply "Progressives." In a speech at Osawatomie, Kansas, during the congressional election of 1910, Roosevelt

658   UNIT 7 Entering a New Century: 1867–1920

Cooperative Learning

Organize students into groups of four or five. Ask each group to consider the accomplishments of Taft's administration. Using one piece of paper per group, have each group member take a turn writing a statement about Taft's achievements. Have each group share its statements with the class. Then discuss any missing information. **L2**

spoke of a new set of policies that he called the "New Nationalism." In words that recalled the Populist platform of the 1890s and foreshadowed the New Deal of the 1930s, Roosevelt said:

> *We are face to face with new conceptions of the relations of property to human welfare. . . . The man who wrongly holds that every human right is secondary to his profit must now give way to the advocate of human welfare, who rightly maintains that every man holds his property subject to the general right of the community to regulate its use to whatever degree the public welfare may require it.*

In his New Nationalism speech, Roosevelt outlined a much more radical program of action than he had ever proposed while in the presidency. He favored both state and federal legislation to actively promote human welfare, including laws to protect women and children in the labor force and workers' compensation for those injured on the job.

Attacking the courts for declaring certain progressive legislation unconstitutional, Roosevelt suggested that state judges be subject to recall and that Supreme Court decisions be reversible by popular vote. By taking such stands, Roosevelt established his position as the natural leader of the Progressive Republicans.

Taft's Successes

Despite Taft's political problems, his administration experienced several successes. Although it was Roosevelt who was nicknamed the "trustbuster," Taft actually prosecuted twice as many antitrust cases in four years as his predecessor had in seven. Taft established the Tariff Board to investigate tariff rates, and under his leadership a federal budget began to take shape. Taft also supported the Sixteenth Amendment, giving Congress power to collect **income taxes,** or taxes on the income of individuals and companies, and the Seventeenth Amendment, calling for direct election of United States senators. In addition, during his administration two new states—New Mexico and Arizona—were admitted to the United States.

Taft genuinely supported Roosevelt's Square Deal policies, but unlike Roosevelt, who claimed an executive right to do anything not forbidden, Taft's judicial background allowed him to use "only those powers expressly authorized by law." Taft also lacked his predecessor's gift for dramatizing issues and enlisting public support. To some degree, Taft brought his political troubles on himself. He had a very different temperament from other politicians, and he had a hard time keeping up with the incessant work of the office. He did not really want to be President; his greatest ambition—later fulfilled—was to sit on the Supreme Court. In addition, he did not enjoy politics, and it is not surprising that he was not a success as a politician. In the end, Taft's administration would be remembered for its failures rather than its achievements.

Section 2 ★ Review

Checking for Understanding

1. **Identify** Payne-Aldrich Tariff, Richard Ballinger, Joseph Cannon, New Nationalism, "the Insurgents."
2. **Define** income tax.
3. **List** the reasons the public thought Taft was destroying the Square Deal.
4. **Explain** Theodore Roosevelt's return to national politics with the New Nationalism program.

Critical Thinking

5. **Making Judgments** Analyze how Taft's leadership led to increasing the power and authority of the federal government.

CHAPTER 24 White House Reformers 1900–1914

CHAPTER 24
SECTION 2

ASSESS

Check Understanding

Assign Section 2 Review as homework or as in-class activity.

Evaluate

Assign the Section 2 Quiz in the TCR, or use the History of a Free Nation Testmaker to create a customized quiz.

Reteach

Have students complete Reteaching Activity 24-2.

Enrich

Have students research how the Mann-Elkins Act increased the power of the Interstate Commerce Commission.

CLOSE

Ask students: Based on what you have learned in this section, do you think Theodore Roosevelt will run in the 1912 presidential election against Taft? Why?

Answers to SECTION 2 REVIEW

1. Payne-Aldrich Tariff, 656; Richard Ballinger, 657; Joseph Cannon, 657; New Nationalism, 658–659; "Insurgent" Senators, 657
2. All vocabulary words are defined in the Glossary.
3. Taft's support of Payne-Aldrich Tariff, of Ballinger's proposal to reclaim land set aside for national forests, and of Joseph Cannon destroyed promises of Square Deal.
4. Announced return to politics in "New Nationalism" speech, which focused on human-welfare needs. Roosevelt was convinced that public wanted progressive reforms to continue under Republican President.
5. Taft prosecuted twice as many cases as Roosevelt; established Tariff Board to investigate tariff rates; supported the Sixteenth and Seventeenth amendments.

LESSON PLAN
SECTION 3, 660–664

FOCUS

Bellringer
Before taking roll at the beginning of the class period, display Focus Activity Transparency 80 on the overhead projector, and assign the accompanying Focus Activity Sheet.

Objectives
Point out the objectives on this page to students in previewing the section content.

Motivating Activity
Ask if any students have ever served as volunteers in an election campaign. Ask those who have to describe the various techniques that are used to get a candidate elected. Then discuss with the class the major elements needed to run a successful political campaign. (money, enthusiasm, campaign staff, publicity, volunteers, and so on) Tell students that Section 3 describes the election of 1912.

Assign students the Chapter 24 Reading on the Progressive party in Primary and Secondary Source Readings.

The following material is available from Glencoe and may be used to enrich Chapter 24:

 CD-ROM
- *The Presidents: A Picture History of Our Nation*

SECTION 3

The Election of 1912

Setting the Scene

Section Focus
With his New Nationalism speech, Theodore Roosevelt returned to the political arena. As the election of 1912 approached, he remained convinced that Taft was unfit for another term as President, and it was not in Roosevelt's nature to sit on the sidelines. Thus the great question in American politics as the campaign began was whether Roosevelt would run again for the presidency.

Objectives
After studying this section, you should be able to
★ relate the events that led to the formation of the Progressive party.
★ explain how a split in the Republican party helped lead to Woodrow Wilson's election in 1912.

Key Term
inheritance tax

◀ **POLITICAL CARTOON, 1912 PRESIDENTIAL ELECTION**

Senator Robert La Follette, a man of great ability and a leader of the recently formed National Progressive Republican League, had the support of many Progressive Republicans for the 1912 presidential nomination. When La Follette suffered a temporary nervous collapse, however, the Progressives turned to Roosevelt. Explaining that his no-third-term pledge referred to a third consecutive term, Roosevelt declared himself a candidate against Taft for the Republican nomination.

■ Roosevelt Challenges Taft

The heated, emotional struggle for control of the Republican party reached its climax at the national convention in June. Conservatives rallied behind Taft, as did many former supporters of the Square Deal who thought Roosevelt too radical or who disliked his running for a third term. Except for some devoted followers of La Follette, the Progressive Republicans lined up for Roosevelt. In states where convention delegates were chosen in primary elections, Roosevelt was generally the choice of the voters.

The Taft forces, however, had the immense advantage of controlling the party machinery. The convention chairperson Elihu Root kept such a tight hold on proceedings that he was accused of driving a steam roller over the Roosevelt forces. The convention's Credentials Committee gave 235 of 254 convention seats to Taft. When Taft received the nomination on the first ballot, Roosevelt charged the Republican party leaders with stealing the nomination. He stood ready, he said, to carry on the battle for progressive principles outside the party.

UNIT 7 Entering a New Century: 1867–1920

Classroom Resources for SECTION 3

Teacher's Classroom Resources
- Reproducible Lesson Plan
- Reteaching Activity 24-3
- Chapter 24 Primary and Secondary Source Readings
- Section Quiz

Multimedia
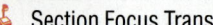
- Section Focus Transparency 80
- Chapter 24 Map Transparency
- Testmaker
- Student Self-Test Software
- Powers of the President
- The Presidents: A Picture History of Our Nation

Formation of Progressive Party

In August a convention met in Chicago to found a new political party—the Progressive party. The delegates were a curious mixture—college professors, social workers, newspaper editors, former Rough Riders, wealthy people motivated by social conscience, and some professional politicians.

Senator Albert J. Beveridge, who had followed Roosevelt out of the Republican party, called on the new party to work for a nobler America. The Progressives, said Beveridge, stood for "social brotherhood" as opposed to "savage individualism," for a "representative government that represents the people," as opposed to invisible government controlled by corrupt bosses and the "robber interest."

The Progressive platform demanded reforms such as a more direct democracy through such means as the initiative and referendum, for conservation of natural resources for the general welfare, for woman suffrage, and for labor reforms such as the prohibition of child labor.

In addition, Progressives called for revision of the currency system and the introduction of an **inheritance tax,** which would be a percentage of the value of an inheritance, levied on the privilege of an heir to receive this property.

The party nominated Theodore Roosevelt for the presidency and immediately acquired a party symbol when the former President announced that he felt "as strong as a bull moose." The Progressive party had a strong enthusiasm and one of the most popular individuals in public life. It also had abundant campaign funds, supplied by wealthy business people who believed that capitalism could survive only if it was reformed.

The Bull Moose crusade was a forlorn hope, however. Most of the Progressives were amateurs with little or no knowledge of practical politics. Party machinery could not be set up in thousands of election districts overnight. All that Roosevelt accomplished by bolting from the Republican party was to give control of the Republican party to the Old Guard, and to ensure the election of a Democratic President.

▼ THE BULL MOOSE, SYMBOL OF THE PROGRESSIVE PARTY

▲ ROOSEVELT THE CAMPAIGNER
Theodore Roosevelt was a vigorous and effective campaigner. The Progressive party platform included a minimum-wage law for women, workers' compensation laws, and strong regulation of child labor. **Who were the Republican and Democratic candidates in the 1912 election?**

Woodrow Wilson and the New Freedom

When the Democratic convention met at Baltimore in June 1912, there was discord between the progressive wing, to which William Jennings Bryan belonged, and the conservative wing, whose delegates represented city political machines. Although

---

Critical Thinking

Analyzing Ideas Point out that during Taft's presidency, Congress passed much progressive legislation, a great deal of it with Taft's backing. For example the Mann-Elkins Act extended the jurisdiction of the ICC to include telegraph and telephone lines, and the Railroad Valuation Act empowered the ICC to establish a basis for fixing fair rates. Furthermore, Congress established postal savings banks to protect the small depositor, and the parcel post to help the small shipper. Ask: Does this legislation conflict with or confirm the image Progressives painted of Taft and the Republicans? **L3**

Taft and Sons Theodore Roosevelt once said, "Taft has the most lovable personality I have ever come in contact with." Their friendship was wrecked, however, on the realities of politics and ambition. *On what ballot was Taft nominated in 1912?*

disclaiming any desire for another nomination, Bryan was influential in seeing that the Democratic platform was as progressive as that of the Bull Moose party itself. After a protracted struggle, Woodrow Wilson, who had won national fame as a reform governor of New Jersey, received the nomination on the 46th ballot, partly through the help of Bryan.

Two Progressive Platforms

In the ensuing campaign Taft was not active, privately expressing the opinion that Wilson was sure to win. The real battle took place between Roosevelt and Wilson. Both men supported progressivism, although under different labels. Wilson countered Roosevelt's New Nationalism with what he called the "New Freedom."

Although there appeared to be little distinction between the philosophies of the two candidates, they did in fact differ. Roosevelt's New Nationalism accepted big business as a fact of life and proposed a more powerful federal government and a strong executive to keep it under control. Wilson's New Freedom viewed monopolies as absolute evils, the antithesis of free competition. He also advocated the use of federal power to ensure more equality of opportunity.

Two Contrasting Candidates

The differences between Wilson and Roosevelt were striking. Roosevelt had long been the best-known political figure in the United States. Wilson, a former university president and college professor, had been active on the American political scene for only three years. Roosevelt, the former Rough Rider, was thought of by the public as a strong fighter in a war on privilege. While Roosevelt enjoyed mixing with all sorts of people, Wilson was aloof.

One writer likened Roosevelt to a great national spectacle, like Niagara Falls. People jammed the halls when he spoke, but it is not certain that they came so much to listen as to gape.

On the campaign platform Wilson's tall, angular figure displayed an ease of manner and his homely face exhibited a warmth he often lacked in personal relations. From his early teens, he had often dreamed of persuading people by using his power of eloquence. Even his strongest enemies had to admit that he could be very persuasive. Although Wilson lacked the magnetism of his rival Roosevelt, he knew how to touch people's conscience and appeal to their sense of reason.

An attempt to assassinate Roosevelt gave him an opportunity to demonstrate his courage and self-possession. On his way to deliver a speech in Milwaukee he was shot in the chest. Pausing only long enough to make sure that his assailant received protection of the police, Roosevelt insisted on delivering his speech before receiving medical attention. Not seriously wounded, he was later able to resume his campaign at full speed.

Results of the Election

The results of the election fulfilled Taft's prediction of victory for Wilson. Although he won the presidency, Wilson actually had fewer popular votes than Roosevelt and Taft combined. Because of the split in the Republican vote, however—and also a surprisingly strong Socialist party vote—Wilson carried 40 of the 48 states, with a total of 435 electoral votes; his opponents together received only 96 electoral votes. So, for the first time since Grover Cleveland's election in 1892, a Democrat became President of the United States.

Wilson's Previous Career

Woodrow Wilson had gained national prominence as a foe of privilege and as an individual with strong powers of leadership. During eight years as president of Princeton University, he not only raised standards and improved teaching, but also fought social privilege as represented by social clubs. As governor of New Jersey he successfully fought political bosses who represented special interests, not the interests of the people as a whole. Under his leadership, the New Jersey legislature enacted an elaborate program of progressive measures.

The extraordinary successes gained by the "scholar in politics" can be explained partly by the fact that from childhood he had been ambitious to hold high office. Not only had he trained himself in public speaking, but he had also devoted much of his life to studying the techniques of effective political leadership. A long-time admirer of the British government, he developed the theory that the President, like the British prime minister, should take the initiative in guiding and promoting legislation. The President alone, in his opinion, stood for the interests of the entire nation.

In addition to books on government, Wilson had written a history of the United States and many articles, mostly on political topics. He was well informed on domestic issues, especially the tariff. A Southerner who had lived his adult life in the North, a Democrat who admired Alexander Hamilton as well as Thomas Jefferson, a scholar who knew the past as well as the present, Wilson was able to see public questions in perspective.

Section 3 ★ Review

Checking for Understanding

1. **Identify** Bull Moose party, New Freedom.
2. **Define** inheritance tax.
3. **Explain** why Roosevelt left the Republicans and helped form the Progressive party.
4. **Describe** the Progressive party platform.

Critical Thinking

5. **Recognizing Stereotypes** Analyze whether supporters of the Progressive party were radical reformers or dreamers.

CHAPTER 24 SECTION 3

ASSESS

Check Understanding
Assign Section 3 Review as homework or an in-class activity.

Evaluate
Assign the Section 3 Quiz in the TCR, or use the History of a Free Nation Testmaker to create a customized quiz.

Reteach
Have students complete Reteaching Activity 24-3.

Enrich
Ask students to construct a flow chart illustrating the history of the Bull Moose party. Then have them describe the impact of the party on the 1912 election.

CLOSE
Ask students to predict the kinds of legislation that Wilson might try to pass during his administration and why. Have them write their predictions in their notebooks.

Answers to SECTION 3 REVIEW

1. Bull Moose party, 661; New Freedom, 661
2. All vocabulary words are defined in the Glossary.
3. Old Guard Republicans nominated Taft. Roosevelt felt cheated and took his supporters, forming the Progressive party.
4. more direct democracy through initiative and referendum, conservation of natural resources, women's suffrage, labor reforms, revision of currency systems, inheritance tax
5. They fitted these stereotypes to a degree, since they were idealists who talked about, wrote about, and crusaded for reform. However, they were not radical activists, and reforms they wanted were realistic.

LESSON PLAN
Mastering Social Studies Skills

Teaching Map and Graph Skills

Remind students that any generalizations made from election maps must be supported. Review the map key. Ask: What information is provided? (popular and electoral votes for Wilson, Roosevelt, and Taft) How are the electoral victories identified on the map? (by color) What generalizations can be drawn from the map? (Wilson won most of the electoral votes in the South and West.)

Discuss the guidelines for making supporting statements. Ask: Why are election maps useful to historians and politicians? (They show areas of support.) What sources could be used to back up information on election maps? (actual election counts)

Did You Know?

Although Wilson led his rivals in the Electoral College by a wide margin (435 to 88 for Roosevelt and 8 for Taft), he got only 41.9 percent of the popular vote. William Jennings Bryan received more votes in 1908.

Social Studies Skills

Map and Graph Skills

Supporting Generalizations

A generalization is a statement that offers a general characteristic rather than a specific one. Sometimes when making a point or offering an interpretation, an author may make a generalization and then give supporting statements. At other times, however, you may be given only a generalization without supporting statements, or supporting statements without a generalization. In such cases you will need to use your understanding of the content and thought processes to supply what's missing—either the generalization or the supporting statement.

As a historian, it is important to back up generalizations with supporting statements or evidence. Here are guidelines for making supporting statements.

- They must relate directly to the generalization.
- They must be logical.
- They must be based on fact.

Study the map of the election of 1912, noting how the two guidelines have been applied to the following generalizations:

- The Southern states had a great influence on the election of the Democratic candidate, Woodrow Wilson.

Supporting statement:
The election map shows that all electoral votes from the Southern states went to Woodrow Wilson. (This statement relates directly to the generalization, is logical, and is based on fact.)

- The citizens who voted preferred Woodrow Wilson.

Supporting statement:
Woodrow Wilson won the election of 1912. (This statement relates directly to the generalization and is logical, but it is not based on fact. The majority of citizens who voted did not vote for Wilson.)

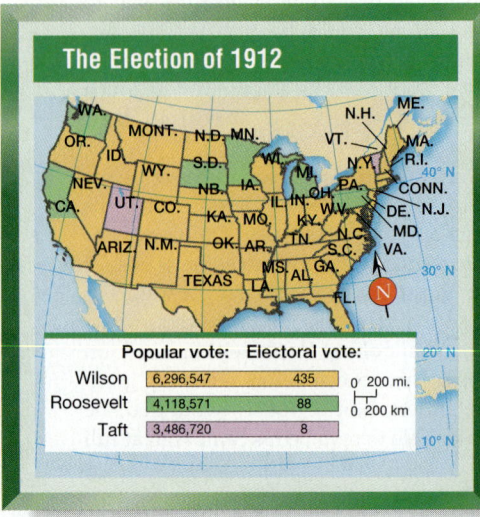

- The Western states did not support any one candidate.

Supporting statement:
California, Nevada, and Utah each gave their electoral votes to a different candidate. (This statement relates directly to the generalization, is logical, and is supported by fact.)

Practicing the Skill

For practice in supporting generalizations, write a supporting statement for the following generalizations. Use information you have learned from this chapter.

1. Theodore Roosevelt, although popular with the public, had difficulty getting "Square Deal" measures through Congress.
2. William Howard Taft continued Roosevelt's reform program, but the public lost confidence in his presidential leadership.

Answers to SOCIAL STUDIES SKILLS

1. Generalization: Theodore Roosevelt, although popular with the public, had difficulty with Congress.
Supporting statements: Roosevelt tried to win public support when Congress failed to pass legislation to regulate big business. (p. 650) Although Roosevelt favored a revision of the tariff, he did not get Congress to act. (p. 654)
2. Generalization: William Howard Taft continued Roosevelt's reform program, but the public lost confidence in his presidential leadership.
Supporting statements: Although it was Roosevelt who was nicknamed the "trust buster," Taft actually prosecuted twice as many antitrust cases in four years as had his predecessor. (p. 659) Unlike Roosevelt, Taft's judicial background allowed him to use "only those powers expressly authorized by law." (p. 659)

SECTION 4

Wilson's Progressivism

Setting the Scene

Section Focus

Before becoming President, Woodrow Wilson had held only one political office, governor of New Jersey from 1910 to 1912. In those two years, he had successfully worked for an elaborate program of progressive laws. Wilson began his first presidential term determined to obtain major social reform at the federal level.

Objectives

After studying this section, you should be able to
★ explain why Wilson had congressional support for his programs.
★ list the accomplishments of Wilson's domestic program, including legislation on tariffs and on trusts.

Key Terms

rediscount, price-cutting, interlocking directorate

◀ NUTCRACKER IN LIKENESS OF WOODROW WILSON

The new President entered office with several handicaps. He was a minority President, chosen by only 42 percent of the voters. With no experience in national politics, he knew few Democratic party leaders. In addition, the Democratic party at the time comprised a loose alliance of local interests not expected to work well together. Long out of office, the Democrats lacked people with experience in government at the federal level.

■ Wilson and Congress

Although inexperienced in national politics, Wilson enjoyed certain advantages upon entering office. The 1912 election results sent Congress a clear message that most Americans demanded progressive legislation. If the Democrats did not support the President in the creation of this legislation, warned a member of Congress, they would be "turned into the wilderness for 40 years more." No prominent Democratic leaders opposed Wilson, as Republicans Cannon and Aldrich had thwarted Taft. On the contrary, Wilson enjoyed the loyal support of most Democrats—including Bryan, the most influential man in the party, whom Wilson appointed secretary of state.

Wilson's first Inaugural Address was one of the shortest and most eloquent ever delivered. He began by asking the meaning of the Democratic triumph at the polls. His answer was that it meant little "except when the Nation is using that party for a large and definite purpose." To Wilson, the purpose was to do away with the evils that, along with many blessings, industrialism had brought. The President described these evils as the "inexcusable waste" of natural resources, the "human cost" of unrestrained individualism, and the use of government "for private and selfish purposes." Wilson

CHAPTER 24 White House Reformers 1900–1914   **665**

CHAPTER 24
SECTION 4

TEACH
Guided Practice

Economics Have students write responses to the following:

If you had been a farmer, business owner, or consumer around 1914, how would each of the following congressional acts have improved your economic situation?

1. Underwood Tariff Act (reduced the price of imported goods to consumers and farmers, opened foreign markets to business owners, put pressure on businesses to be competitive)

2. Federal Reserve Act (provided banks with enough money to extend loans to businesspeople and farmers, assured a steady supply of goods to consumers, protected depositors from bank "runs")

Use students' answers as a starting point for a discussion of the success of Wilson's business reform program. **L3**

Visualizing History Woodrow Wilson had been an attorney and gained eminence as one of the leading experts in political economics and jurisprudence.
Answer to Caption: called for reform of tariff and banking system, equality of business opportuntity, improvements in agriculture, and conservation of natural resources

Visualizing History

▲ **INAUGURATION OF A NEW PRESIDENT** The shortcomings of industrial America were widely recognized when Woodrow Wilson became President in March 1913, so it was no surprise that his brief Inaugural Address was devoted to domestic reform. *What goals did Wilson set forth in his Inaugural Address?*

also stated his goals—not, he said, Democratic or Republican goals but goals for all the nation. After calling for reform of tariffs and banking, equality of business opportunity, improvements in agriculture, and conservation of natural resources, he concluded:

> *This is not a day of triumph. It is a day of dedication. Here muster not the forces of party, but the forces of humanity. . . . I summon all honest men, all patriotic, all forward-looking men to my side. God helping me, I will not fail them, if they will but counsel and sustain me!*

■ The Underwood Tariff

The President lost no time in embarking on his program of reform. Like Taft, Wilson at once called Congress into special session. Appearing in person before Congress—the first President to do so in 100 years—he delivered a special message on the tariff. This short speech made headlines nationwide and illustrated Wilson's long-standing belief that the President's greatest power lay in focusing public attention on important issues.

Wilson's message charged that high tariffs had:

> *. . . built up a set of privileges and exemptions from competition behind which it was easy . . . to organize monopoly; until . . . nothing is obliged to stand the tests of efficiency and economy. . . .*

Lower rates, he claimed, would help businesses by putting them under "constant necessity to be efficient, economical, and enterprising. . . ." Opening the American market to foreign products would at the same time open foreign markets to American goods. Wilson warned, however, against undue haste, making it clear that he did not favor removing protective duties entirely.

666 UNIT 7 Entering a New Century: 1867–1920

Cooperative Learning

Divide students into groups of five, assigning each group member a number between one and five. Then point out that the Aldrich Commission reported that the financial organization of the United States was flawed in four ways. Give groups a certain amount of time for discussion. Select a number, and call on a student with that number to explain one of the ways the financial organization of the United States was flawed. If the answer is incomplete, continue to call on students with the same number. Call another number for another explanation, and so on.
L2, L3

The House of Representatives soon passed a bill, sponsored by Alabama Representative Oscar W. Underwood, embodying the President's recommendations. The real fight occurred in the Senate, where previous attempts to lower the tariff had foundered, and where the Democrats had only a six-vote majority. Lobbyists swarmed to Washington, pressuring senators to alter the bill. But before senatorial opposition could crystallize, Wilson again appealed to the people. He denounced the "insidious" lobbyists and asked an aroused public to insist that Congress put an end to "this unbearable situation." The President then held personal conferences with Democratic senators and wrote letters to those threatening to oppose him. Under such varied and unrelenting pressure from the executive office, the Senate voted to accept the House bill with little change.

The Underwood Tariff Act represented the first substantial drop in import duties since 1857. It attempted to fix duties at a level where costs of production in the United States and abroad would be equalized, thus lowering the duty paid on almost 1,000 articles. It removed protection entirely from industries that already competed successfully with foreign producers.

A most important section of the Underwood Tariff Act was the provision for levying an income tax, now legalized by the Sixteenth Amendment. Originally introduced merely to make up for losses in revenue created by lower tariffs, the income tax became the federal government's chief source of revenue in a very short time.

The Federal Reserve Act

As the tariff debate reached a crescendo, Wilson appeared before Congress to introduce the second major item in his reform program: a revision of the banking and currency system. The purpose of the revision was to provide businesses with cheaper and more available credit. Like the tariff message, Wilson's speech was so brief that many influential newspapers published the entire text.

Flaws in the Banking System

In 1907 a sharp panic had revealed serious weaknesses in the American banking and currency system. There were runs on banks, many of which closed or stopped lending as a result. In 1908 Congress set up the National Monetary Commission, headed

◀ **FEDERAL RESERVE SYMBOL**

▲ **STRUCTURE OF THE FEDERAL RESERVE** By 1994 the United States had more than 11,000 commercial banks. Nearly 40 percent of these were member banks that belonged to the Federal Reserve System. *What flaws in the banking system was the Federal Reserve System set up to correct?*

CHAPTER 24 White House Reformers 1900–1914   667

Sidelights: Baseball Traditions

The tradition of having the President open the baseball season by throwing out the first ball originated with President William Howard Taft. So did the seventh-inning stretch. During a game he was attending, Taft stood up in the middle of the seventh inning because he was uncomfortable—his large, 300-pound frame did not fit too well in the narrow seat. Many people in the crowd thought Taft was about to leave, so, out of respect, they also rose. When he sat back down, so did the crowd. People generally felt that Taft had shown good sense by standing up and stretching, and this action soon became an integral part of the game.

CHAPTER 24 SECTION 4

Independent Practice

Economics To make certain that students understand the meaning of the business and economic terminology in this section, have them write a paragraph in which they correctly use the following terms: *antitrust, price-cutting, contract tying, intercorporate investment, interlocking directorates.* **L1**

Visualizing History When the Federal Reserve takes actions that increase the amount of money in circulation, it is following a *loose money policy*. Conversely the actions it takes to reduce the money supply are called a *tight money policy*.

Answer to Caption: Answers include instability of banks in time of crisis, inflexible currency, no central control, and too much concentration in certain areas to exclusion of rural and isolated districts.

GLENCOE TECHNOLOGY

VIDEODISC
Economics in Action

Disc 2, Side 1, Chapter 21
Title: *The Federal Reserve and Monetary Policy*
Subject: Explains how the Federal Reserve System controls the money supply

CHAPTER 24
SECTION 4

Did You Know?

The law creating the Federal Reserve System was the first reorganization of the banking system since the Civil War.

Linking Across Time

When the Federal Reserve System, or Fed, was established in 1913, its powers were more limited than today. In its early days, the Fed served as the nation's central bank. It cleared the checks of member banks and regulated banking activities. Since the United States went off the gold standard in 1933, the Fed has served as watchdog over the nation's money supply. By controlling the supply of money, the Fed seeks to keep the economy from expanding too fast, or slipping into a recession.

---

by conservative Senator Aldrich, to investigate the situation and propose change. After four years of study, the Aldrich Commission reported that the financial organization of the United States was flawed in four respects.

First, American banking lacked stability in times of crisis. Banks did not keep enough money on reserve to cover sudden withdrawals, and there was not enough cooperation between banks.

Second, America's currency was inflexible. The amount of money in circulation was based on the amount of gold and silver in the treasury, plus the bonds held by the national banks. The present system provided no way to increase or decrease the supply of money according to the investment needs of the country.

Third, there was no central control of banking practices. In other modern industrialized countries, central banks, such as the Bank of England and the Bank of France, directed banking policy. Nothing similar had existed in this nation since Andrew Jackson had destroyed the second Bank.

Finally, the commission found that too much bank capital was concentrated in New York City and on Wall Street. Meanwhile, other parts of the country, especially isolated rural districts, often suffered from a lack of adequate banking facilities and credit.

Although few questioned the list of ills in the banking and currency system, government leaders disputed the cure. Bankers favored a great central bank, privately controlled, like the first and second Banks of the United States. Many progressives, especially Bryan, called for strict federal control of banking and credit. It was Wilson's difficult task to select a plan that would work and at the same time win support from both bankers and Bryan's followers.

Central Banking Authority

The plan Wilson finally chose was called the Federal Reserve Act. Again, under constant pressure from the President, Congress finally passed the law in December 1913. The Federal Reserve Act promptly became one of the most important and useful pieces of legislation in United States history.

The new system provided for 12 Federal Reserve Banks situated throughout the country. All national banks were required to join them, and other banks could join if they wished. The Federal Reserve did not deal directly with individuals but instead serviced member banks. These "banks for bankers" concentrated reserves, so they could provide support to individual banks in times of temporary difficulty such as a "run." They also provided for local investment needs and made it easier to move funds from one part of the country to another.

The Federal Reserve Act provided a compromise between private and public control. The Federal Reserve Banks themselves were privately owned, a majority of their directors being elected by the member banks. Overall control of the Federal Reserve Banks, however, remained in the hands of a Federal Reserve Board, whose 7 members were appointed by the President, subject to approval by the Senate, for 14-year terms. Thus the center of the nation's financial power moved from Wall Street in New York City to Washington, D.C.

Flexible Money Supply

Before passage of the Federal Reserve Act, local banks frequently lacked funds to make sound loans to businesspeople and farmers. For want of adequate funds, stores and factories closed, and crops rotted. The Federal Reserve Act greatly improved this situation by providing for a new form of "flexible" currency known as Federal Reserve notes. The new money went into circulation when local banks needing cash brought businesspeople's promissory notes to Federal Reserve Banks. In return, the Federal Reserve Bank issued Federal Reserve notes, assessing the member bank a small fee called a **rediscount.**

When a Federal Reserve Bank bought promissory notes, it could print and issue more paper money, using those notes as part of the security, or collateral, thereby protecting the value of the currency. Then, when the notes were paid and the money came back to the Bank, the currency was retired.

Critical Thinking

Analyzing Effectiveness The Federal Reserve Act is said to be one of the most important pieces of legislation in the history of the United States. Ask students to explain how this act successfully provided the United States with a banking system responsive to the needs of a great industrial nation. (It set up a new banking system under which the country was divided into 12 banking districts, each with a Federal Reserve Bank that supervised the activities of member banks and controlled credit.) **L3**

The Federal Reserve Banks also controlled the amount of money in circulation by raising or lowering the rediscount rate, or the rate at which they charged for rediscounting. Raising the rate discouraged banks from lending and so "contracted" the currency; lowering the rate encouraged lending and "expanded" the currency. Thus currency and credit in any Federal Reserve District expanded or contracted according to the economic needs of that region.

On the whole, the Federal Reserve Act made the banking system responsive to the needs of a great industrial nation. It succeeded in its first great test, during World War I, when it assisted industrial expansion and helped finance the war effort.

■ Wilson Regulates Trusts

Shortly after signing the Federal Reserve Act, Wilson asked Congress to pass an antitrust law more effective than the Sherman Antitrust Act. Denying any desire to interfere with legitimate business activities, his message to Congress proposed various methods of preventing the "indefensible and intolerable" abuses of private monopoly.

Federal Trade Commission

Late in 1914, Congress responded to Wilson's requests by passing two laws. The first, the Federal Trade Commission Act, established a Federal Trade Commission to

CHAPTER 24
SECTION 4

Map Study — Using Maps

Answer: Twelve districts and Federal Reserve banks within those districts reflect regional centers of finance, industry, and agriculture.

Skills Practice
Describe the regions the following Federal Reserve banks served: San Francisco (West), Dallas (Southwest), Chicago (Great Lakes), Boston (Northeast).

Did You Know?

The President was named Thomas Woodrow Wilson after his maternal grandfather, a Presbyterian minister. After graduating from Princeton, he began calling himself T. Woodrow Wilson. Soon after he dropped the first initial.

Regions of the Federal Reserve System

Legend:
— Federal Reserve District boundaries
★ Federal Reserve Bank
● Federal Reserve Branch Bank

Map Study: The Federal Reserve System divided the nation into 12 districts, each served as a single "bank for bankers." This arrangement made the country's bank system more responsive to local needs and less dominated by financial brokers on Wall Street. *By what criteria do you think the 12 districts and the Federal Reserve Bank cities were chosen?*

CHAPTER 24 White House Reformers 1900–1914

Sidelights: Eugene Debs

The fourth candidate running for President in 1912 was Eugene V. Debs of the Socialist party. Debs campaigned tirelessly, undertaking a whistle-stop tour of the country on which he made as many as 20 appearances a day. He was a powerful and spellbinding speaker, and his speeches were a mixture of socialist idealism and allusions to the greatness of America's past. In the election Debs received almost 900,000 votes—6 percent of all votes cast. It appeared that the Socialist party would become a major force in American politics, but the Red Scare after World War I ended most of its support.

CHAPTER 24 SECTION 4

Teaching American Portraits

In 1909 W.E.B. Du Bois and other members of the Niagara Movement joined with a number of white liberals to form the National Association for the Advancement of Colored People (NAACP). He was named the first editor of the association's journal, *Crisis*.

Although the NAACP's initial aim was to halt the rash of lynchings of African Americans, its long-term goal was to win racial equality and end segregation. Over time the NAACP grew in membership and in influence. Have students research the activities of the NAACP today.

Did You Know?

Before becoming President, Woodrow Wilson had gained national prominence as a foe of privilege. During eight years as president of Princeton University, he not only raised standards and improved teaching, but also fought social privilege as represented by snobbish undergraduate clubs. As governor of New Jersey, he successfully fought the bosses who represented special interests, not the interest of the people as a whole. Under his leadership the New Jersey legislature enacted an elaborate program of progressive measures.

AMERICAN PORTRAITS

W.E.B. Du Bois
1868–1963

The first African American to receive a Harvard Ph.D., W.E.B. Du Bois was a distinguished educator who refused to accept racial inequality. Du Bois initiated the Niagara Movement in 1905 to fight racial discrimination against African Americans in the United States.

For 24 years, Du Bois served as editor of the NAACP's journal, *The Crisis*, using it as a tool to assert demands for racial justice and equality. Between 1910 and 1930, his influence shaped not only the NAACP but a generation of African American intellectuals and activists.

In 1919 he organized the first Pan-African Congress, which promoted the idea that all people of African descent throughout the world should work together to combat the effects of discrimination. *Pan-Africanism* is still strong today among nations in Africa, where Du Bois moved in 1961.

---

investigate and regulate business practices. The commission had power to order companies to "cease and desist" from unfair conduct. In actual practice, though, Wilson's appointees to the commission failed to take strong actions against trusts.

Clayton Antitrust Act

In October 1914, less than a month after passage of the Federal Trade Commission Act, Congress passed the Clayton Antitrust Act. This act forbade several practices that destroyed competition or prevented new businesses from being developed. These practices included ruinous **price-cutting**, whereby a large company deliberately sold goods at a loss to drive weaker competitors out of business; "tying" of contracts, whereby a purchaser of goods from a particular company had to agree not to trade with its competitors; and intercorporate investment, whereby a company bought part ownership in a rival concern. The act also outlawed **"interlocking" directorates** between large corporations and banks, whereby the same people acted as directors in many different companies.

The Clayton Act also contained two sections favorable to trade unions. As noted earlier, the Sherman Act, by forbidding conspiracies, had proven more effective against labor unions than against business monopolies. In the Danbury Hatters' case, fought out in the federal courts from 1903 to 1915, a union had been ruined financially by being forced to pay triple damages to a business concern whose product had been boycotted. To discourage such use of antitrust laws, the Clayton Act stated that "nothing in the antitrust laws shall be construed to forbid the existence and operation of labor . . . organizations."

In addition, ever since the jailing of Eugene V. Debs for contempt of court in the 1894 Pullman strike, labor unions had protested the use of court injunctions forbidding strikes and boycotts. In answer to their protests, the Clayton Act forbade federal courts to issue injunctions against peaceful strikes, picketing, boycotts, or union meetings.

The Clayton Antitrust Act lost most of its effectiveness because of loose wording and unfavorable interpretations by the federal courts. The protection of labor unions from suits under the Sherman Act was limited to unions pursuing their "legitimate" purposes—and it was the courts that defined the word *legitimate*. Injunctions might still be issued when "necessary to prevent irreparable damage to property or to a property right," which again left a large loophole for conservative judges.

Cultural Diversity

In a policy that became known as the Atlanta Compromise, Booker T. Washington, the founder of the Tuskegee Institute, encouraged southern African Americans to accept segregation and to concentrate on quietly uplifting themselves. Some northern African Americans, however, railed against the compromise in general and Washington in particular. W.E.B. Du Bois, for example, said Washington "apologizes for injustice. He belittles the emasculating effects of caste distinctions . . . . The way for people to gain their reasonable rights is not by voluntarily throwing them away." Encourage students to find out more about both men and their impact on American life.

Wilson's Other Accomplishments

The Clayton Act completed the legislative program that Wilson had originally promoted. Wilson, however, did not stop there, turning his attention to other domestic issues.

Domestic Legislation

Additional legislation passed during his first term included the establishment of 12 regional Federal Farm Loan Banks, endowed with public funds in order to provide loans for agriculture. A Federal Highways Act, designed to help farmers get their produce to market, allotted federal funds to states for road construction and development. Wilson also supported the Keating-Owen Child Labor Act, which prohibited the employment of children under age 14 in factories producing goods for interstate commerce. The Adamson Act, passed under threat of a nationwide tie-up in transportation, established an 8-hour day for railroad workers.

Under Wilson's directed eye, much constructive legislation had been passed quickly. Wilson supplied a skillful and dynamic leadership, sometimes keeping Congress in session throughout the hot summer months. Chauncey Depew, a noted conservative Republican, said that for a man regarded as a mere theorist, Wilson had accomplished "the most astonishing practical results."

Segregation in the Capital

The reforms Wilson achieved did not have "practical results" for African Americans, however, as the President brought Jim Crow to Washington. The nation's capital had been desegregated since Reconstruction, but Wilson, a native Virginian, strongly believed in separating the races. Therefore, his administration segregated drinking fountains, rest rooms, and lunch counters in government office buildings and assigned jobs according to race.

A number of prominent African American leaders like W.E.B. Du Bois, who had supported Wilson in 1912, turned against him. African American newspaper editor William Monroe Trotter blamed Wilson's New Freedom for a "new slavery for your Afro-American fellow citizens." Yet the President exemplified the racial prejudice of many other progressive reformers.

Wilson also opposed woman suffrage at first. Later, however, he modified his position. During this second term, the Nineteenth Amendment gave women the right to vote.

Wilson's efforts during the beginning of his first term focused almost exclusively on domestic matters. In fact, foreign affairs did not even receive mention in his first Inaugural Address. But by the end of his term, world events overshadowed these domestic achievements, and soon Wilson's role as architect and promoter of progressive legislation was all but forgotten. It was obscured by growing tensions in foreign affairs that resulted in tragedy for him and for the world.

Section 4 ★ Review

Checking for Understanding

1. **Identify** Underwood Tariff, Federal Reserve Board, Federal Trade Commission, Clayton Antitrust Act.
2. **Define** rediscount, price-cutting, interlocking directorate.
3. **Explain** how the Federal Reserve System works.
4. **Describe** the provisions of the Clayton Antitrust Act that limited the power of monopolies.

Critical Thinking

5. **Making Judgments** Evaluate the effect of Wilson's antitrust legislation and the creation of the Federal Reserve System on the economy of the nation.

Answers to SECTION 4 REVIEW

1. Underwood Tariff, 666; Federal Reserve Board, 668; Federal Trade Commission, 669; Clayton Antitrust Act, 670
2. All vocabulary words are defined in the Glossary.
3. Twelve Federal Reserve banks situated nationwide with reserve funds for local member banks. Had flexible currency system providing loans to local banks as needed. Printed money using notes as collateral; money withdrawn when notes paid. Currency and credit contracted or expanded based on local economy.
4. forbade the following: price-cutting by large companies, tying contracts, intercorporate investment, and interlocking directorates
5. inspired public confidence by reforming banking system, encouraging growth of business through promise of fair trade practices, and generating overall domestic prosperity

REVIEW CHAPTER 24

Answers

Reviewing Facts
1. included government regulation of big business and railroads, trust busting, and conservation of natural resources
2. educators, editors, literary figures, philanthropists, and former Rough Riders who supported progressive reforms
3. Taft's judicial background prevented his going beyond the law. He did not dramatize causes or try to get the support of liberal leaders in Congress, and he did not enlist the public's support.
4. Both wanted to regulate big business through government control and protect the public interest, but Roosevelt saw big business—even monopolies—as necessary; Wilson did not. Wilson believed monopolies and trusts were evil and wanted to eliminate them.

Understanding Concepts
1. The United Mine Workers wanted higher wages, better working conditions, and appointment of a commission to investigate the wage issues. The mine owners refused the idea of a commission, refused to listen to union demands to submit to arbitration or to recognize the United Mine Workers. J.P. Morgan intervened, applying pressure on mine owners to compromise. The conflict was resolved.
2. Price-cutting allowed big companies to sell goods at a loss and wipe out competition;

CHAPTER 24 ★ REVIEW

Using Vocabulary

Write a paragraph describing Wilson's New Freedom program. Use the following terms:

progressivism labor
antitrust monopoly
free competition income tax

Reviewing Facts

1. **Describe** the progressive beliefs of Theodore Roosevelt.
2. **Identify** the sources of support for Roosevelt's Square Deal and New Nationalism.
3. **Cite** two important achievements of William Howard Taft's administration.
4. **Compare** the progressivism of Woodrow Wilson and Theodore Roosevelt based on their respective programs.

Understanding Concepts

Interests and Positions
1. Show how Taft's policies seemed to go against Roosevelt's Square Deal.

Economic Competition
2. In what way did big-business practices and tactics in the early 1900s slow or inhibit economic competition?

Critical Thinking

1. **Linking Past and Present** Compare Theodore Roosevelt's approach to conservation of natural resources with those of Presidents during the 1980s and 1990s.
2. **Analyzing Photographs** Study the photograph on this page, then answer the questions that follow.
   a. During what decade do you think this photograph was taken?

672 UNIT 7 Entering a New Century: 1867–1920

b. Is there an emotional "feeling" present in the photograph? How would you describe it?
c. Do you think the photograph would have a different effect if it were in color? Explain.

Writing About History
Argumentation

Imagine you are a campaign manager for Theodore Roosevelt, William Howard Taft, and Woodrow Wilson during the election of 1912. Write a campaign speech with slogans for Roosevelt, Taft, and Wilson that reflects the views of each candidate and his party.

Cooperative Learning

Organize the class into three debate groups. Each group will then choose one of the following three topics:
1. The Ballinger/Pinchot controversy over protecting wilderness areas
2. The Payne/Aldrich debate over protective tariffs

purchasers of goods from one company agreed not to buy from another; with intercorporate investment, one company bought part ownership in a rival concern; interlocking directorates between large corporations and banks allowed the same people to be directors of different companies.

Critical Thinking
1. The administrations of Roosevelt-Taft and Reagan-Bush differed on conservation issues. Whereas Roosevelt-Taft set aside national parks and other areas for conservation, the Reagan-Bush approach allowed the development and commercial use of wilderness areas.
2. a. Answers will vary, but students should indicate 1900–1925 period.
   b. Answers will vary but

CHAPTER 24 ★ REVIEW

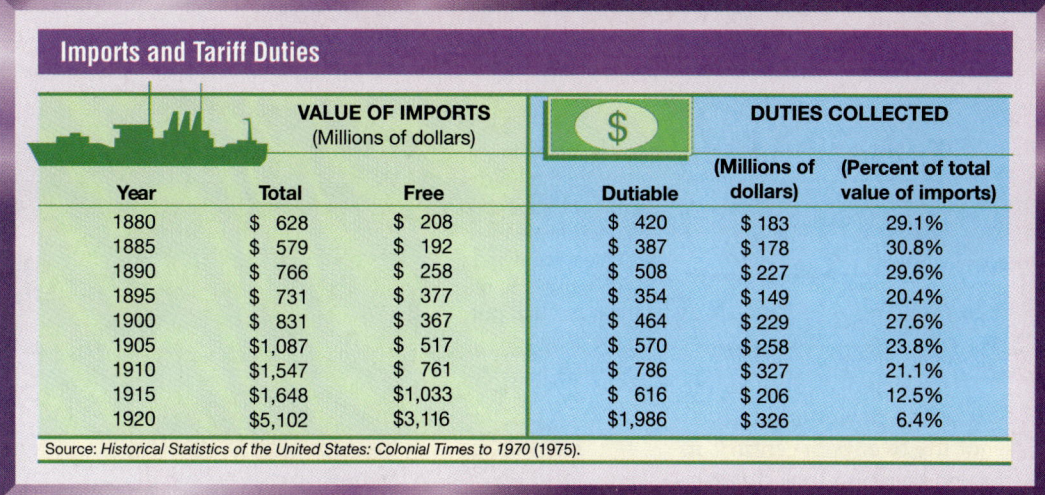

3. The mine workers/mine owners dispute in the coal strike of 1902

You will work within your group to research and prepare arguments on both sides of the issue. Conduct the class debates when each group has completed its preparation.

Social Studies Skills

Analyzing Trends

A table presents statistics in an easily analyzed format. Tables group information into horizontal rows and vertical columns. The table format facilitates quick comparisons, thus helping you recognize and analyze trends. Use the table on this page to help you practice analyzing trends.

Practicing the Skill

1. What years are covered by the table? How many years separate each row of data?
2. Explain the trend in the total value of imports represented on this table.
3. Explain the trend in total duties collected in the time period covered by the table.
4. Explain the trend in percent of total value of imports between 1880 and 1910.
5. Study the columns on the value of imports in the table. Explain the trend in percent of total value of imports between 1910 and 1920.
6. What congressional action affected the collection of duties after 1910? Explain.

Using Your Journal

Read over your journal notes. How successful were the Presidents in making direct appeals to the nation? Do you think the strategy is a good one to use? Explain your response in your journal.

REVIEW CHAPTER 24

Chapter Bonus Test Question

Which of the Progressive era Presidents was the true "trust buster"? Give reasons in support of your answer. (Answers will vary. Theodore Roosevelt was the first to regulate trusts, but Taft prosecuted twice as many cases in four years as Roosevelt did in seven years. Wilson initiated legislation that strengthened the Sherman Anti-Trust Act and established a Federal Trade Commission.)

Using Your Journal

Theodore Roosevelt was successful in his direct appeal to the nation regarding trust regulation; his concern for the environment also stimulated public interest. William Howard Taft, lacking Roosevelt's gift for communication, made few attempts to enlist public support. Woodrow Wilson, although an aloof personality, was a persuasive speaker, and was successful in rallying public opinion in favor of tariff reduction.

On whether or not the strategy is a good one, students will vary in their answers but should offer reasons for their opinions.

---

might include happiness, peace, tranquility.
c. Answers will vary, but students should provide reasons to support their answers.

Practicing the Skill
1. 1880–1920; five years
2. The total value of imports rose in every five-year period, except two. The increase was gradual, until 1915. Between 1915 and 1920 the value of imports more than tripled.
3. increased for every time period, except three
4. fairly constant between 1880 and 1910; only exceptions were in 1895 and 1910
5. dropped dramatically after 1910
6. Underwood Tariff Act; lowered duties on some imports and eliminated others entirely

Cultural Kaleidoscope

Making Connections
History and Government

The increasingly widespread use of the automobile in the early twentieth century led governments at all levels to become involved in a host of new activities. Among them were licensing drivers, registering automobiles, and issuing license plates. Governments also had to build and maintain roads and highways and establish and enforce safety rules. In recent years governments have also concerned themselves with safety and pollution standards of the automobiles themselves.

More About...
Early Cars

Although the United States has long been among the leading nations in car ownership and manufacturing, the pioneers in automobile design were Europeans. Two Germans—Karl Benz and Gottlieb Daimler—invented the first practical internal combustion engines. Louis Renault of France developed the first shaft drive. French influence is indicated by the many French words associated with autos, including chassis, chauffeur, and garage.

Cultural Kaleidoscope

Transportation

Moving Into The Fast Lanes

As America evolved into a world power at the turn of the twentieth century, it also began to look differently at itself. The frontier was nearly gone and in its place, from 1880 to 1914, booming industrial expansion became a hallmark of American culture. No symbol better expresses this period than the automobile. Although the auto was invented in the nineteenth century, it is truly a twentieth-century phenomenon that touched and changed the way Americans lived.

▶ Beginning in 1908, the Ford Model T reached unparalleled sales, justifying its nickname of the car that put the world on wheels.

◀ In the early 1900s, car bodies tended to look similar to each other. By 1912, designers began to create distinctive hood ornaments.

◀ Some automakers outfitted their vehicles with horns operated by hand or by foot. Some luxury cars included two horns—a quiet one for use in the city and a louder one for country driving.

▲ There had been only a handful of automobiles on American highways by 1895. By 1920 there were nearly 5 million, and the automobile was beginning to remake American life.

Cooperative Learning

Divide the class into small groups and ask each to select a car commonly advertised on television. Each group—together or individually—should watch at least one commercial for the car it chose and report on the following: (1) What features does the ad stress? (2) Is the car shown on the road or in a showroom? (3) Who endorses the car? (4) How convincing is the commercial?

▶ No better proof of the impact of the automobile exists than in the popular songs of the day.

▲ Headlights were then called headlamps and were typically constructed of brass.

▼ Modern cars still have four wheels and run on gasoline. Yet they look very different from cars of 80 years ago. Shown is the front compartment of the 1914 Mercer Raceabout.

Cultural Kaleidoscope

Portfolio Project
Ask students to keep a file of the vanity license plates they spot over a two- or three-week period. What vanity plate would they choose for themselves?

The Historian's Craft

Historians are interested in the economic and social effects of important events, including the development of new technology. (One example from earlier times: the invention of the cotton gin.) Over the years, historians have documented a host of sweeping changes that the automobile has produced, including the spread of suburbs, the deterioration of inner cities, the development of a huge network of roads, the decline of railroads, and such phenomena as fast-food restaurants, drive-ins, shopping malls, and motels.

UNIT 7 DIGEST

The Unit 7 Digest can be used to teach unit coverage when time is limited, to review unit content, or to link content of one unit to another.

Unit Digest Transparencies
Use Transparency 13.

■ Chapter 22
Have students work as a group to construct a large world map showing the territories acquired by the United States in the late 1800s. Display the map on the bulletin board and use it as the starting point for a debate on the following: The burdens of imperial rule kept the United States from its true task—the establishment of a fair and equitable society at home.

■ Chapter 23
Ask students to research one of the progressive reforms and write a report. Reports should include the situation before the reform, what the reform changed, and who benefitted from the reform. Invite students to read their reports for a class discussion on the effectiveness of the reforms.

■ Chapter 24
Ask students to compare President Roosevelt's Square Deal with President Wilson's New Freedom. Suggest they focus on such questions as: What were the aims of the two programs? How successful were the programs in accomplishing their aims? Who benefitted from these programs? Then discuss with students who they think was the greater reformer and why.

Chapter 22
Imperialism

In the last decades of the nineteenth century, Americans reassessed and abandoned their traditional isolationist policy. Because of growing industrial power, trade and contacts with Latin America increased. In the Pacific, American interest in Hawaii led to its annexation in 1898.

In 1898 the United States went to war with Spain. Americans sympathized with an independence movement in Cuba seeking to overthrow Spanish control. The Spanish-American War was over in six months.

As a result of the war, the United States gained a colonial empire and with it the challenge of governing overseas territories—Puerto Rico, Guam, and the Philippines. Questions soon arose over whether native people living in colonial possessions were entitled to the same civil rights as American citizens. Eventually the Supreme Court of the United States ruled that the Constitution did not cover overseas possessions.

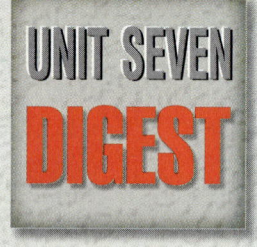

As the United States expanded into the Pacific, Americans were anxious to renew trade opportunities with the Chinese. To protect any potential trade between the two countries, Secretary of State John Hay asked the Chinese in 1899 to grant an "Open Door" trade policy.

President Theodore Roosevelt strengthened American involvement in world affairs. He defended Venezuela from possible European aggression and he issued the Roosevelt Corollary, a statement that attempted to justify United States intervention in Latin America. In addition, Roosevelt negotiated an end to the Russo-Japanese War. Perhaps most important, Roosevelt prevented Colombia from putting down an insurrection in Panama City. This action allowed Panamanians to establish the Republic of Panama. Roosevelt quickly negotiated a treaty for the rights to build a canal across Panama.

Chapter 23
The Progressive Era

Beginning about 1900 a large, loosely organized group of urban, middle-class professionals—including journalists, social workers, educators, ministers, and socially conscious politicians—became concerned about the need for social change in the United States. These reformers—called "progressives"—were the first to thoroughly investigate social problems that they felt were unjust and undemocratic. Progressives were concerned that if society's problems were not solved, democracy and capitalism might be threatened.

The goal of progressives was an efficient, smoothly functioning nation where each social problem could be managed by experts trained in that area. The many areas in which the progressives focused their efforts included the following: reform of the political system, business regulation, consumer protection, limits on immigration, tax reform, protection of working women and children, labor and education reform, and temperance. Journalists called "muckrakers" brought many of these problem areas to public attention, and most Americans supported calls for change. Reform occurred first at local and state levels.

Cooperative Learning

Organize students into three groups to find out more about how their local government works. Suggest that one group do library research to gather information. Ask another group to interview local officials, and the third to attend a board or council meeting. Have groups compare their findings and prepare a report on the impact of progressive reform on the structure and function of their local government.

Although progressives had the nation's best interests at heart, some reforms came at the expense of immigrants and racial minorities. Reformers tried to extinguish immigrant cultures, and they neglected African Americans almost completely.

Chapter 24

White House Reformers

Theodore Roosevelt, William H. Taft, and Woodrow Wilson were reform Presidents. They sought to improve the welfare of the average American citizen, regulate big-business practices, and conserve the nation's natural resources.

Roosevelt supported the progressive movement with his domestic goal to give everyone a "Square Deal." He soon became known as a "trustbuster." Roosevelt also helped settle the coal strike of 1902. Roosevelt's greatest achievement lay in the area of conservation.

During Taft's administration the Constitution was strengthened with the Sixteenth Amendment's passage (providing for an income tax) and the Seventeenth Amendment (allowing direct election of senators). Taft also created the Tariff Board to investigate duties.

One of Wilson's first acts as President was to help pass the Underwood Tariff Act, which lowered import duties and introduced a federal income tax. Wilson achieved a progressive legislative program. He implemented a reform of banking and currency practices, secured passage of a labor reform bill, and engineered legislation regulating trusts.

Understanding Unit Themes

1. **American Democracy** In what ways did reforms in government help the middle class and hinder African Americans?
2. **Economic Development** How did the opening of new markets in East Asia and the acquisition of territories create economic growth in the United States?
3. **The Individual and Family Life** In what ways did social and political reforms improve the quality of life for many?
4. **U.S. Role in World Affairs** How did American foreign policy change around 1900? Give examples of this change.
5. **U.S. Role in World Affairs** How did Roosevelt's role in resolving the Russo-Japanese War show that the United States had become a world leader?

UNIT 7 DIGEST

Understanding Unit Themes

1. The middle class could choose candidates in primaries and had political choices through the initiative, referendum, and recall; reforms in city government gave the middle class more political input. African Americans were still subject to poll taxes, literacy tests, and segregation.
2. There were more goods for new markets, giving more people economic benefits. Investments abroad increased the nation's wealth. New industries developed to process raw materials from new territories.
3. Americans had more voice in government; churches and the temperance movement attempted to bring families together; working conditions improved for women and children.
4. United States abandoned its isolationist policy and began to expand overseas, gaining territories and a colonial empire. Examples may include acquisition of Caribbean and Pacific Ocean lands, Open Door policy in China, intervention in Latin America, building of Panama Canal.
5. In asking to mediate the dispute, Roosevelt believed the U.S. had an obligation to be a world leader, acting responsibly and with restraint.

Student Self-Test Software

Audiocassettes

The Historian's Craft

A major part of studying history is interpreting the statements of historical figures and drawing conclusions about those statements. Read the following statement of W. E. B. Du Bois: "The problem of the twentieth century is the problem of the color line." How do you interpret Du Bois's statement? What does he mean? Based on your own knowledge of past historical events in this century and current events, do you think Du Bois made an accurate prediction? Explain your answer.

INTRODUCING UNIT 8

BEGINNING THE UNIT

Present the cause-and-effect chart to students with the effects omitted. Assign students to complete the chart as they read the chapters in the unit.

Event
- Stock market crashes.

Causes
- U.S. enters World War I.
- U.S. rejects League of Nations.
- Nationalist spirit grows.
- U.S. economy expands.

Effects
- Great Depression
- Crisis in industry and agriculture
- Capitalist system in jeopardy
- "New Deal"

History AND ART

During the Great Depression the federal government established a program to help unemployed artists. The Federal Arts Project employed thousands of artists in many different capacities. It was the beginning of government support of the arts.

00:00 OUT OF TIME? If time does not permit teaching the entire unit, use the Unit Digest on pages 767–768.

UNIT EIGHT
CRUSADE AND DISILLUSION
1914–1932

CHAPTER 25	CHAPTER 26	CHAPTER 27
World War I Era 1914–1920	The Decade of Normalcy 1920–1928	The Depression Begins 1928–1932

▼ WALL TELEPHONE

History AND ART
Third Avenue
by Charles Goeller, 1933–1934

Scenes of city life during the Great Depression were important themes for many artists.

▲ DUSTER COAT

Exploring Unit Themes

Conflict and Cooperation During World War I, the American people readily cooperated with the government in support of the war effort. During the Great Depression, however, many Americans turned against the government. Some became disillusioned when the government failed to stop the country's economic plunge. Others blamed the Great Depression on government policies.

Influence of Technology Technology greatly influenced the lives of Americans in war and in peace. New weapons made war a deadlier game. At home, radio and movies and the advent of the automobile completely revolutionized American life.

INTRODUCING UNIT 8

Setting the Scene

The spirit of progressive reform dwindled as the United States drifted toward the conflict of World War I. Once the war ended, the national mood was no longer progress and optimism but "normalcy" and isolation. During the 1920s, Americans elected conservative Republican leaders.

Themes
- Conflict and Cooperation
- Influence of Technology
- The Individual and Family Life
- United States Role in World Affairs

Key Events
- World War I begins in Europe
- Germany resumes unrestricted submarine warfare
- Congress declares war on Germany
- The Senate rejects the Treaty of Versailles and the League of Nations
- Teapot Dome oil scandal
- Stock market crash
- Bonus Army marches on Washington

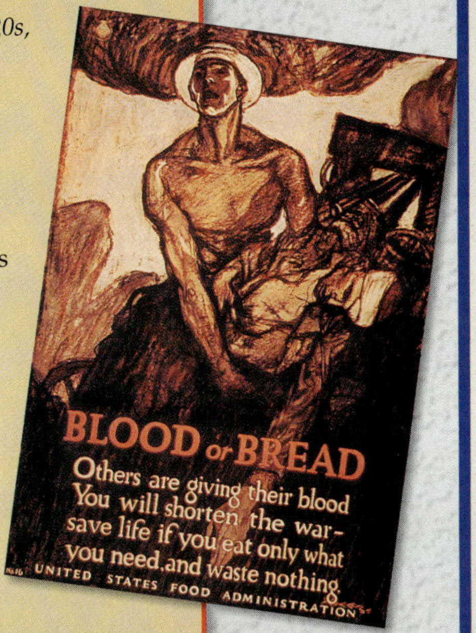

Major Issues
- Violation of neutral rights leads the United States to declare war on Germany.
- Despite Wilson's leadership, an isolationist mood defeats the Treaty of Versailles and the League of Nations.
- Prosperity of the 1920s fails to reach African Americans and farmers.
- Widespread depression and human misery after the crash prompts the federal government to provide direct relief.

▲ GOVERNMENT POSTER, WORLD WAR I

◀ GERMAN HELMET, EARLY 1900s

Portfolio Project
Create a map of Latin America indicating the affairs that involved the United States in the region from 1914 to 1932.

Unit 8 Independent Study Project
Have students work together to create a museum exhibit on the social history of the 1920s. Suggest that they use maps, sketches, pictures from magazines, and so on to illustrate the exhibit.

Unit Digest Transparencies
Use Transparency 15, *Transients Cooking Their Meal in the Snow Near a Coal Chute, DeKalb, Illinois,* by J. Porter.

History and the Humanities
 U.S. History and Art Transparencies 20, 21, 22

Focus on American Fine Art Prints 15, 16

American Music: Cultural Traditions

 Spirit of American Art and Music 25, 26, 27

Portfolio Project
Suggest students review the United States's relations with Latin America in the late 1800s and early 1900s. Have them compare those policies with United States involvement in the region as indicated on their maps.

The Individual and Family Life During the prosperity of the 1920s, the standard of living of many Americans greatly improved, but this good life came to an abrupt end with the onset of the Great Depression.
U.S. Role in World Affairs At first the United States tried to avoid involvement in World War I, but events drew the country into the conflict. The Treaty of Versailles, which ended the war, was rejected by the United States Senate.
Examining Unit Themes Explain that Unit 8 explores events that brought great changes to the United States in the first part of the twentieth century.

LESSON PLAN
Global Perspectives

FOCUS
Motivating Activity

Remind students that World War I resulted in a new world order—old empires were dismantled, and new nations were created. Provide students with maps showing the world before and after World War I. Discuss with students the territorial and political changes that occurred. Then ask them to speculate on what issues might remain unresolved in the future. (new nations created in eastern and central Europe; Middle East changed by breakup of Ottoman Empire; some European nations received territories of others)

TEACH
Guided Practice

Explain that during the early 1900s, rival European nations divided into two major military alliances: Great Britain, France, and Russia; Germany and Austria-Hungary. Ask students how such alliances might lead to conflict in Europe. (A dispute could involve several nations.) In case of a conflict, why might it be difficult for the United States to remain neutral? (U.S. trade and business would be affected; U.S. likely would favor Great Britain and France.)

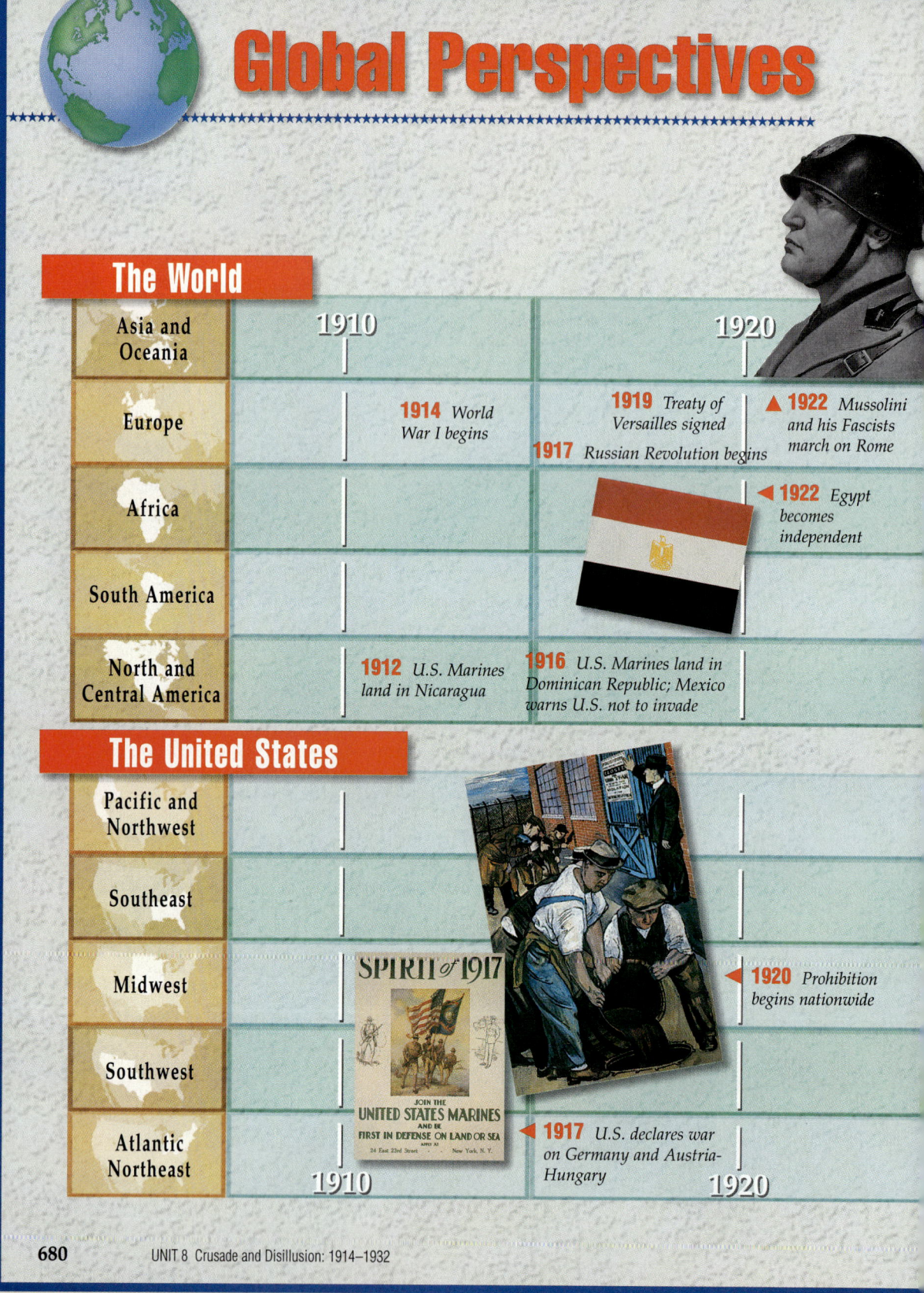

680 UNIT 8 Crusade and Disillusion: 1914–1932

Cultural Diversity

During the 1920s, in what is called the Great Migration, thousands of African Americans left the South for northern cities in hopes of finding a better life. They brought with them a musical form new to the North—jazz. In such cities as New Orleans, African American musicians had for years been adapting old spirituals and work songs to create new rhythms. Jazz musicians such as Louis Armstrong, "King" Oliver, and "Jelly Roll" Morton helped popularize jazz among white Americans. Many music historians think that jazz was the only serious American music to emerge in the early twentieth century, and it continues to leave its mark on popular American music.

Linking Across Time

While the great migration of Eastern Europeans to the United States came at the end of the 1800s, the first Eastern European immigrants arrived nearly 200 years before. John Smith, the leader of Jamestown, wanted to exploit the colony's pine trees for pitch and turpentine. So he sent to Poland, where the manufacturing of naval stores was well established, for skilled workers. The first Polish artisans arrived in 1608, probably as indentured servants. Colony records listed them as free members of the community some 11 years later.

Timeline 1930–1940

- **1928** Chiang Kai-shek and his Kuomintang army win control of China 
- **1930** London Naval Agreement signed
- **1930** Uruguay wins soccer's first World Cup
- **1935** Pope Pius XI condemns Nazi atrocities
- **1935** Bolivia and Paraguay end three-year war 
- **1923** Teapot Dome oil scandal erupts
- **1925** Scopes "Monkey" trial captures national attention
- **1935** Malcolm Campbell sets new land speed record of 301 mph
- **1936** Centennial of Texas Independence celebrated
- **1929** Stock market crashes, triggering the Great Depression
- **1931** Empire State Building opens

UNIT 8 Crusade and Disillusion: 1914–1932

LESSON PLAN
Global Perspectives

Independent Practice
World Events and the U.S.
Have students note the dates of the Russian Revolution. Tell them that when the Bolsheviks seized power in Russia, they called on the workers of the world to revolt. Point out that labor unrest in the United States in 1919 convinced some Americans that a Bolshevik plot existed to overthrow the government. Have students research this "Red Scare" and write an editorial expressing their view of the government's action.

ASSESS
Studying the Time Line

1. Apart from Europe, on what world region did American foreign policy focus in this period?
2. Which foreign nation showed imperialist tendencies during this period? How?
3. What issues seemed to occupy the American people during the 1920s?

Answers to Questions
1. Latin America
2. Japan, occupying Manchuria
3. Political and social issues, women's suffrage, Prohibition, scandal

---

Cooperative Learning

Divide students into three groups, and assign each group one chapter in the unit. Ask each group to skim its chapter and write the headings of the sections in the chapter. Then direct the groups to turn those headings into questions. (Example: What were the results of Wilson's moral diplomacy?) Have groups share their questions and speculate about the answers. When the unit is completed, encourage students to compare their speculations with the text. **L3**

PLANNING GUIDE — Chapter 25 World War I Era

Daily Lesson Objectives	Teacher Classroom Resources	Multimedia
SECTION 1 **Prelude to War** 1 Day pp. 684–688 1. Describe Wilson's foreign policy toward Latin American nations. 2. Identify the causes of World War I. 3. Explain why the United States had difficulty remaining neutral during the war.	Chapter 25 Study Guide Reproducible Lesson Plan Reteaching Activity 25-1 Section Quiz Chapter 25 Cooperative Learning Activity Chapter 25 Concept Mapping Activity Reinforcing Social Studies Skills 31, 32, 36, 59, 61, 67 LEP Chapter 25 Primary and Secondary Source Readings	Student Self-Test Software Testmaker Section Focus Transparency 79 Chapter 25 Skills Transparency Chapter 25 Map Transparencies Lessons of War
SECTION 2 **America Enters the War** 1 Day pp. 690–695 1. Identify the events that led the United States to enter the war. 2. Describe the role of the United States in helping the Allies to achieve victory over the Central Powers.	Reproducible Lesson Plan Reteaching Activity 25-2 Section Quiz American Portrait 47 Reinforcing Social Studies Skills 25, 32, 62, 63, 67 LEP Writer's Guidebook Lesson 6	Student Self-Test Software Testmaker Section Focus Transparency 80 U.S. History and Art Transparency 20 Chapter 25 Map Transparencies Powers of the Supreme Court GTV: A Geographic Perspective on American History
SECTION 3 **War on the Home Front** 1 Day pp. 696–700 1. Explain how the war was financed. 2. Describe how public opinion was shaped by the government. 3. Discuss the goals of Wilson's Fourteen Points.	Reproducible Lesson Plan Reteaching Activity 25-3 Section Quiz American Portrait 50 Reinforcing Social Studies Skills 26, 27, 32, 62	Student Self-Test Software Testmaker Section Focus Transparency 81 Chapter 25 Map Transparencies Lessons of War
SECTION 4 **After the War** 1 Day pp. 701–706 1. Describe the outcome of the Versailles peace conference. 2. Explain why the Senate rejected the Treaty of Versailles. 3. Identify domestic problems that arose after the war.	Reproducible Lesson Plan Reteaching Activity 25-4 Section Quiz Chapter 25 Enrichment Activity Chapter 25 Primary and Secondary Source Readings Reinforcing Social Studies Skills 26, 27, 38, 40, 49, 53 LEP Spanish Summaries & Glossary	Student Self-Test Software Vocabulary Puzzlemaker Section Focus Transparency 82 Chapter 25 Map Transparencies U.S. History and Art Transparency 21 Audiocassette, Chapter 25 GTV: A Geographic Perspective on American History
CHAPTER REVIEW AND EVALUATION 1 Day	Chapter 25 Test Chapter 25 Performance Assessment Activity	Student Self-Test Software Testmaker

00:00 OUT OF TIME? If time does not permit teaching the entire chapter, use the Chapter 25 Summary on pages 766–767 and the Chapter 25 audiocassette (English and Spanish) to point out the main ideas of the chapter.

PLANNING GUIDE

Cultural Diversity Activity

Making Comparisons Have students research and report on the movement of African Americans from the South to the North known as the Great Migration. This massive exodus began during World War I when northern industries needed workers to fill jobs left vacant by workers drafted into the armed forces. It was accelerated by the naval war, which all but stopped immigration from abroad.

Have students identify both "push" and "pull" factors for the Great Migration. Students can also compare the treatment of African American migrants in northern cities with immigrant groups and report on the consequences of the war's end for migrants newly settled in the North.

Performance Assessment Activity

Foreign Policy Recall with students that the United States' foreign policy from 1900 through World War I was based on three different theories: Roosevelt's "Big Stick" diplomacy, Taft's dollar diplomacy, and Wilson's moral diplomacy. Have students individually or in small groups choose a key region of the world and research the current U.S. foreign policy in regard to that region. How is today's policy similar to those of the early 1900s? What differences seem most striking? Suggest students draw conclusions about the effectiveness of today's policies compared with those that characterize the early 1900s. Encourage students to share their findings with the class.

POSSIBLE RUBRIC FEATURES: Content information, research skills, organization, writing and communication skills, critical thinking skills

Chapter Resources

Literature from the Period

Anderson, Sherwood. *Winesburg, Ohio.* 1919.

Norris, George. "Opposition to War." April 4, 1917.

Wilson, Woodrow. "Appeal for Neutrality." August 19, 1914.

_____. "Fourteen Points." January 8, 1918.

Readings for the Student

Carr, Stephen M. "Smidley Butler: Hero or Demagogue?" *American History Illustrated,* Vol. 15, No. 1, April 1980.

McGinty, Brian. "Alvin York." *American History Illustrated,* Vol. 21, No. 7, November 1986.

Readings for the Teacher

Coffman, Edward M. *The War to End All Wars.* University of Wisconsin Press, 1968.

Greenwald, Maurine W. *Women, War and Work.* Greenwood Press, 1980.

Lemann, Nicholas. *The Promised Land: The Great Black Migration and How It Changed America.* Knopf, 1991.

Multimedia Resources

Living American History Series. US History IV: 1915–1960. Priven Learning Systems. (2 Apple diskettes)

Mirror of America. National Archives. (VHS, 36 minutes)

The Ordeal of Woodrow Wilson. NBC. (VHS, 26 minutes)

The United States in World War I: Witness to History. Guidance Associates. (VHS, 15 minutes)

World War I: 1914–1918. Films for the Humanities. (VHS, 52 minutes)

Key to Ability Levels

Teaching strategies have been coded for varying learning styles and abilities.

- **L1** Basic activities for all students
- **L2** Average activities for average to above-average students
- **L3** Challenging activities for above-average students
- **LEP** Limited English Proficiency activities

Glencoe Links to the Humanities

Links to Art
- U.S. History and Art Transparencies 20, 21
- Focus on American Fine Art Prints

Links to Literature
- Macmillan Literature: American Literature Audiotapes Side 4
- Macmillan Literature: American Literature Video—*The Great Gatsby*
- Macmillan Literature: American Literature Text—Langston Hughes, Archibald MacLeish, Marianne Moore, e.e. cummings, Robert Frost

Link to Music
- American Music: Cultural Traditions

CHAPTER 25

BEGINNING THE CHAPTER

Write the following on the chalkboard: Reasons for Using Force.

Have students list a number of reasons for going to war. Then ask the students to be prepared as they read to compare their reasons with the reasons they learn about in Chapter 25, which details the United States's involvement in World War I and its aftermath.

Recording Journal Notes

Encourage students to record their observations under such topics as Outbreak of War in Europe, American Neutrality, United States Declaration of War, and The War Effort.

Linking Across TIME

Explain that World War I spurred technological development, not only in weaponry but also in other areas. Medical advances were made in the treatment of the wounded. The use of the wireless for battlefield communication laid the groundwork for radio broadcasting, which began in 1920. Before the war, aviation was mainly a sport. By the war's end, its potential as a major means of transportation and communication was recognized. The first regular airmail service in the United States

682

CHAPTER 25

World War I Era
1914–1920

▶ CONGRESSIONAL MEDAL OF HONOR

Setting the Scene

Focus

When Europe went to war in 1914, the United States sought to stay out of the conflict. Both sides disregarded American neutrality. Germany's use of unrestricted submarine warfare and economic ties to Great Britain eventually led the United States into the bloody struggle. Mobilization called for many sacrifices by the American people. The Senate, however, rejected Wilson's proposed peace settlement, and wartime fervor led to intolerance.

Concepts to Understand

★ How conflict became evident in American society during and after World War I

★ How Wilson's idealism and American economic interests led to controversy over foreign policy

Read to Discover . . .

★ why the United States declared war on the German Empire in 1917.

★ why the United States did not join the League of Nations.

Journal Notes

What was the general attitude of the American people during World War I? Record your observations as you read the chapter.

CULTURAL
- 1915 First transcontinental telephone is hooked up
- 1917 Temperance movement leads to prohibition laws in 29 states

1914 — 1916

POLITICAL
- 1914 World War I begins when Austria-Hungary declares war on Serbia
- 1916 Germany agrees to restrict submarine warfare
- 1917 United States declares war on Germany

682   UNIT 8 Crusade and Disillusion: 1914–1932

✚ EXTRA CREDIT PROJECT

Explain to students that in 1915 a German submarine sank the British liner *Lusitania*, among whose passengers were more than 100 Americans. The United States responded strongly and even hinted at using force to stop submarine attacks. Events surrounding the sinking were controversial at the time and still are. Interested students might investigate the circumstances and form their own conclusions.

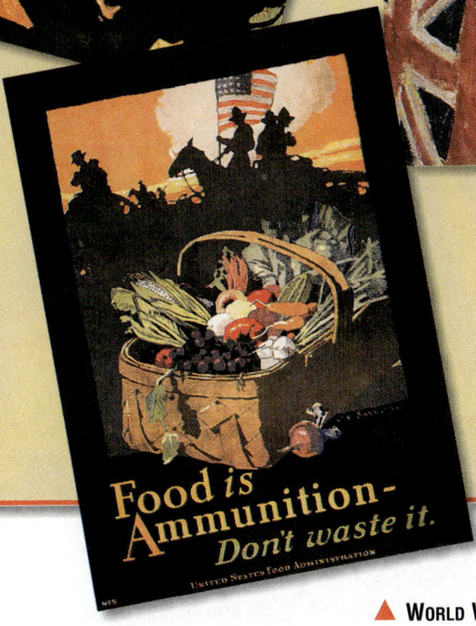

CHAPTER 25 CONCEPTS

Reproduce the concepts map below on the chalkboard, and have students copy it in their notebooks. Ask them to hypothesize about what topics might be covered in Chapter 25, based on this information.

- The conflicting interests of the world powers lead to world war.
  - Conflict
  - Interests

History AND ART

In this painting, Hassam has captured the feelings of patriotism the nation was experiencing after having joined the Allied cause of World War I.

The following material is available from Glencoe and may be used to introduce or enrich Chapter 25:

VIDEODISC
Lessons of War

Side One Chapter 7: Can War Be Justified?

History AND ART

Allies Day by Childe Hassam, 1916

Hassam depicts a vision of the Avenue of the Allies in red, white, and blue brush strokes.

▲ WORLD WAR I POSTERS

- **1918** Daylight savings time is first adopted
- **1918** Wilson proclaims his Fourteen Points

1918

- **1919** Sherwood Anderson publishes *Winesburg, Ohio*
- **1919** Versailles peace conference is held
- **1920** Nineteenth Amendment is ratified

1920

CHAPTER 25 World War I Era 1914–1920 683

Teacher Notes

LESSON PLAN
SECTION 1, 684–689

FOCUS

Bellringer
Before taking roll at the beginning of the class period, display Focus Activity Transparency 83 on the overhead projector, and assign the accompanying Focus Activity Sheet.

Objectives
Point out the objectives on this page to students in previewing the section content.

Motivating Activity
Read to students this statement from President Woodrow Wilson's response to the sinking of the British passenger ship *Lusitania* by a German submarine: "There is such a thing as a nation being so right that it does not need to convince others by force that it is right." What is Wilson's main point? (It is not necessary to go to war to resolve every dispute.)

Use Skills Transparency 25.

Lessons of War

Side One Chapter 5: How Wars Begin—World War I

SECTION 1

Prelude to War

Setting the Scene

Section Focus
On the day he took office, President Woodrow Wilson remarked to a friend that it would be an irony of fate if his administration had to deal mainly with foreign affairs. But Wilson's administration soon was confronted with difficult and complex foreign problems that involved the fate of the world.

Objectives
After studying this section, you should be able to
★ describe Wilson's foreign policy toward Latin American nations.
★ identify the causes of World War I.
★ explain why the United States had difficulty remaining neutral during the war.

Key Term
contraband

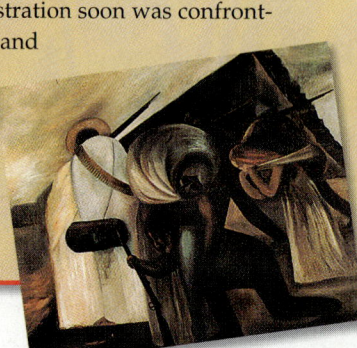

◀ *Revolution* by José Clemente Orozco, 1920

President Wilson's focus on domestic issues was demonstrated in his first Inaugural Address in 1913. He was comfortable with and well-informed on matters such as the tariff and banking. But in foreign affairs neither Wilson nor those he counted on for advice were experienced.

■ Wilson's Moral Diplomacy

As President, Wilson resolved to "strike a new note in international affairs" and to see that "sheer honesty and even unselfishness . . . should prevail over nationalistic self-seeking in American foreign policy." However, other forces at work at home and abroad frustrated his hope to lead the world by moral example.

Political Unrest in Mexico

For nearly 30 years, Mexico had been ruled by a dictator, Porfirio Díaz (pawr•FEE•rih•oh DEE•ahs). He brought stability and encouraged foreign investment in Mexico's economic development. When Díaz was overthrown in 1911, Mexico entered a period of political chaos.

Francisco Madero (frahn•SEES•koh muh•DEHR•oh) came to power. Investors in Mexico feared that the new president would confiscate all property owned by foreigners. Businesspeople and foreign diplomats plotted with units of the Mexican army to overthrow Madero. Before Wilson took office, General Victoriano Huerta (veek•toh•ree•AH•noh WEHR•tuh) seized power, and Madero was murdered—presumably on Huerta's orders.

American capitalists supported Huerta in the belief that he would support business

UNIT 8 Crusade and Disillusion: 1914–1932

Classroom Resources for SECTION 1

Teacher's Classroom Resources
- Chapter 25 Study Guide
- Reproducible Lesson Plan
- Reteaching Activity 25-1
- Chapter 25 Cooperative Learning Activity
- Chapter 25 Primary and Secondary Source Readings
- Section Quiz

Multimedia
- Section Focus Transparency 83
- Chapter 25 Skills Transparency
- Testmaker
- Student Self-Test Software
- Lessons of War

interests. Other countries with large Mexican investments recognized the new ruler. Repulsed by Huerta's brutality, Wilson refused to recognize the new government. He was convinced that without United States support "the unspeakable Huerta" would be overthrown.

Wilson Intervenes

Because Huerta remained in power, Wilson looked for a reason to intervene. In April 1914, American sailors on shore in the city of Tampico (tam•PEE•koh) clashed with Mexican authorities. Seeing a chance to overthrow Huerta, Wilson sent marines to seize the Mexican port of Veracruz (VEHR•uh•KROOZ). Although Wilson expected the Mexican people to welcome his action, anti-American riots broke out in Mexico and throughout Latin America. The President's intervention also was condemned in the European press.

Shocked by world reaction, Wilson accepted an offer from the ABC powers (Argentina, Brazil, and Chile) to mediate the dispute. The ABC powers supported Wilson by recommending that Huerta go into exile.

Venustiano Carranza (vay•noos•TYAH•noh kuh•RAN•zuh) was installed as Mexico's president.

Yet trouble continued between the United States and Mexico. Mexican forces opposed to Carranza conducted raids into the United States. Led by Pancho Villa (PAHN•choh VEE•yuh), guerrillas burned the town of Columbus, New Mexico, and killed 18 Americans. Wilson sent 6,000 troops under General John J. Pershing across the border to find and capture Villa. A year-long expedition failed to capture the guerrillas and resulted in a clash with the Mexican army. Tensions eased in January 1917 when Wilson's growing concern over the war in Europe caused him to recall the troops.

In the Caribbean

Wilson followed Roosevelt's example by ordering marines in Nicaragua, Haiti, and the Dominican Republic to preserve order and set up governments viewed by Americans as more stable than those in control. In 1917 the United States expanded its naval power in the Caribbean by purchasing Denmark's strategically valuable Virgin Islands.

 ▲ **MARINES IN VERACRUZ** In April 1914 President Woodrow Wilson ordered American forces into Mexico to seize the port of Veracruz. *How did Latin American nations respond to American intervention?*

Sidelights: Views of Wilson's Diplomacy

Concerning the Mexican Revolution, President Wilson cautioned "watchful waiting." Interventionists termed his policy "deadly drifting." One critic joked about Wilson's diplomacy when he made up a dance step called the Wilson Tango. It consisted of one step forward, two steps back, one to the side, and then a hesitation.

CHAPTER 25 SECTION 1

Independent Practice

Analyzing Primary Sources Have students read the eyewitness account on this page of German troops marching through Brussels. Ask them to consider the role of primary source documents in the reconstruction of history. Have students write a firsthand account of how they might feel if they watched an army with tanks and weapons approaching their neighborhood. Suggest students read their accounts to the class. Discuss how such eyewitness reports contribute to interpreting and reconstructing history. You might ask if eyewitness accounts are always the most objective sources. **L2**

Visualizing History Emiliano Zapata fought for the poor. He gathered around him tenant farmers or those who had lost their land. The fight for land was one of the key elements in Mexico's civil wars.
Answer to Caption: Wilson sent troops to find and capture Villa.

Did You Know?

For a time Pancho Villa's forces held Mexico City. He finally was defeated by Mexican general Alvaro Obregón, who in 1920 rebelled against Carranza and became Mexico's president.

■ War in Europe

While Wilson was dealing with problems in Mexico and the Caribbean, Europe began one of the bloodiest wars in its history. After almost 50 years of general peace, tensions built up.

Setting the Stage for War

In the late 1800s, as Europe became industrialized and nations sought to establish empires, tensions arose among colonizing nations. Within Europe itself, nationalism also heightened rivalries and tension. Much of central and eastern Europe was ruled by empires that included several nationality groups, each with its own language. Many of these groups wanted to form independent nations by joining with similar groups in other nations. In Austria-Hungary, for example, Slavic groups resented being ruled by the Germans and Magyars (Hungarians). They wanted to join other Slavic peoples to form a South Slav, or Yugoslav, nation in the Balkans.

The Balkans were an area of Slavic peoples in southeastern Europe that for decades had been fought over by three major powers—Russia, Austria-Hungary, and the Ottoman Empire (Turkey and its provinces). In 1908 Austria-Hungary annexed two Balkan territories once ruled by the Turks, Bosnia and Herzegovina (HEHRT•suh•goh•VEE•nuh). Serbia, a Balkan nation on Austria-Hungary's border, called on Russia, its historic protector, for help. The Russians, weakened from their defeat by Japan in 1905 and wanting the Balkans for themselves, did nothing.

This instability and the complex rivalries led to an arms race as each country sought to defend itself. The arms race generated more mistrust and helped military leaders achieve more power and influence in European governments.

Formation of Alliances

The European nations made alliances with one another for mutual self-defense. The Triple Alliance drew together Germany, Austria-Hungary, and Italy. Fearing isolation in Europe, France and Russia agreed to help each other if either became involved in war with Germany or Austria-Hungary. France arranged a separate partnership with Great Britain known as the Entente Cordiale (AHN•TAHNT KAWR•DYAHL), meaning "cordial understanding." After Russia's defeat in 1905 reduced Britain's fear of Russian power, all three nations came together to form the Triple Entente.

War Begins

Tensions were high in June 1914, when Archduke Franz Ferdinand, heir to the throne of Austria-Hungary, visited Bosnia. His assassination by Slavic nationalist Gavrilo Princip provided the incident that ignited Europe into war. Austria-Hungary declared war on Serbia on July 28, 1914.

One month after the assassination, war exploded in Europe. To protect its status as a European power, Russia felt it had to defend Serbia. Believing that Germany would aid Austria-Hungary, Russian armies mobilized along the borders of both nations. Germany demanded that Russia halt its threatening acts and that France pledge neutrality in the event of a war between Russia and Germany. Both Russia and France rejected Germany's demands. On August 1 Germany declared war on Russia;

▶ **PANCHO VILLA** Many Americans viewed Pancho Villa as nothing more than a bandit. To Mexico's poor, however, he was a democratic savior. **What action did Wilson take against Villa?**

686 UNIT 8 Crusade and Disillusion: 1914–1932

Critical Thinking

Explaining Causes Write the following terms on the chalkboard: *imperialism, nationalism, militarism, balance of power.* Have students define each term. Using the text and additional research, ask them to explain how each contributed to war in Europe. Ask if students think any one nation or group of nations was primarily responsible for World War I. Have each give evidence to support his or her opinion. **L3**

on August 3 it declared war on France. The German army crossed neutral Belgium on its way to invade France.

Responding to the invasion of Belgium, Great Britain declared war on Germany. Europe was divided into two camps. Those fighting for the Triple Entente were called the Allies. Italy (which switched sides in 1915) France, Russia, and Great Britain formed the backbone of the Allies. What remained of the Triple Alliance—Germany and Austria-Hungary—joined with the Ottoman Empire and Bulgaria to form the Central Powers.

United States Neutrality

As war consumed Europe, Americans hoped the vast Atlantic Ocean would keep them out of the conflict. President Wilson stated that this was "a war with which we had nothing to do."

Taking of Sides

Despite a neutral stance, America could not help but take sides. Immigrants of European nationality groups gave many Americans roots that influenced their opinions. Many of the 8 million German Americans were sympathetic to their homeland. Many Irish Americans, seething from British domination of Ireland, also hoped for a German victory. In general, however, the common heritage shared by the United States and Britain, and America's historic links with France, put American public opinion on the side of the Allies.

Both Sides Strain Neutrality

America's neutrality did not protect it from either the Allies or the Central Powers. The British imposed a blockade on the Central Powers. They planted mines in the North Sea, forced neutral ships into port for inspection, opened American mail, and redefined **contraband**, or prohibited materials, so that not even food could be shipped to Germany. Trade between the United States and the Central Powers shrank.

At the same time, exports from the United States to the Allies nearly quadrupled, as war materials and food from America helped the Allies. Ties between the United States and the Allies became closer when the United States government lent the Allies $2 billion. The American public purchased another $2 billion in British and French war bonds.

To retaliate against the British blockade, cut off Britain's war supplies, and starve Britain into submission, the Germans relied on a new weapon—the submarine. The "U-boat" broke long-established rules of warfare by sinking unarmed ships. International law required that unarmed ships not be sunk without providing for the safety of passengers and crews.

▲ **ASSASSINATION IN SARAJEVO** The assassination of Archduke Ferdinand and his wife proved to be a fateful event. Within a month, the continent of Europe was ablaze with war. *How did the United States react to the start of war?*

CHAPTER 25 World War I Era 1914–1920

CHAPTER 25
SECTION 1

ASSESS

Check Understanding
Assign Section 1 Review as homework or an in-class activity.

Evaluate
Assign Section 1 Quiz in the TCR, or use the History of a Free Nation Testmaker to create a customized quiz.

Reteach
Have students complete Reteaching Activity 25-1.

Enrich
Suggest that students use primary sources, such as newspaper accounts, to follow the course of the war. Have them present their findings by summarizing them in a feature article with an appropriate headline.

CLOSE

Have students examine the photographs in Section 1. Ask how the photos represent factors that brought the United States into World War I.

Visualizing History Point out that such incidents as this sinking by a U-boat fueled anger in Americans and helped encourage the United States to enter the war.
Answer to Caption: It violated rules of international warfare.

 ▶ **WAR ON THE SEAS** United States neutrality was put to a test when German submarines attacked American vessels in the Atlantic. *Why were submarine attacks considered a barbaric act of war?*

In 1915 the British passenger liner *Lusitania* was sunk. Nearly 1,200 passengers drowned—including 128 Americans. Some Americans felt that this act was grounds for war. But others thought that people who traveled on ships of warring nations did so at their own risk, especially when Germany had taken out newspaper ads warning Americans not to travel on the *Lusitania*.

The Sussex Pledge

Wilson steered a middle course on the issue of the U-boats. He refused to take extreme measures against Germany. However, he sent several messages to Germany insisting that its government safeguard the lives of noncombatants in the war zones.

Late in March 1916, Wilson's policy was tested when a U-boat torpedoed the French passenger ship *Sussex,* injuring several Americans on board. Although Wilson's advisers favored breaking off relations with Germany, the President chose to issue a final warning. He demanded that the German government abandon submarine warfare or risk war with the United States. Germany did not want to strengthen the Allies by drawing the United States into the war. So it offered to compensate Americans injured on the *Sussex* and promised with certain conditions to sink no more merchant ships without warning. The Sussex Pledge, as it was called, met the foreign-policy goals of both Germany and the President by keeping the United States out of war a little longer.

Section 1 ★ Review

Checking for Understanding
1. **Identify** Victoriano Huerta, Pancho Villa, Austria-Hungary, Serbia, Triple Alliance, Triple Entente, *Lusitania*, U-boat.
2. **Define** contraband.
3. **Cite** two causes of World War I.
4. **Describe** two trends that made American neutrality difficult.

Critical Thinking
5. **Evaluating Tactics** Can German U-boat attacks on the *Lusitania* and *Sussex* be justified? Explain your position.

688 UNIT 8 Crusade and Disillusion: 1914–1932

Answers to SECTION 1 REVIEW
1. Victoriano Huerta, 684; Pancho Villa, 685; Austria-Hungary, 686; Serbia, 686; Triple Alliance, 686; Triple Entente, 686; *Lusitania*, 688; U-boat, 688.
2. All vocabulary words are defined in the Glossary.
3. nationalism, imperialism
4. Trade with Britain increased profits for American business, and Germany's submarine warfare threatened maritime commerce.
5. Answers will vary. Yes: There are no rules in war—it was necessary to break the British blockade of Germany. Americans should not travel on ships of warring nations. No: Killing civilians is not justified by military goals.

Social Studies Skills

Map and Graph Skills

Interpreting a Political Map

The ability to read and understand a map is a skill that may be applied in many areas and is useful in the study of history. There are many kinds of maps in use today. In this text, you have studied several different types: historical, physical, thematic, and political.

Historical maps show places and events from the past. Physical maps show natural features such as mountains, valleys, plains, and bodies of water. Thematic maps deal with specialized information, often on a single topic such as population density, land use, languages, and natural resources.

A political map shows the political boundaries or borders of a state, country, and/or region. Political maps change whenever political borders change. A political map of the world today looks very different from one only 10 years old.

Follow these procedures when you evaluate a political map:

- **Determine** the time period covered by the map. This may be given in the title, although some political maps supply the date in the copyright.
- **Read** the map title and scale.
- **Examine** the legend. What information, other than political boundaries, is provided by the map?
- **Analyze** the lines of latitude and longitude. These lines are constant—they do not change. Use them when you compare change in boundaries over time. Boundaries are usually represented by a solid dark line.

Practicing the Skill

Apply the information from the chapter and the guidelines shown as you analyze the map of Europe in 1914.

1. What countries shown on this map maintained neutrality during World War I?
2. How might location have influenced neutrality?
3. Explain this statement: In 1914 the borders of the United Kingdom were determined by geography, not just politics.
4. Compare the map on this page with the map of Europe on page 702. What became of Austria-Hungary?
5. Compare the two maps. What happened to Serbia?
6. Compare the two maps. Before World War I, Finland was part of what nation?
7. Compare the two maps. What became of the Baltic Provinces?

Europe in 1914

LESSON PLAN
Mastering Social Studies Skills

Teaching Map and Graph Skill

Ask what information besides national boundaries the map on page 689 shows. (alignment of nations) Based on information provided on this map, how might war affect Russia? (would be cut off from its allies by the Central Powers)

Use Chapter 25 Map Transparency.

FACT or FICTION?

European nations established alliances because they were continuously in conflict with one another.

FICTION: Europe had not had a major war for 100 years, since the end of the Napoleonic Wars in 1815.

Answers to SOCIAL STUDIES SKILLS

1. Norway, Sweden, Denmark, the Netherlands, Switzerland, Spain, Albania
2. Most neutral nations were on the boundaries of Europe; Switzerland and the Netherlands were caught between the two alliances and might have felt safer being neutral.
3. Great Britain is an island nation, surrounded by water, and is not part of the continent of Europe.
4. The empire was broken up into separate nations—Austria, Hungary, Czechoslovakia, Yugoslavia.
5. part of Yugoslavia
6. Russia
7. became independent nations of Estonia, Latvia, Lithuania

LESSON PLAN
SECTION 2, 690–695

FOCUS

Bellringer
Before taking roll at the beginning of the class period, display Focus Activity Transparency 84 on the overhead projector, and assign the accompanying Focus Activity Sheet.

Objectives
Point out the objectives on this page to students in previewing the section content.

Motivating Activity
Refer students to the list of reasons for going to war that they compiled at the beginning of this chapter. Ask them to speculate about which reasons might bring the United States into World War I. Explain that as they read Section 2, they will be able to compare their speculations with the reasons described in the text.

- *GTV: A Geographic Perspective on American History*

Side 4, Chapter 1
Title: *Modern Times*
Subject: World War I: before and after

See GTV Guide page 57 for complete lesson plan.

SECTION 2

America Enters the War

Setting the Scene

Section Focus

In the presidential election of 1916, the Democrats again chose Woodrow Wilson as their candidate. This time the campaign focused on Wilson's diplomatic skills, using the slogan "He kept us out of the war." Americans, however, gave his policies a less-than-ringing endorsement. When the election votes were counted, Wilson won, but it was a very close race.

Objectives

After studying this section, you should be able to

★ identify the events that led the United States to enter World War I.

★ describe the role of the United States in helping the Allies to achieve victory over the Central Powers.

Key Term

armistice

◀ **DISTINGUISHED SERVICE CROSS**

In 1916 Wilson ran for reelection on a peace ticket under the slogan "He kept us out of the war." Although Wilson never used the slogan himself, he emphasized that he had kept "peace with honor."

Wilson defeated the Republican candidate Charles Evans Hughes in a close election. Following his reelection, Wilson devoted his energies to finding a peaceful solution to the war. The President realized the only sure way to keep Americans out of the European conflict was to end this terrible war altogether.

A quick victory eluded both sides, as defensive weapons proved superior to offensive tactics. The war was especially gruesome. The use of poison gas and such other new weapons as the tank and the machine gun, along with enormous casualty lists, ended the optimism that had pervaded western Europe before the war.

■ "Peace Without Victory"

On December 18, 1916, Wilson asked the warring nations to state their peace terms. As a neutral party, he hoped to negotiate a settlement, but both sides responded with terms that their opponents would not accept. In spite of these replies, Wilson addressed the Senate on January 22, 1917, calling for "peace without victory." "A victor's peace," he argued, "would leave a sting, a resentment, a bitter memory upon which terms of peace would rest only as upon quicksand. Only a peace between equals can last."

Submarine Warfare Resumes

The Germans soon dashed Wilson's hope of mediating an end to the war. German losses on the battlefield and the shortages

690 UNIT 8 Crusade and Disillusion: 1914–1932

Classroom Resources for SECTION 2

Teacher's Classroom Resources
- Reproducible Lesson Plan
- Reteaching Activity 25-2
- Section Quiz

Multimedia
- Section Focus Transparency 83
- Chapter 25 Map Transparency
- Testmaker
- Student Self-Test Software
- A Geographic Perspective on American History

caused by the British blockade forced Germany to resume unrestricted submarine warfare. German naval commanders claimed they could starve Britain into submission in five months if the German government gave U-boats permission to sink ships on sight. The Germans felt that even if this violation of their Sussex Pledge drew the United States into the war, the Americans could not raise an army and transport it to Europe in time to prevent the Allies from collapsing. Therefore, Germany decided to risk American involvement and, on January 31, 1917, announced that all vessels in waters near Great Britain, France, and Italy would be sunk without warning.

On February 3, 1917, Wilson responded to this threat by breaking off diplomatic relations with Germany. When goods piled up in American ports because ships feared to sail, he asked Congress for the power to arm merchant ships. This measure passed the House of Representatives easily, but an 11-person filibuster blocked the bill on the Senate floor. The President refused to be stopped by the effort of this "little group of willful men." Finding the authority in a 1797 law, Wilson armed the merchant ships.

Drawn Into War

Meanwhile, other events caused the nation's antagonism toward Germany to mount. The British government revealed that it had intercepted a cable from the German foreign minister, Arthur Zimmermann, to the German ambassador in Mexico. Zimmermann instructed the ambassador to arrange an alliance between Mexico and Germany in the event that the United States entered the war. To encourage Mexico's cooperation, Germany promised that Mexico would regain Texas, Arizona, and New Mexico upon a German victory. American newspapers published the Zimmermann Note, outraging the public. Then, between March 12 and March 19, four American merchant ships were sunk without warning. Two days later Wilson called a special session of Congress to consider "grave questions of national policy."

On April 2, 1917, Wilson appeared before Congress with a heavy heart. In one of the most eloquent speeches ever delivered in the Capitol, the President asked the members of Congress to declare war on Germany:

▲ **PREPARING FOR WAR** Americans register for the draft in March 1916. The World War I era produced this classic recruitment poster, which has been used ever since. *What percent of American troops went to Europe?*

CHAPTER 25 World War I Era 1914–1920

Critical Thinking

Analyzing Assumptions Write the word *assumption* on the chalkboard. Point out to students that in late 1916 Germany assumed that the United States would not be able to mobilize in time to make any difference to the war in Europe. Ask students to list the actions Germany took that were based on this assumption. Then have them make a list of actions Germany might have taken had it not made this assumption, including any actions that might have ended the war. **L2**

▲ JOHN J. PERSHING

 **Visualizing History** ▲ **AMERICANS IN FRANCE** General John J. Pershing (center), arriving in France at Boulogne in June 1917, commanded the American forces. *What was the status of the conflict when the United States entered the war?*

> " *It is a fearful thing to lead this great, peaceful people into war, into the most terrible and disastrous of all wars, civilization itself seeming to be in the balance. But the right is more precious than peace, and we shall fight for the things which we have always carried nearest our hearts—for democracy, for the right of . . . free peoples as shall bring peace and safety to all nations and make the world itself at last free. To such a task we dedicate our lives and our fortunes, everything we have. . . . [T]he day has come when America is privileged to spend her blood and her might for the principles that gave her birth and happiness and the peace which she has treasured. God helping her, she can do no other.* "

In his war message, the President insisted that the United States's quarrel was only with the "military masters" of Germany, and he expressed friendship for the German people. Maintaining that the United States had "no selfish ends to serve," Wilson stated that the people of the United States would be fighting to make the world "safe for democracy" and to promote "peace and safety to all nations." Four days after Wilson's message, Congress, after a spirited debate, declared war on Germany by the overwhelming margins of 82 votes to 6 in the Senate and 273 to 50 in the House.

■ Status of the Allies

When the United States entered the war, the Allies seemed in danger of defeat. U-boats were sinking ships at a rate that threatened to wipe out the entire merchant tonnage of the world; the British Isles had only a two-month supply of food with no relief in sight. Late in 1917 the Italians suffered a severe defeat at the village of Caporetto. Russia's military effort slackened and then ceased after the overthrow of the czar and the Bolshevik, or communist, revolution. In March 1918, Russia signed the Treaty of Brest-Litovsk, surrendering to Germany immense areas of land including Ukraine.

With one of the richest grain-growing areas in the world now in its possession, Germany hoped to relieve severe food shortages. Russia's withdrawal from the conflict also freed German armies to fight on the Western Front—the area along the French-German border where the war had been stalemated for nearly four years.

UNIT 8 Crusade and Disillusion: 1914–1932

CHAPTER 25 SECTION 2

The World at War: World War I

Map Study — Although most action in World War I occurred in Europe, it was truly a world conflict. Note the battles outside Europe, the intercontinental alliances, and Europe's division of Africa. **Why were so many battles fought in the Middle East?**

Map Study Using Maps

Answer: because the Ottoman Empire was allied with the Central Powers

Map Skills

After students have studied the maps on this page, have them write a paragraph explaining why World War I was not confined to Europe alone. (Students should recognize that worldwide alliances and the colonial empires held by various European countries expanded the conflict.)

Stars and Stripes, the GI newspaper staffed entirely by soldiers, was first published in 1918. In addition to being a source of information and morale for soldiers, it provided many young journalists and cartoonists with their first jobs. Two well-known cartoonists whose work appeared in Stars and Stripes were Milt Caniff ("Terry and the Pirates") and Bill Mauldin, who would win the Pulitzer Prize in 1945 for his Willie and GI Joe cartoons.

CHAPTER 25 World War I Era 1914–1920 693

Sidelights: American Pilots in France

Colonel Stanton's "Lafayette, we are here" declaration was not the first reference to the French general by the Americans. A squadron of American pilots led by French commanders had been flying hundreds of missions against Germany since 1916. Called the Lafayette Escadrille, it consisted mostly of French pilots and well-off Americans who loved flying. Because the United States was officially neutral, American pilots had to reach France in secret, usually through the French Foreign Legion, whose recruitment procedures were notoriously lax.

CHAPTER 25 SECTION 2

Teaching Life of the Times

Theodore Roosevelt, Jr., described the living conditions in the trenches as follows: "Gray dropsical rats ambled around the shelters. Men were soaked from one day's end to the other.... Hands and feet were frost-bitten...." In addition to the miserable conditions, trench warfare took an appalling toll of lives. In the Battle of the Somme, in France, the British lost 60,000 soldiers in the first day's attack. In the entire battle, which lasted from July to October 1916, France, Great Britain, and Germany together lost more than one million men.

Did You Know?

One of the most moving literary works to emerge from World War I is a novel by Erich Maria Remarque. In his book *All Quiet on the Western Front*, Remarque tells the story of the war through the eyes of a young German soldier. At the end of the novel, the young man thinks about what his world will be like after the war, but he is killed only a month before the armistice is signed, on a day so calm that a battlefield report noted: "All quiet on the Western Front."

Life of the Times

Doughboys

After Congress declared war, hundreds of thousands of Americans followed urgings such as "DON'T READ AMERICAN HISTORY, MAKE IT!" which appeared on a recruitment poster designed by James Montgomery Flagg, the leading poster artist of the war. Volunteers gave different reasons for joining the armed services. "Because girls like soldiers"

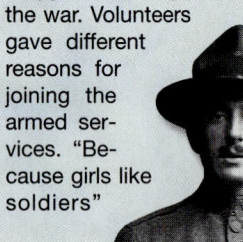

▶ SOLDIER, 1917

was a popular response; "to see the world" was another. Allied troops welcomed the Americans whose shipshape appearance—prior to entering the trenches—inspired the unique nickname "doughboys."

The war was more than the odor of the trenches; the agony of poison gas; and the trauma of violent tremors, which indicated battle shock. To relieve the monotony, soldiers organized musicals and variety shows, betting pools, and holiday celebrations.

Inter-Allied boxing matches and baseball provided additional diversion. Military experience proved a turning point in the lives and attitudes of many young men. For some, the war was the greatest adventure of their lives.

▼ THE ROCK OF THE MARNE BY MAL THOMPSON

Among the doughboys who never lost touch with his wartime friends was Harry Truman, who chose several buddies from Battery D to advise him when he became President in 1945.

Raising an Army

The Allies did not expect the United States to participate in combat because in the spring of 1917 American forces numbered only 200,000. In addition, the army possessed only 1,500 machine guns, 55 obsolete airplanes, and no heavy artillery.

The Draft

Although these numbers looked discouraging, the United States mobilized rapidly. On May 18, 1917, Congress passed the Selective Service Act, requiring all men between the ages of 21 and 30 to register for military service. In June nearly 10 million young men signed up. The draft eventually extended to all men between 18 and 45 and resulted in the induction of 2.8 million men into the armed forces. Another 2 million men and women volunteered for military service.

Twelve weeks after war had been declared, the first United States soldiers landed in France. On July 4, symbolically recalling the American-French partnership during the American Revolution, Colonel Charles E. Stanton stood at the tomb of France's great war hero, Marquis de Lafayette, and said, "Lafayette, we are here." More than 2 million American soldiers comprising 42 infantry divisions reached France before the war ended. This vast new reservoir of military strength was an important factor in the Allied victory.

African Americans

Among those drafted to serve in the war were some 370,000 African Americans; of these, 200,000 served overseas. African American soldiers encountered rampant discrimination and prejudice in the army, where their units were completely segregated from white units. In addition, African Americans were not allowed to serve in the Marine Corps, and the 10,000 in the navy were restricted to the lower ranks.

Critical Thinking

Supporting Opinions Many historians believe that the most significant factors in the defeat of the Central Powers were the entrance of the United States into the war and the collapse of the Russian Empire. Do you agree with this assessment? What evidence can you find to support the conclusion? Is there evidence to refute it? Ask students to write a paragraph explaining their opinion. Have them cite evidence in support. **L1**

Still, in the bitter battles along the Western Front, African American soldiers fought valiantly, winning praise from both the French commander, Marshal Henri Pétain (ahn•REE pay•TAN), and the United States commander, General John Pershing. African American soldiers in one infantry regiment won 21 American Distinguished Service Crosses and 68 French military decorations. The entire 369th Infantry won the highly prized French decoration, the Croix de Guerre (KRWAH dih GEHR), for gallantry.

Victory on Land and Sea

In the spring and early summer of 1918, Germany made a last desperate effort to win the war and nearly succeeded. Starting in March, the Germans almost penetrated the British lines; a second drive in June threatened Paris. United States troops helped to stop the advance, distinguishing themselves in a counterattack at Château-Thierry (SHA•TOH TYEH•REE), a town less than 50 miles from Paris.

The tide turned in mid-July as Marshal Ferdinand Foch (FAWSH), supreme commander of the Allied armies, ordered a great counteroffensive along the Western Front close to the German border. Pershing requested that American troops be assigned a section of the front for themselves—an area near Verdun. In mid-September 550,000 "doughboys"—the nickname given American soldiers—won an overwhelming victory at St.-Mihiel (san mee•yehl). Then an even larger force drove toward the key city of Sedan, breaking through well-defended portions of the German lines.

By early November, the Allies were poised to advance onto German soil. Realizing the war was lost, the Germans signed an **armistice,** or temporary stop to the fighting, on November 11, 1918.

American naval forces joined the British in waging war against Germany's deadly U-boats. The invention of the depth charge, an underwater explosive, provided the Allies with a new weapon, but its effective use demanded hundreds of patrol vessels to watch for U-boats and protect Allied ships by convoying, or escorting, them out of dangerous areas. So, in addition to 79 destroyers, the United States supplied more than 100 small "sub-chasers" plus a variety of former yachts, tugs, and fishing boats—"almost any craft which could carry a wireless, a gun, and depth charges was boldly sent to sea." By the end of 1917, the number of U-boat casualties was slashed in half. In 1918 the United States Navy took the principal role in laying mines across the North Sea, which prevented U-boats from reaching the Atlantic Ocean and isolated those already at sea from ports and supplies.

◀ WORLD WAR I SHELL

Section 2 ★ Review

Checking for Understanding

1. **Identify** Zimmermann Note, Selective Service Act, John Pershing, doughboys.
2. **Define** armistice.
3. **Explain** the meaning of the phrases "peace without victory" and "Lafayette, we are here."
4. **Summarize** the events that brought the United States into the war.

Critical Thinking

5. **Assessing Outcomes** Would Germany have won if the United States had not entered the war? Explain your position.

CHAPTER 25 World War I Era 1914–1920   **695**

Answers to SECTION 2 REVIEW

1. Zimmerman note, 691; Selective Service Act, 694; John Pershing, 694; doughboys, 695.
2. All vocabulary words are defined in the Glossary.
3. no total winners or losers, recognized France's support of American Revolution
4. resumption of submarine warfare, growing antagonism against Germany, Zimmermann note
5. Answers will vary. Although war was stalemated in Europe, until the United States's entrance, German U-boats were threatening Great Britain. American supplies kept Great Britain from starving, and American troops, besides supplying manpower, boosted Allied morale, especially after Russia made a separate peace.

CHAPTER 25 SECTION 2

ASSESS

Check Understanding
Assign Section 2 Review as homework or an in-class activity.

Evaluate
Assign Section 2 Quiz in the TCR, or use the History of a Free Nation Testmaker to create a customized test.

Reteach
Have students identify each of the following and explain his role in World War I: Newton D. Baker (U.S. secretary of war), Henri Pétain (French commander), John J. Pershing (commander of American Expeditionary Forces), Ferdinand Foch (supreme commander of Allied forces), Arthur Zimmermann (German foreign minister).

Have students complete Reteaching Activity 25-2.

Enrich
One of the most significant events of World War I was the Russian Revolution. Have students research the causes of the revolution, its effect on the course of the war, and how it influenced United States policy.

CLOSE
Remind students that Woodrow Wilson ran in 1916 under the slogan "He Kept Us Out of War." Ask students if they would have voted for him and why.

695

LESSON PLAN
SECTION 3, 696–700

FOCUS

Bellringer
Before taking roll at the beginning of the class period, display Focus Activity Transparency 85 on the overhead projector, and assign the accompanying Focus Activity Sheet.

Objectives
Point out the objectives on this page to students in previewing the section content.

Motivating Activity
Ask students to imagine that they are young people at the time of World War I. Have them list some of the things they could do to contribute to the war effort on the home front. Tell them that in this section they will learn how Americans at home contributed to victory abroad.

ABC NEWS INTERACTIVE™

The following material is available from Glencoe and may be used to enrich Chapter 25:

VIDEODISC
Lessons of War

Side Two
Chapter 11: The Enemy

SECTION 3

War on the Home Front

Setting the Scene

Section Focus
In order to raise and equip vast armies, increase the size of the navy elevenfold, and keep munitions and food flowing to the Allies, massive reorganization of American business, industry, and agriculture was needed. Victory in World War I was due, in large part, to the great efforts and sacrifices made on the home front.

Objectives
After studying this section, you should be able to
★ explain how the war was financed.
★ describe how public opinion was shaped by the government.
★ discuss the goals of Wilson's Fourteen Points.

Key Term
victory garden

▲ WORLD WAR I POSTER, 1918

The United States found itself ill-equipped for battle when it entered World War I. The most immediate domestic concern that Congress faced was to keep the United States and Allied armies supplied by gearing United States industry to the war machine. In addition, the federal government needed to raise money to pay for the war and to mobilize the American people to support the war effort.

■ Mobilizing the Economy

To accomplish these goals, Wilson and Congress applied the Progressive Era's ideals of efficiency, control, and conformity in society to the war effort at home. "It is not an army that we must shape and train for war," said the President, "it is a nation."

Organizing Industries

The government's solution to the problem of supplying the troops was to place most industries under the control of federal agencies. The most important of these—the War Industries Board—handled purchasing for both the Allies and the United States. Under the leadership of Bernard Baruch, a Wall Street stockbroker, the War Industries Board attempted "to operate the whole United States as a single factory dominated by one management." Enlisting the most able businesspeople in America to direct the war effort, the government received the cooperation of business to convert factories to war production. Federal officials determined how raw materials would be allocated and what prices should be fixed.

The Fuel Administration was in charge of boosting coal and oil production, while encouraging people to conserve. The agency

UNIT 8 Crusade and Disillusion: 1914–1932

Classroom Resources for SECTION 3

Teacher's Classroom Resources
- Reproducible Lesson Plan
- Reteaching Activity 25-3
- Section Quiz

Multimedia
- Section Focus Transparency 85
- Testmaker
- Student Self-Test Software
-  Lessons of War

introduced such conservation methods as daylight savings time and shortened workweeks for nonwar-related factories. The Railroad Administration took charge of the railroads and ran them as a single system. The War Labor Board worked to prevent labor disputes.

Labor unions generally supported the war effort, hoping that cooperation would result in goodwill from the government and big business. Union leaders saw in the war opportunities for higher pay, better working conditions, and the right to organize and bargain collectively. Membership in unions doubled, and unions won concessions, such as the eight-hour day that industries had long opposed.

Involvement of Women

Wartime also meant increased opportunities for American women. Millions of jobs given up by men who volunteered or were drafted were filled by women. For the first time, women were welcomed in many occupations. Female workers became an essential part of the nation's war effort in war industries and defense plants.

Despite the progress toward social and economic equality the war offered them, many women wondered how the United States could be fighting to save democracy and still deny them the vote at home. Activists for woman suffrage continued to work during the war.

Involvement of African Americans

African Americans might well have asked similar questions because Southern states continued to deny them the right to vote. Also, African American soldiers fighting in Europe encountered far less discrimination from Europeans than they had experienced in their own country.

Nevertheless, the war offered new opportunities for African Americans at home. Job opportunities and high wages during the

 ▲ **AT HOME** During the war more and more women became a vital part of the labor force. In addition, women volunteered for noncombat duty on the war front or for a military Home Guard in the United States. **What happened to the suffrage movement during the war?**

CHAPTER 25 World War I Era 1914–1920   **697**

CHAPTER 25
SECTION 3

Independent Practice
Writing Slogans
Write the following slogans on the chalkboard or duplicate them as a handout.

"Food Will Win the War—Don't Waste It!"

"Every Scout to Save a Soldier"

"Every quarter, every dollar, helps to make the Kaiser holler!"

Discuss with students how slogans like these would help pull Americans together for a common effort. Then ask students to create their own slogans to inspire Americans to get behind the war efforts. **L1**

Food of the Times
Although Americans did not suffer the terrible food shortages that occurred in Europe, they still had to stretch food supplies. There were meatless and breadless days. Across the nation thousands of backyards were turned into "Victory gardens" as Americans supplemented supplies by growing their own vegetables.

▲ POSTER SUPPORTING BONDS

war pulled 500,000 African Americans from Southern farms to munitions-producing Northern factories. Most were offered only unskilled or semiskilled jobs, but by war's end, more than 100,000 African Americans held jobs as skilled workers or factory supervisors.

Although discrimination against African American workers led to race riots in 26 Northern cities in 1919, African Americans in the North made significant economic gains during the war. As a result, migration northward continued after the war ended. One African American wrote a letter to a Chicago newspaper explaining this "great migration." African Americans, he said, were:

> ... compelled to go where there is better wages and sociable conditions, believe me ... many places here in [Alabama] the only thing that a black man gets is a peck of meal and from 3 to 4 lbs. of bacon per week, and he is treated as a slave.

Impact of War on Civilians

The war had a great impact on the lives of all American civilians. Using the slogan "Food Will Win the War—Don't Waste It," the Food Administration, directed by Herbert Hoover, supervised efforts to reduce food consumption. Families were encouraged to "Hooverize" by "serving just enough" and by having Wheatless Mondays and Meatless Tuesdays.

Citizens were also encouraged to plant **victory gardens,** gardens for raising their own vegetables. To increase wheat production, the federally financed Grain Corporation guaranteed farmers first $2.00, then $2.26 per bushel. In 1918 it bought the entire American wheat crop. The combined efforts of the Food Administration and the American public were tremendously successful.

The Cost of War

World War I was costly. By its end the United States was spending about $44 million a day, or a total of about $33 billion. Of that amount, $10 billion went to the Allies as loans. The government raised about one-third of the money to finance the war through taxation. Income taxes were increased, although only wealthier families paid income taxes at that time. Corporations also paid higher taxes, including an "excess profits" tax, designed to return war profits to the government. The government also levied excise duties on items as varied as theater tickets, chewing gum, and phonograph records.

The government borrowed the rest of the money—more than $20 billion—from the American people by selling four issues of Liberty Bonds and a postwar issue of Victory Bonds. Posters, rallies, and "Liberty Loan sermons" encouraged people to buy the bonds.

Purchasing bonds became an act of patriotism. Even children were urged to use their pennies to buy War Savings Stamps. Boy Scouts sold the stamps under the slogan "Every Scout to Save a Soldier." Twenty-one million people—more than one-fifth of the nation's population—subscribed to the Fourth Liberty Loan.

Cooperative Learning

Organize students into small groups, and have them research speeches made by the "four-minute men" or speeches given at "Liberty Loan sermon" rallies. Suggest that each group write a short original speech that could be used by a four-minute man or at a Liberty Loan sermon rally. When the speeches are completed, have group recorders summarize the main ideas for the rest of the class. **L3**

CHAPTER 25
SECTION 3

■ Controlling Public Opinion

Success of the war effort depended heavily on voluntary civilian cooperation. Therefore, the government wanted to make sure that Americans understood and supported the nation's war aims.

Selling the War to Americans

The Committee on Public Information under the leadership of journalist and author George Creel was established to "sell" the war to America. Creel described his job as "the world's greatest adventure in advertising." He recruited advertising people, commercial artists, authors, songwriters, entertainers, public speakers, and motion-picture companies to help him.

Millions of pamphlets were distributed explaining the causes and aims of the war. Thousands of "four-minute men" spoke at movie theaters and public halls and gatherings in support of the war effort. Although this flood of propaganda reinforced the President's image of the war as a moral crusade, it also helped promote widespread intolerance.

Control of War Protesters

To prevent spying and resistance to the war effort, Congress passed the Espionage and Sedition acts. Severe penalties imposed by these laws silenced most war opposition. Loyalty Leagues, organized by Creel, encouraged Americans to spy on their neighbors and to report those who might be "disloyal." In addition, the postmaster general was given authority to ban certain newspapers, magazines, and pamphlets from the mail. Thousands of people were imprisoned, sometimes for opinions expressed in private conversations. People were arrested for criticizing the President, for questioning the American form of government, for criticizing the army or even military uniforms. Socialist leader Eugene Debs was arrested and sentenced to 10 years in prison for merely telling an audience to "resist militarism, wherever found." People were even jailed for criticizing the Red Cross and the YMCA.

War fever was responsible for the vigorous enforcement of these laws, and the courts generally upheld the principle behind them. About 3,000 cases involving convictions under the Espionage and Sedition acts were heard on appeal in federal courts. After the war some of these cases

Teaching American Portraits

George M. Cohan wrote his most famous song, "Over There," on the day war was declared. He sat down at the piano and wrote what he said was just a bugle call. All wars have inspired songs. You might suggest that students research other songs of World War I and study the lyrics. How do they reflect the attitudes of the time? Are they idealistic, humorous, optimistic, patriotic, sentimental?

The mass media of the World War I period consisted only of newsprint. Film had not yet developed as a medium for spreading ideas, nor had the radio. Considering these limitations, World War I propaganda was extremely effective. Decades later, following World War II, an overwhelming media system of radio, television, film, and print was in place, creating a network that helped foster the "cold war" by projecting an image of the Soviet Union and communism as a threat to the security of the United States.

George M. Cohan
1878–1942

★★★★★★★★ AMERICAN PORTRAITS

By the time he wrote "Over There"—the most popular song of World War I—George M. Cohan was already one of America's biggest stars. At the age of 14, he was creating songs and skits for his family's vaudeville act. By his early 20s, he was writing, producing, and starring in hit Broadway shows.

Claiming that he had been born on the 4th of July (actually July 3), Cohan discovered early in his career that he could excite crowds with such patriotic appeals as his "I'm a Yankee Doodle Dandy."

When American troops left for France in 1917, he quickly penned "Over There," touching the chord of nationalistic fervor sweeping the country. His song became America's war anthem. In 1940 Congress awarded Cohan a Medal of Honor for "Over There" and "You're a Grand Old Flag," another patriotic song.

Sidelights: Expanding Role of Women

When men went off to fight, American women began to work at jobs they could not have dreamed of before the war. Necessity drove them into such areas as typesetting and operating linotype machines, and it also opened up jobs as mechanics, bricklayers, and streetcar operators. Some women became blacksmiths or telegraph operators. Thousands worked to keep their family farms going while the men were away. Although these gains were short-lived (many returned to their traditional roles as homemakers after the war), the experience left women with a new sense of their own worth and ability.

reached the Supreme Court. In the landmark case *Schenck v. United States* (1919), Justice Oliver Wendell Holmes, writing for a unanimous Court, stated:

> When a nation is at war, many things that might be said in time of peace are such a hindrance to its efforts that their utterance will not be endured so long as [soldiers] fight and that no Court could regard them as protected by any constitutional right....

The Court refused, however, to support punishment when no "clear and present danger" of hurting the United States existed or when the accused was jailed for unpopular political beliefs.

Persecution of Germans

War fever was also to blame for the mistreatment and persecution of German Americans. Despite Wilson's insistence that Americans were "the sincere friends of the German people," anti-German sentiment ran high. Many school systems banned the teaching of the German language, and orchestras stopped performing the music of Beethoven, Schubert, and Wagner.

■ Wilson's Fourteen Points

While the war was foremost in the President's mind, Wilson never ceased to think ahead to peace. In January 1918, Wilson went before Congress to present his goals

▲ LIBERTY LOAN POSTER

for a lasting peace. With his Fourteen Points (see Appendix), the President hoped to establish a new world order.

The Fourteen Points were based on "the principle of justice to all peoples." The President proposed to eliminate the general causes of war through disarmament, freedom of the seas, and open diplomacy instead of secret agreements. Wilson also addressed the right of peoples to live under a government of their own choosing. Finally, he proposed an international peacekeeping organization.

Although Wilson's words appealed to a world weary of war, other Allied leaders did not support him. They wanted German territory and to punish Germany. A formidable challenge lay ahead for the President if he were to see his dream of peace realized.

Section 3 ★ Review

Checking for Understanding

1. **Identify** Bernard Baruch, George Creel, War Industries Board, Liberty Bonds, Espionage and Sedition acts, Fourteen Points.
2. **Define** victory garden.
3. **Describe** three ways that Americans at home supported the war effort.
4. **List** the two ways the government raised money for the war.

Critical Thinking

5. **Defending an Opinion** Was government action to suppress opposition to the war justified? Formulate your own opinion and use facts to defend it.

SECTION 4

After the War

Setting the Scene

Section Focus

As Kaiser Wilhelm abdicated the German throne and fled, Germany signed an armistice. Now the Allies faced the task of constructing a framework for peace. Wilson still had support at home and enjoyed great popularity abroad. The opportunity to carry out his peace plan seemed at hand. However, his political blunders and the demands of Allied leaders doomed his chances.

Objectives

After studying this section, you should be able to
★ describe the outcome of the Versailles peace conference.
★ explain why the Senate rejected the Treaty of Versailles.
★ identify domestic problems that arose after the war.

Key Terms

covenant, deported

◀ WORLD WAR I HELMET

Midterm elections in the United States in November 1918 showed a changing attitude toward Wilson and his policies. Realizing that Democrats faced heavy losses in the elections, the President appealed to voters to show support for his peace program by returning Democrats to Congress. Instead, voters elected Republican majorities in both houses.

■ The Peace Plan Opposed

Shortly after the election, Wilson announced his intention to head the American delegation to the peace conference. His decision was not received well by those who thought that as President his place was at home. Wilson faltered again when he failed to include any prominent Republicans in the American delegation to the conference.

Peace Conference

The peace conference opened at the palace of Versailles in January 1919, but most of the sessions took place in Paris. Delegates from 27 nations attended. The proceedings, however, were dominated by the leaders of the three most powerful nations—the United States's President Wilson, Britain's Prime Minister David Lloyd George, and France's Premier Georges Clemenceau (KLEH•muhn•SOH). With Vittorio Orlando, the Italian premier, these men became known as "the Big Four." Because their meetings were held in secret, Wilson was robbed of an effective weapon—direct appeal to public opinion. Secrecy also seemed to violate the Fourteen Points, which pledged "open covenants openly arrived at." Nevertheless, the President scored an immediate triumph by forcing plans for a League of Nations into the

CHAPTER 25 World War I Era 1914–1920   **701**

LESSON PLAN
SECTION 4, 701–707

FOCUS

Bellringer

Display Focus Activity Transparency 86 on the overhead projector and assign the accompanying Focus Activity Sheet.

Objectives

Point out the objectives on this page to students in previewing the section content.

Motivating Activity

Read aloud the following words of President Wilson: "It must be a peace without victory.... Victory would mean peace forced upon the loser, a victor's terms imposed upon the vanquished...."

Ask students what the quotation suggests about the way Wilson would treat a defeated Germany.

Assign students the Chapter 25 Reading on Peace Without Victory in Primary and Secondary Source Readings.

NATIONAL GEOGRAPHIC SOCIETY

VIDEODISC
• *GTV: A Geographic Perspective on American History*

Side 4, Chapter 1
Title: *Modern Times*
Subject: World War I: before and after

See GTV Guide page 57 for complete lesson plan.

Classroom Resources for SECTION 4

Teacher's Classroom Resources
- Reproducible Lesson Plan
- Reteaching Activity 25-4
- Chapter 25 Primary and Secondary Source Readings
- Chapter 25 Enrichment Activity
- Chapter 25 Performance Assessment Activity
- Spanish Summaries and Glossary
- Section Quiz

Multimedia
- Section Focus Transparency 86
- Chapter 25 Map Transparency
- Vocabulary Puzzlemaker
- Testmaker
- Student Self-Test Software
- A Geographic Perspective on American History

701

CHAPTER 25 SECTION 4

TEACH

Guided Practice

Economics Write the following on index cards: Economic Controls, Demand for Consumer Goods, Peacetime Production, Wartime Government Spending, Inflation, Government Price Guarantees, Demand for Food, Wartime Crop Prices.

Direct students to take turns drawing a card, and use the phrase written on the card in a sentence that describes the United States economy either during or following the war. Write students' contributions on the board. When all the cards have been used, ask them to form generalizations about whether war is good or bad for the economy and why. **L2**

Map Study Using Maps

Answer: Palestine

Skills Practice

Have students use the map to name the Arab territories that went to Great Britain and France. (Great Britain gained Iraq, Trans-Jordan, Egypt, and Palestine; France gained Syria, Tunisia, Algeria, and French Morocco.) Ask students what generalizations they can form concerning British and French colonization. (Both Great Britain and France expanded their empires as a result of World War I.)

▲ WORLD WAR I BOOTS

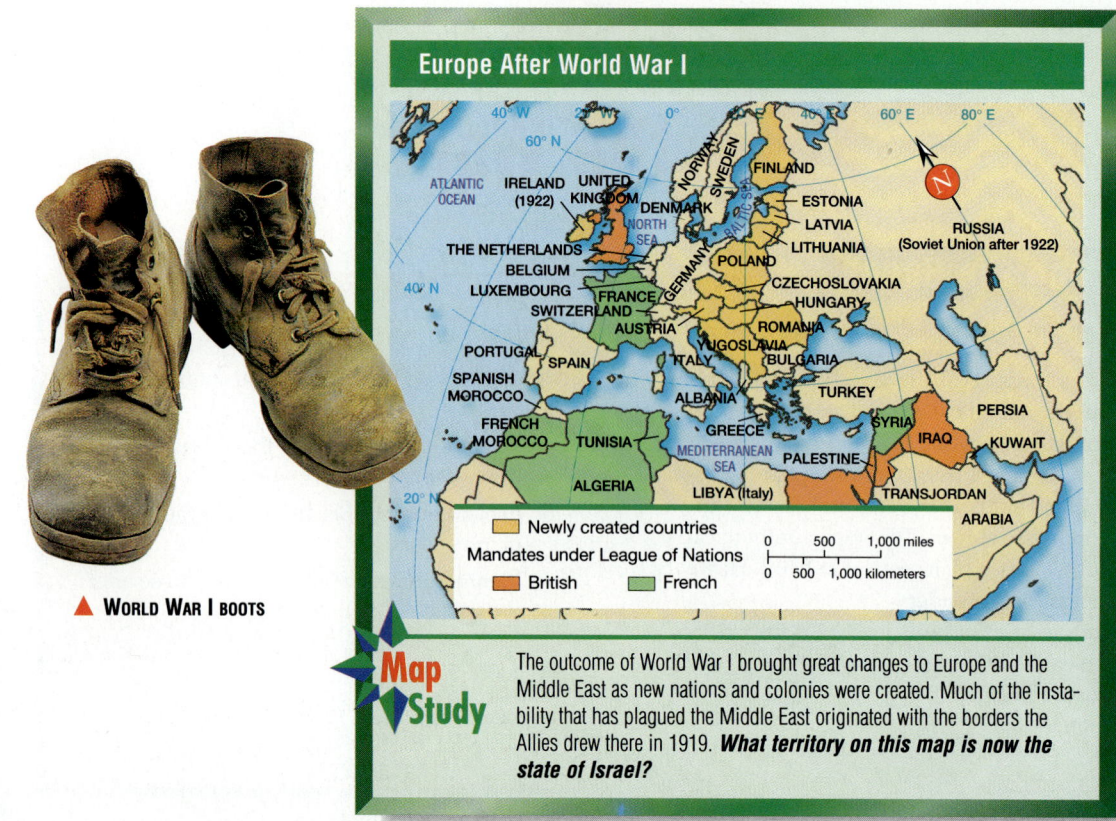

Map Study The outcome of World War I brought great changes to Europe and the Middle East as new nations and colonies were created. Much of the instability that has plagued the Middle East originated with the borders the Allies drew there in 1919. **What territory on this map is now the state of Israel?**

peace treaty. In mid-February the **covenant**, or charter, of the League, written by Wilson himself, was accepted by the conference.

Opposition Grows

During Wilson's absence his political influence in the United States weakened alarmingly. The likelihood that Wilson's peace program would fail became evident when 39 Republican senators and senators-elect—far more than enough to prevent ratification of a treaty—signed a statement opposing the League of Nations. Instead of trying to repair the rift, however, Wilson publicly denounced the "narrow, selfish, provincial purposes" of his opponents and insisted that the League be part of the peace treaty. At the peace table, he tried to appease his critics at home by calling for changes designed to protect American interests. To accept such changes, the Allies required Wilson to make further concessions in their favor.

Treaty of Versailles

Despite Wilson's hopes, it was a victor's peace. In the Middle East, the Ottoman Empire lost territory. In Europe, Austria-Hungary was split up. The greatest humiliation was reserved for the Germans, however. Germany lost territory and was stripped of its colonies. In addition, Germany was required to pay for damage it had done in Europe and to repay the Allies for the cost of the war. Although many of the Fourteen Points were ignored, Wilson trusted the League of Nations to right injustices after the desire for revenge subsided.

Difficulty at Home

The peace settlement complete, in July 1919 President Wilson came home to face his foes. Although he hoped Americans would support the treaty, they criticized it from all sides. In Congress a small group of

UNIT 8 Crusade and Disillusion: 1914–1932

Special Needs

Reading Disability Significant problems often arise because of a lack of decoding skills, and reading comprehension is weakened. By the time the student finishes a paragraph, he or she might have forgotten the beginning. For students who have very poor reading skills, have a good reader tape-record Section 4 so that the student can listen while following along in the text. Remind students to look at all the pictures and maps in the section.

senators branded the League a "treacherous and treasonable scheme," while a much larger group wanted the Senate to ratify the treaty but with amendments that would preserve the nation's freedom to act independently.

Instead of compromising, Wilson insisted that the Senate ratify the treaty without changes. Convinced that he could defeat his opposition by appealing to public opinion, Wilson went directly to the people. Starting in Ohio in September, he traveled 8,000 miles and made 37 major speeches in less than a month on behalf of the treaty. Almost everywhere his reception was warm; he seemed to be regaining popular support. Had his strength held out, he might have won the battle, but the physical strain proved too great for the President. He collapsed in Colorado on September 25 and was forced to abandon his speaking tour. Shortly after returning to the White House, Wilson suffered a stroke that paralyzed one side of his body and impaired his speech. He was bedridden for months, isolated from even his closest advisers.

With the President silenced, in November 1919, and again in March 1920, the Senate refused to ratify the Versailles treaty. Instead, the United States negotiated a separate peace treaty with each of the Central Powers in 1921.

America's Postwar Problems

The fate of the treaty was only one of the problems the United States faced after World War I. Demobilizing the armed forces, returning to a peacetime economy, and coping with fears of espionage presented the country with serious challenges.

Demobilization

The United States began to demobilize as soon as the hostilities ended. Within a short time, the army was reduced to less than 500,000, and economic controls were lifted. The businesspeople left Washington, D.C., and industry converted to peacetime production. With Wilson preoccupied with the peace treaty and later incapacitated, the nation received little overall direction. Industry enjoyed a brief postwar boom, resulting from the increased demand for consumer goods that had been scarce during the war. Unfortunately, government spending during the war brought inflation that nearly doubled the cost of living by 1919, and prices rose to a point where many consumers could not afford to pay for new items. Consequently, after 1920 business activity slowed. Farmers were especially hard-hit. Slackening demands for food and the end of government price guarantees caused agricultural prices to plummet. Many farmers who took advantage of high wartime crop prices and went into debt to expand their farms now faced bankruptcy.

 ▲ **SIGNING OF THE TREATY OF VERSAILLES** by John Johansen, 1919 The greatest obstacle at the peace conference was that many countries were interested chiefly in gaining territory and inflicting punishment on Germany. **Who played major roles in treaty negotiations?**

CHAPTER 25
SECTION 4

Independent Practice
Expressing an Opinion
Have students research the conflict over the ratification of the Treaty of Versailles and the acceptance of the League of Nations. Ask them to write a letter to the editor explaining why they believed the League is to the advantage or disadvantage of the United States. **L2**

Did You Know?
Robert LaFollette, progressive reformer and former governor of Wisconsin, became a senator in 1906. He opposed United States membership in the League of Nations. LaFollette believed that the Treaty of Versailles was unjust and that the United States, if it joined the League, would have to uphold the treaty.

Visualizing History
The demands of European leaders to punish Germany and protect the interests of their own nations did not fit with President Wilson's goals concerning a postwar world. He only agreed to the treaty because it called for a League of Nations.
Answer to Caption: the United States, Great Britain, France, and Italy

---

Cooperative Learning

Organize students into four groups, and have each group draw up a list of interview questions for one of the principals at the Versailles peace conference: David Lloyd George of Great Britain; Vittorio Orlando of Italy; Georges Clemenceau of France; and Woodrow Wilson of the United States. When students have completed their lists, have them compare questions. Which questions would remain the same or similar from man to man? Which would change depending upon the person being interviewed? Have a reporter from each group summarize the main ideas of the interview questions. **L2**

CHAPTER 25
SECTION 4

The labor unrest that followed World War I was repeated after World War II. During the war workers received large increases in wages. After the war, unions wanted to maintain those wages and even increase them. Therefore, miners, auto workers, and railroaders conducted a series of strikes. In response Congress passed the Taft-Hartley Act in 1946. The act made it more difficult for unions to strike and strengthened the ability of the National Labor Relations Board to enforce collective bargaining between labor and management. The Taft-Hartley Act is still in effect.

 During the war, the government fueled antiforeign feelings by warning Americans about spies and foreign agents. These feelings led some to view all immigrants with suspicion.
Answer to Caption: They viewed them as radical and suspected them of plotting revolution.

▲ **ANTI-IMMIGRANT SENTIMENT** A 1920 cartoon shows immigrants taking jobs from Americans. *How did many Americans view labor leaders?*

Labor Unrest

High prices also contributed to labor unrest after the war, and when the War Labor Board disbanded, the truce between employers and organized labor ended. A record number—3,600—strikes occurred in 1919, most meeting with little success. Four of them—the Seattle general strike, the Boston police strike, the steel strike, and the coal strike—were highly disruptive and had effects that lasted well into the 1920s.

In January 1919, only 2 months after the armistice, 35,000 shipyard workers from Seattle, Washington, went on strike to gain an increase in their wages. The next month union workers in all Seattle industries walked off their jobs in support of the shipyard strikers. Many city residents viewed the strike as revolutionary. They responded by hoarding food and fuel and by purchasing guns. Seattle's mayor blamed the situation on dangerous radicals and after 5 days used the state militia to break the strike.

In September 1919, another major city was hit by labor unrest as Boston's police force went on strike for better wages and working conditions. Looters soon were in the streets, smashing windows and stealing goods. When the mayor was unable to restore order, Massachusetts governor Calvin Coolidge called out the state guard. A new police force was hired, and Coolidge received national acclaim for his view that "There is no right to strike against the public safety by anybody, anywhere, anytime."

Later that month more than 350,000 steelworkers went on strike across the nation, demanding better wages, an 8-hour rather than a 12-hour day, and the right to join a union. Two-thirds of the strikers were immigrants. Most of the office workers and supervisors who refused to join the strike were American-born. The companies blamed the strike on radicals who told "these foreigners . . . that if they would join the union they would get Americans' jobs." When the companies hired replacement workers, violence broke out, and federal troops were called in to protect them. After 4 months, the strikers gave up with no gains.

While the steel strike was underway, 450,000 coal miners walked off their jobs nationwide. Overworked and underpaid, the strikers demanded a 60 percent pay increase and a 30-hour week. Since at the time coal was the nation's major energy source, the government responded quickly. Obtaining a court order, it forced the strikers back to work. Eventually, however, coal miners won a large pay increase to an average of $7.50 a day.

Red Scare

Many Americans had long suspected a link between labor unrest and political radicalism. The strikes of 1919 helped fuel a larger "Red Scare" than the United States experienced after the war. When the Bolsheviks seized power in Russia in 1917, they called on workers everywhere to revolt. In 1919 communism seemed to have great appeal among the poverty-stricken peoples of war-torn Europe. Although the overwhelming majority of American labor leaders were not allied with the Communists, nevertheless, many Americans suspected them of planning revolution.

The same laws used to quiet opposition and suppress civil liberties during the war were now turned against radicals. Immigrants—especially those with Russian

---

Critical Thinking

Analyzing Policy Have students debate the following issue: All foreign-born Americans who hold ideas foreign to the United States government, whether or not they advocate the overthrow of the government, should be deported. Ask a class member to keep track of the arguments, both pro and con, by writing them on the board. Suggest that students examine each pro argument in the context of the First Amendment. Ask under what circumstances the First Amendment might not apply. **L3**

names—came under suspicion. Attorney General A. Mitchell Palmer rounded up 6,000 immigrants that the government suspected of being Communists and **deported**—expelled from the country—nearly 600 of them. Some of the immigrants deported had become American citizens, and some were deported without trials.

Racial Tension

Accompanying the Red Scare was a wave of racism. Racial tensions rose as white soldiers returning from Europe found themselves competing for jobs and housing with African Americans who had come north during the war. During the summer of 1919, race riots broke out in many Northern cities. The worst was in Chicago, where nearly 40 people were killed and more than 500 injured. One journalist described the scene:

> *During this wild week mobs of whites pursued and beat and killed [African Americans]. Other mobs of [African Americans] pursued and beat and killed whites.... Armed bands in motor trucks dashed wildly up and down the streets, firing into houses....*

Few cities in the United States escaped racial violence in the early 1920s. Even after the Red Scare died down, racial intolerance lived on in organizations such as the Ku Klux Klan, which spread from the South to become a powerful national force.

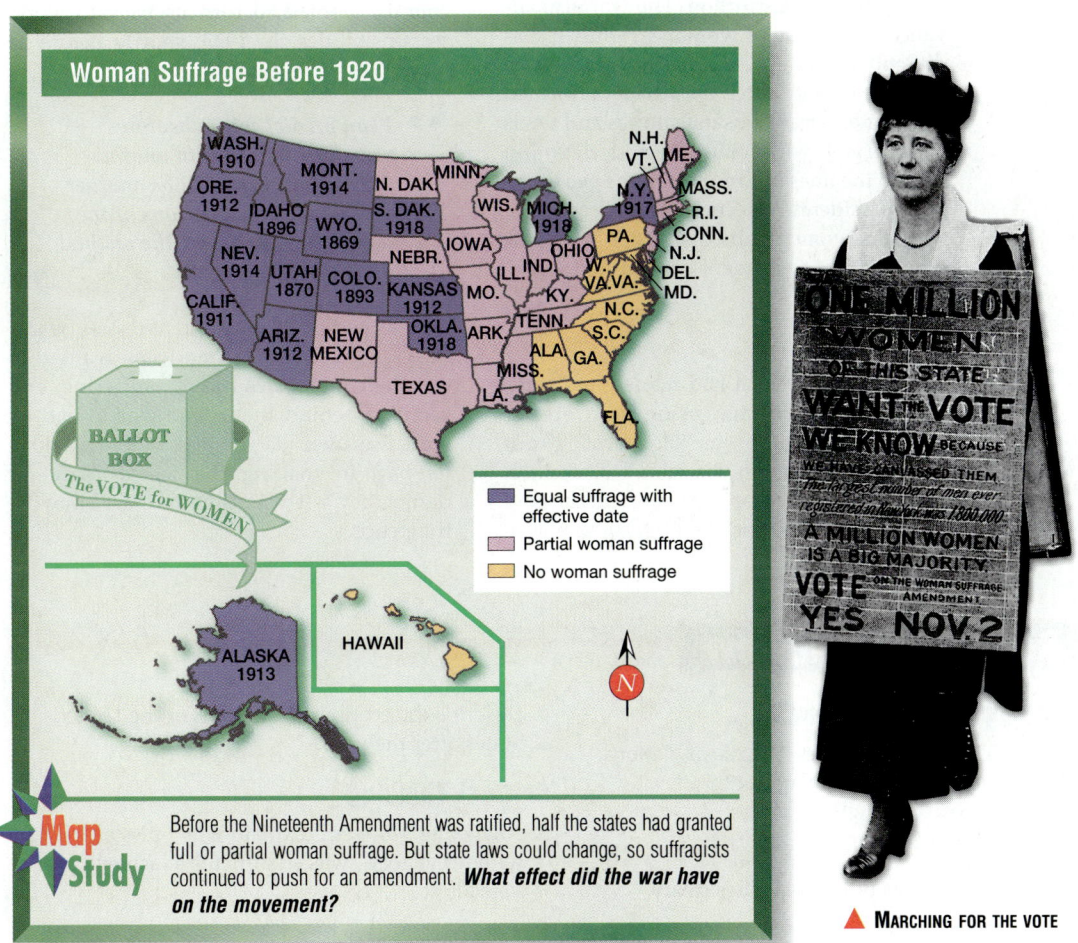

Map Study Before the Nineteenth Amendment was ratified, half the states had granted full or partial woman suffrage. But state laws could change, so suffragists continued to push for an amendment. **What effect did the war have on the movement?**

▲ Marching for the vote

CHAPTER 25 World War I Era 1914–1920   705

CHAPTER 25 SECTION 4

Map Study Using Maps
Answer: encouraged the movement

Map Skills
Ask students which region of the United States was most progressive in granting woman suffrage before 1920. (West) What clues does the map give about attitudes toward equality for women in the various regions of the United States? (Southeast traditional, East and Midwest less so but not ready for full suffrage, West progressive, open to equality for women, at least politically)

Did You Know?

A deadly killer claimed twice as many lives as artillery, machine guns, and poison gas immediately after World War I. An epidemic of influenza probably broke out in an army barracks in Kansas and spread across the United States and to all parts of the world. From 1918 through mid-1919, more than 20 million people died throughout the world.

Sidelights: Carry Nation

Carry Nation, a fiery temperance crusader, is best remembered for smashing up saloons with an axe. Beginning in Kansas, she traveled through the Midwest, lecturing on the evils of liquor and storming barrooms. Nation also tried, unsuccessfully, to alert people to the dangers of smoking tobacco. "I can see," she once said, "where I have made mistakes—many of them—but they were mistakes of the head and not the heart."

CHAPTER 25
SECTION 4

ASSESS

Check Understanding
Assign Section 4 Review as homework or an in-class activity.

Evaluate
Assign the Section 4 Quiz in the TCR, or use the History of a Free Nation Testmaker to create a customized quiz.

Reteach
Have students list the terms of the Treaty of Versailles and also use the maps in this chapter to help answer the following questions: What countries were formed from the Austro-Hungarian Empire? (Austria, Hungary, Czechoslovakia, parts of Poland, Romania, Yugoslavia) What countries were formed from the large western edge of Russia? (Finland, Estonia, Latvia, Lithuania, parts of Poland)

Have students complete Reteaching Activity 25-4.

Enrich
Have students complete the Chapter 25 Enrichment Activity in the TCR.

CLOSE
Have students read Wilson's words that close Section 4. Ask: If Wilson had lived, what do you think he would have done, either as President or as a private citizen, to prevent another outbreak of world war?

■ Wilson's Legacy

Despite a lack of presidential leadership as Wilson's second term drew to a close, Congress and the states implemented important laws. However, Congress would not approve joining the League of Nations.

In 1920 Congress passed the Esch-Cummins Act, which turned the operation of railroads back to their owners. This statute gave the Interstate Commerce Commission almost complete power to fix rates as well as to regulate railroad financing, but the commission was now less concerned with restraining railroad companies than it was with helping them.

The Nineteenth Amendment
World War I helped to add two amendments to the Constitution. The war also advanced the cause of woman's rights. It was difficult to deny demands that women be allowed to vote after they had performed traditionally male jobs in factories and fields and served with courage and devotion behind the lines in Europe. On the eve of the 1920 presidential election, after decades of struggle, women gained suffrage when the Nineteenth Amendment was ratified.

Prohibition
Prohibition, which had made great gains before the war began, made even greater advances during the war. "Hooverizing" put American citizens in the mood to sacrifice, and war needs compelled the federal government to forbid the use of grain to manufacture liquor. By January 1919, two-thirds of the states had ratified the Eighteenth Amendment, which prohibited "the manufacture, sale, or transportation" of intoxicating beverages.

A Warning
Wilson's final year and a half in office left the country virtually leaderless. The President had recovered sufficiently to transact routine business, but his energies still were focused on getting the United States into the League of Nations. Retaining a belief that the American people would not retreat from world leadership, he urged that the election of 1920 be a "great and solemn referendum" on the League issue.

The 1920 election saw Wilson's party and the League repudiated at the polls. The country wanted to turn its back to world responsibilities. In 1923, shortly before he died, Wilson warned:

> *I can predict with absolute certainty that within another generation there will be another world war if the nations of the world do not concert the method by which to prevent it.*

Few people listened to Wilson's warning, however. Most Americans wanted to put their memories of war, suffering, and sacrifice behind them. The war to end all wars was over. The United States had done its part in making the world "safe for democracy." It was time to start enjoying the peace.

Section 4 ★ Review

Checking for Understanding
1. **Identify** Treaty of Versailles, League of Nations, Eighteenth Amendment, Nineteenth Amendment.
2. **Define** covenant, deported.
3. **List** the provisions of the Versailles treaty.
4. **Describe** the economic problems of the United States after the war.

Critical Thinking
5. **Analyzing Motives** Explain why "peace without victory" was so difficult to achieve at Versailles.

---

706   UNIT 8 Crusade and Disillusion: 1914–1932

Answers to SECTION 4 REVIEW
1. Treaty of Versailles, 702; League of Nations, 701–702; Eighteenth Amendment, 706; Nineteenth Amendment, 706.
2. All vocabulary words are defined in the Glossary.
3. a League of Nations, Germany stripped of colonies, reparations from Germany to Allies
4. rising prices, slow business activity, low farm prices, labor unrest
5. Some of the Allies had suffered greatly during the war. They were intent on rewards, revenge, and reparations.

History and Geography Connections

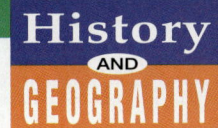

Changing the Map of Europe

Part of President Wilson's peace program following World War I called for self-determination of nations. Before the war Europe was a complex mosaic, or pattern, of distinct ethnic groups. Many of these groups lived within the borders of nations dominated by other ethnic groups. Wilson believed that national boundaries should be drawn to give each ethnic population its own nation.

Other powers at the Versailles peace conference, however, had their own plans. Allied leaders wanted to weaken the Central Powers by dividing their land. Some Allies also wanted their enemies' territory for themselves.

Germany's land area was greatly reduced. Germany's colonies were given over to the Allies as mandates, territories ruled by the Allies with the approval of the League of Nations. Alsace and Lorraine were returned to France. The French also received control of the coal-rich Saar Basin for 15 years.

The Allies signed individual peace treaties with other nations, most of them centering on territorial topics that focused on partitioning the Austro-Hungarian Empire. With the end of the Hapsburg dynasty, Hungary became independent, and Austria was left a small, economically weak country.

From the ashes of the old Russian and Austro-Hungarian empires, new nations emerged in eastern Europe. Among these countries were Finland, Estonia, Lithuania, Latvia, Poland, Czechoslovakia, and Yugoslavia.

▲ The Big Four, December 1918

Wilson's secretary of state, Robert Lansing, noted that the boundaries created after the war were artificial and did not follow ethnic population patterns. Lansing stated that they would last only as long as dissatisfied nations were too weak to change them. He believed that when one nation became confident of its strength and began to seek to remedy these boundaries, a new war would take place. Twenty years later that became the case.

Making the Geography Connection

1. How did Wilson think national boundaries should be determined in Europe after World War I?

Linking Past and Present

2. How did the desire for autonomy among ethnic groups affect the Soviet Union in the 1990s?

CHAPTER 25 CONNECTIONS

Teaching Making Connections

The concept of unifying ethnic groups by redrawing national boundaries was a Wilsonian ideal. Had it actually been done, it might have worked. Instead, artificial boundaries were drawn as the empires of the Central Powers were carved up. For example, the new nation of Czechoslovakia was made up of Czech and Slovak peoples, two distinct ethnic groups. The lands that became Yugoslavia contained people of three different major religions who spoke several different languages and had been hostile to one another for centuries. Though freed from centuries of Austro-Hungarian or Ottoman control, these "nationalities" within a nation were not satisfied. In the 1990s Czechoslovakia divided into two separate nations, and Yugoslavia became a battleground as ethnic groups fought for territory.

Did You Know?

The delegation that accompanied President Wilson to Paris did not include any Republicans. Some were sympathetic to Wilson's aims, but he decided not to invite them. Wilson's lack of tact toward Republicans made many of them angry and resentful.

Answers to CONNECTIONS

1. Wilson believed that nation states should be created based on ethnic population.

2. Soviet states began to demand their independence from the Soviet Union. Civil disturbances occurred in many areas.

REVIEW CHAPTER 25

Answers

Reviewing Facts
1. Wilson based his foreign policy on morality and idealism, and he sent troops into Latin America to protect governments he thought were right for the people.
2. Nationalism created intense allegiances to countries but also fostered unrest among ethnic minorities. Countries pledged to defend their allies if attacked.
3. submarine warfare, the Zimmermann note
4. The economy was largely under government control. Civil liberties were restricted.
5. drove back Germans at St. Mihiel and Sedan (also accept Château-Thierry and Verdun); navy used convoys and depth charges to thwart U-boat attacks
6. The peace terms were punitive to Germany and included reparations payments, loss of territory, and a League of Nations.
7. Congress refused to ratify the Treaty of Versailles.
8. Strikes were unsuccessful; government ordered strikers back to work; the Red Scare made Americans fearful of unions; unemployment was high; prices rose; racial tension led to riots.

Understanding Concepts
1. Nationalism encouraged aggressive growth and expansion, leading to jealousy, distrust, and competition for empires. Internally, the demands of ethnic nationality groups destabilized some nations

CHAPTER 25 ★ REVIEW

Using Vocabulary

Imagine that you have kept a diary of events of World War I. Write headlines of three diary entries using each of the following terms in a headline.

covenant
contraband
armistice
deported
victory garden

Reviewing Facts

1. **Discuss** Wilson's foreign-policy views and how they related to his actions in Latin America.
2. **State** how nationalism and alliances created the conditions that led to World War I.
3. **Identify** two reasons the United States declared war on Germany.
4. **Cite** changes in economic and political policies that were imposed in the United States during World War I.
5. **List** two actions taken by the American military that helped win the war.
6. **Describe** the terms of the Versailles treaty.
7. **Explain** why Wilson was frustrated with Congress after the war.
8. **Summarize** the social difficulties confronting the United States after the war.

Understanding Concepts

Conflict
1. Identify the two types of nationalism that existed in Europe and explain why each was a factor in causing World War I.
2. Explain how Wilson's ideals influenced his actions and made compromise difficult.

Interests
3. Explain how economic and political interests in the United States were factors in its inability to remain neutral in World War I.
4. Analyze how competing interests made the adoption of Wilson's Fourteen Points difficult.

Critical Thinking

1. **Evaluating Foreign Policy** Consider the United States's neutrality policy before entering the war. Evaluate the feasibility of this policy. Consider the events that forced the United States to abandon neutrality and enter the war.
2. **Expressing Viewpoints** During World War I the government worked to control public attitudes about the war. In your opinion, was it necessary for the government to take such actions? Explain your viewpoint.
3. **Analyzing Fine Art** Study the mural by José Clemente Orozco entitled *Revolutionists* on this page, then answer the questions that follow.
   a. What themes are illustrated?
   b. What was happening in Mexico in the early 1900s that may have inspired this work?
   c. Why would a wall mural be a good way to spread a message?

Writing About History

Comparison
Write an essay to compare Woodrow Wilson's ideals with the realities he faced in the world of politics. Before you begin writing, make two lists. In

and caused international rivalry.
2. Wilson insisted on his idealistic goals even when the situation made his success unlikely. His refusal to compromise meant he achieved even fewer goals.
3. The United States was connected to Europe through trade. German and British blockades in Europe also affected commerce and the American economy. British heritage, the fact that the Allies were democracies whereas the Central Powers were not, and anti-German feelings all made neutrality difficult.
4. Wilson's European allies wanted revenge, territorial rewards, and to punish Germans for the war. At home Americans were divided over the role of the United States in European affairs.

CHAPTER 25 ★ REVIEW

one, list Wilson's foreign-policy goals. In the other, enumerate his actions. Use these lists to help you plan and write your essay.

Cooperative Learning

Work with a partner to write two newspaper editorials on the United States government's methods of controlling public opinion during World War I—one supporting the government's policies and the other opposing them. Before writing, collaborate on a list of pros and cons about the government's activities, including the Espionage and Sedition acts and the Committee on Public Information. Then each of you should take opposite positions and write an editorial. When you have finished, exchange your editorials. After reading your partner's work, write a "letter to the editor" as a rebuttal to his or her position.

Social Studies Skills

Analyzing Graphic Data

To successfully analyze complex information, you must first break it into smaller parts that you can examine more easily. By analyzing the information presented in the bar graph on this page, you can obtain a clearer understanding of American military support for its Allies in Europe.

The graph provides information about the United States Army between April 1917 and November 1918. In analyzing its detail you can see that one set of bars shows the growth in total size of the American army from the time the United States entered the war until the armistice was signed. The other set of bars shows how many of those troops were sent to fight in Europe.

Practicing the Skill

Use your analysis of the graph in answering the following questions to better understand American involvement in the war:

1. When the United States declared war, fewer than 250,000 soldiers were ready to fight. When was the first month that the United States had 1 million troops in the army? By what month were there 1 million American soldiers in Europe?

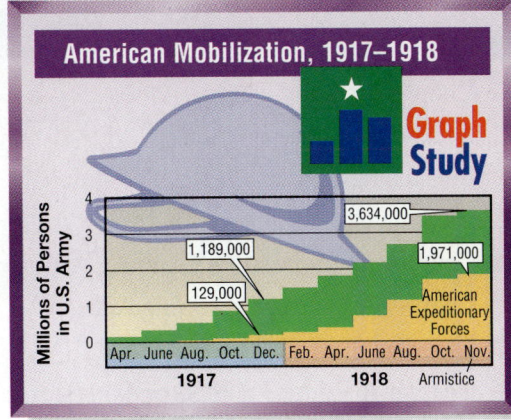

2. Between what months was there the greatest increase in the size of the American army?
3. About what percentage of the United States Army was in Europe by the end of 1917? By the armistice a year later?
4. After reading about America's mobilization to fight the war in the chapter, what information does this graph provide about the efficiency of that effort?

Using Your Journal

From your notes on attitudes during World War I and your knowledge of events in the Persian Gulf in 1990–1991, compare the general feelings during each conflict.

CHAPTER 25 World War I Era 1914–1920   709

REVIEW ★ CHAPTER 25

Practicing the Skill

1. December 1917; August 1918
2. between August and October 1918
3. just over 10 percent; just over 50 percent
4. Students should note from the graph that it took more than a year after the United States declared war for significant American forces to reach Europe. This belies claims of rapid American mobilization.

Chapter Bonus Test Question

This question may be used for extra credit on the chapter test. How did World War I affect the foreign policy of the United States in the years after the war? (United States grew disillusioned with overseas involvement and wanted to stay out of world affairs.)

Using Your Journal

Responses will vary, but in World War I, Americans tried to remain neutral; in the Gulf War, there was little hesitation about stopping Iraqi aggression. In both wars some Americans opposed intervention. Students might note that in both wars, Americans were confident of victory.

Critical Thinking

1. The policy really was not feasible considering German U-boat activity, the blockades of European ports, and the consequences for American interests of a German victory.
2. Some will argue that the suppression of civil rights never is warranted, especially when most Americans had demonstrated their support by personal sacrifice and the lending of money. Others will focus on issues of national security and the unity needed in a national emergency.
3. a. Answers will vary but students might note that the artist is focusing on the plight of the poor.
b. Struggle for power that brought hardships to the people and political chaos.
c. Answers will vary but students might note that the dimensions of a mural provide artists effective and dramatic means to illustrate ideas.

709

PLANNING GUIDE   Chapter 26   The Decade of Normalcy

Daily Lesson Objectives	Teacher Classroom Resources	Multimedia
SECTION 1 **The Harding Years** 1 Day pp. 712–718 1. Describe the accomplishments of the Washington Conference. 2. Explain the provisions of the National Origins Act. 3. Describe the scandals in the Harding administration.	Chapter 26 Study Guide Reproducible Lesson Plan Reteaching Activity 26-1 Section Quiz Chapter 26 Cooperative Learning Activity Chapter 26 Concept Mapping Activity American Portrait 48 Chapter 26 Primary and Secondary Source Readings Reinforcing Social Studies Skills 25, 32, 44, 49, 55, 69–72 Map and Graph Skill Activity 32 Writer's Guidebook Lessons 9–14	Student Self-Test Software Testmaker Section Focus Transparency 83 Chapter 26 Skills Transparency Chapter 26 Map Transparency The Presidents: A Picture History of Our Nation
SECTION 2 **The Coolidge Era** 1 Day pp. 720–725 1. Discuss the changes to industry Henry Ford introduced. 2. Outline the problems of farmers and the government's response. 3. Describe the Kellogg-Briand Pact.	Reproducible Lesson Plan Reteaching Activity 26-2 Section Quiz American Portrait 51 Reinforcing Social Studies Skills 32, 40, 59, 69–72 Writer's Guidebook Lessons 9–14	Student Self-Test Software Testmaker Section Focus Transparency 84 U.S. History Diagraph 5 The Presidents: A Picture History of Our Nation
SECTION 3 **The "Roaring Twenties"** 1 Day pp. 728–734 1. Describe changes in women's lives during the 1920s. 2. Outline developments in the arts and education during this period.	Reproducible Lesson Plan Reteaching Activity 26-3 Section Quiz Chapter 26 Enrichment Activity Chapter 26 Primary and Secondary Source Readings American Portrait 52 Reinforcing Social Studies Skills 6, 32, 55 American Literary Heritage Unit 8 Spanish Summaries & Glossary	Student Self-Test Software Testmaker Section Focus Transparency 85 Vocabulary Puzzlemaker U.S. History and Art Transparency 22 Audiocassette, Chapter 26 The American People: Fabric of a Nation The Presidents: A Picture History of Our Nation
CHAPTER REVIEW AND EVALUATION 1 Day	Chapter 26 Test Chapter 26 Performance Assessment Activity	Student Self-Test Software Testmaker

OUT OF TIME? If time does not permit teaching the entire chapter, use the Chapter 26 Summary on pages 766–767 and the Chapter 26 audiocassette (English and Spanish) to point out the main ideas of the chapter.

PLANNING GUIDE

Cultural Diversity Activity

Expressing Opinions Have students reread pages 716–717 on changes in immigration laws. Note that the 1924 law was biased against immigrants from southern and eastern Europe and from Asia. Under the law each nationality was allowed a quota of immigrants equal to two percent of its percentage of the United States population in 1890. Only the white population was counted. Since British, Scandinavian, Irish, and German Americans were already present in large numbers, these groups received high quotas. By 1927 Britain had 65,721 slots yearly while Italy had less than 6,000 and Poland 6,524. The law did not affect immigration from within the Western Hemisphere.

The editor of a Greek American newspaper said of the law, "The idea of discriminating between foreigners was certainly an imported product, for neither the American Constitution nor the ideals of this country ever allowed such a political conduct." Is he right? Does the Constitution support such discrimination? What does the law suggest about the way Americans in the 1920s regarded immigrants? The way they viewed "real Americans"?

Performance Assessment Activity

History Through Ads The prosperity of the 1920s brought a host of new products to a public eager to buy. To encourage and attract consumers, a new industry developed: the advertising industry. Ask students to work in pairs or small groups to research ads of the period and prepare written or oral reports on their findings. For example, some might focus on foods. What do those ads tell about the American diet? The nation's favorite foods? Eating habits? Another group might explore ads for such household items as refrigerators and vacuum cleaners. Still another might focus on ads for various forms of transportation. Groups might be encouraged to compare their findings with comparable ads today. Their reports should analyze both similarities and differences.

POSSIBLE RUBRIC FEATURES: Research skills, content information, organization, written and oral communication skills, creativity, collaborative skills

Chapter Resources

Literature from the Period

Fitzgerald, F. Scott. *The Great Gatsby.* 1925.

Hughes, Langston. *The Weary Blues.* 1926.

Lewis, Sinclair. *Babbit.* 1922.

Readings for the Student

"The Harlem Renaissance." Cobblestone, Vol. 12, No. 2, February 1991.

Lyons, Mary E. *Sorrow's Kitchen: The Life and Folklore of Zora Neale Hurston.* Charles Scribner's Sons, 1990.

Readings for the Teacher

Nash, Roderick. *The Nervous Generation: American Thought, 1917–1930.* Yale University Press, 1970.

Multimedia Resources

Cultural Contributions of Black Americans: A Literary Renaissance. SVE (color filmstrips)

Living American History Series. US History IV: 1915–1960. Priven Learning Systems. (2 Apple diskettes, guide).

The Spirit of St. Louis. Warners (VHS, 137 minutes)

Key to Ability Levels

Teaching strategies have been coded for varying learning styles and abilities.

- **L1** Basic activities for all students
- **L2** Average activities for average to above-average students
- **L3** Challenging activities for above-average students
- **LEP** Limited English Proficiency activities

Glencoe Links to the Humanities

Links to Art
- U.S. History and Art Transparency 22
- Focus on American Fine Art Prints

Links to Literature
- Macmillan Literature: American Literature Audiotapes Side 4
- Macmillan Literature: American Literature Video— *Our Town*
- Macmillan Literature: Novel guide—*The Great Gatsby*
- Macmillan Literature: American Literature Text— Sherwood Anderson, Sinclair Lewis, Ernest Hemingway

Link to Music
- American Music: Cultural Traditions

CHAPTER 26

BEGINNING THE CHAPTER

Explain that Chapter 26 describes changes that took place during the 1920s. Encourage students to think of names that characterize the decade as they read.

Linking Across Time

Reflecting the sophisticated spirit of the 1920s that many Americans aspired to, magazines such as *Vanity Fair* and *Smart Set*, known as "highbrow" publications, were founded. Both ultimately faded (although *Vanity Fair* was revived in the 1980s). What did not disappear was *Reader's Digest*, with its "digested" articles and positive outlook, founded in 1921. Two other magazines also endured: *Time* (1923), an easy-to-read news magazine, and *The New Yorker* (1925), known for its wit and imaginative writing.

Recording Journal Notes

Suggest students categorize their notes under such headings as music, dance, art, poetry, fiction, nonfiction. Alternatively they might arrange details under the significant people of the Harlem Renaissance and note their contributions.

CHAPTER 26

The Decade of Normalcy
1920–1928

▶ THE CLOCHE, POPULAR WOMAN'S HAT OF THE 1920S

Setting the Scene

Focus

The decade that followed World War I differed considerably from the Progressive years that came before it. Voters turned to conservative leaders who promised to turn the country away from European affairs and inward to "normalcy." For many Americans this shift meant preserving the values of rural America and enjoying prosperity. For others it meant a fascination with a dazzling new assortment of consumer goods, entertainment, and changing fashions.

Concepts to Understand

★ Why shifts in government policies and increased production resulted in economic change

★ How social change affected the arts, the role of women, and minorities

Read to Discover . . .

★ ways United States involvement in international relations changed following World War I.

★ what signs of social tension were evident in the 1920s.

Journal Notes
What was the Harlem Renaissance? Jot down details about it as you read the chapter.

CULTURAL
- 1920 First commercial radio broadcast is aired
- 1922 Lincoln Memorial is dedicated
- 1925 John Scopes trial over teaching evolution in Dayton, Tennessee, occurs

1920 | **1923**

POLITICAL
- 1920 Warren Harding is elected
- 1921 Washington Conference is held
- 1923 Calvin Coolidge becomes President after Harding's death

UNIT 8 Crusade and Disillusion: 1914–1932

✚ EXTRA CREDIT PROJECT

Explain to students that a negative side of the 1920s was the Red Scare, which reflected fears and prejudices often directed at immigrants. One episode was the trial and execution of Nicola Sacco and Bartolomeo Vanzetti, Italian immigrants and confessed anarchists accused of robbery and murder. The Sacco-Vanzetti case attracted worldwide attention. Interested students might research the case. Have them share their findings with the class and offer evidence to support their points of view about the case.

History AND ART
Dance Hall
by Thomas Hart Benton, 1930

Thomas Hart Benton excelled at mural painting, concentrating on Midwestern legend, history, and daily life.

▲ TROMBONE USED IN JAZZ GROUP, 1920S

- **1927** First "talking" motion picture, *The Jazz Singer,* is released
- **1926** United States intervenes in Nicaragua
- **1928** Kellogg-Briand Pact is negotiated

|1926|1929|

- **1929** Chicago mobsters murder seven rival gang members in the St. Valentine's Day Massacre
- **1929** Herbert Hoover becomes President

CHAPTER 26 The Decade of Normalcy 1920–1928

CHAPTER 26 CONCEPTS

Concept Mapping Activity

Reproduce the following generalization and concepts map on the chalkboard, and ask students to copy it in their notebooks. Suggest they predict the effect the events will have on American society.

Rapid social change and political conservatism mark the 1920s.
- Social Change
- Economic Change

History AND ART

Thomas Hart Benton was one of the leaders of regionalism, or art based on depictions of regional themes. Benton celebrated the vital and energetic men and women who tamed the frontier and built new towns and cities. In many of his murals, he divided one scene from another with arbitrary borders. The change in scale and his use of overlapping images give the effect of a photo montage, a picture made by combining several different images. Educated at the Art Institute of Chicago, Benton began his career as a cartoonist for the *Joplin* (Missouri) *American* in 1906.

Teacher Notes

SECTION 1

The Harding Years

Setting the Scene

Section Focus

The internationalism of Woodrow Wilson was reversed under the administrations of the next three Presidents—all Republicans. The party's slogan "America First" hailed the country's unparalleled prosperity, characterized by remarkable achievements in the field of business.

Objectives

After studying this section, you should be able to

★ describe the accomplishments of the Washington Conference.

★ explain the provisions of the National Origins Act.

★ describe the scandals in the Harding administration.

Key Terms

reparation, technological unemployment, open shop, welfare capitalism

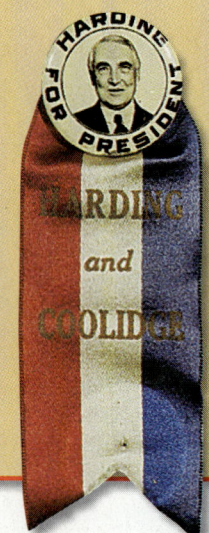

◄ 1920 REPUBLICAN CAMPAIGN PIN

The end of the war created new problems for the United States. After the dismantling of the War Industries Board, business lost the profitable military contracts of the war years. Four million recently demobilized service men and women needed work. In 1920 and 1921, unemployment soared, as did prices. Labor unrest was reflected in the United States Steel strike and the Boston police strike of 1919.

■ The Election of 1920

Several prominent men sought the Republican nomination in 1920, the prize going to a dark horse, Ohio senator Warren G. Harding. Harding's running mate was Massachusetts governor Calvin Coolidge. To oppose Harding, the Democrats chose Ohio governor James M. Cox, a loyal Wilson supporter. Cox's running mate was Franklin D. Roosevelt, who, like his distant cousin, Theodore, had served as assistant secretary of the navy. The strategy chosen by Cox was as Wilson desired—to campaign for the League of Nations.

The Republicans were divided on the issue. Harding said he favored "a society of free nations" to keep peace. Most prominent Republicans took this to mean that Harding supported their decision to join the League, but anti-League Republicans seemed certain that Harding opposed it. Thus, as journalist Walter Lippmann pointed out, Harding received support from "men and women who thought a Republican victory would kill the League, plus those who thought it was the most practical way to procure the League."

The election was an overwhelming Republican victory. Harding carried every Northern and Western state and even broke

UNIT 8 Crusade and Disillusion: 1914–1932

the Democratic Solid South by carrying Tennessee. A key to the election results may be found in the President's reassuring slogan—"a return to normalcy"— coined by Harding during his campaign. It suggested a return to "the good old days," to the conditions that prevailed before the shocks of World War I.

Postwar Foreign Policy

After his election, Harding announced that his administration would not lead the United States into the League of Nations "by the side door, back door, or cellar door." The United States was too powerful, too economically interconnected, and too widely involved in world affairs to retreat into isolationism, however, and participated actively in many League conferences.

War Debt

One international problem that demanded a solution was $10.3 billion in Allied war debts owed to the United States for food and war materials. The debtor nations had difficulty meeting their payments. They argued that high American tariffs had closed the United States market to their imports and slowed their economic recovery. Furthermore, debtor nations argued, because the United States had lost fewer people in the war than the other Allies, it should be willing to pay more of the financial cost. The United States government, however, took the position that the Allies had gained territory and **reparations,** or payments for damages, as a result of the victory while the United States had claimed no reward, and that to cancel these debts would destroy faith in international agreements.

Eventually the United States made agreements with 17 of the 20 debtor nations, reducing the debts by 30 to 80 percent. Most of the money the Allies paid actually came from Germany. To pay its reparations, Germany obtained private bank loans from other countries—especially the United States.

The Washington Conference

At the time of the Harding administration, the United States, Great Britain, and Japan were experiencing costly and competitive naval buildups that originated during the war. There was also friction in East Asia, caused mainly by conflicts over commercial rights in China and by Western suspicion of Japan's recent territorial gains. After World War I, Japan had acquired all of Germany's Pacific islands north of the equator as well as the Chinese port of Kiaochow (jee•OW•JOH). Japan also treated the rest of the Chinese province of Shantung as its own.

In the hope of resolving these problems, the administration hosted an eight-nation conference in Washington, D.C. The negotiations, which lasted from November 1921 to February 1922, led to three important treaties.

The Four-Power Treaty

The Four-Power Treaty, signed by the United States, Great Britain, France, and Japan, was an agreement among the four

Visualizing History ▲ **NOT ROOM FOR BOTH** By showing the League of Nations agreement trying to replace the Constitution in ruling the nation, this artist expressed concern that joining the League would deprive the United States of the freedom to sets its own policies. *What role did the 1920 election play in resolving this issue?*

CHAPTER 26 The Decade of Normalcy 1920–1928   713

CHAPTER 26
SECTION 1

Independent Practice
Comparing Statistics
Have students construct a double bar graph to show the effects of the immigration quota acts of the 1920s. Give students these figures: immigrants from northern/western Europe, average per year from 1907 to 1914—183,301; Act of 1921—138,551; Act of 1924—203,346; Act of 1929—114,469; immigrants from southern/eastern Europe, average per year from 1907 to 1914—474,662; Act of 1921—341,655; Act of 1924—99,487; Act of 1929—27,046.

When students have completed their graphs, ask them to form a generalization about the statistics. (From 1907 to 1914, there were almost three times as many immigrants from southern/eastern Europe as from northern/western Europe. By 1929 there were about five times fewer immigrants from southern/eastern Europe as from northern/western Europe. Accept comparable generalizations.) **L2**

Using Graphs
Answer: Membership declined as unions seemed less necessary to workers.

Skills Practice
Suggest students research statistics for various groups and create a similar graph for each group. How do the earnings of each group compare with the overall earnings of all workers?

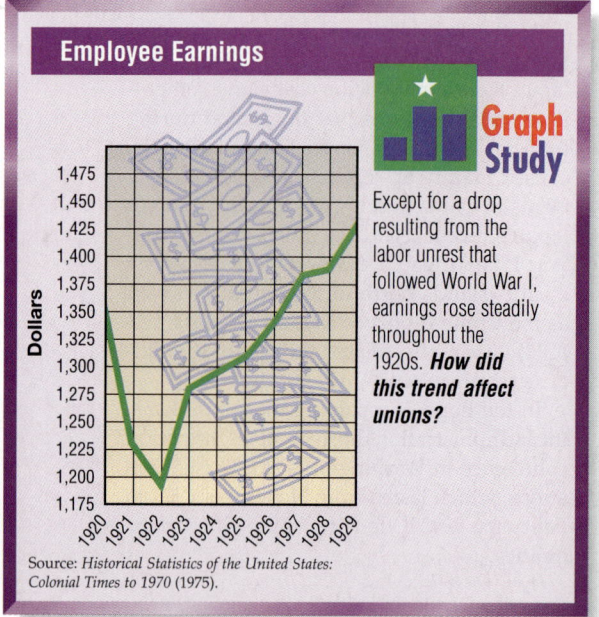

Employee Earnings

Except for a drop resulting from the labor unrest that followed World War I, earnings rose steadily throughout the 1920s. **How did this trend affect unions?**

Source: *Historical Statistics of the United States: Colonial Times to 1970* (1975).

great powers to respect one another's Pacific holdings. In case of disagreements or a threat from another nation, the signers also agreed to confer "fully and frankly."

The Five-Power Treaty
Under the Five-Power Treaty, the 5 naval powers of the United States, Great Britain, Japan, France, and Italy agreed to freeze their navies at 1921 levels and thus avoid the financial strain of further naval buildups. The signers further agreed to halt the building of large warships for 10 years; some ships under construction would even be scrapped. The treaty also included an agreement by the United States and Great Britain not to build new fortifications or naval bases in the western Pacific. This provision gave Japan control of nearby waters in exchange for agreeing to remain at inferior naval strength.

The Nine-Power Treaty
The Nine-Power Treaty—signed by the United States, France, Great Britain, Japan, Italy, Belgium, China, the Netherlands, and Portugal—put the "Open Door" China policies of John Hay into a treaty. The signers agreed to preserve equal commercial rights in China and to refrain from "taking advantage of conditions in China to seek special rights or privileges." Following this policy, Japan soon withdrew from the province of Shantung.

Although the immediate results of the Washington Conference were encouraging, the conference failed to reach an agreement limiting military forces on land. Moreover, the treaties had notable shortcomings. Under the Five-Power Treaty, naval powers could still build unlimited numbers of smaller combat vessels, such as submarines and destroyers. In addition the Four-Power Treaty did not commit the signers to active military defense of their allies; indeed, such a commitment might have been unacceptable to the United States. The Nine-Power Treaty made no provision for enforcement of the Open Door policy.

■ Business Normalcy
From the start Harding's handling of domestic problems made it apparent that normalcy meant a general retreat from government regulation of business. Although the federal government actively aided businesses by levying protective tariffs, promoting foreign trade, and breaking strikes, its policy in other matters was laissez-faire. There was little effort to enforce the antitrust laws that regulated business mergers. Reflecting the dominant feeling of the time, regulatory agencies such as the Interstate Commerce Commission and the Federal Trade Commission were largely unsympathetic to policies restricting private enterprise.

The Fordney-McCumber Act
The new trend was immediately seen in the tariff laws. In 1922 Congress passed the Fordney-McCumber Act, raising import duties to high levels. This protected agriculture as well as certain young industries, such as rayon, china, and the optical-glass and chemical products for which the United States seized patents from Germany during

---

Sidelights: Presidential Gaffes

President Harding's linguistics were a source of both laughter and embarrassment to Americans. The word *normalcy* was his own mispronunciation of the word *normality* and did not exist until he coined it. Democrat William McAdoo, Woodrow Wilson's son-in-law, said the President's speech was like "an army of pompous phrases moving over the landscape in search of an idea." Harding himself said he liked to *bloviate*, a word meaning "to speak bombastically and at length."

the war. Because the Fordney-McCumber Act authorized the President to raise or lower duties by as much as 50 percent, rates often went still higher.

Creating the Bureau of the Budget

Because World War I had raised the national debt from less than $10 per person to over $200, the Harding and Coolidge administrations attempted to lower this burden by making the government more fiscally responsible. In 1921 Congress created the Bureau of the Budget in the Treasury Department.

The efforts of the Bureau of the Budget to introduce savings were especially supported by Coolidge, who felt so strongly about curbing the nation's expenditures that he devoted serious attention to routine federal purchases such as lead pencils and typewriter ribbons. After the Washington Conference, there was no threat of war on the horizon, and even military expenditures were greatly lowered.

Changes in Taxation

Andrew Mellon, secretary of the treasury from 1921 to 1932 and a wealthy man, believed that heavy taxes on excess profits "penalized success" and discouraged investment in productive enterprise. At Mellon's insistence, Congress abolished the wartime excise and excess profits taxes and reduced tax rates on incomes by nearly two-thirds. Even with these cuts, the nation's prosperity produced enough tax revenue to reduce the national debt by $8 billion between 1921 and 1929.

■ Labor and Labor Unions

Between 1921 and 1928, the average annual wage for workers rose from $1,227 to $1,384. However, new manufacturing caused **technological unemployment**—jobs lost when occupations become obsolete. Although people replaced by machines usually found jobs elsewhere, the transition was sometimes difficult. Not only were they often forced to leave home to find employment, but they also frequently lost the benefit of long years spent learning a particular skill.

The introduction of jukeboxes and sound films, to cite an extreme example, caused widespread unemployment among musicians. Although the assembly line lowered the costs of production, many laborers could not stand the monotony and nervous tension caused by working at a speed set by the machine.

Union Decline

The "prosperity decade" saw labor unions decline in strength. Even the American Federation of Labor, one of the largest organizations, had difficulty holding its members in the face of antiunion activities. Employers joined to promote the **open shop**—a shop where workers do not have to

Visualizing History

▲ **KKK** Members of the Ku Klux Klan parade down Pennsylvania Avenue in Washington, D.C., in September 1926. The KKK spread from the South to gain national power in the 1920s. *How did the Klan as well as many other Americans react to increased immigration after World War I?*

CHAPTER 26 SECTION 1

Did You Know?

The individual American's portion of the national debt increased to $200 after World War I. In 1990 the estimated liability for each taxpayer because of the savings and loan scandal (separate from the amount owed on the national debt) was $3,000.

Visualizing History At its height in 1923, the Klan claimed a membership of 4 million. The Klan was politically powerful in Texas, Oregon, Georgia, Oklahoma, Alabama, and Indiana. After 1924 membership began to decline when corruption among its leaders was exposed. **Answer to Caption:** They discriminated against immigrants; the government passed restrictive immigration laws.

Did You Know?

In contrast to Harding's material excess, Vice President Calvin Coolidge's frugality was legendary. His concern for waste continued when he reached the White House. He expected small change from servants sent out to buy newspapers. He also inspected the White House iceboxes and criticized menus that appeared extravagant.

Critical Thinking

Analyzing Viewpoints Have students analyze the financial philosophy of Andrew Mellon, secretary of the treasury. Mellon believed that the wealthy should not be penalized in the form of taxes on excess profits, inheritances, and large incomes. Such taxes would discourage investment, the effects of which would "trickle down" to improve the lot of all. Students may either write individual arguments supporting or challenging this philosophy or divide into groups and debate the question. **L2**

CHAPTER 26
SECTION 1

Linking Across TIME

As in the 1920s, some Americans today resent recent immigrants. In California, where Hispanics make up more than one-fourth of the state's population, resentment is caused by the misguided belief that Hispanics refuse to learn to speak English. A recent study showed, however, that 90 percent of Hispanic children do speak English and that 25 percent of the children speak no Spanish at all.

Graph Study
Answer: 1925

Skills Practice
Suggest students work in pairs or groups to research immigration in the 1980s and create a bar graph similar to this one showing the areas from which immigrants came.

join a union. Labeled the "American Plan," in practice the open shop meant a shop closed to union members. To further reduce the power of unions, companies promoted **welfare capitalism,** a system to make employees feel more a part of the business by enabling them to buy shares of stock, by instituting profit sharing, and by providing such fringe benefits as medical care, retirement pensions, and recreational facilities. Moreover, wages and conditions improved somewhat during the 1920s. With some improvement in their standards of living and the relative weakness of unions, striking seemed pointless to many workers.

Strikebreaking

Although Herbert Hoover, secretary of commerce, persuaded President Harding to make a successful personal appeal to the leaders of the steel industry to abandon the 12-hour day, the federal government was usually on the side of the employers. Thus Attorney General Harry M. Daugherty helped to break railroad and coal strikes in 1922 by obtaining injunctions that prohibited every conceivable union activity, including picketing, making public statements to the press, and jeering at strikebreakers. In 1919 the Indiana State Guard—and eventually federal troops—protected strikebreakers at United States Steel. In addition the Supreme Court continually whittled away at the protections that unions thought they had secured by the Clayton Act of 1914. Once again, injunctions were freely used to stop strikes and boycotts.

■ Restricting Immigration

In the decade before World War I, approximately 1 million persons a year came to live in the United States, over two-thirds of these from countries in southern and eastern Europe. To slow down this tide of immigration, Congress passed in 1917 an act requiring a literacy test, designed to exclude large numbers of immigrants.

The act, however, had little effect. New immigrants congregated in such cities as New York and Chicago, where opportunities for employment were greatest. Established immigrants resented the new immigrants' increasing political power. Even more, they

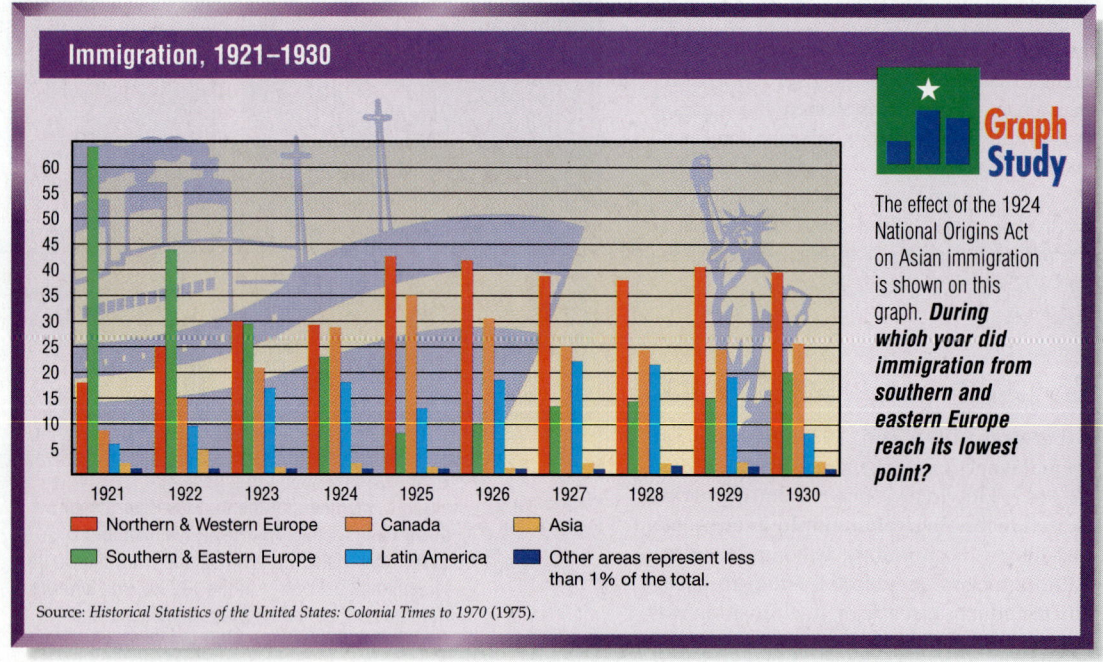

Graph Study

The effect of the 1924 National Origins Act on Asian immigration is shown on this graph. ***During which year did immigration from southern and eastern Europe reach its lowest point?***

UNIT 8 Crusade and Disillusion: 1914–1932

Cooperative Learning

Divide the class into five groups. Have each group represent one of the following: a member of a conservative labor union, a resident of a new immigrant community, an older immigrant from northern or western Europe, an employer of immigrants, and a Japanese businessman. Give each group time to prepare a speech about the immigration acts of the 1920s. Then have each group choose a representative to deliver the speech giving that group's viewpoint about immigration. Conduct a class discussion on the pros and cons of each argument. **L3**

feared that the newcomers, most of whom were Catholic, would overthrow traditional Protestant values. Conservative labor unions were angered by the willingness of poor immigrants to work for very low wages. Employers, who had previously favored unrestricted immigration as a means of hiring cheap labor, now came to fear that the new immigrants were radicals who would fight for a communist revolution.

The National Origins Act

During and after World War I, feeling against "hyphenated-Americans" was stimulated by anti-German hysteria, by the Red Scare, and by the Ku Klux Klan. When immigrants came to the United States, fleeing their war-torn countries in the hopes of finding wealth and opportunity, Congress took quick action. In 1921 Harding signed the Emergency Quota Act, which cut the number of people admitted to the United States. According to this act, only 3 percent of the total number of people in any national group already living in the United States in 1910 would be admitted during a single year.

Three years later the National Origins Act made restriction a permanent policy. This 1924 law temporarily reduced the quota still further. It also provided that after 1927 a total of only 150,000 immigrants would be admitted to the United States per year, their nationalities apportioned on the basis of the 1920 census. This meant that more than 85 percent of the new immigrants would be from Europe—mainly from Great Britain, Ireland, Germany, and Scandinavia.

The intention of the National Origins Act was clearly to discriminate against certain nationalities and races. This became even more apparent when immigrants from Asia and Africa were either assigned very small quotas or barred entirely. Japanese immigration was completely excluded. The Japanese regarded the law as a national insult, and the day it went into effect was declared a day of public mourning and national humiliation in Japan. The incident discredited moderate Japanese politicians who sought to cooperate with the United States and advanced the cause of reactionary militarists in Japan.

▲ **THE PASSION OF SACCO AND VANZETTI** by Ben Shahn, 1932
Many Americans rallied to the defense of Nicola Sacco and Bartolomeo Vanzetti. **Why did this case arouse controversy?**

Sacco and Vanzetti

An event that for many came to symbolize mistrust of immigrants in the United States was the trial of Nicola Sacco and Bartolomeo Vanzetti. These two Italian immigrants and anarchists were accused in 1921 of killing two men during a robbery in Massachusetts. They were convicted, but

CHAPTER 26
SECTION 1

History AND ART

The artist Ben Shahn took many of his subjects from the darker side of life. He was particularly interested in people who were victims of injustices. **Answer to Caption:** Many thought the men had not received a fair trial and were convicted because they were immigrants and radicals.

Scandals in presidential administrations might seem commonplace in contemporary times, but in the 1920s they were rare enough to cause a great deal of concern, and for those involved, a sense of shame and responsibility. Albert Fall was the first cabinet member to serve time in jail. Jesse Smith, a friend of Attorney General Harry Daugherty, committed suicide after it was discovered that he had arranged settlements between the Department of Justice and law violators. Charles Cramer, legal adviser of the Veterans' Bureau, also committed suicide after he was involved in misuse of the bureau's funds.

Sidelights: Religion and Business

The Puritan link between being accepted by God and success in business surfaced again in the 1920s. Bruce Barton, who founded the phenomenally successful advertising agency Batten, Barton, Durstine, and Osborn, claimed that Christians were obligated to build businesses. His book *The Man Nobody Knows* presented Jesus as a businessman. Barton's favorite quote from the Bible was Jesus' response to his parents when they found him in the temple, "Wist [Know] ye not that I must be about my Father's business?" The fact that Jesus was referring to spiritual affairs did not seem to bother Barton. In 1936 Barton was elected to Congress.

many thought they never received a fair trial. It was believed that the trial judge was prejudiced against the defendants because of their ethnic backgrounds and political beliefs. For years attempts were made to obtain a retrial, but in 1927 Sacco and Vanzetti were executed. In his final statement in court, Vanzetti continued to maintain his innocence of the crime, saying:

> ❝ ... [M]y conviction is that I have suffered for things that I am guilty of. I am suffering because I am a radical and indeed I am a radical; I have suffered because I was an Italian and indeed I am an Italian. ... ❞

The question of the guilt or innocence of Sacco and Vanzetti has never been answered with certainty. Their trial made many people think critically about the American justice system, however.

■ Scandals Among Harding's Advisers

Although President Harding was personally honest, there was more corruption in his administration than in any previous one. Harding's poker-playing friends, known as "the Ohio Gang," used their ties to the President and the attorney general to sell government appointments, pardons, and immunity from prosecution.

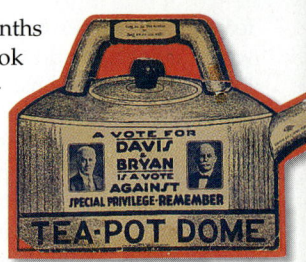

Less than 18 months after Harding took office, his administration was racked by scandal. It was discovered that Charles R. Forbes, the director of the Veterans' Bureau and a close friend of Harding, had made illegal deals that had netted him hundreds of thousands of dollars in commissions. When this fact became public, the attorney for the Bureau, who was also involved, shot himself. His suicide was closely followed by that of Jesse Smith, a close friend of Attorney General Harry M. Daugherty, who himself was later accused of corruption while in office.

The worst scandal involved Harding's secretary of the interior, Albert B. Fall, who secretly leased to private interests some oil lands, which had been set aside for the navy at Teapot Dome, Wyoming, and Elk Hills, California. In return Fall received bribes totaling more than $300,000. Eventually the Senate investigated the Teapot Dome scandal, and Secretary Fall went to prison.

When Harding learned what was going on, he complained privately that he had been betrayed. He said that he had no troubles with his enemies, but his friends—they were a different story. In the summer of 1923, Harding traveled to Alaska, deeply concerned and depressed over the scandals in his administration. On his return he became severely ill. He died on August 2, shortly before news of the scandals broke to the public.

Section 1 ★ Review

Checking for Understanding

1. **Identify** Fordney-McCumber Tariff, Washington Conference, National Origins Act.
2. **Define** reparation, technological unemployment, open shop, welfare capitalism.
3. **Cite** two foreign-policy problems the United States faced after the war.
4. **Summarize** the treaties negotiated at the Washington Conference.

Critical Thinking

5. **Analyzing Changes** Explain why the election of Harding fit America's mood and why this mood had changed since 1917.

History AND Technology CONNECTIONS

Household Technology

". . . [T]he wise woman," proclaimed a 1920s electric company ad, "delegates to electricity all that electricity can do." Inventions such as electric irons, vacuum cleaners, and washing machines changed the lives of urban middle-class housewives in the decade of the 1920s. But these devices changed only the way women spent their time, not how much time they spent.

One study revealed that upper middle-class homemakers employed only half as many full-time servants as their mothers had. These women did work their mothers had hired others to do. Although some women found that laborsaving devices gave them more leisure time, others said that the dirt and soot caused by automobile traffic and nearby factories made their homes dirtier than those of the previous generation. Most of the women surveyed said they spent less time on housework than their mothers, but parenting and other demands had increased. "So many things our mothers didn't know about, we feel that we ought to do for our children," said one woman.

The technological innovations were developed by such creative individuals as Charles Steinmetz. Steinmetz gained recognition in electrical science, and General Electric offered him a job with an excellent salary and superb research facilities.

Known as the "Electrical Genius of GE," Steinmetz made contributions to science and science engineering that sped the nation into an age of electricity. More than 200 patents flowed from his work, which included the study, explanation, and harnessing of alternating current. Before Steinmetz, it had been impossible to transmit electricity more than 3 miles without using multiple generators.

▲ VACUUM CLEANER ADVERTISEMENT, 1920S

Making the Technology Connection

1. What laborsaving devices aided American housewives during the 1920s?
2. How did laborsaving devices and innovations of the period affect American homemakers?

Linking Past and Present

3. What technologies of today have changed the way people spend their time?

CHAPTER 26 CONNECTIONS

Teaching Making Connections

Electric irons, vacuum cleaners, and washing machines had been invented earlier, but they came into widespread use in the 1920s because of the assembly-line technique developed during this decade. By 1926 nearly 16 million homes had been wired for electric lighting. Almost 80 percent of these homes had electric irons, 37 percent had vacuum cleaners, and more than 25 percent had washing machines, toasters, or fans. The following items made their first appearance during this decade: electric food disposal (1920), self-winding wristwatch (1922), spin dryer (1924), automatic potato peeler (1925), embossed and inlaid linoleum (1925), and pop-up toaster (1926).

Ask students to consider the appliances in their homes and decide which are the most time-saving. Ask them if they think modern Americans need all the appliances they can get.

Did You Know?

The technological innovations enjoyed by American households in the 1920s were made possible in part by an increase in the availability of electricity. Before 1914, 20 percent of American homes had electricity. By the end of the 1920s, 70 percent of households enjoyed electric power.

Answers to CONNECTIONS

1. electric iron, vacuum cleaners, washing machines
2. They changed the way women spent their time. Women had fewer servants, and they were more likely to spend time caring for children than cleaning.
3. Answers will vary but may include computers, which can accomplish more work at a faster rate, but standards for productivity and the quality have changed.

LESSON PLAN
SECTION 2, 720–727

FOCUS

Bellringer
Before taking roll at the beginning of the class period, display Focus Activity Transparency 88 on the overhead projector, and assign the accompanying Focus Activity Sheet.

Objectives
Point out the objectives on this page to students in previewing the section content.

Motivating Activity
Read to students President Calvin Coolidge's philosophy concerning business: "The chief business of the American people is business. The man who builds a factory builds a temple. The man who works there worships there." Ask students what Coolidge thought of business. (He related it to religion.) Tell students that Coolidge was firmly convinced that government should be run by businessmen for businessmen. As students read Section 2, ask them to note how Coolidge's philosophy was put into action.

The following material is available from Glencoe and may be used to enrich Chapter 26.

 CD-ROM
- *The Presidents: A Picture History of Our Nation*

SECTION 2

The Coolidge Era

Setting the Scene

Section Focus
When awakened to hear that Harding had died, Vice President Coolidge was at his boyhood home in Vermont. His father, a justice of the peace, administered the oath of office in the flickering light of a kerosene lamp. This homey scene typified the small-town values that the new President held—values which many Americans still shared and cherished.

Objectives
After studying this section, you should be able to
★ discuss the changes to industry Henry Ford introduced.
★ outline the problems of farmers and the government's response.
★ describe the background and details of the Kellogg-Briand Pact.

Key Term
domestic market

◀ AUTOMOBILE ADVERTISEMENT, 1920s

Coolidge had traits often associated with small-town America. He was conservative, cautious, and given to few words. In public speeches and magazine articles, he preached the old-fashioned virtues of honesty, thrift, and hard work. His philosophy of government was simple: economy and laissez-faire. To take as little action as possible was with Coolidge almost a principle of life; he once said, "Four-fifths of all our troubles in this life would disappear if we would only sit down and keep still."

■ The Election of 1924
By 1924 the scandals of the Harding administration had surfaced, hurting the Republican party. This presented the Democratic party with a ready-made issue for the presidential campaign.

The Democrats Are Divided
The Democrats threw away their chances for victory at their national convention, however. The party was deeply divided over two issues: Prohibition—which the rural regions favored and the cities opposed—and more importantly, the Ku Klux Klan.

This secret society, which took its name and ritual from the Southern organization of Reconstruction times, was designed to intimidate African Americans, Catholics, Jews, immigrants, and "foreign ideas," such as the League of Nations. By the mid-1920s the Klan had become a force in American politics, despite its willingness to use terror and violence.

At the 1924 Democratic convention, the rivals for the nomination were William G. McAdoo of California and Governor Alfred E. Smith of New York. McAdoo

720   UNIT 8 Crusade and Disillusion: 1914–1932

Classroom Resources for SECTION 2

Teacher's Classroom Resources
- Reproducible Lesson Plan
- Reteaching Activity 26-2
- Section Quiz

Multimedia
- Section Focus Transparency 88
- Testmaker
- Student Self-Test Software
- The Presidents: A Picture History of Our Nation

favored Prohibition and received most of his support from the western and southern regions of the United States. Governor Smith was a Roman Catholic and opponent of Prohibition. His strongest backing came mostly from urban areas of the Northeast. Smith's supporters wanted an outright condemnation of the Ku Klux Klan, a move that Southern and Western delegates blocked.

The two candidates were deadlocked for so long that the cowboy-humorist Will Rogers suggested that the eventual nominee might be born at the convention. By the time a compromise candidate—John W. Davis of West Virginia—was nominated on the one-hundred-and-third ballot, the Democrats had lost all chance of winning the election.

The Republicans Win

The Republicans campaigned on the slogan "Keep Cool with Coolidge"; the way to keep business thriving, they said, was not to "rock the boat" but to keep in power the party that favored business. This strategy was successful. In an election that attracted only half the eligible voters to the polls, Coolidge won easily.

■ **Business**

During the 1920s many Americans went almost dizzy with prosperity. As business boomed and wages rose, former luxuries became necessities. A combination of increased leisure time for both men and women, new gadgets, new amusements, and more money to spend resulted in something approaching glorification of wealth and of the material comforts that went with it.

The Impact of the Automobile

The outstanding symbol of the new age was the automobile. In the early twentieth century, when the manufacture of automobiles in the United States was just beginning, driving cars was a sport for the wealthy. It was Henry Ford who almost single-handedly changed the automobile from a toy of the wealthy to a necessity for all. Ford's famous "Model T"—affectionately known as the "Tin Lizzie"—was so cheap that most families could afford it. Ford applied many of the familiar techniques of successful industrialists, such as the use of standardized parts and the formation of a vertical organization to combine different

Will Rogers
1879–1935

AMERICAN PORTRAITS

Part Native American, Will Rogers grew up in the West and became a cowboy while in his teens. He landed jobs with Wild West shows, where he would mix in a few jokes while doing his rope-twirling act. Aiming good-natured barbs at famous people, he became known as the "cowboy philosopher."

By 1920 Will Rogers was a star of both stage and screen. Starting in 1926, his daily newspaper column spread his humorous views of life and politics throughout the nation. Claiming "I don't make jokes—I just watch the government and report the facts," he always poked fun in a lighthearted way and was never hostile; one of his favorite sayings was "I never met a man I didn't like."

By the late 1920s audiences were listening to his commentary on radio. To Americans, Rogers had become a national treasure.

Sidelights: Prosperity for Whom?

Although the 1920s was a decade of general prosperity, the percentage of wealth enjoyed by ordinary people declined sharply. The percentage of disposable income received by the top 5 percent of the population rose from 23.96 in 1920 to 34.06 by 1928. (Compare these figures to 16.9 for 1987.) The other 95 percent of the population (approximately 118 million of the nation's 122 million people) actually received more than 10 percent less of the total disposable income in a nine-year span.

CHAPTER 26 SECTION 2

Independent Practice

Technology Have students enlist their families in this activity to see whether a task can be completed more quickly using an assembly-line technique or by having one person do it. Tasks such as washing and drying dishes, setting the table, preparing a meal, and other common household activities might be used. Ask students to time both the family assembly-line completion of an activity and the student's completion. Invite volunteers to report their findings to the class. **L1, LEP**

Using Graphs

Answer: lower auto prices, installment buying, consumer attitudes about prosperity and spending

Skills Practice

Between which years was there a tremendous surge in auto sales? (1921–1923) What might account for that surge? (reduced cost of autos because of efficiency of assembly line)

Did You Know?

Henry Ford was a pacifist and objected to U.S. entrance into World War II. However, after the sneak attack on Pearl Harbor, Ford changed his tune and produced B-24 bombers, armored tanks, and other war vehicles.

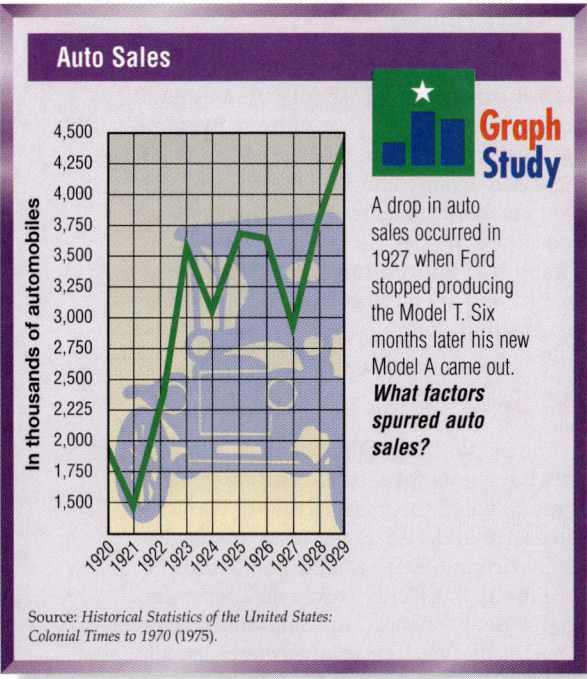

Auto Sales

Graph Study

A drop in auto sales occurred in 1927 when Ford stopped producing the Model T. Six months later his new Model A came out. **What factors spurred auto sales?**

Source: *Historical Statistics of the United States: Colonial Times to 1970* (1975).

---

operations. But Ford's greatest achievement was the assembly line, which divided operations into such simple tasks that most of the work could be done by unskilled labor. Furthermore, by bringing the parts to the workers, assembly lines sped up production so fast that Ford could boast that:

> ... [R]aw iron ore at the docks at 8:00 Monday morning could be marketed as a complete Ford car on Wednesday noon, allowing 15 hours for shipment.

Ford's economies so reduced costs that an American automobile, which sold for an average price of $2,123 in 1907, could be bought for as little as $290 in 1924. While reducing costs, he staved off unionization by nearly doubling wages in 1914 to $5 a day. Other employers resented Ford because his pay scale was so high that it caused discontent among their own workers. It was Ford's belief that mass-production methods and low prices would produce an immense market for goods. This turned out to be correct, and the simplicity of the formula spawned imitators. By the mid-1920s other great trusts, notably General Motors and Chrysler, were competing successfully with Ford.

The impact of the automobile on life in the United States was revolutionary. Although small businesses generally continued to decline, new fields for small enterprises—garages, gas stations, diners, and tourist homes—appeared. Draft animals disappeared from farms as tractors took their places. The isolation of rural areas lessened, as cars put towns within easy reach of many farmers, and put the country within reach of city dwellers.

The Growth of Big Business

It seemed that Americans had discovered a magic formula for producing wealth and fulfilling human wants on a scale never before thought possible. Its ingredients were mass production, standardized products, and a nationwide market. This formula tended to favor big businesses over small because only big businesses could set up assembly lines, do the research necessary for constant development of new products, and afford nationwide advertising. It was natural then that the 1920s should see much concentration of industry. Mergers and holding companies helped to concentrate industry by reducing competition. The chain store soon became a familiar sight on Main Street, capturing one-fourth of the grocery business by 1929.

Whereas many Americans had formerly regarded big business as an enemy, they now relied on it both to supply cheap products and to create new opportunities for wealth. The stock market provided striking evidence of this when, for the first time in history, some members of the general public began to buy securities. The prices of shares of stock, especially those connected with new industries, mounted to dizzying heights. More and more purchasers "invested in the future."

With wealthier Americans speculating in the stock market, money to run business came from more and more diverse sources. Business, on the other hand, was becoming

---

Cooperative Learning

Divide the class into groups of five students each. In each group one student is a minister, another an advertising executive, a third an assembly-line worker, a fourth a farm wife, and a fifth a union leader. Pose this question: How did the automobile industry affect the social, economic, and industrial life in the United States? Have each student answer from the point of view of his or her "character." Ask each group to select a reporter to summarize the group's ideas. **L2**

more and more concentrated. One device used by businesspeople to concentrate financial power was the "pyramiding" of holding companies, whereby it was possible—with a relatively small outlay of capital—for businesspeople to gain control of immense industrial properties.

■ The Plight of Agriculture

Farmers were the one great economic group that did not share in the Coolidge prosperity. The average income for farmers in 1929 was less than one-third of the average income for the rest of the country.

Falling Prices and Shrinking Markets

Technological advances led to greater production, which caused a slump in farm prices even while farmers' costs mounted. As one account puts it:

> *Freight rates, wages, taxes, farm implements, and the like, all of which went into the farmers' cost of production, remained high or came down via the stairway, while farm prices took the elevator.*

Farm prices took disastrous slides in 1920 and 1921 and did not recover. Wheat went from almost $2.50 a bushel to less than $1.50. The foreign market dwindled because the United States had changed from a debtor to a creditor nation. Before World War I, foreign investments in the United States exceeded American investment abroad; the principal means of making up this unfavorable credit balance was for the United States to export agricultural staples, such as wheat and cotton. During the war the balance shifted the other way, principally because of United States loans to the Allies. With the return of peace, countries owing the United States money preferred not to buy its products. Great Britain, for example, often bought wheat from Argentina or Canada, especially after the Fordney-McCumber Tariff reduced the American market for British goods.

The **domestic market,** the market composed of buyers and sellers within the country, also diminished. New fabrics such as rayon lessened the demand for cotton; the

▲ **ON THE ASSEMBLY LINE** Finishing touches are put on a Model A at a Ford plant in Dearborn, Michigan. *What effect did assembly-line production have on the price of automobiles?*

CHAPTER 26 SECTION 2

Research In the 1920s the government gave little if any attention to the plight of American farmers. Point out that in later decades farmers received, and continue to receive, aid from the government. Have students research the kinds of aid the government extends to farmers today. Ask them to draw conclusions about the aid in terms of its effect on farm production and consumer prices. **L2**

Did You Know?

Calvin Coolidge, often referred to as Silent Cal, was an austere, taciturn man. Theodore Roosevelt's daughter, Alice Roosevelt Longworth, once described him as a man who looked as if he "had been weaned on a dill pickle."

Visualizing History Assembly-line production is still the method by which automobiles, as well as many other products, are produced. On some modern assembly lines, robots have replaced workers.
Answer to Caption: reduced the cost of automobiles

Critical Thinking

Supporting Generalizations Write the following sentence on the chalkboard: The business technology of the 1920s created an era of prosperity. Have students find three facts in the section to support this generalization. Write supporting facts on the board as students state them. (Luxuries became necessities; wages rose; most families could afford automobiles; for the first time in history, some members of general public bought securities.) **L1**

CHAPTER 26
SECTION 2

Linking Across Time

The 1980s, like the 1920s, was a time when Presidents vowed to keep government out of business. By the end of the 1980s, however, the lifting of government restriction on investment industries under President Reagan had resulted in hundreds of failed savings and loans businesses because of fraud or bad management. The crisis forced the federal government to undertake a massive cleanup that might end up costing taxpayers $500 million dollars.

Fact or Fiction?

The conservative tide that swept the nation in the 1920s all but wiped out the progressive movement.

FICTION: Robert La Follette ran for President on the Progressive party ticket and received some 1 million votes, 5 percent of the total vote.

History and Art

Thomas Hart Benton belonged to the "American school" of painters. He painted traditional scenes of rural life.
Answer to Caption: Advances in technology led to overproduction, causing a decrease in farm prices.

▼ **FARMING IN THE 1920S**

▲ **WHEAT** by Thomas Hart Benton, 1967 During his later career, Thomas Hart Benton chronicled America's past. **Why did the domestic market for agricultural products diminish during the 1920s?**

substitution of tractors and trucks for draft animals reduced the need for fodder. Faced with decreasing demands for the traditional staples, farmers might have been expected to shift to other products—but that was easier said than done. A Southern tenant farmer usually had no skill at anything but raising cotton. A Dakota wheat farmer usually lacked the capital and the knowledge to change, say, to dairy farming, which in any case was not well suited to that region. Moreover, many farmers had borrowed heavily during the war to buy new land at inflated prices. The only obvious way to pay off the debt was to raise more crops. But more crops meant unsalable surpluses; unsalable surpluses meant low prices. Low prices made the debt burden even heavier.

The Influence of the Farm Bloc

Early in Harding's administration, members of Congress from the Midwest and Plains states formed the Farm Bloc. It included about 25 senators and 100 representatives from both parties. Strong enough to hold a balance of power in Congress, the Farm Bloc forced through several laws favoring farmers. The Capper-Volstead Act of 1922 made farm cooperatives free of antitrust laws; the Intermediate Credits Act of 1923 set up federal banks to make loans to aid farm cooperatives.

None of the laws, however, dealt with the farmers' major problem: surpluses they could not sell. If wheat farmers were to benefit from the 42-cent-a-bushel protective tariff, which eliminated foreign competition, they somehow had to limit the amount of wheat put on that market.

The Farm Bloc supported the McNary-Haugen Bill. This bill proposed that the federal government buy crop surpluses and sell them abroad, while protecting the United States market with a high tariff. This would immediately raise the domestic price. Whatever losses the government suffered would be covered by an equalization fee—a tax

UNIT 8 Crusade and Disillusion: 1914–1932

Sidelights: A New Form of Communication

As the automotive industry expanded, another technology also was spreading its wings. Airmail was common by the early 1920s, although the beginnings of this service were not so auspicious. Started in 1918, the service connected New York City, Philadelphia, and Washington, D.C. When President Wilson one day dropped in to observe, he saw the plane bound for Philadelphia repeatedly fail to take off. Then someone remembered to fill it with gas. Next the pilot flew in the wrong direction and crash-landed in a field. Finally the mail was sent by rail.

▲ FARM LANTERN, 1920s

charged against producers. Supporters of the bill claimed that it would help farmers as the tariff helped manufacturers.

Twice the bill passed Congress, but both times President Coolidge vetoed it. The idea would not work, he insisted, and furthermore, a "healthy economic condition is best maintained through a free play of competition." Thus, farmers failed to obtain protections similar to those many businesses received at the time.

■ Foreign Affairs

During the 1920s both Republican Presidents worked to promote world peace through individual agreements. During Coolidge's administration, France and the United States took the lead in promoting a treaty that attempted to "outlaw war."

Called the Kellogg-Briand Pact after the American secretary of state and the French foreign minister who proposed it, the treaty was eventually ratified by 64 nations, each agreeing to abandon war "as an instrument of national policy" and to settle disputes by peaceful means. The treaty was hailed as a great victory for peace. The pact, often called the Pact of Paris, was signed by most nations only under certain conditions. The primary condition of most was to retain the right to defend themselves against acts of aggression. The United States also stated that the pact did not overrule the principles of the Monroe Doctrine.

A serious weakness of the pact was that it had no means of enforcement. No provisions were set down in the event there were acts of aggression among signer nations.

Although the United States generally participated in talks and treaties with European and Asian nations during this period, its manner toward Latin America remained protective. The Harding and Coolidge administrations—following the Roosevelt Corollary to the Monroe Doctrine—occasionally sent troops to "preserve order" in Caribbean countries. They became increasingly aware, however, that the Latin American people acutely resented such intervention. Although not willing to give up the right to intervene, Secretary of State Charles Evans Hughes believed troops should be sent to Latin America only to promote political stability, not to assist American investors. Accordingly, in the mid-1920s, United States Marines withdrew from the Dominican Republic and Nicaragua, where they had been sent in the previous decade to maintain order.

Section 2 ★ Review

Checking for Understanding

1. **Identify** Henry Ford, assembly line, McNary-Haugen Bill, Farm Bloc.
2. **Define** domestic market.
3. **List** three ways that the automobile changed American life.
4. **Summarize** the farmers' situation in the 1920s and how government reacted.

Critical Thinking

5. **Supporting an Opinion** Would you agree that Coolidge did not regard farming in the same way he viewed big business? Explain.

INTEGRATING Language Arts

American Literary Heritage

Historical Setting

In the 1920s Americans seemed determined to compensate for lost time. The "Roaring Twenties" boasted flourishing jazz musicians and a renewed interest in dance. Radio proved to be a marvel of the era. The movie industry blossomed, and in 1927 the first "talkie" was released. A new emphasis on cultural pride proliferated.

Background

Poetry depends on the creation of a particular mood, which reflects the outlooks and sentiments with which the poet approaches his or her topic. The emotional stance of the poet is essential to mood. The poems here capture the spirit of restlessness, the emphasis upon youthful vigor, and the deepening cultural expansion that characterized the United States during the 1920s.

About the Authors

Edna St. Vincent Millay (1892–1950) was a significant poet in New York City's Greenwich Village, where she embraced a bohemian existence. Langston Hughes (1902–1967) was a central figure in the Harlem Renaissance, which addressed issues of cultural pride while presenting protest pieces. Carl Sandburg (1878–1967) was a product of the Midwest. Before writing in Chicago for *Poetry* magazine, Sandburg worked as a journalist. In addition to writing poetry, he created children's stories and biographies.

▲ EDNA ST. VINCENT MILLAY

After World War I, divergent movements in American literature grew up in New York's Harlem and Greenwich Village and in the nation's heartland. Two poets who typify these movements are Edna St. Vincent Millay and Langston Hughes. In the first of the following selections, Millay captures the tireless energy of youth. In the selection by Hughes, the poet uses rhythms of the jazz age to reflect his African American pride.

▲ FERRY BOAT TRIP BY WILLIAM H. JOHNSON, 1934

Recuerdo by Edna St. Vincent Millay

We were very tired, we were very merry—
We had gone back and forth all night on the ferry.
It was bare and bright, and smelled like a stable—
But we looked into a fire, we leaned across a table,
We lay on a hill-top underneath the moon;
And the whistles kept blowing, and the dawn
   came soon.
We were very tired, we were very merry—
We had gone back and forth all night on the ferry;
And you ate an apple, and I ate a pear,
From a dozen of each we had bought somewhere;
And the sky went wan, and the wind came cold,
And the sun rose dripping, a bucketful of gold.
We were very tired, we were very merry,
We had gone back and forth all night on the ferry.

Cultural Diversity

Point out that in the 1920s both white and African American writers responded to the forces around them. Although African American writers often used literature to protest or to address themes of concern to them, they, like white writers, were influenced by the spirit of restlessness and change that surrounded them.

We hailed, "Good-morrow, mother!" to a
    shawl-covered head,
And bought a morning paper, which neither
    of us read;
And she wept, "God bless you!" for the
    apples and the pears,
And we gave her all our money but our
    subway fares.

Dream Boogie
by Langston Hughes

Ain't you heard
The boogie-woogie rumble
Of a dream deferred?
Listen closely:
You'll hear their feet
Beating out and beating out a—
You think
It's a happy beat?
Listen to it closely:
Ain't you heard
something underneath
like a—
What did I say?
Sure,
I'm happy!
Take it away!
Hey, pop!
Re-bop!
Mop!
Y-e-a-h!

▲ Li'l Sis by William H. Johnson, 1944

▲ Langston Hughes

Interpreting Literature

1. What period of time is covered in the three stanzas of "Recuerdo"?
2. How many speakers are there in "Dream Boogie"? What device is used to set them apart?
3. What differences and similarities in voice can you find between the authors of these selections?

Identifying Viewpoints

4. What views of American life in the 1920s do Millay and Hughes embody?

INTEGRATING
Language Arts

Developing Student Understanding

Invite students to brainstorm names, phrases, and achievements related to the 1920s. (Samples: "Roaring Twenties," the Jazz Age, sheiks, flappers, bobbed hair, short skirts, Rudolph Valentino, Babe Ruth, Charles Lindbergh) Remind students that there was great activity in all areas of society, including the arts. Explain that the new cultural emphasis of the era produced poets of great importance. Inspired and energized by the quick pace of the Jazz Age, these poets placed their fingers on the vigorous pulse of American society.

Other Works by the Authors

Edna St. Vincent Millay's works include *A Few Figs From Thistles* (1920), *Second April* (1921), and *The Harp-Weaver and Other Poems* (1923), for which she was awarded a Pulitzer Prize. Langston Hughes wrote plays, novels, and short stories, in addition to poetry. It was his 1926 collection of poems, *The Weary Blues*, however, that gained him acclaim. Carl Sandburg, another Pulitzer Prize recipient, published several volumes of poetry. Among them are *Smoke and Steel* (1920), *Good Morning, America* (1928), and *Complete Poems* (1950), which earned him the Pulitzer Prize.

Answers to INTERPRETING LITERATURE

1. It covers the space of a single night through dawn of the following morning.
2. There are two. The second voice is represented by the lines in italics.
3. "Recuerdo"—the voice is one of youthful optimism and high spirits; "Dream Boogie"—the dual voice echoes the hope tempered by cynicism that prevails in the African American community to this day; "Jazz Fantasia"—Sandburg celebrates the rich rhythms and beat of jazz.
4. "Recuerdo" contains a view of a nation that is something of a playground. The Hughes piece contains a mixed view of life in a land where black skin remains a barrier to fair and equal treatment. The Sandburg piece celebrates the nation's musical richness.

CHAPTER 26 SECTION 3

FOCUS

 Display Focus Activity Transparency 89 on the overhead projector, and assign the accompanying Focus Activity Sheet.

Objectives

Point out the objectives on this page in previewing the section content.

Motivating Activity

Write the following on the chalkboard and ask students which experiences make them feel more part of a crowd and which make them aware of their individuality:

  reading a book
  watching television
  viewing a film in a theater

Discuss students' responses, and explain that developments during the 1920s changed the lives of individuals and groups of Americans in many ways.

 Assign students the Chapter 26 Reading in Primary and Secondary Source Readings.

VIDEODISC

• *GTV: The American People: Fabric of a Nation*

Side 3, Chapter 7
Title: *Enter the Klan*
Subject: Prejudice and intolerance in America

See GTV Guide page 86 for complete lesson plan.

SECTION 3

The "Roaring Twenties"

Setting the Scene

Section Focus

The 1920s saw striking changes in American society. Radio and film became immensely popular. The arts flowered. "Coolidge prosperity" provided more leisure time and more spending money for new gadgets. The availability of credit helped many to buy more than they could afford. Women adopted new standards of behavior. To many, however, these changes suggested a loss of important traditional values.

Objectives

After studying this section, you should be able to

★ describe changes in women's lives during the 1920s.

★ outline developments in the arts and education during this period.

Key Term

postwar disillusionment

◀ COOLIDGE CAMPAIGN POSTER, 1924

From a Long Island airfield on May 20, 1927, a small plane called the *Spirit of St. Louis* took off for France. Twenty-five-year-old Charles Lindbergh set off to make the first nonstop solo flight across the Atlantic. Thirty-three and one-half hours later, Lindbergh landed near Paris. Huge crowds greeted him. An American naval vessel brought him home, and even greater crowds welcomed him back to the United States. "Lucky Lindy," as he was called, became a hero of the age.

President Coolidge called him "a boy representing the best traditions of his country." In an era when the ideals and heroes of history were questioned, when politics was riddled with graft, and when machines seemed to be replacing people, Lindbergh helped people restore some confidence in themselves. He proved that Americans were still capable of pioneering, even in the machine age. Quiet, courageous, and self-reliant, Lindbergh showed that not all the old values of life had disappeared, despite the changing priorities of modern society.

■ New Directions in Society

The rapid changes caused by the progress of technology in the 1920s brought with them some serious problems. Automobiles, though they offered an exciting new freedom of movement, also killed as many Americans in 1928 and 1929 as had lost their lives in battle during World War I. Cities lost some of their attractiveness as automobiles enabled people and businesses to move to the suburbs. The easily available "canned

---

Classroom Resources for SECTION 3

Teacher's Classroom Resources
- Reproducible Lesson Plan
- Reteaching Activity 26-3
- Chapter 26 Primary and Secondary Source Readings
- Chapter 26 Enrichment Activity
- Chapter 26 Performance Assessment Activity
- Spanish Summaries and Glossary
- Section Quiz

Multimedia
- Section Focus Transparency 89
- Vocabulary Puzzlemaker
- Testmaker
- Student Self-Test Software
- The American People: Fabric of a Nation
- The Presidents: A Picture History of Our Nation

▲ **LINDBERGH'S HISTORIC FLIGHT** Because a huge fuel tank blocked his plane's windshield on his transatlantic flight, Lindbergh used a periscope to see. Lindbergh's heroics inspired other pilots like Amelia Earhart (right). *In what way was Lindbergh a symbol of the 1920s?*

entertainment" provided by radio and motion pictures seemed to discourage Americans from creating their own amusements.

Prohibition

Unfortunately, during the 1920s crime became big business. Gangsters such as Al Capone and Dutch Schultz consolidated the illegal liquor trade on many of the same principles used to consolidate the automobile and steel industries. The Prohibition Bureau, set up to enforce the law against the distilling and sale of liquor, was understaffed, underpaid, graft-ridden, and ineffective. Although liquor consumption dropped substantially during Prohibition, illegal drinking by millions created an illegitimate billion-dollar industry. The entrepreneurs in this illegal business became wealthy enough to buy beautiful homes in Florida, steel-plated limousines, and fabulous jewels, such as Capone's 11.5-carat diamond ring. Some gangsters became powerful enough to corrupt local governments.

Rural America, with its traditional values and churchgoing ways, tended to support Prohibition, but the cities generally opposed it. The customary diets of several urban ethnic groups included liquor, and many city dwellers resisted Prohibition as the work of religious crusaders. Regardless, Prohibition was never fully enforced. Many people supported Prohibition publicly while privately continuing to drink.

CHAPTER 26
SECTION 3

Independent Practice
Identifying Consequences
Have students write a paragraph to describe the "dark side" of each of these 1920s' phenomena, which in general were perceived as social goods: the automobile, Prohibition, new freedom for women, new educational theories. When students have completed their paragraphs, ask them why they think society is willing to tolerate the dangers that accompany technology or the corruption that sometimes accompanies the processes of government and business. **L3**

Did You Know?
The sensationalized case of the kidnapping of Charles Lindbergh's son led Congress to pass the Lindbergh Law, which makes kidnapping a federal offense if the kidnapper takes the victim across state lines.

- **The Presidents: A Picture History of Our Nation**

▲ AL CAPONE

Despite the success of the illegal liquor trade, Prohibition actually gained in popularity during the 1920s. In 1928 voters elected more supporters of Prohibition to Congress than ever before, as well as a "dry" President, Herbert Hoover. The popularity of Prohibition was a sign of continuing faith in the possibility of achieving a better life, of a longing for the ideals that had eroded in the horrors of World War I.

▼ MOVIE POSTER, 1920S

Traditional standards of behavior were changing as Americans left the villages for the cities and the farms for the factories. Prohibition seemed a way to halt this change in values.

Women in the 1920s
The 1920s saw women express greater personal freedom. A dramatic new woman of the 1920s—the "flapper"—demanded the same freedom enjoyed by men. She sometimes smoked cigarettes and drank liquor and dressed in a way her mother and grandmother would not have believed possible. While most women in the 1920s were not flappers, these new women demonstrated how modern behavior was changing.

American family life was also changing. Couples had fewer children because of increased knowledge about family planning, divorce rates increased, and more women than ever before sought employment outside the home.

Women in the Workplace
Having achieved the right to vote, women sought financial independence as well. Many young single women became salesclerks in department stores, secretaries, or telephone operators, for example. In 1920, 25 percent of female workers were in clerical and sales work. Eventually the employees in those particular jobs became almost exclusively female. Graduates of women's colleges began to seek jobs in business rather than in more traditional jobs such as teaching. But many women, especially married women who had to work to support families, were confined to jobs with long hours, poor conditions, and low wages. Women who worked outside the home suffered severe discrimination, often receiving only 50 to 60 percent of a man's wages for the same work. Further, women continued to meet with difficulty when trying to enter prestigious professions such as science and law.

Individual women made great contributions in many fields—often under difficult circumstances. Amelia Earhart learned to fly

UNIT 8 Crusade and Disillusion: 1914–1932

Cooperative Learning
Invite volunteers to form two groups to debate the pros and cons of Prohibition. Give students time to prepare their arguments. As each group presents its argument, summarize it on the chalkboard. Make sure groups cite evidence to support their viewpoints. When the debate is concluded, discuss the arguments with the class. Ask the class to decide which are most valid. **L1**

Life of the Times

Radio

The 1920s ushered in a host of technologies still heavily used today. Among the most significant breakthroughs was commercial radio. In November 1920, radio station KDKA in Pittsburgh broadcast news of Harding's landslide victory, in one of the first commercial broadcasts in history. Within the next two years, almost 600 radio stations began operation. One million Americans tuned in daily to hear their favorite radio programs.

Radio, from its earliest days, was financed through the sale of advertising time and offered a wide variety of information, advice, and entertainment. Farm families particularly appreciated the Department of Agriculture broadcasts of farm market prices. Weather reports were universally popular. Dramas, adventures, and comedies, each with a cast of actors and a sound effects technician, were performed live in the radio studio as the broadcast aired. Sports reached new heights in popularity. News, music, advice, and quiz shows were other early radio programs.

Radio, like so many technologies that emerged in the post–World War I period, served to shrink the world, bringing immediate contact and communication, and a common experience to people in all parts of the world.

▲ ADVERTISEMENT, 1929

◀ RADIO RECEIVER, 1929

planes and became the first woman to complete a solo flight across the Atlantic. Dorothy Thompson became a famous journalist. Mary McLeod Bethune—an African American woman born into poverty—founded her own college, founded the National Council of Negro Women, and served as a government consultant.

Women in the Home

Most Americans—both men and women—continued to believe that a married woman's place was in the home. Thus, in spite of a spirit of independence, most women continued to be bound by the belief that their role was different from that of men, that they were to be mothers and homemakers. With new electric technology, the nature of being a homemaker changed. New household appliances, such as refrigerators and vacuum cleaners, commercial laundries, and canned food made hard, time-consuming domestic duties much easier. Many who stayed at home and became mothers, particularly in middle-class families, managed motherhood by listening to child-rearing experts who promoted regularly scheduled feedings for children and regimented routines for such children's extracurricular activities as music lessons and clubs.

■ Cultural Achievements

American culture thrived in the 1920s. Literature, architecture, music, painting, movies, radio—all flourished during this time.

American Literature

Some writers of the period, such as novelist Willa Cather and poet Robert Frost, tried to recapture the spirit and traditions

CHAPTER 26 The Decade of Normalcy 1920–1928 731

CHAPTER 26 SECTION 3

Teaching Life of the Times

The first commercial broadcasting station was WJW in Detroit, Michigan, which went on the air in August 1920. From then on, radio was a major form of communication. By the mid-1920s, Americans could listen to presidential candidates debating the issues of the day. Radio had an enormous influence on family life as families gathered around the radio to listen to their favorite programs. Although radio has been eclipsed by television, it is still alive and well. Suggest students research radio in their area. How many stations are there? What kinds of broadcasting do they deliver? How does radio influence community life today?

Food of the Times

In the 1920s a native of Brooklyn came home from a trip with an idea that changed the way Americans eat. After Clarence Birdseye watched Native Americans preserve fish and game by freezing it, he hit on a way to turn the idea into a business. He patented his process in 1925. Within three years frozen vegetables could be purchased in hundreds of food stores. Consumers stored their frozen goods in their new electric refrigerators—an invention that became popular in the late 1920s and early 1930s.

Sidelights: A Disillusioning Episode

If the scandals in his cabinet broke Warren Harding's heart, another scandal shattered the idealism of American baseball fans. In 1919 eight members of the Chicago White Sox were accused of taking mob money to throw the World Series to the Cincinnati Reds. The accused, called the Black Sox, were not greedy businessmen but exploited and poorly paid players, some of whom had been promised and then denied raises. The owners, gamblers, and gangsters cleaned up; the players, though formally acquitted in court, were banned from professional baseball for life. The scandal set the tone of disillusionment that would permeate the decade.

CHAPTER 26 SECTION 3

Linking Across Time

The Ku Klux Klan was one of the reactionary forces that manifested itself during the 1920s. The Klan, whose name comes from the Greek word *kyklos*, meaning "circle," has had four periods of influence in the United States. The first was in the post–Civil War period, when it rose as a reaction to Reconstruction. It enjoyed a resurgence in the 1920s, when membership reached more than 3 million, much of it in the Midwest. Membership rose again from the late 1940s to the 1970s. There was yet another rise in the 1980s. Today membership is only about 6,000.

Visualizing History

A well-known educator, Mary McLeod Bethune founded a college for African Americans in Daytona Beach, Florida. Later, in the 1930s, she headed the Division of Negro Affairs of the National Youth Administration, a New Deal agency whose goal was to improve conditions for African Americans. **Answer to Caption:** Increased intolerance of racial or ethnic diversity was general in the 1920s.

▲ **Visualizing History** **WORKING FOR JUSTICE** Activists like Mary McLeod Bethune fought to pass a federal law against lynching. *What attitudes might explain why lynching and other such incidents increased in the 1920s?*

Postwar disillusionment, disappointment or dissatisfaction with the way things were after the war, was often manifested as criticism of American life. Henry Ford said that "history is bunk," and a school of "debunking" historians reexamined the past and reevaluated more accurately the facts behind the myths of many American heroes. Many American writers did the same. In his novels *Main Street* and *Babbitt*, Sinclair Lewis depicted the absurdities of life in small-town America. H. L. Mencken mocked the "vast . . . herd of good-natured animals" who made up most of the machine-age society. Mencken saw no hope for improvement. "If I am convinced of anything," he wrote, "it is that Doing Good is in bad taste."

The Arts

Achievements in American literature were matched in the arts. New city skyscrapers and suburban homes expanded the opportunities of architects like Frank Lloyd Wright, who achieved worldwide fame for his bold use of new materials and for architectural designs free of traditional influence.

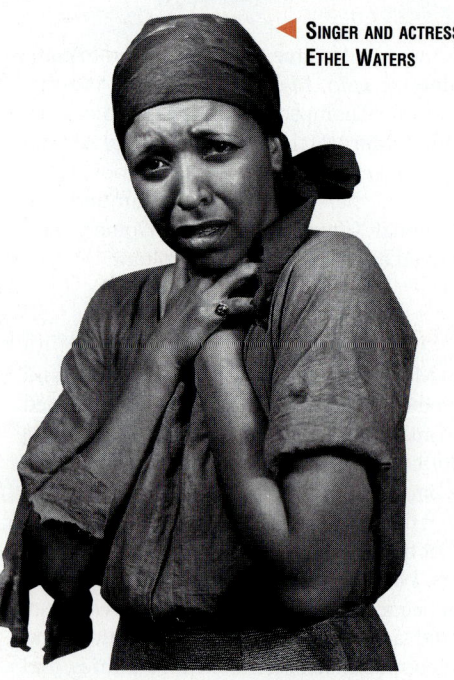

◀ **SINGER AND ACTRESS ETHEL WATERS**

of rural America; others, such as poet Carl Sandburg, examined what was happening in America's cities. In Eugene O'Neill, the United States produced its finest playwright. O'Neill found material in many aspects of American life—from the rage of a worker in the hold of a steamship in *The Hairy Ape*, to family tension in a decaying New England town in *Desire Under the Elms*. Ernest Hemingway, who had driven an ambulance on the Italian front during World War I, wrote about the meaningless violence of war in *A Farewell to Arms*. His fiction created a new literary style characterized by direct, simple, spare prose. The poet T. S. Eliot saw a world filled with "hollow men" and, in *The Wasteland*, one that would end "not with a bang but a whimper."

UNIT 8 Crusade and Disillusion: 1914–1932

Critical Thinking

Classifying On a line across the chalkboard, write the following: Theme, Author/Artist, Work. Invite volunteers to come to the board and fill in entries under Theme. Then have other volunteers classify authors/artists and their works according to the themes. Discuss with the class whether any of the themes expressed in the literature and art of the 1920s are important in society today. **L2**

In jazz, which started with African American Dixieland bands in New Orleans, America produced a new form of music. At first seen as corrupting the morals of young people, jazz was soon accepted as an important art form. In the fine arts, the American scene was brilliantly portrayed by such painters as Reginald Marsh, Thomas Hart Benton, George Bellows, and Edward Hopper. In photography, Alfred Stieglitz achieved an international reputation.

Also during this period, the young motion-picture industry mushroomed. The first feature-length film appeared in 1915. By 1929 there were about 100 million paid admissions to movie theaters every week—proof that moviegoing had gained respectability. During the 1920s the motion-picture industry moved from New York to southern California. Mary Pickford, Charlie Chaplin, Douglas Fairbanks, Gloria Swanson, and Clara Bow were among the first stars of the silent screen. In 1927 Warner Brothers introduced "talking" pictures, which made the movies more popular than ever.

Changes and Challenges in Education

A significant amount of the new wealth of the 1920s went into education, both through taxes for new public schools and through private donations to colleges and universities. The introduction of the school bus made possible the gradual replacement of bare, one-room country schoolhouses with large, well-equipped central schools. High school was no longer the privilege of the well-off but was also attended by the children of farmers and workers—although graduation from high school remained the exception rather than the rule. Both high school and college enrollment increased steadily.

▲ **THE SCOPES TRIAL** Opposing attorneys Clarence Darrow (left) and William Jennings Bryan pose during the Scopes trial. Scopes was later freed on appeal, but the trial proved too much for Bryan, who died a week after it ended. *What basic clash of values in 1920s society did the trial illustrate?*

A philosophy of education, long championed by John Dewey, emphasized learning through direct experience and experiment rather than through memorization. Greater emphasis was placed on science, which Dewey viewed as a way of using both thought and activity to investigate nature.

Some religious groups found these new educational theories threatening and were able to gain laws in some states to prevent the teaching of evolution in public schools. This set the stage for a battle between science and religion. It came in 1925, at the trial of John T. Scopes, a teacher in Dayton, Tennessee, who was willing to be arrested for teaching evolution to his high-school class. The American Civil Liberties Union (ACLU) had raised money to test the new antievolution law in Tennessee and had asked Scopes if he would volunteer for the cause. The famous attorney Clarence Darrow defended Scopes, while William Jennings Bryan aided the prosecution for the antievolution forces. After a sensational trial, Scopes was convicted, but Bryan, who took the witness stand as an expert on the Bible, was made to look foolish through Darrow's penetrating questioning. The Scopes case symbolized the tensions of the

Did You Know?

The annual average salary in 1925 for public school teachers was $1,263, at a time when the average salary for clerical workers was $2,239. Because teachers' salaries were so low, especially at the elementary-school level, most teaching positions were filled by women. In 1925 only about one in five teachers was a man, most of whom were high-school teachers. Rural education, typically inferior to urban education, employed many teachers who had not even graduated from high school. Only about a third as many children in rural areas went to high school as did children in urban areas.

Visualizing History Tennessee's law against the teaching of evolution remained on the books until 1967. One historian noted that the trial was a conflict between rural and urban values.
Answer to Caption: It was a clash between modern emphasis on experiment and experience in education and traditional ideas of education.

Sidelights: Agents of Prohibition

Isador Einstein, known as Izzy, and his partner, Moe Smith, worked as a team to trap lawbreakers during Prohibition. Masters of disguise, they were a flamboyant pair who used any number of methods to enforce the law. Izzy was particularly adept at going through any neighborhood, for he spoke five languages. He once nabbed an unsuspecting speakeasy owner by disguising himself as a pickle salesman. Together Izzy and Moe made some 4,000 arrests and hauled in around 15 million dollars worth of alcohol.

1920s, as some Americans tried to resist the tide of social change and to preserve older values and beliefs.

The Harlem Renaissance

World War I had been a liberating experience for many African Americans. This was especially true of those who went abroad. For the first time they were freed from the second-class citizenship they suffered in the United States. But the prejudice and discrimination that awaited them at home helped to create a spirit of pride and protest, forging a new unity and a new African American:

> ... who had pride in heritage and self and who, through poetry, music, dance, and the theater, was able to create works of beauty out of travail and sufferings, as well as out of the more humorous facts of life.

A striking outcome of this new spirit among African Americans was the "Harlem Renaissance." In New York City, the intellectual capital of the United States, a number of highly talented African Americans rose to fame. Some were in the performing arts, including actors Charles Gilpin and Richard B. Harrison, singers Roland Hayes and Ethel Waters, dancer Bill Robinson, and singer-actor Paul Robeson. Others were scholars, including sociologist E. Franklin Frazier and economist Abram L. Harris. Still others were writers, such as poets Countee Cullen and Langston Hughes and novelists Jessie H. Fauset, Zora Neale Hurston, and Walter White.

▲ WRITER COUNTEE CULLEN

More influential than the intellectuals and artists among African Americans themselves was a dynamic leader from Jamaica, Marcus Garvey. A spokesman for "Negro Nationalism," which exalted African American culture and traditions, Garvey formed the Universal Negro Improvement Association, which soon boasted a million members. Garvey told his followers they would never find justice in America and proposed to lead them to Africa. People were not interested, but Garvey stimulated the pride of African Americans in their history and heritage.

Section 3 ★ Review

Checking for Understanding

1. **Identify** Amelia Earhart, Mary McLeod Bethune, John T. Scopes.
2. **Define** postwar disillusionment.
3. **Cite** the factors that resulted in increased crime in the 1920s.
4. **Summarize** changes in women's personal and economic status during the 1920s.

Critical Thinking

5. **Evaluating Achievements** How are the advances made by women in the 1920s significant to the lives of American women today?

734 UNIT 8 Crusade and Disillusion: 1914–1932

Social Studies Skills

Interpreting Primary Sources

The Harlem Renaissance and Visual Arts

Although the outpouring of literature, art, and music known as the Harlem Renaissance involved only a handful of artists and writers, the power of their work brought international attention and acclaim to Harlem in the 1920s and the 1930s. The visual artists associated with the Harlem Renaissance were a diverse group of people. Some, such as Edwin A. Harleston and Laura Wheeler Waring, painted in a style that was virtually indistinguishable from that of their white European and American peers. Others, such as Lois Mailou Jones and Aaron Douglas, used African design motifs to shape a distinctively African American art.

Aaron Douglas, the best-known visual artist of the Harlem Renaissance, was perhaps also the one most influenced by African design. He developed his style of geometric symbolism as a painter of murals on public buildings. The painting shown here, *The Creation*, shows several elements characteristic of Douglas's style: a figure that represents not a particular person but all humankind; subtle, barely differentiated shades of purple and gray; and shapes such as circles, arches, and waves. Douglas believed that art can be a bridge between different cultures and peoples. He asserted this belief through his paintings, which describe human experience in a streamlined visual language that people of different times, places, genders, and races can easily understand.

Douglas inspired the Harlem Renaissance by actively searching out and training other artists. His efforts were rewarded in 1928 when the first all-African American art show in the United States was held in New York City. Many of the exhibitors became eminent in American art. Their efforts spread the spirit of the Harlem Renaissance well beyond New York.

▲ THE CREATION BY AARON DOUGLAS

Examining the Primary Source

1. Identify one shape, besides the circle, in the painting. What might it stand for?
2. Suggest what the circles represent.
3. What might the hand and figure symbolize?

Critical Thinking

4. **Making Inferences** What emotions might the figure in the painting be experiencing? Explain your viewpoint.
5. **Drawing Conclusions** What foods, clothes, or celebrations reflect the origins of several groups of Americans?

LESSON PLAN
Mastering Social Studies Skills

Teaching Interpreting Primary Sources

Remind students of the power of shape and color—broad strokes versus delicate lines, for example, or bright, bold colors versus pale colors. Ask them to look at *The Creation* with an eye toward discovering what the artist was trying to communicate with the shapes and colors he used. Does the artist represent a person of a particular time or a person of any time? What makes you think as you do? (The stylized drawing of the human figure suggests all people.) Why would an artist choose universal symbols as in *The Creation*? (The artist wanted to speak to people of all times and cultures.)

Discuss the questions together, accepting any responses students can justify.

Did You Know?

During the Harlem Renaissance, Douglas illustrated books written by such writers as Countee Cullen and Langston Hughes.

Answers to SOCIAL STUDIES SKILLS

1. Answers will vary but may include the star, used to represent the heavens; the triangle, used to represent mountains; and the arch, used to represent the rainbow.
2. The title, *The Creation*, suggests that the circles represent the planets of the universe.
3. The hand represents God; the figure represents humanity.
4. Answers will vary, but students may say that the figure is feeling awed in the presence of God and by his handiworks. The hand so much larger implies that humanity is much smaller than God and can know only part of God.
5. Students may mention items of ethnic culture, such as food, clothing, or celebrations.

REVIEW CHAPTER 26

Answers

Reviewing Facts

1. his approachable and warm personality, his position on a return to "normalcy"
2. negotiated the Washington Conference, hammered out a solution to war debts, signed the Kellogg-Briand Pact, continued involvement in Latin America
3. protective tariffs, *laissez-faire* government, lower taxes
4. fear, Red Scare, labor pressure, prejudice
5. High wages, mass production, standardized products, and a nationwide market helped lower prices and make products available to all, thus boosting the economy.
6. Tariffs created a backlash overseas and reduced markets for the oversupply of crops created by new technology. These factors lowered prices.
7. radio, motion pictures, jazz, new literary styles, modern architecture, Harlem Renaissance, improved home products, women feeling more independent, African Americans slowly entering some professions

Understanding Concepts

1. Middle- and lower-income Americans benefited from economic policy in the form of wages, which were rising; products, which were more abundant and cheaper; and jobs, which were plentiful.
2. Answers will vary. Some writers and artists commented on social changes by painting or writing about a slower, simpler past. Others drew upon the rapid and exciting social changes to create new artistic forms, such as jazz.

Critical Thinking

1. Answers will vary. The Washington Conference and Kellogg-Briand Pact were attempts to preclude future wars by disarmament and conflict resolution. These were not very realistic, however, because how these principles would be enforced never was resolved. The goal was peace. Joining the League of Nations might have

---

CHAPTER 26 ★ REVIEW

Using Vocabulary

Imagine that you are the chairperson of a large industrial company in the 1920s. Write a letter to the President using the terms below.

welfare capitalism   open shop

Reviewing Facts

1. **State** two reasons Harding was elected President in 1920.
2. **Summarize** foreign-policy actions of Harding and Coolidge.
3. **List** three ways that Harding and Coolidge helped stimulate business in America.
4. **Explain** why Congress enacted the Emergency Quota Act and the National Origins Act.
5. **Discuss** how Henry Ford's innovations contributed to the growth of the economy.
6. **Describe** ways farmers were affected by tariffs and improved technology.
7. **Cite** evidence that the 1920s changed the arts and the lives of women and African Americans.

Understanding Concepts

Economic Change

1. Explain why urban dwellers of all economic levels would support the economic changes of the 1920s.

Social Change

2. Art, literature, and music thrived in the 1920s. What changes in society do you think inspired artists, writers, and musicians?

Critical Thinking

1. **Drawing Conclusions** Explain how changes in business and manufacturing during the 1920s sparked a revolution in social customs, arts, and entertainment.

---

2. **Analyzing Fine Art** Study the painting of singer and actor Paul Robeson on this page by artist Betsy Graves Reyneau, then answer the questions that follow.
   a. What does the painting tell you about the artist's view of Robeson?
   b. What title would you give this painting?

▲ PAUL ROBESON IN THE ROLE OF OTHELLO

Writing About History

Narration

Choose a topic from Chapter 26 and write an imaginary news report that could be narrated over radio. When you have finished writing, reread your narrative and imagine you are the listener. Rewrite any parts that are unclear or do not adequately convey the sights, sounds, and feelings of the topic.

Cooperative Learning

Work in groups of four to evaluate the changes that took place in the 1920s. One member of each group should assume one of the following roles: business owner, farmer, African American, flapper. The goal of your group is to write four paragraphs

736 UNIT 8 Crusade and Disillusion: 1914–1932

CHAPTER 26 ★ REVIEW

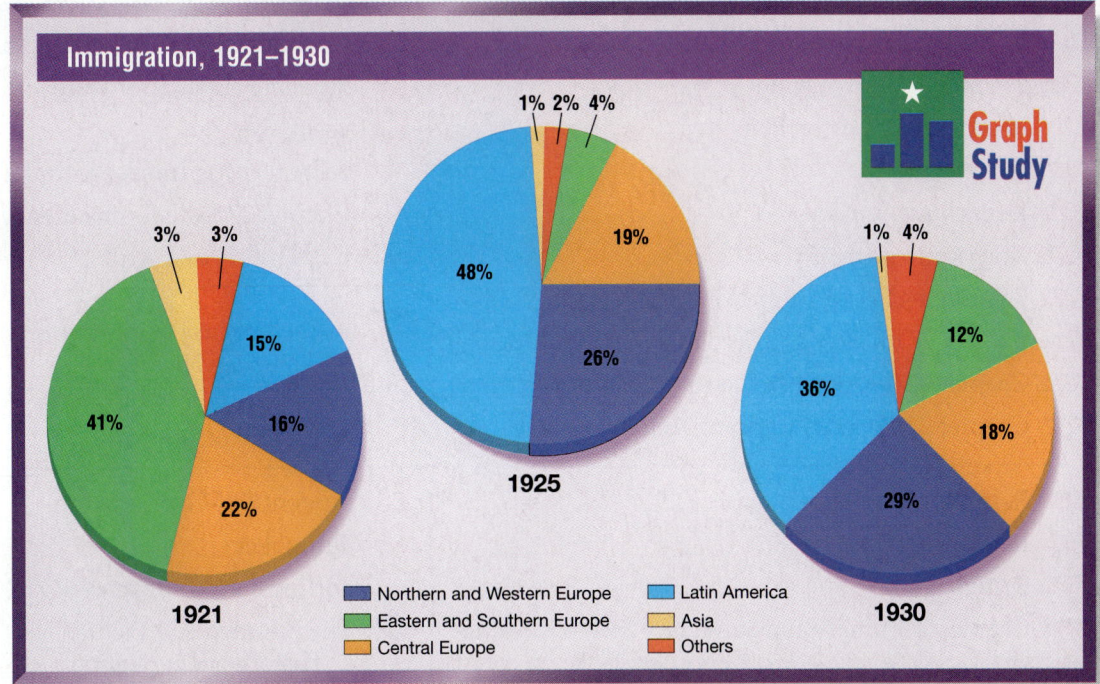

Immigration, 1921–1930

1921 / 1925 / 1930

- Northern and Western Europe
- Eastern and Southern Europe
- Central Europe
- Latin America
- Asia
- Others

Graph Study

that discuss the changes from these four perspectives. Have each group member read the paragraph describing the changes that affected him or her.

Social Studies Skills

Interpreting Graphic Data

When historical information involves numbers and statistics, it is often presented as a graph. Graphs frequently have an advantage over printed text because they make organizing and comparing detailed or complex information much easier.

Practicing the Skill

The circle graphs above provide immigration data. Use the guidelines and information from the chapter to interpret the data shown on them.

1. What is the purpose of these graphs?
2. How do the data in the graphs relate to information in the chapter?
3. What does each part of the graphs represent?
4. What significant changes or other relationships do the graphs show?

Using Your Journal

Why was the burst of creative activity in the African American community called the "Harlem Renaissance"? To answer this, you may have to do outside research. Write your conclusions in your journal.

CHAPTER 26 The Decade of Normalcy 1920–1928

PLANNING GUIDE Chapter 27 The Depression Begins

Daily Lesson Objectives	Teacher Classroom Resources	Multimedia
SECTION 1 **The Stock Market Crashes** 1 Day pp. 740–745 1. Explain how Hoover's philosophy affected his economic policy. 2. Explain the major causes of the Great Depression.	Chapter 27 Study Guide Reproducible Lesson Plan Section Quiz Reteaching Activity 27-1 American Portrait 53 Reinforcing Social Studies Skills 25, 27, 31, 32, 46 Chapter 27 Primary and Secondary Source Readings Chapter 27 Cooperative Learning Activity Chapter 27 Concept Mapping Activity	Student Self-Test Software Testmaker Section Focus Transparency 86 Chapter 27 Skills Transparency U.S. History and Art Transparency 22 A Geographic Perspective on American History The Presidents: A Picture History of Our Nation
SECTION 2 **Hoover's Policies** 1 Day pp. 747–752 1. List the ways in which Hoover tried to end the Depression. 2. Describe the change in policy toward Latin America under Hoover. 3. Describe the Hoover-Stimson Doctrine and evaluate its effectiveness.	Reproducible Lesson Plan Reteaching Activity 27-2 Section Quiz Chapter 27 Primary and Secondary Source Readings Reinforcing Social Studies Skills 25, 32, 49, 55	Student Self-Test Software Testmaker Section Focus Transparency 87 The Presidents: A Picture History of Our Nation
SECTION 3 **The Depression Worsens** 1 Day pp. 754–761 1. Compare the condition of workers and farmers in the early 1930s. 2. Discuss the mood of the country as the election of 1932 approached.	Reproducible Lesson Plan Reteaching Activity 27-3 Section Quiz Chapter 27 Enrichment Activity American Portrait 54 Chapter 27 Primary and Secondary Source Readings American Literary Heritage Unit 8 Reinforcing Social Studies Skills 36, 69–72 Spanish Summaries & Glossary	Student Self-Test Software Testmaker Section Focus Transparency 88 Unit 8 Digest Transparencies Vocabulary Puzzlemaker U.S. History and Art Transparency 24 Audiocassette, Chapter 27 A Geographic Perspective on American History
CHAPTER REVIEW AND EVALUATION 1 Day	Chapter 27 Test Chapter 27 Performance Assessment Activity	Student Self-Test Software Testmaker

OUT OF TIME? If time does not permit teaching the entire chapter, use the Chapter 27 Summary on pages 766–767 and the Chapter 27 audiocassette (English and Spanish) to point out the main ideas of the chapter.

PLANNING GUIDE

Cultural Diversity Activity

Expressing an Opinion From World War I through the 1920s, over 600,000 Mexicans entered the United States either officially or as undocumented aliens. Many found jobs in the Southwest as farm workers. Others went to factories in such cities as Detroit and Chicago. Many companies welcomed the Mexicans and fought efforts to restrict their entry into the United States. During the Depression, however, attitudes toward Mexican Americans shifted sharply. Many thousands lost their jobs and returned to Mexico. Some went willingly; others, especially in southern California, were threatened with deportation if they refused to leave.

Ask: How did the 1924 immigration act affect attitudes toward Mexican immigration? How do you account for the change in attitude during the 1930s? What do your answers suggest about the way people respond to newcomers in times of crisis? Encourage students to test their answers by researching responses to immigrants during periods of economic and political crisis in the past and present.

Performance Assessment Activity

Charting the Economy Have pairs or small groups create a chart by listing signs of prosperity and of economic problems. For each indicator, have students identify its effects. For example, increased production of consumer goods was a sign of prosperity. Effects include both easy credit and overbuying by people who could not afford it. Have students share their charts with the class. Discuss which factors, if any, are at work in the current economy.

POSSIBLE RUBRIC FEATURES: Content information, classifying, organization, collaborative skills, recognizing cause and effect

Chapter Resources

Literature from the Period

Hemingway, Ernest. *A Farewell to Arms*. 1929.

Hoover, Herbert. "Speech at New York City." October 22, 1928.

Readings for the Student

Meltzer, Milton. *Brother, Can You Spare a Dime? The Great Depression 1929–1933*. Mentor, 1977.

Scraff, Anne E. *The Great Depression and the New Deal: America's Economic Collapse and Recovery*. Watts, 1980.

Readings for the Teacher

Terkel, Studs. *Hard Times: An Oral History of the Depression*. Random House, 1980.

Multimedia Resources

Brother, Can You Spare a Dime? History in Action. Films for the Humanities. (VHS, 20 minutes)

Living American History Series. U.S. History IV: 1915–1960. Priven Learning Systems. (2 Apple diskettes, guide).

The 20's and 30's. Westport Media. (5 color filmstrips)

Key to Ability Levels

Teaching strategies have been coded for varying learning styles and abilities.

- **L1** Basic activities for all students
- **L2** Average activities for average to above-average students
- **L3** Challenging activities for above-average students
- **LEP** Limited English Proficiency activities

Glencoe Links to the Humanities

Link to Art
- U.S. History and Art Transparencies 22, 24

Links to Literature
- Macmillan Literature: American Literature Audiotapes Side 5
- Macmillan Literature: American Literature Video—*To Kill a Mockingbird*
- Macmillan Literature: Novel guide—*Of Mice and Men*, *To Kill a Mockingbird*
- Macmillan Literature: American Literature Text—F. Scott Fitzgerald, Willa Cather

Link to Music
- American Music: Cultural Traditions

CHAPTER 27

BEGINNING THE CHAPTER

Write the term *economic depression* on the chalkboard. Call on students to define the term. Write their definitions on the board. Discuss the term with students, and write a class definition. Tell students that Chapter 27 explains the events and issues that led to the Great Depression in the United States in the 1930s.

An economic depression was not a new phenomenon in the United States. Just before World War I, there were signs of economic weakness. The Great Depression of the 1930s, however, was more than a panic and a temporary crisis. Later recessions and economic downturns, such as those of the 1970s and early 1990s, were never as severe as the Great Depression of the 1930s.

Recording Journal Notes

To help organize their information, you might suggest that students record their observations under such headings as Workers, Farmers, Businesspeople, Veterans, The Unemployed, and so on.

CHAPTER 27

The Depression Begins
1928–1932

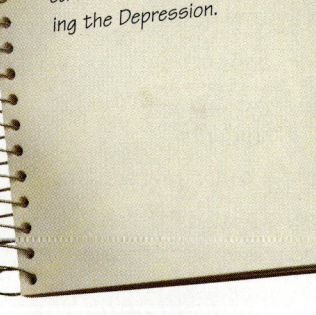

▶ APPLE VENDOR DURING THE DEPRESSION

Setting the Scene

Focus

Most Americans believed that the election of Herbert Hoover as President in 1928 would continue a decade of prosperity. This optimism quickly disappeared. A prolonged slump in agriculture, industrial overproduction, high tariffs, and the stock market crash all contributed to the worst economic depression in the nation's history. By 1932 millions of Americans were out of work. When Hoover's best efforts to revive the economy proved unsuccessful, the nation turned to a new President.

Journal Notes

As you read the chapter, record in your Journal how the American people conflicted with the government during the Depression.

Concepts to Understand

★ Why economic change from prosperity to depression was triggered by the stock market crash
★ How political policy changed as a result of the Depression

Read to Discover . . .

★ how President Hoover tried to lift the country out of the Depression.
★ why Hoover's political leadership was not more successful.

CULTURAL	• First color motion pictures are demonstrated by George Eastman	• Ernest Hemingway publishes *A Farewell to Arms*	• Sinclair Lewis is the first American to win Nobel Prize for Literature
	1928	1929	1930
POLITICAL	• Hoover is elected	• Stock market crashes	• Hawley-Smoot Tariff is passed

738   UNIT 8 Crusade and Disillusion: 1914–1932

✚ EXTRA CREDIT PROJECT

The stock market of the 1920s was largely unregulated. Following the crash of 1929 and the onset of the Great Depression, the federal government stepped in and created the Securities and Exchange Commission (SEC) in 1934 to oversee the stock market. Suggest interested students research the operation and powers of the SEC and evaluate its effectiveness in preventing problems. Discuss student reports with the class, and ask how important the role of the SEC is in keeping the economy on an even keel.

CHAPTER 27 CONCEPTS

Concept Mapping Activity

Reproduce the following generalization and concept map on the chalkboard, and have students copy it in their notebooks. Ask students to hypothesize what topics may be covered in Chapter 27 based on this information.

A chain of economic problems ends prosperity and ushers in a deepening depression that affects all Americans

- Economic Change
- Political Party

History AND ART

Many people lost their homes during the Great Depression because they were unable to meet mortgage payments or pay rent. Millard Sheets's painting depicts life in tenements during this era.

Videodisc

- *GTV: A Geographic Perspective on American History*

Side 4, Chapter 3
Title: *Thinking Big*
Subject: Depression, Dust Bowl, New Deal

See GTV Guide page 59 for complete lesson plan.

History AND ART

Tenement Flats
by Millard Sheets, 1934

Millard Sheets's painting evokes feelings of life during the Great Depression.

◀ PROHIBITION AGENT'S BADGE

- "The Star-Spangled Banner" becomes official U.S. national anthem
- Hoover vetoes Veteran Bonus

1931

- Amelia Earhart is first woman to fly solo across the Atlantic
- RFC is established
- Bonus Army marches on Washington, D.C.

1932

- San Francisco Ballet founded
- Franklin D. Roosevelt becomes President

1933

CHAPTER 27 The Depression Begins 1928–1932   739

Teacher Notes

LESSON PLAN
SECTION 1, 740-746

FOCUS

Bellringer
Before taking roll at the beginning of the class period, display Focus Activity Transparency 90 on the overhead projector, and assign the accompanying Focus Activity Sheet.

Objectives
Point out the objectives on this page to students in previewing the section content.

Motivating Activity
Ask students to think of an event that was so important to them that they have always remembered the day. Discuss how the event affected them. Tell them that the stock market crash of 1929 was such an event.

Use Skills Transparency 27.

Assign students the Chapter 27 Reading on the Problem of Unemployment in Primary and Secondary Source Readings.

NATIONAL GEOGRAPHIC SOCIETY

The following material is available from Glencoe and may be used to enrich Chapter 27.

CD-ROM
- *The Presidents: A Picture History of Our Nation*

SECTION 1

The Stock Market Crashes

Setting the Scene

Section Focus

When Calvin Coolidge declared, "I do not choose to run in 1928," he cleared the way for Herbert Hoover to head the Republican ticket. Many people believed that electing Hoover President would help continue the prosperity. With the great stock market crash of 1929, however, and the chain of economic problems that followed, this optimism disappeared.

Objectives

After studying this section, you should be able to
★ explain how Hoover's philosophy affected his economic policy.
★ explain the major causes of the Great Depression.

Key Terms

armory, securities, speculation, on margin, installment buying

◄ HOOVER CAMPAIGN BUTTON, 1928

Herbert Hoover easily won the Republican nomination in 1928. A successful geologist, he had spent eight years as secretary of commerce in the Harding and Coolidge administrations. The Democrats chose Alfred E. Smith, four-time governor of New York. Their race for the presidency was marked by the influence of a new invention—the radio.

■ The Election of 1928

The most visible issue in the election campaign was Prohibition. Both candidates vowed to continue enforcing Prohibition. The Prohibition issue, however, masked other important differences between the candidates. Hoover represented rural, agrarian interests; Smith represented urban, industrial interests.

Religion was at the core of a smear campaign against Smith's Catholicism. Wild tales circulated alleging that Catholics had turned certain Washington church sites into **armories,** or storehouses for guns. Some believed that the White House under Smith would become a branch of the Vatican. Hoover was embarrassed by these accusations and tried to quash them.

Late in the campaign, Hoover made a speech to offer his ideas on the proper relationship of government to business. Government, Hoover claimed, should be "an umpire instead of a player in the economic game." Government had a part to play—conservation of natural resources, scientific research, and flood control were places where Hoover believed government could

UNIT 8 Crusade and Disillusion: 1914–1932

Classroom Resources for SECTION 1

Teacher's Classroom Resources
- Chapter 27 Study Guide
- Reproducible Lesson Plan
- Reteaching Activity 27-1
- Chapter 27 Cooperative Learning Activity
- Chapter 27 Primary and Secondary Source Readings
- Section Quiz

Multimedia
- Section Focus Transparency 90
- Skills Transparency 27
- Testmaker
- Student Self-Test Software
- A Geographic Perspective on American History
- The Presidents: A Picture History of Our Nation

make useful contributions. To him, personal liberty depended on economic freedom. He reminded his listeners that:

> Our experiment in human welfare has yielded a degree of well-being unparalleled in the world. . . . We are nearer to the ideal of abolition of poverty and fear from the lives of men and women than ever before in any land.

Prosperity was the campaign issue that proved most damaging to the Democrats. The almost uninterrupted prosperity the country had enjoyed during the 1920s was associated in the minds of many voters with the Republican party. Republican campaign slogans such as "two cars in every garage" gave the Democrats no chance of winning the election.

Hoover won an impressive victory in the Electoral College with a vote of 444 to 87, taking 58 percent of the popular vote and carrying all but 8 states. His appeal to rural Protestant voters even broke the Democrats' traditional hold on the Solid South, resulting in a Republican win in 5 Southern states. Although Smith lost the election, he won nearly twice as many votes as had the Democratic candidate in 1924. Of greater significance, Hoover became the first presidential winner to lose in the nation's 12 largest cities. A shift in the rural-urban balance of political power in America was in the wind.

■ **Hoover in the White House**

When he took office in March 1929, Herbert Hoover still radiated optimism. In his Inaugural Address, he predicted that the

▲ **PROHIBITION RAID** by Thomas Hart Benton, 1929 An unwanted result of Prohibition was the stimulus it gave to illegal activity. Thomas Hart Benton's *Prohibition Raid* is symbolic of the time. **What did the Wickersham Commission recommend?**

▲ CRIME FIGHTER ELIOT NESS

CHAPTER 27 The Depression Begins 1928–1932

CHAPTER 27
SECTION 1

TEACH
Guided Practice
Making Comparisons
Have students write on their papers the four Ps that guided the outcome of the 1928 presidential election: personal prestige, prosperity, Prohibition, Protestantism. Ask them to give one example for each, showing how it worked for Hoover and against Al Smith. (Example: personal prestige: Hoover was identified with "old values" of rural America and was a solid, predictable, nonthreatening presence. Smith was a "city" man, linked to immigrants and not as "respectable" as Hoover.) **L1**

History AND ART

The rise of organized crime was due partly to prohibition. Bootleggers, who dealt in the illegal traffic of alcohol, made millions of dollars selling liquor to the public. Eventually the critics of prohibition won out. In 1933 the Twenty-first Amendment repealed national prohibition.
Answer to Caption: recommended that Prohibition should continue

---

Critical Thinking

Comparing Economists today are undecided about the possibility of another Great Depression. Some similarities exist between today's economy and that of the 1920s. Suggest students research elements of the current economy (health of the stock market; problems of industry, business, and wage earners; state of agriculture; and so on) and compare them to those of the 1920s. Ask students to form an opinion about whether or not another such severe depression could occur. **L3**

CHAPTER 27 SECTION 1

Independent Practice

Social Problems Have students research and report on one of the commissions Hoover appointed to investigate housing, retirement pensions, unemployment insurance, child welfare, conservation, and Prohibition. (For example: What was the status of unemployment insurance at this time? Could people who lost their jobs count on any benefits?) In each investigation, ask students to predict how the Depression will affect the situation they have researched. **L2**

 Within a week of the stock market crash, more than $6 billion in stock prices was lost, and thousands of investors like Walter Thornton were ruined. **Answer to Caption:** caused the market to climb rapidly and then crash when many speculators pulled out

• *GTV: A Geographic Perspective on American History*

Side 4, Chapter 3
Title: *Thinking Big*
Subject: Depression, Dust Bowl, New Deal

See GTV Guide page 59 for complete lesson plan.

United States would soon be "in sight of the day when poverty will be banished from this nation."

Prohibition

Hoover did not believe that government should let economic events run their course but rather that it should help people to help themselves. He appointed commissions to investigate problems such as housing, retirement pensions, unemployment insurance, child welfare, and conservation. One commission, headed by former Attorney General George W. Wickersham, devoted 2 years to investigating Prohibition. The 11 members of the commission disagreed among themselves on whether Prohibition should continue. Most felt that the "noble experiment" was ineffective and promoted crime, yet the commission as a whole recommended that Prohibition be continued.

Farmers' Problems

The plight of farmers was an issue that demanded more immediate action. In April 1929, Hoover called Congress into special session to pass farming legislation. Members of Congress from farm states demanded that the federal government buy surplus farm products and sell them abroad. Hoover opposed this on the grounds that "no government agency should engage in buying and selling and price-fixing of products." Instead the President proposed that the federal government help farmers use their own organizations to market produce more efficiently and adjust supply to demand.

Following this recommendation, Congress passed the Agricultural Marketing Act of 1929, which created a Federal Farm Board with $500 million at its disposal to help existing farm organizations and to form new ones. The Farm Board established national cooperatives—such as the National Livestock Marketing Association and the American Cotton Cooperative Association—and then loaned these organizations money to help keep prices stable. It was too little, too late. Farmers were soon worse off than ever.

■ The Crash of 1929

The market value of **securities,** or stocks and bonds, on the New York Stock Exchange more than tripled between 1925 and 1929—from $27 billion to $87 billion. In the summer of 1929, for example, a share of General Motors rose from $268 to $391 and by September 2 rose even higher—to $452 per share.

 ▲ **EFFECTS OF THE CRASH** One day after the stock market crash, Walter Thornton advertised his car for sale. Panic hit the stock market as people frantically tried to sell. *What effect did speculation have on the stock market in 1929?*

UNIT 8 Crusade and Disillusion: 1914–1932

Sidelights: A Get-Rich-Quick Scheme

A popular scheme to make a quick profit in the 1920s was speculation in land. The biggest boom in real estate was in Florida, where the climate and the possibility of vacation resorts attracted scores of speculators. The value of land in Florida soared, and those who were there first realized big profits. Many, however, bought land sight unseen and ended up with swampland. The land rush in Florida ended in 1926 when a devastating hurricane swept the state.

Speculation

As prices rose, more and more people began speculating. **Speculation** is engaging in a risky business venture on the chance that a quick or sizeable profit can be made. People bought shares they thought would rise in price quickly, and after prices went up they would sell the stocks for a profit.

To maximize the potential profits on their investments, speculators commonly bought stock **on margin.** To buy stock in this way one made a small cash down payment and borrowed the rest from a stockbroker. For example, for $2,000 a person could buy 100 shares on margin rather than pay cash for 10 shares of stock at $200 per share. The purchaser simply put down 10 percent of the price (or $20 per share) and borrowed the other $18,000 from a broker, who would then hold the shares of stock as collateral for the loan. So long as prices continued to rise, investors could sell the stock later, repay the loan, and reap the profit.

Stock Market Begins to Decline

Some bankers, brokers, and economists were concerned, however, because they knew the stocks for many companies were greatly overpriced in comparison to the earnings and profits the companies were making. Yet most investors were swept along on the tide of the day's optimism. Meanwhile, the market continued its dizzying climb. By the end of 1929, brokers' loans to those who had bought on margin exceeded $7 billion. The Federal Reserve Board tried to restore stability to the market by advising banks not to loan money for buying stocks on margin, but few banks listened.

In September 1929, the market started to waver as some professional speculators sensed danger and began to pull out, and prices slipped. Late in October real disaster struck. On Thursday, October 24, almost 13 million shares of stocks were frantically traded. As stocks' values dropped below the amounts borrowed to purchase them, brokers demanded that investors repay their loans. If they could not, the brokers offered the stock for sale.

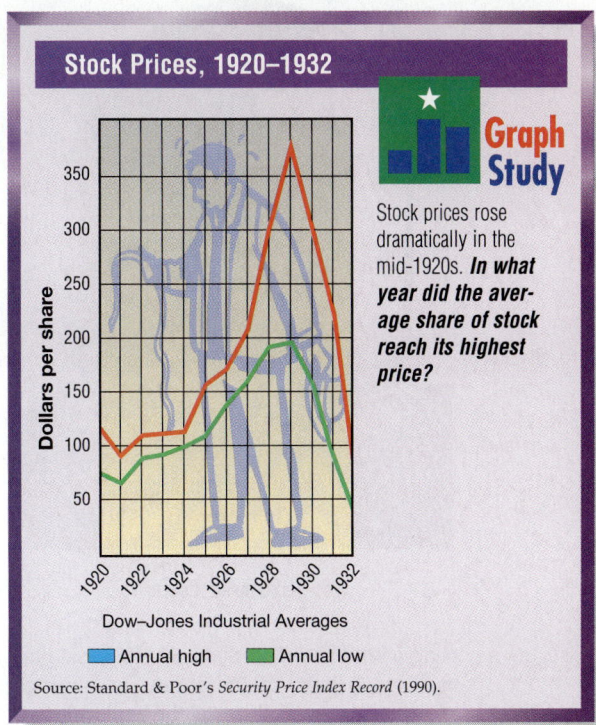

Stock Prices, 1920–1932

Graph Study

Stock prices rose dramatically in the mid-1920s. *In what year did the average share of stock reach its highest price?*

Source: Standard & Poor's *Security Price Index Record* (1990).

Black Tuesday

Recognizing what was going on, investment bankers tried to shore up market prices by purchasing as many shares as they could. The effort was not enough to stabilize an overvalued market. On October 29—Black Tuesday—the bottom fell out. Some 16 million shares were sold, causing such a collapse that by mid-November the average price of securities had been cut nearly in half. This cost investors about $30 billion, a sum that represented almost one-third of the value of all goods and services produced in the United States in 1929. The loss was equal to the total wages of all Americans that year.

About 1.5 million Americans had been involved in purchasing stock. Many investors lost their entire life savings.

It was the failure of banks that hit people the hardest. Banks loaned money to brokerage houses, which in turn bought stock themselves or loaned money to investors for speculative stock purchases. When loan payments were not forthcoming, many banks went bankrupt. In the aftermath, millions of

CHAPTER 27 The Depression Begins 1928–1932

CHAPTER 27
SECTION 1

Using Graphs
Answer: 1929

Skills Practice
Ask students to use the information on the graph and in the text to summarize the course of the American economy in the 1920s.

Did You Know?
The ability of the consumer to obtain easy credit expanded in the 1920s. Between 80 and 90 percent of purchases for large household items were made through time payments.

Did You Know?
In the 1920s the average price for such items as washing machines, refrigerators, and vacuum cleaners was $97.50, $87.50, and $28.95 respectively.

Cooperative Learning

Divide the class into several groups. Assign each group an event or issue covered in Section 1 (for example, the 1928 election, work of the Wickersham Commission, policies of Hoover, speculation on the stock market, problems of farmers, high tariffs, the crash on "Black Tuesday"). Ask each group to compose a headline and write an article examining the issue or event. Have the groups share their articles with the class. **L1, L2**

CHAPTER 27
SECTION 1

ASSESS
Check Understanding

Assign Section 1 Review as homework or an in-class activity.

Evaluate

Assign Section 1 Quiz in the TCR, or use the History of a Free Nation Testmaker to create a customized quiz.

Reteach

Ask students to list the major causes of the Depression and their effects on business, labor, and agriculture.

Have students complete Reteaching Activity 27-1.

Enrich

Suggest students do a "Kelley Chart" to illustrate what would happen to a family caught in a major depression today. Have them imagine that the Kelleys are steelworkers with two children, one in college and one in high school. What items are they likely to be paying for on credit? What assets are they likely to have? What are their major monthly bills? Have students create a chart showing how a depression would affect the Kelleys.

▲ TELEGRAPHIC TICKER

people who had never bought stock but had trustingly kept their money in savings accounts lost everything as the banks closed.

Causes of the Great Depression

The collapse of the stock market was only a prelude to a catastrophic economic decline from which the United States did not recover for 12 years. The causes of the Great Depression were so complex that economists have debated the issue ever since.

Overproduction and Underconsumption

One cause of the Depression was overproduction. Laborsaving machinery had increased the production capacity of the nation's industries so much that far more goods were produced than the American population could consume. For a time, consumer purchasing power was bolstered by **installment buying**—an agreement whereby a purchaser made a down payment and paid the rest of the cost in periodic regular installments to which an interest charge was added. By the late 1920s, most consumers who could afford high-cost items such as refrigerators, cars, or stoves had bought them on an installment plan. Consumer spending began to decrease. From January to September 1929, for example, the number of automobile purchases dropped by one-third.

Another cause of the Depression was underconsumption. In the 1920s the rich got richer much faster than the rest of the people. Some 30,000 families at the top of the economic pyramid had as much income as did the 11 million families at the bottom. Though production increased, employment stood still and workers' wages went up very slowly. In 1929 more than two-thirds of the nation's families were earning less than $2,500 per year, a sum said to be the minimum income for a decent quality of life. About one-fifth of the nation lived in dire poverty. Thus there was insufficient purchasing power to support the nation's mass-production industries.

Agricultural Slump and Surpluses

A prolonged slump in agriculture, which affected the economic life of the entire country, was another factor. Farmers were heavily indebted to banks, which held mortgages on farmlands throughout the nation. The declining value of farms made it harder for farmers to get credit. Banks that had invested heavily in farm mortgages were in danger of failing.

In addition, huge farm surpluses produced a drop in farm prices so great that farmers often spent more money growing and marketing their products than they received in selling them. The resulting loss in farmers' purchasing power further reduced the consumption of manufactured goods—a condition that only added to the problem of underconsumption.

Tariffs and Taxes

The Great Depression was not solely a result of economic practices. Many of the economic policies of the Harding and Coolidge administrations during the 1920s set the stage for problems by the end of the decade. Policies such as the high Fordney-McCumber tariff, combined with an insistence on collecting war debts, interfered with world trade and destroyed

UNIT 8 Crusade and Disillusion: 1914–1932

Critical Thinking

Debating an Issue Have students debate the following proposition: The people who manipulated the stock market and used other means to make money before the crash were just as guilty as those who broke the Prohibition laws and should have been charged and tried as lawbreakers. After students have debated the issue, have them discuss why they think white-collar crime is dealt with so much less severely in this society than other kinds of crime. **L3**

foreign markets for American products, especially in agriculture. The Mellon tax policies, which aided the upper class, contributed to the uneven distribution of wealth. Failure to curb or discourage the stock market's early boom made the ultimate crash more severe.

Once started, the Great Depression took on a momentum of its own. Individuals with mortgages on their homes, who had bought cars and other goods on credit and who had purchased stocks on margin, "lost their shirts." They stopped buying, for example, luxuries like radios, causing radio manufacturers to close down plants or run them only part-time. Thousands of workers were laid off as orders were canceled for copper, wood cabinets, and glass radio tubes. Montana copper miners, Minnesota lumberjacks, and Ohio glassworkers in turn lost their jobs.

Because these jobless workers could not meet mortgage payments or repay loans, they lost their property. Banks that had lent them money failed, wiping out the savings of their depositors. Such chain reactions closed down more and more factories, drove more and more firms into bankruptcy, and put more and more Americans out of work.

Russell Hunter, a brass worker in the Naugatuck Valley region of Connecticut, known as the "Brass Valley," describes what the early years of the Depression were like:

> During Hoover's time, we went on short time. After a while, when things really were bad, in 1932, we were working sometimes five hours a week, one day a week. That was tough, trying to raise a family. Nobody lost their jobs completely. They shared [the work] to give everybody something to do. Still, you had to go on welfare. People got by going on the welfare. At that time, people were losing their homes, automobiles....

The mood of the country was changing. Feelings of optimism were giving way to feelings of fear.

GNP, Stock Values, and Unemployment

Year	Gross National Product (in billions)	Stock Values, New York Stock Exchange (in billions)	Unemployment (Percent)
1920	$140.0	$5.5	5.2
1921	127.8	4.7	11.7
1922	148.0	5.7	6.7
1923	165.9	5.9	2.4
1924	165.5	5.9	5.0
1925	179.4	7.6	3.2
1926	190.0	8.6	1.8
1927	189.8	10.5	3.3
1928	190.9	13.7	4.2
1929	203.6	17.9	3.2
1930	183.5	14.4	8.7
1931	169.3	7.5	15.9
1932	144.2	3.8	23.6

Chart Study Study each column heading, noting the years that show the greatest change. **What was the worst year of the Great Depression for both business and labor?**

Section 1 ★ Review

Checking for Understanding

1. **Identify** Wickersham Commission, Agricultural Marketing Act.
2. **Define** armory, securities, speculation, on margin, installment buying.
3. **Explain** how speculation caused the stock market to rise.
4. **List** four causes of the Great Depression.

Critical Thinking

5. **Synthesizing Ideas** Who was to blame for stock market speculation and the problems it caused—stockbrokers, banks, speculators, or the government? Explain your answer.

CHAPTER 27 The Depression Begins 1928–1932

CHAPTER 27 CONNECTIONS

Teaching Making Connections

The ability to buy on credit has fed the boom-bust cycles of the nation's economy. The Federal Reserve Board's lack of action during the 1920s to keep stock prices from becoming credit-inflated and its subsequent reluctance to inject badly needed cash into the post-crash economy intensified the seeming prosperity of the 1920s and the depths of the Great Depression. Even though these mistakes serve as major influences on current Federal Reserve Board policies, the stock market crash of 1987, the junk-bond collapse, and severe banking problems were not prevented.

Did You Know?

The New York Times index of 25 industrial stocks reached 100 in 1924, 181 in 1925, dropped a little in 1926, and rose to 245 by 1927. In 1928 the index rose to 331 and peaked at 452 in early September 1929. The index lost 31 points on October 31. By mid-November its value was 224.

CONNECTIONS 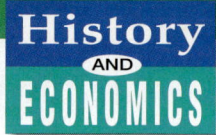 CONNECTIONS

The Stock Market

"Sooner or later," said economist Roger Babson on September 5, 1929, "a crash is coming... factories will be shut down... men will be thrown out of work... the result will be a serious business depression." However, most analysts assured Americans that the stock market was healthy and thriving.

A stock exchange is an organized system for buying and selling shares, or blocks of investments, in corporations. In the late 1920s, the value of stocks on the New York Stock Exchange climbed to dizzying heights. To take advantage of the boom, investors borrowed money to buy stocks, a practice known as buying on margin.

In other words, speculators were using their own money to make a relatively small down payment on the stock and borrowing the remainder of the purchase price from a stockbroker. The broker in turn borrowed the money lent to the speculator from a bank. The brokers' loans were call loans—loans that could be called in at any time by the borrower or lender.

The 1920s seemed to be a period of never-ending prosperity. The values of common stock had been increasing steadily year after year. In 1926 more than 450 million shares of stock were traded on the New York Stock Exchange. In 1927 the total rose to more than 570 million. Speculators believed they could make a quick profit in the market. Bankers knew they could make money by lending to brokers. Brokers knew they could come out ahead by lending to customers. Everyone, it seemed, was trying to get rich quickly.

The boom could last only as long as investors added money to the pool. By 1929 everyone with money to invest had bought into the market, and it ran out of new customers. Prices stopped rising. People sold shares to pay the interest on their loans. As shares were sold, prices fell. Panicked investors tried to minimize their losses.

On October 29, less than two months after Babson's prediction, the market crashed. The crash was a symptom, not a cause, of the Great Depression.

▼ WALL STREET

Making the Economics Connection

1. What series of events occur when the stock market crashes?
2. Why did people begin selling shares of stock in the fall of 1929?

Linking Past and Present

3. Compare the 1929 stock market crash with the savings and loan crisis of the 1980s.

Answers to CONNECTIONS

1. People stop buying stocks, prices stop rising, people sell to pay off loans, prices fall, people panic.
2. People were afraid that they would not get the money they invested back.
3. Both resulted from speculation (investing money that hasn't yet been earned). The 1929 crash resulted from speculation on the stock exchange; the 1980s savings and loan crisis was the result of government deregulation.

SECTION 2

Hoover's Policies

Setting the Scene

Section Focus

Before 1929 the federal government had responded to economic depressions by considering different monetary or tariff policies. During the Great Depression, however, the government was forced to seek more vigorous remedies for the nation's vast economic problems. Failing to succeed in domestic policies, President Herbert Hoover made peace the cornerstone of his administration.

Objectives

After studying this section, you should be able to

★ list the ways in which Hoover tried to end the Depression.

★ describe the change in policy toward Latin America under Hoover.

★ describe the Hoover-Stimson Doctrine and evaluate its effectiveness.

Key Term

moratorium

▲ UNION LABEL SYMBOL

No sooner had the stock market collapsed than President Hoover asked leaders of industry, finance, and labor to come to the White House. The President asked labor leaders to abandon or postpone wage demands, industry leaders to keep employment high, and bankers to continue lending.

Hoover and other leaders tried to restore public confidence by issuing optimistic statements. Their rosy predictions were contradicted by worsening conditions, however, and the phrase "prosperity is just around the corner" became a joke. The Republican campaign slogan "Two cars in every garage" had become "Two families in every garage." The President's position was made all the more difficult because he was blamed for the Depression.

■ Domestic Economic Concerns Loom

In dealing with Congress and the public, Hoover was limited by his inflexible views. A man of great ability and possessing a sincere desire to serve the nation, he lacked the practical political experience that comes from being a legislator or state executive. Even with such skills, his position would have been difficult. Republican party leaders never gave him their wholehearted support, and members of the Farm Bloc were in open revolt. As a result of the midterm elections of 1930, the Democrats made gains in the Senate and won control of the House of Representatives. This shift in power led to a Congress that was hostile to Hoover's policies during the last two years of his administration.

CHAPTER 27 The Depression Begins 1928–1932

LESSON PLAN
SECTION 2, 747–753

FOCUS

Bellringer
Before taking roll at the beginning of the class period, display Focus Activity Transparency 91 on the overhead projector, and assign the accompanying Focus Activity Sheet.

Objectives
Point out the objectives on this page to students in previewing the section content.

Motivating Activity
Write the following on the chalkboard.
Problems
Companies go out of business.
People lose jobs.
Families have no money.
Solutions
Ask students to make a list of things they could expect the government to provide in such a situation today. Then tell them that in Section 2 they will read about the government's response to problems in the early years of the Great Depression.

The following material is available from Glencoe and may be used to enrich Chapter 27.

  CD-ROM

• *The Presidents: A Picture History of Our Nation*

Classroom Resources for SECTION 2

Teacher's Classroom Resources
- Reproducible Lesson Plan
- Reteaching Activity 27-2
- Section Quiz

Multimedia
- Section Focus Transparency 91
- Testmaker
- Student Self-Test Software
- The Presidents: A Picture History of Our Nation

CHAPTER 27 SECTION 2

TEACH
Guided Practice
Expressing an Opinion
Have students write letters to the editor about the plight of American farming during the 1920s and early 1930s. They may write from the point of view of a farmer, a food buyer, a member of the Farm Board, a businessperson. Letters should reflect the writers' beliefs in the importance of farming and suggest solutions to the crisis, while criticizing or approving solutions already being offered. **L2**

Did You Know?
Many sought escape from economic hardship by hopping freight trains to the South and West in hopes of finding work. On one railroad line alone, people living in boxcars increased from 13,000 in 1929 to 200,000 in 1931.

Did You Know?
Despite prejudice and discrimination, an African American leader, Oscar De Priest from Chicago, was elected to Congress in 1928. De Priest was the first African American to attain that position since 1901 and the first northern African American to serve in Congress.

Tariffs

Like President Taft in 1909, Hoover was unable to control Congress on the tariff issue. The Hawley-Smoot Tariff started in the House as a protection for farmers, but by the time it passed the Senate, it had turned into the highest protective tariff in peacetime history. It raised the average duty on raw agricultural materials and other items above the Fordney-McCumber Act levels.

By the time the Hawley-Smoot bill reached the President's desk in 1930, more than 1,000 leading economists had signed a letter urging him to veto it. They argued that it would help inefficient producers, raise consumer prices, reduce foreign markets, and cause ill will toward the United States in other countries. This opinion was voiced by many newspapers, bankers, and even by a number of manufacturers. Now Hoover faced a dilemma. If he used his veto power, he would isolate himself politically by breaking with the Republican values he held so strongly. Furthermore, he would abandon the one feature of the bill he had fought so hard for—a revised Tariff Commission with the authority to raise and lower rates. He therefore signed the bill in spite of the warnings.

Within a year, 25 nations retaliated with laws to restrict purchases of American goods, causing foreign trade with the United States to drop rapidly. Some American corporations managed to avoid international barriers by establishing factories overseas. Ironically, an act designed to promote American economic recovery instead created employment overseas.

Farmers

American farmers, beleaguered throughout the 1920s, were hit even harder. Farmers' income was cut by more than half between 1929 and 1932; their burden of debt became unbearable. During this crisis the Farm Board tried to maintain the price of wheat and cotton by buying up the surplus of these crops. The Farm Board also attempted—without success—to persuade farmers to plant less, in order to reduce the amount of farm produce grown and thus to prevent further surplus crops. The immense quantities of wheat and cotton held by the government actually drove prices down, however, because buyers feared that the government would sell these surpluses as soon as prices rose. Finally, in 1931 the Farm Board acknowledged defeat and stopped its purchases. Immediately prices dropped even lower. By 1932 farmers were receiving only 38 cents a bushel for wheat that in 1929 had sold at $1.04. Even Hoover's relatives in Iowa suffered from the depressed farm economy. Harry Terrell, a farmer who lived in the same neighborhood as President Hoover in Iowa, described conditions in the following way:

> "I was born across the road from the farm of Herbert Hoover's uncle. I knew the Hoover family, distant cousins of the President. Even people like them, they had times just like the rest of us. . . . Corn was going for eight cents a bushel. One county insisted on burning corn to heat the courthouse, 'cause it was cheaper than coal."

■ Hoover's Strong Resolve

Hoover was deeply affected by all the misery and poverty around him, but as a staunch believer in private enterprise, he feared direct government handouts would destroy personal initiative. Hoover therefore offered government help to banks and businesses in the hope that restored financial health at the top of the economic pyramid would eventually trickle down to relieve unemployment at the bottom. Keeping his attitude positive and his resolve strong, Hoover sought to inspire confidence in a people ravaged by hopelessness and despair: "Ninety percent of our difficulty in depression is caused by fear."

Special Needs

Memory Disability New information is learned more quickly and completely when it can be associated with already known information. Memory is aided by activating the "schema" or knowledge frames as underpinnings for the information that presently needs to be remembered. Part of Section 2 deals with American reaction to Japanese aggression in China. Before students read this section, discuss more recent American reactions to aggression by foreign powers. Cite examples such as Iraq's invasion of Kuwait and the struggle for dominance in Bosnia.

▲ DROUGHT-STRICKEN AREA by Alexander Hogue, 1934 The collapse of farm prices was compounded by a terrible drought in 1930. **How did President Hoover feel about providing direct relief to the unemployed?**

In 1932, after Hoover's initial resistance, Congress established the Reconstruction Finance Corporation (RFC). With $2 billion in resources, the RFC made loans to hard-pressed railroads, insurance companies, banks, and even state and local governments—but not to individuals. The RFC favored projects that were "self-liquidating"; that is, projects designed to pay their way so the government would eventually get back its money. Thus projects such as toll bridges and dams that would produce electric power were favored over those that could have been socially useful but brought in no revenue, such as playgrounds, schools, and city halls.

There was a point beyond which Hoover refused to use the power of the federal government. He feared that too much reliance on federal action would result in the "paternalism" and "state socialism" he had warned against in 1928. He opposed direct federal relief for the unemployed because he believed it would weaken the self-respect of those who received it, undercut the efforts of private charity, and that it would destroy the tradition of local responsibility for the unfortunate. Hoover, therefore, vetoed the Garner-Wagner bill in 1932, which would have given direct aid to the unemployed. He also vetoed the Norris bill, which would have put the government in the business of producing and selling electricity in the Tennessee Valley—thus setting up direct competition with private companies.

■ Efforts for Peace

The desire for world peace was strong during these hard times, partly because preparation for war was costly, and partly because few had forgotten the horrors of World War I.

As a Quaker and a pacifist, Herbert Hoover believed that war was morally wrong; as administrator of Belgian relief between 1914 and 1917, he saw firsthand the devastation of World War I. Hoover was committed to world peace. As he stated in 1928:

> ❝ *I think I may say that I have witnessed as much of the horror and suffering of war as any other American. From it I have derived a deep passion for peace. Our foreign policy has one primary objective, and that is peace.* ❞

CHAPTER 27 The Depression Begins 1928–1932

CHAPTER 27 SECTION 2

Visualizing History During the Depression thousands of Americans spent time standing in lines for food, jobs, and relief.
Answer to Caption: direct aid to the unemployed

Did You Know?

On his tour of Latin America, Hoover promised to abstain from intervention in the affairs of Latin American nations. He kept his word. Although about 50 revolutions or attempts at revolution shook the region during his administration, the United States did not intervene.

Did You Know?

Despite cynics' response to what they called "the millionaires' dole," the Reconstruction Finance Corporation turned out to be successful. It also set the stage for the New Deal of Franklin Delano Roosevelt. The Norris bill would also be reborn in the Roosevelt era as the Tennessee Valley Authority.

Hoover's peace efforts were aided by his many years spent overseas. The most widely traveled man ever to occupy the White House, he had visited every continent and knew many foreign leaders personally.

Latin America

As secretary of commerce, Hoover had come to understand Latin America's distrust of the United States. Before his inauguration in March 1929, he made goodwill tours of 10 Latin American countries. Hoover stressed that the United States wished to be a friend to its neighbors in Latin America. Many expressed doubts about how effective Hoover's efforts would be. Hoover's Latin American policies reflected a sincere desire to improve relations. In addition to successfully arbitrating a long-standing boundary dispute between Chile and Peru, Hoover abandoned military intervention in Latin American countries.

The Clark Memorandum, written by Undersecretary of State J. Reuben Clark, argued the position that the Roosevelt Corollary to the Monroe Doctrine had no historical basis. Clark wrote, "The Monroe Doctrine states a case of the United States v. Europe, not of the United States v. Latin America." In other words, the Monroe Doctrine could no longer be used to justify American intervention in Latin America.

In accordance with this principle, Hoover withdrew troops from Nicaragua and refused to intervene in the affairs of Latin American states that, because of political chaos, had repudiated their debts to the United States. While this nonintervention policy helped to convince many Latin Americans that the United States had no aggressive intentions, it won Hoover little goodwill. The Hawley-Smoot Tariff had hurt Latin America's economy, and the region's resentment of the power of the United States did not disappear.

Visualizing History ▲ **Soup Kitchen** People line up at a 1930s Chicago soup kitchen, operated by gangster Al Capone. Government made few efforts to help citizens fight the effects of the Depression. *What was the Garner-Wagner bill intended to provide?*

UNIT 8 Crusade and Disillusion: 1914–1932

Critical Thinking

Analyzing Ideas Remind students that Herbert Hoover was a Quaker, a member of a religious group that believes in pacificism. Suggest students research the Quakers and write a paragraph analyzing the difficulty of following pacifist beliefs in modern times. Encourage students to explore how Hoover's Quaker heritage may have affected his policies. **L3**

Disarmament

Hoover strongly favored disarmament, not only because of his personal beliefs but also because military spending and increased taxes depleted valuable resources. Shortly after taking office, Hoover made arrangements for a new conference in London on naval disarmament. Its goal would be to extend the limits on battleships that had been set in the Five-Power Treaty signed in 1921–1922.

After four months of talks, the London Naval Conference of 1930 produced a treaty fixing ratios for the submarines, cruisers, and destroyers of the United States, British, and Japanese navies. Italy refused to sign. France, fearing aggression by Germany and Italy, said that it favored disarmament only if other powers would agree to give France assurance of protection. In the end, France chose not to sign.

Ever since 1927 a disarmament conference hosted by the League of Nations had been meeting at Geneva. Its work was hampered by the activities of lobbyists for arms manufacturers and by mutual mistrust among the delegates. For five years it had gotten nowhere, focusing on such trivial issues as the influence of fog on war. In 1932 President Hoover proposed to the Geneva Conference that the nations of the world either entirely abandon aggressive weapons or cut existing arms by one-third. No action resulted. With Adolf Hitler's rise to power in Germany, however, and Japanese invasions into China, disarmament now seemed like an invitation to aggression. Hoover's proposal could have succeeded only if the United States had been willing to join an alliance of nations committed to "collective security," whereby members would all agree to come to the aid of any member nation who was threatened with aggression.

War Reparations

By 1931 Germany was in the throes of a serious depression. Germans could not continue paying war reparations to the Allies without defaulting on their debts to American private investors. Hoover, like Harding and Coolidge before him, believed that reparations were "a European problem." But heavy war debts and rising unemployment caused great discontent among the German people and led directly to the rapid growth of two antidemocratic parties—the Communist party and the Nazi party.

▲ **JAPAN AND MANCHURIA** An American cartoon condemns Japan's 1931 seizure of Manchuria. *What was the American response to the Japanese invasion?*

Moratorium

The Allies were unlikely to cancel German reparation payments, which they used to pay off their own war debts to the United States. To address the problem, in 1931 Hoover proposed an international **moratorium,** or suspension, for one year of all war-debt payments to the United States. Hoover's aim was to protect United States investments in Germany and to save the German Republic from collapse, as well as to stimulate international trade. Secretary of State Henry L. Stimson urged that war debts and reparations be canceled completely, but Hoover refused. To do so would have been a highly unpopular measure and would have worsened Hoover's already poor relations with Congress.

Sidelights: Aid to the Soviet Union

Although the United States was hostile to the Communist regime in the Soviet Union, farmers and businesspeople saw the Soviet Union as a new market. Farmers especially wanted to sell their produce to the Soviets. In 1921 Hoover, then secretary of commerce, complied, and some $78 million in food relief was given to the Soviet Union. Hoover believed that some economic relations with the Communists would help make their economy more capitalistic. The aid did not have that effect. It did, however, shore up the Soviet regime and saved millions of Russians from starvation.

CHAPTER 27 SECTION 2

ASSESS

Check Understanding
Assign Section 2 Review as homework or an in-class activity.

Evaluate
▸ Assign Section 2 Quiz in the TCR, or use the History of a Free Nation Testmaker to create a customized quiz.

Reteach
Have students write several paragraphs to show how the Depression, both in the United States and abroad, affected the foreign policy decisions of the Hoover administration.

▸ Have students complete Reteaching Activity 27-2.

Enrich
Suggest students write dialogues between Hoover and the leaders of labor, industry, and finance whom he asked to meet with him at the White House after the 1929 crash. What did Hoover ask of these men? What might their responses have been? Have students dramatize their dialogues.

CLOSE

Have students reread Hoover's statement on page 749, which states the objective of his foreign policy. Ask them to discuss whether Hoover's foreign policy met this objective and tell why or why not.

■ The Hoover-Stimson Doctrine

The Hoover administration encountered problems in the Far East. In September 1931, Japan seized China's rich province of Manchuria. Taking advantage of the civil war in China and the weak condition of the Western nations, Japanese armies speedily overran Manchuria. This action was in direct violation of the Nine-Power Treaty of 1922, which guaranteed China's sovereignty, and the Kellogg-Briand Pact, which outlawed wars of aggression. It also breached the Charter of the League of Nations, to which both China and Japan belonged.

The Intent of the Doctrine

China appealed to the League of Nations, which turned to the United States for help. President Hoover, however, refused to consider either economic or military action. Instead, he sent an army officer to serve on a League commission to investigate Japanese actions in Manchuria. Secretary Stimson proclaimed in 1932 that the United States would refuse to recognize the legality of any territorial arrangement that violated the Kellogg-Briand Pact. The Hoover-Stimson Doctrine, designed to enlist world opinion against aggressor nations, did nothing to aid China and served only to irritate the Japanese.

Although the nonrecognition policy had been worked out by Hoover and Stimson together, it meant different things to each of them. Stimson wanted the policy to act as a warning, which later might be backed up by economic or military aid. According to Hoover, the statement itself was enough. The United States, he said, did not exist to police the world. Economic sanctions might lead to war, he said, and Japanese aggression in Asia did not "imperil the freedom of the American people." Hoover then said that should the United States be obliged to

❝ ... arm and train Chinese, [we would] find ourselves involved in China in a fashion that would excite the suspicions of the whole world. ❞

Nor were the British and French governments willing to apply sanctions. The failure of Western nations to take action only encouraged Japanese expansion into China and Southeast Asia.

Public Opinion

The American public was not prepared to support any interventionist effort that could potentially involve the United States in war once again. This feeling was evident in 1931 when Congress overwhelmingly overrode Hoover's veto and voted to give independence to the Philippines within 10 years. This measure pleased Filipino leaders; it also pleased the United States business community, who wanted to keep Filipino products out of America. However, a major reason for passage of the bill was that the American people no longer wanted to defend the islands, upholding the American anti-imperialist past.

Section 2 ★ Review

Checking for Understanding
1. **Identify** Hawley-Smoot Tariff, Reconstruction Finance Corporation, Clark Memorandum, Naval Conference, Hoover-Stimson Doctrine.
2. **Define** moratorium.
3. **Summarize** why Hoover disapproved of relief programs and direct involvement in business.
4. **List** three actions Hoover took to promote ties with Latin America.

Critical Thinking
5. **Predicting Consequences** What message did the United States and its allies send to leaders such as Adolf Hitler by not taking action against Japan?

---

752 UNIT 8 Crusade and Disillusion: 1914–1932

Answers to SECTION 2 REVIEW

1. Hawley-Smoot Tariff, 748; Reconstruction Finance Corporation, 749; Clark Memorandum, 750; Naval Conference, 751; Hoover-Stimson Doctrine, 752
2. All vocabulary words are defined in the Glossary.
3. suppressed self-initiative, hurt self-respect, destroyed tradition of local responsibility, put government in competition with private business. Creation of RFC, vetoed Garner-Wagner bill and Norris bill
4. trip to Latin America, settled boundary dispute between Chile and Peru, abandoned military intervention in Latin America, withdrew troops from Nicaragua
5. encouraged Japanese and German expansion through nonintervention

Social Studies Skills

Study and Writing Skills

Writing a Persuasive Argument

A persuasive argument is one in which the reader or listener is urged to do something or believe in the same thing as does the writer or speaker.

The following guidelines will help you organize and write a persuasive argument:
a. Before writing, research the topic. What are the facts, and how do people feel about it?
b. Tailor your argument to your audience.
c. Support your argument with solid facts and examples.
d. Save the most persuasive arguments for last, then end your paper by summarizing.

Imagine that the following is a paper that you wrote as Herbert Hoover defending his war debt moratorium. Note how the guidelines were applied:

I am writing to you, the people of France, as you continue to heal the wounds inflicted by the Great War. My heart and thoughts are with you. There is depression, unemployment, and debt. Germany, for all its past offenses, is teetering on the brink of collapse. Europe, like America, is fighting the effects of this demoralizing depression. The time has come to close the gap between how we feel about that Great War. Let us consider our children's future, and not so much our temporary feelings of outrage for a war that is over. Abide with me in my decision to place a one-year, international moratorium on all war debts. It is time to let go of the past and resurrect the quality of life that has been obscured by this spectre of debt.

After reading this, it should be clear to Hoover's audience that:
a. Hoover researched the topic.
b. Hoover tailored this paper for the French people.
c. His remark about America's suffering made the point that all countries were linked by common interests.
d. He mentioned the future of the world's children as perhaps the most persuasive argument, making the reader realize that feelings of revenge could affect the world for years to come. Then he summarized the argument with an appeal to let go of the past and to restore the quality of life that had been lost.

▲ President Herbert Hoover

Practicing the Skill

For practice in this skill, write a persuasive argument against the Hawley-Smoot Tariff. Determine your audience before you begin writing.

LESSON PLAN
Mastering Social Studies Skills

Teaching Study and Writing Skills

Use the guidelines to discuss Herbert Hoover's defense of the war debt moratorium. Ask: At the time of the writing, what was the economic condition of France and the United States? (Both countries were in a depression.) Why does Hoover compare suffering in America with suffering in France? (He wanted to create a feeling of commonality between the nations.) What arguments does Hoover use to persuade the French to go along with his plans? Point out the way Hoover summarizes his argument. Is it persuasive? Why or why not? (Answers will vary, but appeals to future generations and to letting go of the past are powerful.)

Did You Know?

When the moratorium ended, Hoover demanded that European nations resume payments. All but Finland, whose obligation was tiny, had no choice but to default.

Answers to SOCIAL STUDIES SKILLS

Students' papers will vary but should follow the guidelines discussed in the activity. Suggest that they consult the Glencoe Writer's Guidebook before writing their persuasive arguments.

LESSON PLAN
SECTION 3, 754–761

FOCUS

Bellringer
Before taking roll at the beginning of the class period, display Focus Activity Transparency 92 on the overhead projector, and assign the accompanying Focus Activity Sheet.

Objectives
Point out the objectives on this page to students in previewing the section content.

Motivating Activity
Ask students to consider negative emotions and activities a major depression might cause in a nation. Then have them consider what positive emotions and behavior a widespread crisis might precipitate.

Assign students the Chapter 27 Reading on the Bonus March in Primary and Secondary Source Readings.

NATIONAL GEOGRAPHIC SOCIETY

VIDEODISC
- *GTV: A Geographic Perspective on American History*

Side 4, Chapter 3
Title: *Thinking Big*
Subject: Depression, Dust Bowl, New Deal

See GTV Guide page 59 for complete lesson plan.

SECTION 3

The Depression Worsens

Setting the Scene

Section Focus
Between Election Day in November 1932 and Inauguration Day in March 1933, the nation's economy hit rock bottom. National income had dropped from $81 billion to $41 billion. Over 25 percent of the nation's workers were unemployed, and many others worked only part-time. Thousands of businesses were bankrupt, thousands of banks had closed, and farmers were in revolt.

Objectives
After studying this section, you should be able to
★ compare the condition of workers and farmers in the early 1930s.
★ discuss the mood of the country as the election of 1932 approached.

Key Term
lame duck

▶ DEPRESSION SCRIP, EMERGENCY MONEY

The Depression was uneven in its impact. While many people lost their jobs, the majority of Americans did not. Instead many found their hours reduced. The few who kept their jobs and did not have their hours or wages cut actually were better off because prices declined. Even so, for most Americans the mood was gloomy—and for good reason. In 1932 over 30,000 companies closed. In just 2 months in 1931 over 800 banks failed, wiping out the life savings of thousands of depositors.

All over the United States, families not able to pay their rent or mortgages were evicted from their homes. Some ended up in communities of makeshift shacks on the outskirts of cities.

■ Want in the Land of Plenty

As the Depression deepened, fear and despair replaced the buoyant optimism of the 1920s. "I'm afraid, every man is afraid," steel industrialist Charles M. Schwab admitted. "I don't know, we don't know, whether the values we have are going to be real next month or not."

Fear

Loss of confidence affected all sorts of people. Some who lost their jobs suffered such emotional effects that they became unemployable. "My father spent two years

UNIT 8 Crusade and Disillusion: 1914–1932

Classroom Resources for SECTION 3

Teacher's Classroom Resources
- Reproducible Lesson Plan
- Reteaching Activity 27-3
- Chapter 27 Enrichment Activity
- Chapter 27 Performance Assessment Activity
- Chapter 27 Primary and Secondary Source Readings
- Spanish Summaries and Glossary
- Section Quiz

Multimedia
- Section Focus Transparency 92
- U.S. History and Art Transparency
- Unit 8 Digest Transparency
- Vocabulary Puzzlemaker
- Student Self-Test Software
- A Geographic Perspective on American History
- The Presidents: A Picture History of Our Nation

painting his father's house," one man later remembered. "He painted it twice. It gave him something to do."

Business leaders hesitated to build new factories or to bring out new products. Frightened bankers became unwilling to lend money, even to borrowers with good character and ample collateral. On the stock market, security prices dropped dramatically. Stock in Radio Corporation of America (RCA) dropped from $101 per share in 1929 to $2.50 in 1932.

Starvation

One of the great ironies of the Depression was that starvation existed in the midst of plenty. The productive capacity of farmers did not slacken. On the contrary, farmers' problems resulted, in part, from their ability to grow more food than they were able to sell. Already in a depression throughout most of the 1920s, the collapse of the farm economy after 1929 wreaked havoc on rural America. Despite Hoover's programs, grain prices dropped so low that farmers heated their homes by shoveling their crops into their furnaces. They protested low agricultural prices by declaring "farmers' holidays" and tried to prevent food shipments to cities. In Iowa farmers blockaded highways and dumped milk trucks in an attempt to make milk scarce and raise its price. In Oregon they slaughtered sheep because mutton prices were lower than what it cost to ship the animals to market. Meanwhile, in America's cities people picked through garbage looking for scraps of meat.

Virginia Durr, an Alabama activist for tenant farmers' rights, described the suffering when she said, "Have you ever seen a child with rickets shaking, as with palsy? No proteins, no milk. And the companies pouring milk into the gutters. . . . People with nothing to eat and they killed the pigs."

▶ APPLE SELLER, NEW YORK CITY, 1932

▲ "HOOVERVILLES" Many families lost their homes during the Great Depression because they were unable to meet mortgage payments or pay rent. Some of the homeless found living quarters in shacks constructed of tin and old crates. Villages of these makeshift shacks, such as this one in Seattle, Washington, sprouted up throughout the nation. *How did the rate of unemployment change between 1930 and 1933?*

CHAPTER 27 SECTION 3

Independent Practice

Research Have students research photographs and political cartoons from the Depression era and display them on a bulletin board. Ask them to write captions describing the illustrations. Then conduct a class discussion, asking such questions as: What images were used repeatedly as symbols of these times? How were politicians portrayed in cartoons?

Discuss with students the kinds of images used to symbolize problems in today's society. **L3**

Teaching Life of the Times

The Great Depression affected all classes of society. Oscar Ameringer wrote about the "Brokers, bank clerks, counter jumpers, A.B.s, M.D.s, Ph.D.s, D.D.s shoveling snow in the lowly company of bricklayers, cellists, hod carriers, oboists, garment workers, concert masters, stevedores, dramatists, and dock wallopers." Those with the most to lose often took the most drastic way out. Jumping off bridges, from ships, and out of windows became common. This practice gave rise to a morbid sense of humor reflected in a popular joke about hotel clerks asking registering guests if they wanted the room for sleeping or jumping.

Life of the Times

Depression Needy

Counting the families of the unemployed and the underemployed—those who could find only part-time work—34 million Americans were living without enough money to buy adequate food or to pay rent and mortgages.

The tragedies of the Depression became so commonplace that children played games with names like "Eviction" and "Relief." Yet even play was a luxury for some children who, foraging for food, had to fight grown men and women for the garbage in city dumps. Other people survived by eating weeds or dog biscuits that they stole from the local pound. The severe needs of people during the Depression resulted in an increase in health problems. Poor or inadequate nutrition made Americans vulnerable to disease, and the incidence of typhoid, dysentery, tuberculosis, and heart and stomach disorders increased.

The problems of families became acute when they could not pay their rent, and they were evicted from their homes. Homeless people often devised ingenious makeshift shelters. Some built shacks from packing boxes, and others camped in sewer pipes.

▲ **DUST BOWL** BY ALEXANDER HOGUE

The Human Cost of the Depression

Although business leaders promised Hoover that they would not cut wages of remaining workers, as the Depression deepened, their situation changed.

Wage Cuts and Unemployment

In October 1931, United States Steel Corporation cut salaries and wages by 10 percent, and employers in other industries soon followed. By 1933 salaries had decreased 40 percent and hourly wages by 60 percent. The average family's income fell from $2,300 in 1929 to $1,600 in 1932. More layoffs followed the wage cuts. In 1930, 4 million workers were unemployed; by 1933 the number of jobless Americans more than tripled.

In cities throughout the country breadlines and soup kitchens appeared on sidewalks as local governments and private charities struggled to feed the poor. In some cases the lines stretched for blocks as people waited for their only good meal each day.

As unemployment grew, Hoover's Reconstruction Finance Corporation began to loan money to state governments for relief, but these and other relief funds proved woefully inadequate. Toledo, Ohio, for example, could only spend 2 cents for each relief meal it served. New York City provided only $2.39 per week to each family on relief. In many other cities, after private charity was exhausted, there was nothing.

Hoovervilles

Throughout the nation, families who could not pay their rent or make their mortgage payments were evicted from their homes. Some moved in with relatives if they could. The less fortunate ended up in makeshift communities dubbed "Hoovervilles" on the outskirts of cities. One woman later remembered Oklahoma City's Hooverville:

756 UNIT 8 Crusade and Disillusion: 1914–1932

Sidelights: Talking Pictures

Although the first talking pictures were released in 1927, it was not until after the crash that most motion picture theaters were equipped for sound. By then weekly movie attendance reached 110 million out of a population of 121 million. As the Depression grew, the new medium found inventive ways to provide viewers with escape from their troubles. By far the most successful creations were the extravagant musicals. The plots were simple or nonexistent, and the musicals projected upbeat and unreal worlds. Movie musicals could not have existed before the 1930s and have never been more popular since.

> "Here were all these people living in rusted-out car bodies. I mean that was their home. There were people living in shacks made of orange crates. One family with a whole lot of kids were living in a piano box. This wasn't just a little section, this was maybe ten miles wide and ten miles long. People living in whatever they could junk together."

People who were even less fortunate slept in doorways or on park benches. Desperate men grubbed in garbage cans to feed their families. Nearly every street corner had its apple seller. So many apples were available because of a surplus of the fruit in the Pacific Northwest. To reduce the surplus, the International Apple Shippers Association set up a system for unemployed people to sell the apples. A person could get a credit for $1.75 for a crate of 100 to 120 apples, then turn around and sell the apples for 5 cents each, making a small profit. However, as more and more people tried to make money this way, apple vendors reacted by raising the price to $2.25 a crate. Unless a person sold more than half a crate, he or she made no profit.

Other jobless Americans banded together in hunger riots, smashing into grocery stores and grabbing whatever food they could carry. Begging increased dramatically, and the song "Brother, Can You Spare a Dime?" became a bitter testimony to veterans who remembered fighting a war to protect American values and to make the world safe for democracy.

■ The Bonus Army

In May 1932, some 1,500 unemployed army veterans and their families marched on Washington, D.C., to demand early payment of the bonus Congress had promised to pay them in 1945. Within sight of the White House, some set up a Hooverville in an area across the Potomac River known as Anacostia Flats. Others occupied abandoned buildings in the area. As they demonstrated daily in front of the White House and the Capitol, their numbers increased to more than 20,000.

The government tried to keep the protesters peaceful. President Hoover supported their right to express their views and even provided them with army tents, cots, and field kitchens. When Congress

AMERICAN PORTRAITS

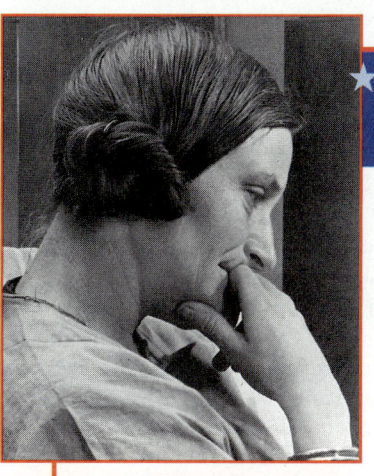

Dorothea Lange
1895–1965

By the time she finished high school, Dorothea Lange had chosen her career. She wanted to be a photographer—even though she had never used a camera.

After taking a photography course, Lange journeyed from New York to San Francisco, where she ran a portrait business for 10 years. Then the Depression struck. Lange became a documentary photographer, her compassion showing clearly in her photos. By the mid-1930s she was documenting the life of California's migrant laborers, work that earned her a position with the Farm Security Administration (FSA). Her FSA photos revealed poverty's brutal effects on rural Americans. Lange later traveled through the dust bowl states, capturing people's suffering in a book called *An American Exodus, A Record of Human Erosion*.

CHAPTER 27 The Depression Begins 1928–1932

CHAPTER 27
SECTION 3

Did You Know?
The first head of the Securities and Exchange Commission was Joseph Kennedy, a wealthy Boston businessperson and father of the future President.

Visualizing History
Although Hoover was blamed for the excessive force used against the Bonus Army, it was General MacArthur who gave the orders and disobeyed Hoover's directive not to use force.
Answer to Caption: with fear and excessive force

Linking Across Time
In 1990 public anger ran high against unscrupulous speculators, much as it had in the 1930s. During the 1980s Wall Street moguls had manipulated stocks to make huge fortunes. In 1986 Ivan Boesky, first of these "raiders," was fined $100 million and sentenced to three years in prison. In 1990 Michael Milken, convicted of similar crimes, received a 10-year sentence, a $600 million fine, and 5,400 hours of public service. Analysts believed the sentence reflected growing public anger at such practices.

---

rejected their demands, most of the veterans left Washington. About 2,000 refused to leave, however. After a clash between the veterans and the local police, Hoover called in the army. General Douglas MacArthur, commander of the troops, carried out the President's orders to clear the veterans from federal buildings. Using tanks, machine guns, and tear gas, his troops drove the veterans out of Washington and burned their camp. Historian Frederick Lewis Allen described the sudden chaos that resulted:

> ❝ Cavalrymen were riding into the crowd, infantrymen were throwing tear-gas bombs, women and children were being trampled and choking from the gas; . . . [People] were running wildly, pell-mell across uneven ground, screaming as they stumbled and fell. The troops moved slowly on, scattering before them veterans and homegoing government clerks alike. . . . That evening, the Washington sky glowed with fire. Even after midnight the troops were still on their way with bayonets and tear-gas bombs. ❞

Many Americans blamed Hoover for the use of brutal and excessive force against the veterans. He seemed more than ever an inflexible leader.

■ Fear of Revolution

During this time of bewilderment and despair, fear of revolution started to spread. Lloyds of London, a British insurance company, began to write policies for riot insurance in the United States. Looking for scapegoats, Americans blamed the Depression on the very people they had admired and willingly followed a few years earlier—industrialists and bankers. Public outrage

▲ **THE BONUS ARMY** Veterans of World War I converged on Washington, D.C., in 1932. They hoped to persuade Congress to grant them immediate payments of a bonus, not due until 1945. **How did the federal government react to the bonus marchers?**

increased when a Senate investigation charged that some of the nation's wealthiest were trying to get away without paying taxes on their huge incomes. Others were accused of using unscrupulous business practices to increase their wealth in the midst of such widespread poverty and suffering.

Radical Alternatives

The unrest in society offered hope to both Socialists and Communists, who preached that the Depression marked the end of capitalism, which would soon be replaced by a system that distributed goods more fairly. Both groups proposed that government control the means of production and distribution. Both promised that a planned economy would result in greater abundance for all. "Folks are restless," observed Mississippi Governor Theodore Bilbo, "communism is gaining a foothold. . . . In fact, I'm getting a little pink myself."

UNIT 8 Crusade and Disillusion: 1914–1932

Sidelights: A Tradition Begun in the Depression

The lighting of the Christmas tree at Rockefeller Center in New York City is a tradition televised for the nation each year. The first Christmas tree in what was to become Rockefeller Center (at the time it was a block of rubble from demolished townhouses) was decorated with tin cans and paper in 1931. The decorators were New York City workers who still had jobs. The official Rockefeller Center tree tradition was inaugurated two years later.

Such radical alternatives were weakened because Socialists and Communists bitterly opposed each other and destroyed each other's credibility. The Socialists proposed to gain their power by persuasion and the ballot box. The Communist party, however, held that capitalism could not be overthrown without violent revolution—what Earl Browder, the general secretary of the party, called the "omelet theory." Just as it was impossible to make an omelet without breaking eggs, Browder explained, it was impossible to make a revolution without breaking heads.

Using the Forces of Democracy

Fears of a revolution in the United States proved to be unfounded, however. Although many Americans were suffering, were angry, and wanted a change, protest movements tended to be splintered. No single leader emerged to galvanize them or act as a unifying force. Most Americans clung to their democratic traditions and expressed their anger at the ballot box.

The Election of 1932

As the presidential election of 1932 approached, the Democrats sensed victory for the first time since 1916.

The Candidates

The Democratic national convention rejected Al Smith's bid for renomination and instead chose New York Governor Franklin D. Roosevelt as their candidate. The former secretary of the navy had run as the Democratic candidate for Vice President in 1920. In 1928, while Smith was losing the presidential election to Hoover, Roosevelt

▲ **HOME RELIEF STATION** by Louis Ribak, 1935–1936 The painting expresses the frustration felt by the American people during the Depression years. **What did the election of 1932 reveal about American public opinion concerning the Hoover administration and its response during the most difficult years of the Depression?**

CHAPTER 27
SECTION 3

After 60 years of government involvement in the economy, millions of Americans are still homeless and jobless. Pictures of homeless men, women, and children huddled in makeshift quarters or of centers to feed the hungry in the 1980s and early 1990s are difficult to distinguish from those of the earlier period.

Ask students if they think government today is doing enough to resolve the problem of homelessness. Ask what suggestions they can offer.

Visualizing History The American people responded enthusiastically at the polls to Roosevelt's call for action to rescue the nation from the Great Depression.
Answer to Caption: The entire country was seized by a banking panic.

had won New York's race for governor and in the process proved himself to be a remarkable vote-getter. In 1930 he had been reelected by a huge majority.

The Democratic Platform

The Democratic platform of 1932—the briefest in United States political history—urged the repeal of Prohibition and made general proposals for reform and recovery. The Democrats' most effective asset, however, was Roosevelt himself. Setting the tone for what became a whirlwind campaign, he flew by plane to the Democratic convention to become the first candidate to accept a presidential nomination in person.

In his acceptance address, he pledged "a new deal for the American people." In later speeches, however, he was vague and described the "New Deal" in broad terms

▲ **INAUGURATION DAY** During the ride to Roosevelt's inauguration, Hoover seemed glum while Roosevelt appeared confident. *What happened to the American economy between Election Day 1932 and Inauguration Day 1933?*

only. It remained clear that Roosevelt intended to take action that would help "the forgotten man at the bottom of the economic pyramid." He summed up the history of the Hoover administration in four sentences:

> *First, it encouraged speculation and overproduction through its false economic policies. Second, it attempted to minimize the crash and misled the people as to its gravity. Third, it erroneously charged the cause to other nations of the world. And finally, it refused to recognize and correct the evils at home which it had brought forth; it delayed reform, it forgot reform.*

The Republicans Nominate Hoover

The Republicans, meanwhile, gloomily renominated Hoover, who suffered the problem of having to defend his policies in the midst of a terrible Depression. He maintained that hard times were the result of economic collapse abroad—for which his administration could not be held responsible. Hoover flatly rejected Roosevelt's position that government had "a positive duty to see that no citizen shall starve." "You cannot," warned Hoover, "extend the mastery of government over the daily life of a people without somewhere making it master of people's souls and thoughts."

Democrats Victorious

On Election Day, the Republican victories of the 1920s were completely reversed as Roosevelt carried 42 of the 48 states. This landslide revealed not only a widespread willingness to blame the Republicans for the Depression but also a desire to use government as an agency for human welfare.

Yet even at the bottom of the worst depression in history, few Americans favored the overthrow of capitalism, either by violent or peaceful means. The election results revealed that the Socialists polled 900,000 votes and

UNIT 8 Crusade and Disillusion: 1914–1932

Sidelights: Hoover Dam

One project undertaken by the Hoover administration that rivaled New Deal programs was the construction of a huge dam on the Colorado River at the Arizona-Nevada border. One of the highest concrete dams in the world, the structure was finished in 1936 at a cost of about $385 million. The dam controls the flooding of the Colorado River and provides hydroelectric power for much of the Southwest. Today environmentalists are concerned that the uneven flow of the Colorado River, controlled by the dam, is causing deterioration of the canyon's walls and beaches.

the Communists only 100,000. This meant that their combined share was a little more than 2 percent of all of the votes cast.

■ Banking Panic

In the time between Roosevelt's election in November and his inauguration in March, the Twentieth Amendment was added to the Constitution, changing the date of the presidential inauguration from March 4 to January 20. Had this amendment gone into effect sooner, it would have been better for the country. For four months Hoover as President was a **lame duck,** an officeholder with little influence, because his term was about to end. During this time the nation was virtually leaderless. The new President—Franklin D. Roosevelt—was without power to act.

Withdrawing Funds

During this short time, the entire banking system disintegrated, and the economy ground almost to a standstill. Although thousands of smaller banks had already failed, most of the larger banks seemed to be able to hold firm during this time. Despite Roosevelt's promise that upon becoming President he would take action to rescue the nation from the Depression, in early 1933 the entire country was seized by a banking panic. Having lost faith in the nation's economy, thousands of depositors withdrew their money from banks and hoarded cash and gold. Given such a situation, even the most stable banks were bound to stop payments eventually because there was not enough gold in circulation to cover all deposits.

 ▲ **DEPRESSION LIFE** These three children, ages 5, 12, and 7, were discovered living in an abandoned house. Many Americans demanded action to escape such economic woes. *What candidate won the 1932 election?*

Bank Closings

As the situation deteriorated, state governors issued proclamations closing the banks of their states until confidence could be restored. By March 4—the day Roosevelt would take the oath of office—almost every private bank in the country was closed or placed under restriction by state regulation. From 1930 to the eve of the inauguration, more than 5,400 banks had shut down. The people of the nation waited anxiously to see what the new President would do.

Section 3 ★ Review

Checking for Understanding

1. **Identify** bonus army, General Douglas MacArthur.
2. **Define** lame duck.
3. **Describe** the mood of the country as the Depression worsened.
4. **Explain** why farmers destroyed crops and livestock even though people were hungry.

Critical Thinking

5. **Identifying Problems** What part did the public's lack of confidence in government play in the banking crisis?

CHAPTER 27 ★ REVIEW

Using Vocabulary

Imagine that you must write a handbook on tips for investing in the stock market. Write an entry about speculation that explains the pros and cons. Use these terms:

speculation   on margin
securities   installment buying

Reviewing Facts

1. **Explain** how overproduction or underconsumption was one cause of the Great Depression.
2. **Describe** the effects of the Hawley-Smoot Tariff.
3. **Summarize** Hoover's actions to combat the Depression and the philosophy behind the actions.
4. **List** two defeats Hoover had in foreign policy.
5. **Cite** reasons for the rise of communism and socialism during the Depression.
6. **State** three reasons Franklin D. Roosevelt won the election of 1932.
7. **Discuss** the banking crisis of 1933 and relate it to the overall mood of Americans.

Understanding Concepts

Economic Change

1. Was America's appetite for money and consumer goods a cause of the Great Depression? Explain how activities such as stock market speculation and installment buying contributed to the crisis.
2. How did economic changes affect American faith and beliefs about the United States? Why do you think some Americans feared a revolution? Explain the increased activity among the Socialists and Communists in America.

Political Policy

3. Explain why Hoover's political beliefs were popular while the economy was doing well but increasingly unpopular during the Depression.

4. Do you think Roosevelt, using the platform he proposed in 1932, would have won the 1928 presidential election? Explain your answer.

Critical Thinking

1. **Contrasting Ideas** Explain the difference between laissez-faire economics and Hoover's beliefs about government in the economy.
2. **Analyzing Fine Art** Study the painting on this page entitled *The Bowery*, by Reginald Marsh, then answer the questions that follow.
   a. Who are the people in the painting?
   b. Would you consider this work a realistic work? Explain.

Writing About History

Cause and Effect

Write an essay on how the Great Depression might have affected a young person your age. Before you begin writing, make a list of the worries, fears,

CHAPTER 27 ★ REVIEW

and hardships the Depression caused. Use this list to write an essay on the effect these factors might have had on an individual your age. Include how the Great Depression would have affected your ideas about careers and school, your self-esteem and way of life, and your hopes for the future.

Cooperative Learning

Work in groups of three to analyze the causes of the Great Depression. Assign each group member two of the causes listed on pages 743–745 of your text. Have each group member make a list of economic and social effects that might have resulted from his or her cause. For example, if your subject is underconsumption, explain how this factor affected store owners, manufacturers, and consumers. When you have finished your individual lists, create a master list entitled "How the Great Depression Changed America."

Social Studies Skills

Reading a Line Graph

A line graph is used to show a relationship between two variables. The independent variable goes on the *x*-axis, and the dependent variable goes on the *y*-axis. By using different colors or different types of lines, a line graph can have two or more curves. Thus, two or more items can be graphed on the same grid.

The three curves shown here are used to show how something changes over time. To interpret the data in a line graph, do the following.

- Read the title of the graph.
- Determine what the *x*-axis and *y*-axis represent.
- Determine what each of the three curves represents.
- Determine the changes or other relationships the graph shows.

Practicing the Skill

Use the graph and your understanding of Chapter 27 to answer the following questions.
1. What is the time period in the graph?
2. What is the independent variable in the graph?
3. What is the dependent variable in the graph?
4. What does each curve show?
5. When were wheat and corn prices the highest? The lowest?
6. What is the overall trend in the prices of wheat, corn, and cotton?
7. How did this trend affect farmers during the Great Depression?

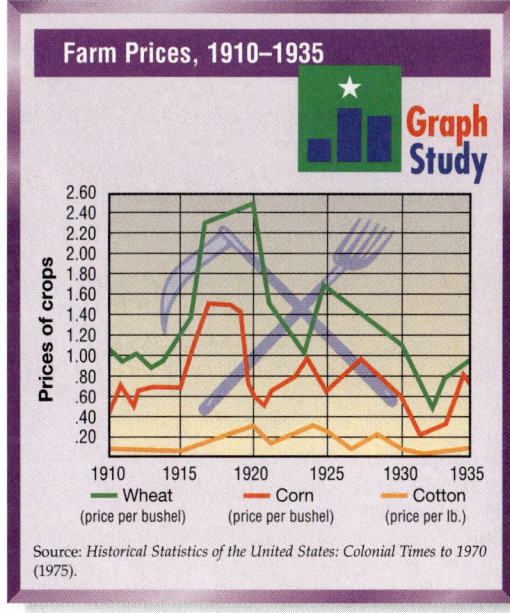

Farm Prices, 1910–1935

Source: *Historical Statistics of the United States: Colonial Times to 1970* (1975).

Using Your Journal

Contrast the conflict of Americans with government during the Depression with the ways they cooperated with government during World War I.

REVIEW
CHAPTER 27

Practicing the Skill
1. 1910–1935
2. years being studied
3. prices of crops
4. the curves show the prices per bushel or pound for each crop per year
5. wheat: 1920, highest; corn: 1931, lowest
6. fluctuates from highs to lows (the overall trend was a decrease)
7. Farmers hit hard because prices were not maintained steadily but fluctuated from highs to lows.

Chapter Bonus Test Question

How did a platform of intervention in the economy help the Democrats win the election of 1932? (Americans wanted government to help alleviate economic conditions, which were growing worse under a Republican administration.)

Using Your Journal

Responses will vary, but students should recognize that people pulled together for a common cause, and the economy was boosted by the war. People were pulled apart by the Depression, and the government did little to alleviate conditions, creating disillusionment and tensions.

---

and some feared starvation. Political ideologies that promised to redistribute wealth were attractive to some.
3. They greatly contributed to both the boom and the bust.
4. Answers will vary. Probably not. In 1928 the economy was booming, and Americans believed in Hoover's pro-business philosophy that stressed individual initiative.

Critical Thinking
1. Hoover did not completely believe in *laissez-faire* policies since it was the role of government to guarantee economic, social, and political justice, but to do so with limited intervention.
2. **a.** They appear to be ordinary people.
   b. Answers will vary. The painting shows people in a realistic setting that reflects urban life.

Cultural Kaleidoscope

Making Connections

History and Literature

Point out that writings of the 1920s offer vivid descriptions of the "new woman" of that era. She plays an important role in the fiction of F. Scott Fitzgerald, especially his novels *This Side of Paradise* (1920) and *The Great Gatsby* (1925). Other fictional characterizations of the flapper can be found in Sinclair Lewis's *Babbitt* (1922) and the short stories of Dorothy Parker.

Other popular fiction of the period, while of less literary value, also provides insights into the ways in which contemporaries viewed the "new woman."

More About... the Flapper

What is the origin of the term "flapper"? No one seems to know for sure. There are two main explanations. According to one, the word comes from a 1920s fad among both men and women—the wearing of floppy galoshes. It's more likely, however, that the word has its origins in eighteenth-century England. At that time it referred to a duck too young to fly.

Cultural Kaleidoscope

The 1920s

Fashions in the 1920s

During the 1920s, postwar America rebelled against many of the social values that were in place at the turn of the century. Nowhere was this revolution more evident than in the fashions of the period. The flapper, embodying independence and social rebellion, became the model for the new woman.

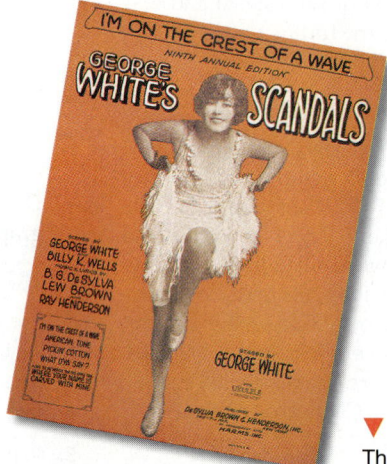

During the 1920s straight, unfitted dresses were in vogue. Skirts seemed to rise and fall with the stock market. When Wall Street boomed during the 1920s, skirt lengths rose above the knee.

The straw hat, or boater, was the common headwear for men.

Poised and chic couples set a sophisticated style of dress in the 1920s.

Many women adopted a new kind of hat style, a drooping, bell-shaped hat called a cloche.

Cooperative Learning

Divide the class into four or five groups. Ask group members to discuss which of the cultural developments covered in this kaleidoscope had the greatest impact on the life of American women. Once selections have been made, ask each group to design and construct a magazine cover illustrating the chosen cultural development. Suggest that they include a message from the publisher explaining why the development is important to American life. Have groups display their completed covers on the bulletin board.

Bow tie

Artist John Held, Jr., helped create the image of youth in the 1920s. His art often appeared on the cover of popular magazines.

Woman's earring

The changes in society gave women a greater measure of intellectual and economic independence.

Cultural Kaleidoscope

Portfolio Project

Ask students to collect advertisements and other illustrations from newspapers and periodicals showing current versions of the items pictured in this kaleidoscope. Ask students to write a brief caption that summarizes the difference between the two styles. They might also write a brief report explaining how contemporary fashions reflect the roles of women in society today. (For example, running shoes might symbolize women's desire for comfort and their interest in keeping fit; they are also a unisex fashion.)

The Historian's Craft

Although popular culture glorified the "new women" of the 1920s, scholars gather evidence to see how much change actually occurred. For instance, statistics show that although men's earning increased in the 1920s, women's earnings fell. Also many firms fired women as soon as they got married. A study of laws passed or enforced during the period reveal that though women could now vote, in many states they could not serve on juries, hold office, or own a business. As one contemporary historian writes: "It is now clear that flappers were the exception rather than the rule in the 1920s."

UNIT 8 DIGEST

Unit 8 Digest can be used to teach unit coverage when time is limited, to review unit content, or to link content of one unit to another.

Unit Digest Transparencies
Show the Unit 8 Digest Transparencies.

■ Chapter 25
Remind students that the United States tried to stay out of World War I. Then ask them to consider what is sufficient provocation for going to war. Have them discuss the following: Why did the United States go to war in 1917? Was war a justifiable step? Why or why not?

■ Chapter 26
Read to the class the following excerpt from Frederick Lewis Allen's *Only Yesterday:* "... [L]ike the suddenly liberated vacationist, the country felt that it ought to be enjoying itself more than it was, and that life was futile and nothing mattered much. But in the meantime it might as well play—follow the crowd, take up the new toys ... go in for the new fads...." Discuss with students whether this is an accurate picture of the United States in the 1920s.

■ Chapter 27
Have students construct an economic time line showing the major developments that took the country from the end of World War I through prosperity to depression. Have them compare their time lines and add any important events.

766

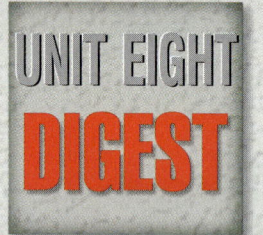

UNIT EIGHT DIGEST

Chapter 25
World War I

Wilson, an idealist who believed in fair play, wanted the United States to stop using military force and economic pressure as a tool of foreign policy. However, he ended up imitating his Republican predecessors by sending American troops into the Caribbean. Latin Americans came to resent his "moral imperialism" as much as Theodore Roosevelt's "Big Stick."

When war erupted in Europe in 1914, the United States declared neutrality. But British and French propaganda, American business interests, and German submarine warfare persuaded Americans to side with the Allies.

An apparent conspiracy between Mexico and Germany against the United States and the sinking of four American merchant ships ended American neutrality. Congress declared war on Germany in April 1917.

Unprepared for war, Americans mobilized with incredible speed. The production of armaments became a top priority, and government agencies such as the War Industries Board reorganized the economy to supply them. The draft was reinstated and propaganda was produced to influence public opinion. The government raised money for the war effort through taxes and selling bonds.

When the balance of the war tipped in favor of the Allies, an armistice was signed in November 1918. The Allies rejected most of Wilson's peace plan. After the war the United States experienced economic and social unrest, punctuated by strikes and race riots.

Chapter 26
The Decade of Normalcy

By the 1920s Americans wanted to get on with their lives, forget about public affairs, and stay out of wars. Warren G. Harding understood this when he promised "normalcy," a return to the values and practices of the past. The United States was now too enmeshed in world affairs to return to isolationism and continued to be involved in foreign diplomacy.

President Harding and his Republican successor Calvin Coolidge eased restrictions on business and looked after business interests. These policies seemed to work as the growth of new, urban industries fueled an economic boom during the 1920s. The growing prosperity was a key factor in the decline of labor unions' strength.

Major social changes and cultural achievements took place during the 1920s. Prohibition brought on a crime wave. The success of radio advertising increased the demand for consumer goods. The automobile affected more than the economy; it seemed to change the American way of life. Along with their newly won suffrage, American women demanded economic opportunity. In the "Harlem Renaissance," African Americans reflected a new spirit of pride and protest.

After World War I, however, feelings against immigrants led Congress to seriously restrict all immigration into the United States.

Chapter 27
The Depression Begins

Herbert Hoover slid into the presidency in 1928 full of optimism. In foreign policy Hoover practiced a "Good Neighbor" policy with Latin American republics. In domestic policy he assured Americans that as long as business thrived, the country would prosper.

766 UNIT 8 Crusade and Disillusion: 1914–1932

Cooperative Learning

Divide the class into small groups, and have students turn to President Wilson's Fourteen Points in the Documents section on page 1118. Ask the groups to read the document and work to rewrite or paraphrase the Fourteen Points, making them readily understandable to junior high–school students. Have groups compare their paraphrased documents. Some groups might like to test the effectiveness of their work by teaching the document to a junior high–school class. **L2**

▲ BONUS ARMY SKIRMISH, 1932

Farmers, however, were already experiencing a depression, and government relief proved ineffective. On Black Tuesday, October 29, 1929, the stock market crashed, losing much of its value. This touched off a business and economic decline from which the country did not recover for more than a decade. The Great Depression was caused not only by stock market speculation but also by the effects of World War I, the depressed condition of agriculture, and unwise government policies.

By the end of the 1920s, thousands of Americans were jobless, and many farmers lost their land. Hoover offered to help banks and businesses but opposed direct federal relief to the unemployed because he feared that government handouts would destroy Americans' drive to work.

The American economy had hit rock bottom by the 1932 presidential election. Signs of instability and rebellion appeared everywhere. In the election, Democrat Franklin D. Roosevelt won the presidency by a wide margin.

Understanding Unit Themes

1. **Conflict and Cooperation** Explain why Americans felt so willing to cooperate with their government during World War I but felt in conflict with it during the Depression. What accounted for these changes in attitude toward the government? Give examples of ways people cooperated with the government and ways they engaged in conflict.

2. **Influence of Technology** How did technological innovation alter the lives of Americans in both war and peace? What was one important technology that revolutionized both?

3. **The Individual and Family Life** Trace the social changes covered in the unit from war to peace, from prosperity to depression. Think about other social changes during the era. How do you think all these changes affected families—for better and for worse?

UNIT 8 Crusade and Disillusion: 1914–1932

UNIT 8 DIGEST

Understanding Unit Themes

1. Concerted efforts produced results during World War I. During the Great Depression, however, many Americans became disillusioned because of the government's inability to make their lives better. Discontent: Bonus Army, increasing support for Socialists and Communists.

2. German submarines provoked Americans into war. Machine guns, tanks, and poison gas were new technologies that prolonged war, made it deadlier. Automobile created migration from cities to suburbs.

3. During World War I Americans made economic sacrifices; more women worked. During 1920s many Americans participated in economic prosperity. The Great Depression was a time of hardship, suffering, anger, and resentment. Families became bigger consumers during the 1920s, had more income, more leisure time. The Depression helped pull families apart, bringing poverty to millions.

🔘 Student Self-Test Software allows students to test their understanding of historical concepts at the unit, chapter, or section levels.

🎧 Have students listen to the Chapter Digests on the audiocassettes.

The Historian's Craft

Writing Persuasive Arguments Recall with students the techniques for presenting arguments to persuade readers of your interpretation or point of view: research your subject thoroughly, know your audience, support your argument with solid facts and evidence, save your most persuasive argument for the end, and then summarize your points. Ask students to use these techniques to write a persuasive argument challenging or supporting one of the following propositions: Prohibition should be ended. Only federal intervention can save the nation from economic disaster. You might have students with opposing views present their arguments to the class.

INTRODUCING UNIT 9

BEGINNING THE UNIT

Provide this cause-and-effect chart to students with the effects omitted. Assign students to complete the chart as they read the chapters in the unit.

Events
- The New Deal

Causes
- The Stock Market crash of 1929
- The Great Depression
- The Dust Bowl
- The election of Franklin Roosevelt

Effects
- The expansion of the federal government
- American involvement in World War II
- Postwar prosperity

History AND ART

This wartime painting of Flying Grumman Wildcat Fighters filling the skies above an old-fashioned hay wagon illustrates the changes that were taking place in the 1930s and 1940. Encourage students to speculate about the causes and effects of those changes.

00:00 OUT OF TIME? If time does not permit teaching the entire unit, use the Unit Digest on pages 890–891.

UNIT NINE
TIMES OF CRISIS
1932–1960

CHAPTER 28
The New Deal
1932–1939

CHAPTER 29
World War II
1933–1945

CHAPTER 30
The Cold War
1945–1952

CHAPTER 31
Search for Stability
1952–1960

▲ WPA PLAY POSTER, 1936

▲ M-1 RIFLE, FIRST USED DURING WORLD WAR II

History AND ART
B-17 Base in England by Peter Hurd, 1943

Less than 25 years after World War I, the United States found itself at war again. This war, however, was far different. It was a fight for survival, and before it was over, it involved almost every nation in the world.

Exploring Unit Themes

American Democracy During the New Deal years, the federal government's role in the economy grew. The government also assumed responsibility for the neediest members of society by providing work, relief, and assistance.

Civil Rights and Liberties While African Americans made some gains during the New Deal and war years, they still did not enjoy equality with whites. And attempts to pass civil rights legislation were defeated. Women's rights followed a similar pattern—gains made during the New Deal and war years were largely rolled back in the 1950s.

Conflict and Cooperation After World War II, the United States entered into a number of mutual defense alliances. It also played a leading role in

Setting the Scene

Several major crises deeply affected the United States between 1930 and 1960. A great depression endangered the nation's economic system, and foreign military power threatened its national security. Americans committed themselves to economic recovery and to fighting—first, the Axis Powers in World War II, later, the spread of communism.

Themes
- American Democracy
- Civil Rights and Liberties
- Conflict and Cooperation
- U.S. Role in World Affairs

Key Events
- New Deal legislation
- Dust Bowl
- Japanese attack Pearl Harbor
- Surrender of Germany and Japan
- United Nations Charter
- Cold War
- Truman Doctrine
- North Atlantic Treaty Organization
- Korean War
- Polio vaccine
- Suez Crisis
- Castro controls Cuba

Major Issues
- New Deal programs attempt to relieve economic hardships and pull the United States out of the Great Depression.
- Aid to the Allies and the Japanese attack on Pearl Harbor pulls the United States into World War II.
- The desire to contain communism leads the United States to assume a more active role in world affairs.

▼ World War II poster

Portfolio Project
Identify something you consider a symbol of the era and describe the ideas and emotions connected with it. Try to include visual materials.

▲ Flying Grumman Wildcat Fighter, 1942

INTRODUCING UNIT 9

UNIT 9 Independent Study Project
Organize students into three groups and assign each group one of the following topics: cultural developments, political developments, economic developments. Ask the groups to construct a major events chart showing the most important events in their topic area for the years covered in Unit 9.

Unit Digest Transparencies
Strategies and Activities
Use Transparency 17, *Interchange* by Wayne Thiebaud.

History and the Humanities
- U.S. History and Art Transparencies 23, 24, 25, 26, 27, 28
- Focus on American Fine Art Prints 17, 18
- American Music: Cultural Traditions
- Spirit of American Art and Music 28, 29, 30, 31

Portfolio Project
After students have chosen their symbols and completed the first draft of their work, ask them to edit one another's writing.

---

the founding of the United Nations, an international organization dedicated to solving conflict through peaceful negotiations.
U.S. Role in World Affairs The Japanese attack on Pearl Harbor drew the United States into a fighting role in World War II. The United States emerged as the major power in the postwar world, assuming leadership in the reconstruction of war-torn Europe and the fight against the spread of communism.
Examining the Themes Point out that this unit describes a series of crises that shook and ultimately transformed the United States. Have students identify the changes each of these crises brought about.

LESSON PLAN
Global Perspectives

FOCUS
Motivating Activity
Have students review the information on the world section of the time line. Then ask them to suggest titles for each of the three decades that sum up the developments of those decades. For example, the 1930s might be titled "The Rise of Totalitarianism." Ask students to do the same thing for the United States section of the time line. Have students compare their titles.

TEACH
Guided Practice
World Events and the U.S.
The Suez Crisis of 1956 had a chilling effect on United States' relations with its allies. American leaders were angered that Britain, France, and Israel took action without consulting them. The British and French governments countered by accusing John Foster Dulles, Eisenhower's secretary of state, of collusion with the Soviet Union. While this bitterness dissipated over time, during 1956 there was serious talk of dismantling NATO. Have students compare the Suez Crisis with the Persian Gulf Crisis in terms of allied relations.

Global Perspectives

The World

- Asia and Oceania
- Europe
- Africa
- South America
- North and Central America

1934 Hitler becomes Der Führer of Germany

1939 World War II begins in Europe

1938 Venezuela becomes the third-largest oil-producing nation in the world

The United States

- Pacific and Northwest
- Southeast
- Midwest
- Southwest
- Atlantic Northeast

1941 Japanese surprise attack on Pearl Harbor brings the United States into World War II

1937 Parts of the Southwest and the Great Plains become a dust bowl

1933 Newly inaugurated President Franklin D. Roosevelt launches New Deal

770 UNIT 9 Times of Crisis: 1932–1960

Cultural Diversity

The Chinese and Japanese have played a major role in American life, especially in California and Hawaii, since the mid-1800s. East Asians arrived in North America many centuries earlier. Some scholars believe that Hui Shen, a Chinese missionary, explored the Pacific Coast of North America as early as the 400s! There is solid evidence to suggest that Chinese sailors regularly visited California in the mid-1500s. Before the closing of Japan in the 1600s, Japanese sailors, too, probably ventured as far as California.

Linking Across Time

The Chinese and Japanese have played a major role in American life, especially in California and Hawaii, since the mid-1800s. They may have set foot on the North American continent hundreds of years before. Some scholars believe that Hui Shen, a Chinese missionary, explored the Pacific coast of North America as early as the 400s! There is solid evidence to suggest that Chinese sailors regularly visited California in the mid-1500s. Before the closing of Japan in the 1600s, Japanese sailors, too, probably ventured as far as California.

▼ **1945** Atomic bombs devastate Hiroshima and Nagasaki

◄ **1956** Revolts in Poland and Hungary

1956 Suez Crisis

1959 Fidel Castro takes over Cuba

1958 First successful launch of a U.S. satellite

1955 AFL-CIO merge to form one union

▲ **1946** United Nations headquarters is established in New York

1953 McCarthyism stirs national interest

UNIT 9 Times of Crisis: 1932–1960   771

LESSON PLAN
Global Perspectives

Independent Practice

U.S. Events and the World Have students research and write a report comparing the first launch of an American satellite with the launch of the Soviet Union's Sputnik I in 1957. Suggest that they include such information as physical dimensions of the satellites, length of flight of each, and impact on world opinion of each flight. Ask for volunteers to read their reports to the class.

ASSESS

1. What 1950s world event had a major impact on the United States? (Castro's takeover in Cuba)

2. How did the balance of power shift after World War II? (European nations lost power; United States and Soviet Union emerged as "super powers".)

3. What cause-effect relationships are there among the events shown on the time line? (World War II begins—UN established; Japanese attack on Pearl Harbor—atomic bombs devastate Hiroshima, Nagasaki)

Cooperative Learning

Divide the class into groups of five. Have half the groups select one event from the world section of the time line and the other half select one event from the United States section of the time line. Ask groups to design a newspaper front page—including a headline, a news story, and illustrations—for their selected events. Display the finished front pages in the class. **L2**

771

PLANNING GUIDE Chapter 28 The New Deal

Daily Lesson Objectives	Teacher Classroom Resources	Multimedia
SECTION 1 **Roosevelt Takes Charge** 1 Day pp. 774–778 1. Identify the traits that made Franklin Roosevelt an effective leader. 2. Describe how Roosevelt gained ideas and support for his New Deal	Chapter 28 Study Guide Reproducible Lesson Plan Reteaching Activity 28-1 Section Quiz Chapter 28 Cooperative Learning Activity Chapter 28 Concept Mapping Activity American Portrait 55 Reinforcing Social Studies Skills 32, 53, 55, 69–72 Chapter 28 Primary and Secondary Source Readings	Student Self-Test Software Testmaker Section Focus Transparency 89 Chapter 28 Skills Transparency Chapter 28 Map Transparencies Unit 9 Digest Transparencies A Geographic Perspective on American History
SECTION 2 **Reform, Relief, and Recovery** 1 Day pp. 779–785 1. Give examples of how Roosevelt's policies helped and hurt the rural poor. 2. Compare the effectiveness of measures aimed at farmers and city workers.	Reproducible Lesson Plan Reteaching Activity 28-2 Section Quiz Reinforcing Social Studies Skills 25, 53, 65 The Living Constitution Writer's Guidebook Lesson 6	Student Self-Test Software Testmaker Section Focus Transparency 90 Powers of the President
SECTION 3 **The Second Deal** 1 Day pp. 787–793 1. List the special interest groups that challenged Roosevelt. 2. Outline the steps the Second New Deal took to achieve reform. 3. Identify the events that led to the end of the New Deal.	Reproducible Lesson Plan Reteaching Activity 28-3 Section Quiz Reinforcing Social Studies Skills 25, 69–72	Student Self-Test Software Testmaker Section Focus Transparency 91 The Presidents: A Picture History of Our Nation
SECTION 4 **The Impact of the New Deal** 1 Day pp. 795–799 1. Identify changes that the New Deal caused in American society. 2. Evaluate the effects of the New Deal on life today.	Reproducible Lesson Plan Reteaching Activity 28-4 Section Quiz Chapter 28 Enrichment Activity American Portrait 53 Reinforcing Social Studies Skills 53, 63 Spanish Summaries & Glossary	Student Self-Test Software Testmaker Vocabulary Puzzlemaker Section Focus Transparency 92 U.S. History and Art Transparency 23, 24 Audiocassette, Chapter 28
CHAPTER REVIEW AND EVALUATION 1 Day	Chapter 28 Test Chapter 28 Performance Assessment Activity	Student Self-Test Software Chapter 28 Testmaker

00:00 OUT OF TIME? If time does not permit teaching the entire chapter, use the Chapter 28 Summary on pages 890–891 and the Chapter 28 audiocassette (English and Spanish) to point out the main ideas of the chapter.

PLANNING GUIDE

Cultural Diversity Activity

Analyzing Ideas Congress passed the Indian Reorganization Act in 1934. It was also known as the Native American New Deal. John Collier, the Commissioner of Indian Affairs, originally proposed the law. However, his original proposal included a plan to set up special courts that took into account Native American traditions and customs in decisions involving a conflict between self-governing Native American communities and state and local governments. Congress rejected that part of Collier's plan.

Ask students why they think lawmakers turned down that part of Collier's proposal. What are some arguments in its favor? Against it? Invite interested students to research recent court battles between groups of Native Americans and state governments over land claims. Discuss how the special courts Collier envisioned might have affected the outcome of those cases.

Performance Assessment Activity

Popular Culture Organize students in groups of four or five to research the popular culture of the Depression years. Each group might focus on a different aspect of culture. For example, one might research films of the time, while another investigates music, literature, radio programs, or the popular magazines of the day. Invite each group to report its findings to the class in the form of an oral report. The reports should explain what students learned about life during the Depression from their research. Encourage groups to compare and contrast their findings.

POSSIBLE RUBRIC FEATURES: Content information, research skills, organization, writing and communication skills, critical thinking skills

Chapter Resources

Literature from the Period

Roosevelt, Franklin D. "First Inaugural Address." March 4, 1933.

Steinbeck, John. *The Grapes of Wrath*. 1939.

Readings for the Student

Dillon, Richard. "Spanning the Golden Gate." *American History Illustrated*, Vol. 22, No. 3, May 1987.

Oxford, Edward. "The Night of the Martians." *American History Illustrated*, Vol. 23, No. 6, October 1988.

Readings for the Teacher

McElvaine, Thomas Gordon. *The Great Depression*. Time Books, 1985.

Sternsher, Bernard, and Judith Sealander, eds. *Women of Valor: The Struggle Against the Great Depression as Told in Their Own Life Stories*. Ivan R. Dee, 1990.

Multimedia Resources

The Grapes of Wrath. 20th Century Fox. (VHS, 129 minutes)

The Great Depression: 1929–1933. Guidance Associates. (2 filmstrip programs)

Industrializing America: A Game of American Industrial Development. Perfection Form. (Apple diskette, backup, guide)

Key to Ability Levels

Teaching strategies have been coded for varying learning styles and abilities.

- **L1** Basic activities for all students
- **L2** Average activities for average to above-average students
- **L3** Challenging activities for above-average students
- **LEP** Limited English Proficiency activities

Glencoe Links to the Humanities

Links to Art
- U.S. History and Art Transparencies 23, 24
- Focus on American Fine Art Prints

Links to Literature
- Macmillan Literature: American Literature Video—*The Glass Menagerie*
- Macmillan Literature: Novel guide—*Where the Red Fern Grows, The Old Man and the Sea*
- Macmillan Literature: American Literature Text—W.H. Auden, Robert Lowell, Gwendolyn Brooks, John Steinbeck, Thomas Wolfe

Link to Music
- American Music: Cultural Traditions

CHAPTER 28

BEGINNING THE CHAPTER

Discuss with students the ways that the federal government is involved in their lives. Ask students if they think the government should be responsible for those who do not have the means to take care of themselves. Discuss the reasons for their opinions. Tell students that in this chapter they will discover the ways that the federal government was involved in combating the Great Depression.

Recording Journal Notes
To help students get started, ask them to watch for accomplishments of Eleanor Roosevelt and Frances Perkins. Encourage them to investigate what each woman contributed to the Roosevelt administration.

Linking Across Time
Point out that the New Deal had its roots in Progressive legislation of the early 1900s. Franklin Roosevelt's activist style resembled that of his cousin, Theodore. Many of the officials who developed New Deal programs had served as officials in the administration of Woodrow Wilson.

CHAPTER 28

The New Deal
1932–1939

▶ SHOVEL, CIVILIAN CONSERVATION CORPS

Setting the Scene

Focus
When Franklin D. Roosevelt took the oath of office, Congress and the American people were eager to follow the President's leadership. Within months, laws were passed to provide relief, recovery, and reform of the economic system. Two years later, however, millions of Americans were still unemployed, and the New Deal came under increasing criticism. Throughout Roosevelt's second term, many programs were reshaped to permanently change the way government relates to its citizens.

Journal Notes
What role did women play in the Roosevelt administration? Note the details in your journal.

Concepts to Understand
★ Why the political leadership of Roosevelt was effective at bringing about New Deal reforms
★ How New Deal economic reform differed from previous policies

Read to Discover . . .
★ how New Deal legislation attempted to end the Depression.
★ what long-term effects the New Deal programs had on American society.

CULTURAL
- 1932 American speed skaters and bobsledders earn medals in the Winter Olympics
- 1934 Severe drought in the Great Plains creates a dust bowl
- 1935 *Middletown* is published

1932 | **1934**

POLITICAL
- 1933 Repeal of Prohibition
- 1933 "Hundred Days" begins after Roosevelt's inauguration
- 1934 Securities and Exchange Commission is established
- 1935 Social Security Act is passed

UNIT 9 Times of Crisis: 1932–1960

✚ EXTRA CREDIT PROJECT

The National Mood Before Franklin Roosevelt took office, many Americans feared that the country would soon erupt in revolution. They believed that the nation's social fabric was weakened by the Great Depression. Ask interested students to interview someone who lived through the early 1930s. Interviewers should encourage their subjects to recall what people were talking about at the time. What were their concerns? Expectations? Hopes for the future? Ask these students to share their findings with the class.

We Demand by Joe Jones, 1934

Depression painter Joe Jones emphasized working people in his art. In *We Demand,* he concentrated on the efforts of workers to organize the protest to improve their wages and conditions of employment.

▲ NEW DEAL POSTERS

- 1936 Tornadoes kill more than 400 Southerners in 5 states
- 1936 Roosevelt is reelected
- 1937 Roosevelt attempts to pack the Supreme Court
- 1938 Thornton Wilder's play Our Town wins Pulitzer Prize
- 1938 Fair Labor Standards Act passes

CHAPTER 28 CONCEPTS

Concept Mapping Activity

Reproduce the following concepts and generalization on the chalkboard and ask students to copy the material into their notebooks. Ask them to speculate how the concepts of economic reform and political leadership might relate to relieving that condition.

> The government attempts to stimulate the national economy and to shelter individuals from the effects of the Depression.
>
> Economic Reform — Political Leadership

History AND ART

Depression-era paintings like "We Demand" by Joe Jones celebrated workers. These paintings suggested the heroic qualities in ordinary people.

 VIDEODISC

- *GTV: The American People: Fabric of a Nation*

Side 3, Chapter 8
Title: *Shoulder to Shoulder*
Subject: Building on America's diversity during the Depression

See GTV Guide page 88 for complete lesson plan.

Teacher Notes

LESSON PLAN
SECTION 1, 774–778

FOCUS

Bellringer

Prior to taking roll at the beginning of the class period, display Focus Activity Transparency 92 on the overhead projector and assign the accompanying Focus Activity Sheet.

Objectives

Point out the objectives on this page to students in previewing the section content.

Motivating Activity

Ask students what they think President Roosevelt meant when he said, "The only thing we have to fear is fear itself." (Fearing what might happen is often far worse than what actually does happen.)

Use Skills Transparency 28. Assign the Chapter 28 Primary and Secondary Source Reading.

VIDEODISC

- *GTV: A Geographic Perspective on American History*

Side 4, Chapter 3
Title: *Thinking Big*
Subject: Depression, Dust Bowl, New Deal

See GTV Guide page 59 for complete lesson plan.

SECTION 1

Roosevelt Takes Charge

Setting the Scene

Section Focus

President Roosevelt's Inaugural Address attempted to lift the gloom and fear that had blanketed the country. At last, a new President promised action against the Depression. Congress and the American public—some in eager anticipation and others out of desperation—were ready to follow the President's lead.

Objectives

After studying this section, you should be able to
★ identify the traits that made Franklin Roosevelt an effective leader.
★ describe how Roosevelt garnered ideas and support for his New Deal.

Key Term

fireside chat

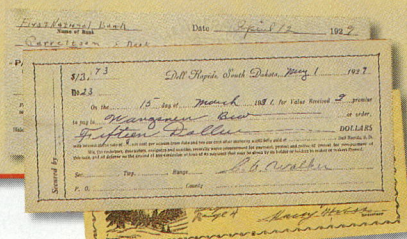

▲ PERSONAL BANK CHECKS

Within his Inaugural Address Franklin D. Roosevelt made the same promises about the nation's recovery that Herbert Hoover and his advisers had been making since 1929. Roosevelt promised that the nation "will endure as it has endured, will revive and will prosper." Unlike Hoover, however, the new President reflected the popular mood of the nation by blaming bankers, "the unscrupulous moneychangers," for allowing starvation in the midst of plenty. The nation was in a kind of war, he said, and strong presidential leadership was needed. Sketching the need for various relief and reform measures, the new President called for immediate legislation. If Congress failed to act quickly, Roosevelt promised to ask for executive authority "as great as the power that would be given to me if we were in fact invaded by a foreign foe."

■ A Strong Leader

Before taking office, Roosevelt displayed little evidence of the leadership he would offer in his 12 years in the White House. One writer described him as "an amiable man ... who without any important qualifications for the office, would very much like to be President." His outstanding attribute was his name, which his cousin Theodore Roosevelt had made well known in American politics.

Early Life

The only son of wealthy parents, FDR, as his friends called him, attended the best schools. At the time of his election, Roosevelt had been in politics for more than 20 years, yet his views on many issues were unknown. Nor did many Americans realize that he had overcome a serious physical handicap.

774 UNIT 9 Times of Crisis: 1932–1960

Classroom Resources for SECTION 1

Teacher's Classroom Resources
- Chapter 28 Study Guide
- Reproducible Lesson Plan
- Reteaching Activity 28-1
- Chapter 28 Cooperative Learning Activity
- Chapter 28 Primary and Secondary Source Readings
- Section Quiz

Multimedia
- Section Focus Transparency 92
- Chapter 28 Skills Transparency
- Unit 9 Digest Transparency
- Chapter 28 Map Transparency
- Testmaker
- Student Self-Test Software
- A Geographic Perspective on American History

In 1921, at age 39, Roosevelt was stricken with polio. Fighting back against the crippling disease, he regained the use of his hands and arms, but he remained paralyzed from the waist down. His painful recovery toughened him and, at the same time, gave him genuine sympathy for the less fortunate. Playwright Robert Sherwood, a close associate, described his toughness and compassion:

> " I tried continually to study him, to try to look beyond his charming and amusing and warmly affectionate surface into his heavily forested interior. But I never understood what was going on in there.... He could be a ruthless politician, but he was the champion of friends and associates who for him were political liabilities ... and of causes which apparently competent observers assured him would be political suicide. "

A Master Politician

Both friends and foes agreed that, despite his complexity, Roosevelt was master of the art of politics. Few Presidents had such varied political training—at local, state, and federal levels—in elected and appointed offices. Elected to the New York legislature in 1910, at the height of the Progressive Era, Roosevelt learned about local government. As assistant secretary of the navy during World War I, he had an insider's view as the Wilson administration organized the federal government to wage war. As governor of New York when the stock market crashed, FDR dealt with many of the same problems he would face as President.

Perhaps Roosevelt's greatest strength as a politician was his warm and understanding approach to people. Where Hoover had withdrawn to the isolation of the White House as the Depression settled in, Roosevelt reached out by radio to the American people in a series of fireside chats. These were informal talks in which the President calmly but confidently explained in simple

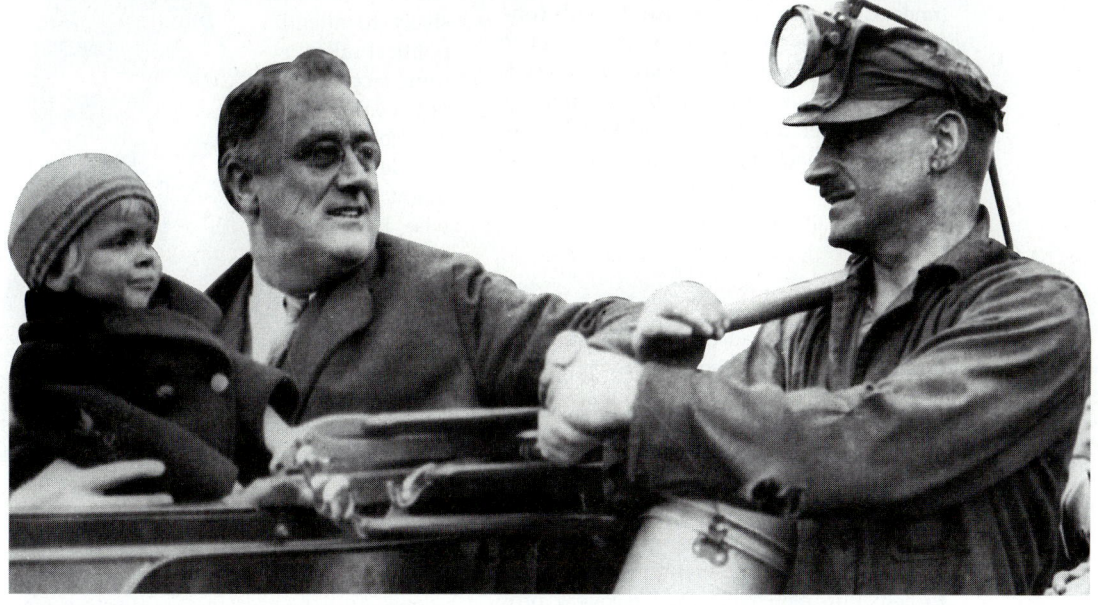

▲ **A Mandate for Change** Farmers in debt, workers without jobs, and bankrupt business owners wanted the government to take bolder action. Americans responded enthusiastically to Franklin D. Roosevelt's call for action to fight the Great Depression. *What personal qualities did Roosevelt bring to the presidency?*

CHAPTER 28 SECTION 1

Independent Practice

Journalism Have students write a newspaper report on President Roosevelt's fireside chat announcing the "bank holiday." Suggest that students focus their reports on Roosevelt's attempt to reassure the American public that the country's financial institutions were sound. Also suggest that they include a concise and interesting headline. **L2**

Did You Know?

Eleanor and Franklin Roosevelt were distant cousins. Eleanor was the niece of Theodore Roosevelt, while Franklin was Theodore's fifth cousin.

Visualizing History At the time Frances Perkins joined Roosevelt's Cabinet, she had been active in labor relations for over 20 years in New York state. **Answer to Caption:** the first woman appointed to a Cabinet post.

---

terms the nation's problems and how the New Deal planned to defeat the Depression. Millions of radio listeners felt that the President was talking directly to them. After a fireside chat, Roosevelt sometimes received as many as 50,000 letters a day.

Roosevelt also knew how to use the press better than his predecessor. Hoover had avoided reporters and refused to answer questions unless they were written out in advance. In contrast, FDR allowed reporters to barrage him with questions during frequent press conferences. This approach made him popular with the press—important shapers of public opinion—and focused public attention on Washington, D.C., and his New Deal programs. "Gone is the fortress that was the White House," wrote one reporter after Roosevelt took office.

Getting Things Done

A product of the Progressive Era, FDR retained the progressives' approach to solving society's problems. As President he was a pragmatist and an experimenter. He sometimes asked three or four people with conflicting opinions to do the same job. FDR compared himself to a quarterback on a football team who called a play, and if it did not work, tried another. Action, he felt, was better than inaction. Most Americans, desperate for relief from the effects of the Depression, agreed with him.

The "Brain Trust"

Roosevelt also had trust in the ability of experts to plan for society. Even before receiving the Democratic nomination for President, he gathered a group of professors from Columbia University to advise him. This group of economists, political scientists, and attorneys was nicknamed the "brain trust" by the press. After Roosevelt became President, the brain trust stayed on to help him plan New Deal recovery programs. In selecting his cabinet, FDR named people who presented a variety of viewpoints and ideas—Northerners and Southerners, liberals and conservatives. He named Republican Harold Ickes as secretary of the interior, and for secretary of agriculture he chose Henry A. Wallace, whose father had the job under Harding. For secretary of labor Roosevelt named the first woman cabinet officer, former child labor reformer Frances Perkins. Other women held important positions in almost every New Deal agency. Like Secretary Perkins, many of these women had been social workers. Now the President was calling upon them to administer the federal government's social and relief programs.

Eleanor Roosevelt as Adviser

Outside the brain trust, the adviser that Roosevelt relied on most was his wife, Eleanor. Because of his paralysis, FDR moved with difficulty in a wheelchair or with heavy braces on his legs. As a result, he asked Eleanor to assume a significant role in his administration. The President called her his "eyes and ears" outside the White House. During the first year of the New Deal, she traveled extensively to attend political rallies, tour factories, visit coal mines, and contact many people that FDR might not otherwise have

Visualizing History ▲ **SECRETARY OF LABOR** Frances Perkins was appointed secretary of labor by Roosevelt. A long-time advocate of minimum wage and maximum hour laws, child-labor restrictions, and other progressive reforms, she was one of only two cabinet members to serve throughout Roosevelt's four terms. *What was unique about her appointment?*

776 UNIT 9 Times of Crisis: 1932–1960

Cooperative Learning

Divide the class into groups of four or five students. Have each group discuss the following statement: The New Deal was a continuation of the Progressive Era. Have group members take turns offering information from Section 1 that supports or opposes the statement. Then have the groups use this information to decide whether or not they agree with the statement. Have a representative from each group report on the group's decision. **L2**

AMERICAN PORTRAITS

Eleanor Roosevelt
1884–1962

Eleanor Roosevelt did not herself hold public office until she was a 61-year-old widow. But as First Lady she fought tenaciously for social justice and added a sense of compassion to the New Deal.

Although painfully shy as a young girl, Eleanor Roosevelt emerged as a vibrant public personality during the 1920s when her husband, FDR, was recovering from polio. She did all she could to keep his name in the public mind. After Roosevelt's election, she spoke for people who otherwise would have been ignored—women, the poor and the underprivileged, and African Americans.

Sensitive to racial injustice, she spoke up so strongly for civil rights that she won African American support for the New Deal. A lecturer and columnist, Eleanor Roosevelt later worked for global human rights in the United Nations.

met. At cabinet meetings, the President would report, "My missus says that people are working for wages well below the minimum . . . in the town she visited last week." Eleanor Roosevelt shared Franklin's concern for the victims of the Depression—close friends thought that her concern was even deeper than his—and the belief that decisive government action was needed to conquer society's ills.

The First New Deal

President Roosevelt fulfilled his promise to provide "action now." Americans waited to see what he would do.

Restoring Faith in Banks

On Sunday, March 5, 1933, the day after his inauguration, Roosevelt called a special session of Congress. On Monday he used an old law still on the books to suspend the nation's banking activity. Many Americans had lost faith in banks after the crash, withdrew their money, and kept it at home. Banks needed depositors' funds to make loans that would help recovery, but, in many areas, the loss of deposits was so great that banks had to close their doors. After a week in office, the President went on the radio with his first fireside chat. He explained that only healthy banks would be allowed to reopen. He assured Americans that it would be "safer to keep money in a reopened bank than under the mattress." The next day most banks began to do business again, and in a few days deposits exceeded withdrawals. As the President's calm assurances restored public confidence in the nation's financial system, the bank crisis ended.

The Hundred Days

That first week was just the beginning of feverish activity. In the "Hundred Days" between March 9 and June 16, 1933, Congress passed 15 major bills, more than had ever been enacted in such a short time. Most were bills that the President submitted and that Congress passed with little debate. Seldom had a President enjoyed such overwhelming support.

Meeting "Each Day's Troubles"

Roosevelt took office with no clear idea of how to solve the nation's economic crisis. "There's nothing to do," he said, "but meet each day's troubles as they come." The New

CHAPTER 28 SECTION 1

Enrich
Have students research the contributions to the New Deal of one of the following members of Roosevelt's "brain trust": Raymond Moley, Rexford Tugwell, Adolph Berle, Eleanor Roosevelt, Harry Hopkins, Harold Ickes, Frances Perkins, or Henry Wallace. Have students present their information in an oral report.

CLOSE
Write the following statement on the chalkboard:
  Franklin Delano Roosevelt was the right person to occupy the presidency at this time.
  Ask students to discuss this statement based on what they learned in Section 1.

Visualizing History In many movies of the period, bank executives were portrayed as cold-hearted figures who foreclosed on mortgages and called in loans. In fact, they had few other choices.
Answer to Caption: suspended the nation's banking activity, thus preventing further runs on banks; reassured Americans that they would not lose their bank deposits.

 ▲ **Bank Closings** Afraid for the safety of their savings, panicked depositors line up outside a bank. Such "runs"—when all depositors tried to withdraw their money at the same time—usually caused those banks to fail, making their depositors' fears come true. *How did Roosevelt handle the bank crisis?*

Deal, therefore, was not a carefully worked out reform plan. Instead, it was a series of measures quickly drawn up to attack the Depression in many ways at once. Some laws were in response to special demands from specific groups in society. Some were even passed against the President's wishes, but he signed them to head off something that he might like even less, or to avoid holding up other legislation. However, New Deal programs had three general purposes: recovery from the Depression, relief for its victims, and reform of the economic system. Much legislation reflected all three goals.

From 1933 to early 1935, the dominating goals of the Roosevelt administration were recovery and relief. During the "First New Deal," as this phase was called, the President and his advisers thought that a series of temporary measures could get the economy moving again. From this beginning, recovery would come on its own momentum. Therefore, little additional legislation followed the Hundred Days of the First New Deal. The administration merely implemented the laws that the Senate and the House had created and waited for recovery to occur.

Section 1 ★ Review

Checking for Understanding
1. **Identify** FDR, brain trust, Frances Perkins, the Hundred Days.
2. **Define** fireside chat.
3. **Cite** the political experience that prepared Roosevelt to lead the nation out of the Depression.
4. **Explain** Roosevelt's approach to solving problems.

Critical Thinking
5. **Making Comparisons** Compare Roosevelt's style in managing the crisis to Hoover's. Why did the public support Roosevelt?

778 UNIT 9 Times of Crisis: 1932–1960

Answers to SECTION 1 REVIEW
1. FDR, 774; brain trust, 776; Frances Perkins, 776; the Hundred Days, 777
2. All vocabulary words are defined in the Glossary.
3. a progressive background, served in New York legislature, assistant secretary of Navy in Wilson administration, Governor of New York
4. a progressive reform approach emphasizing openness to new ideas, experimentation, and action.
5. Roosevelt was informal and warm, more in tune with the nation's mood, and willing to seek public support, such as by blaming the Depression on bankers. He used the media to keep the public informed. Hoover was aloof and isolated, which made him unpopular with the press and public.

SECTION 2

Reform, Relief, and Recovery

Setting the Scene

Section Focus
Many of the laws passed during the Hundred Days were popularly known by their initials—AAA, NRA, TVA, and CCC. People jokingly called them the New Deal's "alphabet soup," yet the programs gave the American people a sense of hope. Many were intended as stopgap measures, but their effects are still felt today.

◀ WPA POSTER, LATE 1930S

Objectives
After studying this section, you should be able to
★ give examples of how Roosevelt's policies helped and hurt the rural poor.
★ compare the effectiveness of measures aimed at farmers and city workers.

Key Terms
deficit spending, pump priming, dole, foreclosure

Both Hoover and Roosevelt believed that prosperity would return with a little help to spark the economy. So, like Hoover, FDR sought the help of the business community and spoke of an alliance of "business and banking, agriculture and industry, and labor and capital." But he differed from Hoover in the amount and variety of legislation he proposed and in his willingness to call on the full powers of the federal government to solve national problems.

■ Financial Reform

In June 1933 Congress passed the Glass-Steagall Act. This law prohibited banks from investing in the stock market and created a Federal Deposit Insurance Corporation (FDIC) to insure depositors' savings. Although the program was opposed by the American Bankers' Association as "unscientific, unjust, and dangerous," federal insurance made people feel that their money would be safe in banks.

Congress also responded to the demand that the government prevent stock market fraud. The Federal Securities Act of 1933 required companies that issued or marketed stocks and bonds to provide complete and truthful information to purchasers. Congress followed this act in 1934 with the Securities and Exchange Commission (SEC) to regulate the stock market.

When Roosevelt took office, he faced strong pressure to inflate the currency. A number of senators and representatives wanted to stimulate recovery by putting into circulation billions of dollars in new paper money. Roosevelt, however, rejected inflation and took a conservative approach in his early efforts to achieve recovery. Still, he realized that to keep relief agencies from

CHAPTER 28 The New Deal 1932–1939

CHAPTER 28
SECTION 2

TEACH
Guided Practice

History Write the following New Deal programs on the chalkboard. Ask students to organize the programs in the following categories: Agriculture Relief, Industrial Relief, and Help for the Unemployed. Students should also indicate the purpose of each program.

Agricultural Adjustment Act (Agriculture; 1933; paid farmers to cut production and so increased prices); Federal Emergency Relief Administration (Unemployed; 1933; provided money to the states for relief programs); Civil Works Administration (Unemployed; 1933; hired the unemployed for public works projects); Farm Security Administration (Agriculture; 1933; gave loans to help farm tenants buy land); Civilian Conservation Corps (Unemployed; 1933; offered outdoor work to unemployed single men between ages of 18 and 25); National Recovery Administration (Industrial; 1933; directed the NIRA, which proposed a partnership of business, labor, and government); Public Works Administration (Unemployed; 1933; set up projects to provide jobs and to stimulate business). **L2**

◀ CHILDREN PICKETING, ST. PAUL, MINNESOTA, 1937

closing and millions of Americans from starving, **deficit spending** was necessary. In other words, the federal government's annual spending would have to exceed its income.

Help for the Jobless

From deficit spending, the New Deal moved to **pump priming**—pouring government money into the economy through loans and federal spending in the hope of stimulating recovery. Roosevelt called for government to give money directly to people who would spend it. Increased spending would increase demand for consumer goods, New Dealers claimed, which would stimulate production and create jobs.

By 1933, 12 million to 15 million Americans—1 of every 4 workers—was unemployed, and many were on the verge of starvation. At first Roosevelt, like Hoover, thought that local agencies should handle relief until industry and agriculture recovered enough to provide jobs. It soon became clear, however, that states, cities, and local charities had exhausted their resources.

The Federal Government Steps In

In May 1933 Congress established a Federal Emergency Relief Administration (FERA). FERA made outright grants to states and municipalities to distribute as they chose. They generally provided a **dole**—direct gifts of money, food, and clothing. Although the dole was the cheapest and quickest form of relief, its critics were concerned that people who received handouts would lose their self-respect and job skills, making them even more unemployable. So once the federal government had met the need for emergency relief, New Dealers searched for alternatives to the dole.

The Public Works Administration (PWA), created in June 1933, offered jobs instead of handouts. Under the direction of Secretary of the Interior Harold Ickes, the program provided jobs on construction projects—improving highways and building dams, sewer systems, waterworks, schools, and other government buildings. The PWA generally worked through private contractors, and Ickes broke down long-standing racial barriers in the construction trades by insisting that contractors hire African Americans.

In the autumn of 1933, Harry Hopkins, head of the FERA, won approval for a Civil Works Administration (CWA) to hire jobless persons. During the winter of 1933–1934, the CWA employed 4 million people—300,000 of them women. The CWA built or improved 1,000 airports, 500,000 miles of roads, 40,000 school buildings, and 3,500 parks, playgrounds, and playing fields. But the cost of all this was tremendous—$1 billion in just five months. In the spring of 1934, Roosevelt gave in to fierce criticism from conservatives and cancelled the program.

The TVA

One early New Deal program combined emergency relief and pump priming with long-term economic and social planning. In May 1933, after Roosevelt's prodding, Congress established the Tennessee Valley Authority (TVA), designed to promote the development of a seven-state region.

Before the TVA, the natural resources of the Tennessee Valley had long been exploited.

Critical Thinking

Relating Past to Present Briefly review the recent savings and loan crisis. Then ask students to compare this crisis with the banking crisis of the 1930s by answering the following questions: How were the two crises the same? How were they different? What approaches used to solve the 1930s crisis might have been used to settle the 1990s crisis? What do we know today that might have helped Roosevelt settle the 1930s crisis? Discuss students' answers. **L2**

Forests were leveled, and heavy rainfalls caused erosion and disastrous floods. Poor farmers attempted to work worn-out land, and many people were on relief.

Employing as many as 40,000 workers at a time, the TVA built 20 dams for flood control and improved 5 others. The TVA also moved farmers from marginal lands, reforested millions of acres, built power plants and fertilizer factories, and even started new towns. But the most notable change was the immense amount of cheap electricity that the TVA produced. Its increased availability allowed farmers to install refrigerators, milking machines, and other equipment. Cheap power also attracted industry.

Despite its obvious benefits, the TVA had its critics. Some charged that funds for the TVA should be used to support programs nationwide. Above all, the TVA was attacked by the power companies. One goal of the TVA was to provide a basis to determine fair electricity rates all over the country. But private power companies argued that to use the TVA for this purpose was unfair because the government charged large parts of the cost of electricity production to the cost of flood control and navigation. For the federal government to take over the production of private power, they argued, was unfair and communistic. Although the power companies were powerful enough to prevent any more regional authorities like the TVA, the New Deal did build other power plants, the most famous of which was the Grand Coulee Dam in Washington state.

The CCC

The most generally admired New Deal relief agency was the Civilian Conservation Corps (CCC), established in March 1933. It offered outdoor work to unemployed single men, 18 to 25 years old, at $30 per month, $22 of which went back to their families. By midsummer the CCC had established 1,500 camps. During its existence, the CCC helped conserve the nation's natural resources by putting 3 million young men to work planting trees, fighting forest fires, building reservoirs, and stopping soil erosion.

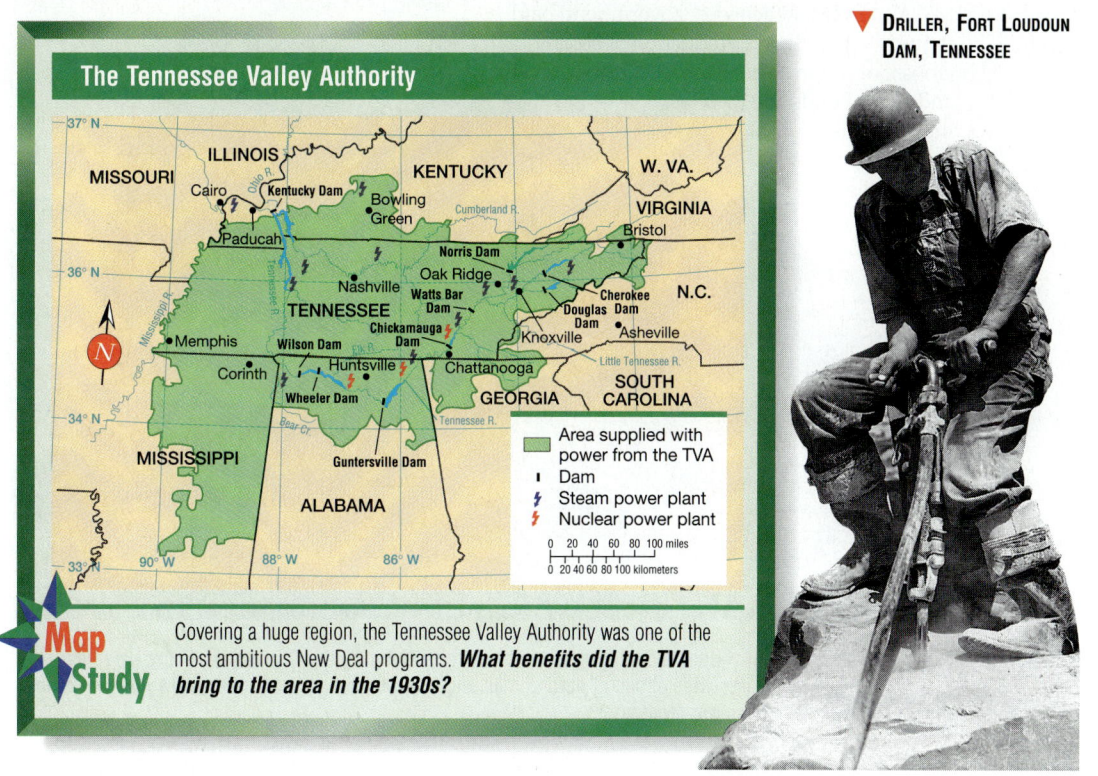

DRILLER, FORT LOUDOUN DAM, TENNESSEE

Map Study Covering a huge region, the Tennessee Valley Authority was one of the most ambitious New Deal programs. **What benefits did the TVA bring to the area in the 1930s?**

CHAPTER 28 SECTION 2

Map Study Using Maps

Answer: flood control, cheap power, economic growth and development, jobs

Skills Practice

Which states were provided with electricity by the Tennessee Valley Authority? (Alabama, Georgia, Kentucky, Mississippi, North Carolina, Tennessee, Virginia)

Did You Know?

The young men who worked in the Civilian Conservation Corps came from all parts of the country, but mostly from the large cities. One of their most important tasks was planting trees. By the time the CCC was phased out in 1942, more than 200 million trees had been planted and 17 million acres of land had been reforested. And some 3 million young men had spent time working in the CCC. It was considered one of the most successful New Deal programs because it aided both human and natural resources.

Cooperative Learning

Organize students into groups of four or five and have group members work together to write an answer to the following question: Were the measures President Roosevelt took to help the unemployed simply "make work" government programs, or did they have a truly positive impact on the economy? Explain your answer.

Answers should be developed in three stages—brainstorming, first draft, and final draft. Call on groups randomly to report their progress. **L1, L2**

CHAPTER 28
SECTION 2

Independent Practice

Analyzing Government Policies Tell students that when someone attacked the New Deal as being too "left wing," Roosevelt shot back, "Why do we have to be 'socialist' or 'capitalist'? The United States is a big enough country to have several systems going at once. It has brains and tolerance enough to accommodate them. We don't have to force everything into some doctrinaire model."

Have students use information from Section 2 to write a brief essay supporting or challenging Roosevelt's view of the New Deal. Select students with opposing views to read their essays to the class. Use these readings as a starting point for a class discussion. **L3**

Visualizing History The young men employed by the CCC, many of whom lacked prior job experience, were most likely to be out of work in an economic downturn. Have students consider why. (lacked seniority, work experience)
Answer to Caption: Spending fuels the economy by encouraging production of goods and services.

Relief for Agriculture

The impoverished condition of farmers in the Tennessee Valley was by no means unique in 1933. Since 1929 banks had foreclosed on the property of 10 percent of the nation's farmers. In **foreclosure** actions, when a borrower cannot make loan payments, the bank seizes the property that was put up as security for the loan. Farmers threatened to stop producing food unless their debt burden and agricultural prices improved. The New Deal provided relief for heavily indebted farmers by placing a five-year moratorium, or freeze, on mortgage foreclosures. But New Dealers recognized that the root of the farmers' plight was low agricultural prices, and that this situation was related to a problem that had plagued farmers since the end of World War I—overproduction.

The Agricultural Adjustment Act

Roosevelt proposed an unusual approach: stop agricultural surpluses by paying farmers to *not* produce crops. In May 1933, Congress passed the Agricultural Adjustment Act (AAA), under which the government paid farmers who reduced production of basic crops like cotton, wheat, tobacco, hogs, and corn. Funds for these payments came from a tax levied on flour mills, slaughterhouses, and other businesses that processed food.

In 1933 cotton farmers plowed under a quarter of their acreage, and hog producers killed 6 million piglets instead of fattening them for market. In 1934 and 1935, farmers withdrew 10 million acres from production and received more than $1 billion in benefit payments. Surpluses were greatly reduced by 1936, and total farm income rose by more than 50 percent.

Large commercial farmers, who concentrated on one crop, benefited more than smaller farmers who raised several. The crop reduction program actually hurt some people. In the West and Southwest, Mexican migrant workers suffered when growers raised less produce and so hired fewer pickers. Tenant farmers and sharecroppers were forced off the land they worked as owners took it out of production. About 150,000 white tenants and almost 195,000 African American tenants left farming during the 1930s. To stop this trend, the New Deal created the Farm Security Administration to give loans to help tenants purchase land.

 **Jobs** Unemployment was a major problem during the Depression. Many New Deal programs were aimed at putting men and women back to work. *Why were jobs important to economic recovery?*

Critical Thinking

Evaluating Tactics Point out that union leaders criticized the NRA because they felt it allowed employers to ignore the right of the unions to collective bargaining. In 1934 workers all over the country struck, demanding the right to organize. Ask students the following question: Did the workers have the right to strike to get their demands met? Why or why not? (Answers will vary. Supporting argument: strikes most effective means of getting employers to meet demands. Opposing argument: strikes hurt economy; ongoing negotiations better tactic.) **L2**

▲ **THE CCC** Many work programs for the unemployed were started during the Roosevelt administration. The CCC offered outdoor work to unemployed single men. *What work did the CCC do?*

CHAPTER 28 SECTION 2

Visualizing History The Civilian Conservation Corps enabled many young men to learn new skills. The CCC became a precedent for a number of government-sponsored jobs programs over the years, including the Job Corps. **Answer to Caption:** built reservoirs, planted trees, fought forest fires, and helped prevent soil erosion

But only 3,400 African American farmers received any of this money. Landless farmers joined other urban and rural migrants who wandered the country in search of jobs.

The Dust Bowl

In 1934 and 1935 a terrible disaster struck the Great Plains and added to the number of farmers on the move. The origins of the disaster arose during World War I, when high crop prices tempted farmers to grow wheat and cotton on what traditionally had been grazing lands. Plows broke up the deep, tough sod that had prevented erosion and conserved moisture in this semiarid region. When the years from 1933 to 1935 were unusually dry, the area began to turn to desert. Dust storms carried away so much topsoil that a haze obscured the sun, sometimes as far away as the Atlantic coast. Between 1934 and 1939, nearly 350,000 farm families left the dust bowl.

To take care of immediate distress, Congress provided the farmers in the dust bowl with funds for new seed and livestock. For long-term solutions, the Department of Agriculture helped farmers plant millions of trees in shelter belts to cut wind velocity and help retain moisture. The government also encouraged farmers to return the land to grazing. Yet there was much criticism of New Deal farm policies. Many farmers did not like being told what to raise or how much to plant. To others, decreasing food supplies when people were hungry seemed immoral. However, the New Deal provided more direct assistance to farmers than to any other group, and saved thousands of farm families from poverty and despair.

Native Americans and the New Deal

The New Deal worked to change long-standing government policies affecting Native Americans, including a reversal of

Fact or Fiction?
Young unemployed women could not take part in the CCC.

FICTION: While women complained that they were excluded, a few special camps were set up for them. But only 8,000 participated in a program that put over 3 million young men to work.

The following material is available from Glencoe and may be used to enrich Chapter 28:

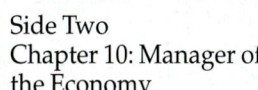
VIDEODISC
Powers of the President

Side Two
Chapter 10: Manager of the Economy

Sidelights: Woody Guthrie

One of those who abandoned the Dust Bowl and headed west for the promised land of California was Woody Guthrie. He soon gave up farm work and devoted his whole time to song writing and performing. Guthrie wrote songs about the everyday lives of working people—the hardships of the migrant workers, the struggle to organize unions, and the fight for racial equality and freedom. Once considered radical and subversive, Guthrie's songs—most notably "This Land Is Your Land"—are now national treasures.

CHAPTER 28
SECTION 2

Using Graphs
Point out the drop in union membership in the 1930s. Ask what may have caused it. (the Great Depression) Then ask what caused the rise in membership in the 1940s. (New Deal legislation)
Caption: Section 7a of the NIRA required that every NRA code recognize workers' right to join unions and to bargain.

Did You Know?
During the New Deal years, people had more time on their hands and less money than they had in the 1920s. This had a great impact on how people used their leisure time. Sports that were rather expensive to play—golf, for instance—declined in popularity. For example, there were as many as 1,155 private golf clubs in the United States in 1930. This number fell to 763 by 1936.

---

the gradual loss of land and tribal authority. Earlier, the federal government had opted for a number of different policies with widely divergent goals.

With the end of the frontier wars in the late 1800s, the federal government had at long last abandoned a policy that could fairly be summarized as expulsion and extermination. The General Allotment Act in 1887 provided for the division of reservation land into plots to be granted to individual Native Americans. This arrangement was based on the idea that the best thing for Native Americans was to make them as much like other Americans as possible.

The education system reinforced this idea: children were taken from home at an early age, crowded into boarding schools, and given some "book learning" before being sent back to the reservation. They acquired little knowledge of the culture of their ancestors. Meanwhile, older people received just enough food to sustain them.

However well-meaning, this policy was scarcely better than the old policy. By 1934 Native Americans held only 48 million of the 133 million acres they had possessed in 1887. Although Native Americans were citizens of the United States, state laws often discriminated against them, and the federal government generally ran their affairs for them.

Some improvement began during the Coolidge administration with a reorganization of health services for Native Americans. Later, President Hoover appointed two dedicated individuals as commissioner and deputy commissioner of Indian Affairs. They began a reform of the workings of the department.

The Indian Reorganization Act

More action on Native American affairs was taken during the New Deal years. The Roosevelt administration promoted a new approach that was made law in the Indian Reorganization Act in 1934. This act repealed the allotment policy and returned to tribal ownership Native American lands previously open to sale.

According to John Collier, commissioner of Indian Affairs, the act had a worthwhile purpose. It would enable Native Americans "to earn a decent livelihood and lead self-respecting, organized lives in harmony with their own aims and ideals."

Instead of promoting individual ownership, the federal government now encouraged Native Americans to revert to their own traditions. Instead of being weakened, tribal organization was strengthened. Native Americans were encouraged to become members of the federal Indian Service. Children were now taught the traditions of their own people in school. Ceremonies, art forms, and handicrafts were revived.

New Benefits

The new arrangements brought benefits that could be seen in the reversal of two disturbing trends: Native American landholdings increased after 1934, and the Native American population once again began to increase. Since then Native Americans, now a rapidly growing minority group, have continued to fight in the courts and legislatures for religious freedom, water rights, and land claims.

■ Industrial Relief

Roosevelt's advisers believed that industry, like agriculture, suffered from overproduction. In June 1933 the New Deal tried to help industry with the National Industrial Recovery Act (NIRA).

The NIRA

To control production, the NIRA provided that representatives of labor and of management from competing companies draw up "codes of fair competition" in each industry. These codes set the prices of products to eliminate discount selling. They shortened workers' hours in order to create more jobs, and they established minimum-wage levels. To spread production among as many firms as possible, factories were limited to two shifts a day. To direct this complex program, the act created the National Recovery Administration (NRA).

Sidelights: Relations with the Soviet Union

Relations between the United States and the Soviet Union began to improve in November 1933 when, at President Roosevelt's request, Soviet Commissar for Foreign Affairs Maxim Litvinov visited Washington, D.C. At a formal ceremony, the United States recognized the Soviet government for the first time. In addition, the Soviets pledged to stop broadcasting anti-American propaganda and interfering in American internal affairs.

Power to enforce the codes was very limited, so the NRA used the power of public opinion to enlist the cooperation of business. Those that signed code agreements were given signs with blue eagles and the words "We Do Our Part." Consumers were encouraged to purchase goods only from businesses that displayed the signs. The NIRA, however, never worked out as planned. Prices rose faster than wages. Businesses complained that large companies wrote the codes to favor themselves and to put small competitors out of business.

Workers Turn to Unions

Probably no group suffered more than people who worked for hourly wages. By 1933 one-third of these workers were unemployed. The earnings of the rest had shrunk as their rates or hours were cut. The idea spread that the best way to restore workers' wages and purchasing power was to strengthen labor unions. Under Section 7a of the NIRA, every NRA code guaranteed workers the right to organize unions and to bargain collectively with their employers. As a result, between May and October 1933, American Federation of Labor (AFL) membership jumped by about a million workers.

In 1934 a wave of strikes swept the nation as workers demanded the right to organize for improved wages and job security. Many of these strikes became violent, and most resulted in defeat for the workers, as police generally sided with employers. Although sympathetic to organized labor, the only way the NRA could punish a company was to take away its Blue Eagle symbol. Workers began to demand stronger labor laws.

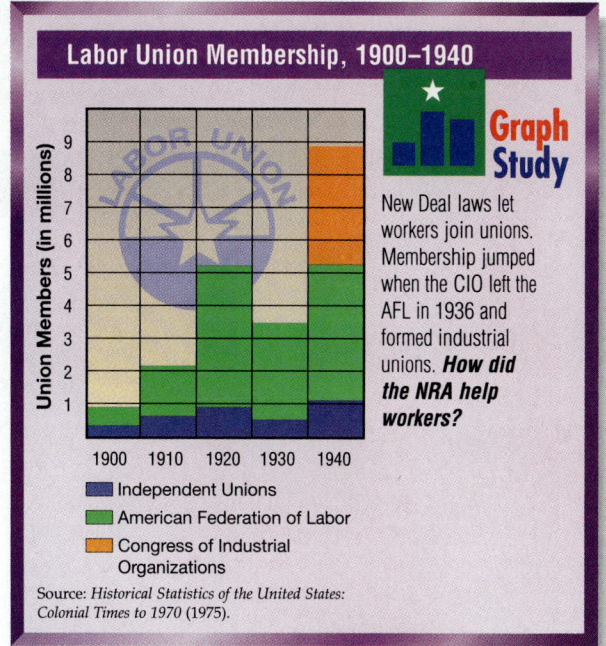

Graph Study

New Deal laws let workers join unions. Membership jumped when the CIO left the AFL in 1936 and formed industrial unions. *How did the NRA help workers?*

New Solutions Needed

As the nation entered 1935, American spirits sagged. Despite the New Deal, farm prices and industrial wages were well below 1929 levels, and workers remained unemployed and poor. To many Americans, the New Deal was taking too long and accomplishing too little. FDR clearly saw that he must find other means to restore prosperity.

Section 2 ★ Review

Checking for Understanding
1. **Identify** FDIC, FERA, PWA, CCC, AAA, NRA, Section 7a.
2. **Define** deficit spending, pump priming, dole, foreclosure.
3. **List** three programs designed to create jobs by employing workers on projects to benefit the nation.
4. **Explain** Roosevelt's theory that giving money directly to people would stimulate economic recovery.

Critical Thinking
5. **Making Judgments** During widespread unemployment, is government money better used as a dole or for more expensive work-relief programs? Why?

CHAPTER 28 CONNECTIONS

Teaching Connections

The term "dust bowl" was first used by Associated Press reporter Robert Geiger in a story published in April 1935. Mention that the dust storms continued on and off for 10 years. The westerly winds carried the dust as much as 300 miles into the Atlantic, depositing it on ships that plied the ocean. Ask students to identify a similar situation to the Dust Bowl going on today. (Most students will suggest the desertification of the Sahel region of Africa.)

Did You Know?

The first of the great dust storms began on November 11, 1933. In South Dakota the sky was pitch dark by noon. Historian William Manchester writes that by the time the sun reappeared "fields had been replaced by sand while roads, trees, sheds, fences, and machinery had disappeared beneath great hanging dunes of soil. By then the wind was headed for Texas. A towering pall darkened Chicago and was visible as far east as Albany."

CONNECTIONS  History AND ENVIRONMENT CONNECTIONS

▲ FARM IN THE DUST BOWL

The Dust Bowl

As the entire nation struggled to cope with the Depression, farmers in Kansas, Oklahoma, and Texas suffered from the scourges of drought and dust. From the 1890s to the 1920s, grasslands in this part of the Great Plains were put to the plow, and when rain fell, they were bountiful. But in the 1930s, the rains failed. As crops withered, leaving bare dirt exposed, the region's high winds lifted the fine topsoil to create dust storms called "dusters."

Large-scale mechanized farming on the plains after 1900 exposed huge areas of soil. Farmers eager to maximize yields overtilled the soil and burned wheat stubble to kill weeds. These poor soil-conservation practices and the long drought created a dust bowl on the plains throughout most of the 1930s, as millions of tons of airborne powdery topsoil buried crops and killed livestock.

The dust bowl took its toll on people too. People sat helpless while their farms blew away. They sometimes lost their way and died in the thick storms while only yards from their houses. Thousands of families abandoned their land to seek work in the fields and orchards of California, Oregon, and Washington. Many migrants, however, could not find work even after they reached their destination. Those who stayed on their land were encouraged to plant crops that conserved the soil.

Making the Environment Connection

1. How did humans change the natural environment of the Great Plains in the early twentieth century?
2. How was a dust bowl created in this region?

Linking Past and Present

3. What soil-conservation practices are used today?

Answers to CONNECTIONS

1. By plowing and planting crops, they broke up the grasslands that covered the topsoil and held it together.
2. The development of large-scale mechanized farming exposed huge areas of soil which dried out in the drought and was carried away by the wind.
3. crop stubble left in place; wind breaks planted; soil-conserving crops rotated into fields

SECTION 3

The Second New Deal

Setting the Scene

Section Focus

Some of Roosevelt's critics planted seeds of dissatisfaction with the New Deal by appealing to the jobless, the displaced, the underpaid, and the elderly. These victims of the Depression were fertile ground for the radical ideas floating about in 1935. FDR recognized that the New Deal must be reassessed and redirected. Yet even after strong voter support in the 1936 presidential election, Roosevelt faced continued opposition.

Objectives

After studying this section, you should be able to

★ list the special interest groups that challenged Roosevelt.

★ outline the steps the Second New Deal took to achieve reform.

★ identify the events that led to the end of the New Deal.

Key Terms

coalition, craft union, industrial union, recession

◀ UNION CARDS

For the 10 million unemployed Americans in 1935, Senator Huey Long's slogan, "Every Man a King," was an appealing fantasy but a far cry from their reality. They received just enough relief to keep themselves and their families alive. Their miserable dole seemed hardly worth the humiliation it caused. Millions of elderly Americans faced a similar stark reality, without savings, without adequate medical care, and without hope.

■ Attacks on the New Deal

The radical critics of the New Deal posed a greater threat to the Roosevelt administration than the Republican party. As time passed, the ranks of New Deal critics grew. Some wanted a more active government. Others felt that the government was interfering too much in American life.

Three Prominent Attackers

Every week Father Charles E. Coughlin, the "Radio Priest" whose broadcasts reached 40 million listeners, bitterly attacked Roosevelt. Originally a New Deal supporter, Coughlin accused the President of turning the New Deal into a "raw deal." His political organization, the National Union for Social Justice, called for such socialistic measures as heavy taxes on the wealthy and a guaranteed income for everyone. Gradually, Coughlin began expressing anti-Semitic, or anti-Jewish, views. In 1942 Catholic leaders ordered him to stop broadcasting.

An even more dangerous rival to Roosevelt was Huey Long, senator from Louisiana. With the backing of the rural poor, he became extremely powerful in his home state and used it as a base on which to build national popularity. With his folksy, humorous manner, Long knew how to win

CHAPTER 28 The New Deal 1932–1939 787

 **NEW DEAL CRITICS** Father Charles Coughlin (left) reached millions of listeners before the Catholic Church made him stop his radio broadcasts. Until his assassination, Senator Huey Long (right) was equally popular. *What idea did these leaders share?*

audiences. He proposed confiscating the property of the rich and giving every family a home, $2,000 a year, and a free college education for their children. His followers organized hundreds of "Share-Our-Wealth" clubs.

Less colorful than Father Coughlin or Senator Long, but just as threatening, was Dr. Francis Townsend. A former public health official, Townsend was shocked by the plight of older Americans who were no longer able to compete for jobs. He proposed a plan that he claimed would provide relief for the elderly and at the same time stimulate economic recovery, calling for the federal government to pay all Americans over age 60 a pension of $200 per month. Recipients would be required to spend their entire pension check within 30 days. Townsend claimed that not only would this plan end the suffering of older Americans, but the money they pumped into the economy would increase consumption and create jobs. The pensions could be financed by a national sales tax on consumer goods, Townsend argued. His innovative plan attracted millions of devoted advocates.

Fighting Back

Roosevelt's annual address to Congress in January 1935 answered his attackers. He admitted that "we have not weeded out the overprivileged and we have not effectively lifted up the underprivileged." The President announced a "Second New Deal" to put recovery on a new course. This new phase showed greater concern for the less fortunate and abandoned efforts to enlist the support of business.

The political groups supporting the New Deal also changed. Roosevelt had played down partisanship to gain the support of moderate and progressive Republicans. Now he devoted his energies to achieving his goals through the Democratic party alone. To strengthen it, he attempted to form a coalition, or combination, of separate groups whose members could be counted on to vote for Democrats. To the traditional source of Democratic political power—the South and Northern urban political machines—Roosevelt attempted to add labor unions, farmers, and African Americans. Many of the Second New Deal's programs were intended to appeal to these groups.

Sidelights: Roosevelt's Press Conferences

Throughout his presidency Franklin Roosevelt averaged about two press conferences a week. These were informal affairs, with as many as 200 reporters cramming into the Oval Office to hear Roosevelt's pronouncements. He would answer questions off the cuff, and he seemed to know each reporter by name. With a mixture of charm, openness, and familiarity, Roosevelt built a working relationship with the press unmatched by any other United States President.

Work Relief and Social Security

The most immediate result of the New Deal's shift in attitude was the President's demand for large-scale work relief. Responding to Roosevelt's request, Congress appropriated funds in April 1935 for "work relief and to increase employment by providing useful projects." An immense new agency, the Works Progress Administration (WPA) was set up under the direction of Harry Hopkins to provide a chance for all people to use their skills to earn an income.

The WPA employed writers, teachers, librarians, actors, musicians, and artists. A "junior WPA," the National Youth Administration (NYA) helped high school and college students stay in school by giving them part-time work, such as typing and library cataloguing. Existing work-relief programs were expanded. The Reconstruction Finance Corporation lent large sums to businesses and to local governments. The Civilian Conservation Corps increased the number it employed. The Public Works Administration finally rolled into high gear and provided hundreds of thousands of jobs.

The unemployable needed help during the Depression as much as the unemployed. Persons with no source of support and no ability to earn an income had no place to go. To remedy this problem, Congress in 1935 passed the Social Security Act. Under this program, the federal government financed state unemployment insurance plans through payroll taxes paid by employers. Federal grants to states provided care for dependent mothers and children. The core of the program was retirement benefits, paid for by taxes on workers and employers, that people could collect when they stopped working at age 65.

The Social Security Act had flaws. For example, the act did not protect some groups who needed it most, such as farm workers and domestic help. Since 65 percent of all African American employees in the 1930s fell into these two categories, the act neglected this group the most. Yet the Social Security Act was a landmark in reforming society. It set the policy that an industrial society was responsible for those who, through no fault of their own, are unable to work.

Business and Labor

Several pieces of legislation demonstrated Roosevelt's efforts to appeal to the political coalition he was forming. Early in the New Deal, taxes remained at levels set in the 1920s. Now Congress passed tax increases on the incomes of wealthy Americans, inheritance taxes on the property of deceased persons, and higher taxes on corporations. Although the law was attacked as communistic, Roosevelt was more interested, some felt, in heading off the various "share-the-wealth" schemes than he was in actually redistributing the nation's wealth.

▲ **Attack on the New Deal** Some Americans thought the New Deal was too restrictive to free enterprise. This cartoonist shows Uncle Sam tied down by New Deal agencies and laws, much as Gulliver was bound by the Lilliputians in the book Gulliver's Travels. **Why might critics have thought this way?**

CHAPTER 28 SECTION 2

Did You Know?
One program financed by the WPA was the Federal Arts Project. Hospitals, schools, and government offices could request loans of works of art created by artists who were members of the project. In the first three years of the project's operation, some 13,000 institutions received loans of 186,452 artworks. Ask students to find out if any government buildings in their community have WPA artworks.

Visualizing History Discuss the way the cartoonist views the government and the American people. Ask: Who today might share the views expressed in this cartoon? (those who would like to reduce the size of the federal government) **Answer to Caption:** The New Deal represented an unprecedented expansion of the government into areas of the private sector. Many Americans were unaccustomed to so high a degree of government regulation of business.

Cooperative Learning
Divide the class into three groups. Assign each group one of the following organizations: Father Coughlin's National Union for Social Justice, Huey Long's Share-Our-Wealth Clubs, Dr. Francis Townsend's Old-Age Revolving Pensions, Inc. Have group members work together to design and construct a poster encouraging people to join their organization. Remind groups that their posters should include strong visual images and catchy slogans. Display finished posters on the bulletin board. **L2**

 **CONCERT AT THE LINCOLN MEMORIAL** by Mitchell Jamieson WPA artists painted murals in many government offices. Mitchell Jamieson's mural of African American opera singer Marian Anderson's famous concert before an integrated audience of 73,000 at the Lincoln Memorial is in the offices of the United States Department of the Interior in Washington, D.C. *What political favor did Roosevelt want from African Americans?*

The Wagner Act

Next to the Social Security Act, the most important and lasting legislation of the Second New Deal was the National Labor Relations Act, also called the Wagner Act, passed in July 1935 after the Supreme Court declared the National Industrial Recovery Act unconstitutional. The Wagner Act set up a National Labor Relations Board (NLRB), which could hold secret elections in factories to find out whether workers wanted to unionize. The board could arbitrate grievances, reinstate workers fired for supporting unions, and order employers to stop antiunion activities.

The Wagner Act stimulated a burst of labor union activity. But the AFL was ill-equipped in both philosophy and structure to organize workers in mass-production industries such as radio, steel, automobiles, and textiles. The AFL was a federation of **craft unions**—unions where all members had the same skill. In mass-production industries, however, workers from many crafts or skills often worked in a single plant. To have several unions undermined unity. So some labor leaders proposed that factory workers be organized in an industrial union—a union to which all workers in a single industry belong, regardless of the job they perform. When the AFL rejected this approach, these leaders abandoned it to form the Congress of Industrial Organizations (CIO).

The CIO

"If I went to work in a factory, the first thing I'd do would be to JOIN A UNION," read the slogan signed by President Roosevelt on union recruiting posters, as the CIO moved into industries that the AFL had long neglected. By 1936 the CIO had signed up enough steelworkers to threaten a nationwide strike. Instead, in March 1937 the nation's largest steel producer, the United States Steel Corporation, recognized the union as bargaining agent for its workers, established a 40-hour workweek, and increased wages. Just beginning to recover from the Depression, the company was not willing to risk a major strike. The smaller producers did not follow this lead, however, and bloody strikes broke out around the country. But by 1941, the steelworkers' union had contracts with the entire industry.

Meanwhile, the CIO moved into the automobile industry, where management discouraged worker unity by exploiting racial and religious tensions among African Americans, Southern whites, and Catholic ethnic groups. Although hourly wages in the industry were high, seasonal layoffs reduced the average worker's annual earnings to less than $1,000. Workers also resented the "speed-ups" that occurred when management increased the rate at which cars moved along the assembly line.

The Autoworkers Strike

The CIO did not want to challenge the auto industry until the struggle with the steel companies had ended. But autoworkers were impatient for change and took matters into their own hands, using a strike strategy called the sit-down strike. Rather than walking off their jobs, strikers remained in the factory. The company could not hire new workers to continue production, nor could it remove the strikers by force without risking violence to the factory. One striker later remembered:

> We were nervous. We didn't know we could do it. Those machines had been kept going as long as we could remember. When we finally pulled the switch and there was some quiet, I finally remembered something. . . . that I was a human being, that I could stop those machines. . . .

The sit-down strike was not originated by the autoworkers, nor was it unique to them. The radical International Workers of the World first used the technique against General Electric in 1906. But in the late 1930s factory workers, taxi drivers, maids, secretaries, and salesclerks sat down at their jobs to protest their pay and working conditions.

Union success in the auto, steel, and other industries swelled the ranks of organized labor during the Second New Deal. The CIO grew especially rapidly because it was willing to organize women workers, whom the AFL had ignored. From less than 3 million in 1933, union membership more than tripled by 1939. Organized labor showed its appreciation for the Wagner Act and other New Deal programs by giving political support to the Democrats.

The 1936 Election

The Democrats renominated Roosevelt for President in 1936, and they enthusiastically endorsed the New Deal. The business community, however, contributed to his 1936 campaign only about one-fifth as much as it contributed in 1932, and many newspapers turned against FDR. The Republican nominee, Kansas governor Alfred M. Landon, denounced Roosevelt for endangering the "American system of free enterprise." He labeled Social Security as "unjust, unworkable, stupidly drafted, and wastefully financed," and attacked many other New Deal programs.

Four years of New Deal programs, however, had forged a new political coalition for the Democrats. Farmers, labor unions, retirees, and many ethnic groups supported Roosevelt and his programs. African American voters abandoned an allegiance to the Republican party that dated back to Reconstruction to support the party of Roosevelt. FDR's New Deal had not offered special programs for African Americans, but it had not tried to exclude them either. African American workers, who often were the first fired when hard times hit, owed much to New Deal relief programs, and they showed their gratitude at the polls. On Election Day, Roosevelt won in a landslide, and Democrats elected huge majorities to the House and Senate.

The New Deal and the Supreme Court

Before he could continue the New Deal in his second term, Roosevelt believed he had to eliminate opposition on the Supreme Court. During 1935 and 1936 the Court struck down New Deal programs, including the NIRA and AAA. Never before had the Court declared so much legislation unconstitutional. Roosevelt and his supporters

CHAPTER 28 The New Deal 1932–1939

CHAPTER 28
SECTION 3

Did You Know?

The social security system set up by the Social Security Act of 1935 is operated by one of the biggest agencies of the federal government. The Social Security Reform Act of 1983 fine-tuned the system's short-range and long-range financing and benefits. These changes were necessary because of the growing number of elderly in the United States.

FACT or FICTION?
As Maine goes, so goes the country.

FACT: Until 1936, results in Maine were such a solid indicator of who would win the presidential election that the saying became a political rule-of-thumb.

NATIONAL GEOGRAPHIC SOCIETY

The following material is available from Glencoe and may be used to enrich Chapter 28.

CD-ROM
- *The Presidents: A Picture History of Our Nation*

Sidelights: The Federal Theater

Among the most exciting and innovative projects of the WPA was the Federal Theater. In 1936 a gifted young director named Orson Welles staged Shakespeare's *Macbeth*, setting it in the West Indies and using an all African American cast. Another all African American production, *Swing Mikado*, was copied extensively by commercial theater companies. Many Federal Theater productions used the "living newspaper" technique—often taking on the style and methods of radio and documentary cinema to build morality plays about current events.

CHAPTER 28
SECTION 3

Teaching Life of the Times

The sit-down strike had been used before, most notably by workers at the rubber factories in Akron, but the Flint strike was the first time it was used on such a large scale. Discipline among the strikers was rigid—no liquor was allowed on the premises and smoking was prohibited on the production floors. A 45-person "police force" made sure these rules were followed. This discipline, and a sense of unity of purpose, helped the workers repel an attempt to evict them by the police. Even a threat to bring in the national guard could not budge them. Ask students to discuss whether or not the sit-down strike is a fair labor practice.

ASSESS

Check Understanding

Assign Section 3 Review as homework or an in-class activity.

Evaluate

Assign the Section 3 Quiz in the TCR, or use the History of a Free Nation Testmaker to create a customized quiz.

Reteach

Have students complete Reteaching Activity 28-3.

Life of the Times

Sit-down Strikes

Passage of the Wagner Act boosted workers' morale and inspired imaginative techniques to bring reluctant managers to the negotiating table. Chief among their strategies was the sit-down strike. On December 30, 1936, the UAW members of General Motors' Fisher Body plant in Flint, Michigan, sat down at their work stations. Meanwhile, workers at other General Motors plants followed suit or struck in more traditional ways: picketing factories, seizing plants by force, and jeering at scabs—workers sent to take their places.

General Motors strike veteran Bob Stinson described how workers managed to get food and keep in touch with their families during the sit-down: "The soup kitchen was outside the plant. The women handled all the cooking, outside of one chef who came from New York. He had anywhere from 10 to 20 women washing dishes and peeling potatoes in the strike kitchen. Mostly stews, pretty good meals. They were put in containers and hoisted up through the window....

We had a ladies' auxiliary. They'd visit the homes of the guys that was in the plant.

They would find out if there was any shortage of coal or food. Then they'd maneuver around amongst themselves until they found some place to get a ton of coal."

Since the strikers were not going to starve, GM decided to freeze them out. It turned off the heat in the plant. But after six weeks, when the strikers still refused to give in, General Motors signed a contract with the UAW.

▼ FLINT, MICHIGAN PLANT STRIKE

---

believed that "9 old men" on the Court, 7 of whom had been appointed by Republican Presidents, were interfering with the New Deal's attempts at recovery. Laws that helped millions of people, passed by large majorities in Congress, were being rejected by the Court, often by margins of 5 to 4.

Roosevelt considered his landslide reelection to be a mandate to curb the Supreme Court. In February 1937 the President presented legislation allowing him to appoint an additional justice to the Supreme Court for each justice over 70 years of age. Although the Court's size would increase from 9 to 15, Roosevelt argued that it needed "an infusion of younger blood." The "court-packing" bill caused a furor even in the President's own party. Many Americans were alarmed by the threat it posed to the system of checks and balances. Enough Democrats joined the Republicans in Congress to defeat Roosevelt's proposal. Although he suffered a major setback and lost many supporters, the President claimed that he had "lost the battle but won the war." While debate on the "court-packing" bill raged in Congress, in two 5-to-4 decisions, the Court upheld the constitutionality of the two major laws of the Second New Deal—the Social Security Act and the Wagner Act.

■ Later New Deal Measures

By 1937 the economy had recovered nearly to 1929 levels, although widespread unemployment still remained. Roosevelt's financial advisers urged a cutback in spending and a balanced federal budget. Federal Reserve banks tightened credit, and the WPA cut the number of its employees in half.

Difficult Times Continue

The economy quickly slumped into a **recession,** a mild downturn in the business cycle, that critics called a "Roosevelt Depression." Huge crop surpluses collapsed agricultural prices, and industrial production

UNIT 9 Times of Crisis: 1932–1960

Sidelights: Dissension in Roosevelt's Cabinet

The recession caused dissension within Roosevelt's cabinet. Secretary of the Treasury Henry Morgenthau argued that the New Deal was not able to bring about economic recovery because businesses feared that continued government spending would cause inflation. Morgenthau felt that the government should balance its budget and let businesses lead the way in economic recovery. However, Harry Hopkins and Harold Ickes argued that Roosevelt's quick spending cuts caused the recession. They felt that an increase in government spending was the only way to bring about economic recovery.

dropped by one-third, almost to 1932 levels. The President blamed the slump on businesses that, he claimed, failed to reinvest profits in production and on monopolies that kept prices artificially high. To meet the economic crisis, the President again expanded the work-relief programs of the WPA and stepped up military spending. People went back to work and prices rose. But the recession proved that hard times were not yet over.

In 1938 Congress passed a number of New Deal measures that carried out earlier policies. A Fair Labor Standards Act abolished child labor and placed a ceiling on hours and a floor under wages, at least for workers in businesses classified as "interstate commerce." A new Farm Security Administration promoted the well-being of impoverished farmers. A new AAA attempted to cope with surpluses by paying farmers not only to produce less but also to improve the soil and to control erosion. In addition, a food-stamp plan helped to distribute farm surplus among those on relief.

The Opposition Succeeds

These were some of the last New Deal programs. In the fall of 1937, when Roosevelt called a special session of Congress, not one of his proposals was enacted. Both in 1937 and in 1938 Congress rejected the President's request to reorganize the executive branch. These defeats were largely the result of a coalition of Republicans and conservative Southern Democrats who increasingly opposed the President in Congress. Roosevelt tried to weaken this coalition by supporting liberal Democrats against incumbents in the 1938 primary.

 ▲ **PACKING THE COURT** Although Roosevelt was overwhelmingly reelected in 1936, most people reacted negatively in 1937 to his attempt to pack the Supreme Court. *In this cartoon, what does the donkey's reaction symbolize?*

Roosevelt's attempted "purge" of his own party ended in defeat. In most cases, the conservative Democrats won. In the November election the Republicans staged a modest comeback, picking up seats in both houses of Congress. The coalition of Republicans and Southern Democrats was growing powerful and could block further extension of the New Deal.

Roosevelt accepted the judgment of the voters in the 1938 election. In January 1939 he announced that he would propose no further New Deal programs. Instead, he turned his attention to the growing threat of war in Europe.

Section 3 ★ Review

Checking for Understanding

1. **Identify** Father Coughlin, Huey Long, WPA, NLRB, CIO, court-packing.
2. **Define** coalition, craft union, industrial union, recession.
3. **Explain** the steps in Dr. Townsend's recovery plan.
4. **Describe** steps the New Deal took toward reform after 1935.

Critical Thinking

5. **Contrasting Ideas** How did the second New Deal differ from the first in its objectives, support base, program focus, and success? Which was more successful?

LESSON PLAN
Mastering Social Studies Skills

Teaching Study and Writing Skills

Encourage students to recall times when they accurately predicted outcomes and to remember the information on which they based their predictions. Why might a predicted outcome, although reasonable, not occur? (An unexpected action changes the course of events.) Then ask volunteers to read the list of actions listed on page 794 and identify the organizing principle of the list (a chronology of events that impacted the labor movement)

Did You Know?

The New Deal's pro-labor position had a dramatic effect on union membership. In 1933 less than 3 million workers belonged to labor unions. Two years later membership rose to 4.5 million.

Social Studies Skills

Study and Writing Skills

Predicting Consequences

Consequences are the effects and repercussions that result from a decision or action. Sometimes the consequences of an action take you by surprise. More often, with a little forethought you can anticipate possible consequences. To help predict consequences you can:

- **Restate** the action or decision under consideration.
- **Link** the action with relevant prior circumstances.
- **Map** out all possible outcomes or consequences.
- **Analyze** the possibilities. Are some consequences more likely to occur than others?

Read the information that follows. Then complete the Practicing the Skill to help you predict consequences.

Much of the government activity of the 1930s revolved around improving economic conditions and employment opportunities. The American labor movement worked toward these goals long before Roosevelt's New Deal. But the progress of the labor movement was impacted, either negatively or positively, by the actions and decisions of employers, Congress, and the courts. Based on your historical understanding, predict the effect of these actions on the labor movement.

- Court interpretation of the Sherman Antitrust Act of 1890 finds that union strikes are "in restraint of trade or commerce."
- Clayton Act of 1914 holds that the courts cannot stop peaceful strikes, pickets, or boycotts.
- Fair Labor Standards Act of 1938 outlaws child labor and limits maximum workday hours.
- Taft-Hartley Act of 1947 halts strikes that might endanger national health and safety.

Practicing the Skill

1. Predict the effect of the Clayton Act on the power of American labor unions.
2. Was the Fair Labor Standards Act a victory for labor or for business? Explain.
3. Predict the effect of the Taft-Hartley Act on police and firefighters.
4. Today the quest for improved worker rights focuses on issues such as sexual harassment, equal opportunity for the disabled, and access to health-care benefits. Why have these issues replaced earlier ones?

794

Answers to SOCIAL STUDIES SKILLS

1. increase union power
2. By limiting immigration, the law made it harder for employers to replace workers with newly arrived immigrants willing to take any job they could find
3. limited their ability to strike
4. Many of the earlier issues have been resolved by legislation or court action. Economic and social conditions also have changed, with more ethnic and gender equity in the workplace and a public more accepting of government involvement in business.

SECTION 4

The Impact of the New Deal

Setting the Scene

Section Focus

Just as Roosevelt's fireside chats over the radio reached the American people, his New Deal programs touched their lives. From relief for the poor, to wages and working conditions, to regulation of the nation's economy and financial markets, programs affected society at every level. The New Deal involved the federal government in American life to an extent unprecedented in the nation's history.

▶ WPA POSTER, 1940

Objectives

After studying this section, you should be able to

★ identify changes that the New Deal caused in American society.

★ evaluate the effects of the New Deal on life today.

Key Term

ethnic group

Sociologists Robert and Helen Lynd in 1929 published a study of values, behaviors, and everyday life in the 1920s in a typical American city that they called "Middletown." (It was actually Muncie, Indiana.) In 1935 they returned to "Middletown" for a follow-up study and found that the Depression and the New Deal had profoundly affected the families living in that community.

■ The New Deal and Society

The Depression affected every part of society. Its impact was felt at home and at work. The New Deal brought relief for some, but problems remained. In 1937 President Roosevelt said, "I see one-third of a nation ill-housed, ill-clad, ill-nourished."

Adapting to the Depression at Home

During the Depression, both births and divorces decreased as people could not afford either event. Older people moved in with working relatives. Many families rented rooms to boarders or moved to smaller and less expensive homes. Housewives took in laundry and sewing to help support their families. Sales of prepared food declined, and many people canned foods at home.

Changes at Work

Competition among adults for jobs resulted in stronger child labor laws, and the number of working children declined during the 1930s. Consequently, the number of high school and college students rose.

In Middletown, the Lynds noted that when a man lost his job and could not find

CHAPTER 28 The New Deal 1932–1939 **795**

LESSON PLAN
SECTION 4, 795–801

FOCUS

Bell Ringer
Prior to taking roll at the beginning of the class period, display Focus Activity Transparency 95 on the overhead projector and assign the accompanying Focus Activity Sheet.

Objectives
Point out the objectives on this page to students in previewing the section content.

Motivating Activity
Display Transparency 23 *Fallingwater* by Frank Lloyd Wright and Transparency 24 *Migrant Mother* by Dorothea Lange from the Glencoe United States History and Art transparency package. Have students describe what is shown in the transparencies, and then have them discuss how the works reflect the times—the 1930s. As they read this section, have students focus on how the culture of the 1930s reflected the changes that the New Deal caused in American society.

Classroom Resources for SECTION 4

Teacher's Classroom Resources
- Reproducible Lesson Plan
- Reteaching Activity 28-4
- Chapter 28 Enrichment Activity
- Chapter 28 Performance Assessment Activity
- Spanish Summaries and Glossary
- Section Quiz

Multimedia
- Section Focus Transparency 95
- U.S. History and Art Transparencies 23, 24
- Vocabulary Puzzlemaker
- Testmaker
- Student Self-Test Software

▲ A. PHILIP RANDOLPH As a young man, A. Philip Randolph quickly became aware of the discrimination African Americans faced in employment. He became a leader in the labor movement. **What civil rights measures were enacted during the New Deal?**

another, traditional family roles often were reversed, "with the woman taking a job for whatever money she could earn and the man caring for the household." Still, women were accused of taking men's jobs, and businesses often refused to hire married women.

Most women who worked outside the home, with the exception of farm and domestic workers, benefited from the New Deal. Women's wages rose and working conditions improved. The greatest direct assistance to women came from the Women's Division of the WPA. It employed between 300,000 and 400,000 women, some in traditionally female white-collar jobs such as teacher, nurse, and librarian. But most worked on canning and sewing projects. Their pay was low, but it often made the difference between food and famine.

■ Minorities

African Americans did not fare well under the New Deal. In addition, the government failed to enact any major civil rights measures during this period.

African Americans Get Mainly the Same Old Deal

As the poorest of the poor, African Americans often fell through the cracks of broad legislation such as the AAA and the Social Security Act. For example, although the AAA gave money to rural landowners, in the South 80 percent of all African American farmers owned no land. In addition, Roosevelt offered no civil rights program and did little to challenge the segregation that continued to exist throughout the nation, and he tolerated job discrimination. Even some government agencies refused to hire African Americans. Those that did, such as the CCC and armed forces, segregated African Americans and whites. In addition, African Americans received lower wages than white workers and were not assigned to certain jobs.

Nevertheless, Roosevelt appointed more African Americans to government posts than any President before him. Although most African American officials filled secondary posts, they influenced the President as an unofficial "black cabinet." Heading the cabinet was Mary McLeod Bethune, director of the Negro Affairs Division of the National Youth Administration. A personal friend of Eleanor Roosevelt, she often expressed the cabinet's concerns to the First Lady, who then carried them to FDR.

One concern of African Americans during the Depression was an increase in lynching and other acts of mob violence against them. Roosevelt supported a 1934 federal antilynching bill that held local sheriffs accountable for the frequent lynchings of African Americans in the South. But he never made the bill a legislative priority, and it finally died in the Senate in 1938.

One reason New Deal programs for African Americans were so limited was the opposition of powerful congressional committee heads who were from the South. As a result Roosevelt accepted NRA codes, for example, that permitted a lower minimum wage in the South than in the rest of the nation. FDR felt that if he pushed these Southern legislators too strongly, he would lose their support.

White Ethnic Groups Do Well

In general, the federal government responded more favorably to white ethnic groups, groups of people who shared the same culture, religion, and customs. During the 1930s the federal Office of Education sponsored a radio series called "Americans All . . . Immigrants All." The show celebrated the cultural vitality of a democracy made up of people from many lands. It also indicated the Democrats' awareness of the political power that ethnic groups could exercise if they were organized. Immigrants and their children made up 40 percent of the white population at that time. They tended to vote in groups and could swing elections, especially in large urban areas. Americans of Irish, Italian, and Polish descent became major partners in the New Deal coalition.

■ Popular Culture

The 1930s were somber years compared to the fads and frivolity of the 1920s. Literature and the arts generally turned to more realistic themes about poverty and human suffering.

Literature

Grim times provided powerful themes for American authors such as John Dos Passos, whose trilogy of novels called *U.S.A.* focused on fictional characters who lost their ideals and became hardened by society. Perhaps the most powerful novel of the era was John Steinbeck's *Grapes of Wrath*, the story of a family who left their Oklahoma farm in the dust bowl and headed to the migrant labor camps of California.

There was also much escapism in popular culture, as people turned to entertainment when things became grim. The best-selling book of the decade was Margaret Mitchell's *Gone with the Wind.* Although set in the South during the Civil War and Reconstruction, it offered a hopeful account of Scarlett

CHAPTER 28
SECTION 4

Did You Know?

During the early months of 1933, the rate of foreclosures on private homes was about 1,000 per week. Congress quickly took action, establishing the Home Owners Loan Corporation (HOLC) on June 13, 1933. The HOLC helped owners refinance their debts into a single mortgage. By 1936 the HOLC had made loans covering 1 million mortgages.

Visualizing History The movies of Fred Astaire and Ginger Rogers offered Depression audiences "escapist" entertainment, frequently presenting the stars in luxurious settings and beautiful costumes. The movies featured witty dialogue, a mixture of romantic and comic dance routines, popular songs, and gifted entertainers.
Answer to Caption: 85 million

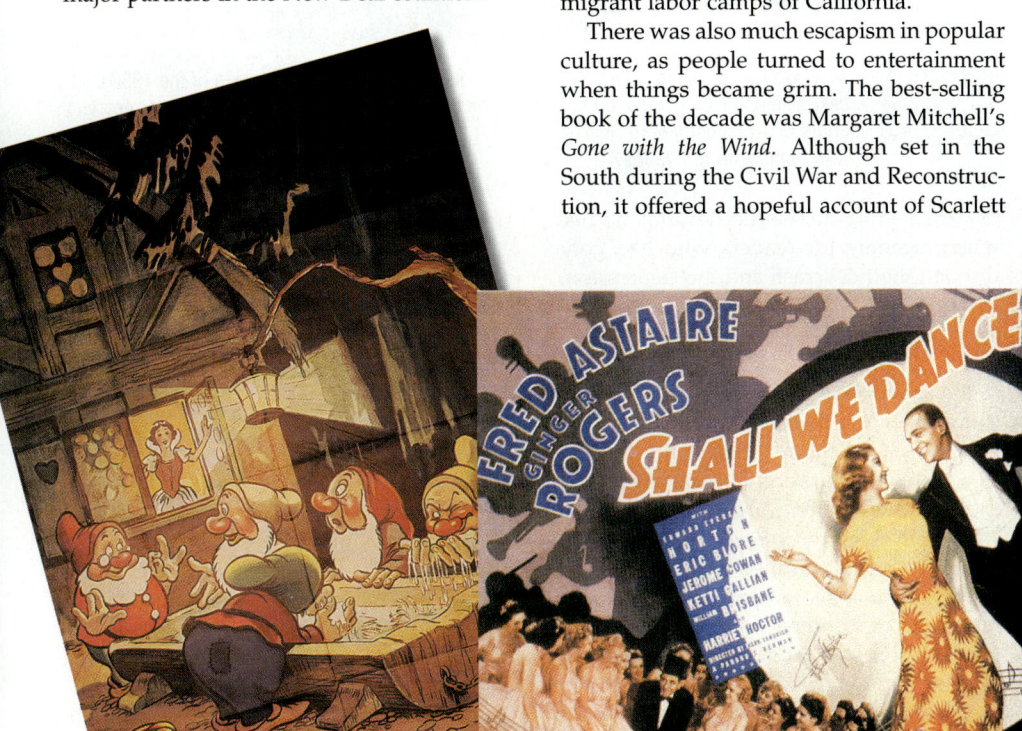

Visualizing History ▲ **AT THE MOVIES** The decade of the 1930s was a golden era for motion pictures. Popular fare included the Fred Astaire and Ginger Rogers musicals and Disney favorites such as *Snow White and the Seven Dwarfs*. **How many Americans attended the movies every week?**

CHAPTER 28 The New Deal 1932–1939

Critical Thinking

Linking Past and Present Tell students that in 1936 about 38 percent of families in the United States—11.7 million families—had annual incomes of less than $1,000. The poverty line at that time was $1,330. Ask students to use sources such as the *Statistical Abstract of the United States* to find the most recent poverty figures. Have students compare the poverty situation today and in the mid-1930s. Then ask them to discuss the following question: What changes made in the 1930s may have helped us in dealing with poverty today? **L2**

 **MASS ENTERTAINMENT** Clark Gable and Vivien Leigh starred in the movie of the 1930s best-selling novel, *Gone With the Wind*. The film was a big hit because people got nearly 4 hours of entertainment for just 10 to 25 cents. *What other mass entertainment medium was popular in the 1930s?*

O'Hara's efforts to rebuild her life and had much meaning for readers who had gone through the 1929 crash and the Depression.

Entertainment

As "talkies"—films with sound—became common during the 1930s, about 85 million people escaped the realities of the Depression for a few hours each week at the movie theater. There they watched movies that were often about the lives of happy and successful people. Continued improvements in sound technology ushered in the era of musicals, and audiences delighted at the dance routines of Fred Astaire and Ginger Rogers. Cartoon characters, such as Mickey Mouse, made audiences laugh, and as color-film technology spread, full-length animated features like Walt Disney's *Snow White and the Seven Dwarfs* provided more fantasy and escape.

At home families could listen to network radio programs broadcast coast-to-coast. Daytime radio offered "soap operas," where characters suffered through daily crises. At night comedy, adventure, and musical variety programs dominated the airwaves. And the performances of Arturo Toscanini conducting the NBC Symphony of the Air brought classical music for the first time to millions of radio listeners.

The Automobile

Just as books, movies, and the radio provided Americans with an emotional outlet from the realities of the Depression, the automobile made them feel that they could physically escape their problems. Americans' love affair with cars, which began during the prosperity of the 1920s, continued throughout the poverty-stricken 1930s. The number of automobiles increased from 26 million in 1933 to 32 million by 1940. During the depths of the Depression, almost half the families in the United States owned a car, even though many could not afford to buy gasoline.

Yet despite the expense, many Americans continued to drive their cars during the 1930s. By late in the decade, thanks to government

Cultural Diversity

Mexican Americans suffered greatly during the Depression, and the New Deal relief agencies provided them with considerable assistance. The Farm Security Administration built permanent migrant camps in areas of large-scale agricultural employment, such as the San Joaquin Valley in California. The FERA provided immediate relief during the worst part of the Depression. And while the WPA provided employment, it also created a renewed interest in Mexican arts and crafts.

work projects, a maze of paved highways crisscrossed the nation. Large numbers of people took off down these two-lane roads, some searching for employment and others pioneering what became an American institution—the family vacation by car.

The Influence of the New Deal

In the arts, as in so many other areas of society, the New Deal played a role. The WPA helped unemployed actors, artists, writers, and musicians. The Federal Theatre Project sponsored performances of Shakespeare as well as children's plays. Some 6,500 writers put together state and regional guidebooks and recorded life stories of formerly enslaved people, immigrants, and Native Americans.

The Federal Arts Project had artists paint murals and sculptors create statues, many of which still can be viewed today. The artistic works of William Gropper, Peter Blume, and Jack Levine reflected social concerns. Photographers like Dorothea Lange and artists like Ben Shahn documented people's lives during the Depression. Arts projects were among the most controversial New Deal programs, however. Critics called them socialistic. In 1939 Congress cut off funds for the theater project, and the other arts programs were discontinued as employment rose during World War II.

To many people who lived through it, the New Deal seemed to have changed American society. Yet it was not the revolutionary assault on capitalism that some of its critics charged. The New Deal changed the lives of farmers through crop subsidies and rural electrification. It changed the lives of industrial workers by strengthening labor unions and expanding collective bargaining. It provided Social Security and welfare programs for the aged, the unemployed, and dependent children. In so doing, it turned a government that previously had responded more to business groups into a government open to labor, farmers, and other interests.

Yet the New Deal did not adopt national planning of the economy, as some of Roosevelt's advisers had expected. Rather than government owning industry, the New Deal emphasized federal regulation of private enterprise. Rather than overturning capitalism, New Dealers believed that they had helped to save it.

▲ LITTLE ORPHAN ANNIE

Section 4 ★ Review

Checking for Understanding

1. **Identify** black cabinet, John Steinbeck, Margaret Mitchell, soap operas, Federal Arts Project.
2. **Define** ethnic group.
3. **Summarize** the impact of the New Deal on African Americans.
4. **Discuss** popular forms of entertainment in the 1930s.

Critical Thinking

5. **Seeing Relationships** Analyze how the Depression influenced themes in American art and literature during the 1930s.

INTEGRATING Language Arts

American Literary Heritage

Historical Setting
The crash of 1929 resulted in bank closings, severe business losses, and 14 million unemployed Americans. Tragically it was during the Depression that the Dust Bowl dried up and blew away. Its tenant farmers, too, were tossed to the wind.

Background
During the Great Depression, radio and film offered escapist fare for Americans who momentarily sought to forget their troubles. Yet, there were artists who chose to reveal the Depression in ugly, gritty terms. With *The Grapes of Wrath*, Steinbeck illustrates the harshness of the Depression.

About the Author
Born in Salinas, California, in 1902, John Steinbeck was to set much of his literature in the Salinas Valley. He had intended to earn a degree in marine biology but interrupted his studies at Stanford University to pursue a writing career. It was not until the 1935 publication of his novel *Tortilla Flat* that he gained any recognition. His 1937 novel, *Of Mice and Men,* which he also turned into a play, portrayed the tragic friendship of two drifters. Considered by many to be his masterpiece, *The Grapes of Wrath* was awarded the Pulitzer Prize. Six years before his death in 1968, Steinbeck was honored with the Nobel Prize for Literature. He is considered one of the greatest American realistic authors.

▲ JOHN STEINBECK

In *The Grapes of Wrath*, John Steinbeck chronicles the hardships of the Joads, an Oklahoma farm family whose plight resembles that of the downtrodden everywhere. As you read the excerpt from Steinbeck's novel, look for statements that reveal the beliefs, concerns, and attitudes of tenant farmers during the 1930s.

The Grapes of Wrath (excerpts)

The owners of the land came onto the land, or more often a spokesman for the owners came. They came in closed cars, and they felt the dry earth with their fingers, and sometimes they drove big earth augers into the ground for soil tests. The tenants, from their sun-beaten dooryards, watched uneasily when the closed cars drove along the fields. And at last the owner men drove into the dooryards and sat in their cars to talk out of the windows....

If a bank or a finance company owned the land, the owner man said, The Bank—or the Company—needs-wants-insists-must have-as though the Bank or the Company were a monster, with thought and feeling, which had ensnared them.... The owner men sat in the cars and explained. You know the land is poor. You've scrabbled at it long enough, God knows.

The squatting tenant men nodded and wondered and drew figures in the dust, and yes, they knew, God knows. If the dust only wouldn't fly. If the top would only stay on the soil, it might not be so bad.

The owner men went on leading to their point: You know the land's getting poorer. You know what cotton does to the land; robs it, sucks all the blood out of it.

The squatters nodded—they knew, God knew. If they could only rotate the crops they might pump blood back into the land. Well, it's too late. And the owner men explained the workings and the thinkings of the monster that was stronger than they were....

The squatting men raised their eyes to understand. Can't we just hang on? Maybe the next year will be a good year. God knows how much cotton next year. And with all the wars—God knows what price cotton will bring. Don't they make explosives out of cotton? And uniforms? Get enough wars and cotton'll hit the ceiling. Next year, maybe. They looked up questioningly.

We can't depend on it. The bank—the monster has to have profits all the time. It can't wait. It'll die....

The squatting men looked down again. What do you want us to do? We can't take less share of the crop—we're half starved now. The kids are hungry all

UNIT 9 Times of Crisis: 1932–1960

Cultural Diversity

John Steinbeck became popular all over the world, because of his ability to tell unforgettable stories and his empathy for disadvantaged people. His socially relevant books made him a favorite author in the former Soviet Union and in developing countries. Later Steinbeck also wrote about life in Russia, England, and France. As an indication of his international popularity, Steinbeck received the Nobel Prize for Literature in 1962. After he received the award President Lyndon Johnson asked him to serve as goodwill ambassador to the United Nations.

the time. We got no clothes, torn an' ragged. If all the neighbors weren't the same, we'd be ashamed to go to meeting.

And at last the owner men came to the point. The tenant system won't work any more. One man on a tractor can take the place of twelve or fourteen families. Pay him a wage and take all the crop. We have to do it. We don't like to do it. But the monster's sick. Something's happened to the monster.

But you'll kill the land with cotton. We know. We've got to take cotton quick before the land dies. Then we'll sell the land. Lots of families in the East would like to own a piece of land.

The tenant men looked up alarmed. But what'll happen to us? How'll we eat?

You'll have to get off the land. The plows'll go through the dooryard.

And now the squatting men stood up angrily. Grampa took up the land, and he had to kill the Indians and drive them away. An Pa was born here, and he killed weeds and snakes. Then a bad year came and he had to borrow a little money. An' we was born here. There in the door—our children born here. And Pa had to borrow money. The bank owned the land then, but we stayed and we got a little bit of what we raised.

We know the—all that. It's not us, it's the bank. A bank isn't like a man. Or an owner with fifty thousand acres, he isn't like a man either. That's the monster.

▲ **COVER OF *THE GRAPES OF WRATH***

▶ **DESTITUTE FAMILY, OZARKS**

Interpreting Literature

1. Locate passages where the tenant men are beseeching or protesting.
2. What is the "monster"? Do you think this is an apt metaphor? Why or why not?

Evaluating Viewpoints

3. Steinbeck clearly sides with the tenant farmers. What arguments could be made for the banks and the owners? Which viewpoint do you favor?

CHAPTER 28 The New Deal 1932–1939   801

INTEGRATING Language Arts

Developing Student Understanding

Challenge students to compare and contrast the displaced tenant farmers of the 1930s with the homeless of today. (Comparison: Both were uprooted and forced to struggle for survival because of their poverty. Contrast: Because of many of the New Deal's programs, today's homeless, in theory, have more options than did the tenant farmers.)

Explain that Steinbeck's novel presents a no-holds-barred look at the grim reality of the tenant farmer's life.

Interpreting Literature

1. The tenants beseech the owner men to allow crop rotation for a better yield and protest when they are told to leave.
2. The monster is the bank. Students probably will find the metaphor apt, because Steinbeck portrays the bank as heartless and unfeeling.
3. Students may answer that many other families depended on the bank. If it did not foreclose and collapsed as a result, they would suffer. Students will most likely favor the tenants' stance.

Other Works of the Period

Ernest Hemingway was a realistic, Nobel Prize-winning author. His terse, economical writing style explored war, danger, and "macho" endeavors—hunting, fishing, and bullfighting. His works include *The Sun Also Rises* (1926), *A Farewell to Arms* (1929), *For Whom the Bell Tolls* (1940), and *The Old Man and the Sea* (1952).

William Faulkner, twice awarded the Pulitzer Prize, is known for his "Southern literature." A nearly lifelong Mississippi resident, he set his novels in the fictional Yoknapatawpha County. His works include *The Sound and the Fury* (1929) and *The Mansion* (1959).

REVIEW CHAPTER 28

Answers

Reviewing Facts

1. to allow time to study which banks were secure to operate so that public confidence in banks could be restored
2. Both had relief and work programs. Before: focus on financial reform and on emergency relief and recovery programs. After: increase work relief programs, focus on lasting business, labor, taxation, and social welfare reform.
3. fireside chats, press conferences, public appearances
4. farmers—Resettlement Administration, AAA, TVA, FSA; workers—NIRA, NLRB; unemployed—CWA, PWA, CCC, TVA, WPA, social security; unemployable—social security
5. AAA paid farmers to reduce production, which raised prices; 5-year moratorium on mortgage foreclosures; FSA provided loans to tenants to buy their own land; Resettlement Administration helped poor farmers get a new start on good land.
6. Government supported labor unions through NIRA and NLRB. CIO organized and achieved contracts in major industries.
7. African Americans, tenant farmers, some private industries like power companies
8. Federal Arts Project hired artists to paint and sculpt; Federal Theater Project sponsored plays; FSA hired photographers to record the Depression; WPA hired writers for guide books and biographies.

CHAPTER 28 ★ REVIEW

Using Vocabulary

Write sentences about Roosevelt's New Deal using these vocabulary words.

deficit spending   pump priming
dole   foreclosure
moratorium   recession

Reviewing Facts

1. **Explain** the purpose of the bank holiday in the first Hundred Days.
2. **Compare** the purposes of New Deal legislation before and after 1935.
3. **Cite** the means Roosevelt used to advocate, promote, and gain public support for his New Deal programs.
4. **Identify** specific New Deal programs that provided help to various types of needy people in society.
5. **Describe** Roosevelt's attempts to help farmers.
6. **Discuss** developments and achievements within organized labor movements during the 1930s and the role that the New Deal played in these developments.
7. **Specify** groups that did not fully share in the benefits of the New Deal.
8. **List** ways the New Deal supported the arts during the Depression.

Understanding Concepts

Economic Reform

1. Which New Deal programs would you classify as achieving lasting economic reform? Explain your reasons for your choices.

Political Leadership

2. Much of the success of the New Deal relied on the charismatic personality and leadership of Franklin Roosevelt. Explain how he used these assets to gain support for his controversial and complicated New Deal policies.

Critical Thinking

1. **Finding Explanations** Though farmers received substantial assistance during the New Deal and have since, many farmers have continued to suffer economically. What problems inherent in farming could possibly account for this recurring difficulty?
2. **Analyzing Fine Art** Study the detail from the painting *City Life* that is on this page, then answer the questions that follow.
   a. What is going on in the painting?
   b. How does the artist give depth to the painting?
   c. Has Arnautoff created a mood in the work? Explain.
   d. If you were to rename this work, what would you entitle it? Explain your choice.

▲ CITY LIFE BY VICTOR ARNAUTOFF, 1934

802 UNIT 9 Times of Crisis: 1932–1960

Understanding Concepts

1. Social Security benefits, labor laws, banking and securities reform, commitment to public assistance
2. appealed to people with fireside chats and media with press conferences, activist approach to solving problems, openness to new ideas, flexibility, and willingness to experiment, sought support from many segments of society

Critical Thinking

1. Continued overproduction has kept prices down; farmers historically have been independent and, unlike workers and business people, do not have as strong a tradition of cooperation for the improvement of the group.
2. a. painting shows a busy street scene
   b. Answers will vary but should include idea of

CHAPTER 28 ★ REVIEW

Writing About History

Argumentation

Assume the nation has entered a depression in the 1990s. As a member of Congress devoted to economic reform, write an argument proposing and supporting deficit spending to stimulate the economy and to finance expanded government assistance programs. Think about what reasons an economist might have to favor such programs. Also think carefully about the reasons why some of your constituents would favor such policies and why others would oppose them.

Cooperative Learning

Working in a group of three, assume roles of government officials during Roosevelt's term. One member should assume the role of a Roosevelt supporter in Congress and present an argument to Congress for enlarging the Supreme Court. The second member should assume the role of an anti-Roosevelt senator and address Congress, refuting the need to enlarge the Court. The third member will listen to both arguments and decide which is the more effective. All group members should then be prepared to argue either position before the class if called upon by the teacher.

Social Studies Skills

Reading a Table

Tables are a useful way to organize information that you want to compare. Use the table on this page and information from the chapter to answer the following questions.

Practicing the Skill

1. How many years does the information presented in the table cover?
2. What is the subject of the table?
3. Which column shows how much money each person in the country would owe if the federal debt were divided equally among all the people?
4. What year was the federal deficit at its highest level? What was happening in the United States at that time?

The Federal Budget and Deficit

	Federal Receipts (in billions of dollars)	Federal Deficit (in billions of dollars)	Gross Federal Debt (in billions of dollars)	Per Capita Federal Debt (total dollar amt.)
1940	6.9	−2.7	43.0	325
1939	6.6	−2.9	40.4	309
1938	7.0	−.1	37.2	286
1937	5.6	−2.8	36.4	283
1936	4.2	−3.5	33.8	264
1935	3.8	−2.4	28.7	226
1934	3.1	−3.3	27.1	214
1933	2.1	−2.6	22.5	179
1932	2.0	−2.7	19.5	156

Source: *Historical Statistics of the United States: Colonial Times to 1970* (1975).

5. During the time period shown, did the federal government ever spend less money than it received?
6. If the federal deficit decreased in 1940, why didn't the federal debt also decrease?

Using Your Journal

Compare the roles women played in the Roosevelt administration with the roles women play in the current administration.

CHAPTER 28 The New Deal 1932–1939   **803**

REVIEW ★ CHAPTER 28

❓ Chapter Bonus Test Question

Many would argue that Franklin Roosevelt was one of this century's greatest presidents. Choose a President among FDR's predecessors to compare and contrast with Roosevelt, in terms of both substance and style. (Answers will vary but should reflect an understanding of Roosevelt's ideology and style of governing.)

Using Your Journal

Students should note that, while Roosevelt's administration included a few prominent women, as well as an activist First Lady, the current administration includes many more women in power—in the cabinet, as heads of agencies, as ambassadors.

---

    perspective.
c. Answers will vary but students might note that there appears to be little friendship or connection among the people.
d. Answers will vary.

Practicing the Skill
1. 9
2. Federal budgets and deficits
3. fourth
4. 1936; Depression—lower tax revenues, expanded federal programs
5. no
6. The debt is cumulative.

PLANNING GUIDE Chapter 29 World War II

Daily Lesson Objectives	Teacher Classroom Resources	Multimedia
SECTION 1 **World Affairs, 1933–1939** 1 Day pp. 806–810 1. Discuss how the Depression influenced American foreign policy. 2. Explain the reasons for Japan's aggression in Asia.	Chapter 29 Study Guide Reproducible Lesson Plan Reteaching Activity 29-1 Section Quiz Chapter 29 Cooperative Learning Activity Chapter 29 Concept Mapping Activity American Portrait 48 Chapter 29 Primary and Secondary Source Readings Reinforcing Social Studies Skills 32-35, 69–72 Map and Graph Skill Activity 14	Student Self-Test Software Testmaker Section Focus Transparency 93 Chapter 29 Skills Transparency
SECTION 2 **Moving Closer to War** 1 Day pp. 811–816 1. Discuss Germany's conquest of Europe. 2. List the steps by which Roosevelt increased support to the Allies.	Reproducible Lesson Plan Reteaching Activity 29-2 Section Quiz Reinforcing Social Studies Skills 25, 46 Map and Graph Skill Activity 18 SAT Practice Tests 9–14	Student Self-Test Software Testmaker Section Focus Transparency 94 Chapter 29 Map Transparencies Lessons of War
SECTION 3 **The United States at War** 1 Day pp. 817–825 1. Discuss the course of the war in Europe and in Asia. 2. Describe the Atlantic Charter and the agreements the Allies reached at the Yalta Conference.	Reproducible Lesson Plan Reteaching Activity 29-3 Section Quiz American Portrait 51 Chapter 29 Primary and Secondary Source Readings Reinforcing Social Studies Skills 32, 40, 59, 69–72 Life Unworthy of Life: A Holocaust Curriculum Outline Map 4 Writer's Handbook	Student Self-Test Software Testmaker Section Focus Transparency 95 Chapter 29 Map Transparencies U.S. History and Art Transparency 25 A Geographic Perspective on American History Lessons of War Focus on Government
SECTION 4 **War on the Home Front** 1 Day pp. 827–832 1. Discuss efforts to mobilize the economy for war production. 2. Explain the war's impact on women, African Americans, and Japanese Americans.	Reproducible Lesson Plan Reteaching Activity 29-4 Section Quiz Chapter 29 Enrichment Activity American Portrait 57, 58 Reinforcing Social Studies Skills 14, 25, 32, 53, 67 Spanish Summaries & Glossary	Student Self-Test Software Testmaker Section Focus Transparency 96 Vocabulary Puzzlemaker Chapter 29 Map Transparencies Audiocassette, Chapter 29 The American People: Fabric of a Nation Lessons of War
CHAPTER REVIEW AND EVALUATION 1 Day	Chapter 29 Test Chapter 29 Performance Assessment Activity	Student Self-Test Software Testmaker

 **OUT OF TIME?** If time does not permit teaching the entire chapter, use the Chapter 29 Summary on pages 890–891 and the Chapter 29 audiocassette (English and Spanish) to point out the main ideas of the chapter.

PLANNING GUIDE

Cultural Diversity Activity

Expressing Opinions In March 1942, United States General John DeWitt ordered the evacuation of all Japanese from the western half of Washington, Oregon, and California and from southern Arizona. Of the 110,000 evacuees, 70,000 were American citizens. In testimony before a congressional committee, General DeWitt explained his views on removal and internment:

"It makes no difference whether a Japanese is theoretically a citizen. He is still a Japanese. Giving him a scrap of paper won't change him. I don't care what they do with the [Japanese] so long as they don't send them back."

Note that thousands of Japanese Americans served in the armed forces during the war. The bravery of the all-Japanese American 442nd Regimental Combat Team made it the most highly decorated unit in U.S. military history. Note too that the 150,000 Japanese who lived in Hawaii were not evacuated. Nor were people of German or Italian descent. Divide the class into groups. Have each group write a response to DeWitt's statement. Encourage groups to share their responses with the class.

Performance Assessment Activity

Shifting Opinions In the 1930s many Americans wanted to keep the nation out of another world war. Gradually attitudes began to change. Working alone or in small groups, have students choose an individual or a group to research. What was the attitude of that individual or group toward the Germans or the Japanese at the time the Olympics were held in Berlin? In 1939, when the war began in Europe? In December 1941, when Pearl Harbor was bombed? During the course of the war? Have students present their findings to the class in the form of a written or oral report. The reports should describe how and why attitudes changed from 1936 through 1945.

POSSIBLE RUBRIC FEATURES: Research skills, content information, organization, written and oral communication skills, creativity, critical thinking skills

Chapter Resources

Literature from the Period

Parker, Dorothy. "Soldiers of the Republic." 1938.

Roosevelt, Franklin D. "Radio Address." September 3, 1939.

Readings for the Student

Berenbaum, Michael. *The World Must Know: The History of the Holocaust as Told in the United States Holocaust Memorial Museum.* Little Brown, 1993.

Gregory, Ross. *America 1941: A Nation at the Crossroads.* The Free Press, 1989.

Readings for the Teacher

Davis, Daniel S. *Behind Barbed Wire: The Imprisonment of Japanese Americans During World War II.* Dutton, 1982.

Multimedia Resources

American Foreign Policy. Focus Media. (Apple diskette, backup, guide)

December 7th. National Archives. (VHS, 34 minutes)

Home Front, World War II. Multi-Media Productions. (2 filmstrips, cassette)

Key to Ability Levels

Teaching strategies have been coded for varying learning styles and abilities.

- **L1** Basic activities for all students
- **L2** Average activities for average to above-average students
- **L3** Challenging activities for above-average students
- **LEP** Limited English Proficiency activities

Glencoe Links to the Humanities

Link to Art
- U.S. History and Art Transparency 25

Links to Literature
- Macmillan Literature: American Literature Video— *A Separate Peace*
- Macmillan Literature: Novel Guides—*The Snow Goose, A Separate Peace*
- Macmillan Literature: American Literature Text— Delmore Schwartz, Eudora Welty, James Agee, William Faulkner

Link to Music
- American Music: Cultural Traditions

CHAPTER 29

BEGINNING THE CHAPTER

Ask students if they would support or oppose U.S. involvement in a conflict between other countries if that involvement might result in a world war. (Students should give reasons for their positions.) Point out that the issue of involvement was very important before the onset of World War II. Tell students that they will discover how that issue was resolved as they study this chapter.

Linking Across Time

By the mid-1930s, it was obvious that war in Europe was again on the way. The U.S. had twice been drawn into European wars, once in 1812 and again in 1917. Fearing that history would repeat itself, Congress passed the Neutrality Acts, forbidding any American action that could lead the United States into war.

Recording Journal Notes

To help students get started, ask them to make a list of the major combatants in World War II—Germany, Japan, and Italy on the Axis side, and Britain, France, the United States, and the Soviet Union on the Allied side.

CHAPTER 29

World War II
1933–1945

▶ SILVER STAR, AWARDED FOR GALLANTRY IN ACTION

Setting the Scene

Focus

The Depression of the 1930s was worldwide. When a new war engulfed Europe, Roosevelt sought to aid the British. After Japan attacked Pearl Harbor in 1941, America entered the war directly. Initially, Allied prospects were bleak, but by 1944 the tide had turned. Victory in the Pacific, however, came only after the use of nuclear weapons.

Concepts to Understand

★ Why international alliances were formed between Germany, Italy, and Japan

★ How the Allies prevented Germany and Italy from winning the military conflict in Europe

Read to Discover . . .

★ what events led the American people to abandon isolationism and neutrality.

★ why Roosevelt was more successful than Wilson in helping to form a world peacekeeping body.

Journal Notes

Consider the interests, fears, and concerns of the nations involved in World War II. Record examples in your journal as you read the chapter.

CULTURAL
- 1931 Pearl Buck publishes *The Good Earth*
- 1936 Babe Ruth and Ty Cobb named to baseball's Hall of Fame

1930 — **1935**

POLITICAL
- 1933 United States recognizes the government of the Soviet Union
- 1939 Germany attacks Poland; war in Europe begins

804 UNIT 9 Times of Crisis: 1932–1960

✚ EXTRA CREDIT PROJECT

Just as many Americans could not locate Middle Eastern countries on a map until the Persian Gulf War began in January 1991, many Americans in the 1940s had not heard of European and Japanese combat locales until the nation took part in World War II. On an outline map of the world, ask interested students to identify the Allied and Axis powers. Also encourage them to provide a thumbnail sketch of each nation including key geographical features, major products, main ethnic groups, and involvement in World War I.

 **Follow Me!**
by Charles McBarron, Jr.

United States forces take the key central Philippine island of Leyte in October 1944.

◀ TANK BOOTS, 1943

- **1940** Color television is demonstrated by the Columbia Broadcasting System
- **1942** Sugar and gasoline are rationed
- **1945** Tennessee Williams's play *The Glass Menagerie* opens in New York

| 1940 | 1945 |

- **1940** Selective Service Act passed
- **1941** Japanese attack Pearl Harbor
- **1944** Allies invade Normandy
- **1945** Nuclear weapons first used

CHAPTER 29 World War II 1933–1945

CHAPTER 29 CONCEPTS

Concept Mapping Activity

Reproduce the concept generalization below on the chalkboard for students as a preview of the chapter content:

> Isolationist America shuns war until aggressive dictators threaten world order and national security

> International Alliances

> Military Conflict

History AND ART

Paintings like *Follow Me* captured the emotion, urgency, and excitement of the battle in a more realistic way than had most paintings of earlier wars. Many of these works were created by soldiers.

 VIDEODISC

- *GTV: A Geographic Perspective on American History*

Side 4, Chapter 6
Title: *Echoes of War*
Subject: Effects of World War II on America

See GTV Guide page 61 for complete lesson plan.

Teacher Notes

LESSON PLAN
SECTION 1, 806–810

FOCUS

Bellringer
Before taking roll at the beginning of the class period, display Focus Activity Transparency 92 on the overhead projector, and assign the accompanying Focus Activity Sheet.

Objectives
Point out the objectives on this page to students in previewing the section content.

Motivating Activity
Ask students if they have ever been at home doing a job that needed to be done when a friend called and asked them for help. Did they drop what they were doing to go to help their friend? Discuss students' answers.

Then point out that President Roosevelt was in a similar situation when he entered the White House in 1933. Direct students to read the Section Focus, and tell them they will learn how Roosevelt attempted to deal with problems both at home and abroad in the late 1930s.

Use Skills Transparency 29.

SECTION 1

World Affairs, 1933–1939

Setting the Scene

Section Focus

Like President Woodrow Wilson, for whom he had worked during World War I, Franklin D. Roosevelt was greatly interested in world affairs. But when he entered the White House in 1933, recovery from the Depression kept most of his energy and attention focused on the United States. As Europe again moved toward war, however, the President experienced growing concern with events overseas.

Objectives

After studying this section, you should be able to
★ discuss how the Depression influenced American foreign policy.
★ explain the reasons for Japan's aggression in Asia.

Key Terms

fascism, totalitarian, appeasement

◀ MILITARY ALUMINUM CANTEEN

Like his distant cousin Theodore, Franklin D. Roosevelt was acquainted with the world beyond the shores of the United States. He had made more than a dozen trips to Europe, and he had first-hand knowledge of the Caribbean area. Through family connections with the China trade, he had acquired an interest in Asia. He resembled Theodore Roosevelt, too, in realizing that as a world power the United States had a commitment to help preserve the peace of the world. As a former associate of Woodrow Wilson, he believed in world organization to promote international cooperation and to solve disputes.

For most of his first two terms, however, Franklin D. Roosevelt focused on domestic affairs. Events in Europe and Asia seemed distant when compared to the crisis of the Depression. In addition, the President recognized that Americans, pressed by hard times at home, cared little about the world at large. So although Roosevelt believed that German expansion posed a threat to the United States, he was cautious in his efforts to alert the nation to this danger. Only when dealing with affairs in the Western Hemisphere did Roosevelt act with his typical bold political style.

■ New Deal Foreign Policy

At his first inaugural in 1933, President Roosevelt pledged that the United States would be a "good neighbor" in the family of nations. He pledged to respect the sovereign rights of all nations in the Western Hemisphere. A few weeks later, he applied the phrase "Good Neighbor" specifically to the administration's Latin American policy.

806   UNIT 9 Times of Crisis: 1932–1960

Classroom Resources for SECTION 1

Teacher's Classroom Resources
- Chapter 29 Study Guide
- Reproducible Lesson Plan
- Reteaching Activity 29-1
- Chapter 29 Performance Assessment Activity
- Chapter 29 Cooperative Activity

Multimedia
- Section Focus Transparency 92
- Chapter 29 Skills Transparency
- Testmaker
- Student Self-Test Software

Peaceful Intentions in Latin America

President Roosevelt and Secretary of State Cordell Hull worked to improve relations with the United States's southern neighbors. Later that year, at the Pan-American Conference at Montevideo, Uruguay, the United States agreed to a resolution that "no state has the right to intervene in the internal affairs of another." Roosevelt demonstrated his commitment to the Good Neighbor policy by recalling American troops from Haiti and Nicaragua, where they had been protecting American property since the 1920s. When Cuba erupted in revolution in 1933, Roosevelt used diplomacy, not troops, to help restore order. When Mexico seized American-owned oil companies in 1938, Roosevelt resisted demands for military action and sought a peaceful settlement.

Domestic Recovery Determines Foreign Decisions

During Roosevelt's first years in office, the United States seemed less inclined to cooperate with Europe. The New Deal adopted a policy of economic isolation, and its recovery programs included attempts to solve agricultural and industrial production problems without considering the rest of the world. In 1933 delegates from more than 60 nations met in London to bring about cooperation in confronting world depression. Roosevelt wrecked the conference by rejecting proposals to peg the value of the dollar to any other currency. He feared that such a move would hurt his efforts to raise American farm prices.

Only when the United States had achieved some recovery from the Depression was the President willing to consider economic cooperation with other nations. Secretary of State Hull believed world prosperity and goodwill could be gained by reducing tariffs. At Hull's urging, Congress passed the Reciprocal Trade Agreements Act of 1934, allowing the State Department to make treaties with other countries to mutually lower import duties. Within six years, the United States had reached such agreements with more than a dozen nations.

Recognition of the Soviet Union

Another change in foreign policy took place when the United States recognized the government of the Soviet Union. Since the Bolshevik Revolution of 1917, the United States had refused to recognize the communist government. After their revolution, the Soviets tried to encourage communism throughout the world. By 1933, however, the USSR was beset by serious economic problems at home and seemed less of a threat. Much more threatening was the rising power of Japan, the Soviets' rival in Asia. The President hoped that a strong Soviet Union could slow Japanese expansion. In addition, Roosevelt saw the Soviets' need for food and industrial equipment as a market for American farmers and manufacturers. "The United States would probably

▲ **JAPANESE EXPANSION** Japanese forces first moved into Manchuria in 1931. Japan established the puppet state of Manchukuo a year later. **How did Roosevelt hope to slow Japan's aggression in Asia?**

CHAPTER 29
SECTION 1

TEACH
Guided Practice

History Divide students into groups of three. Ask each student to play one of the following: Japan's leader, Hitler, or Mussolini. Have each discuss and list reasons for their aggressive policies in the early to mid-1930s and list the countries his armies invaded. During class discussion, have each person share the lists. **L2**

Did You Know?
The word *fascist* comes from the Latin word *fasces*, or the rods and axes that Roman officials carried in ancient times to show that Rome was strong and unified.

Visualizing History Japan had been building its military forces for decades. In the early part of the century, Japanese soldiers won an impressive victory in the Russo-Japanese War (1904–1905). As a result of this war, Japan gained international status as a great military power.
Answer to Caption: Roosevelt hoped that by recognizing the Soviet Union, he could slow Japanese aggression in Asia.

Special Needs

Language Disability It is not unusual for students with language-based learning disabilities to know a variety of strategies for studying text, but to forget to employ these strategies appropriately. Ask students to preview Section 1 to determine the topics presented. List the topics on the board: the Good Neighbor policy, American isolationism, the rise of Hitler and Mussolini. Ask students to think of strategies and skills they have employed throughout this text that might be of help in learning the information in the section.

▲ **MUSSOLINI** Italy's dictator Benito Mussolini gives the Fascist salute during an address. After Italy surrendered to Allied forces, Mussolini was captured and executed by the Italian people. *What plans did Mussolini have in common with Adolf Hitler?*

recognize the Devil," Will Rogers joked, "if it could sell him pitchforks." Recognition of the Soviet Union helped improve relations but did little to increase trade or to check Japanese militarism.

■ Aggression and Appeasement

American hopes to concentrate on domestic affairs, relatively isolated from foreign concerns, were quickly dashed. Events in the world began to send off alarms of trouble ahead.

Japanese Expansion in the Pacific

Between 1872 and 1925, Japan's population nearly doubled, causing severe problems for that small island nation. To sustain industrial growth Japan needed larger markets for its products and more raw materials for its factories. To meet these needs and to ease overcrowding in the home islands, Japan pursued a policy of expansion in the Pacific.

During World War I, Japan supported the Allies but used the war to increase its influence in China. After the war Japan was bitter toward the West. The Washington Conference of 1921 cost Japan most of its gains in China and limited Japan's naval power. When the United States joined other Western nations in 1924 in banning immigrants from Japan, its leaders looked to military solutions for their nation's problems.

In September 1931, Japanese troops invaded and occupied mineral-rich Manchuria in northeastern China. When the League of Nations demanded that Manchuria be returned to China, Japan ignored the order.

Threats From Germany and Italy

On March 5, 1933, the day after Roosevelt took office, the German parliament voted Adolf Hitler, the National Socialist (Nazi) leader, the power he needed to begin a program of conquest in central and eastern Europe. In Italy, dictator Benito Mussolini made similar plans to control the Mediterranean and to expand Italy's empire in Africa.

Mussolini and Hitler followed a new political doctrine known as **fascism** (FASH•ihz•uhm), a form of government in which a dictator and supporters cooperate to seek more power for their nation, usually at the expense of rights for individuals. Each ruler established a **totalitarian** state—a nation that totally controls the life of its people. The Fascists in Italy and the Nazis in Germany set up all-powerful official parties. Both whipped up support with huge patriotic rallies, parades, music, and appeals to national pride and racial hatred, and both used force to silence all opposition.

Each dictator blamed his country's problems after World War I on undesirables in society. Mussolini accused Italy's Communists of causing strikes and social unrest. The Nazis blamed Germany's economic chaos on its Jewish population. They restricted Jews, boycotted Jewish-owned stores, and destroyed synagogues. Both Hitler and Mussolini hinted that another war might be necessary to right the wrongs they felt had been done to their countries by the Treaty of Versailles.

The glorification of war by Italy, Germany, and Japan was not idle talk. In 1935 Mussolini attacked and took control of Ethiopia in Africa. In 1937 Japanese armies invaded the rest of China. In March 1938 Hitler marched into Austria. In 1936 General Francisco Franco rebelled against the republican government of Spain, and German and Italian tanks, bombers, and troops helped Franco win a bitter civil war that lasted until 1939.

Bargaining for Peace

The response of Great Britain and France was **appeasement,** a policy of giving aggressor nations what they wanted in order to avoid war. Like the Americans, the British and French were disillusioned by World War I and wanted peace. Much as they disliked Italian, German, or Japanese expansion, they disliked the thought of war

GERMANY UNDER HITLER In 1935 Adolf Hitler announced that he intended to ignore the Versailles treaty and began to rearm Germany. In 1936 his army reoccupied the Rhineland on Germany's border with France. **How did the Allies respond when Hitler began to act aggressively in Europe?**

CHAPTER 29 SECTION 1

Did You Know?

The American public, unwilling to support Roosevelt's push to abandon isolationism in the late 1930s, turned to celebrating the "blessings of democracy and the wonders of technology" at the New York World's Fair, which opened on April 30, 1939, and cost $150 million. The fairgrounds in Flushing Meadows covered 1,216 acres, was planted with 1 million tulips imported from Holland and 10,000 trees, and sported 300 futuristic exhibit buildings for the Fair's 1,500 exhibitors.

Visualizing History Both Hitler and Mussolini used such gestures as salutes to create a bond of authority between themselves and their public, a sense of solidarity based on discipline and power. **Answer to Caption:** They gave in to Hitler's demand for part of Czechoslovakia in return for a promise to ask for nothing more.

Critical Thinking

Expressing an Opinion Ask students to reread pages 808–809 and write their answers to the following questions: What reasons did the leaders of Great Britain and France have for appeasing Hitler? Do you feel these reasons were justified? How would you have felt if you were a French or British citizen? A citizen of Czechoslovakia? **L2**

CHAPTER 29 SECTION 1

ASSESS
Check Understanding
Assign Section 1 Review as homework or an in-class activity.

Evaluate
Assign the Section 1 Quiz in the TCR, or use the History of a Free Nation Testmaker to create a customized quiz.

Reteach
Have students summarize the reasons for the Neutrality Acts passed in the mid-1930s.
Have students complete Reteaching Activity 29-1.

Enrich
Direct students to select a historical figure mentioned in Section 1. Have them use library resources to find out more about this individual. Then ask them to prepare a short biographical sketch about the person to present to the class.

CLOSE
Ask students to recap the events that led to Roosevelt's calling for the abandonment of U.S. isolationism. Then remind them that public opinion did not support Roosevelt's proposal. Ask students to predict what might change people's minds.

---

even more. Pacifism reached new heights: a majority of the students in the debating union at Britain's Oxford University voted that on no account would they go to war for king or country. Appeasement reached its peak at the Munich Conference of September 1938 when British and French leaders allowed Hitler to annex part of Czechoslovakia in return for his promise to make no further territorial demands. British Prime Minister Neville Chamberlain returned from Germany to tell a jittery world that the Munich Pact meant "peace for our time." Winston Churchill, however, who soon would replace Chamberlain as prime minister, observed that "Britain and France had to choose between war and dishonor. They chose dishonor. They will have war."

Neutrality

The American people were also determined to avoid war. World War I had left the United States with a huge domestic debt and billions of dollars in foreign debts that could not be collected. Americans also wanted to avoid war for a number of other reasons. A congressional investigation of the munitions industry revealed that American manufacturers had made large profits by supplying arms and credit to the Allies during the years 1914–1917. This led to the notion that American participation in World War I had been arranged by "merchants of death," assisted by British propagandists. There was increasing feeling that William Jennings Bryan had been correct in 1914 in urging that the United States supply no arms to the belligerents, make them no loans, and abandon defense of neutral rights on the high seas. To prevent being drawn into war again, Congress passed Neutrality Acts in 1935, 1936, and 1937. These laws barred the transportation or sale of arms to warring nations and banned loans to nations at war outside the Western Hemisphere.

The restrictions of the Neutrality Acts did not please Roosevelt who believed they would "drag us into the war instead of keeping us out." He had wanted legislation that would allow him more discretion—for example, to embargo supplies on one side but not to the other. On October 5, 1937, he warned the American people that war was contagious:

> *Innocent people are being cruelly sacrificed to a greed for power and supremacy. . . . Let no one imagine that America will escape. . . . War is contagion, whether it be declared or not.*

Roosevelt signed the Neutrality Acts without protest. However, he would have preferred some freedom to distinguish between aggressors and victims. The President believed that Germany, Italy, and Japan were "bad neighbors" who were bent on war. In a speech in October 1937, Roosevelt called for the abandonment of isolation, but American public opinion forced him to drop any idea of collective action against aggressor nations. "It's a terrible thing," Roosevelt remarked, "to look over your shoulder when you're trying to lead—and find no one there."

Section 1 ★ Review

Checking for Understanding
1. **Identify** Benito Mussolini, Munich Conference, Neutrality Acts.
2. **Define** fascism, totalitarian, appeasement.
3. **Describe** what influence the Depression had in shaping American foreign policy.
4. **Examine** Japan's objectives in its aggressive expansion in Asia.

Critical Thinking
5. **Evaluating Policy** Should one country intervene militarily in the affairs of another to protect property owned by its citizens? Explain.

---

810   UNIT 9 Times of Crisis: 1932–1960

Answers to SECTION 1 REVIEW

1. Benito Mussolini, 808; Munich Conference, 809; Neutrality Acts, 810
2. All vocabulary words are defined in the Glossary.
3. preoccupation with domestic economic crisis, policy of economic isolation, unwilling to jeopardize recovery by international cooperation
4. ease overcrowding at home, provide raw materials and markets for growing industry
5. Answers will vary. Some may say United States owes protection to American businesses abroad; others may argue that when American companies go to other countries, out of reach of American power, they take their chances; still others may note that the United States would oppose such intervention in its affairs by another country.

SECTION 2

Moving Closer to War

Setting the Scene

Section Focus

As war in Europe became a certainty, a great debate took place among Americans over what role the United States should play. Isolationists opposed any American involvement in European affairs and wanted the United States to act independently in the world. On the other side of the debate, internationalists believed that America's own security was linked to the success of Europe's struggle against Hitler.

Objectives

After studying this section, you should be able to
★ discuss Germany's military conquest of Europe during the late 1930s and early 1940s.
★ list the steps by which the Roosevelt administration increased American support to the Allies and the effects these steps had.

Key Terms

blitzkrieg, lend-lease

◀ BRONZE STAR, AWARDED FOR HEROISM

The most outspoken isolationists in Congress were progressive Republicans mainly from the Midwest and the West. Their primary support came from a number of newspapers, most notably those in the William Randolph Hearst chain. On the radio Roosevelt's New Deal critic, Father Charles Coughlin, also lined up with the isolationists. An America First Committee sponsored rallies around the country against the war. A frequent speaker was the popular pilot Charles Lindbergh who warned that "the only way our American life and ideals can be preserved is by staying out of this war." The internationalists were strongest in the Democratic party and generally represented states in the South and the Northeast. They looked to President Roosevelt for leadership.

■ Europe at War Again

As Churchill had predicted, the Munich agreement failed to appease Hitler, who in March 1939 swallowed up the rest of Czechoslovakia and demanded territory in Poland. Britain and France pledged to defend Poland from Hitler, and they asked the Soviet Union to join in an alliance to contain Germany. In August 1939, however, Soviet dictator Joseph Stalin signed a nonaggression pact with Germany. By removing the threat of war on two fronts, the pact cleared the way for Hitler to invade Poland. Hitler still doubted that Britain and France would resist him, however.

▲ PURPLE HEART

CHAPTER 29 World War II 1933–1945   811

Classroom Resources for SECTION 2

Teacher's Classroom Resources
- Reproducible Lesson Plan
- Reteaching Activity 29-2
- Chapter 29 Primary and Secondary Source Readings
- Section Quiz

Multimedia
- Section Focus Transparency 93
- Chapter 29 Map Transparency
- Testmaker
- Student Self-Test Software
- Lessons of War

LESSON PLAN
SECTION 2, 811–816

FOCUS

Bellringer

Prior to taking roll at the beginning of the class period, display Focus Activity Transparency 93 on the overhead projector, and assign the accompanying Focus Activity Sheet.

Objectives

Point out the objectives on this page to students in previewing the section content.

Motivating Activity

Have students turn to page 812 and direct their attention to Winston Churchill's words from a speech in which he offers his people only "blood, tears, sweat, and toil" and pledges to fight the Germans to the end. Ask: As an American, how would you have responded to these words in 1940? Tell them that they will find out more about the events surrounding this speech in Section 2.

ABC NEWS INTERACTIVE™

The following material is available from Glencoe and may be used to introduce or enrich Chapter 29:

 VIDEODISC
Lessons of War
Side 1
Chapter 7: Can War Be Justified?

811

CHAPTER 29
SECTION 2

TEACH

Guided Practice

History Have students write answers to the following questions: Why was the giving of destroyers to Britain in exchange for bases a dangerous precedent-setting decision? (It expanded the power of the President in international crises.) What was a major reason Roosevelt won reelection in 1940? (Americans did not want to gamble on a leadership change in time of crisis.) What caused Congress to revise the Neutrality Acts? (increased German attacks on American ships supplying Britain) Discuss students' answers. **L2**

Did You Know?

Father Charles Coughlin, better known as the "radio priest," established the newspaper *Social Justice*, which was his forum for espousing anti-Semitic feelings as well as his admiration for fascist doctrines.

Visualizing History The photograph and cartoon illustrate the same idea: the power of the Nazi storm troopers. **Answer to Caption:** The cartoon expresses the idea that the Nazis were a seemingly unstoppable force rolling over conquered nations.

Visualizing History ▲ THE FALL OF POLAND Nazi troops march through the streets of Warsaw after the fall of Poland. The conquest of Poland had taken little more than a month. *What point does the cartoon express?*

Outbreak of War

Before dawn on September 1, 1939, German forces crossed into Poland in an attack so fast and brutal that a new word was coined—**blitzkrieg,** meaning "lightning war." This time Britain and France decided to fight, and on September 3 they declared war on Germany.

President Roosevelt declared that the United States would remain neutral, but he added, "Even a neutral cannot be asked to close his mind or his conscience." Within weeks he asked Congress to lift the Neutrality Acts' arms embargo that prevented Britain and France from buying American weapons. Although Congress was flooded with telegrams urging it to "keep America out of the blood business," after weeks of debate, it agreed to sell arms to the Allies if they paid cash and carried the goods in their own ships.

Near Disaster at Dunkirk

After a lull in the fighting over the winter of 1939–1940, Hitler launched an invasion of Norway and Denmark. Next, the German armies swept into the Netherlands and Belgium, where for the first time they met resistance from British and French troops. In May 1940, German forces defeated the Allied army and drove it to the sea at the French town of Dunkirk on the Belgian border. Cut off from retreat by land, the army was saved when 300,000 British and French troops were evacuated across the English Channel in a heroic nine-day rescue effort aided by 600 private boats.

Battle of Britain

In June 1940, Italy suddenly invaded France and declared war on Great Britain. In response, Roosevelt announced that,

812 UNIT 9 Times of Crisis: 1932–1960

Sidelights: Rationing in Wartime

During the early years of World War II, Germany was one of the best-fed of the European combatant nations. Germany's rationing plan provided its citizens with 2,000 calories per day—95 percent of the calories received in peacetime. Soviet citizens received about 1,800 calories per day, while people in occupied Belgium, the Netherlands, Finland, and Norway received less than 1,800. Citizens of the Baltic states, Poland, France, Italy, and Greece were lucky to get 1,500 calories per day.

although the United States would not enter the war, it would extend as much aid as possible to the democracies. On June 22 France surrendered, and Britain faced Hitler alone.

As the German air force bombed British airfields, factories, and cities to prepare the way for German armies to cross the English Channel, Britain found leadership in its new prime minister, Winston Churchill. Offering only "blood, toil, tears, and sweat," he pledged:

> ... we shall defend our island, whatever the cost may be. We shall fight on the beaches. We shall fight on the landing grounds. We shall fight on the fields and in the streets. We shall fight in the hills. We shall never surrender. ... until, in God's good time, the New World, with all its power and might, steps forth to the rescue and liberation of the Old.

America Abandons Neutrality

Prime Minister Churchill asked the United States for a loan of 50 destroyers to protect British shipping from German submarines. Recognizing that the isolationists in Congress would block approval of the loan, Roosevelt decided to act on his own. In September 1940, by executive order, he transferred 50 old World War I destroyers to Britain in return for the use of bases in Newfoundland and the Caribbean.

Meanwhile, for months London suffered bombing day and night by hundreds of German planes. The fighter pilots of the Royal

▶ WATCHING THE GERMAN ARMY ENTER PARIS

▲ **DUNKIRK** As the trapped British and French armies awaited evacuation at Dunkirk, they were bombarded by German planes and artillery. The largest retreat in military history was accomplished by the British navy and private boats ranging from yachts to tugboats, all protected by the Royal Air Force. Huge amounts of equipment were left behind, but Britain's army was saved from total destruction. *What effect did the fall of France have on American foreign policy?*

CHAPTER 29 World War II 1933–1945   813

CHAPTER 29 SECTION 2

Independent Practice

Debate Divide the class into two groups. One group should represent isolationists; the other group should represent internationalists, or groups who favored aid to our allies and a stronger defense program. After doing further research on isolationist and internationalist movements of the 1930s, have the students debate the following topic: The United States should have entered the war in 1940. The students should present sound arguments for their positions. **L2**

Did You Know?

Besides *blitzkrieg*, Germany used other war tactics such as *sitzkrieg*, in which there existed a lull in hostilities, only to be followed by a series of German attacks against countries without a declaration of war.

Visualizing History This painting highlights the drama of the Dunkirk rescue by focusing on the many small boats that evacuated thousands of British and French soldiers.

Answer to Caption: The fall of France worried many Americans. Although it did not result in a declaration of war, the U.S. did reinstitute the draft and increase its defense spending.

Cooperative Learning

Pose the following question to students: What were some reasons for the shift in American public opinion away from isolation? Give students time to think of a response. Have them pair up and discuss their responses. Ask students to share their responses with the class. (Students might cite that the fall of France and the threat to Britain shook many Americans out of the belief that events outside the Western Hemisphere were none of their business. Students might also include Roosevelt's appropriation for defense and the passage of the Selective Service Act in 1940.) **L2, L3**

813

CHAPTER 29 SECTION 2

Fact or Fiction?

Isolationist sentiment in the United States arose in part from the fact that the nation was an ocean away from the conflict in Europe and Asia.

FACT: In the days before intercontinental missiles and supersonic jet flights, the Atlantic and Pacific oceans made many Americans feel protected within their own borders.

Visualizing History

Point out that the Nazis established major death camps at Auschwitz, Treblinka, and Majdanek in Poland. Two-thirds of the Jewish population in Europe perished at these and other camps.
Answer to Caption: They began to heed Roosevelt's warnings.

Visualizing History ▲ **ARRESTING OPPONENTS** Hitler's secret police, the Gestapo, arrested Jews and other opponents of the government by the thousands. Many were sent to large prisons called concentration camps. Resistance by the imprisoned against Nazi atrocities took many forms, including trying to escape and rebelling against their captors. *How did Americans react to the fall of France and the threat to Britain?*

Air Force, however, kept the Germans from gaining control of the skies over Britain and forced Hitler to abandon his invasion plans. "Never in the field of human conflict," said Churchill, "was so much owed by so many to so few."

America Realizes Its Peril

The fall of France and the threat to Britain shook many Americans out of their belief that events outside the Western Hemisphere were none of their business. The possibility that Hitler and Mussolini might add the British and French fleets to their own made the Atlantic Ocean suddenly seem narrower, and Congress began to heed Roosevelt's warnings. It appropriated billions of dollars for defense and passed a Selective Service Act in September 1940, the first peacetime draft in American history, adding 800,000 men to the armed forces.

Roosevelt's Leadership Endorsed

In the presidential election of 1940, the debate between internationalists and isolationists was carried on in both major parties. The Republicans nominated a newcomer to politics—Wendell Willkie, a Wall Street lawyer and utility company executive, best known for his criticism of the New Deal. For Democrats the question was whether Roosevelt would seek a third term, breaking the precedent set by George Washington. With the United States facing war in Europe and Asia, Roosevelt felt his experience was needed. He kept silent until the Democratic convention, then announced that he would accept the nomination.

At first, both candidates agreed on foreign-policy issues. But when Willkie slipped in the polls, he began to warn that Roosevelt's reelection would mean war. Roosevelt's promise to keep American troops out of war, Willkie said, was no better than

UNIT 9 Times of Crisis: 1932–1960

Critical Thinking

Supporting an Opinion Remind students of the embargo cutting off exports of scrap metal to Japan, ordered by Roosevelt in 1940. The embargo was later extended to include other products with military uses. Discuss the embargo imposed against Iraq in 1990 and Haiti in 1994. Ask students to write their opinions on whether embargoes are successful in preventing war and to explain the reason for their answers. **L1, L2**

his promise to balance the budget. In November 1940, Roosevelt won reelection. With the world in crisis, most American voters did not want to gamble on a change in leadership.

Aid to a Desperate Britain

The British government was running out of money to pay for weapons, so the President proposed that the United States abandon its "cash and carry" policy. But not wanting to revive the old war-debts controversy, Roosevelt suggested a **lend-lease** policy, wherein the United States would merely lend goods to Britain, which the British could return or replace after the war. Lend-lease again stirred debate, but public opinion was shifting in Roosevelt's favor. A poll in January 1941 showed that 60 percent of Americans believed that it was more important to help Britain than to keep out of war. In March 1941, large majorities in both houses of Congress passed lend-lease, authorizing the President to send American supplies and weapons to other nations on any terms he thought would protect the security of the United States.

Battle for the Atlantic

It was one thing to enact lend-lease, however, and another to get supplies across the Atlantic in time to help. When Hitler attacked Yugoslavia and Greece in the spring of 1941, the Nazis overran those countries before lend-lease aid could reach them. When Hitler's bombers failed to knock out Britain, he ordered his submarine fleet to starve that nation into submission.

In trying to make sure that lend-lease supplies reached their destination, the United States was drawn step-by-step into the critical battle of the Atlantic. As German U-boats sank British and American supply ships almost daily, Roosevelt ordered the United States Navy to protect merchant shipping. By the fall of 1941, American and German warships were exchanging fire, and in October a German U-boat sank an American destroyer, killing more than 90 members of its crew. Congress responded by revising the Neutrality Acts to allow merchant ships to be armed.

Germany Turns on a Former Ally

While German-American tensions were escalating in the Atlantic, in June 1941 Hitler, wanting Russia's vast wheat and oil supplies, suddenly attacked the Soviet Union. As German armies quickly advanced into the USSR, Stalin signed an alliance with Great Britain, and the United States offered lend-lease aid. American isolationists were outraged that Roosevelt would aid the Soviets. But Churchill knew that American aid to the Soviet Union would reduce German pressure on Britain. In supporting Roosevelt's decision, he remarked:

> *I have only one purpose, the destruction of Hitler. . . . If Hitler invaded Hell I would at least make a favorable reference to the Devil in the House of Commons.*

▲ **STRATEGY SESSION** Before the United States entered the war, Roosevelt and Churchill met to coordinate Allied strategy and to make peacetime plans. Out of this meeting off the North American coast in August 1941, plans emerged for the United Nations. **How did Churchill feel about helping Stalin?**

CHAPTER 29
SECTION 2

Visualizing History Churchill and Roosevelt formed a strong working partnership in the early years of the war. Some Americans saw that partnership as a threat to U.S. neutrality.
Answer to Caption: Churchill felt that it would reduce German pressure on Britain.

Did You Know?

During the bombing of Great Britain from September 1940 to May 1941, large areas of London and the entire city of Coventry were reduced to rubble.

Sidelights: The U.S.S. *Reuben James*

Several incidents in 1941 increased tensions between the United States and Germany. In September a German submarine attacked an American destroyer, the *Greer*, which was on its way to Iceland. Roosevelt used this incident to order the navy to protect the merchant vessels of all nations. On October 20, 96 American sailors died when the destroyer U.S.S. *Reuben James* sank after being hit by a German torpedo. As a result Roosevelt pushed through Congress a measure that authorized the arming of U.S. merchant ships and permitted these ships to carry war supplies to Britain.

CHAPTER 29 SECTION 2

ASSESS
Check Understanding
Assign Section 2 Review as homework or an in-class activity.

Evaluate
📁 🖥 Assign the Section 2 Quiz in the TCR, or use the History of a Free Nation Testmaker to create a customized quiz.

Reteach
Provide students with the following event: Congress passes the Lend-Lease Act. Ask students to identify a cause and an effect. (Cause: Roosevelt desires new ways to aid Britain's war efforts; Effect: America sends supplies and weapons to Britain.)
📁 Have students complete Reteaching Activity 29-2.

Enrich
Have students use library resources to find more information about the evacuation of Dunkirk. Ask them to share their information in the form of oral reports. They might use statistical information to accompany their reports.

CLOSE
Remind the class that Roosevelt hoped that the United States would become "the great arsenal of democracy." Ask students to discuss the ways in which the United States was fulfilling Roosevelt's hope based on what they learned in Section 2.

By the end of November 1941, very few Americans were preaching isolation. Most agreed with Roosevelt that the United States must be an "arsenal of democracy" to supply Great Britain and the Soviet Union against Hitler. In fact, about 15,000 Americans were already at war, most in British or Canadian uniforms.

■ Aggression in the Pacific

While the American public's attention was fixed on the Atlantic and Europe, events were taking place in the Pacific and Asia that would eventually plunge the United States into war. Already in China, Japan moved against European colonies in Southeast Asia. This vast region contained the rice, rubber, tin, zinc, and oil needed for Japan's expanding industries. With France defeated, Britain on its knees, and the Soviets retreating in front of German armies, the United States was the only remaining obstacle to Japanese ambitions in the Pacific.

Embargo
In September 1940, Japan allied with the Axis Powers, Germany and Italy, and the United States responded by cutting off exports of scrap metal to Japan. As Japan continued its aggression in Asia, Roosevelt extended the embargo to include other products with possible military uses. In July 1941, he told the Japanese that the United States would help them find raw materials if they abandoned their policy of conquest. When Japan rejected his proposal, the President halted all trade with Japan and ordered American forces in the Pacific to prepare for war.

Appeal for Peace
On October 18, 1941, the Japanese prime minister, Prince Fumimaro Konoye, resigned. Konoye had been willing to negotiate with the United States because he did not believe Japan could defeat America in a war. The new prime minister, General Hideki Tojo, did not share Konoye's views. He favored war to eliminate American and British influence in Asia.

By late November, as the United States continued to insist that Japan honor the Open Door policy, Japanese leaders decided that if the dispute did not quickly come to a favorable conclusion, they would attack. Nonetheless, on November 20, negotiations were opened in Washington, D.C. Representing the United States was Secretary of State Cordell Hull. Ambassador Admiral Kichisaburo Nomura and special envoy Saburo Kurusu represented Japan.

The Talks Stall
As negotiations deadlocked, Roosevelt realized that war was inevitable. On December 6, the President appealed for peace directly to Japan's Emperor Hirohito. American officials did not know that, on November 26, a Japanese fleet had put to sea, headed for the United States's main naval base in the Pacific—Pearl Harbor in Hawaii.

Section 2 ★ Review

Checking for Understanding
1. **Identify** Winston Churchill, Selective Service Act, Pearl Harbor.
2. **Define** blitzkrieg, lend-lease.
3. **Describe** why hostilities developed between the United States and Japan.
4. **Explain** the importance of the election of 1940.

Critical Thinking
5. **Citing Evidence** What actions and policies demonstrated that Congress and Roosevelt recognized the possibility that the United States would be drawn into war?

Answers to SECTION 2 REVIEW
1. Winston Churchill, 813; Selective Service Act, 815; Pearl Harbor, 816
2. All vocabulary words are defined in the Glossary.
3. Japan's ambitions and America's Open Door policies in Asia long had clashed. With Europe at war, Japan viewed the United States as its only barrier to expansion. When negotiations failed, Japan attacked.
4. Foreign policy was a campaign issue settled in favor of interventionists by reelection of Roosevelt; this opened way to supplying arms to Allies.
5. Roosevelt appropriated $13 billion for defense. Selective Service Act drafted 800,000 men immediately.

SECTION 3

The United States at War

Setting the Scene

Section Focus

Three days after Congress declared war on Japan, Germany and Italy declared war on the United States. Americans now faced war in both Europe and Asia. Japan's unprovoked attack had ended the public debate over foreign policy. The American people were now united in their determination to win the war.

Objectives

After studying this section, you should be able to
★ discuss the course of the war in Europe and in Asia.
★ describe the Atlantic Charter and the agreements the Allies reached at the Yalta Conference.

Key Term

Holocaust

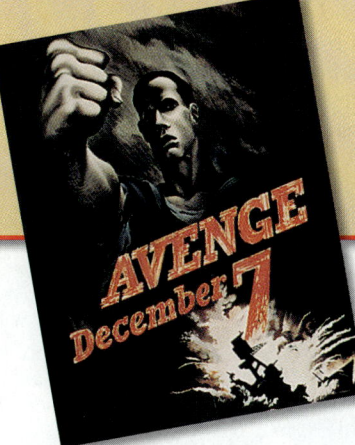

◀ UNITED STATES POSTER AFTER BOMBING OF PEARL HARBOR

With little warning, Japanese bombers attacked the American fleet based at Pearl Harbor. Shortly after noon on Sunday, December 7, 1941, President Roosevelt had just finished lunch when he received an urgent telephone call from Frank Knox, the secretary of the navy. The secretary had just received a wire from Hawaii: "Air Raid on Pearl Harbor. This is no Drill."

In 2 hours, Japanese planes sank many vessels, including 5 battleships and 3 destroyers, and heavily damaged many others. The attack also destroyed about 250 airplanes, and about 4,500 people were killed or wounded. Only the fleet's aircraft carriers, out of the harbor on maneuvers, escaped the devastation.

■ The World at War

However determined the American people were to defeat the Axis Powers—Germany, Italy, and Japan—the immediate outlook was bleak.

Japanese Victories in the Pacific

The destruction of the American fleet removed Japan's only obstacle in the Pacific. For six months the Japanese won victory after victory, capturing American bases at Guam and Wake Island, conquering Britain's colonies at Hong Kong and Singapore, and occupying the independent kingdom of Thailand. In April 1942, American forces on the peninsula of Bataan in the

CHAPTER 29 World War II 1933–1945   817

Classroom Resources for SECTION 3

Teacher's Classroom Resources
- Reproducible Lesson Plan
- Reteaching Activity 29-3
- Chapter 29 Primary and Secondary Source Readings
- Section Quiz

Multimedia
- Section Focus Transparency 94
- Chapter 29 Map Transparency
- U.S. History and Art Transparency 25
- Student Self-Test Software
- A Geographic Perspective on American History
- Lessons of War

LESSON PLAN
SECTION 3, 817–826

FOCUS

Bellringer
Before taking roll at the beginning of the class period, display Focus Transparency 94 on the overhead projector, and assign the accompanying Focus Activity Sheet.

Objectives
Point out the objectives on this page to students in previewing the section content.

Motivating Activity
Ask students what military strategy they think would be most effective in fighting a two-front war. (Some students might indicate that the best way would be to focus on one front at a time. Others might suggest that an all-out effort on both fronts would be the best way to fight and end the war.)

Assign students the Chapter 29 Reading in Primary and Secondary Source Readings.

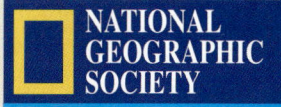

- *GTV: A Geographic Perspective on American History*

Side 4, Chapter 6
Title: *Echoes of War*
Subject: Effects of World War II on America

See GTV Guide page 61 for complete lesson plan.

CHAPTER 29 SECTION 3

TEACH

Guided Practice

Chronology Write the following on the chalkboard or overhead transparency or distribute as a handout:

Place the following events in chronological order and add dates to each entry.

__(4)__ a. The Axis armies in North Africa surrendered. (May 1943)
__(5)__ b. Germany surrendered unconditionally. (May 7, 1945)
__(2)__ c. American warships defeated Japanese fleet in the Battle of the Coral Sea. (May 1942)
__(6)__ d. Americans dropped atomic bomb on Hiroshima. (August 6, 1945)
__(1)__ e. Japanese attacked Americans at Pearl Harbor. (December 7, 1941)
__(3)__ f. Hitler's forces surrendered in Russia after being surrounded by Soviet troops. (February 1943)
__(7)__ g. Japanese surrendered on the battleship *Missouri*. (September 2, 1945)

Hold a discussion on students' sequential choices. **L1**

Visualizing History
The anti-Japanese sentiment implied by the racial epithet in the newspaper headline was widespread during the war.
Answer to Caption: silenced many who had previously opposed involvement in the war and ended support for American isolationism

---

Philippines finally surrendered. Meanwhile, the Japanese forces conquered Burma and the East Indies.

German Success in Europe

Axis forces occupied nearly all of Europe, and Britain was besieged. In North Africa, German General Erwin Rommel, "the Desert Fox," led an Italian-German force toward the Suez Canal, pushing the British back to the borders of Egypt. By summer 1942 the Germans had pushed deep into the Soviet Union, capturing the rich farmland of Ukraine and threatening the cities of Stalingrad, Leningrad, and Moscow. Success or failure of the war in Europe depended on whether the Soviet Union could hold out until the United States and Britain could launch an offensive on the western front.

Even before Japan attacked Pearl Harbor, American strategists had decided that in the event of war, United States forces would concentrate on defeating Hitler before dealing with Japan. Not only did the United States have closer ties with the countries occupied by Germany, but Germany seemed a greater threat to the Western Hemisphere, where Nazi sympathies were strong in several Latin American nations. Churchill agreed with this plan, observing that

> "... [T]he defeat of Germany... will leave Japan exposed to an overwhelming force, whereas the defeat of Japan would by no means bring the World War to an end."

Turning Point of the War

Meanwhile, German troops launched a second attack on the Soviets in 1942. In the spring they moved toward the oil fields near the Caspian Sea, and by midsummer

 **PEARL HARBOR** Japan's surprise attack on Pearl Harbor severely damaged the United States Pacific Fleet. In addition, about 250 warplanes were destroyed and more than 2,400 Americans were killed. *How did the attack affect American public opinion about isolationism?*

Cooperative Learning

Divide the class into groups of three. Have each group analyze the propaganda used by both the Axis Powers and the Allied Powers during World War II. Assign each member of the group one of the following tasks: researching the information, writing descriptions and summaries of the information, and analyzing the propaganda. Have the members of each group combine their tasks to make a presentation to the class. Groups should include visual examples of the propaganda in their presentations. **L2**

CHAPTER 29
SECTION 3

World War II in Europe and Africa

Churchill and Roosevelt delayed an attack in Europe to first fight in the Mediterranean. Some historians believe this was a plan to weaken Soviet power in postwar Europe. **What reasoning might support such a theory?**

Map Study Maps Study

Answers: Originally Stalin had cooperated with Hitler. Churchill's distrust of Stalin's intentions was well known. Delaying the invasion forced the Soviets to face the Germans alone, increased Soviet losses, and weakened them as a postwar power.

Skills Practice

Ask students to identify the major Axis Powers shown on the map. (Germany, Italy)

Did You Know?

The attack on Pearl Harbor repeated Japan's surprise attack on February 8, 1904, against Russian ships lying at anchor in Port Arthur, Manchuria. That attack set off the Russo-Japanese War of 1904–1905.

Side 2, Chapter 8
Title: *At the Front*
Subject: Contributions of minorities in World War II

---

they were more than halfway to their goal. Stalin pleaded with the Allied leaders Roosevelt and Churchill for an invasion of western Europe that would take some pressure off the Soviet Union. Churchill told him that such a second front in Europe was a year away. Soviet troops were left to face the Germans alone.

In September 1942, the Red Army made a desperate and heroic stand at Stalingrad. For four months, Soviet and German troops battled house-to-house for control of the city. Although the German invasion was halted, Stalingrad was reduced to rubble and the Soviets suffered more casualties defending it than the United States did in the entire war. Stalin never forgave Roosevelt and Churchill for allowing this to happen.

In November the Soviet army counterattacked. Taking advantage of the Russian winter, the Red Army surrounded Hitler's freezing forces. In February 1943, the tattered remains of the invading German army, only one-third of its 330,000 men still alive, surrendered.

CHAPTER 29 World War II 1933–1945   819

Critical Thinking

Analyzing Events World War II resulted in the devastation of lives and property. Ask students the following question: Could World War II have been avoided? Why or why not? (Answers will vary. Some students might say that it could have been avoided if the Allies had not used the policy of appeasement with Hitler in the late 1930s; they might also indicate that it could have been avoided if the League of Nations had been given greater powers after World War I. Other students might say that a war could not have been avoided because force was the only way to stop the military aggression of Germany and Japan.) **L2**

CHAPTER 29
SECTION 3

Independent Practice

Mathematics Have students use library resources to compare World War II with World War I. The comparison should include the number of nations participating, the number of soldiers mobilized, the number of lives lost, and the amount of money spent. Students might present their information in the form of an oral report. The oral report should be accompanied by charts and graphs that illustrate the statistics. **L2**

Did You Know?

Poor weather postponed the D-Day operation, named Operation Overlord, for 24 hours, and weather looked unfavorable for the next day as well. Eisenhower knew that if he did not go ahead, the tidal and moon conditions would delay the invasion several months.

Visualizing History The code name for the planned invasion was "Operation Overlord." Most of the Allied troops landed from the water, but large numbers also came from the air on gliders and as paratroopers.

Answer to Caption: forced Hitler to move troops from the eastern front to fight Allied forces in France

German Weak Point Exposed

In North Africa, American and British forces, working first separately and then together, pushed Rommel and his Afrika Korps into Tunisia. Under the command first of Major General Lloyd R. Fredendall and then of Major General George S. Patton, American forces checked Rommel's drive at Kasserine Pass and took El Guettar and Bizerte. Under General Bernard L. Montgomery, the British took Tripoli and Tunis. By May, Rommel had fled, nearly 250,000 Axis troops had surrendered, and the campaign in North Africa was over.

Allied victories in North Africa cleared the way for an attack on what Churchill called "the soft underbelly" of Europe. In August 1943, British and American forces took Sicily, and in September they invaded the Italian mainland. After his defeat in Sicily, Mussolini was overthrown, and the new Italian government quickly surrendered. German troops still occupied Italy, however, and put up fierce resistance in the mountainous terrain. Not until June 1944 did the Allies enter Rome. Axis forces remained in control of northern Italy.

■ Victory in Europe

American and British air forces had already begun round-the-clock bombing of German industrial and transportation centers. But Hitler's armies had to be defeated on the ground.

Normandy Invasion

On June 6, 1944, the greatest amphibious force in history—176,000 troops carried in 5,000 vessels—crossed the English Channel to land along a 60-mile stretch of coastline in France. Planning for the "D-Day" invasion at Normandy had been under way for more than two years.

▲ **D-Day** American troops, under heavy fire from German defenders, stormed the coast of France from Coast Guard landing barges. British, Canadian, and free French forces also participated in the invasion. *How did the Normandy invasion take pressure off Soviet forces?*

Sidelights: Ernie Pyle

Journalist Ernie Pyle was a famous World War II correspondent. He traveled with the U.S. armed forces and covered campaigns in Europe, North Africa, and the Pacific. In 1944 Pyle won the Pulitzer Prize for journalism. The popular motion picture *G.I. Joe* was based on his European campaign in Italy. Ernie Pyle was killed by the Japanese while reporting on the war.

Under the command of American General Dwight D. Eisenhower, a million Allied forces were in France within a month after D-Day. On July 25 the Americans broke through the German line. By early August, General George Patton and his forces were racing across northern France through open countryside. In August American and British troops broke out of Normandy and struck rapidly eastward, entering Paris on August 25, 1944. In September they crossed the western border of Germany.

Rapid Soviet Advance from the East

At the same time, the Soviets closed in from the east. In January 1944, the Red Army freed Leningrad from an 890-day German siege, during which 800,000 residents died. By spring Soviet troops had freed Ukraine, and in July they entered Poland. In August Romania and Bulgaria surrendered, opening the Balkans to the Soviets. In December they entered Hungary. By the end of 1944, most of eastern Europe was in Soviet hands.

Germany Surrenders

In December 1944, Hitler ordered a counterattack in Belgium. Although Allied lines "bulged," the Germans could not break through. The Battle of the Bulge was the last German offensive. In March 1945, the Allies crossed the Rhine River and moved into the heart of Germany. Meanwhile, the Soviets pushed from the east, taking Berlin in April 1945. In April, Hitler committed suicide in his underground shelter in Berlin, and on May 7, 1945, German leaders agreed to an unconditional surrender. Franklin D. Roosevelt, who led the nation through the Depression and the war, however, did not witness this event. Only days before Hitler's suicide, the President died of a massive cerebral hemorrhage.

Crimes Against Humanity

As they entered Germany, Allied armies discovered evidence of one of the most terrible acts of the war—the Nazi **Holocaust,**

Visualizing History ▲ **CONCENTRATION CAMPS** The condition of survivors in Nazi death camps such as Belsen, Auschwitz, and Buchenwald horrified the world. **Why were the death camps created?**

or deliberate extermination of millions of European Jews and other civilians. As early as 1942, the United States government had received reports that Hitler had ordered the murder of all Jews in German-occupied territories. Only in 1944 did Roosevelt respond to criticism within his own administration that the United States was passively accepting the murder of Jews. He created a War Refugee Board, but for 6 out of 10 Jews in Europe, action came too late. Not until Allied troops reached the Nazi death camps—at Auschwitz, Dachau, Buchenwald, and elsewhere—and found the survivors and the gas chambers in which so many had died was the horrible truth fully realized. The Nazis had killed 12 million people, of whom 6 million were Jews.

CHAPTER 29
SECTION 3

Linking Across TIME

One key scientific gain during the war was the improvement and wide use of radar. Allied radar could detect incoming enemy aircraft long before these planes reached their target. As a result Allied fighter planes and antiaircraft were prepared when attacking planes arrived. Radar also provided accurate weather information for Allied aircraft crews.

Visualizing History Many Americans refused to believe the rumors circulating during the war about the systematic exterminations practiced in the concentration camps. Photographs like this awakened many Americans to facts they had tried to ignore.
Answer to Caption: systematically murder Jews and other minorities the Nazis regarded as racially inferior

Did You Know?

On the day following the attack on Pearl Harbor, Congress declared war against Japan. The only member of Congress to vote against war was Jeannette Rankin of Montana, who had also voted against America's entry into World War I.

Sidelights: Human Cost of War

Over 54 million military personnel and civilians died in World War II. The Soviet Union lost over 20 million people, China lost about 13 million, Poland lost 6½ million people (more than 22 percent of its population), Germany lost about 5 million, Japan over 1,800,000, France just under 500,000, Great Britain over 450,000, and the United States just under 300,000.

CHAPTER 29
SECTION 3

Map Study — Using Maps

Answer: They were the two strategic islands closest to Japan and could be used to launch attacks against Japan itself.

Map Skills

Have students use the arrows on the map to follow the drives of the American forces to reconquer the Pacific by tracing the campaign from year to year. The dates show when each campaign started and ended. When did American forces take the islands of Iwo Jima and Okinawa? (March 1945 and June 1945, respectively)

Fact or Fiction?

If it had not been for the Navajos, the marines might never have taken Iwo Jima.

FACT: A group of Navajos in the Marine Signal Corps confused the Japanese with a code based on the Navajo language.

ABC NEWS INTERACTIVE

Videodisc
Lessons of War

Side 1, Chapter 6
Title: *Can a Battle Change History?*
Subject: The Battle of Midway

War in the Pacific

In May 1942, American warships defeated a Japanese fleet in the Battle of the Coral Sea. In June Japanese forces tried to take the Midway Islands, an atoll in the central Pacific about 1,200 miles (1,920 kilometers) northwest of Hawaii. The naval and air Battle of Midway that ensued was a great victory for the Allies, resulting in the first major defeat of the Japanese navy. It slowed the Japanese advance across the central Pacific, brought an end to the threat to Hawaii, and ended Japanese naval superiority in the Pacific. Japan still held many heavily fortified Pacific islands. So the Allies

World War II in the Pacific

Map Study

While a joint British-American force freed Southeast Asia from Japanese occupation, American forces recaptured strategic islands as the forces moved northward toward the Philippines and Japan itself. **What strategic importance does the map show for Iwo Jima and Okinawa?**

822   UNIT 9 Times of Crisis: 1932–1960

Cultural Diversity

The over 16 million men and women who fought for the United States in World War II represented every cultural background, religious affiliation, and ethnic group in the nation. Although many faced discrimination in the armed forces, the overwhelming majority served their country with distinction. Encourage students to choose a particular group and research its contributions to the war effort. Of special interest is the role played by the 10,000 Japanese Americans who volunteered for service in World War II despite the fact that their families were held in "relocation centers."

adopted a military strategy called "island hopping"—to cut Japanese supply lines by capturing key islands and to use them as bases to attack other Japanese strongholds, especially the Philippines and eventually Japan itself.

Guadalcanal

In August 1942, Americans took the first step in the long and bloody road to Tokyo when marines landed on Guadalcanal in the Solomon Islands. The struggle for Guadalcanal was fought on the ground, at sea, and in the air, lasting six months. Not until 1943 did Japan's resistance there come to an end.

In attacking the United States, Japan had failed to realize the industrial power of America and its ability to mobilize that power rapidly. Of the 19 ships sunk at Pearl Harbor, 17 were returned to duty by December 1942, and new ships were constantly added. The navy worked out new ways of fueling and repairing ships at sea, allowing fleets to stay at sea for long periods of time.

During 1943 and 1944, American forces "island-hopped" toward the Philippines and Japan. In October 1944, Allied forces under the leadership of American General Douglas MacArthur landed in the Philippines. MacArthur's advance was matched by amphibious operations directed by Admiral Chester Nimitz against Japanese-held islands in the central Pacific.

Iwo Jima and Okinawa

In 1945 the last of Japan's island outposts fell with the taking of Iwo Jima (EE•woh JEE•muh) in March and Okinawa (oh•kuh•NAH•wuh) in June. Though Iwo Jima measures only a few square miles, American marines suffered more than 20,000 casualties in capturing it. Japan now began to use kamikazes (KAH•mih•KAH•zeez), suicide pilots who flew bomb-laden planes into American ships. During the invasion of Okinawa, kamikazes scored 279 hits on United States vessels.

By the summer of 1945, after Germany was defeated, all Allied power was turned against Japan. The Soviet Union agreed to declare war on Japan and confront Japan's forces in Manchuria. But the conquest of the Japanese islands was left to the United States. America's long-range B-29 bombers had been bombing Japan from bases on recaptured Pacific islands since June 1944. In one raid alone in March 1945, more than 83,000 Tokyo civilians were incinerated by American incendiary bombs. But despite such heavy casualties, Japan's military leaders rejected calls for unconditional surrender. American commanders worried that an invasion of Japan would meet heavy resistance and might cost a million lives.

Hiroshima and Nagasaki

Since early in the war, American scientists had secretly been developing an atomic bomb. First tested in New Mexico in July 1945, it gave Harry Truman, who became President after Roosevelt's death, another choice, and Soviet leader Stalin told Truman to "make good use of it."

After the Japanese government rejected Truman's final warning to surrender or risk "utter destruction," on August 6 an atomic bomb destroyed 60 percent of Hiroshima, a major Japanese industrial city. When Japan still refused to surrender, a second bomb was dropped on the city of Nagasaki on August 9, causing almost as much destruction as the first. The two attacks took about 150,000 Japanese lives. When reports of the death and devastation reached Tokyo, the stunned emperor, telling his people that "the unendurable must be endured," asked for peace. The final surrender took place on September 2, 1945, on the battleship *Missouri* anchored in Tokyo Bay.

◀ AMERICAN MILITARY HELMET NICKNAMED THE "STEEL POT"

CHAPTER 29
SECTION 3

Did You Know?

The U.S.S. *Arizona* was one of the battleships sunk by the Japanese at Pearl Harbor. A memorial structure was placed over the partly sunken ship in tribute to those who died in the attack. The ship remains where it came to rest on December 7, 1941.

GLENCOE
TECHNOLOGY

The following material available from Glencoe may be used to enrich Chapter 29:

VIDEODISC

Focus on Government

The United Nations Videodisc 3, Chapter 55

Sidelights: *Adagio for Strings*

After announcing the death of President Franklin D. Roosevelt from a cerebral hemorrhage, the NBC Radio Network played Samuel Barber's *Adagio for Strings*. Since that time, this sad, serene piece of music has been linked to occasions of public mourning. It has been used as a lament in hundreds of funerals and memorials all over the world.

CHAPTER 29
SECTION 3

Did You Know?

World War II was the first war in which women were given regular military status. About 350,000 women signed up. Most joined the Women's Army Corps (WACS) and the women's branch of the navy (WAVES).

Visualizing History Some Americans believed that the physically weakened Roosevelt, who died two months after the Yalta Conference, gave Stalin too much ground at Yalta.
Answer to Caption: agreed to occupy Germany after the war, encourage representative governments in eastern Europe, establish an organization for world peace, and secretly give the Soviets territories in Japan and China

ASSESS

Check Understanding

Assign Section 3 Review as homework or an in-class activity.

Evaluate

Assign the Section 3 Quiz in the TCR, or use the History of a Free Nation Testmaker to create a customized quiz.

Visualizing History ▲ **MEETING AT YALTA** Looking tired and drawn, Roosevelt (center) poses with Stalin (right) and Churchill during a break in their meetings at Yalta. Two months later, Roosevelt was dead. *What agreements were reached at Yalta?*

■ Wartime Diplomacy

The first planning for peace took place in August 1941 when Roosevelt and Churchill met on a ship off the coast of Newfoundland. At that meeting they issued the Atlantic Charter, a statement of principles on which depended "hopes for a better future for the world." Much like Wilson's Fourteen Points, the Atlantic Charter looked forward to a world where people would have the right to choose their form of government.

After Pearl Harbor, Roosevelt turned his attention to forming an alliance among the nations fighting against Hitler. On January 1, 1942, representatives of the 26 countries at war with the Axis Powers agreed to support the principles of the Atlantic Charter. They promised full economic and military support in the war, and they agreed not to make a separate peace.

In holding the great alliance together, Roosevelt and Churchill kept constantly in touch. Although they often did not agree on strategy, neither wavered in admiration for the other. Working closely with the other major Allies was more difficult. Japanese troops had pushed China's government deep into the interior, and Chinese leaders were unhappy that the war in Europe was the top priority. General Charles de Gaulle (dih•GOHL), leader of the French government in exile, disapproved of the United States's recognizing a government in south France that was friendly to the Nazis.

Cooperation with the Soviet Union proved the most difficult problem. Stalin had almost never been outside of his country and was suspicious of capitalist nations. Even so, the alliance between the United States and Great Britain and the Soviet Union lasted until the end of the war. Germany could not be defeated without Soviet aid, and the Soviets depended on supplies from Britain and the United States.

Planning for War and Peace

Cooperation in plans for war and peace was worked out in a series of international conferences. At Casablanca, Morocco, in January 1943, Roosevelt and Churchill agreed to demand "unconditional surrender" from the Axis Powers, assuring the Soviet Union that its allies would not sign a separate peace treaty with Germany.

Sidelights: Eleanor Roosevelt

President Truman appointed Eleanor Roosevelt one of the first American delegates to the new United Nations. In 1947 she was named chairperson of the UN Commission on Human Rights. After a year and a half of her determined leadership, the commission produced the Universal Declaration of Human Rights. This document states the basic principles of freedom and liberty for the people of the member states and territories under United Nations jurisdiction. The document still serves as a model for democratic governments all over the world.

At Cairo, Egypt, in November 1943, Roosevelt and Churchill met Chinese leader Chiang Kai-shek (jee•AHNG ky•SHEHK) and agreed that Japan should be stripped of its Pacific empire and Korea given independence. From Cairo, Roosevelt and Churchill flew to Tehran, capital of Iran, to meet with Stalin. There they promised that the D-Day invasion of France would be launched the next year. In return Stalin agreed to begin a new offensive against Germany at the same time from the east.

The Yalta Conference

In February 1945, Roosevelt, Churchill, and Stalin met for the last time at Yalta, in the Soviet Union. They agreed publicly that the United States, Britain, and the Soviet Union, along with France, should occupy Germany after the war, but they promised to encourage some form of representative government for the other peoples of Europe. They also agreed on a conference to be held at San Francisco in April 1945 to establish a world peace organization.

Secret agreements at Yalta covered the terms on which the Soviet Union could enter the war against Japan after Germany was defeated. The Soviets were promised Japanese territories, and that they could keep Outer Mongolia, in China, and obtain an ice-free naval port. In return, Stalin agreed to support the Nationalist government of Chiang Kai-shek instead of the Chinese Communists who were challenging Chiang for power.

Although the Yalta agreements later were attacked as a "sellout," at the time it seemed vital to keep the Soviet Union from making a separate peace with Germany when American and British forces were still fighting in the west. Even more important, the United States wanted Soviet support in the war against Japan.

Roosevelt's Death

When he reported to Congress on his Yalta trip, Roosevelt looked tired and pale. Two months later, on April 12, 1945, the President died suddenly at Warm Springs, Georgia. The nation he led for more than 12 years was shocked, and newspapers that printed daily lists of soldiers and sailors who had died in action added the name: "Roosevelt, Franklin D., Commander in Chief."

The United Nations

Two weeks after Roosevelt's death, representatives of 50 nations met at San Francisco to make plans for a new world organization. But the talks at San Francisco were made more difficult by rising suspicions among the Allies. The Soviet Union was keeping a firm hand on Poland and seemed to be breaking its Yalta promises. Still, the meeting at San Francisco produced a charter for the United Nations (UN). The preamble of the UN Charter pledged all the countries signing it to "faith in fundamental human rights," to "justice and respect" for the terms of peace treaties, and to the goal of living together. In July 1945, when the Senate ratified the Charter by a vote of 89 to 2, the United States became the first nation to join the UN.

Section 3 ★ Review

Checking for Understanding

1. **Identify** D-Day, Dwight Eisenhower, Harry Truman, Atlantic Charter, Yalta Conference.
2. **Define** Holocaust.
3. **Summarize** the progression of the war in Asia, Europe, Africa, and the Pacific.
4. **List** the meetings held among Allied leaders between 1941 and 1945.

Critical Thinking

5. **Anticipating Consequences** In a wartime alliance, what risk is carried by each nation that agrees not to make a separate peace?

CHAPTER 29 CONNECTIONS

Teaching Making Connections

Early in 1939 U.S. physicists saw the application of nuclear energy to military weapons. It was German-born physicist Albert Einstein who informed President Roosevelt of the potential military use of nuclear fission. The Manhattan Project was set up in 1942 to build a nuclear bomb, and on July 16, 1945, the first nuclear device was tested in a desert in New Mexico.

Did You Know?

The reconstruction of Hiroshima began about 1950. Today, Hiroshima has a population larger than it was before World War II. An annual "Peace Festival" is held in Hiroshima. Nagasaki has been mostly rebuilt and is the seat of Nagasaki University and many government offices.

Did You Know?

The effects of a nuclear explosion depend on the size of the bomb, weather, terrain, and the point of the explosion in relationship to the earth's surface. Two different types of atomic bombs were dropped on Hiroshima and Nagasaki. The one dropped on Hiroshima was smaller. However, more people—over 100,000—were killed in Hiroshima due to the city's flat terrain.

CONNECTIONS  CONNECTIONS

The Atomic Bomb

"We must not be the most hated and feared people in the world," a physicist wrote, urging President Truman not to use the atomic bombs that would kill some 150,000 mostly civilian Japanese.

Rumors that the Nazis might develop an atomic bomb spurred American and British efforts to build one. Scientist Albert Einstein wrote President Roosevelt urging that a major research program begin at once so that the nation would be the first with the bomb.

The secret project, later called the Manhattan Project, was carried out primarily at facilities in Oak Ridge, Tennessee, and, later, at Los Alamos, New Mexico. American physicist J. Robert Oppenheimer was the director, and he persuaded many top physicists to join the project. On July 16, 1945, the bomb was tested atop a steel tower in a lonely desert track at Alamogordo, New Mexico, called *Jorada del Muerto*, Journey of Death.

President Truman did not know the bomb existed until a few weeks before his decision to use it. Truman, who had taken office after President Roosevelt's death on April 12, received word of the test results in Potsdam, Germany, where he was in conference with Churchill, Stalin, and their top advisors. Roosevelt had told Churchill about the bomb. Although some historians disagree about why atomic bombs were dropped on Japan and about the ethical issues involved, President Truman believed the bombing was justified: "The dropping of the bombs stopped the war, saved millions of lives."

▲ THE DEVASTATION AT HIROSHIMA

Making the Science Connection

1. Why did the United States start the Manhattan Project?

Linking Past and Present

2. Given the present concerns about the dangers of nuclear war, do you think the United States was right to develop nuclear weapons? Why or why not?

826

Answers to CONNECTIONS

1. American leaders were concerned that Nazi Germany was close to creating an atomic bomb.
2. Answers will vary. Some students might argue that under no circumstances should the United States use nuclear weapons. Others may argue that nuclear weapons should be used for defensive purposes only or to save the lives of American military personnel.

SECTION 4

War on the Home Front

Setting the Scene

Section Focus

To fight the Axis Powers, the United States had to mobilize people and resources more quickly than ever before. By 1944 more than 11 million men and women were in uniform. As the number of industrial workers also rose to new heights, the war accomplished what the New Deal had never been able to—it ended the Depression's unemployment.

Objectives

After studying this section, you should be able to
★ discuss efforts to mobilize the economy for war production.
★ explain the war's impact on women, African Americans, and Japanese Americans.

Key Term

wildcat strike

◀ ROSIE THE RIVETER, SYMBOL OF WOMEN WORKERS DURING WORLD WAR II

Americans were amazed at the speed with which industry turned to making war materials. When in May 1940 President Roosevelt talked of producing 50,000 airplanes a year, some thought he was asking the impossible. Yet, by 1944 the number of planes produced annually had risen to about 100,000. Mass production was so effective in the ship industry that the average time for building a freighter dropped from a year to less than 2 months. In 4 years American shipyards put to sea tonnage equal to the entire merchant fleet of all the other countries of the world.

■ The Production Battle

As in World War I, federal agencies took on the direction of private companies doing war work. After a Senate investigation revealed corruption and mismanagement among companies involved in war production, in January 1942 Roosevelt gave a War Production Board strong regulatory power. Its head, Donald Nelson, could seize vital materials, order industrial plants to convert to war production, and prohibit manufacture of products he considered unessential to the war effort.

Rapid Conversion to War Production

Within weeks of Pearl Harbor, production of bicycles, beer cans, refrigerators, toothpaste tubes, and more than 300 other items was cut back or banned. Automobile manufacturers were ordered to convert production to tanks and other war supplies. Entire new industries were created. Synthetic rubber, for example, became important when Japan's conquest of Southeast Asia

CHAPTER 29 World War II 1933–1945   827

LESSON PLAN
SECTION 4, 827-833

FOCUS

Bellringer

Prior to taking roll at the beginning of the class period, display Focus Activity Transparency 95 on the overhead projector, and assign the accompanying Focus Activity Sheet.

Objectives

Point out the objectives on this page to students in previewing the section content.

Motivating Activity

Ask students what they know about the treatment given to Japanese Americans who were living in the United States during World War II. Write their responses on the chalkboard, and tell students they can check the accuracy of their ideas as they read Section 4.

VIDEODISC
Lessons of War

Side 2, Chapter 9
Title: *In the Crossfire*
Subject: Home fronts, here and abroad

Classroom Resources for SECTION 4

Teacher's Classroom Resources
- Reproducible Lesson Plan
- Reteaching Activity 29-4
- Chapter 24 Enrichment Activity
- Chapter 24 Performance Assessment Activity
- Spanish Summaries and Glossary
- Section Quiz

Multimedia
- Section Focus Transparency 95
- Chapter 29 Map Transparency
- Vocabulary Puzzlemaker
- Testmaker
- Student Self-Test Software
- The American People: Fabric of a Nation
- Lessons of War

827

CHAPTER 29
SECTION 4

TEACH

Guided Practice

Determining Cause and Effect Present the cause-and-effect concept map below, omitting the effects. Have students complete the map. **L1**

Event
- inflation due to World War II production

Causes
- increased employment
- increase in workers' earnings
- rise in prices of consumer goods

Effects
- government sets price ceiling on consumer products
- government rations goods
- 1943 act outlaws strikes against war industries

Teaching Life of the Times

Point out that many women during World War II also did volunteer work for the Red Cross, collecting over 13.3 million units of blood from donors during the war. Some of these Red Cross workers contributed over 14,000 hours of work, which amounts to 10 hours for every day of the war—without pay. Ask students to research the role the Red Cross played in the Persian Gulf War in 1991.

---

cut off America's supply of natural rubber. By the end of 1942, nearly 33 percent of American production went to war materials, and by 1944 nearly 50 percent. Production of all goods nearly doubled, and America's production of war materials matched the total output of Germany, Italy, and Japan combined.

In May 1941, Roosevelt set up the Office of Scientific Research and Development to mobilize science and technology for the war effort. Among the many inventions that came from this agency were DDT, which controlled insects and made jungle fighting more tolerable; the bazooka, a weapon that enabled an infantry soldier to destroy a tank; and radar, which determined the position and speed of airplanes and ships.

Financing the War

To raise funds for the war effort, the federal government increased taxes and sold war bonds in amounts ranging from $25 to $10,000. In 1942 the government extended the income tax for the first time to include middle- and lower-income people. To make collection easier, the government in 1943 began to require that employers deduct taxes from workers' paychecks before they received them.

The war increased employment, and workers' earnings rose as war production brought longer workweeks and overtime. As people had more money to spend, and as the shift to war materials made consumer goods scarce, prices rose. To combat inflation, in 1942 Congress created the Office of Price Administration, which set price ceilings on consumer products and began to ration goods that were in short supply. By war's end 20 items—including sugar, meat, butter, coffee, gasoline, fuel oil, and shoes—required government-issued rationing coupons to be presented at the time of purchase. Despite attempts to hold down prices, however, the cost of living rose 29 percent during the war, leading to demands for higher wages.

Life of the Times

The Home Front

Fan magazines reflected the changing role of women during the war. Magazines such as *Modern Screen* and *Photoplay-Movie-Mirror* used the lives of the stars to encourage patriotism, discourage extravagance, and sell products designed with the working woman in mind. In the 1920s and 1930s, fan magazines had emphasized movie stars' extravagant lifestyles, often depicting the stars as carefree, excessive consumers who felt little responsibility for the rest of society. Now *Photoplay* told readers that actress Ann Sheridan used her grocery money to buy Victory Bonds. An advertisement in the same magazine portrayed the use of lipstick as a woman's patriotic duty. Lipstick, the advertisement said, raised wartime morale, enhanced self-confidence, and proved that women could do "men's" work without sacrificing their femininity.

▲ Actress Ann Sheridan

Cooperative Learning

Group students into home teams of four or five, and then have them number off to form "expert groups." Expert groups consist of one member from each home team. Tell students in the expert groups to read Section 4 and find out how the government geared the nation's economy for war production. (Federal government agencies took on the direction of private companies doing war work and obtained promises from unions not to strike during the war.) Students in the expert group should discuss their findings and create a teaching tool that will help in sharing the material with their home teams. **L1, L2**

CHAPTER 29
SECTION 4

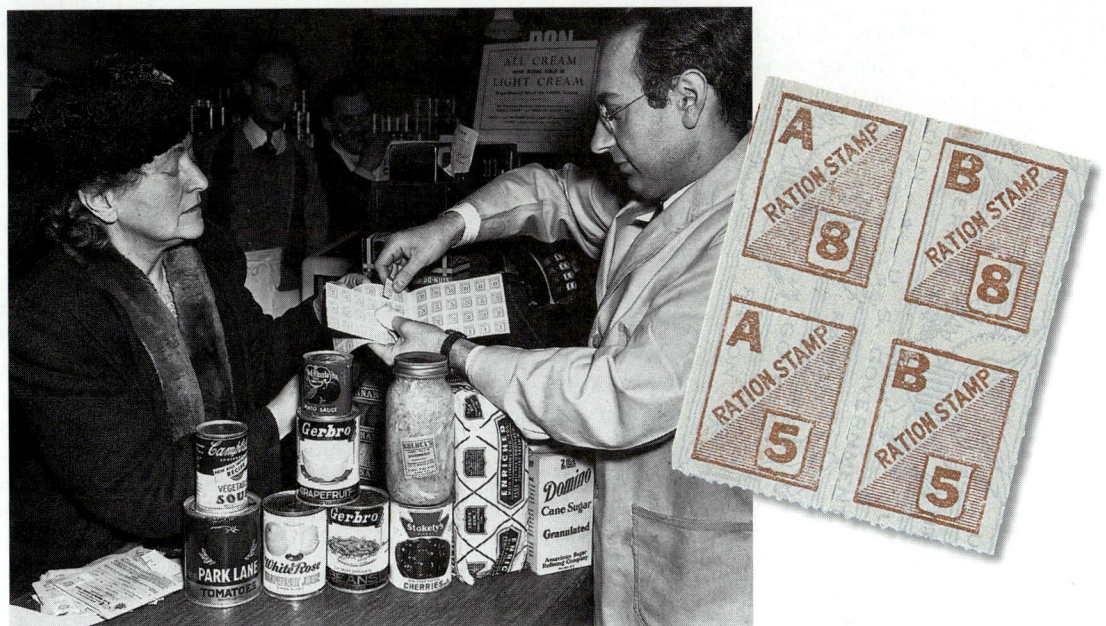

 **RATIONING** Ration stamps were used during World War II in an attempt to distribute essential goods fairly. Meat, butter, sugar, and gasoline were among the items that were rationed. **How did the cost of living change during the war years?**

Food of the Times

During the war sugar, coffee, processed and canned foods, meat, fish, and dairy products were all rationed. To compensate for the scarcity of meat, some homemakers cooked meatless dishes. Others used horse meat, which was unrationed. To make up for shortages of fresh vegetables, many families planted victory gardens. By 1943 they produced 40 percent of the nation's vegetables.

To help prevent strikes, a National War Labor Board was established to settle labor disputes by mediation. Although this task was made easier by the no-strike pledges that both the AFL and the CIO made after Pearl Harbor, there were many small **wildcat strikes**—work stoppages without union approval—and a short national strike by 500,000 coal miners. Even though most labor unions kept their no-strike pledge, an act passed in 1947 outlawed strikes against war industries.

■ The War and Social Change

The need for defense workers altered traditional patterns of American society. As millions of men joined the armed services, more women than ever before entered the labor force. "If you can drive a car, you can run a machine" became an advertising slogan for industries.

Women Assume Nontraditional Roles

The government, newspapers, radio, and newsreels encouraged women to take factory jobs as a patriotic duty, and 5 million American women entered the workforce during the war. "Rosie the Riveter," who first appeared in overalls in a Lockheed Aircraft poster, became a national symbol of the vital contribution women were making to the war effort.

More than ever before, women filled jobs that were not traditional for females. They worked on production lines, in steel mills, on the docks, and in other jobs that required heavy manual labor. Outside war industries, women also took over such traditionally male jobs as driving buses and trucks and working as train conductors, lumberjacks, and barbers. Most of these new workers were married and had children. Yet women still encountered resistance from male workers. As one female aircraft worker described it:

Did You Know?

During World War II rationing affected the clothing industry. Cuffs disappeared from men's trousers, and the vest passed out of style in an effort to conserve cloth.

Visualizing History

Some of the products shown in the photograph are still available today. Interested students could visit a grocery store to look for these brands and check their current prices.
Answer to Caption: The cost of living rose 29% as consumer goods grew scarcer and wages went up.

CHAPTER 29 World War II 1933–1945

Critical Thinking

Evaluating Decisions In 1942 the government removed over 100,000 persons of Japanese birth and ancestry from their homes on the Pacific Coast to poorly constructed relocation centers. Ask students the following question: Do you think the government ever has the right to relocate or keep a group in detention? Why or why not? (Answers will vary. Students who oppose the relocation policy might suggest that it was a violation of the Bill of Rights; those who agree with the policy might indicate that sometimes the country's security takes precedence over the issue of a group's rights.) **L2**

CHAPTER 29
SECTION 4

Independent Practice

Art During World War II, many posters were used to encourage Americans to cooperate in the all-out war effort needed to bring victory. Using the information in Section 4, have students make their own posters in which they encourage the American public to contribute to the war effort. Display students' completed posters. **L2**

Did You Know?

By 1943 the United States was producing twice the amount of war goods as all the enemy countries combined. By the end of the war, American industry had produced 296,000 aircraft, 102,000 tanks, 93,000 naval and cargo vessels, and 373,000 artillery pieces.

Visualizing History

The photographs shown here were probably posed. Women in factories wore overalls so that their clothing would not get caught in equipment. They also tied back their hair or wore nets so that it would not get caught in the machinery.
Answer to Caption: Most were lost to male workers returning from military service. Still, many more women remained in the workforce than before the war.

> *The men really resented the women very much.... [A]fter a while they realized that it was essential that the women worked there, 'cause there wasn't enough men, and the women were doing a good job.*

To encourage women to work, the government offered job-training courses, and Congress appropriated funds for child-care centers, but even this was not enough to meet the need. Federal and state governments suspended laws that limited the hours women could work, and women's wages rose as the concept of equal pay for equal work spread. Although at first most women considered their new employment to be temporary, by war's end 80 percent said they wanted to keep their jobs.

Opportunities for African Americans

The need for workers also speeded the shift of African Americans from farming to manufacturing. Many African Americans left the South and moved to cities in the Northeast, the Midwest, and California to work in war industries. Some companies hired few African Americans before the war, but by 1945 thousands of African Americans had jobs in defense plants.

Resentment Toward Social Change

Between 1941 and 1945, one of every five Americans relocated to another part of the country. The movement of so many Americans to fill jobs in war industries created housing shortages, crowded schools, and heightened social tensions. Old-timers resented the newcomers, regardless of their race. In California there were prejudices against "Okies," white migrants from Oklahoma and Texas who arrived in the 1930s to look for work after losing their farms in the Dust Bowl. In many cities prejudices arose against newly arrived African Americans. The police were needed to help African American families move into public housing in Detroit, when angry mobs tried to block them. It took federal troops to break a strike of streetcar operators in Philadelphia, who protested against the promotion of African American workers.

The federal government's response to racial discrimination during the war was uneven. In 1941 African American labor leader

Visualizing History ▲ **NEW OPPORTUNITIES** World War II offered increased job opportunities for women and for African Americans. Although women's wages rose, they still averaged 60 percent less than men's wages. *What happened to women's jobs when the war ended?*

UNIT 9 Times of Crisis: 1932–1960

Sidelights: Japanese Internment Camps

The Japanese internment camps were bleak and dismal. One in Santa Anita was formerly a race track, and detainees lived in horse stalls along with the stench of manure and the biting of horse flies. In the camp in Puyallup, Washington, the detainees were supplied with only one washroom for every 100 families. In many camps there was no electric lighting, which forced the detainees to use highly flammable kerosene lamps or candles.

American Portraits

Charles Drew
1904–1950

Born and raised in the segregated city of Washington, D.C., Charles Drew refused to let racial prejudice bar him from professional success. After graduating from Amherst College in Massachusetts, he earned his M.D. degree at Canada's McGill University.

In the 1930s Drew conducted pioneering research on blood plasma, and he established a model blood plasma bank. When the United States entered World War II, Drew was asked to head the military's blood plasma program. By collecting, storing, transporting, and transfusing donated blood plasma, this program saved the lives of countless wounded soldiers. But in 1942 Drew resigned when the military refused to accept blood donations from African Americans unless their blood was segregated from the blood of white donors and was given only to black soldiers.

A. Philip Randolph threatened to lead 100,000 protesters on Washington, D.C., to demand an end to discrimination in defense jobs and the armed forces. In order to stop the march, Roosevelt established the Fair Employment Practices Commission to promote minority hiring in government offices and in companies that had war contracts. But while it opposed discrimination, the commission did not reject segregation. Even the military remained segregated, and although hundreds of thousands of African Americans served in uniform in every capacity from cooks to fighter pilots, most served in all-black units.

Detention of Japanese Americans

The most significant racial discrimination of the war involved the removal of Japanese Americans from the West Coast. About 90 percent of all Japanese Americans, outside Hawaii, lived in California and the Pacific Northwest. Because of immigration restrictions after 1924, two-thirds had been born in the United States and were citizens by birth. Yet government officials were suspicious of their loyalty. When war broke out, residents of California, Oregon, and Washington feared that with the Pacific fleet at Pearl Harbor severely damaged, they were vulnerable to invasion at any time. Californians, in particular, were concerned that their neighbors of Japanese descent might engage in sabotage. Army General John DeWitt investigated and reported that:

> The Japanese race is an enemy race and while many second and third generation Japanese born on United States soil have become 'Americanized,' the racial strains are undiluted. . . . It, therefore, follows that along the vital Pacific Coast over 112,000 potential enemies of Japanese extraction are at large today.

Based on such reports, beginning in February 1942, the government moved 110,000 Japanese Americans to detention centers surrounded by barbed wire and patrolled by soldiers and confined them there for the duration of the war.

The order to evacuate Japanese Americans from the West Coast came quickly. Detainees had as little as 48 hours to make arrangements for their homes, businesses, and

CHAPTER 29 World War II 1933–1945 831

CHAPTER 29 SECTION 4

Teaching American Portraits

There is a sad ending to the life of Charles Drew. In 1950, at age 46, he was in a car accident in North Carolina. Drew was taken to a white hospital where he was refused treatment. Before he could be moved to another hospital, he bled to death. Ask students to explain the irony of this event.

Linking Across Time

American industry in World War II would not have been so productive had the American people not fully supported the war effort. Such support was in marked contrast to the detachment with which Americans traditionally had viewed Europe's great conflicts.

VIDEODISC

- *GTV: The American People: Fabric of a Nation*

Side 4, Chapter 2
Title: *United We Stand?*
Subject: Japanese internment during World War II

See GTV Guide page 92 for complete lesson plan.

Critical Thinking

Interpreting Primary Sources Obtain a copy of *Farewell to Manzanar* by Jeanne Wakatsuki-Houston and James D. Houston, which describes Jeanne Wakatsuki's experiences in a Japanese relocation camp. Read excerpts to the students, and discuss with them the conditions in which the Japanese Americans were forced to live. Have them speculate how they might have felt toward the American government if they had been sent to a relocation center like the one to which Wakatsuki was sent. **L2**

▲ **INTERNMENT OF JAPANESE AMERICANS** During World War II, persons of Japanese descent were sent to internment camps. More than 70,000 were Nisei, or American-born. *How did the Supreme Court rule on the detainees' appeal to protect their rights?*

Visualizing History It was not until January 1945 that the policy calling for the mass exclusion from the West Coast of persons of Japanese ancestry was terminated. **Answer to caption:** It upheld the government's policy as necessary to national security.

farms. Many had to sell their property at a loss or abandon it. Bargain hunters descended on them, taking advantage of their plight.

Arriving at one of 10 detention camps in isolated areas of Utah, Wyoming, Arizona, and other sparsely settled Western states, they were put to work at menial, low-paying jobs. Their military guards searched their quarters for "weapons," sometimes confiscating kitchen knives, scissors, and even knitting needles. Entire families lived out the war in a single room in army-style barracks furnished with cots and bare light bulbs. Since the authorities had no plans for running the camps, the detainees established their own camp governments, schools, and newspapers.

Almost immediately detainees appealed to the courts to protect their rights. When the issue came before the Supreme Court in December 1944, in *Korematsu* v. *United States*, the justices upheld the government's policy as necessary for national security.

Despite their unhappy experience, most Japanese Americans remained loyal to the United States. Thousands served in segregated military units. A Japanese American army unit recruited from detention camps fought in the Italian campaign and was the army's most decorated unit in American military history. However, the government's policy toward Japanese Americans at home became a blot on the nation's war record.

ASSESS
Check Understanding
Assign Section 4 Review as homework or an in-class activity.

Evaluate
 Assign the Section 4 Quiz in the TCR, or use the History of a Free Nation Testmaker to create a customized quiz.

Reteach
Have students complete Reteaching Activity 29-4.

Have students complete Chapter 29 Enrichment Activity in the Teacher's Classroom Resources.

CLOSE
Ask students how Americans reacted to the "patriotic challenge" referred to in the opening quotation by Frederich Crawford. Have them compare Americans' World War II patriotism with that during the Persian Gulf War in 1991.

Section 4 ★ Review

Checking for Understanding
1. **Identify** War Production Board.
2. **Define** wildcat strike.
3. **Explain** how the productive capacity of the industries of the United States aided the Allies' war effort.
4. **Contrast** the war's effects on African Americans and on Japanese Americans.

Critical Thinking
5. **Formulating Hypotheses** Why were Japanese Americans detained during the war while Americans of German or Italian descent were not?

Answers to SECTION 4 REVIEW
1. War Production Board, 827
2. All vocabulary words are defined in the Glossary.
3. converted many industries to war production, produced all goods and materials necessary to supply troops, amount of manufactured goods doubled
4. African Americans in defense jobs and armed services, though segregated; shift from farming to manufacturing, migration to North; white resentment and race riots.
5. Japan attacked Pearl Harbor, and Americans feared an attack on the West Coast, where there were high concentrations of Japanese Americans.

Social Studies Skills

Interpreting Primary Sources

Who Is an American?

Peter Ota was 15 when he was interned, or sent to a detention camp for Japanese Americans, in 1942. When he reached draft age, Ota was required to register for military service. He served in an armored division of the United States Army. In the following passage, Ota reflects on the effects of his internment on himself and his children.

From Studs Terkel, "The Good War, An Oral History of World War Two":

We came back to Los Angeles at the end of the war, believing that there was no other way but to be American. We were discouraged with our Japanese culture. My feeling at the time was, I had to prove myself. I don't know why I had to prove myself. Here I am, an ex-GI, born and raised here. Why do I have to prove myself? We all had this feeling. We had to prove that we were Americans, okay?

. . . We moved to a white community near Los Angeles. It was typical American suburb living. We became more American than Americans, very conservative. . . .

My children were denied a lot of the history of what happened. If you think of all those forty years of silence, I think this stems from another Japanese characteristic: when shame is put on you, you try to hide it. We were put into camp, we became victims, it was our fault. We hide it.

My oldest daughter, Cathy, in her senior year at college, wanted to write a thesis about the camp experience. She asked if we knew people she might interview. Strange thing is, many people, even now, didn't want to talk about it. Some of the people she did talk to broke down. Because this was the first time they had told this story.

▶ JAPANESE AMERICAN CHILDREN AT INTERNMENT CAMP

Examining the Primary Source

1. What effect did Peter Ota's experiences during World War II have on his feelings and opinions concerning Japanese culture?
2. How does Ota explain the long silence of Japanese Americans on the internment camps? Do you agree or disagree with Ota's explanation?

Critical Thinking

3. **Drawing Conclusions** What, in your opinion, may have prompted Ota's daughter to write about the camp experience?

LESSON PLAN
Mastering Social Studies Skills

Teaching Study and Writing Skills

Ask students to describe the overall impression of Ota's experience. Compare the information in Ota's account with what students already know about the internment of Japanese Americans during World War II. How does the document support their understanding of this event? (Sample: Ota's statements prove that Japanese Americans were loyal Americans.)

Explain that American law is based on rights of the individual and not rights of a group. American law does not recognize collective guilt. Consequently, the internment was illegal. Ask: How has the Congress dealt with this situation recently? (Appropriating money as reparations for Japanese Americans who were interned.) Could a similar internment policy be instituted in the future? (Answers will vary, but most students will say no because it is illegal.)

Did You Know?

Reparation payments for Japanese Americans placed in relocation camps during World War II have been a political issue since the war ended. In 1988 Congress finally voted to award a specific sum to each survivor of the relocation camps.

Answers to SOCIAL STUDIES SKILLS

1. He became discouraged with Japanese culture and felt that he had to prove that he was an American.
2. Ota attributed the silence to Japanese Americans' tendency to blame themselves and to hide their shame.
3. She wanted to know the history that her parents had withheld from her in order to increase her understanding of her parents and herself.

CHAPTER 29 ★ REVIEW

Using Vocabulary

Use each of the following words in a statement about the aggressor nations in World War II, the kind of warfare they conducted, and world response.

appeasement Holocaust
fascism totalitarian

Reviewing Facts

1. **List** reasons for isolationist policies in the United States and appeasement in Europe.
2. **State** the reasons for Japan's territorial ambitions in Asia.
3. **Chronicle** the steps by which the United States progressed from neutrality to war.
4. **Discuss** the priorities and sequence of the Allies' military campaigns in World War II.
5. **Explain** the difficulties Roosevelt and Churchill faced in dealing with Chiang Kai-shek, de Gaulle, and Stalin.
6. **Describe** how World War II affected women and minorities in the United States.

Understanding Concepts

International Alliances

1. How did World War II underscore the importance of an international organization such as the United Nations?
2. Explain the importance of Germany's 1939 nonaggression treaty with the Soviet Union to Hitler. Why do you suppose the Soviet Union signed it?

Military Conflict

3. Analyze Hitler's strategy for war. After his early victories, where did he go wrong?
4. Why did kamikaze missions pose such a deadly threat to American forces? What does this strategy suggest about the values and patriotism of the Japanese?

Critical Thinking

1. **Evaluating Policy** Economic problems at home was one reason that the United States initially avoided involvement in World War II. What subsequent developments suggest that this policy may have been self-defeating?
2. **Analyzing Fine Art** Study the painting of V-J Day on this page, then answer the questions.
   a. Does the painting have a central focus?
   b. Could you understand the meaning of this painting if it did not have a caption?

▲ V-J DAY—CROWDS CHEERING AT TIMES SQUARE by EDWARD DANCIG, 1947

Writing About History

Description

Write an extended definition of neutrality. Begin with a formal definition, followed by examples of neutrality as demonstrated by the Neutrality Acts. Use comparison and contrast to expand on the definition by showing how later foreign policy began to depart from neutrality as defined.

834 UNIT 9 Times of Crisis: 1932–1960

REVIEW CHAPTER 29

Answers

Reviewing Facts

1. Both Europe and America had economic problems; European nations did not want war and thought if they appeased Hitler, he would be satisfied; Americans believed it was a European problem.
2. wanted raw materials for production, land for rising population, and markets for industry; desired prestige through empire building
3. sold arms to Allies, provided destroyers by executive order, provided lend-lease to Britain, U.S. Navy protected merchant ships, American ships exchanged fire with German ships, extended lend-lease to Soviets, armed merchant ships
4. first focus on Germany and Italy; North Africa, 1942: U.S. and British forces defeat Germans; Mediterranean, 1943: invasion of Sicily, Italy surrenders; Europe, 1944: Allied army invades and liberates France, moves into Germany while Soviets press Germany from the east; Asia, 1942: defeat Japan's fleet in naval battles; Asia, 1942–1945: capture key islands in Pacific, retake Philippines, bomb Japan; Japan,1945: drop atomic bombs on Japan
5. They distrusted Stalin and Soviet intentions in Europe and Asia, and they were not convinced that the other two leaders really represented their people.
6. More women worked outside homes; minorities and women gained jobs and higher wages, served in armed forces, and contributed significantly to the war effort. By contrast, Japanese Americans were rounded up and interned during the war.

Understanding Concepts

1. The world's lack of unity and resolve against aggression allowed widespread conquests by several totalitarian dictators.
2. It freed Hitler to attack in Europe without threat of a two-front war. After their devastation in World War I, the Soviets were eager to avoid war.
3. After removing any Soviet threat with a pact, he blitzed through Europe; he went wrong in that he could not eliminate Britain, attacked Soviet Union, and did not anticipate United States aid to the Allies.
4. Such attacks were difficult to prevent because the pilot

CHAPTER 29 ★ REVIEW

Cooperative Learning

As a class, create a courtroom with students role-playing a panel of judges, a three-member prosecution team, three defense attorneys, a jury, three defendants, and an audience. Put the following people on trial for crimes against humanity: Adolf Hitler—for beginning World War II and establishing the Nazi death camps; a German military officer—for carrying out orders to execute Jews in a death camp; General Hideki Tojo—for ordering kamikaze attacks against Allied forces.

Social Studies Skills

Seeing Relationships on a Line Graph

Line graphs are commonly used to plot change over time. Frequency or quantity is charted on the *y*, or vertical, axis, while time is recorded on the *x*, or horizontal, axis. A line graph may help you see the relationship between a particular date and the frequency of a particular event.

To search for possible relationships, follow these procedures:
   a. Read the title and labels on the graph.
   b. Note any shifts in frequency or quantity at particular time points.
   c. Relate these changes to your knowledge of historical events.

Practicing the Skill

Use the line graph on this page to answer the following questions.
1. Which decade depicted on the graph shows the smallest increase in the number of women joining the labor force?
2. Which decade shows the largest increase in the number of women joining the labor force?
3. World War I was fought during which decade? World War II?
4. Summarize the apparent relationship between each war and the employment of women.
5. The text tells how women moved from higher-paying industrial jobs into clerical ones after World War II. Is this information represented on the graph? Explain.

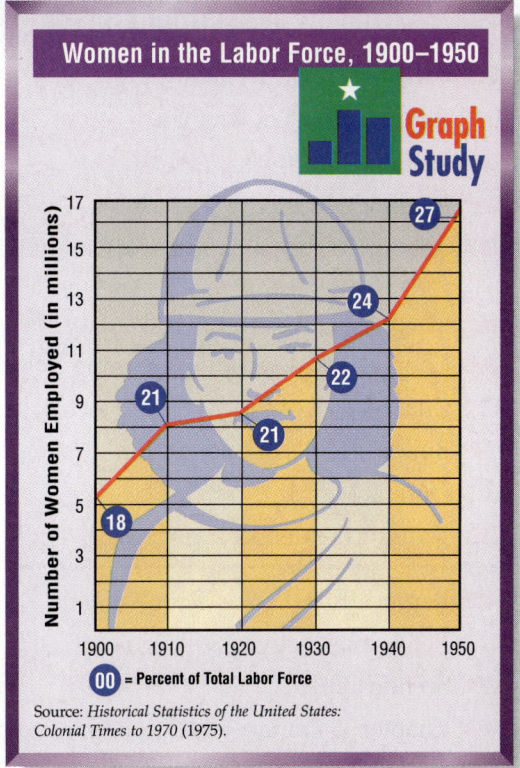

Women in the Labor Force, 1900–1950

Graph Study

Source: *Historical Statistics of the United States: Colonial Times to 1970* (1975).

00 = Percent of Total Labor Force

Using Your Journal

Write a paragraph describing the problems faced by an organization such as the United Nations, when it attempts to resolve international tensions like the ones that touched off World War II.

REVIEW CHAPTER 29

? Chapter Bonus Test Question

Give an example of the way the war heightened prejudices toward and discrimination against minorities. How do you account for that response? (Possible answers include internment of Japanese Americans and discrimination against African Americans.

Using Your Journal

The ideas students present in their paragraphs will vary but should include references to conflicts arising from competing interests. Students may refer also to specific countries and crises.

CHAPTER 29 World War II 1933–1945

---

was determined to sacrifice the plane and his life. Missions demonstrated that the pilots valued their nation, bravery, and national honor before life.

Critical Thinking
1. Although the New Deal did not keep the United States out of the war, the war's demand for goods and workers ended the Great Depression.
2. a. The painting has no central focus.
   b. Even without a caption, the painting suggests joy and celebration.

Practicing the Skill
1. 1910–1920
2. 1940–1950
3. 1910–1920; 1940–1950
4. During wartime more women enter the workforce.
5. No; only numbers of working women are shown.

PLANNING GUIDE

Chapter 30 The Cold War

Daily Lesson Objectives	Teacher Classroom Resources	Multimedia
SECTION 1 **The Beginning of the Cold War** 1 Day pp. 838–843 1. Describe the changes in Eastern Europe and the factors that made communism strong after World War II. 2. Outline the foreign policy goals of the Truman administration. 3. Explain how the United States became a world power after World War II.	Chapter 30 Study Guide Reproducible Lesson Plan Section Quiz Reteaching Activity 30-1 Reinforcing Social Studies Skills 14, 23, 25, 32-34, 37, 48, 53 Chapter 30 Primary and Secondary Source Readings Chapter 30 Cooperative Learning Activity Chapter 30 Concept Mapping Activity Building Skills in Geography Outline Map 37 Writer's Guidebook Lesson 6	Student Self-Test Software Testmaker Section Focus Transparency 97 Chapter 30 Skills Transparency Chapter 30 Map Transparencies Communism and the Cold War
SECTION 2 **The Cold War in Asia** 1 Day pp. 845–849 1. Cite the outcome of the United States' occupation of Japan. 2. Explain the political situation in China after the war. 3. Explain why the United Nations waged a limited war in Korea.	Reproducible Lesson Plan Reteaching Activity 30-2 Section Quiz Chapter 30 Primary and Secondary Source Readings Reinforcing Social Studies Skills 23, 26, 55, 63 Outline Map 33 The Living Constitution	Student Self-Test Software Testmaker Section Focus Transparency 98 Communism and the Cold War
SECTION 3 **Cold War America** 1 Day pp. 850–856 1. Explain changes in the American labor force after the war. 2. Describe the condition of African Americans during the 1940s. 3. Evaluate the Truman presidency.	Reproducible Lesson Plan Reteaching Activity 30-3 Section Quiz Chapter 30 Enrichment Activity American Portraits 59, 60 Reinforcing Social Studies Skills 28, 44, 53, 55 Spanish Summaries & Glossary Writer's Guidebook Lesson 6	Student Self-Test Software Testmaker Section Focus Transparency 99 Chapter 30 Map Transparencies Vocabulary Puzzlemaker Audiocassette, Chapter 30 Communism and the Cold War A Geographic Perspective on American History The American People: Fabric of a Nation
CHAPTER REVIEW AND EVALUATION 1 Day	Chapter 30 Test Chapter 30 Performance Assessment Activity	Student Self-Test Software Testmaker

OUT OF TIME? If time does not permit teaching the entire chapter, use the Chapter 30 Summary on pages 890–891 and the Chapter 30 audiocassette (English and Spanish) to point out the main ideas of the chapter.

PLANNING GUIDE

Cultural Diversity Activity

Analyzing a Conclusion Historian Ronald Takaki writes: "World War II was the transition to the Civil Rights Revolution. The defense of democracy abroad stirred demands for racial justice at home; with peace came new challenges against discrimination and inequality. The winds of democracy began sweeping through American political institutions, especially the courts." He cites as evidence the following events: the Kajiro Oyama case of 1948 (a challenge of California's Alien Land Law by Japanese Americans); Harry Truman's desegregation of the armed forces; the McCarran-Walter Act (which nullified the racial restriction of the 1790 Nationalization Act). Ask interested students to research one of these events to find out whether it supports Takaki's conclusion. Have them share their findings with the class. Ask students to research events described in this chapter that suggest changes would come slowly and reluctantly.

Performance Assessment Activity

Documenting a Life Divide students into small groups and ask each to imagine that its members have been asked to prepare a documentary about a major historical figure of the Cold War. Tell them that before a director shoots a film, he or she creates a storyboard that serves as a guide to the director and the camera crew. Ask them to develop a storyboard for the figure their group chose. Possibilities include Harry Truman, Joseph Stalin, Joseph McCarthy, George Marshall. After groups have completed their research, ask them to assemble their information—including maps, photographs, and other artwork—onto a storyboard. It should describe the individual's life in chronological order, highlight his or her involvement in the Cold War. Encourage groups to present their storyboards to the class.

POSSIBLE RUBRIC FEATURES: Content information, organization, written and visual communication skills, collaborative skills, creativity, research

Chapter Resources

Literature from the Period

Churchill, Winston. "Speech at Fulton, Missouri." March 5, 1946.

Williams, Tennessee. *The Glass Menagerie.* 1945.

Readings for the Student

Caute, David. *The Great Fear.* Simon and Schuster, 1978.

Ingalls, Robert. *Point of Order—A Profile of Senator Joe McCarthy.* Putnam, 1981.

Readings for the Teacher

Fried, Richard M. *Nightmare in Red: The McCarthy Era in Perspective.* Oxford, 1990.

Weisberger, Bernard A. *Cold War, Cold Peace: The United States and Russia since 1945.* American Heritage, 1985.

Multimedia Resources

America and the World Since World War II, 1945–1952: Volume 1. ABC (VHS, 52 minutes)

The Berlin Airlift. Prentice-Hall Media. (color, sound filmstrip)

Foreign Policy: The Burdens of World Power. Tom Snyder. (Apple or IBM diskette)

Key to Ability Levels

Teaching strategies have been coded for varying learning styles and abilities.

- **L1** Basic activities for all students
- **L2** Average activities for average to above-average students
- **L3** Challenging activities for above-average students
- **LEP** Limited English Proficiency activities

Glencoe Links to the Humanities

Links to Literature

- Macmillan Literature: Understanding Literature Audiotapes Side 4
- Macmillan Literature: Appreciating Literature Audiotapes Side 4
- Macmillan Literature: American Literature Audiotapes Side 5
- Macmillan Literature: Appreciating Literature Video—*The Pearl*
- Macmillan Literature: Novel Guide—*A Raisin in the Sun*
- Macmillan Literature: American Literature Text—Jack Kerouac, Carson McCullers

Link to Music

♪ American Music: Cultural Traditions

CHAPTER 30

BEGINNING THE CHAPTER

Discuss with students some of the issues that face the United States today in terms of its relations with Europe and Asia: the political and economic changes in the former Soviet Union and Eastern European countries; the movements in China toward a freer society. Point out to students that many of these issues are responses to situations that originated during the post–World War II era.

Recording Journal Notes

To get students started, discuss the hearings held by the Un-American Activities Committee of the House of Representatives and the Army-McCarthy hearings in the Senate.

Linking Across Time

Point out that the iron curtain effectively isolated Eastern Europe from 1946 until 1989. In that year the Soviet program of *glasnost* flowered, and many Soviet satellites declared their independence from Moscow. The most dramatic of these declarations came when East Germans broke through the Berlin Wall in 1990.

CHAPTER 30

The Cold War
1945–1952

▼ REBUILDING BERLIN, THE MARSHALL PLAN AT WORK

Setting the Scene

Focus

Within months after the end of World War II, the United States and the Soviet Union entered into a period of intense confrontation and rivalry. American leaders sought to maintain workable links with the Soviets while trying to check communism in Europe. Later this containment policy was applied to China, but it could not prevent the outbreak of war in Korea. At home, Americans sought to adjust to a peacetime economy.

Concepts to Understand

★ Why the political and economic power of the United States and the Soviet Union were set against each other

★ How effective presidential leadership resulted in aggressive foreign and domestic policies

Read to Discover . . .

★ ways the United States sought to contain the Soviet Union.
★ the effect the cold war had on Americans at home.

Journal Notes

How did the fear of communism become a serious threat to American democracy during the Truman administration? Record relevant points as you read the chapter.

CULTURAL
- 1945 *Harvey* by Mary Chase wins Pulitzer Prize for plays
- 1947 Jackie Robinson first plays for Brooklyn Dodgers

| 1944 | 1946 |

POLITICAL
- 1945 Harry S Truman becomes President on death of Franklin D. Roosevelt
- 1946 Winston Churchill makes "iron curtain" speech
- 1947 Truman Doctrine announced

UNIT 9 Times of Crisis: 1932–1960

✚ EXTRA CREDIT PROJECT

Several nations in Eastern Europe have a long history of being overrun by more powerful nations. Ask interested students to research the history of one country in the region. Tell them to keep the following questions in mind: At what times in history has the nation been conquered? By whom? How did living under foreign rule affect the nation and its people? What is its status today? Ask students to share their findings with the rest of the class.

CHAPTER 30 CONCEPTS

Concept Mapping Activity

Draw the following diagram on the chalkboard. Ask students to use the generalization to speculate about topics that will be covered in this chapter. Urge them to look for examples of each concept as they read the chapter.

> The United States takes on the challenge of world leadership and the protection of Western Democracy.
>
> - Political and Economic Power
> - Leadership

History AND ART

Norman Rockwell's paintings appeared regularly in the *Saturday Evening Post*. They were enormously popular because they captured the hopes, dreams, and ideals of many Americans.

ABC NEWS INTERACTIVE

VIDEODISC
Communism and the Cold War

Side 1, Chapter 3
Title: *End of Alliance*
Subject: Summary of events near end of World War II which led to the Cold War

History AND ART
The Homecoming
by Norman Rockwell, 1945

New opportunities for housing and education eased the transition from military to civilian life for returning veterans. At the same time, Americans faced new challenges at home and abroad.

▲ **PRESIDENT HARRY S TRUMAN AND GENERAL DOUGLAS MACARTHUR**

- **1948** Largest telescope in the world is dedicated at Mount Palomar Observatory
- **1948** Berlin airlift
- **1948** Communist forces take China
- **1949** NATO created

1948 | **1950**

- **1950** National Council of Churches of Christ is formed, representing 30 denominations
- **1950** North Korea invades South Korea

CHAPTER 30 The Cold War 1945–1952

Teacher Notes

LESSON PLAN
SECTION 1, 838–844

FOCUS
Before taking roll at the beginning of the class period, display Focus Activity Transparency 96 on the overhead projector, and assign the accompanying Focus Activity Sheet.

Objectives
Point out the objectives on this page to students in previewing the section content.

Motivating Activity
Read Harry Truman's statement: "[H]istory will remember my term of office as the years when the cold war began to overshadow our lives." Then ask why they think President Truman's words were effective in describing the effects of World War II.

Use Skills Transparency 30.

VIDEODISC
Communism and the Cold War

Side 1, Chapter 3
Title: *End of Alliance*
Subject: Summary of events near end of World War II which led to the Cold War

---

SECTION 1

The Start of the Cold War

Setting the Scene

Section Focus

The Allies' goal of establishing democratic governments throughout Europe after World War II proved to be elusive. To Churchill and Truman, democracy meant political and economic systems like those in Great Britain and the United States. Western democracy was unacceptable to Stalin, who began to establish Soviet-style communism in Eastern Europe. To implement a policy of containment, the Truman administration provided massive economic aid to war-torn Western Europe, joining with these countries in the first peacetime alliance in United States history.

Objectives

After studying this section, you should be able to

★ describe the changes in Eastern Europe and the factors that made communism strong after World War II.

★ outline the foreign policy goals of the Truman administration.

★ explain how the United States became a world power after World War II.

Key Terms

communism, satellite nation, purge, buffer, guerrilla, containment, collective security

◄ UN FLAG

President Truman's policies from the beginning of his administration showed his determination and the high degree to which he was personally involved in handling both domestic and international affairs. On his desk he kept a sign: "The buck stops here." In times of great crisis, Truman showed an extraordinary capacity for quick, effective, yet restrained action.

■ East-West Suspicions

In 1945, during the first months of his administration, President Truman concentrated his attention on winning the war against Germany and Japan. Like Roosevelt, he supported the creation of the United Nations as a world peacekeeping organization. But Truman was much more suspicious than Roosevelt had been of the Soviet Union and its dictator, Joseph Stalin.

Soviet Control of Eastern Europe

When the war ended, the alliance between the United States, Great Britain, and the Soviet Union unraveled. While there was a common enemy, Western democracies and Soviet leaders had overlooked their political, economic, and social differences. After the war, suspicions returned. Soviet expansion into Eastern Europe heightened American fears of **communism,** a system in which society as a whole, represented by the Communist party, owns and controls property and the means of production.

UNIT 9 Times of Crisis: 1932–1960

Classroom Resources for SECTION 1

Teacher's Classroom Resources
- Chapter 30 Study Guide
- Reproducible Lesson Plan
- Reteaching Activity 30-1
- Chapter 30 Cooperative Learning Activity
- Section Quiz

Multimedia
- Section Focus Transparency 96
- Skills Transparency 30
- Testmaker
- Student Self-Test Software
- Communism and the Cold War

As fighting ended, Soviet troops occupied much of Eastern Europe. The Soviet leaders, who had promised free elections in these nations, did not follow through. In Hungary, where free elections were held in November 1945, communist candidates received only 17 percent of the vote. Unwilling to lose control, Stalin later suppressed elections in Hungary and in the other nations of Eastern Europe. Then, under elections supervised by Soviet troops, voters gave 90 percent of the vote to communist candidates in Poland. This pattern was repeated in all Soviet-occupied areas, helping to establish communist governments throughout Eastern Europe. Nations that were held under Soviet domination came to be called **satellite nations.**

To restore the devastated Soviet economy, the Soviets removed whole factories, transportation equipment, and machinery from the satellite nations. Stalin also ordered **purges,** or forced removals, of leaders of satellite nations who were deemed disloyal.

The Iron Curtain

The leaders of Western Europe and the United States watched with grave concern as the Soviet Union crushed all opposition in the nations of Eastern Europe after 1945. Former Prime Minister Winston Churchill identified the new threat in a speech in March 1946 at Fulton, Missouri. With President Truman on the platform, Churchill warned:

> ... [F]rom Stettin on the Baltic to Trieste on the Adriatic, an iron curtain has descended across the continent. Behind that line lie all the capitals of the ancient states of central and eastern Europe.

The phrase "iron curtain" would be used to describe Soviet policy in Europe from 1945 to 1989. The West, said Churchill, must meet this challenge with force, if needed, because the Communists had no respect for weakness. Truman and his advisers agreed that a "get tough" policy was their only choice.

▲ **AN IRON CURTAIN** Former Prime Minister Winston Churchill and President Truman appear together during Churchill's speech at Fulton, Missouri. *What message did Churchill give to the American people?*

CHAPTER 30 The Cold War 1945–1952

CHAPTER 30 SECTION 1

Independent Practice

Debate Have students debate the following statement: Truman's policy to contain the expansion of communism was too soft. **L3**

Did You Know?

The only two superpowers after World War II were the United States and the Soviet Union. They possessed as much productive capacity as the rest of the world combined. Throughout the cold war era, the two powers would vie for the loyalty and support of the rest of the world.

VIDEODISC
Communism and the Cold War

Side 1, Chapter 25
Title: *Music of the Cold War*
Subject: Montage of music reflecting the political moods during the Cold War

---

■ The Strength of Communism

Following World War II, the United States began to withdraw troops from Europe, leaving the Soviet army as the most powerful military force in Europe. As a result of the German invasion, the Soviet Union had lost 20 million people and suffered devastation of land, property, and industry. Feeling threatened by Western powers, the Soviet Union wanted to create a **buffer,** or safety zone, on its western border. Soviet troops stationed there ensured that the nations of Eastern Europe would remain its allies.

Communism's Promises

The Communists promised to abolish poverty, privilege, and private property. They guaranteed productive work, shelter, education, health care, and a classless society in the new "people's democracies" of war-torn Eastern Europe.

The Communists saw the world as divided between forces of progress and forces of oppression. Soviet rhetoric incited revolts in other impoverished nations, as people living in poverty listened eagerly to the Communists' plans. Communists began to organize resistance to governments they considered to be reactionary and imperialist. Sometimes they organized groups of **guerrilla** forces—armed bands that were not a part of a regular military unit—to foment civil war.

Containment

President Truman responded with a policy of **containment**—preventing the further spread of communism. This policy was based on the belief that foreign policy goals of Soviet leaders included conquering other nations—not simply the securing of their own borders. Containment, however, did not win universal support.

Some who opposed the policy believed that it was too soft. Angry with the advance of communism, they called for a quick and decisive victory over the Soviet Union. Another view was expressed by Walter Lippmann, a newspaper columnist. Lippmann argued that Soviet troops remained in Eastern Europe to protect the Soviets' western border. He warned that the United States could not contain the Soviet Union everywhere. Such a policy, he said, would require the United States to defend all anticommunist governments—no matter how repressive or unpopular they might be.

Lippmann published his newspaper columns on containment in a book called *The Cold War*. The title, a term coined by Lippmann to refer to a state of war that did not involve actual bloodshed, came to be used by everyone, including the President, to describe the icy rivalry that existed between the United States and the Soviet Union.

■ Aid to Europe

The cold war was like no other struggle that had ever engaged the United States. It required a constant state of military preparedness; it called for military support for countries believed to be in danger of a communist takeover. It had other economic costs, as both the United States and the Soviet Union tried to "buy" allies with gifts ranging from food to steel mills.

The Truman Doctrine

The policy of containment began in Europe. Great Britain, in financial trouble, was forced to notify United States officials early in 1947 that it would withdraw its soldiers from Greece and end aid to Turkey. United States diplomats in Greece warned that this could lead to a communist takeover. Already, they said, Soviet-supported guerrillas were controlling much of the country. It was feared that if Greece fell to the Communists, Turkey would be next.

President Truman decided that the United States must act. In March 1947 he told Congress that if the United States was not willing to give aid to Greece and Turkey to contain communism, democratic governments everywhere would be threatened. Truman's warning that the nation faced a crisis was clear:

UNIT 9 Times of Crisis: 1932–1960

Cooperative Learning

Divide the class into two groups. Assign each group member one of the following two topics. Have them answer the question that corresponds to their topic: "East-West Suspicions" (What was the main reason the alliance between the United States and the Soviet Union began to shatter after the war ended?) "The Strength of Communism" (Why did the message of communism sound compelling to the people of Europe?) Randomly call on various group members to share their responses with the remainder of the class. **L2**

> *I believe that it must be the policy of the United States to support free peoples who are resisting attempted subjugation by armed minorities or outside pressures.... If we falter in our leadership, we may endanger the peace of the world—and we shall surely endanger the welfare of our own nation.*

Truman's policy, known as the Truman Doctrine, proposed that the United States provide military and economic aid to Greece and Turkey. Immediately approved by Congress, the Truman Doctrine superseded the Monroe Doctrine, shifting the United States away from peacetime isolationism.

The Marshall Plan

Soon after the Truman Doctrine went into effect, the administration proposed a plan for economic aid to Europe. The situation in Europe was desperate in 1947. There were shortages of food, fuel, and raw materials, and European nations needed money to rebuild industries and transportation systems.

The Truman administration realized that economic woes in France, Italy, and other Western European countries might lead to the election of communist governments. The nation's leaders were also concerned that Europe's faltering economy would affect United States markets.

In June 1947, Secretary of State George C. Marshall went beyond the Truman

Map Study After being invaded twice in less than 30 years, the Soviets especially feared future German power. Thus, after World War II, the Allies agreed to divide and occupy Germany. **What other nation was divided after the war?**

CHAPTER 30 The Cold War 1945–1952   841

CHAPTER 30
SECTION 1

Visualizing History Over 750 years old, Berlin has been a major European cultural center since the 1700s.
Answer to Caption: The Soviets eventually lifted their blockade.

Linking Across Time

Berlin remained a focal point throughout the Cold War. In 1961, the government of East Germany built the Berlin Wall to prevent its people from moving to West Germany. The dismantling of the Berlin Wall in 1989 foreshadowed the end of Communist domination of Eastern Europe.

VIDEODISC
Communism and the Cold War

Side 1, Chapter 4
Title: *Spheres of Influence: NATO and the Warsaw Pact*
Subject: Creation of alliances

Visualizing History ▲ **THE BERLIN AIRLIFT** When the Soviets closed off the routes from the West to Berlin, American and British cargo planes carried on an around-the-clock airlift. Berlin children, standing in the rubble of their shattered city, watch an American bomber fly in with supplies. *What effect did the airlift have on the Soviet blockade?*

Doctrine to propose a massive recovery plan for European nations. Under the Marshall Plan, American aid in the form of money, supplies, and machinery would help to end Europe's "hunger, poverty, desperation, and chaos." The United States offered the Marshall Plan to all nations in Europe—including the Soviet Union. Believing that the plan would promote the interests of United States capitalism, the Soviet Union and Eastern European communist nations turned it down.

The nations of Western Europe, on the other hand, welcomed the Truman administration's offer. Drawing up detailed plans for restoring production and controlling inflation, they also agreed to change trade laws—tariffs and quotas that blocked the flow of commerce.

The Marshall Plan was an enormous success. During the Truman years, the United States gave more than $13 billion in loans and grants to the nations of Western Europe. To administer aid effectively, the 16 Western European nations formed the Organization for European Economic Cooperation, the first step toward European economic unity.

■ The Berlin Airlift

At the end of the war, the Allies had decided on a joint occupation of Germany. The United States, Great Britain, France, and the Soviet Union each controlled a zone, or section, of Germany. They also each controlled a section of the capital, Berlin, in the Soviet-controlled zone.

Failing to reach agreement with the Soviet Union, the Western powers in May 1948 announced plans to join their 3 sections of Germany to form an independent nation. The Soviet Union responded by closing off all traffic from West Germany to Berlin. They thought that this move would force the West to back down from its control of West Berlin. President Truman saw this action as a test of Western determination. Instead of sending troops through the land corridor to Berlin and risking war, Truman ordered a massive airlift to supply Berlin's 2 million people. Night and day for more than 10 months, British and United States cargo planes carried food, medicine, clothing, raw materials, and even coal to Berlin. In May 1949, the Soviet Union finally lifted its blockade. Truman said:

UNIT 9 Times of Crisis: 1932–1960

Cooperative Learning

On an outline map of Europe, have students work in groups of three to show the division between East and West by indicating the European countries that made up the NATO alliance in 1949 and those that made up the Warsaw Pact in 1955. (NATO: Belgium, Denmark, France, Iceland, Italy, Luxembourg, the Netherlands, Norway, Portugal, the United Kingdom. Warsaw Pact: Albania, Bulgaria, Czechoslovakia, East Germany, Hungary, Poland, Romania, the Soviet Union.) **L2**

> *When we refused to be forced out of Berlin, we demonstrated to the people of Europe that with their cooperation we would act, and act resolutely, when their freedom was threatened.*

■ North Atlantic Treaty Organization

Believing that rebuilding their economies without rebuilding their military strength might invite Soviet aggression, five Western European states formed an alliance in March 1948. They invited the United States, the world's only atomic power, to join their alliance. With Senate approval, Truman began talks to create a North Atlantic Treaty Organization (NATO), which formed in April 1949.

NATO linked into a military alliance the United States, Great Britain, Canada, Belgium, Italy, France, the Netherlands, Luxembourg, Iceland, Denmark, Norway, and Portugal. Greece, Turkey, and West Germany joined later. NATO was based on **collective security,** an agreement by which "an armed attack against one or more of them in Europe or North America shall be considered an attack against all of them." Truman appointed General Dwight D. Eisenhower, who exercised sole authority over the atomic weapons that the United States committed to the defense of NATO.

Then, in September 1949, the Soviet Union exploded its first atomic bomb. Much sooner than military experts had expected, the United States had lost its nuclear monopoly. Faced with this new threat, Congress quickly passed the NATO appropriations bill. In 1955 the Soviet Union and its satellites countered NATO by establishing their own military alliance—the Warsaw Pact. The arms race had begun.

Within a few years, both the United States and the Soviet Union developed a new and more powerful weapon—the hydrogen bomb. Later, other nations, including Great Britain, France, and China, also built nuclear weapons.

▲ **General Dwight D. Eisenhower**

Section 1 ★ Review

Checking for Understanding

1. **Identify** cold war, Truman Doctrine, Marshall Plan, NATO, Berlin airlift.
2. **Define** communism, satellite nation, purge, buffer, guerrilla, containment, collective security.
3. **Explain** the threat perceived by the Soviet Union and its response in Eastern Europe.
4. **Summarize** the Truman administration's major foreign policy goals.

Critical Thinking

5. **Analyzing Policies** How did exercising the Truman Doctrine in Greece nullify the Monroe Doctrine of 1823?

CHAPTER 30 The Cold War 1945–1952 843

LESSON PLAN
Mastering Social Studies Skills

Teaching Map and Graph Skills

Point out that maps can chronicle events in a war, the political and economic development of an area, the change in population—almost any collection of facts about a place can be shown on a map.

Review the guidelines for using maps to form hypotheses. Guide practice in writing statements to research. (Vienna was jointly occupied. The territories of eastern East Germany and East Prussia were jointly administered by the Soviets and the Poles.) Discuss how the statements could be proved or disproved.

Did You Know?

During the Berlin airlift, a plane flew into the city every three minutes. Without the supplies those planes carried, West Berliners would have had to back down.

Social Studies Skills

Map and Graph Skills

Hypothesizing

Hypothesizing is the process of forming a tentative explanation based on available evidence. A hypothesis offers a possible answer to a problem, or an explanation for why a situation or condition exists.

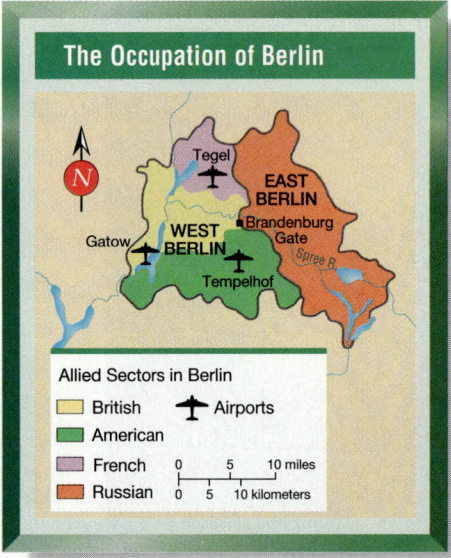

A hypothesis cannot be judged right or wrong until it is confirmed or disproved by additional evidence. The following guidelines will help you form hypotheses from historical maps:

a. **Determine** the situation that the map is showing and write it as a statement.
b. **Form** some possible hypotheses that may explain the statement you have written.
c. **Gather** additional evidence about the situation and test each hypothesis.
d. **Accept** or reject each hypothesis as an explanation for the situation.

Look at the historical map on this page showing the Allied occupation of Berlin. Note how the guidelines on forming hypotheses have been applied.

a. Berlin was divided and occupied by the Allies. The Soviets occupied East Berlin. West Berlin was divided into French, British, and American sectors.

b. Berlin was divided because the Allies wanted to keep the city for themselves.
Hypothesis: Berlin was divided among the Allies because the Western nations did not want the Soviets to have control of it.
Hypothesis: Berlin was divided so that its citizens would have self-government.
Hypothesis: Berlin was divided because the Western Allies feared Soviet intentions in Europe.

c. Gather additional evidence to test these hypotheses. Historians use many sources of information to understand an event. Written primary sources are often the most reliable record of what happened. Diaries, documents, eyewitness accounts, journals, and letters are primary sources. Research additional information in this chapter, other textbooks, encyclopedias, and other sources.

d. Accept or reject each hypothesis based on the evidence gathered. The information provided from reading Chapter 30 and from doing additional research might indicate that the second hypothesis best explains the statement of the situation.

Practicing the Skill

For further practice in hypothesizing, apply the guidelines to the map of the election of 1948 on page 854.

Answers to SOCIAL STUDIES SKILLS

Statement: Three candidates, one from a third party, got electoral votes in the 1948 presidential election.

Hypotheses: (a) Thurmond took votes from Truman because some southern Democrats did not like Truman's civil rights policies. (b) Some farm states supported Dewey because of Truman's lack of concern for farmers. (c) Truman's lopsided victory was aided by a widespread belief that Dewey could not defeat him.

Accept (a); reject (b) and (c).

SECTION 2

The Cold War in Asia

Setting the Scene

Section Focus

In Asia the end of World War II brought peace only to the people of Japan. Under the United States's occupation, the Japanese renounced militarism, disbanded their army, democratized their society, and embarked on a program of economic development that brought them unprecedented prosperity. In contrast, the rest of Asia was caught up in the cold war. As tensions grew, the cold war escalated into a hot war.

Objectives

After studying this section, you should be able to

★ cite the outcome of the United States's occupation of Japan.

★ explain the political situation in China after the war.

★ explain why the United Nations waged a limited war in Korea.

Key Term

defense perimeter

◄ CHINESE COMMUNIST LEADER MAO ZEDONG

At the close of World War II, the aims of the United States in Asia were to restore peace, help Asian peoples to resist foreign rule, and restore Asian trade with the world. The United States felt it had a special commitment to the Philippines, Japan, and China.

On July 4, 1946, the United States carried out its promise of independence for the Philippines. In return for special business rights and the lease of military bases, the United States gave the Philippine nation tariff concessions in American markets and $600 million to repair war damage. Later, when communist-led guerrilla groups revolted against the government, the United States sent money and weapons to put down the rebellion. Despite difficult economic and political problems, the Philippines became an independent, democratic nation.

■ The Occupation of Japan

In July 1945, shortly before the United States dropped atomic bombs on Hiroshima and Nagasaki, the leaders of Great Britain, the United States, and the Soviet Union met in Potsdam, near Berlin. They discussed how they would deal with Germany and Japan after the war.

The agreement regarding Japan provided that Japanese militarists be punished and Japan disarmed, Japanese rule be restricted

CHAPTER 30 The Cold War 1945–1952 **845**

LESSON PLAN
SECTION 2, 845–849

FOCUS

Bellringer

Prior to taking roll at the beginning of the class period, display Focus Activity Transparency 97 on the overhead projector, and assign the accompanying Focus Activity Sheet.

Objectives

Point out the objectives on this page to students in previewing the section content.

Motivating Activity

Recall with students the events that led to the end of World War II in Japan. (the dropping of atomic bombs on Hiroshima and Nagasaki) Then ask them to state how they would deal with postwar Japan.

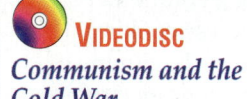

Side 2, Chapter 4
Title: *Revolution in China*
Subject: Transformation of China into a communist country

Classroom Resources for SECTION 2

Teacher's Classroom Resources
- Reproducible Lesson Plan
- Reteaching Activity 30-2
- Chapter 30 Primary and Secondary Source Readings
- Section Quiz

Multimedia
- Section Focus Transparency 97
- Chapter 30 Map Transparency
- Testmaker
- Student Self-Test Software
- Communism and the Cold War

CHAPTER 30
SECTION 2

TEACH
Guided Practice

Chronology Provide the following activity for students:

Place the following events in chronological order.
(6) a. MacArthur was removed from command of the UN forces.
(3) b. North Korea invaded South Korea.
(2) c. Philippines become independent.
(4) d. American forces staged landing at Inchon.
(1) e. The civil war between the Nationalists and Communists in China began again.
(5) f. Chinese troops crossed the border to aid the North Koreans. **L1, L2**

Did You Know?

Matsushita Konoskuke, a Japanese entrepreneur, introduced an electric rice saucepan that revolutionized Japanese cooking. This was the beginning of Panasonic electronics.

Teaching American Portraits

Douglas MacArthur and his father are the only father and son to have both received the Congressional Medal of Honor. This medal is given only to people who perform extraordinary acts of heroism. The army, navy, and air force each has its own medal.

---

to their home islands, and the Japanese be reeducated so that a democratic Japanese nation could be formed. American troops would occupy Japan until these aims were accomplished. To carry out this Potsdam Declaration, General Douglas MacArthur was named Supreme Commander of the Allied Powers.

Under MacArthur's leadership, Japan's military was dismantled. A few militarists were tried and convicted of war crimes and hanged. Under American direction, a new constitution provided for elected representative government and woman suffrage. Most other aspects of Japanese culture remained intact. The emperor remained as a symbol of Japan's unity, but he was no longer to be looked upon as a god.

MacArthur encouraged economic opportunity and trade unionism, and he attempted to redistribute large rural tracts to landless Japanese. A reorganized school system taught democratic values. The Allies had planned to make Japan pay reparations for war damages, but MacArthur realized that the Japanese lacked the resources to pay such compensation. Instead, Japan received nearly $2 billion in aid. The Japanese people accepted the reforms. In a treaty signed in San Francisco in 1951, the country gained back its independence. Japan achieved a remarkable recovery, eventually establishing itself as the leading economy of Asia.

■ Communist Triumph in China

Japan's surrender left China a divided nation. The Communists under Mao Zedong [MOW dzuh•DUNG] controlled the north, the Nationalists led by Chiang Kai-shek held the southwest, and Japanese armies occupied the center. The United States helped the Nationalist armies take the land the Japanese had held. In planning for peace, President Roosevelt had insisted to Churchill and Stalin that China be treated as a power. As a result, China gained a permanent seat on the UN Security Council.

Civil War

Since the early 1930s, a civil war between the nationalist government and the Communists had ravaged China. During World War II, both sides stopped fighting one another and fought the Japanese. In the war against Japan, Mao's Communists grew to

Douglas MacArthur
1880–1964

★★★★★★★★ AMERICAN PORTRAITS

Douglas MacArthur was born into a military family. His father won the Congressional Medal of Honor during the Civil War and later became the army's top-ranking general. Following in his father's footsteps, MacArthur saw action during World War I and was twice wounded. By 1918 he had risen to the rank of general. When Japan attacked Pearl Harbor, MacArthur was stationed in the Philippines, where he led its defense.

Ordered to retreat in 1942, he pledged: "I shall return." He kept his promise in 1944 by leading the liberation of the islands. After the war, as commander of U.S. occupation forces in Japan, he wrote its constitution. From July 1950 until President Truman fired him in April 1951, MacArthur commanded UN forces in Korea. Some Republican leaders urged MacArthur to run for President, but he declined and retired.

Cooperative Learning

After the class has read the material in Section 2, divide it into three or four groups. Ask students to provide examples of how the policy of containment was at work in the United States's relations with Asia. Have them take turns contributing answers by writing their ideas on a sheet of paper and passing the paper to the other members of their group. When all the members of the group have contributed their ideas, ask one member to share the answers with the rest of the class. **L2**

CHAPTER 30
SECTION 2

Americans in Korea President Truman ordered American forces to the Korean peninsula in June 1950 after North Korean troops invaded South Korea. In the conflict with North Korea, the United States was directly fighting a communist nation for the first time. *What was the outcome of the conflict?*

be a strong guerrilla force. Through his promise of land reform, as well as military and political pressure, Mao's forces were able to extend their control over much of mainland China. The civil war of the 1930s had greatly weakened the Nationalists.

After Japan surrendered, the conflict between the Communists and the Nationalists again flared. To prevent the extension of communist power, Truman sent General George C. Marshall to China. Marshall was unsuccessful. As the Communists gained strength, Chiang asked Truman to send military aid. Marshall, now secretary of state, advised that it was more important to spend the limited foreign-aid resources of the United States on saving Western Europe from Stalin rather than on saving China from Mao. In addition, a fact finder Truman sent to China reported no attempt to save it from the Communists could succeed because:

> The only basis on which national Chinese resistance to Soviet aims can be revitalized is through the presently corrupt, reactionary and inefficient Chinese National government.

Having already given Chiang's forces $2 billion in aid, the State Department judged that further help would not save the Nationalists from their own internal weaknesses. By the end of 1949 Mao Zedong's forces had forced Chiang's army off the mainland to Taiwan and a few other small islands.

Aftermath of Communist Victory

Truman's China policy came under bitter political attack. Nationalist supporters accused Truman of "writing off" Chiang and losing China to the Communists. Truman believed, however, that most Americans would not support the massive military intervention needed to save Chiang's government.

The United States recognized the nationalist government in Taiwan as the government of all of China and blocked attempts by Mao's government to gain a seat in the United Nations. To protest the exclusion of the Chinese communist government, the Soviet Union walked out of the United Nations Security Council and boycotted its proceedings.

CHAPTER 30 The Cold War 1945–1952   **847**

Did You Know?

The United States long maintained bases in the Philippines. Late in 1990, at the request of the Philippine government, the United States agreed to remove its fighter aircraft from Clark Air Force Base by September 1991, and to close its other three air bases within 10 to 12 years. The Philippine government made its request on the grounds that U.S. military presence violated Philippine national sovereignty. The agreement was cordial, and ties between the two nations remain strong.

Visualizing History Because Congress never declared war, the U.S. involvement in the struggle in Korea has never been officially called a "war," but rather a "conflict."
Answer to Caption: a stalemate in Korea left a divided country

---

Critical Thinking

Making Judgments The Truman administration's policy toward China was met with criticism. Have the students answer the following questions: Could the United States have saved China from Communist domination? If so, how? If not, why not? (Students' answers will vary. Some might suggest that the United States should have given the Nationalists more military and economic aid to fight communism. Other students might suggest that the conflict in China was a civil war, and as such was beyond the control of the U.S. government.) **L2**

CHAPTER 30
SECTION 2

Independent Practice

Debating Have students write arguments in favor of or against the following statement: President Truman had no choice but to fire General Douglas MacArthur. **L2**

Using Maps

Answer: September 15

Skills Practice

Where was the prewar boundary between North Korea and South Korea? (the 38th parallel)

Communism and the Cold War

Side 2, Chapter 7
Title: *Korean War*
Subject: Images of the Korean War, including newsreel footage

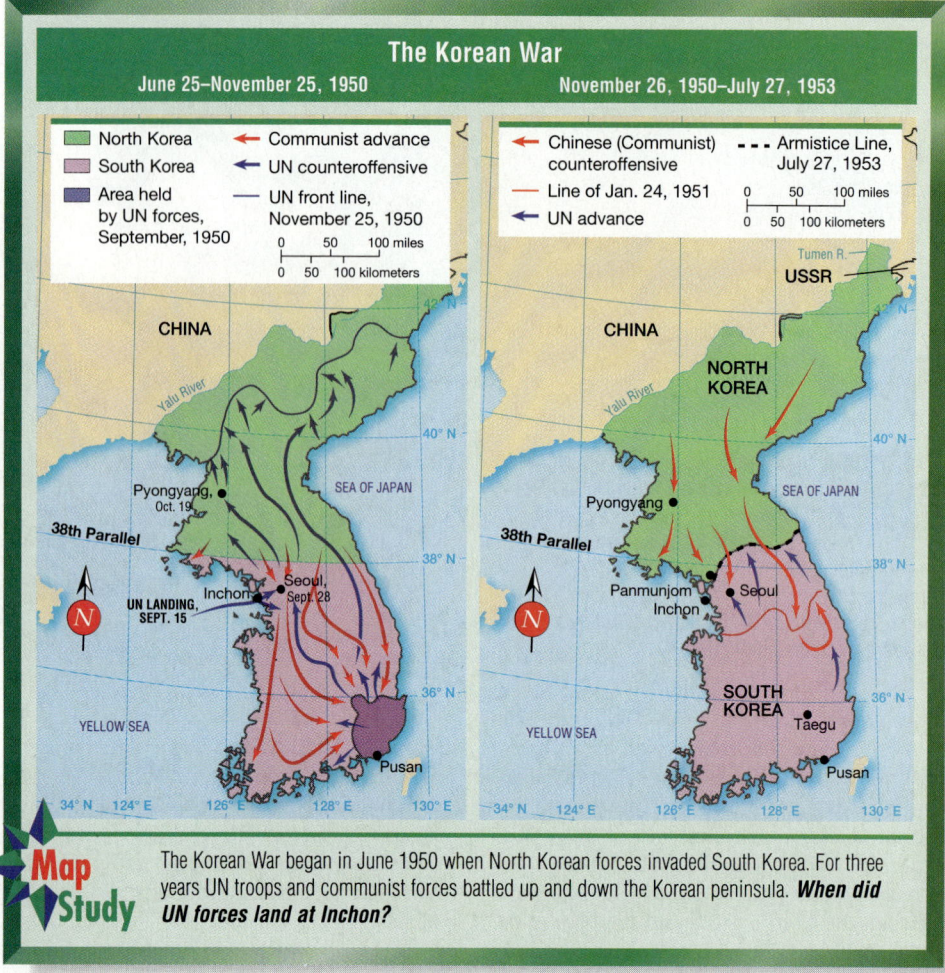

Map Study The Korean War began in June 1950 when North Korean forces invaded South Korea. For three years UN troops and communist forces battled up and down the Korean peninsula. **When did UN forces land at Inchon?**

War in Korea

The Allied nations had promised Korea "independence" at the Cairo conference in 1943. That did not occur. When the Japanese surrendered, Soviet Union troops occupied Korea north of the 38th parallel. Aided by Korean Communists, they set up a communist government. As with other Soviet satellite states, North Korea sealed itself off from other countries of the world. A 1948 UN fact-finding commission was not allowed to travel north of the 38th parallel.

In the south the United States supported the government of Syngman Rhee, who was chosen in UN-supervised elections. In 1948 the UN recognized the South Korean Republic as the government of all Korea.

United States military and diplomatic experts advised that Korea should be viewed as outside the **defense perimeter**, or area that could be protected, of the United States because of the great cost of defending it. The next year the United States withdrew most of its troops from Korea.

Fighting Begins

On June 25, 1950, North Korean troops invaded South Korea. Poorly armed, the South Koreans were no match for the North. The Truman administration was not sure whether North Korea was acting by itself or as the agent of the Soviet Union or China. The invasion, however, became a vital test

848   UNIT 9 Times of Crisis: 1932–1960

Sidelights: TV from Coast to Coast

In the six years following World War II, television grew from a limited East Coast industry into a nationwide series of broadcasting stations linked by networks. By 1951 about 100 stations across the country participated in the first transcontinental television broadcast—Truman's opening address to the delegates of the Japanese Peace Treaty Conference in San Francisco. That year more than 6 million television sets could be tuned to news or special events programs, such as the Kefauver hearings on organized crime, or to lighter programming, such as *I Love Lucy* or a variety of quiz shows.

848

for the UN. Calling an emergency meeting of the Security Council, the United States won a 9-to-0 vote to order North Korea to withdraw its troops. Because of its boycott, the Soviet Union was not present for the vote. On June 27, 1950, as the invasion continued, the Security Council called on all UN members to aid South Korea.

MacArthur in Command

President Truman quickly appointed General MacArthur to command all UN troops in Korea and instructed him to limit the fighting to South Korean territory below the 38th parallel. Truman also ordered United States military forces to Korea without asking Congress to declare war, claiming he was acting under his authority as commander in chief and under the United Nations Charter.

During the summer of 1950, North Korean troops pressed UN forces down the Korean peninsula until they had their backs to the water at Pusan (POO•SAHN), a major port in South Korea. In the fall, however, General MacArthur planned a surprise landing midway up the peninsula at the South Korean port of Inchon.

This landing gave the UN troops the offensive, and MacArthur was given authority by the UN Security Council to liberate North Korea and unite it with the South. By November, UN troops were as far north as the Yalu River valley, bordering communist China, when 200,000 Chinese troops crossed the border to aid the North Koreans. MacArthur's troops were once again pushed back.

Truman Fires MacArthur

A major disagreement soon developed between MacArthur and Truman over the conduct of the war. MacArthur wanted the United States to bomb China and to help Chiang Kai-shek invade China from Taiwan. Truman, however, did not want to risk war with China. In April 1951, Joseph Martin, Republican leader of the House of Representatives, released a letter he had received in which MacArthur criticized the President. MacArthur's letter was a deliberate challenge to the principle that the civilian power of the President must be superior to that of the military. Truman felt he had no choice but to remove MacArthur from command. He explained, "I could do nothing else and still be President of the United States."

The Senate Foreign Relations and Armed Services Committee opened hearings to determine the circumstances of MacArthur's dismissal. Two months of hearings dispelled much of the controversy. Truman's decision emerged as acceptable to the country.

The Conflict Ends

Years of fighting had produced a stalemate in Korea. Presidential candidate Dwight Eisenhower in 1952 pledged to "go to Korea," to settle hostilities. The war continued until 1953, when a cease-fire was declared. Korea was left a divided country, much as it had been before the war began. The Korean struggle was costly for the United States, which lost more than 54,000 troops. But as a result, many neutral nations drew closer to the United States, and noncommunist ones began to arm for their own defense.

Section 2 ★ Review

Checking for Understanding

1. **Identify** Chiang Kai-shek, Mao Zedong, Douglas MacArthur.
2. **Define** defense perimeter.
3. **Explain** why the United States's China policy failed.
4. **Summarize** the important events that led to the Korean War.

Critical Thinking

5. **Choosing a Position** Explain the two positions represented by Truman and MacArthur on Korea. Which position would you have chosen?

LESSON PLAN
SECTION 3, 850–856

FOCUS

Bellringer
Before taking roll at the beginning of the class period, display Focus Activity Transparency 98 on the overhead projector, and assign the accompanying Focus Activity Sheet.

Objectives
Point out the objectives on this page to students in previewing the section content.

Motivating Activity
Read the following quotation, which expresses President Truman's views about a free society.

"I think small business, the small farmer, the small corporation are the backbone of any free society, and when there are too many people on relief and too many people at the top who control the wealth of the country, then we must look out."

- **GTV: A Geographic Perspective on American History**

Side 4, Chapter 8
Title: *Shifting Winds*
Subject: Population movements since the 1940s

See GTV Guide page 62 for complete lesson plan.

SECTION 3

Cold War America

Setting the Scene

Section Focus
Life in cold war America was marked by a search for security. African Americans and women sought to keep the gains they had made during the war, and many Americans struggled to maintain their standard of living in the face of postwar inflation. For some, security meant exposing the subversives they suspected were operating in society and at high levels of their government. In the face of mounting opposition, Truman attempted to pursue policies that addressed these concerns.

Objectives
After studying this section, you should be able to
★ explain changes in the American labor force after the war.
★ describe the condition of African Americans during the 1940s.
★ evaluate the Truman presidency.

Key Terms
jurisdictional strike, featherbedding, subversive

◀ **SENATOR ROBERT TAFT**

World War II brought great changes to the nation's economy. War industries solved the unemployment problem of the Depression. In fact, with 16 million people in the United States armed services, there was actually a shortage of workers in industry. The number of African American workers in defense industries more than tripled. Six million women joined the labor force, a rise of nearly 60 percent.

■ Prosperity Continues

When the war ended in 1945, people were fearful of depression. In the past, when government spending for war materials stopped and soldiers returned home to look for jobs, unemployment spread. Even if the factories kept running, some newly hired African American and women workers now feared that they would be replaced by returning soldiers.

Fears of a depression proved groundless. After a slight drop in business activity, the number of Americans with jobs actually increased. Several factors contributed to the continuing prosperity. As the United States kept feeding not only its own people but millions of people overseas, farm income remained high. During the war Americans, due to rationing and scarcity of consumer goods, had saved $30 billion. Now they spent their savings for postponed purchases. In addition Congress stimulated postwar business by cutting wartime taxes nearly $6 billion. Instead of depression, consumer demand stimulated a sharp rise in prices, or inflation. Defense spending, which had

850 UNIT 9 Times of Crisis: 1932–1960

Classroom Resources for SECTION 3

Teacher's Classroom Resources
- Reproducible Lesson Plan
- Reteaching Activity 30-3
- Chapter 30 Primary and Secondary Source Readings
- Chapter 30 Enrichment Activity
- Chapter 30 Performance Assessment Activity
- Spanish Summaries and Glossary
- Section Quiz

Multimedia
- Section Focus Transparency 98
- Chapter 30 Map Transparency
- Student Self-Test Software
- Communism and the Cold War
- A Geographic Perspective on American History
- The American People: Fabric of a Nation
- The Presidents: A Picture History of Our Nation

dropped to $15 billion by 1949, escalated to $50 billion by 1953, pouring even more money into the economy. In addition the Marshall Plan restored markets in Europe for American goods.

In some ways the cold war economy of the 1950s resembled the wartime economy of the 1940s. The government's military spending continued to stimulate industrial production, while a portion of the labor force continued in military service.

Women

Immediately following World War II, soldiers returning from service took the places of many women who were employed in factories. In the automobile plants the proportion of women on assembly lines dropped from 25 percent in 1944 to 7.5 percent in 1946. The head of the Women's Bureau, a federal agency set up to protect women's interests, stated that "women ought to be delighted to give up any job and return to their proper sphere in the kitchen." Federal and state aid to child-care centers in factories was stopped.

Yet continued prosperity created new job opportunities. By 1952 more than 2 million more women were employed than in 1946. The kinds of work available to women were changing. This change was dramatically reflected in the experience of African American women. Between 1940 and 1950 the percentage of African American women employed as domestic servants dropped from 72 to 48 percent. The number of those working as farm laborers fell from 20 percent to 7 percent. At the same time, the percentage hired by factories rose from 7 percent to 18 percent. The rise in female employment did not mean that women had gained economic equality, however. Women in industries earned less than two-thirds as much as men.

■ Gains for African Americans

As a group, African Americans benefited from the postwar economic boom. Many made the transition from farming to manufacturing, from rural areas to cities, from the South to other regions of the country. The number of African American workers in white-collar, skilled, and supervisory jobs nearly tripled, increasing from about 300,000 to nearly 900,000. As opportunities for African Americans opened up fields such as law, nursing, and professional sports, average income—even adjusted for inflation—almost doubled.

▼ **1953 Packard convertible**

▲ **Purchasing Power** The United States enjoyed an economic boom in the early postwar years. Increasing consumer demand for necessities as well as luxury items fueled inflation, however. **How did many workers react to their loss of purchasing power?**

Cooperative Learning

Divide the class into five groups. Assign each group one of the following topics discussed in Section 4: inflation in the postwar years, the desire of American women for full equality, civil rights for African Americans, resentment of the Taft-Hartley Act by labor unions, the fear of communism at home. The students in each group should discuss the assigned topic, the factors that caused the problem to arise, and the methods used in attempting to solve it. At the end of the discussion, have a representative of each group report the highlights of the group's findings to the rest of the class. **L1, L2**

CHAPTER 30 SECTION 3

Independent Practice

Math Ask students to choose a consumer product, such as food, medical care, fuel, housing, or clothing. Have them research the prices of this product from 1946 to the present and plot their findings on a line graph. Students should also plot the national family income for the same years. Have them draw conclusions about the effects of inflation on consumers. A useful source of information is *The Statistical Abstract of the United States*. **L2**

Did You Know?

Reliable day care facilities were first called for by working women during World War II.

• *GTV: The American People: Fabric of a Nation*

Side 4, Chapter 3
Title: *Up and Out*
Subject: Movement of African Americans to the North

See GTV Guide page 94 for complete lesson plan.

Changing social attitudes helped these advances. The war against Germany and the cold war both played a part. The horrifying racism of the Nazis helped to make some Americans more sensitive to racism in their own country. They began to realize that not only African Americans, but also Asian Americans, Hispanic Americans, and other minorities had been treated unfairly and denied social and economic opportunities.

During this period, African Americans worked hard to gain civil rights. During the war, the membership of the National Association for the Advancement of Colored People (NAACP) rose from 100,000 to 351,000. The NAACP hired teams of able lawyers to bring a series of lawsuits to the federal courts to end violations of the constitutional rights of African American citizens. Like women, however, African Americans fell short of gaining full equality in the 1940s.

In the North, African Americans often lived in crowded inner-city areas. Wages averaged about 60 percent of those paid to white workers. African American workers were still likely to be "last hired, first fired." In the South old patterns of segregation and racism remained. African American Southerners resented that their children had to attend separate schools that were often ill-equipped and understaffed. They objected to Jim Crow laws that forced them to use segregated facilities. Even worse, most African American Southerners were denied the vote, either by custom or by law. Almost none held political office.

■ Inflation in the Postwar Years

Government spending on wartime military programs and for postwar domestic programs brought prosperity and inflation. During periods of inflation the amount of money in circulation increases and prices rise sharply as the demand for goods exceeds the supply.

Because increased taxes were not sufficient to pay the costs of war, the federal government ran a large deficit during World War II. The national debt rose from $50 million to nearly $270 billion. The government borrowed much of this money from Federal Reserve Banks. Using the federal bonds that the government gave as security, the banks issued new money. As a result, there was four times as much money in circulation in 1945 as there was in 1938.

As inflation drove prices up, the purchasing power of paychecks decreased. When consumers could not buy as much, factories slowed production, returning to a 40-hour week, and employers stopped paying overtime. Workers, losing purchasing power, demanded pay raises and often went on strike. In 1946 there were nearly 5,000 strikes, in which nearly 4.6 million workers took part—a record that is unlikely to be surpassed. Some strikes hit industries basic to the national economy such as steel, transportation, and coal. When railroad workers went on strike, President Truman asked Congress for power to draft them into the army. Fortunately, however, the strike ended before this measure was necessary.

■ The Taft-Hartley Act

Union activities were a major issue in the congressional elections of 1946. The anxiety caused by the strikes in basic industries helped conservative, antilabor candidates. The Republicans showed new vigor as they ran on the slogan, "Had enough?" For the first time in 18 years, they gained control of both the Senate and the House.

An immediate result of this swing toward conservatism was the Taft-Hartley Act, passed over President Truman's veto in 1947. Intended to keep unions from abusing their power, the act outlawed practices such as the closed shop, which forced business owners to hire only union members; **jurisdictional strikes**, which forced businesses to recognize one union instead of another; **featherbedding**, which limited workers' output in order to create more jobs; and high fees charged to workers for joining a union. In addition, unions were forbidden to use their money to support political campaigns.

UNIT 9 Times of Crisis: 1932–1960

Critical Thinking

Supporting a Position The Taft-Hartley Act created controversy for the Truman administration. Have the students determine their position on the following statement: The President should have the right to halt economically damaging strikes for a "cooling off" period. Students should provide reasons for their position. (Students' answers will vary, but their positions need to be substantiated with specific reasons.) **L2**

Life of the Times

Veterans Return

After World War II, thousands of military personnel came home. They poured off the troop ships and into the arms of families, wives, and girlfriends. When the celebrating was over, however, these former soldiers faced the task of rebuilding their lives and returning to their jobs or education.

As the nation adjusted to a peacetime economy, there was turmoil in the job market. Thousands of veterans hunted for jobs while wartime industries changed to peacetime production.

Many veterans decided to take advantage of the Servicemen's Readjustment Act of 1944. More popularly known as the G.I. Bill of Rights, this legislation assisted veterans in finding employment, education, and medical care. Many who went to college on G.I. Bill assistance were married men with young children. At most colleges and universities, housing was not sufficient for this increased enrollment. For some veterans the answer was a small mobile home or house trailer.

▲ MEMORIAL OF JAPANESE SURRENDER

During the late 1940s and the early 1950s, many campuses included large trailer parks where "GIs" and their families lived. Lasting relationships developed from the strong sense of community in these parks, which helped veterans adjust to civilian life.

◄ SOLDIERS RETURNING HOME AFTER WORLD WAR II

The Taft-Hartley Act was a very controversial measure. Its supporters claimed the law held irresponsible unions in check the way the Wagner Act of 1935 restrained antiunion activities of employers. Labor leaders called the act a "slave labor" law. They claimed it erased many of the gains that unions had made since 1933. In addition, they deeply resented that union leaders had to swear they were not members of the Communist party.

Election of 1948

As the presidential election of 1948 drew near, the Democratic party was divided. Southern Democrats objected to Truman's civil-rights program, which included proposals to end racial, religious, and ethnic discrimination, to abolish immigration quotas, and to integrate the armed forces.

The Candidates

Many white Southerners left the Democratic party to form the "Dixiecrat" party, which nominated South Carolina Governor Strom Thurmond for President. Other Democrats thought Truman was taking too hard a line against the Soviet Union. They supported the Progressive party ticket led by former Vice President Henry Wallace. Truman appeared certain to lose the election; he had lost the support of both the right wing and the left wing of his party. The Democrats renominated Truman only after party leaders failed to persuade General Eisenhower to accept the nomination.

The Republicans united behind their candidate for President, Governor Thomas E. Dewey of New York. Dewey was so confident that he would win that he avoided discussing issues and simply called on Americans to join him in building unity.

CHAPTER 30 SECTION 3

Teaching of the Times

Since 1944 more than 20 million veterans have received training through the G.I. Bill of Rights. In July 1985, the Montgomery G.I. Bill established two educational benefits programs. One program benefits those who began active duty after June 30, 1985. The other provides benefits for members of the Reserves and the Army and Air National Guard.

Did You Know?

Despite the Taft-Hartley Act, union membership rose from 14.3 million persons (which was 35.5 percent of the labor force) in 1945 to more than 18 million persons by 1955 (which was 33.2 percent of the labor force).

NATIONAL GEOGRAPHIC SOCIETY

The following material is available from Glencoe and may be used to enrich Chapter 30.

CD-ROM
- *The Presidents: A Picture History of Our Nation*

Cultural Diversity

A vivid description of African American life in the postwar years was created by James Baldwin in his novel *Go Tell It on the Mountain*. The novel describes a day in the lives of members of a church in Harlem, and, through flashbacks, their ancestors. Baldwin was recognized as a leading African American novelist noted for his powerful treatment of bigotry and oppression in American society.

CHAPTER 30 SECTION 3

Fact or Fiction?
Harry Truman fought in World War I.

FACT: Harry Truman entered World War I as a private, then became captain of a battery of field artillery and saw action in the famous battles of St. Mihiel and Meuse-Argonne.

Did You Know?
In 1947 Jackie Robinson signed with the Brooklyn Dodgers to become the first African American baseball player in the major leagues. He was named to the Baseball Hall of Fame for his hitting, fielding, and leadership. He continued playing through the 1956 season. Off the field Robinson fought for civil rights. He died in 1972.

Map Study: Using Maps
Answer: the South

Skills Practice
Why did Truman win? (He attacked the "do-nothing" Congress. He made a whistle-stop campaign and made more than 350 speeches.

The Campaign

Far behind in the public-opinion polls, President Truman pursued an aggressive campaign from the beginning. First, he called the Republican Congress back into special session and asked them to carry out the promises of the Republican party platform by passing civil rights and other progressive legislation. When they failed to act, Truman had his campaign theme: The "do-nothing, good for nothing" Republican 80th Congress. Setting out on a "whistle stop" tour of the country by train, Truman covered 30,000 miles, giving some 350 speeches along the way.

Right up to Election Day, the pollsters predicted a Republican victory. But Truman won 2 million more votes than Dewey and piled up a 303-to-189 margin in the Electoral College. Truman had held together the New Deal coalition. He won labor support for his veto of the Taft-Hartley Act. He won support from African American voters for his civil-rights proposals. He won the farmers' vote for his support of high farm price supports. Not only did Truman defeat Dewey, but the Democrats regained their majority in Congress.

The Fair Deal

In his Inaugural Address in January 1949, Truman called for a Fair Deal, a return to and expansion of Roosevelt's New Deal policies. President Truman asked for slum clearance, federal subsidies for public schools, government-backed medical insurance, aid to farmers, and higher minimum wages. Although the Democrats held a majority, the new Congress was still influenced by an alliance of Republicans and conservative Southern Democrats. Together they blocked most of Truman's proposals to Congress.

In 1949 postwar prosperity slipped into a recession. Unemployment reached 7 percent of the labor force. The recession lasted only a few months, however. A tax cut passed in 1948 took effect, making more money available. The New Deal's built-in stabilizers such as price supports for agriculture and social security benefits helped to lessen the effect of the economic downturn. Beginning in 1950, the Korean War changed the economic picture sharply. Rearmament now competed with the demand for consumer goods. The war also fueled anticommunist sentiment at home.

▲ TRUMAN DISPLAYS HEADLINE THAT WRONGLY PROJECTED DEWEY AS THE WINNER

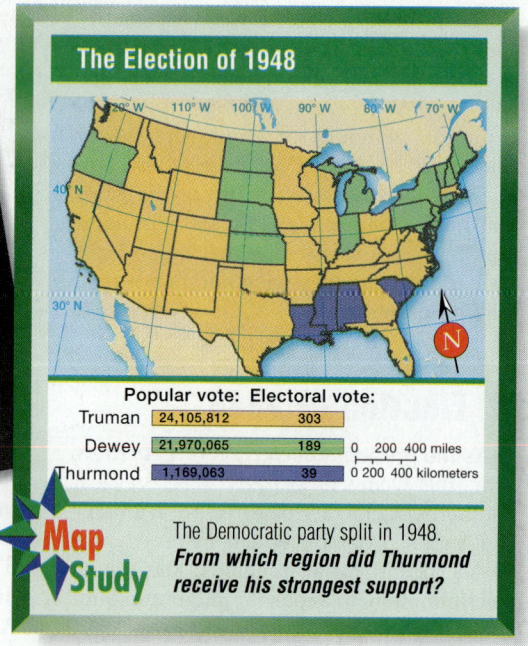

The Election of 1948

Popular vote: Electoral vote:
Truman 24,105,812 — 303
Dewey 21,970,065 — 189
Thurmond 1,169,063 — 39

Map Study
The Democratic party split in 1948. *From which region did Thurmond receive his strongest support?*

Sidelight: Fighting Inflation

To combat inflation President Truman wanted to continue wartime controls on wages, prices, and rents. Business leaders objected, stating that such controls prevented them from putting more factories into full production. They argued that once consumer demand was met prices would stabilize. Under these circumstances there was little the Truman administration could do. During 1946 wholesale prices on 28 basic commodities rose by 25 percent. Prices continued to rise for the next 2 years.

CHAPTER 30
SECTION 3

■ Fear of Communists

The cold war and the Korean War heightened fear of communism in the United States. A communist spy ring, which had been sending atomic secrets to the Soviet Union, was uncovered in Canada. To Americans, this explained the Soviets' success in developing an atomic bomb so early. Americans began to suspect that there might be other communist sympathizers and spies in the government, universities, press, and the arts—all working to undermine American democracy. In a period of international tensions, national insecurity led to a search for scapegoats.

Constitutional Rights

The question arose: Should the rights of Communists be protected by the Constitution? In 1949, 11 members of the Communist party in the United States were convicted of conspiracy. The courts held that since the Communist party was organized to overthrow the United States government by force, its members were not entitled to protection by the free speech rights of the First Amendment. Although there were relatively very few Communist party members in the United States, the suspected communist conspiracy led to extensive precautions. Many people were forced to take loyalty oaths before being hired for jobs. Government officials were subjected to security checks.

Loyalty Oaths

During the postwar period, a tendency grew among many Americans to mistake criticism of American institutions for disloyalty. As Judge Harold Medina told the jury that convicted the 11 Communists of conspiracy, taking away the right to criticize does not make a country stronger. Instead, allowing abuses of rights to go unchecked makes it weaker. In several rulings during this period, however, the Supreme Court found state loyalty oaths to be constitutional. The Court noted that the states had a constitutional right to assurance that an employee was not engaged in subversive activity.

 ▲ **CHARGES OF SUBVERSION** In the early 1950s, Senator Joseph R. McCarthy (left) claimed that Communists had infiltrated educational institutions and high levels of government. **What cold war events stirred McCarthy and others?**

Subversives

The "loss" of China to the Communists and the stalemated Korean War helped to create this mood in the United States that was much like the Red Scare in the years following World War I. Critics of Truman accused the President of having lost China, alleging that his close advisers were Communists or communist tools. Senator Robert A. Taft, Republican leader in the Senate, claimed that the State Department was "riddled" with **subversives,** or individuals attempting to overthrow the government. Taft said that State Department officials had:

> ❝ . . . surrendered to every demand of the Soviet Union and promoted, at every opportunity, the communist cause in China. ❞

In 1948 the House Committee on Un-American Activities heard testimony from Whittaker Chambers, a magazine editor. Chambers admitted that he had been a communist spy in the 1930s and said that he had received secret documents from Alger Hiss, then a high-ranking State Department official. At first, few people believed Chambers's story. However, Richard M. Nixon, a

Did You Know?

In his 1953 play *The Crucible*, playwright Arthur Miller wrote about the witch trials in Salem, Massachusetts, in the 1600s. Despite its seventeenth-century setting, the play was widely recognized as referring to the anti-Communist fervor of the McCarthy era.

Visualizing History Many Americans were afraid to challenge McCarthy. Among the few to do so was Dwight Eisenhower. Before an audience at Columbia University, he warned that if we allow ourselves to be persuaded that every person or party who disagrees with us is "wicked or treasonous—that we are approaching the end of freedom's road." **Answer to Caption:** the "loss" of China and the stalemate in Korea

VIDEODISC
Communism and the Cold War

Side 1, Chapter 11
Title: *Communists in our Midst: McCarthyism*
Subject: McCarthyism

Sidelight: A Boom in Auto Sales

Lack of auto production during World War II created a massive postwar seller's market, which peaked in the 1950s with sales of 6.7 million cars. The producers in 1950 included names such as Nash, Packard, Studebaker, Kaiser-Frazer, Hudson, Willys, and Crosley, as well as General Motors, Ford, and Chrysler. The combined saturation of demand and the Korean War caused a contraction in the auto industry. By the end of the decade, only American Motors (formed by a merger between Nash and Hudson) and Studebaker remained to feebly compete with GM, Ford, and Chrysler.

CHAPTER 30 SECTION 3

ASSESS

Check Understanding

Assign Section 3 Review as homework or an in-class activity.

Evaluate

Assign the Section 3 Quiz in the TCR, or use the History of a Free Nation testmaker to create a customized quiz.

Reteach

Have students write an essay describing the changes that occurred in the United States labor force during the 1940s.

Have students complete Reteaching Activity 30-3.

Enrich

Ask students to write a response with reasons to this question: "Do you think current employees of the federal government should be required to sign loyalty oaths?" Have them explain their answers.

Have students complete Chapter 30 Enrichment Activity in the Teacher's Classroom Resources.

CLOSE

Discuss with students what they think were three of the greatest accomplishments and three of the most serious problems of the Truman administration.

---

young representative from California, pressed the case forward. Finally, Chambers produced several rolls of microfilm of secret documents he claimed to have received from Hiss. Hiss denied these charges. Though not convicted of spying, Hiss was found guilty of lying under oath.

McCarthyism

Increased fears of communist subversion were fertile ground for more reckless voices. At a Lincoln's Day speech in February 1950, Senator Joseph R. McCarthy of Wisconsin accused the Democratic party of "twenty years of treason." McCarthy charged that Roosevelt had deliberately sacrificed the navy at Pearl Harbor and had "sold out" to the Soviet Union at Yalta. In addition, McCarthy claimed to have a list of "card-carrying Communists" in the State Department.

While McCarthy never produced the list, nor a shred of evidence to support his charges, he ruined the careers of many government officials. A growing atmosphere of hysteria inspired other "witch-hunts." Private groups used the communist label to drive liberal professors out of colleges. They made sure books they believed to be subversive were removed from schools. They had many broadcasters, writers, and entertainers barred from television and kept many actors from working on the stage and in films.

Years later a Senate committee determined that McCarthy's accusations and investigations had been groundless. The use of indiscriminate, unfounded political accusations to destroy or assassinate the character of one's opponent came, in time, to be known as McCarthyism.

■ Truman's Legacy

In 1952 President Truman announced that he would not run for reelection. By the time Truman left office, he had become unpopular. The successful Soviet atomic bomb explosion, the defeat of the Nationalists in China, and the problems with carrying out the war in Korea, all contributed to charges that Truman was "soft on communism." Other Americans thought his loyalty program had hurt innocent people.

Instances of corruption in high places were also discovered—some of the President's closest aides had received valuable gifts in return for political favors. Although Truman was not personally involved, the "Truman scandals" gave the Republicans a ready-made issue for the 1952 elections.

The problems Truman faced were new and complex. Congress was often suspicious or hostile, yet Truman got many of his programs enacted. Americans were tired of foreign involvements, yet he managed to keep the nation from retreating into isolationism. Truman's reputation as leader rose after he left the White House. Most of the Fair Deal measures he called for eventually became law. His policy of "containment" was continued by other Presidents. He set the United States on a course that included aid for those in need and an unwavering defense of democracy everywhere.

Section 3 ★ Review

Checking for Understanding

1. **Identify** Taft-Hartley Act, Alger Hiss, Joseph McCarthy.
2. **Define** jurisdictional strike, featherbedding, subversive.
3. **List** reasons why economic growth continued after World War II.
4. **Compare** gains made by African Americans in their struggle for equality with the limitations on their achievements.

Critical Thinking

5. **Drawing Conclusions** Why was Senator McCarthy, with groundless accusations, able to generate mass hysteria about communism?

UNIT 9 Times of Crisis: 1932–1960

Answers to SECTION 3 REVIEW

1. Taft-Hartley Act, p. 853; Alger Hiss, p. 856; Joseph McCarthy, p. 856
2. All vocabulary words are defined in the Glossary.
3. Farm income increased; wartime savings provided buying power; military spending increased; European markets restored through Marshall Plan, employment.
4. more and varied jobs, changing attitudes toward enhanced self-awareness, integrated armed forces, African American organizations
5. Atmosphere of fear; communism indeed spreading; swore had secret lists but could not verify; leak of atomic secrets make plausible; people receptive to scandal and conspiracy theory

CONNECTIONS  CONNECTIONS

▲ FLORIDA FAMILY MOVING NORTH

African American Migration

African American migration from the rural South to Northern and Western cities between 1910 and 1950 was one of the largest migrations in American history. African Americans migrated in search of greater economic opportunity and a better life than the drought, boll weevils, racism, and poverty they were accustomed to in the South. Much of the African American migration took place during the two world wars.

During World War I, industrial agents traveled the South promising jobs with high wages and free transportation to the North. Soon the African American population of cities such as Chicago, Cleveland, and Detroit swelled. Detroit alone saw an increase of over 600 percent.

In the 1940s rural Southern African Americans streamed into Northern and Western cities for two main reasons. First, around 1940 cotton farming became mechanized. Far fewer workers were needed, and many African Americans became jobless. Second, many saw great opportunity in wartime industries.

Although social and economic gains in the cities were limited by racial prejudice, African Americans acquired a political voice. Their migration forever changed the face of American politics and society.

Making the Geography Connection
1. Where did African Americans migrate to from 1910 to 1950?
2. Why did they migrate from the rural South?

Linking Past and Present
3. Where did many people migrate to in the 1970s and 1980s?

CHAPTER 30 CONNECTIONS

Teaching Connections
Between 1941 and 1945, one out of every five Americans moved from one area of the country to another. More than 700,000 African Americans left the South for the North and the West.

Ask students to hypothesize about the kinds of problems such a migration presented.

Did You Know?
In the 1950s Detroit's African American population increased from 16 to 29 percent of the total population. Chicago's African American population increased from 14 to 23 percent of the total.

 VIDEODISC
- *GTV: The American People: Fabric of a Nation*

Side 4, Chapter 3
Title: *Up and Out*
Subject: Movement of African Americans to the North

See GTV Guide page 94 for complete lesson plan.

Answers to CONNECTIONS
1. to northern and western cities
2. in search of greater economic opportunity and a better life
3. from the North and Midwest, south to the Sunbelt

REVIEW CHAPTER 30

Answers

Reviewing Facts

1. Fear for western border, twice invaded in recent years; appeal to poor, antigovernment; control or suppress elections; install Communists
2. Promised to abolish poverty, privilege, private property; guaranteed productive work, classless society
3. Negative: would bankrupt U.S. and weaken UN; would provoke Soviet Union; couldn't contain everywhere, perhaps support corrupt or repressive regimes. Positive: cost of not acting; inability of UN to deal with problems; Russian expansionist ambitions
4. massive economic aid, tariff concessions, establishment of democratic governments, reorganization of education system, development of industry, agrarian reform
5. Did not stop Mao, insufficient aid to Nationalists; pulled troops out of South Korea; limited Korean war, refused to invade China
6. Soviet occupation of North Korea; establishment of People's Republic–like satellite states; U.S. recognized South Korea; withdrew troops in 1949; Soviets trained, equipped North Korean army to attack South Korea
7. more upper-level jobs, increased membership and legal activity of NAACP, desegregation and equal treatment in armed services
8. civil rights proposals—the African American vote; farmers' subsidies—farm vote; veto Taft-Hartley—labor vote

Understanding Concepts

1. Society, as represented by state, controls means of production. State controlled by those with political power.
2. leadership role UN; aid Greece, Turkey, prevent Communist takeover; Marshall Plan; started NATO to protect against Soviet expansion

Critical Thinking

1. cold war—war of nerves, not shooting war; atmosphere of hostility; response to Russian expansionism, Eastern Europe. Moscow built buffer of Communist satellites, opposed with containment.

CHAPTER 30 ★ REVIEW

Using Vocabulary

Using the following vocabulary, write a paragraph describing the Soviet establishment of an iron curtain and the development of the cold war.

communism   satellite nation
containment   subversive
purge   buffer

Reviewing Facts

1. **Discuss** how and why the Soviets created a buffer of satellite states.
2. **Explain** why communism appealed to people in certain parts of the world.
3. **Summarize** arguments for and against containment and the Truman Doctrine.
4. **Cite** actions taken in the Philippines and Japan after World War II that led to successful economic recovery.
5. **Examine** the reasons for the charge that Truman was soft on communism.
6. **Detail** events leading to war in Korea.
7. **List** the advances made by African Americans.
8. **Explain** how the Truman agenda for prosperity at home and abroad enabled him to win in 1948.

Understanding Concepts

Political and Economic Power

1. How did the United States use its position as the strongest and wealthiest nation in the world to shape economic recovery in Europe?

Leadership

2. Analyze the qualities that made President Truman an effective leader.

Critical Thinking

1. **Applying Ideas** What does the term "cold war" mean and how does it apply to this era?

2. **Applying Principles** How was the Truman Doctrine applied in assisting Greece, by the Marshall Plan, and in creating NATO?
3. **Testing Conclusions** According to some experts, the United States failed to save China because of its loyalty to the Nationalists and its ignorance of China's true situation. Test this theory using information from the text.
4. **Analyzing Political Cartoons** Study the political cartoon on this page and answer the questions that follow.
   a. Whom do the individuals in the cartoon represent?
   b. What is the cartoonist saying about Truman's power?

Writing About History

Comparison

Write an essay comparing the purposes and provisions of the Monroe Doctrine and the Truman Doctrine. Address such questions as: What were the foreign policy objectives that the United States tried to accomplish in each case? What commitment of resources was required to support each doctrine? Explain what the differences indicate about fundamental changes in foreign policy between 1823 and 1947.

858 UNIT 9 Times of Crisis: 1932–1960

CHAPTER 30 ★ REVIEW

Cooperative Learning

Working in groups of three, conduct a debate about the possible alternatives of United States foreign policy in Europe after World War II. One member should propose and support pulling troops out of Europe to lessen the Soviets' perceived need for a buffer of satellites. Another should support the contention that the Soviets wanted to conquer other nations as well as secure their own borders, and only a heavy military presence in Europe would contain them. The third member should decide which position was best supported and write an opinion that examines the best points of each argument. All members should be prepared to argue either position in front of the class if called on by the teacher.

Social Studies Skills

Reading and Interpreting Bar Graphs

As in the two bar graphs on this page, a bar graph can take more than one form. Many bar graphs are like the smaller one—vertical bars. The larger bar graph is different in that the bars are horizontal and there are no *x*-axis gradations. However, it still organizes data for easy comparison and analysis.

To interpret the data in a bar graph, do the following:
a. Read the title of the graph.
b. Determine what the bars represent by studying the *x*- and *y*-axes.
c. Determine the changes or other relationships the graph shows.

Practicing the Skill

Use the bar graphs that appear on this page and your understanding of chapter content to answer the following questions.
1. Using the three steps above, explain what is shown in the larger bar graph.
2. What two Western European nations did not receive aid?
3. Using the three steps above, explain what is shown in the smaller bar graph.

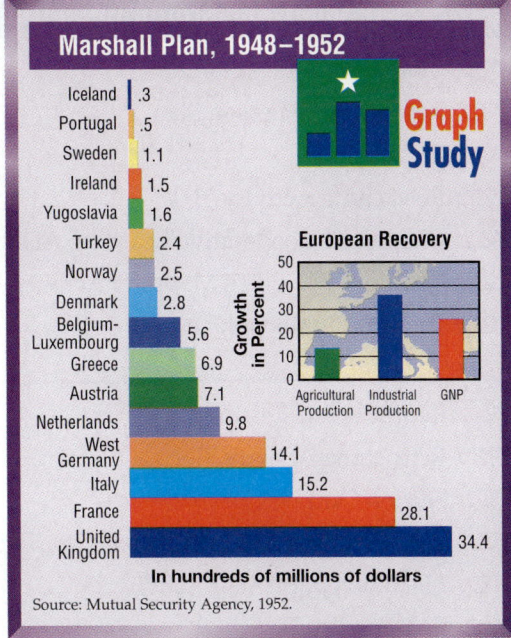

4. Why do you suppose the United Kingdom and France received the largest amounts of aid?
5. What do you think is the relationship between the two bar graphs?

Using Your Journal
Compare the threat of communism after World War II with the threat of communism after World War I.

CHAPTER 30 The Cold War 1945–1952   859

Practicing the Skill

1. the amount of Marshall Plan aid given to each European country between 1948 and 1952
2. Spain and Portugal
3. the percentage growth in agricultural production, industrial production, and gross national product for all of Europe from 1948 to 1952
4. the United States's closest allies during the war
5. shows that Marshall Plan aid did restore the economies of Western Europe, particularly industrial production

Chapter Bonus Test Question

In which location were African Americans most likely to establish a political power base during the years after World War II?
a. small southern towns
b. industrial cities in the North
c. agricultural centers in the Midwest
d. rural communities all around the country
(Answer: b)

Using Your Journal

Responses will vary but should reflect the very different positions of the Soviet Union after each war. It was only after World War II that the Soviets dominated Eastern Europe.

---

2. help free people resist aggressors, Greek civil war; economic aid to strengthen free societies; cooperation in agreeing to coordinate recovery efforts; eliminate hunger, poverty, chaos; collective security against threat of Communist expansion

3. underestimated Mao's strength and appeal to peasants; Chiang government corrupt, out of tune with needs of majority; never supported Nationalists with sufficient aid to combat Communist forces; no real commitment to China

4. a. President Truman and Congress
   b. That he is overextending the powers of the office.

PLANNING GUIDE   Chapter 31   Search for Stability

Daily Lesson Objectives	Teacher Classroom Resources	Multimedia
SECTION 1 **Eisenhower in the White House** **1 Day** pp. 862–865 1. Describe President Eisenhower's style of leadership. 2. Explain how Senator Joseph McCarthy's influence came to an end.	Chapter 31 Study Guide Reproducible Lesson Plan Section Quiz Reteaching Activity 31-1 Chapter 31 Cooperative Learning Activity Chapter 31 Concept Mapping Activity Writer's Guidebook Lessons 3-5	Student Self-Test Software Testmaker Section Focus Transparency 100 Chapter 30 Skills Transparency The Presidents: A Picture History of the Nation
SECTION 2 **The Straight Road Down the Middle** **1 Day** pp. 867–870 1. Explain Eisenhower's economic policies. 2. Discuss the plight of the small farmer in the 1950s.	Reproducible Lesson Plan Reteaching Activity 31-2 Section Quiz Reinforcing Social Studies Skills 23, 53, 59 Map and Graph Skill Activity 28 SAT Practice Tests 5–9	Student Self-Test Software Testmaker Section Focus Transparency 101
SECTION 3 **An Affluent Society** **1 Day** pp. 871–876 1. Describe the effect of affluence on American life. 2. Give examples of advances in medical technology. 3. Explain the pressures of conformity in the 1950s.	Reproducible Lesson Plan Reteaching Activity 31-3 Section Quiz American Portrait 62 Reinforcing Social Studies Skills 23, 53, 59 Chapter 31 Primary and Secondary Source Readings Map and Graph Skill Activities 29, 35, 36 American Literary Heritage Unit 9	Student Self-Test Software Testmaker Section Focus Transparency 102 The American People: Fabric of a Nation
SECTION 4 **Foreign Policy and Developing Nations** **1 Day** pp. 878–885 1. Discuss Eisenhower's approach to foreign policy and the Eisenhower Doctrine. 2. Describe how the fear of nuclear war affected the cold war. 3. Discuss why American relations with Latin America were poor in the 1950s.	Reproducible Lesson Plan Reteaching Activity 31-4 Section Quiz Chapter 31 Enrichment Activity American Portrait 61 Reinforcing Social Studies Skills 25, 28 Map and Graph Skill Activities 4, 5 Spanish Summaries & Glossary Writer's Guidebook Lessons 3–5	Student Self-Test Software Testmaker Section Focus Transparency 103 Chapter 31 Map Transparency Vocabulary Puzzlemaker Chapter Digest Audiocassette, Chapter 31 Communism and the Cold War
CHAPTER REVIEW AND EVALUATION **1 Day**	Chapter 31 Test Chapter 31 Performance Assessment Activity	Student Self-Test Software Testmaker

00:00 OUT OF TIME? If time does not permit teaching the entire chapter, use the Chapter 31 Summary on pages 890–891 and the Chapter 31 audiocassette (English and Spanish) to point out the main ideas of the chapter.

PLANNING GUIDE

Cultural Diversity Activity

Exploring Ideas Discuss with students the link between conformity and racial discrimination in suburban housing noted on page 874. Have students define conformity in their own words. Then tell them that the word is often defined as "acting in accordance with prevailing standards or customs." Ask students to describe the "standards" or customs that would have contributed to discrimination in suburban neighborhoods in the 1950s. Ask: How might living in a community in which conformity is encouraged and valued affect the willingness of white suburbanites to speak out against racial prejudice? Is the pressure for conformity in suburban neighborhoods as great today as in the 1950s? To what extent is the pressure to conform still a factor in prejudice and discrimination?

Performance Assessment Activity

Scientific Breakthroughs Divide students into small groups and ask each to research scientific developments during the 1950s in one of the following fields: medicine, communications, computers, or aviation and space science. Have each group create a poster to highlight achievements in the field it researched. Invite groups to share their posters with the class.

POSSIBLE RUBRIC FEATURES: Content information, organization, visual communication skills, collaborative skills, creativity, research

Chapter Resources

Literature from the Period

Ellison, Ralph. *Invisible Man.* 1952.

Galbraith, John Kenneth. *The Affluent Society.* 1958.

Hansberry, Lorraine. *A Raisin in the Sun.* 1959.

Readings for the Student

Cheney, Glenn Alan. *Television in American Society.* Franklin Watts, 1983.

Divine, Robert. *Eisenhower and the Cold War.* Oxford University Press, 1981.

Readings for the Teacher

Girling, John L. S. *America and the Third World.* Routledge and Kegan, 1980.

Multimedia Resources

Balance of Power. Software Toolworks (Apple, IBM, and MAC diskettes, with guide)

The Cold War. Educational Environment. (VHS, 31 minutes)

Focus on the Fifties. ABC Wide World of Learning. (color film)

Key to Ability Levels

Teaching strategies have been coded for varying learning styles and abilities.

L1 Basic activities for all students

L2 Average activities for average to above-average students

L3 Challenging activities for above-average students

LEP Limited English Proficiency activities

Glencoe Links to the Humanities

Link to Art
- U.S. History and Art Transparencies 26, 27, 28

Links to Literature
- Macmillan Literature: Novel Guide—*A Wrinkle in Time*
- Macmillan Literature: American Literature Text—Thornton Wilder, Tennessee Williams

Link to Music
- American Music: Cultural Traditions

CHAPTER 31

BEGINNING THE CHAPTER

Ask students to describe the changes that took place in the country after the United States entered the war. (Students should include changes in industry, jobs, family life, and farming.) Then ask them to skim the chapter, paying attention to the subheads and photographs. Have students make some generalizations about the economy, technology, lifestyles, and foreign affairs during the 1950s.

Recording Journal Notes

To help students get started, remind them of the various postwar crises of the Truman administration—the Berlin blockade and airlift, the Korean War, and the domestic anti-communist fervor.

Linking Across Time

Point out that the 1950s was a period of relative tranquility after decades of crisis—the Great Depression of the 1930s and World War II and its aftermath. The federal government had grown and met these crises successfully. As they faced the second half of the twentieth century, Americans saw their country as the most prosperous and powerful nation in the world. Yet they remained uneasy, not sure that the peace and prosperity would last.

CHAPTER 31

Search for Stability
1952–1960

▼ 1957 CHEVROLET

Setting the Scene

Focus

A war hero, Dwight D. Eisenhower became one of the most popular Presidents of modern times. His domestic and foreign policies were stable and consistent. At home, the nation was generally prosperous. In foreign policy he continued Truman's efforts at containment. The cold war expanded into the Middle East, Africa, and Latin America. Covert operations increased, and American troops were sent into Lebanon.

Journal Notes

As you read the chapter, record in your Journal the efforts of the United States to contain the spread of communism.

Concepts to Understand

★ Why the United States's international leadership led to the use of covert operations in other countries
★ How economic growth stimulated the economy during the 1950s

Read to Discover . . .

★ how President Eisenhower viewed his role as President.
★ how the lives of most Americans improved following World War II.

CULTURAL
- 1952 Ralph Ellison publishes *Invisible Man*
- 1955 Jonas Salk develops vaccine to prevent polio

1950 ——————— **1953**

POLITICAL
- 1950 McCarthy charges communist influence in government
- 1952 Eisenhower elected President
- 1953 Truce in the Korean War reached
- 1954 Geneva Conference divides Vietnam

860 UNIT 9 Times of Crisis: 1932–1960

✚ EXTRA CREDIT PROJECT

In the 1950s many women married young and were expected to stay at home and care for their children or work at jobs reserved for women. Ask interested students to gather statistical information about women's roles in the years from 1950 to 1960: What was the average age for marriage? How many children did the average woman have? What percentage of women worked outside the home? What jobs did these women hold? Encourage students to share their findings with the class.

History AND ART

Snack Bar
by Isabel Bishop, 1954

The 1950s was an era of social change for many Americans. Artist Isabel Bishop captures the lonely aspects of urban life and the nature of the fast-food culture.

◀ BASEBALL PLAYER JACKIE ROBINSON

- **1957** The musical *West Side Story* premieres in New York
- **1955** Formation of the AFL-CIO
- **1956** Suez crisis erupts

1956

- **1960** There are more than 45 million television sets in American homes
- **1959** Castro comes to power in Cuba
- **1960** Soviets shoot down a United States U-2 surveillance plane

1959

CHAPTER 31 Search for Stability 1952–1960

CHAPTER 31 CONCEPTS

Concept Mapping Activity

Reproduce the following concept map on the chalkboard for students as a preview of the chapter content:

The nation searches for economic and political stability in a world of crisis.
- International Leadership
- Economic Growth

History AND ART

In *Snack Bar* Isabel Bishop captures the lonely aspects of urban life and the nature of our fast-food culture. Bishop was one of many artists employed by federal art projects during the Great Depression.

 VIDEODISC

- *GTV: The American People: Fabric of a Nation*

Side 4, Chapter 4
Title: *Greener Pastures?*
Subject: Development and impact of suburbs

See GTV Guide page 96 for complete lesson plan.

Teacher Notes

LESSON PLAN
SECTION 1, 862–866

FOCUS

Bellringer

Before taking roll at the beginning of the class period, display Focus Activity Transparency 99 on the overhead projector, and assign the accompanying Focus Activity Sheet.

Objectives

Point out the objectives on this page to students in previewing the section content.

Motivating Activity

Ask students what kind of President they think the American people wanted in the early 1950s. (Students might indicate that people wanted someone who would make the country stable and make them feel secure.) As the students read this section, tell them to focus on the type of leadership the American people received from President Eisenhower.

Use Skills Transparency 31.

The following material is available from Glencoe and may be used to introduce or enrich Chapter 31:

CD-ROM
- *The Presidents: A Picture History of Our Nation*

SECTION 1

The Eisenhower Years

Setting the Scene

Section Focus

As the Truman presidency ended, the fear of communism preoccupied the nation. In Asia the United States was engaged in a long and frustrating war with the Communists. In other parts of the world, a dangerous cold war between communism and American interests intensified. The nation was ready for new leadership to guide it through these troubling times.

Objectives

After studying this section, you should be able to

★ describe President Eisenhower's style of leadership.
★ explain how Senator Joseph McCarthy's influence came to an end.

Key Term

presidential succession

◀ EISENHOWER CAMPAIGN BUTTON

After 7 years of the Truman administration and 20 years of Democratic leadership, the Republicans hoped that 1952 would be their year. They knew Americans were worried about the continuing war in Korea and the tense cold war. Americans were also concerned with the charges of communist infiltration in the government. President Truman's reputation was damaged by news reports that some of his officials had accepted bribes. These issues gave the Republicans their rallying cry for the election. They ran against "Korea, communism, and corruption."

■ The Election of 1952

As their candidate, the Republicans picked one of the most popular war heroes, Dwight D. Eisenhower.

When asked to run for President in 1948, Eisenhower refused. By 1952, however, he became concerned that isolationists might regain the White House and agreed to run. He won the Republican nomination after a hotly contested race with Senator Robert A. Taft of Ohio. As his running mate, Eisenhower chose Richard M. Nixon, a 39-year-old senator from California who had made his reputation pursuing alleged Communists in government.

"I Like Ike"

The Republicans adopted the slogan "It's time for a change!" Eisenhower, known as "Ike," promised to end the war in Korea and took a hard line against corruption. "I like Ike" became the Republican rallying cry.

Eisenhower's promise to keep his administration clean was soon regarded with skepticism. Charges were disclosed that Richard

862 UNIT 9 Times of Crisis: 1932–1960

Classroom Resources for SECTION 1

Teacher's Classroom Resources
- Chapter 1 Study Guide
- Reproducible Lesson Plan
- Reteaching Activity 31-1
- Chapter 31 Cooperative Learning Activity
- Section Quiz

Multimedia
- Section Focus Transparency 99
- Chapter 31 Skills Transparency
- Unit 9 Digest Transparency
- Testmaker
- Student Self-Test Software
- The Presidents: A Picture History of Our Nation

Nixon had received gifts from California businesspeople totaling $18,000 while he was a senator. For a while, it looked as though Nixon might be dropped from the ticket. But in a nationwide speech broadcast on radio and television, he insisted the funds had been used for legitimate political purposes. He did admit that his family had kept one gift, a cocker spaniel puppy named "Checkers." The "Checkers speech" saved Nixon, who remained on the Republican ticket.

Eisenhower Defeats Stevenson

The Democrats nominated Adlai Stevenson, governor of Illinois. Stevenson was a thoughtful and eloquent liberal, but his campaign was burdened by the need to defend the actions of the Truman administration.

It is doubtful that Stevenson ever had a chance to win against the popular Eisenhower. If he did, he lost it two weeks before Election Day, when Eisenhower promised to make a trip to Korea if elected. The election was a landslide for Eisenhower. He received in excess of 6 million popular votes more than Stevenson and carried the Electoral College by 442 to 89 votes. The Republicans also gained an eight-seat majority in the House. The Senate was evenly divided between Democrats and Republicans.

■ A New Style of Leadership

Although Eisenhower was a career soldier, he did not run the White House like an officer commanding an army. Instead, he acted as the chief administrator or leader of the White House team.

Hidden-Hand Presidency

Under Eisenhower the cabinet assumed new importance and acted as a genuine advisory board. For the first time in history, the cabinet had a full-time secretary, an agenda, and regularly kept minutes. Eisenhower made Sherman Adams, former governor of

▲ **EISENHOWER BECOMES PRESIDENT** Dwight D. Eisenhower proved to be a popular campaigner and was the first Republican to be elected President since 1928. *How great was his margin of victory over Stevenson in 1952?*

CHAPTER 31
SECTION 1

Independent Practice

Writing Have students write a report explaining the provisions of the Twenty-fifth Amendment. It outlines the procedures for times when the President is disabled as well as how these procedures are to be put into effect. **L2**

Did You Know?

The problem of presidential incapacity was not new. William H. Harrison suffered from pneumonia for a month before his death in 1841. In 1881 James Garfield lingered for two months before he died from an assassin's bullet. In 1919 Woodrow Wilson suffered a paralyzing stroke that rendered him unable to participate in upcoming treaty negotiations.

Visualizing History Lyndon B. Johnson was first elected to the Senate in 1949. He served as minority leader from 1953 to 1955 and as majority leader from 1955 to 1961.

Answer to Caption: "modern Republicans" and moderate-to-liberal Democrats

Visualizing History ▲ **LYNDON JOHNSON** Senate Majority leader Lyndon Johnson (right), shown here meeting with Prime Minister Harold Macmillan of Great Britain, took an active role in domestic and foreign policy issues. **What congressional coalition supported President Eisenhower?**

New Hampshire, his chief of staff. Adams wielded great power by controlling access to the President.

The advantages of Eisenhower's kind of administration were clear. If, for some reason, the President was unable to lead, the government would not come to a standstill. Cabinet members could easily take over day-to-day operations. Indeed, Eisenhower suffered serious illnesses three times during his presidency, and each time the White House staff carried on with little difficulty. Critics claimed that the President was abdicating his responsibilities. At crucial times he seemed unaware of decisions made by his aides. Historians later described Eisenhower's management style as a "hidden-hand presidency."

The Bricker Amendment

Eisenhower hoped to establish good working relations with Congress, but members of his own party sometimes made this difficult. Still angry over the secret agreements that President Roosevelt had made with Stalin and Churchill at Yalta, Republican Senator John Bricker of Ohio introduced a bill to limit presidential power. The Bricker Amendment required Senate ratification of all agreements made by the President with other nations. It also prohibited the President from making a treaty that conflicted with the laws of any state.

Eisenhower believed that the Bricker Amendment would limit the President's power to deal effectively with other nations. It would also allow any state to disrupt United States foreign policy. Although most Republicans in Congress supported the Bricker Amendment, the Eisenhower administration fought hard against it. In February 1954, the bill was defeated by a single vote. Wearily, the President commented:

> *If it is true that when you die the things that bothered you most are engraved on your skull, I am sure I'll have there the mud and dirt of France during the invasion and the name of Senator Bricker.*

■ McCarthy's Influence Ends

Some Americans believed that a Republican President would put an end to Senator Joseph McCarthy's charges that the government was filled with Communists. But McCarthy continued his crusade and subjected many government officials to humiliating investigations.

For a time McCarthy succeeded in giving the impression that he was saving the country from communism. A public opinion poll taken in 1954 reported that 50 percent of the people favored him and 29 percent opposed him. Senators wary of McCarthy's influence with the voters were reluctant to oppose him.

Although the President privately disapproved of McCarthy and his methods, Eisenhower refused to attack him publicly. The President believed that if he fought

UNIT 9 Times of Crisis: 1932–1960

Critical Thinking

Assessing Motivation During the 1950s the fear of Communist subversion hung over the country and was fanned by Senator Joseph McCarthy. Ask students if they think that McCarthyism was a "necessary evil" in order to protect America's vital interests during the cold war. (Some students might indicate that McCarthyism was an overreaction and that it resulted in infringement on the civil rights of many falsely accused people. Other students might indicate that the United States was very vulnerable during that time and couldn't afford to take any chances of Communist subversion.) **L2**

McCarthy, he would only give him more publicity. This tactic, however, deprived McCarthy's opponents in Congress of Eisenhower's leadership.

McCarthy's underhanded tactics were finally exposed to the public in 1954. In televised hearings regarding possible communist subversion in the army, Americans observed McCarthy's callous disregard of law and fairness. After the hearings ended, the Senate passed a resolution condemning McCarthy for his conduct.

Presidential Disability

In September 1955, President Eisenhower suffered a heart attack. Although the President recovered rapidly, the nation's confidence was shaken. The stock market dropped more sharply than it had since 1929. Then, within the next two years, Eisenhower suffered two major illnesses.

The President's health focused attention on the question of **presidential succession,** the order in which others fill the office of President. Although Eisenhower had kept the government running smoothly during his illnesses, Americans wondered what would happen if the President remained ill. The Constitution provides that the Vice President becomes President if the President is unable to handle the duties of office. However, it does not say who is to decide whether the President is, or is not, able to serve.

The matter was addressed in 1967 after ratification of the Twenty-fifth Amendment, which outlines procedures when the President is disabled. Moreover, it deals with the situation when a President feels capable of continuing in office but is thought by others to be incapable.

The Election of 1956

In 1956 the Republicans renominated Eisenhower. The Republicans claimed that the Eisenhower administration had brought peace and prosperity to the nation. Eisenhower had ended the war in Korea and avoided other world conflicts. The Democrats, nominating Adlai Stevenson for a second time, capitalized on fear about the President's health. They played upon the public's concern that Vice President Nixon might become President.

Eisenhower won by a greater margin than in 1952. The President's popularity did not rub off on his party, however. Democrats won control of both the House of Representatives and the Senate.

In his second term, Eisenhower was more independent of his party than any other President in the twentieth century. Many conservative Republicans regarded Eisenhower as too liberal in domestic affairs and too interventionist in foreign affairs. However, "modern Republicans" and some Democrats supported the President. His policies won support from the two Democratic leaders in Congress, House Speaker Sam Rayburn and Senate Majority Leader Lyndon Johnson. On domestic issues, an alliance developed between "modern Republicans" and moderate-to-liberal Democrats.

Section 1 ★ Review

Checking for Understanding

1. **Identify** Adlai Stevenson, Richard Nixon, "Checkers speech," Bricker Amendment.
2. **Define** presidential succession.
3. **Explain** the need for an amendment concerning presidential succession.
4. **State** reasons for Eisenhower's appeal to moderate Democrats.

Critical Thinking

5. **Evaluating Performance** Describe Eisenhower's leadership style and discuss its advantages and disadvantages.

CHAPTER 31 Search for Stability 1952–1960

Answers to SECTION 1 REVIEW

1. Adlai Stevenson, 863; Richard Nixon, 862; "Checkers," 863; Bricker Amendment, 864
2. All vocabulary words are defined in the Glossary.
3. Eisenhower's heart attack and illnesses; need for amendment saying who would succeed if President suffered extended illness or there was disagreement over capacity to serve
4. middle course economics; retained some New Deal assistance; independent of party
5. Decentralized "staff" approach, cabinet, advisers; shared decision making; staff advised on policy matters. Advantages: could carry on in President's absence; use staff expertise. Disadvantages: President isolated; could be unaware of staff decisions; staff not elected to lead.

CHAPTER 31
SECTION 1

ASSESS
Check Understanding
Assign Section 1 Review as homework or an in-class activity.

Evaluate
Assign the Section 1 Quiz in the TCR, or use the History of a Free Nation testmaker to create a customized quiz.

Reteach
Have students write a paragraph describing Eisenhower's style of leadership and how it differed from his predecessors.

Have students complete Reteaching Activity 31-1.

Enrich
Have students look for quotes that show opposing viewpoints by two of the people mentioned in this section.

CLOSE
Have students read the quote that opened the section. Ask them to discuss this quote based on what they learned about President Eisenhower's administration in Section 1.

LESSON PLAN
Mastering Social Studies Skills

Teaching Critical Thinking Skills

Remind students that events can be symbolic. Neil Armstrong's walk on the moon can symbolize modern technology. Have students review the guidelines presented for understanding symbolism. Discuss historical events that have become symbols. For example the Vietnam War has come to symbolize the failure of American diplomacy; Jackie Robinson's integrating baseball has become a symbol of the American struggle to integrate society.

Did You Know?

When asked why he pushed the United States to send an astronaut to the moon, President John F. Kennedy replied, "Because it is there.... The moon and planets are there, and new hopes for knowledge and peace are there."

Social Studies Skills

Critical Thinking Skills

Discovering Symbolism in History

▲ COLD WAR CARTOON

Neil Armstrong was the first person to walk on the moon. This accomplishment had a powerful impact on people all over the world. One reason this event had such an impact was that people saw his walking on the moon as a symbol, and they attached extra meaning to it.

A *symbol* is something used to represent or stand for something else—often an abstract idea, concept, or feeling. Symbols are all around us, even though we often do not recognize them as such. All words, for example, are symbols for objects or ideas.

A familiar symbol is the American flag, which stands for the United States and patriotic pride. Other familiar symbols include the color purple, which stands for royalty; lions, which stand for courage; and the skull and crossbones, which symbolizes death.

Armstrong's moon walk symbolizes human progress, the power of modern technology, and our neverending curiosity about the universe. The following guidelines will help you discover symbolism in history:

- Think about the event or condition being studied. What is the main activity in it?
- What overall condition led to this main activity?
- Who or what situation could be affected by this activity?
- What consequences could there be for those who are affected?
- What statement could be made that would demonstrate the symbolism, or meaning, of this event?

For example, possible statements of the symbolism in McCarthyism include:

a. McCarthyism symbolized a callous disregard for law and fairness.
b. McCarthyism symbolized cold war mistrust between two superpowers.
c. McCarthyism symbolized a pervasive fear of communism.
d. McCarthyism symbolized America's desire to safeguard its values and ideologies.
e. McCarthyism symbolized fanaticism.

Practicing the Skill

1. Analyze the political cartoon on this page. What do the two figures symbolize?
2. Read Section 3 of this chapter. Reread the guidelines that are listed above. Then, use the guidelines to list examples of the symbolism you found in the Eisenhower Doctrine.

866

Answers to SOCIAL STUDIES SKILLS

1. The eagle represents the United States. The bear represents the Soviet Union.

2. Possible statement about symbolism—The Eisenhower Doctrine symbolized the need for the United States to be the police of the world.

SECTION 2

"The Straight Road"

Setting the Scene

Section Focus

Democratic administrations had leaned toward the interests of labor. When Eisenhower accepted the presidential nomination, he promised that in economic matters he would "travel the straight road down the middle." As a result, the nation enjoyed an unprecedented period of prosperity and witnessed the rapid development of big business and agribusiness.

Objectives

After studying this section, you should be able to

★ explain the Eisenhower administration's economic policies.

★ discuss the plight of the small farmer in the 1950s.

Key Term

agribusiness

◀ LABOR UNION SYMBOL

Throughout both of his administrations, Eisenhower steered a course between conservatism and liberalism. Ike's middle course pleased most Americans. At the beginning of his administration it looked as though he might try to undo the New Deal. Like Hoover, Eisenhower believed that the role of government should be limited. Eisenhower advocated cutting the budget, reducing taxes, and ending government regulation of business. He condemned the Tennessee Valley Authority as "creeping socialism" and tried unsuccessfully to arrange for private industry to build new power plants in Tennessee, Alabama, and Kentucky.

Eisenhower and the New Deal

Despite this conservative agenda, Eisenhower recognized that New Deal programs were strongly supported by most Americans. He wrote in a private letter:

> *Should any political party attempt to abolish Social Security, unemployment insurance, and eliminate labor laws and farm programs, you would not hear of that party again in our political history.*

The debate during Eisenhower's presidency was not over ending such New Deal programs as Social Security or the minimum wage, but over how much larger to allow them to become. With President Eisenhower's encouragement, Congress extended Social Security to 7 million more people and increased benefits. Congress also extended unemployment compensation to 4 million more people. Eisenhower tried to persuade Congress to enact a health insurance program partly funded by the federal government, but Congress rejected the legislation.

CHAPTER 31 Search for Stability 1952–1960

LESSON PLAN
SECTION 2, 867–870

FOCUS

Bellringer

Before taking roll at the beginning of the class period, display Focus Activity Transparency 100 on the overhead projector, and assign the accompanying Focus Activity Sheet.

Objectives

Point out the objectives on this page to students in previewing the section content.

Motivating Activity

Have students recall the New Deal programs, especially social security. Ask them how the American people might have felt if these programs were undone. As students read this section, have them focus on Eisenhower's economic policies and on how these policies differed from his predecessors.

Use Skills Transparency 31.

Classroom Resources for SECTION 2

Teacher's Classroom Resources
- Reproducible Lesson Plan
- Reteaching Activity 31-2
- Section Quiz

Multimedia
- Section Focus Transparency 100
- Testmaker
- Student Self-Test Software

CHAPTER 31
SECTION 2

TEACH
Guided Practice
Finding Main Ideas Have students summarize the main ideas in Section 2 by writing a newspaper headline for each subhead in the section. For example, a headline for the first subhead might read "Government Supportive of Big Business." **L1, LEP**

Visualizing History Until his death in 1970, Walter Reuther was the most respected labor leader in the United States. Presidents sought his advice and his support in political campaigns.
Answer to Caption: The merger increased the strength of organized labor and made it easier to form local unions.

■ Business and Labor

Big business also had an ally in the White House. During the 1950s, 3,000 companies merged with the 500 largest corporations without any antitrust challenges by the government. The nation's 100 largest companies controlled more than 30 percent of all industrial production. Some corporations, such as General Motors and American Telephone and Telegraph, had annual budgets that were larger than those of many countries.

The American labor movement grew more slowly than big business, but it continued to gain strength. In 1955 the American Federation of Labor (AFL) and the Congress of Industrial Organizations (CIO) merged, forming the AFL-CIO. The merger increased the strength of organized labor and made it easier for workers to form local unions.

Organized labor tried hard to win pay increases. During the 1950s, take-home pay and buying power rose sharply. Workers also enjoyed longer paid vacations. Walter Reuther, United Auto Workers president, observed that the movement was developing a "whole new middle class."

Organized labor was not very successful in its efforts to organize the lowest-paid factory workers and office workers. Often, these workers were women or minorities. The growth in AFL-CIO membership actually slowed by 1957.

Union growth was also adversely affected by congressional investigations into corrupt union practices. The investigations revealed that strong-arm tactics were used by some unions to force employers into accepting the unions. The Teamsters' Union, accused of misappropriating funds, was expelled from the AFL-CIO. These revelations began to turn public opinion against unions.

■ Farm Problems

Despite the prosperity of the 1950s, it was a difficult time for many of the nation's farmers. Between 1948 and 1956, the farmers' share of the national income dropped from 9 to 4 percent. While the average American enjoyed a per capita income of $1,629, the farm population averaged $632 a year.

 ▲ **LABOR UNIONS MERGE** George Meany (left), president of the AFL, and Walter Reuther (right), president of the CIO, shake hands on the merger of the two unions. *How did the joining of these unions help organized labor?*

UNIT 9 Times of Crisis: 1932–1960

Cooperative Learning

Ask students the following question: How were the economic policies of President Eisenhower more conservative than those of his predecessors? Have students use the information in Section 2 to answer the question. After they think of a response, have them pair up to discuss their responses. Ask volunteers to share their responses with the class. (Student responses should indicate that Eisenhower believed that the role of government should be limited. He advocated cutting the budget, reducing taxes, and ending government regulation of business.) **L2**

American Portraits

Betty Friedan 1921–

Betty Friedan (free•DAN) was one of the first to analyze the lives of women. When she began her analysis, most women were homemakers or worked in low-paying jobs.

In 1957 she began a yearlong study of her Smith College classmates. She discovered that many of these well-educated women were leading unhappy lives. With additional research it became clear to Friedan that American women were failing to find fulfillment in life. Instead, they were succumbing to "the feminine mystique"—a belief that they were supposed to ignore their talents and interests and live only for the achievements of their family.

In 1963 Friedan published *The Feminine Mystique*, a book that sparked the modern women's liberation movement. In 1966 she helped found the National Organization for Women (NOW) to lead the fight for equal rights.

Question of Price Supports

Eisenhower was reluctant to have the government continue to guarantee farmers set prices for their products. The heart of the issue, according to the administration, was

> [W]hether our farms are to continue to be operated by freemen. Or . . . to offset some very real and obvious problems that farmers now face, will government go in the opposite direction and subsidize agriculture in such a manner that it also takes control?

But without strong price supports from the government, the small family farmer faced economic ruin. Overproduction from better seeds, fertilizers, and mechanization kept farm prices low. Legislation reduced but did not end price supports or the farm surplus.

Many small farm families gave up and sold out to large farm owners who raised only a single crop and used the latest machinery and agricultural methods. Because of their efficiency, the large farm owners could cut their costs and still make a profit. More small farmers were unable to compete with the **agribusinesses,** or modern large-scale farms that covered 1,000 acres or more. By 1959 half of the nation's farmland belonged to 4 percent of the farmers.

Seasonal Workers

There were other problems associated with America's changing agricultural patterns. Large farm owners hired seasonal workers to cultivate and harvest their crops. Many of the workers were Mexican Americans from California and the Southwest, but as many as 400,000 workers were Mexicans allowed into the United States on short-term visas. Unprotected by the National Labor Relations Act or federal minimum wage laws, these migrant workers labored long hours for little pay and endured terrible living conditions. Their children grew up with little, if any, education.

■ Prosperity and Recession

Much of the economic growth of the 1950s was due to a tremendous increase in consumer credit. Effective advertising enticed Americans to borrow more and

---

Critical Thinking

Determining Cause and Effect Four solutions to the disposal of the overabundance of production in the 1950s were used in different degrees. They were (1) built-in obsolescence—a new model car every year; (2) the creation of new consumer demand—advertising; (3) shipping excess goods to "needy" nations—food and technology; and (4) government-sponsored public programs—highways, public housing. The space exploration program and the military buildup are other examples of what society could do with an oversupply of production capability. Discuss what changes each solution would undergo if overabundance vanished. **L2**

CHAPTER 31
SECTION 2

ASSESS
Check Understanding
Assign Section 2 Review as homework or an in-class activity.

Evaluate
Assign the Section 2 Quiz in the TCR, or use the History of a Free Nation testmaker to create a customized quiz.

Reteach
Have students summarize the Eisenhower administration's economic policies by making a chart with these headings: Big Business, Labor, and Farmers.

Have students complete Reteaching Activity 31-2.

Enrich
Have students research and report on the Soil-Bank Bill that Congress passed in 1956. The report should include how soil banks started, how they were used, and their effect on farm income today.

CLOSE
Ask students to create a cause and effect chart for the following event: In the mid-1950s, Eisenhower attempted to hold down government spending.

---

more money to buy houses, cars, and consumer goods. This growing demand, in turn, encouraged industries to produce more goods and hire more people.

Economic Slump

President Eisenhower worried that this rapid growth of the economy would lead to inflation, or rapidly rising prices. Because of this he tried to hold down government spending, both for domestic and military projects. But in 1957 and 1958, his attempts to balance the budget set off a recession. Sales dropped and manufacturers laid off workers. Unemployment rose to 7.6 percent of the workforce. Eisenhower resisted congressional pressure for a tax cut to stimulate the economy. Finally, late in 1958, boom times returned again.

Mounting Criticism

Although President Eisenhower remained a popular leader during the late 1950s, he was sharply blamed by some critics for not moving quickly enough. Some detractors charged that the President ignored important national issues such as civil rights and the protection of natural resources.

Scandals

At the same time, the administration also had to deal with a number of scandals. The most publicized scandal revolved around Sherman Adams, the President's closest adviser. In the spring of 1958, congressional hearings disclosed that Adams had received gifts from a wealthy Boston industrialist who was under investigation by the government. Adams was forced to resign. The recession and the scandals hurt the Republican cause during the 1958 elections, and the Democrats strengthened their control of both houses, winning 15 additional seats in the Senate and 48 seats in the House.

Accomplishments

Despite these difficulties, Eisenhower received praise for some of his efforts. In foreign policy, he sought to ease world tensions. During his last year in office, the President visited an unprecedented number of nations on a goodwill tour. He affirmed that

> *Our basic aspiration is to search out methods by which peace in the world can be assured with justice for everybody.*

At home, he backed government grants to help in the building of more schools for the nation's expanding school-age population. Eisenhower also supported the National Defense Education Act of 1958. This law provided a $295-million fund to provide loans to college students for their education.

In 1959 two new states were added to the union. On January 3 Eisenhower issued a proclamation making Alaska the 49th state—the first new state since Arizona and New Mexico joined the Union in 1912. On August 21, Hawaii became the 50th state.

Section 2 ★ Review

Checking for Understanding

1. **Identify** creeping socialism, AFL-CIO, migrant workers.
2. **Define** agribusiness.
3. **Characterize** the economic philosophy and practice of Eisenhower.
4. **List** two problems connected with farming in the 1950s.

Critical Thinking

5. **Comparing Trends** Compare developments in business and agriculture during the 1950s, including the impact on workers.

---

870   UNIT 9 Times of Crisis: 1932–1960

Answers to SECTION 2 REVIEW

1. creeping socialism, 867; AFL-CIO, 868; migrant workers, 869
2. All vocabulary words are defined in the Glossary.
3. Minimal business regulation, allow mergers; taxes and government spending low, but provide assistance for needy, security for citizens; no intervention in farm prices.
4. Farm surplus brought low prices; without price supports small farmers couldn't compete with agribusiness, left land; agribusiness used imported labor, overworked, underpaid.
5. Mergers increased big-business share of market, agribusinesses increased share of farmland. Business profits high, farmers' minimal or none. Business labor gained higher wages, better conditions. Agricultural workers worked under poor conditions for low pay.

SECTION 3

An Affluent Society

Setting the Scene

Section Focus

The economic growth of the 1950s brought great changes to the nation. For the first time, most Americans enjoyed a life of abundance. This prosperity greatly changed the way people lived. Advances in technology and medicine coupled with economic prosperity gave Americans great confidence in the future.

Objectives

After studying this section, you should be able to
★ describe the effect of affluence on American life.
★ give examples of advances in medical technology.
★ explain the pressures of conformity in the 1950s.

Key Term

automation

◀ THE TELEVISION GENERATION

After World War II, Americans were ready to settle down and enjoy a period of peace and prosperity. Industry responded to the demands of Americans by turning out huge quantities of new goods. New communities and housing developments were built as people moved from the cities to the suburbs. Americans were on the move, and they relied heavily on the automobile for this new mobility. People anxiously awaited each year's new car models with their added gadgets and longer "tail fins." Highways stretched across the country carrying more and more traffic. A new suburban lifestyle evolved among middle-class Americans.

New technology and continuing prosperity allowed many Americans to enjoy more leisure time. At the same time, the number of available leisure activities increased.

■ An Economy of Abundance

In 1958 economist John Kenneth Galbraith published *The Affluent Society*, in which he claimed that America's postwar prosperity was a new phenomenon. In the past, Galbraith said, all societies were based on an "economy of scarcity," in which the productivity of the economy was limited by a lack of resources and overpopulation.

In the 1950s, however, the United States and a few other highly industrialized nations were experiencing what Galbraith called an "economy of abundance." Up-to-date technology enabled these nations to produce an endless variety and amount of goods and services for their people. The citizens of these countries were enjoying a standard of living never before thought possible. Poverty was disappearing, except

CHAPTER 31 Search for Stability 1952–1960 **871**

LESSON PLAN
SECTION 3, 871–877

FOCUS

Bellringer
Before taking roll at the beginning of the class period, display Focus Activity Transparency 101 on the overhead projector, and assign the accompanying Focus Activity Sheet.

Objectives
Point out the objectives on this page to students in previewing the section content.

Motivating Activity
Ask students to list 10 things that make them happy. Then ask them to count how many things on their lists are material goods. Discuss with the students the importance of material wealth. As they read this section, have them focus on the ways that affluence affected American life.

Use Skills Transparency 31.

VIDEODISC
• *GTV: The American People: Fabric of a Nation*

Side 4, Chapter 4
Title: *Greener Pastures?*
Subject: Development and impact of suburbs

See GTV Guide page 96 for complete lesson plan.

Classroom Resources for SECTION 3

Teacher's Classroom Resources
- Reproducible Lesson Plan
- Reteaching Activity 31-3
- Chapter 31 Primary and Secondary Source Readings
- Section Quiz

Multimedia
- Section Focus Transparency 101
- Testmaker
- Student Self-Test Software
- The American People: Fabric of a Nation

871

CHAPTER 31 SECTION 3

TEACH

Guided Practice

Debate Have students debate the following point:

Suburbs are better places to live than cities.

(The basic pro argument might include the point that suburbs are often safer than cities and are less crowded. The basic con argument might include the point that cities offer a more diverse way of life, because the people are generally not as homogeneous as people in suburbs. Cities also generally offer a greater variety of cultural activities.) **L2**

Assign students the Chapter 31 Reading in Primary and Secondary Source Readings.

Visualizing History Early computers were large because information was stored on envelope-sized rectangular cards with holes punched in them. Each card could store only a few pieces of information. Today a tiny silicon chip can store millions of pieces of information.
Answer to Caption: for bookkeeping functions like billing and inventory control

 ▲ **COMPUTERS COME OF AGE** Early computers, such as the UNIVAC, occupied entire rooms and used vacuum tubes rather than microchips to process information. *How did businesses first use computers?*

within such groups as the unskilled, uneducated, and new immigrant population.

Some critics accused Galbraith of overstating the situation, but the facts and figures seemed to support it. Americans produced more than they could use, and this new wealth was being distributed throughout the population. During the 1920s the wealthiest 5 percent of the population received 35 percent of the country's income, but by 1960 this group received only 18 percent.

Life for most Americans was easier than ever before. They earned more money than they needed for such necessities as food and housing. With their surplus income, they purchased automobiles, household appliances, and other luxury items. The number of Americans owning their own homes went up from 40 percent to 60 percent between 1940 and 1960. Americans also had more free time as working hours were reduced and they were given holidays with pay. Not only were Americans better off, but they were more secure. Unemployment insurance and social security now covered the majority of jobholders.

■ Technological and Scientific Progress

The United States made spectacular leaps in the field of science. With more money to spend, an increase in the number of university-trained scientists, and a growing commitment to the future, the United States led the world in new technological developments. America's factories and industries began to use **automation,** the technique of operating a production system using mechanical or electronic devices. With automated production methods, goods could be produced more efficiently and quickly than with human workers.

During the 1950s the use of computers began to revolutionize American industry. Businesses used computers for many purposes. Computers took over bookkeeping functions such as billing and inventory control. They were also used for such things as making hotel reservations, sorting bank checks, guiding satellites, predicting election results, forecasting weather conditions, identifying fingerprints, and setting type for printing.

872 UNIT 9 Times of Crisis: 1932–1960

Cooperative Learning

Divide the class into groups of five to six. Have each group report on attitudes toward children and child-rearing practices in the United States from colonial times to the present. The reports should include information on Puritan child-rearing practices and child labor during the 1800s. Each group should assign a specific responsibility to each member in the group, such as research, writing, or graphic presentation. Have each group present their report to the rest of the class. **L2, L3**

Automation and computers in the workplace caused many workers to lose their jobs. In the long run, however, computers and automation created more jobs than they eliminated. And the new jobs usually demanded a higher level of education.

Breakthroughs in medicine during the 1950s were also impressive. In April 1955, Americans learned of one of the most important discoveries in the history of medicine. After many years of research, United States scientist Dr. Jonas Salk had developed a vaccine for preventing the dreaded childhood disease known as polio. The Salk vaccine was proven effective after a huge test run on 1,830,000 schoolchildren. Within a few years, cases of polio nearly disappeared.

By 1960 other major illnesses, including pneumonia, tuberculosis, and diphtheria, were nearly wiped out. Life expectancy in the United States increased. While cancer and heart disease continued to be serious threats to the lives of Americans, researchers made important advances in diagnosing and treating these diseases.

less-crowded places. This migration of city residents caused rapid growth of suburbs. In the years after World War II, cities became ringed by seemingly endless housing developments carved out of the less densely settled country land. Shopping centers with vast parking lots were built to serve the new suburban population. Businesses and factories also began relocating from the cities to the suburbs, where their workers now lived. The Highway Act of 1956 contributed to the growth of the suburbs by adding 41,000 miles to the interstate highway system.

Meanwhile, cities began to experience serious problems. To handle the flood of automobile traffic, new highways had to be built, often destroying whole urban neighborhoods. Those who were left behind to live in the cities often included poor people and the members of minority groups. With a declining population, cities faced growing financial problems. Taxes could no longer keep up with the demands for such services as public transportation, police protection, housing, and education.

■ From Cities to Suburbs

In the 1950s the automobile changed the face of America. No longer did people have to live near their places of work. Those who lived and worked in the city could move to

■ Pressures to Conform

In the affluent 1950s, a new house in the suburbs, a larger television in the living room, and the newest model automobile in the garage represented the fulfillment of the

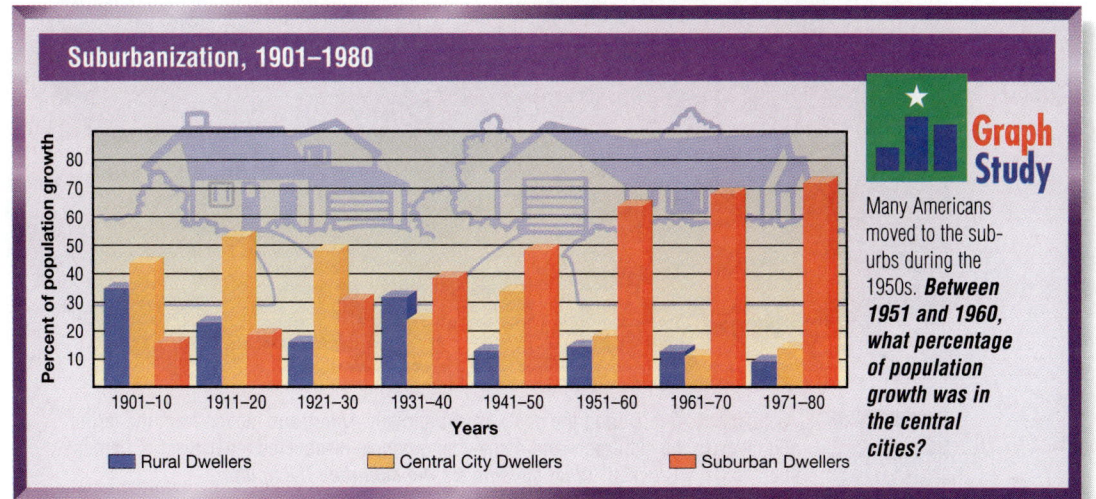

Graph Study

Many Americans moved to the suburbs during the 1950s. **Between 1951 and 1960, what percentage of population growth was in the central cities?**

Cultural Diversity

In 1959 two new states were added to the Union. Alaska became the forty-ninth state and Hawaii the fiftieth. Both states are home to people from many different ethnic groups.

Encourage students to research the ethnic heritage of each state and then share their findings with the class by preparing a poster.

CHAPTER 31
SECTION 3

Independent Practice

History Ask students to use the information in Section 3 to make a chart listing the advances in technology and medicine during the 1950s. (Technology: the use of automation to produce goods; the use of computers in businesses; the use of television for entertainment and communication. Medicine: Salk vaccine against polio; the treatment and near elimination of pneumonia, tuberculosis, and diphtheria.) Have them research other advances in technology and medicine not mentioned in the section and add them to the chart. Hold a class discussion on students' additions. **L2**

Did You Know?

Among the most popular television shows of the 1950s were family situation comedies like *I Love Lucy, Father Knows Best,* and *Leave It to Beaver*; westerns like *Gunsmoke* and *Wagon Train*; and detective shows like *Peter Gunn* and *77 Sunset Strip*.

Using Graphs

Answer: 50 percent

Skills Practice

In what decade did half of all Americans live in suburbs? (1941–50)

CHAPTER 31 SECTION 3

Linking Across Time

Have students find out more about the Hungarian uprising in November 1956 and the Soviet Union's response. Ask students to compare the Hungarian uprising with the disturbances in the Baltic countries after the fall of the Berlin Wall and in the former Soviet republics after the Soviet Union dissolved.

Visualizing History Developers attracted home buyers to the suburbs with promises of fresh air, green lawns, and trees. Many suburbs had "park," "forest," "woods," "grove," or "hill" as part of their name. **Answer to Caption:** comfort, security, and a pleasant place to raise their children

---

"American Dream." For many young couples, the suburbs offered comfort, security, and a pleasant place to raise their children. Yet it soon became clear that this new lifestyle had problems of its own.

Critics noted that a strong pressure to conform characterized American suburban life. Suburban neighborhoods were usually filled with people who were very much alike. They were generally typified as being young, with comfortable incomes, and having jobs in the service industries. Often this conformity led to discrimination or ostracism of those who seemed "different." For example, in many suburbs racial and religious minorities were unable to buy homes. To some extent, the high cost of homes in the suburbs was the reason, but prejudice was an even more important factor. Often suburban residents refused to sell homes to minority families. If minority families did move to the suburbs, others in the community made them feel unwelcome.

Many writers criticized the trend toward conformity in American life in the 1950s. Nonfiction works, such as David Reisman's *The Lonely Crowd* (1950) and William H. Whyte's *The Organization Man* (1956), and novels such as Sloan Wilson's *The Man in the Gray Flannel Suit* (1956) tried to explain the pressure to conform. Sometimes, as represented in *The Man in the Gray Flannel Suit,* these pressures were so subtly pervasive as to make people feel they had little control over their own lives:

> [I]t seemed as though all I could see was a lot of bright young men in gray flannel suits rushing around New York in a frantic parade to go nowhere. They seemed to be pursuing neither ideals nor happiness—they were pursuing a routine.... I thought I was on the sidelines watching that parade.... It was quite a shock to glance down and see that I too was wearing a gray flannel suit.

The pressures to conform in business were especially great. Employees who wanted to advance to better positions took care to adhere to the company's rules. This often meant being loyal to the corporation and being "one of the team." Outside work

Visualizing History ▲ SUBURBAN LIFE During the postwar years, many Americans moved from the farms and cities to the suburbs—and many young people discovered a new cast of heroes such as Davy Crockett. **What advantages did suburban living offer?**

Sidelights: Mies van der Rohe

The most common new buildings of the 1950s were the split-level homes of the suburbs and the steel skyscrapers of the city. Mies van der Rohe probably had the greatest impact on architecture during this time. His tall and straight structures of glass, brick, and steel set the style for new buildings in cities. His idea of "less is more" became the basis for building designs by those who imitated his style. The John Hancock Center in Chicago was based on van der Rohe's style.

Life of the Times

Child Rearing by Spock

Millions of women, voluntarily and involuntarily, left their wartime jobs to make room for returning soldiers. Just as women had received training for the skilled positions they held during the war, they looked to experts for training in their new positions as mothers. Dr. Benjamin Spock obliged them by publishing *Baby and Child Care* in 1946.

Spock urged flexibility in child care, but he also advised mothers to give undivided attention to their infants. "For [a baby's] spirit to grow naturally," Spock admonished, "he needs someone to dote on him. . . ." One mother, a homemaker and career woman, wrote Spock describing her anxiety because she might not be giving her son enough affection. She wondered whether she or her child needed more help.

▼ DR. BENJAMIN SPOCK

▲ BEST-SELLING CHILD CARE BOOK

Many experts on childhood concluded that Spock's permissive methods led to a generation of young people in the next decade who were used to getting their own way.

CHAPTER 31 SECTION 3

Teaching Life of the Times

Dr. Spock did not consider himself permissive. This accusation against him first came in the 1960s, years after his book came out. Spock's opponents said that his advice to parents to give their children "instant gratification" was what made many young men who opposed the war in Vietnam "irresponsible, undisciplined, and unpatriotic." Spock opposed the war and ran for President in 1972 on an antiwar ticket.

Did You Know?

In 1959 the first play appeared on Broadway that was written by a black woman: Lorraine Hansberry's *A Raisin in the Sun*.

Food Through the Ages

As Americans spent more and more time watching TV, many ate their meals in front of the set. The food industry encouraged the trend by developing the TV dinner, a frozen meal that could be quickly heated and eaten.

---

it meant having the "right" type of family life and belonging to the "right" clubs and religious groups. Social critics complained that Americans were in danger of losing their individuality.

Changes in Family Life

During the 1950s there were renewed social pressures on women to remain at home. Women's magazines ran articles such as "Should I Stop Work When We Marry?" and "The Business of Running a Home." The immensely popular *Pocket Book of Baby and Child Care* by Dr. Benjamin Spock said that raising children was more important and rewarding than the extra money or satisfaction that a woman might get from a job. Many women who had gone to college or had careers traded their aspirations and jobs for marriage and motherhood. The number of women who worked continued to rise, but women lost ground in the workplace. They were still paid less than men for doing the same work. They were also shut out of better jobs with higher salaries.

After World War II, more women dropped out of school and married at an early age. The nation's birthrate increased so rapidly that people refer to the period between 1945 and 1961 as the "baby boom." During the baby boom, more than 65 million children were born in the United States.

Parents in the prosperous 1950s wanted their children to have all the things that they had not been able to have during the Depression and war years. They gave their children an increasing amount of material goods and emphasized the benefits of living the "good life." Parents also allowed their children greater freedom than they themselves had known as youngsters. Critics pointed to this new "permissiveness" as the major cause of the rise in juvenile delinquency.

CHAPTER 31 Search for Stability 1952–1960   875

Sidelights: Television and the Movies

One of the greatest effects of television in the 1950s was on the movie industry. Between the late 1940s and 1960, nearly half of the 18,000 movie theaters in the United States closed. This was largely the result of more people turning to television for entertainment. The movies lost more of their audience as improvements in television technology were made. By the end of the 1950s, it was apparent that the great days of the movie industry were over. Ask students what effect the rise of the videotape industry has had on the movie industry today.

CHAPTER 31
SECTION 3

ASSESS
Check Understanding
Assign Section 3 Review as homework or an in-class activity.

Evaluate
📁 Assign the Section 3 Quiz in the TCR, or use the History of a Free Nation testmaker to create a customized quiz.

Reteach
📁 Have students complete Reteaching Activity 31-3.

Enrich
Have students use reference materials to prepare a short biography of a 1950s film star or television personality.

CLOSE
Direct students' attention to the quote on page 874 that opens the section. Ask them to discuss how this statement relates to the lifestyle of Americans in the 1950s.

Visualizing History Invented in the 1930s, television became popular in the late 1940s. By 1960 nearly 90 percent of American families owned at least one set.

Answer to Caption: It was feared that people would expect to be entertained much of the time.

 ▲ **WATCHING TELEVISION** The most popular of the 1950s television shows were comedies, variety shows, and "Westerns" starring Roy Rogers (above), Hopalong Cassidy, and other stars. **Why were some people worried about the effects of watching television?**

■ The Impact of Television

One of the symbols of the prosperity of the 1950s was the television set. In 1945 fewer than 1 in every 20,000 people had a television. But within a few years, televisions were everywhere, and they were almost as common as telephones.

Beginning with the election of 1952, television brought national politics into American living rooms. There were televised broadcasts of political party conventions in which not only the public speeches but the goings-on in committee meetings were recorded. During the campaign, both the Republican party and the Democratic party spent millions on television advertising and broadcasts. Although television stirred greater interest in voting, it also posed disturbing questions. Would television give an unfair advantage to the candidate who used television most effectively and who could afford to buy the most airtime?

Some critics also worried that television would have a negative effect on American culture. In the early 1950s, George Gallup, one of the country's first pollsters, voiced concern that:

> ❝ [O]ne of the real threats to America's future place in the world is a citizenry which daily elects to be entertained and not informed. ❞

Supported by advertisers trying to reach the widest possible audience, television programs often appealed to the lowest common denominator of public taste. In order to avoid offending potential customers, advertisers would not buy time on programs that dealt with controversial issues. As a result, television furnished entertainment that was intended "to fix the attention but not engage the mind."

Yet the 1950s has often been called the "Golden Age of Television." Many of the country's most talented writers, comedians, musicians, and actors flocked to the new medium. There they could reach an audience of millions.

Section 3 ★ Review

Checking for Understanding
1. **Identify** John Kenneth Galbraith, Jonas Salk, Benjamin Spock, baby boom.
2. **Define** automation.
3. **Discuss** changes that occurred in American life as a result of abundance, affluence, and the growth of technology.
4. **Report** how minority groups were adversely affected by pressures to conform.

Critical Thinking
5. **Analyzing Results** Examine the ways the television and the automobile changed the American lifestyle during the 1950s. How would your life be different without them?

Answers to SECTION 3 REVIEW
1. John K. Galbraith, 871; Jonas Salk, 873; Benjamin Spock, 875; baby boom, 875
2. All vocabulary words are defined in the Glossary.
3. Growth of suburbs; increase in home ownership; autos, mobility; luxury items; time-saving devices; more leisure time and activities.
4. Difficult for African Americans and certain religious minorities to buy homes in suburbs; if they did buy, were made to feel unwelcome.
5. Automobile: migration to suburbs, growth of shopping centers, business relocation, mobility. Television: claimed leisure time, dictated taste, products to use, political candidates, replaced games and reading. May devote more time to other recreational activities. Less independence and mobility; less influence by advertising.

CONNECTIONS  CONNECTIONS

◀ ELVIS PRESLEY, ROCK-AND-ROLL STAR OF THE 1950S

▲ CHUCK BERRY

Origins of Rock and Roll

During the Eisenhower years, many teenagers rebelled against the pressure to conform by rejecting the mellow pop music favored by their parents. Teens of the 1950s preferred the heavily accented beats and repetitious lyrics of rock and roll.

Rock and roll developed in the mid-1950s. It was a derivation of the rhythm and blues that African American musicians had created for black audiences years before. It also often had some elements of country music. In rock and roll, the tempo was quicker, the accented beats were moved, and electrically amplified instruments—mostly guitars—were used.

Because rock and roll was such a departure from the sentimental love songs of the past, it shocked and dismayed many parents. Teenagers, however, were sold. One of the first rock hits, recorded in 1955, was Bill Haley and the Comets' *Rock Around the Clock,* which sold 17 million copies. In 1956 Elvis Presley came on the rock scene. In his performances he moved to the beat of the music. Presley set the musical style for a decade. The lyrics of most rock-and-roll music remained about love, although some writers and performers, most notably Chuck Berry, treated the subject with wit and humor.

Making the Music Connection
1. How did rock-and-roll music evolve?
2. Why did rock and roll shock and dismay parents?

Linking Past and Present
3. What conflicts exist in rock and roll today?

CHAPTER 31 CONNECTIONS

Teaching Making Connections
The moral indignation and trend toward censorship directed toward rock and roll was self-defeating. Point out that these forces themselves were causes of the rebellious nature of rock and roll's popularity.

Did You Know?
Elvis Presley's black leather jacket and ducktail haircut became standard dress for young men.

Answers to CONNECTIONS

1. Rock and roll was a derivation of the rhythm and blues of black musicians with some elements of country music. In rock and roll, the tempo was quicker, the accented beats were moved, and electrically amplified instruments (mostly guitars) were used.

2. Rock and roll was such a departure from the sentimental tunes of the past.

3. There is currently a movement to censor lyrics with sexual, violent, or drug-related overtones. Defenders of the lyrics say that censoring deprives them of their First Amendment rights.

LESSON PLAN
SECTION 4, 878–885

FOCUS

Bellringer
Before taking roll at the beginning of the class period, display Focus Activity Transparency 102 on the overhead projector, and assign the accompanying Focus Activity Sheet.

Objectives
Point out the objectives on this page to students in previewing the section content.

Motivating Activity
Review with the class earlier events in the cold war. (Students should recall the Truman Doctrine, the Marshall Plan, and the Korean War.) Review with students the policy of containment adopted by President Truman. As they read this section, tell them to focus on the ways that President Eisenhower continued the policy of containment.

Use Skills Transparency 31.

Side 1, Chapter 6
Title: *The Arms Race*
Subject: Development of the arms race between the United States and the Soviet Union

---

SECTION 4

Foreign Policy

Setting the Scene

Section Focus
In the 1950s affluence at home contrasted sharply with political upheaval abroad. Forces were changing the international landscape. The Eisenhower administration aggressively waged a campaign against communism. Fully aware of the consequences of nuclear war, Eisenhower attempted to manage international conflict through cooperative alliances.

◀ ASTRONAUT JOHN GLENN

Objectives
After studying this section, you should be able to

★ discuss Eisenhower's approach to foreign policy and the Eisenhower Doctrine.
★ describe how the fear of nuclear war affected the cold war.
★ discuss why American relations with Latin America were poor in the 1950s.

Key Term
covert

During the 1950s the Eisenhower administration labored to contain communism, particularly in newly independent nations in Asia and Africa. Eisenhower used diplomacy, military power, and covert activities to achieve these goals.

President Eisenhower and Secretary of State John Foster Dulles (DUH•luhs) expanded the nation's network of alliances in order to contain communism. In Western Europe, the United States took a leading role in NATO. In Southeast Asia, the United States helped to create the Southeast Asian Treaty Organization (SEATO). In the Middle East, the United States counted on the cooperation of the Central Treaty Organization (CENTO), and in Latin America, the United States promoted the Organization of American States (OAS). These alliances created a formidable counterbalance to the influence of the Soviet Union.

■ The Influence of Dulles

President Eisenhower's foreign policy was greatly influenced by Dulles. After serving in the United States Senate in the late 1940s, Dulles had years of experience in high-level diplomacy, particularly with Asian nations. Secretary Dulles favored a vigorous foreign policy, denouncing Truman's "containment" policy as inadequate. Instead, he advocated "liberation" of Eastern European nations that were under Soviet domination:

> *If our policy is to stay where we are, we will be driven back. It is only by keeping alive the hope of liberation, by taking advantage of that wherever opportunity arises, that we will end this terrible peril which dominates the world....*

878 UNIT 9 Times of Crisis: 1932–1960

Classroom Resources for SECTION 4

Teacher's Classroom Resources
- Reproducible Lesson Plan
- Reteaching Activity 31-4
- Chapter 31 Enrichment Activity
- Chapter 31 Performance Assessment Activity
- Spanish Summaries and Glossary
- Section Quiz

Multimedia
- Section Focus Transparency 102
- Chapter 31 Map Transparency
- Vocabulary Puzzlemaker
- Testmaker
- Student Self-Test Software
- Communism and the Cold War

Dulles threatened "massive retaliation" against communist aggression. "If you are scared to go to the brink [of nuclear war], you are lost," he said. Accordingly, the Department of Defense reduced the size of the regular army and increased its nuclear arsenal.

Eisenhower tempered Dulles's tough stance and took a more cautious approach. He insisted that "there is no alternative to peace." A nuclear war might well mean the end of civilization. Therefore, the Eisenhower administration continued Truman's policy of containment.

War and Peace in Asia

Containing communism became a global challenge for Eisenhower. In Asia the end of one conflict was followed by the start of another one.

End of the Korean War

Carrying out his campaign promise, Eisenhower went to Korea in December 1952. Peace negotiations to end the Korean War, however, seemed to go nowhere. Exasperated, Eisenhower threatened the Communists with possible use of nuclear weapons. Finally in July 1953, after long and bloody fighting, the United Nations Command and the North Koreans reached a settlement. Korea was divided along a line close to the 38th parallel.

Southeast Asia

The United States then was faced with a new problem in Southeast Asia. After Japan surrendered Indochina in 1945, France tried to regain control of its colonies. The people, however, wanted to rule themselves. Ho Chi Minh, a Communist, headed an independence movement called the Vietminh to drive the French from Vietnam, one of the countries of Indochina. The United States stayed out of the fighting but supplied weapons and supplies to the French.

In 1954 the Vietminh surrounded French troops at Dien Bien Phu. The French asked the United States to bomb communist positions. Eisenhower believed that a French defeat might lead to communist domination of all of Southeast Asia.

Secretary Dulles favored giving military support to France. But when Eisenhower could get no support from the leaders of Congress or from other Western nations, he decided to stay out of the war. Dien Bien Phu fell in May 1954, and the French soon withdrew from Indochina.

Visualizing History ▲ **EISENHOWER AND DULLES** President Eisenhower delegated much of the conduct of foreign affairs to his secretary of state, John Foster Dulles (left). *What policy did Dulles design to fight communist aggression?*

▲ **THE UNITED STATES AND IRAN** Shah Mohammad Reza Pahlavi came to power in Iran in 1953 with the help of secret American funds. He was later overthrown during the Iranian revolution of 1979. **Why did Eisenhower involve the CIA in Iran?**

At a conference in Geneva, Switzerland, in 1954, Vietnam was divided along the 17th parallel. North of that line, Ho Chi Minh's communist forces took control. To the south, a United States-supported government under Ngo Dinh Diem was set up. Diem's regime was dictatorial, inefficient, and unpopular. Communist-supported guerrillas began to fight against Diem's government. The United States provided most of the money for South Vietnam's defense. President Eisenhower had avoided war in Vietnam, but he had tied American prestige to the survival of Diem's unpopular and dictatorial government.

The Eisenhower Approach

When it came to solving foreign problems, Eisenhower preferred using diplomacy and **covert,** or secret, activities carried out by the Central Intelligence Agency (CIA).

In Iran and Guatemala

In 1953 President Eisenhower became concerned when the Iranian prime minister seized control of the Anglo-American Oil Company. The President feared that Iran was aligning itself with the Soviet Union, which would endanger oil supplies to Western nations. Under Eisenhower's orders, the CIA secretly funded a successful revolt by the young shah of Iran. Later Iran signed an agreement allowing United States, British, and French companies to share in Iranian oil production.

In 1954 the CIA helped to remove another unfriendly government. The Guatemalan government of Colonel Jacobo Arbenz Guzman had seized property of the American-owned United Fruit Company. The United States learned that Guzman was getting weapons from communist nations. Concerned that Guatemala would become a communist foothold in Latin America, the Eisenhower administration funded a coup that overthrew the government.

In both Iran and Guatemala, the revolutions appeared to have been inspired from within the nation. Only later did people learn of the CIA's role.

Secretary Dulles believed the events in Vietnam, Iran, and Guatemala were evidence of the Soviet Union's intention to spread communism. He argued that newly emerging nations should choose sides in the worldwide struggle between communism and democracy.

UNIT 9 Times of Crisis: 1932–1960

"Third World" Neutrality

In 1955 representatives from 29 Asian and African states met and signed an agreement calling for racial equality and self-determination. Two thousand delegates, from countries containing more than half the world's population, saw themselves as the "Third World." They declared their intention to remain independent of both the "First World"—the West—and the "Second World"—the Soviet Union.

The policy of neutralism was hotly debated. Some observers compared neutralism to isolationism and defended it as necessary for new and comparatively weak nations. Others attacked neutralism. Secretary Dulles took the position that no nation had the right to remain neutral in a conflict between "tyranny and freedom."

Middle East Powder Keg

During the 1950s the United States was drawn into the affairs of the Middle East. Before World War II, American businesses had begun to exploit the area's rich oil supplies. After the war the United States became increasingly dependent on Mideast oil. Americans were anxious to protect this oil supply. Many Americans also were interested in the survival of Israel, established in 1948 as a Jewish homeland.

The Middle East was like a "powder keg ready to explode." Arab nations believed that Israel was on land belonging to the Palestinians. They threatened to destroy Israel. Also, deep divisions existed among the Arab nations. Poverty and discontent were widespread. Finally, Soviet expansion posed a threat to Western oil supplies.

The first explosion came in 1956 in Egypt. Egypt's President Gamal Abdel Nasser was anxious to gain military superiority over the Jewish state. To get weapons, Egypt signed a commercial treaty with the Soviet Union, exchanging cotton—Egypt's major cash crop—for tanks and guns. The United States had tried to forge friendly relations with Egypt by offering to loan the nation money to build a giant dam across the Nile River. But Nasser's overtures toward the People's Republic of China and the Soviet bloc forced Dulles to cancel the loan. Nasser responded by seizing the Suez Canal in July 1956.

The British, French, and Israelis decided to attack Egypt and reclaim the Suez Canal, which provided a vital trade link between Europe, the Middle East, and Asia. Acting independently of the United States, they invaded Egypt in October.

The world seemed on the verge of another major war. During a heated debate in the United Nations, the United States voted with the Soviet Union to condemn the actions of Israel, Great Britain, and France. This pressure forced the three nations to agree to withdraw from Egypt.

The Suez crisis greatly embarrassed the United States. Three of its strongest allies had acted alone. The affair might have shattered the Western alliance if Soviet action to crush the Hungarian revolution had not persuaded them to close ranks again.

 ▲ **NASSER AND THE SUEZ CRISIS** Warfare in the Middle East was close at hand after Egyptian leader Nasser seized the Suez Canal. Then Egypt was invaded by Britain, France, and Israel. **What caused Britain, France, and Israel to withdraw?**

CHAPTER 31 SECTION 4

Linking Across Time

Tensions between Egypt and Israel have been the focus of several Middle East conflicts: the Six-Day War in 1967 and the Yom Kippur War in 1973. In 1978, in a dramatic turnabout, Egypt became the first Arab state to make peace with Israel. The 1978 peace accords were engineered by Egypt's Anwar Sadat, Israel's Menachem Begin, and U.S. President Jimmy Carter.

Did You Know?

Gamal Abdel Nasser resigned after Egypt's defeat by Israel in the 1967 Six-Day War but was persuaded to return to power. He died in 1970.

Visualizing History

The Suez Canal, which connects the Mediterranean and Red seas, was opened in 1869. It cut 4,000 miles off voyages between Britain and India.

Answer to Caption: In the United Nations, the U.S. joined the Soviet Union in condemning the invasion.

Critical Thinking

Evaluating an Action The overthrow of the leftist Guatemalan government was made possible by the activities of the CIA. Ask students the following question: Is secret aggression, such as that by the CIA, justifiable? Why or why not? (Answers will vary. Some students might indicate that such action is justifiable because it is necessary for our country's and the world's security. Other students might indicate that such action is not justifiable because it undermines the sovereignty of another country. **L2**

CHAPTER 31
SECTION 4

Did You Know?
Sputnik I, the first artificial satellite, was launched by the Soviet Union in October 1957, promoting concern that U.S. technology had fallen behind that of its superpower rival.

In 1958 U.S. scientists began testing Earth's ozone.

FACT: Scientists wanted to discover what effects, if any, had been caused by atmospheric testing of nuclear weapons and by the growing number of high-altitude flights by military and commercial jet aircraft.

Visualizing History As a result of the Hungarian crisis, the United States dropped its call for the liberation of Eastern Europe.
Answer to Caption: Soviet troops overwhelmed Hungarian fighters.

Visualizing History ▲ **CONFLICT IN HUNGARY** The Hungarian revolt began when workers and students demonstrated for reform in 1956. Here, Hungarian citizens capture a Soviet tank in strife-torn Budapest. *How did the revolt end?*

■ The Eisenhower Doctrine

After the Suez crisis, the Soviets supported Egypt and offered to help build the Aswan Dam. President Eisenhower worried that the Soviets would gain new strength in the region. In January 1957, Eisenhower asked Congress to give him authority to use United States military forces to defend any Middle Eastern country that requested help against the forces of "international communism." Congress overwhelmingly approved the so-called Eisenhower Doctrine.

A year later the president of Lebanon asked Eisenhower to send troops to protect his government. He feared that Nasser and the Soviet Union might encourage a revolt in Lebanon.

In July 1958, American soldiers entered Lebanon. American troops remained in Lebanon until new elections established a stronger government. By taking this action, the United States showed that it intended to play a leading role in the Middle East. Yet the basic problems of the Middle East—poverty, rivalry and strife, and the threat of communist aggression—still defied solution.

■ The NATO Alliance

After President Eisenhower took office in 1953, he attempted to strengthen NATO under a unified command. But France was fearful of German resurgence and strongly opposed the plan. Western defenses were strengthened, however, when West Germany was allowed to rearm and join NATO.

The NATO alliance faced other difficulties. Europeans had mixed feelings about the United States. European Socialists and Communists regarded the United States as a materialistic nation where workers were exploited in order to increase the profits of a few great trusts. Conservatives believed Europe would be Americanized. In Britain and France, many people blamed the United States for their nation's loss of power in the world. But Soviet aggression persuaded Western Europe and the United States to maintain a common front.

Political uprisings in two of its satellites prompted the Soviet Union to reassert its control over Eastern Europe. In October 1956, anti-Soviet riots broke out in some Polish cities. The Soviet Union ultimately agreed to Polish demands for more freedoms. In Hungary, however, what began as

882   UNIT 9 Times of Crisis: 1932–1960

Sidelights: Nationalism and Independence

The years following World War II saw major political change in Africa. A large number of new nations were formed during this time. Once colonies ruled by European powers, many of these new nations found sovereignty difficult. Differences between groups within nations sometimes led to revolution and intertribal war. Many new nations needed help and asked for it but at the same time feared it because of the link between democracy and capitalism and imperialism and colonialism.

peaceful protests ended with open fighting. When communist leaders tried to put down the unrest, the Hungarians turned against them. On October 30, 1956, after less than a week of fighting, Budapest radio told the Hungarians: "You have won!" For five days jubilant Hungarians tasted freedom. Then on November 4, Soviet tanks and troops rolled through Budapest and overwhelmed its defenders. In the United States there was sympathy for the Hungarians, but little could be done without risking war.

Trouble in Latin America

While the United States worried about communist gains in Europe, Asia, and Africa, it ignored Latin America. There, the great poverty of the majority of the people and the concentration of land and power in the hands of a few created a breeding ground for political instability.

Latin Americans had good cause to believe they were "forgotten neighbors." They saw the United States pouring billions of dollars into remaking Europe's economy and strengthening weak governments in Asia. Yet Latin America received little United States foreign aid.

In 1958 Vice President Nixon made a goodwill visit to Latin America. In some of the countries he visited, Nixon faced hostile demonstrations. In Peru and Venezuela, mobs threw stones and beat sticks against Nixon's car. This shocking attack on the Vice President brought home to people of the United States their neglect of Latin America's problems.

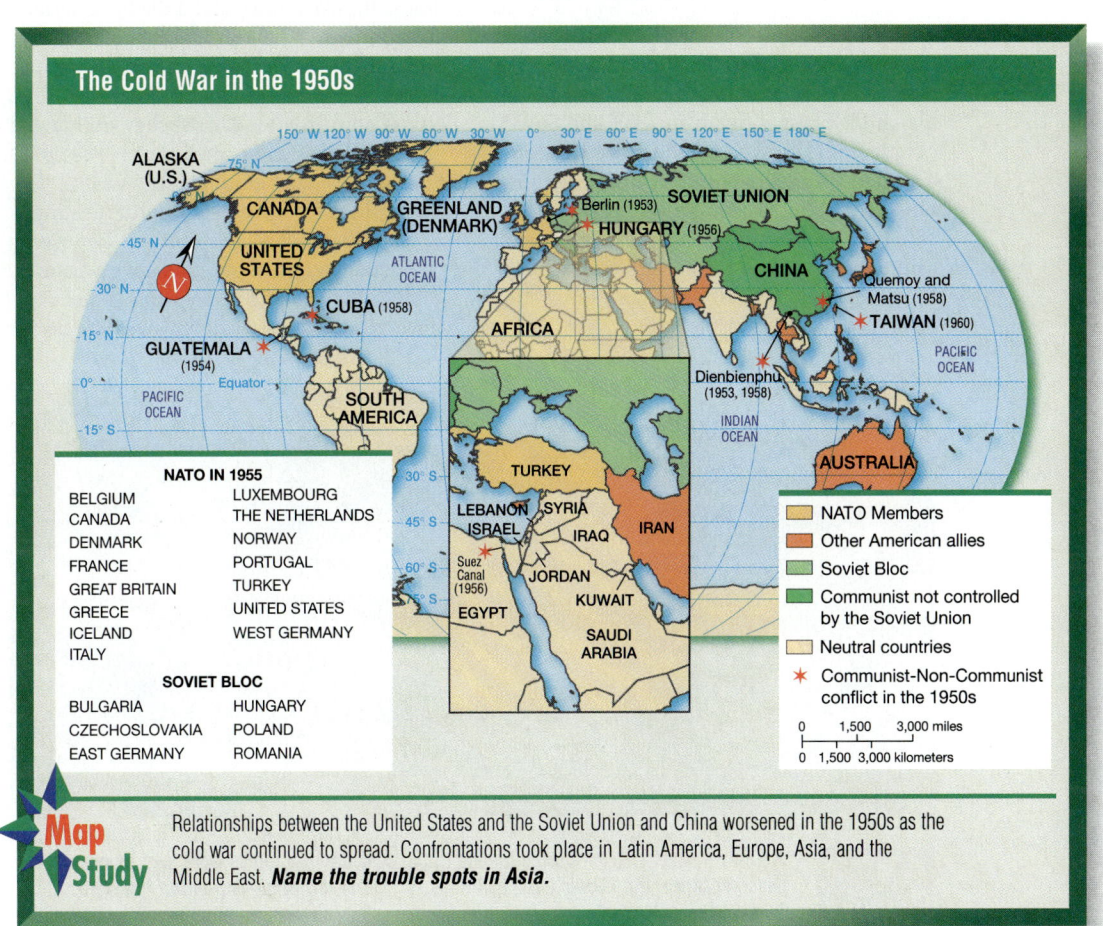

The Cold War in the 1950s

Map Study Relationships between the United States and the Soviet Union and China worsened in the 1950s as the cold war continued to spread. Confrontations took place in Latin America, Europe, Asia, and the Middle East. **Name the trouble spots in Asia.**

CHAPTER 31 Search for Stability 1952–1960

CHAPTER 31
SECTION 4

Visualizing  The "thaw" in the cold war continued despite occasional setbacks. The Communist Chinese challenged the Soviet's leadership of the communist world and accused them of softness toward the West and of "selling out" the Third World. **Answer to Caption:** The Soviet people were allowed a little more freedom. New leaders denounced Stalin. Talk grew of peaceful coexistence. Geneva summit held.

ABC NEWS INTERACTIVE

VIDEODISC
Communism and the Cold War

Side 1, Chapter 18
Title: *Civil Defense*
Subject: 1954 government film on civil defense and fallout shelters

---

Events in Cuba further soured United States-Latin American relations. In 1959 a resistance movement headed by Fidel Castro forced the resignation of Cuba's corrupt dictator, Fulgencio Batista. Castro became a popular figure in the United States, and there was hope that the two nations would establish friendly relations. But American enthusiasm for Castro waned when he made friendly moves toward the Communists, denounced the United States, and seized private property. Castro also sought the military support of the Soviet Union. In response, President Eisenhower cut the quota of sugar the United States imported from Cuba and broke off relations with the Castro government.

■ Thaws in the Cold War

During the Eisenhower administration, the cold war spread to all continents. Yet there were signs that a "thaw" was possible. After Stalin's death in 1953, the Soviet people were allowed a little more freedom. The new premier, Nikita Khrushchev, denounced Stalin as a brutal tyrant. The Soviets now talked of peaceful coexistence and said that war in the atomic age would be so horrible that "the living will envy the dead."

In July 1955, Eisenhower met with the leaders of the Soviet Union, France, and Great Britain in Geneva, Switzerland. He made a strong plea for nuclear disarmament, saying that it would:

> 66 ... ease the fears of war in the anxious hearts of people everywhere. ... It would make [it] possible for every nation, great and small, developed and less developed, to advance the standards of living of its people. ... 99

The summit, however, settled nothing. In 1958 tensions between the superpowers escalated once more, this time over the divided city of Berlin. The Soviets threatened to cut off Western access to Berlin unless the West recognized the East German government. When the crisis cooled down, both sides made new efforts to reduce world tensions. In 1959 Vice President Nixon and Premier Khrushchev exchanged visits. Khrushchev met with President Eisenhower at Camp David, where they made plans for a second summit meeting.

The new thaw was short-lived. Two weeks before the second summit meeting was to be held, in May 1960, an American U-2 surveillance plane was shot down over the Soviet

Visualizing History ▲ **COLD WAR RELATIONS** During the era of the cold war, UN forces were sent to keep peace in Africa, the Middle East, and other hot spots. *What signs pointed toward a thaw in the cold war?*

UNIT 9 Times of Crisis: 1932–1960

Critical Thinking

Seeing Relationships Fear of nuclear war lay behind the offensive and defensive decisions of both the superpowers and provided a background for the machinations of the politics of economically developing nations. The threat of a complete military "solution" to a disagreement led to hostilities played out in specific "theaters," with influence being the objective. Many leaders of economically developing countries recognized this by playing the United States against the Soviet Union. Discuss the shift from military muscle to economic might in fighting the cold war and how the threat of nuclear war influenced this change. **L2**

▲ U-2 PILOT GARY POWERS

■ Eisenhower's Farewell Address

The U-2 incident and the failure of East-West negotiations brought Eisenhower's years in office to a frustrating close. After the death of Secretary Dulles in 1959, Eisenhower took over more of the direction of foreign policy himself. He traveled widely in Europe, Asia, the Middle East, and Latin America to promote "peace and goodwill" and a "better understanding of America." But he was unable to lessen the tensions of the cold war and the threat of nuclear confrontation.

Still, Eisenhower remained a popular President, as near to a "father figure" as any President since George Washington. Like Washington, Eisenhower gave a farewell address. In it he warned against the overpowering influence of the military-industrial complex:

> We must never let the weight of this combination (of the military and industry) endanger our liberties or democratic processes. We should take nothing for granted. Only an alert and knowledgeable citizenry can compel the proper meshing of the huge industrial and military machinery of defense with our peaceful methods and goals, so that security and liberty may prosper together.

The President's message was impressive because it came from a man who had spent most of his life as a soldier.

Union. The CIA had sent it to spy on and photograph Soviet nuclear sites and missile bases. Khrushchev denounced Eisenhower as a prisoner of the "war mongers" and refused to take part in the meeting. Relations between East and West once again turned colder.

Section 4 ★ Review

Checking for Understanding

1. **Identify** John Foster Dulles, Ho Chi Minh, Gamal Abdel Nasser, SEATO, CENTO, OAS, Fulgencio Batista, Fidel Castro, U-2.
2. **Define** covert.
3. **Describe** the Eisenhower administration's foreign policy.
4. **State** reasons why European attitudes toward the United States changed in the 1950s.

Critical Thinking

5. **Locating Evidence** What event described in this section supports the idea that the containment policy might result in supporting unpopular or repressive regimes?

CHAPTER 31 Search for Stability 1952–1960

REVIEW CHAPTER 31

Answers

Reviewing Facts
1. war hero, father figure, smile, optimism, trust, strong, tough, policies consistent, middle course, kept economy strong, no war
2. whether to continue price supports or leave farmer survival at mercy of elements and prices
3. Liberal: extended social security and increased benefits; tried to get health insurance program. Conservative: little regulation of business, low taxes, allow mergers.
4. Automation produced goods faster; electronics revolutionized industry; improved farm machines increased yields, shortened hours. Television opened new medium for advertising plus whole new industry.
5. More Americans moved to suburbs; brought homes, autos, television, luxury goods; leisure time interests, joined clubs.
6. Dulles: no reconciliation with Communists, containment inadequate, take offensive against Soviets to free satellites, aid French against Ho Chi Minh, willing to go to brink of nuclear war. Eisenhower: seek peace, negotiate, avoid military involvement in foreign problems, strengthen European unity, stabilize Far East relations, seek nuclear disarmament and back off from risk of war.
7. (1) house in suburbs like others, big cars, right clubs, schools, correct dress, behavior (2) more discrimination, keep out of suburbs (3) back to home, child-rearing
8. probably shifted focus away from military solutions to diplomacy, formation of alliances, because military conflict carried risk of escalation to nuclear war

Understanding Concepts
1. Answers will vary. Probably more authoritative, less sharing of decision. Military based on obedience and discipline.
2. Answers will vary. Some may say necessary to protect United States; others may say United States has no right to impose system on any other country.
3. nonregulation of business; business mergers increased productivity, profits; technological advances; higher wages increased buying power; peace, confidence

---

CHAPTER 31 ★ REVIEW

Using Vocabulary

Use these vocabulary words in a statement about the influence of technology on business and agriculture.

agribusiness   automation

Reviewing Facts

1. **State** reasons why Americans elected Ike by overwhelming majorities in 1952 and 1956.
2. **Explain** the Eisenhower administration's dilemma regarding the farm problem.
3. **Show** how Eisenhower policies toward health and welfare programs and big business reflected his middle-course economic policy.
4. **Identify** technological advances of the 1950s that contributed to the strength of the American economy.
5. **Describe** the effects of economic growth and affluence on American life.
6. **Cite** the differences between Dulles's and Eisenhower's approaches to foreign policy.
7. **Discuss** how the following groups were affected by the pressure to conform: (1) middle-class families, (2) African Americans, (3) women.
8. **Speculate** about the effects of the nuclear threat on the conduct of the cold war.

Understanding Concepts

International Leadership
1. If you were to examine Eisenhower's leadership style as commander of NATO forces, how would you expect it to differ from his international leadership style as President? Why?
2. What is your opinion of Eisenhower's use of covert operations to remove unfriendly foreign governments? Explain.

Economic Growth
3. What factors stimulated economic growth in the 1950s?
4. How did the growth of the television industry both reflect and stimulate economic growth?

Critical Thinking

1. **Demonstrating Reasoned Judgment** Find an example of Eisenhower's actions that supports both national security and global security. Did he take any steps in the interest of national security at the possible expense of global security? Support your answer.
2. **Locating Examples** What lifestyle changes reflected the "economy of abundance" during the 1950s?
3. **Analyzing Photographs** Study the photograph of the bomb shelter on this page, then answer the questions that follow.
   a. What do you think the photographer was trying to show with this picture?
   b. Do you think this photograph was part of an advertisement, a news story, or for another purpose? Explain.

UNIT 9 Times of Crisis: 1932–1960

CHAPTER 31 ★ REVIEW

Writing About History

Description
Imagine you are a journalist in 1961 just after Eisenhower left office. Write a profile of Eisenhower for a popular publication, focusing on his personal traits, his leadership style, or both. For details, refer to biographies and reference books covering the history of the 1950s.

Cooperative Learning
Working in a group of four, research life in the United States during the Eisenhower administration. Divide the research assignments so that different members are responsible for finding information about news events, movies, television shows, popular music, theater, art achievements, literary publications, advances in science and technology, sports events, and fashion trends for those years. Have members record their findings. Combine the reports to form a history of the Eisenhower years.

Social Studies Skills

Identifying Trends
Tables can draw attention to both the similarities and differences between groups. An analysis of a table may enable you to identify trends and patterns between groups.

To identify a trend, you must carefully compare a table's statistics. Look at each column's data. Look at each row. Are there similarities between columns? Between rows? Are any patterns apparent? What generalizations can you make?

Practicing the Skill
Use the table to answer these questions.

1. Compare income for white families between 1950 and 1960. What income is earned by the largest percent of white families in 1950? 1955? 1960?
2. Compare income distribution for nonwhite families between 1950 and 1960. What income is earned by the largest percent of nonwhite families in 1950? 1955? 1960?
3. Write a generalization that identifies the trend in distribution for minority and white families.

Income Distribution by Families

	1950		1955		1960	
	Whites	African Americans and Others	Whites	African Americans and Others	Whites	African Americans and Others
More than $15,000			1.5	—	4.1	.6
$12,000–$14,999	3.5	.3	2.0	.3	4.6	1.6
$10,000–$11,999			3.2	.3	6.6	2.7
$7,000–$9,999	6.1	1.6	14.0	3.1	21.3	8.7
$5,000–$6,999	15.1	3.4	23.3	10.6	24.5	15.4
$3,000–$4,999	35.7	17.8	30.3	28.3	19.9	24.5
Less than $3,000	39.4	76.9	25.7	57.3	19.2	46.5

Source: Historical Statistics of the United States: Colonial Times to 1970 (1975).

4. What percent of white families earned more than $15,000 in 1960? Nonwhite families?
5. How does income change for most families in the 1950s? State the trend.

Using Your Journal
Write a paragraph discussing the success or failure of the Eisenhower administration to contain communism.

REVIEW CHAPTER 31

Practicing the Skill
1. less than $3,000; $3,000–$4,999; $5,000–$6,999
2. less than $3,000; same; same
3. The income of white families increased at a higher rate than that of African American families.
4. 4.1 percent; 0.6 percent; A much higher percentage of white families than African American families were in the highest income bracket.
5. During the 1950s the income of most families—white and African American—increased.

Chapter Bonus Test Question
This question may be used for extra credit on the chapter test. How did President Eisenhower try to keep the cold war from turning into a shooting war? (tried to reduce tensions, reduce threat of Soviet nuclear war, contain Soviet expansion)

Using Your Journal
Students will present various positions but should review the major East-West crises of the period, including the events in Vietnam, the Suez crisis, the Hungarian uprising, the crisis in Lebanon, the Cuban Revolution, and the U-2 incident.

---

4. Most American homes had TV. Advertisers pitched to wide audience, increased product sales, demand.

Critical Thinking
1. Answers will vary. Summits, good will missions, and plea for nuclear disarmament probably support both. Covert overthrow of unfriendly government may establish dangerous precedent, harm global security.
2. Suburbs, home ownership, autos, television, luxury goods, leisure time interests, joined clubs, education.
3. a. Answers will vary but should include a view of life in a bomb shelter.
b. Answers will vary but students should include valid reasons to support their answers.

Cultural Kaleidoscope

Making Connections
History and Technology

Since its beginnings, the United States has protected innovators by issuing patents. A patent is a grant given an inventor that prevents anyone else from making, using, or selling his or her invention. It usually runs for 17 years. The Constitution provides for patents in Article I, Section 8, and the first one was issued in 1790.

More About...
Credit Cards

Although credit cards were issued in the 1930s by oil companies in order to increase sales at service stations, the first multi-purpose card dates back to 1950. Francis X. McNamara, dining out in New York City with clients, discovered that he'd left his wallet at home. He called his wife, who obligingly drove in from the suburbs with money. McNamara, determined to avoid such embarassment in the future, went home and thought up the Diners Club.

Cultural Kaleidoscope

A Changing Society

Innovations

From important discoveries and innovations like computers, penicillin, open heart surgery, and the polio vaccine to more mundane accomplishments like TV dinners, the period from the 1930s to the 1960s was a time of discovery and unbounded imagination. New technology transformed the nature of work and helped Americans enjoy more leisure time. At the same time, the number of available leisure activities increased. By the 1950s Americans were enjoying a standard of living far beyond any they had previously known.

▶ Progress in electronics began to revolutionize home entertainment. Probably no form of entertainment has matched the effects of television. Developed in the 1930s, television went on the market in the late 1940s. Fewer than 1 million households had a set in 1949. Within four years, the number had soared to 20 million.

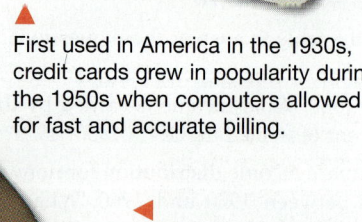

▲ First used in America in the 1930s, credit cards grew in popularity during the 1950s when computers allowed for fast and accurate billing.

◀ The electric iron, such as this 1936 model, became a necessary domestic appliance.

Cooperative Learning

Divide the class into small groups. Assign each one an innovation featured in this spread, such as antibiotics, refrigeration, or television (or others of your choice). Have each group research its innovation and report to the class.

▶ With new means of refrigeration widely available after World War II, Americans could store quantities of food for months on end. By 1956, 9 of 10 American families owned a refrigerator. Other symbols of the affluent society: by 1956, 3 of 4 families owned at least one auto, 3 out of 5 owned their own home. In 1945 only 9,000 private swimming pools were in use. In 1957 alone more than 50,000 pools were installed.

▲ Between the 1920s and the advent of the television age, millions of Americans learned about the important events of the day from radio. By the mid-1930s, two-thirds of American homes had at least one radio—less than half that many had telephones.

▶ More and more Americans, it seems, were eating canned foods. Hormel's Spiced Ham, better known as Spam, quickly established a strong position. Part of the impetus came during World War II when Spam's price and shelf life made it a staple of the soldier's diet. In Korea, Spam is considered an imported luxury item.

Cultural Kaleidoscope

Portfolio Project

Have students keep a log of their leisure activities for a week. Among the specifics they might note: what the activity is, whether they engage in it alone or with others, and how much time they spend on it. They might also speculate about whether their parents and/or grandparents could have spent their leisure time pursuing the same activities.

The Historian's Craft

The innovations shown here were all designed to appeal to, and be purchased by, consumers. Historians study advertisements in order to understand the impact of various innovations. Among other things, they note the audience being targeted and the motives (competition, anxiety, thrift, and so on) to which they appeal.

UNIT 9 DIGEST

The Unit Digest may be used to teach unit coverage when time is limited, to review unit content, or to relate content of one unit to that of another.

Unit Digest Transparencies
Use Transparency 17.

■ Chapter 28
Have students construct a chart showing the New Deal legislation mentioned in Chapter 28. Tell them to use four columns in their charts under the following headings: Name of Program, Date Established, Purpose, Impact. Suggest that students retain their charts for review purposes.

■ Chapter 29
Ask students to list the reasons American leaders gave for entering World War II.

■ Chapter 30
Remind students that the postwar years brought some interesting words and phrases into everyday language—"cold war," "containment," and "iron curtain," for example. Ask students to use political and etymological dictionaries to find and note the meaning and origin of these and other new political terms introduced in Chapter 30.

■ Chapter 31
Remind students that prosperity brought changes in lifestyle for many Americans during the 1950s. Have them research and write a re-

UNIT NINE DIGEST

Chapter 28
The New Deal
Franklin D. Roosevelt's New Deal was a two-part program of emergency measures and long-range planning with three specific aims—recovery from the Depression, relief for victims of the Depression, and reform of the nation's economic system.

During Roosevelt's first days in office, Congress enacted an unprecedented number of new programs. The second phase of the New Deal emphasized social reform rather than short-term emergency measures. Out of these efforts came large-scale public works programs and a social security system.

Roosevelt won reelection in 1936 by a landslide. However, problems with the Supreme Court and other setbacks in Congress slowed the pace of the New Deal. But by then its programs already had altered the role of government in American life.

Chapter 29
World War II
During FDR's first and second administrations, the Good Neighbor policy committed the United States to a policy of nonintervention in Latin America. In Europe, FDR recognized the Soviet Union and sought to maintain neutral relations with other nations.

When war in Europe broke out in 1939, German victories prompted the United States to aid the Allied nations of Britain, France, and the Soviet Union. In 1941, after Japanese planes bombed Pearl Harbor, the United States declared war on Japan and Germany. For the second time in 25 years, the American economy converted to war production and transformed the nation's way of life.

By the time an ailing Roosevelt was reelected to a fourth term, Germany and Japan had suffered major defeats on all fronts. Germany surrendered in May 1945. Japan surrendered after American planes dropped atomic bombs on Hiroshima and Nagasaki. Before the war ended, the United Nations formed in hopes of maintaining international peace and cooperation.

UNIT 9 Times of Crisis: 1932–1960

Cooperative Learning
Divide the class into groups of four or five. Have groups select one of the following topics: Tennessee Valley Authority, social security, United Nations, G.I. Bill, House Committee on Un-American Activities, cold war, affluent society. Have groups write a letter to someone who might have played a part in the early history of their chosen topic. The letters should explain changes concerning their topics that have taken place in the intervening years. Groups should select representatives to read their letters to the class. **L2**

Chapter 30
The Cold War

After World War II, the Soviet Union drew an "iron curtain" between Eastern Europe and the rest of Europe. An intense war of words, rivalry, and confrontation soon developed between the West and the Soviet Union.

Western fear that communism would spread led to a policy of containment. The Marshall Plan also gave massive economic aid to war-torn Western Europe. The United States, Canada, and nations of Western Europe established the North Atlantic Treaty Organization (NATO); Eastern European communist countries responded with the Warsaw Pact.

Meanwhile, the cold war spread to Asia. In 1949 Mao Zedong established a communist government in China, despite American efforts to prevent it. In Korea, Americans fought a "hot war" to stop a communist takeover of the peninsula.

At home the Truman administration pushed for economic and social reform. Inflation was rising, and labor resorted to strikes to increase wages. Fear generated by the cold war led to a search for Communists in the federal government.

In the early 1950s, the country began a long period of economic prosperity. The growing economy created millions of new jobs. Encouraged by their new economic strength, African Americans began to lobby for their civil rights.

Chapter 31
Search for Stability

In 1953, Dwight D. Eisenhower brought a new style of leadership to the White House. Although friendly to corporations, Eisenhower also expanded New Deal programs. Despite inflation and a brief recession, businesses and working men and women prospered. Farmers, however, did not fare well.

For many Americans, affluence and a new confidence in the future came with economic growth. A new way of life evolved as families moved from the cities to the suburbs and wage earners commuted to work.

Under Eisenhower, America's cold war containment policy continued through diplomacy, aid, and covert operations. His efforts to lessen tensions and reduce the Soviet nuclear threat, however, failed.

Understanding Unit Themes

1. **American Democracy** How did the role of government in American democracy change during the Depression and the New Deal? What changes persist to the present?
2. **Civil Rights and Liberties** Throughout the 1930s and 1940s, women gained new employment opportunities and a recognized place in the workforce. How do you account for the ground they lost in the 1950s?
3. **Conflict and Cooperation** How does the purpose of the United Nations differ from that of NATO, the Warsaw Pact, and the alliances of World War II?
4. **U.S. Role in World Affairs** Describe United States efforts to contain the spread of communism worldwide from 1948–1960. What were the results of these efforts?

UNIT 9 DIGEST

port on everyday life in the "affluent society."

Analyzing Unit Themes

Answers

1. More government intervention; supported labor, work relief, and assistance programs; social security benefits; regulated banking and business practices; intervened to stimulate or otherwise adjust economy.
2. 1930s—Roosevelt appointed women to high government positions. New Deal created jobs. 1940s—Continued need for labor in war and postwar industry. 1950s—Labor not needed. Pressure to conform sent women back to homes.
3. United Nations is unaligned international peacekeeping organization. Resolves conflict through cooperation, opposes aggression from any quarter.
4. China—supported Chiang Kai-shek against Mao; failed. Korea—sent troops to help Rhee drive out North Koreans; fought to a draw; country divided. Indochina—supplied Diem against Communist forces. Continued involvement led to Vietnam War. Europe—could not end Soviet control of satellites but contained its further expansion. Middle East—CIA covert operations overthrew Mossadegh's government.

The Historian's Craft

Have students study President Franklin D. Roosevelt's first inaugural speech, which can be found in the Documents section of this textbook. Point out that two major purposes of this speech were to reassure the American people and to restore their confidence in their country and themselves. Ask students to locate and note words and phrases that might fulfill these purposes. Then have them select one sentence or brief passage that best represents the spirit of the speech.

INTRODUCING UNIT 10

BEGINNING THE UNIT

Provide this cause and effect chart to students with effects omitted. Assign students to complete the chart as they read the chapters in the unit.

Event
- War in Vietnam

Causes
- Struggle for civil rights
- U.S. intervention globally against communism
- Beginning of U.S. involvement in southeast Asia

Effects
- Americans divided over war in Vietnam
- War undermines economic and social progress
- Protests and conflict challenge the government
- Government resists policy changes
- Watergate scandal erodes confidence in government
- Challenge to government's role in society brings change
- Struggle to redefine government continues

History AND ART
Ask students to discuss what advantages and disadvantages a mural artist faces.

00:00 OUT OF TIME?
If time does not permit teaching the entire unit, use the Unit Digest on pages 1026–1027.

UNIT TEN
REDEFINING AMERICA
1954–PRESENT

CHAPTER 32	CHAPTER 33	CHAPTER 34	CHAPTER 35	CHAPTER 36
The Civil Rights Era 1954–1975	The Vietnam Era 1954–1975	Camelot to Watergate 1960–1976	Search for Solutions 1976–1992	Toward a New Century 1992–

▲ VIETNAM VETERAN'S HAT

History AND ART

Mural on Building
Davenport, Iowa

Vivid images abound in this colorful mural commemorating American leaders and important events.

892

Exploring Unit Themes

Civil Rights and Liberties During this period, through demonstrations and civil disobedience, African Americans won repeal of discriminatory laws and more opportunities to share in the American dream. Women, too, made progress in their drive for equal rights.

Conflict and Cooperation In the early 1960s the belief grew—especially among young Americans—that by working together people could overcome problems. But bitter feelings over the Vietnam War left young Americans at odds with their government. During the 1980s, however, American confidence was restored.

Cultural Diversity The United States continued to be a haven for immigrants seeking freedom or opportunities for a better life. Today, the new

Setting the Scene

American society from the mid-1950s to the present has been described as a roller coaster. Americans were taken to new heights of optimism and confidence but lows of doubt and frustration as well. In addition, growing awareness of new technology redefined the way Americans lived and worked.

Themes
- Civil Rights and Liberties
- Conflict and Cooperation
- Cultural Diversity
- Role in World Affairs

Key Events
- Desegregation in public schools
- Kennedy's assassination
- War in Vietnam
- Watergate scandal
- Camp David Peace Accords
- Persian Gulf War
- Congress approves NAFTA

Major Issues
- The growing civil rights movement opens the political process for thousands of Americans.
- Involvement in Vietnam polarizes Americans at home and tarnishes the nation's image abroad.
- Illegal activities by high-level government officials result in the Watergate scandal.
- Democratic movements lead to the end of the Soviet Union.
- The United States and allies liberate Kuwait after Iraqi invasion.
- America seeks to redefine its role in the new world order and meet rising challenges at home.

▲ TALL SHIPS, PART OF BICENTENNIAL CELEBRATION

▲ POLITICAL CAMPAIGN BUTTONS

Portfolio Project
Make a poster for an imaginary benefit concert similar to the "Live Aid" concert. Select a topic from the leading challenges facing America in the late 1990s. Make sure to note this topic on the poster, along with the location of the concert and what artists will be performing.

INTRODUCING UNIT 10

UNIT 10 Independent Study Project
Explain to students that the decades from the 1950s to present times saw tremendous changes in the United States. Those changes affected all aspects of society. Have students report on one of the following topics: individuals who have made a difference in American life since the late 1950s; a reform movement that brought about great change in American life during this period; pressing foreign-policy issues that confronted our nation during these decades.

Unit Digest Transparencies
Use Transparency 19.

History and the Humanities
- U.S. History and Art Transparencies 29, 30, 31
- Focus on American Fine Art Prints 19, 20
- American Music: Cultural Traditions
- Spirit of American Art & Music 32, 33, 34, 35, 36

Portfolio Project
Suggest students narrow the focus of their topic. For instance, if they study the environment, ask them to select a specific aspect of the environment that is of particular concern to them.

---

immigrants are mostly from Latin America and Asia.

U.S. Role in World Affairs During most of this period, the United States assumed a cold-war stance. The collapse of communism in the Soviet Union and throughout Eastern Europe beginning in the late 1980s, however, brought much of the cold war to an end.

Examining the Themes
Tell students that this unit traces the many events and issues that have confronted the United States since the 1950s.

LESSON PLAN
Global Perspectives

FOCUS
Motivating Activity

Remind students that on the evening of January 16, 1991, even before the United States government had made any official statements, the American people knew that the Gulf War to repel the invasion of Kuwait by the forces of Iraq had begun. Reporters from the news network CNN provided vivid, live word-pictures of the aerial bombardment of Iraq's capital of Baghdad.

Ask students to draw conclusions about the impact of satellite communications by discussing the following statement: Today, there are no local events, only global events. (Students may suggest that instant communications makes people more aware of global events.)

TEACH
Guided Practice

Exploring the Timeline

Direct students' attention to the World Events section of the timeline and have them note events that reflect changes around the world. Conduct a class discussion about how these changes might affect policies of the United States. (For example, building the Berlin Wall—U.S. might step up cold war policies against USSR; collapse of communism—U.S. redefine policy toward USSR and Eastern Europe.) **L2**

Global Perspectives

The World

	1950		1965	
Asia and Oceania		1954 French are defeated in Vietnam		1966 China's Cultural Revolution begins
Europe				1961 Berlin Wall built
Africa				◀ 1960 "Year of Africa"—many countries become independent
South America				
North and Central America				1959 St. Lawrence Seaway opens

The United States

Pacific and Northwest			◀ 1959 Alaska and Hawaii become states	
Southeast		1955 Rosa Parks inspires Montgomery bus boycott		1965 Freedom March from Selma to Montgomery
Midwest		1954 Brown v. Board of Education decision		
Southwest				◀ 1966 First artificial heart implanted
Atlantic Northeast	1950		1965	

894 UNIT 10 Redefining America: 1954–Present

Cultural Diversity

In the late 1980s, Asia, the Caribbean, and Latin America were the major sources of immigration to the United States. The largest numbers of newcomers were from Colombia, the Dominican Republic, Ecuador, Guyana, Haiti, Jamaica, India, China, the Philippines, and South Korea. At the same time, however, people emigrated from another 150 countries. It is not surprising, then, that the United States has been called the world in microcosm.

Linking Across TIME

The United States has long been known as a nation of immigrants. Throughout its history, people from other countries came to its shores seeking a better way of life. In the late 1980s, the major sources of immigration to the United States were Asia, the Caribbean, and Latin America. Among the countries that sent the most immigrants were China, Colombia, the Dominican Republic, Ecuador, Guyana, Haiti, India, Jamaica, the Philippines, and South Korea. At the same time, however, immigrants came from another 150 countries. It is not surprising then that some people have called the United States the world in microcosm, or miniature.

1980 — **1995**

- **1975** American military evacuate Saigon
- **1993** Israel-PLO treaty signed 
- ◀ **1989** Communism crumbles in Eastern Europe
- **1994** War continues between Bosnia and Serbia
- **1993** Apartheid ends in South Africa
- **1974** Isabel Perón becomes president in Argentina
- **1982** Argentina invades Falkland Islands 
- ◀ **1983** American troops invade Grenada
- **1994** Haitian leader Aristide returns from exile
- ▼ **1989** Exxon Valdez oil spill in Alaska
- **1994** Northridge earthquake hits Southern California 
- **1980** Michigan's unemployment rate is nation's highest
- **1990** Navaho nation elects its first president
- **1974** President Nixon resigns office of the presidency
- **1987** Worst Wall Street stock market plunge in history

1980 — **1995**

UNIT 10 Redefining America: 1954–Present   895

Cooperative Learning

Divide the class into two groups and assign one group the world, the other, the United States. Have each group research and construct a timeline for its area for the last 15 years. Suggest that groups have at least five entries for each region in its area. Display the finished timelines on the bulletin board and use them as a starting point for a class discussion on global interdependence. **L2**

LESSON PLAN
Global Perspectives

Independent Practice

World Events and the U.S. Point out that the opening of the St. Lawrence Seaway in 1959 enabled ocean-going vessels to travel as far inland in the United States as the Great Lakes. Ask students to write a report on how the seaway changed the patterns of trade in the United States. Suggest that they illustrate their reports with maps, graphs, and charts. A useful source of information is *The United States and Canada, Present and Future* by Richard S. Thoman. **L3**

ASSESS
Studying the Time Line

1. Which 1950s entry in the world section of the timeline is related to a 1970s entry in the United States section? (1954—French defeated in Vietnam)

2. In what sense have the events in the Europe column of the world timeline come "full circle?" (Berlin wall symbolic of division between communist and free Europe; crumbling of communism led to fall of Berlin Wall.)

3. "Americans must not be ignorant of the world, for what happens thousands of miles away may have a resounding impact on their lives." Ask students to support this statement with information from the timelines. (Answers will vary but may include that Iraq's invasion of Kuwait threatened American allies and supply of oil.

PLANNING GUIDE   Chapter 32   The Civil Rights Era

Daily Lesson Objectives	Teacher Classroom Resources	Multimedia
SECTION 1 **A New Beginning** 1 Day pp. 898–902 1. Discuss the effects of the *Brown* v. *Board of Education* decision. 2. Describe major events in the early civil rights movement.	Chapter 32 Study Guide Reproducible Lesson Plan Reteaching Activity 32-1 Section Quiz Chapter 32 Cooperative Learning Activity Chapter 32 Concept Mapping Activity American Portrait 63 Reinforcing Social Studies Skills 13, 30, 32, 38, 53, 55, 63 Chapter 32 Primary and Secondary Source Readings	Student Self-Test Software Testmaker Section Focus Transparency 104 Chapter 32 Skills Transparency Chapter 32 Map Transparencies Unit 10 Digest Transparencies Powers of the Supreme Court Martin Luther King, Jr.
SECTION 2 **Successes and Drawbacks** 1 Day pp. 904–908 1. Describe advances made in civil rights during the Kennedy-Johnson administrations. 2. Describe the setbacks and difficulties the civil rights activists faced during the 1960s.	Reproducible Lesson Plan Reteaching Activity 32-2 Section Quiz American Portrait 64 Reinforcing Social Studies Skills 53, 59, 65, 69–72 Chapter 32 Primary and Secondary Source Readings The Living Constitution	Student Self-Test Software Testmaker Section Focus Transparency 105 U.S. History and Art Transparency 29 The American People: Fabric of a Nation Martin Luther King, Jr.
SECTION 3 **New Leaders and Black Power** 1 Day pp. 910–914 1. List some of the factors responsible for discontent among some African Americans. 2. Explain what new philosophies were developed by African Americans to deal with the discontent.	Reproducible Lesson Plan Reteaching Activity 32-3 Section Quiz	Student Self-Test Software Testmaker Section Focus Transparency 106 U.S. History and Art Transparency 30 Martin Luther King, Jr.
SECTION 4 **The Impact of Civil Rights** 1 Day pp. 915–919 1. Describe the gains made by women and minorities. 2. Explain why the Equal Rights Amendment was not ratified.	Reproducible Lesson Plan Reteaching Activity 32-4 Section Quiz Chapter 32 Enrichment Activity American Portrait 68 Reinforcing Social Studies Skills 23, 27, 31, 55, 66 Chapter 32 Primary and Secondary Source Readings Writer's Guidebook Lesson 6 Spanish Summaries & Glossary	Student Self-Test Software Testmaker Vocabulary Puzzlemaker Section Focus Transparency 107 Audiocassette, Chapter 32 The American People: Fabric of a Nation
CHAPTER REVIEW AND EVALUATION 1 Day	Chapter 32 Test Chapter 32 Performance Assessment Activity	Student Self-Test Software Testmaker

 **OUT OF TIME?** If time does not permit teaching the entire chapter, use the Chapter 32 Summary on pages 1028–1029 and the Chapter 32 audiocassette (English and Spanish) to point out the main ideas of the chapter.

PLANNING GUIDE

Cultural Diversity Activity

Cooperative Learning The civil rights movement inspired other minorities to demand social justice. Divide students into small groups and ask each to research the effects of the movement on Hispanics, women, Native Americans, and the disabled. Students might trace the way the Civil Rights Movement inspired leaders of groups, shaped strategies for demanding justice, and influenced the way other Americans responded to those demands. Have each group report its findings to the class. Then discuss similarities and differences among the groups. Which made the greatest gains in the 1960s and 1970s? What work remains to be done?

Performance Assessment Activity

A Chronology of a Movement Organize students in groups of four or five. Have each select six events discussed in this chapter that they consider important to the civil rights movement. For each event, groups should tell when and what happened, how this event contributed to the struggle for equality, and how they think the history of this period might have been different if the event had not occurred. Groups might also suggest a picture or visual image to represent the event. Have groups share their choices with the class. Then as a class, create an illustrated time line of the civil rights movement.

POSSIBLE RUBRIC FEATURES: Content information, research skills, organization, writing and communication skills, critical thinking skills, collaborative skills

Chapter Resources

Literature from the Period

Brown, et. al. v. Board of Education of Topeka, KA. et al. May 17, 1954.

Ellison, Ralph. *Shadow and Act.* Random House, 1964.

King, Jr., Martin Luther. "I Have a Dream." 1963.

Readings for the Student

Durham, Michael S. *Powerful Days: The Civil Rights Photography of Charles Moore.* Stewart, Tabori, and Chang, 1991.

Patterson, Lillie. *Martin Luther King, Jr. and the Freedom Movement.* Facts on File, 1989.

Readings for the Teacher

King, Jr. Martin Luther. *Stride Toward Freedom.* Harper, 1958.

Powledge, Fred. *Free at Last? The Civil Rights Movement and the People Who Made It.* Little, Brown, 1991.

Multimedia Resources

All the Unsung Heroes. American Heritage Group. (VHS, 30 minutes)

The Civil Rights Movement: Witness to History. Guidance Associates. (VHS, 15 minutes)

King. Filmways. (VHS, 254 minutes)

Key to Ability Levels

Teaching strategies have been coded for varying learning styles and abilities.

- **L1** Basic activities for all students
- **L2** Average activities for average to above-average students
- **L3** Challenging activities for above-average students
- **LEP** Limited English Proficiency activities

Glencoe Links to the Humanities

Links to Art
- U.S. History and Art Transparencies 29, 30
- Focus on American Fine Art Prints

Links to Literature
- Macmillan Literature: Understanding Literature Audiotapes Sides 3, 4
- Macmillan Literature: American Literature Video—*The Glass Menagerie*
- Macmillan Literature: Novel Guides—*Where the Red Fern Grows, The Old Man and the Sea*

Link to Music
♪ American Music: Cultural Traditions

CHAPTER 32

BEGINNING THE CHAPTER

Remind students that in the 1950s segregation was the rule in the South and was widespread in the North. Have students suggest ways in which African Americans could secure equal rights. (through protests and demonstrations, court cases that challenge discriminatory laws) Tell students that in this chapter they will learn how African Americans struggled for equality and the impact of their struggle on American society.

Point out that African American leaders had been working toward full equality since the Civil War ended but they made only limited progress until the 1950s. By the 1960s, African Americans had made considerable gains in securing enforcement of their voting rights. During those years a number of African Americans were elected to Congress and served as mayors of large cities.

Recording Journal Notes
Suggest students organize their notes into categories such as demonstrations, boycotts, marches, freedom rides, sit-ins.

CHAPTER 32

The Civil Rights Era
1954–1975

▶ CELEBRATING KWANZAA, HOLIDAY BASED ON TRADITIONAL AFRICAN FESTIVAL

Setting the Scene

Focus
During the 1950s, African Americans rebelled against their second-class status. The ranks of civil rights advocates swelled, and African Americans, joined by some white liberals, began following the nonviolent ideas of Dr. Martin Luther King, Jr. They fought for equality first in the South and eventually in the North. Met with violence at every turn, many African Americans abandoned King's ideas and developed new philosophies. Whatever their ideas, these civil rights activists inspired hope to other minorities.

Concepts to Understand
★ Why efforts to gain civil rights created an effective movement for change
★ How the civil rights movement led to social upheaval

Read to Discover . . .
★ legislation that addressed civil rights issues.
★ the kind of impact the civil rights movement had on other minorities.

Journal Notes
What was life like for civil rights activists during the 1950s and 1960s? Note details about it in your journal as you read the chapter.

CULTURAL	• 1959 *Jazz pioneer Ornette Coleman releases* The Shape of Jazz	• 1962 *Richard Wright pens* Another Country • 1964 *Dr. King wins Nobel Peace Prize*
	1954	**1960**
POLITICAL	• 1955 *Montgomery bus boycott begins* • 1957 *Congress passes the first civil rights legislation since Reconstruction*	• 1964 *Civil Rights Act is passed* • 1965 *"March for Freedom" begins* • 1965 *Voting Rights Act is passed*

896 UNIT 10 Redefining America: 1954–Present

✚ EXTRA CREDIT PROJECT

Explain that the Voting Rights Act of 1965 was a major step in ensuring voting rights for African Americans. The act led to massive voter registration drives in the South. Invite interested students to research the growth in African American voter registration in the southern states following passage of the act. Have students create a chart showing, for example, the years 1960 and 1966. (The *Statistical Abstract of the United States* is a source for such information.) Ask them to present their charts to the class and discuss their findings. Which states showed the greatest increase? The least increase? What might account for the differences among the states?

The March on Washington, 1963

The August 1963 March on Washington for equal rights was the largest and most peaceful protest in the nation's history. Dr. Martin Luther King, Jr., electrified the listeners with his "I Have a Dream" address.

◀ STATUE OF LIBERTY

- **1966** *Soul on Ice* states Black Panther aims

1966

- **1967** Carl Stokes is elected mayor of Cleveland, Ohio
- **1968** Martin Luther King, Jr., is assassinated

- **1972** Joseph Walker publishes *The River Niger*
- **1973** Toni Morrison publishes *Sula*

1972

- **1972** Congress approves Equal Rights Amendment

CHAPTER 32 The Civil Rights Era 1954–1975

CHAPTER 32 CONCEPTS

Concept Mapping Activity

Reproduce the following generalization and concepts map on the chalkboard and have students copy it in their notebooks. Ask students to hypothesize what topics may be covered in Chapter 32 based on this information.

> African American leaders offered a new vision of equality, which brought about reform and change in American society.

- Civil Rights
- Social Change

History AND ART

The civil rights march on Washington, D.C., in 1963 was the culmination of hundreds of protests and demonstrations that took place across the nation.

  VIDEODISC

- *GTV: The American People: Fabric of a Nation*

Side 4, Chapter 5
Title: *The War at Home*
Subject: The Civil Rights movement

See GTV Guide page 98 for complete lesson plan.

Teacher Notes

LESSON PLAN
SECTION 1, 898–903

FOCUS

Bellringer
Prior to taking roll at the beginning of the class period, display Focus Activity Transparency 109 on the overhead projector and assign the accompanying Focus Activity Sheet.

Objectives
Point out the objectives on this page to students in previewing the section content.

Motivating Activity
Read the following song verse to students.
"We shall overcome, we shall overcome,
We shall overcome someday.
Oh, deep in my heart, I do believe,
We shall overcome someday."
Point out that songs were an important aspect of the civil rights movement.

Use Skills Transparency 32.

ABC NEWS INTERACTIVE

VIDEODISC
Powers of the Supreme Court

Side 2, Chapter 22
Title: *Brown v. Board of Education of Topeka (KS)*
Subject: Explains the issues behind the landmark case that ended school segregation

---

SECTION 1

A New Beginning

Setting the Scene

Section Focus

Almost a century after passage of the Fourteenth and Fifteenth amendments, African Americans were still victims of discrimination and segregation. In the South these attitudes were entrenched not only in custom but also in law. The battle to obtain equal rights for African Americans would have to be fought in the courts, in the news media, and in the consciences of the American people. For the civil rights movement, the 1950s marked a new beginning in the ongoing struggle for equality.

Objectives

After studying this chapter, you should be able to
★ discuss the effects of the *Brown* v. *Board of Education* decision.
★ describe major events in the early civil rights movement.

Key Terms

nonviolent resistance, federalized

▶ Dr. Martin Luther King, Jr.

The end of Reconstruction left African Americans economically and politically second-class citizens. The sharecropping system and "Jim Crow" segregation laws worked to deny them their rights as citizens. African American leaders began to work toward restoring their full civil rights in the early decades of the twentieth century, but the movement did not come into full flower until almost 50 years later.

During the 1950s and the early 1960s, African Americans boldly rejected their second-class status and the humiliating practice of forced separation. They fought for equal opportunities in jobs, housing, and education. They fought against segregated schools, buses, and trains; they fought against separate facilities in restaurants, hotels, libraries, and hospitals. They won an important ally when the Supreme Court issued several decisions against racial discrimination. But the main force behind the civil rights movement came from citizens—African American and white—who banded together in an effective protest movement.

■ Brown v. Board of Education

One of the Supreme Court's most significant rulings of the 1950s came in May 1954. Three years earlier, Linda Brown's parents had sued the school board of Topeka, Kansas, for not allowing their daughter to attend an all-white school, miles closer to their home than the segregated elementary school she was assigned to attend.

The Supreme Court ruled in *Brown* v. *Board of Education of Topeka, Kansas* that it was unconstitutional to separate schoolchildren by race. The Brown decision reversed the

898 UNIT 10 Redefining America: 1954–Present

Classroom Resources for SECTION 1

Teacher's Classroom Resources
- Chapter 32 Study Guide
- Reproducible Lesson Plan
- Reteaching Activity 32-1
- Chapter 32 Cooperative Learning Activity
- Chapter 32 Primary and Secondary Source Readings
- Section Quiz

Multimedia
- Section Focus Transparency 109
- Skills Transparency 32
- Testmaker
- Student Self-Test Software
- Powers of the Supreme Court
- Martin Luther King, Jr.

Court's decision in *Plessy* v. *Ferguson*, an 1896 ruling that had upheld the constitutionality of "separate but equal" public accommodations. *Plessy* had become the basis for Jim Crow laws and legal segregation in many states.

The Southern Manifesto

The Supreme Court's ruling in *Brown* v. *Board of Education* called for major changes in many states, especially those in the South. Some border states integrated their schools, but the South remained segregated. The governor of Virginia threatened to close the state's public schools and send white children to private schools. A group of 101 southern members of Congress signed a "Southern Manifesto," which called the Court's ruling "a clear abuse of judicial power" and pledged use of "all lawful means to bring about a reversal of this decision."

Boycotts and Demonstrations

The decisions of the Warren Court gave legal support to African Americans' struggle for civil rights. But most civil rights battles, particularly in the South, were fought by brave men and women who broke down barriers of segregation one by one.

Rosa Parks Takes a Stand

In December 1955, an African American seamstress from Montgomery, Alabama, became one of the first to take a stand. At the end of the workday, Parks boarded a segregated bus in which all the seats allotted for African Americans were filled; she took a seat in the front, which was reserved for white riders. Because Parks refused to give up her seat, she was arrested.

The arrest of Rosa Parks aroused anger in Montgomery's African American community. Many of its leaders believed that now was the time to challenge Alabama's segregation laws. At a meeting held at the Dexter Avenue Baptist Church, a boycott of the city's buses was called. The 26-year-old minister of the church, Dr. Martin Luther King, Jr., was asked to lead the boycott.

On the day of Rosa Parks's trial, almost all the African American riders who usually took the buses began a nearly year-long boycott. Because a majority of the regular bus riders were African American, the bus company lost much of its business.

▲ **ROSA PARKS** Rosa Parks refused to give up her seat to a white bus rider. She meets with her lawyer after she was charged with breaking the law. **What actions did civil rights leaders take to protest Parks's arrest?**

CHAPTER 32 The Civil Rights Era 1954–1975 **899**

CHAPTER 32
SECTION 1

Teaching Life of the Times

Tell students that rather than integrate Arkansas schools, Governor Orval Faubus closed all the public schools. In 1959 the Supreme Court ordered that such "evasive schemes" could not be used to avoid integration, and the schools reopened. Invite a volunteer to read Melba Pattillo Beals' account aloud. Call on students to explain in their own words the "greatest lesson" that Melba learned. Suggest students write accounts of a personal experience they have had related to prejudice or segregation.

Independent Practice

Have students research and construct a timeline of the major developments in African Americans' struggle for equal rights in the twentieth century. (protest movements, formation of groups, court cases, and so forth) Suggest students summarize their findings in a paragraph or two. **L2**

Did You Know?

The lawyer who argued the Brown case before the Supreme Court was Thurgood Marshall, who had been fighting for equal rights in court since the 1930s. In 1967, he became the first African American to be appointed to the Supreme Court, where he served until his retirement in 1991.

Life of the Times

School Desegregation

Melba Patillo Beals was one of the African American teenagers who integrated Little Rock's Central High School in the fall of 1957. Despite the danger, Beals felt proud to participate in what she saw even then as a historic happening.

In the following passage, Melba Beals recalls some of her experiences at the formerly all-white high school.

"I went in not through the side doors but up the front stairs, and there was a feeling of pride and hope that yes, this is the United States; yes, there is a reason I salute the flag. . . . The troops were wonderful. . . . [But] they couldn't be with us everywhere. . . . We'd be showering in gym and someone would turn your shower on to scalding. You'd be walking out to the volleyball court and someone would break a bottle and trip you on the bottle . . . first you're in pain, then you're angry, then you try to fight back, . . . And then you just mellow out and you realize that survival is day-to-day and you start to grasp the depth of the human spirit, you start to understand your own ability to cope no matter what. That is the greatest lesson I learned."

◀ **CENTRAL HIGH SCHOOL, LITTLE ROCK, ARKANSAS, 1957**

Rosa Parks was convicted and fined $10. Dr. King and other African American leaders were arrested for sponsoring an "illegal boycott." Then, in November 1956, the Supreme Court ruled that segregation in public transportation was illegal. The bus company ended its policy of segregation. The African American citizens of Montgomery, assured of equal treatment, resumed riding the buses. The Montgomery bus boycott galvanized the civil rights movement, and in Martin Luther King, Jr., that movement found an inspiring leader.

King Preaches Nonviolence

African American churches and their ministers took the lead in organizing the civil rights movement. Dr. King, a Baptist minister, drew from his own faith and also from techniques of the Indian leader Mohandas Gandhi. Like Gandhi, King encouraged the use of **nonviolent resistance,** or peaceful means to effect change. He told people to disobey unjust laws but asked them to love their oppressors and never fight with them even if provoked. He explained that public opinion, not violence, would force authorities to change unjust laws:

> " *Injustice must be exposed, with all the tension its exposure creates, to the light of human conscience and the air of national opinion before it can be cured.* "

In 1957, to carry on this nonviolent struggle against discrimination in public places all over the South, King and other African American leaders founded the Southern Christian Leadership Conference (SCLC). In addition to the SCLC and its student branch—the Student Nonviolent Coordinating Committee—there were many other groups organized to promote civil rights.

900   UNIT 10 Redefining America: 1954–Present

Sidelights: African Americans in Films

Hattie McDaniel, who won an Academy Award for her role in *Gone with the Wind* in 1939, once noted that she had two choices: she could play a maid for $7,000 a week or be a real one for $7.00 a week. From the early days of film, African Americans were usually shown in movies as servants, clowns, or crooks. In the 1950s and 1960s, the stereotyping began to end. Films such as *Pinky, Lost Boundaries,* and *Imitation of Life* portrayed African Americans as having a range of experiences and emotions. Changes have occurred slowly, however. Not until the 1980s did African Americans break the color barriers in films not only as actors but also as producers and directors.

Among them were such long-established African American organizations as the National Association for the Advancement of Colored People (NAACP), which fought discrimination in many legal cases, including *Brown* v. *Board of Education;* the National Urban League, which established community programs for minorities in cities; and the Congress of Racial Equality (CORE), which worked for economic and political opportunities for African Americans. Dr. King remained at the forefront of the movement as it continued to grow in the 1960s. In 1964 he received the Nobel Peace Prize for his nonviolent leadership.

Crisis in Little Rock

Not wanting to create controversy, the Eisenhower administration and Congress refused to pass civil rights legislation. As a result, civil rights groups turned to the courts for settlement of their grievances.

In 1953 Eisenhower appointed Earl Warren as Chief Justice of the United States Supreme Court. Warren began to move the Court toward a more liberal interpretation of the Constitution in decisions on individual rights. Also in 1953 the NAACP brought a number of civil rights cases before the Court. Thurgood Marshall, the NAACP's leading lawyer, wanted the Court to strike down state laws that required racial segregation in public schools. He argued that African American children were not getting the same quality of education as white children.

On May 17, 1954, the Court handed down a historic decision in *Brown* v. *Board of Education of Topeka*. It overturned the 1896 *Plessy* v. *Ferguson* decision that segregation was constitutional so long as equal facilities were provided for both races. The Court declared

> *We conclude that in the field of public education, the doctrine of "separate but equal" has no place. Separate educational facilities are inherently unequal.*

In *Brown* v. *Board of Education of Topeka*, the Supreme Court did not set a deadline for ending segregation. However, in May 1955, the Court called for the implementation of integration "with all deliberate speed."

Civil Rights Legislation

The ruling needed the active support of President Eisenhower, but the President believed that the federal government should remain neutral concerning controversial issues that affected state and local governments. He remarked, "I don't believe you can change the hearts of men with laws and decisions."

In 1957 Congress passed the first civil rights law since Reconstruction. The act created a civil rights division within the Department of Justice and gave the government the power to seek court injunctions against those who denied any citizen's constitutional rights.

Confrontation

In September 1957, the state of Arkansas tested the federal government's policies on civil rights. A federal court had ordered that

▲ **CRISIS IN LITTLE ROCK** Central High School in Little Rock, Arkansas, became the focus of court-ordered desegregation in 1957. After Governor Orval Faubus used the Arkansas National Guard to prevent nine African American students from attending, Eisenhower sent federal troops to Little Rock. *How was the crisis resolved?*

CHAPTER 32
SECTION 1

Visualizing History Little Rock seemed an unlikely place for a showdown on school segregation. Just five days after the *Brown* decision, the Little Rock school board announced its willingness to obey the new law. Then on September 2, Governor Faubus appeared on statewide television to announce he had ordered state National Guard soldiers to surround the school.

Answer to Caption: Federal troops remained in Little Rock for the rest of the year, and African American students were able to attend school. Central High closed for the 1958–59 academic year.

Did You Know?

In 1989, Linda Brown, now Linda Brown Smith, was concerned that integration was not proceeding quickly enough. To make sure her grandson received an equal education, she attempted to reopen the *Brown* case. It did not get to the courts because she and her local board of education resolved their differences.

Critical Thinking

Comparing Philosophies Martin Luther King, Jr., took many of his nonviolent ideas from those of Mohandas K. Gandhi, leader of India's liberation movement against the British. Ask students to research Gandhi's philosophy and his work. Have them compare the two philosophies. How are they similar? Different? What impact did each leader have on his nation? How successful was each in reaching his goals? Have students present their findings orally for class discussion. **L3**

CHAPTER 32
SECTION 1

ASSESS
Check Understanding
Assign Section 1 Review as homework or an in-class activity.

Evaluate
Assign the Section 1 Quiz in the TCR or use the History of a Free Nation Testmaker to create a customized quiz.

Reteach
For each subsection in Section 1, have students write a statement summarizing the main idea. Invite several students to read their statements aloud. Ask students to pick the statement they think best summarizes each subsection.

Have students complete Reteaching Activity 32-1.

Enrich
Tell students that the Warren Court was highly criticized during the 1950s and 1960s. Have students investigate the groups and events behind the "Impeach Earl Warren" movement and present their findings to the class.

CLOSE
Suggest a volunteer read aloud Martin Luther King's statement on page 901. Ask students to discuss the following questions: Based on what you know of the civil rights movement, how effective was nonviolent direct action? Is breaking the law in a just cause ever acceptable? Why or why not?

▲ PROTESTING FOR RIGHTS

nine African American students be admitted to the all-white Central High School in Little Rock, Arkansas. The state's governor, Orval Faubus, defied federal authority and sent National Guard troops to prevent the students from attending.

President Eisenhower tried to persuade Governor Faubus to obey the court order. The governor withdrew the troops, but without their presence the African American students were exposed to an angry mob that threatened them with physical harm. Forced to act to maintain order, Eisenhower sent in 1,000 paratroopers and **federalized,** or put under the jurisdiction of the federal government, 10,000 members of the Arkansas National Guard to surround the school so that the students could enter safely.

As Daisy Bates, then the president of the Arkansas NAACP, later remembered:

> ❝ . . . the nine [African American] pupils marched solemnly through the doors of Central High School, surrounded by twenty-two soldiers. An Army helicopter circled overhead. Around the massive brick schoolhouse 350 paratroopers stood grimly at attention. . . . Within minutes a world that had been holding its breath learned that the nine pupils . . . had finally entered the 'never-never-land.' ❞

Troops remained in Little Rock for the rest of the year, however, and Central High School was closed for the 1958–1959 academic year.

As the Eisenhower administration drew to a close, the nation remained racially divided. Custom and years of intimidation kept many African Americans from voting. Between 1957 and 1960, the Justice Department brought only 10 suits to secure voting rights for African Americans. Only 25 percent of African American adults voted in states of the deep South, and only 5 percent in Mississippi. The movement for civil rights was just beginning.

Section 1 ★ Review

Checking for Understanding
1. **Identify** Brown v. Board of Education, Earl Warren, Southern Manifesto, Rosa Parks, Martin Luther King, Jr.
2. **Define** nonviolent resistance, federalized.
3. **Explain** Martin Luther King's philosophy of nonviolence.
4. **Describe** why Eisenhower sent federal troops into Little Rock.

Critical Thinking
5. **Analyzing a Viewpoint** How would you evaluate Eisenhower's stand on civil rights? Explain why many African Americans in the South would not be content with this approach.

Answers to SECTION 1 REVIEW
1. Brown v. Board of Education, 898; Earl Warren, 901; Southern Manifesto, 899; Rosa Parks, 900; Martin Luther King, Jr., 899–900; Southern Christian Leadership Conference, 900; National Urban League, 901; Congress of Racial Equality, 901
2. All vocabulary words are defined in the Glossary.
3. King advocated disobeying unjust laws without using violence. Rather, he suggested followers should love their oppressors.
4. to maintain order and protect African American students trying to attend Central High
5. Answers may include that Eisenhower had to take action to enforce federal law. Because desegregation was not a matter of changing "hearts of men"—it was African Americans' legal right to equal opportunity.

CONNECTIONS — History AND Religion — CONNECTIONS

▲ THE BRADFORD SINGERS GOSPEL GROUP
◀ DR. MARTIN LUTHER KING, JR.

African American Churches and the Civil Rights Movement

African Americans in the South had long heard the message of the Christian scriptures that God is on the side of the oppressed. They concluded that if it was true in ancient Israel it could also be true in the American South. From the organization of the Montgomery bus boycott in 1955 until the March on Washington in 1963, African American churches played the central role in devising strategies and mobilizing volunteers for the civil rights movement. The message of the gospel became the message of the movement. The churches called for protest without retaliatory violence, confrontation without conflict.

Many leaders of the Southern Christian Leadership Conference and other organizations were ministers. In 1957 King, Bayard Rustin, and others had founded the SCLC in the wake of the Montgomery bus boycott to work toward full citizenship rights for African Americans and their integration in all aspects of society.

The SCLC took a leading role in the Freedom Rides challenging segregation on public transportation and other public accommodations. Dr. King's first Southern Christian Leadership Conference drive in the North was launched in Chicago in July 1966 for open housing.

Some of them were arrested for taking part in demonstrations. Dr. Martin Luther King, Jr., himself was arrested repeatedly for demonstrating in Birmingham. In response to a group of Birmingham ministers who criticized King as an "outside agitator" he wrote from jail: ". . . just as the apostle Paul left his village of Tarsus and carried the gospel of Jesus Christ to the far corners of the Greco-Roman world, so am I compelled to carry the gospel of freedom beyond my own hometown."

Making the Religion Connection

1. How was the message of the gospel related to the civil rights movement?
2. Why were civil rights leaders sometimes jailed?

Linking Past and Present

3. How are African American churches involved in politics today?

LESSON PLAN
SECTION 2, 904–909

FOCUS

Bellringer
Display Focus Activity Transparency 110 on the overhead projector and assign the accompanying Focus Activity Sheet.

Objectives
Point out the objectives on this page in previewing the section content.

Motivating Activity
Write the terms *New Frontier* and *Great Society* on the chalkboard. Invite students to tell what kind of images these terms evoke (a new beginning, new challenges, new opportunities; progress, prosperity, equality) Explain that as the civil rights movement gained momentum, the government took a more active role in supporting it.

Project Map Transparency 41. Assign the accompanying activity from Map Transparencies: Strategies and Activities.

NATIONAL GEOGRAPHIC SOCIETY

 **VIDEODISC**

- *GTV: The American People: Fabric of a Nation*

Side 4, Chapter 5
Title: *The War at Home*
Subject: The Civil Rights movement

See GTV Guide page 98 for complete lesson plan.

SECTION 2

Successes and Setbacks

Setting the Scene

Section Focus

During the Kennedy-Johnson years, there were successes and setbacks for the civil rights movement. Kennedy moved slowly at first. However, violent events soon forced his hand, and he used the federal courts as well as troops to enforce desegregation in the South. Lyndon Johnson continued the former President's policies and succeeded in getting them passed into law.

Objectives

After studying this section, you should be able to
★ describe advances made in civil rights during the Kennedy-Johnson administrations.
★ describe the setbacks and difficulties the civil rights activists faced during the 1960s.

Key Term

sit-in

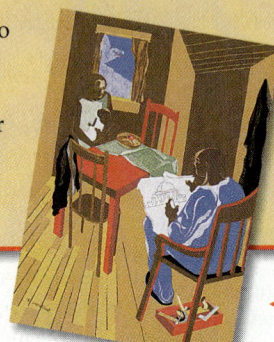

◀ "IN A FREE GOVERNMENT..." BY JACOB LAWRENCE

As the 1960s began, leaders for the civil rights movement—both African Americans and liberal whites—stepped up the tactics of nonviolent resistance throughout the South. Although eventually many of these tactics resulted in great gains for the movement, they generally were met with violence. People were attacked and killed, and only the federal government was strong enough to do something about it.

■ Students Stage Sit-ins

During the winter of 1959 and 1960, civil rights groups held marches, demonstrations, and boycotts to end segregation in public places. They especially challenged the practice of not serving African Americans at many southern lunch counters. In February 1960 four African American students sat down at a segregated lunch counter in a local store in Greensboro, North Carolina. They refused to leave until they were served. Their action was known as a **sit-in,** and before long students were staging sit-ins all over the South. By September 1961, 70,000 students were using this tactic to produce social change.

By 1960 the crusade for civil rights had become a national movement. As a result, many Americans were now beginning to recognize the moral evil of racial discrimination. King wrote:

❝ *The law cannot change the heart—but it can restrain the heartless. It will take education and religion to change bad internal attitudes—but legislation and court orders can control their external aspects.* ❞

UNIT 10 Redefining America: 1954–Present

Classroom Resources for SECTION 2

Teacher's Classroom Resources
- Reproducible Lesson Plan
- Reteaching Activity 32-2
- Chapter 32 Primary and Secondary Source Readings
- Section Quiz

Multimedia
- Section Focus Transparency 110
- Chapter 32 Map Transparency
- Testmaker
- Student Self-Test Software
- The American People: Fabric of a Nation

Kennedy and Civil Rights

In contrast to Eisenhower's cautious stand on civil rights, President Kennedy had promised vigorous support of the movement. Kennedy was aware of the support he needed from African American voters to win the 1960 election. Yet his slim victory over Nixon, coupled with the fear of losing southern Democratic support in Congress, made him act less forcefully than the words of his campaign had seemed to promise.

Kennedy's cautious attitude disappointed white liberals and African American leaders. He waited until 1962 to sign an executive order ending segregation in government-owned housing. And although Kennedy appointed African Americans to his administration as well as to federal judicial positions, he also appointed some judges who supported segregation. Events in the South, however, soon forced Kennedy to take a more active role in civil rights.

The Freedom Riders

In the spring of 1961, civil rights activists volunteered as "Freedom Riders" to ride buses into segregated terminals throughout the South. In May busloads of Freedom Riders were attacked by mobs in the Alabama cities of Anniston and Birmingham. A bus was fire-bombed and riders were beaten and clubbed. As more and more Freedom Riders poured into southern cities, local police were unable or unwilling to protect them from angry racists. The President was forced to use federal marshals to restore order. The Justice Department also pressured the Interstate Commerce Commission to bring lawsuits against those terminals that refused to comply with regulations on desegregation.

While Kennedy was in office, from 1961 to 1963, the Department of Justice brought 6 times as many lawsuits to protect African American voting rights as it did under Eisenhower, from 1958 to 1960. As a result, by 1964, the percentage of African American citizens registered to vote in the deep South had risen from 25 to 40 percent, largely as a result of the work of the Freedom Riders.

Violence in Birmingham

Violence that broke out in Birmingham was the last straw for Kennedy. From that point on, Kennedy wholeheartedly sided

▲ **CHALLENGING SEGREGATION** Civil rights groups challenged the practice of not serving African Americans at many southern diners. Here, two African Americans refuse to leave a segregated Raleigh, North Carolina, lunch counter until they are served. *What was their tactic called?*

CHAPTER 32
SECTION 2

Independent Practice

Music Have students locate recordings or lyrics of such civil rights protest songs as "We Shall Overcome," "Keep Your Eyes on the Prize," and "If You Miss Me From the Back of the Bus." Ask students to note the lyrics and consider what made these songs so powerful among civil rights activists.

Suggest interested students select a current social issue about which to write their own protest song. They might write it in the rap style—today's protest music. Select volunteers to perform their songs for the class. **L2**

Did You Know?

Although the Kennedy administration supported civil rights, it did not always support the tactics used by civil rights activists. Both the President and Robert Kennedy, then Attorney General, tried to dissuade Martin Luther King from proceeding with the march on Washington in 1963. King refused, and the march went forward.

Visualizing History After crossing the Edmund Pettus Bridge outside Selma on the way to Montgomery, the marchers were set upon with tear gas and clubs.
Answer to Caption: because most African Americans who applied to vote there were turned down

Visualizing History ▲ **THE ROAD TO MONTGOMERY** Dr. Martin Luther King, Jr., led a five-day march from Selma to Montgomery, Alabama, in March 1965. Marches were an effective way for African Americans to protest discrimination. *Why was Selma chosen as the march's starting point?*

with Martin Luther King and the civil rights activists. In April 1963, King led a demonstration in Birmingham, Alabama. On the orders of Police Commissioner Eugene "Bull" Connor, police used fire hoses, clubs, and snarling dogs on demonstrators, including women and children. National television carried the sight of this violence into millions of homes across America. Viewers were shocked and outraged. Kennedy sent 3,000 troops to restore peace in the city. In June he proposed a new civil rights bill that would outlaw segregation throughout the nation.

■ Trouble in Southern Universities

During Kennedy's administration the Department of Justice brought numerous suits for desegregation of schools. In September 1962, James Meredith, a 29-year-old African American Air Force veteran, sought entrance to the University of Mississippi. Although Meredith was backed by a court order, Governor Ross Barnett declared, "Never! We will never surrender to the evil and illegal forces of tyranny." Kennedy immediately sent in federal marshals and eventually the Mississippi National Guard to enable Meredith to enter the university safely. Meredith was able to attend classes, but two people were killed in a mob action.

Another confrontation between state and federal powers took place in June 1963—this time in Alabama. Governor George Wallace symbolically stood in a doorway to prevent desegregation of the University of Alabama at Tuscaloosa. Kennedy immediately federalized the Alabama National Guard and ordered the troops to make sure African Americans were allowed to enter. As a result, Wallace backed down.

The violence of such confrontations convinced Kennedy that federal legislation against segregation and discrimination was needed. Kennedy quickly proposed laws that would forbid segregation in stores, restaurants, hotels, and theaters and that would prohibit discrimination in employment. But progress on school desegregation was slow. Most African American school children in the south continued to attend all-black schools.

UNIT 10 Redefining America: 1954–Present

Cultural Diversity

Music of Protest Popular music of the 1960s reflected the mood and temper of the times. Folksingers carried political messages in their lyrics, with such singers as Bob Dylan and Joan Baez. Rock music was revolutionized with the advent of the Beatles, and the Detroit "Motown" sound introduced new African American singers. Music of the 1960s culminated in the rock festival of 1969 at Woodstock, New York, when thousands gathered to display what many Americans thought of as the "counterculture."

CHAPTER 32
SECTION 2

■ The March on Washington

In August 1963, for the 100th anniversary of the Emancipation Proclamation, African American leaders planned to hold the largest civil rights demonstration in the nation's history. This "March on Washington for Jobs and Freedom" would press for the passage of Kennedy's proposed civil rights bill, which was being debated in Congress.

King's Dream of Freedom

More than 200,000 demonstrators, both African American and white, converged on the nation's capital. They sang hymns and spirituals as they gathered near the Lincoln Memorial. As one 15-year-old African American girl described it:

> *There was this sense of hope for the future—the belief that this march was the big step in the right direction. It could be heard in the voices of the people singing and seen in the way they walked. It poured out into smiles.*

At the Lincoln Memorial the marchers heard eloquent speeches, especially from Dr. Martin Luther King, Jr., who, in a famous address, described his dream of freedom and equality for all people:

> *I have a dream that one day this nation will rise up and live out the true meaning of its creed: 'We hold these truths to be self-evident; that all men are created equal' . . . And when this happens, and when we allow freedom to ring, when we let it ring from every village and hamlet, from every state and every city, we will be able to speed up that day when all God's children . . . [will] join hands and sing in the words of the old . . . spiritual: 'Free at last, Free at last, Thank God Almighty, we're free at last.'*

The leaders of the march then left for a meeting with President John F. Kennedy at the White House.

A New Civil Rights Act

The March on Washington was a historic event for the civil rights movement. It not only awakened millions to the plight of African Americans living in the South but also confirmed for Congress the widespread support for a civil rights bill.

Progress was slow. In 1963, 9 years after the *Brown* decision, only one-half of one percent of African American public school children in the 11 former Confederate states were attending desegregated schools. Some southern communities desegregated public facilities only after boycotts and sit-ins. Others refused, however, and some even used violence to intimidate nonviolent protestors.

After President Kennedy's assassination on November 22, 1963, President Johnson was determined to continue Kennedy's civil rights policies. So he accepted

Visualizing History

▲ **JAMES MEREDITH** In 1962, against the wishes of the governor of Mississippi, the Supreme Court ordered that James Meredith (center) be allowed to enroll at the University of Mississippi. **What action did the federal government take to enable Meredith to enter the university safely?**

Linking Across TIME

Reformers and protesters in the United States have always relied on some form of media to get across their messages. Rebelling colonists published cartoons and pamphlets. During the civil rights movement, the medium was television.

Visualizing History James Meredith became the first African American to graduate from the University of Mississippi. **Answer to Caption:** The President ordered federal and state troops to enable Meredith to enter the university in safety.

ABC NEWS INTERACTIVE™

VIDEODISC
Martin Luther King, Jr.

Side 1, Chapter 21
Title: *1963 March on Washington: Newsreel*
Subject: Newsreel account of the August 28, 1963, march on Washington

Side 1, Chapter 22
Title: *1963 March on Washington: "I Have A Dream . . ."*
Subject: Portions of King's speech

Sidelights: Memorial to a Struggle

In 1989, the Southern Poverty Law Center dedicated the Civil Rights Memorial in honor of those who died during the struggle for civil rights in the South. Located in Montgomery, Alabama—the scene of so many of the events in that cause—the memorial serves to inform and educate young people about the civil rights movement. The monument was designed by Maya Lin, the creator of the Vietnam Veterans Memorial in Washington, D.C.

CHAPTER 32 SECTION 2

ASSESS

Check Understanding
Assign Section 2 Review as homework or an in-class activity.

Evaluate
Assign the Section 2 Quiz in the TCR or use the History of a Free Nation Testmaker to create a customized quiz.

Reteach
Have students complete Reteaching Activity 32-2.

Enrich
Have students research and write a report about the activities of the Congress of Racial Equality (CORE).

CLOSE
Summarize the section by referring students to the generalization on the chapter concept map. Ask them to give examples of how the civil rights movement brought social and political change to American society.

Map Study Using Maps
Answer: Texas, Arkansas, Tennessee, and Florida

Skills Practice
Ask students to explain the change in registration of African American voters in Alabama from 1960 to 1966. (Less than 1 in 6 African Americans were registered in 1960. By 1966 nearly 1 in 2 were.)

908

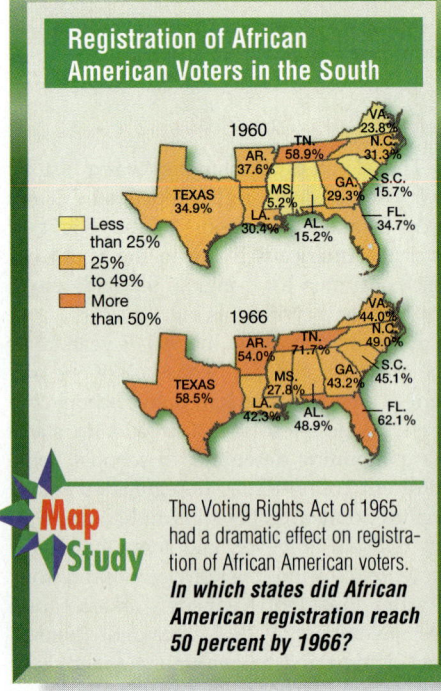

Map Study
The Voting Rights Act of 1965 had a dramatic effect on registration of African American voters. **In which states did African American registration reach 50 percent by 1966?**

the challenge of getting Kennedy's proposed bill passed. It had passed the House of Representatives in February 1964 but was stalled in the Senate where southern segregationists intended to kill it. Even though Johnson himself was from the South, he had broken with the segregationists early in his career. Johnson was aided in his goal by national remorse over Kennedy's assassination. To take advantage of this, the President called for speedy action:

> *No memorial . . . could more eloquently honor President Kennedy's memory than the earliest possible passage of the civil rights bill. . . .*

On July 2, the President signed into law the Civil Rights Act of 1964. The strongest civil rights act since Reconstruction stated that all citizens should have equal access to such public facilities as parks and libraries and to such private businesses serving the public as restaurants and theaters. It forbade discrimination in education and strengthened the right to vote. It also outlawed job discrimination because of race, sex, religion, or national origin. Passage of the Voting Rights Act of 1965 helped pave the way for more African Americans to vote. John Lewis, the head of SNCC, said:

> *These elections signal a new level of maturation in American politics. They demonstrate the willingness of white voters to set aside racial differences, and they reflect the fact that many minorities have gained the broad political experience and skills to make them solid candidates for major office.*

The Voting Rights Act of 1965 also helped other minorities. It set aside a New York state law requiring voters to be able to read English, enabling such groups as Puerto Ricans and Mexican Americans to vote.

Section 2 ★ Review

Checking for Understanding
1. **Identify** Freedom Riders, Eugene "Bull" Connor, James Meredith, March on Washington, Selma.
2. **Define** sit-in.
3. **Summarize** the advances and setbacks of the civil rights movement during Kennedy's presidency.
4. **Describe** the effects of the Voting Rights Act of 1965 on African American political power.

Critical Thinking
5. **Evaluating Events** The March on Washington is seen as one of the major events of the civil rights movement. Why was the march so effective?

908   UNIT 10 Redefining America: 1954–Present

Answers to SECTION 2 REVIEW
1. Freedom Riders, 905; Eugene "Bull" Connor, 906; James Meredith, 906; March on Washington, 907; Selma, 906
2. All vocabulary words are defined in the Glossary.
3. Advances: segregation ended in government-owned housing, blacks appointed to government offices, proposed civil rights bill, federal protection and lawsuits; Setbacks: Kennedy's cautious approach, slow pace of school desegregation, attempts to prevent African Americans from registering at universities, violence against African Americans
4. Thousands of African Americans registered to vote; African Americans elected to offices throughout the South.
5. United people of different races, religions, and backgrounds, giving hope that hatred, prejudice, and discrimination might end.

Social Studies Skills

Critical Thinking Skills

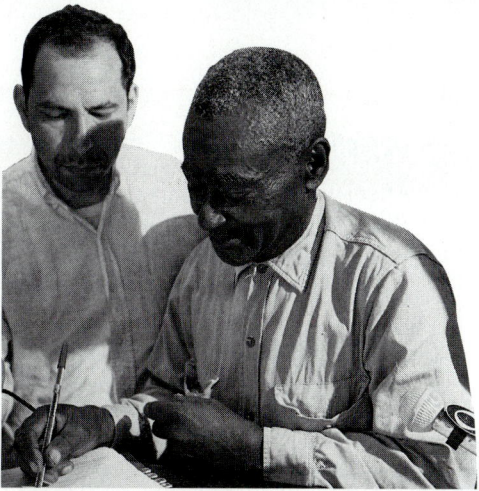
▲ REGISTERING TO VOTE, BATESVILLE, MISSISSIPPI

Identifying Cause and Effect

Passage of the Civil Rights Act of 1964 did not bring an end to the civil rights movement. Though the act had addressed segregation, there was still a battle to fight over voting rights. Despite federal laws that already granted them the vote, many African Americans in the South were deprived of their rights by threats and violence or by unfair eligibility tests.

Dr. Martin Luther King, Jr., decided it was time to push for voting rights, and selected Selma, Alabama, as the starting place for his campaign. This was because in Selma most of the African Americans who applied to vote were turned down. Dr. King wanted to dramatize this injustice.

In January 1965, King organized a voter registration drive in Selma. However, the county sheriff deputized whites and attacked groups of African Americans with dogs and cattle prods as they tried to register.

On March 7, Dr. King organized a "march for freedom" from Selma, Alabama, to the state capitol in Montgomery, 50 miles away. More than 25,000 people from all over the country joined in. Police armed with billy clubs, bullwhips, and tear gas, urged on by angry mobs, met the marchers. Many marchers were injured in the clash that followed, and 2 white demonstrators were killed. The marchers reached Montgomery only after Johnson sent federal troops to provide protection.

National outrage over events in Selma helped speed the passage of the Voting Rights Act of 1965. It did away with literacy tests in many southern states and provided for federal assistance in registering African Americans. Steps were also taken to eliminate the poll tax, forbidden by the Twenty-fourth Amendment yet still used to keep the poor from voting. In a single year, more than 400,000 people, mostly African Americans who had not previously voted, were registered.

As a result, African American candidates began to win election as state legislators, mayors, and members of Congress. Within 25 years after the Voting Rights Act, the number of African American elected officials in the South rose from about 100 to 5,000. Southern politicians who had championed desegregation appealed to African American voters for support in their election campaigns.

Practicing the Skill

1. Why did Dr. Martin Luther King, Jr., select Selma, Alabama, as the starting place for the movement's voting rights campaign?
2. What effect did the events at Selma have on subsequent voting rights legislation?

909

Answers to SOCIAL STUDIES SKILLS

1. to dramatize the injustice of voting discrimination in the city
2. National outrage helped speed passage of the Voting Rights Act of 1965.

LESSON PLAN
Mastering Social Studies Skills

Teaching Critical Thinking Skills

Review *cause* and *effect* by asking students to define these terms. (A cause is any condition, person, or event that makes something happen. What happens as a result of a cause is known as an effect.) Select and discuss with students an instance in which recognizing cause-effect relationships has enhanced their understanding of a situation or event. Discuss whether recognizing cause-effect relationships is crucial to understanding history.

Did You Know?

When many African Americans in the South registered to vote, they were threatened with the loss of their jobs. One woman who was fired as a timekeeper on a cotton plantation in Mississippi was Fannie Lou Hamer. When she lost her job, she immediately joined SNCC and became actively involved in the voter registration drives of the summer of 1961.

ABCNEWS InterACTIVE

 **VIDEODISC**
Martin Luther King, Jr.

Side 1, Chapter 3
Title: *Ted Koppel: MLK Overview*
Subject: Brief overview of the life of Dr. Martin Luther King, Jr.

LESSON PLAN
SECTION 3, 910–914

FOCUS

Bellringer
Prior to taking roll at the beginning of the class period, display Focus Activity Transparency 111 on the overhead projector and assign the accompanying Focus Activity Sheet.

Objectives
Point out the objectives on this page to students in previewing the section content.

Motivating Activity
Explain to students that in 1964, Martin Luther King, Jr., received the Nobel Peace Prize for his use of nonviolent resistance in the civil rights movement. At the same time, more radical African Americans were beginning to question the effectiveness of nonviolence. Ask students to write a paragraph or two speculating on how they think more militant leaders might affect the civil rights movement. Point out that this section describes discontent among African Americans and describes actions they took.

SECTION 3

New Directions

Setting the Scene

Section Focus
As the civil rights movement progressed, African Americans found their situation unchanged in many ways. Laws had not altered prejudice, and improvement in their economic status had practically ceased. As many African Americans were stopped from exercising their rights, some began to change their ideas about how to go about gaining equality.

Objectives
After studying this section, you should be able to
★ list some of the factors responsible for discontent among some African Americans.
★ explain what new philosophies were developed by African Americans to deal with the discontent.

Key Terms
racism, black nationalism, black power, assimilation, busing

◀ MALCOLM X HAT

Despite gains made at the national, state, and local levels through peaceful change in cooperation with whites, progress in civil rights was slow. It was especially slow in social and economic areas. Unemployment for African Americans, for example, was much higher than the national average. As a result, by the mid-1960s a growing number of African Americans adopted a new, more radical approach to the problem of **racism,** that is, racial prejudice or discrimination. They believed in taking immediate action not only to gain political and legal rights, but to end discrimination in housing, education, and employment. Instead of following King's philosophy of integration and nonviolence, radical groups began to put forward a new theory and expressed their willingness to use violence to protect themselves and to achieve just treatment.

■ New Leadership
Many whites reacted with alarm to the new direction in the civil rights movement. They were especially worried about groups that openly preached black revolution. These whites felt the new philosophies African Americans were developing threatened their way of life.

The Black Muslims
The Nation of Islam, known as the Black Muslims, was originally founded in 1930, and was led by Elijah Muhammed. This group appealed to African Americans to embrace the Islamic faith and preached **black nationalism.** This philosophy stated that African Americans should completely separate themselves from whites and form their own self-governing communities—their own

UNIT 10 Redefining America: 1954–Present

Classroom Resources for SECTION 3

Teacher's Classroom Resources
- Reproducible Lesson Plan
- Reteaching Activity 32-3
- Section Quiz

Multimedia
- Section Focus Transparency 111
- Testmaker
- Student Self-Test Software
- Martin Luther King, Jr.

nation. They also advocated a program of self-defense. Their ideas—popularized by a talented speaker and minister known as Malcolm X—received national attention in the early 1960s. In his autobiography, Malcolm X talked about his views:

> ... I'm not for wanton violence, I'm for justice.... I feel that when the law fails to protect [African Americans] from whites' attacks, then those [African Americans] should use arms, if necessary, to defend themselves....

By 1964, however, Malcolm X came to favor an integrated society instead of separatism. Therefore, he broke with the Black Muslims. Apparently as a result of his public disagreements with them, he was shot and killed in February 1965. Although in the end Malcolm X came to favor integration, his earlier ideas continued to influence many young African Americans after his death. By late 1960s, the Student Nonviolent Coordinating Committee (SNCC) and the Congress of Racial Equality (CORE), which had originally supported King's tactics, had become more radical.

Black Power

In May 1966, the head of SNCC, Stokely Carmichael, developed the idea of **black power** to further racial equality. This philosophy stated that blacks should "take back control of all aspects of their lives—social, political, and economic. As expounded by the black nationalists, it meant separation from white society, by violent means if necessary."

The philosophy of black power moved away from the idea of **assimilation**—the policy of incorporating different racial or cultural groups into the dominant society—and preached racial distinctiveness, pride, and leadership.

Many members and leaders of the civil rights movement had been white liberals. Now groups like SNCC and CORE moved whites out of leadership positions. African Americans began to reexamine their African heritage. Some took African names or wore "Afro" hairstyles and African-style clothing. They demanded that schools adopt programs in African-American studies.

Black power created a deep division among civil rights activists. This new idea was firmly rejected by such groups as the NAACP, which saw it as a threat to law and order. However, it would be black power that, from this point on, would more strongly influence the future development of the civil rights movement.

The Black Panthers

One of the most militant black-power groups was the Black Panthers. Founded in 1966 by Huey Newton, Bobby Seale, and Eldridge Cleaver, the Black Panthers urged African Americans to arm themselves and confront white society in order to force whites to grant them equal rights. Cleaver's *Soul on Ice* (1967) served as a statement of Black Panthers' aims:

Visualizing History ▲ **NATION OF ISLAM** The Nation of Islam, founded in Detroit, Michigan, in 1931 by Wali Farad, gained many converts during the 1950s and 1960s. *What were the goals and objectives of black nationalism?*

CHAPTER 32
SECTION 3

Independent Practice

Oral History Have students draw up questions in order to conduct an interview with someone who lived through the civil rights movement. Help students prepare questions that will get the interviewee to tell how his or her life changed as a result of the civil rights movement. Have students present their interviews to the class. Discuss how the interviews compare with information in the text. **L2**

Teaching American Portraits

Tell students that Malcolm X encouraged young people to think of themselves as part of an African majority not an African American minority. He believed that there could be no unity between African Americans and white Americans until African Americans themselves were united. Ask students why they think such a message might appeal to young people. (would give them a sense of pride and belonging, might make some feel superior)

> *What the white man must be brought to understand is that the black man . . . does not intend to be tricked again into another hundred-year forfeit of freedom. Not for a single moment or for any price will the black men now rising up in America settle for anything less than their full . . . share . . . in the sovereignty of America.*

■ The Battle in the North

Although the major battles for civil rights were fought in the South, the movement's leaders recognized that segregation and prejudice also existed in the North. King shifted his demonstrations from the South to such northern cities as Chicago, where he protested housing discrimination, unemployment, and urban poverty. Northern African American populations tended to be concentrated in the inner cities, where poverty was widespread and discontent was high.

Discontent Leads to Riots

Frustration over urban conditions led to a series of riots in many cities. Often occurring in the heat of summer, these riots were sometimes triggered by an incident between police and African American citizens. When riots erupted, looting and burning also broke out.

The first major riot took place in the Harlem section of New York City in July 1964. Other riots broke out that year in Philadelphia and Chicago. In August 1965, a riot in the African American neighborhood of Watts in Los Angeles left 34 people dead, more than 3,000 arrested, and $20 million in property damage. The summer of 1966 brought new disruptions in New York, Atlanta, Cleveland, Detroit, Chicago, San Francisco, and Los Angeles. Federal troops and National Guardsmen entered Detroit in July 1967, after much of the city was in flames. When the riot was over, 40 people had been killed and hundreds more were injured. Thousands were left homeless, and many businesses were in ashes.

Most of the riots took place outside the South, in parts of the United Stated where African Americans supposedly enjoyed

AMERICAN PORTRAITS

Malcolm X
1925–1965

Born Malcolm Little in Omaha, Nebraska, this future religious leader and activist became a member of the Nation of Islam while serving a prison sentence for burglary. As was the custom in this religious sect, Malcolm dropped his "slave" name in favor of the letter X.

Malcolm X became a powerful and eloquent minister in the Nation of Islam. He taught the religious faith while advocating a position of independent African American political action, black power, pride, and self-defense. The Nation of Islam, sometimes referred to as the Black Muslim movement, stressed the need for African American unity, and advocated a position of separation in a time when most civil rights workers dedicated themselves to achieving racial and economic integration.

Malcolm X eventually broke with the Nation of Islam, moderated his separatist stance, and agreed to work with other civil rights activists to fight racism, discrimination, and injustice. However, Malcolm was assassinated shortly thereafter by rival members of the Nation of Islam.

912 UNIT 10 Redefining America: 1954–Present

Critical Thinking

Evaluating Have students write an essay comparing the strategies of the Kennedy administration and those of the Nixon administration concerning the civil rights movement. Ask students to evaluate the two in terms of their effects on the progress of the movement. Have them conclude with a statement describing how government can influence the course of reform and change in a society. **L2**

 **SUMMER OF 1965** Members of the National Guard patrol the streets of the Watts section of Los Angeles in August 1965. Watts was the site of one of many urban racial confrontations to erupt in the United States during the middle and late 1960s. *What event set off a wave of riots in April 1968?*

equal rights. Adam Clayton Powell, Jr., an African American member of Congress from New York City, offered an explanation. In the South, he said, what African Americans wanted was relatively easy for whites to give: the right to sit at a drugstore counter or in the front of a bus. In the North, African Americans had long been able to sit where they pleased. Now they wanted "a bigger piece of the pie"—better jobs, more money, better places to live. Some white jobholders and property owners felt threatened.

The Kerner Commission

In response to the violence spreading across America, President Johnson appointed a National Advisory Commission on Civil Disorders, known as the Kerner Commission, to look into the problem. The Kerner Commission laid responsibility for the ghettos at the feet of white society.

Although African Americans suffered greater loss of life and property, the riots tended to harden white prejudices. The urgently requested commission report was quietly received and produced little change.

The Death of Martin Luther King, Jr.

Despite the Kerner Commission report, violence continued to grow. Then in 1968 the violence reached a climax with the assassination of Dr. Martin Luther King, Jr. In April of that year, King was in Memphis, Tennessee, to support a strike of African American sanitation workers. He was planning a national poor people's campaign to promote economic gains for African Americans and all poor people.

There had been many threats against King's life over the years. Dr. King, however, had always dismissed them. Yet prophetically, King told a church meeting the night of April 3:

> ❝ . . . I've been to the mountain top, and I don't mind. . . . I've looked over and I've seen the Promised Land. I may not get there with you, but I want you to know tonight that we as a people will get to the Promised Land. ❞

CHAPTER 32 The Civil Rights Era 1954–1975   **913**

CHAPTER 32 SECTION 3

ABC NEWS INTERACTIVE

The following materials are available from Glencoe and may be used to enrich Chapter 32:

VIDEODISC
Martin Luther King, Jr.

Side One
Chapter 38: Memphis, the Final Stop

Side One
Chapter 39: His Final Speech April 3

Side One
Chapter 40: ABC Special Report, April 4, 1968

Visualizing History The Watts riot was the first of a series of racial disorders that hit cities throughout the United States in the summers of 1965, 1966, and 1967.
Answer to caption: assassination of Martin Luther King

Special Needs

Study Strategy The development of metacognitive understandings in students is aided by teacher explanation. This means that the teacher describes critical features of the strategy. Summarizing is one strategy that students have practiced before. Have students read the subsection titled *The Kerner Report*. Explain to them that summarizing is a process of restating the information in the text. Then explain each component of summarizing: reading, thinking about essential elements of the text, framing the information in succinct units, and writing it.

◀ STOKELY CARMICHAEL

The next day, he was killed by a sniper. Ironically, the murder of the great teacher of nonviolence set off a week of rioting, arson, and looting in 125 American cities. It was as if King's death swept away the last bit of faith in a peaceful solution. "America," announced Stokely Carmichael, "must be burned down in order for us to survive." Rioting took place in Washington, D.C., just blocks from the White House. President Johnson ordered troops to enforce a curfew and protect government buildings.

■ The Civil Rights Movement After 1968

Between the *Brown* decision and King's death, the civil rights movement made great gains. After King died, however, the movement's leaders feared that they would begin to lose some of their hard-won victories. Richard Nixon, who won the presidency in 1968, had his own agenda. He wanted to make the Republicans so powerful that they would control both the White House and Congress in 1972. To do that, he needed to lure southern Democrats into the Republican ranks.

To this end, Nixon developed a "southern strategy." He appointed a southern justice to the Supreme Court. The President also reversed a Johnson administration policy that cut off federal funds to racially segregated school systems. Although federal policy had been affirmed in 1968 by the Supreme Court in *Green* v. *County School Board*, Nixon ignored the Court's ruling and instructed the Justice Department to support school boards that were seeking to delay desegregation.

Contrary to Nixon's hopes, his appointments to the Supreme Court did not guarantee a reversal of the *Green* decision. Instead, the Court affirmed integration by means of **busing**—transporting children to a school outside their residential area to achieve racial balance in that school. White Americans in the South and most other regions of the nation resisted busing, and Nixon denounced it. The Nixon administration's open opposition to busing for desegregation intensified public controversy over the issue.

Nixon's agenda moved many people and much of government policy to the right, away from the liberal policies of the Kennedy-Johnson years. Many civil rights gains were lost or delayed. However, despite the setback, the movement continued. It would make gains in the future and strongly influence other minorities.

Section 3 ★ Review

Checking for Understanding

1. **Identify** Malcolm X, Stokely Carmichael, Kerner Commission, Watts, "southern strategy."
2. **Define** racism, black nationalism, black power, assimilation, busing.
3. **Summarize** the goals of the black-power movement.
4. **Cite** two reasons for the summer riots during the 1960s.

Critical Thinking

5. **Making Comparisons** Explain how the views of Malcom X on the problem of racism differed from those of Martin Luther King, Jr.

UNIT 10 Redefining America: 1954–Present

SECTION 4

The Impact of Civil Rights

Setting the Scene

Section Focus

All the efforts made by civil rights activists during the 1950s and 1960s had a far greater impact than just to help African Americans gain equality in America. Other disadvantaged groups—women, Hispanics, and Native Americans—found new hope in the African Americans' struggle and formed movements of their own. These movements found support because of the atmosphere in the nation as a whole. Because of the civil rights struggle and the Vietnam War, a great number of people had begun to question the status of American society and the policies of the government.

Objectives

After studying this section, you should be able to
★ describe the gains made by women and minorities.
★ explain why the Equal Rights Amendment was not ratified.

Key Terms

feminist, sexism, bilingualism

▶ Shirley Chisholm

During the 1960s and 1970s, young Americans became leaders in promoting social justice. They were determined to close the gap between the realities of American life—discrimination, poverty, and social inequalities—and the nation's ideal of "liberty and justice for all."

■ The Woman's Rights Movement

Women constituted more than 50 percent of the population in the United States in the 1970s. However, their political, economic, legal, and social status resembled that of a disadvantaged minority. Minority women faced a special problem in that they encountered sexual and racial discrimination at the same time.

Status of Women

In 1977 women held less than 5 percent of the elective offices in the United States. There had been few female senators or governors, no Supreme Court justices, and no mayors of major cities in the history of the republic. Of the 435 members of the House of Representatives, only 18 were women. In her autobiography *Unbought and Unbossed*, Shirley Chisholm, the first African American woman to serve in the House of Representatives, wrote:

 When I decided to run for Congress, I knew I would encounter both anti-black and anti-feminist sentiments. What surprised me was the much greater virulence of the sex discrimination.

CHAPTER 32 The Civil Rights Era 1954–1975   915

Classroom Resources for SECTION 4

Teacher's Classroom Resources
- Reproducible Lesson Plan
- Reteaching Activity 32-4
- Chapter 32 Enrichment Activity
- Chapter 32 Performance Assessment Activity
- Spanish Summaries and Glossary
- Section Quiz

Multimedia
- Section Focus Transparency 112
- Vocabulary Puzzlemaker
- Testmaker
- Student Self-Test Software
- The American People: Fabric of a Nation

LESSON PLAN
SECTION 4, 915–919

FOCUS

Bellringer

Prior to taking roll at the beginning of the class period, display Focus Activity Transparency 112 on the overhead projector and assign the accompanying Focus Activity Sheet.

Objectives

Point out the objectives on this page to students in previewing the section content.

Motivating Activity

Ask students to consider how women and minority groups are portrayed today in television and films. Have them speculate about the ways the movement for equal rights for women and minorities may have affected these portrayals. Explain that Section 4 traces the impact of the struggle for equal rights on women and minorities.

 VIDEODISC

- *GTV: The American People: Fabric of a Nation*

Side 4, Chapter 1
Title: *America's Choir*
Subject: A profile of Americans in the 90s

See GTV Guide page 90 for complete lesson plan.

CHAPTER 32 SECTION 4

TEACH
Guided Practice
Point out to students that the women's movement is often referred to as the "women's liberation movement." Ask students to write a short news feature titled "Women's Liberation," explaining why the movement was so named. **L1**

Did You Know?
In the past, many people lumped women together with minority groups, using such references as "women and other minorities." In fact, women in the United States are not a minority but make up a little more than the majority of the population.

Visualizing History
The same year that Congress voted to submit the ERA, it also passed The Equal Employment Opportunity Act, which provided the power to enforce the sex discrimination provisions of the 1964 Civil Rights Act through the courts.

Answer to Caption: It failed to obtain the votes needed for ratification

▼ GLORIA STEINEM

Visualizing History ▲ ERA MARCHERS The Equal Rights Amendment, submitted to the states in 1972 for ratification, aroused strong feelings among supporters and opponents. *What happened to the Equal Rights Amendment?*

Representative Chisholm was elected for a second term in 1970. In 1972 she ran against George McGovern for the Democratic nomination for President. She served in Congress for the next decade and continued to support equal rights for minorities and women. After serving in Congress, she then turned her talent to teaching on the college level. About her accomplishments, she noted:

> ❝ I hope that my having made it, the hard way, can be some kind of inspiration, particularly to women. ❞

In 1960 women made up one-third of the nation's workforce. Yet, most of their jobs offered less pay and prestige than those positions that men held. For every dollar on average that a man earned on a job in the 1960s, a woman with the same job earned only 59 cents. During the rest of the 1960s and into the next decade the economic situation of women improved slightly.

In 1976 the United States Department of Labor reported that full-time working men averaged 75 percent more pay than full-time working women. Dissatisfied with the slow progress, many women began calling for stronger action.

The publication in 1963 of *The Feminine Mystique* by Betty Friedan had inspired demands for change. Friedan rejected the notion that the destiny of women was only to be wives and mothers. She described how the media had created an image of women that was designed to imprison them in their households and bar serious consideration of them as competitors in the labor market.

National Organization for Women

In 1966 Betty Friedan joined with other **feminists,** or women activists, to establish the National Organization for Women (NOW). The organization's Statement of Purpose read:

> ❝ . . . [To] take action to bring women into full participation in the mainstream of American society now, assuming all the privileges and responsibilities thereof in truly equal partnership with men. ❞

Among its early successes, NOW helped end separate classified employment ads for men and women, and airline rules that required female flight attendants to retire at age 32. In the 1960s and 1970s, NOW and

UNIT 10 Redefining America: 1954–Present

Critical Thinking

Comparing Suggest students compare the women's movements in the nineteenth and early twentieth centuries with that of the 1960s and 1970s. How were the leaders similar? What differences seem most striking? How were their objectives alike? How did each movement influence American society? Which was the more militant or radical? Students might present their comparisons orally or as a report to the class. **L2**

▲ PHYLLIS SCHLAFLY

similar groups helped increasing numbers of women to enter professions. Banks, realtors, and department stores were forced to grant loans, mortgages, leases, and credit that they long had denied to female applicants.

The Equal Rights Amendment

Following intense lobbying by women's groups, in 1972 Congress voted to submit the Equal Rights Amendment (ERA) to the states for ratification. This amendment stated that "equality of rights under the law shall not be denied or abridged by the United States or by any state on account of sex."

Not all women supported ERA, however. Phyllis Schlafly, founder of STOP ERA, dismissed the women's rights movement as "a series of sharp-tongued, high-pitched, whining complaints by unmarried women." STOP ERA supporters contended that the ERA would force women to give up their traditional roles as wives and mothers, and that they would lose certain legal protections in the family and in the workplace. As a result of a vigorous campaign by STOP ERA and other groups, the Equal Rights Amendment failed to obtain the votes needed for ratification.

Women Make Progress

Despite the failure of the ERA, women continued to make progress. **Sexism**—treating people differently because of their gender—was recognized and outlawed in the workplace by 1971. Princeton, Yale, and other traditionally all-male colleges began to open their doors to females.

Women were also becoming increasingly important in the business world. By the mid-1970s, nearly half of all married women worked outside the home; almost all who had graduated from college worked.

Women also were becoming an important force in politics in the 1970s. By the 1980s, there were more women than ever in both the Senate and the House of Representatives, as well as on the Supreme Court, in the cabinet, and in state government offices. In 1984, Representative Geraldine Ferraro became the first female major-party candidate to run for Vice President.

■ Hispanic Activism

At this time, Hispanics also became active in campaigning for equal rights. By the 1970s Hispanic Americans had become the second-largest minority in the United States, next to African Americans. Spanish-speaking people made up almost 8 percent of the population and were the largest minority group in several states. New York City alone had about 2 million Spanish-speaking people. Part of Miami, Florida, became known as "Little Havana" because it was home to hundreds of thousands of Cuban immigrants.

▲ **HISPANIC AMERICANS** By the 1970s Hispanic Americans were the second-largest minority in the United States. **What group made up the largest number of Hispanics?**

CHAPTER 32 The Civil Rights Era 1954–1975

Cooperative Learning

Making a Graph Divide students into three groups and assign one of the following to each: women, Hispanics, Native Americans. Ask each group to research recent economic gains in terms of earnings and employment and create a line or bar graph showing trends in the last 10 years. When the graphs are completed, have groups present them to the class and summarize their findings. **L2**

CHAPTER 32
SECTION 4

Independent Practice

Supporting an Opinion Tell students that the struggle for full civil rights for all Americans continues in the 1990s. Ask students to write an editorial in which they identify groups that still experience discrimination. Have them explain the issues involved, why the prejudice persists, and possible solutions. **L3**

Betty Friedan was a major leader in the women's movement. Her book *The Feminine Mystique* stirred tremendous controversy and became a bible for many women in the struggle for equal rights. In the early 1990s, Friedan again became the center of controversy when she seemed to back away from her earlier, more radical views.

Visualizing History Among Hispanic Americans who worked to secure equal rights was Rodolfo Gonzalis who organized the Crusade for Justice and was active in the Chicano Movement.

Answer to caption: Mexican Americans

CHAPTER 32
SECTION 4

Did You Know?

In 1972, Shirley Chisholm ran as a presidential candidate in the primaries. She got enough votes to put her name on the ballot at the Democratic National Convention. Although Chisholm did not receive enough votes to be nominated, her candidacy showed that a woman and an African American could aspire to the highest office in the land.

Linking Across Time

The struggle of Native Americans for equality and justice has been a long one. From their first encounters with Europeans, they experienced the loss of their lands and their ways of life. The federal government has gone back and forth in its efforts to either assimilate Native Americans or separate them onto reservations. Today, Native Americans are fighting in the courts to regain land rights and have organized to lobby for their cause.

Mexican Americans made up the largest group of Hispanic peoples. For years, thousands of Mexican Americans labored as migrant farm workers, moving from place to place to harvest seasonal crops. They were not protected by federal minimum-wage laws, unemployment insurance, or social security.

In 1965 Cesar Chavez organized a nationwide coalition and asked Americans to boycott California grapes picked by nonunion labor. After enduring five years of such persistent protest, most California grape growers relented and agreed to sign a contract with Chavez's union, the United Farm Workers.

During the 1970s, Hispanic Americans began to organize. The League of United Latin American Citizens (LULAC) won suits in federal courts to guarantee Hispanic Americans the right to serve on juries, to send their children to unsegregated schools, and to be taught in Spanish as well as in English. The use of two languages is called **bilingualism.** As their political strength grew, more Hispanic Americans were elected to local and state offices as well as to Congress.

Native Americans Organize

Like the Hispanics, Native Americans organized during the 1960s and 1970s. Their plight captured national attention when a 1966 study revealed that Native Americans suffered from malnutrition and disease to such an extent that their life expectancy was only 46 years. They had less formal education than any other minority group, and their family income was less than one-half the national average.

Termination Policy

After World War II, the federal government tried to incorporate Native Americans into white society. A new policy called "termination" was established in 1953. This meant that the federal government stopped recognizing Native American nations as legal entities that were separate from state government. Now, the nations would be subject to the same local governments as whites. The government in Washington worked to make Native Americans give up their cultures and adapt to white society.

Native Americans were so angry that they began speaking out more forcibly. A group of younger Native Americans had breathed life into the National Congress of

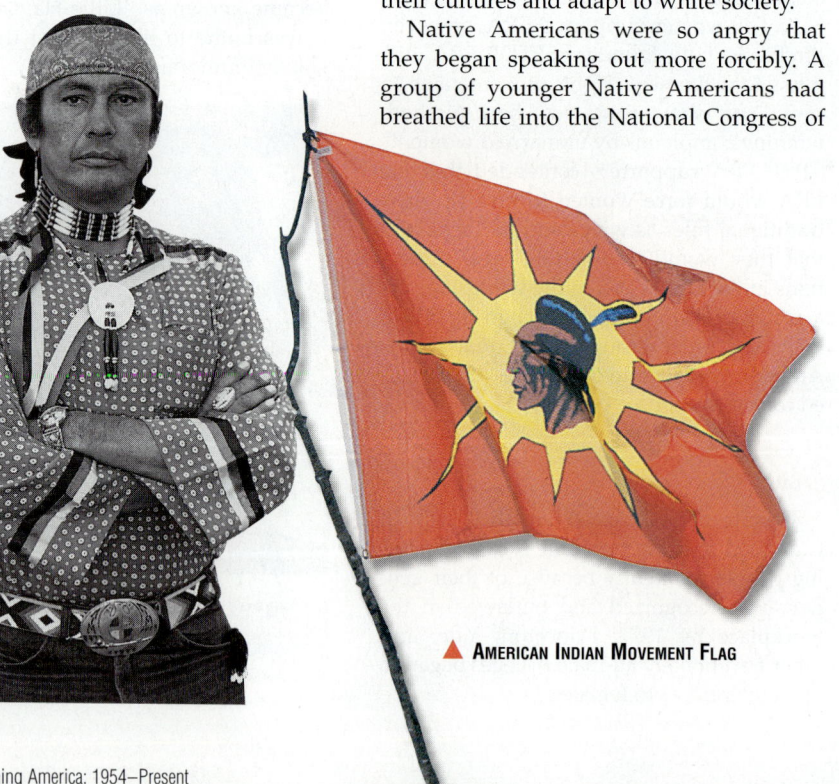

▶ RUSSELL MEANS, AIM LEADER

▲ AMERICAN INDIAN MOVEMENT FLAG

UNIT 10 Redefining America: 1954–Present

Critical Thinking

Analyzing Gains Although women and minorities have gained many rights and opportunities as a result of the civil rights movement, much remains to be done. Ask student to identify areas where they think more could be done to ensure that all Americans have equal rights. Have students write their ideas in the form of a letter to their representative in Congress. Invite volunteers to read their letters and discuss with the class the areas they feel are most important. **L2**

American Indians (NCAI), set up in 1944. As a result of their activity, President Eisenhower put a stop to termination without consent. Later Presidents did not revive it during the 1960s. They made some efforts to provide tribes with government money.

Declaration of Indian Purpose

In 1961, more than 400 representatives of 67 Native American nations met in Chicago to draw up a bill of rights for Native Americans. They called it the Declaration of Indian Purpose, and in it they committed themselves to Indian nationalism and intertribal unity. The delegates also stated their belief in "red power," and demanded an end to federal control of Native American affairs. "We simply want to run our lives our own way," said one young leader.

As a result, in 1968, the Congress passed the Indian Civil Rights Act, which guaranteed Native American reservation dwellers some of the rights provided to other citizens under the Bill of Rights.

However, some Native Americans wanted to take more direct action. In the state of Washington, men from more than 50 Native American groups led a "fish-in." They deliberately broke game laws and risked imprisonment to protest the loss of their former fishing and hunting grounds.

In 1973 a more militant group, the American Indian Movement (AIM), seized the reservation at Wounded Knee, South Dakota. They demanded that lands taken from Native Americans in violation of federal treaties be returned. They also demanded that development programs on reservations be managed by their own governments, and not the federal Bureau of Indian Affairs. The takeover ended after a standoff between federal agents and Native Americans, and federal policies toward Native Americans began to change.

The Pueblo of Taos, New Mexico, regained Blue Lake, a place sacred to their religious life. In 1975 a federal court declared that the Passamaquoddy and the Penobscot nations had a valid claim to more than half the state of Maine and to $25 billion in damages and unpaid rents.

Visualizing History ▲ **NATIVE AMERICANS** Native Americans fought in the nation's wars and honored those who gave their lives for freedom. Many pressed for economic and political equality and compensation for the loss of their land. *What action did Native Americans take at Wounded Knee in 1973?*

Section 4 ★ Review

Checking for Understanding

1. **Identify** Shirley Chisholm, Betty Friedan, NOW, ERA, Phyllis Schlafly, Cesar Chavez, LULAC, "red power," AIM.
2. **Define** feminist, sexism, bilingualism.
3. **List** three inequalities between men and women that existed in the 1970s.
4. **State** two demands that were made by Hispanics and Native Americans.

Critical Thinking

5. **Analyzing Point of View** Analyze the backlash to the women's rights movement in the 1970s. What stereotypes of women continue to exist today?

CHAPTER 32 The Civil Rights Era 1954–1975

REVIEW CHAPTER 32

Answers

Reviewing Facts

1. public schools desegregated; southern resistance created
2. King emerged as leader of civil rights movement; bus company ended segregation on buses.
3. Supreme Court desegregation ruling, 1954; Montgomery bus boycott, 1955; formation of SCLC, 1957; Civil Rights Act, 1957; Little Rock desegregation battle, 1957; sit-in movement, 1960; freedom rides, 1961; James Meredith entered U. of Mississippi, 1962; Birmingham demonstration, 1963; March on Washington, 1963
4. pushed through Voting Rights Act
5. divided civil rights movements into moderates and radicals; helped spark a backlash against African Americans
6. economic, social, and political equality with men
7. Native Americans have gained more control over their own lives and have gained back or been compensated for some of their land.

Understanding Concepts

1. Answers will vary but may include increased incomes and more wages in which African Americans wanted to share; more African Americans attended college, giving them desire to gain professional positions; television, which presented only a white view of society but gave exposure to civil rights movement.

CHAPTER 32 ★ REVIEW

Using Vocabulary

Using the following vocabulary terms, write a paragraph describing the development of the civil rights movement.

nonviolent resistance sit-in
federalized racism
black nationalism black power
assimilation busing

Reviewing Facts

1. **List** two results of the Supreme Court's *Brown v. Board of Education* ruling.
2. **Cite** two results of the Montgomery bus boycott.
3. **Arrange** in chronological order significant events in the civil rights movement that occurred between 1953 and 1963.
4. **Describe** how Johnson followed through on Kennedy's policies regarding civil rights.
5. **List** two results of the black power movement.
6. **Describe** the aims and objectives of the woman's rights movement.
7. **Summarize** advances made by Native American peoples.

Understanding Concepts

Civil Rights

1. Explain the factors in American society that helped the civil rights movement grow.
2. Evaluate the importance of leadership to the civil rights movement in the 1950s and 1960s.

Social Upheaval

3. Compare the results of the late 1960s riots with the goals of the black power movement. Use this information to formulate an opinion of the use of violence in demonstrations.
4. Why did the civil rights movement cause so much turmoil? Explain how the demands of African Americans affected other minorities and what the results were.

Critical Thinking

1. **Evaluating Tactics** Though Martin Luther King, Jr.'s, methods for change were nonviolent, they were not passive. What were some challenges faced by nonviolent civil rights demonstrators? Why was their nonviolence an effective tactic?
2. **Analyzing Fine Art** Study the mural that appears on this page. Then answer the questions that follow.
   a. Describe what the mural is showing.
   b. What can you tell about the artist by looking at the mural?
   c. What can you tell from the mural about the artist's feelings toward African American culture?

Writing About History

Description

Imagine that you are one of the first freedom riders on a bus traveling in the South during the spring of 1961. Write a two-page paper in which you describe your feelings and fears as you take part in this pioneering civil rights tactic. Describe various incidents that occur along the highway and at stops at segregated bus terminals. Describe the human feelings of other African Americans and whites accompanying you on the freedom rides. Include at least one conversation you have with another rider.

UNIT 10 Redefining America: 1954–Present

2. Answers will vary. Possible response: leadership was essential—boycotts, sit-ins, and demonstrations required effective organization. King's leadership and vision supplied the movement with effective tactics and ideas.
3. Responses will vary but students are likely to suggest that the riots led many Americans, both African American and white, to oppose the militant and radical goals of the black power movement.
4. The movement attempted to bring reform and change and threatened the status quo. The gains won by African Americans encouraged other groups to protest and demand equal rights. Results varied, but both Native Americans and Hispanics gained more opportunities and social and political rights.

CHAPTER 32 ★ REVIEW

Cooperative Learning

You will work in a group with two others to analyze three activist movements of the 1970s: the women's rights movement, the Hispanic movement, and the Native American movement. The goal of your group is to find as many similarities between these movements as you can. Each group member should choose one of these movements. First, work individually to make a list of the goals of each group and the methods used to attain them. Next, work with your partners to compile a master list of similarities between the three movements. Present your list to the class and discuss the findings.

Social Studies Skills

Interpreting Demographic Data

Demographics is the data used to show the characteristics of a human population in terms of size, growth, density distribution, and vital statistics. The information can be presented in a number of ways: in circle graphs, bar graphs, or line graphs. One application of demographic data in the study of history or political science is to understand the relative voting strength of different ethnic groups. Candidates for political office need demographic information about their region in order to identify and target voter groups and to devise strategies that will attract those voters.

Practicing the Skill

Study the circle graph on this page, which shows the racial background of United States citizens and the origins of Hispanics according to the 1990 census.

1. What does the circle graph suggest about the problems a small group such as Native Americans might have effecting change through the political process?
2. The Asian American population almost doubled between 1980 and 1990. Hypothesize reasons this rate of growth might be higher than that of other ethnic minorities.
3. Since persons of Hispanic origin could be of any race, they are not identified in the race circle graph. How would inclusion of Hispanics affect the existing percentages in the race chart?
4. What do the numbers in parentheses represent? What changes does this information show?

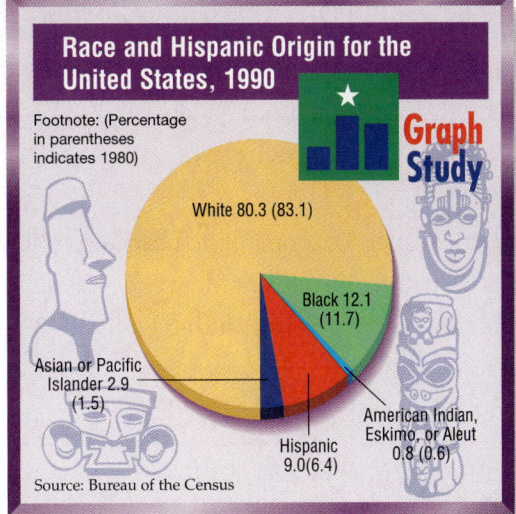

Graph Study

Race and Hispanic Origin for the United States, 1990

Footnote: (Percentage in parentheses indicates 1980)

- White 80.3 (83.1)
- Black 12.1 (11.7)
- Asian or Pacific Islander 2.9 (1.5)
- Hispanic 9.0 (6.4)
- American Indian, Eskimo, or Aleut 0.8 (0.6)

Source: Bureau of the Census

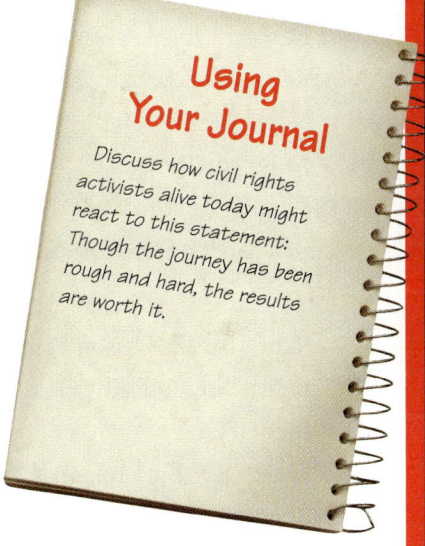

Using Your Journal

Discuss how civil rights activists alive today might react to this statement: Though the journey has been rough and hard, the results are worth it.

REVIEW ★ CHAPTER 32

by how much each would decrease is not known.
4. Politicians who represent a significant Hispanic constituency need to know the issues of these groups.

? Chapter Bonus Test Question

This question may be used for extra credit on the chapter test. What kinds of gains do you think African Americans and other minorities might experience in the first decades of the next century. (Responses will vary but should include political and economic issues.)

Using Your Journal

Most students are likely to agree. Many gains were made and the example of the civil rights movement continues to inspire people to fight for equal rights.

CHAPTER 32 The Civil Rights Era 1954–1975

Critical Thinking

1. Demonstrators faced physical and psychological abuse. Repercussions could have included backlash among sympathetic whites and lessened federal protection for violent activists.

2. a. Answers will vary, but students may note that a celebration is depicted.
   b. Answers will vary but may include artist used bright colors.
   c. Answers may vary but may include the painting shows pride in African American culture.

Practicing the Skill

1. Their small numbers might lead them to pursue political strategies other than running for elective office.
2. Continued immigration from Asian countries might explain a high growth rate.
3. The existing percentages would be reduced. However,

PLANNING GUIDE   Chapter 33   The Vietnam Era

Daily Lesson Objectives	Teacher Classroom Resources	Multimedia
SECTION 1 **Cold War Challenges in the 1960s** **1 Day** pp. 924–928 1. Discuss Kennedy's responses to Soviet and international communism. 2. Explain the purposes of the Alliance for Progress and the Peace Corps.	Chapter 33 Study Guide Reproducible Lesson Plan Reteaching Activity 33-1 Section Quiz Chapter 33 Cooperative Learning Activity Chapter 33 Concept Mapping Activity Reinforcing Social Studies Skills 30–32, 53, 69–72 Building Skills in Geography	Student Self-Test Software Testmaker Section Focus Transparency 108 Chapter 33 Skills Transparency U.S. History and Art Transparencies 26, 27 Communism and the Cold War
SECTION 2 **War in Vietnam** **1 Day** pp. 930–934 1. Explain how the Gulf of Tonkin incident led to the escalation of the war in Vietnam. 2. Explain why the Tet offensive was the turning point of the Vietnam War.	Reproducible Lesson Plan Reteaching Activity 33-2 Section Quiz American Portraits 65, 66 Reinforcing Social Studies Skills 14, 19, 30, 49, 55, 65 Chapter 33 Primary and Secondary Source Readings Writer's Handbook Lessons 9–14 U.S. History Diagraph 12	Student Self-Test Software Testmaker Section Focus Transparency 109 Chapter 33 Map Transparencies Powers of the President Communist and the Cold War
SECTION 3 **Protest and Reaction** **1 Day** pp. 936–940 1. List reasons for opposition to the war. 2. Describe the youth counter-culture.	Reproducible Lesson Plan Reteaching Activity 33-3 Section Quiz American Portrait 63, 64 Chapter 33 Primary and Secondary Source Readings Reinforcing Social Studies Skills 30, 32, 38, 49, 53, 55	Student Self-Test Software Testmaker Section Focus Transparency 110 Chapter 33 Map Transparencies Communism and the Cold War Powers of the President
SECTION 4 **Secrecy, Surprise, and Summitry** **1 Day** pp. 941–945 1. Explain why Nixon pursued detente. 2. List the steps Nixon took to end American involvement in Vietnam.	Reproducible Lesson Plan Reteaching Activity 33-4 Section Quiz Chapter 33 Enrichment Activity Reinforcing Social Studies Skills 27, 31, 37, 55, 69–72 Chapter 33 Primary and Secondary Source Readings Spanish Summaries & Glossary	Student Self-Test Software Testmaker Section Focus Transparency 111 Vocabulary Puzzlemaker Audiocassette, Chapter 33 Communism and the Cold War
CHAPTER REVIEW AND EVALUATION **1 Day**	Chapter 33 Test Chapter 33 Performance Assessment Activity	Student Self-Test Software Testmaker

OUT OF TIME? If time does not permit teaching the entire chapter, use the Chapter 33 Summary on pages 1028–1029 and the Chapter 33 audiocassette (English and Spanish) to point out the main ideas of the chapter.

PLANNING GUIDE

Cultural Diversity Activity

Cooperative Learning In 1975, after the fall of the U.S.-supported South Vietnamese government, the United States agreed to admit those Vietnamese who wanted to settle in the nation. These immigrants were given refugee status and such aid as free English classes, job counseling and training, and day care. These services helped many Vietnamese make a successful transition to American life. Discuss why Americans felt an obligation to help Vietnamese who wished to leave their country. Then divide the class into small groups and ask each to design a brochure that would help the newcomers adjust to life in the United States in the 1970s. Encourage students to share their brochures with the class. Discuss how they might be updated for new arrivals in the 1990s.

Performance Assessment Activity

Foreign Policy Have students choose one of the Presidents highlighted in this chapter and write a speech defining his approach to foreign problems. The speeches should begin by describing his objectives, then outline policies based on those objectives, and conclude with a critical examination of the results of those policies. Students might work alone on the speeches or in small groups. Encourage speechwriters to read their address to the class.

POSSIBLE RUBRIC FEATURES: Research skills, content information, organization, written and oral communication skills, critical thinking skills

Chapter Resources

Literature from the Period
Kennedy, John F. "Inaugural Address." January 20, 1963.

Readings for the Student
Oxford, Edward. "Destiny in Dallas." *American History Illustrated*, Vol. 23, No. 7, November 1988.

Lawson, Don. *The United States in the Vietnam War.* Crowell, 1981.

Readings for the Teacher
Barnet, Richard J. *The Giants: Russia and America.* Touchstone, 1977.

Multimedia Resources
America and the World Since World War II, 1961–1975, Volume III. ABC News. (VHS, 52 minutes)

America and the World Since World War II, 1961–1975, Volume IX. ABC News. (VHS, 52 minutes)

The Cuban Missile Crisis. Prentice-Hall Media. (color sound filmstrip)

Key to Ability Levels

Teaching strategies have been coded for varying learning styles and abilities.

- **L1** Basic activities for all students
- **L2** Average activities for average to above-average students
- **L3** Challenging activities for above-average students
- **LEP** Limited English Proficiency activities

Glencoe Links to the Humanities

Link to Art
- U.S. History and Art Transparencies 29, 30

Link to Literature
- Macmillan Literature: Understanding Literature Audiotapes Side 2

Link to Music
- American Music: Cultural Traditions

CHAPTER 33

BEGINNING THE CHAPTER

Have students look at the illustrations in Chapter 33 and write down the issues that each suggests. Then ask them how many of those issues were carried over from the period before 1961. Are there any new issues? Have students save their notes for reference as they study Chapter 33. After they have read the chapter, have them add to their list of issues.

Recording Journal Notes

To help students get started, suggest that they list the major events of the Vietnam War era as they read the chapter. They can then record details about the role of the President during these events and what his feelings might have been at the time.

Twenty-six senators cosponsored a bill authorizing the fund to build a memorial on public grounds in Washington, D.C. The bill had widespread support and was passed unanimously in both houses of Congress. On July 1, 1980, President Jimmy Carter signed the bill into law.

CHAPTER 33

The Vietnam Era
1954–1975

▶ SOLDIER STANDING GUARD

Setting the Scene

Focus

The President's handling of foreign policy was tested strenuously as cold war challenges arose during the Vietnam Era. Kennedy faced a failed Cuban invasion, a missile crisis, quarrels over nuclear testing, and the beginnings of the war in Vietnam. During the Johnson years, this conflict became the focus of attention for the nation. More and more, the American people became divided over this issue.

Concepts to Understand

★ How social upheaval divided the nation and affected government policy during the Vietnam Era
★ Why public opinion was divided over the conduct of the war in Vietnam

Read to Discover . . .

★ lessons Kennedy learned from his handling of foreign policy.
★ what events set off political turmoil during this period.

Journal Notes

What do you think it would have been like to be President of the United States during the Vietnam War? Note details about it in your journal as you read the chapter.

CULTURAL	• 1955 Ford offers seatbelts as optional equipment	• 1964 The Beatles appear on The Ed Sullivan Show
	1955	**1960**
POLITICAL	• 1959 Castro takes power in Cuba	• 1961 Peace Corps is established • 1962 Cuban Missile Crisis

922 UNIT 10 Redefining America 1954–Present

✚ EXTRA CREDIT PROJECT

Divide interested students into groups of three. Have each group create a magazine cover, its table of contents, and the editorial message for an issue called "The Year in Review." The magazine cover should highlight the articles inside. Ask students to design the cover, to write the "Table of Contents," and to write a short "Message From the Editor" paragraph. The magazine cover should reflect one of the major events mentioned in the chapter, such as the cold war challenges of the 1960s, the war in Vietnam, student protests. Have students present their project to the class. Post their work on the bulletin board.

CHAPTER 33 CONCEPTS

Concept Mapping Activity

Ask students to write these concepts in their notebooks and to list each major event in the chapter under the appropriate concept.

President Kennedy's and President Johnson's attempts to continue New Deal policies at home and cold war containment abroad fell short of expectations; the nation continued at war and was thrown into domestic turmoil.

- Social Upheaval
- War

History AND ART

The statue of the servicemen was sculpted by Frederick Hart. Cast in bronze, it is 7 feet (2.1 meters) tall.

History AND ART
Con Thien by John Gordon, 1967

An American soldier in a Vietnam bunker waits out heavy shelling during an attack near the demilitarized zone.

◀ VIETNAM VETERANS STATUE, WASHINGTON, D.C.

- **1967** Green Bay Packers win first Super Bowl, 35–10, over Kansas City Chiefs
- **1968** Peace talks to end Vietnam War begin in Paris
- **1968** Robert Kennedy is assassinated; Nixon becomes President

1965

- **1970** First Earth Day observed as millions protest pollution
- **1970** Kent State University students riot
- **1971** Pentagon Papers are published
- **1972** President Nixon visits China

1970

CHAPTER 33 The Vietnam Era 1954–1975

ABC NEWS INTERACTIVE

VIDEODISC
Communism and the Cold War

Side 2, Chapter 5
Title: *How We Saw Them*
Subject: American view of communism during the Cold War

Side 2, Chapter 6
Title: *How They Saw Us*
Subject: Soviet perspective of the United States

Teacher Notes

LESSON PLAN
SECTION 1, 924–929

FOCUS

Bellringer

Before taking roll at the beginning of the class period, display Focus Activity Transparency 107 on the overhead projector, and assign the accompanying Focus Activity Sheet.

Objectives

Point out the objectives on this page to students in previewing the section content.

Motivating Activity

Ask students how they think most Americans would respond if the President announced that missiles in Cuba were pointed at the United States. Tell them that this happened in 1962. Ask what they think should be done. Compare with President Kennedy's actions.

Videodisc
Communism and the Cold War

Side 1, Chapter 16
Title: *Cuban Missile Crisis*
Subject: Summary of Cuban Missile Crisis

Use Skills Transparency 33.

SECTION 1

Cold War Challenges

Setting the Scene

Section Focus

President Kennedy entered office with little firsthand experience in international affairs. Yet he had to meet such challenges as the buildup of nuclear arms, anti-United States feeling in Latin America, and instability in economically developing nations in Africa and Asia. He achieved some triumphs, but in other cases his inexperience led him into mistakes.

Objectives

After studying this section, you should be able to

★ discuss Kennedy's responses to Soviet and international communism.

★ explain the purposes of the Alliance for Progress and the Peace Corps.

Key Terms

reactionary government, credibility gap

◀ CUBAN LEADER FIDEL CASTRO

President Kennedy's basic aims in foreign policy were similar to those of Truman and Eisenhower. His major concern was the threat of communism, and he declared that he would not relax efforts to contain it.

■ Crises in Cuba

In 1959 Fidel Castro had led a movement to overthrow Fulgencio Batista—the corrupt dictator then ruling Cuba—and had set up a new government. Castro soon established ties with the Soviet Union and began to adopt Marxist-influenced policies. As a result, the Eisenhower administration began to view Cuba as a threat to democracy in the Western Hemisphere. Eisenhower authorized the Central Intelligence Agency to train and arm Cuban exiles secretly for the overthrow of Castro.

The Bay of Pigs Invasion

The CIA believed that an invasion of Cuba by these exiles would touch off a popular uprising against Castro. Kennedy's military advisers approved the project. In office less than three months, Kennedy agreed that the invasion should proceed.

On April 17, 1961, a force of 1,400 Cuban exiles came ashore at the Bay of Pigs on the south coast of Cuba. From the start the invasion went poorly. There was no popular uprising by the Cuban people. Within hours Castro's forces had the invaders surrounded.

The failed invasion hurt the prestige of the new Kennedy administration and strengthened Castro's position in the world. It also allowed Soviet leader Nikita Khrushchev to pose as the defender of Latin America against United States imperialism.

924   UNIT 10 Redefining America 1954–Present

Classroom Resources for SECTION 1

Teacher's Classroom Resources
- Chapter 33 Study Guide
- Reproducible Lesson Plan
- Reteaching Activity 33-1
- Chapter 33 Cooperative Learning Activity
- Section Quiz

Multimedia
- Section Focus Transparency 107
- Chapter 33 Skills Transparency
- Unit 10 Digest Transparencies
- Testmaker
- Student Self-Test Software
- Communism and the Cold War

The Alliance for Progress

The Castro movement, known as "Fidelismo," threatened to spread to other countries in Latin America. Promoted by Cuban agents, it often found support among the poverty-stricken and those seeking more political power. Kennedy announced a new economic program for Latin America—called the Alliance for Progress—that emphasized social reform and political freedom. Its purpose was to develop long-term economic growth among 19 Latin American nations, thus making it less likely that poverty would drive people in these countries to support communist-inspired revolutions. Over a 10-year period, the United States pledged $20 billion to help Latin American countries provide better schools, housing, and health care, as well as introduce fairer methods of taxation and redistribution of large landholdings to small farmers.

Even though United States aid to Latin America quadrupled, the results were uneven. In some countries—notably Chile, Colombia, Venezuela, and the Central American republics—the Alliance succeeded in promoting reform. In others, however, much of the money was diverted for the benefit of the military and the wealthy.

The Cuban Missile Crisis

On October 22, 1962, President Kennedy appeared on television and made a chilling announcement. U-2 spy planes from the United States had taken photographs proving that the Soviet Union had placed missiles on Cuba. The medium-range missiles were capable of reaching Atlanta and New Orleans; intermediate-range missiles were capable of reaching as far north as Pittsburgh and Detroit and as far west as Denver. Kennedy ordered a naval blockade to keep the Soviets from delivering anymore missiles, and he demanded that the Soviets dismantle all their missile sites in Cuba. As Soviet ships approached, war seemed imminent.

Secretly, the Soviet Union offered to remove the missiles if the United States promised never to invade Cuba. As negotiations continued, Khrushchev added another demand: that the United States remove its own missiles from the Soviet border of Turkey. President Kennedy rejected this demand because it would weaken the NATO alliance. The President's brother, Attorney General Robert Kennedy, suggested they ignore the new proposal and accept the Soviet Union's first offer.

After five agonizing days, when the world appeared on the brink of nuclear disaster, the Soviet ships turned back from the blockade. Soviet leaders also decided to withdraw their missiles from Cuba. President Kennedy won strong public support for his firm stand.

■ The Peace Corps

To help developing nations all over the world fight poverty and disease, Kennedy set up the Peace Corps in 1961. Like the Alliance for Progress, the Peace Corps was organized to help prevent the spread of communism.

Peace Corps Volunteers

The Corps was made up of volunteers from the United States who wanted to help people in developing nations. After a period of rigorous training, Peace Corps volunteers went to countries that had asked for their assistance. There they lived among the people and helped them solve local problems. They laid out sewage systems in Bolivia, trained medical technicians in Chad, and built a model town in Pakistan. A high proportion of volunteers taught English and practical skills. In return they received only a living wage and a small vacation allowance. By late 1963 there were 11,000 Peace Corps volunteers serving in 40 countries.

Peace Corps volunteers in economically developing nations of Africa, Asia, and Latin America witnessed firsthand the problems and potential of newly independent nations. Many countries often lacked the necessary institutions to make the transition from colonial status to political and economic independence.

CHAPTER 33
SECTION 1

TEACH
Guided Practice

Geography Ask students to discuss Kennedy's foreign policy challenges by asking: How did President Kennedy's policy in Latin America change over time? Why did many people consider the Bay of Pigs incident a mistake? How was the Cuban missile crisis resolved? **L2**

FACT or FICTION?
During the Kennedy administration, a "hot line" was installed between the White House and the Kremlin.

FACT: The purpose of this direct telephone line between the government centers of the United States and the Soviet Union was to prevent an accidental nuclear attack.

Did You Know?

At the time of the Cuban missile crisis, the Soviets had already deployed 20 missiles with nuclear warheads in Cuba and had shipped another 20. The Americans admitted that they had developed a contingency plan to invade Cuba if the missiles had not been removed.

Sidelights: Kennedy's Foreign Policy

In 1961 President Kennedy had to set a new path in foreign policy that would accommodate the changes occurring in the world. There had been much talk of "the end of the postwar world." Europe, for example, no longer recognized the United States as the leader of the free world. During his 1960 campaign, Kennedy charged that the United States had lost its "position of pre-eminence" under Eisenhower and stated his intent to regain that position through disarmament and détente with the Soviet Union.

CHAPTER 33 SECTION 1

Independent Practice

Analyzing Point of View
Write the following on the chalkboard:

The Kennedy presidency is sometimes represented as the point in time when the world began to make the great turn toward peace.

Have students write a brief paragraph supporting or opposing this point of view. Ask them to support their arguments with details from this section.

Visualizing History  During its first 29 years, the Peace Corps sent volunteers to work in Africa, Asia, Latin America, and the Pacific islands. Beginning in 1989, however, the Peace Corps sent volunteers to several Eastern European countries.
Answer to Caption: 1963 treaty that banned atomic testing in the atmosphere, outer space, and under water

 **VIDEODISC**
Communism and the Cold War

Side 1, Chapter 15
Title: *Berlin Wall*
Subject: Newsreel reports of the building of the Berlin Wall

 ▲ **SUMMIT MEETING** When Khrushchev and Kennedy met at Vienna in June 1961, the two leaders treated one another with wary politeness. *What agreement did they reach on nuclear testing?*

Nationalism in Africa

By 1961, 27 newly independent nations had been formed from European colonies in Africa. When Europeans established boundary lines of the colonies in the 1800s and early 1900s, they failed to take into account the existing ethnic and cultural divisions. Even decades later, it was difficult to obtain loyalty to the new nation-states.

Since the beginning of colonial rule, nationalist groups in Africa had resisted European control, often violently. Following World War II, these relatively small efforts for freedom swelled into powerful mass movements.

In 1961 ethnic rivalries in the Congo, later renamed Zaire, broke out into civil war. When the mineral-rich province of Katanga attempted to secede because of tribal and regional differences, two Congolese leaders called for Soviet military aid. The United States, however, backed the efforts of the United Nations to arrange a cease-fire. In 1963, after intervention by U. N. troops, the Congo was reunited. Other attempts at superpower intervention were generally rebutted as most African nations developed a policy of nonalignment.

■ Challenges From the Soviet Union

Although holding to the containment policy, Kennedy sought means of relieving the tensions of the cold war. In his inaugural address he had said, "Let us never negotiate out of fear, but let us never fear to negotiate." In June 1961, he met with Khrushchev in the Austrian capital, Vienna. The two men treated each other with wary politeness, but they could find no area of agreement. Khrushchev may have thought that he could intimidate Kennedy, who had recently been embarrassed by the Bay of Pigs disaster. The Russian leader handed Kennedy a near-ultimatum on East Germany and Berlin. He insisted that the Western powers recognize the German puppet state and that the four-power postwar occupation of Berlin, which was completely surrounded by East Germany, come to an end. The President refused.

The Berlin Wall

The communist answer was to build a wall through Berlin, blocking free movement between their section of Berlin and the

926   UNIT 10 Redefining America 1954–Present

Critical Thinking

Analyzing Point of View Ask students to discuss the following statement made by President Kennedy as it applies to his foreign policy and to American foreign policy.

"The United States is neither omnipotent nor omniscient—that we are only six percent of the world's population—that we cannot impose our will upon the other ninety-four percent of mankind—that we cannot right every wrong or reverse every adversity—and that therefore there cannot be an American solution to every world problem." **L2**

rest of the city. This weakened the economy of West Berlin, which had drawn much of its labor from the Russian sector. The wall also prevented the flight of refugees seeking to escape the oppression of East Germany. Those attempting to escape were shot down by East German police.

In June 1963, Kennedy visited West Berlin. A vast, cheering crowd gathered to hear him at the city hall. The President told them:

> *Freedom has many difficulties and democracy is not perfect, but we have never had to put up a wall to keep our people in. . . . All free men, wherever they may live, are citizens of Berlin, and therefore, as a free man I take pride in the words, 'Ich bin ein [I am a] Berliner.'*

The Berlin Wall stood for nearly 30 years as a menacing symbol of the cold war division between East and West.

Quarrels Over Nuclear Testing

In 1961 the Soviet Union broke a three-year moratorium on testing nuclear weapons in the atmosphere. The Soviets exploded more than 40 bombs, one with 3,000 times the power of the bomb that destroyed Hiroshima. Kennedy attempted to persuade the Soviets to ban above-ground testing because nuclear fallout pollutes the atmosphere of the whole world. The Soviets would not agree to a method of inspection satisfactory to Americans. Not wanting the Soviet Union to gain nuclear superiority, the United States also resumed testing.

In August 1963, the United States, the Soviet Union, and Great Britain signed a test-ban treaty that prohibited atomic tests in the atmosphere, in outer space, and underwater. It did not, however, ban underground testing or reduce the total number of nuclear weapons. In September 1963, the Senate ratified the treaty by a vote of 80 to 19.

Dominican Intervention

Cold war tensions were again heightened when the United States intervened in the Dominican Republic. In April 1965, Lyndon Johnson, who was then in the White House,

CHAPTER 33 SECTION 1

Visualizing History Not long after the Berlin Wall was constructed, stories began to emerge about *wall-jumpers*—people who illegally crossed the wall regularly. One told of three East Berliners who were addicted to American movies. Every weekend they would sneak into West Berlin and take in all the latest Hollywood releases, returning in time for work on Monday morning. **Answer to Caption:** to protest the West's refusal to recognize the East German Government and to end the four-power occupation of the city; also prevented East Germans from fleeing to West Germany

Did You Know?

The Vienna summit began with a good-natured exchange of jokes. Khrushchev suggested that he should be credited with Kennedy's victory at the polls, for if he had released Gary Powers—the U-2 pilot shot down over the soviet Union in 1960—before the election, Nixon would have trounced Kennedy by some 200,000 votes. "Don't spread the story around," Kennedy replied. "If you tell everybody that you like me better than Nixon, I'll be ruined at home."

▲ **Barrier to Freedom** The Berlin Wall dividing the East German and West German parts of the city was hastily constructed in August 1961. West Berliners decorated their side and questioned the wall's existence. **Why was the wall built?**

Cultural Diversity

Cubans began arriving in the United States after the Cuban missile crisis in 1962. For several months, 3,000 people a week arrived, largely for political reasons. Between 1965 and 1970, more than 360,000 Cubans immigrated to the United States. Many settled in and around Miami, Florida. Others established large communities in New York and New Jersey.

CHAPTER 33
SECTION 1

ASSESS

Check Understanding
Assign Section 1 as homework or an in-class activity.

Evaluate
Assign the Section 1 Quiz in the TCR, or use the History of a Free Nation Testmaker to create a customized quiz.

Reteach
Have students complete Reteaching Activity 33-1.

Enrich
Have students complete Chapter 33 Enrichment Activity in the Teacher's Classroom Resources.

CLOSE

Tell students that in his popular history of the United States, Samuel Eliot Morison closed the chapter on the Kennedy years with these lines from the musical *Camelot*:
"Don't let it be forgot
That once there was a spot
For one brief shining moment
That was known as Camelot."

Ask students to discuss why they think Morison associated the Arthurian legend with Kennedy.

---

received word that rebels were trying to overthrow the rightist military government that controlled the island country. Fearing that the rebels were controlled by Communists, Johnson ordered 20,000 marines to the Dominican Republic. This was the first time the United States had openly sent troops to the Caribbean since 1926.

Many Latin Americans criticized this military action. They charged that fear of a communist takeover, similar to that of Cuba by Fidel Castro, was leading the United States to support **reactionary governments,** or extremely conservative governments with oppressive policies. Nonetheless, most members of Congress continued to support the President. By a margin of 312 to 52, the House of Representatives voted in support of sending American troops to prevent a communist takeover anywhere in Latin America. But the Dominican incident raised suspicions of a **credibility gap,** a lack of believability growing out of the difference between official statements and practices.

■ Israel and Korea

Two other incidents caused friction with the Soviet Union during the 1960s. One had to do with Israel. The other was the *Pueblo* incident in Korea.

Arab-Israeli War

Hostilities between Israel and the Arab nations in the Middle East were common and continuing. The United States, which had traditionally supported Israel since its founding in 1948, continued that support during the Arab-Israeli War of 1967. The Soviet Union, on the other hand, backed and armed Egypt, Syria, and Jordan, the three Arab nations involved. Being on opposite sides in this conflict heightened cold war tensions between the two superpowers. However, the speed of Israel's victory prevented an out-and-out clash between the two countries.

Later in 1967, President Johnson met with Soviet Premier Aleksey Kosygin at Glassboro, New Jersey, to try to smooth relations between the United States and the Soviet Union. Although they discussed their nations' views and goals, they came to no agreement.

The *Pueblo* Incident

In January 1968, the North Koreans seized a United States ship, the *Pueblo*, and its 83 crew members. The *Pueblo* was a spy vessel, which used electronic equipment to obtain information about communist North Korea. As long as the ship stayed in international waters at least 12 miles from shore, its activities were considered legal. North Korea, however, claimed that the *Pueblo* had illegally entered its waters.

American officials were stunned. Some people wanted to retaliate, but President Johnson could not afford a conflict with North Korea while the United States was involved in the Vietnam War. As a result, the crew members remained prisoners for nearly a year.

Section 1 ★ Review

Checking for Understanding
1. **Identify** Bay of Pigs, Nikita Khrushchev, Alliance for Progress, Peace Corps, Berlin Wall, *Pueblo*.
2. **Define** reactionary government, credibility gap.
3. **Explain** why the Bay of Pigs invasion failed.
4. **State** two possible reasons why Khrushchev sent missiles to Cuba.

Critical Thinking
5. **Making Inferences** Besides being an economic policy, the Alliance for Progress was an attempt to stop communism. Explain this aspect of the program.

Answers to SECTION 1 REVIEW

1. Bay of Pigs, 924; Nikita Khrushchev, 924; Alliance for Progress, 925; Peace Corps, 925; Berlin Wall, 926; *Pueblo*, 928
2. All vocabulary words are defined in the Glossary.
3. No popular uprising against Castro occurred once Cuban exiles invaded.
4. wanted to protect Cuba from invasion; wanted missile-launching site close to United States; wanted to pressure United States into negotiating arms treaty.
5. Promoting economic growth: improving education, housing, and health care; and redistribution of land would alleviate poverty and discontent on which communism thrived.

History and Technology CONNECTIONS

Changing Nature of Warfare

Technology always affects the conduct of war. In fact, changes in the way wars are fought are often the result of changes in technology.

During the Revolutionary War, armies were outfitted with flintlock muskets—notoriously inaccurate. The soldier fired at the enemy when he saw "the whites of his eyes," a distance of less than 50 yards. With the Civil War and the introduction of a more accurate bullet, rifles were deadly up to 300 yards.

In some ways the Civil War was the first modern war. It was the first war in which railroad lines were vital, and the first in which telegraph lines, ironclad ships, and observation balloons were used as a matter of course. It foreshadowed World War I, since the armies often dug in, and sometimes fought from elaborate trenches. It also represented a step toward the concept of "total war," with less and less distinction between civilians and soldiers.

Over time, battles became increasingly impersonal, as soldiers killed and were killed by unseen enemies. Field telephones, first used in World War I, enabled soldiers to direct their fire thousands of feet behind enemy lines. Airplanes were introduced, and pilots dropped bombs by hand from open cockpits. Bombing quickly became more sophisticated, and by World War II, bombers flying over enemy territory in Europe dropped hundreds of bombs in a single mission.

Modern-day warfare has become even more detached. Weapons systems are computer-controlled. Pilots use radar to direct heat-seeking missiles at enemies miles away.

During the Vietnam War, United States pilots flew huge B-52s on bombing raids over North Vietnam. Helicopters supplied food and ammunition to United States field forces, transported troops, and promptly evacuated the wounded.

▶ Marine during Gulf War

 World War I soldiers

Making the Technology Connection
1. How did technological advances affect battlefield tactics? Which advance do you think has had the greatest effect on modern warfare?

Linking Past and Present
2. How do today's radio and television influence the perception of war on the home front? Do you think the media has had too great an influence?

CHAPTER 33 CONNECTIONS

Teaching Making Connections
Due to advances in technology, battles have become increasingly impersonal and deadly. At the same time, the line separating civilians from the military has become more blurred.

Did You Know?
By the late 1960s, television was playing an important role in the war in Vietnam. It brought visual images of burning villages and wounded soldiers into living rooms across the nation. Those images shaped not only the way Americans viewed the war but also their resolve to continue the war.

ABCNEWS INTERACTIVE

VIDEODISC
Lessons of War

Side 1, Chapter 10
Title: *Strategy and Tactics*
Subject: Reviews strategies and tactics used in warfare

Side 1, Chapter 11
Title: *Weapons of War*
Subject: Overview of technological changes in weapons used in wars

---

Answers to CONNECTIONS

1. In general the conduct of battles has grown more and more impersonal as weapons have become more powerful. Now, soldiers kill and get killed by unseen enemies.

2. Radio and television bring the reality of war into each person's home. This can dramatically influence feelings about war, particularly when the reason for participation in the war is complicated or controversial.

LESSON PLAN
SECTION 2, 930–935

FOCUS

Bellringer
Before taking roll at the beginning of the class period, display Focus Activity 108 on the overhead projector, and assign the accompanying Focus Activity Sheet.

Objectives
Point out the objectives on this page to students in previewing the section content.

Motivating Activity
Make a line of dominoes standing on end. Knock the first one over so that the rest fall in turn. Ask students what the "domino theory" meant in relation to Southeast Asia. Ask: How did the domino theory influence Americans? (created fear) Tell students to keep the domino theory in mind as they read Section 2.

Did You Know?
President Eisenhower first coined the phrase "domino theory" in 1954.

VIDEODISC
Communism and the Cold War

Side 2, Chapter 8
Title: *Vietnam War*
Subject: Summary of Vietnam War

SECTION 2

War in Vietnam

Setting the Scene

Section Focus
Perhaps the biggest cold war challenge was the war in Vietnam. Kennedy increased the number of military advisers in South Vietnam, but his tragic death prevented him from finding a solution. Although Kennedy's intentions for the future were not clear, Johnson continued the established policy of containment and honored the commitments made by Eisenhower and Kennedy.

Objectives
After studying this section, you should be able to
★ explain how the Gulf of Tonkin incident led to the escalation of the war in Vietnam.
★ explain why the Tet offensive was the turning point of the Vietnam War.

Key Terms
war of national liberation, escalation, search-and-destroy strategy

◀ SOLDIER'S BOOTS, VIETNAM WAR

In setting United States policy in Vietnam, both Kennedy and Johnson were torn between a wish to limit American involvement in a country halfway around the world and fear of a communist victory that would swallow up all of Southeast Asia. Ultimately, however, involvement increased and, before long, American troops were engaged in combat.

■ Trouble in Southeast Asia

During the Kennedy years, the Soviet Union lent its support to **wars of national liberation.** These were wars to free a nation from the control of another country, and they took place in many economically developing nations.

War in Laos
When Kennedy took office in 1961, the Southeast Asian nation of Laos was in danger of falling to communist guerrilla forces. The CIA and the Joint Chiefs of Staff pressed for a strong defense of Laos. Kennedy, on the other hand, believed a diplomatic solution could be found. In the end Kennedy avoided war by striking a compromise with Khrushchev—first by agreeing to a cease-fire and then by establishing a neutral government. Fighting between the Laos government and the guerrilla forces soon resumed, however.

Kennedy and Vietnam
Another hot spot was Vietnam, a former French colony in Southeast Asia. It had been divided into North and South Vietnam in 1954. North Vietnam was controlled by the

UNIT 10 Redefining America 1954–Present

Classroom Resources for SECTION 2

Teacher's Classroom Resources
📁 Reproducible Lesson Plan
📁 Reteaching Activity 33-2
📁 Chapter 33 Primary and Secondary Source Readings
📁 Section Quiz

Multimedia
Section Focus Transparency 108
Chapter 33 Map Transparency
Testmaker
Student Self-Test Software
Powers of the President
Communism and the Cold War

communist government of Ho Chi Minh. South Vietnam was controlled by a noncommunist government supported first by France and then by the United States. In the late 1950s the Vietcong—South Vietnamese communist guerrillas—began fighting to overthrow the United States-backed government of Ngo Dinh Diem and to reunite South Vietnam with the North. Both Eisenhower and Kennedy responded by sending military aid and advisers to South Vietnam. By late 1963 Kennedy had increased the number of advisers to 16,000.

Kennedy's Vietnam policy was complicated because Diem was a corrupt and unpopular dictator, a French-educated, upper-middle-class Catholic who ruled a largely Buddhist country. Middle- and lower-class Buddhists distrusted both Diem and the West. In his efforts to remain in power, Diem took increasingly harsh and undemocratic measures.

■ Johnson's Choices

During the 1964 campaign Johnson ran as the candidate of peace and restraint. "We seek no wider war," he repeatedly promised.

"We don't want our American boys to do the fighting for Asian boys." At the same time, the President did not want to appear weak or to leave the door open for a communist victory in Vietnam.

As the military situation in Vietnam continued to deteriorate, the war dominated the foreign policy of the administration. When President Johnson entered the White House, South Vietnamese President Ngo Dinh Diem had just been assassinated. Within three months, another revolution took place in South Vietnam. This was followed by a series of governments, as one military faction after another gained power in South Vietnam.

The President faced disagreeable choices. He could admit defeat and pull out. If the "domino theory" was correct, the rest of Southeast Asia would soon fall to the Communists. Another option was continuing limited support of South Vietnam's government, but the instability of that government would probably mean eventual defeat. Finally, he could actively enter the war and attack North Vietnam. This would mean the loss of lives and vast expense, and also the possibility of war with the People's Republic of China.

 **▲ ESCALATION** By the end of 1965, there were nearly 200,000 American troops in Vietnam. By the end of 1968, the total had increased to more than 500,000. *What was the Gulf of Tonkin Resolution?*

CHAPTER 33 The Vietnam Era 1954–1975   931

CHAPTER 33 SECTION 2

TEACH

Guided Practice
Expressing an Opinion
Present the following statement to students:
  The Gulf of Tonkin incident had a long-term and unexpected significance.
  Ask students if they agree or disagree with this statement. Why or why not? Have them explain their answers in a brief paragraph. (The incident moved Johnson to order American forces into the conflict. Involvement escalated at a steady pace. Peace overtures failed, and Americans became divided.) **L2**

Visualizing History The Green Berets were specially trained to infiltrate behind enemy lines and counter guerrilla activity.
Answer to Caption: allowed the President to "take all the necessary steps" to prevent further aggression in Vietnam

📁 Assign students the Chapter 33 Reading entitled "The Reality of Vietnam" in Primary and Secondary Source Readings.

Critical Thinking

Review with students the Gulf of Tonkin incident. Have them identify information that was withheld from Congress and the American people. Then ask students to write newspaper editorials focusing on the effects of misinformation on Congress. Have students predict how the Gulf of Tonkin Resolution might affect the future of U.S. involvement in Vietnam. They should conclude their editorials with recommendations that the President or Congress might take to prevent similar incidents.

CHAPTER 33 SECTION 2

Independent Practice

Oral History Have students conduct a 15-minute interview with a Vietnam veteran from their community. **L2**

Visualizing History GI slang referred to helicopters as TWA—teenie-weenie airlines. They were used on a massive scale during the Vietnam War. With gas turbine replacing piston engines, the helicopters had remarkable range and maneuverability.
Answer to Caption: to counter the Vietcong guerilla tactics

ABC NEWS INTERACTIVE

VIDEODISC
Powers of the President

Side 2, Chapter 15
Title: *The Vietnam War*
Subject: Case study of checks and balances concerning U.S. involvement in Vietnam

Side 2, Chapter 16
Title: *Use of Force*
Subject: President Johnson requests Gulf of Tonkin Resolution

Side 2, Chapter 17
Title: *Gulf of Tonkin Resolution*
Subject: Congressional leaders discuss Gulf of Tonkin Resolution

Visualizing History ▲ **THE AIR WAR** As American involvement in Vietnam grew, helicopters were used extensively because they were effective at pinpointing enemy positions. *What were the goals of search-and-destroy missions?*

By the summer of 1964 Johnson began to move cautiously toward the third alternative. In secrecy the United States began limited bombing of positions held by the Vietcong and supported limited commando raids on North Vietnam's coast.

■ Escalation

Johnson reported that North Vietnamese torpedo boats fired on two American destroyers in the Gulf of Tonkin on August 2 and 4, 1964. Calling these attacks unprovoked, he asked Congress for authorization to bomb North Vietnam.

Gulf of Tonkin Resolution

On August 7 the Senate and House quickly passed the Gulf of Tonkin Resolution, authorizing the President to "take all necessary steps, including the use of armed force" to prevent further aggression. In effect, Congress, with only two dissenting votes, handed its war powers over to the President.

Johnson, however, had kept important information from Congress. The two American destroyers had been assisting the South Vietnamese military in conducting electronic spying on North Vietnam. It was unclear whether the ships had been attacked. Furthermore, Johnson did not reveal that a draft of the resolution had been prepared three months before the attack, in case such an event occurred.

President Johnson regarded the Gulf of Tonkin Resolution as a blanket approval of the war effort from Congress. At the suggestion of his military advisers, he ordered the bombing of bases in North Vietnam.

Until August 1964, the fighting in South Vietnam had been between South Vietnamese government troops and the Vietcong. After the Gulf of Tonkin incident, however, North Vietnam began sending its own troops to fight in the South. As the United States expanded its role, the civil war grew into a major conflict between American and communist forces.

In February 1965, after the Vietcong attacked an American base in South Vietnam, Johnson ordered an **escalation**, or military expansion, of the war. He ordered American planes to begin bombing targets in North Vietnam, and, in April 1965, made the fateful decision that American ground forces should engage in combat.

UNIT 10 Redefining America 1954–Present

Cooperative Learning

To review the Vietnam War, divide the class into groups of three. Have each group discuss how the lack of success in a limited war in Vietnam ultimately divided the nation. Assign each member of the group one of three topics: the significance of the Gulf of Tonkin Resolution, the growing divisions within Johnson's cabinet, and the reasons for American opposition to the war. Ask students to research each topic in the text and teach the other group members the information. Call on students randomly to check each group's progress. **L1**

In the Vietnam War the United States faced a far more difficult situation than it had in Korea. In Korea the United States fought as an agent of the United Nations, with widespread support from noncommunist countries. Now the United States stood almost alone in its military support of South Vietnam's government, and much of world opinion was hostile to American policy in Vietnam. The South Vietnamese communists had strong support in rural areas and military aid from North Vietnam. Most noncommunist South Vietnamese were indifferent or opposed to their government, no matter what group happened to be in power.

A Different Kind of War

Military operations turned into a "dirty, ruthless, wandering war" without a battlefront. The Vietcong guerrillas used hit-and-run tactics. Not as well equipped as the Americans, the Vietcong and North Vietnamese used ambushes, boobytraps, and small-scale attacks. They moved swiftly by night and by day hid in the jungles or in friendly villages. Using terrorism against civilians, the Vietcong controlled much of the countryside.

Search and Destroy

To counter such tactics, American troops adopted a **search-and-destroy strategy.** American forces tried to search out enemy troops, bomb their positions, destroy their supply lines, and force them out into the open for combat. By 1966 American planes had dropped nearly the same tonnage of bombs in Vietnam as had been dropped in the Pacific in World War II.

Napalm, a jellied gasoline that explodes, splatters, and clings to whatever it touches, was dropped from airplanes. In order to improve visibility, American planes sprayed chemical defoliants—Agent Orange, for example—that stripped leaves from trees and shrubs, turning farmland and forest into wasteland. American troops burned villages believed to be hiding communist supporters.

Resistance to Peace

The United States poured increasing numbers of troops into Vietnam. During the height of the conflict, more than 500,000 American soldiers were serving in Vietnam. The number of American dead continued to rise: from 5,008 in 1966 to 9,377 in 1967 and 14,489 in 1968.

Once the United States had escalated the fighting, there seemed to be no way of leaving without damaging its international prestige. North Vietnam's leader, Ho Chi Minh, kept his forces in battle despite the massive bombing of his country, believing that North Vietnam could simply outlast the United States in the war.

Map Study
Throughout the war United States troops and the government of South Vietnam controlled the major cities. **What strategy did the Vietcong use?**

CHAPTER 33 The Vietnam Era 1954–1975

CHAPTER 33
SECTION 2

Linking Across Time

The Vietnam War caused controversy into the 1990s. Still unresolved was whether the American government would compensate war veterans who claimed that exposure to the jungle defoliant Agent Orange was to blame for their high cancer rate. In 1987 the government said that no such connection could be proven because it was impossible to assess a veteran's contact with the herbicide. In 1990 an opposing report said that records of troop movements could establish exposure to Agent Orange.

Did You Know?

During the Vietnam War, African Americans and Mexican Americans made up a large share of the American soldiers fighting in Vietnam.

Map Study Using Maps
Answer: guerrilla tactics, striking and then disappearing

Skills Practice
Where is the border between North and South Vietnam? (17th parallel)

CHAPTER 33 SECTION 2

ASSESS

Check Understanding

Assign the Section 2 Review as homework or an in-class activity.

Evaluate

Assign the Section 2 Quiz in the TCR, or use the History of a Free Nation Testmaker to create a customized quiz.

Reteach

Have students complete Reteaching Activity 33-2.

Enrich

Have students research Agent Orange. Ask them to find out the effects of this defoliant on Vietnam and its effect on the health of American soldiers after the war. Have students report their findings to the class.

CLOSE

Discuss President Johnson's actions during the war. Remind students that President Lincoln did not consult with Congress before the start of the Civil War. Ask: Should the President be permitted to make executive decisions on matters of national defense without the consent of Congress? Have students write a brief editorial defending their point of view and share it with the class.

Between 1965 and 1967, American officials estimated that some 2,000 attempts were made to open direct negotiations, all unsuccessful. Other nations, including Great Britain, Poland, and the Soviet Union, offered plans to negotiate between the two sides. None succeeded.

■ Tet and Retreat

At the end of 1967, General William Westmoreland, American commander in Vietnam, had assured the country that the end of the war was in sight. Vastly enlarged American forces expanded the "search-and-destroy" missions. American bombers destroyed North Vietnamese factories, roads, bridges, and cities. Secretary of State Dean Rusk said the enemy "was hurting very badly."

Vietcong Attack Turns the Tide

January 30, 1968, marked a turning point in the war. The supposedly exhausted communist guerrillas abruptly launched major offensive strikes. Early that morning a handful of Vietcong soldiers attacked the United States Embassy compound in Saigon—the very center of the American presence in South Vietnam. Together, the Vietcong and the North Vietnamese then launched massive attacks on all American bases in South Vietnam and on most of South Vietnam's major cities and provincial capitals. Taken by surprise by the assault during the celebration of Tet, the Vietnamese lunar New Year, Americans and South Vietnamese sustained heavy losses. After fierce fighting, they finally drove back the communist offensive.

Militarily, the communists were defeated. Politically, however, they scored a victory. The American people were shocked that the enemy that was supposedly on the verge of defeat could launch such a large-scale attack. Television coverage of the attack and the destruction that followed shook the nation's confidence. When General Westmoreland requested an additional 209,000 troops for Vietnam—in addition to the 500,000 already there—it seemed like another admission that the United States could not win the war.

Peace Talks Begin

Finally, on March 31, 1968, Johnson announced that he would halt nearly all bombing of North Vietnam. He offered to send special negotiators to hold peace talks with the North Vietnamese and the Vietcong. A few days later, on April 3, North Vietnam accepted Johnson's offer to begin peace negotiations. Diplomats from the United States and North Vietnam met in Paris in May 1968, but they could not agree on terms. Prospects for peace in Vietnam grew dim. After a lull, the war continued, and the number of American troops in Vietnam reached a new high. It would be five long years of continued bitter struggle, however, before the United States left the war in Vietnam behind.

Section 2 ★ Review

Checking for Understanding

1. **Identify** Vietcong, Gulf of Tonkin Resolution, General William Westmoreland.
2. **Define** wars of national liberation, escalation, search-and-destroy strategy.
3. **Explain** what mistake Johnson's military advisers made about the Vietcong and the North Vietnamese.
4. **Explain** why the Tet offensive was the turning point of the Vietnam War.

Critical Thinking

5. **Expressing Problems Clearly** Some political analysts called Vietnam a "quagmire." Write two statements that explain the difficult choices the United States faced in Vietnam.

934 UNIT 10 Redefining America 1954–Present

Answers to SECTION 2 REVIEW

1. Vietcong, 931; Gulf of Tonkin Resolution, 932; General William Westmoreland, 934
2. All vocabulary words are defined in the Glossary.
3. underestimated the will and ability of the Vietcong and the North Vietnamese to keep fighting despite American military escalation
4. It brought home to Americans that the North Vietnamese were not close to crumbling and the United States was not close to winning the war.
5. Answers will vary. President Johnson was torn between his desire to contain and end the war, and his belief that the fall of South Vietnam would lead to a Communist takeover of the entire region. It became increasingly evident that military might alone would not win the war and that other solutions to the conflict had to be found.

Social Studies Skills

Map and Graph Skills

The Tet Offensive, 1968

Interpreting Military Maps

In your study of American history, you often use maps. Maps are especially helpful for studying the progression of war. A military map shows the area where battles occur, where victories have been won, and who controls various sites.

Military maps vary in the level of detail provided. Some military maps show only the major battles fought over the course of a war. Others may show detailed troop movements and defensive positions during a particular battle or over a specific period of time.

To interpret military maps, follow these guidelines:

a. **Read** the map title. This will indicate the location and time period covered on the map.

b. **Read** the items listed in the map key. This tells what the symbols on the map represent. For example, areas under the control of a particular nation or region may be represented by a color. Battle sites may be symbolized by crossed swords, a shell burst, or a star. Military movements and offensives may be illustrated with solid or broken lines and arrows.

c. **Study** the map itself. This will reveal the actual events or sequence of events that took place. Notice the geography of the area and try to determine how it would affect military strategy.

Practicing the Skill

Nearly 8,400 communist troops infiltrated South Vietnam's major cities and government installations during the Tet offensive. Overall, more than thirty cities were attacked, with the heaviest fighting in Saigon and Hue. Before the offensive was over, an estimated 33,000 communist soldiers died.

Look at the military map of Southeast Asia on this page. Then follow the above guidelines to answer these questions.

1. What time period is represented on the map?
2. From the map, can you tell the outcome of the attacks?
3. Where are the attack sites with respect to North Vietnam?
4. The Ho Chi Minh Trail, through Laos and Cambodia, was an important supply line for communist troops and ammunition. Which side do you think Laos and Cambodia favored? Explain.

LESSON PLAN
SECTION 3, 936–940

FOCUS

Bellringer
Before taking roll at the beginning of the class period, display Focus Activity 109 on the overhead projector, and assign the accompanying Focus Activity Sheet.

Objectives
Point out the objectives on this page to students in previewing the section content.

Motivating Activity
Obtain music recordings from the mid-1960s that represented mainstream society (for example, Frank Sinatra) and the counterculture (for example, the Beatles). Play each selection. Ask students to characterize each recording with adjectives. List the adjectives on the board, and discuss student answers. Point out that in the 1960s each type of music was popular among different groups of people, reflecting their conflicting philosophies and lifestyles.

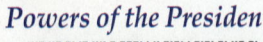
Powers of the President

Side 2, Chapter 18
Title: *Vietnam Protests*
Subject: Sights and sounds of antiwar protests

SECTION 3

Protest and Reaction

Setting the Scene

Section Focus
As casualties mounted, there was strong opposition to the war among a growing number of Americans. They lost confidence in their government. Soon, large numbers of disillusioned youths began demonstrating against United States involvement in Vietnam. In the middle of all the chaos, *Newsweek* reported that the United States was "divided and confused as never since the Great Depression."

Objectives
After studying this section, you should be able to
★ list reasons for opposition to the war.
★ describe the values and beliefs of the youth counterculture.

Key Terms
student deferment, conscientious objector, teach-in, commune, counterculture

◀ ANTIWAR BUTTON

After Tet, criticism of American involvement in Vietnam increased. One of the nation's most trusted news broadcasters, Walter Cronkite, reported:

> *We have too often been disappointed by the optimism of the American leaders to have faith any longer in the silver linings. . . . To say that we are closer to victory today is to believe, in the face of evidence, the optimists who have been wrong in the past. To suggest we are on the edge of defeat is to yield to unreasonable pessimism. To say that we are mired in stalemate seems the only realistic, yet unsatisfactory conclusion.*

Hearing Cronkite's broadcast, President Johnson turned to his aides and said, "It's all over." He recognized that he had lost the battle for public opinion.

■ Growing Opposition to War

Gradually, as America moved deeper into the Vietnam War, opposition grew. The United States's reasons for fighting in Southeast Asia began to be questioned.

Senate Hearings on the War
Beginning in January 1966, the Senate Foreign Relations Committee held "educational" hearings on Vietnam. The televised hearings carried the senators' doubts about the war to millions of American homes.

936 UNIT 10 Redefining America 1954–Present

Classroom Resources for SECTION 3

Teacher's Classroom Resources
- Reproducible Lesson Plan
- Reteaching Activity 33-3
- Chapter 33 Primary and Secondary Source Readings
- Section Quiz

Multimedia
- Section Focus Transparency 109
- Chapter 33 Map Transparency
- Testmaker
- Student Self-Test Software
- Communism and the Cold War
- Powers of the President

Hawks and Doves

Before long, Americans became divided into two groups. Those who supported the war were called "hawks" and those who opposed "doves." For a long time, polls showed that most Americans sided with the "hawks." But doubts began to grow. By May 1967, even the Secretary of Defense Robert McNamara had begun to question America's role in the war.

Student Protests

Many of those opposed to the war were students who openly protested America's involvement in Vietnam. The antiwar movement was centered on college campuses, which had also been the source for activists in the civil rights movement.

Protests Against the Draft

A number of the antiwar protests focused on the draft. Many of those facing the draft did not understand why the war was being fought or why they should go. Students also protested against the government's unfair practices. A person with a limited education from a low-income family was far more likely to be sent to fight in Vietnam than someone with a good education from an upper-income family, and African American soldiers made up a disproportionately large number of American soldiers fighting overseas.

One policy that contributed to this inequity was the practice of giving **student deferments.** Young men were safe from the draft as long as they were enrolled in college. In 1966 alone, there were 1.8 million deferments. Some men who did not serve were **conscientious objectors.** They received this status by belonging to an organized religious body with pacifist views. About 500,000 young men simply refused to report when they were drafted. Some fled to other countries, such as Canada or Sweden. Around 3,000 young men went to prison rather than fight in a war they opposed. Some antiwar protesters used the tactics of civil disobedience and demonstrations that they had learned from the civil rights movement.

▲ **DEMONSTRATIONS AND CONFRONTATION** Reacting against the antiwar demonstrations, many Americans began to counter with demonstrations in support of American troops. Many antiwar demonstrations were accompanied by violence. In May 1970 six students were killed during separate confrontations at Jackson State and Kent State (above right). **Why did many students protest the war?**

Critical Thinking

Analyzing Reactions Tell students that in 1964 the Vietnam War was not a national issue. Two incidents, however, would soon bring it to national attention. The first incident was the controversy surrounding the Gulf of Tonkin incident. The second were campaign speeches in which Johnson pledged he would not "send American boys halfway around the world to do a job that Asian boys ought to be doing for themselves." Have students analyze in writing how both of these events became crucial issues by 1967 and 1968. **L2**

CHAPTER 33
SECTION 3

TEACH
Guided Practice

Debate Tell students that television and newspapers brought the war into homes of Americans and divided the nation. Divide the class into two groups. Appoint one student to be the moderator between the groups. Have the first group advocate the "hawk" viewpoint. Have the second group advocate the "dove" viewpoint. Have the moderator reconcile the differences between groups. **L3**

Visualizing History News of the killings at Kent State traveled quickly to college campuses all over the country. Hundreds of other universities and colleges closed in protest and sympathy. **Answer to Caption:** Answers will vary but might include: questions arose over American involvement, disproportionate number of poor fighting overseas.

Did You Know?

Ho Chi Minh City (formerly Saigon) proclaimed 1990 its "Year of Tourism." The tunnels once used by the Vietcong guerrillas—a network of 200 miles—were one of the featured tourist attractions.

▼ Assign students the Chapter 33 Reading in the Primary and Secondary Source Readings.

CHAPTER 33
SECTION 3

Independent Practice
Sociology Have students interview a parent or an older friend on his or her opinion of the counterculture or black power movements of the late 1960s. **L2**

Teaching Life of the Times
The combat duty of U.S. Army personnel during the Vietnam War was limited to 365 days. Marines served 13 months. Because of this one-year policy, many soldiers carried calendars marked with their DEROS—date of expected return from overseas. As you can see from the letter on this page, soldiers were very conscious of the time they had been overseas. Writing letters was a good way to pass the time, as they looked forward to going home.

VIDEODISC
Communism and the Cold War

Side 1, Chapter 25
Title: *Music of the Cold War*
Subject: Montage of music reflecting the political moods during the Cold War

---

Life of the Times

Letters From Vietnam

A soldier's life is charged with action and danger, but it also holds long periods of tiresome waiting and inactivity. Writing letters to family and friends back home is one way generations of soldiers have fought boredom and loneliness. United States soldiers in Vietnam were no different. They shared their lives, their fears, and their desires through their letters. Here First Lieutenant Robert Michael Murray writes to his fiancée.

6 July [1967]
My Darling Claudia,
It's raining outside. A damp smell in the air and the raindrops slamming onto the plasterboard roof. Sound of cricket and frog, and the rumble of distant bomb explosions shake the earth here many miles away. Lightning flashes bare the heavens for a brief glimpse at a troubled sky watching over a war-torn land. The area is flooded, and mud clings to boots with a slurp-sucking sound. Soaked uniform hanging on chair to dry and shriveling up into a wrinkled mass. A chilling air is coddled by two ceiling fans and swirled through my body. . . .

Sometimes you have to pretend you're not really lonely or else you'd find yourself going out of your mind. But when the day is done, and you're lying alone with your thoughts, then there's no more fooling and that's when it really hurts. The days seem to go by quickly, but the weeks seem forever. Today I have been in Vietnam 73 days, $10\frac{1}{2}$ weeks, a little over $2\frac{1}{2}$ months. The guys who are over here now tell me, looking back, that the time flew by. But right now it seems so very long.

I love you,
Michael

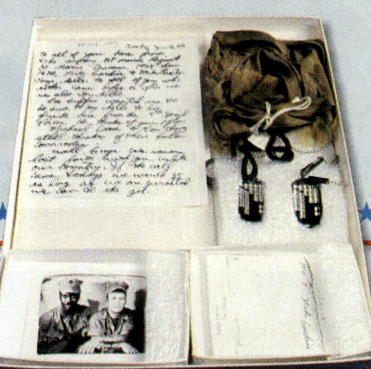
◀ **COLLECTION OF VETERAN'S ITEMS**

Some university students and teachers held **teach-ins** to study the history of the war and to protest against its expansion.

Violence on Campus

While most protests were peaceful, some turned violent. One occurred in April 1968 at Columbia University in New York City. It began when students seized college buildings and ended in a riot marked by both police brutality and student retaliation.

Two of the most tragic episodes of the antiwar movement took place in May 1970. After President Nixon announced the invasion of Cambodia, protests erupted on scores of campuses. At Kent State University in Ohio, rioting reached such an intensity that the National Guard was sent in. On May 4, a contingent of guardsmen, harassed by students, fired into the crowd, killing 4 students and wounding 10. On May 14, at Jackson State University in Mississippi, student protest was suppressed by the state police, who fired randomly into a dormitory. Two students were killed, 9 were wounded. These events precipitated a nationwide student strike. Hundreds of colleges and universities suspended classes or closed down completely.

The campus violence that erupted was not limited to the United States. During this time and before, there were student riots in Rio de Janeiro, London, Paris, Rome, Madrid, Warsaw, and Prague. In Prague, student protests triggered a rebellion that led to the overthrow of the communist regime that had ruled Czechoslovakia since 1948. However, after a few months 200,000 Soviet troops crushed the revolt and reestablished control.

938 UNIT 10 Redefining America 1954–Present

Cooperative Learning

Divide the class into small groups. Have the groups design a museum project on the 1960s counterculture. Groups may select the music, fashion trends, literature, individuals, and events they feel are most significant in the study of this cultural movement. Encourage students to use music, scenarios, photographs, and primary sources in their projects. Have each team present their projects to the class. Emphasize the selection of details as important to the exhibit. **L2**

New Beliefs and Values

Some young people rebelled against established values and searched for a new set of beliefs. They studied different religions and philosophies. In an attempt to achieve expanded awareness, some experimented with drugs that cause hallucinations. They proclaimed their freedom of expression and individuality by wearing long hair and unconventional clothing. Some even left family and comfortable homes to live in **communes**—communities in which living quarters, food, and work were shared.

In their rejection of their parents' values, the "hippies," or "flower children" as they were frequently called, were said to have established a **counterculture**—with values and practices that conflicted with those of established society. The counterculture was symbolized in an outdoor rock concert, the Woodstock festival held in New York in August 1969. More than 400,000 people attended what TIME called "history's biggest happening."

A Conservative Backlash

The actions and protests of the Woodstock generation caused a reaction among a growing number of conservative Americans who had become angry over the demonstrations, the riots, and a war that seemed to be going nowhere. The sight of long-haired draft protesters outraged many who did not hesitate to support their government in time of war. Many working-class Americans were offended by the actions of students they considered privileged. The deep anger these Americans felt soon developed into a backlash against the antiwar movement.

■ 1968: The Turning Point

By 1968, a kind of turning point had been reached in American society. With the Tet offensive and the protests, polls showed that the majority of Americans had turned against the President's handling of the war. Johnson had become so unpopular that he seldom appeared in public for fear of hostile crowds. Even the President's own party was divided over the war.

The Race for President

By this time, Eugene McCarthy, a Democratic senator from Minnesota—and a dove—had announced that he was going to challenge Johnson for the Democratic Party's presidential nomination. Although Johnson won the first primary election in New Hampshire, his margin of victory was narrow. McCarthy received more than 40 percent of the votes. Then, four days after this primary, Democratic Senator Robert Kennedy, who also opposed the war, announced that he too would run for the nomination.

Johnson had always intended to run for reelection in 1968. When he realized just how little support he had, however, he made a decision that was surprising to many. The President decided to drop out of the race. On March 31, 1968, he stunned the nation by announcing, "I shall not seek, and I will not accept, the nomination of my party for another term as your President." With Johnson withdrawn, Vice President

▲ **ASSASSINATION** During the 1968 Democratic primary, Robert F. Kennedy won a number of victories. On June 5, 1968, the night of his victory in the California primary, Kennedy was assassinated. *What two Democratic candidates remained in the race?*

Whether the availability of guns is a cause of violence in America is a bigger issue now than in 1968. Although 225,000 people died from handguns in the 1980s (four times as many as were killed in Vietnam), few gun-control measures were passed. A 1990 poll, however, showed that a large majority of gun owners favored a seven-day waiting period for handgun purchases and registration of semiautomatic weapons; and 50 percent favored registration of rifles and handguns.

Visualizing History Robert Kennedy campaigned so hard that reporters traveling with him complained of the pace. Kennedy was usually up by 7:00 A.M. and often didn't quit shaking hands and meeting people until 3:00 in the morning.
Answer to Caption: McCarthy and Humphrey

Sidelights: Protest Buttons and Patches

Protest buttons were a nearly universal way for young people to express their views of society during this period. This development could have grown out of the long-time American tradition of campaign buttons. The Vietnam War, poverty, racial and gender discrimination, and pollution were all targets of their protests. The message T-shirt also had its beginnings in this era. Cloth patches carried the symbols of the day, including the peace symbol; a rainbow, a symbol of optimism; and the ecology flag designed in 1970 for the first Earth Day.

CHAPTER 33 SECTION 3

ASSESS

Check Understanding
Assign Section 3 Review as homework or an in-class activity.

Evaluate
Assign the Section 3 Quiz in the TCR, or use the History of a Free Nation Testmaker to create a customized quiz.

Reteach
Discuss the vocal opposition during this period. Ask: What methods did student protesters and members of the counterculture use to change American society? How did other Americans respond to these actions?

Have students complete Reteaching Activity 33-3.

Enrich
Interested students might want to find out more about American folk-singers such as Joan Baez, Bob Dylan, and Joan Collins, who used their lyrics for social and political causes. Have students report briefly on these people and why they became the voices of the antiwar movement in the late 1960s.

CLOSE
Summarize this section by asking students what achievements were made by student protesters and counterculture members. Ask: What evidence in our culture shows that changes have taken place?

Hubert Humphrey became the administration candidate and the preferred choice for many longtime Democrats.

Soon it appeared that Kennedy was pulling in front of McCarthy and Humphrey. Kennedy's program and popularity seemed broad enough to rebuild the Democratic coalition shattered by Vietnam. Then on June 5, 1968, just after winning the Democratic primary in California, Kennedy was assassinated by an Arab nationalist, angry at Kennedy for his support of Israel.

In August the Democrats held their national convention in Chicago. Now that Kennedy was dead, Humphrey was expected to win the nomination. However, furious at the Vice President's support of the war, about 10,000 protesters gathered in Chicago. Reflecting the "silent majority's distaste for the protesters, Chicago Mayor Daley, himself a Democrat, advised his police to get tough with the protesters. While violence reigned outside, the convention nominated Hubert Humphrey for President and Senator Edmund Muskie of Maine for Vice President.

The Candidates

The splintering of the Democratic party made the Republican candidate, Richard M. Nixon, the front-runner in the election of 1968. Although defeated in his campaign for President in 1960 and for governor of California in 1962, Nixon had remained active in national politics. For his vice-presidential running mate, Nixon chose Spiro T. Agnew, governor of Maryland.

In his campaign, Nixon promised to unify the nation, return dignity to the presidency, stabilize American foreign policy, and lead a war against crime in the streets. He said he had a plan for ending the war in Vietnam, but he did not provide details.

A third candidate, George Wallace, governor of Alabama, ran as an Independent in all 50 states. He selected General Curtis LeMay as his running mate. Wallace was against federally enforced civil rights, including desegregation and busing; Black Power; "pointy-headed intellectuals"; and social unrest. As a result of his civil rights stand, he attracted support in the South. Wallace also appealed to blue-collar workers in the North as well as the South. Leaders of organized labor, however, campaigned hard for Humphrey and moved much of the blue-collar vote back to the Democrats.

The Election of 1968

On Election Day, Nixon won, though the vote was very close. He received 31.8 million votes, while Humphrey had 31.3 million and Wallace, 9.9 million. In the Electoral College, Nixon won 301 votes to 191 for Humphrey and 46 for Wallace. However, although the people had elected a Republican President, the Democrats kept their majorities in both houses of Congress.

Speaking to reporters after his election, Nixon recalled seeing a young girl carrying a sign at one of his rallies that said: "Bring Us Together." This, he promised, would be his chief effort as President.

Section 3 ★ Review

Checking for Understanding

1. **Identify** hawks, doves, Robert McNamara, Woodstock, Eugene McCarthy, Hubert Humphrey.
2. **Define** student deferment, conscientious objector, teach-in, commune, counterculture.
3. **List** two reasons why some Americans began to oppose United States involvement in Vietnam.
4. **Explain** how the conservative backlash developed.

Critical Thinking

5. **Synthesizing Ideas** How did the war in Vietnam and increasing violence at home affect Americans' confidence in President Johnson?

---

940 UNIT 10 Redefining America 1954–Present

Answers to SECTION 3 REVIEW

1. hawks, 937; doves, 937; Robert McNamara, 937; Woodstock, 939; Eugene McCarthy, 939; Hubert Humphrey, 940
2. All vocabulary words are defined in the Glossary.
3. belief that Vietnam was not strategically important, the realization and horror at American deaths and the deaths of noncombatants.
4. Protests against the war and for civil rights unsettled many people. Fear of radicalism led to defense of conservative values.
5. Answers will vary. American perception that the war in Vietnam was not winnable increased opposition to Johnson's Vietnam policies. Domestic violence led to the perception that there was no law and order in the country.

SECTION 4

Secrecy and Summitry

Setting the Scene

Section Focus

The foreign policy of the Nixon administration was one of secrecy and surprise. Also during his administration, Nixon secretly plotted the bombing of Cambodia and the expansion of the war in Indochina. As opposition to the war heated up, government documents came to light that indicated Nixon, along with Kennedy and Johnson, had deceived the public about what was really going on in the Vietnam War. Finally, Nixon gave in and began withdrawing American troops.

Objectives

After studying this section, you should be able to
★ explain why Nixon pursued détente in foreign policy.
★ list and describe the steps that President Nixon took to end American involvement in Vietnam.

Key Terms

détente, summit, shuttle diplomacy

◀ VIEW AT THE VIETNAM MEMORIAL

Surprising both his supporters and his critics, Richard Nixon as President shed his long-held image as a "cold warrior." He opened a dialogue with the communist leaders of China and entered into a series of agreements with the Soviet Union. Nixon recognized the legitimacy of the communist regimes of Eastern Europe.

■ A New Policy

Like Woodrow Wilson, President Nixon took almost sole charge of foreign policy. To help him handle foreign policy matters, Nixon appointed Henry A. Kissinger, a brilliant political scientist, as his national security adviser. Kissinger's job was to present the President with policy options in which the probable consequences of each policy were outlined. Kissinger also undertook secret missions abroad. In 1973 Nixon appointed Kissinger secretary of state.

Nixon, like Wilson, wanted to be remembered as a peacemaker. In his Inaugural Address he proclaimed:

> *After a period of confrontation, we are entering an era of negotiation. Let all nations know that during this administration our lines of communication will be open. We seek an open world—open to ideas, open to the exchange of goods and people....*

CHAPTER 33 The Vietnam Era 1954–1975 **941**

Classroom Resources for SECTION 4

Teacher's Classroom Resources
- Reproducible Lesson Plan
- Reteaching Activity 33-4
- Chapter 33 Enrichment Activity
- Chapter 33 Performance Assessment Activity
- Spanish Summaries and Glossary
- Section Quiz

Multimedia
- Section Focus Transparency 110
- Vocabulary Puzzlemaker
- Testmaker
- Student Self-Test Software
- Communism and the Cold War

LESSON PLAN
SECTION 4, 941–945

FOCUS

Bellringer
Display Focus Activity 110 on the overhead projector, and assign the accompanying Focus Activity Book.

Objectives
Point out the objectives on this page in previewing the section content.

Motivating Activity
Write the word *détente* on the board. Ask students if they know its meaning. (easing of tensions between the superpowers) Point out that détente was one of the main features of Nixon's foreign policy.

Did You Know?

During the decade of the 1960s, the number of young people increased by 1.3 million a year. The 10-year increase of 13 million in the 14-to-24-age group was greater than the growth in young people during the first half of the twentieth century.

Communism and the Cold War

Side 1, Chapter 20
Title: *Détente*
Subject: Overview of détente between United States and the Soviet Union

CHAPTER 33
SECTION 4

TEACH
Guided Practice
Synthesizing Information
Have students divide a sheet of paper in three columns and head a column with each of these words: Summit, Surprise, Secrecy. Ask students to enter events under the appropriate column as they read the section. Review the completed lists with the class.
L1, LEP

Visualizing History Point out that the word *détente* is derived from the French word for "relaxation."
Answer to Caption: relaxation from tensions between two countries

Did You Know?
American involvement in Vietnam came to an end a week after Nixon's second inauguration. At the peace accords, all American forces were to withdraw from South Vietnam and all U.S. prisoners were to be returned. It was agreed that North Vietnamese forces would remain in areas of South Vietnam they already occupied. These were the same terms offered Nixon four years earlier, which he had rejected.

Visualizing History ▲ **OPENING THE LINES OF COMMUNICATION** President Richard Nixon worked to improve relations with the communist superpowers. The thaw in relations was reflected in the President's visits to the Soviet Union (left) and China (right). **What is détente?**

Nixon Proclaims Détente

Nixon proclaimed a policy of **détente,** or relaxation of tensions between the United States and the communist bloc. He maintained that it would be a "safer world and a better world if we have a strong, healthy United States, Europe, China, Russia, and Japan, each balancing the other."

To achieve this balance Nixon proposed a meeting between the United States and the Soviet Union to discuss strategic arms limitations. The SALT negotiations, as they were called, began in Helsinki, Finland, in 1969. Before the conclusion of SALT I in 1972, the two sides had agreed to ban biological warfare and limit the growth of nuclear weapons.

SALT culminated in the May 1972 Moscow **summit,** or diplomatic meeting, between the superpowers. In addition to signing the SALT agreement, Nixon and the Soviet leader, Leonid Brezhnev, also agreed to increase trade, exchange scientific information, and cooperate in preventing pollution.

Nixon and China

President Nixon also sought improved relations with China. He began by lifting trade and travel restrictions. The President also withdrew the Seventh Fleet from defending Taiwan, an island which China claimed as its own.

The Chinese responded to Nixon's initiatives in a variety of ways. More important, the Chinese accepted Henry Kissinger's proposal that he visit Beijing secretly to open discussions with Chinese leaders. During Kissinger's meeting with Chinese Premier Zhou En-lai (JOH EHN•lye), he arranged for President Nixon to visit China in February 1972. President Nixon's sensational announcement that he would visit Beijing foreshadowed the 1971 admission of the government of the People's Republic of China to the United Nations.

■ War in Vietnam

During the 1968 presidential campaign, Nixon declared that he had a plan for ending the Vietnam War. After his inauguration he resumed negotiations with the North Vietnamese, but they produced little.

The President faced a dilemma: if he continued United States involvement in the war, public opposition would increase. If he withdrew United States troops without a peace agreement, he would be the first President of the United States ever to lose a war.

942   UNIT 10 Redefining America 1954–Present

Sidelights: Nixon's Foreign Policy

Although President Nixon escalated the Vietnam War, he gained stature from his achievements in foreign policy, especially as the sponsor of détente. In 1969 he announced a "Nixon Doctrine" based on his willingness to forgo future military intervention like that in Vietnam. In Moscow he negotiated the limiting of strategic missiles and ended the production of biological weapons. Also, in 1971 the United States relaxed its opposition, and the People's Republic of China was admitted to the United Nations, replacing the Chinese Nationalist government of Taiwan.

The Pentagon Papers

To make matters worse, in June 1971, *The New York Times* published a secret Department of Defense study. *The Pentagon Papers*, as they were called, documented that for two decades, four Presidents had escalated the nation's involvement in Indochina.

The Pentagon Papers were evidence of the growing power of the executive branch. They contained details of decisions made by Presidents and their advisers without the consent of Congress. *The Pentagon Papers* also showed how the administrations acted to deceive Congress and the public about Vietnam.

President Nixon was outraged over the "leaking" of the secret documents. He ordered the Justice Department to go to court to stop further publication of the papers. Nixon hoped the court would affirm the government's right to restrain publication in matters of national security, but the Supreme Court decided that *The Pentagon Papers* were not vital to national security.

The federal government then brought charges against Daniel Ellsberg, one of the authors of *The Pentagon Papers*, for leaking the documents to the press. President Nixon also authorized a group of people who were called "the Plumbers" to break into the office of Ellsberg's psychiatrist to collect information about him. When their activities came to light, the charges against Daniel Ellsberg were dropped.

The United States in Vietnam, 1950–1975

1950	**May 8** President Truman sends U.S. aid and advisers to French forces in Indochina
1954	**May 7** French defeated by Communists at Dien Bien Phu
	July 20–21 Geneva Conference provides cease-fire and divides Vietnam
1957	Vietcong begin attacks in South Vietnam
1960	**Dec. 20** Vietcong form National Front for the Liberation of South Vietnam
1961	**Nov. 16** President Kennedy increases number of U.S. advisers in Vietnam
1963	**Nov. 1** Ngo Dinh Diem assassinated
1964	**July 24** U.S. rejects French President de Gaulle's plan to neutralize all of Indochina
	Aug. 2–4 Gulf of Tonkin—N. Vietnam attacks a U.S. destroyer and U.S. retaliates
	Aug. 7 Gulf of Tonkin Resolution—Congress grants President Johnson authority to use force against aggression
1965	**Feb. 7–8** First U.S. bombing of North Vietnam
	March 2 Rolling Thunder bombing campaign begins against North Vietnam
	March 8–9 President Johnson sends 3,500 Marines (first combat troops) to join 23,500 U.S. advisers
1966	**March 2** U.S. forces number 215,000
	Dec. 31 U.S. forces number 389,000
1967	**May 19** First U.S. air strike against central Hanoi
1968	**Jan. 30–Feb. 24** Tet offensive by Vietcong
	March 31 President Johnson announces cessation of bombing of N. Vietnam north of 20th parallel and that he will not seek reelection
	May 10 Paris Peace Talks begin between U.S. and N. Vietnam
1969	**January 25** First full session of Paris Peace Talks with Vietcong and S. Vietnam also represented
	March 16 My Lai massacre (revealed in November 1969)
	June 8 President Nixon announces the withdrawal of 25,000 U.S. troops from Vietnam
	Sept. 3 Death of Ho Chi Minh
	Oct. 15 Vietnam Moratorium Day—nationwide antiwar demonstrations across the U.S.
1970	**Feb. 20** Presidential adviser Henry A. Kissinger opens secret peace negotiations in Paris
	April 29 U.S. troops invade Cambodia
	May 4 Four antiwar students killed during demonstrations at Kent State University, Ohio
	July 24 Senate votes to repeal Gulf of Tonkin Resolution
1971	**Nov. 12** President Nixon limits U.S. ground forces in Vietnam to a defensive role
1972	**April 15–20** Widespread antiwar demonstrations in U.S.
	June 17–22 Watergate break-in and arrests
	Aug. 12 Last U.S. ground combat troops leave Vietnam
	Dec. 18–30 Bombing of Hanoi and Haiphong resumed to break stalled peace negotiations
1973	**Jan. 27** Cease-fire in Vietnam agreed upon
	Feb. 12 N. Vietnam releases first U.S. prisoners of war
1974	**Aug. 9** President Nixon resigns
1975	**April 29–30** North Vietnamese capture Saigon; American personnel evacuated; Vietnam War ends

Source: *The New York Times*, April 30, 1985; *An Encyclopedia of World History*, 5th ed. (1972); Gorton Carruth, *What Happened When* (1989); James S. Olson, *Dictionary of the Vietnam War* (1988)

Chart Study American involvement in Vietnam grew rapidly after the first combat troops arrived in 1965. In 1975 troops from North Vietnam moved into South Vietnam, and it came under communist control. **When did the Tet offensive take place?**

CHAPTER 33 The Vietnam Era 1954–1975 943

CHAPTER 33
SECTION 4

Teaching American Portraits

The Civil Rights Memorial is inscribed with a quote from Martin Luther King, Jr., which comes from the Bible: "Until justice rolls down like waters and righteousness like a mighty stream." Ask students to discuss the meaning of these words.

Side 2, Chapter 10
Title: *Middle East*
Subject: ABC News reports examine U.S. decision to intervene and assist Israel in the 1973 Yom Kippur War

Did You Know?

In 1973 Henry Kissinger of the United States shared the Nobel Peace Prize with Le Duc Tho of North Vietnam for negotiating a cease-fire in the Vietnam War.

Food of the Times

Nixon's trip to China led to a renewed interest in China—including Chinese food. Chinese restaurants across the United States tried to duplicate many of the dishes served at the many banquets the President attended.

AMERICAN PORTRAITS

Maya Lin
1959–

Maya Lin was a 21-year-old architecture student at Yale University when her design for the Vietnam Veterans Memorial was selected in a national competition. Lin's simple but powerful and unique design joined two gleaming black granite walls inscribed with the names of the war's 58,000 dead and missing. While Maya's work was initially controversial, today the memorial is a symbol of national healing.

Maya was born and raised in Athens, Ohio. Her parents, both of whom had emigrated from China in the 1940s, were college professors. Maya was a good high school student, with a particular aptitude for mathematics.

In 1988, Maya Lin designed the Civil Rights Memorial in Montgomery, Alabama. Recently she completed a memorial at Yale University and designed the interior of the Museum of African Art in New York City.

President Nixon's response to the publication was a further sign that the credibility of his administration was eroding. Nixon himself, it was revealed, had ordered the secret bombing of North Vietnamese sanctuaries in Cambodia in 1969. In April 1970, Nixon, without consulting Congress, ordered an invasion of Cambodia to drive the North Vietnamese out of the country. Protests against the war now intensified.

Nixon Announces Vietnamization

To quiet opposition to the war, Nixon announced a policy of "Vietnamization." Vietnamization consisted of two steps: the phased withdrawal of United States troops, and their replacement by conscripts from Vietnam. Nixon hoped that Vietnamization, combined with saturation bombing of North Vietnam, would allow the United States to withdraw from the war "with honor."

By the end of the war, the total tonnage of bombs dropped by the United States on Vietnam was more than twice that dropped by the United States on all targets in both World War II and the Korean War.

Finally, on January 23, 1973, the United States, South Vietnam, North Vietnam, and the Vietcong signed a cease-fire agreement, ending the military presence of the United States in Vietnam. The war, however, did not end for the people of Vietnam. Although United States troops withdrew from South Vietnam, North Vietnamese troops did not.

The End of the War

In 1974 the weakened forces of South Vietnam abandoned distant outposts they could no longer defend, and North Vietnamese forces captured several provincial capitals. In January 1975, North Vietnam launched a major offensive. By late March they drove South Vietnamese troops from a region known as the Central Highlands, approximately 160 miles north of Saigon. While thousands of civilians retreated with the soldiers, many died in the gunfire or from starvation. The South Vietnamese army soon collapsed, and by early April, the North Vietnamese army had reached the outskirts of Saigon.

Hoping to stall the communist drive, President Gerald Ford, Nixon's successor, requested more than $700 million in military aid for South Vietnam. Congress, however, approved only $300 million, to be used chiefly to evacuate Americans from Saigon. On April 29, as North Vietnamese troops overtook Saigon, the United States carried out an emergency evacuation of all remaining Americans and many South Vietnamese refugees.

944 UNIT 10 Redefining America 1954–Present

Critical Thinking

Expressing an Opinion Ask students to answer the following question: Do you agree or disagree with Nixon's attempt to stop the publication of the *Pentagon Papers* leaked by a Pentagon expert, Daniel Ellsberg, to the press? Why or why not? In their answers, ask students to discuss under what circumstances, if any, the government should misrepresent the atrocities of war and United States participation in order to protect the innocence of the American people. Have students explain their answers in a brief paragraph. **L3**

The war ended when the Saigon government surrendered on April 30, 1975. North and South Vietnam were formally united as the Socialist Republic of Vietnam on July 2, 1976.

War in the Middle East

On October 6, 1973, the Jewish holiday of Yom Kippur, Egyptian and Syrian troops launched surprise attacks against Israeli forces. Their objective was to recapture the territory Egypt and Syria had lost to Israel during the Six-Day War of 1967. Caught by surprise, the Israeli troops were pushed back, but they quickly regrouped and launched their own attack, pushing into Syria and across the Suez Canal into Egypt.

Israel appealed to the United States for help, and President Nixon responded with a massive airlift of $2 billion in military supplies. At the same time, the Soviet Union continued to supply Egypt and Syria. American aid to Israel angered the Arab countries, and quickly they retaliated by placing an embargo on the shipment of oil to the United States and other countries that supported Israel.

Even as the United States and the Soviet Union gave aid to the opposing sides, they worked through the United Nations Security Council to arrange a cease-fire. In late October, the nations of Israel, Egypt, and Syria agreed to terms. By the end of 1973, a UN peacekeeping force had been sent to the Middle East to police the region.

After the conflict, Secretary of State Henry Kissinger worked with Israel and Egypt to reduce tensions in the Middle East. For the next two years, he engaged in **shuttle diplomacy,** flying back and forth between the capitals of the two nations in an effort to produce a lasting peace. Kissinger's efforts yielded two important results. Early in 1974 Golda Meir, the prime minister of Israel, and Anwar el-Sadat, the president of Egypt, agreed to establish diplomatic relations again between their countries. Then in September 1975, Israel and Egypt agreed to withdraw their forces from the cease-fire line. Although significant problems remained, a measure of peace had been achieved in the Middle East.

 ▲ **THE FALL OF SAIGON** On April 28, 1975, President Ford ordered the emergency helicopter evacuation of all Americans remaining in Vietnam. *When did the United States end its military involvement in Vietnam?*

Section 4 ★ Review

Checking for Understanding

1. **Identify** Henry Kissinger, Leonid Brezhnev, SALT, Zhou En-lai, *The Pentagon Papers,* Daniel Ellsberg, Vietnamization.
2. **Define** détente, summit, shuttle diplomacy.
3. **List** three steps taken during Nixon's presidency to end United States involvement in Vietnam.
4. **Describe** how Henry Kissinger's shuttle diplomacy helped to end war in the Middle East.

Critical Thinking

5. **Evaluating Foreign Policy** Evaluate the pros and cons of Nixon's use of secrecy in China and Vietnam.

REVIEW CHAPTER 33

Answers

Reviewing Facts
1. In Vienna Kennedy and Khrushchev quarreled over Berlin, resulting in building of Berlin Wall. In Cuba they came to brink of war over Soviet missiles, resulting in removal of missiles. Both agreed to Nuclear Test Ban Treaty.
2. Communist guerrillas attempted to take over the governments of Laos and Vietnam. Kennedy had to decide on how much the United States should be involved. Negotiated cease-fire in Laos. Sent U.S. advisers to Vietnam.
3. Little popular support for South Vietnamese government; Vietnamese Communists were militarily strong and had widespread support; difficult for American troops to fight against the hit-and-run tactics of the enemy.

Understanding Concepts
1. American policy in Vietnam was founded on containment and the "domino theory" belief that if Vietnam fell, so would the rest of Southeast Asia.
2. Answers will vary. Nonviolent measures had some success in identifying areas of discrimination. Some national legislation was passed to deal with these. The 1960s riots did bring attention to the goals of the black-power movement, but one might question the cost involved, which included deaths and the destruction of property.

CHAPTER 33 ★ REVIEW

Using Vocabulary

Imagine you are a reporter who is covering the diplomatic meeting between the superpowers at Moscow in May 1972. Use the following vocabulary words to write an article describing the history of the United States's cold war struggle against communism.

reactionary government
credibility gap
war of national liberation
search-and-destroy strategy
summit
escalation
détente

Reviewing Facts

1. **Summarize** Kennedy's relations with Khrushchev.
2. **Explain** the many foreign policy challenges that Kennedy faced in Southeast Asia.
3. **State** two reasons why it was difficult for the United States to win the war in Vietnam.

Understanding Concepts

War
1. Explain how Americans' perceptions of communism influenced United States policy to support South Vietnam.

Social Upheaval
2. Evaluate the effectiveness of violent versus nonviolent demonstrations. What were the results of nonviolent demonstrations in the early 1960s?

Critical Thinking

1. **Inferring Results** What lessons about military intervention do you think President Kennedy learned from the Bay of Pigs?
2. **Analyzing Art** Study the photograph on this page of the Vietnam Veterans Memorial, then answer the questions that follow.
   a. Compare the Vietnam Memorial with other national monuments and memorials. In what way is the design of the Memorial unique?

b. The Vietnam Veterans Memorial is one of the most visited of our nation's monuments. Why do you think this is so?

Writing About History

Narration

Imagine that it is 1968 and you have just received a draft notice in the mail. Though you are legally obligated to join the military, many Americans at this time are refusing to be drafted. Write an essay explaining whether or not you will fight in the war.

Cooperative Learning

Work with two other group members to explore the options facing President Kennedy during the Cuban missile crisis. List two potential consequences of each option.

Social Studies Skills

Reading Terrain Maps

Two kinds of terrain maps are shown on page 947—a terrain model and a topographic map. The two maps show roughly the same area of Vietnam. The terrain model is a representation of the shape of the land, with hills and valleys shown. Although the actual model is only two-dimensional, the shading and shapes of the dark areas make the model appear three-dimensional.

946 UNIT 10 Redefining America 1954–Present

Critical Thinking
1. Answers will vary. Kennedy probably learned not to intervene without local support. The Alliance for Progress and Peace Corps attempted to enlist local support to thwart the spread of communism.

2. a. Answers will vary but may include its dimensions and the names printed on it.
b. Answers will vary but may include that many Americans had relatives or friends who served.

Practicing the Skill
1. valleys and relatively flat land
2. For the purpose of the map—show troop movements—distances are not important.
3. No, neither map has any scale or markings for elevation.

CHAPTER 33 ★ REVIEW

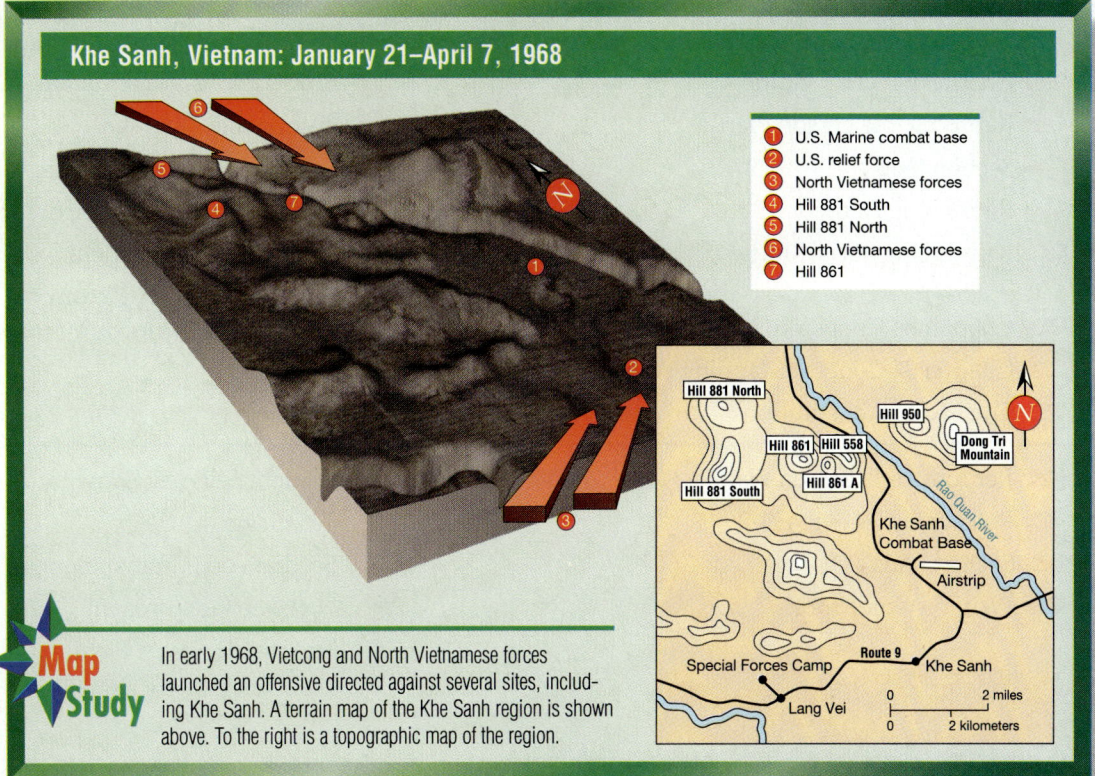

Khe Sanh, Vietnam: January 21–April 7, 1968

1. U.S. Marine combat base
2. U.S. relief force
3. North Vietnamese forces
4. Hill 881 South
5. Hill 881 North
6. North Vietnamese forces
7. Hill 861

Map Study
In early 1968, Vietcong and North Vietnamese forces launched an offensive directed against several sites, including Khe Sanh. A terrain map of the Khe Sanh region is shown above. To the right is a topographic map of the region.

The topographic map is a two-dimensional map showing elevations using contour lines. A contour line represents points that are all at the same elevation. Each contour line represents a successively higher or lower elevation. The vertical distance between contour lines is the same for all lines in a particular topographic map.

Practicing the Skill

Use the two terrain maps to answer the following questions.
1. The 3-D terrain model shows the paths of North Vietnamese forces during one part of the Tet offensive. Over what land features did the North Vietnamese forces travel?
2. Why do you suppose there are no distance or elevation scales on the 3-D model?
3. Can elevation of the hills in either map be determined? Why or why not?

Using Your Journal
From your journal notes and knowledge of how the Vietnam War has been viewed over the years, write a paragraph explaining whether you think the hawks or doves were correct in their views.

CHAPTER 33 The Vietnam Era 1954–1975

REVIEW CHAPTER 33

? Chapter Bonus Test Question
Which of the following events was the most significant to American life? Give reasons in support of your choice.
Cuban missile crisis
Tet offensive
Vietcong signing of the cease-fire agreement
(Answers will vary but should reflect an understanding that significance is measured by an event's long-term effects.)

Using Your Journal
Students' answers should reflect an understanding of the views of the group they choose to support—hawks supported the war, doves opposed it.

PLANNING GUIDE   Chapter 34   Camelot to Watergate

Daily Lesson Objectives	Teacher Classroom Resources	Multimedia
SECTION 1 **Kennedy's New Frontier** 1 Day pp. 950–954 1. Describe important legislation Kennedy proposed during his term of office. 2. Describe the impact of Kennedy's death.	Chapter 34 Study Guide Reproducible Lesson Plan Section Quiz Reteaching Activity 34-1 Reinforcing Social Studies Skills 53, 59, 65, 69–72 Chapter 34 Cooperative Learning Activity Chapter 34 Concept Mapping Activity The Living Constitution	Student Self-Test Software Testmaker Section Focus Transparency 112 Chapter 34 Skills Transparency Powers of the President The Presidents: A Picture History of Our Nation
SECTION 2 **The Great Society** 1 Day pp. 956–960 1. Explain how Johnson's belief in consensus helped win the 1964 election. 2. Discuss Johnson's efforts to fight poverty.	Reproducible Lesson Plan Reteaching Activity 34-2 Section Quiz Writer's Guidebook	Student Self-Test Software Testmaker Section Focus Transparency 113 Focus on Government The Presidents: A Picture History of Our Nation
SECTION 3 **An Imperial Presidency** 1 Day pp. 962–966 1. Describe how Nixon tried to deal with the economic problems of the early 1970s. 2. Explain how Nixon handled the war on crime and the energy crisis.	Reproducible Lesson Plan Reteaching Activity 34-3 Section Quiz American Portraits 64 Chapter 34 Primary and Secondary Source Readings Reinforcing Social Studies Skills 26, 32, 53, 55, 59, 61 Writer's Guidebook	Student Self-Test Software Testmaker Section Focus Transparency 114 Powers of the President The Presidents: A Picture History of Our Nation
SECTION 4 **The Watergate Scandal** 1 Day pp. 967–971 1. Explain how the constitutional process resolved the Watergate crisis. 2. List the ways in which Congress sought to reassert its constitutional powers.	Reproducible Lesson Plan Reteaching Activity 34-4 Section Quiz Chapter 34 Enrichment Activity American Portrait 67 Chapter 34 Primary and Secondary Source Readings Reinforcing Social Studies Skills 49, 55 The Living Constitution Spanish Summaries & Glossary	Student Self-Test Software Testmaker Section Focus Transparency 115 Vocabulary Puzzlemaker Audiocassette, Chapter 34 Powers of the President The Presidents: A Picture History of Our Nation
CHAPTER REVIEW AND EVALUATION 1 Day	Chapter 34 Test Chapter 34 Performance Assessment Activity	Student Self-Test Software Testmaker

OUT OF TIME? If time does not permit teaching the entire chapter, use the Chapter 34 Summary on pages 1028–1029 and the Chapter 34 audiocassette (English and Spanish) to point out the main ideas of the chapter.

PLANNING GUIDE

Cultural Diversity Activity

Comparing Immigration Laws The Immigration Act of 1965 eliminated quotas setting limits on the number of people entering the United States from various countries. In its place lawmakers set an annual limit of 120,000 immigrants for the Western Hemisphere and 170,000 for the Eastern Hemisphere. In 1978 the law was revised to create a single global quota of 290,000. The 1965 law gave priority to immigrants with close relatives in the United States, political refugees, and people with special skills such as doctors, engineers, and scientists.

Ask students to write an essay comparing the 1965 law with the one passed in 1924. The essays should explain how the two laws are similar, what differences seem most striking, and how students account for those differences. Use the essays to stimulate a discussion of the causes and effects of shifts in the nation's immigration policies.

Performance Assessment Activity

Domestic Policy Have students choose one of the Presidents highlighted in this chapter and write a speech defining his approach to domestic problems. The speeches should begin by describing his objectives, then outline policies based on those objectives, and conclude with a critical examination of the results of those policies. Students might work alone on the speeches or in small groups. Encourage speechwriters to read their address to the class. The class might compare the way different Presidents approached the nation's domestic problems. Students might also focus on a single President and compare his domestic policy with his approach to foreign affairs (Chapter 33). What similarities do they detect? What differences seem most striking? How do they account for those differences?

POSSIBLE RUBRIC FEATURES: Research skills, content information, organization, written and oral communication skills, critical thinking skills

Chapter Resources

Literature from the Period
Nixon, Richard M. "Farewell Address." August 1974.

Readings for the Student
Cummins, Duane. *Conflict and Compromise: The 1960's and 1970's.* Glencoe, 1980.

"Energy: Powering Our Nation." *Cobblestone,* Vol. 2, No 10, October 1990.

Readings for the Teacher
Ambrose, Stephen E. *Nixon: The Triumph of a Politician.* Simon and Schuster, 1989.

Goodwin, Richard. *Remembering America: A Voice from the Sixties.* Little, Brown, 1988.

Manchester, William. *The Glory and the Dream.* Little, Brown, 1972.

Multimedia Resources
All the President's Men. Warner. (VHS, 135 minutes)

That Memorable Year: 1963. Media Access Corp. (VHS, 50 minutes)

Television: A Study of Media Ethics. Tom Snyder. (Apple or IBM diskette)

Watergate: Computer Version. Thomas Henderson. (Apple diskette)

Watergate Hearings: Summer of Judgment. WETA (VHS, 120 minutes)

Key to Ability Levels

Teaching strategies have been coded for varying learning styles and abilities.

- **L1** Basic activities for all students
- **L2** Average activities for average to above-average students
- **L3** Challenging activities for above-average students
- **LEP** Limited English Proficiency activities

Glencoe Links to the Humanities

Links to Literature
- Macmillan Literature: Understanding Literature Audiotapes Sides 2, 5
- Macmillan Literature: Appreciating Literature Audiotapes Side 4
- Macmillan Literature: American Literature Audiotapes Side 5
- Macmillan Literature: Appreciating Literature Video—
- Macmillan Literature: American Literature Text— Robert Penn Warren, James Wright, William Stafford, Bernard Malamud, William Saroyan, Truman Capote, A.C. Greene, Anne Tyler, John Updike, William Goyen

Link to Music
- American Music: Cultural Traditions

CHAPTER 34

BEGINNING THE CHAPTER

Explain that this was a time of great hope and great despair. It began with Kennedy's dream of a "New Frontier" and ended with the resignation of Nixon.

ABCNEWS INTERACTIVE

Videodisc
Powers of the President

Side 2, Chapter 23
Title: *Watergate Scandal*
Subject: Montage of news reports about the scandal

Side 2, Chapter 24
Title: *Presidential Denials*
Subject: Nixon denies involvement in Watergate

Side 2, Chapter 25
Title: *Watergate Committee Hearings*
Subject: Montage of statements

Side 2, Chapter 26
Title: *House Judiciary Committee*
Subject: Committee votes articles of impeachment

Side 2, Chapter 27
Title: *The President Resigns*
Subject: Excerpts from Nixon's resignation speech

CHAPTER 34

Camelot to Watergate
1960–1976

▶ HYDRANT DECORATED FOR NATION'S BICENTENNIAL

Setting the Scene

Focus

During the brief administration of John F. Kennedy, his leadership and the American people were repeatedly tested by staggering challenges at home and abroad. During Johnson's administration federal spending for social programs, along with the cost of the war in Vietnam, strained the government's budget. The Nixon administration was troubled by questions about illegal activities that led to Nixon's resignation and left the nation with deep wounds.

Concepts to Understand

★ How election mandates affect a President's ability to govern
★ How presidential power is balanced by the other branches of federal government

Read to Discover . . .

★ how Kennedy's and Johnson's approaches to economic problems differed from Nixon's.
★ what developments caused Nixon to resign the presidency.

Journal Notes
In what ways has corruption affected politics in America? Note details in your journal as you read the chapter.

Timeline

CULTURAL
- 1964 The Beatles come to America
- 1968 Cost of mailing a letter increases to 6 cents
- 1969 Neil Armstrong walks on the moon

1960 — **1965**

POLITICAL
- 1963 Kennedy assassinated; Lyndon Johnson becomes President
- 1968 Nixon appoints Warren Burger head of Supreme Court
- 1969 Nixon announces new federalism

✚ EXTRA CREDIT PROJECT

Ask interested students to write a campaign speech for a presidential candidate in 1960, 1964, or 1968. The speeches should address the issues of the day and offer the candidates' views on those issues. Encourage volunteers to read their speeches to the class. Discuss similarities and differences within a given election and between elections.

CHAPTER 34 CONCEPTS

Concept Mapping Activity
Write the chapter generalization and concepts on the chalkboard. Ask students to copy them into their notebooks and to list each major event in the chapter under the appropriate concept.

> The style of leadership and the domestic policies of President Kennedy and President Johnson differed from those of President Nixon.
> - The New Frontier
> - The Great Society
> - The New Federalism

History AND ART
The Peace Corps in Ethiopia, 1966 by Norman Rockwell

Rockwell's painting depicts a young American volunteer giving instructions on the use of a plow. Peace Corps volunteers worked in many developing countries around the world.

◀ PRESIDENT JOHN F. KENNEDY

History AND ART
Norman Rockwell's *The Peace Corps in Ethiopia* depicts a young American volunteer giving instruction on using a plow.

- **1971** Amtrak passenger service begins
- **1976** Bicentennial celebration of the United States

|1970| |1975|

- **1973** Vice President Agnew resigns
- **1974** Watergate scandal unfolds; Nixon resigns
- **1975** Several of Nixon's aides are convicted

Linking Across TIME
John F. Kennedy was the first President born in the twentieth century.

CHAPTER 34 Camelot to Watergate 1960–1976   **949**

Recording Journal Notes
Suggest that students also include actions by Congress to curb presidential power and future abuses.

Teacher Notes

949

LESSON PLAN
SECTION 1, 950–955

FOCUS
Bellringer
Before taking roll at the beginning of the class period, display Focus Activity 111 on the overhead projector, and assign the accompanying Focus Activity Sheet.

Objectives
Point out the objectives on this page to students in previewing the section content.

Motivating Activity
Read aloud the following excerpt from President Kennedy's Inaugural Address:

"Let the word go forth from this time and place, to friend and foe alike, that the torch has been passed to a new generation of Americans born in this century, tempered by war, disciplined by a cold and bitter peace."

Ask students: What qualities do you associate with the term "new generation of Americans"? (youth, optimism, promise, opportunity, idealism, bravery)

Use Skills Transparency 34.

The following material is available from Glencoe and may be used to enrich Chapter 34:

CD-ROM
- *The Presidents: A Picture History of Our Nation*

SECTION 1

Kennedy's New Frontier

Setting the Scene

Section Focus
By the late 1950s, many people in the United States felt it was time to attack the nation's problems vigorously. Despite the prosperity of the postwar years, poverty was still prevalent. Eisenhower, the first President to be legally limited to two terms, would soon be leaving office. The people looked to his still-unchosen successor to provide strong, active leadership.

Objectives
After studying this section, you should be able to
★ describe important legislation Kennedy proposed during his term of office.
★ describe the impact of Kennedy's death on the nation.

Key Terms
mandate, pragmatist, urban renewal

 DECORATIVE FLAG, COMPUTER ART

Washington, D.C., glittered during the Kennedy years. As never before, millions became familiar with the occupants of the White House. The public's enchantment with Kennedy was not shared by Congress, however. Many of Kennedy's most important legislative efforts would have to wait until after his death to become law.

■ The Election of 1960

In the 1960 presidential campaign, the Republicans chose Vice President Richard M. Nixon and the Democrats chose Senator John F. Kennedy of Massachusetts. As his vice-presidential running mate Nixon chose UN Ambassador Henry Cabot Lodge. To win Southern support, Kennedy chose Texas Senator Lyndon B. Johnson.

The backgrounds of the two presidential candidates presented striking contrasts. Kennedy was a Catholic and the second-oldest son of a wealthy family. Nixon, born in California, was from far more humble origins, and his Quaker mother had struggled to keep the family together.

There were also similarities between the two men. Both were young: Nixon was 47 years old, and Kennedy was 43. Nixon and Kennedy were experienced legislators, both having served in the House of Representatives or in the Senate. Nixon had also served eight years as Eisenhower's Vice President.

The Impact of Television

The political differences between the candidates were small. Both were considered "cold warriors" who believed that communism was the chief threat to the way of life in

950 UNIT 10 Redefining America: 1954–Present

Classroom Resources for SECTION 1

Teacher's Classroom Resources
- Chapter 34 Study Guide
- Reproducible Lesson Plan
- Reteaching Activity 34-1
- Chapter 34 Cooperative Learning Activity
- Section Quiz

Multimedia
- Section Focus Transparency 111
- Chapter 34 Skills Transparency
- Testmaker
- Student Self-Test Software
- Powers of the President
- The Presidents: A Picture History of Our Nation

the United States. Senator Kennedy hoped to take advantage of Republican weaknesses and challenged Nixon to a series of televised debates. Nixon was the more skilled debater, and most who heard the debates on radio declared Nixon the winner. Yet, the millions more who watched on television thought a well-prepared, poised, and youthful Senator Kennedy won the debates. The debates were one of the earliest examples of the strong impact television would have on politics in the United States.

The Issue of Religion

Political observers wondered whether Kennedy's religion would be an obstacle to his election. No Catholic had ever been elected President, and some believed that a Catholic could not make official decisions independent from the Roman Catholic Church. Kennedy answered by stressing his belief in the separation of church and state. He declared he would resign, rather than violate either his conscience or the interests of the nation.

Kennedy won the election, finally laying to rest the idea that a Roman Catholic could not be elected President. Analyzing his victory, Kennedy concluded, "It was TV more than anything else that turned the tide." However, he carried the election by one of the narrowest margins in American history. He won the popular vote by 120,000 out of 68 million votes cast and the Electoral College by 303 to 219. In several states a difference of only a few thousand votes would have swung the electoral votes the other way. As a result, Kennedy did not enter office with a clear **mandate,** or endorsement, of his ideas from the American people. Nevertheless, though he was cautious at first, the new President moved ahead with his domestic program.

▶ KENNEDY-NIXON DEBATE

▲ THE 1960 ELECTION At the start of the 1960 election campaign, polls showed Richard Nixon in the lead. Kennedy, who had been less in the public eye than Nixon, began to draw enthusiastic responses on the campaign trail and revealed that he was highly informed and poised under fire. *What impact did the televised debates have on voters?*

CHAPTER 34 Camelot to Watergate 1960–1976

CHAPTER 34
SECTION 1

TEACH
Guided Practice

Journalism Divide the class into small groups. Have each group produce a newsletter in which it describes the successes and failures of Kennedy's domestic programs. Some topics groups might include are successes—passing the Area Redevelopment Act and the Housing Act of 1961, increased federal funding for education, attention to civil rights, funding for a national space program; failures—difficulties with Congress and business leaders, obstacles in establishing a department of urban affairs and in passing legislation to provide national health insurance for the poor and elderly. **L2**

Did You Know?
John Kennedy, his wife, and their two small children were the youngest family to live in the White House since Theodore Roosevelt's days.

Visualizing History
Nixon and Kennedy were the first presidential candidates to debate on television. **Answer to Caption:** They may have swung the election in Kennedy's favor.

Special Needs

Study Strategy Many students will not use a learning strategy unless they are fully aware of its benefits. Explain the benefits of summarizing by saying: "Summarizing is a way of remaining actively involved in reading by committing yourself to making decisions about information in the text so that it is compact enough to be easily remembered." Then ask these questions about the material on the 1960 presidential election: Which point should be included in a summary—that Kennedy and Nixon took part in a televised debate or that Kennedy was the son of wealthy parents? Why?

CHAPTER 34
SECTION 1

Independent Practice

Research Divide the class into small groups. Assign to each one aspect of Kennedy's domestic policies to research and critique. Sample topics might include the Housing Act of 1961, the Area Redevelopment Act, and increased funding for NASA. Ask groups to describe the program to the class and then assess its successes and failures. **L3**

Map Study Using Maps

Answer: Northeast and the South

Skills Practice
Where did Nixon make his strongest showing? (the West)

Side 2, Chapter 73
Title: *Patronage*
Subject: Robert Kennedy becomes attorney general

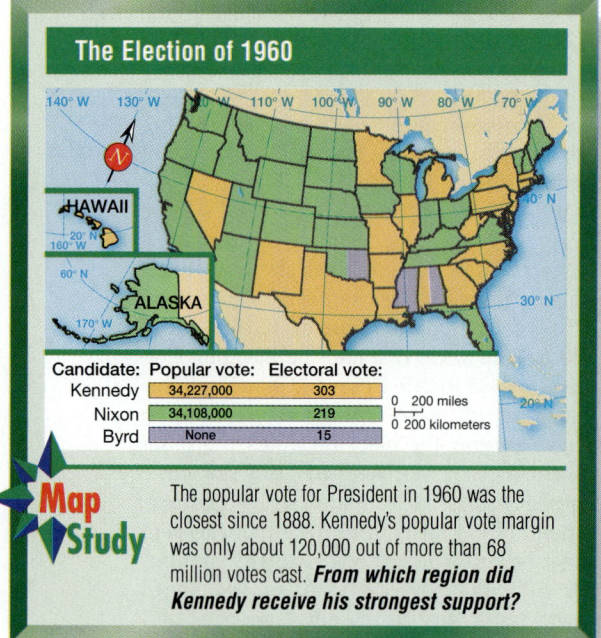

The Election of 1960

Candidate:	Popular vote:	Electoral vote:
Kennedy	34,227,000	303
Nixon	34,108,000	219
Byrd	None	15

Map Study
The popular vote for President in 1960 was the closest since 1888. Kennedy's popular vote margin was only about 120,000 out of more than 68 million votes cast. **From which region did Kennedy receive his strongest support?**

The New Frontier

Kennedy devoted his Inaugural Address to defining the role of the United States in a divided world. The torch, he said, had been "passed to a new generation," committed to the rights for which the United States had stood since the Revolution. He warned the communist world that the United States would remain strong, but he also urged both sides to renew the search for peace. He wanted both to join forces against the common enemies of "tyranny, poverty, disease, and war itself." In ringing tones, he declared:

> My fellow Americans, ask not what your country can do for you: Ask what you can do for your country. My fellow citizens of the world: Ask not what America can do for you, but what together we can do for the freedom of man.

The Kennedy administration became known as the "New Frontier." For the first time, the future of the United States lay in the hands of those born in the twentieth century. The President and his closest advisers were intelligent and tough-minded. They were sure of their ability to make the country and the world better places to live in.

Kennedy and his advisers organized a domestic program—the New Frontier—to meet the challenges of poverty and slow economic growth. After his election, Kennedy named as his advisers the "best and brightest" of his generation.

Although he showed a great deal of idealism, Kennedy was also a **pragmatist** who searched for practical solutions to problems. His gifts of leadership inspired trust and devotion in people throughout the nation.

Kennedy's Economic Program

Essentially, Kennedy's New Frontier was a continuation of Roosevelt's New Deal and Truman's Fair Deal. Kennedy promised to stimulate the economy with tax cuts and increased federal spending.

Promoting Economic Growth

In 1960, though the country was still prosperous, the economy was slowing down. When Kennedy became President, the nation's rate of economic growth was only 3 percent a year. Kennedy looked for ways to increase growth and create more jobs. In stimulating the economy, he chose not to rely on federal spending, which tends to cause inflation. Instead he sought to increase business production and efficiency. His administration also asked businesses to hold down prices and labor leaders to hold down requests for pay increases.

Conflicts With Steel Companies

Prodded by Secretary of Labor Arthur Goldberg, labor unions in the steel industry agreed to reduce their demands for higher wages. Despite this agreement, several steel companies raised prices sharply in 1962. Kennedy denounced the steel company executives and threatened to have the Department of Defense buy cheaper steel from foreign companies. He also instructed

---

Sidelights: Kennedy's Wit

President Kennedy's press conferences were marked by witty asides and friendly banter with reporters. For example, when chided by a reporter for appointing his younger brother, Robert, as attorney general, Kennedy replied, "I can't see that it's wrong to give him a little legal experience before he goes out to practice law." On a visit to France, during which the French press seemed more interested in what his wife was wearing, Kennedy announced, "I am the man who accompanied Jacqueline Kennedy to Paris, and I have enjoyed it."

the Justice Department to investigate whether the steel industry was guilty of price-fixing. The steel companies backed down and cut their prices. To achieve this victory, however, Kennedy had strained his relations with the nation's business leaders. As a result of his actions to stimulate the economy, Kennedy achieved his aim of raising the growth rate, which doubled during his administration.

Legislative Victories

Kennedy was able to win some legislative victories in his domestic program. After getting a bill for federal aid to public schools passed, he tried to wipe out areas of poverty, notably in the Appalachian Mountain region, in much of the South, and in the nation's inner cities. Kennedy supported the Area Redevelopment Act, designed to encourage industries to move into economically depressed areas. His Housing Act of 1961 called for $5 billion for **urban renewal,** or programs to improve homes and neighborhoods in the inner cities.

Perhaps his most significant victory was increased funding for the National Aeronautics and Space Administration (NASA). Kennedy challenged the nation and NASA with the goal of putting an astronaut on the moon by 1970. There were those who objected to spending an estimated $20 billion for the space program, but Kennedy saw space exploration as a challenge to the nation's prestige and a symbol of cold war rivalry with the Soviet Union.

Conflict With Congress

Although Kennedy achieved some legislative victories, conflict with Congress prevented him from getting much of his domestic program passed. Despite the fact that the Democratic party enjoyed large majorities in both houses, a coalition of conservative Southern Democrats dominated Congress, rejecting many New Frontier measures.

CHAPTER 34 SECTION 1

Visualizing History Kennedy had prepared a major speech on U.S. foreign policy. Cut down by an assassin's bullet on the streets of Dallas, he never delivered the speech. By unanimous consent, it was entered into the Congressional Record a few days later. **Answer to Caption:** Theories persist because the Warren Commission's report did not answer all the questions.

Did You Know?

In 1961 Russian cosmonaut Yuri Gagarin became the first man to travel in space. Later that year Alan Shepard became the first American in space.

ABC NEWS INTERACTIVE

VIDEODISC *Powers of the President*

Side 1, Chapter 15
Title: *Presidential Vacancy*
Subject: Kennedy's assassination and Johnson's swearing in—in Dallas

▲ **A NEW PRESIDENT** Lyndon B. Johnson took the oath of office a few hours after the assassination of President Kennedy. The shock and grief on the faces of those present reflected the feelings of the stunned nation. *Why do some questions still remain about the circumstances of Kennedy's death?*

◀ **JOHN F. KENNEDY, JR., AT FUNERAL**

CHAPTER 34 Camelot to Watergate 1960–1976

Sidelights: The Death of a President

The shock and sadness of President Kennedy's untimely death reached far beyond the borders of the United States. In Britain the cast of the irreverent television satire program *That Was the Week That Was* threw out their prepared script and did a show memorializing Kennedy. In the former Soviet Union, young people openly wept on the streets of Moscow. In a remote town in Sudan, a storekeeper etched a dark border on his receipts because "the greatest man in the world is dead today."

CHAPTER 34 SECTION 1

Food of the Times

The research for space travel in the 1960's led to the development of freeze dried foods. Within a short time, they found their way to supermarkets across the nation.

ASSESS

Check Understanding

Assign Section 1 Review as homework or an in-class activity.

Evaluate

Assign the Section 1 Quiz in the TCR, or use the History of a Free Nation Testmaker to create a customized quiz.

Reteach

Have students complete Reteaching Activity 34-1.

Enrich

Have students write a letter to President Kennedy thanking him for his actions on a particular issue or urging him to support some other kind of legislation. Select students to read their letters to the class.

CLOSE

Summarize the section by referring students to the chapter generalization. Ask them to give examples of how President Kennedy offered a new vision and sense of idealism to the American people.

When Kennedy proposed that the government recognize the problems of cities by creating a new cabinet department for urban affairs, Congress voted down the proposal. Kennedy also asked for a national health insurance program, medicare, to help older citizens pay their medical bills. The Senate defeated this bill, which was opposed by many doctors. The President called the Senate's action a "serious defeat for every American family."

■ Tragedy in Dallas

Kennedy hoped to achieve a greater mandate for his domestic program in the election of 1964. To that end, he traveled to Dallas, Texas, to smooth party differences and gather support. In Dallas, on November 22, 1963, the President was assassinated.

The sense of tragedy and grief that many felt was caught by a conversation between the newspaper columnist Mary McGrory and Daniel Moynihan, a member of Kennedy's staff. In response to McGrory's remark that "we'll never laugh again," Moynihan replied, "Heavens, Mary, we'll laugh again. It's just that we'll never be young again." It was this feeling of youth snuffed out, of promise unfulfilled, that made Kennedy's death seem peculiarly tragic to many.

The country and the world were deeply shocked and saddened at this loss. Americans everywhere grieved over the President's death. In Italy, people brought flowers to the gates of the American embassy in Rome. In India, crowds wept in the streets of New Delhi. In Africa, President Sékou Touré of Guinea said, "I have lost my only true friend in the outside world."

The Warren Commission

Kennedy's alleged assassin, Lee Harvey Oswald, was himself shot to death only two days after the assassination. This event led to speculation that Oswald was killed to protect others who may have helped plan the crime. In 1964, a national commission headed by Chief Justice Warren concluded that Oswald was indeed the assassin and that he acted alone. The commission's report did leave important questions unanswered, though, and theories still persist that Oswald acted as part of a conspiracy. None of those theories has gained wide acceptance, however.

Johnson Takes Over

Kennedy was succeeded in office by Vice President Lyndon B. Johnson. Johnson took the oath of office on the plane that carried Kennedy's body from Dallas back to Washington, D.C. From Kennedy, Johnson inherited both unsolved problems and unfulfilled promises.

In domestic policy, Kennedy's New Frontier program was stalled in Congress. Yet, only two years after his death, most of these programs became law. The public reaction to the young President's tragic death, combined with the political skills of Lyndon Johnson, made possible sweeping social reform.

Section 1 ★ Review

Checking for Understanding

1. **Identify** New Frontier, Housing Act of 1961, NASA.
2. **Define** mandate, pragmatist, urban renewal.
3. **List** three economic programs undertaken by President Kennedy.
4. **Explain** why many of Kennedy's domestic programs were not passed.

Critical Thinking

5. **Analyzing Results** How did the lack of an election mandate affect Kennedy's ability to govern?

---

954 UNIT 10 Redefining America: 1954–Present

Answers to SECTION 1 REVIEW

1. New Frontier, 952; Housing Act of 1961, 953; NASA, 953
2. All vocabulary words are defined in the Glossary.
3. tax cuts, requests to business and labor to hold down prices and wages, and poverty-fighting programs like Area Redevelopment Act and Housing Act
4. Congress dominated by conservative coalition of Republicans and Southern Democrats
5. Answers will vary, but many students will suggest the lack of a mandate made him more cautious.

History AND Science CONNECTIONS

▲ ASTRONAUT IN SPACE

▼ PHOTOGRAPH OF EARTH FROM THE MOON

Space Race

Americans were stunned by the news that the Soviets had put a satellite—*Sputnik I*—into orbit around the earth in October 1957. Physicist Edward Teller called the launch a Soviet victory in "a battle more important and greater than Pearl Harbor." President Eisenhower told the panicked nation that only its pride, not its security, was damaged.

Americans, however, were threatened by what they considered Soviet technical superiority. In response, Congress passed the National Defense Education Act, which financed science and foreign-language programs in schools. In addition, the National Science Foundation's curriculum-development budget was dramatically increased. Congress also created the National Aeronautics and Space Administration (NASA) in 1958. Huge sums of money were allocated to develop space technology and compete with the Soviets in space.

In the spring of 1961, Alan Shepard, Jr., became the first American to make a space flight. On February 20, 1962, Lieutenant Colonel John Glenn became the first American to orbit the earth. Shortly after Shepard's flight, Kennedy challenged the nation to a great undertaking. He pledged America to landing an individual on the moon by 1970. In July 1969 Commander Neil A. Armstrong, Colonel Edwin E. Aldrin, Jr., and Lieutenant Colonel Michael Collins took off in Apollo.

When they reached the moon, Collins remained aboard the command spacecraft while Aldrin and Armstrong descended to the surface in a lunar module. Millions watched on television as Armstrong became the first human being to set foot on the surface of the moon.

Making the Science Connection

1. How did Americans feel about the success of *Sputnik*?
2. What actions were taken in response to *Sputnik*?

Linking Past and Present

3. Why do you think the United States space program today has less support than it did in the 1960s?

CHAPTER 34 CONNECTIONS

Teaching Making Connections

The launching of *Sputnik II* a month later caused even more concern in the United States. Much larger than its predecessor and carrying a passenger—a dog named Laika—*Sputnik II* was propelled into space by an incredibly powerful rocket. Such a rocket, American scientists surmised, could be modified to carry missiles against the United States. Ask students to discuss whether they think American security concerns were justified.

Did You Know?

In 1958 the United States sent up its first satellite, *Explorer I*. It marked the beginning of a "space race."

VIDEODISC
Communism and the Cold War

Side 1, Chapter 14
Title: Sputnik *Launches the Space Race*
Subject: The beginning of the space race

Answers to CONNECTIONS

1. They were stunned.
2. Passed the National Defense Education Act, which financed educational, science, and foreign-language programs; increased the National Science Foundation's budget; created NASA; committed to moon landing by 1970.
3. The United States surpassed Soviet space technology long ago. Also, space technology and space exploration's high costs have caused cooperation rather than competition.

LESSON PLAN
SECTION 2, 956–961

FOCUS

Bellringer
Before taking roll at the beginning of the class period, display Focus Activity 112 on the overhead projector, and assign the accompanying Focus Activity Sheet.

Objectives
Point out the objectives on this page to students in previewing the section content.

Motivating Activity
Write the definition of *consensus* on the chalkboard. (general agreement among all sides) Discuss its meaning, and give a few examples. Point out that Johnson tried to get a consensus in favor of his programs. Ask students: What is the advantage of this approach? (broad base of support) Tell students Johnson had much more experience as a politician than Kennedy and was determined to become a national, not a sectional, leader. Remind students that consensus does not mean unanimity but, rather, general agreement.

The following material is available from Glencoe and may be used to enrich Chapter 34:

- *The Presidents: A Picture History of Our Nation*

SECTION 2

The Great Society

Setting the Scene

Section Focus
Lyndon Johnson was a big man, with great energy and ambition. Sharing the same goals as Kennedy, Johnson carried into legislation the former President's war on poverty. As a former Senate leader, Johnson conceived and skillfully guided through Congress more significant domestic legislation than had been passed since the New Deal.

Objectives
After studying this section, you should be able to
★ explain how Johnson's belief in consensus helped him win the 1964 election.
★ discuss Johnson's efforts to fight poverty in the United States.

Key Term
consensus

◀ SILENT SPRING BY RACHEL CARSON

Aided by the Kennedy cabinet and relying on his long experience in government, Lyndon Johnson quickly made the transition from Vice President to President. On November 27, 1963, five days after John F. Kennedy's assassination, Johnson appeared before a joint session of Congress. His words assured the nation's representatives that he intended to carry out Kennedy's programs:

> 66 . . . the ideas and ideals which [Kennedy] so nobly represented must and will be translated into effective action. John Kennedy's death commands what his life conveyed—that America must move forward. 99

Elected to the House of Representatives in 1937 and the Senate in 1948, Johnson was at home in Congress. During the 1950s he was the powerful Democratic Majority Leader of the Senate. Although a Southerner, Johnson had taken a moderate position on most issues and had been a leader in passing the Civil Rights Act of 1957.

■ The Election of 1964

As President, Johnson continued an effective policy of working through **consensus**, or general agreement, that he had developed in Congress. With skilled bargaining, compromising, and even verbal arm-twisting, Johnson reinforced his favorite Biblical quotation, "Come let us reason together." He took over the responsibilities of the chief executive with firmness and strength, determined to pursue the Democratic party's goals of social justice.

In the election of 1964, Johnson used these goals to campaign for President. His campaign plan offered something for everyone: business and labor, rich and poor, young and

UNIT 10 Redefining America: 1954–Present

Classroom Resources for SECTION 2

Teacher's Classroom Resources
- Reproducible Lesson Plan
- Reteaching Activity 34-2
- Section Quiz

Multimedia
- Section Focus Transparency 112
- Testmaker
- Student Self-Test Software
- Focus on Government
- The Presidents: A Picture History of Our Nation

old, African American and white. Known as "the Great Society," Johnson's domestic program was an effort to expand upon Kennedy's ideas as well as to make a contribution of his own. It was designed to fight poverty, discrimination, unemployment, pollution, and other social ills of America. At the same time, he pledged to provide major tax cuts for individuals and corporations.

To offer voters "a choice, not an echo," Republicans selected an outspoken conservative, Barry Goldwater, to run against Johnson and his liberal running mate, Hubert Humphrey. The Arizona senator ran a determined, uncompromising campaign. His opposition to the Civil Rights Act of 1964 turned away African American voters. His coolness to social security made older people fearful. His support of the open shop hurt him with organized labor. Above all, Goldwater's suggestion that military commanders should be allowed to decide for themselves whether to use nuclear weapons made many people nervous.

As predicted, Johnson's wide appeal won him more than 60 percent of the popular vote. Goldwater carried only his home state of Arizona and 5 Southern states, where former "Dixiecrats" switched to the Republican party. In addition, the Democrats increased their majorities in both houses of Congress. The Great Society had won an overwhelming mandate.

War on Poverty

In the mid-1960s the United States had the highest standard of living in the world. But behind the Great Society program was a new awareness that many Americans did not share in the general prosperity.

The Other America

Contributing to this awareness was a book by Michael Harrington entitled *The Other America*, published in 1962. In response to economist John Kenneth Galbraith, who wrote in *The Affluent Society* that only "pockets" of poverty remained, Harrington claimed that as many as 40 million Americans—one-fourth of the population—were poor. He charged:

 ▲ **HELP FOR NEGLECTED AMERICANS** The War on Poverty reached into Appalachia where poor soil and lack of education affected many lives. *Why did some writers and leaders call for the government to help the poor?*

CHAPTER 34 SECTION 2

Independent Practice
Conducting a Survey
Have students conduct a survey of 12 people who live in their communities. Ask them to find out each person's age, employment, and interests. Have them write a paragraph explaining how each person could benefit from the following Great Society programs: 1964 Equal Opportunity Act, 1965 Immigration Act, 1965 Voting Rights Act, 1965 Elementary and Secondary Education Act, and Medicare. **L1, LEP**

Teaching American Portraits
As Cesar Chavez sought support from migrant workers, he reminded them: "No union movement is worth the life of a single grower or his child or a single worker or his child."

Ask students: What turned the tide in Chavez's strike against grape growers?

GLENCOE TECHNOLOGY

VIDEODISC
Focus on Government

Videodisc 1, Chapter 9
Citizenship in the United States

AMERICAN PORTRAITS

Cesar Chavez
1927–1993

Born to Mexican American migrant workers, Cesar Chavez picked crops in the Southwest as a child and young man. At age 25, he began organizing farm workers to win better pay and working conditions.

Early in the 1960s, Chavez founded a union for migrant farm workers and later merged it with another to form the first large-scale organization of farm workers. He then organized a strike against grape growers.

The strike drew national attention as Chavez borrowed tactics from the civil rights movement—marches and a 25-day fast.

Yet the grape growers would not settle. The tide began to turn in 1968 when Chavez asked the American people to boycott grapes. Growers' profits tumbled as consumers began to side with the workers. The strike lasted until 1970, when the growers finally agreed to settle.

> *The United States contains an underdeveloped nation, a culture of poverty. Its inhabitants do not suffer the extreme poverty of the peasants of Asia . . . yet the mechanism of the misery is similar. They are beyond history, beyond progress, sunk in a paralyzing, maiming routine.*

Most of the American people knew little of the great mass of human misery, said Harrington. The poor were hidden away in the slums of central cities, in rural areas—especially in Appalachia and the Deep South—and on Native American reservations. Many of the poor were elderly people leading "lives of quiet desperation" in secluded rooms.

It was not possible for these people to "pull themselves up by their bootstraps," Harrington believed. Automation had done away with the jobs of many workers, and small farmers could no longer compete with agribusiness. Then, too, displaced factory workers and farmers did not have the opportunity for the training and work experience needed for new jobs. Further, pensions and social security did not adequately cover medical expenses for older citizens.

Johnson Declares War

Johnson announced his strategy in his first State of the Union Address on January 8, 1964: "This administration . . . declares unconditional war on poverty in America." A new Office of Economic Opportunity (OEO) aimed its billion-dollar budget at illiteracy, unemployment, and disease. The OEO-sponsored VISTA (Volunteers in Service to America) sent workers to improve conditions in poor neighborhoods. Job Corps provided training for the unskilled, while Project Head Start helped poor children prepare for school. The Elementary and Secondary Education Act of 1965 gave direct massive federal aid to public and parochial schools. A similar act provided college scholarships for needy students.

The Great Society's War on Poverty extended federal influence into areas that had traditionally been handled by local governments, private enterprise, or religious groups. In some cases OEO was granted power to overrule local governments.

The emphasis was not simply on relief but on helping poor people help themselves. For example, community action programs taught people to organize protests and put pressure on landlords, employers, and even government agencies to effect change.

958   UNIT 10 Redefining America: 1954–Present

Cultural Diversity

President Johnson named Robert Weaver as head of the Department of Housing and Urban Development. Weaver was the first African American in United States history to serve in a President's cabinet. Lisle Carter, also an African American, was named as assistant secretary in the Department of Health, Education, and Welfare. Encourage students to research the accomplishments of these and other African Americans who broke political barriers in the 1960s.

Medicare

After nearly 20 years of opposition by those who believed that the government should stay out of health care, Congress passed the Medicare Act. Medicare provided people over age 65 with hospital care. Medical centers were to be set up in areas where such facilities were lacking. The act provided funds for medical schools to increase enrollments and reduce the shortage of doctors.

■ Immigration Reform

To many thousands of immigrants, the United States already represented a "great society"—a land of newfound opportunity and freedom. The doors of this great society had opened wide to immigrants from northwestern Europe and nearly closed to others, because of a quota system that the United States established in 1924.

Out of 157,000 immigrants admitted each year, Great Britain and Ireland were allotted 83,000; India, with a population of 450 million, and Andorra, with a population of 6,400, each were allotted 100. Presidents Truman, Eisenhower, and Kennedy had been unable to persuade Congress to change this system.

Standing beneath the Statue of Liberty, which welcomed immigrants to the country, Johnson signed the Immigration Act of 1965. The law replaced national quotas with global quotas and favored those with special skills. As a result, immigration to the United States from Asia and Latin America increased sharply.

Under Johnson's leadership Congress passed a great number of other important laws in a few months. "We did reach consensus," he concluded. "I think we did convince the vast majority of Americans that the time for procrastinating had passed."

His programs were well-received in part because people saw benefits for themselves. Some businesspeople, for example, benefited from the War on Poverty because of the increased purchasing power of poor people. Johnson's program also included subsidies to farmers.

■ Rising Costs End Great Society

Great Society programs required large sums of money. Federal spending for social purposes rose from $54 billion in 1964 to $98 billion in 1968. Federal budget problems and national inflation made Great Society spending an issue for debate. The $20-billion-a-year cost of the Vietnam War made things worse.

Guns and Butter

At first, Johnson tried to finance the war with taxes, explaining that the nation could afford both guns and butter. New social programs and rising war costs made the federal deficit climb to $28 billion by 1968. The President realized that without additional taxes, either social or military programs would have to be cut. He asked Congress for a tax increase. Congress refused unless the President would cut the budget. Johnson chopped $6 billion out of proposed domestic spending, marking the end of the Great Society.

End of an Era

Lyndon Johnson left office in January 1969 a discouraged man. Unable to build a Great Society at home and wage a war at the same time, he had to waive his chance for another term. The American people had rejected Johnson's policies in Vietnam. Supporters of Nixon, he knew, were not sympathetic to the Great Society programs. The nation had become deeply divided.

The 1960s had begun as a time of youth, optimism, and confidence in the future and ended in war, riots, and violence. Three national heroes—President John F. Kennedy, Dr. Martin Luther King, Jr., and Senator Robert Kennedy—had been assassinated. Tens of thousands of young Americans had been killed or wounded in the most unpopular war the United States had ever fought. The New Frontier and the Great Society programs, designed to make life better for the poor and the needy, had also become casualties of the war.

CHAPTER 34 SECTION 2

Did You Know?

President Johnson signed the Elementary and Secondary Education Act at his one-room schoolhouse in the presence of his first teacher, the Voting Rights Act in the room where Lincoln had signed the Emancipation Proclamation, and the Immigration Act in the shadow of the Statue of Liberty.

FACT or FICTION?

The Highway Beautification Act allocated funds to control and minimize the use of billboards along the nation's highways.

FACT: Lady Bird Johnson played an active role in convincing Congress to enact the law in 1965. It passed by a single vote.

NATIONAL GEOGRAPHIC SOCIETY

The following material is available from Glencoe and may be used to enrich Chapter 34:

CD-ROM
- *The Presidents: A Picture History of Our Nation*

Critical Thinking

Evaluating Policies Tell students that Franklin Roosevelt appointed 27-year-old Lyndon Baines Johnson to serve as the national youth administrator for the state of Texas. Under Johnson's leadership thousands of boys returned to high school, and thousands more found work on government or private projects. Ask students how Johnson's early experiences under Franklin Roosevelt's New Deal influenced his Great Society legislation in the 1960s. Discuss student answers. **L3**

CHAPTER 34
SECTION 2

Visualizing History Johnson was called a "Whirlwind President" by a reporter who noticed his high level of energy.
Answer to Caption: He would not run for reelection.

ASSESS

Check Understanding
Assign Section 2 Review as homework or an in-class activity.

Evaluate
Assign the Section 2 Quiz in the TCR, or use the History of a Free Nation Testmaker to create a customized quiz.

Reteach
Have students complete Reteaching Activity 34-2.

Enrich
Have students think about how they would choose a President if they were eligible to vote in the next election. Ask them to write down three domestic and three global issues that concern them most.

CLOSE
Tell students that President Johnson thought of the Great Society as an extension of the Bill of Rights, because like the Bill of Rights, it reflected the concern of people who fought for freedom in their time. Ask: What rights did the Great Society seek?

Visualizing History ▲ END OF THE GREAT SOCIETY
President Johnson felt increasing criticism because of the growing dissent over the war and increasing opposition within his own party. *What decision did the President make in 1968 regarding his political future?*

After the unhappy events of 1968, the year itself ended on an ironic note of hope and progress. Late in December 1968 the United States succeeded in sending the first astronauts into orbit around the moon. During one of the most difficult years in American history, the nation had scored a great technological achievement. The photographs sent back from space made planet Earth seem small, peaceful, and beautiful. It brought a new feeling to Americans that no matter how difficult, the problems they faced could be solved.

Growing Concern for the Environment

During the 1960s, greater emphasis was placed on the environment. Many conservation projects had been started during the Great Depression, mostly as a means of providing work for the unemployed. During the same period, the dust bowl demonstrated the need for soil conservation. As time went on, scientists discovered more about the effects of pollutants on the environment, and people became more concerned with environmental health.

The individual most responsible for launching the environmental movement and prompting new regulations was Rachel Carson. From her earliest days, Carson had two great loves: nature and books. At first, she planned to be a writer, but she switched majors from English to biology during her junior year of college. Carson was able to combine her twin loves by becoming a science author.

An aquatic biologist by training, Rachel Carson wrote about the sea with great insight. Her most important book, *Silent Spring* (1962), dealt with the environment. Long aware of the threat posed by careless use of toxic chemicals, she researched carefully and wrote movingly about how modern industry and agriculture were poisoning the planet. *Silent Spring* sparked a federal investigation that backed her conclusions and led to tougher laws regarding harmful chemicals. Rachel Carson died soon after publication of *Silent Spring,* unaware of the ecology movement that her work would inspire.

Section 2 ★ Review

Checking for Understanding
1. **Identify** Barry Goldwater, *The Other America,* Office of Economic Opportunity, Medicare Act.
2. **Define** consensus.
3. **Explain** the Great Society.
4. **List** four programs that were part of the War on Poverty.

Critical Thinking
5. **Classifying Information** Do all Americans define poverty the same way? Think of what poverty means to you. Make a list of guidelines that you would use to classify Americans who live in poverty. Would your classification meet government standards?

UNIT 10 Redefining America: 1954–Present

Answers to SECTION 2 REVIEW
1. Barry Goldwater, 957; *The Other America,* 957; Office of Economic Opportunity, 958; Medicare Act, 959
2. All vocabulary words are defined in the Glossary.
3. Johnson's programs for fighting poverty, unemployment, discrimination, pollution, and other social issues
4. VISTA, Job Corps, Head Start, Elementary and Secondary Education Act of 1965
5. Answers will vary. Some will define poverty as not only more than a severe lack of money, but also as a condition in which people are locked into a life of misery, including elderly Americans and inner-city dwellers.

Social Studies Skills

Interpreting Primary Sources

Collage Art in the 1960s

The decade of the 1960s was a fresh period in American art when artists experimented with a variety of media, materials, techniques, and styles. Robert Rauschenberg mastered the technique of *collage*, a two-dimensional art form using a variety of images.

Rauschenberg came into prominence in the mid-1950s when he began to incorporate pieces of discarded cloth, wood, crumpled printed materials, and other manufactured objects, such as tin cans or bottles, onto his canvases. He referred to these works as "combine paintings."

The bold drips and splatters of Rauschenberg's brushwork, as well as his use of geometric shapes and colors, reflect his debt to abstract expressionism, an artistic movement that came into vogue after World War II. Yet his works also point to the emergence of pop art in the 1960s, an artistic style that used commonplace subject matter from popular culture.

Rauschenberg's kaleidoscope-like works often reflect an interesting interplay between reality and art, everyday life and technological achievement. His collages often draw on themes from history. In *Kite* Rauschenberg focuses attention on social unrest in the early 1960s. This is seen in the clash of troops and flags, and an army helicopter poised either to strike or bring assistance. Yet the images of the bald eagle and the military flag parade also stir feelings of patriotism and national pride.

When displayed in 1963, *Kite* may have reminded viewers of American troops in Little Rock or Birmingham, Korea or Vietnam. The eagle, perhaps stained with blood, is positioned at the top of the collage where vertical paint thrusts resemble rocket blasts. This suggests American global power or the will to dominate outer space. The pale blue sky and white areas of the collage are spattered by ominous black markings. *Kite* is thus a statement of discord, a view of America filled with aggression and torn by turmoil.

▼ *Kite* by Robert Rauschenberg, 1963

Examining the Primary Source

1. Which of the images in the collage were probably mass-produced? How can you tell?
2. Describe an image that appears twice in this collage. Why do you think the artist repeated this image?

Critical Thinking

3. **Analyzing Information** Interpret the meaning of Rauschenberg's title *Kite*.
4. **Drawing Conclusions** How does *Kite* capture the dynamic change of a nation?

LESSON PLAN
Mastering Social Studies Skills

Teaching Interpreting Primary Sources

Read the article with students, and discuss the questions. Make sure students understand terms such as *collage*, *assemblage*, and "combine paintings."

Discuss the way Rauschenberg uses these techniques. What themes does he often portray? (events in American history and the interplay between daily life and technology) What themes are evident in *Kite*? (Sample answer: American power, the right to dissent, conflict, military technology) If the artist created *Kite* today, what images might he include to illustrate this theme? (Answers will vary. Students might mention the inclusion of different technologies, a person in place of the eagle, a more or less violent clash.)

Did You Know?

Since the 1960s, Robert Rauschenberg, like many other artists, has used silkscreen transfers to create a kaleidoscope of images deriving from newspapers and films. Rauschenberg has been active not only as an artist but also in dance and theater design.

Answers to SOCIAL STUDIES SKILLS

1. The photographs in the collage were probably mass-produced.
2. An image of troops marching with flags appears twice.
3. The title *Kite* connotes something that flies. The images in the collage reflect the same—the eagle, a helicopter, flags, rocket trails.
4. The collage is full of tension and energy, conflict and pride.

LESSON PLAN
SECTION 3, 962–966

FOCUS

Bellringer
Before taking roll at the beginning of the class period, display Focus Activity 113 on the overhead projector, and assign the accompanying Focus Activity Sheet.

Objectives
Point out the objectives on this page to students in previewing the section.

Motivating Activity
Ask students to list the domestic problems Nixon faced and the methods he used to deal with them.

The following material is available from Glencoe and may be used to enrich Chapter 34:

CD-ROM
- *The Presidents: A Picture History of Our Nation*

SECTION 3

An Imperial Presidency

Setting the Scene

Section Focus

Under Nixon the office of the President became more powerful, threatening the balance among the three branches of government. Although Nixon used presidential powers chiefly in foreign affairs, he also expanded them for his own purposes at home. Although he projected a new image during the campaign, the specter of the ruthless Richard Nixon of his early career haunted the White House. His time in office came to be known as the "imperial presidency."

Objectives

After studying this section, you should be able to
★ describe how Nixon tried to deal with the economic problems of the early 1970s.
★ explain how Nixon handled the war on crime and the energy crisis.

Key Terms

stagflation, balance of payments, new federalism, revenue sharing

◀ SEAL OF THE REPUBLICAN NATIONAL COMMITTEE

To Americans and foreigners alike, the United States in the late 1960s had lost its direction. Not only was it losing the war in Vietnam, but its industries were losing their competitive edge. A sense of defeat and decay became apparent. Deep social, political, and racial divisions were threatening to tear society apart. Richard Nixon claimed that he had a "plan to end the war in Vietnam" and "bring Americans together." His promise of peace in Vietnam and tranquility at home appealed to many.

■ Nixon's Political Career

Richard M. Nixon was the first President in modern times to be elected after having lost a previous bid for the presidency. After losing the 1962 California gubernatorial race, his political career seemed over. In the 1968 campaign, however, he changed his public image. The old Nixon had been intensely partisan and ruthless. When he had run for Congress from California in 1946 as a newly discharged naval officer, he charged that his opponent had strong ties to communist organizations. Political opponents called him opportunistic and self-serving.

The new Nixon, however, impressed observers as calm, broad-minded, and statesmanlike. He promised that his administration would be "open to new ideas, open to men and women of both parties, open to the critics as well as those who support us." Bringing the nation together proved difficult, however. With the Democrats in control of Congress, Nixon saw many of his domestic proposals rejected.

962 UNIT 10 Redefining America: 1954–Present

Classroom Resources for SECTION 3

Teacher's Classroom Resources
- Reproducible Lesson Plan
- Reteaching Activity 34-3
- Chapter 34 Primary and Secondary Source Readings
- Section Quiz

Multimedia
- Section Focus Transparency 113
- Testmaker
- Student Self-Test Software
- Powers of the President
- The Presidents: A Picture History of Our Nation

The War Against Crime

One of Nixon's domestic successes was his war against crime. During the 1968 campaign, Nixon spoke out against permissive attitudes toward the rights of those accused of crimes. Nixon criticized the record of the Supreme Court under Chief Justice Earl Warren. He denounced Supreme Court decisions that curtailed the powers of the police in the interrogation of suspects and that forbade the use of electronic "bugging" equipment for gathering evidence. Such decisions, Nixon maintained, violated "the first civil right of every American to be free of domestic violence." He promised to fill vacancies on the Supreme Court with judges who would not "weaken the peace forces as against the criminal forces."

Nixon eventually succeeded in his campaign to change the liberal thrust of the Court. When Chief Justice Warren resigned shortly after Nixon took office, the President nominated Warren Burger, a respected conservative judge, to take his place. He also placed three other conservative justices on the Court. The Burger Court, known to critics as the Nixon Court, did not abolish the protections of criminal suspects set up by the Warren Court. It did, however, whittle them down. Its harder line against criminals was dramatically revealed when it reversed the opinion of the Warren Court that capital punishment was a violation of the Bill of Rights.

Nixon's Economic Policies

Nixon inherited difficult economic problems. The combined costs of President Johnson's War on Poverty and the Vietnam War had produced a large federal budget deficit and mounting inflation. Between 1964 and 1969, the dollar lost one-fifth of its purchasing power.

Stagflation

The President tackled inflation by curtailing the supply of money. By the end of 1970, however, it was apparent that the plan was not working. Restricting the supply of money drove interest rates up, and higher

 ▲ **THE BURGER COURT** The Supreme Court is generally referred to by the name of its chief justice. Thus, in 1969, when Warren E. Burger became chief justice, the Supreme Court became known as the Burger Court. **Why had President Nixon criticized the Warren Court?**

Life of the Times

Shopping Malls

A 1973 report on New Jersey's Cherry Hill Mall observed that the shopping mall had become to the suburb what Main Street once was to the small town—the focus of community life. The period between 1971 and 1975 was a heyday of mall construction. Cities and suburbs across the United States became home to enclosed malls featuring, under one roof, a fairly predictable array of small specialty stores for books, gifts, and shoes.

Large malls typically included major department stores as dependable "anchors" for sales and customers, as well as several popular restaurants. Some malls also had portable boutique stands that sold everything from perfume to wicker.

Mall managers were enormously successful in not only attracting shoppers, but also walkers, joggers, and vast crowds of teenagers just "hanging out." Malls became such popular gathering places in the early 1970s that a high school in Bethesda, Maryland, held its senior prom at one.

Despite the carefully controlled environment that malls maintain through regulated climate, piped-in music, security personnel, and squeaky cleanliness, they did not escape the social upheaval of the 1970s. Several large malls became sites for Vietnam War protests.

▲ Mall of the Americas, Bloomington, Minne

interest rates discouraged investment. Unemployment increased, and the stock market declined. The slowdown in business activity reduced federal revenues, and inflation accelerated. This economic slowdown, coupled with inflation, was called **stagflation.**

To meet the problem of stagflation, Nixon turned to other, less conservative measures. In August 1971 he announced his New Economic Policy, which called for a 90-day freeze on wages, prices, and rents. This was followed by a system of wage and price controls in November. In January 1973 the President relaxed controls, and prices rose sharply. In response, a new freeze was imposed in June.

President Nixon also took steps to end the recession by stimulating the economy. He proposed tax cuts for both businesses and individuals, hoping that when the demand went up, production would rise and unemployment would fall. After making some revisions in the President's proposals, Congress enacted tax cuts in December 1971. The President also used deficit spending to fight recession.

These measures, however, failed to solve the problem of stagflation. Although the tax cuts and deficit spending helped to ease the recession, they added to inflation. On the other hand, while the controls slowed inflation for a time, they did little to help the economy grow or to lower unemployment.

A Balance of Payments Deficit

Inflation caused prices to rise not only on domestic goods, but on exports. So, fewer exports were purchased. This resulted in a balance of payments deficit. The **balance of payments** is the difference between the money paid to and received from other nations. In this case, the nation was spending more than it received. Between 1970 and 1971, the nation's balance of payments deficit jumped from $4 billion to $22 billion.

The deficit was evidence that the United States had lost its dominance in world markets. Between 1950 and 1970, for example, the United States's share of world automobile production dropped from 76 to 31 percent, and the same phenomenon was occurring in the textile, shoe, and electrical equipment industries.

A serious effect of the balance of payments deficit was that it weakened other nations' confidence in the value of the dollar. Because world trade depends on stable money and because the dollar was the major currency in the world, the dollar crisis threatened to disrupt trade.

Trying to improve the economic situation, Nixon acted decisively. To combat inflation, in August 1971 he announced, as noted earlier, a 90-day freeze on prices and wages. To discourage imports, he placed an additional duty of 10 percent on all goods purchased from abroad. He also allowed the dollar to decline in value in relation to foreign currencies, making it more expensive for Americans to buy goods from other countries. Therefore, goods made in the United States became cheaper than foreign-made goods, and that promoted exports.

Although Nixon's policies brought some relief, inflation, chronic unemployment, and the loss of foreign markets remained a problem throughout his presidency. The measures also caused ill will in nations that depended on American markets for their products.

The New Federalism

Nixon also announced his **new federalism,** which was intended to reduce the federal government's role in the economy and turn many of its tasks over to state and local governments. Following the President's lead, Congress passed a series of **revenue-sharing** bills that granted federal funds to local agencies to use as they saw fit.

The Energy Crisis

Another problem concerned energy. In the fall of 1973, Arab nations placed an embargo on crude oil shipments from the Middle East. The purpose of the embargo was to force the United States to stop supporting Israel in its struggle with the Arab states. Support for Israel did not change, but the embargo produced an energy crisis in America—and near panic. In some areas the price of petroleum shot up nearly 400 percent, and there were shortages of gasoline for cars and heating oil for homes, schools, and businesses.

Although the United States had about one-sixteenth of the world's population, Americans consumed about one-third of the world's energy. Most of this energy came from such nonrenewable resources as oil, gas, and coal. Coal reserves were abundant in America but supplied less than 20 percent of the nation's energy needs. By 1973, the United States was importing about 6 million barrels of oil each day, or about 36 percent of the oil needed to heat homes and to keep factories and automobiles running.

President Nixon announced a plan to make the country self-sufficient in energy by 1980. He called for higher taxes on imported oil and encouraged Americans to take conservation measures, such as lowering their thermostats at home and at work. Congress passed a law requiring states to lower the speed limit on highways to 55 miles per hour to save gasoline and approved the construction of a pipeline in Alaska for the shipment of newly discovered oil to refineries.

▼ SIGN OF THE TIMES

Sidelights: The Moon Landing

During the Nixon administration, the United States reached the moon. On July 16, 1969, the U.S. spacecraft *Apollo 11* left Cape Kennedy. Four days later Neil Armstrong, Edwin Aldrin, and Michael Collins became the first men to reach the moon. As Americans watched on television, two of the astronauts planted an American flag. Neil Armstrong, stepping onto the moon's surface, commented, "That's one small step for a man, one giant leap for mankind." Nixon called the astronauts and said, "Because of what you have done the heavens have become a part of man's world."

CHAPTER 34
SECTION 3

Enrich
Have interested students research Nixon's political comeback. Ask them to collect news articles from Nixon's inauguration and then write a paragraph explaining how various groups of people felt about Nixon's return.

CLOSE
Summarize the section by telling students that Nixon portrayed himself as a promoter of peace. Ask: In what way did he accomplish this at the beginning of his term?

Visualizing History Congress approved construction of an Alaska pipeline to help reduce the nation's dependence on imported oil. Construction of the 800-mile (1,287.2-kilometer) pipeline was completed in 1977. It can transport up to 2 million barrels of crude oil a day from the Arctic Coastal Plain to the port of Valdez. From there the oil is shipped by tanker to refineries.
Answer to Caption: higher taxes on imported oil, new conservation measures

▲ **ENERGY CRISIS** One of the nation's most important concerns during the Nixon administration was the energy crisis. Long lines of cars at gas stations were a sign of the times. *What actions did the administration take to conserve energy?*

Congress provided some tax incentives to encourage energy research and put the nation on year-round daylight saving time for two years.

After the Arab nations lifted the oil embargo in March 1974, most Americans forgot about the energy crisis mentality. They began once again to use fuel in increasing quantities. However, fuel prices began a steep rise as the oil shortage continued. In the 1960s the major oil-exporting nations had formed the Organization of Petroleum Exporting Countries (OPEC). By 1970 OPEC had begun to raise prices, and over the next decade the cost of oil increased from less than $2 a barrel to more than $30 a barrel. The increases in the price of oil by the OPEC members contributed to the problems that plagued the American economy throughout the 1970s.

Section 3 ★ Review

Checking for Understanding
1. **Identify** Warren Burger.
2. **Define** stagflation, balance of payments, new federalism, revenue sharing.
3. **Point out** how Nixon affected the criminal justice system.
4. **Describe** two features of Nixon's economic policies.

Critical Thinking
5. **Evaluating Policy** Write an evaluation of the effectiveness of Nixon's policy for handling inflation.

966   UNIT 10 Redefining America: 1954–Present

Answers to SECTION 3 REVIEW
1. Warren Burger, 963
2. All vocabulary words are defined in the Glossary.
3. He placed conservative justices on Supreme Court, changing the Court's previous liberal thrust and diminishing the rights of criminal suspects.
4. Reduced federal spending and curtailed the supply of money.
5. Answers will vary. Though Nixon's policies brought some relief, inflation, unemployment, and the loss of foreign markets remained problems.

SECTION 4

The Watergate Scandal

Setting the Scene

Section Focus

The public disclosure of Richard Nixon's involvement in the Watergate scandal culminated in his resignation from office. It also led Congress and the Supreme Court to reassert their constitutional powers. Although confidence in the government was shaken by Watergate, the bicentennial, or the 200th anniversary of the American Revolution, was cause for celebration.

Objectives

After studying this section, you should be able to

★ explain how the constitutional process solved the Watergate crisis.

★ list the ways in which Congress sought to reassert its constitutional powers.

Key Terms

executive privilege, impound, deregulation

◀ STREET SIGN, WASHINGTON, D.C.

Not surprisingly, the Republican party nominated President Nixon as its candidate in the election of 1972. Nixon ran against Senator George McGovern of South Dakota, who won the Democratic nomination with the support of a coalition of activists—young people, African Americans, and women.

■ A Crisis in the Presidency

Almost from the beginning, however, the McGovern campaign derailed itself. McGovern's running mate, Senator Thomas Eagleton, was forced to withdraw when it was disclosed that he had been hospitalized for depression. In addition, Democratic party regulars and labor union leaders were cool, if not hostile, toward the liberal McGovern's candidacy.

In contrast, President Nixon conducted a perfect campaign. The almost-complete withdrawal of United States troops from Vietnam defused the war issue, and the summits in Beijing and Moscow signaled an easing of cold war tensions. Moreover, the President solidified his support among "middle Americans" by calling for law and order, by opposing busing, and by making continuous appeals to patriotism.

On Election Day the President received 61 percent of the popular vote and won every electoral vote except those of Massachusetts and the District of Columbia.

CREEP

It was later learned, however, that this tremendous victory was not won entirely fairly. During the campaign the President and his political advisers organized the Committee to Reelect the President (CREEP) and collected more than $50 million for Nixon's reelection campaign, some

---

LESSON PLAN
SECTION 4, 967–971

FOCUS

Bellringer

Before taking roll at the beginning of the class period, display Focus Activity 114 on the overhead projector, and assign the accompanying Focus Activity Sheet.

Objectives

Point out the objectives on this page to students in previewing the section content.

Motivating Activity

Refer students to those parts of the Constitution that deal with impeachment. (Article I, Sections 2 and 3, Article II, Section 4) For what reasons may a President be impeached? (conviction of treason, bribery, or other high crimes and misdemeanors) Who can impeach a President? (House of Representatives) Who tries an impeached President? (Senate) Ask students if they can identify the only President who was ever impeached. (Andrew Johnson) Point out that Nixon was close to being impeached when he resigned.

Side 2, Chapter 23
Title: *Watergate Scandal*
Subject: Montage of news reports about the scandal

Classroom Resources for SECTION 4

Teacher's Classroom Resources
- Reproducible Lesson Plan
- Reteaching Activity 34-4
- Chapter 34 Primary and Secondary Source Readings
- Chapter 34 Enrichment Activity
- Chapter 34 Performance Assessment Activity
- Spanish Summaries and Glossary
- Section Quiz

Multimedia
- Section Focus Transparency 114
- Testmaker
- Student Self-Test Software
- Powers of the President
- The Presidents: A Picture History of Our Nation

CHAPTER 34
SECTION 4

TEACH

Guided Practice

History Remind students that unlike Kennedy and Johnson, Nixon had been more concerned with foreign affairs than with domestic issues. **L2**

ABC NEWS INTERACTIVE

VIDEODISC
Powers of the President

Side 2, Chapter 23
Title: *Watergate Scandal*
Subject: Montage of news reports about the scandal

Side 2, Chapter 24
Title: *Presidential Denials*
Subject: Nixon denies involvement in Watergate

Side 2, Chapter 25
Title: *Watergate Committee Hearings*
Subject: Montage of statements

Side 2, Chapter 26
Title: *House Judiciary Committee*
Subject: Committee votes articles of impeachment

Side 2, Chapter 27
Title: *The President Resigns*
Subject: Excerpts from Nixon's resignation speech

---

of which was illegally received. Some campaign contributions were used to finance "dirty tricks" against the Democrats.

The Watergate Break-in

A group of CREEP employees were caught "bugging" the offices of the Democratic National Committee in the Watergate building in Washington, D.C. Although the President's press secretary dismissed the break-in as a "third-rate burglary," this seemingly insignificant incident had serious consequences for the President.

Rumors began to circulate that the President himself had ordered the Watergate break-in. Stories were published in the *Washington Post* and other newspapers that linked key members of the White House staff and CREEP to the break-in. It was reported that key Nixon advisers had paid the Watergate burglars almost $1 million in "hush money" to plead guilty and say nothing else at their trials. To quiet the rumors, the President ordered his attorney general to appoint a special prosecutor, Harvard law professor Archibald Cox, to investigate the case.

The Investigation

At the same time, a special Senate committee began to hold televised hearings on the break-in and other abuses alleged to have been committed during the campaign of 1972. Starting in May 1973, millions of Americans watched in fascination as a parade of witnesses testified about illegal activities carried out by the White House staff and by CREEP. Perhaps the most startling discovery was that the President tape-recorded most of the conversations he had in the Oval Office.

The Trial

Following these revelations, federal grand juries indicted members of the Nixon administration for their illegal activities, including the unauthorized wiretapping, burglaries, illegal campaign contributions, and the bribing of witnesses. Eventually 25 people connected with the administration—including former Attorney General John Mitchell and two of Nixon's closest White House aides, H. R. Haldeman and John D. Erlichman—were convicted and served prison terms for Watergate-related crimes.

■ The President Answers

Month after month President Nixon continued to deny any involvement in Watergate. Claiming **executive privilege,** or the principle that the President does not have to give information to other branches of the government, Nixon refused to turn over the White House tapes to the special prosecutor. In October 1973, he offered to provide written summaries of the tapes.

The Saturday Night Massacre

When the special prosecutor insisted on having the tapes, Nixon ordered the attorney general to remove Cox. Both the attorney general and his top assistant resigned rather than carry out the President's order. Finally Nixon found a Justice Department official who was willing to fire Cox. The dismissal of the special prosecutor became known as the "Saturday Night Massacre," and it provoked a wave of public protest as well as the first serious calls for Nixon's impeachment.

Agnew Resigns

October 1973 proved to be a disastrous time for Richard Nixon for other reasons as well. His Vice President, Spiro Agnew, was forced to resign in disgrace. A grand jury found that Agnew, while governor of Maryland, had taken bribes from contractors who did business with the state. It was further revealed that Agnew continued to receive such payments while he was Vice President. Nixon nominated Gerald Ford, the Republican leader of the House of Representatives, as the new Vice President.

Nixon Proclaims Innocence

In an effort to quiet public outrage over the Saturday Night Massacre, Nixon appointed another special prosecutor in

UNIT 10 Redefining America: 1954–Present

Cultural Diversity

President Nixon's landslide victory over George McGovern in the 1972 election occurred despite the fact that some 86 percent of the African American vote went to McGovern. However, African Americans did achieve some electoral successes—their number in Congress increased from 12 to 15, and Barbara Jordan of Houston, Texas, and Andrew Young of Atlanta, Georgia, became the first African Americans elected to Congress from the South since Reconstruction.

November 1973. In April 1974, the President released written transcripts of 47 tape-recorded conversations. Even though the transcripts had been heavily edited, many believed the tapes indicated the President had indeed been involved in covering up the Watergate scandal. Nevertheless, the President still continued to proclaim his innocence:

> If read with an open and fair mind and read together with the record of actions I took, these transcripts will show that what I have stated since the beginning to be the truth . . . my actions were directed toward finding the facts and seeing that justice was done, fairly and according to the law.

Tapes Reveal Cover-up

In July the Supreme Court ruled that the President had to turn over the tapes themselves, not just their transcripts. A month later Nixon complied and handed over the tapes. One tape provided direct evidence that on June 23, 1972, only six days after the Watergate break-in, the President had arranged a cover-up. With this news, even the President's strongest supporters conceded that there was sufficient evidence to support impeachment. They advised Nixon that it seemed certain the House would impeach him and that the Senate would find him guilty. On August 8, 1974, Nixon announced on national television that he would resign. He also expressed hope that his departure would begin the process of healing the country.

Ford Becomes President

The next day Gerald Ford was sworn in as the thirty-eighth President. President Ford appointed Nelson Rockefeller, former governor of New York, as his Vice President, making them the first unelected presidential team in the nation's history.

At first, President Ford inspired public confidence. He assured a joint session of Congress that his administration would be free of "illegal tappings, eavesdropping, buggings, or break-ins." The new President seemed to be a decent, candid, and trustworthy man.

A month after entering office, however, Ford damaged his public image by granting Richard Nixon an unconditional pardon for

Visualizing History

▲ **WATERGATE** The Watergate hearings led to criminal charges against several top White House aides, including H. R. Haldeman (left) and Jeb Stuart Magruder (speaking at hearing). President Nixon disavowed knowledge of the break-in. *What is executive privilege?*

CHAPTER 34
SECTION 4

Did You Know?

The House of Representatives started impeachment proceedings against President Nixon in late 1973. In July 1974 the House Judiciary Committee recommended that three charges be made against the President: obstruction of justice, abuse of power, and contempt of Congress. Nixon resigned before the House voted on the impeachment charges. A total of 56 men were convicted of Watergate-related offenses, including 20 members of the cabinet, the White House staff, and CREEP.

ASSESS

Check Understanding

Assign Section 4 Review as homework or an in-class activity.

Evaluate

Assign the Section 4 Quiz in the TCR, or use the History of a Free Nation Testmaker to create a customized quiz.

▲ PRESIDENT NIXON LEAVES THE WHITE HOUSE

all crimes he committed or may have committed while in office. Ford insisted that he was acting not out of sympathy for Nixon, but in the public interest. He wanted to avoid the publicity and national division that a trial would create. Nevertheless, the pardon aroused fierce and widespread criticism of the new President.

Congress Reasserts Its Authority

When he took office, Gerald Ford promised to adopt a policy of "communication, conciliation, compromise, and cooperation" with Congress. He expected good relations with Congress, since he had served for 25 years as a representative and almost a decade as House Republican leader. However, the President and Congress were often at odds because Ford was a conservative, and liberal Democrats controlled both houses of Congress. In addition, the new President confronted a Congress that was determined to reassert its authority over what some critics called the "imperial presidency."

Congress Attacks Executive Privilege

To counter the trend toward greater presidential power and curb future abuses, Congress passed a series of laws. In the last year of the Nixon administration, as Watergate weakened the President, Congress attempted to regain some of its power. In November 1973, it passed the War Powers Act in spite of President Nixon's veto. This law required that the President report to Congress within 48 hours after sending combat troops abroad or after engaging in any military action. Unless Congress approved his action, the President had to withdraw all troops within 60 days. After the Watergate crisis, Congress passed the Congressional Budget and Impoundment Control Act of 1974, which allowed Congress to force the President to spend any appropriations that he attempted to **impound,** or withhold, unless he could justify his action to both houses.

Quarrels Over the Economy

One of the biggest problems facing President Ford and Congress was the economic recession. To Ford, inflation and the nation's dependence on foreign oil were the greatest threats to recovery. The Democratic Congress was more alarmed by the highest rates of unemployment and the lowest levels of productivity since the Great Depression of the 1930s.

Like Nixon, President Ford wanted to cut spending on social welfare programs and adopt an energy program. He favored **deregulation,** or removing price controls, of gas and oil. This would cause a rise in prices so people would use less. Increased profits would go toward helping companies find alternate forms of energy. Congress, however, did not cooperate. Ford, in turn, prevented the enactment of liberal Democratic legislation by the use of the veto power.

Ford's Foreign Policy

At first, Congress allowed the President greater leeway in foreign policy than it had to past officeholders. Ford met with leaders

970 UNIT 10 Redefining America: 1954–Present

Cooperative Learning

To review the events in Section 4, place students into groups of three or four. Have each group write review questions to be used in a class competition. Tell the groups their questions will be used to review the section content. They should include questions on the Watergate scandal, Nixon's impeachment, Ford's ascension to the presidency, economic problems, and the bicentennial. Then have the groups compete with each other one by one. You may want to award the winning team bonus points on the section or chapter review test. **L1**

of NATO and the Warsaw Pact to sign the Helsinki Accords in August 1975. Under the terms of the accords, the parties recognized the borders of the countries of Eastern Europe and committed themselves to respect and protect the human rights of their citizens.

Soon, however, in foreign policy, as in domestic affairs, Ford came into conflict with the Democratic-controlled Congress. In 1975 Congress refused President Ford's request for additional funds to aid South Vietnam and Cambodia in their continuing civil wars. As a result, the Cambodian government surrendered to the repressive Khmer Rouge forces on April 17. Twelve days later the North Vietnamese and the Vietcong overran Saigon and forced the government of South Vietnam to surrender. Communist regimes were now in control everywhere in Indochina except Thailand, which remained an ally.

■ The Bicentennial

Despite difficulties with Congress, President Ford headed for Boston to participate in the opening ceremonies of the bicentennial, celebrating the nation's 200th birthday. As July 4, 1976 approached, most people in the United States caught the bicentennial spirit. Cities, towns, and villages held parades and concerts and displayed fireworks. A procession of Conestoga wagons traveled to Valley Forge, Pennsylvania, and eighteenth-century sailing ships from many countries majestically sailed into New York Harbor on the Fourth of July.

▲ **THE NATION'S BICENTENNIAL** In 1976 Americans were anxious to put the tragedy of the Vietnam War and the Watergate affair behind them. A bicentennial spirit swept the nation as millions participated in parades, fireworks displays, and other activities. **Who was the nation's President during this time?**

As the bicentennial ended, the nation felt a new sense of hopefulness. It knew that the constitutional system had curbed the abuses of the imperial presidency. The people of the United States were proud of achievements such as the space program, and they began to regain their sense of confidence.

Section 4 ★ Review

Checking for Understanding

1. **Identify** George McGovern, CREEP, Archibald Cox, Gerald Ford, War Powers Act, Helsinki Accords.
2. **Define** executive privilege, impound, deregulation.
3. **Explain** why Nixon resigned.
4. **Summarize** actions Congress took to reassert its authority.

Critical Thinking

5. **Interpreting Viewpoints** Explain why many Americans, although dismayed by the Watergate scandal, felt proud of the way their government functioned during the crisis.

CHAPTER 34 ★ REVIEW

REVIEW CHAPTER 34

Answers

Reviewing Facts
1. Kennedy mixed idealism with realism and informality with dignity. He had a gift of leadership that inspired trust and devotion.
2. Legislative victories: Area Redevelopment Act, Housing Act of 1961, increased funding for NASA; legislative setbacks: defeat of proposals for a new cabinet department for urban affairs and a national health insurance program
3. Establishment of the Office of Economic Opportunity, Medicare Act, Immigration Act of 1965, Civil Rights Act of 1957
4. Growing inflation caused prices of American exports to rise, so fewer exports were purchased.
5. Under Nixon's New Federalism, the federal government's role in the economy was reduced, and many of its tasks were turned over to state and local governments.
6. Watergate break-in, appointment of a special prosecutor, Senate hearings, indictments of administration officials, Saturday Night Massacre, release of June 23, 1972, tape transcript.

Understanding Concepts
1. Kennedy did not enter office with a clear mandate, but he inspired trust in the American people, and he achieved some legislative victories. A coalition of conservative southern Democrats, however, prevented him from getting much of his domestic program passed. Johnson's Great Society won a clear mandate in the 1964 election, and under his leadership through consensus, Congress passed many important laws.
2. Johnson's programs offered something for everyone. His programs for the poor and underprivileged were balanced with tax cuts for corporations. To maintain a consensus of this kind is very difficult as seen by the divisions that erupted in America during the last years of Johnson's presidency.
3. Nixon used secrecy to control foreign policy. This tactic caused resentment among members of Congress and some Americans because they disagreed with his policies.
4. Answers will vary. Yes, it is important; Americans pride themselves on an egalitarian system of government in which all members are equally accountable.

Using Vocabulary

Each of the terms below has significance for the concept of presidential power. Use each of these terms in a sentence, describing how it is related to this concept.

mandate   executive privilege
pragmatist   impound
consensus

Reviewing Facts

1. **Describe** Kennedy's presidential style.
2. **State** two legislative victories and two legislative setbacks for Kennedy.
3. **Identify** four achievements of the Johnson administration.
4. **Describe** why there was a decrease in United States dominance of world markets.
5. **Explain** the significance of Nixon's new federalism.
6. **Chart** the sequence of events that led to Nixon's resignation.

Understanding Concepts

Mandates
1. Examine the Kennedy and Johnson presidencies and describe how an election mandate affected each man's ability to govern.
2. Explain the importance of political consensus to President Johnson.

Presidential Power
3. What function did secrecy serve in the Nixon presidency? Why did some Americans and members of Congress resent this tactic?
4. When President Nixon resigned over Watergate, some nations expressed astonishment that Americans would force their highest leader to step down over a "relatively small offense." Is it important for our nation to hold politicians accountable for their actions? Explain.

Critical Thinking

1. **Comparing and Contrasting** Explain how Kennedy and Johnson differed in their relationships with Congress.
2. **Drawing Conclusions** What are the lessons of the Watergate scandal? Would you agree that our system of government was vindicated by this affair? What long-term repercussions do you think Watergate had on Americans' views of government and politicians?
3. **Analyzing Fine Art** Study the painting that appears on this page, then answer the questions that follow.
   a. What do you think the artist is expressing in this painting?
   b. How does the artist lead your eye around the composition?
   c. Do you like this painting? Why or why not?

972   UNIT 10 Redefining America: 1954–Present

CHAPTER 34 ★ REVIEW

Writing About History

Cause and Effect

Imagine you are a reporter for the *Washington Post* and you have discovered evidence of the President's involvement in the Watergate break-in. You are aware of Nixon's tremendous power as well as his denial that he had anything to do with it. Write a follow-up article after the President has resigned, reviewing the importance of the media and its effect on the resignation.

Cooperative Learning

You will work in small groups to investigate testimony before the Senate subcommittee on Watergate. Each group member should select a different witness to research. Use the actual transcripts of the hearings to discover the process the committee really went through. Then meet together and discuss your findings with the class.

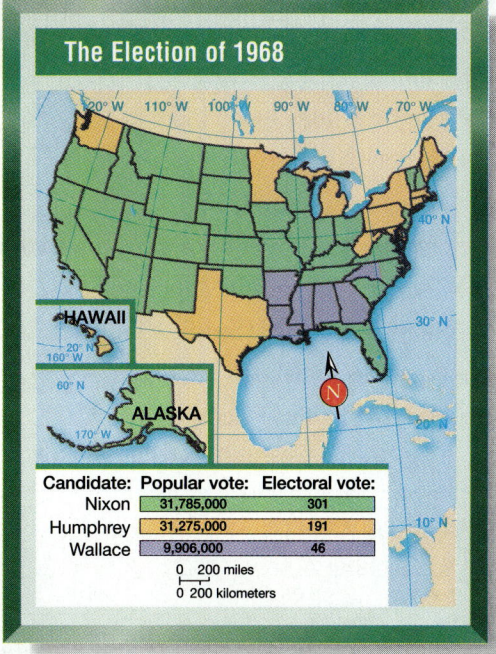

The Election of 1968

Candidate:	Popular vote:	Electoral vote:
Nixon	31,785,000	301
Humphrey	31,275,000	191
Wallace	9,906,000	46

Social Study Skills

Analyzing Political Maps

An election map is a type of political map. It shows how each state voted in an election. The legend indicates which candidate each color represents. Popular vote and electoral vote are sometimes shown on the map with each state.

Practicing the Skill

Use the election map on this page and the election map on page 952 to answer the following questions.
1. What election results does the map show?
2. Who were the candidates in the 1968 election?
3. Speculate on why Wallace won only Southern states.
4. Compare this election map with the election map on page 952. In both, the popular votes are relatively close, but the electoral votes are not so close. How can this be explained?
5. In comparing the two maps, where was Nixon consistently weak?

Using Your Journal

Review your journal notes about corruption in the government as evidenced by the Watergate scandal. Write a paragraph describing how public awareness of that corruption affected people's views during later scandals in government. To answer, you may have to do extra research.

REVIEW CHAPTER 34

Practicing the Skill
1. the presidential election of 1968
2. Nixon, Humphrey, and Wallace
3. As governor of Alabama, Wallace was best known in the South.
4. The margin is larger in the electoral vote because usually all electoral votes of a state go to the winning candidate.
5. Texas, the South, and the Northeast

❓ Chapter Bonus Test Question

List an example of Great Society legislation that makes a difference in your life or the lives of people in your community. (Possible answers include the Office of Economic Opportunity, the Elementary and Secondary Education Act, and Medicare.)

Using Your Journal

Students should mention that people were deeply discouraged with government officials as a result of the Watergate scandal. Many hoped that new leaders would restore their confidence. They might mention scandals during Reagan's administration, such as the Iran-Contra affair in 1986.

Critical Thinking

1. A coalition of conservative southern Democrats prevented Kennedy from getting much of his domestic program passed. Johnson was more comfortable with members of Congress and continued as president to work at getting his programs passed through consensus.
2. Answers will vary. There are many lessons to be learned including abuse of power and the importance of our checks-and-balances system. One possible repercussion of Watergate is a growing cynicism among Americans about politics and government in general.
3. a. Artist is expressing his or her ideas about the U.S. at this time.
   b. Students should note that the flag helps the viewer focus on the open area.
   c. Answers will vary, but students should provide reasons.

PLANNING GUIDE Chapter 35 Search for New Solutions

Daily Lesson Objectives	Teacher Classroom Resources	Multimedia
SECTION 1 **Crisis of Confidence** **1 Day** pp. 976–981 1. State reasons for the American public's crisis of confidence. 2. Explain how moral principles directed President Carter's domestic and foreign policy.	Chapter 35 Study Guide Reproducible Lesson Plan Section Quiz Reteaching Activity 35-1 Chapter 35 Cooperative Learning Activity Chapter 35 Concept Mapping Activity Reinforcing Social Studies Skills 12, 20, 27 Writer's Guidebook Lesson 1 Building Skills in Geography Map and Graph Skills Activities 23, 33	Student Self-Test Software Testmaker Section Focus Transparency 116 Chapter 34 Skills Transparency Powers of the President The Presidents: A Picture History of Our Nation
SECTION 2 **A Conservative Shift** **1 Day** pp. 982–988 1. Explain the conservative shift in Americans' political convictions. 2. Describe President Reagan's economic recovery plan. 3. Describe President Reagan's foreign policy regarding the Soviet Union.	Reproducible Lesson Plan Reteaching Activity 35-2 Section Quiz Chapter 35 Primary & Secondary Source Readings American Portrait 70 Reinforcing Social Studies Skills 36 Building Skills in Geography Map and Graph Skills Activities 29, 31	Student Self-Test Software Testmaker Section Focus Transparency 117 The Presidents: A Picture History of Our Nation Communism and the Cold War
SECTION 3 **A New Presidency** **1 Day** pp. 990–996 1. Explain how the spread of democracy led to the formation of a new world order. 2. Describe America's role in the post–cold-war world. 3. Discuss the reasons for discord between the legislative and executive branches of government under President Bush.	Reproducible Lesson Plan Reteaching Activity 35-3 Section Quiz Chapter 35 Enrichment Activity Reinforcing Social Studies Skills 6, 15 Writer's Guidebook Lessons 6, 8-14 The Living Constitution Map and Graph Skills Activities 29, 31 Spanish Summaries and Glossary	Student Self-Test Software Testmaker Section Focus Transparency 118 Vocabulary Puzzlemaker Audiocassette, Chapter 35 Communism and the Cold War Lessons of War The Presidents: A Picture History of Our Nation
CHAPTER REVIEW AND EVALUATION **1 Day**	Chapter 35 Test Chapter 35 Performance Assessment Activity	Student Self-Test Software Testmaker

OUT OF TIME? If time does not permit teaching the entire chapter, use the Chapter 35 Summary on pages 1028–1029 and the Chapter 35 audiocassette (English and Spanish) to point out the main ideas of the chapter.

PLANNING GUIDE

Cultural Diversity Activity

Cooperative Learning During the Industrial Age most immigrants came from Europe. By the 1970s most newcomers were from Asia, Latin America, and the Caribbean. Yet no matter when they arrived, immigrants faced many of the same problems: finding a job, locating a place to live, learning a new language, and becoming accustomed to a new way of life.

Divide students into groups to prepare a television public service announcement. The ad should offer practical advice to newcomers. Encourage the class to translate their announcements into at least one of the languages spoken by immigrants in their community.

Chapter Resources

Literature from the Period

Bush, George. "The Liberation of Kuwait." January 16, 1991.

Wiesel, Elie. "Nobel Acceptance Speech." December 11, 1986.

Readings for the Student

Kennedy, Caroline, and Ellen Alderman. *In Our Defense: The Bill of Rights in Action*. William Morrow, 1991.

Readings for the Teacher

Blumenthal, Sidney. *Pledging Allegiance: The Last Campaign of the Cold War*. HarperCollins, 1990.

Friedman, Thomas L. *From Beirut to Jerusalem*. Doubleday, 1991.

Multimedia Resources

The Eagle and the Bear. Guidance Associates. (VHS 48 minutes)

The Budget Deficit: A Question of Balance. Tom Snyder. (Apple or IBM diskette)

Performance Assessment Activity

Tracing Major Events Divide the class into small groups and ask each to construct a time line of the major events that shaped American life between 1976 and 1992. The events a group selects can be of national or global significance. Each group should also write a paragraph defending the choices it made. Encourage groups to share their time lines with the class.

POSSIBLE RUBRIC FEATURES: Content information, organization, evaluation of evidence, written and oral communication skills, critical thinking skills, collaborative skills

Key to Ability Levels

Teaching strategies have been coded for varying learning styles and abilities.

- **L1** Basic activities for all students
- **L2** Average activities for average to above-average students
- **L3** Challenging activities for above-average students
- **LEP** Limited English Proficiency activities

Glencoe Links to the Humanities

Link to Art
- U.S. History and Art Transparency 31

Links to Literature
- Macmillan Literature: Appreciating Literature Audiotapes Side 4
- Macmillan Literature: American Literature Text—Raymond Carver, Mark Helprin, Barry Lopez

Link to Music
- American Music: Cultural Traditions

CHAPTER 35

BEGINNING THE CHAPTER

Tell students that the percentage of Americans who vote has steadily declined. The 1960 election between Kennedy and Nixon saw the highest voter turnout in years. Yet even then over one-third of Americans registered to vote did not take part. In the 1976 presidential election, 45 percent of registered voters failed to make it to the polls.

Linking Across Time

A child during the Great Depression, Jimmy Carter had vivid memories of President Roosevelt's fireside chats. Carter decided to adopt similar methods to promote his programs. He made television addresses from the White House residence rather than the formal setting of the Oval Office.

Recording Journal Notes

To get students started, suggest that they use as headings these conservative policies: reduction in taxes, reduction in government spending, higher defense spending.

CHAPTER 35

Search for Solutions
1976–1992

▶ YELLOW RIBBON TREE TIE

Setting the Scene

Focus

Despite success in foreign affairs, Jimmy Carter rapidly lost the people's confidence. In the next election, they turned to the conservative Ronald Reagan to restore their confidence. During his administration, the economy recovered and relations with the Soviet Union improved. But Reagan left a mixed legacy, and problems with the economy were passed on to his successor, George Bush, who also had to redefine America's role in world affairs.

Concepts to Understand

★ How the leadership of Carter, Reagan, and Bush shaped events and policies

★ How reform and change altered the world's political landscape

Read to Discover...

★ what important changes took place in the Soviet Union and Eastern Europe in the late 1980s and early 1990s.

Journal Notes

Why do you think so many Americans were ready for the conservative shift initiated by Ronald Reagan in the 1980s? Note details about it in your journal as you read the chapter.

CULTURAL
- 1979 Inflation reaches unprecedented rates
- 1980 United States boycotts Moscow Olympics
- 1983 Sally Ride is first American woman in space

1975 | **1980**

POLITICAL
- 1978 Camp David Accords are signed
- 1979 Iran seizes 52 American hostages
- 1981 Sandra Day O'Connor is first woman named to Supreme Court
- 1983 Reagan announces Strategic Defense Initiative

974 UNIT 10 Redefining America: 1954–Present

✚ **EXTRA CREDIT PROJECT**

Refer interested students to a world map. Ask them to trace the map and label the countries or regions mentioned in this chapter. Then have them select one of the countries or regions and research the relationship between their selection and the United States. Their reports should include the political, economic, and geographical implications of the relationship.

Three Flags
by Jasper Johns, 1958

The paintings of American artist Jasper Johns typically featured two-dimensional objects of everyday life as subjects. Johns, for example, painted pictures that consisted entirely of flags, maps, numbers, and letters of the alphabet.

◀ UNITED STATES SOLDIERS, ACTION DURING THE GULF WAR

- **1986** Space shuttle *Challenger* explodes
- **1989** Bicentennial of the Constitution
- **1990** Detroit Pistons win National Basketball Association championship

| 1985 | 1990 |

- **1986** Iran-contra scandal
- **1987** Reagan and Gorbachev sign nuclear arms reduction treaty
- **1990** Persian Gulf War begins
- **1991** The Soviet Union collapses

CHAPTER 35 Search for Solutions 1976–1992   975

CHAPTER 35 CONCEPTS

Concept Mapping Activity

Write the following chapter generalization and concepts on the chalkboard. Ask students to write these concepts in their notebooks and to list each major event in the chapter under the appropriate concept.

> Two very different leaders, Carter and Reagan, faced the challenge to create a new national mood despite economic uncertainties and disillusionment.

- Political Ideology
- Leadership

History AND ART

In addition to Johns, Andy Warhol, Roy Lichtenstein, and Claes Oldenburg were artists who monumentalized everyday objects.

ABC NEWS INTERACTIVE

VIDEODISC
Powers of the President

Side 2, Chapter 10
Title: *Manager of the Economy*
Subject: The President's role as manager of the economy

Teacher Notes

LESSON PLAN
SECTION 1, 976–981

FOCUS
Bellringer

Prior to taking roll at the beginning of the class period, display Focus Activity 115 on the overhead projector and assign the accompanying Focus Activity Sheet.

Objectives

Point out the objectives on this page to students in previewing the section content.

Motivating Activity

Tell students that in the mid-1970s many Americans resented presidential authority. Because of the Vietnam War and the Watergate scandal, a lot of people believed that an "imperial presidency" had developed. President Carter tried to develop a more informal approach to government, a style sometimes characterized as "Jacksonian." Ask students: What do you think this means? ("man of the people" or "folksy" manner)

Use Skills Transparency 35.

The following material is available from Glencoe and may be used to enrich Chapter 35.

CD-ROM
- *The Presidents: A Picture History of Our Nation*

SECTION 1

Crisis of Confidence

Setting the Scene

Focus

Americans felt a deep sense of pride and patriotism as they celebrated the Bicentennial in 1976. These feelings, however, could not erase the painful memories of two of the most disillusioning events in United States history—the Vietnam War and the Watergate scandal. Americans were ready for new leadership to bolster the national mood and solve the difficult problems that loomed ahead.

Objectives

After studying this section, you should be able to
★ state reasons for the American public's crisis of confidence.
★ explain how moral principles directed President Carter's domestic and foreign policy.

Key Terms

cartel, double-digit inflation, pork-barrel legislation

◀ HOSTAGE TERRY ANDERSON AFTER HIS RELEASE

At the time of its Bicentennial in 1976, the United States was faced with the grim prospect of diminishing vital natural resources. One result was that the nation was no longer self-sufficient in its production of energy. By then, the United States was importing more than half of its oil. Competition from Japan, Germany, and other countries threatened America's giant automobile and steel industries. With rising inflation and unemployment, the lifestyles of many Americans were critically affected.

There were equally serious problems in foreign affairs. Political turmoil in economically developing nations upset global stability. The Soviet Union pursued an increasingly aggressive foreign policy as the nuclear arms race continued. As the United States began its third century, the American people wondered if the government was capable of meeting these challenges.

Election of 1976

Soon after Gerald Ford became President in 1974, he began to campaign for his election in 1976. The public regarded Ford as a warm, easygoing man of high integrity, but had doubts about his intellectual capabilities and competence as a leader. As a result, conservatives in the Republican party rallied behind Ronald Reagan, the former governor of California. Ford survived the challenge and won the Republican nomination, but only by a few votes.

The Democratic presidential primaries were crowded with candidates including several who were nationally known. One, however, was a political outsider. James Earl "Jimmy" Carter, Jr., a former governor of Georgia, had no previous experience in the federal government. He toured the nation meeting voters face to face. Carter made a virtue of this inexperience:

UNIT 10 Redefining America: 1954–Present

Classroom Resources for SECTION 1

Teacher's Classroom Resources
- Chapter 35 Study Guide
- Reproducible Lesson Plan
- Reteaching Activity 35-1
- Chapter 35 Cooperative Learning Activity
- Section Quiz

Multimedia
- Section Focus Transparency 115
- Skills Transparency 35
- Testmaker
- Student Self-Test Software
- Powers of the President
- The Presidents: A Picture History of Our Nation

> *The people of this country want a fresh face, not one associated with a long series of mistakes at the White House and Capitol Hill.*

To almost everyone's surprise, Carter won many of the primaries and secured the Democratic nomination for President. This was partly because his informal, down-home style appealed to Americans tired of the "imperial presidency."

During the presidential campaign, Jimmy Carter vowed to restore people's faith in the federal government by making it more open and efficient. He promised major new programs for energy development, tax reform, welfare reform, and national medical care. Conservatives liked him because he promised to balance the budget. Liberals supported him because he insisted he would not let unemployment rise as a means of lowering inflation.

Although the vote was close, Carter won the election. He took 51 percent of the popular vote and 297 electoral votes to Ford's 48 percent and 241 electoral votes. Carter achieved his victory by combining the support of the old Democratic coalition of the industrial Northeast and the Solid South (except for Virginia). For the first time since 1848, a candidate from the Deep South had been elected President. To a great extent, Carter owed his margin of victory to African American Southern voters.

Energy and Economic Shocks

President Carter believed that America's most serious domestic problem was its increasing dependence on oil as an energy source. Experts warned that world supplies of oil, a nonrenewable resource, would soon be exhausted. The oil-producing countries belonged to a **cartel,** an association of nations promoting its economic interests, the Organization of Petroleum Exporting Countries (OPEC). They set prices at ever-higher levels. Rising oil prices added substantially to the price of consumer goods.

Carter's Energy Program

To address the problem, Carter proposed a national energy program. He persuaded Congress to create a Department of Energy. In order to conserve oil, he promoted the

▲ **AN INFORMAL PRESIDENCY** Both Jimmy Carter and his wife Rosalyn lived a relatively simple life. Both came from close-knit families that stressed hard work, dedication, and religion. **What electoral group helped Carter win the 1976 election?**

CHAPTER 35 Search for Solutions 1976–1992

Special Needs

Study Strategy Much of the information in this text is tested at comprehension levels that require understanding of main ideas, details, and relationships. Throughout the text, students with learning problems have been taught the skills for acquiring this level of information.

Explain to students that some tests require them to make and defend value judgments. As students read about the presidency of Jimmy Carter, ask them to consider their opinions of his actions. Then inquire: How do you think history will judge his presidency? Why?

CHAPTER 35 SECTION 1

TEACH
Guided Practice

Drama Organize students into small groups to write a scene—set in the 1970s—involving conversations among an American housewife, a manager of an automobile factory, a young unemployed worker, a college student, and a newspaper reporter. Each person should state reasons—energy crisis, foreign competition, rising inflation and unemployment, social and economic inequality—for losing confidence in the nation's future. Have each group dramatize its dialogues. **L1, LEP**

Visualizing History After the inaugural ceremony, Carter and his family walked up Pennsylvania Avenue from the Capitol to the White House instead of riding in the traditional limousine. This gesture symbolized Carter's desire to create a more informal presidency.
Answer to Caption: African Americans

CHAPTER 35 SECTION 1

Independent Practice

Speech Writing Have students assume the role of President Carter's chief speechwriter in 1979. Ask them to write a political speech in which they outline Carter's foreign policy accomplishments and justify his failures. Ask volunteers to read their speeches to the class. **L3**

The United States has done little to develop alternative energy sources, evidenced by continued dependence on Middle East oil. Americans have made a certain amount of progress nevertheless, as shown by recent developments in nuclear and solar energy, more fuel-efficient cars, and better building materials.

Using Charts
Answer: 1974, 1979, 1980

Skills Practice
Why is "NA" indicated in the No Lead column for the year 1973? (Nonleaded gasoline was not available to the public in 1973.)

Gasoline Consumption and Prices

Year	Consumption (billions of gallons)	Reg.	Prem.	No lead
1973	110.5	40	45	NA
1974	106.3	53	57	55
1975	109.0	57	61	60
1976	115.7	59	64	61
1977	119.6	62	67	66
1978	125.1	63	69	67
1979	122.1	86	92	90
1980	115.0	119	128	125

Source: *Statistical Abstract of the United States, 1981*

Chart Study Gasoline prices increased steadily beginning in 1973. *In what years did prices affect consumption?*

use of coal and such renewable energy sources as solar energy. The President wanted Americans to join together in a moral crusade against rising consumption:

> [The nation's] decision about energy will test the character of the American people and the ability of the President and Congress to govern this nation. This difficult decision will be the 'moral equivalent of war'—except that we will be uniting our efforts to build and not to destroy.

The President asked all Americans to make personal sacrifices to reduce their energy consumption. Because the sacrifices he asked people to make were voluntary, however, the public was confused about the seriousness of the crisis. When Carter later proposed stronger methods of restricting consumption, such as a 10 percent tax on all imported oil and emergency authority to impose gasoline rationing, Congress rejected them. Carter did, however, convince Congress to lift controls on domestic oil production and to impose a "windfall profits" tax on the oil companies' huge earnings.

Double-digit Inflation

Sharp rises in the price of oil and gasoline contributed to **double-digit inflation,** or a rise in the general level of prices of 10 percent or more. By 1980 it cost more than $200 to purchase the same goods that $100 would have bought only 10 years earlier. At the same time, the Federal Reserve Board raised interest rates to all-time highs in an effort to discourage borrowing and bring the economy under control. These policies helped reduce inflation but caused a severe business recession.

■ Governmental Disunity

Even though the Democrats held the presidency and had a majority in both houses of Congress, there was a lack of unity between the two branches of government. This was largely because Carter was unwilling to play politics. For example, in 1977 he announced that he would veto appropriation bills for a series of costly dams, canals, and other water projects. Passing such **pork-barrel legislation,** or bills that benefit only a small part of the country, was a common practice. Carter's move saved the nation millions of dollars, but it cost him valuable support.

Carter's inability to sell his political position on important issues puzzled many people. He followed a cautious middle course, promising to reduce government spending while endorsing expensive social programs. The President would not "choose up sides," as newspaper columnist James Reston observed. "Confronted with a series of ambiguous questions, he simply refused to give simple answers." As a result, the public became confused about Carter's goals. By 1979 his popular support had fallen dramatically.

■ Morality in Foreign Policy

In contrast to his leadership in domestic policy, President Carter's foreign policy was clearly defined. Carter denounced past

UNIT 10 Redefining America: 1954–Present

Cooperative Learning

Organize students into small groups to develop scripts for a news magazine program on one of the major events, issues, or policies of the Carter administration. Suggest that the groups use the following structure for their programs: a statement on the subject of the program, a brief report providing background detail on the subject, and a discussion involving a moderator and at least two people with differing views on the subject. Have groups perform their scripts for the rest of the class. **L2**

American foreign policy as "lacking moral principle." A man of strong religious beliefs, Carter argued that instead of relying on military and economic might, the United States must try to be "right and honest and truthful and decent" in its dealings with other nations.

The Panama Canal

Carter demonstrated his new policy over the Panama Canal, which the United States had controlled since 1903. In 1978 he won Senate ratification of the Panama Canal treaties, which transferred control of the canal from the United States to Panama by the end of the century. This action removed a major symbol of United States interventionist policy and signaled a new approach to Latin American relations.

Respect for Human Rights

In his dealings with other nations, Carter expressed a "clear-cut preference for those societies which share with us an abiding respect for human rights." His administration cut off military and economic support to several Latin American governments considered dictatorial and repressive. Carter also strongly condemned the Soviet Union for imprisoning people who protested government policies and for not allowing more of its Jewish citizens to emigrate.

Tension Over Afghanistan

Tension between the United States and the Soviet Union heightened when Soviet troops invaded Afghanistan late in 1979. In keeping with Carter's noninterventionist policy, the United States refrained from sending troops to the area. Instead, the President imposed an embargo on the sale of grain to the Soviet Union and called for a boycott of the 1980 Summer Olympic Games to be held in Moscow.

■ The Troubled Middle East

Carter's greatest foreign policy triumph and his greatest failure involved the Middle East. Since its early history, the region had been troubled by deep political and religious conflicts. Carter acknowledged that:

Visualizing History ▲ **AGREEMENT AT CAMP DAVID** President Carter meets with Egyptian President Anwar el-Sadat (left) and Israeli Prime Minister Menachem Begin (right) to sign the Camp David Peace Accords. **What was the goal of the agreement?**

CHAPTER 35 SECTION 1

Did You Know?

A graduate of the Naval Academy at Annapolis, Jimmy Carter served as an electrical engineer on battleships and submarines. His love of engineering dated from his boyhood when, while watching mechanics repairing his father's farm machinery, he would try to figure out how things worked.

FACT or FICTION?

Unlike previous presidents, Jimmy Carter worked without a chief of staff during the first two years of his presidency.

FACT: Instead, he had several different aides report to him. But this approach proved cumbersome and chaotic and, in part, contributed to his indecisive image and his difficulties with Congress. For the final two years of his term, he returned to the traditional organizational system.

Visualizing History The Camp David Accords were bitterly opposed by some of the other Arab states. Some Arab states, however, refused either to condemn or support Sadat. **Answer to Caption:** to establish peace in the Middle East

---

Critical Thinking

Classifying Information Tell students that interest groups are made up of people who support a common goal and seek to influence government policies. Interest groups have brought their concerns to the notice of public officials since colonial times. Today, they can be classified into a number of categories—labor, business, farm, professional, special population, and public interest, to name a few. Ask students to provide examples of interest groups that would fall into these categories. Upon completion of this task, have them compare their lists. **L3**

CHAPTER 35 SECTION 1

Visualizing History The former Shah of Iran entered the United States in October 1979 seeking medical treatment. When Iranians demanded that Carter surrender the Shah to them to stand trial for the brutality of his regime, Carter refused. Soon after, the American embassy was stormed. **Answer to Caption:** negotiations and a military rescue

VIDEODISC
Powers of the President

Side 2, Chapter 6
Title: *Roles of the President*
Subject: Former President Carter discusses the extraconstitutional roles of the President

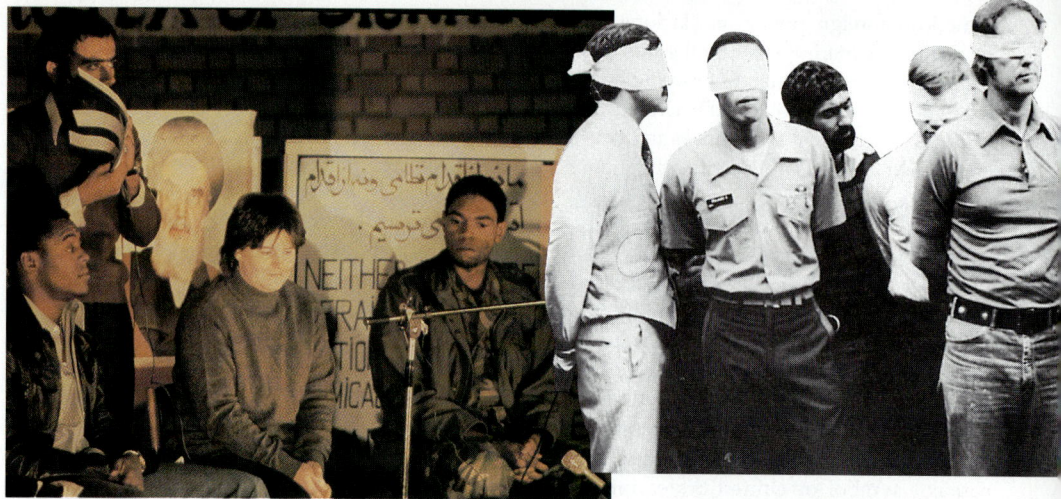

▲ **HOSTAGE CRISIS** In November 1979 Iranian radicals seized more than 50 Americans as hostages. President Carter condemned the action as "an act of terrorism outside the boundaries of international law." **What actions did Carter take to resolve the crisis?**

> *[The Middle East] has long been a textbook for pessimism, a demonstration that diplomatic ingenuity was no match for intractable human conflicts.*

The Camp David Accords

Despite this view, President Carter made a bold move to negotiate a peace treaty between Egypt and Israel, nations that had been bitter enemies for 30 years. In 1978 Carter brought Egypt's President Anwar el-Sadat and Israel's Prime Minister Menachem Begin together at Camp David, the presidential retreat in Maryland. The leaders talked for 14 days. More than once the discussions broke down, but Carter persisted until the leaders reached an agreement on September 17, 1978. In front of a joint session of Congress, with Sadat and Begin in the gallery, Carter announced:

> *This is the first time that an Arab and an Israeli leader have signed a comprehensive framework for peace. It contains the seeds of a time when the Middle East, with all its vast potential, may be a land of human richness and fulfillment, rather than a land of bitterness and continued conflict.*

The Camp David Accords, which were formally signed in 1979, established peace between Egypt and Israel. Most of the other Arab nations expressed strong opposition to the treaty because they felt Egypt should not have acted alone. Also the issue of the Israeli-occupied territories inhabited by Palestinians was yet to be solved. Still, an important first step toward peace in the Middle East had been taken.

Crisis With Iran

This success, however, could not make up for Carter's inability to resolve the crisis with Iran in 1979. The United States had long supported the Shah of Iran. Iran served as a major supplier of oil and as a reliable buffer against Soviet expansion in the Middle East. Yet many Iranians had grown unhappy with the Shah's rule. The Shah had brought Western technology and reform to his people with immense revenues from oil, but these changes had only widened the gap between the wealthy and the extremely poor.

UNIT 10 Redefining America: 1954–Present

Cultural Diversity

Jimmy Carter was a representative of the "New South," a society that would be based on racial harmony rather than conflict and prejudice. Both as governor of Georgia and as President, Carter appointed African Americans to positions of importance, and his belief in racial equality seemed to be a deeply held conviction. As Andrew Young, Carter's ambassador to the United Nations, noted, "Blacks have a kind of radar about white folks and, somewhere along the line, Jimmy passed the test."

Some Islamic leaders objected to the Western social reforms and customs that had been introduced into Iran, claiming that they ran contrary to their religious traditions. Huge protests forced the Shah to flee in 1979, and an Islamic republic replaced the monarchy.

The new regime, headed by the religious leader Ayatollah Ruholla Khomeini (koh•MAY•nee), viewed the United States with deep distrust because of its ties with the Shah. Anti-American feelings were so strong that on November 4, 1979, militants stormed the American embassy in Tehran, the Iranian capital, and took hostage more than 50 Americans. The militants threatened to kill the hostages or try them as spies.

Negotiations for the freedom of the hostages were unsuccessful. As pressure mounted to secure their release, Carter felt he had no choice but to launch a military rescue. One morning in April 1980, Americans awoke to the shocking news that a mission to rescue the hostages had failed. Eight members of the rescue team had died in a helicopter crash in Iran. Despite this setback, Carter persisted in his diplomatic efforts to free the hostages.

Election of 1980

The hostage crisis became a key issue in Carter's bid for reelection. Carter fought off a strong challenge from Senator Edward Kennedy of Massachusetts for the Democratic nomination. As Election Day grew near, however, the American people became increasingly impatient with the situation in Iran.

The Republicans chose former California governor Ronald Reagan as their candidate. Reagan's chief opponents in the primaries were two moderate Republicans, former United Nations Ambassador George Bush and Illinois Representative John Anderson. After his nomination, Reagan picked Bush as his running mate. Anderson decided to run for President as an independent candidate, hoping to appeal to voters who were unhappy with Reagan and Carter.

The Republicans adopted a conservative platform calling for reductions in taxes and government spending in order to restore prosperity. The party did endorse, however, higher defense spending to strengthen the role of the United States in world affairs.

Throughout the campaign, Reagan hammered at Carter's lack of leadership and the nation's weak economy. He promised voters economic growth and development instead of the sacrifices and restraints that Carter advocated. Carter responded by picturing Reagan as unsympathetic to the needs of the poor and minority groups. On Election Day, Reagan claimed victory with 51 percent of the popular vote and 489 electoral votes. Carter won 41 percent, with 49 electoral votes. John Anderson and other candidates of minor parties split the rest of the vote. The conservative tide that elected Reagan resulted in a Republican Senate and reduced the Democratic House of Representatives.

President Carter's failure to obtain release of the hostages sealed his defeat. Only after Ronald Reagan was sworn in on January 20, 1981, did Iran release the Americans, ending their 444 days in captivity.

Section 1 ★ Review

Checking for Understanding

1. **Identify** OPEC, Anwar el-Sadat, Menachem Begin, Camp David Accords, Shah of Iran, Ayatollah Ruhollah Khomeini, John Anderson.
2. **Define** cartel, double-digit inflation, pork-barrel legislation.
3. **List** three features of Carter's energy program.
4. **Summarize** President Carter's successes and failures in negotiations with nations in the Middle East.

Critical Thinking

5. **Evaluating Leaders** Explain why Carter's unwillingness to play politics eroded his support in Congress.

CHAPTER 35 Search for Solutions 1976–1992   981

LESSON PLAN
SECTION 2, 982–988

FOCUS

Bellringer
Prior to taking roll at the beginning of the class period, display Focus Activity 116 on the overhead projector and assign the accompanying Focus Activity Book.

Objectives
Point out the objectives on this page to students in previewing the section content.

Motivating Activity
Present the following excerpt from a Carter campaign speech made at a town meeting in 1980:

"[T]he Republican party now is sharply different from what the Democratic party is. And I might add parenthetically that the Republican party is sharply different under Reagan from what it was under Gerald Ford and Presidents all the way back to Eisenhower."

Ask: What point do you think Carter was trying to make by comparing Reagan to earlier Republican presidents? (Students should reply that Reagan was more radical and conservative than earlier Republicans.)

The following material is available from Glencoe and may be used to enrich Chapter 35.

CD-ROM
- *The Presidents: A Picture History of Our Nation*

SECTION 2

A Conservative Shift

Setting the Scene

Section Focus
Despite the hope they had felt in 1976, Americans became increasingly dissatisfied with the government during Carter's administration. Angered over economic conditions, the energy crisis, and the President's inability to free the hostages, the people turned to a new leader to restore their confidence. The voters were not only reacting against Carter, however, but giving voice to a growing conservative movement that rejected the liberalism of the 1960s and demanded changes in the way the government met challenges at home and abroad.

Objectives
After studying this section, you should be able to
★ explain the conservative shift in Americans' political convictions in the late 1970s and early 1980s.
★ describe President Reagan's economic recovery plan, which included cutting taxes and reducing spending.
★ describe Reagan's foreign policy regarding the Soviet Union.

Key Terms
supply-side economics, federal deficit, glasnost, perestroika, privatized

◀ REPUBLICAN PARTY SYMBOL

Reagan's election indicated a significant conservative shift in Americans' political convictions. In addition to support from traditionally conservative groups such as fundamentalist Christians and antifeminists, many groups that had historically voted Democratic broke with their party and supported Reagan. These included former liberals, blue-collar workers, ethnic voters, and Southerners, who became known as "Reagan Democrats." The 69-year-old Reagan also attracted many older voters.

As a whole, the Reagan conservatives believed that the federal government should withdraw from most areas of domestic life. They were against liberal social programs and government restrictions on business. In foreign policy, they favored a strong military to stand against communism.

■ Reagan's Economic Program

President Reagan acted quickly to limit the size of the federal government. His first act as President was to place a freeze on the hiring of federal employees. At the same time, he began to ease government controls on many business activities. He set up a task force headed by Vice President Bush to

982   UNIT 10 Redefining America: 1954–Present

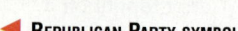

Classroom Resources for SECTION 2

Teacher's Classroom Resources
- Reproducible Lesson Plan
- Reteaching Activity 35-2
- Chapter 35 Primary and Secondary Source Readings
- Section Quiz

Multimedia
- Section Focus Transparency 116
- Testmaker
- Student Self-Test Software
- The Presidents: A Picture History of Our Nation

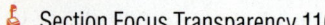

review federal regulations. As President, Reagan moved to fulfill his campaign promise to get the economy going again. In February 1981, he told Americans:

> Since 1960 our government has spent $5.1 trillion. Our debt has grown to $648 billion. Prices have exploded by 178 percent.... [We] know we must act and act now. We must not be timid....

To take care of the problem, Reagan proposed a new economic program, which came to be called "Reaganomics."

Cutting Taxes

The first part of the President's program was to make deep cuts in federal taxes. He predicted that income tax reductions would increase consumer spending and would also encourage investments, especially by the wealthy. Similarly, cuts in corporate taxes would allow companies to expand production and hire more workers. Reagan's beliefs were based on an economic theory called **supply-side economics,** which claimed that the economy could best be stimulated by increasing the supply of goods rather than the demand.

Reducing Government Spending

The second part of Reagan's program was to reduce government spending by ending federal job-training programs and cutting back the amount of federal money going into medicare, food stamps, and education. Critics predicted that Reagan's proposal would cause great suffering for the economically disadvantaged. Reagan denied this, claiming that there would always be a "safety net" of government aid for truly needy Americans.

■ Results of Reaganomics

Although the President faced opposition to his proposals, he had personal qualities that helped to promote his position: a great ability to communicate with his audience and a sense of humor. In March 1981, when he was shot and seriously wounded, the

 ▲ **ASSASSINATION ATTEMPT** In March 1981 President Reagan survived an attempt on his life outside a Washington hotel. His press secretary, a police officer, and a Secret Service agent were also wounded. **What was Reagan's chief concern when he took office?**

CHAPTER 35 Search for Solutions 1976–1992 **983**

Special Needs

Study Strategy To understand and evaluate this section, which describes the reawakening of "conservative" feelings in this country, several political ideologies must be understood. Have students write in their notebooks the words Conservative, Moderate, and Liberal as headings of three columns. Using the categories social policy, foreign policy, and economic policy, see what information can be gained about each heading from their reading of the chapter. Have students work in groups to research the information not included. Discuss their findings.

CHAPTER 35
SECTION 2

Independent Practice

Interviewing Have students conduct interviews with older relatives on how their lives changed during the Reagan years. Ask them to share the results of their interviews with the the class. **L2**

Visualizing History George Bush, Ronald Reagan's running-mate in 1980 and 1984, had been in public life for 30 years. He served two terms in the House of Representatives and later became ambassador to the United Nations, director of the CIA, and chairman of the Republican National Committee.
Answer to Caption: Walter Mondale and Geraldine Ferraro

Did You Know?

A major advantage that Ronald Reagan had in the 1984 election was television. A former actor, Reagan was completely at home in front of the camera. Walter Mondale, on the other hand, came across as awkward and uncomfortable on the screen. After the election Mondale noted, "I never warmed up to television and television never warmed up to me."

 ▲ **A POPULAR PRESIDENT** Some observers noted that President Reagan's strong victories in the 1980 and 1984 elections were due to his personal appeal as well as to growing public support for his conservative policies. *Who were the Democratic candidates in 1984?*

President's aides visited him in the hospital. They assured him that the business of government was continuing as usual. "What makes you think I'd be happy about that?" Reagan quipped.

With his great popularity and shrewd handling of Congress, Reagan soon got much of his economic program passed. The final bill included $39 billion in tax cuts and a 25 percent cut in income taxes. The results of Reaganomics, however, were not quite what the President had hoped. Spending cuts, together with high interest rates, brought inflation down, but at first the cure was painful.

Recession

In 1982 a severe economic recession occurred. Business bankruptcies, factory closings, and farm foreclosures increased at alarming rates. By the end of the year, more than 11 million Americans—10 percent of the workforce—were jobless. Blaming President Reagan's economic programs for the recession, the Democrats won back many seats in the congressional elections.

Recovery

By 1983, however, the economy began to turn around. The Federal Reserve Board lowered interest rates, making it easier for businesses and individuals to borrow money. The inflation rate dropped just as the 25-percent cut in income taxes was putting more money into the hands of consumers. Feeling new confidence in the economy, Americans made purchases they had put off during the recession. Sales of every type of goods and service shot upward, and industries hired back workers who had been laid off during the recession. By the end of Reagan's second term in 1988, unemployment had dropped to 5.5 percent—the lowest in 14 years.

To hail the recovery, President Reagan went before Congress in 1984, saying:

> ❝ . . . America is back—standing tall, looking to the '80s with courage, confidence, and hope. . . . Send away the hand-wringers and doubting Thomases. ❞

984 UNIT 10 Redefining America: 1954–Present

Cooperative Learning

Have students reread the definition of supply-side economics on this page. Then divide the class into three groups and ask group members to work together to write letters to President Reagan on the impact of his economic policies. One group should represent business owners; another should represent workers in manufacturing industries; and the third should represent people on fixed incomes, such as senior citizens or welfare recipients. Have groups select representatives to read their letters to the rest of the class. **L2**

CHAPTER 35
SECTION 2

The Federal Debt Increases

Although Reagan promised to balance the budget, the federal debt greatly increased during his first term. He cut taxes, which meant the government received less revenue. In addition, Congress, now controlled by the Democrats, refused to make the deeper cuts in social programs that Reagan requested. On top of that, Reagan himself increased government spending in certain areas, especially defense. The result was the most unbalanced budget in American history.

By 1984 the **federal deficit,** or the difference between the amount of money the government took in and what it spent, was nearly $200 billion a year. When the government spends more money than it collects, it has to borrow to make up the difference. The more the government borrows, the more interest it owes on its debts. In 1984 the interest alone on the federal debt amounted to $153.8 billion, an increase of more than $55 billion from Reagan's first year in office.

■ Election of 1984

Despite the federal deficit, Reagan was still popular, and the economy had made a healthy recovery. These factors made Reagan a formidable candidate for President in the 1984 election. To run against him, the Democrats nominated a traditional liberal, former Vice President Walter Mondale. Mondale created a precedent by choosing Representative Geraldine Ferraro of New York to run as his Vice President. She was the first woman candidate from a major party to run for this office.

Mondale claimed that Reagan's tax and budget cuts benefited only the wealthy. Reagan countered that his economic program had aided all Americans by sharply reducing inflation. To cut the deficit, Mondale proposed raising taxes, always an unpopular political step. Reagan, however, continued to oppose any increases and insisted that economic expansion and deeper cuts in government spending would reduce the deficit.

In November Americans gave the President an overwhelming vote of confidence. Winning 59 percent of the popular vote, he captured 49 states and took 525 electoral votes to Mondale's 13. Reagan won the biggest electoral margin in history.

■ A Conservative Court

With this tremendous mandate, Reagan began his second term confident in his policies. One of his priorities was to appoint conservative justices to the Supreme Court and the lower federal courts. In 1981, the President had appointed Sandra Day O'Connor, the first woman to serve on the Court. In 1986 Reagan selected Antonin Scalia, and a year later he chose Anthony M. Kennedy.

With Reagan's appointees in place, the Supreme Court began to hand down the kind of conservative rulings for which Reagan had hoped. For example, one decision cut back affirmative action programs that had benefited minorities.

■ Strengthening America's Defenses

President Reagan strongly supported America's space program, both as a means of restoring the nation's self-confidence and as a means of strengthening its defenses. Americans took pride in their successes in space exploration, and the launch of reusable space shuttles marked a new era in the space program.

Support for SDI

Reagan had a special interest in the military aspects of the space program. In 1983 he announced a new research project to create a shield that would intercept and destroy nuclear ballistic missiles. It was called the Strategic Defense Initiative (SDI), nicknamed "Star Wars." Opponents feared that SDI would stimulate an intensified nuclear competition between the United States and the Soviet Union. Reagan and the project's supporters, however, believed SDI would improve chances of nuclear disarmament.

A 1990 magazine interview reported Geraldine Ferraro's belief that, by running for Vice President in 1984, she would make it easier for future women candidates. Said Ferraro in the same interview, "We have a real shot at having a woman President in this . . . decade." Ferraro advised women who aspire to the office to work hard and take risks. To gain the right experience, Ferraro believes that a woman should first be a U.S. Senator or a state governor.

NATIONAL GEOGRAPHIC SOCIETY

The following material is available from Glencoe and may be used to enrich Chapter 35.

 CD-ROM
- *The Presidents: A Picture History of Our Nation*

Sidelights: Reagan's Nicknames

Throughout his time in office, President Reagan's enormous popularity never wavered. All the trials and tribulations of his administration—economic setbacks, foreign policy mishaps, and rumors of scandal and wrongdoing—made little more than a dent in his standing with the American public. Because neither bad news nor personal mistakes seemed to "stick" to him, opponents named Reagan the *Teflon President*—after the nonstick coating applied to cooking utensils.

CHAPTER 35
SECTION 2

Visualizing History The twenty-fifth shuttle flight was the first to have a "civilian observer" aboard. Christa McAuliffe, a teacher from Concord, New Hampshire, was the finalist in a nationwide search for the best example of an American teacher. She was to have taught lessons and provided demonstrations from space that would be beamed live back to earth. **Answer to Caption:** reusable spacecraft

Did You Know?

The superpowers have been holding summit meetings—the 1987 meeting was the sixteenth—since World War II. The results of these meetings have been inconclusive. However, as former President Richard Nixon noted, "when each superpower has the means to destroy... the world... summit meetings have become essential if peace is to be preserved."

Military Buildup

In addition to Star Wars, Reagan also promoted a military buildup, including new bombers, submarines, and missiles and better training for ground troops. Other aspects of his defense program included placing new nuclear missiles in Europe, basing intercontinental missiles in Western states, and developing expensive new B-2 "stealth" bombers. Stealth bombers are military aircraft designed so that radar cannot easily detect them.

The Cost of Defense

Aside from Star Wars, Reagan's military buildup cost $1 trillion. This caused a sharp rise in the federal deficit. As the deficit increased, a greater share of tax revenues went to pay the interest on the national debt. This left less money available for new programs in education, the environment, and public housing.

Congress responded in 1985 by passing the Gramm-Rudman Act, which put greater pressure on Congress and the President to reach agreement on reducing the budget. If they were unable to reduce the annual deficit to certain limits, this legislation set up automatic, across-the-board federal spending cuts.

Reagan, however, still refused to increase income taxes. He was able to maintain this position only because in 1986 a great drop in oil prices occurred. Fear of inflation lessened as interest rates dropped. Nevertheless, by 1988 the national debt had reached $2.3 trillion.

■ Improved Relations With the Soviet Union

Reagan's desire for a strong defense was based on his belief that the Soviet Union, which he called an "evil empire," was a serious threat to the United States. He aimed to contain and counter communism throughout the world, and he followed this policy until relations with the Soviet Union suddenly began to improve.

When Mikhail Gorbachev (GAWR•buh•CHAWF) became Soviet premier, his country's economy, which was highly centralized under the control of the Communist party, was on the verge of collapse. For decades,

Visualizing History ▲ **THE CHALLENGER DISASTER** On January 28, 1986, the space shuttle *Challenger* exploded in space, killing all seven astronauts on board. The tragedy temporarily halted the space program. *What innovation had the shuttle introduced?*

UNIT 10 Redefining America: 1954–Present

Sidelights: "Trickle Down" Presidents

Political opponents slightingly compared Ronald Reagan to Calvin Coolidge, pointing out the similarity between Reaganomics and Coolidge's "trickle down" economic policies. They also noted that Reagan, like Coolidge, seemed rather detached from the process of government. Far from being insulted, Reagan reveled in the comparison. He hung Coolidge's portrait in a prominent place in the White House. He also regularly quoted Coolidge's philosophy on business and government.

Life of the Times

Physical Fitness

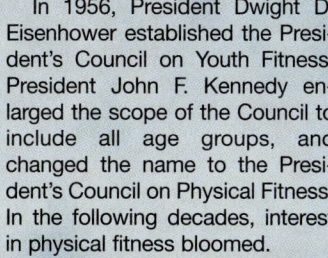

Men and women of early times got plenty of exercise—their lives revolved around the physical tasks involved in the procuring of food and shelter. Beginning with the industrial age and the invention of the steam engine, and continuing into the post-World War II technological age, adults and children became more and more sedentary.

In 1956, President Dwight D. Eisenhower established the President's Council on Youth Fitness. President John F. Kennedy enlarged the scope of the Council to include all age groups, and changed the name to the President's Council on Physical Fitness. In the following decades, interest in physical fitness bloomed.

Tracking individuals over many years, scientists studied the effect of exercise on the body. They concluded that physical inactivity is a significant risk factor for the development of several major illnesses including coronary heart disease. They have also found that regular exercise increases fitness and health. Health professionals of the 1970s and 1980s stressed the benefits of aerobic

exercise. Jogging, aerobic dance, exercise bikes, rowing machines, and mini-trampolines were familiar fitness activities of the time. More recent studies have documented the health benefits of moderate, less intense workouts, and the popularity of bicycling and walking has grown.

---

the party had focused on building up the Soviet Union's position as a superpower and neglected the needs of the people. As a result, farms and factories underproduced and the standard of living was low. The centralized communist system of government was also showing serious strain. The people had no voice and had grown very apathetic in the face of total party control.

Gorbachev Sets New Policy

To save his country and party, Gorbachev set some new policies. First, he introduced **glasnost,** meaning "openness." This policy gave people the right to speak freely—and, Gorbachev hoped, in support of his reforms. Then Gorbachev began **perestroika,** a restructuring of the economy and the government. Instead of party officials deciding everything from Moscow, local farm and factory managers now had the power to make some decisions. The nation's businesses were **privatized,** or transferred from government to private ownership. To lessen the party's control of government, Gorbachev scheduled the first elections in 70 years in which the people had a real choice.

Gorbachev Makes an Astounding Offer

Gorbachev knew that if the arms race could be halted, it would free people and money to produce consumer goods in the Soviet Union. Peace would also allow him to concentrate all his energies on domestic reforms, and could lead to trade agreements and economic aid from the West. So, Gorbachev made the United States an astounding offer, announcing that the Soviet Union would reduce its nuclear weapons.

Reagan and Gorbachev Hold Summit Meeting

When Reagan and Gorbachev met at Reykjavík, Iceland, in 1986, the two leaders tried but could not come to an agreement on the issue of the Strategic Defense Initiative.

CHAPTER 35 SECTION 2

Teaching Life of the Times

According to a recent survey, only 36 percent of school-age children in the United States have daily physical education classes. Fewer than half of all children get enough exercise to develop healthy hearts and lungs. Ask students what they do to keep physically fit.

Food of the Times

Along with the growing interest in physical fitness came a new concern for healthy eating. In the 1950s "meat and potatoes" were the standard dinner in the United States. By the 1970s and 1980s Americans were eating more turkey, chicken and fish and less beef. They were also eating more fruits and vegetables.

VIDEODISC
Communism and the Cold War

Side 2, Chapter 21
Title: *Changing Images*
Subject: Changes in American perceptions of the Soviet Union

Critical Thinking

Verifying Opinions Present this view of Ronald Reagan from his former chief of staff, Donald T. Regan:

"Like [Franklin D.] Roosevelt, Reagan changed the political landscape of the United States—and the way in which Americans saw themselves and their country—in a fundamental and probably permanent way."

Ask students to verify this opinion with facts from the text. Then have them state whether or not they agree with this assessment of Reagan and give reasons for their answers. **L3**

CHAPTER 35
SECTION 2

ASSESS
Check Understanding
Assign Section 2 Review as homework or an in-class activity.

Evaluate
Assign the Section 2 Quiz in the TCR or use the History of a Free Nation Testmaker to create a customized quiz.

Reteach
Have students complete Reteaching Activity 35-2.

Enrich
Have students create an editorial cartoon to illustrate a significant event during President Reagan's first term in office. Suggest that students display their cartoons on the bulletin board.

CLOSE
Point out that President Reagan reduced federal aid on many housing, education, and health programs. Ask students to discuss how this policy affected life in the United States.

Reagan insisted on pursuing it, and Gorbachev opposed it. When they met again a year later at Washington, D.C., however, they signed a treaty calling for the removal of all intermediate-range nuclear weapons from Europe. This was the first agreement that eliminated an entire class of nuclear weapons. Unbelievably, the cold war was slowly coming to an end.

Along with agreeing to limit nuclear weapons, Gorbachev took other surprising steps that affected international relations. Admitting that the Soviet Union's intervention in Afghanistan had been "morally wrong," he withdrew Soviet troops. He also released political prisoners and allowed freer emigration of Soviet Jews.

■ A Hands-Off Presidency

Although Reagan was a strong leader when it came to establishing public policy, he adopted a "hands-off" attitude toward the day-to-day operations of the presidency. This attitude led to scandals that would tarnish Reagan's final years in office, though he remained popular.

A Master of Delegation

Reagan gave far greater responsibilities to his staff than any other recent President had. The President's detachment allowed his subordinates to function independently. Some acted for financial gain. Others made policy on their own.

The Iran-Contra Scandal

The worst fiasco to hit the Reagan administration was the Iran-contra scandal of 1986. Several of the President's national security aides, including John Poindexter, Robert McFarland, and Lieutenant Colonel Oliver North, had schemed to sell weapons to the Iranians to win the release of American hostages in the Middle East. Then they had diverted the profits from these arms sales to the contras, Nicaraguan guerrillas who were fighting to topple the Sandanista government ruling the nation. This was a violation of a congressional ban on such financing.

Critics charged that an undercover foreign policy was being carried out against the express will of Congress. Defenders maintained that the executive branch was forced to take these measures because of congressional interference with the President's authority to conduct foreign policy. A special commission was set up to study the Iran-contra case. Although the commission cleared the President of direct blame, it found fault with Reagan for allowing aides to make policy decisions without his knowledge.

The Iran-contra scandal helped the Democrats win back a Senate majority in 1986. The election produced a divided government—with the presidency held by the Republican party and control of Congress held by the Democrats. Democratic majorities in Congress acted as a brake on the Reagan administration.

Section 2 ★ Review

Checking for Understanding

1. **Identify** Reaganomics, Walter Mondale, Geraldine Ferraro, Sandra Day O'Connor, Gramm-Rudman Act, Strategic Defense Initiative (SDI), Mikhail Gorbachev, Lieutenant Colonel Oliver North, contras.

2. **Define** supply-side economics, federal deficit, glasnost, perestroika, privatized.

3. **List** three measures Reagan took to restore the economy.

4. **Describe** three controversial weapons proposals of the Reagan administration.

Critical Thinking

5. **Evaluating Policies** Evaluate whether technology such as the SDI will help prevent nuclear war.

UNIT 10 Redefining America: 1954–Present

Answers to SECTION 2 REVIEW

1. Reaganomics, 983; Walter Mondale, 985; Geraldine Ferraro, 985; Sandra Day O'Connor, 985; Gramm-Rudman Act, 986; Strategic Defense Initiative (SDI), 985; Mikhail Gorbachev, 986; Lieutenant Colonel Oliver North, 988; contras, 988
2. All vocabulary words are defined in the Glossary.
3. cut income taxes, cut corporate taxes, reduced federal spending
4. SDI, stealth bomber, placing new nuclear missiles in Europe
5. Answers will vary. Supporters will argue that SDI would prevent nuclear attacks due to United States invulnerability and ability to retaliate. Opponents will argue that the system was not feasible and would escalate the arms race into space.

Social Studies Skills

Map and Graph Skills

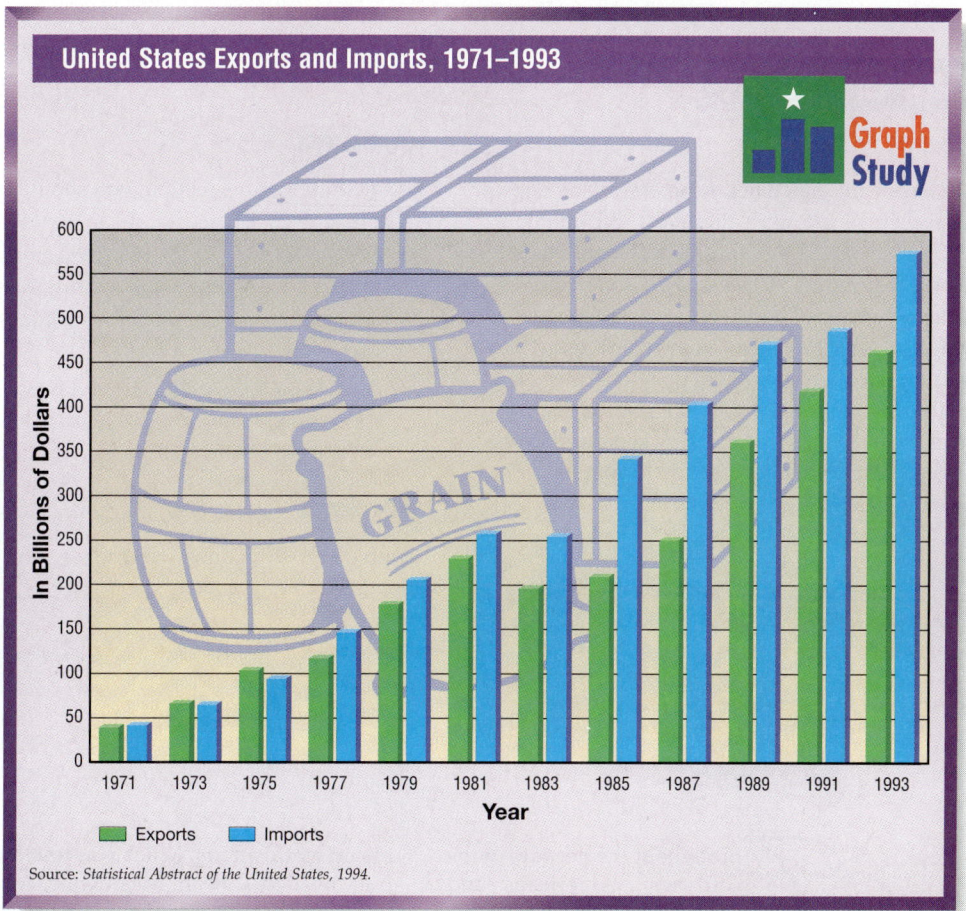

United States Exports and Imports, 1971–1993
Source: Statistical Abstract of the United States, 1994.

Reading a Bar Graph

Exports are the merchandise and materials made or mined in one country and sold or traded to another. Imports are the goods and materials a country buys or trades for from other countries. A surplus balance of trade means that a country exports more than it imports: that is, a nation sells more goods than it purchases from other countries. A deficit balance of trade indicates a greater volume of imports than exports.

Practicing the Skill

Refer to the bar graph to answer these questions.
1. What is the graph's unit of measurement?
2. What year had the largest deficit balance of trade?
3. Analyze the growth trends of both exports and imports from 1971 to 1993.

LESSON PLAN
Mastering Social Studies Skills

Teaching Map and Graph Skills

Have students refer to the graph on page 989. Ask them what the graph shows. Tell them that for much of the 1990s, the United States has had a surplus in its balance of trade. An ever increasing percentage of the economy has been exposed to foreign competition— from 7 percent in the 1960s to more than 70 percent in the 1980s.

Did You Know?

The main factors in the dramatic growth of the trade deficit in the 1980s were the rising cost of imported oil and the dollar's rising value against foreign currencies. Imports, such as cars and electronics, as a result were less expensive.

Answers to SOCIAL STUDIES SKILLS

1. billions of dollars
2. 1987
3. In general, the dollar amount of both exports and imports grew during the time period.

LESSON PLAN
SECTION 3, 990–997

FOCUS

Bellringer
Prior to taking roll at the beginning of the class period, display Focus Activity 117 on the overhead projector and assign the accompanying Focus Activity Sheet.

Objectives
Point out the objectives on this page to students in previewing the section content.

Motivating Activity
Write the phrase *New World Order* on the chalkboard and ask students to express in writing what it means to them. (the new system of international relations in the post–cold war world)

Tell students that in this section they will learn that changes at home and abroad during the late 1980s led our country's leaders to hope that a new, harmonious system of relations among the world's nations could be built. They will also see that as the 1990s dawned, this hope had to be put on hold.

NATIONAL GEOGRAPHIC SOCIETY

The following material is available from Glencoe and may be used to enrich Chapter 35.

CD-Rom
- *The Presidents: A Picture History of Our Nation*

SECTION 3

A New Presidency

Setting the Scene

Section Focus

Despite his difficulties, Reagan was still popular when he left office. Promising to continue Reagan's policies, Vice President George Bush won a resounding victory in 1988. In foreign affairs, Bush acted decisively to meet the challenges of what he called "a new world order" and tried to forge a different path for America in the post-cold war world. Domestically, however, many felt his leadership lacked direction, and problems with the economy continued to plague society.

Objectives

After studying this section, you should be able to
★ explain how the spread of democracy led to the formation of a new world order.
★ describe America's role in the post-cold war world.
★ discuss the reasons for discord between the legislative and executive branches of government under Bush.

Key Terms

coup d'état, drawdown, user taxes, junk bonds, underemployed

◀ ROAD SIGN IN KUWAIT

Throughout the decades of the cold war, Americans and Soviets had lived under the threat of nuclear war as each side built mighty arsenals and viewed almost all disputes around the world in terms of the East-West struggle. Then, with almost surprising suddenness, democratic movements erupted throughout the Soviet Union's Eastern European satellites. Popular demands for political, social, and economic reform toppled one communist government after another. Eventually, even the Soviet Union itself split into independent republics.

Without a Soviet adversary, the United States was the only superpower left. It faced the critical challenge of establishing a new role in world affairs, which was tested when Iraq invaded Kuwait. Meanwhile, America also faced challenges in the domestic arena. Troubled by severe economic problems, a divided government tried to work toward a solution.

■ Election of 1988

In the election of 1988, there was tough competition for both the Republican and Democratic presidential nominations. In the end, the Republicans selected Vice President George Bush. The final Democratic contenders were the Reverend Jesse Jackson and Massachusetts Governor Michael

UNIT 10 Redefining America: 1954–Present

Classroom Resources for SECTION 3

Teacher's Classroom Resources
- Reproducible Lesson Plan
- Reteaching Activity 35-3
- Chapter 35 Performance Assessment Activity
- Chapter 35 Enrichment Activity
- Spanish Summaries and Glossary
- Section Quiz

Multimedia
- Section Focus Transparency 117
- Testmaker
- Student Self-Test Software
- The Presidents: A Picture History of Our Nation
- Communism and the Cold War
- Lessons of War

Dukakis. Jackson, who appealed to a "rainbow coalition" of minorities and reformers, picked up support along the way and ran a much stronger race than expected. Dukakis, however, won the nomination.

Early in the race, Dukakis led Bush in the public polls. Then Bush's campaign team unleashed a string of negative television advertisements that portrayed the liberal Dukakis as unpatriotic and soft on criminals. Dukakis, however, failed to respond strongly to these charges. As a result, Dukakis lost his lead to Bush. Slick television commercials seemed to replace debating real issues.

Saying, "Read my lips," the Vice President pledged not to raise taxes. Bush also promised the nation that if elected he would follow Reagan's economic policies. On Election Day he won a resounding victory, taking 40 of the 50 states, with 49 million popular votes and 426 electoral votes. Dukakis had 42 million popular votes and 112 electoral votes.

A Tidal Wave of Change

George Bush came to the presidency with a great deal of experience in foreign policy. In addition to being Vice President, he had been Ambassador to the United Nations, Ambassador to China, and Director of the CIA. This training served Bush well, for he was immediately confronted with a tidal wave of change around the world.

Change in Eastern Europe

Gorbachev's new policies in the Soviet Union triggered demands for change in Eastern Europe. In 1989 the people of the satellite nations of Poland, Hungary, Czechoslovakia, Bulgaria, Romania, and East Germany overthrew their communist rulers and forced democratic elections. When the East German government fell, crowds tore down the Berlin Wall that had divided Germany and symbolized the "iron curtain" that separated Eastern Europe and Western Europe.

▲ **THE BARRIER FALLS** In November 1989 the Berlin Wall, which had separated the two Germanys since 1961, was opened. On the first weekend after the wall was opened, 3 million visitors crossed from East Berlin to visit West Berlin. *What had the Berlin Wall symbolized?*

Cultural Diversity

In 1988, as in 1976, the black vote was vital to the success of the Democratic party. It did not help the Democrats win the election, although African Americans voted for Democrats over Republicans by a 10-to-1 ratio. Even had 10 percent more blacks than whites voted, the number still would not have pushed Michael Dukakis past George Bush's winning margin of 7 million votes. The black vote was most effective in 1988 in helping Jesse Jackson come closer to winning the presidential nomination than any African American before him.

CHAPTER 35
SECTION 3

TEACH
Guided Practice

Language Arts Have students summarize the major ideas in Section 3 by writing a sentence that expresses the main idea of each subhead. Ask them to share their summaries with the class. **L1**

Visualizing History In November 1989, the Berlin Wall was torn down. In October 1991, East and West Germany were reunified into a single, democratic country.
Answer to Caption: the separation of Eastern and Western Europe

ABC NEWS INTERACTIVE

VIDEODISC
Communism and the Cold War

Side 1, Chapter 22
Title: *Collapse of European Communism*
Subject: Events leading to rapid political change

Side 1, Chapter 23
Title: *Fall of the Wall*
Subject: Fall of the Berlin Wall

Side 1, Chapter 21
Title: *A New Soviet Union: Communist Rule Ends*
Subject: The end of the Soviet Union

CHAPTER 35 SECTION 3

Independent Practice

Making a Map Provide the outline map of the world found in the TCR, and ask students to label the nations of Europe and the Commonwealth of Independent States. **L1, LEP**

Teaching American Portraits

Jesse Jackson suffered prejudice early in life. A star quarterback in high school, he attended the University of Illinois on a football scholarship. However, he was told that African Americans on the team played lineman, not quarterback. After a year he transferred to the all-black North Carolina Agricultural and Technical State College, where he became a star athlete and the student body president. He also gained a reputation as a talented organizer for the civil rights movement. Ask students what qualities Jackson showed as a young man. (determination, ambition, a strong value system)

AMERICAN PORTRAITS

Jesse Jackson
1941–

Born in a segregated city—Greenville, North Carolina—Jesse Jackson became involved in civil rights activities while a college student. He went on to join Dr. Martin Luther King, Jr.'s, protest marches in Selma, Alabama. Later, Jackson was selected to head Operation Breadbasket, a program designed to promote the hiring of more African Americans by major businesses. After Dr. King was killed, Jesse Jackson emerged as the best-known African American leader in America.

In 1971 Jackson launched his own organization: People United to Save Humanity (PUSH). Supported by a "rainbow coalition" he unsuccessfully sought the 1984 Democratic presidential nomination. When he ran again in 1988, he finished a strong second in the primaries, proving that an African American could be a serious presidential contender.

The end of the cold war allowed some countries to renew and rethink relationships. In October 1990, East Germany and West Germany reunited. As Western European nations took steps toward political and economic union, Eastern Europe sought to forge new ties with them—especially economic ones. In July 1991, the Warsaw Pact between Eastern Europe and the Soviet Union was terminated. This left the future of NATO, which was also a military alliance, in doubt.

The Collapse of the Soviet Union

The loss of Eastern Europe was only the beginning. Despite Gorbachev's efforts to save his country, the Soviet Union itself collapsed. Glasnost and perestroika had unleashed two forces that would bring it down. One was the people's demand for democracy. The other was the desire of different ethnic groups for self-rule; the Soviet Union had been organized without regard for ethnic boundaries. As rumblings for independence began, Gorbachev even dispatched troops to preserve the Soviet Union.

The catalyst came in August 1991 when a group of hard-line Communists attempted a **coup d'état,** or a sudden revolt, and proclaimed an old-style communist government. The plotters arrested Gorbachev and ordered troops to Moscow. They failed, however, to take into account Boris Yeltsin, the recently elected president of the Russian Republic. Appearing before crowds gathered in front of the Russian parliament building, Yeltsin condemned the coup and called for the people's help. To protect him, tens of thousands of Moscow's citizens stood guard unarmed, ready to face down an expected attack. The soldiers refused to carry out orders, and the coup collapsed. Gorbachev was back in office, but Yeltsin now held the real power.

Both men knew that the Communist party had been behind the coup. Soon, Gorbachev stepped down as general secretary and abolished the party. Without communism holding the Soviet state together, the country itself shattered. Republic after republic declared its independence.

On December 25, 1991, Gorbachev formally resigned as Soviet president, saying, "We are living in a new world." His resignation marked the end of what was left of the Soviet Union. By this time, 11 of the 15 former republics had organized a loose union called the Commonwealth of Independent States (CIS).

992 UNIT 10 Redefining America: 1954–Present

Critical Thinking

Identifying Alternatives Since the first communist government had been established in Russia in 1917, the economy of the former Soviet Union had been strictly controlled. Gorbachev's main objective under *perestroika* was to reform the economic system, not scrap it. In the Russian Republic, Yeltsin moved more boldly. He set up a 500-day plan to legalize private property, abolish government subsidies, lift price controls, and institutionalize private banks and a stock market. Ask students to analyze whether they think such a massive undertaking should proceed at a moderate pace or quickly. **L3**

Troubles in the New States

All the former Soviet and communist bloc states faced serious economic troubles. In trying to set up capitalist economies, the new governments began lifting state controls on economies already in decline. So production fell, prices rose, and unemployment spread. People suffered from shortages of fuel, food, medicine, and housing.

Another problem was ethnic rivalry. Without tight communist control there was a rise of nationalism, and old hatreds surfaced. These hatreds led to the outbreak of bloody civil wars in many states. The worst was in what was formerly Yugoslavia.

Although western nations, including the United States, quickly recognized the new countries, they were uncertain what kind of aid to send. Some people wanted to send cash to help support the new democracies. Others feared even a non-communist Russia might someday threaten world security and favored increasing trade and sending advisers, along with food and medicine. For the most part the United States government followed the latter course.

Part of the reason the United States was concerned about Russia was that it had most of the former Soviet Union's nuclear weapons. In 1992, Bush and Yeltsin met at Camp David and agreed to drastic reductions. Afterward, the President declared that the meeting marked "a new relationship based on trust, based on a commitment to economic and political freedom."

■ The Persian Gulf War

Meanwhile, the Persian Gulf War gave President Bush an opportunity to further define America's role in the post-cold war world. On August 2, 1990, Iraq's president, Saddam Hussein, sent invasion forces into Kuwait, its oil-rich neighbor. To punish this aggression, Bush froze $20 billion of Iraqi money in American banks and banned imports of Iraqi oil. The United Nations demanded that Saddam Hussein withdraw his forces and called for countries throughout the world to halt all trade with Iraq. But Iraqi troops remained in Kuwait.

Operation Desert Shield

Bush, with assistance from 25 nations around the world, assembled a huge military coalition he called "Operation Desert Shield." The United Nations then authorized military action to restore Kuwait's independence. The coalition waited for 6 months, however, hoping that diplomacy and the threat of force would prevent a war.

Operation Desert Storm

Finally, Bush initiated Operation Desert Storm. He ordered massive air strikes against Iraq on January 16, 1991, rejecting calls for further delay:

▲ **THE PERSIAN GULF WAR** In January 1991 the United States launched a massive air and missile assault on Iraq after Iraq refused to withdraw from Kuwait. **Why had Iraq invaded Kuwait?**

Visualizing History War with Iran left Iraq's economy near collapse. Saddam Hussein needed a strategy for boosting oil revenues and for redirecting the blame for Iraq's worsening economy. He claimed that Kuwait was a historic part of Iraq and that Kuwait had unfairly drilled Iraqi oil. **Answer to Caption:** to gain control of its oil

CHAPTER 35
SECTION 3

Visualizing History By mid-January 1991, the United States had deployed about 540,000 troops. The Desert Storm Coalition also included 118,000 Saudi troops, 43,000 British troops, 40,000 Egyptian troops, 20,000 Syrian troops, and 16,000 French troops. **Answer to Caption:** General Schwarzkopf

Did You Know?

Of the 2 million individuals serving in the United States armed forces in 1990, about 11 percent were women. Women made up 7 percent of U.S. sailors, 35 percent of administrators, and 10 percent of military officers. Although women were barred from combat units, they flew helicopters carrying troops and supplies, worked as mechanics on tanks and trucks, and also worked as paratroopers and ship navigators.

▲ **COMING HOME** American military personnel return after taking part in Operation Desert Storm. Coalition forces took part in the military action after diplomatic efforts failed. *Who was the military leader of the operation?*

> *The world could wait no longer. . . . While the world waited, Saddam Hussein met every overture of peace with open contempt. While the world prayed for peace, Saddam Hussein prepared for war.*

After a month of bombing, General Norman Schwarzkopf led a lightning-swift ground assault. Just 100 hours later, Allied forces had crushed the Iraqi army and freed the Kuwaiti people. "Kuwait is liberated," Bush announced. "America and the world have kept their word."

■ Rethinking America's Military Role

The Persian Gulf War caused people in the United States to begin rethinking America's military role in the world. Some leaders felt the United States should scale down its military. They pointed out that the source of a country's power in the new world order promised to be its economy rather than its military. Examples of just such a change were evident by the emergence of Germany and Japan. So, as the federal deficits skyrocketed, Bush called for cuts in defense spending, and Congress made even greater reductions. The Pentagon planned a **drawdown** that would bring troops home from overseas bases in Europe and Asia.

Other experts, however, warned that the United States should maintain a strong military—and that the cost would be worth it. They pointed out that Cuba, North Korea, Vietnam, and the People's Republic of China remained communist nations. Although China had shown some signs of change by instituting various free-market programs, its Communist party leaders had massacred prodemocracy demonstrators at Beijing's Tiananmen Square in 1989.

■ Divided Government

Whereas President Bush acted decisively in foreign affairs, he was accused of wavering leadership at home. Part of the problem was that the government was divided again, with the presidency held by one

UNIT 10 Redefining America: 1954–Present

Sidelights: What's in a Name?

Iraqi leader Saddam Hussein liked to be called by his first name. For, when pronounced correctly, with the emphasis on the second syllable, *Saddam* means "leader," "learned one," or "he who confronts"—exactly how he wanted to be viewed. During the Persian Gulf Crisis, President Bush insisted on pronouncing the name with the emphasis on the first syllable. Pronounced this way, Saddam means "a boy who fixes or cleans shoes"—a grave insult in many Arab countries. Whether or not this was a conscious act by Bush, it did sum up the way he felt about his adversary.

party and Congress controlled by the other. During the Bush administration, this hindered the process of government.

Bush and Congress in Gridlock

Congress ignored or drastically changed many of the President's proposals. The President, in turn, vetoed many bills, knowing that the Democrats generally lacked the two-thirds vote needed to override his vetoes. The executive and legislative branches of the government quickly became gridlocked over such issues as reforming campaign financing, improving public education, recharging the economy, reducing the federal deficit, and balancing the budget.

Taxation Issues

When the federal deficit rose to a record level of $300 billion, Bush realized he would have to increase revenues. To do so, however, he was forced to break his campaign pledge of "no new taxes." In 1992, after weeks of negotiations with Democratic congressional leaders, Bush agreed to raise some taxes. Among these were gasoline, tobacco, and other **user taxes,** or taxes on products used by consumers. The President also agreed to make deep cuts in medicare and military spending. Although this plan was defeated by conservative Republicans, the President and congressional leaders finally hammered out a compromise bill.

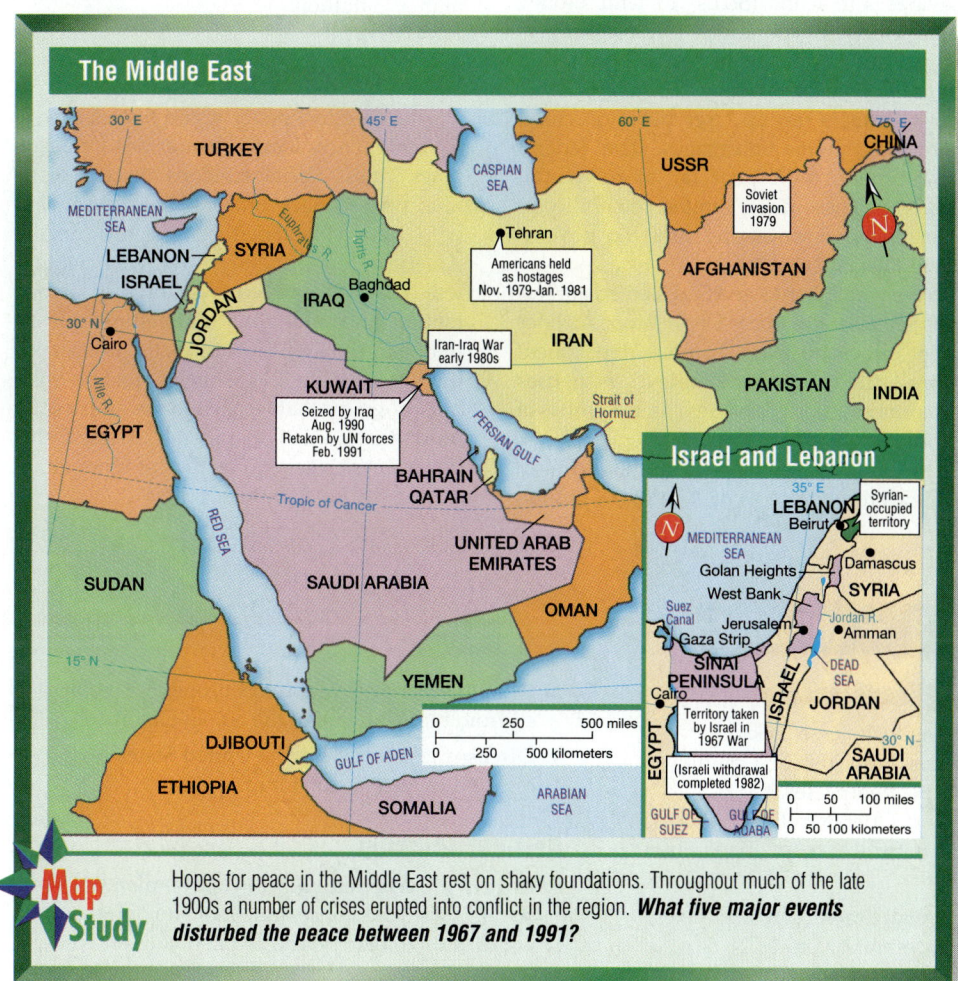

Map Study Hopes for peace in the Middle East rest on shaky foundations. Throughout much of the late 1900s a number of crises erupted into conflict in the region. **What five major events disturbed the peace between 1967 and 1991?**

CHAPTER 35 Search for Solutions 1976–1992   995

Sidelights: Computers

Computer technology has been adapted for many purposes, including guidance systems for weapons. The Tomahawk cruise missile, for example, uses a number of computerized guidance systems. During flight, a scanner matches the landscape to coordinates programmed before the launch and, as the missile approaches the target, a camera matches a picture of the target to data in the memory. Traveling at 550 miles an hour, the missile can hit a target as small as a door from a distance of 1,500 miles.

CHAPTER 35
SECTION 3

Linking Across Time

Some political observers have suggested that the way George Bush viewed the Persian Gulf crisis was deeply influenced by an incident from his high-school graduation ceremony in 1940. In the commencement speech, former Secretary of State Henry Lewis Stimson said that, even though the world was at war and civilization was under attack, it was a time of great opportunity, because people had the chance to choose between good and evil.

Map Study Using Maps
Answer: 1967 war between Israel and Arab states; Americans taken hostage in Iran in 1979; Soviet invasion of Afghanistan in 1979; Iran-Iraq War, 1980–1988; Iraqi invasion of Kuwait in 1990.

Map Skills
Ask students why the United States considers the Persian Gulf an area of great strategic importance. (It is the waterway through which much of the world's supply of oil must travel.)

CHAPTER 35
SECTION 3

ASSESS

Check Understanding

Assign Section 3 Review as homework or an in-class activity.

Evaluate

Assign the Section 3 Quiz in the TCR or use the History of a Free Nation Testmaker to create a customized quiz.

Reteach

Have students complete Reteaching Activity 35-3

Enrich

Have students complete Chapter 35 Enrichment Activity in the TCR.

CLOSE

Discuss with students what they think are two of the greatest accomplishments and two of the most serious failures of the Bush administration.

Economic Woes in the Early 1990s

During the Bush administration, the economy grew more slowly than at any time since the end of World War II. Among other factors, sharply rising oil prices following Iraq's invasion of Kuwait threw America into a recession that persisted longer than expected.

Consumer and Corporate Debt and Unemployment

This was partly because of consumer and corporate debts incurred during the Reagan era. Deregulation had allowed banks and savings and loans (S&Ls) to lend money more freely. Corporations funded mergers with **junk bonds**, or high-risk bonds that offer high yields.

Consumers ran up large debts on credit cards and home mortgages. The federal government, too, spent far more than it received. These debts limited the ability of consumers, corporations, and the government to spend and invest.

As a result, banks and S&Ls failed at rates unseen since the Great Depression. Airlines went out of business. Famous department stores filed for bankruptcy. Industries announced plant closings and layoffs of workers.

By mid-1992, almost 10 million Americans were unemployed. Another 6 million workers were **underemployed.** This means that these people held part-time jobs while looking for full-time work.

The Problem of Homelessness in America

As unemployment rose, people migrated from one state to another in search of jobs, and some found themselves homeless. Homeless people included battered women, runaway children, alcoholics, drug abusers, deinstitutionalized mental patients, and people lacking family support. Homelessness reflected rising rents, lower wages for unskilled workers, and the urgent need for low-cost housing. Estimates of the number of homeless people in America ranged as high as 3 million.

The Los Angeles Riots

The recession, poverty, and homelessness hit particularly hard at minorities living in inner cities. Racial tensions ignited after four white police officers in Los Angeles who were videotaped beating an African American man, Rodney King, were acquitted. The city erupted into days of arson, looting, and rioting that claimed more lives than had the 1965 riots in Watts. Conservatives blamed the Los Angeles riots on welfare programs that weakened the family and individual initiative. Liberals blamed the government's general neglect of inner cities during the Reagan-Bush years.

Section 3 ★ Review

Checking for Understanding

1. **Identify** George Bush, Jesse Jackson, Michael Dukakis, Boris Yeltsin, Commonwealth of Independent States (CIS), Saddam Hussein, Operation Desert Storm, General Norman Schwarzkopf, Tiananmen Square.

2. **Define** coup d'état, drawdown, user taxes, junk bonds, underemployed.

3. **Describe** changes in Eastern Europe that resulted from breaking free of the Soviet Union.

4. **Discuss** the reason why the United States resorted to force against Iraq.

Critical Thinking

5. **Identifying Alternatives** In your opinion, should Presidents concentrate more on domestic issues or on foreign policy? Explain your answer.

UNIT 10 Redefining America: 1954–Present

Answers to SECTION 3 REVIEW

1. George Bush, 990; Jesse Jackson, 990; Michael Dukakis, 990–991; Boris Yeltsin, 992; Commonwealth of Independent States (CIS), 992; Saddam Hussein, 993; Operation Desert Storm, 993; General Norman Schwarzkopf, 994; Tiananmen Square, 995
2. All vocabulary words are defined in the Glossary.
3. Changes included: tearing down of the Berlin Wall; reuniting of East and West Germany; termination of Warsaw Pact; lifting of state controls on economies; rise in nationalism and ethnic rivalry
4. Iraq had refused President Bush's warnings, attempts at negotiation, economic pressure, and threat of warfare.
5. Answers will vary, but students should present logical arguments to defend their positions.

History and Science CONNECTIONS

As the Brain Grows Older

Life expectancy in the United States increased dramatically in the twentieth century. In the early 1900s, most people died before the age of 50. By the year 2000, the average life expectancy will be 80 years for women and 76 for men. Even more significant is the fact that by 2000, 13 percent of all Americans will be 65 years of age or older. By 2025, one-fourth the population will be over age 65.

The aging population has prompted scientists to study the changes that occur in the brain with age. What these studies show is that the brain loses little functioning during most of the adult years. After age 65, deterioration in memory, spatial skills, and reasoning begins. What is most noticeable in the over-65 population, however, is the greater variation in brain function between individuals. That is, some people show only slight mental decline, while others show very noticeable losses. Alzheimer's disease, a condition that limits brain functioning, especially in memory, language, reasoning, and spatial abilities, afflicts millions of older adults in this country.

Research in the 1990s has centered on ways that older individuals can maintain or regain their intellectual strength. Just as diet and exercise have been shown to have a direct impact on physical fitness, researchers hope to identify educational, nutritional, and medical breakthroughs that can build mental fitness.

▲ SENIOR CITIZENS HIKING

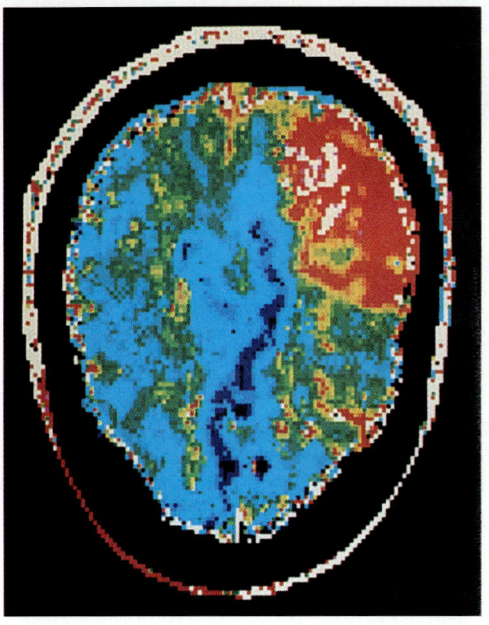

▲ BRAIN SCAN

Making the Science Connection

1. How does brain functioning change with age?
2. Describe two educational or nutritional factors that could be studied in relation to brain function.

Linking Past and Present

3. Why are declines in brain function, and diseases such as Alzheimer's, of particular significance at this time? Identify possible consequences if methods to slow intellectual decline are not identified.

CHAPTER 35 CONNECTIONS

Teaching Making Connections

In the United States alone, 4 million people are afflicted with Alzheimer's disease. Identified by a German doctor named Alois Alzheimer in 1906, the disease has baffled experts, and its causes have been subject to much conjecture. Some think that aluminum brings on symptoms. Others believe that head injuries could lead to the disease. Other possible causes include a chemical imbalance in the brain, the presence of a virus at birth, and a gene defect.

Did You Know?

Former President Reagan was diagnosed with Alzheimer's disease in 1994.

Answers to CONNECTIONS

1. The brain loses few of its functions during most of the adult years. After age 65, deterioration in memory, spatial skills, and reasoning begins.
2. Educational factors could include the amount of schooling an individual completes or the kinds of intellectual stimulation as one ages. Nutritional factors could include kinds of foods eaten or vitamin supplements taken.
3. People are living longer, and if methods to slow intellectual decline are not identified, there will be many older people incapable of caring for themselves.

REVIEW CHAPTER 35

Answers

Reviewing Facts
1. Americans were interested in a political "outsider" after the scandal. Carter's inexperience seemed preferable to a professional politician.
2. Carter emphasized honesty, nonintervention, and selective support based on human rights.
3. Reagan was optimistic, charismatic, and an extremely effective communicator who stressed unifying themes.
4. Gorbachev introduced *glasnost* and *perestroika;* took steps to end the cold war, such as announcing that the Soviet Union would reduce its nuclear weapons.
5. economic crises, relaxation of price controls led to rising prices, low productivity
6. The United States took charge of restoring Kuwait's independence and initiated the assault against Iraq.
7. to increase revenues and reduce the federal deficit

Understanding Concepts
1. Answers will vary. Carter's lack of unifying themes made him seem indecisive and incomprehensible to many Americans. Conversely, Reagan was a master at articulating broad themes that unified Americans.
2. Answers will vary but should include the idea that the government takes a much more active role in the economy today.

Critical Thinking
1. Answers will vary.

CHAPTER 35 ★ REVIEW

Using Vocabulary

On a separate sheet of paper, write three headings: *Carter, Reagan, Bush*. Classify each of the following terms under the Presidents to which they are related. Some terms belong in more than one category.

- double-digit inflation
- supply-side economics
- glasnost
- coup d'état
- user taxes
- pork-barrel legislation
- federal deficit
- perestroika
- drawdown
- junk bond
- underemployed

Reviewing Facts

1. **Explain** how Carter's election was partly a result of Watergate.
2. **Summarize** Carter's foreign policy philosophy.
3. **Describe** why Ronald Reagan appealed to the American people.
4. **Discuss** how Mikhail Gorbachev tried to save the Communist party and the Soviet Union.
5. **Describe** the problems faced by the former Soviet and communist bloc states.
6. **Explain** how the problems between Kuwait and Iraq helped define America's new role in world affairs.
7. **Discuss** the reason for Bush's decision to break his campaign promise and raise taxes.

Understanding Concepts

Leadership
1. Analyze how the image of the President may have affected popular support during the Carter and Reagan administrations.

Reform and Change
2. How does the role of the United States government in the economy during the 1980s and 1990s compare to its role during the early 1900s?

Critical Thinking

1. **Assessing Programs** The United States has had difficulty implementing an energy policy. Evaluate Carter's energy program. Explain why it was only partially successful.
2. **Analyzing Media** Television has exposed Americans to an unprecedented amount of news and information.
   a. In what ways does television benefit society?
   b. Do you think the overall effect of television is a positive one or a negative one? Explain.

Writing About History

Classification
Write an essay on the changing relations between the United States and the Soviet Union during the Carter, Reagan, and Bush administrations. Before you begin writing, divide your information into two classifications: (1) events, policies, and actions that eased tensions between the United States and the Soviet Union, and (2) events, policies, and actions that kept the two nations apart.

Cooperative Learning

Organize into four groups to research and analyze the two ways to reduce the federal deficit. Two groups will research and present arguments for and

---

Unfortunately, few Americans seem willing to pay the price for a strong energy policy. Carter found this out when he met strong opposition to his program, which called for sacrifices.

2. a. Provides coverage of important issues around the world; increases awareness and knowledge about other cultures.
b. Answers will vary, but students should support their opinions.

Practicing the Skill
1. It was the period immediately following the war.
2. Federal outlays have increased steadily just as the gross national debt has risen.
3. U.S. dependence on exporting oil; global competition.
4. difficult to see the ratio of outlays to Gross National Debt.
5. As federal outlays rise, the gross national debt rises.

CHAPTER 35 ★ REVIEW

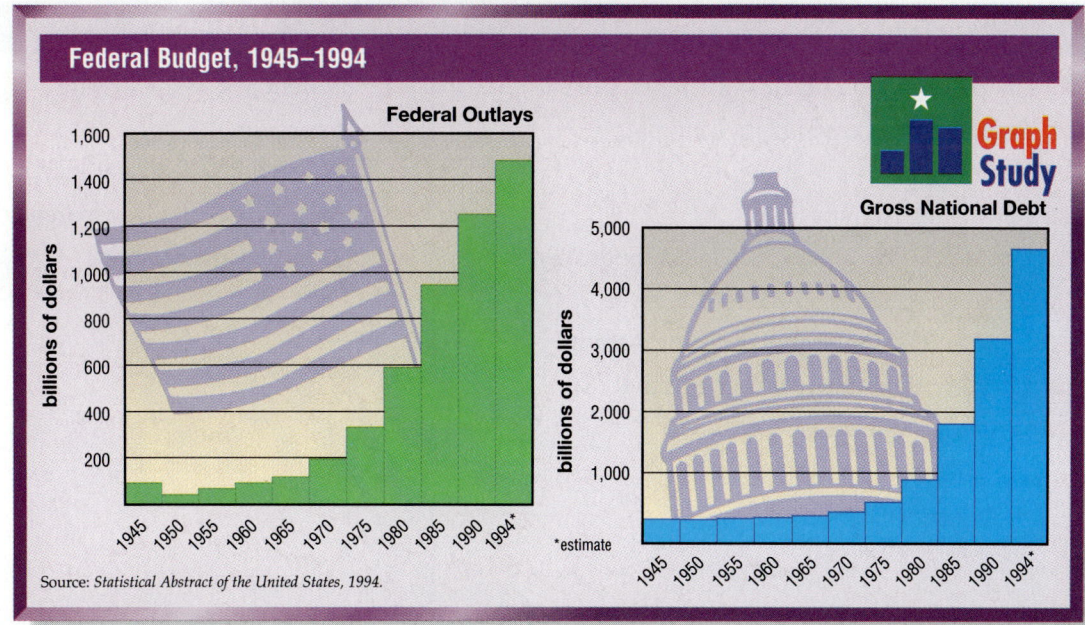

Federal Budget, 1945–1994

Source: *Statistical Abstract of the United States, 1994.*

against raising taxes. The other two groups will research and present arguments for and against reduced government spending. You will have one class period to prepare. Select a representative from your group to report your arguments to the class. The members of the class should evaluate the arguments and decide which method would be best.

Social Studies Skills

Interpreting Economic Data

The graphs on this page show economic information for the United States from 1945 to 1994. The first graph shows total federal expenditures, or outlays. The second graph shows total gross national debt.

Practicing the Skill

Using the two graphs and your understanding of the chapter, answer the following questions.

1. Why do you suppose both outlays and federal gross debt declined between 1945 and 1950?
2. Describe the trend shown in each graph.
3. What do you think may have contributed to the large increase beginning in 1975?
4. How might the difference in the *y*-axis scales cause problems in interpreting the data in the two graphs?
5. How are the two graphs related?

Using Your Journal
After reviewing the chapter and your journal notes, discuss why you believe that those who abandoned their traditional party to vote conservative in 1980 did or did not realize their hopes.

REVIEW CHAPTER 35

? Chapter Bonus Test Question

Explain the effect of one of the following events.
1. Americans taken hostage in Iran. (possible answer: key issue in Carter's reelection campaign)
2. A special commission investigates the Iran-Contra scandal. (possible answers: Democrats win back a Senate majority in 1986; put a brake on Reagan's programs)
3. The Soviet Union collapses. (possible answers: uncertain about how to aid the new countries of the CIS; concern about nuclear weapons in the hands of newly independent states)

Using Your Journal
Answers may vary. Students may base their views on whether conservative philosophies of low taxes and reduced federal spending have been realized.

CHAPTER 35 Search for Solutions 1976–1992

PLANNING GUIDE   Chapter 36   Toward a New Century

Daily Lesson Objectives	Teacher Classroom Resources	Multimedia
SECTION 1 **Reinventing Government** **1 Day** pp. 1002–1007 1. Explain why many Americans demanded a change in government in 1992. 2. Explain how gridlock between Congress and the President affected the process of government. 3. Discuss why criticism of the Clinton administration increased and led to a Republican sweep of the congressional elections of 1994.	Chapter 36 Study Guide Reproducible Lesson Plan Section Quiz Reteaching Activity 36-1 Chapter 36 Primary and Secondary Source Readings Reinforcing Social Studies Skills 51, 55 Chapter 36 Cooperative Learning Activity Chapter 36 Concept Mapping Activity Writer's Guidebook Lessons 1–5	Student Self-Test Software Testmaker Section Focus Transparency 119 Chapter 36 Skills Transparency Focus on Government
SECTION 2 **America in a Changing World** **1 Day** pp. 1008–1013 1. Describe the development of Clinton's foreign policy in the new world order. 2. Explain what key role the United States played in bringing about major breakthroughs between old enemies.	Reproducible Lesson Plan Reteaching Activity 36-2 Section Quiz American Portrait 71 Chapter 36 Primary and Secondary Source Readings Reinforcing Social Studies Skills 28, 51 Writer's Guidebook Lessons 1–5	Student Self-Test Software Testmaker Section Focus Transparency 120
SECTION 3 **Challenges and Opportunities** **1 Day** pp. 1015–1020 1. Identify the challenges facing the United States in the 1990s. 2. Describe some of the proposed solutions to these challenges.	Reproducible Lesson Plan Reteaching Activity 36-3 Section Quiz Chapter 36 Enrichment Activity American Portrait 72 Spanish Summaries & Glossary Writer's Guidebook Lessons 1–5	Student Self-Test Software Testmaker Section Focus Transparency 121 Unit 10 Digest Transparency Vocabulary Puzzlemaker Audiocassette, Chapter 36 Focus on Government A Geographic Perspective on American History
CHAPTER REVIEW AND EVALUATION **1 Day**	Chapter 36 Test Chapter 36 Performance Assessment Activity	Student Self-Test Software Testmaker

OUT OF TIME? If time does not permit teaching the entire chapter, use the Chapter 36 Summary on pages 1028–1029 and the Chapter 36 audiocassette (English and Spanish) to point out the main ideas of the chapter.

PLANNING GUIDE

Cultural Diversity Activity

Cooperative Learning Write the following quotation from *The Uprooted* by historian Oscar Handlin:

"Once I thought to write a history of immigrants in America. Then I discovered that the immigrants were America."

Have students prepare a collage, mural, or bulletin-board display that illustrates Handlin's statement.

Performance Assessment Activity

Looking Ahead Divide the class into small groups. Have each prepare a list of the 10 most critical issues Americans face as they approach the year 2000. Ask groups to conduct a survey to determine if other Americans share their views. Based on the results of their survey, invite each group to present its 5 most critical issues to the class. Then have students compare and contrast the various lists. Which issues seem to be most important to teenagers? To adults in the community?

POSSIBLE RUBRIC FEATURES: Research skills, content information, organization, written and oral communication skills, critical thinking skills, creativity

Chapter Resources

Readings for the Student

Hewett, Ed. A., and Victor H. Winston, eds. *Milestones in Glasnost and Perestroyka: Politics and People.* Brookings, 1991.

Hyde, Margaret O. *The Homeless: Profiling the Problem.* Enslow Publishers, 1989.

Parillo, Vincent N., ed. *Rethinking Today's Minorities.* Greenwood Press, 1991.

Readings for the Teacher

Dinnerstein, Leonard, et al. *Natives and Strangers: Blacks, Indians, and Immigrants in America.* Oxford University Press, 1990.

Takaki, Ronald. *A Different Mirror: A History of Multicultural America.* Little, Brown, 1993.

Multimedia Resources

COPE: A Simulation of Adapting to Change and Anticipating the Future. Interact. (Teaching time frame: 3 weeks)

Energy: The Key to Our Future. United Learning. (VHS, 60 minutes)

Spaceship Earth: Our Global Environment. WORLDLINK. (VHS, 25 minutes)

Key to Ability Levels

Teaching strategies have been coded for varying learning styles and abilities.

L1 Basic activities for all students

L2 Average activities for average to above-average students

L3 Challenging activities for above-average students

LEP Limited English Proficiency activities

Glencoe Links to the Humanities

Link to Art
- U.S. History and Art Transparency 32

Link to Literature
- Macmillan Literature: American Literature Text—Ann Dillard, James Baldwin, Saul Bellow

Link to Music
- American Music: Cultural Traditions

CHAPTER 36

BEGINNING THE CHAPTER

Discuss with students issues that currently present challenges to Americans. (peace, the environment, human rights, role of government, poverty, economic opportunities, education, and so forth) Ask students to list issues they are concerned about and rank them in order of importance. Tell them to compare their lists with issues discussed in Chapter 36.

The last decade of the twentieth century marked the anniversary of Columbus's first voyage to the Americas. It was less a time of celebration than one of reflection on what the voyage meant to the American people. Many insisted that the nation recognize the effects of that event on the inhabitants of the Americas. Others wanted to commemorate the courage and daring of the voyagers. Still, it was a time for all Americans to reflect on the challenges of a changing society and growing global interdependence.

Recording Journal Notes

Suggest that students organize their notes under such headings as education, work opportunities, housing, health care, societal attitudes, and so forth.

CHAPTER 36

Toward a New Century
1992–Present

▶ HAITIAN REFUGEE BOAT

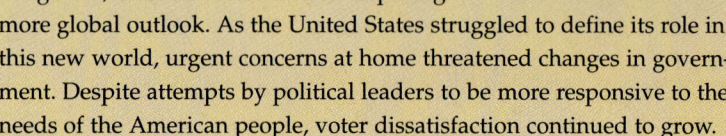

Setting the Scene

Focus

As 1992 dawned, the cold war had ended and a new world order was emerging. Instead of being sharply divided by the East-West conflict, nations were becoming more integrated, and their leaders were acquiring a more global outlook. As the United States struggled to define its role in this new world, urgent concerns at home threatened changes in government. Despite attempts by political leaders to be more responsive to the needs of the American people, voter dissatisfaction continued to grow.

Journal Notes

What do you think it would be like to be an immigrant from another country coming to the United States during the 1990s? Note details about it in your journal as you read the chapter.

Concepts to Understand

★ What changes occurred in government as a result of Clinton's election
★ How Americans were dealing with the challenges they faced

Read to Discover ...

★ how Clinton's policies—both domestic and foreign—affected Americans.
★ what challenges face the American government and people in the future.

CULTURAL
- Eric Clapton's "Unplugged" wins Grammy award
- Americorps helps student education
- Projections show Hispanics as largest minority by 2010

1992 | **1993**

POLITICAL
- Bill Clinton is elected President
- Yugoslav Federation breaks up
- Israel and PLO negotiate peace with American help
- Congress approves NAFTA

✚ EXTRA CREDIT PROJECT

Congress and the President Congress and presidents have often engaged in tugs of war over the powers of the executive and legislative branches, even though the Constitution spells out these powers. Suggest that interested students research examples of conflict between the two branches. Have them present their findings to the class and discuss how and why conflicts arise and how these conflicts reflect both the strengths and weaknesses of each branch.

History AND ART

Earth
by David Lawrence, 1994

New technology has opened new avenues for artists. Computer-manipulated art combines actual photography and computer art to create a new image.

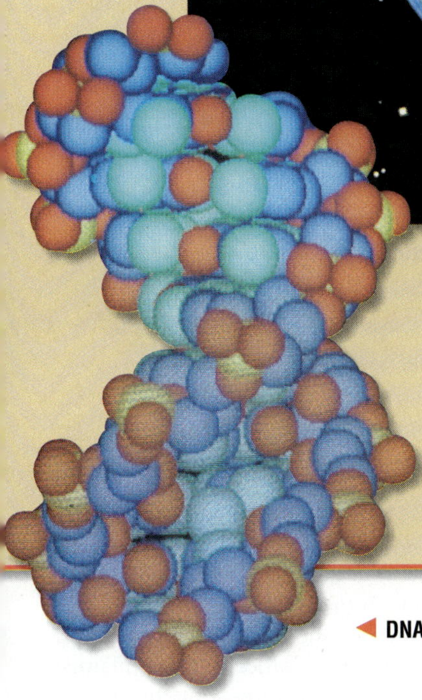

◀ **DNA,** COMPUTER MODEL

- Scientists estimate 1 million Americans have HIV

1994

- Israel and Jordan, assisted by United States, sign peace treaty
- Republicans sweep mid-term elections

- Internet revolutionizes communications
- Myrlie Evers-Williams leads NAACP

1995

- President Clinton authorizes $20 billion in loans and loan guarantees to Mexico

CHAPTER 36 Toward a New Century 1992–Present

CHAPTER 36 CONCEPTS

Concept Mapping Activity

Reproduce the following generalization and concept map on the chalkboard and ask students to copy it in their notebooks. Have them list each major event in the chapter under the appropriate concept.

> Americans face the future with confidence in their democratic institutions to meet the challenges of a changing society and the demands of global interdependence.

- Reform and change
- Challenges

History AND ART

Use the image to prompt discussion of space exploration. Ask students to consider both the benefits and the risks.

 VIDEODISC

- *GTV: A Geographic Perspective on American History*

Side 4, Chapter 14
Title: *You've Grown Accustomed to My Face*
Subject: Coming of age in the Information Age

See GTV Guide page 65 for complete lesson plan.

Teacher Notes

LESSON PLAN
SECTION 1, 1002–1007

FOCUS

Bellringer

Prior to taking roll at the beginning of the class period, display Focus Activity Transparency 119 on the overhead projector and assign the accompanying Focus Activity Sheet.

Objectives

Point out the objectives on this page to students in previewing the section content.

Motivating Activity

Have students give examples of the ways the federal government affects their everyday lives. (taxes on some items, regulation of food products, air and water quality, prescription drugs, automobiles, and so forth) Ask them if they agree or disagree with the idea that the federal government is too large. Discuss responses. Point out that Section 1 explores the reasons many Americans in the 1990s were dissatisfied with the federal government and the ways they expressed that dissatisfaction.

Use Skills Transparency 36.

SECTION 1

Reinventing Government

Setting the Scene

Section Focus

Candidate Bill Clinton and his running mate, Al Gore, promised "to redesign, to reinvent, to reinvigorate the entire national government" by making it more efficient and responsive to the needs of the American people. As time passed, however, citizens expressed growing dissatisfaction. In 1994 Republicans won control of both houses of Congress.

Objectives

After studying this section, you should be able to

★ explain why many Americans demanded a change in government in 1992.

★ explain how gridlock between Congress and the President affected the process of government.

★ discuss why criticism of the Clinton administration increased and led to Republican control of Congress.

Key Terms

incumbent, filibuster, downsizing, line-item veto, appropriations bill

◀ MEMORIAL BUTTON, INAUGURATION DAY 1993

At the beginning of the twentieth century, progressives had worked to strengthen and enlarge the small federal government. Their purpose in moving toward this objective was to equip government to handle the social and economic problems caused by industrialization. Toward the end of the century, government had grown so large that more Americans worked in local, state, and national government than in the manufacturing industries.

Many Americans believed government had grown too large, that it taxed too heavily and spent too much. Leaders from both major political parties promised to renovate government and make it more responsive to the needs of the people.

■ Demands for Change

As the election of 1992 approached, many people in the United States expressed demands for change in government. Public opinion had turned against Washington, D.C., "insiders" and **incumbents,** or people currently holding office. Voters blamed incumbents for the recession, the federal deficit, and government gridlock.

Government Scandals

Scandals deepened Americans' anger at incumbents. Revelations that some members of the House of Representatives had bounced checks repeatedly at the House bank outraged many citizens. They asked

UNIT 10 Redefining America: 1954–Present

Classroom Resources for SECTION 1

Teacher's Classroom Resources
- Study Guide
- Reproducible Lesson Plan
- Reteaching Activity 36-1
- Chapter 36 Cooperative Learning Activity
- Chapter 36 Primary and Secondary Source Reading
- Section Quiz

Multimedia
- Section Focus Transparency 119
- Skills Transparency 36
- Testmaker
- Student Self-Test Software
- Focus on Government

Visualizing History ▲ **HILL AND THOMAS** The Senate delayed the confirmation of Clarence Thomas to the Supreme Court when University of Oklahoma law professor Anita Hill accused Thomas of sexual misconduct. *What was the outcome of the confirmation hearing?*

how these officials could manage the nation's economy when they bungled their personal finances. Further angered when members of Congress voted to raise their own salaries, many political leaders and citizens took action. Ultimately, the movement led to the ratification in 1992 of the Twenty-seventh Amendment to the Constitution. This amendment prohibited any congressional pay raise from taking effect until after the following election, thus giving the voters a chance to act.

Another uproar followed President Bush's nomination of Clarence Thomas to the Supreme Court in 1991. One of Thomas's former coworkers, law professor Anita Hill, testified before the Senate Judiciary Committee that Thomas had sexually harassed her. Thomas strongly denied the charge.

The Senate narrowly confirmed Thomas to the Supreme Court, but many Americans were angry. Noting the absence of any women on the Senate Judiciary Committee and seeing that only 2 of the 100 senators were women, they argued that "2 percent is not enough." Building on the rising discontent, more women ran for political office. As "outsiders" in politics, women candidates drew support from both women and men who demanded change.

The Race for President

After victory in the Persian Gulf War, President Bush's reelection seemed assured. Several Democrats declined to run against him. The lengthening recession, however, raised new doubts about his leadership and encouraged challengers to enter the race.

After a short struggle during the primaries, Bush received his party's nomination. He told voters that having set the world in order during his first term, he intended to begin rebuilding the nation. Blaming the Democrats' long control of Congress for gridlock, Bush called for the election of a Republican Congress.

Among the leading Democratic candidates for President was Governor Bill Clinton of Arkansas. Early in the campaign, the press raised questions about Clinton's character and his failure to serve in the armed forces during the Vietnam War. Yet Clinton emerged

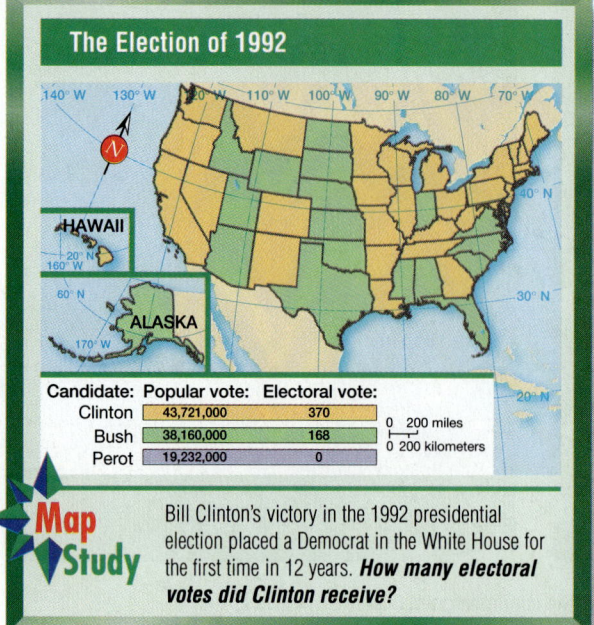

The Election of 1992

Candidate:	Popular vote:	Electoral vote:
Clinton	43,721,000	370
Bush	38,160,000	168
Perot	19,232,000	0

Map Study Bill Clinton's victory in the 1992 presidential election placed a Democrat in the White House for the first time in 12 years. *How many electoral votes did Clinton receive?*

as the leading contender after victories in the South and in Illinois and New York, and he won the nomination.

Texas billionaire H. Ross Perot fashioned a strong third-party challenge. Perot had promised to run if volunteers could collect enough petitions to place his name on all 50 state ballots. The outpouring of volunteers expressed demand for change as well as unhappiness with the two major parties.

A sign in Clinton's campaign headquarters read, "It's the economy, stupid." This blunt message was a strong reminder that, no matter what other topics might be debated, the recession was the number-one issue. Clinton painted the recession as the President's most glaring failure and made a campaign promise to revive the economy.

Election of 1992

About 104 million Americans—the largest number of people ever to go to the polls—voted in the presidential election of 1992. Clinton received 43 percent of the popular vote, while Bush captured 38 percent and Perot 19 percent. Clinton received less than a majority because of Perot's strong showing, the highest for any third-party candidate since 1912.

Although Republicans gained seats in the House of Representatives for the first time since 1984, the Democrats retained control of both houses of Congress. Voters defeated 24 incumbents in House races and 3 running for reelection to the Senate.

Even more significantly, voters elected a record of number women and minority candidates. Twenty-four new women members were elected to the House, and four won Senate seats. Jay Kim was the first Korean American and Nydia Velazquez the first Puerto Rican woman in the House of Representatives. Carol Moseley Braun of Illinois was the first African American woman senator, while Ben Nighthorse Campbell was the first Native American in the Senate in more than 60 years.

A New Democrat

President Clinton identified himself as a "New Democrat" who represented the moderate wing of the party. Only 46 years old, Clinton was a complex person who, at times, presented different images to different people. He embraced middle-class values, playing music, jogging, and exhibiting a taste for fast foods.

Yet Clinton had graduated from such elite institutions as Georgetown University and the Yale Law School and had attended Oxford University as a Rhodes scholar. Reflecting a tension between these two facets of his personality, Clinton changed positions on a number of issues. Critics complained that these shifts showed that Clinton was a pragmatic politician and compromiser rather than a committed leader.

Taxes

One of the more dramatic shifts concerned a middle-class tax cut. As a candidate, Clinton had called for a tax cut along with new spending to stimulate the economy. Soon after he took office, Clinton learned that the federal deficit would be even bigger than estimated. As a result, Clinton concluded that reducing the deficit would put the government in a stronger position to respond to future economic problems. He abandoned plans for the tax cut and instead supported tax increases to raise more revenue.

Congress passed the deficit reduction plan but then defeated the Clinton administration's $16 billion spending plan that had been intended to stimulate the economy. Opponents of the spending plan had successfully argued that increasing spending while trying to cut the deficit sent a mixed message to Americans.

An Anticrime Program

President Clinton moved quickly to deal with the problem of crime, focusing largely on prevention. The administration's crime bill gave grants to cities and states to hire a total of 100,000 new police officers. The program also contained a "3 strikes and you're out" policy that mandated life imprisonment for those convicted of 3 major felonies.

In addition, the crime bill banned many types of assault (military-style) weapons, and the Brady Law established a waiting period for the purchase of hand guns. This waiting period gave authorities a chance to determine whether the buyer had a criminal record. As part of the anticrime package, Congress approved money for such programs as midnight basketball leagues that would keep young people occupied during high-crime hours.

Dealing with the Bureaucracy

The President and Vice President Al Gore planned ways to redesign the national government. They called for greater and more efficient use of computer technology to sustain services with fewer workers, and they launched a National Performance Review to examine each government agency. The purpose of the review was to eliminate outdated and unnecessary functions and to shrink the bureaucracy to create a government that "works better and costs less."

■ Gridlock Continues

With Democratic majorities in both houses of Congress, the President hoped at last to end government gridlock. After an initial "honeymoon," however, during which Congress passed some legislation formerly vetoed by Presidents Reagan and Bush, gridlock reappeared.

CHAPTER 36 SECTION 1

Teaching American Portraits

Point out that women are becoming more influential at all levels of government. The gender barrier was broken in the Supreme Court when President Ronald Reagan appointed Sandra Day O'Connor to the bench, opening the way for Bill Clinton's appointment of Ruth Bader Ginsberg. Ask students what benefits they think women might gain from having two female justices on the Court. (Answers will vary but may include that the two may bring a different perspective to issues of special interest for women, such as abortion, that could come before the Court.)

GLENCOE TECHNOLOGY

VIDEODISC

Focus on Government

Videodisc 1, Chapter 17
Interest Groups

AMERICAN PORTRAITS

Ruth Bader Ginsburg
1933–

On August 10, 1993, Ruth Bader Ginsburg was sworn in as the 107th justice of the United States Supreme Court. The second woman ever to serve on the Court, Justice Ginsburg attended law school at a time when women often suffered discrimination. Ginsburg experienced discrimination firsthand when, in 1960, Supreme Court Justice Frankfurter refused to hire her as his law clerk because she was a woman. Having a keen sense of fairness, Ginsburg successfully argued against a number of laws that treated men and women differently, even when the laws gave women favorable treatment.

When Ginsburg became a judge on the United States Court of Appeals, she carefully thought out her decisions just as she had carefully prepared her cases when she was a lawyer. Largely because of those decisions, the Senate approved her appointment to the Supreme Court.

Sidelights: The Supreme Court

Unlike jurors who decide cases in the lower courts, justices of the Supreme Court have not been representative of the general population in social class, background, gender, or ethnic group. They have come from upper socioeconomic levels. Only two African American justices have been appointed, Thurgood Marshall and Clarence Thomas, and only two women, Sandra Day O'Connor and Ruth Bader Ginsberg.

▲ **CLINTON AND GORE** From the beginning, the Clinton administration worked to streamline government. *What plans did the administration put in place for redesigning the government?*

Gridlock remained a problem partly because Democrats had split into two camps on some issues. Democrats who favored smaller government were uncomfortable with many of Clinton's proposals. They considered ways to cut back some social programs and many environmental and regulatory provisions.

The Republicans, however, remained united in their opposition to most administration programs. In the Senate, Republicans used delaying tactics to block passage of certain bills. The main weapon they used was the **filibuster.** To filibuster means to keep talking for hours until a majority of the Senate either abandons the bill or agrees to modify its most controversial provisions.

The Clinton Health Plan

A central goal for the administration was to set up a system of health care to provide for the 15 percent of Americans with no insurance. The President named his spouse, Hillary Rodham Clinton, an experienced attorney, to lead a task force that would recommend changes in the health-care system. When completed, the Clinton plan guaranteed basic health benefits to all Americans. The plan required employers to shoulder much of the burden for health insurance for their employees. As a result, the plan was opposed by small-business owners who feared that they could not afford it.

The insurance industry, which stood to lose revenue, was also opposed. This industry sponsored a series of television commercials featuring a fictitious couple who worried what impact the Clinton health plan would have on their lives. The majority of Americans already had medical insurance. As a result, the commercials encouraged people to worry that universal health care might increase their costs and reduce the quality of care they were currently receiving in order to pay for the uninsured.

The Republicans also challenged the Clinton health-care plan, deriding it as too big, complicated, and costly. After viewing a chart representing the Republican view of the administration's program, Clinton's White House chief of staff said:

> *It looks more like a New York subway system, and I don't think it represents our health-care plan at all.*

Soon the Democrats, too, deserted the President's plan and proposed a variety of alternatives. None of their plans, however, attracted enough support to be passed into law. Conservative radio talk-show hosts attacked the Clinton health-care plan and criticized the President and his wife, causing Clinton's popularity to dwindle.

Criticism Increases

Accusations against his personal morals and financial ethics also hurt the President. A key issue was the Whitewater scandal. Clinton had invested in Whitewater, an Arkansas land development project that had gone bankrupt. Soon, Republicans demanded a congressional investigation.

Many middle-class Americans who still felt insecure economically also criticized the President. Early in Clinton's term the economy improved as unemployment fell,

UNIT 10 Redefining America: 1954–Present

Critical Thinking

Forming an Opinion Have students review the system of checks and balances set up by the Constitution. Ask them to summarize the powers of the Congress and the powers of the President and form an opinion answering the following questions: Do you think the executive branch has become too powerful? Do you think the Congress has become too powerful? Have students explain their answers to the class. **L1**

inflation remained low, and the federal deficit declined. Many people, however, continued to worry about losing their jobs.

Many men over the age of 50 had lost their jobs because of cutbacks in the defense industry and by corporate **downsizing,** the process by which companies seek to achieve savings by reducing the number of midlevel employees. Many of those who lost their jobs found it hard to locate new employment at comparable salaries. Some had to resort to part-time or temporary jobs with less security, lower income, and no benefits.

■ The 1994 Congressional Elections

Mounting criticism of the Clinton administration was reflected in the results of the 1994 congressional elections. Before the elections, President Clinton had called on voters to keep Democrats in the majority. However, the coalition of liberals, working people, minorities, and Southerners that Franklin D. Roosevelt had put together more than 60 years ago was about to collapse.

Instead, Americans turned control of both the House and Senate over to the Republicans for the first time in 40 years. Every Republican incumbent running for reelection won. Prominent Democrats lost, including House Speaker Tom Foley, who had served in Congress for 30 years.

A key to the Republican victories was their "Contract with America" that proposed lower taxes, stronger restrictions on immigration, tougher anti-crime laws, limits on congressional terms, a balanced budget, and the **line-item veto.** This kind of veto would allow the President to veto particular items in an appropriations bill without having to veto the entire bill. An **appropriations bill** sets aside money for a specific purpose. The new Republican Speaker of the House, Newt Gingrich of Georgia, blamed New Deal and Great Society programs for creating a culture of poverty and violence. Condemning the growth of large government, Gingrich vowed to "erase the slate and start over."

Visualizing History ▲ **THE 100 DAYS** Speaker Newt Gingrich (above) and other House Republican leaders promised that they would bring 10 significant measures to a vote within the first 100 days of the session. Most of the measures were passed. Only term limits and the balanced-budget amendment stalled. *What is the line-item veto?*

Section 1 ★ Review

Checking for Understanding

1. **Identify** Clarence Thomas, H. Ross Perot, Carol Moseley Braun, Hillary Rodham Clinton, Newt Gingrich, Contract with America.
2. **Define** incumbent, filibuster, downsizing, line-item veto, appropriations bill.
3. **List** two reasons for the anti-incumbent mood in the United States during the early 1990s.
4. **Explain** why President Clinton called himself a "New Democrat."

Critical Thinking

5. **Identifying Alternatives** In your opinion, should President Clinton have shifted his political position on key issues, such as the deficit, once he took office? Explain your answer.

LESSON PLAN
SECTION 2, 1008–1014

FOCUS
Prior to taking roll at the beginning of the class period, display Focus Activity Transparency 120 on the overhead projector and assign the accompanying Focus Activity Sheet.

Objectives
Point out the objectives on this page to students in previewing the section content.

Motivating Activity
Point out to students that in economic terms the world is becoming a smaller place. For example, a jacket bought in Chicago could have been made from Chinese cotton, assembled on an English sewing machine in a factory in Taiwan, and transported to the United States by a Norwegian freight line. Ask students to think of other examples of products they use that are made in different parts of the world.

SECTION 2

America in a Changing World

Setting the Scene

Focus
For more than 40 years, the struggle to contain communism determined United States foreign policy and defined America's role in the world. When the Soviet Union dissolved in 1991, the world changed, and America's role changed with it. The United States government now had to consider each country and issue separately.

Objectives
After studying this section, you should be able to
★ describe the development of Clinton's foreign policy in the new world order.
★ explain what key role the United States played in bringing about major breakthroughs between old enemies.

Key Terms
multinational state, genocide, ethnic cleansing, global economy, multinational corporation, trade deficit, creditor nation, debtor nation, globalized corporation

◀ TRAVEL PASSPORT

The struggle between communism and democracy was virtually over. Yet, throughout the world bloody wars erupted over ethnic hatreds, political boundaries, and religious views.

■ Foreign Policy

In his first year in office, President Clinton began to develop a different direction in foreign policy, stating that the United States should seek to enlarge the global community of market-oriented democracies. Clinton generally sought to achieve his goals through diplomacy or by using economic pressures. Whenever the prospect of using military force arose, however, the President tried to work through the United Nations.

Civil War in Somalia

One of the first crises to confront the Clinton administration was civil war in the east African nation of Somalia. While warring factions battled for power, Somalian civilians were dying of hunger by the thousands. When Clinton took office in 1993, more than 28,000 American troops were already in this war-torn land, having been ordered there by President Bush in 1992 to lead a United Nations mission. The force served to protect deliveries of food to the starving Somalians.

Fierce fighting, however, obstructed the task, and the longer American troops remained in Somalia, the more they were drawn into the conflict. When television cameras recorded the body of an American soldier being dragged through the streets,

---

Classroom Resources for SECTION 2

Teacher's Classroom Resources
- Reproducible Lesson Plan
- Reteaching Activity 36-2
- Chapter 36 Primary and Secondary Source Readings
- Section Quiz

Multimedia
- Section Focus Transparency 120
- Testmaker
- Student Self-Test Software

public opinion in the United States, which had favored the Somalia mission, changed. Under fierce criticism for not providing adequate protection for American soldiers, the President set a deadline for withdrawal of all United States troops. In February 1995 American marines returned to ensure safe passage out of Somalia for the remaining American personnel.

Bloodshed in the Balkans

Uneasiness over Somalia made the United States hesitate over involving itself either militarily or via other means in conflict in the Balkans. After World War II had ended, Yugoslavia had been created as a **multinational state,** or a nation with many different ethnic groups. Six republics were part of the new nation—Croatia, Slovenia, Bosnia-Herzegovina, Serbia, Montenegro, and Macedonia.

Although each republic had a dominant ethnic group, the populations were mixed. Dividing the people were centuries-old differences based not only on the ethnic group to which they belonged but on religion and territorial claims as well.

War Begins

In 1991 the republics of Slovenia, Croatia, Bosnia-Herzegovina, and Macedonia declared their independence. They did so after Serbia, the largest of the former republics, refused to agree to a looser confederation that would give the other republics greater autonomy. Under its leader Slobodan Milosevic, Serbia began waging war against the breakaway states.

The most violent fighting occurred in Bosnia-Herzegovina, where Bosnian Serbs wanted to retain ties with Serbia. Bosnian Serb forces followed a policy of **genocide**—the systematic destruction of an ethnic, political, or cultural group—of the Muslims and Croats. The Serbs also engaged in what is known as **ethnic cleansing,** in this case, the expulsion of Bosnian Muslims and other non-Serbs from areas under Bosnian Serb control. As a result of the war, about 300,000 people died and 2.7 million lost their homes.

 ▲ **SOMALIA** By late 1992 anarchy ruled the east African nation of Somalia, plagued by a civil war for more than 3 years. Gangs of rival clans battled for power while civilians starved. American troops served to protect food deliveries to the people. **Why did public opinion about the mission in Somalia change?**

Exploring Options

The United States and western Europe were unable to decide how to reduce the suffering of the besieged people. Initial steps included the UN instituting an arms embargo against all the former Yugoslav states, placing trade sanctions on Serbia, and sending a peacekeeping force into Bosnia.

Throughout the conflict, the United States also tried to persuade its NATO allies to stage air strikes against Bosnian Serb military sites. NATO jets, acting under the authority of the United Nations, attacked several military targets in November 1994. In retaliation, Bosnian Serbs kidnapped 165 United Nations peacekeepers and offered to exchange them for NATO flight plans.

Then, in a sudden and surprising move, Bosnian Serb leader Radovan Karadzic (RAH•doh•vahn ka•RAH•dzihk) requested the diplomatic services of former United States President Jimmy Carter. Carter managed to arrange a shaky truce that turned increasingly fragile as warfare erupted again in early 1995.

CHAPTER 36 Toward a New Century 1992–Present

CHAPTER 36 SECTION 2

Independent Practice

Ask students to research the current status of NAFTA and the results thus far. Have them write a report evaluating the results and draw conclusions about its effects on the economy of the United States. **L3**

Visualizing History  In September 1994, American and Cuban diplomats came to an agreement. The United States would take in at least 20,000 legal Cuban immigrants and Cuban leaders agreed to limit the exodus.
Answer to Caption: The new rulers of Haiti used violent means to put down opposition to their regime.

▲ **REFUGEES** In the 1990s poor conditions in Cuba and Haiti swelled the flow of "boat people" seeking refuge in the United States. *For what other reason did many Haitians leave their homeland?*

Conflict in Chechnya

At the start of the 1990s, relations between the former parts of the Soviet Union were being radically redefined as demands for self-rule grew. By the mid-1990s, tensions were rising in the Russian Federation. The north Caucasus republic of Chechnya attempted to secede from the Federation. Russian leader Boris Yeltsin sent forces into Chechnya both to bring the republic back into the Federation and as a warning against secession to the other Russian republics.

Soon after the invasion, Yeltsin noted, "Everything will be settled soon on the Chechen issue. I am in strict control." Events, however, contradicted Yeltsin's confidence. Vastly outnumbered Chechen forces held off the Russians' superior firepower. Russian looting, torture, and indiscriminate bombing drew sharp criticism from human rights leaders. The Russian government acknowledged only that isolated instances of rights violations had occurred. After the capital city of Grozny fell, Chechen forces vowed to take to the mountains south of the capital and continue the war from there.

Unrest in Haiti

Closer to home, unrest in the Caribbean nation of Haiti posed difficult challenges for the United States. In December 1990, a Roman Catholic priest, Jean-Bertrand Aristide (ah•ree•STEED), had won the presidency of Haiti in the country's first fully democratic elections. In September 1991, however, the Haitian military, headed by Lieutenant General Raoul Cédras (SAY•drahs), overthrew Aristide. The new rulers of Haiti used violence—even murder—to put down opposition, causing thousands of Haitians to flee for their lives to the United States in flimsy boats.

Clinton and the Haitian Refugees

During the presidential campaign, Clinton had criticized the Bush administration's policy of sending Haitians rescued at sea back to their homeland rather than offering them asylum in the United States. Once he took office, however, Clinton also sought to stem the tide of Haitian refugees to the United States. The President accepted the argument of Gulf Coast governors that their states could not absorb large numbers of new and very poor refugees.

Sidelights: The Federal Reserve and the Economy

Many economists are dissatisfied with the policies of the Federal Reserve System. They argue, for example, that in a time of economic growth like the mid-1990s, the Federal Reserve becomes fearful of inflation and tampers with the economy by raising interest rates. Such moves dampen the economy by making it more difficult for businesses and consumers to borrow money for expansion and housing. To these economists, the Federal Reserve is much too concerned about inflation.

Attempts to Restore Democracy

To try to topple the Haitian military government and restore democracy, the UN used economic pressure, imposing an embargo of oil and arms in October 1993 and of all trade seven months later. The United Nations also called for an end to all financial aid to Haiti, which was desperately poor. As a result, in June 1994 Clinton banned all financial transactions between the United States and Haiti. Despite this growing pressure, Haiti's rulers retained their tight grip on the country.

Opting for stronger measures, the United Nations authorized the United States to lead an invasion to drive the military rulers out of Haiti. General Cédras commented, "I am the pin in Haiti's hand grenade—if pulled an explosion will occur." On September 18, 1994, the eve of the planned invasion, President Clinton sent former President Jimmy Carter to negotiate with Haiti's military rulers. The threat of an invasion persuaded the generals to step down peacefully. The next day, 2,000 American troops met no resistance when they landed in Haiti. Joined by soldiers from other countries, they provided stability for the return of President Aristide on October 15, 1994. In February 1995 Carter returned to Haiti to help implement plans for new elections.

Moves Toward Peace in the Middle East

Although bloody wars seemed to be raging all over the post-cold war world, there were also breakthroughs as old enemies moved toward peace. The United States played an important role in several peace efforts in the Middle East.

Israeli-PLO Agreement

Of all the conflicts in the Middle East, the Arab-Israeli conflict had been the most enduring and difficult. When Israel was created from British-occupied Palestine in 1948, Palestinian Arabs had been forced to move to the West Bank of the Jordan River. This area soon came under the control of Jordan, however. In 1964, some of these displaced

▲ **Peace Agreement** After signing a new peace agreement, Israel's Prime Minister Yitzhak Rabin (left) and PLO leader Yasir Arafat (right) congratulate one another as President Clinton looks on. **What were the terms of the agreement?**

CHAPTER 36 SECTION 2

Linking Across Time

Since its emergence as a major industrial power, the United States has usually exported more goods to other nations than it has imported. However, in the 1970s, oil prices rose and the United States imported more oil. The balance of trade shifted, with the United States importing more goods than it exported. This shift was accompanied by the growing economies of Western Europe and Japan, which competed with American companies that wanted to sell their products overseas. In the 1990s the balance was beginning to shift again in favor of the United States.

Visualizing History The Palestine Liberation Organization was forced in 1964 to press for an independent Palestinian homeland.
Answer to Caption: The PLO recognized Israel's right to exist, and Israel recognized the PLO as the representative of the Palestinians.

Critical Thinking

Expressing an Opinion Tell students that many Americans resent the growth of foreign investment in the United States. Some critics advocate limiting foreign investment in U.S. real estate and industry. Others argue that U.S. investment abroad exports American jobs and wages to foreign countries. Ask students to decide whether investors, foreign or U.S., should be allowed to spend their money, or capital, wherever they think it will yield the highest return. Have students explain their answers. **L2**

CHAPTER 36
SECTION 2

Teaching Life of the Times

Many observers believe that some of the incredible damage of the 1993 flood in the Midwest could have been averted. They argue that diverting areas of the river system to increase the water supply for farmlands led to some of the flooding. They also point out that in some places the floodwalls were so high, water could not flow over them and therefore flooded other areas thought to be safe. Discuss with students how such flooding could be avoided in the future.

Did You Know?

While many former communist nations were altering their political and economic fabric in the late 1980s and early 1990s, the People's Republic of China resisted democratic reforms. Leaders of China said they would institute some capitalist-style economic reforms, but they ruled out any Western-style political changes.

Life of the Times

Volunteers

Rain fell on America's Midwest in record levels from April to June 1993. The waters of the vast Mississippi and Missouri river systems spilled over their banks and burst through flood walls and levees. Hundreds of low-lying cities and towns were flooded, at least 50 people were killed, and millions of acres of prime farmland were covered by water. The Great Flood of 1993 caused damage in nine states at a cost of over $10 billion.

Local citizens quickly came together to fight the surging floodwaters. People of all ages and professions volunteered to fill sandbags and raise the flood walls. Others transported personal belongings, livestock, and machinery to safety. Still others assisted at emergency shelters. Federal agencies, the National Guard, and private relief organizations all stepped in to help.

Many volunteers came from outside the flooded area. Some came in groups and fought the flood side by side with the local citizens. Others came singly. One man from Ohio drove a truck loaded with bottled water to Des Moines, Iowa, at his own expense, after the city's water treatment plant had been knocked out by the flood. Several residents from Homestead, Florida, came to the Midwest, offering to help as a way to pay back the help they had received after Hurricane Andrew devastated their city in 1992.

▼ Erecting a Barrier

---

people formed the Palestine Liberation Organization (PLO) to work toward an independent Arab Palestine.

Then in 1967 Israeli troops seized the Gaza Strip from Egypt and Jordanian territory west of the River Jordan, including Jordan's part of the city of Jerusalem. In 1987, after 20 years of smoldering rage, the Palestinians in both areas began an uprising. Finally, in October 1991 the United States, under President Bush, succeeded in getting the two sides to begin peace talks. By the time Clinton took office, however, hostilities had disrupted them.

Although Clinton devoted much of his first year in office to domestic issues, he put together a Middle East policy team and resumed the peace process. Over the next eight months, talks proceeded erratically, breaking down frequently. Then on September 13, 1993, Israeli Prime Minister Yitzhak Rabin (EE•tsahk rah•BEEN) and Palestine Liberation Organization leader Yasir Arafat (YAH•suhr AIR•uh•FAHT) reached an agreement. The PLO recognized Israel's right to exist, and Israel recognized the PLO as the representative of the Palestinians. In addition, both parties agreed on a framework for limited Palestinian self-rule in the Gaza Strip and the West Bank.

Peace Between Israel and Jordan

President Clinton also helped work out a peace agreement between Israel and Jordan a little over a year later. In July 1994, Prime Minister Rabin and Jordan's King Hussein signed a historic peace treaty officially ending the state of war that had existed between their countries for nearly half a century. The treaty also had other objectives. It set up a framework for cooperation in such areas as environmental protection, tourism, and trade. The two former adversaries stated that they supported a "just, lasting, and comprehensive peace between Israel and its neighbors."

New problems, however, endangered the plans. Palestinian leaders contended that the growing Israeli settlements on the West Bank violated the spirit of the agreement.

UNIT 10 Redefining America: 1954–Present

Sidelights: What Does the Public Want?

A poll taken shortly after the congressional elections of 1994 indicates that Americans do not particularly want what either the Republicans or Democrats were proposing. According to the survey, Americans wanted to spend more money to fight crime but also supported federal funding for education and the environment. In addition, while they wanted welfare reform, they also were willing to spend money to help the truly needy. Overall the poll indicated that Americans do not necessarily want less government but more efficient and effective government.

Israeli leaders drew away from implementing the agreement when Islamic forces attacked Israeli settlements.

America in a Global Economy

Innovations in technology and economics have transformed national and regional economies into a **global economy,** an economic world without strict borders where products, personnel, money, and resources intertwine. Wide-ranging developments in transportation and communications have made international trade a booming business and an economic driving force in today's world. Part of this pattern is the growth of **multinational corporations,** companies that produce and market goods in a number of different countries.

The United States had long based its economic prosperity on selling its industrial and agricultural goods abroad. By the 1970s, however, the United States was losing its economic dominance as more and more nations strengthened their own industries and trade. America experienced **trade deficits,** purchasing more from foreign nations than they sold in foreign markets. By the early 1970s, the United States had changed from a **creditor nation,** or a lending nation, to a **debtor nation,** or a borrowing one.

The United States reacted to its declining economic position by working to become more competitive in the global marketplace. In recent years, many American multinational companies have become **globalized corporations,** meaning that they operate throughout the world and not just in specific foreign areas.

The government also pursued ways to strengthen America's economic position in the global marketplace. Just weeks before Clinton took office, the United States, Canada, and Mexico had signed the North American Free Trade Agreement (NAFTA), which lifted all tariffs, making North America the world's largest free trade area.

The agreement offered American manufacturers an opportunity to open factories in Mexico, where wages were lower. At the same time, Mexican and Canadian markets would be more open to American products and services. Critics of the agreement argued, however, that workers would be displaced when nations agree on trade pacts that lower barriers to trade. Congress approved the treaty in November 1993, after an almost year-long battle.

In time the American economic picture improved. From 1990 to 1995, American exports were up 28 percent. As a result, the United States achieved trading surpluses with nearly every nation. For the first time since 1985, the World Economic Forum rated the United States economy as the most competitive in the world.

Section 2 ★ Review

Checking for Understanding

1. **Identify** Jean-Bertrand Aristide, Raoul Cédras, Yitzhak Rabin, Yasir Arafat, General Agreement of Tariffs and Trade (GATT), North American Free Trade Agreement (NAFTA).
2. **Define** multinational state, genocide, ethnic cleansing, global economy, multinational corporation, trade deficit, creditor nation, debtor nation, globalized corporation.
3. **Explain** why President Clinton found it difficult to decide when and how to intervene in another nation's affairs.
4. **Cite** two reasons for the United States's trade deficit.

Critical Thinking

5. **Making Judgments** Weigh the pros and cons of American companies' moving factories to foreign countries to take advantage of lower wages there.

CHAPTER 36 Toward a New Century 1992–Present 1013

CHAPTER 36 SECTION 2

ASSESS

Check Understanding
Assign Section 2 Review as homework or an in-class activity.

Evaluate
Assign the Section 2 Quiz in the TCR or use the History of a Free Nation Testmaker to create a customized quiz.

Reteach
Ask students to summarize the strengths and weaknesses of Clinton's domestic programs and foreign policy initiatives.

Have students complete Reteaching Activity 36-2.

Enrich
Have students research the current balance of trade between the United States and its major competitors. Have them write a report on whether the balance is favorable or unfavorable to the United States and why.

CLOSE
Discuss with students the impact on American society of the major domestic programs the Clinton administration was able to pass.

Answers to SECTION 2 REVIEW

1. Slobodan Milosevic, 1009; Radovan Karadzic, 1009; Jean Bertrand Aristide, 1010; Raoul Cédras, 1010; Yitzhak Rabin, 1012; Yasir Arafat, 1012; North American Free Trade Agreement (NAFTA), 1013
2. All vocabulary words are defined in the Glossary.
3. conflicted over whether to use diplomacy to revolve issues or military force
4. The United States imported more than it exported, spending more money than it earned; foreign investors used money from goods sold in the United States to buy American companies.
5. Answers will vary. Pro: American workers are overpaid, American companies cannot compete in world markets; Con: move has displaced thousands of U.S. workers.

1013

LESSON PLAN
Mastering Social Studies Skills

Teaching Map and Graph Skills

Tell students that you can draw conclusions about a topic by studying a bar graph. Using information from the graphs, ask students to write a statement about the position of U.S. multinational corporations in the global economy.

Did You Know?

Multinational corporations are not a new idea. They began to develop around the turn of the century. By 1969 the combined sales of foreign subsidiaries of U.S companies were larger than the gross national product of France or Britain.

Social Studies Skills

Map and Graph Skills

Reading a Bar Graph

Bar graphs present statistics in a form that is easy to read and that lets you make comparisons at a glance. These graphs are helpful when you want to show financial information about businesses.

Follow these procedures when you read a bar graph:
- **Read** the graph's title or caption.
- **Examine** the graph's key, if one is included (not all graphs have keys).
- **Read** the labels on the horizontal and vertical axes. Determine what quantities the bars represent.
- **Check** the graph for unfamiliar terms. When you find one, look up the term in your book's glossary or in a dictionary.

Practicing the Skill

Use the guidelines above to help you examine the three graphs on this page. Then answer these questions:

1. What subject do all these graphs deal with?
2. What do the graphs' keys tell you?
3. What do the labels on the horizontal axes tell you?
4. Which company has the greatest total assets?
5. Which company has the greatest foreign assets?
6. Which company has the highest percentage of foreign sales?
7. How are assets and sales related?
8. Which companies sell more of their products nationally than internationally?

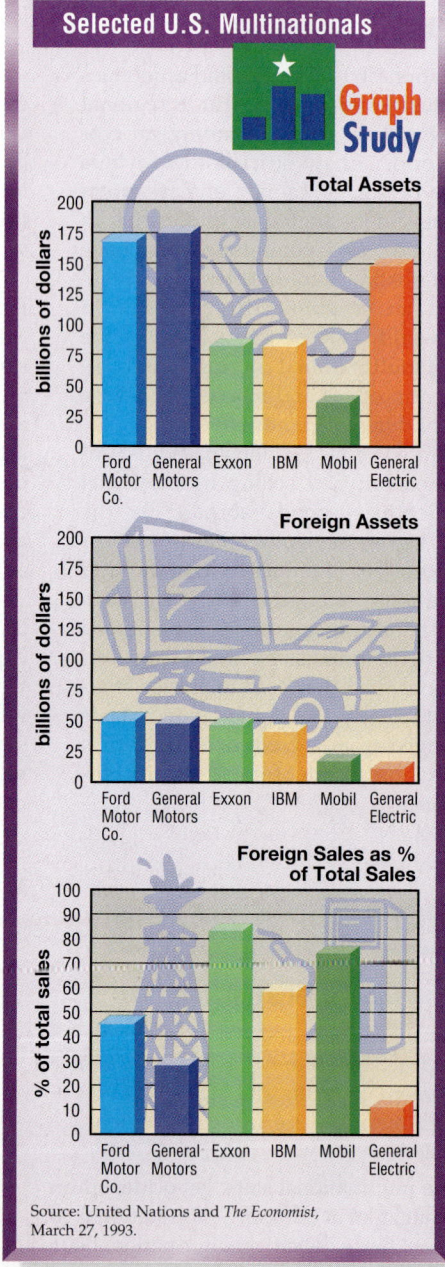

Source: United Nations and *The Economist*, March 27, 1993.

1014

Answers to SOCIAL STUDIES SKILLS

1. U.S. multinational corporations
2. For two of the graphs, total assets and foreign assets in billions of dollars; for one, foreign sales as a percentage of total sales
3. the companies that the different colored bars represent
4. General Motors
5. Ford Motor Co.
6. Exxon
7. Sales are a part of a company's assets.
8. Ford Motor Company, General Motors, and General Electric

SECTION 3

Challenges and Opportunities

Setting the Scene

Section Focus
Even though the threat of the cold war was over and America was taking its place in the new world order, other challenges faced the United States. Worry about their children's future and the challenges facing the nation during the 1990s troubled many Americans.

Objectives
After studying this section, you should be able to
★ identify the challenges facing the United States in the 1990s.
★ describe some of the proposed solutions to these challenges.

Key Terms
acid rain, wetland, crack cocaine, illegal alien, multicultural society, melting-pot society

◀ AIDS RIBBON

The 1994 congressional elections reflected deep unrest in American life. Such issues as poverty, crime and violence, threats to the environment, health risks, and increased immigration all threatened to diminish the quality of life in the United States.

■ Growing Poverty

One of the main challenges facing Americans in the 1990s was poverty. In the past, the federal government had helped many low-income families who had no place to turn. Yet these efforts did little to reduce the growing number of Americans in poverty. By 1994, nearly 14 million Americans were receiving Aid to Families with Dependent Children (AFDC). In 1984 that figure had been 10.9 million and in 1974, 10.8 million.

The Income Gap
Not only did the number of poor people increase, but the income gap between the rich and poor, which had narrowed between 1929 and 1969, grew wider than at any time since the 1930s. Partly responsible were changes in the American economy. In the past, the wide range of good jobs in industry had helped people with a high-school education enter the middle class. In the latter part of the twentieth century, however, low-skill manufacturing declined and high-technology and service companies increased. A high-school diploma was no longer enough to guarantee a good job. Median household income, and with it the standard of living, dropped for four straight years.

Workers who could take advantage of the technological revolution, however, did better. Salaries of college graduates increased steadily, especially for those in the new

CHAPTER 36 Toward a New Century 1992–Present   1015

CHAPTER 36 SECTION 3

TEACH
Guided Practice

History Lead a class discussion on the patterns of twentieth-century immigration. Review the traditional "push-pull" factors that influence immigration, such as economic forces, war, and religious persecution. Then ask students to write a brief answer to the following question: What issues do you think have arisen because of the most recent wave of immigration? **L1**

Did You Know?

In an article in the 1990 January-February *Futurist*, forecasters made predictions about the future of the United States. Among the predictions: the nation's population will peak at about 302 million by the year 2040; the nation will need to care for about 5 million AIDS patients by 2000.

- *GTV: A Geographic Perspective on American History*

Side 4, Chapter 12
Title: *What Goes Around, Comes Around*
Subject: Modern life: an environmental statement

See GTV Guide page 64 for complete lesson plan.

---

high-technology and service companies. More people than ever before entered such professions as education, law, and medicine, including a large number of women. Although women's salaries increased, however, they still remained below men's, leading to continuing calls for equal pay.

Government Response

Both Democratic and Republican leaders called for reforming the welfare system, but they had different reasons. Some sought reform because of welfare's great cost to the government and the need to decrease the deficit. Others argued that the system had to change because it created a "culture of poverty" in which the poor were trapped by their dependence on welfare.

In June 1994, Clinton proposed a sweeping reform plan. It offered increased education and training for welfare recipients and set a two-year limit on benefits. After this limit expired, most recipients would have to go to work. The President's plan also called for a crackdown on "deadbeat parents" by using the Internal Revenue Service to collect overdue child support. The Clinton plan, however, stalled in Congress.

Some members of Congress offered different ideas. Speaker of the House Newt Gingrich argued that the government should cut public assistance and emphasized that it was up to the poor to find work. Gingrich also advocated relying on private charities instead of the federal government to rescue the most impoverished.

Tapping Students as a Resource

Other reform measures addressed poverty indirectly. Seeking to help students who had left school before graduation, such programs as Boston's City Year and New York's City Volunteer Corps launched volunteer programs to provide them with job skills. Volunteers received scholarships in return for performing community services such as assisting disabled children.

In addition, at President Clinton's urging, Congress set up Americorps in 1993. This program employed students as resources to deal with the country's most pressing issues. Volunteers received a salary and, after completing their service, scholarships to continue their education. By bringing young people of different economic, racial, and ethnic backgrounds to work together in a common effort, the program helped break down barriers of mistrust and promote a strong sense of community responsibility.

Concern Over Crime and Violence

For many Americans the troubling aspects of poverty include how it contributes to crime and violence and, in particular, how crime and violence affect the very young. In many cities, gang activity rose, and sometimes very young children became gang members. Approximately 20 percent of all homicides in Los Angeles are witnessed by children. In efforts to protect their children, parents resorted to walking their children to school and keeping them at home after school.

■ The Environment

Threats to the environment also troubled Americans in the last decade of the twentieth century. The battle continued between those who wanted to preserve natural wilderness unchanged and those who favored greater development of natural resources. Concern about the environment heightened after a 1989 tanker accident off the coast of Alaska caused one of the biggest oil spills in history.

Acid Rain

One of the more controversial issues concerned **acid rain,** rain made by acidic gases given off when oil, gas, or coal burn. Environmentalists contended that acid rain kills fish, damages crops, and strips forests, and they called for stricter regulations to prevent it. Developers, on the other hand, warned that more regulations meant higher costs for companies that burn fossil fuels, forcing them either to find other energy sources or to install pollution-control

UNIT 10 Redefining America: 1954–Present

Special Needs

Study Strategy Ask students to think of one specific skill or strategy in these activities that helped them to learn the material in the text. Have them demonstrate the use of this skill or strategy to a classmate using the material in this section. Ask them to consider these questions: What learning procedures continue to be difficult? How can you overcome problems created by your distinct learning style? What effect does the teacher's instructional style have on your learning? Finally, have students complete this sentence: I learn best when I . . .

devices. Accepting either option, they argued, would send costs spiraling upward and lead to loss of jobs.

Speaking for those who believe that businesses have to change their ideas, Douglas Olesen, president of an Ohio research institute, said:

> So far we've focused . . . on eliminating waste only to the very end of the production line. . . . To cut waste at its sources, maybe we'll have to change the way we make products. Maybe we'll even have to change the products themselves.

Clinton and the Environment

When President Clinton took office, he wanted to protect the environment, but he had also promised to "grow the economy." The President tried to placate both developers and environmentalists through a series of compromises. One compromise was between loggers in the Pacific Northwest and environmentalists seeking to preserve the habitat of endangered species, such as the spotted owl. This agreement, although not satisfying either side completely, permitted both the logging industry and the spotted owls to survive.

The President took steps to prevent further loss of America's **wetlands,** or land or areas such as tidal flats or swamps that contain much soil moisture. He also stopped developers from building in areas that would affect migrating birds and other wildlife. In return, the government eased federal restrictions on other land in which developers were interested.

The Clinton administration also pushed for other measures to protect the environment. Some reduced solid and toxic wastes as well as air and water pollution. Others reduced American use of substances that destroy the ozone layer of the atmosphere.

Others Respond

Both state governments and private industry responded to demands to clean up the environment. To combat pollution, California and several Eastern states required that, starting in 1998, an increasing percentage of new cars sold should emit no pollution at all. Private companies tested batteries that break down water to produce electricity and never

▲ **CLEANING UP** The March 1989 *Exxon Valdez* oil spill was costly, both in terms of dollars for the cleanup (left) and lasting injury to wildlife. Young volunteers (right) clean a California beach. **What efforts did state government make to fight pollution?**

CHAPTER 36 Toward a New Century 1992–Present

Sidelights: Family Incomes

Median household income for American families increased between 1989 and 1992. For all households the median income dropped from $31,750 in 1989 to $31,203 in 1990, to $30,126 in 1991. During this period the income for white households fell from $33,398 to $31,569; for African American households from $19,862 to $18,807; for Hispanic-origin households from $24,078 to $22,691, and for Asian and Pacific Islander households from $39,654 to $36,449.

CHAPTER 36
SECTION 3

Historically Asian Americans have experienced considerable discrimination. Therefore they have tended to live together for protection and self-help. Although Asian American political gains have not been as dramatic as those of other minority groups, that may soon change. One writer noted, "As younger Americanized (and American born) Asians enter their adult years, they are likely to become more involved in politics."

Visualizing History Explain that Ryan White was a boy who contracted AIDS through a blood transfusion. His heroic fight against the disease and against the prejudice he encountered because of it encouraged the federal government to increase funding for AIDS and to name the Ryan White Care Act in his honor.
Answer to Caption: an act giving funds to cities for the treatment of AIDS

▲ **THE FIGHT AGAINST AIDS** Artists created an AIDS quilt to call attention to this deadly disease. Since the early 1980s, AIDS has killed 243,000 Americans. An estimated 1 million Americans are infected with HIV. *What is the Ryan White Care Act?*

need recharging. David Ramm, a top official for one of the testing companies, said, "The demand for clean energy will drive the technology."

Increasing Risks to Health

In the 1990s, there were increasing risks to the health of the American people. Diseases such as AIDS (*A*cquired *i*mmune *d*eficiency *s*yndrome) killed thousands and devastated society in the United States. Drug addiction also wreaked havoc and caused many to demand action from the federal government.

The Spread of AIDS

During the 1980s and 1990s, AIDS spread rapidly throughout the United States. By the mid-1990s, AIDS was the third leading cause of death among Americans aged 25 to 44. From 1981 through June 1994, more than 400,000 AIDS cases were diagnosed in the United States. During the early 1990s, there were 20,000 deaths a year and estimates placed the number of Americans infected with HIV (which in many cases leads to AIDS) at 1 million.

Responding to these alarming statistics and the growing demand for action, the federal government launched programs to educate Americans about the dangers of AIDS. It encouraged voluntary behavioral changes that would reduce the spread of the disease. President Clinton appointed a federal AIDS policy coordinator. Acting on his proposals, Congress increased the funding for AIDS research and fully funded the Ryan White Care Act, providing $275 million to cities for AIDS treatment.

Drug Abuse

In the 1990s, drug abuse continued to spread. For a while, the "Just Say No" campaign begun in the 1980s during the Reagan administration seemed to be working to limit drug use among children.

Between 1991 and 1995, however, marijuana use among high-school students nearly doubled. In a 1994 study, 8 percent of eighth graders, 16 percent of tenth graders, and 20 percent of twelfth graders said they had smoked "pot" during the previous 30 days. Joseph Califano, Jr., a former cabinet member and head of Columbia University's Center on Addiction and Substance Abuse, said:

1018 UNIT 10 Redefining America: 1954–Present

Cooperative Learning

The issues addressed in Section 3 unite the world in that they create common concerns, goals, and needs. Point out that students will be involved in the search for solutions to these issues in their adult years. Hold a roundtable discussion on an issue selected by the class. Then organize the class into a number of committees to investigate various aspects of the issue. Have groups report their findings to the class. Ask students to suggest ways in which they as adults would attempt to resolve these issues. **L3**

> "... [T]he most frightening thing is that smoking marijuana is clearly a steppingstone to more serious problems. Children who smoke pot are 85 times more likely to use cocaine."

Cocaine use was also on the rise. **Crack cocaine**, a form of the drug that comes in smokable chunks, proved to be extremely potent and able to cause addiction very quickly. Using cocaine while pregnant can cause addiction in a newborn baby, and hospital reports indicated that more and more newborns were testing positive for cocaine. These children, sometimes called "cocaine babies," often suffered serious and lasting health and behavioral problems.

The Clinton administration also launched a war against the sale and use of illegal drugs, focusing on lowering the demand for drugs. As part of his crime program, the President proposed "drug courts" that would order hard-core abusers to undergo treatment. Republican leaders in Congress, however, disagreed with Clinton's prevention measures. They viewed supply as the principal problem and advocated a continuing emphasis on stopping drug smuggling from South America and on prosecuting drug dealers.

The Issue of Immigration

Economic and political ills around the world brought a new tide of immigration to the United States during the 1990s. Although some Americans called for accepting the immigrants, others expressed alarm. Traditionally known as a "nation of immigrants," the United States was beginning to slam its doors.

Many of the new immigrants were refugees from such places as the former Soviet Union, eastern Europe, Vietnam, Cuba, and Haiti fleeing from political repression and economic hardships in their homelands. Some newcomers were **illegal aliens**, people who enter a country without a legal permit. Many illegal immigrants were from Mexico.

Total legal immigration surpassed 1 million a year during the late 1980s, the highest number since the early 1900s. About 50,000 immigrants a year were allowed in from the former Soviet Union alone.

Illegal Aliens

Threatened by the distasteful choice of losing jobs and services or paying higher taxes, many Americans directed their anger at immigrants. The issue took on an even more emotional tone in states with large concentrations of illegal immigrants such as Florida, Texas, and California. For example, California's governor Pete Wilson blamed much of the state's economic problems on the costs of providing state services for these immigrants. Wilson argued, "We can no longer allow compassion to overrule reason."

New Laws

In November 1994 California voters approved Proposition 187, which banned illegal aliens from using schools, nonemergency medical care, and other social services. Although critics sought to test the law's constitutionality, its passage indicates deep concern. Proposition 187 also stirred anger among legal immigrants, who reacted strongly to what they considered ethnic prejudice.

Because the largest number of illegal immigrants crossed the border from Mexico, the United States sought ways to bolster the Mexican economy to improve conditions there in order to reduce the flow of Mexican immigrants. During the Clinton administration, Congress also approved spending $1.2 billion over 3 years to strengthen patrols along the border with Mexico.

The Treatment of Legal Immigrants

Along with objecting to the presence of illegal aliens, some Americans proposed to change the treatment of legal immigrants by limiting their access to welfare benefits. Even though immigrants used these benefits less often than American citizens, the number of legal immigrants was rising. This

Food of the Times

Like earlier immigrants, newcomers from Asia, Africa, the Caribbean, Mexico, and Latin America have introduced other Americans to a variety of new foods and dishes. Many have tasted these foods for the first time in the scores of ethnic restaurants spread across the nation.

VIDEODISC
Focus on Government

Videodisc 1, Chapter 9 Citizenship in the United States

VIDEODISC
Powers of the Congress

Side 2, Chapter 49
Title: *Becoming a U.S. Citizen*
Subject: Swearing in a new group of American Citizens

Critical Thinking

Making Predictions Remind students of the questions they should ask when making predictions about the outcome of an event or issue: What related prior conditions existed? What caused these conditions? What was the event or issue supposed to accomplish? Based on the answers to the previous questions, what will happen as a result of the event or issue? Have students apply this procedure to make predictions about how the great diversity in our nation may affect society in the future. **L2**

CHAPTER 36 SECTION 3

ASSESS
Check Understanding
Assign Section 3 Review as homework or an in-class activity.

Evaluate
Assign the Section 3 Quiz in the TCR or use the History of a Free Nation Testmaker to create a customized quiz.

Reteach
Ask students to outline the major challenges described under each section heading. Then have them outline solutions they would propose for each challenge.

Have students complete Reteaching Activity 36-3.

Enrich
Suggest the students investigate the cultural diversity of their own community. They might identify foods, holidays, customs, street names, and so forth. Have them report their findings to the class.

CLOSE
Discuss with students whether they think the federal government should concentrate more on domestic issues or on foreign affairs.

---

growth in population increased costs for the government.

Congressional leaders, as part of a welfare reform bill, planned to introduce legislation that would bar the nation's 10 million legal immigrants from 60 different federal programs. These programs included Aid to Families with Dependent Children and food stamps.

President Clinton announced his opposition to across-the-board limitations on welfare benefits for legal immigrants, but he supported curtailing some benefits to those elderly persons who have financially stable relatives.

The Question of Diversity

Tying directly into the debate on immigration was the question of diversity. Some people believed that the many different peoples who make up the United States should retain much of their individual cultural heritages. These people saw the United States as a **multicultural society** in which all people should respect each other's unique identities. As Mayor Sharpe James of Newark, New Jersey, said, "Our diversity is our strength."

Others, however, viewed things quite differently. They believed, as many had in years past, that the United States should be a **melting-pot society** in which immigrants from around the world ought to blend into one unique people. They worried that greater emphasis on diversity and multiculturalism would create a fragmented society.

■ The Search for Equal Rights

One group that asserted themselves dramatically during the 1990s were Americans with disabilities. One aspect of this story began in 1962 on the day James Meredith became the first African American to enter the University of Mississippi. That same day Ed Roberts, a paraplegic in a wheelchair, entered the University of California. Like Meredith, Roberts had gone to court to win the right to attend college. While Meredith's story went out over the national news wires, Roberts's story was largely overlooked.

Even after winning the right to attend school, Roberts found dormitories and classroom buildings almost impossible to enter. To overcome the barriers to their education, Roberts and a group of friends started the Physically Disabled Students' Program to help disabled students get to class and locate accessible apartments.

In 1990 Congress passed the Americans with Disabilities Act. This law prohibited discrimination against the more than 40 million Americans who had physical, hearing, or visual impairments. Television news correspondent John Hockenberry, who himself uses a wheelchair, noted that the struggle for rights in America was a very old story that people with disabilities were just beginning to go through. "Our struggle for inclusion in this society," he noted, "is a test of whether American society truly wants diversity and freedom for all."

Section 3 ★ Review

Checking for Understanding

1. **Identify** Americorps, AIDS, Ryan White Care Act, drug court, Proposition 187, Ed Roberts.
2. **Define** acid rain, wetlands, crack cocaine, illegal alien, multicultural society, melting-pot society.
3. **Describe** how the United States tried in the early 1990s to stop illegal immigration.
4. **Cite** factors that have affected the increase of poverty in the United States.

Critical Thinking

5. **Evaluating Tactics** Do you think the government's efforts in the war on drugs should be focused on stopping the supply of drugs from other countries or on reducing the demand for drugs in this country? Explain your answer.

UNIT 10 Redefining America: 1954–Present

Answers to SECTION 3 REVIEW

1. Americorps, 1016; AIDS, 1018; Ryan White Care Act, 1018; drug court, 1019; Proposition 187, 1019; Ed Roberts, 1020
2. All vocabulary words are defined in the Glossary.
3. California banned illegal aliens from schools, emergency medical care, and other social services. Federal government attempted to bolster Mexico's economy to improve conditions so that Mexicans would not emigrate to the U.S..
4. Many do not have the education to enable them to enter the job market; industry declined, hitting hardest blue-collar workers who lacked technological skills
5. Answers will vary. Students may note that past efforts to stop drugs entering the country have largely failed. Most may argue that reducing the demand through preventive programs and education is the best answer.

CONNECTIONS — History AND Environment — CONNECTIONS

Environmental Issues of the Twenty-first Century

The industrialized world has purchased prosperity at the expense of the environment. The conflict between economic growth and environmental protection may well become the central issue of the twenty-first century.

The disappearing ozone layer—part of the upper atmosphere—is linked to the widespread use of chlorofluorocarbons (CFCs), commonly found in such products as aerosols and foam packaging. Ozone depletion may cause an increase in skin cancer. Another concern is global warming caused by high levels of carbon dioxide and other gases that trap heat from the sun in the atmosphere and cause a greenhouse effect. The destruction of rain forests, which absorb carbon dioxide and release oxygen, compounds the problem. Many scientists believe that global warming could cause polar ice caps to melt, raising ocean levels and flooding coastal cities.

Disposal of wastes, especially toxic and nuclear materials, will also be a continuing issue. The United States alone produces 40 million tons of toxic wastes annually.

▲ Effects of Acid Rain

▲ Scientists taking water samples, Arctic research project

Making the Environment Connection
1. What is the cause of global warming?
2. How do you think future technology will affect environmental problems?

Linking Past and Present
3. What can individuals do to slow down the destruction of the environment?

CHAPTER 36 CONNECTIONS

Teaching Making Connections
Point out that scientists estimate the greenhouse effect will cause a 2 to 7 degrees Fahrenheit (1 to 4 degrees Celsius) rise in average temperatures in the next 75 years. This is way beyond the range of normal temperature change. Ask students to discuss the impact this warming will have on agriculture.

Did You Know?
Some scientists say that although global warming may have little effect at the equator, it will have enormous consequences at the poles. If the polar ice caps begin to melt, sea levels will rise. As a result much of Florida would be flooded.

Answers to CONNECTIONS
1. accumulation of carbon dioxide and other gases in the atmosphere; these gases trap heat from sun
2. Technological developments are largely responsible for today's environmental problems. However, new technology helps scientists understand and combat environmental problems.
3. Answers will vary but may include recycling, car-pooling, using reusable grocery bags.

INTEGRATING Language Arts

American Literary Heritage

Historical Setting

Although the United States remains a unique blend of ethnic, religious, and cultural diversity, immigrants do possess one common thread: Most must adopt a new language. Despite the obvious values of a bilingual upbringing, such an existence poses challenges.

Background

An autobiography is the narrative of a person's life, as written by that particular individual. Most autobiographies possess a chronological narrative; most are psychological in nature. Autobiographies run the gamut from the historical to the kiss-and-tell. Most, however, are similar in emphasis. Analysis, subjectivity, and self-examination are prominent.

About the Author

Born to blue-collar Mexican immigrants, Richard Rodriguez was reared in Sacramento, California. In what he calls "an accident of geography," he attended a Catholic grade school whose students were primarily well-to-do Caucasians. It was there that he embarked on his long journey toward assimilation. A graduate of Stanford University, Rodriguez attended graduate school in London. He now resides in San Francisco, where he works as an essayist. A lecturer on current educational trends, his views on education have resulted in his becoming a rather controversial figure.

▲ RICHARD RODRIGUEZ

Hispanic Americans cherish their heritage, and many speak only Spanish among their friends and family. However, most of their children's teachers speak only English. As a result, Hispanic students often find school confusing and humiliating. Richard Rodriguez describes his struggle to become "educated" in his autobiography, *Hunger of Memory*. As you read this excerpt, notice how the author's attitude toward books changes.

Hunger of Memory (excerpts)

From an early age I knew that my mother and father could read and write both Spanish and English. . . . For both my parents, however, reading was something done out of necessity and as quickly as possible. . . . Their reading consisted of work manuals, prayer books, newspapers, recipes. . . .

. . . I privately wondered: What was the connection between reading and learning? Did one learn something only by reading it? . . . [A sign said:] CONSIDER BOOKS YOUR BEST FRIENDS. Friends? Reading was, at best, only a chore. I needed to look up whole paragraphs of words in a dictionary. Lines of type were dizzying, the eye having to move slowly across the page, then down, and across. . . . What bothered me most, however, was the isolation reading required. To console myself for the loneliness I'd feel when I read, I tried reading in a very soft voice. Until: "Who is doing all that talking to his neighbor?" Shortly after, remedial reading classes were arranged for me with a very old nun.

At the end of each school day, for nearly six months, I would meet with her in the tiny room that served as the school's library. . . . Most of the time we took turns. I began with my elementary text. Sentences of astonishing simplicity seemed to me lifeless and drab: "The boys ran from the rain. . . . She wanted to sing. . . . The kite rose in the blue." Then the old nun would read from her favorite books, usually biographies of early American presidents. Playfully she ran through complex sentences, calling the words alive with her voice, making it seem that the author somehow was speaking directly to me. I smiled just to listen to her. I sat there and sensed for the very first time some possibility of fellowship between a reader and a writer, a communication. . . .

I entered high school having read hundreds of books. My habit of reading made me a confident speaker and writer of English. Reading also enabled me to sense something of the shape, the major

UNIT 10 Redefining America: 1954–Present

Cultural Diversity

Two other autobiographical works by Hispanic authors have gained acclaim since their publications. One such book is Ernesto Galarza's *Barrio Boy* (1971). Born in Mexico, Galarza emigrated to Sacramento's *barrio*. *Barrio Boy* is the story of his assimilation. Other works by Galarza include *Zoo Risa* and *Merchants of Labor*.

Gary Soto, a professor of Chicano Studies at the University of California at Berkeley, wrote a collection of essays, *Living Up the Street*. Like Galarza's work, it depicts a boyhood in the *barrio*. Soto's work earned the American Book Award in 1985.

concerns, of Western thought.... In these various ways books brought me academic success as I hoped that they would. But I was not a good reader. Merely bookish, I lacked a point of view when I read. Rather, I read in order to acquire a point of view. I vacuumed books for epigrams, scraps of information, ideas, themes—anything to fill the hollow within me and make me feel educated....

...One day I came across a newspaper article about the retirement of an English professor at a nearby state college. The article was accompanied by a list of the "hundred most important books of Western Civilization." "More than anything else in my life," the professor told the reporter with finality, "These books have made me all that I am." ... I clipped out the list and kept it for the several months it took me to read all of the titles. Most books, of course, I barely understood. While reading Plato's *Republic*, for instance, I needed to keep looking at the book's jacket comments to remind myself what the text was about. Nevertheless ... I looked at every word of the text. And by the time I reached the last word, relieved, I convinced myself that I had read *The Republic*. In a ceremony of pride, I solemnly crossed Plato off my list.

THE LIBRARY BY JACOB LAWRENCE, 1960

Interpreting Literature
1. How did the writer's attitude toward reading change over time?
2. What benefits from reading do you think the writer especially appreciated because he was Hispanic American?

Making Comparisons
3. Why do you think Rodriguez's parents viewed books differently from his teachers?

INTEGRATING Language Arts

Developing Student Understanding
Encourage bilingual students to share some of the difficulties they have encountered in speaking different languages at home and at school. If there are no bilingual students in the class, ask students to speculate why speaking different languages at different times might prove challenging.

Explain that Richard Rodriguez presents an autobiographical account of such challenges.

Other Works of Richard Rodriguez
Prior to writing *Hunger of Memory,* Rodriguez, in the 1970s, began publishing a series of autobiographical essays dealing with his education. While a graduate student at the University of California at Berkeley, he published essays in *The Columbia Forum* (1973) and *The American Scholar* (1974). He later published essays in *College English* (1978) and *Change* (1978). These essays, first published in scholarly journals and then refined and transformed, became the basis for this autobiography.

Answers to INTERPRETING LITERATURE
1. At first he found reading a chore, but eventually he learned to read for pleasure.
2. He writes that his "habit of reading made me a confident speaker and writer of English."
3. Like many Hispanic Americans, his parents probably spoke and thought in Spanish, so reading in English was a chore for them. However, the teacher's first language was English, so reading was a pleasure.

REVIEW CHAPTER 36

Answers

Reviewing Facts

1. Liberals believe that government should be active and compassionate; conservatives believe in government restraint and more individual initiative.
2. Because, Clinton said, the United States needed a strong economy in order to improve conditions internally and to play a strong role as a world leader.
3. gave grants to cities and states to hire more police, increased prison sentences, banned assault weapons, provided money for athletics to keep young people off the streets; overall focus on prevention
4. Some splits occurred within the Democratic party over the role of government while Republicans remained united.
5. There was initial shock and horror but resistance to sending in American troops. The government supported the UN and established an arms embargo, whose funding was later cut off by the U.S. The U.S. also tried to persuade European allies to stage air attacks, and finally former President Jimmy Carter managed to negotiate a ceasefire.
6. felt he had to enforce the order to stem the flood of Haitian refugees entering the country
7. Beginnings of democracy restored in Haiti; peace accords established between Israel and the PLO and between Israel and Jordan
8. U.S. signed agreements to break down trade barriers while industry downsized to become more efficient. Multinational corporations built factories overseas and sold more and more goods, which decreased the trade deficit.

Understanding Concepts

1. Voters blamed incumbents for the recession, the trade deficit, and government gridlock, and they were angered at scandals within government. Clinton declared that he would reinvent government and bring change and reform. He proposed a deficit-reduction act and developed an anticrime program. Although it was defeated, he proposed a sweeping health-care plan.
2. Poverty, crime and violence, the environment, drugs, health care, and immigration are among the challenges to be faced. Answers will vary but should be reasonable and backed up with facts and evidence.

CHAPTER 36 ★ REVIEW

Using Vocabulary

Assume that you are a magazine reporter covering the state of the economy during the Clinton administration. Write an article detailing your findings using the following vocabulary words.

   global economy
   multinational corporation
   trade deficit
   creditor nation
   debtor nation
   globalized corporation

Reviewing Facts

1. **Discuss** the differences between liberal and conservative approaches to government.
2. **Explain** why Clinton charged that the economic recession was Bush's most glaring failure.
3. **Describe** Clinton's crime program, including its overall focus.
4. **Explain** why gridlock in Congress reappeared despite the fact that the Democrats controlled the Presidency and held majorities in both the House and the Senate.
5. **Summarize** the United States's reaction to the war in Bosnia.
6. **Describe** why President Clinton decided to turn back Haitian refugees instead of granting them asylum after he had criticized Bush for doing the same thing.
7. **Describe** the positive breakthroughs in world affairs in which the United States played a part.
8. **Summarize** how America became more competitive in order to take its place in the new world order.

Understanding Concepts

Change

1. Why did Americans demand that politicians "reinvent government," and how did Clinton proceed to carry out this charge?

Challenge

2. What challenges do the American people face in the future, and what are some possible solutions to them?

Critical Thinking

1. **Synthesizing Information** Were any of the problems the United States faced in the last decade of the twentieth century truly new? Explain your answer.
2. **Analyzing Art** The personal computer has become a common tool in homes, schools, and offices. In addition, the computer has revolutionized graphic, illustrated, and animated art. Study the art on this page and answer the questions that follow.
   a. Does the computer extend the creative capacity of artists? Explain.
   b. What do you think the artist is trying to say in this work?
   c. What title would you give it?

1024 UNIT 10 Redefining America: 1954–Present

CHAPTER 36 ★ REVIEW

Writing About History

Argumentation

Write an argument that supports or opposes the Clinton health-care plan. State the controversy or problem clearly, and give your position or your solution to the problem. Gather relevant facts and statistics that support your position and logically disprove opposing positions.

Cooperative Learning

Form a study group and research news sources to determine recent happenings in Somalia, the Balkans, Haiti, and the Middle East. Evaluate the continuing major problems in each area, the key figures working out solutions, any additional breakthroughs that have occurred, and how these further developments could affect the United States. Present your findings to the class.

Social Studies Skills

Analyzing Trends

Equality in the workplace is an ideal goal for many Americans. Several groups of people have strived for equality for women and/or minority groups in the United States. Analyzing data in a table can help determine these groups' success.

To analyze a table and determine trends, you must carefully examine the title, all the heads, and the data in each row and column of the table. By comparing each row and each column you can determine any similarities and patterns.

Practicing the Skill

Use the table on this page to answer the following questions.

1. What are the three parts of the table?

2. In order for the percentage of women and minorities in the workforce to increase, what group's percentage must decrease? Is this happening?

3. Are minorities and women achieving equality of earnings in the workplace?

The Labor Force, 1983–1993

	1983	1985	1990	1993
Total workforce (in thousands)	70,976	77,002	85,082	85,211
Percentage of total workforce				
Male	59.6	59.2	57.6	56.8
Female	40.4	40.8	42.4	43.2
White	87.0	86.3	85.4	85.0
Black	10.4	10.9	11.3	11.4
of Hispanic origin	NA	NA	8.2	8.3
Ratio of weekly median earnings				
Females to Males	66.7	68.2	71.8	76.8
Blacks to Whites	81.8	78.0	77.0	77.4
Hispanics to Whites	NA	NA	71.9	70.0

Source: *Statistical Abstract of the United States*, 1994.

4. How do the percentages of minorities in the workforce compare with the percentages of those minorities in the population? (See the Chapter Review for Chapter 32.)

Using Your Journal

From your journal notes and knowledge of the immigration issue in America, would you choose to be an immigrant at this time? Explain your answer.

Cultural Kaleidoscope

Making Connections
History and Sociology

Rock music was the first form of popular music in the United States to appeal specifically to teenagers. For many it symbolized rebellion against an older generation devoted to the smooth pop songs of the 1940s and early 1950s. Young people were not only attracted by the strong beat and pulsing sounds of rock 'n' roll, they also had enough money to buy records in quantity in this affluent era, and thus be reckoned with as serious consumers.

More About... Rock Musicals

Rock did not have much impact on Broadway shows until the late 1960s. The first big hit was *Hair* (1967). It was followed by *Tommy* (1968) and *Jesus Christ Superstar* (1971). Another popular musical, *Grease* (1972), spoofed high school life in the rock 'n' roll era of the 1950s.

Cultural Kaleidoscope

The World of Music

ROCKING INTO THE FUTURE

Rock and roll music has been one of the most popular forms of musical expression in the twentieth century. It began as a mixture of styles, borrowing elements from rhythm and blues and country music as well as the popular ballads of the 1950s. Today's rock musicians show the willingness to explore new boundaries. In pushing for new sounds, they have made use of synthesizers and electronic sounds, classical instrumentation, and Latin and African phrasings and rhythms. Rock performers in the late 1900s have created one of the most popular and unique postwar arts.

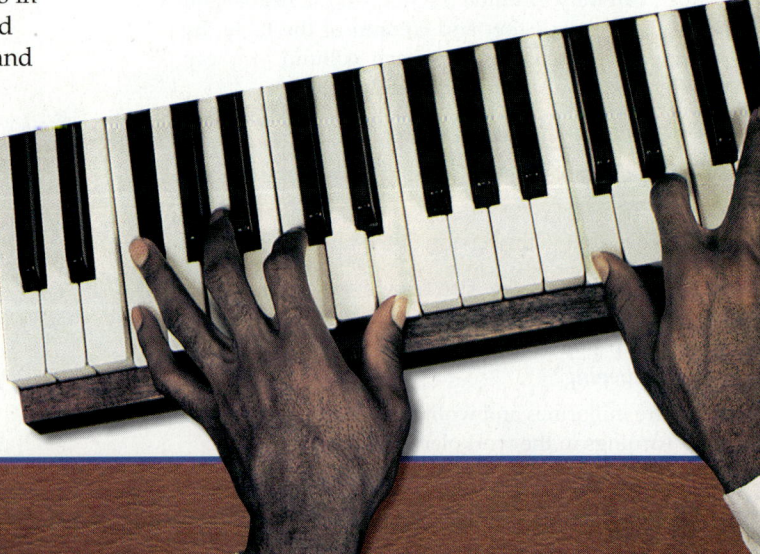

▲ In the late 1970s and early 1980s, Janet Jackson was best known as the sister of Michael Jackson and for her appearances in televised situation comedies. Her musical albums *Rhythm Nation* and *Janet* pushed her to the top echelon of rock performers.

▶ Such keyboard instruments as the piano, organ, and synthesizer add to rock's eclectic appeal.

1026

Cooperative Learning

Divide the class into five groups. Assign each one a pioneering figure from the early days of rock: Elvis Presley, Bill Haley, Chuck Berry, Buddy Holly, and the Beatles. Have each one research its topic and report to the class. **L2**

▶ Innovations ranging from the jukebox to the compact disc have helped the popular appeal of rock and roll.

▼ Whitney Houston's billowy soprano voice made "I Will Always Love You" one of the top-selling singles of the 1990s.

▼ The appeal of Seattle's Pearl Jam is based on the group's hard-rocking sound and the expressive vocals of lead singer Eddie Vedder.

Cultural Kaleidoscope

Portfolio Project

Have students clip articles from newspapers or periodicals about rock performers in the news. In each case they should (a) note who the story is about, and (b) summarize the main idea of the article.

The Historian's Craft

Many social historians are interested in how popular music reflects the spirit of the times. Throughout this century, titles and lyrics have told a story of their own: the jaunty "Over There" from World War I, the sad "Brother, Can You Spare a Dime?" from the Depression years, and the spirited "Praise the Lord and Pass the Ammunition" from World War II. Rock music, too, has mirrored its times. While Bob Dylan's "Blowin' in the Wind" symbolized the socially conscious 1960s, Michael Jackson's "Thriller" typified the excitement and technical sophistication of 1980s rock videos.

UNIT 10 DIGEST

The Unit Digest may be used to teach unit coverage when time is limited, to review unit content, or to relate content of one unit to that of another.

Unit Digest Transparencies
Use Unit 10 Digest Transparency.

■ Chapter 32
Have students construct a time line showing the major events in the struggle for African American civil rights in the 1950s and 1960s. Select time lines to display on the bulletin board. Ask students which event had the greatest impact.

■ Chapter 33
Write the following statement on the chalkboard: But for his involvement in the Vietnam War, Lyndon Johnson would have been considered one of the nation's greatest presidents. Have students use information from the text to write a few paragraphs supporting or challenging the statement.

■ Chapter 34
Ask students to select a major event from Richard Nixon's presidency—his visit to China, for example. Have them imagine they are among Nixon's advisers. Ask them to write a diary expressing their feelings about the event. Invite volunteers to read their entries to the class.

■ Chapter 35
Suggest that the decades of the 1970s, 1980s, and

UNIT TEN DIGEST

Chapter 32
The Civil Rights Era
In the 1950s many African Americans renewed their fight for full equality and an end to segregation and discrimination. Their efforts were aided by the Supreme Court's decision in *Brown v. Board of Education* that stated separation by race was inherently unequal. A quiet pioneer of the civil rights movement was Rosa Parks, who in 1956 refused to give her seat on a Montgomery bus to a white man. Dr. Martin Luther King, Jr., emerged as a powerful and inspiring leader for nonviolent protest against unjust segregation laws. The efforts of the civil rights movement culminated in the March on Washington where hundreds of thousands of Americans gathered to demonstrate peacefully for racial harmony and justice.

Inspired by the energy of civil rights leaders, women and other minority groups began to work for change in their own right.

Chapter 33
The Vietnam Era
In setting United States policy in Vietnam, President Johnson was torn between his wish to limit American involvement and his fear of a communist victory. Passage of the Gulf of Tonkin Resolution gave Johnson the power to wage war on North Vietnam as he saw fit. American planes began bombing North Vietnam targets and in April 1965 the President decided to engage American troops in combat. Unable to end the war quickly, the

United States found itself increasingly drawn into the conflict.

In January 1968 North Vietnam staged the Tet offensive. Though it was turned back, Americans began to question whether or not the war could be won. When Johnson decided not to run for reelection, Republican Richard Nixon, campaigning on the promise to "bring the nation together," was elected President.

Nixon expanded the war into neighboring Cambodia and Laos to stop enemy lines of supply. This effort failed while antiwar protests increased. Finally, Nixon opted for "Vietnamization," the withdrawal of American troops and replacing them with Vietnamese soldiers.

Chapter 34
Camelot to Watergate
After narrowly winning the 1960 election, President Kennedy wanted to stimulate the economy and to improve life for the poor, but he moved cautiously on civil rights legislation. Kennedy was assassinated before many of his goals could be realized.

Vowing to continue the work of John Kennedy, President Johnson set out to implement his domestic program known as the Great Society—a blueprint for the elimination of poverty and discrimination in America. As the United States was drawn more into the Vietnam War, however, Johnson's attention focused on foreign affairs.

President Nixon came to the White House with the hope of bringing America together. A cornerstone of his domestic policy was a greater emphasis on local decision making and revenue sharing.

Nixon easily won reelection in 1972. However, throughout his second term, evidence surfaced linking high officials in his administration to a campaign of illegal activity. Finally, transcripts of secret White House tapes proved that Nixon had attempted a cover-up. Faced with impeachment, the President resigned and was succeeded by Gerald Ford.

1028   UNIT 10 Redefining America: 1954–Present

Cooperative Learning

Divide the class into groups of five. Have the groups create a questionnaire on the major issues confronting the United States today. Point out that the objective of the questionnaire is to discover what Americans think will be the greatest challenges for the nation as the twenty-first century begins. Have groups give the questionnaire to friends and family members. Groups should collate the results and present their findings to the class. Ask groups to combine their results to find the five most important issues.

Chapter 35
Search for Solutions

After Vietnam and Watergate, Americans wanted a change in leadership. Outsider Jimmy Carter barely defeated Gerald Ford in the 1976 election. Carter's domestic policy focused on the energy problem. Poor relations with Congress, however, caused his efforts to falter.

Carter displayed bold initiative in foreign policy. He won Senate ratification of a new Panama Canal treaty and took a tough stand against countries that violated human rights. His greatest triumph was negotiation of a peace treaty between Israel and Egypt. His greatest failure was his inability to secure the release of American hostages in Iran.

Republican Ronald Reagan soundly defeated Carter in the 1980 election. Reagan quickly began to lower taxes and reduce government spending on social programs. Reagan fought communism vigorously, especially in Latin America where he rallied support for contra rebels in Nicaragua. Reagan's overwhelming victory in his 1984 reelection bid demonstrated strong support for his policies.

Reagan began his second term intent on keeping the United States strong. The military buildup added to social spending sent the federal deficit soaring. In foreign affairs changing conditions in the Soviet Union eased strained relations with the United States.

The late 1980s and early 1990s were years of astonishing change. One communist government after another toppled, until even the Soviet Union split into independent republics. When Iraq invaded Kuwait in 1990, President Bush acted decisively. When Iraq refused to meet a deadline for withdrawal, United States-led forces launched a devastating series of attacks on Iraqi defenses.

Chapter 36
Toward a New Century

As the 1992 election drew near, President Bush faced challenges from within his own party as well as from Democratic and independent candidates. After 12 years of Republican rule, voters elected Democrat Bill Clinton President in 1992.

American society faced pressing problems at home and abroad. Environmentalists struggled with opponents who favored greater use of natural resources. Public health issues, such as the AIDS epidemic and drug abuse, continued to take their toll. Migration patterns to the United States changed. Immigration from Europe decreased, and immigration from Latin America and Asia increased.

The American people and government and business leaders pondered ways to deal with the federal deficit and other economic and social problems that troubled the nation.

Federal government attempts to address these problems produced few long-lasting solutions. Partisan politics played a role in the deadlock. The Clinton administration and Congress often were at odds and found it difficult to compromise.

Understanding Unit Themes

Civil Rights and Liberties

1. How have the goals of the civil rights movement evolved?

Conflict and Cooperation

2. What events since World War II helped create a spirit of cooperation between the United States and the Soviet Union? Which events represented low points in their relationship?

Cultural Diversity

3. How have immigration and increased global interdependence contributed to a more culturally diverse American society?

United States Role in World Affairs

4. Why has the United States's relationship with other countries become more interdependent since World War II?

UNIT 10 Redefining America's Role: 1954–Present   1029

UNIT 10 DIGEST

1990s have distinct moods. Ask students to consider what these moods might be. Invite them to write slogans that express these moods and compare.

Chapter 36

In the past, the United States has been called a "melting pot" because of its cultural pluralism. Recently, however, people have revised the metaphor, calling the nation a "cultural quilt." Ask students to discuss which of the two metaphors they feel is more appropriate.

Understanding Unit Themes

1. Answers will vary but may include that goals are geared toward preventing discrimination to gaining economic and social status and power.
2. Cooperation: Nuclear Test Ban Treaty, detente, SALT, Gorbachev, glasnost, summit meetings. Low points: Cuban missile crisis, Vietnam War, Berlin Wall, Middle East wars, war in Nicaragua, Soviet invasion of Afghanistan
3. Recent immigration is increasingly from Latin America and Asia. Global interdependence has forced Americans to increase their knowledge of other cultures.
4. The U.S. has become increasingly dependent on trade with other nations. Foreign investment in the U.S. has increased; U.S. investment abroad has increased.

Student Self-Test Software

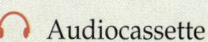 Audiocassette

The Historian's Craft

Remind students that historians analyze points of view of people involved in events in order to draw conclusions. Tell students that President Bush suggested that the United States' victory in the Gulf War had helped the nation "liberate itself from old ghosts and doubts." Have students analyze Bush's point of view by asking: To which old ghosts and doubts was Bush referring? How did victory in the Gulf "liberate" the United States from these ghosts and doubts? Given recent developments at home and in the Middle East, do you think Bush was correct? Why or why not?

Appendix Contents

Atlas

The World	1032
United States	1034
North America	1036
Latin America	1037
Eurasia	1038
The Middle East	1040
Africa	1042
Mainland Southeast Asia	1043

United States Databank	1044
Presidents of the United States	1048
Documents of America's Heritage	1055
Gazetteer	1073
Glossary	1080
Index	1089
Acknowledgments and Credits	1115

Atlas Key

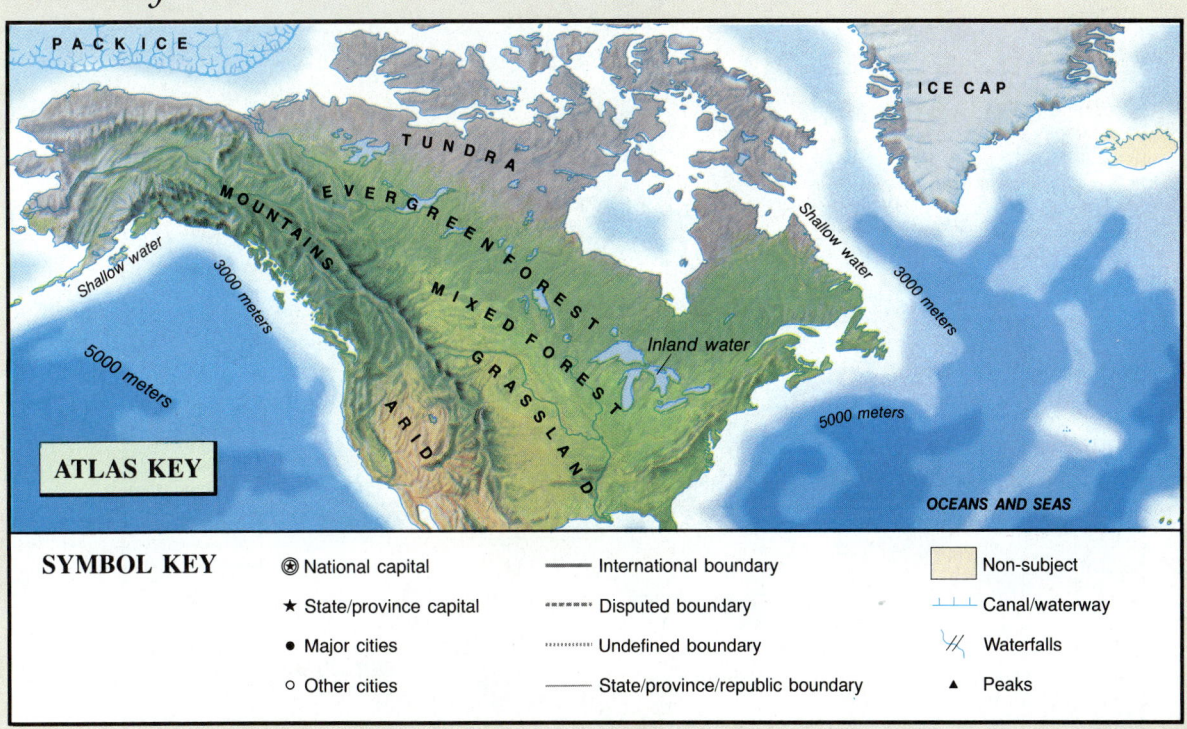

United States Databank

Population of the United States

Year	Population	Pop/sq mi	% increase	Year	Population	Pop/sq mi	% increase
1790	3,929,214	4.5	–	1900	76,212,168	21.5	21.0
1800	5,308,483	6.1	35.1	1910	92,228,496	26.0	21.0
1810	7,239,881	4.3	36.4	1920	106,021,537	29.9	15.0
1820	9,638,453	5.5	33.1	1930	123,202,624	34.7	16.2
1830	12,866,020	7.4	33.5	1940	132,164,569	37.2	7.3
1840	17,069,453	9.8	32.7	1950	151,325,798	42.6	14.5
1850	23,191,876	7.9	35.9	1960	179,323,175	50.6	18.5
1860	31,443,321	10.6	35.6	1970	203,302,031	57.5	13.4
1870	38,558,371	10.9	22.6	1980	226,542,203	64.0	11.4
1880	50,189,209	14.2	30.2	1990	248,709,873	70.3	9.8
1890	62,979,766	17.8	25.5				

Key:
- Population per square mile of land
- Percentage increase over preceding census

Source: U.S. Department of the Census; *Statistical Abstract of the United States*, 1994.

Population Distribution by Age

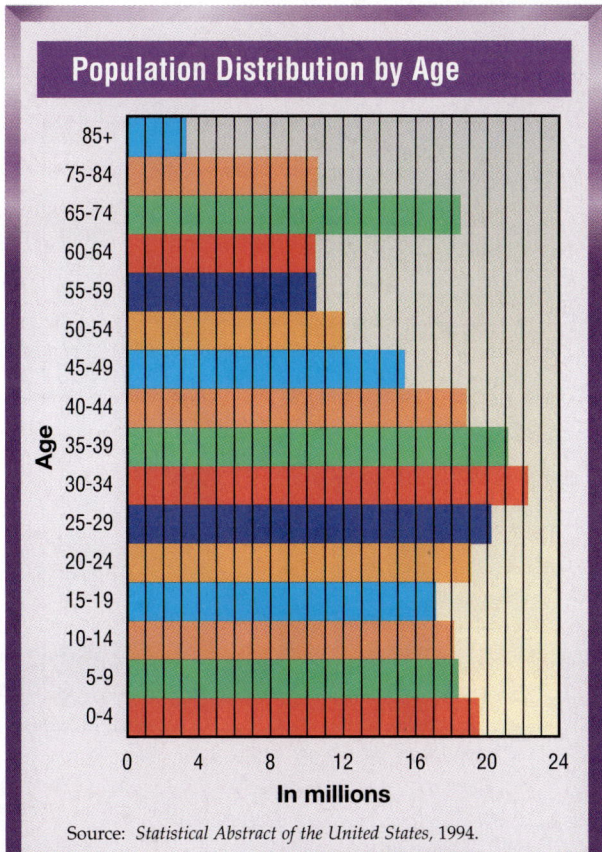

Source: *Statistical Abstract of the United States*, 1994.

Major Religions in the United States

Roman Catholic Church	58,267
Southern Baptist Convention	15,232
United Methodist Church	8,785
National Baptist Convention	3,500
Muslims	6,000
Jews	5,981
Evangelical Lutheran Church	5,245
Church of Jesus Christ of Latter-Day Saints (Mormon)	4,336
Church of God in Christ (Pentecostal)	3,710
Presbyterian Church (U.S.A.)	3,778
National Baptist Convention of America	3,500
Lutheran Church (Missouri Synod)	2,607
Episcopal Church	2,472
African Methodist Episcopal Church	3,500
Assemblies of God	2,235
Greek Orthodox Archdiocese of North and South America	1,950
United Church of Christ	1,584
Churches of Christ	1,690
American Baptist Churches in the U.S.A.	1,528
African Methodist Episcopal Zion Church	1,200
Christian Churches and Churches of Christ	1,071
Christian Church (Disciples of Christ)	1,023
Orthodox Church in America	1,030

In thousands

Source: *Statistical Abstract of the United States*, 1994; *Time* magazine (November 19, 1990).

United States Databank

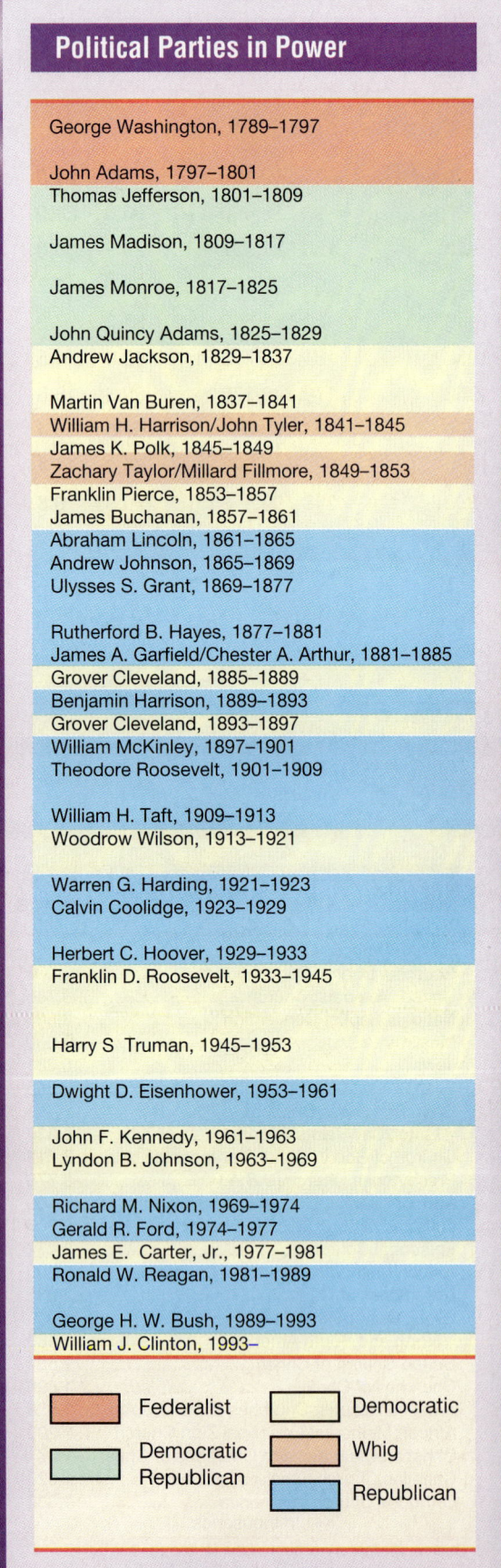

Political Parties in Power

George Washington, 1789–1797

John Adams, 1797–1801
Thomas Jefferson, 1801–1809

James Madison, 1809–1817

James Monroe, 1817–1825

John Quincy Adams, 1825–1829
Andrew Jackson, 1829–1837

Martin Van Buren, 1837–1841
William H. Harrison/John Tyler, 1841–1845
James K. Polk, 1845–1849
Zachary Taylor/Millard Fillmore, 1849–1853
Franklin Pierce, 1853–1857
James Buchanan, 1857–1861
Abraham Lincoln, 1861–1865
Andrew Johnson, 1865–1869
Ulysses S. Grant, 1869–1877

Rutherford B. Hayes, 1877–1881
James A. Garfield/Chester A. Arthur, 1881–1885
Grover Cleveland, 1885–1889
Benjamin Harrison, 1889–1893
Grover Cleveland, 1893–1897
William McKinley, 1897–1901
Theodore Roosevelt, 1901–1909

William H. Taft, 1909–1913
Woodrow Wilson, 1913–1921

Warren G. Harding, 1921–1923
Calvin Coolidge, 1923–1929

Herbert C. Hoover, 1929–1933
Franklin D. Roosevelt, 1933–1945

Harry S Truman, 1945–1953

Dwight D. Eisenhower, 1953–1961

John F. Kennedy, 1961–1963
Lyndon B. Johnson, 1963–1969

Richard M. Nixon, 1969–1974
Gerald R. Ford, 1974–1977
James E. Carter, Jr., 1977–1981
Ronald W. Reagan, 1981–1989

George H. W. Bush, 1989–1993
William J. Clinton, 1993–

Legend: Federalist, Democratic-Republican, Democratic, Whig, Republican

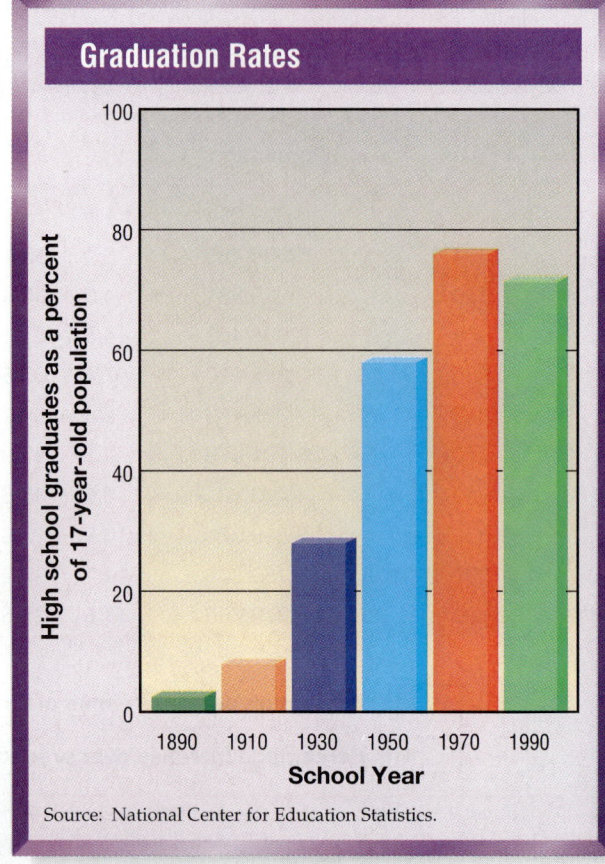

Graduation Rates

High school graduates as a percent of 17-year-old population, School Year 1890–1990.

Source: National Center for Education Statistics.

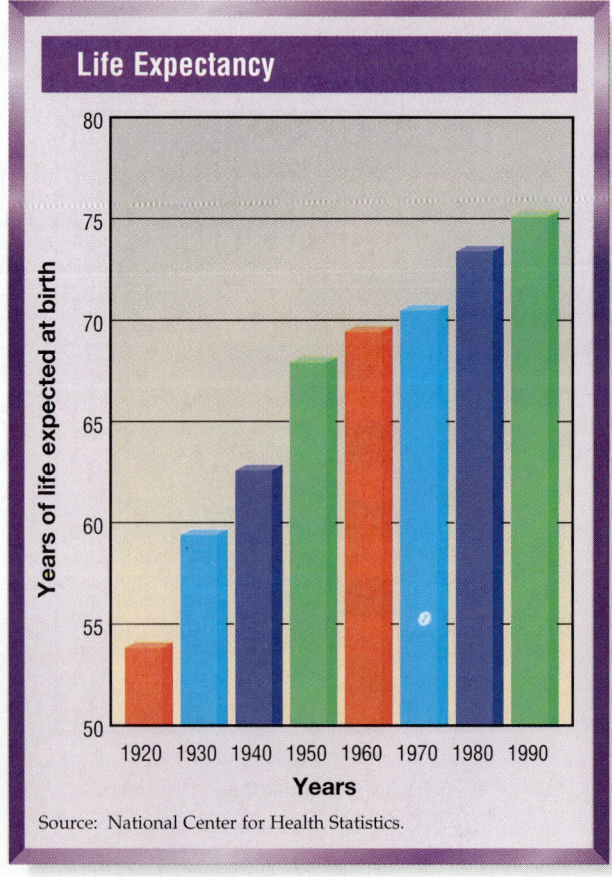

Life Expectancy

Years of life expected at birth, 1920–1990.

Source: National Center for Health Statistics.

1046 United States Databank

The United States

STATE*	YEAR ADMITTED	POPULATION (1990)	LAND AREA (sq mi)	CAPITAL	LARGEST CITY	HOUSE REP. (1990)**
1. Delaware	1787	666,168	1,954	Dover	Wilmington	1
2. Pennsylvania	1787	11,881,643	44,819	Harrisburg	Philadelphia	21
3. New Jersey	1787	7,730,188	7,418	Trenton	Newark	13
4. Georgia	1788	6,478,216	57,918	Atlanta	Atlanta	11
5. Connecticut	1788	3,287,116	4,845	Hartford	Bridgeport	6
6. Massachusetts	1788	6,016,425	7,838	Boston	Boston	10
7. Maryland	1788	4,781,468	9,774	Annapolis	Baltimore	8
8. South Carolina	1788	3,486,703	30,111	Columbia	Columbia	6
9. New Hampshire	1788	1,109,252	8,969	Concord	Manchester	2
10. Virginia	1788	6,187,358	39,597	Richmond	Virginia Beach	11
11. New York	1788	17,990,455	47,223	Albany	New York	31
12. North Carolina	1789	6,628,637	48,718	Raleigh	Charlotte	12
13. Rhode Island	1790	1,003,464	1,045	Providence	Providence	2
14. Vermont	1791	562,758	9,249	Montpelier	Burlington	1
15. Kentucky	1792	3,685,296	39,732	Frankfort	Louisville	6
16. Tennessee	1796	4,877,185	41,219	Nashville	Memphis	9
17. Ohio	1803	10,847,115	40,952	Columbus	Columbus	19
18. Louisiana	1812	4,219,973	43,566	Baton Rouge	New Orleans	7
19. Indiana	1816	5,544,159	35,870	Indianapolis	Indianapolis	10
20. Mississippi	1817	2,573,216	46,913	Jackson	Jackson	5
21. Illinois	1818	11,430,602	55,593	Springfield	Chicago	20
22. Alabama	1819	4,040,587	50,750	Montgomery	Birmingham	7
23. Maine	1820	1,227,928	30,864	Augusta	Portland	2
24. Missouri	1821	5,117,073	68,898	Jefferson City	Kansas City	9
25. Arkansas	1836	2,350,725	52,075	Little Rock	Little Rock	4
26. Michigan	1837	9,295,297	56,809	Lansing	Detroit	16
27. Florida	1845	12,937,926	53,997	Tallahassee	Jacksonville	23
28. Texas	1845	16,986,510	261,194	Austin	Houston	30
29. Iowa	1846	2,776,755	55,874	Des Moines	Des Moines	5
30. Wisconsin	1848	4,891,769	54,313	Madison	Milwaukee	9
31. California	1850	29,760,021	155,973	Sacramento	Los Angeles	52
32. Minnesota	1858	4,375,099	79,616	St. Paul	Minneapolis	8
33. Oregon	1859	2,853,733	96,002	Salem	Portland	5
34. Kansas	1861	2,477,574	81,823	Topeka	Wichita	4
35. West Virginia	1863	1,793,477	24,086	Charleston	Charleston	3
36. Nevada	1864	1,201,833	109,805	Carson City	Las Vegas	2
37. Nebraska	1867	1,578,385,	76,877	Lincoln	Omaha	3
38. Colorado	1876	3,294,394	103,729	Denver	Denver	6
39. North Dakota	1889	638,800	68,994	Bismarck	Fargo	1
40. South Dakota	1889	696,004	75,897	Pierre	Sioux Falls	1
41. Montana	1889	799,065	145,556	Helena	Billings	1
42. Washington	1889	4,887,941	66,581	Olympia	Seattle	9
43. Idaho	1890	1,006,749	82,750	Boise	Boise	2
44. Wyoming	1890	455,975	97,104	Cheyenne	Cheyenne	1
45. Utah	1896	1,727,784	82,168	Salt Lake City	Salt Lake City	3
46. Oklahoma	1907	3,145,585	68,678	Oklahoma City	Oklahoma City	6
47. New Mexico	1912	1,515,069	121,364	Sante Fe	Albuquerque	3
48. Arizona	1912	3,665,228	113,642	Phoenix	Phoenix	6
49. Alaska	1959	550,043	570,373	Juneau	Anchorage	1
50. Hawaii	1959	1,108,229	6,423	Honolulu	Honolulu	2
District of Columbia (Washington, D.C.)	–	606,900	61	–	–	–
United States of America	–	248,709,873	3,536,341	Washington, D.C.	New York	435

* Numbers denote the order in which states were admitted.
** Number of members in House of Representatives

THE PRESIDENTS

The President's power and influence touch the lives of all Americans and the lives of citizens throughout the world. Each of the Presidents has expressed his hopes and views for the nation in dramatic and unique language. The passages that follow are excerpts from presidential statements and addresses.

George Washington

It is our true policy to steer clear of permanent alliances with any portion of the foreign world, so far, I mean, as we are now at liberty to do it; for let me not be understood as capable of patronizing infidelity to existing engagements, I hold the maxim no less applicable to public than to private affairs that honesty is always the best policy.

*Farewell Address
September 17, 1796*

John Adams

Employed in the service of my country . . . I first saw the Constitution of the United States in a foreign country. Irritated by no literary altercation, animated by no public debate, heated by no party animosity, I read it with great satisfaction, as the result of good heads prompted by good hearts, as an experiment better adapted to the genius, character, situation, and relations of this nation and country than any which had ever been proposed or suggested.

*Inaugural Address
March 4, 1797*

Presidents of the United States

** The Republican party during this period developed into today's Democratic party. Today's Republican party originated in 1854.

George Washington

1

1789–1797

Born: 1732
Died: 1799
Born in: Virginia
Elected from: Virginia
Age when elected: 56
Occupations: Planter, Soldier
Party: None
Vice President: John Adams

John Adams

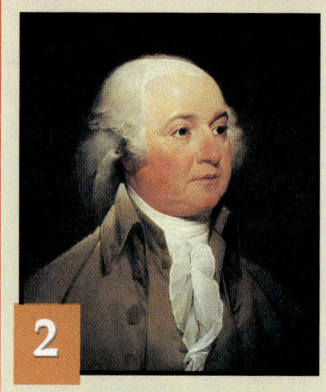

2

1797–1801

Born: 1735
Died: 1826
Born in: Massachusetts
Elected from: Massachusetts
Age when elected: 61
Occupations: Teacher, Lawyer
Party: Federalist
Vice President: Thomas Jefferson

Thomas Jefferson

3

1801–1809

Born: 1743
Died: 1826
Born in: Virginia
Elected from: Virginia
Age when elected: 57
Occupations: Planter, Lawyer
Party: Republican**
Vice Presidents: Aaron Burr, George Clinton

James Madison

4

1809–1817

Born: 1751
Died: 1836
Born in: Virginia
Elected from: Virginia
Age when elected: 57
Occupation: Planter
Party: Republican**
Vice Presidents: George Clinton, Elbridge Gerry

James Monroe

5

1817–1825

Born: 1758
Died: 1831
Born in: Virginia
Elected from: Virginia
Age when elected: 58
Occupation: Lawyer
Party: Republican**
Vice President: Daniel D. Tompkins

Thomas Jefferson

We are all Republicans, we are all Federalists. If there be any among us who would wish to dissolve this Union or to change its republican form, let them stand undisturbed as monuments of the safety with which error of opinion may be tolerated. . . .

*First Inaugural Address
March 4, 1801*

James Madison

If I do not sink under the weight . . . it is because I find some support in a consciousness of the purposes and a confidence in the principles which I bring. . . . To cherish peace and friendly intercourse with all nations. . . .

*First Inaugural Address
March 4, 1809*

James Monroe

[T]he American continents, by the free and independent condition which they have assumed and maintain, are henceforth not to be considered as subjects for future colonization by any European powers. . . .

*Address to Congress
December 2, 1823*

THE PRESIDENTS

John Quincy Adams

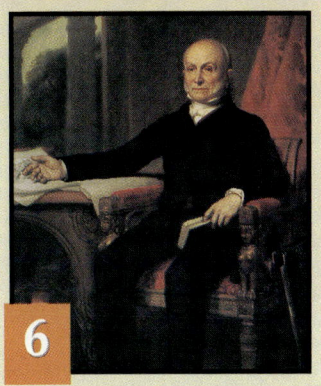

6
1825–1829

Born: 1767
Died: 1848
Born in: Massachusetts
Elected from: Massachusetts
Age when elected: 57
Occupation: Lawyer
Party: Republican**
Vice President: John C. Calhoun

Andrew Jackson

7
1829–1837

Born: 1767
Died: 1845
Born in: South Carolina
Elected from: Tennessee
Age when elected: 61
Occupations: Lawyer, Soldier
Party: Democratic
Vice Presidents: John C. Calhoun, Martin Van Buren

Martin Van Buren

8
1837–1841

Born: 1782
Died: 1862
Born in: New York
Elected from: New York
Age when elected: 54
Occupation: Lawyer
Party: Democratic
Vice President: Richard M. Johnson

William H. Harrison

9
1841

Born: 1773
Died: 1841
Born in: Virginia
Elected from: Ohio
Age when elected: 67
Occupations: Soldier, Planter
Party: Whig
Vice President: John Tyler

John Tyler

10
1841–1845

Born: 1790
Died: 1862
Born in: Virginia
Elected as V.P. from: Virginia
Succeeded Harrison
Age when became President: 51
Occupation: Lawyer
Party: Whig
Vice President: None

James K. Polk

11
1845–1849

Born: 1795
Died: 1849
Born in: North Carolina
Elected from: Tennessee
Age when elected: 49
Occupation: Lawyer
Party: Democratic
Vice President: George M. Dallas

John Quincy Adams

The spirit of improvement is abroad upon the earth. It stimulates the hearts and sharpens the faculties not of our fellow-citizens alone, but of the nations of Europe and of their rulers.... [L]et us not be unmindful that liberty is power; that the nation blessed with the largest portion of liberty must... be the most powerful nation upon earth, and that the tenure of power by man is... to improve the condition of himself and his fellow men.

Address to Congress
December 6, 1825

Andrew Jackson

The time at which I stand before you is full of interest. The eyes of all nations are fixed on our Republic.... Great is the stake placed in our hands; great is the responsibility which must rest upon the people of the United States. Let us realize the importance of the attitude in which we stand before the world. Let us exercise forbearance and firmness.

Second Inaugural Address
March 4, 1833

Martin Van Buren

Position and climate and the bounteous resources that nature has scattered with so liberal a hand... will avail us nothing if we fail sacredly to uphold those political institutions that were wisely and deliberately formed with reference to every circumstance that could preserve or might endanger the blessings we enjoy.

Inaugural Address
March 4, 1837

William H. Harrison

We admit of no government by divine right, believing that so far as power is concerned the Beneficent Creator has made no distinction amongst men; that all are upon an equality,...

Inaugural Address
March 4, 1841

John Tyler

The Constitution itself I regard and cherish as the embodied and written will of the whole people of the United States. It is their fixed and fundamental law....

September 9, 1841

James K. Polk

... the Chief Magistrate must almost of necessity be chosen by a party and stand pledged to its principles... yet in his official action he should not be the President of a part only, but of the whole people of the United States.

Inaugural Address
March 4, 1845

THE PRESIDENTS

Zachary Taylor
Under these circumstances I thought, and still think, that it was my duty to endeavor to put it in the power of Congress, by the admission of California and New Mexico as States, to remove all occasion for the unnecessary agitation of the public mind.
*Address to Congress
January 1850*

Millard Fillmore
The duty of the Executive extends only to the execution of laws and the maintenance of treaties already in force and the protection of all the people of the United States in the enjoyment of the rights which those treaties and laws guarantee.
*Special Message to Congress
August 6, 1850*

Franklin Pierce
The great objects of our pursuit as a people are best to be attained by peace, and are entirely consistent with the tranquillity and interests of the rest of mankind.
*Inaugural Address
March 4, 1853*

James Buchanan
It may be asked, then, Are the people of the States without redress against the tyranny and oppression of the Federal Government? By no means. The right of resistance on the part of the governed against the oppression of their government can not be denied.
*Address to Congress
December 3, 1860*

Zachary Taylor

12
1849–1850
Born: 1784
Died: 1850
Born in: Virginia
Elected from: Louisiana
Age when elected: 63
Occupation: Soldier
Party: Whig
Vice President: Millard Fillmore

Millard Fillmore

13
1850–1853
Born: 1800
Died: 1874
Born in: New York
Elected as V.P. from: New York
Succeeded Taylor
Age when became President: 50
Occupation: Lawyer
Party: Whig
Vice President: None

Franklin Pierce

14
1853–1857
Born: 1804
Died: 1869
Born in: New Hampshire
Elected from: New Hampshire
Age when elected: 47
Occupation: Lawyer
Party: Democratic
Vice President: William R. King

James Buchanan

15
1857–1861
Born: 1791
Died: 1868
Born in: Pennsylvania
Elected from: Pennsylvania
Age when elected: 65
Occupation: Lawyer
Party: Democratic
Vice President: John G. Breckinridge

Abraham Lincoln

16
1861–1865
Born: 1809
Died: 1865
Born in: Kentucky
Elected from: Illinois
Age when elected: 51
Occupation: Lawyer
Party: Republican
Vice Presidents: Hannibal Hamlin, Andrew Johnson

Andrew Johnson

17
1865–1869
Born: 1808
Died: 1875
Born in: North Carolina
Elected as V.P. from: Tennessee
Age when became President: 56
Succeeded Lincoln
Occupation: Tailor
Party: Republican
Vice President: None

Abraham Lincoln
I therefore consider that in view of the Constitution and the laws the Union is unbroken, and to the extent of my ability I shall take care, as the Constitution itself expressly enjoins upon me, that the laws of the Union be faithfully executed in all the States.
*First Inaugural Address
March 4, 1861*

Andrew Johnson
Some persons assume that the success of our arms in crushing the opposition which was made in some of the States . . . reduced those States and all their people — the innocent as well as the guilty — to the condition of vassalage and gave us a power over them which the Constitution does not bestow or define or limit. No fallacy can be more transparent than this.
*Veto Message
March 2, 1867*

THE PRESIDENTS

Ulysses S. Grant

18

1869–1877

Born: 1822
Died: 1885
Born in: Ohio
Elected from: Illinois
Age when elected: 46
Occupations: Farmer, Soldier
Party: Republican
Vice Presidents: Schuyler Colfax, Henry Wilson

Rutherford B. Hayes

19

1877–1881

Born: 1822
Died: 1893
Born in: Ohio
Elected from: Ohio
Age when elected: 54
Occupation: Lawyer
Party: Republican
Vice President: William A. Wheeler

James A. Garfield

20

1881

Born: 1831
Died: 1881
Born in: Ohio
Elected from: Ohio
Age when elected: 49
Occupations: Laborer, Professor
Party: Republican
Vice President: Chester A. Arthur

Chester A. Arthur

21

1881–1885

Born: 1830
Died: 1886
Born in: Vermont
Elected as V.P. from: New York
Succeeded Garfield
Age when became President: 50
Occupations: Teacher, Lawyer
Party: Republican
Vice President: None

Grover Cleveland

22 **24**

1885–89, 1893–97

Born: 1837
Died: 1908
Born in: New Jersey
Elected from: New York
Age when elected: 47; 55
Occupation: Lawyer
Party: Democratic
Vice Presidents: Thomas A. Hendricks, Adlai E. Stevenson

Benjamin Harrison

23

1889–1893

Born: 1833
Died: 1901
Born in: Ohio
Elected from: Indiana
Age when elected: 55
Occupation: Lawyer
Party: Republican
Vice President: Levi P. Morton

Ulysses S. Grant

... [T]he past four years, so far as I could control events, have been consumed in the effort to restore harmony, public credit, commerce, and all the arts of peace and progress. It is my firm conviction that the civilized world is tending toward republicanism, or government by the people through their chosen representatives, and that our own great Republic is destined to be the guiding star to all others.

*Second Inaugural Address
March 4, 1873*

Rutherford B. Hayes

The President of the United States owes his election to office to the ... labors of a political party, ... but he should strive to be always mindful of the fact that he serves his party best who serves the country best.

*Inaugural Address
March 5, 1877*

James A. Garfield

The supremacy of the nation and its laws should be no longer a subject of debate. That ... the Constitution and the laws made in pursuance thereof are and shall continue to be the supreme law of the land....

*Inaugural Address
March 4, 1881*

Chester A. Arthur

For the fourth time in the history of the Republic its Chief Magistrate has been removed by death. All hearts are filled with grief and horror.... Men may die, but the fabrics of our free institutions remain unshaken.

*First Presidential Statement
September 22, 1881*

Grover Cleveland

Amid the din of party strife the people's choice was made, but its attendant circumstances have demonstrated anew the strength and safety of a government by the people. In each succeeding year it more clearly appears that our democratic principle needs no apology, and that in its fearless and faithful application is to be found the surest guaranty of good government.

*First Inaugural Address
March 4, 1885*

Benjamin Harrison

I do not mistrust the future. Dangers have been in frequent ambush along our path, but we have uncovered and vanquished them all. Passion has swept some of our communities, but only to give us a new demonstration that the great body of our people are stable, patriotic, and law-abiding.

*Inaugural Address
March 4, 1889*

THE PRESIDENTS

William McKinley

It is inspiring, too, to remember that no great emergency in the one hundred and eight years of our eventful national life has ever arisen that has not been met with wisdom and courage by the American people....

*First Inaugural Address
March 4, 1897*

Theodore Roosevelt

[W]e have faith that we shall not prove false to the memories of the men of the mighty past. They did their work, they left us the splendid heritage we now enjoy.

*Inaugural Address
March 4, 1905*

William H. Taft

Our international policy is always to promote peace. We shall enter into any war with a full consciousness of the awful consequences that it always entails, whether successful or not, and we, of course, shall make every effort consistent with national honor and the highest national interest to avoid a resort to arms.

*Inaugural Address
March 4, 1909*

Woodrow Wilson

The world must be made safe for democracy. Its peace must be planted upon the tested foundations of political liberty. We have no selfish ends to serve. We desire no conquest, no domination.... We are but one of the champions of the rights of mankind.

*War Message to Congress
April 2, 1917*

William McKinley

25
1897–1901
Born: 1843
Died: 1901
Born in: Ohio
Elected from: Ohio
Age when elected: 53
Occupations: Teacher, Lawyer
Party: Republican
Vice Presidents: Garret Hobart, Theodore Roosevelt

Theodore Roosevelt

26
1901–1909
Born: 1858
Died: 1919
Born in: New York
Elected as V.P. from: New York
Succeeded McKinley
Age when became President: 42
Occupations: Historian, Rancher
Party: Republican
Vice President: Charles W. Fairbanks

William H. Taft

27
1909–1913
Born: 1857
Died: 1930
Born in: Ohio
Elected from: Ohio
Age when elected: 51
Occupation: Lawyer
Party: Republican
Vice President: James S. Sherman

Woodrow Wilson

28
1913–1921
Born: 1856
Died: 1924
Born in: Virginia
Elected from: New Jersey
Age when elected: 55
Occupation: College Professor
Party: Democratic
Vice President: Thomas R. Marshall

Warren G. Harding

29
1921–1923
Born: 1865
Died: 1923
Born in: Ohio
Elected from: Ohio
Age when elected: 55
Occupations: Newspaper Editor, Publisher
Party: Republican
Vice President: Calvin Coolidge

Calvin Coolidge

30
1923–1929
Born: 1872
Died: 1933
Born in: Vermont
Elected as V.P. from: Massachusetts
Succeeded Harding
Age when became President: 51
Occupation: Lawyer
Party: Republican
Vice President: Charles G. Dawes

Warren G. Harding

America is ready to encourage, eager to initiate, anxious to participate in any seemly program likely to lessen the probability of war, and promote that brotherhood of mankind which must be God's highest conception of human relationship.

*Inaugural Address
March 4, 1921*

Calvin Coolidge

We have been, and propose to be, more and more American. We believe that we can best serve our own country and most successfully discharge our obligations to humanity by continuing to be ... American.

*Inaugural Address
March 4, 1925*

Herbert C. Hoover

[I]f we hold the faith of the men in our mighty past who created these ideals, we shall leave them heightened and strengthened for our children.

*Inaugural Address
March 4, 1929*

THE PRESIDENTS

Herbert C. Hoover

31

1929–1933

Born: 1874
Died: 1964
Born in: Iowa
Elected from: California
Age when elected: 54
Occupation: Engineer
Party: Republican
Vice President: Charles Curtis

Franklin D. Roosevelt

32

1933–1945

Born: 1882
Died: 1945
Born in: New York
Elected from: New York
Age when elected: 50
Occupation: Lawyer
Party: Democratic
Vice Presidents: John N. Garner, Henry A. Wallace, Harry S Truman

Harry S Truman

33

1945–1953

Born: 1884
Died: 1972
Born in: Missouri
Elected as V.P. from: Missouri
Succeeded Roosevelt
Age when became President: 60
Occupations: Clerk, Farmer
Party: Democratic
Vice President: Alben W. Barkley

Dwight D. Eisenhower

34

1953–1961

Born: 1890
Died: 1969
Born in: Texas
Elected from: New York
Age when elected: 62
Occupation: Soldier
Party: Republican
Vice President: Richard M. Nixon

John F. Kennedy

35

1961–1963

Born: 1917
Died: 1963
Born in: Massachusetts
Elected from: Massachusetts
Age when elected: 43
Occupations: Author, Reporter
Party: Democratic
Vice President: Lyndon B. Johnson

Lyndon B. Johnson

36

1963–1969

Born: 1908
Died: 1973
Born in: Texas
Elected as V.P. from: Texas
Succeeded Kennedy
Age when became President: 55
Occupation: Teacher
Party: Democratic
Vice President: Hubert H. Humphrey

Franklin D. Roosevelt

I see one-third of a nation ill-housed, ill-clad, ill-nourished. It is not in despair that I paint you that picture. I paint it for you in hope—because the Nation, seeing and understanding the injustice in it, proposes to paint it out. We are determined to make every American citizen the subject of his country's interest and concern....

Second Inaugural Address January 20, 1937

Harry S Truman

The American people stand firm in the faith which has inspired this Nation from the beginning. We believe that all men have a right to equal justice under law and equal opportunity to share in the common good.... We believe that all men are created equal because they are created in the image of God. From this faith, we shall not be moved.

Inaugural Address January 20, 1949

Dwight D. Eisenhower

In the swift rush of great events, we find ourselves groping to know the full sense and meaning of these times in which we live.... We bring all our wit and all our will to meet the question: How far have we come in man's long pilgrimage from darkness toward light? Are we nearing the light—a day of freedom and of peace for all mankind?

First Inaugural Address January 20, 1953

John F. Kennedy

We dare not forget today that we are the heirs of that first revolution. Let the word go forth from this time and place, to friend and foe alike, that the torch has been passed to a new generation of Americans....

Inaugural Address January 20, 1961

Lyndon B. Johnson

At times, history and fate meet at a single time in a single place to shape a turning point in man's unending search for freedom.... So it was at Lexington and Concord. So it was a century ago at Appomattox. So it was last week in Selma, Alabama....

Address to Congress March 15, 1965

THE PRESIDENTS

Richard M. Nixon

Together with the rest of the world, let us resolve to move forward from the beginnings we have made. Let us continue to bring down the walls of hostility, which have divided the world for too long, and to build in their place bridges of understanding—so that despite profound differences between systems of government, the people of the world can be friends.

*Second Inaugural Address
January 20, 1973*

Gerald R. Ford

I believe that truth is the glue that holds governments together, not only our government but civilization itself. That bond, though strained, is unbroken at home and abroad....

My fellow Americans, our long national nightmare is over. Our Constitution works. Our great Republic is a government of laws and not of men. Here, the people rule.

*First Presidential Address
August 9, 1974*

James E. Carter, Jr.

The world itself is now dominated by a new spirit. Peoples more numerous and more politically aware are craving and now demanding their place in the sun.... The passion for freedom is on the rise. Tapping this new spirit, there can be no nobler nor more ambitious task for America to undertake on this day of a new beginning than to help shape a just and peaceful world that is truly humane.

*Inaugural Address
January 20, 1977*

Richard M. Nixon

37
1969–1974

Born: 1913
Died: 1994
Born in: California
Elected from: New York
Age when elected: 55
Occupation: Lawyer
Party: Republican
Vice Presidents: Spiro T. Agnew, Gerald R. Ford

Gerald R. Ford

38
1974–1977

Born: 1913
Born in: Nebraska
Appointed by Nixon as V.P. upon Agnew's resignation; assumed presidency upon Nixon's resignation
Age when became President: 61
Occupation: Lawyer
Party: Republican
Vice President: Nelson R. Rockefeller

James E. Carter, Jr.

39
1977–1981

Born: 1924
Born in: Georgia
Elected from: Georgia
Age when elected: 52
Occupations: Business, Farmer
Party: Democratic
Vice President: Walter F. Mondale

Ronald W. Reagan

40
1981–1989

Born: 1911
Born in: Illinois
Elected from: California
Age when elected: 69
Occupations: Actor, Lecturer
Party: Republican
Vice President: George H.W. Bush

George H.W. Bush

41
1989–1993

Born: 1924
Born in: Massachusetts
Elected from: Texas
Age when elected: 64
Occupation: Business
Party: Republican
Vice President: J. Danforth Quayle

William J. Clinton

42
1993–

Born: 1946
Born in: Arkansas
Elected from: Arkansas
Age when elected: 46
Occupation: Lawyer
Party: Democratic
Vice President: Albert Gore, Jr.

Ronald W. Reagan

History is a ribbon, always unfurling; history is a journey. And as we continue our journey, we think of those who traveled before us.... [W]e hear again the echoes of our past.... It is the American sound. It is hopeful, big-hearted, idealistic, daring, decent, and fair.

*Second Inaugural Address
January 21, 1985*

George H.W. Bush

No President, no government, can teach us to remember what is best in what we are. But if the man you have chosen to lead this government can help make a difference... then he must.

*Inaugural Address
January 20, 1989*

William J. Clinton

[W]e need a new approach to government.... [A] solemn commitment between the people and their government, based not simply on what each of us can take, but on what all of us must give to make America work again.

Address to Democratic Convention, July 16, 1992

Documents of America's Heritage

The Magna Carta

The Magna Carta, signed by King John in 1215, marked a decisive step forward in the development of constitutional government in England. Later, it became a model for colonists who carried the Magna Carta's guarantees of legal and political rights to America.

1. That the English church shall be free, and shall have her rights entire, and her liberties inviolate;. . .

2. We also have granted to all the freemen of our kingdom, for us and for our heirs forever, all the underwritten liberties, to be had and holden by them and their heirs, of us and our heirs forever. . . .

39. No freeman shall be taken or imprisoned, or diseased, or outlawed, or banished, or in any way destroyed, nor will we pass upon him, nor will we send upon him, unless by the lawful judgment of his peers, or by the law of the land.

40. We will sell to no man, we will not deny to any man, either justice or right.

41. All merchants shall have safe and secure conduct to go out of, and to come into, England, and to stay there and to pass as well by land as by water, for buying and selling by the ancient and allowed customs, without any unjust tolls, except in time of war, or when they are of any nation at war with us. . . .

42. It shall be lawful, for the time to come, for any one to go out of our kingdom and return safely and securely by land or by water, saving his allegiance to us (unless in time of war, by some short space, for the common benefit of the realm).

60. All the aforesaid customs and liberties, which we have granted to be holden in our kingdom, as much as it belongs to us, all people of our kingdom, as well clergy as laity, shall observe, as far as they are concerned, towards their dependents.

63. . . . It is also sworn, as well on our part as on the part of the barons, that all the things aforesaid shall be observed in good faith, and without evil duplicity. Given under our hand, in the presence of the witnesses above named, and many others, in the meadow called Runnymede, between Windsor and Staines, the 15th day of June, in the 17th year of our reign.

The Mayflower Compact

On November 21, 1620, 41 colonists aboard the Mayflower *drafted this agreement. The Mayflower Compact was the first plan of self-government ever put in force in the English colonies.*

In ye name of God Amen. We whose names are underwritten, the loyall subjects of our dread soveraigne Lord King James, by ye grace of God, of Great Britaine, Franc, & Ireland king, defender of ye faith, &c. Haveing undertaken, for ye glorie of God, and advancemente of ye Christian faith and honour of our king & countrie, a voyage to plant ye first colonie in ye Northerne parts of Virginia, doe by these presents solemnly & mutualy in ye presence of God, and one of another, covenant, & combine ourselves togeather into a Civill body politick; for our better ordering, & preservation & furtherance of ye ends aforesaid; and by vertue hereof to enacte, constitute, and frame such just & equall Lawes, ordinances, Acts, constitutions, & offices, from time to time, as shall be thought most meete & convenient for ye generall good of ye colonie: unto which we promise all due submission and obedience. In witnes whereof we have hereunder subscribed our names at Cap-Codd ye -11- of November, in ye year of ye raigne of our soveraigne Lord King James of England, France, & Ireland ye eighteenth, and of Scotland ye fiftie fourth. Ano Dom. 1620.

Virginia Statute of Religious Liberty

The concept of separation of church and state had been part of the American fabric since the 1600s. In 1777 Thomas Jefferson drafted a bill to establish religious freedom in Virginia. The bill was made law in 1786.

2. *Be it therefore enacted by the General Assembly,* That no man shall be compelled to frequent or support any religious worship, place of ministry whatsoever, nor shall be enforced, restrained, molested, or burthened in his body or goods, nor shall otherwise suffer on account of his religious opinions or belief; but that all men shall be free to profess, and by argument to maintain, their opinion in matters of religion, and that the same shall in no wise diminish, enlarge or affect their civil capacities.

3. And though we well know that this Assembly, elected by the people for the ordinary purposes of legislation only, have no power to restrain the acts of succeeding Assemblies, constituted with powers equal to our own, and that therefore to declare this act to be irrevocable would be of no effect in law, yet as we are free to declare, and do declare, that the rights hereby asserted are of the natural rights of mankind, and that if any act shall hereafter be passed to repeal the present or to narrow its operation, such act will be an infringement of natural right.

Washington's Farewell Address

At the end of his second term as President, George Washington spoke of the dangers facing the young nation. He warned against the dangers of political parties and sectionalism, and advised the nation against permanent alliances with other nations.

Citizens by birth or choice of a common country, that country has a right to concentrate your affections. The name of American, which belongs to you, in your national capacity, must always exalt the just pride of patriotism more than any appellation derived from local discriminations. With slight shades of difference, you have the same religion, manners, habits, and political principles. You have in a common cause fought and triumphed together. . . .

In contemplating the causes which may disturb our Union, it occurs as matter of serious concern that any ground should have been furnished for characterizing parties by geographical discriminations: Northern and Southern; Atlantic and Western. . . .

No alliances, however strict between the parts, can be an adequate substitute. They must inevitably experience the infractions and interruptions which all alliances in all times have experienced. . . .

The basis of our political systems is the right of the people to make and to alter their constitutions of government. But the constitution which at any time exists, till changed by an explicit and authentic act of the whole people, is sacredly obligatory upon all. . . .

The great rule of conduct for us, in regard to foreign nations, is in extending our commercial relations to have with them as little political connection as possible. So far as we have already formed engagements, let them be fulfilled with perfect good faith. . . .

Relying on its kindness in this as in other things, and actuated by that fervent love toward it which is so natural to a man who views in it the native soil of himself and his progenitors for several generations, I anticipate with pleasing expectations that retreat in which I promise myself to realize, without alloy, the sweet enjoyment of partaking, in the midst of my fellow citizens, the benign influence of good laws under a free government, the ever favorite object of my heart, and the happy reward, as I trust, of our mutual cares, labors, and dangers.

The Star-Spangled Banner

During the British bombardment of Fort McHenry during the War of 1812, a young Baltimore lawyer named Francis Scott Key was inspired to write the words to "The Star-Spangled Banner." Although it became popular immediately, it was not until 1931 that Congress officially declared "The Star-Spangled Banner" as our national anthem.

O! say can you see, by the dawn's early light,
What so proudly we hail'd at the twilight's last gleaming,
Whose broad stripes and bright stars through the perilous fight,
O'er the ramparts we watched, were so gallantly streaming?
And the Rockets' red glare, the Bombs bursting in air,
Gave proof through the night that our Flag was still there;
O! say, does that star-spangled banner yet wave
O'er the Land of the free and the home of the brave!

On the shore, dimly seen through the mists of the deep,
Where the foe's haughty host in dread silence reposes,
What is that, which the breeze o'er the towering steep,
As it fitfully blows, half conceals, half discloses?
Now it catches the gleam of the morning's first beam,
In full glory reflected, now shines on the stream.
'Tis the star-spangled banner; O! long may it wave
O'er the land of the free and the home of the brave.

The Monroe Doctrine

In an 1823 address to Congress, President James Monroe proclaimed what has become known as the Monroe Doctrine. The doctrine was designed to end European influence in the Western Hemisphere. In addition, it showed the world the American spirit of strength and unity, and became a cornerstone of United States foreign policy.

. . . . The citizens of the United States cherish sentiments the most friendly in favor of the liberty and happiness of their fellowmen on that side of the Atlantic. In the wars of the European powers in matters relating to themselves we have never taken any part, nor does it comport with our policy so to do. It is only when our rights are invaded or seriously menaced that we resent injuries or make preparation for our defense.

With the movements in this hemisphere we are of necessity more immediately connected, and by causes which must be obvious to all enlightened and impartial observers. The political system of the allied powers is essentially different in this respect from that of America. This difference proceeds from that which exists in their respective governments; and to the defense of our own, which has been achieved by the loss of so much blood and treasure, and matured by the wisdom of their most enlightened citizens, and under which we have enjoyed unexampled felicity, this whole nation is devoted. We owe it, therefore, to candor and to the amicable relations existing between the United States and those powers to declare that we should consider any attempt on their part to extend their system to any portion of this hemisphere as dangerous to our peace and safety.

With the existing colonies or dependencies of any European power we have not interfered and shall not interfere. But with the governments who have declared their independence and maintained it, and whose independence we have, on great consideration and on just principles, acknowledged, we could not view any interposition for the purpose of oppressing them, or controlling in any other manner their destiny, by any European power in any other light than as the manifestation of any unfriendly disposition toward the United States. . . .

Our policy in regard to Europe, which was adopted at an early stage of the wars which have so long agitated that quarter of the globe, nevertheless remains the same, which is not to interfere in the internal concerns of any of its powers; to consider the government de facto as the legitimate government for us; to cultivate friendly relations with it, and to preserve those relations by a frank, firm, and manly policy, meeting in all instances the just claims of every power, submitting to injuries from none. . . .

Memorial and Protest of the Cherokee Nation

While Native Americans were being forced from their homeland, Cherokee leaders put their protest before the United States Senate. Their call for justice went unheard.

It cannot be concealed that the situation of the Cherokees is peculiarly distressing. In adverting to that situation it is not done to arouse, at this late day, a useless sympathy, but only as matter of history, and from necessity in giving a fair and impartial illustration of their difficulties. It is well known to those who have paid any attention to their history for the last five years, that they have been contending for the faithful execution of treaties between their nation and the United States, and that their distresses have not been mitigated; their efforts seem to have increased their difficulties. It remains for them to seek an adjustment by treaty, and an equitable acknowledgement of their rights and claims, so far as circumstances will permit.

For this purpose, this delegation has been deputed, as the proper organ of the Cherokee people, to settle, by treaty, their difficulties; and they wish, in sincerity, to have them settled, for the good, peace, and harmony of the whole nation.

The Seneca Falls Declaration

One of the first documents to express the desire for equal rights for women is the Declaration of Sentiments and Resolutions, issued in 1848 at the Seneca Falls Convention in New York. Led by Lucretia Mott and Elizabeth Cady Stanton, the delegates adopted a set of resolutions that called for woman suffrage and opportunities in employment and education. Excerpts from the Declaration follow.

When, in the course of human events, it becomes necessary for one portion of the family of man to assume among the people of the earth a position different from that which they have hitherto occupied, but one to which the laws of nature and of nature's God entitle them, a decent respect to the opinions of mankind requires that they should declare the causes that impel them to such a course.

We hold these truths to be self-evident: that all men and women are created equal; that they are endowed by their Creator with certain inalienable rights; that among these are life, liberty, and the pursuit of happiness; that to secure these rights governments are instituted, deriving their just powers from the consent of the governed. Whenever any form of government becomes destructive of these ends, it is the right of those who suffer from it to refuse allegiance to it, and to insist upon the institution of a new government, laying its foundation on such principles, and organizing its powers in such form, as to them shall seem most likely to effect their safety and happiness. Prudence, indeed, will dictate that governments long established should not be changed for light and transient causes; . . . But when a long train of abuses and usurpations, pursuing invariably the same object, evinces a design to reduce them under absolute despotism, it is their duty to throw off such government and to provide new guards for their future security. . . .

The history of mankind is a history of repeated injuries and usurpations on the part of man toward woman, having in direct object the establishment of an absolute tyranny over her. To prove this, let facts be submitted to a candid world. . . .

Now, in view of the entire disfranchisement of one-half the people of this country, their social and religious degradation, in view of the unjust laws above mentioned, and because women do feel themselves aggrieved, oppressed, and fraudulently deprived of their most sacred rights, we insist that they have immediate admission to all the rights and privileges which belong to them as citizens of the United States. . . .

The Emancipation Proclamation

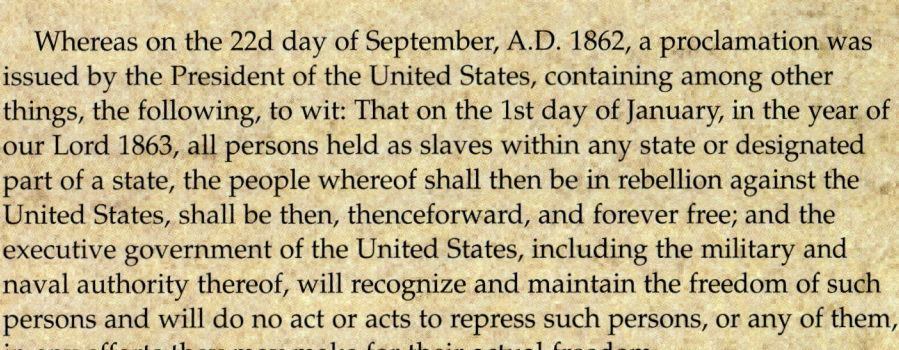

On January 1, 1863, President Abraham Lincoln issued the Emancipation Proclamation, which freed all slaves in states under Confederate control. The Proclamation was a significant step toward the Thirteenth Amendment (1865) that ended slavery in all of the United States.

Whereas on the 22d day of September, A.D. 1862, a proclamation was issued by the President of the United States, containing among other things, the following, to wit: That on the 1st day of January, in the year of our Lord 1863, all persons held as slaves within any state or designated part of a state, the people whereof shall then be in rebellion against the United States, shall be then, thenceforward, and forever free; and the executive government of the United States, including the military and naval authority thereof, will recognize and maintain the freedom of such persons and will do no act or acts to repress such persons, or any of them, in any efforts they may make for their actual freedom.

That the executive will, on the 1st day of January aforesaid, by proclamation, designate the states and parts of states, if any, in which the people thereof, respectively, shall then be in rebellion against the United States; and the fact that any state or the people thereof shall on that day be in good faith represented in the Congress of the United States by members chosen thereto at elections wherein a majority of the qualified voters of such states shall have participated shall, in the absence of strong countervailing testimony, be deemed conclusive evidence that such state and the people thereof are not then in rebellion against the United States. . . .

And, by virtue of the power and for the purpose aforesaid, I do order and declare that all persons held as slaves within said designated states and parts of states are, and henceforward shall be, free; and that the executive government of the United States, including the military and naval authorities thereof, will recognize and maintain the freedom of said persons.

And I hereby enjoin upon the people so declared to be free to abstain from all violence, unless in necessary self-defense; and I recommend to them that, in all cases when allowed, they labor faithfully for reasonable wages.

And I further declare and make known that such persons of suitable condition will be received into the armed service of the United States to garrison forts, positions, stations, and other places, and to man vessels of all sorts in said service. . . .

Documents of America's Heritage

The Gettysburg Address

On November 19, 1863, President Abraham Lincoln gave a short speech at the dedication of a national cemetery on the battlefield of Gettysburg. His simple yet eloquent words expressed his hopes for a nation divided by civil war.

Four score and seven years ago our fathers brought forth on this continent a new nation, conceived in liberty, and dedicated to the proposition that all men are created equal.

Now we are engaged in a great civil war, testing whether that nation or any nation so conceived and so dedicated can long endure. We are met on a great battlefield of that war. We have come to dedicate a portion of that field as a final resting place for those who here gave their lives that that nation might live. It is altogether fitting and proper that we should do this.

But, in a larger sense, we can not dedicate—we can not consecrate—we can not hallow—this ground. The brave men, living and dead, who struggled here have consecrated it far beyond our poor power to add or detract. The world will little note nor long remember what we say here, but it can never forget what they did here. It is for us, the living, rather, to be dedicated here to the unfinished work which they who fought here have thus far so nobly advanced.

It is rather for us to be here dedicated to the great task remaining before us—that from these honored dead we take increased devotion to that cause for which they gave the last full measure of devotion; that we here highly resolve that these dead shall not have died in vain; that this nation, under God, shall have a new birth of freedom; and that government of the people, by the people, and for the people, shall not perish from the earth.

I Will Fight No More

In 1877 the Nez Perce Indians fought the government's attempt to move them to a smaller reservation. After a remarkable attempt to escape to Canada, Chief Joseph realized that resistance was hopeless and advised his people to surrender.

Tell General Howard I know his heart. What he told me before I have in my heart. I am tired of fighting. Our chiefs are killed. Looking Glass is dead. It is the young men who say yes or no. He who led the young men is dead. It is cold and we have no blankets. The little children are freezing to death. My people, some of them have run away to the hills and have no blankets, no food; no one knows where they are—perhaps freezing to death. I want to have time to look for my children and see how many I can find. Maybe I shall find them among the dead. Hear me my chiefs. I am tired; my heart is sick and sad. From where the sun now stands, I will fight no more forever.

The Pledge of Allegiance

In 1892 the nation celebrated the 400th anniversary of Columbus's landing in America. In connection with this celebration, Francis Bellamy, a magazine editor, wrote and published the Pledge of Allegiance.

I pledge allegiance to the Flag of the United States of America and to the Republic for which it stands, one Nation under God, indivisible, with liberty and justice for all.

Documents of America's Heritage

Douglass's Speech to the Congregational Church in Washington, D.C.

Frederick Douglass marked the twentieth anniversary of the emancipation of the enslaved people of the District of Columbia with a speech that probed the relations between African Americans and white Americans.

The sky of the American Negro is dark, but not rayless; it is stormy, but not cheerless . . . As the war for the Union recedes into the misty shadows of the past, and the Negro is no longer needed to assault forts and stop rebel bullets, he is in some sense, of less importance. Peace with the old master class has been war to the Negro. As the one has risen, the other has fallen. The reaction has been sudden, marked, and violent. It has swept the Negro from all the legislative halls of the Southern States, and from those of the Congress of the United States. It has, in many cases, driven him from the ballot box and the jury box. The situation has much in it for serious thought, but nothing to cause despair . . .

Time and events which have done so much for us in the past, will, I trust, not do less for us in the future. The moral government of the universe is on our side, and cooperates, with all honest efforts, to lift up the down-trodden and oppressed in all lands, whether the oppressed be white or black . . .

What is to be the future of the colored people of this country? Some change in their condition seems to be looked for by thoughtful men everywhere; but what that change will be, no one yet has been able with certainty to predict . . .

In every great movement men are prepared by preceding events for those which are to come. We neither know the evil nor the good which may be in store for us. Twenty-five years ago the system of slavery seemed impregnable. Cotton was king, and the civilized world acknowledged his sway. Twenty-five years ago no man could have foreseen that in less than ten years from that time no master would wield a lash and no slave would clank a chain in the United States.

Who at that time dreamed that Negroes would ever be seen as we have seen them to-day marching through the streets of this superb city, the Capital of this great Nation, with eagles on their buttons, muskets on their shoulders and swords by their sides, timing their high footsteps to the Star Spangled Banner and the Red, White and Blue? . . .

The Fourteen Points

On January 8, 1918, President Woodrow Wilson went before Congress to offer a statement of aims called the Fourteen Points. Wilson's plan called for freedom of the seas in peace and war, an end to secret alliances, and equal trading rights for all countries. The excerpt that follows is taken from the President's message.

. . . . We entered this war because violations of right had occurred which touched us to the quick and made the life of our own people impossible unless they were corrected and the world secured once for all against their recurrence. What we demand in this war, therefore, is nothing peculiar to ourselves. It is that the world be made fit and safe to live in; and particularly that it be made safe for every peace-loving nation which, like our own, wishes to live its own life, determine its own institutions, be assured of justice and fair dealings by the other peoples of the world, as against force and selfish aggression. All the peoples of the world are in effect partners in this interest, and for our own part we see very clearly that unless justice be done to others it will not be done to us.

The program of the world's peace, therefore, is our program, and that program, the only possible program, as we see it, is this:

I. Open covenants of peace, openly arrived at, after which there shall be no private international understandings of any kind, but diplomacy shall proceed always frankly and in the public view.

II. Absolute freedom of navigation upon the seas, outside territorial waters, alike in peace and in war, except as the seas may be closed in whole or in part by international action for the enforcement of international covenants.

III. The removal, so far as possible, of all economic barriers and the establishment of an equality of trade conditions among all the nations consenting to the peace and associating themselves for its maintenance.

IV. Adequate guarantees given and taken that national armaments will be reduced to the lowest point consistent with domestic safety.

V. Free, open-minded, and absolutely impartial adjustment of all colonial claims, based upon a strict observance of the principle that in determining all such questions of sovereignty the interests of the population concerned must have equal weight with the equitable claims of the Government whose title is to be determined. . . .

XIV. A general association of nations must be formed under specific covenants for the purpose of affording mutual guarantees of political independence and territorial integrity to great and small states alike. . . .

Franklin D. Roosevelt's First Inaugural Address

The New Deal was launched March 4, 1933, the day that Franklin D. Roosevelt became President. At a time when the nation was in the depths of the Great Depression, the address showed a great sense of leadership and encouraged the American people.

I am certain that my fellow Americans expect that on my induction into the presidency I will address them with a candor and a decision which the present situation of our nation [impels]. This is preeminently the time to speak the truth, the whole truth, frankly and boldly. Nor need we shrink from honestly facing conditions in our country today. This great Nation will endure as it has endured, will revive and will prosper. So, first of all, let me assert my firm belief that the only thing we have to fear is fear itself—nameless, unreasoning, unjustified terror which paralyzes needed efforts to convert retreat into advance. In every dark hour of our national life a leadership of frankness and vigor has met with that understanding and support of the people themselves which is essential to victory. I am convinced that you will again give that support leadership in these critical days.

In such a spirit on my part and on yours we face our common difficulties. They concern, thank God, only material things. Values have shrunken to fantastic levels; taxes have risen; our ability to pay has fallen; government of all kinds is faced by serious curtailment of income; the means of exchange are frozen in the currents of trade; the withered leaves of industrial enterprise lie on every side; farmers find no markets for their produce; the savings of many years in thousands of families are gone.

More important, a host of unemployed citizens face the grim problem of existence, and an equally great number toil with little return. Only a foolish optimist can deny the dark realities of the moment.

Yet our distress comes from no failure of substance. We are stricken by no plague of locusts. Compared with the perils which our [ancestors] conquered because they believed and were not afraid, we have still much to be thankful for. Nature still offers her bounty, and human efforts have multiplied it. Plenty is at our doorstep, but a generous use of it languishes in the very sight of the supply. Primarily this is because the rulers of the exchange of mankind's goods have failed, through their own stubbornness and their own incompetence, . . .

Brown v. Board of Education

On May 17, 1954, the Supreme Court ruled in Brown v. Board of Education *that racial segregation in public schools was unconstitutional. This decision provided the legal basis for court challenges to segregation in every aspect of American life.*

The plaintiffs contend that segregated public schools are not "equal" and cannot be made "equal," and that hence they are deprived of the equal protection of the laws. Because of the obvious importance of the question presented, the Court took jurisdiction. . . .

Our decision . . . cannot turn on merely a comparison of these tangible factors in the Negro and white schools involved in each of the cases. We must look instead to the effect of segregation itself on public education.

In approaching this problem, we cannot turn the clock back to 1868 when the Amendment was adopted, or even to 1896 when *Plessy v. Ferguson* was written. We must consider public education in the light of its full development and its present place in American life throughout the nation. Only in this way can it be determined if segregation in public schools deprives these plaintiffs of the equal protection of the laws.

Today, education is perhaps the most important function of state and local governments. Compulsory school attendance laws and the great expenditures for education both demonstrate our recognition of the importance of education to our democratic society. . . . In these days, it is doubtful that any child may reasonably be expected to succeed in life if he is denied the opportunity of an education. Such an opportunity, where the state has undertaken to provide it, is a right which must be made available to all on equal terms.

We come then to the question presented: Does segregation of children in public schools solely on the basis of race, even though the physical facilities and other "tangible" factors may be equal, deprive the children of the minority group of equal educational opportunities? We believe that it does.

. . . .We conclude that in the field of public education the doctrine of "separate but equal" has no place. Separate educational facilities are inherently unequal. Therefore, we hold that the plaintiffs and others similarly situated for whom the actions have been brought are, by reason of the segregation complained of, deprived of the equal protection of the laws guaranteed by the Fourteenth Amendment. . . .

John F. Kennedy's Inaugural Address

President Kennedy's Inaugural Address on January 20, 1961, set the tone for his administration. In his address Kennedy stirred the nation by calling for "a grand and global alliance" to fight tyranny, poverty, disease, and war.

We observe today not a victory of party but a celebration of freedom—symbolizing an end as well as a beginning—signifying renewal as well as change. For I have sworn before you and Almighty God the same solemn oath our forebears prescribed nearly a century and three-quarters ago.

The world is very different now. For man holds in his mortal hands the power to abolish all forms of human poverty and all forms of human life. And yet the same revolutionary beliefs for which our forebears fought are still at issue around the globe—the belief that the rights of man come not from the generosity of the state but from the hand of God.

We dare not forget today that we are the heirs of that first revolution. Let the word go forth from this time and place, to friend and foe alike, that the torch has been passed to a new generation of Americans born in this century, tempered by war, disciplined by a hard and bitter peace, proud of our ancient heritage—and unwilling to witness or permit the slow undoing of those human rights to which this nation has always been committed, and to which we are committed today at home and around the world.

Let every nation know, whether it wishes us well or ill, that we shall pay any price, bear any burden, meet any hardship, support any friend, oppose any foe to assure the survival and the success of liberty.

This much we pledge—and more.

To those old allies whose cultural and spiritual origins we share, we pledge the loyalty of faithful friends. United, there is little we cannot do in a host of cooperative ventures. Divided, there is little we can do . . .

Let us never negotiate out of fear. But let us never fear to negotiate. . . . Let both sides explore what problems unite us instead of belaboring those problems which divide us. . . . Let both sides seek to invoke the wonders of science instead of its terrors. Together let us explore the stars, conquer the deserts, eradicate disease, tap the ocean depths, and encourage the arts and commerce. . . .

And so, my fellow Americans—ask not what your country can do for you—ask what you can do for your country.

My fellow citizens of the world—ask not what America will do for you but what together we can do for the freedom of man.

I Have a Dream

On August 28, 1963, while Congress debated wide-ranging civil rights legislation, Martin Luther King, Jr., led more than 200,000 people on a march on Washington, D.C. On the steps of the Lincoln Memorial he gave a stirring speech in which he eloquently spoke of his dreams for African Americans and for the United States. Excerpts of the speech follow.

. . . . There are those who are asking the devotees of civil rights, "when will you be satisfied?"

We can never be satisfied as long as the Negro is the victim of the unspeakable horrors of police brutality. . . . We cannot be satisfied as long as the Negro's basic mobility is from a smaller ghetto to a larger one. We can never be satisfied as long as a Negro in Mississippi cannot vote and a Negro in New York believes he has nothing for which to vote. . . .

I say to you today, my friends, that in spite of the difficulties and frustrations of the moment I still have a dream. It is a dream deeply rooted in the American dream.

I have a dream that one day this nation will rise up and live out the true meaning of its creed, "We hold these truths to be self-evident, that all men are created equal."

I have a dream that one day on the red hills of Georgia the sons of former slaves and the sons of former slaveowners will be able to sit down together at the table of brotherhood.

I have a dream that one day even the state of Mississippi, a desert state sweltering with the heat of injustice and oppression, will be transformed into an oasis of freedom and justice.

I have a dream that my four little children will one day live in a nation where they will not be judged by the color of their skin, but by the content of their character. . . .

. . . When we let freedom ring, when we let it ring from every village and every hamlet, from every state and every city, we will be able to speed up that day when all of God's children, black men and white men, Jews and Gentiles, Protestants and Catholics, will be able to join hands and sing in the words of the old Negro spiritual: "Free at last! Free at last! Thank God Almighty, we are free at last!"

Documents of America's Heritage

Peacemaking and Peace-Keeping for the Next Century

In 1945 the United States and other nations helped establish the United Nations to provide a forum for nations to settle their disputes by peaceful means. In March 1995, during the 50th anniversary year of the UN, Boutros Boutros-Ghali, the organization's Secretary General, spoke about the principal issues of international peace and security.

—Most of today's conflicts take place within states. They are fought not only by armies but also by irregular forces. Civilians are the main victims. Humanitarian emergencies are commonplace. State institutions often have collapsed.

—The demands go beyond traditional peace-keeping. Recent operations have demobilized troops; promoted national reconciliation; restored effective government; and organized and monitored elections.

—Civic operations are as important as military operations.

—Long term economic and social programmes may be needed to address the original causes of conflict.

United Nations peace efforts have become more expensive, more complex and more dangerous. . . .

In Somalia, the United Nations responded to a unique situation. All semblance of governmental authority had collapsed. Chaos endangered the lives of innocent people throughout the country. Massive refugee flows took place within and across borders. Infants starved to death before the cameras of the world media.

The aim of the United Nations Operations in Somalia (UNOSOM) was to provide basic security, services and administration to the people, while assisting in a negotiating process to restore legitimate and effective State authority. . . .

The United Nations can only facilitate, encourage and assist; it cannot impose a solution on the parties—even when the solution is one that the parties at one time seemed prepared to accept.

Thus we have learned a lesson: how and when to withdraw.

And perhaps we have taught a lesson as well: that when warring parties reject U.N. help and endanger the U.N. mission, they will find that the U.N.'s patience is not unlimited. They will find that they cannot expect to be supported yet continue to act irresponsibly. . . .

As a workable system of international and human security comes into being, the need for peace operations will decrease. The three pillars of such a system must be: consistent response, adequate human and financial resources, and sustained political resolve.

Responsibility for resolving disputes and conflicts lies with the parties themselves. But the international community, by selecting carefully among the instruments at its disposal, and mobilizing the necessary political and economic support, can play an indispensable role in supporting their efforts.

Gazetteer

Afghanistan—Charleston

The gazetteer is a geographical dictionary that lists political divisions, natural features, and other places and locations. Following each entry is a description, its latitude and longitude, and a page reference that indicates where each entry may be found in this text.

A

Afghanistan country in south central Asia (33°N/63°E) 995

Africa continent of the Eastern Hemisphere south of the Mediterranean Sea and adjoining Asia on its northeastern border (10°N/22°E) 12

Alabama state in the southeastern United States; 22nd state to enter the Union (32°45'N/87°30'W) 213

Alaska state in the United States, located in northwestern North America; territory purchased from Russia in 1867 (64°N/150°W) 610

Albany capital of New York located in the Hudson Valley; site where Albany Congress proposed first formal plan to unite the 13 colonies (40°45'N/73°45'W) 59

Allegheny River river in western Pennsylvania uniting with the Monongahela River at Pittsburgh to form the Ohio River (40°N/82°W) 96

Andes Mountains mountain system extending along western coast of South America (13°S/75°W) 12

Antarctica continent located around the South Pole (80°15'S/127°E) 39

Antietam Civil War battle site in western Maryland (39°45'N/77°30'W) 419

Appalachian Mountains chief mountain system in eastern North America extending from Quebec and New Brunswick to central Alabama (37°N/82°W) 57

Appomattox Court House site in central Virginia where Confederate forces surrendered ending the Civil War (37°N/77°W) 437

Arctic Ocean ocean in the northernmost part of the world (85°N/170°E) 12

Arizona state in the southwestern United States; 48th state to enter the Union (34°N/113°W) 378

Arkansas state in the south central United States; acquired as part of Louisiana Purchase (34°45'N/93°45'W) 265

Aroostook Valley fertile farming region in Maine (47°N/68°W) 367

Asia continent of the Eastern Hemisphere forming a single landmass with Europe (50°N/100°E) 12

Atlanta capital of Georgia located in the northwest central part of the state (33°45'N/84°30'W) 398

Atlantic Ocean ocean separating North and South America from Europe and Africa (5°S/25°W) 12

Australia continent and country southeast of Asia (25°S/125°E) 12

B

Baltimore city on the Chesapeake Bay in central Maryland (39°15'N/76°45'W) 57

Barbary Coast north coast of Africa between Morocco and Tunisia (36°45'N/3°E) 255

Baton Rouge capital of Louisiana located on the Mississippi River in the southeastern part of the state (30°30'N/91°15'W) 275

Bay of Pigs site of 1961 invasion of Cuba by U.S.-trained Cuban exiles (22°N/79°W) 924

Beijing capital of China located in the northeastern part of the country (40°N/116°30'E) 619

Berlin city in east central Germany; former national capital divided into sectors after World War II; city reunited in 1989 (52°31'N/13°30'E) 819

Black Hills mountains in southwestern South Dakota; site of conflict between the Sioux and white settlers during 1870s (44°15'N/103°45'W) 478

Boston capital of Massachusetts located in the eastern part of the state; founded by English Puritans in 1630 (42°15'N/71°W) 57

Brazil country in eastern South America (9°S/53°W) 39

C

California state in the western United States; attracted thousands of miners during gold rush of 1849 (38°15'N/121°15'W) 12

Cambodia country in Southeast Asia bordering Gulf of Siam; official name Democratic Kampuchea (12°N/105°E) 933

Canada country in northern North America (50°N/100°W) 303

Charleston city in South Carolina on the Atlantic coast; original name Charles Town (32°45'N/80°W) 213

Château-Thierry—Greece

Château-Thierry World War I battle site in France (49°N/3°15'E) 693

Chautauqua Lake lake in western New York State (42°15'N/79°45'W) 559

Chesapeake Bay inlet of the Atlantic Ocean in Virginia and Maryland (37°N/76°W) 57

Chicago largest city in Illinois; located in northeastern part of the state along Lake Michigan (41°45'N/87°30'W) 265

China country in eastern Asia; mainland (People's Republic of China) under communist control since 1949 (36°45'N/93°E) 12

Chisholm Trail pioneer cattle trail from Texas to Kansas (34°N/98°W) 478

Cincinnati city in southern Ohio on the Ohio River; grew as result of increasing steamship traffic during the mid-1800s (39°15'N/84°30'W) 153

Cleveland city in northern Ohio on Lake Erie (41°30'N/81°45'W) 265

Colorado state in the western United States (39°30'N/107°W) 378

Columbia River river flowing through southwest Canada and northwestern United States into the Pacific Ocean (46°15'N/124°W) 150

Concord village northwest of Boston, Massachusetts; site of early battle of the American Revolution on April 19, 1775 (42°N/71°W) 113

Connecticut state in the northeastern United States; one of the original 13 states (41°45'N/73°15'W) 57

Cuba country in the West Indies, North America (22°N/79°W) 605

Czechoslovakia former country in central Europe; now two countries, the Czech Republic and Slovakia (49°30'N/16°E) 702

D

Delaware state in the northeastern United States; one of the original 13 states (38°45'N/75°30'W) 57

Detroit city in southeastern Michigan; site of significant battles during the French and Indian War and the War of 1812; center of automobile industry (42°15'N/82°15'W) 150

dust bowl area of the Great Plains where the drought of the 1930s turned the soil to wind-borne dust (37°N/98°W) 783

E

Egypt country in northeastern Africa (27°N/30°E) 693

England division of the United Kingdom of Great Britain and Northern Ireland (56°30'N/1°45'W) 12

Erie Canal waterway connecting the Hudson River with Lake Erie through New York State (43°N/76°W) 265

Erie, Lake one of the Great Lakes between Canada and the United States (42°15'N/81°30'W) 50

Europe continent of the northern part of the Eastern Hemisphere between Asia and the Atlantic Ocean (50°N/15°E) 12

F

Florida state in the southeastern United States (30°30'N/84°45'W) 95

Fort Duquesne French fort on the site of Pittsburgh, Pennsylvania (40°30'N/80°W) 96

Fort Sumter Union fort during the Civil War located on island near Charleston, South Carolina; site of first military engagement of Civil War (32°45'N/80°W) 412

France country in western Europe (49°45'N/0°45'E) 12

Fredericksburg city and Civil War battle site in northeast Virginia (38°15'N/77°30'W) 419

Freeport city in northern Illinois; site of 1858 Lincoln-Douglas debate (42°15'N/89°30'W) 403

G

Galveston city on the Gulf of Mexico coast in Texas; created nation's first commission form of city government (29°15'N/95°W) 632

Georgia state in the southeastern United States (32°45'N/83°45'W) 57

Germany country in central Europe; divided after World War II into East Germany and West Germany; unified in 1989 (50°N/10°E) 689

Gettysburg city and Civil War battle site in south central Pennsylvania; site where Lincoln delivered the Gettysburg Address (39°45'N/77°15'W) 419

Great Basin interior drainage area in Nevada (40°15'N/117°15'W) 376

Great Britain commonwealth comprising England, Scotland, and Wales (56°30'N/1°45'W) 92

Great Lakes chain of five lakes, Superior, Erie, Michigan, Ontario, and Huron, in central North America (45°N/87°W) 95

Great Plains flat grassland in the central United States (45°N/104°W) 376

Great Salt Lake lake in northern Utah with no outlet and strongly saline waters (41°15'N/112°45'W) 238

Greece country in southeastern Europe (39°N/21°30'E) 702

Guadalcanal island in the Solomons east of Australia (9°45'S/158°45'E) 882

Guam United States possession in the western Pacific Ocean (14°N/143°15'E) 610

H

Harlem northern section of Manhattan in New York City; cultural center of African Americans in the early and mid-1900s (40°45'N/74°W) 734

Harpers Ferry town in northern West Virginia on the Potomac River (39°15'N/77°45'W) 403

Hartford capital of Connecticut located on the Connecticut River in the central part of the state (41°45'N/72°45'W) 57

Hawaii state in the United States located in the Pacific Ocean (20°N/157°W) 610

Hiroshima city in southern Japan; site of first military use of atomic bomb, August 6, 1945 (34°15'N/132°30'E) 822

Hispaniola island in the West Indies in North America, where Haiti and the Dominican Republic are located (17°30'N/73°15'W) 50

Hong Kong British colony along the southern coast of China in Asia (21°45'N/115°E) 610

Hudson Bay large bay in northern Canada (60°N/86°W) 12

Hudson River river flowing through New York State into the Atlantic Ocean at New York City (52°45'N/74°W) 57

Hungary country in central Europe (47°N/20°E) 702

Huron, Lake one of the Great Lakes between the United States and Canada in North America (45°15'N/82°45'W) 50

I

Idaho state in the northwestern United States; ranks among top states in silver production (44°N/115°15'W) 478

Illinois state in the north central United States; one of the states formed in the Northwest Territory (40°30'N/90°45'W) 213

India country in southern Asia (23°N/77°30'E) 12

Indian Territory land reserved by the United States government for Native Americans, now the state of Oklahoma (36°N/98°15'W) 316

Indiana state in the north central United States; one of the states formed in the Northwest Territory (39°45'N/86°45'W) 213

Indochina region in Southeast Asia (17°15'N/105°15'E) 879

Iowa state in the north central United States acquired as part of the Louisiana Purchase (42°N/94°15'W) 12

Iran country of the Middle East in southwestern Asia (31°15'N/53°30'E) 702

Iraq country of the Middle East in southwestern Asia (32°N/42°30'E) 883

Israel country of the Middle East in southwestern Asia along the Mediterranean Sea (32°45'N/34°E) 883

Italy country in southern Europe along the Mediterranean Sea (44°N/11°15'E) 689

J

Jamestown first permanent English settlement in North America; located in southeastern Virginia (37°15'N/76°45'W) 57

Japan island country in eastern Asia (36°30'N/133°30'E) 610

K

Kansas state in the central United States; fighting over slavery issue in 1850s gave territory the name "Bleeding Kansas" (38°30'N/98°45'W) 378

Kentucky state in the south central United States; border state that sided with the Union during the Civil War (37°30'N/87°30'W) 212

Kings Mountain Revolutionary War battle site in northern South Carolina (35°15'N/81°15'W) 137

Korea peninsula in eastern Asia between China, Russia, and the Sea of Japan, on which are located the countries of North Korea and South Korea (38°15'N/127°30'E) 822

Kuwait country of the Middle East in southwestern Asia between Iraq and Saudi Arabia (29°N/47°45'E) 702

L

Lebanon country in southwest Asia along the Mediterranean Sea (34°N/34°E) 883

Lexington Revolutionary War battle site in eastern Massachusetts; site of first clash between colonists and British, April 19, 1775 (42°26'N/71°13'W) 113

Little Rock capital of Arkansas located in the center of the state; site of 1957 conflict over public school integration (34°45'N/92°15'W) 398

London capital of United Kingdom located in the southeastern part of England (51°30'N/0°15'W) 12

Los Angeles—North Dakota

Los Angeles city along the Pacific coast in southern California; industrial, financial, and trade center of western United States (34°N/118°15'W) 376

Louisiana state in the south central United States (30°45'N/92°45'W) 213

Louisiana Territory region of west central United States between the Mississippi River and the Rocky Mountains purchased from France in 1803 (40°N/95°W) 95

M

Maine state in the northeastern United States; 23rd state to enter the Union (45°30'N/69°45'W) 57

Maryland state in the eastern United States; one of the original 13 states (39°15'N/76°30'W) 57

Massachusetts state in the northeastern United States; one of the original 13 states (42°15'N/72°30'W) 57

Mediterranean Sea sea between Europe and Africa (36°15'N/13°30'E) 33

Mexico country in North America south of the United States (23°45'N/104°W) 277

Mexico, Gulf of gulf south of the United States and east of Mexico in North America (25°15'N/93°45'W) 12

Michigan state in the north central United States; one of the states formed in the Northwest Territory (45°N/85°W) 265

Michigan, Lake one of the five Great Lakes located in the north central United States (43°15'N/87°15'W) 50

Midway Islands United States possession in the central Pacific Ocean; site of Battle of Midway, June 1942 (28°N/177°W) 610

Milwaukee city in eastern Wisconsin along Lake Michigan (43°N/88°W) 528

Minnesota state in the north central United States; fur trade, good soil, and lumber attracted early settlers (46°15'N/96°15'W) 398

Mississippi state in the southeastern United States; became English territory after French and Indian War (32°30'N/89°45'W) 213

Mississippi River river flowing through the United States from Minnesota to the Gulf of Mexico; explored by French in 1600s (29°N/89°W) 50

Missouri state in the south central United States; petition for statehood resulted in sectional conflict and the Missouri Compromise (40°45'N/93°W) 12

Missouri River river flowing through the United States from the Rocky Mountains to the Mississippi River near St. Louis (38°45'N/90°15'W) 50

Montana state in the northwestern United States; cattle industry grew during 1850s (47°15'N/111°45'W) 378

Montgomery capital of Alabama located in the central part of the state; site of 1955 bus boycott to protest segregation (32°30'N/86°15'W) 398

Montreal city on the St. Lawrence River in southern Quebec, Canada (45°30'N/73°30'W) 50

Moscow capital of former Soviet Union and capital of Russia (55°45'N/37°30'E) 818

N

Nashville capital of Tennessee located in the north central part of the state (36°15'N/86°45'W) 213

Natchez city in western Mississippi along the Mississippi River (31°30'N/91°15'W) 265

National Road road from Baltimore, Maryland, to Vandalia, Illinois (40°N/81°30'W) 265

Nebraska state in the central United States (41°45'N/101°30'W) 378

Netherlands country in northwestern Europe (53°N/4°E) 39

Nevada state in the western United States (39°30'N/117°W) 378

New Amsterdam town founded on Manhattan Island by Dutch settlers in 1625; renamed New York by British settlers (40°45'N/74°W) 57

New Hampshire state in the northeastern United States; one of the original 13 states (44°N/71°45'W) 57

New Jersey state in the northeastern United States; one of the original 13 states (40°30'N/74°45'W) 57

New Mexico state in the southwestern United States; ceded to the United States by Mexico in 1848 (34°30'N/107°15'W) 378

New Orleans city in southern Louisiana in the Mississippi Delta (30°N/90°W) 213

New York state in the northeastern United States; one of the original 13 states (42°45'N/78°W) 57

New York City city in southeastern New York State at the mouth of the Hudson River; largest city in the United States (40°45'N/74°W) 59

Nicaragua country in Central America (12°45'N/86°15'W) 616

Normandy region along French coast and site of D-Day invasion, June 6, 1944 (48°N/2°W) 820

North America continent in the northern part of the Western Hemisphere between the Atlantic and Pacific oceans (45°N/100°W) 39

North Carolina state in the southeastern United States; one of the original 13 states (35°45'N/81°30'W) 57

North Dakota state in the north central United States; Congress created Dakota Territory in 1861 (47°15'N/102°W) 378

Northwest Territory territorial division north of the Ohio River and east of the Mississippi River (47°30'N/87°30'W) 212

O

Oberlin college and town in northern Ohio (41°15'N/82°15'W) 558

Ohio state in the north central United States; first state in the Northwest Territory (40°30'N/83°15'W) 213

Ohio River river flowing from Allegheny and Monongahela rivers in western Pennsylvania into the Mississippi River (39°N/85°W) 50

Ohio Valley valley of the Ohio River, which flows from Pennsylvania to the Mississippi River at Cairo, Illinois (37°30'N/88°W) 11

Oklahoma state in the south central United States; Five Civilized Tribes moved to territory 1830–1842 (36°N/98°15'W) 378

Omaha city in eastern Nebraska on the Missouri River (41°15'N/96°W) 498

Ontario, Lake one of the five Great Lakes between Canada and the United States (43°30'N/79°W) 50

Oregon state in the northwestern United States; adopted woman suffrage in 1912 (43°45'N/123°45'W) 378

Oregon Trail pioneer trail from Independence, Missouri, to the Oregon Territory (42°30'N/110°W) 368

P

Pacific Ocean world's largest ocean located between Asia and the Americas (0°/175°W) 12

Panama country in the southern part of Central America, occupying the Isthmus of Panama (8°N/81°W) 621

Panama Canal canal built across the Isthmus of Panama through Panama to connect the Caribbean Sea and the Pacific Ocean (9°15'N/79°45'W) 621

Pearl Harbor naval base at Honolulu, Hawaii; site of 1941 Japanese attack, leading to United States entry into World War II (21°21'N/157°57'W) 822

Pennsylvania state in the northeastern United States (41°N/78°15'W) 57

Persian Gulf gulf in southwestern Asia between Iran and the Arabian Peninsula (27°45'N/50°30'E) 995

Philadelphia city in eastern Pennsylvania on the Delaware River; Declaration of Independence and the Constitution both adopted in city's Independence Hall (40°N/75°W) 57

Philippines island country in southeast Asia (14°30'N/125°E) 605

Pittsburgh city in western Pennsylvania; one of the great steelmaking centers of the world (40°30'N/80°W) 213

Plymouth town in eastern Massachusetts; first successful English colony in New England (42°N/70°45'W) 57

Portugal country in southwestern Europe (38°15'N/8°15'W) 39

Potomac River river flowing from West Virginia into Chesapeake Bay (38°N/77°W) 57

Promontory Point site in Utah where the first transcontinental railroad was completed (41°45'N/112°15'W) 498

Providence capital of Rhode Island; site of first English settlement in Rhode Island (41°45'N/71°30'W) 57

Puerto Rico United States possession in the West Indies (18°15'N/66°45'W) 50

Pullman company town south of Chicago; site of 1894 railroad strike (41°45'N/87°30'W) 519

Q

Quebec city in Canada, capital of Quebec Province, on the St. Lawrence River; first settlement in New France (46°45'N/71°15'W) 50

R

Raleigh capital of North Carolina located in the north central part of the state (35°45'N/78°45'W) 265

Rhode Island state in the northeastern United States; one of the original 13 states (41°30'N/71°45'W) 57

Richmond capital of Virginia located in the central part of the state; capital of the Confederacy during the Civil War (37°30'N/77°30'W) 137

Rio Grande river between the United States and Mexico in North America; forms the boundary between Texas and Mexico (26°N/97°30'W) 50

Roanoke island off the coast of present-day North Carolina that was site of early British colonizing efforts (35°N/75°39'W) 57

Rocky Mountains mountain range in western United States and Canada in North America (50°N/114°W) 303

Russia name of republic; former empire of eastern Europe and northern Asia coinciding with Soviet Union (60°30'N/64°E) 12

Sacramento—Vermont

S

Sacramento capital of California located in the north central part of the state (38°30'N/121°30'W) 368

St. Augustine city in northeastern Florida on the Atlantic coast; oldest permanent existing European settlement in North America, founded in 1565 (30°N/81°15'W) 50

St. Lawrence River river flowing from Lake Ontario, between Canada and the United States, through Canada to the Atlantic Ocean (48°N/65°15'W) 57

St. Louis city in eastern Missouri on the Mississippi River (38°45'N/90°15'W) 153

St. Mihiel World War I battle site in France (49°N/5°30'E) 693

Salt Lake City capital of Utah located in the northern part of the state; founded by Mormons in 1847 (40°45'N/111°45'W) 368

San Antonio city in south central Texas (29°30'N/98°30'W) 371

San Francisco city in northern California on the Pacific coast (37°45'N/122°30'W) 368

Santa Fe capital of New Mexico located in the north central part of the state (35°45'N/106°W) 368

Saratoga Revolutionary War battle site in the Hudson Valley of eastern New York State (43°N/73°51'W) 131

Savannah city in eastern Georgia (32°N/81°W) 57

Sea Islands group of islands off the coast of Georgia and South Carolina (31°15'N/81°W) 444

Seneca Falls town in New York State; site of woman's rights convention in 1848 (43°N/77°W) 341

Sierra Nevada mountain range in eastern California (39°N/120°W) 478

South Africa country in southern Africa (28°S/24°45'E) 693

South America continent in the southern part of the Western Hemisphere lying between the Atlantic and Pacific oceans (15°S/60°W) 39

South Carolina state in the southeastern United States; one of the original 13 states (34°15'N/81°15'W) 57

South Dakota state in the north central United States; acquired through the Louisiana Purchase (44°15'N/102°W) 378

Soviet Union former country in northern Europe and Asia (60°30'N/64°E) 807

Spain country in southwestern Europe (40°15'N/4°30'W) 12

Stalingrad city in the former Soviet Union on the Volga River; present name Volgograd (48°45'N/42°15'E) 819

Suez Canal canal built between the Mediterranean Sea and the Red Sea through northeastern Egypt (31°N/32°15'E) 883

Superior, Lake one of the five Great Lakes between Canada and the United States in North America (47°45'N/89°15'W) 50

T

Tampa city in west central Florida (28°N/82°30'W) 498

Tennessee state in the south central United States; first state readmitted to the Union after the Civil War (35°45'N/88°W) 213

Tennessee Valley valley of the Tennessee River, which flows from the Appalachian Mountains to the Ohio River (35°30'N/88°15'W) 781

Tenochtitlán Aztec capital on the site of present-day Mexico City (19°30'N/99°15'W) 12

Texas state in the south central United States; Mexican colony that became an independent republic before joining the United States (31°N/101°W) 213

Tokyo capital of Japan located on the eastern coast of Honshu Island (35°45'N/139°45'E) 822

Toronto city in Canada on Lake Ontario; capital of the province of Ontario (43°45'N/79°30'W) 251

Trenton capital of New Jersey located on the Delaware River in the central part of the state; site of Revolutionary War battle in December 1776 (40°15'N/74°45'W) 131

U

Union of Soviet Socialist Republics *See* Soviet Union.

United Kingdom country in northwestern Europe made up of England, Scotland, Wales, and Northern Ireland (56°30'N/1°45'W) 689

United States country in central North America; fourth largest country in the world in both area and population (38°N/110°W) 146

Utah state in the western United States; settled by Mormons in 1840s (39°30'N/112°45'W) 378

V

Valley Forge Revolutionary War winter camp northwest of Philadelphia (40°N/75°30'W) 131

Veracruz city in eastern Mexico on the Gulf of Mexico coast (19°15'N/96°W) 376

Vermont state in the northeastern United States; 14th state to enter the Union (43°45'N/72°45'W) 146

Vicksburg city and Civil War battle site in western Mississippi on the Mississippi River (32°21'N/90°52'W) 421

Vietnam country in southeastern Asia (16°N/108°E) 935

Virginia state in the eastern United States; colony in which first permanent English settlement in the Americas was established (37°N/78°W) 57

W

Wall Street street in New York City at the center of the financial district (40°45'N/74°W) 535

Washington state in the northwestern United States; territory reached by Lewis and Clark in 1805 (47°30'N/121°15'W) 378

Washington, D.C. capital of the United States located on the Potomac River at its confluence with the Anacostia River, between Maryland and Virginia; coinciding with the District of Columbia (38°53'N/77°02'W) 213

West Virginia state in the east central United States (39°N/80°45'W) 378

Willamette River Valley valley of the Willamette River in western Oregon (45°N/123°W) 368

Wisconsin state in the north central United States; passed first state unemployment compensation act, 1932 (44°30'N/91°W) 265

Wounded Knee site of battle between settlers and Native Americans in southern South Dakota in 1890 and of Native American movement protest in 1973 (43°26'N/102°30'W) 478

Wyoming state in the western United States; territory provided women the right to vote, 1869 (42°45'N/108°30'W) 478

Y

Yorktown town in southeastern Virginia and site of final battle of Revolutionary War (37°15'N/76°30'W) 137

Z

Zaire country in central Africa (1°S/22°15'E) 926

Glossary

A

abolitionist 1800s reformer who worked to end slavery (p. 342)

acid rain acid precipitation in the form of rain (p. 1016)

agribusiness large farming operation that includes the cultivation, processing, storage, and distribution of farm products (p. 869)

amendment alteration to the Constitution (p. 160)

amnesty act of a government by which pardon is granted to an individual or groups of persons (p. 445)

anarchism a belief in no direct government authority over society (p. 531)

anarchist one who opposes all forms of government (p. 616)

antebellum customs, manners, and institutions that existed before the Civil War (p. 559)

appeasement policy of compromising or giving in to demands in an attempt to avoid trouble and maintain peace (p. 809)

appropriations bill draft of a law setting aside funds for a specific use (p. 1007)

arbitration hearing and resolution of a disagreement between two parties through an impartial third party (pp. 524, 600)

armistice temporary suspension of hostilities between opponents (p. 695)

armory place or building where arms and military equipment are stored (p. 740)

artillery weapons for discharging missiles (p. 116)

assimilation process of one group or culture absorbing another (p. 911)

astrolabe instrument used to observe positions of celestial bodies (p. 27)

automation technique of operating a machine, manufacturing process, or system that will do a job formerly performed by humans (p. 872)

B

balance of payments difference between the value of a nation's imports and its exports; also known as balance of trade (p. 964)

bicameral political system based on two legislative chambers (p. 144)

bilingualism ability to speak two languages (p. 918)

blacklist record kept by companies of employees or former employees who are disapproved of or are to be punished or boycotted (p. 521)

black nationalism belief of militant blacks who advocate separatism from whites and forming self-governing black communities (p. 910)

black power mobilizing economic and political power of African Americans to improve their condition (p. 911)

blitzkrieg war conducted with great speed or force (p. 812)

blockade to close off something (p. 415)

bond certificate that earns interest and is redeemed for cash on a specific date (p. 209)

bounty money paid to recruit soldiers for military service; payment to encourage an action (p. 427)

boycott refusal to buy goods or have dealings with a country or other entity, usually to express disapproval or force acceptance of certain conditions (p. 100)

buffer area designed to separate and serve as a protective barrier; neutral area separating conflicting forces (p. 840)

business cycle sequence of economic activity, usually consisting of recession, recovery, growth, and decline (p. 520)

busing transportation of children to a school outside their residential area to establish racial integration in that school (p. 914)

C

cabinet a group of advisers to the President (p. 205)

capital money invested in a business (p. 26)

caravel small ship with a broad bow (p. 27)

carrack large merchant ship (p. 27)

charter formal document granting the right of self-rule (p. 17)

classical relating to ancient Greece or Rome (p. 17)

closed shop system where all workers in a particular industry are required to be union members or employer agrees to hire only union members (p. 291)

coalition alliance, combination, or union of parties, people, or states formed for a specific action or purpose (p. 789)

collective bargaining negotiation between organized workers and management to reach an agreement on wages, hours, and working conditions (p. 521)

collective security an agreement to provide for common defense (p. 843)

commodity economic good; product of agriculture; article of commerce (p. 488)

commonwealth self-governing political unit of independent states associated in a common allegiance (p. 65)

commune group of people living together with collective ownership and use of property, often having shared goals, philosophies, and ways of life; large cooperative farms (p. 939)

communism system of government in which the Communist party controls the political, economic, cultural, and social life of the people; economic system in which society as a whole, represented by the Communist party, owns all means of production, distribution, and exchange of goods (p. 838)

compact covenant, agreement, or contract between two or more parties (p. 321)

company town village built and run by a company where workers are required to live (p. 519)

compass device for determining direction by means of a magnetic needle (p. 27)

confederation nonbinding political alliance of independent countries, states, or groups (p. 13)

congregation body of church members; people meeting for worship and religious instruction (p. 65)

conquistador Spanish adventurer in sixteenth-century Americas (p. 42)

conscientious objector person who refuses to perform military service or to bear arms on the grounds of moral or religious principles or beliefs (p. 937)

conscription compulsory enrollment of people for military service (p. 426)

consensus general agreement; judgment arrived at by most of those concerned; group solidarity in sentiment and belief (p. 956)

conservation the planned management of natural resources to prevent destruction or neglect (p. 652)

conspicuous consumption lavish spending for show (p. 584)

constitution plan of government in America; basic principles and laws of a nation, state, or social group that determine the powers and duties of the government and guarantee certain rights to its people (p. 67)

consul official appointed by a government to reside in a foreign country to represent the interests of the citizens of the appointing country (p. 374)

containment policy of preventing the expansion of a hostile power; post-World War II foreign policy stating the United States would hold Soviet influence within its existing limits (p. 840)

Continental American paper money used as currency instead of British coins (p. 126)

contraband goods or merchandise whose importation, exportation, or possession is forbidden (p. 687)

cooperative enterprise or organization owned by and operated for the benefit of those using its services (p. 570)

corollary proposition added to another as a natural consequence or effect (p. 617)

corporation form of business consisting of a group of people authorized by law to act as a single person and having an identity that survives its incorporators (p. 502)

cotton gin a machine that cleans the seeds from cotton fibers (p. 294)

counterculture one with values and mores that run contrary to those of established society (p. 939)

covenant formal and binding agreement between two or more parties (p. 702)

covert secret or undercover; not openly shown or engaged in (p. 880)

crack cocaine purified cocaine in the form of small chips (p. 1019)

craft union labor union in which all members practice the same occupation or skill (p. 790)

credibility gap lack of trust stemming from difference between official government statements and practices (p. 928)

creditor nation a nation that lends money (p. 1013)

creole resident of the Spanish colonies born of Spanish parents (p. 44)

currency paper money that is in circulation as a means of exchange (p. 154)

D

dark horse political candidate unexpectedly nominated, usually as a compromise between groups (p. 372)

debtor nation a country that owes money (p. 1013)

defense perimeter boundary of military protection (p. 848)

deficit spending government practice of borrowing money in order to spend more money than is received from taxes (p. 780)

deflation economic condition in which the volume of available money or credit decreases, resulting in the decline of the price of goods and services (p. 574)

deported remove from a country an alien presence is unlawful (p. 705)

depression economic condition marked by an extended and severe decline in production and sales, and a severe increase in unemployment (p. 153)

deregulation act of removing restrictions and regulations (p. 970)

détente relaxation of cold war tensions between the United States and the Soviet Union that began in the early 1970s (p. 942)

direct primary election in which nominations of candidates for office are made by voters (p. 634)

direct tax one paid directly to the government rather than being included in the price of goods; a tax collected directly from the person on whom the tax burden is expected to fall (p. 100)

disenfranchised having had the legal right to vote taken away (p. 449)

disestablished deprived of the status and privileges of an established position (p. 145)

dissenter protester; one who differs in opinion from the majority (p. 63)

dole money or goods given as charity; grant of government funds to the unemployed (p. 780)

domestic market market composed of buyers and sellers within a nation (p. 723)

downsizing to reduce operations or number of employees (p. 1007)

duty tax on imported goods (p. 92)

dynasty series of rulers from the same family; powerful family that holds its influence for a long time (p. 18)

E

economies of scale ability of large businesses to operate more cheaply and efficiently than smaller ones, resulting in lower per-unit costs for the products of large companies (p. 498)

effigy crude image or representation of a hated person (p. 104)

emancipation freeing of enslaved persons; act or process of freeing from restraint, control, or the power of another; freedom from bondage (p. 145)

emigration departure from one's place of residence or country to live in another (p. 289)

encomienda system of rewarding conquistadores with tracts of land, including the right to tax and demand labor from Native Americans who lived on the land (p. 44)

entrepreneur person who organizes, manages, and assumes the risks of a business or enterprise (p. 495)

enumerated commodity colonial product that Parliament said could be shipped only to Britain (p. 92)

enumerated powers those mentioned specifically one after another in the Constitution (p. 212)

envoy person delegated to represent one government in its dealings with another; a messenger, representative (p. 130)

escalation increase in extent, volume, number, amount, intensity, or scope (p. 932)

ethnic cleansing expulsion or extermination of a group from a country (p. 1009)

ethnic group groups of people who share the same culture, religion, and customs (p. 797)

excise tax one paid by a manufacturer and passed on to those who buy the product; a tax on the manufacture, sale, or consumption of a product within a country (p. 209)

executive privilege principle that the executive branch of government is exempt from disclosing information when such disclosure would adversely affect the functions and decision-making processes of the presidency or national security (p. 968)

expatriate person who leaves his or her native country to live elsewhere (p. 560)

expedition a journey with a specific purpose (p. 239)

extraterritoriality exemption from the application or jurisdiction of local law (p. 382)

F

fascism system of government that is strongly nationalistic and allows private ownership of property while controlling general economic policies; government characterized by racism and militarism; a repressive one-party dictatorship (p. 809)

favorite son presidential candidate supported by the delegates of the candidate's native state at a national political convention (p. 302)

featherbedding requiring of an employer under a union rule or safety statute to hire more employees than are needed (p. 852)

federalism system of government in which power is distributed between national and state governments (p. 159)

federalized brought under federal government jurisdiction (p. 902)

feminist person who acts on behalf of women's rights (p. 916)

feudalism a system in which powerful leaders gave land to nobles in return for pledges of loyalty and service (p. 15)

filibuster the use of delaying tactics to prevent action in a legislative assembly (p. 1006)

fireside chat the name used to describe how former President Franklin D. Roosevelt talked to people by radio (p. 775)

forage to live off the land (p. 432)

foreclosure legal procedure for reclaiming a piece of property when the owner is unable to keep up the mortgage payments (p. 782)

free-trader one that practices or advocates trade without taxes or tariffs (p. 555)

G

frigate medium-sized warship smaller than a destroyer; used for escort and patrol duties (p. 251)

genocide deliberate and systematic destruction of a group (p. 1009)

gentry the upper class of England (p. 73)

global economy economic interdependence among countries of the world (p. 1013)

globalized corporation firms that do business and have offices or factories in many countries (p. 1013)

gold standard monetary system in which a nation's currency is based on the value of gold (p. 574)

graft acquisition of money or power in dishonest or questionable ways while in public office (p. 544)

greenback paper money that was not backed by gold or silver; legal-tender notes issued by the United States government (p. 429)

grievance formal expression of a complaint (p. 116)

guerrilla soldier who barrages the enemy with surprise attacks, harassment, sabotage, and other nontraditional warfare (p. 840)

H

habeas corpus legal principle which requires that people who are arrested be brought to court to show why they should be held; writ inquiring into the lawfulness of retaining a person who is imprisoned or detained in custody (p. 424)

holding company one that gains control of other companies by buying their stock (p. 505)

Holocaust systematic mass murder of 12 million European civilians, especially Jews, by Nazis during World War II (p. 821)

horizontal integration joining together of businesses that are engaged in similar business activities or processes (p. 505)

humanism interest in classical Greek and Roman arts, literature, knowledge, and culture (p. 17)

I

illegal alien noncitizen who is in a country illegally (p. 1019)

impeach to bring charges of a crime against a federal or state public official with the intent of removing the official from office (p. 451)

imperialism act of creating an empire by dominating other nations (p. 598)

implied powers those suggested but not directly stated in the Constitution (p. 212)

impound to refuse to spend congressionally allocated funds; to seize and hold in the custody of the law (p. 970)

impressment form of military and naval conscription, usually by force, practiced by Britain and other European countries (p. 245)

income tax tax on the net income of an individual or business (p. 659)

incumbent current officeholder (p. 1002)

indemnity security or protection against hurt, loss, or damage; exemption from incurred penalties or liabilities (p. 619)

indentured servant person who agreed to work for an employer in colonial America for a specified time in exchange for passage to America (p. 58)

industrial union union that represents every worker in a single industry regardless of his or her job (pp. 526, 790)

inflation decline in money's value when more money is printed, resulting in increased prices of goods and services (p. 573)

inheritance tax tax on an inheritance that an heir must pay to receive the inheritance (p. 661)

initiative procedure enabling citizens to propose a bill by petitioning with a specific number of signatures from registered voters (p. 634)

injunction court order requiring an individual or company to do something or to prohibit a given action; used frequently to stop strikes (p. 527)

installment buying system of paying for goods at regular intervals, usually with interest added to the balance (p. 744)

interlocking directorate system under which the same people serve on the boards of directors of several firms within the same industry (p. 670)

internal improvements roads, canals, and other transportation needs inside a nation's boundaries (p. 259)

isolationism policy or belief that a nation should limit its alliances and involvement in international political and economic affairs (p. 598)

isthmus narrow piece of land connecting two larger land areas (p. 40)

J

joint resolution a resolution passed by both houses of Congress requiring only a simple majority vote (p. 372)

joint-stock company form of business organization; pooled funds of many investors or stockholders who can independently sell their shares of the company (p. 26)

judicial review Supreme Court's power to review all congressional acts and executive actions and reject those it considers unconstitutional (p. 234)

jurisdictional strike one resulting from a dispute between unions over which union should represent the workers in a company or industry (p. 852)

K

kickback payback of a sum received from increased fees because of a confidential agreement or act of coercion (p. 545)

L

laissez-faire government doctrine of noninterference in business practices and in the economic affairs of individuals; literally, "let do" (p. 233)

lame duck elected official who continues to hold office during the period between the election and the inauguration of a successor (p. 761)

land speculator person who purchases land to resell for profit; one who buys or sells land in expectation of profiting from future price changes (p. 99)

lend-lease transfer of goods and services to an ally (p. 815)

line-item veto power to veto a single part of a bill (p. 1007)

line of demarcation north-south line of longitude through the Atlantic Ocean dividing lands in the Americas claimed by Spain and Portugal (p. 38)

literacy test tests to show if immigrants could read (p. 641)

lobbyist person who promotes or secures the passage of legislation by influencing public officials (p. 547)

lock chambers with gates at each end used to raise or lower boats as they pass from a level of higher elevation to a level of lower elevation or the reverse on a river or canal (p. 263)

lockout closed factory or place of employment caused by a strike; withholding of employment by an employer (p. 521)

long drive cattle run in which a large herd is moved across great distances to a railhead, where they are shipped to market (p. 478)

Loyalist American colonist who supported the British government; one who is or remains loyal to a political cause, party, or government (p. 116)

lyceum voluntary organization providing public lectures, concerts, and entertainments to promote the improvement of its members and their useful knowledge (p. 337)

M

maize a large seeded grass cultivated by people in the central valley of Mexico which became the forerunner of corn (p. 8)

mandate clear expression of the wishes of voters, as shown in election results (pp. 448, 951)

manor large estate owned by a noble on which peasants lived and were protected in exchange for their services (p. 15)

martial law form of military rule that suspends Bill of Rights guarantees; law administered by the military in an emergency situation when civilian law-enforcement agencies are not able to maintain order (p. 414)

maverick unbranded range animal or cattle; a motherless calf (p. 477)

mechanics' lien law charge against a bankrupt employer, insuring that wages owed to workers be the first payments made (p. 292)

melting-pot society a place where ethnic, social, and cultural assimilation is going on (p. 1020)

mercantilism the theory that a state's power depended on its wealth (p. 48)

mercenary paid soldier hired for service in the army of a foreign country; one that serves merely for wages (p. 116)

merchandising buying and selling of goods in a business for a profit (p. 537)

meridian line of longitude; a great circle on the surface of the earth passing through the poles (p. 486)

mestizo person in the Spanish colonies born of Spanish and Native American parents (p. 44)

militia group of civilians declared by law to be called to military service and trained as soldiers to fight in emergencies (p. 94)

monopoly exclusive control of a product or service in a particular market by a single company (p. 106)

moratorium official authorization to suspend payments, as with a debt; officially authorized period of waiting (p. 751)

mudslinging making malicious often untrue charges against an opponent (p. 310)

mulatto person of Spanish and African or Native American and African ancestry (p. 44)

multicultural society society in which all people respect unique cultures (p. 1020)

multinational corporation a corporation that operates divisions in more than two countries (p. 1013)

multinational state nation with many different ethnic groups (p. 1009)

N

nationalism feeling of loyalty and devotion to one's country, honoring that nation above all others and promoting its culture and interests rather than those of other nations (p. 258)

naval store products of pine forests used in wooden shipbuilding and maintenance (p. 61)

neutrality refusal to take sides (p. 603)

new federalism Richard Nixon's policy of economic partnership between the federal and state governments whereby states and municipalities received less federal funding (p. 965)

nomadic frequent roaming from place to place without a fixed pattern of movement, usually following a food source (p. 470)

nonimportation agreement one between colonial merchants and planters not to import certain goods (p. 100)

nonpartisan free from party affiliation, bias, or designation (p. 222)

nonviolent resistance objection or demonstration to gain political ends without use of violence (p. 900)

northwest passage water route to Asia through North America sought by European explorers (p. 47)

nullification state declaration of a federal law to be invalid (pp. 225, 320)

O

obiter dictum incidental opinion that is issued by a judge or court but is not binding (p. 400)

on margin method of buying stock with a small cash down payment and the rest borrowed from a stockbroker. Stockbroker holds shares of stock as collateral for the loan; borrower repays broker from stock resale profits (p. 743)

open shop employment practice in which eligibility is not determined by union membership (p. 715)

P

parliament supreme legislative body in Britain made up of nobility, clergy, and commons (p. 16)

partitioned divided into two or more territorial units having separate political status (p. 618)

Patriot American colonist who favored separation before and during the Revolutionary War (p. 116)

patronage practice of elected officials to make appointments to unelected government positions for political advantage or repayment of favors (p. 551)

patroon landowner in the Dutch colonies who received rent, taxes, and labor from tenant farmers (p. 70)

peninsulares government and church officials in Spanish colonial America who had been born in Spain (p. 44)

philanthropy actions to promote human welfare and benefit society (p. 511)

piracy robbery on the high seas (p. 244)

platform declaration of the principles and policies adopted by a political party or candidate (p. 327)

pocket veto indirect rejection of a legislative bill by the President by retaining the bill unsigned until after Congress adjourns (p. 316)

pogrom organized massacres of unarmed people, especially Jews (p. 530)

political machine party organization in big cities that holds power by controlling votes, courts, and police (p. 545)

pooling illegal agreements among individual railroads to divide the total volume of freight among their lines and to keep rates high (p. 570)

popular sovereignty principle that the settlers within a federal territory have the power to decide the legality of slavery within that territory (p. 389)

post-war disillusionment period after a war in which the populace is disenchanted (p. 732)

pragmatism belief that government actions should meet the needs of society; practical approach to problems and affairs (p. 628)

preamble introductory part of a constitution or statute that states the reasons for and intent of the law; introduction to a document (p. 116)

presidential succession the order in which others fill the office of President (p. 865)

presidio Spanish fort in the Americas built to protect mission settlements (p. 45)

price-cutting reduction of prices to a level designed to cripple competition (p. 670)

privateer armed private ship commissioned by the government to attack ships of an enemy (p. 217)

proclamation official formal public announcement (p. 419)

proprietor individual who received legal and exclusive right to American colonial land from the king of England and who was expected to administer the land according to English laws (p. 60)

protectionist one who advocates government protection for domestic producers and manufacturers through restrictions on imports (p. 555)

protective tariff high tax on imports intended to protect domestic products from foreign competition rather than to yield revenue (p. 208)

protectorate—sexism

protectorate country that is technically independent, but whose government and economy are controlled by a stronger power; the nation or region controlled by a stronger nation (p. 613)

public land land belonging to the national government and therefore to the people (p. 146)

pueblo apartment-like buildings of adobe and cut stone built by Native Americans (p. 11)

pump priming government money invested in the economy to stimulate a self-sustaining economic recovery (p. 780)

purge large-scale forced removal of officials who show signs of disloyalty to their superiors (p. 839)

Q

quadrant instrument used to measure altitudes (p. 27)

quorum number of officers or members of a body that must be present to legally transact business (p. 206)

R

racism belief that a particular race is superior to others (p. 910)

ratify to officially approve a proposal (p. 145)

reactionary government government characterized by ultraconservative policies (p. 928)

real wages income adjusted to compensate for reduced earning power due to inflation (p. 518)

realism European-influenced literary movement that strove for accurate representation of nature or real life without idealization (p. 559)

rebate discount in the form of a refund or part of a payment for a product or service (p. 507)

recall removal of an elected official by voters in a special election (p. 634)

recession downturn in the nation's economy marked by reduced economic activity (p. 792)

reciprocity mutual lowering by nations of tariff barriers; recognition by one of two countries of the validity of privileges granted by the other (p. 600)

redcoat derogatory term for British soldiers in the colonies, referring to their red uniforms (p. 101)

rediscount small fee charged to a member bank by the Federal Reserve Bank upon acceptance of a business's promissory note (p. 668)

referendum process by which people can vote directly on a proposed law (p. 634)

Renaissance revival of interest in the arts, literature, culture, and learning of ancient Greece and Rome, c. 1400–1600 (p. 17)

reparation payments made by nations defeated in war as a penalty for damages caused to other countries (p. 713)

revenue sharing plan to share or divide income (p. 965)

revenue tariff low tax on imports intended to provide income for the government rather than protection of domestic products from foreign competition (p. 208)

rider unrelated amendment attached to a bill under legislative consideration (p. 551)

right of deposit right to temporarily put goods ashore for transfer to other ships without paying import duties (p. 150)

right of self-determination right of people to choose their own government and be free from rule by a foreign country (p. 116)

S

saga prose narrative or heroic poem about legendary figures and events from the heroic age of Norway and Iceland (p. 36)

salutary neglect policy of noninterference by a governing nation in order to produce a beneficial effect (p. 93)

samurai member of the military class of feudal Japan (p. 23)

satellite nations East European nations politically and economically under Soviet domination; country dominated or controlled by another more powerful country (p. 839)

scab nonunion replacement workers during a strike or union members who refuse to strike and continue working (p. 521)

scrip money that can only be redeemed at a company store (p. 519)

scurvy sickness caused by lack of ascorbic acid (p. 29)

search-and-destroy strategy military tactic used to force enemy into open combat (p. 933)

seceding withdrawing from a large political body (p. 152)

secession formal withdrawal from an organization (p. 404)

securities stocks, bonds, and other financial instruments traded on a stock exchange (p. 742)

segregation enforced separation of racial groups in schooling, housing, and other public areas (p. 455)

serf peasant of the Middle Ages who was bound to the land (p. 15)

sexism prejudice or discrimination based on gender (p. 917)

sharecropper agricultural worker who cultivates part of another person's land, receives supplies and equipment from the landowner, and in return gives the landowner part of the harvest (p. 441)

shogun one of a line of military governors ruling Japan until the revolution of 1867–1868; Japanese commander in chief (p. 23)

shuttle diplomacy negotiations carried out by an intermediary who shuttles back and forth between the disputants (p. 945)

sit-in occupying seats or sitting on the floor of an establishment as a means of protest (p. 904)

social contract agreement among individuals forming an organized society that defines and limits the rights and duties of each (p. 116)

social Darwinism sociological theory that states only the fittest survive social competition and experience social advancement (p. 510)

social gospel application by religious organizations of Christian principles to social problems (p. 627)

socialism economic system in which government partly owns and controls production and distribution of goods produced (p. 349)

Spanish Armada large fleet of seemingly invincible ships dispatched by King Philip II of Spain to England in retaliation against English piracy (p. 48)

specie money in the form of gold and silver coin (p. 100)

speculation risky business venture involving buying or selling in the hope of making a large, quick profit (p. 743)

sphere of influence area in China during the late 1800s where trade was controlled by a foreign power (p. 618)

spoils system practice of dismissing government job holders affiliated with a defeated party and replacing them with supporters of the winning party (p. 315)

stagflation persistent inflation combined with static consumer demand and relatively high rate of unemployment (p. 964)

stock partial ownership interest in a company sold in the form of shares to raise operating capital (p. 26)

strait narrow passageway connecting two larger bodies of water (p. 40)

student deferment official postponement of military service (p. 937)

subsistence farming level of farming at which farmers produce only enough to feed and maintain their families (p. 61)

subversives people working secretly, attempting to overthrow or undermine a government or political system (p. 855)

suffrage right to vote (p. 214)

summit diplomatic meeting of the superpowers; conference of highest level government officials (p. 942)

T

tariff tax on imported goods (p. 208)

teach-in lecture, debate, and discussion on controversial topic (p. 938)

technological unemployment jobs lost as the result of machines doing the jobs formerly accomplished by humans (p. 715)

tenant farmer agricultural worker who rents and farms land from another person and pays the rent either in cash or with a portion of the crop (p. 441)

textile fabric, especially woven or knitted; cloth (p. 288)

third party minor political party operating in addition to two other major parties in a nation or state normally characterized by a two-party system (p. 575)

toll fee charged for a privilege such as the use of a means of transportation (p. 264)

totalitarian type of government controlled by a single person or party; suppressing freedom and controlling every aspect of life (p. 809)

township local unit of government within a county (p. 548)

trade deficit economic condition in which the value of a nation's imports is more than the value of its exports (p. 1013)

traitor one who commits treason (p. 136)

treason attempt to overthrow the government of the state to which the offender owes allegiance (p. 116)

tribute payment by one nation or ruler to another to acknowledge submission, or as the price of protection (p. 151)

trust combination of companies to gain control of an industry and reduce competition (p. 505)

turnpike road barricaded by spiked poles where travelers stop to pay a fee to use the road (p. 264)

U

ultimatum a demand that would have serious consequences if ignored (p. 272)

Underground Railroad a secret organization that had hiding places throughout the Northern states and Canada to bring enslaved people out of the South and to freedom (p. 343)

U

unicameral legislature consisting of a single chamber (p. 147)

urban renewal construction program to replace or restore a city or urban area (p. 953)

V

vaudeville stage entertainment consisting of various acts (p. 480)

vertical integration joining together of businesses that are involved in different but related activities or processes (p. 505)

veto action by which an executive rejects a bill submitted by a legislature; to refuse to approve (p. 144)

viceroy person who rules a country or province as the representative of the monarch (p. 45)

victory gardens gardens for raising one's own vegetables, especially during wartime (p. 698)

vigilance committee organization of citizens who take the law into their own hands for their protection (p. 480)

W

ward division of a city for representative, electoral, or administrative purposes (p. 546)

war of national liberation conflict with goal of freeing one nation from the control of another (p. 930)

welfare capitalism system of benefit programs offered to workers by employers intended to reduce the appeal of unions (p. 716)

"Western" novel, story or Hollywood motion picture depicting life in the western United States during the latter half of the nineteenth century (p. 481)

wetland land or area containing much soil moisture (p. 1017)

wildcat strike work stoppage initiated by a group of workers without formal union approval or in violation of a contract (p. 829)

writ of assistance written order that allowed officials to conduct unrestricted searches for smuggled or illegal goods (p. 99)

writ of mandamus court order requiring specific action on the part of person or organization served (p. 234)

Y

yellow journalism type of newspaper reporting in the late 1890s that featured sensational headlines and stories (p. 561)

Index

Italicized page numbers refer to illustrations. Preceding the page number, abbreviations refer to a map (m), chart (c), photograph or other picture (p), graph (g) cartoon (crt), or painting (ptg). Quoted material is referenced with the abbreviation (q) before the appropriate page number. Each boldface term is also referenced in the Glossary by the page on which it appears.

A

ABC powers, 685
abolitionist movement, 403; emancipation, 145; Emancipation Proclamation, 419; Frederick Douglass, 343, *ptg342*, 426, *ptg426*; Southern, 296, 342–43, 344; Texas, 371; women in, 344, *ptg344*, 581, *p581*
abolitionists, 342–44, 403
Across the Continent, p499
Adams, Abigail, 134, *ptg134*
Adams, Charles Francis, Jr., *q500*
Adams, John, *ptg107;* Constitutional Convention, 223; Continental Congress (First), 223; Continental Congress (Second), 223; election of 1796, 223; election of 1800, 230–31; Marshall appointment, 234, 260; Minister to Great Britain, 149, 223; presidency of, 223–25, *ptg223,* 251
Adams, John Quincy; election of 1824, 302–04; election of 1828, 310, 311, 313; Monroe Doctrine, 272–74; nationalism of, 274; presidency of, *ptg304,* 304; secretary of state (Monroe), 270, 272–74
Adams, Samuel, 106, 135, *ptg135,* 159
Adams-Onís Treaty of 1819, 272
Adamson Act, 671
Addams, Jane, 534, *p534,* 536–37
Afghanistan, 21, 979
AFL. *See* American Federation of Labor (AFL).
AFL-CIO, 868
Africa; early civilizations, 24; medieval empire of, 20, 24; trading kingdoms, 24, *m33;* World War II, 818, 820. *See also* slavery, enslaved persons; individual countries.
African Americans; abolitionist movement, 296, 342–44, 442; AFL discrimination against, 526; in armed forces, 250, 426, 606; black codes, 447, 456; black revolution, 910–11; Boston Massacre, 106, *ptg106;* in Civil War, 426, 427; Congress, 450, *p450,* 1004; cowhands, 478; culture of, 299; discrimination against, 447, 455, 643; education of, 75, 335, 337, 396, 443; *ptg443, q443, p456;* election of 1936, 791; election of 1988, 990–91; election of 1992, 1004; Fifteenth Amendment, 449, 456; Fourteenth Amendment, 448, 456; Harlem Renaissance, 734, 735, *q734;* integration, 455; Jackson administration, 318; job opportunities for, 441–43, 443–44; Johnson's Great Society, 957–60; Ku Klux Klan, 453, *p454;* Lewis and Clark expedition, 238; lynchings of, 643, 644, 796; medical research, 318, *p831;* migration, *q698,* 857, *p857;* music of, 299, 406–07, *ptg406,* 703; and New Deal, 791, 796; post-Civil War, 441–44, 447; post-Reconstruction, 454–56, 898; post-World War I discrimination against, 705; post-World War II gains, 851–52; Progressive Era, 643–44, 671; recolonization of, 296; Reconstruction, 445–51, 453; Revolutionary War, 133, 144; Roosevelt, F., administration, 796; Roosevelt, F., "black cabinet," 796; sharecroppers, 441–42, *q442,* 782–83; Southern class structure, 296; Spanish-American War, 606; spirituals, 299, 406–07; tenant farmers, 441, 782–83; Thirteenth Amendment, 445; Union soldiers, 427; voting, 144, 450, 902, *m908,* 909; War of 1812, 250; World War I, 694–95, 697–98; World War II, 830–31. *See also* civil rights; discrimination; segregation; slavery, enslaved persons.
Agent Orange, 933
Agnew, Spiro, 968
Agricultural Adjustment Act (AAA), 782
Agricultural Marketing Act, 742
agriculture. *See* farmers, farming; regions; individual names.
Agriculture, Department of, 786
Aguinaldo, Emilio, 605–06, 610
Aid to Families with Dependent Children, 1015
AIDS, 1018, *p1018*
AIM. *See* American Indian Movement.
Alabama; civil rights violence in, 906, 909; cotton agriculture in, 296; Native American conflict, 240; readmission of, *m449;* secession of, 404; statehood, 296; Tuskegee Institute, 643
Alamo, the, 370, *m371*
Alaska, *p600;* acquisition of, 599; Asian land bridge, 8; gold in, *p599;* oil spill in, 1016, *p1016;* pipeline, 965; purchase of, 599; Russia, 367, 599; statehood, 870
Albany, NY, 130; Albany Plan, 94, *crt92;* Erie Canal to, 266–67
Albany Plan of Union, 94, *crt92*
Aldrich, Nelson W., 656–57, 668
Aldrin, Edwin E., 955
Alexander I, Tsar, 599
Al-Fahri, Achbar Ben Nafi, 20, *q20*
Alger, Horatio, 504, 584
Algeria, 819–20, *m819*
Algiers, 244
Algonquin, 48, 49
Alien Act, 224

Allen, Frederick Lewis, *q758*
Alliance for Progress, 925
alliances. *See* Central Treaty Organization (CENTO); North Atlantic Treaty Organization (NATO); Quadruple Alliance; Southeast Asian Treaty Organization (SEATO); Triple Alliance; Triple Entente.
Allied Powers; Japan, World War II, 817–18, 822–23; World War I, 686–715; World War II, 811–833. *See also* World War I; World War II.
Allies, 687
Allies Day, ptg683
Alzheimer's disease, 997
amendments. *See* Constitution, amendments.
America First Committee, 811
American Bankers' Association, 779
American Civil Liberties Union (ACLU), 733
American Colonization Society, 296, *q297*
American Cotton Cooperative Association, 742
The American Crisis, Number 1, q110–11
American Federation of Labor (AFL), 525–26, 785, *g785,* 790, 829, 868
American Indian. *See* Native Americans; individual nations; individual names.
American Indian Movement (AIM), 919
American Library Association, 537
American Oleograph Company, *p567*
American party, 399
American Protective Association, 531–32
American Railway Union, 526
American Red Cross, 428, 429
American Sisters of Charity, 292
American Socialist party, 582
American Sugar Refining Company, 512
Americans With Disabilities Act, 1020
American Telephone and Telegraph, 868
American Tobacco, 504
Americorps, 1016
Among the Sierra Nevada Mountains, *ptg348*
Anasazi, 11
Anderson, John, 981
Anderson, Marian, 790
Anderson, Terry, *p976*
Anglican Church, 63, 145
Annapolis Convention, 155
Anshutz, Thomas Pollock, *ptg441,* 441
Anthony, Susan B., 553, *ptg553,* 581

Antietam, Battle of, 418–19
Anti-Federalists, 160
Anti-Imperialists, 614, *crt614*
Antioch, 558
Anti-Saloon League, 580
antislavery, 296, 342–44, 371–72. *See also* abolitionist movement.
Apache, 471, *p471*
Appomattox Court House, *ptg434*, 435, *q435*
Arapaho, 474
archaeology, 14
architecture; in cities, 537; federal, 348; Greek revival, 349; Victorian, 560; Wright, Frank Lloyd, 732
Area Redevelopment Act, 953
Argentina, 685
Aristotle, 41
Arizona, 11, 471, 659
Arkansas; civil rights in, 901–02; Civil War in, 421, 428; cotton agriculture in, 296; Native American conflict in, 240; readmission of, 446, *m449*; secession of, 413; statehood, 296
armed forces. *See* army; marines; navy; veterans; individual wars; battles; individuals.
Armour (Company), 503, *q503*
arms race. *See* disarmament; nuclear weapons.
army; African Americans in, 427; Civil War, 414–15, 426–27, *q427*, 435; Confederate, 414–15, 426; doughboys, 694, 695; Native American conflict, 473–75; Revolutionary War, 109; Spanish-American War, 605–07; Vietnam War, 933; War of 1812, 247–52. *See also* armed forces; Continental army; battles; wars.
Army Appropriation Act, 450
Arnautuff, Victor, *ptg802*
Arnold, Benedict, 137
Aroostook War, 367
art; African, *p23*, *p24*, *p25*; African Americans, 734, 735, *p735*; architecture, 348–49, 537; computer-manipulated, 1001, *p1001*; Great Depression, 789; Harlem Renaissance, 734, 735, *ptg735*; Hudson River School of, 268, 348; literature, 268, 346–47; medieval, 17; mural, *ptg892*; painters, sculptors, 17, 348; prehistoric, *p2*; realism, 268, 560; Renaissance, 17; Works Progress Administration artists, 789. *See also* music; individual artists.
Arthur, Chester A., 552
Articles of Confederation, 145–47, *p147*, 155, 156
Ashburton, Lord, 367
Asia; cold war in, 845–49; communism in, 846–47; immigrants from, 8, 959; Kennedy administration, 930–31; medieval empire of, 22–23. *See also* individual countries.
Asian Americans. *See* Chinese Americans; Japanese Americans.
Assiniboin (Native Americans), 314
"Association, The," 108
Assumption Act, 210
Assumption Bill, 212

astronauts. *See* space program.
astronomy, 10, 21, 161, *p161*
Atahualpa, 43
Atchison, Topeka, and Santa Fe, 472
Atlanta, GA, 432, *q432*
Atlanta University, 463
Atlantic Charter, 824
Atlantic Monthly, 563
atomic bomb, 823, 826, *p826*. *See also* nuclear weapons.
Attorney General; creation of the office, 206
Attucks, Crispus, 106, *ptg106*
Audubon, John J., *ptg333*
Auschwitz, 821
Austin, Stephen F., 370
Austria, 19, 272, 809
Austria-Hungary, 529, 686, 702
automobile industry; crisis, 965, *p966*; environment, 1017–18; Great Depression, 798–99; Henry Ford, 721–22, *q722*, *p723*; Model T, *p674*, 721; sales, *g722*; suburbs, 873–74; unionization of, 791
Axis Powers. *See* World War II; countries.
Axum, 24
Aztec, 10, 43

B

"baby boom," 875
Bacon, Nathaniel, 60
Baer, George F., 652
Baker, Ray Stannard, 629
Balboa, Vasco Núñez de, 38
Balkans, 821, 1009–10
Ballinger, Richard A., 657
Baltimore, Lord, 60
Baltimore, MD; Catholic schools in, 292; Civil War, 414; colonial, 61; Continental Congress in, 126; growth of, 532; railroad strike of 1877, 522; War of 1812, 249, 250
Bancroft, George, 312
Banjo Lesson, The, *ptg360*
banking, banks; Bank of the United States (first), 210, 212, 259; Bank of the United States (second), 259, 322–26, 329; farmers, 322, 326, 569; Federal Reserve, 329, 668–69, 852; Great Depression, 761, 777, *p778*; Middle Ages, 16; Roosevelt, F., administration, 761–774, 777; savings and loan crisis, 996; stock market crash 1929, 743–44; Wilson administration, 667–69
Bank Bill, 212
Bank of the United States (first), 209, 212, 259
Bank of the United States (second), 259, 323–25, 326, 329, *crt324*
Banneker, Benjamin, *p224*, 224
Bantu nations (Africa), 24
Baptists, 66, 342, 351
Barbary Coast pirates, 151, 244
Barbary States, *m255*

Barnett, Ross, 906
Barton, Clara, 428, *ptg428*, 429
Baruch, Bernard, 696
baseball, 562, *q562*, *p562*
Bataan, 817
Bates, Daisy, *q902*
Bath, The, *ptg557*
Batista, Fulgencio, 884
Baton Rouge, LA, 136
Battle of Fredericksburg, *ptg141*
battles. *See* specific places, wars.
Bay of Pigs, 925
bazooka, 828
Beals, Melba Pattillo, 900
Beecher, Catharine, 317, 337
Beecher, Lyman, 373
Begin, Menachem, *p979*, 980
Belgium, 687, 714, 812, 821
Bell, Alexander Graham, 496
Bell, John, 404
Bell Telephone Company, 496
Bellamy, Edward, 575, 625
Bellows, George, 592, *ptg592*, *ptg623*, 733
Benton, Thomas Hart (senator), *q313*, 320
Benton, Thomas Hart (artist), *ptg711*, *ptg724*, 733, *ptg741*
Berkeley, Lord John, 70
Berlin, Germany, 842–43, *q843*, *m844*, 926, 991
Berlin Wall, 926–27, *p927*, *q927*, 991, *p991*
Berry, Chuck, 877, *p877*
Bessemer process, 498, 509
Bethune, Mary McLeod, 976
Beveridge, Albert J., 661, *q661*
Bicentennial, the, 971
bicycling, 562
Biddle, Nicholas, 324, 325, *ptg325*
Bierstadt, Albert, *ptg348*, *ptg469*
Big Stick policy, 616–19
Bilbo, Theodore, *q758*
Billington, Ray Allen, *q479*
Billion-Dollar Congress, 555–56
Bill of Rights, 207. *See also* Constitution.
Bingham, George Caleb, *ptg151*, *ptg282*, *ptg309*, 348
Birmingham, AL, 455, 533, 905–06
Birney, James G., 342–43
Bishop, Isabel, *ptg861*
bison. *See* buffalo.
Bizerte, 820
"black cabinet," 796
black codes, 447, 456
Black Coat, *ptg308*
Blackfeet, 314, 470, 471
Black Hawk, 297, *ptg315*, 317–18
Black Hills, Dakotas, 474
Black Kettle, Chief, 474
Black Muslims, 910–11
black nationalism, 910
Black Panthers, 911, *q912*
black power, 911

blacks. *See* abolitionist movement; African Americans; discrimination; freedmen; segregation; slavery, enslaved persons; individual groups; names.
Blackwell, Elizabeth, 341, *ptg341*
Blaine, James G., 552, *p552,* 553, *crt554,* 599–600
Bland-Allison Act, 574–75
Blanket Signal, ptg474
blitzkrieg, 812
Bloomer, Amelia, 344, *ptg344*
Blue Eagle, 785
Blue Jacket, Chief, 214
Blue Lake, 919
Blume, Peter, 799
Bly, Nelly, 561
boardinghouses, 583
Board, Ernest, *ptg35*
Bolívar, Simón, 272
Bolshevik Revolution, 692
Bonaparte, Napoleon. *See* Napoleon.
bonds; Civil War, 429; Hamilton, A., 208–11; repayment of, 209, 211–12; Revolutionary War, 209, 210, 211–12; Treasury Department, 206, 577; War of 1812, 252; World War I, II, 687, 698
Bonus Army, 757–58, *p758, q758*
Bonus Bill, 263
Book of Mormon, 350
Boone, Daniel, 101
Booth, John Wilkes, 435, *p435*
Booth, William, 626, *p626*
Bosnia-Herzegovina, 1009–10
Boston, MA; Boston Massacre, 105, *p107;* Boston Police Strike, 704; Boston Tea Party, 106; colonial, 65; growth of, 533; immigrants in, 393, 528; Irish immigrants in, 528; settlement houses in, 536
Boston Massacre, 105
Boston Tea Party, 106
Boughton, George H., *ptg65*
Bow, Clara, 733
Bowdoin College, 337
Bowery, The, ptg762
Boxer Rebellion, 618–19
Boy Scouts of America (BSA), 637
Braddock, Edward, 95
Bradford, William, 64, 66–67, *q66*
Brady, Mathew, *p427*
Bragg, Braxton, 421–22
brain trust, 776
Brandeis, Louis D., 637, 639, 640
Brandywine, Battle of, 130
Braun, Carol Moseley, 1004
Brazil, 685
Breckinridge, John C., 403–04
Breed's Hill, 109
Brent, Margaret, 60, *p60*
Brest-Litovsk, Treaty of, 692
Brezhnev, Leonid, 942
Bricker Amendment, 864
bride ships, 58, *p58*
Bridgman, Laura, 336, *p336*

Britain. *See* Great Britain.
British Army. *See* battles; names; wars.
British West Indies, 92
Brooke, R.N., 439, *ptg439*
Brook Farm, 349
Brooklyn Bridge, 537
Brotherhood of Locomotive Firemen, 526
Browder, Earl, 759, *q759*
Brown, Albert Gallatin, 404, *q404*
Brown, John, 403, *q403, ptg408*
Brown, Linda, 898
Brown University, 77
Brown v. Board of Education, 898–99, 901, *q901*
Bryan, William Jennings; banks, 667; election of 1896, *p576,* 578; election of 1900, 615; election of 1912, 661–62; Philippines annexation, *q614;* Scopes trial, 733–34, *p733;* secretary of state, 665; World War I, 810
Bryant, William Cullen, 347
Bryce, James, *q548*
Bryn Mawr, 558
B-17 Base in England, ptg768
Buchanan, James, 399–400, 412
Buchenwald, 821
Buddhists, 931
Budget, Bureau of the, 715
budget deficit; Bush administration, 994, 995; Eisenhower administration, 870; from World War I, 713, 715; Great Depression, 745; Great Society, 959; Hamilton, Alexander, 208–10; Nixon administration, 964; Reagan administration, 985, 986; Revolutionary War debt, 208–09; Roosevelt, F., administration, *c803*
budget, federal; *g999*
Buena Vista, Battle of, 376
buffalo, 11, *ptg469,* 470, 473, 479
Buffalo, NY, 266–67
Bulfinch, Charles, 348
Bulgaria, 821
Bulge, Battle of the, 821
Bullock, William A., 563
Bull Moose party, 661
Bull Run, Battle of, 417–18, *q417, q418*
Bull Run, Second Battle of, 418
Bulwer, Sir Henry, 381
Bunker Hill, Battle of, *ptg108,* 109. *See also* Breed's Hill.
Burger, Warren, 963
Burgoyne, John, 129, 130–31
Burma, 818
Burnside, Ambrose, 418
Burr, Aaron, 223, 230, 240, *ptg240*
Bush, George, *p984;* domestic policies, 995–96; election of 1980, 981; election of 1984, 985; election of 1988, 990–91; election of 1992, 1003–04; foreign policy of, 991–94; Kuwaiti invasion, 993–94, *q994*
business; benefits of big business, 502–03; computers, 872; consolidation, 499–500, 505, 510, 512; Coolidge administration, 721–25; corporations, 502, 505, 996; cycles, 520; Eisenhower administration, 868;

entrepreneurs, 504, *q504;* global marketplace, 1013; government, 512, 547, 569, 740; Granger laws, 571–72; Great Depression, 742–45, *c745,* 756; Harding administration, 721–25; in Mexico, 684–85, 807; monopolies, 503, 511–12, *crt514,* 669; multinational corporations, 1013, *g1014;* New Deal, 784–85; oil industry, 494–95, 498, 880; Philippines annexation, 609; progressivism reform, 628, 638; regulation, 650–51; Republican party, 548–49; social Darwinism, 510, *q510,* 609; socialism, 581–82, 625–26; tactics, 504, 527; trust regulation, 512, *q512,* 650–51, 669; union opposition by, 521; Wilson administration, 669; World War I, 696, 698. *See also* government; industry; factories; monopolies; trade; trusts; industry names.
busing, 914
Butler, Nicholas Murray, 534

C

Cabot, John, *ptg35,* 47, *m39*
Cabot's Departure, ptg35
Cabral, Pedro Alvares, 38
Cahokia, 11
Calhoun, John C., 259, 263, 302, *ptg303,* 320–21, 322, 371
Califano, Joseph, Jr., 1018, *q1018*
California; acquisition of, 374–77; Chinese Americans in, 532; environmental laws, 1017; gold in, *q379,* 381, 379, 389, 390, 479; illegal aliens, 1019; Japanese American discrimination, 831–832; Mexican Americans in, 1019; Mexican War, 374–77; *m376;* migrant workers in, 918; migration to, 379; missions in, 45; Proposition 187, 1019; statehood, 389–90
Calvert, Cecil, 60–61
Calvert, George. *See* Baltimore, Lord.
Cambodia, 938, 944, 971
Campbell, Ben Nighthorse, 1004
campaigns. *See* elections, congressional; elections, presidential.
Camp David Accords, *p979,* 980, *q980*
Canada; Asian land bridge, 8; disputes with, 271; French colonies, 48, 70; French and Indian War, 95, *m96;* Revolutionary War, 130; Treaty of Paris, 95–96, 366–67; War of 1812, 248–49
canals, *m265,* 266–67, 270, 494, *m621.* *See also* Erie Canal; Panama Canal; Suez Canal.
Canal Zone. *See* Panama; Panama Canal.
Cannon, Joseph G., 657–58
Cape of Good Hope, 29
Cape Town, South Africa, 51
Cape Verde, 28, 606
Capitol, the, *p172*
Capone, Al, 729, 750
Capper-Volstead Act, 724
Caribbean, the, 42, 380, *m610, m685–86,* 725
Carmichael, Stokely, 911, *p914, q914*

Carnegie, Andrew, 509–11, *ptg510*, *q510*, *q511*, *q610*

Carnegie Steel Company, 510, 521

Carolinas; Civil War, 434; settlement of, 60, 61

carpetbaggers, 450

Carranza, Venustiano, 685

Carson, Rachel, 960

Carter, Dennis Malone, *ptg115*

Carter, Jimmy, *p977*, *p979*, 976–77; Balkans, 1009; domestic policy, 978, *q978*; energy policy, 977–78, *q978*; election of 1976, 976–77; election of 1980, 981; foreign policy, 978–81, *q979*; Haiti negotiator, 1011; Middle East, 979–81, *q980*

Carteret, Sir George, 71

Cartier, Jacques, 48

Cassatt, Mary, *ptg557*

Cass, Lewis, 389

Castro, Cipriano, 616–17

Castro, Fidel, 884, *p924*

Cather, Willa, 488, 731

Catholic. *See* Roman Catholicism.

Catlin, George, *ptg266*, *ptg314*, 314

Catt, Carrie Chapman, 628

cattle ranching, 477–79, *q479*

Cayuga, 10, 13

CCC. *See* Civilian Conservation Corps.

Cédras, Raoul, 1010–11

Census Bureau, *q488*

CENTO. *See* Central Treaty Organization.

Central America. *See* Latin America; specific countries.

Central Intelligence Agency (CIA), 880, 885, 924

Central Pacific Company, 472, 532

Central Powers, 687; *See also* World War I; battles; countries.

Central Treaty Organization (CENTO), 878

Cervera, Pascual, 606–07

Challenger, the, 986

Chamberlain, Neville, 810

Chambers, Whittaker, 855–56

Champlain, Samuel de, 48–49, *q49*

Chancellorsville, VA, 418, 419

Chandler, Helen Clark, *ptg143*

Channing, Reverend William Ellery, 350

Chaplin, Charlie, 733

Chapman, Conrad Wise, *ptg413*, 413

Charge of San Juan Hill, ptg620

Charles I, King, (Spain), 40

Charles I, King, (England), 60, 64, 67

Charles II, King, 69, 71

Charleston, SC, 61, 117, 321, 394, 412

Chase, Samuel, 234

Chautauqua Institute, 558–59

Chattanooga, TN, 421–22, *q421*, *ptg422*

Chavez, Cesar, 918

Chechnya, 1010

"Checkers" speech, 863

Checks and balances, *c169*, *q169*, 235. *See also* Congress; Constitution; presidency, President; Supreme Court.

Cherokee, 13, 133, 150, 213, 240, *ptg308*, 317, 428

Chesapeake, 246

Chesapeake Bay, 138, 249

Chesnut, Mary, *ptg387*

Chevalier, Michael, *q266*, 266

Cheyenne, 471, 474, *p490*

Chiang Kai-shek, 825, 846–47

Chicago, IL; 1968 Democratic convention, 940; growth of, 533; Haymarket Square riot, 525, *ptg525*; housing shortage in, 534; Hull House, 534, 536–37; pizza introduced in, 530; race riots in, 705, *q705*, 912; railroad strike of 1877, 522; World's Fair (1893), 537, *ptg543*; Chickamaugas, 213

Chickamauga, Battle of, 421

Chickasaw, 13, 150, 240

Child, Lydia Maria, 347

child labor, 519–20, *q520*, *p519*, 637, 671, 793

Children's Bureau, 628, 637

Chile, 685, 750, 925

China; Boxer Rebellion, 618–19; civil war in, 752, 846–47; Hoover-Stimson Doctrine, 752; immigrants from, 528, 532, *p532*; inventions, 22; Japan, 23, 619, 752, 846; Korean War, 849; medieval empire of, 22–23; Ming rule, 23; Mongols, 22–23; Nine-Power Treaty, 714, 752; Nixon administration, 942, *p942*; Open Door policy, 618–19, 714; Russo-Japanese War, 619; Tiananmen Square, 994; trade with, 22, 382–83; World War II, 824–25. *See also* Taiwan.

Chinese Americans, 472, 532

Chisholm, Shirley, 915–16, *p915*, *q915*, *q916*

Chisholm Trail, 478

Chivington, John, 474

Choctaw, 13

Christianity. *See* religion; individual denominations.

Chrysler, 722

Church, Frederic E., *ptg55*

Church of England. *See* Anglican Church.

Church of Jesus Christ of Latter-day Saints. *See* Mormon Church.

Churchill, Winston, *p815*, *p824*; Atlantic Charter, 824; Chamberlain replacement, 810; iron curtain speech, 839, *p839*, *q839*; Munich agreement, *q810*; war declaration, *q813*; World War II, 813, 824; Yalta Conference, 825

CIA. *See* Central Intelligence Agency.

Cincinnati, OH, 297, *ptg298*, 528, 536

Cincinnati Red Stockings, 562

CIO. *See* Congress of Industrial Organizations.

cities; African American discrimination, 912; beautification of, 537–38; building codes, 635; corruption, 544–46; crime, 535; cultural centers, 562; ethnic neighborhoods, 530; factories, 290; government reform, 538, 546, 632–33; growth of, 533; housing shortage in, 534; immigrants in, 528, 534, 545, 641–43; industrial, 533–34; industry in, 290, 533–34; Middle Ages, 16; political machines, 545–46, 642–43; problems of, 534–36, *p535*, *q536*, 539, 705, 873; Prohibition, 730; public education, 292; public services in, 538, 638; race riots in, 705, 912; settlement houses, 534, 536–37; suburbs, 873–74, *g873*; tenements, 497, 534, *p540*; transportation in, 290, 535; zoning laws, 635

City Life, ptg802

Civilian Conservation Corps (CCC), 781, *p783*, 789

civil rights; Bill (1866), 448; Act (1875), 455; Act (1957), 901; Act (1964), 908; black revolution, 910–12, *q911*, *q912*; boycotts, demonstrations, 899–900, *p902*, *p905*; busing, 914; Civil War, 424, 425; Eisenhower administration, 898–902, *p902*, 904–05; Eleanor Roosevelt, 777, *p777*; Hispanics, *p917*; Johnson's Great Society, 907–08, *q908*; Kennedy administration, 905–07; marches, *p906*; Native Americans, 918–19, *p918*, *p919*; post-World War II, 852; Voting Rights Act of 1965, 908, 909. *See also* African Americans; Bill of Rights; Constitution; discrimination; equality; woman's rights; women; individuals.

civil service, 551–54, 577

Civil Service Commission, 552

Civil War; battles of, 412, 417–22, 423, 431–33, *m437*; civil rights, 424, 425; Emancipation Proclamation, 419; final days of, 434–35, *ptg434*, *m437*; food supplies of, 417, 427; Reconstruction, 445–51, 453–54, 456; strategies, 414–16; veterans' pensions, 554, 556; women in, 428–29. *See also* Confederacy; North; Reconstruction; slavery, enslaved persons; South; Union; battles; individuals.

Civil Works Administration (CWA), 780

Clark, George Rogers, *ptg131*, 217

Clark, J. Reuben, 750

Clark, William, 239, 253

Clark Memorandum, 750

Clay, Cassius Marcellus, 343–44

Clay, Henry, 259, *ptg259*, 555; American System, 259; Bank of the United States, 324; Compromise of 1850, 389–90; election of 1824, 302–04; election of 1832, 325; election of 1844, 371–72; Harrison support, 328; internal improvements, 259, 263, 319; Native Americans, 318; tariff issue, 322; Treaty of Ghent, *q271*; Whig party, 328

Clayton, John M., 382

Clayton Antitrust Act, 670

Clayton-Bulwer Treaty, 382

Cleaver, Eldridge, 911, *q912*

Clemenceau, Georges, 701

Clemens, Samuel, 559. *See also* Twain, Mark.

Clermont, 265

Cleveland, Grover, *ptg554*, *p577*; election of 1884, 553; election of 1888, 555; election of 1890, 556; election of 1892, 556; Hawaii annexation, 600; Philippines annexation, 608; presidency, 554; Pullman Strike of 1894, 527, 577; second term of, 577; Spanish-American War, 603–04; Venezuela border dispute, 601

Cleveland, OH, 633, 912

Cliff Dwellers, ptg592

Clinton, Bill, *p1006, p1011,* 1003–04; domestic policy, 1004–07; election of, 1003–04; foreign policy, 1008–13; image, 1004

Clinton, Henry, 136

Clinton, Hillary Rodham, 1006

clipper ships, 383, 394

coal mining, 494–95; coal strike of 1902, 651–52, *p651;* energy source, 978; industrial growth, 290, *g515;* Pennsylvania, 289–90, 494; strikes, 651–52, 704; working conditions, 651

Coercive Acts, 107

Coffey, Alvin, *q379,* 379

Cohan, George M., 699, *p699*

Cohens v. Virginia, c261

Cold Harbor, 431

cold war, 840; in America, 850–56; in 1950s, *m883,* 884

Collier, John, 784

Collier's, 629, 635

Collins, Michael, 955

Collis, Charles C., 411, *ptg411*

Colombia, 382, 616, 925

colonies; culture of, 68, *ptg68,* 73–79, *m74, p76, ptg77, ptg80, p85,* 94, *p94,* 133, *ptg133,* 164–65; economy, *m59,* 60–61, 77–78, 92–93; education in, 77–78; government of, 60–61, 65–66, *c66,* 69, 79, 101, 144; hardships in, 57, *q57,* 73–74; leisure activities, 94; mind-set of, 76–78; Native American conflict with, 36, 56, 74, 75, 98; newspapers in, 78–79; religious tolerance, 61, 66–67, 145; representation issue, 102; slavery in, 60, 61, 74, 75; women in, 68, *ptg68,* 74–75

colonization; Columbus, 36–37; Dutch exploration, 51; English, Spanish rivalry, 47–48; France, 48–51, 96; Spanish, Portuguese explorations, 38–40, *m39*

Colorado, 11, 473–74, 480, 581

Columbia University, 77, *q77,* 938

Columbus, Christopher, *ptg37,* 36–37, *q37, m39,* 41

Comanche, 470, 471, 474

commerce; African trading kingdoms, 24; Asian exploration, 22–23, 28–29, *q29,* 51, 62; canals, 266–67, *p270,* 494; China, 22; Crusades, 16, 21; industrial revolution, 494; joint-stock companies, 26, 62; Middle Ages, 16, 21; Mississippi River, 150, 394; Portuguese exploration, 27–29; trade laws on, 92, 512; water transportation, 19, 265–67. *See also* industry; trade; transportation.

Commerce and Labor, Department of, 651

Committee on Public Information, 699

Committee to Re-elect the President, 967–68

Common Sense, q110–11, 111, 117

Commonwealth of Independent States (CIS), 992

Commonwealth v. Hunt, 293

communications; American language, 337; Cherokee language, 317; technology, 496; telegraph, 348, 391, 472; telephone, 496, *p496*

communism; in Asia, 846–47, 879; Berlin Wall, 991; in Cambodia, 938, 944, 971; changes in, 991–93; in Cuba, 884, 924; in Eastern Europe, 838–40, 991–93; fall of, 992; fear of, 838, 855–56; Great Depression, 758–59; iron curtain, 839; in Latin America, 883–84, 925; Middle East, 880; in Southeast Asia, 879–80, 971. *See also* Union of Soviet Socialist Republics; specific countries.

Communist Manifesto, The, 582

Communist party, 758–59, 838, 992

Compromise, Missouri. *See* Missouri Compromise.

Compromise of 1850, 389–90, *ptg389,* 397, *m401*

Compromise of 1877, 454

computers, 872, *p872*

Comstock Lode, 479, 574

concentration camps, 821, *p821*

Concert at the Lincoln Memorial, ptg790

Concord, Battle of, 108–09, *m113*

Concord, MA, 108–09

Conestoga wagons, 264, *p264,* 297

Confederate States of America, 405, *m405,* 434. *See also* Confederacy.

Confederacy; army, 413, 426, 427, 429; British alliance with, 416, 600; government of, 412, 434; Native American soldiers, 428; resources of, 415, *g415;* Southern secession, 404–05, 413; states' rights, 404. *See also* Civil War; South.

Confederation Congress, 147, 149, 151–54, 158

Congo, 926

Congregational Church, 65, 121, 145

Congress, *p177;* acquisition of Alaska, 599; African American members of, 450; annexation of Hawaii, 608; Articles of Confederation, 145–47, *p147;* Bank of the United States (second), 259, 324; Billion-Dollar Congress, 555–56; Bill of Rights, 168, 206, 207; business and labor, 495–96, 512, 669; Bush administration, 994–95; Carter administration, 978; checks and balances, *c169;* civil rights legislation, 448, 455, 899, 901; Clinton administration, 1005–06; conservation, 652, 960, 965–66; Constitution, 173–77; Continental, First, 107–08; Second, 109, 116, 127, 132, 133; corruption in, 547; Dawes Act, 475; Democratic party, 549; Eisenhower administration, 864, 865; election of 1872, 454; election of 1884, 388–389; election of 1888, 512; election of 1892, 556; Embargo Act of 1806, 246; energy legislation, 965–66, 976–77; enumerated, implied powers, 168, 169–70, *c169,* 212; Farm Bloc, 724–25, 747; farming legislation, 724, 742; first, 206–07; Ford administration, 970–71; gold standard, 574, 577; immigration, 532; income tax, 789; Interstate Commerce Act, 572; industry supported by, 495; isolationism, 811; Jefferson administration, 233; judicial review of, 171; League of Nations, 702–03; legislative process, *c170;* letters, postage stamps, 268; Maine boundary dispute, 367; Mexican War, 375–76; national bank, 259; National Monetary Commission, 667–68; National Road, 263–64; Naval Act of 1890, 603; naval appropriations, 601; Neutrality Acts, 810; New Deal policies, 778, 779–85, 793; Non-Intercourse Act, 247; nullification, 322; Pacific Railroad, 472; Philippine independence, 611; Platt Amendment, 612–13; Pure Food and Drug Act, 635; Reconstruction, 446, *ptg446,* 447–48, 448–51, 453–56; Reconstruction Finance Corporation (RFC), 749; Roosevelt, F., administration, 777–85; salary increase, 1003; Sherman Antitrust Act, 512, *q512;* Sherman Silver Purchase Act, 556, 577; Spanish-American War, 604; Tariff of 1816, 259–60; tariff laws, 322, 555, 577; Teller Amendment, 604, 612; Treaty of Versailles, 702–03; Truman Doctrine, 840–41; trust regulation, 651; Underwood Tariff, 666–67; unemployment relief, 780–781; Wilson administration, 665, 701–03; women in, 915, 917; World War I legislation, 699; Yellowstone National Park, 649. *See also* Constitution; elections, congressional; government; House of Representatives; Senate; Supreme Court; individual names; specific legislation.

Congressional Budget and Impoundment Control Act, 970

Congressional Pugilists, p225

Congress of Industrial Organizations (CIO), *g785,* 790, 829, 868

Congress of Racial Equality (CORE), 901, 911

Connecticut, 67, *c66,* 153, 154, *c163*

Connor, Eugene "Bull," 906

conquistadors, 42–44, 45, *p46*

conscientious objectors, 937

conscription. *See* draft.

conservation; natural resources, 638; Roosevelt, T., administration, 652–53; soil, 960

Conservative Republicans, 433

conspicuous consumption, 584

Constitution, document, 172–97

Constitution, amendments, 168, 187–97; Eleventh, 189; Twelfth, 189–90, 303; Thirteenth, 190, 445; Fourteenth, 190–92, 448, 456; Fifteenth, 192, 449, 456; Sixteenth, 192, 659; Seventeenth, 192–93, 634, 659; Eighteenth, 193, 638, 706; Nineteenth, 193, 671, 706; Twentieth, 193–94, 761; Twenty-first, 194; Twenty-second, 195; Twenty-third, 195; Twenty-fourth, 196, 909; Twenty-fifth, 196–97, 865; Twenty-sixth, 197; Twenty-seventh, 197, 1002; Bank of the United States (second), 210; Bill of Rights, 160, 187–89, 207; checks and balances, *c169, q169,* 235; division of powers, *c168,* 169–71; document, 172–97; Missouri Compromise, 400; overseas possessions, 612; Preamble to, *p176,* 173; presidential terms, 180; ratification struggle, 158–60, *crt159, c163;* signing of, *ptg143,* 158. *See also* civil rights; equality; states; woman's rights; women; related subjects.

Constitutional Convention. *See* Philadelphia Convention.

Constitution, 319; document, 172–197

Constitution of Five Nations, The, 30, *q30*

Constitutional Union party, 403–04

containment, 840

Con Thien, *p923*

Continental Army, 117, 126–129, 130–33, 136
Continental Congress; First, 107–08; Second, 109, 116, 118, 126–28, 132, 133
continentals (currency), 128, 134
contras. *See* Nicaragua.
Convention of 1818, 272
Coolidge, Calvin, 704, 720; election of 1920, 712; election of 1924, 720–21; foreign policy of, 725; Harding's death, 719; image of, 718
Cooper, Anthony, 61
Cooper, James Fenimore, 242, *q242–43*, 268, 346, *ptg347*
copper, 479
Copperheads, 425
Coral Sea, Battle of, 822
Corinth, MS, 420
Cornwallis, Charles, 127, 137–38, *ptg139*
Coronado, Francisco Vásquez de, *m50*
corporations, 996, *g1014*. *See also* government; industry; monopolies; trusts.
corruption; Grant administration, 544; Harding administration, 718; political machines, 545–46, 550; railroads, 569–70; Truman administration, 856
Cortés, Hernán, *q13*, 13, *q43*, 43
Cosmopolitan, 629
Costa Rica, 611
cotton; Confederacy, 416; cotton culture, 318; from Middle East, 21, 880; gin, 294, *p294*; textile industry, 288–89, 291, *ptg291*; production, 294–95, 296, *ptg299*, 392; Texas, 371. *See also* plantations; slavery, enslaved persons.
Cotton Pickers, *ptg299*
Coughlin, Charles, 787–88, *p788,* 811
Country School, *ptg335*
County Election, *ptg282*
courts. *See* Supreme Court; specific cases.
Cowpens, Battle of, 138, *ptg138*
Cox, Archibald, 968
Cox, James M., 712
craft unions, 291
Crandall, Prudence, 335
Crane, Stephen, 560
Crawford, William, 302, 303
Crazy Horse, Chief, 474
Creation, The, *ptg735*
Credit Mobilier, 547
Creek (Native Americans), 13, 150, 213, 272
Creel, George, 699
CREEP. *See* Committee to Re-elect the President.
crime, 1016
Crisis, The, 126, 644
critical thinking skills; cause and effect, 909; comparisons, 338; fact and value judgment, 215; fallacies in a line of reasoning, 645; historical symbolism, 866, *crt866*; making comparisons, 338; making predictions, 452; predictions, 452; recognizing fallacies in a line of reasoning, 645; recognizing stereotypes, 96; supporting an opinion, 109

Crittenden, John J., 404
Crittenden Compromise, 405
Croatia, 1009
Cronkite, Walter, 936, *q936*
Crow (Native Americans), 471
Crusades, 15–16, *ptg16,* 21
Crystal Palace Exhibition, 395
Cuba; annexation of, 380–81, 612–13; Castro, 884, 924–25, *p924*; immigrants from, 1019; Missile Crisis, 925; Ostend Manifesto, 381, *q381*; as protectorate, 612–13, *q613*; refugees, *p1010*; revolution in, 603, 807, 884; Spanish-American War, 603–05, 606–07, *m605*; Spanish exploration of, 42
Cullen, Countee, 734, *p734*
culture; American language, 237; antebellum, 295–96; archaeology, 14; the Arts, 17, 268, 348–49; automobile, 674–75, *p674–75*; boardinghouses, 583; Boy Scouts, 637; bride ships, 58; child rearing, 875; of cities, 562; classical, 17; colonial, 58, 73–79, *ptg77*, 79, 94, *p94*, 121, 164–65; cowhands, 588–89; doughboys, 694; ethnic neighborhoods, 530; etiquette, 340; fashion, 356–57, 764–65; first Americans, 8–13; "flappers," 730; forty-niners, 390; frontier weddings, 211; Great Depression, 756, 797–99; Harlem Renaissance, 734, 735, *q734*; hippies, counterculture, flower children, 939; home remedies, 152; hygiene, personal, 559, *p559*; imperial fruits, 611; Industrial Revolution, 290, 295–96, innovations, 888–89; Italian cuisine, 530; leisure time, 94, *p94,* 561; letters, from Vietnam, 938; literature, 268, 336, 346–47, 797–798; mess call, 427; mountain men, 370; Muslim influence, 21; Native Americans, 13, 82–83, 473; 1950s, 873–76; Northwest settlers, 297; one-room schoolhouse, 460–61; physical fitness, 987; radio, 731; Reform Judaism, 639; Roaring Twenties, 728–34; school desegregation, 901, *p902*; scientific advances, 347–48; shopping malls, 964, *p964*; social class distinctions, 73; Southern post-Civil War, 447; Southern social classes, 295–96; suburbs, 873–74; telling time, 234, *p234*; time zones, 501; transportation improvements, 268, 278–79, *p278–79*; veterans, return of, 853; volunteers, 1012; women's equality, 236; women's fashions, *p356–57*, working-class tenements, 497; World War II, 829–33; Yankee peddler, 133, *ptg133*. *See also* art; music; sports; individual ethnic groups.
Cumberland Road, 319
currency; Bank of the United States (first), 209, 212; Bank of the United States (second), 323, 329, 259; Civil War, 415, 429; colonial, 79, 100; Federal Reserve Act of 1913, 668; free silver, 573–75; gold standard, 210, 574; "hard money," 323; paper wealth, 323; Revolutionary War, 128, 154; specie, 100, 574; states', 154, *p154*; supply, 573–74, 575, 668–69; whiskey as, 214
Currier and Ives, 268, *p450, p499*
Cushing, Caleb, 383
Custer, George, 474
Czechoslovakia, 810, 811, 938

D

Dachau, 821
Da Gama, Vasco, 29
daily life. *See* culture.
Dakota (Native Americans). *See* Sioux.
Dakota Territory, 474
Daley, Richard J., 940
Dance Hall, *ptg711*
Dancig, Edward, *ptg834*
Daniel Boone Escorting Settlers Through the Cumberland Gap, *ptg151*
Dankers, Jasper, 70, *q70*
Darrow, Clarence, 733–34, *p733*
Dartmouth College, 77, 261
Dartmouth College v. Woodward, 261, *c261*
Darwin, Charles, 510, 584
Das Kapital, 582
Daugherty, Harry M., 716
Daughters of Liberty, 104, 105
da Vinci, Leonardo, 17
Davis, Jefferson, 412, 413, 424, 434, 435
Davis, John W., 721
Dawes, William, 108
Dawes Act, 475
daylight saving time, 697, 966
D-Day, 820–21, *p820*
DDT, 828
Deane, Silas, 130
Death of General Warren at the Battle of Bunker Hill, *ptg108*
de Berry, Jean, Duc, *ptg17*
Debs, Eugene V., 525–26, 527, 582, 670, 699
Decatur, Stephen, 244
Decker, Elizabeth, 628
Declaration of Independence, 118, 119–20, *q119,* 120, 598; document, 122–25
Declaration of Independence in Congress, *ptg123*
Declaration of Indian Purpose, 919
Declaration of Rights and Grievances, 108
Declaration of Sentiments and Resolutions, 341, *q341*
Declaration of the Rights of Man and the Citizen, 216
Declaratory Act, 104
Deere, John, 392
de Galvez, Bernardo, 136
de Gaulle, Charles, 824
de Grasse, Admiral, 138
Dekanawida, 13, 42, *q42*
Delaware, 72, *c66, c163,* 413
DeLeon, Daniel, 625–26, *q625–26*
de León, Juan Ponce, 44, *ptg46*
de Lôme, Enrique Dupuy, 604
democracy; election of 1800, 230–31; election of 1828, 310; Jackson administration, 312–25; Native American, 13; progressivism, 632–34; public education, 334; spoils system, 552–53; Tiananmen Square,

China, 994. *See also* Bill of Rights; civil rights; Constitution; Jackson, Andrew; Roosevelt, Franklin; voting; woman's rights; women.

Democratic party; elections: of 1828, 310; of 1836, 326; of 1840, 327; of 1844, 371–72; of 1848, 388–89; of 1856, 339–40; of 1860, 403–04; of 1864, 433; of 1868, 451; of 1872, 453; of 1876, 454; of 1880, 552; of 1884, 553; of 1888, 512, 554–55; of 1890, 556; of 1892, 556, 576–77; of 1896, 578; of 1900, 615; of 1910, 658; of 1912, 661–63; of 1916, 690; of 1918, 701; of 1920, 712–13; of 1924, 720–21; of 1928, 740–41; of 1932, 759–61; of 1936, 791; of 1940, 814–15; of 1948, 853–54; of 1952, 862–863; of 1956, 865; of 1960, *g952*; of 1964, 956–57; of 1968, 939–940; of 1972, 967; of 1976, 976–77; of 1980, 981; of 1984, 984; of 1988, 990–91; of 1992, 1003–04; Federalist party principles, 258; free silver, 578; internationalism, 811, 814; Jacksonians, 310, 304; Ku Klux Klan, 720–21; labor vote, 293; New Deal opposition, 787–88; Philippines annexation, 608; post-Civil War, 453, 454; Solid South, 549; Tammany Hall, 544–46; union support, 293, 791. *See also* elections; presidency, President; individual names.

Democratic Republicans, 310
Denmark, 812
department store, 537–38
depressions; (1837), 326–27; (1873), 520, 532; (1882), 520; (1893), 520, 575; (1907), 656; (1929), 742–80; (1971), 963–65; (1982), 984; post-Revolutionary War, 153. *See also* Great Depression.
deregulation, 996
desegregation, 900, 901–02, *q902*, 905
Detroit, MI, 249, 633, 912
Dewey, George, 605, 606
Dewey, John, 628, 642, 733
Dewey, Thomas E., 853–54
DeWitt, John, 831, *q831*
de Woiseri, John L. Boqueta, *ptg229*
Dias, Bartholomeu, 29
Díaz, Porfirio, 684
Dickinson, John, 102, *ptg102*, 147
Diem, Ngo Dinh, 880, 931
Dien Bien Phu, 879
dime novels, 561
disabled Americans, 1020
disarmament, 884, *q884*
discrimination. *See* African Americans; immigrants; Japanese Americans; Jewish Americans; Jews; women. *See also* civil rights; education; religion; segregation; woman's rights; specific groups; individual names.
disestablishment, 145
Disney, Walt, 798
District of Columbia. *See* Washington, D.C.
Dix, Dorothea, 339, *q339*, 428–29
Dixiecrats, 957
Dog Swap, ptg439
dollar diplomacy, 617
Dominican Republic, 617, 927
Dos Passos, John, 797

Doubleday, Abner, 412, *q412*
doughboys, 694, 695
Douglas, Aaron, 734, 735, *ptg735*
Douglas, Stephen A., 390, 397, 402–03, *q403*, 403–04
Douglass, Frederick, 341, *ptg342*, 346, 426, *q426*, *ptg442*, 442
doves, 937
draft, 426–27, *p691*, 694, 814, 937
Drago, Luis, 617
Drake, Sir Francis, 47–48
Dream Boogie, q727
Dred Scott decision, 400; effect of, 402–04
Dreiser, Theodore, 630, *q630–31*
Drew, Charles, 831, *p831*
Drought-Stricken Area, ptg749
drug abuse, 1018–19
Du Bois, W.E.B., *p642*, 643–44, 670, *ptg670*, 671
Dukakis, Michael, *p879*, 991
Dulles, John Foster, 878–79, *q878*, *p879*, 880
Dunkirk, France, 812, *p813*
Dunne, Finley Peter, 503, *q503*, 547, *crt547*, *q548*
Dunsmore, John W., *ptg207*
Dust Bowl, ptg756
dust bowl, 783, 786, *p786*
Dutch; colonies, 51, 69, 72; trade, 51; slave trade, 59, 74; immigrants, 393
Dutch Calvinist churches, 70
Dutch United East India Company, 51

E

Eagleton, Thomas, 967
Eakins, Thomas, 560, *ptg560*, *q560*
Earhart, Amelia, *p729*, 730–31
Early, Jubal, 431
Earth, ptg1001
East; confederation period, 153–54; public land policy, 300; tariffs, 301, 328
East Africa, 24
East Asia, 617–19; balance of power, 619
eastern Europe, 1019
East Germany. *See* Berlin; Germany.
East India Company, 51, 106
East Indies, 51, 818
Eaton, Major John, 322
Eaton, Peggy, *ptg321*, 322
economics; banks and the money supply, 329; growth of Southern manufacturing, 457; stock exchanges, 62, *p62*; the stock market, 722, 746
Economic Opportunity, Office of, (OEO), 958
economy; affluent society, 721–22, 871–72; Bush administration, 995–96; Clinton administration, 1015–16; colonial, 79, 92–93; crash of 1929, 742–44; currency standard, 210, 574; 1840–1860, 390–91; Eisenhower administration, 874–76; Era of Good Feelings, 268; Federal Reserve System, 329, 667–68; free silver, 574–75, 577; global, 1013; Great Depression, 807; Great Plains, 487–88, *q488*; Great Society, 957–59; Kennedy administration, 952–53; Nixon administration, 963–64; North v. South, 415; Populist movement, 575–77; post-World War I, 703–04, 721–25; post-World War II, 850–51, 852–53, 854; Reagan administration, 982–85; Roaring Twenties, 721–22; Southern cotton plantations, 415; World War I, 696–98. *See also* depressions; Great Depression; industry; oil; trade; unemployment; individual names; related subjects.

Ecuador, 8–9
Edison, Thomas, *p493*, 497
Edmonds, Francis W., 365, *ptg365*
education; African Americans, 335, 337, 901; busing, 914; desegregation, 901–02, *q901*; cities, 290, 557; colonial, 77–78; federal subsidy to, 558; freedmen, 443; Gilded Age, 557–59; higher education, 76, 77–78, 337, 557–58; high school, 334, 557, 733; Native Americans, 473; one-room school house, 460–61, 733; progressivism, 628–29; Project Head Start, 958; public schools, 334–35, *ptg335*, *c336*, *p338*, 460–61, 557, 642, 733; reform in, 334–37, *q335*, 336, 638, 642; religion and, 76, 77, 292, 335, 556; resistance, 335, 642; science, 77–78, 733; special needs, 336; state reform, 334, 638; teachers, 334, 336, 337; for women, 77, 337, 341, 488, 558. *See also* segregation; individual names; related subjects.
Edwards, Jonathan, 76–77, 121
Egypt; Camp David accords, 980, *p979*; cotton, 416, 881; Israeli conflict, 881, 928, 1011–12; medieval empire of, 24; Soviet Union, 881, 928; Suez Canal, *p880*, 881; World War II, 818
Ehninger, John Whetton, *ptg384*
Einstein, Albert, 826
Eisenhower Doctrine, 882
Eisenhower, Dwight D., *p843*, *p863*, *p879*; Bricker Amendment, 864, *q864*; civil rights, 870, 898–902; cold war, 884; disability of, 864; economic policies of, 868–70; Eisenhower Doctrine, 882; election of 1952, 862–63; election of 1956, 865; farewell address of, *q885*; foreign policy of, 870, *q870*, 878–85; France, 821; image of, 863–64; Korea, 843, 863, 879; NATO, 843, 878; New Deal and, 867, *q867*; scandals, 870; Vietnam, 879–90, 931
El Camino Real, 45
elderly; in Greenwich Village, 658; medicare, 959; New Deal, 789; old age pensions, 789; social security, 789. *See also* social security.
elections, 312, *g548*
elections, congressional; (1800), 233; (1842), 328; (1866), 448; (1878), 574; (1890), 556; (1892), 556–57; (1910), 658; (1918), 701; (1928), 740–41; (1930), 747; (1936), 791; (1938), 793; (1946), 852; (1948), 854; (1952), 863; (1956), 865; (1958), 870; (1980), 981; (1982), 984; (1986), 988; (1992), 1004; (1994), 1007, 1015
elections, presidential; (1796), 223; (1800), 230–31; (1804), 235; (1808), 247; (1816), 258; (1820), 258; (1824), 302–04, *c307*; (1828),

310–12, crt311; (1832), 325; (1836), 326; (1840), 327–28; (1844), 371–72; (1848), 388–89; (1856), 399–400; (1860), 403–04, m404; (1864), 433; (1868), 451; (1872), 453; (1876), 454, m459, 551; (1880), 552, q552; (1884), 553; (1888), 512, 554–55; (1892), 556, 576–77; (1896), 577–78, m587; (1900), 615, 650; (1904), 653; (1912), crt670, 661–63, m664; (1916), 690; (1920), 712–13; (1924), 720–21; (1932), 759–61, p760; (1936), 791; (1948), 853–54, m854, p854; (1952), 862–63; (1956), 865; (1960), g952; (1964), 956–57; (1968), 939–40, m973; (1972), 967; (1976), 976–77; (1980), 981; (1984), 985; (1988), 990–91; (1992), 1002–04, m1004; mudslinging, 310

Electoral College; elections: of 1796, 223; of 1800, 231, m231; of 1804, 235; of 1824, 302–04, c307; of 1828, 311; of 1832, 325; of 1836, 326; of 1840, 328; of 1848, 389; of 1856, 399–400; of 1860, m404, 404; of 1868, 451; of 1872, 454, m459; of 1888, 512, 555; of 1892, 576; of 1896, m587; of 1912, 663, m664; of 1928, 741; of 1952, 863; of 1960, g952; of 1968, 940; of 1972, 967; of 1976, 977; of 1980, 981; of 1984, 985; of 1988, 991; of 1992, 1004, m1004

electricity, 497, 538

Elementary and Secondary Education Act of 1965, 958

Eliot, T.S., 732

Elizabeth I, Queen, 47, ptg48, 56

Elizabeth of York, 18

Ellis Island, p517

Ellsberg, Daniel, 943–44

El Guettar, 820

el-Sadat, Anwar, 945, p979, 980

emancipation. *See* abolitionist movement.

Emancipation Proclamation, 419, q419, 426

Embargo Act, 246

Emergency Quota Act, 717

Emerson, Ralph Waldo, 139, 339, 350

employment. *See* unemployment.

Energy, Department of, 977

England; colonial policy of, 46–47, 92, 93; emergence of, 18; exploration of America by, 19, 26, 47; piracy by, 46–47; Protestantism in, 18; Renaissance in, 17; War of Roses, 18. *See also* Great Britain.

Enlightenment, the, 77–78, 161

enslaved persons. *See* slavery, enslaved persons.

Entente Cordiale, 686

Entering Mexico City, ptg377

entertainment; colonial dance, 94, p94; Gilded Age, 561–62; Great Depression, 798; radio, motion pictures, 798, p797, p798. *See also* culture; sports.

enumerated commodities, 92

environment; acid rain, 1016–17; big business, q1017; Clinton administration, 1016–17; history and, 655; issues of the twenty-first century, 1021, p1021; natural resource conservation, 652–54; soil depletion, 296; urban pollution and public health, 539. *See also* conservation; natural resources.

Episcopalians, 121

Equal Rights Amendment (ERA), p916

equality; African Americans, 144–45; Americans with disabilities, 1020; Declaration of Independence, 119–20; Fourteenth and Fifteenth amendments, 448, 456; post-Reconstruction, 455; women, 236. *See also* African Americans; discrimination; segregation; voting; woman's rights; women; specific groups; related subjects.

ERA. *See* Equal Rights Amendment.

Era of Good Feelings, 258–62

Eratosthenes, 41

Erie Canal, 266–67, 394

Erie Railroad, 394, 547, 570

Erlichman, John D., 968

Esch-Cummins Act, 706

Espionage and Sedition acts, 699–700

Ethiopia, 24, 809

ethnic neighborhoods, 530

ethnic rivalries, 993, 1008

Europe, 684; Asia, search for, 19, 26–29, 36–40, m39; cold war in, 838–43; m841; colonialism, 42–45, 46–51; Confederacy assistance, 415; exploration of the world, m39, m50; immigration from, c392, 528–30; land values, 76, 97; Marshall Plan, 841–42; Middle Ages, 15–17; national boundaries in 1914, m689; nations, emerging of, 18–19; post-World War I, m702, 707; slavery, 426; United States investment by, 569, 692, m693; World War I, II, m693, 692, 818, m819. *See also* immigration; World War I; World War II; countries; related subjects.

Evans, Oliver, q394

executive branch. *See* presidency, President.

Exeter Compact, 67

expansionism; Alaska, g612; California, 374, 377, 378, m478; colonial, 76, 98–99, m99, 101; Cuba, 380–81, 612–13; federal land policy, 320; Florida, g612; Hawaii, 608, g612; Louisiana Purchase, 238, g612; Maine, 366–367; Mexican Cession, g612; Northwest Territory settlement, 297–98, 367–69, 372; Philippines annexation, 608–11; possessions, m610; Puerto Rico, 613; Texas, 372, 376, 477–79, g612; Utah, 369; westward expansion, 101, 151–53, 297–98, 320, 366–67, m368, m378, m478. *See also* frontier; Manifest Destiny.

Ex parte Vallandigham, 425

Expedition Act, 651

Exploration, Age of, 26–29

F

factories; child labor, 519–20, p519, q520, 624–25, 637; depression of 1837, 326–27; immigrant labor, 289, 291, 392–39, 495; labor union development, 291–93, 520–22; women, 291, 292, 340, 428, 624, 636–37; working conditions in, 291, 518–19, q519, 624–25. *See also* industry; specific industry.

Factory Chimneys, ptg493

Factory Girls' Association, 292

Fairbanks, Douglas, 733

Fair Employment Practices Commission, 831

Fair Labor Standards Act, 793

Fall, Albert, 718

Fall of the Aztec Empire, ptg43

Fallen Timbers, Battle of, 214

Falmouth, ME, 116

Farm Bloc, 742, 747

Farm Board, 748

farmers, farming; agribusiness, 869; in ancient civilizations, 9, 10; banks, 323, 487–88, q488, 569, 671; cattle ranching, 477–79; city migration, 533; colonial women, 74, q74; Coolidge administration, 720–25; currency standard, 154, 573–75; Democratic party, 599; depression of 1837, 326–27; Eisenhower administration, 868–69, q869; gold standard, 573–74; Grange, 570–72; grasshoppers, 568, q568, ptg569; Great Depression, 744, 748, q748; Great Plains, 568–69; Great Society, 959; Harding administration, 723–25; Homestead Act, 484; Hoover administration, 742, 748; immigrants, 297, 485, 528; indentured servants, 58, 59–60; industry, 390–92; Interstate Commerce Act, 572; Middle Ages, 16; New Deal, 782–83; organizations, 569–72, p572, 573; overproduction, falling prices, 479, 568–69, g569, 573, 723–24, q723, g763; Populist movement, 573–77; railroads, 484, 486, 487, 569, 575; Republican party, 548; rural electrification, 781; seasonal workers, 869; sharecroppers, tenant farmers, 240–41; Southern, 60, g455; specialization, 487, g491; status, 488; subsistence farming, 61, 487; tariff issue, 320–23; and technology, 390–92, 484, p486; technologic advances, 391–92, 484–85; telling time, 234, p239; Tennessee Valley Authority, 780–81, m781; transportation, 269, 485, 671; westward movement of, 297, 484–88; Wilson administration, 671; women, 428, 488; World War I, 703. *See also* cattle ranching; regions; states; related subjects.

Farm Security Administration (FSA), 783, 793

Farragut, David, 420

fashions, 356–57, 764–65, p764–65

Faubus, Orval, 901–02

Faucet, Jessie H., 734

Federal Arts Project, 799

federal deficit. *See* budget deficit.

Federal Deposit Insurance Corporation (FDIC), 779

Federal Emergency Relief Administration (FERA), 780

Federal Farm Board, 742

Federal Farm Loan Banks, 671

Federal Government. *See* government.

Federal Highways Act, 671

Federalist, The, 160

Federalist party, beginnings of, 159–60, 222–23; decline of, 258; election of 1800, 230–31, q231, 233; Embargo Act, 246; Jefferson administration, 232–35; Louisiana Purchase, 240

**Federalists, ** 159–60
**Federal Reserve Act of 1913, ** 329, 667–69
**Federal Reserve Board, ** 329, 668, 743, 978, 984
**Federal Reserve System, ** 329, 667–68, *m669*
**Federal Securities Act of 1933, ** 779
**Federal Society of Journeymen Cordwainers, ** 293
**Federal Theatre Project, ** 799
**Federal Trade Commission, ** 669–70, 714; Act, 669
*Feminine Mystique, The, * 869
**Ferber, Edna, ** 488
**Ferdinand, King, ** 19, 37
**Ferraro, Geraldine, ** 917, 985
*Ferry Boat Trip, * ptg726
**feudalism, ** 15, 16
**filibusterers, ** 380
**Fifteenth Amendment, ** 456
**Fillmore, Millard, ** 383, *q383*, 390, 399
**Finlay, Carlos, J., ** 613
**fireside chats, ** 775–76
*First at Vicksburg, * ptg423
**First Opium War, ** 382
**Fish, Hamilton, ** 600–01
**Fisk, James J., ** 547, 570
**Fisk University, ** 443
**Five Civilized Tribes, ** 13
**Five-Power Treaty, ** 714
**"flappers," ** 730
*Fletcher v. Peck, * c261
Florida; acquisition of, *m275*, 272; election of 1872, 453; election of 1876, 454; Native Americans in, 272, 273, 318; readmission of, *m449*; secession of, 404; Spanish, 44, 61, 95, 272; War of 1812, 272
**Foch, Marshal Ferdinand, ** 695
**Foley, Tom, ** 1007
*Follow Me!, * ptg805
*Follow the Drinking Gourd, * 406
**food, ** 427, 497, 530, 635
**Food Administration, ** 698
**Food and Drug Administration, ** 635
**Foot, Samuel A., ** 320
**Forbes, Charles R., ** 718
**Force Bill, ** 322
**Ford, Gerald, ** 968–69, 976
**Ford, Henry, ** 721–22
**Fordney-McCumber Act, ** 714–15, 723, 744
foreign aid. *See* cash-and-carry; foreign policy; lend-lease; countries.
foreign policy; Adams, J., administration, 223–25; Bush administration, 991–94; Carter administration, 978–81; Coolidge administration, 725; Eisenhower administration, 870; Ford administration, 971; Jefferson administration, 244–46; Monroe administration, 271–74, 598; Nixon administration, 941–42; right of self-determination, 119, 598; Roosevelt, T., administration, 616–19; Taft administration, 617; Truman administration, 840–41; Washington administration, 216–19, 598. *See also* cold war; countries; individual Presidents; related subjects.

foreign relations; Confederation period, 149–51
**Forest Reserve Act, ** 652, 653
forests. *See* conservation.
**Fort Donelson, ** 420, *q420*
**Fort Duquesne, ** 94–95
**Fort Henry, ** 420
**Fort McHenry, ** 250
**Fort Sumter, ** 412–14, *ptg413*
**Fort Ticonderoga, ** 117, 131
*Fortune, * 64
**Fortune, Amos, ** 75
**forty-niners, ** 389, 390
**Fourier, Charles, ** 349
**Four-Power Treaty, ** 713–14
**Fourteen Points, ** 700
**Fourteenth Amendment, ** 445, 456
*Fourth of July Celebration in Center Square, Philadelphia, * ptg257
France; American colonization, 48–51; British conflict with, 93–95, 96, 118, 216, 217, 245–46; California, 374; Canada, 48–50, 70, 95; China leasehold by, 618; Confederacy assistance, 416; Egyptian invasion, 881; emergence of, 19; Four, Five, Nine-Power Treaties, 713–14; French and Indian War, 93–95; French Revolution, 138, 216; fur trading, 49–50, 95; German resistance, 812; Great Britain, 686; Hundred Years' War, 19; immigrants from, 225, 528; in North America, *m95*; Italian invasion of, 812; Louisiana Purchase, 49, 237–38; Louisiana Territory, 95, 237; Mexican occupation by, 598–99; Middle Ages in, 17, 19; Napoleon, 237, 245; Napoleon III, 598–99; Native Americans, 48–50, 95; NATO, 882; New World exploration, 19, 26, 48–51, *m50*; Oregon, 368; Ostend Manifesto, 381; Panama Canal, 616; Quadruple Alliance, 273; relations in Confederation period, 151; Renaissance in, 17; Revolutionary War (American), 118, 129, 130, 132, 135, 151; Revolutionary War debt, 208, 209; Russia, 686; Spain, 95; trade with, 151; Treaty of Paris, 95–96; Vietnam, 879; World War I, 686–87, 694; World War II, 811–12, 824; World War II peace, 841, *m841*
**franchise, ** 79, 311. *See also* voting rights.
**Francis I, King, ** 48
**Franciscans, ** 373
**Franco, General Francisco, ** 809
**Franklin, Benjamin, ** *ptg130;* Albany Plan of Union, 94, 147; Boston Tea Party, 106; Constitution, 319; Declaration of Independence, 119; envoy to France, 130; on English manufacturing restrictions, *q93;* on English taxes, *ptg93;* Philadelphia Convention, 156, 157, *q158;* Treaty of Paris, 138
**Franz Ferdinand, Archduke, ** 686
**Frazier, E. Franklin, ** 734
**Fredericksburg, Battle of, ** 411, *ptg411*, 418
**free silver, ** 574–75, 577, *q578*
**Free-Soil party, ** 389
free states. *See* slavery, enslaved persons; states.

**free trade agreement, ** 1013
freedmen; discrimination against, 75; education, 443, *q443, ptg443;* Ku Klux Klan, 453, *p453;* Reconstruction, 453–54. *See also* African Americans; Civil War; slavery, enslaved persons.
**Freedmen's Bureau, ** 443–44, 456
**Freedom March, ** 906
**Freedom Riders, ** 905
**Freeport Doctrine, ** 403, *q403*
**Frémont, John C., ** 399
**French and Indian War, ** 93–95, *m96*
**Frick, Henry C., ** 510
**Friedan, Betty, ** 869, *p869*
**Frobisher, Martin, ** 47
frontier; Conestoga wagons, 264, *p264*, 297; disappearance of, *m487*, 488; mining frontier, 479–80; mountain men, 370; Native American conflict, 76, 98, 297; space, 955, 960; weddings, 211; westward expansion, 101, 238, 297–98, 366–77, *m368*, 381, *m478*, 477–81. *See also* individual names; related subjects.
**Frost, Robert, ** 731
**Fuel Administration, ** 696–97
**Fugitive Slave Law, ** 390, 397, 404
**Fuller, Margaret, ** 350, *ptg351*
**Fulton, Robert, ** 265
**Fundamental Constitutions of Carolina, ** 61
**Fundamental Orders of Connecticut, ** 67
**Funding Bill, ** 209, 211–12
**fur trading, ** 49–50, 51, 94, 98–99, 150, 238, *p243*, 370

G

**Gadsden, Christopher, ** 104, *q104*
**Gadsden Purchase, ** 377, *m378*, 471
**Gage, Thomas, ** 108–09, 129, *q129*
**Galbraith, John Kenneth, ** 871, 957
**Gallatin, Albert, ** 258, *q258*
**Gallaudet, Thomas, ** 336
**Gallup, George, ** *q876*
**Galveston, TX, ** 632
**Galvez, Bernardo de, ** 136
Gama, Vasco da. *See* Da Gama, Vasco.
**Garfield, James, ** 552, *ptg552, p552*
**Garner-Wagner bill, ** 749
**Garrison, William Lloyd, ** 342, *q343*, 346
**Garvey, Marcus, ** 734
**gasoline, ** c978
**Gast, John, ** *ptg367*
**Gates, Horatio, ** 131
**General Allotment Act, ** 784
**General Electric, ** 504
**General Federation of Women's Clubs, ** 628
**General Motors, ** 868
**Genet, Edmond, ** 217–18
**Geneva Conference, ** 751
**Gentlemen's Agreement, ** 619

geography; Battle of Vicksburg, 423, *p423, ptg423;* African American migration, 857, *p857;* changing the map of Europe, *m689;* exploring the Louisiana Purchase, 253; the Great American Desert, 489; Native American and European land values, 97; standard time zones, 501; "'Twas a Small World," Columbus Thought, 41

George II, King, 61

George III, King, *ptg108,* 116–17, *ptg118,* 119, 120, 138–39, *q139*

George, Henry, 575, 583, *q583*

George Washington Before Yorktown, 1781, ptg86

Georgia; Civil War in, 422, 432–33; Constitution ratification, 157, *c163;* cotton plantations, 294–95; Native Americans in, 132, 240, 272, 317; readmission of, *m449;* Revolutionary War in, 113, 136, 137; secession of, 404; settlement of, 61, *c66;* slavery in, 61; state government of, 71, 144

German Americans, 74, 700

Germantown, PA, 130

Germany; Austria, 809; Berlin Wall, 926–27; Brest-Litovsk, Treaty of, 692; China leasehold by, 618; Czechoslovakia invasion, 811; division of, *m841;* Hitler, 808, *p809,* 821; Holocaust, 821; Holy Roman Empire, 18; immigrants from, 393, 528; Jewish harassment, *p814;* Mexico, 691; NATO, 843; Nazi party, 751, 808; peace plan, 700, 702; Poland, 811–12; post-World War II, *m841,* 842; Protestantism in, 18; reunification of, *p991,* 992; Soviet Union invasion, 815, 818; Triple Alliance, 686; U-boats, 687–88, *ptg688,* 690–91, 695, 815; Venezuelan blockade by, 617; war reparations, effect of, 751; World War I, 686–88, *m693,* 692, 700; World War II, 818–21, *m819. See also* Hitler, Adolf; World War I; World War II.

Gettysburg, Battle of, 419, *q419*

Gettysburg Address, 419–20

Ghana, 24, *m33*

Ghent, Treaty of, 252, 271

Gibbons v. Ogden, c261, 262

Gilbert, Sir Humphrey, 56

Gilded Age; art, architecture, 560–61; civil service reform, 551–54; Cleveland administration, 553–56; corruption, 544–47; education, 557–59; election of 1888, 554–55; literature, 559–60; political parties, 548–49; sports, entertainment, 561–62; tariffs, 554–55; yellow journalism, 561

Gilpin, Charles, 734

Gingrich, Newt, 1007, *p1007*

Ginsburg, Ruth Bader, 1005, *p1005*

Gladden, Washington, 627

glasnost, 987, 992

Glass-Steagall Act, 779

Glenn, John, 955

Glidden, Joseph, 485

Glorious Revolution, 70

Go Down, Moses, 407

Goeller, Charles, *ptg678*

Goethals, George W., 616

gold; African trade, 24; in California, 379, *ptg379,* 381, 389; in Colorado, 479, *q479;* currency standard, 548; mining, 379, 479–80, *p483;* Spanish explorers, 13, 52–53

Gold Mining in California, ptg379

gold standard, 548, 577

Goldwater, Barry, 957

Gompers, Samuel, 526

Good Neighbor policy, 800, 806

Goodyear, Charles, 391

Gorbachev, Mikhail, 986–88, 992

Gordon, John, *p923*

Gore, Albert, 1005, *p1006*

Gorgas, William C., 613, 616

Gould, Jay, 500, 524, 547, 570

government; Bank of the United States (second), 322–26, 329; business, 547; Civil War power of, 424; colonial, 60–61, 65–66, 67, 69–70, 72, 79; Spanish, 44–45, 144–45; Coolidge administration, 720; corruption, 544–47, 552–53; Era of Good Feelings, 258–62; fascism, 809; federalism, 159, 168; financing of, 157; Harding administration, 714–18; Hoover administration, 740–42; human welfare, 760; Jefferson administration, 231–33; laissez-faire policy, 327; by popular will, 119; of overseas possessions, *m610,* 612–13; powers of, 157, 168–71; progressive reform, 551–54, 632–35; by social contract, 119; Supreme Court decisions supporting federal power over states, 260–62, totalitarian state, 809; Washington administration, 204–11, 216–20. *See also* Articles of Confederation; Constitution; states.

Gramm-Rudman Act, 986

Grand Canyon of the Yellowstone, ptg649

Grand Coulee Dam, 781

Grange, 570–72

Grant, Jehu, 133

Grant, Ulysses S., 552; Civil War, 420, *q420,* 422, 431–33, 434–35; corruption, 544, 547; election of 1868, 451; election of 1872, 453; Johnson, A., 433; administration, 451; Mexican War, 377; spoils system, 552–53

Grapes of Wrath, The, 800, *q800–01, p801*

Grasse, Admiral de, 138

Great American Desert, 302, 317, 470, 489, *p489*

Great Awakening, 76; Second Great Awakening, 350

Great Britain; arbitration of disputes with, 600–01; Battle of Britain, 812–13; Berlin airlift, 842; British Guiana, 601; California, 374; Canada, 95, 366–67, 600–01; canal route, 382; China, leasehold by, 382–83, 618; colonial taxes, trade regulation by, 92–93, 98–101; Confederate alliance of, 416, 600; cotton imports, 92, 294, 295, 416; disarmament, 272; Egyptian invasion, 881; Entente Cordiale, 686; First Opium War, 382; Four, Five, Nine-Power Treaty, 713–14; French conflict with, 93–95, 96, 216–17, 245; French and Indian War, 93–95, *m96;* fur trading, 94, 150, 216, 219; German resistance, 812; Hong Kong, 382; immigrants from, 392, *c392;* in North America, *m95,* 95–96; investments of, 326, 479, 495–96; Italian invasion, 820, *m822;* Jay Treaty, 219; Monroe Doctrine, 273–74; Native Americans, 57, 94, 97, 98, 133, 216; NATO, 882; Navigation Laws, 394; North Africa, 818, 820; Oregon, 272, 366–69; Ostend Manifesto, 381; Quadruple Alliance, 272–74; Revolutionary War, 116–20, 126–33, 136–38, *q129,* effects of, 138–39; slavery, 371; Soviet Union, 815, *q815;* Spanish colonization, 42–45; Texas, 371; trade with, 92–93, 108, 217, 271–72, 284, 295; Treaty of Paris (1763), 95–96, 366; Treaty of Paris (1783), 138, 149–50, 366; United States investment by, 326; Venezuela, 601; War of 1812, 248–52, *q251, m251;* World War I, 686, 687; World War II, 811–13, 815

Great Compromise, 157

Great Depression; African Americans, 780; banks, 745, 761, *p778;* business and labor, *c745, q745, p782;* causes of, 744–45; culture during, 754–57, *p755, q757, p761, p780;* dust bowl, *ptg756,* 786, *p786;* economy, 745, *c745, q745;* election of 1932, 759–61; farmers, 748, *q748,* 755; fear of revolution, 758–59, *q758;* financial reform, 779–80; Hoover administration, 742, 748; industrial relief, 784–85; New Deal, 779; Social Security Act, 789; tariff issue, 744–45; unemployment, *c745,* 780; unions, 785. *See also* New Deal; Roosevelt, Franklin D.

Great Flood of 1993, 1012

Great Lakes, 271, 272, 394, 494; westward expansion, 394

Great Northern Railway, 472, 526

Great Plains, 11, 470–71, *q473,* 473–75, 477–79, 484–88, *p485;* economics, 487–88, *q488,* 489; weather, 486

Great Society, 956–60

Greece, 815, 840, *m841*

Greeley, Horace, 349, 453

greenbacks, 429, 574

Greene, Nathaniel, 138

Greenland, 36, 37

Green v. County School Board, 914

Greenville, Treaty of, 240

Greenwich, Great Britain, 501

Grenville, George, 98–99, 101

Grimké, Sarah and Angelina, 343, *ptg343*

Griswold, Roger, *p225*

Gropper, William, 799

Gross Clinic, ptg560

Guadalcanal, 823

Guadaloupe, 51

Guadalupe Hidalgo, Treaty of, 377–78

Guam, 609, 817

Guatemala, 611, 880

Guerriere, 246

Guilford Courthouse, 138

Guiteau, Charles J., 552, *p552*

Gulf of Tonkin, 932

Gulf of Tonkin Resolution, 932

Gutenberg, Johann, 17
Guzman, Jacobo Arbenz, 880

H

habeas corpus, writ of, 424, 425
Haiti, 237–38, 807, 1010–11, p1010, 1019
Haldeman, H.R., 968, p969
Halfbreeds (political party), 552
Hamburg, SC, 394
Hamilton, Alexander, ptg209; Bank of the United States, 210; Burr, Aaron, 240; election of 1800, 230–31; *The Federalist*, 160; government, 155, 158; implied powers, 212; industry, 210; Jay Treaty, 218–19; Jefferson conflict with, 211, 219; neutrality, 217; opposition to, 211–12; Philadelphia Convention, 155, 158; Report on Manufactures, 209; Report on the Public Credit, 209; treasury, 209–11; view of democracy, q209, 211, q211; Washington's cabinet, 205, ptg205, 206, 209, 219; whiskey excise tax, 209
Hamilton, Andrew, 78
Hamilton, James, ptg354
Hammond, Harry, 441, q441
Hampton Institute, 443
Hancock, John, 159, 160
Hancock, Winfield S., 552
handicapped. See handicapping conditions.
handicapping conditions; Americans With Disabilities Act, 1020
Hanna, Mark, 577–78, 650, q650, 653
Harding, Warren G.; advisers' scandals, 718; business policy, 714–15; death of, 718; election of 1920, 712–13; foreign policy, 713–14, 725; immigration policies, 716–18; unions, 715–16
Harlem, 734, 735
Harlem Renaissance, 734, 735, q734
Harleston, Edwin A., 735
Harpers Ferry, VA, ptg387, 403, 418
Harper's Magazine, 563
Harrington, Michael, 957–58, q958
Harris, Abram L., 734
Harrison, Benjamin, 555
Harrison, Richard B., 555, ptg555, 556, 734
Harrison, William H.; death of, 328; election of 1840, 327; Native Americans, 327, 241; War of 1812, 249
Hartford Convention, 252
Harvard Law School, 628
Harvard University, 77, 558
Hassam, Childe, ptg683
Hat Act, 92
Hatch Family, ptg511
Havermeyer, Henry O., 512
Hawaii, 600, 608, 818, 822, 870
hawks, 937
Hawley-Smoot Tariff, 748, 750
Hawthorne, Nathaniel, ptg332, 346, 349, q349, q434

Hay, John, 605, 618–19
Hayes, Roland, 734
Hayes, Rutherford B., 454, 522, 551–52
Haymarket Square riot, 525, ptg525
Hayne, Robert Y., 320, 322
Hays, Mary Ludwig, 134. See also Pitcher, Molly.
health. See medicine; progressivism.
Hearst, William Randolph, 606, 811
helicopters, p932
Helsinki Accords, 971
Hemingway, Ernest, 732
Henry, Alexander, 97
Henry, Joseph, 347
Henry the Navigator, Prince, 28–29, ptg29
Henry, Patrick, ptg91, ptg101, 102, 116, 159
Henry Street Settlement, 536
Henry VII, King, 18, 47
Hepburn Act of 1906, 654
Hessians, 116–17, 127
Hester Street, ptg517
Hiawatha, 10, ptg10, 13, 347
Hicks, Edward, ptg71
Highway Act of 1956, 873
Hill, Anita, 1003, p1003
Hill, James J., 472, q473, 526
Hinduism, 21
Hirohito, 816
Hiroshima, Japan, 823, p826
Hispanic Americans, 917–18, p917. See also Mexican Americans; individual countries.
Hiss, Alger, 855
Hitchcock, Ethan Allen, 375, q375
Hitler, Adolf, 751, 808, p809. See also Germany; Nazi party; World War II.
Ho Chi Minh, 879–80, 933
Hockenberry, John, 1020, q1020
Hoe, Richard March, 563
Hogue, Alexander, ptg749, ptg756
Hohokam, 11
holding companies, 505
Holland, 528
Holmes, Oliver Wendell, 628–29, 640, q700
Holocaust, 821
Holy Roman Empire, 17, 18, 19
Homecoming, ptg837
homelessness, 996
Homer, Winslow, ptg291, ptg335, 444, ptg444, ptg558, 560
Home Relief Station, ptg759
Homestead Act, 484
Homestead lockout, 521
Hong Kong, 817
Hooker, Joe, 418, q418, 419
Hooker, Thomas, ptg55, 67
Hooker and Company Journeying through the Wilderness from Plymouth to Hartford in 1636, ptg55

Hoover, Herbert, ptg753; Bonus Army, 758; disarmament, 751; election of 1928, 740–41; election of 1932, 759–61; Food Administration, 698; foreign policy, 749–752, q752; government policies of, 740–41, q741, 742, 747–49; Great Depression, 742–45, q745; Hoover-Stimson Doctrine, 752, q752; Prohibition, 733; secretary of commerce, 716; world peace, 749–50, q749
Hopewell, 11
Hopi, 11
Hopkins, Harry, 780, 789
Hopper, Edward, 733
horizontal integration, 505
House of Burgesses, 60, ptg91, 102
House Committee on Un-American Activities, 855
House of Commons, 102
House of Representatives; antislavery issue, 344; balance of power in, 389–90; early years, 206; election of 1800, 231, 233; election of 1824, 303–04; House bank scandal, 1002–03; impeachment, 234; Jay Treaty, 219; Johnson impeachment, 451; Missouri Compromise, 302; presidential election of 1824, 302–04; progressivism, 303; Radical Republicans in, 451–54; Texas statehood, 371–72; Wilmot Proviso, 388
housing, p485. See also cities; discrimination; Great Depression; specific groups.
Houston, Sam, 370, ptg371
Howard, O.O., 443, 444
Howard University, 443
Howe, Elias, 391
Howe, Richard, 126
Howe, Samuel Gridley, 336
Howe, William, 117, 126, 127, 130–31
Howells, William Dean, 560
Hudson, Henry, 51
Hudson River, 51, 130
Hudson River School (art), ptg55, 348
Hudson's Bay Company, 372
Hudson's Bay Territory, 93
Huerta, Victoriano, 684–85
Hughes, Charles Evans, 635, 640, 690, 725
Hughes, Langston, p727, q727, 734
Huguenots, 51, 74
Hull, Cordell, 807, 816
Hull House, 534, 536–37
Humphrey, Hubert, 940
Hundred Days, (First), 777
Hungary, 821, 839, p882
Hunger of Memory, q1022–23
Hunter, Russell, q745
Huntington, Collis, q500
Hurd, Peter, ptg768
Huron (Native Americans), 48
Hurston, Zora Neale, 734
Huss, John, 18
Hussein, King, 1012
Hussein, Saddam, 992

Hutchinson, Anne, 67, p67
hydrogen bomb. *See* arms race; atom bomb; nuclear weapons.
hygiene, personal, 559, p559

I

Ibibio, 25, q25
ibn-Battutu, 23, q23
Ice Age, 8
Iceland, 36, 987
Ickes, Harold, 776, 780
Idaho, 556, 581
I Feed You All, p567
"I Have a Dream," q907
Illinois, 241, 317–18, 369
immigration, immigrants; Act, 959; AFL discrimination against, 526; Alien and Sedition acts, 225; in cities, 393, 528, 530–31, 716–17; colonial, 43, 44, 48, 50, 51, 56, 57, 58, 61, 63, 64, 70, 72, 74, m74, 528; Democratic party, 549; discrimination against, 393, 530–32; education, 642; Ellis Island, 517; farmers, 391, 485; Harding administration, 716–17; Johnson's Great Society, 959; Ku Klux Klan, 720–21; labor force, 289, 291, 393, 495, 521, 528, 641; modern, 1019–20; naturalization, 393; Naturalization, Alien, and Sedition acts, 224; New Deal and, 797; 1980s and 1990s, 1019; patterns of, c392, 528–32, g529, g716, g737; political machines, 642; political power of, 641–42, q642; progressivism, 641–42; public education, 642; Red Scare, 704–05; resentment of, 531–32, 1019–20; settlement houses, 534, 536–37; textile industry, 289; transcontinental railroad, 472; unions, 521, 717. *See also* specific countries; ethnic groups.
Immigration Restriction League, 641
impeachment, 234, 968
imperialism, 598. *See also* China, Cuba, Hawaii, Philippines.
imports, c673
impressment, 245–46, p245, ptg254
In a Free Government . . . , ptg904
Inaugural Address; Franklin Roosevelt's first, 774; John F. Kennedy's, 952, q952
Incas, 9, q13, 43
income distribution, c887
income tax, 638
indentured servants, 58, 60, 73
Independent Treasury Act, 327
Independent Treasury System, 327
India, 21, 382, 416
Indiana, 241, 267
Indian Affairs, Bureau of, 784, 919
Indian Civil Rights Act, 919
Indian Reorganization Act, 784
Indians. *See* Native Americans; individual Native American nations.
indigo, 61, 92

Industrial Revolution, 288–98; early effects in North of, 290; labor movement, 291–93; in South, 294
industrialization, 494–500, 502–12, 518
industry; automobile, 790–91; child labor, 519–20, p519, q520, 637; in cities, 290, 298, 534; clothing, 497–98; cotton, 294–96; and farmers, 297–98, 391–92, 485, 569; efficiency, 503, 518, 722; Hamilton, A., 210; industrial revolution, 288–90, 294, c307, 494; industrial unions, 291–93, 520–22; inequality, 624; innovation, 390–91, 395, 497, 888–89; insurance, 635; labor union development, 291–93, 520–22, 524–27, 790; mass production, 502–03, 504, p504, 722; munitions, 810; natural, human resources, ptg464, m478, 494–95, q513; New Deal relief, 784–85; overproduction, 479, 568–69; public policies, private investment, 495–96; railroad building, 267–68, 471–73, 495, 499–500, q500, 569–70; Southern, 294–95, 455–56, 457; steel, 790; tariffs, 259–60, 301, 556; technology, 390–91, 872–73; textile, 288–89, 391, 497; women labor force, 291, ptg291, 293, 636–37, p645; working conditions in, 291, 510, 518–19, 624–25, c625; World War I, II, 696, 698, 823, 827–28. *See also* business; factories.
inflation. *See* economy.
Inspection of the First U.S. Coins, ptg207
insurgents, 657–58
integration. *See* African Americans; civil rights; discrimination; segregation; groups; related subjects.
Interior, Department of, 474, 551
Intermediate Credits Act, 724
International Apple Shippers Association, 757
International Date Line, 501
internationalists, 811
International Ladies' Garment Workers Union, 581
International Workers of the World, 626
interpreting primary sources; William Jennings Bryan, speech to Democratic National Convention, 614; Reminiscences by Alvin Coffey, 379; "Burning Stamps to Protest the Stamp Act," ptg103; collage art in the 1960s, 961, ptg961; Eliza Southgate, "Female Equality," 236; political cartoons, 550, crt550; women in the colonies, 68, q68
Interstate Commerce Act, 572, q572, 654
Interstate Commerce Commission (ICC), 572, 653, 654, 706, 714
Intolerable Acts, 106–08
inventions. *See* technology; related subjects.
Iowa, 317
Iowa (ship), ptg602
Iran; CIA involvement in, 880; Carter administration, 980–81; hostages, 980–81, p980; Iran-contra scandal, 988; oil company seizures, 880; Persia, 21; Shah of, 880, p880, 980–81; war with Iraq, 993–94
Iraq, 993–94
Ireland, 528. *See also* Irish Americans.
Irish Americans, 74, 225, 267, 393, 472, 528
Iron Act, 98
ironclad ships, ptg414

iron curtain, 839, p839, 991
iron ore mining, 289, 290, 494
iron plow, 392
Iroquois Confederacy, 10, 13, 48–49, 50, 70, 76, 94, 97, 133–34
Irving, Washington, 268, 346
Isabella, Queen, 19, 37
Islam, 20, 24, 981
isolationism, 598; election of 1900, 615; election of 1940, 814–15; Monroe Doctrine, 598, 841; Washington administration, 598; World War II, 811
Israel, 881, m995, 1001–13; Egypt, 881; Jordan, 1012; Palestine Liberation Organization, 1011–12; Six-Day War, 928, 944
Italian Americans; cuisine, 530
Italy; Africa, 809; Allied forces in, 692; Five, Nine-Power Treaty, 714; Holy Roman Empire, 19; immigrants from, 529; Middle Ages in, 16; Mussolini, p809, 820; naval disarmament, 884; post-World War II, 841, m841; Renaissance in, 17; revolution in, 809; trade monopoly, 29, q29; Triple Alliance, 686; World War I, 686, 692; World War II, 820. *See also* Italian Americans.
"I Will Fight No More Forever," q475
Iwo Jima; World War II, 823

J

Jackson, Andrew, q316, crt319, q319; Bank of the United States (second), 322, 324, crt324, q324, q325; "candidate of the people," 311; career, 312–13; Constitution, 320, 325; Democratic party, 304, 310, 549; early life, 313; election of 1824, 302–04; election of 1828, 310, crt311; election of 1832, 325; election of 1836, 326; expansionism, 297–98; image of, 310, 311–13, q312, ptg313, q313, crt319; inauguration, 313; labor vote, 291; Native American policies, 314, 317, 322, m316; nullification crisis, 321–22, q322; presidency, 313–25; reform movement, 339–44; slavery policy, 318–19; Spanish Florida, 272; Texas statehood, 371; War of 1812, 248, ptg252, 312
Jackson, Helen Hunt, 475
Jackson, Jesse, 990–91, 992, p992
Jackson, Rachel, 311
Jackson State University, 938
Jackson, Thomas "Stonewall," 418, q418
Jacksonians, 310
Jamaica, 42
James I, King, 56, 58, 60
James II, King, 69, 70, 71
James, Sharpe, 1020
James, William, 628
Jamestown, VA, 56–57, q57, 58, 59, 60, p84
Jamieson, Mitchell, ptg790
Japan; China (Manchuria), 619, 751, crt751, 752, p807, 808–09; Chinese invasion, attempt at, 23; disarmament, 845; Dutch trade, 51; expansion in the Pacific, 808; Formosa, 619; Four, Five, Nine-Power Treaty, 713–14; Hoover-Stimson Doctrine, 752; immigrants

Japanese Americans—Latinos

from, 717; industrialization, 383; Korea, 619; medieval empire of, 23; mental asylums in, 340; National Origins Act, 717; naval disarmament, 884; Nine-Power Treaty, 714; occupation of, 845–46; Pearl Harbor, 816, 817; Russo-Japanese War, 619; Soviet Union, 807, 823; trade with, 383, 816; World War II, 816, 817–18, 822–23. *See also* Japanese Americans.

Japanese Americans; internment of, 831–33, *q831, p832, p833*

Jay, John, 160, 218–19, *ptg219*

Jay Treaty, 219

Jefferson, Thomas, 156, *ptg156, ptg230;* accomplishments, 231, 232; biography, 156; chief legislator, 233; Declaration of Independence, 119, 120; Democratic party, 549; election of 1796, 223; election of 1800, 230–31, *q230;* election of 1804, 235; election of 1808, 247; election of 1824, 302–04; foreign affairs, 244–46; foreign policy of, 244–46; government principles, 232, 233; Hamilton conflict with, 219; image of, 231–32; Inaugural Address, 232, *q232;* industrial revolution, *q289;* Lewis and Clark expedition, role in, 239; Louisiana Purchase, 237–38; Madison's cabinet, 274; Monticello, 231; national bank, 212; Native American conflict, 240–41; neutrality, 217; opposition to Hamilton, 211, 219; religious freedom, 145, *q145;* republican government, 232; Republican party, 222; Sedition Act, 230; University of Virginia, 231, *ptg231;* Washington's cabinet, 205, *ptg205,* 219

Jesuits, 50, *q50,* 373

Jewish Americans, 145, 531, 639, 720–21

Jews; colonial, 67, 74, 77; culture of, 639; discrimination against, 145, 531; German harassment of, *p814;* Holocaust, 821; immigrants, 528, 529–30, 639; Ku Klux Klan, 720–21; Orthodox, 639; Reform Judaism, 639; Soviet Union, 639; of Spain, 19. *See also* Israel.

Jim Crow laws, 455, 643, 671

Joan of Arc, 19

Job Corps, 958

Johansen, John, *ptg703*

Johns Hopkins University, 628

Johns, Jasper, *ptg975*

Johnson, Andrew, 433, 444, 446–47, 448, 450–51

Johnson, Eastman, *ptg407*

Johnson, Jonathon Eastman, *ptg511*

Johnson, Lyndon B., *p864,* 865, *p953,* 959, *p960;* election of 1960, *g952;* election of 1964, 931, 956–57; election of 1968, 939; Great Society, 956–60; Kennedy assassination, 907; Vietnam War, 931–33

Johnson, Tom, 633

Johnson, William H., *ptg726, ptg727*

Johnston, Albert Sidney, 420

Joint Committee on Reconstruction, 446, *ptg446,* 448

Joliet, Louis, 49

Jones, F.C., *ptg543*

Jones, Joe, *ptg773*

Jones, Lois Mailou, 735

Jones, Samuel "Golden Rule," 633

Jordan, 928, 1012

Joseph, Chief, 475, *q475*

Juárez, Benito, 598

judicial branch, 158, *c169,* 171, 183–85. *See also* Supreme Court.

judicial review, 171, 234

Judiciary Act of 1789, 206, 234, 235

Judiciary Act of 1801, 234

Jungle, The, 635, *q635*

jury, trial by, Quebec Act, 107

Justice, Department of, 651, 905, 906

K

kamikazes, 823

Kansas, 398–99

Kansas-Nebraska Act, 398–99, *m399*

Karadzic, Radovan, 1009

Kasserine Pass, 820

Kearny, Stephen, 376

Keating-Owen Child Labor Act, 671

Kelley, Florence, 628

Kelley, Oliver Hudson, 570

Kellogg-Briand Pact, 725, 752

Kennedy, Anthony M., 985

Kennedy, Edward, 981

Kennedy, John F., *p926, p949;* assassination of, 907, 952; civil rights policies of, 905–07; economic policies of, 952–53; election of 1960, *p951;* foreign policy of, 924–28, 930–31; Inaugural Address, 926, *q926,* 952, *q952;* Cuban missile crisis, 925; Peace Corps, 925; space program, 955, *p955*

Kennedy, John F., Jr., *p953*

Kennedy, Robert, 939–40, *p939*

Kent State University, *p937,* 938

Kentucky; African American recolonization, 296; Civil War in, 414, 420; Cumberland Road, 319; secession from Confederation, 152; settlement of, 152, 213; statehood, 213

Kentucky Resolutions, 225

Kerner Commission, 913

Key, Francis Scott, 250

Khan, Genghis, 22

Khan, Kublai, 22–23

Khmer Rouge, 971

Khomeini, Ayatollah Ruhollah, 981

Khrushchev, Nikita, 884–85, 924–25, 926, *p926*

Kilwa, 24, 29

Kim, Jay, 1004

King, Martin Luther, Jr., *p898,* 899–901, *q900, p903, q904, p906, q913,* 913–914

King, Rodney, 996

King, Rufus, 258

King George's War, 93

King William's War, 93

King's College, 77, *q77*

Kiowa (Native Americans), 474

Kissinger, Henry, 941, 943, 945

Kite, ptg961

Knights of Labor, 524–25

Know-Nothings, 393, 399

Knox, Henry, 205, *ptg205*

Knox, Frank, 817

Knox, Philander C., 617

Korea; communism in, 848; division of, 879; Korean War, 848–49, *p847, m848,* 879; Russia, 848. *See also* Korean War; South Korea.

Korean War, 848–49, *m848, p847,* 879

Korematsu v. United States, 832

Kosygin, Aleksey, 928

Krimmel, John Lewis, *ptg257*

Ku Klux Klan, 453, 705, *p715,* 720–21

Kushites, 24

Kuwait, 993

L

labor force, 1015–16, *c1025;* child labor, 58, 671; immigrants, 289, 495, 530; indentured servants, 58, 60, 73; post-World War I, 704, 715–16; union development, 291–93; women in, 269, 291, 292, 340, *g835,* 851; working conditions of, 291, *q538,* 624–25. *See also* factories; industry; slavery, enslaved persons; strikes; unemployment; unions; industries.

Labrador, 47

Ladies Home Journal, 563

Lafayette, Marquis de, 132, 138, *ptg139*

La Follette, Robert, 633–34, 638, 653, 660

laissez-faire, 232, 327, 495

Lake Erie, 249

land, 444, 484. *See also* Native Americans; countries; territories; related subjects.

Land Ordinance of 1785, 152, *m153*

Landon, Alfred M., 791

Lange, Dorothea, 757, *p757,* 799

Lansing, Robert, 707

Laos, 930

La Salle, Robert de, 49, *m50*

Las Casas, Bartolomé de, 40, *q40,* 45, *ptg52*

Last of the Buffalo, ptg469

Lathrop, Julia, 628

Latin America, *m277,* 600; anti-Americanism of, 883; Carter administration, 979–81; Clark Memorandum, 750; communism in, 884; dollar diplomacy, 617; Eisenhower administration, 878, 880, 883–84; Europeans in, 43–45; Good Neighbor policy, 806; Good Neighbor policy toward, 806–07; Harding and Coolidge, 725; Hoover administration, 750; immigrants from, 959; Kennedy administration, 925, 927–28; Monroe Doctrine, 272–74, 750; Nazi sympathies in, 818; trade with, 273; Wilson administration, 685–86. *See also* Hispanic Americans; Latin Americans; Mexican Americans; individual countries.

Latin Americans, 959. *See also* Mexican Americans; individual country of origin.

Latinos. *See* Hispanic Americans; Latin Americans.

Index **1101**

law. *See* civil rights; Congress; Constitution; Supreme Court; related subjects.
Lawrence, David, *ptg1001*
Lawrence, Jacob, *ptg904, ptg1023*
League of the Five Nations, 10
League of Nations; charter of, 701–02; disarmament conference, 751; election of 1920, 712; Japanese-Manchurian invasion, 808–09; opposition to, 701–03
League of United Latin American Citizens (LULAC), 918
Lease, Mary E., *p575*
Lebanon, 882, *m995*
Lee, Ann Mother, 349
Lee, Richard Henry, 118, 119
Lee, Robert E., 377, 403, 414–15, *q414–15, ptg418,* 418, 422, 431, 434–35
legislative branch. *See* Congress.
Leisler, Jacob, 70
LeMay, Curtis, 940
lend-lease policy, 815
L'Enfant, Pierre, 221, *ptg221,* 224
Leningrad, USSR, 818, 821
Leopard, 246
Leutze, Emanuel Gottlieb, *ptg185*
Levine, Jack, 799
Lewis and Clark expedition, *m235,* 238, *ptg239,* 253
Lewis, John, 908, *q908*
Lewis, Meriwether, 239, *ptg239,* 253
Lewis, Sinclair, 732
Lexington, MA, 108–09, *m113*
Liberal Republican party, 453
Liberia, 296
Liberty Bonds, 698
Liberty in the Form of the Goddess of Youth, p198
Liberty party, 343
libraries, 337, 537, *ptg1023*
Library, The, ptg1023
Li'l Sis, ptg727
Liliuokalani, Queen, *p598,* 600
Lincoln, Abraham, *ptg425;* African American Union soldiers, 426; Antietam, 418–19; assassination of, 435, *q435;* Civil War, *q413;* Confederate blockade, 416; Crittenden Compromise, 405; election of 1860, 404; election of 1864, 433; Emancipation Proclamation, 419, 425–26; first Inaugural Address of, 405, *q405;* Gettysburg, 419–20; image, 434, *q434;* Lincoln-Douglas debates, 402–03; Mexican War, 375; prohibition, 351; Reconstruction, 445–46; Republican party, 402, 549; second Inaugural Address of, *q433,* 433; slavery, 425–26; Southern secession, 404, 413, *q413;* Thirteenth Amendment, 445–46
Lincoln University, 337
Lindbergh, Charles, 728, *p729,* 811
Lin, Maya, 944, *p944*
linotype machines, 563
Lippmann, Walter, 712, 840
liquor, 351
literature; the American Scene, 346–47; Great Depression, 797–98; local-color, 559;

realism, 558–59; Renaissance, 17–19; Roaring Twenties, 726, *q726–27,* 731–32; romanticism, 242; transcendentalism, 350
Little Bighorn, Battle of, 474
Little Rock, AR, 901–02, *p901, q902*
Little Turtle, Chief, 213
Livingston, Robert, 237, 238
Lloyd George, David, 571, 701
Locke, John, 61, 78, 119
Lodge, Henry Cabot, 531, *q531,* 601, 609
London Company, 56–57, 60, 63
London, England, 813–14
London, Jack, 625
London Naval Conference, 751
Lone Star Republic, 370–71
Lone Tenement, ptg623
long drive, 478–79, *q479*
Long, Crawford W., 348
Long, Huey, 787–88, *p788*
Long, John D., 605
Long, Stephen, 470, 489, *q489*
Longfellow, Henry Wadsworth, 347
López, Narciso, 380–81, *ptg381*
Los Angeles, CA, 912, 996
Louis XIV, King, 49
Louis XVI, King, 138
Louisburg, 95
Louisiana; election of 1876, 453; French exploration of, 49; readmission of, 446, *m449;* Revolutionary War, 136; secession of, 404
Louisiana Purchase, *m378,* 302, 237–38, *m238,* 272
Louisiana Territory, 95, 237, 238
Louisville, KY, 297
L'Ouverture, Pierre Toussaint, 237–38
Love, Nat, *p477,* 478
Lowell, Jacqueline Shaw, 538, *q538*
Lowell, James Russell, 347–75
Loyalists, 117, 132, 138
Loyalty Leagues, 699
Lucas, Eliza, 61
Luce, Maximillian, *ptg493, ptg509*
Luks, George, *ptg517*
LULAC. *See* League of United Latin American Citizens.
Lundy, Benjamin, 342
Lusitania, 688
Luther, Martin, 18, *q18*
Lutherans, 18, 556
lynchings, 643
Lynd, Robert and Helen, 795
Lyon, Mary, 317, 337
Lyon, Matthew, *p225*

M

MacArthur, Douglas, *p846;* Bonus Army, 758, *q758;* dismissal, 846, 849; Japanese surrender, 823; World War II, 823, 846

Maclay, William, 206, *q206*
Maclure, William, 345
Macmillan, Harold, 864
McAdoo, William G., 720–21
McBarron, H. Charles, *ptg423*
McBarron, Charles, Jr., *ptg805*
McCarthy, Eugene, 939
McCarthy, Joseph, 856, *p855,* 864–65
McClellan, George, 418, 433
McClure's Magazine, 508, 563, 629
McCormick, Cyrus, 392
McCullough v. Maryland, 260–61
McDowell, Irvin, 418
McFarland, Robert, 988
McGovern, George, 967
McGuffey, William, 337, *p337*
McKim, Mead, and White, 537
McKinley Tariff, 556, 577, 600
McKinley, William, assassination, 616; election of 1896, 577–78; election of 1900, 615; foreign policy, 615, *q615;* Hawaii annexation, 608; Philippines annexation, *q608,* 609, *q609, crt614;* Spanish-American War, 603–04; tariff issue, 577
McNamara, Robert, 937
McNary-Haugen Bill, 724–25
Macedonia, 1009
Macon's Bill No. 2, 247
Macune, C.W., 572
Madero, Francisco, 684
Madison, Dolley, 249, *ptg249,*
Madison, James, *ptg151,* 161; election of 1808, 247; *The Federalist,* 160; Hamilton, Jefferson conflict, 211–12; Jay Treaty, 219; *Marbury v. Madison,* 234–35, *c261;* Monroe's foreign policy, 247, 274; Native Americans, 240; Philadelphia Convention, 156, 158, *q158;* Republican party, 247; Virginia Plan, 156; War of 1812, 247, 248–52
Magafan, Ethel, *ptg299*
Magellan, Ferdinand, 40, *ptg40, q40,* 41
Magruder, Jeb Stuart, *p969*
Mahan, Alfred T., 601, 603
mail-order catalogs, *p570,* 572
Maine, 67; prohibition, 351; boundaries, 366–67; conflict with Britain, 366–67, *m96;* statehood, 302; Native Americans, 919
Maine (ship), 604, *ptg604*
Malcolm X, 911, *q911,* 912, *p912*
Mali, 23, *q23,* 24, *m33*
Malinche, 43
Malindi, 29
malls (shopping), 964, *p964*
Manchuria, 619, 751, *crt751,* 752, *p807,* 808–09
Mandan, 83
Manhattan Island, 51
Manhattan Project, 826
Manifest Destiny, 366–82, *m378,* 603; Alaskan acquisition, 599; Cuban annexation, 380–81; election of 1844, 372; Southern, 380–81; westward expansion, 366–78, *m378, ptg369, m371, m376, m478. See also* expansionism; West.

Manila—Monroe

Manila, 605–06, *ptg607*
Mann, Horace, 334
manufacturing. *See* industry.
Mao Zedong, 846–47
map and graph skills; analyzing map data, 476, *m476*; bar graph, 988, *g988*, 1014, *g1014*; conclusions from maps, *m275*, 275; classifying information, 401; demographic data, 921, *g921*; generalizations, 664, *m664*; hypothesizing, 844, *m844*; information classification, 401, *m401*; line graph, 513, *g513*; military maps, 113, *m113*, 935, *m935*; political map, 689, *m689*; supporting generalizations, 664; thematic maps, 81, *m81*
Marbury v. Madison, 235–36, *c261*
Marbury, William, 238
March on Washington, 1963, p897
March on Washington, 907, *q907*
Marcy, William, 381, 1018–19
marijuana, *q1019*
marines; African American discrimination in, 695; Caribbean instability, 685; Dominican Republic, 617, 685, 725, 928; Hawaii annexation, 600; in Latin America, 617, 685, *p685*; Nicaragua, 617, 685, 725, 807; World War I, 695; World War II, 823
Marion, Francis, 137
Marquette, Jacques, 49
Marryat, Frederick, 340
Marsh, Reginald, 733, *ptg762*
Marshall, George C., 841–42
Marshall, John, 234–35, *ptg235*, 240, 260, 317
Marshall Plan, 841–42, *g859*
Marshall, Thurgood, 901
Martinique, 51
Martinsburg, VA, 522
Marx, Karl, 582
Maryland; African American recolonization, 296; Articles of Confederation, 146, *m146*, 155; Civil War in, 413–14, 418–19; Constitution ratification, *c163*; religious tolerance in, 61; settlement of, 60–61, *c66*; state government of, 60; tobacco, 61
Mason and Dixon Line, 72
Mason Children: David, Joanna, and Abigail, ptg77
Massachusetts; asylums, 340; colonial government of, 65–66; *Commonwealth v. Hunt,* 293; Constitution ratification, 160, *c163*; education in, 77, 334; election of 1848, 389; factories in, 290; industry in, 290, 292; Pilgrims, 63–64; public education, 77, 334; Puritans in, 64–67, 77; settlement in, *c66*; Shays's Rebellion, 154; taxation protest, 102, 106; textile industry in, 290
Massachusetts Bay Colony, 64
Massachusetts Bay Company, 65
Massachusetts Committee of Public Safety, 109
Massachusetts General School Act, 77, 334
Massachusetts Institute of Technology, 558
mathematics, 9, 21; planning Washington, D.C., 221
Maury, Matthew, 347
Maximilian, 599

Maya, 9
Mayflower, 63
Mayflower Compact, 63, *ptg64*
Maysville Road Bill, 319
Meade, George G., 419
Means, Russell, *p918*
Meany, George F., *p868*
Meat Inspection Act, 635, 654
meatpacking industry, 635
medicare, 958
medicine; AIDS, 1018; anesthetics, 348; blood plasma, 831; home remedies, 152; Muslim advances in, 21, *p21*; Native Americans, 152; physical fitness, 987; polio vaccine, 873; women in, 347; yellow fever, 613
Medina, Harold, 855
Meir, Golda, 945
Melchers, Julius Gari, *ptg333*
Mellon, Andrew, 715, 745
Mellon, Thomas, *q495*
Melville, Herman, 347
Memphis, TN, 420, 913
Mencken, H.L., 732
Mennonites, 75
mental illness, 339–40
mercantilism, 48
merchant marine fleet, 815
Meredith, James, 906, *p907*
Merrimac, 414, *ptg414*
Mesoamerica, 9–10
Metacomet, 97
Methodists, 318, 351
Metternich, Klemens von, 273, *q273*
Metys, Quentin, *ptg27*
Mexican Americans, 918. *See also* Hispanic Americans; Latin Americans.
Mexican War, 375–77; *q375*
Mexico; anti-American sentiment in, 374–75, 685; California, 374–77; early cultures, 9–10; France in, 598–99; immigrants, illegal, 1019; Mexican Cession, *m378*, 390; Mexican War, 374–78, 390; migrant workers, 869, 918; oil company seizures by, 807; slavery in, 370; Spain, 370; Texas, 361, 369–72; Utah, 369; Wilson's relations with, 684–85; World War I, 691
Mexico City, Mexico, 10, 43, 45, 376, *p43*, *ptg377*
Miami (Native Americans), 213
Miami, FL, 917
Michelangelo, 17
Michigan; iron ore in, 494
Middle Ages, 15–17, *p16*
middle class, 16
Middle Colonies; education in, 77; government of, 69, 79; religion in, 71, 72; settlement of, 69–72
Middle East, *m995;* Carter administration, 979–81; Clinton administration, 1011–13; Eisenhower administration, 878, 880, 881–82; Iraq-Kuwait Persian Gulf War, 994–95; Nixon administration, 944–45; Reagan administration, 985–86; World War I, *m693*, 702, *m702. See also* foreign policy; communism; countries.

Midway, Battle of, 822
Midway Islands, 822
migrant workers, 869
migrations, 8
Millay, Edna St. Vincent, 726, *p726*, *q726–27*
Milosevic, Slobodan, 1009
Milwaukee, WI, 528
Ming Dynasty, 23
Minh, Ho Chi, 879–80, 933
Miners in the Sierra, ptg464
mining. *See* coal mining; gold; iron ore; silver.
mining towns, 479–81, *q480*, *ptg481*
Minnesota, 474
missionaries; to China, 383; education, 373; Jesuits, 50, *q50*; to Native Americans, 49, 49–50, 52, 76, 368, 373; Protestant, 373; Roman Catholic, 26; Spanish, 44, 45, 50, 52, 373; to West, 373
Mississippi; civil rights violence in, 906; Civil War in, 420; cotton plantations, 296; flood, 1012; Jackson State University, 938; readmission of, *m449*; secession of, 404; statehood, 296
Mississippi River; as boundary, 95, 96; Civil War, 414, 415, 417, 420; commerce, 150, 394; cotton plantations, 296; farmers, farming, 11; Louisiana Territory, 49; Mark Twain, 394, 559; Marquette, Joliet, exploration of, 49; Native Americans of, 11; Spain, control of, 150; steamboats on, 265–66, 394; transportation improvements, 265–66; War of 1812, 250, *m251*
Missouri, 369, 414, 420
Missouri (ship), 823
Missouri Compromise, 318, 344, 302, *m302*, 400
Missouri River, 239
Mitchell, John (UMW leader), 652
Mitchell, John (attorney general), 968
Mitchell, Margaret, 797
Mitchell, Maria, 347, *ptg347*
Moctezuma, 13, 43
Mogul Empire, 22
Mohammed, Askia, 24
Mohawk, 10, 13, 134
Molasses Act, 92, 100
Molly Pitcher at the Battle of Monmouth, ptg115
Mondale, Walter, 985
money. *See* currency.
Moneychanger and His Wife, ptg27
Mongols, 22–23
Monitor, 414, *ptg414*
Monmouth, NJ, Battle of, *ptg115*, 134, 136
monopolies; Bank of the United States, 323; big business, 503, 511–12, *crt514*, 669; colonial tea, 106; oil industry, 508, 511–12; railroads, 570; Sherman Antitrust Act, 512, 669. *See also* business; trusts; industries.
Monroe, James, *ptg274*, *ptg271*; election of 1816, 258; election of 1820, 258; foreign policy of, 271–74; Louisiana Purchase, 237–38; issuance of Monroe Doctrine, 272–74

Index **1103**

Monroe Doctrine, 598; British Guiana boundary dispute, 601, *q601;* California, 374; issuance of, 272–74, *ptg274;* Kellogg-Briand Pact, 725; Mexican-French occupation, 598–99; Roosevelt Corollary to, 617; Truman Doctrine, 841; Venezuela, 601, 616–17; in war with Mexico, 374

Montana, 479, 556

Montcalm, Louis de, 95

Montenegro, 1009

Montgomery, AL, 899

Montreal, Canada, 48, 180, 248

Moors, 19, 28

Moran, Edward, *ptg597*

Moran, Thomas, 649, *ptg649,*

Morgan, Daniel, 138

Morgan, J. Pierpont, 577, 652

Mormon Church, 349, 369

Mormons Move West, ptg369

Morning Bell, ptg291

Morocco, 244

Morrill Act, 488, 558

Morris, Robert, 128

Morse, Samuel F.B., 348

Morton, T.G., 348

Moscow, USSR, 818

Mott, Lucretia, 341, *ptg341*

Mount Holyoke College, 558

Mount Vernon, 128, 155

mountain men, 370

movies, 733, *p797,* 798. *See also* entertainment.

muckrakers, 629

mudslinging, 310

Mugwumps, 553, 554

Muhammad, 20

Muhammed, Elijah, 910

Muller v. Oregon, 636–37

multiculturalism, 1020

Munich Conference, 810

Munn v. Illinois, 571

Murray, Robert Michael, 938, *q938*

music; folk songs of protest, 579; Harlem Renaissance, 734; jazz, 733; patriotism, 699; origins of rock and roll, 877; rocking into the future, 1026–27; songs of slavery, 406–07; Woodstock, 939

Muskie, Edmund, 940

Muslims, 15, 21–22

Mussolini, Benito, *p808,* 809. *See also* Italy; World War II.

N

NAACP. *See* National Association for the Advancement of Colored People.

NAFTA. *See* North American Free Trade Agreement.

Nagasaki, Japan, 823

Nahl, Charles, *ptg464*

napalm, 933

Napoleon, 237, 238, 247, 249, 272

Narragansetts, 67

Nashville, TN, 433

Nasser, Gamal Abdel, 881, *p881*

Nast, Thomas, 546 *p546, q546,* 550, *crt550*

Natchez, MS, 136

National Advisory Commission on Civil Disorders, 913

National Aeronautics and Space Administration (NASA), 955

National Association for the Advancement of Colored People (NAACP), *q644,* 648, 670, 901

national bank. *See* Bank of the United States.

National Child Labor Committee, 637

National Congress of American Indians, 918–19

National Conservation Commission, 653

National Consumers League, 628

National Council of the Churches of Christ, 627

National Council of Negro Women, 731

national debt. *See* budget deficit.

National Defense Education Act, 870, 955

National Farmers' Allliance and Industrial Union, 572

National Guard, 522, 906

National Industrial Recovery Act (NIRA), 784–85

nationalism; Era of Good Feelings, 258–62, *q258;* European, 686; North, 413, *q413;* Republican party, 258; South, 413; Supreme Court decisions, 260–62; transportation, 263–70

National Labor Relations Act, 790

National Labor Relations Board (NLRB), 790

National League, 562

National Liberation Front (NLF). *See* Vietcong.

National Livestock Marketing Association, 742

National Monetary Commission, 667–68

National Organization for Women (NOW), 869, 916–17, *q917*

National Origins Act, 717

National Progressive Republican League, 660

National Recovery Administration (NRA), 784

National Republicans, 304, 310, *q325,* 325

National Road, 263–64

National Science Foundation, 955

National Trades Union, 291

National Union for Social Justice, 787

National Urban League, 901

National War Labor Board, 829

National Woman's Christian Temperance Union (WCTU), 351

National Woman Suffrage Association (NWSA), 581

National Women's Trade Union League, 581

National Youth Administration (NYA), 789

Nation, Carrie, *p580,* 910–11

Nation of Islam, *p911*

Native Americans; archaeology, 14; army removal of, *m316,* 317, 318; art subjects, *ptg7, ptg9, ptg10, ptg314, ptg318, ptg347, ptg469;* Battle of Tippecanoe, 241, 327; civil rights movement, 918–19; Civil War, 428; colonies, 67, 75–76, 98–99; in Congress, 1004; Dawes Act, 475; European explorers, 13, 36, 37, 42–43, 44, 45, 48–50; first Americans, 8–13, *ptg9, m12;* French and Indian War, 94, 95; frontier conflict, 36, 75–76, 97–98, 297, 473–75; fur trading, 49–50, 51; General Allotment Act, 784; Great Britain and, 94, 98–99, 133–34, 212, 218; horses, 470–71; hostilities with, 56, 75–76, 97, 297, 212–14, 473–75; Indian Reorganization Act, 784; Jackson administration, 317; Jefferson administration, 240–41, 317; land values, 76, 97, *q97;* literature subjects, 346–47; Madison administration, 240; medicine, 152; missionaries and, 44, 45, 50, *q50,* 52, 368, 373; New Deal and, 783–84; Pilgrims, 64; Plains Indians, 11, *ptg469,* 470–71, *ptg471,* 473–75; population, 1860–1900, *g472;* Proclamation of 1763, 98–99, 133; public education, 473; removal, 240–41, 317, *m316,* 473; reservations for, 317, 474; return of land to, 919; Revolutionary War, 131, 133–34; Roman Catholicism, 50; Spain, 11, 42–45, 150, 212; sports and games, 82–83; Trail of Tears, 317; Van Buren administration, 317; Washington administration, 212–14; westward expansion, 151, 297, 366–68, 373, 473–75; William Penn, 72; women, 13; Wounded Knee, SD, 475. *See also* specific Native American nations.

NATO. *See* North Atlantic Treaty Organization.

Naturalization Act, 224

natural resources; Civilian Conservation Corps, 781; conservation of, 653; energy, 976; industry, 494–95; soil, 783, 786; water, 484

natural rights, 77, 119

Navajo (Native Americans), *q32, p32,* 471

Naval Act of 1890, 603

Naval Advisory Board, 601

naval stores, 61, 150

navy; Adams, J., administration, 224; African Americans in, 694; Barbary Coast pirates, 244; Civil War, 416; disarmament, 884; Great Lakes, 271; Pearl Harbor, 817; Spanish-American War, *m605,* 606–07; Venezuela, British Guiana boundary dispute, 601; War of 1812, 249, *ptg250,* 251–52, *q251;* World War I, 694, 695; World War II, 822–23

Navy, Department of the, 224

Nazi party, 751, 821. *See also* Germany; Hitler, Adolf; World War II.

Nebraska, 398

Negro Nationalism, 734

Nehru, Jawaharlal, 120

Nelson, Donald, 827

Ness, Elliot, *p741*

Netherlands; exploration, 26, 51, *p70;* German invasion of, 812; New Netherlands colony, 51, 69; Nine-Power Treaty, 714; Protestantism in, 63; Renaissance in, 17; Revolutionary War debt to, 208, 209

neutrality; before War of 1812, 245; before World War I, 687; before World War II, 810, 813. *See also* isolationism; Monroe Doctrine.
Neutrality Acts, 810
Neutrality Proclamation, 217
Nevada, 480
New Amsterdam, 51, 69
New Deal, first, 777–78; second, 788–793; for African Americans, 791, 796; brain trust, 776; business and labor, 789–91; criticism of, 787–88, *crt789*, 793; culture and, 795–99; farmers' relief, 782–83; financial reform, 779–780; First Hundred Days, 777; foreign policy of, 806–10; impact of, 799; industrial relief, 784–85; Native Americans and, 783–84; objectives of, 778; Social Security Act, 789; Supreme Court, 791–92, *crt793*; unemployment relief, 780–81, 789. *See also* Great Depression; Roosevelt, Franklin D.; specific New Deal programs.
New England Colonies; education in, 77; government of, 65–66, 69, 79; Revolutionary War in, 108, 117, 131; settlement of, 63–64, 66–67, *m81*
new federalism, 965
Newfoundland, 36, 48, 93, 147
New Freedom, 661–62
New Frontier, 926
New Granada, 381–82
New Hampshire, 67, 75, *c66*, *c163*, 337, 367
New Harmony, IN, 345, *p345*, 581
New Jersey, 70–71, *c66*, 126–27, *c163*, 404, 519
New Jersey Plan, 156
Newlands Act of 1902, 653
New Mexico, 11, 377, 378, 388, 390, 471, 659
New Nationalism, 658, 662
New Netherland, 69, *c66*
New Orleans, Battle of, 250
New Orleans, LA; Civil War in, 420; France, 237; port of, 237; Spain, 237; War of 1812, 249, 250
Newport, RI, 136
newspapers, 78, 268, 561
Newton, Huey, 911
Newton, Isaac, 161
New York; boundary of, 69, 367; colonial, 69–70, *q70*; Constitution ratification, 160, *c163*; corruption in, 547; election of 1848, 389; election of 1884, 553; Erie Canal, 266–67; industry in, 290; insurance regulation, 635; in literature, 346; prison reform in, 339; Revolutionary War in, 130, 131, 133; Stamp Act Congress, 102; settlement of, 69–70, *c66*; shoemakers strike, 293, *q293*
New York Central Railroad, 500
New York Charity Organization Society, 538, *q538*
New York, NY; Burr, Aaron, 231; Central Park, 537; Civil War draft riots, 426–27, *q427*; Dutch settlement of, 51, 70; elderly in, 658; election of 1800, 231; ethnic neighborhoods of, 530; growth of, 533; harbor of, 70, 267; Harlem Renaissance, 734, *q734*; Harlem riots, 912; health hazards of, 539; Hispanic Americans in, 917; immigrants in, 70, 528; industry in, 290; Irish immigrants in, 528; Jewish immigrants in, 530; pizzeria, 530; Prospect Park, 537; Revolutionary War in, 126, 130; skyscrapers, 535; Stock Exchange, 62, 742–44, *g743*; Tammany Hall, 545–46, 550, *crt550*; tenements, 497; Washington's inauguration, 204; water source for, 535

Nez Percé, 475
Ngo Dinh Diem, 880, 931
Niagara Movement, 670
Nicaragua; canal across, 382; fruit exports from, 671; Iran-contra scandal, 988; marines in, 617, 685, 725, 807; troops in, 750, 807
Nigeria, 25 *q25*
Nile River, 24
Nimitz, Chester, 823
Nine-Power Treaty, 714
Nixon, Richard M.; Alger Hiss, 855–56; "Checkers" speech, 863; civil rights, 914; economic policies of, 963–65; election of 1952, 862–63; election of 1960, *p951*; election of 1968, 940; election of 1972, 967; energy crisis, 965–66; foreign policy of, 941–42, *p942*; Inaugural Address, *q941*; Khrushchev meeting, 884; Latin American goodwill visit, 883; political career of, 962; resignation of, 969; Vietnam, 942–44; Vietnam War, 942–44, *c943*; Watergate scandal, 967–69, *q969*
Nobel Peace Prize, 901
nonimportation agreement, 100
Non-Intercourse Act, 247
Normandy Invasion, 820–21, *p820*
Norris, Frank, 629
Norris bill, 749
Norse, 36
North; advantages, strategies of, 414–16; as market, 477–78; black codes, response to, 447; Civil War preparation, 415; *Dred Scott* decision, 400; economy of, 289–93, 390–91, 415, 494–96, 497–500, 502–12; election of 1800, 230–31; election of 1848, 388–89; election of 1876, 454; federal land policy, 320; industry in, 289–290, 395, 391; internal improvements, 290, 301; Missouri Compromise, 398; public education in, 292, 293; public land policy, 300; railroads, 472; Revolutionary War in, *m131*; slavery issue, 301, 371, 388–89; tariff issue, 301; textile industry, 289; War of 1812, 248–52. *See also* Civil War; sectionalism; Union; individual states; related subjects.
North, Lord, 139
North, Oliver, 988
North, Simeon, 391
North Africa, 818, 820
North America, 95–96, *m96*, 98, *m150*, 598
North Atlantic Treaty Organization (NATO), 843, 882, *m883*
North Carolina; Civil War in, 422; Constitution ratification, *c163*; readmission of, *m449*; Revolutionary War in, 117, 118, 133, 136, 138; secession of, 413; settlement of, 56, 61, *c66*; tobacco, 455
North Dakota, 556
Northern Alliance, 575

Northern Pacific, 472
Northern Securities Company, 651
North Korea, 848–49, *m848*, 928. *See also* Korean War.
Northrup automatic loom, 497
North Star, The, 343
North Vietnam, 880, 932–34. *See also* South Vietnam; Vietnam; Vietnam War.
Northwest Ordinance, 152–53; slavery prohibited in, 153
Northwest Territory, *m153*, 218, 296–98, 394
Norway, 812
Nova Scotia, 47, 93
NOW. *See* National Organization for Women.
nuclear weapons, 843, 987–88, 993
nullification theory, 320, 321–22, 225
nurses, 428–29

O

Oakley, Annie, 480
OAS. *See* Organization of American States.
Oberlin College, 337, 558
O'Connor, Sandra Day, 985
October, 1867, *ptg384*
Ogala Sioux, 474
Oglethorpe, James, 61
Ohio, 214, 267, 369
Ohio River; canal system of, 267; Civil War, 414; Native Americans of, 11; settlement of, 213–14; westward expansion, 213
Ohio Valley, 94, 98
oil industry; conservation, 978; growth of, 494–95, 498, 506–08; industry, 495, 881; Middle East, 881, 945; monopolies, 511; oil embargo, 945, 965, *p966*
Okinawa, 823
Oklahoma, 474
old age. *See* elderly; population; social security.
Olesen, Douglas, q1017
Oliver, Andrew, 104
Olmecs, (Native Americans), 9
Olmsted, Frederick L., 537
Olney, Richard, 572, *q572*, 601, *q601*
Olympia (ship), *ptg597*
Olympics, 979
Omaha (Native Americans), 470
Omaha Platform, 575–76
On the River, ptg266
Oneida (Native Americans), 10, 13
Oneida Community, 349
O'Neill, Eugene, 732
Onondaga, 10, 13
OPEC. *See* Organization of Petroleum Exporting Countries.
Open Door policy, 618–19, 714
Operation Breadbasket, 1008–09
Operation Desert Shield (Storm), 993–94, *p994*

Oppenheimer, J. Robert, 826
Order of "The Star-Spangled Banner," 393
Ordinance of Nullification, 322
Oregon; division of, 372; election of 1844, 372; Great Britain, 368, 369; missionaries, 373; Native Americans, 368; Oregon Territory, 272, 367–69, 372, m378, q368; Russia, 368; Spain, 368, 272; territorial constitution, q368, 368–69; territory of, 367–69, 372
Oregon Trail, 368, m368
Organization of American States (OAS), 878
Organization of Petroleum Exporting Countries (OPEC), 966, 977
Oriskany, NY; ambush, 131
Orlando, Vittorio, 701
Orozco, José Clemente, ptg684
Osage, 470
Osburn, Sarah, 134
Osceola, 318, ptg330
Ostend Manifesto, 381, q381
Ota, Peter, 833, q833
Ottawa (Native Americans), 97, 98
Ottoman Empire, 21, 686, 702
Ottoman Turks, 21
Owen, Robert, 345, 349, 582
Oxford University, 810

P

Pacific Campaign, 817–18, 822–23
Pacific possessions, m618
Pact of Paris, 725
Pahlavi, Shah Mohammad Reza, p880, 880–81
Paine, Thomas, ptg110, q110–11, 117, 127
Palestine, 15, 1011
Palestine Liberation Organization, 1012
Palmer, A. Mitchell, 705
Pan-African Congress, 670
Panama, 38, 381–82, 616, q616, 979
Panama Canal, 381–82, 616, p617, m621, 979
Pan-American Conference, 807
Pan-American Congress, 600
Pan-American Union, 600
Panic of 1837, 326, 532
Panic of 1873, 570
Panic of 1893, 577
Paredes, Mariano, 375
Paris, France, 821
Paris, Treaty of, (1763), 95–96
Paris, Treaty of, (1783), 138
Parks, Rosa, 899–900, p899
Parrington, Vernon L., q504
Passamaquoddy (Native Americans), 919
Parton, James, 312
Passion of Sacco and Vanzetti, ptg717
Paterson, William, 156
Patrick Henry Before the Virginia House of Burgesses, ptg91

Patriots, 117, 132
Patrons of Husbandry. *See* Grange.
patroons, 70
Paul Robeson, ptg736
Patton, George S., 820, 821
Pawnee, (Native Americans), 7, ptg7, 314, 471
Pawtuxet (Native Americans), 64
Payne-Aldrich Tariff, 656–57
Payne, Sereno, 656
Peace Corps, 925
Peace Corps in Ethiopia, 1966, ptg949
Peace Democrats, 433
Peale, Rembrandt, ptg86, 86
Pearl Harbor, 817, p818
Peggy Eaton, ptg321
Pendleton Act, 552–53
Penn, William, 71–72, 75
Pennsylvania; canal system of, 267; Civil War in, 419–20; coal mining in, 494; coal strike of 1902, 651–52, p652; Constitution ratification, 160, c163; corruption, 547; "Frame of Government," 72; Native Americans, 72, ptg77; oil industry in, 495, 547; prison reform in, 339; religious tolerance in, 72; settlement of, c66, 71–72; shoemakers strike, 293; state government of, c66, 72, 144; territorial disputes, 72, 153; Whiskey Rebellion, 214
Pennsylvania Railroad, 500, 522
Penobscot (Native Americans), 919
Pensacola, FL, 136, 272
Pentagon Papers, 943
People's party. *See* Populist party.
People United to Save Humanity (PUSH), 992
Pequot (Native Americans), 97
Percy, George, q57
perestroika, 987, 992
Perkins, Frances, 537, 776, p776
Perot, H. Ross, 1004
Perry, Commodore Matthew, ptg382, 383
Perry, Oliver Hazard, 249, ptg251
Pershing, John J., 685, p692, 695
Persia, 21. *See also* Iran.
Persian Gulf War, p993, 994–95
personal liberty laws, 397
Peru, 8–9, 13, 43, 750, 883
Pétain, Marshal Henri, 695
Philadelphia Convention, 155–59; conflicts in, 156–57
Philadelphia, PA; canal system to, 267; capital location, 212; colonial, 71–72, ptg72; factories in, 290; First Continental Congress in, 108; growth of, 533; Philadelphia Convention, 155–59; race riots in, 912; Revolutionary War in, 127–30; Second Continental Congress, 109, 116, 126; Independence Hall, p158; trade society strikes, 291, 293; trading center, 62, 72
Phillip II, King, 48
Philippines; annexation of, 608–11, q610; independence of, 611, 752; resistance, 610; Roosevelt, T. administration, 611, 617–18; Spanish-American War, 605–06; World War II, 818, 823

Phillips, David, 629
Pickering, John, 234
Pickett, George, 419
Pickford, Mary, 733
Pierce, Franklin, 381
Pigeon's Egg Head Going to and Returning from Washington, ptg314
Pilgrims, 63–64
Pilgrims Going to Church, ptg65
Pinchot, Gifford, 657
Pinckney, Charles, 224, 230, 235, 247
Pinckney, Thomas, 219, 223
Pingree, Hazen, 633
pirates, 151, 244
Pitcher, Molly, p87, ptg115, 115, 134
Pitt, William, 95, 107–08
Pittsburgh, PA, 298; canal system to, 267; coal mining in, 290; growth of, 533; manufacturing in, 290, 298; railroad strike of 1877, 522; steel industry in, 494, 498, 506
Pizarro, Francisco, 43, m50
Plains of Abraham, 95
Plains Wars, 473–75
plantations; collapse of, 441; cotton, 294–95, p295; rice, 74; slavery, 60, 74, 294, 380; sugar, 92, 380, 603; tobacco, 58–60, 74; women in, 75, 60, 428. *See also* Civil War; cotton; slavery, enslaved persons; South; related subjects.
Platt Amendment, 612–13
Plea for the West, 373
Plessy v. Ferguson, 643
Plymouth, MA; settlement of, 63–64, c66
pocket veto, 316
Poe, Edgar Allan, 347
Poindexter, John, 988
Poland; emergence of, 19; German invasion of, 811, 812 p812; immigrants from, 529, 530; Soviet Union, 821, 825, 882; World War II, 811, 821
Polish Americans, 128
political machines, 545–46, 550
political parties; American Socialist, 582, 625; election of 1800, 230–31, 233; favorite sons, 302; formation of, 222–23; Free Soil party, 389; Greenback, 574; growth of, 231; Populist, 573–77; Liberty party, 343; minor political parties, 389; political machines, 545, 546; Progressive party, 627, 661, 853; spoils system, 315–16, q316, 552. *See also* Democratic party; elections, presidential; elections, congressional; Republican party; names of other individual parties; related subjects.
Polk, James K., 372, 374–76, ptg375; war strategy, 376–77
poll tax, 909
pollution, p1017
Polo, Marco, 22–23, q23, 36
Ponce de León, Juan, ptg46
Pontiac, Chief, 97, q97, 98, p100
Pontiac's Rebellion, 98
Pope, John, General, 418
popular consent, 119–120
popular sovereignty, 389, 390, 398

population, g331; colonial trends of, 74, m74; demographics, g921; Native American, g472; Population in Urban and Rural Territory, g355; by state, g541; westward migration, 391

Populist movement, 575–77

Populist party, 573, 575; election of 1892, 552, 575–77; election of 1896, 577–78; free silver, 573–75, 578; Omaha Platform, 575–76, q575. *See also* progressivism; individuals; related subjects.

Port Hudson, 421

Portsmouth, Treaty of, 619

Portugal; exploration by, 19, 26, 27–29, q28, 38–39, m39; independence of, 19; Nine-Power Treaty, 714

Powderly, Terence V., 524

Powell, Adam Clayton, Jr., 913, q913

Powers, Francis Gary, p885

pragmatism, 628

Prairie, The, q242–43

Pre-emption Act of 1841, 328, 391

Presbyterianism, 121

presidency, President; executive branch, 158, c169, 170–71, 180–83; executive privilege, 968; illness, incapacity, 865; powers of, c169, 170–71, 177, 424; Reconstruction, 445–46; succession, 865; terms of, 158, 180–81; Twentieth Amendment, 761

Presidential Succession Act, 554

Presley, Elvis, 877, p877

press, freedom of, 78–79

Price Administration, Office of, 828

Princeton, Battle of, 127

Princeton University, 77, 663, 917

Princip, Gavrilo, 686

printing, 17, 22, 561

prison reform, 339

Proclamation of 1763, 98–99, m99, 101, 133

Proclamation of Neutrality, 217

Proclamation to the People of South Carolina, 322

Progressive party, 627, 661, 853

Progressive Republicans, 659, 660

progressivism; business regulation, 638; conservation, 638; consumer protection, 635, 638; education, 628–29, 642; gains, 644; government reform, 632–34; immigrants, 641–42; inequality, 624–26; labor reform, 635–37; leadership of, 626–28; limits, 640–44; public utility reform, 638; racism, 642–44; Roosevelt, Franklin, 635; Roosevelt, T., administration, 654; segregation, 643; senatorial reform, 634; temperance movement, 351, 638; woman's rights, 628

Prohibition, 580, 638, 706; by state action, 351; crime, 729–30; election of 1924, 720–21; election of 1928, 730; election of 1932, 760–61; Hoover administration, 742; local option, 351

Prohibition Bureau, 729

Prohibition Raid, ptg741

Project Head Start, 958

Promontory Point, UT, 472

property rights, 584

Protestantism; 18, 145; Second Great Awakening, 350. *See also* religion; sects.

Prussia, 132, 272

Ptolemy, 36

public land, 146, 391, 495, 554

public libraries, 534

public utilities, 638

Public Works Administration, 780, 789

Pueblo (ship), 928

Pueblo (Native Americans), 11

pueblo, 11, p11

Puerto Rico, 44, 607, 609, 613. *See also* Hispanic Americans.

Pulaski, Casimir, Count, 132

Pulitzer, Joseph, 561, 606, p606

Pullman Palace Car Company, 519, 526

Pullman strike, 526–27, p527, 577

Pure Food and Drug Act, 635

Puritans, 63, 64, 68, ptg68, 77

Q

Quadruple Alliance, 272–74

Quakers, 66, 318, 342, 553. *See also* religion.

Quartering Act, 101

Quebec Act, 107

Quebec, Canada, 48, 95, 107

Queen Anne's War, 93

Quetzalcoatl, 43

R

Rabin, Yitzhak, p1011, 1012

race riots, 913

racism, 705, q705, 910. *See also* civil rights; discrimination; segregation; groups; related subjects.

radar, 828

Radcliffe, 558

Radical Reconstruction, 448–51, 453–54

Radical Republicans, 425, 433, 456; election of 1868, 451; election of 1872, 454; Reconstruction, 446, 448–51, 453–54, q448

radio, 740, 798

Railroad Administration, 697

railroads; abuses of, 500, q500, 569–70, q653; Adamson Act, 671; Chinese American labor, 472, 528; Congress, 495; consolidation, 499–500; early, 267–68, q268, 394; Esch-Cummins Act, 706; farmers, 394, 485–86, 569; Granger laws, 571; industrial growth, 393–94, 499; Irish American labor, 472; lines, m498; monopolies, 570; Pullman strike of 1894, 526–27; rebates, 507; refrigerated cars, 503; regulation of, 571, 572, 638, 653–54, q654, 671; Southern, 458; standardization, 499; standard time zones, 500, 501, m501; steam locomotive, 394; steel industry, 498; strikes, 522, q522; Supreme Court decisions, 571–72; technology, 394, 498; transcontinental railroad, 398, 471–72; western settlement, 472, m478, 484, 485–96, 569

"Raising the Liberty Pole," p117

Raleigh, Sir Walter, ptg3, 56, ptg84

Rall, Johann Gottlieb, 127

Randolph, A. Philip, p796, 831

Randolph, Edmund, 156, 205, ptg84

Raphael, 17

ratification. *See* Constitution, various treaties.

Rauschenberg, Robert, ptg961

Rauschenbusch, Walter, 627, q627

Rayburn, Sam, 865

Reagan, Ronald, p984; attempted assassination of, p903; economic policies of, 982–85, q983, q984; election of 1976, 976; election of 1980, 981; election of 1984, 985; foreign policy of, 986–88; image, 983–84, 988; legacy, 990, 996; national defense, 985–86

realism, 559–60

reaper, 392, p484, 485

Reaping and Shearing in July, ptg17

rebates, 507

recessions. *See* depressions; economy; Great Depression.

Reciprocal Trade Agreements Act, 807

Reconstruction, ptg439, 445–51, 453–54; Act, 448–49. *See also* Radical Reconstruction; Radical Republicans.

Reconstruction Finance Corporation (RFC), 749, 756, 789

Recuerdo, q726–27

Red Badge of Courage, The, 560

Red Cloud, Chief, 474

Red Cross, 428, 429

Red Scare, 704–05

Reed, Thomas B., 608

Reed, Dr. Walter, 613

reform movement; antislavery crusade, 342–44; consumer protection, 635; literature role, 347; prison reform, 339; Progressives, 627; religious movements, 349–50, 627; socialism, 349, 625–26; temperance, 351, 580; woman's rights, 340–41, 581, 634–35. *See also* New Deal; progressivism; woman's rights; women; names; related subjects.

Reisman, David, 874

religion; abolition movement, 34; African American churches and civil rights, 903; in American Revolution, 121; China missionaries, 383; civil rights movement, 903; colonial, 61, 63, 66–67, 76–77; communal groups, 350; conscientious objectors, 936–38; disestablishment, 145; Dutch Calvinist churches, 70; and education, 77, 290, 556; election of 1928, 740; election of 1960, 951; established churches, 76, 145; freedom of, 61, 67, 145; French Jesuits, 50; Great Awakening, 121; Islam, 15, 24, 20–22; Middle Ages, 15, 18, 19; missionaries, 26, 45, 49–50, 52, 76, q50, 373, 383; Muslim. *See* Islam; New World explorations, 26, 37, 38, 44, 45, 47; Oregon

Territory, 373; Pilgrims, 63; political party affiliation, 549; Protestant Reformation, 18; public education, 335; Puritans, 65, 66–67, 76, 145; Quakers, 66, 71, 76, 350; Reform Judaism, 639; reform movement, 349–50, 627; revival, 76–77, *ptg350;* Revolutionary War, 121; Roger Williams, 66–67; slavery, 342, 343; social gospel, 626, 627, *q627;* temperance movement, 351; transportation improvements, 268; western missionaries, 373. *See also* names; religions; sects; related subjects.

Religious Toleration Act of 1649, 61
Remington, Frederic, *ptg474, ptg620*
Reminiscences, *q379*
Renaissance, 17–19
Report on Manufactures, 209
Report on the Public Credit, 209
Republican party (Jeffersonian), elections: of 1800, 230–31, 233; of 1808, 247; of 1816, 258; of 1820, 258; of 1824, 302–04, *c307;* of 1832, 325; Jefferson administration, 233–35; judiciary and, 233–34
Republican party; business, 577; *Dred Scott* decision, 400; elections: of 1856, 399–400; of 1860, 404–05; of 1864, 433; of 1868, 451; of 1872, 453; of 1876, 454; of 1880, 552; of 1884, 553; of 1888, 554–55; of 1890, 556; of 1892, 556; of 1896, 577–78; of 1900, 615; of 1904, 653; of 1912, 660–61; of 1918, 701; of 1920, 712–13; of 1924, 720–21; of 1928, 740–41; of 1932, 760–61; of 1936, 791; of 1940, 814–15; of 1946, 852; of 1948, 853–54; of 1952, 862–63; of 1956, 865; of 1960, 951; of 1964, 956–57; of 1968, 940; of 1972, 967; of 1976, 976–77; of 1980, 981; of 1984, 985; of 1988, 990–91; of 1992, 1003–04; of 1994, 1007; formation of, 222, 399; isolationism, 811, 814; Lincoln-Douglas debates, 402–03; New Deal opposition, 793; *Old Guard v. Insurgents,* 657–58; Philippines annexation, 608; post-Civil War, 446, 450, 548–49; progressives within, 553, 658–59; Prohibition, 556; tariff issue, 555, 656–57. *See also* elections, congressional; elections, presidential; Reconstruction; names; related subjects.
"Resolution of Independence," 118, 119
Reston, James, 978, *q978*
Return of the Conquerors, ptg597
Reuther, Walter, 868, *p868*
Revels, Hiram R., 450, *p450*
Revere, Paul, *p104,* 108
revivalists, *ptg350*
Revolution, *ptg684*
Revolutionists, ptg708
Revolutionary War; African Americans, 133; American advantages in, 128–29; battles of, 125, 126–27, *m131;* British strategy, 130–31, *m131, m137,* 136–38; as civil war, 132; end of, 137–38, *ptg139;* influence of, 138–39; Patriots v. Loyalists, 132; religion in, 121; women, 134
Reuneau, Betsy Graves, *ptg736*
Rhee, Syngman, 848
Rhode Island, 66–67, 155, 159, *c163*
Ribak, Louis, *ptg759*
Richardson, Henry, 537

Richardt, Ferdinand, *ptg387,* 387
Richmond, VA, 415, 417, 433, 434, 455
Ride for Liberty, ptg407
rights. *See* Bill of Rights; Constitution; civil rights; related subjects.
Riis, Jacob A., 535–36
Ripley, George, 349
Rittenhouse, David, 161
roads, 263–64, *m265, q264*
Roanoke colony, 56
Roaring Twenties, 728–34
Roberts, Ed, 1020
Robeson, Paul, 734
Robinson, Bill, 734
Robinson, Harriet Hanson, 292, *q292*
Robinson, Jackie, *p861*
Rochambeau, Jean Baptiste, 138
Rochling, C., *ptg411*
rock and roll, 877, 1026–27
Rock of the Marne, ptg694
Rockefeller Foundation, 638
Rockefeller, John D., 506–08, *ptg507,* 511. *See also* Standard Oil Company.
Rockefeller, Nelson, 968–69
Rockwell, Norman, *ptg837, ptg949*
Rodko, Konstantin, *ptg287*
Rodriguez, Richard, 1022
Roebling, John and Washington, 537
Rogers, Ginger, 798
Rogers, Roy, *p866*
Rogers, Will, 721, *p721, q721*
Rolfe, John, 58
Rölvaag, Ole, 568, *q568*
Roman Catholicism, Anglican Church from, 63; charities, 350; colonial, 61, 107; discrimination against, 145; immigrants, 529; Ku Klux Klan, 720–21; Middle Ages, 15; Native Americans, 50; Protestant Reformation, 18; religious activity in cities, 350, 290; sainthood in, 290. *See also* religion.
Roman Empire, 15, 20
Romania, 821
Rommel, Erwin, 818, 820
Roosevelt Corollary, 617
Roosevelt, Eleanor, 776–777, *p777*
Roosevelt, Franklin; 774–775, *p775, q775, p815, p824;* Atlantic Charter, 824; "black cabinet" of, 796; "brain trust," 776; business and labor, 789–91; death of, 821, 825; elections: of 1920, 712; of 1932, 759–60, *q760;* of 1936, 791; of 1940, 814–15; financial reform, 779–80; first Inaugural Address, 774; foreign policy of, 806–10; Good Neighbor policy, 806–07; image of, 774–76, *p775, q775;* industrial relief, 784–85; Neutrality Acts, 810, *q810,* 815; New Deal, 778; Supreme Court, 791–92, *crt793;* unemployment relief, 780–81; work relief, 780–81, 789; World War II, 812, 813; Yalta Conference, 825. *See also* Great Depression; New Deal; World War II.

Roosevelt, Theodore; conservation, 652–53, *q655;* domestic policies of, 650–53, *q653;* elections: of 1896, 577–78; of 1900, 615; of 1904, 653; of 1912, 660–61, *p661,* 662–63; expansionism, 605; foreign policy of, 616–19; McKinley assassination, 616, 650; muckrakers, 629; navy readiness, 601; New Nationalism, 658–59, *q659;* Philippines, 605, 611, 617–18; Roosevelt Corollary, 617; Rough Riders, 606, *ptg620;* Russo-Japanese War, 619; Spanish-American War, 604, 605; Square Deal, 650; tariff issue, 654; trusts, 650–51; urban problems, 535
Root, Elihu, 652, 660
Rosecrans, William, 421–22
rotary press, 391
Rothermel, Peter F., *ptg91,* 91
Roughing It, q482–83
Rough Riders, 606, *ptg620*
Royal Air Force, 813–14, *q814*
Royal Navy; Revolutionary War, 30–31, 125–27; Spanish Armada, 48, 56
rubber; vulcanized, 391; synthetic, 827
Rush-Bagot Agreement, 272
Rusk, Dean, 934
Russell, Charles E., *q481,* 481, *p481*
Russell, Charles Marion, 481, *q481, p481*
Russia; Alaska, 273, 367, 599; American colonies, *m96;* Bolshevik Revolution, 692; China, 619; emergence of, 19; immigrants from, 528, 530; in North America, *m95,* 598; Jews from, 529–30, *q530,* 639; Korea, 619; Manchuria, 619; Mongols in, 22; Oregon, 274; Quadruple Alliance, 272–74; Revolutionary War (American), 125–28; Russo-Japanese War, 619; Triple Entente, 686; World War I, 686–87, 692. *See also* communism; Union of Soviet Socialist Republics (USSR); countries; related subjects.
Russian Federation, 1010
Russo-Japanese War, 619
Rustin, Baynard, 903
Rutgers University, 77

S

Sacajawea, 238
Sac and Fox (Native Americans), *ptg314,* 317–18, 83
Sacco, Nicola, 717–18, *p717, ptg717*
Sacramento, CA, 381
Sailor's Wedding, ptg357
St. Augustine, FL, 44
St. Clair, Arthur, 213
St. Lawrence River, 48, 95, 271
St. Leger, Barry, 130–31
St. Louis, MO, 528
St. Marks, FL, 272
Sainte Domingue, 51, 237
Salk, Jonas, 873
Salomon, Haym, 128, *ptg128*

1108 Index

SALT. *See* Strategic Arms Limitation Talks.
Salt Lake City, UT, 369
salutary neglect, 93
Salvation Army, 626, 627
Sampson, Deborah, 134
Sampson, William T., 606–07
San Antonio, TX, 370
San Diego, CA, 44
San Francisco, CA, 44, 374, 912
San Juan Hill, 606
San Martín, José de, 272
Santa Anna, Antonio, 370, *m371*
Santa Fe, NM, 371
Santa Maria Institute, 536
Santee Sioux, 474
Santiago, Cuba, 606–07
Saratoga, Battle of, 131–32, *ptg 132*
Sargent, John Singer, 560, *ptg586*
Saturday Evening Post, 563
Saturday Night Massacre, 968
Saudi Arabia, Persian Gulf conflict, 994–95
Sauk (Native Americans), 297
Savage, Edward, *p198*, *ptg203*
Savannah, GA, 61, 433
savings and loan crisis, 996
Say, Thomas, 345
scalawags, 450
Scalia, Antonin, 985
Scandinavia, 18, 36, 393
Scene on the Hudson, *ptg354*
Schenck v. United States, 700, *q700*
Schultz, Dutch, 729
Schurz, Carl, 551, 555
Schwarzkopf, Norman, 994
science; aging and the brain, 997, *p997*; archaeology and prehistory, 14; atomic bomb, 826; colonial education, 77–78; and the Constitution, 161; Muslim advances in, 21; Smithsonian Institution, 347; space race, 955; Washington, D.C., 221. *See also* technology; names; related subjects.
Scientific Research and Development, Office of, 828
Scopes, John T., 733
Scopes trial, 733–34, *p733*
Scotland, 528
Scott, Dred, 400, *ptg400*
Scott, Winfield, 376, 377, 405, *q405*
Seale, Bobby, 911
SEATO. *See* Southeast Asia Treaty Organization.
Seattle General Strike, 704
Seattle, WA, 704
Second Continental Congress, 109, 127
sectionalism, *m302*; Bank of the United States (second), 322–26; *Dred Scott* decision, 400; election of 1824, 302–04; election of 1828, 325–26; election of 1860, 403–04; expansionism, 380; issues of, 300–01, 320, 548–49; Jackson administration, 320–22; Philadelphia convention, 156–57; railroads, 471–72; slavery dispute, 157, 301, 302–03, 319, *m320*, 388–90, 413; Tariff of 1842, 328; Washington administration, 208, 212

Securities and Exchange Commission (SEC), 779
Sedition Act, 224
segregation; African Americans, 455, 852; post-Reconstruction, 455; progressivism, 642–43; Roosevelt, T., administration, 643, *q643*; Wilson administration, 671
Selective Service Act, 814
self-determination, right of, 119
Seljuk Turks, 15
Selma, AL, 909
Seminole, 13, 272, 273, *ptg273*, *p273*, 318, 322
Senate; antislavery issue, 344, 389; balance of power in, 389; direct election of, 634; early years, 206; impeachment, 234, 451; Jay Treaty, 219; Judiciary Committee, 1003; Louisiana Purchase, 238; Missouri Compromise, 302; Oregon dispute, 372; Philippine annexation, 609; and progressivism, 634; Teapot Dome scandal, 718; Texas statehood, 371, 372; Treaty of Ghent, 252; Treaty of Guadalupe Hidalgo, 377; Treaty of Versailles, 703; Wilmot Proviso, 388. *See also* Congress; individual names; related subjects.
Seneca Falls Convention (Declaration), 341
Seneca Falls Declaration, 341
Seneca (Native Americans), 10, 13, 83
Separatists, 63
Sequoya, 317
Serbia, 1009–10
serfs, 15
Serra, Junípero, 44, *p44*, 45
Sermon, The, *ptg333*
Seton, Elizabeth Ann, 292
Seven Days' Battle, 418
Seward, William H., 599
sewing machine, 391
Seymour, Horatio, 451
Shahn, Ben, *ptg717*, 799
Shakers, 349
sharecroppers, 441–42, 782–83
Sharpsburg, MD, 419
Shawnee (Native Americans), 214–15, 241
Shays, Daniel, 154
Shays's Rebellion, 154, *p154*
Sheets, Millard, *ptg739*
Shepard, Alan, Jr., 955
Sheridan, Ann, *p829*
Sheridan, Philip, 431–32
Sherman Antitrust Act, 512, *q512*, 556
Sherman Silver Purchase Act, 556, 577
Sherman, William T., 422, 432–33, 434, *q434*
Sherwood, Robert, *q775*
Shiloh, Battle of, 420, *q420*
shoemaking industry, 293, 391
Sholes, C. Latham, 496
Shoshone (Native Americans), 238
Sicily, 21, 529, 820
Signing of the Constitution, *ptg143*
Signing of the Treaty of Versailles, *ptg703*
silver, 42–45, 479, 574–75

Sinclair, Upton, 625
Singapore, 817
single tax, 583
Sioux, 314, 317, 470, 474
Sister Carrie, *q630–31*
sitdown strikes, 791, *q791*, 792, *p792*
Sitting Bull, Chief, 474
skills, 25, 33, 46, 53, 68, 113
skyscrapers, 535, 537
Slater, Samuel, *ptg288*, *p289*, 289
slavery, enslaved persons; abolitionist movement, 144–45, 296, 342–44; birth of, 58–59; in California, 388, 389–90; colonial, 58, 59, 60, 61, 74, 75, 79; Compromise of 1850, 389–90; conditions of, 75, 396, 406, *p406*; in Constitution, 157, 178, 185; Cuban annexation, 380–81; Declaration of Independence, 120; *Dred Scott* decision, 400; election of 1848, 387–88; Emancipation Proclamation, 419; in Georgia, 61; Jackson administration, 318; legal status, 75; Lincoln-Douglas debates, 402–03, *q403*; in Mexico, 370; Missouri Compromise, 302, 318, 344, 400; in North, 75, 79; Northwest Ordinance, 153, 296, 301; in Oregon, 367–69; plantations, 60, 61, 75, 294–95, 396, *ptg406*; in Revolutionary War, 133; slave trade, 28–29, 42, 51, 59, 74, *ptg75*, 79, 144–45, 390; songs of, 299, 406; Southern defense of, 397; states representation issue, 302, 389; in Texas, 370–72; tobacco, 38, 60, 294; Virginia, 58, 59, 60; in world history, 20, 24, 28–29, 42, 44, 51, 342. *See also* African Americans; Civil War; freedmen; individual names.
slaves. *See* slavery, enslaved persons.
slave states. *See* slavery, enslaved persons; states; territories.
Slavs, 530
Slidell, John, 374–75
Slovenia, 1008
slums. *See* cities; progressivism; reform movements; tenements.
Smith, Alfred E., 720–21, 740–41, 759
Smith, John, 57
Smith, Joseph, 349, 369
Smith, Reverend Sydney, 346
Smith College, 558
Smithsonian Institution, 347
smuggling, 93, 99, 101, 246, 382
Snack Bar, *ptg861*
Snap the Whip, *ptg558*
soap operas, 798
social contract, 119, *q119*
social Darwinism, 510, *q510*
social gospel, 626, 627, *q627*
socialism, 349, 581–82, 625–26
Socialist party, 582, 625, 758–59
social programs. *See* New Deal; social security; individual programs.
social security, 789; Social Security Act, 789
social studies skills; analyzing graphic data, 709; analyzing political maps, 973; analyzing tabular data, 307; analyzing trends, 673, 1025; cause and effect, 331; describing exact and relative location, 255;

drawing conclusions, 437; identifying trends, 886; interpreting demographic data, 921; interpreting economic data, 999; interpreting an election map, 459; interpreting historical maps, 277; interpreting a table, 141; making comparisons, 515; making inferences, 409; organizing in a table, 163; practicing the skill, 385; preparing notecards for a research report, 385; reading a bar graph, 355; reading a cartogram, 541; reading a line graph, 491, 763; reading and interpreting political cartoons, 565; reading military maps, 113; reading a special-purpose map, 621; reading a table, 803; reading terrain maps, 946–77; reading a thematic map, 81; reading a travel route map, 33; recognizing historical reasoning, 227; reviewing map basics, 587; seeing relationships on a line graph, 835; understanding history through political cartoons, 647; using a gazetteer, 53. *See also* map and graph skills; critical thinking skills; interpreting primary sources; study and writing skills.

Solid South, 549
Solomon Islands, 823
Somalia, 1008–09, *p1009*
Songhai, 24, *m33*
Song of the Rain Chant, 31
Sons of Liberty, 104–05, 108
Soo Canal, 494
South; advantages, strategies of, 412, 414–16; agricultural production, 294–95, 392; antislavery movement in, 342–44, 75, 296; Civil War preparation, 412, 414; cotton economy, 294–96, 318, 392, 415; Democratic party, 453; *Dred Scott* decision, 400; economy of, 294–96, 455; election of 1800, 230–31; election of 1824, 302–04; election of 1848, 388–89; election of 1860, 403–04; election of 1872, 454; election of 1892, 556, 576–77; election of 1896, 577–78; industry, 295, 395, 455–56; internal improvements, 301; Manifest Destiny, 380; Missouri Compromise, 319, 398, 400; post–Civil War, 440–50, 453–56, 457, *q440*, *ptg443*, *ptg444*, *m449*; pride, 447; public education in, 899; public land policy, 300; railroads in, 394, 440, 472; Revolutionary War in, 136–38, *m137*, *ptg138*; secession of, 404–05, *q405*, 413; slavery, 34, 59, 60, 61, 74, 294–95, 295–96, 301, 388–89, 396–97; tariff issue, 301, 320–23. *See also* African Americans; cotton; civil rights; Civil War; Confederacy; plantations; Reconstruction; segregation; states' rights; voting; individual states.
South America, 8–9, 38
South Carolina; Civil War in, 412, 422; Constitution ratification, 157, *c163*; cotton plantations, 294–95; election of 1872, 453; election of 1876, 454; government of, 61; nullification, 322; railroads in, 394; readmission of, *m449*; Revolutionary War in, 117, 133, 136, 137; secession of, 322, 404; settlement of, 61, *c66*; slavery in, 74; state government of, 61; tariff issue, 320, 321, 322
South Carolina Exposition, The, 321
South Dakota; statehood, 556

Southeast Asia, 879–80, 930–34, *m935*. *See also* specific countries.
Southeast Asia Treaty Organization (SEATO), 878
South End House, 536
Southern Alliance, 569, 572, 575
Southern Christian Leadership Conference (SCLC), 900, 903
Southern Colonies; education in, 77; government of, 69, 79; Revolutionary War preparation, 108, 109; settlement of, 56–61; westward expansion, 371
Southern Manifesto, 899
Southern Pacific, 472, 500
Southern Railway, 458
Southgate, Eliza, 236, *q236*
South Korea, 848–49, *m848*. *See also* Korea.
South Vietnam, 880, 930–33, 971. *See also* North Vietnam; Vietnam; Vietnam War.
Southwest Mission, *ptg373*
Soviet Bloc, *m883*
Soviet Union. *See* Union of Soviet Socialist Republics (USSR).
space program, 955, 960, 985
Spain; American colonies, 36, 42–45, *ptg45*; cattle ranching, 477; civil war, 809; Cuban annexation, 380–81, 612–13; emergence of, 19; English colonization rivalry with, 47–48; expulsion of Jews, 19; Ferdinand and Isabella, 19, 37; Florida, 44, 61, 95, 272; in North America, *m95*, 96, 150; Jay Treaty, 219; Latin American colonies, 272–74; Louisiana Territory, 95, 237, 272; Mexican independence, 370; Middle Ages in, 19; missions, 45; Monroe Doctrine, 598; Moors, 19, 21; Native American alliance with, 150; New World exploration, 19, 26, 37, 38, *m39*, 40, 42–45, *m50*; Oregon, 272; Philippines, 605, 609; Pinckney Treaty with, 219; Protestantism in, 18; Revolutionary War, 136; revolution in, 809; rivalry within Confederation period, 150; rivalry with Portugal, 38; Spanish-American War, *ptg597*, 603–07, *m605*; Spanish Armada, 48, 56; trade with, 100; Treaty of Paris, 95, 150
Spain in the Americas, *ptg45*
Spargo, John, 629, 637
specie, 100, 574
Specie Circular, 226
Speculator, The, *ptg365*
speculators, 484, 743
speech, freedom of, 78–79. *See also* amendments; civil rights; Constitution.
Spirit of the Frontier, *ptg367*
Spock, Benjamin, 875, *p875*
spoils system, 315, 316, *q316*, 552–53
sports; Native American, 82–83
Spotsylvania, VA, 431
Sputnik, 955
Squanto, 69
Square Deal, 650–53
Stalingrad, USSR, 818–19
Stalin, Joseph, 811, 819, 824–25, *p824*, 838, 839
Stalwarts, 552

Stamp Act, 100, 103, *p103*, 104
Stamp Act Congress, 102, 103, 104
standard gauge track, 499
Standard Oil Company, 506–08, *q508*, 511, 547. *See also* John D. Rockefeller.
Standard Oil Trust, 508
standard time zones, 500, 501, *m501*
Stanton, Charles E., 694, *q694*
Stanton, Edwin, 451
Stanton, Elizabeth Cady, 341, 581, *ptg581*
Star-Spangled Banner, The, 250
Star Wars, 985
State of Franklin, *m146*, 152
State, Department of, 206
statehood. *See* individual states; related subjects.
states; admission of, 372; Articles of Confederation, 145–46, 147, 153–54; bank closings, 761; Bank of the United States, 320–26; Bill of Rights, 160, 168; black codes, 447, 457; child labor laws, 637; Confederacy, 404–05, 415; conservation, 638, 653; Constitution ratification, 159–60, *crt159*; disputes among, 153–54, 156–57; election of 1860, 403–04, *m404*; environmental legislation, 1017–18; federal dominance over, 168, 186; government reform, 144–45, 633–34, *m633*; industry working conditions, 527, 635–36; interstate trade, 154, 168; legislative corruption, 547; legislatures, 144; nullification theory, 320; population, 1900, *g541*; powers granted by Constitution, *c168*, 168, 185–86; Progressive movement, *m633*; Prohibition, 351, 638; public education, 638; Radical Reconstruction, 448–51, 453–54; readmission of, 445, 446, 448–49, *m449*; Reconstruction, 445–48; Revolutionary War debts, 209–10; secession of, 404–05; states' rights, 159, 168, 320, *crt320*, 415; state universities, 488, 558; Tyler administration, 372; western land claims, *m146*; woman's suffrage, 581, 634–35
steamboats, 265–66, *ptg266*, *q266*, 394
steel industry; growth of, 494, 498, 506; railroads, 498; strikes, 704; technology, 498, 509; working conditions in, 510
Steel Mill, *ptg509*
steel plow, 392
Steffens, Lincoln, 629, *p629*
Steinbeck, John, 797, 800, *p800*, *q800–801*
Steinmetz, Charles, 719
Stephens, John Lloyd, 390, *q390*
Stevens, Thaddeus, 451
Stevenson, Adlai, 863
Stevenson, David, 264, *q264*
Stewart, A.T., 537
Stieglitz, Alfred, 733
Stimson, Henry L., 751, 752
stock exchanges, 62, *p62*, 742
stock market, 746; crash of 1929, 742–44, *g743*, *p742*; Great Depression, 743–44; public participation in, 722; stock exchange, 62, *p62*, 742, 746; stock watering, 570
STOP ERA, 917
Storming the Bastille, *ptg217*

1110 Index

Stowe, Harriet Beecher, 397
Strategic Arms Limitations Talks (SALT), 942
Strategic Defense Initiative (SDI), 985, 987
strikes, *p652,* 852; coal strike of 1902, 651–52, *p652;* migrant workers, 918; post-World War I, 704; Pullman strike of 1894, 526–27; sitdown strikes, 791, *q791,* 792, *p792;* trade societies, 289, 291; women's, 290, *p652*
Strong, Josiah, 609, 627
Student Nonviolent Coordinating Committee (SNCC), 900, 910
study and writing skills; analyzing illustrations, 430; effective questions, 46; gazetteer, 53; identifying alternatives, 135; literature as a historical source, 25; note-taking, 148; persuasive arguments, 753; predicting consequences, 794; recognizing ideologies, 585, *crt585;* research, reference works in, 305; summarizing, 523; using literature as a historical source, 25; using reference works in research, 305; Who is an American, 833
Stump Speaking, ptg309
Stuyvesant, Peter, 69
submarines, 687–88, 690–91, 695, 815. See also Germany, U-boat.
suburbs, 873–74, *g873, p874*
subways, 535
Sudan, 24
Suez Canal, 818
suffrage. See voting rights; women.
sugar, 29, 92, 600
Sugar Act, 99–100
Sullivan, Louis, 537
Sumner, Charles, 600
Sumner, William Graham, 510, *q510*
Sunset at Fort Sumter, ptg413
Supreme Court, *p183, p184, p963; Brown v. Board of Education,* 898–99, 901, *q901;* civil rights decisions, 455, 898–99, 900; Civil War, 425; Clarence, Thomas, 1003, *p1003;* constitutional interpretation, 171, 234; court packing, 234, *crt793;* creation of, 158, 171, 206–07; *Dartmouth College v. Woodward,* 261, *c261; Dred Scott* decision, 400; espionage cases, 700, *q700;* freedom of the press, 78–79; *Gibbons v. Ogden, c261,* 262; *Green v. County School Board,* 914; income tax, 638; Japanese American civil liberties, 832; loyalty oaths, 855; *Marbury v. Madison,* 234–35; *McCulloch v. Maryland,* 260–61; *Muller v. Oregon,* 636–37; *Munn v. Illinois,* 571; nationalism, 260, *c261;* New Deal, 790; Nixon administration, 943, 963; overseas possessions, 612; *Plessy v. Ferguson,* 643, 899; progressivism, 637, 640; railroads, 651; Reagan administration, 985; *Schenck v. United States,* 700, *q700;* segregation, 455; Sixteenth Amendment, 638; states' rights, *c262;* trust regulation, 657; *United States v. E.C. Knight Company,* 512; Watergate break-in, 969; women appointed to, 984, 1005, *p1005;* woman's rights, 636–37. See also individual cases; names; related subjects.
Surrender of Lord Cornwallis at Yorktown, ptg138

Sussex Pledge, 688
Sutter's mill, 381
Swahili, 24
Swanson, Gloria, 732
Sweden, 26, 72, 528
Swedish West India Company, *c66*
Swift (Company), 503
Swift, Gustavus, 503, *ptg503*
Swing Low, Sweet Chariot, 407
Syria, 928

T

Taft, Robert A., 850, 855, 862
Taft, William Howard, 656, *crt657, p662;* election of 1908, 247; election of 1912, 660–61; foreign policy of, 617; Philippines, 611; presidency, 659; Square Deal, 658, 659; Supreme Court justice, 659; tariff issue, 656–57; trust regulation, 659
Taft-Hartley Act, 852–53
Taiwan, 847, 942
Talleyrand, Charles Maurice de, 224, 238
Tallmadge, James, 302
Tammany Hall, 545–46, 550
Tallmadge Amendment, 302, *q302*
Taney, Roger, 400
Tanner, Henry, *ptg360,* 360
Tarbell, Ida, 508, *p508,* 629
Tariff of 1789, 208
Tariff of 1816, 260, 321
Tariff of 1828, 321
Tariff of 1832, 322
Tariff of 1833, 322
Tariff of 1842, 328
Tariff of 1890, 556, 600
Tariff Board, 659
Tariff Commission, 748
tariffs, *t673,* 1013; Cleveland administration, 554–55, *q555;* Harding administration, 714–15, 723; Harrison administration, 556; Hoover administration, 744–45, 748; McKinley, 577, 598; McKinley administration, 556, 577, 600; protective tariff issue, 208, 320, 555; Reciprocal Trade Agreement Act, 807; Republican party, 555, 556; Taft administration, 656–57; Underwood, 666–67; Webster-Hayne debates, 320; Wilson-Gorman Tariff of 1894, 577; Wilson administration, 666–67, *q667*
taxation. See income tax; specific tax act.
Taylor, Frederick W., 503
Taylor, Zachary, 375–76, 389, 390
Teamster's Union, 868
Teapot Dome scandal, 718
technology; canal locks, 270, *p270;* coaling stations, 603; communications, 391, 496–97; computers, 872, *p872;* and farming, 391–92; household, 719; and industry, 390–91, 394; leisure time, 94, 561; navigation, 27; printing, 17, 22, 563; ships, 27; steel industry, 790; television, 876; and

transportation, 27, 390; unemployment from, 715; warfare, 929. See also individual advances; related subjects.
Tecumseh, 241, *p241, q241,* 297
Tehran, Iran, 981
telegraph, 348, 391, 472
telephone, 496, *p496,* 538
television, 876, *q876*
Teller Amendment, 604, 612
Teller, Edward, 955
temperance movement, 351, 580
tenant farmers, 441–42
Tenement Flats, ptg739
tenements, 497, *p540, ptg739*
Tennessee; Civil War in, 420; Jackson, Andrew, 312; Ku Klux Klan, 453; Polk, James K., 372; readmission of, 446, 448, *m449;* secession of, 152, 413; settlement of, 152, 213; statehood, 152, 213
Tennessee Valley Authority (TVA), 780–81, *m781, p781*
Tenochtitlán, 10, 43
Tenure of Office Act, 450–51, 554
Terrell, Harry, *q748*
Territorial Expansion of the United States, *m378, g612*
territories, *m95,* 301
Tet Offensive, 934
Texas; Alamo, 370; American settlement of, 370; annexation of, 371–72, *m378;* cattle ranching, 477–79; Civil War, 421; dust bowl, 783, 786; election of 1844, 371–72; Great Britain, 371; independence of, 369, 370; Lone Star Republic, 370–71; Mexican War, 375–77; Mexico, 369–72, 375–77; oil industry in, 495; readmission of, *m449;* secession of, 404; slavery in, 370–71, 372, 375; statehood, 371–72
Texas A&M, 558
textile industry; child labor, 290; conditions in, 289; Northern, 287, 391; sewing machine, 391; Southern, 457; technology, 286–87; unions, 289–91
Thailand, 817
Thales, 41
Thames, Battle of, 249
Thanksgiving Day, 64
Third Avenue, ptg678
"Third World," 881
Thomas, Clarence, 1003, *p1003*
Thomas, George, 97, *q97,* 433
Thomas, Lorenzo, 451
Thompson, Dorothy, 731
Thompson, Mal, *ptg694*
Thoreau, Henry David, *q267,* 347, 350, *ptg352, q352,* 353
Thorpe, Jim, 83
three-fifths compromise, 157
Three Flags, ptg975
Thurmond, Strom, 853
Tiananmen Square, 994
Tilden, Samuel J., 454
Timbuktu, Mali, 24
time; telling, 234; zones, 501

Tippecanoe—Valley Forge

Tippecanoe, IN, 241, 327
tobacco, 150, *p162*; colonial, 58, 92; Maryland, 61; Southern economy, 457; Virginia, 58–59
Tojo, Hideki, 816
Tokyo, Japan, 383, 823
Toledo, OH, 633
Toleration Act of 1649, 61
Topeka, KS, 898
Tordesillas, Treaty of, 38
Tories. *See* Loyalists.
Toro, Alfonso, 376, *q376*
Toscanini, Arturo, 798
Toussaint-L'Ouverture, Pierre, 237–38
Townsend, Francis, 788
Townshend Acts, 100–01, 104
trade, foreign; agriculture products, 1013; Articles of Confederation, 147; balance of trade, *g989*; British West Indies, 150; China, 382–83; coaling stations, 603; colonial, 61, 79, 92–93; exports, 989, *g989*, 1013; with Great Britain, 92–93, 150, 259–60, 271; imports, *t673*, 965, 989, 1013; Japan, 383; North American Free Trade Agreement, 1013; Marshall Plan, 841–42, 851; piracy, 151; reciprocity, 600, 616; right of deposit, 150; tariffs, 260, *t673*, 714–15, 744, 748, 1013; trade agreements, 1013; trade deficit, 964–65, 1013; trading companies, 62; war debts, 744, 751. *See also* commerce.
trade, interstate. *See* Interstate Commerce Act; states' rights.
Trade and Navigation Acts, 92–93
trade routes, 16, 19, *m22*, *m33*, *m59*
trade societies, 289
Trail of Tears, 317, *ptg318*
transcendentalism, 350, *ptg351*
transcontinental railroad, 398, 471–72
transportation, 278–79, *p278–79*, 393–94; automobiles, 674–75; canals, *ptg262*, *m265*, 266–67, 270, 394, 494; in cities, 288; interstate highway system, 873; oceangoing, 394; railroads, 67–68, *q267*, 287–88, 393, 394, 471–73, 499–500; roads, 263–64, *m265*, 287–88; segregation, 455, 899; technology, 390, 393–94, 498; water, 265–67, *m265*, 270, 394. *See also* farmers, farming; industry; forms of.
Treasury, Department of, 206
Treaty of 1842, 367
Treaty of Paris; 1763, 95–96, 366; 1783, 138, *m150*; Spain, 150; violations, 149–50
Treaty of Tordesillas, 38
Treaty of Ghent, 252, 271
Trenton, Battle of, 126–27, *ptg127*
Triple Alliance, 686–87. *See also* Central Powers; World War I; countries.
Triple Entente, 686–87
Tripoli, 244, 820
Trist, Nicholas P., 377
Troost, Gerard, 345
Trotter, William Monroe, 671
Truman, Harry S, 856, *crt858*; American cold war, 838–43; atomic bomb, 823, 826; Berlin airlift, 843, *q843*; cold war, 840; domestic policy, 853, 854; election of 1948, 853–54; Fair Deal, 854; foreign policy of, 840–41; Korean War, 848–49; MacArthur dismissal, 849; North Atlantic Treaty Organization, 843; Taft-Hartley Act, 852–53; Truman Doctrine, 840, 841, *q841*
Truman Doctrine, 840–841, *q841*
Trumbull, John, *ptg108*, *ptg124*, *ptg139*
trusts, *crt545*; Roosevelt, T., administration, 650–51; Taft administration, 659; Wilson administration, 669–70. *See also* holding companies; industry; monopolies; types of.
Truth, Sojourner, *p339*
Tubman, Harriet, 343, 397, *ptg397*
Tuko-See-Mathla, (Native American), 273, *ptg273*
Tunis, 244, 820
Tunisia, 820
Turkey, 15, 21, 382, 840, *m841*
Turner, Frederick Jackson, 488, 532
Turner, Nat, 343
Tuskegee Institute, 643
TVA. *See* Tennessee Valley Authority.
Twain, Mark, 394, 482, *q482–83*, 544, 559, 611
Tweed Ring, 550
Tweed, William, 545–46, *p546*, *q546*, 550, *crt550*
Tyler, John, 327, 328, 371, 372, 383
typewriter, 496

U

Ukraine, 821
U-2 (airplane), 884–85
UN. *See* United Nations.
Un-American Activities, House Committee on, 855
Uncle Tom's Cabin, 397, *p397*
Underground Railroad, *ptg342*, 343, 390, 397, *m397*
Underwood Tariff, 666–67
unemployment; (1982), 996; depression of 1837, 326–27; Great Depression, 742–80; New Deal, 780–81; Nixon administration, 964; Panic of 1837, 520; Panic of 1873, 520; post-World War I, 715; technological unemployment, 715. *See also* Great Depression; related subjects.
Union, the; African American soldiers in, 427; army, 426–27, *p427*; government of, 424–25; Native Americans, 428; Reconstruction, 445–54; resources of, 415, *g415*; strategy of, 415, 416; wartime diplomacy, 416. *See also* North.
unionization, unions; auto industry, 790–91, 868; big business, 510; Clayton Antitrust Act, 670; craft, industrial unions, 289; demands, 290, *ptg713*; early activity, 290–91; Eisenhower administration, 868; gains, 291, 527; Great Depression, 785; Harding administration, 715–16; immigrants, 289, 521; industrial union, 290–91, 526; membership, 785, *g785*; migrant workers, 918; national, 512, 524–25; Populist party, 576; post-World War I unrest, 704; progressivism, 640; public lands, 293; public schools, 290, 291; steel industry, 510, 521, 790; strikes, 521, *p521*, 522, 526–27, 651–52, 785, 791; Supreme Court, 716; Taft-Hartley Act, 852–53; trade societies, 289, 291; Wagner Act, 853; women, 290, 581; workers' compensation, 635–36; working conditions, 290, 518–19; World War I, 697; World War II, 829. *See also* factories; industry; specific industry.
Union Pacific Company, 472
Union Pacific Railroad, 547
Union party, 433
Union for Social Justice, 787
Union of Soviet Socialist Republics (USSR); Afghanistan, 979, 988; arms race, 843; Berlin, 842, 926–27, 991; Carter administration, 979; civil unrest in, 992–93; cold war, 838–40; Cuba, 824–25; Czechoslovakia, 938; Eastern Europe, 821, 839–41, *m841*, 991–93; Egypt, 881–82; Germany, 811, 815, 991; glasnost, 987, 992; government recognition of, 807; Hungary, 882–83, 991; immigrants from, 1019; Japan, 807, 823; Jews, 979, 988; Middle East, 928; NATO, 882–83; Nixon administration, 942; nuclear weapons in Cuba, 925; perestroika, 987, 992; Poland, 825, 839, 882, 991; Reagan administration, 986–88; Warsaw Pact, 843; World War II, 815, 818–19, 821, 824; Yalta Conference, *p824*, 825. *See also* Russia; specific republics.
Unitarian Church, 350
United Auto Workers, 868
United Farm Workers, 918
United Fruit Company, 504, 611
United Mine Workers, 652
United Nations, 825, 838, 847, 849, *p884*, 926, 993
United States. *See* various subjects.
United States Mint, *ptg207*
United States Sanitary Comission, 429
United States Steel Corporation, 511, 790
United States Temperance Union, 351
United States v. E.C. Knight Company, 512
UNIVAC I, 872, *p872*
Universal Negro Improvement Association, 734
University of Alabama at Tuscaloosa, 906
University of California, 558
University of Chicago, 628
University of Mississippi, 906
University of Virginia, 231
University of Wisconsin, 628
Upland Cotton, *ptg444*
urbanization, 533–34. *See also* cities.
Utah, 11, 369, 390, 581

V

Vallandigham, Clement, 425
Valley Forge, PA, 132

Van Buren—Whistler

Van Buren, Martin, 322, *ptg326;* depression of 1837, 327; elections: of 1836, 326; of 1840, 327–28; of 1844, 371–72; of 1848, 389; independent treasury system, 327; Jackson administration, 322, 326; labor vote, 291; Maine boundary dispute, 367; Native American policy, 317; Texas statehood, 371

Vanderbilt, Cornelius, 500

Vanzetti, Bartolomeo, 717–718, *p717, ptg717, q718*

Vassar, 558

Vaux, Calvert, 537

Veblen, Thorstein, 584

Velazquez, Nydia, 1004

Venezuela, 616–17, 883, 925

Veracruz, 685, *p685*

Vermont, 367, 389

Verrazano, Giovanni da, *m39,* 48

Versailles, Treaty of, 701–03, *ptg703,* 809

vertical integration, 505, 508

Vespucci, Amerigo, 38

veterans; World War II, 853

Veterans' Bureau, 718

Vicksburg, Battle of, 420–21, *q421*

Victory Bonds, 698

victory gardens, 698

Vietcong, 931, 932, 934, 944, 971

Vietnam, *m947;* division of, 880, 930; France, 879, 931; immigrants from, 1019. *See also* North Vietnam; South Vietnam; Vietnam War.

Vietnam Memorial, *p941,* 944, *p946*

Vietnam Veterans' Statue, *p923*

Vietnam War, *p931, p932, m933,* 935, *m935, p945, g943;* Nixon administration, 942–44; opposition to, *p937,* 936–38; peace talks, 934; Vietnamization, 944

View of Harpers Ferry, ptg387

View of New Orleans, ptg229

Villa, Pancho, 685, *p686*

Vinland, 36

Virginia; African American recolonization, 296; Articles of Confederation, 146, *m146,* 155; Civil War in, 417–18, 419, 422; colonial government, 60, *c66;* Constitution ratification, 160, *c163;* naming of, 56; readmission of, *m449;* religious freedom, 145, *q145;* Revolutionary War in, 117, 133, 136, 138; secession of, 413; settlement of, 56–60, *m57, c66;* slavery in, 59, 60; Stamp Act protest, 102; tobacco, 58–59; Tyler, John, 328. *See also* Civil War; plantations; slavery, enslaved persons; related subjects.

Virginia Bill of Rights, 119

Virginia Company, 56, 62

Virginia Plan, 156

Virginia Resolutions, 102

Virgin Islands, 685

virtual representation, 102

V-J Day—Crowds Cheering at Times Square, ptg834

Volunteers in Service to America (VISTA), 958

von Metternich, Klemens, 273, *q273*

von Steuben, Friedrich W.A., Baron, 132

voting; African Americans, 144, 643–44, 852, 902, 905, *m908;* colonial, 65–66, 79; poll tax, 909; property-holding qualifications for, 144, 214, 311; public education, 334; reform, 633–34, 908; voter participation, 302, 328, 1004; woman suffrage, 144, 340, 634–35, *p634,* 671, 706. *See also* elections, congressional; elections, presidential.

Voting Rights Act of 1965, 908, 909

W

Wabash Railway decision, 524, 572

Wade-Davis Bill of 1865, 446

Wagner Act, 790, 853

Wake Island, 817

Walden, q352–53, p353

Wallace, George, 906, 940

Wallace, Henry, 776, 853

Wanamaker, John, 537

War, Department of, 206, 474

War Democrats, 433

War Industries Board, 696

War Labor Board, 697

War of 1812, 247, 248–52, *m251, q252,* 376

War on Poverty, 958–60

War Powers Act, 970

War Production Board, 827

War Refugee Board, 821

Waring, Laura Wheeler, 735

Warner, Charles Dudley, 544

Warner Brothers, 733

Warren Commission, 954

Warren, Earl, 901, 963

Warren, Mercy Otis, 105, *p105,* 159, *q159*

Warsaw Pact, 843

Washington (state), 556

Washington, Booker T., *p642,* 643, *q643*

Washington Conference, 713–14, 808

Washington Crossing the Delaware, ptg111

Washington, D.C.; Bonus Army, 757–58; capital location, 212; Capitol, *ptg222;* Civil War in, 413, 418–19, 431; Emancipation Proclamation, 419, 426; integration in, 455; March on, 907, *q907;* planning of, 212, 221, *ptg221;* rioting in, 914; slavery in, 390; Smithsonian Institution, 347; War of 1812, 249–50

Washington, George, *ptg203;* administration of, 205–06, 220, 222; Articles of Confederation, 152; Battle of Trenton, 126–27, *ptg127;* cabinet of, 205, *ptg205,* 219; Continental Army, 109, 117, 126–27, 128, *ptg129,* 131, 132, 137; Continental Congress, 127; Farewell Address, 219, *p220;* foreign policy of, 216–19; French and Indian War, 94; government establishment, *q203,* 204–06, image of, 128–29, *q129, q205,* Inaugural Address, 204; isolationism, 598; national bank, 209, 212; Philadelphia Convention, 156, 157; planning the capital, 221, *ptg221;* Revolutionary War battles, *ptg86, ptg111,* 126–27, 127, 130, 131, 136, 138; second term of, 219, *q219;* slavery, 296; westward expansion, 152; Whiskey Rebellion, 214

Washington Post, The, 968

Washington, Treaty of, 601

Watergate scandal, 967–69

Waters, Ethel, 734

Watts riots, 912, *p913*

Wayne, Anthony, 138, 214

Way They Live, ptg441

weapons; advances in, 690, 828; atomic bomb, 823, 826; chemical, 690; violence, 1016; napalm, 933; nuclear, 927; radar, 828; in space, 985, 987

Weaver, James B., 556, 575

Webster-Ashburton Treaty, 367

Webster, Daniel, *q313,* 322; Bank of the United States, 323–26; Tyler administration, 327–28; the Union, 320–21; Webster-Ashburton Treaty, 367; Webster-Hayne debate, 320–21, *ptg320;* Whig party, 328

Webster, Noah, 337

We Demand, ptg773

welfare reform, 1016

Wenderoth, Frederick August, *ptg464*

West; Chinese immigrants in, 528, 532; Civil War in, 420; Confederation period, 151–53; election of 1824, 302–04; election of 1892, 576; election of 1896, 577–78; farmers, 269, 297, 391–92, 484–88; federal land policy, 320, 328; frontier weddings, 211; immigrants, 393, 485, 532; internal improvements, 269, 301; Louisiana Purchase, 237–38; mining frontier, *m478,* 479–80, *q479;* missionaries, 373; mountain men, 370; Native American conflict, 212–14, *m212, m478,* 473–75; public education, 335, *q335;* public land policy, 300, 328; railroads, *m478,* 484, 485–86, 487, 532, 569; settlement of, 151–53, *ptg151,* 297–98, *m368, m478,* 484–88; silver, 574–75, 577; slavery issue, 301, 302; Tariff of 1842, 328; tariff issue, 301, 556; secession, threat of, by, 152; universities in, 488, 558; voting rights, 214, 581; Whiskey Rebellion, 214; woman suffrage, 581, 635. *See also* expansionism; frontier; Manifest Destiny; regions; states; related subjects.

West, Samuel, 121

West Indies, 42, 51, 58, 61, 74, 79, 92

Westinghouse air brake, 498, 500

Westmoreland, William, 934

West Point, NY, 137

West Virginia, 420

Weyler, Valeriano, 603

Wharton School of Finance, 558

Wheat, ptg724

Wheelwright, John, 67

Where Cotton Is King, ptg287

Whig party; Clay, Henry, 328, 372, 389; election of 1836, 326; election of 1840, 327–28; election of 1844, 372; election of 1848, 389; election of 1856, 399; election of 1860, 403–04; end of, 399; Mexican War, 375–76

Whiskey Rebellion, 214

Whistler, James Abbott McNeill, 560

Whitefield, George, 121, *ptg121*
White House, 250
White, Walter, 734
White, William Allen, 613, *q613, q653*
Whitman, Marcus and Narcissa, 373
Whitman, Walt, 560
Whitney, Eli, 294, *p296*, 391, 395
Whittier, John Greenleaf, 347
Whyte, William H., 874
Wickersham, George W., 742
Wi-jun-jon, 314, *ptg314*
wildcat strikes, 829
Wilderness, Battle of the, 431
Wilderness Trail, *p296*
Wild West, 478, 479–80, *q479, q480, q481,* 588–89
Wilhelm II, Kaiser, 601
Willard, Emma, 317, 337
Willard, Frances, 580
William and Mary, College of, 77, 156
William Penn's Treaty with the Indians, ptg71
Williams, Roger, 66–67, *q67*, 75
Willkie, Wendell, 815
Wilmot Proviso, 388
Wilson-Gorman Tariff, 577
Wilson, Henry, *q448*, 448
Wilson, Sloan, 874, *q874*
Wilson, Woodrow, *p666, ptg666,* 684, *q706;* Congress and, 665–71, 701–03; death of, 706; early career, 663; election of 1912, 662–63; election of 1916, 690; financial reform, 667–69; Fourteen Points, 700, 701; immigrants, 532; Inaugural Address, 665–66, *q666;* League of Nations, 700, 701–03, *q706;* Mexico, 684–85, *p685;* moral diplomacy of, 684–87; neutrality of, 687–88, 690–91; New Freedom, 662; peace plan, 690, 700, 701–03; segregation, 671; tariff, 666–67, *q666;* trust regulation, 669–70; World War I, 687–88, 690–95, *q692,* 696–700
Winthrop, John, 65, *q65,* 66, 67
Wisconsin, 494, 633–34
Wise, Isaac Mayer, 639
Wolfe, James, 95
Woman's Christian Temperance Union (WCTU), 580, 638
woman's rights, 340-41, 581, 628, 634–35; equality, 236; National Organization for Women, 869, 916-17; Supreme Court, 636–37. *See also* women.
women; abolitionist movement, 343–44, *p359;* Adams, Abigail, 134, *ptg134;* AFL discrimination against, 526; Anthony, Susan B., 553, *p553;* art, 560; cabinet officer, 537, 776; Civil War, 428–29; colonial, 68, *ptg68,* 74–75, *q74;* Declaration of Independence, 120; education, 317, 336–37, 488, 628, 917; effects of transportation improvements on, 269; equal pay for, 340; Equal Rights Amendment, 917; Friedan, Betty, 869, *p869;* Grange, 570; Great Plains life, 488; higher education, 75, 337, 341, 558; household technology, 74–75, 719, 731; industrial working conditions, 519, *p631;* job opportunities for, 74–75, 340–41, 496, *p496;* labor force, 74, 75, 269, 340, 624, *p631,* 730–31, *g835,* 851, 916; in medicine, 341; legal rights, 68, 340, 341; Nineteenth Amendment, 706; New Deal, 795–96; political office, 1003; post-World War II, 851, 875; progressivism, 628; property acts, 317, 341; reform movement, 335, 337, 339–41, 580–81; Revolutionary War, 134; Roaring Twenties, 730–31; role models, 731, 875; in science, 347; Seneca Falls Convention, 236, 341; settlement house movement, 534, 536–37, 628; Supreme Court appointment, 985, 1005, *p1005;* Supreme Court decisions, 636–37; telephone operators, 496, *p496;* temperance movement, 580; in unions, 581, 791; vice presidential candidate, 917; woman suffrage, 144, 340–41, 581, *p581,* 628, 671, 706; working conditions, 519, *q519,* 538, 636–37; World War I, 697; World War II, *p827, p828,* 829–30, *q830. See also* individual names; related subjects.
Women's International League for Peace and Freedom, 534
Wood, Jethro, 391–92
Wood, Leonard, 613
Woolen Act, 92
workers' compensation, 635–36
Workingmen's party, 290
Works Progress Administration (WPA), 789

ptg543
World War I; African Americans in, 694–95; battles of, 692, *m693,* 695; bonds, 698; cost of, 698; doughboys, 694, *p694;* draft for, 694; Eastern Front, *m693;* European beginnings, 686–87; France, 686–87; home front, 696–700; national debt from, 713, 715; neutrality, *m689;* peace plan, 701–02; post-war economic problems, 703–05; postwar foreign policy, 713–14; public opinion, 687–91, 699–700; United States entrance, 691–92, *q692;* war debt, 713; Western Front, 692, *m693,* 695; Wilson's neutrality, 687–88, 690–91; world map, *m689, m693. See also* Allied Powers; Wilson, Woodrow; countries; battles; individual names.
World War II; African Americans in, 830–31; African Theater, 818, 819, *m819,* 820; D-Day, *p820;* European Theater, *m819,* 820–21; financing, 828–29; home front, 828; isolationism, 811; Japanese Americans, 831–32, *p832,* 833, *p833;* neutrality, 811, 812; Pacific Theater, 816, 817, 822–23, *m822;* peace, 823; Pearl Harbor, 816, 817, *p818;* post-war prosperity, 850–51; rationing, 828, *p829;* social change, 829–33; Soviet Union, 815, *q815;* United States involvement in, 811–815; wartime diplomacy, 824–25, *p824;* women in, *p827, p828,* 829–30, *p830, q830*
Wounded Knee, SD, 475, 919
Wright, Frank Lloyd, 537
writs of assistance, 99
Wycliffe, John, 48
Wyoming, 556, 581

X

XYZ Affair, *crt222,* 224, *q224*

Y

Yale University, 77, 917
Yalta Conference, *p824,* 825
Yankee peddler, 133, *ptg133*
Yellowstone National Park, *ptg649,* 652
Yeltsin, Boris, 992–93, 1010
York (African American), 238
York, Duke of, 69, 72
York, PA, 130
Yorktown, VA, 138, *ptg138*
Young, Brigham, 369
Yugoslavia, 815, 992, 1009–10

Z

Zaire, 926
Zenger, John Peter, 78–79
Zhou En-lai, 942
Zimmermann Note, 691

Acknowledgments

30 "Constitution of the Five Nations," from William N. Fenton, ed., *Parker on the Iroquois*, Copyright © 1868 by Syracuse University Press; used by permission. **31** "Navajo Song of the Rain Chant," from Nataline Curtis, ed., *The Indians' Book*, Harper and Brothers, 1907; used by permission. **110** From Thomas Paine, *American Crisis, Number 1*, reprinted in *The Annals of America*, vol. 2, Chicago: Encyclopaedia Britannica, 1968. **236** Southgate letter from James A. Henretta, et al, *America's History*, Chicago: Dorsey Press, 1987. **242** From James Fenimore Cooper, *The Prairie*, Albany: State University of New York Press, 1962. **362** From Henry David Thoreau, *Walden and Other Writings*. New York: Doubleday, 1970. **379** Coffey "Reminiscences" from *Eyewitness: The Negro in American History* by William L. Katz, rev. ed. New York: Pitman Publishing Corp., 1971. **482** From Mark Twain, *Roughing It*. Berkeley: University of California Press, 1972. **614** From *Official Proceedings of the Democratic National Convention. . . . 1890*, reprinted in *The Annals of America*, vol. 12. Chicago: Encyclopaedia Britannica, 1968. **630** From Theodore Dreiser, *Sister Carrie*. New York: W.W. Norton, Critical Ed., 1970. **726** "Recuerdo" by Edna St. Vincent Millay, From *Collected Poems*, Harper & Row, Copyright © 1922, 1950 by Edna St. Vincent Millay. Reprinted by permission of Elizabeth Barnett, Literary Executor. **727** "Dream Boogie," reprinted by permission of Harold Ober Associates, Inc. Copyright © 1932, 1951 by Langston Hughes, Copyright renewed 1979 by George Houston Bass. **800** From John Steinbeck, *The Grapes of Wrath*, Copyright © 1939, renewed © 1967 by John Steinbeck. Used by permission of Viking Penguin, a division of Penguin Books USA, Inc. **833** Ota excerpt from *"The Good War": An Oral History of World War Two* by Studs Terkel. Copyright © 1984. Reprint by permission of Pantheon Books, a division of Random House. **900** Beals excerpt from Henry Hampton and Steve Fayer, *Voices of Freedom*. New York: Bantam Books, 1990. **1022** From *Hunger of Memory* by Richard Rodriguez. Copyright © 1981 by Richard Rodriguez. Reprinted by permission of David R. Godine, Publisher. **1071** "I Have a Dream" copyright © 1963 by Martin Luther King, Jr. Used by permission, Joan Daves Agency.

Photo Credits

COVER, Jim Barber Studio; **x**(l), The Granger Collection, (tr), R. Krubner/H. A. Roberts, (br), The Granger Collection; **xi**(tl), Shelburne Museum, Shelburne, VT, (tr), Henry Ford Museum, (ct), The Granger Collection, (cr), file photo, (cb), Aaron Haupt Photography, (bl), Courtesy Hormel Foods/Aaron Haupt Photography, (br), Reuters/Bettmann; **xii**(tl), The Granger Collection, (tr), North Wind Picture Archives, (b), Courtesy PHYSICS TODAY Magazine; **xiii**(tl)(bl), The Granger Collection, (tr), Ted Wood/Black Star, (br), Bettmann Archive; **xiv**(l), Stock Montage, (r), North Wind Picture Archives; **xv**(tl)(tc), The Granger Collection, (tr)(cl), Brown Brothers, (cr), Bettmann Archive, (bl), UPI/Bettmann, (br), Courtesy David Godine Publishers; **xvi**(l), New York Historical Society, (r), The Time Museum; **xvii**(tl), Rueters/Bettmann, (tr), Mark Burnett/Central Ohio Council of B S A, (bl), Aldo Tutino/Art Resource, (br), FPG, Intl; **xviii**(l), Bettmann Archive, (ct), Courtesy Independence National Historic Park/Eastern National Park and Monument Association, (cb), Archive Photos, (r), American Antiquarian Society; **xix**(tl), UPI/Bettmann, (tc), John Launois/Black Star, (tr), Richard Howard/Black Star, (bl)(bc), Stock Montage, (br), The Granger Collection; **xx**(t), Library of Congress, (b), National Museum of American Art, Washington, DC/Art Resource; **xxi**(t), Library of Congress, (b), The Sonnabend Collection, NY; **xxiv**, William J. Weber; **xxv**(t), The Art Collection of the Boatman's National Bank of St. Louis, (b), Missouri Historical Society; **xxvi**(t), Estate of Mrs. Edsel B. Ford, (b), Metropolitan Museum of Art; **xxvii**(t), The Granger Collection, (b), H. Armstrong Roberts; **xxviii**(t), file photo, (b), Bettmann Archive; **xxix**(t), The Granger Collection, (b), Reuters/Bettmann; **xxx**, General Electric Company; **xxxi**(t), Andy Levin/Photo Researchers, (b), Joseph DiChello; **xxxii**(t), Architect of the Capitol, (b), Alex Maclean/Landslides; **xxxiii**(t), The Granger Collection, (b), Lynn Stone; **xxxiv**(t), Margot Granitsas/Photo Researchers, (b), The Granger Collection; **1**(t), North Wind Picture Archives, (b), Joe Sohm/Photo Researchers; **2**(t), Chuck O'Rear/H. Armstrong Roberts, (b), file photo; **3**(tl)(b), Scala/Art Resource, (tr), The Granger Collection; **4**(t)(c), Boltin Picture Library, (b), Larry Hamill; **5, 6**, Boltin Picture Library; **7**(t), Bettmann Archive, (b), Courtesy of the School of American Research, Santa Fe; **8**, Bettmann Archive; **9**, George C. Page Museum; **10**, Bettmann Archive; **11**, Werner Forman/Art Resource; **13**, George Hunter/H. Armstrong Roberts; **14**(t), Courtesy Museum of Natural History, Raleigh, NC, (b), Mark Burnett; **15**, Erich Lessing/Art Resource; **16**(t), The Granger Collection, (b), North Wind Picture Archives; **17**, The Granger Collection; **18**, Scala/Art Resource; **19, 20**, British Museum; **21**, SEF/Art Resource; **22**, The Granger Collection; **23**(l), Aldo Tutino/Art Resource, (r), British Museum; **24**, Metropolitan Museum of Art; **25**, Boltin Picture Library; **26**, H. Armstrong Roberts; **27**(l), The Granger Collection, (r), Scala/Art Resource; **28**, Giraudon/Art Resource; **29**, The Granger Collection; **30**(t), file photo, (b), Cranbrook Institute of Science; **31**, G. L. French/H. Armstrong Roberts; **32**, The British Museum; **34**, Erich Lessing/Art Resource; **35**(t), Bridgeman Art Library, London, (b), Werner Forman/Art Resource; **36, 37**, The Granger Collection; **38**, Scala/Art Resource; **40**, Giraudon/Art Resource; **41**, Scala/Art Resource; **42**, Peabody Museum of Salem; **43, 44**, The Granger Collection; **45**, North Wind Picture Archives; **46**(t), file photo, (b), The Granger Collection; **47, 48**, The Granger Collection; **49**(l), National Archives of Canada, (r), The Granger Collection; **52**, The Granger Collection; **54**, Boltin Picture Library; **55**(t), Wadsworth Atheneum, Hartford, (b), H. Armstrong Roberts; **56**, H. Armstrong Roberts; **58**, North Wind Picture Archives; **62**, The Granger Collection; **63**, Courtesy of the Pilgrim Society, Plymouth, MA; **64**, Bettmann Archive; **65**, The Pilgrim Society; **67, 68**, The Granger Collection; **69**, Chase Manhattan Bank; **70**, The Granger Collection; **71, 72**, The Granger Collection; **73**, The Shelburne Museum, Shelburne, VT; **75**, Bettmann Archive; **76**, The Granger Collection; **77**, Bettmann Archive; **78**, North Wind Picture Archives; **80**(l), file photo, (r), Bettmann Archive; **82**(t), The Granger Collection, (b), Boltin Picture Library; **82, 83**(b), David McGlynn/FPG, Intl; **83**(tl), Smithsonian Institution, American Museum of Natural History, (tr), Roger K. Burnard, (br), file photo; **84**(l), E. Cooper/H. Armstrong Roberts, (r), Bettmann Archive; **85, 86**(l)(c), The Granger Collection, (r), Folger Shakespeare Library, Washington, D.C.; **87**(l), Bettmann Archive, (r), The Granger Collection; **88**(t), Boltin Picture Library, (bl), Joslyn Art Museum, (br), Laurie Platt Winfrey, Inc; **89**(t), The Granger Collection, (bl), Courtesy American Antiquarian Society, (br), Courtesy Independence National Historic Park/Eastern National Park and Monument Association; **90**, The Granger Collection; **91**(t), Red Hill: The Patrick Henry National Memorial, Brookneal, VA, (b), North Wind Picture Archives; **92, 93**, The Granger Collection; **94**, Stock Montage; **96**, Culver Pictures; **97**, The Art Gallery of Ontario; **98**, The Granger Collection; **100**, Culver Pictures; **101**, National Portrait Gallery, Washington, DC/Art Resource; **102**, Bettmann Archive; **103**, The Library of Congress; **104**, From: Old North Church, Boston; **105**(l),

Bettmann Archive, (r), The Granger Collection; **106**, Archive Photos; **107**(l), Stock Montage, (r), Bettmann Archive; **108**(l), The Granger Collection, (r), Giraudon/Art Resource, NY; **110**, Historical Pictures Service/Stock Montage; **111**(t), The Metropolitan Museum of Art, Gift of John Stewart Kennedy, 1897 (97.34), (b), Stock Montage; **112**, Photograph courtesy of The Concord Museum, Concord MA; **114**, The National Gallery of Art, Washington; **115**(t), Fraunces Tavern Museum, Gift of Herbert P. Whitlock, 1913, (b), file photo; **116, 117, 118**, The Granger Collection; **120**, Stock Montage; **121**, National Portrait Gallery, London; **123**, Architect of the Capitol, Washington, DC; **126**, file photo; **127**, The Granger Collection; **128**, Courtesy American Jewish Historical Society, Waltham MA; **129**, The Granger Collection; **130**, North Wind Picture Archives; **131**, National Portrait Gallery, Smithsonian Institution/Art Resource, NY; **132**, The Granger Collection; **133**, New York Historical Society; **134**(l), Bettmann Archive, (r), Courtesy the Rhode Island Historical Society; **135**, The Granger Collection; **136**, Orbis Book Publishing Corporation Ltd., London; **138**, Painting by Don Troiani, Southbury, CT; **139**(l), Giraudon/Art Resource, (r), Architect of the Capitol, Washington, DC; **140**, The Granger Collection, New York; **142**, Bettmann Archive; **143**(t), Art Resource, NY, (b), Chase Manhattan Archives; **144**, North Wind Picture Archives; **145**, The Metropolitan Museum of Art, Gift of Mrs. A. Wordsworth Thompson, 1899. (99.28); **147**, The Granger Collection; **148**, Smithsonian Institution Photo No. 73-10283; **149, 151**, Bettmann Archive; **152**, Archive Photos; **154**(l), Stock Montage, (r), file photo; **155**, Pictures Unlimited; **156**, Bettmann Archive; **157**, Library of Congress; **158**, Independence National Historical Park; **159**, Bettmann Archive; **161**, Courtesy Princeton University Observatory; **162**, file photo; **164**(t)(br), North Wind Picture Archives, (br), Aaron Haupt Photography; **165**(t), J. R. Schnelzer, (c), The Granger Collection, (b), Richard Gross Photo; **166**, The Granger Collection; **172**, Mark Burnett; **175**, Reuters/Bettmann; **176**, Aaron Haupt; **177**, UPI/Bettmann; **179, 180**, ©1991 Dennis Brack/Black Star; **182**, Reuters/Bettmann; **183**, © 1991 Dennis Brack/Black Star; **184**, Collection, The Supreme Court Historical Society; **188**, Ted Rice; **191**, ©1992 Lisa Quinones/Black Star; **194**, M.L.Uttermohlen; **198**(l), Museum of the American Indian, (r), Worcester Art Museum, Worcester MA, Gift of Mrs. Kingsmill Maars; **199**(tl), file photo, (tr), The Granger Collection, (b), Smithsonian Institution; **200**(t), Bridgeman/Art Resource, (c), The Granger Collection, (bl), Bettmann Archive, (br), Peabody Museum/Harvard University, Photo by Hillel Burger; **201**(tl), Lauros-Giraudon/Art Resource, (tr), Giraudon/Art Resource, (b), Archives Division Texas State Library; **202**, National Gallery of Art; **203**(t), National Gallery of Art, (b), The Granger Collection; **204**, North Wind Picture Archives; **205**(l), North Wind Picture Archives, (r), Superstock; **207**(t), Courtesy Independence National Historic Park/Eastern National Park and Monument Association, (b), Museum of American Political Life; **208, 209, 210, 211**, The Granger Collection; **215**, Free Library of Philadelphia; **216**, Boltin Picture LIbrary; **217, 218**, The Granger Collection; **219**, National Archives; **220**(t), Boltin Picture Library, (b), National Gallery of Art; **221**(t), The Granger Collection, (b), Bettmann Archive; **222**, Lilly Library; **223**, Bettmann Archive; **224**, Russ Lappa; **225, 226, 228**, The Granger Collection; **229**(t), Chicago Historical Society, (b), Peabody Museum/Harvard University, Photo by Hillel Burger; **230**, FPG, Intl; **232**, Courtesy Virginia State Library; **233**, The Granger Collection; **234**, The Time Museum; **235**, file photo; **236**, Courtesy, The Henry Francis du Pont Winterthur Museum; **237**, Erich Lessing/Art Resource; **239, 240**, The Granger Collection; **241**, The Field Museum/John Weinstein, A93851.1c; **242**(t), North Wind Picture Archives, (b), Museum of the American Indian; **243**, The Granger Collection; **244**, North Wind Picture Archives; **245, 246**, The Granger Collection; **247**, North Wind Picture Archives; **248**, West Point Museum, presented by F. Donald Campbell, No.14,874; **249**, Courtesy Independence National Historic Park/Eastern National Park and Monument Association; **250**, North Wind Picture Archives; **251**, The Granger Collection; **252**, FPG, Intl; **253**, Missouri Historical Society; **254**, North Wind Picture Archives; **256**, The Granger Collection; **257**(t), Historical Society of Pennsylvania, (b), Aaron Haupt Photography; **258**, file photo; **259**, National Portrait Gallery, Smithsonian Institution/Art Resource; **260, 262, 263**, The Granger Collection; **264**, H. Armstrong Roberts; **265**, Mark Sexton/Peabody Essex Museum; **266**, National Museum of American Art, Washington, DC/Art Resource; **267**, Courtesy of the Bostonian Society; **268**, North Wind Picture Archives; **269, 270, 271**, The Granger Collection; **273**, Superstock; **274, 276**, Bettmann Archive; **278**(t), D. Logan/H. Armstrong Roberts, (b), H. Armstrong Roberts; **279**(t), R. Krubner/H. Armstrong Roberts, **279**(c)(bl)(br), **280, 281**, The Granger Collection; **282**(t), Bettmann Archive, (b), The Ralph E. Becker Collection, The Smithsonian Institution; **283**(tl), The British Museum, (bl), The Charleston Museum, Charleston, SC, (r), The Wenham Museum; **284**(t), Giraudon/Art Resource, (b), The Fine Arts Museum of San Francisco, Gift of Eleanor Martin, 37573; **285**(t), The Granger Collection, (b), Philbrook Museum of Art, (c), Bettmann Archive; **286**, Lowell National Historical Park; **287**(t), Superstock, (b), Stock Montage; **288**, The Granger Collection; **289**, Rhode Island Historical Society; **290, 291**, Bettmann Archive; **292**, Stock Montage; **294**, file photo; **295**(l), Museum of the City of New York/Scala/Art Resource, (r), Bettmann Archive; **296**, Maryland Historical Society, Baltimore; **297**, Bettmann Archive; **298**, The Granger Collection; **299**, National Museum of American Art, Washington, DC/Art Resource, NY; **300**, Bettmann Archive; **301**(l), Bettmann Archive, (r), MAK-1; **303**, National Portrait Gallery, Washington, DC/Art Resource, NY; **304**, Bettmann Archive; **305**, ©Richard Pasley/Stock Boston; **306**, Bettmann Archive; **308**, National Museum of American Art, Washington, DC/Art Resource, NY; **309**(t), From the art collection of The Boatman's National Bank of St. Louis, (b), The Granger Collection; **310**, National Museum of American History, Smithsonian Institution; **311, 312**, The Granger Collection; **314**, National Museum of American Art, Washington, DC/Art Resource, NY; **315**, Bettmann Archive; **316**, David L. Perry; **317**, Stock Montage; **318**, Superstock; **319, 320, 321**, Bettmann Archive; **323, 324**, The Granger Collection; **325**, National Portrait Gallery, Smithsonian Institution/Art Resource, NY; **326**, Bettmann Archive; **327**(l), The Granger Colllection, (r), National Portrait Gallery, Smithsonian Institution/Art Resource, NY; **328, 329**, The Granger Collection; **330**, Smithsonian Institution, American Museum of Natural History; **332**, National Portrait Gallery, Smithsonian Institution/Art Resource, NY; **333**(t), The National Museum of American Art, Washington, DC, (b), Bridgeman/Art Resource, NY; **334**, The Granger Collection; **335**, Superstock; **336**, Stock Montage; **337**, Bettmann Archive; **338**, The Granger Collection; **339**, Bettmann Archive; **340**, The Granger Collection; **341**(t), The Granger Collection, (b), Bettmann Archive; **342**(t), Bettmann Archive, (b), The Granger Collection; **343**, The Granger Collection, New York; **344**(t), Archive Photos, (b), Bettmann Archive; **345**, Library of Congress; **346**, Stock Montage; **347**, The Granger Collection; **348**, National Museum of American Art, Washington, DC/Art Resource, NY; **350, 351, 352**, The Granger Collection; **353**, Judith J. Cohen; **354**, National Museum of American Art, Washington, DC/Art Resource, NY; **356**(tl), Mark Sexton/Peabody Essex Museum, (tr), Charles Schneider/Photophile, (b), Shelburne Museum, Shelburne, VT; **357**(t), Walter's Art Gallery, (c), Photophile, (bl), National Gallery of Art, (br), **358**, The Granger Collection; **359**(t), National Museum of American Art, Washington, DC/Art Resource, NY, (b), The Granger Collection; **360**(l), Aaron Haupt Photography, (r), Hampton University Museum, Hampton, VA, **360, 361**(b), Chris Sorensen/State Historical Society of Wisconsin/Wisconsin Veterans Museum; **361**(tl), Smithsonian Institution, gift of E. A. Rodgers, (tr), The Burns Archive; **362**(t), Giraudon/Art Resource, (bl), file photo, (br), State Historical Society of Wisconsin; **363**(tl), Laurie Platt Winfrey, Inc, (tr), Bettmann Archive; **364**, Library of Congress; **365**(t), file photo, (b), Texas State Department of Highways and Public Transportation; **366, 367, 369**(l), Library of Congress, (r), Alan Carey; **370**, The Granger Collection; **371**, Archives Division, Texas State Library; **373**, file photo; **374**, Dukes County Historical Society/Robert Schellhammer; **375**, The Corcoran Gallery of Art; **377**, Chicago Historical Society; **379**, Library of Congress; **380**, The Historical Society of Pennsylvania, **381**, The Historic New Orleans Collection; **382**, Library of Congress; **384**, file photo; **386**, Smithsonian Institution; **387**(t), Courtesy Robert M. Hicklin Jr, Inc, (b), National Portrait Gallery, Smithsonian Institution/Art Resource, NY; **388**, New York Historical Society; **389**, National Portrait Gallery; **390**, The Granger Collection; **391**, Bettmann Archive; **393**, Smithsonian Institution; **395**, The Granger Collection; **396**, Bob Mullenix; **397**(t), New York Public Library, (b), Library of Congress; **399**, The Kansas State Historical Society; **400**, Missouri State Historical Society; **402**, Jerry and Sharon Austin/Devaney Stock Photos; **403**(t), The Granger Collection, (b), Library of Congress; **407, 408**, The Granger Collection; **410**, H. Abernathy/H. Armstrong Roberts; **411**(t), The Granger Collection, (b), Mark Burnett; **412**, The New York Historical Society; **413**, Bettmann Archive; **414**, Historical Pictures Service/Stock Montage, Inc; **416**, The Granger Collection; **417**, Photo Network; **418**, The Granger Collection; **421**, Smithsonian Institution; **422**, U.S. Army Center of Military History Art/Exhibits Branch; **423**(l), The Granger Collection, (r), K. Vreeland/H. Armstrong Roberts; **424**, Glasheen Graphics; **425**, Smithsonian Institution; **427**(tl), William B. Folsom, (bl), Cheryl D. Callaman/ Tradd Street Stock,

1116 Credits

(r), The Granger Collection; **428,** file photo; **430,** The Granger Collection; **431,** Mark Burnett; **432**(l), James Blank/FPG, Intl, (r), The Granger Collection; **433,** file photo; **434,** Appomattox Court House National Historical Park; **435**(tl), file photo, (tr), L.L.T. Rhoades/ Devaney Stock Photos, (b), **436,** Library of Congress; **438,** Bettmann Archive; **439**(t), file photo, (b), Boltin Picture Library; **440,** The American Numismatic Society; **441,** The Granger Collection; **442,** National Portrait Gallery, Washington, DC/Art Resource; **443, 444,** The Granger Collection; **445,** file photo; **446**(l), Collection of Nancy Gewirz, Antique Textile Resource, (r), North Wind Picture Archives; **447,** Larry Sherer/Time-Life Books; **450, 452,** Library of Congress; **453,** Smithsonian Institution; **454,** file photo; **456,** Library of Congress; **457**(t), Pembroke Herbert/Picture Research Consultants, (b), Smithsonian Institution; **458,** National Museum of American Art, Washington DC/Art Resource; **460**(t), F. Sieb/H. Armstrong Roberts, (c)(bl), **461**(tr)(c)(bl), The Granger Collection, (br), W. Talarowski/H. Armstrong Roberts; **461**(tl), Shelburne Museum, Shelburne, VT/Photo by Ken Burris; **462**(l), Smithsonian Institution, (r), Library of Congress; **463**(l), Bettmann Archive, (r), Larry Sherer/Time-Life Books; **464**(t), National Museum of American Art/Art Resource, NY, (b), file photo; **465**(tl), Smithsonian Institution photo #744404, (bl)(r), The Granger Collection; **466**(t)(b), Culver Pictures, (c), **467**(t), Library of Congress, (cl), Chicago Historical Society, (cr), Culver Pictures, (b), National Park Service Collection; **468,** Anthracite Museum Complex; **469, 470,** The Granger Collection; **471**(l), National Museum of American Art, Washington, DC/Art Resource, NY, (r), Bettmann Archive; **473,** Stock Montage; **474, 475,** The Granger Collection; **477, 480,** Bettmann Archive; **481,** The Henry Ford Museum, The Edison Institute; **482**(t), The Granger Collection, (b), Randy Trine; **483,** The Granger Collection; **484,** State Historical Society of Wisconsin; **485,** Bettmann Archive; **486**(l), The Granger Collection, (r), Bettmann Archive; **489**(l), Courtesy Sperry/New Holland, (r), **490, 492,** The Granger Collection; **493**(t), Giraudon/Art Resource, NY, (b), National Portrait Gallery, Smithsonian Institution, Washington, DC/Art Resource, NY; **494,** NCR Corporation; **495,** The Granger Collection; **496**(l), Courtesy AT&T, (r), The Granger Collection; **497**(l), National Museum of American Art, Washington, DC/Art Resource, NY, (r), Bettmann Archive; **499,** Scala/Art Resource, NY; **502,** The Granger Collection; **503,** Stock Montage; **504,** Archive Photos; **506, 507, 508,** The Granger Collection; **509,** Giraudon/Art Resource, NY; **510, 511, 514, 516,** The Granger Collection; **517**(t), The Brooklyn Museum, Dick S. Ramsay Fund, (b), The Granger Collection; **518,** Anthracite Museum Complex; **519**(l), The Granger Collection, (r), Bettmann Archive; **520, 521,** The Granger Collection; **523,** Bettmann Archive; **524,** Aaron Haupt; **525,** Bettmann Archive; **526, 527, 528,** The Granger Collection; **530**(l), Bob Mullenix, (r), Arnoldo Mondadori Editore, Milano; **531, 532, 533, 534, 535, 536,** The Granger Collection; **537,** Archive Photos; **539,** Bettmann Archive; **540,** The Granger Collection; **542,** Art Resource, NY; **543**(t), The Granger Collection, (b), Collection of Pembroke Herbert, Picture Research Consultants; **544-551,** The Granger Collection; **552**(l), Archive Photos, (r), **553,** The Granger Collection; **554**(l), Bettmann Archive, (r), **555,** The Granger Collection; **557,** Bettmann Archive; **558,** The Granger Collection; **559,** Bettmann Archive; **560,** Tate Gallery/Art Resource, NY; **561, 562, 563,** The Granger Collection; **564,** Bettmann Archive; **565,** The Granger Collection; **566,** The Ralph E. Becker Collection, Smithsonian Institution; **567**(t), The Granger Collection, (b), B&O Railroad Museum, Baltimore; **568, 569,** The Granger Collection; **570,** Sears, Roebuck and Company; **571, 572,** The Granger Collection; **573,** Library of Congress; **574, 575, 576**(l), The Granger Collection, (r), Bettmann Archive; **577,** The Granger Collection; **579,** From THE DEPRESSION YEARS AS PHOTOGRAPHED BY ARTHUR ROTHSTEIN, Dover Publications, Inc.; **580, 581**(l), National Portrait Gallery, Smithsonian Institution, Art Resource, NY, (r), The Granger Collection; **582,** Courtesy Metropolitan Life Insurance Company; **583,** Archive Photos; **586,** The Granger Collection; **588**(t), Steve Smith/ H. Armstrong Roberts, (bl), M. Roessler/H. Armstrong Roberts, (br), file photo; **589**(t), The Granger Collection, (bl), Bob Mullenix, (br), J. Urwiller/H. Armstrong Roberts; **590,** The Granger Collection; **591**(tl), Collection of Picture Research Consultants Inc, (tr), Library of Congress, (bl), The Granger Collection; **592**(l), David Diaz Guerrero/Collection of Roddy Moore, (r), Los Angeles County Museum of Art, Los Angeles County Fund, CLIFF DWELLERS by George Bellows; **593**(tl), Library of Congress, (tr), Mark Burnett, (bl), Boltin Picture Library; **594**(t), file photo, (bl), Brown Brothers, (br), David Austen/Stock Boston; **595**(t), SEF/Art Resource, (cl), Giraudon/Art Resource, (cr), The Granger Collection, (bl), Bettmann Archive, (br), Courtesy Ford Motor Company; **595,** The Granger Collection; **596,** Mark Sexton/Peabody Essex Museum; **597**(t), Courtesy U.S. Naval Academy Museum, (b), The Granger Collection; **598,** Courtesy Hawaii Visitor's Bureau; **599,** The Granger Collection; **600**(l), file photo, (r), Johnny Johnson; **602,** North Wind Picture Archives; **603,** Collection of David J. and Janice L. Frent; **604**(l), The Granger Collection, (r), file photo; **606,** Brown Brothers; **607, 608, 609,** The Granger Collection; **609,** National Archives; **611**(l), file photo, (r), Mark Burnett; **613,** California Museum of Photography; **614,** Library of Congress; **615,** Smithsonian Institution; **617,** The Granger Collection; **618,** Superstock; **620,** National Guard Bureau; **622,** Boltin Picture Library; **623**(t), The Granger Collection, (b), Larry Hamill; **624,** Courtesy Labor Archives and Research Center, San Francisco State Universtiy; **626**(l), Charles Phelps Cushing/H. Armstrong Roberts, (r), The Granger Collection; **627,** Culver Pictures; **629, 630,** Brown Brothers; **631,** The Granger Collection; **632,** Nebraska State Historical Society; **634**(l), Superstock, (r), Schlesinger Library, Radcliffe College; **636**(l), Library of Congress, (r), UPI/Bettmann; **637,** Mark Burnett/Central Ohio Council of B S A; **639,** Courtesy, American Jewish Historical Society, Waltham, MA; **640,** Smithsonian Institution; **641**(l), Chicago Historical Society, (r), Lewis Hine/International Museum of Photography at George Eastman House; **642**(l), Courtesy of the NAACP, (r), Library of Congress; **643,** The Granger Collection; **644,** H. Armstrong Roberts; **645,** Library of Congress; **646,** North Wind Picture Archives; **647,** Theodore Roosevelt Collection, Harvard College Library; **648,** Courtesy of AT&T; **649**(t), file photo, (b), National Baseball Library; **650,** Devaney Stock Photos; **651, 652,** Brown Brothers; **653**(l), Craig Kramer, (r), Paul Nesbit; **655,** Lloyd Lemmermann; **656,** Theodore Roosevelt Collection, Harvard College Library by permission of the Houghton Library, Harvard University; **657,** file photo; **658,** Library of Congress; **660,** Theodore Roosevelt Collection/The Houghton Library-Harvard University; **661**(t), file photo, (b), **662,** Library of Congress; **665,** Smithsonian Institution; **666**(l), The New York Historical Society, (r), Smithsonian Institution; **667**(l), file photo, (r), Tim Courlas Photography; **668,** Bettmann Archive; **670,** National Portrait Gallery, Smithsonian Institution/Art Resource; **672,** H. Armstrong Roberts; **674**(tr), Henry Ford Museum, (c), W. H. Clark/H. Armstrong Roberts, (bl), H. Armstrong Roberts; **675**(tl), H. Armstrong Roberts, (tr)(br), The Granger Collection, (b), H. Armstrong Roberts; **675,** H. Armstrong Roberts; **676,** The Granger Collection; **677**(t), Lloyd Lemmermann, (b), Library of Congress; **678**(l), file photo, (c), National Museum of American Art, Washington, DC/Art Resource, NY, (r), Collection of Picture Research Consultants, Inc.; **679**(l), Collection of Colonol Stuart S. Corning, photo ©Rob Huntley/Lightstream, (r), The National Archives; **680**(t), SEF/Art Resource, (c), United Nations, (bl), Franklin D. Roosevelt Library, (br), Museum of the City of New York; **681**(t), file photo, (b), H. Armstrong Roberts; **682,** Bettmann Archive; **683,** The Granger Collection; **684,** Bettmann Archive; **685,** UPI/Bettmann; **686,** Bettmann Archive; **687,** The Granger Collection; **688, 690,** Bettmann Archive; **691**(l), UPI/Bettmann, (r), file photo; **692**(l), The Granger Collection, (r), Bettmann Archive; **694**(l), Culver Pictures, (r), The Granger Collection; **695,** Collection of Colonel Stuart S. Corning. Photo by Rob Huntley/Lightstream; **696,** The Granger Collection; **697,** Bettmann Archive; **698,** American Red Cross, Washington, DC; **699, 700,** The Granger Collection; **701, 702,** Collection of Colonel Stuart S. Corning. Photo by Rob Huntley/Lightstream; **703,** National Portrait Gallery, Smithsonian Institution/Art Resource, NY; **704,** Bettmann Archive; **705,** file photo; **707,** The Granger Collection; **708,** Museo Nacional de Arte Moderno, Mexico City; **710,** Private collection, photo by Rob Huntley/Lightstream; **711**(t), Thomas Hart Benton "City Activities with Dance Hall" from America Today, 1930. Distemper and egg tempera with oil glaze on gessoed linen. Size: 92x134" Collection, The Equitable Life Assurance Society of the United States. Photo 1988 by Dorothy Zeidman, (b), ©1992 Jan White Brantley. Courtesy Louisianna Jazz Club Collection, Louisianna State Museum; **712, 713, 715, 717**(b), Bettmann Archive, (t), UPI/Bettmann; **718,** Collection of David J. and Janice L. Frent; **719, 720,** file photo; **721,** The Granger Collection; **723**(l), Ford Motor Company, (r), Collection of Colonel Stuart S. Corning. Photo by Rob Huntley/Lightstream; **724**(l), National Museum of American Art, Smithsonian Institution, Washington, DC/Art Resource, NY, (r), Bettmann Archive; **725,** Superstock; **726**(l), Brown Brothers, (r), National Museum of American Art, Washington, DC/Art Resource; **727**(t), National Museum of American Art, Washington, DC/Art Resource, (b), Bettmann Archive; **728,** Smithsonian Institution; **729**(l), Bettmann Archive, (r), The Granger Collection, New York; **730**(t), Bettmann Archive, (b), **731,** The Granger Collection; **732, 733,** Bettmann Archive; **734,** The Granger Collection; **735,** The

Credits **1117**

Howard University Gallery of Art, Washington, D.C.; **736,** National Portrait Gallery, Smithsonian Institution/Art Resource, NY; **738,** Smithsonian Institution; **739**(t), National Museum of American Art, Washington, DC/Art Resource, NY, (b), Courtesy Department of the Treasury, Bureau of Alcohol, Tobacco and Firearms; **740,** Bettmann Archive; **741**(l), Gerald Peters Gallery, New York, (r), Courtesy Department of the Treasury, Bureau of Alcohol, Tobacco and Firearms; **742,** UPI/Bettmann; **744,** Arthur Beck/Photo Researchers Inc.; **746**(l), Culver Pictures, (r), UPI/Bettmann; **747,** George Meany Memorial Archives; **749,** Dallas Museum of Art; **750,** UPI/Bettmann; **751,** The Granger Collection; **753,** National Portrait Gallery, Washington, DC/Art Resource, NY; **754,** file photo; **755**(l), Bettmann Archive, (r), Culver Pictures; **756**(l), The National Museum of American Art, Washington, D.C., (r), Photo by The Detroit News; **757,** The Oakland Museum; **758,** UPI/Bettmann; **759,** Collection of the Whitney Museum of American Art Purchase; **760,** The Granger Collection; **761,** UPI/Bettmann; **762, 764**(t)(bl)(br), The Granger Collection, (c), **765**(t), Aaron Haupt Photography; (cl), The Granger Collection; (cr)(b), Bettmann Archive; **766, 767**(b), Collection of Colonel Stuart S. Corning. Photo by Rob Huntley/Lightstream, (t), UPI/Bettmann; **768**(l), U. S. Army, (r), Warren Motts Photographic Center, (b), The Granger Collection; **769**(t), The Granger Collection, (b), Bettmann Archive; **770**(tr), Hugo Jaeger/Life Magazine ©Time Warner, Inc, (br), Franklin D. Roosevelt Library, (c), UPI/Bettmann; **771**(tl), Bettmann Archive, (tr), Topham Picture Source/The Image Works, (b), United Nations; **772,** Aaron Haupt Photography; **773**(tl)(bl), The Granger Collection, (r), The Butler Institute of American Art; **774,** Mark Burnett; **775,** file photo; **776,** Wide World Photos; **777,** Franklin D. Roosevelt Library; **778,** Wide World Photo; **779,** The Granger Collection; **780,** Minnesota Historical Society/St. Paul Daily News; **781,** Library of Congress; **782, 783,** FPG, Intl; **786,** Library of Congress; **787,** Ohio Historical Society/Center of Labor and Industry; **788**(l), UPI/Bettmann, (r), Wide World Photos; **789,** ©1935 (renewed 1963) by the Conde Nast Publications, Inc; **790,** The U. S. Department of the Interior, Washington, DC, photographer David Allison; **792,** Library of Congress; **793,** Franklin D. Roosevelt Library; **794**(t), Mark Reinstein/FPG, Intl, (b), Mark Burnett; **795,** The Granger Collection; **796,** file photo; **797**(l), Movie Still Archives, (r), The Granger Collection; **798,** Movie Still Archives; **799,** Collection of Picture Research Consultants; **800,** UPI/Bettmann; **801**(t), The Granger Collection; (b), Library of Congress; **802,** The Granger Collection; **804,** Warren Motts Photographic Center; **805**(t), The Granger Collection, (b), **806,** Warren Motts Photographic Center; **807, 808,** FPG, Intl; **809**(l), The Library of Congress, (r), Hugo Joeger/LIFE Magazine, Time, Inc; **811,** Warren Motts Photographic Center; **812,** The Granger Collection; **813,** UPI/Bettmann; **814,** Yivo Institute of Jewish Research; **815,** Franklin D. Roosevelt Library; **817,** National Archives; **818**(l), Library of Congress, (r), The Granger Collection; **820**(l), Wide World Photo, (r), The Granger Collection; **821,** Bettmann Archive; **823,** Warren Motts Photographic Center; **824,** The Granger Collection; **826**(t), USAF;, (b), Wide World Photo; **827, 828**(l), The Granger Collection, (r), Culver Pictures; **829**(l), Bettmann Archive, (r), UPI/Bettmann Archive; **830**(r), Cobalt Production; **830**(r), The Granger Collection; **831,** AP/Wide World Photos; **832,** Wide World Photo; **833,** FPG, Intl; **834,** Courtesy D. Wigmore Fine Art, Inc, New York; **836,** UPI/Bettmann Archive; **837**(tl), White House Historical Association, (bl), LIFE Magazine (c)Time, Inc, (r), Printed by permission of the Norman Rockwell Family Trust, ©1945 The Norman Rockwell Family Trust; **838,** UN/J. Isaac; **839**(l), AP/Wide World Photos, (r), UPI/Bettmann; **841**(l), FPG, Intl, (r), UPI/Bettmann; **843,** Department of the Army; **845,** Wide World Photos; **846,** U. S. Army Photograph; **847**(l), FPG, Intl, (r), Wide World Photos; **850,** file photo; **852**(l), Robert Reiff/FPG, Intl, (r), **853**(l), FPG, Intl, (r), U.S.Navy; **854,** Harry S Truman Library; **855,** AP/Wide World Photos; **857,** Library of Congress; **858,** Chicago Tribune Cartoon by Carey Orr; **860,** Robert Reiff/FPG, Intl; **861**(t), Isabel Bishop/Howald Fund/The Columbus Museum of Art, #54.47, (b), UPI/Bettmann; **862,** Cobalt Productions; **863,** Bettmann Archive; **864, 866,** file photo; **867,** Courtesy of Ohio AFL-CIO; **868,** UPI/Bettmann; **869,** Magnum Photos; **871,** FPG, Intl; **872,** Erich Hartmann/Magnum Photos; **874**(l), FPG, Intl, (r), **875**(l), UPI/Bettmann, (r), Mark Burnett; **876, 877,** UPI/Bettmann; **878,** Ralph Morse/LIFE Magazine (c)Time, Inc; **879, 880, 881,** UPI/Bettmann; **882,** AP/Wide World Photos; **884,** UPI/Bettmann; **885,** AP/Wide World Photos; **886,** UPI/Bettmann; **888**(t)(b), The Granger Collection, (c), Courtesy American Express; **889**(t)(bl), The Granger Collection, (br), Courtesy Hormel Foods/Aaron Haupt Photography; **890**(tr), Warren Motts Photographic Center, (bl), Minnesota Historical Society/St. Paul Daily News, (br), Wide World Photos; **891**(t), UPI/Bettmann, (b), Wide World Photos; **892**(t), John Eastcott/Yxa Momatiuk/Stock Boston, (b), David J. Sams/Stock Boston; **893**(t), Burt Glinn/Magnum, (b), Bob Mullenix; **894**(t), United Nations, (c), Steve McCutcheon, (b), Hank Morgan/Photo researchers; **895**(t)(c), Peter Turnley/Black Star, (b), file photo; **896,** Lawrence Migdale/Stock Boston; **897**(t), Flip Schulke/Black Star, (b), Tim Courlas; **898,** Bob Daemmrich/Stock Boston; **899**(l), UPI/Bettmann, (r), Topham Picture Source; **900**(l), UPI/Bettmann, (r), Declan Haun/Black Star; **901,** UPI/Bettmann; **902,** Steve Schapiro/Black Star; **903**(l), Flip Schulke/Black Star, (r), UPI/Bettmann; **904,** National Museum of American Art, Washington, DC/Art Resource, NY; **905,** UPI/Bettmann; **906**(l), DeClan Haun/Black Star, (r), Charles Moore/Black Star; **907,** Dan McCoy/Black Star; **909,** UPI/Bettmann; **910,** Mark Burnett; **911,** UPI/Bettmann; **912,** John Launois/Black Star; **913,** AP/Wide World Photos; **914,** Flip Schulke/Black Star; **915,** Peter Southwick/Stock Boston; **916**(l), Allen Zak; (r), Allen Zak; **917**(t), Lynda Gordon/Liaison Intl, (b), Joe Sohm/Image Works; **918**(l), Lionel Delavingne/Stock Boston, (r), Bob Daemmrich/Stock Boston; **919,** J. Jacobson/Image Works; **920,** Richard Pasley/Stock Boston; **922,** David Frazier; **923**(t), John Gordon/Black Star, (b), Joe Lynch/Liaison Intl; **924,** file photo; **926, 927**(l), UPI/Bettmann, (r), Patrick Piel/Liaison Intl; **929**(l), Culver Pictures; **929**(r), UPI/Bettmann; **930,** Dennis Brack/Black Star; **931**(l), Dick Johnson, (r), Robert Ellison/Black Star; **932**(l), UPI/Bettmann, (r), James Pickerell/Black Star; **936,** file photo; **937**(l), L. Kalvoord/Image Works, (r), John Filo; **938,** Dennis Brack/Black Star; **939,** Allen Zak; **941,** Tim Crosby/Liaison Intl; **942**(l), Charlon/Liaison Intl, (r), Liaison Intl; **944,** Richard Howard/Black Star; **945, 946,** UPI/Bettmann; **948,** L.H.Jawitz/Image Bank; **949**(t), Photo courtesy the Archives of the American Illustrator's Gallery, New York; (b), Smithsonian Institute photo #1689; **950,** Joe Sohm/Chromosohm/Stock Boston; **951**(l), Photo Tiffany/Gamma Liaison, (r), **953**(l), UPI/Bettmann, (r), Fred Ward/Black Star; **955,** NASA; **956,** Life Images; **957,** Owen Franken/Stock Boston; **958, 960,** UPI/Bettmann; **961,** The Sonnabend Collection, NY; **962,** Fred Ward/Black Star; **963,** Photo by Robert S. Oakes, National Geographic Society, Collection of the Supreme Court of the United States; **964,** Bill Pugliano/Black Star; **965,** Stock Boston; **966,** Randy Trine; **967,** Dennis Brack/Black Star; **969,** UPI/Bettmann; **970,** Roland Freeman/Magnum; **971,** Bill Foley/Black Star; **972,** R. Hess/Image Bank; **974, 975,** ©Bill Hickey/Image Bank; **975**(t), Collection of the Whitney Museum of American Art, 50th Anniversary Gift of the Gilman Foundation, Inc., The Lauder Foundation, A. Alfred Taubman, an anonymous donor, and purchase, (b), AP/Wide World Photos; **976,** Theo Westenberger/Liaison Intl; **977,** KEZA/Liaison Intl; **979,** Liaison Intl; **981,** UPI/Bettmann; **982,** Stock Boston; **983,** Bresse/Pozarik/Gamma Liaison; **984,** Bill Fitz-Patrick, The White House; **986,** NASA; **987**(l), Aaron Haupt, (r), Nubar Alexanian/Stock Boston; **990,** Liaison Intl; **991,** S. Ferry/Liaison Intl; **992,** Bob Daemmrich/Stock Boston; **993,** C. Hires, G. Merillon/Liaison Intl; **994,** Todd Adank, Photo Op Inc; **997**(t), George H. Matchneer, (b), Courtesy PHYSICS TODAY Magazine; **998,** William Johnson/Stock Boston; **1000,** Nathan Benn/Stock Boston; **1001**(t), David Lawrence/Stock Market, (b), Peter Menzel/Stock Boston; **1002,** Mark Burnett; **1003,** Markel/Liaison Intl; **1005,** Reuters/Bettmann; **1006,** Dennis Brack/Black Star; **1006,** Rueters/Bettmann; **1008,** file photo; **1009,** AP/Wide World Photos; **1010**(l), Miami Herald/Liaison Intl, (r), Todd Sumlin/Liaison Intl; **1011,** AP/Wide World Photos; **1012,** Reuters/Bettmann; **1015,** Aaron Haupt; **1017**(l), Ron Levy/Liaison Intl, (r), Paul Fusco/Magnum; **1018,** Marcel Mikanda III; **1021**(l), Ted Wood/Black Star, (r), Joyce Photographics/Photo Researchers Inc.; **1022,** Courtesy David Godine Publishers; **1023,** National Museum of American Art, Washington, DC/Art Resource; **1024,** Frank Rossotto/Stock Market; **1026**(tl), Reuters/Bettmann, (tr), Skip Comer, (b), Ellen Giamportone/H. Armstrong Roberts; **1027**(tl), C. P. George/H. Armstrong Roberts, (bl), Reuters/Bettmann, (br), Steve Jennings/LGI Photo Agency; **1028,** Declan Haun/Black Star; **1029**(t), Peter Menzel/Stock Boston, (b), AP/Wide World Photos; **1030,** Larry Kunkel/FPG, Intl; **1048-1054,** White House Historical Assn; **1055, 1056,** The Granger Collection; **1057,** FPG, Intl; **1058**(l), Boltin Picture Library, (r), Museum of American Political Life; **1059,** Smithsonian Institution; **1060,** The Granger Collection; **1061,** Superstock; **1062**(t), The Granger Collection, (b), National Portrait Gallery, Smithsonian Institution, Art Resource; **1063**(l), The Granger Collection, (r), Smithsonian Institution; **1064**(l), Photo Network, (r), Mark Burnett; **1065,** The Granger Collection; **1066**(t), National Portrait Gallery, Smithsonian Institution/Art Resource, (b), North Wind Picture Archives; **1067,** The Granger Collection; **1068,** Franklin D. Roosevelt Library; **1069,** UPI/Bettmann Archive; **1070,** Photo Tiffany/Liaison Intl; **1071,** Flip Schulke/Black Star.